PETERSON'S GUIDE TO

MBA

PROGRAMS

1999

*A Comprehensive Directory
of Graduate Business Education at
U.S., Canadian, and Select
International Business Schools*

Peterson's
Princeton, New Jersey

Visit Peterson's Education Center on the Internet (World Wide Web) at www.petersons. com

Editorial inquiries concerning this book should be addressed to the editor at: Peterson's, P.O. Box 2123, Princeton, New Jersey 08543-2123.

ISSN 1080-2533
ISBN 0-7689-0046-8

Printed in the United States of America

10   9   8   7   6   5   4   3   2   1

Contents

How to Use This Book

Peterson's Guide to MBA Programs 1999 provides detailed information on more than 900 schools offering more than 2,900 programs of study leading to a Master of Business Administration (MBA) degree or an equivalent graduate-level degree. These programs are offered by accredited colleges and universities in the United States and its territories and by institutions in Canada, Europe, Mexico, Asia, and Africa that offer equivalent or comparable programs of study.

MBA Programs At-A-Glance

This quick reference chart provides an overview of the programs offered at all the colleges and universities included in this guide. Entries in the chart are arranged geographically under the state, territory, province, or country in which they are located. Use this section to compare key facts about schools as you begin your search for the right MBA program. For additional details on particular programs, refer to the Program Profiles section and the In-Depth Descriptions that many schools have chosen to provide.

Entries in the chart include the following information:
Name of institution
Page reference to Program Profile
AACSB or ACBSP accreditation
Matriculation calendar (fall, winter, spring, summer, deferred)
Admission requirements (minimum GMAT score, minimum undergraduate GPA, minimum TOEFL score)
Full-time tuition
Part-time tuition
Financial aid availability
Distance learning option availability
Executive MBA program availability

Program Profiles

Profiles begin with the official school name, the name of the business unit (if applicable), and main address of the school.

Overview

This section provides general information about the college or university and its MBA and/or master's-level program offerings, including institutional control (i.e., public vs. private, religious affiliation, etc.), the year the institution was founded, campus setting, and total enrollment. Institutions may also be described as one or more of the following:

Coed: coeducational, enrolling both men and women
Comprehensive: awards baccalaureate degrees and offers graduate degree programs primarily at the master's, specialist, or professional level, although some doctoral programs may be offered

Independent: nonprofit
Independent-religious: sponsored by or affiliated with a certain religious group or having a nondenominational or interdenominational religious orientation
Locally supported: may refer to county, district, or city
Proprietary: profit making
Province-supported: applies to Canadian institutions
Specialized: offers degrees in one field only
State-supported: supported by state funding
State-related: funded primarily by the state but administratively autonomous
State and locally supported: supported by state and local funding
Territory-supported: applies to U.S. territories
University: offers four years of undergraduate work plus graduate degrees through the doctorate in more than two academic or professional fields

Program Highlights

This portion of each profile features the following key information for quick reference and comparison: the Enrollment Profile—MBA enrollment figures for the most recent academic year, including average age of MBA students upon entrance; percentage of women, international, and minority students enrolled; average class size for MBA courses; average GMAT score of entering students; and average GPA of entering students. Costs—minimum tuition and fees for full-time study, for both resident and nonresident students. Accreditation—whether the institution is accredited by the AACSB–The International Association for Management Education or by the American Council of Business Schools and Programs (ACBSP). If the MBA or equivalent graduate-level program is offered in conjunction with any other institutions, those institutions will be listed on the last line in the highlights box.

Graduate Business Programs

This section provides information pertaining to the basic MBA program offered by the institution and business school described. Information on other graduate management and master's-level degrees that are considered comparable or equivalent to an MBA, such as a Master of Science in Management, is also provided here.

Keep in mind that basic programs at different schools may vary considerably in academic focus, philosophy, and degree requirements, although each is offering an MBA degree or equivalent graduate-level program. Always contact schools directly for details on their programs, curricula, and individual approaches.

Also note that for consistency and data-management purposes, the names of degree concentrations reported by institutions were sometimes translated to fit under a more generalized name. For example, concentrations such as internal communications, management communication, survey of professional communication, business communication, and business writing would all be placed under the general category of business communications.

Details in this section include minimum and maximum length of the program in months or years; academic calendar (semesters, trimesters, quarters, etc.); number of credits required, including elective credits; special application requirements, if applicable; and areas of concentration or specialization offered (accounting/finance, economics, marketing, operations, etc.).

Admission

The number of business program applicants who applied, were accepted, and enrolled; specific application requirements and what is recommended; and application deadlines and fees are described here.

Application requirements may include letters of recommendation, a written essay, an interview, copies of transcripts of previous college study, a resume/curriculum vitae, a personal statement, computer experience, work experience, or other specific requirements. Application deadlines for spring, fall, or other admission are provided by most schools. Some may process applications on a continuous or rolling basis or offer a deferred entrance plan.

Recommended items to accompany or enhance the application may include a specific bachelor's degree, submission of GMAT (Graduate Management Admission Test) scores, minimum GPA (grade point average), minimum acceptable TOEFL (Test of English as a Foreign Language) score, minimum acceptable IELT (International English Language Test) score, proof of adequate funds, proof of health immunizations (for non–U.S. applicants), and previous work experience.

Academics

Number of full-time and part-time faculty is listed. Teaching methodologies (lecture, team projects, case studies, etc.) are described. Technology, including how many computer terminals are provided on campus for use by students, type of campuswide network in use (if applicable), and whether students are required to own a PC, is described here. Special opportunities, such as the types of education or experience that will qualify for transfer of credits to the MBA program, whether there is an international exchange program, and whether internships are available to students in the MBA program, are detailed here.

Finances

Information on tuition, fees, room and board, and financial aid is provided in this section. Tuition expenses may be indicated separately for full-time or part-time study. Tuition and fees are expressed as dollar amounts per course, credit hour, hour, quarter hour, semester hour, unit, quarter, semester,

trimester, term, academic year, or degree program, as specified by the institution. Fees include only charges that apply to all students—not charges for optional services or specific courses. Figures for tuition and fees are designated as official 1997–98. For public institutions in which tuition differs according to residence, separate figures are given for area or state residents and for nonresidents. Some non–U.S. institutions have chosen to report figures in currencies other than U.S. dollars. In these instances, readers should refer to current exchange rates in determining equivalents in U.S. dollars.

Average room and board expenses are indicated in either U.S. dollars or non–U.S. currencies. Both on-campus and off-campus costs may be indicated, depending upon the types of housing provided and whether or not institutions provided this data.

Financial aid information includes the percentage of MBA students who received college-administered financial aid in 1997–98; what types of aid were granted (grants, scholarships, work-study, loans, etc.); whether or not aid is awarded to part-time students; deadlines for submission of financial aid applications; and contact information, including name, address, phone, fax, and e-mail address.

Facilities

This section contains details on library and information resources and other technical facilities available for use by students. Details include name of the main library, the number of additional libraries on campus, total number of bound volumes, number of microforms in all libraries, total number of periodical subscriptions, available online services, and availability of CD players.

International Students

An international student is defined, in this guide, as a person who is not a citizen of the country in which a particular college, university, or other institution is located but is in that country on a visa or temporary basis and does not have the right to remain indefinitely.

This section provides information regarding entrance and application requirements for international students, international student enrollment as a percentage of the total number of students enrolled in the business school, special services or facilities available to international students, availability of student housing, ESL classes, and the availability of financial aid.

Application requirements for international students may include minimum acceptable TOEFL (Test of English as a Foreign Language) score, minimum acceptable IELT (International English Language Test) score, proof of adequate funds, and proof of health immunizations.

Where applicable, the name, address, phone, fax, and e-mail address of the on-campus adviser or other person responsible for working with international students or exchange students are provided.

Placement

This section provides information on placement services available on campus that may include career placement, career counseling/planning, career fairs, career library, an electronic job bank, arrangement of job interviews, resume preparation, job search courses, referral of resumes to employers, the number of organizations that have participated in on-campus recruiting, how many on-campus job interviews were conducted with MBA students during the previous academic year, what percentage of students had gained employment within three months of graduation, average starting salaries for recent MBA graduates, starting salary range for recent MBA graduates, and types of employment entered such as manufacturing, service, nonprofit, etc.

Business Program(s) URL

The Universal Resource Locator (URL), or what is more commonly known as a Web address, specific to the business school will appear only if the business school has provided it to Peterson's.

Program Contact

The name, title, mailing address, telephone number, fax number, and e-mail address of the person who should receive applications for admission are provided at the end of the profile. Toll-free telephone numbers may also be included.

Additional Information

A special announcement may precede the profile for schools that wish to place additional emphasis on some aspect of their MBA program offerings. In addition, other schools have provided narratives that appear in the In-Depth Descriptions of MBA Programs section immediately following the Program Profiles. These In-Depth Descriptions provide additional information about institutions and their programs.

Data Collection Procedures

Information contained in the Program Profiles, At-A-Glance Chart, and Index sections of the guide was collected in the spring and summer of 1998 through Peterson's Survey of MBA and Other Master's-Level Business Degree Programs. Questionnaires were sent to more than 1,000 U.S. and international institutions offering MBA and equivalent programs. Information was requested from program department contacts, admissions officers, or other appropriate personnel within these institutions in order to ensure accuracy. In some cases, this information was supplemented with data available from school catalogs and brochures and in some instances directly from the institution's Web site on the Internet in order to provide as much detail as possible on a particular school's MBA and/or master's-level degree offerings.

The omission of any particular item from a profile, chart, or index entry indicates that the item was either not applicable, not available at the time of publication, or not provided by the institution. Users of this guide should check with specific colleges and universities at the time of application to verify figures such as tuition and fees that may have changed since the publication of this guide.

Why an MBA? Future Trends and Opportunities in the Twenty-first Century

by John C. Hallenborg

MBA degrees are traditionally pursued in two-year, full-time programs; in more than two years in part-time evening and weekend programs; or in one-year intensive MBA programs, usually for executives or others with substantial work experience or those with undergraduate degrees in business.

Master's degrees of all types are on the rise. The plentiful supply of MBAs has allowed employers to be quite discriminating in hiring in recent years, requiring many MBAs to arrive equipped with specialized training and hands-on experience suited to their particular business niche.

Year	Master's Graduates in all Disciplines	Master's Graduates in Business and Management		
		Male	Female	Total
1990–91	337,168	50,883	27,372	78,255
1991–92	352,838	54,705	29,937	84,642
1992–93	369,585	57,651	31,964	89,615
1993–94	387,070	59,335	34,102	93,437
1994–95	397,629	59,109	34,700	93,809

Source: National Center for Education Statistics, U.S. Department of Education. Figures were unavailable beyond 1995.

In comparing the programs profiled in this volume, careful consideration should be given to the time required for studying, as every school varies in its expectations of students. At first, rather than merely communicating with targeted schools via letter, speak with someone in the admissions office who is familiar with your prospective course of study. Such a conversation will more than likely draw you closer to, or deter you from, participating in their program. Especially if you're holding down a job, it is always prudent to map out your time wisely.

Certainly, there are variations on this theme as the working MBA candidate may, for example, distribute a course load to accommodate a work schedule. There is also the related issue of employer assistance. The candidate's choice of school or program might be determined solely by which programs are endorsed and subsidized by the candidate's employer.

The one-year program has been around long enough for employers to gauge many of its attributes as compared to the two-year counterpart. One consensus is that there are many other issues that are more likely to clearly differentiate one candidate from another. An MBA degree can improve a candidate's chances to approximately the same level as a non-MBA candidate with more years of successful work experience.

Of course, the weight assigned to the MBA degree by prospective employers varies considerably, depending on the industry, company, and job assignment. For the savvy salesperson of copiers at a large firm such as Xerox, for example, the company's in-house training would provide more valuable background than an MBA degree, at least until a promotion incorporated management skills into the position. Conversely, someone applying for a middle-management job in the finance department at a mid-size company may find an MBA degree indispensable. The point is, the two jobs might be represented on the same salary tier, so it is still a maxim in the transitional process from MBA school to the workplace that the degree's importance is job-specific.

There are other key intangibles that have significance. Acquiring an advanced degree may imbue certain candidates with a feeling of confidence that may signal the difference between a lackluster career wandering the halls of a nondescript organization and a robust, life-affirming career full of welcome challenges and even more welcome rewards.

The knowledge gained in acquiring the MBA degree is not to be taken for granted at any point in the hiring process, as MBA holders can expect dedicated human resource executives to grill potential new hires in detail as to their educational experiences. What can the MBA grad do to improve this process? Graduates can apply their newly acquired knowledge to specific corporate examples to show why they should be hired.

Closing the Loop: Business Schools and Corporations

Ambitious MBA candidates in the late 1990s, looking forward to their careers or perhaps to the exciting prospect of entrepreneurship, cannot afford to presume that every MBA program will meet the educational requirements specific to an industry or profession. In today's job market and that of the near future, the MBA graduate will be expected to deliver both technical and nontechnical skills in every business and industrial sector. As in other areas of graduate study and related employment, the focus is, and will continue to be, on specialized expertise in business management. For business, opportunities abound to work with universities to create new MBA programs

4

Peterson's Guide to MBA Programs 1999

that will prepare candidates to fulfill an array of specialized leadership roles. For schools, this phenomenon continues to spur revamping of curricula almost annually to keep pace with the real-world demands that will be placed upon future MBA graduates.

Is it safe to presume that the recruitment managers at most major companies are aware of the changing makeup of the leading business school programs? The answer is most definitely yes and apparent in the variety of degree options, concentrations, and alternative courses of study available to today's MBA student.

How the degree can be obtained today also closely mirrors current business trends—the expectation of an early return on investment, preferably within one to two years. Future MBA programs will likely continue to reflect the choices seen today: the one-year degree, which often dispenses with core programs in favor of specialized courses tailored to specific career paths, and the more traditional two-year and extended MBA programs, which have been the basis of graduate business degrees for decades.

Certainly for the last twenty years or so, benchmark companies and top graduate schools have worked intensively to match academic programs to corporate needs. These relationships are likely to strengthen as more corporations and prospective students, hesitant to invest in two-year programs, are more willing to commit to emerging one-year programs.

Two-Year MBA vs. One-Year MBA

By all accounts, the composition of the MBA degree and how it is acquired will change significantly over the next five to ten years. The perceived value of the MBA degree has changed considerably in the student community and within the corporations that hire MBA graduates by the thousands every year. After a period of flat growth several years ago, the degree now appears dynamic and evolving. Affordable, highly focused, and time-efficient versions of the degree have replaced some multiyear courses of study.

The upsurge seen recently in one-year degrees has been driven, for the most part, by corporate demand, serving mostly experienced professionals and recent undergraduates with some work experience. Although two-year programs are still the norm in most business schools, accelerated and specialized one-year programs are seeing slight increases in enrollment. Business schools have been adversely affected by this trend and are offering degree options that combine an undergraduate business degree with an MBA in a five-year program.

The primary difference between one-year and traditional two-year programs is that with the shorter version, there is little if any overlap with undergraduate business curricula. Thus, it is highly recommended that students who decide on a one-year program enroll soon after receiving their undergraduate degrees and be able to satisfy all core business course requirements. However, some one-year programs require from two to five years' work experience in lieu of the traditional first-year MBA core study courses. In most cases, one-year elective courses are all but tailored to the applicant's career, so that the graduate can reenter the workforce as quickly as possible. Classic

Steven Lavender, President, Morgan/Webber: retained search firm

In answering the one-year versus two-year MBA program question, I have high regard for both programs at top schools such as Harvard, Wharton, Boston University, MIT's Sloan, Stanford, and the University of Chicago.

In the intensive one-year program, the student really lives the program in that time frame. I see it as a firm plus on a resume. A two-year program offers an assignment-oriented course of study, as the student has more time to assert his or her ideas as an individual versus the largely company-oriented slant of one-year programs.

Both of these programs add an attractive package of improved skills to the corporate world, reflecting course study in planning; distribution; the modern structure of marketing; assessments of MIS requirements; and the practical implementation of useful business models.

Right now, I don't have any clients who request an MBA. Work experience is still preferred as background for most positions. The MBA is still making a comeback as a hiring asset.

My searches today indicate that the person with a very general background—with a liberal arts BA and an MBA in management—might command $4000 more in salary than the BA-only candidate, on average—not much considering what acquiring the degree might have cost.

If you are considering an MBA, gear the course work toward a specialization and limit your choice of schools to those that include the targeted curriculum. This way, you will bring a continued focus on a specialty that today's employers find attractive.

You may wonder when, in a career, it's a good time to acquire an MBA. In today's job market, it's best if you work for six or seven years and then go get yourself an MBA. By the time someone has six years' work experience, he or she knows enough to properly shape a course of MBA study that will be beneficial to the employer.

two-year programs most often focus on elective and specialized course work in the second year after completion of core requirements in the first year.

A number of emerging realities will highlight the one-year MBA degree: technology-based information media will replace class time in many cases as students gain access to CD-ROM and online services; fewer faculty members may be required as schools combine resources to teach fewer classes to more students; and distance learning will replace some on-campus classes. For most schools and students of the future, technology will certainly dictate the learning medium.

In the relatively brief period that one-year MBA graduates have been working, corporations have been neutral about recruiting one-year program versus two-year program graduates, as there is no published evidence that graduates of two-year programs outperform their one-year counterparts.

Albert W. Niemi Jr., Dean of Southern Methodist University's Edwin L. Cox School of Business, explains that "I don't see, in the data that we have collected—in terms of starting salaries—that there is any difference in the way one-year people are treated by industry. One-year grads do as well as two-year grads in terms of earning power in the marketplace."

Despite Niemi's findings, to date there has not been significant movement toward the one-year degree, as at present there are relatively few such programs compared to the total number of MBA programs offered nationwide.

Traditional Course Work vs. In-house Training

Rather than sending employees off company premises for continuing education, many companies may choose to hire competent teachers as staff members to provide in-house training. This trend is not yet fully under way, but it is seen as a cost-effective alternative to traditional MBA programs. The one-year MBA and in-house training represent new models for graduate education. "Our dynamic economy is forcing change on all of us, if we are to be competitive and meet new challenges," offers William K. Laidlaw Jr., Executive Vice President of AACSB–The International Association for Management Education.

Among the programs on the horizon are those directed at problem solving within a limited number of companies or even a single company. These programs are tailored to specific company issues. Typically, collaborative tutoring teams are composed of university professors and corporate upper management.

Changes in the Financial Sector

In the top tiers of the financial markets, there have been many changes following the scandals and management excesses of the 1980s. By close association with these events, the reputation of the MBA degree was somewhat tainted, directly or by implication. Today's graduates are under scrutiny to improve the standing of the degree in the academic and corporate worlds. Clearly, teamwork has superseded personal glory in most corporate environments, and the financial community is no exception.

There has been a considerable shakeout in the better sectors of the financial job market, and many large financial organizations are as vigilant in maintaining a positive public image as they are about profit levels. Any MBA candidate seeking a spot at one of the top investment banks, for example, will have to be aware of issues of public relations in addition to more predictable questions about money markets. Expect this sensitivity to public opinion to remain high for many years. In fact, a reputation for aboveboard dealings is nearly as important as bottom-line performance in today's financial sphere.

At present, the MBA degree is still key in the world of investment banking, as recruitment specialists at banks large and small report that about 90 percent of new hires have the degree.

L. Nicholas Deane, former Senior Vice President, Faulkner & Gray, subsidiary of Thomson Financial Services

Faulkner & Gray is a departmentalized organization, and as head of a division that publishes content for professionals in the tax field, I tend to value work experience in that particular area more than a general MBA degree. However, I do recognize the usefulness of MBAs that target disciplines more specifically than, for example, an MBA in marketing, which I do not value very highly. However, in considering my department's needs, I'll flag a resume with an MBA with taxation as a specialty.

My sense is that work experience has more value than an MBA in general business environments, but that as one swings toward the more technical domains, a technically based MBA will look more attractive to an employer. The likelihood is that such a candidate will get up to speed more quickly on what is happening, both good and bad, within a company. And then, there is a greater chance that background in the specific area will serve to provide a base for successful decision making.

The in-depth study of sophisticated financial concepts is the key attribute that sets the MBA degree apart. I like to see well-placed employees armed with this advanced knowledge of finance. All sharp-minded candidates deserve a fair shot. There are experienced people who perform well without an MBA degree. Faulkner & Gray is typical of the high end of the publishing sector that is using technology to migrate from paper-based products to online and other electronically based formats.

As to the one-year degree versus the two-year degree, I have not seen evidence that causes me to prefer a two-year degree over the one-year alternative, but I should stress again that pertinent work background has been a better indicator of good hires than degrees of any sort. It comes down to the individual, really, the candidate's unique mix of experiences and qualifications. One area that I have seen strength in as the MBA relates to job specs is in financial analysis. I have come to expect the MBA holder to be sophisticated in crunching numbers.

The New MBA Attitude

How does this job market realignment affect the MBA holder's chances for a lucrative career in finance? The answer is often more in the attitude of the prospect than in the present and future states of the job market. These behavioral issues resound throughout not only the financial sector but also the finance departments of major corporations. The message is: bring us good grades from a good school but also bring along maturity and a problem-solving attitude.

Despite the fact that compensation at the higher levels in banking is very bonus-oriented, the fresh MBA graduate should avoid being a self-serving maverick. The MBA of tomorrow, more than ever before, will have to display strengths in leadership, teamwork, problem solving, and dealing with people.

Upper management will be looking for well-rounded individuals who offer a balanced perspective and are ready and able to apply their education in a real-life setting.

Working for Smaller Companies

And what about the option of employment by the thousands of small and mid-size firms that populate the American business landscape? The ideal of a "secure job forever" has been replaced by the reality that most Americans will have two or three careers in their lifetimes and may even change jobs every five years or so. Small and middle-market corporations have become the most fertile ground for MBA recruitment in the 1990s and will likely continue to hire more MBAs into the next century. In many instances, it is easier for a talented MBA holder to make a significant contribution to a mid-size firm in a high-growth mode. The key, of course, may be to identify likely high-growth companies that have the potential for continued growth over a three- to five-year period.

Once again, preparation for a specific industry niche, or better yet a specific company or companies, is key to landing those choice spots that feature a daunting 50:1, or 500:1, applicant/position ratio. Most competing MBAs are aware that the key to landing the desired job is to positively differentiate oneself from other equally qualified candidates. Some MBA students have gone so far as to research potential employers at the beginning of their course work, studying the details of annual reports, product brochures, etc., for the duration of the typical two-year MBA program.

Skills learned in MBA core and specialized courses can be especially valuable in helping to transform technical ideas and concepts into tangible, marketable products. In both large and small businesses in the future, managers will certainly be expected to bring not only technical expertise to the table but also the ability to translate new ideas into profit-sustaining products and services.

The small and mid-size firm is often the perfect venue for such creative expression coupled with pragmatic implementation. Smaller firms are already actively recruiting from the ranks of new MBA degree holders to discover the talented individuals whose skills and judgment will drive future growth and product improvement.

MBA candidates should be very selective in targeting small and mid-size companies, however, as many smaller firms are adopting a lean corporate structure by not instituting a middle layer of management until they reach the 1,000-employee mark. For the MBA holder this may mean more responsibility within a flat organizational structure and the need to "wear many hats." High-tech, high-growth, small to mid-size firms such as Dallas Semiconductor (Dallas, TX) with 1,350 employees; software maker Wonderware (Irvine, CA), with 425 employees; and California Micro Devices (Milpitas, CA) with 260 employees are all focused on hiring individuals with variations of the master's degree.

Richard Helfrich, former Vice President at California Micro, a semiconductor maker, considers the MBA to be "a strong plus in our hiring considerations. I weigh the degree as the

Bril Flint, former Vice President, Strategic Planning, EMI-Capital Music

When recruiting management talent for my team, I evaluate candidates across four dimensions: the candidate's long-term career plan and objectives; relevant real-world experience; technical capabilities for the job at hand; and interpersonal skills.

With these parameters in mind, how can a prospective business school student make the best use of an MBA education within the context of overall career advancement?

First, make sure graduate management education really does fit in with your long-term career plan. This may sound like a trivial step, but I have met more people that have not explicitly delineated their objectives than those that have. You can change them as you go along, but make sure the time and money you will spend on business school are really worthwhile.

I also like to see candidates who factor their long-term strategy into their choice of business school. For example, if they want to pursue a career in engineering management, did they pick a school that has a good program in that field, or did they opt for a "name school to get their ticket punched?" I prefer to see the former.

While an MBA from a top school can be a leg up on the competing candidates, I have seen enough successful executives with degrees from middle or lower tier graduate management programs (and many without an MBA degree at all) to know that a degree from a top ten institution is not required to prove and validate the individual's capability. Neither is it a guarantee of success, as I have seen plenty of graduates from top tier schools fail miserably in the working world.

Relevant work experience is really the most important area for me when I look at recruits. Most executives would rather have someone who understands their industry and how it works. I usually prefer the candidate with two years of relevant industry experience over one with two years of business school, no matter how "applied" a business school curriculum claims to be. It simply cannot duplicate the real day-to-day business activity in a particular industry or company.

The bottom line here is: It is better to work several years before you go to business school. (*Editor's Note:* Flint has a master's degree in management from MIT's Sloan School of Management.) If you have identified an industry in which you really want to work long term, go all out to find a job in that line of business before you go to business school. This may mean sacrificing short-term earnings.

I look for candidates who can bring the right "tool box" to the job for which I am recruiting. The appropriate technical skills for the position under consideration can be developed and demonstrated through prior experience, whether in the same industry or in the same functional area in a different line of business.

(continued)

To a lesser, but still important, extent, specific technical skills can be learned in school. To reiterate, if your long-term career strategy should help drive your choice of business school, then developing the appropriate technical capabilities should be the tactical driver in your selection of specific courses to take. In the typical two-year business school program, you have a limited number of elective courses. Make each one count to your advantage; try to leave business school with the appropriate tools at your disposal.

Interpersonal skills have a profound impact on a manager's long-term career path. In every meeting or transaction, others are making assessments of your poise, level of confidence, ability to communicate clearly, your business ethics, competency, and about one hundred other interpersonal traits. As in the other areas, prior work experience is most valuable in developing this skill set. Watch how successful executives interact in a variety of business settings.

Business school is also a good setting to enhance your interpersonal abilities. Working and socializing with classmates from varied backgrounds is good experience and is essential to get the most out of the business school experience.

equivalent of three years of solid work experience. But because our products are so technology-based, the master's degree is still our primary qualifier."

Tomorrow's MBA Entrepreneur

There will also be a place for the ambitious MBA holder who cannot wait for others to bring his or her ideas to the marketplace. For many fearless graduates, starting or buying a business may be a quicker and more lucrative route to success. Those with the best chance of making it this way will most likely combine prior technical training with the marketing and financial knowledge acquired with an MBA degree—for example, the electrical engineering whiz who starts a small, niche-focused circuit design firm.

Still, the appeal of running a small business does not get as much media coverage as it should, if the Harvard MBA Class of 1970 is any indication. In a recent survey of the 723 alumni who are now as a group generally in the peak phases of their careers, only 13 percent worked for *BusinessWeek* 1000 companies. By contrast, 36 percent were self-employed and the majority worked in small businesses (fewer than 500 employees) in one capacity or another.

Opportunities for MBAs in the Year 2000

Because management and finance are functions common to every conceivable type of business or industry, it is difficult to make predictions about job growth for MBAs in particular markets. However, although it may sound simplistic, it is still true that career opportunities will most likely continue to exist for talented MBAs in nearly all areas of the marketplace into

the next century. Although manufacturing and investment firms have experienced somewhat of a downswing in top management positions in the last few years, a tremendous variety of positions still attract MBAs to accounting, commercial banking, management consulting, consumer products, health care, insurance, services, and chemical companies in functions that include marketing, finance, operations, information systems, and long-term planning. Even many nonprofits are recruiting MBAs to help them redefine and reshape their organizations both economically and socially.

So, what are some of the growth areas for the MBA graduates to consider? As in the 1980s and early 1990s, there appears to be no limit to the growth potential in the software and telecommunications industries, particularly in the convergence of data and voice technologies. The number of professional jobs in computer software and hardware development and marketing will also likely only increase over the next ten years, although many companies may start up and then fold or be bought out in these volatile fields.

Telecommunications giants such as AT&T, MCI, and the Regional Bell Companies are already driving much of the development in this sector and will certainly require MBA graduates with a broad range of business and technical skills. MBAs with well-honed analytical and marketing skills will certainly be needed as telecommunications companies continue making forays into the information and entertainment services markets.

Another area for consideration by the eager MBA is publishing and information services. Innumerable products in CD-ROM, CD-I, and online formats are displacing paper equivalents most notably in the professional and academic domains. Books, newspapers, and other information products are certain to follow this trend toward electronic versus paper distribution. Publishing professionals armed with MBA degrees will certainly supply much of the marketing, financial, and strategic expertise needed to help such companies enter these new markets.

Still another high-growth area that may lure many MBAs is the world of entertainment. The creative entrepreneur seeking entry into the television, film, or music industry could be well positioned with an MBA, since bottom-line business issues usually determine if projects are produced. Consulting opportunities for the freelance MBA holder are already numerous in the entertainment industry. This should continue as a promising area of activity for the creative MBA.

For U.S.–based firms in other industry sectors, a significant amount of future growth may come from overseas operations. In the chemicals and polymers sector, for example, many of the management jobs will be in maintaining investments on the Pacific Rim and Eastern Europe, where most of the largest petrochemical conglomerates have joint ventures in place. MBA graduates should be willing to travel abroad to land these types of positions.

Most sources indicate that U.S. industries overall will experience moderate, 3 to 7 percent annual growth in the next ten years. Hiring of MBAs in industries such as construction and real estate, general manufacturing, foods and beverages, and electronics is predicted to be moderate by comparison.

Which sectors will be the toughest to enter, based on a flat industry growth forecast for the next ten years? Aerospace, oil and gas, health care, retail, and apparel are some of the major industries that are likely to experience fluctuating growth at best.

Go Global

By the year 2000, with the continued advance of telecommunications as the primary medium for data transfer, banks and corporations will have permanently erased many commercial barriers between nations. This borderless, global market should be an exciting prospect for the ambitious MBA.

An in-depth review of international trade regulations will serve tomorrow's MBA well since American firms already derive some 50 percent of gross revenues from overseas operations. Given the prodigious growth rate of economies in the developing nations, particularly in Asia and South America, virtually any MBA with skills to lend to those markets should find much success.

There will be more exciting opportunities in the former Eastern Bloc nations as these countries struggle to establish free-market economies. But the challenges are as enormous as the potential rewards. Still, the fearless MBA, armed with street smarts, a good command of the host country's language, and a firm grasp of the cultural keys to market entry, will find plenty of qualified European partners ready to forge ahead.

Similarly, at home, most large companies will be importing and exporting huge quantities of commodities, consumer goods, and financial services. For American MBAs seeking careers at home, the importance of global awareness cannot be overstated. Ten years from now, there will be impressive opportunities for international licensing of technologies, trademarks, and copyrighted products and processes that most Americans take for granted. Clearly, the cosmopolitan MBA will be the first to reap the rewards from emerging international markets in the twenty-first century.

Postgrad Tips

A candidate should zero in on three to five companies that are very attractive, firms wherein one could happily spend the next three to ten years working hard to establish oneself in the business community. If writing is a strong skill, parlay the skill by writing a detailed letter expressing your knowledge of the industry and the company and why you would be an asset to that company.

In the case of public companies, get their latest annual report, analyze it, and have your own views on the company's future ready to share with your interviewer. Do not make the mistake of blindly agreeing with everything the interviewer offers about the firm. If you disagree on a point, assert yourself with an explanation of your perspective on the issue. Never shy away

Willard Anderson, former Director, Management Development and Diversity, ITT Corporation

At ITT, the MBA degree is very important as part of an overall package of attributes a candidate may have to offer. When we hire an MBA, we expect that new hire to hit the ground running, as there is less time in today's competitive marketplace for in-house training.

We presume that an MBA holder emerging from our group of recruitment schools (Harvard, Columbia, Duke, Northwestern, Wharton, and Stanford) will have considerable business acumen. This is part of the skill set we are seeking. Another key element is an undergraduate course of study that integrates well with the curriculum that was chosen in acquiring an MBA.

Also important in terms of middle-management jobs and marketing leadership positions is that the candidate have three to five years' solid work experience. So, we look for people who have a synergistic mix of MBA and relevant undergraduate training, along with some real time spent solving real business problems.

As to the question of one-year versus two-year MBA programs, we are decidedly in favor of two-year programs. In fact, exceptions are very few. Perhaps 1 in 100 MBA holders will come on board with a one-year degree. This conservative approach has paid off in that we have reaped significant rewards from this hiring system.

We also view the MBA degree as more important today than it was five or ten years ago. In order to move easily within the extensive ITT corporate system, a new management employee needs to be familiar with sophisticated business models and other more advanced business concepts that reflect exposure to the rigors of acquiring an MBA degree. Our undergraduate employees are more deterministic in how they go about their jobs. MBA holders are much more likely to get into developmental work right away.

Overall, ITT is a company that all but requires management candidates to have a two-year MBA and three to five years of work experience. In terms of specialties within the MBA degree, we have had notable success with candidates who stressed finance and marketing in their courses of study.

from creating polarized discussion during an interview if you truly believe your position to be correct. Hopefully, your interviewer will recognize your willingness to defend your viewpoint as a trait of a successful executive.

John C. Hallenborg is a writer and business consultant based in Los Angeles, California.

The New MBA: What to Look for in Today's Reinvented Programs

by Carter A. Prescott

Your team's assignment: Climb through different size openings in a massive rope web without touching anything—and do it faster than competing teams. Another assignment: Tell a fellow student about an experience in which you felt odd or left out. Sound like typical MBA fare? If you answered yes, you pass.

Today's graduate business programs are undergoing what some experts tout as nothing less than revolutionary change. In response to new competitive demands on corporations and increasing globalization—both of which require tomorrow's business leaders to be flexible and manage workforces and internal structures that cross cultural and political lines—MBA programs are diversifying and redefining themselves. You'll still graduate with a firm grounding in the staples of business education—finance, strategy, operations management, marketing, and the like—but you'll also learn how to work in teams, how to motivate others, and how to see the "big picture" when solving problems. Strong communication and interpersonal skills are just as important in today's new MBA programs as technical knowledge and the ability to "crunch numbers."

"There's more churning going on right now in management education than at any time in thirty-five years," says Charles W. Hickman, Director of Projects and Services at AACSB–The International Association for Management Education, which accredits MBA programs in the United States. "The emphasis today is changing from teaching to learning," Hickman notes. "The front-end-load module, where you dump two years of education into a student's head and then sew it up, is over. The world is moving too fast. Companies want MBA graduates to know how to learn, because lifelong learning is the key to success for practicing managers and executives. The MBA is not an end in itself. It positions the degree-holder for a variety of general management positions."

What, you may ask, can you expect to learn from the rope exercise? How to plan, pay attention to detail, and how to work in teams. And the lesson behind baring your soul to a colleague? How to become sensitive to gender and ethnic diversity in order to manage it effectively.

The days when MBA graduates could dazzle their bosses with only a few mentions of decision trees, regression analysis, net present value, and gap planning are gone. You'll still learn these concepts, but you'll be synthesizing them into a broader skill set. Dennis J. Weidenaar, Dean of the Krannert Graduate School of Management at Purdue University, calls it the "new

management environment." He says it is characterized by "teamwork and alliances, continuous changes in technologies, globalization, and networks that are in instantaneous communication with each other."

How specifically do today's MBA programs prepare you to succeed in this environment? Here are ten primary ways.

1. Cross-Functional, Interdisciplinary Curricula

You'll hear these phrases so often they'll sound like a mantra. Even the venerable Harvard Business School voted to overhaul its MBA curriculum, effective in 1996, to offer students more interdisciplinary courses and more freedom in choosing electives. Across the country, MBA schools are reshaping curricula to teach students the importance of solving problems by synthesizing a variety of subjects. Faculty members from different disciplines coordinate their syllabi and teach in teams to students who work in teams. When Stanford added a new course in human resource management, for example, it was designed by professors of organizational behavior and economics. A cross-functional approach also has proved resoundingly popular with students. After Wharton tested a dramatically revised curriculum, surveys showed that a full 94 percent of its 1993 graduates who participated in the pilot would do so again, while 60 percent of those who studied under the traditional program would have preferred the new one.

2. New Programs

Whether they are specific sequences or subjects woven into the fabric of an MBA curriculum, you'll find strong mentions of entrepreneurship, ethics, Total Quality Management (TQM), information technology management, and leadership development in nearly all basic MBA programs. Purdue's PL+S Program (Preparing Leaders and Stewards) provides additional course work, community service opportunities, self-assessment, and self-directed team consulting projects with companies, all as avenues for developing leadership skills. Harvard's new "foundations" program will place heavy emphasis on career planning, self-assessment, working in groups, and business ethics. Ethical challenges are constantly reinforced in the Pepperdine University curriculum, says Stanley K. Mann, a professor in the Graduate School of Business. "We are training managers to take on responsibilities and obligations, not to put the dollar ahead of everything else."

A new emphasis on entrepreneurship reflects the reality that "the majority of MBA graduates will not work in Fortune 500 companies, because they have been downsizing the most," notes Charles Hickman of the AACSB. Accordingly, many universities help students develop better job-hunting and career development skills.

3. Global Perspectives

Because U.S. corporations increasingly compete around the world, globalization is serious business in the nation's MBA programs. Stanford offers four times as many internationally focused electives as it did ten years ago. Even though Pace University has featured an international business major for twenty years, "we now view it as a jumping-off point to integrate international issues throughout the curriculum," says Associate Dean Arthur L. Centonze. Pepperdine University in Malibu, California, designed a specific Master of International Business program that features eight months of study and internships in France or Germany. Students are required to find their own internships and to be proficient in French or German. Although 6 percent routinely drop out, another third stay abroad for at least a year, postponing their graduation to gain valuable work experience.

4. Increased Student and Faculty Diversity

Business schools have realized that the best way to teach tomorrow's managers to tap the talents of an increasingly diverse workforce is to surround students with a widely diverse student body. They're also recruiting more faculty members who reflect diverse viewpoints and philosophies as well as national origin. While more and more schools are quick to point to their rising numbers of international students, they also refer to the diverse backgrounds and experiences among their MBA students. Students from diverse countries and backgrounds are viewed as a resource that complements what faculty members know and what other students bring to the program. Women students are swelling the ranks of MBA graduates as well.

5. Teamwork, Teamwork, and More Teamwork

Schools are working hard to encourage the same environment of teamwork that graduates will experience in the working world. "Cohort structures," for example, have gained in popularity. Cohorts means that you are placed with a specified number of fellow students—deliberately chosen for their diversity—either for the first few weeks of class or for the entire first year. Together with other members of your cohort, you'll solve problems as a team, resolve conflicts, sustain morale, achieve accountability, and, it is hoped, learn to reach your goals by becoming interdependent, just as you would in a corporate setting.

Reinvented MBA programs are learning to "pit students against the curriculum and not against one another," says Sam Lundquist, Chief of Staff in the Dean's Office at Wharton. Stanford says its cooperative learning environment is a significant factor in the program's "joy coefficient," as George Parker, Associate Dean for Academic Affairs, describes it.

6. Richer Learning Environment

Hand in hand with curriculum improvements, business schools are finding new ways to strengthen teaching and foster improved student-faculty relationships. Indeed, the "most exciting part" of Wharton's new cross-functional curriculum, Lundquist says, is that teams of faculty now teach the same students for the entire first year, which "drastically improves the quality of relationships between students and faculty members."

As MBA programs bolster the quality of the learning experience, they are focusing a laser beam on how well professors help students learn. Pace University views faculty members as "the managers of the student learning process," says Centonze. As a result, all programs and courses have objectives that are measured by student exit surveys, faculty questionnaires, and yearly performance evaluations for faculty members. Any underperforming teachers are coached at the school's Center for Faculty Development and Teaching Effectiveness, where their syllabi are reviewed and their classes videotaped.

Increasingly, a variety of teaching methods are employed, including lectures, case studies, computer simulations, and consulting projects. Harvard's curriculum reform was notable for adopting alternative teaching methods in addition to its reliance on the traditional case-study approach and for developing ways to have faculty members spend less time teaching basics.

7. Greater Use of Learning Technologies

MBA programs are making increasing use of such state-of-the-art technologies as distance learning, which uses interactive cable television and computers to take courses directly to students' homes. The University of Maryland, for instance, uses distance learning and team teaching to bundle its assets and hire big-name teachers. Distance learning also is "favored heavily" in Europe, where virtually all programs are part-time, according to Roger McCormick, director general of the Association of MBA's in the United Kingdom. Distance learning allows students to learn at their own pace, which is especially helpful for remedial courses and quantitative work, he says.

Business schools are avidly employing other technologies as well, such as interactive cases on CD and real-time data feeds from Wall Street. In fall 1996, the University of Texas at Austin completed a $1.5-million trading room so that its students could experience trading in real time with real dollars from a $2-million investment fund. Purdue is even investigating how to bring virtual reality experiences into the classroom. Meanwhile, videoconferencing is used for classroom presentations or off-site interviews with corporations.

8. More Applied Learning

At the University of Illinois at Chicago, student and faculty teams tackle corporate projects by interviewing corporate executives, writing reports, and presenting recommendations to the company and to their fellow students. They're not alone. Students at the University of Texas at Austin helped Ford Motor Company better segment its Hispanic marketing efforts. The

University of Michigan adopted a medical school model, requiring students to get considerable practical experience working at corporations. At Stanford, corporate leaders such as Andrew S. Grove of Intel team with professors to teach classes on strategy in the high-technology industry.

9. Strategic Alliances

To better leverage their resources, schools are joining forces to teach students and to conduct postgraduate training for corporate executives. The Thunderbird School reserves seats at its learning centers around the world for its partner schools in the United States. Business schools at the University of Florida and Fordham University in New York team up with AT&T and MCI, respectively, to offer customized programs for their executives. Corporate advisory boards, long a staple of most MBA programs, are increasingly relied on to provide advice on curricula as well as hiring opportunities. Corporate partners also contribute other sorely needed resources. Purdue has one of the most extensive computing labs of any business school, thanks to the generosity of such high-tech partners as AT&T, Hewlett Packard, IBM, Microsoft, and PictureTel. "The business environment is moving fast, and even elite schools don't have all the money they need to access new markets, technology, and faculty expertise," says the AACSB's Hickman.

10. Customer Focus

It's not uncommon to hear business school professors routinely refer to students and companies as customers—and to treat their needs with the same respect. Many schools are applying Total Quality Management (TQM) principles to operating the business schools themselves. They're becoming more customer-focused, reducing the cycle time for admissions processing and curriculum development, and becoming more efficient to lower tuition or keep it from rising quickly. Seattle University takes classes to the customers, dispatching faculty members to teach evening and breakfast courses near Seattle's biggest employers.

With such evolution occurring day by day at business schools, more than ever before, today's reinvented MBA programs aim to prepare you for the real world of work, where you will work in teams, take a global view, and analyze problems from a multitude of perspectives. To accomplish these goals, MBA programs intend to equip you with the ability to embrace change, accept ambiguity, and lead others with the vision and confidence gained from continuous learning.

With a newly minted MBA degree, you are better qualified to enter new fields, better able to leverage your prior work experience, and more likely to sustain higher earnings over the course of your career. Equally important, you'll have the opportunity to make a significant difference on as broad a scale as you wish. With finely honed analytical skills, the ability to work well with people, and the desire to keep learning, today's MBA graduates can succeed in a broad range of general management positions and add more value than ever before.

Carter A. Prescott is a management communications consultant in New York City.

Choosing the Right Program for Your Career Needs

by Richard L. White, Director of Career Services, Rutgers University

In recent senior surveys, more than 80 percent of Rutgers University students have indicated that they intend to pursue graduate study at some point in the future. Many are thinking about an MBA. The intentions of Rutgers students reflect a national trend: More and more students want additional education, and, in fact, many feel they will need it to achieve their fullest career potential.

From your first thoughts about graduate school to your actual admission and decision to attend a school, you are engaged in an extensive, complex, competitive process. The emphasis of the program you select will greatly influence the direction of your career. In selecting an MBA program, it is critical to match your strengths, interests, and goals with the specific offerings of the school and program.

To organize and manage the process, develop a strategy for evaluating your choices and developing an action plan. At the heart of your action plan are four basic questions that are simple to ask but require self-exploration and research:

- Why do I want to pursue an MBA?
- When and how do I want to pursue an MBA?
- Where do I want to pursue an MBA?
- What schools and programs are right for me?

1. Why Pursue an MBA?

Typically, you are probably thinking about pursuing an MBA for four basic reasons:

- Your chosen profession demands further study
- You want to enhance your marketability and salary
- You want to change careers
- You are committed to further study in your current discipline or a new discipline

Most applicants fit one of these profiles:

- You're currently working with an employer that you would like to stay with long term. You've talked to your boss and colleagues, and they feel that getting an MBA will improve your business and technical knowledge and thus increase your performance and promotional opportunities with the employer. You understand that there probably won't be a big jump in salary when you complete your degree, but in the long term it will pay off. In addition, your employer will pick up the tab through its tuition reimbursement program.
- You're currently working with an employer who doesn't fit into your longer term plans. You're planning to leave in the near future. You see your MBA as the key to opening new opportunities in the same field or a new field and to increasing your salary prospects. You realize that you're on your own with regard to costs (no employer assistance), but you see the short-term investment paying off in the long run.
- You're a senior in college. You've looked at the job market, but you're really leaning toward an MBA program. You're very interested in pursuing your business education, especially because your bachelor's degree is not in business. You understand that the best business schools accept only a small percentage of applicants directly from undergraduate programs, but you have a strong academic record and some good internship and part-time work experience.

Whatever your profile may be, make sure you can articulate your reasons for pursuing an MBA clearly, succinctly, and persuasively both orally and in writing. Review the evolution of your thinking from first thoughts about an MBA to major influences such as people, courses, positions, and research.

To understand your motivation for pursuing an MBA, follow these action steps:

1. Take notes on yourself.
2. Write or revise your resume.
3. Develop a generic personal statement (2 to 3 typed pages), indicating what makes you special and why you want an MBA degree.
4. Request a sampling of MBA applications and begin crafting sample answers to the questions, using parts of your generic personal statement.
5. Read *How to Write a Winning Personal Statement for Graduate and Professional School* by Richard Stelzer (Peterson's, 1997). Check your college's career services library, your campus bookstore, or a local bookstore in the education/reference section.
6. Determine job prospects for MBAs in your intended field—both short-term and long-term. The best resources for short-term job prospects are individual placement reports from business schools, which you can request from the schools of your choice. For long-term prospects, talk to relatives, family friends, or professors. Another great source is alumni, if your school has an alumni career network.

2. When and How Do You Want to Pursue Your MBA?

There are four fairly clear-cut options about when and how to pursue your MBA:

• *Full-time beginning in the fall after your graduation from college.* Keep in mind that MBA programs typically look for candidates with at least one to two years of full-time work experience. If you are a student early in your undergraduate career, one option to explore is a five-year dual-degree (BS/MBA) program.

• *Full-time after a year or more of work.* MBA programs value the diversity and quality of candidates' work experiences, which bring "real-world" perspectives and new ideas into the classroom. Moreover, many MBA students indicate that their MBA course work has even more significance after they continue their professional and career development.

• *Part-time beginning anytime while working.* In most cases, you will take evening classes. As part of your preliminary research, find out if your employer provides full or partial tuition remission. Also explore whether or not your employer values an MBA and whether it will really contribute to your long-term promotability. Finally, try to determine how flexible your employer may be if, for example, you need to take a 4:30 class or need one or two days off to complete a school project.

• *Part-time beginning anytime while not working.* If you're not working, you can take either day or evening classes. But if you're looking for a daytime job, bear in mind that you might want to remain flexible during the day and therefore take your classes at night. The reverse is true if you have a part-time evening job.

To sort out the different possibilities, take these action steps:
Research the schools of your choice, using this guide. Compare these five key elements: percentage of full-time vs. part-time enrollees; percentage of incoming MBAs who came directly from undergraduate programs; average age; average work experience; and costs.

Research the profession and prospective employers, utilizing corporate recruiters, friends in the corporate world, career services and admissions professionals, professional associations, alumni networks, professors, and publications. Consider these elements: availability of tuition remission programs; value of the MBA within the profession or company; balance between a company's BA/BS hiring and MBA hiring.

Balance all of the above elements with your personal life and lifestyle and those of the people closest to you.

3. Where Do You Want to Pursue Your MBA?

This is the most complex step in the process, because there are many variables. However, by taking these action steps, you can gain firm control of the process and manage it to your advantage.

Note that these steps are in no order of preference. It would be helpful to put them in rank order in terms of importance for you—or at least group them by "very important," "important," and "less important."

Determine the availability of degree programs in your specific field. For example, if you are thinking about an MBA in international business, this guide will tell you which schools offer that program.

Determine the quality and reputation of the programs of your choice. This is a crucial element. Employers often base their recruiting decisions on quality and reputation, and you will be associated with the name of your MBA school for the remainder of your career. Three key factors in assessing quality and reputation are faculty, facilities, and student body. In addition to utilizing this guide and perhaps other resources, talk to professors and professionals and "read between the lines" of the admissions literature and placement reports. Feel free to consult various national rankings, but don't take them too seriously. These are often based on journalistic endeavors rather than hard research and often overlook the special offerings of individual programs.

Determine the costs of graduate programs—the simple part—and your ability to pay through loans, income, savings, financial aid, and parental support—the not-so-simple part. Pursue those programs that are affordable. Consult the "Paying for Your MBA" section in this guide for an overview of the financing process.

Determine the locations of your preferred graduate programs. Do you prefer urban, suburban, or rural locations? Do you have any personal geographical restrictions or preferences? Think about the time and cost of commuting and travel.

Determine the size of the programs and the institutions. Most MBA programs are relatively small but the size of institutions varies considerably. Size is critical to the overall environment, character, academic resources, and student-faculty ratios and relationships.

4. What Schools and Programs Are Right for You?

Here, you are putting it all together and generating a list of five to ten schools where you intend to apply. Typically, you will want one or two "stretch" schools, a handful of "good bets," and one or two "safety" schools. Feel free to rank your preferences at the outset of the admissions process, but remain flexible. As you receive admissions decisions, your preferences will probably change and need to change.

Once your admissions acceptances are in hand, how do you make the final important decision? Consider the following steps.

Rank the five most important features of the MBA experience for you. You might also want a second-tier group of five additional features. Focus on these ten features (feel free to add others to the list):

1. Career and placement services (placement report, number of employers recruiting on campus, quality of operation)
2. Class offerings (day, evening, summer, weekend)
3. Cost (tuition, room, board, travel, living expenses)
4. Curricular focus (ethics, diversity, international, etc.)
5. Facilities (dorms, classrooms, libraries)
6. Faculty (general quality, individual faculty members)
7. Location (geographic, urban, rural)
8. Personal considerations (spouse, family, friends)
9. Quality and reputation (general comments)

10. Teaching methodology (lectures, case studies, team projects)

Systematically compare each school with regard to each feature. Rank schools within each feature, assigning a score if you wish.

Once you have done all of the analysis, make sure your heart agrees with your head. If it's a toss-up, go with your instincts. They're probably right.

Using This Guide to Compare Programs

This guide provides answers to many of the key questions you will have about the numerous MBA programs that are available. Consult the individual program profiles as you research and gather information about schools and their specific MBA offerings. You will find the following topics addressed in each profile.

Overview

1. What are the overall characteristics of the institution (public, private, religious affiliation, establishment date, academic calendar, and location—urban, suburban, or rural)?
2. What is the size of the university at both the graduate and undergraduate level?

Highlights

3. What is the enrollment profile (full-time and part-time students; average age; average GPA; percentages of international, women, and minority students; average class size; average GMAT scores)?
4. What are the costs (full-time and part-time)?
5. Is the school accredited?

Graduate Business Programs

6. What range of graduate business programs is offered (e.g., traditional MBA, full-time, part-time, distance learning, executive MBA, MBA/JD option, MS programs)?

Admission

7. What are the acceptance rates (number of applications vs. number accepted)?
8. What are the application requirements (forms, fees, degrees, transcripts, recommendations, personal statement, GMAT scores, work experience, etc.)?
9. What else is recommended for admission (resume, essay, spreadsheet, computer experience, etc.)?

Academics

10. How large is the faculty, both full-time and part-time?

11. What are the teaching methodologies (case studies, seminars, lectures, research, corporate seminars, student presentations, team projects, etc.)?
12. What technology does the school offer (number of computers available to students, campus network, e-mail, access to the Internet, etc.)?
13. What special credit opportunities are available (transfer credits, credit by examination or portfolio review, international exchange programs, etc.)?

Finances

14. What are the full-time, part-time, day, and evening tuition costs? What are the costs of fees, room, and board?
15. What percentage of students receive financial aid? When is the application deadline?
16. What is the name, title, address, and phone number for the financial aid contact?

Facilities

17. How large is the university library in terms of volumes, microforms, and periodical holdings? Is there a network of libraries? Does the business school have its own library?
18. What computer facilities are available through the libraries?

International Students

19. What is the percentage of international students?
20. What services and facilities are available (international student office, visa services, ESL courses, counseling/support services)?
21. What special application procedures are required (TOEFL test, financial support, immunizations, etc.)?
22. What is the name, title, address, and telephone number of the international student contact?

Placement

23. What placement services are available (alumni networks, career counseling, career fairs, career library, on-campus recruiting, job banks, resume preparation, resume referral, etc.)?
24. How many companies conducted on-campus interviews last year? What are the placement rates, leading employers and industries, and average starting salaries?

Once you have completed your preliminary research and request applications from the schools of your choice, you are ready for the next step: completing your application and getting into the school of your choice.

Getting Admitted to MBA Programs

by Samuel T. Lundquist, Chief of Staff, Dean's Office, The Wharton School, University of Pennsylvania

Applicants to MBA programs often spend more time trying to figure out how to get into business school than researching the program itself. Hence, the prospective student has made the first critical error of the admissions process—seeking the elusive "admissions formula" versus making a quality presentation that demonstrates knowledge of self and graduate business education.

There really is not any formula that can predict admission to an MBA program. Business school applicants must enter the selection process understanding the difference between being admissible and being admitted. The distinction between the two varies considerably among business schools, depending on the level of selectivity in the admissions process. While some MBA programs admit all qualified students, others may deny admission to 4 of every 5 applicants who are qualified to be admitted. Understanding this difference is the first step to a successful application.

The Evaluative Process

Applicants to MBA programs should understand how they will be evaluated during the admissions process. In general, presentation, academic profile, professional work experience, and personal qualities will be the four areas in which each applicant will be evaluated. Admissions officers generally evaluate the factors influencing applicants' educational and professional decisions and the corresponding outcomes. Admissions committees do not spend a lot of time evaluating the labels that tend to categorize applicants into special groups. For instance, candidates for admission often assume that the quality of the undergraduate institution that they attended will affect the outcome of their application. A common misconception is that applicants with undergraduate degrees from Ivy League schools are always more desirable candidates for business schools. In fact, the undergraduate institution one attended may not be a significant variable in the admissions process at some business schools.

Applicants are evaluated as individuals. The environment in which they have studied or worked is relevant only when it is given meaning in the context of their life experiences. How the culture of a campus or workplace has influenced one's success is interesting and important to the admissions committee's ability to fully evaluate an application. Therefore, applicants who provide only factual information about their academic and professional profile miss the opportunity to present the most compelling and distinguishing characteristics of their candidacy.

The MBA degree is not a professional license that is required to practice management. Therefore, people of all ages are known to pursue the degree. Older applicants (32 years old and up) often fear that because they are atypical to the traditional graduate school student profile they will be less desirable to business schools. On the contrary, older students offer professional experience, maturity, and perspective that are highly valued in the classroom. The admissions committee does expect older applicants to have highly developed reasons for pursuing the MBA at this stage of their lives. Post-MBA goals are expected to be clearer and more defined than those of their younger counterparts.

Applicants have much more control of the admissions process than they realize. Prospective students determine all of the information that is presented in the application forms, essays, and interviews. They even get to select the people who will serve as references to support their candidacy. The only aspect of the process that an applicant does not control is the competition; that is, who else applies for admission. It is the competition that will determine the threshold between admissibility and acceptance.

Presentation is obviously one of the most important factors in admission. Four other areas are evaluated during the evaluative process. They include academic profile, GMAT score, professional work experience, and personal qualities.

Academic Profile

Business schools seek students who can survive the demands of a rigorous program, and the best way to show your intellectual strength is to demonstrate strong classroom achievement and high aptitude. Your ability to excel as an undergraduate student is directly related to your ability to succeed in a graduate program.

Your undergraduate specialization will have little effect on admission to business school. It is not necessary to take undergraduate courses in business administration because most MBA programs offer or require a core curriculum of basic business courses as part of the graduate degree. However, it is advisable to have basic skills in economics, calculus, and statistics in preparation for graduate study in business.

The Graduate Management Admission Test (GMAT)

Most business schools require applicants to submit the results of their Graduate Management Admission Test (GMAT). The importance of the GMAT in admissions will vary depending on the school. Minimum score requirements do not exist at some business schools. Test scores are certainly not the sole criterion for admission to an MBA program, but to one degree or another, most business schools use them as part of the admissions process.

The GMAT uses a standardized set of criteria to evaluate the basic skills of college graduates, which allows graduate schools to compare and judge applicants. The test measures general verbal and math skills so that schools can assess an applicant's ability to succeed in a graduate-level environment.

- Quantitative section—this section measures mathematical skills and the ability to solve quantitative problems.
- Qualitative section—this section focuses on verbal skills, the ability to understand and interpret written materials, and basic English writing skills.
- Scoring—total scores range from 200 to 800, but scores lower than 300 and higher than 700 are unusual.
- Analytical Writing Assessment—this section requires test-takers to write two essays that measure the ability to think critically and communicate complex ideas through writing in English. This section is scored on a scale of 0 to 6, but scores lower than 2 and higher than 5 are unusual.
- Taking the test—until recently, the GMAT was available throughout the world as a paper-and-pencil test. Since October 1997, however, the GMAT has been available in North America and many other parts of the world only as a computer-adaptive test. (Research has shown that scores from the paper-based test are comparable to those from the computer-based test.) The GMAT is offered by appointment many times each month at hundreds of locations worldwide. It is possible to schedule a test within a few days of taking it, but popular dates, such as weekends, fill up quickly. You should call the test center as early as possible to increase your chances of getting your preferred date. For more information, contact GMAT, Educational Testing Service, P.O. Box 6103, Princeton, NJ 08541-6103 (telephone: 609-771-7330; fax: 609-883-4349; Web site: http://www.gmat.org).

Professional Work Experience

Admission to selective, international business programs usually requires full-time, professional work experience prior to enrollment. While professional work experience is needed to provide a context for the interpretation and use of classroom material, students must also be able to contribute to class discussions and group projects in meaningful ways. Career success is the most effective way to prove your potential for leadership in a managerial capacity.

Personal Qualities

MBA programs want to enroll students who can lead people. The admissions committee seeks men and women who will eventually be responsible for the management of entire organizations. Leadership is one of the basic ingredients for success. Communication skills, initiative, and motivation can become the most important aspects of the admissions process. Personal qualities set the tone for the entire review of an application. It is the one part of an application that is most likely to distinguish a candidate in a compelling way.

The Interview

The interview is the one aspect of the admissions process that varies the most among schools. Some schools, like the Kellogg School at Northwestern, require all applicants to interview prior to admission. Others, such as Stanford's Graduate School of Business, do not interview any of their applicants. Most schools, like Wharton at the University of Pennsylvania, leave the decision to interview up to the applicant. It is one more part of the admissions process that the applicant can control. For those prospective students who do have the interview available to them, it is a highly recommended experience. It is also a great opportunity to take initiative in the admissions process.

If an interview is part of the admissions process, it can be an invaluable opportunity for the applicant to show the strengths and leadership qualities that most business schools are seeking in MBA candidates. The most effective and interesting interviews are those discussions that go beyond the information provided in the written application. Too often interviews remain focused solely on the candidate's resume. The meeting becomes nothing more than a redundancy in the evaluation of a candidacy. It is up to both the interviewer and the applicant to create an exchange of information that solicits useful information that will help the admissions committee understand the context of the choices that the applicant has made throughout life.

In Summary

Categories and labels do not play as significant a role in the process as most applicants assume. Prospective MBA students should take a high level of initiative during the admissions process, while exercising discretion when determining what information is most important for a school to properly evaluate their candidacy.

These guidelines are the first step in understanding the nature of the admissions process from the perspective of an admissions officer. It is vital to recognize that each school has its own policies and procedures in admissions. Careful research and communication will, fundamentally, have the greatest impact on the success of an MBA application.

GradAdvantage: Applying to Business School Just Got a Whole Lot Easier!

Thanks to a new, cutting-edge service developed by Educational Testing Service and Peterson's, and sponsored by the Graduate Management Admission Council, you can now apply to business schools online. The new service, GradAdvantage, allows you to apply to as many schools as you wish, enter most of your personal data only once, and have your application arrive at the admission office with your secure Graduate Management Admission Test (GMAT) attached.

The GradAdvantage Alliance

GradAdvantage brings together the three major players in the business-school admission arena to develop an online service to make applying to schools easier for you.

Educational Testing Service (ETS), a private, nonprofit corporation headquartered in Princeton, NJ, develops, delivers, scores, and manages score reports for "high-stakes" tests. These tests include the SAT, GRE, GMAT, and TOEFL, to name only a few. For millions of American and international students, the results of these tests have helped determine which institution they attend. Celebrating its fiftieth anniversary this year, ETS is moving in new directions to simplify the admission process for students and institutions alike and to promote its mission of education access for all.

The Graduate Management Admission Council (GMAC), an association of the 130 most prestigious business schools worldwide, provides a variety of services to MBA students and business schools alike. GMAC sponsors diversity programs such as the Ph.D. Project and Destination MBA, outreach programs such as the MBA Forums, and professional development workshops for admission deans. Material both in print and on CD, such as the Web site MBAExplorer, the computer-adaptive GMAT, and the MBA LOANS programs, show GMAC's commitment to promoting business school education and industry professionalism both in the U.S. and around the world.

Peterson's, America's largest education information/communications company, is a leading educational database publisher, the valued publishing partner of admission officers and academic deans at every level, a publisher of books and CDs, and a developer of online services designed to facilitate access to education and career guidance. Peterson's is known globally for the accuracy and breadth of its data first in print, then in software, and now on line with Peterson's Web site, petersons.com. The company is a subsidiary of The Thomson Corporation, a $7.7-billion publishing and information company. At the foundation of most of its activities is the country's largest education data collection, covering kindergarten through executive training and adult education, which is revised and expanded annually.

The GradAdvantage Web Site: gradadvantage.org

At gradadvantage.org, you will find a wealth of information about business schools, financing options, and GMAT registration, as well as a variety of ways to prepare for taking the GMAT and applying to business schools. Click on "New and Registered User Login" to begin applying to business schools on line.

When you click on the "Program Search & Financing" tab at the bottom of the screen, you'll find yourself with two choices: links to mba.petersons.com and to MBAExplorer, the GMAC Web site. In MBAExplorer, you can delve into information about MBA programs around the world and find links to those institutions' Web sites, learn about financing your business school education, buy the Pre-MBA CD and GMAT test-prep products at the GMAC online store, and check out GMAC's calendar of events.

Click on mba.petersons.com and search for the right business school for you by name, concentration, location, average GMAT score, and enrollment size, or do keyword searches to look for particular MBA programs in Peterson's searchable database. Numerous In-Depth Descriptions include detailed program and faculty information. You can join Peterson's MBA discussion board, purchase books and CDs, and find information about distance-learning MBA programs, GMAT test preparation, and financing your education.

The Benefits to You

With GradAdvantage, you can complete your applications on line, save your work, and return to it later. You no longer have to find a typewriter or try to match application spacing with your computer printer. It's easy to revise answers or essays as you rethink the questions during the application process before you submit your application.

GradAdvantage will save you lots of time. You can enter most information into multiple applications at the same time. If, for example, you are applying to four schools, as you fill in data in the "Biographical," "Education," "Activities," and "Employment" tabs, the information automatically cross-fills into the data fields in the other three applications. You will only have to respond to questions on the "Programs" and the "Essay" tabs in each application.

You no longer have to worry about express mail or courier services to have your application arrive at the admission offices on time. On average, most MBA applicants have jobs and work on their applications late at night the week or two before applications are due. Now all you have to do is click on "Submit" and your application is on its way to the institutions you designate. GradAdvantage's modest $12-per-application fee costs less than many express services—and is much less hassle.

You can pay by credit card to further save you time. Just enter your American Express, MasterCard, or Visa credit card number on the "Finish" tab, and your application will arrive with its electronic payment attached.

Your secure GMAT scores will arrive already integrated into your application. ETS has worked closely with Peterson's to guarantee the security of score data. All you have to do is provide information used to ensure that score matching is accurate.

You can work on your application anywhere as long as you can access the Web. All you have to do is remember the URL for the GradAdvantage service: gradadvantage.org. The platform- and browser-independent service works with both PCs and Macs and on both Internet Explorer and Netscape and requires no substantial upgrades in hardware or software.

You can also track the progress of each of your applications using GradAdvantage's "Application Manager" interface.

The Future of GradAdvantage

In the future, you will be able to find a host of new functionalities on GradAdvantage to further streamline the application process. To make your life even easier, on gradadvantage.org you will be able to:

• Request additional GMAT score reports
• Have your college transcripts and letters of recommendation electronically authenticated and sent to designated institutions
• Access international transcript-evaluation services
• Learn more about financing your MBA through a variety of financial aid services
• Discover more in-depth information about business schools you should consider in online MBA Forum events

Welcome to the new world of electronic applications! ETS, Peterson's, GMAC, and GradAdvantage's participating institutions encourage you to save time and money and apply online using GradAdvantage.

Paying for Your MBA

by Bart Astor

Now that you've made a commitment to getting your MBA, the next question is likely to be "How will I pay for it?"

The first thing you will have to decide is whether you will go to school part-time and continue working full-time or go to school full-time while working part-time. About two thirds of MBA students get their degree while they continue working at a full-time job. And though it will take you longer to get your MBA this way, the costs are more manageable and the amount of money you'll need to borrow is kept to a minimum. Furthermore, if you work for one of the many companies that offers either full or partial tuition reimbursement to their employees, this will further reduce your expenses.

Some MBA programs, on the other hand, are only available to full-time students. If you go to one of these schools, it will be impossible for you to work full-time. Therefore, you will have to make some other arrangement to pay the expenses of your schooling and to find the necessary resources for your living expenses.

But it is not only possible to find the resources you will need, it is also quite likely. Unfortunately, though, for most full-time MBA students, most of the money is available through student loans. And the amount of debt an MBA student takes on can be quite sizable.

Most MBA students feel it is worthwhile to take on some debt to pay for a degree that they believe will offer them considerable career advancement. In that sense, then, they view these costs as an investment in their earnings potential. And the numbers have consistently supported this claim. A quick look at Table 1: Average Starting Salary Offers for Non-MBA and MBA Graduates shows that the salary for holders of an MBA is 25 to 40 percent higher than for non-MBA graduates.

TABLE 1: AVERAGE STARTING SALARY OFFERS FOR NON-MBA AND MBA GRADUATES

Degree (field of study)	Starting Salary Offer
BA (Arts & Letters)	$27,608
BA (Business)	31,437
MBA (nontechnical undergraduate degree)	$36,133
MBA (technical undergraduate degree)	47,760

Reprinted from the July 1998 Salary Survey, with permission from the National Association of Colleges and Employers (copyright holder).

Looking only at earnings potential, getting an MBA has certainly proved to be an excellent financial investment. And, of course, this does not even consider career opportunities or quality-of-life issues.

The Costs

Now let's look at the cost of getting your MBA degree. All students are required to pay some sort of tuition or fee to go to school (in some state-supported business schools, this may be called a "fee"). This can be a total amount for the year, regardless of the number of credits you take, or a per-credit amount. The annual tuition for a full-time student can range from $2000 or $4000 at some of the state-supported schools to well over $20,000 at some of the higher-priced business schools. In addition, some business schools require all students to pay fees for such things as student activities, health services, etc., much like you may have paid as an undergraduate.

Most business school students pay a little more for books and supplies than they did as an undergraduate. While the amount will differ at each school, the annual amount for a full-time student ranges from $500 to $800. If you will need a computer, that will naturally add a considerable amount to the total cost. Many business schools make computers available to their students, so be sure to check with the school before you purchase a computer. These are the two obvious additional expense categories you will face when you go to business school, and they are generally referred to as "direct costs."

In addition, however, there are other "indirect costs" you face that you may not think of as business school expenses. Rent and living expenses are certainly the largest two. But indirect costs also include transportation to and from school, travel from your home town to the city in which the school is located, personal expenses, and other expenses if appropriate (such as car loan payments and insurance, child care, summer tuition, medical expenses, etc.). If you are going to business school straight out of college, you may not have had to personally pay for these expenses before (although your parents certainly did). If you have been paying them already, then you know you may need to cut back on the amount you spend on some discretionary items, such as clothing and entertainment. As a student, you will have to budget your expenses as carefully as you budget your time. Most business schools can tell you what the average cost of living will be in the area and may offer subsidized housing or, at the very least, a housing office to help you find a place to live.

Financial Aid

Once you've calculated the total amount it will cost you to go to business school, you may find that the amount of income you receive won't be enough. That's where financial aid comes in. If you received financial aid as an undergraduate, then you have a head start: at least you understand some of the basics.

But financial aid is quite different for graduate students. For one, all graduate students are considered independent for federal financial aid. That means your parents are not required to assist you financially (although if they are willing and able, that would certainly help). Secondly, there is very little grant and scholarship money available to graduate students. The bulk of your expenses will be paid either from money you've already saved, money you will earn while you are attending school, or money you will borrow and pay back out of future earnings.

Most business school students take on considerable debt to pay their expenses since there are very few alternatives. If you're going to school part-time and working full-time, your salary in combination with your savings may be enough to avoid having to borrow very much. However, you may still decide it is better to borrow through a government-subsidized loan program than take the necessary funds out of your savings or current income.

If you've decided to go to school full-time, you will probably need to borrow, although many business schools offer fellowships and teaching and research assistantships to some students. Some of these positions and awards may be awarded based on your previous academic and employment record (merit-based) and some based on how much you need it. While everyone will say they need assistance, the definition of need for financial aid is up to the school, not you.

Applying for Financial Aid

When you apply for financial aid, you are generally applying for both merit-based and need-based aid. The application process has changed significantly in the past year or two, so even if you applied for financial aid as an undergraduate, you should pay close attention to the process described here

To qualify for federal aid, most of which will be in the form of loans, every student is required to complete the Free Application for Federal Student Aid (FAFSA), either in paper or electronic form (either FAFSA Express, a diskette available from the government, or FAFSA on the Web). The paper form is available in both business school and undergraduate school financial aid offices (your local community college or even your local high school guidance office will have them available as well). The computer software, FAFSA Express, can be ordered by calling 800-801-0576. And you can access FAFSA on the Web at the Internet address: http://www.ed.gov

Soon after January 1, 1999 (for students entering in the fall of 1999 or spring 2000), you should complete the FAFSA, which asks about your 1998 income and current assets. The application cannot be completed until after January 1, 1999.

Many business schools require that you complete a different application, the Financial Aid PROFILE, to begin the financial aid process and require the form to be completed much earlier, in October or November of 1998. The paper ver-

Types of Financial Aid

Gift Aid (money you do not have to pay back)
Individual grants, scholarships, and fellowships (may be merit-based or need-based)
Sources: business schools, foundations, private companies, community groups

Tuition waivers (awarded by individual business schools)

Company employee educational benefits (a personnel benefit for employees of many large and some small companies. Generally covers only a portion of tuition)

Federal grants (very limited and based on need)

State grants (also very limited)

Self-Help Aid (money you must earn or pay back later)
Work Programs
Federal Work-Study (need-based and awarded by business school)—Source: federal government

Teaching Assistantships—Source: business school

Resident Assistantships—Source: business school

Research Assistantships—Source: business school

Loans
Federal Perkins Loan (need-based, lender is business school)

Federal Subsidized Stafford Loan (need-based, lender is a bank, savings & loan, etc.)

Federal Unsubsidized Stafford Loan (non-need-based)

Federal Direct Loan (similar to Stafford Loans; lender is the federal government)

Private loan programs (e.g., MBA Loans; Business Access Loans, etc.)

Tuition payment plans (private or school-based)

---

sion of the PROFILE information is available from the same places as the FAFSA. It is also available on the Internet at http://www.collegeboard.org

You can also call a toll-free number (800-778-6888) and "register" your information, including which business schools you are applying to. You must also pay a registration fee of $5 plus $14.50 per school. A few weeks later you will receive your customized application form containing all the questions the particular schools you are applying to require answers to.

You may have to complete both the FAFSA and the PROFILE. The way to find out is check the PROFILE registration packet for the list of schools that require the PROFILE. You should also read the business school literature or ask someone in the business school financial aid office to be certain.

A few business schools will have their own aid application or use yet a third form, called Need Access. This information will be noted in the brochures they send to you, so be sure to check the literature. Make certain you know if there are deadlines when applying for financial aid. Applying after a deadline can hurt your chances of qualifying for aid.

Once you have submitted an application, the business schools you have designated will receive an output showing an amount you can afford to contribute to your education, calculated based on your income and assets. This number is called the "Expected Family Contribution" (EFC). The EFC from the federal form is the official amount that determines whether you will qualify for federal aid. If this amount is less than the total cost of attendance of the MBA program, you have demonstrated need and will qualify for aid, again, usually low-cost, government-subsidized loans. The output from the PROFILE will give the school an estimate of your federal eligibility and will also give an expected contribution based on additional criteria you provided. This contribution will be used by those schools using the PROFILE to award their own funds. And, like the federal EFC, if your contribution is less than the total cost of the school, you qualify for need-based aid.

But even if your family contribution is higher than the cost of the school, you may still qualify for aid. For one, this EFC is based on your previous year's income, which will likely change significantly when you go to school full-time. You can appeal to the business school financial aid office and ask them to recalculate your need based on the amount you will have when you go to school, rather than on your previous year's income. Secondly, there are government, institutional, and private loans available to students regardless of whether they have demonstrated need (such as the Federal Unsubsidized Stafford Loan, MBA Loans, and Business Access Loans). Although these loans ultimately cost borrowers more since they are not subsidized, they are still sources of income for you to pay your business school costs.

Your Credit History

Since most MBA students have to borrow to pay for their education, making sure you qualify for a loan is critical. For the most part that means your credit record must be free of default or delinquency. You can check your credit history with one or more of the following four major credit bureaus and clean up any adverse credit that appears. You can look up the local numbers in your phone book or call the numbers below:

Equifax
P.O. Box 105873
Atlanta, GA 30348
800-685-1111
Fax: 404-612-3150

CSC Credit Services
Consumer Assistance Center
P.O. Box 674402
Houston, TX 77267-4402
800-759-5979

Trans Union Corporation
P.O. Box 390
Springfield, PA 19064-0390
800-888-4213

Experian
P.O. Box 9530
Allen, TX 75013
888-397-3742

Debt Management

Although the limits on borrowing from federal and private programs are quite high, you will want to make sure you are not borrowing more than you will later be able to repay. Use Table 2 below to estimate your MBA school loan monthly payments. Then by estimating your income and the total amount you'll need to borrow for your MBA education, you can use Table 3 to determine whether your loan payments will be affordable.

TABLE 2: ESTIMATED LOAN REPAYMENT SCHEDULE
Monthly Payments for Every $1000 Borrowed

Rate	5 years	10 years	15 years	20 years	25 years
5%	$18.87	$10.61	$ 7.91	$ 6.60	$ 5.85
8%	20.28	12.13	9.56	8.36	7.72
9%	20.76	12.67	10.14	9.00	8.39
10%	21.74	13.77	10.75	9.65	9.09
12%	22.24	14.35	12.00	11.01	10.53
14%	23.27	15.53	13.32	12.44	12.04

You can use this table to estimate your monthly payments on a loan for any of the five repayment periods (5, 10, 15, 20, and 25 years). The amounts listed are the monthly payments for a $1000 loan for each of the interest rates. To estimate your monthly payment, choose the closest interest rate and multiply the amount of the payment listed by the total amount of your loan and then divide by 1,000. For example, for a total loan of $15,000 at 9% to be paid back over 10 years, multiply $12.67 times 15,000 (190,050) divided by 1,000. This yields $190.05 per month.

TABLE 3: DEBT MANAGEMENT GUIDE

Total Outstanding Loan	Years in Repayment	Monthly Payment	Suggested Minimum Monthly Income
$10,000	10	$126	$ 840
20,000	10	253	1,687
30,000	10	380	2,533
40,000	10	506	3,373
50,000	10	633	4,220
20,000	20	179	1,193
30,000	20	270	1,800
40,000	20	360	2,400
50,000	20	450	3,000

International Students

Costs of U.S. business schools for international students are the same as or slightly higher than for U.S. residents. Your Certificate of Eligibility for a student visa will require that you prove that you have sufficient funds for the entire MBA program. United States government aid for international students is virtually nonexistent, and very few business schools make any resources available. You should make sure you have obtained the necessary funds from your own resources, including from your own government.

Additional Information

For more information about financing your education, refer to the personnel office at the company for whom you work and the business school financial aid office. You can also obtain additional information on possible sources of aid from the following Peterson's publications.

• *Grants for Graduate and Postdoctoral Study*
• *Financing Graduate School*

For information about loan options, you can contact the following organizations:

The Access Group
P.O. Box 7400
Wilmington, DE 19803-0400
800-292-1330

Business and Professional Women's Foundation
Loan Programs
2012 Massachusetts Avenue, NW
Washington, DC 20036
202-293-1200

ConSern Loans for Education
205 Van Buren Street, Suite 200
Herndon, VA 22070
800-SOS-LOAN

The Education Resource Institute (TERI)
330 Stuart Street, Suite 500
Boston, MA 02116
800-255-TERI

MBA Loans
2400 Broadway, Suite 230
Santa Monica, CA 90404
800-366-6227

New England Education Loan Marketing Corporation
(Nellie Mae)
50 Braintree Hill Park, Suite 300
Braintree, MA 02184
800-634-9308

USA Group Affinity Loan
P.O. Box 6182
Indianapolis, IN 46206
800-635-3785

Sallie Mae Smart Loan Consolidation
P.O. Box 1304
Merrifield, VA 22116-1304
800-524-9100

U.S. Department of Education
Office of Student Financial Assistance
400 Maryland Avenue
Washington, DC 20202
800-433-3243 (Federal Student Aid Information Center)

Going Abroad for Your MBA

by Richard Edelstein

Students are increasingly going abroad to obtain their MBA education. Why? Individuals seeking a management career must prepare themselves to function in international contexts on a global scale. Studying abroad is one of the most effective ways of obtaining knowledge and developing skills that respond to these new demands. In large measure, this reflects the changing nature of business where the globalization of markets and companies is forcing a rethinking of the types of education and experience necessary to pursue a successful career as a manager.

International mobility, cross-cultural skills, and foreign language proficiency have all increased in value to employers. Technical skills remain critical, but international experience and knowledge are increasingly appreciated by companies. Choosing to pursue your MBA education abroad is an excellent way to acquire knowledge and skills that are necessary for the global economy.

This trend of attaching increased value to international experience is most noteworthy in transnational companies that have operations and management responsibility distributed in numerous countries. Hewlett Packard, for example, reorganized its personal computer division and made Grenoble, France, the location of its top management team. This reflects the reality that most of HP's personal computer sales are outside the U.S. It also may be related to the rapid growth of communications technologies that allow companies to communicate easily with management teams irrespective of geographic location.

Another indication of increased demand for managers with specialized international experience and skills is the growth in importance of the so-called "transitional economies" like China, India, Russia, Brazil, and Indonesia. Many firms want to develop joint ventures or start-up operations in these countries but are constrained by lack of personnel who can manage in such different cultural and linguistic contexts. Demand for MBAs who have experience in these countries and have language skills is very high.

Career Paths in Different Countries

The MBA degree is not recognized as the ideal qualification for a business career in all countries. Its acceptance in the U.S. and by many multinational firms as a primary qualification for future managers sometimes leaves the impression of a universal acceptance worldwide. In fact, the majority of countries outside the U.S. have significantly different educational and career paths for their managers. For example, the most common educational qualification for future managers in many countries is an engineering degree. This is the case in Germany, Switzerland, the Scandinavian countries, and many countries in the developing world, such as India and China. Even in France, Belgium, Italy, and Spain, engineering training is a major source of recruitment of managers. Another educational qualification for a business career quite common in other nations is a law degree.

The lack of universal acceptance of the MBA does not imply that it may not be an excellent way to launch your own career. In a world full of different educational philosophies, cultural values, and economic systems, there cannot be a single form of preparation for becoming a manager. The MBA is still the most common qualification for business managers. Nevertheless, it is important to keep in mind that it may not be met with the same degree of acceptance in all countries. This is important to consider if you have particular aspirations to work in countries where it may not have the same recognition that it does in the U.S. It also is useful information for anyone who plans to work in a multinational enterprise where professional colleagues may come from any country. The MBA is only one way to acquire the knowledge and skills necessary to manage a company.

Markets, Hierarchies, and Prestige

Not all MBAs are created equal! Given the choice between going to Harvard or a correspondence course from an unknown institution for your MBA, the answer is obvious. In reality the choice is never that clear, and many individuals must make compromises between where they would like to pursue their degree and where they have a serious chance of being accepted. This is true whether you are applying to institutions in your home country or abroad.

If you want to pursue an MBA abroad, it is important to do some research about the schools you are considering. Learn about their status in the prestige hierarchy and the types of companies that are likely to employ their graduates. Going to a school of high prestige is not always the best choice, depending upon your own abilities and professional goals. Students applying to American schools from abroad frequently assume that the only schools worth attending are the most elite and prestigious schools with international reputations. In fact, the range of schools offering high-quality MBA programs is much larger in number than the top twenty institutions that make it on the *BusinessWeek* survey. Reputation and prestige are important factors to consider in planning your MBA education, but keep in mind that prestige alone does not assure you of an education that is best suited to your individual needs. This is true abroad as well as at home.

Making the Decision to Study Abroad

Why go abroad for your MBA when you can just as easily enter an American program that has an international dimension built into the program? The answer for many people is that they want and need a more intensive experience abroad that allows them to acquire foreign language and cultural skills and to build professional networks that cannot be obtained through an American program. Traveling and becoming a "citizen of the world" are also appealing, although more romantic, reasons for some students. Before you decide to pursue your MBA in another country, however, it is important to consider a few key points.

Personal Goals and Foreign Language Ability

Personal attributes will define whether or not study abroad for an MBA is the right choice for you. Have you already had extensive experiences abroad? Previous experience may make the added value of doing your graduate business studies abroad less significant. But, what about building on the skills you acquired in your previous experience and developing high levels of language competence and specialized knowledge in the country or region where you would like to study?

Studying abroad is clearly a more intensive international experience than anything you could pursue in the U.S. In the end, it is this intensity that distinguishes getting the MBA abroad from getting it at home. If you are doubtful about the need for this intensity of international experience, then you may want to consider staying in the U.S. and entering a program that includes an international emphasis of less intensive character.

Foreign language proficiency can be a defining criterion in deciding whether or not to consider studying abroad. Although there are an increasing number of MBA programs abroad that are taught in English, many of them require some level of proficiency in foreign languages. The United Kingdom, Australia, New Zealand, Hong Kong, and Singapore have MBA programs in English, but most of them are oriented toward a national employment market. Many of the European English-language MBA programs outside these countries are targeted to foreign nationals and actually include few students from the home country where the school is located. The "flagship" management studies program of the school is often taught in the local language and limits admission to students who can demonstrate language proficiency.

A distinction should be made between international MBA programs taught in English and national MBA programs taught in the local language. Each has its market niche and serves different needs. A good example of an institution offering both types of programs is SDA Bocconi in Italy. Bocconi created an English-language international MBA that responds to the needs of students who seek to develop an international career. However, the traditional Bocconi degree program is taught in Italian, is more prestigious, and has an international reputation for training managers, especially for the Italian market. In considering which program to apply to, an American needs to consider both foreign language proficiency and personal needs and goals.

Structure and Cost of MBA Programs Abroad

MBA programs outside the U.S. are frequently structured differently. In Europe, for example, some MBAs are only one year long. Typically this involves 12 months of intensive study with no summer break. In the U.K., the MBA is most often two years in length, following a more American model. Whatever the length of the program, it may have somewhat different course requirements and curricula. Frequently, teaching approaches are also different. Sometimes they are closely tied to the patterns of university education in the host country. Increasing attention is being paid to teaching skills related to teamwork and working in cross-national groups.

Another point to consider is the tendency of off-shore MBA programs to be more application-oriented and less tied to the research faculty. MBA programs in other countries vary significantly in the emphasis placed on teaching versus research as a major focus of faculty reward systems.

The cost of MBA programs outside the U.S. is generally quite competitive, even when you consider the added cost of airfare. Tuition costs for graduate education in the U.S., especially at elite private universities, are among the highest in the world. All in all, you may find the cost of an MBA abroad surprisingly reasonable by comparison. Keep in mind that there is significant variation among schools, so the generalization that programs are less costly has its exceptions.

Cultural Adjustment

Cultural adjustment is a factor that should be considered in applying to an overseas program. Unless you have spent an extended period of time in the country you plan to study in, you are likely to be affected by this change. Reactions to living in another culture vary considerably depending on the person and on the culture. There is always a greater difference in lifestyle, values, and professional life than expected, no matter which country you go to. As noted earlier, acquiring the skill to work and learn in more than one culture is a primary reason for wanting to study abroad in the first place. Still, do not assume this is an easy adjustment or task. It takes a serious commitment to self-improvement and a willingness to be open to entirely new situations to succeed in cross-cultural settings.

Building Professional Networks

One of the keys to a career as a successful manager is the capacity to develop networks of individuals whom you can work with and learn from. These professional networks may be within your present employer, with colleagues in other firms, and, increasingly, in other nations. By choosing to pursue an MBA abroad, you should recognize that you will build different professional networks than you would in the U.S. Alumni associations that are a fixture in American universities and business schools tend to be less well developed in other countries, but where you went to school is often a critical factor in what job opportunities you may have in the future.

In some cases, Americans have some advantages when it comes to applying to MBA programs abroad. Since the MBA is essentially an American invention, one of the most significant ways of gaining credibility for an MBA program outside the

U.S. is to begin attracting American students who might otherwise attend an American institution. Although poorly qualified candidates will not be admitted no matter what their national origin, all things being equal, Americans sometimes have an advantage in the selection process at some schools. This may not continue to be true for very long as more Americans begin enrolling in foreign programs. But for the time being, many MBA programs abroad are interested in recruiting Americans.

Finding the Right Program

Where Do You Want to Work?

One obvious reason for choosing to study for an MBA abroad is to increase your chances of obtaining employment outside the U.S. If you have your heart set on living and working in France or Indonesia, then it makes sense to seriously consider attending an institution in that country. This is especially true if you select a school and program linked to the national employment market. While global markets are certainly a long-term trend, national employment markets are still the norm for most firms, and doing your studies in a particular country will generally enhance your chances of obtaining employment in that country.

This is accomplished in two ways. First, your degree and school/university will be more easily recognized in that national employment market. Second, the school may have placement services, alumni relations, and other ways of connecting graduates into the labor market for management positions. Even if you elect to work for a transnational firm, there are significant benefits to being able to access this national network of business professionals.

Which Country and What Language?

MBA-type degrees are more prevalent in countries like England, France, Belgium, and the Netherlands than in other European countries. In these countries there may be numerous institutions from which to choose. In the remaining European countries, choices are much more limited and may require significant foreign language skill. One way to increase your options is to consider enrolling in a university program in business and economics. In France, for example, there are many degree programs in universities that offer business degrees that are targeted to the national and European job market, often based in an Institut d'Administration des Enterprises or IAE. University-based options are also available in other European countries but in virtually all cases require host country language fluency and a willingness to be one of few foreigners in a program.

In Latin America, the options are numerous if one includes university-based programs in business and economics. Pure MBA-type options are much more limited and often involve only one or two institutions in the country. Still, Latin American countries have created a number of good business schools that offer MBA programs that have international standing. Gatulio Vargas in São Paulo, ESAN in Peru, IESE in Venezuela, and INCAE in Costa Rica/Nicaragua are examples of institutions that offer programs that may interest prospective American students.

In Asia and the Pacific Rim, options are more limited. This is partly due to distinctly different educational systems that reflect different recruitment practices for managers. Japan is well known for a manager recruitment structure that relies on in-company training rather than professional education in the university. This pattern can also be found in other Asian countries, though to a somewhat lesser degree. In Japan, the language barrier can be significant since very few Japanese universities have programs targeted to foreigners taught in English. Combined with the cultural tendency toward in-company education, this makes Japan especially difficult for foreigners to penetrate. One noteworthy exception is the IUJ, the International University of Japan, which does offer an MBA program in English.

Hong Kong, Australia, and New Zealand have MBA programs that are open to Americans and are taught in English. Most are university-based business schools that follow either the American or British models of university education. The Hong Kong programs tend to be focused on special needs of Hong Kong and China. The Australian programs are frequently oriented toward doing business in Asia, especially Southeast Asia. Schools in the Philippines, Indonesia, Malaysia, Singapore, and Thailand may also be of interest to those interested in working in one of the countries that are developing dynamic economies in the midst of transition and rapid growth. The English-based MBA courses are very limited, however, and careful research needs to be done to ensure that the program is up to international standards. The Asian Institute of Management in Manila and Singapore National University are two programs that have gained international credibility in the last decade.

Foreign language requirements are often significant, even at schools that teach in English. Since the study of foreign languages is more commonplace outside the U.S., you should be prepared to study a foreign language even if you are entering an English language-based program. Be sure to inform yourself about foreign language requirements prior to entering a program as this may be an important consideration in preparing for your experience.

Evaluating Quality

In evaluating the quality of a school you need to go deeper than the promotional piece typically sent to prospective students. Are the school and degree accredited by the Ministry of Education in the country where the degree is offered? Too often the school may be licensed by the department of commerce or industry as a business, but its degrees are not recognized by the country's university-level education authorities, usually in the Ministry of Education. If a program is not recognized as academically legitimate in the country where it operates, it is doubtful that its graduates have credibility in the international employment market. The embassy or consulate of the country in which an institution is located can also provide useful information.

A close, common-sense look at faculty qualifications is also important. Are faculty members qualified to teach at the advanced level of an MBA-type program by virtue of their education and experience? How many are full-time permanent

faculty? How many are part-time or "contact only" faculty? How many faculty members hold a doctoral degree in the field in which they teach? Be cautious of schools that say they have no full-time faculty because they prefer part-time instructors. This can be a ploy to avoid paying qualified people who require higher levels of salary. Have faculty members done any research or published any articles? Do they have corporate or professional experience related to the course work?

It is always useful to speak with some graduates of the school prior to making a commitment to enroll. Schools will usually provide you with the names of several graduates whom you can contact about their experiences with the school. You can usually get a sense of the quality of the experience they had by asking questions about what the classes were like, how good were the faculty, and what kind of placement services the school provided. If it is possible to make a visit to the school and meet with current students, this is even better.

Financing Your International MBA

As noted earlier, tuition costs abroad are rarely more than those found among leading MBA programs in the U.S. That is not saying much since costs in the U.S. can be as high as $25,000 annually for tuition alone! Still, you are likely to find that MBA programs abroad compare favorably to most cost/benefit analyses. This is especially true for some of the less well known programs that may be outside major capital cities. In instances where the program is less than two years in length, this may also be a factor in considering costs.

Where you may run into problems is in obtaining federally subsidized loans such as are commonly available through many American university financial aid offices. Most of these loans have some restrictions regarding the status of institutions and programs that you can attend and still be eligible for the loan program. Although some loan programs have been more flexible than others in allowing foreign study, you should check with your bank or lender regarding the regulations that apply.

Some institutions have their own loan programs and scholarships to help defray the costs of tuition. Less common are work opportunities, since MBA programs generally require a full-time commitment. Still, it is worth asking the school about the potential for working on campus or assisting in research or consulting activity.

Other major costs to consider are round-trip air travel and the costs of living abroad. In some countries, especially in Europe and Asia, the cost of housing and food will be significantly higher than in the U.S., depending on the specific location.

Studying and Living Abroad

Living abroad requires adaptability, an adventurous spirit, and a willingness to adjust to living in another culture. You will acquire a set of skills and experiences that will contribute to your preparation as a manager and a deeper understanding of your strengths, weaknesses, and values, even if you already have some cross-cultural experience.

Cross-cultural experience is always a challenge and an opportunity. It is always useful to do a lot of reading on the country and region you will live in prior to your departure. Knowing something about the history, geography, and culture is critical to learning how to adapt in your new culture. There are many good reference books available at bookstores and libraries that can help prepare you for your experience abroad. You might also explore the Internet for "chat" groups sharing information on studying and working abroad.

There are often support networks that you can take advantage of when you are abroad. Although you may have a desire to "go native" and avoid anything that is American while abroad, you may want to consider joining groups such as churches, university clubs, and alumni groups abroad as a means to enlarge your support system while living abroad.

The important thing to remember is that not only are you adapting to the rigors of pursuing an MBA program, but also that you will need energy and effort to deal with the adaptation required of the foreign visitor. But, again, this is precisely the reason for pursuing this path in the first place.

International Programs at U.S. Schools

If you are still having doubts as to whether or not studying for an MBA abroad is the right choice for you, you can consider attending one of many MBA programs in the U.S. that incorporate some international experience into the curriculum. This is clearly a less intensive option and cannot compare with living abroad but may be preferable depending upon your needs and goals.

This guide includes information on a range of MBA programs that have international dimensions built into their programs. Several schools that offer a master's degree in international business (requiring significant language and cultural knowledge) rather than a classic MBA are the Lauder Program at the University of Pennsylvania (a joint program of the Wharton School and the College of Arts and Science) and the MIBS programs at the University of South Carolina, Columbia University, and the American Graduate School of International Management–Thunderbird in Glendale, Arizona.

An increasing number of MBA programs include an international track or international fellows program that requires advanced foreign language competence and an internship abroad. Institutions offering programs with this type of option include UCLA, University of Washington, University of Michigan, University of Chicago, University of Pittsburgh, University of Memphis, Indiana University, San Diego State University, University of Hawaii, and the University of Southern California.

A few MBA programs include joint-degree or double-degree options in conjunction with a business school in another country. The University of Texas at Austin has several double-degree programs that allow a student to pursue a Texas MBA and with a year abroad also acquire a French, German, or Mexican degree at the same time. NYU's Stern School has one of the most extensive exchange programs with foreign business schools of any U.S. university, and a significant percentage of MBA students take advantage of this option. Also available are joint-degree programs that combine an MBA with a master's or doctoral degree in an area specialty such as Asian studies or Eastern European studies. The University of Pittsburgh, the

University of Michigan, and the University of California at Berkeley are among the business schools offering this type of option.

Many other MBA programs are including international internships and group projects outside the U.S. as a major component of their programs. The University of Pennsylvania's Wharton School has integrated a project abroad into the MBA program for a portion of its students. The same is true for the University of California at Berkeley and the University of Michigan.

Does the trend in American MBA programs to integrate international experience for some students make the case for going abroad for the MBA any less compelling? Probably not. An MBA program in the U.S. can never match the intense learning experience of spending a year or two in another country studying business. Moreover, the personal and professional contacts you make while abroad allow you to create an international network that cannot be easily duplicated when studying in most American MBA programs. In the end, you need to weigh the benefits of gaining an intense international experience along with other factors, such as the quality and prestige of the institutions you are considering.

International Students Considering U.S. Programs

Recent years have seen significant increases in the percentages of foreign student enrollments in MBA programs. It is estimated that 20 percent of all business students studying in American colleges and universities are from countries other than the U.S. It is clear that obtaining an MBA in the U.S. is very attractive for many students. Why?

American higher education continues to have a level of quality that places it among the best in the world. It is also attractive because the MBA was invented in the U.S., and obtaining the "original and genuine article" still has some prestige, especially as viewed from abroad. Perhaps an even more important, but less recognized, factor is that studying in the U.S. gives foreign students many of the same international skills and networks that are described above. This can be a tremendous advantage for students who aspire to work for companies with global markets and international management teams.

Will MBA study in the U.S. continue to be as attractive in the future and will it be for the same reasons? The answer to these questions is less clear for several reasons. As business education becomes more of a global commodity and schools outside the U.S. improve the quality of their programs, it may be less appealing to pay the high cost of studying in the U.S. Second, distance learning capabilities may result in greater possibilities for undertaking MBA education without coming to the U.S. Questions of quality and intensity of interaction with other students and faculty make this option less attractive for now, but this is already changing at some U.S. institutions. Finally, MBA education may increasingly be offered by joint ventures or partnerships among and between institutions in several countries, using faculty and facilities in numerous locations. This internationalization of the postgraduate education market will, if it actually happens, alter many of the structures and processes that are currently considered "normal" for most universities and management education centers.

Returning to School for Your MBA

by Barbara B. Reinhold, Ed.D., Director, Career Development, Smith College

Some decisions can be made and implemented quickly—you can often choose a new car, a new place to live, or even a new relationship rather impetuously and have it work out just fine. For the returning student, however, the process of deciding, applying to school, and then earning an MBA is seldom simple. It has to be done with a great deal of forethought and awareness of the considerable sacrifice required.

The good news about being a more mature student is that you'll probably get much more out of it, because there is more of you to take to the classroom—more experience, better judgment, clearer goals, and more appreciation for learning. The bad news is that your life will be more "squeezed" than it would have been before you took on all of life's responsibilities, particularly balancing work and family. In general, however, later is often better than sooner when it comes to getting an MBA.

For mature women and men alike, there are many things to consider before upending your life to pursue an MBA. First, be sure you really need one. It is silly to waste your time and resources being "retooled" in an MBA program if your career goals could be accomplished just as easily by taking targeted courses, getting more training and supervision through your employer, or using your connections to enter a different field or organization and move up. If you are trying to determine if an MBA is really the key to where you want to go, find ways to network with people whose lives and career goals are similar to yours. You might discover that a variety of routes could lead you to your desired goal.

It's essential that you make your own decision about whether and where to apply, using a blend of logic and intuition. Though an MBA requires strong quantitative skills, you'll also need good organizational, decision-making, and communication skills. For returning students, success in an MBA program is often due more to life and work experience than technical knowledge alone. You have more information, more common sense, and more self-awareness at your disposal than you did as an undergraduate student. Use these assets along with your intuition in deciding whether this is really right for you now.

TEN TIPS FOR RETURNING STUDENTS

DECIDING

1. Be sure an MBA is the best route to where you're going—don't embark on a trip until your destination is clear.
2. Make your own decision, using a blend of logic and intuition.
3. Be a discerning customer; ask hard questions about which programs best meet your specific needs.

ARRIVING

4. Learn to market yourself; don't launch the campaign until you're ready.
5. Be sure your support system is in order—at home and at work.
6. Review your skills—technical, quantitative, written, and oral. If you're not really ready to do well yet, take an extra year to polish those skills.
7. Measure your confidence level—if it's weak, consider counseling to learn how to manage your anxieties and self-doubts.
8. Get your life in good shape before you begin—paying attention to nutrition, exercise, relationships, and all the other things you'll need to sustain you.

THRIVING

9. Ascertain your most effective learning style (from your own self-assessment or more formalized measurements, such as the Learning Styles Inventory or the Myers-Briggs Type Inventory) and design routines and study regimens that best fit your style.
10. Find a group of friends/colleagues right away; collaboration is the key to succeeding and staying healthy through one of the most demanding experiences you'll ever have.

It's important also to be an informed and demanding customer on the front end of the process. Be sure to ask hard questions about how well a school is prepared to respond to the particular concerns you might have, such as being a minority candidate, having children, needing special accommodations of some type, or being in your forties or fifties. The ball will be in their court later; in the first half of the game, however, be aggressive about getting the information you need. For more mature students, the philosophy, resources, and services of the school can be much more important than ranking or reputation.

The application stage is also a great time to practice your marketing skills. This may be the first of many times when you'll have to convince someone of your worth. For returning students this is often frightening. Some have been out of the job market for awhile, while others either want to change careers or are feeling stuck at a career plateau. Any of these situations is likely to leave you feeling less than competitive. This is a good time to figure out what you really have to offer to a particular school and to adjust to the notion of lifelong self-advocacy.

As you begin the difficult task of self-assessment, be honest about your strengths and weaknesses. If your technical, quantitative, or communication competencies are not what they should be in order for you to begin course work in a confident frame of mind, spend a year or so coming up to speed in these areas. Although you'll be taking accounting, statistics, and computer courses as part of the core requirements, it's best to be comfortable with these basic disciplines before you enroll.

Once enrolled, you can do two things to make your life easier. First, take an honest look at your own learning style. Try to determine which methods work best for you; use methods that fit your personality—outlines, memorizing, listening to tapes, discussing concepts with other people, etc. Be proactive and establish a routine. As a returning student with many other life responsibilities, you'll need to take a different approach to studying than you did in undergraduate school.

You'll also find that connecting with classmates is a critical part of doing well. You may be assigned to project teams, but it's a good idea to seek out your own support group as well. Join study groups and relevant student organizations, even though it may seem you can't spare the time. In business school, as in business itself, collaboration and networking are everything!

Becoming a student again is a great adventure—earning an MBA will tax you, test you, stretch you, and reward you. But only you can know if it's right for you. When you applied to college as a high school student, you thought you had all the answers. What's different now is that, although you still don't have all the answers, you probably know much more than you think.

This table includes the names and locations of colleges, universities, and other institutions offering MBA and other master's-level business programs. Schools appear in geographical sequence by U.S. state or territory or by country and then alphabetically by school name. Specific degree information is detailed within the profile for each school. Refer to the page number in the table for the school's profile. If a school submitted incomplete data, one or more columns opposite the school name may be blank.	Page Number	Accreditation (AA=AACSB, AC=ACBSP)	ADMISSION REQUIREMENTS				TUITION (R) State Resident (NR) Non-Resident	OPTIONS		
			Matriculation (spring, summer, fall, winter, deferred)	Minimum GMAT Score	Minimum Undergraduate GPA	Minimum TOEFL Score		Financial Aid	Distance Learning	Executive MBA Program
ALABAMA										
Alabama Agricultural and Mechanical University, Department of Business Administration	85									
Auburn University, College of Business	85	AA	F, W, S, SU, D			550	$3420 per year (R); $71 per credit (R); $10,260 per year (NR); $213 per credit (NR)	•	•	
Auburn University Montgomery, School of Business	86									
Birmingham-Southern College, Division of Graduate Studies	86		D				$9030 per year; $1290 per course	•		
Jacksonville State University, College of Commerce and Business Administration	87	AA	D			550	$100 per credit hour (R); $200 per credit hour (NR)	•		
Samford University, School of Business	87		D			550	$344 per credit	•		
Spring Hill College, Division of Business and Management	88		F, S, SU, D		3.0	550	$245 per credit	•		
Troy State University, Sorrell College of Business	88	AC		450	2.5	525	$57 per credit hour (R); $114 per credit hour (NR)	•		
Troy State University Dothan, School of Business	89	AC			2.75		$61 per quarter hour (R); $122 per quarter hour (NR)			
Troy State University Montgomery, Division of Business	90	AC	D	450	2.5		$350 per course (R); $350 per course (NR)	•		
The University of Alabama, Manderson Graduate School of Business	90	AA	F, D		3.0	550	$2594 per year (R); $6808 per year (NR)	•		•
The University of Alabama at Birmingham, Graduate School of Management	91	AA	F, S, D	450	2.0	550	$96 per semester hour (R); $192 per semester hour (NR)	•		
The University of Alabama in Huntsville, College of Administrative Science	92	AA	D		2.5	550	$5180 per program (R); $521 per course (R); $10,575 per program (NR); $1059 per course (NR)	•		
University of Mobile, School of Business	92		D			550	$155 per credit hour	•		
University of North Alabama, College of Business	93	AC	D			550	$98 per semester hour (R); $98 per semester hour (NR)	•	•	•
University of South Alabama, College of Business and Management Studies	93	AA	F, W, S, SU, D		2.5	525	$68 per credit (R); $136 per credit (NR)	•		
ALASKA										
Alaska Pacific University, Business Administration Department	94									
University of Alaska Anchorage, College of Business and Public Policy	94	AA	D			550	$162 per credit (R); $316 per credit (NR)	•		
University of Alaska Fairbanks, School of Management	95	AA	D		3.0	550	$3726 per year (R); $158 per credit hour (R); $7344 per year (NR); $308 per credit hour (NR)	•		

	Page Number	Accreditation (AA=AACSB, AC=ACBSP)	Matriculation (spring, summer, fall, winter, deferred)	Minimum GMAT Score	Minimum Undergraduate GPA	Minimum TOEFL Score	TUITION (R) State Resident (NR) Non-Resident	Financial Aid	Distance Learning	Executive MBA Program
This table includes the names and locations of colleges, universities, and other institutions offering MBA and other master's-level business programs. Schools appear in geographical sequence by U.S. state or territory or by country and then alphabetically by school name. Specific degree information is detailed within the profile for each school. Refer to the page number in the table for the school's profile. If a school submitted incomplete data, one or more columns opposite the school name may be blank.		**ADMISSION REQUIREMENTS**							**OPTIONS**	
University of Alaska Southeast, Business and Public Administration Academic Programs	95		D		3.0	550	$2916 per year (R); $158 per credit hour (R); $5688 per year (NR); $474 per credit hour (NR)	•	•	
ARIZONA										
Arizona State University, College of Business	96	AA	F, D		3.0	580	$4058 per year (R); $6000 per year (R); $10,710 per year (NR); $10,492 per year (NR)	•		•
Arizona State University West, School of Management	97	AA	F, S, SU, D		3.0		$994 per semester (R); $105 per credit hour (R); $4320 per semester (NR); $360 per credit hour (NR)	•		
Grand Canyon University, College of Business	98	AC	D			550	$2601 per semester; $268 per semester hour	•		
Northern Arizona University, College of Business Administration	98	AA	F, S, SU, D			550	$3588 per year (R); $189 per credit hour (R); $9504 per year (NR); $396 per credit hour (NR)	•	•	
Thunderbird, The American Graduate School of International Management, Master's Program in International Management	99	AA	F, W, S, SU, D		2.7	550	$20,700 per year	•	•	
University of Arizona, Karl Eller Graduate School of Management	100	AA	F, W			600	$4162 per year (R); $2644 per year (R); $11,114 per year (NR); $5584 per year (NR)	•		
University of Phoenix, Department of Graduate Business	101		D				$5712 per year		•	
Western International University, Graduate Programs in Business	101		D		2.75		$215 per credit hour	•		
ARKANSAS										
Arkansas State University, College of Business	102									
Henderson State University, School of Business Administration	102	AA			2.5		$4760 per year (R); $9224 per year (NR)	•		
University of Arkansas, College of Business Administration	103	AA	D	530		550	$161 per credit hour (R); $383 per credit hour (NR)	•		
University of Arkansas at Little Rock, College of Business Administration	104	AA	D	450	2.7	550	$3120 per year (R); $130 per credit (R); $6672 per year (NR); $278 per credit (NR)	•	•	•
University of Central Arkansas, College of Business Administration	104	AA	D		2.7	550	$151 per hour (R); $314 per hour (NR)	•		
CALIFORNIA										
Antioch Southern California/Los Angeles, Program in Organizational Management	105		F, W, S, SU, D			600	$9600 per year; $320 per unit	•		
Antioch Southern California/Santa Barbara, Graduate Program in Organizational Management	105		F, W, S, SU, D			600	$12,400 per year; $310 per credit	•	•	
Armstrong University, Graduate School	106		D		2.5	500	$8400 per year; $350 per unit	•	•	
Azusa Pacific University, School of Business and Management	107		D	450	3.0	550	$405 per unit	•		

This table includes the names and locations of colleges, universities, and other institutions offering MBA and other master's-level business programs. Schools appear in geographical sequence by U.S. state or territory or by country and then alphabetically by school name. Specific degree information is detailed within the profile for each school. Refer to the page number in the table for the school's profile. If a school submitted incomplete data, one or more columns opposite the school name may be blank.

	Page Number	Accreditation (AA=AACSB, AC=ACBSP)	Matriculation (spring, summer, fall, winter, deferred)	Minimum GMAT Score	Minimum Undergraduate GPA	Minimum TOEFL Score	TUITION (R) State Resident (NR) Non-Resident	Financial Aid	Distance Learning	Executive MBA Program
California Baptist College, Graduate Program in Business Administration	107		D		2.75	550	$274 per unit; $274 per unit	•		
California Lutheran University, School of Business Administration	108		D		3.0	570	$7110 per year; $395 per credit	•		
California Polytechnic State University, San Luis Obispo, College of Business	109	AA	F, D	530	2.5	550	$164 per unit	•		
California State Polytechnic University, Pomona, College of Business	109									
California State University, Bakersfield, School of Business and Public Administration	110	AA	F, W, S		2.75	550	$1887 per year (R); $9233 per year (NR)			
California State University, Chico, College of Business	110	AA	D	500	2.75	550	$2006 per year (R); $670 per 6 units (R); $6434 per year (NR); $2146 per 6 units (NR)	•		
California State University, Dominguez Hills, School of Management	111	AC	F, S, D	450	2.75	550	$1821 per year (R); $95 per unit (R); $4773 year (NR); $246 per unit (NR)	•	•	
California State University, Fresno, Sid Craig School of Business	111	AA	F, S		2.5	550	$454 per 6 units (R); $1900 per 6 units (NR)	•		
California State University, Fullerton, School of Business Administration and Economics	112	AA			2.75	500	$246 per unit; $2117 per 6 credit hours	•	•	
California State University, Hayward, School of Business and Economics	113	AA	F, W, S, SU, D		2.75	550	$383 per 4 units (R); $1039 per 4 units (NR)	•		•
California State University, Long Beach, College of Business Administration	114	AA	F, S, D		2.5	550	$246 per unit; $246 per unit			
California State University, Los Angeles, School of Business and Economics	114	AA	F, W, S, SU		3.0	550	$2400 per year (R); $363 per quarter (R); $10,000 per year (NR); $585 per quarter (NR)	•		
California State University, Northridge, College of Business Administration and Economics	115	AA	F, S		3.0	550	$1980 per year (R); $657 per 6 units (R); $3444 year (NR); $246 per unit (NR)	•		
California State University, Sacramento, School of Business Administration	116									
California State University, San Bernardino, School of Business and Public Administration	116	AA	F, W, S, D		2.5	550	$2050 per year (R); $7872 per year (NR); $164 per unit (NR)	•	•	
California State University, San Marcos, Graduate Program in Business Administration	117		F, S, SU, D		2.5	530	$15,671 per program (R); $21,575 per program (NR)	•		
California State University, Stanislaus, School of Business Administration	117			450	2.5	550	$1738 per year (R); $530 per 6 units (R); $8049 per year (NR); $2006 per 6 units (NR)	•	•	•
Chapman University, School of Business and Economics	118		F, S, SU, D		2.5	550	$12,740 per year; $520 per credit	•		•
Claremont Graduate University, Peter F. Drucker Graduate School of Management	118	AA	D				$20,250 per year; $913 per credit	•		•
Coleman College, Information Systems Department, Graduate Division	120				3.0					
College of Notre Dame, Business Programs	120		F, S, SU, D	450	2.5	550	$460 per unit	•		

This table includes the names and locations of colleges, universities, and other institutions offering MBA and other master's-level business programs. Schools appear in geographical sequence by U.S. state or territory or by country and then alphabetically by school name. Specific degree information is detailed within the profile for each school. Refer to the page number in the table for the school's profile. If a school submitted incomplete data, one or more columns opposite the school name may be blank.

	Page Number	Accreditation (AA=AACSB, AC=ACBSP)	Matriculation (spring, summer, fall, winter, deferred)	Minimum GMAT Score	Minimum Undergraduate GPA	Minimum TOEFL Score	TUITION (R) State Resident (NR) Non-Resident	Financial Aid	Distance Learning	Executive MBA Program
Dominican College of San Rafael, School of Business and International Studies	120		F, S		3.0	600	$12,816 per year; $534 per unit	•		
Fielding Institute, Graduate Programs—Organizational Design and Effectiveness	121		F, W				$4254 per term	•	•	
Fresno Pacific University, Fresno Pacific Graduate School	122					550	$3000 per semester	•		
Golden Gate University, School of Business	122		D		2.5	550	$1404 per course	•	•	•
Holy Names College, Department of Business Administration and Economics	123		F, W, S, D		2.6		$375 per unit	•		
Hope International University, Graduate Management Program	123		D			550	$341 per credit	•	•	
Humboldt State University, School of Business and Economics	124		F, S, D		2.5	550	$1916 per year (R); $1250 per year (R); $1916 per year (NR); $1250 per year (NR)	•	•	
John F. Kennedy University, School of Management	125		D		2.0	550	$276 per unit	•		
La Sierra University, School of Business and Management	125		D		2.75	550	$384 per unit	•		
Lincoln University, Graduate Business Administration Program	126		D		2.7		$230 per credit hour	•		
Loyola Marymount University, College of Business Administration	126	AA	D	400		600	$590 per unit; $590 per unit	•		
Monterey Institute of International Studies, Fisher Graduate School of Business Management	127				3.0	550	$18,200 per year; $760 per credit	•		•
National University, School of Management and Technology	128		D		2.0	550	$870 per course	•	•	
Naval Postgraduate School, Department of Systems Management	128		F, W, S, SU, D		2.2		$9600 (R); $9600 (NR)		•	
Pacific States University, College of Business	129				3.0	450	$200 per credit			
Pepperdine University, The George L. Graziadio School of Business and Management	129		F, S, D			550	$11,025 per trimester; $705 per credit	•		•
Saint Mary's College of California, School of Economics and Business Administration	130		D		3.0	550	$340 per quarter unit	•		•
San Diego State University, Graduate School of Business	131	AA	F, S		3.0	570	$1902 per year (R); $1236 per year (R); $7806 per year (NR); $4300 per year (NR)	•		
San Francisco State University, College of Business	132	AA	F, S		2.7	550	$1982 per semester (R); $661 per semester (R); $4934 per semester (NR); $2137 per semester (NR)	•		
San Jose State University, College of Business	132	AA	F, S		3.0	550	$1896 per year (R); $295 per unit (R); $3900 per year (NR); $541 per unit (NR)	•	•	
Santa Clara University, Thomas and Dorothy Leavey School of Business and Administration	133	AA	F, W, S, D			600	$15,552 per year; $432 per unit	•		

This table includes the names and locations of colleges, universities, and other institutions offering MBA and other master's-level business programs. Schools appear in geographical sequence by U.S. state or territory or by country and then alphabetically by school name. Specific degree information is detailed within the profile for each school. Refer to the page number in the table for the school's profile. If a school submitted incomplete data, one or more columns opposite the school name may be blank.

	Page Number	Accreditation (AA=AACSB, AC=ACBSP)	Matriculation (spring, summer, fall, winter, deferred)	Minimum GMAT Score	Minimum Undergraduate GPA	Minimum TOEFL Score	TUITION (R) State Resident (NR) Non-Resident	Financial Aid	Distance Learning	Executive MBA Program
Sonoma State University, School of Business and Economics	134				2.5	550	$2130 per year (R); $732 per semester (R); $732 per semester (NR)	•		
Stanford University, Graduate School of Business	134	AA	F, W, S, D				$2400 per year	•		
United States International University, College of Business Administration	135		D		2.5	550	$3900 per quarter; $1300 per course	•		
University of California, Berkeley, Haas School of Business	136	AA	F		2.0	570	$8984 per year	•		
University of California, Davis, Graduate School of Management	137	AA	F, D			600	$19,452 per year	•		
University of California, Irvine, Graduate School of Management	137	AA	F		3.0	600	$9000 per year	•		•
University of California, Los Angeles, The Anderson School at UCLA	138	AA	F				$8994 per year	•		•
University of California, Riverside, A. Gary Anderson Graduate School of Management	139		F, W, S		3.0	550	$4866 per year (R); $13,854 per year (NR)	•		
University of Judaism, Lieber School of Graduate Studies	140		D			550	$13,910 per year; $580 per unit	•		
University of La Verne, School of Business and Global Studies	141		D			550	$11,340 per program; $315 per credit	•	•	
University of Redlands, Alfred North Whitehead College	141		D		3.0	550	$400 per credit	•		
University of San Diego, School of Business Administration	142	AA	F, S, SU, D		3.0	580	$10,530 per year; $585 per credit	•		
University of San Francisco, McLaren School of Business	143	AA	F, S, SU, D			600	$15,792 per year; $658 per unit	•	•	•
University of Southern California, Marshall School of Business	143	AA	F, D			600	$23,958 per year; $26,775 per year	•	•	•
University of the Pacific, Eberhardt School of Business	144	AA	F, S, SU, D		3.0	550	$17,820 per year; $1731 per course	•		
Woodbury University, School of Business and Management	145	AC	D		2.5	550	$550 per unit	•		
COLORADO										
College for Financial Planning, Program in Financial Planning	146				2.5		$600 per course		•	
Colorado State University, College of Business	146	AA	F, S, D			550	$2154 per semester (R); $106 per credit (R); $7015 per semester (NR); $398 per credit (NR)	•	•	•
Colorado Technical University, Management Department	147		D		3.0	550	$6500 per year; $225 per credit hour	•		
International School of Information Management, Programs in Information Management and Business Administration	148		D				$1125 per course		•	•

This table includes the names and locations of colleges, universities, and other institutions offering MBA and other master's-level business programs. Schools appear in geographical sequence by U.S. state or territory or by country and then alphabetically by school name. Specific degree information is detailed within the profile for each school. Refer to the page number in the table for the school's profile. If a school submitted incomplete data, one or more columns opposite the school name may be blank.

	Page Number	Accreditation (AA=AACSB, AC-ACBSP)	Matriculation (spring, summer, fall, winter, deferred)	ADMISSION REQUIREMENTS Minimum GMAT Score	Minimum Undergraduate GPA	Minimum TOEFL Score	TUITION (R) State Resident (NR) Non-Resident	OPTIONS Financial Aid	Distance Learning	Executive MBA Program
Regis University, School for Professional Studies	148		D			550	$309 per credit hour	•	•	
University of Colorado at Boulder, Graduate School of Business Administration	149	AA	F, D	590		590	$3710 per semester (R); $621 per 3 hours (R); $14,670 per semester (NR); $2445 per 3 hours (NR)	•	•	
University of Colorado at Colorado Springs, Graduate School of Business Administration	150	AA	F, S, SU, D			550	$2824 per year (R); $119 per credit (R); $9194 per year (NR); $407 per credit (NR)	•	•	
University of Colorado at Denver, Graduate School of Business Administration	150	AA	F, S, SU, D			525	$3706 per year (R); $222 per credit (R); $12,548 per year (NR); $752 per credit (NR)	•	•	•
University of Denver, Daniels College of Business	151	AA	D			550	$18,216 per year; $506 per quarter hour	•		•
University of Southern Colorado, Hasan School of Business	152				2.5	550	$872 per semester (R); $87 per semester hour (R); $3994 per semester (NR); $399 per semester hour (NR)	•		
CONNECTICUT										
Albertus Magnus College, Master of Science in Management	153				2.5	550	$9450 per year; $1050 per course	•		
Central Connecticut State University, School of Business	153		F, S		2.7	550	$2069 per semester (R); $175 per credit hour (R); $4811 per semester (NR); $175 per credit hour (NR)	•		
Eastern Connecticut State University, Program in Organizational Management	154									
Fairfield University, School of Business	154	AA	F, S, SU, D			550	$7500 per semester; $450 per credit hour	•		
Quinnipiac College, School of Business	155		D	400	2.5	575	$395 per credit	•		
Rensselaer at Hartford, Lally School of Management and Technology	155		D			570	$525 per credit hour	•	•	
Sacred Heart University, College of Business	156		D		2.8	525	$395 per credit	•		
Southern Connecticut State University, School of Business	157				2.5		$4118 per year (R); $564 per credit (R); $9602 per year (NR); $564 per credit (NR)	•		
University of Bridgeport, School of Business	157	AC	D			575	$340 per credit	•		
University of Connecticut, School of Business Administration	158	AA	D	530	3.0	550	$7600 per year (R); $15,800 per year (NR)	•	•	•
University of Hartford, Barney School of Business and Public Administration	158		D			550	$360 per credit hour	•		
University of New Haven, School of Business	159		D			520	$9720 per year; $360 per credit	•		•
Western Connecticut State University, Ancell School of Business and Public Administration	160		D		3.0	550	$2568 per year (R); $178 per credit (R); $7156 per year (NR); $178 per credit (NR)	•		
Yale University, School of Management	161	AA	F, D			600	$25,250 per year	•		

This table includes the names and locations of colleges, universities, and other institutions offering MBA and other master's-level business programs. Schools appear in geographical sequence by U.S. state or territory or by country and then alphabetically by school name. Specific degree information is detailed within the profile for each school. Refer to the page number in the table for the school's profile. If a school submitted incomplete data, one or more columns opposite the school name may be blank.

	Page Number	Accreditation (AA=AACSB, AC=ACBSP)	Matriculation (spring, summer, fall, winter, deferred)	ADMISSION REQUIREMENTS			TUITION (R) State Resident (NR) Non-Resident	OPTIONS		
				Minimum GMAT Score	Minimum Undergraduate GPA	Minimum TOEFL Score		Financial Aid	Distance Learning	Executive MBA Program
DELAWARE										
Delaware State University, School of Management	161		D			550	$1323 per semester (R); $147 per credit (R); $3159 per semester (NR); $351 per credit (NR)	•		
Goldey-Beacom College, Office of Graduate Studies	162	AC	D	450	2.5	525	$13,065 per program	•		
University of Delaware, College of Business and Economics	163	AA	F, S, D			585	$5360 per year (R); $298 per credit hour (R); $12,250 per year (NR); $681 per credit hour (NR)	•		•
Wilmington College, Business Programs	163					500	$245 per credit hour			
DISTRICT OF COLUMBIA										
American University, Kogod College of Business Administration	164	AA	D			550	$19,080 per year; $687 per credit	•		
The Catholic University of America, Department of Economics and Business	165									
Georgetown University, School of Business	165	AA	F, D			600	$23,880 per year	•		
The George Washington University, School of Business and Public Management	166	AA	F, S, D			550	$680 per credit	•	•	•
Howard University, School of Business	167	AA	F, S, SU, D			500	$10,600 per year	•		
Southeastern University, College of Graduate Studies	167		D		3.0	550	$6156 per year; $228 per credit	•	•	
Strayer University, Graduate School	168		D	450	2.75	400	$6750 per year; $250 per quarter hour credit	•	•	
University of the District of Columbia, College of Professional Studies	168	AC	D		2.5	550	$3574 per year (R); $198 per credit hour (R); $5922 per year (NR); $329 per credit hour (NR)	•		
FLORIDA										
Barry University, School of Business	169			400	3.0	550	$10,800 per year; $450 per credit	•		•
Embry-Riddle Aeronautical University, Department of Aviation Business Administration	170	AC	D		2.5	550	$3825 per semester; $425 per credit hour	•		
Embry-Riddle Aeronautical University, Extended Campus, College of Career Education	170		D			550	$279 per credit hour	•	•	
Florida Agricultural and Mechanical University, School of Business and Industry	171		F, S, SU		3.0		$118 per credit (R); $389 per credit (NR)	•		
Florida Atlantic University, College of Business	171	AA	F, S, SU, D	500	3.0	600	$133 per credit (R); $438 per credit (NR)	•		•
Florida Institute of Technology, School of Business	172		D		3.0	550	$9594 per year; $533 per credit hour	•		

This table includes the names and locations of colleges, universities, and other institutions offering MBA and other master's-level business programs. Schools appear in geographical sequence by U.S. state or territory or by country and then alphabetically by school name. Specific degree information is detailed within the profile for each school. Refer to the page number in the table for the school's profile. If a school submitted incomplete data, one or more columns opposite the school name may be blank.

	Page Number	Accreditation (AA=AACSB, AC=ACBSP)	Matriculation (spring, summer, fall, winter, deferred)	Minimum GMAT Score	Minimum Undergraduate GPA	Minimum TOEFL Score	TUITION (R) State Resident (NR) Non-Resident	Financial Aid	Distance Learning	Executive MBA Program
Florida International University, College of Business Administration	173	AA	D			500	$130 per credit hour (R); $435 per credit hour (NR)	•		•
Florida Metropolitan University-Tampa College, Business and Computer Information Division	173				3.0	550	$6000 per year	•		
Florida Metropolitan University-Orlando College, North, Graduate Program	174		D		3.0	550	$263 per credit hour	•	•	
Florida Southern College, Department of Business and Economics	174		F, S, SU	450		550	$290 per credit hour	•		
Florida State University, College of Business	175	AA	F, S, SU, D		3.1	600	$131 per credit hour (R); $436 per credit hour (NR)	•		
Jacksonville University, College of Business	176		D	450		550	$465 per credit hour	•		•
Lynn University, School of Business	176		D			550	$360 per credit hour	•		
Nova Southeastern University, School of Business and Entrepreneurship	177		F, W, S, SU, D		2.5	550	$9500 per year; $425 per credit	•	•	
Palm Beach Atlantic College, Rinker School of Business	178		D		3.0	550	$280 per credit hour			
Rollins College, Crummer Graduate School of Business	178	AA	D				$10,200 per semester; $627 per credit	•		•
Saint Leo College, Graduate Business Studies	179		F, W			550	$3420 per year; $190 per credit	•		
St. Thomas University, Department of Business Administration	179		D				$7020 per year; $390 per credit	•		
Schiller International University, Business Programs	180		D			550	$14,850 per year; $990 per course	•		
Stetson University, School of Business Administration	181	AA	F, S, SU, D			550	$390 per credit hour	•		
University of Central Florida, College of Business Administration	181	AA	F, S, SU		3.0	575	$130 per hour (R); $434 per hour (NR)	•		•
University of Florida, Warrington College of Business Administration	182	AA	D	500		550	$3354 per year (R); $129 per hour (R); $11,294 per year (NR); $434 per hour (NR)	•	•	•
University of Miami, School of Business Administration	183	AA	D		3.0	550	$815 per credit	•		•
University of North Florida, College of Business Administration	184	AA	D			500	$2124 per year (R); $118 per semester hour (R); $7020 per year (NR); $390 per semester hour (NR)	•		
University of Sarasota, College of Business Administration	185				3.0	500	$9531 per 9 courses; $353 per credit hour	•	•	
University of South Florida, College of Business Administration	185	AA	F, S, D	500	3.0	500	$134 per credit hour (R); $440 per credit hour (NR)	•		•
The University of Tampa, College of Business	186		D	400	2.5	550	$305 per hour	•		

This table includes the names and locations of colleges, universities, and other institutions offering MBA and other master's-level business programs. Schools appear in geographical sequence by U.S. state or territory or by country and then alphabetically by school name. Specific degree information is detailed within the profile for each school. Refer to the page number in the table for the school's profile. If a school submitted incomplete data, one or more columns opposite the school name may be blank.	Page Number	Accreditation (AA=AACSB, AC=ACBSP)	Matriculation (spring, summer, fall, winter, deferred)	ADMISSION REQUIREMENTS			TUITION (R) State Resident (NR) Non-Resident	OPTIONS		
				Minimum GMAT Score	Minimum Undergraduate GPA	Minimum TOEFL Score		Financial Aid	Distance Learning	Executive MBA Program
University of West Florida, College of Business	187	AA	F, S, SU, D			500	$3144 per year (R); $131 per semester hour (R); $10,473 per year (NR); $436 per semester hour (NR)	•		
GEORGIA										
Albany State University, College of Business	187	AC		450	3.0			•	•	
Augusta State University, School of Business Administration	188		F, S, SU, D		2.5	540	$1560 per year (R); $780 per year (R); $5700 per year (NR); $2850 per year (NR)	•		
Berry College, Campbell School of Business	188		F, S, SU	500	2.5		$340 per credit hour	•		
Brenau University, Department of Business Administration	189									
Clark Atlanta University, School of Business Administration	189	AA	F, D			500	$11,460 per year; $382 per credit	•		
Columbus State University, Abbott Turner College of Business	190					550	$90 per quarter hour (R); $228 per quarter hour (NR)	•	•	
Emory University, Roberto C. Goizueta Business School	190	AA	F, D			600	$24,000 per year; $15,999 per year	•		•
Georgia College and State University, J. Whitney Bunting School of Business	191	AA	D			500	$260 per 5 hours (R); $250 per semester hour (NR); $1428 per 5 hours (NR)	•		
Georgia Institute of Technology, DuPree College of Management	192	AA	F, D			600	$3627 per year (R); $12,465 per year (NR)	•		
Georgia Southern University, College of Business Administration	193	AA	D				$228 per course (R); $684 per course (NR)	•	•	
Georgia Southwestern State University, School of Business	193					550	$2468 per year (R); $83 per semester hour (R); $8468 per year (NR); $333 per semester (NR)	•		
Georgia State University, College of Business Administration	194	AA	F, S, SU, D			550	$300 per 5-hour course (R); $1200 per 5-hour course (NR)	•		•
Kennesaw State University, Michael J. Coles College of Business	195	AA	D	475	2.8	550	$1199 per semester (R); $83 per credit hour (R); $4199 per semester (NR); $250 per credit hour (NR)	•	•	•
LaGrange College, Division of Business Administration and Economics	195	AC					$8240 per year; $206 per quarter hour	•		
Mercer University, Stetson School of Business and Economics	196			400	2.75	550	$831 per course	•		
Mercer University, Cecil B. Day Campus, Stetson School of Business and Economics	196		F, S, SU, D		2.75	550	$5580 per semester; $930 per course	•	•	•
Oglethorpe University, Division of Business Administration	197				2.5	500	$1340 per 4-hour course	•		
Southern Polytechnic State University, School of Management	198	AC	F, S, SU, D		2.0	550	$1560 per year (R); $52 per credit hour (R); $5700 per year (NR); $130 per credit hour (NR)	•		
State University of West Georgia, Richards College of Business	198	AA	F, S, SU, D	410	2.5	550	$2756 per year (R); $52 per quarter hour (R); $8188 per year (NR); $166 per quarter hour (NR)	•		

This table includes the names and locations of colleges, universities, and other institutions offering MBA and other master's-level business programs. Schools appear in geographical sequence by U.S. state or territory or by country and then alphabetically by school name. Specific degree information is detailed within the profile for each school. Refer to the page number in the table for the school's profile. If a school submitted incomplete data, one or more columns opposite the school name may be blank.

	Page Number	Accreditation (AA=AACSB, AC=ACBSP)	ADMISSION REQUIREMENTS Matriculation (spring, summer, fall, winter, deferred)	Minimum GMAT Score	Minimum Undergraduate GPA	Minimum TOEFL Score	TUITION (R) State Resident (NR) Non-Resident	OPTIONS Financial Aid	Distance Learning	Executive MBA Program
University of Georgia, Terry College of Business	199	AA	D			585	$3290 per year (R); $11,300 per year (NR)	•		
Valdosta State University, College of Business Administration	200	AA			2.75	550	$1869 per year (R); $210 per quarter (R); $5097 per year (NR); $660 per quarter (NR)	•		
HAWAII										
Chaminade University of Honolulu, School of Business	200									
Hawaii Pacific University, Center for Graduate Studies	201		D		2.7		$7500 per year; $296 per credit	•		
University of Hawaii at Manoa, College of Business Administration	201	AA	F, S	500	3.0	500	$3936 per year (R); $164 per credit (R); $9840 per year (NR); $410 per credit (NR)	•	•	•
IDAHO										
Boise State University, College of Business and Economics	202	AA	F, S			550	$3500 per year (R); $125 per credit (R); $11,000 per year (NR); $125 per credit (NR)	•		
Idaho State University, College of Business	203	AA	D			550	$2940 per year (R); $125 per credit hour (R); $8920 per year (NR); $211 per credit hour (NR)	•	•	
University of Idaho, College of Business and Economics	204	AA	F, S, SU		3.0	550	$2482 per year (R); $124 per credit (R); $7282 per year (NR); $219 per credit (NR)	•		
ILLINOIS										
Aurora University, School of Business and Professional Studies	204		D		2.75	550	$1176 per 3 semester hours	•	•	
Benedictine University, Graduate Programs	205					600	$295 per credit hour	•		•
Bradley University, Foster College of Business Administration	206									
Columbia College, Department of Management	206				3.0		$349 per credit hour	•		
DePaul University, Charles H. Kellstadt Graduate School of Business	206	AA	F, W, S, SU, D			550	$1920 per course	•		
Dominican University, Graduate School of Business	207	AC	D		3.0	550	$13,350 per year; $1335 per 3-hour course	•		
Eastern Illinois University, Lumpkin College of Business and Applied Science	208	AA	F, S, SU, D			550	$1622 per semester (R); $90 per credit hour (R); $3860 per semester (NR); $270 per credit hour (NR)	•		
Governors State University, College of Business and Public Administration	208	AC	D		2.5	550	$1104 per trimester (R); $92 per credit (R); $3312 per trimester (NR); $276 per credit (NR)	•	•	
Illinois Institute of Technology, Stuart School of Business	209		F, W, S, SU, D		2.0	550	$18,360 per year; $1620 per 3-credit course	•		
Illinois State University, College of Business	210	AA	D		2.75	600	$2670 per year (R); $298 per course (R); $6352 per year (NR); $895 per course (NR)	•		

		ADMISSION REQUIREMENTS					OPTIONS		

This table includes the names and locations of colleges, universities, and other institutions offering MBA and other master's-level business programs. Schools appear in geographical sequence by U.S. state or territory or by country and then alphabetically by school name. Specific degree information is detailed within the profile for each school. Refer to the page number in the table for the school's profile. If a school submitted incomplete data, one or more columns opposite the school name may be blank.

School	Page Number	Accreditation (AA=AACSB, AC-ACBSP)	Matriculation (spring, summer, fall, winter, deferred)	Minimum GMAT Score	Minimum Undergraduate GPA	Minimum TOEFL Score	TUITION (R) State Resident (NR) Non-Resident	Financial Aid	Distance Learning	Executive MBA Program
Keller Graduate School of Management, Master of Business Administration Program	211					550	$1235 per course			
Lake Forest Graduate School of Management, Graduate Programs	211		F, W, S				$1575 per course	•		•
Lewis University, College of Business	212		D		2.0	550	$7326 per year; $407 per credit hour	•		
Loyola University Chicago, Graduate School of Business	212	AA	F, W, S, SU, D			550	$17,865 per year; $1985 per course	•		
National-Louis University, College of Management and Business	213		D		3.0	550	$459 per semester hour	•	•	
North Central College, Department of Business Administration	214		D		2.75	600	$1407 per course			
Northeastern Illinois University, College of Business and Management	214		F, S, SU, D		2.75	550	$2148 per year (R); $90 per credit (R); $6444 per year (NR); $269 per credit (NR)	•		
Northern Illinois University, College of Business	215	AA	F, S, SU, D		2.75	550	$1392 per semester (R); $116 per credit hour (R); $4176 per semester (NR); $116 per credit hour (NR)	•		•
North Park University, The Center for Management Education	216		D			550	$970 per course	•		
Northwestern University, J. L. Kellogg Graduate School of Management	216	AA	F, W, S, D		3.0	600	$24,351 per annum; $2402 per course	•		
Olivet Nazarene University, Division of Business	217									
Quincy University, Division of Business	217					600	$1080 per course	•		
Rockford College, Department of Economics, Business, and Accounting	218					550	$14,750 per year; $400 per credit hour	•		
Roosevelt University, Walter E. Heller College of Business Administration	219		D			550	$8010 per year; $445 per credit hour	•		
Saint Xavier University, Graham School of Management	219		D				$8028 per year; $445 per semester hour	•		
Southern Illinois University at Carbondale, College of Business and Administration	220	AA	F, S, SU, D		2.7	550	$1620 per year (R); $90 per hour (R); $4860 per year (NR); $270 per hour (NR)	•		
Southern Illinois University at Edwardsville, School of Business	221	AA	F, S, SU, D	400	2.5	550	$572 per 6 semester hours (R); $1716 per 6 semester hours (NR)	•	•	
University of Chicago, Graduate School of Business	221	AA	D			600	$24,904 per year; $2490 per course	•		•
University of Illinois at Chicago, College of Business Administration	222	AA	F, S, SU, D		2.75	570	$10,436 per year (R); $982 per course (R); $16,878 per year (NR); $1903 per course (NR)	•		
University of Illinois at Springfield, School of Business and Management	223		D		2.5	550	$99 per credit hour (R); $296 per credit hour (NR)	•	•	
University of Illinois at Urbana-Champaign, Illinois MBA	224	AA	F, D		3.0	610	$10,700 per year (R); $17,400 per year (NR)	•	•	•

This table includes the names and locations of colleges, universities, and other institutions offering MBA and other master's-level business programs. Schools appear in geographical sequence by U.S. state or territory or by country and then alphabetically by school name. Specific degree information is detailed within the profile for each school. Refer to the page number in the table for the school's profile. If a school submitted incomplete data, one or more columns opposite the school name may be blank.

	Page Number	Accreditation (AA=AACSB, AC=ACBSP)	Matriculation (spring, summer, fall, winter, deferred)	ADMISSION REQUIREMENTS			TUITION (R) State Resident (NR) Non-Resident	OPTIONS		
				Minimum GMAT Score	Minimum Undergraduate GPA	Minimum TOEFL Score		Financial Aid	Distance Learning	Executive MBA Program
University of St. Francis, College of Graduate Studies	225		D		2.75	550	$370 per credit hour	•	•	
Western Illinois University, College of Business and Technology	225	AA	D	450	2.5	550	$1575 per semester (R); $125 per credit (R); $3807 per semester (NR); $311 per credit (NR)	•	•	
INDIANA										
Ball State University, College of Business	226	AA	D		2.5	550	$5976 per program (R); $5976 per program (R); $13,955 per program (NR); $13,955 per program (NR)	•	•	
Bethel College, Program in Business Administration	227		D	450	2.75	560	$300 per credit hour			
Butler University, College of Business Administration	227	AA	F, S, SU, D			550	$320 per credit hour	•		
Indiana State University, School of Business	228	AA	F, W, S, SU, D		2.7	550	$143 per credit hour (R); $325 per credit hour (NR)	•	•	
Indiana University Bloomington, Kelley School of Business	229	AA	F, D			580	$8775 per year (R); $17,013 per year (NR)	•		
Indiana University Kokomo, Division of Business and Economics	229		F, S, SU, D				$140 per credit hour (R); $315 per credit hour (NR)	•		
Indiana University Northwest, Division of Business and Economics	230	AA	D				$132 per credit hour (R); $303 per credit hour (NR)	•		
Indiana University-Purdue University Fort Wayne, School of Business and Management Sciences	231	AA	F, S, SU, D		2.5	550	$141 per credit hour (R); $302 per credit hour (NR)	•		
Indiana University-Purdue University Indianapolis, Kelley School of Business	231		F, S, D				$239 per credit hour (R); $478 per credit hour (NR)	•		
Indiana University South Bend, Division of Business and Economics	232	AA	F, S, SU, D	450	2.75		$145 per credit hour (R); $346 per credit hour (NR)	•		
Indiana Wesleyan University, Division of Adult and Professional Studies	232		D		2.5		$250 per credit hour	•	•	
Manchester College, Department of Accounting	233				3.0		$13,180 per semester; $440 per semester hour	•		
Oakland City University, School of Adult Programs and Professional Studies	233		D		3.0	500	$285 per semester hour	•		
Purdue University, Krannert Graduate School of Management	234	AA	D			570	$3588 per semester (R); $7712 per semester (NR)	•		
Purdue University Calumet, Department of Management	234				3.0		$118 per credit hour (R); $268 per credit hour (NR)			•
University of Indianapolis, Graduate Business Programs	235		D			550	$244 per hour	•		•
University of Notre Dame, College of Business Administration	235	AA	F, SU, D			600	$21,500 per year	•	•	•
University of Saint Francis, Department of Business Administration	236			400	2.5	550	$3015 per semester; $335 per credit hour	•		

This table includes the names and locations of colleges, universities, and other institutions offering MBA and other master's-level business programs. Schools appear in geographical sequence by U.S. state or territory or by country and then alphabetically by school name. Specific degree information is detailed within the profile for each school. Refer to the page number in the table for the school's profile. If a school submitted incomplete data, one or more columns opposite the school name may be blank.

School	Page Number	Accreditation (AA=AACSB, AC=ACBSP)	Matriculation (spring, summer, fall, winter, deferred)	Minimum GMAT Score	Minimum Undergraduate GPA	Minimum TOEFL Score	TUITION (R) State Resident (NR) Non-Resident	Financial Aid	Distance Learning	Executive MBA Program
University of Southern Indiana, School of Business	237	AA	D	450	2.5	550	$118 per credit hour (R); $235 per credit hour (NR)			
IOWA										
Clarke College, Business Department	237					550	$6344 per semester; $325 per credit	•		
Drake University, College of Business and Public Administration	238	AA	D			550	$340 per hour	•	•	
Iowa State University of Science and Technology, College of Business	239	AA	F, SU, D			570	$3166 per year (R); $230 per credit (R); $9324 per year (NR); $572 per credit (NR)	•		
Maharishi University of Management, School of Business and Public Administration	239		D			575	$15,520 per year	•	•	
St. Ambrose University, H.L. McLaughlin One-Year MBA Program	240		D			550	$1206 per course	•	•	
University of Dubuque, School of Business	241		D			550	$11,700 per program; $975 per 3 credits	•		
The University of Iowa, School of Management	241	AA	F, D	600	3.0	600	$4130 per year (R); $221 per semester hour (R); $11,246 per year (NR); $221 per semester hour (NR)	•		•
University of Northern Iowa, College of Business Administration	242	AA	F, S	500		500	$3046 per year (R); $170 per credit hour (R); $7512 per year (NR); $418 per credit hour (NR)			
Upper Iowa University, Program in Business Leadership	243				2.5	550	$600 per 3 hours			
KANSAS										
Baker University, School of Professional and Graduate Studies	243					600	$13,200 per program; $300 per credit	•		
Emporia State University, School of Business	244				2.5		$1108 per semester (R); $103 per credit hour (R); $2922 per semester (NR); $258 per credit hour (NR)	•		
Fort Hays State University, College of Business	244					550	$94 per credit (R); $249 per credit (NR)	•		
Friends University, Graduate Programs	245		W, SU, D		2.75	550	$445 per credit hour			•
Kansas Newman College, Program in Organizational Leadership	245				3.0		$257 per credit hour			
Kansas State University, College of Business Administration	245	AA	F, S, D	500	3.0	590	$101 per credit hour (R); $329 per credit hour (NR)	•		
Kansas Wesleyan University, MBA Program	246						$340 per credit hour			
MidAmerica Nazarene University, Graduate Studies in Management	247		D		3.0	600	$13,788 per program			
Ottawa University, Department of Human Resources	247				3.0		$275 per credit hour	•	•	

This table includes the names and locations of colleges, universities, and other institutions offering MBA and other master's-level business programs. Schools appear in geographical sequence by U.S. state or territory or by country and then alphabetically by school name. Specific degree information is detailed within the profile for each school. Refer to the page number in the table for the school's profile. If a school submitted incomplete data, one or more columns opposite the school name may be blank.

	Page Number	Accreditation (AA=AACSB, AC=ACBSP)	Matriculation (spring, summer, fall, winter, deferred)	Minimum GMAT Score	Minimum Undergraduate GPA	Minimum TOEFL Score	TUITION (R) State Resident (NR) Non-Resident	Financial Aid	Distance Learning	Executive MBA Program
Pittsburg State University, Gladys A. Kelce School of Business and Economics	247		F, S, SU, D	400		450	$2332 per year (R); $100 per credit hour (R); $5960 per year (NR); $251 per credit hour (NR)	•	•	
Saint Mary College, Department of Business, Economics and Information Technology	248				2.75	550	$207 per semester credit hour	•		
University of Kansas, School of Business	248	AA	F, S, SU, D		3.0	600	$3400 per year (R); $100 per credit hour (R); $11,177 per year (NR); $100 per credit hour (NR)	•	•	
Washburn University of Topeka, School of Business	249		F, S, SU		2.6	550	$131 per credit hour (R); $270 per credit hour (NR)	•		
Wichita State University, W. Frank Barton School of Business	250	AA	F, S, D		2.75	550	$112 per credit (R); $332 per credit (NR)	•		•
KENTUCKY										
Bellarmine College, W. Fielding Rubel School of Business	251		D				$375 per credit hour	•		•
Brescia College, Master of Science in Management Program	251		D			550	$150 per credit hour	•		
Eastern Kentucky University, College of Business	252		F, S, SU, D	400	2.5	550	$124 per hour (R); $344 per hour (NR)	•		
Morehead State University, College of Business	253	AC			2.5	525	$2470 per year (R); $138 per credit hour (R); $6710 per year (NR); $373 per credit hour (NR)	•	•	
Murray State University, College of Business and Public Affairs	253	AA	D			525	$2300 per year (R); $116 per hour (R); $6260 per year (NR); $334 per hour (NR)	•	•	
Northern Kentucky University, College of Business	254	AA	F, S, SU, D		2.3	550	$1150 per semester (R); $125 per semester hour (R); $3130 per semester (NR); $345 per semester hour (NR)	•		
Thomas More College, Department of Business Administration	255		D		2.5	600	$6975 per year			•
University of Kentucky, Carol Martin Gatton College of Business and Economics	255	AA	F, D		2.5	550	$2640 per year (R); $150 per credit hour (R); $7920 per year (NR); $430 per credit hour (NR)	•		
University of Louisville, College of Business and Public Administration	256	AA	D		2.75	550	$175 per semester hour (R); $525 per semester hour (NR)	•		
LOUISIANA										
Louisiana State University and Agricultural and Mechanical College, E. J. Ourso College of Business Administration	257	AA				550	$2708 per year (R); $495 per six hours (R); $6008 per year (NR)	•		
Louisiana State University in Shreveport, College of Business Administration	257	AA	F, S, SU		2.75	550	$150 per hour (R); $315 per hour (NR)	•	•	
Louisiana Tech University, College of Administration and Business	258	AA	F, W, S, SU, D		2.25	550	$3336 per year (R); $574 per 6 hours (R); $6196 per year (NR); $1054 per 6 hours (NR)	•		
Loyola University New Orleans, Joseph A. Butt, SJ, College of Business Administration	258	AA	D		2.75	580	$450 per credit hour	•		
McNeese State University, College of Business	259	AA	D			525	$1987 per year (R); $540 per semester (R); $3530 per year (NR); $882 per semester (NR)	•		

	Page Number	Accreditation (AA=AACSB, AC=ACBSP)	Matriculation (spring, summer, fall, winter, deferred)	Minimum GMAT Score	Minimum Undergraduate GPA	Minimum TOEFL Score	TUITION (R) State Resident (NR) Non-Resident	Financial Aid	Distance Learning	Executive MBA Program
Nicholls State University, College of Business Administration	260	AA			2.0	550	$2025 per year (R); $90 per credit hour (R); $4700 per year (NR); $250 per credit hour (NR)	•		
Northeast Louisiana University, College of Business Administration	261	AA	F, S, SU	400	2.5	600	$825 per semester (R); $177 per semester (R); $3237 per semester (NR); $177 per semester (NR)	•		
Southeastern Louisiana University, College of Business	261	AA	F, S, SU, D	400	2.5	525	$1010 per semester (R); $287 per 3 hours (R); $2234 per semester (NR); $287 per 3 hours (NR)	•		
Southern University and Agricultural and Mechanical College, College of Business	262	AA					$2500 per year (R); $6500 per year (NR)			
Tulane University, A. B. Freeman School of Business	262	AA	F, D				$21,719 per year; $724 per credit hour	•		•
University of New Orleans, College of Business Administration	263	AA	F, S, SU		2.5	550	$373 per 1-3 hours (R); $1500 per 1-3 hours (NR)	•	•	•
University of Southwestern Louisiana, Graduate School	264	AA	D			550	$1100 per semester (R); $530 per 6 credits (R); $3500 per semester (NR); $1695 per 6 credits (NR)	•		
MAINE										
Husson College, Graduate Studies Division	265					550	$550 per 3-credit course			
Maine Maritime Academy, Department of Graduate Studies and Research	265		D				$15,390 per program (R); $342 per credit (R); $15,390 per program (NR); $342 per credit (NR)	•		
Thomas College, Programs in Business	266				3.0		$435 per course	•		
University of Maine, The Maine Business School	266	AA	F, S, SU, D	475	2.6	550	$188 per semester hour (R); $531 per semester hour (NR); $531 per semester hour (NR)	•		
University of Southern Maine, School of Business	267		D	500		550	$173 per credit hour (R); $477 per credit hour (NR)	•		
MARYLAND										
Bowie State University, Business Programs	268				2.5	550	$1521 per semester (R); $169 per credit (R); $2736 per semester (NR); $169 per credit (NR)	•	•	
College of Notre Dame of Maryland, Center for Graduate Studies	268		D		2.8	550	$248 per semester hour	•		
Frostburg State University, School of Business	269		D		2.5	550	$3060 per year (R); $170 per hour (R); $3546 per year (NR); $197 per hour (NR)	•	•	
Hood College, Department of Economics and Management	270				2.5		$270 per credit hour	•		
Johns Hopkins University, School of Continuing Studies, Division of Business and Management	270					650	$420 per credit hour	•		
Loyola College, Sellinger School of Business and Management	271	AA	F, S, SU, D		2.9	550	$6570 per year; $365 per credit	•		•
Morgan State University, School of Business and Management	271	AA	D			600	$145 per credit hour (R); $260 per credit hour (NR)		•	

This table includes the names and locations of colleges, universities, and other institutions offering MBA and other master's-level business programs. Schools appear in geographical sequence by U.S. state or territory or by country and then alphabetically by school name. Specific degree information is detailed within the profile for each school. Refer to the page number in the table for the school's profile. If a school submitted incomplete data, one or more columns opposite the school name may be blank.

ADMISSION REQUIREMENTS

OPTIONS

	Page Number	Accreditation (AA=AACSB, AC=ACBSP)	Matriculation (spring, summer, fall, winter, deferred)	Minimum GMAT Score	Minimum Undergraduate GPA	Minimum TOEFL Score	TUITION (R) State Resident (NR) Non-Resident	Financial Aid	Distance Learning	Executive MBA Program
Mount Saint Mary's College and Seminary, Graduate Program of Business	272					500	$250 per credit	•		
Salisbury State University, Franklin P. Perdue School of Business	272	AA	F, W, S, SU		3.0	550	$158 per credit hour (R); $310 per credit hour (NR)	•		
Towson University, College of Graduate and Extended Education	273	AA	D		2.75	550	$3132 per year (R); $174 per credit hour (R); $6120 per year (NR); $340 per credit hour (NR)	•		
University of Baltimore, Robert G. Merrick School of Business	274	AA	D	400		550	$2359 per semester (R); $239 per credit (R); $3412 per semester (NR); $356 per credit (NR)	•	•	
University of Maryland, College Park, Robert H. Smith School of Business	274	AA	D			600	$9558 per year (R); $272 per credit hour (R); $14,184 per year (NR); $400 per credit hour (NR)	•		
University of Maryland University College, Graduate School of Management and Technology	275		D		2.5	580	$273 per credit (R); $353 per credit (NR)	•	•	
MASSACHUSETTS										
American International College, School of Business Administration	276					550	$343 per semester hour	•		
Anna Maria College, Graduate Program in Business Administration	277				2.6	500	$730 per course	•		
Arthur D. Little School of Management, One-Year Master of Science in Management Program	277		F, D			550	$32,000 per year	•		
Assumption College, Department of Business Studies	278				2.75	500	$297 per credit	•		
Babson College, F. W. Olin Graduate School of Business	279	AA	F, D		2.8	580	$21,940 per year; $2046 per 3-credit course	•		
Bentley College, Graduate School of Business	279	AA	F, S, SU, D			580	$1980 per course	•		
Boston College, Wallace E. Carroll Graduate School of Management	280	AA	F, D			600	$22,134 per year; $714 per credit hour	•		
Boston University, School of Management	281	AA	F, S, D			600	$22,830 per year; $687 per credit	•		•
Brandeis University, Graduate School of International Economics and Finance	282		F, D			600	$23,360 per year; $2100 per course	•		
Cambridge College, Program in Management	283					550	$315 per credit	•		
Clark University, Graduate School of Management	284	AA	F, S, D			550	$19,250 per year; $1925 per course	•		
Emerson College, School of Communication, Management and Public Policy	284		D			550	$13,032 per year; $543 per credit	•		
Emmanuel College, Center for Adult Studies	285					550	$1266 per course	•		
Fitchburg State College, Division of Graduate and Continuing Education	285		D		2.8	500	$140 per credit hour (R); $140 per credit hour (NR)	•		

	Page Number	Accreditation (AA=AACSB, AC=ACBSP)	Matriculation (spring, summer, fall, winter, deferred)	Minimum GMAT Score	Minimum Undergraduate GPA	Minimum TOEFL Score	TUITION (R) State Resident (NR) Non-Resident	Financial Aid	Distance Learning	Executive MBA Program
Framingham State College, Program in Business Administration	286									
Harvard University, Graduate School of Business Administration	286	AA				630	$25,000 per year	•		
Lesley College, School of Management	287		D		2.5	550	$425 per credit	•		
Massachusetts Institute of Technology, Sloan School of Management	288	AA	F, D				$25,800 per year	•		
Nichols College, Graduate School of Business	288		D			550	$1050 per course			
Northeastern University, Graduate School of Business Administration	289	AA	D			600	$19,500 per year; $500 per credit	•		•
Salem State College, Program in Business Administration	290		F, S		2.5	550	$140 per credit hour (R); $230 per credit hour (NR)	•		
Simmons College, Graduate School of Management	290		F, S			550	$596 per credit hour	•		
Suffolk University, Frank Sawyer School of Management	291	AA	F, S, SU, D		2.6	550	$17,490 per year; $1749 per course	•		•
University of Massachusetts Amherst, School of Management	292	AA	F, D		3.0	600	$2080 per semester (R); $335 per credit (R); $6625 per semester (NR); $335 per credit (NR)	•	•	
University of Massachusetts Boston, College of Management	292		F, S, D		2.75	550	$1320 per semester (R); $110 per credit (R); $4422 per semester (NR); $369 per credit (NR)	•		
University of Massachusetts Dartmouth, College of Business and Industry	293		F, S, D			500	$2071 per year (R); $86 per credit (R); $7192 per year (NR); $300 per credit (NR)	•		
University of Massachusetts Lowell, College of Management	294	AA	D			550	$89 per credit hour (R); $306 per credit hour (NR)	•		
Western New England College, School of Business	294		D				$351 per semester hour	•		
Worcester Polytechnic Institute, Graduate Management Programs	295		D			580	$636 per credit	•	•	
MICHIGAN										
Andrews University, School of Business	296		D	400	2.6	550	$272 per quarter credit	•		
Aquinas College, Graduate Management Program	296		D		2.75	550	$310 per credit hour	•		
Baker College Center for Graduate Studies, Center for Graduate Studies	297		D		2.5	550	$6560 per year; $215 per quarter hour	•	•	•
Central Michigan University, College of Business Administration	297	AA	F, W, S, SU, D		2.5	550	$135 per credit hour (R); $269 per credit hour (NR)	•		
Eastern Michigan University, College of Business	298	AA	F, W, S	450	2.5	500	$4800 per year (R); $145 per credit hour (R); $10,800 per year (NR); $336 per credit hour (NR)	•		

	Page Number	Accreditation (AA=AACSB, AC=ACBSP)	Matriculation (spring, summer, fall, winter, deferred)	ADMISSION REQUIREMENTS			TUITION (R) State Resident (NR) Non-Resident	OPTIONS		
				Minimum GMAT Score	Minimum Undergraduate GPA	Minimum TOEFL Score		Financial Aid	Distance Learning	Executive MBA Program
Ferris State University, Graduate Programs, College of Business	299		F, W, SU, D		2.75	500	$206 per credit hour (R); $425 per credit hour (NR)	•	•	
Grand Valley State University, Seidman School of Business	300	AA	F, W, S, D	450		550	$162 per credit (R); $330 per semester credit hour (NR); $330 per credit (NR)	•		
Kettering University, Graduate Studies and Extension Services	300		F, W		3.0	580	$1185 per course	•	•	
Lake Superior State University, School of Business	301		D			550	$168 per credit (R); $168 per credit (NR)		•	
Lawrence Technological University, Graduate College of Management	302	AC	D		2.75	550	$400 per credit hour	•		
Madonna University, Graduate Programs in Business Administration	302		D		3.0	530	$250 per credit hour	•	•	
Michigan State University, Eli Broad Graduate School of Management	303	AA	F, S, D		3.0	600	$8350 per year (R); $12,150 per year (NR)	•		•
Michigan Technological University, School of Business and Economics	304		D			520	$1092 per quarter (R); $182 per credit hour (R); $2502 per quarter (NR); $417 per credit hour (NR)	•		
Northwood University, Richard DeVos Graduate School of Management	304		D				$15,000 per program; $20,000 per program	•		•
Oakland University, School of Business Administration	305	AA	F, W, S, SU, D		2.6	550	$208 per credit (R); $461 per credit (NR)	•	•	
Saginaw Valley State University, College of Business and Management	306					525	$153 per credit hour (R); $302 per credit hour (NR)	•		
Siena Heights University, Office of Graduate Studies and Lifelong Learning	306		D		3.0	550	$278 per semester hour	•		
Spring Arbor College, School of Business and Management	307		D		3.0	550	$265 per credit hour	•		
University of Detroit Mercy, College of Business Administration	308	AA	D		3.0		$448 per credit hour	•		
University of Michigan, University of Michigan Business School	308	AA	F			600	$18,400 per year (R); $600 per credit hour (R); $24,000 per year (NR); $600 per credit hour (NR)	•	•	
University of Michigan-Dearborn, School of Management	309	AA	D			560	$2560 per semester (R); $240 per credit (R); $7432 per semester (NR); $694 per credit (NR)	•		
University of Michigan-Flint, School of Management	310	AA	F, W, D				$5327 per year (R); $5327 per year (NR)	•		•
Walsh College of Accountancy and Business Administration, College of Accountancy and Business Administration	311		D		2.75	550	$263 per semester credit hour	•	•	
Wayne State University, School of Business Administration	311	AA	F, W, S, SU	450	2.75	550	$3816 per year (R); $159 per credit (R); $8184 per year (NR); $341 per credit (NR)	•		
Western Michigan University, Haworth College of Business	312	AA	F, W, S, D	450	3.0	550	$3990 per year (R); $142 per hour (R); $9780 per year (NR); $344 per hour (NR)	•	•	•

This table includes the names and locations of colleges, universities, and other institutions offering MBA and other master's-level business programs. Schools appear in geographical sequence by U.S. state or territory or by country and then alphabetically by school name. Specific degree information is detailed within the profile for each school. Refer to the page number in the table for the school's profile. If a school submitted incomplete data, one or more columns opposite the school name may be blank.

This table includes the names and locations of colleges, universities, and other institutions offering MBA and other master's-level business programs. Schools appear in geographical sequence by U.S. state or territory or by country and then alphabetically by school name. Specific degree information is detailed within the profile for each school. Refer to the page number in the table for the school's profile. If a school submitted incomplete data, one or more columns opposite the school name may be blank.

	Page Number	Accreditation (AA=AACSB, AC=ACBSP)	Matriculation (spring, summer, fall, winter, deferred)	Minimum GMAT Score	Minimum Undergraduate GPA	Minimum TOEFL Score	TUITION (R) State Resident (NR) Non-Resident	Financial Aid	Distance Learning	Executive MBA Program
MINNESOTA										
College of St. Catherine, Business Programs	313		D			500	$456 per credit	•		
College of St. Scholastica, Program in Management	313		D				$332 per quarter credit	•	•	
The Graduate School of America, Management Field	314		F, W, S, SU, D				$1995 per quarter; $845 per course	•	•	
Metropolitan State University, Management and Administration Program	314					550	$83 per credit (R); $131 per credit (NR)	•		
St. Cloud State University, College of Business	315	AA		470	2.75	600	$2500 per year (R); $1250 per year (R); $3200 per year (NR); $1600 per year (NR)	•		
Saint Mary's University of Minnesota, School of Graduate Studies/ School of Business and Social Sciences	316		D		2.75	550	$205 per credit	•		
Southwest State University, Department of Business Administration	316				3.0		$128 per credit (R); $202 per credit (NR)		•	
University of Minnesota, Duluth, School of Business and Economics	317		F, W, S, SU, D	500	3.0	550	$6000 per year (R); $260 per credit (R); $6000 per year (NR); $260 per credit (NR)	•		
University of Minnesota, Twin Cities Campus, Carlson School of Management	317	AA	F, D				$13,036 per year (R); $235 per credit (R); $19,368 per year (NR); $235 per credit (NR)	•		•
University of St. Thomas, Graduate School of Business	318		D			550	$394 per credit hour	•	•	•
Winona State University, College of Business	319		D		2.5	575	$129 per credit (R); $204 per credit (NR)	•		
MISSISSIPPI										
Delta State University, School of Business	320	AC	D		3.0	550	$1295 per semester (R); $124 per semester hour (R); $2474 per semester (NR); $282 per semester hour (NR)	•		•
Jackson State University, School of Business	321	AA	D		2.5	525	$2380 per year (R); $132 per hour (R); $2594 per year (NR); $132 per hour (NR)	•		
Millsaps College, Else School of Management	321	AA	F, S, SU, D				$540 per credit hour	•		
Mississippi College, School of Business	322	AC	D		2.5		$276 per hour	•		
Mississippi State University, College of Business and Industry	323	AA	F, S, SU, D	500	3.0	575	$1237 per semester (R); $111 per hour (R); $2216 per semester (NR); $158 per hour (NR)	•	•	
University of Mississippi, School of Business Administration	323	AA	SU	500	3.0	600	$2662 per three semesters (R); $5648 per three semesters (NR)	•		
University of Southern Mississippi, College of Business Administration	324	AA	F, S, SU				$1295 per semester (R); $378 per 3 hours (R); $2705 per semester (NR); $741 per 3 hours (NR)	•		
William Carey College, School of Business	325		D				$2400 per year; $210 per hour	•		

This table includes the names and locations of colleges, universities, and other institutions offering MBA and other master's-level business programs. Schools appear in geographical sequence by U.S. state or territory or by country and then alphabetically by school name. Specific degree information is detailed within the profile for each school. Refer to the page number in the table for the school's profile. If a school submitted incomplete data, one or more columns opposite the school name may be blank.

	Page Number	Accreditation (AA=AACSB, AC=ACBSP)	Matriculation (spring, summer, fall, winter, deferred)	Minimum GMAT Score	Minimum Undergraduate GPA	Minimum TOEFL Score	TUITION (R) State Resident (NR) Non-Resident	Financial Aid	Distance Learning	Executive MBA Program
MISSOURI										
Avila College, Department of Business and Economics	325			450	3.0	550	$5350 per semester; $280 per credit hour	•		
Central Missouri State University, College of Business and Economics	326									
Columbia College, Program in Business Administration	326		D		3.0	550	$180 per credit hour	•		
Drury College, Breech School of Business Administration	327	AC	F, S, SU			550	$220 per credit hour	•		
Fontbonne College, Business Department	327		D		2.5	600	$325 per hour			
Lincoln University, College of Business	328									
Lindenwood University, Department of Business Administration	328		D			550	$260 per credit	•		
Maryville University of Saint Louis, John E. Simon School of Business	329		D		2.5	550	$11,480 per year; $345 per credit hour	•		
Northwest Missouri State University, College of Professional and Applied Studies	329	AC	F, S, SU		2.5	550	$105 per credit (R); $187 per credit (NR)	•		
Rockhurst College, School of Management	330		D		2.75	550	$325 per credit hour	•		•
Saint Louis University, School of Business and Administration	331	AA	F, S, SU, D			550	$10,836 per year; $602 per credit	•		
Southeast Missouri State University, College of Business	332	AA	D			550	$100 per credit hour (R); $180 per credit hour (NR)	•		
Southwest Baptist University, School of Business	332				2.5		$5220 per program			
Southwest Missouri State University, College of Business Administration	333	AA	D				$2520 per year (R); $105 per hour (R); $5040 per year (NR); $210 per hour (NR)	•	•	
Stephens College, Program in Business Administration	333				3.0	550	$230 per credit hour	•	•	
Truman State University, Division of Business and Accountancy	334		F, S, D		3.0	560	$2466 per year (R); $144 per hour (R); $4464 per year (NR); $255 per hour (NR)	•		
University of Missouri-Columbia, College of Business and Public Administration	335	AA	F, W, SU, D		2.7	550	$158 per credit hour (R); $475 per credit hour (NR)	•		
University of Missouri-Kansas City, Harry W. Block School of Public Administration	335	AA	D			550	$163 per credit hour (R); $489 per credit hour (NR)	•		•
University of Missouri-St. Louis, School of Business Administration	336	AA	D		3.0	550	$4740 per year (R); $158 per credit hour (R); $13,830 per year (NR); $461 per credit hour (NR)	•	•	
Washington University in St. Louis, John M. Olin School of Business	337	AA	F, D				$23,800 per year; $670 per credit hour	•		•

	Page Number	Accreditation (AA=AACSB, AC=ACBSP)	Matriculation (spring, summer, fall, winter, deferred)	Minimum GMAT Score	Minimum Undergraduate GPA	Minimum TOEFL Score	TUITION (R) State Resident (NR) Non-Resident	Financial Aid	Distance Learning	Executive MBA Program
Webster University, School of Business and Technology	338		D				$332 per semester hour	•		
William Woods University, Graduate and Adult Studies	339		D		2.5	550	$9180 per year		•	
MONTANA										
Montana State University-Bozeman, College of Business	339	AA	F, S, SU, D	500	3.0	550	$2677 per year (R); $89 per credit (R); $7776 per year (NR); $259 per credit (NR)	•		
The University of Montana-Missoula, School of Business Administration	340	AA	F, S, SU, D		2.75	580	$1568 per semester (R); $150 per credit (R); $4254 per semester (NR); $370 per credit (NR)	•	•	
NEBRASKA										
Bellevue University, College of Business	341		D				$250 per credit		•	
Chadron State College, Department of Business and Economics	341			400	2.75	550	$1734 per year (R); $72 per credit (R); $3468 per year (NR); $145 per credit (NR)	•	•	
Creighton University, College of Business Administration	342	AA	D	450		550	$7236 per year; $402 per credit	•		
University of Nebraska at Kearney, College of Business and Technology	343		F, S, SU		2.75	550	$78 per credit hour (R); $148 per credit hour (NR)	•	•	
University of Nebraska at Omaha, College of Business Administration	343	AA	F, S, SU, D	450	2.7	550	$88 per credit (R); $212 per credit (NR)	•		
University of Nebraska-Lincoln, College of Business Administration	344	AA	F, S, SU		2.5	500	$2285 per year (R); $104 per credit hour (R); $5000 per year (NR); $256 per credit hour (NR)	•		
Wayne State College, Division of Business	345					550	$250 per course (R); $460 per course (NR)	•	•	
NEVADA										
University of Nevada, Las Vegas, College of Business	345	AA	F, S	475	2.75	550	$90 per credit (R); $90 per credit (NR)	•		
University of Nevada, Reno, College of Business Administration	346	AA	F, S		2.75	550	$93 per credit hour (R); $2750 per semester (NR)	•		
NEW HAMPSHIRE										
Antioch New England Graduate School, Department of Organization and Management	347		D			550	$12,700 per year	•		
Dartmouth College, Amos Tuck School of Business Administration	347	AA	D				$24,900 per year	•		
New England College, Program in Organizational Management	348				3.0		$170 per credit			
New Hampshire College, Graduate School of Business	348	AC	D		2.5	550	$1065 per course; $945 per course	•	•	

This table includes the names and locations of colleges, universities, and other institutions offering MBA and other master's-level business programs. Schools appear in geographical sequence by U.S. state or territory or by country and then alphabetically by school name. Specific degree information is detailed within the profile for each school. Refer to the page number in the table for the school's profile. If a school submitted incomplete data, one or more columns opposite the school name may be blank.

This table includes the names and locations of colleges, universities, and other institutions offering MBA and other master's-level business programs. Schools appear in geographical sequence by U.S. state or territory or by country and then alphabetically by school name. Specific degree information is detailed within the profile for each school. Refer to the page number in the table for the school's profile. If a school submitted incomplete data, one or more columns opposite the school name may be blank.

School	Page Number	Accreditation (AA=AACSB, AC=ACBSP)	Matriculation (spring, summer, fall, winter, deferred)	Minimum GMAT Score	Minimum Undergraduate GPA	Minimum TOEFL Score	TUITION (R) State Resident (NR) Non-Resident	Financial Aid	Distance Learning	Executive MBA Program
Plymouth State College of the University System of New Hampshire, Department of Business Studies	349	AC	F, W, S, SU, D		2.5	500	$9828 per program (R); $273 per credit (R); $10,764 per program (NR); $299 per credit (NR)	•		
Rivier College, Department of Business Administration	349		D			600	$855 per course	•		
University of New Hampshire, Whittemore School of Business and Economics	350	AA	F, D		3.0	550	$5200 per year (R); $1050 per course (R); $14,060 per year (NR); $1275 per course (NR)	•		•
NEW JERSEY										
Fairleigh Dickinson University, Samuel J. Silberman College of Business Administration	351				3.2	500	$522 per credit	•		•
Georgian Court College, Program in Business Administration	351	AC				550	$350 per credit			
Kean University, School of Business, Government, and Technology	352		F, S, D				$248 per credit (R); $305 per credit (NR)	•		
Monmouth University, School of Business Administration	352		F, S, SU, D		2.75	525	$7902 per year; $439 per credit	•		
Montclair State University, School of Business Administration	353				3.0	550	$186 per credit (R); $236 per credit (NR)	•		
New Jersey Institute of Technology, School of Industrial Management	354	AA				525	$6340 per semester (R); $326 per credit (R); $9158 per semester (NR); $451 per credit (NR)	•		
The Richard Stockton College of New Jersey, Program in Business Studies	354		D				$213 per credit (R); $297 per credit (NR)	•		
Rider University, College of Business Administration	355	AA	F, S, SU, D				$9000 per year; $420 per credit	•		
Rowan University, School of Business Administration	355				2.5	550	$2470 per semester (R); $205 per credit (R); $3915 per semester (NR); $326 per credit (NR)	•		
Rutgers, The State University of New Jersey, Camden, School of Business	356	AA	D		2.5	550	$8408 per year (R); $348 per credit (R); $12,600 per year (NR); $520 per credit (NR)	•		
Rutgers, The State University of New Jersey, Newark, Graduate School of Management	357	AA	F, S, D		3.1	600	$8410 per year (R); $348 per credit (R); $12,538 per year (NR); $520 per credit (NR)	•		•
Rutgers, The State University of New Jersey, New Brunswick, School of Management and Labor Relations	358	AA	F, S, SU, D		3.0	575	$6700 per year (R); $250 per credit (R); $9528 per year (NR); $369 per credit (NR)	•		
Saint Peter's College, Graduate Business Programs	359			400		550	$11,448 per year; $477 per credit	•		
Seton Hall University, W. Paul Stillman School of Business	359	AA	D	500	3.0	550	$508 per credit	•	•	
Stevens Institute of Technology, Wesley J. Howe School of Technology Management	360				3.0	550	$650 per credit hour	•		
Thomas Edison State College, Graduate Studies Office	361		D			500	$289 per credit (R); $289 per credit (NR)		•	
William Paterson University of New Jersey, College of Business	361		F, S, D	400	2.0		$210 per credit (R); $298 per credit (NR)	•		

		ADMISSION REQUIREMENTS					OPTIONS		

This table includes the names and locations of colleges, universities, and other institutions offering MBA and other master's-level business programs. Schools appear in geographical sequence by U.S. state or territory or by country and then alphabetically by school name. Specific degree information is detailed within the profile for each school. Refer to the page number in the table for the school's profile. If a school submitted incomplete data, one or more columns opposite the school name may be blank.

School	Page Number	Accreditation (AA=AACSB, AC=ACBSP)	Matriculation (spring, summer, fall, winter, deferred)	Minimum GMAT Score	Minimum Undergraduate GPA	Minimum TOEFL Score	TUITION (R) State Resident (NR) Non-Resident	Financial Aid	Distance Learning	Executive MBA Program
NEW MEXICO										
College of Santa Fe, Department of Business Administration	362		D			550	$237 per credit	•		
Eastern New Mexico University, College of Business	362	AC	D		3.0	550	$960 per year (R); $80 per hour (R); $3285 per year (NR); $274 per hour (NR)	•	•	
New Mexico Highlands University, School of Business	363	AC			3.0	525	$858 per semester (R); $72 per hour (R); $3600 per semester (NR); $72 per hour (NR)	•	•	
New Mexico State University, College of Business Administration and Economics	364	AA	F, S, SU, D	500		550	$2352 per year (R); $98 per credit (R); $7344 per year (NR); $306 per credit (NR)	•		
University of New Mexico, Robert O. Anderson Graduate School of Management	364	AA	F, S, D	500	3.0	550	$928 per semester (R); $99 per credit hour (R); $3271 per semester (NR); $99 per credit hour (NR)	•		•
Western New Mexico University, Department of Business Administration	365	AC	D			550	$1322 per year (R); $55 per credit hour (R); $4388 per year (NR); $55 per credit hour (NR)	•		
NEW YORK										
Adelphi University, School of Management and Business	366		F, S, SU, D	450	2.75	550	$14,850 per year; $465 per credit		•	
Alfred University, College of Business	366	AA	D				$20,376 per year; $405 per credit hour	•		
Audrey Cohen College, School of Business	367		D	550	3.0	550	$18,000 per year	•		
Baruch College of the City University of New York, Zicklin School of Business	367	AA	F, W, S, D		3.0	570	$4350 per year (R); $185 per credit (R); $7600 per year (NR); $320 per credit (NR)	•		•
Canisius College, Wehle School of Business	368	AA	D		3.0	500	$11,976 per year; $499 per credit hour	•		
Clarkson University, School of Business	369	AA	D			600	$20,352 per program; $584 per credit hour	•		
College of Insurance, Business Programs	370		F, S, D	500	3.0	550	$1662 per 3 credits	•		
The College of Saint Rose, School of Business	370	AC	F, S, SU, D		3.0	550	$338 per credit	•	•	
Columbia University, Columbia Business School	371	AA	F, S, SU, D			610	$13,260 per year	•		•
Cornell University, Johnson Graduate School of Management	372	AA	F, W, S, SU, D			600	$23,460 per year	•		
Dowling College, School of Business	373		D		2.8		$5280 per year; $440 per credit	•		
Fordham University, Graduate School of Business Administration	373	AA	F, W, S, D			600	$560 per credit	•		
Hofstra University, Frank G. Zarb School of Business	374	AA	D			580	$442 per credit	•		•

	Page Number	Accreditation (AA=AACSB, AC=ACBSP)	Matriculation (spring, summer, fall, winter, deferred)	Minimum GMAT Score	Minimum Undergraduate GPA	Minimum TOEFL Score	TUITION (R) State Resident (NR) Non-Resident	Financial Aid	Distance Learning	Executive MBA Program
Iona College, Hagan School of Business	375		D		2.7	550	$480 per credit	•		
Le Moyne College, Department of Business	376			500	3.0		$364 per credit hour	•		
Long Island University, Brooklyn Campus, School of Business and Public Administration	376		F, W, SU			600		•		
Long Island University, C.W. Post Campus, College of Management	377		F, S, D			550	$475 per credit	•		
Manhattan College, School of Business	378		F, S, SU		2.8	550	$440 per credit	•		
Manhattanville College, Adult and Special Programs	378		D		2.5	600	$398 per credit			
Marist College, School of Management	379		D			550	$419 per credit hour	•	•	
Mercy College, Program in Human Resource Management	379		D			550	$390 per credit	•		
Mount Saint Mary College, Division of Business	380		D				$367 per credit	•	•	
Nazareth College of Rochester, Business Department	380		D				$396 per credit hour	•		
New School for Social Research, Robert J. Milano Graduate School of Management and Urban Policy	381		D		3.0	600	$588 per credit	•	•	
New York Institute of Technology, School of Management	382		D		2.5	500	$390 per credit	•	•	
New York University, Leonard N. Stern School of Business	382	AA	F			600	$25,486 per year; $900 per credit	•		•
Niagara University, Graduate Division of Business Administration	383		D		2.5	550	$430 per credit hour	•	•	
Pace University, Lubin School of Business	384	AA	F, S, SU, D			550	$545 per credit	•		•
Polytechnic University, Brooklyn Campus, Management Department	385		F, S, SU, D		3.0		$645 per credit hour		•	
Polytechnic University, Farmingdale Campus, Department of Management	385									
Polytechnic University, Westchester Graduate Center, Management Department	385									
Pratt Institute, Program in Facilities Management	386					550	$637 per credit			
Rensselaer Polytechnic Institute, Lally School of Management and Technology	386	AA	F, S, SU, D			570	$18,900 per year; $630 per credit hour	•	•	•
Roberts Wesleyan College, Division of Business and Management	387	AC	D			550	$450 per credit hour	•		

| | ADMISSION REQUIREMENTS | | | | | OPTIONS | | |
This table includes the names and locations of colleges, universities, and other institutions offering MBA and other master's-level business programs. Schools appear in geographical sequence by U.S. state or territory or by country and then alphabetically by school name. Specific degree information is detailed within the profile for each school. Refer to the page number in the table for the school's profile. If a school submitted incomplete data, one or more columns opposite the school name may be blank.	Page Number	Accreditation (AA=AACSB, AC=ACBSP)	Matriculation (spring, summer, fall, winter, deferred)	Minimum GMAT Score	Minimum Undergraduate GPA	Minimum TOEFL Score	TUITION (R) State Resident (NR) Non-Resident	Financial Aid	Distance Learning	Executive MBA Program
Rochester Institute of Technology, College of Business	388	AA	F, W, S, SU, D		2.5	575	$18,765 per year; $527 per credit hour	•		•
Sage Graduate School, Division of Management, Comunications, and Legal Studies	388		D		2.75	550	$360 per credit hour	•		
St. Bonaventure University, School of Business Administration	389		D	450	2.5	600	$7650 per year; $425 per credit hour	•		
St. John Fisher College, Graduate School of Management	390		F, S, SU, D	400		525	$14,700 per year; $490 per credit hour	•		
St. John's University, College of Business Administration	390	AA	D			500	$13,800 per year; $575 per credit	•		
St. Thomas Aquinas College, Division of Business Administration	391		D		2.8	500	$9560 per year; $390 per credit	•		
Siena College, Business Division	392		D			550	$315 per credit hour	•		
State University of New York at Albany, School of Business	392	AA	D			580	$5100 per year (R); $213 per credit hour (R); $8416 per year (NR); $351 per credit hour (NR)	•		
State University of New York at Binghamton, School of Management	393	AA		500	3.0	550	$5100 per year (R); $213 per credit hour (R); $8416 per year (NR); $351 per credit hour (NR)	•		•
State University of New York at Buffalo, School of Management	394	AA	D			550	$5100 per year (R); $213 per credit (R); $8416 per year (NR); $351 per credit (NR)	•		
State University of New York at New Paltz, Department of Business Administration	395				3.0	550	$213 per credit (R); $351 per credit (NR)			
State University of New York at Oswego, School of Business	395				2.5	525	$5100 per year (R); $8416 per year (NR)	•		
State University of New York at Stony Brook, W. Averell Harriman School for Management and Policy	396		F, S, D		3.0	550	$5100 per year (R); $213 per credit hour (R); $8416 per year (NR); $351 per credit hour (NR)	•		
State University of New York College at Oneonta, Department of Economics and Business	396				2.8	500	$2550 per semester (R); $213 per credit (R); $4208 per semester (NR); $351 per credit (NR)			
State University of New York Empire State College, Business and Policy Studies Program	397		F, S, D			600	$213 per credit (R); $351 per credit (NR)	•	•	
State University of New York Institute of Technology at Utica/Rome, School of Business	398		D		3.0	550	$5100 per year (R); $213 per credit hour (R); $8416 per year (NR); $351 per credit hour (NR)	•	•	
State University of New York Maritime College, Graduate Program in Transportation Management	398		D			500	$2550 per year (R); $213 per credit (R); $4208 per year (NR); $351 per credit (NR)			
Syracuse University, School of Management	399	AA	F, D		2.0	580	$16,650 per year; $555 per credit	•	•	•
Union College, Graduate Management Institute	400		D		3.0	550	$12,888 per year; $1432 per course	•		
University of Rochester, William E. Simon Graduate School of Business Administration	401	AA	F, W, D			600	$22,620 per year; $754 per credit hour	•		•
Wagner College, Department of Economics and Business Administration	402	AC			2.7	550	$580 per credit	•		•

This table includes the names and locations of colleges, universities, and other institutions offering MBA and other master's-level business programs. Schools appear in geographical sequence by U.S. state or territory or by country and then alphabetically by school name. Specific degree information is detailed within the profile for each school. Refer to the page number in the table for the school's profile. If a school submitted incomplete data, one or more columns opposite the school name may be blank.	Page Number	Accreditation (AA=AACSB, AC=ACBSP)	Matriculation (spring, summer, fall, winter, deferred)	ADMISSION REQUIREMENTS			TUITION (R) State Resident (NR) Non-Resident	OPTIONS		
				Minimum GMAT Score	Minimum Undergraduate GPA	Minimum TOEFL Score		Financial Aid	Distance Learning	Executive MBA Program
NORTH CAROLINA										
Appalachian State University, John A. Walker College of Business	402									
Campbell University, Lundy-Fetterman School of Business	402				2.7	550	$170 per semester hour			
Duke University, The Fuqua School of Business at Duke University	403	AA	F, D		3.0		$25,250 per year	•	•	
East Carolina University, School of Business	404	AA	D			550	$450 per semester (R); $450 per semester (R); $4014 per semester (NR); $2007 per semester (NR)	•		
Elon College, Martha and Spencer Love School of Business	404					500	$256 per semester hour	•		
Fayetteville State University, Program in Business Administration	405		F, S, SU, D			550	$1334 per year (R); $90 per credit (R); $8176 per year (NR); $478 per credit (NR)	•		
Gardner-Webb University, School of Business	405				2.25	500	$205 per credit hour	•		
High Point University, Graduate Studies	406		F, S, SU, D		3.0	550	$4806 per year; $267 per credit	•		
Lenoir-Rhyne College, Department of Business	407				2.7		$210 per semester hour			
Meredith College, John W. Weems Graduate School	407									
Montreat College, Business Division	407						$14,000 per year; $225 per credit			
North Carolina Central University, School of Business	407	AC					$1754 per year (R); $430 per 3 semester hours (R); $8908 per year (NR); $2218 per 3 semester hours (NR)	•		
North Carolina State University, College of Management	408		F, S, D			550	$2276 per year (R); $819 per semester (R); $11,262 per year (NR); $4188 per semester (NR)	•		
Pfeiffer University, Program in Business Administration	409				3.0		$245 per semester hour	•		
Queens College, McColl School of Business	409	AC	D		2.5	550	$15,000 per year; $260 per credit hour	•		•
University of North Carolina at Chapel Hill, Kenan-Flagler Business School	410	AA	F, D			600	$1428 per year (R); $13,145 per year (NR)	•		•
The University of North Carolina at Charlotte, The Belk College of Business Administration	410	AA	D	500	2.75	550	$891 per semester (R); $339 per course (R); $4460 per semester (NR); $2121 per course (NR)	•		
University of North Carolina at Greensboro, Joseph M. Bryan School of Business and Economics	411	AA	F, S, SU, D			550	$1952 per year (R); $976 per semester (R); $10,270 per year (NR); $5135 per semester (NR)	•		
The University of North Carolina at Pembroke, Graduate Studies	412		D		2.5		$1748 per year (R); $219 per 3 hours (R); $6022 per year (NR); $1004 per 3 hours (NR)	•		
University of North Carolina at Wilmington, Cameron School of Business	413	AA	SU, D		3.0	500	$561 per semester (R); $3244 per semester (NR)	•		

This table includes the names and locations of colleges, universities, and other institutions offering MBA and other master's-level business programs. Schools appear in geographical sequence by U.S. state or territory or by country and then alphabetically by school name. Specific degree information is detailed within the profile for each school. Refer to the page number in the table for the school's profile. If a school submitted incomplete data, one or more columns opposite the school name may be blank.

School	Page Number	Accreditation (AA=AACSB, AC=ACBSP)	Matriculation (spring, summer, fall, winter, deferred)	Minimum GMAT Score	Minimum Undergraduate GPA	Minimum TOEFL Score	TUITION (R) State Resident (NR) Non-Resident	Financial Aid	Distance Learning	Executive MBA Program
Wake Forest University, Babcock Graduate School of Management	413	AA	D			600	$19,200 per year; $1980 per course	•		•
Western Carolina University, College of Business	414	AA	D		2.75	550	$918 per year (R); $230 per 3 semester hours (R); $8188 per year (NR); $2047 per 3 semester hours (NR)	•	•	
Wingate University, School of Business	415	AC	D			550	$750 per course	•		
NORTH DAKOTA										
Minot State University, College of Business	415				2.75	550	$1223 per year (R); $102 per credit (R); $3264 per year (NR); $272 per credit (NR)	•	•	
North Dakota State University, College of Business Administration	416		D		2.8	550	$116 per credit (R); $286 per credit (NR)	•		
University of Mary, Business Division	416		D		2.5	550	$265 per credit	•		
University of North Dakota, College of Business and Public Administration	417	AA	D	450	2.75	550	$2738 per year (R); $133 per credit (R); $6612 per year (NR); $294 per credit (NR)	•	•	
OHIO										
Ashland University, School of Business Administration and Economics	418	AC	F, S, SU, D			550	$350 per credit hour			•
Baldwin-Wallace College, Division of Business Administration	418		F, S, SU, D			500	$20,160 per year; $2016 per course	•		•
Bowling Green State University, College of Business Administration	419	AA	F, S, D		2.7	575	$5004 per year (R); $232 per credit hour (R); $10,018 per year (NR); $471 per credit hour (NR)	•		
Capital University, Graduate School of Administration	420		F, W, S, D	500		550	$12,000 per program; $260 per credit	•		
Case Western Reserve University, Weatherhead School of Management	420	AA	F, S, SU, D			570	$20,900 per year; $873 per credit hour	•		
Cleveland State University, James J. Nance College of Business Administration	422	AA	F, S, SU, D			500	$5050 per year (R); $130 per credit hour (R); $10,101 per year (NR); $259 per hour (NR)	•		
Franciscan University of Steubenville, Business Programs	422			460	2.5	550	$280 per credit	•		
Franklin University, Graduate School of Business	423		F, W, SU, D			550	$5880 per year; $270 per credit	•		
Heidelberg College, Graduate Studies in Business	424		D		2.7	550	$350 per semester hour	•		
John Carroll University, John M. and Mary Jo Boler School of Business	424	AA	D		2.0		$530 per credit hour	•		
Kent State University, Graduate School of Management	425	AA	F, S, SU, D		2.75	550	$2376 per semester (R); $216 per credit (R); $4606 per semester (NR); $419 per credit (NR)	•	•	•
Lake Erie College, Division of Management Studies	425		D		3.0	590	$380 per semester hour			

This table includes the names and locations of colleges, universities, and other institutions offering MBA and other master's-level business programs. Schools appear in geographical sequence by U.S. state or territory or by country and then alphabetically by school name. Specific degree information is detailed within the profile for each school. Refer to the page number in the table for the school's profile. If a school submitted incomplete data, one or more columns opposite the school name may be blank.

School	Page Number	Accreditation (AA=AACSB, AC=ACBSP)	Matriculation (spring, summer, fall, winter, deferred)	Minimum GMAT Score	Minimum Undergraduate GPA	Minimum TOEFL Score	TUITION (R) State Resident (NR) Non-Resident	Financial Aid	Distance Learning	Executive MBA Program
Malone College, Graduate School	426		D		2.5		$334 per semester credit	•		
The McGregor School of Antioch University, Graduate Management Program	426		D				$8992 per year	•		
Miami University, Richard T. Farmer School of Business Administration	427	AA	F, D		2.75	550	$2302 per semester (R); $192 per hour (R); $5352 per semester (NR); $446 per hour (NR)	•		
The Ohio State University, Max M. Fisher College of Business	427	AA	F, D			600	$5067 per year (R); $4079 per 3 quarters (R); $12,582 per year (NR); $10,592 per 3 quarters (NR)	•		
Ohio University, College of Business	428	AA	F, D		3.0	600	$5492 per year (R); $171 per credit hour (R); $11,784 per year (NR); $366 per credit hour (NR)	•	•	•
Otterbein College, Department of Business, Accounting and Economics	429						$5216 per quarter; $195 per credit			
Tiffin University, Program in Business Administration	429	AC	F, S, D		3.0	550	$6000 per year; $1500 per module	•		•
University of Akron, College of Business Administration	430	AA	F, S, SU, D			550	$165 per credit (R); $308 per credit (NR)	•		
University of Cincinnati, Graduate Business Program	431	AA	F, S, SU	550		600	$5418 per year (R); $10,356 per year (NR)	•		
University of Dayton, School of Business Administration	431	AA	D		2.5	550	$7362 per year; $409 per semester hour	•		
The University of Findlay, Business Programs	432				2.5	525	$299 per credit hour	•	•	
University of Toledo, College of Business Administration	433	AA	F, S, SU, D	450	2.7	550	$5505 per year (R); $201 per credit hour (R); $10,790 per year (NR); $434 per credit hour (NR)	•		•
Walsh University, Program in Management	433		D		2.6	500	$363 per credit hour			
Wright State University, College of Business and Administration	434	AA	D			550	$1563 per quarter (R); $148 per credit (R); $2799 per quarter (NR); $263 per credit (NR)	•		
Xavier University, Williams College of Business Administration	435	AA	D		2.0	550	$3420 per semester; $380 per credit	•		•
Youngstown State University, Warren P. Williamson Jr. College of Business Administration	435	AC	F, W, S, SU, D			550	$86 per quarter hour (R); $137 per quarter hour (NR)	•		•
OKLAHOMA										
Cameron University, School of Graduate and Professional Studies	436		D		2.0	550	$1750 per year (R); $73 per credit (R); $4050 per year (NR); $168 per credit (NR)	•	•	
Northeastern State University, College of Business and Industry	437	AC	F, W, S, SU		2.5	550	$327 per 6 hours (R); $816 per 6 hours (NR)	•		
Oklahoma City University, Meinders School of Business	437	AC				550	$310 per credit hour	•	•	•
Oklahoma State University, College of Business Administration	438	AA	F, S, D		2.5	550	$1764 per year (R); $80 per hour (R); $5604 per year (NR); $240 per hour (NR)	•	•	

This table includes the names and locations of colleges, universities, and other institutions offering MBA and other master's-level business programs. Schools appear in geographical sequence by U.S. state or territory or by country and then alphabetically by school name. Specific degree information is detailed within the profile for each school. Refer to the page number in the table for the school's profile. If a school submitted incomplete data, one or more columns opposite the school name may be blank.

	Page Number	Accreditation (AA=AACSB, AC=ACBSP)	Matriculation (spring, summer, fall, winter, deferred)	Minimum GMAT Score	Minimum Undergraduate GPA	Minimum TOEFL Score	TUITION (R) State Resident (NR) Non-Resident	Financial Aid	Distance Learning	Executive MBA Program
Oral Roberts University, School of Business	439		F, S, SU, D		3.0	600	$259 per hour	•		
Phillips University, School of Business	439		D			550	$97 per semester hour	•		
Southeastern Oklahoma State University, School of Business	440		F, S, SU, D		2.75	550	$1044 per year (R); $58 per credit (R); $2754 per year (NR); $153 per credit (NR)	•		
Southern Nazarene University, School of Business	441					550	$12,000 per year			
Southwestern Oklahoma State University, School of Business	441	AC	D		2.5	550	$75 per hour (R); $177 per (NR)	•	•	
University of Central Oklahoma, College of Business Administration	442	AC	D	450	2.75		$220 per 3 hours (R); $501 per 3 hours (NR)	•		
University of Oklahoma, Michael F. Price College of Business	442	AA	D		3.0	550	$92 per credit hour (R); $266 per credit hour (NR)	•		
University of Tulsa, College of Business Administration	443	AA	D	500	3.0	575	$480 per credit hour	•		
OREGON										
George Fox University, Department of Business and Economics	444		F, D		3.0	550	$21,240 per degree program	•		
Marylhurst University, Graduate Department of Management	444		F, W, S, SU, D			550	$250 per credit hour	•	•	
Oregon Graduate Institute of Science and Technology, Department of Management in Science and Technology	445				3.0	650	$4250 per quarter; $425 per credit			
Oregon State University, College of Business	445	AA	F, D		3.0	575	$10,020 per program (R); $986 per 4 credits (R); $17,050 per program (NR); $1607 per 4 credits (NR)	•		
Portland State University, School of Business Administration	446	AA	F, W, D		2.75	550	$6000 per year (R); $1540 per 8 hours (R); $10,086 per year (NR); $1540 per 8 hours (NR)	•	•	
University of Oregon, Charles H. Lundquist College of Business	447	AA	F, SU		2.8		$6150 per year (R); $10,449 per year (NR)	•		
University of Portland, School of Business Administration	447	AA	F, S, SU		2.75	570	$515 per credit hour	•		
Willamette University, George H. Atkinson Graduate School of Management	448	AA	D			550	$14,900 per year; $497 per credit	•		
PENNSYLVANIA										
Allentown College of St. Francis de Sales, Business Programs	449									
American College, Richard D. Irwin Graduate School of Management	449						$490 per course		•	
Bloomsburg University of Pennsylvania, College of Business	450		D		2.5		$3370 per year (R); $187 per credit hour (R); $6054 per year (NR); $336 per credit hour (NR)			

This table includes the names and locations of colleges, universities, and other institutions offering MBA and other master's-level business programs. Schools appear in geographical sequence by U.S. state or territory or by country and then alphabetically by school name. Specific degree information is detailed within the profile for each school. Refer to the page number in the table for the school's profile. If a school submitted incomplete data, one or more columns opposite the school name may be blank.

School	Page Number	Accreditation (AA=AACSB, AC=ACBSP)	Matriculation (spring, summer, fall, winter, deferred)	Minimum GMAT Score	Minimum Undergraduate GPA	Minimum TOEFL Score	TUITION (R) State Resident (NR) Non-Resident	Financial Aid	Distance Learning	Executive MBA Program
California University of Pennsylvania, School of Graduate Studies and Research	450									
Carnegie Mellon University, Graduate School of Industrial Administration	450	AA	D			600	$24,000 per year; $250 per unit	•	•	
Chatham College, Program in Management	451		D		3.0	600	$7529 per semester; $370 per credit	•		
Clarion University of Pennsylvania, College of Business Administration	452	AA	F, S, D		2.75	550	$3368 per year (R); $187 per credit (R); $6054 per year (NR); $336 per credit (NR)	•		
Drexel University, College of Business and Administration	452	AA	F, W, S, SU, D		3.0	570	$477 per credit	•		
Duquesne University, Graduate School of Business Administration	453	AA	F, S, SU, D			550	$470 per credit	•		
Eastern College, Graduate Business Programs	454		D		2.5	550	$368 per credit	•		
Gannon University, Dahlkemper School of Business	455		D			550		•		
Grove City College, Program in Accounting	455						$273 per credit	•		
Indiana University of Pennsylvania, Eberly College of Business	456				2.6	500	$193 per credit (R); $346 per credit (NR)	•		•
King's College, William G. McGowan School of Business	456		D			550	$437 per credit hour	•		
Kutztown University of Pennsylvania, College of Business	457		D		3.0	550	$3968 per year (R); $187 per credit (R); $6654 per year (NR); $336 per credit (NR)	•	•	
La Roche College, Graduate Studies Office	458		D			550	$385 per credit	•		
La Salle University, School of Business Administration	458	AA	F, S, SU, D			550	$497 per credit	•		
Lebanon Valley College, Business Programs	459					550	$277 per credit	•		
Lehigh University, College of Business and Economics	459	AA	F, S, SU, D			570	$16,200 per year; $590 per credit hour	•	•	
Marywood University, Department of Business and Managerial Science	460		D		3.0	550	$7632 per year; $424 per credit	•		•
Moravian College, Department of Economics and Business	461		D			550	$1254 per course			
Pennsylvania State University at Erie, The Behrend College, Program in Business Administration	461		F, S, SU, D			550	$7320 per year (R); $305 per credit (R); $14,160 per year (NR); $590 per credit (NR)	•		
Pennsylvania State University Great Valley Graduate Center, School of Graduate Professional Studies	462		F, S, D		3.0	550	$330 per credit (R); $590 per credit (NR)	•		
Pennsylvania State University Harrisburg Campus of the Capital College, School of Business Administration	462	AA	F, S, SU, D			550	$305 per credit (R); $590 per credit (NR)	•		

This table includes the names and locations of colleges, universities, and other institutions offering MBA and other master's-level business programs. Schools appear in geographical sequence by U.S. state or territory or by country and then alphabetically by school name. Specific degree information is detailed within the profile for each school. Refer to the page number in the table for the school's profile. If a school submitted incomplete data, one or more columns opposite the school name may be blank.

	Page Number	Accreditation (AA=AACSB, AC=ACBSP)	Matriculation (spring, summer, fall, winter, deferred)	Minimum GMAT Score	Minimum Undergraduate GPA	Minimum TOEFL Score	TUITION (R) State Resident (NR) Non-Resident	Financial Aid	Distance Learning	Executive MBA Program
Pennsylvania State University University Park Campus, Mary Jean and Frank P. Smeal College of Business Administration	463	AA	F, D		2.5	580	$3608 per semester (R); $7070 per semester (NR)	•		
Philadelphia College of Bible, Organizational Leadership Program	464				2.5		$275 per credit			
Philadelphia College of Textiles and Science, School of Business Administration	464		D		2.85	550	$421 per credit	•		
Point Park College, Business Programs	465		D		2.75	500	$347 per credit	•		
Robert Morris College, Graduate Programs in Business and Related Professional Areas	465		D	500		500	$315 per credit	•		
Rosemont College, Accelerated Program in Management	466						$1275 per 3-credit course			
Saint Francis College, Business Administration Program	466		D			500	$7272 per year; $404 per credit	•		
Saint Joseph's University, Erivan K. Haub School of Business	467		F, S, SU, D		2.8	550	$16,610 per year; $510 per credit	•	•	•
Slippery Rock University of Pennsylvania, College of Information Science and Business Administration	468				2.75					
Temple University, School of Business and Management	468	AA	F, S, SU, D			575	$7392 per year (R); $308 per credit (R); $10,296 per year (NR); $429 per credit (NR)	•	•	•
University of Pennsylvania, Wharton School	469	AA	D				$24,990 per year	•		•
University of Pittsburgh, Joseph M. Katz Graduate School of Business	470	AA	D		2.4	600	$15,375 per 11-month program (R); $446 per credit (R); $26,190 per 11-month program (NR); $834 per credit (NR)	•		
University of Scranton, Program in Business Administration	471	AA	D		2.75	500	$465 per credit	•		
Villanova University, College of Commerce and Finance	471	AA	F, S, D			600	$11,280 per year; $470 per credit	•		
Waynesburg College, Graduate Program in Business Administration	472		D				$310 per credit hour	•		•
West Chester University of Pennsylvania, School of Business and Public Affairs	472		D		2.75	550	$193 per credit (R); $346 per credit (NR)	•		•
Widener University, School of Business Administration	473	AA	F, S, SU, D		2.5	550	$470 per credit	•		
Wilkes University, School of Business, Society, and Public Policy	474	AC	D		2.5	550	$523 per credit	•		
York College of Pennsylvania, Department of Business Administration	474	AC	F, S, SU	480	2.8		$5300 per semester; $284 per credit hour	•		
RHODE ISLAND										
Bryant College, Graduate School	475	AA	F, S, SU, D	480	3.0	600	$950 per course	•		

	Page Number	Accreditation (AA=AACSB, AC=ACBSP)	Matriculation (spring, summer, fall, winter, deferred)	Minimum GMAT Score	Minimum Undergraduate GPA	Minimum TOEFL Score	TUITION (R) State Resident (NR) Non-Resident	Financial Aid	Distance Learning	Executive MBA Program
Johnson & Wales University, Alan Shawn Feinstein Graduate School	476		D		2.75	550	$1071 per course; $194 per quarter credit	•		
Providence College, Graduate Business Program	476		D		3.0	550	$8640 per year; $729 per 3-credit course	•		
Salve Regina University, Graduate School	477		D			550	$275 per credit	•	•	
University of Rhode Island, College of Business Administration	478	AA	F, S, D		3.0	575	$6700 per year (R); $187 per credit (R); $17,000 per year (NR); $521 per credit (NR)	•		•
SOUTH CAROLINA										
Charleston Southern University, Graduate Program in Business	478					550	$204 per semester hour	•		
The Citadel, College of Graduate and Professional Studies	479	AA	D			550	$129 per credit hour (R); $129 per credit hour (NR)	•		
Clemson University, College of Business and Public Affairs	480	AA	F, D		2.8	550	$1512 per semester (R); $194 per credit hour (R); $3024 per semester (NR); $384 per credit hour (NR)			
Francis Marion University, School of Business	480	AA	D			550	$3370 per year (R); $160 per hour (R); $6740 per year (NR); $321 per hour (NR)	•	•	
South Carolina State University, Department of Agribusiness and Economics	481		F, S, SU		2.8		$2750 per year (R); $155 per credit (R); $2750 per year (NR); $155 per credit (NR)			
Southern Wesleyan University, Program in Management	482		D		2.7	500	$240 per credit hour	•		
University of Charleston, South Carolina, School of Business and Economics, Graduate Studies	482		D			550	$1251 per semester (R); $139 per credit hour (R); $2565 per semester (NR); $285 per credit hour (NR)	•		
University of South Carolina, College of Business Administration	483	AA	F, S, SU	550	3.0	600	$3724 per year (R); $185 per credit hour (R); $7634 per year (NR); $380 per credit hour (NR)	•	•	
Winthrop University, College of Business Administration	484	AA	F, S, SU, D			550	$1899 per semester (R); $160 per semester hour (R); $3420 per semester (NR); $285 per semester hour (NR)	•	•	•
SOUTH DAKOTA										
Huron University, School of Business	485		D		3.0		$11,440 per year; $220 per quarter hour	•		
University of South Dakota, School of Business	485	AA	F, S, SU, D		2.7	550	$82 per credit (R); $241 per credit (NR)	•		
TENNESSEE										
Belmont University, Jack C. Massey Graduate School of Business	486									
Christian Brothers University, School of Business	486		D	450	2.0	550	$325 per credit hour	•		•
Cumberland University, Business and Economics Division	487		F, S, SU, D				$465 per hour	•		

	Page Number	Accreditation (AA=AACSB, AC=ACBSP)	Matriculation (spring, summer, fall, winter, deferred)	Minimum GMAT Score	Minimum Undergraduate GPA	Minimum TOEFL Score	TUITION (R) State Resident (NR) Non-Resident	Financial Aid	Distance Learning	Executive MBA Program
This table includes the names and locations of colleges, universities, and other institutions offering MBA and other master's-level business programs. Schools appear in geographical sequence by U.S. state or territory or by country and then alphabetically by school name. Specific degree information is detailed within the profile for each school. Refer to the page number in the table for the school's profile. If a school submitted incomplete data, one or more columns opposite the school name may be blank.										
East Tennessee State University, College of Business	487	AA	F, S, D	450	2.5	550	$1183 per semester (R); $119 per credit hour (R); $3351 per semester (NR); $309 per credit hour (NR)	•	•	
Lincoln Memorial University, DeBusk School of Business	488					500	$210 per semester hour	•		
Middle Tennessee State University, College of Business	488	AA				525	$2560 per year (R); $129 per credit hour (R); $7386 per year (NR); $340 per credit hour (NR)	•	•	
Rhodes College, Department of Economics and Business Administration	489		F			550	$17,363 per year			
Tennessee State University, College of Business	489	AA	D		2.0	500	$134 per credit (R); $335 per credit (NR)	•		
Tennessee Technological University, College of Business Administration	490	AA	D		2.5	550	$138 per hour (R); $211 per hour (NR)	•		
Trevecca Nazarene University, Major in Organizational Management	491				2.5	500	$287 per credit hour	•		
Tusculum College, Program in Applied Organizational Management	491		D		2.75	550	$240 per credit hour	•		
Union University, McAfee School of Business Administration	492		D			600	$10,175 per program	•		
The University of Memphis, Fogelman College of Business and Economics	492	AA	F, S, SU, D			550	$2630 per year (R); $130 per credit hour (R); $6940 per year (NR); $321 per credit hour (NR)	•	•	•
University of Tennessee at Chattanooga, School of Business Administration	493	AA	D		2.5	500	$2478 per year (R); $384 per 3-hour course (R); $6078 per year (NR); $927 per 3-hour course (NR)	•	•	•
The University of Tennessee at Martin, School of Business Administration	494	AA	D		2.5	525	$2962 per year (R); $165 per credit (R); $4826 per year (NR); $434 per credit (NR)	•	•	
University of Tennessee, Knoxville, College of Business Administration	494	AA	F			550	$3142 per year (R); $8210 per year (NR)	•		•
Vanderbilt University, Owen Graduate School of Management	495	AA	F, W, S, D				$22,900 per year	•	•	•
TEXAS										
Abilene Christian University, College of Business Administration	496	AC	D		2.8	550	$5238 per year; $291 per credit hour	•		
Amber University, Department of Business Administration	497				3.0		$3600 per year; $450 per course		•	
Angelo State University, Department of Business Administration	497	AC	F, S, SU, D	500	2.5	550	$1022 per year (R); $36 per credit (R); $7382 per year (NR); $246 per credit (NR)	•		
Baylor University, Hankamer School of Business	498	AA	F, S, SU, D			600	$11,088 per year; $308 per hour	•		•
Dallas Baptist University, Graduate School of Business	499	AC	D	425	3.0	550	$4860 per year; $270 per semester hour	•		
East Texas Baptist University, Program in Business Administration	500									

This table includes the names and locations of colleges, universities, and other institutions offering MBA and other master's-level business programs. Schools appear in geographical sequence by U.S. state or territory or by country and then alphabetically by school name. Specific degree information is detailed within the profile for each school. Refer to the page number in the table for the school's profile. If a school submitted incomplete data, one or more columns opposite the school name may be blank.

	Page Number	Accreditation (AA=AACSB, AC=ACBSP)	Matriculation (spring, summer, fall, winter, deferred)	Minimum GMAT Score	Minimum Undergraduate GPA	Minimum TOEFL Score	TUITION (R) State Resident (NR) Non-Resident	Financial Aid	Distance Learning	Executive MBA Program
Houston Baptist University, College of Business and Economics	500		F, W, S, SU, D		2.5	550	$900 per 3-hour course	•		•
Lamar University, College of Business	500	AA	F, S, SU, D	400	2.0	525	$576 per year (R); $120 per 3-hour course (R); $4428 per year (NR); $738 per 3-hour course (NR)	•		
LeTourneau University, Program in Business Administration	501		D		2.8	500	$7215 per year; $300 per credit hour			
Midwestern State University, Division of Business Administration	501	AC	F, S, SU, D	400		550	$1000 per semester (R); $42 per hour (R); $7464 per semester (NR); $222 per hour (NR)	•		
Our Lady of the Lake University of San Antonio, School of Business and Public Administration	502	AC	F, S, SU, D			550	$353 per credit hour	•		
Prairie View A&M University, College of Business	503				2.75	550	$206 per credit (R); $415 per credit (NR)	•		
Rice University, Jesse H. Jones Graduate School of Management	503	AA	F				$15,750 per year	•		
St. Edward's University, School of Business	504		F, S, SU, D	500	2.75	500	$377 per credit hour	•		
St. Mary's University of San Antonio, School of Business and Administration	505		D		2.5	550	$383 per credit hour	•		
Sam Houston State University, College of Business Administration	505	AA	D			550	$650 per semester (R); $32 per credit (R); $3000 per semester (NR); $171 per credit (NR)	•	•	
Southern Methodist University, Edwin L. Cox School of Business	506	AA	F, W, S, SU, D			600	$21,244 per year; $645 per hour	•		
Southwest Texas State University, Graduate School of Business	506	AA	F, S, SU, D		2.75	550	$768 per year (R); $192 per 6 hours (R); $5904 per year (NR); $1476 per 6 hours (NR)	•		
Stephen F. Austin State University, College of Business	507	AA	F, S, SU, D			550	$408 per semester (R); $120 per course (R); $2976 per semester (NR); $744 per course (NR)	•		
Sul Ross State University, Department of Business Administration	508	AC			2.75	520	$120 per semester hour (R); $249 per semester hour (NR)	•		
Tarleton State University, College of Business Administration	508	AC			2.5		$42 per semester credit hour (R); $246 per semester credit hour (NR)		•	
Texas A&M International University, Graduate School of International Trade and Business Administration	509		F, S, SU, D			550	$925 per semester (R); $120 per 3 credit hours (R); $3481 per semester (NR); $744 per 3 credit hours (NR)	•		
Texas A&M University, Lowry Mays Graduate School of Business	510	AA	D			600	$3500 per year (R); $68 per credit hour (R); $9200 per year (NR); $282 per credit hour (NR)	•	•	•
Texas A&M University Commerce, College of Business and Technology	511	AA	F, S, SU, D		2.75	500	$2381 per year (R); $612 per 6 hours (R); $8801 per year (NR); $1896 per 6 hours (NR)	•	•	
Texas A&M University-Corpus Christi, College of Business Administration	511		F, S, SU, D			550	$306 per 9 hours (R); $120 per 3-hour course (R); $2232 per 9 hours (NR); $744 per 3 hour course (NR)	•		
Texas A&M University-Kingsville, College of Business Administration	512	AC			2.5	550	$1112 per year (R); $3886 per year (NR)	•		
Texas A&M University-Texarkana, Division of Business Administration	512		F, S, SU, D			550	$1560 per year (R); $52 per credit hour (R); $7980 per year (NR); $266 per credit hour (NR)	•		

	Page Number	Accreditation (AA=AACSB, AC=ACBSP)	Matriculation (spring, summer, fall, winter, deferred)	Minimum GMAT Score	Minimum Undergraduate GPA	Minimum TOEFL Score	TUITION (R) State Resident (NR) Non-Resident	Financial Aid	Distance Learning	Executive MBA Program
Texas Christian University, M. J. Neeley School of Business	513	AA	D			550	$8280 per year; $345 per semester hour	•		
Texas Southern University, Jesse H. Jones School of Business	514		F, S, SU, D		2.5	550	$558 per 9 hours (R); $372 per 6 hours (R); $2268 per 9 hours (NR); $1512 per 6 hours (NR)	•		
Texas Tech University, College of Business Administration	514	AA	D	500	3.0	550	$2600 per year (R); $68 per credit (R); $8200 per year (NR); $282 per credit (NR)	•		
Texas Wesleyan University, School of Business Administration	515		D		2.85	550	$275 per credit hour	•		
Texas Woman's University, Department of Business and Economics	516		F, S, SU		3.0	550	$75 per credit hour (R); $288 per credit hour (NR)	•		
University of Central Texas, Division of Management, Business and Technology	517				2.5	515	$2664 per year; $148 per hour	•		
University of Dallas, Graduate School of Management	517		F, S, D		3.0	520	$9120 per year; $380 per credit hour	•		
University of Houston, College of Business Administration	518	AA	F, S, D		3.0	620	$672 per 6 hours (R); $2968 per 6 hours (NR)	•		•
University of Houston-Clear Lake, College of Business and Public Administration	519	AA	F, S, SU		2.0	550	$52 per semester hour (R); $171 per semester hour (NR)	•		
University of Houston-Victoria, Division of Business Administration	519		D	400	2.5	500	$486 per 9 hours (R); $2232 per 9 hours (NR)	•	•	
University of Mary Hardin-Baylor, School of Business	520						$9720 per year; $270 per semester hour	•		
University of North Texas, College of Business Administration	521	AA	D	450	2.8	550	$146 per credit hour (R); $272 per credit hour (NR)	•		
University of St. Thomas, Cameron School of Business	521	AC	D		2.5	550	$9840 per year; $410 per credit	•		
The University of Texas at Arlington, College of Business Administration	522	AA	F, S, SU, D	480	2.7	550	$3691 per year (R); $110 per hour (R); $10,411 per year (NR); $331 per hour (NR)	•		
University of Texas at Austin, Graduate School of Business	523	AA	F, D		2.0	600	$3060 per year (R); $102 per semester hour (R); $12,360 per year (NR); $412 per semester hour (NR)	•		•
The University of Texas at Brownsville, School of Business	524		D	400	2.8	550	$229 per course (R); $889 per course (NR)	•		
University of Texas at Dallas, School of Management	525		F, S, SU, D			550	$1379 per year (R); $527 per 3 credits (R); $3305 per year (NR); $1169 per course (NR)	•	•	•
University of Texas at El Paso, College of Business Administration	526	AA	F, S, SU		2.75	600	$2350 per year (R); $356 per course (R); $7294 per year (NR); $974 per course (NR)	•		
University of Texas at San Antonio, College of Business	526	AA	F, S, SU, D	500	3.0	500	$1230 per 9 semester hours (R); $99 per semester credit hour (R); $3147 per 9 semester hours (NR); $313 per semester credit hour (NR)	•		•
University of Texas at Tyler, School of Business Administration	527	AA	D			550	$337 per course (R); $967 per course (NR)	•	•	
University of Texas of the Permian Basin, School of Business	528		D		2.5		$227 per hour (R); $356 per hour (NR)	•		

This table includes the names and locations of colleges, universities, and other institutions offering MBA and other master's-level business programs. Schools appear in geographical sequence by U.S. state or territory or by country and then alphabetically by school name. Specific degree information is detailed within the profile for each school. Refer to the page number in the table for the school's profile. If a school submitted incomplete data, one or more columns opposite the school name may be blank.

	Page Number	Accreditation (AA=AACSB, AC=ACBSP)	Matriculation (spring, summer, fall, winter, deferred)	Minimum GMAT Score	Minimum Undergraduate GPA	Minimum TOEFL Score	TUITION (R) State Resident (NR) Non-Resident	Financial Aid	Distance Learning	Executive MBA Program
University of Texas-Pan American, College of Business Administration	528	AA	F, S, SU, D	470		500	$1570 per year (R); $54 per credit hour (R); $6658 per year (NR); $248 per credit hour (NR)	•		
University of the Incarnate Word, College of Professional Studies	529	AC	D	400	2.5	550	$370 per semester hour; $370 per semester hour	•		
Wayland Baptist University, Graduate Studies Office	529					500	$210 per hour	•		
West Texas A&M University, T. Boone Pickens College of Business	530	AC	F, S, SU, D			550	$2160 per year (R); $60 per credit hour (R); $7992 per year (NR); $222 per credit hour (NR)	•		
UTAH										
Brigham Young University, Marriott School of Management	531	AA	F, D	500	3.0	570		•		•
Southern Utah University, School of Business	531		D			500	$1581 per year (R); $47 per hour (R); $5985 per year (NR); $175 per hour (NR)	•		
University of Utah, David Eccles School of Business	532	AA	F, SU		3.0	600	$3046 per year (R); $1891 per year (R); $9457 per year (NR); $5642 per year (NR)	•		
Utah State University, College of Business	533	AA	D	500	3.0	550	$2426 per year (R); $754 per quarter (R); $7438 per year (NR); $2314 per quarter (NR)	•	•	
Weber State University, College of Business and Economics	534	AA	F, S, D				$1716 per year (R); $1036 per year (R); $6006 per year (NR); $3628 per year (NR)	•		
Westminster College of Salt Lake City, Bill and Vieve Gore School of Business	534		D		3.0	550	$5740 per semester; $410 per hour	•		
VERMONT										
Saint Michael's College, Prevel School Graduate Program in Administration and Management	535				2.8	550	$290 per credit hour			
School for International Training, Program in International and Intercultural Management	535		D			550	$18,500 per degree	•		
University of Vermont, School of Business Administration	536	AA	D			550	$7032 per year (R); $293 per credit (R); $17,580 per year (NR); $733 per credit (NR)	•		
VIRGINIA										
Averett College, Program in Business Administration	537									
College of William and Mary, Graduate School of Business Administration	537	AA	D	550		600	$6500 per year (R); $220 per credit hour (R); $16,500 per year (NR); $515 per credit hour (NR)	•		•
George Mason University, School of Management	538	AA	F, S		3.0	600	$6168 per year (R); $257 per credit hour (R); $12,240 per year (NR); $510 per credit hour (NR)	•	•	•
Hampton University, School of Business	539		D		2.5		$4038 per year; $220 per credit hour	•		
James Madison University, College of Business	539	AA			2.75	500	$134 per credit hour (R); $404 per credit hour (NR)	•	•	

	Page Number	Accreditation (AA=AACSB, AC=ACBSP)	Matriculation (spring, summer, fall, winter, deferred)	Minimum GMAT Score	Minimum Undergraduate GPA	Minimum TOEFL Score	TUITION (R) State Resident (NR) Non-Resident	Financial Aid	Distance Learning	Executive MBA Program
			ADMISSION REQUIREMENTS					OPTIONS		
Lynchburg College, School of Business and Economics	540		SU	400	2.5	550	$255 per hour	•	•	
Marymount University, School of Business Administration	540	AC	D			600	$465 per credit hour	•		
Old Dominion University, College of Business and Public Administration	541	AA	F, S, SU, D		2.5	550	$180 per credit (R); $477 per credit (NR)	•	•	
Radford University, College of Business and Economics	542	AA	D		2.7	550	$2240 per year (R); $142 per credit hour (R); $5518 per year (NR); $278 per credit hour (NR)	•		
Regent University, School of Business	543		D		2.75	550	$11,700 per year; $325 per credit hour	•	•	
Shenandoah University, Harry F. Byrd, Jr. School of Business	543		D			550	$450 per hour	•		
University of Richmond, The Richard S. Reynolds Graduate School	544	AA	F, S, SU, D	540		550	$17,670 per year; $870 per course	•		
University of Virginia, Darden Graduate School of Business Administration	545	AA	F, D				$13,835 per year (R); $20,429 per year (NR)	•		
Virginia Commonwealth University, School of Business	545	AA	F, S, SU, D		2.7	600	$3810 per year (R); $212 per credit (R); $12,265 per year (NR); $627 per credit (NR)	•	•	
Virginia Polytechnic Institute and State University, Pamplin College of Business	546	AA	D				$229 per hour (R); $374 per hour (NR)	•	•	
Virginia State University, School of Business	547					500	$133 per credit hour (R); $364 per credit hour (NR)	•		
WASHINGTON										
Antioch University Seattle, Graduate Management Program	547		F, D			600	$12,500 per year; $380 per credit	•		
City University, Graduate School of Business and Management Professions	548		D			540	$6720 per year; $280 per credit hour	•	•	
Eastern Washington University, College of Business Administration and Public Administration	548									
Gonzaga University, School of Business Administration	549	AA	D			550	$395 per credit hour	•		
Pacific Lutheran University, School of Business	549	AA	D		2.75	550	$11,352 per year; $473 per semester hour	•		
Saint Martin's College, Business and Economics Division	550		D			525	$450 per credit hour	•		
Seattle Pacific University, School of Business and Economics	550		F, W, S, SU, D			565	$11,124 per year; $412 per quarter credit hour	•		
Seattle University, Albers School of Business and Economics	551	AA	F, W, S, SU, D		3.0	580	$440 per quarter hour	•		
University of Washington, School of Business Administration	552	AA	F		3.0	600	$5232 per year (R); $1682 per quarter (R); $12,966 per year (NR); $4158 per quarter (NR)	•		•

This table includes the names and locations of colleges, universities, and other institutions offering MBA and other master's-level business programs. Schools appear in geographical sequence by U.S. state or territory or by country and then alphabetically by school name. Specific degree information is detailed within the profile for each school. Refer to the page number in the table for the school's profile. If a school submitted incomplete data, one or more columns opposite the school name may be blank.

	Page Number	Accreditation (AA=AACSB, AC=ACBSP)	Matriculation (spring, summer, fall, winter, deferred)	Minimum GMAT Score	Minimum Undergraduate GPA	Minimum TOEFL Score	TUITION (R) State Resident (NR) Non-Resident	Financial Aid	Distance Learning	Executive MBA Program
Washington State University, College of Business and Economics	553	AA	D		3.0	580	$5334 per year (R); $267 per credit (R); $13,380 per year (NR); $669 per credit (NR)	•		
Western Washington University, College of Business and Economics	553	AA	SU		3.0	565	$1400 per quarter (R); $140 per credit (R); $4260 per quarter (NR); $426 per credit (NR)	•		
Whitworth College, Whitworth Graduate School of International Management	554		F, S, D		3.0	550	$6400 per 20 credits; $320 per credit	•		
WEST VIRGINIA										
Marshall University, College of Business	555	AA	D		2.5	525	$1158 per semester (R); $121 per credit hour (R); $3325 per semester (NR); $361 per credit hour (NR)	•		
Marshall University Graduate College, College of Business and Economics	555		D			550	$158 per credit hour (R); $449 per credit hour (NR)	•	•	•
The University of Charleston, Jones-Benedum Division of Business	556		D			600	$515 per credit hour	•		•
West Virginia University, College of Business and Economics	556	AA	D	500	3.0	550	$2805 per semester (R); $158 per credit hour (R); $8056 per semester (NR); $449 per credit hour (NR)	•	•	•
West Virginia Wesleyan College, Faculty of Business	557					500	$290 per credit hour	•		
Wheeling Jesuit University, Graduate Business Program	557		D		2.75	550	$1130 per 3 credits	•	•	
WISCONSIN										
Cardinal Stritch University, College of Business and Management	558		D		2.5	600	$365 per credit	•		
Concordia University Wisconsin, Business Programs	559		D		3.0	550	$11,700 per program; $300 per credit	•	•	
Edgewood College, Program in Business	559									
Lakeland College, Graduate Studies Division	559		D		2.75	550	$215 per credit	•		
Marian College of Fond du Lac, Business Division	560		D		2.5		$275 per credit	•		
Marquette University, College of Business Administration	561	AA	D			550	$510 per credit hour	•		•
Milwaukee School of Engineering, Program in Engineering Management	561				2.8	550	$365 per credit	•	•	
Silver Lake College, Program in Management and Organizational Behavior	562				3.0		$230 per credit	•		
University of Wisconsin-Eau Claire, School of Business	562	AA	D		2.75	550	$204 per credit (R); $581 per credit (NR)	•	•	
University of Wisconsin-Green Bay, Program in Administrative Sciences	563						$3130 per year (R); $10,358 per year (NR)	•		

	Page Number	Accreditation (AA=AACSB, AC=ACBSP)	Matriculation (spring, summer, fall, winter, deferred)	Minimum GMAT Score	Minimum Undergraduate GPA	Minimum TOEFL Score	TUITION (R) State Resident (NR) Non-Resident	Financial Aid	Distance Learning	Executive MBA Program
University of Wisconsin-La Crosse, College of Business Administration	563	AA	D		2.85	550	$3670 per year (R); $227 per semester credit (R); $10,300 per year (NR); $628 per semester credit (NR)	•	•	
University of Wisconsin-Madison, School of Business	564	AA	F, S		3.0	600	$5666 per year (R); $15,380 per year (NR)	•		•
University of Wisconsin-Milwaukee, School of Business Administration	565	AA	D		2.75	550	$2642 per semester (R); $350 per credit (R); $7478 per semester (NR); $934 per credit (NR)	•		•
University of Wisconsin-Oshkosh, College of Business Administration	565	AA	F, S, SU, D		2.75	550	$1900 per semester (R); $200 per credit (R); $5600 per semester (NR); $600 per credit (NR)	•	•	
University of Wisconsin-Parkside, School of Business and Administrative Science	566	AA	F, S, SU, D		2.75		$521 per course (R); $1559 per course (NR)			
University of Wisconsin-Stout, Program in Training and Development and Program in Management Technology	566				2.75	500	$3129 per year (R); $174 per credit (R); $7229 per year (NR); $402 per credit (NR)	•		
University of Wisconsin-Whitewater, College of Business and Economics	567	AA	F, S, SU, D		2.75	550	$656 per 3-credit class (R); $656 per 3-credit class (R); $1856 per 3-credit class (NR)	•	•	
WYOMING										
University of Wyoming, College of Business	568	AA	F, D		3.0	540	$2812 per year (R); $135 per credit hour (R); $7518 per year (NR); $418 per credit hour (NR)	•	•	
GUAM										
University of Guam, College of Business and Public Administration	569									
PUERTO RICO										
Inter American University of Puerto Rico, Metropolitan Campus, Division of Economics and Business Administration	569		F		2.75					
Inter American University of Puerto Rico, San Germán Campus, Department of Business Administration	569				2.5		$2610 per year; $145 per credit	•		
Pontifical Catholic University of Puerto Rico, College of Business Administration	570									
Universidad del Turabo, Programs in Business Administration	570									
University of Puerto Rico, Mayagüez Campus, College of Business Administration	570		F, S				$75 per credit (R); $1750 per semester (NR)	•		
University of Puerto Rico, Río Piedras, Graduate School of Business Administration	571		F, S	450	3.0			•		
University of the Sacred Heart, Business School	571			500	2.75		$150 per credit	•		
VIRGIN ISLANDS										
University of the Virgin Islands, Division of Business Administration	572									

This table includes the names and locations of colleges, universities, and other institutions offering MBA and other master's-level business programs. Schools appear in geographical sequence by U.S. state or territory or by country and then alphabetically by school name. Specific degree information is detailed within the profile for each school. Refer to the page number in the table for the school's profile. If a school submitted incomplete data, one or more columns opposite the school name may be blank.

ADMISSION REQUIREMENTS

OPTIONS

This table includes the names and locations of colleges, universities, and other institutions offering MBA and other master's-level business programs. Schools appear in geographical sequence by U.S. state or territory or by country and then alphabetically by school name. Specific degree information is detailed within the profile for each school. Refer to the page number in the table for the school's profile. If a school submitted incomplete data, one or more columns opposite the school name may be blank.

	Page Number	Accreditation (AA=AACSB, AC=ACBSP)	Matriculation (spring, summer, fall, winter, deferred)	Minimum GMAT Score	Minimum Undergraduate GPA	Minimum TOEFL Score	TUITION (R) State Resident (NR) Non-Resident	Financial Aid	Distance Learning	Executive MBA Program
AUSTRALIA										
Australian National University, Managing Business in Asia Program	572					570	Aus$27,500 per program (R); Aus$27,500 per program (NR)	•		
Bond University, School of Business	573		D	550		560	Aus$25,800 per program; Aus$2150 per unit			•
Curtin University of Technology, Graduate School of Business	574		D			580	Aus$16,800 per course (R); Aus$26,400 per course (NR)	•	•	
Deakin University, Faculty of Business and Law	574		S, SU	600		580			•	
Edith Cowan University, Faculty of Business	575		D			650	Aus$950 per unit (R); Aus$12,600 per year (NR)	•	•	
La Trobe University, Faculty of Law and Management	575		S			575				
Macquarie University, Macquarie Graduate School of Management	576		W		3.0	550				
Monash University, Monash Mt. Eliza Business School	577		W, SU, D	575	3.0	580				
Murdoch University, School of Business	577		F, D			550	Aus$14,100 per year (R); Aus$4700 per trimester (R); Aus$22,000 per year (NR); Aus$6900 per trimester (NR)	•		
Royal Melbourne Institute of Technology, Graduate School of Business	578		F			580		•	•	
The University of Adelaide, Graduate School of Management	579		F, S, D			580	Aus$22,400 per program (R); Aus$1400 per subject (R); Aus$31,500 per program (NR); Aus$1969 per subject (NR)	•		
University of Melbourne, Melbourne Business School	579		W, D				Aus$40,000 per program; Aus$1650 per subject	•		
University of Newcastle, Graduate School of Business	580		W, SU	500		550	Aus$12,000 per year (R); Aus$17,400 per year (NR)	•		
University of New South Wales, Australian Graduate School of Management	581		W, SU, D	550	3.0			•	•	•
University of Southern Queensland, Faculty of Business	581		W, SU, D			550	Aus$800 per unit (R); Aus$1050 per unit (NR)		•	
The University of Sydney, Graduate School of Business	582		W, SU, D			575	Aus$6000 per semester (R); Aus$10,600 per semester (NR)	•		
University of Technology, Sydney, Graduate School of Business	582		F, S			575		•		
The University of Western Australia, Graduate School of Management	583		F, S, D		2.75	550	Aus$4400 per trimester (R); Aus$1100 per unit (R); Aus$8000 per trimester (NR); Aus$2000 per unit (NR)			
University of Western Sydney, Macarthur, Faculty of Business and Technology	584		F, W, S, SU, D			570				

This table includes the names and locations of colleges, universities, and other institutions offering MBA and other master's-level business programs. Schools appear in geographical sequence by U.S. state or territory or by country and then alphabetically by school name. Specific degree information is detailed within the profile for each school. Refer to the page number in the table for the school's profile. If a school submitted incomplete data, one or more columns opposite the school name may be blank.

	Page Number	Accreditation (AA=AACSB, AC=ACBSP)	Matriculation (spring, summer, fall, winter, deferred)	Minimum GMAT Score	Minimum Undergraduate GPA	Minimum TOEFL Score	TUITION (R) State Resident (NR) Non-Resident	Financial Aid	Distance Learning	Executive MBA Program
AUSTRIA										
Vienna University of Economics and Business Administration, Business Program/International MBA	584		SU, D			550	$25,000 per program (R); $25,000 per program (R); $25,000 per program (NR); $25,000 per program (NR)	•		
BANGLADESH										
International University of Business Agriculture and Technology (IUBAT), College of Business Administration	585		D				$4884 per program	•		
University of Dhaka, Institute of Business Administration	585		W							
BELGIUM										
European University, International Center for Management Studies	586			450		450	$12,000 per program			•
Katholieke Universiteit Leuven, Department of Applied Economic Sciences	587		F, D				18,000 Belgian francs per year (R); 10,000 Belgian francs per year (R); 18,000 Belgian francs per year (NR); 10,000 Belgian francs per year (NR)			
St. Ignatius University Faculty of Antwerp (UFSIA), Center for Business Administration	587		F	550						
CANADA										
Athabasca University, Centre for Innovative Management	588		F, W, S, D				Can$19,550 per program (R); Can$19,550 per program (NR)		•	•
Carleton University, School of Business	588		D		7.0/12 scale	550	Can$3886 per year (R); Can$8786 per year (NR)	•		
Concordia University, Faculty of Commerce and Administration	589	AA	F, W, SU, D		3.0	600	Can$1622 per year (R); Can$155 per credit (R); Can$8262 per year (NR); Can$275 per credit (NR)	•		•
Dalhousie University, Faculty of Management	590		F, W	550	3.0	580	Can$4975 per year (R); Can$1613 per year (R); Can$7925 per year (NR); Can$4675 per year (NR)	•	•	
École des Hautes Études Commerciales, Master of Business Administration Program	591		F, W		70.0/100 scale		Can$3211 per year (R); Can$62 per credit (R); Can$14,651 per year (NR); Can$282 per credit (NR)			
Laurentian University, School of Commerce and Administration	591		F		70.0/100 scale	550	Can$4975 per year (R); Can$995 per 6-credit course (R); Can$9072 per year (NR); Can$1814 per 6 credit course (NR)	•	•	
McGill University, Faculty of Management	592		F		3.0	600	Can$2497 per year (R); Can$16,000 per year (NR)	•		
McMaster University, Michael G. DeGroote School of Business	593		F		3.0		Can$4748 per year (R); Can$431 per course (R); Can$12,000 per year (NR); Can$1500 per course (NR)	•		
Memorial University of Newfoundland, Faculty of Business Administration	593		D	520	2.0/3 scale	580	Can$5800 per program (R); Can$5800 per program (NR)	•		
Queen's University at Kingston, School of Business	594		W		3.0	600		•	•	•
Saint Mary's University, Frank H. Sobey Faculty of Commerce	595		D			600	Can$750 per credit (R); Can$1380 per credit (NR)	•		•

This table includes the names and locations of colleges, universities, and other institutions offering MBA and other master's-level business programs. Schools appear in geographical sequence by U.S. state or territory or by country and then alphabetically by school name. Specific degree information is detailed within the profile for each school. Refer to the page number in the table for the school's profile. If a school submitted incomplete data, one or more columns opposite the school name may be blank.

	Page Number	Accreditation (AA=AACSB, AC=ACBSP)	Matriculation (spring, summer, fall, winter, deferred)	Minimum GMAT Score	Minimum Undergraduate GPA	Minimum TOEFL Score	TUITION (R) State Resident (NR) Non-Resident	Financial Aid	Distance Learning	Executive MBA Program
Simon Fraser University, Faculty of Business Administration	595		F, S, SU, D		3.0	570	Can$2400 per year (R); Can$2400 per year (NR)	•		
Université de Moncton, Faculty d' Administration	596		F, D		3.0		Can$132 per credit (R); Can$176 per credit (NR)	•	•	
Université de Sherbrooke, Faculty of Administration	596									
Université du Québec à Montréal, École des Sciences de la Gestion	597									
Université Laval, Faculty des Sciences de l'Administration	597	AA	F, W, D		3.2			•		
University of Alberta, Faculty of Business	597	AA			3.0	600	Can$3710 per year (R); Can$327 per 3 credits (R); Can$6980 per year (NR); Can$654 per 3 credits (NR)			
University of British Columbia, Faculty of Commerce and Business Administration	598		F		3.2	600	Can$15,000 per program (R); Can$20,000 per program (NR)	•		
The University of Calgary, Faculty of Management	599	AA	F, W	500	3.0	550	Can$10,000 per program (R); Can$454 per credit (R); Can$20,000 per program (NR); Can$908 per credit (NR)	•		•
University of Guelph, Business Programs	600					550	Can$6000 per year (R); Can$6000 per year (NR)	•		
University of Manitoba, Faculty of Management	600		F, D		3.0	550	Can$17,600 per program (R); Can$17,600 per program (NR)	•		
University of New Brunswick, Faculty of Business	601		D		3.0	550	Can$18,000 per year (R); Can$500 per semester (R); Can$18,000 per year (NR); Can$500 per semester (NR)	•		
University of New Brunswick, Faculty of Administration	602		F		3.0	550	Can$3330 per year (R); Can$5630 per year (NR)	•		
University of Ottawa, Faculty of Administration	602		F		2.8	550	Can$1912 per session (R); Can$150 per credit (R); Can$3630 per session (NR); Can$300 per credit (NR)	•		•
University of Regina, Faculty of Administration	603		D		3.0	580	Can$563 per course (R); Can$563 per course (NR)	•		
University of Saskatchewan, College of Commerce	603		F, W, D	500	70.0/100 scale	550	Can$357 per 3-credit course (R); Can$357 per 3-credit course (NR)	•		
University of Toronto, Joseph L. Rotman School of Management	604		F, W, D		3.0	600	Can$7390 per year (R); Can$1890 per year (R); Can$13,610 per year (NR); Can$4327 per year (NR)	•		
University of Victoria, Faculty of Business	605		F		3.0	575	Can$8000 per program (R); Can$8000 per program (NR)	•		
University of Waterloo, School of Accountancy	605								•	
The University of Western Ontario, Richard Ivey School of Business	606		D	560	2.7	600	Can$12,000 per year (R); Can$14,000 per year (NR)	•		
University of Windsor, Faculty of Business Administration	607		D	500	3.0	600	Can$4250 per year (R); Can$707 per term (R); Can$8250 per year (NR); Can$1375 per term (NR)	•		
Wilfrid Laurier University, School of Business and Economics	607		F	550	8.0/12 scale	550	Can$4860 per year (R); Can$876 per term (R); Can$10,500 per year (NR)	•		

This table includes the names and locations of colleges, universities, and other institutions offering MBA and other master's-level business programs. Schools appear in geographical sequence by U.S. state or territory or by country and then alphabetically by school name. Specific degree information is detailed within the profile for each school. Refer to the page number in the table for the school's profile. If a school submitted incomplete data, one or more columns opposite the school name may be blank.	Page Number	Accreditation (AA=AACSB, AC=ACBSP)	ADMISSION REQUIREMENTS				TUITION (R) State Resident (NR) Non-Resident	OPTIONS		
			Matriculation (spring, summer, fall, winter, deferred)	Minimum GMAT Score	Minimum Undergraduate GPA	Minimum TOEFL Score		Financial Aid	Distance Learning	Executive MBA Program
York University, Schulich School of Business	608		F, W, D		3.0	600	Can$2150 per term (R); Can$1100 per term (R); Can$8650 per term (NR); Can$4300 per term (NR)	•		
CAYMAN ISLANDS										
International College of the Cayman Islands, Graduate Studies Program	609		D				$3000 per year; $100 per quarter credit	•		
CHINA										
Fudan University, School of Management	610									
COSTA RICA										
INCAE (Instituto Centroamericano de Administración de Empresas), Graduate Program	610		F, D				$11,500 per year	•		
CZECH REPUBLIC										
Czech Management Center, Graduate School of Business	611		W, D		3.0			•		•
DENMARK										
Copenhagen Business School, Faculty of Economics and Business Administration	611		F, S, D			575		•		
EGYPT										
American University in Cairo, School of Business, Economics and Communication	612		F, S	600	3.0	550		•		
FINLAND										
Helsinki School of Economics and Business Administration, International Center	613		W, D			500	$18,500 per program (R); $18,500 per program (NR)			•
FRANCE										
EAP-European School of Management, School of Management	613		F, D			600	125,000 French francs per year (R); 125,000 French francs per year (NR)	•		•
École Nationale des Ponts et Chaussées, ENPC Graduate School of International Business	614		D			550	110,000 French francs per year	•		
École Supérieure de Commerce de Rouen, Business Programs	615									
École Supérieure des Sciences Économiques et Commerciales, ESSEC School of Management	615	AA	F, D			500	127,500 French francs per program			•
E. M. Lyon, Cesma MBA	616		F, D	550		600	97,000 French francs per year; 30,000 French francs per year	•		

	Page Number	Accreditation (AA=AACSB, AC=ACBSP)	Matriculation (spring, summer, fall, winter, deferred)	Minimum GMAT Score	Minimum Undergraduate GPA	Minimum TOEFL Score	TUITION (R) State Resident (NR) Non-Resident	Financial Aid	Distance Learning	Executive MBA Program
Groupe CERAM, Ceram ESC Nice School of Management	617		D				96,600 French francs per year (R); 96,600 French francs per year (NR)		•	•
Groupe ESC Clermont, Clermont Graduate School of Management	617									
Groupe ESC Nantes Atlantique, Groupe ESC Nantes Atlantique Business Programs	617		D				90,000 French francs per program		•	
Groupe ESC Toulouse, ESC Toulouse Graduate School of Management	618		F, D							
HEC Graduate School of Management, Institute Supérieur des Affaires	619		D		2.5	600	125,000 French francs per program (R); 125,000 French francs per program (NR)	•		
INSEAD (The European Institute of Business Administration), Business Programs	619		D			620	159,000 French francs per year	•		
Institut Superieur de Gestion, ISG International School of Business	620		F, D		3.0	550				•
Reims Graduate Business School, Reims Business School	621									
Schiller International University, Business Programs	621		F, W, S, SU, D						•	
Schiller International University, Business Programs	621		D				6600 French francs per course		•	
THESEUS Institute, International Management Institute	622		F, D				140,000 French francs per program			
GERMANY										
Schiller International University, Business Programs	623		D						•	
WHU Koblenz, Otto-Beisheim Graduate School of Management	623		F	530		530	12,000 German marks per year; 48,000 German marks per program	•		•
GREECE										
Athens University of Economics and Business, Department of Business Administration	624		D				250,000 Greek drachmas per semester	•		
HONG KONG										
The Chinese University of Hong Kong, Faculty of Business Administration	624		F, D		3.0		42,100 Hong Kong dollars per year (R); 42,100 Hong Kong dollars per year (NR)	•		•
Hong Kong Baptist University, School of Business	625		F	500			57,600 Hong Kong dollars per year (R); 57,600 Hong Kong dollars per year (NR)	•		
The Hong Kong University of Science and Technology, School of Business and Management	626		F, D		3.0			•		•
University of Hong Kong, University of Hong Kong School of Business	626		F, D	550		550	57,150 Hong Kong dollars per year (R); 57,150 Hong Kong dollars per year (NR)			

This table includes the names and locations of colleges, universities, and other institutions offering MBA and other master's-level business programs. Schools appear in geographical sequence by U.S. state or territory or by country and then alphabetically by school name. Specific degree information is detailed within the profile for each school. Refer to the page number in the table for the school's profile. If a school submitted incomplete data, one or more columns opposite the school name may be blank.

ADMISSION REQUIREMENTS

OPTIONS

This table includes the names and locations of colleges, universities, and other institutions offering MBA and other master's-level business programs. Schools appear in geographical sequence by U.S. state or territory or by country and then alphabetically by school name. Specific degree information is detailed within the profile for each school. Refer to the page number in the table for the school's profile. If a school submitted incomplete data, one or more columns opposite the school name may be blank.

	Page Number	Accreditation (AA=AACSB, AC=ACBSP)	Matriculation (spring, summer, fall, winter, deferred)	Minimum GMAT Score	Minimum Undergraduate GPA	Minimum TOEFL Score	TUITION (R) State Resident (NR) Non-Resident	Financial Aid	Distance Learning	Executive MBA Program
INDONESIA										
Institut Pengembangan Manajemen Indonesia, Business Programs	627		SU			575				•
IRELAND										
University College Cork, Faculty of Commerce	627		F				4840 Irish pounds per year (R); 4400 Irish pounds per year (NR)			•
University College Dublin, The Michael Smurfit Graduate School of Business	628		F				7500 Irish pounds per year (R); 10,000 Irish pounds per year (NR)			•
University College, Galway, Faculty of Commerce	629			450			3745 Irish pounds per year			•
University of Limerick, College of Business	629				3.0	550	4375 Irish pounds per year (R); 8750 Irish pounds per year (NR)	•		•
ISRAEL										
Bar-Ilan University, S. Daniel Abraham Center of Economics and Business, The Graduate School of Business	630		SU, D							
Hebrew University of Jerusalem, Jerusalem School of Business Administration	630									
Tel Aviv University, Leon Recanati Graduate School of Business Administration	630		F, S		70.0/100 scale			•		•
ITALY										
Bocconi University, SDA Bocconi	631		F, D				32,000,000 Italian lire per year	•		
JAPAN										
International University of Japan, Graduate School of International Management	632		F, D			550	¥1,900,000 per year	•		
Waseda University, Graduate School of Asia-Pacific Studies	633		F, S					•		
MEXICO										
Duxx Graduate School of Business Leadership, Business Programs	633		F, S							
Instituto Tecnológico y de Estudios Superiores de Monterrey, Graduate School of Business Administration and Leadership	634									
Instituto Tecnológico y de Estudios Superiores de Monterrey, Campus Estado de México, Graduate Division	634									
Instituto Tecnológico y de Estudios Superiores de Monterrey, Campus Guadalajara, Program in Business Administration	634		F, W, S, SU, D		8.0/10 scale		24,600 Mexican pesos per trimester; 16,996 Mexican pesos per trimester	•	•	•

This table includes the names and locations of colleges, universities, and other institutions offering MBA and other master's-level business programs. Schools appear in geographical sequence by U.S. state or territory or by country and then alphabetically by school name. Specific degree information is detailed within the profile for each school. Refer to the page number in the table for the school's profile. If a school submitted incomplete data, one or more columns opposite the school name may be blank.	Page Number	Accreditation (AA=AACSB, AC=ACBSP)	ADMISSION REQUIREMENTS			TUITION (R) State Resident (NR) Non-Resident	OPTIONS		
			Matriculation (spring, summer, fall, winter, deferred)	Minimum GMAT Score	Minimum Undergraduate GPA	Minimum TOEFL Score		Financial Aid	Distance Learning	Executive MBA Program
Instituto Tecnológico y de Estudios Superiores de Monterrey, Campus Laguna, Graduate School	635									
Instituto Tecnológico y de Estudios Superiores de Monterrey, Campus León, Program in Business Administration	635									
Instituto Tecnológico y de Estudios Superiores de Monterrey, Campus México City, Programs in Business	635		F, SU, D		8.0/10 scale		75,000 Mexican pesos per year; 6960 Mexican pesos per subject	•	•	•
Instituto Tecnológico y de Estudios Superiores de Monterrey, Campus Querétaro, EGADE School of Business	636		F, W, D		3.0	570	$1000 per course			
Instituto Tecnológico y de Estudios Superiores de Monterrey, Campus Toluca, Graduate Programs	636									
Universidad de las Américas- Puebla, Business and Management School	637		F, S			500	920 Mexican pesos per credit			
MONACO										
University of Southern Europe, Monaco Graduate School	637		F, D			550	96,500 French francs per year	•		
NETHERLANDS										
Erasmus University Rotterdam, Rotterdam School of Management	638	AA	F, D				42,500 Dutch guilders per program	•		
Nijenrode University, Netherlands Business School	638		F, D	550	3.2	600	38,000 Dutch guilders per program; 95,000 Dutch guilders per 18-month program	•	•	•
Open University of the Netherlands, Business Programs	639		F, W, S				7500 European currency units per year (R); 7500 European currency units per year (NR)		•	
University of Twente, TSM Business School	640			500				•		•
NEW ZEALAND										
University of Auckland, Executive Programs	640		S, D				NZ$8156 per year (R); NZ$19,238 per year (NR)	•		
University of Canterbury, Department of Management	641		W	560		600		•		
University of Otago, Advanced Business Programme	641		W			575	NZ$20,000 per year (R); NZ$33,000 per year (NR)	•		
University of Waikato, School of Management Studies	642					630		•		•
Victoria University of Wellington, Graduate School of Business and Government Management	642					600	NZ$4680 per trimester (R); NZ$1040 per course (R); NZ$6375 per trimester (NR); NZ$25,500 per degree (NR)	•		
NORWAY										
Norwegian School of Management, Graduate School	643		F, D				122,000 Norwegian kroner per program; 180,000 Norwegian kroner per program	•		

	Page Number	Accreditation (AA=AACSB, AC=ACBSP)	Matriculation (spring, summer, fall, winter, deferred)	ADMISSION REQUIREMENTS			TUITION (R) State Resident (NR) Non-Resident	OPTIONS		
				Minimum GMAT Score	Minimum Undergraduate GPA	Minimum TOEFL Score		Financial Aid	Distance Learning	Executive MBA Program
This table includes the names and locations of colleges, universities, and other institutions offering MBA and other master's-level business programs. Schools appear in geographical sequence by U.S. state or territory or by country and then alphabetically by school name. Specific degree information is detailed within the profile for each school. Refer to the page number in the table for the school's profile. If a school submitted incomplete data, one or more columns opposite the school name may be blank.										
University of Oslo, Department of Economics	644		F, S				330 Norwegian kroner per semester (R); 330 Norwegian kroner per semester (NR)			
PAKISTAN										
Lahore University of Management Sciences, Graduate School of Business Administration	644		F, D	450			147,000 Pakistani rupees per year	•		
PERU										
Escuela de Administracion de Negocios para Graduados, Programa Magister	645		D				$15,500 per year; $16,000 per program			
PORTUGAL										
Instituto Empresarial Portuense, Business School	646		F						•	
Universidade do Porto, Graduate School of Business	646		F						•	
Universidade Nova de Lisboa, Faculdade de Economia-Gestao	646		W		14.0/20 scale	500	1,400,000 Portugese escudos per year (R); 1,400,000 Portugese escudos per year (NR)			
REPUBLIC OF SINGAPORE										
Nanyang Technological University, Nanyang Business School	647		D		3.0		$1875 per trimester (R); $1250 per trimester (R); $1875 per trimester (NR); $1250 per trimester (NR)	•		
National University of Singapore, Graduate School of Business	648		W, SU, D			580	7170 Singapore dollars per year (R); 12,190 Singapore dollars per year (R); 14,340 Singapore dollars per year (NR); 24,380 Singapore dollars per year (NR)	•		
RUSSIAN FEDERATION										
The International Management Institute of St. Petersburg, Marketing Department	648					500				•
SLOVENIA										
International Executive Development Center, School of Business Administration	649		W, D						•	•
SOUTH AFRICA										
Rhodes University, Management Department	649						4500 South African rand per year			
University of Cape Town, Graduate School of Business	650		D			600	33,000 South African rand per year (R); 33,000 South African rand per year (NR)			
University of the Witwatersrand, Graduate School of Business Administration	650		F, W				35,000 South African rand per program (R); 36,000 South African rand per program (NR)	•		

This table includes the names and locations of colleges, universities, and other institutions offering MBA and other master's-level business programs. Schools appear in geographical sequence by U.S. state or territory or by country and then alphabetically by school name. Specific degree information is detailed within the profile for each school. Refer to the page number in the table for the school's profile. If a school submitted incomplete data, one or more columns opposite the school name may be blank.

	Page Number	Accreditation (AA=AACSB, AC=ACBSP)	Matriculation (spring, summer, fall, winter, deferred)	Minimum GMAT Score	Minimum Undergraduate GPA	Minimum TOEFL Score	TUITION (R) State Resident (NR) Non-Resident	Financial Aid	Distance Learning	Executive MBA Program
SPAIN										
EAP-European School of Management, Business School	651		W			600				
Escola d'Alta Direcció i Administració (EADA), Business Programs	651		D				1,400,000 Spanish pesetas per year; 1,090,000 Spanish pesetas per year	•		•
Escuela Superior de Administración y Dirección de Empresas (ESADE), Business School	652		F	550				•		
IADE, Instituto Universitario de Administracion de Empresas	653		S, SU					•		•
Instituto de Empresa, Business School	653			550				•		
Schiller International University, Business Programs	654		F, W, S, SU					•		
University of Navarra, IESE International Graduate School of Management	654		F, D			600	2,300,000 pesetas per year	•		
SWEDEN										
Göteborg University, School of Economics and Commercial Laws	655									
Stockholm School of Economics, Department of Business Administration	655									
SWITZERLAND										
American Graduate School of Business, Master of International Business Administration Program	655		D		2.7	550	30,000 Swiss francs per year; 2700 Swiss francs per course	•		
Graduate School of Business Administration Zürich, Business Programs	656		D	550		550		•	•	•
International Institute for Management Development (IMD), Business Programs	657						41,000 Swiss francs per program	•		
Schiller International University, American College of Switzerland, Business Programs	657									
Université de Lausanne, École des Hautes Etudes Commerciales	657		F				10,000 Swiss francs per year (R); 17,000 Swiss francs per 2 years (R); 10,000 Swiss francs per year (NR); 17,000 Swiss francs per 2 years (NR)			•
University of St. Gallen, Business School	658									•
THAILAND										
Bangkok University, Graduate School	659		F	450	2.5	550				
Chulalongkorn University, Sasin Graduate Institute of Business Administration	659		S, D				$13,875 per program			•

				ADMISSION REQUIREMENTS				OPTIONS		
This table includes the names and locations of colleges, universities, and other institutions offering MBA and other master's-level business programs. Schools appear in geographical sequence by U.S. state or territory or by country and then alphabetically by school name. Specific degree information is detailed within the profile for each school. Refer to the page number in the table for the school's profile. If a school submitted incomplete data, one or more columns opposite the school name may be blank.	Page Number	Accreditation (AA=AACSB, AC=ACBSP)	Matriculation (spring, summer, fall, winter, deferred)	Minimum GMAT Score	Minimum Undergraduate GPA	Minimum TOEFL Score	TUITION (R) State Resident (NR) Non-Resident	Financial Aid	Distance Learning	Executive MBA Program
TURKEY										
Bilkent University, School of Business Administration	660		F			550	$4350 per year	•		
UKRAINE										
Kyiv State University of Economics, MBA Program	660									•
UNITED KINGDOM										
The American InterContinental University, School of Business	661		D		2.5	550	$5407 per year; $1803 per 5 quarter hours	•	•	
Ashridge Management College, Ashridge Executive MBA Program	661						£17,000 per program			
Aston University, Aston Business School	662					600				•
City University, Business School	662		F, D	550	3.5	650	£13,000 per year (R); £18,000 per program (R); £13,000 per year (NR); £18,000 per program (NR)	•	•	
Cranfield University, Cranfield School of Management	663		D			600	£15,000 per year (R); £10,000 per year (R); £15,000 per year (NR); £10,000 per year (NR)	•		•
De Montfort University, Leicester Business School	664									
EAP–European School of Management, Business Programs	664		F, W, D							•
Henley Management College, Business Programs	665				2.75		£14,000 per year; £15,550 per 2-year program			•
Heriot-Watt University, Edinburgh Business School	665		D			550			•	•
Huron University USA in London, MBA Program	666		D	450	2.75	550	£8700 per academic year; £750 per class	•		
Imperial College, Management School	667		F, D			600				
Kingston University, Kingston Business School	667		F			600				
Lancaster University, Management School	668		F, D			580	£10,500 per program (R); £10,500 per program (NR)	•	•	
London School of Economics and Political Science, The Graduate School	669		F		3.5	600		•		
Loughborough University, Management Development Centre	669		F			550				•
Manchester Metropolitan University, Faculty of Management and Business, Department of Management	670									

This table includes the names and locations of colleges, universities, and other institutions offering MBA and other master's-level business programs. Schools appear in geographical sequence by U.S. state or territory or by country and then alphabetically by school name. Specific degree information is detailed within the profile for each school. Refer to the page number in the table for the school's profile. If a school submitted incomplete data, one or more columns opposite the school name may be blank.

	Page Number	Accreditation (AA=AACSB, AC=ACBSP)	ADMISSION REQUIREMENTS				TUITION (R) State Resident (NR) Non-Resident	OPTIONS		
			Matriculation (spring, summer, fall, winter, deferred)	Minimum GMAT Score	Minimum Undergraduate GPA	Minimum TOEFL Score		Financial Aid	Distance Learning	Executive MBA Program
Middlesex University, Business School	670					550				
Napier University, Napier Business School	671		D						•	
Open University, Business School	671								•	
Oxford Brookes University, School of Business	671		D			550	£7650 per year (R); £7650 per year (NR)		•	
Richmond, The American International University in London, School of Business	672		F, S, SU, D		3.0	550	£5050 per semester; £995 per course	•		
Schiller International University, Business Programs	673		D					•		
Sheffield Hallam University, Business School	673		F, W, D			500	£7750 per program (R); £1300 per semester (R); £7750 per program (NR); £1300 per semester (NR)	•	•	
South Bank University, Business School	674		F, D			600	£6250 per program (R); £7900 per program (NR)			
University of Bath, School of Management	675		F, D			600	£11,000 per year (R); £7000 per year (R); £11,000 per year (NR); £7000 per year (NR)	•		•
University of Birmingham, Birmingham Business School	676					550				•
University of Bradford, Bradford Management Center	677		F, D	550		550	£9250 per year (R); £9750 per year (NR)		•	
University of Brighton, Center for Management Development	677		F, S, D			590	£6360 per year (R); £7350 per year (NR)	•		•
University of Bristol, Graduate School of International Business	678		F, D			600	£13,500 per program (R); £13,500 per program (NR)	•		•
University of Durham, Business School	679		F, D			550			•	
University of Edinburgh, Edinburgh University Management School	679		D			580	£9300 per year (R); £8500 per program (R); £9900 per year (NR); £8500 per program (NR)			
University of Glasgow, University of Glasgow Business School	680		F, D						•	•
University of Hull, School of Management	681		F			550		•		
University of London, London Business School	681		F				£26,000 per program	•		•
The University of Manchester, Manchester Business School	682		F, D			580	£19,000 per year (R); £16,000 per year (NR)			
University of Newcastle upon Tyne, School of Management	682		F, D			580	£7500 per year (R); £9500 per year (NR)			
University of Northumbria, Newcastle Business School	683			550		550			•	

	Page Number	Accreditation (AA=AACSB, AC=ACBSP)	Matriculation (spring, summer, fall, winter, deferred)	Minimum GMAT Score	Minimum Undergraduate GPA	Minimum TOEFL Score	TUITION (R) State Resident (NR) Non-Resident	Financial Aid	Distance Learning	Executive MBA Program
This table includes the names and locations of colleges, universities, and other institutions offering MBA and other master's-level business programs. Schools appear in geographical sequence by U.S. state or territory or by country and then alphabetically by school name. Specific degree information is detailed within the profile for each school. Refer to the page number in the table for the school's profile. If a school submitted incomplete data, one or more columns opposite the school name may be blank.										
University of Nottingham, School of Management and Finance	683		D			600	£7980 per program (R); £665 per course (R); £9000 per program (NR); £750 per course (NR)	•		•
University of Oxford, School of Management Studies	684		D		3.5	600	£15,000 per year (R); £15,000 per year (NR)	•		
University of Plymouth, Business School	685					550		•		
University of Reading, ISMA Centre	686		D	600	3.3	590				
University of Salford, Management School	686		D			550				
University of Sheffield, Management School	687			550	3.5	575				
University of Stirling, School of Management	687		D		2.7	550				
University of Strathclyde, Strathclyde Graduate Business School	688		F, S, D			600	£10,750 per program (R); £8925 per program (R); £10,750 per program (NR); £8925 per program (NR)		•	
University of the West of England, Bristol, Bristol Business School	689		D			570	£7600 per program (R); £7600 per program (NR)			
University of Ulster at Jordanstown, Ulster Business School	689		F	450		550	£3150 per program (R); £7700 per program (NR)			•
University of Wales, Business School	690		F, D			570				
University of Warwick, Warwick Business School	690		D				£14,000 per program (R); £4416 per program (R); £14,000 per program (NR); £4416 per program (NR)	•	•	
University of Westminster, Business School	691					650			•	

Profiles of Business Schools and MBA Programs

This section contains factual profiles of colleges, with a focus on their MBA programs. Each profile covers such items as enrollment, tuition, entrance and admission requirements, financial aid, programs of study, placement, and whom to contact for program information.

The information in each profile was collected via Peterson's MBA and Master's-Level Business Programs Survey, which was sent to the dean or director of the business school or MBA program at each institution.

The profiles are arranged geographically, then alphabetically within the state or country.

ALABAMA

Alabama Agricultural and Mechanical University

Department of Business Administration

Normal, Alabama

OVERVIEW
Alabama Agricultural and Mechanical University is a state-supported, coed university. Enrollment: 5,543 graduate, professional, and undergraduate students; 366 full-time matriculated graduate/professional students; 1,048 part-time matriculated graduate/professional students. Founded: 1875. The graduate business unit is in a suburban setting and is on a semester calendar.

GRADUATE BUSINESS PROGRAMS
Master of Business Administration (MBA)

Master of Economics (MEcon)

ACADEMICS
Faculty Full-time 17; part-time 4.

Teaching Methodologies Case study, computer-aided instruction, group discussion, lecture, research, seminars by members of the business community.

Technology 500 on-campus computer terminals/PCs are available for student use and are linked by a campus-wide network. The network has full access to the Internet. Students are not required to have their own PC.

Special Opportunities Advanced credit may be earned through transfer of credits from another institution. An internship program is available.

FACILITIES
Information Resources J. F. Drake Memorial Learning Resources Center; total holdings of 349,134 volumes, 528,867 microforms, 1,683 current periodical subscriptions. CD player(s) available for graduate student use. Access provided to online bibliographic retrieval services.

Program Contact: Dean of Graduate Studies, PO Box 998, Normal, AL 35762. Phone: 205-851-5266; Fax: 205-859-3641.

Auburn University

College of Business

Auburn University, Alabama

OVERVIEW
Auburn University is a state-supported, coed university. Enrollment: 21,505 graduate, professional, and undergraduate students; 1,382 full-time matriculated graduate/professional students; 1,390 part-time matriculated graduate/professional students. Founded: 1856. The graduate business unit is in a small-town setting and is on a quarter calendar.

HIGHLIGHTS

Enrollment Profile

Full-time: 126	International: 9%
Part-time: 221	Women: 38%
Total: 347	Minorities: 11%
Average Age: 27	Average Class Size: 35
Fall 1997 Average GPA: 3.2	Fall 1997 Average GMAT: 595

Costs
Full-time tuition: $3420 per academic year (resident); $10,260 per academic year (nonresident)
Part-time tuition: $71 per credit (resident); $213 per credit (nonresident)

AACSB – The International Association for Management Education accredited

GRADUATE BUSINESS PROGRAMS
Master of Business Administration (MBA) Full-time, part-time, distance learning option; 87 total credits required; 12 months to 5 years to complete program. Concentrations in economics, finance, human resources, management information systems, operations management, marketing, agribusiness, technology management, resources management.

Master of Business Administration in Agri-Business (MBA) Full-time, part-time; 87 total credits required; 12 months to 5 years to complete program. Concentration in agribusiness.

Master of Business Administration in Natural Resources Management (MBA) Full-time, part-time; 87 total credits required; 12 months to 5 years to complete program. Concentration in resources management.

Video-based Outreach MBA (MBA) Full-time, part-time, distance learning option; 87 total credits required; 12 months to 5 years to complete program. Concentrations in finance, human resources, management information systems, marketing, operations management, technology management.

ADMISSION
Applications For fall 1997 there were 291 applications for admission. Of those applying, 127 were accepted. Of those accepted, 63 enrolled.

Application Requirements GMAT score, application form, application fee, bachelor's degree, essay, minimum GPA, 3 letters of recommendation, personal statement, resume, college transcript(s), computer experience: word processing, spreadsheet, database.

Recommended for Application Interview, work experience.

Application Deadline 8/15 for fall, 11/15 for winter, 2/15 for spring, 5/15 for summer, 7/15 for fall (international), 10/15 for winter (international), 2/15 for spring (international), 5/15 for summer (international). Application fee: $25, $50 (international). Deferred entrance is available.

ACADEMICS
Faculty Full-time 85; part-time 6.

Teaching Methodologies Case study, computer-aided instruction, computer analysis, computer simulations, experiential learning, faculty seminars, field projects, group discussion, lecture, research, role playing, seminars by members of the business community, simulations, student presentations, study groups, team projects.

Technology 750 on-campus computer terminals/PCs are available for student use and are linked by a campus-wide network. The network has full access to the Internet. Students are not required to have their own PC.

Special Opportunities Advanced credit may be earned through credit by examination, transfer of credits from another institution. International exchange programs in Czech Republic, Germany, Hungary, Japan. An internship program is available.

FINANCES
Costs for 1997–98 Tuition: Full-time: $3420 per year (resident); $10,260 per year (nonresident). Part-time: $71 per credit (resident); $213 per credit (nonresident). Cost varies by number of credits taken. Fees: Full-time: $90 per academic year (resident); $90 per academic year (nonresident). Part-time: $90 per orientation (resident); $90 per orientation (nonresident). Average 1997–98 room and board costs were $5040 per academic year (on campus) and $8000 per academic year (off campus). Room and board costs vary by occupancy (e.g., single, double, triple), type of accommodation, type of meal plan.

Financial Aid In 1997–98, 29% of students received some institutionally administered aid in the form of fellowships, research assistantships, teaching assistantships, work study. Financial aid is available to part-time students. Application Deadline: 3/15.

Financial Aid Contact Ms. Kaye Storey, Director—Financial Aid Office, 203 Mary Martin Hall, Auburn University, AL 36849. Phone: 334-844-4723; E-mail: aldricl@auducadm.duc.auburn.edu

FACILITIES
Information Resources Ralph B. Draughon Library plus 2 additional on-campus libraries; total holdings of 2,464,666 volumes, 2,380,772 microforms, 10,708 current periodical subscriptions. CD player(s) available for graduate student use. Access provided to online bibliographic retrieval services and online databases.

INTERNATIONAL STUDENTS
Demographics 9% of students enrolled are international students [Africa, 7%, Asia, 43%, Europe, 7%, North America, 7%, South America, 7%, other, 29%].

Services and Facilities International student office, international student center, international student housing, visa services, ESL courses, counseling/support services.

Applying TOEFL: minimum score of 550, proof of adequate funds, proof of health/immunizations required. Financial aid is available to international students.

International Student Contact Ms. Mary Jo Wear, Assistant Director, International Programs, 201 Hargis Hall, Auburn University, AL 36849. Phone: 334-844-4505; Fax: 334-844-5074; E-mail: mjwear@mail.auburn.edu

PLACEMENT
Services include alumni network, career counseling/planning, career fairs, career library, career placement, electronic job bank, job interviews arranged, job search course, resume referral to employers, and resume preparation. In 1996–97, 115 organizations participated in on-campus recruiting; 600 on-campus interviews were conducted.

Employment Of 1996–97 graduates, 97% were employed within three months of graduation; the average starting salary was $42,000. Types of employ-

Auburn University (continued)

ment entered: accounting, banking, chemical industry, communications, computer-related, consulting, consumer products, education, energy, engineering, finance, financial services, government, health services, high technology, human resources, information systems/technology, insurance, international trade, management, manufacturing, marketing, nonprofit, petrochemical, pharmaceutical, real estate, retail, service industry, telecommunications, transportation, utilities.

Business Program(s) URL: http://www.mba.business.auburn.edu/

Program Contact: Dr. Daniel M. Gropper, MBA Director, Suite 503, Lowder Building, Auburn University, AL 36849. Phone: 334-844-4060; Fax: 344-844-2964; E-mail: dgropper@business.auburn.edu

See full description on page 710.

Auburn University Montgomery

School of Business

Montgomery, Alabama

OVERVIEW
Auburn University Montgomery is a state-supported, coed, comprehensive institution. Enrollment: 6,206 graduate, professional, and undergraduate students; 434 full-time matriculated graduate/professional students; 453 part-time matriculated graduate/professional students. Founded: 1967. The graduate business unit is in an urban setting and is on a quarter calendar.

GRADUATE BUSINESS PROGRAMS
Master of Business Administration (MBA)

ACADEMICS
Faculty Full-time 37; part-time 1.

Teaching Methodologies Case study, computer-aided instruction, computer analysis, computer simulations, experiential learning, faculty seminars, field projects, group discussion, lecture, research, role playing, seminars by members of the business community, simulations, student presentations, study groups, team projects.

Technology 40 on-campus computer terminals/PCs are available for student use and are linked by a campus-wide network. The network has full access to the Internet. Students are not required to have their own PC.

Special Opportunities Advanced credit may be earned through transfer of credits from another institution. An internship program is available.

FACILITIES
Information Resources Library Tower plus 1 additional on-campus library; total holdings of 675,935 volumes, 790,000 microforms, 2,958 current periodical subscriptions. CD player(s) available for graduate student use. Access provided to online bibliographic retrieval services.

Program Contact: MBA Director, School of Business, 7300 University Drive, Montgomery, AL 36117-3596. Phone: 334-244-3565; Fax: 334-244-3792.

Birmingham-Southern College

Division of Graduate Studies

Birmingham, Alabama

OVERVIEW
Birmingham-Southern College is an independent-religious, coed, comprehensive institution. Enrollment: 1,531 graduate, professional, and undergraduate students; 58 full-time matriculated graduate/professional students; 30 part-time matriculated graduate/professional students. Founded: 1856. The graduate business unit is in an urban setting and is on a semester calendar.

HIGHLIGHTS

Enrollment Profile
Full-time: 58
Part-time: 30
Total: 88
Average Age: 36
Fall 1997 Average GPA: 3.0

International: N/R
Women: 47%
Minorities: 30%
Average Class Size: 20
Fall 1997 Average GMAT: N/R

Costs
Full-time tuition: $9030 per academic year
Part-time tuition: $1290 per course

GRADUATE BUSINESS PROGRAMS
Master of Arts in Public and Private Management (MA) Full-time, part-time; 16 total credits required; 2 to 5 years to complete program. Concentration in public and private management.

Master of Accounting (MAcc) Full-time, part-time; 10 total credits required; 2 to 5 years to complete program. Concentration in accounting.

ADMISSION
Applications For fall 1997 there were 19 applications for admission. Of those applying, 18 were accepted. Of those accepted, 18 enrolled.

Application Requirements Application form, application fee, bachelor's degree, essay, interview, 2 letters of recommendation, personal statement, resume, college transcript(s), minimum of 3 years of work experience.

Recommended for Application GMAT score accepted, GRE score accepted, MAT score accepted, minimum GPA: 3.0.

Application Deadline Applications processed on a rolling/continuous basis for both domestic and international students. Application fee: $25. Deferred entrance is available.

ACADEMICS
Faculty Full-time 19; part-time 6.

Teaching Methodologies Case study, computer-aided instruction, computer analysis, computer simulations, experiential learning, faculty seminars, field projects, group discussion, lecture, research, role playing, seminars by members of the business community, simulations, student presentations, study groups, team projects.

Technology 114 on-campus computer terminals/PCs are available for student use and are linked by a campus-wide network. The network has full access to the Internet. Students are not required to have their own PC.

Special Opportunities Advanced credit may be earned through transfer of credits from another institution.

FINANCES
Costs for 1997–98 Tuition: Full-time: $9030 per year. Part-time: $1290 per course. Fees: Full-time: $6 per academic year. Part-time: $6 per course.

Financial Aid Grants, scholarships, loans available. Financial aid is available to part-time students.

Financial Aid Contact Mr. Forest Stuart, Director of Financial Aid, Box 549016, Birmingham, AL 35254. Phone: 205-226-4670; Fax: 205-226-4840.

FACILITIES
Information Resources Charles Andrew Rush Learning Center/N. E. Miles Library; total holdings of 287,756 volumes, 45,636 microforms, 857 current periodical subscriptions. CD player(s) available for graduate student use. Access provided to online bibliographic retrieval services.

INTERNATIONAL STUDENTS
Demographics N/R

Services and Facilities International student office, international student center, counseling/support services.

Applying TOEFL, proof of adequate funds, proof of health/immunizations required. Financial aid is available to international students.

International Student Contact Ms. Pat Kidd, Administrative Secretary to Director of Admissions, Box 549018, Birmingham, AL 35214. Phone: 205-226-4681; Fax: 205-226-3064.

PLACEMENT
Services include alumni network, career counseling/planning, career fairs, career library, career placement, electronic job bank, job interviews arranged, resume referral to employers, and resume preparation.

Employment Of 1996–97 graduates, 99% were employed within three months of graduation; the average starting salary was $55,000. Types of employment entered: accounting, banking, communications, computer-related, consulting, energy, engineering, finance, financial services, government, health services, hospitality management, human resources, information systems/technology, insurance, management, manufacturing, marketing, media, nonprofit, pharmaceutical, real estate, service industry, telecommunications, transportation, utilities.

Business Program(s) URL: http://www.bsc.edu

Program Contact: Ms. Regina Cates, Coordinator of Marketing, Box 54902, Birmingham, AL 35254. Phone: 205-226-4803, 800-523-5293; Fax: 205-226-4843.

Jacksonville State University

College of Commerce and Business Administration

Jacksonville, Alabama

OVERVIEW
Jacksonville State University is a state-supported, coed, comprehensive institution. Enrollment: 7,500 graduate, professional, and undergraduate students; 200 full-time matriculated graduate/professional students; 1,300 part-time matriculated graduate/professional students. Founded: 1883. The graduate business unit is in a small-town setting and is on a semester calendar.

HIGHLIGHTS

Enrollment Profile
Full-time: 20
Part-time: 60
Total: 80
Average Age: N/R
Fall 1997 Average GPA: 3.17

International: 36%
Women: 30%
Minorities: 11%
Average Class Size: 20
Fall 1997 Average GMAT: 450

Costs
Full-time tuition: N/R
Part-time tuition: $100 per credit hour (resident); $200 per credit hour (nonresident)

AACSB – The International Association for Management Education accredited

GRADUATE BUSINESS PROGRAMS
Master of Business Administration (MBA) Full-time, part-time; 30-36 total credits required; 18 months to 6 years to complete program. Concentration in accounting.

ADMISSION
Applications For fall 1997 there were 15 applications for admission. Of those applying, 13 were accepted. Of those accepted, 10 enrolled.

Application Requirements GMAT score, application form, application fee, bachelor's degree, minimum GPA, college transcript(s).

Application Deadline Applications processed on a rolling/continuous basis for both domestic and international students. Application fee: $20. Deferred entrance is available.

ACADEMICS
Faculty Full-time 21.

Teaching Methodologies Case study, computer-aided instruction, computer analysis, computer simulations, experiential learning, faculty seminars, field projects, group discussion, lecture, research, simulations, student presentations, study groups, team projects.

Technology 100 on-campus computer terminals/PCs are available for student use and are linked by a campus-wide network. The network has full access to the Internet. Students are not required to have their own PC.

Special Opportunities Advanced credit may be earned through credit for military training programs, transfer of credits from another institution. An internship program is available.

FINANCES
Costs for 1997–98 Tuition: $100 per credit hour (resident); $200 per credit hour (nonresident). Cost varies by number of credits taken, reciprocity agreements. Average 1997–98 room only costs were $1300 per academic year. Room and board costs vary by campus location, occupancy (e.g., single, double, triple), type of accommodation, type of meal plan.

Financial Aid In 1997–98, 1% of students received some institutionally administered aid in the form of research assistantships.

Financial Aid Contact Larry Smith, Director of Financial Aid, 700 Pelham Road North, Jacksonville, AL 36265-9982. Phone: 205-782-5006.

FACILITIES
Information Resources Houston Cole Library; total holdings of 550,000 volumes, 1,000,000 microforms, 2,000 current periodical subscriptions. CD player(s) available for graduate student use. Access provided to online bibliographic retrieval services.

INTERNATIONAL STUDENTS
Demographics 36% of students enrolled are international students [Asia, 50%, Europe, 5%, South America, 25%, other, 20%].

Services and Facilities International student office, international student housing, visa services, counseling/support services.

Applying TOEFL: minimum score of 550, proof of adequate funds required. Financial aid is not available to international students.

International Student Contact Dr. Adrian Aveni, Director of The Office of International Programs and Studies, 700 Pelham Road North, Jacksonville, AL 36265-9982. Phone: 256-782-5674; E-mail: aaveni@jsucc.jsu.edu

PLACEMENT
Services include career counseling/planning, career fairs, career placement, job interviews arranged, and resume preparation. In 1996–97, 25 organizations participated in on-campus recruiting; 10 on-campus interviews were conducted.

Employment Types of employment entered: accounting, banking, finance, financial services, government, human resources, manufacturing.

Business Program(s) URL: http://jsucc.jsu.edu/depart/ccba/page11.html

Program Contact: Dr. Louise Clark, Associate Dean/MBA Director, 700 Pelham Road, Jacksonville, AL 36265-9982. Phone: 205-782-5780; Fax: 205-782-5312; E-mail: lclark@jsucc.jsu.edu

Samford University

School of Business

Birmingham, Alabama

OVERVIEW
Samford University is an independent-religious, coed university. Enrollment: 4,485 graduate, professional, and undergraduate students; 1,267 full-time matriculated graduate/professional students; 299 part-time matriculated graduate/professional students. Founded: 1841. The graduate business unit is in a suburban setting and is on a term calendar.

HIGHLIGHTS

Enrollment Profile
Full-time: 12
Part-time: 117
Total: 129
Average Age: 31
Fall 1997 Average GPA: 3.0

International: 2%
Women: 42%
Minorities: 9%
Average Class Size: 24
Fall 1997 Average GMAT: 500

Costs
Full-time tuition: N/R
Part-time tuition: $344 per credit

GRADUATE BUSINESS PROGRAMS
Master of Business Administration (MBA) Full-time, part-time; 33-48 total credits required; 12 months to 7 years to complete program. Concentration in management.

Master of Accountancy (MAcc) Part-time; 30 total credits required; 12 months to 6 years to complete program. Concentration in accounting.

Master of Business Administration/Master of Accountancy (MBA/MAcc) Full-time, part-time; 48-60 total credits required; 12 months to 7 years to complete program. Concentrations in management, accounting.

Master of Business Administration/Doctor of Jurisprudence (MBA/JD) Full-time; 92-117 total credits required; 3 to 7 years to complete program.

Master of Accountancy/Doctor of Jurisprudence (MAcc/JD) Full-time; 99 total credits required; 3 to 4 years to complete program.

Master of Business Administration/Master of Divinity (MBA/MDiv) Part-time; 106-118 total credits required; 3 to 7 years to complete program.

Master of Business Administration/Master of Science in Nursing (MBA/MS) Part-time; 106-118 total credits required; 2 to 7 years to complete program.

Master of Business Administration/Master of Science in Environmental Management (MBA/MS) Part-time; 45-59 total credits required; 2 to 7 years to complete program.

ADMISSION
Applications For fall 1997 there were 112 applications for admission. Of those applying, 100 were accepted. Of those accepted, 56 enrolled.

Application Requirements GMAT score, application form, application fee, bachelor's degree, minimum GPA, 2 letters of recommendation, resume, college transcript(s), minimum of 3 years of work experience.

Recommended for Application GRE score accepted, MAT score accepted, computer experience.

Application Deadline Applications processed on a rolling/continuous basis for both domestic and international students. Application fee: $25. Deferred entrance is available.

ACADEMICS
Faculty Full-time 19.

Teaching Methodologies Case study, computer-aided instruction, computer analysis, computer simulations, experiential learning, faculty seminars, field projects, group discussion, lecture, research, seminars by members of the business community, student presentations, study groups, team projects.

Samford University (continued)

Technology 25 on-campus computer terminals/PCs are available for student use and are linked by a campus-wide network. The network has full access to the Internet. Students are not required to have their own PC.

Special Opportunities Advanced credit may be earned through credit for business training programs, transfer of credits from another institution. International exchange program in United Kingdom.

FINANCES
Costs for 1997–98 Tuition: $344 per credit. Cost varies by number of credits taken.

Financial Aid In 1997–98, 31% of students received some institutionally administered aid in the form of teaching assistantships, scholarships, loans. Financial aid is available to part-time students.

Financial Aid Contact Mr. David Long, Assistant Director of Financial Aid , 800 Lakeshore Drive, Birmingham, AL 35229-0002. Phone: 205-870-2857; E-mail: dclong@samford.edu

FACILITIES
Information Resources Davis Library plus 4 additional on-campus libraries; total holdings of 857,460 volumes, 318,336 microforms, 4,683 current periodical subscriptions. CD player(s) available for graduate student use. Access provided to online bibliographic retrieval services and online databases.

INTERNATIONAL STUDENTS
Demographics 2% of students enrolled are international students [Africa, 33%, Asia, 33%, South America, 33%, other, 1%].

Services and Facilities International student office, visa services, counseling/support services.

Applying TOEFL: minimum score of 550, proof of adequate funds, proof of health/immunizations required. Financial aid is not available to international students.

International Student Contact Mr. Phil Kimrey, International Counselor, Admissions Office, 800 Lakeshore Drive, Birmingham, AL 35229-0002. Phone: 205-870-2871.

PLACEMENT
Services include alumni network, career counseling/planning, career library, career placement, and resume referral to employers.

Employment Of 1996–97 graduates, 98% were employed within three months of graduation. Types of employment entered: accounting, banking, chemical industry, communications, consumer products, energy, engineering, finance, financial services, health services, high technology, human resources, information systems/technology, insurance, management, manufacturing, marketing, mining, petrochemical, pharmaceutical, transportation, utilities.

Business Program(s) URL: http://www.samford.edu/schools/business.html

Program Contact: Ms. Francoise Horn, Director of Graduate Programs, School of Business, 800 Lakeshore Drive, Birmingham, AL 35229-2306. Phone: 205-870-2931; Fax: 205-870-2540; E-mail: fhhorn@samford.edu

Spring Hill College

Division of Business and Management
Mobile, Alabama

OVERVIEW
Spring Hill College is an independent-religious, coed, comprehensive institution. Enrollment: 1,450 graduate, professional, and undergraduate students; 20 full-time matriculated graduate/professional students; 251 part-time matriculated graduate/professional students. Founded: 1830. The graduate business unit is in a suburban setting and is on a semester calendar.

HIGHLIGHTS

Enrollment Profile

Full-time: 9	International: 6%
Part-time: 45	Women: 33%
Total: 54	Minorities: 13%
Average Age: 32	Average Class Size: 12
Fall 1997 Average GPA: 3.1	Fall 1997 Average GMAT: 470

Costs
Full-time tuition: N/R
Part-time tuition: $245 per credit

GRADUATE BUSINESS PROGRAMS
Master of Business Administration (MBA) Full-time, part-time; 36 total credits required; 2 to 6 years to complete program. Concentration in accounting.

ADMISSION
Applications For fall 1997 there were 23 applications for admission. Of those applying, 21 were accepted. Of those accepted, 17 enrolled.

Application Requirements Application form, application fee, bachelor's degree, minimum GPA: 3.0, college transcript(s).

Recommended for Application GMAT score accepted, interview, work experience, computer experience.

Application Deadline 8/1 for fall, 12/1 for spring, 5/1 for summer. Application fee: $25. Deferred entrance is available.

ACADEMICS
Faculty Full-time 8; part-time 5.

Teaching Methodologies Case study, computer simulations, group discussion, lecture, research, role playing, simulations, student presentations, study groups, team projects.

Technology 75 on-campus computer terminals/PCs are available for student use and are linked by a campus-wide network. The network has full access to the Internet. Students are not required to have their own PC.

Special Opportunities Advanced credit may be earned through transfer of credits from another institution.

FINANCES
Costs for 1997–98 Tuition: $245 per credit. Fees: $10 per term.

Financial Aid Loans available. Financial aid is available to part-time students.

Financial Aid Contact Mrs. Betty Harlan, Director of Financial Aid, 4000 Dauphin Street, Mobile, AL 36608-1791. Phone: 334-380-3460; Fax: 334-460-2176; E-mail: bharlan@shc.edu

FACILITIES
Information Resources Thomas Byrne Library plus 1 additional on-campus library; total holdings of 150,000 volumes, 14,000 microforms, 650 current periodical subscriptions. Access provided to online bibliographic retrieval services.

INTERNATIONAL STUDENTS
Demographics 6% of students enrolled are international students [Asia, 100%].

Services and Facilities International student office, visa services, ESL courses, counseling/support services.

Applying TOEFL: minimum score of 550, proof of adequate funds required. Proof of health/immunizations recommended.

International Student Contact Mrs. Joyce Genz, Director of Graduate Program Administration, 4000 Dauphin Street, Mobile, AL 36608-1791. Phone: 334-380-3094; Fax: 334-460-2190; E-mail: jgenz@shc.edu

PLACEMENT
Services include alumni network, career counseling/planning, and career library.

Employment Of 1996–97 graduates, 100% were employed within three months of graduation. Types of employment entered: accounting, banking, chemical industry, engineering, health services, management, manufacturing, utilities.

Business Program(s) URL: http://www.shc.edu

Program Contact: Mrs. Joyce Genz, Director of Graduate Program Administration, 4000 Dauphin Street, Mobile, AL 36608-1791. Phone: 334-380-3094; Fax: 334-460-2190; E-mail: grad@shc.edu

Troy State University

Sorrell College of Business
Troy, Alabama

OVERVIEW
Troy State University is a state-supported, coed, comprehensive institution. Enrollment: 11,717 graduate, professional, and undergraduate students; 861 full-time matriculated graduate/professional students; 2,096 part-time matriculated graduate/professional students. Founded: 1887. The graduate business unit is in a small-town setting and is on a quarter calendar.

HIGHLIGHTS

Enrollment Profile

Full-time: 45
Part-time: 15
Total: 60
Average Age: 25
Fall 1997 Average GPA: 3.0

International: 30%
Women: 50%
Minorities: 2%
Average Class Size: 24
Fall 1997 Average GMAT: 510

Costs

Full-time tuition: N/R
Part-time tuition: $57 per credit hour (resident); $114 per credit hour (nonresident)

ACBSP – The American Council of Business Schools and Programs accredited

GRADUATE BUSINESS PROGRAMS

Master of Business Administration (MBA) Full-time, part-time; 50 total credits required; 12 months to 8 years to complete program. Concentration in accounting.

ADMISSION

Applications For fall 1997 there were 36 applications for admission. Of those applying, 36 were accepted. Of those accepted, 24 enrolled.

Application Requirements Application form, application fee, bachelor's degree, minimum GPA: 2.5, 3 letters of recommendation, college transcript(s).

Recommended for Application GMAT score accepted: minimum 450, GRE score accepted: minimum 850, MAT score accepted: minimum 33, work experience, computer experience.

Application Deadline Applications processed on a rolling/continuous basis for both domestic and international students. Application fee: $20.

ACADEMICS

Faculty Full-time 12.

Teaching Methodologies Case study, lecture, team projects.

Technology 90 on-campus computer terminals/PCs are available for student use. The network has full access to the Internet. Students are not required to have their own PC.

Special Opportunities Advanced credit may be earned through transfer of credits from another institution.

FINANCES

Costs for 1997–98 Tuition: $57 per credit hour (resident); $114 per credit hour (nonresident). Fees: $6 per credit hour (resident); $6 per credit hour (nonresident). Average 1997–98 room and board costs were $1779 per academic year (on campus) and $2000 per academic year (off campus). Room and board costs vary by occupancy (e.g., single, double, triple), type of accommodation, type of meal plan.

Financial Aid In 1997–98, 12% of students received some institutionally administered aid in the form of fellowships, research assistantships. Application Deadline: 5/25.

Financial Aid Contact MBA Coordinator, Bibb Graves Hall, Room 131, Troy, AL 36082. Phone: 334-670-3509; Fax: 334-670-3708.

FACILITIES

Information Resources L. B. Wallace Hall plus 3 additional on-campus libraries; total holdings of 236,125 volumes, 708,246 microforms, 1,675 current periodical subscriptions.

INTERNATIONAL STUDENTS

Demographics 30% of students enrolled are international students.

Services and Facilities International student office, international student housing, counseling/support services.

Applying TOEFL: minimum score of 525, proof of adequate funds, proof of health/immunizations required.

International Student Contact Mrs. Helen Hutto, International Student Advisor, Suite 203, Wright Hall, Troy, AL 36082. Phone: 334-670-3736; Fax: 334-670-3735; E-mail: hhutto@trojan.troyst.edu

PLACEMENT

Services include career counseling/planning, and career fairs. In 1996–97, 20 organizations participated in on-campus recruiting.

Employment Of 1996–97 graduates, 70% were employed within three months of graduation. Types of employment entered: accounting, banking.

Program Contact: Mrs. Theresa Rodgers, Graduate Admission Counselor, Bibb Graves Hall, Room O3, Troy, AL 36082. Phone: 334-670-3188, 800-551-9716 (AL only); Fax: 334-670-3774.

Troy State University Dothan

School of Business

Dothan, Alabama

OVERVIEW

Troy State University Dothan is a state-supported, coed, comprehensive institution. Enrollment: 2,150 graduate, professional, and undergraduate students. Founded: 1961. The graduate business unit is in a small-town setting and is on a quarter calendar.

HIGHLIGHTS

Enrollment Profile

Full-time: N/R
Part-time: N/R
Total: 32
Average Age: N/R
Fall 1997 Average GPA: 3.0

International: N/R
Women: 38%
Minorities: 16%
Average Class Size: N/R
Fall 1997 Average GMAT: 500

Costs

Full-time tuition: N/R
Part-time tuition: $61 per quarter hour (resident); $122 per quarter hour (nonresident)

ACBSP – The American Council of Business Schools and Programs accredited

GRADUATE BUSINESS PROGRAMS

Master of Business Administration (MBA) Full-time, part-time; 60-85 total credits required; 15 months to 2 years to complete program. Concentrations in accounting, human resources, management information systems, management.

Master of Science in Human Resources Management (MS) Full-time, part-time; 50 total credits required; 12 to 15 months to complete program. Concentration in human resources.

ADMISSION

Application Requirements Application form, application fee, bachelor's degree, minimum GPA: 2.75, college transcript(s).

Recommended for Application GMAT score accepted, computer experience.

Application Deadline Applications processed on a rolling/continuous basis for both domestic and international students. Application fee: $20.

ACADEMICS

Faculty Full-time 16; part-time 18.

Teaching Methodologies Case study, computer analysis, group discussion, lecture, research, student presentations, team projects.

Technology 80 on-campus computer terminals/PCs are available for student use and are linked by a campus-wide network. The network has full access to the Internet. Students are not required to have their own PC.

Special Opportunities Advanced credit may be earned through transfer of credits from another institution.

FINANCES

Costs for 1997–98 Tuition: $61 per quarter hour (resident); $122 per quarter hour (nonresident).

Financial Aid Contact Ms. Jonua Byrd, Director of Financial Aid, PO Box 8368, Dothan, AL 76304-0368. Phone: 334-983-6556; Fax: 334-983-6322.

FACILITIES

Information Resources University Library; total holdings of 93,692 volumes, 242,134 microforms, 622 current periodical subscriptions. CD player(s) available for graduate student use. Access provided to online bibliographic retrieval services and online databases.

INTERNATIONAL STUDENTS

Demographics N/R

Services and Facilities International student office, counseling/support services, tutoring.

Applying TOEFL, proof of adequate funds, proof of health/immunizations required. Financial aid is not available to international students.

International Student Contact Mrs. Pamela Williamson, Director of Counseling Services, PO Box 8368, Dothan, AL 36304. Phone: 334-983-6556 Ext. 221; Fax: 334-983-6322.

PLACEMENT

Services include alumni network, career counseling/planning, career fairs, career library, career placement, job interviews arranged, resume referral to employers, and resume preparation. In 1996–97, 52 organizations participated in on-campus recruiting.

Employment Types of employment entered: accounting, banking, chemical industry, communications, computer-related, consulting, consumer products, education, energy, engineering, finance, financial services, government, health services, high technology, hospitality management, human resources, information systems/technology, insurance, international trade, law, management, manufacturing, marketing, media, mining, nonprofit, petrochemical, pharmaceutical, real estate, retail, service industry, telecommunications, transportation, utilities.

Program Contact: Ms. Reta Cordell, Director of Graduate Admissions and Records, PO Box 8368, Dothan, AL 36304. Phone: 334-983-6556 Ext. 230; Fax: 334-983-6322; E-mail: rcordell@tsud.edu

Troy State University Montgomery

Division of Business

Montgomery, Alabama

OVERVIEW

Troy State University Montgomery is a state-supported, coed, comprehensive institution. Enrollment: 3,408 graduate, professional, and undergraduate students; 226 full-time matriculated graduate/professional students; 318 part-time matriculated graduate/professional students. Founded: 1966. The graduate business unit is in an urban setting and is on a quarter calendar.

HIGHLIGHTS

Enrollment Profile

Full-time: 94	International: N/R
Part-time: 130	Women: 40%
Total: 224	Minorities: 35%
Average Age: 36	Average Class Size: 20
Fall 1997 Average GPA: N/R	Fall 1997 Average GMAT: N/R

Costs
Full-time tuition: N/R
Part-time tuition: $350 per course (resident); $350 per course (nonresident)

ACBSP – The American Council of Business Schools and Programs accredited

GRADUATE BUSINESS PROGRAMS

Master of Business Administration (MBA) Full-time, part-time; 55 total credits required; 18 months to 8 years to complete program. Concentrations in accounting, human resources, management, management information systems, industrial administration/management.

Master of Science in Human Resources Management (MS) Full-time, part-time; 50 total credits required; 18 months to 8 years to complete program. Concentration in human resources.

ADMISSION

Application Requirements MAT score: minimum 35, application form, application fee, bachelor's degree, minimum GPA: 2.5, interview, resume, college transcript(s), computer experience: computer literacy.

Recommended for Application GMAT score accepted: minimum 450, GRE score accepted: minimum 1,000, personal statement.

Application Deadline Applications processed on a rolling/continuous basis for both domestic and international students. Application fee: $15. Deferred entrance is available.

ACADEMICS

Faculty Full-time 10; part-time 7.

Teaching Methodologies Case study, computer-aided instruction, computer simulations, experiential learning, faculty seminars, field projects, group discussion, lecture, research, role playing, seminars by members of the business community, student presentations, study groups, team projects.

Technology 100 on-campus computer terminals/PCs are available for student use and are linked by a campus-wide network. The network does not have Internet access. Students are not required to have their own PC.

Special Opportunities Advanced credit may be earned through credit for military training programs, credit for business training programs, transfer of credits from another institution. An internship program is available.

FINANCES

Costs for 1997–98 Tuition: $350 per course (resident); $350 per course (nonresident).

Financial Aid In 1997–98, 4% of students received some institutionally administered aid in the form of scholarships. Financial aid is available to part-time students.

Financial Aid Contact Ms. Evelyn McKeithen, Director of Financial Aid, PO Drawer 4419, Montgomery, AL 36103-4419.

FACILITIES

Information Resources Main library; total holdings of 22,410 volumes, 1,473 microforms, 337 current periodical subscriptions. CD player(s) available for graduate student use. Access provided to online bibliographic retrieval services.

INTERNATIONAL STUDENTS

Demographics N/R

Applying TOEFL required.

PLACEMENT

Services include alumni network, career counseling/planning, career fairs, career library, career placement, electronic job bank, job interviews arranged, resume referral to employers, and resume preparation.

Employment Types of employment entered: accounting, banking, chemical industry, communications, computer-related, consulting, consumer products, education, energy, engineering, finance, financial services, government, health services, high technology, hospitality management, human resources, information systems/technology, insurance, international trade, law, management, manufacturing, marketing, media, mining, nonprofit, petrochemical, pharmaceutical, real estate, retail, service industry, telecommunications, transportation, utilities.

Program Contact: Dr. Freda Hartman, Dean, PO Drawer 4419, Montgomery, AL 36103-4419. Phone: 334-241-9703, 800-335-TSUM (AL only), and/or 800-355-TSUM (AL only); Fax: 334-241-9696.

The University of Alabama

Manderson Graduate School of Business

Tuscaloosa, Alabama

OVERVIEW

The University of Alabama is a state-supported, coed university. Enrollment: 18,938 graduate, professional, and undergraduate students. Founded: 1831. The graduate business unit is in a small-town setting and is on a semester calendar.

HIGHLIGHTS

Enrollment Profile

Full-time: 116	International: 11%
Part-time: 26	Women: 24%
Total: 142	Minorities: 6%
Average Age: 25	Average Class Size: 55
Fall 1997 Average GPA: 3.3	Fall 1997 Average GMAT: 610

Costs
Full-time tuition: $2594 per academic year (resident); $6808 per academic year (nonresident)
Part-time tuition: N/R

AACSB – The International Association for Management Education accredited

GRADUATE BUSINESS PROGRAMS

Master of Business Administration (MBA) Full-time; 49 total credits required; 2 years to complete program. Concentrations in accounting, finance, human resources, international business, marketing, production management, strategic management, operations management, management information systems, entrepreneurship.

Executive MBA (MBA) Part-time; 49 total credits required; minimum of 17 months to complete program.

ADMISSION

Applications For fall 1997 there were 162 applications for admission. Of those applying, 83 were accepted. Of those accepted, 56 enrolled.

Application Requirements Application form, application fee, bachelor's degree, essay, minimum GPA: 3.0, interview, 3 letters of recommendation, personal statement, resume, college transcript(s).

Recommended for Application GMAT score accepted, computer experience.

Application Deadline 5/15 for fall. Application fee: $25. Deferred entrance is available.

ACADEMICS

Faculty Full-time 87.

Teaching Methodologies Case study, computer-aided instruction, computer simulations, experiential learning, field projects, group discussion, lecture, simulations, student presentations, study groups, team projects.

Technology 250 on-campus computer terminals/PCs are available for student use and are linked by a campus-wide network. The network has full access to the Internet. Students are not required to have their own PC.

Special Opportunities Advanced credit may be earned through transfer of credits from another institution. An internship program is available.

FINANCES
Costs for 1997–98 Tuition: Full-time: $2594 per year (resident); $6808 per year (nonresident). Average 1997–98 room and board costs were $4000 per academic year. Room and board costs vary by occupancy (e.g., single, double, triple), type of accommodation, type of meal plan.

Financial Aid In 1997–98, 30% of students received some institutionally administered aid in the form of fellowships, research assistantships, scholarships, loans. Financial aid is available to part-time students.

Financial Aid Contact Director, Student Financial Services, Box 870162, 100 East Annex, Tuscaloosa, AL 35487.

FACILITIES
Information Resources Amelia Gayle Gorgas Library plus 8 additional on-campus libraries; total holdings of 2,057,586 volumes, 3,224,111 microforms, 11,425 current periodical subscriptions. CD player(s) available for graduate student use. Access provided to online bibliographic retrieval services.

INTERNATIONAL STUDENTS
Demographics 11% of students enrolled are international students [Asia, 67%, Europe, 27%, South America, 6%].

Services and Facilities International student office, international student center, international student housing, counseling/support services.

Applying TOEFL: minimum score of 550, proof of adequate funds, proof of health/immunizations required.

International Student Contact Ms. Edwina Crawford, Graduate International Admissions Supervisor, Box 870118, Tuscaloosa, AL 35487. Phone: 205-348-5921.

PLACEMENT
Services include alumni network, career counseling/planning, career fairs, career library, career placement, electronic job bank, job interviews arranged, job search course, resume referral to employers, and resume preparation.

Employment Of 1996–97 graduates, 98% were employed within three months of graduation; the average starting salary was $46,800. Types of employment entered: accounting, banking, chemical industry, computer-related, consulting, energy, finance, financial services, high technology, human resources, information systems/technology, insurance, pharmaceutical, real estate, retail, telecommunications, utilities.

Business Program(s) URL: http://www.cba.ua.edu/~mba

Program Contact: Ms. Patti Eggers, Interim Director, MBA Program, Box 870223, 101 Bidgood Hall, Tuscaloosa, AL 35487. Phone: 205-348-6517, 888-863-2622; Fax: 205-348-4504; E-mail: peggers@alston.cba.ua.edu
See full description on page 1030.

The University of Alabama at Birmingham

Graduate School of Management

Birmingham, Alabama

OVERVIEW
The University of Alabama at Birmingham is a state-supported, coed university. Enrollment: 16,000 graduate, professional, and undergraduate students. Founded: 1969. The graduate business unit is in an urban setting and is on a quarter calendar.

HIGHLIGHTS

Enrollment Profile
Full-time: N/R
Part-time: N/R
Total: 510
Average Age: N/R
Fall 1997 Average GPA: 3.0

International: N/R
Women: N/R
Minorities: N/R
Average Class Size: 30
Fall 1997 Average GMAT: 515

Costs
Full-time tuition: N/R
Part-time tuition: $96 per semester hour (resident); $192 per semester hour (nonresident)

AACSB – The International Association for Management Education accredited

GRADUATE BUSINESS PROGRAMS
Master of Business Administration (MBA) Full-time, part-time; 36-54 total credits required; 12 months to 7 years to complete program.

Master of Accountancy (MAcc) Full-time, part-time; 30 total credits required; 12 months to 7 years to complete program. Concentration in accounting.

Master of Business Administration/Master of Public Health (MBA/MPH) Full-time, part-time; 72 total credits required; 2 to 7 years to complete program.

Master of Business Administration/Master of Science in Health Administration (MBA/MS) Full-time; 72 total credits required; 2.8 years to complete program.

ADMISSION
Applications For fall 1997 there were 240 applications for admission. Of those applying, 190 were accepted. Of those accepted, 140 enrolled.

Application Requirements Application form, application fee, bachelor's degree, minimum GPA: 2.0, personal statement, college transcript(s).

Recommended for Application GMAT score accepted: minimum 450.

Application Deadline 8/1 for fall, 2/1 for spring, 8/1 for fall (international), 2/1 for spring (international). Application fee: $50, $55 (international). Deferred entrance is available.

ACADEMICS
Faculty Full-time 44; part-time 3.

Teaching Methodologies Case study, computer simulations, experiential learning, field projects, group discussion, lecture, simulations, student presentations, team projects.

Technology 100 on-campus computer terminals/PCs are available for student use and are linked by a campus-wide network. The network has full access to the Internet. Students are not required to have their own PC.

Special Opportunities Advanced credit may be earned through transfer of credits from another institution. International exchange program in Germany.

FINANCES
Costs for 1997–98 Tuition: $96 per semester hour (resident); $192 per semester hour (nonresident). Cost varies by academic program, number of credits taken. Fees: $41 per semester hour (resident); $41 per semester hour (nonresident). Fees vary by academic program, number of credits taken. Average 1997–98 room only costs were $1948 per academic year (on campus) and $3150 per academic year (off campus). Room and board costs vary by occupancy (e.g., single, double, triple), type of accommodation.

Financial Aid Fellowships available.

Financial Aid Contact Ms. Janet May, Director of Financial Aid, Financial Aid Office, 1400 University Boulevard, 317 HUG, Birmingham, AL 35294-1150. Phone: 205-934-8223; Fax: 205-934-8941.

FACILITIES
Information Resources Mervyn Sterne Library plus 1 additional on-campus library; total holdings of 1,476,168 volumes, 416,175 microforms, 5,390 current periodical subscriptions. CD player(s) available for graduate student use. Access provided to online bibliographic retrieval services and online databases.

INTERNATIONAL STUDENTS
Demographics N/R

Services and Facilities International student office, international student center, visa services, ESL courses, counseling/support services.

Applying TOEFL: minimum score of 550, proof of adequate funds, proof of health/immunizations required. Financial aid is not available to international students.

International Student Contact Ms. Barbara Whitt, Foreign Student Advisor, Center for International Programs, 1400 University Boulevard, Birmingham, AL 35294-1150. Phone: 205-934-3328; Fax: 205-934-8664; E-mail: ucip003@larry.huc.uab.edu

PLACEMENT
Services include alumni network, career counseling/planning, career fairs, career library, career placement, electronic job bank, job interviews arranged, job search course, resume referral to employers, and resume preparation. In 1996–97, 231 organizations participated in on-campus recruiting; 849 on-campus interviews were conducted.

Employment Of 1996–97 graduates, 92% were employed within three months of graduation. Types of employment entered: banking, health services, telecommunications.

Business Program(s) URL: http://www.uab.edu

Program Contact: Ms. Pamela Blaylock, Admissions Coordinator, UAB Graduate School, 1400 University Boulevard, HUC 511, Birmingham, AL 35294-1150. Phone: 205-934-8227, 800-975-GRAD; Fax: 205-934-8413; E-mail: inquire@gradschool.huc.uab.edu

The University of Alabama in Huntsville

College of Administrative Science

Huntsville, Alabama

OVERVIEW

The University of Alabama in Huntsville is a state-supported, coed university. Enrollment: 6,500 graduate, professional, and undergraduate students; 450 full-time matriculated graduate/professional students; 850 part-time matriculated graduate/professional students. Founded: 1950. The graduate business unit is in a suburban setting and is on a semester calendar.

HIGHLIGHTS

Enrollment Profile

Full-time: 32
Part-time: 120
Total: 152
Average Age: 33
Fall 1997 Average GPA: 3.22

International: 10%
Women: 48%
Minorities: 11%
Average Class Size: 25
Fall 1997 Average GMAT: 515

Costs

Full-time tuition: $5180 per academic year (resident); $10,575 per academic year (nonresident)
Part-time tuition: $521 per course (resident); $1059 per course (nonresident)

AACSB – The International Association for Management Education accredited

GRADUATE BUSINESS PROGRAMS

Master of Science in Management of Technology (MS) Full-time, part-time; 33-48 total credits required; 12 months to 6 years to complete program. Concentration in technology management.

Master of Accountancy (MAcc) Full-time, part-time; 33-51 total credits required; 12 months to 6 years to complete program. Concentration in accounting.

ADMISSION

Applications For fall 1997 there were 97 applications for admission. Of those applying, 87 were accepted. Of those accepted, 74 enrolled.

Application Requirements GMAT score, application form, application fee, bachelor's degree, minimum GPA: 2.5, personal statement, college transcript(s).

Application Deadline Applications processed on a rolling/continuous basis for both domestic and international students. Application fee: $20. Deferred entrance is available.

ACADEMICS

Faculty Full-time 32; part-time 2.

Teaching Methodologies Case study, computer analysis, computer simulations, experiential learning, group discussion, lecture, student presentations, team projects.

Technology 200 on-campus computer terminals/PCs are available for student use and are linked by a campus-wide network. The network has full access to the Internet. Students are not required to have their own PC.

Special Opportunities Advanced credit may be earned through credit by examination, credit for military training programs, transfer of credits from another institution. An internship program is available.

FINANCES

Costs for 1997–98 Tuition: Full-time: $5180 per program (resident); $10,575 per program (nonresident). Part-time: $521 per course (resident); $1059 per course (nonresident). Cost varies by number of credits taken. Fees: Full-time: $120 per academic year (resident); $120 per academic year (nonresident). Part-time: $20 per course (resident); $20 per course (nonresident). Fees vary by number of credits taken. Average 1997–98 room and board costs were $5340 per academic year (on campus) and $5940 per academic year (off campus). Room and board costs vary by occupancy (e.g., single, double, triple), type of accommodation, type of meal plan.

Financial Aid In 1997–98, 7% of students received some institutionally administered aid in the form of fellowships, research assistantships, teaching assistantships, grants, scholarships, work study, loans. Financial aid is available to part-time students. Application Deadline: 4/1.

Financial Aid Contact Ms. Doris Lacey, Assistant Director, 301 Sparkman Drive, Huntsville, AL 35899. Phone: 256-890-6241; Fax: 256-890-6073; E-mail: laceyd@email.uah.edu

FACILITIES

Information Resources Lewis M. Salmon Library; total holdings of 426,344 volumes, 613,198 microforms, 3,105 current periodical subscriptions. CD player(s) available for graduate student use. Access provided to online bibliographic retrieval services.

INTERNATIONAL STUDENTS

Demographics 10% of students enrolled are international students [Asia, 54%, Europe, 45%, North America, 1%].

Services and Facilities Visa services, ESL courses, counseling/support services.

Applying TOEFL: minimum score of 550, proof of adequate funds, proof of health/immunizations required. Financial aid is available to international students.

PLACEMENT

Services include alumni network, career counseling/planning, career fairs, career library, career placement, electronic job bank, job interviews arranged, resume referral to employers, and resume preparation.

Employment Types of employment entered: accounting, chemical industry, computer-related, engineering, government, high technology, human resources, information systems/technology, management, manufacturing, marketing, telecommunications.

Business Program(s) URL: http://www.uah.edu/colleges/adminsci/

Program Contact: Dr. John Burnett, Assistant Dean, ASB 102, Huntsville, AL 35899. Phone: 256-890-6024, 800-UAH-CALL; Fax: 256-890-7571; E-mail: msmprog@email.uah.edu

University of Mobile

School of Business

Mobile, Alabama

OVERVIEW

The University of Mobile is an independent-religious, coed, comprehensive institution. Enrollment: 2,117 graduate, professional, and undergraduate students; 136 full-time matriculated graduate/professional students; 125 part-time matriculated graduate/professional students. Founded: 1961. The graduate business unit is in a suburban setting and is on a semester calendar.

HIGHLIGHTS

Enrollment Profile

Full-time: 9
Part-time: 37
Total: 46
Average Age: 33
Fall 1997 Average GPA: 3.08

International: 13%
Women: 43%
Minorities: 17%
Average Class Size: 11
Fall 1997 Average GMAT: 445

Costs

Full-time tuition: N/R
Part-time tuition: $155 per credit hour

GRADUATE BUSINESS PROGRAMS

Master of Business Administration (MBA) Full-time, part-time; 40 total credits required; 12 months to 5 years to complete program.

ADMISSION

Applications For fall 1997 there were 37 applications for admission. Of those applying, 23 were accepted. Of those accepted, 20 enrolled.

Application Requirements GMAT score: minimum 400, application form, application fee, bachelor's degree, minimum GPA, college transcript(s).

Recommended for Application Work experience, computer experience.

Application Deadline Applications processed on a rolling/continuous basis for both domestic and international students. Application fee: $30. Deferred entrance is available.

ACADEMICS

Faculty Full-time 10; part-time 3.

Teaching Methodologies Case study, computer-aided instruction, computer analysis, faculty seminars, field projects, group discussion, lecture, research, student presentations, study groups, team projects.

Technology 60 on-campus computer terminals/PCs are available for student use. The network has full access to the Internet. Students are not required to have their own PC.

Special Opportunities Advanced credit may be earned through credit for experience, transfer of credits from another institution. An internship program is available.

FINANCES

Costs for 1997–98 Tuition: $155 per credit hour. Cost varies by number of credits taken. Fees: $25 per semester. Average 1997–98 room and board costs were $4080 per academic year.

Financial Aid Work study, loans available. Financial aid is available to part-time students. Application Deadline: 8/1.

Financial Aid Contact Mrs. Lydia Husley, Director of Financial Aid, PO Box 12330, Mobile, AL 36663-0220. Phone: 334-675-5990 Ext. 252; Fax: 334-675-6293.

FACILITIES

Information Resources J. L. Bedsole Library; total holdings of 113,663 volumes, 293 microforms, 986 current periodical subscriptions. CD player(s) available for graduate student use. Access provided to online bibliographic retrieval services.

INTERNATIONAL STUDENTS

Demographics 13% of students enrolled are international students [Asia, 17%, Central America, 33%, Europe, 50%].

Services and Facilities ESL courses, counseling/support services.

Applying TOEFL: minimum score of 550, proof of adequate funds, proof of health/immunizations required. Financial aid is not available to international students.

International Student Contact Mrs. Kim Leousis, Director of Admissions, PO Box 13220, Mobile, AL 36663-0220. Phone: 334-675-5990 Ext. 220; Fax: 334-675-6329; E-mail: adminfo@umobile.edu

PLACEMENT

Services include alumni network, career counseling/planning, career fairs, career library, career placement, electronic job bank, job interviews arranged, resume referral to employers, and resume preparation. In 1996–97, 79 organizations participated in on-campus recruiting.

Employment Of 1996–97 graduates, 90% were employed within three months of graduation; the average starting salary was $37,000. Types of employment entered: banking, chemical industry, finance, government, health services, human resources, insurance, management, manufacturing, pharmaceutical, service industry.

Business Program(s) URL: http://www2.acan.net/~adminfo/

Program Contact: Dr. Anne B. Lowery, Dean and MBA Director, School of Business, PO Box 13220, Mobile, AL 36663-0220. Phone: 334-675-5990 Ext. 332, 800-946-7267; Fax: 334-675-9816; E-mail: lowerys@gulftel.com

University of North Alabama

College of Business

Florence, Alabama

OVERVIEW

The University of North Alabama is a state-supported, coed, comprehensive institution. Enrollment: 5,166 graduate, professional, and undergraduate students; 48 full-time matriculated graduate/professional students; 453 part-time matriculated graduate/professional students. Founded: 1830. The graduate business unit is in a suburban setting and is on a semester calendar.

HIGHLIGHTS

Enrollment Profile

Full-time: 25	International: N/R
Part-time: 85	Women: N/R
Total: 110	Minorities: N/R
Average Age: 30	Average Class Size: 18
Fall 1997 Average GPA: 3.0	Fall 1997 Average GMAT: 475

Costs

Full-time tuition: N/R
Part-time tuition: $98 per semester hour (resident); $98 per semester hour (nonresident)

ACBSP – The American Council of Business Schools and Programs accredited

GRADUATE BUSINESS PROGRAMS

Master of Business Administration (MBA) Full-time, part-time, distance learning option; 33 total credits required; 12 months to 8 years to complete program. Concentration in accounting.

Executive MBA (MBA) Full-time, distance learning option; 33 total credits required; up to 22 months to complete program.

ADMISSION

Application Requirements GMAT score, application form, application fee, bachelor's degree, minimum GPA, college transcript(s).

Application Deadline Applications processed on a rolling/continuous basis for both domestic and international students. Application fee: $25. Deferred entrance is available.

ACADEMICS

Faculty Full-time 20.

Teaching Methodologies Case study, computer-aided instruction, computer analysis, computer simulations, field projects, group discussion, lecture, research, role playing, seminars by members of the business community, simulations, student presentations, study groups, team projects.

Technology 50 on-campus computer terminals/PCs are available for student use and are linked by a campus-wide network. The network has full access to the Internet.

Special Opportunities Advanced credit may be earned through transfer of credits from another institution. International exchange program in Netherlands. An internship program is available.

FINANCES

Costs for 1997–98 Tuition: $98 per semester hour (resident); $98 per semester hour (nonresident). Cost varies by number of credits taken. Average 1997–98 room and board costs were $1785 per academic year. Room and board costs vary by campus location, occupancy (e.g., single, double, triple), type of accommodation, type of meal plan.

Financial Aid Work study available. Financial aid is available to part-time students. Application Deadline: 4/1.

Financial Aid Contact Dr. Jo Ann Weaver, Director of Student Financial Services, University Station, Florence, AL 35632-0001. Phone: 205-760-4278.

FACILITIES

Information Resources Collier Library plus 4 additional on-campus libraries; total holdings of 269,354 volumes, 666,857 microforms, 2,517 current periodical subscriptions. CD player(s) available for graduate student use. Access provided to online bibliographic retrieval services.

INTERNATIONAL STUDENTS

Demographics N/R

Services and Facilities International student office.

Applying TOEFL: minimum score of 550, proof of health/immunizations required.

Program Contact: Mrs. Carolyn Austin, Graduate Admissions Record Specialist, Box 5011, Florence, AL 35632. Phone: 205-760-4447; Fax: 205-760-4349.

University of South Alabama

College of Business and Management Studies

Mobile, Alabama

OVERVIEW

The University of South Alabama is a state-supported, coed university. Enrollment: 11,999 graduate, professional, and undergraduate students. Founded: 1963. The graduate business unit is in an urban setting and is on a quarter calendar.

HIGHLIGHTS

Enrollment Profile

Full-time: 36	International: 31%
Part-time: 104	Women: 35%
Total: 140	Minorities: N/R
Average Age: N/R	Average Class Size: 25
Fall 1997 Average GPA: 3.04	Fall 1997 Average GMAT: 490

Costs

Full-time tuition: N/R
Part-time tuition: $68 per credit (resident); $136 per credit (nonresident)

AACSB – The International Association for Management Education accredited

GRADUATE BUSINESS PROGRAMS

Master of Business Administration (MBA) Full-time, part-time; 33 total credits required; 12 months to 5 years to complete program. Concentration in management.

Master of Accounting (MAcc) Full-time, part-time; 33 total credits required; 12 months to 5 years to complete program. Concentration in accounting.

ADMISSION

Applications For fall 1997 there were 69 applications for admission. Of those applying, 64 were accepted. Of those accepted, 42 enrolled.

Application Requirements GMAT score, application form, application fee, bachelor's degree, essay, minimum GPA: 2.5, college transcript(s).

Application Deadline 9/1 for fall, 12/1 for winter, 3/1 for spring, 6/1 for summer. Application fee: $25. Deferred entrance is available.

ACADEMICS

Faculty Full-time 45; part-time 6.

University of South Alabama (continued)

Teaching Methodologies Case study, computer-aided instruction, computer analysis, computer simulations, experiential learning, group discussion, lecture, research, role playing, simulations, student presentations, team projects.

Technology 130 on-campus computer terminals/PCs are available for student use and are linked by a campus-wide network. The network has partial access to the Internet. Students are not required to have their own PC.

Special Opportunities Advanced credit may be earned through transfer of credits from another institution. International exchange programs in France, Germany, Netherlands.

FINANCES

Costs for 1997–98 Tuition: $68 per credit (resident); $136 per credit (nonresident). Cost varies by number of credits taken, reciprocity agreements. Fees: $66 per quarter (resident); $66 per quarter (nonresident). Average 1997–98 room and board costs were $3585 per academic year. Room and board costs vary by campus location, occupancy (e.g., single, double, triple), type of accommodation, type of meal plan.

Financial Aid In 1997–98, 6% of students received some institutionally administered aid in the form of research assistantships. Application Deadline: 4/1.

Financial Aid Contact Mr. Grady Collins, Director, AD 260, 307 University Boulevard, Mobile, AL 36688. Phone: 334-460-6231.

FACILITIES

Information Resources Main library plus 2 additional on-campus libraries; total holdings of 437,451 volumes, 770,645 microforms, 3,695 current periodical subscriptions. CD player(s) available for graduate student use. Access provided to online bibliographic retrieval services.

INTERNATIONAL STUDENTS

Demographics 31% of students enrolled are international students.

Services and Facilities International student office, visa services, ESL courses, counseling/support services.

Applying TOEFL: minimum score of 525, proof of adequate funds, proof of health/immunizations required. Financial aid is not available to international students.

International Student Contact Ms. Brenda Henson, Director—International Admissions, 307 University Boulevard, Mobile, AL 36688. Phone: 334-460-6050.

PLACEMENT

Services include career counseling/planning, career fairs, career library, career placement, electronic job bank, job interviews arranged, job search course, resume referral to employers, and resume preparation.

Employment Of 1996–97 graduates, 92% were employed within three months of graduation. Types of employment entered: accounting, banking, consumer products, finance, financial services, hospitality management, human resources, information systems/technology, insurance, management, manufacturing, marketing, retail, service industry.

Business Program(s) URL: http://bms.usouthal.edu/

Program Contact: Dr. Warren Flynn, Associate Dean, College of Business and Management Studies, 307 University Boulevard, Mobile, AL 36688. Phone: 334-460-6418; Fax: 334-460-6529; E-mail: wflynn@jaguar1.usouthal.edu

ALASKA

Alaska Pacific University

Business Administration Department

Anchorage, Alaska

OVERVIEW

Alaska Pacific University is an independent-nonprofit, coed, comprehensive institution. Enrollment: 513 graduate, professional, and undergraduate students; 71 full-time matriculated graduate/professional students; 76 part-time matriculated graduate/professional students. Founded: 1957. The graduate business unit is in an urban setting and is on a semester calendar.

GRADUATE BUSINESS PROGRAMS

Master of Business Administration (MBA)

Master of Business Administration in Telecommunications Management (MBA)

ACADEMICS

Faculty Full-time 7; part-time 10.

Teaching Methodologies Case study, computer analysis, computer simulations, experiential learning, field projects, group discussion, lecture, research, student presentations, study groups, team projects.

Technology 22 on-campus computer terminals/PCs are available for student use. Students are not required to have their own PC.

Special Opportunities Advanced credit may be earned through transfer of credits from another institution. International exchange programs in Japan, People's Republic of China, Russia. An internship program is available.

FACILITIES

Information Resources Consortium Library; total holdings of 425,801 volumes, 419,314 microforms, 3,841 current periodical subscriptions. CD player(s) available for graduate student use. Access provided to online bibliographic retrieval services.

Program Contact: Assistant Director of Admissions, 4101 University Drive, Anchorage, AK 99508-4672. Phone: 907-564-8248, 800-252-7528 (AK only); Fax: 907-564-8317; E-mail: apu@corecom.net

University of Alaska Anchorage

College of Business and Public Policy

Anchorage, Alaska

OVERVIEW

The University of Alaska Anchorage is a state-supported, coed, comprehensive institution. Enrollment: 14,028 graduate, professional, and undergraduate students; 237 full-time matriculated graduate/professional students; 415 part-time matriculated graduate/professional students. Founded: 1954. The graduate business unit is in a suburban setting and is on a semester calendar.

HIGHLIGHTS

Enrollment Profile

Full-time: 19	International: 5%
Part-time: 84	Women: 40%
Total: 103	Minorities: 10%
Average Age: 35	Average Class Size: 20
Fall 1997 Average GPA: 2.99	Fall 1997 Average GMAT: 530

Costs
Full-time tuition: N/R
Part-time tuition: $162 per credit (resident); $316 per credit (nonresident)

AACSB – The International Association for Management Education accredited

GRADUATE BUSINESS PROGRAMS

Master of Business Administration (MBA) Full-time, part-time; 36-54 total credits required; 12 months to 7 years to complete program. Concentration in management.

ADMISSION

Applications For fall 1997 there were 52 applications for admission. Of those applying, 44 were accepted. Of those accepted, 34 enrolled.

Application Requirements GMAT score, application form, application fee, bachelor's degree, minimum GPA, college transcript(s), computer experience: word processing, spreadsheet, internet.

Recommended for Application Interview, resume, work experience.

Application Deadline Applications processed on a rolling/continuous basis for both domestic and international students. Application fee: $45. Deferred entrance is available.

ACADEMICS

Faculty Full-time 19.

Teaching Methodologies Case study, computer-aided instruction, computer analysis, computer simulations, experiential learning, faculty seminars, field projects, group discussion, lecture, research, role playing, seminars by members of the business community, simulations, student presentations, study groups, team projects.

Technology 175 on-campus computer terminals/PCs are available for student use and are linked by a campus-wide network. The network has full access to the Internet. Students are not required to have their own PC.

Special Opportunities Advanced credit may be earned through transfer of credits from another institution. An internship program is available.

FINANCES

Costs for 1997–98 Tuition: $162 per credit (resident); $316 per credit (nonresident). Fees: $60 per semester (resident); $60 per semester (nonresident). Fees vary by number of credits taken. Average 1997–98 room only costs were $5400 per academic year (off campus). Room and board costs vary by occupancy (e.g., single, double, triple), type of accommodation.

Financial Aid Research assistantships, teaching assistantships, scholarships, work study available. Financial aid is available to part-time students.

Financial Aid Contact Mr. Rick Weems, Student Financial Aid Director, 3211 Providence Drive, Anchorage, AK 99508-8060. Phone: 907-786-1586; Fax: 907-786-6122; E-mail: anrdw1@acad2.alaska.edu

FACILITIES

Information Resources Consortium Library; total holdings of 552,495 volumes, 419,314 microforms, 3,479 current periodical subscriptions. CD player(s) available for graduate student use. Access provided to online bibliographic retrieval services.

INTERNATIONAL STUDENTS

Demographics 5% of students enrolled are international students [Asia, 80%, Europe, 20%].

Services and Facilities International student office, international student housing, visa services, ESL courses, counseling/support services.

Applying TOEFL: minimum score of 550, proof of adequate funds, proof of health/immunizations required. Financial aid is available to international students.

International Student Contact Ms. Leslie Tuovinen, International Student Advisor, 3211 Providence Drive, Anchorage, AK 99508-8060. Phone: 907-786-1573; Fax: 907-786-4888; E-mail: anlat@acad2.alaska.edu

PLACEMENT

Services include alumni network, career counseling/planning, career fairs, career placement, and resume referral to employers.

Employment Of 1996–97 graduates, 100% were employed within three months of graduation.

Business Program(s) URL: http://www.scob.alaska.edu

Program Contact: Mrs. Joy Barbee, MBA Program Assistant, 3211 Providence Drive, Anchorage, AK 99508-8060. Phone: 907-786-4129; Fax: 907-786-4119; E-mail: anjlb2@uaa.alaska.edu

University of Alaska Fairbanks

School of Management
Fairbanks, Alaska

OVERVIEW

The University of Alaska Fairbanks is a state-supported, coed university. Enrollment: 8,360 graduate, professional, and undergraduate students; 466 full-time matriculated graduate/professional students; 325 part-time matriculated graduate/professional students. Founded: 1917. The graduate business unit is in a small-town setting and is on a semester calendar.

HIGHLIGHTS

Enrollment Profile
Full-time: 33
Part-time: 31
Total: 64
Average Age: 32
Fall 1997 Average GPA: 3.32

International: 6%
Women: 47%
Minorities: 17%
Average Class Size: 15
Fall 1997 Average GMAT: 550

Costs
Full-time tuition: $3726 per academic year (resident); $7344 per academic year (nonresident)
Part-time tuition: $158 per credit hour (resident); $308 per credit hour (nonresident)

AACSB – The International Association for Management Education accredited

GRADUATE BUSINESS PROGRAMS

Master of Business Administration (MBA) Full-time, part-time; 30-54 total credits required; 12 months to 7 years to complete program. Concentrations in accounting, resources management.

Master of Science in Resource Economics (MS) Full-time, part-time; 30 total credits required; 12 months to 7 years to complete program.

ADMISSION

Applications For fall 1997 there were 32 applications for admission. Of those applying, 28 were accepted. Of those accepted, 17 enrolled.

Application Requirements GMAT score: minimum 400, application form, application fee, bachelor's degree, essay, minimum GPA: 3.0, interview, 3 letters of recommendation, personal statement, college transcript(s).

Recommended for Application Resume, computer experience.

Application Deadline Applications processed on a rolling/continuous basis for both domestic and international students. Application fee: $35. Deferred entrance is available.

ACADEMICS

Faculty Full-time 19; part-time 5.

Teaching Methodologies Case study, computer-aided instruction, computer analysis, computer simulations, field projects, group discussion, lecture, research, role playing, seminars by members of the business community, simulations, student presentations, team projects.

Technology 300 on-campus computer terminals/PCs are available for student use and are linked by a campus-wide network. The network has full access to the Internet. Students are not required to have their own PC.

Special Opportunities Advanced credit may be earned through credit by examination, credit for experience, credit for business training programs, transfer of credits from another institution. International exchange program in Sweden . An internship program is available.

FINANCES

Costs for 1997–98 Tuition: Full-time: $3726 per year (resident); $7344 per year (nonresident). Part-time: $158 per credit hour (resident); $308 per credit hour (nonresident). Cost varies by class time (e.g., day/evening), number of credits taken, reciprocity agreements. Fees: Full-time: $800 per academic year (resident); $800 per academic year (nonresident). Part-time: $400 per semester (resident); $400 per semester (nonresident). Fees vary by class time (e.g., day/evening), number of credits taken. Average 1997–98 room and board costs were $3800 per academic year (on campus) and $5500 per academic year (off campus). Room and board costs vary by occupancy (e.g., single, double, triple), type of accommodation, type of meal plan.

Financial Aid In 1997–98, 11% of students received some institutionally administered aid in the form of fellowships, research assistantships, teaching assistantships, grants, scholarships, loans. Application Deadline: 3/15.

Financial Aid Contact Mr. Donald Schaeffer, Director, PO Box 756360, Fairbanks, AK 99775-6360. Phone: 907-474-7256; Fax: 907-474-7900; E-mail: fndes@aurora.alaska.edu

FACILITIES

Information Resources Rasmuson Library plus 1 additional on-campus library; total holdings of 1,750,000 volumes, 882,765 microforms, 6,700 current periodical subscriptions. Access provided to online bibliographic retrieval services.

INTERNATIONAL STUDENTS

Demographics 6% of students enrolled are international students [Asia, 75%, Europe, 25%].

Services and Facilities International student office, international student center, visa services, counseling/support services.

Applying TOEFL: minimum score of 550, TSE, proof of adequate funds, proof of health/immunizations required. Financial aid is available to international students.

International Student Contact Ms. Nancy Kuhn, International Student Advisor, PO Box 756340, Division of Student Services, Fairbanks, AK 99775-6340. Phone: 907-474-7317; Fax: 907-474-7900; E-mail: fnnkk@aurora.alaska.edu

PLACEMENT

Services include career counseling/planning, career fairs, career library, career placement, electronic job bank, job interviews arranged, and resume preparation. In 1996–97, 30 organizations participated in on-campus recruiting; 350 on-campus interviews were conducted.

Employment Of 1996–97 graduates, 80% were employed within three months of graduation. Types of employment entered: accounting, banking, computer-related, finance, financial services, government, hospitality management, human resources, insurance, marketing, retail, service industry.

Business Program(s) URL: http://zorba.uafadm.alaska.edu

Program Contact: Dr. Jacob Joseph, Director, MBA Program, PO Box 756080, Fairbanks, AK 99775-6080. Phone: 907-474-6532; Fax: 907-474-5219; E-mail: famba@fortune.uafsom.alaska.edu

University of Alaska Southeast

Business and Public Administration Academic Programs
Juneau, Alaska

OVERVIEW

The University of Alaska Southeast is a state-supported, coed, comprehensive institution. Enrollment: 2,761 graduate, professional, and undergraduate students; 16 full-time matriculated graduate/professional students; 49 part-time matriculated graduate/professional students. Founded: 1956. The graduate business unit

University of Alaska Southeast (continued)

is in a small-town setting and is on a semester calendar.

HIGHLIGHTS

Enrollment Profile
Full-time: 1
Part-time: 31
Total: 32
Average Age: 39
Fall 1997 Average GPA: 3.0

International: 16%
Women: 44%
Minorities: N/R
Average Class Size: 11
Fall 1997 Average GMAT: 540

Costs
Full-time tuition: $2916 per academic year (resident); $5688 per academic year (nonresident)
Part-time tuition: $158 per credit hour (resident); $474 per credit hour (nonresident)

GRADUATE BUSINESS PROGRAMS
Master of Business Administration (MBA) Full-time, part-time, distance learning option; 36 total credits required; up to 7 years to complete program. Concentrations in management, accounting.
Master of Public Administration (MPA) Full-time, part-time, distance learning option; 36 total credits required; up to 7 years to complete program. Concentrations in public management, resources management.

ADMISSION
Application Requirements GMAT score, GRE score, application form, application fee, bachelor's degree, essay, minimum GPA: 3.0, 3 letters of recommendation, personal statement, resume, college transcript(s).
Application Deadline Applications processed on a rolling/continuous basis for both domestic and international students. Application fee: $35. Deferred entrance is available.

ACADEMICS
Faculty Full-time 4; part-time 3.
Teaching Methodologies Case study, computer-aided instruction, faculty seminars, field projects, group discussion, lecture, research, seminars by members of the business community, student presentations, study groups, team projects.
Technology 48 on-campus computer terminals/PCs are available for student use and are linked by a campus-wide network. The network has full access to the Internet. Students are not required to have their own PC.
Special Opportunities Advanced credit may be earned through transfer of credits from another institution. An internship program is available.

FINANCES
Costs for 1997–98 Tuition: Full-time: $2916 per year (resident); $5688 per year (nonresident). Part-time: $158 per credit hour (resident); $474 per credit hour (nonresident). Cost varies by number of credits taken. Average 1997–98 room only costs were $2900 per academic year (on campus) and $6840 per academic year (off campus).
Financial Aid In 1997–98, 22% of students received some institutionally administered aid in the form of work study, loans. Financial aid is available to part-time students. Application Deadline: 3/1.
Financial Aid Contact Ms. Barbara Burnett, Financial Aid Manager, 11120 Glacier Highway, Juneau, AK 99801-8625. Phone: 907-465-6255; Fax: 907-465-6365; E-mail: jyfin@acad1.alaska.edu

FACILITIES
Information Resources Egan Library; total holdings of 77,000 volumes, 250,000 microforms, 780 current periodical subscriptions. CD player(s) available for graduate student use. Access provided to online bibliographic retrieval services and online databases.

INTERNATIONAL STUDENTS
Demographics 16% of students enrolled are international students [North America, 100%].
Services and Facilities International student office, counseling/support services.
Applying TOEFL: minimum score of 550, proof of adequate funds required. Financial aid is available to international students.
International Student Contact Mr. Greg Wagner, Director of Admissions, 11120 Glacier Highway, Juneau, AK 99801-8625. Phone: 907-465-6457; Fax: 907-465-6365; E-mail: jyuas@acad1.alaska.edu

Business Program(s) URL: http://www.jun.alaska.edu/

Program Contact: Mr. Greg Wagner, Director of Admissions, 11120 Glacier Highway, Juneau, AK 99801-8625. Phone: 907-465-6239; Fax: 907-465-6365; E-mail: jyuas@acad1.alaska.edu

ARIZONA

Arizona State University

College of Business
Tempe, Arizona

OVERVIEW
Arizona State University is a state-supported, coed university. Enrollment: 44,255 graduate, professional, and undergraduate students; 5,901 full-time matriculated graduate/professional students; 4,857 part-time matriculated graduate/professional students. Founded: 1885. The graduate business unit is in a suburban setting and is on a trimester calendar.

HIGHLIGHTS

Enrollment Profile
Full-time: 326
Part-time: 578
Total: 904
Average Age: 31
Fall 1997 Average GPA: 3.25

International: 11%
Women: 30%
Minorities: 14%
Average Class Size: 45
Fall 1997 Average GMAT: 609

Costs
Full-time tuition: $4058 per academic year (resident); $10,710 per academic year (nonresident)
Part-time tuition: $6000 per year (resident); $10,492 per year (nonresident)

AACSB – The International Association for Management Education accredited

GRADUATE BUSINESS PROGRAMS
Day MBA (MBA) Full-time; 60 total credits required; 22 months to 2 years to complete program. Concentrations in information management, international business, marketing, logistics, finance, management information systems, production management.
Evening MBA (MBA) Full-time, part-time; 48 total credits required; 2 to 3 years to complete program. Concentrations in accounting, information management, international business, production management, logistics, project management, finance, marketing, economics, information management, operations management.
Technology MBA (MBA) Full-time, part-time; 48 total credits required; 2 to 3 years to complete program. Concentrations in information management, production management, project management, system management.
Executive MBA (MBA) Full-time, part-time; 48 total credits required; 22 months to 2 years to complete program.
Master of Business Administration/Master of Science in Accounting (MBA/MS) Full-time, part-time; 63 total credits required; up to 2 years to complete program.
Master of Business Administration/Master of Science in Taxation (MBA/MS) Full-time, part-time; 63 total credits required; 22 months to 2 years to complete program.
Master of Business Administration/Master of Science in Economics (MBA/MS) Full-time, part-time; 66 total credits required; 22 months to 2 years to complete program.
Master of Business Administration/Doctor of Jurisprudence (MBA/JD) Full-time; 117 total credits required; 4 to 5 years to complete program.
Master of Business Administration/Master of Health Service Administration (MBA/MHSA) Full-time; 72 total credits required; 22 months to 2 years to complete program.
Master of Business Administration/Master of Science in Information Management (MBA/MS) Full-time, part-time; 60 total credits required; 22 months to 2 years to complete program.

ADMISSION
Applications For fall 1997 there were 1,360 applications for admission. Of those applying, 656 were accepted. Of those accepted, 448 enrolled.
Application Requirements Application form, application fee, bachelor's degree, essay, minimum GPA: 3.0, 2 letters of recommendation, personal statement, resume, college transcript(s), minimum of 2 years of work experience, computer experience: word processing, spreadsheet, powerpoint.
Recommended for Application GMAT score accepted, interview.
Application Deadline 5/1 for fall, 3/1 for fall (international). Application fee: $45. Deferred entrance is available.

ACADEMICS
Faculty Full-time 168.

Teaching Methodologies Case study, computer analysis, computer simulations, faculty seminars, field projects, group discussion, lecture, research, role playing, student presentations, study groups, team projects.

Technology 1,000 on-campus computer terminals/PCs are available for student use and are linked by a campus-wide network. The network has full access to the Internet. Students are not required to have their own PC.

Special Opportunities International exchange programs in France, Mexico, Norway, Spain.

FINANCES
Costs for 1997–98 Tuition: Full-time: $4058 per year (resident); $10,710 per year (nonresident). Part-time: $6000 per year (resident); $10,492 per year (nonresident). Cost varies by academic program, class time (e.g., day/evening), number of credits taken. Fees: Full-time: $250 per academic year (resident); $250 per academic year (nonresident). Fees vary by academic program, class time (e.g., day/evening). Average 1997–98 room and board costs were $6800 per academic year (off campus). Room and board costs vary by campus location, occupancy (e.g., single, double, triple), type of accommodation, type of meal plan.

Financial Aid Research assistantships, teaching assistantships, scholarships, loans available. Application Deadline: 3/1.

Financial Aid Contact Ms. Paula Vaughn, Financial Aid Counselor, Graduate College, PO Box 871003, Tempe, AZ 85287-1003. Phone: 602-965-3521; Fax: 602-965-5151.

FACILITIES
Information Resources Charles Trumbull Hayden Library plus 4 additional on-campus libraries; total holdings of 2,922,157 volumes, 5,984,180 microforms, 32,241 current periodical subscriptions. CD player(s) available for graduate student use. Access provided to online bibliographic retrieval services.

INTERNATIONAL STUDENTS
Demographics 11% of students enrolled are international students [Africa, 2%, Asia, 62%, Australia/New Zealand, 1%, Central America, 4%, Europe, 22%, North America, 6%, South America, 2%, other, 1%].

Services and Facilities International student office, international student housing, visa services, ESL courses, counseling/support services.

Applying TOEFL: minimum score of 580, TSE: minimum score of 50, proof of adequate funds, proof of health/immunizations required. TWE recommended. Financial aid is available to international students.

International Student Contact Ms. Suzanne Steadman, Coordinator, Student Services Building, B225, Tempe, AZ 85287-0512. Phone: 602-965-7451; Fax: 602-965-1608.

PLACEMENT
Services include alumni network, career counseling/planning, career fairs, career library, career placement, electronic job bank, job interviews arranged, job search course, resume referral to employers, and resume preparation. In 1996–97, 252 organizations participated in on-campus recruiting.

Employment Of 1996–97 graduates, 98% were employed within three months of graduation; the average starting salary was $62,500. Types of employment entered: accounting, banking, communications, computer-related, consulting, consumer products, finance, financial services, health services, high technology, information systems/technology, management, manufacturing, marketing, petrochemical, pharmaceutical, service industry, telecommunications, transportation.

Business Program(s) URL: http://www.cob.asu.edu/mba

Program Contact: Judith Heilala, Director, Recruiting and Admissions, MBA Program, PO Box 874906, College of Business, Tempe, AZ 85287-4906. Phone: 602-965-3332; Fax: 602-965-8569; E-mail: iacjkh@asuvm.inre.asu.edu

See full description on page 704.

Arizona State University West

School of Management

Phoenix, Arizona

OVERVIEW
Arizona State University West is a state-supported, coed, upper-level institution. Enrollment: 4,700 graduate, professional, and undergraduate students; 300 full-time matriculated graduate/professional students; 900 part-time matriculated graduate/professional students. Founded: 1984. The graduate business unit is in a suburban setting and is on a semester calendar.

HIGHLIGHTS
Enrollment Profile
Full-time: 50
Part-time: 404
Total: 454
Average Age: 33
Fall 1997 Average GPA: 3.2

International: N/R
Women: 31%
Minorities: N/R
Average Class Size: 25
Fall 1997 Average GMAT: 580

Costs
Full-time tuition: $994 per academic year (resident); $4320 per academic year (nonresident)
Part-time tuition: $105 per credit hour (resident); $360 per credit hour (nonresident)

AACSB – The International Association for Management Education accredited

Degree(s) offered in conjunction with Thunderbird, The American Graduate School of International Management

GRADUATE BUSINESS PROGRAMS
Evening Program for Professionals (MBA) Full-time, part-time; 45 total credits required; 18 months to 6 years to complete program.

ASU West/Thunderbird Dual Degree (MBA/MIM) Full-time; 72 total credits required; 20 months to 3.8 years to complete program. Concentration in international management.

The Scottsdale MBA (MBA) Part-time; 45 total credits required; 2.7 years to complete program.

ADMISSION
Application Requirements GMAT score, application form, application fee, bachelor's degree, essay, minimum GPA: 3.0, 2 letters of recommendation, personal statement, resume, college transcript(s), computer experience.

Recommended for Application Work experience.

Application Deadline 6/1 for fall, 11/1 for spring, 4/1 for summer, 4/1 for fall (international), 8/1 for spring (international), 1/1 for summer (international). Application fee: $45. Deferred entrance is available.

ACADEMICS
Teaching Methodologies Case study, computer-aided instruction, computer simulations, experiential learning, field projects, group discussion, lecture, research, seminars by members of the business community, simulations, student presentations, study groups, team projects.

Technology 150 on-campus computer terminals/PCs are available for student use and are linked by a campus-wide network. The network has full access to the Internet. Students are not required to have their own PC.

Special Opportunities Advanced credit may be earned through transfer of credits from another institution. International exchange program available. An internship program is available.

FINANCES
Costs for 1997–98 Tuition: Full-time: $994 per semester (resident); $4320 per semester (nonresident). Part-time: $105 per credit hour (resident); $360 per credit hour (nonresident). Cost varies by academic program, campus location, number of credits taken. Fees: Full-time: $936 per academic year (resident); $744 per academic year (nonresident). Part-time: $234 per course (resident); $186 per course (nonresident). Fees vary by academic program, campus location, number of credits taken. Average 1997–98 room and board costs were $7000 per academic year (off campus).

Financial Aid Research assistantships, scholarships, work study, loans available. Financial aid is available to part-time students.

Financial Aid Contact Financial Aid Services, 4701 West Thunderbird Road, Phoenix, AZ 85069-7100. Phone: 602-543-8178.

FACILITIES
Information Resources Fletcher Library; total holdings of 242,415 volumes, 1,321,962 microforms, 3,389 current periodical subscriptions. CD player(s) available for graduate student use. Access provided to online bibliographic retrieval services and online databases.

INTERNATIONAL STUDENTS
Demographics N/R

Services and Facilities International student office, visa services, counseling/support services.

Applying TOEFL, proof of adequate funds, proof of health/immunizations required. Financial aid is not available to international students.

International Student Contact Ms. Marge Runyan, Graduate Studies Coordinator, 4701 West Thunderbird Road, Phoenix, AZ 85069-7100. Phone: 602-543-4567; Fax: 602-543-4561; E-mail: istmaf@asuvm.inre.asu.edu

PLACEMENT
Services include alumni network, career counseling/planning, career fairs, career library, career placement, electronic job bank, job interviews arranged, job search course, and resume preparation.

Business Program(s) URL: http://www.west.asu.edu/som/mba

Program Contact: Mr. Jon Delany, MBA Program Coordinator, 4701 West Thunderbird Road, Phoenix, AZ 85069-7100. Phone: 602-543-6201 Ext. 6123; Fax: 602-543-6221; E-mail: delany@asu.edu

Grand Canyon University

College of Business

Phoenix, Arizona

OVERVIEW
Grand Canyon University is an independent-religious, coed, comprehensive institution. Enrollment: 2,245 graduate, professional, and undergraduate students; 40 full-time matriculated graduate/professional students; 416 part-time matriculated graduate/professional students. Founded: 1949. The graduate business unit is in an urban setting and is on a trimester calendar.

HIGHLIGHTS

Enrollment Profile

Full-time: 16	International: 14%
Part-time: 47	Women: 43%
Total: 63	Minorities: 33%
Average Age: N/R	Average Class Size: 25
Fall 1997 Average GPA: N/R	Fall 1997 Average GMAT: N/R

Costs
Full-time tuition: $2601 per academic year
Part-time tuition: $268 per semester hour

ACBSP – The American Council of Business Schools and Programs accredited

Degree(s) offered in conjunction with Grand Canyon Education Center (Taiwan)

GRADUATE BUSINESS PROGRAMS
Master of Business Administration (MBA) Full-time, part-time; 36 total credits required; 18 months to 5 years to complete program. Concentrations in accounting, international business, health care.

ADMISSION
Applications For fall 1997 there were 27 applications for admission. Of those applying, 23 were accepted. Of those accepted, 19 enrolled.

Application Requirements GMAT score, application form, application fee, bachelor's degree, minimum GPA, interview, college transcript(s).

Recommended for Application Work experience, computer experience.

Application Deadline Applications processed on a rolling/continuous basis for both domestic and international students. Application fee: $25. Deferred entrance is available.

ACADEMICS
Faculty Full-time 7; part-time 1.

Teaching Methodologies Case study, computer analysis, computer simulations, experiential learning, group discussion, lecture, research, role playing, seminars by members of the business community, student presentations, study groups, team projects.

Technology 119 on-campus computer terminals/PCs are available for student use. The network does not have Internet access. Students are not required to have their own PC.

Special Opportunities Advanced credit may be earned through transfer of credits from another institution. International exchange programs in Brazil, United Kingdom.

FINANCES
Costs for 1997–98 Tuition: Full-time: $2601 per semester. Part-time: $268 per semester hour. Fees: Full-time: $220 per academic year. Part-time: $46 per semester hour. Fees vary by number of credits taken. Average 1997–98 room and board costs were $3720 per academic year (on campus) and $4500 per academic year (off campus). Room and board costs vary by occupancy (e.g., single, double, triple), type of accommodation, type of meal plan.

Financial Aid In 1997–98, 25% of students received some institutionally administered aid in the form of scholarships, work study, loans. Financial aid is available to part-time students. Application Deadline: 3/15.

Financial Aid Contact Rosanna Short, Financial Aid Director, 3300 West Camelback Road, Phoenix, AZ 85017-3030. Phone: 602-589-2885.

FACILITIES
Information Resources Fleming Library; total holdings of 76,011 volumes, 1,139 microforms, 590 current periodical subscriptions. CD player(s) available for graduate student use. Access provided to online bibliographic retrieval services.

INTERNATIONAL STUDENTS
Demographics 14% of students enrolled are international students.

Services and Facilities International student office, international student housing, ESL courses, counseling/support services.

Applying TOEFL: minimum score of 550, proof of adequate funds, proof of health/immunizations required. TWE recommended. Financial aid is available to international students.

International Student Contact Dr. Treva Gibson, Director of International Education and E.A.S.E. Program, 3300 West Camelback Road, Phoenix, AZ 85017-3030. Phone: 602-589-2808; Fax: 602-841-8771.

PLACEMENT
Services include alumni network, career counseling/planning, and career fairs.

Employment Types of employment entered: accounting, banking, communications, computer-related, consulting, finance, financial services, government, health services, high technology, human resources, marketing, media, utilities.

Business Program(s) URL: http://www.grand-canyon.edu/

Program Contact: Dr. Rob Jones, Associate Dean, Graduate Studies, 3300 West Camelback Road, PO Box 11097, Phoenix, AZ 85017-3030. Phone: 602-589-2867, 800-800-9776; Fax: 602-589-2532; E-mail: robjo24@aol.com

Northern Arizona University

College of Business Administration

Flagstaff, Arizona

OVERVIEW
Northern Arizona University is a state-supported, coed university. Enrollment: 19,605 graduate, professional, and undergraduate students; 1,447 full-time matriculated graduate/professional students; 3,908 part-time matriculated graduate/professional students. Founded: 1899. The graduate business unit is in a small-town setting and is on a semester calendar.

HIGHLIGHTS

Enrollment Profile

Full-time: 35	International: 28%
Part-time: 8	Women: 23%
Total: 43	Minorities: 0%
Average Age: 27	Average Class Size: 15
Fall 1997 Average GPA: 3.4	Fall 1997 Average GMAT: 517

Costs
Full-time tuition: $3588 per academic year (resident); $9504 per academic year (nonresident)
Part-time tuition: $189 per credit hour (resident); $396 per credit hour (nonresident)

AACSB – The International Association for Management Education accredited

GRADUATE BUSINESS PROGRAMS
Master of Business Administration (MBA) Full-time, part-time, distance learning option; 31 total credits required; 10 months to 6 years to complete program. Concentrations in management information systems, international business.

ADMISSION
Applications For fall 1997 there were 55 applications for admission. Of those applying, 35 were accepted. Of those accepted, 18 enrolled.

Application Requirements GMAT score, application form, application fee, bachelor's degree, essay, minimum GPA, 3 letters of recommendation, personal statement, resume, college transcript(s), computer experience: programming in COBOL.

Application Deadline 3/1 for fall, 10/15 for spring, 1/15 for summer. Application fee: $40. Deferred entrance is available.

ACADEMICS
Faculty Full-time 53; part-time 1.

Teaching Methodologies Case study, computer-aided instruction, computer analysis, computer simulations, experiential learning, faculty seminars, field projects, group discussion, lecture, research, role playing, seminars by members of the business community, simulations, student presentations, study groups, team projects.

Technology 150 on-campus computer terminals/PCs are available for student use and are linked by a campus-wide network. The network has full access to the Internet. Students are not required to have their own PC.

Special Opportunities Advanced credit may be earned through credit by examination, transfer of credits from another institution. An internship program is available.

FINANCES
Costs for 1997–98 Tuition: Full-time: $3588 per year (resident); $9504 per year (nonresident). Part-time: $189 per credit hour (resident); $396 per credit hour (nonresident). Cost varies by number of credits taken. Fees: Full-time: $70 per academic year (resident); $70 per academic year (nonresident). Part-time: $5 per credit hour (resident); $5 per credit hour (nonresident). Fees vary by number of credits taken. Average 1997–98 room and board costs were $3472 per academic year (on campus) and $5690 per academic year (off campus). Room and board costs vary by occupancy (e.g., single, double, triple), type of accommodation, type of meal plan.

Financial Aid In 1997–98, 77% of students received some institutionally administered aid in the form of research assistantships, teaching assistantships, scholarships, work study, loans. Application Deadline: 4/15.

Financial Aid Contact Mr. James Pritchard, Director, Financial Aid, PO Box 4108, Flagstaff, AZ 86011-4108. Phone: 520-523-4951; Fax: 520-523-1551; E-mail: finaid@nau.edu

FACILITIES
Information Resources Cline Library plus 1 additional on-campus library; total holdings of 999,042 volumes, 336,031 microforms, 3,800 current periodical subscriptions. CD player(s) available for graduate student use. Access provided to online bibliographic retrieval services.

INTERNATIONAL STUDENTS
Demographics 28% of students enrolled are international students [Asia, 60%, Europe, 40%].

Services and Facilities International student office, international student center, visa services, ESL courses, counseling/support services.

Applying TOEFL: minimum score of 550, proof of adequate funds, proof of health/immunizations required. Financial aid is available to international students.

International Student Contact Dr. Joan Fagerburg, Assistant Dean, Student Life, University Union 201, Box 06015, Flagstaff, AZ 86011. Phone: 520-523-6772; E-mail: joan.fagerburg@nau.edu

PLACEMENT
Services include alumni network, career counseling/planning, career fairs, career placement, electronic job bank, resume referral to employers, and resume preparation. In 1996–97, 43 organizations participated in on-campus recruiting.

Employment Of 1996–97 graduates, 92% were employed within three months of graduation; the average starting salary was $51,000. Types of employment entered: communications, computer-related, consulting, education, finance, financial services, high technology, hospitality management, information systems/technology, real estate, telecommunications.

Business Program(s) URL: http://www.cba.nau.edu/website/index.html

Program Contact: Dr. Mason S. Gerety, Director, MBA Program, Box 15066, Flagstaff, AZ 86011. Phone: 520-523-7342; Fax: 520-523-7331; E-mail: cba-mba@mail.cba.nau.edu

Thunderbird, The American Graduate School of International Management

Master's Program in International Management

Glendale, Arizona

OVERVIEW
Thunderbird, The American Graduate School of International Management is an independent-nonprofit, coed, graduate institution. Enrollment: 1,508 graduate, professional, and undergraduate students; 1,508 full-time matriculated graduate/professional students; part-time matriculated graduate/professional students. Founded: 1946. The graduate business unit is in a suburban setting and is on a semester calendar.

HIGHLIGHTS
Enrollment Profile
Full-time: 1,508
Part-time: 0
Total: 1,508
Average Age: 28
Fall 1997 Average GPA: 3.4
International: 44%
Women: 35%
Minorities: 10%
Average Class Size: 40
Fall 1997 Average GMAT: 590

Costs
Full-time tuition: $20,700 per academic year
Part-time tuition: N/R

AACSB – The International Association for Management Education accredited

Degree(s) offered in conjunction with Arizona State University, Arizona Stat University West, Case Western Reserve University, Drury College, University of Colorado at Denver, University of Florida, University of Houston, University of Texas at Arlington

GRADUATE BUSINESS PROGRAMS
Master of International Management (MIM) Full-time, distance learning option; 42 total credits required; 12 months to 5 years to complete program. Concentrations in international management, international marketing, international finance, international trade.

Executive Master of International Management (EMIM) distance learning option; 50 total credits required; minimum of 2 years to complete program. Concentration in international management.

Master of International Health Management (MIHM) Full-time, distance learning option; 30 total credits required; 18 months to 2 years to complete program. Concentration in international management.

Master of International Management of Technology (MIMOT) Full-time, distance learning option; 59 total credits required; 2 to 5 years to complete program. Concentrations in international management, technology management.

Master of Business Administration/Master of International Management (MBA/MIM) Full-time, distance learning option; 30 total credits required; 18 months to 5 years to complete program. Concentration in international management.

Master of International Management Latin America (MIMLA) Full-time, distance learning option; 50 total credits required; minimum of 22 months to complete program.

ADMISSION
Applications For fall 1997 there were 1,333 applications for admission. Of those applying, 745 were accepted. Of those accepted, 428 enrolled.

Application Requirements GMAT score, application form, application fee, bachelor's degree, essay, minimum GPA: 2.7, 3 letters of recommendation, resume, college transcript(s), computer experience: Microsoft Office.

Recommended for Application Work experience.

Application Deadline 1/31 for fall, 7/31 for winter, 7/31 for spring, 1/31 for summer, 1/31 for fall (international), 7/31 for winter (international), 7/31 for spring (international), 1/31 for summer (international). Application fee: $50. Deferred entrance is available.

ACADEMICS
Faculty Full-time 103; part-time 19.

Teaching Methodologies Case study, computer-aided instruction, computer simulations, field projects, group discussion, lecture, research, seminars by members of the business community, student presentations, study groups, team projects.

Technology 187 on-campus computer terminals/PCs are available for student use and are linked by a campus-wide network. The network has full access to the Internet. Students are required to have their own PC.

Special Opportunities Advanced credit may be earned through transfer of credits from another institution. International exchange programs in Austria, Brazil, Chile, Costa Rica, Egypt, Finland, France, Germany, Japan, Mexico, Norway, People's Republic of China, Republic of Korea, Russia, Spain, Taiwan. An internship program is available.

FINANCES
Costs for 1997–98 Tuition: Full-time: $20,700 per year. Cost varies by number of credits taken. Fees: Full-time: $200 per academic year. Average 1997–98 room and board costs were $5380 per academic year. Room and board costs vary by campus location, type of accommodation.

Financial Aid In 1997–98, 67% of students received some institutionally administered aid in the form of fellowships, research assistantships, grants, scholarships, work study. Application Deadline: 4/1.

Financial Aid Contact Ms. Catherine King-Todd, Director of Financial Aid, 15249 North 59th Avenue, Glendale, AZ 85306-3236. Phone: 602-978-7888; Fax: 602-439-5432; E-mail: kingtodc@t-bird.edu

Thunderbird, The American Graduate School of International Management (continued)

FACILITIES

Information Resources The Merle A. Heinrichs International Business Information Centre plus 1 additional on-campus library; total holdings of 72,858 volumes, 4,648 microforms, 1,612 current periodical subscriptions. CD player(s) available for graduate student use. Access provided to online bibliographic retrieval services and online databases.

INTERNATIONAL STUDENTS

Demographics 44% of students enrolled are international students [Africa, 1%, Asia, 52%, Europe, 23%, North America, 4%, South America, 17%, other, 3%].

Services and Facilities International student office, international student housing, visa services, ESL courses, counseling/support services, newsletter, international student orientation.

Applying TOEFL: minimum score of 550, proof of adequate funds required. Financial aid is available to international students.

International Student Contact Ms. Mary Lee Carter, Director, Programs for Foreign Students and Scholars, 15249 North 59th Avenue, Glendale, AZ 85306-3236. Phone: 602-978-7599; Fax: 602-439-5432; E-mail: carterml@t-bird.edu

PLACEMENT

Services include alumni network, career counseling/planning, career fairs, career library, career placement, job interviews arranged, job search course, resume referral to employers, and resume preparation. In 1996–97, 271 organizations participated in on-campus recruiting; 2,954 on-campus interviews were conducted.

Employment Of 1996–97 graduates, 82% were employed within three months of graduation; the average starting salary was $50,319. Types of employment entered: accounting, banking, communications, computer-related, consulting, consumer products, engineering, finance, financial services, government, health services, human resources, insurance, international trade, management, manufacturing, marketing, nonprofit, pharmaceutical, service industry, telecommunications.

Business Program(s) URL: http://www.t-bird.edu

Program Contact: Ms. Judith Johnson, Director of Admissions, 15249 North 59th Avenue, Glendale, AZ 85306-3236. Phone: 602-978-7100, 800-848-9084; Fax: 602-439-5432; E-mail: tbird@t-bird.edu
See full description on page 1022.

University of Arizona

Karl Eller Graduate School of Management

Tucson, Arizona

OVERVIEW

The University of Arizona is a state-supported, coed university. Enrollment: 35,306 graduate, professional, and undergraduate students; 5,597 full-time matriculated graduate/professional students; 3,241 part-time matriculated graduate/professional students. Founded: 1885. The graduate business unit is in a suburban setting and is on a semester calendar.

HIGHLIGHTS

Enrollment Profile

Full-time: 256	International: 10%
Part-time: 66	Women: 28%
Total: 322	Minorities: 17%
Average Age: 27	Average Class Size: 50
Fall 1997 Average GPA: 3.39	Fall 1997 Average GMAT: 610

Costs
Full-time tuition: $4162 per academic year (resident); $11,114 per academic year (nonresident)
Part-time tuition: $2644 per year (resident); $5584 per year (nonresident)

AACSB – The International Association for Management Education accredited

Degree(s) offered in conjunction with Thunderbird, The American Graduate School of International Business

GRADUATE BUSINESS PROGRAMS

Master of Business Administration (MBA) Full-time, part-time; 60 total credits required; 21 months to 2 years to complete program. Concentrations in management information systems, marketing, entrepreneurship, finance, accounting, banking, decision sciences, economics, health care, human resources, management, operations management, marketing research, production management.

Master of Business Administration/Master of Science in Management Information Systems (MBA/MS) Full-time; 75 total credits required; 3.2 to 3.4 years to complete program. Concentrations in accounting, banking, decision sciences, economics, entrepreneurship, finance, health care, management, management information systems, marketing, operations management, marketing research, production management.

Master of Business Administration/Master of Science in Nursing (MBA/MS) Full-time; 75 total credits required; 3.2 to 3.4 years to complete program. Concentrations in accounting, banking, decision sciences, economics, entrepreneurship, finance, health care, management, management information systems, marketing, operations management, marketing research, production management, system management.

Master of Business Administration/Master of International Management (MBA/MIM) Full-time; 75 total credits required; 3.2 to 3.4 years to complete program. Concentrations in international and area business studies, international banking, international business, international development management, international economics, international finance, international logistics, international management, international marketing, international trade, accounting, banking, decision sciences, economics, entrepreneurship, finance, health care, human resources, management, management information systems, marketing, operations management, marketing research, production management.

Master of Business Administration/Doctor of Jurisprudence (MBA/JD) Full-time; 90 total credits required; 3.8 years to complete program. Concentrations in accounting, legal administration, economics, entrepreneurship, finance, health care, human resources, management, management information systems, marketing, operations management, banking, decision sciences, international business, marketing research, production management.

Master of Business Administration/Master of Arts in Journalism (MBA/MA) Full-time; 75 total credits required; 2.8 years to complete program. Concentrations in management information systems, marketing, entrepreneurship, finance, accounting, banking, decision sciences, economics, health care, human resources, management, operations management, marketing research, production management.

ADMISSION

Applications For fall 1997 there were 725 applications for admission. Of those applying, 250 were accepted. Of those accepted, 131 enrolled.

Application Requirements Application form, application fee, bachelor's degree, essay, minimum GPA, interview, 2 letters of recommendation, personal statement, resume, college transcript(s), minimum of 2 years of work experience.

Recommended for Application GMAT score accepted, computer experience.

Application Deadline 3/1 for fall, 12/1 for winter, 2/1 for fall (international). Application fee: $45.

ACADEMICS

Faculty Full-time 45; part-time 10.

Teaching Methodologies Case study, computer-aided instruction, computer analysis, computer simulations, group discussion, lecture, research, seminars by members of the business community, simulations, student presentations, team projects.

Technology 35 on-campus computer terminals/PCs are available for student use and are linked by a campus-wide network. The network has full access to the Internet. Students are not required to have their own PC.

Special Opportunities An internship program is available.

FINANCES

Costs for 1997–98 Tuition: Full-time: $4162 per year (resident); $11,114 per year (nonresident). Part-time: $2644 per year (resident); $5584 per year (nonresident). Cost varies by number of credits taken. Average 1997–98 room and board costs were $5500 per academic year (off campus). Room and board costs vary by occupancy (e.g., single, double, triple), type of accommodation.

Financial Aid In 1997–98, 19% of students received some institutionally administered aid in the form of fellowships, teaching assistantships, scholarships, work study. Application Deadline: 2/1.

Financial Aid Contact Ms. Christina O'Bannon, Program Coordinator, 210 McClelland Hall, PO Box 210108, Tucson, AZ 85721-0108. Phone: 520-621-3915; Fax: 520-621-2606; E-mail: cobannon@bpa.arizona.edu

FACILITIES
Information Resources Main library plus 3 additional on-campus libraries; total holdings of 3,873,408 volumes, 4,705,741 microforms, 26,513 current periodical subscriptions. CD player(s) available for graduate student use. Access provided to online bibliographic retrieval services.

INTERNATIONAL STUDENTS
Demographics 10% of students enrolled are international students.

Services and Facilities International student office, international student center, counseling/support services.

Applying TOEFL: minimum score of 600, proof of adequate funds, proof of health/immunizations required. Financial aid is available to international students.

International Student Contact Mr. David Currey, Assistant Director, 915 North Tyndall Avenue, Tucson, AZ 85721. Phone: 520-621-4627; Fax: 520-621-4069.

PLACEMENT
Services include alumni network, career counseling/planning, career fairs, career library, career placement, electronic job bank, job interviews arranged, resume referral to employers, and resume preparation. In 1996–97, 75 organizations participated in on-campus recruiting; 60 on-campus interviews were conducted.

Employment Of 1996–97 graduates, 78% were employed within three months of graduation; the average starting salary was $56,000. Types of employment entered: accounting, banking, communications, computer-related, consulting, engineering, finance, financial services, health services, high technology, human resources, information systems/technology, manufacturing, marketing, mining, retail, telecommunications.

Business Program(s) URL: http://www.bpa.arizona.edu/

Program Contact: Ms. Susan Salinas Wong, Director of Admissions, Eller Graduate School of Management, 210 McClelland Hall, PO Box 210108, Tucson, AZ 85721-0108. Phone: 520-621-4008; Fax: 520-621-2606; E-mail: ellernet@bpa.arizona.edu

See full description on page 1032.

University of Phoenix

Department of Graduate Business

Phoenix, Arizona

OVERVIEW
The University of Phoenix is a proprietary, coed, comprehensive institution. Enrollment: 42,134 graduate, professional, and undergraduate students; 13,070 full-time matriculated graduate/professional students; part-time matriculated graduate/professional students. Founded: 1976. The graduate business unit is in an urban setting and is on a continuous enrollment—every 6 weeks calendar.

HIGHLIGHTS
Enrollment Profile
Full-time: 9,197
Part-time: 0
Total: 9,197
Average Age: 35
Fall 1997 Average GPA: N/R

International: N/R
Women: 44%
Minorities: 33%
Average Class Size: 13
Fall 1997 Average GMAT: N/R

Costs
Full-time tuition: $5712 per academic year
Part-time tuition: N/R

GRADUATE BUSINESS PROGRAMS
Master of Business Administration (MBA) Full-time, distance learning option; 51 total credits required.

Master of Arts in Organizational Leadership (MA) Full-time, distance learning option; 41 total credits required.

Master of Business Administration in Global Management (MBA) Full-time, distance learning option; 41 total credits required.

Master of Business Administration in Technology Management (MBA) Full-time, distance learning option; 51 total credits required.

Master of Business Administration in Health Care Management (MBA) Full-time, distance learning option; 40 total credits required.

ADMISSION
Application Requirements Application form, bachelor's degree, college transcript(s), work experience.

Application Deadline Applications processed on a rolling/continuous basis for both domestic and international students. Application fee: $50. Deferred entrance is available.

ACADEMICS
Faculty Full-time 33; part-time 2,187.

Teaching Methodologies Case study, experiential learning, group discussion, research, student presentations, study groups, team projects.

Technology Students are not required to have their own PC.

Special Opportunities Advanced credit may be earned through credit by examination, credit for experience, credit for military training programs, transfer of credits from another institution.

FINANCES
Costs for 1997–98 Tuition: Full-time: $5712 per year. Cost varies by academic program, campus location.

Financial Aid Contact Stephanie Schwencer, Director of Financial Aid, 4615 East Elwood Road, PO Box 52069, Phoenix, AZ 85072-2069. Phone: 602-966-9577.

FACILITIES
Information Resources Learning Resource Center. Access provided to online databases.

INTERNATIONAL STUDENTS
Demographics N/R

Applying TOEFL: minimum score of 520 recommended. Financial aid is not available to international students.

Business Program(s) URL: http://www.uophx.edu

Program Contact: Department of Graduate Business, 4615 East Elwood Road, PO Box 52069, Phoenix, AZ 85072-2069. Phone: 602-966-9577.

Western International University

Graduate Programs in Business

Phoenix, Arizona

OVERVIEW
Western International University is a proprietary, coed, comprehensive institution. Enrollment: 1,376 graduate, professional, and undergraduate students. Founded: 1978. The graduate business unit is in an urban setting and is on a semester calendar.

HIGHLIGHTS
Enrollment Profile
Full-time: N/R
Part-time: N/R
Total: 410
Average Age: 35
Fall 1997 Average GPA: 3.0

International: N/R
Women: N/R
Minorities: N/R
Average Class Size: 18
Fall 1997 Average GMAT: N/R

Costs
Full-time tuition: N/R
Part-time tuition: $215 per credit hour

Western International University (WIU) was established on the principle that a global business perspective is vital in the emerging international marketplace. International issues and technology are key themes throughout WIU's programs. Taught by professors with real-world experience, American business techniques are coupled with a comprehensive view of global business. WIU's international emphasis can be found in the faculty, which includes respected industry professionals, and in the students, who come from more than thirty countries, including the United States. WIU's students are primarily working professionals who are serious about assuming leadership roles in the global environment. The diversity of the student body brings a broad range of cultural experiences to the campus and provides future executives with an understanding of cross-cultural communication. WIU recognizes that this high level of diversity necessitates a flexible and practical approach to learning. WIU's flexible schedule enables students to expedite their academic progress. Classes meet once a week over a two-month session. New classes begin every month, which enables students to take one or more classes at a time in order to shorten the length of their degree program. At WIU, the attributes of traditional and nontraditional educational approaches are combined, with an emphasis on practical application.

GRADUATE BUSINESS PROGRAMS
Master of Business Administration in Management (MBA) Full-time, part-time; 39 total credits required; minimum of 15 months to complete program. Concentration in management.

Western International University (continued)

Master of Business Administration in International Business (MBA) Full-time, part-time; 39 total credits required; minimum of 15 months to complete program. Concentration in international business.

Master of Business Administration in Finance (MBA) Full-time, part-time; 39 total credits required; minimum of 15 months to complete program. Concentration in finance.

Master of Business Administration in Health Care Management (MBA) Full-time, part-time; 39 total credits required; minimum of 15 months to complete program. Concentration in health care.

Master of Business Administration in Management Information Systems (MBA) Full-time, part-time; 39 total credits required; minimum of 15 months to complete program. Concentration in management information systems.

Master of Business Administration in Marketing (MBA) Full-time, part-time; 39 total credits required; minimum of 15 months to complete program. Concentration in marketing.

Master of Business Administration in Public Administration (MBA) Full-time, part-time; 39 total credits required; minimum of 15 months to complete program.

Master of Science in Accounting (MS) Full-time, part-time; 39 total credits required; minimum of 15 months to complete program.

Master of Science in Health Care Information Resources Management (MS) Full-time, part-time; 39 total credits required; minimum of 15 months to complete program.

Master of Science in Information Systems (MS) Full-time, part-time; 39 total credits required; minimum of 15 months to complete program.

Master of Science in Information Systems Engineering (MS) Full-time, part-time; 39 total credits required; minimum of 15 months to complete program.

ADMISSION
Applications For fall 1997 there were 1,219 applications for admission.

Application Requirements Application form, application fee, bachelor's degree, minimum GPA: 2.75, personal statement, college transcript(s).

Recommended for Application Interview.

Application Deadline Applications processed on a rolling/continuous basis for both domestic and international students. Application fee: $50, $100 (international). Deferred entrance is available.

ACADEMICS
Faculty Part-time 146.

Teaching Methodologies Case study, computer-aided instruction, experiential learning, field projects, group discussion, lecture, research, student presentations.

Technology 25 on-campus computer terminals/PCs are available for student use and are linked by a campus-wide network. The network has full access to the Internet. Students are not required to have their own PC.

Special Opportunities Advanced credit may be earned through credit by examination, credit for military training programs, transfer of credits from another institution.

FINANCES
Costs for 1997–98 Tuition: $215 per credit hour. Cost varies by academic program, campus location. Average 1997–98 room and board costs were $9000 per academic year (off campus).

Financial Aid In 1997–98, 25% of students received some institutionally administered aid in the form of scholarships, work study, loans. Financial aid is available to part-time students.

Financial Aid Contact Financial Aid Office, 9215 North Black Canyon Highway, Phoenix, AZ 85260. Phone: 602-943-2311 Ext. 141.

FACILITIES
Information Resources Learning Resource Center; total holdings of 16,325 volumes, 125 current periodical subscriptions. CD player(s) available for graduate student use. Access provided to online bibliographic retrieval services.

INTERNATIONAL STUDENTS
Demographics N/R

Services and Facilities International student office, international student center, visa services, ESL courses, counseling/support services.

Applying Proof of adequate funds, proof of health/immunizations required. TOEFL: minimum score of 550 recommended. Financial aid is not available to international students.

International Student Contact Ms. Janet Haning, International Student Advisement, 9215 North Black Canyon Highway, Phoenix, AZ 85021-2718. Phone: 602-943-2311 Ext. 121; Fax: 602-943-3204.

PLACEMENT
Services include alumni network.

Employment Types of employment entered: accounting, banking, communications, energy, finance, financial services, high technology, information systems/

technology, international trade, management, service industry, telecommunications, utilities.

Program Contact: Enrollment Management, 9215 North Black Canyon Highway, Phoenix, AZ 85021. Phone: 602-943-2311; Fax: 602-371-8637.

ARKANSAS

Arkansas State University

College of Business

State University, Arkansas

OVERVIEW
Arkansas State University is a state-supported, coed, comprehensive institution. Enrollment: 9,631 graduate, professional, and undergraduate students; 241 full-time matriculated graduate/professional students; 733 part-time matriculated graduate/professional students. Founded: 1909. The graduate business unit is in a small-town setting and is on a semester calendar.

GRADUATE BUSINESS PROGRAMS
Master of Business Administration (MBA)

ACADEMICS
Faculty Full-time 52; part-time 2.

Teaching Methodologies Case study, computer-aided instruction, computer analysis, computer simulations, faculty seminars, field projects, group discussion, lecture, research, role playing, seminars by members of the business community, simulations, student presentations, study groups, team projects.

Technology 250 on-campus computer terminals/PCs are available for student use and are linked by a campus-wide network. The network has full access to the Internet. Students are not required to have their own PC.

Special Opportunities Advanced credit may be earned through transfer of credits from another institution. International exchange programs in Cyprus, Mexico. An internship program is available.

FACILITIES
Information Resources Dean B. Ellis Library; total holdings of 483,200 volumes, 378,800 microforms, 2,458 current periodical subscriptions. CD player(s) available for graduate student use. Access provided to online bibliographic retrieval services.

Program Contact: Director of Graduate Business Programs, PO Box 2220, State University, AR 72467-1630. Phone: 870-972-3035; Fax: 870-972-3744; E-mail: t.d.roach@cherokee.astate.edu

Henderson State University

School of Business Administration

Arkadelphia, Arkansas

OVERVIEW
Henderson State University is a state-supported, coed, comprehensive institution. Enrollment: 3,754 graduate, professional, and undergraduate students. Founded: 1890. The graduate business unit is in a small-town setting and is on a semester calendar.

HIGHLIGHTS

Enrollment Profile

Full-time: N/R	International: N/R
Part-time: N/R	Women: N/R
Total: 32	Minorities: N/R
Average Age: N/R	Average Class Size: N/R
Fall 1997 Average GPA: N/R	Fall 1997 Average GMAT: N/R

Costs

Full-time tuition: $4760 per academic year (resident); $9224 per academic year (nonresident)

Part-time tuition: N/R

AACSB – The International Association for Management Education accredited

GRADUATE BUSINESS PROGRAMS

Master of Business Administration (MBA) Full-time, part-time. Concentrations in management, accounting, economics, finance, marketing.

ADMISSION

Application Requirements GMAT score: minimum 400, application form, bachelor's degree, minimum GPA: 2.5, college transcript(s).

Application Deadline Applications processed on a rolling/continuous basis for both domestic and international students.

ACADEMICS

Faculty Full-time 8.

Teaching Methodologies Case study, computer analysis, group discussion, lecture, research, student presentations, study groups, team projects.

FINANCES

Costs for 1997–98 Tuition: Full-time: $4760 per year (resident); $9224 per year (nonresident). Cost varies by number of credits taken.

Financial Aid Research assistantships, work study, loans available. Financial aid is available to part-time students. Application Deadline: 7/31.

Financial Aid Contact Lisa Holland, 1100 Henderson Street, Arkadelphia, AR 71999-0001. Phone: 870-230-5094.

FACILITIES

Information Resources Huie Library; total holdings of 250,000 volumes, 192,780 microforms, 1,800 current periodical subscriptions. CD player(s) available for graduate student use. Access provided to online bibliographic retrieval services.

INTERNATIONAL STUDENTS

Demographics N/R

Services and Facilities International student office, visa services, international student orientation.

International Student Contact Katherine Vlassek, 1100 Henderson Street, Arkadelphia, AR 71999-0001. Phone: 870-230-5265.

Business Program(s) URL: http://www.hsu.edu/dept/bus/index.html

Program Contact: Mr. Tom Gattin, Registrar, PO Box 7534, Arkadelphia, AR 71999-0001. Phone: 870-230-5000 Ext. 3293 E-mail: gattint@oak.hsu.edu

University of Arkansas

College of Business Administration

Fayetteville, Arkansas

OVERVIEW

The University of Arkansas is a state-supported, coed university. Enrollment: 14,577 graduate, professional, and undergraduate students; 1,982 full-time matriculated graduate/professional students; 394 part-time matriculated graduate/professional students. Founded: 1871. The graduate business unit is in a small-town setting and is on a semester calendar.

HIGHLIGHTS

Enrollment Profile

Full-time: 65	International: 23%
Part-time: 62	Women: 30%
Total: 127	Minorities: 3%
Average Age: 27	Average Class Size: 25
Fall 1997 Average GPA: 3.1	Fall 1997 Average GMAT: 540

Costs
Full-time tuition: N/R
Part-time tuition: $161 per credit hour (resident); $383 per credit hour (nonresident)

AACSB – The International Association for Management Education accredited

GRADUATE BUSINESS PROGRAMS

Master of Business Administration (MBA) Full-time, part-time; 30 total credits required; GMAT score: minimum 530 required. Concentrations in management information systems, marketing, logistics, finance, economics, accounting.

Master of Accountancy (MAcc) Full-time; 30 total credits required; GMAT score: minimum 530 required.

Master of Arts in Economics (MA) Full-time; 30 total credits required; GRE score required.

Master of Arts in Information System (MA) Full-time; GMAT score: minimum 530 required; minimum of 12 months to complete program.

Master of Arts in Transportation Logistics (MA) Full-time; GMAT score: minimum 530 required; minimum of 12 months to complete program.

ADMISSION

Applications For fall 1997 there were 280 applications for admission. Of those applying, 160 were accepted. Of those accepted, 110 enrolled.

Application Requirements Application form, application fee, bachelor's degree, minimum GPA, letters of recommendation, personal statement, college transcript(s).

Recommended for Application GMAT score accepted: minimum 530, GRE score accepted, work experience.

Application Deadline Applications processed on a rolling/continuous basis for domestic students only. 3/15 for fall (international), 11/1 for spring (international), 3/15 for summer (international). Application fee: $30, $35 (international). Deferred entrance is available.

ACADEMICS

Faculty Full-time 81; part-time 12.

Teaching Methodologies Case study, computer simulations, experiential learning, field projects, group discussion, lecture, seminars by members of the business community, student presentations, team projects.

Technology 485 on-campus computer terminals/PCs are available for student use and are linked by a campus-wide network. The network has full access to the Internet. Students are not required to have their own PC.

Special Opportunities Advanced credit may be earned through transfer of credits from another institution. International exchange programs in Costa Rica, Italy.

FINANCES

Costs for 1997–98 Tuition: $161 per credit hour (resident); $383 per credit hour (nonresident). Cost varies by number of credits taken. Fees vary by academic program, number of credits taken. Average 1997–98 room and board costs were $3731 per academic year (on campus) and $7200 per academic year (off campus). Room and board costs vary by occupancy (e.g., single, double, triple), type of accommodation, type of meal plan.

Financial Aid Research assistantships, teaching assistantships, scholarships, work study available. Application Deadline: 4/1.

Financial Aid Contact Graduate Studies Office, College of Business Administration, Suite 475, Fayetteville, AR 72701. Phone: 501-575-2851; Fax: 501-575-8721.

FACILITIES

Information Resources Mullins Library plus 5 additional on-campus libraries; total holdings of 1,423,667 volumes, 1,721,065 microforms, 16,332 current periodical subscriptions. CD player(s) available for graduate student use. Access provided to online bibliographic retrieval services.

INTERNATIONAL STUDENTS

Demographics 23% of students enrolled are international students [Africa, 3%, Asia, 91%, Europe, 3%, North America, 3%].

Services and Facilities International student office, international student center, international student housing, visa services, ESL courses, counseling/support services.

Applying TOEFL: minimum score of 550, proof of adequate funds, proof of health/immunizations required. Financial aid is not available to international students.

International Student Contact International Admissions, 215 Hunt Hall, Fayetteville, AR 72701. Phone: 501-575-6246; Fax: 501-575-7515; E-mail: lgoza@comp.uark.edu

PLACEMENT

Services include alumni network, career counseling/planning, career fairs, career placement, job interviews arranged, resume referral to employers, and resume preparation. In 1996–97, 80 organizations participated in on-campus recruiting.

Employment Of 1996–97 graduates, 80% were employed within three months of graduation; the average starting salary was $38,700. Types of employment entered: accounting, banking, computer-related, consulting, consumer products, energy, engineering, finance, financial services, government, human resources, information systems/technology, management, manufacturing, marketing, nonprofit, retail, telecommunications, transportation.

Business Program(s) URL: http://www.uark.edu/depts/badminfo/

Program Contact: Graduate Studies Office, College of Business Administration, Suite 475, Fayetteville, AR 72701. Phone: 501-575-2851; Fax: 501-575-8721; E-mail: gso@comp.uark.edu
See full description on page 1034.

University of Arkansas at Little Rock

College of Business Administration

Little Rock, Arkansas

OVERVIEW
The University of Arkansas at Little Rock is a state-supported, coed university. Enrollment: 10,959 graduate, professional, and undergraduate students; 500 full-time matriculated graduate/professional students; 1,347 part-time matriculated graduate/professional students. Founded: 1927. The graduate business unit is in an urban setting and is on a semester calendar.

HIGHLIGHTS

Enrollment Profile

Full-time: 29	International: 13%
Part-time: 187	Women: 43%
Total: 216	Minorities: 9%
Average Age: 29	Average Class Size: 20
Fall 1997 Average GPA: 3.1	Fall 1997 Average GMAT: 520

Costs
Full-time tuition: $3120 per academic year (resident); $6672 per academic year (nonresident)
Part-time tuition: $130 per credit (resident); $278 per credit (nonresident)

AACSB – The International Association for Management Education accredited

Degree(s) offered in conjunction with Arkansas Tech University, Southern Arkansas University, University of Arkansas at Monticello

GRADUATE BUSINESS PROGRAMS
Master of Business Administration (MBA) Full-time, part-time, distance learning option; 30-66 total credits required; 12 months to 5 years to complete program. Concentrations in accounting, finance, management, marketing.

Executive MBA (MBA) Part-time; 46 total credits required; 5 years work experience required; 17 months to complete program.

ADMISSION
Applications For fall 1997 there were 84 applications for admission. Of those applying, 48 were accepted. Of those accepted, 27 enrolled.

Application Requirements Application form, bachelor's degree, minimum GPA: 2.7, college transcript(s), computer experience: spreadsheet.

Recommended for Application GMAT score accepted: minimum 450.

Application Deadline Applications processed on a rolling/continuous basis for both domestic and international students. Deferred entrance is available.

ACADEMICS
Faculty Full-time 42; part-time 10.

Teaching Methodologies Case study, computer-aided instruction, computer analysis, computer simulations, group discussion, lecture, research, student presentations, study groups, team projects.

Technology 60 on-campus computer terminals/PCs are available for student use and are linked by a campus-wide network. The network has full access to the Internet. Students are not required to have their own PC.

Special Opportunities Advanced credit may be earned through transfer of credits from another institution.

FINANCES
Costs for 1997–98 Tuition: Full-time: $3120 per year (resident); $6672 per year (nonresident). Part-time: $130 per credit (resident); $278 per credit (nonresident). Cost varies by number of credits taken. Fees: Full-time: $138 per academic year (resident); $138 per academic year (nonresident). Part-time: $11 per credit (resident); $11 per credit (nonresident). Fees vary by number of credits taken. Average 1997–98 room and board costs were $4900 per academic year (on campus) and $6000 per academic year (off campus). Room and board costs vary by occupancy (e.g., single, double, triple), type of accommodation, type of meal plan.

Financial Aid Research assistantships, scholarships, work study, loans available. Financial aid is available to part-time students. Application Deadline: 7/31.

Financial Aid Contact Ms. Roberta Moore, MBA Advisor, 2801 South University Avenue, Little Rock, AR 72204. Phone: 501-569-3048; Fax: 501-569-8898; E-mail: rmmoore@ualr.edu

FACILITIES
Information Resources Ottenheimer Library plus 1 additional on-campus library; total holdings of 367,648 volumes, 1,019,578 microforms, 2,361 current periodical subscriptions. CD player(s) available for graduate student use. Access provided to online bibliographic retrieval services.

INTERNATIONAL STUDENTS
Demographics 13% of students enrolled are international students.

Services and Facilities International student office, international student center, counseling/support services.

Applying TOEFL: minimum score of 550, proof of adequate funds, proof of health/immunizations required. Financial aid is not available to international students.

International Student Contact Ms. Robbin Fulmore, International English Language Program, 2801 South University Avenue, Little Rock, AR 72204. Phone: 501-569-3583; Fax: 501-569-3581; E-mail: rsfulmore@ualr.edu

PLACEMENT
Services include alumni network, career counseling/planning, career fairs, career library, career placement, and job interviews arranged.

Employment Of 1996–97 graduates, 95% were employed within three months of graduation; the average starting salary was $35,000. Types of employment entered: accounting, banking, consulting, consumer products, education, energy, engineering, finance, financial services, government, health services, human resources, management, manufacturing, marketing, media, retail, service industry, transportation, utilities.

Business Program(s) URL: http://www.ualr.edu/~cbadept/

Program Contact: Ms. Roberta Moore, MBA Advisor, 2801 South University Avenue, Little Rock, AR 72204. Phone: 501-569-8893; Fax: 501-569-8898; E-mail: rmmoore@ualr.edu

University of Central Arkansas

College of Business Administration

Conway, Arkansas

OVERVIEW
The University of Central Arkansas is a state-supported, coed, comprehensive institution. Enrollment: 8,994 graduate, professional, and undergraduate students. Founded: 1907. The graduate business unit is in an urban setting and is on a semester calendar.

HIGHLIGHTS

Enrollment Profile

Full-time: 39	International: 44%
Part-time: 45	Women: 33%
Total: 84	Minorities: 6%
Average Age: 27	Average Class Size: 30
Fall 1997 Average GPA: 3.13	Fall 1997 Average GMAT: 476

Costs
Full-time tuition: N/R
Part-time tuition: $151 per hour (resident); $314 per hour (nonresident)

AACSB – The International Association for Management Education accredited

GRADUATE BUSINESS PROGRAMS
Master of Business Administration (MBA) Full-time, part-time; 30 total credits required; 12 months to 6 years to complete program.

ADMISSION
Applications For fall 1997 there were 122 applications for admission. Of those applying, 83 were accepted. Of those accepted, 31 enrolled.

Application Requirements GMAT score: minimum 400, application form, application fee, bachelor's degree, minimum GPA: 2.7, college transcript(s).

Application Deadline Applications processed on a rolling/continuous basis for domestic students only. 6/15 for fall (international), 11/1 for spring (international), 5/1 for summer (international). Application fee: $15, $30 (international). Deferred entrance is available.

ACADEMICS
Faculty Full-time 15.

Teaching Methodologies Case study, computer-aided instruction, computer simulations, group discussion, lecture, simulations, student presentations, study groups, team projects.

Technology 351 on-campus computer terminals/PCs are available for student use and are linked by a campus-wide network. The network has full access to the Internet. Students are not required to have their own PC.

Special Opportunities Advanced credit may be earned through transfer of credits from another institution.

FINANCES
Costs for 1997–98 Tuition: $151 per hour (resident); $314 per hour (nonresident). Cost varies by number of credits taken. Fees: $15 per semester (resident); $15 per semester (nonresident). Fees vary by number of credits taken. Average 1997–98 room and board costs were $2800 per academic year. Room

and board costs vary by occupancy (e.g., single, double, triple), type of accommodation, type of meal plan.

Financial Aid Work study available. Application Deadline: 2/15.

Financial Aid Contact Mrs. Sherry Byrd, Director of Financial Aid, 201 Bernard, Conway, AR 72035-0001. Phone: 501-450-5000; Fax: 501-329-2403; E-mail: sherryb@ecom.uca.edu

FACILITIES

Information Resources Torreyson Library; total holdings of 503,173 volumes, 82,918 microforms, 2,676 current periodical subscriptions. CD player(s) available for graduate student use. Access provided to online bibliographic retrieval services.

INTERNATIONAL STUDENTS

Demographics 44% of students enrolled are international students [Asia, 95%, Europe, 4%, North America, 1%].

Services and Facilities International student office, international student center, international student housing, ESL courses, counseling/support services.

Applying TOEFL: minimum score of 550, proof of adequate funds, proof of health/immunizations required. Financial aid is not available to international students.

International Student Contact Dr. Brian Bolton, Director of International Program, 109 South Minton Hall, 201 Donaghey Avenue, Conway, AR 72035. Phone: 501-450-5000; Fax: 501-329-2403.

PLACEMENT

Services include alumni network, career counseling/planning, career fairs, career library, career placement, electronic job bank, job interviews arranged, job search course, resume referral to employers, and resume preparation. In 1996–97, 120 organizations participated in on-campus recruiting; 500 on-campus interviews were conducted.

Employment Of 1996–97 graduates, 85% were employed within three months of graduation; the average starting salary was $26,000. Types of employment entered: accounting, banking, communications, computer-related, consumer products, education, energy, finance, financial services, government, health services, human resources, information systems/technology, insurance, law, management, manufacturing, marketing, media, nonprofit, pharmaceutical, real estate, retail, service industry, transportation, utilities.

Business Program(s) URL: http://www.business.uca.edu

Program Contact: Dr. Doug Carter, MBA Coordinator, Burdick 222G, 201 Donaghey Avenue, Conway, AR 72035. Phone: 501-450-3411; Fax: 501-450-5302.

CALIFORNIA

Antioch Southern California/Los Angeles

Program in Organizational Management

Marina del Rey, California

OVERVIEW

Antioch Southern California/Los Angeles is an independent-nonprofit, coed, upper-level institution. Enrollment: 474 graduate, professional, and undergraduate students; 184 full-time matriculated graduate/professional students; 108 part-time matriculated graduate/professional students. Founded: 1972. The graduate business unit is in an urban setting and is on a quarter calendar.

HIGHLIGHTS

Enrollment Profile

Full-time: 5	International: 4%
Part-time: 23	Women: 82%
Total: 28	Minorities: 36%
Average Age: 36	Average Class Size: 6
Fall 1997 Average GPA: N/R	Fall 1997 Average GMAT: N/R

Costs
Full-time tuition: $9600 per academic year
Part-time tuition: $320 per unit

GRADUATE BUSINESS PROGRAMS

Master of Arts in Organizational Management (MA) Full-time, part-time; 60 total credits required; 15 months to 5 years to complete program. Concentrations in human resources, organizational behavior/development, organizational management, leadership.

ADMISSION

Applications For fall 1997 there were 11 applications for admission. Of those applying, 9 were accepted. Of those accepted, 3 enrolled.

Application Requirements Application form, application fee, bachelor's degree, essay, interview, 2 letters of recommendation, personal statement, resume, college transcript(s).

Recommended for Application Work experience, computer experience.

Application Deadline 8/7 for fall, 11/5 for winter, 2/5 for spring, 5/1 for summer, 8/7 for fall (international), 11/5 for winter (international), 2/5 for spring (international), 5/1 for summer (international). Application fee: $50. Deferred entrance is available.

ACADEMICS

Faculty Full-time 2; part-time 5.

Teaching Methodologies Case study, experiential learning, faculty seminars, field projects, group discussion, lecture, research, role playing, seminars by members of the business community, simulations, student presentations, study groups, team projects.

Technology 8 on-campus computer terminals/PCs are available for student use and are linked by a campus-wide network. The network has full access to the Internet. Students are not required to have their own PC.

Special Opportunities Advanced credit may be earned through transfer of credits from another institution. An internship program is available.

FINANCES

Costs for 1997–98 Tuition: Full-time: $9600 per year. Part-time: $320 per unit. Cost varies by academic program, number of credits taken. Fees: Full-time: $200 per academic year. Part-time: $200 per enrollment. Average 1997–98 room and board costs were $9675 per academic year (off campus).

Financial Aid Grants, scholarships, work study, loans available. Financial aid is available to part-time students. Application Deadline: 8/15.

Financial Aid Contact Mr. Larry Brickman, Director of Financial Aid, 13274 Fiji Way, Marina del Rey, CA 90292-7090. Phone: 310-578-1080 Ext. 402; Fax: 310-822-4824.

FACILITIES

Information Resources Instructional Resources Center. CD player(s) available for graduate student use. Access provided to online bibliographic retrieval services and online databases.

INTERNATIONAL STUDENTS

Demographics 4% of students enrolled are international students [Europe, 100%].

Services and Facilities Counseling/support services.

Applying TOEFL: minimum score of 600, proof of adequate funds required. Financial aid is not available to international students.

International Student Contact Dr. Mehee Hyun, Director of Admissions, 13274 Fiji Way, Marina del Rey, CA 90292-7090. Phone: 310-578-1080 Ext. 101; Fax: 310-301-8403.

PLACEMENT

Services include career counseling/planning, career library, and resume preparation.

Business Program(s) URL: http://www.antiochla.edu

Program Contact: Dr. Mehee Hyun, Director of Admissions, 13274 Fiji Way, Marina del Rey, CA 90292-7090. Phone: 310-578-1080 Ext. 101; Fax: 310-822-4824.

Antioch Southern California/Santa Barbara

Graduate Program in Organizational Management

Santa Barbara, California

OVERVIEW

Antioch Southern California/Santa Barbara is an independent-nonprofit, coed, upper-level institution. Founded: 1852. The graduate business unit is in a small-town setting and is on a quarter calendar.

Antioch Southern California/Santa Barbara (continued)

HIGHLIGHTS

Enrollment Profile

Full-time: 13	International: 4%
Part-time: 10	Women: 70%
Total: 23	Minorities: 22%
Average Age: 38	Average Class Size: 15
Fall 1997 Average GPA: N/R	Fall 1997 Average GMAT: N/R

Costs
Full-time tuition: $12,400 per academic year
Part-time tuition: $310 per credit

GRADUATE BUSINESS PROGRAMS

Master of Arts in Organizational Management (MA) Full-time, part-time, distance learning option; 60 total credits required; minimum of 15 months to complete program. Concentrations in managerial economics, management, international management, public and private management, business ethics, human resources, nonprofit management, nonprofit organization.

ADMISSION

Application Requirements Application form, application fee, bachelor's degree, essay, interview, 2 letters of recommendation, personal statement, resume, college transcript(s), minimum of 2 years of work experience, computer experience: word processing, spreadsheet.

Application Deadline 9/2 for fall, 12/1 for winter, 2/25 for spring, 5/27 for summer. Application fee: $50. Deferred entrance is available.

ACADEMICS

Faculty Full-time 1; part-time 9.

Teaching Methodologies Case study, computer analysis, faculty seminars, group discussion, student presentations, team projects.

Technology 12 on-campus computer terminals/PCs are available for student use and are linked by a campus-wide network. The network has full access to the Internet. Students are required to have their own PC.

Special Opportunities Advanced credit may be earned through transfer of credits from another institution. International exchange programs in Hong Kong, Italy, United Kingdom. An internship program is available.

FINANCES

Costs for 1997–98 Tuition: Full-time: $12,400 per year. Part-time: $310 per credit. Cost varies by academic program, campus location, class time (e.g., day/evening), number of credits taken, reciprocity agreements. Fees vary by academic program, campus location, class time (e.g., day/evening), number of credits taken, reciprocity agreements.

Financial Aid In 1997–98, 87% of students received some institutionally administered aid in the form of work study, loans. Financial aid is available to part-time students. Application Deadline: 9/1.

Financial Aid Contact Karen Morgan, Financial Aid Director, 801 Garden Street, #101, Santa Barbara, CA 93101. Phone: 805-962-8779; Fax: 805-962-4786.

FACILITIES

Information Resources Instructional Resources Center. CD player(s) available for graduate student use. Access provided to online bibliographic retrieval services and online databases.

INTERNATIONAL STUDENTS

Demographics 4% of students enrolled are international students.

Applying TOEFL: minimum score of 600, proof of adequate funds required.

International Student Contact Ms. Rose Chrynko, Admissions Associate, 801 Garden Street, Santa Barbara, CA 93101-1580. Phone: 805-962-8179 Ext. 112; Fax: 805-962-4786; E-mail: rchrynko@antiochsb.edu

PLACEMENT

Services include alumni network.

Employment Types of employment entered: communications, consulting, finance, financial services, health services, human resources, insurance, management, marketing, nonprofit, pharmaceutical.

Business Program(s) URL: http://www.antiochsb.edu

Program Contact: Ms. Rose Chrynko, Admissions Associate, 801 Garden Street, Santa Barbara, CA 93101-1580. Phone: 805-962-8179 Ext. 112; Fax: 805-962-4786; E-mail: rchrynko@antiochsb.edu

Armstrong University

Graduate School

Oakland, California

OVERVIEW

Armstrong University is an independent-nonprofit, coed, comprehensive institution. Enrollment: 1,028 graduate, professional, and undergraduate students; 658 full-time matriculated graduate/professional students; part-time matriculated graduate/professional students. Founded: 1918. The graduate business unit is in an urban setting and is on a quarter calendar.

HIGHLIGHTS

Enrollment Profile

Full-time: 658	International: N/R
Part-time: 0	Women: 40%
Total: 658	Minorities: N/R
Average Age: 26	Average Class Size: 7
Fall 1997 Average GPA: 3.5	Fall 1997 Average GMAT: N/R

Costs
Full-time tuition: $8400 per academic year
Part-time tuition: $350 per unit

GRADUATE BUSINESS PROGRAMS

Master of Business Administration (MBA) Full-time, distance learning option; 36 total credits required; 12 months to 2 years to complete program. Concentrations in accounting, finance, international business, management, marketing.

ADMISSION

Application Requirements Application form, application fee, bachelor's degree, minimum GPA: 2.5, interview, college transcript(s).

Recommended for Application Essay, letters of recommendation, personal statement, resume, computer experience.

Application Deadline Applications processed on a rolling/continuous basis for both domestic and international students. Application fee: $50. Deferred entrance is available.

ACADEMICS

Faculty Full-time 11; part-time 8.

Teaching Methodologies Case study, computer-aided instruction, computer analysis, computer simulations, field projects, group discussion, lecture, research, role playing, seminars by members of the business community, student presentations, study groups, team projects.

Technology 27 on-campus computer terminals/PCs are available for student use and are linked by a campus-wide network. The network has full access to the Internet. Students are not required to have their own PC.

Special Opportunities Advanced credit may be earned through transfer of credits from another institution. An internship program is available.

FINANCES

Costs for 1997–98 Tuition: Full-time: $8400 per year. Part-time: $350 per unit. Cost varies by number of credits taken. Fees: Full-time: $120 per academic year. Part-time: $120 per year. Fees vary by number of credits taken. Average 1997–98 room and board costs were $7500 per academic year (on campus) and $5550 per academic year (off campus).

Financial Aid Work study, loans available.

Financial Aid Contact Mr. Larry Guo, Dean of Students/Registrar, 1608 Webster Street, Oakland, CA 94612. Phone: 510-835-7900 Ext. 16; Fax: 510-835-8935; E-mail: admin@armstrong-u.edu

FACILITIES

Information Resources Main library; total holdings of 12,000 volumes, 500 microforms, 150 current periodical subscriptions. CD player(s) available for graduate student use.

INTERNATIONAL STUDENTS

Demographics N/R

Services and Facilities International student office, international student center, counseling/support services.

Applying TOEFL: minimum score of 500, proof of adequate funds, proof of health/immunizations required. Financial aid is not available to international students.

International Student Contact Mr. Larry Guo, Dean of Students/Registrar, 1608 Webster Street, Oakland, CA 94612. Phone: 510-835-7900 Ext. 16; Fax: 510-835-8935; E-mail: admin@armstrong-u.edu

PLACEMENT

Services include alumni network, career counseling/planning, career library, electronic job bank, and resume preparation.

Employment Types of employment entered: accounting, banking, consulting, finance, human resources, information systems/technology, insurance, international trade, management, manufacturing, marketing, media, telecommunications.

Business Program(s) URL: http://www.armstrong-u.edu/DEGREE/mba/mbaindex.htm

Program Contact: Ms. Judy Battle, Director of Admissions, 1608 Webster Street, Oakland, CA 94612. Phone: 510-835-7900 Ext. 11; Fax: 510-835-8935; E-mail: admin@armstrong-u.edu

See full description on page 706.

Azusa Pacific University

School of Business and Management

Azusa, California

OVERVIEW

Azusa Pacific University is an independent-religious, coed, comprehensive institution. Enrollment: 5,069 graduate, professional, and undergraduate students; 455 full-time matriculated graduate/professional students; 2,019 part-time matriculated graduate/professional students. Founded: 1899. The graduate business unit is in a suburban setting and is on a trimester calendar.

HIGHLIGHTS

Enrollment Profile

Full-time: 55	International: 46%
Part-time: 60	Women: 44%
Total: 115	Minorities: 46%
Average Age: 26	Average Class Size: 15
Fall 1997 Average GPA: 3.0	Fall 1997 Average GMAT: 450

Costs
Full-time tuition: N/R
Part-time tuition: $405 per unit

The School of Business and Management at Azusa Pacific University (APU) is committed to preparing tomorrow's leaders of change, developing excellent management skills, and enhancing personal integrity. Its M.B.A. program has been preparing managers and executives for more than twenty-five years in the areas of international business, finance, management information systems, marketing, and strategic management.

The APU School of Business and Management is an integral part of the Los Angeles and San Gabriel Valley business communities. These areas are focal points of international business entrepreneurship. The diverse nature of the local business community and the international business climate help provide a unique climate for advanced study. The School provides a stimulating environment for study and employs a dynamic faculty that is actively involved in and devoted to quality education.

Other distinguishing elements of the graduate program at Azusa Pacific University include a relationship-based education, small classes tailored to students' career interests, evening class schedules, emphasis on ethical decisions and actions, and an accessible faculty of mentor-scholars whose experience is firmly rooted in years of industry leadership and broadened through active consulting. Those who meet the admission requirements are prepared for a gratifying career.

GRADUATE BUSINESS PROGRAMS

Master of Business Administration (MBA) Full-time, part-time; 36-42 total credits required; 12 months to 5 years to complete program. Concentrations in human resources, international business, leadership, management, management information systems.

Master of Science in Human Resource Development (MS) Full-time, part-time; 36 total credits required; 12 months to 5 years to complete program.

ADMISSION

Application Requirements Application form, application fee, bachelor's degree, minimum GPA: 3.0, resume, college transcript(s).

Recommended for Application GMAT score accepted: minimum 450, GRE score accepted, MAT score accepted, personal statement.

Application Deadline Applications processed on a rolling/continuous basis for both domestic and international students. Application fee: $45. Deferred entrance is available.

ACADEMICS

Faculty Full-time 11; part-time 6.

Teaching Methodologies Case study, computer simulations, experiential learning, field projects, group discussion, lecture, research, role playing, student presentations, study groups, team projects.

Technology 285 on-campus computer terminals/PCs are available for student use and are linked by a campus-wide network. The network has full access to the Internet. Students are not required to have their own PC.

Special Opportunities Advanced credit may be earned through transfer of credits from another institution.

FINANCES

Costs for 1997–98 Tuition: $405 per unit.

Financial Aid Scholarships available.

Financial Aid Contact Ms. Debbie Serano, Account Counselor, 901 East Alosta Avenue, PO Box 7000, Azusa, CA 91702-7000. Phone: 626-815-5440.

FACILITIES

Information Resources Marshburn Memorial Library plus 2 additional on-campus libraries; total holdings of 140,000 volumes, 535,000 microforms, 1,156 current periodical subscriptions. CD player(s) available for graduate student use. Access provided to online bibliographic retrieval services.

INTERNATIONAL STUDENTS

Demographics 46% of students enrolled are international students.

Services and Facilities International student office, visa services, ESL courses, counseling/support services.

Applying TOEFL: minimum score of 550, proof of adequate funds, proof of health/immunizations required. Financial aid is available to international students.

International Student Contact Ms. Mary Grams, Director, International Student Affairs, 901 East Alosta Avenue, PO Box 7000, Azusa, CA 91702-7000. Phone: 626-815-6000 Ext. 3055; E-mail: mgrams@apu.edu

PLACEMENT

Services include alumni network, career counseling/planning, career fairs, career library, and resume preparation. In 1996–97, 10 organizations participated in on-campus recruiting.

Employment Of 1996–97 graduates, 90% were employed within three months of graduation; the average starting salary was $28,000. Types of employment entered: computer-related, consumer products, financial services, human resources, management, manufacturing, marketing, retail, service industry.

Business Program(s) URL: http://www.apu.edu/academics/business/grad.html

Program Contact: Dr. Tomas Parks, Chair, Graduate Business Studies, 901 East Alosta Avenue, PO Box 7000, Azusa, CA 91702-7000. Phone: 626-815-3820; Fax: 626-815-3802.

California Baptist College

Graduate Program in Business Administration

Riverside, California

OVERVIEW

California Baptist College is an independent-religious, coed, comprehensive institution. Enrollment: 2,009 graduate, professional, and undergraduate students; 85 full-time matriculated graduate/professional students; 249 part-time matriculated graduate/professional students. Founded: 1950. The graduate business unit is in an urban setting and is on a 2-4-4-2 calendar.

HIGHLIGHTS

Enrollment Profile

Full-time: 23	International: N/R
Part-time: 0	Women: 35%
Total: 23	Minorities: 22%
Average Age: 35	Average Class Size: 18
Fall 1997 Average GPA: N/R	Fall 1997 Average GMAT: N/R

Costs
Full-time tuition: $274 per academic year
Part-time tuition: $274 per unit

GRADUATE BUSINESS PROGRAMS

MBA with emphasis in Information Technology (MBA) Full-time, part-time; 48 total credits required; 18 months to 5 years to complete program. Concentration in management.

ADMISSION

Applications For fall 1997 there were 22 applications for admission. Of those applying, 19 were accepted. Of those accepted, 16 enrolled.

Application Requirements Application form, application fee, bachelor's degree, essay, minimum GPA: 2.75, interview, 3 letters of recommendation, personal statement, resume, college transcript(s), computer experience.

Recommended for Application GMAT score accepted, GRE score accepted, work experience.

California Baptist College (continued)

Application Deadline Applications processed on a rolling/continuous basis for both domestic and international students. Application fee: $40. Deferred entrance is available.

ACADEMICS
Faculty Full-time 4; part-time 7.

Teaching Methodologies Case study, computer-aided instruction, group discussion, lecture, research, simulations, student presentations, team projects.

Technology 60 on-campus computer terminals/PCs are available for student use and are linked by a campus-wide network. The network has full access to the Internet. Students are not required to have their own PC.

Special Opportunities Advanced credit may be earned through transfer of credits from another institution.

FINANCES
Costs for 1997-98 Tuition: Full-time: $274 per unit. Part-time: $274 per unit. Cost varies by academic program, number of credits taken. Fees: Full-time: $195 per academic year. Part-time: $70 per semsester.

Financial Aid Work study, loans available. Financial aid is available to part-time students.

Financial Aid Contact Mrs. Alicia Ramirez, Graduate Financial Aid Counselor, 8432 Magnolia Avenue, Riverside, CA 92504-3206. Phone: 909-343-4236; Fax: 909-343-4518.

FACILITIES
Information Resources Annie Gabriel Library. CD player(s) available for graduate student use. Access provided to online bibliographic retrieval services and online databases.

INTERNATIONAL STUDENTS
Demographics N/R

Services and Facilities International student office, international student housing, ESL courses, counseling/support services.

Applying TOEFL: minimum score of 550, proof of adequate funds, proof of health/immunizations required. Financial aid is not available to international students.

International Student Contact Mrs. Gail Ronveaux, Director of Graduate Services, 8432 Magnolia Avenue, Riverside, CA 92504-3206. Phone: 909-343-4249; Fax: 909-351-1808.

PLACEMENT
Services include career counseling/planning, career fairs, career placement, job search course, resume referral to employers, and resume preparation.

Business Program(s) URL: http://www.calbaptist.edu

Program Contact: Mrs. Gail Ronveaux, Director of Graduate Services, 8432 Magnolia Avenue, Riverside, CA 92504-3206. Phone: 909-343-4249; Fax: 909-351-1808.

California Lutheran University

School of Business Administration

Thousand Oaks, California

OVERVIEW
California Lutheran University is an independent-religious, coed, comprehensive institution. Enrollment: 2,750 graduate, professional, and undergraduate students; 150 full-time matriculated graduate/professional students; 798 part-time matriculated graduate/professional students. Founded: 1959. The graduate business unit is in a suburban setting and is on a semester calendar.

HIGHLIGHTS
Enrollment Profile

Full-time: 10	International: 3%
Part-time: 301	Women: 46%
Total: 311	Minorities: 19%
Average Age: 30	Average Class Size: 15
Fall 1997 Average GPA: N/R	Fall 1997 Average GMAT: 525

Costs
Full-time tuition: $7110 per academic year
Part-time tuition: $395 per credit

*T*he curriculum at California Lutheran University (CLU) is based on skills relevant to the current business environment—analytical and leadership skills, technological know-how, human resource strategies, and strategic planning techniques.

Innovation and relevance are the hallmarks of the program, as illustrated by the seven distinctive professional tracks. They combine the value of the general M.B.A. with the opportunity to gain specialized knowledge in a specific area. The University monitors current and emerging trends and builds its curriculum accordingly. Staying current with the changing business environment ensures that CLU's M.B.A. graduates are well prepared not only to be successful in today's business world but are also able to cope and succeed in the future.

The program is designed to develop competencies and skills for innovative and responsible leadership. CLU's M.B.A. program has helped professionals equip themselves to cope with new challenges in a changing world, acquire leadership skills to prepare for promotion into management, make a smooth transition into a new career field, stand out in a job search with enhanced skills and an advanced degree, gain satisfaction from personal and professional growth, make smart financial decisions in personal and professional life, form a strong network with professional peers and faculty experts, and succeed as an entrepreneur.

GRADUATE BUSINESS PROGRAMS
Master of Business Administration (MBA) Full-time, part-time; 42 total credits required; 15 months to 7 years to complete program. Concentrations in finance, entrepreneurship, information management, international business, management, marketing, organizational behavior/development, health care.

ADMISSION
Applications For fall 1997 there were 90 applications for admission. Of those applying, 81 were accepted. Of those accepted, 60 enrolled.

Application Requirements GMAT score: minimum 500, application form, application fee, bachelor's degree, minimum GPA: 3.0, interview, 3 letters of recommendation, personal statement, college transcript(s).

Recommended for Application Resume, minimum of 2 years of work experience, computer experience.

Application Deadline Applications processed on a rolling/continuous basis for both domestic and international students. Application fee: $50. Deferred entrance is available.

ACADEMICS
Faculty Full-time 8; part-time 29.

Teaching Methodologies Case study, computer-aided instruction, computer analysis, computer simulations, experiential learning, field projects, group discussion, lecture, research, role playing, seminars by members of the business community, simulations, student presentations, study groups, team projects.

Technology 125 on-campus computer terminals/PCs are available for student use and are linked by a campus-wide network. The network has full access to the Internet. Students are not required to have their own PC.

Special Opportunities Advanced credit may be earned through transfer of credits from another institution.

FINANCES
Costs for 1997-98 Tuition: Full-time: $7110 per year. Part-time: $395 per credit. Average 1997-98 room only costs were $8100 per academic year (off campus).

Financial Aid In 1997-98, 1% of students received some institutionally administered aid in the form of teaching assistantships, scholarships, loans. Financial aid is available to part-time students. Application Deadline: 3/2.

Financial Aid Contact Ms. Betsy Kocher, Director, Student Financial Planning, 60 West Olsen Road, Thousand Oaks, CA 91360-2787. Phone: 805-493-3115; Fax: 805-493-3114; E-mail: kocher@robles.callutheran.edu

FACILITIES
Information Resources Pearson Library; total holdings of 101,000 volumes. Access provided to online bibliographic retrieval services.

INTERNATIONAL STUDENTS
Demographics 3% of students enrolled are international students.

Services and Facilities International student office, international student center, visa services, counseling/support services.

Applying TOEFL: minimum score of 570, proof of adequate funds, proof of health/immunizations required. Financial aid is not available to international students.

International Student Contact Miss Paula Avery, International Coordinator, 60 West Olsen Road, Thousand Oaks, CA 91360-2787. Phone: 805-493-3491; Fax: 805-493-3114; E-mail: avery@clunet.edu

PLACEMENT
Services include alumni network, career counseling/planning, career fairs, career library, career placement, electronic job bank, job interviews arranged, job search course, resume referral to employers, and resume preparation. In

1996–97, 30 organizations participated in on-campus recruiting; 8 on-campus interviews were conducted.

Employment Of 1996–97 graduates, the average starting salary was $50,000. Types of employment entered: accounting, banking, communications, computer-related, education, finance, financial services, government, health services, high technology, information systems/technology, insurance, management, pharmaceutical, telecommunications.

Business Program(s) URL: http://www.clunet.edu

Program Contact: Mrs. Anita Hanney, MBA Admission Counselor, School of Business Administration, 60 West Olsen Road, Thousand Oaks, CA 91360-2787. Phone: 805-493-3127; Fax: 805-493-3542; E-mail: hanney@clunet. edu

California Polytechnic State University, San Luis Obispo

College of Business

San Luis Obispo, California

OVERVIEW

California Polytechnic State University, San Luis Obispo is a state-supported, coed, comprehensive institution. Enrollment: 16,735 graduate, professional, and undergraduate students; 591 full-time matriculated graduate/professional students; 355 part-time matriculated graduate/professional students. Founded: 1901. The graduate business unit is in a small-town setting and is on a quarter calendar.

HIGHLIGHTS

Enrollment Profile

Full-time: 85	International: N/R
Part-time: 21	Women: 28%
Total: 106	Minorities: 31%
Average Age: 27	Average Class Size: 45
Fall 1997 Average GPA: 3.16	Fall 1997 Average GMAT: 539

Costs
Full-time tuition: $164 per academic year (nonresident)
Part-time tuition: N/R

AACSB – The International Association for Management Education accredited

GRADUATE BUSINESS PROGRAMS

Master of Business Administration (MBA) Full-time; 96 total credits required; 2 to 7 years to complete program. Concentrations in agribusiness, management.

Master of Business Administration/Master of Science in Engineering Management (MBA/MS) Full-time; 107-111 total credits required; 2 to 7 years to complete program. Concentrations in agribusiness, manufacturing management.

Master of Business Administration/Master of Science in Computer Science (MBA/MS) Full-time; 105 total credits required; 2 to 7 years to complete program. Concentrations in agribusiness, manufacturing management.

Master of Business Administration/Master of Science in Electrical Engineering (MBA/MS) Full-time; 101 total credits required; 2 to 7 years to complete program. Concentrations in agribusiness, manufacturing management.

Master of Business Administration/Master of Science in Mechanical Engineering (MBA/MS) Full-time; 101 total credits required; 2 to 7 years to complete program. Concentrations in agribusiness, manufacturing management.

ADMISSION

Applications For fall 1997 there were 112 applications for admission. Of those applying, 65 were accepted. Of those accepted, 50 enrolled.

Application Requirements Application form, application fee, bachelor's degree, essay, minimum GPA: 2.5, 2 letters of recommendation, resume, college transcript(s).

Recommended for Application GMAT score accepted: minimum 530.

Application Deadline 7/1 for fall, 6/1 for fall (international). Application fee: $55. Deferred entrance is available.

ACADEMICS

Faculty Full-time 53; part-time 32.

Teaching Methodologies Case study, computer-aided instruction, computer analysis, computer simulations, experiential learning, field projects, group discussion, lecture, research, seminars by members of the business community, simulations, student presentations, team projects.

Technology 1,880 on-campus computer terminals/PCs are available for student use and are linked by a campus-wide network. The network has full access to the Internet. Students are not required to have their own PC.

Special Opportunities Advanced credit may be earned through credit by examination, transfer of credits from another institution. International exchange programs in Hungary, Israel, Mexico, Taiwan. An internship program is available.

FINANCES

Costs for 1997–98 Tuition: Full-time: $164 per unit (nonresident). Cost varies by number of credits taken. Fees: Full-time: $2231 per academic year (resident); $2231 per academic year (nonresident). Average 1997–98 room and board costs were $5553 per academic year (on campus) and $4779 per academic year (off campus). Room and board costs vary by type of meal plan.

Financial Aid Research assistantships, teaching assistantships, grants, scholarships, work study, loans available. Financial aid is available to part-time students. Application Deadline: 3/1.

Financial Aid Contact Mr. John Anderson, Director, Financial Aid Office, San Luis Obispo, CA 93407. Phone: 805-756-2927; Fax: 805-756-7243; E-mail: anderson@calpoly.edu

FACILITIES

Information Resources Robert F. Kennedy Library; total holdings of 625,044 volumes, 3,179,258 microforms, 3,500 current periodical subscriptions. CD player(s) available for graduate student use. Access provided to online bibliographic retrieval services and online databases.

INTERNATIONAL STUDENTS

Demographics N/R

Services and Facilities International student office, ESL courses, counseling/ support services, language tutoring.

Applying TOEFL: minimum score of 550, TWE: minimum score of 4.5, proof of adequate funds, proof of health/immunizations required. Financial aid is not available to international students.

International Student Contact Ms. Barbara Andre, International Student Advisor, Global Affairs, San Luis Obispo, CA 93407. Phone: 805-756-5837; Fax: 805-756-5484; E-mail: bandre@calpoly.edu

PLACEMENT

Services include career counseling/planning, career fairs, career placement, job interviews arranged, resume referral to employers, and resume preparation. In 1996–97, 520 organizations participated in on-campus recruiting.

Employment Of 1996–97 graduates, 99% were employed within three months of graduation; the average starting salary was $47,375. Types of employment entered: accounting, banking, communications, computer-related, consulting, consumer products, engineering, finance, financial services, high technology, human resources, information systems/technology, insurance, management, manufacturing, marketing, media, retail, service industry, telecommunications, utilities.

Business Program(s) URL: http://www.cob.calpoly.edu/

Program Contact: Dr. David Peach, Director, Graduate Programs, College of Business, San Luis Obispo, CA 93407. Phone: 805-756-2637; Fax: 805-756-0110; E-mail: dpeach@calpoly.edu

California State Polytechnic University, Pomona

College of Business

Pomona, California

OVERVIEW

California State Polytechnic University, Pomona is a state-supported, coed, comprehensive institution. Enrollment: 16,304 graduate, professional, and undergraduate students; 191 full-time matriculated graduate/professional students; 755 part-time matriculated graduate/professional students. Founded: 1938. The graduate business unit is in an urban setting and is on a quarter calendar.

GRADUATE BUSINESS PROGRAMS

Master of Business Administration (MBA)

Master of Science in Business Administration (MS)

ACADEMICS

Faculty Full-time 135.

Teaching Methodologies Case study, lecture, research, seminars by members of the business community, student presentations, team projects.

Technology 450 on-campus computer terminals/PCs are available for student use and are linked by a campus-wide network. The network has full access to the Internet. Students are not required to have their own PC.

Special Opportunities Advanced credit may be earned through transfer of credits from another institution. International exchange program in Mexico. An internship program is available.

California State Polytechnic University, Pomona (continued)

FACILITIES
Information Resources University Library; total holdings of 592,433 volumes, 2,003,847 microforms, 2,964 current periodical subscriptions. CD player(s) available for graduate student use. Access provided to online bibliographic retrieval services.

Program Contact: Director, Graduate Business Programs, 3801 West Temple Avenue, Pomona, CA 91768-2557. Phone: 909-869-2363; Fax: 909-869-4559; E-mail: rrhodes@csupomona.edu

California State University, Bakersfield

School of Business and Public Administration

Bakersfield, California

OVERVIEW
California State University, Bakersfield is a state-supported, coed, comprehensive institution. Enrollment: 4,820 graduate, professional, and undergraduate students; 750 full-time matriculated graduate/professional students; 658 part-time matriculated graduate/professional students. Founded: 1965. The graduate business unit is in an urban setting and is on a quarter calendar.

HIGHLIGHTS

Enrollment Profile

Full-time: N/R	International: 6%
Part-time: N/R	Women: 50%
Total: 718	Minorities: 4%
Average Age: 30	Average Class Size: 25
Fall 1997 Average GPA: 3.0	Fall 1997 Average GMAT: 525

Costs
Full-time tuition: $1887 per academic year (resident); $9233 per academic year (nonresident)
Part-time tuition: N/R

AACSB – The International Association for Management Education accredited

GRADUATE BUSINESS PROGRAMS
Master of Business Administration (MBA) Full-time, part-time; 45 total credits required; 12 months to 7 years to complete program. Concentration in management.
Master of Public Administration (MPA) Full-time, part-time.
Master of Science in Health Care Management (MS) Full-time, part-time.

ADMISSION
Applications For fall 1997 there were 80 applications for admission. Of those applying, 67 were accepted. Of those accepted, 64 enrolled.
Application Requirements GMAT score: minimum 500, application form, application fee, bachelor's degree, minimum GPA: 2.75, college transcript(s).
Application Deadline 7/1 for fall, 11/1 for winter, 3/1 for spring. Application fee: $55.

ACADEMICS
Faculty Full-time 24; part-time 17.
Teaching Methodologies Case study, computer simulations, faculty seminars, lecture, student presentations, team projects.
Technology 50 on-campus computer terminals/PCs are available for student use and are linked by a campus-wide network. The network has full access to the Internet. Students are not required to have their own PC.
Special Opportunities Advanced credit may be earned through transfer of credits from another institution.

FINANCES
Costs for 1997–98 Tuition: Full-time: $1887 per year (resident); $9233 per year (nonresident). Average 1997–98 room and board costs were $4603 per academic year (on campus) and $4340 per academic year (off campus). Room and board costs vary by type of meal plan.
Financial Aid Contact Financial Aid Office, 9001 Stockdale Highway, Bakersfield, CA 93311-1022. Phone: 805-664-3016; Fax: 805-664-6800.

FACILITIES
Information Resources Walter Stiern Library; total holdings of 250,204 volumes, 343,653 microforms, 2,663 current periodical subscriptions. Access provided to online bibliographic retrieval services and online databases.

INTERNATIONAL STUDENTS
Demographics 6% of students enrolled are international students [Africa, 5%, Asia, 75%, Australia/New Zealand, 2%, Europe, 10%, North America, 3%, South America, 5%].
Services and Facilities International student office, ESL courses, counseling/support services.
Applying TOEFL: minimum score of 550, proof of adequate funds, proof of health/immunizations required.
International Student Contact Dr. Fabien Fang, Director, Center for International Education, 9001 Stockdale Highway, Bakersfield, CA 93311-1022. Phone: 805-664-2354.

PLACEMENT
Services include career fairs, and career placement.

Business Program(s) URL: http://www.csubak.edu

Program Contact: Thomas Mishoe, MBA Coordinator, 9001 Stockdale Highway, Bakersfield, CA 93311-1022. Phone: 805-664-2326; Fax: 805-664-2438; E-mail: dkirk@csubak.edu

California State University, Chico

College of Business

Chico, California

OVERVIEW
California State University, Chico is a state-supported, coed, comprehensive institution. Enrollment: 14,232 graduate, professional, and undergraduate students; 480 full-time matriculated graduate/professional students; 322 part-time matriculated graduate/professional students. Founded: 1887. The graduate business unit is in a suburban setting and is on a semester calendar.

HIGHLIGHTS

Enrollment Profile

Full-time: 40	International: 17%
Part-time: 20	Women: 30%
Total: 60	Minorities: N/R
Average Age: 27	Average Class Size: 25
Fall 1997 Average GPA: 3.3	Fall 1997 Average GMAT: 530

Costs
Full-time tuition: $2006 per academic year (resident); $6434 per academic year (nonresident)
Part-time tuition: $670 per 6 units (resident); $2146 per 6 units (nonresident)

AACSB – The International Association for Management Education accredited

GRADUATE BUSINESS PROGRAMS
Master of Business Administration (MBA) Full-time, part-time; 30 total credits required; 12 months to 5 years to complete program. Concentrations in finance, human resources, management, management information systems, production management, marketing.
Master of Science in Accountancy (MS) Full-time, part-time; 30 total credits required; 12 months to 5 years to complete program. Concentrations in accounting, management information systems.

ADMISSION
Applications For fall 1997 there were 50 applications for admission. Of those applying, 25 were accepted. Of those accepted, 15 enrolled.
Application Requirements Application form, application fee, bachelor's degree, minimum GPA: 2.75, 3 letters of recommendation, personal statement, resume, college transcript(s), computer experience: word processing, spreadsheet, database.
Recommended for Application GMAT score accepted: minimum 500, minimum of 2 years of work experience.
Application Deadline Applications processed on a rolling/continuous basis for domestic students only. 3/1 for fall (international), 10/1 for spring (international). Application fee: $55. Deferred entrance is available.

ACADEMICS
Faculty Full-time 60; part-time 15.
Teaching Methodologies Case study, computer-aided instruction, computer analysis, computer simulations, experiential learning, field projects, lecture, research, simulations, student presentations, team projects.
Technology 300 on-campus computer terminals/PCs are available for student use and are linked by a campus-wide network. The network has full access to the Internet. Students are not required to have their own PC.

Special Opportunities Advanced credit may be earned through transfer of credits from another institution. An internship program is available.

FINANCES
Costs for 1997–98 Tuition: Full-time: $2006 per year (resident); $6434 per year (nonresident). Part-time: $670 per 6 units (resident); $2146 per 6 units (nonresident). Cost varies by number of credits taken. Average 1997–98 room and board costs were $4700 per academic year (on campus) and $5200 per academic year (off campus). Room and board costs vary by occupancy (e.g., single, double, triple), type of accommodation, type of meal plan.
Financial Aid In 1997–98, 25% of students received some institutionally administered aid in the form of fellowships, teaching assistantships, work study. Financial aid is available to part-time students. Application Deadline: 3/1.
Financial Aid Contact Financial Aid, 408 West First Street, Chico, CA 95929-0705. Phone: 530-898-6451; Fax: 530-898-6824.

FACILITIES
Information Resources Meriam Library; total holdings of 1,436,072 volumes, 927,111 microforms, 3,698 current periodical subscriptions. CD player(s) available for graduate student use. Access provided to online bibliographic retrieval services.

INTERNATIONAL STUDENTS
Demographics 17% of students enrolled are international students [Asia, 85%, Europe, 14%, other, 1%].
Services and Facilities International student office, ESL courses, counseling/support services.
Applying TOEFL: minimum score of 550, proof of adequate funds, proof of health/immunizations required. TWE recommended. Financial aid is available to international students.
International Student Contact Mr. James Luyirika-Sewagudde, Jr., Advisor, Center for International Studies, 408 West First Street, Chico, CA 95929-0875. Phone: 530-898-6880; Fax: 530-898-6889; E-mail: gs_student@macgate.csuchico.edu

PLACEMENT
Services include alumni network, career counseling/planning, career fairs, career library, career placement, job interviews arranged, resume referral to employers, and resume preparation. In 1996–97, 300 organizations participated in on-campus recruiting.
Employment Of 1996–97 graduates, 85% were employed within three months of graduation; the average starting salary was $43,000. Types of employment entered: accounting, computer-related, consulting, engineering, financial services, health services, information systems/technology, international trade, manufacturing, utilities.

Business Program(s) URL: http://www.cob.csuchico.edu/

Program Contact: Ms. Sandy Jensen, Secretary, Business Graduate Programs, 408 West First Street, Chico, CA 95929-0041. Phone: 530-898-4425; Fax: 530-898-5889; E-mail: sjensen@busipo.csuchico.edu

California State University, Dominguez Hills

School of Management
Carson, California

OVERVIEW
California State University, Dominguez Hills is a state-supported, coed, comprehensive institution. Enrollment: 9,660 graduate, professional, and undergraduate students; 425 full-time matriculated graduate/professional students; 1,335 part-time matriculated graduate/professional students. Founded: 1960. The graduate business unit is in an urban setting and is on a semester calendar.

HIGHLIGHTS

Enrollment Profile
Full-time: 60
Part-time: 400
Total: 460
Average Age: 34
Fall 1997 Average GPA: 3.03

International: 9%
Women: 49%
Minorities: N/R
Average Class Size: 22
Fall 1997 Average GMAT: 493

Costs
Full-time tuition: $1821 per academic year (resident); $4773 per academic year (nonresident)
Part-time tuition: $95 per unit (resident); $246 per unit (nonresident)

ACBSP – The American Council of Business Schools and Programs accredited

GRADUATE BUSINESS PROGRAMS
Master of Business Administration (MBA) Full-time, part-time, distance learning option; 30-57 total credits required; 12 months to 2 years to complete program. Concentrations in international business, management.

ADMISSION
Applications For fall 1997 there were 125 applications for admission. Of those applying, 80 were accepted. Of those accepted, 65 enrolled.
Application Requirements Application form, application fee, minimum GPA: 2.75, personal statement, college transcript(s).
Recommended for Application GMAT score accepted: minimum 450, 2 letters of recommendation, resume, computer experience.
Application Deadline 6/1 for fall, 12/1 for spring, 5/1 for fall (international), 11/1 for spring (international). Application fee: $55. Deferred entrance is available.

ACADEMICS
Faculty Full-time 39; part-time 25.
Teaching Methodologies Case study, computer-aided instruction, computer simulations, experiential learning, group discussion, lecture, simulations, student presentations, study groups, team projects.
Technology 150 on-campus computer terminals/PCs are available for student use and are linked by a campus-wide network. The network has full access to the Internet. Students are not required to have their own PC.
Special Opportunities Advanced credit may be earned through transfer of credits from another institution.

FINANCES
Costs for 1997–98 Tuition: Full-time: $1821 per year (resident); $4773 per year (nonresident). Part-time: $95 per unit (resident); $246 per unit (nonresident). Cost varies by number of credits taken. Fees: Full-time: $242 per academic year (resident); $242 per academic year (nonresident). Part-time: $242 per 6 units. Fees vary by number of credits taken. Average 1997–98 room only costs were $4348 per academic year. Room and board costs vary by occupancy (e.g., single, double, triple).
Financial Aid In 1997–98, 3% of students received some institutionally administered aid. Financial aid is available to part-time students.
Financial Aid Contact Mr. James Woods, Director, Financial Aid, Office of Financial Aid, Carson, CA 90742. Phone: 310-243-3691; Fax: 310-516-4498; E-mail: jwood@dhvx20.csudh.edu

FACILITIES
Information Resources Educational Resources Center; total holdings of 411,297 volumes, 572,221 microforms, 2,222 current periodical subscriptions. CD player(s) available for graduate student use. Access provided to online bibliographic retrieval services.

INTERNATIONAL STUDENTS
Demographics 9% of students enrolled are international students.
Services and Facilities International student office, international student center, international student housing, visa services, ESL courses, counseling/support services.
Applying TOEFL: minimum score of 550, proof of adequate funds, proof of health/immunizations required. Financial aid is not available to international students.
International Student Contact Ms. Zepur Solakian, International Student Officer, School Of Management, Carson, CA 90747-0001. E-mail: intstlid@dhvxz0.csudh.edu

PLACEMENT
Services include alumni network, career counseling/planning, career fairs, career library, career placement, job interviews arranged, and resume preparation.

Business Program(s) URL: http://som.csudh.edu

Program Contact: Ms. Eileen Hall, MBA Coordinator, School of Management, 1000 East Victoria Street, Carson, CA 90747-0001. Phone: 310-243-3465; Fax: 310-516-4178; E-mail: ehall@soma.csudh.edu

California State University, Fresno

Sid Craig School of Business
Fresno, California

OVERVIEW
California State University, Fresno is a state-supported, coed, comprehensive institution. Enrollment: 17,277 graduate, professional, and undergraduate students; 942 full-time matriculated graduate/professional students; 886 part-

California State University, Fresno (continued)

time matriculated graduate/professional students. Founded: 1911. The graduate business unit is in an urban setting and is on a semester calendar.

HIGHLIGHTS

Enrollment Profile
Full-time: 42
Part-time: 168
Total: 210
Average Age: 31
Fall 1997 Average GPA: 3.3

International: 14%
Women: 38%
Minorities: N/R
Average Class Size: 22
Fall 1997 Average GMAT: 540

Costs
Full-time tuition: N/R
Part-time tuition: $454 per 6 units (resident); $1900 per 6 units (nonresident)

AACSB – The International Association for Management Education accredited

GRADUATE BUSINESS PROGRAMS
Master of Business Administration (MBA) Full-time, part-time; 33 total credits required; 18 months to 5 years to complete program. Concentrations in accounting, finance, information management, international business, marketing.

ADMISSION
Applications For fall 1997 there were 174 applications for admission. Of those applying, 93 were accepted. Of those accepted, 73 enrolled.

Application Requirements Application form, application fee, bachelor's degree, essay, minimum GPA: 2.5, letters of recommendation, personal statement, resume, college transcript(s).

Recommended for Application GMAT score accepted.

Application Deadline 6/1 for fall, 10/1 for spring, 4/1 for fall (international), 9/1 for spring (international). Application fee: $55.

ACADEMICS
Faculty Full-time 30.

Teaching Methodologies Case study, computer analysis, computer simulations, faculty seminars, lecture, research, student presentations, team projects.

Technology 700 on-campus computer terminals/PCs are available for student use and are linked by a campus-wide network. The network has full access to the Internet. Students are not required to have their own PC.

Special Opportunities Advanced credit may be earned through transfer of credits from another institution.

FINANCES
Costs for 1997–98 Tuition: $454 per 6 units (resident); $1900 per 6 units (nonresident). Fees: $119 per semester (resident); $119 per semester (nonresident). Average 1997–98 room and board costs were $5500 per academic year. Room and board costs vary by occupancy (e.g., single, double, triple), type of accommodation, type of meal plan.

Financial Aid Fellowships, research assistantships, teaching assistantships, work study available. Application Deadline: 3/1.

Financial Aid Contact Dr. Joseph Heuston, Director, 5241 North Maple Avenue, Fresno, CA 93740-0064. Phone: 209-278-2182; Fax: 209-278-4833.

FACILITIES
Information Resources Henry Madden Library; total holdings of 882,433 volumes, 1,170,769 microforms, 2,888 current periodical subscriptions. CD player(s) available for graduate student use. Access provided to online bibliographic retrieval services.

INTERNATIONAL STUDENTS
Demographics 14% of students enrolled are international students.

Services and Facilities International student office, international student center, visa services, ESL courses, counseling/support services.

Applying TOEFL: minimum score of 550, proof of adequate funds, proof of health/immunizations required. Financial aid is not available to international students.

International Student Contact Ms. Carol Munshower, Director, 5241 North Maple Avenue, Fresno, CA 93740-0056. Phone: 209-278-2782; Fax: 209-278-7879.

PLACEMENT
Services include career counseling/planning, career fairs, and career placement.

Program Contact: Ms. Penny Lacy, Administrative Assistant, 5245 North Backer Avenue, Fresno, CA 93740-0008. Phone: 209-278-2107; Fax: 209-278-4911.

California State University, Fullerton

School of Business Administration and Economics
Fullerton, California

OVERVIEW
California State University, Fullerton is a state-supported, coed, comprehensive institution. Enrollment: 24,906 graduate, professional, and undergraduate students; 326 full-time matriculated graduate/professional students; 2,351 part-time matriculated graduate/professional students. Founded: 1957. The graduate business unit is in an urban setting and is on a semester calendar.

HIGHLIGHTS

Enrollment Profile
Full-time: 43
Part-time: 454
Total: 497
Average Age: 29
Fall 1997 Average GPA: 3.16

International: 32%
Women: 44%
Minorities: 27%
Average Class Size: 24
Fall 1997 Average GMAT: 522

Costs
Full-time tuition: $246 per academic year (nonresident)
Part-time tuition: $2117 per 6 credit hours (nonresident)

AACSB – The International Association for Management Education accredited

GRADUATE BUSINESS PROGRAMS
Master of Business Administration, Specialist (MBA) Part-time; 33 total credits required; 12 months to 5 years to complete program. Concentrations in accounting, finance, management, management science, management information systems, marketing.

Master of Business Administration (MBA) Part-time, distance learning option; 57 total credits required; 2 to 5 years to complete program.

Master of Science in Taxation (MS) Full-time, part-time; 30 total credits required; 12 months to 5 years to complete program.

Master of Science in Management Science (MS) Full-time, part-time; 33 total credits required; 12 months to 5 years to complete program. Concentration in management information systems.

Master of Science in Accountancy (MS) Full-time, part-time; 30 total credits required; 12 months to 5 years to complete program.

ADMISSION
Applications For fall 1997 there were 332 applications for admission. Of those applying, 212 were accepted. Of those accepted, 119 enrolled.

Application Requirements GMAT score: minimum 400, application form, application fee, bachelor's degree, essay, minimum GPA: 2.75, personal statement, college transcript(s), computer experience: introductory computer course.

Recommended for Application Letters of recommendation, resume.

Application Deadline Applications processed on a rolling/continuous basis for both domestic and international students. Application fee: $55.

ACADEMICS
Faculty Full-time 124; part-time 120.

Teaching Methodologies Case study, computer analysis, computer simulations, experiential learning, field projects, group discussion, lecture, research, role playing, simulations, student presentations, study groups, team projects.

Technology 1,200 on-campus computer terminals/PCs are available for student use and are linked by a campus-wide network. The network has full access to the Internet. Students are not required to have their own PC.

Special Opportunities Advanced credit may be earned through transfer of credits from another institution.

FINANCES
Costs for 1997–98 Tuition: Full-time: $246 per unit (nonresident). Part-time: $2117 per 6 credit hours (nonresident). Fees: Full-time: $974 per academic year (resident); $974 per academic year (nonresident). Part-time: $641 per unit (resident); $641 per unit (nonresident). Fees vary by number of credits taken. Average 1997–98 room and board costs were $5330 per academic year (on campus) and $6768 per academic year (off campus). Room and board costs vary by type of meal plan.

Financial Aid In 1997–98, 6% of students received some institutionally administered aid in the form of fellowships, teaching assistantships, grants, scholarships, work study, loans. Financial aid is available to part-time students. Application Deadline: 3/1.

Financial Aid Contact Ms. Deborah Gordon, Director of Financial Aid, PO Box 6804, Fullerton, CA 92834-6804. Phone: 714-278-3125; Fax: 714-278-7090.

FACILITIES
Information Resources Main library; total holdings of 684,912 volumes, 947,096 microforms, 3,986 current periodical subscriptions. CD player(s) available for graduate student use. Access provided to online bibliographic retrieval services.

INTERNATIONAL STUDENTS
Demographics 32% of students enrolled are international students.

Services and Facilities International student office, international student center, ESL courses, counseling/support services.

Applying TOEFL: minimum score of 500, proof of adequate funds, proof of health/immunizations required. Financial aid is not available to international students.

International Student Contact Mr. Robert Ericksen, Director of International Education and Exchange, PO Box 34080, Fullerton, CA 92834-6830. Phone: 714-278-2787; Fax: 714-278-7292; E-mail: bericksen@fullerton.edu

PLACEMENT
Services include alumni network, career counseling/planning, career fairs, career library, career placement, job interviews arranged, and resume preparation. In 1996–97, 208 organizations participated in on-campus recruiting.

Employment Of 1996–97 graduates, the average starting salary was $48,260. Types of employment entered: accounting, banking, communications, computer-related, consulting, consumer products, education, energy, engineering, finance, financial services, government, health services, high technology, hospitality management, human resources, information systems/technology, insurance, international trade, management, manufacturing, marketing, media, nonprofit, petrochemical, pharmaceutical, real estate, retail, service industry, telecommunications, transportation, utilities.

Business Program(s) URL: http://sbaeweb.fullerton.edu/

Program Contact: Dr. Dorothy Heide, Associate Dean, PO Box 34080, Fullerton, CA 92834-6848. Phone: 714-278-2592; Fax: 714-278-7101; E-mail: dheide@fullerton.edu

California State University, Hayward

School of Business and Economics
Hayward, California

OVERVIEW
California State University, Hayward is a state-supported, coed, comprehensive institution. Enrollment: 12,855 graduate, professional, and undergraduate students; 714 full-time matriculated graduate/professional students; 1,321 part-time matriculated graduate/professional students. Founded: 1957. The graduate business unit is in a suburban setting and is on a quarter calendar.

HIGHLIGHTS

Enrollment Profile
Full-time: 159
Part-time: 445
Total: 604
Average Age: 33
Fall 1997 Average GPA: 3.05

International: 14%
Women: 50%
Minorities: 36%
Average Class Size: 24
Fall 1997 Average GMAT: 515

Costs
Full-time tuition: N/R
Part-time tuition: $383 per 4 units (resident); $1039 per 4 units (nonresident)

AACSB – The International Association for Management Education accredited

Degree(s) offered in conjunction with Academy of National Economy, International Management Development Consulting, United Institute of International Education

GRADUATE BUSINESS PROGRAMS
Master of Business Administration (MBA) Part-time; 45 total credits required; 12 months to 5 years to complete program. Concentrations in accounting, economics, entrepreneurship, finance, human resources, international business, management information systems, management science, marketing, operations management, taxation, management, materials management, new venture management, strategic management, telecommunications management.

Executive MBA in Vienna (EMBA) Part-time; 47 total credits required; 12 months to complete program.

Master of Science in Taxation (MS) Part-time; 45 total credits required; 12 months to 5 years to complete program. Concentration in taxation.

Master of Science in Business Administration: Computer Information Systems/Quantitative (MS) Part-time; 45 total credits required; 12 months to 5 years to complete program. Concentrations in decision sciences, management information systems.

Master of Arts in Economics (MA) Part-time; 45 total credits required; 12 months to 5 years to complete program. Concentration in economics.

ADMISSION
Applications For fall 1997 there were 268 applications for admission. Of those applying, 205 were accepted. Of those accepted, 128 enrolled.

Application Requirements Application form, application fee, bachelor's degree, minimum GPA: 2.75, personal statement, college transcript(s), computer experience: word processing, spreadsheet, database.

Recommended for Application GMAT score accepted, letters of recommendation.

Application Deadline 6/1 for fall, 9/1 for winter, 1/1 for spring, 4/1 for summer, 4/1 for fall (international), 10/1 for spring (international). Application fee: $55. Deferred entrance is available.

ACADEMICS
Faculty Full-time 75.

Teaching Methodologies Case study, computer analysis, computer simulations, experiential learning, field projects, group discussion, lecture, research, role playing, simulations, student presentations, study groups, team projects.

Technology 570 on-campus computer terminals/PCs are available for student use and are linked by a campus-wide network. The network has full access to the Internet. Students are not required to have their own PC.

Special Opportunities Advanced credit may be earned through credit by examination, transfer of credits from another institution. International exchange programs in Australia, Canada, Denmark, France, Germany, Japan, Philippines, Thailand, United Kingdom. An internship program is available.

FINANCES
Costs for 1997–98 Tuition: Part-time: $383 per 4 units (resident); $1039 per 4 units (nonresident). Cost varies by number of credits taken. Average 1997–98 room only costs were $3200 per academic year (on campus) and $5000 per academic year (off campus). Room and board costs vary by occupancy (e.g., single, double, triple), type of accommodation, type of meal plan.

Financial Aid Fellowships, teaching assistantships, grants, scholarships, work study, loans available. Financial aid is available to part-time students. Application Deadline: 3/1.

Financial Aid Contact Ms. Betty Harris, Director, Financial Aid Office, 25800 Carlos Bee Boulevard, Hayward, CA 94542-3000. Phone: 510-885-3018; Fax: 510-885-4627; E-mail: bharris@csuhayward.edu

FACILITIES
Information Resources University Library; total holdings of 726,504 volumes, 684,473 microforms, 2,023 current periodical subscriptions. CD player(s) available for graduate student use. Access provided to online bibliographic retrieval services.

INTERNATIONAL STUDENTS
Demographics 14% of students enrolled are international students [Africa, 3%, Asia, 40%, South America, 5%, other, 16%].

Services and Facilities Visa services, ESL courses.

Applying TOEFL: minimum score of 550, proof of adequate funds, proof of health/immunizations required. Financial aid is not available to international students.

International Student Contact Ms. Lynn Clement, Enrollment Services, 25800 Carlos Bee Boulevard, Hayward, CA 94542-3000. Phone: 510-885-3260; Fax: 510-885-3816; E-mail: lclement@csuhayward.edu

PLACEMENT
Services include alumni network, career counseling/planning, career fairs, career library, career placement, electronic job bank, job interviews arranged, job search course, resume referral to employers, and resume preparation. In 1996–97, 250 organizations participated in on-campus recruiting; 2,500 on-campus interviews were conducted.

Employment Of 1996–97 graduates, 99% were employed within three months of graduation. Types of employment entered: accounting, banking, computer-related, consulting, consumer products, education, energy, finance, financial services, government, health services, high technology, human resources, information systems/technology, insurance, international trade, management, manufacturing, marketing, media, nonprofit, pharmaceutical, real estate, retail, service industry, telecommunications, transportation, utilities.

Business Program(s) URL: http://www.sbe.csuhayward.edu/grdstdy/

Program Contact: Dr. Donna Wiley, Director of School of Business and Economics Graduate Programs, School of Business and Economics, Hayward, CA 94542-3000. Phone: 510-885-3964; Fax: 510-885-2176; E-mail: dwiley@csuhayward.edu

California State University, Long Beach

College of Business Administration

Long Beach, California

OVERVIEW

California State University, Long Beach is a state-supported, coed, comprehensive institution. Enrollment: 27,000 graduate, professional, and undergraduate students. Founded: 1948. The graduate business unit is in an urban setting and is on a semester calendar.

HIGHLIGHTS

Enrollment Profile

Full-time: 85	International: 18%
Part-time: 345	Women: 37%
Total: 430	Minorities: 21%
Average Age: 32	Average Class Size: 25
Fall 1997 Average GPA: 3.2	Fall 1997 Average GMAT: 540

Costs
Full-time tuition: $246 per academic year (nonresident)
Part-time tuition: $246 per unit (nonresident)

AACSB – The International Association for Management Education accredited

GRADUATE BUSINESS PROGRAMS

Master of Business Administration (MBA) Full-time, part-time; 33-60 total credits required; 12 months to 7 years to complete program. Concentrations in finance, human resources, management, management information systems, marketing.

Fully Employed MBA (MBA) Part-time; up to 2 years to complete program.

ADMISSION

Applications For fall 1997 there were 322 applications for admission. Of those applying, 145 were accepted. Of those accepted, 97 enrolled.

Application Requirements GMAT score, application form, application fee, bachelor's degree, essay, minimum GPA: 2.5, 2 letters of recommendation, personal statement, resume, college transcript(s).

Recommended for Application Work experience, computer experience.

Application Deadline 7/1 for fall, 11/1 for spring, 7/11 for fall (international), 11/1 for spring (international). Application fee: $55. Deferred entrance is available.

ACADEMICS

Faculty Full-time 105; part-time 115.

Teaching Methodologies Case study, computer-aided instruction, computer analysis, group discussion, lecture, research, seminars by members of the business community, student presentations, study groups, team projects.

Technology 60 on-campus computer terminals/PCs are available for student use and are linked by a campus-wide network. The network has full access to the Internet. Students are not required to have their own PC.

Special Opportunities Advanced credit may be earned through credit by examination, transfer of credits from another institution.

FINANCES

Costs for 1997–98 Tuition: Full-time: $246 per unit (nonresident). Part-time: $246 per unit (nonresident). Cost varies by number of credits taken. Fees: Full-time: $923 per academic year (resident); $923 per academic year (nonresident). Part-time: $580 per semester (resident); $580 per semester (nonresident). Fees vary by number of credits taken. Average 1997–98 room and board costs were $7800 per academic year. Room and board costs vary by occupancy (e.g., single, double, triple), type of accommodation, type of meal plan.

Financial Aid Application Deadline: 3/2.

Financial Aid Contact Gloria Kapp, 1250 Bellflower Boulevard, Long Beach, CA 90840-0119. Phone: 562-985-8403; E-mail: gkapp@csulb.edu

FACILITIES

Information Resources Total library holdings of 1,052,551 volumes, 1,502,068 microforms, 6,015 current periodical subscriptions. CD player(s) available for graduate student use. Access provided to online bibliographic retrieval services.

INTERNATIONAL STUDENTS

Demographics 18% of students enrolled are international students.

Services and Facilities International student office, international student center, international student housing, visa services, ESL courses, counseling/support services.

Applying TOEFL: minimum score of 550 required.

International Student Contact Robert Prather, Assistant Director, International Admissions, 1250 Bellflower Boulevard, Long Beach, CA 90840-0119. Phone: 562-985-5476; Fax: 562-985-1725; E-mail: rprather@csulb.edu

PLACEMENT

Services include career counseling/planning, career fairs, career library, career placement, electronic job bank, job interviews arranged, resume referral to employers, and resume preparation.

Employment Types of employment entered: accounting, banking, computer-related, consulting, finance, financial services, health services, human resources, information systems/technology, management, marketing, media, pharmaceutical.

Business Program(s) URL: http://www.csulb.edu/~cba/

Program Contact: Paula Gloeckner, MBA Evaluator, 1250 Bellflower Boulevard, Long Beach, CA 90840-0119. Phone: 562-985-1797; Fax: 562-985-5742; E-mail: paula@csulb.edu

California State University, Los Angeles

School of Business and Economics

Los Angeles, California

OVERVIEW

California State University, Los Angeles is a state-supported, coed, comprehensive institution. Enrollment: 18,849 graduate, professional, and undergraduate students; 875 full-time matriculated graduate/professional students; 1,981 part-time matriculated graduate/professional students. Founded: 1947. The graduate business unit is in an urban setting and is on a quarter calendar.

HIGHLIGHTS

Enrollment Profile

Full-time: 0	International: 27%
Part-time: 330	Women: 54%
Total: 330	Minorities: 49%
Average Age: 31	Average Class Size: 25
Fall 1997 Average GPA: 3.3	Fall 1997 Average GMAT: 560

Costs
Full-time tuition: $2400 per academic year (resident); $10,000 per academic year (nonresident)
Part-time tuition: $363 per quarter (resident); $585 per quarter (nonresident)

AACSB – The International Association for Management Education accredited

GRADUATE BUSINESS PROGRAMS

Master of Business Administration (MBA) Full-time, part-time; 48 total credits required; 18 months to 4 years to complete program. Concentrations in accounting, business information science, economics, finance, international business, management, marketing.

Master of Science in Business Administration (MS) Full-time, part-time; 45 total credits required; 18 months to 4 years to complete program. Concentrations in economics, finance, international business, management, management information systems, marketing.

Master of Science in Accountancy (MS) Full-time, part-time; 45 total credits required; 18 months to 4 years to complete program. Concentration in accounting.

Master of Science in Health Care Management (MS) Full-time, part-time; 45 total credits required; 18 months to 4 years to complete program. Concentration in health care.

ADMISSION

Applications For fall 1997 there were 388 applications for admission. Of those applying, 166 were accepted. Of those accepted, 87 enrolled.

Application Requirements GMAT score: minimum 550, application form, application fee, bachelor's degree, essay, minimum GPA: 3.0, 3 letters of recommendation, personal statement, resume, college transcript(s), minimum of 2 years of work experience.

Recommended for Application Interview, computer experience.

Application Deadline 6/15 for fall, 10/1 for winter, 12/1 for spring, 3/1 for summer, 3/1 for fall (international), 9/1 for winter (international), 10/1 for spring (international). Application fee: $55.

ACADEMICS

Faculty Full-time 80; part-time 39.

Teaching Methodologies Case study, computer-aided instruction, computer analysis, computer simulations, experiential learning, faculty seminars, field projects, group discussion, lecture, research, role playing, seminars by members of the business community, simulations, student presentations, study groups, team projects.

Technology 600 on-campus computer terminals/PCs are available for student use and are linked by a campus-wide network. The network has full access to the Internet. Students are not required to have their own PC.

Special Opportunities Advanced credit may be earned through credit by examination, credit for experience, transfer of credits from another institution. An internship program is available.

FINANCES
Costs for 1997–98 Tuition: Full-time: $2400 per year (resident); $10,000 per year (nonresident). Part-time: $363 per quarter (resident); $585 per quarter (nonresident). Cost varies by number of credits taken. Fees: Full-time: $164 per academic year. Part-time: $164 per unit. Average 1997–98 room only costs were $4800 per academic year (on campus) and $7200 per academic year (off campus). Room and board costs vary by campus location, occupancy (e.g., single, double, triple), type of accommodation.

Financial Aid In 1997–98, 10% of students received some institutionally administered aid in the form of fellowships, teaching assistantships, grants, scholarships, work study. Financial aid is available to part-time students. Application Deadline: 3/1.

Financial Aid Contact Mr. Vu Tran, Director of Student Financial Services, 5151 State University Drive, Los Angeles, CA 90032-4221. Phone: 213-343-3245; Fax: 213-343-3166; E-mail: tru@calstatela.edu

FACILITIES
Information Resources John F. Kennedy Memorial Library; total holdings of 1,147,573 volumes, 814,721 microforms, 2,134 current periodical subscriptions. CD player(s) available for graduate student use. Access provided to online bibliographic retrieval services and online databases.

INTERNATIONAL STUDENTS
Demographics 27% of students enrolled are international students [Asia, 80%, South America, 5%, other, 15%].

Services and Facilities International student office, international student center, international student housing, visa services, ESL courses, counseling/support services, language tutoring.

Applying TOEFL: minimum score of 550, proof of adequate funds, proof of health/immunizations required. Financial aid is not available to international students.

International Student Contact Mr. Harold Martin, International Student Advisor, 5151 State University Drive, Los Angeles, CA 90032-4221. Phone: 213-343-3170; Fax: 213-343-6478; E-mail: hmartin@calstatela.edu

PLACEMENT
Services include alumni network, career counseling/planning, career fairs, career library, career placement, electronic job bank, job interviews arranged, resume referral to employers, and resume preparation.

Employment Of 1996–97 graduates, 95% were employed within three months of graduation. Types of employment entered: accounting, computer-related, consulting, education, finance, government, health services, information systems/ technology, international trade, management, marketing, nonprofit, retail, utilities.

Business Program(s) URL: http://sbela.calstatela.edu/sbe/graduate/index. htm

Program Contact: Ms. Mary Ellen Hoskanson, Admissions Officer, 5151 State University Drive, Los Angeles, CA 90032-4221. Phone: 213-343-5156; Fax: 213-343-5480; E-mail: mhokans@calstatela.edu

California State University, Northridge

College of Business Administration and Economics

Northridge, California

OVERVIEW
California State University, Northridge is a state-supported, coed, comprehensive institution. Enrollment: 27,189 graduate, professional, and undergraduate students; 887 full-time matriculated graduate/professional students; 4,553 part-time matriculated graduate/professional students. Founded: 1958. The graduate business unit is in a suburban setting and is on a semester calendar.

HIGHLIGHTS

Enrollment Profile

Full-time: 25	International: 4%
Part-time: 325	Women: 41%
Total: 350	Minorities: 19%
Average Age: 30	Average Class Size: 20
Fall 1997 Average GPA: N/R	Fall 1997 Average GMAT: N/R

Costs
Full-time tuition: $1980 per academic year (resident); $3444 per academic year (nonresident)
Part-time tuition: $657 per 6 units (resident); $246 per unit (nonresident)

AACSB – The International Association for Management Education accredited

GRADUATE BUSINESS PROGRAMS
Evening MBA (MBA) Full-time, part-time; 33 total credits required; 12 months to 5 years to complete program. Concentrations in business law, economics, finance, international business, management, management science, marketing, management information systems.

Master of Science in Accountancy (MS) Full-time, part-time; 30 total credits required; 12 months to 5 years to complete program. Concentration in accounting.

Master of Science in Taxation (MS) Full-time, part-time; 30 total credits required; 12 months to 5 years to complete program. Concentration in taxation.

ADMISSION
Applications For fall 1997 there were 150 applications for admission. Of those applying, 140 were accepted. Of those accepted, 84 enrolled.

Application Requirements Application form, application fee, bachelor's degree, minimum GPA: 3.0, college transcript(s).

Recommended for Application GMAT score accepted, essay, 3 letters of recommendation, personal statement, resume, work experience, computer experience.

Application Deadline 4/1 for fall, 11/1 for spring, 4/30 for fall (international), 11/30 for spring (international). Application fee: $55.

ACADEMICS
Faculty Full-time 120; part-time 18.

Teaching Methodologies Case study, computer-aided instruction, computer analysis, faculty seminars, field projects, group discussion, lecture, research, role playing, seminars by members of the business community, simulations, student presentations, study groups, team projects.

Technology 100 on-campus computer terminals/PCs are available for student use and are linked by a campus-wide network. The network has full access to the Internet. Students are not required to have their own PC.

Special Opportunities Advanced credit may be earned through credit by examination, credit for experience, transfer of credits from another institution. An internship program is available.

FINANCES
Costs for 1997–98 Tuition: Full-time: $1980 per year (resident); $3444 per year (nonresident). Part-time: $657 per 6 units (resident); $246 per unit (nonresident). Cost varies by number of credits taken. Average 1997–98 room and board costs were $5763 per academic year (on campus) and $6000 per academic year (off campus). Room and board costs vary by occupancy (e.g., single, double, triple), type of accommodation, type of meal plan.

Financial Aid Teaching assistantships, work study available. Financial aid is available to part-time students. Application Deadline: 3/1.

Financial Aid Contact CSUN Financial Aid Office, 18111 Nordhoff Street, Northridge, CA 91330. Phone: 818-885-3000.

FACILITIES
Information Resources Oviatt Library plus 1 additional on-campus library; total holdings of 990,938 volumes, 7,566 current periodical subscriptions. Access provided to online bibliographic retrieval services.

INTERNATIONAL STUDENTS
Demographics 4% of students enrolled are international students.

Services and Facilities International student office, international student center, visa services, ESL courses, counseling/support services.

Applying TOEFL: minimum score of 550, proof of adequate funds, proof of health/immunizations required. Financial aid is not available to international students.

International Student Contact Ms. Mary Baxton, Associate Director, International Admissions, 18111 Nordhoff Street, Northridge, CA 91330. Phone: 818-677-3778; E-mail: mbaxton@csun.edu

PLACEMENT
Services include alumni network, career counseling/planning, career fairs, career library, and electronic job bank.

Business Program(s) URL: http://www.csun.edu/cobaegrad

Program Contact: Ms. Kristen Walker, Assistant Director of Graduate Programs, 18111 Nordhoff Street, Northridge, CA 91330-8380. Phone: 818-677-2467; Fax: 818-677-3188; E-mail: hfbus033@csun.edu

California State University, Sacramento

School of Business Administration

Sacramento, California

OVERVIEW
California State University, Sacramento is a state-supported, coed, comprehensive institution. Enrollment: 23,420 graduate, professional, and undergraduate students; 2,199 full-time matriculated graduate/professional students; 2,508 part-time matriculated graduate/professional students. Founded: 1947. The graduate business unit is in a suburban setting and is on a semester calendar.

GRADUATE BUSINESS PROGRAMS
Master of Business Administration (MBA)
Master of Science in Accountancy (MS)
Master of Science in Business Administration (MS)

ACADEMICS
Faculty Full-time 80; part-time 30.
Teaching Methodologies Case study, computer-aided instruction, field projects, group discussion, research, seminars by members of the business community, student presentations, team projects.
Technology 300 on-campus computer terminals/PCs are available for student use and are linked by a campus-wide network. The network has full access to the Internet. Students are not required to have their own PC.
Special Opportunities Advanced credit may be earned through transfer of credits from another institution. International exchange programs in Argentina, Belgium, Brazil, Canada, Denmark, France, Germany, Japan, Mexico, New Zealand, Republic of Korea, Taiwan. An internship program is available.

FACILITIES
Information Resources Main library; total holdings of 806,455 volumes, 32,596 microforms, 5,264 current periodical subscriptions. Access provided to online bibliographic retrieval services.

Program Contact: Director, Graduate Programs, School of Business Administration, Sacramento, CA 95819-6088. Phone: 916-278-6772; Fax: 916-278-4979; E-mail: sbagrad@csus.edu

California State University, San Bernardino

School of Business and Public Administration

San Bernardino, California

OVERVIEW
California State University, San Bernardino is a state-supported, coed, comprehensive institution. Enrollment: 13,300 graduate, professional, and undergraduate students; 939 full-time matriculated graduate/professional students; 737 part-time matriculated graduate/professional students. Founded: 1960. The graduate business unit is in an urban setting and is on a quarter calendar.

HIGHLIGHTS

Enrollment Profile
Full-time: 186
Part-time: 146
Total: 332
Average Age: 29
Fall 1997 Average GPA: 3.1

International: 50%
Women: 48%
Minorities: 20%
Average Class Size: 20
Fall 1997 Average GMAT: 482

Costs
Full-time tuition: $2050 per academic year (resident); $7872 per academic year (nonresident)
Part-time tuition: $164 per unit (nonresident)

AACSB – The International Association for Management Education accredited

Degree(s) offered in conjunction with Claremont McKenna College

GRADUATE BUSINESS PROGRAMS
Master of Business Administration (MBA) Full-time, part-time, distance learning option; 48-96 total credits required; 15 months to 7 years to complete program. Concentrations in accounting, finance, management, human resources, operations management, marketing, information management.

ADMISSION
Applications For fall 1997 there were 233 applications for admission. Of those applying, 211 were accepted. Of those accepted, 125 enrolled.
Application Requirements GMAT score: minimum 430, application form, application fee, bachelor's degree, essay, minimum GPA: 2.5, personal statement, college transcript(s).
Application Deadline 7/1 for fall, 11/1 for winter, 2/1 for spring, 7/1 for fall (international), 11/1 for winter (international), 2/1 for spring (international). Application fee: $55. Deferred entrance is available.

ACADEMICS
Faculty Full-time 31; part-time 5.
Teaching Methodologies Case study, computer-aided instruction, computer analysis, computer simulations, faculty seminars, field projects, group discussion, lecture, research, role playing, seminars by members of the business community, simulations, student presentations, study groups, team projects.
Technology 300 on-campus computer terminals/PCs are available for student use and are linked by a campus-wide network. The network has full access to the Internet. Students are not required to have their own PC.
Special Opportunities Advanced credit may be earned through transfer of credits from another institution. International exchange programs in France, Germany. An internship program is available.

FINANCES
Costs for 1997–98 Tuition: Full-time: $2050 per year (resident); $7872 per year (nonresident). Part-time: $164 per unit (nonresident). Average 1997–98 room only costs were $4965 per academic year (on campus) and $4500 per academic year (off campus). Room and board costs vary by occupancy (e.g., single, double, triple), type of accommodation.
Financial Aid Research assistantships, grants, scholarships, work study, loans available. Financial aid is available to part-time students. Application Deadline: 3/1.
Financial Aid Contact Mr. Ted Krug, Financial Aid Director, 5500 University Parkway, San Bernardino, CA 94207-2392. Phone: 909-880-5000; Fax: 909-880-5903; E-mail: tkrug@wiley.csusb.edu

FACILITIES
Information Resources Pfau Library; total holdings of 596,890 volumes, 605,664 microforms, 1,493 current periodical subscriptions. CD player(s) available for graduate student use. Access provided to online bibliographic retrieval services and online databases.

INTERNATIONAL STUDENTS
Demographics 50% of students enrolled are international students.
Services and Facilities International student office, international student center, counseling/support services.
Applying TOEFL: minimum score of 550 required.
International Student Contact Elsa Ochoa-Fernandez, 5500 University Parkway, San Bernardino, CA 92407-2397. Phone: 909-880-5197; Fax: 909-880-5903.

PLACEMENT
Services include alumni network, career counseling/planning, career fairs, career placement, job interviews arranged, resume referral to employers, and resume preparation. In 1996–97, 95 organizations participated in on-campus recruiting.
Employment Types of employment entered: accounting, banking, communications, computer-related, consulting, consumer products, education, energy, finance, financial services, government, high technology, human resources, information systems/technology, insurance, management, manufacturing, nonprofit, real estate, retail, service industry, telecommunications, transportation.
Business Program(s) URL: http://www.sbpa.csusb.edu

Program Contact: Dr. Sue Greenfeld, MBA Director, School of Business and Public Administration, 5500 University Parkway, Bernardino, CA 92407-2397. Phone: 909-880-5703; Fax: 909-880-7026; E-mail: sgreenfe@wiley.csusb.edu

California State University, San Marcos

Graduate Program in Business Administration

San Marcos, California

OVERVIEW
California State University, San Marcos is a state-supported, coed, comprehensive institution. Enrollment: 4,500 graduate, professional, and undergraduate students; 150 full-time matriculated graduate/professional students; 350 part-time matriculated graduate/professional students. Founded: 1990. The graduate business unit is in a suburban setting and is on a semester calendar.

HIGHLIGHTS

Enrollment Profile
Full-time: 150
Part-time: 0
Total: 150
Average Age: 35
Fall 1997 Average GPA: 3.1

International: 7%
Women: 40%
Minorities: N/R
Average Class Size: 30
Fall 1997 Average GMAT: 535

Costs
Full-time tuition: $15,671 per academic year (resident); $21,575 per academic year (nonresident)
Part-time tuition: N/R

GRADUATE BUSINESS PROGRAMS
Fully-employed MBA (MBA) Full-time; 36-48 total credits required; 3 years work experience required; 16 to 21 months to complete program. Concentration in management.

ADMISSION
Applications For fall 1997 there were 160 applications for admission. Of those applying, 83 were accepted. Of those accepted, 78 enrolled.

Application Requirements GMAT score, application form, application fee, bachelor's degree, essay, minimum GPA: 2.5, 3 letters of recommendation, college transcript(s), minimum of 3 years of work experience.

Recommended for Application Resume, computer experience.

Application Deadline 5/1 for fall, 11/1 for spring, 2/1 for summer, 5/1 for fall (international), 11/1 for spring (international), 3/1 for summer (international). Application fee: $55. Deferred entrance is available.

ACADEMICS
Faculty Full-time 30; part-time 20.

Teaching Methodologies Case study, computer analysis, computer simulations, experiential learning, field projects, group discussion, lecture, research, seminars by members of the business community, student presentations, study groups, team projects.

Technology 120 on-campus computer terminals/PCs are available for student use and are linked by a campus-wide network. The network has full access to the Internet. Students are not required to have their own PC.

Special Opportunities Advanced credit may be earned through transfer of credits from another institution.

FINANCES
Costs for 1997–98 Tuition: Full-time: $15,671 per program (resident); $21,575 per program (nonresident).

Financial Aid In 1997–98, 17% of students received some institutionally administered aid in the form of fellowships, teaching assistantships, scholarships, loans. Financial aid is available to part-time students. Application Deadline: 4/1.

Financial Aid Contact Mr. Paul Phillips, Director of Financial Aid, San Marcos, CA 92096-0001. Phone: 760-750-4850; Fax: 760-750-3047; E-mail: finaid@csusm.edu

FACILITIES
Information Resources Main library; total holdings of 80,000 volumes, 950 current periodical subscriptions. CD player(s) available for graduate student use. Access provided to online bibliographic retrieval services.

INTERNATIONAL STUDENTS
Demographics 7% of students enrolled are international students [Asia, 50%, Central America, 30%, Europe, 10%, South America, 10%].

Services and Facilities International student office, ESL courses.

Applying TOEFL: minimum score of 530, proof of health/immunizations required.

International Student Contact Ms. Kiera Friedrich, Coordinator, MBA Program, San Marcos, CA 92096-0001. Phone: 760-750-4267; Fax: 760-750-4263; E-mail: mba@csusm.edu

PLACEMENT
Services include alumni network, career counseling/planning, career fairs, career library, career placement, electronic job bank, job interviews arranged, job search course, resume referral to employers, and resume preparation. In 1996–97, 181 organizations participated in on-campus recruiting.

Employment Of 1996–97 graduates, 98% were employed within three months of graduation.

Business Program(s) URL: http://www.csusm.edu/CBA

Program Contact: Ms. Kiera Friedrich, Coordinator, MBA Program, San Marcos, CA 92096-0001. Phone: 760-750-4267; Fax: 760-750-4263; E-mail: mba@csusm.edu

California State University, Stanislaus

School of Business Administration

Turlock, California

OVERVIEW
California State University, Stanislaus is a state-supported, coed, comprehensive institution. Enrollment: 6,213 graduate, professional, and undergraduate students. Founded: 1957. The graduate business unit is in a small-town setting and is on a semester calendar.

HIGHLIGHTS

Enrollment Profile
Full-time: N/R
Part-time: N/R
Total: 90
Average Age: 31
Fall 1997 Average GPA: 2.87

International: N/R
Women: N/R
Minorities: N/R
Average Class Size: 20
Fall 1997 Average GMAT: 500

Costs
Full-time tuition: $1738 per academic year (resident); $8049 per academic year (nonresident)
Part-time tuition: $530 per 6 units (resident); $2006 per 6 units (nonresident)

GRADUATE BUSINESS PROGRAMS
Master of Business Administration (MBA) Full-time, part-time, distance learning option; 63 total credits required; 12 months to 7 years to complete program.

ADMISSION
Applications For fall 1997 there were 55 applications for admission. Of those applying, 50 were accepted. Of those accepted, 36 enrolled.

Application Requirements Application form, application fee, bachelor's degree, minimum GPA: 2.5, 3 letters of recommendation, personal statement, college transcript(s).

Recommended for Application GMAT score accepted: minimum 450, essay, resume.

Application Deadline Applications processed on a rolling/continuous basis for both domestic and international students. Application fee: $55.

ACADEMICS
Faculty Full-time 27; part-time 13.

Teaching Methodologies Case study, computer-aided instruction, computer analysis, computer simulations, experiential learning, faculty seminars, field projects, group discussion, lecture, research, role playing, seminars by members of the business community, simulations, student presentations, study groups, team projects.

Technology 110 on-campus computer terminals/PCs are available for student use and are linked by a campus-wide network. The network has full access to the Internet. Students are not required to have their own PC.

Special Opportunities Advanced credit may be earned through transfer of credits from another institution.

FINANCES
Costs for 1997–98 Tuition: Full-time: $1738 per year (resident); $8049 per year (nonresident). Part-time: $530 per 6 units (resident); $2006 per 6 units (nonresident). Cost varies by number of credits taken. Fees vary by number of credits taken. Average 1997–98 room and board costs were $5600 per academic year (on campus) and $6500 per academic year (off campus). Room and board costs vary by campus location, occupancy (e.g., single, double, triple), type of accommodation, type of meal plan.

Financial Aid Work study available. Application Deadline: 3/2.

Financial Aid Contact Ms. Joan Hillery, Director, Financial Aid, 801 West Monte Vista Avenue, Turlock, CA 95382. Phone: 209-667-3336; Fax: 209-667-3080.

FACILITIES
Information Resources Vasche Library; total holdings of 290,000 volumes, 770,000 microforms, 4,000 current periodical subscriptions. CD player(s) avail-

California State University, Stanislaus (continued)

able for graduate student use. Access provided to online bibliographic retrieval services.

INTERNATIONAL STUDENTS

Demographics N/R

Services and Facilities International student office, international student center, international student housing, visa services, ESL courses, counseling/support services.

Applying TOEFL: minimum score of 550, proof of adequate funds, proof of health/immunizations required. Financial aid is not available to international students.

International Student Contact Dr. Robert Santos, Coordinator of International Student Programs, 801 West Monte Vista Avenue, Turlock, CA 95382. Phone: 209-667-3381; Fax: 209-667-3333; E-mail: santos_bob@macmail.csustan. edu

PLACEMENT

Services include alumni network, career counseling/planning, career fairs, career library, career placement, job interviews arranged, job search course, resume referral to employers, and resume preparation. In 1996–97, 37 organizations participated in on-campus recruiting; 156 on-campus interviews were conducted.

Employment Of 1996–97 graduates, 99% were employed within three months of graduation; the average starting salary was $42,000. Types of employment entered: accounting, banking, education, finance, government, health services, insurance, management, manufacturing, marketing, real estate, retail, utilities.

Business Program(s) URL: http://www.csustan.edu/

Program Contact: Dr. Randall Brown, Director, MBA Programs, 801 West Monte Vista Avenue, Turlock, CA 95382. Phone: 209-667-3280, 800-300-7420; Fax: 209-667-3080; E-mail: kcravinh@toto.csustan.edu

Chapman University

School of Business and Economics

Orange, California

OVERVIEW

Chapman University is an independent-religious, coed, comprehensive institution. Enrollment: 3,800 graduate, professional, and undergraduate students. Founded: 1861. The graduate business unit is in a suburban setting and is on a semester calendar.

HIGHLIGHTS

Enrollment Profile

Full-time: 54	International: 15%
Part-time: 163	Women: 40%
Total: 217	Minorities: 25%
Average Age: 30	Average Class Size: 22
Fall 1997 Average GPA: 3.03	Fall 1997 Average GMAT: 504

Costs
Full-time tuition: $12,740 per academic year
Part-time tuition: $520 per credit

GRADUATE BUSINESS PROGRAMS

Master of Business Administration (MBA) Full-time, part-time; 49 total credits required; 18 months to 7 years to complete program.

Executive MBA (MBA) Part-time; 48 total credits required; minimum of 21 months to complete program.

ADMISSION

Applications For fall 1997 there were 104 applications for admission. Of those applying, 99 were accepted. Of those accepted, 67 enrolled.

Application Requirements GMAT score: minimum 400, application form, application fee, bachelor's degree, minimum GPA: 2.5, letters of recommendation, personal statement, college transcript(s).

Recommended for Application Interview, resume, work experience, computer experience.

Application Deadline 6/15 for fall, 11/15 for spring, 4/15 for summer, 5/15 for fall (international), 12/15 for spring (international), 4/15 for summer (international). Application fee: $40. Deferred entrance is available.

ACADEMICS

Faculty Full-time 23; part-time 6.

Teaching Methodologies Case study, computer-aided instruction, experiential learning, field projects, group discussion, lecture, research, seminars by members of the business community, student presentations, study groups, team projects.

Technology 60 on-campus computer terminals/PCs are available for student use and are linked by a campus-wide network. The network has full access to the Internet. Students are not required to have their own PC.

Special Opportunities Advanced credit may be earned through credit by examination, transfer of credits from another institution. An internship program is available.

FINANCES

Costs for 1997–98 Tuition: Full-time: $12,740 per year. Part-time: $520 per credit. Cost varies by academic program. Average 1997–98 room and board costs were $7000 per academic year.

Financial Aid In 1997–98, 27% of students received some institutionally administered aid in the form of research assistantships, grants, loans. Financial aid is available to part-time students. Application Deadline: 3/1.

Financial Aid Contact Greg Ball, Director, Financial Aid, 333 North Glassell Street, Orange, CA 92866-1011. Phone: 714-997-6741; Fax: 714-997-6743.

FACILITIES

Information Resources Thurmond Clarke Memorial Library; total holdings of 220,000 volumes, 13,000 microforms, 1,914 current periodical subscriptions. CD player(s) available for graduate student use. Access provided to online bibliographic retrieval services and online databases.

INTERNATIONAL STUDENTS

Demographics 15% of students enrolled are international students [Asia, 80%, Europe, 13%, North America, 2%, South America, 5%].

Services and Facilities International student office, visa services, ESL courses, counseling/support services.

Applying TOEFL: minimum score of 550, proof of adequate funds required. Proof of health/immunizations recommended.

International Student Contact Mrs. Vicky Koerner, Director, International Student Services and Study Abroad, Argyros Forum, Orange, CA 92866. Phone: 714-997-6829; Fax: 714-997-6825; E-mail: koerner@nexus.chapman.edu

PLACEMENT

Services include alumni network, career counseling/planning, career fairs, career library, electronic job bank, and resume preparation. In 1996–97, 60 organizations participated in on-campus recruiting; 362 on-campus interviews were conducted.

Employment Types of employment entered: accounting, communications, computer-related, consumer products, financial services, marketing, pharmaceutical, retail, service industry.

Business Program(s) URL: http://www.chapman.edu/sbe/index.html

Program Contact: Ms. Debra Gonda, Associate Director, School of Business and Economics, Orange, CA 92866. Phone: 714-997-6745; Fax: 714-532-6081; E-mail: gonda@chapman.edu
See full description on page 744.

Claremont Graduate University

Peter F. Drucker Graduate School of Management

Claremont, California

OVERVIEW

Claremont Graduate University is an independent-nonprofit, coed, graduate institution. Enrollment: 2,018 graduate, professional, and undergraduate students; 511 full-time matriculated graduate/professional students; 1,507 part-time matriculated graduate/professional students. Founded: 1925. The graduate business unit is in a suburban setting and is on a semester calendar.

HIGHLIGHTS

Enrollment Profile

Full-time: 200	International: 29%
Part-time: 195	Women: 35%
Total: 395	Minorities: 18%
Average Age: 38	Average Class Size: 30
Fall 1997 Average GPA: 3.2	Fall 1997 Average GMAT: 582

Costs
Full-time tuition: $20,250 per academic year
Part-time tuition: $913 per credit

AACSB – The International Association for Management Education accredited

Degree(s) offered in conjunction with Claremont McKenna College, Pitzer College, Scropps College, Pomona College, Harvey Mudd College, Thunderbird, The American Graduate School of International Management, Groupe ESC Toulouse

The Drucker M.B.A. offers students a world-class education that features state-of-the-art facilities, an outstanding faculty, and small class sizes. Students, who are the top priority at Drucker, are offered a program that prepares tomorrow's leaders by providing the elements that allow students not only to learn but also to develop and excel.

The Drucker School is a learning community in which education is a process of exchange that is facilitated by the faculty. Students learn from faculty members and each other. Students are drawn from diverse backgrounds in terms of ethnicity, education, and job history. This diversity enriches the Drucker experience in preparing graduates for positions in the global marketplace. The emphasis is on general management and equipping students with a wide range of cross-functional tools and a sound understanding of management-related topics that is unsurpassed. Concentrations are available in strategy, marketing, information management, and finance

GRADUATE BUSINESS PROGRAMS

Drucker MBA (MBA) Full-time, part-time; 60 total credits required; 16 months to 5 years to complete program. Concentrations in marketing, strategic management, finance.

PhD in Executive Management (PhD) Part-time; 72 total credits required; 4 to 7 years to complete program. Concentrations in organizational behavior/development, strategic management, management systems analysis.

Master of Arts in Management (MA) Part-time; 32 total credits required; 12 months to 5 years to complete program. Concentrations in leadership, strategic management.

Executive Master of Business Administration (EMBA) Part-time; 48 total credits required; 2 to 5 years to complete program. Concentrations in leadership, strategic management.

Master of Science in Financial Engineering (MS) Full-time, part-time; 48 total credits required; 2 to 5 years to complete program.

Master of Business Administration/Master of Information Systems (MBA/MIS) Full-time, part-time; 80 total credits required; 3 to 5 years to complete program. Concentrations in marketing, strategic management, finance.

Master of Business Administration/Master of Science in Management of Information Science (MBA/MS) Full-time, part-time; 104 total credits required; 3 to 5 years to complete program. Concentrations in marketing, strategic management, finance.

Master of Business Administration/PhD in Management of Information Systems (MBA/PhD) Full-time, part-time; 124 total credits required; 5 to 7 years to complete program. Concentrations in marketing, strategic management, finance.

Master of Business Administration/Master of Science in Human Resources Design (MBA/MS) Full-time, part-time; 84 total credits required; 3 to 5 years to complete program. Concentrations in marketing, strategic management, finance.

Master of Business Administration/Master of Arts in Psychology (MBA/MA) Full-time, part-time; 80 total credits required; 3 to 5 years to complete program. Concentrations in marketing, strategic management, finance.

Master of Business Administration/PhD in Psychology (MBA/PhD) Full-time, part-time; 120 total credits required; 5 to 7 years to complete program. Concentrations in marketing, strategic management, finance.

Master of Business Administration/PhD in Philosophy (MBA/PhD) Full-time, part-time; 120 total credits required; 5 to 7 years to complete program. Concentrations in marketing, strategic management, finance.

Master of Business Administration/Master of Arts in Economics (MBA/MA) Full-time, part-time; 96 total credits required; 3 to 5 years to complete program. Concentrations in marketing, strategic management, finance.

Master of Business Administration/PhD in Economics (MBA/PhD) Full-time, part-time; 120 total credits required; 5 to 7 years to complete program. Concentrations in marketing, strategic management, finance.

Master of Business Administration/Master of Arts in Politics and Policy (MBA/MA) Full-time, part-time; 96 total credits required; 3 to 5 years to complete program. Concentrations in marketing, strategic management, finance.

Master of Business Administration/PhD in Politics and Policy (MBA/PhD) Full-time, part-time; 120 total credits required; 5 to 7 years to complete program. Concentrations in marketing, strategic management, finance.

ADMISSION

Applications For fall 1997 there were 430 applications for admission. Of those applying, 241 were accepted. Of those accepted, 105 enrolled.

Application Requirements GMAT score, application form, application fee, bachelor's degree, essay, 3 letters of recommendation, personal statement, resume, college transcript(s).

Recommended for Application Minimum GPA: 3.2, interview, work experience, computer experience.

Application Deadline Applications processed on a rolling/continuous basis for both domestic and international students. Application fee: $40. Deferred entrance is available.

ACADEMICS

Faculty Full-time 15; part-time 30.

Teaching Methodologies Case study, computer-aided instruction, computer analysis, computer simulations, experiential learning, faculty seminars, field projects, group discussion, lecture, research, role playing, seminars by members of the business community, simulations, student presentations, study groups, team projects, workshops.

Technology 100 on-campus computer terminals/PCs are available for student use and are linked by a campus-wide network. The network has full access to the Internet. Students are not required to have their own PC.

Special Opportunities Advanced credit may be earned through transfer of credits from another institution. International exchange programs in Argentina, Austria, Belgium, Chile, Finland, France, Germany, Japan, Kenya, Liberia, Mexico, Norway, Peru, Republic of South Africa, Spain, Switzerland, Taiwan, United Arab Emirates.

FINANCES

Costs for 1997–98 Tuition: Full-time: $20,250 per year. Part-time: $913 per credit. Cost varies by class time (e.g., day/evening), number of credits taken. Average 1997–98 room and board costs were $9082 per academic year. Room and board costs vary by occupancy (e.g., single, double, triple), type of accommodation, type of meal plan.

Financial Aid In 1997–98, 21% of students received some institutionally administered aid in the form of fellowships, research assistantships, teaching assistantships, scholarships, work study, loans. Financial aid is available to part-time students. Application Deadline: 2/15.

Financial Aid Contact Ms. Donna Espinoza, Director of Financial Aid, 170 East 10th Street, Claremont, CA 91711. Phone: 909-621-8337; Fax: 909-607-7285; E-mail: finaid@cgu.edu

FACILITIES

Information Resources Honnold Library plus 4 additional on-campus libraries; total holdings of 2,000,000 volumes, 1,200,000 microforms, 5,922 current periodical subscriptions. CD player(s) available for graduate student use. Access provided to online bibliographic retrieval services.

INTERNATIONAL STUDENTS

Demographics 29% of students enrolled are international students [Africa, 1%, Asia, 81%, Australia/New Zealand, 1%, Central America, 6%, Europe, 4%, North America, 4%, South America, 3%].

Services and Facilities International student office, international student center, international student housing, visa services, ESL courses, counseling/support services.

Applying TOEFL, proof of adequate funds, proof of health/immunizations required. Financial aid is available to international students.

International Student Contact Ms. Leslie Rusch, Admissions Counselor/International Student Advisor, McManus 131, 170 East Tenth Street, Claremont, CA 91745-6163. Phone: 909-621-8069; Fax: 909-607-7285; E-mail: admiss@cgu.edu

PLACEMENT

Services include alumni network, career counseling/planning, career fairs, career library, career placement, electronic job bank, job interviews arranged, job search course, resume referral to employers, and resume preparation. In 1996–97, 15 organizations participated in on-campus recruiting.

Employment Of 1996–97 graduates, 70% were employed within three months of graduation; the average starting salary was $51,000. Types of employment entered: accounting, banking, computer-related, consulting, consumer products, energy, finance, financial services, health services, high technology, human resources, information systems/technology, international trade, management, manufacturing, marketing, nonprofit, pharmaceutical, service industry, utilities.

Business Program(s) URL: http://www.cgu.edu/drucker

Program Contact: Mr. Jack Day, Educational Counselor, Office of Educational Counseling and Recruiting, 165 East Tenth Street, Claremont, CA 91711. Phone: 909-607-7811, 800-944-4312; Fax: 909-607-9104; E-mail: mba@cgu.edu

See full description on page 748.

Coleman College

Information Systems Department, Graduate Division

La Mesa, California

OVERVIEW
Coleman College is an independent-nonprofit, coed, comprehensive institution. Founded: 1963.

HIGHLIGHTS

Enrollment Profile

Full-time: N/R	International: N/R
Part-time: N/R	Women: N/R
Total: N/R	Minorities: N/R
Average Age: 39	Average Class Size: N/R
Fall 1997 Average GPA: N/R	Fall 1997 Average GMAT: N/R

Costs
Full-time tuition: N/R
Part-time tuition: N/R

GRADUATE BUSINESS PROGRAMS
Master of Science Degree, Information Systems (MS)

ADMISSION
Application Requirements Application form, application fee, bachelor's degree, essay, minimum GPA: 3.0, 3 letters of recommendation, college transcript(s), minimum of 2 years of work experience.
Application Deadline Application fee: $100.

FINANCES
Financial Aid Contact Financial Aid Office, 7380 Parkway Drive, La Mesa, CA 91942-1500.

FACILITIES
Information Resources CD player(s) available for graduate student use. Access provided to online bibliographic retrieval services.

INTERNATIONAL STUDENTS
Demographics N/R
Services and Facilities International student office.
International Student Contact International Student Advisor, 7380 Parkway Drive, La Mesa, CA 91942-1500. E-mail: intladvisor@coleman.edu

Business Program(s) URL: http://www.coleman.edu/Academic/infosys.html

Program Contact: Graduate Admissions Office, 7380 Parkway Drive, La Mesa, CA 91942-1500. E-mail: admissions@coleman.edu

College of Notre Dame

Business Programs

Belmont, California

OVERVIEW
College of Notre Dame is an independent-religious, coed, comprehensive institution. Enrollment: 1,743 graduate, professional, and undergraduate students; 255 full-time matriculated graduate/professional students; 551 part-time matriculated graduate/professional students. The graduate business unit is in a suburban setting and is on a trimester calendar.

HIGHLIGHTS

Enrollment Profile

Full-time: 18	International: 6%
Part-time: 163	Women: 55%
Total: 181	Minorities: 22%
Average Age: 33	Average Class Size: 14
Fall 1997 Average GPA: 2.8	Fall 1997 Average GMAT: 458

Costs
Full-time tuition: N/R
Part-time tuition: $460 per unit

GRADUATE BUSINESS PROGRAMS
Master of Business Administration (MBA) Full-time, part-time; 36 total credits required; work experience required; 12 months to 4 years to complete program. Concentrations in finance, international business, management information systems, marketing, organizational management, human resources.
Master of Science in Systems Management (MS) Full-time, part-time; 36 total credits required; 12 months to 4 years to complete program.

ADMISSION
Applications For fall 1997 there were 91 applications for admission. Of those applying, 62 were accepted. Of those accepted, 43 enrolled.
Application Requirements Application form, application fee, bachelor's degree, minimum GPA: 2.5, 2 letters of recommendation, college transcript(s).
Recommended for Application GMAT score accepted: minimum 450, minimum of 1 year of work experience, computer experience.
Application Deadline 8/1 for fall, 12/1 for spring, 4/1 for summer, 8/1 for fall (international), 12/1 for spring (international), 4/1 for summer (international). Application fee: $55. Deferred entrance is available.

ACADEMICS
Faculty Full-time 4; part-time 22.
Teaching Methodologies Case study, computer-aided instruction, field projects, lecture, role playing, seminars by members of the business community, simulations, student presentations, study groups, team projects.
Technology 30 on-campus computer terminals/PCs are available for student use and are linked by a campus-wide network. The network has partial access to the Internet. Students are not required to have their own PC.
Special Opportunities Advanced credit may be earned through transfer of credits from another institution.

FINANCES
Costs for 1997–98 Tuition: $460 per unit. Average 1997–98 room and board costs were $8000 per academic year (on campus) and $8500 per academic year (off campus). Room and board costs vary by occupancy (e.g., single, double, triple), type of accommodation, type of meal plan.
Financial Aid Financial aid is available to part-time students. Application Deadline: 3/1.
Financial Aid Contact Ms. Kathleen Kelly, Director of Financial Aid, 1500 Ralston Avenue, Belmont, CA 94002-1997. Phone: 650-508-3580; Fax: 650-508-3736.

FACILITIES
Information Resources Main library; total holdings of 100,461 volumes, 16,487 microforms, 550 current periodical subscriptions. CD player(s) available for graduate student use. Access provided to online bibliographic retrieval services.

INTERNATIONAL STUDENTS
Demographics 6% of students enrolled are international students [Africa, 1%, Asia, 96%, Central America, 1%, Europe, 1%, South America, 1%].
Services and Facilities International student office, visa services, ESL courses, counseling/support services.
Applying TOEFL: minimum score of 550 required. Proof of adequate funds, proof of health/immunizations recommended. Financial aid is not available to international students.
International Student Contact Ms. Virginia Spinelli, Coordinator, 1500 Ralston Avenue, Belmont, CA 94002. Phone: 650-508-3512; Fax: 650-508-3736.

PLACEMENT
Services include alumni network, career counseling/planning, and resume preparation.
Employment Of 1996–97 graduates, 95% were employed within three months of graduation. Types of employment entered: accounting, banking, computer-related, consumer products, finance, financial services, human resources, information systems/technology, insurance, law, marketing, nonprofit, service industry, telecommunications.

Program Contact: Ms. Barbara Sterner, Assistant to the Graduate Dean for Admissions, 1500 Ralston Avenue, Belmont, CA 94002-1997. Phone: 650-508-3527; Fax: 650-508-3736; E-mail: barbara@cnd.edu

Dominican College of San Rafael

School of Business and International Studies

San Rafael, California

OVERVIEW
Dominican College of San Rafael is an independent-nonprofit, coed, comprehensive institution. Enrollment: 1,452 graduate, professional, and undergraduate students; 252 full-time matriculated graduate/professional students; 180 part-time

matriculated graduate/professional students. Founded: 1889. The graduate business unit is in a suburban setting and is on a semester calendar.

HIGHLIGHTS

Enrollment Profile
Full-time: 39
Part-time: 53
Total: 92
Average Age: 35
Fall 1997 Average GPA: N/R

International: 26%
Women: 48%
Minorities: 17%
Average Class Size: 20
Fall 1997 Average GMAT: N/R

Costs
Full-time tuition: $12,816 per academic year
Part-time tuition: $534 per unit

GRADUATE BUSINESS PROGRAMS

Master of Business Administration in International Business, Pacific Basin (MBA) Full-time, part-time; 58 total credits required; minimum of 2 years to complete program. Concentrations in international business, asian business studies, international and area business studies.

Master of Arts in International Economic and Political Assessment in the Pacific Basin (MA) Full-time, part-time; 45 total credits required; minimum of 18 months to complete program. Concentrations in international and area business studies, international business, asian business studies.

Strategic Leadership (MBA) Part-time; 36 total credits required; minimum of 2 years to complete program. Concentrations in human resources, strategic management.

ADMISSION

Applications For fall 1997 there were 65 applications for admission. Of those applying, 53 were accepted. Of those accepted, 34 enrolled.

Application Requirements Application form, application fee, bachelor's degree, essay, minimum GPA: 3.0, 3 letters of recommendation, college transcript(s).

Recommended for Application Resume, work experience, computer experience.

Application Deadline 8/15 for fall, 12/15 for spring, 7/15 for fall (international), 11/15 for spring (international). Application fee: $50.

ACADEMICS

Faculty Full-time 5; part-time 8.

Teaching Methodologies Case study, group discussion, lecture, student presentations, team projects.

Technology 29 on-campus computer terminals/PCs are available for student use and are linked by a campus-wide network. The network has full access to the Internet. Students are not required to have their own PC.

Special Opportunities Advanced credit may be earned through transfer of credits from another institution. An internship program is available.

FINANCES

Costs for 1997–98 Tuition: Full-time: $12,816 per year. Part-time: $534 per unit. Cost varies by academic program. Fees: Full-time: $320 per academic year. Part-time: $320 per year. Fees vary by academic program. Average 1997–98 room and board costs were $7246 per academic year. Room and board costs vary by type of meal plan.

Financial Aid Research assistantships, grants, work study available. Financial aid is available to part-time students. Application Deadline: 3/15.

Financial Aid Contact Ms. Susan Gutierrez, Director of Financial Aid, 50 Acacia Avenue, San Rafael, CA 94901-2298. Phone: 415-485-3294; Fax: 415-485-3205; E-mail: gutierrez@dominican.edu

FACILITIES

Information Resources Archbishop Alemany Library; total holdings of 96,890 volumes, 2,559 microforms, 421 current periodical subscriptions. CD player(s) available for graduate student use. Access provided to online bibliographic retrieval services.

INTERNATIONAL STUDENTS

Demographics 26% of students enrolled are international students [Asia, 79%, Europe, 13%, South America, 4%, other, 4%].

Services and Facilities Visa services, ESL courses, counseling/support services.

Applying TOEFL: minimum score of 600, proof of adequate funds required. Financial aid is available to international students.

International Student Contact Ms. Signe Sugiyama, Admissions Officer, School of Business and International Studies, 50 Acacia Avenue, San Rafael, CA 94901-2298. Phone: 415-257-1359; Fax: 415-459-3206; E-mail: pbsadm@dominican.edu

PLACEMENT

Services include alumni network, career counseling/planning, career library, electronic job bank, job interviews arranged, resume referral to employers, and resume preparation.

Employment Of 1996–97 graduates, 75% were employed within three months of graduation; the average starting salary was $45,000. Types of employ-

ment entered: banking, computer-related, consulting, education, finance, financial services, high technology, human resources, insurance, international trade, management, manufacturing, marketing, nonprofit, telecommunications, transportation.

Business Program(s) URL: http://www.dominican.edu/Schools/BIS/PBS/

Program Contact: Ms. Signe Sugiyama, Admissions Officer, School of Business and International Studies, 50 Acacia Avenue, San Rafael, CA 94901-2298. Phone: 415-257-1359; Fax: 415-459-3206; E-mail: pbsadm@dominican.edu

See full description on page 780.

Fielding Institute

Graduate Programs—Organizational Design and Effectiveness

Santa Barbara, California

OVERVIEW

Fielding Institute is an independent-nonprofit, coed, graduate institution. Enrollment: 1,112 graduate, professional, and undergraduate students; 1,112 full-time matriculated graduate/professional students; part-time matriculated graduate/professional students. Founded: 1974. The graduate business unit is on a terms calendar.

HIGHLIGHTS

Enrollment Profile
Full-time: 51
Part-time: 0
Total: 51
Average Age: N/R
Fall 1997 Average GPA: N/R

International: 0%
Women: 67%
Minorities: N/R
Average Class Size: 12
Fall 1997 Average GMAT: N/R

Costs
Full-time tuition: $4254 per academic year
Part-time tuition: N/R

GRADUATE BUSINESS PROGRAMS

MA in Organizational Design and Effectiveness (MA) Full-time, distance learning option; 52 total credits required; 20 months to complete program. Concentration in organizational behavior/development.

ADMISSION

Applications For fall 1997 there were 62 applications for admission. Of those applying, 58 were accepted. Of those accepted, 51 enrolled.

Application Requirements Application form, bachelor's degree, essay, letters of recommendation, personal statement, resume, college transcript(s), work experience, computer experience: computer literacy.

Application Deadline 6/1 for fall, 11/1 for winter, 6/1 for fall (international). Application fee: $75.

ACADEMICS

Teaching Methodologies Case study, computer-aided instruction, experiential learning, faculty seminars, group discussion, research, role playing, seminars by members of the business community, simulations, student presentations, study groups, Capstone Seminar and Grand Rounds.

Technology The network has full access to the Internet. Students are required to have their own PC.

FINANCES

Costs for 1997–98 Tuition: Full-time: $4254 per term.

Financial Aid Scholarships, loans available.

Financial Aid Contact Raul Aldama, Financial Aid Officer, Santa Barbara, CA 93105. Phone: 805-687-1099 Ext. 4008; Fax: 805-687-9793; E-mail: rmaldama@fielding.edu

FACILITIES

Information Resources Access provided to online bibliographic retrieval services.

INTERNATIONAL STUDENTS

Demographics N/R

Applying Financial aid is not available to international students.

Program Contact: Mrs. Sylvia Williams, Director, Enrollment Management Services, Santa Barbara, CA 93105. Phone: 805-687-1099 Ext. 4008, 800-340-1099 (CA only); Fax: 805-687-9793; E-mail: sawilliams@fielding.edu

Fresno Pacific University

Fresno Pacific Graduate School

Fresno, California

OVERVIEW

Fresno Pacific University is an independent-religious, coed, comprehensive institution. Enrollment: 1,579 graduate, professional, and undergraduate students; full-time matriculated graduate/professional students; 701 part-time matriculated graduate/professional students. Founded: 1944. The graduate business unit is in an urban setting and is on a trimester calendar.

HIGHLIGHTS

Enrollment Profile

Full-time: 0	International: 5%
Part-time: 40	Women: 25%
Total: 40	Minorities: N/R
Average Age: 34	Average Class Size: 8
Fall 1997 Average GPA: N/R	Fall 1997 Average GMAT: N/R

Costs
Full-time tuition: N/R
Part-time tuition: $3000 per semester

GRADUATE BUSINESS PROGRAMS

Master of Arts in Administrative Leadership (MA) Part-time; 37 total credits required; 16 months to 3 years to complete program. Concentrations in management, health care, entrepreneurship, nonprofit management, health care.

ADMISSION

Applications For fall 1997 there were 96 applications for admission. Of those applying, 60 were accepted. Of those accepted, 40 enrolled.

Application Requirements Application form, application fee, bachelor's degree, essay, interview, 3 letters of recommendation, personal statement, college transcript(s), minimum of 2 years of work experience.

Recommended for Application GMAT score accepted, GRE score accepted, computer experience.

Application Deadline Applications processed on a rolling/continuous basis for both domestic and international students. Application fee: $65.

ACADEMICS

Faculty Full-time 4; part-time 3.

Teaching Methodologies Case study, computer analysis, computer simulations, faculty seminars, field projects, group discussion, lecture, research, role playing, seminars by members of the business community, simulations, student presentations, team projects.

Technology 100 on-campus computer terminals/PCs are available for student use and are linked by a campus-wide network. The network has full access to the Internet. Students are not required to have their own PC.

Special Opportunities Advanced credit may be earned through transfer of credits from another institution.

FINANCES

Costs for 1997–98 Tuition: Part-time: $3000 per semester. Average 1997–98 room and board costs were $7200 per academic year (off campus). Room and board costs vary by type of accommodation.

Financial Aid In 1997–98, 90% of students received some institutionally administered aid. Financial aid is available to part-time students.

Financial Aid Contact Office of Financial Aid, 1717 South Chestnut Avenue, Fresno, CA 93702. Phone: 209-453-2016; Fax: 209-453-2001.

FACILITIES

Information Resources Hiebert Library; total holdings of 139,500 volumes, 102,000 microforms, 1,015 current periodical subscriptions. CD player(s) available for graduate student use. Access provided to online bibliographic retrieval services.

INTERNATIONAL STUDENTS

Demographics 5% of students enrolled are international students [Europe, 50%, South America, 50%].

Services and Facilities International student office, ESL courses, counseling/support services.

Applying TOEFL: minimum score of 550, proof of adequate funds, proof of health/immunizations required.

International Student Contact Philip Hofer, Director of International Programs and Services, 1717 South Chestnut Avenue, Fresno, CA 93702. Phone: 209-453-2069; Fax: 209-453-2001; E-mail: plhofer@fresno.edu

PLACEMENT

Services include alumni network, career counseling/planning, career library, and electronic job bank.

Business Program(s) URL: http://www.fresno.edu/grad

Program Contact: Dr. James Holm, Jr., MAAL Program Director, 1717 South Chestnut Avenue, Fresno, CA 93702. Phone: 209-453-3668; Fax: 209-453-2001; E-mail: jnholm@fresno.edu

Golden Gate University

School of Business

San Francisco, California

OVERVIEW

Golden Gate University is an independent-nonprofit, coed university. Enrollment: 5,646 graduate, professional, and undergraduate students; 1,400 full-time matriculated graduate/professional students; 2,759 part-time matriculated graduate/professional students. Founded: 1853. The graduate business unit is in an urban setting and is on a trimester calendar.

HIGHLIGHTS

Enrollment Profile

Full-time: 550	International: 24%
Part-time: 915	Women: 46%
Total: 1,465	Minorities: 26%
Average Age: 33	Average Class Size: 20
Fall 1997 Average GPA: N/R	Fall 1997 Average GMAT: N/R

Costs
Full-time tuition: N/R
Part-time tuition: $1404 per course

GRADUATE BUSINESS PROGRAMS

Master of Business Administration (MBA) Full-time, part-time, distance learning option; 36-48 total credits required; up to 6 years to complete program. Concentrations in accounting, entrepreneurship, finance, human resources, international business, management, marketing, organizational behavior/development, operations management.

Executive MBA (MBA) Full-time, part-time, distance learning option; 36 total credits required; up to 6 years to complete program.

Master of Science (MS) Full-time, part-time, distance learning option; 30-48 total credits required; up to 6 years to complete program. Concentrations in finance, human resources, marketing.

Master of Arts in Arts Administration (MA) Full-time, part-time, distance learning option; 36-42 total credits required; up to 6 years to complete program.

Master of Accountancy (MAcc) Full-time, part-time, distance learning option; 30-51 total credits required; up to 6 years to complete program. Concentration in accounting.

ADMISSION

Applications For fall 1997 there were 761 applications for admission. Of those applying, 567 were accepted. Of those accepted, 390 enrolled.

Application Requirements Application form, application fee, bachelor's degree, essay, minimum GPA: 2.5, interview, personal statement, resume, college transcript(s), minimum of 5 years of work experience.

Recommended for Application GMAT score accepted.

Application Deadline Applications processed on a rolling/continuous basis for domestic students only. 7/1 for fall (international), 11/1 for spring (international), 3/1 for summer (international). Application fee: $55, $70 (international). Deferred entrance is available.

ACADEMICS

Teaching Methodologies Case study, computer-aided instruction, computer simulations, faculty seminars, group discussion, research, role playing, seminars by members of the business community, student presentations.

Technology 150 on-campus computer terminals/PCs are available for student use and are linked by a campus-wide network. The network has full access to the Internet. Students are not required to have their own PC.

Special Opportunities Advanced credit may be earned through credit for military training programs, transfer of credits from another institution. An internship program is available.

FINANCES

Costs for 1997–98 Tuition: $1404 per course. Cost varies by academic program, campus location. Average 1997–98 room and board costs were $7200 per academic year (off campus).

Financial Aid Work study, loans available. Financial aid is available to part-time students.

Financial Aid Contact Financial Aid Officer, 536 Mission Street, San Francisco, CA 94105-2968. Phone: 415-442-7270; Fax: 415-442-7807; E-mail: info@ggu.edu

FACILITIES

Information Resources Golden Gate University Library plus 1 additional on-campus library; total holdings of 126,486 volumes, 709,319 microforms, 1,500 current periodical subscriptions. CD player(s) available for graduate student use. Access provided to online bibliographic retrieval services.

INTERNATIONAL STUDENTS

Demographics 24% of students enrolled are international students.

Services and Facilities International student office, international student center, ESL courses, counseling/support services.

Applying TOEFL: minimum score of 550, proof of adequate funds, proof of health/immunizations required. Financial aid is available to international students.

International Student Contact Mr. Arthur Levine, Assistant Dean, International Student Services, 536 Mission Street, San Francisco, CA 94105-2968. Phone: 415-442-7291; Fax: 415-442-7284.

PLACEMENT

Services include alumni network, career counseling/planning, career fairs, career library, and resume preparation.

Employment Types of employment entered: accounting, banking, communications, computer-related, consulting, finance, financial services, government, health services, hospitality management, human resources, information systems/technology, insurance, international trade, management, marketing, media, real estate, retail, service industry, telecommunications.

Business Program(s) URL: http://www.ggu.edu/schools/business/business.html

Program Contact: Enrollment Services, 536 Mission Street, San Francisco, CA 94105-2968. Phone: 415-442-7800, 800-448-4968; Fax: 415-442-7807; E-mail: info@ggu.edu

See full description on page 834.

Holy Names College

Department of Business Administration and Economics

Oakland, California

OVERVIEW

Holy Names College is an independent-religious, coed, comprehensive institution. Enrollment: 950 graduate, professional, and undergraduate students. Founded: 1868. The graduate business unit is in an urban setting and is on a trimester calendar.

HIGHLIGHTS

Enrollment Profile
Full-time: N/R
Part-time: N/R
Total: 30
Average Age: N/R
Fall 1997 Average GPA: 3.0

International: N/R
Women: N/R
Minorities: N/R
Average Class Size: 15
Fall 1997 Average GMAT: N/R

Costs
Full-time tuition: N/R
Part-time tuition: $375 per unit

GRADUATE BUSINESS PROGRAMS

Master of Business Administration (MBA) Full-time, part-time; 23 total credits required; 15 months to 6 years to complete program. Concentrations in management, finance, marketing.

ADMISSION

Applications For fall 1997 there were 25 applications for admission.

Application Requirements Application form, application fee, bachelor's degree, minimum GPA: 2.6, 3 letters of recommendation, college transcript(s).

Recommended for Application Interview, work experience, computer experience.

Application Deadline 8/1 for fall, 12/1 for winter, 3/1 for spring, 8/1 for fall (international), 11/15 for winter (international), 2/15 for spring (international). Application fee: $35. Deferred entrance is available.

ACADEMICS

Faculty Full-time 4.

Teaching Methodologies Case study, computer-aided instruction, faculty seminars, group discussion, lecture, research, seminars by members of the business community, student presentations, study groups, team projects.

Technology 25 on-campus computer terminals/PCs are available for student use and are linked by a campus-wide network. The network has full access to the Internet. Students are not required to have their own PC.

Special Opportunities Advanced credit may be earned through transfer of credits from another institution. An internship program is available.

FINANCES

Costs for 1997–98 Tuition: $375 per unit. Fees: $100 per trimester. Average 1997–98 room and board costs were $5000 per academic year (on campus) and $6000 per academic year (off campus). Room and board costs vary by occupancy (e.g., single, double, triple), type of meal plan.

Financial Aid Work study available. Financial aid is available to part-time students. Application Deadline: 3/2.

Financial Aid Contact Director of Financial Aid, 3500 Mountain Boulevard, Oakland, CA 94619-1699. Phone: 510-436-1328; Fax: 510-436-1199.

FACILITIES

Information Resources Paul J. Cushing Library; total holdings of 109,067 volumes, 45,500 microforms, 448 current periodical subscriptions. CD player(s) available for graduate student use. Access provided to online bibliographic retrieval services.

INTERNATIONAL STUDENTS

Demographics N/R

Services and Facilities International student office, international student center, ESL courses.

Applying TOEFL, proof of adequate funds required.

International Student Contact Mr. Xavier Romano, Vice President for Student Services, 3500 Mountain Boulevard, Oakland, CA 94619-1699. Phone: 510-436-1113; Fax: 510-436-1199.

PLACEMENT

Services include career counseling/planning, career fairs, career placement, resume referral to employers, and resume preparation.

Employment Types of employment entered: accounting, banking, computer-related, consumer products, energy, finance, financial services, government, human resources, international trade, management, manufacturing, marketing, media, nonprofit, retail, service industry, telecommunications, transportation, utilities.

Program Contact: Dr. David Angrisani, Director of MBA Programs, 3500 Mountain Boulevard, Oakland, CA 94619-1699. Phone: 510-436-1465; Fax: 510-436-1199.

Hope International University

Graduate Management Program

Fullerton, California

OVERVIEW

Hope International University is an independent-religious, coed, comprehensive institution. Enrollment: 1,100 graduate, professional, and undergraduate students; 100 full-time matriculated graduate/professional students; 200 part-time matriculated graduate/professional students. Founded: 1928. The graduate business unit is in a suburban setting and is on a semester calendar.

HIGHLIGHTS

Enrollment Profile
Full-time: N/R
Part-time: N/R
Total: 80
Average Age: N/R
Fall 1997 Average GPA: N/R

International: N/R
Women: N/R
Minorities: N/R
Average Class Size: 8
Fall 1997 Average GMAT: N/R

Costs
Full-time tuition: N/R
Part-time tuition: $341 per credit

GRADUATE BUSINESS PROGRAMS

Master of Business Administration (MBA) Full-time, part-time, distance learning option; 48 total credits required; minimum of 2 years to complete program. Concentrations in nonprofit management, international development management.

Master of Science in Management (MS) Full-time, part-time, distance learning option; 36 total credits required; minimum of 2 years to complete program. Concentrations in international development management, nonprofit management.

ADMISSION

Application Requirements Application form, application fee, bachelor's degree, essay, 2 letters of recommendation, personal statement, college transcript(s).

Recommended for Application Work experience.

Application Deadline Applications processed on a rolling/continuous basis for both domestic and international students. Application fee: $100. Deferred entrance is available.

Hope International University (continued)

ACADEMICS

Faculty Full-time 5; part-time 11.

Teaching Methodologies Case study, computer-aided instruction, computer analysis, computer simulations, experiential learning, faculty seminars, field projects, group discussion, lecture, research, role playing, seminars by members of the business community, simulations, student presentations, study groups, team projects.

Technology 15 on-campus computer terminals/PCs are available for student use and are linked by a campus-wide network. The network has partial access to the Internet. Students are required to have their own PC.

Special Opportunities Advanced credit may be earned through transfer of credits from another institution. International exchange programs in Bolivia, Kenya, Philippines, United Kingdom. An internship program is available.

FINANCES

Costs for 1997–98 Tuition: $341 per credit.

Financial Aid Grants, scholarships available.

Financial Aid Contact Karen Adams, Financial Aid Office, 2500 East Nutwood Avenue, Fullerton, CA 92631-3138. Phone: 800-762-1294 Ext. 230.

FACILITIES

Information Resources Hurst Memorial Library; total holdings of 665,000 volumes. CD player(s) available for graduate student use. Access provided to online bibliographic retrieval services.

INTERNATIONAL STUDENTS

Demographics N/R

Services and Facilities International student office, international student center, international student housing, visa services, ESL courses, counseling/support services.

Applying TOEFL: minimum score of 550 required. Proof of adequate funds, proof of health/immunizations recommended.

PLACEMENT

Services include alumni network.

Employment Of 1996–97 graduates, 90% were employed within three months of graduation. Types of employment entered: information systems/technology, management, manufacturing, nonprofit.

Business Program(s) URL: http://www.hiu.edu/grad/programs.html

Program Contact: Connie Born, Admissions Director, 2500 East Nutwood Avenue, Fullerton, CA 92631-3138. Phone: 800-762-1294, 800-762-1294; E-mail: grad-office@hiu.edu

Humboldt State University

School of Business and Economics

Arcata, California

OVERVIEW

Humboldt State University is a state-supported, coed, comprehensive institution. Enrollment: 7,492 graduate, professional, and undergraduate students; 577 full-time matriculated graduate/professional students; 244 part-time matriculated graduate/professional students. Founded: 1913. The graduate business unit is in a small-town setting and is on a semester calendar.

HIGHLIGHTS

Enrollment Profile

Full-time: 6
Part-time: 16
Total: 22
Average Age: 33
Fall 1997 Average GPA: 3.2

International: 9%
Women: 55%
Minorities: 5%
Average Class Size: 10
Fall 1997 Average GMAT: 521

Costs

Full-time tuition: $1916 per academic year (resident); $1916 per academic year (nonresident)
Part-time tuition: $1250 per year (resident); $1250 per year (nonresident)

GRADUATE BUSINESS PROGRAMS

Master of Business Administration (MBA) Full-time, part-time; 31 total credits required; 2 to 7 years to complete program. Concentration in management.

ADMISSION

Applications For fall 1997 there were 8 applications for admission. Of those applying, 7 were accepted. Of those accepted, 5 enrolled.

Application Requirements Application form, application fee, bachelor's degree, minimum GPA: 2.5, personal statement, college transcript(s).

Recommended for Application GMAT score accepted, computer experience.

Application Deadline 5/15 for fall, 12/4 for spring, 11/30 for fall (international), 8/31 for spring (international). Application fee: $55. Deferred entrance is available.

ACADEMICS

Faculty Full-time 10; part-time 12.

Teaching Methodologies Case study, computer analysis, computer simulations, field projects, group discussion, lecture, research, simulations, student presentations, study groups, team projects.

Technology 50 on-campus computer terminals/PCs are available for student use and are linked by a campus-wide network. The network has full access to the Internet. Students are not required to have their own PC.

Special Opportunities Advanced credit may be earned through transfer of credits from another institution. International exchange programs in Australia, Brazil, Canada, Denmark, France, Germany, Israel, Italy, Japan, Mexico, New Zealand, Spain, Sweden, Taiwan, United Kingdom, Zimbabwe.

FINANCES

Costs for 1997–98 Tuition: Full-time: $1916 per year (resident); $1916 per year (nonresident). Part-time: $1250 per year (resident); $1250 per year (nonresident). Fees: Full-time: $246 per academic year. Part-time: $246 per unit. Fees vary by number of credits taken. Average 1997–98 room and board costs were $5391 per academic year (on campus) and $4888 per academic year (off campus). Room and board costs vary by occupancy (e.g., single, double, triple), type of accommodation, type of meal plan.

Financial Aid In 1997–98, 14% of students received some institutionally administered aid in the form of fellowships, work study. Financial aid is available to part-time students. Application Deadline: 3/1.

Financial Aid Contact Kay Burgess, Director, Financial Aid, Arcata, CA 95521-8299. Phone: 707-826-4321; Fax: 707-826-5360.

FACILITIES

Information Resources Main library; total holdings of 750,000 volumes, 460,000 microforms, 2,200 current periodical subscriptions. CD player(s) available for graduate student use. Access provided to online bibliographic retrieval services and online databases.

INTERNATIONAL STUDENTS

Demographics 9% of students enrolled are international students.

Services and Facilities International student office, visa services, ESL courses, counseling/support services.

Applying TOEFL: minimum score of 550, proof of adequate funds, proof of health/immunizations required. Financial aid is not available to international students.

International Student Contact Ms. Meryl Jewell, International Student Admissions Officer, Siemens Hall 210, Arcata, CA 95521-8299. Phone: 707-826-6199; Fax: 707-826-6194; E-mail: jewell@laurel.humboldt.edu

PLACEMENT

Services include alumni network, career counseling/planning, career fairs, career library, career placement, electronic job bank, job interviews arranged, job search course, resume referral to employers, and resume preparation. In 1996–97, 36 organizations participated in on-campus recruiting; 403 on-campus interviews were conducted.

Employment Of 1996–97 graduates, the average starting salary was $24,000. Types of employment entered: accounting, banking, computer-related, consulting, consumer products, education, finance, financial services, government, health services, human resources, information systems/technology, management, marketing.

Business Program(s) URL: http://sorrel.humboldt.edu/~sbe

Program Contact: Dr. Saeed Mortazavi, Director of MBA Program, School of Business and Economics, Arcata, CA 95521-8299. Phone: 707-826-3224; Fax: 707-826-6666; E-mail: sm5@axe.humboldt.edu

John F. Kennedy University

School of Management

Orinda, California

OVERVIEW
John F. Kennedy University is an independent-nonprofit, coed, comprehensive institution. Enrollment: 1,895 graduate, professional, and undergraduate students; 697 full-time matriculated graduate/professional students; 815 part-time matriculated graduate/professional students. Founded: 1964. The graduate business unit is in a suburban setting and is on a quarter calendar.

HIGHLIGHTS

Enrollment Profile

Full-time: 50	International: 2%
Part-time: 118	Women: 66%
Total: 168	Minorities: 24%
Average Age: 40	Average Class Size: 12
Fall 1997 Average GPA: N/R	Fall 1997 Average GMAT: N/R

Costs
Full-time tuition: N/R
Part-time tuition: $276 per unit

GRADUATE BUSINESS PROGRAMS
Master of Business Administration (MBA) Full-time, part-time; 52 total credits required; 2 to 3 years to complete program. Concentrations in management, financial management/planning, international business, leadership.

Master of Arts in Management (MA) Full-time; 54 total credits required; 2 years to complete program. Concentration in management.

ADMISSION
Applications For fall 1997 there were 52 applications for admission. Of those applying, 45 were accepted. Of those accepted, 34 enrolled.

Application Requirements Application form, application fee, bachelor's degree, minimum GPA: 2.0, interview, 2 letters of recommendation, personal statement, resume, college transcript(s).

Recommended for Application Minimum of 5 years of work experience.

Application Deadline Applications processed on a rolling/continuous basis for domestic students only. 6/30 for fall (international), 9/30 for winter (international), 12/30 for spring (international), 4/30 for summer (international). Application fee: $50. Deferred entrance is available.

ACADEMICS
Faculty Full-time 4; part-time 115.

Teaching Methodologies Case study, field projects, group discussion, lecture, student presentations, study groups, team projects.

Technology 10 on-campus computer terminals/PCs are available for student use. The network has full access to the Internet. Students are not required to have their own PC.

Special Opportunities Advanced credit may be earned through transfer of credits from another institution.

FINANCES
Costs for 1997–98 Tuition: $276 per unit. Cost varies by academic program. Fees: $9 per quarter. Fees vary by academic program. Average 1997–98 room and board costs were $9900 per academic year (off campus).

Financial Aid In 1997–98, 36% of students received some institutionally administered aid in the form of fellowships, loans. Financial aid is available to part-time students. Application Deadline: 3/2.

Financial Aid Contact Director of Financial Aid, 12 Altarinda Road, Orinda, CA 94563-2689. Phone: 925-258-2385; Fax: 925-254-6964.

FACILITIES
Information Resources Robert M. Fisher Library plus 4 additional on-campus libraries; total holdings of 77,587 volumes, 11 microforms, 1,212 current periodical subscriptions. CD player(s) available for graduate student use. Access provided to online bibliographic retrieval services.

INTERNATIONAL STUDENTS
Demographics 2% of students enrolled are international students.

Services and Facilities International student office, counseling/support services.

Applying TOEFL: minimum score of 550, TWE: minimum score of 3, proof of adequate funds, proof of health/immunizations required. Financial aid is not available to international students.

International Student Contact Susan Sermeno, International Student Advisor, 12 Altarinda Road, Orinda, CA 94563-2689. Phone: 925-258-2339; Fax: 925-254-6964.

PLACEMENT
Services include career counseling/planning, career library, job search course, and resume preparation.

Program Contact: Ellena Bloedorn, Director of Admissions and Records, 12 Altarinda Road, Orinda, CA 94563-2689. Phone: 925-258-2213; Fax: 925-254-6964.

La Sierra University

School of Business and Management

Riverside, California

OVERVIEW
La Sierra University is an independent-religious, coed, comprehensive institution. Enrollment: 1,602 graduate, professional, and undergraduate students; 24 full-time matriculated graduate/professional students; 205 part-time matriculated graduate/professional students. Founded: 1922. The graduate business unit is in a suburban setting and is on a quarter calendar.

HIGHLIGHTS

Enrollment Profile

Full-time: 23	International: 88%
Part-time: 1	Women: 21%
Total: 24	Minorities: 4%
Average Age: 28	Average Class Size: 12
Fall 1997 Average GPA: 3.2	Fall 1997 Average GMAT: 500

Costs
Full-time tuition: N/R
Part-time tuition: $384 per unit

GRADUATE BUSINESS PROGRAMS
Master of Business Administration (MBA) Full-time, part-time; 56 total credits required; 15 months to 5 years to complete program. Concentrations in accounting, finance, human resources, management, marketing.

ADMISSION
Application Requirements Application form, application fee, bachelor's degree, minimum GPA: 2.75, 2 letters of recommendation, personal statement, college transcript(s).

Recommended for Application GMAT score accepted, interview, resume, computer experience.

Application Deadline Applications processed on a rolling/continuous basis for both domestic and international students. Application fee: $30. Deferred entrance is available.

ACADEMICS
Faculty Full-time 5; part-time 6.

Teaching Methodologies Case study, computer-aided instruction, computer analysis, group discussion, lecture, research, seminars by members of the business community, student presentations, study groups, team projects.

Technology 50 on-campus computer terminals/PCs are available for student use and are linked by a campus-wide network. Students are not required to have their own PC.

Special Opportunities Advanced credit may be earned through transfer of credits from another institution.

FINANCES
Costs for 1997–98 Tuition: $384 per unit. Average 1997–98 room and board costs were $3882 per academic year. Room and board costs vary by occupancy (e.g., single, double, triple), type of accommodation, type of meal plan.

Financial Aid In 1997–98, 46% of students received some institutionally administered aid in the form of scholarships, work study. Application Deadline: 5/15.

Financial Aid Contact Financial Aid Office, 4700 Pierce Street, Riverside, CA 92515. Phone: 909-785-2175.

FACILITIES
Information Resources Main library; total holdings of 223,791 volumes, 285,572 microforms, 1,331 current periodical subscriptions. CD player(s) available for graduate student use. Access provided to online bibliographic retrieval services.

INTERNATIONAL STUDENTS
Demographics 88% of students enrolled are international students.

Services and Facilities International student office, ESL courses, counseling/support services.

Applying TOEFL: minimum score of 550, proof of adequate funds, proof of health/immunizations required.

International Student Contact Mrs. Jennifer Tyner, International Student Office, 4700 Pierce Street, Riverside, CA 92515. Phone: 909-785-2237.

La Sierra University (continued)

PLACEMENT

Services include career counseling/planning, career fairs, and resume preparation. In 1996–97, 40 organizations participated in on-campus recruiting.

Employment Of 1996–97 graduates, 100% were employed within three months of graduation. Types of employment entered: accounting, banking, communications, computer-related, consumer products, finance, hospitality management, human resources, information systems/technology, insurance, management, marketing.

Program Contact: Dr. Myrna Costa, Director of Admissions, 4700 Pierce Street, Riverside, CA 92515. Phone: 909-785-2176.

Lincoln University

Graduate Business Administration Program

San Francisco, California

OVERVIEW

Lincoln University is an independent-nonprofit, coed, comprehensive institution. Enrollment: 311 graduate, professional, and undergraduate students; 137 full-time matriculated graduate/professional students; part-time matriculated graduate/professional students. Founded: 1919. The graduate business unit is in an urban setting and is on a semester calendar.

HIGHLIGHTS

Enrollment Profile

Full-time: 137	International: 92%
Part-time: 0	Women: 45%
Total: 137	Minorities: 8%
Average Age: 26	Average Class Size: 30
Fall 1997 Average GPA: 3.1	Fall 1997 Average GMAT: N/R

Costs
Full-time tuition: N/R
Part-time tuition: $230 per credit hour

GRADUATE BUSINESS PROGRAMS

Master of Business Administration (MBA) Full-time, part-time; 36-60 total credits required; 12 months to 2 years to complete program. Concentrations in international business, asian business studies, management information systems, management.

ADMISSION

Applications For fall 1997 there were 87 applications for admission. Of those applying, 61 were accepted. Of those accepted, 31 enrolled.

Application Requirements Application form, application fee, bachelor's degree, minimum GPA: 2.7, college transcript(s).

Recommended for Application Letters of recommendation.

Application Deadline Applications processed on a rolling/continuous basis for both domestic and international students. Application fee: $50. Deferred entrance is available.

ACADEMICS

Faculty Full-time 5; part-time 8.

Teaching Methodologies Case study, computer-aided instruction, computer analysis, computer simulations, experiential learning, faculty seminars, field projects, group discussion, lecture, research, role playing, simulations, student presentations, study groups, team projects.

Technology 27 on-campus computer terminals/PCs are available for student use. The network has full access to the Internet. Students are not required to have their own PC.

Special Opportunities Advanced credit may be earned through transfer of credits from another institution. An internship program is available.

FINANCES

Costs for 1997–98 Tuition: $230 per credit hour. Cost varies by academic program, number of credits taken. Fees: $150 per semester. Fees vary by academic program. Average 1997–98 room and board costs were $5600 per academic year (off campus). Room and board costs vary by type of accommodation.

Financial Aid Scholarships available.

Financial Aid Contact Dr. Clarence Rippel, President, 281 Masonic Avenue, San Francisco, CA 94118-4498. Phone: 415-221-1212 Ext. 134; Fax: 415-387-9730.

FACILITIES

Information Resources Main library; total holdings of 17,532 volumes, 5,270 microforms, 642 current periodical subscriptions. CD player(s) available for graduate student use. Access provided to online bibliographic retrieval services.

INTERNATIONAL STUDENTS

Demographics 92% of students enrolled are international students [Asia, 87%, other, 13%].

Services and Facilities International student office, visa services, ESL courses, counseling/support services.

Applying Proof of adequate funds required. TOEFL recommended. Financial aid is available to international students.

International Student Contact Dr. Pete Bogue, Director of Admissions/Registrar, 281 Masonic Avenue, San Francisco, CA 94118-4498. Phone: 415-221-1212 Ext. 116; Fax: 415-387-9730.

PLACEMENT

Services include career counseling/planning, career fairs, career library, job search course, resume referral to employers, and resume preparation.

Employment Of 1996–97 graduates, 75% were employed within three months of graduation. Types of employment entered: accounting, banking, computer-related, consumer products, finance, financial services, hospitality management, human resources, information systems/technology, international trade, management, marketing, real estate, retail.

Business Program(s) URL: http://www.lincolnuca.edu

Program Contact: Maria Delos Reyes, Admissions Officer, 281 Masonic Avenue, San Francisco, CA 94118-4498. Phone: 415-221-1212 Ext. 115; Fax: 415-387-9730.

Loyola Marymount University

College of Business Administration

Los Angeles, California

OVERVIEW

Loyola Marymount University is an independent-religious, coed, comprehensive institution. Enrollment: 5,400 graduate, professional, and undergraduate students; 817 full-time matriculated graduate/professional students; 470 part-time matriculated graduate/professional students. Founded: 1911. The graduate business unit is in a suburban setting and is on a semester calendar.

HIGHLIGHTS

Enrollment Profile

Full-time: 333	International: 5%
Part-time: 130	Women: 46%
Total: 463	Minorities: 28%
Average Age: 28	Average Class Size: 25
Fall 1997 Average GPA: 3.2	Fall 1997 Average GMAT: 550

Costs
Full-time tuition: $590 per academic year
Part-time tuition: $590 per unit

AACSB – The International Association for Management Education accredited

Degree(s) offered in conjunction with Loyola Law School

T *he flexibility of Loyola Marymount University's M.B.A. program attracts both fully employed professionals who attend on a part-time basis and full-time students. Classes are offered year-round, with all classes scheduled in the late afternoon and evening. The M.B.A. program is accredited by the American Assembly of Collegiate Schools of Business. More than 90 percent of all classes are taught by faculty members with doctorates from prestigious universities.*

Classes are held in a variety of state-of-the-art student-centered classrooms in the magnificent Conrad N. Hilton Center for Business. The facility offers M.B.A. students access to many advanced technological features.

M.B.A. students participate in case competitions during the annual Business Ethics Fortnight. Loyola Marymount's commitment to business ethics has been enhanced by the recent appointment of Dr. Thomas White to the Hilton Chair in Business Ethics.

The international program has been enhanced by the addition of a semester-long foreign experience available through an exchange program with the EDHEC Graduate School of Business in Lille, France. In addition, students find the comparative-management-systems sequence, featuring visits to a number of foreign companies over a three-week period, to be very valuable.

GRADUATE BUSINESS PROGRAMS

Master of Business Administration (MBA) Full-time, part-time; 30 total credits required; 12 months to 5 years to complete program. Concentrations in entrepreneurship, finance, human resources, international business, international finance, international management, international marketing, management, management information systems, marketing, accounting, business policy/strategy.

Master of Business Administration/Doctor of Jurisprudence (MBA/JD) Full-time; 30 total credits required; 12 months to 5 years to complete program. Concentration in business law.

Master of Business Administration for International Managers (MBA) Full-time; 45 total credits required; 12 months to complete program.

ADMISSION

Applications For fall 1997 there were 346 applications for admission. Of those applying, 243 were accepted. Of those accepted, 142 enrolled.

Application Requirements Application form, application fee, bachelor's degree, essay, 2 letters of recommendation, personal statement, resume, college transcript(s).

Recommended for Application GMAT score accepted: minimum 400, work experience, computer experience.

Application Deadline Applications processed on a rolling/continuous basis for both domestic and international students. Application fee: $35. Deferred entrance is available.

ACADEMICS

Faculty Full-time 42; part-time 10.

Teaching Methodologies Case study, computer analysis, computer simulations, field projects, group discussion, lecture, research, role playing, simulations, student presentations, team projects.

Technology 200 on-campus computer terminals/PCs are available for student use and are linked by a campus-wide network. The network has full access to the Internet. Students are not required to have their own PC.

Special Opportunities Advanced credit may be earned through credit by examination, transfer of credits from another institution. International exchange program in France.

FINANCES

Costs for 1997–98 Tuition: Full-time: $590 per unit. Part-time: $590 per unit. Fees: Full-time: $403 per academic year. Part-time: $69 per year. Fees vary by number of credits taken.

Financial Aid In 1997–98, 22% of students received some institutionally administered aid in the form of research assistantships, grants, scholarships, work study, loans. Financial aid is available to part-time students.

Financial Aid Contact Mr. Wil Del Pilar, Graduate Financial Aid Counselor, 7900 Loyola Boulevard, Los Angeles, CA 90045-8350. Phone: 310-338-2753; Fax: 310-338-2793.

FACILITIES

Information Resources Charles Von der Ahe Library; total holdings of 351,000 volumes, 101,000 microforms, 2,900 current periodical subscriptions. CD player(s) available for graduate student use. Access provided to online bibliographic retrieval services and online databases.

INTERNATIONAL STUDENTS

Demographics 5% of students enrolled are international students [Africa, 1%, Asia, 63%, Central America, 5%, Europe, 26%, North America, 2%, South America, 3%].

Services and Facilities International student office, international student center, visa services, counseling/support services.

Applying TOEFL: minimum score of 600, proof of adequate funds, proof of health/immunizations required. Financial aid is available to international students.

International Student Contact Ms. Sandrell Doerr, International Services Coordinator, 7900 Loyola Boulevard, Los Angeles, CA 90045. Phone: 310-338-2937; Fax: 310-338-5976; E-mail: sdoerr@lmumail.lmu.edu

PLACEMENT

Services include alumni network, career counseling/planning, career fairs, career library, career placement, electronic job bank, job interviews arranged, resume referral to employers, and resume preparation.

Employment Types of employment entered: accounting, banking, communications, computer-related, consulting, consumer products, finance, financial services, health services, high technology, human resources, information systems/technology, insurance, international trade, law, management, manufacturing, marketing, media, nonprofit, pharmaceutical, real estate, service industry, telecommunications.

Business Program(s) URL: http://www.lmu.edu/colleges/cba/mba

Program Contact: Ms. Charisse Woods, Coordinator, MBA Program, 7900 Loyola Boulevard, Los Angeles, CA 90045-8387. Phone: 310-338-2848, 888-946-5681 (CA only); Fax: 310-338-2899; E-mail: cwoods@lmumail.lmu.edu
See full description on page 876.

Monterey Institute of International Studies

Fisher Graduate School of Business Management

Monterey, California

OVERVIEW

Monterey Institute of International Studies is an independent-nonprofit, coed, upper-level institution. Enrollment: 770 graduate, professional, and undergraduate students. Founded: 1955. The graduate business unit is in a small-town setting and is on a semester calendar.

HIGHLIGHTS

Enrollment Profile

Full-time: 180	International: 19%
Part-time: 10	Women: 39%
Total: 190	Minorities: N/R
Average Age: 28	Average Class Size: 20
Fall 1997 Average GPA: 3.2	Fall 1997 Average GMAT: 550

Costs
Full-time tuition: $18,200 per academic year
Part-time tuition: $760 per credit

GRADUATE BUSINESS PROGRAMS

Master of Business Administration (MBA) Full-time, part-time; 64 total credits required; 10 months to 2 years to complete program. Concentrations in international trade, international marketing, entrepreneurship, human resources, international economics, international finance, decision sciences, nonprofit management.

ADMISSION

Applications For fall 1997 there were 120 applications for admission. Of those applying, 91 were accepted. Of those accepted, 48 enrolled.

Application Requirements GMAT score, application form, application fee, bachelor's degree, essay, minimum GPA: 3.0, 2 letters of recommendation, personal statement, resume, college transcript(s).

Recommended for Application Interview, computer experience.

Application Deadline Applications processed on a rolling/continuous basis for both domestic and international students. Application fee: $50.

ACADEMICS

Faculty Full-time 35; part-time 30.

Teaching Methodologies Case study, computer analysis, computer simulations, experiential learning, field projects, group discussion, lecture, research, role playing, simulations, student presentations, study groups, team projects.

Technology 70 on-campus computer terminals/PCs are available for student use and are linked by a campus-wide network. The network has full access to the Internet. Students are not required to have their own PC.

Special Opportunities Advanced credit may be earned through credit by examination, transfer of credits from another institution. International exchange programs in France, Japan, Mexico, People's Republic of China, Russia.

FINANCES

Costs for 1997–98 Tuition: Full-time: $18,200 per year. Part-time: $760 per credit. Average 1997–98 room and board costs were $7500 per academic year (off campus).

Financial Aid In 1997–98, 63% of students received some institutionally administered aid in the form of research assistantships, grants, scholarships, work study, loans. Application Deadline: 3/15.

Financial Aid Contact Mr. Michael Benson, Director of Financial Aid, 425 Van Buren Street, Monterey, CA 93940. Phone: 408-647-4119; Fax: 408-647-4199; E-mail: mbenson@miis.edu

FACILITIES

Information Resources Barnet J. Segal Library; total holdings of 68,000 volumes, 550 current periodical subscriptions. CD player(s) available for graduate student use. Access provided to online bibliographic retrieval services.

INTERNATIONAL STUDENTS

Demographics 19% of students enrolled are international students [Africa, 2%, Asia, 68%, Central America, 2%, Europe, 24%, North America, 2%, South America, 2%].

Services and Facilities International student office, international student housing, visa services, ESL courses, counseling/support services.

Applying TOEFL: minimum score of 550, proof of adequate funds required. Financial aid is available to international students.

International Student Contact Mrs. Jane Roberts, International Admissions Officer, 425 Van Buren Street, Monterey, CA 93940-2691. Phone: 408-647-4124; Fax: 408-647-4188; E-mail: jroberts@miis.edu

PLACEMENT

Services include alumni network, career counseling/planning, career fairs, career library, career placement, resume referral to employers, and resume

Monterey Institute of International Studies (continued)

preparation. In 1996–97, 35 organizations participated in on-campus recruiting; 85 on-campus interviews were conducted.

Employment Of 1996–97 graduates, 60% were employed within three months of graduation; the average starting salary was $45,000. Types of employment entered: accounting, consulting, finance, government, human resources, international trade, management, marketing, nonprofit.

Business Program(s) URL: http://www.miis.edu

Program Contact: Ms. Berta Aug, Director of Recruiting and Admissions, 425 Van Buren Street, Monterey, CA 93940-2691. Phone: 408-647-3530; Fax: 408-647-6405; E-mail: baug@miis.edu
See full description on page 888.

National University

School of Management and Technology

La Jolla, California

OVERVIEW
National University is an independent-nonprofit, coed, comprehensive institution. Enrollment: 11,303 graduate, professional, and undergraduate students; 5,307 full-time matriculated graduate/professional students; 2,165 part-time matriculated graduate/professional students. Founded: 1971. The graduate business unit is in an urban setting and is on a quarter calendar.

HIGHLIGHTS

Enrollment Profile

Full-time: 1,026	International: N/R
Part-time: 0	Women: N/R
Total: 1,026	Minorities: N/R
Average Age: 34	Average Class Size: 17
Fall 1997 Average GPA: 3.5	Fall 1997 Average GMAT: N/R

Costs
Full-time tuition: N/R
Part-time tuition: $870 per course

GRADUATE BUSINESS PROGRAMS
Master of Business Administration (MBA) Full-time, part-time; 70 total credits required; minimum of 13 months to complete program. Concentrations in accounting, health care, human resources, marketing, public policy and administration, technology management, telecommunications management, environmental economics/management, entrepreneurship, international business, international management.

Global MBA (GMBA) Full-time, part-time, distance learning option; 60 total credits required; minimum of 12 months to complete program.

Master of Arts in International Business Administration (MA) Full-time, part-time; 60 total credits required; minimum of 12 months to complete program. Concentration in international business.

Master of Science in Technology Management (MS) Full-time, part-time; 60 total credits required; minimum of 12 months to complete program. Concentration in technology management.

Master of Arts in Human Resources Management (MA) Full-time, part-time; 60 total credits required; minimum of 12 months to complete program. Concentration in human resources.

Master of Arts in Management (MA) Full-time, part-time; 60 total credits required; minimum of 12 months to complete program. Concentration in management.

Master of Science in Telecommunication Systems Management (MS) Full-time, part-time; 60 total credits required; minimum of 12 months to complete program. Concentration in telecommunications management.

Master of Environmental Management (MEM) Full-time, part-time; 60 total credits required; minimum of 12 months to complete program. Concentration in environmental economics/management.

Master of Health Care Administration (MHCA) Full-time, part-time; 75 total credits required; minimum of 15 months to complete program. Concentration in health care.

ADMISSION
Applications For fall 1997 there were 198 applications for admission. Of those applying, 198 were accepted. Of those accepted, 198 enrolled.

Application Requirements Application form, application fee, bachelor's degree, minimum GPA: 2.0, interview, college transcript(s), minimum of 4 years of work experience.

Application Deadline Applications processed on a rolling/continuous basis for both domestic and international students. Application fee: $60, $100 (international). Deferred entrance is available.

ACADEMICS
Faculty Full-time 25; part-time 113.

Teaching Methodologies Case study, group discussion, lecture, research, seminars by members of the business community, student presentations, study groups, team projects.

Technology 500 on-campus computer terminals/PCs are available for student use and are linked by a campus-wide network. The network has full access to the Internet. Students are not required to have their own PC.

Special Opportunities Advanced credit may be earned through transfer of credits from another institution.

FINANCES
Costs for 1997–98 Tuition: $870 per course. Cost varies by number of credits taken.

Financial Aid Fellowships, work study, loans available. Application Deadline: 5/1.

Financial Aid Contact Mr. Matt Levine, Director of Financial Aid, 11255 North Torrey Pines Road, La Jolla, CA 92037-1011. Phone: 619-642-8512; Fax: 619-642-8720.

FACILITIES
Information Resources Main library; total holdings of 154,942 volumes, 1,366,000 microforms, 2,540 current periodical subscriptions. CD player(s) available for graduate student use. Access provided to online bibliographic retrieval services.

INTERNATIONAL STUDENTS
Demographics N/R

Services and Facilities International student office, ESL courses, counseling/support services, international student orientation.

Applying TOEFL: minimum score of 550, proof of adequate funds required. Financial aid is not available to international students.

International Student Contact Ms. Tuey Carte, Director of International Student Services, 4121 Camino Del Rio South, San Diego, CA 92108-4107. Phone: 619-563-7206; Fax: 619-563-7393.

PLACEMENT
Services include electronic job bank, job search course, and resume preparation.

Business Program(s) URL: http://www.nu.edu

Program Contact: Mr. Terry Flanagan, Associate Director of Student Services, 4121 Camino Del Rio South, San Diego, CA 92108-4107. Phone: 619-563-7208, 800-628-8648; Fax: 619-563-2650; E-mail: kjones@nunic.nu.edu
See full description on page 890.

Naval Postgraduate School

Department of Systems Management

Monterey, California

OVERVIEW
Naval Postgraduate School is a federally supported, primarily male, graduate institution. Enrollment: 1,714 graduate, professional, and undergraduate students; 1,328 full-time matriculated graduate/professional students; part-time matriculated graduate/professional students. Founded: 1909. The graduate business unit is in a small-town setting and is on a quarter calendar.

HIGHLIGHTS

Enrollment Profile

Full-time: 403	International: 10%
Part-time: 0	Women: 16%
Total: 403	Minorities: 12%
Average Age: 28	Average Class Size: 23
Fall 1997 Average GPA: N/R	Fall 1997 Average GMAT: N/R

Costs
Full-time tuition: $9600 per academic year (resident); $9600 per academic year (nonresident)
Part-time tuition: N/R

GRADUATE BUSINESS PROGRAMS

Master of Science in Management (MS) Full-time, distance learning option; 112 total credits required; 18 months to 2 years to complete program. Concentrations in contract management, financial management/planning, leadership, logistics, management, management science, management systems analysis, manpower administration, materials management, project management, resources management, system management.

Master of Science in Information Technology Management (MS) Full-time, distance learning option; 128 total credits required; 21 months to 2 years to complete program. Concentrations in information management, management information systems, system management, technology management, telecommunications management.

Master of Science in International Resource Planning and Management (MS) Full-time, distance learning option; 96 total credits required; 18 to 21 months to complete program. Concentrations in international development management, international economics, managerial economics, resources management.

ADMISSION

Application Requirements Bachelor's degree, minimum GPA: 2.2, college transcript(s).

Recommended for Application Application form, computer experience.

Application Deadline 7/1 for fall, 10/1 for winter, 1/1 for spring, 5/1 for summer. Deferred entrance is available.

ACADEMICS

Faculty Full-time 75; part-time 5.

Teaching Methodologies Case study, computer-aided instruction, computer analysis, computer simulations, experiential learning, faculty seminars, field projects, group discussion, lecture, research, role playing, seminars by members of the business community, simulations, student presentations, study groups, team projects.

Technology 185 on-campus computer terminals/PCs are available for student use and are linked by a campus-wide network. The network has full access to the Internet. Students are not required to have their own PC.

Special Opportunities Advanced credit may be earned through credit by examination, transfer of credits from another institution. International exchange program in United Kingdom. An internship program is available.

FINANCES

Costs for 1997–98 Tuition: Full-time: $9600. Cost varies by academic program, number of credits taken. Average 1997–98 room and board costs were $10,000 per academic year (off campus).

FACILITIES

Information Resources Dudley Knox Library; total holdings of 400,000 volumes, 500,000 microforms, 1,200 current periodical subscriptions. CD player(s) available for graduate student use. Access provided to online bibliographic retrieval services.

INTERNATIONAL STUDENTS

Demographics 10% of students enrolled are international students [Africa, 10%, Asia, 25%, Australia/New Zealand, 5%, Europe, 25%, North America, 3%, South America, 20%, other, 12%].

Services and Facilities International student office, international student center, international student housing, visa services, ESL courses, counseling/support services.

Applying TOEFL, proof of health/immunizations required. TWE recommended. Financial aid is not available to international students.

International Student Contact Gary Roser, International Programs Officer, 699 Dyer Road, M-5, Monterey, CA 93943. Phone: 408-656-2186; E-mail: groser@nps.navy.mil

PLACEMENT

Services include alumni network, career counseling/planning, and career placement.

Employment Of 1996–97 graduates, 100% were employed within three months of graduation; the average starting salary was $42,000. Types of employment entered: accounting, education, financial services, government, high technology, information systems/technology, management, telecommunications.

Business Program(s) URL: http://web.nps.navy.mil/~sm/welcome.html

Program Contact: Theodore Calhoon, Director of Admissions, 589 Dyer Road, Room 103C, Monterey, CA 93943. Phone: 408-656-3093; Fax: 408-656-2891; E-mail: tcalhoon@nps.navy.mil

Pacific States University

College of Business

Los Angeles, California

OVERVIEW

Pacific States University is an independent-nonprofit, comprehensive institution. Enrollment: 103 graduate, professional, and undergraduate students.

HIGHLIGHTS

Enrollment Profile

Full-time: N/R	International: N/R
Part-time: N/R	Women: N/R
Total: 40	Minorities: N/R
Average Age: N/R	Average Class Size: N/R
Fall 1997 Average GPA: N/R	Fall 1997 Average GMAT: N/R

Costs
Full-time tuition: N/R
Part-time tuition: $200 per credit

GRADUATE BUSINESS PROGRAMS

Master of Business Administration (MBA) Full-time, part-time; 60 total credits required; minimum of 2 years to complete program. Concentrations in international business, finance, technology management.

ADMISSION

Application Requirements Application form, bachelor's degree, essay, minimum GPA: 3.0, college transcript(s).

Recommended for Application GMAT score accepted, resume.

Application Deadline Applications processed on a rolling/continuous basis for both domestic and international students. Application fee: $50, $100 (international).

ACADEMICS

Teaching Methodologies Case study, computer-aided instruction, computer analysis, experiential learning, faculty seminars, field projects, group discussion, lecture, research, role playing, seminars by members of the business community, student presentations, study groups, team projects.

FINANCES

Costs for 1997–98 Tuition: $200 per credit.

Financial Aid Contact Darren Kim, Admissions Officer, Los Angeles, CA 90006. Phone: 213-731-2383.

INTERNATIONAL STUDENTS

Demographics N/R

Services and Facilities International student center, international student housing, ESL courses, counseling/support services.

Applying TOEFL: minimum score of 450 required.

International Student Contact Darren Kim, Admissions Officer, Los Angeles, CA 90006. Phone: 213-731-2383.

Program Contact: Darren Kim, Admissions Officer, Los Angeles, CA 90006. Phone: 213-731-2383.

Pepperdine University

The George L. Graziadio School of Business and Management

Malibu, California

OVERVIEW

Pepperdine University is an independent-religious, coed, upper-level institution. Enrollment: 7,802 graduate, professional, and undergraduate students; 1,594 full-time matriculated graduate/professional students; 2,767 part-time matriculated graduate/professional students. Founded: 1937. The graduate business unit is in a suburban setting and is on a trimester calendar.

HIGHLIGHTS

Enrollment Profile

Full-time: 358	International: 5%
Part-time: 1,715	Women: 38%
Total: 2,073	Minorities: 23%
Average Age: 32	Average Class Size: 25
Fall 1997 Average GPA: 3.15	Fall 1997 Average GMAT: 580

Costs
Full-time tuition: $11,025 per academic year
Part-time tuition: $705 per credit

Pepperdine University (continued)

Degree(s) offered in conjunction with Pepperdine University School of Law

GRADUATE BUSINESS PROGRAMS

One-year MBA (MBA) Full-time; 48 total credits required; business undergraduate degree and minimum of 2 years full-time work experience required; 11 months to complete program. Concentrations in finance, marketing.

Two-year MBA (MBA) Full-time; 60 total credits required; 20 months to complete program. Concentrations in finance, marketing.

Master of Business Administration/Doctor of Jurisprudence (MBA/JD) Full-time; 130 total credits required; must apply separately to law school; 3.8 years to complete program. Concentrations in finance, marketing.

Master of International Business (MIB) Full-time; 56 total credits required; 20 months to complete program.

Professional MBA (MBA) Part-time; 48 total credits required; 2 to 7 years to complete program. Concentrations in finance, marketing.

Executive MBA (MBA) Part-time; 50 total credits required; 20 months to complete program. Concentration in strategic management.

Master of Science in Organization Development (MS) Part-time; 40 total credits required; 2 to 3 years to complete program.

Master of Science in Technology Management (MS) Part-time; 40 total credits required; 20 months to complete program.

Presidential/Key Executive MBA (MBA) Part-time; 50 total credits required; 20 months to complete program. Concentration in strategic management.

ADMISSION

Applications For fall 1997 there were 1,977 applications for admission. Of those applying, 1,366 were accepted. Of those accepted, 903 enrolled.

Application Requirements GMAT score, application form, application fee, bachelor's degree, essay, minimum GPA, 2 letters of recommendation, personal statement, resume, college transcript(s).

Recommended for Application Interview, work experience, computer experience.

Application Deadline 5/1 for fall, 2/15 for spring, 5/1 for fall (international), 2/15 for spring (international). Application fee: $45. Deferred entrance is available.

ACADEMICS

Faculty Full-time 67; part-time 72.

Teaching Methodologies Case study, computer analysis, computer simulations, experiential learning, field projects, group discussion, lecture, research, role playing, seminars by members of the business community, simulations, student presentations, study groups, team projects.

Technology 35 on-campus computer terminals/PCs are available for student use and are linked by a campus-wide network. The network has full access to the Internet. Students are not required to have their own PC.

Special Opportunities Advanced credit may be earned through transfer of credits from another institution. International exchange programs in Belgium, France, Germany, Hong Kong, Italy, Mexico, Netherlands, People's Republic of China, Philippines, Spain, Thailand. An internship program is available.

FINANCES

Costs for 1997–98 Tuition: Full-time: $11,025 per trimester. Part-time: $705 per credit. Cost varies by academic program, campus location, class time (e.g., day/evening), number of credits taken. Fees: Full-time: $25 per academic year. Fees vary by academic program, campus location, class time (e.g., day/evening), number of credits taken. Average 1997–98 room and board costs were $7400 per academic year (on campus) and $6500 per academic year (off campus). Room and board costs vary by occupancy (e.g., single, double, triple), type of accommodation, type of meal plan.

Financial Aid In 1997–98, 63% of students received some institutionally administered aid in the form of scholarships, loans. Financial aid is available to part-time students.

Financial Aid Contact Ms. Sandi Ford, Associate Director for Financial Aid, 400 Corporate Pointe, Culver City, CA 90230. Phone: 310-568-5530; Fax: 310-568-5779.

FACILITIES

Information Resources Payson Library plus 6 additional on-campus libraries; total holdings of 475,579 volumes, 315,542 microforms, 3,159 current periodical subscriptions. CD player(s) available for graduate student use. Access provided to online bibliographic retrieval services and online databases.

INTERNATIONAL STUDENTS

Demographics 5% of students enrolled are international students.

Services and Facilities International student office, international student center, international student housing, visa services, ESL courses, counseling/support services, tax filing seminar.

Applying TOEFL: minimum score of 550, proof of adequate funds, proof of health/immunizations required. Financial aid is available to international students.

International Student Contact Mr. Richard Dawson, Director, International Student Services, 24255 Pacific Coast Highway, Malibu, CA 90263-4246. Phone: 310-456-4246; Fax: 310-317-7403; E-mail: rdawson@pepperdine.edu

PLACEMENT

Services include alumni network, career counseling/planning, career fairs, career library, career placement, electronic job bank, job interviews arranged, resume referral to employers, and resume preparation. In 1996–97, 62 organizations participated in on-campus recruiting; 350 on-campus interviews were conducted.

Employment Of 1996–97 graduates, 70% were employed within three months of graduation; the average starting salary was $57,500. Types of employment entered: banking, communications, computer-related, consulting, consumer products, engineering, finance, financial services, health services, high technology, hospitality management, human resources, information systems/technology, international trade, law, management, manufacturing, marketing, media, pharmaceutical, retail, service industry, telecommunications.

Business Program(s) URL: http://bschool.pepperdine.edu

Program Contact: Ms. Stacie Rathel, Associate Director of Marketing, 24255 Pacific Coast Highway, Malibu, CA 90263-4100. Phone: 310-456-4858, 800-726-9283 (CA only); Fax: 310-456-4876; E-mail: gsbmadm@pepperdine.edu

See full description on page 924.

Saint Mary's College of California

School of Economics and Business Administration

Moraga, California

OVERVIEW

Saint Mary's College of California is an independent-religious, coed, comprehensive institution. Enrollment: 4,100 graduate, professional, and undergraduate students; 1,200 full-time matriculated graduate/professional students; 800 part-time matriculated graduate/professional students. Founded: 1863. The graduate business unit is in a small-town setting and is on a quarter calendar.

HIGHLIGHTS

Enrollment Profile

Full-time: 197	International: 2%
Part-time: 155	Women: 32%
Total: 351	Minorities: 15%
Average Age: 32	Average Class Size: 23
Fall 1997 Average GPA: 3.0	Fall 1997 Average GMAT: 570

Costs
Full-time tuition: N/R
Part-time tuition: $340 per quarter unit

GRADUATE BUSINESS PROGRAMS

Master of Business Administration (MBA) Full-time, part-time; 72 total credits required; 12 months to 6 years to complete program. Concentrations in finance, international business, management, marketing.

Executive MBA (MBA) Part-time; 56 total credits required; 5 years work experience required; 21 months to complete program. Concentration in management.

Master of Business Administration in International Business (MBA) Full-time; 72 total credits required; 13 months to complete program. Concentration in international business.

ADMISSION

Applications For fall 1997 there were 183 applications for admission. Of those applying, 119 were accepted. Of those accepted, 106 enrolled.

Application Requirements GMAT score: minimum 500, application form, application fee, bachelor's degree, minimum GPA: 3.0, interview, 2 letters of recommendation, personal statement, college transcript(s).

Recommended for Application Resume, computer experience.

Application Deadline Applications processed on a rolling/continuous basis for both domestic and international students. Application fee: $40. Deferred entrance is available.

ACADEMICS

Faculty Full-time 10; part-time 35.

Teaching Methodologies Case study, computer-aided instruction, computer analysis, group discussion, lecture, research, role playing, simulations, student presentations, study groups, team projects.

Technology 200 on-campus computer terminals/PCs are available for student use and are linked by a campus-wide network. The network has full access to the Internet. Students are not required to have their own PC.

Special Opportunities Advanced credit may be earned through credit by examination, transfer of credits from another institution. International exchange programs in Czech Republic, France, Mexico, United Kingdom.

FINANCES
Costs for 1997–98 Tuition: $340 per quarter unit. Cost varies by academic program, class time (e.g., day/evening). Average 1997–98 room and board costs were $13,000 per academic year (off campus).

Financial Aid Grants available. Financial aid is available to part-time students. Application Deadline: 3/2.

Financial Aid Contact Ms. Billie Jones, Director of Financial Aid, PO Box 4530, Moraga, CA 94575. Phone: 925-631-4370.

FACILITIES
Information Resources St. Albert Library; total holdings of 185,000 volumes, 1,131 current periodical subscriptions. CD player(s) available for graduate student use. Access provided to online bibliographic retrieval services and online databases.

INTERNATIONAL STUDENTS
Demographics 2% of students enrolled are international students [Asia, 60%, Europe, 20%, North America, 20%].

Services and Facilities International student office, ESL courses, counseling/support services.

Applying TOEFL: minimum score of 550, proof of adequate funds required. Financial aid is not available to international students.

International Student Contact Mr. Louis Gecenok, Director, International Student Programs, PO Box 3091, Moraga, CA 94575. Phone: 925-631-4352; Fax: 925-631-4651.

PLACEMENT
Services include alumni network, career counseling/planning, career library, resume referral to employers, and resume preparation.

Employment Of 1996–97 graduates, 95% were employed within three months of graduation.

Business Program(s) URL: http://www.stmarys-ca.edu/MBA/index.html

Program Contact: Ms. Tracey Steever Fanelli, Director of Admissions and External Relations, 1928 Saint Mary's Road, PO Box 4240, Moraga, CA 94575-4240. Phone: 925-631-4500, 800-332-4622 (CA only); Fax: 925-376-6521; E-mail: smcmba@st.marys-ca.edu
See full description on page 970.

San Diego State University

Graduate School of Business

San Diego, California

OVERVIEW
San Diego State University is a state-supported, coed university. Enrollment: 25,000 graduate, professional, and undergraduate students; 2,490 full-time matriculated graduate/professional students; 2,994 part-time matriculated graduate/professional students. Founded: 1897. The graduate business unit is in a suburban setting and is on a semester calendar.

HIGHLIGHTS

Enrollment Profile

Full-time: 278	International: 15%
Part-time: 467	Women: 36%
Total: 745	Minorities: 16%
Average Age: 28	Average Class Size: 25
Fall 1997 Average GPA: 3.04	Fall 1997 Average GMAT: 570

Costs
Full-time tuition: $1902 per academic year (resident); $7806 per academic year (nonresident)
Part-time tuition: $1236 per year (resident); $4300 per year (nonresident)

AACSB – The International Association for Management Education accredited

GRADUATE BUSINESS PROGRAMS
Master of Business Administration (MBA) Full-time, part-time; 49 total credits required; 2 to 4 years to complete program. Concentrations in entrepreneurship, finance, international management, management, management information systems, marketing, real estate, taxation, management science.

Master of Science in Business Administration (MS) Full-time, part-time; 30 total credits required; minimum of 12 months to complete program. Concentrations in finance, management information systems, international management, production management, management, marketing, entrepreneurship, real estate, financial management/planning, human resources, taxation.

Master of Science in Accountancy (MS) Full-time, part-time; 30 total credits required; minimum of 12 months to complete program. Concentration in accounting.

Master of Business Administration/Master of Arts in Latin American Studies (MBA/MA) Full-time; 70 total credits required; minimum of 3 years to complete program.

ADMISSION
Applications For fall 1997 there were 884 applications for admission. Of those applying, 350 were accepted. Of those accepted, 218 enrolled.

Application Requirements GMAT score, application form, application fee, bachelor's degree, minimum GPA: 3.0, college transcript(s).

Recommended for Application Essay, letters of recommendation, personal statement, resume, work experience, computer experience.

Application Deadline 4/15 for fall, 10/1 for spring, 4/15 for fall (international), 8/31 for spring (international). Application fee: $55.

ACADEMICS
Faculty Full-time 73; part-time 24.

Teaching Methodologies Case study, computer analysis, computer simulations, experiential learning, field projects, group discussion, lecture, research, role playing, seminars by members of the business community, simulations, student presentations, study groups, team projects.

Technology 1,000 on-campus computer terminals/PCs are available for student use and are linked by a campus-wide network. The network has full access to the Internet. Students are not required to have their own PC.

Special Opportunities Advanced credit may be earned through transfer of credits from another institution. International exchange programs in Australia, Brazil, Canada, Denmark, France, Germany, Israel, Italy, Japan, Mexico, New Zealand, Spain, Sweden, Taiwan, United Kingdom, Zimbabwe. An internship program is available.

FINANCES
Costs for 1997–98 Tuition: Full-time: $1902 per year (resident); $7806 per year (nonresident). Part-time: $1236 per year (resident); $4300 per year (nonresident). Cost varies by class time (e.g., day/evening), number of credits taken. Average 1997–98 room and board costs were $5624 per academic year (on campus) and $6456 per academic year (off campus). Room and board costs vary by occupancy (e.g., single, double, triple), type of accommodation, type of meal plan.

Financial Aid Fellowships, research assistantships, teaching assistantships, grants, scholarships, work study, loans available. Financial aid is available to part-time students.

Financial Aid Contact Financial Aid Office, 5500 Campanile Drive, San Diego, CA 92182-8228. Phone: 619-594-6323; Fax: 619-594-1863.

FACILITIES
Information Resources Malcolm A. Love Library plus 1 additional on-campus library; total holdings of 1,095,581 volumes, 3,554,052 microforms, 5,979 current periodical subscriptions. CD player(s) available for graduate student use. Access provided to online bibliographic retrieval services.

INTERNATIONAL STUDENTS
Demographics 15% of students enrolled are international students.

Services and Facilities International student office, international student center, international student housing, visa services, ESL courses, counseling/support services.

Applying TOEFL: minimum score of 570, proof of adequate funds, proof of health/immunizations required. Financial aid is not available to international students.

International Student Contact Mr. Ron Moffatt, Director of International Programs, 5500 Campanile Drive, San Diego, CA 92182-5101. Phone: 619-594-1982; Fax: 619-594-1973; E-mail: isc.resources@sdsu.edu

PLACEMENT
Services include alumni network, career counseling/planning, career fairs, career library, career placement, electronic job bank, resume referral to employers, and resume preparation. In 1996–97, 132 organizations participated in on-campus recruiting; 10,000 on-campus interviews were conducted.

San Diego State University (continued)

Employment Of 1996–97 graduates, 72% were employed within three months of graduation; the average starting salary was $38,000. Types of employment entered: accounting, banking, chemical industry, communications, computer-related, consulting, consumer products, education, energy, engineering, finance, financial services, government, health services, high technology, hospitality management, human resources, information systems/technology, insurance, international trade, law, management, manufacturing, marketing, media, nonprofit, petrochemical, pharmaceutical, real estate, retail, service industry, telecommunications, transportation, utilities.

Business Program(s) URL: http://www.sdsu.edu/

Program Contact: Ms. Patricia M. Martin, Director of Admissions-Graduate School of Business, 5500 Campanile Drive, San Diego, CA 92182-8228. Phone: 619-594-5217; Fax: 619-594-1863; E-mail: sdsumba@mail.sdsu.edu

San Francisco State University

College of Business

San Francisco, California

OVERVIEW

San Francisco State University is a state-supported, coed, comprehensive institution. Enrollment: 27,004 graduate, professional, and undergraduate students. Founded: 1899. The graduate business unit is in an urban setting and is on a semester calendar.

HIGHLIGHTS

Enrollment Profile

Full-time: 323	International: 30%
Part-time: 533	Women: 47%
Total: 856	Minorities: 38%
Average Age: 29	Average Class Size: 22
Fall 1997 Average GPA: 3.2	Fall 1997 Average GMAT: 522

Costs
Full-time tuition: $1982 per academic year (resident); $4934 per academic year (nonresident)
Part-time tuition: $661 per semester (resident); $2137 per semester (nonresident)

AACSB – The International Association for Management Education accredited

GRADUATE BUSINESS PROGRAMS

Master of Business Administration (MBA) Full-time, part-time; 30-54 total credits required; 12 months to 7 years to complete program. Concentrations in accounting, entrepreneurship, human resources, international business, management, management information systems, marketing, operations management, organizational behavior/development, quantitative analysis, strategic management, business information science, business policy/strategy, finance, information management, port/maritime management, taxation, international finance, japanese business studies, leadership, marketing research.

Master of Science in Business Administration (MSBA) Full-time, part-time; 30-57 total credits required; 12 months to 7 years to complete program. Concentrations in accounting, entrepreneurship, human resources, international business, management, management information systems, marketing, operations management, organizational behavior/development, quantitative analysis, strategic management, business information science, business policy/strategy, finance, information management, port/maritime management, taxation, international finance, japanese business studies, leadership, new venture management.

Master of Science in Taxation (MST) Full-time, part-time; 30-57 total credits required; 12 months to 7 years to complete program. Concentration in taxation.

ADMISSION

Applications For fall 1997 there were 562 applications for admission. Of those applying, 399 were accepted. Of those accepted, 206 enrolled.

Application Requirements GMAT score: minimum 470, application form, application fee, bachelor's degree, minimum GPA: 2.7, college transcript(s).

Recommended for Application Essay, letters of recommendation, personal statement, resume, work experience, computer experience.

Application Deadline 6/1 for fall, 11/16 for spring, 3/14 for fall (international), 10/16 for spring (international). Application fee: $55.

ACADEMICS

Faculty Full-time 102; part-time 40.

Teaching Methodologies Case study, computer analysis, computer simulations, experiential learning, faculty seminars, group discussion, lecture, research,

seminars by members of the business community, simulations, student presentations, study groups, team projects.

Technology 1,000 on-campus computer terminals/PCs are available for student use. The network has full access to the Internet. Students are not required to have their own PC.

Special Opportunities Advanced credit may be earned through credit by examination, transfer of credits from another institution. International exchange programs in Denmark, France, Germany, Japan, Spain, United Kingdom. An internship program is available.

FINANCES

Costs for 1997–98 Tuition: Full-time: $1982 per semester (resident); $4934 per semester (nonresident). Part-time: $661 per semester (resident); $2137 per semester (nonresident). Cost varies by number of credits taken. Average 1997–98 room and board costs were $7000 per academic year (on campus) and $9600 per academic year (off campus).

Financial Aid Fellowships, research assistantships, work study, loans available. Application Deadline: 3/1.

Financial Aid Contact Ms. Barbara Hubler, Director, Financial Aid, 1600 Holloway Avenue, San Francisco, CA 94132-1722. Phone: 415-338-2437.

FACILITIES

Information Resources J. Paul Leonard Library; total holdings of 900,000 volumes, 2,000,000 microforms, 4,300 current periodical subscriptions. CD player(s) available for graduate student use. Access provided to online bibliographic retrieval services and online databases.

INTERNATIONAL STUDENTS

Demographics 30% of students enrolled are international students.

Services and Facilities International student office, international student center, visa services, ESL courses, counseling/support services.

Applying TOEFL: minimum score of 550, proof of adequate funds, proof of health/immunizations required. TWE: minimum score of 4 recommended. Financial aid is not available to international students.

International Student Contact Ms. Marilyn Cheuna, Coordinator, International Outreach Services, Office of International Programs, 1600 Holloway Avenue, San Francisco, CA 94132. Phone: 415-338-1362; E-mail: mcheung@sfsu.edu

PLACEMENT

Services include alumni network, career counseling/planning, career library, career placement, resume referral to employers, and resume preparation.

Employment Of 1996–97 graduates, 95% were employed within three months of graduation. Types of employment entered: accounting, banking, communications, computer-related, consulting, consumer products, education, energy, finance, financial services, government, health services, high technology, hospitality management, human resources, information systems/technology, insurance, international trade, management, manufacturing, marketing, media, nonprofit, pharmaceutical, real estate, retail, service industry, telecommunications, transportation, utilities.

Business Program(s) URL: http://www.sfsu.edu/~mba

Program Contact: Mr. Albert Koo, Admissions Coordinator, College of Business 325, San Francisco, CA 94132. Phone: 415-338-1935; Fax: 415-338-6237; E-mail: mba@sfsu.edu

San Jose State University

College of Business

San Jose, California

OVERVIEW

San Jose State University is a state-supported, coed, comprehensive institution. Enrollment: 26,897 graduate, professional, and undergraduate students; 2,167 full-time matriculated graduate/professional students; 2,977 part-time matriculated graduate/professional students. Founded: 1857. The graduate business unit is in an urban setting and is on a semester calendar.

HIGHLIGHTS

Enrollment Profile

Full-time: 318	International: N/R
Part-time: 407	Women: N/R
Total: 725	Minorities: N/R
Average Age: 32	Average Class Size: 35
Fall 1997 Average GPA: 3.25	Fall 1997 Average GMAT: 560

Costs
Full-time tuition: $1896 per academic year (resident); $3900 per academic year (nonresident)
Part-time tuition: $295 per unit (resident); $541 per unit (nonresident)

AACSB – The International Association for Management Education accredited

GRADUATE BUSINESS PROGRAMS

Traditional MBA (MBA) Part-time; 39-48 total credits required; 12 months to 7 years to complete program.

Accelerated Off-campus MBA (MBA) Part-time; 39-48 total credits required; 16 months to 7 years to complete program.

Master of Science in Accountancy (MS) Full-time; 45 total credits required; 12 months to complete program.

Master of Science in Taxation (MS) Part-time; 39-48 total credits required; 12 months to 7 years to complete program.

Master of Science in Transportation Management (MS) Part-time, distance learning option; 30 total credits required; 15 months to 7 years to complete program.

ADMISSION

Applications For fall 1997 there were 751 applications for admission. Of those applying, 393 were accepted. Of those accepted, 142 enrolled.

Application Requirements GMAT score: minimum 500, application form, application fee, bachelor's degree, minimum GPA: 3.0, personal statement, college transcript(s).

Application Deadline 5/1 for fall, 9/15 for spring, 3/1 for fall (international), 8/31 for spring (international). Application fee: $59.

ACADEMICS

Faculty Full-time 95; part-time 65.

Teaching Methodologies Case study, computer-aided instruction, computer analysis, computer simulations, experiential learning, faculty seminars, field projects, group discussion, lecture, research, role playing, seminars by members of the business community, simulations, student presentations, study groups, team projects.

Technology 250 on-campus computer terminals/PCs are available for student use and are linked by a campus-wide network. The network has full access to the Internet. Students are not required to have their own PC.

Special Opportunities Advanced credit may be earned through credit by examination, transfer of credits from another institution. An internship program is available.

FINANCES

Costs for 1997–98 Tuition: Full-time: $1896 per year (resident); $3900 per year (nonresident). Part-time: $295 per unit (resident); $541 per unit (nonresident). Cost varies by academic program, number of credits taken. Fees: Full-time: $250 per academic year (resident); $250 per academic year (nonresident). Part-time: $250 per year (resident); $250 per year (nonresident). Fees vary by academic program. Average 1997–98 room and board costs were $10,000 per academic year (on campus) and $15,000 per academic year (off campus). Room and board costs vary by occupancy (e.g., single, double, triple), type of accommodation.

Financial Aid In 1997–98, 34% of students received some institutionally administered aid in the form of fellowships, grants, scholarships, work study, loans. Financial aid is available to part-time students. Application Deadline: 3/2.

Financial Aid Contact Financial Aid Office, One Washington Square, San Jose, CA 95192-0036. Phone: 408-924-6100; Fax: 408-924-5978.

FACILITIES

Information Resources Clark Library plus 1 additional on-campus library; total holdings of 700,000 volumes, 650,000 microforms, 11,000 current periodical subscriptions. Access provided to online bibliographic retrieval services.

INTERNATIONAL STUDENTS
Demographics N/R

Services and Facilities International student office, international student center, international student housing, visa services, ESL courses, counseling/support services.

Applying TOEFL: minimum score of 550, proof of health/immunizations required. Financial aid is available to international students.

International Student Contact Mr. Louie Barozzi, Director, International Student Services, One Washington Square, San Jose, CA 95192-0221. Phone: 408-924-5920; Fax: 408-924-5978; E-mail: barozzi@sjsuvm1.sjsu.edu

PLACEMENT

Services include alumni network, career counseling/planning, career fairs, career placement, electronic job bank, job interviews arranged, resume referral to employers, and resume preparation. In 1996–97, 100 organizations participated in on-campus recruiting; 250 on-campus interviews were conducted.

Employment Of 1996–97 graduates, 98% were employed within three months of graduation; the average starting salary was $60,000. Types of employment entered: accounting, banking, chemical industry, communications, computer-related, consulting, consumer products, energy, engineering, finance, financial services, government, health services, high technology, hospitality management, human resources, information systems/technology, insurance, international trade,

management, manufacturing, marketing, media, nonprofit, petrochemical, pharmaceutical, real estate, retail, service industry, telecommunications, transportation, utilities.

Business Program(s) URL: http://www.cob.sjsu.edu/graduate

Program Contact: Ms. Amy Kassing, Assistant Director, Advising and Admission, One Washington Square, San Jose, CA 95192-0162. Phone: 408-924-3420; Fax: 408-924-3426; E-mail: kassing_a@cob.sjsu.edu

See full description on page 976.

Santa Clara University

Thomas and Dorothy Leavey School of Business and Administration

Santa Clara, California

OVERVIEW

Santa Clara University is an independent-religious, coed, comprehensive institution. Enrollment: 7,946 graduate, professional, and undergraduate students; 1,397 full-time matriculated graduate/professional students; 2,267 part-time matriculated graduate/professional students. Founded: 1851. The graduate business unit is in a suburban setting and is on a quarter calendar.

HIGHLIGHTS

Enrollment Profile

Full-time: N/R	International: 8%
Part-time: N/R	Women: 35%
Total: 1,168	Minorities: 36%
Average Age: 29	Average Class Size: 35
Fall 1997 Average GPA: 3.25	Fall 1997 Average GMAT: 632

Costs
Full-time tuition: $15,552 per academic year
Part-time tuition: $432 per unit

AACSB – The International Association for Management Education accredited

GRADUATE BUSINESS PROGRAMS

Master of Business Administration (MBA) Full-time, part-time; 45-72 total credits required; 15 months to 6 years to complete program. Concentrations in finance, management information systems, international business, technology management, marketing, quantitative analysis, marketing research, operations management.

Master of Business Administration in Agribusiness (MBA) Full-time, part-time; 45-72 total credits required; 15 months to 6 years to complete program. Concentrations in finance, management information systems, international business, technology management, marketing, quantitative analysis, marketing research, operations management.

Doctor of Jurisprudence/Master of Business Administration/Law Program (JD/MBA) Full-time; 120-135 total credits required; 3 to 6 years to complete program. Concentrations in finance, management information systems, international business, technology management, marketing, quantitative analysis, marketing research, operations management.

ADMISSION

Applications For fall 1997 there were 530 applications for admission. Of those applying, 212 were accepted. Of those accepted, 153 enrolled.

Application Requirements GMAT score, application form, application fee, bachelor's degree, essay, minimum GPA, 2 letters of recommendation, college transcript(s), computer experience: word processing, spreadsheet.

Recommended for Application Resume, work experience.

Application Deadline 6/1 for fall, 9/1 for winter, 12/1 for spring, 6/1 for fall (international), 9/1 for winter (international), 12/1 for spring (international). Application fee: $55, $75 (international). Deferred entrance is available.

ACADEMICS

Faculty Full-time 62; part-time 20.

Teaching Methodologies Case study, computer-aided instruction, computer analysis, computer simulations, group discussion, lecture, research, role playing, seminars by members of the business community, simulations, student presentations, study groups, team projects.

Technology 300 on-campus computer terminals/PCs are available for student use and are linked by a campus-wide network. The network has full access to the Internet. Students are not required to have their own PC.

Special Opportunities Advanced credit may be earned through credit by examination, transfer of credits from another institution. International exchange

Santa Clara University (continued)

programs in Hong Kong, Italy, Japan, Korea, Republic of Singapore, Thailand, United Kingdom.

FINANCES
Costs for 1997–98 Tuition: Full-time: $15,552 per year. Part-time: $432 per unit. Cost varies by academic program, number of credits taken. Fees: Full-time: $66 per academic year. Part-time: $22 per quarter. Average 1997–98 room and board costs were $8946 per academic year (off campus).

Financial Aid Fellowships, research assistantships, scholarships, work study, loans available. Financial aid is available to part-time students. Application Deadline: 7/1.

Financial Aid Contact Ms. Donna Hunting, MBA Financial Aid Coordinator, MBA Office, Kenna 323, Santa Clara, CA 95053-0001. Phone: 408-554-4500; Fax: 408-554-4571; E-mail: dhunting@mailer.scu.edu

FACILITIES
Information Resources Michel Orradre Library plus 1 additional on-campus library; total holdings of 626,000 volumes, 633,000 microforms, 4,800 current periodical subscriptions. CD player(s) available for graduate student use. Access provided to online bibliographic retrieval services.

INTERNATIONAL STUDENTS
Demographics 8% of students enrolled are international students.

Services and Facilities International student office, international student center, counseling/support services.

Applying TOEFL: minimum score of 600, TWE: minimum score of 4, proof of adequate funds required. Financial aid is not available to international students.

International Student Contact Mr. Vidalino Raatior, Assistant Director, International Students, Benson 203, Santa Clara, CA 95053. Phone: 408-554-4109; Fax: 408-554-5136; E-mail: vraatior@mailer.scu.edu

PLACEMENT
Services include alumni network, career counseling/planning, career fairs, career library, electronic job bank, job interviews arranged, resume referral to employers, and resume preparation. In 1996–97, 98 organizations participated in on-campus recruiting.

Employment Of 1996–97 graduates, 95% were employed within three months of graduation. Types of employment entered: accounting, banking, communications, computer-related, consulting, consumer products, education, engineering, finance, financial services, government, health services, high technology, human resources, information systems/technology, law, management, manufacturing, marketing, media, pharmaceutical, service industry, telecommunications.

Business Program(s) URL: http://lsb.scu.edu

Program Contact: Ms. Elizabeth Ford, Director, MBA Admissions and Recruitment, MBA Office, Kenna Hall #323, Santa Clara, CA 95053-0001. Phone: 408-554-4500; Fax: 408-554-4571; E-mail: mbaadmissions@scu.edu
See full description on page 978.

Sonoma State University

School of Business and Economics
Rohnert Park, California

OVERVIEW
Sonoma State University is a state-supported, coed, comprehensive institution. Enrollment: 7,077 graduate, professional, and undergraduate students. Founded: 1960. The graduate business unit is in a small-town setting and is on a semester calendar.

HIGHLIGHTS

Enrollment Profile
Full-time: 3
Part-time: 57
Total: 60
Average Age: 32
Fall 1997 Average GPA: 3.1

International: N/R
Women: 50%
Minorities: 5%
Average Class Size: 15
Fall 1997 Average GMAT: 525

Costs
Full-time tuition: $2130 per academic year (resident)
Part-time tuition: $732 per semester (resident); $732 per semester (nonresident)

GRADUATE BUSINESS PROGRAMS
Master of Business Administration (MBA) Full-time, part-time; 30-32 total credits required; 2 to 7 years to complete program.

ADMISSION
Application Requirements GMAT score, application form, application fee, bachelor's degree, minimum GPA: 2.5, personal statement, college transcript(s).

Recommended for Application Letters of recommendation, work experience, computer experience.

Application Deadline Applications processed on a rolling/continuous basis for both domestic and international students. Application fee: $55.

ACADEMICS
Faculty Full-time 10.

Teaching Methodologies Faculty seminars.

Technology 100 on-campus computer terminals/PCs are available for student use and are linked by a campus-wide network. The network has full access to the Internet. Students are required to have their own PC.

Special Opportunities An internship program is available.

FINANCES
Costs for 1997–98 Tuition: Full-time: $2130 per year (resident). Part-time: $732 per semester (resident); $732 per semester (nonresident). Fees: $246 per unit. Average 1997–98 room and board costs were $5430 per academic year.

Financial Aid Fellowships, work study, loans available. Financial aid is available to part-time students. Application Deadline: 3/2.

Financial Aid Contact Financial Aid Office, 1801 East Cotati Avenue, Rohnert Park, CA 94928-3609. Phone: 707-664-2389.

FACILITIES
Information Resources Ruben Salazar Library; total holdings of 453,462 volumes, 1,380,049 microforms, 1,596 current periodical subscriptions. CD player(s) available for graduate student use. Access provided to online bibliographic retrieval services.

INTERNATIONAL STUDENTS
Demographics N/R

Services and Facilities International student office, counseling/support services.

Applying TOEFL: minimum score of 550, proof of adequate funds, proof of health/immunizations required.

PLACEMENT
Services include alumni network, career fairs, and career placement.

Program Contact: Office of Admissions, 1801 East Cotati Avenue, Rohnert Park, CA 94928-3609. Phone: 707-664-2778; Fax: 707-664-2060.

Stanford University

Graduate School of Business
Stanford, California

OVERVIEW
Stanford University is an independent-nonprofit, coed university. Enrollment: 14,084 graduate, professional, and undergraduate students; 6,095 full-time matriculated graduate/professional students; 1,350 part-time matriculated graduate/professional students. Founded: 1885. The graduate business unit is in a suburban setting and is on a quarter calendar.

HIGHLIGHTS

Enrollment Profile
Full-time: 745
Part-time: 0
Total: 745
Average Age: 26
Fall 1997 Average GPA: 3.59

International: 29%
Women: 29%
Minorities: 24%
Average Class Size: 60
Fall 1997 Average GMAT: 711

Costs
Full-time tuition: $2400 per academic year
Part-time tuition: N/R

AACSB – The International Association for Management Education accredited

GRADUATE BUSINESS PROGRAMS

Master of Business Administration (MBA) Full-time; 100 total credits required; 18 months to complete program. Concentrations in health care, international management, nonprofit management.

Master of Science in Management (MS) Full-time; 52 total credits required; 10 months to complete program.

ADMISSION

Applications For fall 1997 there were 6,559 applications for admission.

Application Requirements Application form, application fee, bachelor's degree, essay, minimum GPA, 3 letters of recommendation, personal statement, resume, college transcript(s).

Recommended for Application GMAT score accepted, minimum of 2 years of work experience.

Application Deadline 11/5 for fall, 1/7 for winter, 3/18 for spring, 11/5 for fall (international), 1/7 for winter (international), 3/18 for spring (international). Application fee: $140. Deferred entrance is available.

ACADEMICS

Faculty Full-time 84; part-time 30.

Teaching Methodologies Case study, computer-aided instruction, computer analysis, computer simulations, experiential learning, faculty seminars, field projects, group discussion, lecture, research, seminars by members of the business community, student presentations, study groups, team projects.

Technology 500 on-campus computer terminals/PCs are available for student use and are linked by a campus-wide network. The network has full access to the Internet. Students are not required to have their own PC.

FINANCES

Costs for 1997–98 Tuition: Full-time: $2400 per year. Cost varies by academic program. Fees vary by academic program. Average 1997–98 room and board costs were $11,202 per academic year (on campus) and $12,885 per academic year (off campus). Room and board costs vary by campus location, occupancy (e.g., single, double, triple), type of accommodation, type of meal plan.

Financial Aid In 1997–98, 60% of students received some institutionally administered aid in the form of fellowships, research assistantships, loans.

Financial Aid Contact Ms. Ursula Kaiser, Financial Aid Office, Graduate School of Business, Stanford, CA 94305-9991. Phone: 650-723-3282; Fax: 650-725-3328; E-mail: finaid@gsb.stanford.edu

FACILITIES

Information Resources Cecil H. Green Library plus 16 additional on-campus libraries; total holdings of 6,409,239 volumes, 4,263,916 microforms, 47,320 current periodical subscriptions. CD player(s) available for graduate student use. Access provided to online bibliographic retrieval services and online databases.

INTERNATIONAL STUDENTS

Demographics 29% of students enrolled are international students.

Services and Facilities International student office, international student center, counseling/support services.

Applying TOEFL, proof of adequate funds required. TWE recommended. Financial aid is not available to international students.

International Student Contact Ms. Seda Mansour, Assistant Director, MBA Admissions, Stanford, CA 94305-9991. Phone: 650-723-2766; Fax: 650-725-7831; E-mail: mbainquiries@gsb.stanford.edu

PLACEMENT

Services include alumni network, career counseling/planning, career fairs, career library, career placement, electronic job bank, job interviews arranged, job search course, resume referral to employers, and resume preparation. In 1996–97, 392 organizations participated in on-campus recruiting; 6,228 on-campus interviews were conducted.

Employment Of 1996–97 graduates, 99% were employed within three months of graduation; the average starting salary was $80,000. Types of employment entered: accounting, banking, chemical industry, communications, computer-related, consulting, consumer products, education, energy, engineering, finance, financial services, government, health services, high technology, hospitality management, human resources, information systems/technology, insurance, international trade, law, management, manufacturing, marketing, media, mining, nonprofit, petrochemical, pharmaceutical, real estate, retail, service industry, telecommunications, transportation, utilities.

Business Program(s) URL: http://www-gsb.stanford.edu

Program Contact: Dr. Marie Mookini, Director of Admissions, Graduate School of Business, Stanford, CA 94305-5015. Phone: 650-723-2766; Fax: 650-725-7831; E-mail: mbainquiries@gsb.stanford.edu

United States International University

College of Business Administration

San Diego, California

OVERVIEW

United States International University is an independent-nonprofit, coed university. Enrollment: 1,459 graduate, professional, and undergraduate students; 609 full-time matriculated graduate/professional students; 445 part-time matriculated graduate/professional students. Founded: 1952. The graduate business unit is in a suburban setting and is on a quarter calendar.

HIGHLIGHTS

Enrollment Profile
Full-time: 155
Part-time: 85
Total: 240
Average Age: 28
Fall 1997 Average GPA: 3.21

International: 62%
Women: 33%
Minorities: 21%
Average Class Size: 18
Fall 1997 Average GMAT: 450

Costs
Full-time tuition: $3900 per academic year
Part-time tuition: $1300 per course

GRADUATE BUSINESS PROGRAMS

Master of Business Administration (MBA) Full-time, part-time; 48-70 total credits required; 12 months to 3 years to complete program. Concentrations in finance, marketing, strategic management, information management.

Master of International Business Administration (MIBA) Full-time, part-time; 48-70 total credits required; 12 months to 3 years to complete program. Concentrations in finance, marketing, strategic management, information management.

ADMISSION

Applications For fall 1997 there were 268 applications for admission. Of those applying, 136 were accepted. Of those accepted, 52 enrolled.

Application Requirements GMAT score, application form, application fee, bachelor's degree, essay, minimum GPA: 2.5, letters of recommendation, personal statement, college transcript(s).

Recommended for Application Resume, computer experience.

Application Deadline Applications processed on a rolling/continuous basis for both domestic and international students. Application fee: $35. Deferred entrance is available.

ACADEMICS

Faculty Full-time 15; part-time 12.

Teaching Methodologies Case study, computer-aided instruction, experiential learning, faculty seminars, field projects, group discussion, lecture, research, role playing, seminars by members of the business community, simulations, student presentations, study groups, team projects.

Technology 80 on-campus computer terminals/PCs are available for student use and are linked by a campus-wide network. The network has full access to the Internet. Students are not required to have their own PC.

Special Opportunities Advanced credit may be earned through transfer of credits from another institution. International exchange programs in Kenya, Mexico. An internship program is available.

FINANCES

Costs for 1997–98 Tuition: Full-time: $3900 per quarter. Part-time: $1300 per course. Cost varies by academic program, campus location, number of credits taken. Fees: Full-time: $100 per academic year. Part-time: $93 per quarter. Average 1997–98 room and board costs were $4800 per academic year (on campus) and $7065 per academic year (off campus). Room and board costs vary by campus location, occupancy (e.g., single, double, triple), type of accommodation.

Financial Aid In 1997–98, 20% of students received some institutionally administered aid in the form of research assistantships, teaching assistantships, work study, loans. Financial aid is available to part-time students. Application Deadline: 4/2.

Financial Aid Contact Ms. Tina Moncada, Director, Financial Aid, 10455 Pomerado Road, San Diego, CA 92131-1799. Phone: 619-635-4700; Fax: 619-635-4848; E-mail: tmoncada@usiu.edu

FACILITIES

Information Resources Walter Library; total holdings of 205,000 volumes, 209,700 microforms, 1,200 current periodical subscriptions. CD player(s) available for graduate student use. Access provided to online bibliographic retrieval services and online databases.

United States International University *(continued)*

INTERNATIONAL STUDENTS

Demographics 62% of students enrolled are international students [Africa, 8%, Asia, 38%, Europe, 18%, North America, 31%, South America, 2%, other, 3%].

Services and Facilities International student office, international student center, international student housing, visa services, ESL courses, counseling/support services.

Applying TOEFL: minimum score of 550, proof of adequate funds required. Financial aid is available to international students.

International Student Contact Dr. Bijan Massrour, Director, International Scholars and Students Office, 10455 Pomerado Road, San Diego, CA 92131-1799. Phone: 619-635-4564; Fax: 619-635-4843; E-mail: bmassrour@usiu.edu

PLACEMENT

Services include alumni network, career counseling/planning, career fairs, career library, career placement, electronic job bank, job interviews arranged, job search course, resume referral to employers, and resume preparation. In 1996–97, 38 organizations participated in on-campus recruiting; 58 on-campus interviews were conducted.

Employment Of 1996–97 graduates, 96% were employed within three months of graduation; the average starting salary was $42,000. Types of employment entered: accounting, banking, chemical industry, communications, computer-related, consulting, consumer products, education, energy, engineering, finance, financial services, government, health services, high technology, hospitality management, human resources, information systems/technology, insurance, international trade, law, management, manufacturing, marketing, media, mining, nonprofit, petrochemical, pharmaceutical, real estate, retail, service industry, telecommunications, transportation, utilities.

Business Program(s) URL: http://www.usiu.edu

Program Contact: Ms. Susan Topham, Assistant Director of Admissions, 10455 Pomerado Road, San Diego, CA 92131-1799. Phone: 619-635-4885; Fax: 619-635-4739; E-mail: stopham@usiu.edu

University of California, Berkeley

Haas School of Business

Berkeley, California

OVERVIEW

The University of California, Berkeley is a state-supported, coed university. Enrollment: 30,000 graduate, professional, and undergraduate students; 8,284 full-time matriculated graduate/professional students; 268 part-time matriculated graduate/professional students. Founded: 1868. The graduate business unit is in an urban setting and is on a semester calendar.

HIGHLIGHTS

Enrollment Profile
Full-time: 496
Part-time: 277
Total: 773
Average Age: 28
Fall 1997 Average GPA: 3.4

International: 21%
Women: 29%
Minorities: 20%
Average Class Size: 45
Fall 1997 Average GMAT: 675

Costs
Full-time tuition: $8984 per academic year (nonresident)
Part-time tuition: N/R

AACSB – The International Association for Management Education accredited

GRADUATE BUSINESS PROGRAMS

Master of Business Administration (MBA) Full-time; 56 total credits required; 21 months to complete program. Concentrations in accounting, entrepreneurship, financial economics, information management, international and area business studies, management, management information systems, marketing, nonprofit management, operations management, organizational behavior/development, real estate, strategic management, technology management.

Evening MBA (MBA) Part-time; 36 total credits required; 2.3 to 3.8 years to complete program. Concentrations in finance, management, marketing, strategic management, technology management.

Master of Business Administration/Master of Public Health in Health Services Management (MBA/MPH) Full-time; 80 total credits required; 2.8 to 4.5 years to complete program. Concentrations in management, nonprofit management, nonprofit organization.

Doctor of Jurisprudence/Master of Business Administration (JD/MBA) Full-time; 125 total credits required; 3.8 to 4.5 years to complete program. Concentrations in business information science, entrepreneurship, finance, financial economics, information management, international and area business studies, international business, management, management information systems, marketing, nonprofit management, operations management, organizational behavior/development, real estate, strategic management, technology management.

Master of Business Administration/Master of Arts in Asian Studies (MBA/MA) Full-time; 79 total credits required; 2.8 to 4.5 years to complete program. Concentrations in business information science, entrepreneurship, finance, financial economics, information management, international and area business studies, international business, management, management information systems, marketing, nonprofit management, operations management, organizational behavior/development, real estate, strategic management, technology management.

Master of Business Administration/Master of International Area Studies (MBA/MIAS) Full-time; 80 total credits required; 2.8 to 4.5 years to complete program. Concentrations in accounting, entrepreneurship, finance, financial economics, information management, international and area business studies, international business, management, management information systems, marketing, nonprofit management, operations management, organizational behavior/development, real estate, strategic management, technology management.

ADMISSION

Applications For fall 1997 there were 4,227 applications for admission. Of those applying, 501 were accepted. Of those accepted, 296 enrolled.

Application Requirements Application form, application fee, bachelor's degree, essay, minimum GPA: 2.0, 2 letters of recommendation, personal statement, resume, college transcript(s), minimum of 2 years of work experience.

Recommended for Application GMAT score accepted, interview, computer experience.

Application Deadline 3/31 for fall, 2/15 for fall (international). Application fee: $40.

ACADEMICS

Faculty Full-time 68; part-time 93.

Teaching Methodologies Case study, computer-aided instruction, computer analysis, computer simulations, experiential learning, faculty seminars, field projects, group discussion, lecture, research, role playing, seminars by members of the business community, simulations, student presentations, study groups, team projects.

Technology 200 on-campus computer terminals/PCs are available for student use and are linked by a campus-wide network. The network has full access to the Internet. Students are required to have their own PC.

Special Opportunities International exchange programs in Austria, Belgium, Brazil, France, Hong Kong, Italy, Japan, Mexico, Netherlands, Spain, Sweden, United Kingdom.

FINANCES

Costs for 1997–98 Tuition: Full-time: $8984 per year (nonresident). Fees: Full-time: $10,394 per academic year (resident); $10,394 per academic year (nonresident). Part-time: $7242 per semester (resident); $9496 per semester (nonresident). Fees vary by number of credits taken. Average 1997–98 room and board costs were $12,000 per academic year (off campus). Room and board costs vary by occupancy (e.g., single, double, triple), type of accommodation, type of meal plan.

Financial Aid In 1997–98, 40% of students received some institutionally administered aid in the form of fellowships, research assistantships, teaching assistantships, grants, scholarships, work study, loans. Financial aid is available to part-time students. Application Deadline: 3/1.

Financial Aid Contact Ms. Debi Fidler, Financial Aid Coordinator, Haas School of Business, Room F449, Berkeley, CA 94720-1900. Phone: 510-643-1680; Fax: 510-643-6659; E-mail: fidler@haas.berkeley.edu

FACILITIES

Information Resources Doe Library plus 37 additional on-campus libraries; total holdings of 8,000,000 volumes, 5,000,000 microforms, 90,000 current periodical subscriptions. CD player(s) available for graduate student use. Access provided to online bibliographic retrieval services and online databases.

INTERNATIONAL STUDENTS

Demographics 21% of students enrolled are international students [Africa, 2%, Asia, 33%, Australia/New Zealand, 2%, Central America, 6%, Europe, 35%, North America, 2%, South America, 20%].

Services and Facilities International student office, international student center, international student housing, visa services, ESL courses, counseling/support services.

Applying TOEFL: minimum score of 570, proof of adequate funds required. Financial aid is available to international students.

International Student Contact Mr. John Pliska, MBA Admissions Advisor, Haas School of Business , 440 Student Services Building, #1902, Berkeley, CA

94720-1902. Phone: 510-642-1405; Fax: 510-643-6659; E-mail: mbaadms@haas.berkeley.edu

PLACEMENT

Services include alumni network, career counseling/planning, career fairs, career library, career placement, electronic job bank, job interviews arranged, job search course, resume referral to employers, and resume preparation. In 1996–97, 500 organizations participated in on-campus recruiting; 2,500 on-campus interviews were conducted.

Employment Of 1996–97 graduates, 96% were employed within three months of graduation; the average starting salary was $76,364. Types of employment entered: accounting, banking, chemical industry, communications, computer-related, consulting, consumer products, education, energy, engineering, finance, financial services, government, health services, high technology, hospitality management, human resources, information systems/technology, insurance, international trade, law, management, manufacturing, marketing, media, mining, nonprofit, petrochemical, pharmaceutical, real estate, retail, service industry, telecommunications, transportation, utilities.

Business Program(s) URL: http://www.haas.berkeley.edu

Program Contact: Ms. Fran Hill, Director, MBA Admissions, Haas School of Business, 440 Student Services Building, #1902, Berkeley, CA 94720-1902. Phone: 510-642-1405; Fax: 510-643-6659; E-mail: mbaadms@haas.berkeley.edu

University of California, Davis

Graduate School of Management

Davis, California

OVERVIEW

The University of California, Davis is a state-supported, coed university. Enrollment: 24,299 graduate, professional, and undergraduate students; 5,167 full-time matriculated graduate/professional students; part-time matriculated graduate/professional students. Founded: 1905. The graduate business unit is in a small-town setting and is on a quarter calendar.

HIGHLIGHTS

Enrollment Profile
Full-time: 126
Part-time: 0
Total: 126
Average Age: 27
Fall 1997 Average GPA: 3.2

International: 6%
Women: 37%
Minorities: 6%
Average Class Size: 35
Fall 1997 Average GMAT: 660

Costs
Full-time tuition: $19,452 per academic year (nonresident)
Part-time tuition: N/R

AACSB – The International Association for Management Education accredited

GRADUATE BUSINESS PROGRAMS

Master of Business Administration (MBA) Full-time; 72 total credits required; 2 years to complete program. Concentrations in accounting, finance, international business, management, management information systems, management science, marketing, nonprofit management, public management, technology management.

ADMISSION

Applications For fall 1997 there were 345 applications for admission. Of those applying, 104 were accepted. Of those accepted, 57 enrolled.

Application Requirements GMAT score, application form, application fee, bachelor's degree, essay, 3 letters of recommendation, personal statement, resume, college transcript(s).

Recommended for Application Interview, work experience, computer experience.

Application Deadline 2/1 for fall, 2/1 for fall (international). Application fee: $40. Deferred entrance is available.

ACADEMICS

Faculty Full-time 24; part-time 15.

Teaching Methodologies Case study, computer-aided instruction, computer analysis, computer simulations, faculty seminars, group discussion, lecture, research, seminars by members of the business community, student presentations, study groups, team projects.

Technology 319 on-campus computer terminals/PCs are available for student use and are linked by a campus-wide network. The network has full access to the Internet. Students are not required to have their own PC.

Special Opportunities Advanced credit may be earned through transfer of credits from another institution. International exchange programs in Finland, Mexico, Netherlands.

FINANCES

Costs for 1997–98 Tuition: Full-time: $19,452 per year (nonresident). Fees: Full-time: $10,468 per academic year. Fees vary by academic program, number of credits taken. Average 1997–98 room and board costs were $6994 per academic year. Room and board costs vary by campus location, occupancy (e.g., single, double, triple), type of accommodation, type of meal plan.

Financial Aid In 1997–98, 48% of students received some institutionally administered aid in the form of research assistantships, teaching assistantships, work study, loans. Financial aid is available to part-time students. Application Deadline: 3/1.

Financial Aid Contact Patricia Kearney, Graduate Financial Aid Office, One Shields Avenue, Davis, CA 95616. Phone: 530-752-9246; Fax: 530-752-7337; E-mail: gradfinaid@ucdavis.edu

FACILITIES

Information Resources Peter J. Shields Library plus 5 additional on-campus libraries; total holdings of 2,655,600 volumes, 3,315,000 microforms, 49,098 current periodical subscriptions. CD player(s) available for graduate student use. Access provided to online bibliographic retrieval services.

INTERNATIONAL STUDENTS

Demographics 6% of students enrolled are international students.

Services and Facilities International student office, international student center, visa services, ESL courses, counseling/support services.

Applying TOEFL: minimum score of 600, proof of adequate funds, proof of health/immunizations required. Financial aid is not available to international students.

International Student Contact Dorothy Hicks, International Student Assistant, Services for International Students and Scholars, One Shields Avenue, Davis, CA 95616. Phone: 530-752-0864; Fax: 530-752-5822; E-mail: siss@ucdavis.edu

PLACEMENT

Services include alumni network, career counseling/planning, career fairs, career library, career placement, electronic job bank, job interviews arranged, job search course, resume referral to employers, and resume preparation. In 1996–97, 316 organizations participated in on-campus recruiting; 352 on-campus interviews were conducted.

Employment Of 1996–97 graduates, 95% were employed within three months of graduation; the average starting salary was $60,000. Types of employment entered: accounting, computer-related, consulting, engineering, finance, information systems/technology, management.

Business Program(s) URL: http://www.gsm.ucdavis.edu

Program Contact: Mr. Donald A. Blodger, Assistant Dean of Admissions and Student Services, 107 AOB IV, Davis, CA 95616. Phone: 530-752-7661; Fax: 530-752-2924; E-mail: gsm@ucdavis.edu

See full description on page 1044.

University of California, Irvine

Graduate School of Management

Irvine, California

OVERVIEW

The University of California, Irvine is a state-supported, coed university. Enrollment: 17,258 graduate, professional, and undergraduate students; 3,077 full-time matriculated graduate/professional students; 456 part-time matriculated graduate/professional students. Founded: 1965. The graduate business unit is in a suburban setting and is on a quarter calendar.

HIGHLIGHTS

Enrollment Profile
Full-time: 242
Part-time: 0
Total: 242
Average Age: 27
Fall 1997 Average GPA: 3.25

International: 29%
Women: 32%
Minorities: 7%
Average Class Size: 18
Fall 1997 Average GMAT: 637

Costs
Full-time tuition: $9000 per academic year (nonresident)
Part-time tuition: N/R

University of California, Irvine (continued)

AACSB – The International Association for Management Education accredited

GRADUATE BUSINESS PROGRAMS

Master of Business Administration (MBA) Full-time; 92 total credits required; 21 months to 2 years to complete program. Concentration in accounting.

Executive MBA (MBA) Part-time; 92 total credits required; 2 years to complete program.

Health Care Executive MBA (MBA) Part-time; 92 total credits required; 2 years to complete program.

Fully-employed MBA (MBA) Part-time; 92 total credits required; 2.8 to 3 years to complete program.

ADMISSION

Applications For fall 1997 there were 693 applications for admission. Of those applying, 201 were accepted. Of those accepted, 128 enrolled.

Application Requirements GMAT score, application form, application fee, bachelor's degree, essay, minimum GPA: 3.0, 2 letters of recommendation, personal statement, resume, college transcript(s).

Recommended for Application Work experience.

Application Deadline 5/1 for fall, 5/1 for fall (international). Application fee: $40.

ACADEMICS

Faculty Full-time 40; part-time 30.

Teaching Methodologies Case study, computer-aided instruction, computer analysis, computer simulations, field projects, group discussion, lecture, seminars by members of the business community, student presentations, study groups, team projects.

Technology 210 on-campus computer terminals/PCs are available for student use and are linked by a campus-wide network. The network has full access to the Internet. Students are required to have their own PC.

Special Opportunities Advanced credit may be earned through credit by examination, credit for experience, transfer of credits from another institution. International exchange programs in Austria, Belgium, Finland, France, Hong Kong, Hungary, Italy, Mexico, People's Republic of China. An internship program is available.

FINANCES

Costs for 1997–98 Tuition: Full-time: $9000 per year (nonresident). Cost varies by academic program. Fees: Full-time: $11,010 per academic year (resident); $11,010 per academic year (nonresident). Fees vary by academic program, number of credits taken. Average 1997–98 room and board costs were $7074 per academic year (on campus) and $8485 per academic year (off campus). Room and board costs vary by occupancy (e.g., single, double, triple), type of accommodation, type of meal plan.

Financial Aid In 1997–98, 70% of students received some institutionally administered aid in the form of fellowships, research assistantships, teaching assistantships, grants, scholarships, work study, loans. Application Deadline: 3/2.

Financial Aid Contact Ms. Alda Ruggiero, Financial Aid Advisor, 250 Graduate School of Management, Irvine, CA 92697-3125. Phone: 949-824-5728; Fax: 949-824-2235.

FACILITIES

Information Resources Main library plus 2 additional on-campus libraries; total holdings of 1,598,488 volumes, 2,009,936 microforms, 17,550 current periodical subscriptions. CD player(s) available for graduate student use. Access provided to online bibliographic retrieval services and online databases.

INTERNATIONAL STUDENTS

Demographics 29% of students enrolled are international students [Asia, 18%, Europe, 1%, North America, 73%, South America, 1%, other, 7%].

Services and Facilities International student office, international student center, international student housing, visa services, ESL courses, counseling/support services.

Applying TOEFL: minimum score of 600, proof of adequate funds required. Financial aid is not available to international students.

International Student Contact Ms. Victoria Lester, Academic Advising Assistant, 250 Graduate School of Management, Irvine, CA 92697-3125. Phone: 949-824-5232; Fax: 949-824-2235.

PLACEMENT

Services include alumni network, career counseling/planning, career fairs, career library, career placement, electronic job bank, job interviews arranged, job search course, resume referral to employers, and resume preparation. In 1996–97, 90 organizations participated in on-campus recruiting; 952 on-campus interviews were conducted.

Employment Of 1996–97 graduates, 98% were employed within three months of graduation; the average starting salary was $55,477. Types of employment entered: accounting, banking, communications, computer-related, consulting, consumer products, finance, financial services, health services, high technology, human resources, information systems/technology, management, manufacturing, marketing, pharmaceutical, real estate, telecommunications.

Business Program(s) URL: http://www.gsm.uci.edu

Program Contact: Ms. Victoria Lester, Academic Advising Assistant, 250 Graduate School of Management, Irvine, CA 92697-3125. Phone: 949-824-5232; Fax: 949-824-2235; E-mail: gsm-mba@uci.edu

See full description on page 1046.

University of California, Los Angeles

The Anderson School at UCLA

Los Angeles, California

OVERVIEW

The University of California, Los Angeles is a state-supported, coed university. Enrollment: 35,558 graduate, professional, and undergraduate students. Founded: 1919. The graduate business unit is in an urban setting and is on a quarter calendar.

HIGHLIGHTS

Enrollment Profile

Full-time: 640	International: 23%
Part-time: 534	Women: 26%
Total: 1,174	Minorities: 24%
Average Age: 28	Average Class Size: 35
Fall 1997 Average GPA: 3.5	Fall 1997 Average GMAT: 670

Costs
Full-time tuition: $8994 per academic year (nonresident)
Part-time tuition: N/R

AACSB – The International Association for Management Education accredited

GRADUATE BUSINESS PROGRAMS

Full-time MBA (MBA) Full-time; 96 total credits required; 21 months to 2 years to complete program. Concentrations in accounting, production management, entrepreneurship, real estate, finance, strategic management, human resources, technology management, industrial/labor relations, international business, international economics, international finance, international management, international marketing, management, management information systems, management science, managerial economics, marketing, nonprofit management, operations management, organizational behavior/development.

Fully-employed MBA (MBA) Part-time; 84 total credits required; 2.3 to 2.8 years to complete program.

Executive MBA (MBA) Part-time; 66 total credits required; 23 months to complete program.

Master of Business Administration/Doctor of Jurisprudence (MBA/JD) Full-time; 185 total credits required; 3.8 to 4 years to complete program. Concentrations in accounting, production management, entrepreneurship, real estate, finance, strategic management, human resources, technology management, industrial/labor relations, international business, international economics, international finance, international management, international marketing, management, management information systems, management science, managerial economics, marketing, nonprofit management, operations management, organizational behavior/development.

Master of Business Administration/Master of Science in Public Health (MBA/MS) Full-time; 132 total credits required; 2.8 to 3 years to complete program. Concentrations in accounting, production management, entrepreneurship, real estate, finance, strategic management, human resources, technology management, industrial/labor relations, international business, international economics, international finance, international management, international marketing, management, management information systems, management science, managerial economics, marketing, nonprofit management, operations management, organizational behavior/development.

Master of Business Administration/Master of Science in Library Science (MBA/MS) Full-time; 124 total credits required; 2.8 to 3 years to complete program. Concentrations in accounting, production management, entrepreneurship, real estate, finance, strategic management, human resources, technology management, industrial/labor relations, international business, international economics, international finance, international management, international marketing, management, management information systems, management science, managerial economics, marketing, nonprofit management, operations management, organizational behavior/development.

Master of Business Administration/Master of Arts in Urban Studies (MBA/MA) Full-time; 144 total credits required; 2.8 to 3 years to complete program. Concentrations in accounting, production management, entrepreneurship, real estate, finance, strategic management, human resources, technology management, industrial/labor relations, international business, international economics, international finance, international management, international marketing, management, management information systems, management science, managerial economics, marketing, nonprofit management, operations management, organizational behavior/development.

Master of Business Administration/Master of Science in Computer Science (MBA/MS) Full-time; 96 total credits required; 2.8 to 3 years to complete program. Concentrations in accounting, production management, entrepreneurship, real estate, finance, strategic management, human resources, technology management, industrial/labor relations, international business, international economics, international finance, international management, international marketing, management, management information systems, management science, managerial economics, marketing, nonprofit management, operations management, organizational behavior/development.

Master of Business Administration/Master of Arts in Latin American Studies (MBA/MA) Full-time; 120 total credits required; 2.5 to 3 years to complete program. Concentrations in accounting, production management, entrepreneurship, real estate, finance, strategic management, human resources, technology management, industrial/labor relations, international business, international economics, international finance, international management, international marketing, management, management information systems, management science, managerial economics, marketing, nonprofit management, operations management, organizational behavior/development.

Master of Business Administration/Master of Nursing (MBA/MN) Full-time; 129 total credits required; 2.8 to 3 years to complete program. Concentrations in accounting, production management, entrepreneurship, real estate, finance, strategic management, human resources, technology management, industrial/labor relations, international business, international economics, international finance, international management, international marketing, management, management information systems, management science, managerial economics, marketing, nonprofit management, operations management, organizational behavior/development.

Master of Business Administration/Doctor of Medicine (MBA/MD) Full-time; 96 total credits required; 5 to 5.3 years to complete program. Concentrations in accounting, production management, entrepreneurship, real estate, finance, strategic management, human resources, technology management, industrial/labor relations, international business, international economics, international finance, international management, international marketing, management, management information systems, management science, managerial economics, marketing, nonprofit management, operations management, organizational behavior/development.

ADMISSION

Applications For fall 1997 there were 3,871 applications for admission. Of those applying, 617 were accepted. Of those accepted, 323 enrolled.

Application Requirements Application form, application fee, bachelor's degree, essay, minimum GPA, letters of recommendation, personal statement, resume, college transcript(s), computer experience: knowledge of basic operations of MAC or MS DOS.

Recommended for Application GMAT score accepted, interview, work experience.

Application Deadline 4/3 for fall, 1/30 for fall (international). Application fee: $90.

ACADEMICS

Faculty Full-time 94; part-time 48.

Teaching Methodologies Case study, computer-aided instruction, computer analysis, field projects, group discussion, lecture, seminars by members of the business community, student presentations, study groups, team projects.

Technology 2,467 on-campus computer terminals/PCs are available for student use and are linked by a campus-wide network. The network has full access to the Internet. Students are required to have their own PC.

Special Opportunities Advanced credit may be earned through transfer of credits from another institution. International exchange programs in Argentina, Australia, Austria, Belgium, Chile, Denmark, France, Germany, Hong Kong, Italy, Japan, Mexico, Netherlands, Norway, Peru, Philippines, South Africa, Spain, Sweden, Switzerland, UK, Venezuela. An internship program is available.

FINANCES

Costs for 1997–98 Tuition: Full-time: $8994 per year (nonresident). Cost varies by academic program. Fees: Full-time: $11,309 per academic year (resident); $11,309 per academic year (nonresident). Average 1997–98 room and board costs were $6490 per academic year (on campus) and $8801 per academic year (off campus). Room and board costs vary by occupancy (e.g., single, double, triple), type of accommodation.

Financial Aid In 1997–98, 70% of students received some institutionally administered aid in the form of fellowships, research assistantships, teaching assistantships, grants, scholarships, work study, loans. Financial aid is available to part-time students. Application Deadline: 3/2.

Financial Aid Contact Mrs. Marta Klock, Financial Aid Director, 110 Westwood Plaza, Box 951481, Los Angeles, CA 90095-1481. Phone: 310-825-6944; Fax: 310-825-8582; E-mail: mba.admissions@anderson.ucla.edu

FACILITIES

Information Resources University Research Library plus 13 additional on-campus libraries; total holdings of 6,772,851 volumes, 5,815,667 microforms, 101,581 current periodical subscriptions. CD player(s) available for graduate student use. Access provided to online bibliographic retrieval services.

INTERNATIONAL STUDENTS

Demographics 23% of students enrolled are international students.

Services and Facilities International student office, international student center, international student housing, visa services, ESL courses, counseling/support services.

Applying TOEFL required. Financial aid is available to international students.

International Student Contact Mr. Randy Rutledge, Assistant Director, MBA Admissions, 110 Westwood Plaza, Box 951481, Los Angeles, CA 90095-1481. Phone: 310-825-6944; Fax: 310-825-8582; E-mail: mba.admissions@anderson.ucla.edu

PLACEMENT

Services include alumni network, career counseling/planning, career library, career placement, electronic job bank, job interviews arranged, job search course, resume referral to employers, and resume preparation. In 1996–97, 191 organizations participated in on-campus recruiting; 5,100 on-campus interviews were conducted.

Employment Of 1996–97 graduates, 99% were employed within three months of graduation; the average starting salary was $75,000. Types of employment entered: accounting, banking, computer-related, consulting, finance, financial services, high technology, human resources, information systems/technology, management, marketing, nonprofit, real estate.

Business Program(s) URL: http://www.anderson.ucla.edu/

Program Contact: Mrs. Linda Baldwin, Director of MBA Admissions, 110 Westwood Plaza, Box 951481, Los Angeles, CA 90095-1481. Phone: 310-825-6944; Fax: 310-825-8582; E-mail: mba.admissions@anderson.ucla.edu

See full description on page 1048.

University of California, Riverside

A. Gary Anderson Graduate School of Management

Riverside, California

OVERVIEW

The University of California, Riverside is a state-supported, coed university. Enrollment: 9,536 graduate, professional, and undergraduate students; 1,280 full-time matriculated graduate/professional students; 39 part-time matriculated graduate/professional students. Founded: 1954. The graduate business unit is in an urban setting and is on a quarter calendar.

HIGHLIGHTS

Enrollment Profile

Full-time: 130	International: 44%
Part-time: 21	Women: 44%
Total: 151	Minorities: 27%
Average Age: 27	Average Class Size: 30
Fall 1997 Average GPA: 3.3	Fall 1997 Average GMAT: 560

Costs

Full-time tuition: $4866 per academic year (resident); $13,854 per academic year (nonresident)
Part-time tuition: N/R

GRADUATE BUSINESS PROGRAMS

Master of Business Administration (MBA) Full-time, part-time; 92 total credits required; 18 months to 2 years to complete program. Concentrations in accounting, entrepreneurship, finance, human resources, international management, management, marketing, organizational behavior/development, production management, management information systems, operations management, management science.

ADMISSION

Applications For fall 1997 there were 298 applications for admission. Of those applying, 165 were accepted. Of those accepted, 71 enrolled.

Application Requirements GMAT score, application form, application fee, bachelor's degree, essay, minimum GPA: 3.0, 2 letters of recommendation, college transcript(s).

University of California, Riverside (continued)

Recommended for Application Interview, personal statement, resume, computer experience.

Application Deadline 5/1 for fall, 9/1 for winter, 12/1 for spring, 2/1 for fall (international), 7/1 for winter (international), 10/1 for spring (international). Application fee: $40.

ACADEMICS

Faculty Full-time 25; part-time 7.

Teaching Methodologies Case study, computer-aided instruction, computer simulations, faculty seminars, field projects, lecture, research, seminars by members of the business community, student presentations, team projects.

Technology 154 on-campus computer terminals/PCs are available for student use and are linked by a campus-wide network. The network has full access to the Internet. Students are not required to have their own PC.

Special Opportunities Advanced credit may be earned through credit by examination, transfer of credits from another institution. International exchange program available. An internship program is available.

FINANCES

Costs for 1997–98 Tuition: Full-time: $4866 per year (resident); $13,854 per year (nonresident). Cost varies by number of credits taken. Fees vary by number of credits taken. Average 1997–98 room and board costs were $9155 per academic year (on campus) and $9155 per academic year (off campus). Room and board costs vary by occupancy (e.g., single, double, triple), type of accommodation, type of meal plan.

Financial Aid In 1997–98, 100% of students received some institutionally administered aid in the form of fellowships, research assistantships, teaching assistantships, grants, scholarships, work study, loans. Financial aid is available to part-time students. Application Deadline: 2/1.

Financial Aid Contact Mr. Gary Kuzas, Director of MBA Admissions—Graduate School of Management, Anderson Hall, Riverside, CA 92521-0203. Phone: 909-787-4551 Ext. 2525; Fax: 909-787-3970; E-mail: gary.kuzas@ucr.edu

FACILITIES

Information Resources Tomas Rivera Library plus 4 additional on-campus libraries; total holdings of 1,801,200 volumes, 1,556,200 microforms, 13,300 current periodical subscriptions. CD player(s) available for graduate student use. Access provided to online bibliographic retrieval services and online databases.

INTERNATIONAL STUDENTS

Demographics 44% of students enrolled are international students.

Services and Facilities International student office, international student center, ESL courses, counseling/support services.

Applying TOEFL: minimum score of 550, proof of adequate funds required. Financial aid is available to international students.

International Student Contact Mr. Horst Hoffmann, Assistant Director—International Service Center, 900 University Avenue, Riverside, CA 92521-0102. Phone: 909-787-4113; Fax: 909-787-3778.

PLACEMENT

Services include alumni network, career counseling/planning, career fairs, career library, career placement, electronic job bank, job interviews arranged, resume referral to employers, and resume preparation. In 1996–97, 135 organizations participated in on-campus recruiting; 307 on-campus interviews were conducted.

Employment Of 1996–97 graduates, 85% were employed within three months of graduation; the average starting salary was $48,812. Types of employment entered: accounting, banking, communications, computer-related, consulting, engineering, finance, financial services, government, health services, high technology, human resources, information systems/technology, insurance, international trade, management, marketing, pharmaceutical, retail.

Business Program(s) URL: http://www.agsm.ucr.edu

Program Contact: Mr. Gary Kuzas, Director of MBA Admissions, Anderson Hall, Riverside, CA 92521-0203. Phone: 909-787-4551 Ext. 2525; Fax: 909-787-3970; E-mail: gary.kuzas@ucr.edu
See full description on page 1050.

University of Judaism

Lieber School of Graduate Studies

Bel Air, California

OVERVIEW

The University of Judaism is an independent-religious, coed, comprehensive institution. Enrollment: 212 graduate, professional, and undergraduate students;

70 full-time matriculated graduate/professional students; 26 part-time matriculated graduate/professional students. Founded: 1947. The graduate business unit is in an urban setting and is on a semester calendar.

HIGHLIGHTS

Enrollment Profile

Full-time: 14	International: 3%
Part-time: 16	Women: 77%
Total: 30	Minorities: N/R
Average Age: 33	Average Class Size: 10
Fall 1997 Average GPA: 3.5	Fall 1997 Average GMAT: N/R

Costs
Full-time tuition: $13,910 per academic year
Part-time tuition: $580 per unit

GRADUATE BUSINESS PROGRAMS

Master of Business Administration in Nonprofit Management (MBA) Full-time, part-time; 51 total credits required; 2 to 5 years to complete program. Concentrations in nonprofit management, nonprofit organization, resources management, marketing.

Master of Arts in Nonprofit Management (MA) Full-time, part-time; 32 total credits required; minimum of 12 months to complete program. Concentrations in nonprofit management, nonprofit organization, resources management, marketing.

ADMISSION

Applications For fall 1997 there were 14 applications for admission. Of those applying, 14 were accepted. Of those accepted, 8 enrolled.

Application Requirements Application form, application fee, bachelor's degree, essay, 2 letters of recommendation, personal statement, college transcript(s).

Recommended for Application GMAT score accepted, GRE score accepted, minimum GPA: 3.0, interview, resume, work experience, computer experience.

Application Deadline Applications processed on a rolling/continuous basis for both domestic and international students. Application fee: $35. Deferred entrance is available.

ACADEMICS

Faculty Full-time 3; part-time 10.

Teaching Methodologies Case study, computer-aided instruction, computer analysis, experiential learning, faculty seminars, field projects, group discussion, lecture, research, role playing, seminars by members of the business community, simulations, student presentations, study groups, team projects.

Technology 26 on-campus computer terminals/PCs are available for student use and are linked by a campus-wide network. The network has full access to the Internet. Students are required to have their own PC.

Special Opportunities Advanced credit may be earned through credit by examination, transfer of credits from another institution. An internship program is available.

FINANCES

Costs for 1997–98 Tuition: Full-time: $13,910 per year. Part-time: $580 per unit. Fees: Full-time: $400 per academic year. Part-time: $400 per year. Average 1997–98 room and board costs were $7200 per academic year (on campus) and $6750 per academic year (off campus). Room and board costs vary by occupancy (e.g., single, double, triple), type of accommodation, type of meal plan.

Financial Aid In 1997–98, 40% of students received some institutionally administered aid in the form of fellowships, grants, scholarships, work study, loans. Financial aid is available to part-time students. Application Deadline: 3/2.

Financial Aid Contact Ms. Jodi Ehrenberg, Director of Financial Aid, 15600 Mulholland Drive, Bel Air, CA 90077. Phone: 310-476-9777 Ext. 252; Fax: 310-471-3657.

FACILITIES

Information Resources Ostrow Library; total holdings of 105,000 volumes, 2,000 microforms, 400 current periodical subscriptions. CD player(s) available for graduate student use. Access provided to online bibliographic retrieval services.

INTERNATIONAL STUDENTS

Demographics 3% of students enrolled are international students [North America, 100%].

Applying TOEFL: minimum score of 550, proof of health/immunizations required. Financial aid is available to international students.

International Student Contact Mr. Richard Scaffidi, Dean of Admissions and Financial Aid, 15600 Mulholland Drive, Bel Air, CA 90077. Phone: 310-476-9777 Ext. 241; Fax: 310-471-3657; E-mail: admissions@uj.edu

PLACEMENT

Services include alumni network, career counseling/planning, career library, resume referral to employers, and resume preparation.

Employment Of 1996–97 graduates, 95% were employed within three months of graduation; the average starting salary was $48,000. Types of employment entered: accounting, communications, consulting, education, finance, government, human resources, law, management, marketing, nonprofit.

Business Program(s) URL: http://www.uj.edu

Program Contact: Mr. Richard Scaffidi, Dean of Admissions and Financial Aid, 15600 Mulholland Drive, Bel Air, CA 90077. Phone: 310-476-9777 Ext. 250, 800-853-6763; Fax: 310-471-3657.

University of La Verne

School of Business and Global Studies
La Verne, California

OVERVIEW
The University of La Verne is an independent-nonprofit, coed university. Enrollment: 5,889 graduate, professional, and undergraduate students; 1,486 full-time matriculated graduate/professional students; 1,377 part-time matriculated graduate/professional students. Founded: 1891. The graduate business unit is in a suburban setting and is on a 4-1-4 calendar.

HIGHLIGHTS

Enrollment Profile
Full-time: 291
Part-time: 425
Total: 716
Average Age: 35
Fall 1997 Average GPA: N/R
International: 11%
Women: 44%
Minorities: 42%
Average Class Size: 17
Fall 1997 Average GMAT: 520

Costs
Full-time tuition: $11,340 per academic year
Part-time tuition: $315 per credit

GRADUATE BUSINESS PROGRAMS
Master of Business Administration (MBA) Full-time, part-time; 36-54 total credits required; 12 months to 5 years to complete program. Concentrations in accounting, finance, health care, information management, international management, leadership, management, marketing.

MBA for Experienced Professionals (MBA) Full-time, part-time; 33-51 total credits required; 12 months to 5 years to complete program. Concentrations in accounting, finance, health care, information management, international management, leadership, management, marketing.

Master of Science in Business Organizational Management (MS) Full-time, part-time; 36-45 total credits required; 2 to 5 years to complete program. Concentrations in health care, human resources.

Master of Business Administration/Doctor of Jurisprudence (MBA/JD) Full-time, part-time; 4 to 8 years to complete program. Concentrations in accounting, finance, health care, information management, international management, leadership, management, marketing, contract management, legal administration.

ADMISSION
Application Requirements Application form, application fee, bachelor's degree, essay, minimum GPA, 3 letters of recommendation, personal statement, college transcript(s).

Recommended for Application GMAT score accepted, resume, minimum of 3 years of work experience, computer experience.

Application Deadline Applications processed on a rolling/continuous basis for both domestic and international students. Application fee: $25. Deferred entrance is available.

ACADEMICS
Teaching Methodologies Case study, computer analysis, computer simulations, faculty seminars, group discussion, lecture, research, role playing, simulations, student presentations, study groups, team projects.

Technology 250 on-campus computer terminals/PCs are available for student use and are linked by a campus-wide network.

Special Opportunities Advanced credit may be earned through transfer of credits from another institution. International exchange program in Greece. An internship program is available.

FINANCES
Costs for 1997–98 Tuition: Full-time: $11,340 per program. Part-time: $315 per credit. Cost varies by academic program, campus location, number of credits taken. Fees: Full-time: $210 per academic year. Fees vary by academic program. Average 1997–98 room and board costs were $2800 per academic year. Room and board costs vary by occupancy (e.g., single, double, triple).

Financial Aid Fellowships, scholarships, work study available. Financial aid is available to part-time students.

Financial Aid Contact Director of Financial Aid, 1950 Third Street, LaVerne, CA 91750. Phone: 909-593-3511; Fax: 909-392-2704.

FACILITIES
Information Resources Elvin and Betty Wilson Library plus 1 additional on-campus library; total holdings of 265,000 volumes, 2,000 current periodical subscriptions. CD player(s) available for graduate student use. Access provided to online bibliographic retrieval services.

INTERNATIONAL STUDENTS
Demographics 11% of students enrolled are international students.

Services and Facilities International student office, international student center, international student housing, visa services, ESL courses, counseling/support services.

Applying TOEFL: minimum score of 550, proof of adequate funds required. Financial aid is not available to international students.

International Student Contact Dr. Julius Walecki, Director of Program Development, 1950 Third Street, La Verne, CA 91750. Phone: 909-593-3511 Ext. 4192; Fax: 909-392-2704; E-mail: waleckij@uw.edu

PLACEMENT
Services include alumni network, career counseling/planning, career fairs, career library, career placement, electronic job bank, job search course, resume referral to employers, and resume preparation.

Employment Types of employment entered: accounting, banking, communications, computer-related, consulting, education, finance, financial services, government, health services, high technology, human resources, information systems/technology, insurance, international trade, management, marketing, media, real estate, service industry, telecommunications, transportation.

Business Program(s) URL: http://www.ulv.edu

Program Contact: Dr. Julius Walecki, Director of Program Development, 1950 Third Street, La Verne, CA 91750-4443. Phone: 909-593-3511 Ext. 4192, 800-955-4858 (CA only); Fax: 909-392-2704; E-mail: waleckij@ulv.edu

University of Redlands

Alfred North Whitehead College
Redlands, California

OVERVIEW
The University of Redlands is an independent-nonprofit, coed, comprehensive institution. Enrollment: 3,810 graduate, professional, and undergraduate students; 863 full-time matriculated graduate/professional students; 25 part-time matriculated graduate/professional students. Founded: 1907. The graduate business unit is in a small-town setting and is on a 4-1-4 calendar.

HIGHLIGHTS

Enrollment Profile
Full-time: 500
Part-time: 0
Total: 500
Average Age: 38
Fall 1997 Average GPA: 3.2
International: N/R
Women: 40%
Minorities: N/R
Average Class Size: 15
Fall 1997 Average GMAT: N/R

Costs
Full-time tuition: N/R
Part-time tuition: $400 per credit

GRADUATE BUSINESS PROGRAMS
Master of Business Administration (MBA) Full-time; 45 total credits required; 2 years to complete program.

Master of Arts in Management (MA) Full-time; 32 total credits required; minimum of 18 months to complete program. Concentrations in human resources, management information systems, quality management, industrial/labor relations.

ADMISSION
Application Requirements Application form, application fee, bachelor's degree, essay, minimum GPA: 3.0, 2 letters of recommendation, personal statement, college transcript(s), minimum of 5 years of work experience.

Application Deadline Applications processed on a rolling/continuous basis for both domestic and international students. Application fee: $40. Deferred entrance is available.

ACADEMICS
Teaching Methodologies Case study, lecture, simulations.

Special Opportunities International exchange program in United Kingdom.

FINANCES
Costs for 1997–98 Tuition: $400 per credit. Cost varies by number of credits taken.

University of Redlands (continued)

Financial Aid Contact Director of Financial Aid, PO Box 3080, Redlands, CA 92373-0999. Phone: 909-793-2121 Ext. 4047.

FACILITIES

Information Resources Armacost Library plus 2 additional on-campus libraries; total holdings of 219,364 volumes, 162,244 microforms, 1,623 current periodical subscriptions. CD player(s) available for graduate student use. Access provided to online bibliographic retrieval services.

INTERNATIONAL STUDENTS

Demographics N/R

Applying TOEFL: minimum score of 550 required.

PLACEMENT

Services include alumni network, job search course, and resume preparation.

Employment Types of employment entered: health services, utilities.

Program Contact: Admissions Office, PO Box 3080, Redlands, CA 92373-0999. Phone: 909-335-4060, 888-999-9844 (CA only); Fax: 909-335-3400.

University of San Diego

School of Business Administration

San Diego, California

OVERVIEW

The University of San Diego is an independent-religious, coed university. Enrollment: 6,694 graduate, professional, and undergraduate students. Founded: 1949. The graduate business unit is in an urban setting and is on a semester calendar.

HIGHLIGHTS

Enrollment Profile

Full-time: 217	International: 28%
Part-time: 171	Women: 37%
Total: 388	Minorities: N/R
Average Age: 27	Average Class Size: 26
Fall 1997 Average GPA: 3.23	Fall 1997 Average GMAT: 542

Costs
Full-time tuition: $10,530 per academic year
Part-time tuition: $585 per credit

AACSB – The International Association for Management Education accredited

Degree(s) offered in conjunction with Instituto Tecnologico y de Estudios Superiores de Monterrey

GRADUATE BUSINESS PROGRAMS

Master of Business Administration (MBA) Full-time, part-time; 30-60 total credits required; 12 months to 3 years to complete program. Concentrations in finance, management, marketing, entrepreneurship, project management, international business, real estate, materials management.

Master of International Business (MIB) Full-time, part-time; 30-60 total credits required; 12 months to 3 years to complete program.

Master of Business Administration/Doctor of Jurisprudence (MBA/JD) Full-time, part-time; 103-133 total credits required; 3 to 4 years to complete program. Concentrations in finance, management, marketing, entrepreneurship, project management, international business, real estate, materials management.

Master of International Business/Doctor of Jurisprudence (MIB/JD) Full-time, part-time; 103-133 total credits required; 3 to 4 years to complete program.

Master of Business Administration/Master of Science in Nursing (MBA/MS) Full-time, part-time; 60 total credits required; 12 months to 3 years to complete program.

Joint MBA conferred in conjunction with ITESM (MBA) Full-time, part-time; 20 months to 2.2 years to complete program. Concentrations in finance, management, marketing, entrepreneurship, project management, international business, real estate, materials management.

Master of Business Administration at USD/Master of Science Finance at ITESM (MBA/MSF) Full-time, part-time; 19 months to 2 years to complete program.

Master of Business Administration at USD/Master of Marketing at ITESM (MBA/MSMT) Full-time, part-time; 19 months to 2 years to complete program.

Master of International Business at USD/Master of Business Administration at ITESM (MIB/MBA) Full-time, part-time; 20 months to 2.3 years to complete program.

Master of International Businessat USD/Master of Science Finance at ITESM (MIB/MSF) Full-time, part-time; 19 months to 2.2 years to complete program.

Master of International Business/Master of Science in Marketing (MIB/MSMT) Full-time, part-time; 19 months to 2.2 years to complete program.

ADMISSION

Applications For fall 1997 there were 490 applications for admission. Of those applying, 279 were accepted. Of those accepted, 133 enrolled.

Application Requirements GMAT score, application form, application fee, bachelor's degree, essay, minimum GPA: 3.0, 3 letters of recommendation, personal statement, resume, college transcript(s).

Application Deadline 5/1 for fall, 11/15 for spring, 3/15 for summer, 5/1 for fall (international), 11/15 for spring (international), 3/15 for summer (international). Application fee: $45. Deferred entrance is available.

ACADEMICS

Faculty Full-time 59; part-time 29.

Teaching Methodologies Case study, computer-aided instruction, computer analysis, computer simulations, experiential learning, faculty seminars, field projects, group discussion, lecture, research, role playing, seminars by members of the business community, simulations, student presentations, study groups, team projects.

Technology 160 on-campus computer terminals/PCs are available for student use and are linked by a campus-wide network. The network has full access to the Internet. Students are not required to have their own PC.

Special Opportunities Advanced credit may be earned through credit by examination, credit for military training programs, transfer of credits from another institution. International exchange programs in Argentina, France, Germany, Hong Kong, Mexico, United Kingdom. An internship program is available.

FINANCES

Costs for 1997–98 Tuition: Full-time: $10,530 per year. Part-time: $585 per credit. Cost varies by number of credits taken. Fees: Full-time: $50 per academic year. Part-time: $30 per year. Fees vary by number of credits taken. Average 1997–98 room and board costs were $7620 per academic year (on campus) and $5900 per academic year (off campus). Room and board costs vary by occupancy (e.g., single, double, triple), type of accommodation, type of meal plan.

Financial Aid In 1997–98, 34% of students received some institutionally administered aid in the form of fellowships, research assistantships, grants, work study, loans. Financial aid is available to part-time students. Application Deadline: 5/1.

Financial Aid Contact Ms. Judith Lewis Logue, Director of Financial Aid Services, 5998 Alcala Park, San Diego, CA 92110-2492. Phone: 619-260-4600.

FACILITIES

Information Resources Copley Library plus 1 additional on-campus library; total holdings of 853,852 volumes, 1,036,557 microforms, 7,640 current periodical subscriptions. CD player(s) available for graduate student use. Access provided to online bibliographic retrieval services and online databases.

INTERNATIONAL STUDENTS

Demographics 28% of students enrolled are international students [Africa, 5%, Asia, 40%, Europe, 45%, North America, 5%, South America, 5%].

Services and Facilities International student office, international student center, international student housing, visa services, counseling/support services, orientation, publications, alumni, network campus activities, health insurance information.

Applying TOEFL: minimum score of 580, TWE: minimum score of 4.5, proof of adequate funds required. Financial aid is not available to international students.

International Student Contact Ms. Yvette Fontaine, Director of International Resources, 5998 Alcala Park, San Diego, CA 92110-2492. Phone: 619-260-4678; E-mail: yvette@acusd.edu

PLACEMENT

Services include alumni network, career counseling/planning, career fairs, career library, electronic job bank, job interviews arranged, resume referral to employers, and resume preparation. In 1996–97, 38 organizations participated in on-campus recruiting.

Employment Of 1996–97 graduates, 80% were employed within three months of graduation; the average starting salary was $46,700. Types of employment entered: accounting, banking, chemical industry, communications, computer-related, consulting, consumer products, education, engineering, finance, financial services, government, health services, high technology, hospitality management, human resources, information systems/technology, insurance, international trade, law, management, manufacturing, marketing, media, nonprofit, pharmaceutical, real estate, retail, service industry, telecommunications, transportation.

Business Program(s) URL: http://business.acusd.edu/

Program Contact: Ms. Mary Jane Tiernan, Director of Graduate Admissions, 5998 Alcala Park, San Diego, CA 92110-2492. Phone: 619-260-4524, 800-248-4873; Fax: 619-260-4158; E-mail: grads@acusd.edu

See full description on page 1136.

University of San Francisco

McLaren School of Business

San Francisco, California

OVERVIEW
The University of San Francisco is an independent-religious, coed university. Enrollment: 7,488 graduate, professional, and undergraduate students; 2,266 full-time matriculated graduate/professional students; 770 part-time matriculated graduate/professional students. Founded: 1855. The graduate business unit is in an urban setting and is on a semester calendar.

HIGHLIGHTS

Enrollment Profile

Full-time: 311	International: 38%
Part-time: 216	Women: 45%
Total: 527	Minorities: 28%
Average Age: 27	Average Class Size: 25
Fall 1997 Average GPA: 3.1	Fall 1997 Average GMAT: 545

Costs
Full-time tuition: $15,792 per academic year
Part-time tuition: $658 per unit

AACSB – The International Association for Management Education accredited

Degree(s) offered in conjunction with several Jesuit MBA programs in the U.S.

GRADUATE BUSINESS PROGRAMS
Master of Business Administration (MBA) Full-time, part-time, distance learning option; 48 total credits required; 18 months to 2 years to complete program. Concentrations in finance, international business, management, marketing, telecommunications management.

Doctor of Jurisprudence/Master of Business Administration (JD/MBA) Full-time, part-time; 48 total credits required; up to 4 years to complete program.

Master of Science in Nursing/Master of Business Administration (MS/MBA) Full-time, part-time; 48 total credits required; up to 2.5 years to complete program.

Executive Master of Rehabilitation Administration (EMRA) Full-time, part-time; 48 total credits required; up to 2.5 years to complete program.

Executive MBA (EMBA) Full-time, part-time; 48 total credits required; up to 22 months to complete program.

ADMISSION
Applications For fall 1997 there were 598 applications for admission. Of those applying, 340 were accepted. Of those accepted, 218 enrolled.

Application Requirements Application form, application fee, bachelor's degree, essay, minimum GPA, 2 letters of recommendation, personal statement, college transcript(s).

Recommended for Application GMAT score accepted, work experience, computer experience.

Application Deadline 6/1 for fall, 11/10 for spring, 4/1 for summer, 6/1 for fall (international), 11/10 for spring (international), 4/1 for summer (international). Application fee: $40, $50 (international). Deferred entrance is available.

ACADEMICS
Faculty Full-time 45; part-time 40.

Teaching Methodologies Case study, computer-aided instruction, computer analysis, computer simulations, experiential learning, faculty seminars, field projects, group discussion, lecture, research, role playing, seminars by members of the business community, simulations, student presentations, study groups, team projects.

Technology 225 on-campus computer terminals/PCs are available for student use and are linked by a campus-wide network. The network has full access to the Internet. Students are not required to have their own PC.

Special Opportunities Advanced credit may be earned through credit by examination, credit for experience, transfer of credits from another institution.

FINANCES
Costs for 1997–98 Tuition: Full-time: $15,792 per year. Part-time: $658 per unit. Cost varies by number of credits taken. Fees: Full-time: $200 per academic year. Part-time: $100 per year. Fees vary by academic program, reciprocity agreements. Average 1997–98 room and board costs were $7643 per academic year (on campus) and $6500 per academic year (off campus). Room and board costs vary by occupancy (e.g., single, double, triple), type of meal plan.

Financial Aid In 1997–98, 38% of students received some institutionally administered aid in the form of fellowships, research assistantships, work study, loans. Financial aid is available to part-time students. Application Deadline: 3/2.

Financial Aid Contact Scott Reynolds, Financial Aid Counselor, 2130 Fulton Street, San Francisco, CA 94117. Phone: 415-422-6303; Fax: 415-422-2502.

FACILITIES
Information Resources Gleeson Library plus 2 additional on-campus libraries; total holdings of 755,080 volumes, 845,280 microforms, 4,900 current periodical subscriptions. CD player(s) available for graduate student use. Access provided to online bibliographic retrieval services.

INTERNATIONAL STUDENTS
Demographics 38% of students enrolled are international students.

Services and Facilities International student office, international student center, ESL courses, counseling/support services.

Applying TOEFL: minimum score of 600, proof of adequate funds, proof of health/immunizations required. Financial aid is not available to international students.

International Student Contact Mr. Suresh Appavoo, International Student Advisor, 2130 Fulton Street, Lower Level, Gillson Hall, San Francisco, CA 94117-1080. Phone: 415-422-2654; Fax: 415-422-2502.

PLACEMENT
Services include alumni network, career counseling/planning, career fairs, career library, career placement, electronic job bank, job interviews arranged, resume referral to employers, and resume preparation. In 1996–97, 75 organizations participated in on-campus recruiting.

Employment Of 1996–97 graduates, 80% were employed within three months of graduation; the average starting salary was $51,000. Types of employment entered: accounting, banking, communications, computer-related, consulting, consumer products, education, finance, financial services, government, high technology, human resources, information systems/technology, insurance, international trade, law, management, marketing, nonprofit, pharmaceutical, real estate, service industry, telecommunications, transportation.

Business Program(s) URL: http://www.usfca.edu/mclaren

Program Contact: Ms. Cathy Fusco, MBA Program Director, 2130 Fulton Street, San Francisco, CA 94117. Phone: 415-422-6314; Fax: 415-422-2502; E-mail: mbausf@usfca.edu

See full description on page 1138.

University of Southern California

Marshall School of Business

Los Angeles, California

OVERVIEW
The University of Southern California is an independent-nonprofit, coed university. Enrollment: 28,000 graduate, professional, and undergraduate students; 8,102 full-time matriculated graduate/professional students; 4,572 part-time matriculated graduate/professional students. Founded: 1880. The graduate business unit is in an urban setting and is on a semester calendar.

HIGHLIGHTS

Enrollment Profile

Full-time: 510	International: 23%
Part-time: 1,075	Women: 30%
Total: 1,585	Minorities: 15%
Average Age: 30	Average Class Size: 45
Fall 1997 Average GPA: 3.2	Fall 1997 Average GMAT: 640

Costs
Full-time tuition: $23,958 per academic year
Part-time tuition: $26,775 per year

AACSB – The International Association for Management Education accredited

*I*n addition to its full-time, two-year program, the USC Marshall School of Business Administration offers a unique, intensive one-year international M.B.A. program for managers who are pursuing international and Pacific Rim-related careers. The USC International Business Education and Research (IBEAR) M.B.A. Program begins in mid-August each year and includes a preparatory program and nineteen courses in four 11-week terms. It includes special features such as international consulting projects for major multinational firms, a team-building retreat, optional language courses, attendance at off-campus international business events, and an extensive international guest executive speaker series. Participants have access to the extensive resources of the

<u>*University of Southern California (continued)*</u>

Marshall School of Business Administration, which has 174 full-time faculty members.

IBEAR M.B.A. participants average 33 years of age and 10 years of work experience. They come from thirteen or more countries each year. Approximately 50 percent are corporate-sponsored, while the remainder are self-sponsored. Enrollment is limited to 48 participants. Graduates join a network of more than 700 well-placed IBEAR alumni and 50,000 USC business school alumni. Scholarships are available to domestic and international applicants. For information contact the International Business Education and Research (IBEAR) Program at 213-740-7140, fax: 213-740-7559, or e-mail: ibear@usc.edu

GRADUATE BUSINESS PROGRAMS

Full-time MBA (MBA) Full-time; 61 total credits required; 2 to 5 years to complete program. Concentrations in entrepreneurship, banking, finance, marketing, financial management/planning, human resources, information management, management, management information systems, operations management, real estate, technology management, international and area business studies.

MBA Program for Professionals and Managers (MBA) Part-time; 63 total credits required; 2.8 to 5 years to complete program. Concentrations in entrepreneurship, banking, finance, marketing, financial management/planning, human resources, information management, management, management information systems, operations management, real estate, technology management.

Executive MBA (EMBA) Part-time; 63 total credits required; 22 months to complete program. Concentration in management.

Master of Science in Information and Operations Management (MS) Full-time, part-time; 30 total credits required; 12 months to 5 years to complete program. Concentrations in information management, operations management.

Master of Science in Business Administration (MS) Full-time, part-time; 26 total credits required; 12 months to 5 years to complete program.

Master of Accounting (MAcc) Full-time, part-time; 33 total credits required; 10 months to 5 years to complete program. Concentration in accounting.

Master of Business Taxation (MBT) Full-time, part-time; 45 total credits required; 10 months to 5 years to complete program. Concentration in taxation.

Doctor of Jurisprudence/Master of Business Administration (JD/MBA) Full-time; 91 total credits required; 4 to 5 years to complete program.

Doctor of Jurisprudence/Master of Business Taxation (JD/MBTax) Full-time; 91 total credits required; 4 to 5 years to complete program. Concentration in taxation.

Master of Business Administration/Master of Real Estate Development (MBA/MRED) Full-time, part-time; 80 total credits required; 3 to 5 years to complete program.

Master of Business Administration in International Business Education and Research (MBA) Full-time; 56 total credits required; 11 months to complete program. Concentration in international business.

Master of Business Administration/Master of Arts in East Asian Area Studies (MBA/MA) Full-time, part-time, distance learning option; 72 total credits required; 3 to 5 years to complete program.

Master of Business Administration/Master of Science of Gerontology (MBA/MS) Full-time, part-time; 66 total credits required; 3 to 5 years to complete program.

ADMISSION

Applications For fall 1997 there were 2,900 applications for admission. Of those applying, 1,300 were accepted. Of those accepted, 800 enrolled.

Application Requirements GMAT score, application form, application fee, bachelor's degree, essay, 2 letters of recommendation, personal statement, resume, college transcript(s).

Recommended for Application Minimum GPA, interview, work experience, computer experience.

Application Deadline 4/1 for fall, 4/1 for fall (international). Application fee: $90, $125 (international). Deferred entrance is available.

ACADEMICS

Faculty Full-time 173; part-time 42.

Teaching Methodologies Case study, computer-aided instruction, computer analysis, computer simulations, experiential learning, field projects, group discussion, lecture, research, seminars by members of the business community, simulations, student presentations, study groups, team projects.

Technology 750 on-campus computer terminals/PCs are available for student use and are linked by a campus-wide network. The network has full access to the Internet. Students are required to have their own PC.

Special Opportunities International exchange programs in Australia and various countries in Asia, Europe, and South America. An internship program is available.

FINANCES

Costs for 1997–98 Tuition: Full-time: $23,958 per year. Part-time: $26,775 per year. Cost varies by academic program, number of credits taken. Fees: Full-time: $894 per academic year. Fees vary by academic program, number of credits taken. Average 1997–98 room and board costs were $11,000 per academic year (on campus) and $11,000 per academic year (off campus). Room and board costs vary by campus location, occupancy (e.g., single, double, triple), type of accommodation, type of meal plan.

Financial Aid Fellowships, research assistantships, teaching assistantships, work study, loans available. Financial aid is available to part-time students. Application Deadline: 2/15.

Financial Aid Contact Grace Kim, Assistant Director of Admissions, Bridge Hall 101, Los Angeles, CA 90089-1421. Phone: 213-740-0685; Fax: 213-740-8520.

FACILITIES

Information Resources Doheny Memorial Library plus 19 additional on-campus libraries; total holdings of 2,800,000 volumes, 3,600,000 microforms, 20,000 current periodical subscriptions. CD player(s) available for graduate student use. Access provided to online bibliographic retrieval services and online databases.

INTERNATIONAL STUDENTS

Demographics 23% of students enrolled are international students.

Services and Facilities International student office, international student center, visa services, ESL courses, counseling/support services.

Applying TOEFL: minimum score of 600, proof of adequate funds, proof of health/immunizations required. Financial aid is not available to international students.

International Student Contact Ms. Lisa Miller, Manager, International Exchange Programs, Bridge Hall 200, Los Angeles, CA 90089-1421. Phone: 213-740-6878; Fax: 213-740-1037; E-mail: lmiller@marshall.usc.edu

PLACEMENT

Services include alumni network, career counseling/planning, career fairs, career library, career placement, electronic job bank, job interviews arranged, resume referral to employers, and resume preparation. In 1996–97, 153 organizations participated in on-campus recruiting; 3,024 on-campus interviews were conducted.

Employment Of 1996–97 graduates, 96% were employed within three months of graduation; the average starting salary was $70,000. Types of employment entered: accounting, banking, communications, computer-related, consulting, consumer products, energy, finance, financial services, health services, high technology, human resources, information systems/technology, international trade, management, manufacturing, marketing, petrochemical, real estate, retail, service industry, telecommunications.

Business Program(s) URL: http://www.marshall.usc.edu

Program Contact: Keith Vaughn, Director of Admissions, Bridge Hall 101, USC, Los Angeles, CA 90089-1421. Phone: 213-740-7846; Fax: 213-749-8520; E-mail: uscmba@sba.usc.edu

See full descriptions on pages 1142 and 1144.

University of the Pacific

Eberhardt School of Business

Stockton, California

OVERVIEW

The University of the Pacific is an independent-nonprofit, coed university. Enrollment: 5,100 graduate, professional, and undergraduate students; 1,900 full-time matriculated graduate/professional students; 500 part-time matriculated graduate/professional students. Founded: 1851. The graduate business unit is in an urban setting and is on a semester calendar.

HIGHLIGHTS

Enrollment Profile

Full-time: 34	International: 3%
Part-time: 54	Women: 45%
Total: 88	Minorities: 30%
Average Age: 30	Average Class Size: 18
Fall 1997 Average GPA: 3.15	Fall 1997 Average GMAT: 520

Costs
Full-time tuition: $17,820 per academic year
Part-time tuition: $1731 per course

AACSB – The International Association for Management Education accredited

Established in 1851 as California's first chartered institution of higher education, the University of the Pacific (UOP) is an independent university known for its diversity of academic programs and outstanding teaching faculty. The University draws its students from more than forty states and fifty other countries.

The UOP M.B.A. is committed to the cultivation of leadership skills and the innovative spirit of its students. The M.B.A. program was designed with the conviction that leadership and innovation are the managerial ingredients necessary to create the products, services, and processes needed to compete effectively in the global economy.

To achieve these objectives, UOP's M.B.A. program designers have had to rethink traditional assumptions about business education. The curriculum goes beyond courses in the basic skills of finance, accounting, marketing, and production by incorporating newly designed courses that encourage students to tackle business problems in the context and form in which they actually occur.

Integrative problem-focused courses like global business competition, managing innovation and change, strategic management, leadership effectiveness, and managing quality and productivity dominate the M.B.A.'s advanced phase. By emphasizing the focus on leadership and innovation, a unique specialization in entrepreneurship is available to interested students.

GRADUATE BUSINESS PROGRAMS
Master of Business Administration (MBA) Full-time, part-time; 30-54 total credits required; 10 months to 2 years to complete program. Concentrations in management, entrepreneurship.

ADMISSION
Applications For fall 1997 there were 88 applications for admission. Of those applying, 70 were accepted. Of those accepted, 33 enrolled.

Application Requirements Application form, application fee, bachelor's degree, essay, minimum GPA: 3.0, 3 letters of recommendation, college transcript(s), computer experience: introduction to computer science or equivalent experience.

Recommended for Application GMAT score accepted, personal statement, resume, work experience.

Application Deadline 5/1 for fall, 11/1 for spring, 3/1 for summer, 5/1 for fall (international), 11/1 for spring (international), 3/1 for summer (international). Application fee: $50. Deferred entrance is available.

ACADEMICS
Faculty Full-time 26; part-time 3.

Teaching Methodologies Case study, computer-aided instruction, computer simulations, field projects, group discussion, lecture, role playing, seminars by members of the business community, simulations, student presentations, study groups, team projects.

Technology 50 on-campus computer terminals/PCs are available for student use and are linked by a campus-wide network. The network has full access to the Internet. Students are not required to have their own PC.

Special Opportunities Advanced credit may be earned through transfer of credits from another institution. An internship program is available.

FINANCES
Costs for 1997–98 Tuition: Full-time: $17,820 per year. Part-time: $1731 per course. Cost varies by number of credits taken. Fees: Full-time: $250 per academic year. Fees vary by number of credits taken. Average 1997–98 room and board costs were $5840 per academic year (on campus) and $6500 per academic year (off campus). Room and board costs vary by occupancy (e.g., single, double, triple), type of accommodation, type of meal plan.

Financial Aid Fellowships, research assistantships, scholarships, work study, loans available. Financial aid is available to part-time students. Application Deadline: 3/1.

Financial Aid Contact Financial Aid Office, 3601 Pacific Avenue, Stockton, CA 95211-0197. Phone: 209-946-2629; Fax: 209-946-2586.

FACILITIES
Information Resources William Knox Holt Library plus 1 additional on-campus library; total holdings of 437,742 volumes, 531,129 microforms, 2,652 current periodical subscriptions. CD player(s) available for graduate student use. Access provided to online bibliographic retrieval services and online databases.

INTERNATIONAL STUDENTS
Demographics 3% of students enrolled are international students [Europe, 66%, other, 34%].

Services and Facilities International student office, international student center, visa services, ESL courses, counseling/support services.

Applying TOEFL: minimum score of 550, proof of adequate funds required. Financial aid is available to international students.

International Student Contact Director, International Services, 3601 Pacific Avenue, Stockton, CA 95211-0197. Phone: 209-946-2629; Fax: 209-946-2586.

PLACEMENT
Services include alumni network, career counseling/planning, career fairs, career library, career placement, job interviews arranged, and resume referral to employers. In 1996–97, 100 organizations participated in on-campus recruiting; 25 on-campus interviews were conducted.

Employment Of 1996–97 graduates, 95% were employed within three months of graduation; the average starting salary was $45,000. Types of employment entered: accounting, banking, computer-related, consulting, engineering, finance, financial services, health services, human resources, information systems/technology, international trade, law, management, manufacturing, marketing, media, retail, service industry.

Business Program(s) URL: http://www.uop.edu/esb/docs/mba/index.htm

Program Contact: Mr. Christopher Lozano, Director, Student Recruitment, Weber Hall—Suite 206, 3601 Pacific Avenue, Stockton, CA 95211. Phone: 209-946-2629; Fax: 209-946-2586; E-mail: mba@uop.edu

See full description on page 1158.

Woodbury University

School of Business and Management

Burbank, California

OVERVIEW
Woodbury University is an independent-nonprofit, coed, comprehensive institution. Enrollment: 1,045 graduate, professional, and undergraduate students; 76 full-time matriculated graduate/professional students; 95 part-time matriculated graduate/professional students. Founded: 1884. The graduate business unit is in a suburban setting and is on a semester calendar.

HIGHLIGHTS

Enrollment Profile

Full-time: 76	International: 31%
Part-time: 95	Women: 43%
Total: 171	Minorities: 36%
Average Age: 31	Average Class Size: 18
Fall 1997 Average GPA: 3.4	Fall 1997 Average GMAT: 527

Costs
Full-time tuition: N/R
Part-time tuition: $550 per unit

ACBSP – The American Council of Business Schools and Programs accredited

GRADUATE BUSINESS PROGRAMS
Master of Business Administration (MBA) Full-time, part-time; 36-54 total credits required; 2 to 6 years to complete program. Concentrations in accounting, finance, international business, management, marketing, asian business studies, economics, entrepreneurship, international and area business studies, organizational management.

ADMISSION
Applications For fall 1997 there were 68 applications for admission. Of those applying, 48 were accepted. Of those accepted, 45 enrolled.

Application Requirements Application form, application fee, bachelor's degree, essay, minimum GPA: 2.5, 2 letters of recommendation, college transcript(s).

Recommended for Application GMAT score accepted, interview, resume.

Application Deadline Applications processed on a rolling/continuous basis for both domestic and international students. Application fee: $35, $50 (international). Deferred entrance is available.

ACADEMICS
Faculty Full-time 8; part-time 9.

Teaching Methodologies Case study, computer-aided instruction, experiential learning, group discussion, lecture, research, role playing, seminars by members of the business community, student presentations, study groups, team projects.

Technology 65 on-campus computer terminals/PCs are available for student use and are linked by a campus-wide network. The network has full access to the Internet. Students are not required to have their own PC.

Special Opportunities Advanced credit may be earned through credit by examination, credit for experience, credit for business training programs, transfer of credits from another institution.

FINANCES
Costs for 1997–98 Tuition: $550 per unit. Fees: $180 per semester. Fees vary by academic program. Average 1997–98 room and board costs were

Woodbury University (continued)

$6084 per academic year (on campus) and $6384 per academic year (off campus). Room and board costs vary by occupancy (e.g., single, double, triple), type of meal plan.

Financial Aid In 1997–98, 33% of students received some institutionally administered aid. Financial aid is available to part-time students. Application Deadline: 6/30.

Financial Aid Contact Mr. William Wagoner, Director of Financial Aid, 7500 Glenoaks Boulevard, Burbank, CA 91510-7846. Phone: 818-767-0888 Ext. 273; Fax: 818-767-4816; E-mail: wagoner@vaxb.woodbury.edu

FACILITIES

Information Resources The Los Angeles Times Library; total holdings of 70,249 volumes, 87,421 microforms, 626 current periodical subscriptions. CD player(s) available for graduate student use. Access provided to online bibliographic retrieval services and online databases.

INTERNATIONAL STUDENTS

Demographics 31% of students enrolled are international students [Africa, 2%, Asia, 87%, Central America, 1%, Europe, 3%, South America, 1%, other, 8%].

Services and Facilities International student office, international student housing, visa services, ESL courses, counseling/support services.

Applying TOEFL: minimum score of 550, proof of adequate funds required. Financial aid is not available to international students.

International Student Contact Jocelyn Chong , Director, International Student Services, 7500 Glenoaks Boulevard, Burbank, CA 91510-7846. Phone: 818-767-0888 Ext. 261; Fax: 818-767-0032; E-mail: jchong@vaxb.woodbury. edu

PLACEMENT

Services include alumni network, career counseling/planning, career fairs, career library, career placement, job interviews arranged, resume referral to employers, and resume preparation. In 1996–97, 40 organizations participated in on-campus recruiting.

Employment Of 1996–97 graduates, 70% were employed within three months of graduation; the average starting salary was $47,000. Types of employment entered: accounting, banking, communications, computer-related, consulting, consumer products, finance, financial services, health services, high technology, hospitality management, human resources, information systems/technology, insurance, international trade, management, manufacturing, marketing, media, nonprofit, real estate, retail, telecommunications, utilities.

Business Program(s) URL: http://www.woodburyu.edu

Program Contact: Ms. Roxanne Rafii, Assistant Dean, 7500 Glenoaks Boulevard, Burbank, CA 91510-7846. Phone: 818-767-0888 Ext. 260; Fax: 818-767-0032; E-mail: wec6@vaxb.woodbury.edu
See full description on page 1198.

COLORADO

College for Financial Planning

Program in Financial Planning

Denver, Colorado

OVERVIEW
College for Financial Planning is an independent-nonprofit, coed, graduate institution. Enrollment: 22,638 graduate, professional, and undergraduate students; full-time matriculated graduate/professional students; 1,033 part-time matriculated graduate/professional students. Founded: 1972. The graduate business unit is in a suburban setting and is on a trimester calendar.

HIGHLIGHTS

Enrollment Profile
Full-time: 0	International: 0%
Part-time: 1,033	Women: 33%
Total: 1,033	Minorities: N/R
Average Age: 44	Average Class Size: 20
Fall 1997 Average GPA: 2.85	Fall 1997 Average GMAT: N/R

Costs
Full-time tuition: N/R
Part-time tuition: $600 per course

GRADUATE BUSINESS PROGRAMS
Master of Science in Financial Planning (MS) Part-time, distance learning option; 36 total credits required; 18 months to 7 years to complete program. Concentrations in financial management/planning, finance.

ADMISSION
Applications For fall 1997 there were 227 applications for admission. Of those applying, 147 were accepted. Of those accepted, 129 enrolled.

Application Requirements Application form, application fee, bachelor's degree, minimum GPA: 2.5, personal statement, college transcript(s).

Recommended for Application Essay, resume.

Application Deadline Applications processed on a rolling/continuous basis for both domestic and international students. Application fee: $225, $275 (international).

ACADEMICS
Faculty Full-time 8.

Teaching Methodologies Case study, computer analysis, research, distance education: print based.

Technology Students are not required to have their own PC.

Special Opportunities Advanced credit may be earned through transfer of credits from another institution.

FINANCES
Costs for 1997–98 Tuition: Part-time: $600 per course.

FACILITIES
Information Resources Main library; total holdings of 2,000 volumes, 200 current periodical subscriptions.

INTERNATIONAL STUDENTS
Demographics 0% of students enrolled are international students.

Applying Financial aid is not available to international students.

PLACEMENT
Employment Types of employment entered: accounting, banking, finance, financial services, insurance.

Business Program(s) URL: http://www.fp.edu

Program Contact: Mr. Glen Steelman, Registrar, 4695 South Monaco Street, Denver, CO 80237. Phone: 303-220-1200 Ext. 4861.

Colorado State University

College of Business

Fort Collins, Colorado

OVERVIEW
Colorado State University is a state-supported, coed university. Enrollment: 22,344 graduate, professional, and undergraduate students; 2,396 full-time matriculated graduate/professional students; 1,497 part-time matriculated graduate/professional students. Founded: 1870. The graduate business unit is in a suburban setting and is on a semester calendar.

HIGHLIGHTS

Enrollment Profile
Full-time: 152	International: N/R
Part-time: 114	Women: 46%
Total: 266	Minorities: 7%
Average Age: 29	Average Class Size: 35
Fall 1997 Average GPA: 3.2	Fall 1997 Average GMAT: 606

Costs
Full-time tuition: $2154 per academic year (resident); $7015 per academic year (nonresident)
Part-time tuition: $106 per credit (resident); $398 per credit (nonresident)

AACSB – The International Association for Management Education accredited

GRADUATE BUSINESS PROGRAMS
Accelerated MBA (MBA) Full-time; 36 total credits required; minimum of 11 months to complete program.

Evening MBA (MBA) Part-time, distance learning option; 36 total credits required; minimum of 4 years work experience required; minimum of 2 years to complete program.

Executive MBA (MBA) Part-time; 36 total credits required; minimum of 8 years work experience required; minimum of 21 months to complete program.

Master of Science in Business Administration (MS) Full-time, part-time; 32 total credits required; minimum of 12 months to complete program. Concentrations in accounting, finance, human resources, information management, management, marketing, production management, taxation.

ADMISSION
Applications For fall 1997 there were 408 applications for admission. Of those applying, 198 were accepted. Of those accepted, 123 enrolled.

Application Requirements Application form, application fee, bachelor's degree, minimum GPA, 3 letters of recommendation, personal statement, college transcript(s).

Recommended for Application GMAT score accepted, resume, computer experience.

Application Deadline 4/1 for fall, 9/1 for spring, 2/15 for fall (international). Application fee: $30. Deferred entrance is available.

ACADEMICS
Faculty Full-time 55.

Teaching Methodologies Case study, computer-aided instruction, computer analysis, computer simulations, experiential learning, field projects, group discussion, lecture, research, seminars by members of the business community, student presentations, team projects.

Technology 107 on-campus computer terminals/PCs are available for student use and are linked by a campus-wide network. The network has full access to the Internet. Students are not required to have their own PC.

FINANCES
Costs for 1997–98 Tuition: Full-time: $2154 per semester (resident); $7015 per semester (nonresident). Part-time: $106 per credit (resident); $398 per credit (nonresident). Cost varies by academic program, number of credits taken. Fees: $28 per credit (resident); $28 per credit (nonresident). Fees vary by academic program, number of credits taken. Room and board costs vary by occupancy (e.g., single, double, triple), type of accommodation, type of meal plan.

Financial Aid In 1997–98, 45% of students received some institutionally administered aid in the form of fellowships, research assistantships, teaching assistantships, work study. Application Deadline: 2/1.

Financial Aid Contact Director of Enrollment Services, 103 Administration Annex, Fort Collins, CO 80523-8024. Phone: 970-491-6321; Fax: 970-491-5010.

FACILITIES
Information Resources Morgan Library; total holdings of 1,708,109 volumes, 2,374,794 microforms, 21,455 current periodical subscriptions. CD player(s) available for graduate student use. Access provided to online bibliographic retrieval services and online databases.

INTERNATIONAL STUDENTS
Demographics N/R

Services and Facilities International student office, international student center, international student housing, ESL courses, counseling/support services.

Applying TOEFL: minimum score of 550, proof of adequate funds, proof of health/immunizations required.

International Student Contact International Student Services, 315 Aylesworth, Fort Collins, CO 80523-8009. Phone: 970-491-5917; Fax: 970-491-5501.

PLACEMENT
Services include career counseling/planning, career fairs, career library, career placement, electronic job bank, job interviews arranged, job search course, resume referral to employers, and resume preparation. In 1996–97, 146 organizations participated in on-campus recruiting; 1,328 on-campus interviews were conducted.

Employment Of 1996–97 graduates, 93% were employed within three months of graduation; the average starting salary was $48,500. Types of employment entered: accounting, banking, communications, computer-related, consulting, consumer products, education, engineering, finance, financial services, government, high technology, hospitality management, human resources, information systems/technology, insurance, international trade, management, manufacturing, marketing, nonprofit, petrochemical, pharmaceutical, real estate, retail, service industry, telecommunications, transportation, utilities.

Business Program(s) URL: http://www.csu-business.net

Program Contact: Dr. Jon Clark, Associate Dean, College of Business, Fort Collins, CO 80523. Phone: 970-491-6471; Fax: 970-491-0596.

See full description on page 764.

Colorado Technical University

Management Department

Colorado Springs, Colorado

OVERVIEW
Colorado Technical University is a proprietary, coed, comprehensive institution. Enrollment: 1,700 graduate, professional, and undergraduate students; 435 full-time matriculated graduate/professional students; part-time matriculated graduate/professional students. Founded: 1965. The graduate business unit is in an urban setting and is on a quarter calendar.

HIGHLIGHTS

Enrollment Profile

Full-time: 261	International: 4%
Part-time: 0	Women: 22%
Total: 261	Minorities: 28%
Average Age: 33	Average Class Size: 19
Fall 1997 Average GPA: 3.25	Fall 1997 Average GMAT: N/R

Costs
Full-time tuition: $6500 per academic year
Part-time tuition: $225 per credit hour

GRADUATE BUSINESS PROGRAMS
Master of Science in Management (MS) Full-time, part-time; 48-52 total credits required; 12 months to 3 years to complete program. Concentrations in management, logistics, management information systems, system management.

ADMISSION
Applications For fall 1997 there were 98 applications for admission. Of those applying, 91 were accepted. Of those accepted, 90 enrolled.

Application Requirements Application form, application fee, bachelor's degree, essay, minimum GPA: 3.0, college transcript(s).

Recommended for Application Interview, resume, work experience, computer experience.

Application Deadline Applications processed on a rolling/continuous basis for both domestic and international students. Application fee: $100. Deferred entrance is available.

ACADEMICS
Faculty Full-time 7; part-time 11.

Teaching Methodologies Case study, computer analysis, experiential learning, field projects, group discussion, lecture, research, role playing, seminars by members of the business community, simulations, student presentations, study groups, team projects.

Technology 177 on-campus computer terminals/PCs are available for student use. The network has full access to the Internet. Students are not required to have their own PC.

Special Opportunities Advanced credit may be earned through transfer of credits from another institution.

FINANCES
Costs for 1997–98 Tuition: Full-time: $6500 per year. Part-time: $225 per credit hour. Cost varies by number of credits taken. Fees: Full-time: $168 per academic year. Part-time: $28 per course. Fees vary by academic program, number of credits taken. Average 1997–98 room and board costs were $10,000 per academic year (off campus).

Financial Aid In 1997–98, 14% of students received some institutionally administered aid in the form of grants, work study, loans.

Financial Aid Contact Ms. Marjorie Davis, Financial Aid Department, 4435 North Chestnut Street, Colorado Springs, CO 80907-3896. Phone: 719-598-0200 Ext. 204; Fax: 719-598-3740.

FACILITIES
Information Resources Resource Center; total holdings of 14,000 volumes, 1,650 microforms, 1,200 current periodical subscriptions. CD player(s) available for graduate student use. Access provided to online bibliographic retrieval services and online databases.

INTERNATIONAL STUDENTS
Demographics 4% of students enrolled are international students [Asia, 50%, other, 50%].

Services and Facilities Counseling/support services.

Applying TOEFL: minimum score of 550, proof of adequate funds required. Financial aid is not available to international students.

International Student Contact Ms. Judith Galante, Graduate Admissions, 4435 North Chestnut Street, Colorado Springs, CO 82907-3896. Phone: 719-598-0200 Ext. 204; Fax: 719-598-3740; E-mail: cotech@iex.net

PLACEMENT
Services include alumni network, career counseling/planning, career fairs, career library, career placement, electronic job bank, job interviews arranged, job search course, resume referral to employers, and resume preparation. In 1996–97, 51 organizations participated in on-campus recruiting; 44 on-campus interviews were conducted.

Employment Of 1996–97 graduates, 95% were employed within three months of graduation; the average starting salary was $35,000. Types of employment entered: banking, communications, computer-related, consulting, engineering, government, high technology, information systems/technology, management, manufacturing, nonprofit, telecommunications, utilities.

Colorado Technical University (continued)

Business Program(s) URL: http://www.colotechu.edu

Program Contact: Ms. Judith Galante, Graduate Admissions, 4435 North Chestnut Street, Colorado Springs, CO 80907-3896. Phone: 719-598-0200 Ext. 204; Fax: 719-598-3740.

International School of Information Management

Programs in Information Management and Business Administration

Denver, Colorado

OVERVIEW
International School of Information Management is an independent-nonprofit, coed, graduate institution. Enrollment: 124 graduate, professional, and undergraduate students. Founded: 1987. The graduate business unit is on a term calendar.

HIGHLIGHTS

Enrollment Profile
Full-time: 0
Part-time: 124
Total: 124
Average Age: 37
Fall 1997 Average GPA: 3.2

International: 30%
Women: 19%
Minorities: N/R
Average Class Size: 8
Fall 1997 Average GMAT: N/R

Costs
Full-time tuition: N/R
Part-time tuition: $1125 per course

GRADUATE BUSINESS PROGRAMS
Executive MBA (MBA) Full-time, part-time, distance learning option; 36 total credits required; 18 months to 2.5 years to complete program. Concentrations in accounting, management systems analysis, system management.

Master of Science in Information Management (MS) Full-time, part-time, distance learning option; 36 total credits required; 18 months to 2.5 years to complete program.

Master of Business Administration (MBA) Full-time, part-time, distance learning option; 30 total credits required; 18 months to 2.5 years to complete program.

ADMISSION
Applications For fall 1997 there were 59 applications for admission. Of those applying, 24 were accepted. Of those accepted, 9 enrolled.

Application Requirements Application form, application fee, bachelor's degree, essay, 3 letters of recommendation, personal statement, resume, college transcript(s).

Recommended for Application Work experience, computer experience.

Application Deadline Applications processed on a rolling/continuous basis for both domestic and international students. Application fee: $50. Deferred entrance is available.

ACADEMICS
Faculty Part-time 16.

Teaching Methodologies Case study, experiential learning, group discussion, team projects.

Technology The network has full access to the Internet. Students are required to have their own PC.

Special Opportunities Advanced credit may be earned through credit by examination, credit for experience, credit for military training programs, credit for business training programs, transfer of credits from another institution.

FINANCES
Costs for 1997–98 Tuition: $1125 per course. Fees: $100 per course.

FACILITIES
Information Resources Access provided to online bibliographic retrieval services.

INTERNATIONAL STUDENTS
Demographics 30% of students enrolled are international students.

Applying Proof of adequate funds recommended. Financial aid is not available to international students.

Business Program(s) URL: http://www.isimu.edu

Program Contact: Admissions Office, 501 South Cherry Street, Room #350, Denver, CO 80246. Phone: 303-333-4224, 800-441-4746; Fax: 303-336-1144; E-mail: admissions@isimu.edu

Regis University

School for Professional Studies

Denver, Colorado

OVERVIEW
Regis University is an independent-religious, coed, comprehensive institution. Enrollment: 7,837 graduate, professional, and undergraduate students; 1,221 full-time matriculated graduate/professional students; 1,090 part-time matriculated graduate/professional students. Founded: 1877. The graduate business unit is in a suburban setting and is on a semester calendar.

HIGHLIGHTS

Enrollment Profile
Full-time: 755
Part-time: 759
Total: 1,514
Average Age: 36
Fall 1997 Average GPA: N/R

International: N/R
Women: N/R
Minorities: 11%
Average Class Size: 15
Fall 1997 Average GMAT: 500

Costs
Full-time tuition: N/R
Part-time tuition: $309 per credit hour

GRADUATE BUSINESS PROGRAMS
Master of Business Administration (MBA) Full-time, part-time, distance learning option; 30-45 total credits required; 2 years full-time business work experience required; 18 months to 6 years to complete program. Concentrations in accounting, international business, management information systems, marketing, operations management, finance, information management.

Master of Science in Management (MS) Full-time, part-time; 36 total credits required; 2 admissions essays required; 2 to 6 years to complete program. Concentrations in management, management science, leadership.

Master of Science in Computer Information Systems (MS) Full-time, part-time; 36 total credits required; 2 to 6 years to complete program. Concentrations in information management, management information systems, system management, technology management.

Master of Non-Profit Management (MNM) Full-time, part-time, distance learning option; 36 total credits required; admissions essay required; 2 to 6 years to complete program. Concentrations in nonprofit management, nonprofit organization.

ADMISSION
Application Requirements Application form, application fee, bachelor's degree, essay, interview, 2 letters of recommendation, resume, college transcript(s), minimum of 2 years of work experience.

Recommended for Application GMAT score accepted, minimum GPA, personal statement, computer experience.

Application Deadline Applications processed on a rolling/continuous basis for domestic students only. 7/1 for fall (international), 10/15 for spring (international), 3/1 for summer (international). Application fee: $75. Deferred entrance is available.

ACADEMICS
Faculty Full-time 10; part-time 400.

Teaching Methodologies Case study, computer-aided instruction, computer analysis, computer simulations, experiential learning, faculty seminars, field projects, group discussion, lecture, research, role playing, seminars by members of the business community, student presentations, study groups, team projects.

Technology 221 on-campus computer terminals/PCs are available for student use and are linked by a campus-wide network. The network has full access to the Internet. Students are not required to have their own PC.

Special Opportunities Advanced credit may be earned through transfer of credits from another institution.

FINANCES
Costs for 1997–98 Tuition: $309 per credit hour. Cost varies by academic program. Fees: $80 per graduation.

Financial Aid Fellowships, work study, loans available. Financial aid is available to part-time students.

Financial Aid Contact Ms. Lydia MacMillan, Director of Financial Aid, 3333 Regis Boulevard, Mail Stop A-8, Denver, CO 80221. Phone: 303-458-4066; Fax: 303-964-5538; E-mail: regisfa@regis.edu

FACILITIES
Information Resources Dayton Memorial Library plus 3 additional on-campus libraries; total holdings of 420,799 volumes, 136,379 microforms, 3,979 current periodical subscriptions. CD player(s) available for graduate student use. Access provided to online bibliographic retrieval services.

INTERNATIONAL STUDENTS
Demographics N/R

Services and Facilities Visa services, admissions advisor.

Applying TOEFL: minimum score of 550, TWE: minimum score of 4.5, proof of adequate funds required. TSE recommended.

International Student Contact Ms. Karla Nostas, Graduate Admissions Coordinator, 3333 Regis Boulevard, Denver, CO 80221. Phone: 303-458-4341; Fax: 303-964-5538; E-mail: admarg@regis.edu

PLACEMENT
Services include alumni network, career counseling/planning, career fairs, career library, career placement, electronic job bank, job interviews arranged, job search course, resume referral to employers, and resume preparation. In 1996–97, 300 organizations participated in on-campus recruiting.

Employment Types of employment entered: accounting, banking, communications, computer-related, consulting, consumer products, education, energy, engineering, finance, financial services, government, health services, high technology, hospitality management, human resources, information systems/technology, insurance, international trade, management, manufacturing, marketing, media, mining, nonprofit, pharmaceutical, real estate, retail, service industry, telecommunications, transportation, utilities.

Business Program(s) URL: http://www.regis.edu

Program Contact: Mr. Richard Boorem, Director of Marketing and Admissions, Mail Stop L-16, 3333 Regis Boulevard, Denver, CO 80211-1099. Phone: 303-458-4080, 800-677-9270; Fax: 303-964-5538; E-mail: admarg@regis.edu

University of Colorado at Boulder

Graduate School of Business Administration

Boulder, Colorado

OVERVIEW
The University of Colorado at Boulder is a state-supported, coed university. Enrollment: 25,109 graduate, professional, and undergraduate students. Founded: 1876. The graduate business unit is in a suburban setting and is on a semester calendar.

HIGHLIGHTS

Enrollment Profile
Full-time: 150
Part-time: 115
Total: 265
Average Age: 30
Fall 1997 Average GPA: 3.12

International: 8%
Women: 29%
Minorities: 11%
Average Class Size: 25
Fall 1997 Average GMAT: 615

Costs
Full-time tuition: $3710 per academic year (resident); $14,670 per academic year (nonresident)
Part-time tuition: $621 per 3 hours (resident); $2445 per 3 hours (nonresident)

AACSB – The International Association for Management Education accredited

GRADUATE BUSINESS PROGRAMS
Master of Business Administration (MBA) Full-time, part-time; 51 total credits required; 2 to 5 years to complete program. Concentrations in accounting, entrepreneurship, finance, management, marketing, organizational management, technology management, real estate.

Master of Business Administration/Master of Science in Telecommunications (MBA/MS) Full-time, part-time, distance learning option; 66 total credits required; must submit separate applications to both MBA and Telecommunications programs; 2 to 5 years to complete program. Concentrations in accounting, entrepreneurship, finance, management, marketing, organizational management, technology management, real estate, telecommunications management.

Master of Business Administration/Doctor of Jurisprudence (MBA/JD) Full-time; 141 total credits required; must submit separate applications to both MBA and School of Law; 4 years to complete program. Concentrations in accounting, entrepreneurship, finance, management, marketing, organizational management, technology management, real estate.

Master of Science in Business Administration (MS) Full-time, part-time; 30 total credits required; 12 months to 5 years to complete program. Concentrations in accounting, taxation.

ADMISSION
Applications For fall 1997 there were 435 applications for admission. Of those applying, 220 were accepted. Of those accepted, 127 enrolled.

Application Requirements Application form, application fee, bachelor's degree, essay, 3 letters of recommendation, personal statement, resume, college transcript(s), minimum of 2 years of work experience, computer experience: Microsoft Excel, Microsoft Powerpoint, Microsoft Word.

Recommended for Application GMAT score accepted: minimum 590, minimum GPA: 3.2, interview.

Application Deadline 2/15 for fall, 12/1 for fall (international). Application fee: $40, $60 (international). Deferred entrance is available.

ACADEMICS
Faculty Full-time 66; part-time 33.

Teaching Methodologies Case study, computer-aided instruction, computer analysis, experiential learning, faculty seminars, field projects, group discussion, lecture, research, role playing, seminars by members of the business community, student presentations, study groups, team projects.

Technology 650 on-campus computer terminals/PCs are available for student use and are linked by a campus-wide network. The network has full access to the Internet. Students are not required to have their own PC.

FINANCES
Costs for 1997–98 Tuition: Full-time: $3710 per semester (resident); $14,670 per semester (nonresident). Part-time: $621 per 3 hours (resident); $2445 per 3 hours (nonresident). Cost varies by academic program, campus location, class time (e.g., day/evening), number of credits taken. Fees: Full-time: $294 per academic year (resident); $294 per academic year (nonresident). Part-time: $294 per year (resident); $294 per year (nonresident). Fees vary by class time (e.g., day/evening), number of credits taken. Average 1997–98 room and board costs were $5750 per academic year (on campus) and $6273 per academic year (off campus). Room and board costs vary by campus location, occupancy (e.g., single, double, triple), type of accommodation, type of meal plan.

Financial Aid In 1997–98, 80% of students received some institutionally administered aid in the form of fellowships, research assistantships, teaching assistantships, grants, scholarships, work study, loans. Financial aid is available to part-time students. Application Deadline: 3/1.

Financial Aid Contact Mr. Paul Waskiewicz, Financial Aid Counselor, Office of Financial Aid, Campus Box 106, Boulder, CO 80309. Phone: 303-492-5091; Fax: 303-492-0838.

FACILITIES
Information Resources Norlin Library plus 6 additional on-campus libraries; total holdings of 2,575,290 volumes, 5,319,494 microforms, 28,444 current periodical subscriptions. CD player(s) available for graduate student use. Access provided to online bibliographic retrieval services.

INTERNATIONAL STUDENTS
Demographics 8% of students enrolled are international students [Asia, 80%, Central America, 5%, Europe, 10%, North America, 5%].

Services and Facilities International student office, visa services, ESL courses, counseling/support services.

Applying TOEFL: minimum score of 590, proof of adequate funds, proof of health/immunizations required. Financial aid is not available to international students.

International Student Contact Mr. James Morfeld, International Admissions, Campus Box 65, Boulder, CO 80309-0065. Phone: 303-492-7536; E-mail: james.morfeld@colorado.edu

PLACEMENT
Services include alumni network, career counseling/planning, career fairs, career library, career placement, electronic job bank, job interviews arranged, job search course, resume referral to employers, and resume preparation. In 1996–97, 94 organizations participated in on-campus recruiting.

Employment Of 1996–97 graduates, 84% were employed within three months of graduation; the average starting salary was $49,756. Types of employment entered: accounting, banking, communications, computer-related, consulting, consumer products, engineering, finance, financial services, government, health services, high technology, human resources, information systems/technology, law, management, marketing, pharmaceutical, real estate, telecommunications, transportation, utilities.

Business Program(s) URL: http://www-bus.colorado.edu

Program Contact: Ms. Diana Marinaro, Director, Graduate Student Services and Admissions, Graduate Student Services, Campus Box 419, Boulder, CO 80309-0419. Phone: 303-492-1831; Fax: 303-492-1727; E-mail: busgrad@colorado.edu

See full description on page 1054.

University of Colorado at Colorado Springs

Graduate School of Business Administration

Colorado Springs, Colorado

OVERVIEW

The University of Colorado at Colorado Springs is a state-supported, coed, comprehensive institution. Enrollment: 5,866 graduate, professional, and undergraduate students; 664 full-time matriculated graduate/professional students; 445 part-time matriculated graduate/professional students. Founded: 1965. The graduate business unit is in an urban setting and is on a semester calendar.

HIGHLIGHTS

Enrollment Profile

Full-time: 197	International: 1%
Part-time: 125	Women: 42%
Total: 322	Minorities: 13%
Average Age: 29	Average Class Size: 30
Fall 1997 Average GPA: 3.08	Fall 1997 Average GMAT: 539

Costs

Full-time tuition: $2824 per academic year (resident); $9194 per academic year (nonresident)

Part-time tuition: $119 per credit (resident); $407 per credit (nonresident)

AACSB – The International Association for Management Education accredited

The M.B.A. program at the University of Colorado at Colorado Springs allows students the opportunity to explore cutting-edge issues that challenge businesses today. The College of Business holds AACSB–The International Association for Management Education accreditation, which places the University among the top 20 percent of business schools nationally. Courses are taught by full-time, doctorally qualified faculty members who enrich students' classroom experience with their own experience in research, academic publishing, community involvement, and industry consulting. The M.B.A. program fits the needs of working professionals by offering opportunities for both full- and part-time study. Classes are held in the evening, generally one night per week, at either 4:30 or 7:15. Approximately 80 percent of all M.B.A. students at CU–Colorado Springs work full-time and attend classes part-time.

In addition to the resident M.B.A. program, CU–Colorado Springs offers a distance M.B.A. program. The distance M.B.A. program holds the same accreditation as the residence program, which allows these students to earn the same degree as resident students. Courses, delivered via the Internet and videotape, cater particularly to students whose schedules prevent them from attending regularly scheduled classes. Forbes magazine ranks the distance M.B.A. at CU–Colorado Springs as one of the nation's top twenty Cyber University programs.

GRADUATE BUSINESS PROGRAMS

Master of Business Administration (MBA) Full-time, part-time, distance learning option; 31 total credits required; 12 months to 5 years to complete program. Concentrations in accounting, finance, international business, management information systems, marketing, technology management, human resources, leadership, operations management, production management.

ADMISSION

Applications For fall 1997 there were 105 applications for admission. Of those applying, 91 were accepted. Of those accepted, 58 enrolled.

Application Requirements Application form, application fee, bachelor's degree, minimum GPA, resume, college transcript(s).

Recommended for Application GMAT score accepted, letters of recommendation, personal statement.

Application Deadline 6/1 for fall, 11/1 for spring, 4/1 for summer, 6/1 for fall (international), 11/1 for spring (international), 4/1 for summer (international). Application fee: $40, $50 (international). Deferred entrance is available.

ACADEMICS

Faculty Full-time 21.

Teaching Methodologies Case study, computer-aided instruction, computer simulations, experiential learning, field projects, group discussion, lecture, research, seminars by members of the business community, simulations, student presentations, team projects.

Technology 126 on-campus computer terminals/PCs are available for student use and are linked by a campus-wide network. The network has full access to the Internet. Students are not required to have their own PC.

Special Opportunities Advanced credit may be earned through transfer of credits from another institution. International exchange program in Finland.

FINANCES

Costs for 1997–98 Tuition: Full-time: $2824 per year (resident); $9194 per year (nonresident). Part-time: $119 per credit (resident); $407 per credit (nonresident). Cost varies by academic program, number of credits taken. Fees: Full-time: $160 per academic year (resident); $160 per academic year (nonresident). Part-time: $19 per credit hour (resident); $19 per credit hour (nonresident). Fees vary by number of credits taken. Average 1997–98 room and board costs were $5020 per academic year. Room and board costs vary by occupancy (e.g., single, double, triple), type of accommodation, type of meal plan.

Financial Aid Fellowships, research assistantships, teaching assistantships, grants, scholarships, work study, loans available. Financial aid is available to part-time students.

Financial Aid Contact Mr. Doug Nelson, Counseling Coordinator, Financial Aid/Student Employment, PO Box 7150, Colorado Springs, CO 80933-7150. Phone: 719-262-3460; Fax: 719-262-3650; E-mail: finaidse@mail.uccs.edu

FACILITIES

Information Resources Kramer Family Library; total holdings of 290,649 volumes, 431,382 microforms, 2,440 current periodical subscriptions. Access provided to online bibliographic retrieval services.

INTERNATIONAL STUDENTS

Demographics 1% of students enrolled are international students.

Applying TOEFL: minimum score of 550, proof of adequate funds required. Financial aid is not available to international students.

International Student Contact Roy Rimstad, International Student Coordinator, PO Box 7150, Colorado Springs, CO 80933-7150. Phone: 719-262-3587; Fax: 719-262-3494; E-mail: rrimstad@mail.uccs.edu

PLACEMENT

Services include career fairs, and resume referral to employers.

Employment Types of employment entered: accounting, computer-related, finance, financial services, government, health services, high technology, human resources, information systems/technology, insurance, management, manufacturing, marketing, nonprofit, service industry, telecommunications.

Business Program(s) URL: http://www.uccs.edu/~collbus

Program Contact: Mrs. Barbara Neiberg, MBA Program Director, 1420 Austin Bluffs Parkway, PO Box 7150, Colorado Springs, CO 80933-7150. Phone: 719-262-3408, 800-990-8227; Fax: 719-262-3494; E-mail: busadvsr@mail.uccs.edu

University of Colorado at Denver

Graduate School of Business Administration

Denver, Colorado

OVERVIEW

The University of Colorado at Denver is a state-supported, coed university. Enrollment: 10,871 graduate, professional, and undergraduate students; 1,582 full-time matriculated graduate/professional students; 3,460 part-time matriculated graduate/professional students. Founded: 1912. The graduate business unit is in an urban setting and is on a semester calendar.

HIGHLIGHTS

Enrollment Profile

Full-time: 446	International: 16%
Part-time: 975	Women: 43%
Total: 1,421	Minorities: 10%
Average Age: 33	Average Class Size: 35
Fall 1997 Average GPA: 3.04	Fall 1997 Average GMAT: 530

Costs

Full-time tuition: $3706 per academic year (resident); $12,548 per academic year (nonresident)

Part-time tuition: $222 per credit (resident); $752 per credit (nonresident)

AACSB – The International Association for Management Education accredited

Degree(s) offered in conjunction with Thunderbird, The American Graduate School of International Management

GRADUATE BUSINESS PROGRAMS
Master of Business Administration (MBA) Full-time, part-time, distance learning option; 48 total credits required; 16 months to 5 years to complete program.

Executive MBA (EMBA) Part-time; 48 total credits required; minimum of 22 months to complete program.

Master of Business Administration/Master of Science (MBA/MS) Full-time, part-time; 66 total credits required; 2.3 to 7.2 years to complete program. Concentrations in accounting, finance, information management, international business, management, management information systems, marketing.

Master of Business Administration/Master of International Management (MBA/MIM) Full-time, part-time; 66 total credits required; 2 to 3 years to complete program. Concentration in international business.

Master of Science (MS) Full-time, part-time; 30-48 total credits required; 9 months to 5 years to complete program. Concentrations in accounting, finance, international business, management information systems, marketing, management, health care.

11-Month MBA (MBA) Full-time; 48 total credits required; 11 months to complete program.

ADMISSION
Applications For fall 1997 there were 677 applications for admission. Of those applying, 478 were accepted. Of those accepted, 307 enrolled.

Application Requirements GMAT score: minimum 400, application form, application fee, bachelor's degree, essay, minimum GPA, 3 letters of recommendation, personal statement, college transcript(s).

Recommended for Application Resume, work experience, computer experience.

Application Deadline 7/1 for fall, 11/1 for spring, 4/1 for summer, 3/1 for fall (international), 7/1 for spring (international), 12/1 for summer (international). Application fee: $50, $60 (international). Deferred entrance is available.

ACADEMICS
Faculty Full-time 64; part-time 30.

Teaching Methodologies Case study, computer-aided instruction, computer simulations, experiential learning, field projects, group discussion, lecture, research, seminars by members of the business community, simulations, student presentations, study groups, team projects.

Technology 230 on-campus computer terminals/PCs are available for student use and are linked by a campus-wide network. The network has full access to the Internet. Students are not required to have their own PC.

Special Opportunities Advanced credit may be earned through transfer of credits from another institution. International exchange programs in Belgium, France. An internship program is available.

FINANCES
Costs for 1997–98 Tuition: Full-time: $3706 per year (resident); $12,548 per year (nonresident). Part-time: $222 per credit (resident); $752 per credit (nonresident). Cost varies by number of credits taken. Fees: Full-time: $310 per academic year (resident); $310 per academic year (nonresident). Part-time: $155 per semester (resident); $155 per semester (nonresident). Average 1997–98 room and board costs were $12,000 per academic year (off campus). Room and board costs vary by occupancy (e.g., single, double, triple), type of accommodation.

Financial Aid In 1997–98, 29% of students received some institutionally administered aid in the form of research assistantships, scholarships, work study, loans. Financial aid is available to part-time students. Application Deadline: 4/1.

Financial Aid Contact Ms. Ellie Miller, Director of Financial Aid, Campus Box 125, PO Box 173364, Denver, CO 80217-3364. Phone: 303-556-2886; Fax: 303-556-2325.

FACILITIES
Information Resources Auraria Library; total holdings of 522,303 volumes, 751,762 microforms, 3,581 current periodical subscriptions. CD player(s) available for graduate student use. Access provided to online bibliographic retrieval services and online databases.

INTERNATIONAL STUDENTS
Demographics 16% of students enrolled are international students.

Services and Facilities International student office, international student center, visa services, ESL courses, counseling/support services.

Applying TOEFL: minimum score of 525, proof of adequate funds required. TSE, TWE recommended. Financial aid is available to international students.

International Student Contact Ms. Lucy C. Daley, Director of International Student Programs, Campus Box 165, PO Box 173364, Denver, CO 80217-3364. Phone: 303-556-5941; Fax: 303-556-5904; E-mail: ldaley@castle.cudenver.edu

PLACEMENT
Services include alumni network, career counseling/planning, career fairs, career library, career placement, electronic job bank, job interviews arranged, job search course, resume referral to employers, and resume preparation.

Employment Of 1996–97 graduates, 90% were employed within three months of graduation; the average starting salary was $51,000. Types of employment entered: accounting, banking, communications, computer-related, consulting, consumer products, finance, financial services, health services, high technology, hospitality management, human resources, information systems/technology, insurance, international trade, management, manufacturing, marketing, media, mining, nonprofit, petrochemical, pharmaceutical, real estate, retail, service industry, telecommunications, transportation, utilities.

Business Program(s) URL: http://www.cudenver.edu/public/business

Program Contact: Lori Cain, Graduate Admissions Coordinator, Campus Box 165, PO Box 173364, Denver, CO 80217-3364. Phone: 303-556-5900; Fax: 303-556-5904.

See full description on page 1056.

University of Denver

Daniels College of Business

Denver, Colorado

OVERVIEW
The University of Denver is an independent-nonprofit, coed university. Enrollment: 8,667 graduate, professional, and undergraduate students; 2,703 full-time matriculated graduate/professional students; 2,508 part-time matriculated graduate/professional students. Founded: 1864. The graduate business unit is in a suburban setting and is on a quarter calendar.

HIGHLIGHTS

Enrollment Profile
Full-time: 408
Part-time: 272
Total: 680
Average Age: 28
Fall 1997 Average GPA: 3.2

International: 24%
Women: 39%
Minorities: 11%
Average Class Size: 30
Fall 1997 Average GMAT: 540

Costs
Full-time tuition: $18,216 per academic year
Part-time tuition: $506 per quarter hour

AACSB – The International Association for Management Education accredited

Founded in 1908, the University of Denver Daniels College of Business is the nation's eighth-oldest collegiate school of business. It has been accredited by the AACSB–The International Association for Management Education since 1923. Located in the heart of Denver, Colorado, the Daniels College of Business is an integral part of the city that is the business, cultural, and recreational center of the Rocky Mountain West.

The Daniels College of Business M.B.A. Program reflects the real-world decision making that is required of today's managers and prepares men and women for leadership in a vast range of careers and industries. The heart of the M.B.A. program is the integrated core curriculum, where courses mirror the cross-functional involvement found in business decision making. Instead of separate courses for each discipline, the Daniels M.B.A. program uses seven major courses to present business fundamentals, such as accounting, financial management, marketing, statistics, and current business issues, in an interrelated format that provides a comprehensive view of business the way it actually operates.

The program focuses on flexibility. Day and evening courses are available for both full- and part-time schedules, and numerous specialization options are available. The Daniels College of Business M.B.A. Program provides an outstanding learning experience that is the cornerstone of achievement for career success

GRADUATE BUSINESS PROGRAMS
Executive MBA (MBA) Part-time; 70 total credits required; up to 18 months to complete program.

Master of Business Administration (MBA) Full-time, part-time; 72 total credits required; 15 months to 5 years to complete program. Concentrations in accounting, construction management, entrepreneurship, finance, management information systems, marketing, real estate, international business.

Master of International Management (MIM) Full-time, part-time; 79 total credits required; 18 months to 5 years to complete program. Concentrations in account-

University of Denver (continued)

ing, construction management, entrepreneurship, finance, management information systems, marketing, real estate.

Master of Accountancy (MAcc) Full-time, part-time; 56 total credits required; 15 months to 5 years to complete program.

Master of Science in Finance (MS) Full-time, part-time; 64 total credits required; 18 months to 5 years to complete program.

Master of Real Estate and Construction Management (MRECM) Full-time, part-time; 64 total credits required; 15 months to 5 years to complete program.

Master of Science in Resort and Tourism Management (MS) Full-time, part-time; 60 total credits required; 12 months to 5 years to complete program.

Master of Science in Management (MS) Full-time, part-time; 54-66 total credits required; 15 months to 5 years to complete program. Concentrations in health care, sports/entertainment management, telecommunications management, legal administration.

ADMISSION

Applications For fall 1997 there were 711 applications for admission. Of those applying, 528 were accepted. Of those accepted, 256 enrolled.

Application Requirements Application form, application fee, bachelor's degree, essay, minimum GPA, 2 letters of recommendation, resume, college transcript(s).

Recommended for Application GMAT score accepted, GRE score accepted, interview, work experience, computer experience.

Application Deadline Applications processed on a rolling/continuous basis for both domestic and international students. Application fee: $50. Deferred entrance is available.

ACADEMICS

Faculty Full-time 75; part-time 15.

Teaching Methodologies Case study, computer-aided instruction, computer analysis, computer simulations, experiential learning, faculty seminars, field projects, group discussion, lecture, research, role playing, seminars by members of the business community, simulations, student presentations, study groups, team projects.

Technology 125 on-campus computer terminals/PCs are available for student use. The network has full access to the Internet. Students are not required to have their own PC.

Special Opportunities Advanced credit may be earned through credit by examination, transfer of credits from another institution. International exchange program in various countries. An internship program is available.

FINANCES

Costs for 1997–98 Tuition: Full-time: $18,216 per year. Part-time: $506 per quarter hour. Cost varies by number of credits taken. Fees: Full-time: $695 per academic year. Part-time: $695 per program. Average 1997–98 room and board costs were $8100 per academic year (on campus) and $8100 per academic year (off campus). Room and board costs vary by occupancy (e.g., single, double, triple), type of accommodation, type of meal plan.

Financial Aid Research assistantships, teaching assistantships, work study, loans available. Financial aid is available to part-time students. Application Deadline: 2/15.

Financial Aid Contact Ms. Laurel Shurtlef, Financial Aid Coordinator, University Park, Denver, CO 80208. Phone: 303-871-4193; Fax: 303-871-4466; E-mail: dcb@du.edu

FACILITIES

Information Resources Penrose Library plus 2 additional on-campus libraries; total holdings of 1,835,021 volumes, 879,857 microforms, 5,102 current periodical subscriptions. CD player(s) available for graduate student use. Access provided to online bibliographic retrieval services.

INTERNATIONAL STUDENTS

Demographics 24% of students enrolled are international students [Africa, 3%, Asia, 64%, Australia/New Zealand, 2%, Central America, 1%, Europe, 11%, North America, 3%, South America, 10%, other, 6%].

Services and Facilities International student office, international student center, visa services, ESL courses, counseling/support services.

Applying TOEFL: minimum score of 550, proof of adequate funds required. Financial aid is not available to international students.

International Student Contact Ms. Elke Breker, International Student Advisor, 2200 South Josephine Street, Denver, CO 80208. Phone: 303-871-4193; Fax: 303-733-6122; E-mail: ebreker@du.edu

PLACEMENT

Services include alumni network, career counseling/planning, career fairs, career library, career placement, electronic job bank, job interviews arranged, job search course, resume referral to employers, and resume preparation. In 1996–97, 86 organizations participated in on-campus recruiting; 500 on-campus interviews were conducted.

Employment Of 1996–97 graduates, 90% were employed within three months of graduation; the average starting salary was $45,186. Types of employment entered: accounting, banking, communications, computer-related, consulting, consumer products, education, engineering, finance, financial services, government, high technology, hospitality management, information systems/technology, international trade, management, manufacturing, marketing, nonprofit, real estate, service industry, telecommunications.

Business Program(s) URL: http://www.dcb.du.edu

Program Contact: Ms. Jan Johnsen, Executive Director, Student Services, University Park, 2020 South Race Street, BA-122, Denver, CO 80208. Phone: 303-871-2161, 800-622-4723; Fax: 303-871-4466; E-mail: dcb@du.edu

See full description on page 1064.

University of Southern Colorado

Hasan School of Business

Pueblo, Colorado

OVERVIEW

The University of Southern Colorado is a state-supported, coed, comprehensive institution. Enrollment: 4,069 graduate, professional, and undergraduate students; 88 full-time matriculated graduate/professional students; 233 part-time matriculated graduate/professional students. Founded: 1933. The graduate business unit is in a suburban setting and is on a semester calendar.

HIGHLIGHTS

Enrollment Profile

Full-time: 59	International: 44%
Part-time: 72	Women: 50%
Total: 131	Minorities: 8%
Average Age: 31	Average Class Size: 25
Fall 1997 Average GPA: 3.0	Fall 1997 Average GMAT: 500

Costs
Full-time tuition: $872 per academic year (resident); $3994 per academic year (nonresident)
Part-time tuition: $87 per semester hour (resident); $399 per semester hour (nonresident)

GRADUATE BUSINESS PROGRAMS

Master of Business Administration (MBA) Full-time, part-time; 36 total credits required; 12 months to 6 years to complete program. Concentration in management.

Master of Business Administration/Bachelor of Science in Business Administration in Management (MBA/BS) Full-time, part-time; 146-149 total credits required; 5 to 6 years to complete program. Concentration in management.

Master of Business Administration/Bachelor of Science in Business Administration in Accounting (MBA/BS) Full-time, part-time; 154 total credits required; 5 to 6 years to complete program. Concentration in accounting.

ADMISSION

Applications For fall 1997 there were 80 applications for admission. Of those applying, 70 were accepted. Of those accepted, 59 enrolled.

Application Requirements GMAT score, application form, application fee, bachelor's degree, minimum GPA: 2.5, college transcript(s), computer experience: word processing, spreadsheet, statistical analysis.

Application Deadline Applications processed on a rolling/continuous basis for both domestic and international students. Application fee: $15.

ACADEMICS

Faculty Full-time 10.

Teaching Methodologies Case study, computer-aided instruction, computer analysis, computer simulations, field projects, group discussion, lecture, research, seminars by members of the business community, student presentations, study groups, team projects.

Technology 390 on-campus computer terminals/PCs are available for student use and are linked by a campus-wide network. The network has full access to the Internet. Students are not required to have their own PC.

Special Opportunities Advanced credit may be earned through transfer of credits from another institution. International exchange programs in France, Mexico. An internship program is available.

FINANCES

Costs for 1997–98 Tuition: Full-time: $872 per semester (resident); $3994 per semester (nonresident). Part-time: $87 per semester hour (resident); $399 per semester hour (nonresident). Cost varies by number of credits taken. Fees: Full-time: $214 per academic year (resident); $214 per academic year (nonresident). Part-time: $21 per semester hour (resident); $21 per semester hour (nonresident).

Fees vary by number of credits taken. Average 1997–98 room and board costs were $5444 per academic year (on campus) and $4200 per academic year (off campus). Room and board costs vary by occupancy (e.g., single, double, triple), type of accommodation, type of meal plan.

Financial Aid In 1997–98, 6% of students received some institutionally administered aid in the form of research assistantships, scholarships, work study, loans. Financial aid is available to part-time students.

Financial Aid Contact Ms. Linda DiPrince, Associate Director, 2200 Bonforte Boulevard, Pueblo, CO 81001-4901. Phone: 719-549-2753; Fax: 719-549-2088.

FACILITIES
Information Resources University of Southern Colorado Library; total holdings of 190,000 volumes, 6,500 microforms, 1,300 current periodical subscriptions. CD player(s) available for graduate student use. Access provided to online bibliographic retrieval services.

INTERNATIONAL STUDENTS
Demographics 44% of students enrolled are international students [Africa, 2%, Asia, 60%, Europe, 38%].

Services and Facilities International student office, international student center, international student housing, visa services, ESL courses, counseling/support services.

Applying TOEFL: minimum score of 550, proof of adequate funds, proof of health/immunizations required. Financial aid is not available to international students.

International Student Contact Ms. Annie Williams, Coordinator of the International Student Center, 2200 Bonforte Boulevard, Pueblo, CO 81001-4901. Phone: 719-549-2116; Fax: 719-549-2938; E-mail: annewill@uscolo.edu

PLACEMENT
Services include career counseling/planning, career fairs, career library, career placement, job interviews arranged, job search course, resume referral to employers, and resume preparation. In 1996–97, 167 organizations participated in on-campus recruiting; 706 on-campus interviews were conducted.

Employment Of 1996–97 graduates, 75% were employed within three months of graduation; the average starting salary was $55,000. Types of employment entered: accounting, banking, consulting, education, engineering, finance, financial services, government, health services, human resources, information systems/technology, insurance, international trade, management, manufacturing, marketing, nonprofit, real estate, retail, service industry, transportation.

Business Program(s) URL: http://www.uscolo.edu

Program Contact: Mr. Jon Valdez, Admissions Administrative Assistant III, 2200 Bonforte Boulevard, Pueblo, CO 81001-4901. Phone: 719-549-2997, 800-872-4769; Fax: 719-549-2419; E-mail: jvaldez@uscolo.edu

CONNECTICUT

Albertus Magnus College

Master of Science in Management

New Haven, Connecticut

OVERVIEW
Albertus Magnus College is an independent-religious, coed, comprehensive institution. Enrollment: 1,600 graduate, professional, and undergraduate students; 185 full-time matriculated graduate/professional students; part-time matriculated graduate/professional students. Founded: 1925. The graduate business unit is in an urban setting and is on a semester calendar.

HIGHLIGHTS

Enrollment Profile
Full-time: 185
Part-time: 0
Total: 185
Average Age: 35
Fall 1997 Average GPA: 3.0
International: N/R
Women: N/R
Minorities: N/R
Average Class Size: 20
Fall 1997 Average GMAT: N/R

Costs
Full-time tuition: $9450 per academic year
Part-time tuition: $1050 per course

GRADUATE BUSINESS PROGRAMS
Master of Science in Management (MSM) Full-time; 36 total credits required; 18 months to 2 years to complete program.

ADMISSION
Applications For fall 1997 there were 110 applications for admission. Of those applying, 95 were accepted. Of those accepted, 95 enrolled.

Application Requirements Application form, bachelor's degree, essay, minimum GPA: 2.5, letters of recommendation, personal statement, college transcript(s), minimum of 3 years of work experience, computer experience.

Application Deadline Applications processed on a rolling/continuous basis for both domestic and international students. Application fee: $35.

ACADEMICS
Faculty Full-time 4; part-time 12.

Teaching Methodologies Computer-aided instruction, computer analysis, group discussion, research, student presentations, study groups, team projects.

Technology 48 on-campus computer terminals/PCs are available for student use and are linked by a campus-wide network. The network has full access to the Internet. Students are required to have their own PC.

FINANCES
Costs for 1997–98 Tuition: Full-time: $9450 per year. Part-time: $1050 per course. Fees: Full-time: $900 per academic year. Part-time: $100 per course.

Financial Aid Loans available. Financial aid is available to part-time students.

Financial Aid Contact Office of Financial Aid, New Dimensions Office, New Haven, CT 06511. Phone: 203-773-8550.

FACILITIES
Information Resources Main library; total holdings of 110,006 volumes, 682 microforms, 1,100 current periodical subscriptions. CD player(s) available for graduate student use. Access provided to online bibliographic retrieval services and online databases.

INTERNATIONAL STUDENTS
Demographics N/R

Applying TOEFL: minimum score of 550 required. Financial aid is not available to international students.

PLACEMENT
Services include career counseling/planning, and career fairs.

Employment Of 1996–97 graduates, 100% were employed within three months of graduation. Types of employment entered: banking, computer-related, high technology, human resources, information systems/technology, law, management, marketing.

Program Contact: Admission Office, New Dimensions, One Long Wharf, Room 216, New Haven, CT 06511. Phone: 203-773-8550.

Central Connecticut State University

School of Business

New Britain, Connecticut

OVERVIEW
Central Connecticut State University is a state-supported, coed, comprehensive institution. Enrollment: 11,959 graduate, professional, and undergraduate students; 394 full-time matriculated graduate/professional students; 2,101 part-time matriculated graduate/professional students. Founded: 1849. The graduate business unit is in an urban setting and is on a semester calendar.

HIGHLIGHTS

Enrollment Profile
Full-time: 12
Part-time: 41
Total: 53
Average Age: 32
Fall 1997 Average GPA: 3.24
International: 21%
Women: 68%
Minorities: 2%
Average Class Size: 25
Fall 1997 Average GMAT: 516

Costs
Full-time tuition: $2069 per academic year (resident); $4811 per academic year (nonresident)
Part-time tuition: $175 per credit hour (resident); $175 per credit hour (nonresident)

Central Connecticut State University (continued)

GRADUATE BUSINESS PROGRAMS

International Master of Business Administration (IMBA) Full-time, part-time; 33 total credits required; 14 months to 6 years to complete program. Concentrations in accounting, finance, international business, management, marketing, international management, international marketing.

ADMISSION

Application Requirements GMAT score: minimum 500, application form, application fee, bachelor's degree, essay, minimum GPA: 2.7, 2 letters of recommendation, personal statement, resume, college transcript(s), computer experience: MS Office.

Recommended for Application GRE score accepted, work experience.

Application Deadline 5/1 for fall, 10/1 for spring. Application fee: $40.

ACADEMICS

Faculty Full-time 9; part-time 4.

Teaching Methodologies Case study, computer-aided instruction, computer analysis, computer simulations, field projects, group discussion, lecture, research, seminars by members of the business community, simulations, student presentations, team projects.

Technology 200 on-campus computer terminals/PCs are available for student use and are linked by a campus-wide network. The network has full access to the Internet. Students are not required to have their own PC.

Special Opportunities Advanced credit may be earned through transfer of credits from another institution. International exchange programs in Germany, People's Republic of China, Poland, Russia, Spain. An internship program is available.

FINANCES

Costs for 1997–98 Tuition: Full-time: $2069 per semester (resident); $4811 per semester (nonresident). Part-time: $175 per credit hour (resident); $175 per credit hour (nonresident). Fees: Full-time: $256 per academic year (resident); $256 per academic year (nonresident). Part-time: $44 per registration (resident); $44 per registration (nonresident). Average 1997–98 room and board costs were $10,000 per academic year (off campus).

Financial Aid In 1997–98, 57% of students received some institutionally administered aid in the form of research assistantships, work study, loans. Application Deadline: 3/15.

Financial Aid Contact Financial Aid Office, 1615 Stanley Street, New Britain, CT 06050. Phone: 860-832-2205.

FACILITIES

Information Resources Elihu Burritt Library plus 1 additional on-campus library; total holdings of 534,224 volumes, 430,567 microforms, 3,027 current periodical subscriptions. CD player(s) available for graduate student use. Access provided to online bibliographic retrieval services.

INTERNATIONAL STUDENTS

Demographics 21% of students enrolled are international students.

Services and Facilities International student office, international student center, international student housing, ESL courses, counseling/support services.

Applying TOEFL: minimum score of 550, proof of adequate funds, proof of health/immunizations required. Financial aid is available to international students.

International Student Contact Ms. Susan Lesser, Director of International Affairs Center, International Affairs Center, 1615 Stanley Street, New Britain, CT 06050. Phone: 860-832-2050; Fax: 860-832-2047.

PLACEMENT

Services include career fairs.

Business Program(s) URL: http://wwwsb.ccsu.ctstateu.edu

Program Contact: Dr. George Claffey, Director of Graduate Business Programs, School of Business, 1615 Stanley Street, New Britain, CT 06050. Phone: 860-832-3210; Fax: 860-832-3219; E-mail: claffey@ccsu.edu

Eastern Connecticut State University

Program in Organizational Management

Willimantic, Connecticut

OVERVIEW

Eastern Connecticut State University is a state-supported, coed, comprehensive institution. Founded: 1889.

GRADUATE BUSINESS PROGRAMS

Master of Science in Organizational Relations (MS)

ACADEMICS

Faculty Full-time 7.

FACILITIES

Information Resources J. Eugene Smith Library; total holdings of 200,243 volumes, 21,464 microforms, 1,831 current periodical subscriptions. CD player(s) available for graduate student use. Access provided to online bibliographic retrieval services.

Program Contact: Educational Leadership Department, 83 Windham Street, Willimantic, CT 06226-2295. Phone: 860-392-5342.

Fairfield University

School of Business

Fairfield, Connecticut

OVERVIEW

Fairfield University is an independent-religious, coed, comprehensive institution. Enrollment: 5,179 graduate, professional, and undergraduate students; 134 full-time matriculated graduate/professional students; 740 part-time matriculated graduate/professional students. Founded: 1942. The graduate business unit is in a suburban setting and is on a semester calendar.

HIGHLIGHTS

Enrollment Profile

Full-time: 15	International: 4%
Part-time: 270	Women: 41%
Total: 285	Minorities: 1%
Average Age: 27	Average Class Size: 25
Fall 1997 Average GPA: 3.2	Fall 1997 Average GMAT: 530

Costs
Full-time tuition: $7500 per academic year
Part-time tuition: $450 per credit hour

AACSB – The International Association for Management Education accredited

GRADUATE BUSINESS PROGRAMS

Master of Business Administration (MBA) Full-time, part-time; 62 total credits required; 18 months to 5 years to complete program. Concentrations in accounting, finance, human resources, international business, marketing, management information systems, taxation.

Master of Science in Financial Management (MS) Full-time, part-time; 68 total credits required; 2 to 5 years to complete program. Concentration in financial management/planning.

ADMISSION

Applications For fall 1997 there were 93 applications for admission. Of those applying, 82 were accepted. Of those accepted, 77 enrolled.

Application Requirements GMAT score: minimum 500, application form, application fee, bachelor's degree, minimum GPA, 2 letters of recommendation, personal statement, college transcript(s), computer experience: undergraduate introductory course to computer information systems.

Recommended for Application Work experience.

Application Deadline 8/15 for fall, 12/15 for spring, 5/15 for summer, 5/15 for fall (international), 10/15 for spring (international). Application fee: $40. Deferred entrance is available.

ACADEMICS

Faculty Full-time 37; part-time 2.

Teaching Methodologies Case study, experiential learning, faculty seminars, group discussion, lecture, research, seminars by members of the business community, student presentations, team projects.

Technology 150 on-campus computer terminals/PCs are available for student use and are linked by a campus-wide network. The network has full access to the Internet. Students are not required to have their own PC.

Special Opportunities Advanced credit may be earned through transfer of credits from another institution. International exchange programs in Germany, Japan, Netherlands, Russia, United Kingdom.

FINANCES

Costs for 1997–98 Tuition: Full-time: $7500 per semester. Part-time: $450 per credit hour. Cost varies by number of credits taken. Fees: Full-time: $40 per academic year. Part-time: $20 per semester. Average 1997–98 room and board costs were $7500 per academic year. Room and board costs vary by occupancy (e.g., single, double, triple), type of meal plan.

Financial Aid Research assistantships, scholarships available.

Financial Aid Contact Director of Financial Aid, Fairfield University, Fairfield, CT 06430-5195. Phone: 203-254-4000.

FACILITIES
Information Resources Nyselius Library; total holdings of 325,000 volumes, 500,000 microforms, 1,849 current periodical subscriptions. CD player(s) available for graduate student use. Access provided to online bibliographic retrieval services.

INTERNATIONAL STUDENTS
Demographics 4% of students enrolled are international students [Asia, 10%, Europe, 50%, North America, 40%].

Services and Facilities International student office, visa services, counseling/support services.

Applying TOEFL: minimum score of 550, proof of adequate funds, proof of health/immunizations required. Financial aid is not available to international students.

International Student Contact Dr. Barbara Waters, Assistant to Academic Vice President, International Programs, Fairfield University, Fairfield, CT 06430-5195. Phone: 203-254-2957.

PLACEMENT
Services include alumni network, career counseling/planning, career library, resume referral to employers, and resume preparation.

Business Program(s) URL: http://www.fairfield.edu/academic/business/business.htm

Program Contact: Cynthia Chegwidden, Graduate Admissions, School of Business, Fairfield, CT 06430. Phone: 203-254-4180; Fax: 203-254-4105; E-mail: mba@fair1.fairfield.edu

See full description on page 812.

Quinnipiac College

School of Business

Hamden, Connecticut

OVERVIEW
Quinnipiac College is an independent-nonprofit, coed, comprehensive institution. Enrollment: 5,571 graduate, professional, and undergraduate students; 712 full-time matriculated graduate/professional students; 662 part-time matriculated graduate/professional students. Founded: 1929. The graduate business unit is in a suburban setting and is on a semester calendar.

HIGHLIGHTS

Enrollment Profile

Full-time: 58	International: 3%
Part-time: 150	Women: 50%
Total: 208	Minorities: 6%
Average Age: 29	Average Class Size: 20
Fall 1997 Average GPA: 3.04	Fall 1997 Average GMAT: N/R

Costs
Full-time tuition: N/R
Part-time tuition: $395 per credit

GRADUATE BUSINESS PROGRAMS
Master of Business Administration (MBA) Full-time, part-time; 39 total credits required; 14 months to 3 years to complete program. Concentrations in accounting, taxation, management information systems, economics, finance, international business, management, marketing, health care.

Master of Health Administration in General Health Administration (MHA) Full-time, part-time; 39 total credits required; 14 months to 3 years to complete program.

Master of Health Administration in Long-term Care Administration (MHA) Full-time, part-time; 45 total credits required; 20 months to 4 years to complete program.

Master of Business Administration/Doctor of Jurisprudence (MBA/JD) Full-time, part-time.

Master of Health Administration/Doctor of Jurisprudence (MHA/JD) Full-time, part-time.

ADMISSION
Applications For fall 1997 there were 103 applications for admission. Of those applying, 69 were accepted. Of those accepted, 55 enrolled.

Application Requirements Application form, application fee, bachelor's degree, minimum GPA: 2.5, 2 letters of recommendation, resume, college transcript(s).

Recommended for Application GMAT score accepted: minimum 400, essay, interview, personal statement, work experience.

Application Deadline Applications processed on a rolling/continuous basis for domestic students only. 8/1 for fall (international), 12/1 for spring (inter-

national), 5/1 for summer (international). Application fee: $45. Deferred entrance is available.

ACADEMICS
Faculty Full-time 19; part-time 8.

Teaching Methodologies Case study, computer-aided instruction, computer analysis, experiential learning, faculty seminars, field projects, group discussion, lecture, research, role playing, seminars by members of the business community, student presentations, study groups, team projects.

Technology 280 on-campus computer terminals/PCs are available for student use and are linked by a campus-wide network. The network has full access to the Internet. Students are not required to have their own PC.

Special Opportunities Advanced credit may be earned through credit by examination, transfer of credits from another institution.

FINANCES
Costs for 1997-98 Tuition: $395 per credit. Cost varies by number of credits taken. Fees: Full-time: $370 per academic year. Part-time: $20 per semester. Fees vary by number of credits taken.

Financial Aid Research assistantships available. Financial aid is available to part-time students.

Financial Aid Contact Ms. Louise Craco, Assistant Director of Graduate Admissions and Financial Aid, 275 Mount Carmel Avenue, Hamden, CT 06518-1904. Phone: 203-287-5221; Fax: 203-287-5238.

FACILITIES
Information Resources Quinnipiac College Library plus 1 additional on-campus library; total holdings of 275,008 volumes, 188,523 microforms, 3,963 current periodical subscriptions. CD player(s) available for graduate student use. Access provided to online bibliographic retrieval services and online databases.

INTERNATIONAL STUDENTS
Demographics 3% of students enrolled are international students.

Services and Facilities Counseling/support services.

Applying TOEFL: minimum score of 575, proof of adequate funds, proof of health/immunizations required. Financial aid is not available to international students.

International Student Contact Ms. Leonora Campbell, Associate Dean of Student Affairs, 275 Mount Carmel Avenue, Hamden, CT 06518-1904. Phone: 203-281-8723; Fax: 203-281-8796; E-mail: campbell@quinnipiac.edu

PLACEMENT
Services include alumni network, career counseling/planning, career fairs, career library, career placement, job interviews arranged, and resume preparation.

Employment Types of employment entered: accounting, banking, communications, consulting, consumer products, education, engineering, finance, financial services, government, health services, human resources, information systems/technology, insurance, law, management, manufacturing, marketing, media, nonprofit, pharmaceutical, real estate, retail, service industry, telecommunications, transportation, utilities.

Business Program(s) URL: http://www.quinnipiac.edu

Program Contact: Mr. Scott Farber, Director of Graduate Admissions, 275 Mount Carmel Avenue, Hamden, CT 06518-1904. Phone: 203-281-8795, 800-462-1944; Fax: 203-281-8906; E-mail: qcgradadmi@quinnipiac.edu

See full description on page 938.

Rensselaer at Hartford

Lally School of Management and Technology

Hartford, Connecticut

OVERVIEW
Rensselaer at Hartford is an independent-nonprofit, coed, graduate institution. Enrollment: 1,885 graduate, professional, and undergraduate students; 23 full-time matriculated graduate/professional students; 1,862 part-time matriculated graduate/professional students. Founded: 1955. The graduate business unit is in an urban setting and is on a semester calendar.

Rensselaer at Hartford (continued)

HIGHLIGHTS

Enrollment Profile
Full-time: 18
Part-time: 1,362
Total: 1,380
Average Age: 31
Fall 1997 Average GPA: 3.0

International: N/R
Women: N/R
Minorities: N/R
Average Class Size: 21
Fall 1997 Average GMAT: N/R

Costs
Full-time tuition: N/R
Part-time tuition: $525 per credit hour

GRADUATE BUSINESS PROGRAMS
Master of Business Administration (MBA) Full-time, part-time, distance learning option; 60 total credits required; 2 to 5 years to complete program. Concentrations in finance, international management, marketing, health care, manufacturing management, entrepreneurship, environmental economics/management, management information systems, research and development administration.

Master of Science in Management (MS) Full-time, part-time, distance learning option; 31 total credits required; 2 to 5 years to complete program. Concentrations in finance, international management, marketing, health care, manufacturing management, entrepreneurship, environmental economics/management, management information systems, research and development administration.

Master of Science in Environmental Management and Policy (MS) Full-time, part-time, distance learning option; 45 total credits required; 2 to 5 years to complete program.

ADMISSION
Applications For fall 1997 there were 435 applications for admission. Of those applying, 401 were accepted. Of those accepted, 355 enrolled.

Application Requirements Application form, application fee, bachelor's degree, 2 letters of recommendation, resume, college transcript(s).

Recommended for Application GMAT score accepted.

Application Deadline Applications processed on a rolling/continuous basis for both domestic and international students. Application fee: $25. Deferred entrance is available.

ACADEMICS
Faculty Full-time 18; part-time 63.

Teaching Methodologies Case study, faculty seminars, lecture, research, seminars by members of the business community, student presentations, team projects.

Technology 110 on-campus computer terminals/PCs are available for student use and are linked by a campus-wide network. The network has full access to the Internet. Students are not required to have their own PC.

Special Opportunities Advanced credit may be earned through transfer of credits from another institution.

FINANCES
Costs for 1997–98 Tuition: $525 per credit hour.

Financial Aid In 1997–98, 4% of students received some institutionally administered aid in the form of research assistantships. Financial aid is available to part-time students. Application Deadline: 8/8.

Financial Aid Contact Ms. Gayle Hoffman, Financial Aid Officer, 275 Windsor Street, Hartford, CT 06120. Phone: 860-548-2421; Fax: 860-548-7823.

FACILITIES
Information Resources Main library; total holdings of 30,000 volumes, 43,141 microforms, 490 current periodical subscriptions. CD player(s) available for graduate student use. Access provided to online bibliographic retrieval services.

INTERNATIONAL STUDENTS
Demographics N/R

Services and Facilities Counseling/support services.

Applying TOEFL: minimum score of 570, proof of adequate funds, proof of health/immunizations required. Financial aid is not available to international students.

International Student Contact Ms. Linda Gilbert, Admissions Coordinator and Financial Aid Officer, 257 Windsor Street, Hartford, CT 06120. Phone: 860-548-2422; Fax: 860-548-7823.

PLACEMENT
Services include alumni network, career counseling/planning, and resume referral to employers.

Employment Of 1996–97 graduates, 98% were employed within three months of graduation. Types of employment entered: banking, government, insurance.

Business Program(s) URL: http://www.hgc.edu

Program Contact: Ms. Rebecca Danchak, Director of Admissions, 275 Windsor Street, Hartford, CT 06120. Phone: 860-548-2421; Fax: 860-548-7823; E-mail: beckyd@hgc.edu

Sacred Heart University

College of Business

Fairfield, Connecticut

OVERVIEW
Sacred Heart University is an independent-religious, coed, comprehensive institution. Enrollment: 5,606 graduate, professional, and undergraduate students; 150 full-time matriculated graduate/professional students; 1,284 part-time matriculated graduate/professional students. Founded: 1963. The graduate business unit is in a suburban setting and is on a trimester calendar.

HIGHLIGHTS

Enrollment Profile
Full-time: 35
Part-time: 554
Total: 589
Average Age: 32
Fall 1997 Average GPA: N/R

International: 3%
Women: 50%
Minorities: 12%
Average Class Size: 20
Fall 1997 Average GMAT: N/R

Costs
Full-time tuition: N/R
Part-time tuition: $395 per credit

GRADUATE BUSINESS PROGRAMS
Master of Business Administration (MBA) Full-time, part-time; 30 total credits required; 12 months to 6 years to complete program. Concentrations in accounting, economics, finance, human resources, international business, management, management information systems, marketing.

Master of Business Administration in Health Care (MBA) Full-time, part-time; 30-60 total credits required; 12 months to 6 years to complete program. Concentration in health care.

Master of Business Administration/Master of Science in Nursing (MBA/MS) Full-time, part-time; 48-75 total credits required; 15 months to 6 years to complete program.

ADMISSION
Applications For fall 1997 there were 120 applications for admission. Of those applying, 98 were accepted. Of those accepted, 82 enrolled.

Application Requirements GMAT score: minimum 450, application form, application fee, bachelor's degree, minimum GPA: 2.8, 2 letters of recommendation, resume, college transcript(s), computer experience: word processing, spreadsheet, database.

Recommended for Application Interview, work experience.

Application Deadline Applications processed on a rolling/continuous basis for both domestic and international students. Application fee: $40, $100 (international). Deferred entrance is available.

ACADEMICS
Faculty Full-time 30; part-time 28.

Teaching Methodologies Case study, computer-aided instruction, computer analysis, group discussion, lecture, research, student presentations, team projects.

Technology 250 on-campus computer terminals/PCs are available for student use and are linked by a campus-wide network. The network has full access to the Internet. Students are not required to have their own PC.

Special Opportunities Advanced credit may be earned through transfer of credits from another institution. International exchange program in Luxembourg. An internship program is available.

FINANCES
Costs for 1997–98 Tuition: $395 per credit. Cost varies by number of credits taken. Fees: $75 per semester. Average 1997–98 room and board costs were $6500 per academic year. Room and board costs vary by occupancy (e.g., single, double, triple), type of accommodation, type of meal plan.

Financial Aid Research assistantships available.

Financial Aid Contact Mr. Andrew Foster, Financial Assistance Counselor, 5151 Park Avenue, Fairfield, CT 06432-1000. Phone: 203-371-7980; Fax: 203-371-7889.

FACILITIES
Information Resources Ryan Matura Library; total holdings of 172,500 volumes, 81,400 microforms, 1,700 current periodical subscriptions. CD player(s) available for graduate student use. Access provided to online bibliographic retrieval services and online databases.

INTERNATIONAL STUDENTS
Demographics 3% of students enrolled are international students [Africa, 25%, Asia, 50%, Europe, 15%, South America, 10%].

Services and Facilities International student office, visa services, ESL courses, counseling/support services.

Applying TOEFL: minimum score of 525, proof of adequate funds, proof of health/immunizations required. Financial aid is not available to international students.

International Student Contact Mr. John Gerlach, Advisor and Associate Professor of Finance, 5151 Park Avenue, Fairfield, CT 06432-1000. Phone: 203-396-8017; Fax: 203-365-7538; E-mail: gerlachj@sacredheart.edu

PLACEMENT
Services include alumni network, career counseling/planning, career fairs, career library, career placement, and resume preparation.

Employment Types of employment entered: accounting, banking, communications, computer-related, consumer products, finance, financial services, health services, human resources, information systems/technology, manufacturing, marketing, media, mining, nonprofit, retail, telecommunications.

Program Contact: Scott R. Colvin, Director, MBA Program, 5151 Park Avenue, Fairfield, CT 06432-1000. Phone: 203-371-7850; Fax: 203-371-7538; E-mail: colvins@sacredheart.edu

See full description on page 958.

Southern Connecticut State University

School of Business
New Haven, Connecticut

OVERVIEW
Southern Connecticut State University is a state-supported, comprehensive institution. Enrollment: 11,395 graduate, professional, and undergraduate students; 768 full-time matriculated graduate/professional students; 3,060 part-time matriculated graduate/professional students.

HIGHLIGHTS

Enrollment Profile
Full-time: 86
Part-time: 0
Total: 86
Average Age: N/R
Fall 1997 Average GPA: N/R

International: N/R
Women: N/R
Minorities: N/R
Average Class Size: N/R
Fall 1997 Average GMAT: N/R

Costs
Full-time tuition: $4118 per academic year (resident); $9602 per academic year (nonresident)
Part-time tuition: $564 per credit (resident); $564 per credit (nonresident)

GRADUATE BUSINESS PROGRAMS
Master of Business Administration (MBA) Full-time; 60 total credits required.
MBA in Accounting (MBA) Full-time; 60 total credits required; application deadline: 4/15.

ADMISSION
Application Requirements GMAT score, application form, bachelor's degree, minimum GPA: 2.5, 3 letters of recommendation, resume, college transcript(s), work experience.
Application Deadline Applications processed on a rolling/continuous basis for both domestic and international students.

FINANCES
Costs for 1997–98 Tuition: Full-time: $4118 per year (resident); $9602 per year (nonresident). Part-time: $564 per credit (resident); $564 per credit (nonresident). Cost varies by number of credits taken.
Financial Aid Contact Financial Aid Office, New Haven, CT 06515-1355. Phone: 203-392-5222.

INTERNATIONAL STUDENTS
Demographics N/R
Services and Facilities International student office, counseling/support services.
Applying TOEFL, proof of adequate funds required.
International Student Contact International Student Advisors, New Haven, CT 06515-1355. Phone: 203-392-6821.

PLACEMENT
Services include career counseling/planning.

Program Contact: Dan Mitchell, Assistant Director, MBA Admissions, New Haven, CT 06515-1355. Phone: 203-392-5881.

University of Bridgeport

School of Business
Bridgeport, Connecticut

OVERVIEW
The University of Bridgeport is an independent-nonprofit, coed, comprehensive institution. Enrollment: 2,427 graduate, professional, and undergraduate students; 713 full-time matriculated graduate/professional students; 616 part-time matriculated graduate/professional students. Founded: 1927. The graduate business unit is in an urban setting and is on a semester calendar.

HIGHLIGHTS

Enrollment Profile
Full-time: 65
Part-time: 120
Total: 185
Average Age: 31
Fall 1997 Average GPA: 3.1

International: 57%
Women: 43%
Minorities: 18%
Average Class Size: 15
Fall 1997 Average GMAT: 500

Costs
Full-time tuition: N/R
Part-time tuition: $340 per credit

ACBSP – The American Council of Business Schools and Programs accredited

GRADUATE BUSINESS PROGRAMS
Master of Business Administration (MBA) Full-time, part-time; 54 total credits required; 12 months to 5 years to complete program. Concentrations in accounting, economics, finance, management, marketing, management information systems, international business.

ADMISSION
Applications For fall 1997 there were 297 applications for admission. Of those applying, 241 were accepted. Of those accepted, 58 enrolled.
Application Requirements GMAT score, application form, application fee, bachelor's degree, essay, 2 letters of recommendation, personal statement, resume, college transcript(s).
Recommended for Application Minimum GPA, interview, work experience, computer experience.
Application Deadline Applications processed on a rolling/continuous basis for domestic students only. 8/1 for fall (international), 1/1 for spring (international), 5/1 for summer (international). Application fee: $40, $50 (international). Deferred entrance is available.

ACADEMICS
Faculty Full-time 13; part-time 15.
Teaching Methodologies Case study, computer-aided instruction, computer analysis, computer simulations, experiential learning, faculty seminars, field projects, group discussion, lecture, research, role playing, seminars by members of the business community, simulations, student presentations, study groups, team projects.
Technology 250 on-campus computer terminals/PCs are available for student use and are linked by a campus-wide network. The network has full access to the Internet. Students are not required to have their own PC.
Special Opportunities Advanced credit may be earned through transfer of credits from another institution. An internship program is available.

FINANCES
Costs for 1997–98 Tuition: $340 per credit. Cost varies by academic program, class time (e.g., day/evening), number of credits taken. Fees: $50 per semester. Fees vary by class time (e.g., day/evening), number of credits taken. Average 1997–98 room and board costs were $6810 per academic year. Room and board costs vary by occupancy (e.g., single, double, triple), type of meal plan.
Financial Aid In 1997–98, 24% of students received some institutionally administered aid in the form of fellowships, research assistantships, teaching assistantships, grants, scholarships, work study, loans. Financial aid is available to part-time students. Application Deadline: 6/1.
Financial Aid Contact Mr. Dominic Yoia, Director of Financial Aid, 380 University Avenue, Bridgeport, CT 06601. Phone: 203-576-4568; Fax: 203-576-4941.

FACILITIES
Information Resources Magnus Wahlstom Library plus 1 additional on-campus library; total holdings of 273,489 volumes, 1,101,708 microforms, 1,630 current periodical subscriptions. CD player(s) available for graduate student use. Access provided to online bibliographic retrieval services.

INTERNATIONAL STUDENTS
Demographics 57% of students enrolled are international students [Africa, 3%, Asia, 90%, Europe, 4%, South America, 3%].

University of Bridgeport (continued)

Services and Facilities International student office, ESL courses, counseling/support services.

Applying TOEFL: minimum score of 575, proof of adequate funds, proof of health/immunizations required. Financial aid is available to international students.

International Student Contact Ms. Dawn Valenti, Director of International Affairs, 380 University Avenue, Bridgeport, CT 06601. Phone: 203-576-4395; Fax: 203-576-4941.

PLACEMENT

Services include alumni network, career counseling/planning, career fairs, career library, career placement, electronic job bank, job interviews arranged, job search course, resume referral to employers, and resume preparation.

Program Contact: Dr. Llewellyn M. Mullings, Director of the MBA Program, School of Business, 230 Park Avenue, Bridgeport, CT 06601. Phone: 203-576-4363; Fax: 203-576-4388.

See full description on page 1038.

University of Connecticut

School of Business Administration

Storrs, Connecticut

OVERVIEW

The University of Connecticut is a state-supported, coed university. Enrollment: 23,585 graduate, professional, and undergraduate students; 4,911 full-time matriculated graduate/professional students; 2,593 part-time matriculated graduate/professional students. Founded: 1881. The graduate business unit is in an urban setting and is on a semester calendar.

HIGHLIGHTS

Enrollment Profile

Full-time: 132	International: N/R
Part-time: 1,046	Women: 45%
Total: 1,178	Minorities: N/R
Average Age: 32	Average Class Size: 30
Fall 1997 Average GPA: 3.3	Fall 1997 Average GMAT: 555

Costs
Full-time tuition: $7600 per academic year (resident); $15,800 per academic year (nonresident)
Part-time tuition: N/R

AACSB – The International Association for Management Education accredited

Degree(s) offered in conjunction with E.M. Lyon, Laval Université

GRADUATE BUSINESS PROGRAMS

Master of Business Administration (MBA) Full-time, part-time, distance learning option; 57 total credits required; 2 to 6 years to complete program. Concentrations in finance, marketing, international business, technology management, real estate, health care, management, accounting.

Master of Business Administration/Doctor of Jurisprudence (MBA/JD) Full-time; 116 total credits required; 4 to 5 years to complete program.

Master of Business Administration/Master of Science in Nursing (MBA/MS) Full-time, part-time, distance learning option; 63 total credits required; 18 months to 5 years to complete program.

Executive MBA (MBA) Full-time, distance learning option; 48 total credits required; 21 months to complete program.

Master of Business Administration/Master of Social Work (MBA/MSW) Full-time, part-time; minimum of 2.5 years to complete program.

Master of Business Administration/Master of Arts in European Studies (MBA/MA) Full-time; 72 total credits required; minimum of 2.5 years to complete program. Concentrations in asian business studies, european business studies.

Master of Business Administration/Master of Arts in African Studies (MBA/MA) Full-time; 72 total credits required; minimum of 2.5 years to complete program.

Master of Business Administration/Master of Arts in Latin American and Caribbean Studies (MBA/MA) Full-time; 72 total credits required; minimum of 2.5 years to complete program.

Master of Business Administration/Master of Public Health (MBA/MPH) Full-time, part-time; up to 2.8 years to complete program.

Master of Business Administration/Master of Public Affairs (MBA/MPA) Full-time, part-time; up to 2.8 years to complete program.

Master of Business Administration/Doctor of Medicine (MBA/MD) Full-time, part-time; up to 2.8 years to complete program.

ADMISSION

Applications For fall 1997 there were 244 applications for admission. Of those applying, 133 were accepted. Of those accepted, 48 enrolled.

Application Requirements Application form, application fee, bachelor's degree, essay, minimum GPA: 3.0, 2 letters of recommendation, personal statement, resume, college transcript(s), minimum of 2 years of work experience, computer experience: Microsoft Office 97.

Recommended for Application GMAT score accepted: minimum 530.

Application Deadline Applications processed on a rolling/continuous basis for both domestic and international students. Application fee: $40, $45 (international). Deferred entrance is available.

ACADEMICS

Faculty Full-time 82; part-time 16.

Teaching Methodologies Case study, computer-aided instruction, computer analysis, computer simulations, experiential learning, faculty seminars, field projects, group discussion, lecture, research, role playing, seminars by members of the business community, simulations, student presentations, study groups, team projects.

Technology 500 on-campus computer terminals/PCs are available for student use and are linked by a campus-wide network. The network has full access to the Internet. Students are required to have their own PC.

Special Opportunities International exchange programs in France, Netherlands. An internship program is available.

FINANCES

Costs for 1997–98 Tuition: Full-time: $7600 per year (resident); $15,800 per year (nonresident). Average 1997–98 room and board costs were $5800 per academic year. Room and board costs vary by occupancy (e.g., single, double, triple), type of accommodation, type of meal plan.

Financial Aid Fellowships, research assistantships, teaching assistantships available. Application Deadline: 3/2.

Financial Aid Contact Mona Lucas, Director, Student Financial Aid Office, 233 Glenbrook Road, U-116, Wilbur Cross Building, Storrs, CT 06269-4116. Phone: 860-486 2819; Fax: 860-486 0945.

FACILITIES

Information Resources Homer D. Babbidge Library plus 3 additional on-campus libraries; total holdings of 1,946,784 volumes, 2,829,795 microforms, 9,747 current periodical subscriptions. CD player(s) available for graduate student use. Access provided to online bibliographic retrieval services.

INTERNATIONAL STUDENTS

Demographics N/R

Services and Facilities International student office, international student center, ESL courses, counseling/support services.

Applying TOEFL: minimum score of 550, proof of adequate funds, proof of health/immunizations required. Financial aid is not available to international students.

PLACEMENT

Services include alumni network, career counseling/planning, career fairs, career library, career placement, electronic job bank, job interviews arranged, resume referral to employers, and resume preparation. In 1996–97, 55 organizations participated in on-campus recruiting; 500 on-campus interviews were conducted.

Employment Of 1996–97 graduates, 88% were employed within three months of graduation; the average starting salary was $50,000. Types of employment entered: accounting, banking, computer-related, consulting, consumer products, education, finance, financial services, government, health services, high technology, hospitality management, human resources, information systems/technology, insurance, international trade, management, manufacturing, marketing, nonprofit, pharmaceutical, real estate, service industry, transportation.

Business Program(s) URL: http://www.sba.uconn.edu

Program Contact: Mr. Paul Mason, Director, Storrs MBA Program, 368 Fairfield Road, U-41 MBA, Storrs, CT 06269-2041. Phone: 860-486-2872; Fax: 860-486-5222.

See full description on page 1058.

University of Hartford

Barney School of Business and Public Administration

West Hartford, Connecticut

OVERVIEW

The University of Hartford is an independent-nonprofit, coed, comprehensive institution. Enrollment: 7,089 graduate, professional, and undergraduate students;

592 full-time matriculated graduate/professional students; 1,110 part-time matriculated graduate/professional students. Founded: 1877. The graduate business unit is in a suburban setting and is on a semester calendar.

HIGHLIGHTS

Enrollment Profile
Full-time: 182
Part-time: 310
Total: 492
Average Age: 30
Fall 1997 Average GPA: 2.5

International: 28%
Women: 44%
Minorities: 5%
Average Class Size: 23
Fall 1997 Average GMAT: 480

Costs
Full-time tuition: N/R
Part-time tuition: $360 per credit hour

GRADUATE BUSINESS PROGRAMS

Master of Business Administration (MBA) Full-time, part-time; 48 total credits required; 12 months to 5 years to complete program. Concentrations in accounting, finance, insurance, international business, management, management information systems, marketing, organizational behavior/development, public management, taxation.

Master of Science in Taxation (MST) Full-time, part-time; 30 total credits required; 12 months to 5 years to complete program. Concentration in taxation.

Master of Science in Organizational Behavior (MS) Full-time, part-time; 36 total credits required; 15 months to 5 years to complete program. Concentration in organizational behavior/development.

Master of Science in Insurance (MS) Full-time, part-time; 36 total credits required; 12 months to 5 years to complete program. Concentrations in insurance, finance, management.

Master of Science in Professional Accountancy (MS) Full-time, part-time; 30 total credits required; 12 months to 5 years to complete program. Concentrations in accounting, taxation.

Accelerated Master of Science in Professional Accountancy (MS) Full-time; 48 total credits required; 15 months to complete program. Concentration in accounting.

Master of Business Administration/Master of Engineering (MBA/ME) Full-time, part-time; 60 total credits required; 18 months to 5 years to complete program. Concentration in management.

ADMISSION

Applications For fall 1997 there were 301 applications for admission. Of those applying, 207 were accepted. Of those accepted, 149 enrolled.

Application Requirements Application form, application fee, bachelor's degree, minimum GPA, 2 letters of recommendation, personal statement, resume, college transcript(s).

Recommended for Application GMAT score accepted.

Application Deadline Applications processed on a rolling/continuous basis for both domestic and international students. Application fee: $40, $55 (international). Deferred entrance is available.

ACADEMICS

Faculty Full-time 40; part-time 30.

Teaching Methodologies Case study, computer-aided instruction, computer analysis, computer simulations, experiential learning, field projects, group discussion, lecture, research, role playing, student presentations, study groups, team projects.

Technology 150 on-campus computer terminals/PCs are available for student use and are linked by a campus-wide network. The network has full access to the Internet. Students are not required to have their own PC.

Special Opportunities Advanced credit may be earned through transfer of credits from another institution. International exchange program available. An internship program is available.

FINANCES

Costs for 1997–98 Tuition: $360 per credit hour. Fees: $30 per semester. Average 1997–98 room and board costs were $5250 per academic year. Room and board costs vary by occupancy (e.g., single, double, triple), type of meal plan.

Financial Aid Research assistantships, loans available. Financial aid is available to part-time students. Application Deadline: 5/1.

Financial Aid Contact Joseph Martinkovic, Director of SFA, 200 Bloomfield Avenue, West Hartford, CT 06117-1500. Phone: 860-768-4904; Fax: 860-768-4961.

FACILITIES

Information Resources W. H. Mortensen Library plus 2 additional on-campus libraries; total holdings of 405,000 volumes, 59,535 microforms, 2,300 current periodical subscriptions. CD player(s) available for graduate student use. Access provided to online bibliographic retrieval services and online databases.

INTERNATIONAL STUDENTS

Demographics 28% of students enrolled are international students.

Services and Facilities International student office, international student center, ESL courses.

Applying TOEFL: minimum score of 550, proof of adequate funds, proof of health/immunizations required. Financial aid is not available to international students.

International Student Contact Mr. Richard Lazzerini, Associate Director of International Programs, 200 Bloomfield Avenue, West Hartford, CT 06117-1500. Phone: 860-768-4873; Fax: 860-768-4726.

PLACEMENT

Services include alumni network, career counseling/planning, career fairs, career placement, job interviews arranged, resume referral to employers, and resume preparation. In 1996–97, 65 organizations participated in on-campus recruiting.

Employment Of 1996–97 graduates, 97% were employed within three months of graduation; the average starting salary was $40,000. Types of employment entered: accounting, banking, communications, computer-related, consulting, consumer products, education, energy, engineering, finance, financial services, government, health services, high technology, hospitality management, human resources, information systems/technology, insurance, international trade, management, manufacturing, marketing, media, nonprofit, pharmaceutical, real estate, retail, service industry, telecommunications, transportation, utilities.

Business Program(s) URL: http://www.hartford.edu

Program Contact: Ms. Claire Silverstein, Assistant Director of Graduate Programs, 200 Bloomfield Avenue, West Hartford, CT 06117-1500. Phone: 860-768-4900; Fax: 860-768-4821; E-mail: silverste@mail.hartford.edu

University of New Haven

School of Business

West Haven, Connecticut

OVERVIEW

The University of New Haven is an independent-nonprofit, coed university. Enrollment: 4,849 graduate, professional, and undergraduate students; 585 full-time matriculated graduate/professional students; 1,379 part-time matriculated graduate/professional students. Founded: 1920. The graduate business unit is in a suburban setting and is on a trimester plus abbreviated summer session calendar.

HIGHLIGHTS

Enrollment Profile
Full-time: 140
Part-time: 512
Total: 652
Average Age: 29
Fall 1997 Average GPA: N/R

International: 22%
Women: 42%
Minorities: 10%
Average Class Size: 21
Fall 1997 Average GMAT: N/R

Costs
Full-time tuition: $9720 per academic year
Part-time tuition: $360 per credit

GRADUATE BUSINESS PROGRAMS

Master of Business Administration (MBA) Full-time, part-time; 51 total credits required; GMAT score required; 12 months to 5 years to complete program. Concentrations in accounting, finance, human resources, international business, logistics, management, management science, marketing, public relations, technology management, business policy/strategy, health care, sports/entertainment management, business information science, industrial administration/management, operations management.

Master of Science in Accounting (MS) Full-time, part-time; 42 total credits required; 15 months to 5 years to complete program.

Master of Business Administration/Master of Science in Industrial Engineering (MBA/MS) Full-time, part-time; 72 total credits required; 2 to 5 years to complete program.

Master of Business Administration/Master of Public Administration (MBA/MPA) Full-time, part-time; 72 total credits required; 2 to 5 years to complete program.

Executive MBA (MBA) Part-time; 30 total credits required; 22 months to complete program.

Master of Science in Finance and Financial Services (MS) Full-time, part-time; 42 total credits required; 15 months to 5 years to complete program.

Master of Science in Health Care Administration (MS) Full-time, part-time; 42 total credits required; 15 months to 5 years to complete program.

University of New Haven (continued)

Master of Science in Industrial Relations (MS) Full-time, part-time; 39 total credits required; 12 months to 5 years to complete program.

Master of Public Administration (MPA) Full-time, part-time; 42 total credits required; 15 months to 5 years to complete program.

Master of Science in Taxation (MS) Full-time, part-time; 36 total credits required; 15 months to 5 years to complete program.

ADMISSION
Applications For fall 1997 there were 220 applications for admission. Of those applying, 209 were accepted. Of those accepted, 121 enrolled.

Application Requirements Application form, application fee, bachelor's degree, 2 letters of recommendation, college transcript(s).

Recommended for Application Minimum GPA, computer experience.

Application Deadline Applications processed on a rolling/continuous basis for both domestic and international students. Application fee: $50. Deferred entrance is available.

ACADEMICS
Faculty Full-time 44.

Teaching Methodologies Case study, computer-aided instruction, computer analysis, computer simulations, experiential learning, faculty seminars, field projects, group discussion, lecture, research, role playing, seminars by members of the business community, student presentations, study groups, team projects.

Technology 260 on-campus computer terminals/PCs are available for student use and are linked by a campus-wide network. The network has full access to the Internet. Students are not required to have their own PC.

Special Opportunities Advanced credit may be earned through credit by examination, transfer of credits from another institution. An internship program is available.

FINANCES
Costs for 1997–98 Tuition: Full-time: $9720 per year. Part-time: $360 per credit. Cost varies by academic program, number of credits taken. Fees: Full-time: $139 per academic year. Part-time: $13 per trimester. Fees vary by academic program. Average 1997–98 room and board costs were $10,000 per academic year (on campus) and $10,000 per academic year (off campus). Room and board costs vary by type of meal plan.

Financial Aid In 1997–98, 78% of students received some institutionally administered aid in the form of research assistantships, teaching assistantships, work study, loans. Financial aid is available to part-time students. Application Deadline: 5/1.

Financial Aid Contact Ms. Jane Sangeloty, Director of Financial Aid, 300 Orange Avenue, West Haven, CT 06516-1916. Phone: 800-DIAL-UNH Ext. 7315; Fax: 203-932-7137.

FACILITIES
Information Resources Marvin K. Peterson Library; total holdings of 300,000 volumes. CD player(s) available for graduate student use. Access provided to online bibliographic retrieval services and online databases.

INTERNATIONAL STUDENTS
Demographics 22% of students enrolled are international students.

Services and Facilities International student office, international student center, international student housing, ESL courses, counseling/support services.

Applying TOEFL: minimum score of 520, proof of adequate funds, proof of health/immunizations required. Financial aid is not available to international students.

International Student Contact Ms. Lisa Carraretto, Director, International Services, 300 Orange Avenue, West Haven, CT 06516-1916. Phone: 800-DIAL-UNH Ext. 7338; Fax: 203-932-7343; E-mail: lisacarr@charger.newhaven.edu

PLACEMENT
Services include career counseling/planning, career fairs, career library, career placement, and resume preparation.

Business Program(s) URL http://www.mba.newhaven.edu

Program Contact: Mr. Joseph F. Spellman, Director of Graduate Admissions, 300 Orange Avenue, West Haven, CT 06516-1916. Phone: 203-932-7133, 800-DIAL-UNH; Fax: 203-932-7137; E-mail: gradinfo@charger.newhaven.edu

See full description on page 1114.

Western Connecticut State University

Ancell School of Business and Public Administration
Danbury, Connecticut

OVERVIEW
Western Connecticut State University is a state-supported, coed, comprehensive institution. Enrollment: 5,421 graduate, professional, and undergraduate students; 30 full-time matriculated graduate/professional students; 580 part-time matriculated graduate/professional students. Founded: 1903. The graduate business unit is in a suburban setting and is on a semester calendar.

HIGHLIGHTS
Enrollment Profile
Full-time: 17
Part-time: 121
Total: 138
Average Age: 32
Fall 1997 Average GPA: 3.0

International: 3%
Women: N/R
Minorities: N/R
Average Class Size: 15
Fall 1997 Average GMAT: 475

Costs
Full-time tuition: $2568 per academic year (resident); $7156 per academic year (nonresident)
Part-time tuition: $178 per credit (resident); $178 per credit (nonresident)

GRADUATE BUSINESS PROGRAMS
Master of Business Administration (MBA) Full-time, part-time; 45-57 total credits required; 2 to 8 years to complete program. Concentrations in accounting, management.

Master of Health Administration (MHA) Full-time, part-time; 36 total credits required; 18 months to 6 years to complete program. Concentrations in management, health care.

ADMISSION
Application Requirements Application form, application fee, bachelor's degree, minimum GPA: 3.0, 2 letters of recommendation, personal statement, college transcript(s).

Recommended for Application GMAT score accepted, resume, computer experience.

Application Deadline Applications processed on a rolling/continuous basis for both domestic and international students. Application fee: $40. Deferred entrance is available.

ACADEMICS
Faculty Full-time 14; part-time 2.

Teaching Methodologies Case study, computer analysis, computer simulations, experiential learning, field projects, group discussion, lecture, research, role playing, seminars by members of the business community, simulations, student presentations, study groups, team projects.

Technology 300 on-campus computer terminals/PCs are available for student use and are linked by a campus-wide network. The network has full access to the Internet. Students are not required to have their own PC.

Special Opportunities Advanced credit may be earned through transfer of credits from another institution.

FINANCES
Costs for 1997–98 Tuition: Full-time: $2568 per year (resident); $7156 per year (nonresident). Part-time: $178 per credit (resident); $178 per credit (nonresident). Fees: Full-time: $1559 per academic year (resident); $2425 per academic year (nonresident). Part-time: $25 per semester (resident); $25 per semester (nonresident). Average 1997–98 room and board costs were $4758 per academic year. Room and board costs vary by type of meal plan.

Financial Aid Fellowships, work study available. Financial aid is available to part-time students. Application Deadline: 5/1.

Financial Aid Contact Mr. William Hawkins, Director of Financial Aid, 181 White Street, Danbury, CT 06810-6885. Phone: 203-837-8586; Fax: 203-837-8528; E-mail: hawkinsw@wcsu.ctstateu.edu

FACILITIES
Information Resources Ruth A. Haas Library plus 1 additional on-campus library; total holdings of 147,670 volumes, 62,926 microforms, 1,347 current periodical subscriptions. CD player(s) available for graduate student use. Access provided to online bibliographic retrieval services and online databases.

INTERNATIONAL STUDENTS
Demographics 3% of students enrolled are international students.

Applying TOEFL: minimum score of 550, proof of adequate funds, proof of health/immunizations required.

PLACEMENT

Services include alumni network, career counseling/planning, career fairs, career library, career placement, electronic job bank, job interviews arranged, and resume preparation.

Employment Of 1996–97 graduates, 99% were employed within three months of graduation. Types of employment entered: accounting, banking, communications, computer-related, consulting, consumer products, education, finance, financial services, government, health services, high technology, human resources, information systems/technology, insurance, management, manufacturing, marketing, nonprofit, petrochemical, pharmaceutical, retail, service industry, telecommunications, transportation, utilities.

Business Program(s) URL: http://www.wcsu.ctstateu.edu/mba

Program Contact: Mr. Chris Shankle, Assistant Director of University Admissions, 181 White Street, Danbury, CT 06810-6885. Phone: 203-837-9005; Fax: 203-837-8338.

Yale University

School of Management

New Haven, Connecticut

OVERVIEW

Yale University is an independent-nonprofit, coed university. Enrollment: 11,085 graduate, professional, and undergraduate students; 5,646 full-time matriculated graduate/professional students; part-time matriculated graduate/professional students. Founded: 1701. The graduate business unit is in an urban setting and is on a semester calendar.

HIGHLIGHTS

Enrollment Profile
Full-time: 439	International: 32%
Part-time: 0	Women: 28%
Total: 439	Minorities: 20%
Average Age: 27	Average Class Size: 49
Fall 1997 Average GPA: 3.4	Fall 1997 Average GMAT: 679

Costs
Full-time tuition: $25,250 per academic year
Part-time tuition: N/R

AACSB – The International Association for Management Education accredited

GRADUATE BUSINESS PROGRAMS
Master of Public and Private Management (MPPM) Full-time; 54 total credits required; minimum of 2 years to complete program. Concentrations in management, finance, marketing, operations management, strategic management, nonprofit management, public management.

ADMISSION
Applications For fall 1997 there were 1,620 applications for admission. Of those applying, 416 were accepted. Of those accepted, 214 enrolled.

Application Requirements Application form, application fee, bachelor's degree, essay, 3 letters of recommendation, personal statement, resume, college transcript(s), minimum of 4 years of work experience.

Recommended for Application GMAT score accepted, GRE score accepted, minimum GPA, computer experience.

Application Deadline 3/15 for fall, 3/15 for fall (international). Application fee: $120. Deferred entrance is available.

ACADEMICS
Faculty Full-time 43; part-time 39.

Teaching Methodologies Case study, experiential learning, faculty seminars, field projects, group discussion, lecture, research, role playing, seminars by members of the business community, simulations, student presentations, study groups, team projects.

Technology 41 on-campus computer terminals/PCs are available for student use and are linked by a campus-wide network. The network has full access to the Internet. Students are required to have their own PC.

Special Opportunities Advanced credit may be earned through credit by examination. An internship program is available.

FINANCES
Costs for 1997–98 Tuition: Full-time: $25,250 per year. Fees: Full-time: $105 per academic year. Average 1997–98 room and board costs were $8675 per academic year (on campus) and $8675 per academic year (off campus).

Financial Aid In 1997–98, 62% of students received some institutionally administered aid in the form of grants, loans. Financial aid is available to part-time students. Application Deadline: 3/1.

Financial Aid Contact Karen Wellman, Director, Financial Aid Office, Box 208200, New Haven, CT 06520-8200. Phone: 203-432-5173; Fax: 203-432-9916.

FACILITIES
Information Resources Sterling Memorial Library plus 40 additional on-campus libraries; total holdings of 11,000,000 volumes, 4,700,000 microforms, 54,600 current periodical subscriptions. Access provided to online bibliographic retrieval services.

INTERNATIONAL STUDENTS
Demographics 32% of students enrolled are international students.

Services and Facilities International student office, visa services, ESL courses.

Applying TOEFL: minimum score of 600, proof of adequate funds, proof of health/immunizations required. Financial aid is available to international students.

International Student Contact Director, Office of Foreign Students and Scholars, 442 Temple Street, New Haven, CT 06520. Phone: 203-432-2305.

PLACEMENT
Services include alumni network, career counseling/planning, career fairs, career library, career placement, electronic job bank, job interviews arranged, job search course, resume referral to employers, and resume preparation. In 1996–97, 125 organizations participated in on-campus recruiting; 1,360 on-campus interviews were conducted.

Employment Of 1996–97 graduates, 97% were employed within three months of graduation; the average starting salary was $75,000. Types of employment entered: accounting, banking, consulting, engineering, finance, government, health services, high technology, management, manufacturing, marketing, media, nonprofit, pharmaceutical, service industry.

Business Program(s) URL: http://www.yale.edu/som

Program Contact: Mr. Richard Silverman, Executive Director of Admissions, Box 208200, 135 Prospect Street, New Haven, CT 06520-8200. Phone: 203-432-5932; Fax: 203-432-9991; E-mail: som.admissions@yale.edu

DELAWARE

Delaware State University

School of Management

Dover, Delaware

OVERVIEW

Delaware State University is a state-supported, coed, comprehensive institution. Enrollment: 3,320 graduate, professional, and undergraduate students; 107 full-time matriculated graduate/professional students; 156 part-time matriculated graduate/professional students. Founded: 1891. The graduate business unit is in a small-town setting and is on a semester calendar.

HIGHLIGHTS

Enrollment Profile
Full-time: N/R	International: N/R
Part-time: N/R	Women: N/R
Total: N/R	Minorities: N/R
Average Age: N/R	Average Class Size: 10
Fall 1997 Average GPA: N/R	Fall 1997 Average GMAT: N/R

Costs
Full-time tuition: $1323 per academic year (resident); $3159 per academic year (nonresident)
Part-time tuition: $147 per credit (resident); $351 per credit (nonresident)

GRADUATE BUSINESS PROGRAMS
Master of Business Administration (MBA) Full-time, part-time; 30 total credits required; 12 months to 7 years to complete program.

ADMISSION
Applications For fall 1997 there were 35 applications for admission. Of those applying, 28 were accepted. Of those accepted, 26 enrolled.

Application Requirements Application form, application fee, bachelor's degree, minimum GPA, 3 letters of recommendation, college transcript(s).

Recommended for Application GMAT score accepted, computer experience.

Application Deadline Applications processed on a rolling/continuous basis for both domestic and international students. Application fee: $25. Deferred entrance is available.

Delaware State University (continued)

ACADEMICS
Faculty Part-time 5.

Teaching Methodologies Case study, computer-aided instruction, computer analysis, computer simulations, experiential learning, field projects, group discussion, lecture, research, seminars by members of the business community, simulations, student presentations, study groups, team projects.

Technology Computer terminals/PCs are available for student use and are linked by a campus-wide network. The network has full access to the Internet. Students are not required to have their own PC.

Special Opportunities Advanced credit may be earned through transfer of credits from another institution. An internship program is available.

FINANCES
Costs for 1997–98 Tuition: Full-time: $1323 per semester (resident); $3159 per semester (nonresident). Part-time: $147 per credit (resident); $351 per credit (nonresident). Cost varies by number of credits taken. Fees: $40 per semester.

Financial Aid Fellowships, work study, loans available. Financial aid is available to part-time students.

FACILITIES
Information Resources William C. Jason Library plus 1 additional on-campus library; total holdings of 173,756 volumes, 73,266 microforms, 2,850 current periodical subscriptions. CD player(s) available for graduate student use.

INTERNATIONAL STUDENTS
Demographics N/R

Services and Facilities International student office, international student center, counseling/support services.

Applying TOEFL: minimum score of 550, proof of adequate funds required.

PLACEMENT
Services include alumni network, career fairs, career placement, and resume referral to employers.

Employment Types of employment entered: banking, finance, transportation.

Business Program(s) URL: http://som.dsc.edu/

Program Contact: Dr. John Stith, School of Management, 1200 North DuPont Highway, Dover, DE 19901-2277. Phone: 302-739-4972; Fax: 302-739-3517; E-mail: jstith@dsc.edu

Goldey-Beacom College

Office of Graduate Studies

Wilmington, Delaware

OVERVIEW
Goldey-Beacom College is an independent-nonprofit, coed, comprehensive institution. Enrollment: 1,900 graduate, professional, and undergraduate students; 18 full-time matriculated graduate/professional students; 171 part-time matriculated graduate/professional students. Founded: 1886. The graduate business unit is in a suburban setting and is on a trimester calendar.

HIGHLIGHTS

Enrollment Profile
Full-time: 18
Part-time: 171
Total: 189
Average Age: 33
Fall 1997 Average GPA: 3.0

International: 20%
Women: 51%
Minorities: 24%
Average Class Size: 30
Fall 1997 Average GMAT: 504

Costs
Full-time tuition: N/R
Part-time tuition: $13,065 per program

ACBSP – The American Council of Business Schools and Programs accredited

Located in the suburbs of Wilmington, Delaware, Goldey-Beacom College is a small, private college with a tradition of excellence, specializing exclusively in business education since 1886. The College is accredited nationally by ACBSP and regionally by the Commission on Higher Education of the Middle States Association of Colleges and Schools.

The M.B.A. Program is specifically aimed at the working professional and manager. It combines a convenient location, convenient course schedule, small class size, friendly atmosphere, teaching-oriented and experienced faculty members, and an open-minded administration.

The M.B.A. Program develops skills needed to successfully manage in tomorrow's global marketplace. The thirteen required courses build upon a basic foundation of business knowledge gained through formal education, work experience, or specialized training. With all courses offered in the evening, the M.B.A. can be earned in two years, on a part-time basis, by taking courses in the fall, spring, and summer semesters. Students may pursue the Comprehensive M.B.A. or concentrations in human resource management, financial management, and accounting.

The M.B.A. Program features case studies, team projects, small group seminars, research, and practical experience led and taught by an outstanding faculty, the members of which all have both the Ph.D. and significant business experience. Formal instruction is enhanced through interaction with dynamic executives from both large corporations and small businesses, who share their business expertise and acumen.

GRADUATE BUSINESS PROGRAMS
Master of Business Administration (MBA) Full-time, part-time; 39 total credits required; 2 to 7 years to complete program. Concentrations in human resources, finance, accounting.

ADMISSION
Applications For fall 1997 there were 60 applications for admission. Of those applying, 50 were accepted. Of those accepted, 45 enrolled.

Application Requirements Application form, application fee, bachelor's degree, minimum GPA: 2.5, interview, 3 letters of recommendation, personal statement, college transcript(s).

Recommended for Application GMAT score accepted: minimum 450.

Application Deadline Applications processed on a rolling/continuous basis for both domestic and international students. Application fee: $30. Deferred entrance is available.

ACADEMICS
Faculty Full-time 6; part-time 4.

Teaching Methodologies Case study, computer-aided instruction, computer analysis, computer simulations, experiential learning, faculty seminars, field projects, group discussion, lecture, research, role playing, seminars by members of the business community, student presentations, study groups, team projects.

Technology 129 on-campus computer terminals/PCs are available for student use and are linked by a campus-wide network. The network has full access to the Internet. Students are not required to have their own PC.

Special Opportunities Advanced credit may be earned through transfer of credits from another institution. An internship program is available.

FINANCES
Costs for 1997–98 Tuition: $13,065 per program. Cost varies by academic program, number of credits taken. Fees: $300 per program. Average 1997–98 room only costs were $4865 per academic year.

Financial Aid In 1997–98, 5% of students received some institutionally administered aid in the form of research assistantships. Financial aid is available to part-time students.

Financial Aid Contact Jane Lysle, Director of Financial Aid, 4701 Limestone Road, Wilmington, DE 19808-1999. Phone: 800-833-4877; Fax: 302-998-8631.

FACILITIES
Information Resources J. Wilbur Hirons Library; total holdings of 50,000 volumes, 34 microforms, 750 current periodical subscriptions. CD player(s) available for graduate student use. Access provided to online bibliographic retrieval services.

INTERNATIONAL STUDENTS
Demographics 20% of students enrolled are international students [Africa, 33%, Asia, 41%, Europe, 9%, South America, 17%].

Services and Facilities International student office, visa services, counseling/support services.

Applying TOEFL: minimum score of 525, proof of adequate funds, proof of health/immunizations required. Financial aid is not available to international students.

International Student Contact Irina Skowronski, International Student Advisor, 4701 Limestone Road, Wilmington, DE 19808-1999. Phone: 800-833-4877 Ext. 311; Fax: 302-998-1139.

PLACEMENT
Services include alumni network, career counseling/planning, career fairs, career library, career placement, electronic job bank, job interviews arranged, resume referral to employers, and resume preparation. In 1996–97, 63 organizations participated in on-campus recruiting; 150 on-campus interviews were conducted.

Employment Of 1996–97 graduates, 100% were employed within three months of graduation; the average starting salary was $28,000. Types of employment entered: accounting, banking, chemical industry, consulting, finance, financial services, government, health services, high technology, human resources, information systems/technology, insurance, international trade, manufacturing, marketing, nonprofit, petrochemical, pharmaceutical, service industry, telecommunications.

Business Program(s) URL: http://goldey.gbc.edu/mba

Program Contact: Bruce D. Marsland, Director of Graduate Programs, 4701 Limestone Road, Wilmington, DE 19808-1999. Phone: 302-998-8814 Ext. 276, 800-883-4877 (DE only); Fax: 302-998-8631; E-mail: graduate@goldey.gbc. edu

University of Delaware

College of Business and Economics

Newark, Delaware

OVERVIEW

The University of Delaware is a state-related, coed university. Enrollment: 18,814 graduate, professional, and undergraduate students; 1,711 full-time matriculated graduate/professional students; 1,575 part-time matriculated graduate/professional students. Founded: 1833. The graduate business unit is in a small-town setting and is on a semester calendar.

HIGHLIGHTS

Enrollment Profile

Full-time: 130	International: 8%
Part-time: 450	Women: 34%
Total: 580	Minorities: 11%
Average Age: 26	Average Class Size: 30
Fall 1997 Average GPA: 3.1	Fall 1997 Average GMAT: 595

Costs
Full-time tuition: $5360 per academic year (resident); $12,250 per academic year (nonresident)
Part-time tuition: $298 per credit hour (resident); $681 per credit hour (nonresident)

AACSB – The International Association for Management Education accredited

GRADUATE BUSINESS PROGRAMS

Master of Business Administration (MBA) Full-time, part-time; 36-48 total credits required; 11 months to 5 years to complete program. Concentrations in accounting, economics, finance, international business, management, marketing, operations management, technology management, arts administration/management, information management.

Executive MBA (EMBA) Full-time; 48 total credits required; 19 months to complete program.

Master of Science in Accounting (MSA) Full-time, part-time; 36-48 total credits required; 11 months to 5 years to complete program. Concentration in accounting.

ADMISSION

Applications For fall 1997 there were 259 applications for admission. Of those applying, 120 were accepted. Of those accepted, 60 enrolled.

Application Requirements GMAT score: minimum 500, application form, application fee, bachelor's degree, essay, minimum GPA, interview, 2 letters of recommendation, personal statement, resume, college transcript(s), computer experience.

Recommended for Application Work experience.

Application Deadline 5/1 for fall, 11/1 for spring, 5/1 for fall (international), 11/1 for spring (international). Application fee: $45. Deferred entrance is available.

ACADEMICS

Faculty Full-time 90; part-time 5.

Teaching Methodologies Case study, computer-aided instruction, computer analysis, computer simulations, faculty seminars, field projects, group discussion, lecture, research, role playing, simulations, student presentations, study groups, team projects.

Technology 100 on-campus computer terminals/PCs are available for student use and are linked by a campus-wide network. The network has full access to the Internet. Students are not required to have their own PC.

Special Opportunities Advanced credit may be earned through transfer of credits from another institution. An internship program is available.

FINANCES

Costs for 1997–98 Tuition: Full-time: $5360 per year (resident); $12,250 per year (nonresident). Part-time: $298 per credit hour (resident); $681 per credit hour (nonresident). Cost varies by academic program. Fees: Full-time: $320 per academic year (resident); $320 per academic year (nonresident). Average 1997–98 room and board costs were $7200 per academic year (on

campus) and $7200 per academic year (off campus). Room and board costs vary by occupancy (e.g., single, double, triple), type of accommodation, type of meal plan.

Financial Aid In 1997–98, 4% of students received some institutionally administered aid in the form of fellowships, research assistantships, teaching assistantships, work study. Application Deadline: 2/1.

Financial Aid Contact Mr. Alex Brown, Assistant Director of MBA Programs, 103 MBNA America Hall, Newark, DE 19716. Phone: 302-831-4596; Fax: 302-831-3329; E-mail: mba@udel.edu

FACILITIES

Information Resources Hugh M. Morris Library plus 4 additional on-campus libraries; total holdings of 2,100,000 volumes, 2,600,000 microforms, 24,000 current periodical subscriptions. Access provided to online bibliographic retrieval services.

INTERNATIONAL STUDENTS

Demographics 8% of students enrolled are international students.

Services and Facilities International student office, international student center, ESL courses, counseling/support services.

Applying TOEFL: minimum score of 585, proof of adequate funds, proof of health/immunizations required. Financial aid is available to international students.

International Student Contact Ms. Mary Politakis, Staff Assistant, Foreign Student and Scholar Services, 4 Kent Way, Newark, DE 19716. Phone: 302-831-2115; Fax: 302-831-8000; E-mail: mary.politakis@mvs.udel.edu

PLACEMENT

Services include alumni network, career counseling/planning, career fairs, career library, career placement, job interviews arranged, and resume referral to employers. In 1996–97, 30 organizations participated in on-campus recruiting.

Employment Of 1996–97 graduates, the average starting salary was $42,700. Types of employment entered: accounting, banking, chemical industry, consulting, finance, human resources, information systems/technology, management, manufacturing, service industry, transportation, utilities.

Business Program(s) URL: http://www.mba.udel.edu

Program Contact: Mr. Alex Brown, Assistant Director of MBA Programs, 103 MBNA America Hall, Newark, DE 19716. Phone: 302-831-4596; Fax: 302-831-3329; E-mail: mba@udel.edu

See full description on page 1062.

Wilmington College

Business Programs

New Castle, Delaware

OVERVIEW

Wilmington College is an independent-nonprofit, coed, comprehensive institution. Enrollment: 5,600 graduate, professional, and undergraduate students; 1,050 full-time matriculated graduate/professional students; 450 part-time matriculated graduate/professional students. Founded: 1967. The graduate business unit is in an urban setting and is on a semester calendar.

HIGHLIGHTS

Enrollment Profile

Full-time: N/R	International: N/R
Part-time: N/R	Women: N/R
Total: 650	Minorities: N/R
Average Age: 33	Average Class Size: 20
Fall 1997 Average GPA: N/R	Fall 1997 Average GMAT: N/R

Costs
Full-time tuition: N/R
Part-time tuition: $245 per credit hour

GRADUATE BUSINESS PROGRAMS

Master of Business Administration (MBA) Full-time, part-time; 36 total credits required; 12 months to 5 years to complete program.

Master of Science in Management (MS) Full-time, part-time; 36 total credits required; 12 months to 5 years to complete program. Concentrations in human resources, public policy and administration, health care.

ADMISSION

Application Requirements Application form, application fee, bachelor's degree, interview, 2 letters of recommendation, personal statement, college transcript(s), minimum of 3 years of work experience, computer experience: basic computer skills.

Application Deadline Applications processed on a rolling/continuous basis for both domestic and international students. Application fee: $25.

ACADEMICS

Teaching Methodologies Case study, experiential learning, faculty seminars, field projects, group discussion, lecture, research, role playing, seminars by members of the business community, simulations, student presentations, study groups, team projects.

FINANCES

Costs for 1997–98 Tuition: $245 per credit hour. Cost varies by campus location. Fees: $25 per semester.

Financial Aid Contact Lynn Iocono, Director, Financial Aid, 320 DuPont Highway, New Castle, DE 19720-6491. Phone: 302-328-9407 Ext. 106.

FACILITIES

Information Resources Main library; total holdings of 78,000 volumes, 17,516 microforms, 317 current periodical subscriptions. CD player(s) available for graduate student use. Access provided to online bibliographic retrieval services.

INTERNATIONAL STUDENTS

Demographics N/R

Applying TOEFL: minimum score of 500, proof of adequate funds, proof of health/immunizations required.

International Student Contact Mr. Dennis Huffman, International Student Advisor, 320 DuPont Highway, New Castle, DE 19720-6491. Phone: 302-328-9407 Ext. 151.

PLACEMENT

Services include career counseling/planning, and career placement.

Employment Types of employment entered: banking, insurance, petrochemical.

Program Contact: Dr. Clinton D. Robertson, Coordinator of MBA Program, 518 North King Street, Wilmington, DE 19801. Phone: 302-655-5400; Fax: 302-655-7360.

DISTRICT OF COLUMBIA

American University

Kogod College of Business Administration

Washington, District of Columbia

OVERVIEW

American University is an independent-religious, coed university. Enrollment: 10,821 graduate, professional, and undergraduate students; 2,458 full-time matriculated graduate/professional students; 2,454 part-time matriculated graduate/professional students. Founded: 1893. The graduate business unit is in an urban setting and is on a semester calendar.

HIGHLIGHTS

Enrollment Profile

Full-time: 239	International: 28%
Part-time: 267	Women: 46%
Total: 506	Minorities: 17%
Average Age: 26	Average Class Size: 25
Fall 1997 Average GPA: 3.1	Fall 1997 Average GMAT: 560

Costs

Full-time tuition: $19,080 per academic year
Part-time tuition: $687 per credit

AACSB – The International Association for Management Education accredited

GRADUATE BUSINESS PROGRAMS

Master of Business Administration (MBA) Full-time, part-time; 41-54 total credits required; minimum of 18 months to complete program. Concentrations in accounting, developmental economics, entrepreneurship, finance, human resources, international business, management, management information systems, marketing, real estate, international finance, international marketing.

Master of Science in Accounting (MS) Full-time, part-time; 60 total credits required; 12 months to 2 years to complete program.

Master of Science in Taxation (MS) Full-time, part-time; 30 total credits required; 12 months to 2 years to complete program.

Master of Science in Finance (MS) Full-time, part-time; 30 total credits required; 12 months to 2 years to complete program.

ADMISSION

Applications For fall 1997 there were 581 applications for admission. Of those applying, 445 were accepted. Of those accepted, 145 enrolled.

Application Requirements GMAT score, application form, application fee, bachelor's degree, essay, minimum GPA, letters of recommendation, personal statement, college transcript(s).

Recommended for Application Resume, work experience, computer experience.

Application Deadline Applications processed on a rolling/continuous basis for domestic students only. 6/1 for fall (international), 10/1 for spring (international). Application fee: $50. Deferred entrance is available.

ACADEMICS

Faculty Full-time 57; part-time 21.

Teaching Methodologies Case study, computer-aided instruction, computer analysis, computer simulations, experiential learning, field projects, group discussion, lecture, research, simulations, student presentations, study groups, team projects.

Technology 500 on-campus computer terminals/PCs are available for student use and are linked by a campus-wide network. The network has full access to the Internet. Students are not required to have their own PC.

Special Opportunities Advanced credit may be earned through transfer of credits from another institution. International exchange program in France. An internship program is available.

FINANCES

Costs for 1997–98 Tuition: Full-time: $19,080 per year. Part-time: $687 per credit. Cost varies by academic program, number of credits taken. Average 1997–98 room and board costs were $9000 per academic year (on campus) and $12,000 per academic year (off campus). Room and board costs vary by campus location, occupancy (e.g., single, double, triple), type of accommodation, type of meal plan.

Financial Aid In 1997–98, 28% of students received some institutionally administered aid in the form of fellowships, research assistantships, work study, loans. Financial aid is available to part-time students. Application Deadline: 2/1.

Financial Aid Contact Judith Sugarman, Director of Graduate Admissions and Financial Aid, Kogod College of Business Administration, 4400 Massachusetts Avenue, NW, Washington, DC 20016. Phone: 202-885-1913; Fax: 202-885-1078; E-mail: aumbams@american.edu

FACILITIES

Information Resources University Library plus 1 additional on-campus library; total holdings of 966,974 volumes, 1,884,538 microforms, 11,554 current periodical subscriptions. CD player(s) available for graduate student use. Access provided to online bibliographic retrieval services.

INTERNATIONAL STUDENTS

Demographics 28% of students enrolled are international students [Africa, 3%, Asia, 30%, Australia/New Zealand, 2%, Central America, 5%, Europe, 40%, North America, 5%, South America, 5%, other, 10%].

Services and Facilities International student office, international student housing, visa services, ESL courses, counseling/support services.

Applying TOEFL: minimum score of 550, proof of adequate funds, proof of health/immunizations required. Financial aid is available to international students.

International Student Contact Fanta Aw, Associate Director, Intercultural Services, Butler Pavillion, Room 408, 4400 Massachusetts Avenue, NW, Washington, DC 20016. Phone: 202-885-3357; Fax: 202-885-3354.

PLACEMENT

Services include alumni network, career counseling/planning, career fairs, career library, career placement, job interviews arranged, resume referral to employers, and resume preparation. In 1996–97, 15 organizations participated in on-campus recruiting; 180 on-campus interviews were conducted.

Employment Of 1996–97 graduates, 82% were employed within three months of graduation; the average starting salary was $49,000. Types of employment entered: accounting, banking, computer-related, consulting, finance, financial services, government, high technology, human resources, information systems/technology, international trade, management, marketing, nonprofit, real estate, service industry, telecommunications, utilities.

Business Program(s) URL: http://www.kogod.american.edu/

Program Contact: Judith Sugarman, Director of Graduate Admissions and Financial Aid, Kogod College of Business Administration, 4400 Massachusetts Avenue, NW, Washington, DC 20016. Phone: 202-885-1913, 800-AN-AU-MBA; Fax: 202-885-1078; E-mail: aumbams@american.edu

See full description on page 702.

The Catholic University of America

Department of Economics and Business

Washington, District of Columbia

OVERVIEW
The Catholic University of America is an independent-religious, coed university. Enrollment: 6,128 graduate, professional, and undergraduate students; 1,634 full-time matriculated graduate/professional students; 2,129 part-time matriculated graduate/professional students. Founded: 1887. The graduate business unit is in an urban setting and is on a semester calendar.

GRADUATE BUSINESS PROGRAMS
Master of Arts in Accounting (MA)

Master of Arts in Financial Management (MA)

Master of Arts in Human Resources Management (MA)

Master of Arts in International Political Economics (MA)

Master of Arts in Economics (MA)

ACADEMICS
Faculty Full-time 14; part-time 7.

Teaching Methodologies Case study, computer-aided instruction, experiential learning, group discussion, lecture, research, seminars by members of the business community, student presentations, team projects.

Technology 100 on-campus computer terminals/PCs are available for student use and are linked by a campus-wide network. The network has full access to the Internet. Students are not required to have their own PC.

Special Opportunities Advanced credit may be earned through credit by examination, transfer of credits from another institution. An internship program is available.

FACILITIES
Information Resources Mullen Library plus 7 additional on-campus libraries; total holdings of 1,342,339 volumes, 1,125,635 microforms, 9,310 current periodical subscriptions. CD player(s) available for graduate student use. Access provided to online bibliographic retrieval services.

Program Contact: Graduate Admissions, Cardinal Station Post Office, Washingtaon, DC 20064. Phone: 202-319-5305.

Georgetown University

School of Business

Washington, District of Columbia

OVERVIEW
Georgetown University is an independent-religious, coed university. Enrollment: 12,532 graduate, professional, and undergraduate students; 5,072 full-time matriculated graduate/professional students; 963 part-time matriculated graduate/professional students. Founded: 1789. The graduate business unit is in an urban setting and is on a six week modules calendar.

HIGHLIGHTS

Enrollment Profile

Full-time: 477	International: 31%
Part-time: 0	Women: 32%
Total: 477	Minorities: 14%
Average Age: 28	Average Class Size: 40
Fall 1997 Average GPA: 3.19	Fall 1997 Average GMAT: 631

Costs
Full-time tuition: $23,880 per academic year
Part-time tuition: N/R

AACSB – The International Association for Management Education accredited

GRADUATE BUSINESS PROGRAMS
Master of Business Administration (MBA) Full-time; 60 total credits required; minimum of 21 months to complete program.

Master of Business Administration/Master of Science in Foreign Service (MBA/MS) Full-time; 90 total credits required; minimum of 3 years to complete program.

Master of Business Administration/Master of Public Policy (MBA/MPP) Full-time; 87 total credits required; minimum of 3 years to complete program.

Doctor of Jurisprudence/Master of Business Administration (JD/MBA) Full-time; 122 total credits required; minimum of 4 years to complete program.

Doctor of Medicine/Master of Business Administration (MD/MBA) Full-time; minimum of 5 years to complete program.

International Executive MBA (MBA) Full-time; 60 total credits required; minimum of 18 months to complete program.

ADMISSION
Applications For fall 1997 there were 2,129 applications for admission. Of those applying, 731 were accepted. Of those accepted, 249 enrolled.

Application Requirements GMAT score, application form, application fee, bachelor's degree, essay, minimum GPA, 2 letters of recommendation, resume, college transcript(s).

Recommended for Application Interview, minimum of 2 years of work experience, computer experience.

Application Deadline 4/15 for fall, 2/1 for fall (international). Application fee: $75. Deferred entrance is available.

ACADEMICS
Faculty Full-time 67; part-time 25.

Teaching Methodologies Case study, computer-aided instruction, computer analysis, computer simulations, experiential learning, faculty seminars, field projects, group discussion, lecture, research, role playing, seminars by members of the business community, simulations, student presentations, study groups, team projects, international projects.

Technology 100 on-campus computer terminals/PCs are available for student use and are linked by a campus-wide network. The network has full access to the Internet. Students are required to have their own PC.

Special Opportunities Advanced credit may be earned through transfer of credits from another institution. International exchange programs in Australia, Belguim, Czech Republic, France, Germany, Hong Kong, Italy, Japan, Mexico, Republic of South Africa, Spain, Sweden, United Kingdom.

FINANCES
Costs for 1997–98 Tuition: Full-time: $23,880 per year. Cost varies by academic program, number of credits taken. Fees: Full-time: $2500 per academic year. Fees vary by academic program. Average 1997–98 room and board costs were $10,000 per academic year (off campus). Room and board costs vary by occupancy (e.g., single, double, triple), type of accommodation.

Financial Aid In 1997–98, 26% of students received some institutionally administered aid in the form of research assistantships, scholarships, work study, loans. Application Deadline: 2/1.

Financial Aid Contact Mr. Bill Brosseau, Counselor, Main Campus, Office of Student Financial Services—MBA Contact, G-19 Healy Building, Washington, DC 20057. Phone: 202-687-4547; Fax: 202-687-6542; E-mail: brosseab@ gunet.georgetown.edu

FACILITIES
Information Resources Lauinger Library plus 5 additional on-campus libraries; total holdings of 2,017,927 volumes, 2,605,469 microforms, 26,036 current periodical subscriptions. CD player(s) available for graduate student use. Access provided to online bibliographic retrieval services and online databases.

INTERNATIONAL STUDENTS
Demographics 31% of students enrolled are international students [Africa, 4%, Asia, 28%, Australia/New Zealand, 1%, Central America, 8%, Europe, 30%, North America, 3%, South America, 23%, other, 3%].

Services and Facilities International student office, international student center, visa services, ESL courses, counseling/support services.

Applying TOEFL: minimum score of 600, proof of adequate funds, proof of health/immunizations required. Financial aid is available to international students.

International Student Contact Ms. Karla Stillwell, Assistant Director, International Programs and Student Services, 105 Old North, Box 571148, Washington, DC 20057-1148. Phone: 202-687-4200; Fax: 202-687-7809; E-mail: stillwk@gunet.georgetown.edu

PLACEMENT
Services include alumni network, career counseling/planning, career fairs, career library, career placement, electronic job bank, job interviews arranged, job search course, resume referral to employers, and resume preparation. In 1996–97, 102 organizations participated in on-campus recruiting; 906 on-campus interviews were conducted.

Employment Of 1996–97 graduates, 95% were employed within three months of graduation; the average starting salary was $63,857. Types of employment entered: accounting, banking, communications, computer-related, consulting, consumer products, education, energy, finance, financial services, government, health services, high technology, hospitality management, human resources, information systems/technology, insurance, international trade, law, management, manufacturing, marketing, media, nonprofit, petrochemical, pharmaceutical, real estate, retail, service industry, telecommunications, transportation, utilities.

Business Program(s) URL: http://www.gsb.georgetown.edu

Georgetown University (continued)

Program Contact: Ms. Nancy Moncrief, Assistant Dean, Graduate Business Programs, 105 Old North, Box 571148, Washington, DC 20057-1148. Phone: 202-687-4200; Fax: 202-687-7809; E-mail: moncrien@gunet.georgetown. edu
See full description on page 826.

The George Washington University

School of Business and Public Management

Washington, District of Columbia

OVERVIEW
The George Washington University is an independent-nonprofit, coed university. Enrollment: 19,356 graduate, professional, and undergraduate students; 5,355 full-time matriculated graduate/professional students; 6,171 part-time matriculated graduate/professional students. Founded: 1821. The graduate business unit is in an urban setting and is on a semester calendar.

HIGHLIGHTS
Enrollment Profile
Full-time: 988
Part-time: 1,076
Total: 2,064
Average Age: 31
Fall 1997 Average GPA: 3.09

International: 28%
Women: 40%
Minorities: 14%
Average Class Size: 30
Fall 1997 Average GMAT: 569

Costs
Full-time tuition: N/R
Part-time tuition: $680 per credit

AACSB – The International Association for Management Education accredited

GRADUATE BUSINESS PROGRAMS
Full-time and Professional MBA (MBA) Full-time, part-time; 50-54 total credits required; GMAT required, minimum of 1-3 years work experience preferred; 12 months to 5 years to complete program. Concentrations in accounting, entrepreneurship, finance, human resources, international business, logistics, management, management information systems, management science, marketing, operations management, organizational behavior/development, real estate, travel industry/tourism management, decision sciences, health care, strategic management, public policy and administration, marketing research.
Executive MBA (MBA) Part-time; 60 total credits required; interview, GMAT score, and 10 years work experience typically required (5 years in mid- to upper-level management or senior professional experience); 21 months to complete program. Concentration in management.
Accelerated MBA (MBA) Part-time; 40-48 total credits required; GMAT, interview, and 4 years work experience typically required; 2 years to complete program. Concentrations in accounting, entrepreneurship, finance, human resources, international business, logistics, management, management information systems, management science, marketing, operations management, real estate, travel industry/tourism management, decision sciences, health care, strategic management, public policy and administration, marketing research, organizational behavior/development.
Master of Business Administration/Master of Arts in International Affairs (MBA/MA) Full-time, part-time; 56 total credits required; GMAT, GRE, and application to joint degree program required; 20 months to 5 years to complete program. Concentration in international business.
Master of Business Administration/Doctor of Jurisprudence (MBA/JD) Full-time, part-time; 108 total credits required; GMAT, LSAT, and dual application required; 3.8 years to complete program. Concentrations in accounting, entrepreneurship, finance, human resources, international business, logistics, management, management information systems, management science, marketing, operations management, organizational behavior/development, real estate, travel industry/tourism management, decision sciences, health care, strategic management, public policy and administration.
Master of Science in Finance (MSF) Full-time, part-time; 48-69 total credits required; GRE or GMAT score required, interview preferred; 12 months to 2 years to complete program.
Master of Science in Project Management (MSPM) Full-time, part-time, distance learning option; 27-36 total credits required; GRE or GMAT scores and an interview are recommended; minimum of 12 months to complete program.
Master of Tourism Administration (MTA) Full-time, part-time; 36 total credits required; GMAT or GRE score required; minimum of 12 months to complete program.

Master of Accountancy (MAcc) Full-time, part-time; 35-40 total credits required; GMAT score required; minimum of 12 months to complete program. Concentrations in accounting, taxation.
Master of Science in Acquistion Management (MSAM) Full-time, part-time; 33-36 total credits required; GRE or GMAT score required; minimum of 12 months to complete program.
Master of Science in Information Science Technology (MSIST) Full-time, part-time; 30-33 total credits required; minimum of 12 months to complete program. Concentrations in technology management, management information systems, project management.
Master of Public Administration (MPA) Full-time, part-time; GRE score required; 18 months to 5 years to complete program. Concentrations in finance, public policy and administration, public management.

ADMISSION
Applications For fall 1997 there were 2,958 applications for admission. Of those applying, 1,728 were accepted. Of those accepted, 666 enrolled.
Application Requirements Application form, application fee, bachelor's degree, 3 letters of recommendation, personal statement, resume, college transcript(s).
Recommended for Application GMAT score accepted, GRE score accepted, minimum GPA: 3.0, work experience, computer experience.
Application Deadline 4/1 for fall, 10/1 for spring, 4/1 for fall (international), 10/1 for spring (international). Application fee: $60. Deferred entrance is available.

ACADEMICS
Faculty Full-time 128; part-time 53.
Teaching Methodologies Case study, computer-aided instruction, computer analysis, computer simulations, experiential learning, faculty seminars, field projects, group discussion, lecture, research, role playing, seminars by members of the business community, simulations, student presentations, study groups, team projects.
Technology Computer terminals/PCs are available for student use and are linked by a campus-wide network. The network has full access to the Internet. Students are not required to have their own PC.
Special Opportunities Advanced credit may be earned through transfer of credits from another institution. International exchange programs in Chile, Denmark, France, Germany, Hungary, Portugal, Republic of Korea, Spain, Sweden, Thailand. An internship program is available.

FINANCES
Costs for 1997–98 Tuition: $680 per credit. Cost varies by academic program, campus location, number of credits taken. Fees: $33 per credit. Fees vary by academic program, campus location, number of credits taken. Average 1997–98 room and board costs were $11,000 per academic year (off campus).
Financial Aid Fellowships, teaching assistantships, work study, loans available. Financial aid is available to part-time students. Application Deadline: 2/1.
Financial Aid Contact Mr. Daniel Small, Director, Student Financial Assistance, 2121 I Street, NW Suite 310, Washington, DC 20052. Phone: 202-994-6620.

FACILITIES
Information Resources Melvin Gelman Library plus 2 additional on-campus libraries; total holdings of 1,776,848 volumes, 2,266,349 microforms, 17,111 current periodical subscriptions. CD player(s) available for graduate student use. Access provided to online bibliographic retrieval services.

INTERNATIONAL STUDENTS
Demographics 28% of students enrolled are international students [Africa, 4%, Asia, 81%, Europe, 7%, North America, 2%, South America, 5%, other, 1%].
Services and Facilities International student office, international student center, visa services, ESL courses, counseling/support services.
Applying TOEFL: minimum score of 550, proof of adequate funds, proof of health/immunizations required. TSE, TWE recommended. Financial aid is available to international students.
International Student Contact Graduate Admissions, School of Business and Public Management, 710 21st Street, NW, Government Hall 209, Washington, DC 20052. Phone: 202-994-6584; Fax: 202-994-6382; E-mail: sbpmapp@ gwu.edu

PLACEMENT
Services include alumni network, career counseling/planning, career fairs, career library, career placement, electronic job bank, job interviews arranged, job search course, resume referral to employers, and resume preparation. In 1996–97, 75 organizations participated in on-campus recruiting; 750 on-campus interviews were conducted.
Employment Of 1996–97 graduates, 88% were employed within three months of graduation; the average starting salary was $56,500. Types of employment entered: accounting, banking, chemical industry, communications, computer-related, consulting, consumer products, education, energy, engineering, finance, financial services, government, health services, high technology, hospitality man-

agement, human resources, information systems/technology, insurance, international trade, law, management, manufacturing, marketing, media, nonprofit, petrochemical, pharmaceutical, real estate, retail, service industry, telecommunications, transportation, utilities.

Business Program(s) URL: http://www.sbpm.gwu.edu

Program Contact: Ms. Dorothy J. Umans, Director, Graduate Admissions, School of Business and Public Management, 710 21st Street, NW, Washington, DC 20052. Phone: 202-994-6584; Fax: 202-994-6382; E-mail: sbpmapp@gwis2.circ.gwu.edu

See full description on page 828.

Howard University

School of Business

Washington, District of Columbia

OVERVIEW
Howard University is an independent-nonprofit, coed university. Enrollment: 10,248 graduate, professional, and undergraduate students. Founded: 1867. The graduate business unit is in an urban setting and is on a semester calendar.

HIGHLIGHTS

Enrollment Profile

Full-time: N/R	International: N/R
Part-time: N/R	Women: N/R
Total: 128	Minorities: N/R
Average Age: N/R	Average Class Size: 'N/R
Fall 1997 Average GPA: N/R	Fall 1997 Average GMAT: N/R

Costs
Full-time tuition: $10,600 per academic year
Part-time tuition: N/R

AACSB – The International Association for Management Education accredited

GRADUATE BUSINESS PROGRAMS
Master of Business Administration (MBA) Full-time, part-time; 39-63 total credits required; 18 months to 6 years to complete program. Concentrations in health care, finance.

Master of Finance (MF) Full-time, part-time; 39-63 total credits required; 18 months to 6 years to complete program.

Doctor of Jurisprudence/Master of Business Administration (JD/MBA) Full-time; 127 total credits required; minimum of 4 years to complete program.

ADMISSION
Application Requirements GMAT score, application form, application fee, bachelor's degree, minimum GPA, 2 letters of recommendation, personal statement, resume, college transcript(s).

Application Deadline 4/1 for fall, 11/1 for spring, 3/15 for summer, 4/1 for fall (international), 11/1 for spring (international), 3/15 for summer (international). Application fee: $25. Deferred entrance is available.

ACADEMICS
Teaching Methodologies Case study, group discussion, student presentations, team projects.

Special Opportunities Advanced credit may be earned through transfer of credits from another institution. An internship program is available.

FINANCES
Costs for 1997–98 Tuition: Full-time: $10,600 per year. Cost varies by number of credits taken.

Financial Aid Fellowships, research assistantships, teaching assistantships, grants, scholarships, work study, loans available.

Financial Aid Contact Director of Financial Aid and Student Employment, 2400 Sixth Street, NW, Washington, DC 20059-0002. Phone: 202-806-2800.

FACILITIES
Information Resources Founders Library plus 10 additional on-campus libraries; total holdings of 1,729,875 volumes, 1,453,542 microforms. CD player(s) available for graduate student use. Access provided to online bibliographic retrieval services.

INTERNATIONAL STUDENTS
Demographics N/R

Applying TOEFL: minimum score of 500 required.

PLACEMENT
Services include career counseling/planning, career fairs, resume referral to employers, and resume preparation.

Business Program(s) URL: http://www.bschool.howard.edu

Program Contact: MBA Program Office, 2400 Sixth Street, Washington, DC 20059-0002. Phone: 202-806-1514; Fax: 202-797-9363.

Southeastern University

College of Graduate Studies

Washington, District of Columbia

OVERVIEW
Southeastern University is an independent-nonprofit, coed, comprehensive institution. Enrollment: 806 graduate, professional, and undergraduate students; 180 full-time matriculated graduate/professional students; 176 part-time matriculated graduate/professional students. Founded: 1879. The graduate business unit is in an urban setting and is on a quadmester calendar.

HIGHLIGHTS

Enrollment Profile

Full-time: 115	International: 50%
Part-time: 117	Women: 50%
Total: 232	Minorities: 98%
Average Age: N/R	Average Class Size: N/R
Fall 1997 Average GPA: N/R	Fall 1997 Average GMAT: N/R

Costs
Full-time tuition: $6156 per academic year
Part-time tuition: $228 per credit

Degree(s) offered in conjunction with various institutions in the Washington, DC area

GRADUATE BUSINESS PROGRAMS
Master of Business Administration (MBA) Full-time, part-time; 45 total credits required; 12 months to 7 years to complete program. Concentrations in accounting, finance, marketing, financial management/planning, international management, information management, management.

Master of Public Administration (MPA) Full-time, part-time; 45 total credits required; 12 months to 7 years to complete program. Concentration in health care.

Master of Science (MS) Full-time, part-time; 45 total credits required; 12 months to 7 years to complete program. Concentration in taxation.

ADMISSION
Applications For fall 1997 there were 76 applications for admission. Of those applying, 62 were accepted. Of those accepted, 59 enrolled.

Application Requirements Application form, application fee, bachelor's degree, minimum GPA: 3.0, interview, 2 letters of recommendation, personal statement, resume, college transcript(s).

Recommended for Application GRE score accepted, essay, minimum of 3 years of work experience, computer experience.

Application Deadline Applications processed on a rolling/continuous basis for domestic students only. 7/1 for fall (international), 10/1 for winter (international), 12/1 for spring (international), 4/1 for summer (international). Application fee: $45. Deferred entrance is available.

ACADEMICS
Faculty Full-time 9; part-time 60.

Teaching Methodologies Case study, computer-aided instruction, computer analysis, group discussion, lecture, research, student presentations, study groups, team projects.

Technology 80 on-campus computer terminals/PCs are available for student use. The network has full access to the Internet. Students are not required to have their own PC.

Special Opportunities Advanced credit may be earned through credit by examination, credit for experience, credit for military training programs, transfer of credits from another institution. International exchange programs in Turkey, United Kingdom. An internship program is available.

FINANCES
Costs for 1997–98 Tuition: Full-time: $6156 per year. Part-time: $228 per credit. Cost varies by number of credits taken. Fees: $200 per quadmester.

Financial Aid Work study, loans available. Financial aid is available to part-time students.

Financial Aid Contact Willis Parker, Director of Financial Aid, 501 Eye Street, Washington, DC 20024. Phone: 202-488-8162; Fax: 202-488-8093; E-mail: willis@admin.seu.edu

FACILITIES
Information Resources Total library holdings of 45,000 volumes, 2,000 current periodical subscriptions. CD player(s) available for graduate student use. Access provided to online bibliographic retrieval services.

Southeastern University (continued)

INTERNATIONAL STUDENTS
Demographics 50% of students enrolled are international students [Africa, 2%, Asia, 52%, North America, 46%].

Services and Facilities International student office, visa services, ESL courses, counseling/support services.

Applying TOEFL: minimum score of 550 required. Financial aid is not available to international students.

International Student Contact Gayle Damelin, International Student Advisor, 501 Eye Street, Washington, DC 20024. Phone: 202-488-8162; Fax: 202-488-8093; E-mail: gayle@admin.seu.edu

PLACEMENT
Services include career counseling/planning, career fairs, career library, and resume preparation. In 1996–97, 12 organizations participated in on-campus recruiting.

Employment Of 1996–97 graduates, 90% were employed within three months of graduation. Types of employment entered: accounting, banking, computer-related, consulting, education, finance, financial services, government, health services, high technology, hospitality management, human resources, information systems/technology, insurance, international trade, management, marketing, nonprofit, real estate, retail, service industry, telecommunications.

Program Contact: Jack Flinter, Jr., Director of Admissions, 501 Eye Street, Washington, DC 20024. Phone: 202-265-5343 Ext. 211; Fax: 202-488-8093; E-mail: jackf@admin.seu.edu

Strayer University

Graduate School

Washington, District of Columbia

OVERVIEW
Strayer University is a proprietary, coed, comprehensive institution. Enrollment: 9,419 graduate, professional, and undergraduate students; 656 full-time matriculated graduate/professional students; 574 part-time matriculated graduate/professional students. Founded: 1892. The graduate business unit is in an urban setting and is on a quarter calendar.

HIGHLIGHTS

Enrollment Profile
Full-time: 656
Part-time: 574
Total: 1,230
Average Age: 33
Fall 1997 Average GPA: N/R

International: 15%
Women: 46%
Minorities: 39%
Average Class Size: 20
Fall 1997 Average GMAT: N/R

Costs
Full-time tuition: $6750 per academic year
Part-time tuition: $250 per quarter hour credit

GRADUATE BUSINESS PROGRAMS
Master of Science in Business Administration (MSBA) Full-time, part-time, distance learning option; 54 total credits required; 12 months to 10 years to complete program. Concentration in management.

Master of Science in Professional Accounting (MSA) Full-time, part-time, distance learning option; 54 total credits required; 12 months to 10 years to complete program. Concentration in accounting.

Master of Science in Information Systems (MSIS) Full-time, part-time, distance learning option; 54 total credits required; 12 months to 10 years to complete program. Concentration in management information systems.

ADMISSION
Application Requirements Application form, application fee, bachelor's degree, minimum GPA: 2.75, college transcript(s).

Recommended for Application GMAT score accepted: minimum 450, GRE score accepted: minimum 1,000, interview, letters of recommendation, work experience, computer experience.

Application Deadline Applications processed on a rolling/continuous basis for both domestic and international students. Application fee: $25. Deferred entrance is available.

ACADEMICS
Faculty Full-time 39; part-time 49.

Teaching Methodologies Case study, computer-aided instruction, faculty seminars, group discussion, lecture, research, role playing, seminars by members of the business community, simulations, student presentations, study groups, team projects.

Technology 780 on-campus computer terminals/PCs are available for student use and are linked by a campus-wide network. The network has full access to the Internet. Students are not required to have their own PC.

Special Opportunities Advanced credit may be earned through transfer of credits from another institution.

FINANCES
Costs for 1997–98 Tuition: Full-time: $6750 per year. Part-time: $250 per quarter hour credit. Average 1997–98 room and board costs were $6000 per academic year (off campus).

Financial Aid Scholarships, work study, loans available. Financial aid is available to part-time students.

Financial Aid Contact Ms. Marjorie Arrington, Director of Financial Aid, 3045 Columbia Pike, Arlington, VA 22204. Phone: 703-892-5100; Fax: 703-769-2640; E-mail: ma@strayer.edu

FACILITIES
Information Resources Wilkes Library plus 8 additional on-campus libraries; total holdings of 25,000 volumes, 3,000 microforms, 450 current periodical subscriptions. CD player(s) available for graduate student use. Access provided to online bibliographic retrieval services and online databases.

INTERNATIONAL STUDENTS
Demographics 15% of students enrolled are international students [Africa, 29%, Asia, 59%, Central America, 4%, Europe, 5%, North America, 1%, South America, 2%].

Services and Facilities International student office, counseling/support services.

Applying TOEFL: minimum score of 400, proof of adequate funds, proof of health/immunizations required. Financial aid is not available to international students.

International Student Contact Ms. Cyndi Wastler, Manager of Student Certification, 3045 Columbia Pike, Arlington, VA 22204. Phone: 703-769-3778; Fax: 703-769-2640; E-mail: clw@net.strayer.edu

PLACEMENT
Services include alumni network, career counseling/planning, career fairs, career placement, resume referral to employers, and resume preparation. In 1996–97, 1,000 organizations participated in on-campus recruiting.

Employment Of 1996–97 graduates, 89% were employed within three months of graduation. Types of employment entered: accounting, banking, communications, computer-related, consulting, consumer products, engineering, finance, government, health services, hospitality management, human resources, information systems/technology, law, management, retail, telecommunications, transportation.

Business Program(s) URL: http://www.strayer.edu/

Program Contact: Mr. Michael Williams, Campus Coordinator, 1025 15th Street, NW, Washington, DC 20005-2603. Phone: 202-408-2400; Fax: 202-289-1831; E-mail: mw@strayer.edu

University of the District of Columbia

College of Professional Studies

Washington, District of Columbia

OVERVIEW
The University of the District of Columbia is a locally supported, coed, comprehensive institution. Enrollment: 5,000 graduate, professional, and undergraduate students; 200 full-time matriculated graduate/professional students; 433 part-time matriculated graduate/professional students. Founded: 1975. The graduate business unit is in an urban setting and is on a semester calendar.

HIGHLIGHTS

Enrollment Profile
Full-time: 22
Part-time: 130
Total: 152
Average Age: 28
Fall 1997 Average GPA: 2.7

International: 33%
Women: 47%
Minorities: 76%
Average Class Size: 17
Fall 1997 Average GMAT: 450

Costs
Full-time tuition: $3574 per academic year (resident); $5922 per academic year (nonresident)
Part-time tuition: $198 per credit hour (resident); $329 per credit hour (nonresident)

ACBSP – The American Council of Business Schools and Programs accredited

GRADUATE BUSINESS PROGRAMS
Master of Business Administration (MBA) Full-time, part-time; 36 total credits required; 2 to 5 years to complete program. Concentrations in accounting, international business, management, marketing, finance.

Master of Public Administration (MPA) Full-time, part-time; 36 total credits required; 2 to 5 years to complete program. Concentrations in public management, public policy and administration.

ADMISSION
Applications For fall 1997 there were 70 applications for admission. Of those applying, 50 were accepted. Of those accepted, 40 enrolled.

Application Requirements Application form, application fee, bachelor's degree, essay, minimum GPA: 2.5, 2 letters of recommendation, personal statement, college transcript(s).

Recommended for Application GMAT score accepted, GRE score accepted, computer experience.

Application Deadline Applications processed on a rolling/continuous basis for both domestic and international students. Application fee: $20. Deferred entrance is available.

ACADEMICS
Faculty Full-time 8; part-time 5.

Teaching Methodologies Case study, computer-aided instruction, computer analysis, computer simulations, faculty seminars, field projects, group discussion, lecture, research, role playing, seminars by members of the business community, simulations, student presentations, study groups, team projects.

Technology 100 on-campus computer terminals/PCs are available for student use. The network has full access to the Internet. Students are not required to have their own PC.

Special Opportunities Advanced credit may be earned through transfer of credits from another institution. An internship program is available.

FINANCES
Costs for 1997–98 Tuition: Full-time: $3574 per year (resident); $5922 per year (nonresident). Part-time: $198 per credit hour (resident); $329 per credit hour (nonresident). Cost varies by number of credits taken. Fees: Full-time: $110 per academic year (resident); $110 per academic year (nonresident). Part-time: $105 per semester (resident); $105 per semester (nonresident).

Financial Aid Work study, loans available.

Financial Aid Contact Ken Howard, Director of Financial Aid, 4200 Connecticut Avenue, NW, Washington, DC 20008-1175. Phone: 202-274-5060; Fax: 202-274-7022.

FACILITIES
Information Resources Main library plus 3 additional on-campus libraries; total holdings of 522,123 volumes, 605,281 microforms, 1,434 current periodical subscriptions. CD player(s) available for graduate student use. Access provided to online bibliographic retrieval services and online databases.

INTERNATIONAL STUDENTS
Demographics 33% of students enrolled are international students [Africa, 80%, Asia, 10%, South America, 10%].

Services and Facilities ESL courses, counseling/support services.

Applying TOEFL: minimum score of 550, proof of adequate funds, proof of health/immunizations required.

International Student Contact Dr. Hany Makhlouf, Director of MBA and MPA, 4200 Connecticut Avenue, NW, Washington, DC 20008-1175. Phone: 202-274-7040; Fax: 202-274-7022.

PLACEMENT
Services include career fairs, job interviews arranged, resume referral to employers, and resume preparation. In 1996–97, 20 organizations participated in on-campus recruiting; 30 on-campus interviews were conducted.

Employment Types of employment entered: accounting, banking, finance, government, management, marketing.

Program Contact: Dr. Hany Makhlouf, Director of MBA and MPA, 4200 Connecticut Avenue, NW, Washington, DC 20008-1175. Phone: 202-274-7001; Fax: 202-274-7022.

FLORIDA

Barry University

School of Business
Miami Shores, Florida

OVERVIEW
Barry University is an independent-religious, coed, comprehensive institution. Enrollment: 6,899 graduate, professional, and undergraduate students; 886 full-time matriculated graduate/professional students; 1,328 part-time matriculated graduate/professional students. Founded: 1940. The graduate business unit is in a suburban setting and is on a semester calendar.

HIGHLIGHTS

Enrollment Profile
Full-time: 38
Part-time: 124
Total: 162
Average Age: N/R
Fall 1997 Average GPA: N/R

International: N/R
Women: 43%
Minorities: N/R
Average Class Size: 19
Fall 1997 Average GMAT: 440

Costs
Full-time tuition: $10,800 per academic year
Part-time tuition: $450 per credit

GRADUATE BUSINESS PROGRAMS
Master of Business Administration (MBA) Full-time, part-time; 36 total credits required; 20 months to 5 years to complete program. Concentrations in accounting, finance, management, marketing, health care, management information systems, international business.

Master of Business Administration (MBA) Part-time; 45 total credits required; 20 months to 5 years to complete program. Concentrations in international business, management information systems.

ADMISSION
Applications For fall 1997 there were 132 applications for admission. Of those applying, 104 were accepted. Of those accepted, 68 enrolled.

Application Requirements Application form, application fee, bachelor's degree, essay, minimum GPA: 3.0, personal statement, college transcript(s).

Recommended for Application GMAT score accepted: minimum 400, 2 letters of recommendation, computer experience.

Application Deadline Applications processed on a rolling/continuous basis for both domestic and international students. Application fee: $30.

ACADEMICS
Faculty Full-time 20; part-time 3.

Teaching Methodologies Case study, computer-aided instruction, computer analysis, computer simulations, experiential learning, group discussion, lecture, role playing, seminars by members of the business community, student presentations, study groups, team projects.

Technology 250 on-campus computer terminals/PCs are available for student use and are linked by a campus-wide network. The network has full access to the Internet. Students are not required to have their own PC.

Special Opportunities Advanced credit may be earned through transfer of credits from another institution. An internship program is available.

FINANCES
Costs for 1997–98 Tuition: Full-time: $10,800 per year. Part-time: $450 per credit. Fees vary by number of credits taken. Average 1997–98 room and board costs were $6750 per academic year. Room and board costs vary by occupancy (e.g., single, double, triple), type of meal plan.

Financial Aid In 1997–98, 34% of students received some institutionally administered aid in the form of research assistantships, loans. Financial aid is available to part-time students.

Financial Aid Contact Ms. Celia Melis, Associate Director, Financial Aid, 11300 Northeast Second Avenue, Miami Shores, FL 33161-6695. Phone: 305-899-3673; Fax: 305-899-3104; E-mail: melis@jeanne.barry.edu

FACILITIES
Information Resources Monsignor William A. Barry Memorial Library; total holdings of 214,665 volumes, 475,781 microforms, 1,674 current periodical subscriptions. CD player(s) available for graduate student use. Access provided to online bibliographic retrieval services.

INTERNATIONAL STUDENTS
Demographics N/R

Services and Facilities International student office, international student center, counseling/support services.

169

Barry University (continued)

Applying TOEFL: minimum score of 550, proof of adequate funds, proof of health/immunizations required. Financial aid is not available to international students.

International Student Contact Ms. Joy DeMarchis, Director, International Student Services, 11300 Northeast Second Avenue, Miami Shores, FL 33161-6695. Phone: 305-899-3082 Ext. 3082; Fax: 305-899-3083; E-mail: demarchis@ jeanne.barry.edu

PLACEMENT

Services include alumni network, career counseling/planning, career fairs, career library, electronic job bank, job interviews arranged, resume referral to employers, and resume preparation. In 1996–97, 125 organizations participated in on-campus recruiting.

Employment Types of employment entered: accounting, banking, computer-related, consumer products, education, financial services, government, health services, hospitality management, human resources, information systems/ technology, insurance, law, management, marketing, media, real estate, telecommunications, transportation, utilities.

Program Contact: Mr. Jose Poza, Director of Marketing, Andreas School of Business, 11300 Northeast Second Avenue, Miami Shores, FL 33161-6695. Phone: 305-899-3535, 800-289-1111; Fax: 305-899-6412; E-mail: poza@ aquinas.barry.edu

Embry-Riddle Aeronautical University

Department of Aviation Business Administration

Daytona Beach, Florida

OVERVIEW

Embry-Riddle Aeronautical University is an independent-nonprofit, coed, comprehensive institution. Enrollment: 4,586 graduate, professional, and undergraduate students; 135 full-time matriculated graduate/professional students; 115 part-time matriculated graduate/professional students. Founded: 1926. The graduate business unit is in a suburban setting and is on a semester calendar.

HIGHLIGHTS

Enrollment Profile

Full-time: 51	International: 42%
Part-time: 37	Women: 19%
Total: 88	Minorities: 6%
Average Age: 28	Average Class Size: 12
Fall 1997 Average GPA: 2.93	Fall 1997 Average GMAT: 458

Costs
Full-time tuition: $3825 per academic year
Part-time tuition: $425 per credit hour

ACBSP – The American Council of Business Schools and Programs accredited

GRADUATE BUSINESS PROGRAMS

MBA in Aviation Business Administration (MBA) Full-time, part-time; 36-39 total credits required; 18 months to 7 years to complete program.

ADMISSION

Applications For fall 1997 there were 54 applications for admission. Of those applying, 43 were accepted. Of those accepted, 29 enrolled.

Application Requirements Application form, application fee, bachelor's degree, minimum GPA: 2.5, 3 letters of recommendation, personal statement, college transcript(s).

Recommended for Application GMAT score accepted.

Application Deadline Applications processed on a rolling/continuous basis for both domestic and international students. Application fee: $30, $50 (international). Deferred entrance is available.

ACADEMICS

Faculty Full-time 13; part-time 1.

Teaching Methodologies Case study, computer-aided instruction, computer analysis, computer simulations, group discussion, lecture, research, student presentations, study groups, team projects.

Technology 720 on-campus computer terminals/PCs are available for student use and are linked by a campus-wide network. The network has full access to the Internet. Students are not required to have their own PC.

Special Opportunities Advanced credit may be earned through credit by examination, credit for experience, transfer of credits from another institution. An internship program is available.

FINANCES

Costs for 1997–98 Tuition: Full-time: $3825 per semester. Part-time: $425 per credit hour. Cost varies by academic program, campus location, number of credits taken. Fees: Full-time: $25 per academic year. Part-time: $25 per semester. Average 1997–98 room and board costs were $4600 per academic year (on campus) and $5050 per academic year (off campus). Room and board costs vary by campus location, occupancy (e.g., single, double, triple), type of accommodation, type of meal plan.

Financial Aid In 1997–98, 5% of students received some institutionally administered aid in the form of fellowships, research assistantships, teaching assistantships, scholarships, work study, loans. Financial aid is available to part-time students.

Financial Aid Contact Garry Vance, Director, Financial Aid Office, 600 South Clyde Morris Boulevard, Daytona Beach, FL 32114-3900. Phone: 904-226-6300; Fax: 904-226-6307; E-mail: vanceg@cts.db.erau.edu

FACILITIES

Information Resources Jack R. Hunt Memorial Library; total holdings of 61,581 volumes, 60,579 microforms, 712 current periodical subscriptions. CD player(s) available for graduate student use. Access provided to online bibliographic retrieval services and online databases.

INTERNATIONAL STUDENTS

Demographics 42% of students enrolled are international students [Asia, 24%, Europe, 43%, South America, 10%, other, 23%].

Services and Facilities International student office, ESL courses, counseling/ support services.

Applying TOEFL: minimum score of 550, TSE, proof of adequate funds, proof of health/immunizations required. Financial aid is not available to international students.

International Student Contact Judith Assad, Director, International Student Services, 600 South Clyde Morris Boulevard, Daytona Beach, FL 32114-3900. Phone: 904-226-6579; Fax: 904-226-7920; E-mail: assadj@cts.db. erau.edu

PLACEMENT

Services include alumni network, career counseling/planning, career fairs, career library, career placement, electronic job bank, job interviews arranged, resume referral to employers, and resume preparation. In 1996–97, 35 organizations participated in on-campus recruiting; 400 on-campus interviews were conducted.

Employment Types of employment entered: banking, communications, computer-related, engineering, finance, financial services, government, high technology, hospitality management, information systems/technology, insurance, management, manufacturing, marketing, nonprofit, telecommunications, transportation.

Business Program(s) URL: http://www.db.erau.edu

Program Contact: Ginny Tait, Graduate Admissions Specialist, 600 South Clyde Morris Boulevard, Daytona Beach, FL 32114-3900. Phone: 904-226-6115, 800-862-2416; Fax: 904-226-6299; E-mail: taitg.@cts.db.erau.edu

See full description on page 798.

Embry-Riddle Aeronautical University, Extended Campus

College of Career Education

Daytona Beach, Florida

OVERVIEW

Embry-Riddle Aeronautical University, Extended Campus is an independent-nonprofit, coed, comprehensive institution. Enrollment: 6,623 graduate, professional, and undergraduate students; 48 full-time matriculated graduate/ professional students; 2,212 part-time matriculated graduate/professional students. Founded: 1970. The graduate business unit is on a term calendar.

HIGHLIGHTS

Enrollment Profile

Full-time: 13	International: 1%
Part-time: 431	Women: 16%
Total: 444	Minorities: 23%
Average Age: 35	Average Class Size: 6
Fall 1997 Average GPA: N/R	Fall 1997 Average GMAT: N/R

Costs
Full-time tuition: N/R
Part-time tuition: $279 per credit hour

GRADUATE BUSINESS PROGRAMS
MBA in Aviation Business Administration (MBA) Full-time, part-time, distance learning option; 36-39 total credits required; up to 7 years to complete program.

Master of Science in Technical Management (MS) Full-time, part-time, distance learning option; 39 total credits required; up to 7 years to complete program.

ADMISSION
Applications For fall 1997 there were 90 applications for admission. Of those applying, 90 were accepted. Of those accepted, 90 enrolled.

Application Requirements Application form, application fee, bachelor's degree, essay, 3 letters of recommendation, personal statement, college transcript(s).

Recommended for Application Interview.

Application Deadline Applications processed on a rolling/continuous basis for both domestic and international students. Application fee: $30, $50 (international). Deferred entrance is available.

ACADEMICS
Faculty Full-time 97; part-time 2,103.

Teaching Methodologies Case study, computer-aided instruction, computer analysis, experiential learning, faculty seminars, group discussion, lecture, research, role playing, simulations, student presentations, team projects.

Technology 235 on-campus computer terminals/PCs are available for student use and are linked by a campus-wide network. The network has full access to the Internet. Students are not required to have their own PC.

Special Opportunities Advanced credit may be earned through credit by examination, credit for experience, credit for military training programs, credit for business training programs, transfer of credits from another institution.

FINANCES
Costs for 1997–98 Tuition: $279 per credit hour.

Financial Aid In 1997–98, 13% of students received some institutionally administered aid in the form of loans. Financial aid is available to part-time students.

Financial Aid Contact Garry Vance, Financial Aid Counselor, 600 South Clyde Morris Boulevard, Daytona Beach, FL 32114-3900. Phone: 904-226-6300; Fax: 904-226-6307; E-mail: vanceg@cts.db.erau.edu

FACILITIES
Information Resources Jack R. Hunt Memorial Library; total holdings of 61,581 volumes, 60,579 microforms, 712 current periodical subscriptions. CD player(s) available for graduate student use. Access provided to online bibliographic retrieval services.

INTERNATIONAL STUDENTS
Demographics 1% of students enrolled are international students [Asia, 60%, Europe, 20%, North America, 20%].

Services and Facilities ESL courses, counseling/support services.

Applying TOEFL: minimum score of 550, TSE, proof of adequate funds required. Financial aid is not available to international students.

International Student Contact Pam Thomas, Director of Admissions and Records, 600 South Clyde Morris Boulevard, Daytona Beach, FL 32114-3900. Phone: 904-226-6909; Fax: 904-226-6984; E-mail: ecinfo@ec.db.erau.edu

PLACEMENT
Services include alumni network, career counseling/planning, career fairs, career library, career placement, electronic job bank, job interviews arranged, resume referral to employers, and resume preparation. In 1996–97, 35 organizations participated in on-campus recruiting; 400 on-campus interviews were conducted.

Employment Types of employment entered: banking, communications, computer-related, engineering, finance, financial services, government, high technology, hospitality management, information systems/technology, insurance, management, manufacturing, marketing, nonprofit, telecommunications, transportation.

Business Program(s) URL: http://www.ec.erau.edu

Program Contact: Pam Thomas, Director of Admissions and Records, 600 South Clyde Morris Boulevard, Daytona Beach, FL 32114-3900. Phone: 904-226-6909; Fax: 904-226-6984; E-mail: ecinfo@ec.db.erau.edu

Florida Agricultural and Mechanical University

School of Business and Industry
Tallahassee, Florida

OVERVIEW
Florida Agricultural and Mechanical University is a state-supported, coed university. Enrollment: 10,998 graduate, professional, and undergraduate students. Founded: 1887. The graduate business unit is on a semester calendar.

HIGHLIGHTS

Enrollment Profile

Full-time: N/R	International: N/R
Part-time: N/R	Women: N/R
Total: 80	Minorities: N/R
Average Age: N/R	Average Class Size: N/R
Fall 1997 Average GPA: N/R	Fall 1997 Average GMAT: N/R

Costs
Full-time tuition: N/R
Part-time tuition: $118 per credit (resident); $389 per credit (nonresident)

GRADUATE BUSINESS PROGRAMS
Master of Business Administration (MBA) minimum of 5 years to complete program. Concentrations in accounting, finance, management, management information systems.

ADMISSION
Application Requirements GMAT score: minimum 550, application form, bachelor's degree, minimum GPA: 3.0, 3 letters of recommendation, resume, college transcript(s), computer experience.

Application Deadline 5/15 for fall, 11/10 for spring, 3/1 for summer, 5/15 for fall (international), 11/10 for spring (international), 3/1 for summer (international).

ACADEMICS
Teaching Methodologies Case study, group discussion, lecture.

FINANCES
Costs for 1997–98 Tuition: Part-time: $118 per credit (resident); $389 per credit (nonresident).

Financial Aid Fellowships, grants, work study available.

Financial Aid Contact Financial Aid, Tallahassee, FL 32307. Phone: 850-599-3730.

FACILITIES
Information Resources Coleman Library plus 2 additional on-campus libraries; total holdings of 485,985 volumes, 82,000 microforms, 3,639 current periodical subscriptions. Access provided to online bibliographic retrieval services.

INTERNATIONAL STUDENTS
Demographics N/R

Services and Facilities International student office, international student center, counseling/support services.

International Student Contact International Programs, Tallahassee, FL 32307. Phone: 850-599-3000.

PLACEMENT
Services include alumni network, and career counseling/planning.

Employment Types of employment entered: accounting, banking, consulting, finance, financial services, insurance, marketing.

Program Contact: Office of Admissions, Tallahassee, FL 32307. Phone: 850-599-3796.

Florida Atlantic University

College of Business
Boca Raton, Florida

OVERVIEW
Florida Atlantic University is a state-supported, coed university. Enrollment: 19,421 graduate, professional, and undergraduate students; 990 full-time matriculated graduate/professional students; 3,189 part-time matriculated graduate/professional students. Founded: 1961. The graduate business unit is in an urban setting and is on a semester calendar.

HIGHLIGHTS

Enrollment Profile

Full-time: 139	International: 17%
Part-time: 469	Women: 47%
Total: 608	Minorities: 15%
Average Age: 30	Average Class Size: 25
Fall 1997 Average GPA: 3.32	Fall 1997 Average GMAT: 537

Costs
Full-time tuition: N/R
Part-time tuition: $133 per credit (resident); $438 per credit (nonresident)

Florida Atlantic University (continued)

AACSB – The International Association for Management Education accredited

GRADUATE BUSINESS PROGRAMS

Master of Business Administration (MBA) Full-time, part-time; 39-51 total credits required; 12 months to 7 years to complete program. Concentrations in accounting, decision sciences, finance, human resources, management, management information systems, marketing, operations management.

Executive MBA (MBA) Full-time; 48 total credits required; 20 months to complete program. Concentrations in management, entrepreneurship.

Weekend MBA (MBA) Full-time; 39 total credits required; 2 years to complete program. Concentrations in management, entrepreneurship.

Master of Accounting (MAcc) Full-time, part-time; 33 total credits required; 12 months to 5 years to complete program. Concentration in accounting.

Master of Taxation (MTax) Full-time, part-time; 33 total credits required; 12 months to 5 years to complete program. Concentration in taxation.

ADMISSION

Applications For fall 1997 there were 207 applications for admission. Of those applying, 135 were accepted. Of those accepted, 80 enrolled.

Application Requirements Application form, application fee, bachelor's degree, minimum GPA: 3.0, college transcript(s), computer experience: PC literacy.

Recommended for Application GMAT score accepted: minimum 500, work experience.

Application Deadline 6/15 for fall, 10/15 for spring, 3/15 for summer, 5/15 for fall (international), 9/15 for spring (international), 2/15 for summer (international). Application fee: $20. Deferred entrance is available.

ACADEMICS

Faculty Full-time 107; part-time 5.

Teaching Methodologies Case study, computer-aided instruction, computer analysis, computer simulations, experiential learning, faculty seminars, field projects, group discussion, lecture, research, role playing, seminars by members of the business community, simulations, student presentations, study groups, team projects.

Technology Computer terminals/PCs are available for student use and are linked by a campus-wide network. The network has full access to the Internet. Students are not required to have their own PC.

Special Opportunities Advanced credit may be earned through transfer of credits from another institution. International exchange programs in Australia, Chile, Ecuador, China, Denmark, Finland, France, Germany, Greece, Israel, Japan, Lithuania, Mexico, Russia, Spain, Sweden, United Kingdom.

FINANCES

Costs for 1997–98 Tuition: $133 per credit (resident); $438 per credit (nonresident). Cost varies by reciprocity agreements. Fees: $100 per semester (resident); $100 per semester (nonresident). Fees vary by number of credits taken. Average 1997–98 room and board costs were $5000 per academic year (on campus) and $7000 per academic year (off campus). Room and board costs vary by occupancy (e.g., single, double, triple), type of accommodation, type of meal plan.

Financial Aid In 1997–98, 12% of students received some institutionally administered aid in the form of fellowships, research assistantships, teaching assistantships, work study, loans. Financial aid is available to part-time students. Application Deadline: 3/1.

Financial Aid Contact Ms. Carole Pfeilsticker, Director of Student Financial Aid, 777 Glades Road, PO Box 3091, Boca Raton, FL 33431-0991. Phone: 561-297-3530; Fax: 561-297-3517; E-mail: pfeilsti@acc.fau.edu

FACILITIES

Information Resources S. E. Wimberly Library; total holdings of 715,431 volumes, 2,183,733 microforms, 4,180 current periodical subscriptions. CD player(s) available for graduate student use. Access provided to online bibliographic retrieval services.

INTERNATIONAL STUDENTS

Demographics 17% of students enrolled are international students [Asia, 40%, Central America, 10%, Europe, 20%, North America, 10%, South America, 20%].

Services and Facilities International student office, international student center, international student housing, visa services, ESL courses, counseling/support services.

Applying TOEFL: minimum score of 600, proof of adequate funds, proof of health/immunizations required. TSE: minimum score of 250 recommended. Financial aid is available to international students.

International Student Contact Ms. Susan D'Amico, Director, Student Affairs; International Student and Scholars, SO 301, Boca Raton, FL 33431-0991. Phone: 561-297-3049; Fax: 561-297-2447; E-mail: damicos@acc.fau.edu

PLACEMENT

Services include alumni network, career counseling/planning, career fairs, career library, career placement, electronic job bank, job interviews arranged, and resume preparation. In 1996–97, 99 organizations participated in on-campus recruiting.

Employment Of 1996–97 graduates, 95% were employed within three months of graduation; the average starting salary was $35,000. Types of employment entered: accounting, banking, computer-related, consulting, engineering, finance, financial services, government, health services, hospitality management, human resources, insurance, international trade, management, manufacturing, marketing, nonprofit, pharmaceutical, real estate, retail, telecommunications.

Business Program(s) URL: http://www.fau.edu/divdept/cobus/cobhome.htm

Program Contact: Mrs. Ella Smith, Graduate Advisor, College of Business, Bue 126, Boca Raton, FL 33461-0991. Phone: 561-297-3650; Fax: 561-297-3978; E-mail: smith@acc.fau.edu

Florida Institute of Technology

School of Business

Melbourne, Florida

OVERVIEW

Florida Institute of Technology is an independent-nonprofit, coed university. Enrollment: 4,135 graduate, professional, and undergraduate students; 409 full-time matriculated graduate/professional students; 1,883 part-time matriculated graduate/professional students. Founded: 1958. The graduate business unit is in a small-town setting and is on a semester calendar.

HIGHLIGHTS

Enrollment Profile

Full-time: 23	International: 26%
Part-time: 45	Women: 37%
Total: 68	Minorities: 10%
Average Age: 33	Average Class Size: 10
Fall 1997 Average GPA: 3.7	Fall 1997 Average GMAT: 463

Costs
Full-time tuition: $9594 per academic year
Part-time tuition: $533 per credit hour

GRADUATE BUSINESS PROGRAMS

Master of Business Administration (MBA) Full-time, part-time; 36 total credits required; minimum of 12 months to complete program.

ADMISSION

Applications For fall 1997 there were 37 applications for admission. Of those applying, 18 were accepted. Of those accepted, 8 enrolled.

Application Requirements GMAT score: minimum 425, application form, application fee, bachelor's degree, minimum GPA: 3.0, college transcript(s).

Recommended for Application Letters of recommendation, personal statement, resume, computer experience.

Application Deadline Applications processed on a rolling/continuous basis for both domestic and international students. Application fee: $50. Deferred entrance is available.

ACADEMICS

Faculty Full-time 12; part-time 13.

Teaching Methodologies Case study, computer-aided instruction, computer analysis, computer simulations, faculty seminars, group discussion, lecture, research, role playing, seminars by members of the business community, student presentations, team projects.

Technology 400 on-campus computer terminals/PCs are available for student use and are linked by a campus-wide network. The network has full access to the Internet. Students are not required to have their own PC.

Special Opportunities Advanced credit may be earned through credit by examination, transfer of credits from another institution. International exchange programs in France, United Kingdom.

FINANCES

Costs for 1997–98 Tuition: Full-time $9594 per year. Part-time $533 per credit hour. Fees: Full-time $250 per academic year. Part-time $250 per enrollment. Average 1997–98 room and board costs were $4640 per academic year (on campus) and $4640 per academic year (off campus). Room and board costs vary by occupancy (e.g., single, double, triple), type of accommodation, type of meal plan.

Financial Aid In 1997–98, 9% of students received some institutionally administered aid in the form of research assistantships, teaching assistantships. Application Deadline: 3/1.

Financial Aid Contact Mr. John Lally, Director, Financial Aid, 150 West University Boulevard, Melbourne, FL 32901-6975. Phone: 800-666-4348; Fax: 407-724-2778; E-mail: lally@fit.edu

FACILITIES
Information Resources Evans Library; total holdings of 323,068 volumes, 203,465 microforms, 1,524 current periodical subscriptions. CD player(s) available for graduate student use. Access provided to online bibliographic retrieval services and online databases.

INTERNATIONAL STUDENTS
Demographics 26% of students enrolled are international students [Asia, 47%, Central America, 6%, Europe, 12%, South America, 12%, other, 23%].

Services and Facilities International student office, international student center, ESL courses, counseling/support services.

Applying TOEFL: minimum score of 550, proof of adequate funds, proof of health/immunizations required. TSE: minimum score of 230, TWE recommended. Financial aid is not available to international students.

International Student Contact Ms. Christine Frank, International Student Director, 150 West University Boulevard, Melbourne, FL 32901-6975. Phone: 407-674-8053; Fax: 407-728-4570; E-mail: cfrank@fit.edu

PLACEMENT
Services include alumni network, career counseling/planning, career fairs, job interviews arranged, and resume preparation. In 1996–97, 54 organizations participated in on-campus recruiting; 250 on-campus interviews were conducted.

Employment Of 1996–97 graduates, 67% were employed within three months of graduation. Types of employment entered: accounting, consulting, engineering, finance, financial services, management, manufacturing, marketing, nonprofit.

Business Program(s) URL: http://www.fit.edu

Program Contact: Ms. Carolyn Farrior, Associate Dean, Graduate Admission, 150 West University Boulevard, Melbourne, FL 32901-6975. Phone: 407-674-7118, 800-944-4348; Fax: 407-723-9468; E-mail: cfarrior@fit.edu

Florida International University

College of Business Administration

Miami, Florida

OVERVIEW
Florida International University is a state-supported, coed university. Enrollment: 30,000 graduate, professional, and undergraduate students. Founded: 1965. The graduate business unit is in an urban setting and is on a semester calendar.

HIGHLIGHTS

Enrollment Profile

Full-time: 656	International: 10%
Part-time: 164	Women: 51%
Total: 820	Minorities: N/R
Average Age: 28	Average Class Size: 40
Fall 1997 Average GPA: 3.4	Fall 1997 Average GMAT: 530

Costs
Full-time tuition: N/R
Part-time tuition: $130 per credit hour (resident); $435 per credit hour (nonresident)

AACSB – The International Association for Management Education accredited

GRADUATE BUSINESS PROGRAMS
Master of Business Administration (MBA) Full-time, part-time; 40-61 total credits required; 12 months to 5 years to complete program. Concentrations in accounting, finance, human resources, international business, management information systems, marketing, organizational behavior/development.

Master of Science in Finance (MS) Full-time, part-time; 36-67 total credits required; 12 months to 5 years to complete program. Concentration in finance.

Master of Accountancy (MAcc) Full-time, part-time; 30 total credits required; 12 months to 6 years to complete program. Concentration in accounting.

Executive MBA (EMBA) Full-time, part-time; 42 total credits required; 21 months to complete program.

Master of Science in Taxation (MST) Full-time, part-time; 30 total credits required; 11 months to 6 years to complete program. Concentration in taxation.

Executive Master of Science in Taxation (EMST) Part-time; 30 total credits required; 12 months to 6 years to complete program. Concentration in taxation.

ADMISSION
Applications For fall 1997 there were 537 applications for admission. Of those applying, 215 were accepted.

Application Requirements GMAT score: minimum 500, application form, application fee, bachelor's degree, minimum GPA, personal statement, resume, college transcript(s).

Recommended for Application Interview, 3 letters of recommendation, minimum of 2 years of work experience, computer experience.

Application Deadline Applications processed on a rolling/continuous basis for both domestic and international students. Application fee: $20. Deferred entrance is available.

ACADEMICS
Faculty Full-time 82; part-time 13.

Teaching Methodologies Case study, computer-aided instruction, computer analysis, computer simulations, experiential learning, faculty seminars, field projects, group discussion, lecture, research, role playing, seminars by members of the business community, simulations, student presentations, study groups, team projects.

Technology Computer terminals/PCs are available for student use and are linked by a campus-wide network. The network has full access to the Internet. Students are required to have their own PC.

Special Opportunities Advanced credit may be earned through transfer of credits from another institution. International exchange programs in France, Spain. An internship program is available.

FINANCES
Costs for 1997–98 Tuition: $130 per credit hour (resident); $435 per credit hour (nonresident). Cost varies by number of credits taken. Fees: $46 per semester (resident); $46 per semester (nonresident). Fees vary by number of credits taken. Average 1997–98 room and board costs were $7908 per academic year (on campus) and $7908 per academic year (off campus). Room and board costs vary by occupancy (e.g., single, double, triple), type of accommodation, type of meal plan.

Financial Aid Research assistantships, teaching assistantships, scholarships, work study, loans available. Financial aid is available to part-time students.

Financial Aid Contact Ms. Ana Sarasti, Director, Financial Aid Office, University Park, Miami, FL 33199. Phone: 305-348-2489; Fax: 305-348-2346; E-mail: sarastia@fiu.edu

FACILITIES
Information Resources University Park Campus Library; total holdings of 1,054,000 volumes, 2,800,000 microforms, 11,930 current periodical subscriptions. CD player(s) available for graduate student use. Access provided to online bibliographic retrieval services and online databases.

INTERNATIONAL STUDENTS
Demographics 10% of students enrolled are international students.

Services and Facilities International student office, international student center, ESL courses, counseling/support services.

Applying TOEFL: minimum score of 500, proof of adequate funds, proof of health/immunizations required. Financial aid is not available to international students.

International Student Contact Ms. Ana Sippin, Director, International Student Services, University Park, Miami, FL 33199. Phone: 305-348-2421; Fax: 305-348-1521; E-mail: sippina@fiu.edu

PLACEMENT
Services include career counseling/planning, career fairs, career placement, electronic job bank, job interviews arranged, job search course, resume referral to employers, and resume preparation.

Employment Types of employment entered: banking, finance, financial services, mining.

Business Program(s) URL: http://www.fiu.edu/~cba/

Program Contact: Ms. Eleanor Polster, Graduate Coordinator, FIU University Park Campus, Miami, FL 33199. Phone: 305-348-3256; Fax: 305-348-1763; E-mail: polstere@fiu.edu

See full description on page 820.

Florida Metropolitan University-Tampa College

Business and Computer Information Division

Tampa, Florida

OVERVIEW
Florida Metropolitan University-Tampa College is a proprietary, coed, comprehensive institution. Enrollment: 1,000 graduate, professional, and undergraduate students; 65 full-time matriculated graduate/professional students; 25 part-time matriculated graduate/professional students. Founded: 1890. The graduate business unit is in a suburban setting and is on a quarter calendar.

HIGHLIGHTS

Enrollment Profile
Full-time: 65
Part-time: 25
Total: 90
Average Age: 32
Fall 1997 Average GPA: N/R

International: 22%
Women: 47%
Minorities: N/R
Average Class Size: 20
Fall 1997 Average GMAT: N/R

Costs
Full-time tuition: $6000 per academic year
Part-time tuition: N/R

GRADUATE BUSINESS PROGRAMS

Master of Business Administration (MBA) Full-time, part-time; 54 total credits required; 15 months to 5 years to complete program. Concentrations in accounting, international business, human resources.

ADMISSION

Application Requirements Application form, application fee, bachelor's degree, minimum GPA: 3.0, interview, personal statement, resume, college transcript(s).

Recommended for Application GMAT score accepted.

Application Deadline Applications processed on a rolling/continuous basis for both domestic and international students. Application fee: $25.

ACADEMICS

Faculty Full-time 1; part-time 5.

Teaching Methodologies Case study, computer-aided instruction, computer analysis, experiential learning, faculty seminars, field projects, group discussion, lecture, research, role playing, seminars by members of the business community, simulations, student presentations, study groups, team projects.

Technology 50 on-campus computer terminals/PCs are available for student use and are linked by a campus-wide network. The network has full access to the Internet. Students are not required to have their own PC.

Special Opportunities Advanced credit may be earned through credit for military training programs, credit for business training programs, transfer of credits from another institution.

FINANCES

Costs for 1997–98 Tuition: Full-time: $6000 per year. Cost varies by number of credits taken.

Financial Aid Financial aid is available to part-time students.

Financial Aid Contact Mr. Rod Kirkwood, Director of Financial Aid, 3319 West Hillsborough Avenue, Tampa, FL 33614-5899. Phone: 813-879-6000; Fax: 813-871-2483.

FACILITIES

Information Resources Main library plus 1 additional on-campus library; total holdings of 15,000 volumes, 100 current periodical subscriptions. Access provided to online bibliographic retrieval services.

INTERNATIONAL STUDENTS

Demographics 22% of students enrolled are international students.

Applying TOEFL: minimum score of 550 required.

International Student Contact Mr. Patrick Burch, Registrar, 3319 West Hillsborough Avenue, Tampa, FL 33614-5899. Phone: 813-879-6000; Fax: 813-871-2483.

PLACEMENT

Services include career counseling/planning, career fairs, career library, career placement, resume referral to employers, and resume preparation. In 1996–97, 35 organizations participated in on-campus recruiting.

Employment Of 1996–97 graduates, 94% were employed within three months of graduation. Types of employment entered: accounting, banking, communications, computer-related, education, finance, financial services, government, health services, high technology, human resources, information systems/technology, international trade, management, marketing, nonprofit, pharmaceutical, service industry, telecommunications.

Program Contact: Mr. Foster Thomas, Director of Admissions, 3319 West Hillsborough Avenue, Tampa, FL 33614. Phone: 813-879-6000; Fax: 813-871-2483.

Florida Metropolitan University-Orlando College, North

Graduate Program

Orlando, Florida

OVERVIEW
Florida Metropolitan University-Orlando College, North is a proprietary, coed, comprehensive institution. Enrollment: 650 graduate, professional, and undergraduate students; 100 full-time matriculated graduate/professional students; part-time matriculated graduate/professional students. Founded: 1953. The graduate business unit is in an urban setting and is on a quarter calendar.

HIGHLIGHTS

Enrollment Profile
Full-time: 100
Part-time: 0
Total: 100
Average Age: 30
Fall 1997 Average GPA: N/R

International: N/R
Women: 60%
Minorities: N/R
Average Class Size: 20
Fall 1997 Average GMAT: N/R

Costs
Full-time tuition: N/R
Part-time tuition: $263 per credit hour

GRADUATE BUSINESS PROGRAMS

Master of Business Administration (MBA) Full-time, distance learning option; 54-56 total credits required; 18 months to 2 years to complete program. Concentrations in marketing, management, accounting, information management, international business.

ADMISSION

Application Requirements Application form, application fee, bachelor's degree, minimum GPA: 3.0, college transcript(s).

Recommended for Application Computer experience.

Application Deadline Applications processed on a rolling/continuous basis for both domestic and international students. Application fee: $25. Deferred entrance is available.

ACADEMICS

Faculty Full-time 4; part-time 3.

Teaching Methodologies Case study, computer-aided instruction, computer analysis, computer simulations, experiential learning, faculty seminars, field projects, group discussion, lecture, research, role playing, seminars by members of the business community, simulations, student presentations, study groups, team projects.

FINANCES

Costs for 1997–98 Tuition: $263 per credit hour. Cost varies by number of credits taken.

Financial Aid Work study available. Financial aid is available to part-time students.

Financial Aid Contact Linda Kaisrlik, 5421 Diplomat Circle, Orlando, FL 32810-5674. Phone: 407-628-5870.

FACILITIES

Information Resources Main library. Access provided to online bibliographic retrieval services.

INTERNATIONAL STUDENTS

Demographics N/R

Applying TOEFL: minimum score of 550, proof of adequate funds required.

Program Contact: Ms. Charlene Donnelly-Meyer, Director of Admissions, 5421 Diplomat Circle, Orlando, FL 32810-5674. Phone: 407-628-5870, 800-628-5870 (FL only); Fax: 407-628-1344.

Florida Southern College

Department of Business and Economics

Lakeland, Florida

OVERVIEW
Florida Southern College is an independent-religious, coed, comprehensive institution. Enrollment: 1,800 graduate, professional, and undergraduate students. Founded: 1885. The graduate business unit is in a suburban setting and is on a semester calendar.

HIGHLIGHTS

Enrollment Profile
Full-time: 0
Part-time: 75
Total: 75
Average Age: 31
Fall 1997 Average GPA: N/R

International: N/R
Women: N/R
Minorities: N/R
Average Class Size: 14
Fall 1997 Average GMAT: N/R

Costs
Full-time tuition: N/R
Part-time tuition: $290 per credit hour

GRADUATE BUSINESS PROGRAMS
Master of Business Administration (MBA) Part-time; 39-52 total credits required; 18 months to 7 years to complete program. Concentration in accounting.

ADMISSION
Applications For fall 1997 there were 75 applications for admission. Of those applying, 65 were accepted. Of those accepted, 52 enrolled.

Application Requirements Application form, application fee, bachelor's degree, minimum GPA, 3 letters of recommendation, college transcript(s).

Recommended for Application GMAT score accepted: minimum 450, GRE score accepted: minimum 850, work experience, computer experience.

Application Deadline 8/1 for fall, 12/1 for spring, 4/1 for summer, 8/1 for fall (international), 12/1 for spring (international), 4/1 for summer (international). Application fee: $30.

ACADEMICS
Faculty Full-time 14; part-time 6.

Teaching Methodologies Case study, computer-aided instruction, computer analysis, computer simulations, faculty seminars, group discussion, lecture, research, role playing, seminars by members of the business community, simulations, student presentations, study groups, team projects.

Technology Computer terminals/PCs are available for student use and are linked by a campus-wide network. The network has partial access to the Internet. Students are not required to have their own PC.

Special Opportunities Advanced credit may be earned through transfer of credits from another institution.

FINANCES
Costs for 1997-98 Tuition: Part-time: $290 per credit hour.

Financial Aid Financial aid is available to part-time students.

Financial Aid Contact Mr. David Bodwell, Director of Financial Aid, 111 Lake Hollingsworth Drive, Lakeland, FL 33801-5698. Phone: 941-680-4142; Fax: 941-680-4567.

FACILITIES
Information Resources Roux Library; total holdings of 158,143 volumes, 335,062 microforms, 746 current periodical subscriptions. CD player(s) available for graduate student use. Access provided to online bibliographic retrieval services.

INTERNATIONAL STUDENTS
Demographics N/R

Services and Facilities Counseling/support services.

Applying TOEFL: minimum score of 550, proof of adequate funds, proof of health/immunizations required. Financial aid is not available to international students.

International Student Contact Ms. Missy Sheldon, International Student Advisor, 111 Lake Hollingsworth Drive, Lakeland, FL 33801-5698. Phone: 941-680-3912; Fax: 941-680-4120.

PLACEMENT
Services include alumni network, career counseling/planning, and career placement.

Employment Types of employment entered: accounting, banking, consumer products, finance, financial services, human resources, management, manufacturing, marketing, transportation.

Program Contact: Mrs. Kim Pickering, Graduate Counselor, Department of Business and Economics, 111 Lake Hollingsworth Drive, Lakeland, FL 33801-5698. Phone: 941-680-4131, 800-274-4131 (FL only); Fax: 941-680-4120.

Florida State University

College of Business

Tallahassee, Florida

OVERVIEW
Florida State University is a state-supported, coed university. Enrollment: 29,630 graduate, professional, and undergraduate students; 3,699 full-time matriculated graduate/professional students; 1,950 part-time matriculated graduate/professional students. Founded: 1851. The graduate business unit is in an urban setting and is on a semester calendar.

HIGHLIGHTS

Enrollment Profile
Full-time: 66
Part-time: 123
Total: 189
Average Age: 28
Fall 1997 Average GPA: 3.25

International: 0%
Women: 46%
Minorities: 13%
Average Class Size: 30
Fall 1997 Average GMAT: 550

Costs
Full-time tuition: N/R
Part-time tuition: $131 per credit hour (resident); $436 per credit hour (nonresident)

AACSB – The International Association for Management Education accredited

GRADUATE BUSINESS PROGRAMS
Master of Business Administration (MBA) Full-time, part-time; 39 total credits required; 12 months to 2.5 years to complete program. Concentrations in international business, entrepreneurship.

Master of Business Administration/Doctor of Jurisprudence (MBA/JD) Full-time; 107 total credits required; 12 months to 4 years to complete program.

Master of Accounting (MAcc) Full-time, part-time; 33 total credits required; 12 months to 3 years to complete program. Concentrations in accounting, taxation.

Master of Science in Management Information Systems (MS) Full-time, part-time; 32 total credits required; 12 months to 3 years to complete program. Concentration in management information systems.

ADMISSION
Applications For fall 1997 there were 275 applications for admission. Of those applying, 194 were accepted. Of those accepted, 100 enrolled.

Application Requirements GMAT score: minimum 510, application form, application fee, bachelor's degree, minimum GPA: 3.1, 3 letters of recommendation, personal statement, resume, college transcript(s), minimum of 2 years of work experience, computer experience: Microsoft Excel, Microsoft Word, Powerpoint, Microsoft Office 95, Microsoft Office 97, Microsoft Windows 95.

Application Deadline 6/1 for fall, 10/1 for spring, 3/1 for summer, 3/1 for fall (international), 7/1 for spring (international), 11/1 for summer (international). Application fee: $20. Deferred entrance is available.

ACADEMICS
Faculty Full-time 85.

Teaching Methodologies Case study, computer-aided instruction, computer analysis, computer simulations, group discussion, lecture, research, seminars by members of the business community, simulations, student presentations, team projects.

Technology 16 on-campus computer terminals/PCs are available for student use and are linked by a campus-wide network. The network has full access to the Internet. Students are not required to have their own PC.

Special Opportunities Advanced credit may be earned through transfer of credits from another institution.

FINANCES
Costs for 1997-98 Tuition: $131 per credit hour (resident); $436 per credit hour (nonresident). Cost varies by campus location. Average 1997–98 room only costs were $3372 per academic year (on campus) and $4524 per academic year (off campus). Room and board costs vary by campus location, occupancy (e.g., single, double, triple), type of accommodation, type of meal plan.

Financial Aid In 1997–98, 39% of students received some institutionally administered aid in the form of fellowships, research assistantships, teaching assistantships, grants, scholarships, loans.

Financial Aid Contact Office of Financial Aid, Tallahassee, FL 32306-1023. Phone: 850-644-5871; Fax: 850-644-6404.

FACILITIES
Information Resources Robert Manning Strozier Library plus 6 additional on-campus libraries; total holdings of 2,065,664 volumes, 4,253,629 microforms. Access provided to online bibliographic retrieval services.

INTERNATIONAL STUDENTS
Demographics N/R

Services and Facilities International student office, international student center, international student housing, visa services, ESL courses, counseling/support services.

Applying TOEFL: minimum score of 600, proof of adequate funds, proof of health/immunizations required. Financial aid is not available to international students.

Florida State University (continued)

International Student Contact Ms. Roberta Christie, Director of Student Affairs, International Student Center, Room 107 ISH, Tallahassee, FL 32306-4240. Phone: 850-644-3050; Fax: 850-644-9951; E-mail: rchristi@admin.fsu.edu

PLACEMENT

Services include alumni network, career counseling/planning, career fairs, career library, career placement, electronic job bank, job interviews arranged, job search course, resume referral to employers, and resume preparation. In 1996–97, 25 organizations participated in on-campus recruiting; 54 on-campus interviews were conducted.

Employment Of 1996–97 graduates, 100% were employed within three months of graduation; the average starting salary was $44,000. Types of employment entered: accounting, banking, communications, computer-related, consulting, consumer products, education, engineering, finance, financial services, government, health services, hospitality management, information systems/technology, insurance, management, marketing, telecommunications.

Business Program(s) URL: http://www.cob.fsu.edu/

Program Contact: Dr. Pamela L. Perrewe, Associate Dean for Graduate Programs, Graduate Office, College of Business, Tallahassee, FL 32306-1110. Phone: 850-644-6458; Fax: 850-644-0915; E-mail: pperrew@garnet. acns.fsu.edu

Jacksonville University

College of Business

Jacksonville, Florida

OVERVIEW

Jacksonville University is an independent-nonprofit, coed, comprehensive institution. Enrollment: 2,321 graduate, professional, and undergraduate students; 38 full-time matriculated graduate/professional students; 73 part-time matriculated graduate/professional students. Founded: 1934. The graduate business unit is in a suburban setting and is on a semester calendar.

HIGHLIGHTS

Enrollment Profile
Full-time: 38
Part-time: 73
Total: 111
Average Age: 32
Fall 1997 Average GPA: N/R

International: 4%
Women: 40%
Minorities: 11%
Average Class Size: 15
Fall 1997 Average GMAT: N/R

Costs
Full-time tuition: N/R
Part-time tuition: $465 per credit hour

GRADUATE BUSINESS PROGRAMS

Master of Business Administration (MBA) Full-time, part-time; 30 total credits required; 12 months to 5 years to complete program. Concentrations in management, marketing, international business, health care.

Executive Master of Business Administration (EMBA) Full-time; 40 total credits required; 2 years to complete program.

ADMISSION

Application Requirements Application form, application fee, bachelor's degree, minimum GPA, interview, 2 letters of recommendation, college transcript(s), computer experience: basic computer course.

Recommended for Application GMAT score accepted: minimum 450.

Application Deadline Applications processed on a rolling/continuous basis for both domestic and international students. Application fee: $25. Deferred entrance is available.

ACADEMICS

Faculty Full-time 8; part-time 2.

Teaching Methodologies Case study, lecture, student presentations, team projects.

Technology 200 on-campus computer terminals/PCs are available for student use. The network has full access to the Internet.

Special Opportunities Advanced credit may be earned through transfer of credits from another institution.

FINANCES

Costs for 1997–98 Tuition: $465 per credit hour. Cost varies by academic program, class time (e.g., day/evening), number of credits taken. Fees: $80 per semester. Average 1997–98 room and board costs were $4750 per academic year.

Financial Aid Scholarships, work study, loans available. Financial aid is available to part-time students.

Financial Aid Contact Director of Financial Aid, 2800 University Boulevard North, Jacksonville, FL 32211. Phone: 904-745-7060.

FACILITIES

Information Resources Swisher Library; total holdings of 274,175 volumes, 147,270 microforms, 715 current periodical subscriptions. CD player(s) available for graduate student use. Access provided to online bibliographic retrieval services.

INTERNATIONAL STUDENTS

Demographics 4% of students enrolled are international students.

Services and Facilities International student office, international student housing, visa services, ESL courses, counseling/support services, 6 days of orientation, extensive ESL courses.

Applying TOEFL: minimum score of 550 required.

International Student Contact Ms. Sally Myers, International Advisor, Assistant Dean of Students, 2800 University Boulevard North, Jacksonville, FL 32211. Phone: 904-745-7070; Fax: 904-745-7066.

PLACEMENT

Services include career counseling/planning, career fairs, and career library.

Program Contact: Director of Graduate Programs, College of Business, 2800 University Boulevard North, Jacksonville, FL 32211. Phone: 904-745-7459; Fax: 904-745-7463.

Lynn University

School of Business

Boca Raton, Florida

OVERVIEW

Lynn University is an independent-nonprofit, coed, comprehensive institution. Enrollment: 1,782 graduate, professional, and undergraduate students; 72 full-time matriculated graduate/professional students; 72 part-time matriculated graduate/professional students. The graduate business unit is in a suburban setting and is on a four 10-week terms calendar.

HIGHLIGHTS

Enrollment Profile
Full-time: 29
Part-time: 21
Total: 50
Average Age: N/R
Fall 1997 Average GPA: N/R

International: 12%
Women: 54%
Minorities: 12%
Average Class Size: 20
Fall 1997 Average GMAT: 450

Costs
Full-time tuition: N/R
Part-time tuition: $360 per credit hour

GRADUATE BUSINESS PROGRAMS

Master of Business Administration (MBA) Full-time, part-time; 36 total credits required; 12 months to 5 years to complete program. Concentrations in international management, health care, sports/entertainment management, travel industry/tourism management.

ADMISSION

Applications For fall 1997 there were 53 applications for admission. Of those applying, 39 were accepted. Of those accepted, 35 enrolled.

Application Requirements GMAT score, application form, bachelor's degree, essay, minimum GPA, 2 letters of recommendation, personal statement, resume, college transcript(s), computer experience: prerequisite computer applications course.

Recommended for Application Interview.

Application Deadline Applications processed on a rolling/continuous basis for both domestic and international students. Application fee: $50. Deferred entrance is available.

ACADEMICS

Faculty Full-time 5; part-time 2.

Teaching Methodologies Case study, computer analysis, computer simulations, experiential learning, field projects, group discussion, lecture, research, role playing, seminars by members of the business community, simulations, student presentations, study groups, team projects.

Technology 125 on-campus computer terminals/PCs are available for student use and are linked by a campus-wide network. The network has full access to the Internet. Students are not required to have their own PC.

Special Opportunities Advanced credit may be earned through transfer of credits from another institution. International exchange programs in Argentina, Ireland, Japan, Sweden.

FINANCES
Costs for 1997–98 Tuition: $360 per credit hour. Fees: $30 per term. Average 1997–98 room and board costs were $6250 per academic year (on campus) and $7500 per academic year (off campus). Room and board costs vary by occupancy (e.g., single, double, triple).

Financial Aid Work study available.

Financial Aid Contact Ms. Barrie Tripp, Associate Director/Financial Aid, Boca Raton, FL 33431-5598. Phone: 561-994-0770 Ext. 114; Fax: 561-241-3552.

FACILITIES
Information Resources The Lynn Library; total holdings of 89,341 volumes, 821 microforms, 899 current periodical subscriptions. CD player(s) available for graduate student use. Access provided to online bibliographic retrieval services and online databases.

INTERNATIONAL STUDENTS
Demographics 12% of students enrolled are international students [Central America, 50%, Europe, 33%, South America, 17%].

Services and Facilities International student office, international student center, visa services, ESL courses, counseling/support services.

Applying TOEFL: minimum score of 550, proof of adequate funds required. Proof of health/immunizations recommended. Financial aid is not available to international students.

International Student Contact Ms. Shelia Sheppard-Sciarra, International Student Affairs Coordinator, Boca Raton, FL 33431-5598. Phone: 561-994-0770 Ext. 433; Fax: 561-241-3552.

PLACEMENT
Services include alumni network, career counseling/planning, career fairs, career library, career placement, electronic job bank, job interviews arranged, resume referral to employers, and resume preparation. In 1996–97, 120 organizations participated in on-campus recruiting.

Employment Types of employment entered: finance, human resources, management, marketing, telecommunications.

Business Program(s) URL: http://www.lynn.edu

Program Contact: Ms. Pat Sieredzki, Graduate Admission Coordinator, Boca Raton, FL 33431-5598. Phone: 561-994-0770 Ext. 193; Fax: 561-241-3552; E-mail: psieredzki@lynn.edu

Nova Southeastern University

School of Business and Entrepreneurship
Fort Lauderdale, Florida

OVERVIEW
Nova Southeastern University is an independent-nonprofit, coed university. Enrollment: 16,501 graduate, professional, and undergraduate students; 8,741 full-time matriculated graduate/professional students; 3,553 part-time matriculated graduate/professional students. Founded: 1964. The graduate business unit is in an urban setting and is on a quarter calendar.

HIGHLIGHTS

Enrollment Profile
Full-time: 182
Part-time: 2,022
Total: 2,204
Average Age: 35
Fall 1997 Average GPA: 3.0

International: 17%
Women: 46%
Minorities: 37%
Average Class Size: 15
Fall 1997 Average GMAT: 480

Costs
Full-time tuition: $9500 per academic year
Part-time tuition: $425 per credit

GRADUATE BUSINESS PROGRAMS
Master of Business Administration (MBA) Full-time, part-time, distance learning option; 41 total credits required; 12 months to 5 years to complete program. Concentrations in finance, marketing, accounting, international business, public management, human resources, management information systems, sports/entertainment management, health care, system management, entrepreneurship.

Master of Accounting (MAcc) Part-time, distance learning option; 37 total credits required; 18 months to 5 years to complete program. Concentration in taxation.

Master of Science in Health Services Administration (MS) Part-time, distance learning option; 41 total credits required; 18 months to 5 years to complete program.

Master of Public Administration (MPA) Part-time; 40 total credits required; 18 months to 5 years to complete program.

Master of Science in Human Resource Management (MS) Part-time; 41 total credits required; 18 months to 5 years to complete program.

Master of International Business Administration (MIBA) Full-time, part-time, distance learning option; 41 total credits required; 12 months to 5 years to complete program.

ADMISSION
Applications For fall 1997 there were 628 applications for admission. Of those applying, 461 were accepted. Of those accepted, 392 enrolled.

Application Requirements GMAT score: minimum 450, GRE score: minimum 1,000, application form, application fee, bachelor's degree, minimum GPA: 2.5, college transcript(s), computer experience: computer literacy.

Application Deadline 3/1 for fall, 5/31 for winter, 11/30 for spring, 8/30 for summer, 3/1 for fall (international), 5/31 for winter (international), 11/30 for spring (international), 8/30 for summer (international). Application fee: $50. Deferred entrance is available.

ACADEMICS
Faculty Full-time 24; part-time 200.

Teaching Methodologies Case study, computer simulations, group discussion, lecture, research, seminars by members of the business community, student presentations, team projects.

Technology 50 on-campus computer terminals/PCs are available for student use and are linked by a campus-wide network. The network has full access to the Internet. Students are required to have their own PC.

Special Opportunities Advanced credit may be earned through transfer of credits from another institution. An internship program is available.

FINANCES
Costs for 1997–98 Tuition: Full-time: $9500 per year. Part-time: $425 per credit. Cost varies by academic program, number of credits taken. Fees: Full-time: $120 per academic year. Part-time: $20 per term. Fees vary by campus location. Average 1997–98 room and board costs were $9000 per academic year (on campus) and $7200 per academic year (off campus). Room and board costs vary by occupancy (e.g., single, double, triple), type of accommodation, type of meal plan.

Financial Aid In 1997–98, 36% of students received some institutionally administered aid in the form of work study, loans. Financial aid is available to part-time students. Application Deadline: 4/1.

Financial Aid Contact Office of Student Financial Aid, 3301 College Avenue, Fort Lauderdale, FL 33314. Phone: 800-522-3243; Fax: 954-262-3966.

FACILITIES
Information Resources Einstein Library plus 6 additional on-campus libraries; total holdings of 340,000 volumes, 1,200,000 microforms, 8,192 current periodical subscriptions. CD player(s) available for graduate student use. Access provided to online bibliographic retrieval services and online databases.

INTERNATIONAL STUDENTS
Demographics 17% of students enrolled are international students.

Services and Facilities International student office, visa services, counseling/support services.

Applying TOEFL: minimum score of 550, proof of adequate funds required. Financial aid is not available to international students.

International Student Contact Ms. Debra Puzzo, International Student Advisor, 3301 College Avenue, Fort Lauderdale, FL 33314. Phone: 800-541-6682 Ext. 7240; Fax: 954-262-7265; E-mail: puzzo@nsu.nova.edu

PLACEMENT
Services include alumni network, career counseling/planning, career fairs, electronic job bank, job interviews arranged, job search course, resume referral to employers, and resume preparation.

Employment Types of employment entered: accounting, banking, communications, computer-related, consulting, engineering, finance, financial services, government, health services, human resources, information systems/technology, insurance, international trade, law, management, manufacturing, marketing, nonprofit, real estate, retail, telecommunications.

Business Program(s) URL: http://www.sbe.nova.edu

Program Contact: Office of Marketing and Student Recruitment, 3100 SW 9th Avenue, Fort Lauderdale, FL 33315-3025. Phone: 800-672-7223 Ext. 5100; Fax: 954-262-3964.

See full description on page 912.

Palm Beach Atlantic College

Rinker School of Business

West Palm Beach, Florida

OVERVIEW
Palm Beach Atlantic College is an independent-religious, coed, comprehensive institution. Enrollment: 1,941 graduate, professional, and undergraduate students; 100 full-time matriculated graduate/professional students; 191 part-time matriculated graduate/professional students. Founded: 1968. The graduate business unit is in an urban setting and is on a semester calendar.

HIGHLIGHTS

Enrollment Profile
Full-time: 62
Part-time: 50
Total: 112
Average Age: 32
Fall 1997 Average GPA: 3.0

International: 6%
Women: 37%
Minorities: 12%
Average Class Size: 20
Fall 1997 Average GMAT: 440

Costs
Full-time tuition: N/R
Part-time tuition: $280 per credit hour

GRADUATE BUSINESS PROGRAMS
Master of Business Administration (MBA) Full-time, part-time; 36 total credits required; 12 months to 6 years to complete program.

ADMISSION
Applications For fall 1997 there were 47 applications for admission. Of those applying, 41 were accepted. Of those accepted, 35 enrolled.

Application Requirements GMAT score: minimum 450, application form, application fee, bachelor's degree, essay, minimum GPA: 3.0, interview, 3 letters of recommendation, resume, college transcript(s).

Recommended for Application Work experience, computer experience.

Application Deadline Applications processed on a rolling/continuous basis for both domestic and international students. Application fee: $35. Deferred entrance is available.

ACADEMICS
Faculty Full-time 3; part-time 4.

Teaching Methodologies Case study, computer-aided instruction, computer analysis, computer simulations, experiential learning, field projects, group discussion, lecture, research, role playing, simulations, student presentations, study groups, team projects.

Technology 100 on-campus computer terminals/PCs are available for student use and are linked by a campus-wide network. The network has full access to the Internet. Students are not required to have their own PC.

Special Opportunities Advanced credit may be earned through transfer of credits from another institution.

FINANCES
Costs for 1997–98 Tuition: $280 per credit hour. Cost varies by academic program, number of credits taken. Average 1997–98 room only costs were $4100 per academic year (off campus).

Financial Aid Contact Ms. Kathy Frugé, Director of Student Financial Planning, PO Box 24708, West Palm Beach, FL 33416-4708. Phone: 561-803-2110; Fax: 561-803-2115; E-mail: fruge@pbac.edu

FACILITIES
Information Resources E. C. Blomeyer Library; total holdings of 101,000 volumes, 2,000 microforms, 580 current periodical subscriptions. Access provided to online bibliographic retrieval services.

INTERNATIONAL STUDENTS
Demographics 6% of students enrolled are international students.

Services and Facilities International student office, ESL courses, counseling/support services.

Applying TOEFL: minimum score of 550, proof of adequate funds, proof of health/immunizations required. Financial aid is available to international students.

International Student Contact Cybelle Seeds, School of Arts and Sciences, PO Box 24708, West Palm Beach, FL 33416-4708. Phone: 561-803-2355.

PLACEMENT
Services include alumni network, career counseling/planning, career fairs, career library, career placement, electronic job bank, job interviews arranged, job search course, resume referral to employers, and resume preparation. In 1996–97, 55 organizations participated in on-campus recruiting.

Employment Types of employment entered: accounting, banking, communications, computer-related, consumer products, education, energy, engineering,

finance, financial services, government, health services, high technology, human resources, information systems/technology, management, manufacturing, marketing, nonprofit, real estate, retail, service industry, telecommunications, transportation, utilities.

Business Program(s) URL: http://www.pbac.edu

Program Contact: Mrs. Carolanne Brown, Coordinator, Graduate Studies, PO Box 24708, West Palm Beach, FL 33416-4708. Phone: 561-803-2121, 800-281-3466 (FL only); Fax: 561-803-2115; E-mail: grad@pbac.edu

Rollins College

Crummer Graduate School of Business

Winter Park, Florida

OVERVIEW
Rollins College is an independent-nonprofit, coed, comprehensive institution. Enrollment: 3,345 graduate, professional, and undergraduate students; 327 full-time matriculated graduate/professional students; 395 part-time matriculated graduate/professional students. Founded: 1885. The graduate business unit is in a suburban setting and is on a semester calendar.

HIGHLIGHTS

Enrollment Profile
Full-time: 168
Part-time: 143
Total: 311
Average Age: 29
Fall 1997 Average GPA: 3.22

International: 9%
Women: 30%
Minorities: 11%
Average Class Size: 24
Fall 1997 Average GMAT: 595

Costs
Full-time tuition: $10,200 per academic year
Part-time tuition: $627 per credit

AACSB – The International Association for Management Education accredited

GRADUATE BUSINESS PROGRAMS
Executive MBA (MBA) Full-time; 49 total credits required; 21 months to 6 years to complete program. Concentrations in accounting, finance, international and area business studies, management, marketing, operations management.

Professional MBA (MBA) Part-time; 50 total credits required; 2.7 to 6 years to complete program. Concentrations in accounting, finance, international and area business studies, management, marketing, operations management.

Accelerated MBA (MBA) Full-time; 59 total credits required; 21 months to 6 years to complete program. Concentrations in accounting, finance, international and area business studies, management, marketing, operations management.

Early Advantage MBA (MBA) Full-time; 59 total credits required; 21 months to 6 years to complete program. Concentrations in accounting, finance, international and area business studies, management, marketing, operations management.

ADMISSION
Applications For fall 1997 there were 591 applications for admission. Of those applying, 290 were accepted. Of those accepted, 205 enrolled.

Application Requirements GMAT score, application form, application fee, bachelor's degree, essay, interview, 2 letters of recommendation, personal statement, resume, college transcript(s), minimum of 3 years of work experience.

Application Deadline Applications processed on a rolling/continuous basis for both domestic and international students. Application fee: $40. Deferred entrance is available.

ACADEMICS
Faculty Full-time 20; part-time 4.

Teaching Methodologies Case study, computer analysis, computer simulations, experiential learning, field projects, group discussion, lecture, student presentations, study groups, team projects.

Technology 30 on-campus computer terminals/PCs are available for student use and are linked by a campus-wide network. The network has full access to the Internet. Students are required to have their own PC.

Special Opportunities Advanced credit may be earned through transfer of credits from another institution.

FINANCES
Costs for 1997–98 Tuition: Full-time: $10,200 per semester. Part-time: $627 per credit. Cost varies by academic program, number of credits taken. Average 1997–98 room and board costs were $13,200 per academic year (off campus).

Financial Aid In 1997–98, 47% of students received some institutionally administered aid in the form of fellowships, research assistantships, work study.

Financial Aid Contact Ms. Linda Downing, Assistant Dean, 1000 Holt Avenue, Winter Park, FL 32789-4499. Phone: 407-646-2395; Fax: 407-646-2402.

FACILITIES
Information Resources Olin Library; total holdings of 269,287 volumes, 38,916 microforms, 2,649 current periodical subscriptions. CD player(s) available for graduate student use. Access provided to online bibliographic retrieval services and online databases.

INTERNATIONAL STUDENTS
Demographics 9% of students enrolled are international students [Asia, 58%, Central America, 14%, Europe, 14%, North America, 7%, South America, 7%].

Services and Facilities Visa services, counseling/support services.

Applying TOEFL, proof of adequate funds required. Financial aid is available to international students.

International Student Contact Ms. Bobbie Ayala, International Advisor, 1000 Holt Avenue—2722, Winter Park, FL 32789-4499. Phone: 407-646-2405; Fax: 407-646-2402; E-mail: bayala@rollins.edu

PLACEMENT
Services include alumni network, career counseling/planning, career fairs, career library, career placement, electronic job bank, job interviews arranged, job search course, resume referral to employers, and resume preparation. In 1996–97, 55 organizations participated in on-campus recruiting; 440 on-campus interviews were conducted.

Employment Of 1996–97 graduates, 90% were employed within three months of graduation; the average starting salary was $62,000. Types of employment entered: accounting, banking, computer-related, consulting, consumer products, finance, financial services, hospitality management, human resources, information systems/technology, management, marketing, telecommunications, utilities.

Business Program(s) URL: http://www.crummer.rollins.edu

Program Contact: Mr. Stephen Gauthier, Assistant Dean, Crummer Graduate School of Business, 1000 Holt Avenue—2722, Winter Park, FL 32789-4499. Phone: 407-646-2405, 800-866-2405 (FL only); Fax: 407-646-2402.

See full description on page 952.

Saint Leo College

Saint Leo, Florida

OVERVIEW
Saint Leo College is an independent-religious, coed, comprehensive institution. Enrollment: 1,675 graduate, professional, and undergraduate students; 162 full-time matriculated graduate/professional students; 53 part-time matriculated graduate/professional students. Founded: 1889. The graduate business unit is in a rural setting and is on a semester calendar.

HIGHLIGHTS

Enrollment Profile

Full-time: 129	International: 1%
Part-time: 18	Women: 56%
Total: 147	Minorities: 9%
Average Age: 35	Average Class Size: 20
Fall 1997 Average GPA: 3.3	Fall 1997 Average GMAT: 464

Costs
Full-time tuition: $3420 per academic year
Part-time tuition: $190 per credit

GRADUATE BUSINESS PROGRAMS
Master of Business Administration (MBA) Full-time, part-time; 36 total credits required; 2 to 5 years to complete program.

ADMISSION
Application Requirements Application form, application fee, bachelor's degree, interview, 2 letters of recommendation, resume, college transcript(s), computer experience.

Recommended for Application GMAT score accepted, work experience.

Application Deadline 8/1 for fall, 12/1 for winter. Application fee: $45.

ACADEMICS
Faculty Full-time 5; part-time 6.

Teaching Methodologies Case study, computer analysis, computer simulations, experiential learning, faculty seminars, field projects, group discussion, lecture,

research, role playing, seminars by members of the business community, simulations, student presentations, study groups, team projects.

Technology 120 on-campus computer terminals/PCs are available for student use and are linked by a campus-wide network. The network has full access to the Internet. Students are not required to have their own PC.

Special Opportunities Advanced credit may be earned through transfer of credits from another institution.

FINANCES
Costs for 1997–98 Tuition: Full-time: $3420 per year. Part-time: $190 per credit. Fees: Full-time: $60 per academic year. Part-time: $60 per year.

Financial Aid Financial aid is available to part-time students.

Financial Aid Contact Mr. Richard Ritzman, Director, Financial Aid and Veterans Affairs, PO Box 6665, MC 2228, Saint Leo, FL 33574-2228. Phone: 352-588-8270; Fax: 352-588-8403.

FACILITIES
Information Resources Cannon Memorial Library; total holdings of 71,541 volumes, 288 microforms, 750 current periodical subscriptions. CD player(s) available for graduate student use. Access provided to online bibliographic retrieval services.

INTERNATIONAL STUDENTS
Demographics 1% of students enrolled are international students [Europe, 100%].

Services and Facilities International student housing, visa services, counseling/support services.

Applying TOEFL: minimum score of 550, proof of adequate funds required. Financial aid is not available to international students.

International Student Contact Mr. Gary Bracken, Dean of Admissions and Financial Aid, PO Box 6665 MC 20008, Saint Leo, FL 33574-2008. Phone: 352-588-8200; Fax: 352-588-8257; E-mail: admissns@saintleo.edu

PLACEMENT
Services include alumni network, career counseling/planning, career library, and resume preparation.

Employment Of 1996–97 graduates, 100% were employed within three months of graduation. Types of employment entered: accounting, banking, communications, computer-related, consulting, consumer products, education, energy, engineering, finance, government, health services, human resources, insurance, management, manufacturing, marketing, nonprofit, pharmaceutical, retail, service industry, telecommunications, utilities.

Business Program(s) URL: http://www.saintleo.edu/

Program Contact: Mr. Gary Bracken, Dean of Admissions and Financial Aid, PO Box 6665, MC2008, Saint Leo, FL 33574-2008. Phone: 352-588-8283, 800-334-5532 (FL only), and/or 800-247-6559 (FL only); Fax: 352-588-8257; E-mail: admissns@saintleo.edu

St. Thomas University

Miami, Florida

OVERVIEW
St. Thomas University is an independent-religious, coed, comprehensive institution. Enrollment: 2,262 graduate, professional, and undergraduate students; 900 full-time matriculated graduate/professional students; 234 part-time matriculated graduate/professional students. Founded: 1962. The graduate business unit is in a suburban setting and is on a semester calendar.

HIGHLIGHTS

Enrollment Profile

Full-time: 143	International: 9%
Part-time: 121	Women: 52%
Total: 264	Minorities: 58%
Average Age: 27	Average Class Size: 25
Fall 1997 Average GPA: N/R	Fall 1997 Average GMAT: 500

Costs
Full-time tuition: $7020 per academic year
Part-time tuition: $390 per credit

St. Thomas University (continued)

GRADUATE BUSINESS PROGRAMS

Master of Business Administration (MBA) Full-time, part-time; 42-51 total credits required; 18 months to 5 years to complete program. Concentrations in accounting, health care, international business, management, sports/entertainment management.

Master of Accounting (MAcc) Full-time, part-time; 30 total credits required; 12 months to 3 years to complete program.

Master of Science in Management (MS) Full-time, part-time; 36 total credits required; 12 months to 5 years to complete program. Concentrations in human resources, management, international business, public management.

Master of Science in Sports Administration (MS) Full-time, part-time; 36 total credits required; 12 months to 5 years to complete program.

ADMISSION

Application Requirements Application form, application fee, bachelor's degree, essay, minimum GPA, interview, 2 letters of recommendation, personal statement, resume, college transcript(s).

Recommended for Application GMAT score accepted, GRE score accepted, work experience.

Application Deadline Applications processed on a rolling/continuous basis for both domestic and international students. Application fee: $35. Deferred entrance is available.

ACADEMICS

Faculty Full-time 23; part-time 34.

Teaching Methodologies Case study, computer-aided instruction, field projects, group discussion, lecture, research, role playing, seminars by members of the business community, student presentations, study groups, team projects.

Technology 115 on-campus computer terminals/PCs are available for student use and are linked by a campus-wide network. The network has full access to the Internet. Students are not required to have their own PC.

Special Opportunities Advanced credit may be earned through transfer of credits from another institution. An internship program is available.

FINANCES

Costs for 1997–98 Tuition: Full-time: $7020 per year. Part-time: $390 per credit. Cost varies by number of credits taken. Fees: Full-time: $70 per academic year. Part-time: $70 per year. Average 1997–98 room and board costs were $5400 per academic year. Room and board costs vary by occupancy (e.g., single, double, triple), type of meal plan.

Financial Aid Scholarships, work study, loans available. Financial aid is available to part-time students. Application Deadline: 4/15.

Financial Aid Contact Ms. Patricia Bisciotti, Acting Director of Financial Aid, 16400 Northeast 32nd Avenue, Miami, FL 33054-6459.

FACILITIES

Information Resources Main library; total holdings of 140,000 volumes, 190,000 microforms, 990 current periodical subscriptions. Access provided to online bibliographic retrieval services.

INTERNATIONAL STUDENTS

Demographics 9% of students enrolled are international students [Africa, 4%, Asia, 4%, Central America, 32%, Europe, 24%, North America, 16%, South America, 20%].

Services and Facilities International student office, international student housing, visa services, ESL courses, counseling/support services.

Applying TOEFL, TWE required. Financial aid is available to international students.

International Student Contact Ms. Maria A. Burke, Associate Director of Graduate Admissions, 16400 Northwest 32nd Avenue, Miami, FL 33054-6459. Phone: 305-628-6614; Fax: 305-628-6591.

PLACEMENT

Services include alumni network, career counseling/planning, career fairs, career library, career placement, electronic job bank, job interviews arranged, resume referral to employers, and resume preparation. In 1996–97, 70 organizations participated in on-campus recruiting.

Business Program(s) URL: http://www.stu.edu

Program Contact: Ms. Maria A. Burke, Associate Director of Graduate Admissions, 16400 Northwest 32nd Avenue, Miami, FL 33054-6459. Phone: 305-628-6614, 800-367-9006 (FL only), and/or 800-367-9010 (FL only); Fax: 305-628-6591.

See full description on page 974.

Schiller International University

Business Programs

Dunedin, Florida

OVERVIEW

Schiller International University is an independent-nonprofit, coed, comprehensive institution. Enrollment: 265 graduate, professional, and undergraduate students. Founded: 1964. The graduate business unit is in a suburban setting and is on a semester calendar.

HIGHLIGHTS

Enrollment Profile

Full-time: N/R	International: N/R
Part-time: N/R	Women: N/R
Total: 37	Minorities: N/R
Average Age: N/R	Average Class Size: 15
Fall 1997 Average GPA: N/R	Fall 1997 Average GMAT: N/R

Costs
Full-time tuition: $14,850 per academic year
Part-time tuition: $990 per course

Degree(s) offered in conjunction with Schiller Germany, Schiller Spain, Schiller Switzerland, Schiller United Kingdom

GRADUATE BUSINESS PROGRAMS

Master of Business Administration in International Business (MBA) Full-time, part-time; 45 total credits required; 12 to 18 months to complete program. Concentration in international business.

International Hotel and Tourism Management (MBA) Full-time, part-time; 45 total credits required; 12 to 18 months to complete program. Concentration in travel industry/tourism management.

Master of International Management in International Business (MIM) Full-time, part-time; 45 total credits required; 12 to 18 months to complete program. Concentration in international management.

Master of Arts in International Hotel and Tourism Management (MA) Full-time, part-time; 45 total credits required; 12 to 18 months to complete program. Concentration in international management.

Master of Arts in Business Communciation (MA)

MBA in Public Administration (MBA)

Master of Arts in Infomation Technology Management (MA)

ADMISSION

Application Requirements GMAT score, application form, application fee, bachelor's degree (must be in field of business), essay, college transcript(s).

Recommended for Application Minimum GPA: 3.0, resume, work experience.

Application Deadline Applications processed on a rolling/continuous basis for both domestic and international students. Application fee: $35. Deferred entrance is available.

ACADEMICS

Faculty Part-time 50.

Teaching Methodologies Case study, computer-aided instruction, field projects, group discussion, lecture, research, role playing, seminars by members of the business community, student presentations, study groups, team projects.

Technology 15 on-campus computer terminals/PCs are available for student use and are linked by a campus-wide network. The network has partial access to the Internet. Students are not required to have their own PC.

Special Opportunities Advanced credit may be earned through credit for military training programs, credit for business training programs, transfer of credits from another institution. International exchange programs in France, Germany, Spain, Switzerland, United Kingdom.

FINANCES

Costs for 1997–98 Tuition: Full-time: $14,850 per year. Part-time: $990 per course. Cost varies by campus location, number of credits taken. Average 1997–98 room and board costs were $4250 per academic year. Room and board costs vary by campus location, occupancy (e.g., single, double, triple).

Financial Aid Financial aid is available to part-time students. Application Deadline: 3/30.

Financial Aid Contact Mr. James Sutherland, Financial Aid Officer, 453 Edgewater Drive, Dunedin, FL 34698-7532. Phone: 813-736-5082 Ext. 253; Fax: 813-738-8405.

FACILITIES

Information Resources Main library; total holdings of 10,000 volumes, 100 current periodical subscriptions.

INTERNATIONAL STUDENTS

Demographics N/R

Services and Facilities International student office, international student housing, visa services, ESL courses, counseling/support services.

Applying TOEFL: minimum score of 550, proof of adequate funds required. Financial aid is available to international students.

International Student Contact Dr. Christoph Leibrecht, Director of Admissions, 453 Edgewater Drive, Dunedin, FL 34698-7532. Phone: 813-736-5082 Ext. 222; Fax: 813-734-0359.

PLACEMENT
Services include alumni network, career counseling/planning, career library, resume referral to employers, and resume preparation.

Employment Of 1996–97 graduates, 95% were employed within three months of graduation. Types of employment entered: banking, chemical industry, computer-related, financial services, government, hospitality management, information systems/technology, international trade, management, marketing, pharmaceutical.

Business Program(s) URL: http://www.schiller.edu/

Program Contact: Dr. Christoph Leibrecht, Director of Admissions, 453 Edgewater Drive, Dunedin, FL 34698-7532. Phone: 813-736-5082 Ext. 236, 800-336-4133 (FL only); Fax: 813-734-0359; E-mail: christof@campus.schiller.edu
See full description on page 980.

Stetson University

School of Business Administration

DeLand, Florida

OVERVIEW
Stetson University is an independent-nonprofit, coed, comprehensive institution. Enrollment: 3,210 graduate, professional, and undergraduate students; 790 full-time matriculated graduate/professional students; 340 part-time matriculated graduate/professional students. Founded: 1883. The graduate business unit is in a suburban setting and is on a semester calendar.

HIGHLIGHTS

Enrollment Profile
Full-time: 70
Part-time: 80
Total: 150
Average Age: 25
Fall 1997 Average GPA: 2.9

International: 7%
Women: 44%
Minorities: N/R
Average Class Size: 18
Fall 1997 Average GMAT: 540

Costs
Full-time tuition: N/R
Part-time tuition: $390 per credit hour

AACSB – The International Association for Management Education accredited

GRADUATE BUSINESS PROGRAMS
Master of Business Administration (MBA) Full-time, part-time; 30-60 total credits required; 12 months to 8 years to complete program. Concentration in finance.

Master of Accountancy (MAcc) Full-time, part-time; 30-60 total credits required; 12 months to 8 years to complete program.

Master of Business Administration/Doctor of Jurisprudence (MBA/JD) Full-time; 12 months to 8 years to complete program.

ADMISSION
Applications For fall 1997 there were 400 applications for admission. Of those applying, 175 were accepted. Of those accepted, 110 enrolled.

Application Requirements Application form, application fee, bachelor's degree, minimum GPA, 3 letters of recommendation, college transcript(s).

Recommended for Application GMAT score accepted, interview, personal statement, resume, computer experience.

Application Deadline 7/15 for fall, 12/15 for spring, 4/15 for summer, 6/15 for fall (international), 11/15 for spring (international), 3/15 for summer (international). Application fee: $25. Deferred entrance is available.

ACADEMICS
Faculty Full-time 36.

Teaching Methodologies Case study, computer-aided instruction, computer analysis, computer simulations, experiential learning, field projects, group discussion, lecture, research, role playing, seminars by members of the business community, simulations, student presentations, study groups, team projects.

Technology 60 on-campus computer terminals/PCs are available for student use and are linked by a campus-wide network. The network has full access to the Internet. Students are not required to have their own PC.

Special Opportunities Advanced credit may be earned through transfer of credits from another institution. An internship program is available.

FINANCES
Costs for 1997–98 Tuition: $390 per credit hour. Cost varies by academic program, campus location, number of credits taken. Average 1997–98 room and board costs were $6000 per academic year. Room and board costs vary by campus location, occupancy (e.g., single, double, triple), type of meal plan.

Financial Aid In 1997–98, 17% of students received some institutionally administered aid in the form of research assistantships, work study, loans. Financial aid is available to part-time students. Application Deadline: 3/15.

Financial Aid Contact Douglas Minter, Director of Student Financial Planning, 421 North Woodland Boulevard, DeLand, FL 32720-3781. Phone: 904-822-7120; Fax: 904-822-7126.

FACILITIES
Information Resources DuPont Ball Library plus 2 additional on-campus libraries; total holdings of 491,647 volumes, 131,056 microforms, 1,400 current periodical subscriptions. CD player(s) available for graduate student use. Access provided to online bibliographic retrieval services.

INTERNATIONAL STUDENTS
Demographics 7% of students enrolled are international students [Asia, 20%, Europe, 40%, South America, 60%].

Services and Facilities International student office, international student center, counseling/support services.

Applying TOEFL: minimum score of 550, proof of adequate funds, proof of health/immunizations required.

International Student Contact Dr. Frank A. DeZoort, Director, Graduate Business Programs, 421 North Woodland Boulevard, Unit 8398, DeLand, FL 32720-3374. Phone: 904-822-7410; Fax: 904-822-7413; E-mail: f.dezoort@stetson.edu

PLACEMENT
Services include alumni network, career counseling/planning, career fairs, electronic job bank, and resume preparation.

Employment Of 1996–97 graduates, 90% were employed within three months of graduation; the average starting salary was $35,000. Types of employment entered: accounting, banking, computer-related, consulting, finance, financial services, government, health services, hospitality management, human resources, information systems/technology, insurance, international trade, law, management, manufacturing, marketing, nonprofit, retail.

Program Contact: Dr. Frank A. DeZoort, Director, Graduate Business Programs, 421 North Woodland Boulevard, Unit 8398, DeLand, FL 32720-3774. Phone: 904-822-7410; Fax: 904-822-7407.

University of Central Florida

College of Business Administration

Orlando, Florida

OVERVIEW
The University of Central Florida is a state-supported, coed university. Enrollment: 25,978 graduate, professional, and undergraduate students. Founded: 1963. The graduate business unit is in a suburban setting and is on a semester calendar.

HIGHLIGHTS

Enrollment Profile
Full-time: 0
Part-time: 698
Total: 698
Average Age: 30
Fall 1997 Average GPA: 3.4

International: 17%
Women: 44%
Minorities: 7%
Average Class Size: 30
Fall 1997 Average GMAT: 535

Costs
Full-time tuition: N/R
Part-time tuition: $130 per hour (resident); $434 per hour (nonresident)

AACSB – The International Association for Management Education accredited

University of Central Florida (continued)

GRADUATE BUSINESS PROGRAMS
Master of Business Administration (MBA) Part-time; 33 total credits required; 12 months to 3 years to complete program. Concentrations in entrepreneurship, finance, international and area business studies, management information systems, marketing, real estate, travel industry/tourism management.

Master of Arts in Applied Economics (MA) Part-time; 33 total credits required; 12 months to 3 years to complete program.

Master of Science in Accounting (MS) Part-time; 30 total credits required; 12 months to 2 years to complete program.

Master of Science in Taxation (MS) Part-time; 30 total credits required; 12 months to 2 years to complete program.

Executive MBA (EMBA) Part-time; 33 total credits required; 16 months to complete program.

ADMISSION
Applications For fall 1997 there were 327 applications for admission. Of those applying, 206 were accepted. Of those accepted, 164 enrolled.

Application Requirements GMAT score: minimum 500, application form, application fee, bachelor's degree, essay, minimum GPA: 3.0, 3 letters of recommendation, resume, college transcript(s).

Recommended for Application Work experience, computer experience.

Application Deadline 6/15 for fall, 11/1 for spring, 3/15 for summer, 3/1 for fall (international), 8/1 for spring (international), 12/1 for summer (international). Application fee: $20.

ACADEMICS
Faculty Full-time 58.

Teaching Methodologies Case study, computer-aided instruction, computer analysis, computer simulations, experiential learning, faculty seminars, field projects, group discussion, lecture, research, role playing, seminars by members of the business community, simulations, student presentations, study groups, team projects.

Technology 550 on-campus computer terminals/PCs are available for student use and are linked by a campus-wide network. The network has full access to the Internet. Students are not required to have their own PC.

Special Opportunities Advanced credit may be earned through transfer of credits from another institution. An internship program is available.

FINANCES
Costs for 1997–98 Tuition: Part-time: $130 per hour (resident); $434 per hour (nonresident). Average 1997–98 room and board costs were $3500 per academic year. Room and board costs vary by occupancy (e.g., single, double, triple), type of accommodation, type of meal plan.

Financial Aid Research assistantships, teaching assistantships, work study, loans available. Financial aid is available to part-time students.

Financial Aid Contact Ms. Mary McKinney, Director, Financial Aid Office, PO Box 25000, AD 120, Orlando, FL 32816. Phone: 407-823-2827; E-mail: mckinney@ucf1vm.cc.ucf.edu

FACILITIES
Information Resources University of Central Florida Library; total holdings of 864,415 volumes, 1,191,233 microforms, 4,981 current periodical subscriptions. CD player(s) available for graduate student use. Access provided to online bibliographic retrieval services.

INTERNATIONAL STUDENTS
Demographics 17% of students enrolled are international students [Asia, 40%, Europe, 15%, North America, 10%, South America, 20%, other, 15%].

Services and Facilities International student office, international student center, visa services, ESL courses, counseling/support services.

Applying TOEFL: minimum score of 575, proof of adequate funds, proof of health/immunizations required. Financial aid is not available to international students.

International Student Contact Director, International Student Services, PO Box 25000, Ying International Center, Orlando, FL 32816. Phone: 407-823-2337; Fax: 407-823-2526.

PLACEMENT
Services include alumni network, career counseling/planning, career fairs, career library, career placement, electronic job bank, job interviews arranged, resume referral to employers, and resume preparation.

Business Program(s) URL: http://www.bus.ucf.edu

Program Contact: Ms. Stacey Bush, Graduate Admissions, PO Box 25000, Orlando, FL 32816. Phone: 407-823-5693; Fax: 407-823-6442; E-mail: sbush@mail.ucf.edu

University of Florida

Warrington College of Business Administration
Gainesville, Florida

OVERVIEW
The University of Florida is a state-supported, coed university. Enrollment: 41,713 graduate, professional, and undergraduate students; 7,322 full-time matriculated graduate/professional students; 2,856 part-time matriculated graduate/professional students. Founded: 1853. The graduate business unit is in a small-town setting and is on a semester calendar.

HIGHLIGHTS

Enrollment Profile

Full-time: 302	International: 13%
Part-time: 0	Women: 24%
Total: 302	Minorities: 13%
Average Age: 27	Average Class Size: 25
Fall 1997 Average GPA: 3.21	Fall 1997 Average GMAT: 605

Costs
Full-time tuition: $3354 per academic year (resident); $11,294 per academic year (nonresident)
Part-time tuition: $129 per hour (resident); $434 per hour (nonresident)

AACSB – The International Association for Management Education accredited

Degree(s) offered in conjunction with Vanderbilt University

For more than 50 years, the University of Florida has developed successful leaders and managers for a challenging business environment. That commitment will be carried into the next century with renewed ambition, focus, and spirit.

The Florida M.B.A. is consistently rated a "best buy" in business education. The combination of a nationally ranked program, high quality of life, and low cost of attendance offers tremendous value. Continuous refinement of the programs strengthens the value of the degree.

Innovative new programs and a modular curriculum provide greater flexibility and accessibility. With nearly 50 degree options, concentrations, and international exchanges, students can customize their learning experience. The Florida M.B.A. degree is available to full-time, in-residence students as well as working professionals. The latest creation, the Internet-Based Flexible Program, incorporates leading-edge technology, periodic classroom interaction, and a European trip to deliver a fully accredited, high-caliber degree via distance education.

The Florida M.B.A. programs integrate distinguished faculty members, talented students, a dedicated staff, and successful alumni to form a cooperative, team-oriented, and supportive community. Leading researchers and high-quality teachers provide a solid academic foundation. Small class sizes, a low student-faculty ratio, and expanded program staff ensure that individual needs are met throughout the M.B.A. experience. Qualified candidates are invited to explore these exciting opportunities with the Florida M.B.A. programs.

GRADUATE BUSINESS PROGRAMS
Traditional MBA (MBA) Full-time; 48 total credits required; 2 years to complete program. Concentrations in decision sciences, entrepreneurship, finance, human resources, information management, management, marketing, operations management, real estate, technology management, arts administration/management, international and area business studies, sports/entertainment management, public policy and administration.

Executive MBA (MBA) Full-time; 48 total credits required; 20 months to complete program. Concentration in management.

Master of Business Administration/Master of Science in Business and Biotechnology (MBA/MS) Full-time; 68 total credits required; 2 to 6 years to complete program.

Master of Business Administration/Master of Hospital Administration (MBA/MHS) Full-time; 69 total credits required; 2 to 3 years to complete program.

Master of Business Administration/Doctor of Jurisprudence (MBA/JD) Full-time; 124 total credits required; 3.5 to 4 years to complete program.

Accelerated MBA (MBA) Full-time; 32 total credits required; 11 months to complete program. Concentrations in arts administration/management, decision sciences, entrepreneurship, finance, human resources, information management, international and area business studies, management, marketing, operations management, real estate, sports/entertainment management, technology management, public policy and administration.

Master of Business Administration/Doctor of Pharmacy (MBA/PharmD) Full-time; 164 total credits required; 2 to 6 years to complete program.

FLORIDA

Managers MBA (MBA) Full-time; 32 total credits required; 12 months to complete program. Concentration in management.

Flexible MBA (MBA) Full-time, distance learning option; 48 total credits required; 20 months to complete program. Concentration in management.

Weekend MBA (MBA) Part-time; 48 total credits required; 2.5 years to complete program. Concentration in management.

Master of Business Administration/Master of Exercise Sport Science (MBA/MESS) Full-time; 66 total credits required; 2 to 3 years to complete program.

Master of Business Administration/Bachelor of Science in Industrial and Systems Engineering (MBA/BSISE) 152 total credits required; 2 to 6 years to complete program.

ADMISSION
Applications For fall 1997 there were 507 applications for admission. Of those applying, 200 were accepted. Of those accepted, 122 enrolled.

Application Requirements Application form, application fee, bachelor's degree, essay, interview, letters of recommendation, resume, college transcript(s), work experience.

Recommended for Application GMAT score accepted: minimum 500, minimum GPA: 3.0, computer experience.

Application Deadline Applications processed on a rolling/continuous basis for both domestic and international students. Application fee: $20. Deferred entrance is available.

ACADEMICS
Faculty Full-time 90.

Teaching Methodologies Case study, computer-aided instruction, computer analysis, computer simulations, experiential learning, group discussion, lecture, research, role playing, seminars by members of the business community, simulations, student presentations, study groups, team projects.

Technology 40 on-campus computer terminals/PCs are available for student use and are linked by a campus-wide network. The network has full access to the Internet. Students are required to have their own PC.

Special Opportunities International exchange programs in Denmark, Finland, France, Germany, Hong Kong, Italy, Netherlands, Norway, Spain, United Kingdom, Venezuela.

FINANCES
Costs for 1997–98 Tuition: Full-time: $3354 per year (resident); $11,294 per year (nonresident). Part-time: $129 per hour (resident); $434 per hour (nonresident). Cost varies by number of credits taken. Average 1997–98 room and board costs were $2960 per academic year (on campus) and $5000 per academic year (off campus). Room and board costs vary by occupancy (e.g., single, double, triple), type of accommodation, type of meal plan.

Financial Aid Fellowships, research assistantships, teaching assistantships, work study, loans available. Financial aid is available to part-time students. Application Deadline: 3/16.

Financial Aid Contact Office for Student Financial Affairs, P.O. Box 114025, S107 Criser Hall, Gainesville, FL 32611-4025. Phone: 352-392-1275; Fax: 352-392-2861.

FACILITIES
Information Resources George A. Smathers Libraries plus 8 additional on-campus libraries; total holdings of 3,000,000 volumes, 4,200,000 microforms. CD player(s) available for graduate student use. Access provided to online bibliographic retrieval services.

INTERNATIONAL STUDENTS
Demographics 13% of students enrolled are international students [Asia, 58%, Australia/New Zealand, 2%, Central America, 10%, North America, 2%, South America, 13%, other, 15%].

Services and Facilities International student office, international student center.

Applying TOEFL: minimum score of 550, proof of adequate funds, proof of health/immunizations required. Financial aid is not available to international students.

International Student Contact Mr. Brian Ray, Director, Student Services, 134 Bryan Hall, PO Box 117152, Gainesville, FL 32611-7152. Phone: 352-392-7992; Fax: 352-392-8791; E-mail: bray@notes.cba.ufl.edu

PLACEMENT
Services include alumni network, career counseling/planning, career fairs, career library, career placement, electronic job bank, job interviews arranged, job search course, resume referral to employers, and resume preparation. In 1996–97, 176 organizations participated in on-campus recruiting; 460 on-campus interviews were conducted.

Employment Of 1996–97 graduates, 95% were employed within three months of graduation; the average starting salary was $53,517. Types of employment entered: banking, chemical industry, communications, computer-related, consulting, consumer products, engineering, finance, financial services, government, health services, high technology, human resources, information systems/technology, insurance, international trade, law, management, manufacturing, marketing, media, nonprofit, pharmaceutical, real estate, retail, service industry, telecommunications, transportation, utilities.

Business Program(s) URL: http://www.cba.ufl.edu/mba

Program Contact: Mr. Todd Reale, Director, Admissions and Marketing, 134 Bryan Hall, Box 117152, Gainesville, FL 32611-7152. Phone: 352-392-7992; Fax: 352-392-8791; E-mail: treale@notes.cba.ufl.edu

See full description on page 1070.

University of Miami

School of Business Administration
Coral Gables, Florida

OVERVIEW
The University of Miami is an independent-nonprofit, coed university. Enrollment: 13,651 graduate, professional, and undergraduate students; 4,458 full-time matriculated graduate/professional students; 798 part-time matriculated graduate/professional students. Founded: 1925. The graduate business unit is in a suburban setting and is on a semester calendar.

HIGHLIGHTS

Enrollment Profile
Full-time: 858	International: 14%
Part-time: 101	Women: 40%
Total: 959	Minorities: 10%
Average Age: 25	Average Class Size: 20
Fall 1997 Average GPA: 3.1	Fall 1997 Average GMAT: 601

Costs
Full-time tuition: N/R
Part-time tuition: $815 per credit

AACSB – The International Association for Management Education accredited

GRADUATE BUSINESS PROGRAMS
MBA Track I or II (MBA) Full-time, part-time; 36-58 total credits required; 12 months to 6 years to complete program. Concentrations in accounting, economics, finance, human resources, international business, management, management information systems, management science, marketing, quality management, strategic management, taxation, financial management/planning, public policy and administration, business law, leadership, telecommunications management, logistics.

Executive MBA (MBA) Full-time; 51 total credits required; 23 months to complete program. Concentrations in international business, management.

Master of Professional Accountancy (MPA) Full-time, part-time; 30 total credits required; 12 months to 6 years to complete program.

Master of Science in Computer Information Systems (MS) Full-time, part-time; 30 total credits required; 12 months to 6 years to complete program.

Master of Science in Taxation (MS) Full-time, part-time; 30 total credits required; 12 months to 6 years to complete program.

Master of Arts in Economics (MA) Full-time, part-time; 30 total credits required; 12 months to 6 years to complete program.

Master of Science in Management Science (MS) Full-time, part-time; 30 total credits required; 12 months to 6 years to complete program. Concentration in quality management.

Master of Public Administration (MPA) Full-time, part-time; 36-48 total credits required; 12 months to 6 years to complete program.

Master of Business Administration/Doctor of Jurisprudence (MBA/JD) Full-time; 142 total credits required; 3 to 6 years to complete program.

Master of Business Administration/Master of Science in Industrial Engineering (MBA/MS) Full-time; 63 total credits required; 2.1 years to complete program.

ADMISSION
Applications For fall 1997 there were 749 applications for admission. Of those applying, 271 were accepted. Of those accepted, 149 enrolled.

Application Requirements Application form, application fee, bachelor's degree, essay, minimum GPA: 3.0, resume, college transcript(s).

Recommended for Application GMAT score accepted, GRE score accepted: minimum 1,000.

Application Deadline Applications processed on a rolling/continuous basis for both domestic and international students. Application fee: $35. Deferred entrance is available.

ACADEMICS
Faculty Full-time 119; part-time 70.

Peterson's Guide to MBA Programs 1999

183

University of Miami (continued)

Teaching Methodologies Case study, group discussion, lecture, seminars by members of the business community, student presentations, study groups, team projects.

Technology 150 on-campus computer terminals/PCs are available for student use and are linked by a campus-wide network. The network has full access to the Internet. Students are not required to have their own PC.

Special Opportunities Advanced credit may be earned through transfer of credits from another institution. An internship program is available.

FINANCES

Costs for 1997–98 Tuition: $815 per credit. Fees: $87 per semester. Fees vary by number of credits taken. Average 1997–98 room and board costs were $8320 per academic year. Room and board costs vary by occupancy (e.g., single, double, triple), type of accommodation, type of meal plan.

Financial Aid In 1997–98, 9% of students received some institutionally administered aid in the form of fellowships, research assistantships, work study, loans. Application Deadline: 3/1.

Financial Aid Contact Mr. Martin Carney, Director, Financial Assistance Services, PO Box 248187, Coral Gables, FL 33124-5240. Phone: 305-284-5212; Fax: 305-284-4082; E-mail: ofas@umiamivm.ir.miami.edu

FACILITIES

Information Resources Otto G. Richter Library plus 6 additional on-campus libraries; total holdings of 2,080,000 volumes, 3,100,000 microforms, 19,600 current periodical subscriptions. CD player(s) available for graduate student use. Access provided to online bibliographic retrieval services.

INTERNATIONAL STUDENTS

Demographics 14% of students enrolled are international students.

Services and Facilities International student office, international student center, ESL courses, counseling/support services.

Applying TOEFL: minimum score of 550, proof of adequate funds, proof of health/immunizations required. Financial aid is available to international students.

International Student Contact Ms. Teresa De la Guardia, Director, International Student Services, Building 21-F, Coral Gables, FL 33124-5550. Phone: 305-284-2928; Fax: 305-284-3409; E-mail: tdelagua@umiamivm.ir.miami.edu

PLACEMENT

Services include alumni network, career counseling/planning, career fairs, career library, career placement, electronic job bank, job interviews arranged, resume referral to employers, and resume preparation. In 1996–97, 94 organizations participated in on-campus recruiting; 687 on-campus interviews were conducted.

Employment Of 1996–97 graduates, 64% were employed within three months of graduation; the average starting salary was $50,500. Types of employment entered: accounting, banking, communications, computer-related, consulting, consumer products, finance, financial services, health services, high technology, human resources, information systems/technology, international trade, management, manufacturing, marketing, pharmaceutical, retail, service industry, telecommunications, transportation.

Business Program(s) URL: http://www.bus.miami.edu/grad

Program Contact: Ms. Dierdre Lacativa, Director, Graduate Business Recruiting and Admissions, PO Box 248505, Coral Gables, FL 33124-6524. Phone: 305-284-2510, 800-531-7137; Fax: 305-284-1878; E-mail: dlacativa@exchange.sba.miami.edu

See full description on page 1098.

University of North Florida

College of Business Administration

Jacksonville, Florida

OVERVIEW

The University of North Florida is a state-supported, coed, comprehensive institution. Enrollment: 11,000 graduate, professional, and undergraduate students; 354 full-time matriculated graduate/professional students; 1,183 part-time matriculated graduate/professional students. Founded: 1965. The graduate business unit is in an urban setting and is on a semester calendar.

HIGHLIGHTS

Enrollment Profile

Full-time: 136	International: 9%
Part-time: 413	Women: 43%
Total: 549	Minorities: 14%
Average Age: 28	Average Class Size: 30
Fall 1997 Average GPA: 2.95	Fall 1997 Average GMAT: 520

Costs

Full-time tuition: $2124 per academic year (resident); $7020 per academic year (nonresident)

Part-time tuition: $118 per semester hour (resident); $390 per semester hour (nonresident)

AACSB – The International Association for Management Education accredited

GRADUATE BUSINESS PROGRAMS

Master of Business Administration (MBA) Full-time, part-time; 64 total credits required; 12 months to 5 years to complete program. Concentrations in accounting, economics, finance, human resources, logistics, management, marketing.

Master of Accountancy (MAcc) Full-time, part-time; 66 total credits required; 12 months to 5 years to complete program. Concentrations in accounting, taxation.

Master of Human Resource Management (MHRM) Full-time, part-time; 66 total credits required; 12 months to 5 years to complete program. Concentrations in human resources, industrial/labor relations.

ADMISSION

Applications For fall 1997 there were 211 applications for admission. Of those applying, 143 were accepted. Of those accepted, 121 enrolled.

Application Requirements GMAT score, application form, application fee, bachelor's degree, minimum GPA, college transcript(s), computer experience: spreadsheet, word processing.

Application Deadline Applications processed on a rolling/continuous basis for both domestic and international students. Application fee: $20. Deferred entrance is available.

ACADEMICS

Faculty Full-time 51; part-time 7.

Teaching Methodologies Case study, computer-aided instruction, computer analysis, field projects, group discussion, lecture, student presentations, study groups, team projects.

Technology 91 on-campus computer terminals/PCs are available for student use and are linked by a campus-wide network. The network has full access to the Internet. Students are required to have their own PC.

Special Opportunities Advanced credit may be earned through transfer of credits from another institution.

FINANCES

Costs for 1997–98 Tuition: Full-time: $2124 per year (resident); $7020 per year (nonresident). Part-time: $118 per semester hour (resident); $390 per semester hour (nonresident). Average 1997–98 room and board costs were $4800 per academic year (on campus) and $6000 per academic year (off campus). Room and board costs vary by occupancy (e.g., single, double, triple), type of accommodation, type of meal plan.

Financial Aid Fellowships, work study available. Financial aid is available to part-time students. Application Deadline: 3/15.

Financial Aid Contact Ms. Janice Nowak, Director, Financial Aid, 4567 St. Johns Bluff Road South, Jacksonville, FL 32224-2645. Phone: 904-620-2604; Fax: 904-620-2594; E-mail: jnowak@unf.edu

FACILITIES

Information Resources Thomas G. Carpenter Library; total holdings of 661,000 volumes, 1,200,000 microforms, 3,000 current periodical subscriptions. CD player(s) available for graduate student use. Access provided to online bibliographic retrieval services and online databases.

INTERNATIONAL STUDENTS

Demographics 9% of students enrolled are international students [Africa, 4%, Asia, 58%, Central America, 6%, Europe, 20%, North America, 4%, South America, 8%].

Services and Facilities International student office, international student housing, visa services, ESL courses, counseling/support services.

Applying TOEFL: minimum score of 500, proof of adequate funds, proof of health/immunizations required. Financial aid is not available to international students.

International Student Contact Ms. Nancy Messer, Coordinator, International Student Affairs, 4567 St. Johns Bluff Road South, Jacksonville, FL 32224-2645. Phone: 904-626-2768; Fax: 904-620-3525; E-mail: nmesser@unf.edu

PLACEMENT

Services include alumni network, career counseling/planning, career fairs, career library, career placement, electronic job bank, job interviews arranged, resume referral to employers, and resume preparation. In 1996–97, 700 organizations participated in on-campus recruiting; 1,600 on-campus interviews were conducted.

Employment Of 1996–97 graduates, 95% were employed within three months of graduation. Types of employment entered: accounting, banking, computer-related, energy, finance, financial services, health services, hospitality management, human resources, insurance, marketing, real estate, service industry, transportation, utilities.

Business Program(s) URL: http://www.unf.edu/coba/

Program Contact: Dr. Donald Graham, Graduate Advisor, College of Business Administration, 4567 St. Johns Bluff Road South, Jacksonville, FL 32224-2645. Phone: 904-620-2575; Fax: 904-620-2594; E-mail: unfmba@unf.edu

University of Sarasota

College of Business Administration

Sarasota, Florida

OVERVIEW

The University of Sarasota is an independent-nonprofit, coed, graduate institution. Enrollment: 1,350 graduate, professional, and undergraduate students. Founded: 1974. The graduate business unit is in a suburban setting and is on a semester calendar.

HIGHLIGHTS

Enrollment Profile

Full-time: 310	International: 10%
Part-time: 0	Women: 40%
Total: 310	Minorities: N/R
Average Age: 43	Average Class Size: 13
Fall 1997 Average GPA: 3.6	Fall 1997 Average GMAT: N/R

Costs
Full-time tuition: $9531 per academic year
Part-time tuition: $353 per credit hour

GRADUATE BUSINESS PROGRAMS

Master of Business Administration (MBA) Full-time, part-time, distance learning option; 45 total credits required; 12 months to 3 years to complete program. Concentrations in finance, human resources, international trade, marketing, health care.

Doctor of Business Administration (DBA) Full-time, part-time, distance learning option; 60 total credits required; 2 to 4 years to complete program. Concentrations in management information systems, management, international business, marketing, finance, accounting.

ADMISSION

Application Requirements Application form, application fee, bachelor's degree, essay, minimum GPA: 3.0, 3 letters of recommendation, personal statement, resume, college transcript(s), computer experience: computer literacy.

Recommended for Application Interview, work experience.

Application Deadline Applications processed on a rolling/continuous basis for both domestic and international students. Application fee: $50.

ACADEMICS

Faculty Full-time 5; part-time 5.

Teaching Methodologies Case study, computer analysis, computer simulations, experiential learning, group discussion, lecture, seminars by members of the business community, student presentations, team projects.

Technology 15 on-campus computer terminals/PCs are available for student use. The network does not have Internet access. Students are not required to have their own PC.

Special Opportunities Advanced credit may be earned through transfer of credits from another institution. An internship program is available.

FINANCES

Costs for 1997–98 Tuition: Full-time: $9531 per 9 courses. Part-time: $353 per credit hour. Cost varies by academic program. Fees: $11 per course. Average 1997–98 room and board costs were $9600 per academic year (off campus).

Financial Aid In 1997–98, 19% of students received some institutionally administered aid in the form of loans. Financial aid is available to part-time students.

Financial Aid Contact Diane Gifford, Admissions Director, 5250 17th Street, Sarasota, FL 34235-8242. Phone: 941-379-0404; Fax: 941-379-9464; E-mail: 102556.2652@compuserv.com

FACILITIES

Information Resources Main library; total holdings of 5,000 volumes, 100 current periodical subscriptions. CD player(s) available for graduate student use. Access provided to online bibliographic retrieval services.

INTERNATIONAL STUDENTS

Demographics 10% of students enrolled are international students.

Services and Facilities International student office, visa services, counseling/support services.

Applying TOEFL: minimum score of 500, proof of adequate funds required. Proof of health/immunizations recommended. Financial aid is not available to international students.

International Student Contact Dr. Gordana Pesakovic, International Student Coordinator, 5250 17th Street, Sarasota, FL 34235-8242. Phone: 941-379-0404 Ext. 251; Fax: 941-379-9464; E-mail: 102556.2652@compuserve.com

PLACEMENT

Services include alumni network, and electronic job bank.

Employment Types of employment entered: accounting, banking, communications, consulting, consumer products, financial services, health services, hospitality management, human resources, international trade, management, manufacturing, marketing, retail, service industry.

Business Program(s) URL: http://www.sarasota.edu

Program Contact: Dr. Carol Todd, Admissions Director, 5250 17th Street, Sarasota, FL 34235-8242. Phone: 941-379-0404 Ext. 251, 800-331-5995 (FL only); Fax: 941-379-9464; E-mail: 102556.2652@compuserve.com

University of South Florida

College of Business Administration

Tampa, Florida

OVERVIEW

The University of South Florida is a state-supported, coed university. Enrollment: 34,066 graduate, professional, and undergraduate students; 2,714 full-time matriculated graduate/professional students; 3,606 part-time matriculated graduate/professional students. Founded: 1956. The graduate business unit is in an urban setting and is on a semester calendar.

HIGHLIGHTS

Enrollment Profile

Full-time: 400	International: 13%
Part-time: 556	Women: 40%
Total: 956	Minorities: 9%
Average Age: 32	Average Class Size: 30
Fall 1997 Average GPA: 3.2	Fall 1997 Average GMAT: 542

Costs
Full-time tuition: N/R
Part-time tuition: $134 per credit hour (resident); $440 per credit hour (nonresident)

AACSB – The International Association for Management Education accredited

GRADUATE BUSINESS PROGRAMS

Master of Business Administration (MBA) Full-time, part-time; 36-57 total credits required; 12 months to 5 years to complete program. Concentrations in entrepreneurship, finance, health care, international business, management, management information systems, marketing, quality management.

Executive MBA (MBA) Full-time; 57 total credits required; 8 years work experience required; 20 months to complete program.

MBA Program for Physicians (MBA) Full-time; 57 total credits required; 21 months to complete program.

Master of Accountancy (MAcc) Full-time, part-time; 30 total credits required; minimum of 12 months to complete program. Concentrations in accounting, taxation.

Master of Arts in Economics (MA) Full-time, part-time; 30 total credits required; minimum of 12 months to complete program.

Information Systems (MS) Full-time, part-time; 32 total credits required; minimum of 12 months to complete program.

Leadership and Organizational Effectiveness (MS) Full-time, part-time; 32 total credits required; minimum of 12 months to complete program.

University of South Florida (continued)

ADMISSION

Applications For fall 1997 there were 594 applications for admission. Of those applying, 396 were accepted. Of those accepted, 215 enrolled.

Application Requirements Application form, application fee, bachelor's degree, minimum GPA: 3.0, college transcript(s).

Recommended for Application GMAT score accepted: minimum 500, GRE score accepted: minimum 1,050, computer experience.

Application Deadline 5/15 for fall, 10/15 for spring, 3/2 for fall (international), 8/3 for spring (international). Application fee: $20. Deferred entrance is available.

ACADEMICS

Faculty Full-time 108; part-time 6.

Teaching Methodologies Case study, computer analysis, experiential learning, field projects, lecture, role playing, seminars by members of the business community, student presentations, team projects.

Technology 547 on-campus computer terminals/PCs are available for student use and are linked by a campus-wide network. The network has full access to the Internet. Students are not required to have their own PC.

Special Opportunities Advanced credit may be earned through transfer of credits from another institution. International exchange programs in Brazil, Costa Rica, England, France, Mexico.

FINANCES

Costs for 1997–98 Tuition: $134 per credit hour (resident); $440 per credit hour (nonresident). Cost varies by campus location, reciprocity agreements. Average 1997–98 room and board costs were $4830 per academic year (on campus) and $7200 per academic year (off campus). Room and board costs vary by occupancy (e.g., single, double, triple), type of accommodation, type of meal plan.

Financial Aid In 1997–98, 7% of students received some institutionally administered aid in the form of fellowships, research assistantships, teaching assistantships, scholarships. Application Deadline: 3/1.

Financial Aid Contact Wendy Baker, Assistant Director of Graduate Studies, 4202 East Fowler Avenue, Tampa, FL 33620. Phone: 813-974-4516; Fax: 813-974-5530.

FACILITIES

Information Resources Main library plus 4 additional on-campus libraries; total holdings of 1,565,573 volumes, 3,763,280 microforms, 9,342 current periodical subscriptions. CD player(s) available for graduate student use. Access provided to online bibliographic retrieval services.

INTERNATIONAL STUDENTS

Demographics 13% of students enrolled are international students.

Services and Facilities International student office, international student center, visa services, ESL courses, counseling/support services.

Applying TOEFL, proof of adequate funds, proof of health/immunizations required.

International Student Contact Wendy Baker, Assistant Director of Graduate Studies, 4202 East Fowler Avenue, Tampa, FL 33620. Phone: 813-974-3335; Fax: 813-974-4518.

PLACEMENT

Services include career counseling/planning, career fairs, career placement, electronic job bank, job interviews arranged, resume referral to employers, and resume preparation. In 1996–97, 175 organizations participated in on-campus recruiting.

Employment Of 1996–97 graduates, the average starting salary was $48,800. Types of employment entered: banking, communications, computer-related, consulting, consumer products, education, finance, financial services, government, health services, high technology, information systems/technology, insurance, law, management, manufacturing, marketing, nonprofit, service industry, telecommunications, transportation, utilities.

Business Program(s) URL: http://www.coba.usf.edu

Program Contact: Wendy Baker, Assistant Director of Graduate Studies, 4202 East Fowler Avenue, Tampa, FL 33620. Phone: 813-974-4516; Fax: 813-974-4518.

The University of Tampa

College of Business

Tampa, Florida

OVERVIEW

The University of Tampa is an independent-nonprofit, coed, comprehensive institution. Enrollment: 2,896 graduate, professional, and undergraduate students; 94 full-time matriculated graduate/professional students; 468 part-time matriculated graduate/professional students. Founded: 1931. The graduate business unit is in an urban setting and is on a semester calendar.

HIGHLIGHTS

Enrollment Profile

Full-time: 90	International: 16%
Part-time: 347	Women: 45%
Total: 437	Minorities: 13%
Average Age: 31	Average Class Size: 20
Fall 1997 Average GPA: 3.275	Fall 1997 Average GMAT: 504

Costs
Full-time tuition: N/R
Part-time tuition: $305 per hour

GRADUATE BUSINESS PROGRAMS

Master of Business Administration (MBA) Full-time, part-time; 39-60 total credits required; 16 months to 7 years to complete program. Concentrations in accounting, finance, information management, international business, leadership, marketing, quality management, health care, management information systems.

ADMISSION

Applications For fall 1997 there were 196 applications for admission. Of those applying, 153 were accepted. Of those accepted, 111 enrolled.

Application Requirements Application form, application fee, bachelor's degree, minimum GPA: 2.5, 2 letters of recommendation, college transcript(s), computer experience: word processing, spreadsheet.

Recommended for Application GMAT score accepted: minimum 400, essay, interview, personal statement, resume.

Application Deadline Applications processed on a rolling/continuous basis for both domestic and international students. Application fee: $35. Deferred entrance is available.

ACADEMICS

Faculty Full-time 37; part-time 5.

Teaching Methodologies Case study, computer-aided instruction, experiential learning, field projects, group discussion, lecture, research, role playing, seminars by members of the business community, simulations, student presentations, study groups, team projects.

Technology 160 on-campus computer terminals/PCs are available for student use. The network has full access to the Internet. Students are not required to have their own PC.

Special Opportunities Advanced credit may be earned through transfer of credits from another institution. International exchange programs in France, Mexico, Netherlands, Spain, Sweden, Switzerland, United Kingdom.

FINANCES

Costs for 1997–98 Tuition: $305 per hour. Fees: Full-time: $70 per academic year. Part-time: $35 per semester. Average 1997–98 room and board costs were $6250 per academic year (on campus) and $5600 per academic year (off campus). Room and board costs vary by occupancy (e.g., single, double, triple), type of accommodation, type of meal plan.

Financial Aid In 1997–98, 37% of students received some institutionally administered aid in the form of grants, scholarships, loans. Financial aid is available to part-time students.

Financial Aid Contact Ms. JoEllen Soucier, Director, Financial Aid, Box #, 401 West Kennedy Boulevard, Tampa, FL 33606-1490. Phone: 813-253-6219; Fax: 813-258-7439; E-mail: jsoucier@alpha.utampa.edu

FACILITIES

Information Resources Merl Kelce Library; total holdings of 275,000 volumes, 50,422 microforms, 1,850 current periodical subscriptions. CD player(s) available for graduate student use. Access provided to online bibliographic retrieval services.

INTERNATIONAL STUDENTS

Demographics 16% of students enrolled are international students [Africa, 4%, Asia, 26%, Australia/New Zealand, 1%, Central America, 12%, Europe, 22%, North America, 9%, South America, 26%].

Services and Facilities International student office, ESL courses, counseling/support services.

Applying TOEFL: minimum score of 550, proof of adequate funds, proof of health/immunizations required. Financial aid is not available to international students.

International Student Contact Mrs. Sally Moorehead, Coordinator, International Student Affairs, Box 70F, 401 West Kennedy Boulevard, Tampa, FL 33606-1490. Phone: 813-258-7433 Ext. 3659.

PLACEMENT

Services include alumni network, career counseling/planning, career fairs, career library, career placement, electronic job bank, job interviews arranged, job search course, resume referral to employers, and resume preparation. In

1996–97, 80 organizations participated in on-campus recruiting; 30 on-campus interviews were conducted.

Employment Of 1996–97 graduates, 75% were employed within three months of graduation; the average starting salary was $42,500. Types of employment entered: accounting, banking, computer-related, consulting, finance, financial services, information systems/technology, management, marketing.

Business Program(s) URL: http://www.utampa.edu

Program Contact: Mr. Fernando Nolasco, Associate Director, MBA Program, Box 128-F, 401 West Kennedy Boulevard, Tampa, FL 33606-1490. Phone: 813-258-7409, 800-733-4773 (FL only); Fax: 813-259-5403; E-mail: fnolasco@alpha.utampa.edu

See full description on page 1146.

University of West Florida

College of Business

Pensacola, Florida

OVERVIEW

The University of West Florida is a state-supported, coed, comprehensive institution. Enrollment: 8,085 graduate, professional, and undergraduate students; 387 full-time matriculated graduate/professional students; 937 part-time matriculated graduate/professional students. Founded: 1963. The graduate business unit is in a suburban setting and is on a semester calendar.

HIGHLIGHTS

Enrollment Profile
Full-time: 85
Part-time: 193
Total: 278
Average Age: 32
Fall 1997 Average GPA: 3.12

International: 4%
Women: 47%
Minorities: 13%
Average Class Size: 25
Fall 1997 Average GMAT: 550

Costs
Full-time tuition: $3144 per academic year (resident); $10,473 per academic year (nonresident)
Part-time tuition: $131 per semester hour (resident); $436 per semester hour (nonresident)

AACSB – The International Association for Management Education accredited

GRADUATE BUSINESS PROGRAMS
Master of Business Administration (MBA) Full-time, part-time; 36 total credits required; minimum of 12 months to complete program. Concentrations in management, leadership, finance, marketing, accounting.

Master of Accounting (MAcc) Full-time, part-time; 30 total credits required; minimum of 12 months to complete program. Concentration in accounting.

ADMISSION
Applications For fall 1997 there were 122 applications for admission. Of those applying, 102 were accepted. Of those accepted, 72 enrolled.

Application Requirements GMAT score: minimum 450, application form, application fee, bachelor's degree, essay, interview, 2 letters of recommendation, personal statement, resume, college transcript(s).

Recommended for Application Minimum GPA, work experience, computer experience.

Application Deadline 7/1 for fall, 11/1 for spring, 4/1 for summer, 5/15 for fall (international), 10/15 for spring (international), 2/14 for summer (international). Application fee: $20. Deferred entrance is available.

ACADEMICS
Faculty Full-time 25; part-time 8.

Teaching Methodologies Case study, computer simulations, experiential learning, faculty seminars, field projects, group discussion, lecture, research, role playing, seminars by members of the business community, simulations, student presentations, study groups, team projects.

Technology 95 on-campus computer terminals/PCs are available for student use and are linked by a campus-wide network. The network has full access to the Internet. Students are not required to have their own PC.

Special Opportunities Advanced credit may be earned through transfer of credits from another institution. International exchange programs in Austria, Belgium, Canada, Finland, Germany, Japan, Mexico, Netherlands, United Kingdom.

FINANCES
Costs for 1997–98 Tuition: Full-time: $3144 per year (resident); $10,473 per year (nonresident). Part-time: $131 per semester hour (resident); $436 per semester hour (nonresident). Cost varies by campus location. Average 1997–98 room only costs were $2200 per academic year. Room and board costs vary

by occupancy (e.g., single, double, triple), type of accommodation, type of meal plan.

Financial Aid Fellowships, research assistantships, grants, scholarships, work study available. Financial aid is available to part-time students. Application Deadline: 4/1.

Financial Aid Contact Dr. C. Raymond Bennett, Director, Student Financial Aid, 11000 University Parkway, Pensacola, FL 32514-5750. Phone: 850-474-2400; Fax: 850-474-3360.

FACILITIES
Information Resources Pace Library; total holdings of 570,769 volumes, 1,061,599 microforms, 3,333 current periodical subscriptions. CD player(s) available for graduate student use. Access provided to online bibliographic retrieval services.

INTERNATIONAL STUDENTS
Demographics 4% of students enrolled are international students [Africa, 10%, Asia, 60%, Europe, 30%].

Services and Facilities International student office, visa services, ESL courses, counseling/support services.

Applying TOEFL: minimum score of 500, proof of adequate funds, proof of health/immunizations required. Financial aid is available to international students.

International Student Contact Ms. Kay Mackenzie, Assistant Director, Student Affairs, 11000 University Parkway, Pensacola, FL 32514. Phone: 850-474-2384; Fax: 850-474-3145; E-mail: 5mackenz@uwf.edu

PLACEMENT
Services include alumni network, career counseling/planning, career fairs, career library, career placement, job interviews arranged, resume referral to employers, and resume preparation. In 1996–97, 56 organizations participated in on-campus recruiting; 373 on-campus interviews were conducted.

Employment Types of employment entered: accounting, banking, chemical industry, consumer products, finance, government, health services, human resources, management, marketing, petrochemical, telecommunications, utilities.

Business Program(s) URL: http://www.uwf.edu/~enrserv/b.htm

Program Contact: Ms. Francy Dowhal, Admissions/Registrar Officer, 11000 University Parkway, Pensacola, FL 32514-5750. Phone: 850-474-2352; Fax: 850-474-3360; E-mail: fdowhal@uwf.edu

GEORGIA

Albany State University

College of Business

Albany, Georgia

OVERVIEW
Albany State University is a state-supported, coed, comprehensive institution. Enrollment: 3,062 graduate, professional, and undergraduate students; 107 full-time matriculated graduate/professional students; 214 part-time matriculated graduate/professional students. Founded: 1903. The graduate business unit is in an urban setting and is on a semester calendar.

HIGHLIGHTS

Enrollment Profile
Full-time: 22
Part-time: 42
Total: 64
Average Age: 28
Fall 1997 Average GPA: 3.0

International: 2%
Women: 61%
Minorities: 42%
Average Class Size: 15
Fall 1997 Average GMAT: 450

Costs
Full-time tuition: N/R
Part-time tuition: N/R

ACBSP – The American Council of Business Schools and Programs accredited

GRADUATE BUSINESS PROGRAMS
Master of Business Administration (MBA) Full-time, part-time, distance learning option; 36 total credits required; 18 months to 5 years to complete program.

ADMISSION
Application Requirements Application form, application fee, bachelor's degree, minimum GPA: 3.0, resume, college transcript(s), computer experience: word processing, spreadsheet, database.

Recommended for Application GMAT score accepted: minimum 450, work experience.

Application Deadline Applications processed on a rolling/continuous basis for both domestic and international students. Application fee: $10.

ACADEMICS
Faculty Full-time 10.

Teaching Methodologies Case study, computer-aided instruction, computer analysis, computer simulations, experiential learning, faculty seminars, field projects, group discussion, lecture, research, role playing, seminars by members of the business community, simulations, student presentations, study groups, team projects.

Technology 50 on-campus computer terminals/PCs are available for student use and are linked by a campus-wide network. The network has full access to the Internet. Students are not required to have their own PC.

Special Opportunities Advanced credit may be earned through transfer of credits from another institution.

FINANCES
Financial Aid Scholarships, work study available. Financial aid is available to part-time students. Application Deadline: 4/1.

Financial Aid Contact Financial Aid Office, 504 College Avenue, Albany, GA 31705. Phone: 912-430-4650.

FACILITIES
Information Resources Pendergrast Memorial Library; total holdings of 147,908 volumes, 447,284 microforms, 635 current periodical subscriptions. CD player(s) available for graduate student use. Access provided to online bibliographic retrieval services and online databases.

INTERNATIONAL STUDENTS
Demographics 2% of students enrolled are international students.

Applying TOEFL, proof of health/immunizations required. Financial aid is not available to international students.

International Student Contact Graduate School, 504 College Drive, Albany, GA 31705-2717.

PLACEMENT
Services include career placement.

Employment Types of employment entered: banking, education, finance, government, human resources, management, marketing.

Program Contact: Dr. John Kooti, MBA Coordinator, College of Business, 504 College Avenue, Albany, GA 31705. Phone: 912-430-4771; Fax: 912-430-5119.

Augusta State University

School of Business Administration

Augusta, Georgia

OVERVIEW
Augusta State University is a state-supported, coed, comprehensive institution. Enrollment: 5,510 graduate, professional, and undergraduate students; 266 full-time matriculated graduate/professional students; 487 part-time matriculated graduate/professional students. Founded: 1925. The graduate business unit is in a small-town setting and is on a trimester calendar.

HIGHLIGHTS

Enrollment Profile

Full-time: 44	International: 2%
Part-time: 37	Women: 38%
Total: 81	Minorities: 15%
Average Age: 29	Average Class Size: 20
Fall 1997 Average GPA: 2.93	Fall 1997 Average GMAT: 500

Costs
Full-time tuition: $1560 per academic year (resident); $5700 per academic year (nonresident)
Part-time tuition: $780 per year (resident); $2850 per year (nonresident)

GRADUATE BUSINESS PROGRAMS
Master of Business Administration (MBA) Full-time, part-time; 36 total credits required; 16 months to 4 years to complete program. Concentration in management.

ADMISSION
Applications For fall 1997 there were 45 applications for admission. Of those applying, 33 were accepted. Of those accepted, 25 enrolled.

Application Requirements GMAT score: minimum 450, application form, application fee, bachelor's degree, minimum GPA: 2.5, college transcript(s), computer experience: word processing, spreadsheet, database.

Recommended for Application Work experience.

Application Deadline 7/15 for fall, 12/1 for spring, 5/15 for summer, 7/1 for fall (international), 11/15 for spring (international), 5/1 for summer (international). Application fee: $10. Deferred entrance is available.

ACADEMICS
Faculty Full-time 22.

Teaching Methodologies Case study, computer analysis, computer simulations, field projects, group discussion, lecture, student presentations, team projects.

Technology 150 on-campus computer terminals/PCs are available for student use and are linked by a campus-wide network. The network has full access to the Internet. Students are not required to have their own PC.

Special Opportunities Advanced credit may be earned through transfer of credits from another institution.

FINANCES
Costs for 1997–98 Tuition: Full-time: $1560 per year (resident); $5700 per year (nonresident). Part-time: $780 per year (resident); $2850 per year (nonresident). Cost varies by number of credits taken, reciprocity agreements. Fees: Full-time: $246 per academic year (resident); $246 per academic year (nonresident). Part-time: $246 per year (resident); $246 per year (nonresident). Average 1997–98 room and board costs were $9501 per academic year (off campus).

Financial Aid Research assistantships, work study, loans available. Financial aid is available to part-time students. Application Deadline: 6/1.

Financial Aid Contact Kevin Wellwood, Director of Financial Aid, 2500 Walton Way, Augusta, GA 30904-2200. Phone: 706-737-1431; Fax: 706-737-1767.

FACILITIES
Information Resources Reese Library; total holdings of 458,503 volumes, 896,141 microforms, 2,014 current periodical subscriptions. CD player(s) available for graduate student use. Access provided to online bibliographic retrieval services.

INTERNATIONAL STUDENTS
Demographics 2% of students enrolled are international students [Europe, 100%].

Services and Facilities Counseling/support services.

Applying TOEFL: minimum score of 540, proof of adequate funds, proof of health/immunizations required. Financial aid is not available to international students.

International Student Contact Dr. Frank Chou, 2500 Walton Way, Augusta, GA 30904-2200. Phone: 706-737-4196; Fax: 706-667-4064.

PLACEMENT
Services include career counseling/planning, career fairs, career library, career placement, job interviews arranged, resume referral to employers, and resume preparation.

Employment Of 1996–97 graduates, 90% were employed within three months of graduation. Types of employment entered: accounting, banking, computer-related, consulting, education, engineering, finance, financial services, government, health services, human resources, information systems/technology, management, manufacturing, marketing, nonprofit, service industry.

Business Program(s) URL: http://www.aug.edu/school_of_business_administration/

Program Contact: Miyoko Jackson, Graduate Degree Program Specialist, School of Business Administration, 2500 Walton Way, Augusta, GA 30904-2200. Phone: 706-737-1565; Fax: 706-667-4064; E-mail: mbainfo@.aug.edu

Berry College

Campbell School of Business

Mount Berry, Georgia

OVERVIEW
Berry College is an independent-nonprofit, coed, comprehensive institution. Enrollment: 2,000 graduate, professional, and undergraduate students; 8 full-time matriculated graduate/professional students; 90 part-time matriculated

graduate/professional students. Founded: 1902. The graduate business unit is in a small-town setting and is on a semester calendar.

HIGHLIGHTS

Enrollment Profile

Full-time: 0
Part-time: 31
Total: 31
Average Age: 32
Fall 1997 Average GPA: 2.81

International: 3%
Women: 45%
Minorities: N/R
Average Class Size: 11
Fall 1997 Average GMAT: 547

Costs

Full-time tuition: N/R
Part-time tuition: $340 per credit hour

GRADUATE BUSINESS PROGRAMS

General Business MBA (MBA) Part-time; 36 total credits required; 12 months to 6 years to complete program. Concentration in management.

ADMISSION

Application Requirements Application form, application fee, bachelor's degree, minimum GPA: 2.5, letters of recommendation, college transcript(s).

Recommended for Application GMAT score accepted: minimum 500, interview, work experience.

Application Deadline 7/26 for fall, 12/6 for spring, 4/19 for summer, 2/26 for fall (international), 7/6 for spring (international), 11/19 for summer (international). Application fee: $25, $30 (international).

ACADEMICS

Faculty Part-time 10.

Teaching Methodologies Case study, computer-aided instruction, computer analysis, field projects, group discussion, lecture, role playing, seminars by members of the business community, student presentations, study groups, team projects.

Technology 50 on-campus computer terminals/PCs are available for student use and are linked by a campus-wide network. The network has full access to the Internet. Students are not required to have their own PC.

Special Opportunities Advanced credit may be earned through transfer of credits from another institution.

FINANCES

Costs for 1997–98 Tuition: Part-time: $340 per credit hour. Cost varies by number of credits taken. Average 1997–98 room only costs were $3600 per academic year (off campus). Room and board costs vary by type of accommodation.

Financial Aid Research assistantships available. Financial aid is available to part-time students.

Financial Aid Contact Mr. William Fron, Director of Financial Aid, 5007 Berry College, Mount Berry, GA 30149-5007. Phone: 706-236-2244; Fax: 706-290-2160.

FACILITIES

Information Resources Memorial Library plus 1 additional on-campus library; total holdings of 167,000 volumes, 604,000 microforms, 1,441 current periodical subscriptions. CD player(s) available for graduate student use. Access provided to online bibliographic retrieval services and online databases.

INTERNATIONAL STUDENTS

Demographics 3% of students enrolled are international students.

Services and Facilities International student office, visa services, counseling/support services.

Applying TOEFL, proof of adequate funds, proof of health/immunizations required. Financial aid is not available to international students.

International Student Contact Dr. Carol Willis, Associate Dean of Students, 159 Mount Berry Station, Mount Berry, GA 30149-0159. Phone: 706-236-2207; Fax: 706-290-2649; E-mail: cwillis@berry.edu

PLACEMENT

Services include alumni network, career counseling/planning, career fairs, career placement, job interviews arranged, resume referral to employers, and resume preparation. In 1996–97, 116 organizations participated in on-campus recruiting; 28 on-campus interviews were conducted.

Employment Of 1996–97 graduates, 60% were employed within three months of graduation. Types of employment entered: accounting, banking, communications, computer-related, consumer products, education, finance, financial services, government, hospitality management, human resources, information systems/technology, insurance, management, manufacturing, marketing, media, nonprofit, pharmaceutical, retail, service industry, telecommunications.

Business Program(s) URL: http://www.campbell.berry.edu

Program Contact: Mrs. Madalyn McLeod, Secretary for Graduate Studies in Business, Campbell School of Business, 5024 Mount Berry Station, Mount Berry, GA 30149-5024. Phone: 706-236-1751, 800-BERRYGA; Fax: 706-238-7926.

Brenau University

Department of Business Administration

Gainesville, Georgia

OVERVIEW

Brenau University is an independent-nonprofit, coed, comprehensive institution. Enrollment: 2,241 graduate, professional, and undergraduate students; 378 full-time matriculated graduate/professional students; 411 part-time matriculated graduate/professional students. Founded: 1878. The graduate business unit is in a small-town setting and is on a semester calendar.

GRADUATE BUSINESS PROGRAMS

Master of Business Administration (MBA)

ACADEMICS

Faculty Full-time 11; part-time 40.

Teaching Methodologies Case study, computer-aided instruction, computer analysis, computer simulations, field projects, group discussion, lecture, research, role playing, seminars by members of the business community, simulations, student presentations, study groups, team projects.

Technology 100 on-campus computer terminals/PCs are available for student use and are linked by a campus-wide network. The network has full access to the Internet.

FACILITIES

Information Resources Brenau Trustee Library; total holdings of 86,217 volumes, 190,457 microforms, 1,190 current periodical subscriptions. CD player(s) available for graduate student use. Access provided to online bibliographic retrieval services.

Program Contact: Director of Graduate Admissions, One Centennial Circle, Gainesville, GA 30501. Phone: 770-534-6162; Fax: 770-538-4306.

Clark Atlanta University

School of Business Administration

Atlanta, Georgia

OVERVIEW

Clark Atlanta University is an independent-religious, coed university. Enrollment: 5,616 graduate, professional, and undergraduate students; 765 full-time matriculated graduate/professional students; 652 part-time matriculated graduate/professional students. Founded: 1865. The graduate business unit is in an urban setting and is on a semester calendar.

HIGHLIGHTS

Enrollment Profile

Full-time: 130
Part-time: 10
Total: 140
Average Age: 28
Fall 1997 Average GPA: 2.89

International: 4%
Women: 60%
Minorities: 96%
Average Class Size: 70
Fall 1997 Average GMAT: N/R

Costs

Full-time tuition: $11,460 per academic year
Part-time tuition: $382 per credit

AACSB – The International Association for Management Education accredited

GRADUATE BUSINESS PROGRAMS

Master of Business Administration (MBA) Full-time, part-time; 60 total credits required; 21 months to 5 years to complete program. Concentrations in decision sciences, finance, marketing, health care.

ADMISSION

Applications For fall 1997 there were 300 applications for admission. Of those applying, 117 were accepted. Of those accepted, 65 enrolled.

Application Requirements GMAT score, application form, application fee, bachelor's degree, essay, minimum GPA, 3 letters of recommendation, resume, college transcript(s).

Recommended for Application Work experience, computer experience.

Application Deadline 4/1 for fall. Application fee: $40, $55 (international). Deferred entrance is available.

ACADEMICS

Faculty Full-time 22; part-time 3.

Teaching Methodologies Case study, computer-aided instruction, computer simulations, experiential learning, faculty seminars, field projects, group discus-

GEORGIA

Clark Atlanta University (continued)

sion, lecture, research, seminars by members of the business community, student presentations, study groups, team projects.

Technology The network has full access to the Internet. Students are not required to have their own PC.

Special Opportunities Advanced credit may be earned through transfer of credits from another institution.

FINANCES
Costs for 1997–98 Tuition: Full-time: $11,460 per year. Part-time: $382 per credit. Fees: Full-time: $100 per academic year. Part-time: $100 per year. Average 1997–98 room and board costs were $4500 per academic year (on campus) and $6750 per academic year (off campus). Room and board costs vary by occupancy (e.g., single, double, triple), type of accommodation, type of meal plan.

Financial Aid In 1997–98, 13% of students received some institutionally administered aid in the form of scholarships, work study. Application Deadline: 4/1.

Financial Aid Contact Ms. Cele Echols, Director of Admissions and Financial Aid, James P. Brawley Drive, Atlanta, GA 30314. Phone: 404-880-8479; Fax: 404-880-6159.

FACILITIES
Information Resources Robert W. Woodruff Library plus 3 additional on-campus libraries; total holdings of 346,137 volumes, 189,245 microforms, 49,481 current periodical subscriptions. CD player(s) available for graduate student use. Access provided to online bibliographic retrieval services.

INTERNATIONAL STUDENTS
Demographics 4% of students enrolled are international students [Africa, 26%, Europe, 8%, South America, 8%, other, 58%].

Services and Facilities International student office, international student center, visa services, counseling/support services.

Applying TOEFL: minimum score of 500, proof of adequate funds, proof of health/immunizations required. Financial aid is available to international students.

International Student Contact Mr. Calvin Macklin, Program Coordinator, International Student Services, James P. Brawley Drive at Fair Street, SW, Atlanta, GA 30314. Phone: 404-880-8884; Fax: 404-880-8625.

PLACEMENT
Services include alumni network, career counseling/planning, career fairs, career library, career placement, job interviews arranged, job search course, resume referral to employers, and resume preparation. In 1996–97, 45 organizations participated in on-campus recruiting; 1,110 on-campus interviews were conducted.

Employment Of 1996–97 graduates, 89% were employed within three months of graduation; the average starting salary was $59,025. Types of employment entered: accounting, banking, communications, computer-related, consulting, consumer products, energy, finance, financial services, health services, hospitality management, human resources, law, marketing, nonprofit, pharmaceutical, service industry, telecommunications, transportation, utilities.

Business Program(s) URL: http://www.cau.edu/cau/ctsps.html

Program Contact: Ms. Cele Echols, Director of Admissions and Financial Aid, James P. Brawley Drive at Fair Street, SW, Atlanta, GA 30314. Phone: 404-880-8479; Fax: 404-880-6159.

Columbus State University

Abbott Turner College of Business
Columbus, Georgia

OVERVIEW
Columbus State University is a state-supported, coed, comprehensive institution. Enrollment: 5,405 graduate, professional, and undergraduate students; 377 full-time matriculated graduate/professional students; 444 part-time matriculated graduate/professional students. Founded: 1958. The graduate business unit is in an urban setting and is on a semester calendar.

HIGHLIGHTS

Enrollment Profile
Full-time: 43
Part-time: 29
Total: 72
Average Age: N/R
Fall 1997 Average GPA: N/R
International: N/R
Women: N/R
Minorities: N/R
Average Class Size: N/R
Fall 1997 Average GMAT: N/R

Costs
Full-time tuition: N/R
Part-time tuition: $90 per quarter hour (resident); $228 per quarter hour (nonresident)

GRADUATE BUSINESS PROGRAMS
Master of Business Administration (MBA) Full-time, part-time, distance learning option; 60 total credits required; 18 months to 6 years to complete program.

ADMISSION
Application Requirements GMAT score, application form, application fee, bachelor's degree, essay, minimum GPA, resume, college transcript(s).

Application Deadline Applications processed on a rolling/continuous basis for both domestic and international students. Application fee: $20.

ACADEMICS
Teaching Methodologies Case study, computer simulations, experiential learning, group discussion, lecture, role playing, seminars by members of the business community, student presentations, team projects.

Technology Computer terminals/PCs are available for student use and are linked by a campus-wide network. The network has full access to the Internet. Students are not required to have their own PC.

Special Opportunities Advanced credit may be earned through transfer of credits from another institution.

FINANCES
Costs for 1997–98 Tuition: $90 per quarter hour (resident); $228 per quarter hour (nonresident). Cost varies by number of credits taken, reciprocity agreements. Average 1997–98 room and board costs were $3560 per academic year. Room and board costs vary by type of meal plan.

Financial Aid Research assistantships, scholarships, work study, loans available. Financial aid is available to part-time students. Application Deadline: 7/1.

Financial Aid Contact Al Pinckney, Director, Financial Aid, 4225 University Avenue, Columbus, GA 31907-5645. Phone: 706-568-2036; Fax: 706-568-2230.

FACILITIES
Information Resources Schwob Memorial Library; total holdings of 254,479 volumes, 842,170 microforms, 1,460 current periodical subscriptions. CD player(s) available for graduate student use. Access provided to online bibliographic retrieval services.

INTERNATIONAL STUDENTS
Demographics N/R

Services and Facilities International student office, international student housing, ESL courses, counseling/support services.

Applying TOEFL: minimum score of 550, proof of adequate funds, proof of health/immunizations required. Financial aid is available to international students.

International Student Contact Dr. Charlotte Stephens, Director, MBA Program, 4225 University Avenue, Columbus, GA 31907. Phone: 706-568-2129; Fax: 706-568-2184; E-mail: grad_studies@colstate.edu

PLACEMENT
Services include alumni network, career counseling/planning, career fairs, career library, career placement, electronic job bank, job interviews arranged, job search course, resume referral to employers, and resume preparation.

Employment Types of employment entered: accounting, banking, financial services, government, hospitality management, human resources, information systems/technology, insurance, management, manufacturing, marketing.

Business Program(s) URL: http://earth.colstate.edu/atcob/

Program Contact: Dr. Charlotte Stephens, Director, MBA Program, 4225 University Avenue, Columbus, GA 31907-5645. Phone: 706-568-2129; Fax: 706-568-2184; E-mail: grad_studies@colstate.edu

Emory University

Roberto C. Goizueta Business School
Atlanta, Georgia

OVERVIEW
Emory University is an independent-religious, coed university. Enrollment: 11,270 graduate, professional, and undergraduate students; 3,889 full-time matriculated

graduate/professional students; 1,354 part-time matriculated graduate/ professional students. Founded: 1836. The graduate business unit is in a suburban setting and is on a semester calendar.

HIGHLIGHTS

Enrollment Profile
Full-time: 290
Part-time: 200
Total: 490
Average Age: 26
Fall 1997 Average GPA: 3.2

International: 15%
Women: 33%
Minorities: 10%
Average Class Size: 35
Fall 1997 Average GMAT: 626

Costs
Full-time tuition: $24,000 per academic year
Part-time tuition: $15,999 per year

AACSB – The International Association for Management Education accredited

GRADUATE BUSINESS PROGRAMS

Day MBA (MBA) Full-time; 63 total credits required; 21 months to complete program. Concentrations in accounting, entrepreneurship, finance, human resources, international business, management, management information systems, marketing, operations management, organizational behavior/development, quantitative analysis, strategic management.

One-year MBA (MBA) Full-time; 43 total credits required; 12 months to complete program.

Master of Business Administration/Doctor of Jurisprudence (MBA/JD) Full-time, part-time; 77 total credits required; 4 years to complete program.

Master of Business Administration/Master of Public Health (MBA/MPH) Full-time, part-time; 81 total credits required; up to 2.3 years to complete program.

Master of Business Administration/Master of Divinity (MBA/MDiv) Full-time, part-time; 115 total credits required; up to 4 years to complete program.

Master of Business Administration/Master of Nursing (MBA/MN) Full-time, part-time; 92 total credits required; minimum of 23 months to complete program.

Executive MBA (MBA) Part-time; 54 total credits required; 16 months to complete program.

Evening MBA (MBA) Part-time; 57 total credits required; 2.8 years to complete program.

ADMISSION

Applications For fall 1997 there were 1,025 applications for admission. Of those applying, 326 were accepted. Of those accepted, 144 enrolled.

Application Requirements GMAT score, application form, application fee, bachelor's degree, essay, 3 letters of recommendation, personal statement, resume, college transcript(s).

Recommended for Application Interview, work experience, computer experience.

Application Deadline 4/15 for fall, 4/15 for fall (international). Application fee: $45. Deferred entrance is available.

ACADEMICS

Faculty Full-time 49; part-time 15.

Teaching Methodologies Case study, computer-aided instruction, computer analysis, computer simulations, experiential learning, field projects, group discussion, lecture, research, role playing, seminars by members of the business community, simulations, student presentations, study groups, team projects.

Technology 50 on-campus computer terminals/PCs are available for student use and are linked by a campus-wide network. The network has full access to the Internet. Students are not required to have their own PC.

Special Opportunities Advanced credit may be earned through credit by examination. International exchange programs in Austria, Chile, Costa Rica, Finland, France, Germany, Italy, Mexico, People's Republic of China, Republic of Singapore, Spain, United Kingdom, Venezuela. An internship program is available.

FINANCES

Costs for 1997–98 Tuition: Full-time: $24,000 per year. Part-time: $15,999 per year. Cost varies by academic program, number of credits taken. Fees: Full-time: $200 per academic year. Part-time: $180 per year. Fees vary by academic program. Average 1997–98 room only costs were $8000 per academic year (on campus) and $15,000 per academic year (off campus). Room and board costs vary by campus location, occupancy (e.g., single, double, triple), type of accommodation.

Financial Aid In 1997–98, 44% of students received some institutionally administered aid in the form of fellowships, research assistantships, scholarships, work study, loans. Financial aid is available to part-time students. Application Deadline: 3/1.

Financial Aid Contact Ms. Brenda Hill, Associate Director, Financial Aid, Office of Financial Aid, Atlanta, GA 30322. Phone: 404-727-1141; Fax: 404-727-6709.

FACILITIES

Information Resources Robert W. Woodruff Library plus 6 additional on-campus libraries; total holdings of 2,200,000 volumes, 2,421,282 microforms, 22,287 current periodical subscriptions. Access provided to online bibliographic retrieval services.

INTERNATIONAL STUDENTS

Demographics 15% of students enrolled are international students [Africa, 9%, Asia, 63%, Central America, 5%, Europe, 13%, North America, 2%, South America, 6%, other, 2%].

Services and Facilities International student office, international student center, visa services, counseling/support services, language tutoring.

Applying TOEFL: minimum score of 600, proof of adequate funds, proof of health/immunizations required. Financial aid is not available to international students.

International Student Contact Nancy Roth Remington, Director of International Programs, 1300 Clifton Road, NE, Atlanta, GA 30322-2710. Phone: 404-727-2553; Fax: 404-727-0868; E-mail: nancy_remington@bus.emory.edu

PLACEMENT

Services include alumni network, career counseling/planning, career fairs, career library, career placement, electronic job bank, job interviews arranged, job search course, resume referral to employers, and resume preparation. In 1996–97, 92 organizations participated in on-campus recruiting; 1,456 on-campus interviews were conducted.

Employment Of 1996–97 graduates, 96% were employed within three months of graduation; the average starting salary was $61,086. Types of employment entered: accounting, banking, communications, computer-related, consulting, consumer products, education, finance, financial services, health services, high technology, hospitality management, human resources, information systems/technology, international trade, management, manufacturing, marketing, media, nonprofit, pharmaceutical, service industry, telecommunications.

Business Program(s) URL: http://www.emory.edu/BUS/

Program Contact: Julie Barefoot, Assistant Dean of Admissions and Student Services, 1300 Clifton Road, NE, Atlanta, GA 30322-2712. Phone: 404-727-6311; Fax: 404-727-4612; E-mail: admissions@bus.emory.edu

See full description on page 804.

Georgia College and State University

J. Whitney Bunting School of Business

Milledgeville, Georgia

OVERVIEW

Georgia College and State University is a state-supported, coed, comprehensive institution. Enrollment: 5,500 graduate, professional, and undergraduate students; 336 full-time matriculated graduate/professional students; 577 part-time matriculated graduate/professional students. Founded: 1889. The graduate business unit is in a small-town setting and is on a semester calendar.

HIGHLIGHTS

Enrollment Profile
Full-time: 66
Part-time: 150
Total: 216
Average Age: 32
Fall 1997 Average GPA: N/R

International: 9%
Women: 41%
Minorities: 18%
Average Class Size: 18
Fall 1997 Average GMAT: 500

Costs
Full-time tuition: $250 per academic year (nonresident)
Part-time tuition: $260 per 5 hours (resident); $1428 per 5 hours (nonresident)

AACSB – The International Association for Management Education accredited

GRADUATE BUSINESS PROGRAMS

Master of Business Administration (MBA) Full-time, part-time; 36-57 total credits required; 12 months to 7 years to complete program.

Master of Management Information Systems (MMIS) Full-time, part-time; 36-60 total credits required; 12 months to 7 years to complete program. Concentration in accounting.

ADMISSION

Applications For fall 1997 there were 125 applications for admission. Of those applying, 92 were accepted.

Application Requirements GMAT score, application form, application fee, bachelor's degree, college transcript(s).

Recommended for Application Computer experience.

Application Deadline Applications processed on a rolling/continuous basis for both domestic and international students. Application fee: $10. Deferred entrance is available.

ACADEMICS
Faculty Full-time 31.

Teaching Methodologies Case study, computer-aided instruction, computer simulations, group discussion, lecture, research, seminars by members of the business community, simulations, student presentations, study groups, team projects.

Technology 250 on-campus computer terminals/PCs are available for student use and are linked by a campus-wide network. The network has full access to the Internet. Students are not required to have their own PC.

Special Opportunities Advanced credit may be earned through credit by examination, credit for military training programs, transfer of credits from another institution. International exchange programs in Brazil, Hungary, Mexico, People's Republic of China, Spain, United Kingdom.

FINANCES
Costs for 1997–98 Tuition: Full-time: $250 per semester hour (nonresident). Part-time: $260 per 5 hours (resident); $1428 per 5 hours (nonresident). Cost varies by number of credits taken. Fees: $5 per semester (resident); $5 per semester (nonresident). Fees vary by campus location. Average 1997–98 room and board costs were $4635 per academic year. Room and board costs vary by occupancy (e.g., single, double, triple), type of accommodation, type of meal plan.

Financial Aid Research assistantships, work study available. Financial aid is available to part-time students. Application Deadline: 3/15.

Financial Aid Contact Ms. Suzanne Price, Director of Financial Aid, CBX 030, Milledgeville , GA 31061. Phone: 912-445-5149; Fax: 912-445-0729; E-mail: sprice@mail.gac.peachnet.edu

FACILITIES
Information Resources Ina Dillard Russell Library; total holdings of 170,834 volumes, 515,123 microforms, 1,137 current periodical subscriptions. CD player(s) available for graduate student use. Access provided to online bibliographic retrieval services and online databases.

INTERNATIONAL STUDENTS
Demographics 9% of students enrolled are international students.

Services and Facilities International student office, visa services, counseling/support services.

Applying TOEFL: minimum score of 500, proof of adequate funds required. Financial aid is available to international students.

International Student Contact Dr. Dwight Call, Assistant Vice President for International Education, CBX 046, Milledgeville, GA 31061. Phone: 912-445-4789; Fax: 912-445-2623; E-mail: dwither@mail.gac.peachnet.edu

PLACEMENT
Services include alumni network, career counseling/planning, career fairs, career library, career placement, job interviews arranged, resume referral to employers, and resume preparation. In 1996–97, 67 organizations participated in on-campus recruiting.

Employment Types of employment entered: accounting, banking, chemical industry, communications, computer-related, consulting, energy, finance, financial services, government, health services, high technology, hospitality management, human resources, information systems/technology, insurance, management, manufacturing, marketing, mining, pharmaceutical, real estate, retail, service industry, utilities.

Business Program(s) URL: http://www.gac.peachnet.edu

Program Contact: Dr. Melinda McCannon, Director, Graduate Programs in Business, CBX 019, Milledgeville, GA 31061. Phone: 912-471-2992, 800-342-0471 (GA only); Fax: 912-445-5249; E-mail: mmccanno@mail.gac.peachnet.edu

Georgia Institute of Technology

DuPree College of Management

Atlanta, Georgia

OVERVIEW
Georgia Institute of Technology is a state-supported, coed university. Enrollment: 13,109 graduate, professional, and undergraduate students; 2,755 full-time matriculated graduate/professional students; 733 part-time matriculated graduate/professional students. Founded: 1885. The graduate business unit is in an urban setting and is on a quarter calendar.

HIGHLIGHTS

Enrollment Profile
Full-time: 230	International: 15%
Part-time: 0	Women: 30%
Total: 230	Minorities: 10%
Average Age: 27	Average Class Size: 40
Fall 1997 Average GPA: 3.2	Fall 1997 Average GMAT: 632

Costs
Full-time tuition: $3627 per academic year (resident); $12,465 per academic year (nonresident)
Part-time tuition: N/R

AACSB – The International Association for Management Education accredited

GRADUATE BUSINESS PROGRAMS
Master of Science in Management (MSM) Full-time; 81 total credits required; 18 to 21 months to complete program. Concentrations in accounting, entrepreneurship, finance, human resources, international and area business studies, management information systems, marketing, operations management, organizational behavior/development, strategic management, technology management, business policy/strategy, information management, international business, management consulting, manufacturing management, marketing research, strategic management.

Master of Science in Management of Technology (MS) Full-time; 81 total credits required; 18 months to complete program. Concentration in technology management.

ADMISSION
Applications For fall 1997 there were 500 applications for admission. Of those applying, 225 were accepted. Of those accepted, 87 enrolled.

Application Requirements Application form, application fee, bachelor's degree, essay, minimum GPA, 2 letters of recommendation, resume, college transcript(s).

Recommended for Application GMAT score accepted, interview, personal statement, work experience, computer experience.

Application Deadline 4/15 for fall, 2/15 for fall (international). Application fee: $50. Deferred entrance is available.

ACADEMICS
Faculty Full-time 55.

Teaching Methodologies Case study, computer-aided instruction, computer analysis, computer simulations, experiential learning, faculty seminars, field projects, group discussion, lecture, research, role playing, seminars by members of the business community, simulations, student presentations, study groups, team projects.

Technology 200 on-campus computer terminals/PCs are available for student use and are linked by a campus-wide network. The network has full access to the Internet. Students are not required to have their own PC.

Special Opportunities Advanced credit may be earned through transfer of credits from another institution. International exchange programs in Brazil, Colombia, Denmark, France, Germany, Japan, Netherlands, People's Republic of China, United Kingdom. An internship program is available.

FINANCES
Costs for 1997–98 Tuition: Full-time: $3627 per year (resident); $12,465 per year (nonresident). Cost varies by academic program, number of credits taken. Fees: Full-time: $400 per academic year (resident); $400 per academic year (nonresident). Average 1997–98 room and board costs were $5400 per academic year (on campus) and $6500 per academic year (off campus). Room and board costs vary by campus location, occupancy (e.g., single, double, triple), type of accommodation, type of meal plan.

Financial Aid Fellowships, research assistantships, teaching assistantships, work study, loans available. Application Deadline: 2/15.

Financial Aid Contact Mr. Jerry McTier, Director of Financial Aid, Student and Financial Planning and Services, Atlanta, GA 30332-0460. Phone: 404-894-0460; Fax: 404-894-7412.

FACILITIES
Information Resources Price Gilbert Memorial Library; total holdings of 2,700,000 volumes, 3,187,633 microforms, 12,000 current periodical subscriptions. CD player(s) available for graduate student use. Access provided to online bibliographic retrieval services.

INTERNATIONAL STUDENTS
Demographics 15% of students enrolled are international students.

Services and Facilities International student office, international student center, international student housing, visa services, ESL courses, counseling/support services.

Applying TOEFL: minimum score of 600, proof of adequate funds, proof of health/immunizations required. Financial aid is not available to international students.

International Student Contact Mr. Miller Templeton, International Student Services, 225 North Avenue, NW, Atlanta, GA 30332-001. Phone: 404-894-7475.

PLACEMENT

Services include alumni network, career counseling/planning, career fairs, career library, career placement, electronic job bank, job interviews arranged, resume referral to employers, and resume preparation. In 1996–97, 175 organizations participated in on-campus recruiting; 1,200 on-campus interviews were conducted.

Employment Of 1996–97 graduates, 98% were employed within three months of graduation; the average starting salary was $56,100. Types of employment entered: accounting, banking, chemical industry, communications, computer-related, consulting, consumer products, energy, engineering, finance, financial services, government, health services, high technology, human resources, information systems/technology, management, manufacturing, marketing, media, nonprofit, petrochemical, pharmaceutical, real estate, retail, service industry, telecommunications, transportation, utilities.

Business Program(s) URL: http://www.iac.gatech.edu/dupree

Program Contact: Ms. Carita Reynolds, Admissions and Student Services Coordinator, 755 Ferst Avenue, Room 212, DuPree College of Management, Atlanta, GA 30332-0520. Phone: 404-894-8722, 800-869-1014 (GA only); Fax: 404-894-4199; E-mail: msm@mgt.gatech.edu
See full description on page 830.

Georgia Southern University

College of Business Administration

Statesboro, Georgia

OVERVIEW

Georgia Southern University is a state-supported, coed, comprehensive institution. Enrollment: 14,138 graduate, professional, and undergraduate students; 650 full-time matriculated graduate/professional students; 1,243 part-time matriculated graduate/professional students. Founded: 1906. The graduate business unit is in a small-town setting and is on a quarter calendar.

HIGHLIGHTS

Enrollment Profile

Full-time: 97	International: 14%
Part-time: 90	Women: 47%
Total: 187	Minorities: 10%
Average Age: 28	Average Class Size: 20
Fall 1997 Average GPA: 3.12	Fall 1997 Average GMAT: 492

Costs
Full-time tuition: N/R
Part-time tuition: $228 per course (resident); $684 per course (nonresident)

AACSB – The International Association for Management Education accredited

GRADUATE BUSINESS PROGRAMS

Master of Business Administration (MBA) Full-time, part-time; 48-80 total credits required; 15 months to 7 years to complete program. Concentration in accounting.

Master of Accountancy (MAcc) Full-time, part-time, distance learning option; 48 total credits required; 15 months to 7 years to complete program. Concentration in accounting.

ADMISSION

Applications For fall 1997 there were 52 applications for admission. Of those applying, 52 were accepted. Of those accepted, 52 enrolled.

Application Requirements Application form, bachelor's degree, minimum GPA, college transcript(s).

Recommended for Application GMAT score accepted.

Application Deadline Applications processed on a rolling/continuous basis for both domestic and international students. Deferred entrance is available.

ACADEMICS

Faculty Full-time 36; part-time 19.

Teaching Methodologies Case study, computer-aided instruction, computer analysis, computer simulations, faculty seminars, group discussion, lecture, research, role playing, seminars by members of the business community, simulations, student presentations, study groups, team projects.

Technology 150 on-campus computer terminals/PCs are available for student use and are linked by a campus-wide network. The network has full access to the Internet. Students are not required to have their own PC.

Special Opportunities Advanced credit may be earned through transfer of credits from another institution.

FINANCES

Costs for 1997–98 Tuition: $228 per course (resident); $684 per course (nonresident). Cost varies by number of credits taken.

Financial Aid Research assistantships, teaching assistantships, work study available. Financial aid is available to part-time students. Application Deadline: 4/15.

Financial Aid Contact Ms. Pamela Pierce, Director of Financial Aid, PO Box 8065, Statesboro, GA 30460-8065. Phone: 912-681-5413; Fax: 912-682-0573.

FACILITIES

Information Resources Henderson Library plus 1 additional on-campus library; total holdings of 463,102 volumes, 759,072 microforms, 3,531 current periodical subscriptions. CD player(s) available for graduate student use. Access provided to online bibliographic retrieval services and online databases.

INTERNATIONAL STUDENTS

Demographics 14% of students enrolled are international students.

Services and Facilities International student office, international student center, international student housing, visa services, ESL courses, counseling/support services.

Applying TOEFL, proof of adequate funds, proof of health/immunizations required.

International Student Contact Mr. Maher Tubbeh, Director, International Student Program, PO Box 8063, Statesboro, GA 30460-8063. Phone: 912-681-0382; Fax: 912-681-0694.

PLACEMENT

Services include alumni network, career counseling/planning, career fairs, career placement, job interviews arranged, resume referral to employers, and resume preparation.

Employment Types of employment entered: consumer products, engineering, marketing, media.

Business Program(s) URL: http://www2.gasou.edu/mba/main.htm

Program Contact: Dr. J. Michael McDonald, Director of Graduate Studies, Landrum Box 8125, Statesboro, GA 30460. Phone: 912-681-5767; Fax: 912-681-0292; E-mail: mmcdonal@gsaix2.cc.gasou.edu

Georgia Southwestern State University

School of Business

Americus, Georgia

OVERVIEW

Georgia Southwestern State University is a state-supported, comprehensive institution. Enrollment: 2,500 graduate, professional, and undergraduate students.

HIGHLIGHTS

Enrollment Profile

Full-time: N/R	International: N/R
Part-time: N/R	Women: N/R
Total: 55	Minorities: N/R
Average Age: N/R	Average Class Size: N/R
Fall 1997 Average GPA: N/R	Fall 1997 Average GMAT: N/R

Costs
Full-time tuition: $2468 per academic year (resident); $8468 per academic year (nonresident)
Part-time tuition: $83 per semester hour (resident); $333 per semester (nonresident)

GRADUATE BUSINESS PROGRAMS

Master of Science in Administration (MSA) Full-time, part-time; 30 total credits required; minimum of 12 months to complete program.

ADMISSION

Application Requirements GMAT score: minimum 500, application form, bachelor's degree, minimum GPA, letters of recommendation, college transcript(s).

Recommended for Application Interview.

Application Deadline Applications processed on a rolling/continuous basis for both domestic and international students.

ACADEMICS

Teaching Methodologies Case study, computer-aided instruction, computer analysis, field projects, group discussion, lecture, research, role playing, seminars by members of the business community, simulations, student presentations, study groups, team projects.

Georgia Southwestern State University (continued)

FINANCES

Costs for 1997–98 Tuition: Full-time: $2468 per year (resident); $8468 per year (nonresident). Part-time: $83 per semester hour (resident); $333 per semester (nonresident).

Financial Aid Contact Freida Jones, Director of Financial Aid, Americus, GA 31709-4693. Phone: 912-928-1378.

INTERNATIONAL STUDENTS

Demographics N/R

Services and Facilities International student office, counseling/support services.

Applying TOEFL: minimum score of 550 required.

International Student Contact Angela Walker, Americus, GA 31709-4693. Phone: 912-928-1387.

Program Contact: Chris Laney, Graduate Specialist, Americus, GA 31709-4693. Phone: 912-928-2027.

Georgia State University

College of Business Administration

Atlanta, Georgia

OVERVIEW

Georgia State University is a state-supported, coed university. Enrollment: 24,300 graduate, professional, and undergraduate students; 4,322 full-time matriculated graduate/professional students; 3,150 part-time matriculated graduate/professional students. Founded: 1913. The graduate business unit is in an urban setting and is on a quarter calendar.

HIGHLIGHTS

Enrollment Profile

Full-time: 1,535	International: 15%
Part-time: 1,090	Women: 37%
Total: 2,625	Minorities: 22%
Average Age: 28	Average Class Size: 30
Fall 1997 Average GPA: 3.05	Fall 1997 Average GMAT: 560

Costs
Full-time tuition: N/R
Part-time tuition: $300 per 5-hour course (resident); $1200 per 5-hour course (nonresident)

AACSB – The International Association for Management Education accredited

GRADUATE BUSINESS PROGRAMS

Master of Business Administration (MBA) Full-time, part-time; 85 total credits required; 12 months to 5 years to complete program. Concentrations in accounting, decision sciences, economics, finance, international business, management, marketing, real estate, risk management, information management.

Master of Science (MS) Full-time, part-time; 75 total credits required; 12 months to 4 years to complete program. Concentrations in decision sciences, finance, management, marketing, financial management/planning, risk management, economics.

Master of Actuarial Science (MAS) Full-time; 50 total credits required; 15 months to 2.5 years to complete program. Concentration in actuarial science.

Master of Business Administration/Doctor of Jurisprudence (MBA/JD) Full-time, part-time; 95 total credits required; 12 months to 5 years to complete program.

Master of Business Administration/Master of Health Administration (MBA/MHA) Full-time; 110 total credits required; 2.8 to 6 years to complete program.

Master of Professional Accountancy (MPA) Full-time, part-time; 45 total credits required; 12 months to 2.3 years to complete program.

Master of Science in Real Estate (MS) Full-time, part-time; 60 total credits required; 12 months to 3 years to complete program.

Master of Taxation (MTax) Full-time, part-time; 50 total credits required; 12 months to 2.5 years to complete program.

Executive MBA (MBA) Full-time; 66 total credits required; 18 months to complete program.

Concentrated MBA (MBA) Full-time; 80 total credits required; 12 months to complete program.

Master of Science in Health Administration (MS) Full-time, part-time; 55 total credits required; 12 months to 2.8 years to complete program. Concentrations in finance, information management, management, marketing, risk management, human resources.

Master of International Business (MIB) Full-time, part-time; 60 total credits required; 12 months to 3 years to complete program.

ADMISSION

Applications For fall 1997 there were 1,077 applications for admission. Of those applying, 652 were accepted. Of those accepted, 497 enrolled.

Application Requirements GMAT score, application form, application fee, bachelor's degree, essay, minimum GPA, college transcript(s).

Recommended for Application Letters of recommendation, work experience.

Application Deadline 8/1 for fall, 10/1 for spring, 6/1 for summer, 8/1 for fall (international), 10/1 for spring (international), 6/1 for summer (international). Application fee: $25. Deferred entrance is available.

ACADEMICS

Faculty Full-time 177; part-time 29.

Teaching Methodologies Case study, computer-aided instruction, computer analysis, computer simulations, group discussion, lecture, research, role playing, simulations, student presentations, study groups, team projects.

Technology 155 on-campus computer terminals/PCs are available for student use and are linked by a campus-wide network. The network has full access to the Internet. Students are not required to have their own PC.

Special Opportunities Advanced credit may be earned through transfer of credits from another institution. International exchange programs in France, Germany.

FINANCES

Costs for 1997–98 Tuition: $300 per 5-hour course (resident); $1200 per 5-hour course (nonresident). Cost varies by number of credits taken. Fees: $141 per quarter (resident); $141 per quarter (nonresident). Average 1997–98 room only costs were $3990 per academic year (on campus) and $5000 per academic year (off campus).

Financial Aid Fellowships, research assistantships, teaching assistantships available. Financial aid is available to part-time students.

Financial Aid Contact Student Financial Aid, University Plaza, Atlanta, GA 30303. Phone: 404-651-2227.

FACILITIES

Information Resources William R. Pullen Library plus 1 additional on-campus library; total holdings of 1,215,397 volumes, 1,973,138 microforms, 11,283 current periodical subscriptions. CD player(s) available for graduate student use. Access provided to online bibliographic retrieval services.

INTERNATIONAL STUDENTS

Demographics 15% of students enrolled are international students [Africa, 5%, Asia, 72%, Central America, 5%, Europe, 11%, North America, 3%, South America, 4%].

Services and Facilities International student office, international student center, international student housing, visa services, ESL courses, counseling/support services.

Applying TOEFL: minimum score of 550, proof of adequate funds, proof of health/immunizations required. Financial aid is available to international students.

International Student Contact Mr. Douglas Podoll, Director, International Student Services, Office of International Services and Programs, University Plaza, Atlanta, GA 30303. Phone: 404-651-2209.

PLACEMENT

Services include alumni network, career counseling/planning, career fairs, career library, career placement, electronic job bank, job interviews arranged, job search course, resume referral to employers, and resume preparation. In 1996–97, 124 organizations participated in on-campus recruiting; 664 on-campus interviews were conducted.

Employment Of 1996–97 graduates, 85% were employed within three months of graduation; the average starting salary was $49,550. Types of employment entered: accounting, banking, chemical industry, computer-related, consulting, consumer products, finance, financial services, government, health services, high technology, hospitality management, human resources, information systems/technology, insurance, international trade, management, manufacturing, marketing, media, nonprofit, pharmaceutical, real estate, retail, service industry, telecommunications, transportation, utilities.

Business Program(s) URL: http://www.cba.gsu.edu

Program Contact: Office of Academic Assistance and Master's Admissions, College of Business Administration, University Plaza, Atlanta, GA 30303-3087. Phone: 404-651-1913; Fax: 404-651-0219.
See full description on page 832.

Kennesaw State University

Michael J. Coles College of Business

Kennesaw, Georgia

OVERVIEW
Kennesaw State University is a state-supported, coed, comprehensive institution. Enrollment: 13,000 graduate, professional, and undergraduate students. Founded: 1963. The graduate business unit is in a suburban setting and is on a semester calendar.

HIGHLIGHTS

Enrollment Profile

Full-time: 485
Part-time: 459
Total: 944
Average Age: 34
Fall 1997 Average GPA: 3.0

International: 7%
Women: 44%
Minorities: 17%
Average Class Size: 30
Fall 1997 Average GMAT: 510

Costs

Full-time tuition: $1199 per academic year (resident); $4199 per academic year (nonresident)
Part-time tuition: $83 per credit hour (resident); $250 per credit hour (nonresident)

AACSB – The International Association for Management Education accredited

*D*uring the past year, U.S. News & World Report, Business Week, Entrepreneur Magazine, *and* Success Magazine, *have heralded the leadership in innovation and entrepreneurship programs developed by the* Michael J. Coles College of Business. *The M.B.A. program now features the opportunity to major in this most important discipline that is the mainstay of private enterprise systems and economic growth and development worldwide. Course-work in entrepreneurship, innovation and creativity, new venture analysis, entrepreneurial finance, the award-winning consulting services class, and family business make this program unique and appealing. This expertise combined with what the* Wall Street Journal *has called one of the finest family enterprise programs in the nation makes the Coles School a true leader in the field of small, family, and emerging enterprises. Entrepreneurship is but one of ten formal majors in this American Assembly of Collegiate Schools of Business (AACSB)–accredited program. The Coles School, situated in suburban Atlanta, is committed to supporting the academic and professional needs of the more than 800 students enrolled in graduate business programs. The School combines new, state-of-the-art facilities and 85 committed faculty members for a global educational experience.*

GRADUATE BUSINESS PROGRAMS
Executive MBA (MBA) Full-time, distance learning option; 36 total credits required; 5 years work experience required; 18 months to complete program.

Master of Business Administration (MBA) Full-time, part-time, distance learning option; 36 total credits required; 12 months to 6 years to complete program. Concentrations in accounting, economics, information management, entrepreneurship, finance, human resources, marketing, operations management, international business, management.

Master of Accounting (MAcc) Full-time, part-time, distance learning option; 36 total credits required; 18 months to 6 years to complete program. Concentrations in management, taxation.

ADMISSION
Application Requirements Application form, application fee, bachelor's degree, minimum GPA: 2.8, interview, letters of recommendation, resume, college transcript(s).

Recommended for Application GMAT score accepted: minimum 475, GRE score accepted: minimum 1,425, work experience.

Application Deadline Applications processed on a rolling/continuous basis for both domestic and international students. Application fee: $20. Deferred entrance is available.

ACADEMICS
Faculty Full-time 92; part-time 3.

Teaching Methodologies Case study, computer-aided instruction, computer analysis, computer simulations, experiential learning, field projects, group discussion, lecture, research, role playing, seminars by members of the business community, simulations, student presentations, study groups, team projects.

Technology 60 on-campus computer terminals/PCs are available for student use and are linked by a campus-wide network. The network has full access to the Internet. Students are not required to have their own PC.

Special Opportunities Advanced credit may be earned through transfer of credits from another institution.

FINANCES
Costs for 1997–98 Tuition: Full-time: $1199 per semester (resident); $4199 per semester (nonresident). Part-time: $83 per credit hour (resident); $250 per credit hour (nonresident). Cost varies by number of credits taken. Fees: $199 per semester (resident); $199 per semester (nonresident).

Financial Aid In 1997–98, 4% of students received some institutionally administered aid in the form of work study. Financial aid is available to part-time students. Application Deadline: 8/1.

Financial Aid Contact Ms. Cheryl Matson, Office of Financial Aid, 1000 Chastain Road, Kennesaw, GA 30144-5591. Phone: 770-423-6074; E-mail: cmatson@ksumail.kennesaw.edu

FACILITIES
Information Resources Horace W. Sturgis Library; total holdings of 555,000 volumes, 850,000 microforms, 3,500 current periodical subscriptions. CD player(s) available for graduate student use. Access provided to online bibliographic retrieval services.

INTERNATIONAL STUDENTS
Demographics 7% of students enrolled are international students.

Services and Facilities International student office, counseling/support services.

Applying TOEFL: minimum score of 550, proof of adequate funds, proof of health/immunizations required. Financial aid is not available to international students.

International Student Contact Mr. Julio D. España, Sr., International Admissions Counselor, Office of Admissions, Kennesaw, GA 30144-5591.

PLACEMENT
Services include alumni network, career counseling/planning, career fairs, career library, career placement, electronic job bank, job interviews arranged, job search course, resume referral to employers, and resume preparation. In 1996–97, 100 organizations participated in on-campus recruiting.

Employment Types of employment entered: accounting, banking, communications, computer-related, consulting, consumer products, education, engineering, finance, financial services, government, health services, high technology, hospitality management, human resources, information systems/technology, insurance, international trade, law, management, manufacturing, marketing, media, nonprofit, pharmaceutical, real estate, retail, service industry, telecommunications, transportation, utilities.

Business Program(s) URL: http://wwwcoles.kennesaw.edu/

Program Contact: Ms. Susan Cochran, Administrative Coordinator, Coles College of Business, 1000 Chastain Road, Kennesaw, GA 30144-5591. Phone: 770-423-6472; Fax: 770-423-6141; E-mail: scochran@ksumail.kennesaw.edu

See full description on page 866.

LaGrange College

Division of Business Administration and Economics

LaGrange, Georgia

OVERVIEW
LaGrange College is an independent-religious, coed, comprehensive institution. Enrollment: 971 graduate, professional, and undergraduate students; 15 full-time matriculated graduate/professional students; 36 part-time matriculated graduate/professional students. Founded: 1831. The graduate business unit is in a small-town setting and is on a quarter calendar.

HIGHLIGHTS

Enrollment Profile

Full-time: 9
Part-time: 26
Total: 35
Average Age: 33
Fall 1997 Average GPA: 3.5

International: N/R
Women: 23%
Minorities: 17%
Average Class Size: 14
Fall 1997 Average GMAT: N/R

Costs

Full-time tuition: $8240 per academic year
Part-time tuition: $206 per quarter hour

LaGrange College (continued)

ACBSP – The American Council of Business Schools and Programs accredited

GRADUATE BUSINESS PROGRAMS

Master of Business Administration (MBA) Full-time, part-time; 60 total credits required; 18 months to 5 years to complete program.

ADMISSION

Applications For fall 1997 there were 25 applications for admission. Of·those applying, 20 were accepted. Of those accepted, 16 enrolled.

Application Requirements Application form, application fee, bachelor's degree, minimum GPA, interview, personal statement, college transcript(s), minimum of 2 years of work experience.

Recommended for Application GMAT score accepted, essay, letters of recommendation, resume, computer experience.

Application Deadline Applications processed on a rolling/continuous basis for both domestic and international students. Application fee: $25.

ACADEMICS

Faculty Full-time 5.

Teaching Methodologies Case study, computer-aided instruction, computer analysis, computer simulations, experiential learning, faculty seminars, field projects, group discussion, lecture, research, role playing, simulations, student presentations, study groups, team projects.

Technology 434 on-campus computer terminals/PCs are available for student use and are linked by a campus-wide network. The network has partial access to the Internet. Students are not required to have their own PC.

Special Opportunities International exchange programs in Canada, France, Mexico, United Kingdom. An internship program is available.

FINANCES

Costs for 1997–98 Tuition: Full-time: $8240 per year. Part-time: $206 per quarter hour.

Financial Aid In 1997–98, 34% of students received some institutionally administered aid in the form of loans. Financial aid is available to part-time students. Application Deadline: 6/1.

Financial Aid Contact Marjorie Belton, 601 Broad Street, LaGrange, GA 30240. Phone: 706-812-7249.

FACILITIES

Information Resources Banks Library; total holdings of 110,000 volumes, 8,000 microforms, 475 current periodical subscriptions. CD player(s) available for graduate student use. Access provided to online bibliographic retrieval services.

INTERNATIONAL STUDENTS

Demographics N/R

Applying Financial aid is not available to international students.

PLACEMENT

Services include career counseling/planning, and resume referral to employers.

Business Program(s) URL: http://www.lgc.peachnet.edu

Program Contact: Mr. Andy Geeter, Director of Admission, 601 Broad Street, La Grange, GA 30240. Phone: 706-812-7253; Fax: 706-812-7354; E-mail: ageeter@mentor.lgc.peachnet.edu

Mercer University

Stetson School of Business and Economics

Macon, Georgia

OVERVIEW

Mercer University is an independent-religious, coed, comprehensive institution. Enrollment: 6,086 graduate, professional, and undergraduate students; 442 full-time matriculated graduate/professional students; 1,164 part-time matriculated graduate/professional students. Founded: 1833. The graduate business unit is in a suburban setting and is on a semester calendar.

HIGHLIGHTS

Enrollment Profile
Full-time: 3	International: 10%
Part-time: 117	Women: 50%
Total: 120	Minorities: 5%
Average Age: 32	Average Class Size: 28
Fall 1997 Average GPA: 3.3	Fall 1997 Average GMAT: 482

Costs
Full-time tuition: N/R
Part-time tuition: $831 per course

GRADUATE BUSINESS PROGRAMS

Master of Business Administration (MBA) Full-time, part-time; 36-54 total credits required; 12 months to 5 years to complete program. Concentrations in finance, management, international business.

Master of Science in Health Care Administration (MS) Part-time; 39 total credits required; 15 months to 5 years to complete program.

ADMISSION

Application Requirements Application form, application fee, bachelor's degree, minimum GPA: 2.75, college transcript(s).

Recommended for Application GMAT score accepted: minimum 400, GRE score accepted, computer experience: word processing, spreadsheet.

Application Deadline Applications processed on a rolling/continuous basis for both domestic and international students. Application fee: $35, $50 (international).

ACADEMICS

Faculty Full-time 14; part-time 2.

Teaching Methodologies Case study, computer simulations, group discussion, lecture, student presentations, study groups, team projects.

Technology 100 on-campus computer terminals/PCs are available for student use and are linked by a campus-wide network. The network has full access to the Internet. Students are not required to have their own PC.

Special Opportunities Advanced credit may be earned through transfer of credits from another institution. International exchange programs in Belgium, Chile.

FINANCES

Costs for 1997–98 Tuition: $831 per course. Cost varies by campus location, class time (e.g., day/evening). Average 1997–98 room and board costs were $6000 per academic year (on campus) and $4800 per academic year (off campus). Room and board costs vary by type of meal plan.

Financial Aid In 1997–98, 33% of students received some institutionally administered aid in the form of loans. Financial aid is available to part-time students.

Financial Aid Contact Financial Aid Office, 1400 Coleman Avenue, Macon, GA 31207-0003.

FACILITIES

Information Resources Stetson Memorial Library plus 2 additional on-campus libraries; total holdings of 450,000 volumes, 241,010 microforms, 3,346 current periodical subscriptions. CD player(s) available for graduate student use. Access provided to online bibliographic retrieval services and online databases.

INTERNATIONAL STUDENTS

Demographics 10% of students enrolled are international students.

Services and Facilities ESL courses.

Applying TOEFL: minimum score of 550, proof of adequate funds, proof of health/immunizations required. Financial aid is not available to international students.

PLACEMENT

Services include career counseling/planning, career fairs, career placement, and resume preparation. In 1996–97, 100 organizations participated in on-campus recruiting.

Employment Of 1996–97 graduates, 95% were employed within three months of graduation. Types of employment entered: accounting, finance, government, information systems/technology, insurance, marketing, retail.

Program Contact: Ms. Shirley Ralph, MBA Coordinator, Stetson School of Business and Economics, 1400 Coleman Avenue, Macon, GA 31207-0003. Phone: 912-752-2832.

Mercer University, Cecil B. Day Campus

Stetson School of Business and Economics

Atlanta, Georgia

OVERVIEW

Mercer University, Cecil B. Day Campus is an independent-religious, coed, upper-level institution. Enrollment: 1,926 graduate, professional, and undergraduate students; 543 full-time matriculated graduate/professional students; 1,148 part-time matriculated graduate/professional students. Founded: 1964. The graduate business unit is in a suburban setting and is on a eight-week sessions calendar.

HIGHLIGHTS

Enrollment Profile
Full-time: 368
Part-time: 298
Total: 666
Average Age: 30
Fall 1997 Average GPA: N/R

International: 23%
Women: 52%
Minorities: 27%
Average Class Size: 30
Fall 1997 Average GMAT: N/R

Costs
Full-time tuition: $5580 per academic year
Part-time tuition: $930 per course

GRADUATE BUSINESS PROGRAMS
Master of Business Administration (MBA) Full-time, part-time; 36 total credits required; 21 months to 5 years to complete program. Concentrations in accounting, finance, international business, management, marketing, management information systems.

Executive MBA (EMBA) Full-time; 36 total credits required; 21 months to complete program. Concentration in international business.

Master of Science in Technology Management (MS) Full-time, part-time; 39 total credits required; 21 months to 5 years to complete program. Concentration in technology management.

Master of Science in Health Care Policy and Administration (MS) Full-time, part-time; 39 total credits required; 21 months to 5 years to complete program. Concentration in health care.

ADMISSION
Applications For fall 1997 there were 343 applications for admission. Of those applying, 274 were accepted. Of those accepted, 182 enrolled.

Application Requirements GMAT score: minimum 400, application form, application fee, bachelor's degree, essay, minimum GPA: 2.75, letters of recommendation, college transcript(s).

Recommended for Application Interview, personal statement, resume, work experience, computer experience.

Application Deadline Applications processed on a rolling/continuous basis for both domestic and international students. Application fee: $35, $50 (international). Deferred entrance is available.

ACADEMICS
Faculty Full-time 21; part-time 13.

Teaching Methodologies Case study, computer-aided instruction, computer analysis, computer simulations, experiential learning, group discussion, lecture, research, seminars by members of the business community, simulations, student presentations, study groups, team projects.

Technology Computer terminals/PCs are available for student use and are linked by a campus-wide network. The network has full access to the Internet. Students are not required to have their own PC.

Special Opportunities Advanced credit may be earned through transfer of credits from another institution. International exchange program in Belgium.

FINANCES
Costs for 1997–98 Tuition: Full-time: $5580 per semester. Part-time: $930 per course. Cost varies by academic program, campus location.

Financial Aid Grants, scholarships, work study, loans available.

Financial Aid Contact Margaret McGinnis, Financial Aid Director, 3000 Mercer University Drive, Atlanta, GA 30341-4155. Phone: 770-986-3134.

FACILITIES
Information Resources Monroe F. Swilley Jr. Library plus 1 additional on-campus library; total holdings of 81,668 volumes, 351,241 microforms, 742 current periodical subscriptions. CD player(s) available for graduate student use. Access provided to online bibliographic retrieval services.

INTERNATIONAL STUDENTS
Demographics 23% of students enrolled are international students [Africa, 3%, Asia, 58%, Central America, 1%, Europe, 20%, North America, 3%, South America, 15%].

Services and Facilities International student office, ESL courses, counseling/support services.

Applying TOEFL: minimum score of 550, proof of adequate funds, proof of health/immunizations required.

PLACEMENT
Services include career counseling/planning, career fairs, career library, career placement, electronic job bank, resume referral to employers, and resume preparation.

Employment Types of employment entered: accounting, banking, communications, computer-related, consulting, consumer products, education, engineering, finance, financial services, government, health services, high technology, hospitality management, human resources, information systems/technology, insurance, international trade, law, management, manufacturing, marketing, media, nonprofit, pharmaceutical, real estate, retail, service industry, telecommunications, transportation, utilities.

Business Program(s) URL: http://www.mercer.edu/ssbeatl/index.html

Program Contact: Mr. Andrew Bouldin, Director of Graduate Admissions, Stetson School of Business and Economics, 3001 Mercer University Drive, Atlanta, GA 30341. Phone: 770-986-3417; Fax: 770-986-3160; E-mail: bouldin_a@mercer.edu

Oglethorpe University

Division of Business Administration

Atlanta, Georgia

OVERVIEW
Oglethorpe University is an independent-nonprofit, coed, comprehensive institution. Enrollment: 1,230 graduate, professional, and undergraduate students; 17 full-time matriculated graduate/professional students; 102 part-time matriculated graduate/professional students. The graduate business unit is on a semester calendar.

HIGHLIGHTS

Enrollment Profile
Full-time: 11
Part-time: 31
Total: 42
Average Age: N/R
Fall 1997 Average GPA: N/R

International: 7%
Women: N/R
Minorities: N/R
Average Class Size: N/R
Fall 1997 Average GMAT: N/R

Costs
Full-time tuition: N/R
Part-time tuition: $1340 per 4-hour course

GRADUATE BUSINESS PROGRAMS
Master of Business Administration (MBA) Full-time, part-time; 40 total credits required; minimum of 2 years to complete program. Concentration in accounting.

ADMISSION
Application Requirements GMAT score, application form, bachelor's degree, essay, minimum GPA: 2.5, 2 letters of recommendation, college transcript(s).

Recommended for Application Interview, personal statement, resume, work experience.

Application Deadline Applications processed on a rolling/continuous basis for both domestic and international students.

ACADEMICS
Teaching Methodologies Case study, computer-aided instruction, computer analysis, computer simulations, experiential learning, faculty seminars, field projects, group discussion, lecture, research, role playing, seminars by members of the business community, simulations, student presentations, study groups, team projects.

FINANCES
Costs for 1997–98 Tuition: $1340 per 4-hour course.

Financial Aid Contact Patrick Bonones, Director of Financial Aid, Atlanta, GA 30319. Phone: 404-364-8354.

INTERNATIONAL STUDENTS
Demographics 7% of students enrolled are international students.

Services and Facilities International student office, international student center, international student housing, counseling/support services.

Applying TOEFL: minimum score of 500 required.

International Student Contact Marshall Nathon, Associate Dean—Community Life, Atlanta, GA 30319. Phone: 404-364-8424; E-mail: mnathon@facstaff.oglethorpe.edu

Program Contact: Bill Price, Associate Dean for Graduate Enrollment Management, Atlanta, GA 30319. Phone: 404-364-8314.

GEORGIA

Southern Polytechnic State University

School of Management

Marietta, Georgia

OVERVIEW
Southern Polytechnic State University is a state-supported, coed, comprehensive institution. Enrollment: 3,921 graduate, professional, and undergraduate students; 231 full-time matriculated graduate/professional students; 346 part-time matriculated graduate/professional students. Founded: 1948. The graduate business unit is in a suburban setting and is on a semester calendar.

HIGHLIGHTS

Enrollment Profile
Full-time: 38
Part-time: 63
Total: 101
Average Age: 35
Fall 1997 Average GPA: 2.8
International: 22%
Women: 45%
Minorities: 35%
Average Class Size: 20
Fall 1997 Average GMAT: 450

Costs
Full-time tuition: $1560 per academic year (resident); $5700 per academic year (nonresident)
Part-time tuition: $52 per credit hour (resident); $130 per credit hour (nonresident)

ACBSP – The American Council of Business Schools and Programs accredited

GRADUATE BUSINESS PROGRAMS
Master of Science in Management (MS) Full-time, part-time; 36 total credits required; 12 months to 5 years to complete program. Concentrations in marketing, management information systems, operations management, technology management.

ADMISSION
Applications For fall 1997 there were 36 applications for admission. Of those applying, 36 were accepted. Of those accepted, 22 enrolled.

Application Requirements Application form, bachelor's degree, minimum GPA: 2.0, 3 letters of recommendation, college transcript(s).

Recommended for Application GMAT score accepted, work experience, computer experience.

Application Deadline 7/15 for fall, 12/1 for spring, 5/1 for summer, 7/15 for fall (international), 12/1 for spring (international), 5/1 for summer (international). Deferred entrance is available.

ACADEMICS
Faculty Full-time 8; part-time 4.

Teaching Methodologies Case study, computer-aided instruction, computer analysis, computer simulations, experiential learning, faculty seminars, field projects, group discussion, lecture, research, role playing, seminars by members of the business community, simulations, student presentations, study groups, team projects.

Technology 100 on-campus computer terminals/PCs are available for student use and are linked by a campus-wide network. The network has full access to the Internet. Students are not required to have their own PC.

Special Opportunities Advanced credit may be earned through transfer of credits from another institution.

FINANCES
Costs for 1997–98 Tuition: Full-time: $1560 per year (resident); $5700 per year (nonresident). Part-time: $52 per credit hour (resident); $130 per credit hour (nonresident). Cost varies by number of credits taken. Fees: Full-time: $318 per academic year (resident); $318 per academic year (nonresident). Part-time: $318 per year (resident); $318 per year (nonresident). Fees vary by number of credits taken. Average 1997–98 room and board costs were $3450 per academic year (on campus) and $5000 per academic year (off campus). Room and board costs vary by occupancy (e.g., single, double, triple), type of accommodation, type of meal plan.

Financial Aid In 1997–98, 30% of students received some institutionally administered aid in the form of teaching assistantships, grants, scholarships, work study, loans. Financial aid is available to part-time students. Application Deadline: 3/15.

Financial Aid Contact Dr. Emerelle McNair, Director of Financial Aid, 1100 South Marietta Parkway, Marietta, GA 30060-2896. Phone: 770-528-7290; Fax: 770-528-7483; E-mail: emcnair@spsu.edu

FACILITIES
Information Resources Main library; total holdings of 105,000 volumes, 42,900 microforms, 1,500 current periodical subscriptions. CD player(s) available for graduate student use. Access provided to online bibliographic retrieval services.

INTERNATIONAL STUDENTS
Demographics 22% of students enrolled are international students.

Services and Facilities International student office, counseling/support services.

Applying TOEFL: minimum score of 550, proof of adequate funds, proof of health/immunizations required. Financial aid is available to international students.

International Student Contact Ms. Charlotte Janis, Director of International Services , 1100 South Marietta Parkway, Marietta, GA 30060-2896. Phone: 770-528-7226; Fax: 770-528-7409; E-mail: cjanis@spsu.edu

PLACEMENT
Services include career counseling/planning, career fairs, career placement, job interviews arranged, resume referral to employers, and resume preparation.

Business Program(s) URL: http://www2.SPSU.edu/tmgt/

Program Contact: Dr. Robert Yancy, Dean, School of Management, 1100 South Marietta Parkway, Marietta, GA 30060-2896. Phone: 770-528-7440; Fax: 770-528-4967; E-mail: ryancy@spsu.edu

State University of West Georgia

Richards College of Business

Carrollton, Georgia

OVERVIEW
State University of West Georgia is a state-supported, coed, comprehensive institution. Enrollment: 8,650 graduate, professional, and undergraduate students; 734 full-time matriculated graduate/professional students; 1,586 part-time matriculated graduate/professional students. Founded: 1933. The graduate business unit is in a small-town setting and is on a semester calendar.

HIGHLIGHTS

Enrollment Profile
Full-time: 38
Part-time: 53
Total: 91
Average Age: 29
Fall 1997 Average GPA: 3.21
International: 15%
Women: 48%
Minorities: 13%
Average Class Size: 19
Fall 1997 Average GMAT: 520

Costs
Full-time tuition: $2756 per academic year (resident); $8188 per academic year (nonresident)
Part-time tuition: $52 per quarter hour (resident); $166 per quarter hour (nonresident)

AACSB – The International Association for Management Education accredited

GRADUATE BUSINESS PROGRAMS
General MBA (MBA) Full-time, part-time; 30-33 total credits required; minimum of 12 months to complete program.

Master of Professional Accountancy (MPA) Full-time, part-time; 30 total credits required; minimum of 12 months to complete program.

ADMISSION
Application Requirements Application form, application fee, bachelor's degree, minimum GPA: 2.5, 3 letters of recommendation, college transcript(s).

Recommended for Application GMAT score accepted: minimum 410, personal statement, resume, work experience, computer experience.

Application Deadline 8/1 for fall, 12/1 for spring, 4/1 for summer, 7/1 for fall (international), 11/1 for spring (international), 3/1 for summer (international). Application fee: $15. Deferred entrance is available.

ACADEMICS
Faculty Full-time 28.

Teaching Methodologies Case study, computer-aided instruction, computer analysis, computer simulations, experiential learning, group discussion, lecture, research, seminars by members of the business community, student presentations, study groups, team projects.

Technology 150 on-campus computer terminals/PCs are available for student use and are linked by a campus-wide network. The network has full access to the Internet. Students are not required to have their own PC.

Special Opportunities Advanced credit may be earned through transfer of credits from another institution.

FINANCES
Costs for 1997–98 Tuition: Full-time: $2756 per year (resident); $8188 per year (nonresident). Part-time: $52 per quarter hour (resident); $166 per quarter hour (nonresident). Cost varies by number of credits taken, reciprocity agreements. Average 1997–98 room and board costs were $4320 per academic year.

Room and board costs vary by occupancy (e.g., single, double, triple), type of accommodation, type of meal plan.

Financial Aid In 1997–98, 16% of students received some institutionally administered aid in the form of research assistantships, scholarships. Financial aid is available to part-time students. Application Deadline: 3/1.

Financial Aid Contact Dr. Jack Jenkins, Dean, Graduate School, Carrollton, GA 30118. Phone: 770-836-6419; Fax: 770-830-2301; E-mail: jjenkins@westga.edu

FACILITIES
Information Resources Irvine Sullivan Ingram Library plus 1 additional on-campus library; total holdings of 312,504 volumes, 882,096 microforms, 1,534 current periodical subscriptions. CD player(s) available for graduate student use. Access provided to online bibliographic retrieval services and online databases.

INTERNATIONAL STUDENTS
Demographics 15% of students enrolled are international students [Africa, 15%, Asia, 30%, Central America, 5%, Europe, 45%, North America, 5%].

Services and Facilities International student office, international student center, international student housing, counseling/support services.

Applying TOEFL: minimum score of 550, proof of adequate funds, proof of health/immunizations required. Financial aid is available to international students.

International Student Contact Ms. Sylvia E. Shortt, Assistant Director, Student Development, Student Development Center, 137 Parker Hall, Carrollton, GA 30118. Phone: 770-836-6428; Fax: 770-836-4502; E-mail: sshortt@westga.edu

PLACEMENT
Services include career counseling/planning, career fairs, career placement, electronic job bank, job interviews arranged, resume referral to employers, and resume preparation.

Employment Of 1996–97 graduates, 98% were employed within three months of graduation; the average starting salary was $40,000. Types of employment entered: accounting, banking, consumer products, engineering, finance, health services, hospitality management, human resources, information systems/technology, management, manufacturing, marketing, nonprofit, service industry, telecommunications, utilities.

Business Program(s) URL: http://www.westga.edu/~busn/

Program Contact: Mr. John R. Wells, Director, MBA Program, Richards College of Business, Back Campus Drive, Carrollton, GA 30118-3000. Phone: 770-836-6467; Fax: 770-836-6774; E-mail: jwells@sbf.bus.westga.edu

University of Georgia

Terry College of Business
Athens, Georgia

OVERVIEW
The University of Georgia is a state-supported, coed university. Enrollment: 29,693 graduate, professional, and undergraduate students; 4,909 full-time matriculated graduate/professional students; 1,548 part-time matriculated graduate/professional students. Founded: 1785. The graduate business unit is in a small-town setting and is on a semester calendar.

HIGHLIGHTS

Enrollment Profile
Full-time: 239
Part-time: 2
Total: 241
Average Age: 27
Fall 1997 Average GPA: 3.12

International: 21%
Women: 38%
Minorities: 7%
Average Class Size: 35
Fall 1997 Average GMAT: 630

Costs
Full-time tuition: $3290 per academic year (resident); $11,300 per academic year (nonresident)
Part-time tuition: N/R

AACSB – The International Association for Management Education accredited

GRADUATE BUSINESS PROGRAMS
Master of Business Administration (MBA) Full-time; 41-66 total credits required; 12 to 20 months to complete program. Concentrations in accounting, economics, entrepreneurship, finance, insurance, international business, management information systems, marketing, production management, quantitative analysis, real estate, risk management, strategic management, materials management, organizational management, technology management.

Master of Business Administration/Doctor of Jurisprudence (MBA/JD) Full-time; 126 total credits required; 3.3 years to complete program. Concentrations in accounting, economics, entrepreneurship, finance, insurance, international business, management information systems, marketing, production management, quantitative analysis, real estate, risk management, strategic management, materials management, organizational management, technology management.

Master of Accountancy (MAcc) Full-time, part-time; 37 total credits required; 9 months to 3 years to complete program. Concentrations in accounting, taxation.

Master of Arts in Economics (MA) Full-time; 30-36 total credits required; 9 months to 3 years to complete program. Concentrations in economics, financial economics, international economics.

ADMISSION
Applications For fall 1997 there were 905 applications for admission. Of those applying, 200 were accepted. Of those accepted, 95 enrolled.

Application Requirements GMAT score, application form, application fee, bachelor's degree, essay, 3 letters of recommendation, college transcript(s), computer experience: word processing, spreadsheet, database, presentation.

Recommended for Application Minimum GPA, interview, resume, minimum of 2 years of work experience.

Application Deadline Applications processed on a rolling/continuous basis for both domestic and international students. Application fee: $30. Deferred entrance is available.

ACADEMICS
Faculty Full-time 101; part-time 10.

Teaching Methodologies Case study, computer-aided instruction, computer analysis, computer simulations, experiential learning, faculty seminars, field projects, group discussion, lecture, research, role playing, seminars by members of the business community, simulations, student presentations, study groups, team projects.

Technology 500 on-campus computer terminals/PCs are available for student use and are linked by a campus-wide network. The network has full access to the Internet. Students are not required to have their own PC.

Special Opportunities International exchange program in Netherlands.

FINANCES
Costs for 1997–98 Tuition: Full-time: $3290 per year (resident); $11,300 per year (nonresident). Cost varies by number of credits taken. Fees: Full-time: $579 per academic year (resident); $579 per academic year (nonresident). Fees vary by number of credits taken. Average 1997–98 room and board costs were $4470 per academic year (on campus) and $6150 per academic year (off campus). Room and board costs vary by occupancy (e.g., single, double, triple), type of meal plan.

Financial Aid In 1997–98, 64% of students received some institutionally administered aid in the form of fellowships, research assistantships, teaching assistantships, scholarships, work study, loans. Application Deadline: 8/1.

Financial Aid Contact Student Financial Aid, Academic Building, Athens, GA 30602-6114. Phone: 706-542-6147.

FACILITIES
Information Resources Ilah Dunlap Little Memorial Library plus 2 additional on-campus libraries; total holdings of 3,458,298 volumes, 5,643,843 microforms, 45,258 current periodical subscriptions. CD player(s) available for graduate student use. Access provided to online bibliographic retrieval services.

INTERNATIONAL STUDENTS
Demographics 21% of students enrolled are international students [Africa, 4%, Asia, 63%, Europe, 21%, North America, 1%, South America, 10%, other, 1%].

Services and Facilities International student office, international student center, visa services, ESL courses, counseling/support services.

Applying TOEFL: minimum score of 585, proof of adequate funds, proof of health/immunizations required. Financial aid is available to international students.

International Student Contact Foreign Student Advisors, Office of International Education, 201 Barrow Hall, Athens, GA 30602-2407. Phone: 706-542-7903; Fax: 706-542-6622.

PLACEMENT
Services include alumni network, career counseling/planning, career fairs, career library, career placement, electronic job bank, job interviews arranged,

University of Georgia (continued)

job search course, resume referral to employers, and resume preparation. In 1996–97, 63 organizations participated in on-campus recruiting; 630 on-campus interviews were conducted.

Employment Of 1996–97 graduates, 94% were employed within three months of graduation; the average starting salary was $55,601. Types of employment entered: accounting, banking, communications, computer-related, consulting, consumer products, engineering, finance, financial services, health services, high technology, information systems/technology, insurance, international trade, law, management, manufacturing, marketing, media, real estate, service industry, telecommunications, transportation.

Business Program(s) URL: http://www.cba.uga.edu

Program Contact: Mr. Donald Perry, Jr., Director, MBA Admissions, 346 Brooks Hall, Athens, GA 30602-6264. Phone: 706-542-5671; Fax: 706-542-5351; E-mail: ugamba@cba.uga.edu

See full description on page 1072.

Valdosta State University

College of Business Administration
Valdosta, Georgia

OVERVIEW
Valdosta State University is a state-supported, coed university. Enrollment: 9,126 graduate, professional, and undergraduate students; 635 full-time matriculated graduate/professional students; 788 part-time matriculated graduate/professional students. Founded: 1906. The graduate business unit is in a small-town setting and is on a semester calendar.

HIGHLIGHTS
Enrollment Profile

Full-time: 0	International: 10%
Part-time: 21	Women: 33%
Total: 21	Minorities: N/R
Average Age: 35	Average Class Size: N/R
Fall 1997 Average GPA: 3.15	Fall 1997 Average GMAT: 534

Costs
Full-time tuition: $1869 per academic year (resident); $5097 per academic year (nonresident)
Part-time tuition: $210 per quarter (resident); $660 per quarter (nonresident)

AACSB – The International Association for Management Education accredited

GRADUATE BUSINESS PROGRAMS
Master of Business Administration (MBA) Part-time; 60 total credits required; 21 months to 7 years to complete program.
Master of Accountancy (MAcc) Full-time, part-time; 30 total credits required; 12 months to 7 years to complete program. Concentration in accounting.

ADMISSION
Applications For fall 1997 there were 50 applications for admission. Of those applying, 30 were accepted. Of those accepted, 19 enrolled.
Application Requirements Application form, application fee, bachelor's degree, essay, minimum GPA: 2.75, resume, college transcript(s).
Recommended for Application GMAT score accepted, work experience, computer experience.
Application Deadline Applications processed on a rolling/continuous basis for both domestic and international students. Application fee: $10.

ACADEMICS
Faculty Full-time 12.
Teaching Methodologies Case study, computer-aided instruction, computer analysis, computer simulations, experiential learning, field projects, group discussion, lecture, research, role playing, seminars by members of the business community, student presentations, team projects.
Technology 55 on-campus computer terminals/PCs are available for student use and are linked by a campus-wide network. The network has full access to the Internet. Students are not required to have their own PC.
Special Opportunities Advanced credit may be earned through transfer of credits from another institution.

FINANCES
Costs for 1997–98 Tuition: Full-time: $1869 per year (resident); $5097 per year (nonresident). Part-time: $210 per quarter (resident); $660 per quarter

(nonresident). Cost varies by academic program, number of credits taken, reciprocity agreements. Fees: Full-time: $393 per academic year (resident); $393 per academic year (nonresident). Fees vary by academic program, number of credits taken. Average 1997–98 room and board costs were $3090 per academic year (on campus) and $2700 per academic year (off campus). Room and board costs vary by type of accommodation, type of meal plan.

Financial Aid Scholarships, work study, loans available. Application Deadline: 3/1.

Financial Aid Contact Mr. Tommy Moore, Director of Financial Aid, Office of Financial Aid, Valdosta, GA 31698. Phone: 912-333-5935; Fax: 912-333-5430; E-mail: tmoore@.valdosta.edu

FACILITIES
Information Resources Odom Library plus 2 additional on-campus libraries; total holdings of 367,718 volumes, 821,877 microforms, 2,887 current periodical subscriptions. CD player(s) available for graduate student use. Access provided to online bibliographic retrieval services.

INTERNATIONAL STUDENTS
Demographics 10% of students enrolled are international students [Central America, 50%, South America, 50%].
Services and Facilities International student office, international student center, visa services, counseling/support services.
Applying TOEFL: minimum score of 550, proof of adequate funds, proof of health/immunizations required. Financial aid is not available to international students.
International Student Contact Miss Daphne Durham, Foreign Student Advisor, Office of International Programs, Valdosta, GA 31698. Phone: 912-333-7410; Fax: 912-245-3849; E-mail: ddurham@grits.valdosta.peachnet.edu

PLACEMENT
Services include career counseling/planning, career fairs, career placement, resume referral to employers, and resume preparation. In 1996–97, 129 organizations participated in on-campus recruiting.
Employment Of 1996–97 graduates, 100% were employed within three months of graduation; the average starting salary was $52,000. Types of employment entered: accounting, banking, communications, computer-related, education, finance, financial services, government, health services, human resources, insurance, management, manufacturing, marketing, retail, service industry.

Business Program(s) URL: http://www.valdosta.peachnet.edu/vsu/dept/coba/

Program Contact: Dr. Jacqueline Eastman, MBA Director, College of Business Administration, Valdosta, GA 31698. Phone: 912-245-3848; Fax: 912-245-6498; E-mail: jeastman@valdosta.edu

HAWAII

Chaminade University of Honolulu

School of Business
Honolulu, Hawaii

OVERVIEW
Chaminade University of Honolulu is an independent-religious, coed, comprehensive institution. Enrollment: 2,513 graduate, professional, and undergraduate students; 245 full-time matriculated graduate/professional students; 140 part-time matriculated graduate/professional students. Founded: 1955. The graduate business unit is in an urban setting and is on a term calendar.

GRADUATE BUSINESS PROGRAMS
Master of Business Administration (MBA)

ACADEMICS
Faculty Full-time 31; part-time 40.
Teaching Methodologies Case study, computer-aided instruction, computer analysis, computer simulations, experiential learning, field projects, group discussion, lecture, research, role playing, seminars by members of the business community, student presentations, study groups, team projects.
Technology 36 on-campus computer terminals/PCs are available for student use. The network has full access to the Internet. Students are not required to have their own PC.
Special Opportunities Advanced credit may be earned through credit for business training programs, transfer of credits from another institution. International exchange programs in Australia, Japan. An internship program is available.

FACILITIES
Information Resources Sullivan Library; total holdings of 65,000 volumes, 120,000 microforms, 704 current periodical subscriptions. CD player(s) available for graduate student use. Access provided to online bibliographic retrieval services.

Program Contact: Assistant MBA Program Director, 3140 Waialae Avenue, Honolulu, HI 96816-1578. Phone: 808-739-4612; Fax: 808-735-4734; E-mail: mba@chaminade.edu

Hawaii Pacific University

Center for Graduate Studies
Honolulu, Hawaii

OVERVIEW
Hawaii Pacific University is an independent-nonprofit, coed, comprehensive institution. Enrollment: 8,390 graduate, professional, and undergraduate students; 640 full-time matriculated graduate/professional students; 464 part-time matriculated graduate/professional students. Founded: 1965. The graduate business unit is in an urban setting and is on a 4-1-4 calendar.

HIGHLIGHTS

Enrollment Profile
Full-time: 640
Part-time: 464
Total: 1,104
Average Age: 31
Fall 1997 Average GPA: 2.89

International: 44%
Women: 43%
Minorities: 31%
Average Class Size: 20
Fall 1997 Average GMAT: 630

Costs
Full-time tuition: $7500 per academic year
Part-time tuition: $296 per credit

GRADUATE BUSINESS PROGRAMS
Master of Business Administration (MBA) Full-time, part-time; 45 total credits required; minimum of 18 months to complete program. Concentrations in accounting, finance, human resources, information management, international business, management, marketing, nonprofit management, travel industry/tourism management.

Master of Science in Information Systems (MS) Full-time, part-time; 42 total credits required; minimum of 18 months to complete program. Concentration in information management.

Master of Arts in Human Resource Management (MA) Full-time, part-time; 42 total credits required; minimum of 18 months to complete program. Concentration in human resources.

Master of Arts in Management (MA) Full-time, part-time; 42 total credits required; minimum of 18 months to complete program. Concentration in management.

Master of Arts in Organizational Change (MA) Full-time, part-time; 42 total credits required; minimum of 18 months to complete program. Concentration in organizational behavior/development.

ADMISSION
Applications For fall 1997 there were 513 applications for admission. Of those applying, 434 were accepted. Of those accepted, 218 enrolled.

Application Requirements GMAT score, GRE score, application form, application fee, bachelor's degree, minimum GPA: 2.7, 2 letters of recommendation, college transcript(s).

Recommended for Application Essay, personal statement, resume, work experience, computer experience.

Application Deadline Applications processed on a rolling/continuous basis for both domestic and international students. Application fee: $50. Deferred entrance is available.

ACADEMICS
Faculty Full-time 30; part-time 12.

Teaching Methodologies Case study, computer-aided instruction, computer analysis, computer simulations, faculty seminars, group discussion, lecture, research, role playing, seminars by members of the business community, simulations, student presentations, study groups, team projects.

Technology 300 on-campus computer terminals/PCs are available for student use. The network has full access to the Internet. Students are not required to have their own PC.

Special Opportunities Advanced credit may be earned through credit by examination, credit for military training programs, credit for business training programs, transfer of credits from another institution. An internship program is available.

FINANCES
Costs for 1997–98 Tuition: Full-time: $7500 per year. Part-time: $296 per credit. Cost varies by number of credits taken. Average 1997–98 room and board costs were $6900 per academic year (on campus) and $5000 per academic year (off campus). Room and board costs vary by occupancy (e.g., single, double, triple), type of accommodation.

Financial Aid In 1997–98, 15% of students received some institutionally administered aid in the form of research assistantships, scholarships, work study, loans. Financial aid is available to part-time students. Application Deadline: 3/15.

Financial Aid Contact Ms. Donna Lubong, Director of Financial Aid, 1164 Bishop Street, Honolulu, HI 96813. Phone: 808-544-0253; Fax: 808-544-1136; E-mail: dlubong@hpu.edu

FACILITIES
Information Resources Meader Library plus 2 additional on-campus libraries; total holdings of 160,000 volumes, 72,327 microforms, 1,834 current periodical subscriptions. CD player(s) available for graduate student use. Access provided to online bibliographic retrieval services and online databases.

INTERNATIONAL STUDENTS
Demographics 44% of students enrolled are international students [Africa, 3%, Asia, 60%, Australia/New Zealand, 2%, Central America, 3%, Europe, 20%, North America, 5%, South America, 3%, other, 4%].

Services and Facilities International student office, international student center, visa services, ESL courses, counseling/support services, international student organization.

Applying Proof of adequate funds required. TOEFL: minimum score of 550, TWE, proof of health/immunizations recommended. Financial aid is not available to international students.

International Student Contact Ms. Anne Newton, Director, International Student Office, 1132 Bishop Street, Honolulu, HI 96813. Phone: 808-544-0230; Fax: 808-544-1136; E-mail: anewton@hpu.edu

PLACEMENT
Services include alumni network, career counseling/planning, career fairs, career library, career placement, electronic job bank, job interviews arranged, job search course, resume referral to employers, and resume preparation. In 1996–97, 200 organizations participated in on-campus recruiting; 300 on-campus interviews were conducted.

Employment Of 1996–97 graduates, 65% were employed within three months of graduation; the average starting salary was $30,000. Types of employment entered: accounting, banking, communications, computer-related, consulting, consumer products, education, finance, financial services, government, health services, high technology, hospitality management, human resources, information systems/technology, insurance, international trade, management, marketing, media, nonprofit, real estate, retail, service industry, telecommunications, transportation.

Business Program(s) URL: http://www.hpu.edu

Program Contact: Mr. George Moyer, Associate Dean, Graduate Service Center, 1164 Bishop Street, Suite 1510, Honolulu, HI 96813. Phone: 808-544-1120, 800-669-4724; Fax: 808-544-0280; E-mail: gradservctr@hpu.edu
See full description on page 836.

University of Hawaii at Manoa

College of Business Administration
Honolulu, Hawaii

OVERVIEW
The University of Hawaii at Manoa is a state-supported, coed university. Enrollment: 16,296 graduate, professional, and undergraduate students; 3,517 full-time matriculated graduate/professional students; 2,066 part-time matriculated graduate/professional students. Founded: 1907. The graduate business unit is in an urban setting and is on a semester calendar.

University of Hawaii at Manoa (continued)

HIGHLIGHTS

Enrollment Profile

Full-time: 141	International: 21%
Part-time: 139	Women: 44%
Total: 280	Minorities: N/R
Average Age: N/R	Average Class Size: 30
Fall 1997 Average GPA: 3.44	Fall 1997 Average GMAT: 561

Costs

Full-time tuition: $3936 per academic year (resident); $9840 per academic year (nonresident)

Part-time tuition: $164 per credit (resident); $410 per credit (nonresident)

AACSB – The International Association for Management Education accredited

Degree(s) offered in conjunction with Japan-American Institute of Management Science

GRADUATE BUSINESS PROGRAMS

Master of Business Administration (MBA) Full-time, part-time; 42-48 total credits required; 2 to 7 years to complete program.

Executive MBA (EMBA) Full-time; 48 total credits required; 5 years full-time work experience required; 22 months to complete program.

Master of Accounting (MAcc) Full-time, part-time; 30 total credits required; 12 months to 7 years to complete program. Concentration in accounting.

Japan-focused Executive MBA (MBA) Full-time; 48 total credits required; 15 months to complete program.

China-focused Executive MBA (MBA) Full-time; 48 total credits required; 15 months to complete program.

PhD in Communication and Information Science (PhD) Full-time, part-time; 3 to 7 years to complete program.

Dual Degree MBA/JD (MBA/JD) Full-time, part-time; 122-128 total credits required; must submit separate applications to both programs; 5 to 7 years to complete program.

PhD in International Management (PhD) Full-time, part-time; 3 to 7 years to complete program.

ADMISSION

Applications For fall 1997 there were 376 applications for admission. Of those applying, 198 were accepted. Of those accepted, 70 enrolled.

Application Requirements Application form, application fee, bachelor's degree, essay, minimum GPA: 3.0, personal statement, resume, college transcript(s), computer experience: ICS 101 or equivalent.

Recommended for Application GMAT score accepted: minimum 500, work experience.

Application Deadline 3/1 for fall, 9/1 for spring, 1/15 for fall (international), 8/1 for spring (international). Application fee: $25, $50 (international).

ACADEMICS

Faculty Full-time 59; part-time 14.

Teaching Methodologies Case study, computer analysis, computer simulations, field projects, group discussion, lecture, research, role playing, simulations, student presentations, study groups.

Technology 80 on-campus computer terminals/PCs are available for student use and are linked by a campus-wide network. The network has full access to the Internet. Students are not required to have their own PC.

Special Opportunities Advanced credit may be earned through transfer of credits from another institution. International exchange programs in Denmark, Germany, Hong Kong, Japan, Korea, Saipan, Thailand. An internship program is available.

FINANCES

Costs for 1997–98 Tuition: Full-time: $3936 per year (resident); $9840 per year (nonresident). Part-time: $164 per credit (resident); $410 per credit (nonresident). Cost varies by number of credits taken, reciprocity agreements. Fees: Full-time: $116 per academic year (resident); $116 per academic year (nonresident). Part-time: $50 per semester (resident); $50 per semester (nonresident). Average 1997–98 room and board costs were $14,200 per academic year (off campus).

Financial Aid Research assistantships, teaching assistantships available. Financial aid is available to part-time students.

Financial Aid Contact Ms. Gayle Koki, Interim Director of Financial Aid, 2600 Campus Road, Student Services Center, Room 112, Honolulu, HI 96822. Phone: 808-956-7251; Fax: 808-956-3985; E-mail: gkoki@kala.ssc.hawaii.edu

FACILITIES

Information Resources Hamilton Library plus 1 additional on-campus library; total holdings of 2,718,618 volumes, 5,488,805 microforms, 35,000 current periodical subscriptions. CD player(s) available for graduate student use. Access provided to online bibliographic retrieval services and online databases.

INTERNATIONAL STUDENTS

Demographics 21% of students enrolled are international students [Asia, 84%, Australia/New Zealand, 2%, Europe, 2%, North America, 2%, other, 10%].

Services and Facilities International student office, visa services, ESL courses, counseling/support services.

Applying TOEFL: minimum score of 500, proof of adequate funds, proof of health/immunizations required. Financial aid is available to international students.

International Student Contact Ms. June Naughton, Director, International Student Office, 2600 Campus Road, Student Services Center, Room 414, Honolulu, HI 96822. Phone: 808-956-8613; Fax: 808-956-5076; E-mail: jnaught@hawaii.edu

PLACEMENT

Services include career counseling/planning, career fairs, career library, career placement, electronic job bank, job interviews arranged, resume referral to employers, and resume preparation. In 1996–97, 69 organizations participated in on-campus recruiting.

Employment Of 1996–97 graduates, 80% were employed within three months of graduation; the average starting salary was $28,000. Types of employment entered: accounting, banking, communications, computer-related, engineering, finance, government, hospitality management, human resources, information systems/technology, law, management, manufacturing, marketing, media, service industry, telecommunications, utilities.

Business Program(s) URL: http://www.cba.hawaii.edu

Program Contact: Assistant Dean, College of Business Administration, 2404 Maile Way, Business Administration A303, Honolulu, HI 96822. Phone: 808-956-8266; Fax: 808-956-9890; E-mail: osas@busadm.cba.hawaii.edu

See full description on page 1074.

IDAHO

Boise State University

College of Business and Economics

Boise, Idaho

OVERVIEW

Boise State University is a state-supported, coed, comprehensive institution. Enrollment: 14,883 graduate, professional, and undergraduate students; 108 full-time matriculated graduate/professional students; 1,790 part-time matriculated graduate/professional students. Founded: 1932. The graduate business unit is in an urban setting and is on a semester calendar.

HIGHLIGHTS

Enrollment Profile

Full-time: 51	International: 16%
Part-time: 206	Women: 44%
Total: 257	Minorities: 15%
Average Age: 32	Average Class Size: 35
Fall 1997 Average GPA: 3.11	Fall 1997 Average GMAT: 535

Costs

Full-time tuition: $3500 per academic year (resident); $11,000 per academic year (nonresident)

Part-time tuition: $125 per credit (resident); $125 per credit (nonresident)

AACSB – The International Association for Management Education accredited

GRADUATE BUSINESS PROGRAMS

Master of Business Administration (MBA) Full-time, part-time; 33-54 total credits required; 12 months to 7 years to complete program. Concentrations in accounting, entrepreneurship, finance, financial management/planning, management, marketing, organizational management, public policy and administration.

Master of Science in Taxation (MS) Part-time; 30 total credits required; 12 months to 7 years to complete program. Concentration in taxation.

Master of Science in Accountancy (MS) Full-time; 30 total credits required; 12 months to 7 years to complete program. Concentration in accounting.

Master of Science in Management Information Systems (MS) Part-time; 30 total credits required.

ADMISSION

Applications For fall 1997 there were 119 applications for admission. Of those applying, 80 were accepted. Of those accepted, 72 enrolled.

Application Requirements GMAT score: minimum 475, application form, application fee, bachelor's degree, essay, 2 letters of recommendation, personal statement, resume, college transcript(s), computer experience: word processing, spreadsheet, database.

Recommended for Application Minimum GPA: 2.9, work experience.

Application Deadline 3/1 for fall, 10/1 for spring, 2/1 for fall (international), 9/1 for spring (international). Application fee: $20, $30 (international).

ACADEMICS

Faculty Full-time 54; part-time 1.

Teaching Methodologies Case study, computer-aided instruction, computer analysis, computer simulations, experiential learning, group discussion, lecture, research, role playing, seminars by members of the business community, simulations, student presentations, study groups, team projects.

Technology 300 on-campus computer terminals/PCs are available for student use and are linked by a campus-wide network. The network has full access to the Internet. Students are not required to have their own PC.

Special Opportunities Advanced credit may be earned through credit by examination, credit for business training programs, transfer of credits from another institution. International exchange programs in France, Germany, Spain. An internship program is available.

FINANCES

Costs for 1997–98 Tuition: Full-time: $3500 per year (resident); $11,000 per year (nonresident). Part-time: $125 per credit (resident); $125 per credit (nonresident). Cost varies by class time (e.g., day/evening), number of credits taken. Fees vary by class time (e.g., day/evening), number of credits taken. Average 1997–98 room and board costs were $5600 per academic year (on campus) and $11,800 per academic year (off campus). Room and board costs vary by occupancy (e.g., single, double, triple), type of accommodation, type of meal plan.

Financial Aid In 1997–98, 6% of students received some institutionally administered aid in the form of research assistantships, teaching assistantships, scholarships, work study. Application Deadline: 3/1.

Financial Aid Contact Mrs. J. Renee Anchustegui, Program Coordinator, Business Graduate Studies, 1910 University Drive, B310, Boise , ID 83725-1600. Phone: 208-385-1126; Fax: 208-385-4989; E-mail: abuanchu@cobfac.idbsu.edu

FACILITIES

Information Resources Albertson's Library; total holdings of 455,951 volumes, 1,223,235 microforms, 4,702 current periodical subscriptions. CD player(s) available for graduate student use. Access provided to online bibliographic retrieval services.

INTERNATIONAL STUDENTS

Demographics 16% of students enrolled are international students [Asia, 94%, Central America, 3%, Europe, 3%].

Services and Facilities International student office, international student center, visa services, ESL courses, counseling/support services, international student organization.

Applying TOEFL: minimum score of 550, proof of adequate funds required. TSE, TWE, proof of health/immunizations recommended. Financial aid is available to international students.

International Student Contact Mrs. Brenda Ross, Foreign Student Services Coordinator, Admissions, 1910 University Drive, Boise, ID 83725. Phone: 208-385-1737; Fax: 208-385-3765; E-mail: bross@bsu.idbsu.edu

PLACEMENT

Services include alumni network, career counseling/planning, career fairs, career library, career placement, electronic job bank, and resume preparation.

Employment Of 1996–97 graduates, 95% were employed within three months of graduation. Types of employment entered: accounting, banking, computer-related, consulting, consumer products, education, engineering, finance, financial services, government, health services, high technology, information systems/technology, international trade, management, manufacturing, marketing, real estate, retail, utilities.

Business Program(s) URL: http://cobe.idbsu.edu/

Program Contact: Mrs. J. Renee Anchustegui, Program Coordinator, Graduate Business Studies, 1910 University Drive, B610, Boise, ID 83725-1600. Phone: 208-385-1126, 800-632-6586 Ext. 1126 (ID only), and/or 800-824-7017 Ext. 1126 (ID only); Fax: 208-385-4989; E-mail: abuanchu@cobfac.idbsu.edu

See full description on page 724.

Idaho State University

College of Business

Pocatello, Idaho

OVERVIEW

Idaho State University is a state-supported, coed university. Enrollment: 12,155 graduate, professional, and undergraduate students; 890 full-time matriculated graduate/professional students; 1,438 part-time matriculated graduate/professional students. Founded: 1901. The graduate business unit is in a small-town setting and is on a semester calendar.

HIGHLIGHTS

Enrollment Profile

Full-time: 27	International: 7%
Part-time: 93	Women: 35%
Total: 120	Minorities: 3%
Average Age: 34	Average Class Size: 20
Fall 1997 Average GPA: 3.17	Fall 1997 Average GMAT: 520

Costs
Full-time tuition: $2940 per academic year (resident); $8920 per academic year (nonresident)
Part-time tuition: $125 per credit hour (resident); $211 per credit hour (nonresident)

AACSB – The International Association for Management Education accredited

GRADUATE BUSINESS PROGRAMS

Master of Business Administration (MBA) Full-time, part-time, distance learning option; 30 total credits required; minimum of 12 months to complete program.

Master of Business Administration in Accounting (MBA) Full-time, part-time, distance learning option; 30 total credits required; 12 months to 3 years to complete program.

ADMISSION

Applications For fall 1997 there were 170 applications for admission. Of those applying, 140 were accepted. Of those accepted, 75 enrolled.

Application Requirements Application form, application fee, bachelor's degree, minimum GPA, 3 letters of recommendation, resume, college transcript(s).

Recommended for Application GMAT score accepted.

Application Deadline Applications processed on a rolling/continuous basis for both domestic and international students. Application fee: $35. Deferred entrance is available.

ACADEMICS

Faculty Full-time 41; part-time 3.

Teaching Methodologies Case study, computer-aided instruction, computer analysis, computer simulations, experiential learning, faculty seminars, field projects, group discussion, lecture, role playing, seminars by members of the business community, simulations, student presentations, study groups, team projects.

Technology 700 on-campus computer terminals/PCs are available for student use and are linked by a campus-wide network. The network has full access to the Internet. Students are not required to have their own PC.

Special Opportunities Advanced credit may be earned through credit by examination, credit for military training programs, credit for business training programs, transfer of credits from another institution.

FINANCES

Costs for 1997–98 Tuition: Full-time: $2940 per year (resident); $8920 per year (nonresident). Part-time: $125 per credit hour (resident); $211 per credit hour (nonresident). Cost varies by academic program, number of credits taken, reciprocity agreements. Average 1997–98 room and board costs were $2980 per academic year. Room and board costs vary by occupancy (e.g., single, double, triple), type of accommodation, type of meal plan.

Financial Aid In 1997–98, 8% of students received some institutionally administered aid in the form of teaching assistantships, work study. Financial aid is available to part-time students.

Financial Aid Contact Douglas Severs, Financial Aid Office, Campus Box 8077, Pocatello, ID 83209-8077. Phone: 208-236-2756; Fax: 208-236-4755; E-mail: sevedoug@isu.edu

FACILITIES

Information Resources Eli M. Oboler Library; total holdings of 482,793 volumes, 1,293,361 microforms, 3,326 current periodical subscriptions. CD player(s) available for graduate student use. Access provided to online bibliographic retrieval services.

INTERNATIONAL STUDENTS

Demographics 7% of students enrolled are international students.

Idaho State University (continued)

Services and Facilities International student office, international student center, international student housing, counseling/support services.

Applying TOEFL: minimum score of 550 required. Financial aid is available to international students.

International Student Contact Raymond Wallace, International Student Advisor, Box 8123, Pocatello, ID 83209. Phone: 208-236-2941; Fax: 208-236-3719; E-mail: wallraym@isu.edu

PLACEMENT

Services include career counseling/planning, career library, career placement, job interviews arranged, and job search course.

Employment Of 1996–97 graduates, 90% were employed within three months of graduation. Types of employment entered: accounting, banking, computer-related, finance, government.

Program Contact: Mr. George Johnson, MBA Director, Box 8020, Pocatello, ID 83204. Phone: 208-236-2504; Fax: 208-236-4367; E-mail: johngeor@isu.edu

University of Idaho

College of Business and Economics

Moscow, Idaho

OVERVIEW

The University of Idaho is a state-supported, coed university. Enrollment: 11,027 graduate, professional, and undergraduate students; 1,073 full-time matriculated graduate/professional students; 1,109 part-time matriculated graduate/professional students. Founded: 1889. The graduate business unit is in a small-town setting and is on a semester calendar.

HIGHLIGHTS

Enrollment Profile

Full-time: 5	International: 27%
Part-time: 6	Women: 36%
Total: 11	Minorities: N/R
Average Age: 35	Average Class Size: 8
Fall 1997 Average GPA: 3.5	Fall 1997 Average GMAT: 520

Costs

Full-time tuition: $2482 per academic year (resident); $7282 per academic year (nonresident)

Part-time tuition: $124 per credit (resident); $219 per credit (nonresident)

AACSB – The International Association for Management Education accredited

GRADUATE BUSINESS PROGRAMS

Master of Accountancy (MAcc) Full-time, part-time; 30 total credits required. Concentration in accounting.

ADMISSION

Applications For fall 1997 there were 7 applications for admission. Of those applying, 7 were accepted. Of those accepted, 7 enrolled.

Application Requirements GMAT score, GRE score, application form, application fee, bachelor's degree, minimum GPA: 3.0, college transcript(s).

Application Deadline 7/1 for fall, 11/1 for spring, 4/1 for summer, 6/1 for fall (international), 10/1 for spring (international), 3/1 for summer (international). Application fee: $35, $45 (international).

ACADEMICS

Faculty Full-time 33; part-time 12.

Teaching Methodologies Case study, computer-aided instruction, computer simulations, experiential learning, lecture, research, role playing, student presentations, team projects.

Technology 400 on-campus computer terminals/PCs are available for student use and are linked by a campus-wide network. The network has full access to the Internet. Students are not required to have their own PC.

Special Opportunities Advanced credit may be earned through transfer of credits from another institution. International exchange programs in Denmark, France, Germany, Netherlands. An internship program is available.

FINANCES

Costs for 1997–98 Tuition: Full-time: $2482 per year (resident); $7282 per year (nonresident). Part-time: $124 per credit (resident); $219 per credit (nonresident). Cost varies by number of credits taken, reciprocity agreements. Average 1997–98 room and board costs were $3680 per academic year (on campus) and $4000 per academic year (off campus). Room and board

costs vary by campus location, occupancy (e.g., single, double, triple), type of accommodation, type of meal plan.

Financial Aid In 1997–98, 45% of students received some institutionally administered aid in the form of research assistantships, teaching assistantships, scholarships, work study. Application Deadline: 2/15.

Financial Aid Contact Student Financial Aid, Moscow, ID 83844-4291. Phone: 208-885-6312; Fax: 208-885-5592.

FACILITIES

Information Resources Main library plus 1 additional on-campus library; total holdings of 944,813 volumes, 1,333,614 microforms, 11,547 current periodical subscriptions. CD player(s) available for graduate student use. Access provided to online bibliographic retrieval services and online databases.

INTERNATIONAL STUDENTS

Demographics 27% of students enrolled are international students [Africa, 67%, Asia, 33%].

Services and Facilities International student office, international student center, counseling/support services.

Applying TOEFL: minimum score of 550, proof of adequate funds required.

International Student Contact International Programs Office, Moscow, ID 83844-3013. Phone: 208-885-8984; Fax: 208-885-2859.

PLACEMENT

Services include alumni network, career placement, and resume referral to employers. In 1996–97, 30 organizations participated in on-campus recruiting; 33 on-campus interviews were conducted.

Employment Of 1996–97 graduates, 100% were employed within three months of graduation. Types of employment entered: accounting, computer-related.

Business Program(s) URL: http://www.uidaho.edu/cbe/college/

Program Contact: Graduate Admissions Office, Moscow, ID 83844-3019. Phone: 208-885-4001, 800-422-6013 (ID only); Fax: 208-885-8939.

ILLINOIS

Aurora University

School of Business and Professional Studies

Aurora, Illinois

OVERVIEW

Aurora University is an independent-nonprofit, coed, comprehensive institution. Enrollment: 2,122 graduate, professional, and undergraduate students; 316 full-time matriculated graduate/professional students; 595 part-time matriculated graduate/professional students. Founded: 1893. The graduate business unit is in a suburban setting and is on a trimester calendar.

HIGHLIGHTS

Enrollment Profile

Full-time: 80	International: 3%
Part-time: 121	Women: 36%
Total: 201	Minorities: 11%
Average Age: 35	Average Class Size: 15
Fall 1997 Average GPA: 3.0	Fall 1997 Average GMAT: N/R

Costs

Full-time tuition: N/R

Part-time tuition: $1176 per 3 semester hours

GRADUATE BUSINESS PROGRAMS

Master of Business Administration (MBA) Full-time, part-time, distance learning option; 45 total credits required; 2 to 3.2 years to complete program.

ADMISSION

Applications For fall 1997 there were 80 applications for admission. Of those applying, 64 were accepted. Of those accepted, 44 enrolled.

Application Requirements Application form, application fee, bachelor's degree, minimum GPA: 2.75, 2 letters of recommendation, college transcript(s), computer experience.

Recommended for Application Interview, work experience.

Application Deadline Applications processed on a rolling/continuous basis for both domestic and international students. Application fee: $25. Deferred entrance is available.

ACADEMICS

Faculty Full-time 10; part-time 8.

Teaching Methodologies Case study, computer-aided instruction, computer analysis, computer simulations, group discussion, lecture, seminars by members of the business community, student presentations, study groups, team projects.

Technology 100 on-campus computer terminals/PCs are available for student use and are linked by a campus-wide network. The network has full access to the Internet. Students are not required to have their own PC.

Special Opportunities Advanced credit may be earned through transfer of credits from another institution. An internship program is available.

FINANCES

Costs for 1997–98 Tuition: $1176 per 3 semester hours. Average 1997–98 room and board costs were $4500 per academic year.

Financial Aid In 1997–98, 5% of students received some institutionally administered aid in the form of fellowships, teaching assistantships, loans. Financial aid is available to part-time students.

Financial Aid Contact Ms. Heather Gutierrez, Director of Financial Aid, 347 South Gladstone Avenue, Aurora, IL 60506-4892. Phone: 630-844-5448; Fax: 630-844-7830.

FACILITIES

Information Resources Charles B. Phillips Library; total holdings of 130,000 volumes, 79,000 microforms, 762 current periodical subscriptions. CD player(s) available for graduate student use. Access provided to online bibliographic retrieval services.

INTERNATIONAL STUDENTS

Demographics 3% of students enrolled are international students [Asia, 34%, South America, 66%].

Services and Facilities Counseling/support services.

Applying TOEFL: minimum score of 550, proof of adequate funds, proof of health/immunizations required. Financial aid is not available to international students.

International Student Contact Dr. Leo Loughead, MBA Program Manager, 347 South Gladstone Avenue, Aurora, IL 60506-4892. Phone: 630-844-3830; Fax: 630-844-7830.

PLACEMENT

Services include alumni network, career counseling/planning, career fairs, career library, career placement, electronic job bank, job interviews arranged, job search course, resume referral to employers, and resume preparation.

Employment Of 1996–97 graduates, 98% were employed within three months of graduation.

Business Program(s) URL: http://www.aurora.edu

Program Contact: Dr. Leo Loughead, MBA Program Manager, 347 South Gladstone Avenue, Aurora, IL 60506-4892. Phone: 630-844-3830; Fax: 630-844-7830.

Benedictine University

Graduate Programs

Lisle, Illinois

OVERVIEW

Benedictine University is an independent-religious, coed, comprehensive institution. Enrollment: 2,842 graduate, professional, and undergraduate students; 269 full-time matriculated graduate/professional students; 826 part-time matriculated graduate/professional students. Founded: 1887. The graduate business unit is in a suburban setting and is on a quarter calendar.

HIGHLIGHTS

Enrollment Profile

Full-time: 73	International: 0%
Part-time: 238	Women: 39%
Total: 311	Minorities: 8%
Average Age: 33	Average Class Size: 24
Fall 1997 Average GPA: 2.75	Fall 1997 Average GMAT: 500

Costs
Full-time tuition: N/R
Part-time tuition: $295 per credit hour

GRADUATE BUSINESS PROGRAMS

Evening MBA (MBA) Full-time, part-time; 64 total credits required; 12 months to 6 years to complete program. Concentrations in finance, human resources, international business, leadership, management, management information systems, marketing, operations management, technology management, accounting.

Master of Business Administration/Master of Science in Management and Organizational Behavior (MBA/MSMOB) Full-time, part-time; 96 total credits required; 2 to 6 years to complete program. Concentrations in human resources, organizational behavior/development.

Master of Business Administration/Master of Science in Management Information Systems (MBA/MSMIS) Full-time, part-time; 96 total credits required; 2 to 6 years to complete program. Concentration in management information systems.

Master of Business Administration/Master of Public Health (MBA/MPH) Full-time, part-time; 96 total credits required; 2 to 6 years to complete program.

Executive MBA for Health Care Professionals (EMBA) Part-time; 64 total credits required; 18 months to complete program. Concentration in health care.

ADMISSION

Applications For fall 1997 there were 135 applications for admission. Of those applying, 107 were accepted. Of those accepted, 100 enrolled.

Application Requirements Application form, application fee, bachelor's degree, essay, 2 letters of recommendation, personal statement, college transcript(s).

Recommended for Application GMAT score accepted, GRE score accepted, MAT score accepted, minimum GPA, interview, work experience, computer experience.

Application Deadline Applications processed on a rolling/continuous basis for both domestic and international students. Application fee: $30.

ACADEMICS

Faculty Full-time 10; part-time 86.

Teaching Methodologies Case study, computer-aided instruction, computer analysis, computer simulations, experiential learning, field projects, group discussion, lecture, role playing, simulations, student presentations, study groups, team projects.

Technology 80 on-campus computer terminals/PCs are available for student use and are linked by a campus-wide network. The network has full access to the Internet. Students are not required to have their own PC.

Special Opportunities Advanced credit may be earned through credit by examination, credit for experience, credit for military training programs, credit for business training programs, transfer of credits from another institution. International exchange program in United Kingdom.

FINANCES

Costs for 1997–98 Tuition: $295 per credit hour.

Financial Aid In 1997–98, 50% of students received some institutionally administered aid in the form of work study, loans. Financial aid is available to part-time students.

Financial Aid Contact Bryant Anderson, Director of Benedictine Central, 5700 College Road, Lisle, IL 60532-0900. Phone: 630-829-6500; Fax: 630-829-6456.

FACILITIES

Information Resources Lownik Library plus 1 additional on-campus library; total holdings of 162,874 volumes, 109,591 microforms, 700 current periodical subscriptions. CD player(s) available for graduate student use. Access provided to online bibliographic retrieval services.

INTERNATIONAL STUDENTS

Demographics 0% of students enrolled are international students [Asia, 100%].

Services and Facilities International student office, ESL courses.

Applying TOEFL: minimum score of 600 required. Financial aid is not available to international students.

International Student Contact Ms. Anna Cuomo, Director of International Student Affairs, 5700 College Road, Lisle, IL 60532-0900. Phone: 630-829-6342; Fax: 630-829-6584.

PLACEMENT

Services include alumni network, career counseling/planning, career library, career placement, job interviews arranged, resume referral to employers, and resume preparation.

Business Program(s) URL: http://www.ben.edu

Program Contact: Ms. Amy Graham, Director of Graduate Admissions, 5700 College Road, Lisle, IL 60532-0900. Phone: 630-829-6200; Fax: 630-829-6584; E-mail: gradadm@ben.edu

Bradley University

Foster College of Business Administration

Peoria, Illinois

OVERVIEW
Bradley University is an independent-nonprofit, coed, comprehensive institution. Enrollment: 5,882 graduate, professional, and undergraduate students; 135 full-time matriculated graduate/professional students; 686 part-time matriculated graduate/professional students. Founded: 1897. The graduate business unit is in an urban setting and is on a semester calendar.

GRADUATE BUSINESS PROGRAMS
Master of Business Administration (MBA)

Master of Science in Accounting (MS)

ACADEMICS
Faculty Full-time 34; part-time 6.

Teaching Methodologies Case study, computer analysis, computer simulations, experiential learning, field projects, group discussion, lecture, research, role playing, simulations, student presentations, study groups, team projects.

Technology 194 on-campus computer terminals/PCs are available for student use and are linked by a campus-wide network. The network has full access to the Internet. Students are not required to have their own PC.

Special Opportunities Advanced credit may be earned through transfer of credits from another institution.

FACILITIES
Information Resources Cullom-Davis Library; total holdings of 531,744 volumes, 762,581 microforms, 1,833 current periodical subscriptions. Access provided to online bibliographic retrieval services.

Program Contact: Director of Graduate Programs, Foster College of Business Administration, 123 Baker Hall, Peoria, IL 61625. Phone: 309-677-2253; Fax: 309-677-3374; E-mail: ade@bradley.bradley.edu

Columbia College

Department of Management

Chicago, Illinois

OVERVIEW
Columbia College is an independent-nonprofit, coed, comprehensive institution. Enrollment: 8,473 graduate, professional, and undergraduate students; 216 full-time matriculated graduate/professional students; 371 part-time matriculated graduate/professional students. The graduate business unit is in an urban setting and is on a semester calendar.

HIGHLIGHTS

Enrollment Profile

Full-time: N/R	International: N/R
Part-time: N/R	Women: N/R
Total: 72	Minorities: N/R
Average Age: 32	Average Class Size: 8
Fall 1997 Average GPA: N/R	Fall 1997 Average GMAT: N/R

Costs
Full-time tuition: N/R
Part-time tuition: $349 per credit hour

GRADUATE BUSINESS PROGRAMS
Arts, Entertainment and Media Management (MA) Full-time, part-time; 42 total credits required. Concentration in arts administration/management.

ADMISSION
Application Requirements Application form, bachelor's degree, essay, minimum GPA: 3.0, letters of recommendation, personal statement, college transcript(s), computer experience: computer applications.

Recommended for Application Interview, work experience.

Application Deadline Application fee: $30.

ACADEMICS
Technology Students are not required to have their own PC.

Special Opportunities An internship program is available.

FINANCES
Costs for 1997-98 Tuition: $349 per credit hour. Fees: $40 per semester.

Financial Aid Financial aid is available to part-time students.

Financial Aid Contact Ms. Diane Brazier, Financial Aid Advisor, Chicago, IL 60605. Phone: 312-663-1600.

FACILITIES
Information Resources Columbia College Library; total holdings of 178,928 volumes, 118,123 microforms, 981 current periodical subscriptions.

INTERNATIONAL STUDENTS
Demographics N/R

Services and Facilities ESL courses.

Applying TOEFL required. Financial aid is available to international students.

International Student Contact Admissions—Graduate School, Chicago, IL 60605. Phone: 312-663-1600.

Business Program(s) URL: http://www.colum.edu

Program Contact: Admissions—Graduate School, Chicago, IL 60605. Phone: 312-663-1600.

DePaul University

Charles H. Kellstadt Graduate School of Business

Chicago, Illinois

OVERVIEW
DePaul University is an independent-religious, coed university. Enrollment: 17,804 graduate, professional, and undergraduate students; 3,579 full-time matriculated graduate/professional students; 3,528 part-time matriculated graduate/professional students. Founded: 1898. The graduate business unit is in an urban setting and is on a quarter calendar.

HIGHLIGHTS

Enrollment Profile

Full-time: 1,236	International: 3%
Part-time: 1,301	Women: 36%
Total: 2,537	Minorities: N/R
Average Age: 29	Average Class Size: 27
Fall 1997 Average GPA: 3.2	Fall 1997 Average GMAT: 570

Costs
Full-time tuition: N/R
Part-time tuition: $1920 per course

AACSB – The International Association for Management Education accredited

GRADUATE BUSINESS PROGRAMS
Day MBA (MBA) Full-time; 88 total credits required; 18 months to complete program. Concentrations in international finance, international marketing.

Evening MBA (MBA) Full-time, part-time; 60-84 total credits required; 18 months to 6 years to complete program. Concentrations in accounting, economics, entrepreneurship, finance, human resources, international business, management information systems, marketing, operations management.

Weekend MBA (MBA) Full-time, part-time; 60-80 total credits required; 22 months to 2.8 years to complete program. Concentration in strategic management.

Master of Business Administration/Doctor of Jurisprudence (MBA/JD) Full-time, part-time; 140 total credits required; 2.8 to 3.8 years to complete program. Concentrations in accounting, economics, entrepreneurship, finance, human resources, international business, management information systems, marketing, operations management.

Master of Accountancy (MAcc) Full-time, part-time; 52-72 total credits required; 18 months to 6 years to complete program. Concentration in accounting.

Master of Science in Accountancy (MS) Full-time, part-time; 60-64 total credits required; 15 months to 6 years to complete program. Concentration in accounting.

Master of Science in Finance (MS) Full-time, part-time; 52 total credits required; 18 months to 6 years to complete program. Concentration in finance.

Master of Science in Taxation (MS) Full-time, part-time; 52-64 total credits required; 18 months to 6 years to complete program. Concentration in taxation.

Master of Science in Management Information Systems (MS) Full-time, part-time; 116 total credits required; 2 to 6 years to complete program. Concentration in management information systems.

ADMISSION
Applications For fall 1997 there were 1,197 applications for admission. Of those applying, 713 were accepted. Of those accepted, 478 enrolled.

Application Requirements GMAT score, application form, application fee, bachelor's degree, minimum GPA, personal statement, college transcript(s), computer experience.

Recommended for Application Interview, 2 letters of recommendation, resume, work experience.

Application Deadline 8/1 for fall, 11/1 for winter, 3/1 for spring, 5/1 for summer, 6/1 for fall (international), 9/1 for winter (international), 1/1 for spring (international), 3/1 for summer (international). Application fee: $40. Deferred entrance is available.

ACADEMICS
Faculty Full-time 103; part-time 117.

Teaching Methodologies Case study, computer-aided instruction, computer analysis, computer simulations, faculty seminars, group discussion, lecture, research, role playing, seminars by members of the business community, student presentations, study groups, team projects.

Technology 600 on-campus computer terminals/PCs are available for student use and are linked by a campus-wide network. The network has full access to the Internet. Students are not required to have their own PC.

Special Opportunities Advanced credit may be earned through transfer of credits from another institution. International exchange program available. An internship program is available.

FINANCES
Costs for 1997–98 Tuition: $1920 per course. Cost varies by academic program. Fees: $10 per term. Average 1997–98 room and board costs were $10,000 per academic year (off campus).

Financial Aid Research assistantships, scholarships, work study available. Financial aid is available to part-time students. Application Deadline: 4/30.

Financial Aid Contact Ms. Christine Munoz, Director of Admissions, 1 East Jackson Boulevard, Chicago, IL 60604-2287. Phone: 312-362-8810; Fax: 312-362-6677; E-mail: mbainfo@wppost.depaul.edu

FACILITIES
Information Resources Main library plus 3 additional on-campus libraries; total holdings of 738,072 volumes, 309,701 microforms, 10,136 current periodical subscriptions. CD player(s) available for graduate student use. Access provided to online bibliographic retrieval services.

INTERNATIONAL STUDENTS
Demographics 3% of students enrolled are international students.

Services and Facilities International student office, visa services, ESL courses, counseling/support services.

Applying TOEFL: minimum score of 550, proof of adequate funds required. TSE, TWE recommended. Financial aid is available to international students.

International Student Contact Ms. Christine Munoz, Director of Admissions, 1 East Jackson Boulevard, Chicago, IL 60604-2287. Phone: 312-362-8810; Fax: 312-362-6677; E-mail: mbainfo@wppost.depaul.edu

PLACEMENT
Services include alumni network, career counseling/planning, career fairs, career library, career placement, electronic job bank, job interviews arranged, job search course, resume referral to employers, and resume preparation.

Employment Types of employment entered: accounting, banking, communications, computer-related, consulting, consumer products, engineering, finance, financial services, government, health services, high technology, hospitality management, human resources, information systems/technology, insurance, international trade, management, manufacturing, marketing, media, nonprofit, petrochemical, pharmaceutical, real estate, retail, service industry, telecommunications, transportation, utilities.

Business Program(s) URL: http://www.depaul.edu/kellstadt

Program Contact: Ms. Christine Munoz, Director of Admissions, 1 East Jackson Boulevard, Chicago, IL 60604-2287. Phone: 312-362-8810; Fax: 312-362-6677; E-mail: mbainfo@wppost.depaul.edu
See full description on page 778.

Dominican University

Graduate School of Business
River Forest, Illinois

OVERVIEW
Dominican University is an independent-religious, coed, comprehensive institution. Enrollment: 2,000 graduate, professional, and undergraduate students; 160 full-time matriculated graduate/professional students; 829 part-time matriculated graduate/professional students. Founded: 1901. The graduate business unit is in a suburban setting and is on a semester calendar.

HIGHLIGHTS
Enrollment Profile
Full-time: 60
Part-time: 298
Total: 358
Average Age: 29
Fall 1997 Average GPA: 3.2

International: 21%
Women: 48%
Minorities: N/R
Average Class Size: 14
Fall 1997 Average GMAT: 500

Costs
Full-time tuition: $13,350 per academic year
Part-time tuition: $1335 per 3-hour course

ACBSP – The American Council of Business Schools and Programs accredited

Degree(s) offered in conjunction with Concordia University

GRADUATE BUSINESS PROGRAMS
Master of Business Administration (MBA) Full-time, part-time; 30 total credits required; minimum of 12 months to complete program. Concentrations in accounting, finance, management information systems, marketing, entrepreneurship, international business, management, health care, human resources.

Master of Science in Accounting (MS) Full-time, part-time; 30 total credits required; minimum of 12 months to complete program. Concentration in accounting.

Master of Science in Management Information Systems (MS) Full-time, part-time; 30 total credits required; minimum of 12 months to complete program.

Master of Science in Organization Management (MS) Full-time, part-time; 30 total credits required; minimum of 12 months to complete program. Concentrations in human resources, health care.

Master of Business Administration/Doctor of Jurisprudence (MBA/JD) Full-time, part-time; 77-98 total credits required; minimum of 3 years to complete program. Concentrations in accounting, finance, management information systems, marketing, entrepreneurship, international business, management, health care, human resources.

Master of Business Administration/Master of Library and Information Science (MBA/MLIS) Full-time, part-time; 54-75 total credits required; 2 to 6 years to complete program. Concentrations in accounting, finance, management information systems, marketing, entrepreneurship, international business, management, health care, human resources.

ADMISSION
Applications For fall 1997 there were 100 applications for admission. Of those applying, 75 were accepted. Of those accepted, 65 enrolled.

Application Requirements Application form, application fee, bachelor's degree, essay, minimum GPA: 3.0, 3 letters of recommendation, personal statement, college transcript(s).

Recommended for Application GMAT score accepted, computer experience.

Application Deadline Applications processed on a rolling/continuous basis for both domestic and international students. Application fee: $25. Deferred entrance is available.

ACADEMICS
Faculty Full-time 15; part-time 40.

Teaching Methodologies Case study, computer-aided instruction, computer analysis, computer simulations, experiential learning, faculty seminars, field projects, group discussion, lecture, research, role playing, seminars by members of the business community, simulations, student presentations, study groups, team projects.

Technology 200 on-campus computer terminals/PCs are available for student use and are linked by a campus-wide network. The network has full access to the Internet. Students are not required to have their own PC.

Special Opportunities Advanced credit may be earned through transfer of credits from another institution. International exchange programs in France, Germany. An internship program is available.

FINANCES
Costs for 1997–98 Tuition: Full-time: $13,350 per year. Part-time: $1335 per 3-hour course. Cost varies by number of credits taken. Fees: Full-time: $10 per academic year. Part-time: $10 per course. Fees vary by academic program, number of credits taken. Average 1997–98 room and board costs were $5000 per academic year (on campus) and $6500 per academic year (off campus). Room and board costs vary by occupancy (e.g., single, double, triple), type of meal plan.

Financial Aid Grants available. Financial aid is available to part-time students.

Financial Aid Contact Mr. Howard Florine, Director of Financial Aid, 7900 West Division Street, River Forest, IL 60305. Phone: 708-524-6809; Fax: 708-366-5360; E-mail: florineh@email.dom.edu

FACILITIES
Information Resources Rebecca Crown Library plus 1 additional on-campus library; total holdings of 280,000 volumes, 1,100 current periodical

Dominican University (continued)

subscriptions. CD player(s) available for graduate student use. Access provided to online bibliographic retrieval services.

INTERNATIONAL STUDENTS
Demographics 21% of students enrolled are international students.

Services and Facilities International student office, international student housing, visa services, ESL courses, counseling/support services.

Applying TOEFL: minimum score of 550, proof of adequate funds, proof of health/immunizations required. Financial aid is available to international students.

International Student Contact Dr. Sue Ponremy, International Student Advisor, 7900 West Division Street, River Forest, IL 60305. Phone: 708-524-6965; Fax: 708-366-5360; E-mail: sponremy@email.dom.edu

PLACEMENT
Services include alumni network, career counseling/planning, career fairs, career library, career placement, electronic job bank, job interviews arranged, job search course, resume referral to employers, and resume preparation. In 1996–97, 110 organizations participated in on-campus recruiting.

Employment Types of employment entered: accounting, banking, chemical industry, communications, computer-related, consulting, consumer products, education, finance, financial services, government, health services, high technology, hospitality management, human resources, information systems/technology, insurance, international trade, law, management, manufacturing, marketing, media, nonprofit, petrochemical, pharmaceutical, real estate, retail, service industry, telecommunications, transportation, utilities.

Business Program(s) URL: http://www.dom.edu/Academic/Business.html

Program Contact: Dr. Daniel Condon, Director of Admissions, 7900 West Division Street, River Forest, IL 60305. Phone: 708-524-6233; Fax: 708-366-5360; E-mail: condondp@email.dom.edu
See full description on page 782.

Eastern Illinois University

Lumpkin College of Business and Applied Science

Charleston, Illinois

OVERVIEW
Eastern Illinois University is a state-supported, coed, comprehensive institution. Enrollment: 11,878 graduate, professional, and undergraduate students; 531 full-time matriculated graduate/professional students; 1,021 part-time matriculated graduate/professional students. Founded: 1895. The graduate business unit is in a small-town setting and is on a semester calendar.

HIGHLIGHTS

Enrollment Profile

Full-time: 47	International: 9%
Part-time: 149	Women: 45%
Total: 196	Minorities: 5%
Average Age: 28	Average Class Size: 25
Fall 1997 Average GPA: 3.1	Fall 1997 Average GMAT: 528

Costs
Full-time tuition: $1622 per academic year (resident); $3860 per academic year (nonresident)
Part-time tuition: $90 per credit hour (resident); $270 per credit hour (nonresident)

AACSB – The International Association for Management Education accredited

GRADUATE BUSINESS PROGRAMS
Master of Business Administration (MBA) Full-time, part-time; 33 total credits required; 12 months to 6 years to complete program. Concentration in management.

ADMISSION
Applications For fall 1997 there were 96 applications for admission. Of those applying, 90 were accepted. Of those accepted, 78 enrolled.

Application Requirements Application form, application fee, bachelor's degree, 2 letters of recommendation, personal statement, resume, college transcript(s).

Recommended for Application GMAT score accepted, minimum GPA.

Application Deadline 7/1 for fall, 12/1 for spring, 4/15 for summer, 6/1 for fall (international), 10/15 for spring (international), 4/1 for summer (international). Application fee: $25. Deferred entrance is available.

ACADEMICS
Faculty Full-time 42.

Teaching Methodologies Case study, lecture, team projects.

Technology 450 on-campus computer terminals/PCs are available for student use and are linked by a campus-wide network. The network has full access to the Internet. Students are not required to have their own PC.

Special Opportunities Advanced credit may be earned through transfer of credits from another institution. An internship program is available.

FINANCES
Costs for 1997–98 Tuition: Full-time: $1622 per semester (resident); $3860 per semester (nonresident). Part-time: $90 per credit hour (resident); $270 per credit hour (nonresident). Fees: $15 per credit hour (resident); $15 per credit hour (nonresident). Average 1997–98 room only costs were $3000 per academic year. Room and board costs vary by occupancy (e.g., single, double, triple), type of accommodation, type of meal plan.

Financial Aid In 1997–98, 8% of students received some institutionally administered aid in the form of research assistantships, work study, loans. Financial aid is available to part-time students. Application Deadline: 2/15.

Financial Aid Contact Mr. John Flynn, Director of Financial Aid, 600 Lincoln Avenue, Charleston, IL 61920-3099. Phone: 216-581-3713.

FACILITIES
Information Resources Booth Library; total holdings of 97,000 volumes, 1,600,000 microforms, 3,100 current periodical subscriptions. CD player(s) available for graduate student use. Access provided to online bibliographic retrieval services.

INTERNATIONAL STUDENTS
Demographics 9% of students enrolled are international students.

Services and Facilities International student office, international student center, international student housing, ESL courses, counseling/support services, language tutoring.

Applying TOEFL: minimum score of 550, proof of adequate funds, proof of health/immunizations required. Financial aid is available to international students.

International Student Contact International Student Advisor, International Programs, 600 Lincoln Avenue, Charleston, IL 61920-3099. Phone: 217-581-2321; Fax: 217-581-7207.

PLACEMENT
Services include alumni network, career counseling/planning, career fairs, career library, career placement, job interviews arranged, job search course, and resume preparation. In 1996–97, 120 organizations participated in on-campus recruiting.

Employment Of 1996–97 graduates, 95% were employed within three months of graduation; the average starting salary was $41,000. Types of employment entered: consulting, financial services, management, marketing.

Business Program(s) URL: http://www.eiu.edu/~mba/

Program Contact: Dr. Jane Wayland, Coordinator of Graduate Business Studies, 600 Lincoln Avenue, Charleston, IL 61920-3099. Phone: 217-581-3028; Fax: 217-581-6029; E-mail: cfjpw@eiu.edu

Governors State University

College of Business and Public Administration

University Park, Illinois

OVERVIEW
Governors State University is a state-supported, coed, upper-level institution. Enrollment: 6,500 graduate, professional, and undergraduate students; 200 full-time matriculated graduate/professional students; 3,300 part-time matriculated graduate/professional students. Founded: 1969. The graduate business unit is in a suburban setting and is on a trimester calendar.

HIGHLIGHTS

Enrollment Profile

Full-time: 15	International: 6%
Part-time: 255	Women: 44%
Total: 270	Minorities: 39%
Average Age: 36	Average Class Size: 10
Fall 1997 Average GPA: 3.2	Fall 1997 Average GMAT: 450

Costs
Full-time tuition: $1104 per academic year (resident); $3312 per academic year (nonresident)
Part-time tuition: $92 per credit (resident); $276 per credit (nonresident)

ACBSP – The American Council of Business Schools and Programs accredited

GRADUATE BUSINESS PROGRAMS

Master of Business Administration (MBA) Full-time, part-time; 33-45 total credits required; 12 months to 5 years to complete program. Concentrations in accounting, finance, health care, human resources, international business, management, management information systems, marketing, public management.

ADMISSION
Applications For fall 1997 there were 420 applications for admission. Of those applying, 250 were accepted. Of those accepted, 180 enrolled.

Application Requirements GMAT score, application form, bachelor's degree, minimum GPA: 2.5, college transcript(s).

Recommended for Application Computer experience.

Application Deadline Applications processed on a rolling/continuous basis for both domestic and international students. Deferred entrance is available.

ACADEMICS
Faculty Full-time 33; part-time 14.

Teaching Methodologies Case study, computer-aided instruction, computer analysis, computer simulations, experiential learning, field projects, group discussion, lecture, research, seminars by members of the business community, simulations, student presentations, study groups, team projects.

Technology 75 on-campus computer terminals/PCs are available for student use and are linked by a campus-wide network. The network has full access to the Internet. Students are not required to have their own PC.

Special Opportunities Advanced credit may be earned through credit by examination, transfer of credits from another institution. International exchange programs in Egypt, Germany, Mexico, People's Republic of China. An internship program is available.

FINANCES
Costs for 1997–98 Tuition: Full-time: $1104 per trimester (resident); $3312 per trimester (nonresident). Part-time: $92 per credit (resident); $276 per credit (nonresident). Cost varies by number of credits taken. Fees: Full-time: $85 per academic year (resident); $85 per academic year (nonresident). Part-time: $85 per trimester (resident); $85 per trimester (nonresident). Fees vary by campus location, number of credits taken. Average 1997–98 room and board costs were $6000 per academic year (off campus). Room and board costs vary by campus location, occupancy (e.g., single, double, triple), type of accommodation, type of meal plan.

Financial Aid In 1997–98, 19% of students received some institutionally administered aid in the form of fellowships, research assistantships, grants, scholarships, work study, loans. Financial aid is available to part-time students. Application Deadline: 5/1.

Financial Aid Contact Ms. Judith Gustawson, Coordinator of Academic Advising, College of Business and Public Administration, University Park, IL 60466-0975. Phone: 708-534-4391; Fax: 708-534-8457; E-mail: j-gustaw@govst.edu

FACILITIES
Information Resources University Library; total holdings of 235,000 volumes, 644,000 microforms, 2,530 current periodical subscriptions. CD player(s) available for graduate student use. Access provided to online bibliographic retrieval services and online databases.

INTERNATIONAL STUDENTS
Demographics 6% of students enrolled are international students [Africa, 7%, Asia, 52%, Central America, 7%, Europe, 27%, other, 7%].

Services and Facilities International student office, visa services, ESL courses, counseling/support services, housing location assistance.

Applying TOEFL: minimum score of 550, proof of adequate funds required. Financial aid is available to international students.

International Student Contact Ms. Vreni Mendoza, Coordinator of Office of International Services, Office of International Services, University Park, IL 60466-0975. Phone: 708-534-3087; Fax: 708-534-8951; E-mail: v-mendoz@govst.edu

PLACEMENT
Services include alumni network, career counseling/planning, career fairs, career library, career placement, job search course, resume referral to employers, and resume preparation. In 1996–97, 100 organizations participated in on-campus recruiting; 500 on-campus interviews were conducted.

Employment Of 1996–97 graduates, 75% were employed within three months of graduation; the average starting salary was $40,000. Types of employment entered: accounting, banking, communications, computer-related, consulting, consumer products, financial services, government, human resources, information systems/technology, insurance, international trade, management, manufacturing, marketing, nonprofit, retail, service industry, telecommunications, utilities.

Business Program(s) URL: http://www.govst.edu/users/gcbpa

Program Contact: Ms. Judith Gustawson, Coordinator of Academic Advising, College of Business and Public Administration, University Park, IL 60466-0975. Phone: 708-534-4391; Fax: 708-534-8457; E-mail: j-gustaw@govst.edu

Illinois Institute of Technology

Stuart School of Business

Chicago, Illinois

OVERVIEW
Illinois Institute of Technology is an independent-nonprofit, coed university. Enrollment: 6,100 graduate, professional, and undergraduate students; 1,556 full-time matriculated graduate/professional students; 2,696 part-time matriculated graduate/professional students. Founded: 1891. The graduate business unit is in an urban setting and is on a quarter calendar.

HIGHLIGHTS

Enrollment Profile

Full-time: 138	International: 12%
Part-time: 510	Women: 24%
Total: 648	Minorities: 10%
Average Age: 30	Average Class Size: 18
Fall 1997 Average GPA: 3.0	Fall 1997 Average GMAT: 550

Costs
Full-time tuition: $18,360 per academic year
Part-time tuition: $1620 per 3-credit course

GRADUATE BUSINESS PROGRAMS
Master of Business Administration (MBA) Full-time, part-time; 72 total credits required; 12 months to 6 years to complete program. Concentrations in finance, information management, international business, management science, marketing, operations management, organizational management, quality management, risk management, telecommunications management, strategic management.

Master of Science in Financial Markets and Trading (MS) Full-time, part-time; 50 total credits required; 12 months to 6 years to complete program.

Master of Science in Environmental Management (MS) Full-time, part-time; 50 total credits required; 12 months to 6 years to complete program.

Master of Science in Operations and Technology Management (MS) Part-time; 48 total credits required; 18 months to complete program.

PhD in Management (PHD) Full-time, part-time; 94 total credits required; 3 to 6 years to complete program.

Master of Science in Marketing Communication (MS) Part-time; 50 total credits required; 12 months to 6 years to complete program.

ADMISSION
Applications For fall 1997 there were 328 applications for admission. Of those applying, 275 were accepted. Of those accepted, 142 enrolled.

Application Requirements Application form, application fee, bachelor's degree, essay, minimum GPA: 2.0, 2 letters of recommendation, personal statement, college transcript(s).

Recommended for Application GMAT score accepted, GRE score accepted, interview, resume, work experience, computer experience.

Application Deadline 7/15 for fall, 10/1 for winter, 1/15 for spring, 4/15 for summer, 6/1 for fall (international), 8/1 for winter (international), 12/15 for spring (international), 3/1 for summer (international). Application fee: $30. Deferred entrance is available.

ACADEMICS
Faculty Full-time 21; part-time 49.

Teaching Methodologies Case study, computer-aided instruction, computer analysis, computer simulations, experiential learning, faculty seminars, field projects, group discussion, lecture, research, role playing, seminars by members of the business community, simulations, student presentations, study groups, team projects.

Technology 70 on-campus computer terminals/PCs are available for student use and are linked by a campus-wide network. The network has full access to the Internet. Students are not required to have their own PC.

Special Opportunities Advanced credit may be earned through transfer of credits from another institution.

FINANCES
Costs for 1997–98 Tuition: Full-time: $18,360 per year. Part-time: $1620 per 3-credit course. Cost varies by academic program, number of credits taken. Average 1997–98 room and board costs were $8900 per academic year. Room and board costs vary by campus location, occupancy (e.g., single, double, triple), type of accommodation, type of meal plan.

209

Illinois Institute of Technology (continued)

Financial Aid Scholarships, work study, loans available. Application Deadline: 3/1.

Financial Aid Contact Virginia Foster, Director of Financial Aid, Student Finance Center, IIT, 3300 South Federal Street, Room 104, Main Building, Chicago, IL 60616-3793. Phone: 312-567-7219; Fax: 312-567-3313.

FACILITIES
Information Resources Paul V. Galvin Library plus 2 additional on-campus libraries; total holdings of 1,067,084 volumes, 794,085 microforms, 9,346 current periodical subscriptions. CD player(s) available for graduate student use. Access provided to online bibliographic retrieval services and online databases.

INTERNATIONAL STUDENTS
Demographics 12% of students enrolled are international students [Africa, 4%, Asia, 80%, Central America, 1%, Europe, 13%, South America, 1%, other, 1%].

Services and Facilities International student office, international student center, international student housing, visa services, ESL courses, counseling/support services.

Applying TOEFL: minimum score of 550, proof of adequate funds, proof of health/immunizations required. Financial aid is available to international students.

International Student Contact Ms. Vanita Misquita, Director, International Students and Scholars Center, Room 406, Farr Hall, 3300 South Michigan Avenue, Chicago, IL 60616-3793. Phone: 312-808-7104; Fax: 312-808-7133.

PLACEMENT
Services include alumni network, career counseling/planning, career fairs, career library, career placement, electronic job bank, job interviews arranged, job search course, resume referral to employers, and resume preparation. In 1996–97, 60 organizations participated in on-campus recruiting; 50 on-campus interviews were conducted.

Employment Of 1996–97 graduates, 88% were employed within three months of graduation. Types of employment entered: accounting, banking, computer-related, consulting, consumer products, energy, engineering, finance, financial services, government, high technology, hospitality management, human resources, information systems/technology, insurance, international trade, law, management, manufacturing, marketing, media, nonprofit, pharmaceutical, retail, service industry, telecommunications, transportation, utilities.

Business Program(s) URL: http://www.stuart.iit.edu

Program Contact: Dr. Lynn Miller, Assistant Dean, Admission and MBA Program, 565 West Adams Street, Chicago, IL 60661-3691. Phone: 312-906-6544, 800-MBA NEXT (IL only); Fax: 312-906-6549; E-mail: lmiller@stuart.iit.edu
See full description on page 842.

Illinois State University

College of Business
Normal, Illinois

OVERVIEW
Illinois State University is a state-supported, coed university. Enrollment: 19,722 graduate, professional, and undergraduate students; 1,064 full-time matriculated graduate/professional students; 1,901 part-time matriculated graduate/professional students. Founded: 1857. The graduate business unit is in an urban setting and is on a semester calendar.

HIGHLIGHTS
Enrollment Profile
Full-time: 72
Part-time: 121
Total: 193
Average Age: 31
Fall 1997 Average GPA: 3.3

International: 15%
Women: 44%
Minorities: 8%
Average Class Size: 17
Fall 1997 Average GMAT: 545

Costs
Full-time tuition: $2670 per academic year (resident); $6352 per academic year (nonresident)
Part-time tuition: $298 per course (resident); $895 per course (nonresident)

AACSB – The International Association for Management Education accredited

GRADUATE BUSINESS PROGRAMS
Master of Business Administration (MBA) Full-time, part-time; 36-53 total credits required; 12 months to 6 years to complete program. Concentrations in accounting, finance, insurance, agribusiness, international business, management, marketing, organizational behavior/development, human resources, business education, business law, management information systems, entrepreneurship.
Master of Science in Accounting (MS) Full-time, part-time; 33-71 total credits required; 12 months to 6 years to complete program.

ADMISSION
Applications For fall 1997 there were 102 applications for admission. Of those applying, 67 were accepted. Of those accepted, 38 enrolled.

Application Requirements GMAT score: minimum 450, application form, bachelor's degree, essay, minimum GPA: 2.75, 2 letters of recommendation, personal statement, resume, college transcript(s).

Application Deadline Applications processed on a rolling/continuous basis for domestic students only. 5/1 for fall (international), 10/1 for spring (international), 2/1 for summer (international). Deferred entrance is available.

ACADEMICS
Faculty Full-time 46; part-time 2.

Teaching Methodologies Case study, computer analysis, computer simulations, experiential learning, lecture, research, student presentations, team projects.

Technology 493 on-campus computer terminals/PCs are available for student use and are linked by a campus-wide network. The network has full access to the Internet. Students are not required to have their own PC.

Special Opportunities Advanced credit may be earned through transfer of credits from another institution. International exchange programs in France, Mexico, United Kingdom. An internship program is available.

FINANCES
Costs for 1997–98 Tuition: Full-time: $2670 per year (resident); $6352 per year (nonresident). Part-time: $298 per course (resident); $895 per course (nonresident). Fees: Full-time: $806 per academic year (resident); $806 per academic year (nonresident). Part-time: $105 per course (resident); $105 per course (nonresident). Average 1997–98 room and board costs were $4178 per academic year.

Financial Aid In 1997–98, 57% of students received some institutionally administered aid in the form of research assistantships, teaching assistantships, work study, loans. Financial aid is available to part-time students. Application Deadline: 4/1.

Financial Aid Contact Ms. Jennifer Fissel, Financial Aid Advisor, Campus Box 2320, Normal, IL 61790-2320. Phone: 309-438-2231; Fax: 309-438-3755.

FACILITIES
Information Resources Milner Library; total holdings of 1,360,000 volumes, 1,880,000 microforms, 5,700 current periodical subscriptions. CD player(s) available for graduate student use. Access provided to online bibliographic retrieval services.

INTERNATIONAL STUDENTS
Demographics 15% of students enrolled are international students [Africa, 4%, Asia, 76%, Central America, 3%, Europe, 7%, North America, 7%, South America, 3%].

Services and Facilities International student office, international student center, international student housing, ESL courses, counseling/support services.

Applying TOEFL: minimum score of 600, proof of adequate funds, proof of health/immunizations required. Financial aid is available to international students.

International Student Contact Ms. Sara Jome, Coordinator, Foreign Student and Scholar Services, International Studies, Campus Box 6120, Normal, IL 61790-6120. Phone: 309-438-5365; Fax: 309-438-3987; E-mail: sjjome@rs6000.cmp.ilstu.edu

PLACEMENT
Services include alumni network, career counseling/planning, career fairs, career library, career placement, job interviews arranged, resume referral to employers, and resume preparation.

Employment Of 1996–97 graduates, 95% were employed within three months of graduation; the average starting salary was $37,000. Types of employment entered: banking, consumer products, financial services, health services, human resources, insurance, manufacturing, marketing, nonprofit.

Business Program(s) URL: http://gilbreth.cob.ilstu.edu/MBA

Program Contact: Dr. Tim Longfellow, Director of MBA Program, Campus Box 5500, Normal, IL 61790-5500. Phone: 309-438-8388; Fax: 309-438-5510; E-mail: isumba@ilstu.edu
See full description on page 844.

Keller Graduate School of Management

Master of Business Administration Program

Oak Brook Terrace, Illinois

OVERVIEW
Keller Graduate School of Management is a proprietary, coed, graduate institution. Enrollment: 15,224 graduate, professional, and undergraduate students. Founded: 1973. The graduate business unit is in an urban setting and is on a term calendar.

HIGHLIGHTS

Enrollment Profile
Full-time: N/R
Part-time: N/R
Total: 5,000
Average Age: 33
Fall 1997 Average GPA: N/R

International: N/R
Women: N/R
Minorities: N/R
Average Class Size: 17
Fall 1997 Average GMAT: N/R

Costs
Full-time tuition: N/R
Part-time tuition: $1235 per course

GRADUATE BUSINESS PROGRAMS
Master of Business Administration (MBA) Full-time, part-time; 64 total credits required; 18 months to 5 years to complete program. Concentrations in accounting, marketing, finance, information management, management, human resources, project management.
Master of Project Management (MPM) Full-time, part-time; 52 total credits required; 18 months to 5 years to complete program. Concentration in project management.
Master of Human Resources Management (MHRM) Full-time, part-time; 60 total credits required; 18 months to 5 years to complete program.
Master of Telecommunication Management (MTM) Full-time, part-time; 60 total credits required.
Master of Accounting and Financial Management (MAFM) Full-time, part-time; 60 total credits required.
Master of Information Systems Management (MISM) Full-time, part-time; 60 total credits required.

ADMISSION
Application Requirements Application form, bachelor's degree, minimum GPA, interview, resume, college transcript(s).
Recommended for Application GMAT score accepted, GRE score accepted, computer experience.
Application Deadline Applications processed on a rolling/continuous basis for both domestic and international students.

ACADEMICS
Faculty Full-time 6; part-time 193.
Teaching Methodologies Case study, computer-aided instruction, group discussion, lecture, student presentations, team projects.
Technology Students are not required to have their own PC.
Special Opportunities Advanced credit may be earned through transfer of credits from another institution.

FINANCES
Costs for 1997–98 Tuition: $1235 per course. Cost varies by academic program, campus location, number of credits taken, reciprocity agreements.
Financial Aid Contact Financial Aid Office, 1 Tower Lane, Oak Brook Terrace, IL 60181. Phone: 630-571-7700 Ext. 4015.

FACILITIES
Information Resources Access provided to online bibliographic retrieval services.

INTERNATIONAL STUDENTS
Demographics N/R
Applying TOEFL: minimum score of 550 required. Financial aid is not available to international students.
International Student Contact Ms. Martha Gershun, Director of Marketing, 1100 Main Street, Kansas City, MO 64105. Phone: 816-221-8015; Fax: 816-474-0318.

PLACEMENT
Services include career counseling/planning.
Employment Types of employment entered: management.

Program Contact: One Tower Lane, 9th Floor, Oakbrook Terrace, IL 60181. Phone: 630-571-1818.
See full description on page 864.

Lake Forest Graduate School of Management

Graduate Programs

Lake Forest, Illinois

OVERVIEW
Lake Forest Graduate School of Management is an independent-nonprofit, coed, graduate institution. Enrollment: 875 graduate, professional, and undergraduate students; full-time matriculated graduate/professional students; 875 part-time matriculated graduate/professional students. Founded: 1946. The graduate business unit is in a suburban setting and is on a quarter calendar.

HIGHLIGHTS

Enrollment Profile
Full-time: 0
Part-time: 875
Total: 875
Average Age: 32
Fall 1997 Average GPA: 3.0

International: N/R
Women: 34%
Minorities: 10%
Average Class Size: 20
Fall 1997 Average GMAT: N/R

Costs
Full-time tuition: N/R
Part-time tuition: $1575 per course

GRADUATE BUSINESS PROGRAMS
Executive MBA (MBA) Part-time; 64 total credits required; 4 years work experience required; 22 months to 6 years to complete program.

ADMISSION
Application Requirements Application form, application fee, bachelor's degree, essay, minimum GPA, interview, letter of recommendation, college transcript(s), minimum of 4 years of work experience, computer experience.
Recommended for Application GMAT score accepted, GRE score accepted, resume.
Application Deadline 8/7 for fall, 1/8 for winter, 3/26 for spring. Application fee: $35.

ACADEMICS
Faculty Part-time 140.
Teaching Methodologies Case study, computer-aided instruction, computer analysis, computer simulations, experiential learning, field projects, group discussion, research, role playing, seminars by members of the business community, simulations, student presentations, study groups, team projects.
Technology 15 on-campus computer terminals/PCs are available for student use. The network has full access to the Internet. Students are required to have their own PC.
Special Opportunities Advanced credit may be earned through transfer of credits from another institution.

FINANCES
Costs for 1997–98 Tuition: Part-time: $1575 per course. Cost varies by number of credits taken.
Financial Aid In 1997–98, 12% of students received some institutionally administered aid in the form of scholarships, loans. Financial aid is available to part-time students.
Financial Aid Contact Mr. Renato Umali, Financial Aid Advisor, 280 North Sheridan Road, Lake Forest , IL 60045. Phone: 847-234-5005 Ext. 241; Fax: 847-295-3666; E-mail: rumali@lfgsm.edu

FACILITIES
Information Resources Donnelley Library; total holdings of 250,000 volumes. Access provided to online bibliographic retrieval services.

INTERNATIONAL STUDENTS
Demographics N/R
Applying Financial aid is not available to international students.

PLACEMENT
Services include alumni network.
Business Program(s) URL: http://www.lfgsm.edu

Program Contact: Ms. Kristin Kraai-Keely, Director of Admissions, Chicago Campus, 176 West Jackson Boulevard, Chicago, IL 60604. Phone: 312-435-5330; Fax: 312-435-5333; E-mail: admiss@lfgsm.edu
See full description on page 868.

Lewis University

College of Business

Romeoville, Illinois

OVERVIEW

Lewis University is an independent-religious, coed, comprehensive institution. Enrollment: 4,399 graduate, professional, and undergraduate students; 12 full-time matriculated graduate/professional students; 563 part-time matriculated graduate/professional students. Founded: 1932. The graduate business unit is in a suburban setting and is on a semester calendar.

HIGHLIGHTS

Enrollment Profile

Full-time: 12

Part-time: 563

Total: 575

Average Age: 33

Fall 1997 Average GPA: 3.0

International: 1%

Women: 33%

Minorities: N/R

Average Class Size: 17

Fall 1997 Average GMAT: 500

Costs

Full-time tuition: $7326 per academic year

Part-time tuition: $407 per credit hour

GRADUATE BUSINESS PROGRAMS

Master of Business Administration (MBA) Full-time, part-time; 36-54 total credits required; 12 months to 5 years to complete program. Concentrations in accounting, finance, human resources, management information systems, marketing, operations management, health care.

Master of Science in Nursing/Master of Business Administration (MS/MBA) Full-time, part-time; 72 total credits required; 2.5 to 7 years to complete program.

ADMISSION

Applications For fall 1997 there were 135 applications for admission. Of those applying, 120 were accepted. Of those accepted, 110 enrolled.

Application Requirements Application form, application fee, bachelor's degree, minimum GPA: 2.0, personal statement, college transcript(s), minimum of 3 years of work experience.

Recommended for Application GMAT score accepted, letters of recommendation, resume.

Application Deadline Applications processed on a rolling/continuous basis for both domestic and international students. Application fee: $35. Deferred entrance is available.

ACADEMICS

Faculty Full-time 16; part-time 46.

Teaching Methodologies Case study, computer-aided instruction, computer analysis, computer simulations, faculty seminars, field projects, group discussion, lecture, research, role playing, seminars by members of the business community, student presentations, study groups, team projects.

Technology 100 on-campus computer terminals/PCs are available for student use and are linked by a campus-wide network. The network has full access to the Internet. Students are not required to have their own PC.

Special Opportunities Advanced credit may be earned through credit by examination, transfer of credits from another institution.

FINANCES

Costs for 1997–98 Tuition: Full-time: $7326 per year. Part-time: $407 per credit hour. Average 1997–98 room and board costs were $5800 per academic year. Room and board costs vary by occupancy (e.g., single, double, triple), type of meal plan.

Financial Aid Financial aid is available to part-time students.

Financial Aid Contact Ms. Sally Floyd, Director, Route 53, Romeoville, IL 60446. Phone: 815-838-0500 Ext. 5263; Fax: 815-838-9456.

FACILITIES

Information Resources Lewis University Library; total holdings of 163,040 volumes, 8,292 microforms, 593 current periodical subscriptions. CD player(s) available for graduate student use. Access provided to online bibliographic retrieval services.

INTERNATIONAL STUDENTS

Demographics 1% of students enrolled are international students.

Services and Facilities International student office, visa services, ESL courses, counseling/support services.

Applying TOEFL: minimum score of 550, proof of health/immunizations required. Financial aid is not available to international students.

International Student Contact Ms. Suzanne Benson, Executive Director, Graduate School of Management, Route 53, Romeoville, IL 60446. Phone: 815-838-0500 Ext. 5339; Fax: 815-838-3330.

PLACEMENT

Services include alumni network, career counseling/planning, career fairs, career library, career placement, job interviews arranged, job search course, resume referral to employers, and resume preparation. In 1996–97, 125 organizations participated in on-campus recruiting; 90 on-campus interviews were conducted.

Employment Of 1996–97 graduates, 90% were employed within three months of graduation; the average starting salary was $30,000. Types of employment entered: accounting, banking, chemical industry, communications, computer-related, consulting, consumer products, finance, financial services, government, health services, high technology, hospitality management, human resources, information systems/technology, insurance, international trade, management, manufacturing, marketing, nonprofit, petrochemical, pharmaceutical, real estate, retail, service industry, telecommunications, transportation, utilities.

Business Program(s) URL: http://www.lewisu.edu

Program Contact: Ms. Suzanne Benson, Executive Director, Graduate School of Management, Route 53, Romeoville, IL 60446. Phone: 815-838-0500 Ext. 5339, 800-897-9000 (IL only); Fax: 815-838-3330.

Loyola University Chicago

Graduate School of Business

Chicago, Illinois

OVERVIEW

Loyola University Chicago is an independent-religious, coed university. Enrollment: 13,604 graduate, professional, and undergraduate students; 2,437 full-time matriculated graduate/professional students; 3,647 part-time matriculated graduate/professional students. Founded: 1870. The graduate business unit is in an urban setting and is on a quarter calendar.

HIGHLIGHTS

Enrollment Profile

Full-time: 225

Part-time: 747

Total: 972

Average Age: 27

Fall 1997 Average GPA: 3.2

International: 17%

Women: 45%

Minorities: 14%

Average Class Size: 34

Fall 1997 Average GMAT: 530

Costs

Full-time tuition: $17,865 per academic year

Part-time tuition: $1985 per course

AACSB – The International Association for Management Education accredited

GRADUATE BUSINESS PROGRAMS

Master of Business Administration (MBA) Full-time, part-time; 42-54 total credits required; 12 months to 5 years to complete program. Concentrations in accounting, finance, international business, management, management information systems, management science, managerial economics, marketing, operations management, health care.

Master of Business Administration/Doctor of Jurisprudence (MBA/JD) Full-time, part-time; 128-140 total credits required; 4 to 8 years to complete program. Concentrations in accounting, business law, finance, international business, management, management information systems, management science, managerial economics, marketing, operations management, health care.

Master of Business Administration/Master of Science in Nursing (MBA/MSN) Full-time, part-time; 69-81 total credits required; 3 to 7 years to complete program. Concentrations in accounting, business law, finance, health care, international business, management, management information systems, management science, managerial economics, marketing, operations management.

Master of Science in Accounting (MSA) Full-time, part-time; 36 total credits required; 12 months to 5 years to complete program.

Master of Science in Information Systems Management (MSISM) Full-time, part-time; 36 total credits required; 12 months to 5 years to complete program.

ADMISSION

Applications For fall 1997 there were 594 applications for admission. Of those applying, 362 were accepted. Of those accepted, 187 enrolled.

Application Requirements Application form, application fee, bachelor's degree, minimum GPA, 3 letters of recommendation, college transcript(s).

Recommended for Application GMAT score accepted, essay, interview, personal statement, resume, minimum of 3 years of work experience.

Application Deadline 7/1 for fall, 9/1 for winter, 12/1 for spring, 3/1 for summer, 6/1 for fall (international), 8/1 for winter (international), 11/1 for spring (international), 2/1 for summer (international). Application fee: $50. Deferred entrance is available.

ACADEMICS
Faculty Full-time 72; part-time 15.

Teaching Methodologies Case study, computer analysis, computer simulations, field projects, group discussion, lecture, role playing, simulations, student presentations, team projects.

Technology 400 on-campus computer terminals/PCs are available for student use and are linked by a campus-wide network. The network has full access to the Internet. Students are not required to have their own PC.

Special Opportunities Advanced credit may be earned through transfer of credits from another institution. International exchange programs in Greece, Italy, Korea, Thailand. An internship program is available.

FINANCES
Costs for 1997–98 Tuition: Full-time: $17,865 per year. Part-time: $1985 per course. Cost varies by academic program. Fees: Full-time: $117 per academic year. Part-time: $39 per quarter. Average 1997–98 room and board costs were $6000 per academic year (on campus) and $7500 per academic year (off campus). Room and board costs vary by occupancy (e.g., single, double, triple), type of accommodation, type of meal plan.

Financial Aid In 1997–98, 31% of students received some institutionally administered aid in the form of research assistantships, work study, loans. Financial aid is available to part-time students. Application Deadline: 4/15.

Financial Aid Contact Student Financial Assistance, 6525 North Sheridan Road, Chicago, IL 60626-5208. Phone: 312-508-3155; Fax: 312-508-3397; E-mail: lufinaid@luc.edu

FACILITIES
Information Resources Elizabeth M. Cudahy Memorial Library plus 5 additional on-campus libraries; total holdings of 1,400,000 volumes, 1,100,000 microforms, 12,000 current periodical subscriptions. CD player(s) available for graduate student use. Access provided to online bibliographic retrieval services and online databases.

INTERNATIONAL STUDENTS
Demographics 17% of students enrolled are international students [Africa, 1%, Asia, 53%, Central America, 4%, Europe, 16%, North America, 5%, South America, 4%, other, 17%].

Services and Facilities International student office, international student center, international student housing, visa services, ESL courses, counseling/support services.

Applying TOEFL: minimum score of 550, proof of adequate funds, proof of health/immunizations required. Financial aid is available to international students.

International Student Contact Mr. John Heise, Director, International Services, 6525 North Sheridan Road, Chicago, IL 60626-5208. Phone: 312-508-3899; Fax: 312-508-3895; E-mail: csteber@luc.edu

PLACEMENT
Services include alumni network, career counseling/planning, career fairs, career library, career placement, electronic job bank, job interviews arranged, job search course, and resume referral to employers. In 1996–97, 36 organizations participated in on-campus recruiting; 288 on-campus interviews were conducted.

Employment Of 1996–97 graduates, 92% were employed within three months of graduation; the average starting salary was $48,673. Types of employment entered: accounting, banking, computer-related, consulting, consumer products, education, energy, finance, financial services, government, health services, high technology, human resources, information systems/technology, insurance, international trade, management, manufacturing, marketing, media, nonprofit, pharmaceutical, real estate, retail, service industry, telecommunications, transportation, utilities.

Business Program(s) URL: http://www.luc.edu/depts/mba

Program Contact: Mr. Paul Davidovitch, Director, Graduate School of Business, 820 North Michigan Avenue, Chicago, IL 60611-2196. Phone: 312-915-6120; Fax: 312-915-7207; E-mail: mba-loyola@luc.edu
See full description on page 878.

National-Louis University

College of Management and Business

Evanston, Illinois

OVERVIEW
National-Louis University is an independent-nonprofit, coed university. Enrollment: 7,100 graduate, professional, and undergraduate students; 1,179 full-time matriculated graduate/professional students; 2,590 part-time matriculated graduate/professional students. Founded: 1886. The graduate business unit is in a suburban setting and is on a year-round cluster calendar.

HIGHLIGHTS

Enrollment Profile

Full-time: 265	International: N/R
Part-time: 27	Women: 61%
Total: 292	Minorities: 49%
Average Age: 39	Average Class Size: 15
Fall 1997 Average GPA: 3.1	Fall 1997 Average GMAT: N/R

Costs
Full-time tuition: N/R
Part-time tuition: $459 per semester hour

GRADUATE BUSINESS PROGRAMS
Master of Science in Managerial Leadership (MS) Full-time, part-time, distance learning option; 33 total credits required; 18 months to complete program.

Master of Science in Human Resource Management and Development (MS) Full-time, part-time, distance learning option; 33 total credits required; 18 months to complete program.

ADMISSION
Applications For fall 1997 there were 106 applications for admission. Of those applying, 104 were accepted. Of those accepted, 90 enrolled.

Application Requirements Application form, application fee, bachelor's degree, essay, minimum GPA: 3.0, letters of recommendation, resume, college transcript(s).

Recommended for Application Work experience.

Application Deadline Applications processed on a rolling/continuous basis for both domestic and international students. Application fee: $25. Deferred entrance is available.

ACADEMICS
Faculty Full-time 26.

Teaching Methodologies Case study, experiential learning, field projects, group discussion, research, role playing, seminars by members of the business community, simulations, student presentations.

Technology 215 on-campus computer terminals/PCs are available for student use and are linked by a campus-wide network. The network has full access to the Internet. Students are not required to have their own PC.

Special Opportunities Advanced credit may be earned through credit by examination, credit for experience, credit for military training programs, credit for business training programs, transfer of credits from another institution.

FINANCES
Costs for 1997–98 Tuition: $459 per semester hour. Cost varies by academic program. Average 1997–98 room and board costs were $5727 per academic year. Room and board costs vary by occupancy (e.g., single, double, triple), type of meal plan.

Financial Aid Grants, scholarships, work study, loans available. Financial aid is available to part-time students. Application Deadline: 4/15.

Financial Aid Contact Ms. Judith Seebach, Financial Aid Department, 1000 Capitol Drive, Wheeling, IL 60090. Phone: 847-475-1100 Ext. 4565.

FACILITIES
Information Resources N. Dwight Harris College Library Center plus 1 additional on-campus library; total holdings of 160,000 volumes, 1,200,000 microforms, 1,524 current periodical subscriptions. CD player(s) available for graduate student use. Access provided to online bibliographic retrieval services and online databases.

INTERNATIONAL STUDENTS
Demographics N/R

Services and Facilities ESL courses.

Applying TOEFL: minimum score of 550, proof of adequate funds required. Financial aid is not available to international students.

International Student Contact Ms. Ewa Luowiczuk, 2840 Sheridan Road, Evanston, IL 60201-1730. Phone: 800-443-5522 Ext. 3417.

PLACEMENT
Services include career counseling/planning, career fairs, career library, career placement, electronic job bank, job search course, resume referral to employers, and resume preparation.

Business Program(s) URL: http://www.nl.edu/cmb/index.html

Program Contact: Mr. Mark Buck, Enrollment Representative, 2840 Sheridan Road, Evanston, IL 60201-1730. Phone: 847-475-1100 Ext. 5111, 800-443-5522

North Central College

Department of Business Administration

Naperville, Illinois

OVERVIEW

North Central College is an independent-religious, coed, comprehensive institution. Enrollment: 2,498 graduate, professional, and undergraduate students; 50 full-time matriculated graduate/professional students; 400 part-time matriculated graduate/professional students. Founded: 1861. The graduate business unit is in a suburban setting and is on a quarter calendar.

HIGHLIGHTS

Enrollment Profile

Full-time: 15	International: 3%
Part-time: 175	Women: 47%
Total: 190	Minorities: N/R
Average Age: 33	Average Class Size: 14
Fall 1997 Average GPA: 2.85	Fall 1997 Average GMAT: 470

Costs
Full-time tuition: N/R
Part-time tuition: $1407 per course

North Central College has been a pioneer in developing degree programs for adults with full-time careers. North Central understands the demands facing students who dedicate themselves to pursuing an advanced degree while simultaneously fulfilling family and career obligations. The M.B.A. program at North Central is designed to allow participants to gain the benefits of obtaining a master's degree without interrupting their careers. All M.B.A. courses are offered in the evenings and some on weekends.

The features that were originally created with the adult student in mind and that have been responsible for the success of the adult programs, continue to hold true in the M.B.A. program: personal attention from expert academic advisers and professors; multiple entry points for students throughout the year; convenient class schedules; highly qualified faculty members, the majority of whom have earned doctoral degrees; a comprehensive approach that develops strong communication and critical thinking skills; and a learning environment based on innovation and problem identification as well as problem solving.

The M.B.A. is open to qualified students from all undergraduate majors, and the curriculum is flexible enough to meet the special needs of those aspiring to leadership positions in business, government, or education.

GRADUATE BUSINESS PROGRAMS

Master of Business Administration (MBA) Full-time, part-time; 52 total credits required; 12 months to 5 years to complete program. Concentrations in financial management/planning, human resources, information management, leadership, management, marketing.

Master of Science in Management Information Systems (MS) Full-time, part-time; 52 total credits required; 12 months to 5 years to complete program. Concentration in management information systems.

ADMISSION

Applications For fall 1997 there were 30 applications for admission. Of those applying, 30 were accepted. Of those accepted, 30 enrolled.

Application Requirements GMAT score, application form, application fee, bachelor's degree, minimum GPA: 2.75, interview, 2 letters of recommendation, personal statement, college transcript(s).

Recommended for Application Resume, work experience, computer experience.

Application Deadline Applications processed on a rolling/continuous basis for both domestic and international students. Application fee: $25. Deferred entrance is available.

ACADEMICS

Faculty Full-time 14.

Teaching Methodologies Case study, computer analysis, computer simulations, field projects, group discussion, lecture, role playing, seminars by members of the business community, student presentations, study groups, team projects.

Technology 36 on-campus computer terminals/PCs are available for student use and are linked by a campus-wide network. The network has full access to the Internet. Students are not required to have their own PC.

Special Opportunities Advanced credit may be earned through credit for experience, credit for military training programs, credit for business training programs, transfer of credits from another institution. International exchange program in United Kingdom.

FINANCES

Costs for 1997–98 Tuition: $1407 per course. Cost varies by academic program. Average 1997–98 room and board costs were $12,000 per academic year (off campus).

Financial Aid Contact Katherine Edmunds, Director of Financial Aid, 30 North Brainard Street, PO Box 3063, Naperville, IL 60566-7063. Phone: 630-637-5600.

FACILITIES

Information Resources Oesterle Library; total holdings of 121,000 volumes, 425 microforms, 730 current periodical subscriptions. CD player(s) available for graduate student use. Access provided to online bibliographic retrieval services.

INTERNATIONAL STUDENTS

Demographics 3% of students enrolled are international students [Asia, 100%].

Services and Facilities International student office, ESL courses, counseling/support services.

Applying TOEFL: minimum score of 600, proof of adequate funds, proof of health/immunizations required. Financial aid is not available to international students.

International Student Contact Dr. John Shindler, Coordinator of International Programs, 30 North Brainard Street, Naperville, IL 60566-7063. Phone: 630-637-5287.

PLACEMENT

Services include career counseling/planning, career fairs, career placement, job interviews arranged, and resume preparation.

Business Program(s) URL: http://www.noctrl.edu

Program Contact: Mr. Steve Sanchez, 30 North Brainard Street, PO Box 3063, Naperville, IL 60566-7063. Phone: 630-637-5840; Fax: 630-637-5844.

Northeastern Illinois University

College of Business and Management

Chicago, Illinois

OVERVIEW

Northeastern Illinois University is a state-supported, coed, comprehensive institution. Enrollment: 10,386 graduate, professional, and undergraduate students; 228 full-time matriculated graduate/professional students; 1,364 part-time matriculated graduate/professional students. Founded: 1961. The graduate business unit is in an urban setting and is on a semester calendar.

HIGHLIGHTS

Enrollment Profile

Full-time: 20	International: 21%
Part-time: 58	Women: 40%
Total: 78	Minorities: 19%
Average Age: 33	Average Class Size: 14
Fall 1997 Average GPA: 3.28	Fall 1997 Average GMAT: 535

Costs
Full-time tuition: $2148 per academic year (resident); $6444 per academic year (nonresident)
Part-time tuition: $90 per credit (resident); $269 per credit (nonresident)

GRADUATE BUSINESS PROGRAMS

Master of Business Administration (MBA) Full-time, part-time; 48 total credits required; 15 months to 4 years to complete program. Concentrations in accounting, finance, management, marketing, international business.

ADMISSION

Applications For fall 1997 there were 72 applications for admission. Of those applying, 31 were accepted. Of those accepted, 27 enrolled.

Application Requirements GMAT score: minimum 450, application form, bachelor's degree, essay, minimum GPA: 2.75, 2 letters of recommendation, personal statement, college transcript(s).

Recommended for Application Resume, work experience, computer experience.

Application Deadline 7/15 for fall, 12/10 for spring, 6/1 for summer, 7/1 for fall (international), 12/1 for spring (international), 5/15 for summer (international). Deferred entrance is available.

ACADEMICS

Faculty Full-time 27.

Teaching Methodologies Case study, computer-aided instruction, computer analysis, computer simulations, field projects, group discussion, lecture, research, student presentations, study groups, team projects.

Technology 340 on-campus computer terminals/PCs are available for student use and are linked by a campus-wide network. The network has full access to the Internet. Students are not required to have their own PC.

Special Opportunities Advanced credit may be earned through transfer of credits from another institution. An internship program is available.

FINANCES

Costs for 1997–98 Tuition: Full-time: $2148 per year (resident); $6444 per year (nonresident). Part-time: $90 per credit (resident); $269 per credit (nonresident). Cost varies by number of credits taken. Fees: Full-time: $312 per academic year (resident); $312 per academic year (nonresident). Part-time: $39 per semester (resident); $39 per semester (nonresident). Fees vary by number of credits taken. Average 1997–98 room only costs were $3000 per academic year (off campus).

Financial Aid In 1997–98, 49% of students received some institutionally administered aid in the form of research assistantships, teaching assistantships, grants, scholarships, work study, loans. Financial aid is available to part-time students.

Financial Aid Contact Dr. Peter Stonebraker, Coordinator of Graduate Programs, 5500 North St. Louis Avenue, Chicago, IL 60625-4699. Phone: 773-794-2642; Fax: 773-794-6288; E-mail: p-stonebraker@neiu.edu

FACILITIES

Information Resources Ronald Williams University Library; total holdings of 676,713 volumes, 820,758 microforms, 3,668 current periodical subscriptions. CD player(s) available for graduate student use. Access provided to online bibliographic retrieval services and online databases.

INTERNATIONAL STUDENTS

Demographics 21% of students enrolled are international students [Africa, 1%, Asia, 6%, Central America, 1%, Europe, 6%, North America, 84%, South America, 2%].

Services and Facilities Visa services, ESL courses.

Applying TOEFL: minimum score of 550, proof of adequate funds required. Financial aid is available to international students.

International Student Contact Dr. Peter Stonebraker, Coordinator of Graduate Programs, 5500 North St. Louis Avenue, Chicago, IL 60625-4699. Phone: 773-794-2642; Fax: 773-794-6288; E-mail: p-stonebraker@neiu.edu

PLACEMENT

Services include alumni network, career counseling/planning, career fairs, career library, career placement, electronic job bank, job interviews arranged, resume referral to employers, and resume preparation.

Employment Of 1996–97 graduates, 100% were employed within three months of graduation. Types of employment entered: accounting, banking, communications, computer-related, consulting, consumer products, engineering, finance, financial services, government, health services, high technology, hospitality management, human resources, information systems/technology, insurance, international trade, management, manufacturing, marketing, media, pharmaceutical, service industry, telecommunications, transportation, utilities.

Business Program(s) URL: http://www.neiu.edu/~bschool

Program Contact: Dr. Peter Stonebraker, Coordinator of Graduate Programs, 5500 North St. Louis Avenue, Chicago, IL 60625-4699. Phone: 773-794-2642; Fax: 773-794-6288; E-mail: p-stonebraker@neiu.edu

Northern Illinois University

College of Business

De Kalb, Illinois

OVERVIEW

Northern Illinois University is a state-supported, coed university. Enrollment: 22,082 graduate, professional, and undergraduate students; 2,584 full-time matriculated graduate/professional students; 3,643 part-time matriculated graduate/professional students. Founded: 1895. The graduate business unit is in a suburban setting and is on a semester calendar.

HIGHLIGHTS

Enrollment Profile

Full-time: 162	International: 6%
Part-time: 623	Women: 36%
Total: 785	Minorities: 8%
Average Age: 32	Average Class Size: 27
Fall 1997 Average GPA: 3.16	Fall 1997 Average GMAT: 547

Costs

Full-time tuition: $1392 per academic year (resident); $4176 per academic year (nonresident)

Part-time tuition: $116 per credit hour (resident); $116 per credit hour (nonresident)

AACSB – The International Association for Management Education accredited

GRADUATE BUSINESS PROGRAMS

Evening MBA (MBA) Part-time; 31-49 total credits required; 2 years work experience and GMAT score: minimum 450 required; 12 months to 6 years to complete program.

Master of Accounting Science (MAS) Full-time, part-time; 30-66 total credits required; GMAT score: minimum 475 required; 12 months to 6 years to complete program.

Master of Science in Finance (MS) Full-time, part-time; 30-48 total credits required; GMAT score: minimum 500 required; 12 months to 6 years to complete program.

Master of Science in Management Information Systems (MS) Full-time, part-time; 30-51 total credits required; GMAT score: minimum 500 required; 12 months to 6 years to complete program.

Executive MBA (MBA) Full-time; 49 total credits required; 5 years work experience and GMAT score: minimum 450 required; 2 years to complete program.

Master of Science in Taxation (MST) 30 total credits required; 12 months to 6 years to complete program.

ADMISSION

Applications For fall 1997 there were 590 applications for admission. Of those applying, 482 were accepted. Of those accepted, 289 enrolled.

Application Requirements Application form, application fee, bachelor's degree, minimum GPA: 2.75, 2 letters of recommendation, personal statement, resume, college transcript(s), minimum of 2 years of work experience.

Recommended for Application GMAT score accepted, computer experience.

Application Deadline 6/1 for fall, 11/1 for spring, 4/1 for summer, 5/1 for fall (international), 10/1 for spring (international). Application fee: $30. Deferred entrance is available.

ACADEMICS

Faculty Full-time 64; part-time 6.

Teaching Methodologies Case study, computer analysis, computer simulations, group discussion, lecture, research, seminars by members of the business community, simulations, student presentations, study groups, team projects.

Technology 137 on-campus computer terminals/PCs are available for student use and are linked by a campus-wide network. The network has full access to the Internet. Students are not required to have their own PC.

Special Opportunities Advanced credit may be earned through credit by examination, transfer of credits from another institution. An internship program is available.

FINANCES

Costs for 1997–98 Tuition: Full-time: $1392 per semester (resident); $4176 per semester (nonresident). Part-time: $116 per credit hour (resident); $116 per credit hour (nonresident). Cost varies by academic program, campus location, class time (e.g., day/evening). Fees: Full-time: $456 per academic year (resident); $456 per academic year (nonresident). Part-time: $150 per credit hour (resident); $150 per credit hour (nonresident). Fees vary by academic program, campus location. Average 1997–98 room and board costs were $4841 per academic year. Room and board costs vary by campus location, occupancy (e.g., single, double, triple), type of accommodation, type of meal plan.

Financial Aid Fellowships, research assistantships, teaching assistantships, work study available. Financial aid is available to part-time students.

Financial Aid Contact Jerry D. Augsberger, Director, Student Financial Aid Office, Swen Parsons 245, DeKalb, IL 60115-2872. Phone: 815-753-1395; Fax: 815-753-9475.

FACILITIES

Information Resources Founders Library plus 3 additional on-campus libraries; total holdings of 1,500,000 volumes, 3,200,000 microforms, 15,000 current periodical subscriptions. CD player(s) available for graduate student use. Access provided to online bibliographic retrieval services and online databases.

INTERNATIONAL STUDENTS

Demographics 6% of students enrolled are international students.

Services and Facilities International student office, international student center, visa services, ESL courses, counseling/support services.

Applying TOEFL: minimum score of 550, proof of adequate funds, proof of health/immunizations required. Financial aid is not available to international students.

International Student Contact Mark D. Thackberry, Director, International Student and Faculty Office, Knetsch House, 515 Garden Road, DeKalb, IL 60115. Fax: 815-753-3300; E-mail: ca0mtd1@niu.edu

PLACEMENT

Services include career counseling/planning, career fairs, career library, career placement, resume referral to employers, and resume preparation.

Northern Illinois University (continued)

Employment Of 1996–97 graduates, 93% were employed within three months of graduation; the average starting salary was $64,399. Types of employment entered: accounting, banking, communications, computer-related, consulting, consumer products, education, energy, engineering, finance, financial services, government, health services, high technology, human resources, information systems/technology, insurance, international trade, law, management, manufacturing, marketing, media, nonprofit, pharmaceutical, real estate, retail, service industry, telecommunications, transportation, utilities.

Business Program(s) URL: http://www.cob.niu.edu/grad/grad.html

Program Contact: Larry Jacobs, Director, Graduate Studies in Business and Research, NIU College of Business, Wirtz Hall 140, DeKalb, IL 60115-2897. Phone: 815-753-1245, 800-323-8714 (IL only); Fax: 815-753-3300; E-mail: cobgrads@niu.edu
See full description on page 906.

North Park University

The Center for Management Education

Chicago, Illinois

OVERVIEW
North Park University is an independent-religious, coed, comprehensive institution. Enrollment: 2,150 graduate, professional, and undergraduate students; 25 full-time matriculated graduate/professional students; 425 part-time matriculated graduate/professional students. Founded: 1891. The graduate business unit is in an urban setting and is on a 8-week quad calendar.

HIGHLIGHTS

Enrollment Profile

Full-time: 14	International: 16%
Part-time: 240	Women: 49%
Total: 254	Minorities: 33%
Average Age: 33	Average Class Size: 20
Fall 1997 Average GPA: 3.2	Fall 1997 Average GMAT: 510

Costs
Full-time tuition: N/R
Part-time tuition: $970 per course

GRADUATE BUSINESS PROGRAMS
Master of Business Administration (MBA) Full-time, part-time; 32-40 total credits required; 12 months to 6 years to complete program. Concentrations in management, entrepreneurship, human resources, organizational behavior/development.

Master of Business Administration/Master of Science in Nursing (MBA/MS) Full-time, part-time; 62 total credits required; 2 to 6 years to complete program.

Master of Business Administration/Master of Divinity (MBA/MDiv) Full-time, part-time; 165 total credits required; 3 to 6 years to complete program.

Master of Business Administration/Master of Arts in Theological Studies (MBA/MA) Full-time, part-time; 114 total credits required; 3 to 6 years to complete program.

Master of Management (MMgt) Full-time, part-time; 36 total credits required; 12 months to 6 years to complete program. Concentrations in management, entrepreneurship, human resources, organizational behavior/development.

ADMISSION
Applications For fall 1997 there were 114 applications for admission. Of those applying, 90 were accepted. Of those accepted, 72 enrolled.

Application Requirements Application form, application fee, bachelor's degree, 2 letters of recommendation, resume, college transcript(s).

Recommended for Application GMAT score accepted, GRE score accepted, MAT score accepted, interview, work experience, computer experience.

Application Deadline Applications processed on a rolling/continuous basis for both domestic and international students. Application fee: $20. Deferred entrance is available.

ACADEMICS
Faculty Full-time 6; part-time 8.

Teaching Methodologies Case study, computer analysis, group discussion, lecture, research, role playing, seminars by members of the business community, simulations, student presentations, study groups, team projects.

Technology 100 on-campus computer terminals/PCs are available for student use and are linked by a campus-wide network. The network has full access to the Internet. Students are not required to have their own PC.

Special Opportunities Advanced credit may be earned through transfer of credits from another institution. An internship program is available.

FINANCES
Costs for 1997–98 Tuition: $970 per course. Cost varies by academic program. Fees vary by academic program. Average 1997–98 room only costs were $6000 per academic year (off campus). Room and board costs vary by occupancy (e.g., single, double, triple), type of accommodation, type of meal plan.

Financial Aid In 1997–98, 59% of students received some institutionally administered aid in the form of grants, scholarships, loans. Financial aid is available to part-time students.

Financial Aid Contact Mr. Christopher Nicholson, Associate Director of Admissions, Graduate and Continuing Education, 3225 West Foster Avenue, Chicago, IL 60625-4895. Phone: 773-244-4953; Fax: 773-244-4953; E-mail: cln@northpark.edu

FACILITIES
Information Resources Wallgren Library plus 4 additional on-campus libraries; total holdings of 225,101 volumes, 1,600 microforms, 1,099 current periodical subscriptions. CD player(s) available for graduate student use. Access provided to online bibliographic retrieval services.

INTERNATIONAL STUDENTS
Demographics 16% of students enrolled are international students [Asia, 66%, Central America, 9%, Europe, 19%, South America, 6%].

Services and Facilities International student office, international student center, international student housing, visa services, ESL courses, counseling/support services.

Applying TOEFL: minimum score of 550, proof of adequate funds, proof of health/immunizations required. Financial aid is available to international students.

International Student Contact Mr. Charles Olcese, Director, Office of International Studies, 3225 West Foster Avenue, Chicago, IL 60625-4895. Phone: 773-244-5738; Fax: 773-244-4953; E-mail: cao@northpark.edu

PLACEMENT
Services include alumni network, career counseling/planning, career library, career placement, job search course, and resume preparation.

Business Program(s) URL: http://www.northpark.edu/acad/mba/

Program Contact: Mr. Christopher Nicholson, Associate Director of Admissions, Graduate and Continuing Education, 3225 West Foster Avenue, Chicago, IL 60625-4895. Phone: 773-244-5518, 800-888-6728 (IL only); Fax: 773-244-4953; E-mail: cln@northpark.edu
See full description on page 908.

Northwestern University

J. L. Kellogg Graduate School of Management

Evanston, Illinois

OVERVIEW
Northwestern University is an independent-nonprofit, coed university. Enrollment: 16,018 graduate, professional, and undergraduate students; 4,424 full-time matriculated graduate/professional students; 1,771 part-time matriculated graduate/professional students. Founded: 1851. The graduate business unit is in a suburban setting and is on a quarter calendar.

HIGHLIGHTS

Enrollment Profile

Full-time: 1,209	International: 19%
Part-time: 1,291	Women: 32%
Total: 2,500	Minorities: 16%
Average Age: 29	Average Class Size: 40
Fall 1997 Average GPA: 3.4	Fall 1997 Average GMAT: 673

Costs
Full-time tuition: $24,351 per academic year
Part-time tuition: $2402 per course

AACSB – The International Association for Management Education accredited

GRADUATE BUSINESS PROGRAMS

Master of Management (MMgt) Full-time, part-time; 23 total credits required; 21 months to 2 years to complete program. Concentrations in accounting, information management, entrepreneurship, organizational behavior/development, managerial economics, real estate, business law, human resources, finance, industrial/labor relations, marketing, operations management, decision sciences, international business, nonprofit organization, management, health care, .

Master of Management/Doctor of Jurisprudence (MMgt/JD) Full-time; up to 4 years to complete program.

Master of Management/Doctor of Medicine (MMgt/MD) Full-time; 66 total credits required; up to 5 years to complete program.

Master of Management/Master of Science in Nursing (MMgt/MS) Full-time; 30 total credits required; up to 2 years to complete program.

Master of Management in Manufacturing (MMgt) Full-time; 23 total credits required; 22 months to 2 years to complete program.

ADMISSION

Applications For fall 1997 there were 6,107 applications for admission. Of those applying, 990 were accepted. Of those accepted, 627 enrolled.

Application Requirements Application form, application fee, bachelor's degree (must be in field of business), essay, minimum GPA: 3.0, interview, letter of recommendation, personal statement, resume, college transcript(s), minimum of 4 years of work experience, computer experience: Microsoft Office.

Recommended for Application GMAT score accepted.

Application Deadline 11/14 for fall, 1/15 for winter, 3/16 for spring, 11/14 for fall (international), 1/15 for winter (international). Application fee: $125. Deferred entrance is available.

ACADEMICS

Faculty Full-time 165; part-time 35.

Teaching Methodologies Case study, computer-aided instruction, computer analysis, computer simulations, experiential learning, field projects, group discussion, lecture, research, role playing, seminars by members of the business community, simulations, student presentations, study groups, team projects.

Technology 65 on-campus computer terminals/PCs are available for student use and are linked by a campus-wide network. The network has full access to the Internet. Students are required to have their own PC.

Special Opportunities International exchange programs in Australia, Austria, Belgium, Chile, Denmark, France, Germany, Hong Kong, Israel, Italy, Japan, Mexico, Netherlands, Norway, Spain, Thailand, United Kingdom. An internship program is available.

FINANCES

Costs for 1997–98 Tuition: Full-time: $24,351 per annum. Part-time: $2402 per course. Cost varies by class time (e.g., day/evening). Average 1997–98 room and board costs were $10,116 per academic year. Room and board costs vary by occupancy (e.g., single, double, triple), type of accommodation, type of meal plan.

Financial Aid In 1997–98, 35% of students received some institutionally administered aid in the form of fellowships, research assistantships, grants, scholarships, work study, loans. Application Deadline: 4/15.

Financial Aid Contact Ms. Michele Rogers, Associate Director of Financial Aid, 2001 North Sheridan Road, Evanston , IL 60208. Phone: 847-491-3308; Fax: 847-491-4960.

FACILITIES

Information Resources University Library plus 3 additional on-campus libraries; total holdings of 3,932,339 volumes, 2,296,503 microforms, 28,424 current periodical subscriptions. CD player(s) available for graduate student use. Access provided to online bibliographic retrieval services.

INTERNATIONAL STUDENTS

Demographics 19% of students enrolled are international students [Africa, 1%, Asia, 7%, Australia/New Zealand, 4%, Central America, 3%, Europe, 7%, North America, 76%, South America, 2%].

Services and Facilities Visa services, counseling/support services.

Applying TOEFL: minimum score of 600, proof of adequate funds required. Financial aid is not available to international students.

International Student Contact Office of Admissions, Kellogg Graduate School of Management, 2001 North Sheridan Road, Evanston, IL 60208. Phone: 847-491-3308; Fax: 847-491-4960; E-mail: kellogg-admissions@nwu.edu

PLACEMENT

Services include alumni network, career counseling/planning, career fairs, career library, career placement, electronic job bank, job interviews arranged, job search course, resume referral to employers, and resume preparation. In 1996–97, 313 organizations participated in on-campus recruiting; 14,260 on-campus interviews were conducted.

Employment Of 1996–97 graduates, 98% were employed within three months of graduation; the average starting salary was $70,000. Types of employ-

ment entered: accounting, banking, chemical industry, communications, computer-related, consulting, consumer products, education, energy, engineering, finance, financial services, government, health services, high technology, hospitality management, human resources, information systems/technology, insurance, international trade, law, management, manufacturing, marketing, media, nonprofit, petrochemical, pharmaceutical, real estate, retail, service industry, telecommunications, transportation, utilities.

Business Program(s) URL: http://www.kellogg.nwu.edu

Program Contact: Office of Admissions, Kellogg Graduate School of Business, 2001 North Sheridan Road, Evanston, IL 60208. Phone: 847-491-3308; Fax: 847-491-4960; E-mail: kellogg-admissions@nwu.edu

Olivet Nazarene University

Division of Business

Kankakee, Illinois

OVERVIEW

Olivet Nazarene University is an independent-religious, coed, comprehensive institution. Founded: 1907. The graduate business unit is in a suburban setting and is on a semester calendar.

GRADUATE BUSINESS PROGRAMS
Master of Business Administration (MBA)

ACADEMICS

Faculty Full-time 5; part-time 8.

Teaching Methodologies Case study, faculty seminars, lecture, seminars by members of the business community, student presentations, team projects.

Technology Computer terminals/PCs are available for student use and are linked by a campus-wide network. The network has partial access to the Internet. Students are required to have their own PC.

Special Opportunities Advanced credit may be earned through transfer of credits from another institution.

FACILITIES

Information Resources Benner Library; total holdings of 155,000 volumes, 88,000 microforms, 950 current periodical subscriptions. CD player(s) available for graduate student use. Access provided to online bibliographic retrieval services.

Program Contact: School of Graduate Adult Studies, PO Box 592, Kankakee, IL 60901-0592. Phone: 815-939-5186; Fax: 815-939-5028.

Quincy University

Division of Business

Quincy, Illinois

OVERVIEW

Quincy University is an independent-religious, coed, comprehensive institution. Enrollment: 1,164 graduate, professional, and undergraduate students; full-time matriculated graduate/professional students; 57 part-time matriculated graduate/professional students. Founded: 1860. The graduate business unit is in a small-town setting and is on a semester calendar.

HIGHLIGHTS

Enrollment Profile

Full-time: 0	International: N/R
Part-time: 57	Women: 46%
Total: 57	Minorities: N/R
Average Age: 28	Average Class Size: 25
Fall 1997 Average GPA: N/R	Fall 1997 Average GMAT: 535

Costs
Full-time tuition: N/R
Part-time tuition: $1080 per course

GRADUATE BUSINESS PROGRAMS

Master of Business Administration (MBA) Full-time, part-time; 30 total credits required; 12 months to 5 years to complete program.

ADMISSION

Applications For fall 1997 there were 20 applications for admission. Of those applying, 17 were accepted. Of those accepted, 17 enrolled.

Application Requirements Application form, application fee, bachelor's degree, minimum GPA, 2 letters of recommendation, college transcript(s).

Recommended for Application GMAT score accepted, work experience.

Quincy University (continued)

Application Deadline Applications processed on a rolling/continuous basis for both domestic and international students. Application fee: $25.

ACADEMICS

Faculty Full-time 6; part-time 1.

Teaching Methodologies Case study, computer-aided instruction, computer analysis, computer simulations, field projects, group discussion, lecture, research, role playing, seminars by members of the business community, simulations, student presentations, study groups, team projects.

Technology 64 on-campus computer terminals/PCs are available for student use and are linked by a campus-wide network. The network has full access to the Internet. Students are not required to have their own PC.

Special Opportunities Advanced credit may be earned through transfer of credits from another institution.

FINANCES

Costs for 1997–98 Tuition: $1080 per course. Cost varies by class time (e.g., day/evening), number of credits taken.

Financial Aid Financial aid is available to part-time students.

FACILITIES

Information Resources Brenner Library; total holdings of 229,742 volumes, 147,395 microforms, 645 current periodical subscriptions. CD player(s) available for graduate student use. Access provided to online bibliographic retrieval services.

INTERNATIONAL STUDENTS

Demographics N/R

Applying TOEFL: minimum score of 600, proof of adequate funds, proof of health/immunizations required. Financial aid is not available to international students.

PLACEMENT

Services include career placement. In 1996–97, 25 organizations participated in on-campus recruiting.

Employment Of 1996–97 graduates, 100% were employed within three months of graduation. Types of employment entered: accounting, banking, chemical industry, communications, computer-related, education, energy, finance, financial services, health services, high technology, hospitality management, human resources, information systems/technology, insurance, law, management, manufacturing, marketing, media, nonprofit, pharmaceutical, real estate, retail, service industry, telecommunications, utilities.

Business Program(s) URL: http://www.quincy.edu/divisions/business/MBA/

Program Contact: Dr. Richard Magliari, Professor of Business, 1800 College Avenue, Quincy, IL 62301-2699. 800-688-4295; Fax: 217-228-5651; E-mail: mba-director@quincy.edu

Rockford College

Department of Economics, Business, and Accounting

Rockford, Illinois

OVERVIEW

Rockford College is an independent-nonprofit, coed, comprehensive institution. Enrollment: 1,500 graduate, professional, and undergraduate students; 48 full-time matriculated graduate/professional students; 383 part-time matriculated graduate/professional students. Founded: 1847. The graduate business unit is in a suburban setting and is on a semester calendar.

HIGHLIGHTS

Enrollment Profile
Full-time: 5
Part-time: 95
Total: 100
Average Age: 32
Fall 1997 Average GPA: 3.2

International: 10%
Women: 50%
Minorities: N/R
Average Class Size: 15
Fall 1997 Average GMAT: 500

Costs
Full-time tuition: $14,750 per academic year
Part-time tuition: $400 per credit hour

GRADUATE BUSINESS PROGRAMS

Master of Business Administration (MBA) Full-time, part-time; 36-50 total credits required; 2 to 5 years to complete program. Concentrations in accounting, marketing, international management, management, finance, nonprofit organization, public management.

ADMISSION

Applications For fall 1997 there were 30 applications for admission. Of those applying, 26 were accepted. Of those accepted, 25 enrolled.

Application Requirements GMAT score, application form, application fee, bachelor's degree, essay, 3 letters of recommendation, personal statement, college transcript(s).

Recommended for Application Minimum GPA, interview, resume, minimum of 5 years of work experience.

Application Deadline Applications processed on a rolling/continuous basis for both domestic and international students. Application fee: $35.

ACADEMICS

Faculty Full-time 12; part-time 2.

Teaching Methodologies Case study, computer-aided instruction, computer simulations, experiential learning, faculty seminars, field projects, group discussion, lecture, research, role playing, simulations, student presentations, team projects.

Technology 75 on-campus computer terminals/PCs are available for student use and are linked by a campus-wide network. The network has full access to the Internet. Students are not required to have their own PC.

Special Opportunities Advanced credit may be earned through credit by examination, transfer of credits from another institution. An internship program is available.

FINANCES

Costs for 1997–98 Tuition: Full-time: $14,750 per year. Part-time: $400 per credit hour. Cost varies by number of credits taken. Average 1997–98 room and board costs were $4800 per academic year. Room and board costs vary by campus location, occupancy (e.g., single, double, triple), type of accommodation, type of meal plan.

Financial Aid In 1997–98, 10% of students received some institutionally administered aid in the form of research assistantships, grants, loans. Financial aid is available to part-time students. Application Deadline: 4/1.

Financial Aid Contact Mrs. Judy Seebach, Director of Financial Aid, 5050 East State Street, Rockford, IL 61108-2393. Phone: 815-226-3385; Fax: 815-226-4119.

FACILITIES

Information Resources Howard Colman Library; total holdings of 165,995 volumes, 7,410 microforms, 826 current periodical subscriptions. CD player(s) available for graduate student use. Access provided to online bibliographic retrieval services and online databases.

INTERNATIONAL STUDENTS

Demographics 10% of students enrolled are international students [Asia, 30%, Central America, 10%, Europe, 30%, South America, 30%].

Services and Facilities International student office, international student center, international student housing, visa services, ESL courses, counseling/support services.

Applying TOEFL: minimum score of 550, proof of adequate funds, proof of health/immunizations required.

International Student Contact Mr. Brad Lauman, International Student Coordinator, 5050 East State Street, Rockford, IL 61108-2393. Phone: 815-226-3336; Fax: 815-226-4119.

PLACEMENT

Services include alumni network, career counseling/planning, career fairs, career library, career placement, electronic job bank, and resume preparation. In 1996–97, 50 organizations participated in on-campus recruiting.

Employment Of 1996–97 graduates, 98% were employed within three months of graduation. Types of employment entered: accounting, banking, consumer products, engineering, finance, health services, hospitality management, human resources, information systems/technology, insurance, international trade, management, manufacturing, marketing, nonprofit, real estate, retail, service industry, telecommunications, utilities.

Program Contact: Mr. Jeffrey Fahrenwald, Director, MBA Program, 5050 East State Street, Rockford, IL 61108-2393. Phone: 815-226-4178; Fax: 815-226-4119; E-mail: jfahrenwald@rockford.edu

Roosevelt University

Walter E. Heller College of Business Administration

Chicago, Illinois

OVERVIEW
Roosevelt University is an independent-nonprofit, coed, comprehensive institution. Enrollment: 6,800 graduate, professional, and undergraduate students; 374 full-time matriculated graduate/professional students; 1,611 part-time matriculated graduate/professional students. Founded: 1945. The graduate business unit is in an urban setting and is on a semester calendar.

HIGHLIGHTS

Enrollment Profile
Full-time: 30
Part-time: 570
Total: 600
Average Age: 32
Fall 1997 Average GPA: 2.9

International: 10%
Women: 50%
Minorities: N/R
Average Class Size: 17
Fall 1997 Average GMAT: 460

Costs
Full-time tuition: $8010 per academic year
Part-time tuition: $445 per credit hour

GRADUATE BUSINESS PROGRAMS
Master of Business Administration (MBA) Full-time, part-time; 36 total credits required; 12 months to 6 years to complete program. Concentrations in accounting, economics, finance, international business, management, management information systems, marketing, quantitative analysis, human resources, health care, telecommunications management.

Master of Science in Accounting (MS) Full-time, part-time; 30 total credits required; 12 months to 6 years to complete program.

Master of Science in Information Systems (MS) Full-time, part-time; 30 total credits required; 12 months to 6 years to complete program. Concentrations in finance, financial management/planning, management, marketing, accounting.

Master of Science in International Business (MS) Full-time, part-time; 30 total credits required; 12 months to 6 years to complete program. Concentrations in accounting, economics, finance, management information systems, marketing, management.

ADMISSION
Applications For fall 1997 there were 216 applications for admission. Of those applying, 153 were accepted. Of those accepted, 120 enrolled.

Application Requirements GMAT score, application form, application fee, bachelor's degree, college transcript(s).

Recommended for Application Minimum GPA: 2.7, letters of recommendation, personal statement, resume.

Application Deadline Applications processed on a rolling/continuous basis for both domestic and international students. Application fee: $25, $35 (international). Deferred entrance is available.

ACADEMICS
Faculty Full-time 25; part-time 40.

Teaching Methodologies Case study, computer analysis, group discussion, lecture, research, seminars by members of the business community, student presentations, study groups, team projects.

Technology 150 on-campus computer terminals/PCs are available for student use and are linked by a campus-wide network. The network has full access to the Internet. Students are not required to have their own PC.

Special Opportunities Advanced credit may be earned through transfer of credits from another institution. An internship program is available.

FINANCES
Costs for 1997–98 Tuition: Full-time: $8010 per year. Part-time: $445 per credit hour. Cost varies by number of credits taken. Fees: Full-time: $100 per academic year. Part-time: $100 per semester. Average 1997–98 room and board costs were $5800 per academic year. Room and board costs vary by occupancy (e.g., single, double, triple), type of meal plan.

Financial Aid Scholarships, work study available. Financial aid is available to part-time students. Application Deadline: 2/15.

Financial Aid Contact Mr. Walter O'Neill, Director of Financial Aid, 430 South Michigan Avenue, Chicago, IL 60605-1394. Phone: 312-341-3612.

FACILITIES
Information Resources Murray-Green Library plus 1 additional on-campus library; total holdings of 400,000 volumes, 115,000 microforms, 1,500 current periodical subscriptions. CD player(s) available for graduate student use. Access provided to online bibliographic retrieval services.

INTERNATIONAL STUDENTS
Demographics 10% of students enrolled are international students.

Services and Facilities International student office, international student center, visa services, ESL courses, counseling/support services, language tutoring.

Applying TOEFL: minimum score of 550, TWE: minimum score of 3.5, proof of adequate funds required. Financial aid is available to international students.

International Student Contact Ms. Claudia McNamara, International Admissions Coordinator, 430 South Michigan Avenue, Chicago, IL 60605-1394. Phone: 312-341-3581 Ext. 423; Fax: 312-341-6377.

PLACEMENT
Services include alumni network, career counseling/planning, career fairs, career library, career placement, electronic job bank, job interviews arranged, resume referral to employers, and resume preparation. In 1996–97, 75 organizations participated in on-campus recruiting.

Employment Types of employment entered: accounting, banking, consulting, energy, finance, government, health services, hospitality management, human resources, information systems/technology, insurance, management, marketing, nonprofit, transportation.

Business Program(s) URL: http://www.roosevelt.edu

Program Contact: Ms. Marilyn Nance, Director, MBA Program, Walter E. Heller College of Business Administration, 430 South Michigan Avenue, Chicago, IL 60605-1394. Phone: 312-341-3820; Fax: 312-341-3827.
See full description on page 954.

Saint Xavier University

Graham School of Management

Chicago, Illinois

OVERVIEW
Saint Xavier University is an independent-religious, coed, comprehensive institution. Enrollment: 4,408 graduate, professional, and undergraduate students; 100 full-time matriculated graduate/professional students; 1,723 part-time matriculated graduate/professional students. Founded: 1847. The graduate business unit is in a suburban setting and is on a quarter calendar.

HIGHLIGHTS

Enrollment Profile
Full-time: 13
Part-time: 124
Total: 137
Average Age: 28
Fall 1997 Average GPA: N/R

International: 27%
Women: N/R
Minorities: 18%
Average Class Size: 15
Fall 1997 Average GMAT: N/R

Costs
Full-time tuition: $8028 per academic year
Part-time tuition: $445 per semester hour

GRADUATE BUSINESS PROGRAMS
Master of Business Administration (MBA) Full-time, part-time; 39 total credits required; 12 months to 5 years to complete program. Concentrations in finance, management, marketing, health care.

Master of Business Administration/Master of Science in Nursing (MBA/MS) Full-time, part-time; 39 total credits required; 12 months to 5 years to complete program. Concentrations in health care, management, marketing, finance.

ADMISSION
Application Requirements Application form, application fee, bachelor's degree, 2 letters of recommendation, college transcript(s).

Recommended for Application Minimum GPA, personal statement, work experience, computer experience.

Application Deadline Applications processed on a rolling/continuous basis for both domestic and international students. Application fee: $35. Deferred entrance is available.

ACADEMICS
Faculty Full-time 15; part-time 6.

Teaching Methodologies Case study, computer-aided instruction, computer analysis, computer simulations, experiential learning, field projects, group discussion, lecture, research, role playing, seminars by members of the business community, simulations, student presentations, study groups, team projects.

Technology 75 on-campus computer terminals/PCs are available for student use and are linked by a campus-wide network. The network has full access to the Internet. Students are not required to have their own PC.

Special Opportunities Advanced credit may be earned through transfer of credits from another institution. International exchange program in England. An internship program is available.

Saint Xavier University (continued)

FINANCES
Costs for 1997–98 Tuition: Full-time: $8028 per year. Part-time: $445 per semester hour. Fees: Full-time: $65 per academic year. Part-time: $60 per semester.

Financial Aid Research assistantships, work study, loans available. Financial aid is available to part-time students.

Financial Aid Contact Financial Aid Office, 3700 West 103rd Street, Chicago, IL 60655-3105. Phone: 773-298-3070.

FACILITIES
Information Resources Byrne Memorial Library; total holdings of 153,000 volumes, 116,981 microforms, 877 current periodical subscriptions. CD player(s) available for graduate student use. Access provided to online bibliographic retrieval services.

INTERNATIONAL STUDENTS
Demographics 27% of students enrolled are international students [Asia, 50%, Europe, 50%].

Services and Facilities International student office, international student housing, counseling/support services.

Applying TOEFL, proof of adequate funds required. Financial aid is available to international students.

International Student Contact Colleen Durken Early, Coordinator of International Students and Studies, 3700 West 103rd Street, Chicago, IL 60655-3105. Phone: 773-298-3061.

PLACEMENT
Services include alumni network, career counseling/planning, and career placement.

Employment Types of employment entered: accounting, banking, computer-related, consumer products, finance, government, health services, hospitality management, human resources, information systems/technology, insurance, management, marketing, nonprofit, pharmaceutical, real estate, telecommunications, transportation.

Business Program(s) URL: http://www.sxu.edu/academ/manage.htm

Program Contact: Anne Hurley, Admissions, 3700 West 103rd Street, Chicago, IL 60655-3105. Phone: 773-298-3051.

Southern Illinois University at Carbondale

College of Business and Administration

Carbondale, Illinois

OVERVIEW
Southern Illinois University at Carbondale is a state-supported, coed university. Enrollment: 22,000 graduate, professional, and undergraduate students; 3,055 full-time matriculated graduate/professional students; 668 part-time matriculated graduate/professional students. Founded: 1869. The graduate business unit is in a small-town setting and is on a semester calendar.

HIGHLIGHTS

Enrollment Profile
Full-time: 94
Part-time: 40
Total: 134
Average Age: 26
Fall 1997 Average GPA: 3.2

International: 50%
Women: 38%
Minorities: 5%
Average Class Size: 38
Fall 1997 Average GMAT: 526

Costs
Full-time tuition: $1620 per academic year (resident); $4860 per academic year (nonresident)
Part-time tuition: $90 per hour (resident); $270 per hour (nonresident)

AACSB – The International Association for Management Education accredited

Degree(s) offered in conjunction with Group ESC Grenoble

GRADUATE BUSINESS PROGRAMS
Master of Business Administration (MBA) Full-time, part-time; 32 total credits required; 12 months to 2 years to complete program. Concentrations in accounting, finance, management, management information systems, marketing, organizational behavior/development, production management, international business.

Master of Business Administration/Doctor of Jurisprudence (MBA/JD) Full-time; 104 total credits required; 3 to 4 years to complete program.

Master of Business Administration/Master of Science in Agribusiness Economics (MBA/MS) Full-time, part-time; 12 months to 2.5 years to complete program.

Master of Business Administration/Master of Arts in Mass Communication (MBA/MA) Full-time, part-time; 12 months to 2.5 years to complete program.

ADMISSION
Applications For fall 1997 there were 142 applications for admission. Of those applying, 80 were accepted. Of those accepted, 37 enrolled.

Application Requirements GMAT score, application form, application fee, bachelor's degree, essay, minimum GPA: 2.7, 3 letters of recommendation, college transcript(s).

Recommended for Application Personal statement.

Application Deadline 6/15 for fall, 11/15 for spring, 4/15 for summer, 4/15 for fall (international), 9/15 for spring (international), 2/15 for summer (international). Application fee: $20. Deferred entrance is available.

ACADEMICS
Faculty Full-time 47.

Teaching Methodologies Case study, computer-aided instruction, faculty seminars, group discussion, lecture, research, seminars by members of the business community, student presentations, team projects.

Technology 300 on-campus computer terminals/PCs are available for student use and are linked by a campus-wide network. The network has full access to the Internet. Students are not required to have their own PC.

Special Opportunities Advanced credit may be earned through transfer of credits from another institution. International exchange program in France. An internship program is available.

FINANCES
Costs for 1997–98 Tuition: Full-time: $1620 per year (resident); $4860 per year (nonresident). Part-time: $90 per hour (resident); $270 per hour (nonresident). Cost varies by number of credits taken, reciprocity agreements. Fees: Full-time: $878 per academic year (resident); $878 per academic year (nonresident). Average 1997–98 room and board costs were $3472 per academic year (on campus) and $4800 per academic year (off campus). Room and board costs vary by occupancy (e.g., single, double, triple), type of accommodation, type of meal plan.

Financial Aid Fellowships, research assistantships, teaching assistantships, work study, loans available. Financial aid is available to part-time students. Application Deadline: 3/15.

Financial Aid Contact Ms. Pamela Britton, Director, Financial Aid, Woody Hall B326, Carbondale, IL 62901. Phone: 618-453-4334; Fax: 618-453-7305.

FACILITIES
Information Resources Morris Library; total holdings of 2,000,000 volumes, 2,400,000 microforms, 15,000 current periodical subscriptions. Access provided to online bibliographic retrieval services.

INTERNATIONAL STUDENTS
Demographics 50% of students enrolled are international students.

Services and Facilities International student office, international student housing, visa services, ESL courses, counseling/support services, international student council.

Applying TOEFL: minimum score of 550, proof of adequate funds, proof of health/immunizations required. Financial aid is available to international students.

International Student Contact Mr. Joe Pineau, Jr., Coordinator, MBA Program, Rehn 133, Carbondale, IL 62901-4625. Phone: 618-453-3030; Fax: 618-453-7961; E-mail: mbag@siu.edu

PLACEMENT
Services include alumni network, career counseling/planning, career fairs, career library, career placement, electronic job bank, job interviews arranged, resume referral to employers, and resume preparation. In 1996–97, 82 organizations participated in on-campus recruiting.

Employment Of 1996–97 graduates, 60% were employed within three months of graduation; the average starting salary was $35,000. Types of employment entered: accounting, banking, chemical industry, computer-related, consumer products, education, engineering, finance, financial services, government, high technology, human resources, information systems/technology, insurance, international trade, law, management, manufacturing, marketing, pharmaceutical, real estate, retail, service industry, telecommunications, transportation.

Business Program(s) URL: http://www.siu.edu/departments/coba/mba

Program Contact: Mr. Joe Pineau, Jr., Coordinator, MBA Program, Rehn Hall 133, Carbondale, IL 62901-4625. Phone: 618-453-3030; Fax: 618-453-7961; E-mail: mbagp@siu.edu

See full description on page 990.

Southern Illinois University at Edwardsville

School of Business

Edwardsville, Illinois

OVERVIEW
Southern Illinois University at Edwardsville is a state-supported, coed, comprehensive institution. Enrollment: 11,207 graduate, professional, and undergraduate students; 725 full-time matriculated graduate/professional students; 1,775 part-time matriculated graduate/professional students. Founded: 1957. The graduate business unit is in a suburban setting and is on a four 10-week sessions calendar.

HIGHLIGHTS

Enrollment Profile
Full-time: 92
Part-time: 224
Total: 316
Average Age: 32
Fall 1997 Average GPA: 2.9

International: 9%
Women: 45%
Minorities: 7%
Average Class Size: 35
Fall 1997 Average GMAT: 512

Costs
Full-time tuition: N/R
Part-time tuition: $572 per 6 semester hours (resident); $1716 per 6 semester hours (nonresident)

AACSB – The International Association for Management Education accredited

The School of Business at Southern Illinois University Edwardsville prepares students to be leaders in today's global economy. Faculty members provide the benefit of their real-world experience and impressive academic credentials through a curriculum that is focused on knowledge-based leadership. The M.B.A. degree requires 30 hours for those with appropriate undergraduate foundation courses in business. The program consists of four required and six elective courses. Up to 24 hours of foundation courses may be required. Program courses include External Environment of Business; International Business Environment: Leadership, Influence, and Managerial Effectiveness; and Strategic Management. Electives are in finance, management information systems, and marketing, with additional electives also available in accounting, economics, and management. A specialization in MIS is available. Learning formats are flexible, with courses meeting one night a week for ten weeks or courses available concentrated into two weekends. These formats allow rapid completion of the degree. The School also offers master's degrees in accounting, computing and information science, economics and finance, and marketing research.

GRADUATE BUSINESS PROGRAMS
Master of Business Administration (MBA) Full-time, part-time, distance learning option; 60 total credits required; 12 months to 6 years to complete program. Concentrations in business information science, decision sciences, economics, finance, human resources, information management, international business, management, marketing, manpower administration, organizational management.

Master of Science in Accountancy (MS) Full-time, part-time; 60 total credits required; 12 months to 6 years to complete program. Concentration in accounting.

Master of Science in Economics and Finance (MS) Full-time, part-time; 39 total credits required; 12 months to 6 years to complete program. Concentrations in economics, financial economics, finance.

Master of Arts in Economics and Finance (MA) Full-time, part-time; 39 total credits required; 12 months to 6 years to complete program. Concentrations in economics, financial economics, finance.

Master of Science in Computing and Information Systems (MS) Full-time, part-time; 60 total credits required; 12 months to 6 years to complete program. Concentrations in management information systems, management systems analysis, business information science, system management.

Master of Science in Marketing Research (MS) Full-time, part-time; 60 total credits required; 12 months to 6 years to complete program. Concentrations in marketing, marketing research.

ADMISSION
Applications For fall 1997 there were 130 applications for admission. Of those applying, 94 were accepted. Of those accepted, 82 enrolled.

Application Requirements Application form, application fee, bachelor's degree, minimum GPA: 2.5, college transcript(s).

Recommended for Application GMAT score accepted: minimum 400.

Application Deadline 7/24 for fall, 12/11 for spring, 4/27 for summer, 7/24 for fall (international), 12/11 for spring (international), 4/27 for summer (international). Application fee: $25. Deferred entrance is available.

ACADEMICS
Faculty Full-time 63; part-time 13.

Teaching Methodologies Case study, computer-aided instruction, computer analysis, computer simulations, faculty seminars, group discussion, lecture, research, role playing, seminars by members of the business community, simulations, student presentations, study groups, team projects.

Technology 400 on-campus computer terminals/PCs are available for student use and are linked by a campus-wide network. The network has full access to the Internet. Students are not required to have their own PC.

Special Opportunities Advanced credit may be earned through transfer of credits from another institution. International exchange programs in France, Germany, Mexico, Netherlands, United Kingdom. An internship program is available.

FINANCES
Costs for 1997–98 Tuition: $572 per 6 semester hours (resident); $1716 per 6 semester hours (nonresident). Cost varies by reciprocity agreements. Fees: $231 per 6 semester hours (resident); $231 per 6 semester hours (nonresident). Average 1997–98 room and board costs were $4150 per academic year (on campus) and $4150 per academic year (off campus). Room and board costs vary by occupancy (e.g., single, double, triple), type of accommodation, type of meal plan.

Financial Aid In 1997–98, 19% of students received some institutionally administered aid in the form of fellowships, research assistantships, teaching assistantships, scholarships, work study, loans. Financial aid is available to part-time students.

Financial Aid Contact Ms. Marion Smithson, Director of Student Work and Financial Aid, Box 1060, Edwardsville, IL 62026. Phone: 618-692-3880; Fax: 618-692-3885; E-mail: msmiths@siue.edu

FACILITIES
Information Resources Lovejoy Library; total holdings of 734,478 volumes, 1,477,469 microforms, 6,515 current periodical subscriptions. CD player(s) available for graduate student use. Access provided to online bibliographic retrieval services and online databases.

INTERNATIONAL STUDENTS
Demographics 9% of students enrolled are international students [Asia, 6%, Central America, 1%, Europe, 2%, North America, 91%, South America, 1%].

Services and Facilities International student office, international student housing, ESL courses, counseling/support services.

Applying TOEFL: minimum score of 550, proof of adequate funds, proof of health/immunizations required. Financial aid is not available to international students.

International Student Contact Ms. Antoinette Liston, Advisor, Box 1616, Edwardsville, IL 62026. Phone: 618-692-3785; E-mail: aliston@siue.edu

PLACEMENT
Services include alumni network, career counseling/planning, career fairs, career library, career placement, electronic job bank, job interviews arranged, job search course, resume referral to employers, and resume preparation. In 1996–97, 350 organizations participated in on-campus recruiting; 125 on-campus interviews were conducted.

Employment Of 1996–97 graduates, 94% were employed within three months of graduation. Types of employment entered: accounting, banking, chemical industry, communications, computer-related, consulting, consumer products, energy, finance, financial services, government, health services, high technology, human resources, information systems/technology, insurance, international trade, management, manufacturing, marketing, nonprofit, real estate, retail, service industry, telecommunications, transportation, utilities.

Business Program(s) URL: http://www.siue.edu/BUSINESS

Program Contact: Dr. Maurice L. Hirsch, Jr., Associate Dean for Academic Affairs, Box 1051, Edwardsville, IL 62026-1051. Phone: 618-692-3412; Fax: 618-692-3979; E-mail: mhirsch@siue.edu

See full description on page 992.

University of Chicago

Graduate School of Business

Chicago, Illinois

OVERVIEW
The University of Chicago is an independent-nonprofit, coed university. Enrollment: 12,233 graduate, professional, and undergraduate students; 6,487 full-time matriculated graduate/professional students; 1,974 part-time matriculated graduate/professional students. Founded: 1890. The graduate business unit is in an urban setting and is on a quarter calendar.

University of Chicago (continued)

HIGHLIGHTS

Enrollment Profile
Full-time: 1,108
Part-time: 1,654
Total: 2,762
Average Age: 28
Fall 1997 Average GPA: 3.42

International: 12%
Women: 24%
Minorities: 17%
Average Class Size: 53
Fall 1997 Average GMAT: 676

Costs
Full-time tuition: $24,904 per academic year
Part-time tuition: $2490 per course

AACSB – The International Association for Management Education accredited

GRADUATE BUSINESS PROGRAMS

Full-time MBA (MBA) Full-time; 66 total credits required; 18 months to 5 years to complete program. Concentrations in accounting, organizational behavior/development, managerial economics, international business, management science, management, marketing, production management, quality management, economics, financial management/planning, industrial/labor relations, business policy/strategy, entrepreneurship.

International MBA (IMBA) Full-time; 76 total credits required; 2 to 5 years to complete program. Concentrations in accounting, organizational behavior/development, managerial economics, financial management/planning, international business, management science, management, marketing, production management, quality management, economics, industrial/labor relations, business policy/strategy, entrepreneurship.

Evening and Weekend MBA Program (MBA) Part-time; 66 total credits required; 2.5 to 5 years to complete program. Concentrations in accounting, organizational behavior/development, managerial economics, financial management/planning, international business, management science, management, marketing, production management, quality management, economics, industrial/labor relations, business policy/strategy, entrepreneurship.

Executive MBA (MBA) Part-time; 53 total credits required; 16 months to complete program. Concentrations in accounting, organizational behavior/development, managerial economics, financial management/planning, international business, management science, management, marketing, production management, quality management, economics, industrial/labor relations, business policy/strategy, entrepreneurship.

International Executive MBA (MBA) Part-time; 53 total credits required; 16 months to complete program. Concentrations in accounting, organizational behavior/development, managerial economics, financial management/planning, international business, management science, management, marketing, production management, quality management, economics, industrial/labor relations, business policy/strategy, entrepreneurship.

ADMISSION

Applications For fall 1997 there were 3,432 applications for admission. Of those applying, 907 were accepted. Of those accepted, 479 enrolled.

Application Requirements Application form, application fee, bachelor's degree, essay, minimum GPA, 2 letters of recommendation, personal statement, college transcript(s).

Recommended for Application GMAT score accepted, GRE score accepted, interview, resume, work experience, computer experience.

Application Deadline Applications processed on a rolling/continuous basis for both domestic and international students. Application fee: $125. Deferred entrance is available.

ACADEMICS

Faculty Full-time 114; part-time 48.

Teaching Methodologies Case study, computer-aided instruction, computer analysis, computer simulations, experiential learning, faculty seminars, field projects, group discussion, lecture, research, role playing, simulations, student presentations, study groups, team projects.

Technology 80 on-campus computer terminals/PCs are available for student use and are linked by a campus-wide network. The network has full access to the Internet. Students are not required to have their own PC.

Special Opportunities International exchange programs in Australia, Austria, Belgium, Brazil, Chile, France, Hong Kong, Israel, Italy, Japan, Mexico, Netherlands, People's Republic of China, Spain, Sweden, Switzerland, United Kingdom. An internship program is available.

FINANCES

Costs for 1997–98 Tuition: Full-time: $24,904 per year. Part-time: $2490 per course. Fees: Full-time: $351 per academic year. Fees vary by academic program. Average 1997–98 room and board costs were $10,210 per academic year (on campus) and $10,210 per academic year (off campus).

Room and board costs vary by campus location, occupancy (e.g., single, double, triple), type of accommodation.

Financial Aid Grants, scholarships, work study, loans available. Financial aid is available to part-time students. Application Deadline: 1/15.

Financial Aid Contact Associate Director, Financial Aid, 1101 East 58th Street, Chicago, IL 60637-1513. Phone: 773-702-3076; Fax: 773-702-9085.

FACILITIES

Information Resources Joseph Regenstein Library plus 6 additional on-campus libraries; total holdings of 5,710,003 volumes, 2,039,956 microforms, 46,730 current periodical subscriptions. CD player(s) available for graduate student use. Access provided to online bibliographic retrieval services.

INTERNATIONAL STUDENTS

Demographics 12% of students enrolled are international students.

Services and Facilities International student office, international student housing, visa services, counseling/support services.

Applying TOEFL: minimum score of 600, proof of adequate funds, proof of health/immunizations required. Financial aid is not available to international students.

International Student Contact Mr. Donald Martin, Director of Admissions, Graduate School of Business, 1101 East 58th Street, Chicago, IL 60637-1513. Phone: 773-702-7438; Fax: 773-702-9085.

PLACEMENT

Services include alumni network, career counseling/planning, career fairs, career library, career placement, electronic job bank, job interviews arranged, resume referral to employers, and resume preparation. In 1996–97, 437 organizations participated in on-campus recruiting; 12,000 on-campus interviews were conducted.

Employment Of 1996–97 graduates, 99% were employed within three months of graduation; the average starting salary was $89,400. Types of employment entered: accounting, banking, chemical industry, computer-related, consulting, consumer products, energy, finance, financial services, government, health services, high technology, information systems/technology, insurance, law, management, manufacturing, marketing, petrochemical, pharmaceutical, real estate, retail, service industry, telecommunications, transportation, utilities.

Business Program(s) URL: http://gsbwww.uchicago.edu

Program Contact: Mr. Donald Martin, Director of Admissions, Graduate School of Business, 1101 East 58th Street, Chicago, IL 60637-1513. Phone: 773-702-7369; Fax: 773-702-9085.

See full description on page 1052.

University of Illinois at Chicago

College of Business Administration
Chicago, Illinois

OVERVIEW
The University of Illinois at Chicago is a state-supported, coed university. Enrollment: 24,865 graduate, professional, and undergraduate students; 4,997 full-time matriculated graduate/professional students; 3,047 part-time matriculated graduate/professional students. Founded: 1946. The graduate business unit is in an urban setting and is on a semester calendar.

HIGHLIGHTS

Enrollment Profile
Full-time: 101
Part-time: 296
Total: 397
Average Age: 26
Fall 1997 Average GPA: 3.0

International: 13%
Women: 38%
Minorities: 19%
Average Class Size: 20
Fall 1997 Average GMAT: 550

Costs
Full-time tuition: $10,436 per academic year (resident); $16,878 per academic year (nonresident)
Part-time tuition: $982 per course (resident); $1903 per course (nonresident)

AACSB – The International Association for Management Education accredited

GRADUATE BUSINESS PROGRAMS

Master of Business Administration/Master of Science in Accounting (MBA/MS) Full-time, part-time; 66 total credits required; 2.5 to 6 years to complete program. Concentration in accounting.

Master of Business Administration (MBA) Full-time, part-time; 54 total credits required; 2 to 6 years to complete program. Concentrations in entrepreneurship, finance, marketing, management systems analysis, accounting, economics, management, management information systems.

Master of Business Administration/Master of Public Health (MBA/MPH) Full-time, part-time; 68 total credits required; 2.5 to 6 years to complete program. Concentration in health care.

Master of Business Administration/Master of Science in Nursing (MBA/MS) Full-time, part-time; 67 total credits required; 2 to 6 years to complete program. Concentration in health care.

Master of Business Administration/Master of Arts in Economics (MBA/MA) Full-time, part-time; 72 total credits required; 2.5 to 6 years to complete program. Concentration in economics.

ADMISSION

Applications For fall 1997 there were 392 applications for admission. Of those applying, 237 were accepted. Of those accepted, 99 enrolled.

Application Requirements Application form, application fee, bachelor's degree, minimum GPA: 2.75, 2 letters of recommendation, college transcript(s).

Recommended for Application GMAT score accepted, essay, personal statement, resume, work experience, computer experience.

Application Deadline 6/16 for fall, 11/17 for spring, 4/4 for summer, 3/26 for fall (international). Application fee: $40, $50 (international). Deferred entrance is available.

ACADEMICS

Faculty Full-time 70; part-time 39.

Teaching Methodologies Case study, computer simulations, field projects, group discussion, lecture, student presentations, team projects.

Technology 300 on-campus computer terminals/PCs are available for student use and are linked by a campus-wide network. The network has full access to the Internet. Students are not required to have their own PC.

Special Opportunities Advanced credit may be earned through transfer of credits from another institution. International exchange programs in Austria, France, United Kingdom.

FINANCES

Costs for 1997–98 Tuition: Full-time: $10,436 per year (resident); $16,878 per year (nonresident). Part-time: $982 per course (resident); $1903 per course (nonresident). Cost varies by number of credits taken. Fees vary by number of credits taken. Average 1997–98 room and board costs were $4500 per academic year. Room and board costs vary by campus location, occupancy (e.g., single, double, triple), type of accommodation, type of meal plan.

Financial Aid In 1997–98, 6% of students received some institutionally administered aid in the form of fellowships, research assistantships, teaching assistantships, work study, loans. Financial aid is available to part-time students.

Financial Aid Contact Ms. Marsha Weiss, Director, 1200 West Harrison, Suite 1892, Chicago, IL 60607. Phone: 312-996-3126.

FACILITIES

Information Resources University Library plus 4 additional on-campus libraries; total holdings of 1,600,000 volumes. CD player(s) available for graduate student use. Access provided to online bibliographic retrieval services.

INTERNATIONAL STUDENTS

Demographics 13% of students enrolled are international students [Asia, 41%, Europe, 36%, North America, 18%, South America, 5%].

Services and Facilities International student office, visa services, ESL courses, counseling/support services.

Applying TOEFL: minimum score of 570, proof of adequate funds, proof of health/immunizations required. Financial aid is available to international students.

International Student Contact John Binder, Director, MBA Programs, 815 West Van Buren, Suite 220, Chicago, IL 60607. Phone: 312-996-7000; E-mail: mba@uic.edu

PLACEMENT

Services include alumni network, career counseling/planning, career fairs, career library, career placement, job interviews arranged, job search course, resume referral to employers, and resume preparation. In 1996–97, 72 organizations participated in on-campus recruiting; 360 on-campus interviews were conducted.

Employment Of 1996–97 graduates, 82% were employed within three months of graduation; the average starting salary was $46,400. Types of employment entered: accounting, banking, chemical industry, computer-related, consulting, consumer products, education, engineering, finance, financial services, government, health services, high technology, human resources, information systems/technology, insurance, management, manufacturing, marketing, nonprofit, pharmaceutical, service industry, telecommunications.

Business Program(s) URL: http://www.uic.edu/cba/mba

Program Contact: Ms. Linda Casanova-Pineda, Admissions Officer, 815 West Van Buren, Suite 220, Chicago, IL 60607. Phone: 312-996-4573; Fax: 312-413-0338; E-mail: mba@uic.edu

See full description on page 1078.

University of Illinois at Springfield

School of Business and Management

Springfield, Illinois

OVERVIEW

The University of Illinois at Springfield is a state-supported, coed, upper-level institution. Enrollment: 4,611 graduate, professional, and undergraduate students. Founded: 1969. The graduate business unit is in an urban setting and is on a semester calendar.

HIGHLIGHTS

Enrollment Profile
Full-time: N/R
Part-time: N/R
Total: 382
Average Age: 32
Fall 1997 Average GPA: 3.13

International: N/R
Women: N/R
Minorities: N/R
Average Class Size: 30
Fall 1997 Average GMAT: 400

Costs
Full-time tuition: N/R
Part-time tuition: $99 per credit hour (resident); $296 per credit hour (nonresident)

GRADUATE BUSINESS PROGRAMS

Master of Business Administration (MBA) Full-time, part-time, distance learning option; 48 total credits required; 2 to 6 years to complete program.

Master of Arts in Economics (MA) Full-time, part-time, distance learning option; 38 total credits required; 18 months to 5 years to complete program.

Master of Arts in Management Information Systems (MA) Full-time, part-time, distance learning option; 44 total credits required; 2 to 6 years to complete program.

Master of Arts in Accountancy (MA) Full-time, part-time, distance learning option; 36 total credits required; minimum of 18 months to complete program.

ADMISSION

Application Requirements GMAT score, application form, bachelor's degree, minimum GPA: 2.5, college transcript(s), computer experience.

Application Deadline Applications processed on a rolling/continuous basis for domestic students only. 6/1 for fall (international), 11/1 for spring (international), 4/1 for summer (international). Deferred entrance is available.

ACADEMICS

Faculty Full-time 36; part-time 6.

Teaching Methodologies Case study, computer-aided instruction, computer analysis, computer simulations, experiential learning, faculty seminars, field projects, group discussion, lecture, research, seminars by members of the business community, simulations, student presentations, study groups, team projects.

Technology 125 on-campus computer terminals/PCs are available for student use and are linked by a campus-wide network. The network has full access to the Internet. Students are not required to have their own PC.

Special Opportunities Advanced credit may be earned through transfer of credits from another institution. An internship program is available.

FINANCES

Costs for 1997–98 Tuition: $99 per credit hour (resident); $296 per credit hour (nonresident). Cost varies by number of credits taken. Fees: $86 per semester (resident); $86 per semester (nonresident). Fees vary by number of credits taken. Average 1997–98 room only costs were $1692 per academic year. Room and board costs vary by occupancy (e.g., single, double, triple), type of accommodation.

Financial Aid Research assistantships, scholarships, work study available. Financial aid is available to part-time students. Application Deadline: 6/1.

Financial Aid Contact Ms. Rebecca A. Waltrip, Director, Financial Assistance, F-20E, Springfield, IL 62794-9243. Phone: 217-206-6724; Fax: 217-206-6620.

FACILITIES

Information Resources Norris L. Brookens Library; total holdings of 499,536 volumes, 140,557 microforms, 3,126 current periodical subscriptions. CD

University of Illinois at Springfield (continued)

player(s) available for graduate student use. Access provided to online bibliographic retrieval services.

INTERNATIONAL STUDENTS
Demographics N/R

Services and Facilities International student office, international student center, visa services, ESL courses, counseling/support services.

Applying TOEFL: minimum score of 550, proof of adequate funds, proof of health/immunizations required. Financial aid is available to international students.

International Student Contact Ms. Gerlinde B. Coates, Director, International Student Services, International Student Services J-167, Springfield, IL 62794-9243. Phone: 217-206-6678; Fax: 217-206-7280; E-mail: coates.gerlinde@uis.edu

PLACEMENT
Services include career counseling/planning, career fairs, career library, career placement, and resume preparation. In 1996–97, 98 organizations participated in on-campus recruiting; 300 on-campus interviews were conducted.

Program Contact: Office of Enrollment Services, University of Illinois at Springfield, Springfield, IL 62794-9243. Phone: 217-206-6626, 800-252-8533; Fax: 217-206-6620.

University of Illinois at Urbana-Champaign

Illinois MBA

Urbana, Illinois

OVERVIEW
The University of Illinois at Urbana-Champaign is a state-supported, coed university. Enrollment: 36,436 graduate, professional, and undergraduate students; 9,426 full-time matriculated graduate/professional students; part-time matriculated graduate/professional students. Founded: 1867. The graduate business unit is in an urban setting and is on a semester calendar.

HIGHLIGHTS

Enrollment Profile

Full-time: 643	International: 45%
Part-time: 0	Women: 32%
Total: 643	Minorities: 20%
Average Age: 26	Average Class Size: 45
Fall 1997 Average GPA: 3.26	Fall 1997 Average GMAT: 600

Costs
Full-time tuition: $10,700 per academic year (resident); $17,400 per academic year (nonresident)
Part-time tuition: N/R

AACSB – The International Association for Management Education accredited

GRADUATE BUSINESS PROGRAMS
Master of Business Administration (MBA) Full-time; 18 total credits required; minimum of 21 months to complete program. Concentrations in accounting, agribusiness, entrepreneurship, finance, financial economics, financial management/planning, health care, information management, management systems analysis, international economics, marketing, operations management, organizational management, human resources, risk management, strategic management, technology management, international finance, system management, environmental economics/management, international management.

Executive MBA (MBA) Full-time; 18 total credits required; minimum of 18 months to complete program.

Master of Business Administration/Master of Arts in Architecture (MBA/MA) Full-time; 20 total credits required; minimum of 21 months to complete program.

Master of Business Administration/Master of Science in Civil Engineering (MBA/MS) Full-time; 18-19 total credits required; 21 months to 2.3 years to complete program.

Master of Business Administration/Master of Science in Computer Science (MBA/MS) Full-time; 19-20 total credits required; 21 months to 2.3 years to complete program.

Master of Business Administration/Master of Science in Electrical Engineering (MBA/MS) Full-time; 18-19 total credits required; 21 months to 2.3 years to complete program.

Master of Business Administration/Master of Science in General Engineering (MBA/MS) Full-time; 18 total credits required; 21 months to 2.3 years to complete program.

Master of Business Administration/Master of Science in Industrial Engineering (MBA/MS) Full-time; 18-19 total credits required; 21 months to 2.3 years to complete program.

Master of Business Administration/Master of Science (MBA/MS) Full-time; 18-19 total credits required; 21 months to 2.3 years to complete program.

Master of Business Administration/Doctor of Jurisprudence (MBA/JD) Full-time; 85-86 total credits required; minimum of 3.8 years to complete program.

Master of Business Administration/Master of Science in Mechanical Engineering (MBA/MS) Full-time; 18-19 total credits required; 21 months to 2.3 years to complete program.

Master of Business Administration/Doctor of Medicine (MBA/MD) Full-time; 196 total credits required; minimum of 4.8 years to complete program.

ADMISSION
Applications For fall 1997 there were 1,322 applications for admission. Of those applying, 705 were accepted. Of those accepted, 295 enrolled.

Application Requirements Application form, application fee, bachelor's degree, essay, minimum GPA: 3.0, 3 letters of recommendation, personal statement, resume, college transcript(s).

Recommended for Application GMAT score accepted, interview, minimum of 3 years of work experience, computer experience.

Application Deadline 4/1 for fall, 2/1 for fall (international). Application fee: $40, $50 (international). Deferred entrance is available.

ACADEMICS
Faculty Full-time 131; part-time 33.

Teaching Methodologies Case study, computer-aided instruction, computer analysis, computer simulations, experiential learning, faculty seminars, field projects, group discussion, lecture, research, role playing, seminars by members of the business community, simulations, student presentations, study groups, team projects.

Technology 23,000 on-campus computer terminals/PCs are available for student use and are linked by a campus-wide network. The network has full access to the Internet. Students are required to have their own PC.

Special Opportunities International exchange programs in Brazil, Canada, Denmark, France, Germany, Mexico, Netherlands, Norway, Spain, United Kingdom. An internship program is available.

FINANCES
Costs for 1997–98 Tuition: Full-time: $10,700 per year (resident); $17,400 per year (nonresident). Cost varies by academic program. Fees vary by academic program. Average 1997–98 room and board costs were $9000 per academic year (on campus) and $9000 per academic year (off campus). Room and board costs vary by campus location, occupancy (e.g., single, double, triple), type of accommodation, type of meal plan.

Financial Aid In 1997–98, 53% of students received some institutionally administered aid in the form of fellowships, research assistantships, teaching assistantships, grants, scholarships, loans. Application Deadline: 4/1.

Financial Aid Contact Ms. Leela Cheryan, Financial Aid Counselor, Turner Student Services Building, 4th Floor, 610 East John Street, Champaign, IL 61820. Phone: 217-333-0100; Fax: 217-333-1156.

FACILITIES
Information Resources University Library plus 40 additional on-campus libraries; total holdings of 15,900,000 volumes, 4,500,000 microforms, 91,000 current periodical subscriptions. CD player(s) available for graduate student use. Access provided to online bibliographic retrieval services.

INTERNATIONAL STUDENTS
Demographics 45% of students enrolled are international students [Africa, 1%, Asia, 72%, Australia/New Zealand, 1%, Central America, 1%, Europe, 15%, North America, 4%, South America, 7%].

Services and Facilities International student office, international student center, visa services, ESL courses, counseling/support services.

Applying TOEFL: minimum score of 610, proof of adequate funds, proof of health/immunizations required. TSE: minimum score of 45 recommended. Financial aid is not available to international students.

International Student Contact Ms. Melanie Jarocki, Assistant Director of Admissions, 410 David Kinley Hall, 1407 West Gregory Drive, Urbana, IL 61801. Phone: 217-244-7602; Fax: 217-333-1156; E-mail: mba@uiuc.edu

PLACEMENT
Services include alumni network, career counseling/planning, career fairs, career library, career placement, electronic job bank, job interviews arranged, job search course, resume referral to employers, and resume preparation. In 1996–97, 103 organizations participated in on-campus recruiting; 1,056 on-campus interviews were conducted.

Employment Of 1996–97 graduates, 91% were employed within three months of graduation; the average starting salary was $51,893. Types of employment entered: accounting, banking, communications, computer-related, consulting, consumer products, education, engineering, finance, financial services, government, health services, high technology, human resources, information systems/technology, insurance, international trade, law, management, manufacturing, marketing, nonprofit, pharmaceutical, real estate, retail, service industry, telecommunications, transportation, utilities.

Business Program(s) URL: http://www.mba.uiuc.edu

Program Contact: Ms. Melanie Jarocki, Assistant Director of Admissions, 410 David Kinley Hall, 1407 West Gregory Drive, Urbana, IL 61801. Phone: 217-244-7602, 800-MBA-UIUC; Fax: 217-333-1156; E-mail: mba@uiuc.edu

See full description on page 1080.

University of St. Francis

College of Graduate Studies

Joliet, Illinois

OVERVIEW

The University of St. Francis is an independent-religious, coed, comprehensive institution. Enrollment: 4,000 graduate, professional, and undergraduate students. Founded: 1925. The graduate business unit is in a suburban setting and is on a trimester calendar.

HIGHLIGHTS

Enrollment Profile

Full-time: 0
Part-time: 1,000
Total: 1,000
Average Age: 30
Fall 1997 Average GPA: 3.0

International: N/R
Women: N/R
Minorities: N/R
Average Class Size: 17
Fall 1997 Average GMAT: N/R

Costs

Full-time tuition: N/R
Part-time tuition: $370 per credit hour

The M.B.A. at the University of St. Francis (USF) is for business professionals who seek top-management career advancement. The program has three concentrations: management, continuing education and training, and health services. The faculty has both academic credentials and real-world experience, and the curriculum includes theory but emphasizes application to the business world. A Business Advisory Board of executives, entrepreneurs, and educators assures a current and relevant program. Technology is used by faculty members and students in class. Free computer training is available to students as are online research services. The M.B.A. is 36–48 credit hours, depending on a student's undergraduate major and business experience. It can be completed in one to three years. All courses are offered in the evening or on weekends, with an average class size of 15 to 20 students. GRE or GMAT scores may not be required if the applicant has two years of business experience. The application process is simple and can proceed while a student begins the first class. Graduate assistantships and location coordinator positions are available to defray tuition costs. Student loans are available. Tuition can be paid in three interest-free installments or can be delayed for employment reimbursement. Some courses are available online through the USF Web site at http://www. stfrancis.edu

GRADUATE BUSINESS PROGRAMS

Master of Business Administration (MBA) Full-time, part-time, distance learning option; 36-48 total credits required; 2 years management experience required; 12 months to 6 years to complete program. Concentrations in management, health care, organizational behavior/development.

Master of Science in Management (MS) Full-time, part-time; 36 total credits required; 2 years management experience required; 12 months to 6 years to complete program. Concentrations in management, health care, organizational behavior/development.

Master of Science in Continuing Education and Training Management (MS) Full-time, part-time; 36 total credits required; 2 years work experience required; 12 months to 6 years to complete program.

Master of Science in Health Services Administration (MS) Full-time, part-time; 36 total credits required; 2 years health care experience required; 12 months to 6 years to complete program.

ADMISSION

Application Requirements Application form, application fee, bachelor's degree, essay, minimum GPA: 2.75, 2 letters of recommendation, personal statement, college transcript(s), minimum of 2 years of work experience, computer experience: basic operating system, word processing, spreadsheet.

Recommended for Application Interview.

Application Deadline Applications processed on a rolling/continuous basis for both domestic and international students. Application fee: $25. Deferred entrance is available.

ACADEMICS

Faculty Full-time 5; part-time 150.

Teaching Methodologies Case study, computer-aided instruction, computer analysis, computer simulations, group discussion, lecture, research, role playing, seminars by members of the business community, simulations, student presentations, study groups, team projects.

Technology 110 on-campus computer terminals/PCs are available for student use and are linked by a campus-wide network. The network has full access to the Internet. Students are not required to have their own PC.

Special Opportunities Advanced credit may be earned through transfer of credits from another institution. An internship program is available.

FINANCES

Costs for 1997–98 Tuition: $370 per credit hour. Cost varies by academic program.

Financial Aid Research assistantships, loans available. Financial aid is available to part-time students.

Financial Aid Contact Mr. Bruce Foote, Director, Financial Aid Office, 500 Wilcox, Joliet, IL 60435. Phone: 815-740-3403; Fax: 815-740-3537.

FACILITIES

Information Resources University of St. Francis Library; total holdings of 100,000 volumes, 2,676 microforms, 694 current periodical subscriptions. CD player(s) available for graduate student use. Access provided to online bibliographic retrieval services and online databases.

INTERNATIONAL STUDENTS

Demographics N/R

Applying TOEFL: minimum score of 550, proof of adequate funds, proof of health/immunizations required. Financial aid is not available to international students.

PLACEMENT

Services include alumni network, career counseling/planning, career fairs, career library, career placement, job interviews arranged, resume referral to employers, and resume preparation. In 1996–97, 710 organizations participated in on-campus recruiting.

Employment Of 1996–97 graduates, 100% were employed within three months of graduation. Types of employment entered: accounting, banking, computer-related, consulting, consumer products, education, energy, finance, financial services, government, health services, hospitality management, human resources, information systems/technology, insurance, international trade, management, manufacturing, marketing, nonprofit, pharmaceutical, real estate, retail, service industry, telecommunications, transportation, utilities.

Business Program(s) URL: http://www.stfrancis.edu/grd/

Program Contact: Dr. Joy Thompson, Associate Dean, 500 Wilcox, Joliet, IL 60435. Phone: 800-735-4723; Fax: 815-740-3537; E-mail: jthompson@ stfrancis.edu

Western Illinois University

College of Business and Technology

Macomb, Illinois

OVERVIEW

Western Illinois University is a state-supported, coed, comprehensive institution. Enrollment: 12,599 graduate, professional, and undergraduate students; 697 full-time matriculated graduate/professional students; 975 part-time matriculated graduate/professional students. Founded: 1899. The graduate business unit is in a rural setting and is on a semester calendar.

HIGHLIGHTS

Enrollment Profile

Full-time: 83
Part-time: 40
Total: 123
Average Age: 24
Fall 1997 Average GPA: 3.35

International: 25%
Women: 37%
Minorities: 2%
Average Class Size: 20
Fall 1997 Average GMAT: 530

Costs

Full-time tuition: $1575 per academic year (resident); $3807 per academic year (nonresident)
Part-time tuition: $125 per credit (resident); $311 per credit (nonresident)

Western Illinois University (continued)

AACSB – The International Association for Management Education accredited

GRADUATE BUSINESS PROGRAMS
Master of Business Administration (MBA) Full-time, part-time, distance learning option; 33-60 total credits required; 12 months to 2 years to complete program. Concentrations in accounting, decision sciences, economics, entrepreneurship, finance, human resources, information management, international business, management, management information systems, marketing, project management, taxation, logistics.

ADMISSION
Applications For fall 1997 there were 250 applications for admission. Of those applying, 100 were accepted. Of those accepted, 75 enrolled.

Application Requirements Application form, bachelor's degree, minimum GPA: 2.5, college transcript(s).

Recommended for Application GMAT score accepted: minimum 450.

Application Deadline Applications processed on a rolling/continuous basis for both domestic and international students. Deferred entrance is available.

ACADEMICS
Faculty Full-time 87.

Teaching Methodologies Case study, computer analysis, experiential learning, field projects, group discussion, lecture, research, student presentations, team projects.

Technology 600 on-campus computer terminals/PCs are available for student use and are linked by a campus-wide network. The network has full access to the Internet. Students are not required to have their own PC.

Special Opportunities Advanced credit may be earned through transfer of credits from another institution. International exchange programs in Germany, Netherlands, United Kingdom. An internship program is available.

FINANCES
Costs for 1997–98 Tuition: Full-time: $1575 per semester (resident); $3807 per semester (nonresident). Part-time: $125 per credit (resident); $311 per credit (nonresident). Cost varies by number of credits taken. Fees: Full-time: $916 per academic year (resident); $916 per academic year (nonresident). Part-time: $32 per credit (resident); $32 per credit (nonresident). Fees vary by number of credits taken. Average 1997–98 room and board costs were $4193 per academic year. Room and board costs vary by occupancy (e.g., single, double, triple), type of accommodation, type of meal plan.

Financial Aid In 1997–98, 37% of students received some institutionally administered aid in the form of research assistantships, teaching assistantships, scholarships.

Financial Aid Contact Mr. William Bushaw, Director of Financial Aid, 1 University Circle, Macomb, IL 61455-1390. Phone: 309-298-2446; Fax: 309-298-1039.

FACILITIES
Information Resources University Library plus 3 additional on-campus libraries; total holdings of 1,000,000 volumes, 200,000 microforms, 3,500 current periodical subscriptions. CD player(s) available for graduate student use. Access provided to online bibliographic retrieval services.

INTERNATIONAL STUDENTS
Demographics 25% of students enrolled are international students [Asia, 45%, Europe, 55%].

Services and Facilities International student office, international student housing, visa services, ESL courses, counseling/support services.

Applying TOEFL: minimum score of 550, proof of adequate funds, proof of health/immunizations required. Financial aid is not available to international students.

International Student Contact Mr. Sheldon Gary, Director of International Admissions, School of Graduate and International Studies, 1 University Circle, Macomb, IL 61455-1309. Phone: 309-298-1806; Fax: 309-298-1039.

PLACEMENT
Services include career counseling/planning, career fairs, career library, career placement, electronic job bank, job interviews arranged, and resume referral to employers.

Employment Types of employment entered: accounting, banking, computer-related, education, finance, information systems/technology, management, marketing.

Program Contact: Dr. David Bloomberg, Director of MBA Program, College of Business and Technology, 1 University Circle, Macomb, IL 61455-1390. Phone: 309-298-2442; Fax: 309-298-1039; E-mail: dj_bloomberg@wiu.edu

INDIANA

Ball State University

College of Business

Muncie, Indiana

OVERVIEW
Ball State University is a state-supported, coed university. Enrollment: 18,528 graduate, professional, and undergraduate students; 933 full-time matriculated graduate/professional students; 1,016 part-time matriculated graduate/professional students. Founded: 1918. The graduate business unit is in an urban setting and is on a semester calendar.

HIGHLIGHTS

Enrollment Profile

Full-time: 35	International: 8%
Part-time: 279	Women: 28%
Total: 314	Minorities: 5%
Average Age: 28	Average Class Size: 30
Fall 1997 Average GPA: 3.12	Fall 1997 Average GMAT: 543

Costs
Full-time tuition: $5976 per academic year (resident); $13,955 per academic year (nonresident)
Part-time tuition: $5976 per program (resident); $13,955 per program (nonresident)

AACSB – The International Association for Management Education accredited

GRADUATE BUSINESS PROGRAMS
Master of Business Administration in Entrepreneurship (MBA) Full-time, part-time, distance learning option; 36 total credits required; 12 months to 6 years to complete program. Concentration in entrepreneurship.

Master of Business Administration in Operations and Manufacturing (MBA) Full-time, part-time, distance learning option; 36 total credits required; 12 months to 6 years to complete program. Concentrations in operations management, production management, manufacturing management.

Master of Business Administration in Finance (MBA) Full-time, part-time, distance learning option; 36 total credits required; 12 months to 6 years to complete program. Concentrations in finance, financial management/planning.

Master of Business Administration in Human Resource Management (MBA) Full-time, part-time; 36 total credits required; 12 months to 6 years to complete program. Concentration in human resources.

Master of Business Administration in Applied Business Economics (MBA) Full-time, part-time; 36 total credits required; 12 months to 6 years to complete program. Concentrations in economics, managerial economics.

Master of Business Administration in Information Systems (MBA) Full-time, part-time; 36 total credits required; 12 months to 6 years to complete program. Concentrations in management information systems, management systems analysis, information management.

ADMISSION
Applications For fall 1997 there were 144 applications for admission. Of those applying, 114 were accepted. Of those accepted, 58 enrolled.

Application Requirements GMAT score: minimum 400, application form, application fee, bachelor's degree, minimum GPA: 2.5, resume, college transcript(s).

Recommended for Application Personal statement, computer experience.

Application Deadline Applications processed on a rolling/continuous basis for domestic students only. 7/13 for fall (international), 11/30 for spring (international). Application fee: $15. Deferred entrance is available.

ACADEMICS
Faculty Full-time 91; part-time 15.

Teaching Methodologies Case study, computer-aided instruction, computer analysis, field projects, group discussion, lecture, research, student presentations, study groups, team projects.

Technology 600 on-campus computer terminals/PCs are available for student use and are linked by a campus-wide network. The network has full access to the Internet. Students are not required to have their own PC.

Special Opportunities Advanced credit may be earned through transfer of credits from another institution.

FINANCES
Costs for 1997–98 Tuition: Full-time: $5976 per program (resident); $13,955 per program (nonresident). Part-time: $5976 per program (resident); $13,955

per program (nonresident). Cost varies by campus location, number of credits taken. Average 1997–98 room and board costs were $4316 per academic year (on campus) and $3900 per academic year (off campus). Room and board costs vary by campus location, occupancy (e.g., single, double, triple), type of accommodation, type of meal plan.

Financial Aid Research assistantships, teaching assistantships, scholarships, loans available. Financial aid is available to part-time students.

Financial Aid Contact Clarence Casazza, Director of Scholarships and Financial Aid, Scholarships and Financial Aid, LU 245, Muncie, IN 47306. Phone: 765-285-5600; Fax: 765-285-2464; E-mail: 00ccasazza@bsu.edu

FACILITIES
Information Resources Bracken Library plus 2 additional on-campus libraries; total holdings of 182,876 volumes, 967,720 microforms, 3,558 current periodical subscriptions. CD player(s) available for graduate student use. Access provided to online bibliographic retrieval services and online databases.

INTERNATIONAL STUDENTS
Demographics 8% of students enrolled are international students.

Services and Facilities International student office, international student center, visa services, ESL courses, counseling/support services.

Applying TOEFL: minimum score of 550, proof of adequate funds, proof of health/immunizations required. Financial aid is available to international students.

International Student Contact Jim Coffin, Director of International Programs, 708 North Calvert, Muncie, IN 47306. Phone: 765-285-5422; Fax: 765-285-3710; E-mail: jlcoffin@bsu.edu

PLACEMENT
Services include alumni network, career counseling/planning, career fairs, career library, electronic job bank, job interviews arranged, job search course, resume referral to employers, and resume preparation.

Employment Types of employment entered: accounting, banking, communications, computer-related, consulting, engineering, finance, financial services, high technology, human resources, information systems/technology, insurance, management, manufacturing, marketing, nonprofit, service industry.

Business Program(s) URL: http://www.bsu.edu/UP/cover.html

Program Contact: Tamara Estep, Director of Graduate Business Programs, Graduate Business Programs, College of Business, WB 146, Muncie, IN 47306. Phone: 765-285-1931; Fax: 765-285-8818; E-mail: bsumba@bsuvc.bsu.edu

Bethel College

Program in Business Administration

Mishawaka, Indiana

OVERVIEW
Bethel College is an independent-religious, coed, comprehensive institution. Enrollment: 1,550 graduate, professional, and undergraduate students; full-time matriculated graduate/professional students; 70 part-time matriculated graduate/professional students. Founded: 1947. The graduate business unit is in a suburban setting and is on a module calendar.

HIGHLIGHTS
Enrollment Profile
Full-time: 0
Part-time: 50
Total: 50
Average Age: 32
Fall 1997 Average GPA: 2.8

International: 14%
Women: 48%
Minorities: 22%
Average Class Size: 20
Fall 1997 Average GMAT: 460

Costs
Full-time tuition: N/R
Part-time tuition: $300 per credit hour

GRADUATE BUSINESS PROGRAMS
Master of Business Administration (MBA) Part-time; 36 total credits required; 2 to 4 years to complete program. Concentration in management.

ADMISSION
Applications For fall 1997 there were 30 applications for admission. Of those applying, 26 were accepted. Of those accepted, 20 enrolled.

Application Requirements Application form, application fee, bachelor's degree, minimum GPA: 2.75, interview, personal statement, college transcript(s), minimum of 2 years of work experience.

Recommended for Application GMAT score accepted: minimum 450, computer experience.

Application Deadline Applications processed on a rolling/continuous basis for both domestic and international students. Application fee: $25. Deferred entrance is available.

ACADEMICS
Faculty Full-time 6.

Teaching Methodologies Case study, computer-aided instruction, computer analysis, field projects, group discussion, lecture, research, student presentations.

Technology 40 on-campus computer terminals/PCs are available for student use and are linked by a campus-wide network. The network has full access to the Internet. Students are not required to have their own PC.

Special Opportunities Advanced credit may be earned through transfer of credits from another institution.

FINANCES
Costs for 1997–98 Tuition: Part-time: $300 per credit hour. Fees: Part-time: $30 per credit hour.

Financial Aid Contact Mr. Guy Fisher, Director of Financial Aid, 1001 West McKinley Avenue, Mishawaka, IN 46545-5591. Phone: 219-257-3317; Fax: 219-257-3326; E-mail: fisherg@bethel-in.edu

FACILITIES
Information Resources Bowen Library; total holdings of 85,000 volumes, 1,900 microforms, 600 current periodical subscriptions. Access provided to online bibliographic retrieval services.

INTERNATIONAL STUDENTS
Demographics 14% of students enrolled are international students.

Services and Facilities International student office, visa services, counseling/support services.

Applying TOEFL: minimum score of 560 required. Financial aid is not available to international students.

International Student Contact Mr. Steven Matteson, Dean of Admissions, 1001 West McKinley Avenue, Mishawaka, IN 46545-5591. Phone: 219-257-3319; Fax: 219-257-3326; E-mail: mattess@bethel-in.edu

PLACEMENT
Services include alumni network, and career counseling/planning.

Business Program(s) URL: http://www.bethel-in.edu/dept/business/index.htm

Program Contact: Dr. Murray Young, Director of MBA Program, 1001 West McKinley Avenue, Mishawaka, IN 46545-5591. Phone: 219-257-3360, 800-422-4251; Fax: 219-257-7617; E-mail: youngm@bethel-in.edu

Butler University

College of Business Administration

Indianapolis, Indiana

OVERVIEW
Butler University is an independent-nonprofit, coed, comprehensive institution. Enrollment: 3,700 graduate, professional, and undergraduate students; 83 full-time matriculated graduate/professional students; 705 part-time matriculated graduate/professional students. Founded: 1855. The graduate business unit is in a suburban setting and is on a semester calendar.

HIGHLIGHTS
Enrollment Profile
Full-time: 20
Part-time: 385
Total: 405
Average Age: 31
Fall 1997 Average GPA: N/R

International: 8%
Women: 38%
Minorities: 4%
Average Class Size: 27
Fall 1997 Average GMAT: N/R

Costs
Full-time tuition: N/R
Part-time tuition: $320 per credit hour

AACSB – The International Association for Management Education accredited

GRADUATE BUSINESS PROGRAMS
Master of Business Administration (MBA) Full-time, part-time; 30-58 total credits required; 12 months to 5 years to complete program. Concentrations in finance, marketing, accounting, leadership.

ADMISSION
Application Requirements GMAT score, application form, application fee, bachelor's degree, 2 letters of recommendation, resume, college transcript(s).

Butler University (continued)

Application Deadline 8/1 for fall, 12/1 for spring, 5/1 for summer, 8/1 for fall (international), 12/1 for spring (international), 5/1 for summer (international). Application fee: $25. Deferred entrance is available.

ACADEMICS

Faculty Full-time 29; part-time 10.

Teaching Methodologies Case study, computer analysis, computer simulations, faculty seminars, lecture, research, seminars by members of the business community, simulations, student presentations, team projects.

Technology Computer terminals/PCs are available for student use and are linked by a campus-wide network. The network has full access to the Internet. Students are not required to have their own PC.

Special Opportunities Advanced credit may be earned through transfer of credits from another institution. An internship program is available.

FINANCES

Costs for 1997–98 Tuition: $320 per credit hour. Cost varies by academic program.

Financial Aid Loans available. Financial aid is available to part-time students. Application Deadline: 7/15.

Financial Aid Contact Mr. Richard Bellows, Director, Financial Aid, 4600 Sunset Avenue, Indianapolis, IN 46208-3485. Phone: 317-940-9278; Fax: 317-940-9930.

FACILITIES

Information Resources Irwin Library plus 1 additional on-campus library; total holdings of 286,112 volumes, 235,280 microforms, 2,903 current periodical subscriptions. CD player(s) available for graduate student use. Access provided to online bibliographic retrieval services.

INTERNATIONAL STUDENTS

Demographics 8% of students enrolled are international students.

Services and Facilities International student office, visa services, ESL courses, counseling/support services.

Applying TOEFL: minimum score of 550, proof of adequate funds, proof of health/immunizations required. Financial aid is not available to international students.

International Student Contact Mr. David Clapp, Director, International Studies, 4600 Sunset Avenue, Indianapolis, IN 46208-3185. Phone: 317-940-9888; Fax: 317-940-6421.

PLACEMENT

Services include alumni network, career counseling/planning, electronic job bank, job interviews arranged, and resume preparation.

Business Program(s) URL: http://www.butler.edu/www/cba/

Program Contact: Dr. William Rieber, Director of Graduate Studies, 4600 Sunset Avenue, Indianapolis, IN 46208-3485. Phone: 317-940-9221; Fax: 317-940-9455.

Indiana State University

School of Business

Terre Haute, Indiana

OVERVIEW

Indiana State University is a state-supported, coed university. Enrollment: 10,800 graduate, professional, and undergraduate students; 656 full-time matriculated graduate/professional students; 584 part-time matriculated graduate/professional students. Founded: 1865. The graduate business unit is in an urban setting and is on a trimester calendar.

HIGHLIGHTS

Enrollment Profile

Full-time: 30	International: 21%
Part-time: 115	Women: 48%
Total: 145	Minorities: N/R
Average Age: 37	Average Class Size: 20
Fall 1997 Average GPA: 3.1	Fall 1997 Average GMAT: 550

Costs
Full-time tuition: N/R
Part-time tuition: $143 per credit hour (resident); $325 per credit hour (nonresident)

AACSB – The International Association for Management Education accredited

GRADUATE BUSINESS PROGRAMS

Master of Business Administration (MBA) Full-time, part-time, distance learning option; 36 total credits required; 16 months to 5 years to complete program. Concentrations in management, accounting, finance, insurance, marketing.

ADMISSION

Applications For fall 1997 there were 150 applications for admission. Of those applying, 75 were accepted.

Application Requirements GMAT score: minimum 470, application form, application fee, bachelor's degree, minimum GPA: 2.7, personal statement, college transcript(s), computer experience: word processing, spreadsheet, database.

Application Deadline Applications processed on a rolling/continuous basis for both domestic and international students. Application fee: $20. Deferred entrance is available.

ACADEMICS

Faculty Full-time 30; part-time 2.

Teaching Methodologies Case study, computer-aided instruction, computer simulations, experiential learning, lecture, research, student presentations, team projects.

Technology 245 on-campus computer terminals/PCs are available for student use and are linked by a campus-wide network. The network has full access to the Internet. Students are not required to have their own PC.

Special Opportunities Advanced credit may be earned through transfer of credits from another institution.

FINANCES

Costs for 1997–98 Tuition: $143 per credit hour (resident); $325 per credit hour (nonresident). Fees: Full-time: $10 per academic year (resident); $10 per academic year (nonresident). Part-time: $10 per year (resident); $10 per year (nonresident). Average 1997–98 room and board costs were $8539 per academic year.

Financial Aid In 1997–98, 12% of students received some institutionally administered aid in the form of research assistantships, teaching assistantships. Application Deadline: 3/1.

Financial Aid Contact Dr. William Moates, MBA Coordinator, School of Business, Terre Haute, IN 47809-5402. Phone: 812-237-2000; Fax: 812-237-7631; E-mail: mba@befac.indstate.edu

FACILITIES

Information Resources Cunningham Memorial Library plus 3 additional on-campus libraries; total holdings of 2,000,000 volumes, 712,734 microforms, 5,867 current periodical subscriptions. CD player(s) available for graduate student use. Access provided to online bibliographic retrieval services.

INTERNATIONAL STUDENTS

Demographics 21% of students enrolled are international students [Africa, 10%, Asia, 60%, Central America, 10%, Europe, 10%, North America, 5%, South America, 5%].

Services and Facilities International student office, ESL courses, counseling/support services.

Applying TOEFL: minimum score of 550, proof of adequate funds, proof of health/immunizations required. Financial aid is available to international students.

International Student Contact Mr. Christos Iordanidis, Director, International Student and Scholar Services, Terre Haute, IN 47809-1401. Phone: 812-237-2440; Fax: 812-237-3602; E-mail: saslehr@amber.indstate.edu

PLACEMENT

Services include career counseling/planning, career fairs, career library, job interviews arranged, and resume preparation.

Employment Of 1996–97 graduates, 95% were employed within three months of graduation; the average starting salary was $42,000. Types of employment entered: banking, education, finance, financial services, information systems/technology, insurance, management, manufacturing, marketing, nonprofit, pharmaceutical, utilities.

Program Contact: Dr. William Moates, MBA Coordinator, School of Business, Terre Haute, IN 47809-5402. Phone: 812-237-2000; Fax: 812-237-7631; E-mail: mba@befac.indstate.edu

Indiana University Bloomington

Kelley School of Business

Bloomington, Indiana

OVERVIEW
Indiana University Bloomington is a state-supported, coed university. Enrollment: 34,937 graduate, professional, and undergraduate students; 4,539 full-time matriculated graduate/professional students; 2,528 part-time matriculated graduate/professional students. Founded: 1820. The graduate business unit is in a small-town setting and is on a semester calendar.

HIGHLIGHTS

Enrollment Profile

Full-time: 538

Part-time: 0

Total: 538

Average Age: 27

Fall 1997 Average GPA: 3.3

International: 21%

Women: 26%

Minorities: 13%

Average Class Size: 31

Fall 1997 Average GMAT: 630

Costs

Full-time tuition: $8775 per academic year (resident); $17,013 per academic year (nonresident)

Part-time tuition: N/R

AACSB – The International Association for Management Education accredited

Many M.B.A. programs give the impression that business is tidy, that it is neatly divided up into functional categories, that business decisions come with ample time frames built in, and that management problems lend themselves easily to textbook solutions. The Indiana M.B.A. is different. Business is not about theory and abstractions. It is about fast-paced life in the marketplace. The Indiana M.B.A. program takes the focus out of the classroom and puts it in the boardroom, or on the trading floor, or in the corridor after a high-powered meeting, or in the quiet of an office at 11 p.m. as solutions are finally discovered. That is business, and Indiana M.B.A. graduates are prepared to deal with it.

M.B.A. students at Indiana participate in a breakthrough M.B.A. curriculum. There are no academic barriers. Students maneuver within an M.B.A. structure that is based on integration, not fragmentation. Practically and philosophically, the program is about synthesis: gathering information, linking it together, and finding the connections. Teamwork—a common way of working in corporations these days—is a major focus among both the faculty members and the students.

The Indiana M.B.A. program is a leader in graduate management education—an innovator preparing for the twenty-first century of business.

GRADUATE BUSINESS PROGRAMS
Master of Business Administration (MBA) Full-time; 54 total credits required; 15 months to 7 years to complete program. Concentrations in human resources, finance, marketing, management, operations management, entrepreneurship, international business, information management.

Master of Business Administration/Doctor of Jurisprudence (MBA/JD) Full-time; 118 total credits required; 4 to 7 years to complete program. Concentrations in human resources, finance, marketing, management, operations management, entrepreneurship, international business, information management.

Master of Business Administration/Master of Science in East Asian Studies (MBA/MS) Full-time; 64 total credits required; 3 to 7 years to complete program.

Master of Business Administration/Master of Science in Russian and East European Studies (MBA/MS) Full-time; 64 total credits required; 3 to 7 years to complete program.

Master of Business Administration/Master of Science in West European Studies (MBA/MS) Full-time; 64 total credits required; 3 to 7 years to complete program.

ADMISSION
Applications For fall 1997 there were 1,790 applications for admission. Of those applying, 665 were accepted. Of those accepted, 260 enrolled.

Application Requirements Application form, application fee, bachelor's degree, essay, 2 letters of recommendation, personal statement, resume, college transcript(s).

Recommended for Application GMAT score accepted, interview, work experience.

Application Deadline 3/1 for fall, 2/1 for fall (international). Application fee: $50, $65 (international). Deferred entrance is available.

ACADEMICS
Faculty Full-time 109; part-time 20.

Teaching Methodologies Case study, computer-aided instruction, computer analysis, computer simulations, experiential learning, field projects, group discussion, lecture, research, seminars by members of the business community, simulations, student presentations, team projects.

Technology 1,049 on-campus computer terminals/PCs are available for student use and are linked by a campus-wide network. The network has full access to the Internet. Students are required to have their own PC.

Special Opportunities Advanced credit may be earned through transfer of credits from another institution. International exchange programs in Australia, Chile, Finland, France, Germany, Mexico, Norway, Singapore, Spain, Switzerland, United Kingdom.

FINANCES
Costs for 1997–98 Tuition: Full-time: $8775 per year (resident); $17,013 per year (nonresident). Cost varies by academic program, number of credits taken. Fees: Full-time: $543 per academic year (resident); $543 per academic year (nonresident). Fees vary by academic program, number of credits taken. Average 1997–98 room and board costs were $5548 per academic year (on campus) and $5548 per academic year (off campus). Room and board costs vary by occupancy (e.g., single, double, triple), type of accommodation, type of meal plan.

Financial Aid In 1997–98, 82% of students received some institutionally administered aid in the form of fellowships, research assistantships, teaching assistantships, scholarships, loans. Application Deadline: 3/1.

Financial Aid Contact Ms. Thao Nelson, Assistant Director of Financial Aid, MBA, School of Business, Room 254, 1309 East 10th Street, Bloomington, IN 47405-1701. Phone: 812-855-8006; Fax: 812-855-9039; E-mail: thaon@indiana.edu

FACILITIES
Information Resources Main library plus 19 additional on-campus libraries; total holdings of 5,916,291 volumes, 3,981,111 microforms, 41,939 current periodical subscriptions. CD player(s) available for graduate student use. Access provided to online bibliographic retrieval services.

INTERNATIONAL STUDENTS
Demographics 21% of students enrolled are international students [Asia, 75%, Australia/New Zealand, 3%, Europe, 6%, North America, 3%, South America, 7%, other, 6%].

Services and Facilities International student office, international student center, international student housing, visa services, ESL courses, counseling/support services.

Applying TOEFL: minimum score of 580, proof of adequate funds, proof of health/immunizations required. Financial aid is available to international students.

International Student Contact Ms. Roberta Larson, Director of Graduate Student Services, School of Business, Room 254, 1309 East 10th Street, Bloomington, IN 47405-1701. Phone: 812-855-8006; Fax: 812-855-9039; E-mail: rlarson@indiana.edu

PLACEMENT
Services include alumni network, career counseling/planning, career fairs, career library, career placement, electronic job bank, job interviews arranged, job search course, resume referral to employers, and resume preparation. In 1996–97, 210 organizations participated in on-campus recruiting; 3,512 on-campus interviews were conducted.

Employment Of 1996–97 graduates, 94% were employed within three months of graduation; the average starting salary was $65,000. Types of employment entered: banking, chemical industry, computer-related, consulting, consumer products, energy, finance, high technology, human resources, information systems/technology, insurance, international trade, manufacturing, marketing, petrochemical, pharmaceutical, telecommunications, utilities.

Business Program(s) URL: http://www.bus.indiana.edu/mba

Program Contact: Mr. James Holmen, Director of Admissions and Financial Aid, School of Business, Room 254, 1309 East 10th Street, Bloomington, IN 47405-1701. Phone: 812-855-8006, 800-994-8622; Fax: 812-855-9039; E-mail: jholmen@indiana.edu

See full description on page 846.

Indiana University Kokomo

Division of Business and Economics

Kokomo, Indiana

OVERVIEW
Indiana University Kokomo is a state-supported, coed, comprehensive institution. Enrollment: 3,260 graduate, professional, and undergraduate students; 17 full-time matriculated graduate/professional students; 142 part-time matriculated

Indiana University Kokomo (continued)

graduate/professional students. Founded: 1945. The graduate business unit is in an urban setting and is on a semester calendar.

HIGHLIGHTS

Enrollment Profile
Full-time: N/R
Part-time: N/R
Total: 105
Average Age: 31
Fall 1997 Average GPA: 3.1

International: N/R
Women: N/R
Minorities: N/R
Average Class Size: 15
Fall 1997 Average GMAT: 505

Costs
Full-time tuition: N/R
Part-time tuition: $140 per credit hour (resident); $315 per credit hour (nonresident)

GRADUATE BUSINESS PROGRAMS
Master of Business Administration (MBA) Full-time, part-time; 58 total credits required; 2 to 4 years to complete program. Concentration in management.

ADMISSION
Application Requirements GMAT score, application form, application fee, bachelor's degree, essay, minimum GPA, college transcript(s).

Recommended for Application Computer experience: word processing, spreadsheet.

Application Deadline 8/1 for fall, 12/15 for spring, 4/15 for summer, 8/1 for fall (international), 12/15 for spring (international), 4/15 for summer (international). Application fee: $35, $50 (international). Deferred entrance is available.

ACADEMICS
Faculty Full-time 15.

Teaching Methodologies Case study, computer-aided instruction, computer analysis, computer simulations, experiential learning, field projects, group discussion, lecture, research, role playing, seminars by members of the business community, simulations, student presentations, study groups, team projects.

Technology 140 on-campus computer terminals/PCs are available for student use and are linked by a campus-wide network. The network has full access to the Internet. Students are not required to have their own PC.

Special Opportunities Advanced credit may be earned through credit by examination, transfer of credits from another institution.

FINANCES
Costs for 1997–98 Tuition: $140 per credit hour (resident); $315 per credit hour (nonresident). Cost varies by academic program, number of credits taken. Fees vary by academic program, number of credits taken. Average 1997–98 room and board costs were $5000 per academic year (off campus). Room and board costs vary by occupancy (e.g., single, double, triple), type of accommodation, type of meal plan.

Financial Aid Scholarships available.

Financial Aid Contact Jackie Kennedy-Fletcher, Director-Financial Aid, PO Box 9003, Kokomo, IN 46904-9003. Phone: 765-455-9431.

FACILITIES
Information Resources IUK Library; total holdings of 185,128 volumes, 340,621 microforms, 1,461 current periodical subscriptions. CD player(s) available for graduate student use. Access provided to online bibliographic retrieval services.

INTERNATIONAL STUDENTS
Demographics N/R

Services and Facilities International student office, international student center, visa services, ESL courses, counseling/support services.

Applying TOEFL, proof of adequate funds, proof of health/immunizations required. Financial aid is not available to international students.

International Student Contact Kenneth Rogers, Associate Dean and Director, 306 Franklin, Bloomington, IN 46904-9003. Phone: 812-855-5099; Fax: 812-855-4418; E-mail: intlserv@indiana.edu

PLACEMENT
Services include alumni network, career counseling/planning, career fairs, career library, career placement, job search course, resume referral to employers, and resume preparation.

Employment Of 1996–97 graduates, 100% were employed within three months of graduation.

Business Program(s) URL: http://www.iuk.edu/academic_program/business/index.html

Program Contact: Dr. Dilip Pendse, MBA Director, PO Box 9003, Kokomo, IN 46904-9003. Phone: 765-455-9279; Fax: 765-455-9348; E-mail: dpendse@iukfs1.iuk.indiana.edu

Indiana University Northwest

Division of Business and Economics

Gary, Indiana

OVERVIEW
Indiana University Northwest is a state-supported, coed, comprehensive institution. Enrollment: 5,298 graduate, professional, and undergraduate students; 46 full-time matriculated graduate/professional students; 483 part-time matriculated graduate/professional students. Founded: 1922. The graduate business unit is in an urban setting and is on a semester calendar.

HIGHLIGHTS

Enrollment Profile
Full-time: 4
Part-time: 255
Total: 259
Average Age: 30
Fall 1997 Average GPA: 3.1

International: 0%
Women: 40%
Minorities: 8%
Average Class Size: 25
Fall 1997 Average GMAT: 500

Costs
Full-time tuition: N/R
Part-time tuition: $132 per credit hour (resident); $303 per credit hour (nonresident)

AACSB – The International Association for Management Education accredited

GRADUATE BUSINESS PROGRAMS
Evening MBA (MBA) Full-time, part-time; 54 total credits required; 2.5 to 6 years to complete program. Concentrations in finance, marketing, human resources, organizational behavior/development.

Evening Master of Accountancy (MAcc) Part-time; 30 total credits required; 2 to 6 years to complete program. Concentration in accounting.

ADMISSION
Applications For fall 1997 there were 72 applications for admission. Of those applying, 61 were accepted. Of those accepted, 55 enrolled.

Application Requirements GMAT score, application form, application fee, bachelor's degree, letter of recommendation, personal statement, college transcript(s).

Application Deadline Applications processed on a rolling/continuous basis for both domestic and international students. Application fee: $25, $40 (international). Deferred entrance is available.

ACADEMICS
Faculty Full-time 20; part-time 2.

Teaching Methodologies Case study, computer-aided instruction, computer analysis, computer simulations, group discussion, lecture, research, role playing, seminars by members of the business community, simulations, student presentations, study groups, team projects.

Technology 150 on-campus computer terminals/PCs are available for student use and are linked by a campus-wide network. The network has full access to the Internet. Students are not required to have their own PC.

Special Opportunities Advanced credit may be earned through credit by examination, transfer of credits from another institution.

FINANCES
Costs for 1997–98 Tuition: $132 per credit hour (resident); $303 per credit hour (nonresident). Cost varies by academic program. Fees: $9 per credit (resident); $9 per credit (nonresident).

Financial Aid In 1997–98, 3% of students received some institutionally administered aid in the form of work study, loans. Financial aid is available to part-time students. Application Deadline: 7/15.

Financial Aid Contact William Lee, Director, Financial Aid, 3400 Broadway, Gary, IN 46408-1197. Phone: 219-980-6778; Fax: 219-980-6916.

FACILITIES
Information Resources Total library holdings of 206,600 volumes, 190,222 microforms, 1,200 current periodical subscriptions. CD player(s) available for graduate student use. Access provided to online bibliographic retrieval services.

INTERNATIONAL STUDENTS
Demographics N/R

Services and Facilities Visa services.

Applying TOEFL, proof of adequate funds, proof of health/immunizations required. Financial aid is not available to international students.

PLACEMENT
Services include career counseling/planning, career fairs, career library, career placement, electronic job bank, resume referral to employers, and resume preparation.

Business Program(s) URL: http://www.bus.iun.indiana.edu

Program Contact: Kathryn Lantz, Director, Undergraduate and Graduate Programs in Business, Division of Business and Economics, 3400 Broadway, Gary, IN 46408-1197. Phone: 219-980-6630, 800-437-5409 (IN only); Fax: 219-980-6916; E-mail: kathryn@iunbus1.iun.indiana.edu

Indiana University-Purdue University Fort Wayne

School of Business and Management Sciences

Fort Wayne, Indiana

OVERVIEW
Indiana University-Purdue University Fort Wayne is a state-supported, coed, comprehensive institution. Enrollment: 10,749 graduate, professional, and undergraduate students; 33 full-time matriculated graduate/professional students; 639 part-time matriculated graduate/professional students. Founded: 1964. The graduate business unit is in a suburban setting and is on a semester calendar.

HIGHLIGHTS

Enrollment Profile
Full-time: 8
Part-time: 267
Total: 275
Average Age: 32
Fall 1997 Average GPA: 3.2

International: 2%
Women: 31%
Minorities: 9%
Average Class Size: 35
Fall 1997 Average GMAT: 540

Costs
Full-time tuition: N/R
Part-time tuition: $141 per credit hour (resident); $302 per credit hour (nonresident)

AACSB – The International Association for Management Education accredited

GRADUATE BUSINESS PROGRAMS
Master of Business Administration (MBA) Full-time, part-time; 33-54 total credits required; 18 months to 6 years to complete program. Concentration in management.

ADMISSION
Applications For fall 1997 there were 49 applications for admission. Of those applying, 37 were accepted. Of those accepted, 33 enrolled.

Application Requirements GMAT score: minimum 450, application form, application fee, bachelor's degree, essay, minimum GPA: 2.5, 2 letters of recommendation, personal statement, college transcript(s).

Application Deadline 7/1 for fall, 11/1 for spring, 4/1 for summer, 5/1 for fall (international), 10/1 for spring (international), 3/1 for summer (international). Application fee: $30, $40 (international). Deferred entrance is available.

ACADEMICS
Faculty Full-time 20; part-time 2.

Teaching Methodologies Case study, group discussion, lecture, research, student presentations, team projects.

Technology 400 on-campus computer terminals/PCs are available for student use and are linked by a campus-wide network. The network has full access to the Internet. Students are not required to have their own PC.

Special Opportunities Advanced credit may be earned through transfer of credits from another institution.

FINANCES
Costs for 1997–98 Tuition: $141 per credit hour (resident); $302 per credit hour (nonresident). Fees: $3 per credit hour (resident); $3 per credit hour (nonresident). Average 1997–98 room only costs were $4050 per academic year (off campus).

Financial Aid In 1997–98, 3% of students received some institutionally administered aid in the form of research assistantships. Application Deadline: 5/1.

Financial Aid Contact Office of Financial Aid, 2101 Coliseum Boulevard East, Fort Wayne, IN 46805-1499. Phone: 219-481-6820.

FACILITIES
Information Resources Walter E. Helmke Library; total holdings of 295,115 volumes, 428,570 microforms, 2,160 current periodical subscriptions. CD player(s) available for graduate student use. Access provided to online bibliographic retrieval services.

INTERNATIONAL STUDENTS
Demographics 2% of students enrolled are international students.

Services and Facilities International student office, visa services, ESL courses, counseling/support services.

Applying TOEFL: minimum score of 550, proof of adequate funds required. Financial aid is not available to international students.

International Student Contact Dr. Ali Rassuli, Director of Graduate Studies in Business, School of Business and Management Sciences, Neff 366, 2101 Coliseum Boulevard East, Fort Wayne, IN 46805-1499. Phone: 219-481-6498; Fax: 219-481-5472; E-mail: rassuli@cvax.ipfw.indiana.edu

PLACEMENT
Services include alumni network, career placement, and resume preparation.

Employment Types of employment entered: engineering, finance, financial services, high technology, information systems/technology, management, telecommunications.

Business Program(s) URL: http://www.ipfw.indiana.edu

Program Contact: Ms. Lorrie Williams, Secretary, MBA Program, School of Business and Management Sciences, Neff 366, 2101 Coliseum Boulevard East, Fort Wayne, IN 46805-1499. Phone: 219-481-6498; Fax: 219-481-5472; E-mail: williaml@smtplink.ipfw.indiana.edu

Indiana University-Purdue University Indianapolis

Kelley School of Business

Indianapolis, Indiana

OVERVIEW
Indiana University-Purdue University Indianapolis is a state-supported, coed university. Founded: 1969. The graduate business unit is in an urban setting and is on a semester calendar.

HIGHLIGHTS

Enrollment Profile
Full-time: 0
Part-time: 360
Total: 360
Average Age: 29
Fall 1997 Average GPA: 3.3

International: N/R
Women: N/R
Minorities: N/R
Average Class Size: 60
Fall 1997 Average GMAT: 600

Costs
Full-time tuition: N/R
Part-time tuition: $239 per credit hour (resident); $478 per credit hour (nonresident)

GRADUATE BUSINESS PROGRAMS
Master of Business Administration (MBA) Part-time; 50 total credits required; 3 to 5 years to complete program.

Master of Business Administration/Doctor of Jurisprudence (MBA/JD) Full-time; 119 total credits required; 4 to 5 years to complete program.

ADMISSION
Application Requirements GMAT score, application form, application fee, bachelor's degree, essay, minimum GPA, 2 letters of recommendation, personal statement, resume, college transcript(s), computer experience: word processing, spreadsheet.

Recommended for Application Minimum of 2 years of work experience.

Application Deadline 5/1 for fall, 11/1 for spring, 4/1 for fall (international), 10/1 for spring (international). Application fee: $25, $50 (international). Deferred entrance is available.

ACADEMICS
Faculty Full-time 25; part-time 1.

Teaching Methodologies Case study, computer-aided instruction, computer analysis, computer simulations, experiential learning, faculty seminars, field projects, group discussion, lecture, research, role playing, seminars by members of the business community, simulations, student presentations, study groups, team projects.

Technology 100 on-campus computer terminals/PCs are available for student use and are linked by a campus-wide network. The network has full access to the Internet. Students are required to have their own PC.

Special Opportunities Advanced credit may be earned through transfer of credits from another institution.

FINANCES
Costs for 1997–98 Tuition: $239 per credit hour (resident); $478 per credit hour (nonresident). Fees: $38 per semester (resident); $38 per semester (nonresident). Fees vary by number of credits taken.

Indiana University-Purdue University Indianapolis (continued)

Financial Aid In 1997–98, 3% of students received some institutionally administered aid in the form of work study, loans. Financial aid is available to part-time students. Application Deadline: 3/1.

Financial Aid Contact Financial Aid, 425 University Boulevard, Room 103, Indianapolis, IN 46202. Phone: 317-278-3277; Fax: 317-274-5930.

FACILITIES
Information Resources University Library plus 4 additional on-campus libraries; total holdings of 700,000 volumes, 970,000 microforms, 7,000 current periodical subscriptions. CD player(s) available for graduate student use. Access provided to online bibliographic retrieval services.

INTERNATIONAL STUDENTS
Demographics N/R

Services and Facilities International student office, international student center, international student housing, visa services, ESL courses, counseling/support services.

Applying TOEFL, proof of adequate funds, proof of health/immunizations required. Financial aid is not available to international students.

International Student Contact International Affairs, 620 Union Drive, Room 207, Indianapolis, IN 46202-5167. Phone: 317-274-7294; Fax: 317-278-2213.

PLACEMENT
Services include alumni network, career counseling/planning, career fairs, career library, career placement, electronic job bank, job interviews arranged, resume referral to employers, and resume preparation.

Business Program(s) URL: http://www.iupui.edu/~business/

Program Contact: Admissions, 801 West Michigan Street, #3028, Indianapolis, IN 46202-5151. Phone: 317-274-4895; Fax: 317-274-2483.

Indiana University South Bend

Division of Business and Economics

South Bend, Indiana

OVERVIEW
Indiana University South Bend is a state-supported, coed, comprehensive institution. Enrollment: 7,162 graduate, professional, and undergraduate students. Founded: 1922. The graduate business unit is in a small-town setting and is on a semester calendar.

HIGHLIGHTS

Enrollment Profile

Full-time: 45	International: 17%
Part-time: 222	Women: 31%
Total: 267	Minorities: 4%
Average Age: 33	Average Class Size: 25
Fall 1997 Average GPA: 2.85	Fall 1997 Average GMAT: 513

Costs
Full-time tuition: N/R
Part-time tuition: $145 per credit hour (resident); $346 per credit hour (nonresident)

AACSB – The International Association for Management Education accredited

GRADUATE BUSINESS PROGRAMS
Master of Business Administration (MBA) Full-time, part-time; 36-51 total credits required; 2 to 5 years to complete program.

Master of Science in Accounting (MS) Full-time, part-time; 30 total credits required; 2 to 5 years to complete program.

ADMISSION
Applications For fall 1997 there were 64 applications for admission. Of those applying, 60 were accepted. Of those accepted, 46 enrolled.

Application Requirements Application form, application fee, bachelor's degree, minimum GPA: 2.75, 3 letters of recommendation, college transcript(s), computer experience: proficiency in business application software.

Recommended for Application GMAT score accepted: minimum 450, interview, personal statement, resume, work experience.

Application Deadline 7/1 for fall, 11/1 for spring, 4/1 for summer, 7/1 for fall (international), 11/1 for spring (international), 4/1 for summer (international). Application fee: $35, $40 (international). Deferred entrance is available.

ACADEMICS
Faculty Full-time 30; part-time 7.

Teaching Methodologies Case study, computer-aided instruction, computer analysis, computer simulations, field projects, group discussion, lecture, role playing, simulations, student presentations, team projects.

Technology 150 on-campus computer terminals/PCs are available for student use and are linked by a campus-wide network. The network has full access to the Internet. Students are not required to have their own PC.

Special Opportunities Advanced credit may be earned through credit by examination, transfer of credits from another institution.

FINANCES
Costs for 1997–98 Tuition: $145 per credit hour (resident); $346 per credit hour (nonresident). Cost varies by academic program, campus location, number of credits taken.

Financial Aid Work study, loans available. Application Deadline: 3/1.

Financial Aid Contact Ms. Sally Schnakenberg, Receptionist, Financial Aid Office, IUSB, PO Box 7111, South Bend, IN 46634-7111. Phone: 219-237-2223; Fax: 219-237-4599.

FACILITIES
Information Resources Schurz Library; total holdings of 534,683 volumes, 356,051 microforms, 2,180 current periodical subscriptions. CD player(s) available for graduate student use. Access provided to online bibliographic retrieval services.

INTERNATIONAL STUDENTS
Demographics 17% of students enrolled are international students.

Services and Facilities International student office, international student center, international student housing, visa services, ESL courses, counseling/support services.

Applying TOEFL, proof of adequate funds required. TSE, TWE, proof of health/immunizations recommended.

International Student Contact Ms. Julie Williams, International Center, IUSB, PO Box 7111, South Bend, IN 46634-7111. Phone: 219-237-4111; Fax: 219-237-4599.

Program Contact: Dr. Fred Naffziger, Director, Graduate Business Studies, IUSB PO Box 7111, South Bend, IN 46634-7111. Phone: 219-237-4138; Fax: 219-237-4866.

Indiana Wesleyan University

Division of Adult and Professional Studies

Marion, Indiana

OVERVIEW
Indiana Wesleyan University is an independent-religious, coed, comprehensive institution. Enrollment: 6,063 graduate, professional, and undergraduate students; 1,594 full-time matriculated graduate/professional students; 126 part-time matriculated graduate/professional students. Founded: 1920. The graduate business unit is in a small-town setting and is on a 4-4-1 calendar.

HIGHLIGHTS

Enrollment Profile

Full-time: 892	International: 0%
Part-time: 0	Women: N/R
Total: 892	Minorities: N/R
Average Age: 36	Average Class Size: 17
Fall 1997 Average GPA: N/R	Fall 1997 Average GMAT: N/R

Costs
Full-time tuition: N/R
Part-time tuition: $250 per credit hour

GRADUATE BUSINESS PROGRAMS
Master of Business Administration (MBA) Full-time, distance learning option; 41 total credits required; 2 to 5 years to complete program. Concentration in management.

Master of Science in Management (MS) Full-time; 36 total credits required; 2 to 5 years to complete program.

ADMISSION
Application Requirements Application form, bachelor's degree, essay, minimum GPA: 2.5, 2 letters of recommendation, personal statement, college transcript(s), minimum of 3 years of work experience.

Recommended for Application Computer experience.

Application Deadline Applications processed on a rolling/continuous basis for domestic students only. Application fee: $20. Deferred entrance is available.

ACADEMICS
Teaching Methodologies Case study, lecture, student presentations, team projects.

Technology The network does not have Internet access. Students are required to have their own PC.

FINANCES
Costs for 1997–98 Tuition: $250 per credit hour. Cost varies by academic program, campus location.

Financial Aid In 1997–98, 34% of students received some institutionally administered aid. Financial aid is available to part-time students.

Financial Aid Contact Ms. Paula Cook, Assistant Director of Financial Aid, 4201 South Washington Street, Marion, IN 46953-4999. Phone: 765-674-6901.

FACILITIES
Information Resources Woodrow Goodman Library plus 1 additional on-campus library; total holdings of 130,000 volumes, 10,086 microforms, 856 current periodical subscriptions. Access provided to online bibliographic retrieval services.

INTERNATIONAL STUDENTS
Demographics N/R

PLACEMENT
Employment Of 1996–97 graduates, 98% were employed within three months of graduation.

Business Program(s) URL: http://www.indwes.edu

Program Contact: Division of Adult and Professional Studies, 4406 South Harmon Street, Marion, IN 46953. Phone: 765-677-2350.

Manchester College

Department of Accounting

North Manchester, Indiana

OVERVIEW
Manchester College is an independent-religious, coed, comprehensive institution. Enrollment: 1,050 graduate, professional, and undergraduate students; 15 full-time matriculated graduate/professional students; part-time matriculated graduate/professional students. Founded: 1889. The graduate business unit is in a small-town setting and is on a 4-1-4 calendar.

HIGHLIGHTS

Enrollment Profile

Full-time: 15	International: 27%
Part-time: 0	Women: 20%
Total: 15	Minorities: N/R
Average Age: 22	Average Class Size: 12
Fall 1997 Average GPA: 3.4	Fall 1997 Average GMAT: 520

Costs
Full-time tuition: $13,180 per academic year
Part-time tuition: $440 per semester hour

GRADUATE BUSINESS PROGRAMS
Master of Accountancy (MAcc) Full-time, part-time; 33 total credits required; 12 months to 6 years to complete program. Concentration in accounting.

ADMISSION
Applications For fall 1997 there were 23 applications for admission. Of those applying, 21 were accepted. Of those accepted, 21 enrolled.

Application Requirements GMAT score: minimum 500, application form, application fee, bachelor's degree, minimum GPA: 3.0, 2 letters of recommendation, college transcript(s).

Recommended for Application Computer experience.

Application Deadline Applications processed on a rolling/continuous basis for both domestic and international students. Application fee: $20.

ACADEMICS
Faculty Part-time 9.

Teaching Methodologies Case study, computer-aided instruction, experiential learning, faculty seminars, field projects, group discussion, lecture, research, role playing, student presentations, study groups, team projects.

Technology 120 on-campus computer terminals/PCs are available for student use and are linked by a campus-wide network. The network has full access to the Internet. Students are not required to have their own PC.

Special Opportunities Advanced credit may be earned through transfer of credits from another institution. An internship program is available.

FINANCES
Costs for 1997–98 Tuition: Full-time: $13,180 per semester. Part-time: $440 per semester hour. Cost varies by class time (e.g., day/evening). Average 1997–98 room and board costs were $4430 per academic year. Room and board costs vary by occupancy (e.g., single, double, triple), type of accommodation, type of meal plan.

Financial Aid In 1997–98, 93% of students received some institutionally administered aid in the form of teaching assistantships, scholarships, work study, loans. Application Deadline: 5/1.

Financial Aid Contact Financial Aid Office, 604 College Avenue, North Manchester, IN 46962-1225. Phone: 219-982-5066.

FACILITIES
Information Resources Funderburg Library; total holdings of 170,000 volumes, 20,000 microforms, 750 current periodical subscriptions. CD player(s) available for graduate student use. Access provided to online bibliographic retrieval services.

INTERNATIONAL STUDENTS
Demographics 27% of students enrolled are international students [Asia, 50%, Europe, 50%].

Services and Facilities International student office, ESL courses, counseling/support services.

Applying TOEFL, proof of adequate funds, proof of health/immunizations required.

PLACEMENT
Services include alumni network, career counseling/planning, career fairs, career library, career placement, job interviews arranged, resume referral to employers, and resume preparation. In 1996–97, 10 organizations participated in on-campus recruiting; 100 on-campus interviews were conducted.

Employment Of 1996–97 graduates, 98% were employed within three months of graduation; the average starting salary was $30,000. Types of employment entered: accounting, banking, finance, government, manufacturing, nonprofit.

Business Program(s) URL: http://www.manchester.edu

Program Contact: Janis Fahs, Assistant Professor of Accounting, 604 College Avenue, North Manchester, IN 46962-1225. Phone: 219-982-5300; Fax: 219-982-5043.

Oakland City University

School of Adult Programs and Professional Studies

Oakland City, Indiana

OVERVIEW
Oakland City University is an independent-religious, coed, comprehensive institution. Enrollment: 1,159 graduate, professional, and undergraduate students. Founded: 1885.

HIGHLIGHTS

Enrollment Profile

Full-time: 69	International: N/R
Part-time: 0	Women: N/R
Total: 69	Minorities: 3%
Average Age: 35	Average Class Size: 12
Fall 1997 Average GPA: 3.2	Fall 1997 Average GMAT: N/R

Costs
Full-time tuition: N/R
Part-time tuition: $285 per semester hour

GRADUATE BUSINESS PROGRAMS
Master of Science in Management (MS) Full-time, distance learning option; 36 total credits required; 18 months to complete program. Concentration in management.

ADMISSION
Application Requirements GMAT score, application form, application fee, bachelor's degree, minimum GPA: 3.0, interview, 3 letters of recommendation, resume, college transcript(s), computer experience: basic computer skills.

Recommended for Application GRE score accepted, MAT score accepted, personal statement, work experience.

Application Deadline Applications processed on a rolling/continuous basis for both domestic and international students. Application fee: $25. Deferred entrance is available.

ACADEMICS
Faculty Full-time 3.

Teaching Methodologies Case study, faculty seminars, group discussion, lecture, research, seminars by members of the business community, student presentations, team projects.

Technology 24 on-campus computer terminals/PCs are available for student use. The network has full access to the Internet.

Special Opportunities Advanced credit may be earned through transfer of credits from another institution.

FINANCES
Costs for 1997–98 Tuition: $285 per semester hour. Cost varies by number of credits taken.
Financial Aid In 1997–98, 9% of students received some institutionally administered aid in the form of grants, scholarships. Application Deadline: 3/1.
Financial Aid Contact Caren Richeson, Director, Financial Aid, 143 North Lucretia Street, Oakland City, IN 47660-1099.

FACILITIES
Information Resources Founder's Memorial Library plus 1 additional on-campus library; total holdings of 72,550 volumes, 67,366 microforms, 392 current periodical subscriptions. CD player(s) available for graduate student use. Access provided to online bibliographic retrieval services.

INTERNATIONAL STUDENTS
Demographics N/R
Applying TOEFL: minimum score of 500 required. Proof of adequate funds, proof of health/immunizations recommended. Financial aid is available to international students.

PLACEMENT
Services include alumni network, career counseling/planning, and career placement.
Employment Types of employment entered: accounting, banking.

Program Contact: James Jump, Director, Master of Science in Management, 143 North Lucretia Street, Oakland City, IN 47660-1099. E-mail: ejump@comsource.net

Purdue University

Krannert Graduate School of Management

West Lafayette, Indiana

OVERVIEW
Purdue University is a state-supported, coed university. Enrollment: 33,269 graduate, professional, and undergraduate students; 4,477 full-time matriculated graduate/professional students; 1,515 part-time matriculated graduate/professional students. Founded: 1869. The graduate business unit is in a small-town setting and is on a 8-week module calendar.

HIGHLIGHTS

Enrollment Profile

Full-time: 359	International: 26%
Part-time: 0	Women: 23%
Total: 359	Minorities: 7%
Average Age: 27	Average Class Size: 50
Fall 1997 Average GPA: 3.11	Fall 1997 Average GMAT: 615

Costs
Full-time tuition: $3588 per academic year (resident); $7712 per academic year (nonresident)
Part-time tuition: N/R

AACSB – The International Association for Management Education accredited

GRADUATE BUSINESS PROGRAMS
Master of Science in Management (MS) Full-time; 60 total credits required; minimum of 2 years to complete program. Concentrations in accounting, finance, human resources, marketing, organizational behavior/development, operations management, management information systems, strategic management, international management, manufacturing management.
Master of Science in Human Resource Management (MS) Full-time; 62 total credits required; minimum of 2 years to complete program. Concentrations in human resources, organizational behavior/development.
Master of Science in Industrial Administration (MS) Full-time; 48 total credits required; minimum of 11 months to complete program. Concentration in industrial administration/management.

ADMISSION
Applications For fall 1997 there were 1,575 applications for admission. Of those applying, 416 were accepted. Of those accepted, 179 enrolled.

Application Requirements GMAT score, application form, application fee, bachelor's degree, essay, minimum GPA, 2 letters of recommendation, personal statement, resume, college transcript(s).
Recommended for Application Interview, work experience.
Application Deadline Applications processed on a rolling/continuous basis for domestic students only. 2/1 for fall (international). Application fee: $30. Deferred entrance is available.

ACADEMICS
Faculty Full-time 110.
Teaching Methodologies Case study, computer-aided instruction, computer analysis, computer simulations, experiential learning, group discussion, lecture, seminars by members of the business community, simulations, student presentations, study groups, team projects.
Technology 160 on-campus computer terminals/PCs are available for student use and are linked by a campus-wide network. The network has full access to the Internet. Students are not required to have their own PC.
Special Opportunities International exchange programs in Finland, Netherlands.

FINANCES
Costs for 1997–98 Tuition: Full-time: $3588 per semester (resident); $7712 per semester (nonresident). Average 1997–98 room only costs were $4300 per academic year (on campus) and $4000 per academic year (off campus). Room and board costs vary by campus location, occupancy (e.g., single, double, triple), type of accommodation, type of meal plan.
Financial Aid Fellowships, research assistantships, teaching assistantships available. Application Deadline: 2/15.
Financial Aid Contact Ms. Joyce Hall, Director, Division of Financial Aid, 1102 Schleman Hall, Room 305, West Lafayette, IN 47907-1102. Phone: 765-494-5050; Fax: 765-494-6707.

FACILITIES
Information Resources Hicks Library plus 16 additional on-campus libraries; total holdings of 2,107,229 volumes, 2,136,218 microforms, 14,331 current periodical subscriptions. CD player(s) available for graduate student use. Access provided to online bibliographic retrieval services.

INTERNATIONAL STUDENTS
Demographics 26% of students enrolled are international students [Asia, 55%, Central America, 3%, Europe, 18%, North America, 5%, South America, 19%].
Services and Facilities International student office, counseling/support services.
Applying TOEFL: minimum score of 570, proof of adequate funds, proof of health/immunizations required. Financial aid is not available to international students.
International Student Contact Mr. Michael A. Brzezinski, Director, International Students and Scholars Office, 1101 Schleman Hall, Room 136, West Lafayette, IN 47907-1101. Phone: 765-494-5770; Fax: 765-494-6859.

PLACEMENT
Services include alumni network, career counseling/planning, career fairs, career library, career placement, electronic job bank, job interviews arranged, resume referral to employers, and resume preparation. In 1996–97, 100 organizations participated in on-campus recruiting; 3,582 on-campus interviews were conducted.
Employment Of 1996–97 graduates, 98% were employed within three months of graduation; the average starting salary was $68,000. Types of employment entered: accounting, banking, chemical industry, communications, computer-related, consulting, consumer products, energy, engineering, finance, financial services, health services, high technology, hospitality management, human resources, information systems/technology, insurance, management, manufacturing, marketing, nonprofit, petrochemical, pharmaceutical, telecommunications, utilities.

Business Program(s) URL: http://www.mgmt.purdue.edu

Program Contact: Dr. Ward Snearly, Associate Director of Masters Programs, 1310 Krannert Building, West Lafayette, IN 47907-1310. Phone: 765-494-4365; Fax: 765-494-9841.

See full description on page 934.

Purdue University Calumet

Department of Management

Hammond, Indiana

OVERVIEW
Purdue University Calumet is a state-supported, coed, comprehensive institution. Enrollment: 9,287 graduate, professional, and undergraduate students; 126 full-time matriculated graduate/professional students; 824 part-time matriculated graduate/professional students. Founded: 1943. The graduate business unit

is on a semester calendar.

HIGHLIGHTS

Enrollment Profile
Full-time: 0
Part-time: 130
Total: 130
Average Age: 32
Fall 1997 Average GPA: N/R

International: N/R
Women: N/R
Minorities: N/R
Average Class Size: N/R
Fall 1997 Average GMAT: 540

Costs
Full-time tuition: N/R
Part-time tuition: $118 per credit hour (resident); $268 per credit hour (nonresident)

GRADUATE BUSINESS PROGRAMS
Master of Accountancy (MAcc) Part-time; 30 total credits required; minimum of 2 years to complete program.
Master of Business Administration (MBA) Part-time; 36-45 total credits required; 2.5 to 3.5 years to complete program.
Executive MBA (MBA) Part-time; 42 total credits required; 5 years business experience required; minimum of 18 months to complete program.

ADMISSION
Application Requirements GMAT score, bachelor's degree, minimum GPA: 3.0, 3 letters of recommendation, personal statement, college transcript(s).
Recommended for Application Interview.
Application Deadline Applications processed on a rolling/continuous basis for both domestic and international students.

ACADEMICS
Teaching Methodologies Case study, computer-aided instruction, computer analysis, computer simulations, faculty seminars, group discussion, lecture, research, simulations, student presentations, study groups, team projects.

FINANCES
Costs for 1997–98 Tuition: Part-time: $118 per credit hour (resident); $268 per credit hour (nonresident).
Financial Aid Contact Mary Ann Bishel, Director of Financial Aid, Hammond, IN 46323-2094. Phone: 219-989-2301.

FACILITIES
Information Resources Total library holdings of 205,000 volumes, 1,361 current periodical subscriptions. Access provided to online bibliographic retrieval services.

INTERNATIONAL STUDENTS
Demographics N/R

Program Contact: Janet Knight, School of Management, Hammond, IN 46323-2094. Phone: 219-989-2388.

University of Indianapolis

Graduate Business Programs

Indianapolis, Indiana

OVERVIEW
The University of Indianapolis is an independent-religious, coed, comprehensive institution. Enrollment: 4,337 graduate, professional, and undergraduate students; 292 full-time matriculated graduate/professional students; 540 part-time matriculated graduate/professional students. Founded: 1902. The graduate business unit is in a suburban setting and is on a semester calendar.

HIGHLIGHTS

Enrollment Profile
Full-time: 78
Part-time: 210
Total: 288
Average Age: 32
Fall 1997 Average GPA: 2.9

International: 2%
Women: 35%
Minorities: N/R
Average Class Size: 19
Fall 1997 Average GMAT: 436

Costs
Full-time tuition: N/R
Part-time tuition: $244 per hour

GRADUATE BUSINESS PROGRAMS
Master of Business Administration (MBA) Part-time; 42 total credits required; 2 to 5 years to complete program. Concentration in management.
Executive MBA (MBA) Full-time; 40 total credits required; 20 to 22 months to complete program.
Master of Accounting (MAcc) Part-time; 30 total credits required; 12 months to 5 years to complete program. Concentration in accounting.

ADMISSION
Application Requirements Application form, application fee, bachelor's degree, minimum GPA, interview, 2 letters of recommendation, college transcript(s).
Recommended for Application GMAT score accepted.
Application Deadline Applications processed on a rolling/continuous basis for both domestic and international students. Application fee: $30. Deferred entrance is available.

ACADEMICS
Faculty Full-time 1; part-time 17.
Teaching Methodologies Case study, computer simulations, experiential learning, field projects, group discussion, lecture, role playing, simulations, student presentations, study groups, team projects.
Technology 120 on-campus computer terminals/PCs are available for student use and are linked by a campus-wide network. The network has full access to the Internet. Students are not required to have their own PC.
Special Opportunities Advanced credit may be earned through transfer of credits from another institution.

FINANCES
Costs for 1997–98 Tuition: $244 per hour. Cost varies by number of credits taken. Fees: $10 per semester.
Financial Aid Work study available. Application Deadline: 5/1.
Financial Aid Contact Mrs. Linda Handy, Director of Financial Aid, 1400 East Hanna Avenue, Indianapolis, IN 46227. Phone: 317-788-3217; Fax: 317-788-3300.

FACILITIES
Information Resources Krannert Memorial Library; total holdings of 153,500 volumes, 9,475 microforms, 1,119 current periodical subscriptions. CD player(s) available for graduate student use. Access provided to online bibliographic retrieval services.

INTERNATIONAL STUDENTS
Demographics 2% of students enrolled are international students.
Services and Facilities International student office, ESL courses, counseling/support services.
Applying TOEFL: minimum score of 550, proof of adequate funds, proof of health/immunizations required. Financial aid is available to international students.
International Student Contact Ms. Mimi Chase, International Student Officer, 1400 East Hanna Avenue, Indianapolis, IN 46227. Phone: 317-778-3394; Fax: 317-788-3300.

PLACEMENT
Services include alumni network, career counseling/planning, career fairs, career library, career placement, electronic job bank, and resume preparation.

Program Contact: Dr. Gerald Speth, Director, Graduate Business Programs, 1400 East Hanna Avenue, Indianapolis, IN 46227. Phone: 317-788-3396; Fax: 312-788-3300.

University of Notre Dame

College of Business Administration

Notre Dame, Indiana

OVERVIEW
The University of Notre Dame is an independent-religious, coed university. Enrollment: 10,275 graduate, professional, and undergraduate students; 2,437 full-time matriculated graduate/professional students; part-time matriculated graduate/professional students. Founded: 1842. The graduate business unit is in a suburban setting and is on a semester calendar.

University of Notre Dame (continued)

HIGHLIGHTS

Enrollment Profile

Full-time: 487	International: N/R
Part-time: 61	Women: 31%
Total: 548	Minorities: 11%
Average Age: 26	Average Class Size: 60
Fall 1997 Average GPA: 3.11	Fall 1997 Average GMAT: 615

Costs

Full-time tuition: $21,500 per academic year
Part-time tuition: N/R

AACSB – The International Association for Management Education accredited

Degree(s) offered in conjunction with The EDHEC Graduate School of Management of the Catholic University of Lille (France)

GRADUATE BUSINESS PROGRAMS

Master of Business Administration (MBA) Full-time; 44-63 total credits required; 2 years work experience required (3 preferred); 11 months to 2 years to complete program. Concentrations in accounting, finance, human resources, marketing, international business, management, banking, management information systems, manufacturing management, management consulting, marketing research.

Executive MBA (MBA) Full-time, distance learning option; 48 total credits required; up to 2 years to complete program.

Master of Science in Administration (MS) Full-time, part-time; 48 total credits required; up to 5 years to complete program. Concentration in nonprofit management.

MBA/JD Joint Degree Program (MBA/JD) Full-time; 123 total credits required; minimum of 4 years to complete program. Concentrations in accounting, banking, finance, human resources, international business, management, management consulting, management information systems, manufacturing management, marketing, marketing research.

Master of Science in Accountancy (MS) Full-time, part-time; 30-36 total credits required; minimum of 9 months to complete program. Concentrations in accounting, taxation.

ADMISSION

Applications For fall 1997 there were 624 applications for admission. Of those applying, 302 were accepted. Of those accepted, 151 enrolled.

Application Requirements GMAT score, application form, application fee, bachelor's degree, essay, minimum GPA, 2 letters of recommendation, college transcript(s), minimum of 2 years of work experience.

Recommended for Application Interview, resume, computer experience.

Application Deadline 5/8 for fall, 3/6 for summer, 5/8 for fall (international), 3/6 for summer (international). Application fee: $75. Deferred entrance is available.

ACADEMICS

Teaching Methodologies Case study, computer-aided instruction, computer analysis, computer simulations, faculty seminars, field projects, group discussion, lecture, research, role playing, seminars by members of the business community, simulations, student presentations, study groups, team projects.

Technology 550 on-campus computer terminals/PCs are available for student use and are linked by a campus-wide network. The network has full access to the Internet. Students are not required to have their own PC.

Special Opportunities International exchange programs in Chile, France, Mexico, United Kingdom.

FINANCES

Costs for 1997–98 Tuition: Full-time: $21,500 per year. Cost varies by academic program. Fees: Full-time: $250 per academic year. Fees vary by academic program. Average 1997–98 room and board costs were $4600 per academic year (on campus) and $4600 per academic year (off campus). Room and board costs vary by campus location, occupancy (e.g., single, double, triple), type of accommodation, type of meal plan.

Financial Aid In 1997–98, 23% of students received some institutionally administered aid in the form of fellowships, research assistantships, teaching assistantships, grants, scholarships, work study. Application Deadline: 2/20.

Financial Aid Contact Mr. Brian Lohr, Assistant Director of Admissions, 276 College of Business Administration, Notre Dame, IN 46556-0399. Phone: 219-631-8488; Fax: 219-631-8800; E-mail: brian.lohr.1@nd.edu

FACILITIES

Information Resources Theodore M. Hesburgh Library plus 9 additional on-campus libraries; total holdings of 2,500,000 volumes, 2,600,000 microforms, 23,000 current periodical subscriptions. CD player(s) available for graduate student use. Access provided to online bibliographic retrieval services and online databases.

INTERNATIONAL STUDENTS

Demographics N/R

Services and Facilities International student office, international student center, visa services, ESL courses, counseling/support services, Host Family Program.

Applying TOEFL: minimum score of 600, proof of adequate funds required. Proof of health/immunizations recommended. Financial aid is available to international students.

International Student Contact Ms. Maureen A. Fitzgibbon, Director of International Student Affairs, 205 La Fortune, Notre Dame, IN 46556. Phone: 219-631-3824; Fax: 219-631-3162.

PLACEMENT

Services include alumni network, career counseling/planning, career fairs, career library, career placement, electronic job bank, job interviews arranged, job search course, resume referral to employers, and resume preparation. In 1996–97, 92 organizations participated in on-campus recruiting; 150 on-campus interviews were conducted.

Employment Of 1996–97 graduates, 93% were employed within three months of graduation; the average starting salary was $57,052. Types of employment entered: accounting, banking, chemical industry, communications, computer-related, consulting, consumer products, energy, engineering, finance, financial services, government, health services, high technology, human resources, information systems/technology, insurance, law, management, manufacturing, marketing, media, nonprofit, petrochemical, pharmaceutical, real estate, retail, service industry, telecommunications, transportation, utilities.

Business Program(s) URL: http://www.nd.edu/~cba/

Program Contact: Mr. Brian Lohr, Assistant Director of Admissions, 276 College of Business Administration, Notre Dame, IN 46556-0399. Phone: 219-631-8488, 800-631-8488; Fax: 219-631-8800; E-mail: brian.lohr.1@nd.edu
See full description on page 1118.

University of Saint Francis

Department of Business Administration

Fort Wayne, Indiana

OVERVIEW

The University of Saint Francis is an independent-religious, coed, comprehensive institution. Enrollment: 998 graduate, professional, and undergraduate students; 50 full-time matriculated graduate/professional students; 157 part-time matriculated graduate/professional students. Founded: 1890. The graduate business unit is in an urban setting and is on a semester calendar.

HIGHLIGHTS

Enrollment Profile

Full-time: 21	International: 25%
Part-time: 31	Women: 38%
Total: 52	Minorities: 10%
Average Age: 33	Average Class Size: 15
Fall 1997 Average GPA: 2.96	Fall 1997 Average GMAT: 511

Costs

Full-time tuition: $3015 per academic year
Part-time tuition: $335 per credit hour

GRADUATE BUSINESS PROGRAMS

Master of Business Administration (MBA) Full-time, part-time; 30-51 total credits required; 2 to 5 years to complete program. Concentrations in finance, international business, management, marketing.

Master of Science in Business Administration (MS) Full-time, part-time; 30-45 total credits required; 18 months to 5 years to complete program.

ADMISSION

Applications For fall 1997 there were 23 applications for admission. Of those applying, 20 were accepted. Of those accepted, 16 enrolled.

Application Requirements MAT score: minimum 36, application form, application fee, bachelor's degree, minimum GPA: 2.5, college transcript(s).

Recommended for Application GMAT score accepted: minimum 400.

Application Deadline Applications processed on a rolling/continuous basis for domestic students only. 5/1 for fall (international), 9/15 for spring (international). Application fee: $20.

ACADEMICS

Faculty Full-time 5; part-time 5.

Teaching Methodologies Case study, computer-aided instruction, computer analysis, computer simulations, experiential learning, faculty seminars, field projects, group discussion, lecture, research, role playing, seminars by members of the business community, simulations, student presentations, study groups, team projects.

Technology 45 on-campus computer terminals/PCs are available for student use and are linked by a campus-wide network. The network has full access to the Internet. Students are not required to have their own PC.

Special Opportunities Advanced credit may be earned through credit for experience, transfer of credits from another institution.

FINANCES
Costs for 1997–98 Tuition: Full-time: $3015 per semester. Part-time: $335 per credit hour. Fees: Full-time: $180 per academic year. Part-time: $16 per credit hour. Fees vary by number of credits taken. Average 1997–98 room and board costs were $4350 per academic year. Room and board costs vary by occupancy (e.g., single, double, triple).

Financial Aid In 1997–98, 29% of students received some institutionally administered aid in the form of research assistantships, work study, loans. Financial aid is available to part-time students. Application Deadline: 7/1.

Financial Aid Contact Ms. Christina Miller, Student Financial Services, 2701 Spring Street, Fort Wayne, IN 46808-3994. Phone: 219-434-3184; Fax: 219-434-3183; E-mail: cmiller@sfc.edu

FACILITIES
Information Resources Bass Mansion; total holdings of 76,000 volumes, 43,200 microforms, 494 current periodical subscriptions. CD player(s) available for graduate student use. Access provided to online bibliographic retrieval services and online databases.

INTERNATIONAL STUDENTS
Demographics 25% of students enrolled are international students [Asia, 100%].
Services and Facilities Visa services, ESL courses, language tutoring.
Applying TOEFL: minimum score of 550, proof of adequate funds, proof of health/immunizations required. Financial aid is not available to international students.
International Student Contact Mr. Scott Flanagan, Assistant Vice President for Enrollment Services, 2701 Spring Street, Fort Wayne, IN 46808-3994. Phone: 219-434-3279; Fax: 219-434-3183; E-mail: sflanaga@sfc.edu

PLACEMENT
Services include alumni network, career counseling/planning, career fairs, career library, career placement, resume referral to employers, and resume preparation. In 1996–97, 5 organizations participated in on-campus recruiting.
Employment Of 1996–97 graduates, 99% were employed within three months of graduation.

Business Program(s) URL: http://www.sfc.edu/

Program Contact: Mr. Derek Sheafer, Admissions Counselor, 2701 Spring Street, Fort Wayne, IN 46808-3994. Phone: 219-434-7485, 800-729-4732; Fax: 219-434-3183; E-mail: dsheafer@sfc.edu

University of Southern Indiana

School of Business
Evansville, Indiana

OVERVIEW
The University of Southern Indiana is a state-supported, coed, comprehensive institution. Enrollment: 7,666 graduate, professional, and undergraduate students; 63 full-time matriculated graduate/professional students; 367 part-time matriculated graduate/professional students. Founded: 1965. The graduate business unit is in a suburban setting and is on a semester calendar.

HIGHLIGHTS
Enrollment Profile
Full-time: 4
Part-time: 109
Total: 113
Average Age: 30
Fall 1997 Average GPA: 3.1

International: 2%
Women: 30%
Minorities: 5%
Average Class Size: 25
Fall 1997 Average GMAT: 528

Costs
Full-time tuition: N/R
Part-time tuition: $118 per credit hour (resident); $235 per credit hour (nonresident)

AACSB – The International Association for Management Education accredited

GRADUATE BUSINESS PROGRAMS
Master of Business Administration (MBA) Full-time, part-time; 36 total credits required; 2.4 to 4 years to complete program.

ADMISSION
Applications For fall 1997 there were 29 applications for admission. Of those applying, 21 were accepted. Of those accepted, 21 enrolled.
Application Requirements Application form, application fee, bachelor's degree, minimum GPA: 2.5, resume, college transcript(s), computer experience: word processing, spreadsheet.
Recommended for Application GMAT score accepted: minimum 450.
Application Deadline Applications processed on a rolling/continuous basis for both domestic and international students. Application fee: $25. Deferred entrance is available.

ACADEMICS
Faculty Full-time 24.
Teaching Methodologies Case study, computer-aided instruction, computer analysis, computer simulations, field projects, group discussion, lecture, research, student presentations, study groups, team projects.
Technology 360 on-campus computer terminals/PCs are available for student use and are linked by a campus-wide network. The network has full access to the Internet. Students are not required to have their own PC.
Special Opportunities Advanced credit may be earned through transfer of credits from another institution. International exchange programs in Germany, Jordan, Poland, Republic of Korea.

FINANCES
Costs for 1997–98 Tuition: $118 per credit hour (resident); $235 per credit hour (nonresident). Cost varies by reciprocity agreements. Average 1997–98 room and board costs were $7956 per academic year (off campus). Room and board costs vary by occupancy (e.g., single, double, triple), type of accommodation.
Financial Aid In 1997–98, 2% of students received some institutionally administered aid.
Financial Aid Contact James Patton, Director of Student Financial Assistance, 8600 University Boulevard, Evansville, IN 47712. Phone: 812-464-1767; Fax: 812-465-1044.

FACILITIES
Information Resources David L. Rice Library; total holdings of 196,419 volumes, 433,996 microforms, 962 current periodical subscriptions. CD player(s) available for graduate student use. Access provided to online bibliographic retrieval services.

INTERNATIONAL STUDENTS
Demographics 2% of students enrolled are international students.
Services and Facilities ESL courses, counseling/support services, multi-cultural center.
Applying TOEFL: minimum score of 550, proof of adequate funds, proof of health/immunizations required. Financial aid is not available to international students.
International Student Contact Pamela Hopson, Director of Multicultural Center, 8600 University Boulevard, Evansville, IN 47712. Phone: 812-465-7188; Fax: 812-464-1960.

PLACEMENT
Services include career library, career placement, resume referral to employers, and resume preparation.

Program Contact: Dr. Marwan Wafa, Director of MBA Program, 8600 University Boulevard, Evansville, IN 47712. Phone: 812-464-1926; Fax: 812-465-1044; E-mail: dwade.ucs@smtp.usi.edu

IOWA

Clarke College

Business Department
Dubuque, Iowa

OVERVIEW
Clarke College is an independent-religious, coed, comprehensive institution. Enrollment: 1,160 graduate, professional, and undergraduate students; 29 full-time matriculated graduate/professional students; 52 part-time matriculated

Clarke College (continued)

graduate/professional students. Founded: 1843. The graduate business unit is in an urban setting and is on a semester calendar.

HIGHLIGHTS

Enrollment Profile
Full-time: 0
Part-time: 18
Total: 18
Average Age: 38
Fall 1997 Average GPA: N/R

International: 0%
Women: 33%
Minorities: 6%
Average Class Size: 18
Fall 1997 Average GMAT: N/R

Costs
Full-time tuition: $6344 per academic year
Part-time tuition: $325 per credit

GRADUATE BUSINESS PROGRAMS
Master of Science in Management (MSM) Full-time, part-time; 36 total credits required; 18 months to 2 years to complete program. Concentrations in human resources, operations management.

ADMISSION
Applications For fall 1997 there were 27 applications for admission. Of those applying, 24 were accepted. Of those accepted, 18 enrolled.

Application Requirements MAT score, application form, bachelor's degree, essay, minimum GPA, 2 letters of recommendation, personal statement, resume, college transcript(s).

Recommended for Application GMAT score accepted, GRE score accepted, interview, work experience, computer experience.

Application Deadline Applications processed on a rolling/continuous basis for both domestic and international students. Application fee: $25.

ACADEMICS
Teaching Methodologies Case study, computer-aided instruction, computer analysis, computer simulations, experiential learning, field projects, group discussion, lecture, research, role playing, seminars by members of the business community, student presentations, team projects.

Technology 137 on-campus computer terminals/PCs are available for student use and are linked by a campus-wide network. The network has full access to the Internet. Students are not required to have their own PC.

Special Opportunities Advanced credit may be earned through transfer of credits from another institution. An internship program is available.

FINANCES
Costs for 1997–98 Tuition: Full-time: $6344 per semester. Part-time: $325 per credit. Cost varies by academic program, class time (e.g., day/evening), number of credits taken. Fees: Full-time: $120 per academic year. Average 1997–98 room and board costs were $4846 per academic year (on campus) and $6000 per academic year (off campus). Room and board costs vary by occupancy (e.g., single, double, triple), type of accommodation, type of meal plan.

Financial Aid Financial aid is available to part-time students.

Financial Aid Contact Mr. Mike Pope, Director of Financial Aid, Dubuque, IA 52001-3198. Phone: 319-588-6327; Fax: 319-588-6789; E-mail: mpope@clarke.edu

FACILITIES
Information Resources Nicholas J. Schrupp Library; total holdings of 120,514 volumes, 8,953 microforms, 523 current periodical subscriptions. CD player(s) available for graduate student use. Access provided to online bibliographic retrieval services and online databases.

INTERNATIONAL STUDENTS
Demographics N/R

Services and Facilities International student office, international student housing, ESL courses, counseling/support services.

Applying TOEFL: minimum score of 550, proof of adequate funds, proof of health/immunizations required. Financial aid is not available to international students.

International Student Contact Mr. Camilo Tamayo, Coordinator of International Admissions, Dubuque, IA 52001-3198. Phone: 319-588-6316; Fax: 319-588-6789; E-mail: jtamayo@clarke.edu

PLACEMENT
Services include alumni network, career counseling/planning, career library, career placement, electronic job bank, job interviews arranged, and resume preparation. In 1996–97, 15 organizations participated in on-campus recruiting.

Business Program(s) URL: http://www.clarke.edu/admissions/graduate/MSM.htm

---

Program Contact: Gayle Schou, Director of Graduate and Corporate Educational Services, Dubuque, IA 52001-3198. Phone: 319-588-8147, 800-383-2345 (IA only); Fax: 319-588-6789; E-mail: gschou@clarke.edu

Drake University

College of Business and Public Administration

Des Moines, Iowa

OVERVIEW
Drake University is an independent-nonprofit, coed university. Enrollment: 4,785 graduate, professional, and undergraduate students; 43 full-time matriculated graduate/professional students; 1,325 part-time matriculated graduate/professional students. Founded: 1881. The graduate business unit is in an urban setting and is on a semester calendar.

HIGHLIGHTS

Enrollment Profile
Full-time: 14
Part-time: 498
Total: 512
Average Age: 29
Fall 1997 Average GPA: 3.23

International: 5%
Women: 44%
Minorities: 3%
Average Class Size: 31
Fall 1997 Average GMAT: 523

Costs
Full-time tuition: N/R
Part-time tuition: $340 per hour

AACSB – The International Association for Management Education accredited

GRADUATE BUSINESS PROGRAMS
Master of Business Administration (MBA) Full-time, part-time, distance learning option; 36 total credits required; 16 months to 5 years to complete program.

ADMISSION
Applications For fall 1997 there were 210 applications for admission. Of those applying, 205 were accepted. Of those accepted, 133 enrolled.

Application Requirements GMAT score, application form, application fee, bachelor's degree, minimum GPA, college transcript(s), computer experience: word processing, spreadsheet.

Recommended for Application Work experience.

Application Deadline Applications processed on a rolling/continuous basis for both domestic and international students. Application fee: $25. Deferred entrance is available.

ACADEMICS
Faculty Full-time 30.

Teaching Methodologies Case study, computer-aided instruction, computer analysis, computer simulations, group discussion, lecture, student presentations, study groups, team projects.

Technology 300 on-campus computer terminals/PCs are available for student use and are linked by a campus-wide network. The network has full access to the Internet. Students are not required to have their own PC.

Special Opportunities Advanced credit may be earned through transfer of credits from another institution.

FINANCES
Costs for 1997–98 Tuition: $340 per hour. Average 1997–98 room and board costs were $6000 per academic year (off campus). Room and board costs vary by occupancy (e.g., single, double, triple), type of accommodation, type of meal plan.

Financial Aid In 1997–98, 5% of students received some institutionally administered aid in the form of loans. Financial aid is available to part-time students. Application Deadline: 3/1.

Financial Aid Contact Dr. John Parker, Assistant Vice President, Business and Finance, 2507 University Avenue, Des Moines, IA 50311-4516. Phone: 515-271-2905.

FACILITIES
Information Resources Cowles Library plus 1 additional on-campus library; total holdings of 700,000 volumes, 1,060,000 microforms, 3,220 current periodical subscriptions. CD player(s) available for graduate student use. Access provided to online bibliographic retrieval services and online databases.

INTERNATIONAL STUDENTS
Demographics 5% of students enrolled are international students.

Services and Facilities International student office, international student center, international student housing, visa services, ESL courses, counseling/support services.

Applying TOEFL: minimum score of 550, proof of adequate funds, proof of health/immunizations required. Financial aid is not available to international students.

International Student Contact Ms. Ann Martin, Graduate Admission Coordinator, 2507 University Avenue—Office of Graduate Admission, Des Moines, IA 50311. Phone: 515-271-3871; Fax: 515-271-2831; E-mail: ajm@admin.drake.edu

PLACEMENT

Services include career counseling/planning, career fairs, career library, career placement, job interviews arranged, and resume preparation. In 1996–97, 110 organizations participated in on-campus recruiting.

Employment Of 1996–97 graduates, 100% were employed within three months of graduation. Types of employment entered: accounting, banking, computer-related, consumer products, education, engineering, finance, financial services, government, health services, human resources, information systems/technology, insurance, law, management, manufacturing, pharmaceutical, service industry, utilities.

Program Contact: Dr. Thomas Pursel, Director of Graduate Programs, College of Business and Public Administration, 2507 University Avenue, Des Moines, IA 50311-4516. Phone: 515-271-2188, 800-44-DRAKE Ext. 2188

Iowa State University of Science and Technology

College of Business

Ames, Iowa

OVERVIEW

Iowa State University of Science and Technology is a state-supported, coed university. Enrollment: 25,384 graduate, professional, and undergraduate students; 2,386 full-time matriculated graduate/professional students; 1,874 part-time matriculated graduate/professional students. Founded: 1858. The graduate business unit is in a small-town setting and is on a semester calendar.

HIGHLIGHTS

Enrollment Profile
Full-time: 104
Part-time: 115
Total: 219
Average Age: 32
Fall 1997 Average GPA: 3.36

International: 26%
Women: 29%
Minorities: 3%
Average Class Size: 30
Fall 1997 Average GMAT: 581

Costs
Full-time tuition: $3166 per academic year (resident); $9324 per academic year (nonresident)
Part-time tuition: $230 per credit (resident); $572 per credit (nonresident)

AACSB – The International Association for Management Education accredited

GRADUATE BUSINESS PROGRAMS

Full-time MBA (MBA) Full-time; 48 total credits required; 21 months to complete program. Concentrations in accounting, agribusiness, finance, manufacturing management, management information systems, marketing.

Saturday MBA (MBA) Part-time; 48 total credits required; 3 years to complete program. Concentrations in accounting, agribusiness, finance, manufacturing management, management information systems, marketing.

Master of Business Administration/Master of Science in Statistics (MBA/MS) Full-time; 72 total credits required; 2.8 years to complete program.

Master of Business Administration/Master of Science in Community and Regional Planning (MBA/MS) Full-time; 73 total credits required; 2.8 years to complete program.

Master of Science in Business Administrative Sciences (MS) Full-time, part-time; 31 total credits required; 12 months to 3 years to complete program. Concentrations in accounting, agribusiness, finance, management information systems, marketing, production management.

Master of Science in Industrial Relations (MS) Full-time, part-time; 36 total credits required; 12 months to 3 years to complete program. Concentration in industrial/labor relations.

ADMISSION

Applications For fall 1997 there were 289 applications for admission. Of those applying, 187 were accepted. Of those accepted, 99 enrolled.

Application Requirements GMAT score, application form, application fee, bachelor's degree, essay, 3 letters of recommendation, resume, college transcript(s).

Recommended for Application Minimum of 3 years of work experience.

Application Deadline 5/1 for fall, 5/1 for summer, 3/1 for fall (international). Application fee: $20, $30 (international). Deferred entrance is available.

ACADEMICS

Faculty Full-time 53.

Teaching Methodologies Case study, computer-aided instruction, computer analysis, experiential learning, faculty seminars, field projects, group discussion, lecture, research, seminars by members of the business community, student presentations, study groups, team projects.

Technology 2,300 on-campus computer terminals/PCs are available for student use and are linked by a campus-wide network. The network has full access to the Internet. Students are not required to have their own PC.

Special Opportunities Advanced credit may be earned through transfer of credits from another institution. International exchange program in United Kingdom. An internship program is available.

FINANCES

Costs for 1997–98 Tuition: Full-time: $3166 per year (resident); $9324 per year (nonresident). Part-time: $230 per credit (resident); $572 per credit (nonresident). Cost varies by class time (e.g., day/evening), number of credits taken. Fees: Full-time: $208 per academic year (resident); $208 per academic year (nonresident). Part-time: $38 per semester (resident); $38 per semester (nonresident). Fees vary by number of credits taken. Average 1997–98 room and board costs were $4100 per academic year. Room and board costs vary by occupancy (e.g., single, double, triple), type of accommodation, type of meal plan.

Financial Aid Research assistantships, scholarships, work study, loans available. Financial aid is available to part-time students. Application Deadline: 3/1.

Financial Aid Contact Mr. Earl Dowling, Director, Student Financial Aid Office, 12 Beardshear Hall, Ames, IA 50011. Phone: 515-294-2223; Fax: 515-294-0851.

FACILITIES

Information Resources Parks Library plus 5 additional on-campus libraries; total holdings of 2,124,964 volumes, 2,954,805 microforms, 21,775 current periodical subscriptions. CD player(s) available for graduate student use. Access provided to online bibliographic retrieval services and online databases.

INTERNATIONAL STUDENTS

Demographics 26% of students enrolled are international students [Africa, 5%, Asia, 69%, Europe, 22%, North America, 4%].

Services and Facilities International student office, international student center, visa services, ESL courses, counseling/support services.

Applying TOEFL: minimum score of 570, proof of adequate funds required. Financial aid is available to international students.

International Student Contact Mr. Dennis Peterson, Director, Office of International Students and Scholars, 4 Hamilton Hall , Ames, IA 50011. Phone: 515-294-1120; Fax: 515-294-8263; E-mail: intlserv@iastate.edu

PLACEMENT

Services include career counseling/planning, career fairs, career library, career placement, electronic job bank, job interviews arranged, job search course, resume referral to employers, and resume preparation. In 1996–97, 27 organizations participated in on-campus recruiting.

Employment Of 1996–97 graduates, 87% were employed within three months of graduation; the average starting salary was $42,463.

Business Program(s) URL: http://www.public.iastate.edu/~isubuscoll/

Program Contact: Mr. Ronald Ackerman, Director of Graduate Admissions, College of Business, 218 Carver Hall, Ames, IA 50011-2063. Phone: 515-294-8118, 800-433-3452; Fax: 515-294-2446; E-mail: busgrad@iastate.edu
See full description on page 856.

Maharishi University of Management

School of Business and Public Administration

Fairfield, Iowa

OVERVIEW

Maharishi University of Management is an independent-nonprofit, coed university. Enrollment: 1,434 graduate, professional, and undergraduate students; 310 full-time matriculated graduate/professional students; 282 part-time matriculated graduate/professional students. Founded: 1971. The graduate business unit is in a small-town setting and is on a semester calendar.

Maharishi University of Management (continued)

HIGHLIGHTS

Enrollment Profile
Full-time: 301
Part-time: 168
Total: 469
Average Age: 25
Fall 1997 Average GPA: N/R

International: 97%
Women: 23%
Minorities: N/R
Average Class Size: 15
Fall 1997 Average GMAT: N/R

Costs
Full-time tuition: $15,520 per academic year
Part-time tuition: N/R

Degree(s) offered in conjunction with Maharishi Institutes of Management (India)

GRADUATE BUSINESS PROGRAMS
Master of Business Administration (MBA) Full-time, part-time, distance learning option; 60-80 total credits required; 23 months to 5 years to complete program.

ADMISSION
Applications For fall 1997 there were 601 applications for admission. Of those applying, 426 were accepted. Of those accepted, 278 enrolled.

Application Requirements Application form, application fee, bachelor's degree, essay, 2 letters of recommendation, personal statement, college transcript(s).

Recommended for Application GMAT score accepted, minimum GPA, interview, resume, work experience, computer experience.

Application Deadline Applications processed on a rolling/continuous basis for both domestic and international students. Application fee: $40. Deferred entrance is available.

ACADEMICS
Faculty Full-time 13; part-time 2.
Teaching Methodologies Case study, experiential learning, field projects, group discussion, lecture, research, seminars by members of the business community, student presentations, study groups, team projects.
Technology 70 on-campus computer terminals/PCs are available for student use and are linked by a campus-wide network. The network has full access to the Internet. Students are not required to have their own PC.
Special Opportunities Advanced credit may be earned through transfer of credits from another institution. An internship program is available.

FINANCES
Costs for 1997–98 Tuition: Full-time: $15,520 per year. Cost varies by academic program. Fees: Full-time: $230 per academic year. Average 1997–98 room and board costs were $4960 per academic year (on campus) and $4960 per academic year (off campus). Room and board costs vary by occupancy (e.g., single, double, triple).
Financial Aid In 1997–98, 17% of students received some institutionally administered aid in the form of scholarships, work study, loans. Financial aid is available to part-time students.
Financial Aid Contact Tom Rowe, Director, Financial Aid, 1000 North 4th Street, DB 1155, Fairfield, IA 52557-1155. Phone: 515-472-1156; Fax: 515-472-1131; E-mail: finaid@mum.edu

FACILITIES
Information Resources Main library plus 1 additional on-campus library; total holdings of 147,000 volumes, 60,000 microforms, 1,040 current periodical subscriptions. CD player(s) available for graduate student use. Access provided to online bibliographic retrieval services.

INTERNATIONAL STUDENTS
Demographics 97% of students enrolled are international students [Africa, 5%, Asia, 82%, Australia/New Zealand, 1%, Central America, 1%, Europe, 10%, South America, 1%].
Services and Facilities Visa services, ESL courses.
Applying TOEFL: minimum score of 575, proof of adequate funds required. Financial aid is available to international students.
International Student Contact Ms. Elaine Christensen, Director of International Admissions, Office of Admissions, Fairfield, IA 52557. Phone: 515-472-1110; Fax: 515-472-1179.

PLACEMENT
Services include alumni network, career counseling/planning, career placement, and resume preparation. In 1996–97, 3 organizations participated in on-campus recruiting; 20 on-campus interviews were conducted.

Business Program(s) URL: http://www.mum.edu

Program Contact: Mr. Paul Handelman, MBA Admissions Officer, Office of Admissions, Fairfield, IA 52557. Phone: 515-472-1110; Fax: 515-472-1179.

St. Ambrose University

H.L. McLaughlin One-Year MBA Program
Davenport, Iowa

OVERVIEW
St. Ambrose University is an independent-religious, coed, comprehensive institution. Enrollment: 2,776 graduate, professional, and undergraduate students; 217 full-time matriculated graduate/professional students; 589 part-time matriculated graduate/professional students. Founded: 1882. The graduate business unit is in an urban setting and is on a semester calendar.

HIGHLIGHTS
Enrollment Profile
Full-time: 30
Part-time: 570
Total: 600
Average Age: 32
Fall 1997 Average GPA: 2.5

International: 4%
Women: 48%
Minorities: 17%
Average Class Size: 25
Fall 1997 Average GMAT: 540

Costs
Full-time tuition: N/R
Part-time tuition: $1206 per course

GRADUATE BUSINESS PROGRAMS
H.L. McLaughlin MBA (MBA) Full-time, part-time, distance learning option; 45 total credits required; 12 months to 5 years to complete program. Concentrations in finance, human resources, management information systems, marketing, technology management.
Master of Accountancy (MAcc) Part-time; 30 total credits required; 2.5 to 5 years to complete program.
Master of Health Care Administration (MHCA) Part-time; 45 total credits required; 2.5 to 5 years to complete program.

ADMISSION
Applications For fall 1997 there were 230 applications for admission. Of those applying, 228 were accepted. Of those accepted, 213 enrolled.
Application Requirements GMAT score, application form, application fee, bachelor's degree, 2 letters of recommendation, personal statement, college transcript(s).
Application Deadline Applications processed on a rolling/continuous basis for both domestic and international students. Application fee: $25. Deferred entrance is available.

ACADEMICS
Faculty Full-time 41; part-time 31.
Teaching Methodologies Case study, computer-aided instruction, computer analysis, computer simulations, experiential learning, field projects, group discussion, lecture, research, role playing, seminars by members of the business community, simulations, student presentations, study groups, team projects.
Technology 90 on-campus computer terminals/PCs are available for student use and are linked by a campus-wide network. The network has full access to the Internet. Students are not required to have their own PC.
Special Opportunities Advanced credit may be earned through credit by examination, credit for military training programs, credit for business training programs, transfer of credits from another institution.

FINANCES
Costs for 1997–98 Tuition: $1206 per course. Fees: $10 per year. Fees vary by campus location. Average 1997–98 room and board costs were $4310 per academic year (on campus) and $6300 per academic year (off campus). Room and board costs vary by campus location, occupancy (e.g., single, double, triple), type of accommodation, type of meal plan.
Financial Aid Research assistantships available.
Financial Aid Contact Mrs. Rita O'Connor, Director, Financial Aid Office, 518 West Locust Street, Davenport, IA 52803-2898. Phone: 319-333-6314; Fax: 319-333-6297; E-mail: finaid@saunix.sau.edu

FACILITIES
Information Resources O'Keefe Library plus 1 additional on-campus library; total holdings of 179,403 volumes, 31,139 microforms, 600 current periodical subscriptions. CD player(s) available for graduate student use. Access provided to online bibliographic retrieval services.

INTERNATIONAL STUDENTS
Demographics 4% of students enrolled are international students [Africa, 1%, Asia, 57%, Central America, 4%, Europe, 19%, North America, 8%, South America, 8%, other, 3%].
Services and Facilities International student office, international student center, ESL courses, counseling/support services.

Applying TOEFL: minimum score of 550, proof of adequate funds, proof of health/immunizations required. Financial aid is not available to international students.

International Student Contact Mr. Alan Aubbel, International Student Counselor, Admissions Office, 518 West Locust Street, Davenport, IA 52803-2898. Phone: 319-333-6309; Fax: 319-333-6297.

PLACEMENT
Services include alumni network, career counseling/planning, career fairs, career library, career placement, electronic job bank, job interviews arranged, job search course, resume referral to employers, and resume preparation.

Employment Of 1996–97 graduates, 95% were employed within three months of graduation. Types of employment entered: banking, computer-related, consumer products, education, energy, engineering, financial services, manufacturing, marketing.

Business Program(s) URL: http://www.sau.edu/

Program Contact: Dr. John Collis, Dean, College of Business, 518 West Locust Street, Davenport, IA 52803-2898. Phone: 319-333-6270, 888-MBA-1-SAU (IA only); Fax: 319-333-6268; E-mail: jcollis@saunix.sau.edu
See full description on page 962.

University of Dubuque

School of Business
Dubuque, Iowa

OVERVIEW
The University of Dubuque is an independent-religious, coed, comprehensive institution. Enrollment: 1,186 graduate, professional, and undergraduate students; 258 full-time matriculated graduate/professional students; 231 part-time matriculated graduate/professional students. Founded: 1852. The graduate business unit is in an urban setting and is on a semester calendar.

HIGHLIGHTS
Enrollment Profile
Full-time: 108
Part-time: 147
Total: 255
Average Age: 33
Fall 1997 Average GPA: N/R

International: 73%
Women: 35%
Minorities: N/R
Average Class Size: 15
Fall 1997 Average GMAT: N/R

Costs
Full-time tuition: $11,700 per academic year
Part-time tuition: $975 per 3 credits

GRADUATE BUSINESS PROGRAMS
Master of Business Administration (MBA) Full-time, part-time; 36 total credits required; 12 months to 6 years to complete program. Concentrations in finance, quality management, management.

ADMISSION
Application Requirements GMAT score: minimum 400, application form, application fee, bachelor's degree, minimum GPA, 3 letters of recommendation, college transcript(s), computer experience: spreadsheet, database, word processing.

Recommended for Application Interview, personal statement, resume, work experience.

Application Deadline Applications processed on a rolling/continuous basis for both domestic and international students. Application fee: $25. Deferred entrance is available.

ACADEMICS
Faculty Full-time 10; part-time 18.

Teaching Methodologies Case study, computer-aided instruction, computer analysis, computer simulations, experiential learning, faculty seminars, group discussion, lecture, research, role playing, seminars by members of the business community, simulations, student presentations, study groups, team projects.

Technology 75 on-campus computer terminals/PCs are available for student use and are linked by a campus-wide network. The network has full access to the Internet. Students are not required to have their own PC.

Special Opportunities Advanced credit may be earned through transfer of credits from another institution. An internship program is available.

FINANCES
Costs for 1997–98 Tuition: Full-time: $11,700 per program. Part-time: $975 per 3 credits. Cost varies by number of credits taken. Fees: Full-time: $60 per academic year. Part-time: $60 per graduation. Average 1997–98 room and board costs were $4440 per academic year (on campus) and $3825 per

academic year (off campus). Room and board costs vary by occupancy (e.g., single, double, triple), type of accommodation, type of meal plan.

Financial Aid Financial aid is available to part-time students. Application Deadline: 4/1.

Financial Aid Contact Timothy Kremer, Director, 2000 University Avenue, Dubuque, IA 52001-5050. Phone: 319-589-3396.

FACILITIES
Information Resources Ficke-Laird Library; total holdings of 164,859 volumes, 20,739 microforms, 801 current periodical subscriptions. CD player(s) available for graduate student use. Access provided to online bibliographic retrieval services.

INTERNATIONAL STUDENTS
Demographics 73% of students enrolled are international students [Asia, 95%, other, 5%].

Services and Facilities International student office, international student center, international student housing, visa services, ESL courses, counseling/support services.

Applying TOEFL: minimum score of 550, proof of adequate funds, proof of health/immunizations required. Financial aid is not available to international students.

International Student Contact Ms. Raydora Drummer, Director of Multicultural Services, 2000 University Avenue, Dubuque, IA 52001-5050. Phone: 319-589-3253.

PLACEMENT
Services include alumni network, career counseling/planning, career fairs, career library, career placement, job interviews arranged, resume referral to employers, and resume preparation.

Employment Of 1996–97 graduates, 99% were employed within three months of graduation. Types of employment entered: banking, education, energy, health services, manufacturing, marketing, service industry, utilities.

Business Program(s) URL: http://www.dbq.edu

Program Contact: Mr. Thomas A. Tully, MBA Director, 2000 University Avenue, Dubuque, IA 52001-5050. Phone: 319-589-3198, 800-722-5583; Fax: 319-589-3417; E-mail: ttully@univ.dbq.edu

The University of Iowa

School of Management
Iowa City, Iowa

OVERVIEW
The University of Iowa is a state-supported, coed university. Enrollment: 27,871 graduate, professional, and undergraduate students. Founded: 1847. The graduate business unit is in a small-town setting and is on a semester calendar.

HIGHLIGHTS
Enrollment Profile
Full-time: 181
Part-time: 425
Total: 606
Average Age: 30
Fall 1997 Average GPA: 3.29

International: 12%
Women: 35%
Minorities: 4%
Average Class Size: 45
Fall 1997 Average GMAT: 610

Costs
Full-time tuition: $4130 per academic year (resident); $11,246 per academic year (nonresident)
Part-time tuition: $221 per semester hour (resident); $221 per semester hour (nonresident)

AACSB – The International Association for Management Education accredited

GRADUATE BUSINESS PROGRAMS
Full-time MBA (MBA) Full-time; 60 total credits required; 2 years to complete program. Concentrations in accounting, entrepreneurship, finance, human resources, management information systems, operations management, marketing, production management.

Executive MBA (MBA) Part-time; 48 total credits required; 21 months to complete program.

Evening MBA (MBA) Part-time; 45 total credits required; minimum of 3 years to complete program.

Master of Business Administration/Doctor of Jurisprudence (MBA/JD) Full-time; 123 total credits required; 4 years to complete program.

Master of Business Administration/Master of Arts in Hospital Health Administration (MBA/MA) Full-time; 72 total credits required; 3 years to complete program.

The University of Iowa (continued)

Master of Business Administration/Master of Science in Nursing (MBA/MS) Full-time, part-time; 61 total credits required; 4 years to complete program.

Master of Business Administration/Master of Arts in Library Science and Information Science (MBA/MA) Full-time, part-time; 3 years to complete program.

Master of Accountancy (MAcc) Full-time, part-time; 30-61 total credits required; 12 months to 2 years to complete program. Concentration in accounting.

Master of Arts in Management Information Systems (MA) Full-time, part-time; 35 total credits required; 2 years to complete program. Concentration in management information systems.

ADMISSION

Applications For fall 1997 there were 917 applications for admission. Of those applying, 372 were accepted. Of those accepted, 188 enrolled.

Application Requirements Application form, application fee, bachelor's degree, essay, minimum GPA: 3.0, 3 letters of recommendation, personal statement, resume, college transcript(s), minimum of 3 years of work experience.

Recommended for Application GMAT score accepted: minimum 600, interview, computer experience.

Application Deadline 4/15 for fall, 4/15 for fall (international). Application fee: $30, $50 (international). Deferred entrance is available.

ACADEMICS

Faculty Full-time 93; part-time 26.

Teaching Methodologies Case study, computer-aided instruction, group discussion, lecture, seminars by members of the business community, student presentations, study groups, team projects.

Technology 100 on-campus computer terminals/PCs are available for student use and are linked by a campus-wide network. The network has full access to the Internet. Students are not required to have their own PC.

Special Opportunities Advanced credit may be earned through transfer of credits from another institution. International exchange program in Germany.

FINANCES

Costs for 1997-98 Tuition: Full-time: $4130 per year (resident); $11,246 per year (nonresident). Part-time: $221 per semester hour (resident); $221 per semester hour (nonresident). Cost varies by academic program, class time (e.g., day/evening), number of credits taken. Fees: $75 per course (resident); $75 per course (nonresident). Fees vary by academic program. Average 1997-98 room and board costs were $5148 per academic year (off campus). Room and board costs vary by type of accommodation, type of meal plan.

Financial Aid In 1997-98, 12% of students received some institutionally administered aid in the form of fellowships, research assistantships, teaching assistantships, scholarships, work study. Financial aid is available to part-time students. Application Deadline: 4/15.

Financial Aid Contact Ms. Mary Spreen, Director of MBA Admissions and Financial Aid, School of Management, 108 Pappajohn Business Administration Building, Suite C140, Iowa City, IA 52242-1000. Phone: 319-335-1039; Fax: 319-335-3604; E-mail: mary-spreen@uiowa.edu

FACILITIES

Information Resources Main library plus 12 additional on-campus libraries; total holdings of 3,822,656 volumes, 5,934,537 microforms, 39,138 current periodical subscriptions. CD player(s) available for graduate student use. Access provided to online bibliographic retrieval services and online databases.

INTERNATIONAL STUDENTS

Demographics 12% of students enrolled are international students [Africa, 3%, Asia, 64%, Europe, 31%, North America, 1%, South America, 1%].

Services and Facilities International student office, international student center, ESL courses, counseling/support services.

Applying TOEFL: minimum score of 600, proof of adequate funds, proof of health/immunizations required. Financial aid is available to international students.

International Student Contact Ms. Jane Van Voorhis, Director, International Program, 108 Pappajohn Business Administration Building, Suite 5178, Iowa City, IA 52242-1000. Phone: 319-335-1379; Fax: 319-335-3604; E-mail: jvanvoor@scout-po.biz.uiowa.edu

PLACEMENT

Services include alumni network, career counseling/planning, career fairs, career library, career placement, electronic job bank, job interviews arranged, job search course, resume referral to employers, and resume preparation. In 1996-97, 112 organizations participated in on-campus recruiting; 361 on-campus interviews were conducted.

Employment Of 1996-97 graduates, 91% were employed within three months of graduation; the average starting salary was $55,228. Types of employment entered: accounting, banking, computer-related, consulting, consumer products, finance, financial services, health services, human resources, informa-

tion systems/technology, insurance, international trade, management, manufacturing, marketing, service industry, telecommunications, utilities.

Business Program(s) URL: http://www.biz.uiowa.edu/mba

Program Contact: Ms. Mary Spreen, Director of MBA Admissions and Financial Aid, School of Management, 108 Pappajohn Business Administration Building, Suite C140, Iowa City, IA 52242-1000. Phone: 319-335-1039, 800-MBA-IOWA; Fax: 319-335-3604; E-mail: mary-spreen@uiowa.edu

See full description on page 1082.

University of Northern Iowa

College of Business Administration

Cedar Falls, Iowa

OVERVIEW

The University of Northern Iowa is a state-supported, coed, comprehensive institution. Enrollment: 13,108 graduate, professional, and undergraduate students; 511 full-time matriculated graduate/professional students; 943 part-time matriculated graduate/professional students. Founded: 1876. The graduate business unit is in a small-town setting and is on a semester calendar.

HIGHLIGHTS

Enrollment Profile

Full-time: 38	International: 18%
Part-time: 51	Women: 43%
Total: 89	Minorities: 6%
Average Age: 33	Average Class Size: 25
Fall 1997 Average GPA: 3.5	Fall 1997 Average GMAT: 500

Costs
Full-time tuition: $3046 per academic year (resident); $7512 per academic year (nonresident)
Part-time tuition: $170 per credit hour (resident); $418 per credit hour (nonresident)

AACSB – The International Association for Management Education accredited

GRADUATE BUSINESS PROGRAMS

Master of Business Administration (MBA) Full-time, part-time; 33 total credits required; 18 months to 7 years to complete program. Concentration in management.

ADMISSION

Applications For fall 1997 there were 35 applications for admission. Of those applying, 32 were accepted. Of those accepted, 26 enrolled.

Application Requirements Application form, application fee, bachelor's degree, personal statement, college transcript(s).

Recommended for Application GMAT score accepted: minimum 500.

Application Deadline 7/20 for fall, 12/15 for spring, 5/1 for fall (international), 11/1 for spring (international). Application fee: $20.

ACADEMICS

Faculty Full-time 33.

Teaching Methodologies Case study, faculty seminars, lecture, research, seminars by members of the business community, student presentations, team projects.

Technology 100 on-campus computer terminals/PCs are available for student use and are linked by a campus-wide network. The network has full access to the Internet. Students are not required to have their own PC.

Special Opportunities Advanced credit may be earned through transfer of credits from another institution. International exchange programs in Austria, Denmark, France.

FINANCES

Costs for 1997-98 Tuition: Full-time: $3046 per year (resident); $7512 per year (nonresident). Part-time: $170 per credit hour (resident); $418 per credit hour (nonresident). Fees: Full-time: $186 per academic year (resident); $186 per academic year (nonresident). Part-time: $24 per semester (resident); $24 per semester (nonresident). Average 1997-98 room and board costs were $3452 per academic year. Room and board costs vary by occupancy (e.g., single, double, triple).

Financial Aid Scholarships, work study available. Financial aid is available to part-time students. Application Deadline: 3/1.

Financial Aid Contact Mr. Roland Carrillo, Director of Financial Aid, Financial Office, Gilchrist 116, Cedar Falls, IA 50614-0024. Phone: 319-273-2701; Fax: 319-273-6950.

FACILITIES

Information Resources Donald O. Rod Library; total holdings of 765,000 volumes, 690,512 microforms, 3,033 current periodical subscriptions. CD player(s) available for graduate student use. Access provided to online bibliographic retrieval services.

INTERNATIONAL STUDENTS
Demographics 18% of students enrolled are international students.

Services and Facilities International student office, visa services, ESL courses.

Applying TOEFL: minimum score of 500, proof of adequate funds, proof of health/immunizations required. Financial aid is available to international students.

International Student Contact Ms. Germana Nijim, Director, International Student Office, Admissions, H33, Cedar Falls, IA 50614-0521. Phone: 319-273-6421; Fax: 319-273-2921; E-mail: germana.nijim@uni.edu

PLACEMENT
Services include alumni network, career counseling/planning, career fairs, career library, career placement, electronic job bank, job interviews arranged, job search course, resume referral to employers, and resume preparation. In 1996–97, 152 organizations participated in on-campus recruiting.

Employment Types of employment entered: accounting, banking, communications, computer-related, consulting, consumer products, education, engineering, finance, financial services, government, health services, high technology, hospitality management, human resources, information systems/technology, insurance, international trade, management, manufacturing, marketing, media, nonprofit, real estate, retail, service industry, telecommunications, transportation.

Business Program(s) URL: http://www.cba.uni.edu

Program Contact: MBA Office, College of Business, Suite 325, Cedar Falls, IA 50614-0123. Phone: 319-273-6243; Fax: 319-273-2922.

Upper Iowa University

Program in Business Leadership

Fayette, Iowa

OVERVIEW
Upper Iowa University is an independent-nonprofit, comprehensive institution. Enrollment: 8,000 graduate, professional, and undergraduate students.

HIGHLIGHTS

Enrollment Profile

Full-time: 38	International: 28%
Part-time: 87	Women: 60%
Total: 125	Minorities: 40%
Average Age: N/R	Average Class Size: N/R
Fall 1997 Average GPA: N/R	Fall 1997 Average GMAT: N/R

Costs
Full-time tuition: N/R
Part-time tuition: $600 per 3 hours

GRADUATE BUSINESS PROGRAMS
Master of Arts in Business Leadership (MA) Full-time, part-time; 36 total credits required. Concentrations in organizational behavior/development, quality management, health care.

ADMISSION
Application Requirements Application form, bachelor's degree, minimum GPA: 2.5, 3 letters of recommendation, college transcript(s).

Recommended for Application GMAT score accepted, GRE score accepted.

Application Deadline Applications processed on a rolling/continuous basis for both domestic and international students.

ACADEMICS
Teaching Methodologies Case study, computer-aided instruction, group discussion, lecture, research, seminars by members of the business community, student presentations, study groups, team projects.

FINANCES
Costs for 1997–98 Tuition: $600 per 3 hours.

Financial Aid Contact Financial Aid Office, Fayette, IA 52142-1857. Phone: 319-425-5350.

INTERNATIONAL STUDENTS
Demographics 28% of students enrolled are international students.

Services and Facilities International student office, counseling/support services.

Applying TOEFL: minimum score of 550, proof of adequate funds, proof of health/immunizations required.

International Student Contact International Student Advisor, Fayette, IA 52142-1857. Phone: 319-425-5229.

PLACEMENT
Services include alumni network, career counseling/planning, electronic job bank, job interviews arranged, job search course, resume referral to employers, and resume preparation.

Employment Types of employment entered: banking, communications, computer-related, consulting, consumer products, education, energy, finance, financial services, government, health services, high technology, hospitality management, human resources, information systems/technology, management, manufacturing, marketing, nonprofit, real estate, retail, service industry, telecommunications, transportation, utilities.

Program Contact: Graduate Business Director, Fayette, IA 52142-1857. Phone: 319-425-5200.

KANSAS

Baker University

School of Professional and Graduate Studies

Baldwin City, Kansas

OVERVIEW
Baker University is an independent-religious, coed, comprehensive institution. Enrollment: 2,012 graduate, professional, and undergraduate students; 433 full-time matriculated graduate/professional students; 105 part-time matriculated graduate/professional students. Founded: 1858. The graduate business unit is in a suburban setting and is on a continuous lock step calendar.

HIGHLIGHTS

Enrollment Profile

Full-time: 433	International: 1%
Part-time: 105	Women: 53%
Total: 538	Minorities: 12%
Average Age: 35	Average Class Size: 16
Fall 1997 Average GPA: 3.2	Fall 1997 Average GMAT: N/R

Costs
Full-time tuition: $13,200 per academic year
Part-time tuition: $300 per credit

GRADUATE BUSINESS PROGRAMS
Master of Business Administration (MBA) Full-time; 44 total credits required; 2 to 6 years to complete program.

Master of Science in Management (MS) Full-time; 36 total credits required; 18 months to 6 years to complete program.

ADMISSION
Applications For fall 1997 there were 181 applications for admission. Of those applying, 179 were accepted. Of those accepted, 179 enrolled.

Application Requirements Application form, application fee, bachelor's degree, letters of recommendation, college transcript(s), minimum of 3 years of work experience.

Application Deadline Applications processed on a rolling/continuous basis for both domestic and international students. Application fee: $20.

ACADEMICS
Faculty Full-time 35; part-time 173.

Teaching Methodologies Computer-aided instruction, computer simulations, group discussion, lecture, research, role playing, seminars by members of the business community, student presentations, study groups, team projects.

Technology The network has full access to the Internet. Students are required to have their own PC.

FINANCES
Costs for 1997–98 Tuition: Full-time: $13,200 per program. Part-time: $300 per credit. Cost varies by academic program. Fees: Full-time: $50 per academic year. Part-time: $50 per degree program.

Financial Aid In 1997–98, 46% of students received some institutionally administered aid. Financial aid is available to part-time students.

Financial Aid Contact Sylvia Ellis, Associate Director of Financial Aid, 6600 College Boulevard, Suite 340, Overland Park, KS 66211. Phone: 913-491-4432; Fax: 913-491-0470.

FACILITIES
Information Resources Collins Library; total holdings of 60,000 volumes, 14,000 microforms, 452 current periodical subscriptions. CD player(s) available for graduate student use. Access provided to online bibliographic retrieval services.

Baker University (continued)

INTERNATIONAL STUDENTS
Demographics 1% of students enrolled are international students [Asia, 100%].
Applying TOEFL: minimum score of 600, proof of adequate funds required. Financial aid is not available to international students.

PLACEMENT
Services include alumni network, career fairs, career placement, resume referral to employers, and resume preparation.

Program Contact: Mr. Jeff Driskill, Director of Marketing, 6600 College Boulevard, Suite 340, Overland Park, KS 66211. Phone: 913-491-4432; Fax: 913-491-0470.

Emporia State University

School of Business

Emporia, Kansas

OVERVIEW
Emporia State University is a state-supported, coed, comprehensive institution. Enrollment: 5,320 graduate, professional, and undergraduate students; 292 full-time matriculated graduate/professional students; 983 part-time matriculated graduate/professional students. Founded: 1863. The graduate business unit is in a suburban setting and is on a semester calendar.

HIGHLIGHTS

Enrollment Profile
Full-time: 48
Part-time: 20
Total: 68
Average Age: 30
Fall 1997 Average GPA: 3.1

International: 41%
Women: 25%
Minorities: 3%
Average Class Size: 20
Fall 1997 Average GMAT: 450

Costs
Full-time tuition: $1108 per academic year (resident); $2922 per academic year (nonresident)
Part-time tuition: $103 per credit hour (resident); $258 per credit hour (nonresident)

GRADUATE BUSINESS PROGRAMS
Master of Business Administration (MBA) Full-time, part-time; 36 total credits required; 12 months to 7 years to complete program. Concentration in accounting.

ADMISSION
Applications For fall 1997 there were 75 applications for admission.
Application Requirements GMAT score, application form, application fee, bachelor's degree, minimum GPA: 2.5, college transcript(s).
Recommended for Application 3 letters of recommendation, personal statement.
Application Deadline Applications processed on a rolling/continuous basis for both domestic and international students. Application fee: $30, $75 (international).

ACADEMICS
Faculty Full-time 30.
Teaching Methodologies Case study, computer analysis, computer simulations, experiential learning, field projects, group discussion, lecture, research, role playing, seminars by members of the business community, student presentations, study groups, team projects.
Technology 200 on-campus computer terminals/PCs are available for student use and are linked by a campus-wide network. The network has full access to the Internet. Students are not required to have their own PC.
Special Opportunities Advanced credit may be earned through transfer of credits from another institution. An internship program is available.

FINANCES
Costs for 1997–98 Tuition: Full-time: $1108 per semester (resident); $2922 per semester (nonresident). Part-time: $103 per credit hour (resident); $258 per credit hour (nonresident). Average 1997–98 room and board costs were $3560 per academic year. Room and board costs vary by occupancy (e.g., single, double, triple), type of accommodation, type of meal plan.
Financial Aid In 1997–98, 24% of students received some institutionally administered aid in the form of fellowships, research assistantships, teaching assistantships, work study, loans. Application Deadline: 3/15.
Financial Aid Contact Wilma Kasnic, Director of Financial Aid, 1200 Commercial Street, Emporia, KS 66801-5087. Phone: 316-341-5456; Fax: 316-341-5892.

FACILITIES
Information Resources William Allen White Library; total holdings of 726,966 volumes, 1,074,848 microforms, 1,536 current periodical subscriptions. CD player(s) available for graduate student use. Access provided to online bibliographic retrieval services.

INTERNATIONAL STUDENTS
Demographics 41% of students enrolled are international students.
Services and Facilities International student office, international student center, international student housing, visa services, ESL courses, counseling/support services.
Applying Proof of adequate funds, proof of health/immunizations required. TOEFL recommended. Financial aid is available to international students.
International Student Contact James Harter, Assistant Vice President for International Education, 1200 Commercial Street, ESU Box 4041, Emporia, KS 66801-5087. Phone: 316-341-5374; Fax: 316-341-5884; E-mail: oisa@esumail.emporia.edu

PLACEMENT
Services include alumni network, career counseling/planning, career fairs, career library, career placement, electronic job bank, job interviews arranged, resume referral to employers, and resume preparation. In 1996–97, 60 organizations participated in on-campus recruiting.
Employment Of 1996–97 graduates, 90% were employed within three months of graduation; the average starting salary was $32,000. Types of employment entered: accounting, banking, computer-related, consumer products, education, finance, financial services, government, human resources, information systems/technology, management, manufacturing, marketing, nonprofit, retail, service industry.

Business Program(s) URL: http://www.emporia.edu/business

Program Contact: Dr. Donald S. Miller, Director, MBA Program, School of Business, Emporia, KS 66801. Phone: 316-341-5456; Fax: 316-341-5892; E-mail: millerdo@emporia.edu
See full description on page 806.

Fort Hays State University

College of Business

Hays, Kansas

OVERVIEW
Fort Hays State University is a state-supported, coed, comprehensive institution. Enrollment: 5,616 graduate, professional, and undergraduate students. Founded: 1902. The graduate business unit is in a small-town setting and is on a semester calendar.

HIGHLIGHTS

Enrollment Profile
Full-time: 39
Part-time: 20
Total: 59
Average Age: 31
Fall 1997 Average GPA: N/R

International: 64%
Women: 44%
Minorities: 2%
Average Class Size: 20
Fall 1997 Average GMAT: 500

Costs
Full-time tuition: N/R
Part-time tuition: $94 per credit (resident); $249 per credit (nonresident)

GRADUATE BUSINESS PROGRAMS
Master of Business Administration (MBA) Full-time, part-time; 33 total credits required; 18 months to 2 years to complete program. Concentrations in management, accounting.

ADMISSION
Applications For fall 1997 there were 54 applications for admission.
Application Requirements GMAT score, application form, application fee, bachelor's degree, minimum GPA, 3 letters of recommendation, personal statement, college transcript(s).
Recommended for Application Computer experience.
Application Deadline Applications processed on a rolling/continuous basis for both domestic and international students. Application fee: $35.

ACADEMICS
Faculty Full-time 9.
Teaching Methodologies Case study, group discussion, lecture, research, student presentations.
Technology 100 on-campus computer terminals/PCs are available for student use and are linked by a campus-wide network. The network has full access to the Internet. Students are not required to have their own PC.

Special Opportunities An internship program is available.

FINANCES
Costs for 1997–98 Tuition: $94 per credit (resident); $249 per credit (nonresident).
Financial Aid Research assistantships, teaching assistantships, loans available. Financial aid is available to part-time students.
Financial Aid Contact Financial Aid Office, 600 Park Street, Hays, KS 67601-4099. Phone: 785-628-4408; Fax: 785-628-4014.

FACILITIES
Information Resources Forsyth Library plus 1 additional on-campus library; total holdings of 502,760 volumes, 1,095 current periodical subscriptions. CD player(s) available for graduate student use. Access provided to online bibliographic retrieval services.

INTERNATIONAL STUDENTS
Demographics 64% of students enrolled are international students.
Services and Facilities International student office, ESL courses, counseling/support services.
Applying TOEFL: minimum score of 550, proof of adequate funds, proof of health/immunizations required. Financial aid is available to international students.
International Student Contact Mr. Joe Potts, International Student Advisor, SH 208, Hays, KS 67601-4099. Phone: 785-628-4276.

PLACEMENT
Services include alumni network, career counseling/planning, job interviews arranged, job search course, resume referral to employers, and resume preparation.
Employment Types of employment entered: accounting, banking, chemical industry, communications, computer-related, consulting, consumer products, energy, engineering, finance, financial services, government, health services, high technology, hospitality management, human resources, information systems/technology, international trade, management, manufacturing, marketing, nonprofit, petrochemical, retail, service industry, telecommunications, transportation, utilities.

Business Program(s) URL: http://www.fhsu.edu

Program Contact: Dr. James Forsythe, Dean, Graduate School, 600 Park Street, Hays, KS 67601-4099. Phone: 785-628-4236; Fax: 785-628-4046; E-mail: gocs@fhsuvm.fhsu.edu

Friends University

Graduate Programs

Wichita, Kansas

OVERVIEW
Friends University is an independent-nonprofit, comprehensive institution. Enrollment: 2,700 graduate, professional, and undergraduate students.

HIGHLIGHTS

Enrollment Profile
Full-time: 55
Part-time: 0
Total: 55
Average Age: 37
Fall 1997 Average GPA: N/R

International: N/R
Women: 40%
Minorities: 5%
Average Class Size: N/R
Fall 1997 Average GMAT: N/R

Costs
Full-time tuition: N/R
Part-time tuition: $445 per credit hour

GRADUATE BUSINESS PROGRAMS
Executive MBA (MBA) Full-time; 36 total credits required; 22 months to complete program.
Master of Science in Management (MS) Full-time; 36 total credits required; minimum of 2 years to complete program.
Master of Management Information Systems (MMIS) Full-time; 36 total credits required; minimum of 2 years to complete program.

ADMISSION
Application Requirements Minimum GPA: 2.75.
Application Deadline 1/1 for winter, 6/1 for summer, 1/1 for winter (international), 6/1 for summer (international). Deferred entrance is available.

ACADEMICS
Teaching Methodologies Case study, computer-aided instruction, computer analysis, computer simulations, group discussion, lecture, student presentations, study groups, team projects.

FINANCES
Costs for 1997–98 Tuition: $445 per credit hour. Fees: $33 per credit hour.
Financial Aid Contact Scott Kingrey, Wichita, KS 67213. Phone: 800-794-6945 Ext. 5658.

INTERNATIONAL STUDENTS
Demographics N/R
Applying TOEFL: minimum score of 550 required.

PLACEMENT
Services include career fairs, career library, and resume referral to employers.
Program Contact: Wichita, KS 67213.

Kansas Newman College

Program in Organizational Leadership

Wichita, Kansas

OVERVIEW
Kansas Newman College is an independent-religious, comprehensive institution. Enrollment: 2,000 graduate, professional, and undergraduate students. The graduate business unit is on a lock step cohort calendar.

HIGHLIGHTS

Enrollment Profile
Full-time: N/R
Part-time: N/R
Total: 8
Average Age: N/R
Fall 1997 Average GPA: N/R

International: N/R
Women: N/R
Minorities: N/R
Average Class Size: N/R
Fall 1997 Average GMAT: N/R

Costs
Full-time tuition: N/R
Part-time tuition: $257 per credit hour

GRADUATE BUSINESS PROGRAMS
MS in Organization Leadership (MS) Full-time; 33 total credits required.

ADMISSION
Application Requirements GMAT score, GRE score, application form, bachelor's degree, minimum GPA: 3.0, interview, letters of recommendation, college transcript(s), computer experience: prerequisite courses.
Application Deadline Applications processed on a rolling/continuous basis for both domestic and international students.

ACADEMICS
Teaching Methodologies Case study, experiential learning, faculty seminars, field projects, group discussion, lecture, research, student presentations, team projects.

FINANCES
Costs for 1997–98 Tuition: $257 per credit hour.
Financial Aid Contact Financial Aid, Wichita, KS 67213-2084. Phone: 316-942-4291 Ext. 121.

INTERNATIONAL STUDENTS
Demographics N/R
Services and Facilities International student office, international student center.
Applying TOEFL required.
International Student Contact Kathy Samuels-Nomm, Wichita, KS 67213-2084. Phone: 316-942-4291 Ext. 160.

PLACEMENT
Services include career counseling/planning.

Program Contact: Dale Shubert, Wichita, KS 67213-2084. Phone: 316-942-4291 Ext. 355.

Kansas State University

College of Business Administration

Manhattan, Kansas

OVERVIEW
Kansas State University is a state-supported, coed university. Enrollment: 21,507 graduate, professional, and undergraduate students; 46 full-time matriculated graduate/professional students; 23 part-time matriculated graduate/professional students. Founded: 1863. The graduate business unit is in a small-town setting and is on a semester calendar.

Kansas State University (continued)

HIGHLIGHTS

Enrollment Profile
Full-time: 47
Part-time: 22
Total: 69
Average Age: 33
Fall 1997 Average GPA: 3.57

International: 33%
Women: 45%
Minorities: 14%
Average Class Size: 30
Fall 1997 Average GMAT: 540

Costs
Full-time tuition: N/R
Part-time tuition: $101 per credit hour (resident); $329 per credit hour (nonresident)

AACSB – The International Association for Management Education accredited

GRADUATE BUSINESS PROGRAMS
Master of Business Administration (MBA) Full-time, part-time; 40-52 total credits required; 2 years to complete program. Concentrations in management, agri-business, finance, international business, marketing.

Master of Science in Accountancy (MS) Full-time, part-time; 30 total credits required; 12 to 18 months to complete program. Concentration in accounting.

ADMISSION
Applications For fall 1997 there were 42 applications for admission. Of those applying, 26 were accepted. Of those accepted, 23 enrolled.

Application Requirements Application form, application fee, bachelor's degree (must be in field of business), essay, minimum GPA: 3.0, 3 letters of recommendation, resume, college transcript(s).

Recommended for Application GMAT score accepted: minimum 500, work experience, computer experience: personal computing, spreadsheets, databases, word processing.

Application Deadline 8/1 for fall, 1/1 for spring, 6/1 for fall (international), 11/1 for spring (international). Application fee: $45. Deferred entrance is available.

ACADEMICS
Faculty Full-time 20.

Teaching Methodologies Case study, computer-aided instruction, computer analysis, computer simulations, experiential learning, field projects, group discussion, lecture, research, role playing, seminars by members of the business community, simulations, student presentations, study groups, team projects.

Technology 40 on-campus computer terminals/PCs are available for student use and are linked by a campus-wide network. The network has full access to the Internet. Students are not required to have their own PC.

Special Opportunities Advanced credit may be earned through credit by examination, transfer of credits from another institution. International exchange programs in France, Germany, Italy. An internship program is available.

FINANCES
Costs for 1997–98 Tuition: $101 per credit hour (resident); $329 per credit hour (nonresident). Cost varies by academic program, number of credits taken, reciprocity agreements. Fees: $64 per credit hour (resident); $64 per credit hour (nonresident). Fees vary by academic program, number of credits taken, reciprocity agreements. Average 1997–98 room only costs were $3400 per academic year. Room and board costs vary by occupancy (e.g., single, double, triple), type of accommodation, type of meal plan.

Financial Aid Fellowships, research assistantships, teaching assistantships, grants, scholarships, work study, loans available. Financial aid is available to part-time students. Application Deadline: 3/1.

Financial Aid Contact Dr. Cynthia S. McCahon, Director of Graduate Studies, Calvin Hall #107, Manhattan, KS 66506-0501. Phone: 913-532-7190; Fax: 913-532-7216; E-mail: cmccahon@business.cba.ksu.edu

FACILITIES
Information Resources Hale Library plus 4 additional on-campus libraries; total holdings of 1,175,000 volumes, 2,175,000 microforms, 7,500 current periodical subscriptions. CD player(s) available for graduate student use. Access provided to online bibliographic retrieval services.

INTERNATIONAL STUDENTS
Demographics 33% of students enrolled are international students.

Services and Facilities International student office, international student center, international student housing, visa services, ESL courses, counseling/support services.

Applying TOEFL: minimum score of 590, proof of adequate funds required. Financial aid is not available to international students.

International Student Contact Dr. Cynthia S. McCahon, Director of Graduate Studies, Calvin Hall #107, Manhattan, KS 66506-0501. Phone: 913-532-7190; Fax: 913-532-7216; E-mail: cmccahon@business.cba.ksu.edu

PLACEMENT
Services include alumni network, career counseling/planning, career fairs, career library, career placement, electronic job bank, job interviews arranged, job search course, resume referral to employers, and resume preparation. In 1996–97, 769 organizations participated in on-campus recruiting; 5,593 on-campus interviews were conducted.

Employment Of 1996–97 graduates, 85% were employed within three months of graduation; the average starting salary was $29,400. Types of employment entered: accounting, banking, communications, consulting, finance, financial services, information systems/technology, insurance, management, telecommunications, transportation.

Business Program(s) URL: http://www.cba.ksu.edu/

Program Contact: Dr. Cynthia S. McCahon, Director of Graduate Studies, 110 Calvin Hall, Manhattan, KS 66506-0501. Phone: 913-532-7190; Fax: 913-532-7216; E-mail: cmccahon@business.cba.ksu.edu
See full description on page 862.

Kansas Wesleyan University

MBA Program

Salina, Kansas

OVERVIEW
Kansas Wesleyan University is an independent-religious, comprehensive institution. Enrollment: 700 graduate, professional, and undergraduate students. Founded: 1885.

HIGHLIGHTS

Enrollment Profile
Full-time: 45
Part-time: 0
Total: 45
Average Age: 30
Fall 1997 Average GPA: N/R

International: 33%
Women: 49%
Minorities: N/R
Average Class Size: N/R
Fall 1997 Average GMAT: N/R

Costs
Full-time tuition: N/R
Part-time tuition: $340 per credit hour

GRADUATE BUSINESS PROGRAMS
Master of Business Administration (MBA) Full-time; 30 total credits required; 18 months to 7 years to complete program. Concentration in health care.

ADMISSION
Application Requirements Application form, application fee, bachelor's degree, minimum GPA, interview, 3 letters of recommendation, resume, college transcript(s), computer experience: computer literacy.

Recommended for Application GMAT score accepted, GRE score accepted.

Application Deadline Applications processed on a rolling/continuous basis for both domestic and international students. Application fee: $30.

ACADEMICS
Teaching Methodologies Case study, computer-aided instruction, faculty seminars, group discussion, lecture, research, role playing, seminars by members of the business community, student presentations, study groups, team projects.

FINANCES
Costs for 1997–98 Tuition: $340 per credit hour.

Financial Aid Contact Glenna Alexander, 100 East Claflin, Salina, KS 67401-6196. Phone: 913-827-5541.

INTERNATIONAL STUDENTS
Demographics 33% of students enrolled are international students.

Services and Facilities International student office, counseling/support services.

Applying TOEFL, proof of adequate funds, proof of health/immunizations required.

International Student Contact International Office, 100 East Claflin, Salina, KS 67401-6196. Phone: 913-827-5541.

PLACEMENT
Services include alumni network.

Employment Types of employment entered: accounting, education, health services, management, manufacturing, transportation.

Program Contact: Dr. Carol Ahlvers, Director, 100 East Claflin, Salina, KS 67401-6196. Phone: 913-827-5541 Ext. 2214 E-mail: carol@diamond.kwu.edu

MidAmerica Nazarene University

Graduate Studies in Management

Olathe, Kansas

OVERVIEW
MidAmerica Nazarene University is an independent-religious, coed, comprehensive institution. Enrollment: 1,400 graduate, professional, and undergraduate students; 171 full-time matriculated graduate/professional students; part-time matriculated graduate/professional students. Founded: 1966. The graduate business unit is in a suburban setting and is on a year round; modules of 6-8 weeks in length calendar.

HIGHLIGHTS

Enrollment Profile
Full-time: 94
Part-time: 0
Total: 94
Average Age: 36
Fall 1997 Average GPA: 3.36

International: 3%
Women: 34%
Minorities: 9%
Average Class Size: 20
Fall 1997 Average GMAT: N/R

Costs
Full-time tuition: $13,788 per academic year
Part-time tuition: N/R

GRADUATE BUSINESS PROGRAMS
Master of Business Administration (MBA) Full-time; 40 total credits required; 22 months to 2.1 years to complete program.

ADMISSION
Application Requirements Application form, application fee, bachelor's degree, essay, minimum GPA: 3.0, 2 letters of recommendation, personal statement, college transcript(s), minimum of 2 years of work experience.
Recommended for Application Interview, computer experience.
Application Deadline Applications processed on a rolling/continuous basis for both domestic and international students. Application fee: $75. Deferred entrance is available.

ACADEMICS
Faculty Full-time 3; part-time 1.
Teaching Methodologies Case study, computer-aided instruction, computer simulations, group discussion, lecture, research, seminars by members of the business community, student presentations, team projects.
Technology 70 on-campus computer terminals/PCs are available for student use and are linked by a campus-wide network. The network has full access to the Internet. Students are required to have their own PC.

FINANCES
Costs for 1997–98 Tuition: Full-time: $13,788 per program.
Financial Aid In 1997–98, 32% of students received some institutionally administered aid.
Financial Aid Contact Ms. Rhonda Cole, Assistant Director of Fiscal Operations, 2030 East College Way, Olathe, KS 66062-1899. Phone: 913-791-3298; Fax: 913-791-3401; E-mail: rcole@oz.manc.edu

FACILITIES
Information Resources Mabee Library; total holdings of 79,237 volumes, 137,797 microforms, 1,000 current periodical subscriptions. CD player(s) available for graduate student use.

INTERNATIONAL STUDENTS
Demographics 3% of students enrolled are international students.
Services and Facilities International student office, visa services, ESL courses, counseling/support services.
Applying TOEFL: minimum score of 600, proof of adequate funds required. Proof of health/immunizations recommended. Financial aid is available to international students.
International Student Contact Dr. Jim Main, International Student Advisor, 2030 East College Way, Olathe, KS 66062-1899. Phone: 913-791-3296; Fax: 913-791-3290; E-mail: jmain@oz.manc.edu

PLACEMENT
Services include alumni network, career counseling/planning, career fairs, career library, career placement, job interviews arranged, and resume preparation.
Business Program(s) URL: http://www.mnu.edu/http://www/mba/

Program Contact: Dr. Mark Stenger, Director, Graduate Studies in Management, 2030 East College Way, Olathe, KS 66062-1899. Phone: 913-791-3276; Fax: 913-791-3409; E-mail: mstenger@oz.manc.edu

Ottawa University

Department of Human Resources

Ottawa, Kansas

OVERVIEW
Ottawa University is an independent-religious, coed, comprehensive institution. Enrollment: 994 graduate, professional, and undergraduate students; full-time matriculated graduate/professional students; 75 part-time matriculated graduate/professional students. Founded: 1865.

HIGHLIGHTS

Enrollment Profile
Full-time: 0
Part-time: 75
Total: 75
Average Age: N/R
Fall 1997 Average GPA: N/R

International: 0%
Women: N/R
Minorities: N/R
Average Class Size: N/R
Fall 1997 Average GMAT: N/R

Costs
Full-time tuition: N/R
Part-time tuition: $275 per credit hour

GRADUATE BUSINESS PROGRAMS
Master of Arts in Human Resources (MA) Part-time, distance learning option; 36 total credits required; minimum of 2 years to complete program. Concentration in human resources.

ADMISSION
Applications For fall 1997 there were 44 applications for admission.
Application Requirements Application form, bachelor's degree, essay, minimum GPA: 3.0, interview, 3 letters of recommendation, personal statement, resume, college transcript(s).
Application Deadline Applications processed on a rolling/continuous basis for both domestic and international students.

ACADEMICS
Faculty Full-time 1; part-time 13.
Teaching Methodologies Case study, computer-aided instruction, computer analysis, computer simulations, faculty seminars, field projects, group discussion, lecture, research, role playing, seminars by members of the business community, simulations, student presentations, team projects.

FINANCES
Costs for 1997–98 Tuition: Part-time: $275 per credit hour.
Financial Aid Financial aid is available to part-time students.
Financial Aid Contact Tricia Giltner, Financial Aid, 1001 South Cedar, Ottawa, KS 66067-3399. Phone: 913-451-1431.

INTERNATIONAL STUDENTS
Demographics N/R

Program Contact: David Leiter, Admissions Office, 1001 South Cedar, Ottawa, KS 66067-3399. Phone: 913-451-1431.

Pittsburg State University

Gladys A. Kelce School of Business and Economics

Pittsburg, Kansas

OVERVIEW
Pittsburg State University is a state-supported, coed, comprehensive institution. Enrollment: 5,955 graduate, professional, and undergraduate students; 315 full-time matriculated graduate/professional students; 474 part-time matriculated graduate/professional students. Founded: 1903. The graduate business unit is in a small-town setting and is on a semester calendar.

HIGHLIGHTS

Enrollment Profile
Full-time: 64
Part-time: 54
Total: 118
Average Age: 28
Fall 1997 Average GPA: 3.13

International: 36%
Women: 47%
Minorities: N/R
Average Class Size: 20
Fall 1997 Average GMAT: 498

Costs
Full-time tuition: $2332 per academic year (resident); $5960 per academic year (nonresident)
Part-time tuition: $100 per credit hour (resident); $251 per credit hour (nonresident)

Pittsburg State University (continued)

GRADUATE BUSINESS PROGRAMS
Master of Business Administration (MBA) Full-time, part-time, distance learning option; 33 total credits required; 12 months to 3 years to complete program. Concentrations in management, accounting, industrial administration/management.

ADMISSION
Applications For fall 1997 there were 52 applications for admission. Of those applying, 51 were accepted. Of those accepted, 19 enrolled.

Application Requirements Application form, application fee, bachelor's degree, college transcript(s).

Recommended for Application GMAT score accepted: minimum 400, letters of recommendation, work experience, computer experience.

Application Deadline 7/15 for fall, 12/15 for spring, 5/1 for summer, 7/15 for fall (international), 12/15 for spring (international), 5/1 for summer (international). Application fee: 40 (international). Deferred entrance is available.

ACADEMICS
Faculty Full-time 35.

Teaching Methodologies Case study, computer analysis, group discussion, lecture, research, role playing, simulations, student presentations, team projects.

Technology 300 on-campus computer terminals/PCs are available for student use and are linked by a campus-wide network. The network has full access to the Internet. Students are not required to have their own PC.

Special Opportunities Advanced credit may be earned through transfer of credits from another institution.

FINANCES
Costs for 1997–98 Tuition: Full-time: $2332 per year (resident); $5960 per year (nonresident). Part-time: $100 per credit hour (resident); $251 per credit hour (nonresident). Fees vary by academic program. Average 1997–98 room and board costs were $3356 per academic year (on campus) and $3800 per academic year (off campus). Room and board costs vary by occupancy (e.g., single, double, triple), type of accommodation, type of meal plan.

Financial Aid Research assistantships, teaching assistantships, work study available. Application Deadline: 4/1.

Financial Aid Contact Ms. Joanna McCormick, Director, Financial Aid, 1701 South Broadway, Pittsburg, KS 66762. Phone: 316-235-4240; Fax: 316-232-7515.

FACILITIES
Information Resources Axe Library; total holdings of 350,000 volumes, 327,074 microforms, 1,575 current periodical subscriptions. Access provided to online bibliographic retrieval services.

INTERNATIONAL STUDENTS
Demographics 36% of students enrolled are international students.

Services and Facilities International student office, ESL courses, counseling/support services, international student organization.

Applying TOEFL: minimum score of 450 required. Financial aid is not available to international students.

International Student Contact Mr. Khalil Mekkaoui, Director, International Student Services, 1701 South Broadway, Pittsburg, KS 66762. Phone: 316-235-4680; Fax: 316-235-4962.

PLACEMENT
Services include career counseling/planning, career fairs, career library, career placement, electronic job bank, job interviews arranged, and resume referral to employers.

Employment Types of employment entered: accounting, banking, chemical industry, consumer products, education, finance, financial services, government, information systems/technology, insurance, management, real estate, retail.

Business Program(s) URL: http://www.pittstate.edu/academics/sb.html

Program Contact: Dr. Kenneth Clow, Director of MBA Program, School of Business, Pittsburg, KS 66762. Phone: 316-235-4594 E-mail: keclow@pittstate.edu

Saint Mary College

Department of Business, Economics and Information Technology

Leavenworth, Kansas

OVERVIEW
Saint Mary College is an independent-religious, coed, comprehensive institution. Enrollment: 555 graduate, professional, and undergraduate students; 28 full-time matriculated graduate/professional students; 75 part-time matriculated graduate/professional students. Founded: 1923. The graduate business unit is in a suburban setting and is on a semester calendar.

HIGHLIGHTS
Enrollment Profile

Full-time: 25	International: 6%
Part-time: 11	Women: 33%
Total: 36	Minorities: 14%
Average Age: 38	Average Class Size: N/R
Fall 1997 Average GPA: 3.5	Fall 1997 Average GMAT: N/R

Costs
Full-time tuition: $207 per academic year
Part-time tuition: N/R

GRADUATE BUSINESS PROGRAMS
Master of Science in Management (MS) Full-time, part-time; 36 total credits required; 18 months to 2 years to complete program. Concentrations in health care, management.

ADMISSION
Applications For fall 1997 there were 38 applications for admission. Of those applying, 38 were accepted. Of those accepted, 36 enrolled.

Application Requirements Application form, bachelor's degree (must be in field of business), essay, minimum GPA: 2.75, interview, 3 letters of recommendation, college transcript(s).

Recommended for Application Personal statement.

Application Deadline Applications processed on a rolling/continuous basis for both domestic and international students. Application fee: $20.

ACADEMICS
Faculty Full-time 6; part-time 12.

Teaching Methodologies Group discussion, lecture, research, student presentations.

Special Opportunities Advanced credit may be earned through credit for experience, credit for military training programs, transfer of credits from another institution.

FINANCES
Costs for 1997–98 Tuition: Full-time: $207 per semester credit hour. Fees: Full-time: $50 per academic year.

Financial Aid Loans available.

Financial Aid Contact Ms. Judy Wiedower, Director of Financial Aid, Leavenworth, KS 66048-5082. Phone: 913-758-6314; Fax: 913-758-6140; E-mail: wiedower@hub.smcks.edu

FACILITIES
Information Resources De Paul Library; total holdings of 112,970 volumes, 56,926 microforms, 384 current periodical subscriptions. CD player(s) available for graduate student use. Access provided to online bibliographic retrieval services and online databases.

INTERNATIONAL STUDENTS
Demographics 6% of students enrolled are international students [Asia, 100%].

Applying TOEFL: minimum score of 550, proof of adequate funds, proof of health/immunizations required.

International Student Contact Mrs. Minda Whiteside, Registrar, Leavenworth, KS 66048-5082. Phone: 913-758-6110; Fax: 913-758-6140; E-mail: whitesdm@hub.smcks.edu913

Program Contact: Mr. David Jones, Instructor in Business, Overland Park, KS 66215. Phone: 913-345-8288; Fax: 913-345-2802; E-mail: jonesd@hub.smcks.edu

University of Kansas

School of Business

Lawrence, Kansas

OVERVIEW
The University of Kansas is a state-supported, coed university. Enrollment: 27,567 graduate, professional, and undergraduate students; 4,573 full-time matriculated graduate/professional students; 4,102 part-time matriculated graduate/professional students. Founded: 1864. The graduate business unit is in a suburban setting and is on a semester calendar.

HIGHLIGHTS

Enrollment Profile
Full-time: 219
Part-time: 310
Total: 529
Average Age: 29
Fall 1997 Average GPA: 3.25

International: 11%
Women: 35%
Minorities: 4%
Average Class Size: 21
Fall 1997 Average GMAT: 590

Costs
Full-time tuition: $3400 per academic year (resident); $11,177 per academic year (nonresident)
Part-time tuition: $100 per credit hour (resident); $100 per credit hour (nonresident)

AACSB – The International Association for Management Education accredited

Degree(s) offered in conjunction with École Superieure de Commerce, Clermont-Ferrand

GRADUATE BUSINESS PROGRAMS
Full-time MBA (MBA) Full-time; 60 total credits required; 2 years to complete program. Concentrations in international business, technology management, information management, marketing, human resources, finance, management, management science, strategic management.

Part-time MBA (MBA) Part-time; 48 total credits required; 3 to 5 years to complete program. Concentrations in international business, technology management, information management, marketing, human resources, finance, management, management science, strategic management.

Master of Science in Business I (MS) Full-time, part-time; 30 total credits required; 12 months to 2 years to complete program. Concentrations in human resources, organizational behavior/development, information management.

Master of Accounting and Information Systems I (MAIS I) Full-time, part-time; 30 total credits required; 12 months to 2 years to complete program. Concentrations in information management, taxation, accounting.

Master of Accounting and Information Systems II (MAIS II) Full-time; 72 total credits required; 2 to 4 years to complete program. Concentrations in information management, taxation, accounting.

Master of Science in Business II (MS) Full-time, part-time; 64 total credits required; 2 to 4 years to complete program. Concentration in information management.

ADMISSION
Applications For fall 1997 there were 413 applications for admission. Of those applying, 232 were accepted. Of those accepted, 167 enrolled.

Application Requirements GMAT score: minimum 500, application form, application fee, bachelor's degree, essay, minimum GPA: 3.0, interview, 2 letters of recommendation, personal statement, resume, college transcript(s).

Recommended for Application Work experience, computer experience.

Application Deadline 5/1 for fall, 10/1 for spring, 3/1 for summer, 5/1 for fall (international), 10/1 for spring (international), 3/1 for summer (international). Application fee: $50. Deferred entrance is available.

ACADEMICS
Faculty Full-time 56; part-time 4.

Teaching Methodologies Case study, computer-aided instruction, computer simulations, experiential learning, faculty seminars, field projects, group discussion, lecture, research, role playing, seminars by members of the business community, simulations, student presentations, team projects.

Technology 500 on-campus computer terminals/PCs are available for student use and are linked by a campus-wide network. The network has full access to the Internet. Students are not required to have their own PC.

Special Opportunities Advanced credit may be earned through transfer of credits from another institution. International exchange programs in France, Italy, Japan, United Kingdom. An internship program is available.

FINANCES
Costs for 1997–98 Tuition: Full-time: $3400 per year (resident); $11,177 per year (nonresident). Part-time: $100 per credit hour (resident); $100 per credit hour (nonresident). Cost varies by campus location, number of credits taken. Fees: Full-time: $428 per academic year (resident); $428 per academic year (nonresident). Part-time: $96 per credit hour (resident); $96 per credit hour (nonresident). Fees vary by campus location, number of credits taken. Average 1997–98 room and board costs were $3736 per academic year (on campus) and $4500 per academic year (off campus). Room and board costs vary by occupancy (e.g., single, double, triple), type of accommodation, type of meal plan.

Financial Aid In 1997–98, 8% of students received some institutionally administered aid in the form of fellowships, research assistantships, teaching assistantships, scholarships. Application Deadline: 3/1.

Financial Aid Contact Office of Student Financial Aid, 50 Strong Hall, Lawrence, KS 66045. Phone: 785-864-4700; Fax: 785-864-5469; E-mail: sfa@st37.eds.ukans.edu

FACILITIES
Information Resources Watson Library plus 12 additional on-campus libraries; total holdings of 3,292,923 volumes, 2,797,658 microforms, 33,051 current periodical subscriptions. CD player(s) available for graduate student use. Access provided to online bibliographic retrieval services.

INTERNATIONAL STUDENTS
Demographics 11% of students enrolled are international students.

Services and Facilities International student office, visa services, ESL courses, counseling/support services.

Applying TOEFL: minimum score of 600, proof of adequate funds required. Financial aid is available to international students.

International Student Contact Mr. David Collins, Associate Director of Masters Programs, 206 Summerfield Hall, School of Business, Lawrence, KS 66045. Phone: 785-864-4254; Fax: 785-864-5328; E-mail: dcollins@bschool.wpo.ukans.edu

PLACEMENT
Services include alumni network, career counseling/planning, career fairs, career library, career placement, electronic job bank, job interviews arranged, job search course, resume referral to employers, and resume preparation. In 1996–97, 205 organizations participated in on-campus recruiting; 454 on-campus interviews were conducted.

Employment Of 1996–97 graduates, 95% were employed within three months of graduation; the average starting salary was $44,518. Types of employment entered: accounting, banking, chemical industry, communications, computer-related, consulting, consumer products, education, energy, engineering, finance, financial services, government, health services, high technology, hospitality management, human resources, information systems/technology, insurance, law, management, manufacturing, petrochemical, pharmaceutical, retail, service industry, telecommunications, transportation, utilities.

Business Program(s) URL: http://www.bschool.ukans.edu/mba/mbalaw/info.htm

Program Contact: Mr. David Collins, Associate Director of Masters Programs, 206 Summerfield Hall, School of Business, Lawrence, KS 66045. Phone: 785-864-4254, 800-642-2425 (KS only); Fax: 785-864-5328; E-mail: grad@bschool.wpo.ukans.edu

See full description on page 1084.

Washburn University of Topeka

School of Business
Topeka, Kansas

OVERVIEW
Washburn University of Topeka is a locally supported, coed, comprehensive institution. Enrollment: 6,281 graduate, professional, and undergraduate students; 591 full-time matriculated graduate/professional students; 409 part-time matriculated graduate/professional students. Founded: 1865. The graduate business unit is in an urban setting and is on a semester calendar.

HIGHLIGHTS

Enrollment Profile
Full-time: 46
Part-time: 132
Total: 178
Average Age: 32
Fall 1997 Average GPA: 3.0

International: 17%
Women: 50%
Minorities: 17%
Average Class Size: 20
Fall 1997 Average GMAT: 500

Costs
Full-time tuition: N/R
Part-time tuition: $131 per credit hour (resident); $270 per credit hour (nonresident)

GRADUATE BUSINESS PROGRAMS
Master of Business Administration (MBA) Full-time, part-time; 30-55 total credits required; 12 months to 6 years to complete program. Concentration in accounting.

ADMISSION
Applications For fall 1997 there were 49 applications for admission. Of those applying, 34 were accepted. Of those accepted, 30 enrolled.

Application Requirements GMAT score: minimum 400, application form, application fee, bachelor's degree, minimum GPA: 2.6, 2 letters of recommendation, college transcript(s).

Recommended for Application GRE score accepted, interview, personal statement, resume, work experience, computer experience.

Washburn University of Topeka (continued)

Application Deadline 7/1 for fall, 11/15 for spring, 5/1 for summer, 7/1 for fall (international), 11/15 for spring (international), 5/1 for summer (international). Application fee: 40 (international).

ACADEMICS
Faculty Full-time 19; part-time 5.

Teaching Methodologies Case study, computer-aided instruction, computer analysis, computer simulations, faculty seminars, field projects, group discussion, lecture, research, role playing, student presentations, study groups, team projects.

Technology 100 on-campus computer terminals/PCs are available for student use and are linked by a campus-wide network. The network has full access to the Internet. Students are not required to have their own PC.

Special Opportunities Advanced credit may be earned through transfer of credits from another institution.

FINANCES
Costs for 1997–98 Tuition: $131 per credit hour (resident); $270 per credit hour (nonresident). Cost varies by number of credits taken. Fees: $13 per semester (resident); $13 per semester (nonresident). Fees vary by number of credits taken.

Financial Aid In 1997–98, 22% of students received some institutionally administered aid in the form of scholarships, work study, loans. Financial aid is available to part-time students. Application Deadline: 3/1.

Financial Aid Contact Ms. Annita Huff, Director, Financial Aid, 1700 SW College Avenue, Topeka, KS 66621. Phone: 785-231-1151; Fax: 785-231-1079.

FACILITIES
Information Resources Mabee Library plus 2 additional on-campus libraries; total holdings of 540,820 volumes, 579,441 microforms, 5,300 current periodical subscriptions. CD player(s) available for graduate student use. Access provided to online bibliographic retrieval services and online databases.

INTERNATIONAL STUDENTS
Demographics 17% of students enrolled are international students [Africa, 7%, Asia, 87%, Europe, 7%].

Services and Facilities International student office, international student center, international student housing, visa services, ESL courses, counseling/support services.

Applying TOEFL: minimum score of 550, proof of adequate funds required. TSE, TWE recommended. Financial aid is not available to international students.

International Student Contact Dr. William A. Langdon, Chair, International Studies Department and Director, International Programs, 1700 SW College Avenue, Topeka, KS 66621. Phone: 785-231-1010 Ext. 1714; Fax: 785-233-2780; E-mail: zzlang@washburn.edu

PLACEMENT
Services include alumni network, career counseling/planning, career fairs, career library, career placement, electronic job bank, job interviews arranged, job search course, resume referral to employers, and resume preparation. In 1996–97, 63 organizations participated in on-campus recruiting; 619 on-campus interviews were conducted.

Employment Of 1996–97 graduates, 80% were employed within three months of graduation; the average starting salary was $32,610. Types of employment entered: accounting, banking, communications, consumer products, education, finance, financial services, government, human resources, management, manufacturing, marketing, nonprofit, retail, service industry, telecommunications.

Business Program(s) URL: http://www.washburn.edu/sobu/mba

Program Contact: Dr. Russell Smith, Director, Graduate Programs, School of Business, 1700 SW College Avenue, Topeka, KS 66621. Phone: 785-231-1010 Ext. 1307; Fax: 785-231-1063; E-mail: zzsmir@washburn.edu

See full description on page 1186.

Wichita State University

W. Frank Barton School of Business

Wichita, Kansas

OVERVIEW
Wichita State University is a state-supported, coed university. Enrollment: 14,264 graduate, professional, and undergraduate students; 957 full-time matriculated graduate/professional students; 2,137 part-time matriculated graduate/professional students. Founded: 1892. The graduate business unit is in an urban setting and is on a semester calendar.

HIGHLIGHTS

Enrollment Profile

Full-time: 99	International: 23%
Part-time: 240	Women: 38%
Total: 339	Minorities: 3%
Average Age: 35	Average Class Size: 30
Fall 1997 Average GPA: 3.19	Fall 1997 Average GMAT: 514

Costs
Full-time tuition: N/R
Part-time tuition: $112 per credit (resident); $332 per credit (nonresident)

AACSB – The International Association for Management Education accredited

The W. Frank Barton School of Business strives to be the best source of high-quality business education and prospective employees in the Midwest region. By building exciting partnerships with industry-leading companies, utilizing cutting-edge technology, and attracting high-quality students, the Barton School's graduate educational programs provide students with a superior academic experience. Barton School M.B.A. students have the benefit of an updated curriculum that not only teaches necessary business knowledge but also challenges students to enhance their leadership and communication skills. The more than 50 M.B.A. faculty members bring diverse perspectives to the classroom. Many have real-world experience; they also have earned recognition for excellence in both teaching and research at local, state, and national levels. In addition to the M.B.A., the Barton School also offers M.S. in business, Master of Professional Accountancy, and M.A. in economics degree programs. New to the Barton School offerings are the Executive M.B.A. program, offered exclusively to high-potential professionals, and the M.B.A./M.S.N., a dual-degree program that combines nursing and business administration. A broad range of programs and convenient course scheduling options signify the W. Frank Barton School's commitment to meeting the needs of today's graduate business student

GRADUATE BUSINESS PROGRAMS
Master of Business Administration (MBA) Full-time, part-time; 30 total credits required; 12 months to 6 years to complete program.

Master of Science in Business (MS) Full-time, part-time; 31-62 total credits required; 15 months to 6 years to complete program. Concentrations in entrepreneurship, finance, human resources, management, marketing.

Master of Science in Business/Master of Science in Nursing (MBA/MS) Full-time, part-time; 63 total credits required; 3 to 6 years to complete program.

Master of Public Accounting (MPA) Full-time, part-time; 31 total credits required; 12 months to 6 years to complete program. Concentration in accounting.

Master of Arts in Economics (MA) Full-time, part-time; 30-39 total credits required; 18 months to 6 years to complete program. Concentration in managerial economics.

Executive MBA (MBA) Part-time; 36 total credits required; 22 months to complete program.

ADMISSION
Applications For fall 1997 there were 239 applications for admission. Of those applying, 135 were accepted. Of those accepted, 54 enrolled.

Application Requirements GMAT score, application form, application fee, bachelor's degree, minimum GPA: 2.75, college transcript(s), computer experience: word processing, spreadsheet, database.

Recommended for Application Interview, resume, work experience.

Application Deadline 7/1 for fall, 11/1 for spring, 4/30 for fall (international), 8/31 for spring (international). Application fee: $25, $40 (international). Deferred entrance is available.

ACADEMICS
Faculty Full-time 50; part-time 3.

Teaching Methodologies Case study, computer analysis, computer simulations, experiential learning, group discussion, lecture, research, seminars by members of the business community, simulations, student presentations, study groups, team projects.

Technology 500 on-campus computer terminals/PCs are available for student use and are linked by a campus-wide network. The network has full access to the Internet. Students are not required to have their own PC.

Special Opportunities Advanced credit may be earned through transfer of credits from another institution. An internship program is available.

FINANCES
Costs for 1997–98 Tuition: $112 per credit (resident); $332 per credit (nonresident). Cost varies by academic program, reciprocity agreements. Average 1997–98 room and board costs were $3600 per academic year (on campus) and $4000 per academic year (off campus). Room and board costs vary by occupancy (e.g., single, double, triple), type of accommodation, type of meal plan.

Financial Aid Fellowships, teaching assistantships, loans available.

Financial Aid Contact Larry Rector, Director, Office of Career Services, 1845 North Fairmount, Wichita, KS 67260. Phone: 316-978-3430.

FACILITIES

Information Resources Ablah Library; total holdings of 938,817 volumes, 907,837 microforms, 6,319 current periodical subscriptions. CD player(s) available for graduate student use. Access provided to online bibliographic retrieval services and online databases.

INTERNATIONAL STUDENTS

Demographics 23% of students enrolled are international students.

Services and Facilities International student office, international student center, visa services, ESL courses, counseling/support services.

Applying TOEFL: minimum score of 550, proof of adequate funds required. Financial aid is not available to international students.

International Student Contact Mr. John Koppenhaver, Director, Office of International Program, 1845 North Fairmount, Wichita, KS 67260-0088. Phone: 316-689-3730; E-mail: koppenha@twsuvm.uc.twsu.edu

PLACEMENT

Services include alumni network, career counseling/planning, career fairs, career library, career placement, electronic job bank, job interviews arranged, job search course, resume referral to employers, and resume preparation. In 1996–97, 40 organizations participated in on-campus recruiting; 40 on-campus interviews were conducted.

Employment Of 1996–97 graduates, 86% were employed within three months of graduation; the average starting salary was $37,000. Types of employment entered: accounting, banking, communications, computer-related, education, engineering, finance, financial services, government, health services, high technology, human resources, insurance, management, manufacturing, marketing, nonprofit, petrochemical, pharmaceutical, real estate, retail, service industry, telecommunications, utilities.

Business Program(s) URL: http://www.mrc.twsu.edu/gradinfo

Program Contact: Dr. Donald Christensen, Director, Graduate Studies in Business, 1845 North Fairmount, Wichita, KS 67260. Phone: 316-978-3230; Fax: 316-978-3767; E-mail: christen@twsuvm.uc.twsu.edu

KENTUCKY

Bellarmine College

W. Fielding Rubel School of Business

Louisville, Kentucky

OVERVIEW

Bellarmine College is an independent-religious, coed, comprehensive institution. Enrollment: 2,411 graduate, professional, and undergraduate students; 12 full-time matriculated graduate/professional students; 533 part-time matriculated graduate/professional students. Founded: 1950. The graduate business unit is in a suburban setting and is on a semester calendar.

HIGHLIGHTS

Enrollment Profile

Full-time: 8	International: 2%
Part-time: 277	Women: 38%
Total: 285	Minorities: 2%
Average Age: 28	Average Class Size: 20
Fall 1997 Average GPA: 3.15	Fall 1997 Average GMAT: 495

Costs
Full-time tuition: N/R
Part-time tuition: $375 per credit hour

GRADUATE BUSINESS PROGRAMS

Weeknight MBA (MBA) Full-time, part-time; 40 total credits required; 2.5 to 6 years to complete program.

Executive MBA (MBA) Part-time; 40 total credits required; 17 months to complete program.

Weekend MBA (MBA) Full-time, part-time; 40 total credits required; 22 months to complete program.

ADMISSION

Application Requirements Application form, application fee, bachelor's degree, essay, minimum GPA, 2 letters of recommendation, personal statement, resume, college transcript(s).

Recommended for Application GMAT score accepted, work experience, computer experience.

Application Deadline Applications processed on a rolling/continuous basis for both domestic and international students. Application fee: $25. Deferred entrance is available.

ACADEMICS

Teaching Methodologies Case study, computer analysis, faculty seminars, field projects, lecture, research, seminars by members of the business community, student presentations, study groups, team projects.

Technology 100 on-campus computer terminals/PCs are available for student use and are linked by a campus-wide network. The network has full access to the Internet. Students are required to have their own PC.

Special Opportunities Advanced credit may be earned through credit by examination, credit for experience, credit for military training programs, credit for business training programs, transfer of credits from another institution. International exchange programs in Czech Republic, France, Nicaragua, Russia. An internship program is available.

FINANCES

Costs for 1997–98 Tuition: $375 per credit hour.

Financial Aid Work study available. Financial aid is available to part-time students. Application Deadline: 7/1.

Financial Aid Contact Mr. David Wuinee, Director of Financial Aid, 2001 Newburg Road, Louisville, KY 40205-0671. Phone: 502-452-8131; Fax: 502-452-8002.

FACILITIES

Information Resources W. L. Brown Library; total holdings of 125,000 volumes, 1,880 current periodical subscriptions. CD player(s) available for graduate student use. Access provided to online bibliographic retrieval services.

INTERNATIONAL STUDENTS

Demographics 2% of students enrolled are international students.

Services and Facilities Counseling/support services.

Applying TOEFL, proof of adequate funds required. Financial aid is not available to international students.

International Student Contact Laura Richardson, Director, MBA Programs, 2001 Newburg Road, Louisville, KY 40205-0671. Phone: 502-452-8258; Fax: 502-452-8013.

PLACEMENT

Services include alumni network, career counseling/planning, career fairs, career library, and job interviews arranged. In 1996–97, 30 organizations participated in on-campus recruiting.

Employment Of 1996–97 graduates, 100% were employed within three months of graduation. Types of employment entered: health services, manufacturing, utilities.

Program Contact: Laura Richardson, Director, MBA Programs, 2001 Newburg Road, Louisville, KY 40205-0671. Phone: 502-452-8258; Fax: 502-452-8013.

Brescia College

Master of Science in Management Program

Owensboro, Kentucky

OVERVIEW

Brescia College is an independent-religious, coed, comprehensive institution. Enrollment: 711 graduate, professional, and undergraduate students; full-time matriculated graduate/professional students; 42 part-time matriculated graduate/professional students. Founded: 1950. The graduate business unit is in an urban setting and is on a weekend module calendar.

HIGHLIGHTS

Enrollment Profile

Full-time: 0	International: N/R
Part-time: 42	Women: 55%
Total: 42	Minorities: 2%
Average Age: 38	Average Class Size: 17
Fall 1997 Average GPA: 3.04	Fall 1997 Average GMAT: 463

Costs
Full-time tuition: N/R
Part-time tuition: $150 per credit hour

KENTUCKY

Brescia College (continued)

GRADUATE BUSINESS PROGRAMS
Master of Science in Management (MS) Part-time; 30 total credits required; 21 months to 3 years to complete program.

ADMISSION
Applications For fall 1997 there were 27 applications for admission. Of those applying, 21 were accepted. Of those accepted, 20 enrolled.

Application Requirements Application form, application fee, bachelor's degree, resume, college transcript(s).

Recommended for Application GMAT score accepted, interview, work experience, computer experience: computer literacy.

Application Deadline Applications processed on a rolling/continuous basis for both domestic and international students. Application fee: $35. Deferred entrance is available.

ACADEMICS
Faculty Full-time 5; part-time 1.

Teaching Methodologies Case study, computer-aided instruction, computer analysis, computer simulations, experiential learning, field projects, group discussion, lecture, role playing, simulations, student presentations, study groups, team projects.

Technology 25 on-campus computer terminals/PCs are available for student use and are linked by a campus-wide network. The network has full access to the Internet. Students are not required to have their own PC.

FINANCES
Costs for 1997–98 Tuition: Part-time: $150 per credit hour. Cost varies by number of credits taken. Fees: Part-time: $40 per year. Average 1997–98 room and board costs were $3684 per academic year.

Financial Aid In 1997–98, 5% of students received some institutionally administered aid in the form of loans. Financial aid is available to part-time students. Application Deadline: 3/15.

Financial Aid Contact Ms. Vivian Pearson, Student Financial Aid Director, 717 Frederica Street, Owensboro, KY 42301-3023. Phone: 502-686-4290 Ext. 290; Fax: 502-686-4266; E-mail: vivianp@brescia.edu

FACILITIES
Information Resources Brescia College Library; total holdings of 85,486 volumes, 65,653 microforms, 1,743 current periodical subscriptions. CD player(s) available for graduate student use.

INTERNATIONAL STUDENTS
Demographics N/R

Services and Facilities International student housing, counseling/support services.

Applying TOEFL: minimum score of 550, proof of adequate funds required. Financial aid is not available to international students.

International Student Contact Dr. Barry McArdle, Dean of Student Development, 717 Frederica Street, Owensboro, KY 42301-3023. Phone: 502-686-4332 Ext. 332; Fax: 502-686-4266; E-mail: barrym@brescia.edu

PLACEMENT
Services include alumni network, career counseling/planning, career placement, electronic job bank, and job interviews arranged.

Employment Of 1996–97 graduates, 99% were employed within three months of graduation.

Business Program(s) URL: http://brescia.edu/msm/intro.htm

Program Contact: Mr. Rick Eber, Director of Admissions, Admissions Office, 717 Frederica Street, Owensboro, KY 42301-3023. Phone: 502-686-4241 Ext. 241, 800-264-1234; Fax: 502-686-4201; E-mail: admissions@brescia.edu

Eastern Kentucky University

College of Business

Richmond, Kentucky

OVERVIEW
Eastern Kentucky University is a state-supported, coed, comprehensive institution. Enrollment: 15,895 graduate, professional, and undergraduate students; 412 full-time matriculated graduate/professional students; 903 part-time matriculated graduate/professional students. Founded: 1906. The graduate business unit is in a small-town setting and is on a semester calendar.

HIGHLIGHTS

Enrollment Profile
Full-time: 29
Part-time: 106
Total: 135
Average Age: 30
Fall 1997 Average GPA: 3.04
International: 7%
Women: 38%
Minorities: 1%
Average Class Size: 28
Fall 1997 Average GMAT: 480

Costs
Full-time tuition: N/R
Part-time tuition: $124 per hour (resident); $344 per hour (nonresident)

GRADUATE BUSINESS PROGRAMS
Master of Business Administration (MBA) Full-time, part-time; 30-48 total credits required; 12 months to 7 years to complete program.

ADMISSION
Applications For fall 1997 there were 60 applications for admission. Of those applying, 60 were accepted. Of those accepted, 51 enrolled.

Application Requirements Application form, bachelor's degree, essay, minimum GPA: 2.5, personal statement, college transcript(s).

Recommended for Application GMAT score accepted: minimum 400.

Application Deadline 7/20 for fall, 11/20 for spring, 5/20 for summer. Deferred entrance is available.

ACADEMICS
Faculty Full-time 53; part-time 7.

Teaching Methodologies Case study, computer analysis, computer simulations, experiential learning, faculty seminars, field projects, group discussion, lecture, research, seminars by members of the business community, simulations, student presentations, study groups, team projects.

Technology 200 on-campus computer terminals/PCs are available for student use and are linked by a campus-wide network. The network has full access to the Internet. Students are not required to have their own PC.

Special Opportunities Advanced credit may be earned through transfer of credits from another institution.

FINANCES
Costs for 1997–98 Tuition: $124 per hour (resident); $344 per hour (nonresident). Cost varies by number of credits taken. Average 1997–98 room and board costs were $5000 per academic year (on campus) and $6000 per academic year (off campus). Room and board costs vary by campus location, occupancy (e.g., single, double, triple), type of accommodation, type of meal plan.

Financial Aid In 1997–98, 7% of students received some institutionally administered aid in the form of research assistantships, teaching assistantships, work study. Financial aid is available to part-time students.

Financial Aid Contact Ms. Susan Luhman, Director, Student Financial Assistance , Coates Box 4A, Richmond, KY 40475-3101. Phone: 606-622-2361; Fax: 606-622-1020.

FACILITIES
Information Resources John Grant Crabbe Library plus 2 additional on-campus libraries; total holdings of 811,067 volumes, 1,151,125 microforms, 4,006 current periodical subscriptions. CD player(s) available for graduate student use. Access provided to online bibliographic retrieval services.

INTERNATIONAL STUDENTS
Demographics 7% of students enrolled are international students [Africa, 12%, Asia, 50%, Europe, 13%, other, 25%].

Services and Facilities International student office, ESL courses, counseling/support services.

Applying TOEFL: minimum score of 550, proof of adequate funds required. Financial aid is available to international students.

International Student Contact Dr. Neil Wright, Director of International Education, Case Annex, Room 181, Richmond, KY 40475-3140. Phone: 606-622-1478; Fax: 606-622-1020.

PLACEMENT
Services include alumni network, career counseling/planning, career fairs, career library, career placement, electronic job bank, job interviews arranged, job search course, resume referral to employers, and resume preparation. In 1996–97, 10 organizations participated in on-campus recruiting; 20 on-campus interviews were conducted.

Employment Of 1996–97 graduates, 90% were employed within three months of graduation. Types of employment entered: accounting, banking, computer-related, consulting, consumer products, education, finance, financial services, government, health services, high technology, hospitality management, information systems/technology, insurance, management, manufacturing, marketing, nonprofit, pharmaceutical, retail, service industry, telecommunications, utilities.

Business Program(s) URL: http://www.cob.eku.edu/mba/

Program Contact: Dr. Jack L. Dyer, MBA Director, 317 Combs Classroom Building, Richmond, KY 40475-3111. Phone: 606-622-1775, 800-465-9191 (KY only); Fax: 606-622-1413; E-mail: cbomba@acs.eku.edu

Morehead State University

College of Business

Morehead, Kentucky

OVERVIEW
Morehead State University is a state-supported, coed, comprehensive institution. Enrollment: 8,208 graduate, professional, and undergraduate students. Founded: 1923. The graduate business unit is in a small-town setting and is on a semester calendar.

HIGHLIGHTS

Enrollment Profile
Full-time: N/R
Part-time: N/R
Total: 202
Average Age: 25
Fall 1997 Average GPA: 3.2
International: N/R
Women: N/R
Minorities: N/R
Average Class Size: 25
Fall 1997 Average GMAT: 489

Costs
Full-time tuition: $2470 per academic year (resident); $6710 per academic year (nonresident)
Part-time tuition: $138 per credit hour (resident); $373 per credit hour (nonresident)

ACBSP – The American Council of Business Schools and Programs accredited

GRADUATE BUSINESS PROGRAMS
Master of Business Administration in Human Resource Management (MBA) Full-time, part-time, distance learning option; 36 total credits required; minimum of 12 months to complete program. Concentrations in management, health care, human resources, banking.

Master of Business Administration in Bank Management (MBA) Full-time, part-time, distance learning option; 36 total credits required; minimum of 12 months to complete program.

Master of Business Administration in Health Care Administration (MBA) Full-time, part-time, distance learning option; 36 total credits required; minimum of 12 months to complete program.

ADMISSION
Application Requirements GMAT score: minimum 400, application form, bachelor's degree, minimum GPA: 2.5, college transcript(s), computer experience: spreadsheet, word processing.

Application Deadline Applications processed on a rolling/continuous basis for both domestic and international students.

ACADEMICS
Faculty Full-time 26; part-time 2.

Teaching Methodologies Case study, computer simulations, group discussion, lecture, student presentations, team projects.

Technology 830 on-campus computer terminals/PCs are available for student use and are linked by a campus-wide network. The network has full access to the Internet. Students are not required to have their own PC.

Special Opportunities Advanced credit may be earned through transfer of credits from another institution.

FINANCES
Costs for 1997–98 Tuition: Full-time: $2470 per year (resident); $6710 per year (nonresident). Part-time: $138 per credit hour (resident); $373 per credit hour (nonresident). Cost varies by campus location. Average 1997–98 room only costs were $1476 per academic year. Room and board costs vary by occupancy (e.g., single, double, triple), type of accommodation.

Financial Aid Research assistantships, teaching assistantships, scholarships, work study available. Application Deadline: 4/1.

Financial Aid Contact Mr. Tim Rhodes, Director of Financial Aid, HM 305, Morehead, KY 40351. Phone: 606-783-2011; Fax: 606-783-2293.

FACILITIES
Information Resources Camden-Carroll Library plus 1 additional on-campus library; total holdings of 400,000 volumes, 650,000 microforms, 2,000 current periodical subscriptions. CD player(s) available for graduate student use. Access provided to online bibliographic retrieval services.

INTERNATIONAL STUDENTS
Demographics N/R

Services and Facilities International student office, counseling/support services, language tutoring.

Applying TOEFL: minimum score of 525 required. Financial aid is available to international students.

International Student Contact Mr. Clement Liew, International Student Coordinator, UPO 330, Morehead, KY 40351. Phone: 606-783-2759.

PLACEMENT
Services include alumni network, career counseling/planning, career fairs, career library, career placement, electronic job bank, job interviews arranged, resume referral to employers, and resume preparation. In 1996–97, 60 organizations participated in on-campus recruiting; 53 on-campus interviews were conducted.

Employment Types of employment entered: accounting, communications, computer-related, education, health services, human resources, information systems/technology, management, retail.

Business Program(s) URL: http://www.morehead-st.edu

Program Contact: Dr. Marc Glasser, Dean, Graduate Studies, University Boulevard, Morehead, KY 40351. Phone: 606-783-2039; Fax: 606-783-5061.

Murray State University

College of Business and Public Affairs

Murray, Kentucky

OVERVIEW
Murray State University is a state-supported, coed, comprehensive institution. Enrollment: 9,000 graduate, professional, and undergraduate students. Founded: 1922. The graduate business unit is in a small-town setting and is on a semester calendar.

HIGHLIGHTS

Enrollment Profile
Full-time: 78
Part-time: 87
Total: 165
Average Age: 31
Fall 1997 Average GPA: 3.1
International: 36%
Women: 44%
Minorities: 17%
Average Class Size: 20
Fall 1997 Average GMAT: 516

Costs
Full-time tuition: $2300 per academic year (resident); $6260 per academic year (nonresident)
Part-time tuition: $116 per hour (resident); $334 per hour (nonresident)

AACSB – The International Association for Management Education accredited

GRADUATE BUSINESS PROGRAMS
Master of Business Administration (MBA) Full-time, part-time, distance learning option; 67 total credits required; 12 months to 8 years to complete program. Concentration in accounting.

Master of Science in Economics (MS) Full-time, part-time; 30 total credits required; 18 months to 8 years to complete program.

Master of Public Administration (MPA) Full-time, part-time, distance learning option; 36 total credits required; 18 months to 8 years to complete program.

ADMISSION
Applications For fall 1997 there were 116 applications for admission. Of those applying, 94 were accepted. Of those accepted, 44 enrolled.

Application Requirements GMAT score, application form, application fee, bachelor's degree, minimum GPA, college transcript(s).

Application Deadline Applications processed on a rolling/continuous basis for both domestic and international students. Application fee: $20. Deferred entrance is available.

ACADEMICS
Faculty Full-time 26.

Teaching Methodologies Case study, computer-aided instruction, computer analysis, computer simulations, group discussion, lecture, research, seminars by members of the business community, simulations, student presentations, team projects.

Technology 200 on-campus computer terminals/PCs are available for student use and are linked by a campus-wide network. The network has full access to the Internet. Students are not required to have their own PC.

Special Opportunities Advanced credit may be earned through transfer of credits from another institution. International exchange programs in Australia, Belize, Finland, France, People's Republic of China, United Kingdom. An internship program is available.

FINANCES

Costs for 1997–98 Tuition: Full-time: $2300 per year (resident); $6260 per year (nonresident). Part-time: $116 per hour (resident); $334 per hour (nonresident). Cost varies by number of credits taken, reciprocity agreements. Fees: $65 per semester (resident); $65 per semester (nonresident). Fees vary by number of credits taken. Average 1997–98 room and board costs were $2360 per academic year. Room and board costs vary by occupancy (e.g., single, double, triple), type of accommodation, type of meal plan.

Financial Aid In 1997–98, 12% of students received some institutionally administered aid in the form of research assistantships, teaching assistantships, scholarships, work study. Application Deadline: 4/1.

Financial Aid Contact Mr. Charles Vinson, Director, Student Financial Aid, PO Box 9, Murray, KY 42071. Phone: 502-762-2596; Fax: 502-762-3050; E-mail: charles.vinson@murraystate.edu

FACILITIES

Information Resources Waterfield Library plus 2 additional on-campus libraries; total holdings of 375,952 volumes, 179,044 microforms, 2,361 current periodical subscriptions. CD player(s) available for graduate student use. Access provided to online bibliographic retrieval services and online databases.

INTERNATIONAL STUDENTS

Demographics 36% of students enrolled are international students [Africa, 3%, Asia, 58%, Central America, 2%, Europe, 27%, other, 10%].

Services and Facilities International student office, international student center, visa services, ESL courses, counseling/support services.

Applying TOEFL: minimum score of 525, proof of adequate funds required. Financial aid is not available to international students.

International Student Contact Ms. Marcie Johnson, Director, Center for International Programs, PO Box 9, Murray, KY 42071. Phone: 502-762-4411; Fax: 502-762-3237; E-mail: marcie.johnson@murraystate.edu

PLACEMENT

Services include alumni network, career counseling/planning, career fairs, career library, career placement, electronic job bank, job interviews arranged, job search course, resume referral to employers, and resume preparation. In 1996–97, 170 organizations participated in on-campus recruiting; 441 on-campus interviews were conducted.

Employment Of 1996–97 graduates, the average starting salary was $30,000. Types of employment entered: accounting, banking, computer-related, finance, financial services, health services, information systems/technology, insurance, management, manufacturing, marketing, retail, service industry, telecommunications.

Program Contact: Ms. LaDonna McCuan, MBA Coordinator, PO Box 9, Murray, KY 42071. Phone: 502-762-6970, 800-272-4678; Fax: 502-762-3482; E-mail: ladonna.mccuan@murraystate.edu

Northern Kentucky University

College of Business

Highland Heights, Kentucky

OVERVIEW

Northern Kentucky University is a state-supported, coed, comprehensive institution. Enrollment: 11,785 graduate, professional, and undergraduate students; 247 full-time matriculated graduate/professional students; 913 part-time matriculated graduate/professional students. Founded: 1968. The graduate business unit is in a suburban setting and is on a semester calendar.

HIGHLIGHTS

Enrollment Profile

Full-time: 10	International: 2%
Part-time: 174	Women: 35%
Total: 184	Minorities: 5%
Average Age: 33	Average Class Size: 20
Fall 1997 Average GPA: 2.99	Fall 1997 Average GMAT: 537

Costs
Full-time tuition: $1150 per academic year (resident); $3130 per academic year (nonresident)
Part-time tuition: $125 per semester hour (resident); $345 per semester hour (nonresident)

AACSB – The International Association for Management Education accredited

GRADUATE BUSINESS PROGRAMS

Master of Business Administration (MBA) Full-time, part-time; 39-51 total credits required; 21 months to 8 years to complete program. Concentrations in finance, management, management information systems, marketing.

Doctor of Jurisprudence/Master of Business Administration (JD/MBA) Full-time, part-time; 106-118 total credits required; seperate admission to the Chase College of Law required; minimum of 2.8 years to complete program.

ADMISSION

Applications For fall 1997 there were 84 applications for admission. Of those applying, 60 were accepted. Of those accepted, 49 enrolled.

Application Requirements GMAT score: minimum 450, application form, application fee, bachelor's degree, minimum GPA: 2.3, college transcript(s).

Recommended for Application Minimum of 2 years of work experience, computer experience.

Application Deadline 8/1 for fall, 12/1 for spring, 5/1 for summer, 6/1 for fall (international), 10/1 for spring (international), 4/1 for summer (international). Application fee: $25. Deferred entrance is available.

ACADEMICS

Faculty Full-time 19; part-time 6.

Teaching Methodologies Case study, group discussion, lecture, student presentations, team projects.

Technology 380 on-campus computer terminals/PCs are available for student use and are linked by a campus-wide network. The network has full access to the Internet. Students are not required to have their own PC.

Special Opportunities Advanced credit may be earned through transfer of credits from another institution.

FINANCES

Costs for 1997–98 Tuition: Full-time: $1150 per semester (resident); $3130 per semester (nonresident). Part-time: $125 per semester hour (resident); $345 per semester hour (nonresident). Cost varies by academic program, reciprocity agreements. Average 1997–98 room and board costs were $6160 per academic year. Room and board costs vary by occupancy (e.g., single, double, triple), type of accommodation, type of meal plan.

Financial Aid Research assistantships, work study, loans available. Financial aid is available to part-time students. Application Deadline: 4/1.

Financial Aid Contact Dr. Peg Griffin, Coordinator of Graduate Programs, Louie B Nunn Drive, Highland Heights, KY 41099. Phone: 606-572-6364; Fax: 606-572-6670; E-mail: griffinp@nku.edu

FACILITIES

Information Resources W. Frank Steely Library plus 1 additional on-campus library; total holdings of 290,643 volumes, 763,443 microforms, 1,561 current periodical subscriptions. CD player(s) available for graduate student use. Access provided to online bibliographic retrieval services and online databases.

INTERNATIONAL STUDENTS

Demographics 2% of students enrolled are international students [Asia, 75%, other, 25%].

Services and Facilities International student office, international student center, visa services, ESL courses, counseling/support services, language tutoring.

Applying TOEFL: minimum score of 550, proof of adequate funds, proof of health/immunizations required. Financial aid is available to international students.

International Student Contact Ms. Sandra Baumgartner, Director, International Student Affairs Office, Louie B Nunn Drive, Highland Heights, KY 41099. Phone: 606-572-6517; Fax: 606-572-5566.

PLACEMENT

Services include career counseling/planning, career fairs, career library, career placement, electronic job bank, job interviews arranged, resume referral to employers, and resume preparation.

Employment Types of employment entered: accounting, banking, computer-related, energy, engineering, finance, financial services, information systems/technology, law, management, manufacturing, marketing, utilities.

Business Program(s) URL: http://www.nku.edu/~mbusiness

Program Contact: Ms. Nina Thomas, Assistant Dean/MBA Program Director, College of Business, BEP Center 401, Highland Heights, KY 41099. Phone: 606-572-5165; Fax: 606-572-6177; E-mail: mbusiness@nku.edu

Thomas More College

Crestview Hills, Kentucky

OVERVIEW
Thomas More College is an independent-religious, coed, comprehensive institution. Enrollment: 1,400 graduate, professional, and undergraduate students. Founded: 1921. The graduate business unit is in a suburban setting and is on a continuous calendar.

HIGHLIGHTS

Enrollment Profile
Full-time: 105
Part-time: 0
Total: 105
Average Age: 35
Fall 1997 Average GPA: N/R

International: N/R
Women: N/R
Minorities: N/R
Average Class Size: 14
Fall 1997 Average GMAT: N/R

Costs
Full-time tuition: $6975 per academic year
Part-time tuition: N/R

GRADUATE BUSINESS PROGRAMS
Accelerated MBA (MBA) Full-time; 45 total credits required; 2 years to complete program.

ADMISSION
Application Requirements GMAT score, application form, application fee, bachelor's degree, essay, minimum GPA: 2.5, 3 letters of recommendation, personal statement, resume, college transcript(s), minimum of 2 years of work experience.
Application Deadline Applications processed on a rolling/continuous basis for both domestic and international students. Deferred entrance is available.

ACADEMICS
Faculty Full-time 12; part-time 58.
Teaching Methodologies Case study, computer-aided instruction, computer analysis, computer simulations, field projects, group discussion, lecture, research, role playing, seminars by members of the business community, simulations, student presentations, study groups, team projects.
Technology Computer terminals/PCs are available for student use and are linked by a campus-wide network. The network has full access to the Internet. Students are required to have their own PC.

FINANCES
Costs for 1997–98 Tuition: Full-time: $6975 per year. Fees: Full-time: $850 per academic year.
Financial Aid Contact Suzanne Sewell, Assistant Director of Financial Aid, 2670 Chancellor Drive, Crestview Hills, KY 41017. Phone: 606-341-5800.

FACILITIES
Information Resources Thomas More College Library. CD player(s) available for graduate student use. Access provided to online bibliographic retrieval services.

INTERNATIONAL STUDENTS
Demographics N/R
Services and Facilities International student office, visa services, counseling/support services.
Applying TOEFL: minimum score of 600 required. Financial aid is not available to international students.
International Student Contact Mary Campbell, Foreign Student Advisor, 333 Thomas More Parkway, Crestview Hills, KY 41017-3495. Phone: 606-344-3337.

PLACEMENT
Services include career counseling/planning, resume referral to employers, and resume preparation.
Employment Types of employment entered: accounting, financial services, pharmaceutical, telecommunications.
Business Program(s) URL: http://www.thomasmore.edu

Program Contact: TAP Program Representative, 2670 Chancellor Drive, Crestview Hills, KY 41017. Phone: 606-341-4554.

University of Kentucky

Lexington, Kentucky

OVERVIEW
The University of Kentucky is a state-supported, coed university. Enrollment: 24,171 graduate, professional, and undergraduate students; 4,404 full-time matriculated graduate/professional students; 2,752 part-time matriculated graduate/professional students. Founded: 1865. The graduate business unit is in an urban setting and is on a semester calendar.

HIGHLIGHTS

Enrollment Profile
Full-time: 153
Part-time: 110
Total: 263
Average Age: 28
Fall 1997 Average GPA: 3.2

International: 17%
Women: 40%
Minorities: 9%
Average Class Size: 32
Fall 1997 Average GMAT: 590

Costs
Full-time tuition: $2640 per academic year (resident); $7920 per academic year (nonresident)
Part-time tuition: $150 per credit hour (resident); $430 per credit hour (nonresident)

AACSB – The International Association for Management Education accredited

GRADUATE BUSINESS PROGRAMS
Master of Business Administration (MBA) Full-time, part-time; 36 total credits required; 18 months to 8 years to complete program. Concentrations in accounting, international business, marketing, management information systems, production management.
Master of Business Administration/Doctor of Jurisprudence (MBA/JD) Full-time; 111 total credits required; 4 to 8 years to complete program.
Bachelor of Science in Engineering/Master of Business Administration (BS/MBA) Full-time, part-time; 165 total credits required; 5 to 8 years to complete program.
Master of Science in Accountancy (MS) Full-time, part-time; 30 total credits required; 12 months to 8 years to complete program.
Master of Business Administration/Doctor of Medicine (MBA/MD) Full-time; 204 total credits required; 5 to 8 years to complete program.
Doctor of Pharmacy/Master of Business Administration (PharmD/MBA) Full-time; 148 total credits required; minimum of 4 years to complete program.

ADMISSION
Applications For fall 1997 there were 370 applications for admission. Of those applying, 171 were accepted. Of those accepted, 104 enrolled.
Application Requirements GMAT score: minimum 500, application form, application fee, bachelor's degree, minimum GPA: 2.5, 3 letters of recommendation, personal statement, resume, college transcript(s).
Recommended for Application Work experience, computer experience.
Application Deadline 7/1 for fall, 2/1 for fall (international). Application fee: $30, $35 (international). Deferred entrance is available.

ACADEMICS
Faculty Full-time 74; part-time 1.
Teaching Methodologies Case study, computer simulations, group discussion, lecture, seminars by members of the business community, simulations, student presentations, study groups, team projects.
Technology 150 on-campus computer terminals/PCs are available for student use and are linked by a campus-wide network. The network has full access to the Internet. Students are not required to have their own PC.
Special Opportunities Advanced credit may be earned through credit by examination, transfer of credits from another institution. International exchange programs in Austria, Australia, France, Germany, Russia, United Kingdom.

FINANCES
Costs for 1997–98 Tuition: Full-time: $2640 per year (resident); $7920 per year (nonresident). Part-time: $150 per credit hour (resident); $430 per credit hour (nonresident). Cost varies by academic program, reciprocity agreements. Fees: Full-time: $336 per academic year (resident); $336 per academic year (nonresident). Part-time: $6 per credit hour (resident); $6 per credit hour (nonresident). Average 1997–98 room and board costs were $5834 per academic year (on campus) and $6234 per academic year (off campus). Room and board costs vary by occupancy (e.g., single, double, triple), type of accommodation, type of meal plan.
Financial Aid In 1997–98, 46% of students received some institutionally administered aid in the form of fellowships, research assistantships, teaching

University of Kentucky (continued)

assistantships, scholarships, work study. Financial aid is available to part-time students. Application Deadline: 3/1.

Financial Aid Contact Dr. Michael Tearney, Associate Dean, 237 Gatton College of Business and Economics, Lexington, KY 40506-0034. Phone: 606-257-3592; Fax: 606-257-3293; E-mail: tearney@ukcc.uky.edu

FACILITIES

Information Resources William T. Young Library plus 14 additional on-campus libraries; total holdings of 2,600,000 volumes, 5,500,000 microforms, 26,000 current periodical subscriptions. CD player(s) available for graduate student use. Access provided to online bibliographic retrieval services and online databases.

INTERNATIONAL STUDENTS

Demographics 17% of students enrolled are international students [Asia, 90%, Europe, 7%, South America, 1%, other, 2%].

Services and Facilities International student office, international student center, international student housing, visa services, ESL courses, counseling/support services.

Applying TOEFL: minimum score of 550, TWE: minimum score of 4.5, proof of adequate funds, proof of health/immunizations required. Financial aid is available to international students.

International Student Contact Ms. Carolyn Holmes, International Student Advisor, 204 Bradley Hall—Office of International Affairs, Lexington, KY 40506. Phone: 606-257-4067 Ext. 237; E-mail: holmes@ukcc.uky.edu

PLACEMENT

Services include alumni network, career counseling/planning, career fairs, career library, career placement, electronic job bank, job interviews arranged, job search course, resume referral to employers, and resume preparation. In 1996–97, 128 organizations participated in on-campus recruiting.

Employment Of 1996–97 graduates, 93% were employed within three months of graduation; the average starting salary was $44,769. Types of employment entered: accounting, banking, consulting, finance, government, information systems/technology, marketing, nonprofit, real estate, service industry, transportation.

Business Program(s) URL: http://gatton.gws.uky.edu

Program Contact: Ms. Donna Ballos, Graduate Center, Carol Martin Gatton College of Business and Economics, Lexington, KY 40506-0034. Phone: 606-257-3592; Fax: 606-257-3273.

See full description on page 1086.

University of Louisville

College of Business and Public Administration

Louisville, Kentucky

OVERVIEW

The University of Louisville is a state-supported, coed university. Enrollment: 22,145 graduate, professional, and undergraduate students; 2,772 full-time matriculated graduate/professional students; 1,943 part-time matriculated graduate/professional students. Founded: 1798. The graduate business unit is in an urban setting and is on a semester calendar.

HIGHLIGHTS

Enrollment Profile

Full-time: 105	International: 5%
Part-time: 421	Women: 40%
Total: 526	Minorities: N/R
Average Age: 29	Average Class Size: 35
Fall 1997 Average GPA: 3.3	Fall 1997 Average GMAT: 530

Costs
Full-time tuition: N/R
Part-time tuition: $175 per semester hour (resident); $525 per semester hour (nonresident)

AACSB – The International Association for Management Education accredited

GRADUATE BUSINESS PROGRAMS

Master of Business Administration (MBA) Full-time, part-time; 48 total credits required; 12 months to 6 years to complete program. Concentrations in health care, entrepreneurship.

Master of Engineering/Master of Business Administration (ME/MBA) Full-time, part-time; minimum of 3 years to complete program.

ADMISSION

Application Requirements GMAT score, application form, application fee, bachelor's degree, minimum GPA: 2.75, 2 letters of recommendation, college transcript(s).

Application Deadline Applications processed on a rolling/continuous basis for both domestic and international students. Application fee: $25. Deferred entrance is available.

ACADEMICS

Faculty Full-time 77; part-time 41.

Teaching Methodologies Case study, computer-aided instruction, computer simulations, field projects, group discussion, lecture, research, seminars by members of the business community, simulations, student presentations, study groups, team projects.

Technology 150 on-campus computer terminals/PCs are available for student use and are linked by a campus-wide network. The network has full access to the Internet. Students are required to have their own PC.

Special Opportunities Advanced credit may be earned through transfer of credits from another institution. International exchange program in Germany.

FINANCES

Costs for 1997–98 Tuition: $175 per semester hour (resident); $525 per semester hour (nonresident). Cost varies by number of credits taken, reciprocity agreements. Fees: $8 per semester (resident); $8 per semester (nonresident). Fees vary by number of credits taken, reciprocity agreements. Room and board costs vary by campus location, occupancy (e.g., single, double, triple), type of accommodation, type of meal plan.

Financial Aid In 1997–98, 2% of students received some institutionally administered aid in the form of research assistantships, teaching assistantships.

Financial Aid Contact Financial Aid Office, 2301 South Third Street, Louisville, KY 40292-0001. Phone: 502-852-5511.

FACILITIES

Information Resources Ekstrom Library plus 4 additional on-campus libraries; total holdings of 1,232,945 volumes, 12,263 current periodical subscriptions. CD player(s) available for graduate student use. Access provided to online bibliographic retrieval services.

INTERNATIONAL STUDENTS

Demographics 5% of students enrolled are international students.

Services and Facilities International student office, international student center, international student housing, visa services, ESL courses, counseling/support services.

Applying TOEFL: minimum score of 550, proof of adequate funds, proof of health/immunizations required. Financial aid is not available to international students.

International Student Contact Ms. Sharolyn Pepper, International Student Coordinator, International Center, Louisville, KY 40292. Phone: 502-852-6602.

PLACEMENT

Services include career counseling/planning, career fairs, career library, career placement, job search course, resume referral to employers, and resume preparation. In 1996–97, 70 organizations participated in on-campus recruiting; 300 on-campus interviews were conducted.

Employment Of 1996–97 graduates, 90% were employed within three months of graduation; the average starting salary was $35,000. Types of employment entered: accounting, banking, chemical industry, communications, computer-related, consulting, consumer products, energy, engineering, finance, financial services, health services, hospitality management, human resources, information systems/technology, insurance, international trade, law, management, manufacturing, marketing, media, nonprofit, petrochemical, pharmaceutical, real estate, retail, service industry, telecommunications, transportation, utilities.

Business Program(s) URL: http://www.louisville.edu

Program Contact: Dolores Calebs, Academic Counselor: Graduate Programs, CBPA Student Academic Support Services, Louisville, KY 40292. Phone: 502-852-7439; Fax: 502-852-4721.

See full description on page 1088.

LOUISIANA

Louisiana State University and Agricultural and Mechanical College

E. J. Ourso College of Business Administration

Baton Rouge, Louisiana

OVERVIEW

Louisiana State University and Agricultural and Mechanical College is a state-supported, coed university. Enrollment: 28,000 graduate, professional, and undergraduate students. Founded: 1855. The graduate business unit is in an urban setting and is on a semester calendar.

HIGHLIGHTS

Enrollment Profile

Full-time: 318	International: 13%
Part-time: 219	Women: 35%
Total: 537	Minorities: 12%
Average Age: 30	Average Class Size: 35
Fall 1997 Average GPA: 3.038	Fall 1997 Average GMAT: 590

Costs
Full-time tuition: $2708 per academic year (resident); $6008 per academic year (nonresident)
Part-time tuition: $495 per six hours (resident)

AACSB – The International Association for Management Education accredited

GRADUATE BUSINESS PROGRAMS

Master of Business Administration (MBA) Full-time, part-time; 60 total credits required; 2 to 5 years to complete program. Concentrations in decision sciences, economics, finance, economics, management, marketing, real estate.

Master of Science (MS) Full-time, part-time; 30-36 total credits required; 12 months to 5 years to complete program. Concentrations in accounting, decision sciences, information management, management, marketing, economics, finance.

Master of Public Administration (MPA) Full-time, part-time; 42 total credits required; 2 to 5 years to complete program. Concentration in public policy and administration.

ADMISSION

Applications For fall 1997 there were 506 applications for admission. Of those applying, 202 were accepted.

Application Requirements GMAT score, application form, application fee, bachelor's degree, essay, minimum GPA, interview, 3 letters of recommendation, personal statement, college transcript(s).

Recommended for Application Resume, work experience, computer experience.

Application Deadline Applications processed on a rolling/continuous basis for domestic students only. 5/15 for fall (international). Application fee: $25.

ACADEMICS

Faculty Full-time 108; part-time 2.

Teaching Methodologies Case study, computer-aided instruction, computer analysis, computer simulations, group discussion, lecture, role playing, seminars by members of the business community, student presentations, team projects.

Technology 100 on-campus computer terminals/PCs are available for student use and are linked by a campus-wide network. The network has full access to the Internet. Students are not required to have their own PC.

Special Opportunities Advanced credit may be earned through credit by examination, transfer of credits from another institution. An internship program is available.

FINANCES

Costs for 1997–98 Tuition: Full-time: $2708 per year (resident); $6008 per year (nonresident). Part-time: $495 per six hours (resident). Cost varies by number of credits taken. Average 1997–98 room only costs were $5000 per academic year (off campus).

Financial Aid In 1997–98, 38% of students received some institutionally administered aid in the form of fellowships, research assistantships, teaching assistantships, work study, loans.

Financial Aid Contact Student Aid and Scholarships, 202 Himes Hall, Baton Rouge, LA 70803. Phone: 504-388-3103; Fax: 504-388-6300.

FACILITIES

Information Resources Troy H. Middleton Library plus 4 additional on-campus libraries; total holdings of 2,778,482 volumes, 4,891,220 microforms, 14,537 current periodical subscriptions. CD player(s) available for graduate student use. Access provided to online bibliographic retrieval services.

INTERNATIONAL STUDENTS

Demographics 13% of students enrolled are international students.

Services and Facilities International student office, international student center, ESL courses, counseling/support services.

Applying TOEFL: minimum score of 550, proof of adequate funds, proof of health/immunizations required. Financial aid is available to international students.

International Student Contact International Student Office, 111 Johnston Hall, Baton Rouge, LA 70803. Phone: 504-388-3191; Fax: 504-388-4820.

PLACEMENT

Services include alumni network, career counseling/planning, career fairs, career placement, job interviews arranged, resume referral to employers, and resume preparation. In 1996–97, 850 organizations participated in on-campus recruiting.

Employment Types of employment entered: accounting, banking, computer-related, consulting, education, energy, finance, financial services, government, health services, hospitality management, information systems/technology, marketing.

Business Program(s) URL: http://www.bus.lsu.edu

Program Contact: Dr. Deb Ghosh, Director, MBA Programs, Office of Graduate Studies, College of Business Administration, Baton Rouge, LA 70803-6302. Phone: 504-388-8867; Fax: 504-388-5256; E-mail: busmba@lsu.edu

Louisiana State University in Shreveport

College of Business Administration

Shreveport, Louisiana

OVERVIEW

Louisiana State University in Shreveport is a state-supported, coed, comprehensive institution. Enrollment: 4,237 graduate, professional, and undergraduate students; 50 full-time matriculated graduate/professional students; 375 part-time matriculated graduate/professional students. Founded: 1965. The graduate business unit is in a suburban setting and is on a semester calendar.

HIGHLIGHTS

Enrollment Profile

Full-time: 5	International: 1%
Part-time: 130	Women: 48%
Total: 135	Minorities: 15%
Average Age: 32	Average Class Size: 20
Fall 1997 Average GPA: 3.0	Fall 1997 Average GMAT: 490

Costs
Full-time tuition: N/R
Part-time tuition: $150 per hour (resident); $315 per hour (nonresident)

AACSB – The International Association for Management Education accredited

GRADUATE BUSINESS PROGRAMS

Master of Business Administration (MBA) Full-time, part-time; 30-54 total credits required; 12 months to 8 years to complete program.

ADMISSION

Applications For fall 1997 there were 60 applications for admission. Of those applying, 55 were accepted. Of those accepted, 50 enrolled.

Application Requirements GMAT score, application form, application fee, bachelor's degree, essay, minimum GPA: 2.75, college transcript(s).

Recommended for Application Computer experience.

Application Deadline 7/15 for fall, 12/15 for spring, 5/1 for summer, 5/15 for fall (international), 10/15 for spring (international), 3/15 for summer (international). Application fee: $10.

ACADEMICS

Faculty Full-time 27.

Teaching Methodologies Case study, computer simulations, group discussion, lecture, research, student presentations, team projects.

Technology 200 on-campus computer terminals/PCs are available for student use and are linked by a campus-wide network. The network has full access to the Internet. Students are not required to have their own PC.

Special Opportunities Advanced credit may be earned through transfer of credits from another institution. An internship program is available.

FINANCES

Costs for 1997–98 Tuition: $150 per hour (resident); $315 per hour (nonresident). Cost varies by reciprocity agreements. Fees: $50 per semester (resident); $50 per semester (nonresident). Average 1997–98 room only costs were $4800 per academic year (off campus).

Financial Aid Loans available. Financial aid is available to part-time students.

Financial Aid Contact Mr. Ed Chase, Director of Financial Aid, 1 University Place, Shreveport, LA 71115-2399. Phone: 318-797-5363.

FACILITIES

Information Resources Noel Library; total holdings of 225,207 volumes, 229,511 microforms, 2,220 current periodical subscriptions. Access provided to online bibliographic retrieval services and online databases.

INTERNATIONAL STUDENTS

Demographics 1% of students enrolled are international students [Asia, 100%].

Applying TOEFL: minimum score of 550, proof of adequate funds, proof of health/immunizations required. Financial aid is not available to international students.

PLACEMENT

Services include career counseling/planning, career fairs, career library, and career placement. In 1996–97, 20 organizations participated in on-campus recruiting.

Employment Of 1996–97 graduates, 98% were employed within three months of graduation. Types of employment entered: accounting, banking, computer-related, education, energy, engineering, finance, financial services, government, health services, human resources, information systems/technology, insurance, management, manufacturing, marketing, pharmaceutical, real estate, service industry, utilities.

Business Program(s) URL: http://www.lsus.edu/ba/

Program Contact: Dr. Lorraine Krajewski, MBA Director, 1 University Place, Shreveport, LA 71115-2399. Phone: 318-797-5017; Fax: 318-797-5208; E-mail: lkrajews@pilot.lsus.edu

Louisiana Tech University

College of Administration and Business

Ruston, Louisiana

OVERVIEW

Louisiana Tech University is a state-supported, coed university. Enrollment: 9,546 graduate, professional, and undergraduate students; 827 full-time matriculated graduate/professional students; 693 part-time matriculated graduate/professional students. Founded: 1894. The graduate business unit is in a small-town setting and is on a quarter calendar.

HIGHLIGHTS

Enrollment Profile

Full-time: 56	International: 29%
Part-time: 26	Women: 37%
Total: 82	Minorities: 5%
Average Age: 28	Average Class Size: 25
Fall 1997 Average GPA: 3.2	Fall 1997 Average GMAT: 511

Costs
Full-time tuition: $3336 per academic year (resident); $6196 per academic year (nonresident)
Part-time tuition: $574 per 6 hours (resident); $1054 per 6 hours (nonresident)

AACSB – The International Association for Management Education accredited

GRADUATE BUSINESS PROGRAMS

Master of Business Administration (MBA) Full-time, part-time; 33 total credits required; 12 months to 6 years to complete program. Concentrations in accounting, economics, finance, management, marketing, quantitative analysis.

Master of Professional Accountancy (MPA) Full-time; 30 total credits required; 12 months to 6 years to complete program. Concentration in accounting.

ADMISSION

Applications For fall 1997 there were 112 applications for admission. Of those applying, 99 were accepted. Of those accepted, 63 enrolled.

Application Requirements GMAT score: minimum 400, application form, application fee, bachelor's degree, minimum GPA: 2.25, college transcript(s).

Application Deadline 8/1 for fall, 11/1 for winter, 2/1 for spring, 5/1 for summer, 6/1 for fall (international), 9/1 for winter (international), 12/1 for spring (international), 3/1 for summer (international). Application fee: $20, $30 (international). Deferred entrance is available.

ACADEMICS

Faculty Full-time 46; part-time 7.

Teaching Methodologies Case study, computer-aided instruction, computer analysis, computer simulations, field projects, group discussion, lecture, research, student presentations, team projects.

Technology 100 on-campus computer terminals/PCs are available for student use and are linked by a campus-wide network. The network has full access to the Internet. Students are not required to have their own PC.

Special Opportunities Advanced credit may be earned through transfer of credits from another institution.

FINANCES

Costs for 1997–98 Tuition: Full-time: $3336 per year (resident); $6196 per year (nonresident). Part-time: $574 per 6 hours (resident); $1054 per 6 hours (nonresident). Cost varies by academic program, campus location, number of credits taken. Fees: Full-time: $40 per academic year (resident); $40 per academic year (nonresident). Part-time: $40 per quarter (resident); $40 per quarter (nonresident). Fees vary by academic program, campus location. Average 1997–98 room and board costs were $3740 per academic year (on campus) and $6000 per academic year (off campus). Room and board costs vary by occupancy (e.g., single, double, triple), type of accommodation, type of meal plan.

Financial Aid Fellowships, research assistantships, teaching assistantships, grants, loans available. Financial aid is available to part-time students. Application Deadline: 2/1.

Financial Aid Contact Mr. Roger Vick, Director of Financial Aid, PO Box 7925 TS, Ruston, LA 71272. Phone: 318-257-2641; Fax: 318-257-2628.

FACILITIES

Information Resources Prescott Memorial Library; total holdings of 370,867 volumes, 480,006 microforms, 2,615 current periodical subscriptions. CD player(s) available for graduate student use. Access provided to online bibliographic retrieval services and online databases.

INTERNATIONAL STUDENTS

Demographics 29% of students enrolled are international students [Asia, 96%, North America, 4%].

Services and Facilities International student office, international student housing, counseling/support services.

Applying TOEFL: minimum score of 550, proof of adequate funds, proof of health/immunizations required. Financial aid is not available to international students.

International Student Contact Mr. Daniel Erickson, International Student Advisor, PO Box 3177 TS, Ruston, LA 71272. Phone: 318-257-4321; Fax: 318-257-4750; E-mail: daniel@vm.cc.latech.edu

PLACEMENT

Services include career counseling/planning, career fairs, career placement, job interviews arranged, and resume preparation. In 1996–97, 258 organizations participated in on-campus recruiting.

Employment Types of employment entered: accounting, banking, computer-related, finance, financial services, government, manufacturing, marketing, pharmaceutical.

Business Program(s) URL: http://www.cab.latech.edu/graduate.htm

Program Contact: Dr. Gene H. Johnson, Associate Dean of Graduate Affairs and Academic Research, PO Box 10318, Ruston, LA 71272. Phone: 318-257-4528; Fax: 318-257-4253; E-mail: johnson@cab.latech.edu

Loyola University New Orleans

Joseph A. Butt, SJ, College of Business Administration

New Orleans, Louisiana

OVERVIEW

Loyola University New Orleans is an independent-religious, coed, comprehensive institution. Enrollment: 5,499 graduate, professional, and undergraduate students. Founded: 1912. The graduate business unit is in an urban setting and is on a semester calendar.

HIGHLIGHTS

Enrollment Profile

Full-time: 28
Part-time: 55
Total: 183
Average Age: 35
Fall 1997 Average GPA: 3.15

International: 8%
Women: 34%
Minorities: 19%
Average Class Size: 14
Fall 1997 Average GMAT: 540

Costs

Full-time tuition: N/R
Part-time tuition: $450 per credit hour

AACSB – The International Association for Management Education accredited

Degree(s) offered in conjunction with STAT-A-MATRIX Institute for the MQM program

The *Joseph A. Butt, S.J., College of Business Administration (CBA) at Loyola University New Orleans has developed a new M.B.A. curriculum to meet the challenges of the new millennium. The result is an integrated, rigorous curriculum that emphasizes the tools necessary to analyze complex issues, the ability to communicate that analysis, and an understanding that the world is a marketplace. A program highlight is the crucial recognition of the global nature of business. The program's grounding is its ethical underpinning, which is characteristic of Jesuit education.*

The M.B.A. program is flexible. It accommodates students with or without an undergraduate business major and those who prefer to study on a full- or part-time basis. Depending on the student's undergraduate background, the degree can be earned in as few as twelve months of full-time study. Courses are offered in the evening and occasionally on Saturday. For students eager to earn their degree in a shorter time, summer classes are available. Part-time students can finish comfortably in three years.

Loyola's business programs have received the prestigious accreditation of AACSB–The International Association for Management Education by meeting exacting standards on program quality, teaching excellence, continuous improvement, doctoral status of faculty members, state-of-the-art technology, and recognized faculty research.

GRADUATE BUSINESS PROGRAMS

Master of Business Administration (MBA) Full-time, part-time; 33-56 total credits required; 12 months to 7 years to complete program. Concentrations in management, accounting, finance, international business, quality management.

Master of Quality Management (MQM) Part-time; 36 total credits required; 5 years work experience and TOEFL score: minimum 600 required; 3 years to complete program.

Master of Business Administration/Doctor of Jurisprudence (MBA/JD) Full-time, part-time; 105 total credits required; up to 5 years to complete program.

ADMISSION

Applications For fall 1997 there were 52 applications for admission. Of those applying, 31 were accepted. Of those accepted, 21 enrolled.

Application Requirements GMAT score, application form, application fee, bachelor's degree, essay, minimum GPA: 2.75, 2 letters of recommendation, resume, college transcript(s).

Recommended for Application Work experience, computer experience.

Application Deadline Applications processed on a rolling/continuous basis for domestic students only. 6/15 for fall (international), 11/30 for spring (international). Application fee: $20. Deferred entrance is available.

ACADEMICS

Faculty Full-time 30; part-time 9.

Teaching Methodologies Case study, computer simulations, faculty seminars, group discussion, lecture, research, seminars by members of the business community, simulations, student presentations, team projects.

Technology 240 on-campus computer terminals/PCs are available for student use and are linked by a campus-wide network. The network has full access to the Internet. Students are not required to have their own PC.

Special Opportunities Advanced credit may be earned through credit by examination, transfer of credits from another institution. International exchange programs in Belgium, Spain. An internship program is available.

FINANCES

Costs for 1997–98 Tuition: $450 per credit hour. Cost varies by academic program. Fees: $82 per semester. Fees vary by academic program. Average 1997–98 room and board costs were $5850 per academic year. Room and board costs vary by occupancy (e.g., single, double, triple), type of meal plan.

Financial Aid In 1997–98, 24% of students received some institutionally administered aid in the form of research assistantships, work study, loans. Financial aid is available to part-time students. Application Deadline: 5/1.

Financial Aid Contact Dr. E.P. Seybold, Jr., Director of Scholarships and Financial Aid, 6363 Saint Charles Avenue, Box 206, New Orleans, LA 70118. Phone: 504-865-3231; Fax: 504-865-3233.

FACILITIES

Information Resources University Library plus 4 additional on-campus libraries; total holdings of 460,784 volumes, 777,934 microforms, 4,519 current periodical subscriptions. CD player(s) available for graduate student use. Access provided to online bibliographic retrieval services.

INTERNATIONAL STUDENTS

Demographics 8% of students enrolled are international students [Asia, 15%, Central America, 7%, Europe, 21%, North America, 57%].

Services and Facilities International student office, international student center, international student housing, visa services, ESL courses, counseling/support services, language tutoring.

Applying TOEFL: minimum score of 580, proof of adequate funds, proof of health/immunizations required. Financial aid is not available to international students.

International Student Contact Ms. Debbie Danna, Director, International Student Affairs, 6363 Saint Charles Avenue, Box 205, New Orleans, LA 70118. Phone: 504-865-3526; Fax: 504-865-2035; E-mail: danna@beta.loyno.edu

PLACEMENT

Services include alumni network, career counseling/planning, career fairs, career library, career placement, job interviews arranged, resume referral to employers, and resume preparation. In 1996–97, 200 organizations participated in on-campus recruiting.

Employment Of 1996–97 graduates, 96% were employed within three months of graduation; the average starting salary was $43,000. Types of employment entered: accounting, banking, computer-related, consulting, energy, finance, financial services, law, management, marketing, retail.

Business Program(s) URL: http://www.cba.loyno.edu

Program Contact: Dr. Pamela Van Epps, Coordinator of Graduate Programs, 6363 Saint Charles Avenue, New Orleans, LA 70118. Phone: 504-865-3544; Fax: 504-865-3496; E-mail: vanepps@beta.loyno.edu

McNeese State University

College of Business

Lake Charles, Louisiana

OVERVIEW

McNeese State University is a state-supported, coed, comprehensive institution. Enrollment: 7,282 graduate, professional, and undergraduate students; 217 full-time matriculated graduate/professional students; 894 part-time matriculated graduate/professional students. Founded: 1939. The graduate business unit is in a suburban setting and is on a semester calendar.

HIGHLIGHTS

Enrollment Profile

Full-time: 16
Part-time: 85
Total: 101
Average Age: 34
Fall 1997 Average GPA: 2.8

International: 9%
Women: 52%
Minorities: 7%
Average Class Size: 15
Fall 1997 Average GMAT: 530

Costs

Full-time tuition: $1987 per academic year (resident); $3530 per academic year (nonresident)
Part-time tuition: $540 per semester (resident); $882 per semester (nonresident)

AACSB – The International Association for Management Education accredited

GRADUATE BUSINESS PROGRAMS

Master of Business Administration (MBA) Full-time, part-time; 57 total credits required; 18 months to 4 years to complete program.

ADMISSION

Applications For fall 1997 there were 32 applications for admission. Of those applying, 32 were accepted. Of those accepted, 27 enrolled.

Application Requirements Application form, application fee, bachelor's degree, minimum GPA, college transcript(s).

Recommended for Application GMAT score accepted.

Application Deadline Applications processed on a rolling/continuous basis for domestic students only. 5/15 for fall (international), 10/15 for spring (international), 3/15 for summer (international). Application fee: $10, $25 (international). Deferred entrance is available.

ACADEMICS

Faculty Full-time 16.

Teaching Methodologies Case study, computer-aided instruction, computer analysis, computer simulations, group discussion, lecture, research, seminars by members of the business community, student presentations, team projects.

Technology 40 on-campus computer terminals/PCs are available for student use. The network has full access to the Internet. Students are not required to have their own PC.

Special Opportunities Advanced credit may be earned through credit by examination, transfer of credits from another institution.

FINANCES

Costs for 1997–98 Tuition: Full-time: $1987 per year (resident); $3530 per year (nonresident). Part-time: $540 per semester (resident); $882 per semester (nonresident). Cost varies by number of credits taken. Fees vary by number of credits taken. Average 1997–98 room and board costs were $2310 per academic year. Room and board costs vary by occupancy (e.g., single, double, triple), type of accommodation.

Financial Aid Research assistantships, teaching assistantships, work study available. Financial aid is available to part-time students. Application Deadline: 5/1.

Financial Aid Contact Ms. Taina Savoit, Director of Financial Aid, PO Box 93260, Lake Charles, LA 70609. Phone: 318-475-5065; Fax: 318-475-5068.

FACILITIES

Information Resources Lether E. Frazar Memorial Library; total holdings of 257,562 volumes, 1,188,476 microforms, 1,639 current periodical subscriptions. CD player(s) available for graduate student use. Access provided to online bibliographic retrieval services and online databases.

INTERNATIONAL STUDENTS

Demographics 9% of students enrolled are international students [Asia, 5%, Europe, 1%, North America, 91%, South America, 2%, other, 1%].

Services and Facilities Counseling/support services.

Applying TOEFL: minimum score of 525, proof of adequate funds, proof of health/immunizations required. Financial aid is available to international students.

International Student Contact Ms. Kathryn Bond, Admissions Counselor, PO Box 92495 , Lake Charles, LA 70609. Phone: 318-475-5148; Fax: 318-475-5189.

PLACEMENT

Services include career counseling/planning, career fairs, career placement, and job interviews arranged.

Employment Of 1996–97 graduates, 90% were employed within three months of graduation. Types of employment entered: accounting, banking, chemical industry, computer-related, consulting, consumer products, energy, engineering, finance, financial services, government, health services, high technology, human resources, information systems/technology, insurance, management, manufacturing, marketing, nonprofit, petrochemical, retail, service industry, telecommunications, utilities.

Business Program(s) URL: http://www.mcneese.edu/colleges/business/contents.htm

Program Contact: Dr. Bruce Swindle, MBA Program Director, PO Box 91660, Lake Charles, LA 70609. Phone: 318-475-5576, 800-662-3352; Fax: 318-475-5986; E-mail: mbaprog@mail.mcneese.edu

Nicholls State University

College of Business Administration

Thibodaux, Louisiana

OVERVIEW

Nicholls State University is a state-supported, coed, comprehensive institution. Enrollment: 7,184 graduate, professional, and undergraduate students; 115 full-time matriculated graduate/professional students; 662 part-time matriculated graduate/professional students. Founded: 1948. The graduate business unit is in a small-town setting and is on a semester calendar.

HIGHLIGHTS

Enrollment Profile

Full-time: 52	International: 26%
Part-time: 89	Women: 42%
Total: 141	Minorities: 2%
Average Age: 34	Average Class Size: 15
Fall 1997 Average GPA: 3.1	Fall 1997 Average GMAT: 470

Costs

Full-time tuition: $2025 per academic year (resident); $4700 per academic year (nonresident)

Part-time tuition: $90 per credit hour (resident); $250 per credit hour (nonresident)

AACSB – The International Association for Management Education accredited

GRADUATE BUSINESS PROGRAMS

Master of Business Administration (MBA) Full-time, part-time; 33 total credits required; 18 months to 6 years to complete program.

ADMISSION

Applications For fall 1997 there were 71 applications for admission. Of those applying, 68 were accepted. Of those accepted, 37 enrolled.

Application Requirements Application form, application fee, bachelor's degree, minimum GPA: 2.0, college transcript(s).

Recommended for Application GMAT score accepted.

Application Deadline Applications processed on a rolling/continuous basis for both domestic and international students. Application fee: $10, $25 (international).

ACADEMICS

Faculty Full-time 37.

Teaching Methodologies Case study, computer analysis, computer simulations, faculty seminars, field projects, group discussion, lecture, research, role playing, seminars by members of the business community, simulations, student presentations, study groups, team projects.

Technology Computer terminals/PCs are available for student use and are linked by a campus-wide network. The network has full access to the Internet. Students are not required to have their own PC.

Special Opportunities Advanced credit may be earned through transfer of credits from another institution. International exchange program in France.

FINANCES

Costs for 1997–98 Tuition: Full-time: $2025 per year (resident); $4700 per year (nonresident). Part-time: $90 per credit hour (resident); $250 per credit hour (nonresident). Cost varies by number of credits taken. Average 1997–98 room and board costs were $2700 per academic year.

Financial Aid Research assistantships available. Application Deadline: 8/17.

Financial Aid Contact Allison Kleinpeter, Director of Financial Aid, PO Box 2004, Thibodaux, LA 70310. Phone: 504-448-4507; Fax: 504-448-4929; E-mail: fa-aak@nich-nsunet.nich.edu

FACILITIES

Information Resources Allen Ellender Memorial Library plus 1 additional on-campus library; total holdings of 400,000 volumes, 350,000 microforms, 1,777 current periodical subscriptions. CD player(s) available for graduate student use. Access provided to online bibliographic retrieval services.

INTERNATIONAL STUDENTS

Demographics 26% of students enrolled are international students [Africa, 16%, Asia, 33%, Central America, 6%, Europe, 39%, North America, 3%, South America, 3%].

Services and Facilities International student office, ESL courses, counseling/support services.

Applying TOEFL: minimum score of 550, proof of adequate funds, proof of health/immunizations required. Financial aid is not available to international students.

International Student Contact Marilyn Gonzalez, Coordinator, International Student Affairs, PO Box 2004, Thibodaux, LA 70310. Phone: 504-448-4145; Fax: 504-448-4929; E-mail: esap-yip@nich-nsunet.nich.edu

PLACEMENT

Services include career counseling/planning, career fairs, job interviews arranged, resume referral to employers, and resume preparation.

Business Program(s) URL: http://server.nich.edu/ba.html

Program Contact: Dr. J.B. Stroud, Jr., Director of Graduate Studies, PO Box 2015, Thibodaux, LA 70310. Phone: 504-449-7014; Fax: 504-448-4922; E-mail: ba-mba@nich-nsunet.nich.edu

Northeast Louisiana University

College of Business Administration

Monroe, Louisiana

OVERVIEW
Northeast Louisiana University is a state-supported, coed, comprehensive institution. Enrollment: 10,942 graduate, professional, and undergraduate students; 548 full-time matriculated graduate/professional students; 594 part-time matriculated graduate/professional students. Founded: 1931. The graduate business unit is in an urban setting and is on a semester calendar.

HIGHLIGHTS

Enrollment Profile

Full-time: 44	International: 30%
Part-time: 38	Women: 38%
Total: 82	Minorities: 6%
Average Age: 31	Average Class Size: 20
Fall 1997 Average GPA: 3.07	Fall 1997 Average GMAT: 500

Costs
Full-time tuition: $825 per academic year (resident); $3237 per academic year (nonresident)
Part-time tuition: $177 per semester (resident); $177 per semester (nonresident)

AACSB – The International Association for Management Education accredited

Degree(s) offered in conjunction with Hong Kong Shue Yan College

GRADUATE BUSINESS PROGRAMS
Master of Business Administration (MBA) Full-time, part-time; 66 total credits required; 12 months to 6 years to complete program. Concentrations in entrepreneurship, health care.

ADMISSION
Applications For fall 1997 there were 48 applications for admission. Of those applying, 41 were accepted. Of those accepted, 28 enrolled.

Application Requirements Application form, application fee, bachelor's degree, minimum GPA: 2.5, college transcript(s).

Recommended for Application GMAT score accepted: minimum 400, letters of recommendation, personal statement, resume, work experience, computer experience.

Application Deadline 7/1 for fall, 11/1 for spring, 4/1 for summer, 7/1 for fall (international), 11/1 for spring (international), 4/1 for summer (international). Application fee: $15, $25 (international).

ACADEMICS
Faculty Full-time 35.

Teaching Methodologies Case study, computer-aided instruction, computer simulations, group discussion, lecture, research, student presentations, study groups, team projects.

Technology 250 on-campus computer terminals/PCs are available for student use and are linked by a campus-wide network. The network has full access to the Internet. Students are not required to have their own PC.

Special Opportunities Advanced credit may be earned through transfer of credits from another institution.

FINANCES
Costs for 1997–98 Tuition: Full-time: $825 per semester (resident); $3237 per semester (nonresident). Part-time: $177 per semester (resident); $177 per semester (nonresident). Fees: Full-time: $189 per academic year (resident); $189 per academic year (nonresident). Part-time: $63 per semester (resident); $63 per semester (nonresident). Average 1997–98 room and board costs were $2160 per academic year. Room and board costs vary by occupancy (e.g., single, double, triple).

Financial Aid In 1997–98, 45% of students received some institutionally administered aid in the form of research assistantships, teaching assistantships, work study. Application Deadline: 7/1.

Financial Aid Contact Mr. Charles R. Dobrinick, Director of Financial Aid, 700 University Drive, Monroe, LA 71209. Phone: 318-342-5320; Fax: 318-342-1101.

FACILITIES
Information Resources Sandel Library; total holdings of 595,351 volumes, 526,222 microforms, 2,902 current periodical subscriptions. CD player(s) available for graduate student use. Access provided to online bibliographic retrieval services and online databases.

INTERNATIONAL STUDENTS
Demographics 30% of students enrolled are international students.

Services and Facilities International student office, ESL courses, counseling/support services.

Applying TOEFL: minimum score of 600, proof of adequate funds, proof of health/immunizations required. Financial aid is available to international students.

International Student Contact Ms. Telitha Doke, International Student Coordinator, 700 University Drive, Monroe, LA 71209. Phone: 318-342-5223; Fax: 318-342-1101.

PLACEMENT
Services include career counseling/planning, career fairs, career library, career placement, job interviews arranged, resume referral to employers, and resume preparation. In 1996–97, 35 organizations participated in on-campus recruiting.

Employment Types of employment entered: accounting, banking, chemical industry, computer-related, education, engineering, finance, financial services, government, health services, human resources, information systems/technology, insurance, management, manufacturing, marketing, real estate, telecommunications, transportation.

Business Program(s) URL: http://198.79.216.222/

Program Contact: Ms. Jacqueline O'Neal, Director, MBA Program, 700 University Drive, Monroe, LA 71209-0100. Phone: 318-342-1100, 800-372-5127; Fax: 318-342-1101; E-mail: econeal@alpha.nlu.edu

Southeastern Louisiana University

College of Business

Hammond, Louisiana

OVERVIEW
Southeastern Louisiana University is a state-supported, coed, comprehensive institution. Enrollment: 15,330 graduate, professional, and undergraduate students; 361 full-time matriculated graduate/professional students; 1,184 part-time matriculated graduate/professional students. Founded: 1925. The graduate business unit is in a small-town setting and is on a semester calendar.

HIGHLIGHTS

Enrollment Profile

Full-time: 85	International: 25%
Part-time: 76	Women: 35%
Total: 161	Minorities: 12%
Average Age: 29	Average Class Size: 30
Fall 1997 Average GPA: 3.1	Fall 1997 Average GMAT: 475

Costs
Full-time tuition: $1010 per academic year (resident); $2234 per academic year (nonresident)
Part-time tuition: $287 per 3 hours (resident); $287 per 3 hours (nonresident)

AACSB – The International Association for Management Education accredited

GRADUATE BUSINESS PROGRAMS
MBA Program (MBA) Full-time, part-time; 33 total credits required; 12 months to 6 years to complete program. Concentrations in accounting, marketing.

ADMISSION
Application Requirements Application form, application fee, bachelor's degree, minimum GPA: 2.5, college transcript(s).

Recommended for Application GMAT score accepted: minimum 400, computer experience.

Application Deadline 7/15 for fall, 12/1 for spring, 5/1 for summer, 6/1 for fall (international), 10/1 for spring (international), 3/1 for summer (international). Application fee: $10, $25 (international). Deferred entrance is available.

ACADEMICS
Faculty Full-time 22; part-time 2.

Teaching Methodologies Case study, computer-aided instruction, computer analysis, computer simulations, experiential learning, faculty seminars, field projects, group discussion, lecture, research, role playing, seminars by members of the business community, simulations, student presentations, study groups, team projects.

Technology 637 on-campus computer terminals/PCs are available for student use and are linked by a campus-wide network. The network has full access to the Internet. Students are not required to have their own PC.

Special Opportunities Advanced credit may be earned through transfer of credits from another institution. International exchange programs in Austria, France, Germany.

Southeastern Louisiana University (continued)

FINANCES

Costs for 1997–98 Tuition: Full-time: $1010 per semester (resident); $2234 per semester (nonresident). Part-time: $287 per 3 hours (resident); $287 per 3 hours (nonresident). Cost varies by number of credits taken. Fees: Full-time: $87 per academic year (resident); $228 per academic year (nonresident). Part-time: $29 per course (resident); $29 per course (nonresident). Fees vary by number of credits taken. Average 1997–98 room only costs were $1640 per academic year (on campus) and $2700 per academic year (off campus). Room and board costs vary by campus location, occupancy (e.g., single, double, triple), type of accommodation, type of meal plan.

Financial Aid In 1997–98, 21% of students received some institutionally administered aid in the form of research assistantships. Financial aid is available to part-time students. Application Deadline: 5/1.

Financial Aid Contact Mr. Sal Loria, Director, Financial Aid, SLU 505, Hammond, LA 70402. Phone: 504-549-2244; Fax: 504-549-5077; E-mail: xaid1530@selu.edu

FACILITIES

Information Resources Linus A. Sims Memorial Library plus 1 additional on-campus library; total holdings of 323,275 volumes, 606,941 microforms, 2,146 current periodical subscriptions. CD player(s) available for graduate student use. Access provided to online bibliographic retrieval services.

INTERNATIONAL STUDENTS

Demographics 25% of students enrolled are international students.

Services and Facilities International student office, international student center, international student housing, visa services, counseling/support services, international student organization.

Applying TOEFL: minimum score of 525, proof of adequate funds, proof of health/immunizations required. Financial aid is not available to international students.

International Student Contact Dr. Bradley S. O'Hara, Director, MBA Program, SLU 735, Hammond, LA 70402. Phone: 504-549-2146; Fax: 504-549-3977; E-mail: bohara@selu.edu

PLACEMENT

Services include alumni network, career counseling/planning, career fairs, career library, career placement, electronic job bank, job interviews arranged, resume referral to employers, and resume preparation. In 1996–97, 144 organizations participated in on-campus recruiting; 102 on-campus interviews were conducted.

Employment Of 1996–97 graduates, 85% were employed within three months of graduation; the average starting salary was $40,000. Types of employment entered: accounting, banking, communications, computer-related, consulting, education, energy, finance, financial services, government, health services, human resources, information systems/technology, insurance, international trade, management, marketing, petrochemical, pharmaceutical, retail, service industry, telecommunications, utilities.

Business Program(s) URL: http://www.selu.edu/Academics/Business/

Program Contact: Mrs. Edna Smiley, University Records Specialist, Graduate Admissions Office, SLU 752, Hammond, LA 70402. Phone: 504-549-5619, 800-222-7358 (LA only); Fax: 504-549-5632; E-mail: esmiley@selu.edu

Southern University and Agricultural and Mechanical College

College of Business

Baton Rouge, Louisiana

OVERVIEW

Southern University and Agricultural and Mechanical College is a state-supported, comprehensive institution. Enrollment: 9,000 graduate, professional, and undergraduate students.

HIGHLIGHTS

Enrollment Profile

Full-time: N/R	International: N/R
Part-time: N/R	Women: N/R
Total: 15	Minorities: N/R
Average Age: N/R	Average Class Size: N/R
Fall 1997 Average GPA: N/R	Fall 1997 Average GMAT: N/R

Costs
Full-time tuition: $2500 per academic year (resident); $6500 per academic year (nonresident)
Part-time tuition: N/R

AACSB – The International Association for Management Education accredited

GRADUATE BUSINESS PROGRAMS

Master of Public Accounting (MPA) Full-time, part-time; 30 total credits required; minimum of 12 months to complete program.

ADMISSION

Application Requirements GMAT score, application form, bachelor's degree (must be in field of business), minimum GPA, letters of recommendation, resume, college transcript(s).

Application Deadline Applications processed on a rolling/continuous basis for both domestic and international students.

ACADEMICS

Teaching Methodologies Computer-aided instruction, computer analysis, computer simulations, group discussion, lecture, student presentations, team projects.

FINANCES

Costs for 1997–98 Tuition: Full-time: $2500 per year (resident); $6500 per year (nonresident).

Financial Aid Contact Graduate School, Baton Rouge, LA 70813. Phone: 541-771-5642.

INTERNATIONAL STUDENTS

Demographics N/R

Services and Facilities International student office, counseling/support services.

Applying TOEFL required.

PLACEMENT

Services include alumni network, career counseling/planning, career fairs, career library, career placement, job interviews arranged, resume referral to employers, and resume preparation.

Employment Types of employment entered: accounting, finance, financial services, government.

Program Contact: Baton Rouge, LA 70813.

Tulane University

A. B. Freeman School of Business

New Orleans, Louisiana

OVERVIEW

Tulane University is an independent-nonprofit, coed university. Enrollment: 11,362 graduate, professional, and undergraduate students; 4,296 full-time matriculated graduate/professional students; 465 part-time matriculated graduate/professional students. Founded: 1834. The graduate business unit is in an urban setting and is on a semester calendar.

HIGHLIGHTS

Enrollment Profile

Full-time: 206	International: 18%
Part-time: 197	Women: 31%
Total: 403	Minorities: 15%
Average Age: 29	Average Class Size: 48
Fall 1997 Average GPA: 3.4	Fall 1997 Average GMAT: 637

Costs
Full-time tuition: $21,719 per academic year
Part-time tuition: $724 per credit hour

AACSB – The International Association for Management Education accredited

Degree(s) offered in conjunction with Xavier University

GRADUATE BUSINESS PROGRAMS

Master of Business Administration/Doctor of Jurisprudence (MBA/JD) Full-time; 130 total credits required; admittance to Tulane Law School required; 3.8 to 7 years to complete program. Concentrations in accounting, management, entrepreneurship, finance, human resources, international management, management information systems, marketing, operations management, organizational behavior/development, business policy/strategy.

Master of Business Administration/Master of Arts in Latin American Studies (MBA/MA) Full-time; 75 total credits required; admittance to Tulane Master of Arts Program required; 2.3 to 7 years to complete program. Concentrations in accounting, finance, human resources, international management, management, marketing, organizational behavior/development, operations management, management information systems, entrepreneurship, business policy/strategy.

Master of Business Administration (MBA) Full-time; 63 total credits required; 21 months to 7 years to complete program. Concentrations in accounting, entrepreneurship, finance, human resources, international management, management, management information systems, marketing, operations management, organizational behavior/development, business policy/strategy.

Professional MBA (MBA) Part-time; 55 total credits required; 3 to 7 years to complete program. Concentrations in management, accounting, entrepreneurship, finance, human resources, international management, marketing, operations management, organizational behavior/development, management information systems, business policy/strategy.

Executive MBA (MBA) Full-time; 48 total credits required; 19 months to 7 years to complete program. Concentration in management.

Master of Business Administration/Master of Public Health in Health Systems Management (MBA/MPH) Full-time; 93 total credits required; 2.8 to 7 years to complete program. Concentrations in accounting, entrepreneurship, finance, human resources, international management, management, management information systems, marketing, operations management, organizational behavior/development, business policy/strategy.

Master of Accounting (MAcc) Full-time, part-time; 30 total credits required; 9 months to 7 years to complete program. Concentrations in accounting, taxation, management information systems.

ADMISSION

Applications For fall 1997 there were 778 applications for admission. Of those applying, 262 were accepted. Of those accepted, 94 enrolled.

Application Requirements GMAT score, application form, application fee, bachelor's degree, essay, minimum GPA, interview, 2 letters of recommendation, personal statement, resume, college transcript(s).

Recommended for Application Work experience, computer experience.

Application Deadline 5/1 for fall, 4/1 for fall (international). Application fee: $40, $50 (international). Deferred entrance is available.

ACADEMICS

Faculty Full-time 41; part-time 36.

Teaching Methodologies Case study, computer-aided instruction, computer analysis, computer simulations, experiential learning, faculty seminars, field projects, group discussion, lecture, research, role playing, seminars by members of the business community, simulations, student presentations, study groups, team projects.

Technology 236 on-campus computer terminals/PCs are available for student use and are linked by a campus-wide network. The network has full access to the Internet. Students are not required to have their own PC.

Special Opportunities International exchange programs in Argentina, Austria, Brazil, Chile, China, Colombia, Czech Republic, Ecuador, Finland, France, Germany, Hong Kong, Hungary, Mexico, Spain, Taiwan, United Kingdom. An internship program is available.

FINANCES

Costs for 1997–98 Tuition: Full-time: $21,719 per year. Part-time: $724 per credit hour. Cost varies by academic program, campus location, class time (e.g., day/evening), number of credits taken. Fees: Full-time: $1576 per academic year. Part-time: $33 per credit hour. Fees vary by academic program, campus location, class time (e.g., day/evening), number of credits taken. Average 1997–98 room and board costs were $6920 per academic year (on campus) and $6920 per academic year (off campus). Room and board costs vary by campus location, occupancy (e.g., single, double, triple), type of accommodation, type of meal plan.

Financial Aid In 1997–98, 42% of students received some institutionally administered aid in the form of fellowships, research assistantships, teaching assistantships, scholarships, work study. Financial aid is available to part-time students. Application Deadline: 4/15.

Financial Aid Contact Mr. John Silbernagel, Assistant Dean for Admissions and Financial Aid, 7 McAlister Drive, Suite 400, New Orleans, LA 70118-5669.

Phone: 504-865-5410; Fax: 504-865-6770; E-mail: admissions@freeman. tulane.edu

FACILITIES

Information Resources Howard Tilton Library plus 7 additional on-campus libraries; total holdings of 2,001,142 volumes, 2,346,152 microforms, 15,112 current periodical subscriptions. CD player(s) available for graduate student use. Access provided to online bibliographic retrieval services.

INTERNATIONAL STUDENTS

Demographics 18% of students enrolled are international students [Asia, 63%, Central America, 7%, Europe, 9%, North America, 14%, South America, 7%].

Services and Facilities International student office, international student center, international student housing, visa services, ESL courses, counseling/support services.

Applying TOEFL, proof of adequate funds, proof of health/immunizations required. Financial aid is available to international students.

International Student Contact Ms. Janice Hughes, Director, International Programs, 7 McAlister Drive, Suite 451, New Orleans, LA 70118-5669. Phone: 504-865-5438; Fax: 504-862-8770; E-mail: jhughes@freeman.tulane.edu

PLACEMENT

Services include alumni network, career counseling/planning, career fairs, career library, career placement, electronic job bank, job interviews arranged, job search course, resume referral to employers, and resume preparation. In 1996–97, 282 organizations participated in on-campus recruiting; 712 on-campus interviews were conducted.

Employment Of 1996–97 graduates, 96% were employed within three months of graduation; the average starting salary was $60,625. Types of employment entered: accounting, banking, chemical industry, communications, computer-related, consulting, consumer products, education, energy, engineering, finance, financial services, health services, high technology, human resources, information systems/technology, international trade, law, management, manufacturing, marketing, nonprofit, petrochemical, pharmaceutical, real estate, retail, service industry, telecommunications, transportation, utilities.

Business Program(s) URL: http://freeman.tulane.edu

Program Contact: Mr. John Silbernagel, Assistant Dean for Admissions and Financial Aid, 7 McAlister Drive, Suite 400, New Orleans, LA 70118-5669. Phone: 504-865-5410, 800-223-5402; Fax: 504-865-6770; E-mail: admissions@ freeman.tulane.edu

See full description on page 1026.

University of New Orleans

College of Business Administration

New Orleans, Louisiana

OVERVIEW

The University of New Orleans is a state-supported, coed university. Enrollment: 15,833 graduate, professional, and undergraduate students. Founded: 1956. The graduate business unit is in an urban setting and is on a semester calendar.

HIGHLIGHTS

Enrollment Profile

Full-time: 248	International: 13%
Part-time: 558	Women: 44%
Total: 806	Minorities: 16%
Average Age: 28	Average Class Size: 35
Fall 1997 Average GPA: 2.9	Fall 1997 Average GMAT: 500

Costs

Full-time tuition: N/R

Part-time tuition: $373 per 1-3 hours (resident); $1500 per 1-3 hours (nonresident)

AACSB – The International Association for Management Education accredited

GRADUATE BUSINESS PROGRAMS

Master of Business Administration (MBA) Full-time, part-time; 33-54 total credits required; 16 months to 8 years to complete program. Concentrations in finance, international business, marketing, real estate, human resources, travel industry/tourism management, management information systems.

Executive MBA (MBA) Full-time; 48 total credits required; 5 years work experience required; 18 months to complete program.

Master of Science in Accounting (MS) Full-time, part-time; 33-75 total credits required; 2.8 undergraduate GPA required; 16 months to 8 years to complete program.

University of New Orleans (continued)

Master of Science in Accounting/Taxation Option (MS) Full-time, part-time; 33-72 total credits required; 16 months to 8 years to complete program.

Doctor of Philosophy in Financial Economics (PHD) Full-time, part-time; 60 total credits required; 3 to 10 years to complete program.

Master in Health Care Management (MS) Full-time, part-time; 33 total credits required; 18 months to 8 years to complete program.

ADMISSION
Applications For fall 1997 there were 395 applications for admission. Of those applying, 324 were accepted. Of those accepted, 193 enrolled.

Application Requirements GMAT score: minimum 400, application form, application fee, bachelor's degree, minimum GPA: 2.5, college transcript(s).

Recommended for Application Computer experience.

Application Deadline 7/1 for fall, 11/15 for spring, 5/1 for summer, 6/1 for fall (international), 10/1 for spring (international), 3/1 for summer (international). Application fee: $20.

ACADEMICS
Faculty Full-time 71; part-time 10.

Teaching Methodologies Case study, computer analysis, computer simulations, faculty seminars, field projects, group discussion, lecture, research, seminars by members of the business community, student presentations, study groups, team projects.

Technology 250 on-campus computer terminals/PCs are available for student use and are linked by a campus-wide network. The network has full access to the Internet. Students are not required to have their own PC.

Special Opportunities Advanced credit may be earned through transfer of credits from another institution. International exchange program in Austria.

FINANCES
Costs for 1997–98 Tuition: $373 per 1-3 hours (resident); $1500 per 1-3 hours (nonresident). Cost varies by academic program, campus location, number of credits taken, reciprocity agreements. Fees vary by academic program, campus location. Average 1997–98 room and board costs were $6525 per academic year (on campus) and $6525 per academic year (off campus). Room and board costs vary by occupancy (e.g., single, double, triple), type of accommodation, type of meal plan.

Financial Aid In 1997–98, 19% of students received some institutionally administered aid in the form of fellowships, research assistantships, teaching assistantships, scholarships, work study, loans. Application Deadline: 3/15.

Financial Aid Contact Darryl Hankel, Director, Student Financial Aid, Student Financial Aid, AD-1005, New Orleans, LA 70148. Phone: 504-280-6603; Fax: 504-280-3973.

FACILITIES
Information Resources Earl K. Long Library plus 1 additional on-campus library, 3,800 current periodical subscriptions. CD player(s) available for graduate student use. Access provided to online bibliographic retrieval services and online databases.

INTERNATIONAL STUDENTS
Demographics 13% of students enrolled are international students [Africa, 25%, Asia, 20%, Australia/New Zealand, 5%, Central America, 10%, Europe, 20%, North America, 5%, South America, 10%, other, 5%].

Services and Facilities International student office, international student center, international student housing, visa services, ESL courses, counseling/support services.

Applying TOEFL: minimum score of 550, proof of adequate funds, proof of health/immunizations required. Financial aid is not available to international students.

International Student Contact Janice M. Thomas, Director of Office of International Students, University of New Orleans, University Center Room 260, Lakefront, New Orleans, LA 70148. Phone: 504-280-6222; Fax: 504-280-3975; E-mail: jmtsa@uno.edu

PLACEMENT
Services include alumni network, career counseling/planning, career fairs, career library, career placement, electronic job bank, job interviews arranged, job search course, resume referral to employers, and resume preparation. In 1996–97, 250 organizations participated in on-campus recruiting; 500 on-campus interviews were conducted.

Employment Of 1996–97 graduates, 95% were employed within three months of graduation; the average starting salary was $32,000. Types of employment entered: accounting, banking, chemical industry, communications, computer-related, consulting, consumer products, education, energy, engineering, finance, financial services, government, health services, high technology, hospitality management, human resources, information systems/technology, insurance, international trade, law, management, manufacturing, marketing, media, mining,

nonprofit, petrochemical, pharmaceutical, real estate, retail, service industry, telecommunications, transportation, utilities.

Business Program(s) URL: http://www.uno.edu/~coba/

Program Contact: Roslyn Sheley, Director of Admissions, Admissions, Room AD-103, Lakefront, New Orleans, LA 70148. Phone: 504-280-7013, 800-256-5866; Fax: 504-280-5522; E-mail: rssad@uno.edu

University of Southwestern Louisiana

Graduate School
Lafayette, Louisiana

OVERVIEW
The University of Southwestern Louisiana is a state-supported, coed university. Enrollment: 16,000 graduate, professional, and undergraduate students. Founded: 1898. The graduate business unit is in an urban setting and is on a semester calendar.

HIGHLIGHTS

Enrollment Profile

Full-time: 56	International: 16%
Part-time: 95	Women: 42%
Total: 151	Minorities: 4%
Average Age: 30	Average Class Size: 35
Fall 1997 Average GPA: 3.1	Fall 1997 Average GMAT: 500

Costs
Full-time tuition: $1100 per academic year (resident); $3500 per academic year (nonresident)
Part-time tuition: $530 per 6 credits (resident); $1695 per 6 credits (nonresident)

AACSB – The International Association for Management Education accredited

GRADUATE BUSINESS PROGRAMS
Master of Business Administration (MBA) Full-time, part-time; 33-60 total credits required; 12 months to 6 years to complete program. Concentrations in accounting, economics, finance, management, marketing.

Master of Business Administration in Health Care Administration (MBA) Full-time, part-time; 33-60 total credits required; 12 months to 6 years to complete program. Concentrations in accounting, economics, finance, management, marketing, health care.

ADMISSION
Applications For fall 1997 there were 72 applications for admission. Of those applying, 58 were accepted. Of those accepted, 43 enrolled.

Application Requirements Application form, application fee, bachelor's degree, minimum GPA, 3 letters of recommendation, resume, college transcript(s).

Recommended for Application GMAT score accepted, interview, personal statement, work experience, computer experience.

Application Deadline Applications processed on a rolling/continuous basis for both domestic and international students. Application fee: $5, $15 (international). Deferred entrance is available.

ACADEMICS
Faculty Full-time 39.

Teaching Methodologies Case study, computer-aided instruction, computer analysis, faculty seminars, field projects, group discussion, lecture, research, seminars by members of the business community, student presentations, team projects.

Technology 400 on-campus computer terminals/PCs are available for student use and are linked by a campus-wide network. The network has full access to the Internet. Students are not required to have their own PC.

Special Opportunities Advanced credit may be earned through transfer of credits from another institution. An internship program is available.

FINANCES
Costs for 1997–98 Tuition: Full-time: $1100 per semester (resident); $3500 per semester (nonresident). Part-time: $530 per 6 credits (resident); $1695 per 6 credits (nonresident). Cost varies by number of credits taken, reciprocity agreements. Average 1997–98 room and board costs were $1500 per academic year. Room and board costs vary by occupancy (e.g., single, double, triple), type of accommodation, type of meal plan.

Financial Aid In 1997–98, 10% of students received some institutionally administered aid in the form of research assistantships, loans. Application Deadline: 5/1.

Financial Aid Contact Dr. Lewis Pyenson, Dean, Graduate School, USL Box 44610, Lafayette, LA 70504-4610. Phone: 318-482-6965; Fax: 318-482-6195; E-mail: lrp6914@usl.edu

FACILITIES
Information Resources Dupre Library; total holdings of 720,000 volumes, 1,800,000 microforms. CD player(s) available for graduate student use. Access provided to online bibliographic retrieval services.

INTERNATIONAL STUDENTS
Demographics 16% of students enrolled are international students.

Services and Facilities International student office, international student center, international student housing, visa services, counseling/support services.

Applying TOEFL: minimum score of 550, proof of adequate funds, proof of health/immunizations required. Financial aid is available to international students.

International Student Contact Mr. Sekaran Murugaiah, Director, USL Box 43932, Lafayette, LA 70504-3932. Phone: 318-482-6819.

PLACEMENT
Services include alumni network, career counseling/planning, career fairs, career placement, job interviews arranged, and resume preparation. In 1996–97, 80 organizations participated in on-campus recruiting; 880 on-campus interviews were conducted.

Employment Of 1996–97 graduates, 100% were employed within three months of graduation; the average starting salary was $45,000. Types of employment entered: accounting, banking, computer-related, consulting, finance, financial services, government, health services, hospitality management, human resources, information systems/technology, insurance, international trade, management, manufacturing, marketing, nonprofit, petrochemical, pharmaceutical, real estate, retail, service industry, telecommunications.

Business Program(s) URL: http://www.usl.edu

Program Contact: Dr. Lewis Pyenson, Dean, Graduate School, USL Box 44610, Lafayette, LA 70504-4610. Phone: 318-482-6965; Fax: 318-482-6195; E-mail: lrp6914@usl.edu

MAINE

Husson College

Graduate Studies Division

Bangor, Maine

OVERVIEW
Husson College is an independent-nonprofit, coed, comprehensive institution. Enrollment: 1,950 graduate, professional, and undergraduate students. Founded: 1898. The graduate business unit is in a suburban setting and is on a semester calendar.

HIGHLIGHTS
Enrollment Profile
Full-time: 31
Part-time: 197
Total: 228
Average Age: N/R
Fall 1997 Average GPA: N/R

International: 7%
Women: 45%
Minorities: N/R
Average Class Size: 17
Fall 1997 Average GMAT: N/R

Costs
Full-time tuition: N/R
Part-time tuition: $550 per 3-credit course

GRADUATE BUSINESS PROGRAMS
Master of Science in Business (MS) Full-time, part-time; 36 total credits required; 12 months to 5 years to complete program. Concentration in health care.

ADMISSION
Application Requirements GMAT score, application form, application fee, bachelor's degree, essay, minimum GPA, interview, 2 letters of recommendation, personal statement, resume, college transcript(s).

Recommended for Application Minimum of 3 years of work experience.

Application Deadline Applications processed on a rolling/continuous basis for both domestic and international students. Application fee: $25.

ACADEMICS
Teaching Methodologies Case study, computer analysis, experiential learning, faculty seminars, field projects, group discussion, lecture, research, role playing, student presentations, team projects.

Technology 50 on-campus computer terminals/PCs are available for student use.

Special Opportunities Advanced credit may be earned through transfer of credits from another institution. An internship program is available.

FINANCES
Costs for 1997–98 Tuition: $550 per 3-credit course.

Financial Aid Contact Cathy Kimball, Graduate Office, One College Circle, Bangor, ME 04401-2999. Phone: 800-477-4723.

FACILITIES
Information Resources Husson College Library; total holdings of 35,500 volumes. CD player(s) available for graduate student use. Access provided to online bibliographic retrieval services.

INTERNATIONAL STUDENTS
Demographics 7% of students enrolled are international students.

Services and Facilities International student office, counseling/support services.

Applying TOEFL: minimum score of 550 required.

International Student Contact Paul Husson, One College Circle, Bangor, ME 04401-2999. Phone: 207-941-7074.

PLACEMENT
Services include career counseling/planning, career fairs, career library, career placement, job interviews arranged, job search course, resume referral to employers, and resume preparation.

Program Contact: Office of Graduate Studies, 1 College Circle, Bangor, ME 04401. Phone: 207-941-7062, 800-477-4723 (ME only)

Maine Maritime Academy

Department of Graduate Studies and Research

Castine, Maine

OVERVIEW
Maine Maritime Academy is a state-supported, coed, comprehensive institution. Enrollment: 673 graduate, professional, and undergraduate students; 25 full-time matriculated graduate/professional students; 15 part-time matriculated graduate/professional students. Founded: 1941. The graduate business unit is in a small-town setting and is on a 5-week module calendar.

HIGHLIGHTS
Enrollment Profile
Full-time: 24
Part-time: 13
Total: 37
Average Age: 35
Fall 1997 Average GPA: 3.2

International: 35%
Women: 3%
Minorities: N/R
Average Class Size: 12
Fall 1997 Average GMAT: 340

Costs
Full-time tuition: $15,390 per academic year (resident); $15,390 per academic year (nonresident)
Part-time tuition: $342 per credit (resident); $342 per credit (nonresident)

GRADUATE BUSINESS PROGRAMS
Master of Science in Maritime Management (MS) Full-time, part-time; 45 total credits required; 11 months to 5 years to complete program. Concentrations in international logistics, international management, international trade, logistics, management.

Master of Science in Port Management (MS) Full-time, part-time; 45 total credits required; 11 months to 5 years to complete program. Concentrations in international logistics, international trade, logistics, management.

Master of Science in Logistics Management (MS) Full-time, part-time; 45 total credits required; 11 months to 5 years to complete program.

ADMISSION
Applications For fall 1997 there were 10 applications for admission. Of those applying, 6 were accepted. Of those accepted, 6 enrolled.

Application Requirements Application form, application fee, bachelor's degree, 2 letters of recommendation, college transcript(s), computer experience.

Recommended for Application GMAT score accepted, GRE score accepted, essay, interview, personal statement, resume.

Application Deadline Applications processed on a rolling/continuous basis for both domestic and international students. Application fee: $40. Deferred entrance is available.

ACADEMICS
Faculty Full-time 5; part-time 11.

Maine Maritime Academy (continued)

Teaching Methodologies Case study, computer-aided instruction, computer analysis, faculty seminars, field projects, group discussion, lecture, research, seminars by members of the business community, simulations, student presentations, study groups, team projects.

Technology 35 on-campus computer terminals/PCs are available for student use and are linked by a campus-wide network. The network has full access to the Internet. Students are not required to have their own PC.

Special Opportunities Advanced credit may be earned through transfer of credits from another institution. An internship program is available.

FINANCES
Costs for 1997–98 Tuition: Full-time: $15,390 per program (resident); $15,390 per program (nonresident). Part-time: $342 per credit (resident); $342 per credit (nonresident). Fees: Full-time: $360 per academic year (resident); $360 per academic year (nonresident). Part-time: $45 per module (resident); $45 per module (nonresident). Average 1997–98 room only costs were $5750 per academic year (on campus) and $6600 per academic year (off campus).

Financial Aid In 1997–98, 5% of students received some institutionally administered aid in the form of fellowships, research assistantships, teaching assistantships, work study, loans. Financial aid is available to part-time students.

Financial Aid Contact Ms. Gail Ryan, Director of Financial Aid, Castine, ME 04420. Phone: 207-326-2206; Fax: 207-326-2515; E-mail: admissns@ball.mma.edu

FACILITIES
Information Resources Nutting Memorial Library; total holdings of 86,000 volumes, 36,000 microforms, 650 current periodical subscriptions. CD player(s) available for graduate student use. Access provided to online bibliographic retrieval services and online databases.

INTERNATIONAL STUDENTS
Demographics 35% of students enrolled are international students [Asia, 47%, Europe, 8%, North America, 15%, other, 30%].

Services and Facilities International student office, visa services, counseling/support services.

Applying TOEFL, proof of adequate funds, proof of health/immunizations required. Financial aid is not available to international students.

International Student Contact Mr. Harry Kaiserian, Jr., Registrar, Castine, ME 04420. Phone: 207-326-2441; Fax: 207-326-2510.

PLACEMENT
Services include alumni network, career counseling/planning, career library, career placement, job interviews arranged, and resume preparation. In 1996–97, 20 organizations participated in on-campus recruiting; 100 on-campus interviews were conducted.

Employment Of 1996–97 graduates, 100% were employed within three months of graduation. Types of employment entered: computer-related, consulting, energy, engineering, financial services, government, insurance, international trade, management, transportation.

Business Program(s) URL: http://www.mainemaritime.edu

Program Contact: Ms. Carolyn Ulrich, Administrative Assistant, Graduate Studies, Castine, ME 04420. Phone: 207-326-2485, 800-464-6565 (ME only), and/or 800-227-8465 (ME only); Fax: 207-326-2411; E-mail: cjulrich@bell.mma.edu

---

HIGHLIGHTS

Enrollment Profile
Full-time: 0	International: N/R
Part-time: 105	Women: N/R
Total: 105	Minorities: N/R
Average Age: 31	Average Class Size: 20
Fall 1997 Average GPA: 3.2	Fall 1997 Average GMAT: 514

Costs
Full-time tuition: N/R
Part-time tuition: $435 per course

GRADUATE BUSINESS PROGRAMS
Master of Business Administration (MBA) Part-time; 36 total credits required.

Master of Science in Taxation (MS) Part-time; 30 total credits required; minimum of 18 months to complete program. Concentration in taxation.

ADMISSION
Application Requirements Application fee, bachelor's degree, minimum GPA: 3.0, letters of recommendation, personal statement, resume, college transcript(s).

Recommended for Application GMAT score accepted, application form, essay, computer experience.

Application Deadline Applications processed on a rolling/continuous basis for both domestic and international students. Application fee: $40.

ACADEMICS
Faculty Full-time 13; part-time 17.

Teaching Methodologies Case study, computer-aided instruction, computer analysis, faculty seminars, group discussion, lecture, research, student presentations, study groups, team projects.

Technology 50 on-campus computer terminals/PCs are available for student use and are linked by a campus-wide network. The network has full access to the Internet. Students are not required to have their own PC.

Special Opportunities Advanced credit may be earned through transfer of credits from another institution.

FINANCES
Costs for 1997–98 Tuition: Part-time: $435 per course. Cost varies by academic program. Fees vary by academic program.

Financial Aid Financial aid is available to part-time students.

Financial Aid Contact Ms. Lisa Vashon, Director of Financial Aid, 180 West River Road, Waterville, ME 04901. Phone: 207-873-0771 Ext. 323; Fax: 207-877-0114.

FACILITIES
Information Resources Mariner Library; total holdings of 21,500 volumes, 2,744 microforms, 230 current periodical subscriptions. CD player(s) available for graduate student use. Access provided to online bibliographic retrieval services.

INTERNATIONAL STUDENTS
Demographics N/R

Applying TOEFL, proof of health/immunizations required. Financial aid is not available to international students.

PLACEMENT
Services include career counseling/planning, and career placement.

Program Contact: Dr. Robert Whitcomb, Dean, 180 West River Road, Waterville, ME 04901. Phone: 207-877-0102, 800-339-7001; Fax: 207-877-0114.

Thomas College

Programs in Business
Waterville, Maine

OVERVIEW
Thomas College is an independent-nonprofit, coed, comprehensive institution. Enrollment: 1,100 graduate, professional, and undergraduate students; 20 full-time matriculated graduate/professional students; 132 part-time matriculated graduate/professional students. Founded: 1894. The graduate business unit is in a small-town setting and is on a trimester calendar.

University of Maine

The Maine Business School
Orono, Maine

OVERVIEW
The University of Maine is a state-supported, coed university. Enrollment: 8,917 graduate, professional, and undergraduate students; 930 full-time matriculated graduate/professional students; 1,025 part-time matriculated graduate/professional students. Founded: 1865. The graduate business unit is in a small-town setting and is on a semester calendar.

HIGHLIGHTS

Enrollment Profile
Full-time: 30
Part-time: 45
Total: 75
Average Age: 30
Fall 1997 Average GPA: 3.1

International: 15%
Women: 24%
Minorities: 3%
Average Class Size: 15
Fall 1997 Average GMAT: 525

Costs
Full-time tuition: $531 per academic year (nonresident)
Part-time tuition: $188 per semester hour (resident); $531 per semester hour (nonresident)

AACSB – The International Association for Management Education accredited

GRADUATE BUSINESS PROGRAMS
Master of Business Administration (MBA) Full-time, part-time; 30-48 total credits required; 12 months to 6 years to complete program. Concentrations in management, finance, marketing.

ADMISSION
Applications For fall 1997 there were 52 applications for admission. Of those applying, 41 were accepted. Of those accepted, 23 enrolled.

Application Requirements Application form, application fee, bachelor's degree, essay, minimum GPA: 2.6, 3 letters of recommendation, personal statement, college transcript(s).

Recommended for Application GMAT score accepted: minimum 475, resume, computer experience.

Application Deadline 7/15 for fall, 12/1 for spring, 3/15 for summer, 7/15 for fall (international), 12/1 for spring (international), 3/15 for summer (international). Application fee: $50. Deferred entrance is available.

ACADEMICS
Faculty Full-time 14.

Teaching Methodologies Case study, computer analysis, group discussion, lecture, student presentations, team projects.

Technology 200 on-campus computer terminals/PCs are available for student use and are linked by a campus-wide network. The network has full access to the Internet. Students are not required to have their own PC.

Special Opportunities Advanced credit may be earned through transfer of credits from another institution.

FINANCES
Costs for 1997–98 Tuition: Full-time: $531 per semester hour (nonresident). Part-time: $188 per semester hour (resident); $531 per semester hour (nonresident). Cost varies by number of credits taken, reciprocity agreements. Fees: Full-time: $377 per academic year. Part-time: $28 per semester (resident); $28 per semester (nonresident). Fees vary by number of credits taken. Average 1997–98 room and board costs were $4906 per academic year. Room and board costs vary by occupancy (e.g., single, double, triple).

Financial Aid Research assistantships, scholarships, work study, loans available. Application Deadline: 3/1.

Financial Aid Contact Ms. Peggy Crawford, Director of Student Aid, 5781 Wingate Hall, Orono, ME 04469-5781. Phone: 207-581-1324; Fax: 207-587-3261.

FACILITIES
Information Resources Fogler Library; total holdings of 900,000 volumes, 1,250,000 microforms, 5,600 current periodical subscriptions. CD player(s) available for graduate student use. Access provided to online bibliographic retrieval services.

INTERNATIONAL STUDENTS
Demographics 15% of students enrolled are international students [Asia, 55%, Europe, 36%, South America, 9%].

Services and Facilities International student office, international student housing, visa services, ESL courses, counseling/support services.

Applying TOEFL: minimum score of 550, proof of adequate funds, proof of health/immunizations required. Financial aid is available to international students.

International Student Contact Mrs. Karen Boucias, Director of International Programs, 100 Winslow Hall, Orono, ME 04469-5782. Phone: 207-581-2905; Fax: 207-581-2920; E-mail: umintprg@maine.maine.edu

PLACEMENT
Services include alumni network, career counseling/planning, career fairs, career library, career placement, electronic job bank, job interviews arranged, resume referral to employers, and resume preparation. In 1996–97, 100 organizations participated in on-campus recruiting.

Employment Of 1996–97 graduates, 85% were employed within three months of graduation. Types of employment entered: banking, communications, consumer products, education, engineering, financial services, government, health services,

high technology, hospitality management, information systems/technology, manufacturing, marketing, pharmaceutical, real estate, retail, service industry, telecommunications, transportation, utilities.

Business Program(s) URL: http://www.maine.edu/~gibson/umocba.html

Program Contact: Ms. Caroline Dane, Assistant to the Director of the Graduate Program, 5723 Donald P. Corbett Business Building, Orono, ME 04469-5723. Phone: 207-581-1973; Fax: 207-581-1930; E-mail: mba@maine.maine.edu

See full description on page 1090.

University of Southern Maine

School of Business
Portland, Maine

OVERVIEW
The University of Southern Maine is a state-supported, coed, comprehensive institution. Enrollment: 10,230 graduate, professional, and undergraduate students; 951 full-time matriculated graduate/professional students; 975 part-time matriculated graduate/professional students. Founded: 1878. The graduate business unit is in an urban setting and is on a semester calendar.

HIGHLIGHTS

Enrollment Profile
Full-time: 60
Part-time: 58
Total: 118
Average Age: 32
Fall 1997 Average GPA: 3.29

International: 4%
Women: 42%
Minorities: N/R
Average Class Size: 15
Fall 1997 Average GMAT: 550

Costs
Full-time tuition: N/R
Part-time tuition: $173 per credit hour (resident); $477 per credit hour (nonresident)

GRADUATE BUSINESS PROGRAMS
Master of Business Administration (MBA) Full-time, part-time; 30-48 total credits required; 2 to 6 years to complete program. Concentrations in accounting, management, marketing, finance, operations management.

ADMISSION
Applications For fall 1997 there were 56 applications for admission. Of those applying, 44 were accepted. Of those accepted, 34 enrolled.

Application Requirements Application form, application fee, bachelor's degree, essay, minimum GPA, 3 letters of recommendation, resume, college transcript(s).

Recommended for Application GMAT score accepted: minimum 500.

Application Deadline Applications processed on a rolling/continuous basis for both domestic and international students. Application fee: $25. Deferred entrance is available.

ACADEMICS
Faculty Full-time 15; part-time 1.

Teaching Methodologies Case study, computer-aided instruction, computer analysis, computer simulations, experiential learning, group discussion, lecture, simulations, student presentations, team projects.

Technology 280 on-campus computer terminals/PCs are available for student use and are linked by a campus-wide network. The network has full access to the Internet. Students are not required to have their own PC.

Special Opportunities Advanced credit may be earned through transfer of credits from another institution. An internship program is available.

FINANCES
Costs for 1997–98 Tuition: $173 per credit hour (resident); $477 per credit hour (nonresident). Cost varies by academic program. Fees: $12 per credit (resident); $12 per credit (nonresident). Fees vary by number of credits taken. Average 1997–98 room and board costs were $5000 per academic year. Room and board costs vary by campus location, occupancy (e.g., single, double, triple), type of accommodation, type of meal plan.

Financial Aid Research assistantships, teaching assistantships, scholarships, work study, loans available. Financial aid is available to part-time students. Application Deadline: 3/15.

Financial Aid Contact Mr. Keith Dubois, Financial Aid Director, 96 Falmouth Street, PO Box 9300, Portland, ME 04104-9300. Phone: 207-780-5250; Fax: 207-780-4662.

FACILITIES
Information Resources Main library plus 2 additional on-campus libraries; total holdings of 553,977 volumes, 1,140,826 microforms, 8,154 current periodi-

cal subscriptions. CD player(s) available for graduate student use. Access provided to online bibliographic retrieval services.

INTERNATIONAL STUDENTS
Demographics 4% of students enrolled are international students [Asia, 100%].

Services and Facilities International student office, international student housing, visa services, ESL courses, counseling/support services, international student organization.

Applying TOEFL: minimum score of 550, proof of adequate funds, proof of health/immunizations required.

International Student Contact Ms. Domenica Cipollone, Director, International Programs, 96 Falmouth Street, PO Box 9300, Portland, ME 04104-9300. Phone: 207-780-4954; Fax: 207-780-4933; E-mail: domenica@usm.maine.edu

PLACEMENT
Services include career library, and electronic job bank.

Employment Types of employment entered: accounting, banking, finance, management, manufacturing, nonprofit.

Business Program(s) URL: http://www-dept.usm.edu/~cba/

Program Contact: Ms. Alice Cash, MBA Program Manager, PO Box 9300, 96 Falmont Street, Portland, ME 04104-9300. Phone: 207-780-4184, 800-800-4USM Ext. 4184; Fax: 207-780-4662; E-mail: mba@usm.maine.edu

MARYLAND

Bowie State University

Business Programs

Bowie, Maryland

OVERVIEW
Bowie State University is a state-supported, coed, comprehensive institution. Enrollment: 5,167 graduate, professional, and undergraduate students; 347 full-time matriculated graduate/professional students; 1,663 part-time matriculated graduate/professional students. Founded: 1865. The graduate business unit is in a suburban setting and is on a semester calendar.

HIGHLIGHTS

Enrollment Profile

Full-time: 43	International: 9%
Part-time: 154	Women: 49%
Total: 197	Minorities: 88%
Average Age: 34	Average Class Size: 30
Fall 1997 Average GPA: N/R	Fall 1997 Average GMAT: N/R

Costs
Full-time tuition: $1521 per academic year (resident); $2736 per academic year (nonresident)
Part-time tuition: $169 per credit (resident); $169 per credit (nonresident)

Degree(s) offered in conjunction with University of Maryland

GRADUATE BUSINESS PROGRAMS
Master of Science in Management Information Systems (MS) Full-time, part-time, distance learning option; 36 total credits required; up to 7 years to complete program.

Master of Arts in Human Resource Development (MA) Full-time, part-time; 39 total credits required; up to 7 years to complete program.

Master of Arts in Organizational Communications (MA) Full-time, part-time; 36 total credits required; up to 7 years to complete program.

Master of Arts in Administrative Management (MA) Full-time, part-time; 36 total credits required; up to 7 years to complete program. Concentrations in accounting, human resources, public management.

ADMISSION
Application Requirements Application form, application fee, bachelor's degree, minimum GPA: 2.5, college transcript(s).

Recommended for Application Work experience, computer experience.

Application Deadline Applications processed on a rolling/continuous basis for both domestic and international students. Application fee: $35.

ACADEMICS
Faculty Full-time 6; part-time 6.

Teaching Methodologies Case study, computer-aided instruction, computer analysis, computer simulations, experiential learning, faculty seminars, field projects, group discussion, lecture, research, role playing, seminars by members of the business community, student presentations, study groups, team projects.

Technology 150 on-campus computer terminals/PCs are available for student use and are linked by a campus-wide network. The network has full access to the Internet. Students are not required to have their own PC.

Special Opportunities Advanced credit may be earned through transfer of credits from another institution. An internship program is available.

FINANCES
Costs for 1997–98 Tuition: Full-time: $1521 per semester (resident); $2736 per semester (nonresident). Part-time: $169 per credit (resident); $169 per credit (nonresident). Fees: Full-time: $86 per academic year (resident); $86 per academic year (nonresident). Part-time: $86 per semester (resident); $86 per semester (nonresident). Average 1997–98 room and board costs were $4750 per academic year. Room and board costs vary by occupancy (e.g., single, double, triple), type of accommodation, type of meal plan.

Financial Aid Fellowships, grants, scholarships, work study, loans available. Financial aid is available to part-time students. Application Deadline: 4/1.

Financial Aid Contact Mindy Schaffer, Acting Director of Financial Aid, 14000 Jericho Park Road, Bowie, MD 20715-3318. Phone: 301-464-6546; Fax: 301-464-7234; E-mail: mindy.schaffer@bowiestate.edu

FACILITIES
Information Resources Thurgood Marshall Library; total holdings of 208,680 volumes, 633,317 microforms, 1,364 current periodical subscriptions. CD player(s) available for graduate student use. Access provided to online bibliographic retrieval services.

INTERNATIONAL STUDENTS
Demographics 9% of students enrolled are international students.

Services and Facilities International student office, international student center, visa services, counseling/support services.

Applying TOEFL: minimum score of 550, TWE: minimum score of 4, proof of adequate funds required. Financial aid is not available to international students.

International Student Contact Glennis Bacchus, Director of Special Populations, 14000 Jericho Park Road, Bowie, MD 20715-3318. Phone: 301-464-6039; Fax: 301-464-7521; E-mail: glennis.bacchus@bowiestate.edu

PLACEMENT
Services include alumni network, career counseling/planning, career fairs, career library, career placement, job interviews arranged, job search course, resume referral to employers, and resume preparation. In 1996–97, 250 organizations participated in on-campus recruiting; 221 on-campus interviews were conducted.

Business Program(s) URL: http://www.bowiestate.edu

Program Contact: Shawna Acker, Graduate Admissions Coordinator, Office of Enrollment, Recruitment, and Registration, Bowie, MD 20715-3318. Phone: 301-464-6561; Fax: 301-464-7521; E-mail: shawna.acker@bowiestate.edu

College of Notre Dame of Maryland

Center for Graduate Studies

Baltimore, Maryland

OVERVIEW
College of Notre Dame of Maryland is an independent-religious, coed, comprehensive institution. Enrollment: 3,400 graduate, professional, and undergraduate students; 46 full-time matriculated graduate/professional students; 701 part-time matriculated graduate/professional students. Founded: 1873. The graduate business unit is in a suburban setting and is on a 4-1-4 calendar.

HIGHLIGHTS

Enrollment Profile

Full-time: 13	International: 4%
Part-time: 236	Women: 76%
Total: 249	Minorities: 20%
Average Age: 38	Average Class Size: 21
Fall 1997 Average GPA: 3.0	Fall 1997 Average GMAT: N/R

Costs
Full-time tuition: N/R
Part-time tuition: $248 per semester hour

GRADUATE BUSINESS PROGRAMS
Master of Arts in Management (MA) Full-time, part-time; 42 total credits required; 15 months to 7 years to complete program. Concentrations in financial management/planning, human resources, management.

ADMISSION
Applications For fall 1997 there were 60 applications for admission. Of those applying, 54 were accepted. Of those accepted, 51 enrolled.

Application Requirements Application form, application fee, essay, minimum GPA: 2.8, interview, college transcript(s).

Recommended for Application Resume, work experience, computer experience.

Application Deadline Applications processed on a rolling/continuous basis for both domestic and international students. Application fee: $25. Deferred entrance is available.

ACADEMICS
Faculty Full-time 15; part-time 10.

Teaching Methodologies Case study, computer analysis, computer simulations, experiential learning, faculty seminars, field projects, group discussion, lecture, research, role playing, student presentations, study groups, team projects.

Technology 36 on-campus computer terminals/PCs are available for student use and are linked by a campus-wide network. The network has full access to the Internet. Students are not required to have their own PC.

Special Opportunities Advanced credit may be earned through transfer of credits from another institution. An internship program is available.

FINANCES
Costs for 1997–98 Tuition: $248 per semester hour. Fees vary by campus location.

Financial Aid Loans available. Financial aid is available to part-time students. Application Deadline: 5/15.

Financial Aid Contact Ms. Teresa Drzewiecki, Director, Financial Aid, 4701 North Charles Street, Baltimore, MD 21210-2476. E-mail: drzewie@ndm.edu

FACILITIES
Information Resources Loyola/Notre Dame Library; total holdings of 273,336 volumes, 60,555 microforms, 1,600 current periodical subscriptions. CD player(s) available for graduate student use. Access provided to online bibliographic retrieval services and online databases.

INTERNATIONAL STUDENTS
Demographics 4% of students enrolled are international students.

Services and Facilities International student office, international student center, ESL courses, counseling/support services.

Applying TOEFL: minimum score of 550 required. Financial aid is not available to international students.

International Student Contact Sr. Miriam Jansen, Director, International Programs, 4701 North Charles Street, Baltimore, MD 21210-2476. Phone: 410-532-3183; E-mail: mjansen@ndm.edu

PLACEMENT
Services include alumni network, career counseling/planning, career fairs, career library, career placement, electronic job bank, and resume preparation.

Employment Types of employment entered: government, hospitality management, human resources, management, nonprofit.

Program Contact: Ms. Irma Kalkowski, Graduate Admissions Secretary, 4701 North Charles Street, Baltimore, MD 21210-2476. Phone: 410-532-5317; Fax: 410-532-5793; E-mail: gradadm@ndm.edu

Frostburg State University

School of Business
Frostburg, Maryland

OVERVIEW
Frostburg State University is a state-supported, coed, comprehensive institution. Enrollment: 5,199 graduate, professional, and undergraduate students; 154 full-time matriculated graduate/professional students; 740 part-time matriculated graduate/professional students. Founded: 1898. The graduate business unit is in a small-town setting and is on a semester calendar.

HIGHLIGHTS

Enrollment Profile
Full-time: 36
Part-time: 382
Total: 418
Average Age: 34
Fall 1997 Average GPA: N/R
International: 2%
Women: 42%
Minorities: 11%
Average Class Size: 13
Fall 1997 Average GMAT: N/R

Costs
Full-time tuition: $3060 per academic year (resident); $3546 per academic year (nonresident)
Part-time tuition: $170 per hour (resident); $197 per hour (nonresident)

Degree(s) offered in conjunction with University of Maryland at Baltimore

GRADUATE BUSINESS PROGRAMS
Master of Business Administration (MBA) Full-time, part-time; 45 total credits required; 12 months to 6 years to complete program. Concentration in management.

Master of Business Administration/Master of Science in Nursing Administration (MBA/MS) Full-time, part-time, distance learning option; 63 total credits required; 2 to 6 years to complete program. Concentration in management.

ADMISSION
Applications For fall 1997 there were 157 applications for admission. Of those applying, 136 were accepted. Of those accepted, 104 enrolled.

Application Requirements Application form, application fee, bachelor's degree, minimum GPA: 2.5, college transcript(s).

Recommended for Application Work experience, computer experience.

Application Deadline Applications processed on a rolling/continuous basis for both domestic and international students. Application fee: $30. Deferred entrance is available.

ACADEMICS
Faculty Full-time 14; part-time 9.

Teaching Methodologies Case study, experiential learning, field projects, group discussion, lecture, role playing, student presentations, team projects.

Technology 150 on-campus computer terminals/PCs are available for student use and are linked by a campus-wide network. The network has full access to the Internet. Students are not required to have their own PC.

Special Opportunities Advanced credit may be earned through credit by examination, transfer of credits from another institution.

FINANCES
Costs for 1997–98 Tuition: Full-time: $3060 per year (resident); $3546 per year (nonresident). Part-time: $170 per hour (resident); $197 per hour (nonresident). Cost varies by campus location, reciprocity agreements. Fees: Full-time: $60 per academic year (resident); $60 per academic year (nonresident). Part-time: $23 per hour (resident); $23 per hour (nonresident). Fees vary by campus location, reciprocity agreements. Average 1997–98 room and board costs were $2600 per academic year (on campus) and $3450 per academic year (off campus). Room and board costs vary by occupancy (e.g., single, double, triple), type of accommodation, type of meal plan.

Financial Aid In 1997–98, 2% of students received some institutionally administered aid in the form of research assistantships, work study.

Financial Aid Contact Mr. Robert Smith, Assistant Dean for Graduate Admissions and Records, Room 133, Hitchins Administration Building, Frostburg, MD 21532. Phone: 301-687-7053; Fax: 301-687-4597; E-mail: d2pcsmi@fac00.fsu.umd.edu

FACILITIES
Information Resources Lewis Ort Library; total holdings of 453,383 volumes, 154,604 microforms, 1,329 current periodical subscriptions. Access provided to online bibliographic retrieval services.

INTERNATIONAL STUDENTS
Demographics 2% of students enrolled are international students [Africa, 10%, Asia, 22%, Europe, 14%, other, 54%].

Services and Facilities International student office, visa services, counseling/support services.

Applying TOEFL: minimum score of 550, proof of adequate funds, proof of health/immunizations required. Financial aid is available to international students.

International Student Contact Mr. Robert Smith, Assistant Dean for Graduate Admissions and Records, Room 133, Hitchins Administration Building, Frostburg, MD 21532. Phone: 301-687-7053; Fax: 301-687-4597; E-mail: d2pcsmi@fra00.fsu.umd.edu

PLACEMENT
Services include alumni network, career counseling/planning, career fairs, career library, career placement, electronic job bank, and resume preparation.

Frostburg State University (continued)

Business Program(s) URL: http://www.fsu.umd.edu/grad/degree.htm

Program Contact: Dr. David Nicol, Chair, MBA Department, School of Business, Frostburg, MD 21532-1099. Phone: 301-687-4375; Fax: 301-687-4486; E-mail: mba@fre.fsu.umd.edu

Hood College

Department of Economics and Management

Frederick, Maryland

OVERVIEW
Hood College is an independent-religious, primarily women, comprehensive institution. Enrollment: 1,856 graduate, professional, and undergraduate students. Founded: 1893. The graduate business unit is in an urban setting and is on a semester calendar.

HIGHLIGHTS

Enrollment Profile

Full-time: N/R
Part-time: N/R
Total: 131
Average Age: 33
Fall 1997 Average GPA: N/R

International: N/R
Women: N/R
Minorities: N/R
Average Class Size: 20
Fall 1997 Average GMAT: N/R

Costs
Full-time tuition: N/R
Part-time tuition: $270 per credit hour

GRADUATE BUSINESS PROGRAMS
Master of Business Administration (MBA) Full-time, part-time; 36 total credits required; up to 7 years to complete program. Concentrations in finance, accounting, marketing, human resources, public management, information management.

ADMISSION
Application Requirements GMAT score, application form, application fee, bachelor's degree, minimum GPA: 2.5, college transcript(s).
Recommended for Application Letters of recommendation, resume, work experience, computer experience.
Application Deadline Applications processed on a rolling/continuous basis for both domestic and international students. Application fee: $30.

ACADEMICS
Teaching Methodologies Case study, computer-aided instruction, computer analysis, computer simulations, faculty seminars, field projects, group discussion, lecture, research, role playing, seminars by members of the business community, simulations, student presentations, study groups, team projects.

FINANCES
Costs for 1997–98 Tuition: $270 per credit hour.
Financial Aid Loans available. Financial aid is available to part-time students.
Financial Aid Contact Financial Aid Office, 401 Rosemont Avenue, Frederick, MD 21701-8575. Phone: 301-696-3411.

FACILITIES
Information Resources Beneficial-Hodson Library; total holdings of 165,000 volumes, 384,500 microforms, 930 current periodical subscriptions. CD player(s) available for graduate student use. Access provided to online bibliographic retrieval services.

INTERNATIONAL STUDENTS
Demographics N/R

PLACEMENT
Services include career counseling/planning.
Business Program(s) URL: http://www.hood.edu

Program Contact: Admissions Office, 401 Rosemont Avenue, Frederick, MD 21701-8575. Phone: 301-696-3600.

Johns Hopkins University

School of Continuing Studies, Division of Business and Management

Baltimore, Maryland

OVERVIEW
Johns Hopkins University is an independent-nonprofit, coed university. Enrollment: 16,356 graduate, professional, and undergraduate students; 3,111 full-time matriculated graduate/professional students; 8,535 part-time matriculated graduate/professional students. Founded: 1876. The graduate business unit is in an urban setting and is on a semester calendar.

HIGHLIGHTS

Enrollment Profile

Full-time: 43
Part-time: 2,446
Total: 2,489
Average Age: 33
Fall 1997 Average GPA: 3.2

International: 1%
Women: 49%
Minorities: 21%
Average Class Size: 15
Fall 1997 Average GMAT: N/R

Costs
Full-time tuition: N/R
Part-time tuition: $420 per credit hour

GRADUATE BUSINESS PROGRAMS
Master of Science in Business (MS) Part-time; 48 total credits required; 2 to 6 years to complete program. Concentrations in management, management information systems, international business, finance, marketing.
Master of Science in Information and Telecommunications Systems (MS) Part-time; 45 total credits required; 2 to 6 years to complete program.
Master of Science in Marketing (MS) Part-time; 45 total credits required; 2 to 6 years to complete program. Concentration in marketing.
Master of Science in Organization Development and Human Resources (MS) Part-time; 39 total credits required; 2 to 6 years to complete program. Concentrations in organizational behavior/development, human resources.
Master of Science in Real Estate (MS) Part-time; 40 total credits required; 2 to 6 years to complete program. Concentration in real estate.

ADMISSION
Application Requirements Application form, application fee, bachelor's degree, essay, resume, college transcript(s).
Recommended for Application Minimum GPA: 3.0, interview, work experience, computer experience.
Application Deadline Applications processed on a rolling/continuous basis for both domestic and international students. Application fee: $50.

ACADEMICS
Faculty Full-time 12; part-time 267.
Teaching Methodologies Case study, computer-aided instruction, experiential learning, field projects, group discussion, lecture, research, role playing, seminars by members of the business community, simulations, student presentations, study groups, team projects.
Technology Computer terminals/PCs are available for student use and are linked by a campus-wide network. The network has full access to the Internet. Students are not required to have their own PC.
Special Opportunities Advanced credit may be earned through transfer of credits from another institution.

FINANCES
Costs for 1997–98 Tuition: Part-time: $420 per credit hour. Cost varies by campus location. Fees: Part-time: $50 per semester.
Financial Aid Scholarships, work study, loans available. Financial aid is available to part-time students. Application Deadline: 7/1.
Financial Aid Contact Laura Donnelly, Director of Financial Aid, 7150 Gateway Drive, Suite A/B, Columbia, MD 21046-2101. Phone: 410-872-1230; Fax: 410-872-1250.

FACILITIES
Information Resources Eisenhower Library plus 3 additional on-campus libraries; total holdings of 3,224,741 volumes, 2,481,525 microforms, 20,390 current periodical subscriptions. CD player(s) available for graduate student use. Access provided to online bibliographic retrieval services.

INTERNATIONAL STUDENTS
Demographics 1% of students enrolled are international students.
Services and Facilities International student office, visa services.
Applying TOEFL: minimum score of 650, proof of adequate funds required. Financial aid is not available to international students.

International Student Contact Ms. Barbara Shaffer, Director, Student Services, 7150 Gateway Drive, Suite A/B, Columbia, MD 21046-2101. Phone: 410-872-1200.

PLACEMENT
Services include alumni network, career counseling/planning, career fairs, career library, electronic job bank, and resume preparation.

Business Program(s) URL: http://www.scs.jhu.edu/business/

Program Contact: Ms. Barbara Shaffer, Director, Student Services, 7150 Gateway Drive, Suite A/B, Columbia, MD 21046-2101. Phone: 410-872-1200; Fax: 410-872-1250; E-mail: scsinfo@jhu.edu

See full description on page 858.

Loyola College

Sellinger School of Business and Management

Baltimore, Maryland

OVERVIEW
Loyola College is an independent-religious, coed, comprehensive institution. Enrollment: 6,241 graduate, professional, and undergraduate students; 610 full-time matriculated graduate/professional students; 2,347 part-time matriculated graduate/professional students. Founded: 1852. The graduate business unit is in a suburban setting and is on a semester calendar.

HIGHLIGHTS

Enrollment Profile

Full-time: 36	International: 4%
Part-time: 722	Women: 39%
Total: 758	Minorities: 8%
Average Age: 31	Average Class Size: 25
Fall 1997 Average GPA: 3.06	Fall 1997 Average GMAT: 533

Costs
Full-time tuition: $6570 per academic year
Part-time tuition: $365 per credit

AACSB – The International Association for Management Education accredited

GRADUATE BUSINESS PROGRAMS
Master of Business Administration (MBA) Full-time, part-time; 51 total credits required; 12 months to 7 years to complete program. Concentrations in accounting, marketing, economics, finance, international business, management, management information systems, health care.

Executive MBA (MBA) Part-time; 51 total credits required; 21 months to complete program.

MBA Fellows (MBA) Part-time; 51 total credits required; 2.8 years to complete program.

Master of Science in Finance (MSF) Full-time, part-time; 42 total credits required; 12 months to 7 years to complete program.

ADMISSION
Applications For fall 1997 there were 265 applications for admission. Of those applying, 207 were accepted. Of those accepted, 175 enrolled.

Application Requirements Application form, application fee, bachelor's degree, essay, minimum GPA: 2.9, personal statement, resume, college transcript(s), computer experience: spreadsheet, word processing.

Recommended for Application GMAT score accepted, letters of recommendation, minimum of 2 years of work experience.

Application Deadline 7/20 for fall, 11/20 for spring, 4/20 for summer, 5/15 for fall (international), 8/15 for spring (international), 1/15 for summer (international). Application fee: $35. Deferred entrance is available.

ACADEMICS
Faculty Full-time 48; part-time 7.

Teaching Methodologies Case study, computer-aided instruction, computer simulations, field projects, group discussion, lecture, research, seminars by members of the business community, simulations, student presentations, study groups, team projects.

Technology 367 on-campus computer terminals/PCs are available for student use and are linked by a campus-wide network. The network has full access to the Internet. Students are not required to have their own PC.

Special Opportunities Advanced credit may be earned through transfer of credits from another institution. An internship program is available.

FINANCES
Costs for 1997–98 Tuition: Full-time: $6570 per year. Part-time: $365 per credit. Cost varies by academic program, number of credits taken. Fees: Full-

time: $50 per academic year. Part-time: $25 per semester. Fees vary by academic program, number of credits taken.

Financial Aid In 1997–98, 11% of students received some institutionally administered aid in the form of scholarships, loans. Financial aid is available to part-time students.

Financial Aid Contact Mr. Mark Lindenmeyer, Director of Financial Aid, 4501 North Charles Street, Baltimore, MD 21210-2699. Phone: 410-617-2576; Fax: 410-617-5149.

FACILITIES
Information Resources Loyola/Notre Dame Library; total holdings of 349,238 volumes, 435,091 microforms, 2,075 current periodical subscriptions. CD player(s) available for graduate student use. Access provided to online bibliographic retrieval services and online databases.

INTERNATIONAL STUDENTS
Demographics 4% of students enrolled are international students [Asia, 56%, Europe, 26%, South America, 11%, other, 7%].

Services and Facilities International student office, visa services, ESL courses, counseling/support services.

Applying TOEFL: minimum score of 550, proof of adequate funds, proof of health/immunizations required. Financial aid is not available to international students.

International Student Contact Dr. Joseph Healy, Director, International Program, 4501 North Charles Street, Baltimore, MD 21210-2699. Phone: 410-617-2910; Fax: 410-617-2005.

PLACEMENT
Services include alumni network, career counseling/planning, career fairs, career library, career placement, electronic job bank, job interviews arranged, job search course, resume referral to employers, and resume preparation. In 1996–97, 214 organizations participated in on-campus recruiting.

Employment Types of employment entered: accounting, banking, consulting, consumer products, education, energy, engineering, finance, financial services, government, health services, human resources, information systems/technology, manufacturing, marketing, media, nonprofit, pharmaceutical, retail, service industry, telecommunications, transportation, utilities.

Business Program(s) URL: http://www.loyola.edu

Program Contact: Ms. Carol Gebhardt, Director, Graduate Business Programs, 4501 North Charles Street, Baltimore, MD 21210-2699. Phone: 410-617-5067, 800-221-9107 Ext. 5067 (MD only); Fax: 410-617-2005; E-mail: mba@loyola.edu

See full description on page 874.

Morgan State University

School of Business and Management

Baltimore, Maryland

OVERVIEW
Morgan State University is a state-supported, coed university. Enrollment: 5,900 graduate, professional, and undergraduate students; 450 full-time matriculated graduate/professional students; 600 part-time matriculated graduate/professional students. Founded: 1867. The graduate business unit is in an urban setting and is on a semester calendar.

HIGHLIGHTS

Enrollment Profile

Full-time: 63	International: 30%
Part-time: 62	Women: 44%
Total: 125	Minorities: 61%
Average Age: 28	Average Class Size: 12
Fall 1997 Average GPA: N/R	Fall 1997 Average GMAT: N/R

Costs
Full-time tuition: N/R
Part-time tuition: $145 per credit hour (resident); $260 per credit hour (nonresident)

AACSB – The International Association for Management Education accredited

Morgan State University (continued)

GRADUATE BUSINESS PROGRAMS
Master of Business Administration (MBA) Full-time, part-time, distance learning option; 30-60 total credits required; 16 months to 5 years to complete program.

ADMISSION
Applications For fall 1997 there were 137 applications for admission. Of those applying, 105 were accepted. Of those accepted, 77 enrolled.

Application Requirements GMAT score, application form, application fee, bachelor's degree, essay, minimum GPA, 3 letters of recommendation, personal statement, college transcript(s).

Recommended for Application Interview, resume.

Application Deadline Applications processed on a rolling/continuous basis for both domestic and international students. Application fee: $20. Deferred entrance is available.

ACADEMICS
Faculty Full-time 45; part-time 5.

Teaching Methodologies Case study, computer-aided instruction, computer analysis, computer simulations, faculty seminars, field projects, group discussion, lecture, research, role playing, seminars by members of the business community, simulations, student presentations, study groups, team projects.

Technology Computer terminals/PCs are available for student use and are linked by a campus-wide network. The network has full access to the Internet.

Special Opportunities An internship program is available.

FINANCES
Costs for 1997–98 Tuition: $145 per credit hour (resident); $260 per credit hour (nonresident). Cost varies by number of credits taken.

Financial Aid Application Deadline: 4/1.

FACILITIES
Information Resources Soper Library; total holdings of 652,000 volumes, 300,000 microforms, 2,600 current periodical subscriptions. CD player(s) available for graduate student use. Access provided to online bibliographic retrieval services and online databases.

INTERNATIONAL STUDENTS
Demographics 30% of students enrolled are international students [Africa, 5%, Asia, 2%, North America, 90%, other, 3%].

Services and Facilities International student office, international student center, visa services, ESL courses, counseling/support services.

Applying TOEFL: minimum score of 600, proof of adequate funds required.

International Student Contact Mr. Charles Egbe, International Student Services, Carter-Grant Wilson Building 326, Cold Spring Lane Hillen Road, Baltimore, MD 21251. Phone: 410-319-3078; Fax: 410-319-3358.

Program Contact: Dr. Mildred Glover, Assistant Dean and Director of Graduate Program, School of Business and Management, Cold Spring Lane and Hillen Road, Baltimore, MD 21239. Phone: 410-319-3396; Fax: 410-319-3358; E-mail: mba@moac.morgan.edu

Mount Saint Mary's College and Seminary

Graduate Program of Business

Emmitsburg, Maryland

OVERVIEW
Mount Saint Mary's College and Seminary is an independent-religious, coed, comprehensive institution. Enrollment: 1,867 graduate, professional, and undergraduate students. Founded: 1808. The graduate business unit is in a rural setting and is on a semester calendar.

HIGHLIGHTS

Enrollment Profile
Full-time: 20
Part-time: 200
Total: 220
Average Age: 32
Fall 1997 Average GPA: 3.0

International: 9%
Women: 50%
Minorities: N/R
Average Class Size: 17
Fall 1997 Average GMAT: 500

Costs
Full-time tuition: N/R
Part-time tuition: $250 per credit

GRADUATE BUSINESS PROGRAMS
Master of Business Administration (MBA) Full-time, part-time; 37 total credits required; up to 5 years to complete program. Concentrations in finance, marketing, management, human resources, economics, accounting, nonprofit management, international business, health care.

ADMISSION
Application Requirements GMAT score: minimum 400, application form, application fee, bachelor's degree, minimum GPA, letters of recommendation, college transcript(s).

Recommended for Application Work experience, computer experience.

Application Deadline Applications processed on a rolling/continuous basis for both domestic and international students. Application fee: $25.

ACADEMICS
Faculty Full-time 13; part-time 17.

Teaching Methodologies Case study, computer-aided instruction, computer analysis, group discussion, lecture, research, role playing, seminars by members of the business community, student presentations, study groups, team projects.

FINANCES
Costs for 1997–98 Tuition: $250 per credit.

Financial Aid Research assistantships available.

FACILITIES
Information Resources Phillips Library plus 1 additional on-campus library; total holdings of 189,000 volumes, 19,000 microforms, 1,000 current periodical subscriptions. CD player(s) available for graduate student use. Access provided to online bibliographic retrieval services.

INTERNATIONAL STUDENTS
Demographics 9% of students enrolled are international students.

Services and Facilities International student center, international student housing, ESL courses, counseling/support services.

Applying TOEFL: minimum score of 500 required.

Program Contact: Sandy Kauffman, Director, Graduate Program, Mount Saint Mary's College, Emmitsburg, MD 21727-7799. Phone: 301-447-5326 E-mail: kauffman@msmary.edu

Salisbury State University

Franklin P. Perdue School of Business

Salisbury, Maryland

OVERVIEW
Salisbury State University is a state-supported, coed, comprehensive institution. Enrollment: 6,022 graduate, professional, and undergraduate students; 118 full-time matriculated graduate/professional students; 513 part-time matriculated graduate/professional students. Founded: 1925. The graduate business unit is in a small-town setting and is on a semester calendar.

HIGHLIGHTS

Enrollment Profile
Full-time: N/R
Part-time: 92
Total: 116
Average Age: N/R
Fall 1997 Average GPA: 3.12

International: 10%
Women: N/R
Minorities: 10%
Average Class Size: 20
Fall 1997 Average GMAT: 455

Costs
Full-time tuition: N/R
Part-time tuition: $158 per credit hour (resident); $310 per credit hour (nonresident)

AACSB – The International Association for Management Education accredited

GRADUATE BUSINESS PROGRAMS
Master of Business Administration (MBA) Full-time, part-time; 63 total credits required; 12 months to 7 years to complete program. Concentration in accounting.

ADMISSION
Applications For fall 1997 there were 32 applications for admission. Of those applying, 29 were accepted.

Application Requirements GMAT score, application form, application fee, bachelor's degree, minimum GPA: 3.0, 2 letters of recommendation, personal statement, resume, college transcript(s).

Recommended for Application Work experience, computer experience.

Application Deadline 7/15 for fall, 11/15 for winter, 12/15 for spring, 5/1 for summer, 4/1 for fall (international), 9/1 for winter (international), 10/1 for spring (international), 2/1 for summer (international). Application fee: $30.

ACADEMICS
Faculty Full-time 26; part-time 7.

Teaching Methodologies Case study, computer-aided instruction, computer simulations, lecture, student presentations, team projects.

Technology 80 on-campus computer terminals/PCs are available for student use and are linked by a campus-wide network. The network has full access to the Internet. Students are not required to have their own PC.

Special Opportunities Advanced credit may be earned through credit by examination, transfer of credits from another institution. International exchange programs in Chile, France. An internship program is available.

FINANCES
Costs for 1997–98 Tuition: $158 per credit hour (resident); $310 per credit hour (nonresident). Cost varies by academic program. Fees: $3 per credit hour. Fees vary by academic program. Room and board costs vary by occupancy (e.g., single, double, triple), type of accommodation, type of meal plan.

Financial Aid In 1997–98, 4% of students received some institutionally administered aid in the form of research assistantships, loans. Financial aid is available to part-time students.

Financial Aid Contact Director of Financial Aid, 1101 Camden Avenue, Salisbury, MD 21801-6837. Phone: 410-543-6165; Fax: 410-546-6208.

FACILITIES
Information Resources Blackwell Library; total holdings of 235,336 volumes, 587,802 microforms, 1,673 current periodical subscriptions. CD player(s) available for graduate student use. Access provided to online bibliographic retrieval services.

INTERNATIONAL STUDENTS
Demographics 10% of students enrolled are international students [Asia, 50%, Europe, 50%].

Services and Facilities International student office, international student center, international student housing, counseling/support services.

Applying TOEFL: minimum score of 550, proof of adequate funds, proof of health/immunizations required. Financial aid is not available to international students.

International Student Contact Janine Vienna, Global Programs Administrator, 1101 Camden Avenue, Salisbury, MD 21801-6837. Phone: 410-548-3983; Fax: 410-546-6208; E-mail: jmvienna@ssu.edu

PLACEMENT
Services include alumni network, career counseling/planning, career fairs, career placement, electronic job bank, job interviews arranged, resume referral to employers, and resume preparation.

Employment Types of employment entered: banking, consulting, consumer products, financial services, health services, international trade, manufacturing, marketing, service industry.

Business Program(s) URL: http://www.ssu.edu/Schools/Perdue.html

Program Contact: Mr. Wayne Bradford, Director, Graduate Business Program, Perdue School of Business, 1101 Camden Avenue, Salisbury, MD 21801-6837. Phone: 410-546-6215; Fax: 410-546-6208; E-mail: wabradford@ssu.edu

Towson University

College of Graduate and Extended Education
Towson, Maryland

OVERVIEW
Towson University is a state-supported, coed, comprehensive institution. Enrollment: 15,524 graduate, professional, and undergraduate students; 492 full-time matriculated graduate/professional students; 1,289 part-time matriculated graduate/professional students. Founded: 1866. The graduate business unit is in a suburban setting and is on a semester calendar.

HIGHLIGHTS
Enrollment Profile

Full-time: 23	International: 5%
Part-time: 133	Women: 85%
Total: 136	Minorities: 21%
Average Age: 29	Average Class Size: N/R
Fall 1997 Average GPA: N/R	Fall 1997 Average GMAT: N/R

Costs
Full-time tuition: $3132 per academic year (resident); $6120 per academic year (nonresident)
Part-time tuition: $174 per credit hour (resident); $340 per credit hour (nonresident)

AACSB – The International Association for Management Education accredited

Degree(s) offered in conjunction with University of Baltimore

GRADUATE BUSINESS PROGRAMS
Master of Science in Human Resource Development (MS) Full-time, part-time; 36 total credits required; 18 months to 7 years to complete program. Concentration in human resources.

Master of Science in Information Technology (MS) Full-time, part-time; 36 total credits required; 18 months to 7 years to complete program. Concentrations in information management, technology management.

Master of Science in Accountancy (MS) Full-time, part-time; 30 total credits required; GMAT score: minimum 450 required; 18 months to 7 years to complete program. Concentration in accounting.

ADMISSION
Applications For fall 1997 there were 88 applications for admission.

Application Requirements Application form, application fee, bachelor's degree, essay, minimum GPA: 2.75, college transcript(s).

Application Deadline Applications processed on a rolling/continuous basis for both domestic and international students. Application fee: $40, $100 (international). Deferred entrance is available.

ACADEMICS
Faculty Full-time 10.

Teaching Methodologies Case study, experiential learning, faculty seminars, group discussion, lecture, role playing, student presentations, team projects.

Technology The network has full access to the Internet.

Special Opportunities Advanced credit may be earned through transfer of credits from another institution. An internship program is available.

FINANCES
Costs for 1997–98 Tuition: Full-time: $3132 per year (resident); $6120 per year (nonresident). Part-time: $174 per credit hour (resident); $340 per credit hour (nonresident). Cost varies by academic program. Fees: Full-time: $648 per academic year (resident); $648 per academic year (nonresident). Part-time: $36 per credit hour (resident); $36 per credit hour (nonresident). Fees vary by academic program. Average 1997–98 room and board costs were $4280 per academic year. Room and board costs vary by occupancy (e.g., single, double, triple), type of accommodation, type of meal plan.

Financial Aid In 1997–98, 7% of students received some institutionally administered aid in the form of grants, scholarships, work study, loans. Financial aid is available to part-time students. Application Deadline: 4/1.

Financial Aid Contact Ms. Fran Musotto, 8000 York Road, Towson, MD 21252-0001. Phone: 410-830-2501; Fax: 410-830-4675; E-mail: petgrad@towson.edu

FACILITIES
Information Resources Albert S. Cook Library; total holdings of 536,976 volumes, 400,045 microforms, 1,995 current periodical subscriptions. CD player(s) available for graduate student use. Access provided to online bibliographic retrieval services and online databases.

INTERNATIONAL STUDENTS
Demographics 5% of students enrolled are international students.

Services and Facilities International student office, visa services, ESL courses, counseling/support services.

Applying TOEFL: minimum score of 550, proof of adequate funds, proof of health/immunizations required.

International Student Contact Ms. Jan Schmitt, 8000 York Road, Towson, MD 21252-0001. Phone: 410-830-2501; Fax: 410-830-4675; E-mail: petgrad@towson.edu

PLACEMENT
Services include alumni network, career counseling/planning, career fairs, career library, career placement, electronic job bank, job interviews arranged, job search course, resume referral to employers, and resume preparation. In 1996–97, 200 organizations participated in on-campus recruiting.

Towson University (continued)

Business Program(s) URL: http://www.towson.edu

Program Contact: Ms. Fran Musotto, 8000 York Road, Towson, MD 21252-0001. Phone: 410-830-2501, 888-486-9766 (MD only); Fax: 410-830-4675; E-mail: petgrad@towson.edu

University of Baltimore

Robert G. Merrick School of Business

Baltimore, Maryland

OVERVIEW
The University of Baltimore is a state-supported, coed, upper-level institution. Enrollment: 4,306 graduate, professional, and undergraduate students; 1,208 full-time matriculated graduate/professional students; 1,912 part-time matriculated graduate/professional students. Founded: 1925. The graduate business unit is in an urban setting and is on a semester calendar.

HIGHLIGHTS

Enrollment Profile

Full-time: 133	International: 13%
Part-time: 723	Women: 46%
Total: 856	Minorities: 17%
Average Age: 28	Average Class Size: 25
Fall 1997 Average GPA: 3.2	Fall 1997 Average GMAT: 513

Costs
Full-time tuition: $2359 per academic year (resident); $3412 per academic year (nonresident)
Part-time tuition: $239 per credit (resident); $356 per credit (nonresident)

AACSB – The International Association for Management Education accredited

Degree(s) offered in conjunction with University of Maryland

GRADUATE BUSINESS PROGRAMS
Advantage MBA (MBA) Full-time; 48 total credits required; 12 months to complete program. Concentrations in decision sciences, entrepreneurship, finance, international business, marketing, technology management, management information systems, human resources, health care.

Flex MBA (MBA) Full-time, part-time, distance learning option; 30-51 total credits required; 12 months to 7 years to complete program. Concentrations in decision sciences, entrepreneurship, finance, international business, marketing, technology management, management information systems, human resources, health care.

Master of Science in Finance (MS) Full-time, part-time; 30-42 total credits required; 12 months to 7 years to complete program. Concentration in finance.

Master of Science in Information Systems (MS) Full-time, part-time; 33-45 total credits required; 12 months to 7 years to complete program. Concentration in management information systems.

Master of Science in Taxation (MS) Full-time, part-time; 30 total credits required; 12 months to 7 years to complete program. Concentration in taxation.

Saturday MBA (MBA) Part-time; 48 total credits required; 23 months to complete program. Concentration in management.

Master of Business Administration/Master of Science in Nursing (MBA/MS) Full-time, part-time; 66 total credits required; 2 to 7 years to complete program. Concentration in health care.

Master of Business Administration/Doctor of Philosophy in Nursing (MBA/PhD) Full-time, part-time; 85 total credits required; 2 to 7 years to complete program. Concentration in health care.

Master of Business Administration/Doctor of Pharmacy (MBA/PharmD) Full-time, part-time; 155 total credits required; 2 to 7 years to complete program. Concentration in health care.

Master of Business Administration/Doctor of Jurisprudence (MBA/JD) Full-time, part-time; 102-123 total credits required; 3 to 7 years to complete program. Concentrations in entrepreneurship, finance, international business, marketing, technology management, management information systems, human resources.

Master of Science in Accounting (MS) Full-time, part-time; 30-51 total credits required; 12 months to 7 years to complete program. Concentration in accounting.

ADMISSION
Applications For fall 1997 there were 396 applications for admission. Of those applying, 250 were accepted. Of those accepted, 125 enrolled.

Application Requirements Application form, application fee, bachelor's degree, 2 letters of recommendation, personal statement, resume, college transcript(s).
Recommended for Application GMAT score accepted: minimum 400, minimum GPA, work experience, computer experience.
Application Deadline Applications processed on a rolling/continuous basis for both domestic and international students. Application fee: $30. Deferred entrance is available.

ACADEMICS
Faculty Full-time 50; part-time 25.
Teaching Methodologies Case study, computer-aided instruction, field projects, group discussion, lecture, seminars by members of the business community, student presentations, study groups, team projects.
Technology Computer terminals/PCs are available for student use and are linked by a campus-wide network. The network has full access to the Internet. Students are not required to have their own PC.
Special Opportunities Advanced credit may be earned through transfer of credits from another institution. International exchange program in France. An internship program is available.

FINANCES
Costs for 1997–98 Tuition: Full-time: $2359 per semester (resident); $3412 per semester (nonresident). Part-time: $239 per credit (resident); $356 per credit (nonresident). Cost varies by academic program, number of credits taken, reciprocity agreements. Fees: $16 per credit (resident); $16 per credit (nonresident). Fees vary by academic program, number of credits taken, reciprocity agreements.
Financial Aid Research assistantships, scholarships, work study, loans available. Financial aid is available to part-time students. Application Deadline: 4/1.
Financial Aid Contact Ms. Anna Breland, Director of Financial Aid, 1420 North Charles Street, Baltimore, MD 21201-5779. Phone: 410-837-4763; Fax: 410-837-4820.

FACILITIES
Information Resources Langsdale Library plus 1 additional on-campus library; total holdings of 389,175 volumes, 278,303 microforms, 1,394 current periodical subscriptions. CD player(s) available for graduate student use. Access provided to online bibliographic retrieval services.

INTERNATIONAL STUDENTS
Demographics 13% of students enrolled are international students [Asia, 60%, Europe, 30%, other, 10%].
Services and Facilities International student office, international student center, visa services, counseling/support services.
Applying TOEFL: minimum score of 550, proof of adequate funds required. Proof of health/immunizations recommended. Financial aid is available to international students.
International Student Contact Ms. Wendy Burgess, International Student Advisor, 1420 North Charles Street, Baltimore, MD 21201-5779. Phone: 410-837-4758; Fax: 410-837-4875; E-mail: admissions@ubmail.ubalt.edu

PLACEMENT
Services include alumni network, career counseling/planning, career fairs, career library, career placement, electronic job bank, job interviews arranged, job search course, resume referral to employers, and resume preparation. In 1996–97, 97 organizations participated in on-campus recruiting; 563 on-campus interviews were conducted.
Employment Types of employment entered: accounting, banking, communications, computer-related, consumer products, education, finance, financial services, government, health services, high technology, hospitality management, human resources, information systems/technology, insurance, international trade, law, management, manufacturing, marketing, media, nonprofit, pharmaceutical, real estate, retail, service industry, telecommunications, transportation, utilities.

Business Program(s) URL: http://www.ubalt.edu/www/msb/msb.html

Program Contact: Ms. Tracey M. Jamison, Assistant Director of Admissions, 1420 North Charles Street, Baltimore, MD 21201-5779. Phone: 410-837-4777; Fax: 410-837-4820; E-mail: admissions@ubmail.ubalt.edu
See full description on page 1036.

University of Maryland, College Park

Robert H. Smith School of Business

College Park, Maryland

OVERVIEW
The University of Maryland, College Park is a state-supported, coed university. Enrollment: 33,000 graduate, professional, and undergraduate students; 4,296 full-time matriculated graduate/professional students; 3,961 part-time matriculated

graduate/professional students. Founded: 1856. The graduate business unit is in a suburban setting and is on a semester calendar.

HIGHLIGHTS

Enrollment Profile
Full-time: 497
Part-time: 428
Total: 925
Average Age: 27
Fall 1997 Average GPA: 3.37

International: 23%
Women: 36%
Minorities: 13%
Average Class Size: 47
Fall 1997 Average GMAT: 640

Costs
Full-time tuition: $9558 per academic year (resident); $14,184 per academic year (nonresident)
Part-time tuition: $272 per credit hour (resident); $400 per credit hour (nonresident)

AACSB – The International Association for Management Education accredited

Degree(s) offered in conjunction with Johns Hopkins University

GRADUATE BUSINESS PROGRAMS
Master of Business Administration (MBA) Full-time, part-time; 54 total credits required; 18 months to 5 years to complete program. Concentrations in accounting, entrepreneurship, finance, management information systems, international business, human resources, management science, marketing, logistics.

Master of Science (MS) Full-time, part-time; 30 total credits required; 12 months to 5 years to complete program. Concentrations in accounting, management information systems, organizational behavior/development, management science, financial information systems, finance.

Master of Business Administration/Master of Science (MBA/MS) Full-time, part-time; 66 total credits required; 21 months to 5 years to complete program. Concentrations in business information science, logistics, management science, finance.

Master of Business Administration/Doctor of Jurisprudence (MBA/JD) Full-time, part-time; 108 total credits required; 3 to 5 years to complete program.

Master of Business Administration/Master of Public Management (MBA/MPM) Full-time, part-time; 66 total credits required; 2.3 to 5 years to complete program.

Master of Business Administration/Master of Social Work (MBA/MSW) Full-time, part-time; 88 total credits required; 2.3 to 5 years to complete program.

ADMISSION
Applications For fall 1997 there were 1,937 applications for admission. Of those applying, 620 were accepted. Of those accepted, 366 enrolled.

Application Requirements Application form, application fee, bachelor's degree, essay, minimum GPA, 2 letters of recommendation, personal statement, resume, college transcript(s), computer experience.

Recommended for Application GMAT score accepted, GRE score accepted, work experience.

Application Deadline Applications processed on a rolling/continuous basis for domestic students only. 2/15 for fall (international). Application fee: $50, $70 (international). Deferred entrance is available.

ACADEMICS
Faculty Full-time 88; part-time 22.

Teaching Methodologies Case study, computer-aided instruction, computer analysis, computer simulations, experiential learning, faculty seminars, field projects, group discussion, lecture, research, role playing, seminars by members of the business community, simulations, student presentations, study groups, team projects.

Technology 1,600 on-campus computer terminals/PCs are available for student use and are linked by a campus-wide network. The network has full access to the Internet. Students are not required to have their own PC.

Special Opportunities Advanced credit may be earned through transfer of credits from another institution. International exchange programs in Australia, Belgium, France, Hong Kong, Ireland, Norway, Venezuela.

FINANCES
Costs for 1997–98 Tuition: Full-time: $9558 per year (resident); $14,184 per year (nonresident). Part-time: $272 per credit hour (resident); $400 per credit hour (nonresident). Cost varies by campus location, number of credits taken. Fees: Full-time: $1011 per academic year (resident); $1011 per academic year (nonresident). Part-time: $90 per semester. Fees vary by campus location, number of credits taken. Average 1997–98 room and board costs were $12,000 per academic year (off campus). Room and board costs vary by occupancy (e.g., single, double, triple), type of accommodation, type of meal plan.

Financial Aid In 1997–98, 16% of students received some institutionally administered aid in the form of fellowships, research assistantships, teaching assistantships, grants, scholarships, work study. Application Deadline: 4/30.

Financial Aid Contact Financial Aid Department, Lee Building, College Park, MD 20742. Phone: 301-314-8313.

FACILITIES
Information Resources T. R. McKeldin Library plus 7 additional on-campus libraries; total holdings of 2,453,970 volumes, 4,939,215 microforms, 18,675 current periodical subscriptions. CD player(s) available for graduate student use. Access provided to online bibliographic retrieval services and online databases.

INTERNATIONAL STUDENTS
Demographics 23% of students enrolled are international students [Africa, 3%, Asia, 48%, Australia/New Zealand, 2%, Central America, 1%, Europe, 11%, North America, 8%, South America, 10%, other, 17%].

Services and Facilities International student office, visa services, ESL courses, counseling/support services.

Applying TOEFL: minimum score of 600, proof of adequate funds, proof of health/immunizations required. TWE: minimum score of 4 recommended. Financial aid is available to international students.

International Student Contact Ms. Valerie Woolston, Director of International Education Services, Mitchell Building, 3rd Floor, College Park, MD 20742. Phone: 301-314-7740; Fax: 301-314-9347.

PLACEMENT
Services include alumni network, career counseling/planning, career fairs, career library, career placement, electronic job bank, job interviews arranged, job search course, resume referral to employers, and resume preparation.

Employment Of 1996–97 graduates, 97% were employed within three months of graduation; the average starting salary was $55,000. Types of employment entered: accounting, banking, chemical industry, communications, computer-related, consulting, consumer products, engineering, finance, financial services, government, health services, high technology, hospitality management, human resources, information systems/technology, insurance, law, management, manufacturing, marketing, nonprofit, pharmaceutical, real estate, service industry, telecommunications, transportation, utilities.

Business Program(s) URL: http://www.rhsmith.umd.edu

Program Contact: Ms. Sabrina White, Director MBA/MS Admission, The Robert H. Smith School of Business, 2308 Van Munching Hall, College Park, MD 20742. Phone: 301-405-2278; Fax: 301-314-9862; E-mail: mba-info@rhsmith. umd.edu

See full description on page 1094.

University of Maryland University College

Graduate School of Management and Technology

College Park, Maryland

OVERVIEW
The University of Maryland University College is a state-supported, coed, comprehensive institution. Enrollment: 13,786 graduate, professional, and undergraduate students; 233 full-time matriculated graduate/professional students; 3,308 part-time matriculated graduate/professional students. Founded: 1947. The graduate business unit is in a suburban setting and is on a semester calendar.

HIGHLIGHTS

Enrollment Profile
Full-time: 233
Part-time: 3,308
Total: 3,541
Average Age: 36
Fall 1997 Average GPA: 2.9

International: 4%
Women: 49%
Minorities: 38%
Average Class Size: 28
Fall 1997 Average GMAT: N/R

Costs
Full-time tuition: N/R
Part-time tuition: $273 per credit (resident); $353 per credit (nonresident)

Degree(s) offered in conjunction with University of Maryland, Baltimore County, University of Maryland, College Park

GRADUATE BUSINESS PROGRAMS
Master of General Administration (MGA) Full-time, part-time, distance learning option; 36-39 total credits required; 16 months to 7 years to complete program. Concentrations in management, finance, human resources, management information systems, marketing, nonprofit management, contract management, health care.

University of Maryland University College (continued)

Master of Science in Computer Systems Management (MS) Full-time, part-time, distance learning option; 36-39 total credits required; 16 months to 7 years to complete program. Concentration in information management.

Master of Science in Engineering Management (MS) Full-time, part-time; 36-39 total credits required; 16 months to 7 years to complete program.

Master of International Management (MIM) Full-time, part-time, distance learning option; 36-39 total credits required; 16 months to 7 years to complete program. Concentrations in international finance, international marketing, international trade.

Master of Science in Technology Management (MS) Full-time, part-time, distance learning option; 36-39 total credits required; 16 months to 7 years to complete program. Concentration in technology management.

Executive Master of Science in Technology Management (MS) Full-time, part-time; 36 total credits required; 16 months to complete program.

Master of Science in Environmental Management (MS) Full-time, part-time; 36-39 total credits required; 16 months to 7 years to complete program. Concentration in environmental economics/management.

Master of Science in Telecommunications Management (MS) Full-time, part-time; 36-39 total credits required; 16 months to 7 years to complete program. Concentration in telecommunications management.

Executive Master of General Administration (MGA) Full-time, part-time; 36 total credits required; 16 months to complete program.

Executive Master of International Management (MIM) Part-time; 36 total credits required; 18 months to complete program.

ADMISSION
Applications For fall 1997 there were 900 applications for admission. Of those applying, 873 were accepted. Of those accepted, 707 enrolled.

Application Requirements Application form, application fee, bachelor's degree, minimum GPA: 2.5, personal statement, college transcript(s).

Recommended for Application Work experience, computer experience.

Application Deadline Applications processed on a rolling/continuous basis for both domestic and international students. Application fee: $50. Deferred entrance is available.

ACADEMICS
Faculty Part-time 121.

Teaching Methodologies Case study, computer-aided instruction, computer analysis, computer simulations, experiential learning, faculty seminars, field projects, group discussion, lecture, research, role playing, seminars by members of the business community, simulations, student presentations, study groups, team projects.

Technology 375 on-campus computer terminals/PCs are available for student use and are linked by a campus-wide network. The network has full access to the Internet. Students are not required to have their own PC.

Special Opportunities Advanced credit may be earned through credit for military training programs, credit for business training programs, transfer of credits from another institution.

FINANCES
Costs for 1997–98 Tuition: $273 per credit (resident); $353 per credit (nonresident). Cost varies by academic program.

Financial Aid Grants, scholarships, work study, loans available. Financial aid is available to part-time students. Application Deadline: 5/1.

Financial Aid Contact Coordinator, Graduate Services, Graduate Admissions and Advising, University Boulevard at Adelphi Road, College Park, MD 20742-1600. Phone: 301-985-7155; Fax: 301-985-7175; E-mail: gradinfo@nova.umuc.edu

FACILITIES
Information Resources Access provided to online bibliographic retrieval services.

INTERNATIONAL STUDENTS
Demographics 4% of students enrolled are international students.

Services and Facilities International student office, visa services, counseling/support services.

Applying TOEFL: minimum score of 580, TWE: minimum score of 4, proof of adequate funds required. Financial aid is not available to international students.

International Student Contact Ms. Raissa Mallinger, Coordinator, Graduate Services, Graduate Admissions and Advising, University Boulevard at Adelphi Road, College Park, MD 20742-1600. Phone: 301-985-7155; Fax: 301-985-7175; E-mail: gradinfo@nova.umuc.edu

PLACEMENT
Services include alumni network, career counseling/planning, career library, electronic job bank, and job search course.

Business Program(s) URL: http://www.umuc.edu

Program Contact: Coordinator, Graduate Services, Graduate Admissions and Advising, University Boulevard at Adelphi Road, College Park, MD 20742-1600. Phone: 301-985-7155; Fax: 301-985-7175; E-mail: gradinfo@nova.umuc.edu

MASSACHUSETTS

American International College

School of Business Administration
Springfield, Massachusetts

OVERVIEW
American International College is an independent-nonprofit, coed, comprehensive institution. Enrollment: 1,905 graduate, professional, and undergraduate students; 158 full-time matriculated graduate/professional students; 339 part-time matriculated graduate/professional students. Founded: 1885. The graduate business unit is in an urban setting and is on a semester calendar.

HIGHLIGHTS

Enrollment Profile

Full-time: N/R	International: N/R
Part-time: N/R	Women: N/R
Total: 100	Minorities: N/R
Average Age: 25	Average Class Size: 15
Fall 1997 Average GPA: 3.3	Fall 1997 Average GMAT: N/R

Costs
Full-time tuition: N/R
Part-time tuition: $343 per semester hour

GRADUATE BUSINESS PROGRAMS
Master of Business Administration (MBA) Full-time, part-time; 36-54 total credits required; 12 to 18 months to complete program. Concentrations in accounting, finance, management, marketing, materials management, international business.

Master of Science in Accounting and Taxation (MS) Full-time, part-time; 30 total credits required; minimum of 12 months to complete program.

ADMISSION
Application Requirements Application form, application fee, bachelor's degree, 2 letters of recommendation, college transcript(s).

Application Deadline Applications processed on a rolling/continuous basis for both domestic and international students. Application fee: $15, $25 (international).

ACADEMICS
Faculty Full-time 18.

Teaching Methodologies Case study, experiential learning, field projects, group discussion, lecture, seminars by members of the business community, student presentations, team projects.

Technology 90 on-campus computer terminals/PCs are available for student use and are linked by a campus-wide network. The network has full access to the Internet. Students are not required to have their own PC.

Special Opportunities Advanced credit may be earned through transfer of credits from another institution.

FINANCES
Costs for 1997–98 Tuition: $343 per semester hour. Fees: $20 per semester.

Financial Aid Fellowships, work study available. Financial aid is available to part-time students.

Financial Aid Contact Dr. Lee C. Sirois, Director of Financial Aid, 1000 State Street, Springfield, MA 01109-3189. Phone: 413-747-6259; Fax: 413-737-2803.

FACILITIES
Information Resources James J. Shea Memorial Library; total holdings of 105,000 volumes, 660 current periodical subscriptions. CD player(s) available for graduate student use. Access provided to online bibliographic retrieval services.

INTERNATIONAL STUDENTS
Demographics N/R

Services and Facilities International student office, ESL courses, counseling/support services.

Applying TOEFL: minimum score of 550, proof of adequate funds, proof of health/immunizations required. Financial aid is not available to international students.

International Student Contact Dr. Adam Zielinski, Dean, School of Business Administration, 1000 State Street, Box 21A, Springfield, MA 01109-3189. Phone: 413-747-6230; Fax: 413-737-2803; E-mail: business@www.aic. edu

PLACEMENT

Services include career fairs, career placement, job interviews arranged, and resume preparation.

Program Contact: Dr. Adam Zielinski, Dean, School of Business Administration, 1000 State Street, Box 21A, Springfield, MA 01109-3189. Phone: 413-747-6230; Fax: 413-737-2803; E-mail: business@www.aic.edu

Anna Maria College

Graduate Program in Business Administration

Paxton, Massachusetts

OVERVIEW

Anna Maria College is an independent-religious, coed, comprehensive institution. Enrollment: 1,611 graduate, professional, and undergraduate students; 66 full-time matriculated graduate/professional students; 988 part-time matriculated graduate/professional students. Founded: 1946. The graduate business unit is in a small-town setting and is on a 9-week sessions calendar.

HIGHLIGHTS

Enrollment Profile

Full-time: 0	International: N/R
Part-time: 350	Women: N/R
Total: 350	Minorities: N/R
Average Age: N/R	Average Class Size: 18
Fall 1997 Average GPA: 2.6	Fall 1997 Average GMAT: 550

Costs
Full-time tuition: N/R
Part-time tuition: $730 per course

GRADUATE BUSINESS PROGRAMS

Master of Business Administration in Health Care Administration (MBA) Part-time; 36 total credits required; 14 months to 5 years to complete program.

Master of Business Administration (MBA) Part-time; 36 total credits required; 14 months to 5 years to complete program. Concentrations in marketing, finance, entrepreneurship.

ADMISSION

Application Requirements Application form, application fee, bachelor's degree, minimum GPA: 2.6, interview, 3 letters of recommendation, personal statement, resume, college transcript(s).

Recommended for Application GMAT score accepted.

Application Deadline Applications processed on a rolling/continuous basis for both domestic and international students. Application fee: $30.

ACADEMICS

Teaching Methodologies Case study, computer-aided instruction, computer analysis, experiential learning, faculty seminars, field projects, group discussion, lecture, research, role playing, seminars by members of the business community, simulations, student presentations, study groups, team projects.

Technology 45 on-campus computer terminals/PCs are available for student use and are linked by a campus-wide network. Students are not required to have their own PC.

Special Opportunities Advanced credit may be earned through transfer of credits from another institution.

FINANCES

Costs for 1997–98 Tuition: Part-time: $730 per course. Average 1997–98 room and board costs were $5000 per academic year.

Financial Aid Financial aid is available to part-time students.

Financial Aid Contact Ms. Laurie Pelletier, 50 Sunset Lane, Paxton, MA 01612.

FACILITIES

Information Resources Mondor-Eagen Library; total holdings of 91,543 volumes, 1,418 microforms, 450 current periodical subscriptions.

INTERNATIONAL STUDENTS

Demographics N/R

Services and Facilities International student office, international student center, ESL courses, counseling/support services.

Applying TOEFL: minimum score of 500, proof of adequate funds, proof of health/immunizations required. Financial aid is not available to international students.

International Student Contact Ms. Cynthia Ebert, Director of Business Programs, 50 Sunset Lane, Paxton, MA 06612-1198. Phone: 508-849-3344; Fax: 508-849-3362; E-mail: cebert@anna-maria.edu

PLACEMENT

Services include alumni network, career counseling/planning, career fairs, career library, career placement, job interviews arranged, job search course, resume referral to employers, and resume preparation. In 1996–97, 25 organizations participated in on-campus recruiting.

Employment Types of employment entered: accounting, banking, chemical industry, communications, computer-related, consulting, consumer products, education, energy, engineering, finance, financial services, government, health services, high technology, hospitality management, human resources, information systems/technology, insurance, international trade, law, management, manufacturing, marketing, media, mining, nonprofit, pharmaceutical, real estate, retail, service industry, telecommunications, transportation, utilities.

Program Contact: Ms. Christine Soverow, Director of Admissions, 50 Sunset Lane, Paxton, MA 01612-1198. Phone: 508-849-3300, 800-344-4586 Ext. 360; Fax: 508-849-3362; E-mail: cebert@anna-maria.edu

Arthur D. Little School of Management

One-Year Master of Science in Management Program

Chestnut Hill, Massachusetts

OVERVIEW

Arthur D. Little School of Management is a proprietary, coed, graduate institution. Enrollment: 63 graduate, professional, and undergraduate students; 63 full-time matriculated graduate/professional students; part-time matriculated graduate/professional students. Founded: 1973. The graduate business unit is in an urban setting and is on a phase calendar.

HIGHLIGHTS

Enrollment Profile

Full-time: 63	International: 90%
Part-time: 0	Women: 14%
Total: 63	Minorities: 2%
Average Age: 34	Average Class Size: 63
Fall 1997 Average GPA: N/R	Fall 1997 Average GMAT: 475

Costs
Full-time tuition: $32,000 per academic year
Part-time tuition: N/R

*A*rthur D. Little (ADL), a leading international consulting firm, is the only corporation to create an accredited graduate business program. Beginning in 1964, the Arthur D. Little School of Management developed a Master of Science in Management Program especially designed for experienced international managers. This intensive one-year program provides 65 participants with a curriculum distinguished by its practical, problem-solving orientation and multicultural learning environment. The program is further distinguished by its use of actual ADL consulting projects and business simulation exercises.

Students work side by side with the faculty, which is composed of Boston-area business school professors and ADL senior consultants. The faculty's working knowledge of leading-edge business issues reinforces the importance of blending leading academic theory with actual management practice. The professional experience of the participants, typically seven to eight years, futher complements the learning.

With a truly international class (90 percent of students are international and come from twenty-two countries), the M.S.M. program emphasizes global issues, cross-cultural awareness, and team building. Graduates are equipped with the knowledge base and problem-solving skills that will allow them to lead their organizations into the future.

As a result of the School's strategic alliance with Boston College's (BC) Carroll School of Management, the program is housed on BC's 148-acre Chestnut Hill campus and at ADL headquarters in Cambridge. Metropolitan Boston, the educational capital of the U.S., provides participants with a wide array of cultural and recreational activities. The area offers a wide variety of housing to suit any lifestyle

GRADUATE BUSINESS PROGRAMS

Master of Science in Management (MSM) Full-time; 53 total credits required; 11 months to complete program. Concentration in management science.

ADMISSION

Applications For fall 1997 there were 149 applications for admission. Of those applying, 127 were accepted. Of those accepted, 63 enrolled.

Arthur D. Little School of Management (continued)

Application Requirements GMAT score: minimum 550, application form, application fee, bachelor's degree, essay, 2 letters of recommendation, personal statement, resume, college transcript(s), minimum of 5 years of work experience.

Recommended for Application Interview, computer experience.

Application Deadline 5/1 for fall, 5/1 for fall (international). Application fee: $50. Deferred entrance is available.

ACADEMICS

Faculty Full-time 1; part-time 24.

Teaching Methodologies Case study, computer simulations, experiential learning, field projects, group discussion, lecture, research, seminars by members of the business community, simulations, student presentations, study groups, team projects.

Technology 200 on-campus computer terminals/PCs are available for student use and are linked by a campus-wide network. The network has full access to the Internet. Students are required to have their own PC.

Special Opportunities Advanced credit may be earned through transfer of credits from another institution. International exchange programs in France, Germany, Switzerland.

FINANCES

Costs for 1997–98 Tuition: Full-time: $32,000 per year. Cost varies by class time (e.g., day/evening). Average 1997–98 room and board costs were $19,825 per academic year (off campus). Room and board costs vary by occupancy (e.g., single, double, triple), type of accommodation.

Financial Aid Fellowships, grants available. Application Deadline: 6/1.

Financial Aid Contact Mr. Mark Challis, Finance Administrator, 194 Beacon Street, Chestnut Hill, MA 02167. Phone: 617-498-6347; Fax: 617-498-7086.

FACILITIES

Information Resources O'Neill Library plus 5 additional on-campus libraries; total holdings of 1,600,000 volumes, 2,500,000 microforms, 17,500 current periodical subscriptions. CD player(s) available for graduate student use. Access provided to online bibliographic retrieval services.

INTERNATIONAL STUDENTS

Demographics 90% of students enrolled are international students [Africa, 2%, Asia, 25%, Central America, 5%, Europe, 17%, North America, 11%, South America, 40%].

Services and Facilities International student office, international student center, visa services, counseling/support services.

Applying TOEFL: minimum score of 550, proof of adequate funds, proof of health/immunizations required. Financial aid is available to international students.

International Student Contact Admissions Office, 194 Beacon Street, Chestnut Hill, MA 02167. Phone: 617-552-2877; Fax: 617-552-2051; E-mail: adlschool.mgmt@adlittle.com

PLACEMENT

Services include alumni network, career counseling/planning, career fairs, career placement, job interviews arranged, resume referral to employers, and resume preparation.

Employment Of 1996–97 graduates, 80% were employed within three months of graduation; the average starting salary was $70,000. Types of employment entered: banking, consulting, manufacturing, service industry.

Business Program(s) URL: http://www.arthurdlittle.com/som/som.html

Program Contact: Mr. William Makris, Director of Marketing, 194 Beacon Street, Chestnut Hill, MA 02167. Phone: 617-552-2877; Fax: 617-552-2051; E-mail: adlschool.mgmt@adlittle.com

See full description on page 708.

Assumption College

Department of Business Studies

Worcester, Massachusetts

OVERVIEW

Assumption College is an independent-religious, coed, comprehensive institution. Founded: 1904. The graduate business unit is in a suburban setting and is on a semester calendar.

HIGHLIGHTS

Enrollment Profile
Full-time: N/R	International: N/R
Part-time: N/R	Women: N/R
Total: N/R	Minorities: N/R
Average Age: N/R	Average Class Size: 15
Fall 1997 Average GPA: N/R	Fall 1997 Average GMAT: 450

Costs
Full-time tuition: N/R
Part-time tuition: $297 per credit

The Assumption M.B.A. Program has been designed to provide professional preparation for men and women currently employed who wish to study on a part-time basis (typically one or two courses per semester). The primary goal of the program is to provide an opportunity for qualified persons to develop the knowledge, skills, abilities, and competencies that constitute a foundation for career growth and development in business, government, or other organizational environments.

In the program, stress is placed on effective decision making and the development and implementation of organized strategy at all levels. While including required study in the key functional areas of management, the program offers ample flexibility so that students can concentrate their study in a chosen area by completing one of the available concentrations. Alternatively, students may design a package of elective courses that tailor the program to their individual needs.

Small classes taught by full-time Assumption faculty members, each of whom has practical business experience, and by adjunct instructors who actively practice in their fields provide a rich and personally focused graduate learning experience.

GRADUATE BUSINESS PROGRAMS

Master of Business Administration (MBA) Part-time; 36 total credits required; 2.5 to 7 years to complete program. Concentrations in accounting, finance, human resources, international business, management, management information systems, marketing, management science.

ADMISSION

Application Requirements GMAT score, application form, application fee, bachelor's degree, essay, minimum GPA: 2.75, 2 letters of recommendation, personal statement, resume, college transcript(s), computer experience.

Recommended for Application Work experience.

Application Deadline Applications processed on a rolling/continuous basis for both domestic and international students. Application fee: $20.

ACADEMICS

Faculty Full-time 16; part-time 4.

Teaching Methodologies Case study, computer-aided instruction, computer analysis, computer simulations, experiential learning, faculty seminars, field projects, group discussion, research, simulations, student presentations, study groups, team projects.

Technology 50 on-campus computer terminals/PCs are available for student use. The network has full access to the Internet. Students are not required to have their own PC.

Special Opportunities Advanced credit may be earned through credit by examination, transfer of credits from another institution.

FINANCES

Costs for 1997–98 Tuition: Part-time: $297 per credit.

Financial Aid Financial aid is available to part-time students.

Financial Aid Contact Ms. Dana Mignogna, Administrative Secretary of Graduate Studies, Department of Business Studies, 500 Salisbury Street, PO Box 15005, Worcester, MA 01615-0005. Phone: 508-767-7387; Fax: 508-799-4412; E-mail: dmignogn@assumption.edu

FACILITIES

Information Resources Emmanuel D'Alzon Library; total holdings of 199,000 volumes, 1,199 current periodical subscriptions. Access provided to online bibliographic retrieval services.

INTERNATIONAL STUDENTS

Demographics N/R

Applying TOEFL: minimum score of 500, proof of adequate funds, proof of health/immunizations required. Financial aid is not available to international students.

PLACEMENT

Services include career library.

Business Program(s) URL: http://www.assumption.edu/acad/ii/Grad/MBA/

Program Contact: Mr. William Sadd, MBA Advisor, Department of Business Studies, 500 Salisbury Street, PO Box 15005, Worcester, MA 01615-0005. Phone: 508-767-7255; Fax: 508-756-1780.

Babson College

F. W. Olin Graduate School of Business

Babson Park, Massachusetts

OVERVIEW
Babson College is an independent-nonprofit, coed, comprehensive institution. Enrollment: 3,378 graduate, professional, and undergraduate students; 390 full-time matriculated graduate/professional students; 1,254 part-time matriculated graduate/professional students. Founded: 1919. The graduate business unit is in a suburban setting and is on a semester calendar.

HIGHLIGHTS

Enrollment Profile

Full-time: 390	International: 9%
Part-time: 1,254	Women: 34%
Total: 1,644	Minorities: 5%
Average Age: 29	Average Class Size: 27
Fall 1997 Average GPA: 3.0	Fall 1997 Average GMAT: 622

Costs
Full-time tuition: $21,940 per academic year
Part-time tuition: $2046 per 3-credit course

AACSB – The International Association for Management Education accredited

Babson's graduate school building (Olin Hall) opened in the fall of 1996. The building was designed to meet the requirements of the new Two-Year M.B.A. curriculum. The facility includes designated rooms for each first-year mentor team, where the team members can work on their group assignments and, on occasion, host their business mentor representatives. In addition, there are six interactive classrooms, one large classroom for 100 students, a lecture hall for 200, and a computer lab. An adjacent area containing temporary offices for faculty members to use while they teach in a module enhances faculty communication.

Entrepreneurial lab space is used by students for business start-ups and new product development. Other rooms are designed for group study, seminars, and the Graduate Student Association (GSA).

Babson's long tradition of emphasizing the global aspects of business continues today with the international concentration and the thriving International Management Internship Program (IMIP). The international concentration is available to all M.B.A. program participants. The IMIP has inspired M.B.A. graduates to start their careers overseas, some having accepted jobs directly with their IMIP companies, others through connections made while on an IMIP.

GRADUATE BUSINESS PROGRAMS
Two-year MBA (MBA) Full-time; 62 total credits required; minimum of 21 months to complete program. Concentration in international business.

One-year MBA (MBA) Full-time; 45 total credits required; minimum of 12 months to complete program. Concentration in international business.

Evening MBA (MBA) Full-time, part-time; 60 total credits required; 4 to 8 years to complete program. Concentration in international business.

ADMISSION
Applications For fall 1997 there were 900 applications for admission. Of those applying, 395 were accepted. Of those accepted, 145 enrolled.

Application Requirements GMAT score, application form, application fee, bachelor's degree, essay, minimum GPA: 2.8, interview, 2 letters of recommendation, personal statement, resume, college transcript(s), minimum of 2 years of work experience, computer experience: Microsoft Word, Microsoft Excel.

Application Deadline 3/1 for fall, 3/1 for fall (international). Application fee: $50. Deferred entrance is available.

ACADEMICS
Faculty Full-time 151; part-time 53.

Teaching Methodologies Case study, computer-aided instruction, computer analysis, computer simulations, experiential learning, faculty seminars, field projects, group discussion, lecture, research, role playing, seminars by members of the business community, simulations, student presentations, study groups, team projects.

Technology 211 on-campus computer terminals/PCs are available for student use and are linked by a campus-wide network. The network has full access to the Internet. Students are not required to have their own PC.

Special Opportunities Advanced credit may be earned through credit by examination, transfer of credits from another institution. International exchange programs in Ecuador, France, Japan, Norway, Spain, United Kingdom, Venezuela. An internship program is available.

FINANCES
Costs for 1997–98 Tuition: Full-time: $21,940 per year. Part-time: $2046 per 3-credit course. Cost varies by academic program. Fees: Full-time: $660 per academic year. Fees vary by academic program. Average 1997–98 room and board costs were $9810 per academic year (on campus) and $9810 per academic year (off campus). Room and board costs vary by occupancy (e.g., single, double, triple), type of accommodation, type of meal plan.

Financial Aid In 1997–98, 5% of students received some institutionally administered aid in the form of fellowships, research assistantships, scholarships, work study. Application Deadline: 3/15.

Financial Aid Contact Ms. Melissa Shaak, Director, Financial Aid, Babson College, Nichols, Babson Park, MA 02157-0310. Phone: 781-239-4219; Fax: 781-239-5295; E-mail: shaak@babson.edu

FACILITIES
Information Resources Horn Library; total holdings of 129,027 volumes, 339,705 microforms, 1,448 current periodical subscriptions. CD player(s) available for graduate student use. Access provided to online bibliographic retrieval services and online databases.

INTERNATIONAL STUDENTS
Demographics 9% of students enrolled are international students [Asia, 11%, Europe, 7%, North America, 75%, South America, 6%, other, 1%].

Services and Facilities International student office, international student housing, visa services, counseling/support services.

Applying TOEFL: minimum score of 580, proof of adequate funds, proof of health/immunizations required. Financial aid is available to international students.

International Student Contact Mrs. Carmen Ward, Assistant Director, International Programs, Babson Park, MA 02157-0310. Phone: 781-239-4005; Fax: 781-239-5232; E-mail: wardc@babson.edu

PLACEMENT
Services include alumni network, career counseling/planning, career fairs, career library, career placement, electronic job bank, job interviews arranged, job search course, resume referral to employers, and resume preparation. In 1996–97, 286 organizations participated in on-campus recruiting.

Employment Of 1996–97 graduates, 89% were employed within three months of graduation; the average starting salary was $59,670. Types of employment entered: accounting, banking, communications, computer-related, consulting, consumer products, engineering, finance, financial services, government, high technology, human resources, information systems/technology, insurance, international trade, management, manufacturing, marketing, media, nonprofit, pharmaceutical, real estate, retail, service industry, telecommunications.

Business Program(s) URL: http://www.babson.edu/mba

Program Contact: Ms. Rita Edmunds, Director, MBA Admissions, F. W. Olin Graduate School of Business, Olin Hall, Babson Park, MA 02157-0310. Phone: 781-239-5591, 800-488-4512; Fax: 781-239-4194; E-mail: mbaadmission@babson.edu

See full description on page 712.

Bentley College

Graduate School of Business

Waltham, Massachusetts

OVERVIEW
Bentley College is an independent-nonprofit, coed, comprehensive institution. Enrollment: 5,946 graduate, professional, and undergraduate students; 277 full-time matriculated graduate/professional students; 1,537 part-time matriculated graduate/professional students. Founded: 1917. The graduate business unit is in a suburban setting and is on a semester calendar.

HIGHLIGHTS

Enrollment Profile

Full-time: 277	International: 8%
Part-time: 1,537	Women: 44%
Total: 1,814	Minorities: 5%
Average Age: 31	Average Class Size: 27
Fall 1997 Average GPA: 3.2	Fall 1997 Average GMAT: 540

Costs
Full-time tuition: N/R
Part-time tuition: $1980 per course

Bentley College (continued)

AACSB – The International Association for Management Education accredited

Bentley College Graduate School of Business offers both a Full-Time M.B.A. program and a Self-Paced M.B.A. program. The Full-Time M.B.A. is a two-year program that provides an integrated view of the entire enterprise while developing key managerial skills to create a competitive advantage in today's information economy. The Self-Paced M.B.A. provides a strong foundation in business concepts as well as the analytical and practical techniques crucial to management. It allows students to draw on previous business knowledge to customize their curriculum through a flexible format and selection of one of fifteen areas of concentration, including accountancy, advanced accountancy, business communication, business data analysis, business economics, business ethics, entrepreneurial studies, finance, international business, management, management information systems, management of technology, marketing, operations management, and taxation. A full-time student in the Self-Paced M.B.A. program with full advanced-standing credit may complete his or her degree in one year. The College also offers an advanced graduate business certificate.

GRADUATE BUSINESS PROGRAMS

Master of Business Administration (MBA) Full-time, part-time; 30-57 total credits required; 12 months to 7 years to complete program. Concentrations in accounting, business ethics, economics, entrepreneurship, finance, international business, management, management information systems, marketing, operations management, taxation, environmental economics/management, technology management, quantitative analysis.

Master of Science in Accountancy (MS) Full-time, part-time; 30-60 total credits required; 12 months to 7 years to complete program.

Master of Science in Computer Information Systems (MS) Full-time, part-time; 30-36 total credits required; 12 months to 7 years to complete program.

Master of Science in Business Economics (MS) Full-time, part-time; 30-42 total credits required; 12 months to 7 years to complete program.

Master of Science in Finance (MS) Full-time, part-time; 30-57 total credits required; 12 months to 7 years to complete program.

Master of Science in Taxation (MS) Full-time, part-time; 30 total credits required; 12 months to 5 years to complete program.

Master of Science in Personal Financial Planning (MS) Full-time, part-time; 30 total credits required; 12 months to 5 years to complete program.

ADMISSION

Applications For fall 1997 there were 1,271 applications for admission. Of those applying, 852 were accepted. Of those accepted, 443 enrolled.

Application Requirements GMAT score, application form, application fee, bachelor's degree, essay, minimum GPA, 2 letters of recommendation, personal statement, college transcript(s), computer experience.

Recommended for Application Interview, resume.

Application Deadline 6/1 for fall, 11/1 for spring, 3/1 for summer, 3/1 for fall (international), 10/1 for spring (international), 3/1 for summer (international). Application fee: $50. Deferred entrance is available.

ACADEMICS

Faculty Full-time 140; part-time 52.

Teaching Methodologies Case study, computer-aided instruction, computer analysis, computer simulations, experiential learning, faculty seminars, field projects, group discussion, lecture, research, role playing, seminars by members of the business community, simulations, student presentations, study groups, team projects.

Technology 130 on-campus computer terminals/PCs are available for student use and are linked by a campus-wide network. The network has full access to the Internet. Students are not required to have their own PC.

Special Opportunities Advanced credit may be earned through credit by examination, transfer of credits from another institution. International exchange programs in Australia, Austria, Estonia, France, Japan, Netherlands. An internship program is available.

FINANCES

Costs for 1997–98 Tuition: $1980 per course. Fees: $15 per semester. Fees vary by number of credits taken. Average 1997–98 room and board costs were $8155 per academic year (on campus) and $11,000 per academic year (off campus). Room and board costs vary by occupancy (e.g., single, double, triple), type of accommodation, type of meal plan.

Financial Aid In 1997–98, 17% of students received some institutionally administered aid in the form of research assistantships, grants, scholarships, work study. Financial aid is available to part-time students. Application Deadline: 4/15.

Financial Aid Contact Ms. Katherine Nolan, Director of Financial Assistance, Rauch 108, Waltham, MA 02154-4705. Phone: 781-891-3168; Fax: 781-891-2448; E-mail: knolan@bentley.edu

FACILITIES

Information Resources Solomon R. Baker Library; total holdings of 200,000 volumes, 220,000 microforms, 2,000 current periodical subscriptions. CD player(s) available for graduate student use. Access provided to online bibliographic retrieval services and online databases.

INTERNATIONAL STUDENTS

Demographics 8% of students enrolled are international students [Africa, 3%, Asia, 61%, Central America, 3%, Europe, 20%, North America, 2%, South America, 5%, other, 6%].

Services and Facilities International student office, international student center, international student housing, visa services, ESL courses, counseling/support services, one-on-one tutoring.

Applying TOEFL: minimum score of 580, proof of adequate funds, proof of health/immunizations required. Financial aid is available to international students.

International Student Contact Mr. Douglas Gill, Director of International Student and Scholar Services, AGC 161, Waltham, MA 02154-4705. Phone: 781-891-2829; Fax: 781-891-2819; E-mail: dgill@bentley.edu

PLACEMENT

Services include alumni network, career counseling/planning, career fairs, career library, career placement, electronic job bank, job interviews arranged, job search course, resume referral to employers, and resume preparation. In 1996–97, 251 organizations participated in on-campus recruiting; 512 on-campus interviews were conducted.

Employment Of 1996–97 graduates, 90% were employed within three months of graduation; the average starting salary was $49,500. Types of employment entered: accounting, banking, chemical industry, communications, computer-related, consulting, consumer products, education, engineering, finance, financial services, government, health services, high technology, human resources, information systems/technology, insurance, international trade, management, manufacturing, marketing, nonprofit, pharmaceutical, retail, service industry, telecommunications, utilities.

Business Program(s) URL: http://www.bentley.edu

Program Contact: Ms. Sharon Oliver, Director of Graduate Admissions, Graduate School of Business, 175 Forest Street, Waltham, MA 02154-4705. Phone: 781-891-2108, 800-442-4723; Fax: 781-891-2464; E-mail: soliver@bentley.edu

See full description on page 722.

Boston College

Wallace E. Carroll Graduate School of Management

Chestnut Hill, Massachusetts

OVERVIEW

Boston College is an independent-religious, coed university. Enrollment: 14,652 graduate, professional, and undergraduate students; 2,291 full-time matriculated graduate/professional students; 2,428 part-time matriculated graduate/professional students. Founded: 1863. The graduate business unit is in a suburban setting and is on a semester calendar.

HIGHLIGHTS

Enrollment Profile

Full-time: 232	International: 6%
Part-time: 696	Women: 34%
Total: 928	Minorities: 7%
Average Age: 27	Average Class Size: 40
Fall 1997 Average GPA: 3.12	Fall 1997 Average GMAT: 610

Costs
Full-time tuition: $22,134 per academic year
Part-time tuition: $714 per credit hour

AACSB – The International Association for Management Education accredited

GRADUATE BUSINESS PROGRAMS

Master of Business Administration (MBA) Full-time, part-time; 55 total credits required; 15 months to 6 years to complete program. Concentrations in accounting, finance, management, marketing, operations management, organizational behavior/development, strategic management, entrepreneurship, international management, management consulting, management information systems.

Master of Science in Finance (MS) Full-time, part-time; 30 total credits required; 11 months to 3 years to complete program. Concentration in finance.

Master of Business Administration/Master of Science in Biology (MBA/MS) Full-time; 73 total credits required; minimum of 2.8 years to complete program.

Master of Business Administration/Master of Science in Geology/Geophysics (MBA/MS) Full-time; 73 total credits required; minimum of 2.8 years to complete program.

Master of Business Administration/Master of Arts in Mathematics (MBA/MA) Full-time; 73 total credits required; minimum of 2.8 years to complete program.

Master of Business Administration/Juris Doctor (MBA/JD) Full-time; 116 total credits required; must take LSAT; minimum of 3.8 years to complete program.

Master of Business Administration/Master of Social Work (MBA/MSW) Full-time; 110 total credits required; minimum of 2.8 years to complete program.

Master of Business Administration/Doctor of Philosophy in Sociology (MBA/PhD) Full-time; 83 total credits required; minimum of 4.8 years to complete program.

Master of Business Administration/Master of Science in Finance (MBA/MSF) Full-time; 65 total credits required; minimum of 2 years to complete program.

Master of Business Administration/Master of Arts in Slavic Studies (MBA/MA) Full-time; 73 total credits required; minimum of 2.8 years to complete program.

Master of Business Administration/Master of Arts in Russian (MBA/MA) Full-time; 73 total credits required; minimum of 2.8 years to complete program.

Master of Business Administration/Master of Arts in Linguistics (MBA/MA) Full-time; 73 total credits required; minimum of 2.8 years to complete program.

Master of Business Administration/Master of Science in Nursing (MBA/MS) Full-time; 80 total credits required; 3 years to complete program.

ADMISSION

Applications For fall 1997 there were 980 applications for admission. Of those applying, 415 were accepted. Of those accepted, 191 enrolled.

Application Requirements GMAT score, application form, application fee, bachelor's degree, essay, minimum GPA, 2 letters of recommendation, resume, college transcript(s).

Recommended for Application Work experience, computer experience.

Application Deadline 4/1 for fall, 3/1 for fall (international). Application fee: $45. Deferred entrance is available.

ACADEMICS

Faculty Full-time 87; part-time 45.

Teaching Methodologies Case study, computer simulations, experiential learning, faculty seminars, field projects, group discussion, lecture, research, role playing, seminars by members of the business community, student presentations, study groups, team projects, consulting projects.

Technology 165 on-campus computer terminals/PCs are available for student use and are linked by a campus-wide network. The network has full access to the Internet. Students are not required to have their own PC.

Special Opportunities Advanced credit may be earned through credit by examination, transfer of credits from another institution. International exchange programs in France, Ireland, Netherlands, New Zealand, Spain, United Kingdom.

FINANCES

Costs for 1997–98 Tuition: Full-time: $22,134 per year. Part-time: $714 per credit hour. Cost varies by number of credits taken. Fees: Full-time: $900 per academic year. Part-time: $80 per course. Fees vary by number of credits taken. Average 1997–98 room and board costs were $11,325 per academic year (off campus).

Financial Aid Fellowships, research assistantships, grants, scholarships, work study, loans available. Application Deadline: 3/1.

Financial Aid Contact Mr. Stephen Elias, Program Director, Graduate and Law Financial Aid, Lyons Hall 120, 140 Commonwealth Avenue, Chestnut Hill, MA 02167. Phone: 617-552-3320.

FACILITIES

Information Resources O'Neill Library plus 7 additional on-campus libraries; total holdings of 1,600,000 volumes, 2,500,000 microforms, 17,000 current periodical subscriptions. CD player(s) available for graduate student use. Access provided to online bibliographic retrieval services.

INTERNATIONAL STUDENTS

Demographics 6% of students enrolled are international students [Asia, 57%, Australia/New Zealand, 2%, Central America, 6%, Europe, 13%, North America, 6%, South America, 9%, other, 7%].

Services and Facilities International student office, international student center, visa services, counseling/support services.

Applying TOEFL: minimum score of 600, proof of adequate funds, proof of health/immunizations required. Financial aid is available to international students.

International Student Contact Ms. Margaret Shea, Assistant Director of Admissions, Fulton Hall 315, 140 Commonwealth Avenue, Chestnut Hill, MA 02167. Phone: 617-552-3920; Fax: 617-552-8078.

PLACEMENT

Services include alumni network, career counseling/planning, career fairs, career library, career placement, electronic job bank, job interviews arranged, resume referral to employers, and resume preparation. In 1996–97, 117 organizations participated in on-campus recruiting.

Employment Of 1996–97 graduates, 80% were employed within three months of graduation; the average starting salary was $61,567. Types of employment entered: accounting, banking, chemical industry, communications, computer-related, consulting, consumer products, finance, financial services, government, health services, high technology, human resources, information systems/technology, insurance, law, management, manufacturing, marketing, media, nonprofit, pharmaceutical, real estate, retail, service industry, telecommunications.

Business Program(s) URL: http://www.bc.edu/mba

Program Contact: Ms. Simone P. Marthers, Director, MBA Admissions, Carroll School of Management, 140 Commonwealth Avenue, Fulton 315, Chestnut Hill, MA 02167-3808. Phone: 617-552-3920; Fax: 617-552-8078.
See full description on page 726.

Boston University

School of Management

Boston, Massachusetts

OVERVIEW

Boston University is an independent-nonprofit, coed university. Enrollment: 29,857 graduate, professional, and undergraduate students; 7,616 full-time matriculated graduate/professional students; 3,134 part-time matriculated graduate/professional students. Founded: 1869. The graduate business unit is in an urban setting and is on a semester calendar.

HIGHLIGHTS

Enrollment Profile

Full-time: 526	International: 16%
Part-time: 732	Women: 36%
Total: 1,258	Minorities: 8%
Average Age: 27	Average Class Size: 29
Fall 1997 Average GPA: 3.1	Fall 1997 Average GMAT: 580

Costs
Full-time tuition: $22,830 per academic year
Part-time tuition: $687 per credit

AACSB – The International Association for Management Education accredited

GRADUATE BUSINESS PROGRAMS

Master of Business Administration (MBA) Full-time, part-time; 64 total credits required; 14 months to 6 years to complete program. Concentrations in entrepreneurship, international business, finance, management information systems, marketing, operations management, organizational behavior/development, international management.

Executive MBA (MBA) Full-time; 64 total credits required; 10 years work experience and company sponsorship required; 17 months to complete program.

Accelerated MBA with Concentration in Accounting (MBA) Full-time; 64 total credits required; 15 months to complete program. Concentration in accounting.

Master of Science in Management Information Systems (MS) Full-time; 48 total credits required; 12 months to complete program.

Doctor of Business Administration (DBA) Full-time; 64 total credits required; GMAT or GRE score required; 4 to 6 years to complete program. Concentrations in accounting, finance, management information systems, marketing, operations management, organizational behavior/development, strategic management.

Master of Business Administration/Master of Arts in Economics (MBA/MA) Full-time, part-time; 80 total credits required; 2 to 6 years to complete program.

Master of Business Administration/Master of Arts in International Relations (MBA/MA) Full-time, part-time; 80 total credits required; 2 to 6 years to complete program.

Boston University (continued)

Master of Business Administration/Master of Arts in Medical Sciences (MBA/MA) Full-time, part-time; 80 total credits required; 2 to 6 years to complete program. Concentration in health care.

Master of Business Administration/Master of Science in Television Management (MBA/MS) Full-time, part-time; 80 total credits required; 2 to 6 years to complete program.

Master of Business Administration/Master of Science in Manufacturing Engineering (MBA/MS) Full-time, part-time; 80 total credits required; 2 to 6 years to complete program.

Master of Business/Master of Science in Management Information Systems (MBA/MS) Full-time; 84 total credits required; 2 to 6 years to complete program.

Master of Business Administration/Doctor of Jurisprudence (MBA/JD) Full-time; 124 total credits required; 3 to 6 years to complete program. Concentration in health care.

Master of Business with Concentration in Health Care Management (MBA) Full-time, part-time; 64 total credits required; 14 months to 6 years to complete program.

Master of Business with Concentration in Public and Nonprofit Management (MBA) Full-time, part-time; 64 total credits required; 14 months to 6 years to complete program.

ADMISSION
Applications For fall 1997 there were 1,368 applications for admission. Of those applying, 643 were accepted. Of those accepted, 358 enrolled.

Application Requirements Application form, application fee, bachelor's degree, essay, 3 letters of recommendation, resume, college transcript(s).

Recommended for Application GMAT score accepted, minimum GPA: 2.0, interview, work experience, computer experience.

Application Deadline 3/15 for fall, 11/15 for spring, 3/1 for fall (international). Application fee: $50. Deferred entrance is available.

ACADEMICS
Faculty Full-time 110; part-time 54.

Teaching Methodologies Case study, experiential learning, field projects, group discussion, lecture, research, student presentations, study groups, team projects.

Technology 110 on-campus computer terminals/PCs are available for student use and are linked by a campus-wide network. The network has full access to the Internet. Students are not required to have their own PC.

Special Opportunities Advanced credit may be earned through credit by examination, transfer of credits from another institution. International exchange programs in France, Japan, United Kingdom.

FINANCES
Costs for 1997–98 Tuition: Full-time: $22,830 per year. Part-time: $687 per credit. Cost varies by academic program, number of credits taken. Fees: Full-time: $244 per academic year. Part-time: $52 per semester. Fees vary by academic program, number of credits taken. Average 1997–98 room and board costs were $7870 per academic year (on campus) and $8635 per academic year (off campus). Room and board costs vary by occupancy (e.g., single, double, triple), type of accommodation, type of meal plan.

Financial Aid In 1997–98, 16% of students received some institutionally administered aid in the form of scholarships, work study, loans. Financial aid is available to part-time students. Application Deadline: 3/15.

Financial Aid Contact Ms. Ia Vang, Assistant Director of Graduate Admissions and Financial Aid, 595 Commonwealth Avenue, Boston, MA 02215. Phone: 617-353-2670; Fax: 617-353-7368; E-mail: mba@bu.edu

FACILITIES
Information Resources Mugar Memorial Library plus 16 additional on-campus libraries; total holdings of 1,895,723 volumes, 3,328,569 microforms, 28,795 current periodical subscriptions. CD player(s) available for graduate student use. Access provided to online bibliographic retrieval services.

INTERNATIONAL STUDENTS
Demographics 16% of students enrolled are international students [Africa, 1%, Asia, 37%, Australia/New Zealand, 1%, Central America, 4%, Europe, 15%, North America, 9%, South America, 27%, other, 6%].

Services and Facilities International student office, international student center, visa services, ESL courses, counseling/support services.

Applying TOEFL: minimum score of 600, proof of adequate funds, proof of health/immunizations required. Financial aid is not available to international students.

International Student Contact Ms. Dawn Galolo, Assistant Director of Graduate Admissions, 595 Commonwealth Avenue, Boston, MA 02215. Phone: 617-353-2670; Fax: 617-353-7368; E-mail: mba@bu.edu

PLACEMENT
Services include alumni network, career counseling/planning, career fairs, career library, career placement, job interviews arranged, job search course, resume referral to employers, and resume preparation. In 1996–97, 241 on-campus interviews were conducted.

Employment Of 1996–97 graduates, 82% were employed within three months of graduation; the average starting salary was $63,115. Types of employment entered: accounting, banking, chemical industry, communications, computer-related, consulting, consumer products, education, energy, engineering, finance, financial services, government, health services, high technology, hospitality management, human resources, information systems/technology, insurance, international trade, law, management, manufacturing, marketing, media, mining, nonprofit, pharmaceutical, real estate, retail, service industry, telecommunications, transportation, utilities.

Business Program(s) URL: http://management.bu.edu

Program Contact: Mr. Peter Kelly, Director of Graduate Admissions and Financial Aid, 595 Commonwealth Avenue, Boston, MA 02215. Phone: 617-353-9112; Fax: 617-353-7368; E-mail: mba@bu.edu
See full description on page 728.

Brandeis University

Graduate School of International Economics and Finance

Waltham, Massachusetts

OVERVIEW
Brandeis University is an independent-nonprofit, coed university. Enrollment: 4,008 graduate, professional, and undergraduate students; 1,022 full-time matriculated graduate/professional students; 109 part-time matriculated graduate/professional students. Founded: 1947. The graduate business unit is in a suburban setting and is on a semester calendar.

HIGHLIGHTS

Enrollment Profile

Full-time: 139	International: 60%
Part-time: 25	Women: 43%
Total: 164	Minorities: 9%
Average Age: 25	Average Class Size: 50
Fall 1997 Average GPA: 3.5	Fall 1997 Average GMAT: 580

Costs
Full-time tuition: $23,360 per academic year
Part-time tuition: $2100 per course

The Brandeis University Graduate School of International Economics and Finance Master of Business Administration/International (MBAi) Program offers an education in business administration with a strong international focus and solid analytical foundations. Intended for students with several years' work experience, the MBAi prepares students for careers in a wide variety of international areas, such as multinational enterprises, small- and medium-sized firms operating across borders, or consulting firms that service international companies. Many graduates are employed in finance by leading financial services firms, securities companies, and commercial and investment banks. Students receive deep training in technical analysis and strategic issues and gain an understanding of managerial issues. Students must show mastery of a major language other than English and spend a semester studying outside of the United States at one of twenty-two exchange schools. During their studies, they work in multicultural teams; emphasis is placed on acquiring an appreciation for international differences in values and behavior, which are critically important in today's workplace.

The internationally focused curriculum, language requirement, study-abroad component, and multicultural aspects of the Brandeis MBAi distinguish it sharply from "generic" M.B.A. degrees. MBAi students receive training in all the major subjects included in a traditional M.B.A., such as economics, accounting, control, finance, marketing, operations, organizational behavior, and business policy. But they learn these subjects in an international context. Case examples are derived from international firms, and analytical models involve international applications.

GRADUATE BUSINESS PROGRAMS
Master of Arts in International Economics and Finance (MA) Full-time; 64 total credits required; 12 months to 2 years to complete program. Concentrations in international business, international economics, international finance.

PhD in International Economics and Finance (PhD) Full-time; 68 total credits required; 3 to 7 years to complete program. Concentrations in international finance, international business, international trade, developmental economics.

Mid-Career Master of Arts in International Economics and Finance (MA) Full-time; 64 total credits required; 12 months to complete program. Concentrations in international business, international economics, international finance.

International MBA (MBA) Full-time; 64 total credits required; 2-3 years work experience required; minimum of 2 years to complete program.

Master of Science in Finance (MS) Part-time; 2-3 years work experience required; minimum of 15 months to complete program. Concentrations in finance, international finance.

ADMISSION

Applications For fall 1997 there were 334 applications for admission. Of those applying, 120 were accepted. Of those accepted, 75 enrolled.

Application Requirements Application form, application fee, bachelor's degree, essay, 3 letters of recommendation, personal statement, resume, college transcript(s), work experience.

Recommended for Application GMAT score accepted, GRE score accepted, interview.

Application Deadline 2/15 for fall, 2/15 for fall (international). Application fee: $50. Deferred entrance is available.

ACADEMICS

Faculty Full-time 20; part-time 13.

Teaching Methodologies Case study, computer-aided instruction, computer analysis, computer simulations, experiential learning, faculty seminars, field projects, group discussion, lecture, research, role playing, seminars by members of the business community, simulations, student presentations, study groups, team projects.

Technology 24 on-campus computer terminals/PCs are available for student use and are linked by a campus-wide network. The network has full access to the Internet. Students are not required to have their own PC.

Special Opportunities Advanced credit may be earned through credit by examination, transfer of credits from another institution. International exchange programs in Belgium, Brazil, Denmark, France, Germany, Holland, Israel, Italy, Japan, Mexico, People's Republic of China, Republic of Korea, Republic of Singapore, Spain. An internship program is available.

FINANCES

Costs for 1997–98 Tuition: Full-time: $23,360 per year. Part-time: $2100 per course. Cost varies by academic program. Fees: Full-time: $45 per academic year. Average 1997–98 room only costs were $3500 per academic year (on campus) and $4500 per academic year (off campus). Room and board costs vary by occupancy (e.g., single, double, triple), type of accommodation.

Financial Aid In 1997–98, 29% of students received some institutionally administered aid in the form of scholarships, loans. Application Deadline: 2/15.

Financial Aid Contact Marsha Ginn, Associate Dean for Admissions, MS-032, PO Box 9110, Waltham, MA 02254-9110. Phone: 781-736-2252; Fax: 781-736-2263.

FACILITIES

Information Resources Goldfarb Library plus 3 additional on-campus libraries; total holdings of 966,000 volumes, 815,000 microforms, 3,900 current periodical subscriptions. CD player(s) available for graduate student use. Access provided to online bibliographic retrieval services.

INTERNATIONAL STUDENTS

Demographics 60% of students enrolled are international students [Africa, 7%, Asia, 37%, Central America, 3%, Europe, 44%, South America, 7%, other, 2%].

Services and Facilities International student office, international student center, international student housing, visa services, counseling/support services.

Applying TOEFL: minimum score of 600, proof of adequate funds, proof of health/immunizations required. Financial aid is available to international students.

International Student Contact Ms. Susan Mack, Director, International Students and Scholars Office, Kutz Hall, 415 South Street, Waltham, MA 02254-9110. Phone: 781-736-3480; Fax: 781-736-3484.

PLACEMENT

Services include alumni network, career counseling/planning, career fairs, career library, career placement, job interviews arranged, job search course, resume referral to employers, and resume preparation.

Employment Of 1996–97 graduates, 85% were employed within three months of graduation; the average starting salary was $62,000. Types of employment entered: accounting, banking, consulting, finance, financial services, government, information systems/technology, insurance, international trade, management, marketing, nonprofit, telecommunications.

Business Program(s) URL: http://www.brandeis.edu/ief/iefweb.html

Program Contact: Marsha Ginn, Associate Dean for Admissions, MS-032, PO Box 9110, Waltham, MA 02254-9110. Phone: 781-736-2252, 800-878-8866; Fax: 781-736-2263; E-mail: admissions@lemberg.brandeis.edu
See full descriptions on pages 732 and 734.

Cambridge College

Program in Management

Cambridge, Massachusetts

OVERVIEW

Cambridge College is an independent-nonprofit, coed, comprehensive institution. Enrollment: 1,745 graduate, professional, and undergraduate students; 1,448 full-time matriculated graduate/professional students; 92 part-time matriculated graduate/professional students. Founded: 1971. The graduate business unit is in an urban setting and is on a semester calendar.

HIGHLIGHTS

Enrollment Profile

Full-time: 109	International: 16%
Part-time: 10	Women: 55%
Total: 119	Minorities: 22%
Average Age: 38	Average Class Size: 20
Fall 1997 Average GPA: N/R	Fall 1997 Average GMAT: N/R

Costs
Full-time tuition: N/R
Part-time tuition: $315 per credit

GRADUATE BUSINESS PROGRAMS

Master of Management (MMgt) Full-time, part-time; 26-35 total credits required; 12 months to 2.9 years to complete program. Concentrations in entrepreneurship, human resources, leadership, nonprofit management.

ADMISSION

Applications For fall 1997 there were 52 applications for admission. Of those applying, 47 were accepted. Of those accepted, 36 enrolled.

Application Requirements Application form, application fee, bachelor's degree, essay, interview, letter of recommendation, personal statement, resume, college transcript(s), minimum of 5 years of work experience.

Recommended for Application Minimum GPA, computer experience.

Application Deadline Applications processed on a rolling/continuous basis for both domestic and international students. Application fee: $30.

ACADEMICS

Faculty Full-time 9; part-time 9.

Teaching Methodologies Case study, computer-aided instruction, experiential learning, faculty seminars, group discussion, lecture, role playing, seminars by members of the business community, simulations, student presentations, study groups, team projects.

Technology 40 on-campus computer terminals/PCs are available for student use. The network has full access to the Internet. Students are required to have their own PC.

Special Opportunities Advanced credit may be earned through credit by examination, transfer of credits from another institution.

FINANCES

Costs for 1997–98 Tuition: $315 per credit. Cost varies by academic program, campus location, class time (e.g., day/evening). Fees: $180 per year. Fees vary by academic program, campus location, class time (e.g., day/evening).

Financial Aid Teaching assistantships, work study available. Application Deadline: 9/10.

Financial Aid Contact Ms. Genni Major, Director of Financial Aid, 1000 Massachusetts Avenue, Cambridge, MA 02138. Phone: 617-868-1000 Ext. 137; Fax: 617-349-3545.

FACILITIES

Information Resources CD player(s) available for graduate student use. Access provided to online bibliographic retrieval services.

INTERNATIONAL STUDENTS

Demographics 16% of students enrolled are international students [Africa, 2%, Asia, 10%, Europe, 1%, North America, 84%, South America, 1%, other, 2%].

Services and Facilities International student office, ESL courses, counseling/support services.

Applying TOEFL: minimum score of 550, proof of adequate funds, proof of health/immunizations required. TSE recommended.

International Student Contact Ms. Jacqueline Tynes, Senior Enrollment Representative, 1000 Massachusetts Avenue, Cambridge, MA 02138. Phone: 617-868-1000 Ext. 140; Fax: 617-349-3545; E-mail: admitt@idea.cambridge.edu

PLACEMENT

Services include alumni network, and career counseling/planning.

Business Program(s) URL: http://www.cambridge.edu

Cambridge College (continued)

Program Contact: Ms. Jacqueline Tynes, Senior Enrollment Representative, 1000 Massachusetts Avenue, Cambridge, MA 02138. Phone: 617-868-1000 Ext. 140, 800-877-GRAD; Fax: 617-349-3545; E-mail: admitt@idea.cambridge.edu

Clark University

Graduate School of Management

Worcester, Massachusetts

OVERVIEW

Clark University is an independent-nonprofit, coed university. Enrollment: 3,083 graduate, professional, and undergraduate students; 297 full-time matriculated graduate/professional students; 372 part-time matriculated graduate/professional students. Founded: 1887. The graduate business unit is in an urban setting and is on a semester calendar.

HIGHLIGHTS

Enrollment Profile

Full-time: 126
Part-time: 218
Total: 344
Average Age: N/R
Fall 1997 Average GPA: 3.2

International: 26%
Women: 44%
Minorities: 6%
Average Class Size: 22
Fall 1997 Average GMAT: 565

Costs

Full-time tuition: $19,250 per academic year
Part-time tuition: $1925 per course

AACSB – The International Association for Management Education accredited

GRADUATE BUSINESS PROGRAMS

Master of Business Administration (MBA) Full-time, part-time; 57 total credits required; 12 months to 6 years to complete program. Concentrations in accounting, entrepreneurship, finance, human resources, international business, marketing, environmental economics/management, health care, management information systems.

Master of Science in Finance (MSF) Full-time, part-time; 60 total credits required; 12 months to 6 years to complete program.

Master of Business Administration in Health Services (MBA/HS) Full-time, part-time; 57 total credits required; 12 months to 6 years to complete program. Concentration in health care.

ADMISSION

Applications For fall 1997 there were 353 applications for admission. Of those applying, 242 were accepted. Of those accepted, 91 enrolled.

Application Requirements Application form, application fee, bachelor's degree, essay, 2 letters of recommendation, personal statement, resume, college transcript(s).

Recommended for Application GMAT score accepted, minimum GPA: 3.0, interview.

Application Deadline 6/1 for fall, 12/1 for spring, 6/1 for fall (international), 12/1 for spring (international). Application fee: $40. Deferred entrance is available.

ACADEMICS

Faculty Full-time 18; part-time 7.

Teaching Methodologies Case study, computer-aided instruction, computer analysis, computer simulations, experiential learning, faculty seminars, field projects, group discussion, lecture, research, role playing, seminars by members of the business community, simulations, student presentations, study groups, team projects.

Technology 120 on-campus computer terminals/PCs are available for student use and are linked by a campus-wide network. The network has full access to the Internet. Students are not required to have their own PC.

Special Opportunities Advanced credit may be earned through credit by examination, transfer of credits from another institution. International exchange programs in Canada, France, Sweden.

FINANCES

Costs for 1997–98 Tuition: Full-time: $19,250 per year. Part-time: $1925 per course. Fees: Full-time: $50 per academic year. Average 1997–98 room and board costs were $9150 per academic year (off campus). Room and board costs vary by occupancy (e.g., single, double, triple), type of accommodation, type of meal plan.

Financial Aid In 1997–98, 17% of students received some institutionally administered aid in the form of research assistantships, teaching assistantships, scholarships, work study, loans. Financial aid is available to part-time students. Application Deadline: 5/31.

Financial Aid Contact Mr. John Brandon, Associate Director of Admissions, Graduate School of Management, 950 Main Street, Worcester, MA 01610-1477. Phone: 508-793-7406; Fax: 508-793-8822; E-mail: clarkmba@vax.clarku.edu

FACILITIES

Information Resources Goddard Library plus 3 additional on-campus libraries; total holdings of 575,000 volumes, 58,327 microforms, 1,800 current periodical subscriptions. CD player(s) available for graduate student use. Access provided to online bibliographic retrieval services and online databases.

INTERNATIONAL STUDENTS

Demographics 26% of students enrolled are international students [Africa, 5%, Asia, 24%, Central America, 8%, Europe, 20%, North America, 30%, South America, 13%].

Services and Facilities International student office, international student housing, visa services, ESL courses, counseling/support services.

Applying TOEFL: minimum score of 550, proof of adequate funds, proof of health/immunizations required. Financial aid is available to international students.

International Student Contact Mr. David Elwell, Director, International Students and Scholars Office, 950 Main Street, Worcester, MA 01610-1477. Phone: 508-793-7750; Fax: 508-793-8822; E-mail: jdavis@vax.clarku.edu

PLACEMENT

Services include alumni network, career counseling/planning, career fairs, career library, career placement, electronic job bank, job interviews arranged, job search course, resume referral to employers, and resume preparation. In 1996–97, 150 organizations participated in on-campus recruiting.

Employment Of 1996–97 graduates, 95% were employed within three months of graduation. Types of employment entered: accounting, banking, communications, computer-related, consulting, consumer products, finance, financial services, health services, high technology, information systems/technology, insurance, nonprofit, pharmaceutical, retail, service industry, telecommunications.

Business Program(s) URL: http://www.mba.clarku.edu

Program Contact: Mr. John Brandon, Director of Admissions, Graduate School of Management, 950 Main Street, Worcester, MA 01610-1477. Phone: 508-793-7406; Fax: 508-793-8822; E-mail: clarkmba@vax.clarku.edu

See full description on page 754.

Emerson College

School of Communication, Management and Public Policy

Boston, Massachusetts

OVERVIEW

Emerson College is an independent-nonprofit, coed, comprehensive institution. Enrollment: 3,515 graduate, professional, and undergraduate students; 637 full-time matriculated graduate/professional students; 265 part-time matriculated graduate/professional students. Founded: 1880. The graduate business unit is in an urban setting and is on a semester calendar.

HIGHLIGHTS

Enrollment Profile

Full-time: 256
Part-time: 108
Total: 364
Average Age: 26
Fall 1997 Average GPA: 3.1

International: 34%
Women: 72%
Minorities: N/R
Average Class Size: 18
Fall 1997 Average GMAT: N/R

Costs

Full-time tuition: $13,032 per academic year
Part-time tuition: $543 per credit

Degree(s) offered in conjunction with Tufts University School of Medicine

GRADUATE BUSINESS PROGRAMS

Master of Arts in Integrated Marketing Communications (MA) Full-time, part-time; 44 total credits required; 12 months to 2 years to complete program. Concentrations in marketing, advertising, public relations, sports/entertainment management.

Master of Arts in Global Marketing Communication and Advertising (MA) Full-time; 40 total credits required; 12 months to complete program. Concentrations in public relations, marketing, advertising, international marketing.

Communication Industries Management (MA) Full-time, part-time; 44 total credits required; 12 months to 2 years to complete program. Concentration in arts administration/management.

Health Communication (MA) Full-time, part-time; 48 total credits required; 18 months to 2.5 years to complete program. Concentration in health care.

ADMISSION

Applications For fall 1997 there were 402 applications for admission. Of those applying, 343 were accepted. Of those accepted, 184 enrolled.

Application Requirements Application form, application fee, bachelor's degree, essay, minimum GPA, 3 letters of recommendation, personal statement, resume, college transcript(s).

Recommended for Application GMAT score accepted, GRE score accepted.

Application Deadline Applications processed on a rolling/continuous basis for both domestic and international students. Application fee: $45, $75 (international). Deferred entrance is available.

ACADEMICS

Faculty Full-time 27; part-time 15.

Teaching Methodologies Case study, computer-aided instruction, computer analysis, experiential learning, faculty seminars, field projects, group discussion, lecture, research, role playing, seminars by members of the business community, simulations, student presentations, study groups, team projects.

Technology 39 on-campus computer terminals/PCs are available for student use and are linked by a campus-wide network. The network has full access to the Internet. Students are not required to have their own PC.

Special Opportunities Advanced credit may be earned through transfer of credits from another institution. An internship program is available.

FINANCES

Costs for 1997–98 Tuition: Full-time: $13,032 per year. Part-time: $543 per credit. Cost varies by number of credits taken. Fees: Full-time: $80 per academic year. Fees vary by number of credits taken. Average 1997–98 room and board costs were $7875 per academic year (off campus).

Financial Aid Fellowships, research assistantships, teaching assistantships, work study available. Financial aid is available to part-time students. Application Deadline: 3/1.

Financial Aid Contact Director of Financial Aid and Student Employment, 100 Beacon Street, Boston, MA 02116-1511. Phone: 617-824-8655.

FACILITIES

Information Resources Main library; total holdings of 167,000 volumes, 10,000 microforms, 1,300 current periodical subscriptions. CD player(s) available for graduate student use. Access provided to online bibliographic retrieval services and online databases.

INTERNATIONAL STUDENTS

Demographics 34% of students enrolled are international students [Africa, 2%, Asia, 38%, Europe, 24%, South America, 12%, other, 24%].

Services and Facilities International student office, international student center, visa services, counseling/support services, English Summer Language Program.

Applying TOEFL: minimum score of 550, proof of adequate funds, proof of health/immunizations required. Financial aid is available to international students.

International Student Contact Ms. Lynn Terrell, Director of Graduate Admission, 100 Beacon Street, Boston, MA 02116. Phone: 617-824-8610; Fax: 617-824-8614; E-mail: gradapp@emerson.edu

PLACEMENT

Services include alumni network, career counseling/planning, career fairs, career library, electronic job bank, job search course, resume referral to employers, and resume preparation.

Employment Of 1996–97 graduates, 96% were employed within three months of graduation. Types of employment entered: communications, consulting, education, government, health services, international trade, marketing, media, nonprofit, service industry.

Business Program(s) URL: http://www.emerson.edu/gradapp

Program Contact: Ms. Lynn Terrell, Director, Office of Graduate Admission, 100 Beacon Street, Boston, MA 02116-1511. Phone: 617-824-8610; Fax: 617-824-8614; E-mail: gradapp@emerson.edu
See full description on page 800.

Emmanuel College

Center for Adult Studies

Boston, Massachusetts

OVERVIEW

Emmanuel College is an independent-religious, coed, comprehensive institution. Enrollment: 1,500 graduate, professional, and undergraduate students. Founded: 1919.

HIGHLIGHTS

Enrollment Profile

Full-time: 0	International: 5%
Part-time: 180	Women: 60%
Total: 180	Minorities: N/R
Average Age: 32	Average Class Size: N/R
Fall 1997 Average GPA: N/R	Fall 1997 Average GMAT: N/R

Costs
Full-time tuition: N/R
Part-time tuition: $1266 per course

GRADUATE BUSINESS PROGRAMS

Master of Science in Management (MS) Part-time; 36 total credits required; 2 to 5 years to complete program.

Master of Science in Human Resources Management (MS) Part-time; 39 total credits required; must submit GMAT score; 2 to 5 years to complete program.

ADMISSION

Application Requirements Application form, application fee, bachelor's degree, essay, minimum GPA, interview, 2 letters of recommendation, personal statement, resume, college transcript(s), minimum of 3 years of work experience.

Recommended for Application GMAT score accepted, computer experience.

Application Deadline Applications processed on a rolling/continuous basis for both domestic and international students. Application fee: $50.

ACADEMICS

Teaching Methodologies Case study, computer-aided instruction, computer analysis, experiential learning, faculty seminars, field projects, lecture, research, role playing, seminars by members of the business community, student presentations, study groups, team projects.

FINANCES

Costs for 1997–98 Tuition: Part-time: $1266 per course.

Financial Aid Contact Financial Aid Office, 400 The Fenway, Boston, MA 02115. Phone: 617-735-9725.

FACILITIES

Information Resources Cardinal Cushing Library; total holdings of 134,000 volumes, 1,370 microforms, 600 current periodical subscriptions. CD player(s) available for graduate student use. Access provided to online bibliographic retrieval services.

INTERNATIONAL STUDENTS

Demographics 5% of students enrolled are international students.

Services and Facilities International student office, counseling/support services.

Applying TOEFL: minimum score of 550, proof of adequate funds, proof of health/immunizations required.

International Student Contact International Student Office, 400 The Fenway, Boston, MA 02115. Phone: 617-735-9884.

PLACEMENT

Services include alumni network.

Program Contact: Center for Adult Studies, 400 The Fenway, Boston, MA 02115. Phone: 617-735-9700.

Fitchburg State College

Division of Graduate and Continuing Education

Fitchburg, Massachusetts

OVERVIEW

Fitchburg State College is a state-supported, coed, comprehensive institution. Enrollment: 3,644 graduate, professional, and undergraduate students; 114 full-time matriculated graduate/professional students; 460 part-time matriculated graduate/professional students. Founded: 1894. The graduate business unit is in a small-town setting and is on a semester calendar.

Fitchburg State College (continued)

HIGHLIGHTS

Enrollment Profile
Full-time: 0
Part-time: 28
Total: 28
Average Age: 36
Fall 1997 Average GPA: N/R

International: N/R
Women: 46%
Minorities: 18%
Average Class Size: 16
Fall 1997 Average GMAT: N/R

Costs
Full-time tuition: N/R
Part-time tuition: $140 per credit hour (resident); $140 per credit hour (nonresident)

GRADUATE BUSINESS PROGRAMS
Master of Business Administration (MBA) Part-time; 30-54 total credits required; 2 to 6 years to complete program. Concentrations in accounting, management, human resources.

ADMISSION
Application Requirements GMAT score: minimum 400, application form, application fee, bachelor's degree, minimum GPA: 2.8, 3 letters of recommendation, college transcript(s).
Recommended for Application Interview.
Application Deadline Applications processed on a rolling/continuous basis for both domestic and international students. Application fee: $10. Deferred entrance is available.

ACADEMICS
Faculty Full-time 8; part-time 1.
Teaching Methodologies Case study, computer-aided instruction, computer analysis, experiential learning, faculty seminars, field projects, group discussion, lecture, research, role playing, seminars by members of the business community, student presentations, study groups, team projects.
Technology 150 on-campus computer terminals/PCs are available for student use and are linked by a campus-wide network. The network has full access to the Internet. Students are not required to have their own PC.
Special Opportunities Advanced credit may be earned through credit for experience, transfer of credits from another institution.

FINANCES
Costs for 1997–98 Tuition: Part-time: $140 per credit hour (resident); $140 per credit hour (nonresident). Fees: Part-time: $62 per semester (resident); $62 per semester (nonresident). Average 1997–98 room and board costs were $4410 per academic year. Room and board costs vary by occupancy (e.g., single, double, triple), type of meal plan.
Financial Aid Grants, scholarships, work study, loans available. Financial aid is available to part-time students.
Financial Aid Contact Ms. Jennifer Porter, Director of Financial Aid, 160 Pearl Street, Fitchburg, MA 01420-2697. Phone: 978-665-3422; Fax: 978-665-3559.

FACILITIES
Information Resources Hammond Library; total holdings of 213,571 volumes, 445,511 microforms, 1,861 current periodical subscriptions. CD player(s) available for graduate student use. Access provided to online bibliographic retrieval services and online databases.

INTERNATIONAL STUDENTS
Demographics N/R
Services and Facilities International student office, international student housing, visa services, counseling/support services.
Applying TOEFL: minimum score of 500, TSE, proof of adequate funds, proof of health/immunizations required. Financial aid is not available to international students.
International Student Contact Coordinator of International Education, 160 Pearl Street, Fitchburg, MA 01420-2697. Phone: 978-665-3089; Fax: 978-665-4040.

PLACEMENT
Services include alumni network, career counseling/planning, career fairs, career library, electronic job bank, job interviews arranged, resume referral to employers, and resume preparation. In 1996–97, 55 organizations participated in on-campus recruiting.
Employment Types of employment entered: accounting, health services, hospitality management, management.
Business Program(s) URL: http://www.fsc.edu/www/academics_graduate.html

Program Contact: Dr. Jannette Purcell, MBA Program Chair, 160 Pearl Street, Fitchburg, MA 01420-2697. Phone: 978-665-3567; Fax: 978-665-3658; E-mail: dgce@fsc.edu
See full description on page 818.

Framingham State College

Program in Business Administration

Framingham, Massachusetts

OVERVIEW
Framingham State College is a state-supported, coed, comprehensive institution. Enrollment: 40 full-time matriculated graduate/professional students; 645 part-time matriculated graduate/professional students. Founded: 1839. The graduate business unit is in a suburban setting.

HIGHLIGHTS

Enrollment Profile
Full-time: 0
Part-time: 151
Total: 151
Average Age: N/R
Fall 1997 Average GPA: N/R

International: N/R
Women: N/R
Minorities: N/R
Average Class Size: 20
Fall 1997 Average GMAT: N/R

Costs
Full-time tuition: N/R
Part-time tuition: N/R

GRADUATE BUSINESS PROGRAMS
Master of Arts in Business Administration (MA) Part-time.

ACADEMICS
Faculty Full-time 4; part-time 4.
Technology 200 on-campus computer terminals/PCs are available for student use and are linked by a campus-wide network. Students are not required to have their own PC.

FACILITIES
Information Resources Henry Whittemore Library.

INTERNATIONAL STUDENTS
Demographics N/R

PLACEMENT
Services include career counseling/planning, career library, and resume preparation.

Program Contact: Program in Business Administration, 100 State Street, Framingham, MA 01701-9101. Phone: 508-620-1220; Fax: 508-620-4592.

Harvard University

Graduate School of Business Administration

Cambridge, Massachusetts

OVERVIEW
Harvard University is an independent-nonprofit, coed university. Enrollment: 18,628 graduate, professional, and undergraduate students; 11,397 full-time matriculated graduate/professional students; 596 part-time matriculated graduate/professional students. Founded: 1636. The graduate business unit is in an urban setting and is on a semester calendar.

HIGHLIGHTS

Enrollment Profile
Full-time: 1,784
Part-time: 0
Total: 1,784
Average Age: 27
Fall 1997 Average GPA: 3.5

International: 26%
Women: 24%
Minorities: 18%
Average Class Size: 80
Fall 1997 Average GMAT: N/R

Costs
Full-time tuition: $25,000 per academic year
Part-time tuition: N/R

AACSB – The International Association for Management Education accredited

GRADUATE BUSINESS PROGRAMS

Master of Business Administration (MBA) Full-time; 16 to 21 months to complete program. Concentration in management.

Master of Business Administration/Doctor of Jurisprudence (MBA/JD) Full-time; 4 years to complete program. Concentration in management.

ADMISSION

Applications For fall 1997 there were 7,469 applications for admission. Of those applying, 1,032 were accepted. Of those accepted, 894 enrolled.

Application Requirements GMAT score, application form, application fee, essay, 3 letters of recommendation, resume, college transcript(s).

Recommended for Application Bachelor's degree, work experience.

Application Deadline Applications processed on a rolling/continuous basis for both domestic and international students. Application fee: $160.

ACADEMICS

Faculty Full-time 194.

Teaching Methodologies Case study, computer-aided instruction, computer analysis, computer simulations, faculty seminars, field projects, group discussion, research, role playing, simulations, student presentations, study groups, team projects.

Technology 180 on-campus computer terminals/PCs are available for student use and are linked by a campus-wide network. The network has full access to the Internet. Students are required to have their own PC.

Special Opportunities An internship program is available.

FINANCES

Costs for 1997–98 Tuition: Full-time: $25,000 per year. Fees: Full-time: $2540 per academic year. Average 1997–98 room only costs were $7073 per academic year. Room and board costs vary by occupancy (e.g., single, double, triple), type of accommodation.

Financial Aid Fellowships, loans available.

Financial Aid Contact Harvard Business School, Financial Aid Office, Baker Library 6, Soldiers Field , Boston, MA 02163. Phone: 617-495-6640; Fax: 617-496-3955; E-mail: finaid@hbs.edu

FACILITIES

Information Resources Widener Library plus 90 additional on-campus libraries; total holdings of 12,850,000 volumes, 677,500 microforms. CD player(s) available for graduate student use. Access provided to online bibliographic retrieval services and online databases.

INTERNATIONAL STUDENTS

Demographics 26% of students enrolled are international students.

Services and Facilities International student office, visa services, ESL courses.

Applying TOEFL: minimum score of 630, proof of adequate funds, proof of health/immunizations required. TWE recommended. Financial aid is available to international students.

International Student Contact Harvard Business School, MBA Admissions, Dillon House, Soldiers Field , Boston, MA 02163. Phone: 617-495-1000; E-mail: admissions@hbs.edu

PLACEMENT

Services include alumni network, career counseling/planning, career fairs, career library, career placement, electronic job bank, job interviews arranged, job search course, resume referral to employers, and resume preparation.

Business Program(s) URL: http://www.hbs.edu

Program Contact: Harvard Business School, MBA Admissions, Dillon House, Soldiers Field, Boston, MA 02163. Phone: 617-495-6127; Fax: 617-496-9272; E-mail: admissions@hbs.edu

Lesley College

School of Management

Cambridge, Massachusetts

OVERVIEW

Lesley College is an independent-nonprofit, coed, comprehensive institution. Enrollment: 6,128 graduate, professional, and undergraduate students; 581 full-time matriculated graduate/professional students; 4,069 part-time matriculated graduate/professional students. Founded: 1909. The graduate business unit is in an urban setting and is on a semester-based and accelerated programs; 6-8-11 week accelerated courses calendar.

HIGHLIGHTS

Enrollment Profile
Full-time: 224
Part-time: 283
Total: 507
Average Age: 36
Fall 1997 Average GPA: N/R

International: 1%
Women: 67%
Minorities: 12%
Average Class Size: 18
Fall 1997 Average GMAT: N/R

Costs
Full-time tuition: N/R
Part-time tuition: $425 per credit

GRADUATE BUSINESS PROGRAMS

Accelerated Master of Science in Management (MS) Full-time; 40 total credits required; minimum of 17 months to complete program. Concentration in management.

Master of Science in Management (MS) Full-time, part-time; 40 total credits required; 15 months to 3 years to complete program. Concentrations in management, human resources, management information systems, nonprofit management, health care.

Master of Science in Training and Development (MS) Full-time, part-time; 36 total credits required; minimum of 2 years to complete program.

ADMISSION

Applications For fall 1997 there were 170 applications for admission. Of those applying, 162 were accepted.

Application Requirements Application form, application fee, bachelor's degree, essay, minimum GPA: 2.5, interview, 2 letters of recommendation, personal statement, resume, college transcript(s), minimum of 3 years of work experience.

Application Deadline Applications processed on a rolling/continuous basis for both domestic and international students. Application fee: $45. Deferred entrance is available.

ACADEMICS

Faculty Full-time 11; part-time 150.

Teaching Methodologies Case study, computer analysis, computer simulations, experiential learning, faculty seminars, field projects, group discussion, lecture, research, role playing, seminars by members of the business community, simulations, student presentations, study groups, team projects.

Technology 125 on-campus computer terminals/PCs are available for student use and are linked by a campus-wide network. The network has full access to the Internet. Students are not required to have their own PC.

Special Opportunities An internship program is available.

FINANCES

Costs for 1997–98 Tuition: $425 per credit. Cost varies by campus location. Fees: $80 per course. Fees vary by academic program. Average 1997–98 room only costs were $6500 per academic year (off campus).

Financial Aid Research assistantships, grants, work study, loans available. Financial aid is available to part-time students. Application Deadline: 5/1.

Financial Aid Contact Ms. Lois Fitzpatrick, Associate Director of Financial Aid, 29 Everett Street, Cambridge, MA 02138-2790. Phone: 617-349-8710; Fax: 617-349-8717.

FACILITIES

Information Resources Eleanor DeWolfe Ludcke Library; total holdings of 64,500 volumes, 900,000 microforms, 717 current periodical subscriptions. CD player(s) available for graduate student use. Access provided to online bibliographic retrieval services and online databases.

INTERNATIONAL STUDENTS

Demographics 1% of students enrolled are international students.

Services and Facilities International student office, visa services, counseling/support services.

Applying TOEFL: minimum score of 550, proof of adequate funds, proof of health/immunizations required. Financial aid is not available to international students.

International Student Contact Ms. Andrea Stultz, Foreign Student Advisor, 29 Everett Street, Cambridge, MA 02138. Phone: 617-349-8524; Fax: 617-349-8558.

PLACEMENT

Services include alumni network, career counseling/planning, career fairs, career library, career placement, resume referral to employers, and resume preparation. In 1996–97, 150 organizations participated in on-campus recruiting.

Employment Of 1996–97 graduates, 92% were employed within three months of graduation; the average starting salary was $40,000. Types of employment entered: communications, computer-related, consulting, education, engineering, finance, financial services, government, health services, high technology, human resources, information systems/technology, insurance, management,

Lesley College (continued)

manufacturing, marketing, nonprofit, real estate, retail, service industry, telecommunications, transportation, utilities.

Business Program(s) URL: http://www.lesley.edu/som.html

Program Contact: Mr. Rob Elkin, Director of School of Management Admissions, 29 Everett Street, Cambridge, MA 02138-2790. Phone: 617-349-8300, 800-999-1959 Ext. 8300; Fax: 617-349-8313.

Massachusetts Institute of Technology

Sloan School of Management

Cambridge, Massachusetts

OVERVIEW
Massachusetts Institute of Technology is an independent-nonprofit, coed university. Enrollment: 9,947 graduate, professional, and undergraduate students; 5,327 full-time matriculated graduate/professional students; 172 part-time matriculated graduate/professional students. Founded: 1861. The graduate business unit is in an urban setting and is on a semester calendar.

HIGHLIGHTS

Enrollment Profile

Full-time: 711	International: 38%
Part-time: 0	Women: 27%
Total: 711	Minorities: 9%
Average Age: 28	Average Class Size: 58
Fall 1997 Average GPA: 3.5	Fall 1997 Average GMAT: 675

Costs
Full-time tuition: $25,800 per academic year
Part-time tuition: N/R

AACSB – The International Association for Management Education accredited

GRADUATE BUSINESS PROGRAMS
Master of Business Administration (MBA) Full-time; 18 months to 2 years to complete program. Concentrations in management, strategic management, management information systems, management science, operations management, entrepreneurship, finance, financial management/planning, new venture management.

Master of Science (MS) Full-time; 18 months to 2 years to complete program. Concentrations in management, strategic management, management information systems, management science, operations management.

Master of Science in Management/Master of Science in Engineering (Leaders for Manufacturing) (MS/MS) Full-time; 2 years to complete program.

Executive Master of Science in Management of Technology (MS) Full-time; 12 months to complete program. Concentration in technology management.

ADMISSION
Applications For fall 1997 there were 3,394 applications for admission. Of those applying, 469 were accepted. Of those accepted, 350 enrolled.

Application Requirements GMAT score: minimum 600, application form, application fee, bachelor's degree, essay, minimum GPA, 2 letters of recommendation, personal statement, resume, college transcript(s), computer experience.

Recommended for Application Work experience.

Application Deadline 1/31 for fall. Application fee: $150, $175 (international). Deferred entrance is available.

ACADEMICS
Faculty Full-time 100.

Teaching Methodologies Case study, computer-aided instruction, computer analysis, computer simulations, experiential learning, faculty seminars, field projects, group discussion, lecture, research, role playing, seminars by members of the business community, simulations, student presentations, team projects.

Technology 77 on-campus computer terminals/PCs are available for student use and are linked by a campus-wide network. The network has full access to the Internet. Students are required to have their own PC.

Special Opportunities International exchange programs in Spain, United Kingdom.

FINANCES
Costs for 1997–98 Tuition: Full-time: $25,800 per year. Average 1997–98 room and board costs were $16,000 per academic year (on campus) and $16,000 per academic year (off campus). Room and board costs vary by campus location, occupancy (e.g., single, double, triple), type of accommodation, type of meal plan.

Financial Aid Fellowships, research assistantships, teaching assistantships, loans available.

Financial Aid Contact Ms. Liz Barnes, Financial Aid Representative, 77 Massachusetts Avenue, 5-119, Cambridge, MA 02139. Phone: 617-258-5775; Fax: 617-258-8301.

FACILITIES
Information Resources Main institution library plus 11 additional on-campus libraries; total holdings of 2,493,927 volumes, 2,208,996 microforms, 17,359 current periodical subscriptions. Access provided to online bibliographic retrieval services and online databases.

INTERNATIONAL STUDENTS
Demographics 38% of students enrolled are international students.

Services and Facilities International student office, ESL courses, counseling/support services.

Applying TOEFL, proof of adequate funds required. Financial aid is not available to international students.

International Student Contact Ms. Milena Levak, Director of International Student Office, 77 Massachusetts Avenue, 5-106, Cambridge, MA 02139. Phone: 617-253-3795; Fax: 617-253-8000.

PLACEMENT
Services include alumni network, career counseling/planning, career fairs, career library, career placement, electronic job bank, job interviews arranged, job search course, resume referral to employers, and resume preparation. In 1996–97, 214 organizations participated in on-campus recruiting; 5,200 on-campus interviews were conducted.

Employment Of 1996–97 graduates, 98% were employed within three months of graduation; the average starting salary was $78,200. Types of employment entered: accounting, banking, communications, computer-related, consulting, consumer products, education, energy, engineering, finance, financial services, government, health services, high technology, hospitality management, information systems/technology, international trade, management, manufacturing, marketing, media, nonprofit, petrochemical, pharmaceutical, real estate, service industry, telecommunications, transportation, utilities.

Business Program(s) URL: http://web.mit.edu/sloan/www/

Program Contact: Mr. Rod Garcia, Director of Master's Admissions, 50 Memorial Drive, E52-126, Cambridge, MA 02142. Phone: 617-253-3730; Fax: 617-253-6405; E-mail: masters@sloan.mit.edu

Nichols College

Graduate School of Business

Dudley, Massachusetts

OVERVIEW
Nichols College is an independent-nonprofit, coed, comprehensive institution. Enrollment: 3,300 graduate, professional, and undergraduate students; 6 full-time matriculated graduate/professional students; 377 part-time matriculated graduate/professional students. Founded: 1931. The graduate business unit is in a suburban setting and is on a semester calendar.

HIGHLIGHTS

Enrollment Profile

Full-time: 6	International: 2%
Part-time: 377	Women: 46%
Total: 383	Minorities: 7%
Average Age: 29	Average Class Size: 16
Fall 1997 Average GPA: 3.2	Fall 1997 Average GMAT: 480

Costs
Full-time tuition: N/R
Part-time tuition: $1050 per course

GRADUATE BUSINESS PROGRAMS
Master of Business Administration (MBA) Full-time, part-time; 36 total credits required; 15 months to 6 years to complete program. Concentrations in finance, international business, management, marketing, accounting.

ADMISSION
Applications For fall 1997 there were 80 applications for admission. Of those applying, 78 were accepted. Of those accepted, 65 enrolled.

Application Requirements GMAT score, application form, application fee, bachelor's degree, essay, minimum GPA, 2 letters of recommendation, personal statement, college transcript(s).

Application Deadline Applications processed on a rolling/continuous basis for both domestic and international students. Application fee: $25. Deferred entrance is available.

ACADEMICS
Faculty Full-time 21; part-time 6.

Teaching Methodologies Case study, lecture, research, student presentations, team projects.

Technology 30 on-campus computer terminals/PCs are available for student use and are linked by a campus-wide network. The network has full access to the Internet. Students are not required to have their own PC.

Special Opportunities Advanced credit may be earned through transfer of credits from another institution.

FINANCES
Costs for 1997–98 Tuition: $1050 per course. Cost varies by campus location. Average 1997–98 room only costs were $4500 per academic year (off campus).

Financial Aid Contact Ms. Diane Gillespie, Director of Financial Aid, Dudley, MA 01571-5000. Phone: 508-943-0099 Ext. 207; Fax: 508-943-1560.

FACILITIES
Information Resources Conant Library; total holdings of 65,000 volumes, 2,200 microforms, 450 current periodical subscriptions.

INTERNATIONAL STUDENTS
Demographics 2% of students enrolled are international students.

Services and Facilities Counseling/support services, language tutoring.

Applying TOEFL: minimum score of 550, proof of adequate funds required. Financial aid is not available to international students.

International Student Contact Mr. William F. Keith, Director, MBA Program, Dudley, MA 01571. Phone: 800-943-4893; Fax: 508-943-1560 Ext. 102.

PLACEMENT
Services include alumni network, career fairs, career placement, electronic job bank, job interviews arranged, and resume preparation. In 1996–97, 60 organizations participated in on-campus recruiting; 300 on-campus interviews were conducted.

Employment Types of employment entered: accounting, consumer products, energy, finance, financial services, high technology, insurance, telecommunications.

Program Contact: Mr. William F. Keith, Director, MBA Program, Dudley, MA 01571. Phone: 508-943-0099; Fax: 508-943-1560 Ext. 102.

Northeastern University

Graduate School of Business Administration

Boston, Massachusetts

OVERVIEW
Northeastern University is an independent-nonprofit, coed university. Enrollment: 26,999 graduate, professional, and undergraduate students; 2,696 full-time matriculated graduate/professional students; 1,938 part-time matriculated graduate/professional students. Founded: 1898. The graduate business unit is in an urban setting and is on a quarter calendar.

HIGHLIGHTS

Enrollment Profile
Full-time: 314
Part-time: 824
Total: 1,138
Average Age: 28
Fall 1997 Average GPA: 3.2

International: 8%
Women: 45%
Minorities: 4%
Average Class Size: 35
Fall 1997 Average GMAT: 540

Costs
Full-time tuition: $19,500 per academic year
Part-time tuition: $500 per credit

AACSB – The International Association for Management Education accredited

Degree(s) offered in conjunction with Brandeis University, Tufts University

GRADUATE BUSINESS PROGRAMS
Executive MBA (MBA) Part-time; 84 total credits required; 18 months to complete program.

Full-Time MBA (MBA) Full-time; 84 total credits required; 18 months to 2 years to complete program.

Cooperative Education MBA (MBA) Full-time; 84 total credits required; 21 months to complete program.

Part-Time MBA (MBA) Part-time; 74 total credits required; 2.5 to 7 years to complete program.

High Technology MBA (MBA) Part-time; 2 years to complete program.

Master of Science in Finance (MS) Full-time, part-time; 42 total credits required; 12 months to 4 years to complete program.

ADMISSION
Application Requirements Application form, application fee, bachelor's degree, essay, minimum GPA, interview, 2 letters of recommendation, personal statement, resume, college transcript(s).

Recommended for Application GMAT score accepted, work experience, computer experience.

Application Deadline Applications processed on a rolling/continuous basis for both domestic and international students. Application fee: $50. Deferred entrance is available.

ACADEMICS
Faculty Full-time 118; part-time 30.

Teaching Methodologies Case study, experiential learning, faculty seminars, field projects, group discussion, lecture, research, role playing, seminars by members of the business community, simulations, student presentations, study groups, team projects.

Technology Computer terminals/PCs are available for student use and are linked by a campus-wide network. The network has full access to the Internet. Students are not required to have their own PC.

Special Opportunities Advanced credit may be earned through transfer of credits from another institution. International exchange programs in Czech Republic, France, Republic of Singapore. An internship program is available.

FINANCES
Costs for 1997–98 Tuition: Full-time: $19,500 per year. Part-time: $500 per credit. Cost varies by academic program, number of credits taken. Average 1997–98 room and board costs were $10,380 per academic year. Room and board costs vary by campus location, occupancy (e.g., single, double, triple), type of accommodation, type of meal plan.

Financial Aid Fellowships, research assistantships, teaching assistantships, work study, loans available. Financial aid is available to part-time students. Application Deadline: 3/1.

Financial Aid Contact Mr. Keith Conant, Associate Director, Graduate Financial Aid, 410 Richards Hall, Boston, MA 02115. Phone: 617-373-5899; Fax: 617-373-8564.

FACILITIES
Information Resources Snell Library plus 5 additional on-campus libraries; total holdings of 777,252 volumes, 1,803,915 microforms, 8,831 current periodical subscriptions. CD player(s) available for graduate student use. Access provided to online bibliographic retrieval services.

INTERNATIONAL STUDENTS
Demographics 8% of students enrolled are international students [Africa, 7%, Asia, 52%, Central America, 4%, Europe, 20%, North America, 7%, South America, 10%].

Services and Facilities International student office, international student center, international student housing, visa services, ESL courses, counseling/support services.

Applying TOEFL: minimum score of 600, proof of adequate funds, proof of health/immunizations required. Financial aid is not available to international students.

International Student Contact Mr. David Enderlin, Associate Director, International Student Office, 203 E11 Building, 360 Huntington Avenue, Boston, MA 02115. Phone: 617-373-2318; Fax: 617-373-8564.

PLACEMENT
Services include alumni network, career counseling/planning, career fairs, career library, career placement, electronic job bank, job interviews arranged, job search course, resume referral to employers, and resume preparation. In 1996–97, 117 organizations participated in on-campus recruiting; 524 on-campus interviews were conducted.

Employment Of 1996–97 graduates, 86% were employed within three months of graduation; the average starting salary was $54,457. Types of employment entered: accounting, banking, chemical industry, communications, computer-related, consulting, consumer products, energy, engineering, finance, financial services, government, health services, high technology, hospitality management, human resources, information systems/technology, insurance, international trade, law, management, manufacturing, marketing, media, nonprofit, petrochemical, pharmaceutical, real estate, retail, service industry, telecommunications, transportation, utilities.

Business Program(s) URL: http://www.cba.neu.edu/gsba

Program Contact: Graduate School of Business Administration, 350 Dodge Hall, Boston, MA 02115. Phone: 617-373-2714; Fax: 617-373-8564; E-mail: gsba@cba.neu.edu

See full description on page 904.

Salem State College

Program in Business Administration

Salem, Massachusetts

OVERVIEW

Salem State College is a state-supported, coed, comprehensive institution. Enrollment: 9,227 graduate, professional, and undergraduate students; 195 full-time matriculated graduate/professional students; 798 part-time matriculated graduate/professional students. Founded: 1854. The graduate business unit is in a suburban setting and is on a semester calendar.

HIGHLIGHTS

Enrollment Profile
Full-time: 0
Part-time: 116
Total: 116
Average Age: N/R
Fall 1997 Average GPA: 2.82

International: N/R
Women: 39%
Minorities: N/R
Average Class Size: 9
Fall 1997 Average GMAT: 433

Costs
Full-time tuition: N/R
Part-time tuition: $140 per credit hour (resident); $230 per credit hour (nonresident)

GRADUATE BUSINESS PROGRAMS

Master of Business Administration (MBA) Part-time; 54 total credits required; 2 to 6 years to complete program.

ADMISSION

Applications For fall 1997 there were 37 applications for admission. Of those applying, 31 were accepted. Of those accepted, 23 enrolled.

Application Requirements GMAT score, application form, application fee, bachelor's degree, minimum GPA: 2.5, interview, 3 letters of recommendation, personal statement, resume, college transcript(s), computer experience: computer literacy.

Application Deadline 7/1 for fall, 11/1 for spring, 7/1 for fall (international), 11/1 for spring (international). Application fee: $25.

ACADEMICS

Faculty Full-time 18; part-time 4.

Teaching Methodologies Case study, computer-aided instruction, computer analysis, computer simulations, experiential learning, field projects, group discussion, lecture, research, role playing, student presentations, team projects.

Technology 350 on-campus computer terminals/PCs are available for student use and are linked by a campus-wide network. The network has full access to the Internet. Students are not required to have their own PC.

Special Opportunities Advanced credit may be earned through transfer of credits from another institution.

FINANCES

Costs for 1997–98 Tuition: Part-time: $140 per credit hour (resident); $230 per credit hour (nonresident). Fees: Part-time: $20 per credit hour (resident); $20 per credit hour (nonresident).

Financial Aid Research assistantships, work study, loans available. Financial aid is available to part-time students. Application Deadline: 4/15.

Financial Aid Contact Ms. Janet Lundstrom, Director, Financial Aid, 352 Lafayette Street, Salem, MA 01970-5353. Phone: 978-542-6112; Fax: 508-741-6876.

FACILITIES

Information Resources Salem State College Library plus 1 additional on-campus library; total holdings of 190,695 volumes, 169,530 microforms, 1,432 current periodical subscriptions. CD player(s) available for graduate student use. Access provided to online bibliographic retrieval services.

INTERNATIONAL STUDENTS

Demographics N/R

Services and Facilities International student office, international student center, visa services, ESL courses, counseling/support services, cultural programming.

Applying TOEFL: minimum score of 550, proof of adequate funds, proof of health/immunizations required. Financial aid is not available to international students.

International Student Contact Dr. Donald Ross, Director, Center for International Education, 352 Lafayette Street, Salem, MA 01970. Phone: 978-542-6351; Fax: 978-542-7104; E-mail: donald.ross@salem.mass.edu

PLACEMENT

Services include career counseling/planning, career fairs, career library, career placement, electronic job bank, resume referral to employers, and resume preparation. In 1996–97, 69 organizations participated in on-campus recruiting; 55 on-campus interviews were conducted.

Business Program(s) URL: http://www.salem-ma.edu

Program Contact: A. Richard Anderson, Coordinator, Graduate Programs in Business, 352 Lafayette Street, Salem, MA 01970. Phone: 978-542-6320; Fax: 978-542-7215.

Simmons College

Graduate School of Management

Boston, Massachusetts

OVERVIEW

Simmons College is an independent-nonprofit, women only, comprehensive institution. Enrollment: 3,596 graduate, professional, and undergraduate students. Founded: 1899. The graduate business unit is in an urban setting and is on a semester calendar.

HIGHLIGHTS

Enrollment Profile
Full-time: 50
Part-time: 207
Total: 257
Average Age: 32
Fall 1997 Average GPA: 3.2

International: 4%
Women: 100%
Minorities: 9%
Average Class Size: 45
Fall 1997 Average GMAT: 560

Costs
Full-time tuition: N/R
Part-time tuition: $596 per credit hour

GRADUATE BUSINESS PROGRAMS

Master of Business Administration (MBA) Full-time, part-time; 45 total credits required; 11 months to 5 years to complete program. Concentration in management.

ADMISSION

Applications For fall 1997 there were 209 applications for admission.

Application Requirements GMAT score, application form, application fee, essay, 3 letters of recommendation, personal statement, resume, college transcript(s), minimum of 2 years of work experience.

Recommended for Application Interview, computer experience.

Application Deadline 6/30 for fall, 11/15 for spring, 6/30 for fall (international), 11/15 for spring (international). Application fee: $75.

ACADEMICS

Faculty Full-time 11; part-time 2.

Teaching Methodologies Case study, computer simulations, experiential learning, field projects, group discussion, lecture, research, role playing, seminars by members of the business community, simulations, student presentations, study groups, team projects.

Technology 60 on-campus computer terminals/PCs are available for student use and are linked by a campus-wide network. The network has full access to the Internet. Students are not required to have their own PC.

Special Opportunities An internship program is available.

FINANCES

Costs for 1997–98 Tuition: $596 per credit hour. Average 1997–98 room and board costs were $9300 per academic year.

Financial Aid Grants, scholarships, work study, loans available. Financial aid is available to part-time students. Application Deadline: 3/1.

Financial Aid Contact Mr. Brian Hodge, Director of Financial Aid, 300 The Fenway, Boston, MA 02115. Phone: 617-521-3840; Fax: 617-738-2099.

FACILITIES

Information Resources Beatley Library plus 4 additional on-campus libraries; total holdings of 266,417 volumes, 1,400 microforms, 2,027 current periodical subscriptions. CD player(s) available for graduate student use. Access provided to online bibliographic retrieval services.

INTERNATIONAL STUDENTS

Demographics 4% of students enrolled are international students [Africa, 3%, Asia, 25%, Australia/New Zealand, 2%, Central America, 5%, Europe, 50%, North America, 5%, South America, 10%].

Services and Facilities International student office, international student housing, visa services, ESL courses, counseling/support services, language tutoring.

Applying TOEFL: minimum score of 550, proof of adequate funds, proof of health/immunizations required. TSE, TWE recommended. Financial aid is available to international students.

International Student Contact MBA Admissions Office, 409 Commonwealth Avenue, Boston, MA 02215. Phone: 617-521-3840; Fax: 617-521-3880.

PLACEMENT

Services include alumni network, career counseling/planning, career fairs, career library, career placement, electronic job bank, job interviews arranged, job search course, resume referral to employers, and resume preparation.

Employment Of 1996–97 graduates, 80% were employed within three months of graduation. Types of employment entered: accounting, banking, communications, computer-related, consulting, consumer products, education, engineering, finance, financial services, government, health services, high technology, hospitality management, human resources, information systems/technology, insurance, law, management, manufacturing, marketing, media, nonprofit, pharmaceutical, real estate, service industry, telecommunications, transportation, utilities.

Business Program(s) URL: http://www.simmons.edu/gsm

Program Contact: Ms. Shelley Conley, Director of Admissions, MBA Program, 409 Commonwealth Avenue, Boston, MA 02215. Phone: 617-521-3840; Fax: 617-521-3880; E-mail: sburt@simmons.edu
See full description on page 988.

Suffolk University

Frank Sawyer School of Management

Boston, Massachusetts

OVERVIEW

Suffolk University is an independent-nonprofit, coed, comprehensive institution. Enrollment: 6,290 graduate, professional, and undergraduate students; 1,236 full-time matriculated graduate/professional students; 1,994 part-time matriculated graduate/professional students. Founded: 1906. The graduate business unit is in an urban setting and is on a semester calendar.

HIGHLIGHTS

Enrollment Profile
Full-time: 150
Part-time: 998
Total: 1,148
Average Age: 30
Fall 1997 Average GPA: 3.11

International: 10%
Women: 45%
Minorities: 6%
Average Class Size: 19
Fall 1997 Average GMAT: 500

Costs
Full-time tuition: $17,490 per academic year
Part-time tuition: $1749 per course

AACSB – The International Association for Management Education accredited

GRADUATE BUSINESS PROGRAMS

Master of Business Administration (MBA) Full-time, part-time; 54 total credits required; 10 months to 5 years to complete program. Concentrations in accounting, business law, entrepreneurship, finance, human resources, financial economics, management, management information systems, marketing, nonprofit management, organizational behavior/development, organizational management, public management, public policy and administration.

Executive MBA (MBA) Full-time; 54 total credits required; 15 months to 2.5 years to complete program. Concentrations in accounting, business law, entrepreneurship, finance, human resources, international business, management, management information systems, marketing, nonprofit management, organizational behavior/development, organizational management, public management, public policy and administration.

Master of Business Administration in Health (MBA) Full-time, part-time; 54 total credits required; 10 months to 5 years to complete program.

Master of Business Administration/Doctor of Jurisprudence (MBA/JD) Full-time; 117 total credits required; 4 years to complete program.

Master of Science in Entrepreneurial Studies (MS) Full-time, part-time; 48 total credits required; 10 months to 5 years to complete program. Concentration in entrepreneurship.

Master of Science in Finance (MS) Full-time, part-time; 30-48 total credits required; 12 months to 5 years to complete program. Concentration in finance.

Master of Science in Financial Services and Banking (MS) Full-time, part-time; 30-48 total credits required; 12 months to 5 years to complete program. Concentrations in banking, finance.

Master of Science in Accounting (MS) Full-time, part-time; 30-60 total credits required; 10 months to 5 years to complete program. Concentration in accounting.

Master of Science in Taxation (MS) Full-time, part-time; 30 total credits required; 10 months to 5 years to complete program. Concentration in taxation.

ADMISSION

Applications For fall 1997 there were 606 applications for admission. Of those applying, 474 were accepted. Of those accepted, 257 enrolled.

Application Requirements Application form, application fee, bachelor's degree, minimum GPA: 2.6, 2 letters of recommendation, personal statement, resume, college transcript(s).

Recommended for Application GMAT score accepted, work experience.

Application Deadline 6/15 for fall, 11/15 for spring, 4/15 for summer, 6/15 for fall (international), 11/15 for spring (international), 4/15 for summer (international). Application fee: $50. Deferred entrance is available.

ACADEMICS

Faculty Full-time 67; part-time 80.

Teaching Methodologies Case study, computer-aided instruction, computer analysis, computer simulations, experiential learning, faculty seminars, field projects, group discussion, lecture, research, role playing, seminars by members of the business community, simulations, student presentations, study groups, team projects.

Technology 250 on-campus computer terminals/PCs are available for student use and are linked by a campus-wide network. The network has full access to the Internet. Students are not required to have their own PC.

Special Opportunities Advanced credit may be earned through credit by examination, transfer of credits from another institution. International exchange programs in Czech Republic, France, Ireland, Italy, Spain. An internship program is available.

FINANCES

Costs for 1997–98 Tuition: Full-time: $17,490 per year. Part-time: $1749 per course. Cost varies by academic program, number of credits taken. Fees: Full-time: $120 per academic year. Part-time: $60 per year. Fees vary by number of credits taken. Average 1997–98 room and board costs were $9000 per academic year (off campus).

Financial Aid In 1997–98, 30% of students received some institutionally administered aid in the form of fellowships, grants, work study, loans. Financial aid is available to part-time students. Application Deadline: 3/15.

Financial Aid Contact Christine Perry, Director of Financial Aid, 8 Ashburton Place, Boston, MA 02108-2770. Phone: 617-573-8470; Fax: 617-742-4291; E-mail: cperry@acad.suffolk.edu

FACILITIES

Information Resources Sawyer Library plus 2 additional on-campus libraries; total holdings of 285,047 volumes, 307,533 microforms, 5,320 current periodical subscriptions. CD player(s) available for graduate student use. Access provided to online bibliographic retrieval services.

INTERNATIONAL STUDENTS

Demographics 10% of students enrolled are international students [Africa, 3%, Asia, 50%, Europe, 29%, North America, 6%, South America, 3%, other, 9%].

Services and Facilities International student office, visa services, ESL courses, counseling/support services.

Applying TOEFL: minimum score of 550, proof of adequate funds, proof of health/immunizations required. Financial aid is available to international students.

International Student Contact Margaret Loret, Director, Center for International Education, 8 Ashburton Place, Boston, MA 02108-2770. Phone: 617-573-8072; Fax: 617-742-2651; E-mail: mloret@admin.suffolk.edu

PLACEMENT

Services include alumni network, career counseling/planning, career fairs, career library, career placement, electronic job bank, job interviews arranged, resume referral to employers, and resume preparation. In 1996–97, 90 organizations participated in on-campus recruiting; 200 on-campus interviews were conducted.

Employment Of 1996–97 graduates, 95% were employed within three months of graduation; the average starting salary was $60,200. Types of employment entered: accounting, banking, computer-related, consulting, consumer products, finance, financial services, health services, high technology, human resources, information systems/technology, insurance, international trade, law, management, manufacturing, marketing, pharmaceutical, retail, service industry, telecommunications, utilities.

Business Program(s) URL: http://www.sawyer.suffolk.edu/

Program Contact: Judy Reynolds, Director of Graduate Admission, 8 Ashburton Place, Boston, MA 02108-2770. Phone: 617-573-8302; Fax: 617-523-0116; E-mail: grad.admission@admin.suffolk.edu
See full description on page 1004.

University of Massachusetts Amherst

School of Management

Amherst, Massachusetts

OVERVIEW

The University of Massachusetts Amherst is a state-supported, coed university. Enrollment: 25,509 graduate, professional, and undergraduate students; 2,366 full-time matriculated graduate/professional students; 3,589 part-time matriculated graduate/professional students. Founded: 1863. The graduate business unit is in a small-town setting and is on a semester calendar.

HIGHLIGHTS

Enrollment Profile
Full-time: 67
Part-time: 306
Total: 373
Average Age: 27
Fall 1997 Average GPA: 3.27

International: 6%
Women: 44%
Minorities: 4%
Average Class Size: 35
Fall 1997 Average GMAT: 593

Costs
Full-time tuition: $2080 per academic year (resident); $6625 per academic year (nonresident)
Part-time tuition: $335 per credit (resident); $335 per credit (nonresident)

AACSB – The International Association for Management Education accredited

GRADUATE BUSINESS PROGRAMS

Master of Business Administration/Master of Science in Accounting (MBA/MS) Full-time, distance learning option; 55 total credits required; 2 years to complete program. Concentrations in accounting, finance, human resources, management, marketing, health care, nonprofit organization.

Professional Master of Business Administration (MBA) Full-time, part-time, distance learning option; 37 total credits required; 12 months to 4 years to complete program. Concentrations in management, health care, nonprofit organization.

ADMISSION

Applications For fall 1997 there were 390 applications for admission. Of those applying, 148 were accepted. Of those accepted, 103 enrolled.

Application Requirements GMAT score: minimum 600, application form, application fee, bachelor's degree, minimum GPA: 3.0, 2 letters of recommendation, personal statement, resume, college transcript(s), minimum of 3 years of work experience.

Recommended for Application Interview, computer experience.

Application Deadline 3/1 for fall, 3/1 for fall (international). Application fee: $25, $40 (international). Deferred entrance is available.

ACADEMICS

Faculty Full-time 57.

Teaching Methodologies Case study, computer-aided instruction, computer analysis, computer simulations, experiential learning, field projects, group discussion, lecture, research, role playing, seminars by members of the business community, student presentations, study groups, team projects.

Technology 350 on-campus computer terminals/PCs are available for student use and are linked by a campus-wide network. The network has full access to the Internet. Students are not required to have their own PC.

Special Opportunities Advanced credit may be earned through credit by examination, transfer of credits from another institution. International exchange programs in France, Sweden. An internship program is available.

FINANCES

Costs for 1997–98 Tuition: Full-time: $2080 per semester (resident); $6625 per semester (nonresident). Part-time: $335 per credit (resident); $335 per credit (nonresident). Cost varies by reciprocity agreements. Fees: Full-time: $2820 per academic year (resident); $2820 per academic year (nonresident). Average 1997–98 room and board costs were $4230 per academic year (on campus) and $6500 per academic year (off campus). Room and board costs vary by occupancy (e.g., single, double, triple), type of accommodation, type of meal plan.

Financial Aid In 1997–98, 5% of students received some institutionally administered aid in the form of fellowships, research assistantships, teaching assistantships, scholarships, work study, loans. Financial aid is available to part-time students. Application Deadline: 3/1.

Financial Aid Contact Financial Aid Services, 255 Whitmore Building, Amherst, MA 01003. Phone: 413-545-0801; Fax: 313-545-3858; E-mail: a.peramba@dpc.umassp.edu

FACILITIES

Information Resources W. E. B. DuBois Library plus 2 additional on-campus libraries; total holdings of 2,647,000 volumes, 1,839,000 microforms, 8,750 current periodical subscriptions. CD player(s) available for graduate student use. Access provided to online bibliographic retrieval services.

INTERNATIONAL STUDENTS

Demographics 6% of students enrolled are international students [Asia, 5%, Europe, 3%, North America, 92%].

Services and Facilities International student office, international student center, international student housing, visa services, counseling/support services.

Applying TOEFL: minimum score of 600, proof of adequate funds, proof of health/immunizations required. Financial aid is not available to international students.

International Student Contact Patricia Vokbus, Deputy Director of International Programs Office, William S. Clark International Center, Amherst, MA 01003. Phone: 413-545-2843; Fax: 413-545-1201; E-mail: fso@ipo.umass.edu

PLACEMENT

Services include alumni network, career counseling/planning, career fairs, career library, career placement, electronic job bank, job interviews arranged, job search course, resume referral to employers, and resume preparation.

Employment Of 1996–97 graduates, 90% were employed within three months of graduation. Types of employment entered: accounting, banking, computer-related, consulting, consumer products, finance, financial services, government, health services, high technology, human resources, information systems/technology, insurance, international trade, management, manufacturing, marketing, nonprofit, retail, service industry, telecommunications.

Business Program(s) URL: http://www.som.umass.edu

Program Contact: Heather Miller, Director of Admissions, MBA Programs Office, 209 School of Management, Amherst, MA 01003-4910. Phone: 413-545-5608; Fax: 413-545-3858; E-mail: gradprog@som.umass.edu

University of Massachusetts Boston

College of Management

Boston, Massachusetts

OVERVIEW

The University of Massachusetts Boston is a state-supported, coed university. Enrollment: 11,800 graduate, professional, and undergraduate students; 667 full-time matriculated graduate/professional students; 1,698 part-time matriculated graduate/professional students. Founded: 1965. The graduate business unit is in an urban setting and is on a semester calendar.

HIGHLIGHTS

Enrollment Profile
Full-time: 70
Part-time: 316
Total: 386
Average Age: 28
Fall 1997 Average GPA: 3.22

International: 12%
Women: 45%
Minorities: 12%
Average Class Size: 25
Fall 1997 Average GMAT: 540

Costs
Full-time tuition: $1320 per academic year (resident); $4422 per academic year (nonresident)
Part-time tuition: $110 per credit (resident); $369 per credit (nonresident)

GRADUATE BUSINESS PROGRAMS

Master of Business Administration/Master of Science in Nursing (MBA/MS) Full-time, part-time; 48-69 total credits required; 2 to 5 years to complete program. Concentrations in health care, accounting, finance, human resources, international management, management information systems, marketing, operations management, environmental economics/management.

Master of Business Administration/Baccalaureate (MBA/BA/BS) Full-time, part-time; 150 total credits required; 5 to 8 years to complete program. Concentrations in accounting, finance, human resources, international management, management information systems, marketing, operations management, environmental economics/management, health care.

ADMISSION

Applications For fall 1997 there were 325 applications for admission. Of those applying, 150 were accepted. Of those accepted, 80 enrolled.

Application Requirements Application form, application fee, bachelor's degree, essay, minimum GPA: 2.75, 3 letters of recommendation, personal statement, resume, college transcript(s).

Recommended for Application GMAT score accepted, computer experience.

Application Deadline 6/1 for fall, 11/1 for spring, 5/1 for fall (international), 10/1 for spring (international). Application fee: $25, $40 (international). Deferred entrance is available.

ACADEMICS
Faculty Full-time 46; part-time 15.

Teaching Methodologies Case study, computer-aided instruction, computer analysis, computer simulations, experiential learning, field projects, group discussion, lecture, research, role playing, seminars by members of the business community, simulations, student presentations, study groups, team projects.

Technology 500 on-campus computer terminals/PCs are available for student use and are linked by a campus-wide network. The network has full access to the Internet. Students are not required to have their own PC.

Special Opportunities Advanced credit may be earned through credit by examination, transfer of credits from another institution. International exchange programs in Haiti, United Kingdom, Vietnam. An internship program is available.

FINANCES
Costs for 1997–98 Tuition: Full-time: $1320 per semester (resident); $4422 per semester (nonresident). Part-time: $110 per credit (resident); $369 per credit (nonresident). Cost varies by number of credits taken. Fees: Full-time: $1155 per academic year (resident); $1155 per academic year (nonresident). Part-time: $85 per credit (resident); $85 per credit (nonresident). Fees vary by number of credits taken. Average 1997–98 room only costs were $6500 per academic year (off campus).

Financial Aid Research assistantships, teaching assistantships, loans available. Financial aid is available to part-time students. Application Deadline: 3/1.

Financial Aid Contact Ms. Ernestine Whiting, Director of Financial Aid, 100 Morrissey Boulevard, Boston, MA 02125-3393. Phone: 617-287-6300; Fax: 617-287-6323.

FACILITIES
Information Resources Joseph P. Healey Library plus 1 additional on-campus library; total holdings of 600,000 volumes, 701,529 microforms, 3,400 current periodical subscriptions. CD player(s) available for graduate student use. Access provided to online bibliographic retrieval services and online databases.

INTERNATIONAL STUDENTS
Demographics 12% of students enrolled are international students [Africa, 9%, Asia, 61%, Australia/New Zealand, 1%, Central America, 1%, Europe, 21%, North America, 1%, South America, 3%, other, 3%].

Services and Facilities International student office, international student center, visa services, ESL courses, counseling/support services.

Applying TOEFL: minimum score of 550, proof of adequate funds, proof of health/immunizations required. Financial aid is not available to international students.

International Student Contact Mrs. Peggy Roldan, Admissions Officer, 100 Morrissey Boulevard, Boston, MA 02125-3393. Phone: 617-287-6401; Fax: 617-287-6236.

PLACEMENT
Services include alumni network, career counseling/planning, career fairs, career library, career placement, electronic job bank, job interviews arranged, job search course, resume referral to employers, and resume preparation. In 1996–97, 65 organizations participated in on-campus recruiting.

Employment Of 1996–97 graduates, 90% were employed within three months of graduation. Types of employment entered: accounting, banking, communications, computer-related, consulting, consumer products, education, energy, engineering, finance, financial services, government, health services, high technology, hospitality management, human resources, information systems/technology, insurance, international trade, law, management, manufacturing, marketing, media, nonprofit, pharmaceutical, real estate, retail, service industry, telecommunications, transportation, utilities.

Business Program(s) URL: http://www.mgmt.umb.edu

Program Contact: Mr. Daniel Robb, MBA Office, 100 Morrissey Boulevard, Boston, MA 02125-3393. Phone: 617-287-7720; Fax: 617-287-7725.

University of Massachusetts Dartmouth

College of Business and Industry

North Dartmouth, Massachusetts

OVERVIEW
The University of Massachusetts Dartmouth is a state-supported, coed, comprehensive institution. Enrollment: 5,034 graduate, professional, and undergraduate students; 188 full-time matriculated graduate/professional students; 352 part-time matriculated graduate/professional students. Founded: 1895. The graduate business unit is in a rural setting and is on a semester calendar.

HIGHLIGHTS
Enrollment Profile

Full-time: 29	International: 31%
Part-time: 51	Women: 55%
Total: 80	Minorities: 1%
Average Age: 30	Average Class Size: 18
Fall 1997 Average GPA: N/R	Fall 1997 Average GMAT: 495

Costs
Full-time tuition: $2071 per academic year (resident); $7192 per academic year (nonresident)
Part-time tuition: $86 per credit (resident); $300 per credit (nonresident)

GRADUATE BUSINESS PROGRAMS
Master of Business Administration (MBA) Full-time, part-time; 30 total credits required; 2 to 5 years to complete program. Concentration in management.

ADMISSION
Applications For fall 1997 there were 72 applications for admission. Of those applying, 60 were accepted. Of those accepted, 31 enrolled.

Application Requirements GMAT score, application form, application fee, bachelor's degree, 2 letters of recommendation, personal statement, resume, college transcript(s).

Application Deadline 4/20 for fall, 11/15 for spring, 2/20 for fall (international), 9/15 for spring (international). Application fee: $20, $40 (international). Deferred entrance is available.

ACADEMICS
Faculty Full-time 28; part-time 10.

Teaching Methodologies Case study, lecture, research, student presentations, team projects.

Technology 300 on-campus computer terminals/PCs are available for student use and are linked by a campus-wide network. The network has full access to the Internet. Students are not required to have their own PC.

Special Opportunities Advanced credit may be earned through transfer of credits from another institution.

FINANCES
Costs for 1997–98 Tuition: Full-time: $2071 per year (resident); $7192 per year (nonresident). Part-time: $86 per credit (resident); $300 per credit (nonresident). Cost varies by class time (e.g., day/evening), number of credits taken, reciprocity agreements. Fees: Full-time: $2768 per academic year (resident); $3783 per academic year (nonresident). Part-time: $138 per credit (resident); $189 per credit (nonresident). Fees vary by academic program, class time (e.g., day/evening), number of credits taken, reciprocity agreements. Average 1997–98 room only costs were $3184 per academic year. Room and board costs vary by occupancy (e.g., single, double, triple), type of meal plan.

Financial Aid Research assistantships, teaching assistantships, loans available. Financial aid is available to part-time students. Application Deadline: 3/15.

Financial Aid Contact Mr. Gerald Coutinho, Director of Financial Aid, 285 Old Westport Road, North Dartmouth, MA 02747-2300. Phone: 508-999-8632; Fax: 508-999-8983; E-mail: gcoutinho@umassd.edu

FACILITIES
Information Resources UMass Dartmouth University Library; total holdings of 430,194 volumes, 694,827 microforms, 3,118 current periodical subscriptions. CD player(s) available for graduate student use. Access provided to online bibliographic retrieval services and online databases.

INTERNATIONAL STUDENTS
Demographics 31% of students enrolled are international students [Africa, 4%, Asia, 80%, Europe, 8%, other, 8%].

Services and Facilities International student office, visa services, ESL courses, counseling/support services.

Applying TOEFL: minimum score of 500, proof of adequate funds required. Financial aid is available to international students.

International Student Contact Dr. Richard Panofsky, Associate Vice Chancellor for Academic Affairs, 285 Old Westport Road, North Dartmouth, MA 02747-2300. Phone: 508-999-8029; Fax: 508-999-8183; E-mail: rpanofsky@umassd.edu

PLACEMENT
Services include alumni network, career counseling/planning, career fairs, career library, career placement, electronic job bank, job interviews arranged, and resume preparation.

Business Program(s) URL: http://www.umassd.edu/

Program Contact: Ms. Carol Novo, Coordinator of Graduate Admissions, 285 Old Westport Road, North Dartmouth, MA 02747-2300. Phone: 508-999-8604; Fax: 508-999-8183; E-mail: cnovo@umassd.edu

University of Massachusetts Lowell

College of Management

Lowell, Massachusetts

OVERVIEW
The University of Massachusetts Lowell is a state-supported, coed university. Enrollment: 12,350 graduate, professional, and undergraduate students; 803 full-time matriculated graduate/professional students; 1,982 part-time matriculated graduate/professional students. Founded: 1894. The graduate business unit is in an urban setting and is on a semester calendar.

HIGHLIGHTS

Enrollment Profile

Full-time: 30	International: 6%
Part-time: 292	Women: 32%
Total: 322	Minorities: 4%
Average Age: 25	Average Class Size: 25
Fall 1997 Average GPA: 3.0	Fall 1997 Average GMAT: 520

Costs
Full-time tuition: N/R
Part-time tuition: $89 per credit hour (resident); $306 per credit hour (nonresident)

AACSB – The International Association for Management Education accredited

GRADUATE BUSINESS PROGRAMS
Master of Business Administration (MBA) Full-time, part-time; 42 total credits required; 2.5 to 4 years to complete program. Concentrations in management, management information systems, marketing, finance.

Master of Management Science in Manufacturing (MMS) Full-time, part-time; 33 total credits required; 2 to 4 years to complete program. Concentrations in profit management, technology management.

ADMISSION
Applications For fall 1997 there were 181 applications for admission. Of those applying, 150 were accepted. Of those accepted, 126 enrolled.

Application Requirements GMAT score, application fee, bachelor's degree, 3 letters of recommendation, personal statement, college transcript(s).

Application Deadline Applications processed on a rolling/continuous basis for domestic students only. 4/1 for fall (international), 11/1 for spring (international). Application fee: $20, $35 (international). Deferred entrance is available.

ACADEMICS
Faculty Full-time 31; part-time 4.

Teaching Methodologies Case study, lecture, seminars by members of the business community, student presentations, team projects.

Technology 400 on-campus computer terminals/PCs are available for student use and are linked by a campus-wide network. The network has full access to the Internet. Students are not required to have their own PC.

Special Opportunities Advanced credit may be earned through transfer of credits from another institution.

FINANCES
Costs for 1997–98 Tuition: $89 per credit hour (resident); $306 per credit hour (nonresident). Fees: $125 per credit hour (resident); $126 per credit hour (nonresident). Average 1997–98 room and board costs were $4066 per academic year.

Financial Aid In 1997–98, 2% of students received some institutionally administered aid in the form of fellowships, research assistantships, teaching assistantships, work study, loans. Financial aid is available to part-time students. Application Deadline: 4/1.

Financial Aid Contact Ms. Carole King, Program Coordinator, 1 University Avenue, Lowell, MA 01854-2881. Phone: 978-934-4237; E-mail: keyes@rgang.ulowell.edu

FACILITIES
Information Resources Lydon Library plus 1 additional on-campus library; total holdings of 383,712 volumes, 611,799 microforms, 3,425 current periodical subscriptions. CD player(s) available for graduate student use. Access provided to online bibliographic retrieval services.

INTERNATIONAL STUDENTS
Demographics 6% of students enrolled are international students.

Services and Facilities International student office, ESL courses, counseling/support services.

Applying TOEFL: minimum score of 550, proof of adequate funds, proof of health/immunizations required. Financial aid is available to international students.

International Student Contact Ms. Anne Dean, Staff Assistant, Graduate School International Office, 1 University Avenue, Lowell, MA 01854-2881. Phone: 978-934-2386.

PLACEMENT
Services include alumni network, career counseling/planning, career fairs, job interviews arranged, and resume preparation.

Employment Of 1996–97 graduates, 85% were employed within three months of graduation.

Business Program(s) URL: http://www.uml.edu/College/Management/

Program Contact: Ms. Kathleen Rourke, Assistant Director of MBA Program, 1 University Avenue, Lowell, MA 01854-2881. Phone: 978-934-2848; Fax: 978-934-3011; E-mail: rourkek@woods.uml.edu

Western New England College

School of Business

Springfield, Massachusetts

OVERVIEW
Western New England College is an independent-nonprofit, coed, comprehensive institution. Enrollment: 4,200 graduate, professional, and undergraduate students; 485 full-time matriculated graduate/professional students; 1,121 part-time matriculated graduate/professional students. Founded: 1919. The graduate business unit is in a suburban setting and is on a semester calendar.

HIGHLIGHTS

Enrollment Profile

Full-time: 0	International: N/R
Part-time: 763	Women: 40%
Total: 763	Minorities: 5%
Average Age: 29	Average Class Size: 25
Fall 1997 Average GPA: 2.9	Fall 1997 Average GMAT: N/R

Costs
Full-time tuition: N/R
Part-time tuition: $351 per semester hour

GRADUATE BUSINESS PROGRAMS
Master of Business Administration (MBA) Part-time; 36 total credits required; 2 to 8 years to complete program. Concentrations in accounting, finance, human resources, management information systems, international business, marketing, health care.

Weekend MBA (MBA) Part-time; 30 total credits required; 12 months to complete program.

Master of Science in Information Systems (MS) Part-time; 33 total credits required; 3 to 8 years to complete program. Concentration in management information systems.

Master of Science in Accounting (MS) Part-time; 51 total credits required; 3 to 8 years to complete program. Concentration in accounting.

ADMISSION
Applications For fall 1997 there were 125 applications for admission. Of those applying, 100 were accepted.

Application Requirements Application form, application fee, bachelor's degree, minimum GPA, personal statement, resume, college transcript(s).

Recommended for Application GMAT score accepted.

Application Deadline Applications processed on a rolling/continuous basis for both domestic and international students. Application fee: $30. Deferred entrance is available.

ACADEMICS
Faculty Full-time 28; part-time 17.

Teaching Methodologies Case study, computer analysis, computer simulations, faculty seminars, group discussion, lecture, research, seminars by members of the business community, simulations, student presentations, study groups, team projects.

Technology 125 on-campus computer terminals/PCs are available for student use and are linked by a campus-wide network. The network has full access to the Internet. Students are not required to have their own PC.

Special Opportunities Advanced credit may be earned through credit by examination, transfer of credits from another institution.

FINANCES
Costs for 1997–98 Tuition: Part-time: $351 per semester hour. Cost varies by campus location, class time (e.g., day/evening). Fees: Part-time: $25 per semester.

Financial Aid Financial aid is available to part-time students.

Financial Aid Contact Mr. Rodney Pease, Director of Student Administrative Services, 1215 Wilbraham Road, Springfield, MA 01119-2654. Phone: 413-796-2080; Fax: 413-796-2068.

FACILITIES
Information Resources D'Amour Library plus 1 additional on-campus library; total holdings of 289,451 volumes, 3,098,750 microforms, 4,293 current periodical subscriptions. CD player(s) available for graduate student use. Access provided to online bibliographic retrieval services.

INTERNATIONAL STUDENTS
Demographics N/R

Services and Facilities International student office, counseling/support services.

Applying TOEFL, proof of adequate funds required. Financial aid is not available to international students.

International Student Contact Mr. Harold Neunder, Administrative Director of Continuing Education, 1215 Wilbraham Road, Springfield, MA 01119-2654. Phone: 413-782-1750; Fax: 413-782-1779.

PLACEMENT
Services include alumni network, career placement, electronic job bank, and resume preparation.

Employment Types of employment entered: accounting, banking, communications, computer-related, consulting, consumer products, education, energy, engineering, finance, financial services, government, health services, high technology, human resources, information systems/technology, law, management, manufacturing, marketing, nonprofit, pharmaceutical, real estate, retail, service industry, telecommunications, transportation, utilities.

Business Program(s) URL: http://www.wnec.edu

Program Contact: Mr. Harold Neunder, Administrative Director of Continuing Education, 1215 Wilbraham Road, Springfield, MA 01119-2654. Phone: 413-782-1750, 800-325-1122; Fax: 413-782-1779.

Worcester Polytechnic Institute

Graduate Management Programs

Worcester, Massachusetts

OVERVIEW
Worcester Polytechnic Institute is an independent-nonprofit, coed university. Enrollment: 3,648 graduate, professional, and undergraduate students; 401 full-time matriculated graduate/professional students; 636 part-time matriculated graduate/professional students. Founded: 1865. The graduate business unit is in a suburban setting and is on a semester calendar.

HIGHLIGHTS

Enrollment Profile
Full-time: 20
Part-time: 180
Total: 200
Average Age: 33
Fall 1997 Average GPA: 3.1

International: 10%
Women: 25%
Minorities: 4%
Average Class Size: 15
Fall 1997 Average GMAT: 563

Costs
Full-time tuition: N/R
Part-time tuition: $636 per credit

V*irtually every company relies on technology—to manage complexity, reduce costs, improve quality, and bring new products to market faster. Sometimes they even create new technologies. Worcester Polytechnic Institute (WPI), the nation's third-oldest private technological university, has been offering highly flexible, highly relevant M.B.A. and master's programs in management for more than two decades. Each is distinguished by a strong technology management focus and a global perspective. WPI graduates know how to leverage technological innovation to grow their companies, and in doing so, they leverage their own career growth. This is why WPI management graduates have an outstanding record of success in the business community.*

In addition to the Master of Business Administration, WPI offers Master of Science in Marketing and Technological Innovation and Master of Science in Operations and Information Technology degrees as well as a variety of graduate certificate programs.

WPI's student-friendly options include full- or part-time study at WPI campuses in Worcester and Waltham, Massachusetts, and world wide via its Advanced Distance Learning Network. Curriculum and career planning, through a committed, involved academic adviser, are an integral part of the WPI experience and help prepare graduates for the unique management challenges of a technology-driven environment.

GRADUATE BUSINESS PROGRAMS
Master of Business Administration (MBA) Full-time, part-time, distance learning option; 31-49 total credits required; 11 months to 8 years to complete program. Concentrations in construction management, entrepreneurship, management, management information systems, manufacturing management, project management, technology management, operations management, marketing.

Master of Science in Marketing and Technological Innovation (MS) Full-time, part-time, distance learning option; 30 total credits required; 11 months to 8 years to complete program. Concentrations in technology management, marketing.

Master of Science in Operations and Information Technology (MS) Full-time, part-time, distance learning option; 30 total credits required; 11 months to 8 years to complete program. Concentrations in management information systems, operations management, production management.

ADMISSION
Applications For fall 1997 there were 59 applications for admission. Of those applying, 50 were accepted. Of those accepted, 32 enrolled.

Application Requirements GMAT score, application form, application fee, bachelor's degree, essay, minimum GPA, 3 letters of recommendation, personal statement, college transcript(s), computer experience: e-mail, word processing.

Recommended for Application GRE score accepted, resume, work experience.

Application Deadline Applications processed on a rolling/continuous basis for both domestic and international students. Application fee: $50. Deferred entrance is available.

ACADEMICS
Faculty Full-time 16; part-time 4.

Teaching Methodologies Case study, computer-aided instruction, computer analysis, computer simulations, experiential learning, faculty seminars, field projects, group discussion, lecture, research, role playing, seminars by members of the business community, simulations, student presentations, study groups, team projects.

Technology 350 on-campus computer terminals/PCs are available for student use and are linked by a campus-wide network. The network has full access to the Internet. Students are not required to have their own PC.

Special Opportunities Advanced credit may be earned through credit by examination, transfer of credits from another institution. International exchange program available. An internship program is available.

FINANCES
Costs for 1997–98 Tuition: $636 per credit. Cost varies by number of credits taken. Fees vary by number of credits taken. Average 1997–98 room and board costs were $6300 per academic year (off campus). Room and board costs vary by occupancy (e.g., single, double, triple), type of accommodation, type of meal plan.

Financial Aid In 1997–98, 2% of students received some institutionally administered aid in the form of fellowships, research assistantships, loans. Application Deadline: 2/15.

Financial Aid Contact Mr. Norm Wilkinson, Director, Graduate Management Programs, 100 Institute Road, Worcester, MA 01609-2280. Phone: 508-831-5218; Fax: 508-831-5720; E-mail: wpigmp@wpi.edu

FACILITIES
Information Resources Gordon Library; total holdings of 345,000 volumes, 77,053 microforms, 1,200 current periodical subscriptions. CD player(s) available for graduate student use. Access provided to online bibliographic retrieval services and online databases.

INTERNATIONAL STUDENTS
Demographics 10% of students enrolled are international students [Asia, 35%, Central America, 25%, Europe, 15%, South America, 25%].

Services and Facilities International student office, international student center, international student housing, visa services, ESL courses, counseling/support services.

Applying TOEFL: minimum score of 580, proof of adequate funds, proof of health/immunizations required. Financial aid is available to international students.

International Student Contact Dr. Tom Thomsen, Director, International Students and Scholars, 28 Trowbridge Road, Worcester, MA 01609-2280. Phone: 508-831-6030; Fax: 508-831-6032; E-mail: hartvig@wpi.edu

PLACEMENT
Services include alumni network, career counseling/planning, career fairs, career library, career placement, electronic job bank, job interviews arranged, job search course, resume referral to employers, and resume preparation. In 1996–97, 300 organizations participated in on-campus recruiting.

Employment Of 1996–97 graduates, 98% were employed within three months of graduation; the average starting salary was $50,000. Types of employment entered: chemical industry, communications, computer-related, consulting, consumer products, education, energy, engineering, financial services, government, high technology, information systems/technology, international

Worcester Polytechnic Institute (continued)

trade, management, manufacturing, marketing, nonprofit, petrochemical, pharmaceutical, telecommunications, transportation, utilities.

Business Program(s) URL: http://mgnt.wpi.edu/graduate.htm

Program Contact: Mr. Norman D. Wilkinson, Director of Graduate Management Programs, 100 Institute Road, Worcester, MA 01609-2280. Phone: 508-831-5218; Fax: 508-831-5720; E-mail: wpigmp@wpi.edu

See full description on page 1200.

MICHIGAN

Andrews University

School of Business

Berrien Springs, Michigan

OVERVIEW

Andrews University is an independent-religious, coed university. Enrollment: 2,952 graduate, professional, and undergraduate students; 788 full-time matriculated graduate/professional students; 492 part-time matriculated graduate/professional students. Founded: 1874. The graduate business unit is in a small-town setting and is on a quarter calendar.

HIGHLIGHTS

Enrollment Profile

Full-time: 76	International: 67%
Part-time: 32	Women: 29%
Total: 108	Minorities: 19%
Average Age: N/R	Average Class Size: 18
Fall 1997 Average GPA: 3.0	Fall 1997 Average GMAT: 500

Costs
Full-time tuition: N/R
Part-time tuition: $272 per quarter credit

GRADUATE BUSINESS PROGRAMS

Master of Business Administration (MBA) Full-time, part-time; 48 total credits required; 12 months to 4 years to complete program. Concentrations in management, management information systems, accounting, health care.

Master of Science in Administration (MS) Full-time, part-time; 48 total credits required; 12 months to 4 years to complete program. Concentration in nonprofit management.

ADMISSION

Application Requirements Application form, application fee, minimum GPA: 2.6, 3 letters of recommendation, personal statement, college transcript(s), computer experience.

Recommended for Application GMAT score accepted: minimum 400, GRE score accepted, bachelor's degree.

Application Deadline Applications processed on a rolling/continuous basis for both domestic and international students. Application fee: $30. Deferred entrance is available.

ACADEMICS

Faculty Full-time 18; part-time 4.

Teaching Methodologies Case study, computer analysis, computer simulations, group discussion, lecture, research, role playing, seminars by members of the business community, simulations, student presentations, study groups, team projects.

Technology 156 on-campus computer terminals/PCs are available for student use and are linked by a campus-wide network. The network has full access to the Internet. Students are not required to have their own PC.

Special Opportunities Advanced credit may be earned through transfer of credits from another institution.

FINANCES

Costs for 1997–98 Tuition: $272 per quarter credit. Fees: $60 per quarter. Average 1997–98 room and board costs were $3510 per academic year. Room and board costs vary by occupancy (e.g., single, double, triple), type of accommodation.

Financial Aid In 1997–98, 70% of students received some institutionally administered aid in the form of fellowships, research assistantships, scholarships, work study.

Financial Aid Contact Mr. Douglas Miller, Director of Financial Aid, Berrien Springs, MI 49104-0310. Phone: 800-253-2874; Fax: 616-471-6161.

FACILITIES

Information Resources James White Library plus 2 additional on-campus libraries; total holdings of 658,744 volumes, 68,217 microforms, 2,259 current periodical subscriptions. CD player(s) available for graduate student use. Access provided to online bibliographic retrieval services and online databases.

INTERNATIONAL STUDENTS

Demographics 67% of students enrolled are international students.

Services and Facilities International student office, counseling/support services.

Applying TOEFL: minimum score of 550, proof of adequate funds, proof of health/immunizations required.

International Student Contact Mr. Najeeb Nakhle, Director of International Student Affairs, Berrien Springs, MI 49104-0300. Phone: 800-253-2874; Fax: 616-471-6203; E-mail: nakhle@andrews.edu

PLACEMENT

Services include career counseling/planning, career fairs, career placement, job interviews arranged, resume referral to employers, and resume preparation. In 1996–97, 64 organizations participated in on-campus recruiting; 314 on-campus interviews were conducted.

Employment Types of employment entered: accounting, education, finance, financial services, health services, human resources, information systems/technology, management, marketing, nonprofit, retail.

Business Program(s) URL: http://www.andrews.edu/SBA/

Program Contact: Mr. Allen Stembridge, Graduate Advisor, School of Business, Berrien Springs, MI 49104. Phone: 616-471-3584, 800-253-2874; Fax: 616-471-6158; E-mail: stemb@andrews.edu

Aquinas College

Graduate Management Program

Grand Rapids, Michigan

OVERVIEW

Aquinas College is an independent-religious, coed, comprehensive institution. Enrollment: 2,458 graduate, professional, and undergraduate students; 130 full-time matriculated graduate/professional students; 447 part-time matriculated graduate/professional students. Founded: 1923. The graduate business unit is in a suburban setting and is on a semester calendar.

HIGHLIGHTS

Enrollment Profile

Full-time: 20	International: 1%
Part-time: 277	Women: 52%
Total: 297	Minorities: 6%
Average Age: 34	Average Class Size: 25
Fall 1997 Average GPA: 2.9	Fall 1997 Average GMAT: 448

Costs
Full-time tuition: N/R
Part-time tuition: $310 per credit hour

GRADUATE BUSINESS PROGRAMS

Master of Management (MMgt) Full-time, part-time; 39 total credits required; 18 months to 4 years to complete program. Concentrations in international business, marketing, organizational behavior/development, health care, arts administration/management.

ADMISSION

Applications For fall 1997 there were 117 applications for admission. Of those applying, 117 were accepted. Of those accepted, 53 enrolled.

Application Requirements GMAT score, application form, application fee, bachelor's degree, essay, minimum GPA: 2.75, interview, 3 letters of recommendation, personal statement, college transcript(s), minimum of 2 years of work experience.

Application Deadline Applications processed on a rolling/continuous basis for both domestic and international students. Application fee: $35. Deferred entrance is available.

ACADEMICS

Faculty Full-time 11; part-time 11.

Teaching Methodologies Case study, experiential learning, faculty seminars, field projects, group discussion, lecture, research, student presentations, study groups, team projects.

Technology 450 on-campus computer terminals/PCs are available for student use and are linked by a campus-wide network. The network has full access to the Internet. Students are not required to have their own PC.

Special Opportunities Advanced credit may be earned through transfer of credits from another institution. An internship program is available.

FINANCES
Costs for 1997–98 Tuition: $310 per credit hour.

Financial Aid In 1997–98, 12% of students received some institutionally administered aid. Financial aid is available to part-time students. Application Deadline: 6/15.

Financial Aid Contact Mr. David Steffee, Director of Financial Aid, 1607 Robinson Road, SE, Grand Rapids, MI 49506-1799. Phone: 616-459-8281 Ext. 5127; Fax: 616-732-4435.

FACILITIES
Information Resources Woodhouse Learning Resource Center; total holdings of 109,000 volumes, 138,805 microforms, 800 current periodical subscriptions. CD player(s) available for graduate student use. Access provided to online bibliographic retrieval services and online databases.

INTERNATIONAL STUDENTS
Demographics 1% of students enrolled are international students [Europe, 100%].

Services and Facilities Visa services.

Applying TOEFL: minimum score of 550, proof of adequate funds, proof of health/immunizations required. Financial aid is not available to international students.

International Student Contact Mr. Michael Gantt, Transfer/International Student Representative, 1607 Robinson Road, SE, Grand Rapids, MI 49506-1799. Phone: 616-459-8281 Ext. 5208; Fax: 616-732-4435.

PLACEMENT
Services include alumni network, career counseling/planning, career fairs, career library, career placement, resume referral to employers, and resume preparation.

Employment Of 1996–97 graduates, 83% were employed within three months of graduation; the average starting salary was $38,715. Types of employment entered: accounting, banking, communications, computer-related, consulting, consumer products, education, energy, finance, financial services, government, health services, human resources, information systems/technology, insurance, management, manufacturing, marketing, media, nonprofit, pharmaceutical, retail, service industry, telecommunications, utilities.

Business Program(s) URL: http://www.aquinas.edu

Program Contact: Dr. Joyce McNally, Dean of Graduate Studies, 1607 Robinson Road, SE, Grand Rapids, MI 49506-1799. Phone: 616-459-8281 Ext. 5426, 800-748-0350 (MI only); Fax: 616-732-4431; E-mail: mcnaljoy@aquinas.edu

Baker College Center for Graduate Studies

Center for Graduate Studies

Flint, Michigan

OVERVIEW
Baker College Center for Graduate Studies is an independent-nonprofit, coed, graduate institution. Enrollment: 16,020 graduate, professional, and undergraduate students; 102 full-time matriculated graduate/professional students; 614 part-time matriculated graduate/professional students. Founded: 1888. The graduate business unit is in a suburban setting and is on a quarter calendar.

HIGHLIGHTS

Enrollment Profile

Full-time: 102	International: N/R
Part-time: 614	Women: N/R
Total: 716	Minorities: N/R
Average Age: 38	Average Class Size: 12
Fall 1997 Average GPA: 3.06	Fall 1997 Average GMAT: 520

Costs
Full-time tuition: $6560 per academic year
Part-time tuition: $215 per quarter hour

GRADUATE BUSINESS PROGRAMS
Executive MBA (MBA) Full-time, part-time, distance learning option; 50 total credits required; 15 months to 4 years to complete program. Concentrations in human resources, industrial administration/management, international business, leadership, management, health care, marketing.

Master of Business Administration (MBA) Full-time, part-time, distance learning option; 60 total credits required; 2 to 5 years to complete program. Concentrations in human resources, industrial administration/management, international business, leadership, management, sports/entertainment management, health care, marketing.

ADMISSION
Application Requirements Application form, application fee, bachelor's degree, essay, minimum GPA: 2.5, 3 letters of recommendation, personal statement, resume, college transcript(s), minimum of 3 years of work experience, computer experience: word processing.

Recommended for Application GMAT score accepted, GRE score accepted.

Application Deadline Applications processed on a rolling/continuous basis for both domestic and international students. Application fee: $25. Deferred entrance is available.

ACADEMICS
Faculty Full-time 6; part-time 117.

Teaching Methodologies Case study, computer-aided instruction, computer analysis, computer simulations, experiential learning, faculty seminars, field projects, group discussion, lecture, research, role playing, seminars by members of the business community, simulations, student presentations, study groups, team projects.

Technology 1,460 on-campus computer terminals/PCs are available for student use and are linked by a campus-wide network. The network has full access to the Internet. Students are required to have their own PC.

Special Opportunities Advanced credit may be earned through transfer of credits from another institution.

FINANCES
Costs for 1997–98 Tuition: Full-time: $6560 per year. Part-time: $215 per quarter hour. Fees: Full-time: $100 per academic year.

Financial Aid In 1997–98, 61% of students received some institutionally administered aid in the form of grants, loans. Financial aid is available to part-time students.

Financial Aid Contact Mr. Cliff Leavitt, Graduate Director of Financial Aid, 1050 West Bristol Road, Flint, MI 48507-5508. Phone: 800-469-3165 Ext. 4205; Fax: 810-766-4399; E-mail: gradschl@baker.edu

FACILITIES
Information Resources Jewell Memorial Library plus 8 additional on-campus libraries; total holdings of 152,261 volumes, 134,625 microforms, 1,057 current periodical subscriptions. CD player(s) available for graduate student use. Access provided to online bibliographic retrieval services and online databases.

INTERNATIONAL STUDENTS
Demographics N/R

Services and Facilities International student housing, visa services, counseling/support services.

Applying TOEFL: minimum score of 550, proof of adequate funds required. Proof of health/immunizations recommended. Financial aid is not available to international students.

International Student Contact Ms. Dawn Prueter, Registrar, 1050 West Bristol Road, Flint, MI 48507-5508. Phone: 810-766-4390; Fax: 810-766-4399.

PLACEMENT
Services include alumni network, career counseling/planning, career placement, job interviews arranged, resume referral to employers, and resume preparation.

Employment Of 1996–97 graduates, 99% were employed within three months of graduation. Types of employment entered: accounting, banking, consulting, education, finance, financial services, health services, management, manufacturing, marketing, nonprofit, real estate, service industry, transportation.

Business Program(s) URL: http://www.baker.edu

Program Contact: Mr. Chuck Gurden, Director of Graduate Admissions, 1050 West Bristol Road, Flint, MI 48507-5508. Phone: 810-766-4390, 800-469-3165; Fax: 810-766-4399; E-mail: gurden_c@corpfl.baker.edu
See full description on page 714.

Central Michigan University

College of Business Administration

Mount Pleasant, Michigan

OVERVIEW
Central Michigan University is a state-supported, coed university. Enrollment: 16,613 graduate, professional, and undergraduate students; 839 full-time matriculated graduate/professional students; 1,154 part-time matriculated graduate/professional students. Founded: 1892. The graduate business unit is in a small-town setting and is on a semester calendar.

Central Michigan University (continued)

HIGHLIGHTS

Enrollment Profile
Full-time: 237
Part-time: 234
Total: 471
Average Age: 28
Fall 1997 Average GPA: 3.23

International: 34%
Women: 41%
Minorities: 1%
Average Class Size: 31
Fall 1997 Average GMAT: 513

Costs
Full-time tuition: N/R
Part-time tuition: $135 per credit hour (resident); $269 per credit hour (nonresident)

AACSB – The International Association for Management Education accredited

GRADUATE BUSINESS PROGRAMS
Master of Business Administration (MBA) Full-time, part-time; 30 total credits required; 12 months to 4.2 years to complete program. Concentrations in accounting, finance, human resources, international business, management information systems, marketing.

Master of Business Education (MBE) Full-time, part-time; 36 total credits required; 12 months to 7 years to complete program.

ADMISSION
Applications For fall 1997 there were 151 applications for admission. Of those applying, 121 were accepted.

Application Requirements GMAT score: minimum 400, application form, application fee, bachelor's degree, essay, minimum GPA: 2.5, personal statement, college transcript(s), computer experience: spreadsheet, database, presentation graphics.

Recommended for Application Work experience.

Application Deadline Applications processed on a rolling/continuous basis for both domestic and international students. Application fee: $30. Deferred entrance is available.

ACADEMICS
Faculty Full-time 69.

Teaching Methodologies Case study, faculty seminars, lecture, research, role playing, student presentations, team projects.

Technology Computer terminals/PCs are available for student use and are linked by a campus-wide network. The network has full access to the Internet. Students are not required to have their own PC.

Special Opportunities Advanced credit may be earned through transfer of credits from another institution. An internship program is available.

FINANCES
Costs for 1997–98 Tuition: $135 per credit hour (resident); $269 per credit hour (nonresident). Cost varies by number of credits taken. Average 1997–98 room and board costs were $4320 per academic year. Room and board costs vary by occupancy (e.g., single, double, triple), type of accommodation, type of meal plan.

Financial Aid Fellowships, research assistantships, teaching assistantships, work study available. Application Deadline: 3/7.

Financial Aid Contact Office of Scholarships and Financial Aid, 204 Warriner Hall, Mt. Pleasant, MI 48859. Phone: 517-774-3674; Fax: 517-774-3634.

FACILITIES
Information Resources Park Library; total holdings of 697,546 volumes, 1,143,156 microforms, 5,285 current periodical subscriptions. CD player(s) available for graduate student use. Access provided to online bibliographic retrieval services.

INTERNATIONAL STUDENTS
Demographics 34% of students enrolled are international students.

Services and Facilities International student office, visa services, ESL courses, counseling/support services.

Applying TOEFL: minimum score of 550, proof of adequate funds, proof of health/immunizations required. Financial aid is not available to international students.

International Student Contact Christopher Viers, Associate Director, Center for Education, Bovee University Center, Mt. Pleasant, MI 48859. Phone: 517-774-4308; Fax: 517-774-3690.

PLACEMENT
Services include career counseling/planning, career library, career placement, electronic job bank, job interviews arranged, resume referral to employers, and resume preparation.

Employment Of 1996–97 graduates, 100% were employed within three months of graduation.

Business Program(s) URL: http://www.cba.cmich.edu

Program Contact: Dr. Daniel Vetter, Director, Graduate Business Studies, College of Business Administration, 112 Grawn Hall, Mount Pleasant, MI 48859. Phone: 517-774-3150; Fax: 517-774-2372; E-mail: pamela.stambersky@cmich.edu

Eastern Michigan University

College of Business
Ypsilanti, Michigan

OVERVIEW
Eastern Michigan University is a state-supported, coed, comprehensive institution. Enrollment: 23,000 graduate, professional, and undergraduate students; 1,200 full-time matriculated graduate/professional students; 4,600 part-time matriculated graduate/professional students. Founded: 1849. The graduate business unit is in a suburban setting and is on a trimester calendar.

HIGHLIGHTS

Enrollment Profile
Full-time: 222
Part-time: 572
Total: 794
Average Age: 30
Fall 1997 Average GPA: 3.01

International: 31%
Women: 48%
Minorities: 5%
Average Class Size: 21
Fall 1997 Average GMAT: 525

Costs
Full-time tuition: $4800 per academic year (resident); $10,800 per academic year (nonresident)
Part-time tuition: $145 per credit hour (resident); $336 per credit hour (nonresident)

AACSB – The International Association for Management Education accredited

Degree(s) offered in conjunction with Escuela Superior de Gestion Commercial y Marketing (Spain)

Eastern Michigan University's M.B.A. program provides students with a broad understanding of business functions, including the relationship of business to society as a whole, the impact of legal and environmental forces on business, and the internationalization of today's business climate. The College of Business offers many opportunities that enhance and strengthen students' perspectives on the global business environment, including double master's degree programs in conjunction with institutions in France, Germany, and Spain. The College has established a number of strong partnerships with corporations in southeastern Michigan, affording students a variety of opportunities for fieldwork and networking with business leaders.

The program is designed to provide a general M.B.A. or a specialized M.B.A. in finance, financial accounting, human resource management, information systems management, international business, marketing, organizational development, production/operations management, strategic quality management, or tax accounting. This program requires 54 to 63 semester hours of graduate-level courses; however, students with undergraduate business degrees may need as few as 33 semester hours of graduate-level course work to complete the program. Courses are offered in the evenings and on weekends.

In addition to the M.B.A. degree, the College also offers master of science programs in accounting, computer-based information systems, and human resource and organizational development. All graduate programs are accredited by the AACSB–The International Association of Management Education

GRADUATE BUSINESS PROGRAMS
Master of Business Administration (MBA) Full-time, part-time; 33-57 total credits required; 12 months to 6 years to complete program. Concentrations in accounting, finance, management information systems, strategic management, operations management, international business, human resources, management, marketing, organizational behavior/development, production management.

Master of Science in Information Systems (MS) Full-time, part-time; 30-60 total credits required; 12 months to 6 years to complete program. Concentration in management information systems.

Master of Science in Accounting (MS) Full-time, part-time; 30-60 total credits required; 12 months to 6 years to complete program. Concentration in accounting.

Master of Science in Human Resources/Organizational Development (MS) Full-time, part-time; 30-60 total credits required; 12 months to 6 years to complete program. Concentrations in human resources, organizational behavior/development.

ADMISSION

Applications For fall 1997 there were 710 applications for admission. Of those applying, 575 were accepted. Of those accepted, 225 enrolled.

Application Requirements Application form, application fee, bachelor's degree, essay, minimum GPA: 2.5, personal statement, college transcript(s).

Recommended for Application GMAT score accepted: minimum 450, work experience, computer experience.

Application Deadline 5/15 for fall, 11/15 for winter, 3/15 for spring, 5/1 for fall (international), 11/1 for winter (international), 3/1 for spring (international). Application fee: $30.

ACADEMICS

Faculty Full-time 71; part-time 1.

Teaching Methodologies Case study, computer-aided instruction, computer analysis, computer simulations, faculty seminars, field projects, group discussion, lecture, research, seminars by members of the business community, simulations, student presentations, team projects.

Technology 500 on-campus computer terminals/PCs are available for student use and are linked by a campus-wide network. The network has full access to the Internet. Students are not required to have their own PC.

Special Opportunities Advanced credit may be earned through credit by examination, credit for experience, transfer of credits from another institution. International exchange programs in Canada, France, Germany, Mexico, Spain.

FINANCES

Costs for 1997–98 Tuition: Full-time: $4800 per year (resident); $10,800 per year (nonresident). Part-time: $145 per credit hour (resident); $336 per credit hour (nonresident). Cost varies by reciprocity agreements. Fees: Full-time: $495 per academic year (resident); $495 per academic year (nonresident). Part-time: $15 per credit hour (resident); $15 per credit hour (nonresident). Average 1997–98 room and board costs were $6600 per academic year (on campus) and $6000 per academic year (off campus). Room and board costs vary by occupancy (e.g., single, double, triple), type of accommodation, type of meal plan.

Financial Aid In 1997–98, 13% of students received some institutionally administered aid in the form of fellowships, research assistantships, work study. Financial aid is available to part-time students. Application Deadline: 3/15.

Financial Aid Contact Office of Financial Aid, 403 Pierce Hall, Ypsilanti, MI 48197. Phone: 313-487-0455.

FACILITIES

Information Resources University Library; total holdings of 645,765 volumes, 794,534 microforms, 4,370 current periodical subscriptions. CD player(s) available for graduate student use. Access provided to online bibliographic retrieval services and online databases.

INTERNATIONAL STUDENTS

Demographics 31% of students enrolled are international students [Africa, 2%, Asia, 77%, Europe, 8%, North America, 5%, South America, 2%, other, 6%].

Services and Facilities International student office, international student center, international student housing, visa services, ESL courses, counseling/support services.

Applying TOEFL: minimum score of 500, TWE: minimum score of 4, proof of adequate funds, proof of health/immunizations required. Financial aid is not available to international students.

International Student Contact Mr. Paul Webb, Director, Foreign Student Affairs Office, 208 Goodison, Ypsilanti, MI 48197. Phone: 313-487-3116.

PLACEMENT

Services include alumni network, career counseling/planning, career fairs, career library, career placement, electronic job bank, job interviews arranged, job search course, resume referral to employers, and resume preparation.

Employment Of 1996–97 graduates, 98% were employed within three months of graduation; the average starting salary was $48,000. Types of employment entered: accounting, banking, chemical industry, computer-related, consulting, consumer products, energy, engineering, finance, financial services, government, health services, high technology, hospitality management, human resources, information systems/technology, insurance, international trade, management, manufacturing, marketing, media, nonprofit, petrochemical, pharmaceutical, real estate, retail, service industry, telecommunications, transportation, utilities.

Business Program(s) URL: http://www.emich.edu/public/gradcatalog

Program Contact: Mr. William Whitmire, Coordinator, Graduate Business Programs, 401 Gary M. Owen Building, Ypsilanti, MI 48197. Phone: 313-487-4444; Fax: 313-480-0618; E-mail: bill.whitmire@emich.edu

See full description on page 794.

Ferris State University

Graduate Programs, College of Business

Big Rapids, Michigan

OVERVIEW

Ferris State University is a state-supported, coed, comprehensive institution. Enrollment: 9,495 graduate, professional, and undergraduate students; 200 full-time matriculated graduate/professional students; 75 part-time matriculated graduate/professional students. Founded: 1884. The graduate business unit is in a small-town setting and is on a semester calendar.

HIGHLIGHTS

Enrollment Profile

Full-time: 67	International: 30%
Part-time: 42	Women: 40%
Total: 109	Minorities: 14%
Average Age: 28	Average Class Size: 20
Fall 1997 Average GPA: 3.1	Fall 1997 Average GMAT: N/R

Costs
Full-time tuition: N/R
Part-time tuition: $206 per credit hour (resident); $425 per credit hour (nonresident)

GRADUATE BUSINESS PROGRAMS

Master of Science in Information Systems Management (MS) Full-time, part-time, distance learning option; 31-34 total credits required; 12 months to 5 years to complete program. Concentrations in information management, quality management.

Master of Science in Accounting (MS) Full-time, part-time, distance learning option; 31 total credits required. Concentration in accounting.

ADMISSION

Applications For fall 1997 there were 60 applications for admission. Of those applying, 55 were accepted. Of those accepted, 42 enrolled.

Application Requirements Application form, application fee, bachelor's degree, essay, minimum GPA: 2.75, personal statement, resume, college transcript(s).

Recommended for Application Computer experience.

Application Deadline 7/1 for fall, 11/1 for winter, 4/1 for summer, 7/1 for fall (international), 11/1 for winter (international), 6/1 for summer (international). Application fee: $20. Deferred entrance is available.

ACADEMICS

Faculty Full-time 4; part-time 3.

Teaching Methodologies Case study, computer-aided instruction, field projects, group discussion, lecture, research, student presentations, team projects.

Technology 55 on-campus computer terminals/PCs are available for student use and are linked by a campus-wide network. The network has full access to the Internet. Students are not required to have their own PC.

Special Opportunities Advanced credit may be earned through credit by examination, credit for military training programs, credit for business training programs, transfer of credits from another institution. International exchange program in Netherlands. An internship program is available.

FINANCES

Costs for 1997–98 Tuition: $206 per credit hour (resident); $425 per credit hour (nonresident). Cost varies by academic program, number of credits taken, reciprocity agreements. Fees vary by number of credits taken, reciprocity agreements. Average 1997–98 room and board costs were $4792 per academic year (on campus) and $5000 per academic year (off campus). Room and board costs vary by campus location, type of accommodation, type of meal plan.

Financial Aid In 1997–98, 18% of students received some institutionally administered aid in the form of fellowships, research assistantships, teaching assistantships, grants, scholarships, work study. Financial aid is available to part-time students. Application Deadline: 4/1.

Financial Aid Contact Robert Bopp, Financial Aid Director, 901 State Street, Big Rapids, MI 49307. Phone: 616-592-2110.

FACILITIES

Information Resources Timme Library plus 1 additional on-campus library; total holdings of 240,000 volumes, 825,500 microforms, 3,502 current periodical subscriptions. CD player(s) available for graduate student use. Access provided to online bibliographic retrieval services and online databases.

INTERNATIONAL STUDENTS

Demographics 30% of students enrolled are international students [Africa, 6%, Asia, 72%, Central America, 3%, Europe, 12%, North America, 1%, South America, 6%].

Ferris State University (continued)

Services and Facilities International student office, international student center, visa services, ESL courses, counseling/support services.

Applying TOEFL: minimum score of 500, proof of adequate funds, proof of health/immunizations required. Financial aid is available to international students.

International Student Contact Mr. Tom Stoffer, Coordinator, International Student Support, 901 State Street, Big Rapids, MI 49307. Phone: 616-592-3916; Fax: 616-592-2400.

PLACEMENT
Services include alumni network, career counseling/planning, career fairs, career library, career placement, electronic job bank, job interviews arranged, job search course, resume referral to employers, and resume preparation. In 1996–97, 10 organizations participated in on-campus recruiting; 22 on-campus interviews were conducted.

Employment Of 1996–97 graduates, 95% were employed within three months of graduation; the average starting salary was $46,000. Types of employment entered: accounting, banking, communications, computer-related, consulting, engineering, finance, health services, high technology, hospitality management, information systems/technology, management, manufacturing, marketing, nonprofit, telecommunications.

Business Program(s) URL: http://ism.ferris.edu

Program Contact: Coordinator, MSISM, 1420 Knollview Drive, Big Rapids, MI 49307-2289. Phone: 616-592-2168, 800-433-7747; Fax: 616-592-2973; E-mail: goc@bus02.ferris.edu
See full description on page 816.

Grand Valley State University

Seidman School of Business
Allendale, Michigan

OVERVIEW
Grand Valley State University is a state-supported, coed, comprehensive institution. Enrollment: 15,676 graduate, professional, and undergraduate students; 541 full-time matriculated graduate/professional students; 2,521 part-time matriculated graduate/professional students. Founded: 1960. The graduate business unit is in an urban setting and is on a semester calendar.

HIGHLIGHTS

Enrollment Profile
Full-time: 19
Part-time: 324
Total: 343
Average Age: 33
Fall 1997 Average GPA: 3.2

International: 5%
Women: 35%
Minorities: 5%
Average Class Size: 22
Fall 1997 Average GMAT: 540

Costs
Full-time tuition: $330 per academic year (nonresident)
Part-time tuition: $162 per credit (resident); $330 per credit (nonresident)

AACSB – The International Association for Management Education accredited

GRADUATE BUSINESS PROGRAMS
Master of Business Administration (MBA) Full-time, part-time; 33-53 total credits required; 12 months to 8 years to complete program.
Master of Science in Taxation (MS) Full-time, part-time; 33-51 total credits required; 12 months to 8 years to complete program.

ADMISSION
Applications For fall 1997 there were 98 applications for admission. Of those applying, 80 were accepted. Of those accepted, 75 enrolled.
Application Requirements Application form, application fee, bachelor's degree, essay, college transcript(s).
Recommended for Application GMAT score accepted: minimum 450.
Application Deadline 8/1 for fall, 12/1 for winter, 4/1 for spring, 6/1 for fall (international), 12/1 for winter (international), 4/1 for spring (international). Application fee: $20. Deferred entrance is available.

ACADEMICS
Faculty Full-time 30; part-time 2.
Teaching Methodologies Case study, computer analysis; computer simulations, faculty seminars, field projects, group discussion, lecture, research, seminars

by members of the business community, student presentations, study groups, team projects.
Technology 791 on-campus computer terminals/PCs are available for student use and are linked by a campus-wide network. The network has full access to the Internet. Students are not required to have their own PC.
Special Opportunities Advanced credit may be earned through transfer of credits from another institution. International exchange programs in France, Poland, Russia, United Kingdom.

FINANCES
Costs for 1997–98 Tuition: Full-time: $330 per semester credit hour (nonresident). Part-time: $162 per credit (resident); $330 per credit (nonresident). Cost varies by number of credits taken. Fees vary by number of credits taken. Average 1997–98 room and board costs were $4800 per academic year.
Financial Aid In 1997–98, 5% of students received some institutionally administered aid in the form of fellowships, research assistantships, scholarships, work study, loans. Financial aid is available to part-time students. Application Deadline: 4/1.
Financial Aid Contact Mr. Ken Fridsma, Director, Financial Aid, 100 STU, Allendale, MI 49401. Phone: 616-895-3234; Fax: 616-895-3180; E-mail: fridsmak@gvsu.edu

FACILITIES
Information Resources Zumberge Library; total holdings of 463,376 volumes, 722,447 microforms, 2,835 current periodical subscriptions. CD player(s) available for graduate student use. Access provided to online bibliographic retrieval services and online databases.

INTERNATIONAL STUDENTS
Demographics 5% of students enrolled are international students [Asia, 56%, Europe, 13%, North America, 31%].
Services and Facilities International student office, visa services, ESL courses, counseling/support services.
Applying TOEFL: minimum score of 550, proof of adequate funds, proof of health/immunizations required. Financial aid is not available to international students.
International Student Contact Ms. Marche Haddad, Director, Global Programs, International Affairs, 104 STU, Allendale, MI 49401. Phone: 616-895-3898; Fax: 616-895-3899; E-mail: haddadm@gvsu.edu

PLACEMENT
Services include career counseling/planning, career fairs, career library, resume referral to employers, and resume preparation.
Employment Of 1996–97 graduates, 98% were employed within three months of graduation. Types of employment entered: accounting, banking, chemical industry, communications, computer-related, consulting, consumer products, education, energy, engineering, finance, financial services, government, health services, high technology, hospitality management, human resources, information systems/technology, international trade, management, manufacturing, marketing, nonprofit, retail, service industry, telecommunications, utilities.

Business Program(s) URL: http://www.gvsu.edu/ssb/grad/

Program Contact: Ms. Claudia Bajema, MBA Program Director, 301 West Fulton, Grand Rapids, MI 49504. Phone: 616-771-6675; Fax: 616-771-6642; E-mail: bajemac@gvsu.edu

Kettering University

Graduate Studies and Extension Services
Flint, Michigan

OVERVIEW
Kettering University is an independent-nonprofit, coed, comprehensive institution. Enrollment: 3,239 graduate, professional, and undergraduate students; 12 full-time matriculated graduate/professional students; 757 part-time matriculated graduate/professional students. Founded: 1919. The graduate business unit is in an urban setting and is on a quarter calendar.

HIGHLIGHTS

Enrollment Profile
Full-time: 12
Part-time: 757
Total: 769
Average Age: 32
Fall 1997 Average GPA: N/R

International: 2%
Women: 22%
Minorities: N/R
Average Class Size: 15
Fall 1997 Average GMAT: N/R

Costs
Full-time tuition: N/R
Part-time tuition: $1185 per course

GRADUATE BUSINESS PROGRAMS

Master of Science in Manufacturing Management (MS) Part-time, distance learning option; 54 total credits required; 3 to 6 years to complete program. Concentration in manufacturing management.

ADMISSION

Applications For fall 1997 there were 350 applications for admission. Of those applying, 267 were accepted. Of those accepted, 173 enrolled.

Application Requirements GMAT score: minimum 500, application form, minimum GPA: 3.0, 2 letters of recommendation, personal statement, college transcript(s).

Recommended for Application GRE score accepted: minimum 1,200.

Application Deadline 7/15 for fall, 11/1 for winter, 7/15 for fall (international), 11/1 for winter (international).

ACADEMICS

Faculty Part-time 14.

Teaching Methodologies Case study, computer-aided instruction, computer simulations, group discussion, lecture, research, simulations, delayed videotape.

Technology 100 on-campus computer terminals/PCs are available for student use and are linked by a campus-wide network. The network has full access to the Internet. Students are not required to have their own PC.

Special Opportunities Advanced credit may be earned through credit by examination, transfer of credits from another institution.

FINANCES

Costs for 1997–98 Tuition: Part-time: $1185 per course. Fees: Part-time: $45 per course. Average 1997–98 room and board costs were $7500 per academic year.

Financial Aid In 1997–98, 2% of students received some institutionally administered aid in the form of fellowships, research assistantships, teaching assistantships, loans. Financial aid is available to part-time students.

Financial Aid Contact Melissa Ruterbusch, Director of Financial Aid, 1700 West Third Avenue, Flint, MI 48504-4898. Phone: 810-762-7859; Fax: 810-762-9807; E-mail: mruterbu@elite.gmi.edu

FACILITIES

Information Resources Main library; total holdings of 54,000 volumes, 15,000 microforms, 815 current periodical subscriptions. CD player(s) available for graduate student use. Access provided to online bibliographic retrieval services.

INTERNATIONAL STUDENTS

Demographics 2% of students enrolled are international students.

Services and Facilities International student office, visa services.

Applying TOEFL: minimum score of 580, proof of adequate funds, proof of health/immunizations required. Financial aid is available to international students.

International Student Contact Celia Bandl, Coordinator, 1700 West Third Avenue, Flint, MI 48504-4898. Phone: 810-762-9869; E-mail: cbandl@elite.gmi.edu

PLACEMENT

Employment Of 1996–97 graduates, 100% were employed within three months of graduation.

Business Program(s) URL: http://www.gmi.edu/official/acad/grad

Program Contact: Ms. Betty Bedore, Coordinator of Publicity and Special Projects—Graduate Department, 1700 West Third Avenue, Flint, MI 48504-4898. Phone: 810-762-7494, 888-464-4723; Fax: 810-762-9935; E-mail: bbedore@kettering.edu

Lake Superior State University

School of Business

Sault Sainte Marie, Michigan

OVERVIEW

Lake Superior State University is a state-supported, coed, comprehensive institution. Enrollment: 3,369 graduate, professional, and undergraduate students; 3 full-time matriculated graduate/professional students; 142 part-time matriculated graduate/professional students. Founded: 1946. The graduate business unit is in a small-town setting and is on a semester calendar.

HIGHLIGHTS

Enrollment Profile

Full-time: 1	International: 5%
Part-time: 103	Women: 50%
Total: 104	Minorities: 6%
Average Age: 34	Average Class Size: 15
Fall 1997 Average GPA: N/R	Fall 1997 Average GMAT: N/R

Costs
Full-time tuition: N/R
Part-time tuition: $168 per credit (resident); $168 per credit (nonresident)

*L*ake Superior State University offers a rigorous, practitioner-based Master of Business Administration degree. The campus, overlooking the St. Mary's Rapids, gateway to the pristine wilderness of Lake Superior, provides a stunning site for graduate studies. The city of Sault Sainte Marie, whose foundation in 1668 predates the United States and Canada, is a historic cultural crossroads, where ancient Indian tribes met European explorers and traders and began a long history of business exchange.

The M.B.A. students at Lake Superior State are drawn from Michigan and its neighboring states; northern Ontario, Canada; and the Sault tribe of Chippewa Indians, the largest Native American tribe east of the Mississippi.

LSSU M.B.A. graduates can be found throughout the north-central United States and Canada, serving in business, manufacturing, governmental agencies, educational institutions, tribal administration, and nonprofit corporations.

The M.B.A. program at Lake Superior State is designed for working adults, with classes scheduled in the evenings and on weekends. The program is also offered at regional sites across northern Michigan in Escanaba, Petoskey, Traverse City, and Alpena.

GRADUATE BUSINESS PROGRAMS

General MBA (MBA) Full-time, part-time, distance learning option; 36 total credits required; 2.5 to 8 years to complete program.

ADMISSION

Application Requirements GMAT score: minimum 530, application form, application fee, bachelor's degree, minimum GPA, 2 letters of recommendation, personal statement, resume, college transcript(s).

Application Deadline Applications processed on a rolling/continuous basis for both domestic and international students. Application fee: $25. Deferred entrance is available.

ACADEMICS

Faculty Full-time 15; part-time 10.

Teaching Methodologies Case study, computer-aided instruction, computer analysis, computer simulations, experiential learning, faculty seminars, field projects, group discussion, lecture, research, role playing, seminars by members of the business community, simulations, student presentations, study groups, team projects.

Technology 200 on-campus computer terminals/PCs are available for student use and are linked by a campus-wide network. The network has full access to the Internet. Students are not required to have their own PC.

Special Opportunities Advanced credit may be earned through transfer of credits from another institution. International exchange programs in Canada, Taiwan.

FINANCES

Costs for 1997–98 Tuition: $168 per credit (resident); $168 per credit (nonresident). Cost varies by reciprocity agreements. Average 1997–98 room and board costs were $4800 per academic year. Room and board costs vary by occupancy (e.g., single, double, triple), type of accommodation, type of meal plan.

Financial Aid Application Deadline: 4/1.

Financial Aid Contact Financial Aid Office, 650 West Easterday Avenue, Sault Sainte Marie, MI 49783. Phone: 906-635-2678; Fax: 906-635-2111.

FACILITIES

Information Resources Kenneth Shouldice Library; total holdings of 128,000 volumes, 79,000 microforms, 1,100 current periodical subscriptions. CD player(s) available for graduate student use. Access provided to online bibliographic retrieval services and online databases.

INTERNATIONAL STUDENTS

Demographics 5% of students enrolled are international students [Asia, 20%, North America, 80%].

Services and Facilities International student office, ESL courses, counseling/support services.

Applying TOEFL: minimum score of 550 required. Financial aid is not available to international students.

International Student Contact Ms. Susan Camp, Director of Continuing Education, 650 West Easterday Avenue, Sault Sainte Marie, MI 49783-1699. Phone: 906-635-2554; Fax: 906-635-2762; E-mail: scamp@lakers.lssu.edu

Lake Superior State University (continued)

PLACEMENT

Services include alumni network, career counseling/planning, career fairs, career placement, electronic job bank, job interviews arranged, resume referral to employers, and resume preparation.

Employment Of 1996–97 graduates, 100% were employed within three months of graduation. Types of employment entered: accounting, banking, computer-related, education, government, health services, human resources, management, marketing, nonprofit, service industry.

Business Program(s) URL: http://www.lssu.edu

Program Contact: MBA Program Admissions, 650 West Easterday Avenue, Sault Sainte Marie, MI 49783-1699. Phone: 906-635-2426, 888-800-LSSU Ext. 2231; Fax: 906-635-6669.
See full description on page 870.

Lawrence Technological University

Graduate College of Management

Southfield, Michigan

OVERVIEW

Lawrence Technological University is an independent-nonprofit, coed, comprehensive institution. Enrollment: 3,645 graduate, professional, and undergraduate students; 60 full-time matriculated graduate/professional students; 510 part-time matriculated graduate/professional students. Founded: 1932. The graduate business unit is in a suburban setting and is on a semester calendar.

HIGHLIGHTS

Enrollment Profile

Full-time: 60	International: 17%
Part-time: 385	Women: 36%
Total: 445	Minorities: 27%
Average Age: 33	Average Class Size: 20
Fall 1997 Average GPA: N/R	Fall 1997 Average GMAT: N/R

Costs
Full-time tuition: N/R
Part-time tuition: $400 per credit hour

ACBSP – The American Council of Business Schools and Programs accredited

GRADUATE BUSINESS PROGRAMS

Master of Business Administration (MBA) Full-time, part-time; 36 total credits required; 18 months to 7 years to complete program. Concentrations in human resources, international business, management information systems, operations management.

Master of Science in Industrial Operations (MS) Full-time, part-time; 30 total credits required; 18 months to 7 years to complete program.

Master of Science in Information Systems (MS) Full-time, part-time; 30 total credits required; 18 months to 7 years to complete program.

ADMISSION

Applications For fall 1997 there were 159 applications for admission. Of those applying, 137 were accepted. Of those accepted, 98 enrolled.

Application Requirements GMAT score: minimum 550, application form, application fee, bachelor's degree, minimum GPA: 2.75, interview, resume, college transcript(s).

Application Deadline Applications processed on a rolling/continuous basis for both domestic and international students. Application fee: $50. Deferred entrance is available.

ACADEMICS

Faculty Full-time 6; part-time 17.

Teaching Methodologies Case study, faculty seminars, group discussion, lecture, student presentations, team projects.

Technology 200 on-campus computer terminals/PCs are available for student use and are linked by a campus-wide network. The network has full access to the Internet. Students are not required to have their own PC.

Special Opportunities Advanced credit may be earned through transfer of credits from another institution.

FINANCES

Costs for 1997–98 Tuition: $400 per credit hour. Fees: $100 per semester. Average 1997–98 room only costs were $3780 per academic year. Room and board costs vary by occupancy (e.g., single, double, triple).

Financial Aid In 1997–98, 37% of students received some institutionally administered aid in the form of loans. Financial aid is available to part-time students. Application Deadline: 3/1.

Financial Aid Contact Mr. Paul Kinder, Director, Financial Aid, 21000 West Ten Mile Road, Southfield, MI 48075. Phone: 248-204-2120 Ext. 2126; Fax: 248-204-2118; E-mail: paul@ltu.edu

FACILITIES

Information Resources Main library; total holdings of 68,000 volumes, 24,000 microforms, 650 current periodical subscriptions. CD player(s) available for graduate student use. Access provided to online bibliographic retrieval services.

INTERNATIONAL STUDENTS

Demographics 17% of students enrolled are international students [Asia, 90%, Central America, 2%, Europe, 2%, North America, 5%, South America, 1%].

Services and Facilities ESL courses.

Applying TOEFL: minimum score of 550, proof of adequate funds required.

International Student Contact Mr. Frank de Hesselle, Director, International Student Affairs, 21000 West Ten Mile Road, Southfield, MI 48075. Phone: 248-204-3160 Ext. 3179; Fax: 248-204-3188; E-mail: dehesselle@ltu.edu

PLACEMENT

Services include career counseling/planning, career fairs, career library, career placement, electronic job bank, job interviews arranged, resume referral to employers, and resume preparation. In 1996–97, 50 organizations participated in on-campus recruiting.

Employment Of 1996–97 graduates, 96% were employed within three months of graduation. Types of employment entered: accounting, banking, communications, computer-related, consulting, energy, engineering, finance, financial services, government, high technology, human resources, information systems/technology, insurance, international trade, management, manufacturing, marketing, nonprofit, telecommunications, transportation, utilities.

Business Program(s) URL: http://www.ltu.edu/management/

Program Contact: Ms. Patricia Leto, Graduate Admissions Counselor, 21000 West Ten Mile Road, Southfield, MI 48075-1058. Phone: 248-204-3160 Ext. 3187, 800-CALL-LTU (MI only); Fax: 248-204-3188; E-mail: leto@ltu.edu

Madonna University

Graduate Programs in Business Administration

Livonia, Michigan

OVERVIEW

Madonna University is an independent-religious, coed, comprehensive institution. Enrollment: 4,000 graduate, professional, and undergraduate students; 98 full-time matriculated graduate/professional students; 500 part-time matriculated graduate/professional students. Founded: 1947. The graduate business unit is in a suburban setting and is on a semester calendar.

HIGHLIGHTS

Enrollment Profile

Full-time: 54	International: N/R
Part-time: 161	Women: 54%
Total: 218	Minorities: N/R
Average Age: 36	Average Class Size: 20
Fall 1997 Average GPA: 3.1	Fall 1997 Average GMAT: 400

Costs
Full-time tuition: N/R
Part-time tuition: $250 per credit hour

GRADUATE BUSINESS PROGRAMS

Master of Science in Business Administration in Leadership Studies (MSBA) Full-time, part-time, distance learning option; 36 total credits required; 2 to 6 years to complete program. Concentrations in leadership, international business.

Master of Science in Business Administration in Quality and Operations Management (MSBA) Full-time, part-time, distance learning option; 36 total credits required; 2 to 6 years to complete program.

ADMISSION

Applications For fall 1997 there were 60 applications for admission. Of those applying, 48 were accepted. Of those accepted, 40 enrolled.

Application Requirements Application form, bachelor's degree, minimum GPA: 3.0, interview, 2 letters of recommendation, personal statement, college transcript(s).

Recommended for Application GMAT score accepted, GRE score accepted: minimum 1,200, resume, work experience, computer experience.

Application Deadline Applications processed on a rolling/continuous basis for both domestic and international students. Deferred entrance is available.

ACADEMICS

Faculty Full-time 14; part-time 18.

Teaching Methodologies Case study, computer-aided instruction, group discussion, lecture, research, student presentations, team projects.

Technology 75 on-campus computer terminals/PCs are available for student use and are linked by a campus-wide network. The network has full access to the Internet. Students are not required to have their own PC.

Special Opportunities Advanced credit may be earned through transfer of credits from another institution. International exchange program in Mexico. An internship program is available.

FINANCES

Costs for 1997–98 Tuition: $250 per credit hour. Average 1997–98 room and board costs were $4168 per academic year.

Financial Aid Grants, scholarships available. Application Deadline: 8/1.

Financial Aid Contact Kathy Durham, Secretary, 36600 Schoolcraft Road, Livonia, MI 48150-1173. Phone: 734-432-5663; Fax: 734-432-5393.

FACILITIES

Information Resources Main library; total holdings of 109,101 volumes, 23,097 microforms, 1,298 current periodical subscriptions. Access provided to online bibliographic retrieval services.

INTERNATIONAL STUDENTS

Demographics N/R

Services and Facilities International student office, international student housing, visa services, ESL courses, counseling/support services.

Applying TOEFL: minimum score of 530, proof of adequate funds, proof of health/immunizations required. Financial aid is not available to international students.

International Student Contact Mr. Doug Julius, Director, Center for International Studies, 36600 Schoolcraft Road, Livonia, MI 48150-1173. Phone: 734-432-5636; Fax: 734-432-5393; E-mail: julius@smtp.munet.edu

PLACEMENT

Employment Of 1996–97 graduates, 75% were employed within three months of graduation; the average starting salary was $40,000. Types of employment entered: accounting, banking, chemical industry, communications, computer-related, consulting, consumer products, education, energy, engineering, finance, financial services, government, health services, high technology, hospitality management, human resources, information systems/technology, insurance, international trade, law, management, manufacturing, marketing, media, mining, nonprofit, petrochemical, pharmaceutical, real estate, retail, service industry, telecommunications, transportation, utilities.

Program Contact: Mrs. Sandra Kellums, Coordinator of Graduate Admissions, 36600 Schoolcraft Road, Livonia, MI 48150-1173. Phone: 734-432-5666; Fax: 734-432-5393; E-mail: kellums@smtp.munet.edu

Michigan State University

Eli Broad Graduate School of Management

East Lansing, Michigan

OVERVIEW

Michigan State University is a state-supported, coed university. Enrollment: 42,603 graduate, professional, and undergraduate students; 3,733 full-time matriculated graduate/professional students; 4,200 part-time matriculated graduate/professional students. Founded: 1855. The graduate business unit is in a small-town setting and is on a semester calendar.

HIGHLIGHTS

Enrollment Profile

Full-time: 325	International: 33%
Part-time: 0	Women: 31%
Total: 325	Minorities: 12%
Average Age: 27	Average Class Size: 40
Fall 1997 Average GPA: 3.31	Fall 1997 Average GMAT: N/R

Costs

Full-time tuition: $8350 per academic year (resident); $12,150 per academic year (nonresident)
Part-time tuition: N/R

AACSB – The International Association for Management Education accredited

GRADUATE BUSINESS PROGRAMS

Full-time MBA (MBA) Full-time; 54 total credits required; up to 21 months to complete program. Concentrations in accounting, finance, human resources, logistics, management, management information systems, marketing, operations management, entrepreneurship, travel industry/tourism management.

Master of Business Administration in Integrative Management (MBA) Part-time; 45 total credits required; up to 17 months to complete program.

Executive Master of Business Administration in Advanced Management (EMBA) Part-time; 43 total credits required; up to 21 months to complete program.

Professional Accounting (MS) Full-time; 31 total credits required; up to 21 months to complete program. Concentrations in accounting, taxation, management information systems.

Food Service Management (MS) Full-time; 30 total credits required; up to 21 months to complete program.

Business Management of Manufacturing (MS) Full-time; 39 total credits required; up to 21 months to complete program. Concentration in management.

ADMISSION

Applications For fall 1997 there were 655 applications for admission. Of those applying, 279 were accepted. Of those accepted, 141 enrolled.

Application Requirements GMAT score, application form, application fee, bachelor's degree, essay, minimum GPA: 3.0, interview, 3 letters of recommendation, resume, college transcript(s), minimum of 1 year of work experience, computer experience: word processing, spreadsheets, database.

Application Deadline 5/15 for fall, 11/1 for spring, 5/15 for fall (international), 11/1 for spring (international). Application fee: $30, $40 (international). Deferred entrance is available.

ACADEMICS

Faculty Full-time 130.

Teaching Methodologies Case study, computer-aided instruction, computer analysis, computer simulations, field projects, group discussion, lecture, seminars by members of the business community, simulations, student presentations, study groups, team projects.

Technology 110 on-campus computer terminals/PCs are available for student use and are linked by a campus-wide network. The network has full access to the Internet. Students are required to have their own PC.

Special Opportunities International exchange program in Japan. An internship program is available.

FINANCES

Costs for 1997–98 Tuition: Full-time: $8350 per year (resident); $12,150 per year (nonresident). Cost varies by academic program, campus location, class time (e.g., day/evening), number of credits taken. Average 1997–98 room and board costs were $3640 per academic year (on campus) and $6190 per academic year (off campus). Room and board costs vary by campus location, occupancy (e.g., single, double, triple), type of accommodation, type of meal plan.

Financial Aid Fellowships, research assistantships, teaching assistantships, scholarships, work study, loans available. Financial aid is available to part-time students. Application Deadline: 4/1.

Financial Aid Contact Office of Financial Aid, 252 Student Services Building, East Lansing, MI 48824-1113. Phone: 517-353-5940; Fax: 517-432-1155; E-mail: ofa00@msu.edu

FACILITIES

Information Resources Main library plus 15 additional on-campus libraries; total holdings of 4,050,000 volumes, 4,883,791 microforms, 16,000 current periodical subscriptions. CD player(s) available for graduate student use. Access provided to online bibliographic retrieval services and online databases.

INTERNATIONAL STUDENTS

Demographics 33% of students enrolled are international students [Africa, 3%, Asia, 79%, Europe, 8%, North America, 2%, South America, 8%].

Services and Facilities International student office, international student center, international student housing, visa services, ESL courses, counseling/support services.

Applying TOEFL: minimum score of 600, proof of adequate funds required. Financial aid is available to international students.

International Student Contact Office of International Students and Scholars, 103 International Center, East Lansing, MI 48824. Phone: 517-353-1720; Fax: 517-355-4657.

PLACEMENT

Services include alumni network, career counseling/planning, career fairs, career library, career placement, electronic job bank, job interviews arranged, job search course, resume referral to employers, and resume preparation. In 1996–97, 161 organizations participated in on-campus recruiting; 1,504 on-campus interviews were conducted.

Employment Of 1996–97 graduates, 95% were employed within three months of graduation; the average starting salary was $62,303. Types of employment entered: accounting, banking, chemical industry, communications, computer-related, consulting, consumer products, education, finance, financial services, government, health services, high technology, hospitality management, human resources, information systems/technology, insurance, management, manufacturing, marketing, petrochemical, pharmaceutical, real estate, retail, service industry, telecommunications, transportation, utilities.

Business Program(s) URL: http://www.bus.msu.edu/

Program Contact: Ms. Jennifer Chizuk, Director, Admissions and Academic Services, 215 Eppley Center, East Lansing, MI 48824-1121. Phone: 517-355-7604, 800-4-MSU-MBA; Fax: 517-353-1649; E-mail: mba@pilot.msu.edu

Michigan Technological University

School of Business and Economics

Houghton, Michigan

OVERVIEW
Michigan Technological University is a state-supported, coed university. Enrollment: 6,302 graduate, professional, and undergraduate students; 601 full-time matriculated graduate/professional students; 27 part-time matriculated graduate/professional students. Founded: 1885. The graduate business unit is in a small-town setting and is on a quarter calendar.

HIGHLIGHTS

Enrollment Profile

Full-time: 4	International: 50%
Part-time: 0	Women: 25%
Total: 4	Minorities: N/R
Average Age: 29	Average Class Size: N/R
Fall 1997 Average GPA: N/R	Fall 1997 Average GMAT: N/R

Costs
Full-time tuition: $1092 per academic year (resident); $2502 per academic year (nonresident)
Part-time tuition: $182 per credit hour (resident); $417 per credit hour (nonresident)

GRADUATE BUSINESS PROGRAMS
Master of Science in Mineral Economics (MS) Full-time, part-time; 45 total credits required; 9 months to 5 years to complete program. Concentration in resources management.

ADMISSION
Applications For fall 1997 there were 7 applications for admission. Of those applying, 6 were accepted. Of those accepted, 2 enrolled.

Application Requirements GMAT score, GRE score, application form, application fee, bachelor's degree, 3 letters of recommendation, resume.

Recommended for Application Minimum GPA: 2.7.

Application Deadline Applications processed on a rolling/continuous basis for both domestic and international students. Application fee: $35. Deferred entrance is available.

ACADEMICS
Faculty Full-time 24.

Teaching Methodologies Computer simulations, group discussion, lecture, research, student presentations.

Technology Computer terminals/PCs are available for student use and are linked by a campus-wide network. The network has full access to the Internet. Students are not required to have their own PC.

Special Opportunities Advanced credit may be earned through transfer of credits from another institution.

FINANCES
Costs for 1997–98 Tuition: Full-time: $1092 per quarter (resident); $2502 per quarter (nonresident). Part-time: $182 per credit hour (resident); $417 per credit hour (nonresident). Cost varies by number of credits taken, reciprocity agreements. Fees: Full-time: $650 per academic year (resident); $650 per academic year (nonresident). Fees vary by academic program. Average 1997–98 room and board costs were $4420 per academic year. Room and board costs vary by occupancy (e.g., single, double, triple), type of accommodation, type of meal plan.

Financial Aid In 1997–98, 100% of students received some institutionally administered aid in the form of work study. Financial aid is available to part-time students.

Financial Aid Contact Dr. Gary Campbell, Professor of Mineral Economics, 1400 Townsend Drive, Houghton, MI 49931-1295. Phone: 906-487-2808; Fax: 906-487-2944; E-mail: gacampbe@mtu.edu

FACILITIES
Information Resources J. Robert Van Pelt Library; total holdings of 786,267 volumes, 415,801 microforms, 10,007 current periodical subscriptions. CD player(s) available for graduate student use. Access provided to online bibliographic retrieval services.

INTERNATIONAL STUDENTS
Demographics 50% of students enrolled are international students [Asia, 50%, North America, 50%].

Services and Facilities International student office, international student center, visa services, counseling/support services.

Applying TOEFL: minimum score of 520, proof of adequate funds required. Financial aid is available to international students.

International Student Contact Ms. Mary Brunner, Associate Director, International Services, 1400 Townsend Drive, Houghton, MI 49931-1295. Phone: 906-487-2160; E-mail: mbrunner@mtu.edu

PLACEMENT
Services include career counseling/planning, career fairs, career library, career placement, and job interviews arranged.

Employment Of 1996–97 graduates, 100% were employed within three months of graduation. Types of employment entered: engineering, government, management, manufacturing, mining, petrochemical.

Business Program(s) URL: http://www.sbea.mtu.edu

Program Contact: Dr. Gary Campbell, Professor of Mineral Economics, 1400 Townsend Drive, Houghton, MI 49931-1295. Phone: 906-487-2808; Fax: 906-487-2944; E-mail: gacampbe@mtu.edu

Northwood University

Richard DeVos Graduate School of Management

Midland, Michigan

OVERVIEW
Northwood University is an independent-nonprofit, coed, comprehensive institution. Enrollment: 2,903 graduate, professional, and undergraduate students; 44 full-time matriculated graduate/professional students; 165 part-time matriculated graduate/professional students. Founded: 1959. The graduate business unit is in a small-town setting and is on a trimester calendar.

HIGHLIGHTS

Enrollment Profile

Full-time: 44	International: 12%
Part-time: 165	Women: 29%
Total: 209	Minorities: 17%
Average Age: 33	Average Class Size: 25
Fall 1997 Average GPA: 3.0	Fall 1997 Average GMAT: 550

Costs
Full-time tuition: $15,000 per academic year
Part-time tuition: $20,000 per program

The DeVos Graduate School is looking for candidates that value education. There are other business programs, even M.B.A. options, that are easier and faster. The DeVos M.B.A. programs are specifically designed for serious students who recognize the need for additional management training and plan to use this opportunity to aid in advancing their careers and organizations.

DeVos faculty members aspire to provide candidates with the highest standard of personal and professional growth. They combine their premier academic credentials with significant business experience. They also realize that, in the real world, managers are put to the test. That is why the faculty embraces Northwood's policy of no tenure. They are measured as businesses will measure the M.B.A. graduates—through a continual critique of their performance.

The DeVos Graduate School is housed within a state-of-the-art complex on the Northwood University campus in Midland, Michigan. This facility houses breakout rooms, a computer lab, faculty and administrative offices, and multimedia classrooms designed specifically to suit the M.B.A. program's highly interactive environment.

For further information, contact the Graduate School by telephone at 800-MBA-9000 (toll-free) or e-mail at mba@northwood.edu or visit its Web site at http://www.northwood.edu/mba.

GRADUATE BUSINESS PROGRAMS

Executive MBA (MBA) Part-time; 40 total credits required; interview and 5 years work experience required; minimum of 2.5 years to complete program.

Full-time MBA (MBA) Full-time; 65 total credits required; minimum of 15 months to complete program.

ADMISSION

Applications For fall 1997 there were 200 applications for admission. Of those applying, 130 were accepted. Of those accepted, 95 enrolled.

Application Requirements GMAT score, application form, application fee, bachelor's degree, essay, interview, personal statement, resume, college transcript(s), work experience.

Application Deadline Applications processed on a rolling/continuous basis for both domestic and international students. Application fee: $25. Deferred entrance is available.

ACADEMICS

Faculty Full-time 6; part-time 5.

Teaching Methodologies Case study, computer simulations, experiential learning, group discussion, simulations, student presentations, study groups, team projects.

Technology 80 on-campus computer terminals/PCs are available for student use and are linked by a campus-wide network. The network has full access to the Internet. Students are not required to have their own PC.

Special Opportunities An internship program is available.

FINANCES

Costs for 1997–98 Tuition: Full-time: $15,000 per program. Part-time: $20,000 per program. Average 1997–98 room and board costs were $9000 per academic year (on campus) and $10,400 per academic year (off campus).

Financial Aid In 1997–98, 11% of students received some institutionally administered aid in the form of fellowships, scholarships, work study. Application Deadline: 2/15.

Financial Aid Contact Ms. Nancy Vaughn, 3225 Cook Road, Midland, MI 48640-2398. Phone: 517-837-4454.

FACILITIES

Information Resources Strosacker Library plus 1 additional on-campus library; total holdings of 50,000 volumes, 550 current periodical subscriptions. CD player(s) available for graduate student use. Access provided to online bibliographic retrieval services and online databases.

INTERNATIONAL STUDENTS

Demographics 12% of students enrolled are international students [Africa, 8%, Asia, 23%, Central America, 3%, Europe, 31%, North America, 27%, South America, 8%].

Services and Facilities International student office, visa services, ESL courses, counseling/support services.

Applying Proof of adequate funds required. Financial aid is available to international students.

International Student Contact Ms. Lisa Marie Boyd, Director of Graduate Admissions, 3225 Cook Road, Midland, MI 48640-2398. Phone: 517-837-4888; Fax: 517-837-4800; E-mail: mba@northwood.edu

PLACEMENT

Services include alumni network, career counseling/planning, career fairs, career library, career placement, job interviews arranged, job search course, resume referral to employers, and resume preparation.

Employment Of 1996–97 graduates, 100% were employed within three months of graduation; the average starting salary was $75,000. Types of employment entered: accounting, banking, chemical industry, communications, computer-related, consumer products, engineering, finance, high technology, information systems/technology, international trade, management, manufacturing, marketing, retail, service industry, telecommunications.

Business Program(s) URL: http://www.northwood.edu/mba

Program Contact: Ms. Rhonda Anderson, Associate Dean, 3225 Cook Road, Midland, MI 48640. Phone: 517-837-4488, 800-MBA-9000 (MI only); Fax: 517-837-4800; E-mail: mba@northwood.edu

See full description on page 910.

Oakland University

School of Business Administration

Rochester, Michigan

OVERVIEW

Oakland University is a state-supported, coed university. Enrollment: 14,379 graduate, professional, and undergraduate students; 736 full-time matriculated graduate/professional students; 2,465 part-time matriculated graduate/professional students. Founded: 1957. The graduate business unit is in a suburban setting and is on a semester calendar.

HIGHLIGHTS

Enrollment Profile

Full-time: 30	International: 5%
Part-time: 464	Women: 35%
Total: 494	Minorities: 5%
Average Age: 30	Average Class Size: 30
Fall 1997 Average GPA: 3.06	Fall 1997 Average GMAT: 557

Costs

Full-time tuition: N/R

Part-time tuition: $208 per credit (resident); $461 per credit (nonresident)

AACSB – The International Association for Management Education accredited

O*akland University is a comprehensive, state-assisted institution of approximately 14,000 students that offers a diverse set of academic programs, from baccalaureate to doctoral levels. Located between the cities of Pontiac and Rochester (at the intersection of I-75 and M-59), Oakland University is easily accessible to millions of Detroit metropolitan area residents. Undergraduate programs and the M.B.A. are accredited by AACSB—The International Association for Management Education. Oakland University is among four universities in Michigan that have also achieved AACSB accreditation for their undergraduate accounting program.*

The M.B.A. program provides a solid foundation in the functional areas of business, with special emphasis on the management of information resources. Eight concentrations allow students to tailor the program to their career goals. Course work includes real-life cases and applications to assist students with the development of problem-solving skills. A Master of Accounting and post-master's certificate programs are also offered through the School of Business Administration . Classes are held in the evening in Rochester and Birmingham or on Saturday mornings (Rochester only) to accommodate the working adult. Oakland University's graduate business programs are open to both individuals who hold bachelor's degrees in business and nonbusiness majors. Women and minorities are encouraged to apply.

GRADUATE BUSINESS PROGRAMS

Master of Business Administration (MBA) Part-time, distance learning option; 36-60 total credits required; 12 months to 6 years to complete program. Concentrations in accounting, economics, finance, human resources, international business, management information systems, marketing, operations management.

Master of Accounting (MAcc) Part-time; 33 total credits required; 12 months to 6 years to complete program.

Post-Master Certificate (PMC) Full-time, part-time; 15 total credits required; 8 months to 6 years to complete program. Concentrations in accounting, economics, finance, human resources, international business, management information systems, marketing, operations management.

ADMISSION

Applications For fall 1997 there were 173 applications for admission. Of those applying, 151 were accepted. Of those accepted, 107 enrolled.

Application Requirements GMAT score, application form, application fee, bachelor's degree, minimum GPA: 2.6, college transcript(s), computer experience: basic computer workstation course.

Recommended for Application Personal statement, resume, minimum of 2 years of work experience.

Application Deadline 8/1 for fall, 12/1 for winter, 4/1 for spring, 6/1 for summer, 5/1 for fall (international), 9/1 for winter (international). Application fee: $30. Deferred entrance is available.

ACADEMICS

Faculty Full-time 45; part-time 21.

Teaching Methodologies Case study, computer-aided instruction, computer analysis, group discussion, lecture, research, role playing, seminars by members of the business community, student presentations, study groups, team projects.

Technology 310 on-campus computer terminals/PCs are available for student use and are linked by a campus-wide network. The network has full access to the Internet. Students are not required to have their own PC.

Special Opportunities Advanced credit may be earned through transfer of credits from another institution.

FINANCES

Costs for 1997–98 Tuition: $208 per credit (resident); $461 per credit (nonresident). Cost varies by number of credits taken. Fees: $194 per semester (resident); $194 per semester (nonresident). Fees vary by academic program, campus location, number of credits taken. Average 1997–98 room and board costs were $4555 per academic year (on campus) and $5562 per academic year (off campus). Room and board costs vary by occupancy (e.g., single, double, triple), type of accommodation, type of meal plan.

Financial Aid Research assistantships, work study, loans available. Application Deadline: 3/1.

Financial Aid Contact Mr. Lee Anderson, Director, Financial Aid, 161 North Foundation Hall, Rochester, MI 48309-4401. Phone: 248-370-3370.

FACILITIES

Information Resources Kresge Library plus 1 additional on-campus library; total holdings of 593,868 volumes, 1,070,000 microforms, 2,040 current periodical subscriptions. CD player(s) available for graduate student use. Access provided to online bibliographic retrieval services.

INTERNATIONAL STUDENTS

Demographics 5% of students enrolled are international students.

Services and Facilities International student office, visa services, counseling/support services.

Applying TOEFL: minimum score of 550, proof of adequate funds required. Proof of health/immunizations recommended. Financial aid is not available to international students.

International Student Contact Lisa McGill, Director, Disability Support and International Student Services, 157 North Foundation Hall, Rochester, MI 48309-4401. Phone: 248-370-3266.

PLACEMENT

Services include alumni network, career counseling/planning, career fairs, career library, career placement, electronic job bank, job interviews arranged, resume referral to employers, and resume preparation.

Employment Of 1996–97 graduates, 98% were employed within three months of graduation. Types of employment entered: accounting, banking, computer-related, consulting, engineering, finance, financial services, health services, human resources, information systems/technology, management, manufacturing, marketing, retail, service industry.

Business Program(s) URL: http://www.sba.oakland.edu

Program Contact: Ms. Gloria Schatz, Program Assistant, Office of Graduate Business Programs, 416 Varner Hall, Rochester, MI 48309-4493. Phone: 248-370-3287; Fax: 248-370-4275; E-mail: gbp@oak.oakland.edu

Saginaw Valley State University

College of Business and Management

University Center, Michigan

OVERVIEW

Saginaw Valley State University is a state-supported, coed, comprehensive institution. Enrollment: 7,338 graduate, professional, and undergraduate students; 41 full-time matriculated graduate/professional students; 890 part-time matriculated graduate/professional students. Founded: 1963. The graduate business unit is in a suburban setting and is on a semester calendar.

HIGHLIGHTS

Enrollment Profile

Full-time: 14	International: 10%
Part-time: 108	Women: 42%
Total: 122	Minorities: 8%
Average Age: 29	Average Class Size: 20
Fall 1997 Average GPA: 3.16	Fall 1997 Average GMAT: 474

Costs

Full-time tuition: N/R

Part-time tuition: $153 per credit hour (resident); $302 per credit hour (nonresident)

GRADUATE BUSINESS PROGRAMS

Master of Business Administration (MBA) Full-time, part-time; 31-47 total credits required; 12 months to 6 years to complete program. Concentrations in accounting, finance, economics, international business, management, marketing.

ADMISSION

Applications For fall 1997 there were 43 applications for admission. Of those applying, 37 were accepted. Of those accepted, 30 enrolled.

Application Requirements GMAT score, application form, application fee, bachelor's degree, essay, 2 letters of recommendation, personal statement, resume, college transcript(s), computer experience.

Recommended for Application Minimum GPA, interview, work experience.

Application Deadline Applications processed on a rolling/continuous basis for both domestic and international students. Application fee: $25.

ACADEMICS

Faculty Full-time 26.

Teaching Methodologies Case study, computer-aided instruction, computer analysis, computer simulations, group discussion, lecture, seminars by members of the business community, student presentations, team projects.

Technology 300 on-campus computer terminals/PCs are available for student use and are linked by a campus-wide network. The network has full access to the Internet. Students are not required to have their own PC.

Special Opportunities Advanced credit may be earned through credit by examination, transfer of credits from another institution.

FINANCES

Costs for 1997–98 Tuition: $153 per credit hour (resident); $302 per credit hour (nonresident). Cost varies by number of credits taken. Fees: $9 per credit hour (resident); $9 per credit hour (nonresident). Fees vary by number of credits taken. Average 1997–98 room only costs were $1920 per academic year. Room and board costs vary by occupancy (e.g., single, double, triple), type of accommodation, type of meal plan.

Financial Aid In 1997–98, 6% of students received some institutionally administered aid in the form of fellowships, work study, loans. Financial aid is available to part-time students.

Financial Aid Contact Ms. Cindy Munger, Acting Director, Scholarships and Student Financial Aid, 7400 Bay Road, 160 Wickes Hall, University Center, MI 48710. Phone: 517-790-4103; Fax: 517-790-0180; E-mail: wlh@tardis.svsu.edu

FACILITIES

Information Resources Melvin J. Zahnow Library; total holdings of 212,865 volumes, 330,242 microforms, 3,046 current periodical subscriptions. CD player(s) available for graduate student use. Access provided to online bibliographic retrieval services and online databases.

INTERNATIONAL STUDENTS

Demographics 10% of students enrolled are international students [Asia, 100%].

Services and Facilities International student office, international student center, visa services, ESL courses, counseling/support services.

Applying TOEFL: minimum score of 525, proof of adequate funds, proof of health/immunizations required. Financial aid is not available to international students.

International Student Contact Mr. Lee H. Pelton, Special Assistant to the President for International Programs, 7400 Bay Road, University Center, MI 48710. Phone: 517-790-4268; Fax: 517-249-1666; E-mail: pelton@tardis.svsu.edu

PLACEMENT

Services include career fairs, career placement, job interviews arranged, and resume preparation.

Business Program(s) URL: http://www.svsu.edu

Program Contact: Dr. Severin Carlson, Dean, College of Business Administration, 320 Curtiss Hall, University Center, MI 48710. Phone: 517-790-4064; Fax: 517-249-1960; E-mail: cbmdean@tardis.svsu.edu

See full description on page 960.

Siena Heights University

Office of Graduate Studies and Lifelong Learning

Adrian, Michigan

OVERVIEW

Siena Heights University is an independent-religious, coed, comprehensive institution. Enrollment: 1,876 graduate, professional, and undergraduate students; 41 full-time matriculated graduate/professional students; 206 part-time matriculated graduate/professional students. Founded: 1919. The graduate business unit is in a suburban setting and is on a semester calendar.

HIGHLIGHTS

Enrollment Profile

Full-time: 14	International: 1%
Part-time: 84	Women: 65%
Total: 98	Minorities: 23%
Average Age: 35	Average Class Size: 15
Fall 1997 Average GPA: 3.2	Fall 1997 Average GMAT: N/R

Costs

Full-time tuition: N/R

Part-time tuition: $278 per semester hour

GRADUATE BUSINESS PROGRAMS
Master of Arts in Human Resource Development (MA) Full-time, part-time; 36 total credits required; 2 to 7 years to complete program. Concentration in human resources.

ADMISSION
Applications For fall 1997 there were 72 applications for admission. Of those applying, 69 were accepted. Of those accepted, 61 enrolled.

Application Requirements Application form, application fee, bachelor's degree, essay, minimum GPA: 3.0, interview, 3 letters of recommendation, personal statement, resume, college transcript(s), minimum of 5 years of work experience.

Recommended for Application Computer experience.

Application Deadline Applications processed on a rolling/continuous basis for both domestic and international students. Application fee: $25, $50 (international). Deferred entrance is available.

ACADEMICS
Faculty Full-time 4; part-time 14.

Teaching Methodologies Case study, computer-aided instruction, computer analysis, computer simulations, experiential learning, faculty seminars, field projects, group discussion, lecture, research, role playing, seminars by members of the business community, simulations, student presentations, study groups, team projects.

Technology 80 on-campus computer terminals/PCs are available for student use. The network has full access to the Internet. Students are required to have their own PC.

Special Opportunities Advanced credit may be earned through credit for experience, credit for business training programs, transfer of credits from another institution. An internship program is available.

FINANCES
Costs for 1997–98 Tuition: $278 per semester hour. Cost varies by campus location, class time (e.g., day/evening). Fees vary by academic program, campus location. Average 1997–98 room and board costs were $5730 per academic year. Room and board costs vary by occupancy (e.g., single, double, triple), type of accommodation, type of meal plan.

Financial Aid Work study available. Application Deadline: 8/1.

Financial Aid Contact Mr. Kevin Kucera, Dean of Admissions and Enrollment Services, 1247 East Siena Heights Drive, Adrian, MI 49221-1796. Phone: 517-264-7183; Fax: 517-264-7704.

FACILITIES
Information Resources Main library plus 1 additional on-campus library; total holdings of 95,926 volumes, 22,735 microforms, 545 current periodical subscriptions. CD player(s) available for graduate student use. Access provided to online bibliographic retrieval services.

INTERNATIONAL STUDENTS
Demographics 1% of students enrolled are international students [Europe, 100%].

Services and Facilities International student office, international student center, counseling/support services.

Applying TOEFL: minimum score of 550, proof of adequate funds required. Financial aid is not available to international students.

International Student Contact Director of Non-traditional Student Services, 1247 East Siena Heights Drive, Adrian, MI 49221-1796. Phone: 517-264-7666; Fax: 517-264-7704.

PLACEMENT
Services include alumni network, career counseling/planning, career fairs, career library, career placement, and resume referral to employers.

Employment Of 1996–97 graduates, 100% were employed within three months of graduation. Types of employment entered: consulting, consumer products, education, energy, engineering, finance, government, health services, high technology, hospitality management, human resources, information systems/technology, insurance, law, management, manufacturing, marketing, media, nonprofit, retail, service industry, telecommunications, transportation, utilities.

Business Program(s) URL: http://www.sienahts.edu

Program Contact: C. Patrick Palmer, Associate Professor of Human Resource Development, 1247 East Sienna Heights, Adrian, MI 49221-1796. Phone: 517-264-7606 Ext. 7606, 800-521-0009 (MI only); Fax: 517-264-7704.

Spring Arbor College

School of Business and Management

Spring Arbor, Michigan

OVERVIEW
Spring Arbor College is an independent-religious, coed, comprehensive institution. Enrollment: 2,437 graduate, professional, and undergraduate students; 50 full-time matriculated graduate/professional students; 166 part-time matriculated graduate/professional students. Founded: 1873. The graduate business unit is in a small-town setting and is on a semester calendar.

HIGHLIGHTS

Enrollment Profile

Full-time: 30	International: 1%
Part-time: 46	Women: 49%
Total: 76	Minorities: 4%
Average Age: 38	Average Class Size: 15
Fall 1997 Average GPA: 3.02	Fall 1997 Average GMAT: N/R

Costs
Full-time tuition: N/R
Part-time tuition: $265 per credit hour

GRADUATE BUSINESS PROGRAMS
Master of Business Administration (MBA) Full-time, part-time; 36-54 total credits required; 20 months to 6 years to complete program.

ADMISSION
Applications For fall 1997 there were 17 applications for admission. Of those applying, 17 were accepted. Of those accepted, 15 enrolled.

Application Requirements Application form, application fee, bachelor's degree, essay, minimum GPA: 3.0, interview, 2 letters of recommendation, college transcript(s), minimum of 3 years of work experience.

Application Deadline Applications processed on a rolling/continuous basis for both domestic and international students. Application fee: $45. Deferred entrance is available.

ACADEMICS
Faculty Full-time 3; part-time 11.

Teaching Methodologies Case study, computer-aided instruction, computer simulations, experiential learning, group discussion, lecture, role playing, seminars by members of the business community, simulations, student presentations, study groups, team projects.

Technology 20 on-campus computer terminals/PCs are available for student use and are linked by a campus-wide network. The network has full access to the Internet. Students are not required to have their own PC.

Special Opportunities Advanced credit may be earned through credit by examination, credit for business training programs, transfer of credits from another institution.

FINANCES
Costs for 1997–98 Tuition: $265 per credit hour. Fees: $22 per credit hour. Fees vary by number of credits taken.

Financial Aid In 1997–98, 17% of students received some institutionally administered aid in the form of work study. Financial aid is available to part-time students. Application Deadline: 8/25.

Financial Aid Contact Lois Hardy, Director of Financial Aid, 106 East Main, Spring Arbor, MI 49283. Phone: 517-750-6463; Fax: 517-750-1604.

FACILITIES
Information Resources Hugh A. White Library; total holdings of 86,145 volumes, 63,875 microforms, 1,409 current periodical subscriptions. CD player(s) available for graduate student use. Access provided to online bibliographic retrieval services.

INTERNATIONAL STUDENTS
Demographics 1% of students enrolled are international students [South America, 100%].

Services and Facilities International student office, counseling/support services.

Applying TOEFL: minimum score of 550, proof of adequate funds required.

International Student Contact Carla Koontz, Director of International Students, 106 East Main, Spring Arbor, MI 49283. Phone: 517-750-1200; Fax: 517-750-1604.

PLACEMENT
Services include alumni network, career counseling/planning, career placement, and resume preparation.

Program Contact: Denise Schonhard, Admissions Representative, 106 East Main, Spring Arbor, MI 49283. Phone: 800-968-9103 Ext. 1536; Fax: 517-750-1604; E-mail: schonard@admin.arbor.edu

University of Detroit Mercy

College of Business Administration

Detroit, Michigan

OVERVIEW
The University of Detroit Mercy is an independent-religious, coed university. Enrollment: 7,236 graduate, professional, and undergraduate students; 1,124 full-time matriculated graduate/professional students; 1,530 part-time matriculated graduate/professional students. Founded: 1877. The graduate business unit is in an urban setting and is on a semester calendar.

HIGHLIGHTS

Enrollment Profile
Full-time: 132
Part-time: 502
Total: 634
Average Age: 30
Fall 1997 Average GPA: 3.1

International: 25%
Women: 41%
Minorities: 26%
Average Class Size: 30
Fall 1997 Average GMAT: 520

Costs
Full-time tuition: N/R
Part-time tuition: $448 per credit hour

AACSB – The International Association for Management Education accredited

Degree(s) offered in conjunction with Peking University

GRADUATE BUSINESS PROGRAMS
Master of Business Administration (MBA) Full-time, part-time; 36-60 total credits required; 12 months to 5 years to complete program. Concentrations in accounting, decision sciences, developmental economics, economics, finance, human resources, international and area business studies, international trade, management, management information systems, management science, marketing, operations management, quantitative analysis.

Master of Science in Computer and Information Systems (MS) Full-time, part-time; 30-36 total credits required; 12 months to 5 years to complete program.

ADMISSION
Applications For fall 1997 there were 300 applications for admission. Of those applying, 225 were accepted. Of those accepted, 166 enrolled.

Application Requirements GMAT score: minimum 450, application form, application fee, bachelor's degree, minimum GPA: 3.0, college transcript(s).

Recommended for Application Essay, letters of recommendation, personal statement, resume.

Application Deadline Applications processed on a rolling/continuous basis for domestic students only. 5/1 for fall (international), 9/1 for spring (international), 1/1 for summer (international). Application fee: $30, $50 (international). Deferred entrance is available.

ACADEMICS
Faculty Full-time 33; part-time 20.

Teaching Methodologies Case study, computer-aided instruction, computer analysis, computer simulations, faculty seminars, field projects, group discussion, lecture, research, role playing, seminars by members of the business community, simulations, student presentations, study groups, team projects.

Technology 600 on-campus computer terminals/PCs are available for student use and are linked by a campus-wide network. The network has full access to the Internet. Students are not required to have their own PC.

Special Opportunities Advanced credit may be earned through transfer of credits from another institution. International exchange programs in Brazil, Mexico, People's Republic of China, United Kingdom. An internship program is available.

FINANCES
Costs for 1997–98 Tuition: $448 per credit hour. Cost varies by number of credits taken. Fees: $75 per semester. Fees vary by number of credits taken. Average 1997–98 room and board costs were $5000 per academic year. Room and board costs vary by occupancy (e.g., single, double, triple), type of accommodation, type of meal plan.

Financial Aid Research assistantships, work study, loans available. Financial aid is available to part-time students. Application Deadline: 8/1.

Financial Aid Contact Ms. Anne Watson, Director of Financial Aid, 4001 West McNichols Road, Detroit, MI 48219-0900. Phone: 313-993-3350.

FACILITIES
Information Resources McNichols Library; total holdings of 645,039 volumes, 773,225 microforms, 5,505 current periodical subscriptions. CD player(s) available for graduate student use. Access provided to online bibliographic retrieval services.

INTERNATIONAL STUDENTS
Demographics 25% of students enrolled are international students [Africa, 5%, Asia, 68%, Central America, 5%, North America, 8%, South America, 5%, other, 9%].

Services and Facilities International student office, international student center, international student housing, visa services, ESL courses, counseling/support services.

Applying Proof of adequate funds, proof of health/immunizations required. Financial aid is not available to international students.

International Student Contact Dr. David Kent, Director for International Admissions, 4001 West McNichols Road, Detroit, MI 48219-0900. Phone: 313-993-1205; Fax: 313-993-1192.

PLACEMENT
Services include alumni network, career counseling/planning, career fairs, career library, career placement, electronic job bank, job interviews arranged, job search course, resume referral to employers, and resume preparation. In 1996–97, 110 organizations participated in on-campus recruiting.

Employment Of 1996–97 graduates, 95% were employed within three months of graduation; the average starting salary was $57,000. Types of employment entered: accounting, banking, communications, computer-related, consulting, consumer products, engineering, finance, financial services, government, health services, high technology, hospitality management, human resources, information systems/technology, insurance, international trade, law, management, manufacturing, marketing, media, nonprofit, pharmaceutical, real estate, retail, service industry, telecommunications, transportation, utilities.

Program Contact: Dr. Bahman Mirshab, Director of Graduate Business Programs, College of Business Administration, 4001 West McNichols Road, Detroit, MI 48219-0900. Phone: 313-993-1202; Fax: 313-993-1673; E-mail: mirshabb@udmercy.edu
See full description on page 1066.

University of Michigan

University of Michigan Business School

Ann Arbor, Michigan

OVERVIEW
The University of Michigan is a state-supported, coed university. Enrollment: 51,293 graduate, professional, and undergraduate students; 13,925 full-time matriculated graduate/professional students; 1,050 part-time matriculated graduate/professional students. Founded: 1817. The graduate business unit is in an urban setting and is on a semester calendar.

HIGHLIGHTS

Enrollment Profile
Full-time: 424
Part-time: 171
Total: 595
Average Age: 29
Fall 1997 Average GPA: 3.3

International: 17%
Women: 25%
Minorities: 23%
Average Class Size: 45
Fall 1997 Average GMAT: 662

Costs
Full-time tuition: $18,400 per academic year (resident); $24,000 per academic year (nonresident)
Part-time tuition: $600 per credit hour (resident); $600 per credit hour (nonresident)

AACSB – The International Association for Management Education accredited

GRADUATE BUSINESS PROGRAMS
Full-time MBA (MBA) Full-time; 60 total credits required; 2 years to complete program. Concentrations in accounting, asian business studies, entrepreneurship, finance, human resources, international and area business studies, international business, international management, japanese business studies, management information systems, marketing, operations management, production management, public policy and administration, real estate, strategic management.

Evening MBA (MBA) Part-time; 60 total credits required; 3 to 10 years to complete program. Concentrations in accounting, asian business studies, entrepreneurship, finance, human resources, international and area business studies, international business, international management, management information systems, marketing, operations management, organizational behavior/development, production management, public policy and administration, real estate, strategic management.

Master of Business Administration/Master of Architecture (MBA/MArch) Full-time; 90 total credits required; 3 years to complete program.

Master of Business Administration/Master of Arts in Chinese Studies (MBA/MA) Full-time; 70 total credits required; 3 years to complete program.

Master of Business Administration/Master of Science in Construction Engineering & Management (MBA/MS) Full-time; 69 total credits required; 2.5 years to complete program.

Master of Business Administration/Master of Science in Industrial and Operations Engineering (MBA/MS) Full-time; 65 total credits required; 2.5 years to complete program.

Master of Business Administration/Master of Arts in Japanese Studies (MBA/MA) Full-time; 70 total credits required; 3 years to complete program.

Master of Business Administration/Master of Arts in Japanese Studies (MBA/MA) Full-time; 120 total credits required; 4 years to complete program.

Master of Business Administration/Master of Engineering in Manufacturing (MBA/MEM) Full-time; 66 total credits required; 2.5 years to complete program.

Master of Business Administration/Master of Arts in Modern Middle Eastern and North African Studies (MBA/MA) Full-time; 81 total credits required; 3 years to complete program.

Master of Business Administration/Master of Health Service Administration (MBA/MHSA) Full-time; 90 total credits required; 3 years to complete program.

Master of Business Administration/Master of Public Policy (MBA/MPP) Full-time; 84 total credits required; 3 years to complete program.

Master of Business Administration/Master of Social Work (MBA/MSW) Full-time; 85 total credits required; 3 years to complete program.

Master of Business Administration/Master of Music (MBA/MM) Full-time; 65 total credits required; 2 years to complete program.

Master of Business Administration/Master of Science in Engineering (MBA/MS) Full-time; 69 total credits required; 2 to 2.5 years to complete program.

Master of Business Administration/Master of Science in Nursing Administration (MBA/MS) Full-time; 70 total credits required; 2.5 years to complete program.

Master of Business Administration/Master of Arts in South and Southeast Asian Studies (MBA/MA) Full-time; 69 total credits required; 2.5 to 3 years to complete program.

Master of Business Administration/Master of Arts in Russian and East European Studies (MBA/MA) Full-time; 75 total credits required; 2.5 to 3 years to complete program.

ADMISSION
Applications For fall 1997 there were 4,145 applications for admission. Of those applying, 925 were accepted. Of those accepted, 424 enrolled.

Application Requirements GMAT score, application form, application fee, bachelor's degree, essay, 2 letters of recommendation, personal statement, resume, college transcript(s).

Recommended for Application Interview, minimum of 3 years of work experience, computer experience.

Application Deadline 3/1 for fall, 3/1 for fall (international). Application fee: $100.

ACADEMICS
Faculty Full-time 121; part-time 57.

Teaching Methodologies Case study, computer-aided instruction, computer analysis, computer simulations, experiential learning, faculty seminars, field projects, group discussion, lecture, research, role playing, seminars by members of the business community, simulations, student presentations, study groups, team projects.

Technology Computer terminals/PCs are available for student use and are linked by a campus-wide network. The network has full access to the Internet. Students are not required to have their own PC.

Special Opportunities Advanced credit may be earned through credit by examination, credit for experience. International exchange programs in Australia, Austria, Costa Rica, Denmark, Finland, France, Germany, Italy, Netherlands, Republic of Singapore, Spain, Sweden, United Kingdom. An internship program is available.

FINANCES
Costs for 1997–98 Tuition: Full-time: $18,400 per year (resident); $24,000 per year (nonresident). Part-time: $600 per credit hour (resident); $600 per credit hour (nonresident). Cost varies by academic program, class time (e.g., day/evening). Fees: Full-time: $370 per academic year (resident); $370 per academic year (nonresident). Part-time: $185 per semester (resident); $185 per semester (nonresident). Average 1997–98 room and board costs were $5000 per academic year (on campus) and $5000 per academic year (off campus). Room and board costs vary by campus location, occupancy (e.g., single, double, triple), type of accommodation, type of meal plan.

Financial Aid In 1997–98, 47% of students received some institutionally administered aid in the form of fellowships, research assistantships, teaching assistantships, scholarships, work study, loans. Financial aid is available to part-time students. Application Deadline: 3/1.

Financial Aid Contact Ms. Lorie Jager, Senior Financial Aid Officer, 701 Tappan Street, Ann Arbor, MI 48109-1234. Phone: 734-764-5139; Fax: 734-763-7804; E-mail: umbusmba@umich.edu

FACILITIES
Information Resources Hatcher Graduate Library plus 18 additional on-campus libraries; total holdings of 6,900,000 volumes, 3,472,083 microforms, 67,530 current periodical subscriptions. CD player(s) available for graduate student use. Access provided to online bibliographic retrieval services and online databases.

INTERNATIONAL STUDENTS
Demographics 17% of students enrolled are international students [Africa, 1%, Asia, 10%, Australia/New Zealand, 1%, Central America, 2%, Europe, 4%, North America, 76%, South America, 6%].

Services and Facilities International student office, international student center, international student housing, visa services, ESL courses, counseling/support services.

Applying TOEFL: minimum score of 600, proof of adequate funds required. TSE, TWE recommended. Financial aid is available to international students.

International Student Contact Ms. Ellen Schaefer, Associate Director and Administrative Director of MBA Programs, 701 Tappan Street, Ann Arbor, MI 48109-1234. Phone: 734-763-5796; Fax: 734-763-7804; E-mail: umbusmba@umich.edu

PLACEMENT
Services include alumni network, career counseling/planning, career fairs, career library, career placement, electronic job bank, job interviews arranged, job search course, resume referral to employers, and resume preparation. In 1996–97, 350 organizations participated in on-campus recruiting; 9,500 on-campus interviews were conducted.

Employment Of 1996–97 graduates, 100% were employed within three months of graduation. Types of employment entered: accounting, banking, chemical industry, communications, computer-related, consulting, consumer products, education, energy, engineering, finance, financial services, government, health services, high technology, hospitality management, human resources, information systems/technology, insurance, international trade, law, management, manufacturing, marketing, media, mining, nonprofit, petrochemical, pharmaceutical, real estate, retail, service industry, telecommunications, transportation, utilities.

Business Program(s) URL: http://www.bus.umich.edu

Program Contact: Ms. Jeanne Wilt, Director, Admissions and Placement, 701 Tappan Street, Ann Arbor, MI 48109-1234. Phone: 734-763-5796; Fax: 734-763-7804; E-mail: umbusmba@umich.edu

University of Michigan-Dearborn

School of Management
Dearborn, Michigan

OVERVIEW
The University of Michigan-Dearborn is a state-supported, coed, comprehensive institution. Enrollment: 8,350 graduate, professional, and undergraduate students; 43 full-time matriculated graduate/professional students; 1,547 part-time matriculated graduate/professional students. Founded: 1959. The graduate business unit is in an urban setting and is on a trimester calendar.

HIGHLIGHTS

Enrollment Profile
Full-time: 15
Part-time: 336
Total: 351
Average Age: 31
Fall 1997 Average GPA: 3.12

International: N/R
Women: 24%
Minorities: 17%
Average Class Size: 35
Fall 1997 Average GMAT: 563

Costs
Full-time tuition: $2560 per academic year (resident); $7432 per academic year (nonresident)
Part-time tuition: $240 per credit (resident); $694 per credit (nonresident)

University of Michigan-Dearborn (continued)

AACSB – The International Association for Management Education accredited

Degree(s) offered in conjunction with University of Michigan

GRADUATE BUSINESS PROGRAMS

MBA Program (MBA) Full-time, part-time; 60 total credits required; 20 months to 10 years to complete program. Concentration in management.

Master of Business Administration/Master of Science in Engineering (MBA/MS) Full-time, part-time; 66 total credits required; 2 to 5 years to complete program. Concentration in management.

ADMISSION

Applications For fall 1997 there were 114 applications for admission. Of those applying, 81 were accepted. Of those accepted, 55 enrolled.

Application Requirements Application form, application fee, bachelor's degree, minimum GPA, letter of recommendation, personal statement, resume, college transcript(s), computer experience: computer application knowledge.

Recommended for Application GMAT score accepted.

Application Deadline Applications processed on a rolling/continuous basis for both domestic and international students. Application fee: $55. Deferred entrance is available.

ACADEMICS

Faculty Full-time 29; part-time 10.

Teaching Methodologies Case study, computer-aided instruction, computer analysis, computer simulations, faculty seminars, group discussion, lecture, research, seminars by members of the business community, simulations, student presentations, study groups, team projects.

Technology 210 on-campus computer terminals/PCs are available for student use and are linked by a campus-wide network. The network has full access to the Internet. Students are not required to have their own PC.

Special Opportunities Advanced credit may be earned through credit by examination, transfer of credits from another institution. An internship program is available.

FINANCES

Costs for 1997–98 Tuition: Full-time: $2560 per semester (resident); $7432 per semester (nonresident). Part-time: $240 per credit (resident); $694 per credit (nonresident). Cost varies by number of credits taken. Fees: Full-time: $380 per academic year (resident); $380 per academic year (nonresident). Part-time: $145 per semester (resident); $145 per semester (nonresident). Fees vary by academic program, number of credits taken.

Financial Aid Scholarships, work study, loans available. Financial aid is available to part-time students. Application Deadline: 2/1.

Financial Aid Contact Mr. John Mason, Director, Financial Aid Office, 4901 Evergreen Road, Dearborn, MI 48128-1491. Phone: 313-593-5300.

FACILITIES

Information Resources Mardigian Library; total holdings of 299,792 volumes, 432,298 microforms, 1,169 current periodical subscriptions. CD player(s) available for graduate student use. Access provided to online bibliographic retrieval services.

INTERNATIONAL STUDENTS

Demographics N/R

Services and Facilities Visa services, ESL courses, counseling/support services.

Applying TOEFL: minimum score of 560, proof of adequate funds, proof of health/immunizations required. Financial aid is not available to international students.

International Student Contact Ms. Margaret Flannery, Assistant Director Counseling, 4901 Evergreen Road, Dearborn, MI 48128-1491. Phone: 313-593-5430; E-mail: mflanner@um-fl.umd.umich.edu

PLACEMENT

Services include alumni network, career counseling/planning, career fairs, career library, career placement, job interviews arranged, resume referral to employers, and resume preparation.

Employment Types of employment entered: consulting, manufacturing.

Business Program(s) URL: http://www.umd.umich.edu/dept/acad/som/degree.html

Program Contact: MBA Program Director, School of Management, 4901 Evergreen Road, Dearborn, MI 48128-1491. Phone: 313-593-5460; Fax: 313-593-5636; E-mail: mba_umd@fob-fl.umd.umich.edu

University of Michigan-Flint

School of Management

Flint, Michigan

OVERVIEW

The University of Michigan-Flint is a state-supported, coed, comprehensive institution. Enrollment: 6,444 graduate, professional, and undergraduate students. Founded: 1956. The graduate business unit is in an urban setting and is on a semester calendar.

HIGHLIGHTS

Enrollment Profile

Full-time: 0	International: N/R
Part-time: 288	Women: 32%
Total: 288	Minorities: 14%
Average Age: 30	Average Class Size: 30
Fall 1997 Average GPA: 3.0	Fall 1997 Average GMAT: 530

Costs
Full-time tuition: N/R
Part-time tuition: $5327 per year (resident); $5327 per year (nonresident)

AACSB – The International Association for Management Education accredited

GRADUATE BUSINESS PROGRAMS

Executive MBA (MBA) Part-time; 48 total credits required; 3 to 6 years to complete program.

ADMISSION

Applications For fall 1997 there were 73 applications for admission. Of those applying, 67 were accepted. Of those accepted, 51 enrolled.

Application Requirements GMAT score, application form, application fee, bachelor's degree, minimum GPA, 3 letters of recommendation, personal statement, resume, college transcript(s), minimum of 3 years of work experience.

Application Deadline 7/1 for fall, 11/1 for winter, 7/1 for fall (international), 11/1 for winter (international). Application fee: $20. Deferred entrance is available.

ACADEMICS

Faculty Full-time 14; part-time 9.

Teaching Methodologies Case study, computer-aided instruction, computer analysis, computer simulations, experiential learning, field projects, group discussion, lecture, research, role playing, seminars by members of the business community, simulations, student presentations, study groups, team projects.

Technology 150 on-campus computer terminals/PCs are available for student use and are linked by a campus-wide network. The network has full access to the Internet. Students are not required to have their own PC.

Special Opportunities Advanced credit may be earned through credit by examination, transfer of credits from another institution.

FINANCES

Costs for 1997–98 Tuition: Part-time: $5327 per year (resident); $5327 per year (nonresident).

Financial Aid In 1997–98, 9% of students received some institutionally administered aid in the form of grants, scholarships, work study, loans. Financial aid is available to part-time students. Application Deadline: 4/15.

Financial Aid Contact Mr. Mark Delorey, Financial Aid Director, 277 University Pavilion, Flint, MI 48502-2186. Phone: 810-762-3444; Fax: 810-762-3346.

FACILITIES

Information Resources Francis Willson Thompson Library; total holdings of 147,000 volumes, 513,991 microforms, 21,000 current periodical subscriptions. CD player(s) available for graduate student use. Access provided to online bibliographic retrieval services.

INTERNATIONAL STUDENTS

Demographics N/R

Applying TOEFL required. Financial aid is not available to international students.

PLACEMENT

Services include career counseling/planning, career fairs, career library, career placement, electronic job bank, resume referral to employers, and resume preparation.

Business Program(s) URL: http://www.flint.umich.edu/departments/SOM/MBA/

Program Contact: Janet McIntire, Interim MBA Program Coordinator, School of Management, Flint, MI 48502-2186. Phone: 810-762-3163, 800-942-5636 (MI only); Fax: 810-762-3282; E-mail: jmcintir@flint.umich.edu

See full description on page 1100.

Walsh College of Accountancy and Business Administration

College of Accountancy and Business Administration

Troy, Michigan

OVERVIEW

Walsh College of Accountancy and Business Administration is an independent-nonprofit, coed, upper-level institution. Enrollment: 3,335 graduate, professional, and undergraduate students; 87 full-time matriculated graduate/professional students; 1,684 part-time matriculated graduate/professional students. Founded: 1968. The graduate business unit is in a suburban setting and is on a semester calendar.

HIGHLIGHTS

Enrollment Profile
Full-time: 87
Part-time: 1,684
Total: 1,771
Average Age: 33
Fall 1997 Average GPA: 3.131

International: 5%
Women: 47%
Minorities: 13%
Average Class Size: 28
Fall 1997 Average GMAT: N/R

Costs
Full-time tuition: N/R
Part-time tuition: $263 per semester credit hour

GRADUATE BUSINESS PROGRAMS

Master of Science in Professional Accountancy (MS) Full-time, part-time; 36 total credits required; 12 months to 5 years to complete program. Concentration in accounting.

Master of Science in Finance (MS) Full-time, part-time; 36 total credits required; 12 months to 5 years to complete program. Concentrations in banking, finance, financial economics, financial management/planning, international finance.

Master of Science in Management (MS) Full-time, part-time; 36 total credits required; 12 months to 5 years to complete program. Concentrations in human resources, international management, marketing, operations management, technology management.

Master of Science in Information Management and Communication (MS) Full-time, distance learning option; 36 total credits required; 2 years to complete program. Concentration in information management.

Master of Science in Taxation (MS) Full-time, part-time; 35 total credits required; 12 months to 5 years to complete program. Concentration in taxation.

Master of Business Administration (MBA) Full-time, part-time; 36-51 total credits required; GMAT score required; 12 months to 5 years to complete program.

ADMISSION

Applications For fall 1997 there were 493 applications for admission. Of those applying, 480 were accepted. Of those accepted, 316 enrolled.

Application Requirements Application form, application fee, bachelor's degree, minimum GPA: 2.75, resume, college transcript(s), minimum of 2 years of work experience, computer experience.

Application Deadline Applications processed on a rolling/continuous basis for both domestic and international students. Application fee: $25. Deferred entrance is available.

ACADEMICS

Faculty Full-time 11; part-time 82.

Teaching Methodologies Case study, computer-aided instruction, computer analysis, computer simulations, faculty seminars, field projects, group discussion, lecture, research, role playing, seminars by members of the business community, simulations, student presentations, study groups, team projects.

Technology 250 on-campus computer terminals/PCs are available for student use and are linked by a campus-wide network. The network has full access to the Internet. Students are not required to have their own PC.

Special Opportunities Advanced credit may be earned through transfer of credits from another institution.

FINANCES

Costs for 1997-98 Tuition: $263 per semester credit hour. Fees: $75 per semester.

Financial Aid Work study available. Financial aid is available to part-time students.

Financial Aid Contact Ms. Josephine Cassar, Director, Student Financial Resources, 3838 Livernois Road, PO Box 7006, Troy, MI 48007-7006. Phone: 248-689-8282 Ext. 285; Fax: 248-524-2520; E-mail: jcassar@walshcol.edu

FACILITIES

Information Resources Vollbrecht Library; total holdings of 26,000 volumes, 9 microforms, 495 current periodical subscriptions. CD player(s) available for graduate student use. Access provided to online bibliographic retrieval services.

INTERNATIONAL STUDENTS

Demographics 5% of students enrolled are international students.

Services and Facilities Counseling/support services.

Applying TOEFL: minimum score of 550, proof of adequate funds required. Financial aid is available to international students.

International Student Contact Ms. Sherree Hyde, Dean of Enrollment Services, 3838 Livernois Road, PO Box 7006, Troy, MI 48007-7006. Phone: 248-689-8282 Ext. 215; Fax: 248-524-2520; E-mail: shyde@walshcol.edu

PLACEMENT

Services include alumni network, career counseling/planning, career fairs, career library, career placement, job interviews arranged, resume referral to employers, and resume preparation. In 1996-97, 106 organizations participated in on-campus recruiting; 1,480 on-campus interviews were conducted.

Employment Of 1996-97 graduates, 85% were employed within three months of graduation; the average starting salary was $36,000. Types of employment entered: accounting, banking, chemical industry, communications, computer-related, consulting, consumer products, education, finance, financial services, government, health services, high technology, hospitality management, human resources, information systems/technology, insurance, management, manufacturing, marketing, media, nonprofit, pharmaceutical, real estate, retail, service industry, telecommunications, transportation, utilities.

Business Program(s) URL: http://www.walshcol.edu

Program Contact: Ms. Sherree Hyde, Dean of Enrollment Services, 3838 Livernois Road, PO Box 7006, Troy, MI 48007-7006. Phone: 248-689-8282 Ext. 215; Fax: 248-524-2520; E-mail: shyde@walshcol.edu

See full description on page 1182.

Wayne State University

School of Business Administration

Detroit, Michigan

OVERVIEW

Wayne State University is a state-supported, coed university. Enrollment: 30,729 graduate, professional, and undergraduate students. Founded: 1868. The graduate business unit is in an urban setting and is on a semester calendar.

HIGHLIGHTS

Enrollment Profile
Full-time: 191
Part-time: 1,457
Total: 1,648
Average Age: 28
Fall 1997 Average GPA: 3.1

International: N/R
Women: 40%
Minorities: N/R
Average Class Size: 35
Fall 1997 Average GMAT: 525

Costs
Full-time tuition: $3816 per academic year (resident); $8184 per academic year (nonresident)
Part-time tuition: $159 per credit (resident); $341 per credit (nonresident)

AACSB – The International Association for Management Education accredited

*T*he School of Business Administration at Wayne State University offers a nationally (AACSB–The International Association for Management Education) accredited, high-impact M.B.A. program that emphasizes real-world applicability of theoretical concepts and creative problem-solving skills. Open to students with any academic background, this twelve-course program features streamlined foundation and core requirements and extensive elective options designed to help students meet their professional goals and objectives while developing critical leadership, communication, and teamwork skills. Elective subject areas include accounting, business economics, entrepreneurship, finance, industrial relations, international business, management and organizational behavior, management information systems, marketing, personnel/human resources management, quality management, and taxation. The degree can be completed on a full- or part-time basis in the evenings and on Saturdays at campuses in Oakland, Macomb, and Wayne counties. The School of Business also offers an eleven-course M.S. in Taxation degree, also available in the evenings in Oakland and Wayne counties

GRADUATE BUSINESS PROGRAMS
Master of Business Administration (MBA) Full-time, part-time; 36 total credits required; 12 months to 6 years to complete program. Concentrations in accounting, entrepreneurship, finance, human resources, industrial/labor relations, international business, management, management information systems, managerial economics, marketing, quality management, taxation.

Master of Science in Taxation (MS) Full-time, part-time; 36 total credits required; 12 months to 6 years to complete program. Concentration in taxation.

ADMISSION
Applications For fall 1997 there were 494 applications for admission. Of those applying, 407 were accepted. Of those accepted, 285 enrolled.

Application Requirements Application form, application fee, bachelor's degree, minimum GPA: 2.75; college transcript(s).

Recommended for Application GMAT score accepted: minimum 450.

Application Deadline 8/1 for fall, 12/1 for winter, 4/1 for spring, 4/1 for summer, 7/1 for fall (international), 11/1 for winter (international), 3/1 for spring (international), 3/1 for summer (international). Application fee: $20, $30 (international).

ACADEMICS
Faculty Full-time 56; part-time 38.

Teaching Methodologies Case study, computer analysis, computer simulations, group discussion, lecture, research, seminars by members of the business community, simulations, student presentations, study groups, team projects.

Technology 125 on-campus computer terminals/PCs are available for student use and are linked by a campus-wide network. The network has full access to the Internet. Students are not required to have their own PC.

Special Opportunities Advanced credit may be earned through credit by examination, transfer of credits from another institution. An internship program is available.

FINANCES
Costs for 1997–98 Tuition: Full-time: $3816 per year (resident); $8184 per year (nonresident). Part-time: $159 per credit (resident); $341 per credit (nonresident). Cost varies by number of credits taken. Fees: Full-time: $69 per academic year (resident); $69 per academic year (nonresident). Part-time: $69 per semester (resident); $69 per semester (nonresident). Average 1997–98 room only costs were $5000 per academic year (on campus) and $6100 per academic year (off campus). Room and board costs vary by occupancy (e.g., single, double, triple), type of accommodation.

Financial Aid Research assistantships, teaching assistantships, scholarships, work study available. Financial aid is available to part-time students.

Financial Aid Contact Mr. Al Andino, Director, 3 West Helen Newberry Joy Student Services Center, Detroit, MI 48202. Phone: 313-577-3378; Fax: 313-577-6648.

FACILITIES
Information Resources Purdy/Kresge Library plus 5 additional on-campus libraries; total holdings of 2,833,977 volumes, 3,346,213 microforms, 24,574 current periodical subscriptions. CD player(s) available for graduate student use. Access provided to online bibliographic retrieval services and online databases.

INTERNATIONAL STUDENTS
Demographics N/R

Services and Facilities International student office, international student center, international student housing, ESL courses, counseling/support services.

Applying TOEFL: minimum score of 550, proof of adequate funds, proof of health/immunizations required. Financial aid is not available to international students.

International Student Contact Ms. Annette Vitale-Salajanu, Director, International Services Office, 5460 Cass, 2nd Floor, Detroit, MI 48202. Phone: 313-577-3422; Fax: 313-577-2962.

PLACEMENT
Services include career counseling/planning, career fairs, career library, career placement, job interviews arranged, resume referral to employers, and resume preparation.

Employment Of 1996–97 graduates, 95% were employed within three months of graduation; the average starting salary was $47,692. Types of employment entered: accounting, banking, computer-related, consulting, education, engineering, finance, financial services, government, health services, high technology, human resources, information systems/technology, insurance, international trade, management, marketing, media, nonprofit, pharmaceutical, real estate, retail, service industry, telecommunications, transportation, utilities.

Business Program(s) URL: http://www.busadm.wayne.edu

Program Contact: Ms. Linda Zaddach, Assistant Dean of Student Affairs, 5201 Cass, Room 103, Prentis Building, Detroit, MI 48202. Phone: 313-577-4510, 800-910-EARN; Fax: 313-577-5299; E-mail: lzaddach@cms.cc.wayne.edu
See full description on page 1188.

Western Michigan University

Haworth College of Business
Kalamazoo, Michigan

OVERVIEW
Western Michigan University is a state-supported, coed university. Enrollment: 25,699 graduate, professional, and undergraduate students. Founded: 1903. The graduate business unit is in an urban setting and is on a semester calendar.

HIGHLIGHTS

Enrollment Profile

Full-time: 120	International: 19%
Part-time: 473	Women: 42%
Total: 593	Minorities: 4%
Average Age: 29	Average Class Size: 25
Fall 1997 Average GPA: 3.2	Fall 1997 Average GMAT: 530

Costs
Full-time tuition: $3990 per academic year (resident); $9780 per academic year (nonresident)
Part-time tuition: $142 per hour (resident); $344 per hour (nonresident)

AACSB – The International Association for Management Education accredited

GRADUATE BUSINESS PROGRAMS
Master of Business Administration (MBA) Full-time, part-time, distance learning option; 48 total credits required; minimum of 15 months to complete program. Concentrations in accounting, economics, management, management information systems, marketing, finance.

Master of Science in Accountancy (MS) Full-time, part-time; 66 total credits required; minimum of 18 months to complete program.

Professional MBA (MBA) Full-time, part-time, distance learning option; 48 total credits required; 12 months to 3 years to complete program.

ADMISSION
Applications For fall 1997 there were 400 applications for admission. Of those applying, 275 were accepted. Of those accepted, 200 enrolled.

Application Requirements Application form, application fee, bachelor's degree, minimum GPA: 3.0, college transcript(s), computer experience.

Recommended for Application GMAT score accepted: minimum 450, letters of recommendation.

Application Deadline 7/1 for fall, 11/1 for winter, 3/15 for spring, 7/1 for fall (international), 11/1 for winter (international), 3/15 for spring (international). Application fee: $25. Deferred entrance is available.

ACADEMICS
Faculty Full-time 86; part-time 10.

Teaching Methodologies Case study, computer-aided instruction, computer simulations, faculty seminars, group discussion, lecture, research, simulations, student presentations, study groups, team projects.

Technology 800 on-campus computer terminals/PCs are available for student use and are linked by a campus-wide network. The network has full access to the Internet. Students are not required to have their own PC.

Special Opportunities Advanced credit may be earned through transfer of credits from another institution. International exchange programs in Germany, Japan, Mexico. An internship program is available.

FINANCES
Costs for 1997–98 Tuition: Full-time: $3990 per year (resident); $9780 per year (nonresident). Part-time: $142 per hour (resident); $344 per hour (nonresident). Cost varies by campus location, number of credits taken. Fees: Full-time: $578 per academic year (resident); $578 per academic year (nonresident). Part-time: $120 per semester (resident); $120 per semester (nonresident). Fees vary by campus location, number of credits taken. Average 1997–98 room and board costs were $4257 per academic year. Room and board costs vary by campus location, occupancy (e.g., single, double, triple), type of accommodation, type of meal plan.

Financial Aid Fellowships, research assistantships, teaching assistantships, work study available. Application Deadline: 2/15.

Financial Aid Contact Director of Financial Aid, 1000 Oliver Street, Kalamazoo, MI 49008. Phone: 616-387-6000; Fax: 616-387-0958.

FACILITIES

Information Resources Waldo Library plus 3 additional on-campus libraries; total holdings of 1,649,454 volumes, 609,529 microforms, 5,444 current periodical subscriptions. CD player(s) available for graduate student use. Access provided to online bibliographic retrieval services.

INTERNATIONAL STUDENTS

Demographics 19% of students enrolled are international students [Asia, 85%, Europe, 3%, North America, 1%, South America, 1%, other, 10%].

Services and Facilities International student office, international student center, international student housing, visa services, ESL courses, counseling/support services.

Applying TOEFL: minimum score of 550, proof of adequate funds, proof of health/immunizations required. TWE recommended. Financial aid is not available to international students.

International Student Contact Ms. Jolene Jackson, Director, International Student Services, 414 Ellsworth Hall, Kalamazoo, MI 49008. Phone: 616-387-5865; Fax: 616-387-5899; E-mail: jolene.jackson@wmich.edu

PLACEMENT

Services include alumni network, career counseling/planning, career fairs, career library, career placement, electronic job bank, job interviews arranged, resume referral to employers, and resume preparation. In 1996–97, 60 organizations participated in on-campus recruiting.

Employment Types of employment entered: accounting, banking, chemical industry, computer-related, consulting, engineering, finance, information systems/technology, pharmaceutical, utilities.

Business Program(s) URL: http://spider.hcob.wmich.edu

Program Contact: Michele M. Moe, Director, HCOB Academic Advising and Admissions, 2130 Arnold Schneider Hall, Kalamazoo, MI 49008. Phone: 616-387-5075, 800-387-4968; Fax: 616-387-5710; E-mail: michele.moe@wmich.edu

MINNESOTA

College of St. Catherine

Business Programs

St. Paul, Minnesota

OVERVIEW

College of St. Catherine is an independent-religious, primarily women, comprehensive institution. Enrollment: 2,803 graduate, professional, and undergraduate students; 235 full-time matriculated graduate/professional students; 226 part-time matriculated graduate/professional students. Founded: 1905. The graduate business unit is in an urban setting and is on a trimester calendar.

HIGHLIGHTS

Enrollment Profile

Full-time: 10	International: N/R
Part-time: 48	Women: 83%
Total: 58	Minorities: 9%
Average Age: 40	Average Class Size: 13
Fall 1997 Average GPA: N/R	Fall 1997 Average GMAT: N/R

Costs
Full-time tuition: N/R
Part-time tuition: $456 per credit

GRADUATE BUSINESS PROGRAMS

Master of Arts in Organizational Leadership (MA) Full-time, part-time; 36 total credits required; minimum of 2.5 years to complete program.

ADMISSION

Applications For fall 1997 there were 29 applications for admission. Of those applying, 25 were accepted. Of those accepted, 18 enrolled.

Application Requirements Application form, application fee, bachelor's degree, essay, 2 letters of recommendation, personal statement, resume, college transcript(s), minimum of 2 years of work experience.

Recommended for Application GMAT score accepted, GRE score accepted, MAT score accepted.

Application Deadline Applications processed on a rolling/continuous basis for both domestic and international students. Application fee: $25. Deferred entrance is available.

ACADEMICS

Faculty Full-time 6; part-time 5.

Teaching Methodologies Experiential learning, faculty seminars, lecture, research, student presentations.

Technology 250 on-campus computer terminals/PCs are available for student use and are linked by a campus-wide network. The network has full access to the Internet. Students are not required to have their own PC.

Special Opportunities Advanced credit may be earned through credit for experience, transfer of credits from another institution. International exchange program available. An internship program is available.

FINANCES

Costs for 1997–98 Tuition: $456 per credit. Cost varies by academic program, number of credits taken. Fees: $20 per trimester. Average 1997–98 room and board costs were $4700 per academic year. Room and board costs vary by occupancy (e.g., single, double, triple), type of accommodation, type of meal plan.

Financial Aid In 1997–98, 22% of students received some institutionally administered aid in the form of research assistantships, grants, loans. Financial aid is available to part-time students. Application Deadline: 4/1.

Financial Aid Contact Ms. Pamela Johnson, Director, Enrollment, Student Services and Financial Aid, Mailstop F-11, St. Paul, MN 55105. Phone: 612-690-6540; Fax: 612-690-6024; E-mail: pjohnson@stkate.edu

FACILITIES

Information Resources Main library plus 1 additional on-campus library; total holdings of 231,021 volumes, 104,232 microforms, 1,165 current periodical subscriptions. CD player(s) available for graduate student use. Access provided to online bibliographic retrieval services.

INTERNATIONAL STUDENTS

Demographics N/R

Services and Facilities International student office, international student center, international student housing, visa services, ESL courses, counseling/support services.

Applying TOEFL: minimum score of 500, proof of adequate funds, proof of health/immunizations required. Financial aid is available to international students.

International Student Contact Ms. June Noronha, Associate Dean for Multicultural Education, 2004 Randolph Avenue #F-29, Saint Paul, MN 55105. Phone: 612-690-6784; Fax: 612-690-8824; E-mail: jnoronha@stkate.edu

PLACEMENT

Services include alumni network, career counseling/planning, career fairs, job search course, and resume preparation.

Business Program(s) URL: http://www.stkate.edu

Program Contact: Admissions Office, 2004 Randolph Avenue, St. Paul, MN 55105-1789. Phone: 612-690-6505; Fax: 612-690-6024.

College of St. Scholastica

Program in Management

Duluth, Minnesota

OVERVIEW

College of St. Scholastica is an independent-religious, coed, comprehensive institution. Enrollment: 2,015 graduate, professional, and undergraduate students; 178 full-time matriculated graduate/professional students; 469 part-time matriculated graduate/professional students. Founded: 1912. The graduate business unit is in an urban setting and is on a quarter calendar.

HIGHLIGHTS

Enrollment Profile

Full-time: 0	International: N/R
Part-time: 75	Women: 55%
Total: 75	Minorities: 8%
Average Age: 35	Average Class Size: 15
Fall 1997 Average GPA: N/R	Fall 1997 Average GMAT: N/R

Costs
Full-time tuition: N/R
Part-time tuition: $332 per quarter credit

College of St. Scholastica (continued)

GRADUATE BUSINESS PROGRAMS
Master of Arts in Management (MA) Full-time, part-time, distance learning option; 50-53 total credits required; 2 to 7 years to complete program. Concentrations in management, organizational behavior/development, strategic management.

ADMISSION
Applications For fall 1997 there were 8 applications for admission. Of those applying, 6 were accepted. Of those accepted, 6 enrolled.

Application Requirements Application form, application fee, bachelor's degree, essay, interview, college transcript(s), minimum of 2 years of work experience.

Recommended for Application Minimum GPA: 2.8.

Application Deadline Applications processed on a rolling/continuous basis for both domestic and international students. Application fee: $50. Deferred entrance is available.

ACADEMICS
Faculty Full-time 9; part-time 3.

Teaching Methodologies Case study, computer-aided instruction, experiential learning, group discussion, lecture, research, role playing, simulations, student presentations, study groups, team projects.

Technology 150 on-campus computer terminals/PCs are available for student use and are linked by a campus-wide network. The network has full access to the Internet. Students are not required to have their own PC.

Special Opportunities Advanced credit may be earned through transfer of credits from another institution.

FINANCES
Costs for 1997–98 Tuition: $332 per quarter credit. Cost varies by academic program. Average 1997–98 room and board costs were $4134 per academic year (on campus) and $3600 per academic year (off campus). Room and board costs vary by occupancy (e.g., single, double, triple), type of accommodation, type of meal plan.

Financial Aid In 1997–98, 43% of students received some institutionally administered aid in the form of loans. Financial aid is available to part-time students.

Financial Aid Contact Mr. Ben Safratowich, Student Financial Planning Counselor, 1200 Kenwood Avenue, Duluth, MN 55811. Phone: 218-723-6397; Fax: 218-723-5991; E-mail: bsafrato@css.edu

FACILITIES
Information Resources The College of St. Scholastica Library; total holdings of 127,355 volumes, 12,008 microforms, 795 current periodical subscriptions. CD player(s) available for graduate student use. Access provided to online bibliographic retrieval services.

INTERNATIONAL STUDENTS
Demographics N/R

Services and Facilities Counseling/support services.

Applying TOEFL, proof of adequate funds, proof of health/immunizations required. Financial aid is not available to international students.

International Student Contact Ms. Joan Goossens, Coordinator of Admissions Projects, 1200 Kenwood Avenue, Duluth, MN 55811. Phone: 218-723-6180; Fax: 218-723-6290; E-mail: jgoossen@css.edu

PLACEMENT
Services include alumni network, and career counseling/planning.

Employment Of 1996–97 graduates, 99% were employed within three months of graduation. Types of employment entered: accounting, banking, consulting, engineering, finance, government, health services, hospitality management, human resources, information systems/technology, insurance, management, manufacturing, marketing, mining, nonprofit, pharmaceutical, retail, service industry, transportation, utilities.

Business Program(s) URL: http://www.css.edu/depts/grad/gradmgt.html

Program Contact: Dr. Barbara Edwards, Program Director, Management Department, 1200 Kenwood Avenue, Duluth, MN 55811. Phone: 218-723-6150, 800-447-5444; Fax: 218-723-5991; E-mail: bedwards@css.edu

The Graduate School of America

Management Field

Minneapolis, Minnesota

OVERVIEW
The Graduate School of America is a proprietary, coed, graduate institution. Enrollment: 332 graduate, professional, and undergraduate students. Founded: 1993. The graduate business unit is in an urban setting and is on a quarter calendar.

HIGHLIGHTS

Enrollment Profile

Full-time: N/R	International: N/R
Part-time: N/R	Women: N/R
Total: 140	Minorities: N/R
Average Age: N/R	Average Class Size: N/R
Fall 1997 Average GPA: N/R	Fall 1997 Average GMAT: N/R

Costs
Full-time tuition: $1995 per academic year
Part-time tuition: $845 per course

GRADUATE BUSINESS PROGRAMS
Master of Science in Management (MS) Full-time, part-time, distance learning option; 48 total credits required; 12 months to 5 years to complete program. Concentration in management.

Master of Science in Management, Telecommunications Emphasis (MS) Full-time, part-time, distance learning option; 48 total credits required; 12 months to 5 years to complete program. Concentration in telecommunications management.

Master of Science in Organization and Management (MS) Full-time, part-time, distance learning option; 48 total credits required; 12 months to 5 years to complete program.

ADMISSION
Application Requirements Application form, essay, minimum GPA, personal statement, resume, college transcript(s).

Recommended for Application Interview, work experience, computer experience.

Application Deadline 9/5 for fall, 12/5 for winter, 3/5 for spring, 6/5 for summer, 9/5 for fall (international), 12/5 for winter (international), 3/5 for spring (international), 6/5 for summer (international). Application fee: $50, $150 (international). Deferred entrance is available.

ACADEMICS
Teaching Methodologies Case study, computer-aided instruction, experiential learning, faculty seminars, group discussion, research, online discussion forums.

Technology Students are required to have their own PC.

Special Opportunities Advanced credit may be earned through transfer of credits from another institution. An internship program is available.

FINANCES
Costs for 1997–98 Tuition: Full-time: $1995 per quarter. Part-time: $845 per course.

Financial Aid Loans available. Financial aid is available to part-time students.

Financial Aid Contact Ms. Bonnie Clayton, Director of Financial Aid, Minneapolis, MN 55401.

INTERNATIONAL STUDENTS
Demographics N/R

Applying TOEFL, proof of adequate funds required. Financial aid is not available to international students.

Business Program(s) URL: http://www.tgsa.edu

Program Contact: Mr. Thomas Larson, Director of Admissions, Minneapolis, MN 55401. Phone: 800-987-1133 Ext. 221, 800-987-1133 (MN only); Fax: 613-339-8022; E-mail: tlarson@tgsa.edu

Metropolitan State University

Management and Administration Program

St. Paul, Minnesota

OVERVIEW
Metropolitan State University is a state-supported, coed, comprehensive institution. Enrollment: 7,200 graduate, professional, and undergraduate students. Founded: 1971. The graduate business unit is in an urban setting and is on a semester calendar.

HIGHLIGHTS

Enrollment Profile
Full-time: 77
Part-time: 241
Total: 318
Average Age: 36
Fall 1997 Average GPA: 2.9

International: 13%
Women: 52%
Minorities: 30%
Average Class Size: 17
Fall 1997 Average GMAT: 510

Costs
Full-time tuition: N/R
Part-time tuition: $83 per credit (resident); $131 per credit (nonresident)

GRADUATE BUSINESS PROGRAMS
Master of Business Administration (MBA) Full-time, part-time; 40 total credits required; 12 months to 5 years to complete program. Concentrations in accounting, economics, entrepreneurship, finance, human resources, international and area business studies, management information systems, management science, marketing, organizational behavior/development, management.

Master of Management and Administration (MMA) Full-time, part-time; 40 total credits required; 12 months to 5 years to complete program. Concentrations in nonprofit management, public policy and administration.

ADMISSION
Applications For fall 1997 there were 42 applications for admission. Of those applying, 35 were accepted. Of those accepted, 26 enrolled.

Application Requirements GMAT score, application form, application fee, bachelor's degree, essay, 2 letters of recommendation, personal statement, resume, college transcript(s).

Recommended for Application Minimum GPA, minimum of 3 years of work experience, computer experience.

Application Deadline Applications processed on a rolling/continuous basis for both domestic and international students. Application fee: $20.

ACADEMICS
Faculty Full-time 15; part-time 25.

Teaching Methodologies Case study, computer-aided instruction, computer analysis, computer simulations, experiential learning, faculty seminars, field projects, group discussion, lecture, research, seminars by members of the business community, simulations, student presentations, study groups, team projects.

Technology 115 on-campus computer terminals/PCs are available for student use and are linked by a campus-wide network. The network has full access to the Internet. Students are not required to have their own PC.

Special Opportunities Advanced credit may be earned through credit by examination, credit for experience, credit for military training programs, credit for business training programs, transfer of credits from another institution. International exchange programs in Poland, Sweden, Taiwan. An internship program is available.

FINANCES
Costs for 1997–98 Tuition: $83 per credit (resident); $131 per credit (nonresident). Cost varies by reciprocity agreements. Fees: $2 per credit (resident); $2 per credit (nonresident).

Financial Aid In 1997–98, 11% of students received some institutionally administered aid in the form of research assistantships, work study. Financial aid is available to part-time students. Application Deadline: 6/30.

Financial Aid Contact Jim Cleaveland, Director, Financial Aid, 700 East 7th Street, St. Paul, MN 55106-5000. Phone: 612-772-7670; Fax: 612-772-3716; E-mail: jim-cleavland@metro2.metro.msus.edu

FACILITIES
Information Resources CD player(s) available for graduate student use.

INTERNATIONAL STUDENTS
Demographics 13% of students enrolled are international students.

Services and Facilities International student office, visa services, ESL courses, counseling/support services.

Applying TOEFL: minimum score of 550, proof of adequate funds, proof of health/immunizations required. Financial aid is available to international students.

International Student Contact Saleha Suleman, International Student Coordinator/Advisor, 700 East 7th Street, St. Paul, MN 55106-5000. Phone: 612-772-7720; Fax: 612-772-3716; E-mail: suleman@musu1.msus.edu

PLACEMENT
Services include alumni network, career counseling/planning, career fairs, career library, career placement, job interviews arranged, resume referral to employers, and resume preparation.

Employment Types of employment entered: accounting, banking, chemical industry, communications, computer-related, consulting, consumer products, education, energy, engineering, finance, financial services, government, health services, high technology, hospitality management, human resources, information systems/technology, insurance, international trade, law, management, manufacturing, marketing, media, nonprofit, pharmaceutical, real estate, service industry, transportation, utilities.

Business Program(s) URL: http://www.metro.msus.edu/comfact.html

Program Contact: Gloria Marcus, 730 Hennepin Avenue #818, Minneapolis, MN 55403-1896. Phone: 612-373-2724; Fax: 612-373-2888; E-mail: gloria_marcus@metro2.msus.edu

St. Cloud State University

College of Business

St. Cloud, Minnesota

OVERVIEW
St. Cloud State University is a state-supported, coed, comprehensive institution. Enrollment: 15,387 graduate, professional, and undergraduate students; 284 full-time matriculated graduate/professional students; 648 part-time matriculated graduate/professional students. Founded: 1869. The graduate business unit is in a suburban setting and is on a quarter calendar.

HIGHLIGHTS

Enrollment Profile
Full-time: 65
Part-time: 40
Total: 105
Average Age: N/R
Fall 1997 Average GPA: 3.36

International: 31%
Women: 32%
Minorities: N/R
Average Class Size: 25
Fall 1997 Average GMAT: 506

Costs
Full-time tuition: $2500 per academic year (resident); $3200 per academic year (nonresident)
Part-time tuition: $1250 per year (resident); $1600 per year (nonresident)

AACSB – The International Association for Management Education accredited

GRADUATE BUSINESS PROGRAMS
Master of Business Administration (MBA) Full-time, part-time; 48 total credits required; 18 months to 5.3 years to complete program. Concentrations in accounting, business information science, economics, finance, insurance, international business, management, marketing, real estate, taxation.

Master of Science in Accounting (MSA) Full-time, part-time; 48 total credits required; 18 months to 5.3 years to complete program. Concentration in accounting.

ADMISSION
Applications For fall 1997 there were 31 applications for admission. Of those applying, 24 were accepted. Of those accepted, 24 enrolled.

Application Requirements Application form, application fee, bachelor's degree, minimum GPA: 2.75, 3 letters of recommendation, college transcript(s).

Recommended for Application GMAT score accepted: minimum 470, personal statement.

Application Deadline Applications processed on a rolling/continuous basis for both domestic and international students. Application fee: $15, $100 (international).

ACADEMICS
Faculty Full-time 66; part-time 12.

Teaching Methodologies Case study, computer-aided instruction, group discussion, lecture, research, student presentations, team projects.

Technology 62 on-campus computer terminals/PCs are available for student use and are linked by a campus-wide network. The network has full access to the Internet. Students are not required to have their own PC.

Special Opportunities Advanced credit may be earned through transfer of credits from another institution. An internship program is available.

FINANCES
Costs for 1997–98 Tuition: Full-time: $2500 per year (resident); $3200 per year (nonresident). Part-time: $1250 per year (resident); $1600 per year (nonresident). Fees: Full-time: $15 per academic year (resident); $15 per academic year (nonresident). Part-time: $15 per year (resident); $15 per year (nonresident). Average 1997–98 room and board costs were $2937 per academic year.

Financial Aid Work study available. Application Deadline: 3/1.

Financial Aid Contact Frank Loncorich, Director, Financial Aid, 720 4th Avenue South, St. Cloud, MN 56301-4498. Phone: 320-255-2047.

FACILITIES
Information Resources Centennial Hall Learning Resource Center; total holdings of 775,827 volumes, 1,602,700 microforms, 2,082 current periodical

subscriptions. CD player(s) available for graduate student use. Access provided to online bibliographic retrieval services.

INTERNATIONAL STUDENTS

Demographics 31% of students enrolled are international students [Africa, 1%, Asia, 25%, Europe, 16%, other, 58%].

Services and Facilities International student office, international student center.

Applying TOEFL: minimum score of 600, proof of adequate funds, proof of health/immunizations required. Financial aid is available to international students.

International Student Contact Roland Fischer, Director, Center for International Studies , 720 4th Avenue South, St. Cloud, MN 56301-4498. Phone: 320-255-4287.

PLACEMENT

Services include career counseling/planning, career fairs, career library, and resume preparation. In 1996–97, 90 organizations participated in on-campus recruiting.

Employment Of 1996–97 graduates, the average starting salary was $30,000. Types of employment entered: accounting, banking, computer-related, finance, human resources, information systems/technology, insurance, management, marketing, real estate, retail.

Business Program(s) URL: http://www.stcloudstate.edu

Program Contact: Graduate Studies Office, 720 4th Avenue South, St. Cloud, MN 56301-4498. Phone: 320-255-2113.

Saint Mary's University of Minnesota

School of Graduate Studies/School of Business and Social Sciences

Winona, Minnesota

OVERVIEW

Saint Mary's University of Minnesota is an independent-religious, coed, comprehensive institution. Enrollment: 4,350 graduate, professional, and undergraduate students; 350 full-time matriculated graduate/professional students; 2,700 part-time matriculated graduate/professional students. Founded: 1912. The graduate business unit is in an urban setting and is on a trimester calendar.

HIGHLIGHTS

Enrollment Profile

Full-time: 0	International: N/R
Part-time: 300	Women: 45%
Total: 300	Minorities: N/R
Average Age: 32	Average Class Size: 15
Fall 1997 Average GPA: N/R	Fall 1997 Average GMAT: N/R

Costs
Full-time tuition: N/R
Part-time tuition: $205 per credit

GRADUATE BUSINESS PROGRAMS

Master of Arts in Management (MA) Full-time, part-time; 35 total credits required; 2 to 5 years to complete program. Concentration in management.

Master of Arts in International Business (MA) Full-time, part-time; 41 total credits required; GMAT score required; 15 months to 5 years to complete program. Concentrations in international and area business studies, international business, international management.

Master of Arts in Management/Health Human Services Administration (MA) Full-time, part-time; 48 total credits required; 2.3 to 5 years to complete program. Concentrations in management, public policy and administration, public management, health care.

Master of Arts in Management/Master of Science in Telecommunications (MA/MS) Full-time, part-time; 57 total credits required; 2.3 to 5 years to complete program. Concentrations in management, technology management, telecommunications management.

ADMISSION

Application Requirements Application form, application fee, bachelor's degree, minimum GPA: 2.75, interview, 2 letters of recommendation, personal statement, resume, college transcript(s).

Recommended for Application Work experience, computer experience.

Application Deadline Applications processed on a rolling/continuous basis for both domestic and international students. Application fee: $20. Deferred entrance is available.

ACADEMICS

Faculty Full-time 1; part-time 40.

Teaching Methodologies Case study, computer analysis, experiential learning, faculty seminars, field projects, group discussion, lecture, research, role playing, simulations, student presentations, study groups, team projects.

Technology 24 on-campus computer terminals/PCs are available for student use and are linked by a campus-wide network. The network has full access to the Internet. Students are not required to have their own PC.

Special Opportunities Advanced credit may be earned through transfer of credits from another institution.

FINANCES

Costs for 1997–98 Tuition: $205 per credit. Cost varies by academic program, campus location. Fees vary by academic program, campus location. Average 1997–98 room and board costs were $7500 per academic year. Room and board costs vary by campus location, type of meal plan.

Financial Aid Financial aid is available to part-time students.

Financial Aid Contact Ms. Tracey Steine, Assistant Director, Financial Aid, 700 Terrace Heights, Winona, MN 55987-1399. Phone: 507-457-1790; E-mail: tsteine@smumn.edu

FACILITIES

Information Resources Fitzgerald Library. CD player(s) available for graduate student use. Access provided to online bibliographic retrieval services.

INTERNATIONAL STUDENTS

Demographics N/R

Services and Facilities International student office.

Applying TOEFL: minimum score of 550, proof of adequate funds, proof of health/immunizations required. Financial aid is not available to international students.

International Student Contact Dr. Roxanne Eubank, International Student Advisor, 2500 Park Avenue, Minneapolis, MN 55404-4403. Phone: 612-874-9877 Ext. 123; Fax: 612-870-7666.

PLACEMENT

Services include alumni network.

Employment Of 1996–97 graduates, 95% were employed within three months of graduation. Types of employment entered: accounting, banking, communications, computer-related, consulting, consumer products, education, finance, financial services, government, health services, high technology, hospitality management, human resources, information systems/technology, insurance, international trade, management, manufacturing, marketing, media, nonprofit, retail, service industry, telecommunications, transportation, utilities.

Business Program(s) URL: http://www.smumn.edu

Program Contact: Ms. Carolyn Verret, Director, School of Graduate Studies, 2500 Park Avenue, Minneapolis, MN 55404-4403. Phone: 612-728-5135, 800-328-4827; Fax: 612-870-7666; E-mail: cverret@smumn.edu

Southwest State University

Department of Business Administration

Marshall, Minnesota

OVERVIEW

Southwest State University is a state-supported, comprehensive institution. Enrollment: 3,500 graduate, professional, and undergraduate students.

HIGHLIGHTS

Enrollment Profile

Full-time: N/R	International: N/R
Part-time: N/R	Women: N/R
Total: 25	Minorities: N/R
Average Age: N/R	Average Class Size: N/R
Fall 1997 Average GPA: N/R	Fall 1997 Average GMAT: N/R

Costs
Full-time tuition: N/R
Part-time tuition: $128 per credit (resident); $202 per credit (nonresident)

GRADUATE BUSINESS PROGRAMS
Master of Science in Management (MS) Part-time, distance learning option; up to 2.5 years to complete program.

ADMISSION
Application Requirements GMAT score, application form, bachelor's degree, essay, minimum GPA: 3.0, 2 letters of recommendation, college transcript(s), minimum of 2 years of work experience.

Recommended for Application Interview.

Application Deadline Applications processed on a rolling/continuous basis for both domestic and international students.

ACADEMICS
Teaching Methodologies Case study, computer-aided instruction, computer analysis, group discussion, lecture, simulations, student presentations, study groups, team projects.

FINANCES
Costs for 1997–98 Tuition: Part-time: $128 per credit (resident); $202 per credit (nonresident).

Financial Aid Contact Director of Financial Aid, Marshall, MN 56258-1598. Phone: 507-537-6281.

INTERNATIONAL STUDENTS
Demographics N/R

Services and Facilities International student office, international student center, visa services, ESL courses, counseling/support services.

Applying TOEFL required.

International Student Contact Director of Admissions, Marshall, MN 56258-1598. Phone: 507-537-6286.

PLACEMENT
Services include career counseling/planning, job search course, and resume preparation.

Employment Types of employment entered: banking, manufacturing.

Program Contact: Director of Admissions, Marshall, MN 56258-1598. Phone: 507-537-6286.

University of Minnesota, Duluth

School of Business and Economics

Duluth, Minnesota

OVERVIEW
The University of Minnesota, Duluth is a state-supported, coed, comprehensive institution. Enrollment: 7,600 graduate, professional, and undergraduate students. Founded: 1947. The graduate business unit is in an urban setting and is on a quarter calendar.

HIGHLIGHTS

Enrollment Profile
Full-time: 6
Part-time: 47
Total: 53
Average Age: 30
Fall 1997 Average GPA: 3.25

International: 2%
Women: 36%
Minorities: N/R
Average Class Size: 12
Fall 1997 Average GMAT: 550

Costs
Full-time tuition: $6000 per academic year (resident); $6000 per academic year (nonresident)
Part-time tuition: $260 per credit (resident); $260 per credit (nonresident)

GRADUATE BUSINESS PROGRAMS
Evening MBA (MBA) Full-time, part-time; 45 total credits required; 2 to 7 years to complete program.

ADMISSION
Applications For fall 1997 there were 12 applications for admission. Of those applying, 8 were accepted. Of those accepted, 7 enrolled.

Application Requirements Application form, application fee, bachelor's degree, minimum GPA: 3.0, personal statement, college transcript(s), computer experience: word processing, spreadsheet.

Recommended for Application GMAT score accepted: minimum 500, GRE score accepted, work experience.

Application Deadline 7/15 for fall, 10/1 for winter, 1/15 for spring, 5/1 for summer, 7/15 for fall (international), 10/1 for winter (international), 1/15 for spring (international), 5/1 for summer (international). Application fee: $40, $50 (international). Deferred entrance is available.

ACADEMICS
Faculty Full-time 32; part-time 1.

Teaching Methodologies Case study, computer-aided instruction, computer simulations, field projects, group discussion, lecture, simulations, student presentations, team projects.

Technology 250 on-campus computer terminals/PCs are available for student use and are linked by a campus-wide network. The network has full access to the Internet. Students are not required to have their own PC.

Special Opportunities Advanced credit may be earned through transfer of credits from another institution.

FINANCES
Costs for 1997–98 Tuition: Full-time: $6000 per year (resident); $6000 per year (nonresident). Part-time: $260 per credit (resident); $260 per credit (nonresident). Cost varies by number of credits taken. Fees: Full-time: $250 per academic year (resident); $250 per academic year (nonresident). Part-time: $2 per credit (resident); $2 per credit (nonresident). Fees vary by number of credits taken. Average 1997–98 room and board costs were $6000 per academic year (on campus) and $6500 per academic year (off campus). Room and board costs vary by campus location, occupancy (e.g., single, double, triple), type of accommodation, type of meal plan.

Financial Aid In 1997–98, 28% of students received some institutionally administered aid in the form of fellowships, loans.

Financial Aid Contact Ms. Brenda Herzig, Director of Financial Aid, 184 Darland Administration Building, Duluth, MN 55812-2496. Phone: 218-726-8786; E-mail: finaid@d.umn.edu

FACILITIES
Information Resources UMD Library plus 3 additional on-campus libraries; total holdings of 412,100 volumes, 373,150 microforms, 3,075 current periodical subscriptions. Access provided to online bibliographic retrieval services.

INTERNATIONAL STUDENTS
Demographics 2% of students enrolled are international students [Asia, 100%].

Services and Facilities International student office, international student center, counseling/support services.

Applying TOEFL: minimum score of 550, TWE: minimum score of 4, proof of adequate funds, proof of health/immunizations required. Financial aid is not available to international students.

International Student Contact Ms. Karin Robbins, International Student Advisor, 60 Campus Center, 10 University Drive, Duluth, MN 55812-2496. Phone: 218-726-8962; E-mail: krobbin1@d.umn.edu

PLACEMENT
Services include alumni network, career fairs, career library, career placement, and resume preparation.

Business Program(s) URL: http://sbe.d.umn.edu/

Program Contact: Ms. M. J. Leone, 431 Darland Administration Building, Duluth, MN 55812-2496. Phone: 218-726-7523, 800-232-1339; Fax: 218-726-6970; E-mail: grad@d.umn.edu

University of Minnesota, Twin Cities Campus

Carlson School of Management

Minneapolis, Minnesota

OVERVIEW
The University of Minnesota, Twin Cities Campus is a state-supported, coed university. Enrollment: 37,018 graduate, professional, and undergraduate students. Founded: 1851. The graduate business unit is in an urban setting and is on a quarter calendar.

HIGHLIGHTS

Enrollment Profile
Full-time: 282
Part-time: 864
Total: 1,146
Average Age: 27
Fall 1997 Average GPA: 3.3

International: 20%
Women: 27%
Minorities: N/R
Average Class Size: 35
Fall 1997 Average GMAT: 600

Costs
Full-time tuition: $13,036 per academic year (resident); $19,368 per academic year (nonresident)
Part-time tuition: $235 per credit (resident); $235 per credit (nonresident)

University of Minnesota, Twin Cities Campus (continued)

AACSB – The International Association for Management Education accredited

The Carlson School of Management is strategically poised to provide one of the best M.B.A. experiences money can buy. With its state-of-the-art building scheduled for completion in January 1998, the School leaps into the 21st century well equipped to handle the technological demands of the business community located as close as its own backyard. The Twin Cities business community, a powerhouse of Fortune 500 companies, had a direct influence on the School's strategic goals, ranging from curriculum considerations to the building itself. The School's ties with the business community are very close, with CEOs and Executive Vice Presidents participating in the Executive Mentor program and Top Management Perspectives course. Internationally and nationally renowned companies participate in the nation's oldest Consulting Field Project. The School's MIS area consistently ranks 2nd in the nation (U.S. News & World Report, with marketing and finance also receiving special recognition from peers. Quality guru Dr. Joseph M. Juran recently awarded his foundation's assets to the School's Quality Leadership Center. Faculty members bring their international experiences into the classroom. Furthermore, the School has strategically aligned itself with 12 top business schools around the world. Opportunities that are available abroad are quarterly exchanges, summer programs, and 2 weeks at the end of a course. With a 94 percent employment success rate after completing the M.B.A. program, the Carlson School is an excellent investment*

GRADUATE BUSINESS PROGRAMS

Day MBA (MBA) Full-time; 90 total credits required; up to 18 months to complete program. Concentrations in accounting, entrepreneurship, finance, information management, international business, marketing, operations management, strategic management.

Evening MBA (MBA) Part-time; 64-80 total credits required; up to 7 years to complete program. Concentrations in accounting, entrepreneurship, finance, information management, international business, marketing, operations management, strategic management.

Master of Business Taxation (MBT) Full-time, part-time; 47 total credits required; 12 months to 7 years to complete program. Concentration in taxation.

Master of Arts in Human Resources and Industrial Relations (MA) Full-time, part-time; 64 total credits required; 12 months to 7 years to complete program. Concentration in industrial/labor relations.

Master of Healthcare Administration (MHA) 82 total credits required; 21 months to complete program.

Carlson Executive Development MBA (EMBA) 8 years work experience required.

Master of Science in Management of Technology (MS) Full-time.

PhD in Human Resources and Industrial Relations (PhD)

PhD in Health Service Administration (PhD)

ADMISSION

Application Requirements GMAT score, application form, application fee, bachelor's degree, essay, minimum GPA, letters of recommendation, personal statement, resume, college transcript(s), computer experience: word processing, spreadsheet.

Recommended for Application Interview, work experience.

Application Deadline 1/1 for fall, 2/15 for fall (international). Application fee: $60, $90 (international). Deferred entrance is available.

ACADEMICS

Faculty Full-time 102; part-time 59.

Teaching Methodologies Case study, computer-aided instruction, computer analysis, computer simulations, experiential learning, faculty seminars, field projects, group discussion, lecture, research, role playing, seminars by members of the business community, simulations, student presentations, study groups, team projects.

Technology 75 on-campus computer terminals/PCs are available for student use and are linked by a campus-wide network. The network has full access to the Internet. Students are not required to have their own PC.

Special Opportunities International exchange programs in Austria, Australia, Belgium, Brazil, France, Italy, Japan, Spain, Sweden, Switzerland, United Kingdom. An internship program is available.

FINANCES

Costs for 1997–98 Tuition: Full-time: $13,036 per year (resident); $19,368 per year (nonresident). Part-time: $235 per credit (resident); $235 per credit (nonresident). Cost varies by academic program, class time (e.g., day/evening), number of credits taken, reciprocity agreements. Fees: $25 per quarter (resident); $25 per quarter (nonresident). Fees vary by academic program, class time (e.g., day/evening), number of credits taken. Average 1997–98 room and board costs were $5500 per academic year (on campus) and $5500 per academic year (off campus). Room and board costs vary by campus location, occupancy (e.g., single, double, triple), type of accommodation, type of meal plan.

Financial Aid Fellowships, research assistantships, teaching assistantships, grants, scholarships, work study, loans available. Financial aid is available to part-time students. Application Deadline: 3/1.

Financial Aid Contact Ms. Sheryl Spivey, Director, Financial Aid, 210 Fraser Hall, 106 Pleasant Street, SE, Minneapolis, MN 55455-0422. Phone: 612-624-1665; Fax: 612-624-9584.

FACILITIES

Information Resources O. Meredith Wilson Library plus 15 additional on-campus libraries; total holdings of 5,000,000 volumes, 3,000,000 microforms, 35,000 current periodical subscriptions. CD player(s) available for graduate student use. Access provided to online bibliographic retrieval services.

INTERNATIONAL STUDENTS

Demographics 20% of students enrolled are international students.

Services and Facilities International student office, international student center, international student housing, visa services, ESL courses, counseling/support services.

Applying TOEFL, proof of adequate funds, proof of health/immunizations required. Financial aid is not available to international students.

International Student Contact Ms. Kay Thomas, Director, International Student and Scholar Services, 20 Nicholson Hall, Minneapolis, MN 55455. Phone: 612-625-5000; Fax: 612-624-6369; E-mail: kthomas@maroon.tc.umn.edu

PLACEMENT

Services include alumni network, career counseling/planning, career fairs, career library, career placement, electronic job bank, job interviews arranged, job search course, resume referral to employers, and resume preparation. In 1996–97, 94 organizations participated in on-campus recruiting; 1,048 on-campus interviews were conducted.

Employment Of 1996–97 graduates, 93% were employed within three months of graduation; the average starting salary was $66,000. Types of employment entered: accounting, banking, chemical industry, communications, computer-related, consulting, consumer products, education, engineering, finance, financial services, health services, high technology, hospitality management, human resources, information systems/technology, insurance, international trade, management, manufacturing, marketing, mining, nonprofit, pharmaceutical, service industry, telecommunications, transportation.

Business Program(s) URL: http://www.csom.umn.edu

Program Contact: Ms. Ruth Pechauer, MBA Recruiting Coordinator, 2-210 Carlson School of Management, 321-19th Avenue South, Minneapolis, MN 55455. Phone: 612-625-5555, 800-926-9431; Fax: 612-626-7785; E-mail: rpechauer@csom.umn.edu

University of St. Thomas

Graduate School of Business

St. Paul, Minnesota

OVERVIEW

The University of St. Thomas is an independent-religious, coed university. Enrollment: 10,436 graduate, professional, and undergraduate students; 480 full-time matriculated graduate/professional students; 4,829 part-time matriculated graduate/professional students. Founded: 1885. The graduate business unit is in an urban setting and is on a semester calendar.

HIGHLIGHTS

Enrollment Profile

Full-time: 188	International: 5%
Part-time: 2,858	Women: 46%
Total: 3,046	Minorities: 5%
Average Age: 32	Average Class Size: 22
Fall 1997 Average GPA: 3.0	Fall 1997 Average GMAT: 517

Costs
Full-time tuition: N/R
Part-time tuition: $394 per credit hour

Degree(s) offered in conjunction with Confederation College, Universidad de Catholica, National Chengchi University

GRADUATE BUSINESS PROGRAMS

Evening MBA (MBA) Part-time; 37-44 total credits required; 2 years work experience required; minimum of 18 months to complete program. Concentrations in accounting, contract management, finance, information management, insurance, management, marketing, nonprofit management, health care, environmental economics/management, risk management, manufacturing management, sports/entertainment management, new venture management, real estate.

MBA in Human Resource Management (MBA) Part-time; 46-53 total credits required; 2 years work experience required; minimum of 2 years to complete program. Concentrations in human resources, organizational behavior/development.

MBA in Medical Group Management (MBA) Part-time, distance learning option; 50 total credits required; 2 years work experience required; 2.9 years to complete program.

MBA in Accounting (MBA) Full-time; 57 total credits required; 15 months to complete program.

Executive MBA (MBA) Part-time; 42 total credits required; 4 years work experience required; 2.5 years to complete program.

Master of Business Communication (MBC) Part-time; 42 total credits required; 2 years work experience required; minimum of 3 years to complete program. Concentration in public relations.

Master of International Management (MIM) Full-time, part-time; 42 total credits required; minimum of 2 years to complete program. Concentration in international marketing.

Master of Science in Real Estate Appraisal (MS) Part-time; 39 total credits required; minimum of 3 years to complete program.

Day MBA (MBA) Full-time; 48 total credits required; minimum of 2 years to complete program. Concentrations in accounting, commerce, finance, information management, insurance, management, marketing, nonprofit management, health care, environmental economics/management, risk management, manufacturing management, sports/entertainment management, new venture management, real estate.

ADMISSION

Application Requirements Application form, application fee, bachelor's degree, essay, personal statement, resume, college transcript(s), minimum of 2 years of work experience.

Recommended for Application GMAT score accepted, GRE score accepted, MAT score accepted, minimum GPA, computer experience.

Application Deadline Applications processed on a rolling/continuous basis for both domestic and international students. Application fee: $30. Deferred entrance is available.

ACADEMICS

Faculty Full-time 22; part-time 165.

Teaching Methodologies Case study, computer-aided instruction, computer analysis, computer simulations, experiential learning, faculty seminars, field projects, group discussion, lecture, research, role playing, seminars by members of the business community, simulations, student presentations, study groups, team projects.

Technology 100 on-campus computer terminals/PCs are available for student use and are linked by a campus-wide network. The network has full access to the Internet. Students are not required to have their own PC.

Special Opportunities Advanced credit may be earned through credit by examination, transfer of credits from another institution. International exchange programs in Costa Rica, France, Germany, Peoples Republic of China.

FINANCES

Costs for 1997–98 Tuition: $394 per credit hour. Cost varies by academic program.

Financial Aid Grants, scholarships, loans available. Financial aid is available to part-time students.

Financial Aid Contact Mr. Wayne Vernon, Graduate Financial Aid Counselor, 2115 Summit Avenue, AQU 201, St. Paul, MN 55105. Phone: 612-962-6594; Fax: 612-962-6599; E-mail: wrvernon@stthomas.edu

FACILITIES

Information Resources O'Shaughnessy Frey Library plus 2 additional on-campus libraries; total holdings of 421,230 volumes, 553,813 microforms, 2,426 current periodical subscriptions. CD player(s) available for graduate student use. Access provided to online bibliographic retrieval services.

INTERNATIONAL STUDENTS

Demographics 5% of students enrolled are international students.

Services and Facilities International student office, international student center, international student housing, visa services, ESL courses, counseling/support services.

Applying TOEFL: minimum score of 550, proof of adequate funds, proof of health/immunizations required. Financial aid is not available to international students.

International Student Contact Mrs. Eleni Hoffhines, Coordinator, International Admissions, 2115 Summit Avenue, St. Paul, MN 55105-1089. Phone: 612-962-6454; Fax: 612-962-5199; E-mail: evhoffhines@stthomas.edu

PLACEMENT

Services include alumni network, career counseling/planning, career fairs, career library, electronic job bank, job search course, resume referral to employers, and resume preparation.

Employment Of 1996–97 graduates, 98% were employed within three months of graduation; the average starting salary was $50,000. Types of employment entered: accounting, banking, chemical industry, communications, computer-related, consulting, consumer products, education, energy, engineering, finance, financial services, government, health services, high technology, hospitality management, human resources, information systems/technology, insurance, international trade, law, management, manufacturing, marketing, media, mining, nonprofit, petrochemical, pharmaceutical, real estate, retail, service industry, telecommunications, transportation, utilities.

Business Program(s) URL: http://www.gsb.stthomas.edu

Program Contact: Ms. Martha Ballard, Director, Student and Faculty Services, 1000 LaSalle Avenue, MPL 251, Minneapolis, MN 55403-2005. Phone: 612-962-4200, 800-328-6819; Fax: 612-962-4260; E-mail: mba@stthomas.edu

See full description on page 1134.

Winona State University

College of Business

Winona, Minnesota

OVERVIEW

Winona State University is a state-supported, coed, comprehensive institution. Enrollment: 6,851 graduate, professional, and undergraduate students; 73 full-time matriculated graduate/professional students; 343 part-time matriculated graduate/professional students. Founded: 1858. The graduate business unit is in a small-town setting and is on a quarter calendar.

HIGHLIGHTS

Enrollment Profile

Full-time: N/R	International: N/R
Part-time: N/R	Women: N/R
Total: 32	Minorities: N/R
Average Age: N/R	Average Class Size: 20
Fall 1997 Average GPA: 3.0	Fall 1997 Average GMAT: N/R

Costs
Full-time tuition: N/R
Part-time tuition: $129 per credit (resident); $204 per credit (nonresident)

GRADUATE BUSINESS PROGRAMS

Master of Business Administration (MBA) Full-time, part-time; 45 total credits required; up to 7 years to complete program.

Master of Science in Training and Development (MS) Part-time; 51 total credits required; up to 7 years to complete program.

ADMISSION

Applications For fall 1997 there were 15 applications for admission. Of those applying, 12 were accepted. Of those accepted, 10 enrolled.

Application Requirements GMAT score, application form, application fee, bachelor's degree, minimum GPA: 2.5, personal statement, college transcript(s), minimum of 2 years of work experience.

Application Deadline Applications processed on a rolling/continuous basis for both domestic and international students. Application fee: $20. Deferred entrance is available.

ACADEMICS

Faculty Full-time 44.

Teaching Methodologies Case study, lecture, research, student presentations, team projects.

Technology 500 on-campus computer terminals/PCs are available for student use and are linked by a campus-wide network. The network has full access to the Internet. Students are not required to have their own PC.

Special Opportunities Advanced credit may be earned through transfer of credits from another institution.

<u>Winona State University (continued)</u>

FINANCES

Costs for 1997–98 Tuition: $129 per credit (resident); $204 per credit (nonresident). Cost varies by reciprocity agreements. Fees: $14 per credit (resident); $14 per credit (nonresident). Fees vary by number of credits taken. Average 1997–98 room only costs were $3000 per academic year (off campus). Room and board costs vary by occupancy (e.g., single, double, triple), type of accommodation.

Financial Aid Research assistantships, teaching assistantships, work study, loans available. Financial aid is available to part-time students.

Financial Aid Contact Mr. Brigg Peterson, Director of Financial Aid, PO Box 5838, Winona, MN 55987-5838. Phone: 507-457-5090; Fax: 507-457-5586; E-mail: blietzav@winona.msus.edu

FACILITIES

Information Resources Maxwell Library; total holdings of 244,681 volumes, 831,255 microforms, 1,700 current periodical subscriptions. CD player(s) available for graduate student use. Access provided to online bibliographic retrieval services.

INTERNATIONAL STUDENTS

Demographics N/R

Services and Facilities International student office, international student housing, visa services, ESL courses, counseling/support services.

Applying TOEFL: minimum score of 575, proof of adequate funds, proof of health/immunizations required.

International Student Contact Ms. Terri Markos, Director of International Studies, PO Box 5838, Winona, MN 55987-5838. Phone: 507-457-2394; Fax: 507-457-5263; E-mail: tmarkos@winona.msus.edu

PLACEMENT

Services include career counseling/planning, career fairs, career library, career placement, electronic job bank, job interviews arranged, resume referral to employers, and resume preparation. In 1996–97, 59 organizations participated in on-campus recruiting; 299 on-campus interviews were conducted.

Employment Types of employment entered: computer-related, education, engineering, health services.

Business Program(s) URL: http://www.Winona.MSUS.EDU/college_business/

Program Contact: Dr. Kenneth Gorman, Director of MBA, Dean of Business, PO Box 5838, Winona, MN 55987-5838. Phone: 507-457-5014; Fax: 507-457-5586.

MISSISSIPPI

Delta State University

School of Business

Cleveland, Mississippi

OVERVIEW

Delta State University is a state-supported, coed, comprehensive institution. Enrollment: 3,443 graduate, professional, and undergraduate students; 236 full-time matriculated graduate/professional students; 333 part-time matriculated graduate/professional students. Founded: 1924. The graduate business unit is in a small-town setting and is on a semester calendar.

HIGHLIGHTS

Enrollment Profile

Full-time: 40	International: 1%
Part-time: 88	Women: 49%
Total: 128	Minorities: 27%
Average Age: 30	Average Class Size: 25
Fall 1997 Average GPA: 3.2	Fall 1997 Average GMAT: 500

Costs
Full-time tuition: $1295 per academic year (resident); $2474 per academic year (nonresident)
Part-time tuition: $124 per semester hour (resident); $282 per semester hour (nonresident)

ACBSP – The American Council of Business Schools and Programs accredited

GRADUATE BUSINESS PROGRAMS

Master of Business Administration (MBA) Full-time, part-time; 36 total credits required; 12 months to 6 years to complete program. Concentrations in management, marketing, finance, information management, sports/entertainment management, human resources.

Executive MBA (MBA) Full-time; 33 total credits required; 2 years to complete program. Concentration in management.

Master of Professional Accountancy (MPA) Full-time, part-time; 36 total credits required; 12 months to 6 years to complete program. Concentration in accounting.

Master of Commercial Aviation (MCA) Full-time; 36 total credits required; 12 months to 6 years to complete program. Concentration in travel industry/tourism management.

ADMISSION

Applications For fall 1997 there were 63 applications for admission. Of those applying, 62 were accepted. Of those accepted, 56 enrolled.

Application Requirements GMAT score, application form, bachelor's degree, minimum GPA: 3.0, resume, college transcript(s), computer experience: database, spreadsheet, word processing.

Recommended for Application GRE score accepted, MAT score accepted.

Application Deadline Applications processed on a rolling/continuous basis for both domestic and international students. Deferred entrance is available.

ACADEMICS

Faculty Full-time 30; part-time 3.

Teaching Methodologies Case study, computer-aided instruction, computer simulations, group discussion, lecture, research, seminars by members of the business community, simulations, student presentations, study groups, team projects.

Technology 200 on-campus computer terminals/PCs are available for student use and are linked by a campus-wide network. The network has full access to the Internet. Students are not required to have their own PC.

Special Opportunities Advanced credit may be earned through transfer of credits from another institution.

FINANCES

Costs for 1997–98 Tuition: Full-time: $1295 per semester (resident); $2474 per semester (nonresident). Part-time: $124 per semester hour (resident); $282 per semester hour (nonresident). Cost varies by class time (e.g., day/evening), number of credits taken. Fees vary by class time (e.g., day/evening), number of credits taken. Average 1997–98 room and board costs were $2596 per academic year (on campus) and $5400 per academic year (off campus). Room and board costs vary by campus location, occupancy (e.g., single, double, triple), type of accommodation.

Financial Aid In 1997–98, 26% of students received some institutionally administered aid in the form of fellowships, scholarships, work study, loans. Financial aid is available to part-time students. Application Deadline: 6/1.

Financial Aid Contact Mrs. Ann Margaret Mullins, Director of Student Financial Assistance, Box 3154, Cleveland, MS 38733. Phone: 601-846-4670; Fax: 601-846-4215.

FACILITIES

Information Resources W. B. Roberts Library; total holdings of 215,539 volumes, 756,561 microforms, 1,215 current periodical subscriptions. CD player(s) available for graduate student use. Access provided to online bibliographic retrieval services.

INTERNATIONAL STUDENTS

Demographics 1% of students enrolled are international students [Africa, 100%].

Applying TOEFL: minimum score of 550, proof of adequate funds, proof of health/immunizations required. Financial aid is not available to international students.

PLACEMENT

Services include career counseling/planning, career fairs, career placement, job interviews arranged, and resume referral to employers. In 1996–97, 112 organizations participated in on-campus recruiting; 336 on-campus interviews were conducted.

Employment Of 1996–97 graduates, 90% were employed within three months of graduation; the average starting salary was $28,000. Types of employment entered: accounting, banking, communications, computer-related, consulting, finance, government, health services, human resources, information systems/technology, insurance, management, manufacturing, marketing, pharmaceutical, real estate, retail, service industry, telecommunications, transportation.

Program Contact: Dr. Mary Jean Lush, Director of Graduate Studies-School of Business, Box 3295, Cleveland, MS 38733. Phone: 601-846-4234; Fax: 601-846-4215; E-mail: gradbus@dsu.deltast.edu

Jackson State University

School of Business

Jackson, Mississippi

OVERVIEW
Jackson State University is a state-supported, coed university. Enrollment: 6,313 graduate, professional, and undergraduate students; 413 full-time matriculated graduate/professional students; 661 part-time matriculated graduate/professional students. Founded: 1877. The graduate business unit is in an urban setting and is on a semester calendar.

HIGHLIGHTS

Enrollment Profile
Full-time: N/R
Part-time: N/R
Total: 126
Average Age: N/R
Fall 1997 Average GPA: 3.5

International: N/R
Women: N/R
Minorities: N/R
Average Class Size: 15
Fall 1997 Average GMAT: 450

Costs
Full-time tuition: $2380 per academic year (resident); $2594 per academic year (nonresident)
Part-time tuition: $132 per hour (resident); $132 per hour (nonresident)

AACSB – The International Association for Management Education accredited

GRADUATE BUSINESS PROGRAMS
Master of Business Administration (MBA) Full-time, part-time; 36 total credits required; 12 months to 8 years to complete program.

Master of Professional Accountancy (MPA) Full-time, part-time; 30 total credits required; 12 months to 8 years to complete program.

ADMISSION
Application Requirements GMAT score, application form, application fee, bachelor's degree (must be in field of business), minimum GPA: 2.5, 3 letters of recommendation, college transcript(s).

Recommended for Application Computer experience.

Application Deadline Applications processed on a rolling/continuous basis for both domestic and international students. Application fee: 20 (international). Deferred entrance is available.

ACADEMICS
Faculty Full-time 18.

Teaching Methodologies Case study, computer-aided instruction, faculty seminars, group discussion, lecture, research, seminars by members of the business community, student presentations, study groups, team projects.

FINANCES
Costs for 1997–98 Tuition: Full-time: $2380 per year (resident); $2594 per year (nonresident). Part-time: $132 per hour (resident); $132 per hour (nonresident). Cost varies by number of credits taken.

Financial Aid Fellowships, research assistantships, teaching assistantships, work study available. Application Deadline: 5/1.

Financial Aid Contact Dr. Jesse Pennington, 1400 John R Lynch Street, Jackson, MS 39217. Phone: 601-982-6315.

FACILITIES
Information Resources H. T. Sampson Library plus 1 additional on-campus library; total holdings of 364,628 volumes, 472,770 microforms, 4,925 current periodical subscriptions. CD player(s) available for graduate student use. Access provided to online bibliographic retrieval services.

INTERNATIONAL STUDENTS
Demographics N/R

Services and Facilities International student office, ESL courses, counseling/support services.

Applying TOEFL: minimum score of 525 required.

International Student Contact Kathy Sims, 1400 John R Lynch Street, Jackson, MS 39217. Phone: 601-973-3792.

PLACEMENT
Services include alumni network, and resume referral to employers.

Employment Types of employment entered: accounting, banking, finance, management.

Program Contact: Ms. May Robinson, Graduate Admissions Coordinator, PO Box 17095, Jackson, MS 39217. Phone: 601-968-2455; Fax: 601-968-8246.

Millsaps College

Else School of Management

Jackson, Mississippi

OVERVIEW
Millsaps College is an independent-religious, coed, comprehensive institution. Enrollment: 1,362 graduate, professional, and undergraduate students; 43 full-time matriculated graduate/professional students; 100 part-time matriculated graduate/professional students. Founded: 1890. The graduate business unit is in an urban setting and is on a semester calendar.

HIGHLIGHTS

Enrollment Profile
Full-time: 43
Part-time: 100
Total: 143
Average Age: 27
Fall 1997 Average GPA: 3.31

International: 4%
Women: 45%
Minorities: 10%
Average Class Size: 16
Fall 1997 Average GMAT: 553

Costs
Full-time tuition: N/R
Part-time tuition: $540 per credit hour

AACSB – The International Association for Management Education accredited

*T*he Else School of Management at Millsaps represents the perfect blend: top-notch, rigorous graduate business programs housed in an intimate school setting and learning environment. The M.B.A. and Master of Accountancy (M.Acc.) degrees at Millsaps provide serious students the chance to learn strategies and concepts in an interactive setting. The core courses of the M.B.A. program include an average of 20 to 25 students per class, and many elective courses are even smaller. The Else School considers team projects and case work to be a cornerstone of the curriculum; thus, students learn to communicate, delegate, and build relationships along with the concepts and strategies of business. A flexible curriculum provides the opportunity for choices of elective courses and focus areas.

Accredited by AACSB–The International Association for Management Education, Millsaps also offers an expert faculty with academic prestige and real-world experience. While most faculty members do research and consulting to stay current with the business world, their primary focus is the instruction of students in the program. Millsaps is known for having alumni whose quality is unsurpassed, and professors are charged with the task of ensuring that graduates of the M.B.A. and M.Acc. programs are no exception.

Students from all academic majors and all business backgrounds are encouraged to apply.

GRADUATE BUSINESS PROGRAMS
Master of Business Administration (MBA) Full-time, part-time; 30-48 total credits required; 12 months to 6 years to complete program. Concentrations in finance, marketing, management, accounting, decision sciences, health care.

Master of Accountancy (MAcc) Full-time, part-time; 30-48 total credits required; 12 months to 6 years to complete program. Concentration in accounting.

ADMISSION
Applications For fall 1997 there were 90 applications for admission. Of those applying, 74 were accepted. Of those accepted, 53 enrolled.

Application Requirements GMAT score, application form, application fee, bachelor's degree, essay, minimum GPA, 2 letters of recommendation, personal statement, college transcript(s).

Recommended for Application Interview, work experience, computer experience.

Application Deadline 7/1 for fall, 11/15 for spring, 4/15 for summer, 5/30 for fall (international), 10/1 for spring (international), 3/1 for summer (international). Application fee: $25. Deferred entrance is available.

ACADEMICS
Faculty Full-time 21; part-time 5.

Teaching Methodologies Case study, computer-aided instruction, computer analysis, computer simulations, experiential learning, field projects, group discussion, lecture, research, role playing, seminars by members of the business community, simulations, student presentations, study groups, team projects.

Technology 50 on-campus computer terminals/PCs are available for student use and are linked by a campus-wide network. The network has full access to the Internet. Students are not required to have their own PC.

Special Opportunities Advanced credit may be earned through transfer of credits from another institution. An internship program is available.

FINANCES
Costs for 1997–98 Tuition: $540 per credit hour. Cost varies by number of credits taken. Fees: $10 per semester hour. Fees vary by number of credits

Millsaps College (continued)

taken. Average 1997–98 room and board costs were $5500 per academic year (on campus) and $4500 per academic year (off campus). Room and board costs vary by occupancy (e.g., single, double, triple), type of accommodation, type of meal plan.

Financial Aid In 1997–98, 36% of students received some institutionally administered aid in the form of research assistantships, scholarships, work study, loans. Financial aid is available to part-time students. Application Deadline: 7/1.

Financial Aid Contact Mr. Bart Herridge, Director of Graduate Business Admissions, 1701 North State Street, Jackson, MS 39110. Phone: 601-974-1253; Fax: 601-974-1260.

FACILITIES
Information Resources Millsaps Wilson Library; total holdings of 154,957 volumes, 52,205 microforms, 834 current periodical subscriptions. CD player(s) available for graduate student use. Access provided to online bibliographic retrieval services.

INTERNATIONAL STUDENTS
Demographics 4% of students enrolled are international students [Asia, 100%].

Applying TOEFL, proof of adequate funds required. Financial aid is available to international students.

International Student Contact Mr. Bart Herridge, Director of Graduate Business Admissions, 1701 North State Street, Jackson, MS 39210. Phone: 601-974-1253; Fax: 601-974-1260; E-mail: mbamacc@okra.millsaps.edu

PLACEMENT
Services include alumni network, career counseling/planning, career fairs, career library, career placement, electronic job bank, job interviews arranged, job search course, resume referral to employers, and resume preparation. In 1996–97, 60 organizations participated in on-campus recruiting.

Employment Of 1996–97 graduates, 80% were employed within three months of graduation; the average starting salary was $44,000. Types of employment entered: accounting, banking, communications, computer-related, consulting, consumer products, energy, engineering, financial services, government, health services, hospitality management, human resources, information systems/technology, insurance, manufacturing, marketing, media, nonprofit, pharmaceutical, real estate, retail, telecommunications, transportation, utilities.

Business Program(s) URL: http://www.millsaps.edu/www/esom/

Program Contact: Mr. Bart Herridge, Director of Graduate Business Admissions, 1701 North State Street, Jackson, MS 39110. Phone: 601-974-1253, 800-352-1050 Ext. 1253; Fax: 601-974-1260; E-mail: mbamacc@okra. millsaps.edu

Mississippi College

School of Business

Clinton, Mississippi

OVERVIEW
Mississippi College is an independent-religious, coed, comprehensive institution. Enrollment: 3,532 graduate, professional, and undergraduate students; 540 full-time matriculated graduate/professional students; 671 part-time matriculated graduate/professional students. Founded: 1826. The graduate business unit is in a suburban setting and is on a semester calendar.

HIGHLIGHTS

Enrollment Profile
Full-time: 48
Part-time: 195
Total: 243
Average Age: N/R
Fall 1997 Average GPA: N/R

International: N/R
Women: 40%
Minorities: N/R
Average Class Size: 20
Fall 1997 Average GMAT: 443

Costs
Full-time tuition: N/R
Part-time tuition: $276 per hour

ACBSP – The American Council of Business Schools and Programs accredited

GRADUATE BUSINESS PROGRAMS
Master of Business Administration (MBA) Part-time; 30 total credits required; 12 months to 5 years to complete program. Concentrations in accounting, taxation.

Master of Health Services Administration (MHSA) Part-time; 30 total credits required; 12 months to 5 years to complete program.

JD/MBA program (MBA/JD) Full-time; 103 total credits required; minimum of 3.5 years to complete program. Concentrations in accounting, commerce.

ADMISSION
Applications For fall 1997 there were 128 applications for admission. Of those applying, 123 were accepted. Of those accepted, 102 enrolled.

Application Requirements GMAT score: minimum 350, application form, application fee, bachelor's degree, essay, minimum GPA: 2.5, personal statement, college transcript(s), computer experience: business software class.

Application Deadline Applications processed on a rolling/continuous basis for both domestic and international students. Application fee: $25, $75 (international). Deferred entrance is available.

ACADEMICS
Faculty Full-time 15; part-time 12.

Teaching Methodologies Case study, computer-aided instruction, computer analysis, computer simulations, group discussion, lecture, research, role playing, seminars by members of the business community, simulations, student presentations, study groups, team projects.

Technology 60 on-campus computer terminals/PCs are available for student use and are linked by a campus-wide network. The network has full access to the Internet. Students are not required to have their own PC.

Special Opportunities Advanced credit may be earned through credit for military training programs, credit for business training programs, transfer of credits from another institution. International exchange programs in Austria, United Kingdom. An internship program is available.

FINANCES
Costs for 1997–98 Tuition: $276 per hour. Fees: $35 per 5 hours or less. Fees vary by number of credits taken. Average 1997–98 room and board costs were $2000 per academic year. Room and board costs vary by type of accommodation, type of meal plan.

Financial Aid Financial aid is available to part-time students.

Financial Aid Contact Ms. Mary Givhan, Director of Financial Aid, Box 4066, Clinton, MS 39058. Phone: 601-925-3319; E-mail: givhan@mc.edu

FACILITIES
Information Resources Leland Speed Library; total holdings of 249,500 volumes, 224 microforms, 1,804 current periodical subscriptions. CD player(s) available for graduate student use. Access provided to online bibliographic retrieval services and online databases.

INTERNATIONAL STUDENTS
Demographics N/R

Services and Facilities ESL courses, counseling/support services.

Applying TOEFL, proof of health/immunizations required. Proof of adequate funds recommended. Financial aid is not available to international students.

International Student Contact Dr. Debbie Norris, Dean of Graduate School, Box 4029, Clinton, MS 39058. Phone: 601-925-3260; E-mail: dnorris@mc.edu

PLACEMENT
Services include career counseling/planning, career fairs, career placement, job interviews arranged, resume referral to employers, and resume preparation. In 1996–97, 25 organizations participated in on-campus recruiting; 20 on-campus interviews were conducted.

Employment Of 1996–97 graduates, 98% were employed within three months of graduation. Types of employment entered: accounting, banking, communications, computer-related, consumer products, education, energy, finance, financial services, government, health services, hospitality management, human resources, information systems/technology, insurance, law, management, manufacturing, marketing, nonprofit, pharmaceutical, real estate, retail, service industry, telecommunications, transportation, utilities.

Business Program(s) URL: http://www.mc.edu

Program Contact: Dr. Gerald Lee, Director, MBA Program, Box 4014, Clinton, MS 39058. Phone: 601-925-3220; Fax: 601-925-3954; E-mail: glee@mc. edu

Mississippi State University

College of Business and Industry

Mississippi State, Mississippi

OVERVIEW

Mississippi State University is a state-supported, coed university. Enrollment: 15,694 graduate, professional, and undergraduate students. Founded: 1878. The graduate business unit is in a small-town setting and is on a semester calendar.

HIGHLIGHTS

Enrollment Profile

Full-time: 108
Part-time: 73
Total: 181
Average Age: 30
Fall 1997 Average GPA: 3.4

International: 19%
Women: 37%
Minorities: 7%
Average Class Size: 15
Fall 1997 Average GMAT: 520

Costs

Full-time tuition: $1237 per academic year (resident); $2216 per academic year (nonresident)
Part-time tuition: $111 per hour (resident); $158 per hour (nonresident)

AACSB – The International Association for Management Education accredited

GRADUATE BUSINESS PROGRAMS

Master of Business Administration (MBA) Full-time, part-time; 30 total credits required; 12 months to 6 years to complete program. Concentrations in accounting, business information science, economics, finance, management, management information systems, marketing, real estate, taxation.

Master of Science in Business Administration in Information Systems Program (MS) Full-time, part-time; 30 total credits required; 12 months to 6 years to complete program. Concentrations in accounting, business information science, economics, finance, management, management information systems, marketing, real estate, taxation.

Master of Professional Accountancy (MPA) Full-time, part-time; 30 total credits required; 12 months to 6 years to complete program. Concentration in accounting.

Master of Taxation (MTax) Full-time, part-time; 30 total credits required; 12 months to 6 years to complete program. Concentration in taxation.

Master of Science in Systems Management (MS) Full-time, part-time, distance learning option; 30 total credits required; 12 months to 6 years to complete program. Concentrations in information management, business information science.

ADMISSION

Applications For fall 1997 there were 147 applications for admission. Of those applying, 68 were accepted. Of those accepted, 60 enrolled.

Application Requirements Application form, application fee, bachelor's degree, minimum GPA: 3.0, 3 letters of recommendation, personal statement, college transcript(s).

Recommended for Application GMAT score accepted: minimum 500.

Application Deadline 7/1 for fall, 11/1 for spring, 4/1 for summer, 7/1 for fall (international), 11/1 for spring (international), 4/1 for summer (international). Application fee: 25 (international). Deferred entrance is available.

ACADEMICS

Faculty Full-time 50; part-time 1.

Teaching Methodologies Case study, computer-aided instruction, computer analysis, field projects, group discussion, lecture, student presentations, study groups, team projects.

Technology 210 on-campus computer terminals/PCs are available for student use and are linked by a campus-wide network. The network has full access to the Internet. Students are not required to have their own PC.

Special Opportunities Advanced credit may be earned through transfer of credits from another institution.

FINANCES

Costs for 1997–98 Tuition: Full-time: $1237 per semester (resident); $2216 per semester (nonresident). Part-time: $111 per hour (resident); $158 per hour (nonresident). Cost varies by number of credits taken. Fees: Full-time: $368 per academic year (resident); $368 per academic year (nonresident). Part-time: $41 per hour (resident); $41 per hour (nonresident). Fees vary by number of credits taken. Average 1997–98 room only costs were $2500 per academic year (on campus) and $4200 per academic year (off campus). Room and board costs vary by occupancy (e.g., single, double, triple), type of accommodation, type of meal plan.

Financial Aid In 1997–98, 38% of students received some institutionally administered aid in the form of fellowships, research assistantships, teaching assistantships, work study, loans. Financial aid is available to part-time students. Application Deadline: 3/15.

Financial Aid Contact Ms. Audrey Lambert, Director of Financial Aid, PO Box 9501, Mississippi State, MS 39762. Phone: 601-325-2450; Fax: 601-325-0702; E-mail: teresa@sfa.msstate.edu

FACILITIES

Information Resources Mitchell Memorial Library plus 2 additional on-campus libraries; total holdings of 850,067 volumes, 2,067,127 microforms, 7,387 current periodical subscriptions. CD player(s) available for graduate student use. Access provided to online bibliographic retrieval services.

INTERNATIONAL STUDENTS

Demographics 19% of students enrolled are international students [Asia, 60%, Central America, 10%, Europe, 10%, South America, 20%].

Services and Facilities International student office, international student center, counseling/support services.

Applying TOEFL: minimum score of 575, proof of adequate funds, proof of health/immunizations required. Financial aid is not available to international students.

International Student Contact Ms. Helen Zuercher, Director of International Services, PO Box 9742, Mississippi State, MS 39762-9742. Phone: 601-325-8929; Fax: 601-325-8583; E-mail: zuercher@cvmfaculty-msstate.edu

PLACEMENT

Services include alumni network, career counseling/planning, career fairs, career library, career placement, job interviews arranged, resume referral to employers, and resume preparation. In 1996–97, 221 organizations participated in on-campus recruiting; 853 on-campus interviews were conducted.

Employment Of 1996–97 graduates, 85% were employed within three months of graduation; the average starting salary was $35,000. Types of employment entered: accounting, banking, communications, computer-related, consulting, education, engineering, finance, human resources, information systems/technology, insurance, management, marketing, pharmaceutical, real estate, retail, service industry, transportation, utilities.

Business Program(s) URL: http://gsb.cbi.msstate.edu

Program Contact: Dr. Barbara Spencer, Director of Graduate Studies in Business, PO Box 5288, Mississippi State, MS 39762. Phone: 601-325-1891; Fax: 601-325-8161; E-mail: bspencer@cobilan.msstate.edu

See full description on page 886.

University of Mississippi

School of Business Administration

University, Mississippi

OVERVIEW

The University of Mississippi is a state-supported, coed university. Enrollment: 10,534 graduate, professional, and undergraduate students; 1,627 full-time matriculated graduate/professional students; 487 part-time matriculated graduate/professional students. Founded: 1844. The graduate business unit is in a small-town setting and is on a semester calendar.

HIGHLIGHTS

Enrollment Profile

Full-time: 65
Part-time: 0
Total: 65
Average Age: 25
Fall 1997 Average GPA: 3.4

International: 22%
Women: 17%
Minorities: 6%
Average Class Size: 24
Fall 1997 Average GMAT: 560

Costs

Full-time tuition: $2662 per academic year (resident); $5648 per academic year (nonresident)
Part-time tuition: N/R

AACSB – The International Association for Management Education accredited

University of Mississippi (continued)

GRADUATE BUSINESS PROGRAMS

Master of Business Administration (MBA) Full-time; 49 total credits required; 18 months to 2.2 years to complete program. Concentrations in management, accounting, banking, economics, finance, international business, management information systems, marketing, operations management, organizational behavior/development, quantitative analysis, real estate, financial management/planning, human resources, information management, insurance, managerial economics, system management.

Master of Arts in Economics (MA) Full-time, part-time; 30 total credits required; 12 months to 5 years to complete program.

ADMISSION

Applications For fall 1997 there were 144 applications for admission. Of those applying, 58 were accepted. Of those accepted, 26 enrolled.

Application Requirements Application form, application fee, bachelor's degree, minimum GPA: 3.0, 2 letters of recommendation, personal statement, college transcript(s), computer experience: familiarity with spreadsheet, word processing.

Recommended for Application GMAT score accepted: minimum 500, essay, resume, work experience.

Application Deadline 4/15 for summer. Application fee: $25.

ACADEMICS

Faculty Full-time 58.

Teaching Methodologies Case study, computer analysis, computer simulations, experiential learning, field projects, group discussion, lecture, seminars by members of the business community, student presentations, study groups, team projects.

Technology 200 on-campus computer terminals/PCs are available for student use and are linked by a campus-wide network. The network has full access to the Internet. Students are required to have their own PC.

Special Opportunities Advanced credit may be earned through transfer of credits from another institution. International exchange programs in Germany, United Kingdom. An internship program is available.

FINANCES

Costs for 1997–98 Tuition: Full-time: $2662 per three semesters (resident); $5648 per three semesters (nonresident). Cost varies by number of credits taken. Fees: Full-time: $680 per academic year (resident); $680 per academic year (nonresident). Fees vary by number of credits taken. Average 1997–98 room only costs were $2670 per academic year (on campus) and $4200 per academic year (off campus). Room and board costs vary by campus location, occupancy (e.g., single, double, triple), type of accommodation.

Financial Aid In 1997–98, 54% of students received some institutionally administered aid in the form of fellowships, research assistantships, work study. Application Deadline: 4/1.

Financial Aid Contact Mr. Larry Ridgeway, Director of Financial Aid, Old Chemistry Building, Room 25, University, MS 38677. Phone: 601-232-7175; Fax: 601-234-8155.

FACILITIES

Information Resources John Davis Williams Library plus 1 additional on-campus library; total holdings of 844,253 volumes, 2,301,543 microforms, 6,760 current periodical subscriptions. CD player(s) available for graduate student use. Access provided to online bibliographic retrieval services.

INTERNATIONAL STUDENTS

Demographics 22% of students enrolled are international students [Africa, 5%, Asia, 25%, Europe, 5%, North America, 65%].

Services and Facilities International student office, international student center, visa services, counseling/support services.

Applying TOEFL: minimum score of 600, proof of adequate funds, proof of health/immunizations required. Financial aid is available to international students.

International Student Contact Ms. Tanta Owen, Foreign Student Advisor, Office of International Programs, Room 23, Y Building, University, MS 38677. Phone: 601-232-7404.

PLACEMENT

Services include alumni network, career counseling/planning, career fairs, career library, career placement, electronic job bank, job interviews arranged, job search course, resume referral to employers, and resume preparation. In 1996–97, 89 organizations participated in on-campus recruiting.

Employment Of 1996–97 graduates, 90% were employed within three months of graduation; the average starting salary was $42,000. Types of employment entered: accounting, banking, communications, computer-related, consulting, consumer products, education, engineering, finance, financial services, government, high technology, human resources, information systems/technology, insurance, law, management, manufacturing, marketing, pharmaceutical, real estate, retail, service industry.

Business Program(s) URL: http://www.bus.olemiss.edu

Program Contact: Dr. Delvin D. Hawley, Associate Dean, School of Business Administration, Office of the Dean, University, MS 38677. Phone: 601-232-5820; Fax: 601-232-5821; E-mail: hawley@bus.olemiss.edu

See full description on page 1102.

University of Southern Mississippi

College of Business Administration

Hattiesburg, Mississippi

OVERVIEW

The University of Southern Mississippi is a state-supported, coed university. Enrollment: 14,000 graduate, professional, and undergraduate students; 1,307 full-time matriculated graduate/professional students; 1,459 part-time matriculated graduate/professional students. Founded: 1910. The graduate business unit is in a small-town setting and is on a semester calendar.

HIGHLIGHTS

Enrollment Profile

Full-time: 69	International: 10%
Part-time: 32	Women: 50%
Total: 101	Minorities: 14%
Average Age: 28	Average Class Size: 30
Fall 1997 Average GPA: 3.14	Fall 1997 Average GMAT: 492

Costs
Full-time tuition: $1295 per academic year (resident); $2705 per academic year (nonresident)
Part-time tuition: $378 per 3 hours (resident); $741 per 3 hours (nonresident)

AACSB – The International Association for Management Education accredited

GRADUATE BUSINESS PROGRAMS

Master of Business Administration (MBA) Full-time, part-time; 36 total credits required; $25 application fee required for out-of-state applicants; 12 months to 6 years to complete program. Concentrations in finance, marketing, management, management information systems, accounting, international business.

Professional MBA (MBA) Full-time, part-time; 36 total credits required; $25 application fee required for out-of-state applicants; 2 to 6 years to complete program.

Master of Professional Accountancy (MPA) Full-time, part-time; 30 total credits required; $25 application fee required for out-of-state applicants; 12 months to 6 years to complete program.

ADMISSION

Applications For fall 1997 there were 134 applications for admission. Of those applying, 105 were accepted. Of those accepted, 59 enrolled.

Application Requirements GMAT score, application form, bachelor's degree, essay, minimum GPA, letters of recommendation, personal statement, college transcript(s), computer experience: word processing, spreadsheet.

Recommended for Application Resume, work experience.

Application Deadline 7/15 for fall, 11/15 for spring, 4/15 for summer, 7/15 for fall (international), 11/15 for spring (international), 4/15 for summer (international).

ACADEMICS

Faculty Full-time 57; part-time 11.

Teaching Methodologies Case study, computer-aided instruction, computer analysis, field projects, group discussion, lecture, research, role playing, student presentations, study groups, team projects.

Technology 8 on-campus computer terminals/PCs are available for student use and are linked by a campus-wide network. The network has full access to the Internet. Students are not required to have their own PC.

Special Opportunities Advanced credit may be earned through transfer of credits from another institution.

FINANCES

Costs for 1997–98 Tuition: Full-time: $1295 per semester (resident); $2705 per semester (nonresident). Part-time: $378 per 3 hours (resident); $741 per 3 hours (nonresident). Cost varies by number of credits taken. Average 1997–98 room and board costs were $5000 per academic year (on campus) and $8000 per academic year (off campus). Room and board costs vary by campus location, occupancy (e.g., single, double, triple), type of accommodation, type of meal plan.

Financial Aid In 1997–98, 37% of students received some institutionally administered aid in the form of research assistantships, scholarships, work study, loans. Financial aid is available to part-time students. Application Deadline: 3/15.

Financial Aid Contact Ms. Vernetta Fairley, Director of Financial Aid, Box 5101, Hattiesburg, MS 39406-5101. Phone: 601-266-4774.

FACILITIES
Information Resources Cook Memorial Library plus 1 additional on-campus library; total holdings of 920,921 volumes, 2,526,837 microforms, 7,091 current periodical subscriptions. CD player(s) available for graduate student use. Access provided to online bibliographic retrieval services.

INTERNATIONAL STUDENTS
Demographics 10% of students enrolled are international students [Asia, 35%, Europe, 18%, North America, 29%, South America, 18%].

Services and Facilities International student office, international student center, ESL courses, counseling/support services.

Applying TOEFL, proof of health/immunizations required. Financial aid is available to international students.

International Student Contact Ms. Barbara Whitt, Director, International Student Affairs, Box 5151, Hattiesburg, MS 39406-5151. Phone: 601-266-4841; Fax: 601-266-5839; E-mail: barbara_whitt@bull.cc.usm.edu

PLACEMENT
Services include alumni network, career counseling/planning, career fairs, career library, career placement, job interviews arranged, job search course, resume referral to employers, and resume preparation.

Employment Types of employment entered: accounting, banking, computer-related, consulting, finance, financial services, government, health services, human resources, information systems/technology, law, management, marketing, pharmaceutical.

Business Program(s) URL: http://www.usm.edu

Program Contact: Dr. Ernest W. King, Director, Graduate Business Programs, Box 5096, Hattiesburg, MS 39406-5096. Phone: 601-266-4653; Fax: 601-266-4639; E-mail: kinge@cba.usm.edu

William Carey College

School of Business

Hattiesburg, Mississippi

OVERVIEW
William Carey College is an independent-religious, coed, comprehensive institution. Enrollment: 2,200 graduate, professional, and undergraduate students; 20 full-time matriculated graduate/professional students; 330 part-time matriculated graduate/professional students. Founded: 1906. The graduate business unit is in a small-town setting and is on a trimester calendar.

HIGHLIGHTS

Enrollment Profile

Full-time: 3	International: 0%
Part-time: 117	Women: 40%
Total: 120	Minorities: 23%
Average Age: 35	Average Class Size: 18
Fall 1997 Average GPA: 3.2	Fall 1997 Average GMAT: N/R

Costs
Full-time tuition: $2400 per academic year
Part-time tuition: $210 per hour

GRADUATE BUSINESS PROGRAMS
Master of Business Administration (MBA) Full-time, part-time; 30-51 total credits required; 12 months to 4 years to complete program. Concentrations in entrepreneurship, project management, health care.

ADMISSION
Applications For fall 1997 there were 45 applications for admission. Of those applying, 40 were accepted. Of those accepted, 40 enrolled.

Application Requirements Application form, application fee, bachelor's degree, essay, minimum GPA, interview, 3 letters of recommendation, resume, college transcript(s), minimum of 3 years of work experience.

Recommended for Application GMAT score accepted.

Application Deadline Applications processed on a rolling/continuous basis for both domestic and international students. Application fee: $25. Deferred entrance is available.

ACADEMICS
Faculty Full-time 10.

Teaching Methodologies Faculty seminars, lecture, research, seminars by members of the business community, student presentations, team projects.

Technology 60 on-campus computer terminals/PCs are available for student use and are linked by a campus-wide network. The network does not have Internet access. Students are not required to have their own PC.

Special Opportunities Advanced credit may be earned through transfer of credits from another institution.

FINANCES
Costs for 1997–98 Tuition: Full-time: $2400 per year. Part-time: $210 per hour.

Financial Aid In 1997–98, 53% of students received some institutionally administered aid in the form of research assistantships, teaching assistantships, work study. Financial aid is available to part-time students. Application Deadline: 6/15.

Financial Aid Contact Mr. Bill Curry, Director of Financial Aid, 498 Tuscan Avenue, Hattiesburg, MS 39401-5499. Phone: 601-582-6153; Fax: 601-582-6454.

FACILITIES
Information Resources Rouse Library; total holdings of 104,822 volumes, 30,761 microforms, 628 current periodical subscriptions. CD player(s) available for graduate student use.

INTERNATIONAL STUDENTS
Demographics N/R

PLACEMENT
Services include career counseling/planning, and resume preparation.

Employment Of 1996–97 graduates, 100% were employed within three months of graduation. Types of employment entered: banking, education, health services, hospitality management, management, manufacturing, marketing.

Program Contact: Dr. Ben Hawkins, Dean, School of Business, 498 Tuscan Avenue, Hattiesburg, MS 39401-5499. Phone: 601-582-6199; Fax: 601-582-6281.

MISSOURI

Avila College

Department of Business and Economics

Kansas City, Missouri

OVERVIEW
Avila College is an independent-religious, coed, comprehensive institution. Enrollment: 1,246 graduate, professional, and undergraduate students; 32 full-time matriculated graduate/professional students; 147 part-time matriculated graduate/professional students. Founded: 1916. The graduate business unit is in a suburban setting and is on a semester calendar.

HIGHLIGHTS

Enrollment Profile

Full-time: 13	International: 9%
Part-time: 78	Women: 55%
Total: 91	Minorities: 5%
Average Age: 32	Average Class Size: 20
Fall 1997 Average GPA: 3.3	Fall 1997 Average GMAT: 495

Costs
Full-time tuition: $5350 per academic year
Part-time tuition: $280 per credit hour

GRADUATE BUSINESS PROGRAMS
Master of Business Administration (MBA) Full-time, part-time; 30-48 total credits required; 12 months to 7 years to complete program. Concentrations in accounting, finance, international business, management information systems, marketing, health care, management.

ADMISSION
Applications For fall 1997 there were 17 applications for admission. Of those applying, 14 were accepted. Of those accepted, 14 enrolled.

Application Requirements Application form, application fee, bachelor's degree, minimum GPA: 3.0, interview, personal statement, college transcript(s).

Recommended for Application GMAT score accepted: minimum 450.

Application Deadline Applications processed on a rolling/continuous basis for both domestic and international students. Application fee: $20.

ACADEMICS
Faculty Full-time 8; part-time 10.

Avila College (continued)

Teaching Methodologies Case study, computer-aided instruction, computer simulations, group discussion, lecture, research, student presentations, study groups, team projects.

Technology 50 on-campus computer terminals/PCs are available for student use and are linked by a campus-wide network. The network has full access to the Internet. Students are not required to have their own PC.

Special Opportunities Advanced credit may be earned through transfer of credits from another institution. An internship program is available.

FINANCES
Costs for 1997–98 Tuition: Full-time: $5350 per semester. Part-time: $280 per credit hour. Cost varies by number of credits taken. Fees: Full-time: $80 per academic year. Part-time: $3 per credit hour. Fees vary by class time (e.g., day/evening). Average 1997–98 room and board costs were $5300 per academic year. Room and board costs vary by occupancy (e.g., single, double, triple), type of accommodation, type of meal plan.

Financial Aid In 1997–98, 33% of students received some institutionally administered aid in the form of loans. Financial aid is available to part-time students. Application Deadline: 7/31.

Financial Aid Contact Christal Williams, Financial Aid Specialist, 11901 Wornall Road, Kansas City, MO 54145-1698. Phone: 816-942-8400 Ext. 2347; Fax: 816-942-3362; E-mail: borderscd@mail.avila.edu

FACILITIES
Information Resources Hooley-Bundschu Library; total holdings of 65,000 volumes, 383,874 microforms, 545 current periodical subscriptions. CD player(s) available for graduate student use. Access provided to online bibliographic retrieval services.

INTERNATIONAL STUDENTS
Demographics 9% of students enrolled are international students [Asia, 99%, Europe, 1%].

Services and Facilities International student office, ESL courses, counseling/support services.

Applying TOEFL: minimum score of 550, proof of adequate funds required. Financial aid is not available to international students.

International Student Contact Bruce Inwards, ILCP Coordinator and ESL Lecturer, 11901 Wornall Road, Kansas City, MO 64145-1698. Phone: 816-942-8400 Ext. 2372; Fax: 816-942-3362.

PLACEMENT
Services include alumni network, career counseling/planning, career fairs, and resume preparation.

Employment Types of employment entered: accounting, banking, computer-related, finance, financial services, health services, information systems/technology, law, management, nonprofit, retail, service industry, telecommunications.

Program Contact: Wendy Acker, MBA Director, 11901 Wornall Road, Kansas City, MO 64145-1698. Phone: 816-942-8400 Ext. 2321; Fax: 816-942-3362; E-mail: ackerwl@mail.avila.edu

Central Missouri State University

College of Business and Economics
Warrensburg, Missouri

OVERVIEW
Central Missouri State University is a state-supported, coed, comprehensive institution. Enrollment: 10,805 graduate, professional, and undergraduate students; 80 full-time matriculated graduate/professional students; 40 part-time matriculated graduate/professional students. Founded: 1871. The graduate business unit is in a small-town setting and is on a semester calendar.

GRADUATE BUSINESS PROGRAMS
Master of Business Administration (MBA)
Master of Arts in Economics (MA)

ACADEMICS
Faculty Full-time 65; part-time 3.

Teaching Methodologies Case study, computer-aided instruction, computer analysis, computer simulations, experiential learning, field projects, group discussion, lecture, research, seminars by members of the business community, simulations, student presentations, study groups, team projects.

Technology 250 on-campus computer terminals/PCs are available for student use and are linked by a campus-wide network. The network has full access to the Internet.

Special Opportunities International exchange programs in Hungary, Mexico, Netherlands, Sweden, United Kingdom. An internship program is available.

FACILITIES
Information Resources Ward Edwards Library; total holdings of 966,692 volumes, 508,223 microforms, 2,890 current periodical subscriptions. CD player(s) available for graduate student use. Access provided to online bibliographic retrieval services.

Program Contact: Director of Graduate Programs, College of Business and Economics, Warrensburg, MO 64093. Phone: 816-543-8597; Fax: 816-543-8885; E-mail: harmon@cmsuvmb.cmsu.edu

Columbia College

Program in Business Administration
Columbia, Missouri

OVERVIEW
Columbia College is an independent-religious, coed, comprehensive institution. Enrollment: 7,435 graduate, professional, and undergraduate students; 51 part-time matriculated graduate/professional students. Founded: 1851. The graduate business unit is in a small-town setting and is on a five 8-week sessions calendar.

HIGHLIGHTS

Enrollment Profile
Full-time: 6	International: 5%
Part-time: 15	Women: 43%
Total: 21	Minorities: N/R
Average Age: 34	Average Class Size: 5
Fall 1997 Average GPA: N/R	Fall 1997 Average GMAT: N/R

Costs
Full-time tuition: N/R
Part-time tuition: $180 per credit hour

GRADUATE BUSINESS PROGRAMS
Master of Business Administration (MBA) Full-time, part-time; 36 total credits required.

ADMISSION
Applications For fall 1997 there were 38 applications for admission. Of those applying, 30 were accepted. Of those accepted, 21 enrolled.

Application Requirements Application form, bachelor's degree, essay, minimum GPA: 3.0, 3 letters of recommendation, personal statement, college transcript(s).

Recommended for Application Work experience.

Application Deadline Applications processed on a rolling/continuous basis for both domestic and international students. Application fee: $25, $50 (international). Deferred entrance is available.

ACADEMICS
Faculty Full-time 4; part-time 2.

Teaching Methodologies Case study, field projects, group discussion, lecture, research, role playing, student presentations, study groups, team projects.

Technology 100 on-campus computer terminals/PCs are available for student use and are linked by a campus-wide network. The network has full access to the Internet. Students are not required to have their own PC.

Special Opportunities Advanced credit may be earned through transfer of credits from another institution.

FINANCES
Costs for 1997–98 Tuition: $180 per credit hour.

Financial Aid In 1997–98, 48% of students received some institutionally administered aid in the form of loans. Financial aid is available to part-time students.

Financial Aid Contact Ms. Carol Zablocki, Director, Financial Aid, Columbia, MO 65216. Phone: 573-875-7360; Fax: 573-875-7209.

FACILITIES
Information Resources Stafford Library; total holdings of 55,043 volumes, 22,001 microforms, 533 current periodical subscriptions. CD player(s) available for graduate student use. Access provided to online bibliographic retrieval services and online databases.

INTERNATIONAL STUDENTS
Demographics 5% of students enrolled are international students [Asia, 100%].

Services and Facilities International student office, ESL courses.

Applying TOEFL: minimum score of 550, proof of adequate funds required. Financial aid is not available to international students.

International Student Contact Ms. Britta Wright, International Programs Coordinator, Columbia, MO 65216. Phone: 573-875-8700; Fax: 573-875-7209.

PLACEMENT

Services include career counseling/planning, career fairs, career placement, electronic job bank, and resume preparation.

Business Program(s) URL: http://www.ccis.edu

Program Contact: Ms. Virginia Wilson, Assistant Director Evening and Graduate Division, Columbia, MO 65216. Phone: 573-875-7339; Fax: 573-875-7209.

Drury College

Breech School of Business Administration

Springfield, Missouri

OVERVIEW

Drury College is an independent-nonprofit, coed, comprehensive institution. Enrollment: 4,063 graduate, professional, and undergraduate students. Founded: 1873. The graduate business unit is in a suburban setting and is on a semester calendar.

HIGHLIGHTS

Enrollment Profile

Full-time: 4	International: 8%
Part-time: 48	Women: 50%
Total: 52	Minorities: N/R
Average Age: 30	Average Class Size: 30
Fall 1997 Average GPA: 3.2	Fall 1997 Average GMAT: 530

Costs
Full-time tuition: N/R
Part-time tuition: $220 per credit hour

ACBSP – The American Council of Business Schools and Programs accredited

GRADUATE BUSINESS PROGRAMS

Master of Business Administration (MBA) Full-time, part-time; 55 total credits required; 12 months to 4 years to complete program.

ADMISSION

Applications For fall 1997 there were 70 applications for admission. Of those applying, 40 were accepted. Of those accepted, 32 enrolled.

Application Requirements GMAT score, application form, application fee, bachelor's degree, minimum GPA, personal statement, college transcript(s).

Recommended for Application Interview, letters of recommendation, resume, work experience.

Application Deadline 7/15 for fall, 11/15 for spring, 4/15 for summer, 10/15 for spring (international), 6/1 for summer (international). Application fee: $25.

ACADEMICS

Faculty Full-time 10.

Teaching Methodologies Case study, computer-aided instruction, computer simulations, experiential learning, faculty seminars, field projects, group discussion, lecture, research, role playing, seminars by members of the business community, simulations, student presentations, study groups, team projects.

Technology 95 on-campus computer terminals/PCs are available for student use and are linked by a campus-wide network. The network has full access to the Internet. Students are not required to have their own PC.

Special Opportunities Advanced credit may be earned through transfer of credits from another institution. International exchange programs in Croatia, Slovenia, United Kingdom.

FINANCES

Costs for 1997–98 Tuition: $220 per credit hour. Fees: $225 per enrollment. Average 1997–98 room and board costs were $4000 per academic year (on campus) and $4200 per academic year (off campus). Room and board costs vary by occupancy (e.g., single, double, triple), type of accommodation, type of meal plan.

Financial Aid In 1997–98, 6% of students received some institutionally administered aid in the form of research assistantships. Financial aid is available to part-time students. Application Deadline: 9/1.

Financial Aid Contact Dr. William Rohlf, Interim Director/Professor of Economics, Breech School of Business Administration, 900 North Benton Avenue, Springfield, MO 65802-3791. Phone: 417-873-7241; Fax: 417-873-7537.

FACILITIES

Information Resources Olin Library plus 1 additional on-campus library; total holdings of 175,000 volumes, 3,100 microforms, 940 current periodical subscriptions. CD player(s) available for graduate student use. Access provided to online bibliographic retrieval services.

INTERNATIONAL STUDENTS

Demographics 8% of students enrolled are international students [Africa, 25%, Central America, 25%, Europe, 50%].

Services and Facilities International student office, international student center, visa services, ESL courses, counseling/support services.

Applying TOEFL: minimum score of 550, proof of adequate funds, proof of health/immunizations required. Financial aid is not available to international students.

International Student Contact Ms. Cheryl Jones, Director of International Student Services, 900 North Benton Avenue, Springfield, MO 65802-3791. Phone: 417-873-7825; E-mail: xliu@lib.drury.edu

PLACEMENT

Services include alumni network, career counseling/planning, career fairs, career placement, and resume referral to employers.

Employment Of 1996–97 graduates, 100% were employed within three months of graduation. Types of employment entered: banking, chemical industry, communications, consulting, education, finance, financial services, health services, human resources, management, manufacturing, marketing, media, pharmaceutical, real estate, service industry, telecommunications, transportation, utilities.

Business Program(s) URL: http://www.drury.edu

Program Contact: Mr. Alan Foltz, Assistant Director, Breech School of Business Administration, 900 North Benton Avenue, Springfield, MO 65802-3791. Phone: 417-873-7385; Fax: 417-873-7537.

Fontbonne College

Business Department

St. Louis, Missouri

OVERVIEW

Fontbonne College is an independent-religious, coed, comprehensive institution. Enrollment: 1,777 graduate, professional, and undergraduate students; 344 full-time matriculated graduate/professional students; 180 part-time matriculated graduate/professional students. Founded: 1917. The graduate business unit is in a suburban setting and is on a 8-week session; classes run 51 weeks per year calendar.

HIGHLIGHTS

Enrollment Profile

Full-time: N/R	International: N/R
Part-time: N/R	Women: N/R
Total: 374	Minorities: N/R
Average Age: N/R	Average Class Size: 20
Fall 1997 Average GPA: N/R	Fall 1997 Average GMAT: N/R

Costs
Full-time tuition: N/R
Part-time tuition: $325 per hour

GRADUATE BUSINESS PROGRAMS

Traditional MBA (MBA) Part-time; 30 total credits required; 12 months to 6 years to complete program.

Options Accelerated MBA (MBA) Part-time; 43 total credits required; 2 to 6 years to complete program.

Master of Management (MMgt) Part-time; 36 total credits required; 17 months to 6 years to complete program.

ADMISSION

Application Requirements Application form, application fee, bachelor's degree, minimum GPA: 2.5, 2 letters of recommendation, college transcript(s).

Application Deadline Applications processed on a rolling/continuous basis for both domestic and international students. Application fee: $20. Deferred entrance is available.

ACADEMICS

Faculty Full-time 5; part-time 76.

Teaching Methodologies Case study, computer-aided instruction, computer analysis, computer simulations, group discussion, lecture, research, role playing, student presentations, study groups, team projects.

Technology 50 on-campus computer terminals/PCs are available for student use.

Special Opportunities Advanced credit may be earned through transfer of credits from another institution.

FINANCES

Costs for 1997–98 Tuition: Part-time: $325 per hour. Cost varies by academic program. Fees: Part-time: $35 per semester. Fees vary by academic program.

Fontbonne College (continued)

Financial Aid Contact Ms. Nicole Moore, Director of Financial Aid, 6800 Wydown Boulevard, St. Louis, MO 63130. Phone: 314-889-1496; Fax: 314-889-1451; E-mail: nmoore@fontbonne.edu

FACILITIES
Information Resources Main library; total holdings of 96,103 volumes, 1,643 microforms, 527 current periodical subscriptions. CD player(s) available for graduate student use. Access provided to online bibliographic retrieval services and online databases.

INTERNATIONAL STUDENTS
Demographics N/R

Services and Facilities International student office, visa services, ESL courses, counseling/support services.

Applying TOEFL: minimum score of 600, proof of adequate funds required. Financial aid is not available to international students.

International Student Contact Bert Barry, Coordinator of International Students, 6800 Wydown Boulevard, St. Louis, MO 63105-3098. Phone: 314-889-4509; Fax: 314-889-1451; E-mail: bbarry@fontbonne.edu

PLACEMENT
Services include career counseling/planning, career fairs, career library, and resume preparation.

Business Program(s) URL: http://www.fontbonne.edu/

Program Contact: Ms. Cindy Bluestone, Program Representative, Options, 6800 Wydown Boulevard, St. Louis, MO 63105-3098. Phone: 314-863-2220; Fax: 314-863-0917; E-mail: cbbushue@apollogrp.edu

Lincoln University

College of Business

Jefferson City, Missouri

OVERVIEW
Lincoln University is a state-supported, coed, comprehensive institution. Enrollment: 2,979 graduate, professional, and undergraduate students; 23 full-time matriculated graduate/professional students; 321 part-time matriculated graduate/professional students. Founded: 1866. The graduate business unit is in a small-town setting and is on a semester calendar.

GRADUATE BUSINESS PROGRAMS
Master of Business Administration in Management (MBA)

ACADEMICS
Faculty Part-time 6.

Teaching Methodologies Case study, computer-aided instruction, group discussion, lecture, research, student presentations, study groups, team projects.

Technology 125 on-campus computer terminals/PCs are available for student use and are linked by a campus-wide network. The network has full access to the Internet. Students are not required to have their own PC.

Special Opportunities An internship program is available.

FACILITIES
Information Resources Page Library; total holdings of 141,640 volumes, 27,109 microforms, 823 current periodical subscriptions.

Program Contact: Dean, Graduate and Adult Studies, 820 Chestnut, Jefferson City, MO 65102. Phone: 573-681-5207; Fax: 573-681-5209.

Lindenwood University

Department of Business Administration

St. Charles, Missouri

OVERVIEW
Lindenwood University is an independent-religious, coed, comprehensive institution. Enrollment: 5,300 graduate, professional, and undergraduate students; 500 full-time matriculated graduate/professional students; 973 part-time matriculated graduate/professional students. Founded: 1827. The graduate business unit is in a suburban setting and is on a quarter calendar.

HIGHLIGHTS

Enrollment Profile
Full-time: N/R
Part-time: N/R
Total: 450
Average Age: 34
Fall 1997 Average GPA: 3.0

International: 22%
Women: N/R
Minorities: N/R
Average Class Size: 25
Fall 1997 Average GMAT: N/R

Costs
Full-time tuition: N/R
Part-time tuition: $260 per credit

GRADUATE BUSINESS PROGRAMS
Traditional MBA (MBA) Full-time, part-time; 36-48 total credits required; 12 months to 5 years to complete program. Concentrations in accounting, finance, human resources, international business, management, management information systems, marketing, nonprofit management.

Master of Business Administration/Master of Science in Administration (MBA/MS) Full-time, part-time; 42 total credits required; 12 months to 5 years to complete program. Concentrations in marketing, management.

Master of Science in Human Resource Management (MS) Full-time, part-time; 48 total credits required; 12 months to 5 years to complete program.

Master of Science in Health Management (MS) Full-time, part-time; 48 total credits required; 12 months to 5 years to complete program.

Master of Science in Management (MS) Full-time, part-time; 36 total credits required; 12 months to 5 years to complete program. Concentrations in financial management/planning, management, marketing, public management, international business.

Master of Science in Marketing (MS) Full-time, part-time; 36 total credits required; 12 months to 5 years to complete program.

Master of Arts in Human Service Agency Management (MA) Full-time, part-time; 39 total credits required; minimum of 12 months to complete program.

ADMISSION
Applications For fall 1997 there were 60 applications for admission. Of those applying, 55 were accepted. Of those accepted, 52 enrolled.

Application Requirements Application form, application fee, bachelor's degree, letter of recommendation, resume, college transcript(s).

Recommended for Application Minimum GPA: 2.5, interview.

Application Deadline Applications processed on a rolling/continuous basis for both domestic and international students. Application fee: $25. Deferred entrance is available.

ACADEMICS
Faculty Full-time 12; part-time 57.

Teaching Methodologies Case study, computer analysis, group discussion, lecture, research, role playing, seminars by members of the business community, student presentations, study groups.

Technology 100 on-campus computer terminals/PCs are available for student use and are linked by a campus-wide network. The network has full access to the Internet. Students are not required to have their own PC.

Special Opportunities Advanced credit may be earned through transfer of credits from another institution.

FINANCES
Costs for 1997–98 Tuition: $260 per credit. Cost varies by number of credits taken. Average 1997–98 room and board costs were $8200 per academic year. Room and board costs vary by type of accommodation, type of meal plan.

Financial Aid Grants, scholarships, work study, loans available. Financial aid is available to part-time students. Application Deadline: 6/30.

Financial Aid Contact Mr. John Guffey, Associate Director of Graduate and Adult Professional Admissions and MBA Program, 209 South Kingshighway, St. Charles, MO 63301. Phone: 314-949-4933; Fax: 314-949-4910.

FACILITIES
Information Resources Margaret Leggat Butler Memorial Library; total holdings of 138,371 volumes, 32,879 microforms, 523 current periodical subscriptions. CD player(s) available for graduate student use. Access provided to online bibliographic retrieval services.

INTERNATIONAL STUDENTS
Demographics 22% of students enrolled are international students.

Services and Facilities International student office, international student housing.

Applying TOEFL: minimum score of 550, proof of adequate funds required. Financial aid is available to international students.

International Student Contact Ms. Jeanne Murabito, Director, Student Services, 209 South Kingshighway, St. Charles, MO 63301. Phone: 314-949-4978; Fax: 314-949-4910.

PLACEMENT

Services include alumni network, career counseling/planning, career fairs, career library, career placement, job search course, resume referral to employers, and resume preparation. In 1996–97, 75 organizations participated in on-campus recruiting.

Employment Of 1996–97 graduates, 95% were employed within three months of graduation. Types of employment entered: accounting, banking, communications, computer-related, education, finance, health services, human resources, insurance, management, marketing, media, nonprofit, retail, telecommunications.

Program Contact: Mr. John Guffey, Associate Director of Graduate and Adult Professional Admissions and MBA Program, 209 South Kingshighway, St. Charles, MO 63301. Phone: 314-949-4933; Fax: 314-949-4910; E-mail: jdrisk@lc.lindenwood.edu

Maryville University of Saint Louis

John E. Simon School of Business

St. Louis, Missouri

OVERVIEW

Maryville University of Saint Louis is an independent-nonprofit, coed, comprehensive institution. Enrollment: 3,055 graduate, professional, and undergraduate students; 64 full-time matriculated graduate/professional students; 443 part-time matriculated graduate/professional students. Founded: 1872. The graduate business unit is in a suburban setting and is on a semester calendar.

HIGHLIGHTS

Enrollment Profile

Full-time: 38	International: 9%
Part-time: 179	Women: 51%
Total: 217	Minorities: 5%
Average Age: 34	Average Class Size: 16
Fall 1997 Average GPA: 3.15	Fall 1997 Average GMAT: 530

Costs
Full-time tuition: $11,480 per academic year
Part-time tuition: $345 per credit hour

GRADUATE BUSINESS PROGRAMS

Master of Business Administration (MBA) Full-time, part-time; 36 total credits required; up to 5 years to complete program. Concentrations in accounting, management, marketing, international business.

ADMISSION

Applications For fall 1997 there were 68 applications for admission. Of those applying, 68 were accepted. Of those accepted, 54 enrolled.

Application Requirements GMAT score, application form, application fee, bachelor's degree, minimum GPA: 2.5, personal statement, college transcript(s).

Recommended for Application Work experience, computer experience.

Application Deadline Applications processed on a rolling/continuous basis for both domestic and international students. Application fee: $35. Deferred entrance is available.

ACADEMICS

Faculty Full-time 15; part-time 10.

Teaching Methodologies Case study, computer-aided instruction, computer analysis, computer simulations, experiential learning, field projects, group discussion, lecture, research, role playing, seminars by members of the business community, simulations, student presentations, study groups, team projects.

Technology 220 on-campus computer terminals/PCs are available for student use and are linked by a campus-wide network. The network has full access to the Internet. Students are not required to have their own PC.

Special Opportunities Advanced credit may be earned through transfer of credits from another institution. An internship program is available.

FINANCES

Costs for 1997–98 Tuition: Full-time: $11,480 per year. Part-time: $345 per credit hour. Cost varies by number of credits taken. Fees: Full-time: $120 per academic year. Part-time: $30 per semester. Fees vary by number of credits taken. Average 1997–98 room and board costs were $5200 per academic year (on campus) and $13,890 per academic year (off campus). Room and board costs vary by occupancy (e.g., single, double, triple).

Financial Aid Grants available.

Financial Aid Contact Ms. Martha Harbaugh, Director of Financial Aid, 13550 Conway Road, St. Louis, MO 63141-7299. Phone: 314-529-9360; Fax: 314-529-9919; E-mail: fin_aid@maryville.edu

FACILITIES

Information Resources Main library; total holdings of 147,444 volumes, 373,709 microforms, 894 current periodical subscriptions. CD player(s) available for graduate student use. Access provided to online bibliographic retrieval services and online databases.

INTERNATIONAL STUDENTS

Demographics 9% of students enrolled are international students [Africa, 5%, Asia, 60%, Central America, 10%, Europe, 10%, South America, 5%, other, 10%].

Services and Facilities International student office, international student center, international student housing, visa services, ESL courses, counseling/support services, health services, international club.

Applying TOEFL: minimum score of 550, proof of adequate funds, proof of health/immunizations required. Financial aid is not available to international students.

International Student Contact Ms. Liga Abolins, Director of International Programs and ESL, 13550 Conway Road, St. Louis, MO 63141-7299. Phone: 314-529-9502; Fax: 314-529-9384; E-mail: intl@maryville.edu

PLACEMENT

Services include alumni network, career counseling/planning, career fairs, career library, career placement, electronic job bank, job interviews arranged, resume referral to employers, and resume preparation. In 1996–97, 31 organizations participated in on-campus recruiting; 36 on-campus interviews were conducted.

Employment Of 1996–97 graduates, 95% were employed within three months of graduation. Types of employment entered: accounting, banking, chemical industry, communications, computer-related, consulting, consumer products, energy, engineering, finance, financial services, government, health services, high technology, human resources, information systems/technology, insurance, management, manufacturing, marketing, media, nonprofit, pharmaceutical, retail, service industry, telecommunications, transportation, utilities.

Business Program(s) URL: http://www.maryvillestl.edu

Program Contact: Dr. Patricia Parker, MBA Admissions and Enrollment Director, 13550 Conway Road, St. Louis, MO 63141-7299. Phone: 314-529-9382; Fax: 314-529-9975; E-mail: business@maryville.edu

Northwest Missouri State University

College of Professional and Applied Studies

Maryville, Missouri

OVERVIEW

Northwest Missouri State University is a state-supported, coed, comprehensive institution. Enrollment: 6,280 graduate, professional, and undergraduate students; 125 full-time matriculated graduate/professional students; 550 part-time matriculated graduate/professional students. Founded: 1905. The graduate business unit is in a small-town setting and is on a semester calendar.

HIGHLIGHTS

Enrollment Profile

Full-time: 25	International: 11%
Part-time: 48	Women: 49%
Total: 73	Minorities: 11%
Average Age: 30	Average Class Size: 15
Fall 1997 Average GPA: 3.1	Fall 1997 Average GMAT: 476

Costs
Full-time tuition: N/R
Part-time tuition: $105 per credit (resident); $187 per credit (nonresident)

ACBSP – The American Council of Business Schools and Programs accredited

Degree(s) offered in conjunction with Missouri Western State College

GRADUATE BUSINESS PROGRAMS

Master of Business Administration (MBA) Full-time, part-time; 33 total credits required; 12 months to 8 years to complete program.

Master of Business Administration in Accounting (MBA) Full-time, part-time; 33 total credits required; 12 months to 8 years to complete program.

Master of Business Administration in Agricultural Economics (MBA) Full-time, part-time; 36 total credits required; 12 months to 8 years to complete program.

ADMISSION

Applications For fall 1997 there were 30 applications for admission. Of those applying, 29 were accepted. Of those accepted, 18 enrolled.

Northwest Missouri State University (continued)

Application Requirements GMAT score, application form, application fee, bachelor's degree, essay, minimum GPA: 2.5, personal statement, college transcript(s).

Application Deadline 7/1 for fall, 12/1 for spring, 5/1 for summer, 5/15 for fall (international), 11/1 for spring (international), 4/1 for summer (international). Application fee: 50 (international).

ACADEMICS

Faculty Full-time 14.

Teaching Methodologies Case study, computer-aided instruction, computer analysis, experiential learning, field projects, group discussion, lecture, research, role playing, seminars by members of the business community, student presentations, study groups, team projects.

Technology 3,400 on-campus computer terminals/PCs are available for student use and are linked by a campus-wide network. The network has full access to the Internet. Students are not required to have their own PC.

Special Opportunities Advanced credit may be earned through transfer of credits from another institution.

FINANCES

Costs for 1997–98 Tuition: $105 per credit (resident); $187 per credit (nonresident). Cost varies by number of credits taken. Fees: $3 per credit (resident); $3 per credit (nonresident). Fees vary by number of credits taken. Average 1997–98 room and board costs were $3780 per academic year (on campus) and $4300 per academic year (off campus). Room and board costs vary by occupancy (e.g., single, double, triple), type of meal plan.

Financial Aid In 1997–98, 34% of students received some institutionally administered aid in the form of research assistantships, teaching assistantships, scholarships, work study, loans. Application Deadline: 3/1.

Financial Aid Contact Mr. Del Morley, Director of Financial Assistance, 800 University Drive, Maryville, MO 64468. Phone: 660-562-1363; Fax: 660-562-1900; E-mail: 0700277@acad.nwmissouri.edu

FACILITIES

Information Resources B. D. Owens Library plus 1 additional on-campus library; total holdings of 361,200 volumes, 840,914 microforms, 1,350 current periodical subscriptions. CD player(s) available for graduate student use. Access provided to online bibliographic retrieval services and online databases.

INTERNATIONAL STUDENTS

Demographics 11% of students enrolled are international students [Africa, 16%, Asia, 84%].

Services and Facilities International student office, visa services, ESL courses, counseling/support services.

Applying TOEFL: minimum score of 550, proof of adequate funds required. Financial aid is not available to international students.

International Student Contact Mr. Kent Porterfield, Assistant Vice-President, Student Affairs, 800 University Drive, Maryville, MO 64468. Phone: 660-562-1219; Fax: 660-562-1439; E-mail: 0700415@acad.nwmissouri.edu

PLACEMENT

Services include alumni network, career counseling/planning, career fairs, career library, career placement, job interviews arranged, job search course, resume referral to employers, and resume preparation. In 1996–97, 105 organizations participated in on-campus recruiting; 442 on-campus interviews were conducted.

Employment Of 1996–97 graduates, 95% were employed within three months of graduation; the average starting salary was $27,000. Types of employment entered: accounting, banking, communications, computer-related, consulting, consumer products, education, finance, financial services, government, health services, high technology, human resources, information systems/technology, insurance, international trade, management, manufacturing, marketing, media, nonprofit, pharmaceutical, real estate, retail, service industry, telecommunications, utilities.

Business Program(s) URL: http://www.nwmissouri.edu

Program Contact: Mrs. Becky Smith, Administrative Secretary-College of Professional and Applied Studies, 800 University Drive, Maryville, MO 64468. Phone: 660-562-1277, 800-633-1175; Fax: 660-562-1484; E-mail: beckys@acad. nwmissouri.edu

Rockhurst College

School of Management

Kansas City, Missouri

OVERVIEW

Rockhurst College is an independent-religious, coed, comprehensive institution. Enrollment: 2,792 graduate, professional, and undergraduate students; 231 full-time matriculated graduate/professional students; 512 part-time matriculated graduate/professional students. Founded: 1910. The graduate business unit is in an urban setting and is on a semester calendar.

HIGHLIGHTS

Enrollment Profile

Full-time: 51	International: 1%
Part-time: 473	Women: 40%
Total: 524	Minorities: 4%
Average Age: 32	Average Class Size: 25
Fall 1997 Average GPA: 3.216	Fall 1997 Average GMAT: 504

Costs
Full-time tuition: N/R
Part-time tuition: $325 per credit hour

GRADUATE BUSINESS PROGRAMS

Master of Business Administration (MBA) Full-time, part-time; 36 total credits required; 12 months to 6 years to complete program. Concentrations in finance, human resources, industrial/labor relations, international management, management, marketing, accounting.

Executive MBA (EMBA) Part-time; 36 total credits required; 2 years to complete program. Concentration in management.

ADMISSION

Applications For fall 1997 there were 193 applications for admission. Of those applying, 130 were accepted. Of those accepted, 111 enrolled.

Application Requirements GMAT score: minimum 450, application form, bachelor's degree, minimum GPA: 2.75, college transcript(s).

Recommended for Application Interview, work experience, computer experience.

Application Deadline Applications processed on a rolling/continuous basis for both domestic and international students. Deferred entrance is available.

ACADEMICS

Faculty Full-time 22; part-time 7.

Teaching Methodologies Case study, computer-aided instruction, computer analysis, computer simulations, experiential learning, faculty seminars, field projects, group discussion, lecture, research, role playing, seminars by members of the business community, simulations, student presentations, study groups, team projects.

Technology 160 on-campus computer terminals/PCs are available for student use and are linked by a campus-wide network. The network has full access to the Internet. Students are not required to have their own PC.

Special Opportunities Advanced credit may be earned through credit for business training programs, transfer of credits from another institution.

FINANCES

Costs for 1997–98 Tuition: $325 per credit hour. Fees: $15 per semester. Average 1997–98 room and board costs were $4750 per academic year. Room and board costs vary by occupancy (e.g., single, double, triple), type of accommodation, type of meal plan.

Financial Aid In 1997–98, 14% of students received some institutionally administered aid in the form of loans. Financial aid is available to part-time students. Application Deadline: 4/1.

Financial Aid Contact Mr. Keith Jaloma, Director of Financial Aid , 1100 Rockhurst Road, Kansas City, MO 64110-2561. Phone: 816-501-4100; Fax: 816-501-4588.

FACILITIES

Information Resources Greenlease Library; total holdings of 106,880 volumes, 695 microforms, 720 current periodical subscriptions. CD player(s) available for graduate student use. Access provided to online bibliographic retrieval services.

INTERNATIONAL STUDENTS

Demographics 1% of students enrolled are international students.

Services and Facilities International student office, visa services, counseling/support services.

Applying TOEFL: minimum score of 550, proof of adequate funds, proof of health/immunizations required. Financial aid is not available to international students.

International Student Contact Sr. Donette Alonzo, Director of International Student Services, 1100 Rockhurst Road, Kansas City, MO 64110-2561. Phone: 816-501-4821; Fax: 816-501-4588; E-mail: alonzo@vax2.rockhurst.edu

PLACEMENT

Services include alumni network, career counseling/planning, career fairs, career library, career placement, electronic job bank, job interviews arranged, job search course, resume referral to employers, and resume preparation. In 1996–97, 68 organizations participated in on-campus recruiting; 10 on-campus interviews were conducted.

Business Program(s) URL: http://www.rockhurst.edu

Program Contact: Ms. Pamela Kerr, Administrative Assistant-Graduate Studies, 1100 Rockhurst Road, Kansas City, MO 64110-2561. Phone: 816-501-4090; Fax: 816-501-4650; E-mail: kerr@vax2.rockhurst.edu

Saint Louis University

School of Business and Administration

St. Louis, Missouri

OVERVIEW

Saint Louis University is an independent-religious, coed university. Enrollment: 11,038 graduate, professional, and undergraduate students; 2,112 full-time matriculated graduate/professional students; 2,331 part-time matriculated graduate/professional students. Founded: 1818. The graduate business unit is in an urban setting and is on a semester calendar.

HIGHLIGHTS

Enrollment Profile
Full-time: 167
Part-time: 429
Total: 596
Average Age: 27
Fall 1997 Average GPA: 3.15

International: 24%
Women: 40%
Minorities: 7%
Average Class Size: 25
Fall 1997 Average GMAT: 524

Costs
Full-time tuition: $10,836 per academic year
Part-time tuition: $602 per credit

AACSB – The International Association for Management Education accredited

Saint Louis University's School of Business and Administration has a long and proud tradition of providing a sound academic foundation for the professional practice of business. The M.B.A. program provides students with important analytical skills and functional principles, but today's environment demands more. Business learning today is about teamwork and seeing business problems as a whole rather than as a collection of individual parts. The program brings this perspective to the classroom as well as a hands-on, real-world orientation to business problem solving. This is the Saint Louis University advantage.

Managers of tomorrow must be prepared to deal with business problems that are increasingly complex, global, and entrepreneurial in nature. The M.B.A. program at Saint Louis University was redesigned in 1995 to meet the needs of future business managers and to incorporate the latest thinking in business education. The result is a curriculum that emphasizes leadership, written and oral communication skills, and solving business problems through teamwork and experiential learning. Throughout the program, global issues are woven into the course work. Through electives, the School offers students the opportunity to select areas of emphasis, which range from entrepreneurship to international business topics to a specialization in a functional area.

GRADUATE BUSINESS PROGRAMS

Master of Business Administration (MBA) Full-time, part-time; 39-57 total credits required; 12 months to 5 years to complete program. Concentrations in accounting, decision sciences, economics, finance, industrial/labor relations, international business, management, management information systems, marketing.

Master of Finance (MF) Full-time, part-time; 30-48 total credits required; 12 months to 5 years to complete program.

Master of Professional Accountancy (MPA) Full-time, part-time; 30-63 total credits required; 12 months to 5 years to complete program.

Master of Decision Sciences (MDSC) Full-time, part-time; 30-48 total credits required; 12 months to 5 years to complete program.

Master of Management (MMgt) Full-time, part-time; 30-48 total credits required; 12 months to 5 years to complete program.

Executive Master of International Business (EMIB) Part-time; 36 total credits required; 2 years to complete program.

Doctor of Jurisprudence/Master of Business Administration (JD/MBA) Full-time, part-time; 130 total credits required; 3.5 to 5 years to complete program.
Master of Health Administration/Master of Business Administration (MHA/MBA) Full-time; 91 total credits required; 3 years to complete program.
Master of Science in Nursing/Master of Business Administration (MS/MBA) Full-time, part-time; 73 total credits required; 3 to 5 years to complete program.
Master of International Business (MIB) Full-time; 45 total credits required; up to 5 years to complete program.

ADMISSION

Applications For fall 1997 there were 349 applications for admission. Of those applying, 219 were accepted. Of those accepted, 115 enrolled.

Application Requirements GMAT score, application form, application fee, bachelor's degree, 2 letters of recommendation, personal statement, college transcript(s).

Recommended for Application Essay, resume.

Application Deadline 7/15 for fall, 12/1 for spring, 4/15 for summer, 1/15 for fall (international), 6/1 for spring (international), 11/15 for summer (international). Application fee: $40. Deferred entrance is available.

ACADEMICS

Faculty Full-time 55; part-time 15.

Teaching Methodologies Case study, computer simulations, group discussion, lecture, research, simulations, student presentations, study groups, team projects.

Technology 100 on-campus computer terminals/PCs are available for student use and are linked by a campus-wide network. The network has full access to the Internet. Students are not required to have their own PC.

Special Opportunities Advanced credit may be earned through credit by examination, transfer of credits from another institution. An internship program is available.

FINANCES

Costs for 1997–98 Tuition: Full-time: $10,836 per year. Part-time: $602 per credit. Cost varies by academic program. Fees: Full-time: $110 per academic year. Part-time: $10 per semester. Fees vary by number of credits taken. Average 1997–98 room and board costs were $5790 per academic year (on campus) and $5780 per academic year (off campus). Room and board costs vary by campus location, occupancy (e.g., single, double, triple), type of accommodation, type of meal plan.

Financial Aid Fellowships, research assistantships, teaching assistantships, work study available. Financial aid is available to part-time students.

Financial Aid Contact Mr. Hal Deuser, Director, Financial Aid, 221 North Grand, St. Louis, MO 63103-9945. Phone: 314-977-2350; Fax: 314-977-3874.

FACILITIES

Information Resources Pius XII Memorial Library plus 5 additional on-campus libraries; total holdings of 1,460,000 volumes, 1,100,000 microforms, 12,800 current periodical subscriptions. CD player(s) available for graduate student use. Access provided to online bibliographic retrieval services.

INTERNATIONAL STUDENTS

Demographics 24% of students enrolled are international students.

Services and Facilities International student office, international student center, international student housing, visa services, ESL courses, counseling/support services.

Applying TOEFL: minimum score of 550, TWE: minimum score of 4.5, proof of adequate funds, proof of health/immunizations required. Financial aid is not available to international students.

International Student Contact Dr. Young Kim, Director, International Programs, 221 North Grand, St. Louis, MO 63103-9945. Phone: 314-977-2318; Fax: 314-977-3874.

PLACEMENT

Services include alumni network, career counseling/planning, career fairs, career library, career placement, electronic job bank, job interviews arranged, job search course, resume referral to employers, and resume preparation. In 1996–97, 218 organizations participated in on-campus recruiting; 708 on-campus interviews were conducted.

Employment Of 1996–97 graduates, 99% were employed within three months of graduation; the average starting salary was $46,872. Types of employment entered: accounting, banking, communications, computer-related, consulting, consumer products, education, energy, engineering, finance, financial services, government, health services, high technology, human resources, information systems/technology, insurance, international trade, law, management, manufacturing, marketing, nonprofit, pharmaceutical, retail, service industry, telecommunications, utilities.

Business Program(s) URL: http://www.slu.edu

Saint Louis University (continued)

Program Contact: Ms. Alquinston Johnson, Applications Coordinator, School of Business, 3674 Lindell Boulevard, St. Louis, MO 63108. Phone: 314-977-3800; Fax: 314-977-3897; E-mail: johnsonab@slusva.edu
See full description on page 968.

Southeast Missouri State University

College of Business

Cape Girardeau, Missouri

OVERVIEW
Southeast Missouri State University is a state-supported, coed, comprehensive institution. Enrollment: 9,000 graduate, professional, and undergraduate students; 400 full-time matriculated graduate/professional students; 600 part-time matriculated graduate/professional students. Founded: 1873. The graduate business unit is in a small-town setting and is on a semester calendar.

HIGHLIGHTS

Enrollment Profile
Full-time: 20	International: 29%
Part-time: 50	Women: 50%
Total: 70	Minorities: 14%
Average Age: 32	Average Class Size: 20
Fall 1997 Average GPA: 3.4	Fall 1997 Average GMAT: 550

Costs
Full-time tuition: N/R
Part-time tuition: $100 per credit hour (resident); $180 per credit hour (nonresident)

AACSB – The International Association for Management Education accredited

GRADUATE BUSINESS PROGRAMS
Master of Business Administration (MBA) Full-time, part-time; 33-63 total credits required; 12 months to 6 years to complete program. Concentrations in accounting, management.

ADMISSION
Applications For fall 1997 there were 85 applications for admission. Of those applying, 65 were accepted. Of those accepted, 50 enrolled.
Application Requirements Application form, bachelor's degree, minimum GPA, college transcript(s).
Recommended for Application GMAT score accepted.
Application Deadline Applications processed on a rolling/continuous basis for both domestic and international students. Application fee: $20, $50 (international). Deferred entrance is available.

ACADEMICS
Faculty Full-time 45.
Teaching Methodologies Case study, computer analysis, computer simulations, experiential learning, field projects, group discussion, lecture, research, seminars by members of the business community, student presentations, study groups, team projects.
Technology 1,000 on-campus computer terminals/PCs are available for student use and are linked by a campus-wide network. The network has full access to the Internet. Students are not required to have their own PC.
Special Opportunities Advanced credit may be earned through transfer of credits from another institution. International exchange program in various countries in Western Europe. An internship program is available.

FINANCES
Costs for 1997–98 Tuition: $100 per credit hour (resident); $180 per credit hour (nonresident). Cost varies by number of credits taken. Average 1997–98 room and board costs were $5000 per academic year (on campus) and $5000 per academic year (off campus). Room and board costs vary by occupancy (e.g., single, double, triple), type of accommodation, type of meal plan.
Financial Aid In 1997–98, 36% of students received some institutionally administered aid in the form of research assistantships, grants, scholarships, work study, loans. Financial aid is available to part-time students.

FACILITIES
Information Resources Kent Library. CD player(s) available for graduate student use. Access provided to online bibliographic retrieval services and online databases.

INTERNATIONAL STUDENTS
Demographics 29% of students enrolled are international students [Africa, 5%, Asia, 35%, Central America, 10%, Europe, 40%, South America, 10%].
Services and Facilities International student office, international student center, visa services, ESL courses, counseling/support services.
Applying TOEFL: minimum score of 550, proof of adequate funds required.

PLACEMENT
Services include career counseling/planning, career fairs, career library, career placement, electronic job bank, job interviews arranged, job search course, and resume preparation. In 1996–97, 100 organizations participated in on-campus recruiting.
Employment Of 1996–97 graduates, 100% were employed within three months of graduation. Types of employment entered: accounting, banking, consumer products, education, finance, financial services, international trade, management, pharmaceutical, retail, telecommunications.
Business Program(s) URL: http://www.semo.edu

Program Contact: Kenneth Heischmidt, Director, MBA Program, MBA Office, Cape Girardeau, MO 63701. Phone: 573-651-5116; Fax: 573-651-5032; E-mail: mba@semdvm.semd.edu

Southwest Baptist University

School of Business

Bolivar, Missouri

OVERVIEW
Southwest Baptist University is an independent-religious, comprehensive institution. Enrollment: 3,000 graduate, professional, and undergraduate students.

HIGHLIGHTS

Enrollment Profile
Full-time: N/R	International: N/R
Part-time: N/R	Women: N/R
Total: 110	Minorities: N/R
Average Age: N/R	Average Class Size: N/R
Fall 1997 Average GPA: N/R	Fall 1997 Average GMAT: N/R

Costs
Full-time tuition: $5220 per academic year
Part-time tuition: N/R

GRADUATE BUSINESS PROGRAMS
Master of Science (MS) Full-time, part-time; 36 total credits required; minimum of 14 months to complete program. Concentration in accounting.

ADMISSION
Application Requirements Bachelor's degree, minimum GPA: 2.5, 3 letters of recommendation, resume, computer experience: computer literacy.
Recommended for Application Work experience.
Application Deadline Applications processed on a rolling/continuous basis for both domestic and international students.

ACADEMICS
Teaching Methodologies Case study, computer-aided instruction, computer analysis, computer simulations, experiential learning, field projects, group discussion, lecture, research, role playing, seminars by members of the business community, student presentations, study groups, team projects.

FINANCES
Costs for 1997–98 Tuition: Full-time: $5220 per program. Fees: Full-time: $60 per academic year.
Financial Aid Contact Office of Financial Aid, Bolivar, MO 65613-2597. Phone: 417-326-1820.

INTERNATIONAL STUDENTS
Demographics N/R
Applying TOEFL required.

Program Contact: Dr. Rod Oglesby, Bolivar, MO 65613-2597. Phone: 417-326-1756.

Southwest Missouri State University

College of Business Administration

Springfield, Missouri

OVERVIEW

Southwest Missouri State University is a state-supported, coed, comprehensive institution. Enrollment: 16,234 graduate, professional, and undergraduate students; 422 full-time matriculated graduate/professional students; 1,033 part-time matriculated graduate/professional students. Founded: 1905. The graduate business unit is in an urban setting and is on a semester calendar.

HIGHLIGHTS

Enrollment Profile

Full-time: 114
Part-time: 96
Total: 210
Average Age: 25
Fall 1997 Average GPA: 3.0

International: 26%
Women: 49%
Minorities: 4%
Average Class Size: 20
Fall 1997 Average GMAT: 500

Costs

Full-time tuition: $2520 per academic year (resident); $5040 per academic year (nonresident)
Part-time tuition: $105 per hour (resident); $210 per hour (nonresident)

AACSB – The International Association for Management Education accredited

Southwest Missouri State University's (SMSU) M.B.A. degree, which is accredited by AACSB–The International Association for Management Education, integrates a variety of courses offered by the five departments of the College of Business Administration. The program is designed specifically for students who hold undergraduate degrees in the arts, the sciences, engineering, and law, as well as business administration. Students with little or no undergraduate work in business normally require five semesters to complete the program. Students with appropriate prior academic preparation in business and economics and a strong work ethic may complete the program in one calendar year.

A strength of the SMSU M.B.A. program is its emphasis on the individual. The case method is only one of a variety of teaching methods used in M.B.A. courses. Simulation exercises, business games, research, role playing, videos, collateral readings, report writing, and lectures are all used where deemed most appropriate and effective. High educational productivity for each student is the criterion followed. M.B.A. faculty members recognize that their major responsibilities are teaching and working with students, and they also are actively involved in their areas of professional expertise.

State-of-the-art David D. Glass Hall, home of the College of Business Administration, includes a variety of special-purpose classrooms as well as six computer laboratories.

GRADUATE BUSINESS PROGRAMS

Master of Business Administration (MBA) Full-time, part-time; 33-57 total credits required; 12 months to 2.5 years to complete program. Concentrations in accounting, finance, financial management/planning, information management, international business, management, management information systems, marketing.

Master of Accountancy (MAcc) Full-time, part-time; 33-57 total credits required; 12 months to 2.5 years to complete program. Concentration in accounting.

Master of Science in Computer Information Systems (MS) Part-time, distance learning option; 33 total credits required; up to 2 years to complete program. Concentrations in information management, management information systems.

Master of Health Administration (MHA) Full-time, part-time; 54-60 total credits required; minimum of 2 years to complete program.

ADMISSION

Application Requirements GMAT score: minimum 400, application form, application fee, bachelor's degree, minimum GPA, college transcript(s).

Recommended for Application Computer experience.

Application Deadline Applications processed on a rolling/continuous basis for domestic students only. 4/15 for fall (international), 9/1 for spring (international), 4/1 for summer (international). Application fee: $25. Deferred entrance is available.

ACADEMICS

Faculty Full-time 53.

Teaching Methodologies Case study, computer analysis, computer simulations, experiential learning, faculty seminars, field projects, group discussion, lecture, research, role playing, seminars by members of the business community, simulations, student presentations, study groups, team projects.

Technology 400 on-campus computer terminals/PCs are available for student use and are linked by a campus-wide network. The network has full access to the Internet. Students are not required to have their own PC.

Special Opportunities Advanced credit may be earned through transfer of credits from another institution. International exchange programs in Australia, Belgium, Finland, France, Germany, Netherlands, People's Republic of China, United Kingdom. An internship program is available.

FINANCES

Costs for 1997–98 Tuition: Full-time: $2520 per year (resident); $5040 per year (nonresident). Part-time: $105 per hour (resident); $210 per hour (nonresident). Cost varies by academic program, number of credits taken. Fees: Full-time: $270 per academic year (resident); $270 per academic year (nonresident). Part-time: $73 per semester (resident); $73 per semester (nonresident). Fees vary by academic program, number of credits taken. Average 1997–98 room and board costs were $3200 per academic year. Room and board costs vary by occupancy (e.g., single, double, triple), type of accommodation, type of meal plan.

Financial Aid Research assistantships, scholarships, work study, loans available. Financial aid is available to part-time students.

Financial Aid Contact Mr. Todd Morriss, Director, Office of Student Financial Aid, Springfield, MO 65804. Phone: 417-836-5262; Fax: 417-836-8392; E-mail: rtm290t@vma.smsu.edu

FACILITIES

Information Resources Meyer Library plus 2 additional on-campus libraries; total holdings of 487,247 volumes, 737,866 microforms, 4,229 current periodical subscriptions. CD player(s) available for graduate student use. Access provided to online bibliographic retrieval services.

INTERNATIONAL STUDENTS

Demographics 26% of students enrolled are international students.

Services and Facilities International student office, international student center, international student housing, visa services, ESL courses, counseling/support services.

Applying TOEFL, proof of adequate funds, proof of health/immunizations required. Financial aid is available to international students.

International Student Contact Ms. Jan Swann, Coordinator—International Student Services, CAMU 309, 901 South National, Springfield, MO 65804. Phone: 417-836-6618; Fax: 417-836-7656; E-mail: jss679t@vma.smsu.edu

PLACEMENT

Services include career counseling/planning, career fairs, career library, career placement, electronic job bank, job interviews arranged, resume referral to employers, and resume preparation. In 1996–97, 116 organizations participated in on-campus recruiting; 1,102 on-campus interviews were conducted.

Employment Types of employment entered: accounting, banking, communications, computer-related, consulting, consumer products, education, energy, finance, financial services, government, health services, high technology, hospitality management, human resources, information systems/technology, insurance, international trade, management, manufacturing, marketing, media, nonprofit, petrochemical, real estate, retail, service industry, telecommunications, transportation, utilities.

Business Program(s) URL: http://www.COBA.smsu.edu/index.html

Program Contact: Dr. Michael Fields, MBA Program Director, 901 South National, Springfield, MO 65804-0094. Phone: 417-836-5646; Fax: 417-836-4407; E-mail: dmf603f@um2.smsu.edu

Stephens College

Program in Business Administration

Columbia, Missouri

OVERVIEW

Stephens College is an independent-nonprofit, comprehensive institution. Enrollment: 819 graduate, professional, and undergraduate students; 11 full-time matriculated graduate/professional students; part-time matriculated graduate/professional students. Founded: 1833. The graduate business unit is on a 4 ten-week terms calendar.

Stephens College (continued)

HIGHLIGHTS

Enrollment Profile
Full-time: N/R
Part-time: N/R
Total: N/R
Average Age: N/R
Fall 1997 Average GPA: N/R

International: N/R
Women: N/R
Minorities: N/R
Average Class Size: 11
Fall 1997 Average GMAT: N/R

Costs
Full-time tuition: N/R
Part-time tuition: $230 per credit hour

GRADUATE BUSINESS PROGRAMS
Master of Business Administration (MBA) Full-time, part-time, distance learning option; 36 total credits required; 18 months to 7 years to complete program. Concentrations in entrepreneurship, management, information management, health care.

ADMISSION
Application Requirements GMAT score: minimum 500, application form, bachelor's degree (must be in field of business), essay, minimum GPA: 3.0, letters of recommendation, college transcript(s), computer experience: word processing, Internet, e-mail.

Recommended for Application Interview, personal statement, resume, work experience.

Application Deadline Applications processed on a rolling/continuous basis for both domestic and international students. Application fee: $25.

ACADEMICS
Faculty Full-time 5.

Teaching Methodologies Case study, group discussion, research, student presentations, study groups, team projects.

Technology The network has full access to the Internet. Students are required to have their own PC.

Special Opportunities Advanced credit may be earned through credit by examination, credit for experience, credit for military training programs, credit for business training programs, transfer of credits from another institution.

FINANCES
Costs for 1997-98 Tuition: $230 per credit hour.

Financial Aid Loans available. Financial aid is available to part-time students.

Financial Aid Contact Gloria Wright, Director of Financial Aid, 1200 East Broadway, Columbia, MO 65215. Phone: 573-876-7106; Fax: 573-876-7237; E-mail: gloria@wc.stephens.edu

FACILITIES
Information Resources Hugh Stephens Library; total holdings of 125,000 volumes, 10,938 microforms, 375 current periodical subscriptions. CD player(s) available for graduate student use. Access provided to online databases.

INTERNATIONAL STUDENTS
Demographics N/R

Applying TOEFL: minimum score of 550 required. Financial aid is not available to international students.

International Student Contact Dr. Joan Rines, Director of Graduate Programs, 1200 East Broadway, Campus Box 2083, Columbia, MO 65215. Phone: 573-876-7283; Fax: 573-876-7248; E-mail: grad@wc.stephens.edu

PLACEMENT
Services include alumni network.

Business Program(s) URL: http://www.stephens.edu

Program Contact: Dr. Joan Rines, Director of Graduate Programs, 1200 East Broadway, Campus Box 2083, Columbia, MO 65215. Phone: 573-876-7283, 800-388-7579; Fax: 573- 876-7248; E-mail: grad@wc.stephens.edu

Truman State University

Division of Business and Accountancy

Kirksville, Missouri

OVERVIEW
Truman State University is a state-supported, coed, comprehensive institution. Enrollment: 6,200 graduate, professional, and undergraduate students; 170 full-time matriculated graduate/professional students; 54 part-time matriculated graduate/professional students. Founded: 1867. The graduate business unit is in a small-town setting and is on a semester calendar.

HIGHLIGHTS

Enrollment Profile
Full-time: 18
Part-time: 0
Total: 18
Average Age: 23
Fall 1997 Average GPA: 3.6

International: 28%
Women: 72%
Minorities: N/R
Average Class Size: 10
Fall 1997 Average GMAT: 592

Costs
Full-time tuition: $2466 per academic year (resident); $4464 per academic year (nonresident)
Part-time tuition: $144 per hour (resident); $255 per hour (nonresident)

GRADUATE BUSINESS PROGRAMS
Master of Accountancy (MAcc) Full-time, part-time; 30-42 total credits required; 12 months to 2 years to complete program. Concentrations in accounting, taxation.

ADMISSION
Applications For fall 1997 there were 10 applications for admission. Of those applying, 7 were accepted. Of those accepted, 5 enrolled.

Application Requirements GMAT score, application form, bachelor's degree, minimum GPA: 3.0, 3 letters of recommendation, personal statement, resume, college transcript(s).

Application Deadline 6/1 for fall, 11/1 for spring, 6/1 for fall (international), 11/1 for spring (international). Deferred entrance is available.

ACADEMICS
Faculty Full-time 16.

Teaching Methodologies Case study, computer analysis, computer simulations, group discussion, lecture, research, role playing, student presentations, study groups, team projects.

Technology 300 on-campus computer terminals/PCs are available for student use and are linked by a campus-wide network. The network has full access to the Internet. Students are not required to have their own PC.

FINANCES
Costs for 1997-98 Tuition: Full-time: $2466 per year (resident); $4464 per year (nonresident). Part-time: $144 per hour (resident); $255 per hour (nonresident). Cost varies by number of credits taken. Average 1997-98 room and board costs were $3808 per academic year (on campus) and $4200 per academic year (off campus). Room and board costs vary by occupancy (e.g., single, double, triple), type of accommodation.

Financial Aid In 1997-98, 56% of students received some institutionally administered aid in the form of research assistantships, teaching assistantships, work study. Application Deadline: 5/1.

Financial Aid Contact Ms. Melinda Wood, Financial Aid Director, East Normal Street, Kirksville, MO 63501-4221. Phone: 660-785-4130; Fax: 660-785-4221.

FACILITIES
Information Resources Pickler Library; total holdings of 661,465 volumes, 1,215,972 microforms, 3,317 current periodical subscriptions. CD player(s) available for graduate student use. Access provided to online bibliographic retrieval services.

INTERNATIONAL STUDENTS
Demographics 28% of students enrolled are international students [Asia, 40%, Europe, 60%].

Services and Facilities International student office, international student center, international student housing, counseling/support services.

Applying TOEFL: minimum score of 560, proof of adequate funds, proof of health/immunizations required. Financial aid is not available to international students.

International Student Contact Melanee Crist, International Student Advisor, East Normal Street, Kirksville, MO 63501-4221. Phone: 660-785-4215; Fax: 660-785-4221.

PLACEMENT
Services include alumni network, career counseling/planning, career fairs, career placement, electronic job bank, resume referral to employers, and resume preparation.

Employment Of 1996-97 graduates, 100% were employed within three months of graduation; the average starting salary was $35,000. Types of employment entered: accounting, banking, chemical industry, communications, consulting, consumer products, education, finance, financial services, government, health services, high technology, hospitality management, insurance, management, manufacturing, nonprofit, petrochemical, pharmaceutical, real estate, retail, service industry, telecommunications, transportation.

Business Program(s) URL: http://www.truman.edu

Program Contact: Dr. Scott Fouch, Coordinator of Graduate Studies, Division of Business and Accountancy, East Normal Street, Kirksville, MO 63501-4221. Phone: 660-785-4371; Fax: 660-785-4221; E-mail: bu58@truman.edu

See full description on page 1024.

University of Missouri-Columbia

College of Business and Public Administration

Columbia, Missouri

OVERVIEW
The University of Missouri-Columbia is a state-supported, coed university. Enrollment: 22,500 graduate, professional, and undergraduate students; 3,097 full-time matriculated graduate/professional students; 2,057 part-time matriculated graduate/professional students. Founded: 1839. The graduate business unit is in a small-town setting and is on a semester calendar.

HIGHLIGHTS

Enrollment Profile

Full-time: 111	International: 25%
Part-time: 19	Women: 29%
Total: 130	Minorities: 4%
Average Age: 27	Average Class Size: 20
Fall 1997 Average GPA: 3.25	Fall 1997 Average GMAT: 585

Costs
Full-time tuition: N/R
Part-time tuition: $158 per credit hour (resident); $475 per credit hour (nonresident)

AACSB – The International Association for Management Education accredited

GRADUATE BUSINESS PROGRAMS
Master of Business Administration (MBA) Full-time, part-time; 33-55 total credits required; 12 months to 2 years to complete program. Concentrations in advertising, agricultural economics, economics, finance, human resources, legal administration, management, management information systems, management science, marketing, public relations, quality management.

Master of Business Administration/Master of Science in Industrial Engineering (MBA/MS) Full-time, part-time.

Master of Business Administration/Doctor of Jurisprudence (MBA/JD) Full-time, part-time; 4 to 4.5 years to complete program.

Master of Business Administration/Master of Health Administration (MBA/MHA) Full-time, part-time.

ADMISSION
Applications For fall 1997 there were 165 applications for admission. Of those applying, 90 were accepted. Of those accepted, 38 enrolled.

Application Requirements GMAT score, application form, application fee, bachelor's degree, minimum GPA: 2.7, resume, college transcript(s).

Application Deadline 8/1 for fall, 12/1 for winter, 5/1 for summer, 7/1 for fall (international), 11/1 for winter (international), 4/1 for summer (international). Application fee: $25, $50 (international). Deferred entrance is available.

ACADEMICS
Faculty Full-time 47; part-time 2.

Teaching Methodologies Case study, computer-aided instruction, computer simulations, experiential learning, faculty seminars, field projects, group discussion, lecture, seminars by members of the business community, simulations, student presentations, team projects.

Technology 1,000 on-campus computer terminals/PCs are available for student use and are linked by a campus-wide network. The network has full access to the Internet. Students are not required to have their own PC.

Special Opportunities Advanced credit may be earned through transfer of credits from another institution. International exchange programs in France, Italy, Mexico, Romania.

FINANCES
Costs for 1997–98 Tuition: $158 per credit hour (resident); $475 per credit hour (nonresident). Cost varies by academic program, number of credits taken, reciprocity agreements. Fees: $25 per credit hour (resident); $25 per credit hour (nonresident). Fees vary by academic program, campus location, number of credits taken. Average 1997–98 room only costs were $6600 per academic year (on campus) and $6000 per academic year (off campus). Room and board costs vary by campus location, occupancy (e.g., single, double, triple), type of accommodation, type of meal plan.

Financial Aid In 1997–98, 58% of students received some institutionally administered aid in the form of fellowships, research assistantships, teaching assistantships, scholarships, work study, loans.

Financial Aid Contact Ms. Barbara Schneider, Senior Academic Advisor, 303 Middlebush Hall, Columbia, MO 65211. Phone: 573-882-2750; Fax: 573-882-0365; E-mail: grad@bpa.missouri.edu

FACILITIES
Information Resources Ellis Library plus 9 additional on-campus libraries; total holdings of 2,500,000 volumes, 4,800,000 microforms, 13,018 current periodical subscriptions. CD player(s) available for graduate student use. Access provided to online bibliographic retrieval services and online databases.

INTERNATIONAL STUDENTS
Demographics 25% of students enrolled are international students [Asia, 56%, Europe, 38%, North America, 6%].

Services and Facilities International student office, international student center, international student housing, visa services, ESL courses, counseling/support services.

Applying TOEFL: minimum score of 550, proof of adequate funds, proof of health/immunizations required. Financial aid is available to international students.

International Student Contact Ms. Becky Brandt, Assistant Director of Admissions, 123 Jesse Hall, Columbia, MO 65211. Phone: 573-882-3754; Fax: 573-882-9907.

PLACEMENT
Services include alumni network, career counseling/planning, career fairs, career library, career placement, job interviews arranged, resume referral to employers, and resume preparation. In 1996–97, 25 organizations participated in on-campus recruiting; 130 on-campus interviews were conducted.

Employment Of 1996–97 graduates, 96% were employed within three months of graduation; the average starting salary was $41,000. Types of employment entered: accounting, banking, chemical industry, communications, computer-related, consulting, consumer products, finance, financial services, health services, high technology, information systems/technology, insurance, law, management, manufacturing, marketing, pharmaceutical, real estate, retail, telecommunications.

Business Program(s) URL: http://tiger.bpa.missouri.edu

Program Contact: Ms. Barbara Schneider, Senior Academic Advisor, 303 Middlebush Hall, Columbia, MO 65211. Phone: 573-882-2750; Fax: 573-882-0365; E-mail: grad@bpa.missouri.edu

See full description on page 1104.

University of Missouri-Kansas City

Harry W. Bloch School of Public Administration

Kansas City, Missouri

OVERVIEW
The University of Missouri-Kansas City is a state-supported, coed university. Enrollment: 10,444 graduate, professional, and undergraduate students. Founded: 1929. The graduate business unit is in an urban setting and is on a semester calendar.

HIGHLIGHTS

Enrollment Profile

Full-time: 228	International: 18%
Part-time: 499	Women: 49%
Total: 727	Minorities: 10%
Average Age: 31	Average Class Size: 25
Fall 1997 Average GPA: 3.2	Fall 1997 Average GMAT: 541

Costs
Full-time tuition: N/R
Part-time tuition: $163 per credit hour (resident); $489 per credit hour (nonresident)

AACSB – The International Association for Management Education accredited

University of Missouri-Kansas City (continued)

Degree(s) offered in conjunction with Inti College

GRADUATE BUSINESS PROGRAMS

Executive MBA (MBA) Part-time; 48 total credits required; 21 months to complete program. Concentration in management.

Master of Business Administration (MBA) Full-time, part-time; 30-60 total credits required; 12 months to 7 years to complete program. Concentrations in entrepreneurship, finance, human resources, international business, management, management information systems, marketing, operations management, organizational behavior/development, quantitative analysis.

Master of Science in Accounting (MS) Full-time, part-time; 30-60 total credits required; 12 months to 7 years to complete program. Concentration in accounting.

Master of Public Administration (MPA) Full-time, part-time; 36 total credits required; 12 months to 7 years to complete program. Concentrations in nonprofit management, organizational behavior/development, human resources, city/urban administration, health care.

ADMISSION

Applications For fall 1997 there were 483 applications for admission. Of those applying, 282 were accepted. Of those accepted, 212 enrolled.

Application Requirements Application form, application fee, bachelor's degree, personal statement, college transcript(s), computer experience: word processing, spreadsheet, database.

Recommended for Application GMAT score accepted, GRE score accepted.

Application Deadline Applications processed on a rolling/continuous basis for both domestic and international students. Application fee: $25. Deferred entrance is available.

ACADEMICS

Faculty Full-time 42; part-time 14.

Teaching Methodologies Case study, computer-aided instruction, computer analysis, computer simulations, experiential learning, faculty seminars, field projects, group discussion, lecture, research, seminars by members of the business community, simulations, student presentations, study groups, team projects.

Technology 450 on-campus computer terminals/PCs are available for student use and are linked by a campus-wide network. The network has full access to the Internet. Students are not required to have their own PC.

Special Opportunities Advanced credit may be earned through transfer of credits from another institution. International exchange programs in Germany, Japan, Malaysia, Republic of Singapore, United Kingdom.

FINANCES

Costs for 1997–98 Tuition: $163 per credit hour (resident); $489 per credit hour (nonresident). Cost varies by number of credits taken, reciprocity agreements. Fees: $19 per credit hour (resident); $19 per credit hour (nonresident). Fees vary by number of credits taken. Average 1997–98 room and board costs were $4395 per academic year (on campus) and $5000 per academic year (off campus). Room and board costs vary by occupancy (e.g., single, double, triple), type of meal plan.

Financial Aid Fellowships, research assistantships, teaching assistantships, scholarships, work study, loans available. Financial aid is available to part-time students. Application Deadline: 3/1.

Financial Aid Contact Mr. Patrick McTee, Director of Financial Aid, 5100 Rockhill Road, Kansas City, MO 64110-2499. Phone: 816-235-1154; Fax: 816-235-5511.

FACILITIES

Information Resources Miller Nichols Library plus 3 additional on-campus libraries; total holdings of 942,116 volumes, 1,773,026 microforms, 8,764 current periodical subscriptions. CD player(s) available for graduate student use. Access provided to online bibliographic retrieval services.

INTERNATIONAL STUDENTS

Demographics 18% of students enrolled are international students [Asia, 94%, Europe, 3%, North America, 3%].

Services and Facilities International student office, international student center, visa services, ESL courses, counseling/support services.

Applying TOEFL: minimum score of 550, proof of adequate funds, proof of health/immunizations required. Financial aid is available to international students.

International Student Contact Mr. Thomas Burns, Director of International Student Affairs Office, 5100 Rockhill Road, Kansas City, MO 64110-2499. Phone: 816-235-1017; Fax: 816-235-1717; E-mail: tburns@cctr.umkc.edu

PLACEMENT

Services include career counseling/planning, career fairs, career library, career placement, electronic job bank, job interviews arranged, job search course, resume referral to employers, and resume preparation. In 1996–97, 170 organizations participated in on-campus recruiting; 275 on-campus interviews were conducted.

Employment Of 1996–97 graduates, 90% were employed within three months of graduation; the average starting salary was $35,000. Types of employment entered: accounting, banking, communications, computer-related, consulting, education, finance, financial services, government, health services, human resources, information systems/technology, international trade, management, manufacturing, marketing, media, nonprofit, retail, service industry, telecommunications, transportation, utilities.

Business Program(s) URL: http://www.umkc.edu/

Program Contact: Ms. Kathleen Wolfe, 5100 Rockhill Road, Kansas City, MO 64110-2499. Phone: 816-235-2215; Fax: 816-235-2312; E-mail: kwolfe@cctr.umkc.edu

University of Missouri-St. Louis

School of Business Administration

St. Louis, Missouri

OVERVIEW

The University of Missouri-St. Louis is a state-supported, coed university. Enrollment: 11,858 graduate, professional, and undergraduate students; 354 full-time matriculated graduate/professional students; 2,044 part-time matriculated graduate/professional students. Founded: 1963. The graduate business unit is in a suburban setting and is on a semester calendar.

HIGHLIGHTS

Enrollment Profile

Full-time: 63	International: 10%
Part-time: 273	Women: 40%
Total: 336	Minorities: 5%
Average Age: 27	Average Class Size: 18
Fall 1997 Average GPA: 3.2	Fall 1997 Average GMAT: 559

Costs

Full-time tuition: $4740 per academic year (resident); $13,830 per academic year (nonresident)

Part-time tuition: $158 per credit hour (resident); $461 per credit hour (nonresident)

AACSB – The International Association for Management Education accredited

T he M.B.A. program at the University of Missouri (UM)–St. Louis is designed to educate a well-rounded business professional rather than a narrowly trained specialist. The underlying philosophy of all of the graduate business programs at UM–St. Louis is to combine high-quality students with an active and well-trained faculty in a rigorous course of study. The result is a challenging educational program with demanding instruction in state-of-the-art research-based management education. UM–St. Louis has a truly excellent and diverse business school faculty that understands and accepts the importance of blending research with teaching and theory with practice.

In the traditional program, full-time students can complete the 39- to 54-hour M.B.A. degree in eighteen months to two years. Part-time students generally take two to five years to complete the program. Students who earned their undergraduate degree in a nonbusiness discipline will have a degree program length approaching the 54-hour maximum. Students with a recent business degree from a school accredited by AACSB–The International Association for Management Education are likely to have a 39-hour program.

A new Professional MBA On-Line offers part-time students the opportunity to complete an M.B.A. in twenty-three months by attending classes one weekend per month. The remainder of each course is completed over the Internet.

GRADUATE BUSINESS PROGRAMS

Master of Business Administration (MBA) Full-time, part-time; 39-54 total credits required; 18 months to 6 years to complete program. Concentrations in accounting, finance, human resources, management information systems, management science, marketing.

Master of Science in Management Information Systems (MS) Full-time, part-time; 30-60 total credits required; 18 months to 6 years to complete program. Concentration in management information systems.

Master of Accounting (MAcc) Full-time, part-time; 30-69 total credits required; 18 months to 6 years to complete program. Concentrations in accounting, taxation.

Professional MBA On-Line (MBA) Part-time, distance learning option; 48 total credits required; 23 months to complete program.

ADMISSION

Applications For fall 1997 there were 221 applications for admission. Of those applying, 136 were accepted. Of those accepted, 79 enrolled.

Application Requirements GMAT score: minimum 500, application form, bachelor's degree, minimum GPA: 3.0, 2 letters of recommendation, personal statement, college transcript(s).

Recommended for Application Essay, interview, resume, work experience, computer experience.

Application Deadline Applications processed on a rolling/continuous basis for domestic students only. 5/1 for fall (international), 10/1 for winter (international), 3/1 for summer (international). Application fee: $25, $40 (international). Deferred entrance is available.

ACADEMICS

Faculty Full-time 33; part-time 4.

Teaching Methodologies Case study, computer-aided instruction, computer analysis, computer simulations, faculty seminars, field projects, group discussion, lecture, research, role playing, seminars by members of the business community, simulations, student presentations, study groups, team projects.

Technology 306 on-campus computer terminals/PCs are available for student use and are linked by a campus-wide network. The network has full access to the Internet. Students are not required to have their own PC.

Special Opportunities Advanced credit may be earned through credit by examination, transfer of credits from another institution. International exchange programs in France, Germany, Spain.

FINANCES

Costs for 1997–98 Tuition: Full-time: $4740 per year (resident); $13,830 per year (nonresident). Part-time: $158 per credit hour (resident); $461 per credit hour (nonresident). Cost varies by academic program. Fees: Full-time: $660 per academic year (resident); $660 per academic year (nonresident). Part-time: $22 per credit hour (resident); $22 per credit hour (nonresident). Fees vary by academic program. Average 1997–98 room and board costs were $5500 per academic year. Room and board costs vary by occupancy (e.g., single, double, triple), type of accommodation.

Financial Aid Research assistantships available. Financial aid is available to part-time students. Application Deadline: 4/1.

Financial Aid Contact Mr. Anthony Georges, Director, Financial Aid, 8001 Natural Bridge Road, St. Louis, MO 63121-4499. Phone: 314-516-5526; Fax: 314-516-5310; E-mail: sfinaid@umslvma.umsl.edu

FACILITIES

Information Resources Thomas Jefferson Library plus 2 additional on-campus libraries; total holdings of 625,000 volumes, 1,500,000 microforms, 3,000 current periodical subscriptions. CD player(s) available for graduate student use. Access provided to online bibliographic retrieval services and online databases.

INTERNATIONAL STUDENTS

Demographics 10% of students enrolled are international students [Africa, 1%, Asia, 80%, Europe, 19%].

Services and Facilities International student office, international student center, international student housing, visa services, ESL courses, counseling/support services.

Applying TOEFL: minimum score of 550, proof of adequate funds, proof of health/immunizations required. Financial aid is not available to international students.

International Student Contact Mr. Leonard Trudo, International Admissions Officer, Office of International Student Services, 8001 Natural Bridge Road, St. Louis, MO 63121-4499. Phone: 314-516-5229; Fax: 314-516-5636; E-mail: intelstu@umslvma.umsl.edu

PLACEMENT

Services include career counseling/planning, career fairs, career library, career placement, job interviews arranged, resume referral to employers, and resume preparation. In 1996–97, 37 organizations participated in on-campus recruiting.

Employment Of 1996–97 graduates, 93% were employed within three months of graduation; the average starting salary was $37,000. Types of employment entered: accounting, banking, computer-related, consulting, consumer products, finance, financial services, information systems/technology, insurance, management, manufacturing, marketing, nonprofit, pharmaceutical, retail, service industry.

Business Program(s) URL: http://www.umsl.edu/business/busgrad/sobagrad.htm

Program Contact: Director, Graduate Programs in Business, 8001 Natural Bridge Road, St. Louis, MO 63121-4499. Phone: 314-516-5885; Fax: 314-516-6420; E-mail: mba@umsl.edu

Washington University in St. Louis

John M. Olin School of Business

St. Louis, Missouri

OVERVIEW

Washington University in St. Louis is an independent-nonprofit, coed university. Enrollment: 11,606 graduate, professional, and undergraduate students; 4,294 full-time matriculated graduate/professional students; 1,231 part-time matriculated graduate/professional students. Founded: 1853. The graduate business unit is in a suburban setting and is on a mini-semester calendar.

HIGHLIGHTS

Enrollment Profile

Full-time: 296	International: N/R
Part-time: 345	Women: 27%
Total: 641	Minorities: 8%
Average Age: 27	Average Class Size: 35
Fall 1997 Average GPA: 3.2	Fall 1997 Average GMAT: 606

Costs
Full-time tuition: $23,800 per academic year
Part-time tuition: $670 per credit hour

AACSB – The International Association for Management Education accredited

GRADUATE BUSINESS PROGRAMS

Full-time MBA (MBA) Full-time; 60 total credits required; 18 to 21 months to complete program. Concentrations in accounting, finance, international business, management, marketing, operations management, organizational behavior/development, strategic management.

Professional MBA (MBA) Part-time; 54 total credits required; 3 to 5 years to complete program. Concentrations in accounting, finance, international business, management, marketing, operations management, organizational behavior/development, strategic management.

Executive MBA (MBA) Part-time; 60 total credits required; 21 months to complete program.

Executive Master of Manufacturing Management (EMMM) Part-time; 60 total credits required; 2 years to complete program.

Executive MBA in Health Services (MBA) Part-time; 60 total credits required; 21 months to complete program.

ADMISSION

Applications For fall 1997 there were 1,165 applications for admission. Of those applying, 459 were accepted. Of those accepted, 229 enrolled.

Application Requirements GMAT score, application form, application fee, bachelor's degree, essay, minimum GPA, 2 letters of recommendation, personal statement, resume, college transcript(s).

Recommended for Application Interview, work experience, computer experience.

Application Deadline 3/30 for fall, 3/30 for fall (international). Application fee: $80. Deferred entrance is available.

ACADEMICS

Faculty Full-time 69; part-time 27.

Teaching Methodologies Case study, computer-aided instruction, computer analysis, computer simulations, experiential learning, field projects, group discussion, lecture, research, role playing, seminars by members of the business community, simulations, student presentations, study groups, team projects.

Technology 65 on-campus computer terminals/PCs are available for student use and are linked by a campus-wide network. The network has full access to the Internet. Students are not required to have their own PC.

Special Opportunities Advanced credit may be earned through credit by examination, transfer of credits from another institution. International exchange programs in France, Germany, United Kingdom, Venezuela. An internship program is available.

FINANCES

Costs for 1997–98 Tuition: Full-time: $23,800 per year. Part-time: $670 per credit hour. Cost varies by academic program, class time (e.g., day/evening), number of credits taken. Fees vary by academic program, class time (e.g., day/evening), number of credits taken. Average 1997–98 room only costs were $5355 per academic year (off campus). Room and board costs vary by type of accommodation.

Financial Aid In 1997–98, 63% of students received some institutionally administered aid in the form of fellowships, research assistantships, teaching assistantships, grants, scholarships, work study. Financial aid is available to part-time students. Application Deadline: 3/31.

Washington University in St. Louis (continued)

Financial Aid Contact Ms. Konnie Henning, Assistant Director of Financial Aid, 1 Brookings Drive, Campus Box 1133, St. Louis, MO 63130-4899. Phone: 314-935-7301; Fax: 314-935-6309; E-mail: mba@olin.wustl.edu

FACILITIES
Information Resources John M. Olin Library plus 12 additional on-campus libraries; total holdings of 3,164,136 volumes, 2,809,952 microforms, 18,601 current periodical subscriptions. CD player(s) available for graduate student use. Access provided to online bibliographic retrieval services.

INTERNATIONAL STUDENTS
Demographics N/R

Services and Facilities International student office, international student center, international student housing, visa services, ESL courses, counseling/support services.

Applying TOEFL, proof of adequate funds, proof of health/immunizations required. Financial aid is available to international students.

International Student Contact Ms. Kathy Steiner-Lang, Director, International Office, Campus Box 1083, One Brookings Drive, St. Louis, MO 63130-4899. Phone: 314-935-5910; Fax: 314-935-4075; E-mail: stix@artsci.wustl.edu

PLACEMENT
Services include alumni network, career counseling/planning, career fairs, career library, career placement, electronic job bank, job interviews arranged, job search course, resume referral to employers, and resume preparation. In 1996–97, 125 organizations participated in on-campus recruiting; 1,088 on-campus interviews were conducted.

Employment Of 1996–97 graduates, 88% were employed within three months of graduation; the average starting salary was $59,200. Types of employment entered: accounting, banking, chemical industry, communications, computer-related, consulting, consumer products, energy, finance, financial services, health services, high technology, human resources, information systems/technology, insurance, international trade, management, manufacturing, marketing, nonprofit, petrochemical, pharmaceutical, real estate, retail, service industry, telecommunications, transportation.

Business Program(s) URL: http://www.olin.wustl.edu

Program Contact: Ms. Deborah Booker, Director of MBA Admissions, 1 Brookings Drive, Campus Box 1133, St. Louis, MO 63130-4899. Phone: 314-935-7301; Fax: 314-935-4464; E-mail: mba@olin.wustl.edu

Webster University

School of Business and Technology

St. Louis, Missouri

OVERVIEW
Webster University is an independent-nonprofit, coed, comprehensive institution. Enrollment: 11,756 graduate, professional, and undergraduate students. Founded: 1915. The graduate business unit is in a suburban setting and is on a term calendar.

HIGHLIGHTS

Enrollment Profile
Full-time: 5,860
Part-time: 2,906
Total: 8,766
Average Age: 35
Fall 1997 Average GPA: N/R

International: 4%
Women: 44%
Minorities: 30%
Average Class Size: 25
Fall 1997 Average GMAT: N/R

Costs
Full-time tuition: N/R
Part-time tuition: $332 per semester hour

GRADUATE BUSINESS PROGRAMS
Master of Business Administration (MBA) Full-time, part-time; 3 to 4 years to complete program.

Bachelor/Master of Science in Accounting (BS/MS) Full-time, part-time; 152 total credits required. Concentration in accounting.

Master of Science in Computer Science/Distributed Systems (MS) Full-time, part-time; 36 total credits required.

Doctor of Management (DMgt) Full-time, part-time; 42 total credits required. Concentration in management.

Master of Arts in Marketing Management/Master of Business Administration (MA/MBA) Full-time, part-time; 36-57 total credits required. Concentration in marketing.

Master of Arts in Procurement and Acquisitions/Master of Business Administration (MA/MBA) Full-time, part-time; 36-48 total credits required.

Master of Arts in Public Administration (MA) Full-time, part-time; 36 total credits required. Concentration in public policy and administration.

Master of Arts in Real Estate/Master of Business Administration (MA/MBA) Full-time, part-time; 36-48 total credits required. Concentration in real estate.

Master of Arts in Security Management/Master of Business Administration (MA/MBA) Full-time, part-time; 36-51 total credits required.

Master of Arts in Health Services Management/Master of Business Administration (MA/MBA) Full-time, part-time; 39-51 total credits required. Concentration in health care.

Master of Arts in Human Resources Development/Master of Business Administration (MA/MBA) Full-time, part-time; 36-48 total credits required. Concentration in human resources.

Master of Arts in Human Resources Management (MA) Full-time, part-time; 36 total credits required. Concentration in human resources.

Master of Arts in International Business/Master of Business Administration (MA/MBA) Full-time, part-time; 36-48 total credits required. Concentration in international business.

Master of Arts in Management/Master of Business Administration (MA/MBA) Full-time, part-time; 36-48 total credits required. Concentration in management.

Master of Arts in Computer Resources and Information Management/Master of Business Administration (MA/MBA) Full-time, part-time; 36-48 total credits required.

Master of Arts in Telecommunication/Master of Business Administration (MA/MBA) Full-time, part-time; 36-48 total credits required. Concentration in telecommunications management.

Master of Arts in Finance/Master of Business Administration (MA/MBA) Full-time, part-time; 36-48 total credits required. Concentration in finance.

Master of Arts in Health Care Management/Master of Business Administration (MA/MBA) Full-time, part-time; 36-48 total credits required. Concentration in health care.

Master of Arts in Space Systems Management/Master of Business Administration (MA/MBA) Full-time, part-time; 36-48 total credits required.

Master of Arts in Business (MA) Full-time, part-time; 36 total credits required.

ADMISSION
Applications For fall 1997 there were 2,883 applications for admission. Of those applying, 2,698 were accepted. Of those accepted, 2,363 enrolled.

Application Requirements Application form, application fee, bachelor's degree, interview, college transcript(s).

Application Deadline Applications processed on a rolling/continuous basis for both domestic and international students. Application fee: $25, $50 (international). Deferred entrance is available.

ACADEMICS
Faculty Full-time 14; part-time 96.

Teaching Methodologies Case study, computer-aided instruction, computer analysis, computer simulations, experiential learning, faculty seminars, field projects, group discussion, lecture, research, role playing, seminars by members of the business community, simulations, student presentations, study groups, team projects, collaborative teaching and learning project.

Technology 175 on-campus computer terminals/PCs are available for student use and are linked by a campus-wide network. The network has full access to the Internet. Students are not required to have their own PC.

Special Opportunities Advanced credit may be earned through credit for military training programs, credit for business training programs, transfer of credits from another institution. International exchange programs in Austria, Bermuda, Netherlands, People's Republic of China, Switzerland, United Kingdom. An internship program is available.

FINANCES
Costs for 1997–98 Tuition: $332 per semester hour. Cost varies by campus location. Fees: $50 per program. Average 1997–98 room and board costs were $5030 per academic year. Room and board costs vary by occupancy (e.g., single, double, triple), type of accommodation, type of meal plan.

Financial Aid Research assistantships, teaching assistantships, scholarships, work study, loans available. Financial aid is available to part-time students.

Financial Aid Contact Mr. Jonathan Gruett, Director, Kirk House, 211 Edgar Road, Webster Groves, MO 63119-3194. Phone: 314-968-6903; Fax: 314-968-7125; E-mail: gruettjo@webster.edu

FACILITIES
Information Resources Eden-Webster Library; total holdings of 240,774 volumes, 134,251 microforms, 1,300 current periodical subscriptions. CD player(s) available for graduate student use. Access provided to online bibliographic retrieval services and online databases.

INTERNATIONAL STUDENTS
Demographics 4% of students enrolled are international students.

Services and Facilities International student office, international student center, visa services, ESL courses, international student orientation, international student advisor.

Applying TOEFL, proof of adequate funds, proof of health/immunizations required. TSE, TWE recommended. Financial aid is available to international students.

International Student Contact Mr. Charlie Beech, Assistant Vice President, International Enrollment Center, 538 Garden, West, Webster Groves, MO 63119-3194. Phone: 314-961-2660 Ext. 7609; Fax: 314-968-7119; E-mail: beechce@websteruniv.edu

PLACEMENT

Services include alumni network, career counseling/planning, career fairs, career library, career placement, electronic job bank, job interviews arranged, resume referral to employers, and resume preparation. In 1996–97, 27 organizations participated in on-campus recruiting.

Employment Of 1996–97 graduates, 95% were employed within three months of graduation; the average starting salary was $55,000. Types of employment entered: accounting, banking, chemical industry, communications, computer-related, consulting, consumer products, education, energy, engineering, finance, financial services, government, health services, high technology, hospitality management, human resources, information systems/technology, insurance, international trade, law, management, manufacturing, marketing, media, nonprofit, petrochemical, pharmaceutical, real estate, retail, service industry, telecommunications, transportation, utilities.

Business Program(s) URL: http://www.webster.edu

Program Contact: Marcella Dill, Director, Enrollment Services Center, 107 Sverdrup, 8300 Big Bend Boulevard, Webster Groves, MO 63119-3194. Phone: 314-968-7473, 800-981-9801; Fax: 314-968-7166; E-mail: dillma@ websteruniv.edu

William Woods University

Graduate and Adult Studies

Fulton, Missouri

OVERVIEW

William Woods University is an independent-religious, coed, comprehensive institution. Enrollment: 950 graduate, professional, and undergraduate students; 500 full-time matriculated graduate/professional students; 50 part-time matriculated graduate/professional students. Founded: 1870. The graduate business unit is in a small-town setting and is on a year-round calendar.

HIGHLIGHTS

Enrollment Profile

Full-time: 330	International: 12%
Part-time: 0	Women: 45%
Total: 330	Minorities: 21%
Average Age: 29	Average Class Size: 22
Fall 1997 Average GPA: 2.97	Fall 1997 Average GMAT: N/R

Costs
Full-time tuition: $9180 per academic year
Part-time tuition: N/R

GRADUATE BUSINESS PROGRAMS
Master of Business Administration (MBA) Full-time; 36 total credits required; 18 months to complete program. Concentration in management.

ADMISSION
Applications For fall 1997 there were 450 applications for admission. Of those applying, 385 were accepted. Of those accepted, 330 enrolled.

Application Requirements Application form, application fee, bachelor's degree, essay, minimum GPA: 2.5, 2 letters of recommendation, college transcript(s), minimum of 2 years of work experience.

Application Deadline Applications processed on a rolling/continuous basis for both domestic and international students. Application fee: $25. Deferred entrance is available.

ACADEMICS
Faculty Full-time 20; part-time 150.

Teaching Methodologies Case study, computer-aided instruction, group discussion, lecture, research, student presentations, study groups, team projects.

Technology 24 on-campus computer terminals/PCs are available for student use and are linked by a campus-wide network. The network has partial access to the Internet. Students are not required to have their own PC.

Special Opportunities Advanced credit may be earned through transfer of credits from another institution.

FINANCES
Costs for 1997–98 Tuition: Full-time: $9180 per year. Fees: Full-time: $90 per academic year.

Financial Aid Contact Ms. Laura Archuleta, Director of Financial Aid, 200 West 12th Street, Fulton, MO 65251. Phone: 573-592-4232; Fax: 573-592-1164.

FACILITIES
Information Resources William H. Dulany Library plus 1 additional on-campus library; total holdings of 77,853 volumes, 900 microforms, 422 current periodical subscriptions. CD player(s) available for graduate student use. Access provided to online bibliographic retrieval services.

INTERNATIONAL STUDENTS
Demographics 12% of students enrolled are international students [Asia, 92%, other, 8%].

Services and Facilities International student office, international student housing, ESL courses.

Applying TOEFL: minimum score of 550, proof of adequate funds required. Financial aid is not available to international students.

International Student Contact Ms. Stephanie Thomas, Director of Academic Affairs, 200 West 12th Street, Fulton, MO 65251. Phone: 573-592-1149; Fax: 573-592-1164.

PLACEMENT
Services include alumni network, career counseling/planning, career fairs, resume referral to employers, and resume preparation.

Employment Of 1996–97 graduates, 100% were employed within three months of graduation. Types of employment entered: accounting, banking, chemical industry, communications, computer-related, consulting, consumer products, energy, engineering, finance, financial services, government, health services, human resources, information systems/technology, insurance, management, manufacturing, marketing, media, nonprofit, petrochemical, pharmaceutical, real estate, retail, service industry, telecommunications, utilities.

Program Contact: Ms. Julie Howar, Recruitment Representative, 200 West 12th Street, Fulton, MO 65251. Phone: 800-995-3199, 800-995-3199; Fax: 573-592-1164.

MONTANA

Montana State University-Bozeman

College of Business

Bozeman, Montana

OVERVIEW
Montana State University-Bozeman is a state-supported, coed university. Enrollment: 11,662 graduate, professional, and undergraduate students; 452 full-time matriculated graduate/professional students; 450 part-time matriculated graduate/professional students. Founded: 1893. The graduate business unit is in a small-town setting and is on a semester calendar.

HIGHLIGHTS

Enrollment Profile

Full-time: 14	International: 0%
Part-time: 7	Women: 67%
Total: 21	Minorities: 10%
Average Age: 34	Average Class Size: N/R
Fall 1997 Average GPA: 3.3	Fall 1997 Average GMAT: 501

Costs
Full-time tuition: $2677 per academic year (resident); $7776 per academic year (nonresident)
Part-time tuition: $89 per credit (resident); $259 per credit (nonresident)

AACSB – The International Association for Management Education accredited

GRADUATE BUSINESS PROGRAMS
Master of Professional Accountancy (MPA) Full-time, part-time; 30 total credits required; 12 months to 4 years to complete program. Concentration in accounting.

ADMISSION
Application Requirements Application form, application fee, bachelor's degree, minimum GPA: 3.0, 3 letters of recommendation, personal statement, college transcript(s).

Montana State University-Bozeman (continued)

Recommended for Application GMAT score accepted: minimum 500, GRE score accepted: minimum 850.

Application Deadline 6/1 for fall, 11/1 for spring, 3/1 for summer, 5/1 for fall (international), 10/1 for spring (international), 2/1 for summer (international). Application fee: $50. Deferred entrance is available.

ACADEMICS
Faculty Full-time 24; part-time 6.

Teaching Methodologies Case study, computer-aided instruction, computer analysis, computer simulations, lecture, research, seminars by members of the business community, student presentations, team projects.

Technology 750 on-campus computer terminals/PCs are available for student use and are linked by a campus-wide network. The network has full access to the Internet. Students are not required to have their own PC.

Special Opportunities Advanced credit may be earned through transfer of credits from another institution. An internship program is available.

FINANCES
Costs for 1997–98 Tuition: Full-time: $2677 per year (resident); $7776 per year (nonresident). Part-time: $89 per credit (resident); $259 per credit (nonresident). Cost varies by number of credits taken, reciprocity agreements. Fees: Full-time: $311 per academic year (resident); $311 per academic year (nonresident). Part-time: $40 per credit (resident); $45 per credit (nonresident). Fees vary by number of credits taken. Average 1997–98 room and board costs were $4025 per academic year. Room and board costs vary by occupancy (e.g., single, double, triple), type of accommodation, type of meal plan.

Financial Aid In 1997–98, 24% of students received some institutionally administered aid in the form of fellowships, teaching assistantships, scholarships. Application Deadline: 3/1.

Financial Aid Contact Financial Aid Services, Strand Union Building 135, PO Box 174160, Bozeman, MT 59717-4160. Phone: 406-994-2845; Fax: 406-994-6206.

FACILITIES
Information Resources Renne Library plus 1 additional on-campus library; total holdings of 585,571 volumes, 1,403,413 microforms, 3,700 current periodical subscriptions. CD player(s) available for graduate student use. Access provided to online bibliographic retrieval services and online databases.

INTERNATIONAL STUDENTS
Demographics N/R

Services and Facilities International student office, international student center, international student housing, visa services, ESL courses, counseling/support services, job finding service, financial services assistance.

Applying TOEFL: minimum score of 550, TSE: minimum score of 50, proof of adequate funds, proof of health/immunizations required. Financial aid is not available to international students.

International Student Contact Office of International Programs, 400 Culbertson Hall, PO Box 170226, Bozeman, MT 59717-0226. Phone: 406-994-4031; Fax: 406-994-6206.

PLACEMENT
Services include career counseling/planning, career fairs, career library, career placement, electronic job bank, job interviews arranged, resume referral to employers, and resume preparation. In 1996–97, 17 organizations participated in on-campus recruiting.

Employment Of 1996–97 graduates, the average starting salary was $29,075. Types of employment entered: accounting, banking, computer-related, education, engineering, finance, government, health services, management, marketing, media, nonprofit, retail.

Business Program(s) URL: http://www.montana.edu/cob/

Program Contact: Office of Student Services, College of Business, 338 Reid Hall, PO Box 173040, Bozeman, MT 59717-3040. Phone: 406-994-4681; Fax: 406-994-6206; E-mail: busgrad@montana.edu

The University of Montana-Missoula

School of Business Administration

Missoula, Montana

OVERVIEW
The University of Montana-Missoula is a state-supported, coed university. Enrollment: 12,124 graduate, professional, and undergraduate students; 913 full-time matriculated graduate/professional students; 388 part-time matriculated graduate/professional students. Founded: 1893. The graduate business unit is in a small-town setting and is on a semester calendar.

HIGHLIGHTS

Enrollment Profile

Full-time: 37	International: 5%
Part-time: 94	Women: 50%
Total: 131	Minorities: 5%
Average Age: 30	Average Class Size: 18
Fall 1997 Average GPA: 3.2	Fall 1997 Average GMAT: 590

Costs
Full-time tuition: $1568 per academic year (resident); $4254 per academic year (nonresident)
Part-time tuition: $150 per credit (resident); $370 per credit (nonresident)

AACSB – The International Association for Management Education accredited

GRADUATE BUSINESS PROGRAMS
Master of Business Administration (MBA) Full-time, part-time; 30 total credits required; 9 months to 5 years to complete program. Concentration in management.

Master of Accountancy (MAcc) Full-time, part-time; 30 total credits required; 12 months to 5 years to complete program. Concentration in accounting.

Off-campus MBA (MBA) Part-time, distance learning option; 30 total credits required; 2 to 5 years to complete program. Concentration in management.

ADMISSION
Applications For fall 1997 there were 133 applications for admission. Of those applying, 116 were accepted. Of those accepted, 107 enrolled.

Application Requirements GMAT score, application form, application fee, bachelor's degree, minimum GPA: 2.75, 3 letters of recommendation, college transcript(s), computer experience: word processing, spreadsheet.

Recommended for Application Resume.

Application Deadline 3/1 for fall, 9/1 for spring, 3/1 for summer, 3/1 for fall (international), 9/1 for spring (international), 3/1 for summer (international). Application fee: $30. Deferred entrance is available.

ACADEMICS
Faculty Full-time 31; part-time 6.

Teaching Methodologies Case study, computer-aided instruction, computer simulations, experiential learning, faculty seminars, group discussion, lecture, research, role playing, seminars by members of the business community, student presentations, study groups, team projects.

Technology 420 on-campus computer terminals/PCs are available for student use and are linked by a campus-wide network. The network has full access to the Internet. Students are not required to have their own PC.

Special Opportunities Advanced credit may be earned through transfer of credits from another institution. International exchange programs in Australia, Austria, Belize, Brazil, France, Germany, Italy, Mexico, New Zealand, Spain, United Kingdom. An internship program is available.

FINANCES
Costs for 1997–98 Tuition: Full-time: $1568 per semester (resident); $4254 per semester (nonresident). Part-time: $150 per credit (resident); $370 per credit (nonresident). Cost varies by class time (e.g., day/evening), number of credits taken. Fees: Full-time: $250 per academic year (resident); $250 per academic year (nonresident). Fees vary by class time (e.g., day/evening). Average 1997–98 room and board costs were $5050 per academic year. Room and board costs vary by campus location, occupancy (e.g., single, double, triple), type of accommodation, type of meal plan.

Financial Aid Fellowships, research assistantships, teaching assistantships, scholarships, work study, loans available. Application Deadline: 3/1.

Financial Aid Contact Mr. Myron Hanson, Director, Financial Aid Office, Financial Aid Office, Missoula, MT 59812. Phone: 406-243-5373; Fax: 406-243-4930; E-mail: hanson@selway.umt.edu

FACILITIES
Information Resources Maureen and Mike Mansfield Library; total holdings of 800,000 volumes, 100,000 microforms. CD player(s) available for graduate student use.

INTERNATIONAL STUDENTS
Demographics 5% of students enrolled are international students.

Services and Facilities International student office, international student center, ESL courses, counseling/support services.

Applying TOEFL: minimum score of 580, proof of adequate funds, proof of health/immunizations required. Financial aid is available to international students.

International Student Contact Ms. Eftychia Koehn, Director, Foreign Student Office, Foreign Student Office, Missoula, MT 59812-0002. Phone: 406-243-2226; Fax: 406-243-6115; E-mail: ekoehn@selway.umt.edu

PLACEMENT

Services include alumni network, career counseling/planning, career fairs, career library, career placement, job interviews arranged, and resume preparation.

Employment Of 1996–97 graduates, 78% were employed within three months of graduation; the average starting salary was $30,107. Types of employment entered: accounting.

Business Program(s) URL: http://www.business.umt.edu

Program Contact: Ms. Kathleen Spritzer, Administrative Assistant, School of Business Administration, Missoula, MT 59812-1216. Phone: 406-243-4983; Fax: 406-243-2086; E-mail: spritzer@selway.umt.edu

NEBRASKA

Bellevue University

College of Business

Bellevue, Nebraska

OVERVIEW

Bellevue University is an independent-nonprofit, coed, comprehensive institution. Enrollment: 2,600 graduate, professional, and undergraduate students; 357 full-time matriculated graduate/professional students; 153 part-time matriculated graduate/professional students. Founded: 1965. The graduate business unit is in a small-town setting and is on a semester calendar.

HIGHLIGHTS

Enrollment Profile

Full-time: 357
Part-time: 153
Total: 510
Average Age: 35
Fall 1997 Average GPA: N/R

International: 15%
Women: 40%
Minorities: 31%
Average Class Size: 35
Fall 1997 Average GMAT: N/R

Costs

Full-time tuition: N/R
Part-time tuition: $250 per credit

GRADUATE BUSINESS PROGRAMS

Master of Business Administration (MBA) Full-time, part-time, distance learning option; 36 total credits required; 16 months to 2.7 years to complete program. Concentrations in accounting, international business, management information systems.

ADMISSION

Applications For fall 1997 there were 110 applications for admission. Of those applying, 110 were accepted. Of those accepted, 100 enrolled.

Application Requirements Application form, application fee, bachelor's degree, essay, 2 letters of recommendation, personal statement, college transcript(s).

Recommended for Application GMAT score accepted, GRE score accepted, MAT score accepted, minimum of 3 years of work experience.

Application Deadline Applications processed on a rolling/continuous basis for both domestic and international students. Application fee: $50. Deferred entrance is available.

ACADEMICS

Faculty Full-time 10; part-time 16.

Teaching Methodologies Case study, computer-aided instruction, computer analysis, computer simulations, experiential learning, faculty seminars, field projects, group discussion, lecture, research, simulations, student presentations, study groups, team projects.

Technology 30 on-campus computer terminals/PCs are available for student use and are linked by a campus-wide network. The network has full access to the Internet. Students are not required to have their own PC.

Special Opportunities Advanced credit may be earned through transfer of credits from another institution. An internship program is available.

FINANCES

Costs for 1997–98 Tuition: $250 per credit. Fees: $25 per term.

Financial Aid Contact Mr. Jon Dotterer, 1000 Galvin Road South, Bellevue, NE 68005. Phone: 402-293-3763; Fax: 402-293-3730.

FACILITIES

Information Resources Freeman/Lozier Library; total holdings of 113,000 volumes, 7,144 microforms, 1,090 current periodical subscriptions. CD player(s) available for graduate student use. Access provided to online bibliographic retrieval services.

INTERNATIONAL STUDENTS

Demographics 15% of students enrolled are international students [Asia, 100%].

Services and Facilities International student office, international student housing, visa services, ESL courses, counseling/support services.

Applying TOEFL, proof of adequate funds required. Financial aid is not available to international students.

International Student Contact Mr. Ron Psota, International Student Coordinator, 1000 Galvin Road South, Bellevue, NE 68005. Phone: 402-293-3759; Fax: 402-293-3730.

PLACEMENT

Services include alumni network, career counseling/planning, career fairs, and resume preparation. In 1996–97, 100 organizations participated in on-campus recruiting.

Employment Types of employment entered: accounting, banking, communications, computer-related, education, government, health services, information systems/technology, insurance, management, marketing, real estate, retail, telecommunications, transportation.

Business Program(s) URL: http://bruins.bellevue.edu/Trad/Grad/mba.htm

Program Contact: Ms. Elizabeth Wall, Graduate Enrollment Coordinator, 1000 Galvin Road South, Bellevue, NE 68005. Phone: 402-293-3702, 800-756-7920 (NE only); Fax: 402-293-3730.

Chadron State College

Department of Business and Economics

Chadron, Nebraska

OVERVIEW

Chadron State College is a state-supported, coed, comprehensive institution. Enrollment: 3,003 graduate, professional, and undergraduate students; 37 full-time matriculated graduate/professional students; 393 part-time matriculated graduate/professional students. Founded: 1911. The graduate business unit is in a small-town setting and is on a semester calendar.

HIGHLIGHTS

Enrollment Profile

Full-time: 5
Part-time: 8
Total: 13
Average Age: 34
Fall 1997 Average GPA: 3.272

International: 8%
Women: 31%
Minorities: 8%
Average Class Size: 8
Fall 1997 Average GMAT: N/R

Costs

Full-time tuition: $1734 per academic year (resident); $3468 per academic year (nonresident)
Part-time tuition: $72 per credit (resident); $145 per credit (nonresident)

Degree(s) offered in conjunction with University of Nebraska at Lincoln

GRADUATE BUSINESS PROGRAMS

Master of Business Administration (MBA) Full-time, part-time, distance learning option; 36 total credits required; 12 months to 7 years to complete program.

ADMISSION

Applications For fall 1997 there were 14 applications for admission. Of those applying, 6 were accepted. Of those accepted, 5 enrolled.

Application Requirements Application form, application fee, bachelor's degree, minimum GPA: 2.75, 3 letters of recommendation, personal statement, college transcript(s).

Recommended for Application GMAT score accepted: minimum 400.

Application Deadline Applications processed on a rolling/continuous basis for domestic students only. 6/1 for fall (international), 10/1 for spring (international). Application fee: $15.

ACADEMICS

Faculty Full-time 4.

Teaching Methodologies Case study, computer-aided instruction, experiential learning, field projects, group discussion, lecture, research, student presentations, team projects.

Technology 120 on-campus computer terminals/PCs are available for student use and are linked by a campus-wide network. The network has full access to the Internet. Students are not required to have their own PC.

Special Opportunities Advanced credit may be earned through transfer of credits from another institution. An internship program is available.

FINANCES

Costs for 1997–98 Tuition: Full-time: $1734 per year (resident); $3468 per year (nonresident). Part-time: $72 per credit (resident); $145 per credit (nonresident). Cost varies by number of credits taken, reciprocity agreements. Fees: Full-time: $325 per academic year (resident); $325 per academic year (nonresident). Part-time: $14 per credit (resident); $14 per credit (nonresident). Average 1997–98 room and board costs were $3438 per academic year (on campus) and $3600 per academic year (off campus). Room and board costs vary by occupancy (e.g., single, double, triple), type of accommodation, type of meal plan.

Financial Aid Research assistantships, teaching assistantships, scholarships, loans available. Financial aid is available to part-time students. Application Deadline: 6/1.

Financial Aid Contact Ms. Sherry Douglas, Director of Financial Aid, 1000 Main Street, Chadron, NE 69337. Phone: 308-432-6230; Fax: 308-432-6229; E-mail: sdouglas@csc1.csc.edu

FACILITIES
Information Resources Reta King Library; total holdings of 195,489 volumes, 312,555 microforms, 876 current periodical subscriptions. CD player(s) available for graduate student use. Access provided to online bibliographic retrieval services.

INTERNATIONAL STUDENTS
Demographics 8% of students enrolled are international students.

Services and Facilities International student office, counseling/support services.

Applying TOEFL: minimum score of 550, proof of adequate funds, proof of health/immunizations required. Financial aid is available to international students.

International Student Contact Mr. Dale Williamson, Registrar, 1000 Main Street, Chadron, NE 69337. Phone: 308-432-6221; Fax: 308-432-6229; E-mail: dwilliamson@csc1.csc.edu

PLACEMENT
Services include career counseling/planning, career fairs, career library, career placement, electronic job bank, job interviews arranged, resume referral to employers, and resume preparation.

Employment Types of employment entered: accounting, banking, education, financial services, government, hospitality management, insurance, management, marketing, retail, service industry.

Business Program(s) URL: http://www.csc.edu

Program Contact: Ms. Mary Burke, Graduate Office, 1000 Main Street, Chadron, NE 69337. Phone: 308-432-6214; Fax: 308-432-6454; E-mail: mburke@csc1.csc.edu

Creighton University

College of Business Administration
Omaha, Nebraska

OVERVIEW
Creighton University is an independent-religious, coed university. Enrollment: 6,292 graduate, professional, and undergraduate students; 2,035 full-time matriculated graduate/professional students; 375 part-time matriculated graduate/professional students. Founded: 1878. The graduate business unit is in an urban setting and is on a semester calendar.

HIGHLIGHTS

Enrollment Profile

Full-time: 31	International: 6%
Part-time: 130	Women: 38%
Total: 161	Minorities: N/R
Average Age: 28	Average Class Size: 20
Fall 1997 Average GPA: 3.1	Fall 1997 Average GMAT: 540

Costs
Full-time tuition: $7236 per academic year
Part-time tuition: $402 per credit

AACSB – The International Association for Management Education accredited

GRADUATE BUSINESS PROGRAMS
Master of Business Administration (MBA) Full-time, part-time; 33 total credits required; 12 months to 6 years to complete program. Concentration in management.

Master of Science in Information Technology Management (MS) Full-time, part-time; 33 total credits required; 12 months to 6 years to complete program. Concentrations in information management, management information systems, technology management, technology management.

Master of Business Administration/Doctor of Jurisprudence (MBA/JD) Full-time, part-time; 33 total credits required; 2 to 6 years to complete program. Concentration in management.

Information Technology Management (MBA/MS) Full-time, part-time; 48 total credits required; 2 to 6 years to complete program. Concentrations in management, information management, management information systems, technology management.

ADMISSION
Application Requirements Application form, application fee, bachelor's degree, essay, 3 letters of recommendation, college transcript(s).

Recommended for Application GMAT score accepted: minimum 450, minimum GPA: 2.5, resume, computer experience.

Application Deadline Applications processed on a rolling/continuous basis for both domestic and international students. Application fee: $40. Deferred entrance is available.

ACADEMICS
Faculty Full-time 16; part-time 1.

Teaching Methodologies Case study, computer-aided instruction, computer analysis, experiential learning, faculty seminars, group discussion, lecture, research, role playing, seminars by members of the business community, student presentations, team projects.

Technology 100 on-campus computer terminals/PCs are available for student use and are linked by a campus-wide network. The network has full access to the Internet. Students are not required to have their own PC.

Special Opportunities Advanced credit may be earned through credit for military training programs, transfer of credits from another institution. International exchange programs in India, Germany, Japan, People's Republic of China. An internship program is available.

FINANCES
Costs for 1997–98 Tuition: Full-time: $7236 per year. Part-time: $402 per credit. Fees: Full-time: $536 per academic year. Part-time: $28 per semester. Average 1997–98 room and board costs were $6182 per academic year (on campus) and $3685 per academic year (off campus). Room and board costs vary by occupancy (e.g., single, double, triple), type of accommodation, type of meal plan.

Financial Aid In 1997–98, 16% of students received some institutionally administered aid in the form of research assistantships, scholarships. Financial aid is available to part-time students. Application Deadline: 5/1.

Financial Aid Contact Mr. Robert Walker, Director, Financial Aid, 2500 California Plaza, Omaha, NE 68178. Phone: 402-280-2731; Fax: 402-280-2895; E-mail: rwalker@creighton.edu

FACILITIES
Information Resources Alumni Memorial Library plus 2 additional on-campus libraries; total holdings of 766,875 volumes, 1,396,422 microforms, 1,565 current periodical subscriptions. CD player(s) available for graduate student use. Access provided to online bibliographic retrieval services.

INTERNATIONAL STUDENTS
Demographics 6% of students enrolled are international students.

Services and Facilities International student office, visa services, ESL courses, counseling/support services.

Applying TOEFL: minimum score of 550, proof of adequate funds, proof of health/immunizations required. TSE recommended. Financial aid is available to international students.

International Student Contact Ms. Susi Rachovh, Assistant Director of International Programs, 2500 California Plaza, Omaha, NE 68178. Phone: 402-280-2592; Fax: 402-280-2172.

PLACEMENT
Services include alumni network, career counseling/planning, career fairs, career library, career placement, electronic job bank, job interviews arranged, resume referral to employers, and resume preparation. In 1996–97, 104 organizations participated in on-campus recruiting; 334 on-campus interviews were conducted.

Employment Of 1996–97 graduates, 97% were employed within three months of graduation; the average starting salary was $35,000. Types of employment entered: accounting, banking, communications, computer-related, consulting, consumer products, education, finance, financial services, government, health services, high technology, hospitality management, human resources, information systems/technology, insurance, law, management, manufacturing, marketing, media, nonprofit, pharmaceutical, retail, telecommunications, transportation, utilities.

Business Program(s) URL: http://cobweb.creighton.edu

Program Contact: Ms. Michele O'Connor, Coordinator of Graduate Business Programs, College of Business Administration, 2500 California Plaza, Omaha, NE 68178. Phone: 402-280-2853; Fax: 402-280-2172; E-mail: cobagrad@creighton.edu

University of Nebraska at Kearney

College of Business and Technology

Kearney, Nebraska

OVERVIEW
The University of Nebraska at Kearney is a state-supported, coed, comprehensive institution. Enrollment: 7,133 graduate, professional, and undergraduate students. Founded: 1903. The graduate business unit is in a small-town setting and is on a semester calendar.

HIGHLIGHTS

Enrollment Profile

Full-time: 25	International: 17%
Part-time: 75	Women: 48%
Total: 100	Minorities: 1%
Average Age: 25	Average Class Size: 18
Fall 1997 Average GPA: 3.4	Fall 1997 Average GMAT: 506

Costs
Full-time tuition: N/R
Part-time tuition: $78 per credit hour (resident); $148 per credit hour (nonresident)

GRADUATE BUSINESS PROGRAMS
Master of Business Administration (MBA) Full-time, part-time; 36 total credits required; minimum of 2 years to complete program. Concentration in accounting.

ADMISSION
Application Requirements GMAT score: minimum 400, application form, application fee, bachelor's degree, minimum GPA: 2.75, 2 letters of recommendation, personal statement, college transcript(s).

Recommended for Application Work experience, computer experience.

Application Deadline 8/1 for fall, 12/1 for spring, 4/15 for summer, 3/1 for fall (international), 6/1 for spring (international), 12/1 for summer (international). Application fee: $35.

ACADEMICS
Faculty Full-time 17.

Teaching Methodologies Case study, computer-aided instruction, computer analysis, computer simulations, experiential learning, group discussion, lecture, research, student presentations, team projects.

Technology 85 on-campus computer terminals/PCs are available for student use and are linked by a campus-wide network. The network has full access to the Internet. Students are not required to have their own PC.

Special Opportunities Advanced credit may be earned through credit by examination, transfer of credits from another institution.

FINANCES
Costs for 1997–98 Tuition: $78 per credit hour (resident); $148 per credit hour (nonresident). Fees vary by campus location, number of credits taken. Average 1997–98 room and board costs were $3180 per academic year (on campus) and $3600 per academic year (off campus). Room and board costs vary by campus location, occupancy (e.g., single, double, triple), type of accommodation, type of meal plan.

Financial Aid Research assistantships, teaching assistantships available. Financial aid is available to part-time students. Application Deadline: 3/1.

Financial Aid Contact Financial Aid Office, MSAB , Kearney, NE 68849. Phone: 308-865-8520; Fax: 308-865-8096.

FACILITIES
Information Resources Calvin T. Ryan Library; total holdings of 289,057 volumes, 992,757 microforms, 1,644 current periodical subscriptions. CD player(s) available for graduate student use. Access provided to online bibliographic retrieval services and online databases.

INTERNATIONAL STUDENTS
Demographics 17% of students enrolled are international students [Africa, 4%, Asia, 80%, Central America, 4%, Europe, 4%, North America, 4%, other, 4%].

Services and Facilities International student office, international student center, international student housing, counseling/support services.

Applying TOEFL: minimum score of 550, proof of adequate funds, proof of health/immunizations required. Financial aid is not available to international students.

International Student Contact Mr. Jerald Fox, Director, International Education, Mens Hall, Kearney, NE 68849. Phone: 308-865-8246; E-mail: fox@platte.unk.edu

PLACEMENT
Services include career counseling/planning, career fairs, career library, career placement, electronic job bank, job interviews arranged, job search course, resume referral to employers, and resume preparation.

Employment Types of employment entered: accounting, banking, chemical industry, computer-related, education, engineering, finance, financial services, government, health services, human resources, information systems/technology, management, manufacturing, marketing, nonprofit, petrochemical, transportation, utilities.

Business Program(s) URL: http://www.unk.edu

Program Contact: MBA Office, West Center E106, Kearney, NE 68849-4580. Phone: 308-865-8346; Fax: 308-865-8310; E-mail: mbaoffice@platte.unk.edu

University of Nebraska at Omaha

College of Business Administration

Omaha, Nebraska

OVERVIEW
The University of Nebraska at Omaha is a state-supported, coed university. Enrollment: 14,297 graduate, professional, and undergraduate students; 576 full-time matriculated graduate/professional students; 2,059 part-time matriculated graduate/professional students. Founded: 1908. The graduate business unit is in a suburban setting and is on a semester calendar.

HIGHLIGHTS

Enrollment Profile

Full-time: 37	International: 10%
Part-time: 249	Women: 40%
Total: 286	Minorities: 2%
Average Age: 28	Average Class Size: 28
Fall 1997 Average GPA: 3.31	Fall 1997 Average GMAT: 555

Costs
Full-time tuition: N/R
Part-time tuition: $88 per credit (resident); $212 per credit (nonresident)

AACSB – The International Association for Management Education accredited

The University of Nebraska at Omaha is a comprehensive public university located on a beautiful 88.5-acre campus in the heart of Nebraska's largest city. Faculty members have achieved national and international distinction through their writing and research.

The University of Nebraska at Omaha offers a dynamic, challenging M.B.A. program. It is designed to help students acquire the knowledge, perspective, and skills necessary for success in the marketplace. The goal of the program is to develop leaders who have the ability to incorporate change, use information technology to resolve problems, and make sound business decisions. The M.B.A. program received two prestigious Exxon Awards for innovative programming and was nationally recognized for excellence in computing resources.

The curriculum contains a unique blend of theory, experience, and application. It focuses on results, with an emphasis on how to excel in a rapidly changing world. Through a team-oriented approach and interaction with area businesses, students learn to think on their feet and recognize challenges and opportunities.

M.B.A. students must complete a minimum of 36 hours of graduate-level courses that provide a strong interdisciplinary foundation in business yet allow students to explore areas of individual interest. Elective courses are available in accounting, economics, finance, management, international business, management information systems, marketing, and quantitative analysis.

GRADUATE BUSINESS PROGRAMS
Master of Business Administration (MBA) Full-time, part-time; 36-51 total credits required; 15 months to 6 years to complete program.

ADMISSION
Applications For fall 1997 there were 82 applications for admission. Of those applying, 61 were accepted. Of those accepted, 51 enrolled.

Application Requirements Application form, application fee, bachelor's degree, minimum GPA: 2.7, resume, college transcript(s).

Recommended for Application GMAT score accepted: minimum 450, GRE score accepted: minimum 900, minimum of 2 years of work experience, computer experience.

Application Deadline 7/1 for fall, 12/1 for spring, 4/1 for summer, 7/1 for fall (international), 12/1 for spring (international), 4/1 for summer (international). Application fee: $25. Deferred entrance is available.

ACADEMICS
Faculty Full-time 57; part-time 10.

Teaching Methodologies Case study, computer-aided instruction, computer analysis, computer simulations, experiential learning, field projects, group discussion, lecture, research, simulations, student presentations, team projects.

Technology 210 on-campus computer terminals/PCs are available for student use and are linked by a campus-wide network. The network has full access to the Internet. Students are not required to have their own PC.

Special Opportunities Advanced credit may be earned through transfer of credits from another institution.

FINANCES
Costs for 1997–98 Tuition: $88 per credit (resident); $212 per credit (nonresident). Fees: $102 per semester (resident); $102 per semester (nonresident). Fees vary by number of credits taken.

Financial Aid In 1997–98, 6% of students received some institutionally administered aid in the form of research assistantships, scholarships, work study, loans. Financial aid is available to part-time students. Application Deadline: 3/1.

Financial Aid Contact Mr. Randy Sell, Director, Financial Aid, 60th and Dodge Streets, Omaha, NE 68182. Phone: 402-554-2327; Fax: 402-554-3555.

FACILITIES
Information Resources University Library; total holdings of 698,161 volumes, 1,616,590 microforms, 2,938 current periodical subscriptions. CD player(s) available for graduate student use. Access provided to online bibliographic retrieval services.

INTERNATIONAL STUDENTS
Demographics 10% of students enrolled are international students [Asia, 5%, Europe, 3%, North America, 90%, other, 2%].

Services and Facilities International student office, international student center, ESL courses, counseling/support services.

Applying TOEFL: minimum score of 550, proof of adequate funds, proof of health/immunizations required. TWE recommended. Financial aid is not available to international students.

International Student Contact Ms. Sharon Emery, International Student Advisor, 60th and Dodge Streets, Omaha, NE 68182. Phone: 402-554-2442; Fax: 402-554-3555; E-mail: sem@unomaha.edu

PLACEMENT
Services include career counseling/planning, career fairs, career placement, resume referral to employers, and resume preparation. In 1996–97, 95 organizations participated in on-campus recruiting; 407 on-campus interviews were conducted.

Business Program(s) URL: http://cbaweb.unomaha.edu

Program Contact: Ms. Lex Kaczmarek, Assistant Director, MBA Program, 60th and Dodge Streets, Omaha, NE 68182-0048. Phone: 402-554-2303, 800-858-8648 (NE only); Fax: 402-554-3747; E-mail: lkaczmar@cbafaculty.unomaha.edu

University of Nebraska-Lincoln

College of Business Administration

Lincoln, Nebraska

OVERVIEW
The University of Nebraska-Lincoln is a state-supported, coed university. Enrollment: 22,827 graduate, professional, and undergraduate students; 2,383 full-time matriculated graduate/professional students; 2,198 part-time matriculated graduate/professional students. Founded: 1869. The graduate business unit is in an urban setting and is on a semester calendar.

HIGHLIGHTS

Enrollment Profile

Full-time: 112	International: 18%
Part-time: 122	Women: 40%
Total: 234	Minorities: 4%
Average Age: 28	Average Class Size: 25
Fall 1997 Average GPA: 3.42	Fall 1997 Average GMAT: 580

Costs
Full-time tuition: $2285 per academic year (resident); $5000 per academic year (nonresident)
Part-time tuition: $104 per credit hour (resident); $256 per credit hour (nonresident)

AACSB – The International Association for Management Education accredited

The University of Nebraska–Lincoln (UNL) now offers an M.B.A. with an emphasis in agribusiness. The program is a unique combination of the expertise from the faculty of the College of Business Administration and the College of Agricultural Sciences and Natural Resources. Students complete core courses in each college, gaining knowledge in both areas of study. The UNL Agribusiness Program, which started in 1984, is one of the first of its kind in the nation and is a model in agribusiness education.

As students earn their M.B.A. in agribusiness, they develop an understanding of the global economy and build strong analytical and decision-making skills. They also learn about agribusiness opportunities, information technology, business and competitive strategies, the functional components of business administration, and international trade. Nonbusiness undergraduates with an agricultural major or undergraduates with a rural background and a nonagricultural major are good candidates for the program. Agribusiness is an extremely diverse, exciting, and rapidly changing field of employment. The program is excellent preparation for a career in agribusiness. Additional information about the program can be found at UNL's Web site at http://www.cba.unl.edu

GRADUATE BUSINESS PROGRAMS
Master of Business Administration (MBA) Full-time, part-time, distance learning option; 48 total credits required; 18 months to 6 years to complete program. Concentrations in agribusiness, finance, human resources, international business, management information systems, marketing, strategic management.

Master of Arts in Business (MA) Full-time, part-time; 36 total credits required; 12 months to 6 years to complete program. Concentrations in finance, management, marketing.

Master of Professional Accountancy (MPA) Full-time, part-time; 36 total credits required; 12 months to 6 years to complete program.

Master of Business Administration/Master of Architecture (MBA/MArch) Full-time, part-time; 72 total credits required; 3 to 5 years to complete program.

Master of Business Administration/Doctor of Jurisprudence (MBA/JD) Full-time, part-time; 100 total credits required; 4 to 6 years to complete program.

ADMISSION
Applications For fall 1997 there were 222 applications for admission. Of those applying, 83 were accepted. Of those accepted, 56 enrolled.

Application Requirements GMAT score: minimum 450, application form, application fee, bachelor's degree, minimum GPA: 2.5, 3 letters of recommendation, college transcript(s), computer experience: word processing, spreadsheet.

Recommended for Application Work experience.

Application Deadline 6/15 for fall, 11/15 for spring, 4/15 for summer, 5/15 for fall (international), 10/15 for spring (international), 3/15 for summer (international). Application fee: $25.

ACADEMICS
Faculty Full-time 48.

Teaching Methodologies Case study, computer simulations, faculty seminars, lecture, student presentations, team projects.

Technology 70 on-campus computer terminals/PCs are available for student use and are linked by a campus-wide network. The network has full access to the Internet. Students are not required to have their own PC.

Special Opportunities Advanced credit may be earned through transfer of credits from another institution. International exchange programs in France, Japan, Mexico, People's Republic of China, Turkey, United Kingdom. An internship program is available.

FINANCES
Costs for 1997–98 Tuition: Full-time: $2285 per year (resident); $5000 per year (nonresident). Part-time: $104 per credit hour (resident); $256 per credit hour (nonresident). Cost varies by campus location, number of credits taken, reciprocity agreements. Fees: Full-time: $414 per academic year (resident); $414 per academic year (nonresident). Fees vary by campus location, number of credits taken. Average 1997–98 room and board costs were $4150 per

academic year (on campus) and $4150 per academic year (off campus). Room and board costs vary by occupancy (e.g., single, double, triple), type of meal plan.

Financial Aid Fellowships, research assistantships, teaching assistantships, work study available. Financial aid is available to part-time students.

Financial Aid Contact Scholarships and Financial Aid, 16 Administration Building, Lincoln, NE 68588-0411. Phone: 402-472-2030; E-mail: scholsa@cwis.unl.edu

FACILITIES
Information Resources Love Memorial Library plus 12 additional on-campus libraries; total holdings of 2,278,154 volumes, 3,829,379 microforms, 18,387 current periodical subscriptions. CD player(s) available for graduate student use. Access provided to online bibliographic retrieval services and online databases.

INTERNATIONAL STUDENTS
Demographics 18% of students enrolled are international students [Africa, 3%, Asia, 81%, Europe, 16%].

Services and Facilities International student office, international student center, international student housing, visa services, ESL courses, counseling/support services, travel services.

Applying TOEFL: minimum score of 500, proof of adequate funds required.

International Student Contact Mr. Peter Levitov, Associate Dean of International Affairs, 14th and R Streets, Lincoln, NE 68588. Phone: 402-472-5358; E-mail: plevitov@unlinfo.unl.edu

PLACEMENT
Services include alumni network, career counseling/planning, career fairs, career library, career placement, job interviews arranged, resume referral to employers, and resume preparation. In 1996–97, 90 organizations participated in on-campus recruiting.

Employment Of 1996–97 graduates, 95% were employed within three months of graduation; the average starting salary was $45,000. Types of employment entered: accounting, banking, computer-related, consulting, financial services, health services, human resources, information systems/technology, insurance, law, management, manufacturing, marketing, pharmaceutical.

Business Program(s) URL: http://www.cba.unl.edu

Program Contact: Judith Shutts, Graduate Advisor, CBA 126, Lincoln, NE 68588-0405. Phone: 402-472-2338; Fax: 402-472-5180; E-mail: gradadv@cbamail.unl.edu

Wayne State College

Division of Business
Wayne, Nebraska

OVERVIEW
Wayne State College is a state-supported, coed, comprehensive institution. Enrollment: 3,839 graduate, professional, and undergraduate students; 51 full-time matriculated graduate/professional students; 587 part-time matriculated graduate/professional students. Founded: 1909. The graduate business unit is in a small-town setting and is on a semester calendar.

HIGHLIGHTS

Enrollment Profile
Full-time: 7
Part-time: 63
Total: 70
Average Age: 35
Fall 1997 Average GPA: 3.0

International: 3%
Women: 46%
Minorities: 7%
Average Class Size: 15
Fall 1997 Average GMAT: 500

Costs
Full-time tuition: N/R
Part-time tuition: $250 per course (resident); $460 per course (nonresident)

GRADUATE BUSINESS PROGRAMS
Master of Business Administration (MBA) Full-time, part-time, distance learning option; 36 total credits required; 18 months to 7 years to complete program.

ADMISSION
Application Requirements Application form, application fee, bachelor's degree, college transcript(s).

Recommended for Application GMAT score accepted.

Application Deadline Applications processed on a rolling/continuous basis for both domestic and international students. Application fee: $10.

ACADEMICS
Faculty Full-time 19.

Teaching Methodologies Case study, lecture, seminars by members of the business community, student presentations, team projects.

Technology 100 on-campus computer terminals/PCs are available for student use and are linked by a campus-wide network. The network has full access to the Internet. Students are not required to have their own PC.

Special Opportunities Advanced credit may be earned through transfer of credits from another institution.

FINANCES
Costs for 1997–98 Tuition: $250 per course (resident); $460 per course (nonresident). Room and board costs vary by type of accommodation, type of meal plan.

Financial Aid In 1997–98, 14% of students received some institutionally administered aid in the form of teaching assistantships. Financial aid is available to part-time students. Application Deadline: 5/1.

Financial Aid Contact Bonnie Scranton, Director of Financial Aid, 1111 Main Street, Wayne, NE 68787. Phone: 402-375-7000.

FACILITIES
Information Resources U. S. Conn Library; total holdings of 170,000 volumes, 544,000 microforms, 1,000 current periodical subscriptions. CD player(s) available for graduate student use. Access provided to online bibliographic retrieval services and online databases.

INTERNATIONAL STUDENTS
Demographics 3% of students enrolled are international students.

Services and Facilities International student office, counseling/support services.

Applying TOEFL: minimum score of 550 required.

International Student Contact Lin Brummels, Director of International Students, 1111 Main Street, Wayne, NE 68787. Phone: 402-375-7000.

PLACEMENT
Services include career counseling/planning, career fairs, career library, and career placement. In 1996–97, 40 organizations participated in on-campus recruiting.

Employment Of 1996–97 graduates, 95% were employed within three months of graduation. Types of employment entered: accounting, banking, computer-related, education, finance, government, health services, human resources, information systems/technology, management, manufacturing, marketing, utilities.

Business Program(s) URL: http://www.wsc.edu

Program Contact: MBA Office, 1111 Main Street, Wayne, NE 68787. Phone: 402-375-7245.

NEVADA

University of Nevada, Las Vegas

College of Business
Las Vegas, Nevada

OVERVIEW
The University of Nevada, Las Vegas is a state-supported, coed university. Enrollment: 20,272 graduate, professional, and undergraduate students. Founded: 1955. The graduate business unit is in an urban setting and is on a semester calendar.

HIGHLIGHTS

Enrollment Profile
Full-time: 55
Part-time: 179
Total: 234
Average Age: N/R
Fall 1997 Average GPA: 3.15

International: 3%
Women: 40%
Minorities: 23%
Average Class Size: 20
Fall 1997 Average GMAT: 555

Costs
Full-time tuition: N/R
Part-time tuition: $90 per credit (resident); $90 per credit (nonresident)

AACSB – The International Association for Management Education accredited

GRADUATE BUSINESS PROGRAMS

Master of Business Administration (MBA) Full-time, part-time; 30 total credits required; 12 months to 6 years to complete program.

Master of Science in Accountancy (MS) Full-time, part-time; 30 total credits required; 12 months to 6 years to complete program.

Master of Arts in Economics (MA) Full-time, part-time; 30 total credits required; 12 months to 6 years to complete program.

ADMISSION

Application Requirements Application form, application fee, bachelor's degree, essay, minimum GPA: 2.75, 2 letters of recommendation, personal statement, resume, college transcript(s).

Recommended for Application GMAT score accepted: minimum 475.

Application Deadline 6/1 for fall, 11/1 for spring, 5/1 for fall (international), 10/1 for spring (international). Application fee: $25.

ACADEMICS

Faculty Full-time 90.

Teaching Methodologies Case study, computer simulations, experiential learning, group discussion, lecture, research, simulations, student presentations, team projects.

Technology 200 on-campus computer terminals/PCs are available for student use and are linked by a campus-wide network. The network has full access to the Internet. Students are not required to have their own PC.

Special Opportunities Advanced credit may be earned through transfer of credits from another institution.

FINANCES

Costs for 1997–98 Tuition: $90 per credit (resident); $90 per credit (nonresident). Cost varies by number of credits taken, reciprocity agreements. Fees: $76 per credit.

Financial Aid Fellowships, research assistantships, teaching assistantships, grants, scholarships available. Application Deadline: 3/1.

Financial Aid Contact Financial Aid Office, 4505 Maryland Parkway, Las Vegas, NV 89154-6031. Phone: 702-895-3697.

FACILITIES

Information Resources James R. Dickinson Library; total holdings of 772,913 volumes, 1,325,196 microforms, 7,000 current periodical subscriptions. CD player(s) available for graduate student use. Access provided to online bibliographic retrieval services.

INTERNATIONAL STUDENTS

Demographics 3% of students enrolled are international students.

Services and Facilities International student office, visa services, ESL courses, counseling/support services, language tutoring.

Applying TOEFL: minimum score of 550, proof of adequate funds, proof of health/immunizations required. Financial aid is not available to international students.

International Student Contact MBA Office, 4505 Maryland Parkway, Las Vegas, NV 89154-6031. Phone: 702-895-3655.

PLACEMENT

Services include career counseling/planning, career fairs, career library, career placement, electronic job bank, job interviews arranged, job search course, and resume preparation.

Employment Types of employment entered: accounting, banking, communications, computer-related, energy, engineering, finance, financial services, government, health services, high technology, hospitality management, human resources, information systems/technology, insurance, marketing, media, nonprofit, pharmaceutical, real estate, retail, service industry, telecommunications, transportation, utilities.

Program Contact: MBA Office, 4505 Maryland Parkway, Las Vegas, NV 89154-6031. Phone: 702-895-3655.

See full description on page 1108.

University of Nevada, Reno

College of Business Administration

Reno, Nevada

OVERVIEW

The University of Nevada, Reno is a state-supported, coed university. Enrollment: 12,100 graduate, professional, and undergraduate students; 1,128 full-time matriculated graduate/professional students; 872 part-time matriculated graduate/professional students. Founded: 1864. The graduate business unit is in an urban setting and is on a semester calendar.

HIGHLIGHTS

Enrollment Profile

Full-time: 44	International: 12%
Part-time: 123	Women: 43%
Total: 167	Minorities: 5%
Average Age: 27	Average Class Size: 30
Fall 1997 Average GPA: 3.2	Fall 1997 Average GMAT: 500

Costs
Full-time tuition: N/R
Part-time tuition: $93 per credit hour (resident); $2750 per semester (nonresident)

AACSB – The International Association for Management Education accredited

GRADUATE BUSINESS PROGRAMS

Master of Business Administration (MBA) Full-time, part-time; 51 total credits required; 2 years work experience required; 3 to 6 years to complete program.

Master of Arts in Economics (MA) Full-time, part-time; 32 total credits required; 2 to 6 years to complete program.

Master of Science in Economics (MS) Full-time, part-time; 32 total credits required; 2 to 6 years to complete program.

ADMISSION

Application Requirements GMAT score: minimum 450, application form, application fee, bachelor's degree, minimum GPA: 2.75, 2 letters of recommendation, personal statement, resume, college transcript(s), work experience.

Recommended for Application Computer experience.

Application Deadline 2/1 for fall, 10/1 for spring, 2/1 for fall (international), 10/1 for spring (international). Application fee: $20.

ACADEMICS

Faculty Full-time 28; part-time 4.

Teaching Methodologies Case study, faculty seminars, group discussion, lecture, research, student presentations, team projects.

FINANCES

Costs for 1997–98 Tuition: $93 per credit hour (resident); $2750 per semester (nonresident).

Financial Aid In 1997–98, 7% of students received some institutionally administered aid in the form of research assistantships, teaching assistantships. Application Deadline: 2/1.

FACILITIES

Information Resources Getchell Library plus 7 additional on-campus libraries; total holdings of 861,096 volumes, 2,720,024 microforms, 6,775 current periodical subscriptions. CD player(s) available for graduate student use. Access provided to online bibliographic retrieval services.

INTERNATIONAL STUDENTS

Demographics 12% of students enrolled are international students.

Services and Facilities International student office, international student housing, visa services, ESL courses, counseling/support services.

Applying TOEFL: minimum score of 550, proof of adequate funds, proof of health/immunizations required. Financial aid is available to international students.

International Student Contact Office of International Students and Scholars, Reno, NV 89557. Phone: 702-784-6874.

PLACEMENT

Services include career counseling/planning, career fairs, job interviews arranged, job search course, resume referral to employers, and resume preparation.

Program Contact: Vicki Krentz, Associate Director of Graduate Studies, Reno, NV 89557. Phone: 702-784-4912; Fax: 702-784-1773.

See full description on page 1110.

NEW HAMPSHIRE

Antioch New England Graduate School

Department of Organization and Management

Keene, New Hampshire

OVERVIEW

Antioch New England Graduate School is an independent-nonprofit, coed, graduate institution. Enrollment: 842 graduate, professional, and undergraduate students; 694 full-time matriculated graduate/professional students; 148 part-time matriculated graduate/professional students. Founded: 1964. The graduate business unit is in a small-town setting and is on a trimester calendar.

HIGHLIGHTS

Enrollment Profile

Full-time: 62	International: 0%
Part-time: 28	Women: 70%
Total: 90	Minorities: 2%
Average Age: 41	Average Class Size: 18
Fall 1997 Average GPA: 3.0	Fall 1997 Average GMAT: N/R

Costs
Full-time tuition: $12,700 per academic year
Part-time tuition: N/R

GRADUATE BUSINESS PROGRAMS

Master of Science in Management (MS) Full-time, part-time; 50 total credits required; up to 20 months to complete program. Concentrations in human resources, leadership, management, organizational behavior/development, organizational management.

Master of Human Service Administration (MHSA) Full-time, part-time; 40 total credits required; up to 15 months to complete program. Concentrations in human resources, leadership, management, nonprofit management, organizational behavior/development, organizational management.

Master of Education in Administration and Supervision (MEd) Full-time, part-time; 40 total credits required; up to 15 months to complete program. Concentrations in leadership, management, management consulting, nonprofit management, organizational behavior/development, organizational management.

ADMISSION

Applications For fall 1997 there were 72 applications for admission. Of those applying, 67 were accepted. Of those accepted, 51 enrolled.

Application Requirements Application form, application fee, bachelor's degree, essay, interview, letters of recommendation, personal statement, resume, college transcript(s), work experience.

Application Deadline Applications processed on a rolling/continuous basis for both domestic and international students. Application fee: $40. Deferred entrance is available.

ACADEMICS

Faculty Full-time 1; part-time 18.

Teaching Methodologies Case study, computer simulations, experiential learning, faculty seminars, field projects, group discussion, lecture, research, role playing, simulations, student presentations, study groups, team projects.

Technology 18 on-campus computer terminals/PCs are available for student use and are linked by a campus-wide network. The network has full access to the Internet. Students are not required to have their own PC.

Special Opportunities Advanced credit may be earned through credit for experience, transfer of credits from another institution. An internship program is available.

FINANCES

Costs for 1997–98 Tuition: Full-time: $12,700 per year. Cost varies by academic program, campus location, class time (e.g., day/evening), number of credits taken.

Financial Aid In 1997–98, 60% of students received some institutionally administered aid in the form of fellowships, scholarships, work study, loans.

Financial Aid Contact Michelle Chamley, Director, Financial Aid Office, 40 Avon Street, Keene, NH 03431-3516. Phone: 603-357-3122 Ext. 279; Fax: 603-357-0718; E-mail: mchamley@antiochne.edu

FACILITIES

Information Resources Main library; total holdings of 25,222 volumes, 73,002 microforms, 737 current periodical subscriptions. CD player(s) available for graduate student use. Access provided to online bibliographic retrieval services.

INTERNATIONAL STUDENTS

Demographics N/R

Services and Facilities Counseling/support services.

Applying TOEFL: minimum score of 550, proof of adequate funds, proof of health/immunizations required.

International Student Contact Diane K. Hewitt, Co-Director of Admissions, 40 Avon Street, Keene, NH 03431-3516. Phone: 603-357-3122; Fax: 603-357-0718; E-mail: dhewitt@antiochne.edu

PLACEMENT

Services include alumni network.

Employment Of 1996–97 graduates, 95% were employed within three months of graduation; the average starting salary was $35,000. Types of employment entered: accounting, banking, communications, consulting, consumer products, education, financial services, government, health services, hospitality management, human resources, management, manufacturing, marketing, media, nonprofit, retail, service industry, telecommunications.

Business Program(s) URL: http://www.antiochne.edu

Program Contact: Diane K. Hewitt, Co-Director of Admissions, 40 Avon Street, Keene, NH 03431-3516. Phone: 603-357-6265; Fax: 603-357-0718; E-mail: dhewitt@antiochne.edu

Dartmouth College

Amos Tuck School of Business Administration

Hanover, New Hampshire

OVERVIEW

Dartmouth College is an independent-nonprofit, coed university. Enrollment: 5,303 graduate, professional, and undergraduate students; 1,211 full-time matriculated graduate/professional students; 76 part-time matriculated graduate/professional students. Founded: 1769. The graduate business unit is in a rural setting and is on a trimester calendar.

HIGHLIGHTS

Enrollment Profile

Full-time: 374	International: 19%
Part-time: 0	Women: 28%
Total: 374	Minorities: 16%
Average Age: 27	Average Class Size: 60
Fall 1997 Average GPA: 3.4	Fall 1997 Average GMAT: 667

Costs
Full-time tuition: $24,900 per academic year
Part-time tuition: N/R

AACSB – The International Association for Management Education accredited

Degree(s) offered in conjunction with Tufts University

GRADUATE BUSINESS PROGRAMS

Master of Business Administration (MBA) Full-time; 2 to 5 years to complete program.

Master of Business Administration/Doctor of Medicine (MBA/MD) Full-time; 6 to 7 years to complete program.

Master of Business Administration/Master of Engineering (MBA/ME) Full-time; 3 to 5 years to complete program.

Master of Business Administration/Master of Arts, Law, and Diplomacy (MBA/MALD) Full-time; 3 to 5 years to complete program.

ADMISSION

Applications For fall 1997 there were 3,194 applications for admission. Of those applying, 367 were accepted. Of those accepted, 184 enrolled.

Application Requirements GMAT score, application form, application fee, bachelor's degree, essay, minimum GPA, 2 letters of recommendation, personal statement, resume, college transcript(s), minimum of 1 year of work experience.

Recommended for Application Interview, computer experience.

Application Deadline Applications processed on a rolling/continuous basis for both domestic and international students. Application fee: $100. Deferred entrance is available.

ACADEMICS

Faculty Full-time 35; part-time 7.

Teaching Methodologies Case study, computer-aided instruction, computer analysis, computer simulations, experiential learning, faculty seminars, field projects, group discussion, lecture, research, role playing, simulations, student presentations, study groups, team projects.

Dartmouth College (continued)

Technology 450 on-campus computer terminals/PCs are available for student use and are linked by a campus-wide network. The network has full access to the Internet. Students are not required to have their own PC.

Special Opportunities Advanced credit may be earned through credit by examination. International exchange programs in France, Germany, Japan, Spain, United Kingdom. An internship program is available.

FINANCES
Costs for 1997–98 Tuition: Full-time: $24,900 per year. Fees: Full-time: $1500 per academic year. Average 1997–98 room and board costs were $13,600 per academic year (on campus) and $13,600 per academic year (off campus). Room and board costs vary by campus location, occupancy (e.g., single, double, triple), type of accommodation.

Financial Aid In 1997–98, 64% of students received some institutionally administered aid in the form of fellowships, scholarships, work study, loans. Application Deadline: 3/1.

Financial Aid Contact Dr. Macdonald, Executive Officer, Hanover, NH 03755. Phone: 603-646-3504.

FACILITIES
Information Resources Baker Library plus 8 additional on-campus libraries; total holdings of 2,057,421 volumes, 2,378,886 microforms, 20,764 current periodical subscriptions. CD player(s) available for graduate student use. Access provided to online bibliographic retrieval services.

INTERNATIONAL STUDENTS
Demographics 19% of students enrolled are international students [Africa, 4%, Asia, 21%, Australia/New Zealand, 4%, Central America, 9%, Europe, 27%, North America, 9%, South America, 14%, other, 12%].

Services and Facilities Counseling/support services.

Applying TOEFL required. Financial aid is available to international students.

PLACEMENT
Services include alumni network, career counseling/planning, career fairs, career library, career placement, electronic job bank, job interviews arranged, resume referral to employers, and resume preparation. In 1996–97, 140 organizations participated in on-campus recruiting; 4,000 on-campus interviews were conducted.

Employment Of 1996–97 graduates, 100% were employed within three months of graduation; the average starting salary was $120,000. Types of employment entered: accounting, banking, chemical industry, communications, computer-related, consulting, consumer products, engineering, finance, financial services, health services, high technology, human resources, information systems/technology, international trade, management, manufacturing, marketing, media, pharmaceutical, real estate, retail, telecommunications.

Business Program(s) URL: http://www.tuck.dartmouth.edu

Program Contact: Ms. Sally O. Jaeger, Director of Admissions, Amos Tuck School of Business, 100 Tuck Hall, Hanover, NH 03755. Phone: 603-646-3162; Fax: 603-646-1308; E-mail: tuck.admissions@dartmouth.edu
See full description on page 776.

New England College

Program in Organizational Management

Henniker, New Hampshire

OVERVIEW
New England College is an independent-nonprofit, comprehensive institution.

HIGHLIGHTS
Enrollment Profile

Full-time: N/R	International: N/R
Part-time: N/R	Women: N/R
Total: 35	Minorities: N/R
Average Age: N/R	Average Class Size: N/R
Fall 1997 Average GPA: N/R	Fall 1997 Average GMAT: N/R

Costs
Full-time tuition: N/R
Part-time tuition: $170 per credit

GRADUATE BUSINESS PROGRAMS
Master of Science in Organizational Management (MS) Full-time, part-time; 40 total credits required; minimum of 2 years to complete program.

ADMISSION
Application Requirements Application form, bachelor's degree, essay, minimum GPA: 3.0, interview, 3 letters of recommendation, personal statement, resume, college transcript(s).

Application Deadline Applications processed on a rolling/continuous basis for both domestic and international students.

ACADEMICS
Teaching Methodologies Case study, computer-aided instruction, faculty seminars, group discussion, lecture, research, role playing, simulations, student presentations, study groups, team projects.

FINANCES
Costs for 1997–98 Tuition: $170 per credit.

Financial Aid Contact Linda Connor, Administrative Assistant, Henniker, NH 03242-3293. Phone: 603-428-2252; E-mail: lcc@nec1.nec.edu

INTERNATIONAL STUDENTS
Demographics N/R

Program Contact: Graduate and Continuing Studies, Henniker, NH 03242-3293. Phone: 603-428-2252 E-mail: lcc@nec1.nec.edu

New Hampshire College

Graduate School of Business

Manchester, New Hampshire

OVERVIEW
New Hampshire College is an independent-nonprofit, coed, comprehensive institution. Enrollment: 5,766 graduate, professional, and undergraduate students; 315 full-time matriculated graduate/professional students; 1,485 part-time matriculated graduate/professional students. Founded: 1932. The graduate business unit is in a small-town setting and is on a quarter calendar.

HIGHLIGHTS
Enrollment Profile

Full-time: 315	International: 10%
Part-time: 1,485	Women: 41%
Total: 1,800	Minorities: N/R
Average Age: 32	Average Class Size: 21
Fall 1997 Average GPA: N/R	Fall 1997 Average GMAT: N/R

Costs
Full-time tuition: $1065 per academic year
Part-time tuition: $945 per course

ACBSP – The American Council of Business Schools and Programs accredited

GRADUATE BUSINESS PROGRAMS
Master of Business Administration (MBA) Full-time, part-time, distance learning option; 39 total credits required; 12 months to 8 years to complete program. Concentrations in accounting, finance, industrial/labor relations, international business, management information systems, manufacturing management, marketing, taxation, health care.

Master of Science in Accounting (MS) Full-time, part-time; 48 total credits required; 18 months to 8 years to complete program.

Master of Science in Business Education (MS) Full-time, part-time; 30 total credits required; 9 months to 8 years to complete program.

Master of Science in Computer Information Systems (MS) Full-time, part-time; 48 total credits required; 18 months to 8 years to complete program.

Master of Science in Finance (MS) Full-time, part-time; 57 total credits required; 18 months to 8 years to complete program.

Master of Science in International Business (MS) Full-time, part-time; 39 total credits required; 12 months to 8 years to complete program.

ADMISSION
Application Requirements Application form, bachelor's degree, minimum GPA: 2.5, college transcript(s).

Recommended for Application GMAT score accepted.

Application Deadline Applications processed on a rolling/continuous basis for both domestic and international students. Deferred entrance is available.

ACADEMICS
Faculty Full-time 25; part-time 107.

Teaching Methodologies Case study, computer simulations, group discussion, lecture, research, simulations, student presentations, study groups, team projects.

Technology 200 on-campus computer terminals/PCs are available for student use and are linked by a campus-wide network. The network has full access to the Internet. Students are not required to have their own PC.

Special Opportunities Advanced credit may be earned through credit for military training programs, transfer of credits from another institution. An internship program is available.

FINANCES
Costs for 1997–98 Tuition: Full-time: $1065 per course. Part-time: $945 per course. Fees: Full-time: $530 per academic year. Average 1997–98 room and board costs were $7516 per academic year. Room and board costs vary by type of accommodation.

Financial Aid Fellowships, research assistantships, work study, loans available. Financial aid is available to part-time students.

Financial Aid Contact Ms. Christine McGuire, Financial Aid Administrator, 2500 North River Road, Manchester, NH 03106-1045. Phone: 603-645-9645; Fax: 603-645-9665.

FACILITIES
Information Resources H. A. B. Shapiro Memorial Library; total holdings of 77,000 volumes, 6,000 microforms, 850 current periodical subscriptions. CD player(s) available for graduate student use. Access provided to online bibliographic retrieval services.

INTERNATIONAL STUDENTS
Demographics 10% of students enrolled are international students.

Services and Facilities International student office, international student center, visa services, ESL courses, counseling/support services.

Applying TOEFL: minimum score of 550, proof of adequate funds, proof of health/immunizations required. Financial aid is available to international students.

International Student Contact Dr. George Commenator, 2500 North River Road, Manchester, NH 03106-1045. E-mail: commonge@nhc.edu

PLACEMENT
Services include alumni network, career counseling/planning, career fairs, career library, career placement, electronic job bank, job interviews arranged, job search course, resume referral to employers, and resume preparation. In 1996–97, 180 organizations participated in on-campus recruiting.

Employment Of 1996–97 graduates, 92% were employed within three months of graduation. Types of employment entered: accounting, computer-related, education, finance, financial services, government, health services, human resources, management, marketing, nonprofit.

Business Program(s) URL: http://www.nhc.edu

Program Contact: Ms. Ann McCormick, 2500 North River Road, Manchester, NH 03106-1045. Phone: 603-644-3102 Ext. 3338 E-mail: mccorman@nhc.edu
See full description on page 892.

Plymouth State College of the University System of New Hampshire

Department of Business Studies

Plymouth, New Hampshire

OVERVIEW
Plymouth State College of the University System of New Hampshire is a state-supported, coed, comprehensive institution. Enrollment: 3,779 graduate, professional, and undergraduate students. Founded: 1871. The graduate business unit is in a small-town setting and is on a quarter calendar.

HIGHLIGHTS
Enrollment Profile
Full-time: 37
Part-time: 195
Total: 232
Average Age: 35
Fall 1997 Average GPA: 2.99
International: 7%
Women: 42%
Minorities: N/R
Average Class Size: 20
Fall 1997 Average GMAT: 469

Costs
Full-time tuition: $9828 per academic year (resident); $10,764 per academic year (nonresident)
Part-time tuition: $273 per credit (resident); $299 per credit (nonresident)

ACBSP – The American Council of Business Schools and Programs accredited

GRADUATE BUSINESS PROGRAMS
Master of Business Administration in General Management (MBA) Full-time, part-time; 36 total credits required; 9 months to 3 years to complete program. Concentration in management.

ADMISSION
Applications For fall 1997 there were 59 applications for admission. Of those applying, 45 were accepted. Of those accepted, 45 enrolled.

Application Requirements Application form, application fee, bachelor's degree, essay, minimum GPA: 2.5, 3 letters of recommendation, personal statement, resume, college transcript(s), computer experience: spreadsheet.

Recommended for Application GMAT score accepted.

Application Deadline 5/15 for fall, 5/15 for winter, 10/15 for spring, 10/15 for summer. Application fee: $35. Deferred entrance is available.

ACADEMICS
Faculty Full-time 23.

Teaching Methodologies Case study, computer analysis, group discussion, lecture, research, role playing, student presentations, study groups, team projects.

Technology 200 on-campus computer terminals/PCs are available for student use and are linked by a campus-wide network. The network has full access to the Internet. Students are not required to have their own PC.

Special Opportunities Advanced credit may be earned through transfer of credits from another institution.

FINANCES
Costs for 1997–98 Tuition: Full-time: $9828 per program (resident); $10,764 per program (nonresident). Part-time: $273 per credit (resident); $299 per credit (nonresident). Cost varies by number of credits taken. Average 1997–98 room and board costs were $4500 per academic year. Room and board costs vary by occupancy (e.g., single, double, triple), type of accommodation, type of meal plan.

Financial Aid Work study, loans available. Financial aid is available to part-time students.

Financial Aid Contact Mr. David Belenger, Assistant Director, Speare Administration Building, Room 108, Plymouth, NH 03264. Phone: 603-535-2359; Fax: 603-535-2627; E-mail: dbelanger@mail.plymouth.edu

FACILITIES
Information Resources Lamson Library; total holdings of 265,000 volumes, 600,000 microforms, 1,150 current periodical subscriptions. CD player(s) available for graduate student use. Access provided to online bibliographic retrieval services.

INTERNATIONAL STUDENTS
Demographics 7% of students enrolled are international students.

Services and Facilities Visa services, ESL courses, counseling/support services.

Applying TOEFL: minimum score of 500, proof of adequate funds required. Financial aid is not available to international students.

International Student Contact Ms. Karen Hammond, Assistant to the Director, Office of Graduate Studies in Business, Mary Taylor House, MSC #11, Plymouth, NH 03264. Phone: 603-535-2835; Fax: 603-535-2648; E-mail: khammond@mail.plymouth.edu

PLACEMENT
Services include career counseling/planning, career fairs, career library, career placement, and resume preparation.

Employment Types of employment entered: accounting, computer-related, energy, engineering, finance, government, health services, information systems/technology, insurance, management, manufacturing, marketing, real estate, telecommunications, utilities.

Business Program(s) URL: http://www.plymouth.edu

Program Contact: Karen Hammond, Assistant to the Director, Graduate Studies in Business, Plymouth, NH 03264. Phone: 603-535-2835, 800-367-4723; Fax: 603-535-2648; E-mail: khammond@mail.plymouth.edu
See full description on page 928.

Rivier College

Department of Business Administration

Nashua, New Hampshire

OVERVIEW
Rivier College is an independent-religious, coed, comprehensive institution. Enrollment: 2,768 graduate, professional, and undergraduate students; 43 full-time

Rivier College (continued)

matriculated graduate/professional students; 944 part-time matriculated graduate/professional students. Founded: 1933. The graduate business unit is in an urban setting and is on a semester calendar.

HIGHLIGHTS

Enrollment Profile

Full-time: 11
Part-time: 298
Total: 309
Average Age: 30
Fall 1997 Average GPA: 2.8

International: 2%
Women: 45%
Minorities: 6%
Average Class Size: 17
Fall 1997 Average GMAT: N/R

Costs

Full-time tuition: N/R
Part-time tuition: $855 per course

GRADUATE BUSINESS PROGRAMS

Master of Business Administration (MBA) Full-time, part-time; 36-45 total credits required; 2 to 5 years to complete program. Concentrations in accounting, marketing, quality management, health care.

Master of Science in Human Resources Management (MS) Full-time, part-time; 39-48 total credits required; 2 to 5 years to complete program. Concentration in human resources.

ADMISSION

Applications For fall 1997 there were 122 applications for admission. Of those applying, 119 were accepted. Of those accepted, 119 enrolled.

Application Requirements Application form, application fee, bachelor's degree, interview, college transcript(s).

Recommended for Application Minimum GPA, work experience.

Application Deadline Applications processed on a rolling/continuous basis for domestic students only. 7/1 for fall (international), 11/1 for spring (international), 4/1 for summer (international). Application fee: $25. Deferred entrance is available.

ACADEMICS

Faculty Full-time 6; part-time 29.

Teaching Methodologies Case study, computer-aided instruction, computer analysis, computer simulations, experiential learning, field projects, group discussion, lecture, research, role playing, seminars by members of the business community, simulations, student presentations, study groups, team projects.

Technology 100 on-campus computer terminals/PCs are available for student use. The network has partial access to the Internet. Students are not required to have their own PC.

Special Opportunities Advanced credit may be earned through credit for military training programs, credit for business training programs, transfer of credits from another institution.

FINANCES

Costs for 1997-98 Tuition: $855 per course. Cost varies by number of credits taken. Fees: $50 per course.

Financial Aid In 1997-98, 7% of students received some institutionally administered aid in the form of loans. Financial aid is available to part-time students.

Financial Aid Contact Paul Henderson, Director, 420 Main Street, Nashua, NH 03060-5086. Phone: 603-888-1311 Ext. 8534; Fax: 603-888-0237.

FACILITIES

Information Resources Regina Library; total holdings of 135,500 volumes, 40,060 microforms, 945 current periodical subscriptions. CD player(s) available for graduate student use. Access provided to online bibliographic retrieval services and online databases.

INTERNATIONAL STUDENTS

Demographics 2% of students enrolled are international students [Africa, 1%, Asia, 5%, North America, 94%].

Services and Facilities ESL courses, counseling/support services.

Applying TOEFL: minimum score of 600, proof of adequate funds required.

PLACEMENT

Services include career counseling/planning, career placement, and resume preparation.

Program Contact: Dr. George Shagory, Chair, Department of Business Administration, 420 Main Street, Nashua, NH 03060-5086. Phone: 603-888-1311 Ext. 8237; Fax: 603-888-0237.

University of New Hampshire

Whittemore School of Business and Economics

Durham, New Hampshire

OVERVIEW

The University of New Hampshire is a state-supported, coed university. Enrollment: 13,210 graduate, professional, and undergraduate students; 931 full-time matriculated graduate/professional students; 1,171 part-time matriculated graduate/professional students. Founded: 1866. The graduate business unit is in a small-town setting and is on a semester calendar.

HIGHLIGHTS

Enrollment Profile

Full-time: 97
Part-time: 63
Total: 160
Average Age: 32
Fall 1997 Average GPA: 3.1

International: 10%
Women: 32%
Minorities: 2%
Average Class Size: 35
Fall 1997 Average GMAT: 553

Costs

Full-time tuition: $5200 per academic year (resident); $14,060 per academic year (nonresident)
Part-time tuition: $1050 per course (resident); $1275 per course (nonresident)

AACSB – The International Association for Management Education accredited

GRADUATE BUSINESS PROGRAMS

Full-time Day MBA (MBA) Full-time; 60 total credits required; 2 to 3 years to complete program. Concentrations in accounting, finance, management, production management, operations management, marketing, finance.

Part-time Evening MBA (MBA) Part-time; 60 total credits required; 3 to 6 years to complete program. Concentrations in management, accounting, finance, production management, operations management, marketing, finance.

Executive MBA (MBA) Full-time; 54 total credits required; 22 months to complete program. Concentration in management.

ADMISSION

Applications For fall 1997 there were 146 applications for admission. Of those applying, 132 were accepted. Of those accepted, 66 enrolled.

Application Requirements Application form, application fee, bachelor's degree, essay, minimum GPA: 3.0, letters of recommendation, personal statement, college transcript(s), minimum of 2 years of work experience.

Recommended for Application GMAT score accepted.

Application Deadline 7/1 for fall, 4/1 for fall (international). Application fee: $50. Deferred entrance is available.

ACADEMICS

Faculty Full-time 48.

Teaching Methodologies Case study, computer simulations, experiential learning, field projects, group discussion, lecture, seminars by members of the business community, simulations, student presentations, study groups, team projects.

Technology 225 on-campus computer terminals/PCs are available for student use and are linked by a campus-wide network. The network has full access to the Internet. Students are not required to have their own PC.

Special Opportunities Advanced credit may be earned through transfer of credits from another institution. International exchange programs in Canada, France. An internship program is available.

FINANCES

Costs for 1997-98 Tuition: Full-time: $5200 per year (resident); $14,060 per year (nonresident). Part-time: $1050 per course (resident); $1275 per course (nonresident). Cost varies by academic program, class time (e.g., day/evening), number of credits taken, reciprocity agreements. Fees: Full-time: $789 per academic year (resident); $789 per academic year (nonresident). Fees vary by academic program, class time (e.g., day/evening), number of credits taken. Average 1997-98 room and board costs were $4858 per academic year. Room and board costs vary by occupancy (e.g., single, double, triple), type of accommodation, type of meal plan.

Financial Aid In 1997-98, 19% of students received some institutionally administered aid in the form of research assistantships, teaching assistantships, scholarships, work study. Financial aid is available to part-time students. Application Deadline: 3/1.

Financial Aid Contact Mr. George Abraham, Director, Graduate and Executive Programs, McConnell Hall, Room 110, Durham, NH 03824. Phone: 603-862-1367; Fax: 603-862-4468; E-mail: wsbe.grad.program@unh.edu

FACILITIES

Information Resources Dimond Library plus 4 additional on-campus libraries; total holdings of 1,034,946 volumes, 6,500 current periodical subscriptions. Access provided to online bibliographic retrieval services.

INTERNATIONAL STUDENTS

Demographics 10% of students enrolled are international students.

Services and Facilities International student office, international student center, international student housing, visa services, ESL courses, counseling/support services.

Applying TOEFL: minimum score of 550, proof of adequate funds, proof of health/immunizations required. TWE recommended. Financial aid is available to international students.

International Student Contact Dr. Leila Paje-Manalo, Office for International Students and Scholars, Hood House, Durham, NH 03824-3593. Phone: 603-862-2398; Fax: 603-862-0169.

PLACEMENT

Services include alumni network, career counseling/planning, career fairs, career library, career placement, job interviews arranged, resume referral to employers, and resume preparation. In 1996–97, 230 organizations participated in on-campus recruiting; 843 on-campus interviews were conducted.

Employment Of 1996–97 graduates, 85% were employed within three months of graduation; the average starting salary was $49,500. Types of employment entered: accounting, communications, computer-related, high technology, information systems/technology, insurance, manufacturing, pharmaceutical.

Business Program(s) URL: http://www.unh.edu/wsbe/index.html

Program Contact: Mr. George Abraham, Director, Graduate and Executive Programs, Box PI, McConnell Hall, 15 College Road, Durham, NH 03824. Phone: 603-862-1367; Fax: 603-862-4468; E-mail: wsbe.grad.program@unh.edu

See full description on page 1112.

NEW JERSEY

Fairleigh Dickinson University

Samuel J. Silberman College of Business Administration

Teaneck and Madison, New Jersey

OVERVIEW

Fairleigh Dickinson University is an independent-nonprofit, coed, comprehensive institution. Founded: 1954. The graduate business unit is in a suburban setting and is on a semester calendar.

HIGHLIGHTS

Enrollment Profile
Full-time: 246
Part-time: 1,241
Total: 1,487
Average Age: 32
Fall 1997 Average GPA: 3.44

International: 9%
Women: 54%
Minorities: N/R
Average Class Size: 20
Fall 1997 Average GMAT: N/R

Costs
Full-time tuition: N/R
Part-time tuition: $522 per credit

GRADUATE BUSINESS PROGRAMS

Master of Business Administration (MBA) Full-time, part-time; 34-60 total credits required. Concentrations in accounting, finance, human resources, international business, entrepreneurship, management, marketing, quantitative analysis.

Executive Master of Business Administration (EMBA) Full-time, part-time; 48 total credits required.

Master of Science in Taxation (MS) Full-time, part-time; 36 total credits required. Concentration in taxation.

Master of Business Administration in Global Management (MBA) Full-time, part-time; 48 total credits required; 12 months to complete program.

ADMISSION

Applications For fall 1997 there were 633 applications for admission. Of those applying, 446 were accepted. Of those accepted, 299 enrolled.

Application Requirements GMAT score: minimum 525, application form, bachelor's degree, minimum GPA: 3.2, college transcript(s), minimum of 7 years of work experience.

Recommended for Application Computer experience.

Application Deadline Applications processed on a rolling/continuous basis for domestic students only. 7/1 for fall (international), 8/15 for spring (international). Application fee: $35.

ACADEMICS

Faculty Full-time 20; part-time 13.

Teaching Methodologies Case study, computer-aided instruction, computer simulations, faculty seminars, field projects, lecture, research, role playing, seminars by members of the business community, simulations, student presentations.

Technology Computer terminals/PCs are available for student use and are linked by a campus-wide network. The network has full access to the Internet. Students are not required to have their own PC.

Special Opportunities Advanced credit may be earned through credit by examination, transfer of credits from another institution. An internship program is available.

FINANCES

Costs for 1997–98 Tuition: $522 per credit. Cost varies by academic program, class time (e.g., day/evening). Fees: $69 per semester. Average 1997–98 room and board costs were $3020 per academic year.

Financial Aid Research assistantships available.

Financial Aid Contact Ms. Dale Herold, University Director of Admissions, 1000 River Road, Teaneck and Madison, NJ 07666-1914. Phone: 800-338-8803; Fax: 201-460-5467.

FACILITIES

Information Resources Weiner Library plus 1 additional on-campus library; total holdings of 274,188 volumes, 190,181 microforms, 1,613 current periodical subscriptions. Access provided to online bibliographic retrieval services.

INTERNATIONAL STUDENTS

Demographics 9% of students enrolled are international students.

Services and Facilities International student office, international student housing, visa services, ESL courses, counseling/support services.

Applying TOEFL: minimum score of 500, proof of adequate funds, proof of health/immunizations required.

International Student Contact Jane Bush, Director of International Affairs, 1000 River Road, Teaneck and Madison, NJ 07666-1914. Phone: 201-692-2745; Fax: 201-460-5467.

PLACEMENT

Services include career fairs, career placement, job interviews arranged, and resume preparation.

Employment Types of employment entered: chemical industry, financial services, hospitality management, insurance, media, pharmaceutical, telecommunications.

Business Program(s) URL: http://www.fdu.edu/academic/coba

Program Contact: Office of Adult and Graduate Admission, 1000 River Road, Teaneck, NJ 07666. Phone: 201-692-2000, 800-338-8803; Fax: 201-460-5467.

See full description on page 814.

Georgian Court College

Program in Business Administration

Lakewood, New Jersey

OVERVIEW

Georgian Court College is an independent-religious, comprehensive institution. Enrollment: 2,350 graduate, professional, and undergraduate students.

HIGHLIGHTS

Enrollment Profile
Full-time: N/R
Part-time: N/R
Total: 101
Average Age: N/R
Fall 1997 Average GPA: N/R

International: N/R
Women: N/R
Minorities: N/R
Average Class Size: N/R
Fall 1997 Average GMAT: N/R

Costs
Full-time tuition: N/R
Part-time tuition: $350 per credit

Georgian Court College (continued)

ACBSP – The American Council of Business Schools and Programs accredited

GRADUATE BUSINESS PROGRAMS
Master of Business Administration (MBA) Full-time, part-time; 64 total credits required.

ADMISSION
Application Requirements GMAT score, application form, bachelor's degree, minimum GPA, 3 letters of recommendation, college transcript(s), computer experience: PC, spreadsheet, word processing.

Recommended for Application Interview.

Application Deadline Applications processed on a rolling/continuous basis for both domestic and international students.

ACADEMICS
Teaching Methodologies Case study, group discussion, lecture, student presentations.

FINANCES
Costs for 1997–98 Tuition: $350 per credit.

Financial Aid Contact Susan Barshou, Director of Financial Aid, Lakewood, NJ 08701-2697. Phone: 732-364-2200 Ext. 258.

INTERNATIONAL STUDENTS
Demographics N/R

Applying TOEFL: minimum score of 550 required.

International Student Contact Sr. Mary Arthur Beal, Lakewood, NJ 08701-2697. Phone: 732-367-1717.

PLACEMENT
Services include alumni network, career counseling/planning, and career fairs.

Employment Types of employment entered: accounting, banking, chemical industry, consumer products, education, finance, financial services, government, health services, hospitality management, insurance, management, manufacturing, marketing, nonprofit, pharmaceutical, retail, service industry, telecommunications, utilities.

Program Contact: Sr. Mary Arthur Beal, Lakewood, NJ 08701-2697.

Kean University

School of Business, Government, and Technology

Union, New Jersey

OVERVIEW
Kean University is a state-supported, coed, comprehensive institution. Enrollment: 11,537 graduate, professional, and undergraduate students. Founded: 1855. The graduate business unit is in a suburban setting and is on a semester calendar.

HIGHLIGHTS

Enrollment Profile

Full-time: N/R	International: N/R
Part-time: N/R	Women: N/R
Total: 78	Minorities: N/R
Average Age: N/R	Average Class Size: 15
Fall 1997 Average GPA: 3.25	Fall 1997 Average GMAT: 50

Costs
Full-time tuition: N/R
Part-time tuition: $248 per credit (resident); $305 per credit (nonresident)

Degree(s) offered in conjunction with New Jersey Institute of Technology

GRADUATE BUSINESS PROGRAMS
Master of Science in Management Systems Analysis (MS) Full-time, part-time; 36 total credits required; 16 months to 6 years to complete program. Concentrations in management information systems, management science, management systems analysis.

ADMISSION
Application Requirements GMAT score, GRE score, application form, application fee, bachelor's degree, essay, minimum GPA, letters of recommendation, personal statement, college transcript(s).

Recommended for Application Interview, resume, computer experience.

Application Deadline 6/1 for fall, 11/1 for spring, 3/1 for fall (international). Application fee: $35. Deferred entrance is available.

ACADEMICS
Faculty Full-time 65; part-time 30.

Teaching Methodologies Case study, computer-aided instruction, computer analysis, computer simulations, experiential learning, faculty seminars, group discussion, lecture, research, seminars by members of the business community, student presentations, study groups, team projects.

Technology Computer terminals/PCs are available for student use and are linked by a campus-wide network. The network has full access to the Internet. Students are not required to have their own PC.

Special Opportunities Advanced credit may be earned through credit by examination, transfer of credits from another institution. An internship program is available.

FINANCES
Costs for 1997–98 Tuition: $248 per credit (resident); $305 per credit (nonresident). Cost varies by number of credits taken.

Financial Aid Loans available. Financial aid is available to part-time students.

Financial Aid Contact Office of Financial Aid, East Campus, Room 212, Union, NJ 07083. Phone: 908-527-2018.

FACILITIES
Information Resources Nancy Thompson Library plus 1 additional on-campus library; total holdings of 256,908 volumes, 28,445 microforms, 1,350 current periodical subscriptions. Access provided to online bibliographic retrieval services.

INTERNATIONAL STUDENTS
Demographics N/R

Services and Facilities International student housing, ESL courses, counseling/support services.

Applying TOEFL recommended.

International Student Contact William DeGarcia, Associate Director of Admissions, 1000 Morris Avenue, Union, NJ 07083. Phone: 908-527-2195.

PLACEMENT
Services include alumni network, career counseling/planning, career fairs, career library, and career placement.

Business Program(s) URL: http://www.kean.edu

Program Contact: Thomas Abraham, Program Coordinator, 1000 Morris Avenue, Union, NJ 07083. Phone: 908-527-2492 E-mail: tabraham@turbo.kean.edu

Monmouth University

School of Business Administration

West Long Branch, New Jersey

OVERVIEW
Monmouth University is an independent-nonprofit, coed, comprehensive institution. Enrollment: 5,311 graduate, professional, and undergraduate students; 242 full-time matriculated graduate/professional students; 1,032 part-time matriculated graduate/professional students. Founded: 1933. The graduate business unit is in a suburban setting and is on a semester calendar.

HIGHLIGHTS

Enrollment Profile

Full-time: 16	International: 2%
Part-time: 294	Women: 43%
Total: 310	Minorities: 5%
Average Age: 33	Average Class Size: 19
Fall 1997 Average GPA: N/R	Fall 1997 Average GMAT: N/R

Costs
Full-time tuition: $7902 per academic year
Part-time tuition: $439 per credit

GRADUATE BUSINESS PROGRAMS
Master of Business Administration (MBA) Full-time, part-time; 30-48 total credits required; 12 months to 5 years to complete program.

Master of Business Administration in Health Care Management (MBA) Full-time, part-time; 51 total credits required; 12 months to 5 years to complete program.

ADMISSION
Applications For fall 1997 there were 164 applications for admission. Of those applying, 112 were accepted. Of those accepted, 77 enrolled.

Application Requirements GMAT score, application form, application fee, bachelor's degree, minimum GPA: 2.75, college transcript(s), computer experience: word processing, spreadsheet.

Recommended for Application Resume.

Application Deadline 8/1 for fall, 12/15 for spring, 5/7 for summer, 7/15 for fall (international), 11/15 for spring (international), 4/7 for summer (international). Application fee: $35, $40 (international). Deferred entrance is available.

ACADEMICS

Faculty Full-time 23; part-time 3.

Teaching Methodologies Case study, computer-aided instruction, computer analysis, computer simulations, experiential learning, faculty seminars, field projects, group discussion, lecture, research, role playing, seminars by members of the business community, student presentations, team projects.

Technology 400 on-campus computer terminals/PCs are available for student use and are linked by a campus-wide network. The network has full access to the Internet. Students are not required to have their own PC.

Special Opportunities Advanced credit may be earned through transfer of credits from another institution.

FINANCES

Costs for 1997–98 Tuition: Full-time: $7902 per year. Part-time: $439 per credit. Cost varies by number of credits taken. Fees: Full-time: $548 per academic year. Part-time: $137 per semester. Fees vary by number of credits taken.

Financial Aid In 1997–98, 19% of students received some institutionally administered aid. Application Deadline: 3/1.

Financial Aid Contact Ms. Claire Alasio, Director, Financial Aid, Cedar Avenue, West Long Branch, NJ 07764-1898. Phone: 732-571-3463; Fax: 732-263-5577.

FACILITIES

Information Resources Guggenheim Memorial Library; total holdings of 252,497 volumes, 331,970 microforms, 1,250 current periodical subscriptions. CD player(s) available for graduate student use. Access provided to online bibliographic retrieval services and online databases.

INTERNATIONAL STUDENTS

Demographics 2% of students enrolled are international students [Asia, 100%].

Services and Facilities International student office, visa services, ESL courses, counseling/support services.

Applying TOEFL: minimum score of 525, proof of adequate funds, proof of health/immunizations required. Financial aid is available to international students.

International Student Contact Office of Graduate and Adult Enrollment Services, Cedar Avenue, West Long Branch, NJ 07764-1898. Phone: 732-571-3452; Fax: 732-263-5123.

PLACEMENT

Services include career counseling/planning, career fairs, career library, career placement, electronic job bank, job search course, and resume preparation.

Employment Types of employment entered: accounting, banking, chemical industry, communications, computer-related, consulting, human resources, information systems/technology, insurance, management, manufacturing, marketing, media, real estate, retail, telecommunications.

Business Program(s) URL: http://www.monmouth.edu/monmouth/academic/business

Program Contact: Office of Graduate and Adult Enrollment Services, Cedar Avenue, West Long Branch, NJ 07764-1898. Phone: 732-571-3452.

Montclair State University

School of Business Administration

Upper Montclair, New Jersey

OVERVIEW

Montclair State University is a state-supported, coed, comprehensive institution. Enrollment: 12,993 graduate, professional, and undergraduate students; 558 full-time matriculated graduate/professional students; 2,533 part-time matriculated graduate/professional students. Founded: 1908. The graduate business unit is in a suburban setting and is on a semester calendar.

HIGHLIGHTS

Enrollment Profile
Full-time: N/R
Part-time: N/R
Total: 237
Average Age: 31
Fall 1997 Average GPA: 3.35

International: 12%
Women: N/R
Minorities: 13%
Average Class Size: 20
Fall 1997 Average GMAT: 535

Costs
Full-time tuition: N/R
Part-time tuition: $186 per credit (resident); $236 per credit (nonresident)

GRADUATE BUSINESS PROGRAMS

Master of Business Administration (MBA) Part-time; 63 total credits required; 2 to 8 years to complete program. Concentrations in international business, accounting, economics, finance, management, marketing, management information systems.

Master of Science in Accounting (MS) Part-time; 33 total credits required; 2 to 8 years to complete program.

Master of Arts in Social Science and Economics (MA) Part-time; 33 total credits required; 2 to 8 years to complete program.

ADMISSION

Applications For fall 1997 there were 165 applications for admission. Of those applying, 60 were accepted. Of those accepted, 18 enrolled.

Application Requirements GMAT score, application form, application fee, bachelor's degree, essay, minimum GPA: 3.0, 2 letters of recommendation, personal statement, college transcript(s).

Recommended for Application Interview, work experience, computer experience.

Application Deadline Applications processed on a rolling/continuous basis for both domestic and international students. Application fee: $40.

ACADEMICS

Faculty Full-time 57.

Teaching Methodologies Case study, computer-aided instruction, computer analysis, computer simulations, experiential learning, faculty seminars, field projects, group discussion, lecture, research, role playing, seminars by members of the business community, simulations, student presentations, study groups, team projects.

Technology 450 on-campus computer terminals/PCs are available for student use and are linked by a campus-wide network. The network has full access to the Internet. Students are not required to have their own PC.

Special Opportunities Advanced credit may be earned through credit by examination, transfer of credits from another institution.

FINANCES

Costs for 1997–98 Tuition: Part-time: $186 per credit (resident); $236 per credit (nonresident). Fees: Part-time: $17 per credit (resident); $18 per credit (nonresident). Average 1997–98 room and board costs were $5334 per academic year (on campus) and $7200 per academic year (off campus). Room and board costs vary by occupancy (e.g., single, double, triple), type of accommodation, type of meal plan.

Financial Aid Research assistantships, teaching assistantships, work study, loans available. Financial aid is available to part-time students. Application Deadline: 3/1.

Financial Aid Contact Dr. Randall W. Richards, Director, Financial Aid, Valley Road and Normal Avenue, Upper Montclair, NJ 07043-1624. Phone: 973-655-4461; Fax: 973-655-7828.

FACILITIES

Information Resources Sprague Library; total holdings of 418,547 volumes, 1,134,242 microforms, 3,793 current periodical subscriptions. CD player(s) available for graduate student use. Access provided to online bibliographic retrieval services.

INTERNATIONAL STUDENTS

Demographics 12% of students enrolled are international students.

Services and Facilities International student office, international student center, counseling/support services.

Applying TOEFL: minimum score of 550, proof of adequate funds, proof of health/immunizations required.

International Student Contact Ms. Jacqueline Leighton, Director, International Services, Valley Road and Normal Avenue, Upper Montclair, NJ 07043-1624. Phone: 973-655-4253; Fax: 973-655-7726.

PLACEMENT

Services include alumni network, career counseling/planning, career fairs, career library, career placement, job interviews arranged, resume referral to employers, and resume preparation.

Business Program(s) URL: http://www.montclair.edu

Montclair State University (continued)

Program Contact: Dr. Carla M. Narrett, Dean, Graduate Studies and Research, Office of Graduate Studies, One Normal Avenue, Upper Montclair, NJ 07043-1624. Phone: 973-655-5147, 800-331-9207; Fax: 973-655-7828; E-mail: gradstudies@saturn.montclair.edu

New Jersey Institute of Technology

School of Industrial Management

Newark, New Jersey

OVERVIEW
New Jersey Institute of Technology is a state-supported, coed university. Enrollment: 7,504 graduate, professional, and undergraduate students; 615 full-time matriculated graduate/professional students; 1,465 part-time matriculated graduate/professional students. Founded: 1881. The graduate business unit is in an urban setting and is on a semester calendar.

HIGHLIGHTS

Enrollment Profile

Full-time: 66	International: 6%
Part-time: 336	Women: 37%
Total: 402	Minorities: 25%
Average Age: 27	Average Class Size: 22
Fall 1997 Average GPA: 3.2	Fall 1997 Average GMAT: 500

Costs
Full-time tuition: $6340 per academic year (resident); $9158 per academic year (nonresident)
Part-time tuition: $326 per credit (resident); $451 per credit (nonresident)

AACSB – The International Association for Management Education accredited

Degree(s) offered in conjunction with Rutgers, The State University of New Jersey, Newark

GRADUATE BUSINESS PROGRAMS
Executive Master of Science in Management (MS) Part-time; 39 total credits required; 14 months to complete program. Concentrations in management information systems, strategic management.

Master of Science in Management (MS) Full-time, part-time; 30-48 total credits required; 12 months to 7 years to complete program. Concentrations in finance, accounting, marketing, management information systems, management, human resources, technology management.

ADMISSION
Applications For fall 1997 there were 94 applications for admission. Of those applying, 77 were accepted. Of those accepted, 61 enrolled.

Application Requirements GMAT score, application form, application fee, bachelor's degree, minimum GPA, interview, college transcript(s), minimum of 5 years of work experience.

Recommended for Application GRE score accepted: minimum 525, letters of recommendation.

Application Deadline Applications processed on a rolling/continuous basis for domestic students only. 6/5 for fall (international), 11/5 for spring (international). Application fee: $50.

ACADEMICS
Faculty Full-time 23; part-time 15.

Teaching Methodologies Case study, computer-aided instruction, experiential learning, faculty seminars, field projects, group discussion, lecture, research, role playing, seminars by members of the business community, simulations, student presentations, study groups, team projects.

Technology 150 on-campus computer terminals/PCs are available for student use and are linked by a campus-wide network. The network has full access to the Internet.

Special Opportunities Advanced credit may be earned through transfer of credits from another institution. International exchange program in Germany.

FINANCES
Costs for 1997–98 Tuition: Full-time: $6340 per semester (resident); $9158 per semester (nonresident). Part-time: $326 per credit (resident); $451 per credit (nonresident). Cost varies by academic program. Fees: Full-time: $551 per academic year (resident); $551 per academic year (nonresident). Average 1997–98 room and board costs were $5922 per academic year.

Financial Aid In 1997–98, 4% of students received some institutionally administered aid in the form of fellowships, research assistantships, teaching assistantships, work study, loans. Application Deadline: 3/15.

Financial Aid Contact Director, Financial Aid Department, University Heights, Newark, NJ 07102-1982. Phone: 973-596-3479.

FACILITIES
Information Resources Van Houten Library plus 1 additional on-campus library; total holdings of 204,471 volumes, 4,725 microforms, 1,271 current periodical subscriptions. CD player(s) available for graduate student use. Access provided to online bibliographic retrieval services.

INTERNATIONAL STUDENTS
Demographics 6% of students enrolled are international students.

Services and Facilities International student office, international student center, visa services, ESL courses, counseling/support services.

Applying TOEFL: minimum score of 525, proof of adequate funds, proof of health/immunizations required.

International Student Contact Jinan Jaber-Linsalata, Director, International Student and Faculty Services, University Heights, Newark, NJ 07102-1982. Phone: 973-596-2451.

PLACEMENT
Services include alumni network, career counseling/planning, career fairs, career library, career placement, job interviews arranged, job search course, resume referral to employers, and resume preparation. In 1996–97, 60 organizations participated in on-campus recruiting.

Employment Of 1996–97 graduates, 100% were employed within three months of graduation. Types of employment entered: accounting, banking, chemical industry, communications, computer-related, consulting, consumer products, education, energy, engineering, finance, financial services, government, health services, high technology, hospitality management, human resources, information systems/technology, insurance, international trade, law, manufacturing, marketing, media, nonprofit, petrochemical, pharmaceutical, real estate, retail, service industry, telecommunications, transportation, utilities.

Program Contact: George Albright, Director of Special Programs, University Heights, Newark, NJ 07102-1982. Phone: 973-596-6378.

The Richard Stockton College of New Jersey

Program in Business Studies

Pomona, New Jersey

OVERVIEW
The Richard Stockton College of New Jersey is a state-supported, coed, comprehensive institution. Enrollment: 5,647 graduate, professional, and undergraduate students; 20 full-time matriculated graduate/professional students; 28 part-time matriculated graduate/professional students.

HIGHLIGHTS

Enrollment Profile

Full-time: 0	International: 0%
Part-time: 27	Women: 59%
Total: 27	Minorities: 19%
Average Age: N/R	Average Class Size: 14
Fall 1997 Average GPA: N/R	Fall 1997 Average GMAT: N/R

Costs
Full-time tuition: N/R
Part-time tuition: $213 per credit (resident); $297 per credit (nonresident)

GRADUATE BUSINESS PROGRAMS
Master of Business Studies (MBS) 36 total credits required.

ADMISSION
Applications For fall 1997 there were 45 applications for admission. Of those applying, 30 were accepted. Of those accepted, 27 enrolled.

Application Requirements GMAT score, application form, bachelor's degree, minimum GPA, letters of recommendation, resume, college transcript(s).

Application Deadline Applications processed on a rolling/continuous basis for both domestic and international students. Application fee: $35. Deferred entrance is available.

ACADEMICS
Faculty Full-time 24.

Teaching Methodologies Case study, computer analysis, computer simulations, faculty seminars, group discussion, lecture, research, seminars by members of the business community, student presentations, study groups, team projects.

Technology 441 on-campus computer terminals/PCs are available for student use and are linked by a campus-wide network. The network has full access to the Internet. Students are not required to have their own PC.

Special Opportunities Advanced credit may be earned through transfer of credits from another institution. International exchange programs in England, France, Germany, Japan, Sweden, various other countries.

FINANCES

Costs for 1997–98 Tuition: Part-time: $213 per credit (resident); $297 per credit (nonresident). Fees: Part-time: $33 per credit (resident); $33 per credit (nonresident).

Financial Aid Loans available.

Financial Aid Contact Ms. Jeanne Lewis, Director of Financial Aid, Pomona, NJ 08240-0195. Phone: 609-652-4201; Fax: 609-748-5517.

INTERNATIONAL STUDENTS

Demographics N/R

Services and Facilities International student office, counseling/support services.

Applying TOEFL, proof of adequate funds, proof of health/immunizations required.

International Student Contact Dr. Lewis Leitner, Head of the MBA Program, Pomona, NJ 08240-0195. Phone: 609-652-4519; Fax: 609-652-4858; E-mail: lewis.leitner@stockton.edu

PLACEMENT

Services include alumni network, career counseling/planning, career fairs, career library, career placement, electronic job bank, job interviews arranged, job search course, resume referral to employers, and resume preparation.

Program Contact: Dr. Lewis Leitner, Head of the MBS Program, Pomona, NJ 08240-0195. Phone: 609-652-4519; Fax: 609-652-4858.

Rider University

College of Business Administration

Lawrenceville, New Jersey

OVERVIEW

Rider University is an independent-nonprofit, coed, comprehensive institution. Enrollment: 5,006 graduate, professional, and undergraduate students; 123 full-time matriculated graduate/professional students; 964 part-time matriculated graduate/professional students. Founded: 1865. The graduate business unit is in a suburban setting and is on a semester calendar.

HIGHLIGHTS

Enrollment Profile

Full-time: 50	International: 3%
Part-time: 379	Women: 45%
Total: 429	Minorities: 7%
Average Age: 28	Average Class Size: 21
Fall 1997 Average GPA: 3.3	Fall 1997 Average GMAT: 519

Costs
Full-time tuition: $9000 per academic year
Part-time tuition: $420 per credit

AACSB – The International Association for Management Education accredited

GRADUATE BUSINESS PROGRAMS

Master of Business Administration (MBA) Full-time, part-time; 30-57 total credits required; 12 months to 5 years to complete program. Concentrations in accounting, economics, finance, international business, management, health care, marketing, organizational management.

Master of Accountancy (MAcc) Full-time, part-time; 30-57 total credits required; 12 months to 5 years to complete program. Concentrations in accounting, finance, health care, international banking, management, marketing.

ADMISSION

Applications For fall 1997 there were 125 applications for admission. Of those applying, 99 were accepted. Of those accepted, 67 enrolled.

Application Requirements GMAT score, application form, application fee, bachelor's degree, minimum GPA, college transcript(s).

Recommended for Application Essay, interview, letters of recommendation, personal statement, resume, work experience, computer experience.

Application Deadline 8/1 for fall, 12/1 for spring, 5/1 for summer, 8/1 for fall (international), 12/1 for spring (international), 5/1 for summer (international). Application fee: $35. Deferred entrance is available.

ACADEMICS

Faculty Full-time 47; part-time 8.

Teaching Methodologies Case study, computer-aided instruction, computer analysis, computer simulations, experiential learning, faculty seminars, field projects, group discussion, lecture, research, role playing, seminars by members of the business community, simulations, student presentations, study groups, team projects.

Technology 300 on-campus computer terminals/PCs are available for student use and are linked by a campus-wide network. The network has full access to the Internet. Students are not required to have their own PC.

Special Opportunities Advanced credit may be earned through credit by examination, transfer of credits from another institution.

FINANCES

Costs for 1997–98 Tuition: Full-time: $9000 per year. Part-time: $420 per credit. Cost varies by number of credits taken. Fees: Full-time: $150 per academic year. Part-time: $10 per 3 credits. Fees vary by number of credits taken. Average 1997–98 room and board costs were $6270 per academic year. Room and board costs vary by occupancy (e.g., single, double, triple), type of accommodation, type of meal plan.

Financial Aid Research assistantships available. Application Deadline: 4/1.

Financial Aid Contact Ms. Audrey MacKellar, Associate Director—Student Financial Services, 2083 Lawrenceville Road, Lawrenceville, NJ 08648-3099. Phone: 609-896-5360; Fax: 609-895-6645.

FACILITIES

Information Resources Franklin Moore Library; total holdings of 378,000 volumes, 400,000 microforms, 2,542 current periodical subscriptions. CD player(s) available for graduate student use. Access provided to online bibliographic retrieval services and online databases.

INTERNATIONAL STUDENTS

Demographics 3% of students enrolled are international students.

Services and Facilities Visa services.

Applying TOEFL, proof of adequate funds, proof of health/immunizations required. Financial aid is not available to international students.

International Student Contact Mr. Tom Kelly, Associate Dean, College of Business Administration, 2083 Lawrenceville Road, Lawrenceville, NJ 08648-3099. Phone: 609-896-5127; Fax: 609-896-5304 Ext. ; E-mail: kelly@rider.edu

PLACEMENT

Services include alumni network, career counseling/planning, career fairs, career library, career placement, electronic job bank, resume referral to employers, and resume preparation.

Employment Of 1996–97 graduates, 96% were employed within three months of graduation. Types of employment entered: accounting, banking, chemical industry, communications, computer-related, consulting, consumer products, education, energy, engineering, finance, financial services, government, health services, high technology, hospitality management, human resources, information systems/technology, insurance, international trade, management, manufacturing, marketing, nonprofit, pharmaceutical, real estate, retail, service industry, telecommunications, utilities.

Business Program(s) URL: http://www.rider.edu

Program Contact: Dr. John Carpenter, Dean, 2083 Lawrenceville Road, Lawrenceville, NJ 08648-3099. Phone: 609-896-5036; Fax: 609-896-5261.

Rowan University

School of Business Administration

Glassboro, New Jersey

OVERVIEW

Rowan University is a state-supported, coed, comprehensive institution. Enrollment: 9,367 graduate, professional, and undergraduate students; 84 full-time matriculated graduate/professional students; 1,228 part-time matriculated graduate/professional students. Founded: 1923. The graduate business unit is in a small-town setting and is on a semester calendar.

Rowan University (continued)

HIGHLIGHTS

Enrollment Profile

Full-time: 5	International: 3%
Part-time: 95	Women: 43%
Total: 100	Minorities: 3%
Average Age: 31	Average Class Size: 20
Fall 1997 Average GPA: 2.94	Fall 1997 Average GMAT: 528

Costs
Full-time tuition: $2470 per academic year (resident); $3915 per academic year (nonresident)
Part-time tuition: $205 per credit (resident); $326 per credit (nonresident)

The Master of Business Administration (M.B.A.) Program at Rowan University provides a contemporary graduate business education to professionals of diverse fields and academic backgrounds. The M.B.A. curriculum emphasizes communication skills, critical thinking, information technology, quantitative analysis, and the international nature of business. Students learn to be team leaders and team players.

There is an average student/teacher ratio of 20:1 and the convenience of evening and Saturday classes. Classes are taught by professors, not teaching assistants. The campus is easily accessible to students in the southern New Jersey, northern Delaware, and Philadelphia, Pennsylvania areas. Rowan's College of Business has one of the finest computer facilities in this tristate area.

Students enrolled in the M.B.A. Program are required to complete a total of eleven graduate courses, nine required and two elective. Prospective M.B.A. students who do not have the required foundation courses may enroll as pre-M.B.A. students while completing the necessary foundation courses. The maximum number of foundation courses required of pre-M.B.A. students is six.

All M.B.A. students must maintain a 3.0 GPA. Students are expected to make steady progress toward the completion of their degree. A full-time student may complete the degree requirements in one year. Part-time students are allowed a maximum of six years to complete all graduate courses.

GRADUATE BUSINESS PROGRAMS
Master of Business Administration (MBA) Full-time, part-time; 36 total credits required; 12 months to 6 years to complete program.

ADMISSION
Applications For fall 1997 there were 37 applications for admission. Of those applying, 24 were accepted. Of those accepted, 10 enrolled.

Application Requirements GMAT score: minimum 450, application form, application fee, bachelor's degree, essay, minimum GPA: 2.5, 2 letters of recommendation, personal statement, resume, college transcript(s), computer experience.

Recommended for Application Work experience.

Application Deadline Applications processed on a rolling/continuous basis for both domestic and international students. Application fee: $50.

ACADEMICS
Faculty Full-time 16.

Teaching Methodologies Case study, computer-aided instruction, computer analysis, computer simulations, experiential learning, faculty seminars, field projects, group discussion, lecture, research, role playing, seminars by members of the business community, simulations, student presentations, study groups, team projects.

Technology 400 on-campus computer terminals/PCs are available for student use and are linked by a campus-wide network. The network has full access to the Internet. Students are not required to have their own PC.

Special Opportunities Advanced credit may be earned through credit by examination, transfer of credits from another institution.

FINANCES
Costs for 1997–98 Tuition: Full-time: $2470 per semester (resident); $3915 per semester (nonresident). Part-time: $205 per credit (resident); $326 per credit (nonresident). Cost varies by number of credits taken. Fees: Full-time: $369 per academic year (resident); $369 per academic year (nonresident). Part-time: $33 per credit (resident); $33 per credit (nonresident). Average 1997–98 room and board costs were $5200 per academic year. Room and board costs vary by occupancy (e.g., single, double, triple), type of accommodation.

Financial Aid Research assistantships, work study available. Financial aid is available to part-time students.

Financial Aid Contact Financial Aid Office, Memorial Hall, 201 Mullica Hill Road, Glassboro, NJ 08028-1701. Phone: 609-256-4250.

FACILITIES
Information Resources The Library; total holdings of 346,000 volumes, 140,500 microforms, 2,000 current periodical subscriptions. CD player(s) available for graduate student use. Access provided to online bibliographic retrieval services and online databases.

INTERNATIONAL STUDENTS
Demographics 3% of students enrolled are international students [Asia, 34%, Europe, 66%].

Services and Facilities International student office, ESL courses, counseling/support services.

Applying TOEFL: minimum score of 550, proof of adequate funds, proof of health/immunizations required. Financial aid is not available to international students.

International Student Contact Dr. Dilip Mirchandani, MBA Program Director, Bunce Hall, 201 Mullica Hill Road, Glassboro, NJ 08028-1701. Phone: 609-256-4048; Fax: 609-256-4439.

PLACEMENT
Services include alumni network, career counseling/planning, career fairs, career placement, electronic job bank, job interviews arranged, resume referral to employers, and resume preparation.

Employment Types of employment entered: banking, finance, health services, hospitality management, information systems/technology, insurance, manufacturing.

Business Program(s) URL: http://charlotte.rowan.edu/business/soba.htm

Program Contact: 201 Mullica Hill Road, Glassboro, NJ 08028-1701. Phone: 609-256-4050; Fax: 609-256-4436.

Rutgers, The State University of New Jersey, Camden

School of Business

Camden, New Jersey

OVERVIEW
Rutgers, The State University of New Jersey, Camden is a state-supported, coed university. Enrollment: 5,052 graduate, professional, and undergraduate students; 770 full-time matriculated graduate/professional students; 725 part-time matriculated graduate/professional students. Founded: 1927. The graduate business unit is in an urban setting and is on a semester calendar.

HIGHLIGHTS

Enrollment Profile

Full-time: 24	International: 9%
Part-time: 225	Women: 26%
Total: 249	Minorities: 12%
Average Age: 27	Average Class Size: 23
Fall 1997 Average GPA: 3.21	Fall 1997 Average GMAT: 558

Costs
Full-time tuition: $8408 per academic year (resident); $12,600 per academic year (nonresident)
Part-time tuition: $348 per credit (resident); $520 per credit (nonresident)

AACSB – The International Association for Management Education accredited

GRADUATE BUSINESS PROGRAMS
Master of Business Administration (MBA) Full-time, part-time; 60 total credits required; 18 months to 2 years to complete program. Concentrations in accounting, finance, international business, management, management information systems, marketing, human resources, health care.

Master of Business Administration/Doctor of Jurisprudence (MBA/JD) Full-time, part-time; 108-120 total credits required; LSAT score required; 3 to 5 years to complete program. Concentration in business law.

ADMISSION
Applications For fall 1997 there were 106 applications for admission. Of those applying, 82 were accepted. Of those accepted, 68 enrolled.

Application Requirements GMAT score: minimum 500, application form, application fee, bachelor's degree, minimum GPA: 2.5, 3 letters of recommendation, personal statement, college transcript(s).

Recommended for Application Work experience, computer experience.

Application Deadline Applications processed on a rolling/continuous basis for both domestic and international students. Application fee: $40. Deferred entrance is available.

ACADEMICS

Faculty Full-time 32; part-time 6.

Teaching Methodologies Case study, computer-aided instruction, computer analysis, computer simulations, faculty seminars, field projects, group discussion, lecture, research, role playing, seminars by members of the business community, simulations, student presentations, study groups, team projects.

Technology 220 on-campus computer terminals/PCs are available for student use and are linked by a campus-wide network. The network has full access to the Internet. Students are not required to have their own PC.

Special Opportunities Advanced credit may be earned through transfer of credits from another institution. An internship program is available.

FINANCES

Costs for 1997–98 Tuition: Full-time: $8408 per year (resident); $12,600 per year (nonresident). Part-time: $348 per credit (resident); $520 per credit (nonresident). Cost varies by academic program, reciprocity agreements. Fees: Full-time: $391 per academic year (resident); $391 per academic year (nonresident). Part-time: $174 per term (resident); $174 per term (nonresident). Fees vary by academic program, campus location. Average 1997–98 room and board costs were $4846 per academic year (on campus) and $10,000 per academic year (off campus). Room and board costs vary by campus location, occupancy (e.g., single, double, triple), type of accommodation, type of meal plan.

Financial Aid In 1997–98, 9% of students received some institutionally administered aid in the form of research assistantships, work study, loans. Financial aid is available to part-time students.

Financial Aid Contact Mr. Richard Woodland, Director, Financial Aid, Camden Campus, 401 Cooper Street, Camden, NJ 08102-1401. Phone: 609-225-6039; Fax: 609-225-6074; E-mail: rwoodlan@camden.rutgers.edu

FACILITIES

Information Resources Paul Robeson Library plus 1 additional on-campus library; total holdings of 226,700 volumes, 133,000 microforms, 342 current periodical subscriptions. CD player(s) available for graduate student use. Access provided to online bibliographic retrieval services and online databases.

INTERNATIONAL STUDENTS

Demographics 9% of students enrolled are international students [Africa, 5%, Asia, 65%, Central America, 5%, Europe, 25%].

Services and Facilities International student office, international student center, international student housing, visa services, counseling/support services.

Applying TOEFL: minimum score of 550, proof of adequate funds, proof of health/immunizations required. Financial aid is available to international students.

International Student Contact Ms. Janice Edwards, Associate Director of Graduate Admissions, Camden Campus, Office of Graduate Admissions, Camden, NJ 08102-1401. Phone: 609-225-6471; Fax: 609-225-6498.

PLACEMENT

Services include alumni network, career counseling/planning, career fairs, career library, career placement, electronic job bank, job interviews arranged, job search course, resume referral to employers, and resume preparation. In 1996–97, 52 organizations participated in on-campus recruiting; 38 on-campus interviews were conducted.

Employment Of 1996–97 graduates, 98% were employed within three months of graduation; the average starting salary was $57,000. Types of employment entered: accounting, banking, chemical industry, communications, computer-related, consulting, consumer products, energy, finance, financial services, government, health services, high technology, human resources, information systems/technology, insurance, international trade, management, manufacturing, marketing, nonprofit, petrochemical, pharmaceutical, real estate, retail, service industry, telecommunications, transportation, utilities.

Business Program(s) URL: http://camden-www.rutgers.edu/

Program Contact: Dr. Izzet Kenis, MBA Program Director, Rutgers University, School of Business, MBA Program, Camden, NJ 08102-1401. Phone: 609-225-6216; Fax: 609-225-6231; E-mail: kenis@crab.rutgers.edu

Rutgers, The State University of New Jersey, Newark

Graduate School of Management

Newark, New Jersey

OVERVIEW

Rutgers, The State University of New Jersey, Newark is a state-supported, coed university. Enrollment: 9,056 graduate, professional, and undergraduate students; 1,180 full-time matriculated graduate/professional students; 2,315 part-time matriculated graduate/professional students. Founded: 1892. The graduate business unit is in an urban setting and is on a trimester calendar.

HIGHLIGHTS

Enrollment Profile

Full-time: 342	International: 18%
Part-time: 1,150	Women: 35%
Total: 1,492	Minorities: 29%
Average Age: 27	Average Class Size: 30
Fall 1997 Average GPA: 3.1	Fall 1997 Average GMAT: 581

Costs
Full-time tuition: $8410 per academic year (resident); $12,538 per academic year (nonresident)
Part-time tuition: $348 per credit (resident); $520 per credit (nonresident)

AACSB – The International Association for Management Education accredited

GRADUATE BUSINESS PROGRAMS

Master of Business Administration in Management (MBA) Full-time, part-time; 60 total credits required; 15 months to 2 years to complete program. Concentrations in accounting, banking, decision sciences, marketing, finance, economics, real estate, international business, human resources, technology management, entrepreneurship, operations management, information management, management, marketing research, nonprofit organization.

Master of Accountancy in Taxation (MAcc) Part-time; 30 total credits required; 10 months to 2.5 years to complete program. Concentration in taxation.

PhD in Management (PhD) Full-time; 72 total credits required; 2 to 6 years to complete program. Concentrations in accounting, management information systems, operations management, economics, finance, marketing, management, international business.

MBA in Professional Accounting (MBA) Full-time; 62 total credits required; 14 months to complete program. Concentration in accounting.

Executive MBA (MBA) Full-time; 54 total credits required; 20 months to complete program. Concentrations in accounting, economics, entrepreneurship, finance, human resources, information management, international business, management, management information systems, management science, marketing, operations management.

ADMISSION

Applications For fall 1997 there were 1,388 applications for admission. Of those applying, 468 were accepted. Of those accepted, 385 enrolled.

Application Requirements GMAT score: minimum 580, application form, application fee, bachelor's degree, essay, minimum GPA: 3.1, 2 letters of recommendation, personal statement, college transcript.

Recommended for Application Resume, work experience, computer experience.

Application Deadline 6/1 for fall, 11/1 for spring, 3/1 for fall (international). Application fee: $40. Deferred entrance is available.

ACADEMICS

Faculty Full-time 136; part-time 62.

Teaching Methodologies Case study, computer-aided instruction, computer analysis, computer simulations, experiential learning, faculty seminars, field projects, group discussion, lecture, research, role playing, seminars by members of the business community, student presentations, study groups, team projects.

Technology 100 on-campus computer terminals/PCs are available for student use and are linked by a campus-wide network. The network has full access to the Internet. Students are not required to have their own PC.

Special Opportunities Advanced credit may be earned through credit by examination, transfer of credits from another institution. International exchange programs in France, Italy, Netherlands, United Kingdom.

FINANCES

Costs for 1997–98 Tuition: Full-time: $8410 per year (resident); $12,538 per year (nonresident). Part-time: $348 per credit (resident); $520 per credit (nonresident). Cost varies by academic program, number of credits taken. Fees: Full-time: $244 per academic year (resident); $244 per academic year (nonresident). Part-time: $119 per term (resident); $119 per term (nonresident). Fees vary by academic program, number of credits taken. Average 1997–98 room only costs were $8330 per academic year. Room and board costs vary by campus location, occupancy (e.g., single, double, triple), type of accommodation, type of meal plan.

Financial Aid In 1997–98, 14% of students received some institutionally administered aid in the form of fellowships, grants, scholarships, work study, loans. Application Deadline: 3/15.

Financial Aid Contact Dr. Carol Ruskin, Director of Admissions, 81 New Street, Newark, NJ 07102-1895. Phone: 973-648-1234; Fax: 973-648-1592.

Rutgers, The State University of New Jersey, Newark (continued)

FACILITIES

Information Resources John Cotton Dana Library; total holdings of 357,000 volumes, 517,000 microforms. Access provided to online bibliographic retrieval services.

INTERNATIONAL STUDENTS

Demographics 18% of students enrolled are international students.

Services and Facilities International student office, international student center, international student housing, visa services, ESL courses, counseling/support services.

Applying TOEFL: minimum score of 600, proof of adequate funds, proof of health/immunizations required. Financial aid is not available to international students.

International Student Contact Ms. Patricia Rotonda, Assistant Dean, Student Services, Engelhard Hall, 92 New Street, Newark, NJ 07102-1895. Phone: 973-353-5482; Fax: 973-353-1057; E-mail: protonda@gsmack.rutgers.edu

PLACEMENT

Services include alumni network, career counseling/planning, career fairs, career library, career placement, electronic job bank, job interviews arranged, job search course, resume referral to employers, and resume preparation. In 1996–97, 35 organizations participated in on-campus recruiting; 253 on-campus interviews were conducted.

Employment Of 1996–97 graduates, 74% were employed within three months of graduation; the average starting salary was $53,500. Types of employment entered: accounting, banking, communications, computer-related, consulting, consumer products, energy, finance, financial services, human resources, information systems/technology, management, marketing, pharmaceutical, telecommunications.

Business Program(s) URL: http://www.rutgers.edu

Program Contact: Dr. Carol Ruskin, Director of Admissions, 92 New Street, Newark, NJ 07102-1895. Phone: 973-353-5651; Fax: 973-353-1592.

Rutgers, The State University of New Jersey, New Brunswick

School of Management and Labor Relations

New Brunswick, New Jersey

OVERVIEW

Rutgers, The State University of New Jersey, New Brunswick is a state-supported, coed university. Enrollment: 47,697 graduate, professional, and undergraduate students; 2,788 full-time matriculated graduate/professional students; 5,751 part-time matriculated graduate/professional students. Founded: 1766. The graduate business unit is in a suburban setting and is on a semester calendar.

HIGHLIGHTS

Enrollment Profile

Full-time: 46	International: 30%
Part-time: 179	Women: 72%
Total: 225	Minorities: 9%
Average Age: 30	Average Class Size: 20
Fall 1997 Average GPA: 3.32	Fall 1997 Average GMAT: 495

Costs
Full-time tuition: $6700 per academic year (resident); $9528 per academic year (nonresident)
Part-time tuition: $250 per credit (resident); $369 per credit (nonresident)

AACSB – The International Association for Management Education accredited

Degree(s) offered in conjunction with Singapore Institute of Management

GRADUATE BUSINESS PROGRAMS

Master of Human Resource Management (MHRM) Full-time, part-time; 48 total credits required; 18 months to 5 years to complete program. Concentration in human resources.

Master of Labor and Industrial Relations (MLIR) Full-time, part-time; 39 total credits required; 12 months to 5 years to complete program. Concentration in industrial/labor relations.

PhD in Industrial Relations and Human Resources (PhD) Full-time; 72 total credits required; 4 to 5 years to complete program. Concentrations in human resources, industrial/labor relations.

ADMISSION

Applications For fall 1997 there were 169 applications for admission. Of those applying, 147 were accepted. Of those accepted, 100 enrolled.

Application Requirements Application form, application fee, bachelor's degree, minimum GPA: 3.0, 3 letters of recommendation, personal statement, college transcript(s).

Recommended for Application GMAT score accepted, GRE score accepted, resume, work experience, computer experience.

Application Deadline 5/1 for fall, 11/1 for spring, 3/1 for summer, 4/1 for fall (international), 11/1 for spring (international). Application fee: $40. Deferred entrance is available.

ACADEMICS

Faculty Full-time 21; part-time 5.

Teaching Methodologies Case study, computer-aided instruction, computer analysis, computer simulations, experiential learning, faculty seminars, field projects, group discussion, lecture, research, role playing, seminars by members of the business community, simulations, student presentations, study groups, team projects.

Technology 35 on-campus computer terminals/PCs are available for student use and are linked by a campus-wide network. The network has full access to the Internet. Students are not required to have their own PC.

Special Opportunities Advanced credit may be earned through transfer of credits from another institution. International exchange programs in Indonesia, Republic of Singapore.

FINANCES

Costs for 1997–98 Tuition: Full-time: $6700 per year (resident); $9528 per year (nonresident). Part-time: $250 per credit (resident); $369 per credit (nonresident). Cost varies by academic program, number of credits taken. Fees: Full-time: $783 per academic year (resident); $783 per academic year (nonresident). Part-time: $240 per year (resident); $240 per year (nonresident). Average 1997–98 room and board costs were $6884 per academic year. Room and board costs vary by occupancy (e.g., single, double, triple), type of accommodation, type of meal plan.

Financial Aid Fellowships, research assistantships, teaching assistantships, work study available.

Financial Aid Contact Office of Financial Aid, Records Hall, New Brunswick, NJ 08903. Phone: 732-932-7755; Fax: 732-932-7385.

FACILITIES

Information Resources Alexander Library plus 18 additional on-campus libraries; total holdings of 5,418,327 volumes, 3,662,034 microforms, 24,891 current periodical subscriptions. Access provided to online bibliographic retrieval services.

INTERNATIONAL STUDENTS

Demographics 30% of students enrolled are international students [Asia, 88%, North America, 6%, other, 6%].

Services and Facilities International student office, international student center, ESL courses, counseling/support services.

Applying TOEFL: minimum score of 575, proof of adequate funds, proof of health/immunizations required. Financial aid is available to international students.

International Student Contact Ms. Gail Szenes, Director, International Faculty and Student Services Center, 180 College Avenue, New Brunswick, NJ 08903. Phone: 732-932-7015; Fax: 732-932-7992.

PLACEMENT

Services include alumni network, career counseling/planning, career fairs, career library, career placement, electronic job bank, job interviews arranged, job search course, resume referral to employers, and resume preparation. In 1996–97, 100 organizations participated in on-campus recruiting.

Employment Of 1996–97 graduates, 91% were employed within three months of graduation; the average starting salary was $47,000. Types of employment entered: accounting, banking, chemical industry, computer-related, consulting, consumer products, finance, financial services, health services, high technology, hospitality management, human resources, information systems/technology, insurance, management, manufacturing, mining, petrochemical, pharmaceutical, retail, service industry, telecommunications.

Program Contact: Ms. Judy von Loewe, Graduate Program Coordinator, Janice Levin Building, 94 Rockefeller Road, Piscataway, NJ 08854-8054. Phone: 732-445-5973; Fax: 732-445-2830; E-mail: mhrm@rci.rutgers.edu

See full description on page 956.

Saint Peter's College

Graduate Business Programs

Jersey City, New Jersey

OVERVIEW
Saint Peter's College is an independent-religious, coed, comprehensive institution. Enrollment: 3,393 graduate, professional, and undergraduate students; 84 full-time matriculated graduate/professional students; 359 part-time matriculated graduate/professional students. Founded: 1872. The graduate business unit is in an urban setting and is on a trimester calendar.

HIGHLIGHTS

Enrollment Profile
Full-time: 59
Part-time: 197
Total: 256
Average Age: 31
Fall 1997 Average GPA: N/R

International: 15%
Women: 39%
Minorities: 25%
Average Class Size: 15
Fall 1997 Average GMAT: 400

Costs
Full-time tuition: $11,448 per academic year
Part-time tuition: $477 per credit

GRADUATE BUSINESS PROGRAMS
Master of Business Administration in Management (MBA) Full-time, part-time; 48 total credits required; 12 months to 5 years to complete program. Concentration in management.

Master of Business Administration in Management Information Systems (MBA) Full-time, part-time; 48 total credits required; 12 months to 5 years to complete program. Concentration in management information systems.

Master of Business Administration in International Business (MBA) Full-time, part-time; 48 total credits required; 12 months to 5 years to complete program. Concentration in international business.

Master of Science in Accountancy (MS) Full-time, part-time; 30 total credits required; 10 months to 5 years to complete program. Concentration in accounting.

ADMISSION
Applications For fall 1997 there were 140 applications for admission. Of those applying, 125 were accepted. Of those accepted, 74 enrolled.

Application Requirements Application form, application fee, bachelor's degree, 3 letters of recommendation, college transcript(s).

Recommended for Application GMAT score accepted: minimum 400, MAT score accepted: minimum 40.

Application Deadline Applications processed on a rolling/continuous basis for domestic students only. 7/1 for fall (international), 9/1 for winter (international), 12/1 for spring (international). Application fee: $20.

ACADEMICS
Faculty Full-time 16; part-time 17.

Teaching Methodologies Computer-aided instruction, computer analysis, field projects, group discussion, lecture, research, seminars by members of the business community, student presentations.

Technology 150 on-campus computer terminals/PCs are available for student use. The network has full access to the Internet. Students are not required to have their own PC.

Special Opportunities Advanced credit may be earned through transfer of credits from another institution.

FINANCES
Costs for 1997–98 Tuition: Full-time: $11,448 per year. Part-time: $477 per credit.

Financial Aid In 1997–98, 64% of students received some institutionally administered aid in the form of work study, loans. Financial aid is available to part-time students. Application Deadline: 3/15.

Financial Aid Contact Nancy Campbell, Associate Vice President for Enrollment, 2641 Kennedy Boulevard, Jersey City, NJ 07306-5997. Phone: 201-915-9308; Fax: 201-434-6878.

FACILITIES
Information Resources O'Toole Library plus 1 additional on-campus library; total holdings of 258,500 volumes, 62,279 microforms, 1,704 current periodical subscriptions. CD player(s) available for graduate student use. Access provided to online bibliographic retrieval services and online databases.

INTERNATIONAL STUDENTS
Demographics 15% of students enrolled are international students [Asia, 13%, North America, 49%, other, 38%].

Services and Facilities International student office, counseling/support services.

Applying TOEFL: minimum score of 550, proof of adequate funds, proof of health/immunizations required. Financial aid is available to international students.

International Student Contact Stephanie Decker, Acting Co-Director of Admissions, 2641 Kennedy Boulevard, Jersey City, NJ 07306-5997. Phone: 201-915-9213; Fax: 201-432-5860; E-mail: admissions@spcvxa.spc.edu

PLACEMENT
Services include alumni network, career counseling/planning, career fairs, career library, career placement, job interviews arranged, resume referral to employers, and resume preparation. In 1996–97, 175 organizations participated in on-campus recruiting; 200 on-campus interviews were conducted.

Employment Of 1996–97 graduates, 91% were employed within three months of graduation; the average starting salary was $55,000. Types of employment entered: accounting, banking, communications, computer-related, consulting, education, finance, financial services, health services, high technology, human resources, information systems/technology, international trade, management, marketing, media, pharmaceutical, retail, service industry, telecommunications.

Business Program(s) URL: http://www.spc.edu

Program Contact: Ms. Barbara Bertsch, Graduate Admissions Representative, 2641 Kennedy Boulevard, Jersey City, NJ 07306-5997. Phone: 201-915-9213, 888-772-9933; Fax: 201-432-5860; E-mail: admissions@spcvxa.spc.edu

See full description on page 972.

Seton Hall University

W. Paul Stillman School of Business

South Orange, New Jersey

OVERVIEW
Seton Hall University is an independent-religious, coed university. Enrollment: 9,706 graduate, professional, and undergraduate students; 1,399 full-time matriculated graduate/professional students; 2,411 part-time matriculated graduate/professional students. Founded: 1856. The graduate business unit is in a suburban setting and is on a semester calendar.

HIGHLIGHTS

Enrollment Profile
Full-time: 94
Part-time: 771
Total: 865
Average Age: 27
Fall 1997 Average GPA: 3.2

International: N/R
Women: 39%
Minorities: N/R
Average Class Size: 25
Fall 1997 Average GMAT: 560

Costs
Full-time tuition: N/R
Part-time tuition: $508 per credit

AACSB – The International Association for Management Education accredited

GRADUATE BUSINESS PROGRAMS
Evening MBA (MBA) Full-time, part-time; 30-60 total credits required; 2 to 5 years to complete program. Concentrations in accounting, economics, finance, human resources, management, management information systems, marketing, quantitative analysis, sports/entertainment management.

Master of Science in International Business (MS) Part-time; 33 total credits required; 18 months to 5 years to complete program.

Master of Science in Information Systems (MS) Part-time; 30 total credits required; 18 months to 5 years to complete program.

Master of Science in Human Resource Management (MS) Part-time; 30 total credits required; 12 months to 5 years to complete program.

Master of Science in Financial Planning (MS) Part-time; 30 total credits required; 18 months to 5 years to complete program.

Master of Science in Taxation (MS) Full-time, part-time, distance learning option; 30 total credits required; 12 months to 5 years to complete program.

Master of Science in Accounting (MS) Full-time, part-time; 30 total credits required; 12 months to 5 years to complete program.

Master of Science in Professional Accounting (MS) Full-time, part-time; 30 total credits required; 12 months to 5 years to complete program.

Master of Business Administration/Master of Science in International Business (MBA/MS) Full-time, part-time; 78 total credits required; 2.5 to 5 years to complete program. Concentrations in accounting, economics, finance, human resources, management, management information systems, marketing, quantitative analysis, sports/entertainment management.

<u>Seton Hall University (continued)</u>

Master of Business Administration/Master of Science in Financial Planning (MBA/MS) Full-time, part-time; 75 total credits required; 2.5 to 5 years to complete program. Concentrations in accounting, economics, finance, human resources, management, management information systems, marketing, quantitative analysis, sports/entertainment management.

Master of Business Administration/Doctor of Jurisprudence (MBA/JD) Full-time; 4 to 5 years to complete program. Concentrations in accounting, economics, finance, human resources, management, management information systems, marketing, quantitative analysis, sports/entertainment management.

Master of Business Administration (MBA) Full-time; 48 total credits required; 16 months to complete program.

ADMISSION
Applications For fall 1997 there were 421 applications for admission. Of those applying, 265 were accepted.

Application Requirements Application form, application fee, bachelor's degree, essay, minimum GPA: 3.0, 3 letters of recommendation, personal statement, resume, college transcript(s).

Recommended for Application GMAT score accepted: minimum 500, interview, work experience, computer experience.

Application Deadline Applications processed on a rolling/continuous basis for both domestic and international students. Application fee: $50. Deferred entrance is available.

ACADEMICS
Faculty Full-time 54; part-time 32.

Teaching Methodologies Case study, computer-aided instruction, computer analysis, computer simulations, experiential learning, faculty seminars, field projects, group discussion, lecture, research, role playing, seminars by members of the business community, simulations, student presentations, study groups, team projects.

Technology 250 on-campus computer terminals/PCs are available for student use and are linked by a campus-wide network. The network has full access to the Internet. Students are not required to have their own PC.

Special Opportunities Advanced credit may be earned through credit by examination, transfer of credits from another institution. International exchange programs in Dominican Republic, France, Netherlands, People's Republic of China, Spain, Russia. An internship program is available.

FINANCES
Costs for 1997–98 Tuition: $508 per credit. Cost varies by number of credits taken. Fees: $85 per semester. Fees vary by number of credits taken. Average 1997–98 room and board costs were $6500 per academic year (on campus) and $6500 per academic year (off campus). Room and board costs vary by occupancy (e.g., single, double, triple), type of accommodation, type of meal plan.

Financial Aid Fellowships, research assistantships, teaching assistantships, scholarships, work study, loans available. Financial aid is available to part-time students.

Financial Aid Contact Mr. Michael Menendez, Director, Financial Aid Office, Financial Aid Office, Bayley Hall, South Orange, NJ 07079. Phone: 973-761-9348; Fax: 973-761-7954; E-mail: menendmi@lanmail.shu.edu

FACILITIES
Information Resources Walsh Library plus 1 additional on-campus library; total holdings of 503,000 volumes, 500,000 microforms, 3,300 current periodical subscriptions. CD player(s) available for graduate student use. Access provided to online bibliographic retrieval services.

INTERNATIONAL STUDENTS
Demographics N/R

Services and Facilities International student office, visa services, ESL courses, counseling/support services.

Applying TOEFL: minimum score of 550, proof of adequate funds, proof of health/immunizations required. Financial aid is not available to international students.

International Student Contact Ms. Kathleen Reilly, Director/International Programs, Presidents Hall, South Orange, NJ 07079. Phone: 973-761-9081; Fax: 973-275-2383; E-mail: reillyka@shu.edu

PLACEMENT
Services include alumni network, career counseling/planning, career fairs, career library, career placement, electronic job bank, job interviews arranged, job search course, resume referral to employers, and resume preparation. In 1996–97, 200 organizations participated in on-campus recruiting.

Business Program(s) URL: http://www.shu.edu:80/

Program Contact: Student Information Office, W. Paul Stillman School of Business, 400 South Orange Avenue, South Orange, NJ 07079-2692. Phone: 973-761-9222; Fax: 973-761-9217; E-mail: busgrad@shu.edu
See full description on page 986.

Stevens Institute of Technology

Wesley J. Howe School of Technology Management
Hoboken, New Jersey

OVERVIEW
Stevens Institute of Technology is an independent-nonprofit, coed university. Enrollment: 2,800 graduate, professional, and undergraduate students; 403 full-time matriculated graduate/professional students; 1,137 part-time matriculated graduate/professional students. Founded: 1870.

HIGHLIGHTS

Enrollment Profile
Full-time: 66
Part-time: 502
Total: 568
Average Age: 26
Fall 1997 Average GPA: N/R

International: 9%
Women: 32%
Minorities: N/R
Average Class Size: N/R
Fall 1997 Average GMAT: N/R

Costs
Full-time tuition: N/R
Part-time tuition: $650 per credit hour

GRADUATE BUSINESS PROGRAMS
Master of Science in Management (MS) Full-time, part-time; 30 total credits required; up to 3 years to complete program.

Technology Management PhD Program (PhD) Full-time, part-time; 60 total credits required.

Information Management PhD Program (PhD) Full-time, part-time; 60 total credits required.

Master of Engineering/Master of Management (ME/MM) Full-time, part-time; 30 total credits required.

Master of Science in Telecommunications (MS) Full-time, part-time; 30 total credits required.

Master of Technology Management (MTM) Part-time; 32 total credits required; 20 months to complete program.

ADMISSION
Application Requirements Application form, bachelor's degree, minimum GPA: 3.0, 2 letters of recommendation, college transcript(s).

Recommended for Application Personal statement, resume, work experience, computer experience.

Application Deadline Applications processed on a rolling/continuous basis for both domestic and international students.

ACADEMICS
Teaching Methodologies Case study, faculty seminars, group discussion, lecture, research, student presentations, team projects.

FINANCES
Costs for 1997–98 Tuition: $650 per credit hour.

Financial Aid Fellowships, research assistantships, teaching assistantships, work study, loans available.

Financial Aid Contact David Sheridan, Castle Point on Hudson, Hoboken, NJ 07030. Phone: 201-216-5201.

FACILITIES
Information Resources Samuel C. Williams Library; total holdings of 94,847 volumes, 10,461 microforms, 2,622 current periodical subscriptions. CD player(s) available for graduate student use. Access provided to online bibliographic retrieval services.

INTERNATIONAL STUDENTS
Demographics 9% of students enrolled are international students.

Services and Facilities International student office, international student center, visa services, ESL courses, counseling/support services.

Applying TOEFL: minimum score of 550 required.

International Student Contact Laura Arthur, Manager of International Student Services, Castle Point on Hudson, Hoboken, NJ 07030. Phone: 201-216-5189.

PLACEMENT
Services include alumni network, and career library.

Employment Types of employment entered: communications, computer-related, consulting, engineering, finance, financial services, information systems/

technology, management, manufacturing, marketing, pharmaceutical, telecommunications.

Business Program(s) URL: http://www.stevens-tech.edu

Program Contact: James Tietjen, Dean, Wesley J. Howe School of Technology Management, Castle Point on the Hudson, Hoboken, NJ 07030. Phone: 201-216-5386; Fax: 201-216-5385.

Thomas Edison State College

Graduate Studies Office

Trenton, New Jersey

OVERVIEW
Thomas Edison State College is a state-supported, coed, comprehensive institution. Enrollment: 8,564 graduate, professional, and undergraduate students; full-time matriculated graduate/professional students; 49 part-time matriculated graduate/professional students. Founded: 1972. The graduate business unit is in an urban setting and is on a semester calendar.

HIGHLIGHTS

Enrollment Profile
Full-time: 0
Part-time: 49
Total: 49
Average Age: 42
Fall 1997 Average GPA: N/R

International: N/R
Women: 47%
Minorities: 22%
Average Class Size: 20
Fall 1997 Average GMAT: N/R

Costs
Full-time tuition: N/R
Part-time tuition: $289 per credit (resident); $289 per credit (nonresident)

GRADUATE BUSINESS PROGRAMS
Master of Science in Management (MSM) Part-time, distance learning option; 36 total credits required; minimum of 18 months to complete program. Concentration in management.

ADMISSION
Application Requirements Application form, application fee, bachelor's degree, essay, 2 letters of recommendation, personal statement, college transcript(s), minimum of 3 years of work experience, computer experience.

Recommended for Application Resume.

Application Deadline Applications processed on a rolling/continuous basis for both domestic and international students. Application fee: $75. Deferred entrance is available.

ACADEMICS
Faculty Part-time 10.

Teaching Methodologies Case study, computer-aided instruction, experiential learning, faculty seminars, group discussion, lecture, research, role playing, simulations, student presentations, study groups, team projects.

Technology The network has full access to the Internet. Students are required to have their own PC.

Special Opportunities Advanced credit may be earned through credit for experience, credit for military training programs, credit for business training programs, transfer of credits from another institution.

FINANCES
Costs for 1997–98 Tuition: Part-time: $289 per credit (resident); $289 per credit (nonresident). Fees: Part-time: $1500 per 2 years (resident); $1500 per 2 years (nonresident).

Financial Aid Contact Dr. Esther Taitsman, Director of Graduate Studies, 101 West State Street, Trenton, NJ 08608-1176. Phone: 609-292-5143; Fax: 609-777-2956.

FACILITIES
Information Resources The NJ State Library.

INTERNATIONAL STUDENTS
Demographics N/R

Services and Facilities Counseling/support services.

Applying TOEFL: minimum score of 500 required. Financial aid is not available to international students.

International Student Contact Dr. Esther Taitsman, Director of Graduate Studies, 101 West State Street, Trenton, NJ 08608-1176. Phone: 609-292-5143; Fax: 609-984-8447; E-mail: msm@call.tesc.edu

PLACEMENT
Services include alumni network. In 1996–97, 2 organizations participated in on-campus recruiting.

Business Program(s) URL: http://www.tesc.edu

Program Contact: Dr. Esther Taitsman, Director of Graduate Studies, 101 West State Street, Trenton, NJ 08608-1176. Phone: 609-292-5143; Fax: 609-777-2956; E-mail: msm@call.tesc.edu

William Paterson University of New Jersey

College of Business

Wayne, New Jersey

OVERVIEW
William Paterson University of New Jersey is a state-supported, coed, comprehensive institution. Enrollment: 9,207 graduate, professional, and undergraduate students; 117 full-time matriculated graduate/professional students; 522 part-time matriculated graduate/professional students. Founded: 1855. The graduate business unit is in a suburban setting and is on a semester calendar.

HIGHLIGHTS

Enrollment Profile
Full-time: 8
Part-time: 88
Total: 96
Average Age: 34
Fall 1997 Average GPA: 2.861

International: N/R
Women: 40%
Minorities: 9%
Average Class Size: 15
Fall 1997 Average GMAT: 464

Costs
Full-time tuition: N/R
Part-time tuition: $210 per credit (resident); $298 per credit (nonresident)

GRADUATE BUSINESS PROGRAMS
Master of Business Administration (MBA) Full-time, part-time; 60 total credits required; 2 to 7 years to complete program. Concentrations in marketing, business policy/strategy, management, finance.

ADMISSION
Applications For fall 1997 there were 35 applications for admission. Of those applying, 32 were accepted. Of those accepted, 25 enrolled.

Application Requirements Application form, application fee, bachelor's degree, minimum GPA: 2.0, 2 letters of recommendation, personal statement, college transcript(s).

Recommended for Application GMAT score accepted: minimum 400, essay, interview, resume, work experience.

Application Deadline 4/1 for fall, 10/15 for spring, 4/1 for fall (international), 10/15 for spring (international). Application fee: $35. Deferred entrance is available.

ACADEMICS
Faculty Full-time 7; part-time 4.

Teaching Methodologies Case study, computer simulations, experiential learning, group discussion, lecture, research, student presentations, team projects.

Technology 250 on-campus computer terminals/PCs are available for student use and are linked by a campus-wide network. The network has full access to the Internet. Students are not required to have their own PC.

Special Opportunities Advanced credit may be earned through transfer of credits from another institution.

FINANCES
Costs for 1997–98 Tuition: $210 per credit (resident); $298 per credit (nonresident). Average 1997–98 room and board costs were $4800 per academic year. Room and board costs vary by campus location, occupancy (e.g., single, double, triple), type of accommodation, type of meal plan.

Financial Aid In 1997–98, 3% of students received some institutionally administered aid in the form of research assistantships, teaching assistantships, loans. Financial aid is available to part-time students. Application Deadline: 4/1.

Financial Aid Contact Ms. Ann Marie Duffy, Director, Graduate Services, 300 Pompton Road, Wayne, NJ 07470-8420. Phone: 973-720-2237; Fax: 973-720-2035; E-mail: duffya@gw.wilpaterson.edu

FACILITIES
Information Resources Sarah Byrd Askew Library; total holdings of 317,000 volumes, 1,029,000 microforms, 1,650 current periodical subscriptions. CD player(s) available for graduate student use. Access provided to online bibliographic retrieval services.

INTERNATIONAL STUDENTS
Demographics N/R

<u>*William Paterson University of New Jersey (continued)*</u>

Services and Facilities International student office, international student housing, visa services, ESL courses, counseling/support services.

Applying TOEFL, proof of adequate funds, proof of health/immunizations required. Financial aid is not available to international students.

International Student Contact Ms. Ann Marie Duffy, Director, Graduate Services , 300 Pompton Road, Wayne, NJ 07470. Phone: 973-720-2237; Fax: 973-720-2035; E-mail: duffya@gw.wilpaterson.edu

PLACEMENT

Services include alumni network, career counseling/planning, career library, career placement, job search course, and resume preparation.

Employment Of 1996–97 graduates, 100% were employed within three months of graduation. Types of employment entered: banking, consumer products, financial services, insurance, marketing, pharmaceutical, retail, service industry.

Program Contact: Ms. Ann Marie Duffy, Director, Graduate Services, 300 Pompton Road, Wayne, NJ 07470-8420. Phone: 973-720-2237, 800-494-5728; Fax: 973-720-2035; E-mail: duffya@gw.wilpaterson.edu

NEW MEXICO

College of Santa Fe

Department of Business Administration

Santa Fe, New Mexico

OVERVIEW

College of Santa Fe is an independent-nonprofit, coed, comprehensive institution. Enrollment: 1,417 graduate, professional, and undergraduate students; 32 full-time matriculated graduate/professional students; 235 part-time matriculated graduate/professional students. The graduate business unit is in a small-town setting and is on a terms—5 per year (2 fall, 2 spring, 1 summer); each 9 weeks long calendar.

HIGHLIGHTS

Enrollment Profile

Full-time: 32	International: 2%
Part-time: 69	Women: 55%
Total: 101	Minorities: N/R
Average Age: 38	Average Class Size: 12
Fall 1997 Average GPA: 3.2	Fall 1997 Average GMAT: N/R

Costs
Full-time tuition: N/R
Part-time tuition: $237 per credit

GRADUATE BUSINESS PROGRAMS

Master of Business Administration (MBA) Full-time, part-time; 36 total credits required; 12 months to 5 years to complete program. Concentrations in human resources, management information systems, finance.

ADMISSION

Applications For fall 1997 there were 23 applications for admission. Of those applying, 23 were accepted. Of those accepted, 14 enrolled.

Application Requirements Application form, application fee, bachelor's degree, interview, 2 letters of recommendation, college transcript(s).

Recommended for Application Minimum GPA: 3.0, work experience, computer experience.

Application Deadline Applications processed on a rolling/continuous basis for both domestic and international students. Application fee: $25. Deferred entrance is available.

ACADEMICS

Faculty Full-time 4; part-time 7.

Teaching Methodologies Case study, computer-aided instruction, computer analysis, group discussion, lecture, research, role playing, simulations, student presentations, team projects.

Technology 39 on-campus computer terminals/PCs are available for student use and are linked by a campus-wide network. The network has full access to the Internet. Students are not required to have their own PC.

Special Opportunities Advanced credit may be earned through transfer of credits from another institution.

FINANCES

Costs for 1997–98 Tuition: $237 per credit. Fees: $5 per term. Fees vary by academic program. Average 1997–98 room and board costs were $4565 per academic year (on campus) and $4500 per academic year (off campus). Room and board costs vary by occupancy (e.g., single, double, triple), type of meal plan.

Financial Aid Scholarships, work study available. Financial aid is available to part-time students. Application Deadline: 6/15.

Financial Aid Contact Mr. Dale Reinhart, Director of Admissions and Enrollment Management, 1600 St. Michael's Drive, Santa Fe, NM 87505. Phone: 505-473-6133; Fax: 505-473-6127; E-mail: mruzicka@fogelson.csf.com

FACILITIES

Information Resources Fogelson Library; total holdings of 150,000 volumes, 76,300 microforms, 398 current periodical subscriptions. CD player(s) available for graduate student use. Access provided to online bibliographic retrieval services and online databases.

INTERNATIONAL STUDENTS

Demographics 2% of students enrolled are international students [Europe, 100%].

Services and Facilities International student office, counseling/support services.

Applying TOEFL: minimum score of 550, proof of adequate funds required. Financial aid is not available to international students.

International Student Contact Mr. Andy Lovato, Director, Career Placement/ International Student Advisor, 1600 Saint Michael's Drive, Santa Fe, NM 87505-7634. Phone: 505-473-6294; Fax: 505-473-6121.

PLACEMENT

Services include career counseling/planning, career fairs, career library, career placement, electronic job bank, job interviews arranged, and resume preparation. In 1996–97, 75 organizations participated in on-campus recruiting.

Employment Of 1996–97 graduates, 95% were employed within three months of graduation. Types of employment entered: accounting, banking, computer-related, education, finance, government, human resources, management, marketing, nonprofit.

Business Program(s) URL: http://www.csf.edu/busadm/index.html

Program Contact: Ms. Debbie Aragon, Administrative, 1600 Saint Michael's Drive, Santa Fe, NM 87505-7634. Phone: 505-473-6211, 800-456-2673; Fax: 505-473-6504; E-mail: aarshad@csf.edu

Eastern New Mexico University

College of Business

Portales, New Mexico

OVERVIEW

Eastern New Mexico University is a state-supported, coed, comprehensive institution. Enrollment: 3,900 graduate, professional, and undergraduate students; 174 full-time matriculated graduate/professional students; 421 part-time matriculated graduate/professional students. Founded: 1927. The graduate business unit is in a rural setting and is on a semester calendar.

HIGHLIGHTS

Enrollment Profile

Full-time: 14	International: 14%
Part-time: 30	Women: 55%
Total: 44	Minorities: 18%
Average Age: 35	Average Class Size: 22
Fall 1997 Average GPA: 3.2	Fall 1997 Average GMAT: 530

Costs
Full-time tuition: $960 per academic year (resident); $3285 per academic year (nonresident)
Part-time tuition: $80 per hour (resident); $274 per hour (nonresident)

ACBSP – The American Council of Business Schools and Programs accredited

GRADUATE BUSINESS PROGRAMS

Master of Business Administration (MBA) Full-time, part-time, distance learning option; 33 total credits required; 2 years work experience required; 15 months to 5 years to complete program. Concentration in management.

ADMISSION

Applications For fall 1997 there were 20 applications for admission. Of those applying, 18 were accepted. Of those accepted, 10 enrolled.

Application Requirements Application form, application fee, bachelor's degree, minimum GPA: 3.0, personal statement, college transcript(s), minimum of 2 years of work experience.

Recommended for Application GMAT score accepted.

Application Deadline Applications processed on a rolling/continuous basis for both domestic and international students. Application fee: $10. Deferred entrance is available.

ACADEMICS
Faculty Full-time 20; part-time 5.

Teaching Methodologies Case study, computer-aided instruction, computer analysis, computer simulations, group discussion, lecture, research, role playing, simulations, student presentations, study groups, team projects.

Technology 200 on-campus computer terminals/PCs are available for student use and are linked by a campus-wide network. The network has full access to the Internet. Students are not required to have their own PC.

Special Opportunities Advanced credit may be earned through credit for military training programs, transfer of credits from another institution.

FINANCES
Costs for 1997–98 Tuition: Full-time: $960 per year (resident); $3285 per year (nonresident). Part-time: $80 per hour (resident); $274 per hour (nonresident). Cost varies by campus location, reciprocity agreements. Average 1997–98 room and board costs were $2838 per academic year (on campus) and $2700 per academic year (off campus). Room and board costs vary by campus location, occupancy (e.g., single, double, triple), type of accommodation, type of meal plan.

Financial Aid In 1997–98, 30% of students received some institutionally administered aid in the form of fellowships, research assistantships, teaching assistantships, work study. Financial aid is available to part-time students. Application Deadline: 4/1.

Financial Aid Contact Ms. Julie Poorman, Student Financial Aid, Station 20, Portales, NM 88130. Phone: 505-562-2194; Fax: 505-562-2566.

FACILITIES
Information Resources Golden Library plus 1 additional on-campus library; total holdings of 271,935 volumes, 688,895 microforms, 2,756 current periodical subscriptions. CD player(s) available for graduate student use. Access provided to online bibliographic retrieval services.

INTERNATIONAL STUDENTS
Demographics 14% of students enrolled are international students [Asia, 75%, North America, 25%].

Services and Facilities International student office, international student center, counseling/support services.

Applying TOEFL: minimum score of 550, proof of adequate funds, proof of health/immunizations required. Financial aid is not available to international students.

International Student Contact Mrs. Pat Dodd, Admissions Specialist III, Station 7, Portales, NM 88130. Phone: 505-562-2225; Fax: 505-562-2168; E-mail: doddp@email.enmu.edu

PLACEMENT
Services include alumni network, career fairs, career library, career placement, job interviews arranged, and resume referral to employers. In 1996–97, 91 organizations participated in on-campus recruiting; 1,500 on-campus interviews were conducted.

Employment Of 1996–97 graduates, 100% were employed within three months of graduation; the average starting salary was $36,000. Types of employment entered: accounting, banking, computer-related, energy, finance, government, management, marketing.

Business Program(s) URL: http://www.enmu.edu/~glandont/cob/cobhome.htm

Program Contact: Dr. Gerry Huybregts, Graduate Coordinator, College of Business, Station 49, Portales, NM 88130. Phone: 505-562-2702; Fax: 505-562-4331; E-mail: gerry.huybregts@enmu.edu

New Mexico Highlands University

School of Business

Las Vegas, New Mexico

OVERVIEW
New Mexico Highlands University is a state-supported, coed, comprehensive institution. Enrollment: 2,797 graduate, professional, and undergraduate students; 254 full-time matriculated graduate/professional students; 180 part-time matriculated graduate/professional students. Founded: 1893. The graduate business unit is in a small-town setting and is on a semester calendar.

HIGHLIGHTS
Enrollment Profile

Full-time: 26	International: 6%
Part-time: 26	Women: 58%
Total: 52	Minorities: 67%
Average Age: 30	Average Class Size: 15
Fall 1997 Average GPA: 3.3	Fall 1997 Average GMAT: 450

Costs
Full-time tuition: $858 per academic year (resident); $3600 per academic year (nonresident)
Part-time tuition: $72 per hour (resident); $72 per hour (nonresident)

ACBSP – The American Council of Business Schools and Programs accredited

GRADUATE BUSINESS PROGRAMS
Master of Business Administration (MBA) Full-time, part-time, distance learning option; 36 total credits required; 2 to 3 years to complete program. Concentration in management.

ADMISSION
Application Requirements GMAT score, application form, application fee, bachelor's degree, minimum GPA: 3.0, 3 letters of recommendation, resume, college transcript(s), computer experience.

Recommended for Application Essay, interview, personal statement.

Application Deadline Applications processed on a rolling/continuous basis for both domestic and international students. Application fee: $15.

ACADEMICS
Faculty Full-time 13.

Teaching Methodologies Case study, computer-aided instruction, computer analysis, computer simulations, faculty seminars, field projects, lecture, research, seminars by members of the business community, simulations, student presentations, study groups, team projects.

Technology 42 on-campus computer terminals/PCs are available for student use and are linked by a campus-wide network. The network has full access to the Internet. Students are not required to have their own PC.

Special Opportunities Advanced credit may be earned through transfer of credits from another institution.

FINANCES
Costs for 1997–98 Tuition: Full-time: $858 per semester (resident); $3600 per semester (nonresident). Part-time: $72 per hour (resident); $72 per hour (nonresident). Cost varies by academic program, number of credits taken. Fees: Full-time: $20 per academic year (resident); $20 per academic year (nonresident). Part-time: $20 per year (resident); $20 per year (nonresident). Fees vary by academic program. Average 1997–98 room and board costs were $3500 per academic year (on campus) and $3150 per academic year (off campus). Room and board costs vary by type of accommodation, type of meal plan.

Financial Aid Work study available. Application Deadline: 3/1.

Financial Aid Contact Director of Financial Aid, Felix Martinez Building, Las Vegas, NM 87701. Phone: 505-454-0584.

FACILITIES
Information Resources Donnelly Library; total holdings of 49,263 volumes, 143,937 microforms, 1,431 current periodical subscriptions. Access provided to online bibliographic retrieval services.

INTERNATIONAL STUDENTS
Demographics 6% of students enrolled are international students.

Services and Facilities International student office, international student center, ESL courses, counseling/support services.

Applying TOEFL: minimum score of 525 required. Financial aid is not available to international students.

International Student Contact Lyn DeMartin, Director of International Programs, Las Vegas, NM 87701. Phone: 505-454-3344 Ext. 3058.

PLACEMENT
Services include alumni network, career counseling/planning, career fairs, career library, career placement, job interviews arranged, resume referral to employers, and resume preparation.

Employment Types of employment entered: accounting, banking, consumer products, education, finance, government.

Business Program(s) URL: http://www.nmhu.edu/academics/schbusiness/

Program Contact: Dr. Margaret Young, Graduate Coordinator, School of Business, Las Vegas, NM 87701. Phone: 505-454-3115; Fax: 505-454-3354.

New Mexico State University

College of Business Administration and Economics

Las Cruces, New Mexico

OVERVIEW

New Mexico State University is a state-supported, coed university. Enrollment: 15,067 graduate, professional, and undergraduate students; 1,419 full-time matriculated graduate/professional students; 988 part-time matriculated graduate/professional students. Founded: 1888. The graduate business unit is in a small-town setting and is on a semester calendar.

HIGHLIGHTS

Enrollment Profile

Full-time: 51	International: 9%
Part-time: 62	Women: 46%
Total: 113	Minorities: 19%
Average Age: 32	Average Class Size: 18
Fall 1997 Average GPA: 3.169	Fall 1997 Average GMAT: 464

Costs

Full-time tuition: $2352 per academic year (resident); $7344 per academic year (nonresident)

Part-time tuition: $98 per credit (resident); $306 per credit (nonresident)

AACSB – The International Association for Management Education accredited

GRADUATE BUSINESS PROGRAMS

Master of Business Administration (MBA) Full-time, part-time; 36-55 total credits required; 18 months to 3.3 years to complete program. Concentrations in agribusiness, economics, finance, human resources, international business, manufacturing management, marketing, health care, management information systems.

ADMISSION

Applications For fall 1997 there were 99 applications for admission. Of those applying, 57 were accepted. Of those accepted, 21 enrolled.

Application Requirements Application form, application fee, bachelor's degree, minimum GPA, resume.

Recommended for Application GMAT score accepted: minimum 500, college transcript(s).

Application Deadline 7/1 for fall, 11/1 for spring, 4/1 for summer, 3/1 for fall (international), 10/1 for spring (international). Application fee: $15, $35 (international). Deferred entrance is available.

ACADEMICS

Faculty Full-time 62; part-time 1.

Teaching Methodologies Case study, computer-aided instruction, computer analysis, computer simulations, experiential learning, faculty seminars, group discussion, lecture, research, role playing, seminars by members of the business community, student presentations, study groups, team projects.

Technology 600 on-campus computer terminals/PCs are available for student use and are linked by a campus-wide network. The network has full access to the Internet. Students are required to have their own PC.

Special Opportunities Advanced credit may be earned through credit for experience, transfer of credits from another institution. An internship program is available.

FINANCES

Costs for 1997–98 Tuition: Full-time: $2352 per year (resident); $7344 per year (nonresident). Part-time: $98 per credit (resident); $306 per credit (nonresident). Cost varies by number of credits taken, reciprocity agreements. Fees vary by number of credits taken, reciprocity agreements. Average 1997–98 room and board costs were $5700 per academic year (on campus) and $8500 per academic year (off campus). Room and board costs vary by occupancy (e.g., single, double, triple), type of accommodation, type of meal plan.

Financial Aid In 1997–98, 18% of students received some institutionally administered aid in the form of fellowships, research assistantships, teaching assistantships, scholarships, work study. Financial aid is available to part-time students. Application Deadline: 3/1.

Financial Aid Contact Mr. Greeley W. Myers, Director, Financial Aid, PO Box 30001/Dept 5100, Las Cruces, NM 88003. Phone: 505-646-4593; Fax: 505-646-7977.

FACILITIES

Information Resources New Library plus 1 additional on-campus library; total holdings of 929,494 volumes, 1,269,869 microforms, 6,846 current periodical subscriptions. CD player(s) available for graduate student use. Access provided to online bibliographic retrieval services.

INTERNATIONAL STUDENTS

Demographics 9% of students enrolled are international students [Africa, 7%, Asia, 44%, Europe, 22%, North America, 11%, South America, 11%, other, 5%].

Services and Facilities International student office, international student center, international student housing, visa services, ESL courses, counseling/support services, sponsored student assistances, Foreign Student Organization services.

Applying TOEFL: minimum score of 550 required. Financial aid is not available to international students.

International Student Contact Sharon Urtaza, Coordinator, Foreign Students/Immigration Services, Center for International Programs-Box 3567, Las Cruces, NM 88003. Phone: 505-646-2017; Fax: 505-646-5117; E-mail: surtaza@nmsu.edu

PLACEMENT

Services include alumni network, career counseling/planning, career fairs, career library, career placement, electronic job bank, job interviews arranged, job search course, resume referral to employers, and resume preparation. In 1996–97, 378 organizations participated in on-campus recruiting; 3,424 on-campus interviews were conducted.

Employment Of 1996–97 graduates, 40% were employed within three months of graduation; the average starting salary was $36,723. Types of employment entered: accounting, banking, chemical industry, communications, computer-related, consumer products, education, engineering, finance, financial services, government, health services, high technology, human resources, information systems/technology, insurance, management, manufacturing, marketing, petrochemical, retail, telecommunications, transportation, utilities.

Business Program(s) URL: http://cbae.nmsu.edu/

Program Contact: Dr. Joe Benson, Director, MBA Program, PO Box 30001/Dept 3GSP, Las Cruces, NM 88003-8001. Phone: 505-646-8003; Fax: 505-646-7977; E-mail: mbaprog@nmsu.edu

University of New Mexico

Robert O. Anderson Graduate School of Management

Albuquerque, New Mexico

OVERVIEW

The University of New Mexico is a state-supported, coed university. Enrollment: 22,265 graduate, professional, and undergraduate students; 2,818 full-time matriculated graduate/professional students; 2,292 part-time matriculated graduate/professional students. Founded: 1889. The graduate business unit is in an urban setting and is on a semester calendar.

HIGHLIGHTS

Enrollment Profile

Full-time: N/R	International: N/R
Part-time: N/R	Women: N/R
Total: 461	Minorities: 11%
Average Age: 33	Average Class Size: 40
Fall 1997 Average GPA: 3.3	Fall 1997 Average GMAT: 540-550

Costs

Full-time tuition: $928 per academic year (resident); $3271 per academic year (nonresident)

Part-time tuition: $99 per credit hour (resident); $99 per credit hour (nonresident)

AACSB – The International Association for Management Education accredited

GRADUATE BUSINESS PROGRAMS

Master of Business Administration (MBA) Full-time, part-time; 48 total credits required; 12 months to 5 years to complete program.

Master of Business Administration (MBA) Full-time, part-time; 57 total credits required; 12 months to 5 years to complete program. Concentrations in accounting, entrepreneurship, finance, human resources, international business, management information systems, marketing, operations management, public policy and administration, taxation, technology management.

Master of Science in Accounting (MS) Full-time, part-time; 33 total credits required; 2 to 5 years to complete program. Concentration in accounting.

Master of Business Administration/Master of Arts in Latin American Studies (MBA/MA) Full-time, part-time; 72 total credits required; 4.4 to 6 years to complete program. Concentration in international management.

Master of Business Administration/Doctor of Jurisprudence (MBA/JD) Full-time; 129 total credits required; 5 to 8 years to complete program.

Executive MBA (MBA) Full-time; 50 total credits required; 2 years to complete program.

ADMISSION
Applications For fall 1997 there were 180 applications for admission. Of those applying, 132 were accepted. Of those accepted, 99 enrolled.

Application Requirements Application form, application fee, bachelor's degree, essay, minimum GPA: 3.0, 3 letters of recommendation, personal statement, resume, college transcript(s).

Recommended for Application GMAT score accepted: minimum 500, work experience, computer experience: working knowledge of PC software.

Application Deadline 7/17 for fall, 11/13 for spring, 5/1 for fall (international), 10/1 for spring (international). Application fee: $25. Deferred entrance is available.

ACADEMICS
Faculty Full-time 48; part-time 48.

Teaching Methodologies Case study, computer-aided instruction, computer analysis, computer simulations, experiential learning, faculty seminars, field projects, group discussion, lecture, research, role playing, seminars by members of the business community, simulations, student presentations, study groups, team projects.

Technology 110 on-campus computer terminals/PCs are available for student use and are linked by a campus-wide network. The network has full access to the Internet. Students are not required to have their own PC.

Special Opportunities Advanced credit may be earned through transfer of credits from another institution. International exchange programs in Brazil, France, Mexico, United Kingdom.

FINANCES
Costs for 1997–98 Tuition: Full-time: $928 per semester (resident); $3271 per semester (nonresident). Part-time: $99 per credit hour (resident); $99 per credit hour (nonresident). Cost varies by class time (e.g., day/evening), number of credits taken. Fees: Full-time: $16 per academic year (resident); $16 per academic year (nonresident). Part-time: $32 per semester (resident); $32 per semester (nonresident). Average 1997–98 room and board costs were $5000 per academic year (on campus) and $5400 per academic year (off campus). Room and board costs vary by occupancy (e.g., single, double, triple), type of accommodation, type of meal plan.

Financial Aid In 1997–98, 10% of students received some institutionally administered aid in the form of fellowships, research assistantships, teaching assistantships, scholarships, work study, loans.

Financial Aid Contact Ms. Ida Romero, Director, Mesa Vista Hall, Room 1030, Albuquerque, NM 87131. Phone: 505-277-5017; Fax: 505-277-6326; E-mail: iromero@unm.edu

FACILITIES
Information Resources Zimmerman Library plus 7 additional on-campus libraries; total holdings of 4,000,000 volumes, 1,500,000 microforms, 15,000 current periodical subscriptions. CD player(s) available for graduate student use. Access provided to online bibliographic retrieval services.

INTERNATIONAL STUDENTS
Demographics N/R

Services and Facilities International student office, international student center, visa services, ESL courses, counseling/support services.

Applying TOEFL: minimum score of 550, proof of adequate funds, proof of health/immunizations required. Financial aid is not available to international students.

International Student Contact Mr. Gary Kuykendall, Associate Director of Admissions, Student Services Center, Room 140, Albuquerque, NM 87131. Phone: 505-277-5829; Fax: 505-277-6686; E-mail: gkuyken@unm.edu

PLACEMENT
Services include alumni network, career counseling/planning, career fairs, career library, career placement, electronic job bank, job interviews arranged, job search course, resume referral to employers, and resume preparation. In 1996–97, 70 organizations participated in on-campus recruiting; 910 on-campus interviews were conducted.

Employment Of 1996–97 graduates, 70% were employed within three months of graduation; the average starting salary was $38,500. Types of employment entered: accounting, banking, communications, computer-related, consulting, consumer products, engineering, finance, financial services, government, health services, high technology, human resources, information systems/technology, insurance, international trade, law, management, manufacturing, marketing, nonprofit, pharmaceutical, real estate, retail, service industry, telecommunications.

Business Program(s) URL: http://asm.unm.edu/

Program Contact: Ms. Sue Podeyn, MBA Program Director, Anderson Graduate School of Management, Albuquerque, NM 87112-1221. Phone: 505-277-3147; Fax: 505-277-9356; E-mail: podeyn@anderson.unm.edu

Western New Mexico University

Department of Business Administration
Silver City, New Mexico

OVERVIEW
Western New Mexico University is a state-supported, coed, comprehensive institution. Enrollment: 2,474 graduate, professional, and undergraduate students; 22 full-time matriculated graduate/professional students; 444 part-time matriculated graduate/professional students. Founded: 1893. The graduate business unit is in a small-town setting and is on a semester calendar.

HIGHLIGHTS
Enrollment Profile

Full-time: N/R	International: N/R
Part-time: N/R	Women: N/R
Total: 45	Minorities: N/R
Average Age: 30	Average Class Size: 5
Fall 1997 Average GPA: 3.42	Fall 1997 Average GMAT: 495

Costs
Full-time tuition: $1322 per academic year (resident); $4388 per academic year (nonresident)
Part-time tuition: $55 per credit hour (resident); $55 per credit hour (nonresident)

ACBSP – The American Council of Business Schools and Programs accredited

GRADUATE BUSINESS PROGRAMS
Master of Business Administration (MBA) Full-time, part-time; 36 total credits required; 18 months to 7 years to complete program.

ADMISSION
Applications For fall 1997 there were 7 applications for admission. Of those applying, 4 were accepted. Of those accepted, 4 enrolled.

Application Requirements GMAT score: minimum 400, application form, application fee, bachelor's degree, minimum GPA, college transcript(s).

Recommended for Application Computer experience.

Application Deadline Applications processed on a rolling/continuous basis for both domestic and international students. Application fee: $10. Deferred entrance is available.

ACADEMICS
Faculty Full-time 7; part-time 2.

Teaching Methodologies Case study, computer-aided instruction, group discussion, lecture, research, seminars by members of the business community, student presentations, study groups, team projects.

Technology 110 on-campus computer terminals/PCs are available for student use and are linked by a campus-wide network. The network has full access to the Internet. Students are not required to have their own PC.

Special Opportunities Advanced credit may be earned through transfer of credits from another institution. An internship program is available.

FINANCES
Costs for 1997–98 Tuition: Full-time: $1322 per year (resident); $4388 per year (nonresident). Part-time: $55 per credit hour (resident); $55 per credit hour (nonresident). Cost varies by campus location, number of credits taken, reciprocity agreements. Average 1997–98 room and board costs were $2686 per academic year. Room and board costs vary by occupancy (e.g., single, double, triple), type of accommodation, type of meal plan.

Financial Aid Fellowships, work study, loans available. Application Deadline: 4/1.

Financial Aid Contact Charles Kelly, Financial Aid Director, PO Box 680, Silver City, NM 88062. Phone: 505-538-6173; Fax: 505-538-6155.

FACILITIES
Information Resources J. Cloyd Miller Library plus 1 additional on-campus library; total holdings of 112,000 volumes, 44,000 microforms, 800 current periodical subscriptions. CD player(s) available for graduate student use. Access provided to online bibliographic retrieval services.

INTERNATIONAL STUDENTS
Demographics N/R

Services and Facilities International student advisor.

Applying TOEFL: minimum score of 550, proof of adequate funds, proof of health/immunizations required. Financial aid is available to international students.

International Student Contact Mr. Michael Alecksen, Director of Admissions, PO Box 680, Silver City, NM 88062. Phone: 505-538-6106; Fax: 505-538-6155.

PLACEMENT

Services include alumni network, career counseling/planning, career fairs, career placement, job interviews arranged, and resume preparation. In 1996–97, 10 organizations participated in on-campus recruiting; 6 on-campus interviews were conducted.

Employment Of 1996–97 graduates, 80% were employed within three months of graduation. Types of employment entered: accounting, banking, computer-related, education, finance, financial services, government, health services, hospitality management, human resources, information systems/technology, insurance, management, manufacturing, marketing, real estate, retail.

Business Program(s) URL: http://www.wnmu.edu

Program Contact: Mr. Michael Alecksen, Director of Admissions, PO Box 680, Silver City, NM 88062. Phone: 505-538-6106; Fax: 505-538-6155.

NEW YORK

Adelphi University

School of Management and Business

Garden City, New York

OVERVIEW

Adelphi University is an independent-nonprofit, coed university. Enrollment: 5,693 graduate, professional, and undergraduate students; 765 full-time matriculated graduate/professional students; 2,379 part-time matriculated graduate/professional students. Founded: 1896. The graduate business unit is in a suburban setting and is on a semester calendar.

HIGHLIGHTS

Enrollment Profile

Full-time: 26	International: 10%
Part-time: 354	Women: 49%
Total: 380	Minorities: N/R
Average Age: 28	Average Class Size: 20
Fall 1997 Average GPA: 2.8	Fall 1997 Average GMAT: 450

Costs
Full-time tuition: $14,850 per academic year
Part-time tuition: $465 per credit

GRADUATE BUSINESS PROGRAMS

Master of Science in Accounting (MS) Full-time, part-time; 30-42 total credits required; 18 months to 3.5 years to complete program. Concentration in accounting.

Master of Science in Finance and Banking (MS) Full-time, part-time; 30-48 total credits required; 18 months to 4 years to complete program. Concentrations in banking, finance.

Master of Business Administration (MBA) Full-time, part-time; 39-66 total credits required; 18 months to 5 years to complete program. Concentrations in accounting, banking, finance, human resources, international business, management, marketing, health care.

MBA-CPA Program (MBA) Full-time, part-time, distance learning option; 2.5 to 6 years to complete program. Concentration in accounting.

ADMISSION

Applications For fall 1997 there were 105 applications for admission. Of those applying, 96 were accepted. Of those accepted, 77 enrolled.

Application Requirements Application form, application fee, bachelor's degree, essay, minimum GPA: 2.75, 2 letters of recommendation, college transcript(s).

Recommended for Application GMAT score accepted: minimum 450, personal statement, resume.

Application Deadline 8/15 for fall, 12/15 for spring, 5/15 for summer, 5/1 for fall (international), 3/1 for summer (international). Application fee: $50. Deferred entrance is available.

ACADEMICS

Faculty Full-time 23; part-time 17.

Teaching Methodologies Case study, computer-aided instruction, computer simulations, faculty seminars, field projects, group discussion, lecture, research, role playing, seminars by members of the business community, simulations, student presentations, team projects.

Technology 500 on-campus computer terminals/PCs are available for student use and are linked by a campus-wide network. The network has full access to the Internet. Students are not required to have their own PC.

Special Opportunities Advanced credit may be earned through credit by examination, credit for business training programs, transfer of credits from another institution. An internship program is available.

FINANCES

Costs for 1997–98 Tuition: Full-time: $14,850 per year. Part-time: $465 per credit. Fees: Full-time: $250 per academic year. Part-time: $150 per semester. Fees vary by campus location. Average 1997–98 room only costs were $4500 per academic year. Room and board costs vary by type of accommodation, type of meal plan.

Financial Aid Application Deadline: 3/1.

Financial Aid Contact Ms. Gloria Gebhardt, Manager, Office of Student Financial Services, Garden City, NY 11530. Phone: 516-877-3070; Fax: 516-877-3039.

FACILITIES

Information Resources Swirbul Library plus 1 additional on-campus library; total holdings of 461,673 volumes, 647,346 microforms, 5,114 current periodical subscriptions. CD player(s) available for graduate student use. Access provided to online bibliographic retrieval services.

INTERNATIONAL STUDENTS

Demographics 10% of students enrolled are international students.

Services and Facilities International student office, international student housing, visa services, ESL courses, counseling/support services.

Applying TOEFL: minimum score of 550, proof of adequate funds, proof of health/immunizations required. Financial aid is not available to international students.

International Student Contact Ms. Renate Las Manis, Director, International Student Service, South Avenue, Garden City, NY 11530. Phone: 516-877-4990; E-mail: debeir@adlibv.adelphia.edu

PLACEMENT

Services include alumni network, career counseling/planning, career fairs, career library, career placement, electronic job bank, job interviews arranged, and resume preparation.

Employment Types of employment entered: accounting, banking, communications, computer-related, consumer products, finance, health services, human resources, insurance, international trade, management, manufacturing, marketing, nonprofit, pharmaceutical, real estate, retail, service industry, telecommunications.

Business Program(s) URL: http://www.adelphi.edu/~mgtbus/

Program Contact: Ms. Jennifer Spiegel, Associate Director of Graduate Admissions, Office of Admission, Garden City, NY 11530. Phone: 516-877-3055, 800-Adelphi (NY only); Fax: 516-877-3039; E-mail: spiegel@adlibv.adelphi. edu

See full description on page 696.

Alfred University

College of Business

Alfred, New York

OVERVIEW

Alfred University is an independent-nonprofit, coed university. Enrollment: 2,326 graduate, professional, and undergraduate students; 205 full-time matriculated graduate/professional students; 149 part-time matriculated graduate/professional students. Founded: 1836. The graduate business unit is in a rural setting and is on a semester calendar.

HIGHLIGHTS

Enrollment Profile

Full-time: 14	International: 2%
Part-time: 35	Women: 35%
Total: 49	Minorities: N/R
Average Age: 25	Average Class Size: 18
Fall 1997 Average GPA: 3.02	Fall 1997 Average GMAT: 477

Costs
Full-time tuition: $20,376 per academic year
Part-time tuition: $405 per credit hour

AACSB – The International Association for Management Education accredited

GRADUATE BUSINESS PROGRAMS
Master of Business Administration (MBA) Full-time, part-time; 30-55 total credits required; 10 months to 7 years to complete program.

ADMISSION
Applications For fall 1997 there were 24 applications for admission. Of those applying, 16 were accepted. Of those accepted, 14 enrolled.

Application Requirements GMAT score, application form, bachelor's degree, minimum GPA, 2 letters of recommendation, personal statement, college transcript(s), computer experience.

Recommended for Application Work experience.

Application Deadline Applications processed on a rolling/continuous basis for both domestic and international students. Application fee: $50. Deferred entrance is available.

ACADEMICS
Faculty Full-time 15; part-time 2.

Teaching Methodologies Case study, computer-aided instruction, computer analysis, computer simulations, experiential learning, faculty seminars, field projects, group discussion, lecture, research, seminars by members of the business community, simulations, student presentations, study groups, team projects.

Technology 50 on-campus computer terminals/PCs are available for student use and are linked by a campus-wide network. The network has full access to the Internet. Students are not required to have their own PC.

Special Opportunities Advanced credit may be earned through credit by examination, transfer of credits from another institution.

FINANCES
Costs for 1997–98 Tuition: Full-time: $20,376 per year. Part-time: $405 per credit hour. Cost varies by number of credits taken. Fees: Full-time: $440 per academic year. Average 1997–98 room and board costs were $6407 per academic year (on campus) and $5000 per academic year (off campus). Room and board costs vary by campus location, occupancy (e.g., single, double, triple), type of accommodation, type of meal plan.

Financial Aid In 1997–98, 16% of students received some institutionally administered aid in the form of research assistantships, teaching assistantships.

Financial Aid Contact Mr. Earl Pierce, Financial Aid Office, Alumni Hall, 26 North Main Street, Alfred, NY 14802. Phone: 607-871-2159.

FACILITIES
Information Resources Herrick Library plus 1 additional on-campus library; total holdings of 410,000 volumes, 70,000 microforms, 1,900 current periodical subscriptions. CD player(s) available for graduate student use. Access provided to online bibliographic retrieval services.

INTERNATIONAL STUDENTS
Demographics 2% of students enrolled are international students.

PLACEMENT
Services include alumni network, career counseling/planning, career fairs, and career placement.

Employment Types of employment entered: accounting, education, information systems/technology, management, marketing.

Business Program(s) URL: http://business.alfred.edu/

Program Contact: Dr. David Szczerbacki, Dean, College of Business, Saxon Drive, Alfred, NY 14802. Phone: 607-871-2646; Fax: 607-871-2114; E-mail: fszczerbacki@bigvax.alfred.edu
See full description on page 698.

HIGHLIGHTS

Enrollment Profile
Full-time: 12	International: N/R
Part-time: 0	Women: N/R
Total: 12	Minorities: N/R
Average Age: 37	Average Class Size: N/R
Fall 1997 Average GPA: N/R	Fall 1997 Average GMAT: N/R

Costs
Full-time tuition: $18,000 per academic year
Part-time tuition: N/R

GRADUATE BUSINESS PROGRAMS
MBA in Media Management (MBA) Full-time; 48 total credits required; 12 months to complete program.

ADMISSION
Application Requirements Application form, application fee, bachelor's degree, essay, minimum GPA: 3.0, interview, 2 letters of recommendation, personal statement, resume, college transcript(s), computer experience: Windows or MAC skills.

Recommended for Application GMAT score accepted: minimum 550, GRE score accepted.

Application Deadline Applications processed on a rolling/continuous basis for both domestic and international students. Application fee: $45. Deferred entrance is available.

ACADEMICS
Faculty Full-time 5; part-time 9.

Teaching Methodologies Case study, computer-aided instruction, computer analysis, computer simulations, experiential learning, faculty seminars, field projects, group discussion, lecture, research, role playing, seminars by members of the business community, simulations, student presentations, study groups, team projects.

Special Opportunities An internship program is available.

FINANCES
Costs for 1997–98 Tuition: Full-time: $18,000 per year. Cost varies by academic program.

Financial Aid Scholarships available.

Financial Aid Contact Mr. Steven Lenhart, Director of Admissions, 75 Varick Street, New York, NY 10013-1919. Phone: 212-343-1234 Ext. 2700.

FACILITIES
Information Resources Main library plus 1 additional on-campus library; total holdings of 22,067 volumes, 943 microforms, 52,850 current periodical subscriptions. CD player(s) available for graduate student use. Access provided to online bibliographic retrieval services.

INTERNATIONAL STUDENTS
Demographics N/R

Services and Facilities Visa services, counseling/support services.

Applying TOEFL: minimum score of 550 required.

International Student Contact Mr. Steven Lenhart, Director of Admissions, 75 Varick Street, New York, NY 10013-1919. Phone: 212-343-1234 Ext. 2700.

Program Contact: Mr. Steven Lenhart, Director of Admissions, 75 Varick Street, New York, NY 10013-1919. Phone: 212-343-1234 Ext. 2700.

Audrey Cohen College

School of Business
New York, New York

OVERVIEW
Audrey Cohen College is an independent-nonprofit, coed, comprehensive institution. Enrollment: 1,100 graduate, professional, and undergraduate students; 104 full-time matriculated graduate/professional students; part-time matriculated graduate/professional students. Founded: 1964. The graduate business unit is in an urban setting and is on a semester calendar.

Baruch College of the City University of New York

Zicklin School of Business
New York, New York

OVERVIEW
Baruch College of the City University of New York is a state and locally supported, coed, comprehensive institution. Founded: 1919. The graduate business unit is in an urban setting and is on a semester and trimester calendar.

Baruch College of the City University of New York (continued)

HIGHLIGHTS

Enrollment Profile
Full-time: N/R
Part-time: N/R
Total: N/R
Average Age: 28
Fall 1997 Average GPA: 3.2

International: N/R
Women: N/R
Minorities: N/R
Average Class Size: 40
Fall 1997 Average GMAT: 580

Costs
Full-time tuition: $4350 per academic year (resident); $7600 per academic year (nonresident)
Part-time tuition: $185 per credit (resident); $320 per credit (nonresident)

AACSB – The International Association for Management Education accredited

GRADUATE BUSINESS PROGRAMS

Executive MBA (EMBA) Full-time; 54 total credits required; 2 years to complete program.

Master of Science in Operations Research (MS) Full-time, part-time; 36-52 total credits required; 18 months to 6 years to complete program.

Master of Science in Statistics (MS) Full-time, part-time; 36-55 total credits required; 18 months to 6 years to complete program.

Master of Science in Taxation (MS) Full-time, part-time; 36 total credits required; 18 months to 6 years to complete program.

Executive Master of Science in Taxation (MS) Full-time; 48 total credits required; 2 years to complete program.

Master of Business Administration/Doctor of Jurisprudence (MBA/JD) Full-time; 131 total credits required; 3.5 to 4 years to complete program.

Master of Business Administration (MBA) Full-time, part-time; 54 total credits required; 2 to 6 years to complete program. Concentrations in accounting, decision sciences, finance, health care, organizational behavior/development, international business, management, marketing, operations management, taxation, management information systems, economics, entrepreneurship, human resources, advertising, international marketing, quantitative analysis.

Master of Science in Accountancy (MS) Full-time, part-time; 30-54 total credits required; 18 months to 6 years to complete program.

Master of Science in Computer Information Systems (MS) Full-time, part-time; 36-52 total credits required; 18 months to 6 years to complete program.

Master of Science in Industrial Organizational Psychology (MS) Full-time, part-time; 36 total credits required; 18 months to 6 years to complete program.

Master of Science in Marketing (MS) Full-time, part-time; 30-54 total credits required; 18 months to 6 years to complete program.

ADMISSION

Application Requirements GMAT score: minimum 550, application form, application fee, bachelor's degree, essay, minimum GPA: 3.0, 2 letters of recommendation, personal statement, resume, college transcript(s).

Recommended for Application GRE score accepted, work experience, computer experience.

Application Deadline 6/15 for fall, 11/1 for winter, 21/1 for spring, 5/1 for fall (international), 11/1 for spring (international). Application fee: $40. Deferred entrance is available.

ACADEMICS

Faculty Full-time 127; part-time 59.

Teaching Methodologies Case study, computer-aided instruction, computer analysis, computer simulations, experiential learning, faculty seminars, field projects, group discussion, lecture, research, role playing, seminars by members of the business community, simulations, student presentations, study groups, team projects.

Technology 650 on-campus computer terminals/PCs are available for student use and are linked by a campus-wide network. The network has full access to the Internet. Students are not required to have their own PC.

Special Opportunities Advanced credit may be earned through credit by examination, credit for experience, credit for business training programs, transfer of credits from another institution. International exchange programs in France, Germany. An internship program is available.

FINANCES

Costs for 1997–98 Tuition: Full-time: $4350 per year (resident); $7600 per year (nonresident). Part-time: $185 per credit (resident); $320 per credit (nonresident). Cost varies by academic program, number of credits taken.

Financial Aid Fellowships, research assistantships, scholarships, work study, loans available. Financial aid is available to part-time students. Application Deadline: 5/3.

Financial Aid Contact Mr. James Murphy, Director of Financial Aid, 17 Lexington Avenue, Box H-0725, New York, NY 10010. Phone: 212-802-2240.

FACILITIES

Information Resources William and Anita Newman Library; total holdings of 410,000 volumes, 1,740,000 microforms, 1,500 current periodical subscriptions. CD player(s) available for graduate student use. Access provided to online bibliographic retrieval services.

INTERNATIONAL STUDENTS
Demographics N/R

Services and Facilities International student office, international student center, visa services, ESL courses, counseling/support services.

Applying TOEFL: minimum score of 570, TWE: minimum score of 4.5, proof of adequate funds, proof of health/immunizations required. Financial aid is available to international students.

International Student Contact Mr. Stephen Goldberg, Director, International Students Office, 17 Lexington Avenue, Box F-1711, New York, NY 10010. Phone: 212-802-2350.

PLACEMENT

Services include alumni network, career counseling/planning, career fairs, career library, career placement, electronic job bank, job interviews arranged, resume referral to employers, and resume preparation. In 1996–97, 62 organizations participated in on-campus recruiting.

Employment Types of employment entered: accounting, banking, chemical industry, communications, computer-related, consulting, consumer products, engineering, finance, financial services, government, high technology, human resources, information systems/technology, insurance, international trade, management, marketing, media, nonprofit, pharmaceutical, real estate, retail, service industry, telecommunications.

Business Program(s) URL: http://bus.baruch.cuny.edu

Program Contact: Mr. Michael Wynne, Office of Graduate Admissions, 17 Lexington Avenue, Box H-0880, New York, NY 10010-5585. Phone: 212-802-2330; Fax: 212-802-2335; E-mail: graduate_admissions@baruch.cuny.edu
See full description on page 718.

Canisius College

Wehle School of Business

Buffalo, New York

OVERVIEW
Canisius College is an independent-religious, coed, comprehensive institution. Enrollment: 4,789 graduate, professional, and undergraduate students; 490 full-time matriculated graduate/professional students; 940 part-time matriculated graduate/professional students. Founded: 1870. The graduate business unit is in an urban setting and is on a semester calendar.

HIGHLIGHTS

Enrollment Profile
Full-time: 28
Part-time: 409
Total: 437
Average Age: 31
Fall 1997 Average GPA: 3.0

International: 4%
Women: 41%
Minorities: 2%
Average Class Size: 40
Fall 1997 Average GMAT: 500

Costs
Full-time tuition: $11,976 per academic year
Part-time tuition: $499 per credit hour

AACSB – The International Association for Management Education accredited

GRADUATE BUSINESS PROGRAMS

Master of Business Administration (MBA) Full-time, part-time; 51 total credits required; 2 to 5 years to complete program. Concentrations in accounting, finance, human resources, management, management information systems, marketing, public management.

Master of Business Administration in Professional Accounting (MBA) Part-time; 61 total credits required; up to 6 years to complete program.

ADMISSION

Application Requirements GMAT score: minimum 460, application form, application fee, bachelor's degree, essay, minimum GPA: 3.0, personal statement, college transcript(s).

Recommended for Application Letters of recommendation, resume, computer experience.

Application Deadline Applications processed on a rolling/continuous basis for both domestic and international students. Application fee: $20. Deferred entrance is available.

ACADEMICS

Faculty Full-time 29.

Teaching Methodologies Case study, computer-aided instruction, computer analysis, group discussion, lecture, student presentations, study groups, team projects.

Technology 150 on-campus computer terminals/PCs are available for student use and are linked by a campus-wide network. The network has full access to the Internet. Students are not required to have their own PC.

Special Opportunities Advanced credit may be earned through credit by examination, credit for experience, transfer of credits from another institution.

FINANCES

Costs for 1997–98 Tuition: Full-time: $11,976 per year. Part-time: $499 per credit hour. Fees: $10 per credit hour. Average 1997–98 room and board costs were $5500 per academic year.

Financial Aid Research assistantships, loans available. Financial aid is available to part-time students. Application Deadline: 6/15.

Financial Aid Contact Mr. Curt Gaume, 2001 Main Street, Buffalo, NY 14208-1098. Phone: 716-888-2300.

FACILITIES

Information Resources Bouwhuis Library; total holdings of 280,507 volumes, 502,789 microforms, 1,167 current periodical subscriptions. CD player(s) available for graduate student use. Access provided to online bibliographic retrieval services.

INTERNATIONAL STUDENTS

Demographics 4% of students enrolled are international students.

Services and Facilities International student office, international student center, ESL courses, counseling/support services.

Applying TOEFL: minimum score of 500, proof of adequate funds, proof of health/immunizations required. Financial aid is not available to international students.

International Student Contact Ms. Ester Northman, Director, International Student Programs, 2001 Main Street, Buffalo, NY 14208-1098. E-mail: northman@canisius.edu

PLACEMENT

Services include alumni network, career counseling/planning, and resume preparation.

Business Program(s) URL: http://www.canisius.edu

Program Contact: Mr. Daniel Sullivan, Associate Dean, 2001 Main Street, Buffalo, NY 14208-1098. Phone: 716-888-2140, 800-543-7906 (NY only); Fax: 716-888-2525; E-mail: dsully@canisius.edu

Clarkson University

School of Business

Potsdam, New York

OVERVIEW

Clarkson University is an independent-nonprofit, coed university. Enrollment: 2,601 graduate, professional, and undergraduate students; 296 full-time matriculated graduate/professional students; 25 part-time matriculated graduate/professional students. Founded: 1896. The graduate business unit is in a small-town setting and is on a semester calendar.

HIGHLIGHTS

Enrollment Profile

Full-time: 83	International: 13%
Part-time: 46	Women: 36%
Total: 129	Minorities: 6%
Average Age: 25	Average Class Size: 33
Fall 1997 Average GPA: 3.3	Fall 1997 Average GMAT: 540

Costs
Full-time tuition: $20,352 per academic year
Part-time tuition: $584 per credit hour

AACSB – The International Association for Management Education accredited

GRADUATE BUSINESS PROGRAMS

Master of Business Administration (MBA) Full-time, part-time; 32 total credits required; 12 months to 2 years to complete program.

Master of Science in Management Systems (MS) Full-time, part-time; 30 total credits required; 12 months to 2 years to complete program. Concentrations in business information science, manufacturing management, marketing, human resources.

ADMISSION

Applications For fall 1997 there were 172 applications for admission. Of those applying, 98 were accepted. Of those accepted, 83 enrolled.

Application Requirements Application form, application fee, bachelor's degree, 3 letters of recommendation, college transcript(s).

Recommended for Application GMAT score accepted, essay, interview, personal statement, resume, work experience, computer experience.

Application Deadline Applications processed on a rolling/continuous basis for domestic students only. 5/15 for fall (international). Application fee: $25, $35 (international). Deferred entrance is available.

ACADEMICS

Faculty Full-time 30; part-time 3.

Teaching Methodologies Case study, computer-aided instruction, computer analysis, computer simulations, experiential learning, faculty seminars, field projects, group discussion, lecture, research, role playing, seminars by members of the business community, simulations, student presentations, study groups, team projects.

Technology 75 on-campus computer terminals/PCs are available for student use and are linked by a campus-wide network. The network has full access to the Internet. Students are not required to have their own PC.

Special Opportunities Advanced credit may be earned through transfer of credits from another institution. International exchange program available. An internship program is available.

FINANCES

Costs for 1997–98 Tuition: Full-time: $20,352 per program. Part-time: $584 per credit hour. Fees: Full-time: $178 per academic year. Part-time: $175 per year. Average 1997–98 room and board costs were $5500 per academic year (on campus) and $5500 per academic year (off campus). Room and board costs vary by campus location, type of accommodation, type of meal plan.

Financial Aid In 1997–98, 80% of students received some institutionally administered aid in the form of research assistantships, teaching assistantships. Financial aid is available to part-time students.

Financial Aid Contact Dr. Fredric Menz, Director of Graduate Business Programs, CU Box 5770, 207 Snell Hall, Potsdam, NY 13699-5770. Phone: 315-268-6613; Fax: 315-268-3810; E-mail: menzf@icarus.som.clarkson.edu

FACILITIES

Information Resources Andrew S. Schuler Educational Resources Center; total holdings of 219,948 volumes, 264,777 microforms, 2,835 current periodical subscriptions. CD player(s) available for graduate student use. Access provided to online bibliographic retrieval services.

INTERNATIONAL STUDENTS

Demographics 13% of students enrolled are international students [Africa, 10%, Asia, 30%, Europe, 10%, North America, 50%].

Services and Facilities International student office, international student center, visa services, ESL courses, counseling/support services.

Applying TOEFL: minimum score of 600, TSE: minimum score of 50, proof of adequate funds, proof of health/immunizations required. Financial aid is available to international students.

International Student Contact Ms. Mary Theis, Director, International Student and Women's Programs, Box 5645, Potsdam, NY 13699. Phone: 315-268-6400; E-mail: theis@agent.edu

PLACEMENT

Services include alumni network, career counseling/planning, career fairs, career library, career placement, electronic job bank, job interviews arranged, job search course, resume referral to employers, and resume preparation. In 1996–97, 60 organizations participated in on-campus recruiting; 109 on-campus interviews were conducted.

Employment Of 1996–97 graduates, 84% were employed within three months of graduation; the average starting salary was $47,000. Types of employment entered: accounting, banking, communications, computer-related, consulting, consumer products, engineering, finance, financial services, government, health services, high technology, human resources, information systems/technology, insurance, international trade, management, manufacturing, marketing, nonprofit, retail, service industry, telecommunications, utilities.

Business Program(s) URL: http://phoenix.som.clarkson.edu

Clarkson University (continued)

Program Contact: Dr. Farzad Mahmoodi, Director of Graduate Business Programs, CU Box 5770, 207 Snell Hall, Potsdam, NY 13699-5770. Phone: 315-268-6613; Fax: 315-268-3810; E-mail: mahmoodi@icarus.som.clarkson. edu

See full description on page 752.

College of Insurance

Business Programs

New York, New York

OVERVIEW
College of Insurance is an independent-nonprofit, coed, comprehensive institution. Enrollment: 43 full-time matriculated graduate/professional students; 56 part-time matriculated graduate/professional students. Founded: 1929. The graduate business unit is in an urban setting and is on a semester calendar.

HIGHLIGHTS

Enrollment Profile

Full-time: 43	International: 31%
Part-time: 56	Women: 41%
Total: 99	Minorities: N/R
Average Age: 28	Average Class Size: 15
Fall 1997 Average GPA: 3.0	Fall 1997 Average GMAT: 500

Costs
Full-time tuition: N/R
Part-time tuition: $1662 per 3 credits

GRADUATE BUSINESS PROGRAMS
Traditional MBA (MBA) Full-time, part-time; 51 total credits required; 12 months to 5 years to complete program. Concentrations in finance, insurance, actuarial science, risk management.

Non-traditional MBA (MBA) Part-time; 51 total credits required; 12 months to 5 years to complete program. Concentration in risk management.

Traditional MS (MS) Full-time, part-time; 36 total credits required; 12 months to 4 years to complete program. Concentration in insurance.

ADMISSION
Applications For fall 1997 there were 87 applications for admission. Of those applying, 54 were accepted. Of those accepted, 37 enrolled.

Application Requirements Application form, application fee, bachelor's degree, minimum GPA: 3.0, 2 letters of recommendation, personal statement, college transcript(s).

Recommended for Application GMAT score accepted: minimum 500, interview, resume.

Application Deadline 7/15 for fall, 11/1 for spring. Applications processed on a rolling/continuous basis for international students only. Application fee: $30, $50 (international). Deferred entrance is available.

ACADEMICS
Faculty Full-time 11; part-time 12.

Teaching Methodologies Case study, computer simulations, field projects, group discussion, lecture, research, seminars by members of the business community, student presentations, study groups, team projects.

Technology 22 on-campus computer terminals/PCs are available for student use. The network has full access to the Internet. Students are not required to have their own PC.

Special Opportunities Advanced credit may be earned through transfer of credits from another institution.

FINANCES
Costs for 1997–98 Tuition: $1662 per 3 credits. Cost varies by number of credits taken. Fees: $45 per 3 credits. Fees vary by number of credits taken. Average 1997–98 room and board costs were $8500 per academic year. Room and board costs vary by occupancy (e.g., single, double, triple), type of meal plan.

Financial Aid In 1997–98, 55% of students received some institutionally administered aid in the form of research assistantships, grants, work study, loans. Financial aid is available to part-time students. Application Deadline: 5/15.

Financial Aid Contact Ms. Margaret Montano, Director of Financial Aid, 101 Murray Street, New York, NY 10007. Phone: 212-815-9221; Fax: 212-964-3381.

FACILITIES
Information Resources Kathy and Shelby Cullom Davis Library; total holdings of 98,666 volumes, 49,378 microforms, 429 current periodical subscriptions.

INTERNATIONAL STUDENTS
Demographics 31% of students enrolled are international students [Africa, 2%, Asia, 53%, Central America, 12%, Europe, 3%, North America, 2%, South America, 3%, other, 25%].

Services and Facilities International student office, international student housing, visa services, ESL courses, counseling/support services.

Applying TOEFL: minimum score of 550, proof of adequate funds, proof of health/immunizations required. Financial aid is not available to international students.

International Student Contact Ms. Theresa C. Marro, Director of Admissions, 101 Murray Street, New York, NY 10007. Phone: 212-815-9232; Fax: 212-964-3381.

PLACEMENT
Services include alumni network, career counseling/planning, career fairs, resume referral to employers, and resume preparation.

Employment Of 1996–97 graduates, 87% were employed within three months of graduation; the average starting salary was $37,500. Types of employment entered: consulting, financial services, insurance.

Business Program(s) URL: http://www.tci.edu/

Program Contact: Ms. Theresa C. Marro, Director of Admissions, 101 Murray Street, New York, NY 10007. Phone: 212-815-9232, 800-242-9548 (NY only); Fax: 212-964-3381.

The College of Saint Rose

School of Business

Albany, New York

OVERVIEW
The College of Saint Rose is an independent-nonprofit, coed, comprehensive institution. Enrollment: 3,973 graduate, professional, and undergraduate students; 210 full-time matriculated graduate/professional students; 1,126 part-time matriculated graduate/professional students. Founded: 1920. The graduate business unit is in an urban setting and is on a semester calendar.

HIGHLIGHTS

Enrollment Profile

Full-time: 8	International: N/R
Part-time: 102	Women: 49%
Total: 110	Minorities: 10%
Average Age: 32	Average Class Size: 14
Fall 1997 Average GPA: 3.1	Fall 1997 Average GMAT: 497

Costs
Full-time tuition: N/R
Part-time tuition: $338 per credit

ACBSP – The American Council of Business Schools and Programs accredited

Degree(s) offered in conjunction with Albany Law School of Union University

GRADUATE BUSINESS PROGRAMS
Master of Business Administration/Doctor of Jurisprudence (MBA/JD) Full-time, part-time; 102 total credits required; 3 to 4 years to complete program. Concentrations in finance, human resources, leadership, managerial economics, marketing, production management, technology management, strategic management.

One-year MBA (MBA) Full-time; 36 total credits required; 12 months to complete program. Concentrations in finance, human resources, leadership, managerial economics, marketing, production management, technology management.

Master of Science in Accounting (MS) Full-time, part-time; 30 total credits required; 12 months to 8 years to complete program. Concentrations in finance, human resources, leadership, managerial economics, marketing, production management, technology management, accounting, taxation.

Accelerated MBA (MBA) Part-time; 36 total credits required; 2 years to complete program. Concentrations in finance, human resources, leadership, managerial economics, marketing, production management, technology management.

Part-time MBA (MBA) Part-time; 36 total credits required; 2 to 8 years to complete program. Concentrations in finance, human resources, leadership, managerial economics, marketing, production management, technology management.

ADMISSION

Application Requirements Application form, application fee, bachelor's degree, essay, minimum GPA: 3.0, 2 letters of recommendation, resume, college transcript(s), computer experience: word processing, spreadsheet.

Recommended for Application GMAT score accepted.

Application Deadline 7/15 for fall, 12/1 for spring, 4/1 for summer, 7/15 for fall (international), 12/1 for spring (international), 4/1 for summer (international). Application fee: $30. Deferred entrance is available.

ACADEMICS

Faculty Full-time 17; part-time 2.

Teaching Methodologies Case study, computer-aided instruction, computer analysis, experiential learning, faculty seminars, group discussion, lecture, research, seminars by members of the business community, student presentations, team projects.

Technology 202 on-campus computer terminals/PCs are available for student use and are linked by a campus-wide network. The network has full access to the Internet. Students are not required to have their own PC.

Special Opportunities Advanced credit may be earned through credit for experience, transfer of credits from another institution. An internship program is available.

FINANCES

Costs for 1997–98 Tuition: $338 per credit. Fees: $30 per semester. Average 1997–98 room and board costs were $5966 per academic year (on campus) and $6174 per academic year (off campus). Room and board costs vary by type of meal plan.

Financial Aid In 1997–98, 28% of students received some institutionally administered aid in the form of research assistantships, scholarships, work study, loans. Financial aid is available to part-time students. Application Deadline: 3/1.

Financial Aid Contact Mr. Christopher Moore, Director of Financial Aid, 432 Western Avenue, Albany, NY 12203-1419. Phone: 518-454-5168.

FACILITIES

Information Resources Neil Hellman Library plus 1 additional on-campus library; total holdings of 197,703 volumes, 199,836 microforms, 1,035 current periodical subscriptions. CD player(s) available for graduate student use. Access provided to online bibliographic retrieval services and online databases.

INTERNATIONAL STUDENTS

Demographics N/R

Services and Facilities International student office, visa services, ESL courses, counseling/support services, international student organization.

Applying TOEFL: minimum score of 550, proof of adequate funds, proof of health/immunizations required. Financial aid is available to international students.

International Student Contact Ms. Alice Torda, Director of International Programs, 432 Western Avenue, Albany, NY 12203-1419. Phone: 518-454-5111.

PLACEMENT

Services include alumni network, career counseling/planning, career fairs, career library, career placement, electronic job bank, job interviews arranged, and resume preparation. In 1996–97, 135 organizations participated in on-campus recruiting.

Employment Of 1996–97 graduates, 95% were employed within three months of graduation; the average starting salary was $39,000. Types of employment entered: accounting, banking, computer-related, consulting, consumer products, education, energy, finance, financial services, government, health services, human resources, management, manufacturing, marketing, nonprofit, utilities.

Business Program(s) URL: http://www.strose.edu/Academic/GR_MBA.HTM

Program Contact: Ann Tully, Director of Graduate Admissions, Adult and Continuing Education, 432 Western Avenue, Albany, NY 12203-1419. Phone: 518-454-5143 E-mail: mba@rosnet.strose.edu

See full description on page 760.

Columbia University

Columbia Business School

New York, New York

OVERVIEW

Columbia University is an independent-nonprofit, coed university. Enrollment: 19,019 graduate, professional, and undergraduate students; 10,762 full-time matriculated graduate/professional students; 2,197 part-time matriculated graduate/professional students. Founded: 1754. The graduate business unit is in an urban setting and is on a semester calendar.

HIGHLIGHTS

Enrollment Profile

Full-time: 1,394	International: 28%
Part-time: 0	Women: 37%
Total: 1,394	Minorities: 23%
Average Age: 27	Average Class Size: 60
Fall 1997 Average GPA: 3.45	Fall 1997 Average GMAT: 670

Costs
Full-time tuition: $13,260 per academic year
Part-time tuition: N/R

AACSB – The International Association for Management Education accredited

GRADUATE BUSINESS PROGRAMS

Master of Business Administration (MBA) Full-time; 60 total credits required; 16 to 20 months to complete program. Concentrations in accounting, construction management, human resources, international business, management science, marketing, operations management, real estate, economics, public management, nonprofit management, management information systems, management, entrepreneurship, finance, information management, sports/entertainment management, telecommunications management.

Executive MBA (MBA) Full-time; 60 total credits required; must have company sponsorship and 8 or more years of organizational experience; minimum of 21 months to complete program.

Summer MBA (MBA) Full-time, part-time; 60 total credits required; must have company sponsorship and 8 or more years of organizational experience; minimum of 2.3 years to complete program.

Master of Business Administration/Master of Science in Urban Planning (MBA/MS) Full-time; 90 total credits required; must apply and be admitted to both schools; minimum of 2.3 years to complete program.

Master of Business Administration/Master of Science in Nursing (MBA/MS) Full-time; 75 total credits required; must apply and be admitted to both schools; minimum of 21 months to complete program.

Master of Business Administration/Master of Public Health (MBA/MPH) Full-time; 80 total credits required; must apply and be admitted to both schools.

Master of Business Administration/Doctor of Education, Education Administration (MBA/EdD) Full-time; 90 total credits required; must apply and be admitted to both schools.

Master of Business Administration/Master of Arts or Doctor of Education, Higher Learning (MBA/MA or EdD) Full-time; 90 total credits required; must apply and be admitted to both schools.

Master of Business Administration/Baccalaureate (MBA/BA/BS) Full-time; 154 total credits required; must apply and be admitted to both schools; minimum of 3.8 years to complete program.

Master of Business Administration/Master of International Affairs (MBA/MIA) Full-time; 90 total credits required; must apply and be admitted to both schools; minimum of 2.3 years to complete program.

Master of Business Administration/Master of Science in Industrial Engineering (MBA/MS) Full-time; 75 total credits required; must apply and be admitted to both schools; minimum of 21 months to complete program.

Master of Business Administration/Master of Science in Computer Science (MBA/MS) Full-time; 75 total credits required; must apply and be admitted to both schools; minimum of 2.5 years to complete program.

Master of Business Administration/Master of Science in Mining Engineering (MBA/MS) Full-time; 75 total credits required; must apply and be admitted to both schools; minimum of 21 months to complete program.

Master of Business Administration/Master of Science in Operations Research (MBA/MS) Full-time; 69 total credits required; must apply and be admitted to both schools; minimum of 21 months to complete program.

Master of Business Administration/Master of Science in Social Work (MBA/MS) Full-time; 90 total credits required; must apply and be admitted to both schools; minimum of 2.3 years to complete program.

Master of Business Administration/Master of Science in Journalism (MBA/MS) Full-time; 75 total credits required; must apply and be admitted to both schools; minimum of 21 months to complete program.

Master of Business Administration/Doctor of Jurisprudence (MBA/JD) Full-time; 118 total credits required; must apply and be admitted to both schools; minimum of 21 months to complete program.

ADMISSION

Applications For fall 1997 there were 5,257 applications for admission. Of those applying, 687 were accepted. Of those accepted, 488 enrolled.

Application Requirements GMAT score, application form, application fee, bachelor's degree, essay, letters of recommendation, personal statement, resume, college transcript(s), minimum of 2 years of work experience.

Recommended for Application Interview, computer experience.

Columbia University (continued)

Application Deadline 4/20 for fall, 10/1 for spring, 2/1 for summer, 3/1 for fall (international), 10/1 for spring (international), 2/1 for summer (international). Application fee: $125, $150 (international). Deferred entrance is available.

ACADEMICS

Faculty Full-time 105; part-time 86.

Teaching Methodologies Case study, computer-aided instruction, computer analysis, computer simulations, experiential learning, faculty seminars, field projects, group discussion, lecture, seminars by members of the business community, simulations, student presentations, study groups, team projects.

Technology 210 on-campus computer terminals/PCs are available for student use and are linked by a campus-wide network. The network has full access to the Internet. Students are required to have their own PC.

Special Opportunities Advanced credit may be earned through credit by examination. International exchange programs in Australia, Austria, Belgium, Brazil, Finland, Germany, Hong Kong, Israel, Italy, Netherlands, Philippines, Singapore, Spain, Sweden, Switzerland, United Kingdom.

FINANCES

Costs for 1997–98 Tuition: Full-time: $13,260 per year. Cost varies by number of credits taken. Fees: Full-time: $1040 per academic year. Average 1997–98 room and board costs were $9648 per academic year (on campus) and $9648 per academic year (off campus).

Financial Aid In 1997–98, 54% of students received some institutionally administered aid in the form of fellowships, grants, scholarships, work study, loans. Application Deadline: 2/1.

Financial Aid Contact Ms. Eileen Potash, Office of Financial Aid, Graduate School of Business , 218 Uris Hall, 3022 Broadway, New York, NY 10027. Phone: 212-854-4057; Fax: 212-678-0171; E-mail: epotash@admin.gsb. columbia.edu

FACILITIES

Information Resources Butler Library plus 22 additional on-campus libraries; total holdings of 6,792,274 volumes, 5,217,558 microforms, 64,924 current periodical subscriptions. CD player(s) available for graduate student use. Access provided to online bibliographic retrieval services.

INTERNATIONAL STUDENTS

Demographics 28% of students enrolled are international students.

Services and Facilities International student office, international student center, international student housing, visa services, counseling/support services.

Applying TOEFL: minimum score of 610, proof of adequate funds, proof of health/immunizations required. Financial aid is not available to international students.

International Student Contact Mr. Thomas Fernandez, Assistant Dean, Graduate School of Business, 213 Uris Hall, 3022 Broadway, New York, NY 10027. Phone: 212-854-4750; Fax: 212-222-9821; E-mail: chazen@claven. gsb.columbia.edu

PLACEMENT

Services include alumni network, career counseling/planning, career fairs, career library, career placement, electronic job bank, job interviews arranged, job search course, resume referral to employers, and resume preparation. In 1996–97, 393 organizations participated in on-campus recruiting; 11,900 on-campus interviews were conducted.

Employment Of 1996–97 graduates, 98% were employed within three months of graduation; the average starting salary was $130,000. Types of employment entered: accounting, banking, chemical industry, communications, computer-related, consulting, consumer products, education, energy, finance, financial services, government, health services, high technology, hospitality management, human resources, information systems/technology, insurance, international trade, law, management, manufacturing, marketing, media, nonprofit, petrochemical, pharmaceutical, real estate, retail, service industry, telecommunications, transportation.

Business Program(s) URL: http://www.columbia.edu/cu/business/

Program Contact: Ms. Linda Meehan, Assistant Dean and Director of Admissions and Financial Aid, Graduate School of Business, 105 Uris Hall, 3022 Broadway, New York, NY 10027. Phone: 212-854-1961; Fax: 212-662-6754; E-mail: gohermes@claven.gsb.columbia.edu

See full description on page 766.

Cornell University

Johnson Graduate School of Management

Ithaca, New York

OVERVIEW

Cornell University is an independent-nonprofit, coed university. Enrollment: 18,428 graduate, professional, and undergraduate students; 5,134 full-time matriculated graduate/professional students; part-time matriculated graduate/professional students. Founded: 1865. The graduate business unit is in a small-town setting and is on a semester calendar.

HIGHLIGHTS

Enrollment Profile

Full-time: 570	International: 23%
Part-time: 0	Women: 30%
Total: 570	Minorities: 9%
Average Age: 28	Average Class Size: 40
Fall 1997 Average GPA: 3.2	Fall 1997 Average GMAT: 638

Costs
Full-time tuition: $23,460 per academic year
Part-time tuition: N/R

AACSB – The International Association for Management Education accredited

GRADUATE BUSINESS PROGRAMS

Master of Business Administration (MBA) Full-time; 60 total credits required; 12 months to 2 years to complete program. Concentrations in accounting, economics, entrepreneurship, human resources, international management, management, management information systems, marketing, operations management, organizational behavior/development.

Master of Business Administration/Master of Engineering (MBA/ME) Full-time; minimum of 5 years to complete program.

Master of Business Administration/Doctor of Jurisprudence (MBA/JD) Full-time; minimum of 4 years to complete program.

Master of Business Administration/Master of Industrial and Labor Relations (MBA/MILR) Full-time; minimum of 4 years to complete program.

Master of Business Administration/Master of Arts in Asian Studies (MBA/MA) Full-time; minimum of 6 years to complete program.

ADMISSION

Applications For fall 1997 there were 2,082 applications for admission. Of those applying, 609 were accepted. Of those accepted, 289 enrolled.

Application Requirements GMAT score, application form, application fee, bachelor's degree, essay, 2 letters of recommendation, personal statement, resume, college transcript(s), minimum of 3 years of work experience.

Recommended for Application Minimum GPA, computer experience: Microsoft Office, spreadsheet, word processing.

Application Deadline 11/15 for fall, 1/15 for winter, 3/1 for spring, 4/15 for summer, 11/15 for fall (international), 1/15 for winter (international), 3/1 for spring (international). Application fee: $90, $120 (international). Deferred entrance is available.

ACADEMICS

Faculty Full-time 51; part-time 7.

Teaching Methodologies Case study, computer-aided instruction, computer analysis, computer simulations, experiential learning, field projects, group discussion, lecture, research, seminars by members of the business community, simulations, student presentations, study groups, team projects.

Technology 300 on-campus computer terminals/PCs are available for student use and are linked by a campus-wide network. The network has full access to the Internet. Students are required to have their own PC.

Special Opportunities Advanced credit may be earned through credit by examination. International exchange programs in Australia, Belgium, China, Denmark, England, France, Italy, Netherlands, Spain, Sweden, Switzerland, Thailand, Venezuela.

FINANCES

Costs for 1997–98 Tuition: Full-time: $23,460 per year. Average 1997–98 room and board costs were $7300 per academic year (on campus) and $7300 per academic year (off campus). Room and board costs vary by campus location, occupancy (e.g., single, double, triple), type of accommodation, type of meal plan.

Financial Aid Fellowships, grants, scholarships, loans available. Application Deadline: 2/15.

Financial Aid Contact Ms. Ann Richards, Director of Financial Aid, Sage Hall, Ithaca, NY 14853-6201. Phone: 607-255-9395; Fax: 607-254-8886.

FACILITIES

Information Resources Olin Library plus 16 additional on-campus libraries; total holdings of 611,346 volumes, 7,164,967 microforms, 71,783 current periodical subscriptions. CD player(s) available for graduate student use. Access provided to online bibliographic retrieval services.

INTERNATIONAL STUDENTS

Demographics 23% of students enrolled are international students [Africa, 3%, Asia, 53%, Australia/New Zealand, 1%, Central America, 5%, Europe, 26%, North America, 6%, South America, 5%, other, 1%].

Services and Facilities International student office, international student center, counseling/support services.

Applying TOEFL: minimum score of 600, proof of adequate funds, proof of health/immunizations required. TWE: minimum score of 4 recommended. Financial aid is available to international students.

International Student Contact Ms. Harriet Peters, Director of Advising and Student Activities, Ithaca, NY 14853-0001. Phone: 607-255-2000.

PLACEMENT

Services include alumni network, career counseling/planning, career fairs, career library, career placement, electronic job bank, job interviews arranged, job search course, resume referral to employers, and resume preparation. In 1996–97, 147 organizations participated in on-campus recruiting; 2,698 on-campus interviews were conducted.

Employment Of 1996–97 graduates, 95% were employed within three months of graduation; the average starting salary was $69,000. Types of employment entered: accounting, banking, chemical industry, communications, computer-related, consulting, consumer products, energy, engineering, finance, financial services, government, health services, high technology, hospitality management, human resources, information systems/technology, insurance, international trade, law, management, manufacturing, marketing, media, nonprofit, petrochemical, pharmaceutical, real estate, retail, service industry, telecommunications, transportation, utilities.

Business Program(s) URL: http://www.johnson.cornell.edu

Program Contact: Director of Admissions, 111 Sage Hall, Ithaca, NY 14853-6201. Phone: 607-255-4526, 800-847-2082; Fax: 607-255-0065.
See full description on page 770.

Dowling College

School of Business

Oakdale, New York

OVERVIEW

Dowling College is an independent-nonprofit, coed, comprehensive institution. Enrollment: 6,186 graduate, professional, and undergraduate students. Founded: 1955. The graduate business unit is in a suburban setting and is on a semester calendar.

HIGHLIGHTS

Enrollment Profile

Full-time: N/R	International: 11%
Part-time: N/R	Women: N/R
Total: 880	Minorities: N/R
Average Age: 33	Average Class Size: 20
Fall 1997 Average GPA: N/R	Fall 1997 Average GMAT: N/R

Costs
Full-time tuition: $5280 per academic year
Part-time tuition: $440 per credit

GRADUATE BUSINESS PROGRAMS

Public Management MBA (MBA) Full-time, part-time; 36 total credits required; 12 months to 3 years to complete program. Concentration in public management.

Total Quality Management MBA (MBA) Full-time, part-time; 36 total credits required; 12 months to 3 years to complete program. Concentration in quality management.

General Management MBA (MBA) Full-time, part-time; 36 total credits required; 12 months to 3 years to complete program. Concentration in management.

Aviation Management MBA (MBA) Full-time, part-time; 36 total credits required; 12 months to 3 years to complete program.

Banking and Finance MBA (MBA) Full-time, part-time; 36 total credits required; 12 months to 3 years to complete program. Concentrations in international finance, international banking, finance, banking.

Saturday Accelerated MBA (MBA) Full-time; 36 total credits required; 16 months to complete program. Concentrations in management, international finance, international banking, finance, banking.

ADMISSION

Application Requirements Application form, bachelor's degree, minimum GPA: 2.8, 2 letters of recommendation, resume, college transcript(s).

Recommended for Application GMAT score accepted, work experience, computer experience.

Application Deadline Applications processed on a rolling/continuous basis for both domestic and international students. Deferred entrance is available.

ACADEMICS

Faculty Full-time 22; part-time 65.

Teaching Methodologies Case study, computer-aided instruction, computer simulations, faculty seminars, group discussion, lecture, seminars by members of the business community, simulations, student presentations, study groups, team projects.

Technology 100 on-campus computer terminals/PCs are available for student use and are linked by a campus-wide network. The network has full access to the Internet. Students are required to have their own PC.

Special Opportunities Advanced credit may be earned through credit for military training programs, credit for business training programs, transfer of credits from another institution. An internship program is available.

FINANCES

Costs for 1997–98 Tuition: Full-time: $5280 per year. Part-time: $440 per credit. Cost varies by academic program. Fees: Full-time: $260 per academic year. Fees vary by campus location. Average 1997–98 room only costs were $3350 per academic year (on campus) and $4970 per academic year (off campus). Room and board costs vary by campus location, occupancy (e.g., single, double, triple), type of accommodation.

Financial Aid Research assistantships, grants, scholarships, work study available. Financial aid is available to part-time students. Application Deadline: 4/30.

Financial Aid Contact Ms. Nancy Brewer, Director, Enrollment Services for Financial Aid, Idle Hour Boulevard, Oakdale, NY 11769-1999. Phone: 800-369-5464; Fax: 516-563-3827; E-mail: brewern@dowling.edu

FACILITIES

Information Resources Total library holdings of 122,661 volumes, 577,097 microforms, 1,259 current periodical subscriptions. CD player(s) available for graduate student use. Access provided to online bibliographic retrieval services and online databases.

INTERNATIONAL STUDENTS

Demographics 11% of students enrolled are international students.

Services and Facilities Visa services, ESL courses, counseling/support services.

Applying TOEFL, TSE, TWE, proof of adequate funds, proof of health/immunizations required. Financial aid is not available to international students.

International Student Contact Mirka Pangracova, Foreign Student Associate, Enrollment Services—Fortunoff Hall, Oakdale, NY 11769-1999. Phone: 516-244-3030; Fax: 516-563-3827; E-mail: mirkap@dowling.edu

PLACEMENT

Services include alumni network, career counseling/planning, career fairs, career library, career placement, job interviews arranged, resume referral to employers, and resume preparation. In 1996–97, 150 organizations participated in on-campus recruiting; 50 on-campus interviews were conducted.

Employment Types of employment entered: banking, computer-related, consulting, education, finance, government, high technology, hospitality management, human resources, information systems/technology, management, marketing, nonprofit, pharmaceutical, service industry, telecommunications, transportation.

Business Program(s) URL: http://www.dowling.edu/academic/programs/business.htm

Program Contact: Mr. Herbert Armstrong, Assistant Dean, Idle Hour Boulevard, Oakdale, NY 11769-5098. Phone: 516-244-3193, 800-DOWLING; Fax: 516-244-5098; E-mail: armstroh@dowling.edu
See full description on page 784.

Fordham University

Graduate School of Business Administration

New York, New York

OVERVIEW

Fordham University is an independent-religious, coed university. Enrollment: 13,158 graduate, professional, and undergraduate students; 235 full-time matriculated graduate/professional students; 1,355 part-time matriculated graduate/professional students. Founded: 1841. The graduate business unit is in an urban setting and is on a trimester calendar.

Fordham University (continued)

HIGHLIGHTS

Enrollment Profile
Full-time: 235
Part-time: 1,355
Total: 1,590
Average Age: 27
Fall 1997 Average GPA: 3.0

International: 8%
Women: 41%
Minorities: 12%
Average Class Size: 28
Fall 1997 Average GMAT: 570

Costs
Full-time tuition: N/R
Part-time tuition: $560 per credit

AACSB – The International Association for Management Education accredited

GRADUATE BUSINESS PROGRAMS
Master of Business Administration (MBA) Full-time, part-time; 45-69 total credits required; 12 months to 6 years to complete program. Concentrations in accounting, finance, information management, management, marketing, quality management.

Global Professional MBA (MBA) Full-time, part-time; 45-78 total credits required; 12 months to 6 years to complete program. Concentrations in accounting, finance, information management, management, marketing, quality management.

Master of Science in Taxation (MS) Full-time, part-time; 39-54 total credits required; 12 months to 6 years to complete program. Concentration in taxation.

Master of Taxation and Accounting (MTaxA) Full-time; 66-99 total credits required; 18 months to 2 years to complete program. Concentrations in accounting, taxation.

Deming Scholars MBA (MBA) Full-time; 60 total credits required; 18 months to complete program. Concentration in quality management.

ADMISSION
Applications For fall 1997 there were 924 applications for admission. Of those applying, 560 were accepted. Of those accepted, 308 enrolled.

Application Requirements Application form, application fee, bachelor's degree (must be in field of business), essay, minimum GPA, 2 letters of recommendation, personal statement, resume, college transcript(s).

Recommended for Application GMAT score accepted, interview, work experience.

Application Deadline 6/1 for fall, 11/1 for winter, 3/1 for spring, 5/1 for fall (international), 10/1 for winter (international), 2/1 for spring (international). Application fee: $50. Deferred entrance is available.

ACADEMICS
Faculty Full-time 85; part-time 180.

Teaching Methodologies Case study, computer-aided instruction, computer analysis, computer simulations, experiential learning, faculty seminars, field projects, group discussion, lecture, research, role playing, seminars by members of the business community, simulations, student presentations, study groups, team projects.

Technology 100 on-campus computer terminals/PCs are available for student use and are linked by a campus-wide network. The network has full access to the Internet. Students are not required to have their own PC.

Special Opportunities Advanced credit may be earned through credit by examination, credit for business training programs, transfer of credits from another institution. International exchange programs in Belgium, France. An internship program is available.

FINANCES
Costs for 1997–98 Tuition: $560 per credit. Cost varies by number of credits taken. Fees: $80 per term. Fees vary by number of credits taken. Average 1997–98 room only costs were $7400 per academic year.

Financial Aid In 1997–98, 12% of students received some institutionally administered aid in the form of fellowships, research assistantships, teaching assistantships, scholarships, loans. Financial aid is available to part-time students. Application Deadline: 5/1.

Financial Aid Contact Ms. Kathy Pattison, Assistant Dean, Admissions and Financial Aid, 113 West 60th Street, Room 619, New York, NY 10023. Phone: 212-636-6200; Fax: 212-636-7076; E-mail: gbaadmin@mary.fordham.edu

FACILITIES
Information Resources Duane Library plus 5 additional on-campus libraries; total holdings of 1,233,575 volumes, 1,420,920 microforms, 5,505 current periodical subscriptions. CD player(s) available for graduate student use. Access provided to online bibliographic retrieval services.

INTERNATIONAL STUDENTS
Demographics 8% of students enrolled are international students [Africa, 2%, Asia, 44%, Central America, 3%, Europe, 38%, South America, 9%, other, 4%].

Services and Facilities International student office, international student center, visa services, ESL courses, counseling/support services.

Applying TOEFL: minimum score of 600, proof of adequate funds, proof of health/immunizations required. Financial aid is not available to international students.

International Student Contact Ms. Kathy Pattison, Assistant Dean, Admissions and Financial Aid, 113 West 60th Street, Room 619, New York, NY 10023. Phone: 212-636-6200; Fax: 212-636-7076; E-mail: gbaadmin@mary.fordham.edu

PLACEMENT
Services include alumni network, career counseling/planning, career library, career placement, job interviews arranged, and resume preparation. In 1996–97, 17 organizations participated in on-campus recruiting; 86 on-campus interviews were conducted.

Employment Of 1996–97 graduates, 77% were employed within three months of graduation; the average starting salary was $57,900. Types of employment entered: accounting, banking, communications, consulting, consumer products, finance, health services, information systems/technology, insurance, international trade, management, marketing, media, pharmaceutical, real estate, retail, telecommunications.

Business Program(s) URL: http://www.bnet.fordham.edu

Program Contact: Ms. Kathy Pattison, Assistant Dean, Admissions and Financial Aid, 113 West 60th Street, Room 619, New York, NY 10023. Phone: 212-636-6200, 800-825-4422 (NY only); Fax: 212-636-7076; E-mail: gbaadmin@mary.fordham.edu

See full description on page 822.

Hofstra University

Frank G. Zarb School of Business

Hempstead, New York

OVERVIEW
Hofstra University is an independent-nonprofit, coed university. Enrollment: 12,591 graduate, professional, and undergraduate students; 1,259 full-time matriculated graduate/professional students; 2,403 part-time matriculated graduate/professional students. Founded: 1935. The graduate business unit is in a suburban setting and is on a 4-1-4 calendar.

HIGHLIGHTS

Enrollment Profile
Full-time: 160
Part-time: 550
Total: 710
Average Age: 26
Fall 1997 Average GPA: 3.2

International: 7%
Women: 37%
Minorities: 8%
Average Class Size: 22
Fall 1997 Average GMAT: 570

Costs
Full-time tuition: N/R
Part-time tuition: $442 per credit

AACSB – The International Association for Management Education accredited

GRADUATE BUSINESS PROGRAMS
Master of Business Administration (MBA) Full-time, part-time; 42-66 total credits required; 12 months to 5 years to complete program. Concentrations in accounting, system management, international business, management, marketing, finance, taxation.

Master of Science in Accounting (MS) Full-time, part-time; 30-36 total credits required; 12 months to 3 years to complete program. Concentration in accounting.

Executive MBA (MBA) Part-time; 48 total credits required; 7 years work experience required; 20 months to complete program. Concentration in management.

Master of Science in Accounting Information Systems (MS) Full-time, part-time; 30-36 total credits required; 12 months to 3 years to complete program. Concentration in financial information systems.

Master of Science in Taxation (MS) Full-time, part-time; 30-36 total credits required; 12 months to 3 years to complete program. Concentration in taxation.

Master of Science in Accounting and Taxation (MS) Full-time, part-time; 30-36 total credits required; 12 months to 3 years to complete program. Concentrations in accounting, taxation.

ADMISSION

Applications For fall 1997 there were 696 applications for admission. Of those applying, 397 were accepted. Of those accepted, 220 enrolled.

Application Requirements GMAT score, application form, application fee, bachelor's degree, essay, minimum GPA, 2 letters of recommendation, personal statement, resume, college transcript(s).

Application Deadline Applications processed on a rolling/continuous basis for both domestic and international students. Application fee: $40, $75 (international). Deferred entrance is available.

ACADEMICS

Faculty Full-time 48; part-time 2.

Teaching Methodologies Case study, computer-aided instruction, computer analysis, computer simulations, experiential learning, faculty seminars, field projects, group discussion, lecture, research, role playing, seminars by members of the business community, simulations, student presentations, study groups, team projects.

Technology 1,000 on-campus computer terminals/PCs are available for student use and are linked by a campus-wide network. The network has full access to the Internet. Students are not required to have their own PC.

Special Opportunities Advanced credit may be earned through transfer of credits from another institution. International exchange programs in Finland, France, Netherlands. An internship program is available.

FINANCES

Costs for 1997–98 Tuition: $442 per credit. Fees: $182 per semester. Average 1997–98 room and board costs were $7500 per academic year (on campus) and $9000 per academic year (off campus). Room and board costs vary by campus location, occupancy (e.g., single, double, triple), type of accommodation, type of meal plan.

Financial Aid In 1997–98, 7% of students received some institutionally administered aid in the form of fellowships, research assistantships, scholarships, work study. Application Deadline: 4/1.

Financial Aid Contact Ms. Susan McTiernan, Senior Assistant Dean, 134 Hofstra University, Hempstead, NY 11549-1090. Phone: 516-463-5683; Fax: 516-463-5268; E-mail: humba@hofstra.edu

FACILITIES

Information Resources Axinn Library plus 1 additional on-campus library; total holdings of 1,360,603 volumes, 1,009,816 microforms, 5,637 current periodical subscriptions. CD player(s) available for graduate student use. Access provided to online bibliographic retrieval services and online databases.

INTERNATIONAL STUDENTS

Demographics 7% of students enrolled are international students [Africa, 5%, Asia, 45%, Central America, 10%, Europe, 20%, South America, 10%, other, 10%].

Services and Facilities International student office, international student housing, visa services, ESL courses, counseling/support services, language tutoring.

Applying TOEFL: minimum score of 580, proof of adequate funds, proof of health/immunizations required. Financial aid is not available to international students.

International Student Contact Ann Nastasi, Director of International Students' Office, 200 Hofstra University, Hempstead, NY 11549. Phone: 516-467-6796; Fax: 516-463-6921; E-mail: dnsamn@hofstra.edu

PLACEMENT

Services include alumni network, career counseling/planning, career fairs, career library, career placement, electronic job bank, job interviews arranged, resume referral to employers, and resume preparation. In 1996–97, 45 organizations participated in on-campus recruiting.

Employment Of 1996–97 graduates, 92% were employed within three months of graduation; the average starting salary was $51,300. Types of employment entered: accounting, banking, communications, computer-related, consulting, consumer products, education, energy, engineering, finance, financial services, government, health services, high technology, human resources, information systems/technology, insurance, international trade, law, management, marketing, media, nonprofit, pharmaceutical, real estate, retail, service industry, telecommunications, transportation, utilities.

Business Program(s) URL: http://www.hofstra.edu

Program Contact: Office of Graduate Admissions, 100 Hofstra University, Hempstead, NY 11549-1090. Phone: 516-463-6707; Fax: 516-560-7660; E-mail: hofstra@hofstra.edu
See full description on page 838.

Iona College

Hagan School of Business

New Rochelle, New York

OVERVIEW

Iona College is an independent-nonprofit, coed, comprehensive institution. Enrollment: 5,600 graduate, professional, and undergraduate students; 74 full-time matriculated graduate/professional students; 1,129 part-time matriculated graduate/professional students. Founded: 1940. The graduate business unit is in a suburban setting and is on a trimester calendar.

HIGHLIGHTS

Enrollment Profile
Full-time: 27
Part-time: 377
Total: 404
Average Age: 29
Fall 1997 Average GPA: 3.2

International: 2%
Women: 45%
Minorities: 14%
Average Class Size: 20
Fall 1997 Average GMAT: 490

Costs
Full-time tuition: N/R
Part-time tuition: $480 per credit

GRADUATE BUSINESS PROGRAMS

Master of Business Administration (MBA) Full-time, part-time; 33-57 total credits required; 18 months to 6 years to complete program. Concentrations in finance, management, management information systems, marketing, human resources.

ADMISSION

Applications For fall 1997 there were 166 applications for admission. Of those applying, 100 were accepted. Of those accepted, 62 enrolled.

Application Requirements GMAT score: minimum 450, application form, application fee, bachelor's degree, essay, minimum GPA: 2.7, 2 letters of recommendation, personal statement, college transcript(s).

Recommended for Application Resume, work experience, computer experience.

Application Deadline Applications processed on a rolling/continuous basis for both domestic and international students. Application fee: $50. Deferred entrance is available.

ACADEMICS

Faculty Full-time 35; part-time 15.

Teaching Methodologies Case study, computer-aided instruction, computer analysis, computer simulations, experiential learning, faculty seminars, field projects, group discussion, lecture, research, role playing, seminars by members of the business community, simulations, student presentations, study groups, team projects.

Technology 500 on-campus computer terminals/PCs are available for student use and are linked by a campus-wide network. The network has full access to the Internet. Students are not required to have their own PC.

Special Opportunities Advanced credit may be earned through credit by examination, transfer of credits from another institution.

FINANCES

Costs for 1997–98 Tuition: $480 per credit. Fees: $45 per year. Average 1997–98 room and board costs were $7100 per academic year (off campus). Room and board costs vary by type of accommodation.

Financial Aid In 1997–98, 9% of students received some institutionally administered aid in the form of work study. Financial aid is available to part-time students.

Financial Aid Contact Ms. Laurie Schaffler, Student Financial Services, 715 North Avenue, New Rochelle, NY 10801-1890. Phone: 914-633-2497.

FACILITIES

Information Resources Ryan Library; total holdings of 313,134 volumes, 26,000 microforms, 1,350 current periodical subscriptions. CD player(s) available for graduate student use. Access provided to online bibliographic retrieval services.

INTERNATIONAL STUDENTS

Demographics 2% of students enrolled are international students.

Services and Facilities International student office, international student center, counseling/support services.

Applying TOEFL: minimum score of 550, proof of adequate funds, proof of health/immunizations required. Financial aid is not available to international students.

International Student Contact Sr. Rita Dougherty, Associate Dean for Undergraduate Admissions, 715 North Avenue, New Rochelle, NY 10801. Phone: 914-633-2504.

Iona College (continued)

PLACEMENT

Services include alumni network, career counseling/planning, career fairs, career library, career placement, electronic job bank, resume referral to employers, and resume preparation.

Employment Of 1996–97 graduates, 96% were employed within three months of graduation; the average starting salary was $40,000. Types of employment entered: accounting, banking, chemical industry, communications, computer-related, consulting, consumer products, engineering, finance, financial services, government, health services, high technology, human resources, information systems/technology, insurance, international trade, management, manufacturing, marketing, media, nonprofit, petrochemical, pharmaceutical, real estate, telecommunications, utilities.

Business Program(s) URL: http://www.iona.edu/academic/hagan

Program Contact: Mr. Dan Saraceno, Director of MBA Marketing, 715 North Avenue, New Rochelle, NY 10801-1890. Phone: 914-633-2288; Fax: 914-637-7720; E-mail: dsaraceno@iona.edu

See full description on page 854.

Le Moyne College

Department of Business

Syracuse, New York

OVERVIEW

Le Moyne College is an independent-religious, coed, comprehensive institution. Enrollment: 2,757 graduate, professional, and undergraduate students; 80 full-time matriculated graduate/professional students; 596 part-time matriculated graduate/professional students. Founded: 1946. The graduate business unit is in a suburban setting and is on a semester calendar.

HIGHLIGHTS

Enrollment Profile
Full-time: 0
Part-time: 367
Total: 367
Average Age: 33
Fall 1997 Average GPA: 3.0

International: 1%
Women: 29%
Minorities: 5%
Average Class Size: 29
Fall 1997 Average GMAT: 500

Costs
Full-time tuition: N/R
Part-time tuition: $364 per credit hour

GRADUATE BUSINESS PROGRAMS

Master of Business Administration (MBA) Part-time; 51 total credits required; up to 5 years to complete program. Concentrations in accounting, management information systems, human resources.

ADMISSION

Applications For fall 1997 there were 87 applications for admission. Of those applying, 80 were accepted. Of those accepted, 74 enrolled.

Application Requirements Application form, bachelor's degree, essay, minimum GPA: 3.0, interview, 2 letters of recommendation, resume, college transcript(s), minimum of 2 years of work experience.

Recommended for Application GMAT score accepted: minimum 500, computer experience.

Application Deadline Applications processed on a rolling/continuous basis for both domestic and international students.

ACADEMICS

Faculty Full-time 26; part-time 2.

Teaching Methodologies Case study, computer-aided instruction, computer analysis, computer simulations, experiential learning, faculty seminars, field projects, group discussion, lecture, research, role playing, seminars by members of the business community, simulations, student presentations, study groups, team projects.

Technology 60 on-campus computer terminals/PCs are available for student use and are linked by a campus-wide network. The network has full access to the Internet. Students are not required to have their own PC.

Special Opportunities Advanced credit may be earned through transfer of credits from another institution. International exchange program in People's Republic of China. An internship program is available.

FINANCES

Costs for 1997–98 Tuition: Part-time: $364 per credit hour. Cost varies by number of credits taken.

Financial Aid In 1997–98, 4% of students received some institutionally administered aid in the form of research assistantships, loans. Financial aid is available to part-time students.

Financial Aid Contact Financial Aid Director, Syracuse, NY 13214-1399. Phone: 315-445-4400.

FACILITIES

Information Resources Main library; total holdings of 210,191 volumes, 37,670 microforms, 1,683 current periodical subscriptions. CD player(s) available for graduate student use. Access provided to online bibliographic retrieval services.

INTERNATIONAL STUDENTS

Demographics 1% of students enrolled are international students.

Services and Facilities Visa services, counseling/support services.

Applying TOEFL, proof of adequate funds, proof of health/immunizations required.

PLACEMENT

Services include alumni network, career counseling/planning, career fairs, career placement, electronic job bank, job interviews arranged, and resume preparation.

Employment Of 1996–97 graduates, 99% were employed within three months of graduation. Types of employment entered: banking, computer-related, energy, engineering, finance, health services, information systems/technology, management, marketing, pharmaceutical, service industry, utilities.

Business Program(s) URL: http://maple.lemoyne.edu

Program Contact: Dr. Wally J. Elmer, Professor and MBA Director, Le Moyne Heights, Syracuse, NY 13214-1399. Phone: 315-445-4785; Fax: 315-445-4787; E-mail: elmer@palm.lemoyne.edu

Long Island University, Brooklyn Campus

School of Business and Public Administration

Brooklyn, New York

OVERVIEW

Long Island University, Brooklyn Campus is an independent-nonprofit, coed, comprehensive institution. Founded: 1926. The graduate business unit is in an urban setting and is on a semester calendar.

HIGHLIGHTS

Enrollment Profile
Full-time: N/R
Part-time: N/R
Total: N/R
Average Age: N/R
Fall 1997 Average GPA: 3.0

International: N/R
Women: N/R
Minorities: N/R
Average Class Size: 19
Fall 1997 Average GMAT: 480

Costs
Full-time tuition: N/R
Part-time tuition: N/R

GRADUATE BUSINESS PROGRAMS

Generic MBA (MBA) Full-time, part-time; 30-54 total credits required; 18 months to 6 years to complete program.

Master of Business Administration (MBA) Full-time, part-time; 30-54 total credits required; 18 months to 6 years to complete program. Concentrations in management, marketing, finance, accounting, international business, taxation.

Master of Science in Taxation (MS) Full-time, part-time; 36 total credits required; 18 months to 6 years to complete program.

Master of Science in Accounting (MS) Full-time, part-time; 36 total credits required; 18 months to 6 years to complete program.

MBA for Certified Public Accountants (MBA) Full-time, part-time; 30-78 total credits required; 18 months to 6 years to complete program.

Master of Public Administration (MPA) Full-time, part-time; 36-48 total credits required; 18 months to 6 years to complete program.

ADMISSION

Application Requirements GMAT score, application form, application fee, bachelor's degree, minimum GPA, college transcript(s).

Application Deadline 8/15 for fall, 1/1 for winter, 5/15 for summer, 8/1 for fall (international), 12/15 for winter (international), 5/1 for summer (international). Application fee: $30.

ACADEMICS

Faculty Full-time 25; part-time 27.

Teaching Methodologies Case study, computer-aided instruction, computer simulations, experiential learning, faculty seminars, field projects, group discus-

NEW YORK

sion, lecture, research, role playing, seminars by members of the business community, simulations, student presentations, study groups, team projects.

Technology 100 on-campus computer terminals/PCs are available for student use and are linked by a campus-wide network. The network has full access to the Internet. Students are not required to have their own PC.

Special Opportunities Advanced credit may be earned through transfer of credits from another institution. International exchange programs in Republic of Korea, Switzerland. An internship program is available.

FINANCES
Costs for 1997–98 Cost varies by number of credits taken.
Financial Aid Scholarships available. Financial aid is available to part-time students.
Financial Aid Contact Rose Iannicelli, Director of Financial Aid, One University Plaza, Brooklyn, NY 11201-8423. Phone: 718-488-3320.

FACILITIES
Information Resources Salena Library Learning Center; total holdings of 300,000 volumes. CD player(s) available for graduate student use. Access provided to online bibliographic retrieval services.

INTERNATIONAL STUDENTS
Demographics N/R
Services and Facilities International student office, international student center, international student housing, ESL courses, counseling/support services.
Applying TOEFL: minimum score of 600, proof of adequate funds, proof of health/immunizations required. Financial aid is not available to international students.
International Student Contact Steven Chin, Director of International Student Services, One University Plaza, Brooklyn, NY 11201-8423. Phone: 718-488-1216.

PLACEMENT
Services include career counseling/planning, career fairs, career placement, resume referral to employers, and resume preparation. In 1996–97, 50 organizations participated in on-campus recruiting; 300 on-campus interviews were conducted.
Employment Types of employment entered: accounting, banking, communications, computer-related, consulting, consumer products, education, energy, finance, financial services, government, health services, high technology, hospitality management, human resources, information systems/technology, insurance, international trade, management, manufacturing, marketing, nonprofit, pharmaceutical, real estate, retail, service industry, telecommunications, transportation, utilities.
Business Program(s) URL: http://www.liunet.edu/

Program Contact: Alan Chaves, Dean of Admissions, One University Plaza, Brooklyn, NY 11201-8423. Phone: 800-LIUPLAN.

Long Island University, C.W. Post Campus

College of Management
Brookville, New York

OVERVIEW
Long Island University, C.W. Post Campus is an independent-nonprofit, coed, comprehensive institution. Enrollment: 8,406 graduate, professional, and undergraduate students; 827 full-time matriculated graduate/professional students; 2,292 part-time matriculated graduate/professional students. Founded: 1954. The graduate business unit is in a suburban setting and is on a semester calendar.

HIGHLIGHTS

Enrollment Profile
Full-time: 200
Part-time: 500
Total: 700
Average Age: 29
Fall 1997 Average GPA: 2.8

International: 20%
Women: 40%
Minorities: N/R
Average Class Size: 17
Fall 1997 Average GMAT: 500

Costs
Full-time tuition: N/R
Part-time tuition: $475 per credit

Degree(s) offered in conjunction with Franklin College, Touro Law School
GRADUATE BUSINESS PROGRAMS
Master of Business Administration (MBA) Full-time, part-time; 60 total credits required; 2.5 to 5 years to complete program. Concentrations in finance, human resources, international business, management, management information systems, marketing.
Accelerated International MBA (MBA) Full-time; 36 total credits required; minimum of 12 months to complete program. Concentration in international business.
Master of Science in Accountancy (MS) Full-time, part-time; 36-60 total credits required; 12 months to 5 years to complete program. Concentrations in accounting, taxation.

ADMISSION
Applications For fall 1997 there were 587 applications for admission. Of those applying, 150 were accepted. Of those accepted, 100 enrolled.
Application Requirements GMAT score, application form, application fee, bachelor's degree (must be in field of business), essay, minimum GPA, 2 letters of recommendation, resume, college transcript(s).
Recommended for Application Interview, work experience, computer experience.
Application Deadline 7/30 for fall, 11/30 for spring, 5/30 for fall (international), 12/1 for spring (international). Application fee: $30. Deferred entrance is available.

ACADEMICS
Faculty Full-time 56; part-time 96.
Teaching Methodologies Case study, computer-aided instruction, computer simulations, experiential learning, faculty seminars, field projects, group discussion, lecture, research, role playing, seminars by members of the business community, simulations, student presentations, study groups, team projects.
Technology 400 on-campus computer terminals/PCs are available for student use and are linked by a campus-wide network. The network has full access to the Internet. Students are not required to have their own PC.
Special Opportunities Advanced credit may be earned through credit by examination, transfer of credits from another institution. International exchange program in Switzerland.

FINANCES
Costs for 1997–98 Tuition: $475 per credit. Cost varies by academic program, number of credits taken. Fees: $115 per semester. Fees vary by number of credits taken. Average 1997–98 room and board costs were $5890 per academic year. Room and board costs vary by occupancy (e.g., single, double, triple), type of accommodation, type of meal plan.
Financial Aid In 1997–98, 40% of students received some institutionally administered aid in the form of fellowships, research assistantships, teaching assistantships, work study, loans. Financial aid is available to part-time students.
Financial Aid Contact Mrs. Joanne Graziano, Director, Financial Aid, 720 Northern Boulevard, Brookville, NY 11548-1300. Phone: 516-299-2338; Fax: 516-299-3833.

FACILITIES
Information Resources B. Davis Schwartz Memorial Library; total holdings of 2,297,679 volumes, 678,216 microforms, 9,604 current periodical subscriptions. CD player(s) available for graduate student use. Access provided to online bibliographic retrieval services.

INTERNATIONAL STUDENTS
Demographics 20% of students enrolled are international students.
Services and Facilities International student office, international student center, international student housing, visa services, ESL courses, counseling/support services.
Applying TOEFL: minimum score of 550, proof of adequate funds, proof of health/immunizations required. Financial aid is not available to international students.
International Student Contact Renee' Olson, Director, International Admissions, 720 Northern Boulevard, Brookville, NY 11548-1300. Phone: 516-299-2067; Fax: 516-299-2137.

PLACEMENT
Services include alumni network, career counseling/planning, career fairs, career library, career placement, electronic job bank, job interviews arranged, job search course, resume referral to employers, and resume preparation.
Employment Of 1996–97 graduates, 95% were employed within three months of graduation. Types of employment entered: accounting, banking, communications, computer-related, consulting, consumer products, education, engineering, finance, financial services, government, health services, high technology, hospitality management, human resources, information systems/technology, insurance, international trade, law, management, manufacturing, marketing, media, nonprofit, pharmaceutical, real estate, retail, service industry, telecommunications.
Business Program(s) URL: http://www.cwpost.liunet.edu/cwis/cwp/colofman/colofman.html

Long Island University, C.W. Post Campus (continued)

Program Contact: Ms. Sally Luzader, Coordinator, Graduate Admissions, 720 Northern Boulevard, Brookville, NY 11548-1300. Phone: 516-299-3017, 800-LIUPLAN; Fax: 516-299-2137; E-mail: admissions@collegehall.liunet.edu

Manhattan College

School of Business

Riverdale, New York

OVERVIEW
Manhattan College is an independent-religious, coed, comprehensive institution. Enrollment: 3,204 graduate, professional, and undergraduate students; 67 full-time matriculated graduate/professional students; 430 part-time matriculated graduate/professional students. Founded: 1853. The graduate business unit is in an urban setting and is on a 4-1-4 calendar.

HIGHLIGHTS

Enrollment Profile
Full-time: 7
Part-time: 148
Total: 155
Average Age: 28
Fall 1997 Average GPA: N/R

International: 4%
Women: 38%
Minorities: N/R
Average Class Size: 17
Fall 1997 Average GMAT: 483

Costs
Full-time tuition: N/R
Part-time tuition: $440 per credit

GRADUATE BUSINESS PROGRAMS
Master of Business Administration (MBA) Full-time, part-time; 39-57 total credits required; 12 months to 5 years to complete program. Concentrations in finance, international business, management, marketing.

ADMISSION
Applications For fall 1997 there were 90 applications for admission. Of those applying, 76 were accepted. Of those accepted, 57 enrolled.

Application Requirements GMAT score: minimum 440, application form, application fee, bachelor's degree, minimum GPA: 2.8, letter of recommendation, college transcript(s).

Application Deadline 8/10 for fall, 1/7 for spring, 6/10 for summer. Application fee: $50.

ACADEMICS
Faculty Full-time 20; part-time 7.

Teaching Methodologies Case study, computer-aided instruction, computer simulations, experiential learning, field projects, group discussion, lecture, research, seminars by members of the business community, simulations, student presentations, team projects.

Technology Computer terminals/PCs are available for student use and are linked by a campus-wide network. The network has full access to the Internet. Students are not required to have their own PC.

Special Opportunities Advanced credit may be earned through transfer of credits from another institution.

FINANCES
Costs for 1997–98 Tuition: $440 per credit.
Financial Aid In 1997–98, 3% of students received some institutionally administered aid in the form of scholarships. Application Deadline: 2/1.
Financial Aid Contact Mr. Alfred R. Manduley, Director, MBA Program, Manhattan College Parkway, Riverdale, NY 10471. Phone: 718-862-7290; E-mail: amandule@manhattan.edu

FACILITIES
Information Resources Cardinal Hayes Library plus 1 additional on-campus library; total holdings of 244,680 volumes, 347,290 microforms, 2,540 current periodical subscriptions. CD player(s) available for graduate student use. Access provided to online bibliographic retrieval services.

INTERNATIONAL STUDENTS
Demographics 4% of students enrolled are international students.
Services and Facilities International student office, international student center.
Applying TOEFL: minimum score of 550, proof of adequate funds, proof of health/immunizations required.
International Student Contact Debra Damico, Manhattan College Parkway, Riverdale, NY 10471.

PLACEMENT
Services include career placement.

Business Program(s) URL: http://www.manhattan.edu/business/buspage.html
Program Contact: Mr. Alfred R. Manduley, Director, MBA Program, Manhattan College Parkway, Riverdale, NY 10471. Phone: 718-862-7222; Fax: 718-862-8023; E-mail: amandule@manhattan.edu
See full description on page 880.

Manhattanville College

Adult and Special Programs

Purchase, New York

OVERVIEW
Manhattanville College is an independent-nonprofit, coed, comprehensive institution. Enrollment: 1,652 graduate, professional, and undergraduate students; full-time matriculated graduate/professional students; 800 part-time matriculated graduate/professional students. Founded: 1841. The graduate business unit is in a suburban setting and is on a quarter calendar.

HIGHLIGHTS

Enrollment Profile
Full-time: 0
Part-time: 235
Total: 235
Average Age: 36
Fall 1997 Average GPA: 3.1

International: 4%
Women: 87%
Minorities: 17%
Average Class Size: 20
Fall 1997 Average GMAT: N/R

Costs
Full-time tuition: N/R
Part-time tuition: $398 per credit

GRADUATE BUSINESS PROGRAMS
Master of Science in Organizational Management and Human Resource Development (MS) Part-time; 36 total credits required; 18 months to 5 years to complete program. Concentrations in human resources, organizational management.
Master of Science in Leadership and Strategic Management (MS) Part-time; 39 total credits required; 2 to 5 years to complete program. Concentrations in leadership, strategic management.

ADMISSION
Applications For fall 1997 there were 60 applications for admission. Of those applying, 50 were accepted. Of those accepted, 45 enrolled.

Application Requirements Application form, application fee, bachelor's degree, essay, minimum GPA: 2.5, interview, 2 letters of recommendation, personal statement, resume, college transcript(s), minimum of 2 years of work experience.

Recommended for Application Computer experience.

Application Deadline Applications processed on a rolling/continuous basis for both domestic and international students. Application fee: $45. Deferred entrance is available.

ACADEMICS
Faculty Full-time 4; part-time 38.

Teaching Methodologies Case study, computer-aided instruction, experiential learning, field projects, group discussion, lecture, research, role playing, seminars by members of the business community, simulations, student presentations, team projects.

Technology 50 on-campus computer terminals/PCs are available for student use. The network has full access to the Internet. Students are not required to have their own PC.

Special Opportunities Advanced credit may be earned through credit for experience, transfer of credits from another institution. An internship program is available.

FINANCES
Costs for 1997–98 Tuition: Part-time: $398 per credit. Fees: Part-time: $30 per semester.
Financial Aid Contact Mr. Peter Brennan, Director of Financial Aid, 2900 Purchase Street, Purchase, NY 10577-2132. Phone: 914-323-5357.

FACILITIES
Information Resources Main library; total holdings of 244,178 volumes, 224,383 microforms, 1,020 current periodical subscriptions. CD player(s) available for graduate student use. Access provided to online bibliographic retrieval services and online databases.

INTERNATIONAL STUDENTS
Demographics 4% of students enrolled are international students [Africa, 14%, Asia, 14%, Central America, 29%, Europe, 43%].
Services and Facilities International student office, ESL courses, counseling/support services.

Applying TOEFL: minimum score of 600, proof of adequate funds, proof of health/immunizations required. Financial aid is not available to international students.

International Student Contact Dr. Mary Hines, English Language Institute, 2900 Purchase Street, Purchase, NY 10577-2132. Phone: 914-323-5271.

PLACEMENT

Services include alumni network, career counseling/planning, career fairs, career library, career placement, resume referral to employers, and resume preparation.

Business Program(s) URL: http://www.mville.edu

Program Contact: Dr. Donald Richards, Director of MS Program and Associate Dean, 2900 Purchase Street, Purchase, NY 10577-2132. Phone: 914-694-3425; Fax: 914-694-3488.

Marist College

School of Management

Poughkeepsie, New York

OVERVIEW

Marist College is an independent-nonprofit, coed, comprehensive institution. Enrollment: 4,465 graduate, professional, and undergraduate students; 95 full-time matriculated graduate/professional students; 450 part-time matriculated graduate/professional students. Founded: 1929. The graduate business unit is in a suburban setting and is on a semester and trimester calendar.

HIGHLIGHTS

Enrollment Profile
Full-time: 3
Part-time: 101
Total: 104
Average Age: 29
Fall 1997 Average GPA: 3.3

International: N/R
Women: 38%
Minorities: N/R
Average Class Size: 15
Fall 1997 Average GMAT: 544

Costs
Full-time tuition: N/R
Part-time tuition: $419 per credit hour

GRADUATE BUSINESS PROGRAMS

Master of Business Administration (MBA) Full-time, part-time, distance learning option; 30-51 total credits required; 16 months to 7 years to complete program. Concentrations in accounting, finance, human resources, management, management information systems, health care.

ADMISSION

Applications For fall 1997 there were 39 applications for admission. Of those applying, 25 were accepted. Of those accepted, 14 enrolled.

Application Requirements GMAT score, application form, application fee, bachelor's degree, minimum GPA, college transcript(s), computer experience: spreadsheet.

Recommended for Application Resume, work experience.

Application Deadline Applications processed on a rolling/continuous basis for both domestic and international students. Application fee: $30. Deferred entrance is available.

ACADEMICS

Faculty Full-time 25; part-time 4.

Teaching Methodologies Case study, computer analysis, computer simulations, experiential learning, faculty seminars, field projects, group discussion, lecture, research, role playing, seminars by members of the business community, simulations, student presentations, study groups, team projects.

Technology 250 on-campus computer terminals/PCs are available for student use and are linked by a campus-wide network. The network has full access to the Internet. Students are not required to have their own PC.

Special Opportunities Advanced credit may be earned through credit by examination, transfer of credits from another institution. International exchange program in Germany. An internship program is available.

FINANCES

Costs for 1997–98 Tuition: $419 per credit hour. Fees: $25 per semester. Average 1997–98 room and board costs were $5524 per academic year (off campus).

Financial Aid In 1997–98, 10% of students received some institutionally administered aid in the form of grants, work study. Financial aid is available to part-time students. Application Deadline: 8/15.

Financial Aid Contact Ms. Corinne Schell, Associate Director of Financial Aid, 290 North Road, Poughkeepsie, NY 12601-1387. Phone: 914-575-3230; Fax: 914-471-6213.

FACILITIES

Information Resources The Spellman Library; total holdings of 157,500 volumes, 204,397 microforms, 1,795 current periodical subscriptions. CD player(s) available for graduate student use. Access provided to online bibliographic retrieval services.

INTERNATIONAL STUDENTS

Demographics N/R

Services and Facilities International student office, visa services, ESL courses, counseling/support services.

Applying TOEFL: minimum score of 550, TWE: minimum score of 4, proof of adequate funds required. Financial aid is not available to international students.

International Student Contact Ms. Eileen Bull, Director, Graduate Admissions, 290 North Road, Poughkeepsie, NY 12601-1387. Phone: 914-575-3530; Fax: 914-575-3640; E-mail: graduate@marist.edu

PLACEMENT

Services include alumni network, career counseling/planning, career fairs, career library, career placement, electronic job bank, job interviews arranged, job search course, resume referral to employers, and resume preparation.

Employment Of 1996–97 graduates, 100% were employed within three months of graduation; the average starting salary was $45,000. Types of employment entered: accounting, banking, communications, computer-related, education, energy, engineering, finance, financial services, government, health services, high technology, human resources, information systems/technology, insurance, law, management, manufacturing, marketing, nonprofit, pharmaceutical, retail, telecommunications, transportation, utilities.

Business Program(s) URL: http://www.marist.edu

Program Contact: Ms. Eileen Bull, Director, Graduate Admissions, 290 North Road, Poughkeepsie, NY 12601-1387. Phone: 914-575-3530; Fax: 914-575-3640; E-mail: graduate@marist.edu

See full description on page 882.

Mercy College

Program in Human Resource Management

Dobbs Ferry, New York

OVERVIEW

Mercy College is an independent-nonprofit, coed, comprehensive institution. Enrollment: 5,027 graduate, professional, and undergraduate students. Founded: 1950. The graduate business unit is in a suburban setting and is on a quarter calendar.

HIGHLIGHTS

Enrollment Profile
Full-time: 8
Part-time: 198
Total: 206
Average Age: 35
Fall 1997 Average GPA: N/R

International: 2%
Women: 69%
Minorities: 17%
Average Class Size: 15
Fall 1997 Average GMAT: N/R

Costs
Full-time tuition: N/R
Part-time tuition: $390 per credit

GRADUATE BUSINESS PROGRAMS

Master of Science in Human Resource Management (MS) Full-time, part-time; 36 total credits required; 12 months to 5 years to complete program. Concentrations in human resources, organizational management.

ADMISSION

Application Requirements GMAT score, application form, application fee, bachelor's degree, essay, minimum GPA, interview, 2 letters of recommendation, personal statement, college transcript(s).

Recommended for Application Resume, work experience, computer experience.

Application Deadline Applications processed on a rolling/continuous basis for both domestic and international students. Application fee: $35. Deferred entrance is available.

ACADEMICS

Faculty Full-time 1; part-time 18.

Teaching Methodologies Case study, computer-aided instruction, computer analysis, computer simulations, experiential learning, field projects, group discussion, lecture, research, role playing, seminars by members of the business community, student presentations, study groups, team projects.

Technology 100 on-campus computer terminals/PCs are available for student use and are linked by a campus-wide network. The network does not have Internet access. Students are not required to have their own PC.

Mercy College (continued)

Special Opportunities Advanced credit may be earned through credit for business training programs, transfer of credits from another institution.

FINANCES
Costs for 1997–98 Tuition: $390 per credit.

Financial Aid Research assistantships, work study available. Financial aid is available to part-time students.

Financial Aid Contact Director of Financial Aid, 555 Broadway, Dobbs Ferry, NY 10522-1189. Phone: 914-674-7328.

FACILITIES
Information Resources Main library plus 3 additional on-campus libraries; total holdings of 311,499 volumes, 532,310 microforms, 1,170 current periodical subscriptions. CD player(s) available for graduate student use. Access provided to online bibliographic retrieval services.

INTERNATIONAL STUDENTS
Demographics 2% of students enrolled are international students.

Services and Facilities International student office, international student housing, visa services, ESL courses, counseling/support services.

Applying TOEFL: minimum score of 550, proof of adequate funds, proof of health/immunizations required. Financial aid is not available to international students.

International Student Contact Ms. Joan Murphy, International Student Advisor, 555 Broadway, Dobbs Ferry, NY 10522-1189. Phone: 914-674-7233.

PLACEMENT
Services include alumni network, career counseling/planning, career fairs, career library, career placement, job interviews arranged, resume referral to employers, and resume preparation.

Employment Of 1996–97 graduates, 90% were employed within three months of graduation. Types of employment entered: accounting, banking, chemical industry, communications, computer-related, consulting, consumer products, education, energy, engineering, finance, financial services, government, health services, high technology, hospitality management, human resources, information systems/technology, insurance, international trade, law, management, manufacturing, marketing, media, mining, nonprofit, petrochemical, pharmaceutical, real estate, retail, service industry, telecommunications, transportation, utilities.

Program Contact: Ms. Linda A. Jerris, Director, Graduate Program in Human Resource Management, 555 Broadway, Dobbs Ferry, NY 10522-1189. Phone: 914-674-9331 Ext. 500; Fax: 914-674-9457.

Mount Saint Mary College

Division of Business

Newburgh, New York

OVERVIEW
Mount Saint Mary College is an independent-nonprofit, coed, comprehensive institution. Enrollment: 2,089 graduate, professional, and undergraduate students; 22 full-time matriculated graduate/professional students; 380 part-time matriculated graduate/professional students. Founded: 1960. The graduate business unit is in a suburban setting and is on a accelerated six week sections calendar.

HIGHLIGHTS

Enrollment Profile

Full-time: 1	International: 5%
Part-time: 74	Women: 48%
Total: 75	Minorities: 11%
Average Age: 36	Average Class Size: 14
Fall 1997 Average GPA: 3.15	Fall 1997 Average GMAT: 450

Costs
Full-time tuition: N/R
Part-time tuition: $367 per credit

GRADUATE BUSINESS PROGRAMS
Master of Business Administration (MBA) Full-time, part-time, distance learning option; 55 total credits required; 2 to 6 years to complete program.

ADMISSION
Application Requirements Application form, application fee, bachelor's degree, minimum GPA, interview, 3 letters of recommendation, personal statement, college transcript(s), computer experience: spreadsheet.

Recommended for Application GMAT score accepted, resume, work experience.

Application Deadline Applications processed on a rolling/continuous basis for both domestic and international students. Application fee: $20. Deferred entrance is available.

ACADEMICS
Faculty Full-time 7; part-time 4.

Teaching Methodologies Case study, computer-aided instruction, computer analysis, computer simulations, experiential learning, group discussion, lecture, research, seminars by members of the business community, student presentations, team projects.

Technology 120 on-campus computer terminals/PCs are available for student use and are linked by a campus-wide network. The network has full access to the Internet. Students are not required to have their own PC.

Special Opportunities Advanced credit may be earned through transfer of credits from another institution.

FINANCES
Costs for 1997–98 Tuition: $367 per credit.

Financial Aid In 1997–98, 5% of students received some institutionally administered aid in the form of work study, loans. Financial aid is available to part-time students. Application Deadline: 3/15.

FACILITIES
Information Resources Curtin Memorial Library; total holdings of 116,113 volumes, 269 microforms, 1,281 current periodical subscriptions. CD player(s) available for graduate student use. Access provided to online bibliographic retrieval services.

INTERNATIONAL STUDENTS
Demographics 5% of students enrolled are international students [Africa, 1%, Asia, 2%, Central America, 1%, North America, 95%, South America, 1%].

Services and Facilities Counseling/support services.

Applying TOEFL, proof of adequate funds, proof of health/immunizations required. Financial aid is not available to international students.

International Student Contact Dr. Mattson Atsunyo, Coordinator, MBA Program, 330 Powell Avenue, Newburgh, NY 12550-3494. Phone: 914-569-3121; Fax: 914-562-6762; E-mail: atsunyo@msmc.edu

PLACEMENT
Services include alumni network, career counseling/planning, electronic job bank, job interviews arranged, resume referral to employers, and resume preparation.

Employment Of 1996–97 graduates, 96% were employed within three months of graduation. Types of employment entered: accounting, banking, finance, government, human resources, management, manufacturing, marketing, nonprofit.

Business Program(s) URL: http://www.msmc.edu

Program Contact: Dr. Mattson Atsunyo, Coordinator, MBA Program, 330 Powell Avenue, Newburgh, NY 12550-3494. Phone: 914-569-3582, 800-558-0942 (NY only); Fax: 914-562-6762; E-mail: atsunyo@msmc.edu

Nazareth College of Rochester

Business Department

Rochester, New York

OVERVIEW
Nazareth College of Rochester is an independent-nonprofit, coed, comprehensive institution. Enrollment: 2,920 graduate, professional, and undergraduate students; 84 full-time matriculated graduate/professional students; 907 part-time matriculated graduate/professional students. Founded: 1924. The graduate business unit is in a suburban setting and is on a semester calendar.

HIGHLIGHTS

Enrollment Profile

Full-time: 2	International: 1%
Part-time: 68	Women: 54%
Total: 70	Minorities: 7%
Average Age: 37	Average Class Size: 18
Fall 1997 Average GPA: 3.0	Fall 1997 Average GMAT: 500

Costs
Full-time tuition: N/R
Part-time tuition: $396 per credit hour

GRADUATE BUSINESS PROGRAMS

Master of Science in Management (MS) Part-time; 33 total credits required; 15 months to 5 years to complete program. Concentration in management.

ADMISSION

Applications For fall 1997 there were 22 applications for admission. Of those applying, 22 were accepted. Of those accepted, 18 enrolled.

Application Requirements Application form, application fee, bachelor's degree, essay, interview, 2 letters of recommendation, personal statement, resume, college transcript(s), computer experience: basic computer experience.

Recommended for Application GMAT score accepted, minimum GPA: 2.7, work experience.

Application Deadline Applications processed on a rolling/continuous basis for both domestic and international students. Application fee: $40. Deferred entrance is available.

ACADEMICS

Faculty Full-time 6; part-time 8.

Teaching Methodologies Case study, computer analysis, field projects, group discussion, lecture, research, role playing.

Technology 100 on-campus computer terminals/PCs are available for student use and are linked by a campus-wide network. The network has full access to the Internet. Students are not required to have their own PC.

Special Opportunities Advanced credit may be earned through transfer of credits from another institution.

FINANCES

Costs for 1997–98 Tuition: Part-time: $396 per credit hour.

Financial Aid In 1997–98, 10% of students received some institutionally administered aid. Financial aid is available to part-time students.

Financial Aid Contact Dr. Bruce Woolley, Director of Financial Aid, 4245 East Avenue, Rochester, NY 14618-3790. Phone: 716-389-2310; Fax: 716-586-2452; E-mail: bcwoolle@naz.edu

FACILITIES

Information Resources Lorette Wilmont Library plus 1 additional on-campus library; total holdings of 217,397 volumes, 162,816 microforms, 1,709 current periodical subscriptions. CD player(s) available for graduate student use. Access provided to online bibliographic retrieval services.

INTERNATIONAL STUDENTS

Demographics 1% of students enrolled are international students.

Services and Facilities Counseling/support services.

Applying TOEFL, proof of adequate funds, proof of health/immunizations required.

International Student Contact Shirley Pilot, Graduate Student Advisor, 4245 East Avenue, Rochester, NY 14618-3790. Phone: 716-389-2525; Fax: 716-586-2452.

PLACEMENT

Services include alumni network, career counseling/planning, career placement, job search course, and resume preparation.

Business Program(s) URL: http://www.naz.edu

Program Contact: Mr. Gerard Zappia, Chairperson, Business Department, 4245 East Avenue, Rochester, NY 14618-3790. Phone: 716-389-2570; Fax: 716-586-2452; E-mail: gfzappia@naz.edu

New School for Social Research

Robert J. Milano Graduate School of Management and Urban Policy

New York, New York

OVERVIEW

New School for Social Research is an independent-nonprofit, coed university. Enrollment: 6,941 graduate, professional, and undergraduate students; 1,828 full-time matriculated graduate/professional students; 1,122 part-time matriculated graduate/professional students. Founded: 1919. The graduate business unit is in an urban setting and is on a semester calendar.

HIGHLIGHTS

Enrollment Profile
Full-time: 181
Part-time: 602
Total: 783
Average Age: 29
Fall 1997 Average GPA: 3.2

International: 4%
Women: 83%
Minorities: 38%
Average Class Size: 15
Fall 1997 Average GMAT: N/R

Costs
Full-time tuition: N/R
Part-time tuition: $588 per credit

GRADUATE BUSINESS PROGRAMS

Master of Science in Nonprofit Management (MS) Full-time, part-time, distance learning option; 42 total credits required.

Master of Science in Urban Policy Analysis and Management (MS) Full-time, part-time, distance learning option; 42 total credits required.

Master of Science in Health Services Management and Policy (MS) Full-time, part-time, distance learning option; 42 total credits required.

Master of Science in Human Resources Management (MS) Full-time, part-time, distance learning option; 42 total credits required.

ADMISSION

Applications For fall 1997 there were 227 applications for admission. Of those applying, 199 were accepted. Of those accepted, 149 enrolled.

Application Requirements Application form, application fee, bachelor's degree, essay, minimum GPA: 3.0, interview, 2 letters of recommendation, personal statement, college transcript(s).

Recommended for Application Resume, computer experience.

Application Deadline Applications processed on a rolling/continuous basis for both domestic and international students. Application fee: $30. Deferred entrance is available.

ACADEMICS

Faculty Full-time 26; part-time 90.

Teaching Methodologies Case study, computer-aided instruction, computer analysis, computer simulations, faculty seminars, field projects, group discussion, lecture, research, role playing, seminars by members of the business community, simulations, student presentations, study groups, team projects.

Technology 200 on-campus computer terminals/PCs are available for student use and are linked by a campus-wide network. The network has full access to the Internet.

Special Opportunities Advanced credit may be earned through credit by examination, transfer of credits from another institution. An internship program is available.

FINANCES

Costs for 1997–98 Tuition: $588 per credit. Cost varies by academic program, number of credits taken. Fees: $95 per semester. Fees vary by academic program, number of credits taken. Average 1997–98 room and board costs were $9100 per academic year.

Financial Aid In 1997–98, 26% of students received some institutionally administered aid in the form of fellowships, teaching assistantships, scholarships, work study, loans. Financial aid is available to part-time students. Application Deadline: 3/1.

Financial Aid Contact Mr. Harvey Willis, Office of Financial Aid, 66 Fifth Avenue, 7th Floor, New York, NY 10011. Phone: 212-229-5462; Fax: 212-229-8935; E-mail: hwillis@newschool.edu

FACILITIES

Information Resources Raymond Fogelman Library plus 5 additional on-campus libraries; total holdings of 4,063,725 volumes, 1,849,567 microforms, 21,348 current periodical subscriptions. CD player(s) available for graduate student use. Access provided to online bibliographic retrieval services.

INTERNATIONAL STUDENTS

Demographics 4% of students enrolled are international students.

Services and Facilities International student office, visa services, ESL courses, counseling/support services.

Applying TOEFL: minimum score of 600, proof of adequate funds, proof of health/immunizations required. Financial aid is available to international students.

International Student Contact Mr. Gary St. Fleur, International Student Advisor, 65 Fifth Avenue, Office of Student Affairs, New York, NY 10003. Phone: 212-229-5712.

PLACEMENT

Services include career counseling/planning, career fairs, career library, career placement, electronic job bank, job interviews arranged, resume referral to employers, and resume preparation. In 1996–97, 21 organizations participated in on-campus recruiting; 21 on-campus interviews were conducted.

New School for Social Research (continued)

Employment Of 1996–97 graduates, 46% were employed within three months of graduation; the average starting salary was $36,967. Types of employment entered: banking, finance, government, health services, human resources, management, nonprofit.

Business Program(s) URL: http://www.newschool.edu/milano

Program Contact: Ms. Emily Woolf Economou, Office of Admissions, 66 Fifth Avenue, 7th Floor, New York, NY 10011. Phone: 212-229-5462; Fax: 212-229-8935; E-mail: economoue@newschool.edu

See full description on page 894.

New York Institute of Technology

School of Management

Old Westbury, New York

OVERVIEW
New York Institute of Technology is an independent-nonprofit, coed, comprehensive institution. Enrollment: 8,982 graduate, professional, and undergraduate students; 1,666 full-time matriculated graduate/professional students; 1,659 part-time matriculated graduate/professional students. Founded: 1955. The graduate business unit is in a suburban setting and is on a semester calendar.

HIGHLIGHTS

Enrollment Profile

Full-time: 253	International: N/R
Part-time: 424	Women: 41%
Total: 677	Minorities: 22%
Average Age: 31	Average Class Size: 26
Fall 1997 Average GPA: 2.92	Fall 1997 Average GMAT: 443

Costs
Full-time tuition: N/R
Part-time tuition: $390 per credit

GRADUATE BUSINESS PROGRAMS
Master of Business Administration (MBA) Full-time, part-time, distance learning option; 36-54 total credits required; 12 months to 5 years to complete program. Concentrations in accounting, finance, human resources, international business, management, management information systems, health care, marketing.

Master of Business Administration/Bachelor of Architecture (MBA/BArch) Full-time, distance learning option; 5 years to complete program. Concentrations in accounting, finance, human resources, international business, management, management information systems, health care, marketing.

Master of Business Administration/Doctor of Osteopathic Medicine (MBA/DO) Full-time, distance learning option.

Master of Science in Human Resource Management and Labor Relations (MS) Full-time, part-time; 12 months to 5 years to complete program. Concentrations in industrial/labor relations, human resources.

ADMISSION
Applications For fall 1997 there were 392 applications for admission. Of those applying, 321 were accepted. Of those accepted, 199 enrolled.

Application Requirements GMAT score: minimum 400, application form, application fee, bachelor's degree, essay, minimum GPA: 2.5, college transcript(s).

Recommended for Application Work experience, computer experience.

Application Deadline Applications processed on a rolling/continuous basis for both domestic and international students. Application fee: $50. Deferred entrance is available.

ACADEMICS
Faculty Full-time 17; part-time 21.

Teaching Methodologies Case study, computer-aided instruction, computer analysis, computer simulations, experiential learning, faculty seminars, group discussion, lecture, research, seminars by members of the business community, simulations, student presentations, study groups, team projects.

Technology 550 on-campus computer terminals/PCs are available for student use and are linked by a campus-wide network. The network has full access to the Internet. Students are not required to have their own PC.

Special Opportunities Advanced credit may be earned through transfer of credits from another institution.

FINANCES
Costs for 1997–98 Tuition: $390 per credit. Cost varies by academic program, number of credits taken. Average 1997–98 room and board costs were

$5800 per academic year. Room and board costs vary by occupancy (e.g., single, double, triple), type of meal plan.

Financial Aid In 1997–98, 51% of students received some institutionally administered aid in the form of fellowships, research assistantships, loans. Financial aid is available to part-time students.

Financial Aid Contact Mrs. Doreen Meyer, Director of Financial Aid, PO Box 8000, Old Westbury, NY 11568. Phone: 516-686-7680; Fax: 516-686-7997; E-mail: dmeyer@iris.nyit.edu

FACILITIES
Information Resources Wisser Library plus 2 additional on-campus libraries; total holdings of 204,803 volumes, 626,117 microforms, 4,012 current periodical subscriptions. CD player(s) available for graduate student use. Access provided to online bibliographic retrieval services.

INTERNATIONAL STUDENTS
Demographics N/R

Services and Facilities International student office, international student housing, visa services, ESL courses, counseling/support services.

Applying TOEFL: minimum score of 500, proof of adequate funds, proof of health/immunizations required. Financial aid is available to international students.

International Student Contact Ms. Barbara Multari, International Student Advisor, PO Box 8000, Old Westbury, NY 11568. Phone: 516-686-7585; Fax: 516-626-0419.

PLACEMENT
Services include career counseling/planning, career fairs, and resume preparation. In 1996–97, 105 organizations participated in on-campus recruiting.

Employment Of 1996–97 graduates, 90% were employed within three months of graduation. Types of employment entered: accounting, banking, chemical industry, communications, computer-related, consulting, consumer products, education, energy, engineering, finance, financial services, government, health services, high technology, hospitality management, human resources, information systems/technology, international trade, law, management, manufacturing, marketing, media, nonprofit, real estate, telecommunications, transportation, utilities.

Business Program(s) URL: http://www.nyit.edu

Program Contact: Mr. Glenn S. Berman, Executive Director of Graduate Admissions, PO Box 8000, Old Westbury, NY 11568. Phone: 516-686-7519, 800-345-NYIT; Fax: 516-626-0419.

See full description on page 896.

New York University

Leonard N. Stern School of Business

New York, New York

OVERVIEW
New York University is an independent-nonprofit, coed university. Enrollment: 36,056 graduate, professional, and undergraduate students; 9,985 full-time matriculated graduate/professional students; 9,066 part-time matriculated graduate/professional students. Founded: 1831. The graduate business unit is in an urban setting and is on a semester calendar.

HIGHLIGHTS

Enrollment Profile

Full-time: 1,242	International: 17%
Part-time: 2,324	Women: 32%
Total: 3,566	Minorities: 15%
Average Age: 28	Average Class Size: 60
Fall 1997 Average GPA: 3.3	Fall 1997 Average GMAT: 657

Costs
Full-time tuition: $25,486 per academic year
Part-time tuition: $900 per credit

AACSB – The International Association for Management Education accredited

GRADUATE BUSINESS PROGRAMS

Master of Business Administration (MBA) Full-time, part-time; 60 total credits required; 16 months to 6 years to complete program. Concentrations in accounting, economics, finance, management, marketing, taxation, management information systems, operations management, international business, quantitative analysis.

Executive MBA (MBA) Full-time; 72 total credits required; 22 months to complete program. Concentrations in finance, management.

Master of Science (MS) Full-time, part-time; 36-58 total credits required; 18 months to 4 years to complete program. Concentrations in accounting, management information systems, quantitative analysis.

Doctor of Jurisprudence/Master of Business Administration (JD/MBA) Full-time; 122 total credits required; 4 to 6 years to complete program. Concentrations in accounting, economics, finance, management, management information systems, marketing, taxation, operations management, international business, quantitative analysis.

Master of Arts in French Studies/Master of Business Administration (MA/MBA) Full-time, part-time; 80 total credits required; 2.3 to 6 years to complete program. Concentrations in accounting, economics, finance, management, management information systems, marketing, taxation, operations management, international business, quantitative analysis.

Master of Arts in Politics/Master of Business Administration (MA/MBA) Full-time, part-time; 76 total credits required; 2.3 to 6 years to complete program. Concentrations in accounting, economics, finance, management, management information systems, marketing, taxation, operations management, international business, quantitative analysis.

Master of Arts in Journalism/Master of Business Administration (MA/MBA) Full-time, part-time; 76 total credits required; 2.3 to 6 years to complete program. Concentrations in accounting, economics, finance, management, management information systems, marketing, taxation, operations management, international business, quantitative analysis.

ADMISSION

Applications For fall 1997 there were 4,244 applications for admission. Of those applying, 838 were accepted. Of those accepted, 410 enrolled.

Application Requirements GMAT score, application form, application fee, bachelor's degree, essay, minimum GPA, 2 letters of recommendation, resume, college transcript(s), minimum of 2 years of work experience.

Recommended for Application Interview, computer experience.

Application Deadline 3/15 for fall, 3/15 for fall (international). Application fee: $75.

ACADEMICS

Faculty Full-time 175; part-time 211.

Teaching Methodologies Case study, computer-aided instruction, computer analysis, computer simulations, experiential learning, faculty seminars, field projects, group discussion, lecture, research, role playing, seminars by members of the business community, simulations, student presentations, study groups, team projects.

Technology 300 on-campus computer terminals/PCs are available for student use and are linked by a campus-wide network. The network has full access to the Internet. Students are not required to have their own PC.

Special Opportunities International exchange programs in Australia, Austria, Belgium, Brazil, Chile, Costa Rica, Denmark, France, Germany, Hong Kong, Israel, Italy, Japan, Mexico, Netherlands, Norway, Republic of Korea, Spain, Switzerland, United Kingdom.

FINANCES

Costs for 1997-98 Tuition: Full-time: $25,486 per year. Part-time: $900 per credit. Fees: $30 per credit. Average 1997-98 room and board costs were $10,355 per academic year.

Financial Aid In 1997-98, 39% of students received some institutionally administered aid in the form of fellowships, research assistantships, teaching assistantships, scholarships, work study. Application Deadline: 1/15.

Financial Aid Contact Meghan Cummings, Associate Director, 44 West 4th Street, MEC 10-160, New York, NY 10012-1126. Phone: 212-998-0790; Fax: 212-995-4231; E-mail: sternmba@stern.nyu.edu

FACILITIES

Information Resources Elmer H. Bobst Library plus 6 additional on-campus libraries; total holdings of 3,653,477 volumes, 3,236,036 microforms, 28,689 current periodical subscriptions. CD player(s) available for graduate student use. Access provided to online bibliographic retrieval services.

INTERNATIONAL STUDENTS

Demographics 17% of students enrolled are international students [Asia, 13%, Europe, 6%, North America, 67%, South America, 9%, other, 5%].

Services and Facilities International student office, international student center, international student housing, visa services, ESL courses, counseling/support services.

Applying TOEFL: minimum score of 600, proof of adequate funds, proof of health/immunizations required. Financial aid is available to international students.

International Student Contact Jonathan Beverly, Manager, International Programs and Services, 44 West 4 Street, Suite 10-50, New York, NY 10012. Phone: 212-998-0924; Fax: 212-995-4225; E-mail: jbeverly@stern.nyu.edu

PLACEMENT

Services include alumni network, career counseling/planning, career fairs, career library, career placement, electronic job bank, job interviews arranged, job search course, resume referral to employers, and resume preparation. In 1996-97, 250 organizations participated in on-campus recruiting; 7,400 on-campus interviews were conducted.

Employment Of 1996-97 graduates, 97% were employed within three months of graduation; the average starting salary was $92,503. Types of employment entered: accounting, banking, chemical industry, communications, computer-related, consulting, consumer products, education, energy, engineering, finance, financial services, government, health services, high technology, hospitality management, human resources, information systems/technology, insurance, international trade, law, management, manufacturing, marketing, media, mining, nonprofit, petrochemical, pharmaceutical, real estate, retail, service industry, telecommunications, transportation, utilities.

Business Program(s) URL: http://www.stern.nyu.edu

Program Contact: Ms. Mary Miller, Director, Admissions and Financial Aid, 44 West 4th Street, Suite 10-160, Management Education Center, New York, NY 10012-1126. Phone: 212-998-0600, 800-272-7373; Fax: 212-995-4231; E-mail: sternmba@stern.nyu.edu

See full description on page 898.

Niagara University

Graduate Division of Business Administration

Niagara University, New York

OVERVIEW

Niagara University is an independent-nonprofit, coed, comprehensive institution. Enrollment: 2,862 graduate, professional, and undergraduate students; 271 full-time matriculated graduate/professional students; 317 part-time matriculated graduate/professional students. Founded: 1856. The graduate business unit is in a suburban setting and is on a semester calendar.

HIGHLIGHTS

Enrollment Profile

Full-time: 35	International: 25%
Part-time: 110	Women: 34%
Total: 145	Minorities: 6%
Average Age: 30	Average Class Size: 17
Fall 1997 Average GPA: 3.0	Fall 1997 Average GMAT: 510

Costs
Full-time tuition: N/R
Part-time tuition: $430 per credit hour

GRADUATE BUSINESS PROGRAMS

Master of Business Administration in Management (MBA) Full-time, part-time; 51 total credits required; 22 months to 5 years to complete program. Concentrations in accounting, strategic management, management, travel industry/tourism management.

Accelerated MBA (MBA) Full-time; 51 total credits required; 22 months to complete program.

ADMISSION

Applications For fall 1997 there were 70 applications for admission. Of those applying, 55 were accepted. Of those accepted, 35 enrolled.

Application Requirements GMAT score: minimum 400, application form, application fee, bachelor's degree, minimum GPA: 2.5, 2 letters of recommendation, college transcript(s).

Recommended for Application Interview, personal statement, resume, work experience, computer experience.

Application Deadline Applications processed on a rolling/continuous basis for both domestic and international students. Application fee: $25. Deferred entrance is available.

ACADEMICS

Faculty Full-time 10; part-time 3.

Teaching Methodologies Case study, computer-aided instruction, computer analysis, computer simulations, experiential learning, field projects, group discussion, lecture, research, role playing, seminars by members of the business community, simulations, student presentations, study groups, team projects, community service.

Technology 150 on-campus computer terminals/PCs are available for student use and are linked by a campus-wide network. The network has full access to the Internet. Students are not required to have their own PC.

Special Opportunities Advanced credit may be earned through credit by examination, credit for experience, credit for military training programs, credit for business training programs, transfer of credits from another institution. International exchange programs in Germany, United Kingdom. An internship program is available.

FINANCES

Costs for 1997–98 Tuition: $430 per credit hour. Average 1997–98 room only costs were $3150 per academic year (off campus). Room and board costs vary by occupancy (e.g., single, double, triple), type of meal plan.

Financial Aid In 1997–98, 6% of students received some institutionally administered aid in the form of research assistantships, scholarships, work study, loans. Financial aid is available to part-time students. Application Deadline: 8/1.

Financial Aid Contact Ms. Jennifer Garey, Financial Aid, Associate Director, Niagara University, NY 14109. Phone: 716-286-8686; Fax: 716-286-8206.

FACILITIES

Information Resources Main library; total holdings of 288,986 volumes, 74,379 microforms, 1,311 current periodical subscriptions. CD player(s) available for graduate student use. Access provided to online bibliographic retrieval services.

INTERNATIONAL STUDENTS

Demographics 25% of students enrolled are international students [Asia, 2%, Europe, 8%, North America, 90%].

Services and Facilities International student office, visa services, ESL courses, counseling/support services.

Applying TOEFL: minimum score of 550, proof of adequate funds, proof of health/immunizations required. Financial aid is available to international students.

International Student Contact Ms. Christine Schwartz, International Student Advisor, Niagara University, NY 14109. Phone: 716-286-8724; Fax: 716-286-8206; E-mail: cds@niagara.edu

PLACEMENT

Services include alumni network, career counseling/planning, career fairs, career library, career placement, electronic job bank, job interviews arranged, resume referral to employers, and resume preparation. In 1996–97, 95 organizations participated in on-campus recruiting.

Employment Of 1996–97 graduates, 100% were employed within three months of graduation.

Business Program(s) URL: http://www.niagara.edu

Program Contact: Dr. Charles Smith, MBA Director, Graduate Division of Business Administration, Niagara University, NY 14109. Phone: 716-286-8051; Fax: 716-286-8206; E-mail: csmith@niagara.edu

Pace University

Lubin School of Business

New York and Westchester, New York

OVERVIEW

Pace University is an independent-nonprofit, coed university. Enrollment: 13,317 graduate, professional, and undergraduate students; 850 full-time matriculated graduate/professional students; 2,605 part-time matriculated graduate/professional students. Founded: 1906. The graduate business unit is in an urban setting and is on a semester calendar.

HIGHLIGHTS

Enrollment Profile

Full-time: 467	International: 13%
Part-time: 1,485	Women: 41%
Total: 1,952	Minorities: 11%
Average Age: 30	Average Class Size: 24
Fall 1997 Average GPA: 3.13	Fall 1997 Average GMAT: 511

Costs
Full-time tuition: N/R
Part-time tuition: $545 per credit

AACSB – The International Association for Management Education accredited

GRADUATE BUSINESS PROGRAMS

Master of Business Administration (MBA) Full-time, part-time; 61 total credits required; 2 to 5.8 years to complete program. Concentrations in accounting, economics, finance, international business, management, management information systems, management science, marketing, taxation.

Doctor of Jurisprudence/Master of Business Administration (JD/MBA) Full-time, part-time; 129 total credits required; 4 to 6.8 years to complete program.

One-year MBA in Finance (MBA) Full-time; 36 total credits required; 12 months to complete program. Concentration in finance.

Master of Science (MS) Full-time, part-time; up to 5.8 years to complete program. Concentrations in asian business studies, contract management, finance, taxation.

Advanced Professional Certificate (APC) Full-time, part-time; 18 total credits required. Concentrations in accounting, economics, finance, international business, management, management information systems, management science, marketing, taxation.

Doctor of Professional Studies (DPS) Full-time, part-time; 57 total credits required; up to 10 years to complete program. Concentrations in accounting, economics, finance, international business, management, management information systems, management science, marketing.

Executive MBA (MBA) Full-time; 21 months to complete program. Concentration in management.

ADMISSION

Applications For fall 1997 there were 1,233 applications for admission. Of those applying, 844 were accepted. Of those accepted, 425 enrolled.

Application Requirements Application form, application fee, bachelor's degree, essay, minimum GPA, 2 letters of recommendation, personal statement, resume, college transcript(s).

Recommended for Application GMAT score accepted.

Application Deadline 8/1 for fall, 12/1 for spring, 5/1 for summer, 7/1 for fall (international), 11/1 for spring (international), 4/1 for summer (international). Application fee: $60. Deferred entrance is available.

ACADEMICS

Faculty Full-time 55; part-time 42.

Teaching Methodologies Case study, computer-aided instruction, computer analysis, computer simulations, experiential learning, faculty seminars, field projects, group discussion, lecture, research, role playing, seminars by members of the business community, simulations, student presentations, study groups, team projects.

Technology 700 on-campus computer terminals/PCs are available for student use and are linked by a campus-wide network. The network has full access to the Internet. Students are not required to have their own PC.

Special Opportunities Advanced credit may be earned through credit by examination, transfer of credits from another institution. International exchange programs in France, Germany. An internship program is available.

FINANCES

Costs for 1997–98 Tuition: $545 per credit. Fees vary by number of credits taken. Average 1997–98 room and board costs were $5800 per academic year. Room and board costs vary by occupancy (e.g., single, double, triple), type of meal plan.

Financial Aid Research assistantships, grants, scholarships, work study, loans available. Financial aid is available to part-time students.

Financial Aid Contact Ms. Regina Robinson, University Director of Financial Aid, 1 Pace Plaza, New York, NY 10038. Phone: 212-346-1300; Fax: 212-346-1750.

FACILITIES

Information Resources Pace University Library plus 3 additional on-campus libraries; total holdings of 765,431 volumes, 64,678 microforms, 6,668 current periodical subscriptions. CD player(s) available for graduate student use. Access provided to online bibliographic retrieval services and online databases.

INTERNATIONAL STUDENTS

Demographics 13% of students enrolled are international students.

Services and Facilities International student office, visa services, ESL courses, counseling/support services.

Applying TOEFL: minimum score of 550, proof of adequate funds, proof of health/immunizations required. Financial aid is available to international students.

International Student Contact Ms. Deirdre Colby Sato, Director of International Students and Scholars, 861 Bedford Road-Campus Center, Pleasantville, NY 10570-2799. Phone: 914-773-3447; Fax: 914-773-3783; E-mail: dsato@fsmail.pace.edu

PLACEMENT

Services include alumni network, career counseling/planning, career fairs, career library, career placement, electronic job bank, job interviews arranged, job search course, resume referral to employers, and resume preparation. In 1996–97, 108 organizations participated in on-campus recruiting; 500 on-campus interviews were conducted.

Employment Of 1996–97 graduates, 95% were employed within three months of graduation; the average starting salary was $45,000. Types of employment entered: accounting, banking, communications, computer-related, consulting, consumer products, energy, finance, financial services, government, health services, high technology, hospitality management, human resources, information systems/technology, insurance, international trade, management, manufacturing, marketing, media, nonprofit, pharmaceutical, real estate, retail, service industry, telecommunications, transportation, utilities.

Business Program(s) URL: http://www.pace.edu

Program Contact (New York): Richard Alvarez, Office of Graduate Admission, 1 Pace Plaza, New York, NY 10038-1598. Phone: 212-346-1531; Fax: 212-346-1585; E-mail: gradny@pace.edu

Program Contact (White Plains): Joanna Broda, Office of Graduate Admission, 1 Martine Avenue, White Plains, NY 10606-1909. Phone: 914-422-4283; Fax: 914-422-4287; E-mail: gradwp@pace.edu

See full description on page 916.

Polytechnic University, Brooklyn Campus

Management Department

Brooklyn, New York

OVERVIEW

Polytechnic University, Brooklyn Campus is an independent-nonprofit, coed university. Founded: 1854. The graduate business unit is in an urban setting and is on a semester calendar.

HIGHLIGHTS

Enrollment Profile
Full-time: N/R
Part-time: N/R
Total: N/R
Average Age: N/R
Fall 1997 Average GPA: N/R

International: N/R
Women: N/R
Minorities: N/R
Average Class Size: 15
Fall 1997 Average GMAT: N/R

Costs
Full-time tuition: N/R
Part-time tuition: $645 per credit hour

GRADUATE BUSINESS PROGRAMS

Master of Science in Management (MS) Full-time, part-time, distance learning option; 42 total credits required; 3 to 5 years to complete program.

Master of Science in Organizational Behavior (MS) Full-time, part-time, distance learning option; 36 total credits required; 3 to 5 years to complete program.

Master of Science in Financial Engineering (MS) Full-time, part-time; 36 total credits required; 3 to 5 years to complete program.

Master of Science in Management of Technology (MS) Full-time; 36 total credits required; 2 to 5 years to complete program.

Master of Science in Telecommunications and Computing Management (MS) Full-time; 36 total credits required; 2 to 5 years to complete program.

ADMISSION

Application Requirements Application form, application fee, bachelor's degree, essay, minimum GPA: 3.0, interview, 2 letters of recommendation, college transcript(s), computer experience: computer literacy.

Recommended for Application Work experience.

Application Deadline Applications processed on a rolling/continuous basis for both domestic and international students. Application fee: $45. Deferred entrance is available.

ACADEMICS

Teaching Methodologies Case study, computer-aided instruction, computer analysis, experiential learning, faculty seminars, group discussion, lecture, research, role playing, seminars by members of the business community, simulations, student presentations, study groups, team projects.

Technology Students are not required to have their own PC.

Special Opportunities Advanced credit may be earned through transfer of credits from another institution.

FINANCES

Costs for 1997–98 Tuition: $645 per credit hour. Cost varies by academic program. Fees: $85 per semester.

Financial Aid Contact Office of Financial Aid, Six Metrotech Center, Brooklyn, NY 11201. Phone: 718-260-3300.

FACILITIES

Information Resources Bern Dibner Library of Science and Technology; total holdings of 192,738 volumes, 375 microforms, 1,762 current periodical subscriptions. Access provided to online bibliographic retrieval services.

INTERNATIONAL STUDENTS

Demographics N/R

Services and Facilities International student office, international student center, visa services, counseling/support services.

Applying TOEFL, proof of health/immunizations required. Financial aid is available to international students.

International Student Contact Director of International Student Development Office, Six Metrotech Center, Brooklyn, NY 11201. Phone: 718-260-3805.

PLACEMENT

Services include alumni network, career counseling/planning, career fairs, career placement, job interviews arranged, resume referral to employers, and resume preparation.

Employment Types of employment entered: banking, communications, computer-related, energy, finance, high technology, information systems/technology, pharmaceutical, service industry, telecommunications.

Business Program(s) URL: http://www.poly.edu

Program Contact: Evelyn Lombardo, Administrative Assistant, Six Metrotech Center, Brooklyn, NY 11201. Phone: 718-260-3254 E-mail: elombard@duke.poly.edu

See full description on page 930.

Polytechnic University, Farmingdale Campus

Department of Management

Farmingdale, New York

OVERVIEW

Polytechnic University, Farmingdale Campus is an independent-nonprofit, coed university. The graduate business unit is in an urban setting and is on a semester calendar.

GRADUATE BUSINESS PROGRAMS

Master of Science in Management (MS)

Master of Science in Organizational Behavior (MS)

Master of Science in Financial Engineering (MS)

Master of Science in Management of Technology (MS)

Master of Science in Telecommunications and Computing Management (MS)

ACADEMICS

Teaching Methodologies Case study, computer-aided instruction, computer analysis, experiential learning, faculty seminars, lecture, research, role playing, seminars by members of the business community, simulations, student presentations, study groups, team projects.

Technology Students are not required to have their own PC.

Special Opportunities Advanced credit may be earned through transfer of credits from another institution.

FACILITIES

Information Resources Long Island Center Library plus 1 additional on-campus library; total holdings of 192,738 volumes, 375 microforms, 1,762 current periodical subscriptions. Access provided to online bibliographic retrieval services.

Program Contact: Office of Graduate Admissions, Six Metrotech Center, Brooklyn, NY 11201. Phone: 718-260-3254.

Polytechnic University, Westchester Graduate Center

Management Department

Hawthorne, New York

OVERVIEW

Polytechnic University, Westchester Graduate Center is an independent-nonprofit, coed, graduate institution. The graduate business unit is in an urban setting and is on a semester calendar.

GRADUATE BUSINESS PROGRAMS

Master of Science in Management (MS)

Master of Science in Organizational Behavior (MS)

Master of Science in Financial Engineering (MS)
Master of Science in Management of Technology (MS)
Master of Science in Telecommunications and Computing Management (MS)

ACADEMICS
Teaching Methodologies Case study, computer-aided instruction, computer analysis, experiential learning, faculty seminars, group discussion, lecture, research, role playing, seminars by members of the business community, simulations, student presentations, study groups, team projects.

Technology Students are not required to have their own PC.

Special Opportunities Advanced credit may be earned through transfer of credits from another institution.

FACILITIES
Information Resources Richard Laster Library plus 2 additional on-campus libraries; total holdings of 192,738 volumes, 375 microforms, 1,762 current periodical subscriptions. Access provided to online bibliographic retrieval services.

Program Contact: Office of Graduate Admissions, Six Metrotech Center, Brooklyn, NY 11201. Phone: 718-260-3254.

Pratt Institute

Program in Facilities Management

Brooklyn, New York

OVERVIEW
Pratt Institute is an independent-nonprofit, comprehensive institution.

HIGHLIGHTS

Enrollment Profile

Full-time: 15	International: 23%
Part-time: 29	Women: 23%
Total: 44	Minorities: N/R
Average Age: N/R	Average Class Size: N/R
Fall 1997 Average GPA: N/R	Fall 1997 Average GMAT: N/R

Costs
Full-time tuition: N/R
Part-time tuition: $637 per credit

GRADUATE BUSINESS PROGRAMS
Master of Science in Facilities Management (MS) Full-time, part-time; 50 total credits required; minimum of 2 years to complete program.

ADMISSION
Application Requirements GMAT score, application form, bachelor's degree, essay, minimum GPA, interview, 3 letters of recommendation, personal statement, resume, college transcript(s).

Application Deadline Applications processed on a rolling/continuous basis for both domestic and international students.

ACADEMICS
Teaching Methodologies Experiential learning, faculty seminars, group discussion, lecture, research, seminars by members of the business community, student presentations, study groups, team projects.

FINANCES
Costs for 1997–98 Tuition: $637 per credit.

INTERNATIONAL STUDENTS
Demographics 23% of students enrolled are international students.

Applying TOEFL: minimum score of 550 required.

Program Contact: Brooklyn, NY 11205-3899.

Rensselaer Polytechnic Institute

Lally School of Management and Technology

Troy, New York

OVERVIEW
Rensselaer Polytechnic Institute is an independent-nonprofit, coed university. Enrollment: 6,225 graduate, professional, and undergraduate students; 1,577 full-time matriculated graduate/professional students; 352 part-time matriculated graduate/professional students. Founded: 1824. The graduate business unit is in an urban setting and is on a semester calendar.

HIGHLIGHTS

Enrollment Profile

Full-time: 177	International: 28%
Part-time: 151	Women: 23%
Total: 328	Minorities: 11%
Average Age: 28	Average Class Size: 35
Fall 1997 Average GPA: 3.2	Fall 1997 Average GMAT: 590

Costs
Full-time tuition: $18,900 per academic year
Part-time tuition: $630 per credit hour

AACSB – The International Association for Management Education accredited

GRADUATE BUSINESS PROGRAMS
Master of Business Administration (MBA) Full-time, part-time, distance learning option; 60 total credits required; 12 months to 2 years to complete program. Concentrations in entrepreneurship, finance, financial information systems, management information systems, manufacturing management, operations management, production management, research and development administration, technology management, information management, business information science, business policy/strategy, environmental economics/management, management, management consulting, management science, marketing, new venture management, quality management.

Accelerated Bachelor of Science/Master of Business Administration (BS/MBA) Full-time; 154 total credits required; 5 years to complete program. Concentrations in entrepreneurship, finance, financial information systems, management information systems, operations management, production management, research and development administration, technology management, information management, business information science, business policy/strategy, environmental economics/management, management, management science, marketing, quality management, management consulting, new venture management.

Master of Business Administration/Doctor of Jurisprudence (MBA/JD) Full-time, part-time; 60 total credits required; 4 to 5 years to complete program. Concentrations in entrepreneurship, finance, financial information systems, management information systems, manufacturing management, operations management, production management, research and development administration, technology management, information management, business information science, business policy/strategy, environmental economics/management, management, management consulting, marketing, new venture management, quality management, management science.

Master of Business Administration/Master of Science in Engineering (MBA/MS) Full-time, part-time; 72 total credits required; 2.3 to 3 years to complete program. Concentrations in entrepreneurship, finance, financial information systems, management information systems, manufacturing management, marketing, production management, research and development administration, technology management, business information science, business policy/strategy, environmental economics/management, management, management science, marketing, new venture management, quality management, management consulting.

Master of Science in Management (MS) Full-time, part-time, distance learning option; 30 total credits required; 12 months to complete program. Concentrations in financial information systems, management information systems, management, finance, management systems analysis, information management, operations management, production management, quantitative analysis, business information science, business policy/strategy, environmental economics/management, management, management consulting, management science, marketing, new venture management, quality management.

Executive MBA (MBA) Part-time; 2 years to complete program. Concentrations in management, leadership.

ADMISSION
Applications For fall 1997 there were 312 applications for admission. Of those applying, 223 were accepted. Of those accepted, 140 enrolled.

Application Requirements GMAT score, application form, application fee, bachelor's degree, essay, minimum GPA, 2 letters of recommendation, personal statement, resume, college transcript(s).

Recommended for Application GRE score accepted, interview, work experience, computer experience.

Application Deadline 2/1 for fall, 11/1 for spring, 4/1 for summer, 2/1 for fall (international), 11/1 for spring (international), 4/1 for summer (international). Application fee: $35. Deferred entrance is available.

ACADEMICS
Faculty Full-time 33; part-time 6.

Teaching Methodologies Case study, computer-aided instruction, computer analysis, computer simulations, experiential learning, faculty seminars, field projects, group discussion, lecture, research, seminars by members of the business community, simulations, student presentations, study groups, team projects.

Technology 600 on-campus computer terminals/PCs are available for student use and are linked by a campus-wide network. The network has full access to the Internet. Students are not required to have their own PC.

Special Opportunities Advanced credit may be earned through transfer of credits from another institution. International exchange programs in Australia, Denmark, France, Japan, Spain, Switzerland. An internship program is available.

FINANCES
Costs for 1997–98 Tuition: Full-time: $18,900 per year. Part-time: $630 per credit hour. Cost varies by number of credits taken. Fees: Full-time: $1045 per academic year. Part-time: $275 per semester. Average 1997–98 room and board costs were $7125 per academic year. Room and board costs vary by occupancy (e.g., single, double, triple), type of accommodation, type of meal plan.

Financial Aid In 1997–98, 25% of students received some institutionally administered aid in the form of fellowships, research assistantships, teaching assistantships, scholarships, loans. Financial aid is available to part-time students. Application Deadline: 2/1.

Financial Aid Contact Mr. David J. Bohan, Director, Masters Programs, Lally School of Management and Technology, Lally 204, Troy, NY 12180-3590. Phone: 518-276-4800; Fax: 518-276-8661; E-mail: management@rpi.edu

FACILITIES
Information Resources Richard G. Folsom Library plus 1 additional on-campus library; total holdings of 469,024 volumes, 615,477 microforms, 3,283 current periodical subscriptions. CD player(s) available for graduate student use. Access provided to online bibliographic retrieval services.

INTERNATIONAL STUDENTS
Demographics 28% of students enrolled are international students [Africa, 1%, Asia, 77%, Central America, 1%, Europe, 9%, North America, 2%, South America, 10%].

Services and Facilities International student office, international student center, international student housing, visa services, ESL courses, counseling/support services, pre-MBA program through LCP International.

Applying TOEFL: minimum score of 570, proof of adequate funds, proof of health/immunizations required. Financial aid is available to international students.

International Student Contact Ms. Jane Havis, Assistant Dean, International Student Services, RPI 200 Troy Building, Troy, NY 12180-3590. Phone: 518-276-6266; Fax: 518-276-4839; E-mail: havisj@rpi.edu

PLACEMENT
Services include alumni network, career counseling/planning, career fairs, career library, career placement, electronic job bank, job interviews arranged, job search course, resume referral to employers, and resume preparation. In 1996–97, 329 organizations participated in on-campus recruiting; 6,241 on-campus interviews were conducted.

Employment Of 1996–97 graduates, 98% were employed within three months of graduation; the average starting salary was $55,934. Types of employment entered: banking, chemical industry, communications, computer-related, consulting, consumer products, engineering, finance, financial services, health services, high technology, human resources, information systems/technology, international trade, law, manufacturing, marketing, pharmaceutical, service industry, telecommunications, transportation.

Business Program(s) URL: http://lallyschool.rpi.edu

Program Contact: Mr. David J. Bohan, Director, Masters Programs, Lally School of Management and Technology, Lally 204, Troy, NY 12180-3590. Phone: 518-276-4800; Fax: 518-276-8661; E-mail: management@rpi.edu
See full description on page 942.

Roberts Wesleyan College

Division of Business and Management

Rochester, New York

OVERVIEW
Roberts Wesleyan College is an independent-religious, coed, comprehensive institution. Enrollment: 1,414 graduate, professional, and undergraduate students; 171 full-time matriculated graduate/professional students; 107 part-time matriculated graduate/professional students. Founded: 1866. The graduate business unit is in a suburban setting.

HIGHLIGHTS

Enrollment Profile
Full-time: 67
Part-time: 0
Total: 67
Average Age: 37
Fall 1997 Average GPA: 3.15

International: N/R
Women: 48%
Minorities: N/R
Average Class Size: 15
Fall 1997 Average GMAT: 523

Costs
Full-time tuition: N/R
Part-time tuition: $450 per credit hour

ACBSP – The American Council of Business Schools and Programs accredited

GRADUATE BUSINESS PROGRAMS
MS in Management (MS) Full-time, part-time; 36 total credits required; minimum of 17 months to complete program. Concentrations in organizational management, nonprofit organization, entrepreneurship.

ADMISSION
Applications For fall 1997 there were 32 applications for admission. Of those applying, 32 were accepted. Of those accepted, 30 enrolled.

Application Requirements Application form, bachelor's degree, essay, 2 letters of recommendation, college transcript(s), minimum of 2 years of work experience, computer experience: spreadsheet and word processing proficiency.

Recommended for Application GMAT score accepted, GRE score accepted, minimum GPA: 2.75.

Application Deadline Applications processed on a rolling/continuous basis for both domestic and international students. Application fee: $35. Deferred entrance is available.

ACADEMICS
Faculty Full-time 14; part-time 7.

Teaching Methodologies Case study, computer-aided instruction, computer analysis, computer simulations, experiential learning, field projects, group discussion, research, role playing, seminars by members of the business community, simulations, student presentations, study groups, team projects.

Technology 60 on-campus computer terminals/PCs are available for student use and are linked by a campus-wide network. The network has full access to the Internet. Students are not required to have their own PC.

Special Opportunities Advanced credit may be earned through transfer of credits from another institution.

FINANCES
Costs for 1997–98 Tuition: $450 per credit hour. Fees: $90 per year. Average 1997–98 room only costs were $4500 per academic year (off campus).

Financial Aid In 1997–98, 34% of students received some institutionally administered aid in the form of loans. Financial aid is available to part-time students.

Financial Aid Contact Mr. Steve Field, Director of Financial Aid, Rochester, NY 14624-1997. Phone: 716-594-6150; Fax: 716-594-6036; E-mail: fields@roberts.edu

FACILITIES
Information Resources Ora A. Sprague Library; total holdings of 103,376 volumes, 93,760 microforms, 797 current periodical subscriptions. CD player(s) available for graduate student use. Access provided to online bibliographic retrieval services and online databases.

INTERNATIONAL STUDENTS
Demographics N/R

Services and Facilities Visa services, ESL courses, counseling/support services.

Applying TOEFL: minimum score of 550, proof of adequate funds, proof of health/immunizations required. Financial aid is available to international students.

PLACEMENT
Services include alumni network, career counseling/planning, career fairs, career library, career placement, electronic job bank, and resume preparation. In 1996–97, 47 organizations participated in on-campus recruiting.

Business Program(s) URL: http://www.rwc.edu

Program Contact: Mr. Steven Hutchison, MSM Admissions Coordinator, Rochester, NY 14624-1997. Phone: 716-594-6400, 800-777-4RWC; Fax: 716-594-6371; E-mail: hutchisons@roberts.edu

Rochester Institute of Technology

College of Business

Rochester, New York

OVERVIEW

Rochester Institute of Technology is an independent-nonprofit, coed, comprehensive institution. Enrollment: 13,230 graduate, professional, and undergraduate students; 775 full-time matriculated graduate/professional students; 1,405 part-time matriculated graduate/professional students. Founded: 1829. The graduate business unit is in a suburban setting and is on a quarter calendar.

HIGHLIGHTS

Enrollment Profile

Full-time: 136	International: 20%
Part-time: 305	Women: 41%
Total: 441	Minorities: 4%
Average Age: 27	Average Class Size: 24
Fall 1997 Average GPA: 3.1	Fall 1997 Average GMAT: 562

Costs
Full-time tuition: $18,765 per academic year
Part-time tuition: $527 per credit hour

AACSB – The International Association for Management Education accredited

GRADUATE BUSINESS PROGRAMS

Master of Business Administration (MBA) Full-time, part-time; 72 total credits required; 12 months to 7 years to complete program. Concentrations in management, accounting, finance, human resources, leadership, management information systems, marketing, operations management, quality management, technology management, international business.

Master of Science (MS) Full-time, part-time; 48 total credits required; 12 months to 7 years to complete program. Concentrations in finance, manufacturing management.

Executive MBA (EMBA) Part-time; 72 total credits required; 2 years to complete program.

ADMISSION

Applications For fall 1997 there were 444 applications for admission. Of those applying, 329 were accepted. Of those accepted, 123 enrolled.

Application Requirements GMAT score, application form, application fee, bachelor's degree, minimum GPA: 2.5, personal statement, college transcript(s).

Application Deadline 8/7 for fall, 10/31 for winter, 2/6 for spring, 5/1 for summer, 7/24 for fall (international), 10/17 for winter (international), 1/23 for spring (international), 4/17 for summer (international). Application fee: $40. Deferred entrance is available.

ACADEMICS

Faculty Full-time 30; part-time 10.

Teaching Methodologies Case study, computer-aided instruction, computer analysis, computer simulations, experiential learning, field projects, group discussion, lecture, research, simulations, student presentations, team projects.

Technology 800 on-campus computer terminals/PCs are available for student use and are linked by a campus-wide network. The network has full access to the Internet. Students are not required to have their own PC.

Special Opportunities Advanced credit may be earned through credit by examination, transfer of credits from another institution. International exchange programs in Czech Republic, United Kingdom.

FINANCES

Costs for 1997–98 Tuition: Full-time: $18,765 per year. Part-time: $527 per credit hour. Fees: Full-time: $138 per academic year. Average 1997–98 room and board costs were $6645 per academic year. Room and board costs vary by occupancy (e.g., single, double, triple), type of accommodation, type of meal plan.

Financial Aid In 1997–98, 14% of students received some institutionally administered aid in the form of research assistantships, grants, scholarships, loans. Financial aid is available to part-time students. Application Deadline: 8/1.

Financial Aid Contact Ms. Verna Hazen, Director of Financial Aid, One Lomb Memorial Drive, Rochester, NY 14623-5604. Phone: 716-475-5520; E-mail: ujhsfa@rit.edu

FACILITIES

Information Resources Wallace Memorial Library; total holdings of 306,020 volumes, 230,421 microforms, 3,600 current periodical subscriptions. CD player(s) available for graduate student use. Access provided to online bibliographic retrieval services and online databases.

INTERNATIONAL STUDENTS

Demographics 20% of students enrolled are international students.

Services and Facilities International student office, international student center, international student housing, visa services, ESL courses, counseling/support services.

Applying TOEFL: minimum score of 575, proof of adequate funds, proof of health/immunizations required. Financial aid is available to international students.

International Student Contact Ms. Mary Ann Campbell, Program Coordinator, International Students, One Lomb Memorial Drive, Rochester, NY 14623-5604. Phone: 716-475-6876; E-mail: mac9954@rit.edu

PLACEMENT

Services include alumni network, career counseling/planning, career fairs, career library, career placement, electronic job bank, job interviews arranged, job search course, resume referral to employers, and resume preparation.

Employment Of 1996–97 graduates, 92% were employed within three months of graduation; the average starting salary was $42,500. Types of employment entered: accounting, banking, computer-related, finance, financial services, high technology, information systems/technology, insurance, management, manufacturing, marketing, pharmaceutical.

Business Program(s) URL: http://www.cob.rit.edu

Program Contact: Dr. Mildred Portela, Graduate Business Programs, 105 Lomb Memorial Drive, Rochester, NY 14623-5604. Phone: 716-475-6221; Fax: 716-475-7450; E-mail: gradbus@rit.edu
See full description on page 950.

Sage Graduate School

Division of Management, Comunications, and Legal Studies

Troy, New York

OVERVIEW

Sage Graduate School is an independent-nonprofit, coed, graduate institution. Enrollment: 1,123 graduate, professional, and undergraduate students; 334 full-time matriculated graduate/professional students; 789 part-time matriculated graduate/professional students. Founded: 1949. The graduate business unit is in an urban setting and is on a semester calendar.

HIGHLIGHTS

Enrollment Profile

Full-time: 10	International: 2%
Part-time: 105	Women: 51%
Total: 115	Minorities: N/R
Average Age: 33	Average Class Size: 14
Fall 1997 Average GPA: 2.8	Fall 1997 Average GMAT: N/R

Costs
Full-time tuition: N/R
Part-time tuition: $360 per credit hour

Degree(s) offered in conjunction with Albany Law School

GRADUATE BUSINESS PROGRAMS

Professional MBA (MBA) Full-time, part-time; 36-48 total credits required; 2 to 6 years to complete program. Concentrations in finance, human resources, management, marketing.

Combined MBA/JD (Albany Law) (MBA/JD) Full-time, part-time; 75-87 total credits required; 5 to 6 years to complete program. Concentrations in human resources, strategic management, management, marketing.

ADMISSION

Applications For fall 1997 there were 42 applications for admission. Of those applying, 36 were accepted. Of those accepted, 21 enrolled.

Application Requirements Application form, application fee, bachelor's degree, essay, minimum GPA: 2.75, interview, 2 letters of recommendation, personal statement, resume, college transcript(s).

Application Deadline Applications processed on a rolling/continuous basis for both domestic and international students. Application fee: $40. Deferred entrance is available.

ACADEMICS

Faculty Full-time 5; part-time 10.

Teaching Methodologies Case study, computer-aided instruction, computer analysis, computer simulations, field projects, group discussion, lecture, research, role playing, simulations, student presentations, team projects.

Technology 101 on-campus computer terminals/PCs are available for student use and are linked by a campus-wide network. The network has full access to the Internet. Students are not required to have their own PC.

Special Opportunities Advanced credit may be earned through transfer of credits from another institution. An internship program is available.

FINANCES

Costs for 1997–98 Tuition: $360 per credit hour. Fees: $100 per year. Average 1997–98 room and board costs were $4570 per academic year. Room and board costs vary by occupancy (e.g., single, double, triple), type of meal plan.

Financial Aid Fellowships, research assistantships, teaching assistantships, grants, scholarships, work study, loans available. Financial aid is available to part-time students.

Financial Aid Contact Mr. Kenneth Clough, Director of Student Financial Services, 140 New Scotland Avenue, Albany, NY 12208. Phone: 518-292-1786; Fax: 518-292-5414; E-mail: clougk@sage.edu

FACILITIES

Information Resources James Wheelock Clark Library; total holdings of 255,878 volumes, 27,754 microforms, 1,336 current periodical subscriptions. CD player(s) available for graduate student use. Access provided to online bibliographic retrieval services.

INTERNATIONAL STUDENTS

Demographics 2% of students enrolled are international students.

Services and Facilities International student office, visa services.

Applying TOEFL: minimum score of 550, proof of adequate funds, proof of health/immunizations required. TSE: minimum score of 109 recommended. Financial aid is not available to international students.

International Student Contact Ms. Tonia Blackwell, Director, Multicultural Affairs , 45 Ferry Street, Troy, NY 12180-4115. Phone: 518-244-2008; Fax: 518-244-2460; E-mail: blackt@sage.edu

PLACEMENT

Services include alumni network, career counseling/planning, career fairs, career library, career placement, and resume preparation. In 1996–97, 40 organizations participated in on-campus recruiting.

Employment Of 1996–97 graduates, the average starting salary was $35,000. Types of employment entered: accounting, banking, communications, computer-related, consulting, consumer products, education, finance, financial services, government, health services, high technology, human resources, information systems/technology, insurance, international trade, law, management, manufacturing, marketing, media, nonprofit, pharmaceutical, retail, service industry, telecommunications, transportation, utilities.

Business Program(s) URL: http://www.sage.edu

Program Contact: Melissa Robertson, Assistant Director of Admissions, 45 Ferry Street, Troy, NY 12180-4115. Phone: 518-244-2264, 800-999-3772; Fax: 518-244-2460.

St. Bonaventure University

School of Business Administration

St. Bonaventure, New York

OVERVIEW

St. Bonaventure University is an independent-religious, coed, comprehensive institution. Enrollment: 2,822 graduate, professional, and undergraduate students; 299 full-time matriculated graduate/professional students; 385 part-time matriculated graduate/professional students. Founded: 1858. The graduate business unit is in a small-town setting and is on a semester calendar.

HIGHLIGHTS

Enrollment Profile

Full-time: 79	International: 1%
Part-time: 109	Women: 46%
Total: 188	Minorities: N/R
Average Age: 34	Average Class Size: 25
Fall 1997 Average GPA: 3.5	Fall 1997 Average GMAT: 478

Costs
Full-time tuition: $7650 per academic year
Part-time tuition: $425 per credit hour

GRADUATE BUSINESS PROGRAMS

One-year MBA (MBA) Full-time; 51 total credits required; 12 months to 6 years to complete program. Concentrations in accounting, finance, management, marketing, international business.

Evening MBA (MBA) Part-time; 51 total credits required; 12 months to 6 years to complete program. Concentrations in accounting, finance, management, marketing, international business.

Weekend MBA (MBA) Part-time; 51 total credits required; 12 months to 6 years to complete program. Concentrations in accounting, finance, management, marketing, international business.

ADMISSION

Applications For fall 1997 there were 80 applications for admission. Of those applying, 79 were accepted. Of those accepted, 57 enrolled.

Application Requirements Application form, application fee, bachelor's degree, minimum GPA: 2.5, 2 letters of recommendation, college transcript(s).

Recommended for Application GMAT score accepted: minimum 450, interview, computer experience.

Application Deadline Applications processed on a rolling/continuous basis for both domestic and international students. Application fee: $35. Deferred entrance is available.

ACADEMICS

Faculty Full-time 19; part-time 4.

Teaching Methodologies Case study, computer-aided instruction, computer analysis, computer simulations, group discussion, lecture, seminars by members of the business community, simulations, student presentations, study groups, team projects.

Technology 120 on-campus computer terminals/PCs are available for student use and are linked by a campus-wide network. The network has full access to the Internet. Students are not required to have their own PC.

Special Opportunities Advanced credit may be earned through transfer of credits from another institution. An internship program is available.

FINANCES

Costs for 1997–98 Tuition: Full-time: $7650 per year. Part-time: $425 per credit hour. Cost varies by number of credits taken. Average 1997–98 room and board costs were $5200 per academic year. Room and board costs vary by campus location, occupancy (e.g., single, double, triple), type of accommodation, type of meal plan.

Financial Aid In 1997–98, 3% of students received some institutionally administered aid in the form of research assistantships, work study. Financial aid is available to part-time students.

Financial Aid Contact Ms. Mary Piccioli, Director of Financial Aid, School of Business Administration, St. Bonaventure, NY 14778. Phone: 716-375-2528; Fax: 716-375-2005; E-mail: mpiccioli@sbu.edu

FACILITIES

Information Resources Friedsam Memorial Library; total holdings of 267,000 volumes, 690,000 microforms, 1,533 current periodical subscriptions. CD player(s) available for graduate student use. Access provided to online bibliographic retrieval services.

INTERNATIONAL STUDENTS

Demographics 1% of students enrolled are international students.

Services and Facilities International student office, counseling/support services.

Applying TOEFL: minimum score of 600, proof of adequate funds, proof of health/immunizations required. Financial aid is not available to international students.

International Student Contact Ms. Alice Sayegh, Director of Foreign Studies, RC 221B, St. Bonaventure, NY 14778. Phone: 716-375-2574; Fax: 716-375-2381; E-mail: asayegh@sbu.edu

PLACEMENT

Services include alumni network, career counseling/planning, career fairs, career library, job interviews arranged, and resume preparation. In 1996–97, 20 organizations participated in on-campus recruiting; 200 on-campus interviews were conducted.

Employment Of 1996–97 graduates, 100% were employed within three months of graduation.

Business Program(s) URL: http://www.sbu.edu/academics/departments/mba/mba_programs.html

Program Contact: Brian C. McAllister, Director, MBA Program, PO Box BS, St. Bonaventure, NY 14778. Phone: 716-375-2098; Fax: 716-375-2191; E-mail: bmac@sbu.edu

St. John Fisher College

Graduate School of Management

Rochester, New York

OVERVIEW

St. John Fisher College is an independent-religious, coed, comprehensive institution. Enrollment: 2,000 graduate, professional, and undergraduate students; 12 full-time matriculated graduate/professional students; 226 part-time matriculated graduate/professional students. Founded: 1948. The graduate business unit is in a suburban setting and is on a semester calendar.

HIGHLIGHTS

Enrollment Profile

Full-time: 12	International: 3%
Part-time: 226	Women: 51%
Total: 238	Minorities: 9%
Average Age: 31	Average Class Size: 20
Fall 1997 Average GPA: 2.67	Fall 1997 Average GMAT: 478

Costs

Full-time tuition: $14,700 per academic year
Part-time tuition: $490 per credit hour

S*t. John Fisher College awards an M.B.A. with an emphasis on general management, with concentrations in accounting or in industrial and labor relations in conjunction with Cornell University's Rochester district office. The M.B.A. program is structured as an evening program, with some courses offered on Saturday mornings. It attracts both full-time and part-time students, although part-time students are the majority. The faculty has a strong international orientation. The purpose of the program is to educate qualified students from any background for successful careers in management in private or public and domestic or international settings. The curriculum provides an integrated program of studies incorporating liberal learning with various functional areas of management. The objective is not to produce specialists but to give students an opportunity to acquire the mix of advanced skills most useful in dealing with the broadest problems at all levels of managerial responsibility. The School believes that theoretical, quantitative, and technical skills have to be integrated with humanistic values, and the program is designed to help the student develop and refine them and express them effectively and responsibly through the use of skills developed in various courses. Among the key strengths of the program are the offering of a well-balanced education; an emphasis on communication, as well as theory and implementation; diagnosis and decision; a small college community, with a small, select, diverse student body that provides a close, people-oriented, friendly atmosphere for learning; and a strong faculty, distinguished for both intellectual rigor and work experience, that is dedicated to teaching excellence and helping students.*

GRADUATE BUSINESS PROGRAMS

Master of Business Administration (MBA) Full-time, part-time; 54 total credits required; 12 months to 4 years to complete program. Concentrations in accounting, industrial/labor relations, management.

ADMISSION

Applications For fall 1997 there were 132 applications for admission. Of those applying, 116 were accepted. Of those accepted, 98 enrolled.

Application Requirements Application form, application fee, bachelor's degree, minimum GPA, 2 letters of recommendation, personal statement, college transcript(s).

Recommended for Application GMAT score accepted: minimum 400, interview, resume.

Application Deadline 8/15 for fall, 12/15 for spring, 5/15 for summer, 7/15 for fall (international), 11/15 for spring (international), 4/15 for summer (international). Application fee: $30. Deferred entrance is available.

ACADEMICS

Faculty Full-time 11; part-time 8.

Teaching Methodologies Case study, computer-aided instruction, experiential learning, group discussion, lecture, student presentations, study groups, team projects.

Technology 175 on-campus computer terminals/PCs are available for student use and are linked by a campus-wide network. The network has full access to the Internet. Students are not required to have their own PC.

Special Opportunities Advanced credit may be earned through credit by examination, credit for experience, transfer of credits from another institution.

FINANCES

Costs for 1997–98 Tuition: Full-time: $14,700 per year. Part-time: $490 per credit hour. Fees: Full-time: $100 per academic year. Part-time: $100 per year. Average 1997–98 room and board costs were $6500 per academic

year (on campus) and $4000 per academic year (off campus). Room and board costs vary by occupancy (e.g., single, double, triple).

Financial Aid In 1997–98, 29% of students received some institutionally administered aid in the form of work study, loans. Financial aid is available to part-time students. Application Deadline: 8/15.

Financial Aid Contact Mrs. Anne Steger, Director of Financial Aid, 3690 East Avenue, Rochester, NY 14618-3597. Phone: 716-385-8042; Fax: 716-385-8094.

FACILITIES

Information Resources Charles J. Lavery Library; total holdings of 180,000 volumes, 27,000 microforms, 1,300 current periodical subscriptions. CD player(s) available for graduate student use. Access provided to online bibliographic retrieval services and online databases.

INTERNATIONAL STUDENTS

Demographics 3% of students enrolled are international students [Asia, 100%].

Services and Facilities ESL courses, counseling/support services.

Applying TOEFL: minimum score of 525, proof of adequate funds, proof of health/immunizations required. Financial aid is not available to international students.

International Student Contact Mr. Steven Hoskins, Director of Graduate Admissions, 3690 East Avenue, Rochester, NY 14618-3597. Phone: 716-385-8161; Fax: 716-385-8344; E-mail: hoskins@sjfc.edu

PLACEMENT

Services include alumni network, career counseling/planning, career fairs, career library, career placement, resume referral to employers, and resume preparation. In 1996–97, 2 organizations participated in on-campus recruiting; 15 on-campus interviews were conducted.

Employment Of 1996–97 graduates, 100% were employed within three months of graduation; the average starting salary was $31,000. Types of employment entered: accounting, banking, computer-related, consulting, education, financial services, marketing, real estate.

Business Program(s) URL: http://www.sjfc.edu

Program Contact: Mr. Steven Hoskins, Director of Graduate Admissions, 3690 East Avenue, Rochester, NY 14618-3597. Phone: 716-385-8161; Fax: 716-385-8344; E-mail: hoskins@sjfc.edu

St. John's University

College of Business Administration

Jamaica, New York

OVERVIEW

St. John's University is an independent-religious, coed university. Enrollment: 18,523 graduate, professional, and undergraduate students; 1,527 full-time matriculated graduate/professional students; 3,107 part-time matriculated graduate/professional students. Founded: 1870. The graduate business unit is in an urban setting and is on a semester calendar.

HIGHLIGHTS

Enrollment Profile

Full-time: 133	International: 10%
Part-time: 1,003	Women: 40%
Total: 1,136	Minorities: 15%
Average Age: 29	Average Class Size: 26
Fall 1997 Average GPA: 3.1	Fall 1997 Average GMAT: 490

Costs

Full-time tuition: $13,800 per academic year
Part-time tuition: $575 per credit

AACSB – The International Association for Management Education accredited

GRADUATE BUSINESS PROGRAMS

Master of Business Administration in Accounting (MBA) Full-time, part-time; 39-79 total credits required; 16 months to 5 years to complete program. Concentration in accounting.

Master of Business Administration in Computer Information Systems (MBA) Full-time, part-time; 39-72 total credits required; 16 months to 5 years to complete program. Concentration in management information systems.

Master of Business Administration in Decision Sciences (MBA) Full-time, part-time; 39-72 total credits required; 16 months to 5 years to complete program. Concentration in decision sciences.

Master of Business Administration in Economics (MBA) Full-time, part-time; 34-72 total credits required; 16 months to 5 years to complete program. Concentration in economics.

Master of Business Administration in Executive Management (MBA) Full-time, part-time; 39-72 total credits required; 16 months to 5 years to complete program. Concentration in management.

Master of Business Administration in Finance (MBA) Full-time, part-time; 39-72 total credits required; 16 months to 5 years to complete program. Concentration in finance.

Master of Business Administration in Financial Services (MBA) Full-time, part-time; 39-72 total credits required; 16 months to 5 years to complete program. Concentration in finance.

Master of Business Administration in International Finance (MBA) Full-time, part-time; 39-72 total credits required; 16 months to 5 years to complete program. Concentration in international finance.

Master of Business Administration in Marketing (MBA) Full-time, part-time; 39-72 total credits required; 16 months to 5 years to complete program. Concentration in marketing.

Master of Business Administration in Marketing Management (MBA) Full-time, part-time; 39-72 total credits required; 16 months to 5 years to complete program. Concentration in marketing.

Master of Business Administration in Taxation (MBA) Full-time, part-time; 39-72 total credits required; 16 months to 5 years to complete program. Concentration in taxation.

Bachelor of Science/Master of Science in Accounting (BS/MS) Full-time, part-time; 153 total credits required; minimum of 5 years to complete program. Concentration in accounting.

Master of Business Administration/Doctor of Jurisprudence (MBA/JD) Full-time; 115-155 total credits required; minimum of 3 years to complete program. Concentrations in accounting, management information systems, decision sciences, economics, management, finance, international finance, marketing, taxation.

ADMISSION
Applications For fall 1997 there were 592 applications for admission. Of those applying, 411 were accepted. Of those accepted, 230 enrolled.

Application Requirements Application form, application fee, bachelor's degree, essay, minimum GPA, 2 letters of recommendation, personal statement, college transcript(s).

Recommended for Application GMAT score accepted, computer experience.

Application Deadline Applications processed on a rolling/continuous basis for both domestic and international students. Application fee: $40. Deferred entrance is available.

ACADEMICS
Faculty Full-time 104; part-time 23.

Teaching Methodologies Case study, computer-aided instruction, computer analysis, experiential learning, faculty seminars, group discussion, lecture, research, role playing, seminars by members of the business community, student presentations, study groups, team projects.

Technology 800 on-campus computer terminals/PCs are available for student use and are linked by a campus-wide network. The network has full access to the Internet. Students are not required to have their own PC.

Special Opportunities Advanced credit may be earned through credit by examination, transfer of credits from another institution.

FINANCES
Costs for 1997–98 Tuition: Full-time: $13,800 per year. Part-time: $575 per credit. Fees: Full-time: $75 per academic year. Average 1997–98 room only costs were $8100 per academic year (off campus). Room and board costs vary by campus location, occupancy (e.g., single, double, triple), type of accommodation, type of meal plan.

Financial Aid In 1997–98, 38% of students received some institutionally administered aid in the form of research assistantships, scholarships, work study, loans. Financial aid is available to part-time students. Application Deadline: 4/1.

Financial Aid Contact Mr. Jorge Rodriguez, Assistant Vice President and Executive Director, 8000 Utopia Parkway, Jamaica, NY 11439. Phone: 718-990-6403; Fax: 718-990-5945.

FACILITIES
Information Resources St. Augustine Hall plus 2 additional on-campus libraries; total holdings of 1,000,589 volumes, 2,416,627 microforms, 6,876 current periodical subscriptions. CD player(s) available for graduate student use. Access provided to online bibliographic retrieval services and online databases.

INTERNATIONAL STUDENTS
Demographics 10% of students enrolled are international students [Africa, 3%, Asia, 74%, Central America, 1%, Europe, 15%, North America, 1%, South America, 1%, other, 5%].

Services and Facilities International student office, visa services, ESL courses, counseling/support services.

Applying TOEFL: minimum score of 500, proof of adequate funds, proof of health/immunizations required. Financial aid is not available to international students.

International Student Contact Mrs. June Sadowski-Devarez, Assistant Dean-International Student Services, 8000 Utopia Parkway, Jamaica, NY 11439. Phone: 718-990-6083; Fax: 718-990-2070; E-mail: mcgowank@stjohns.edu

PLACEMENT
Services include alumni network, career counseling/planning, career fairs, career library, career placement, job interviews arranged, job search course, resume referral to employers, and resume preparation. In 1996–97, 209 organizations participated in on-campus recruiting; 1,802 on-campus interviews were conducted.

Employment Of 1996–97 graduates, 82% were employed within three months of graduation; the average starting salary was $51,000. Types of employment entered: accounting, banking, communications, computer-related, consulting, consumer products, energy, finance, financial services, government, health services, high technology, human resources, information systems/technology, insurance, international trade, management, marketing, nonprofit, pharmaceutical, retail, service industry, telecommunications, utilities.

Business Program(s) URL: http://www.stjohns.edu/cba/

Program Contact: Br. Shamus McGrenra, Associate Director of Admissions, 8000 Utopia Parkway, Jamaica, NY 11439. Phone: 718-990-6114 Ext. 5736, 800-232-4758 (NY only); Fax: 718-990-2096.

See full description on page 964.

St. Thomas Aquinas College

Division of Business Administration
Sparkill, New York

OVERVIEW
St. Thomas Aquinas College is an independent-nonprofit, coed, comprehensive institution. Enrollment: 2,215 graduate, professional, and undergraduate students; 29 full-time matriculated graduate/professional students; 148 part-time matriculated graduate/professional students. Founded: 1952. The graduate business unit is in a suburban setting and is on a trimester calendar.

HIGHLIGHTS

Enrollment Profile

Full-time: 0	International: 0%
Part-time: 59	Women: 36%
Total: 59	Minorities: 10%
Average Age: 28	Average Class Size: 8
Fall 1997 Average GPA: 3.2	Fall 1997 Average GMAT: 500

Costs
Full-time tuition: $9560 per academic year
Part-time tuition: $390 per credit

GRADUATE BUSINESS PROGRAMS
Master of Business Administration (MBA) Full-time, part-time; 60 total credits required; 12 months to 5 years to complete program. Concentrations in finance, management, marketing.

ADMISSION
Applications For fall 1997 there were 28 applications for admission. Of those applying, 23 were accepted. Of those accepted, 22 enrolled.

Application Requirements Application form, application fee, bachelor's degree, essay, minimum GPA: 2.8, 3 letters of recommendation, personal statement, resume, college transcript(s).

Recommended for Application GMAT score accepted, interview.

Application Deadline Applications processed on a rolling/continuous basis for both domestic and international students. Application fee: $35. Deferred entrance is available.

ACADEMICS
Faculty Full-time 7; part-time 8.

Teaching Methodologies Case study, computer-aided instruction, computer analysis, computer simulations, field projects, group discussion, lecture, research, role playing, seminars by members of the business community, simulations, student presentations, study groups, team projects.

Technology 60 on-campus computer terminals/PCs are available for student use and are linked by a campus-wide network. The network has full access to the Internet. Students are not required to have their own PC.

Special Opportunities Advanced credit may be earned through credit by examination, transfer of credits from another institution.

St. Thomas Aquinas College (continued)

FINANCES

Costs for 1997–98 Tuition: Full-time: $9560 per year. Part-time: $390 per credit. Cost varies by number of credits taken. Fees: $100 per semester.

Financial Aid In 1997–98, 12% of students received some institutionally administered aid. Financial aid is available to part-time students. Application Deadline: 2/15.

Financial Aid Contact Ms. Margaret McGrail, Director of Financial Aid, 125 Route 340, Sparkill, NY 10976-1050. Phone: 914-398-4097; Fax: 914-398-4224.

FACILITIES

Information Resources Lougheed Library; total holdings of 150,000 volumes, 183,900 microforms, 935 current periodical subscriptions. CD player(s) available for graduate student use. Access provided to online bibliographic retrieval services.

INTERNATIONAL STUDENTS

Demographics N/R

Services and Facilities International student office, international student center, visa services, counseling/support services.

Applying TOEFL: minimum score of 500, proof of adequate funds, proof of health/immunizations required. Financial aid is not available to international students.

International Student Contact Ms. Elizabeth Ward, Director of International Student Center, 125 Route 340, Sparkill, NY 10976-1050. Phone: 914-398-4100; Fax: 914-398-4224.

PLACEMENT

Services include alumni network, career counseling/planning, career fairs, career library, career placement, and resume preparation. In 1996–97, 30 organizations participated in on-campus recruiting.

Employment Of 1996–97 graduates, 100% were employed within three months of graduation. Types of employment entered: accounting, banking, communications, computer-related, consulting, consumer products, finance, financial services, government, health services, human resources, information systems/technology, insurance, management, manufacturing, marketing, media, nonprofit, pharmaceutical, real estate, retail, service industry, telecommunications, utilities.

Business Program(s) URL: http://www.stac.edu

Program Contact: Mr. Joseph Chillo, Executive Director of Enrollment Services, 125 Route 340, Sparkill, NY 10976-1050. Phone: 914-398-4100, 800-999-STAC (NY only); Fax: 914-398-4224; E-mail: jchillo@stacmail.stac.edu

Siena College

Business Division

Loudonville, New York

OVERVIEW

Siena College is an independent-religious, coed, comprehensive institution. Enrollment: 3,011 graduate, professional, and undergraduate students; 3 full-time matriculated graduate/professional students; 36 part-time matriculated graduate/professional students. Founded: 1937. The graduate business unit is in a suburban setting and is on a semester calendar.

HIGHLIGHTS

Enrollment Profile
Full-time: 3
Part-time: 36
Total: 39
Average Age: 32
Fall 1997 Average GPA: 3.1

International: 0%
Women: 62%
Minorities: 3%
Average Class Size: 12
Fall 1997 Average GMAT: 516

Costs
Full-time tuition: N/R
Part-time tuition: $315 per credit hour

GRADUATE BUSINESS PROGRAMS

Master of Business Administration in Professional Accountancy (MBA) Full-time, part-time; 33 total credits required; 12 months to 2.5 years to complete program. Concentration in accounting.

ADMISSION

Applications For fall 1997 there were 15 applications for admission. Of those applying, 14 were accepted. Of those accepted, 14 enrolled.

Application Requirements Application form, application fee, bachelor's degree (must be in field of business), essay, 2 letters of recommendation, personal statement, resume, college transcript(s).

Recommended for Application GMAT score accepted, interview, computer experience.

Application Deadline Applications processed on a rolling/continuous basis for domestic students only. 5/31 for fall (international), 10/31 for spring (international). Application fee: $50. Deferred entrance is available.

ACADEMICS

Faculty Part-time 10.

Teaching Methodologies Case study, computer analysis, computer simulations, experiential learning, faculty seminars, field projects, group discussion, lecture, research, role playing, student presentations, study groups, team projects.

Technology 350 on-campus computer terminals/PCs are available for student use and are linked by a campus-wide network. The network has full access to the Internet. Students are not required to have their own PC.

Special Opportunities Advanced credit may be earned through credit by examination, credit for experience, transfer of credits from another institution. International exchange program in Ukraine.

FINANCES

Costs for 1997–98 Tuition: $315 per credit hour. Fees: $25 per semester.

Financial Aid In 1997–98, 18% of students received some institutionally administered aid in the form of loans. Financial aid is available to part-time students. Application Deadline: 4/15.

Financial Aid Contact Ms. Ann White, Director, Financial Aid Office, 515 Loudon Road, Loudonville, NY 12211-1462. Phone: 518-783-2427; Fax: 518-783-7410; E-mail: white@siena.edu

FACILITIES

Information Resources Jerome Dawson Memorial Library; total holdings of 271,002 volumes, 30,868 microforms, 1,709 current periodical subscriptions. CD player(s) available for graduate student use. Access provided to online bibliographic retrieval services.

INTERNATIONAL STUDENTS

Demographics N/R

Services and Facilities Visa services, counseling/support services.

Applying TOEFL: minimum score of 550, proof of adequate funds, proof of health/immunizations required. TSE, TWE recommended. Financial aid is not available to international students.

International Student Contact Ms. Allison Hastings, Assistant Director, MBA Program, 515 Loudon Road, Loudonville, NY 12211-1462. Phone: 518-786-5015; Fax: 518-786-5040; E-mail: hastings@siena.edu

PLACEMENT

Services include alumni network, career counseling/planning, career fairs, career library, and career placement.

Business Program(s) URL: http://www.siena.edu

Program Contact: Ms. Allison Hastings, Assistant Director, MBA Program, 515 Loudon Road, Loudonville, NY 12211-1462. Phone: 518-786-5015; Fax: 518-786-5040; E-mail: hastings@siena.edu

State University of New York at Albany

School of Business

Albany, New York

OVERVIEW

State University of New York at Albany is a state-supported, coed university. Enrollment: 16,651 graduate, professional, and undergraduate students; 1,969 full-time matriculated graduate/professional students; 2,137 part-time matriculated graduate/professional students. Founded: 1844. The graduate business unit is in a suburban setting and is on a semester calendar.

HIGHLIGHTS

Enrollment Profile
Full-time: 186
Part-time: 168
Total: 354
Average Age: 24
Fall 1997 Average GPA: 3.3

International: 10%
Women: 45%
Minorities: 5%
Average Class Size: 30
Fall 1997 Average GMAT: 540

Costs
Full-time tuition: $5100 per academic year (resident); $8416 per academic year (nonresident)
Part-time tuition: $213 per credit hour (resident); $351 per credit hour (nonresident)

AACSB – The International Association for Management Education accredited

GRADUATE BUSINESS PROGRAMS

Master of Business Administration (MBA) Full-time; 63 total credits required; 21 months to complete program. Concentrations in finance, management information systems, marketing.

Evening MBA (MBA) Part-time; 49 total credits required; 3 to 6 years to complete program. Concentration in management.

Master of Science in Accounting (MS) Part-time; 63 total credits required; 21 months to complete program. Concentration in accounting.

Master of Science in Accounting (MS) Full-time, part-time; 30 total credits required; 9 months to 6 years to complete program. Concentration in accounting.

Master of Science in Taxation (MS) Full-time, part-time; 39 total credits required; 12 months to 6 years to complete program. Concentration in taxation.

Weekend MBA (MBA) Part-time; 39 total credits required; 21 months to 6 years to complete program.

ADMISSION

Applications For fall 1997 there were 405 applications for admission. Of those applying, 211 were accepted. Of those accepted, 115 enrolled.

Application Requirements Application form, application fee, bachelor's degree, essay, minimum GPA, 3 letters of recommendation, personal statement, college transcript(s).

Recommended for Application GMAT score accepted, resume, work experience, computer experience.

Application Deadline Applications processed on a rolling/continuous basis for both domestic and international students. Application fee: $50. Deferred entrance is available.

ACADEMICS

Faculty Full-time 48; part-time 15.

Teaching Methodologies Case study, computer analysis, computer simulations, experiential learning, field projects, group discussion, lecture, research, simulations, student presentations, team projects.

Technology 475 on-campus computer terminals/PCs are available for student use and are linked by a campus-wide network. The network has full access to the Internet. Students are not required to have their own PC.

Special Opportunities Advanced credit may be earned through transfer of credits from another institution. An internship program is available.

FINANCES

Costs for 1997–98 Tuition: Full-time: $5100 per year (resident); $8416 per year (nonresident). Part-time: $213 per credit hour (resident); $351 per credit hour (nonresident). Fees: Full-time: $205 per academic year (resident); $205 per academic year (nonresident). Part-time: $90 per semester (resident); $90 per semester (nonresident). Fees vary by number of credits taken. Average 1997–98 room and board costs were $5400 per academic year (on campus) and $5000 per academic year (off campus). Room and board costs vary by occupancy (e.g., single, double, triple), type of accommodation, type of meal plan.

Financial Aid Fellowships, research assistantships, work study available. Application Deadline: 4/1.

Financial Aid Contact Mr. Dennis Tillman, Director of Financial Aid, Office of Financial Aid, CCB52—1400 Washington Avenue, Albany, NY 12222. Phone: 518-442-5480; Fax: 518-442-5295; E-mail: faodbt@safnet.albany.edu

FACILITIES

Information Resources University Library plus 12 additional on-campus libraries; total holdings of 1,800,000 volumes, 2,614,699 microforms, 7,000 current periodical subscriptions. CD player(s) available for graduate student use. Access provided to online bibliographic retrieval services.

INTERNATIONAL STUDENTS

Demographics 10% of students enrolled are international students [Asia, 71%, Central America, 3%, Europe, 11%, North America, 3%, South America, 3%, other, 9%].

Services and Facilities International student office, international student housing, visa services, ESL courses, counseling/support services.

Applying TOEFL: minimum score of 580, proof of adequate funds, proof of health/immunizations required. Financial aid is not available to international students.

International Student Contact Mr. Steven Thomson, Director of International Student Services, ULB-66 1400 Washington Avenue , Albany, NY 12222. Phone: 518-442-5495; Fax: 518-442-5390; E-mail: ssvsat@safnet.albany.edu

PLACEMENT

Services include career counseling/planning, career fairs, career library, electronic job bank, job interviews arranged, resume referral to employers, and resume preparation. In 1996–97, 112 organizations participated in on-campus recruiting; 2,366 on-campus interviews were conducted.

Employment Types of employment entered: accounting, banking, communications, computer-related, consulting, consumer products, education, finance, financial services, government, high technology, human resources, information systems/technology, insurance, management, marketing, nonprofit, retail, service industry.

Business Program(s) URL: http://www.albany.edu/business

Program Contact: Albina Grignon, Assistant Dean for Student Services, BA361 A 1400 Washington Avenue, Albany, NY 12222. Phone: 518-442-4961, 800-UALBANY; Fax: 518-442-5418; E-mail: grigs@cnsibm.albany.edu

See full description on page 996.

State University of New York at Binghamton

School of Management

Binghamton, New York

OVERVIEW

State University of New York at Binghamton is a state-supported, coed university. Enrollment: 11,976 graduate, professional, and undergraduate students; 1,087 full-time matriculated graduate/professional students; 1,540 part-time matriculated graduate/professional students. Founded: 1946. The graduate business unit is in a suburban setting and is on a semester calendar.

HIGHLIGHTS

Enrollment Profile

Full-time: 133	International: 24%
Part-time: 98	Women: 40%
Total: 231	Minorities: 9%
Average Age: 26	Average Class Size: 30
Fall 1997 Average GPA: 3.3	Fall 1997 Average GMAT: 556

Costs
Full-time tuition: $5100 per academic year (resident); $8416 per academic year (nonresident)
Part-time tuition: $213 per credit hour (resident); $351 per credit hour (nonresident)

AACSB – The International Association for Management Education accredited

GRADUATE BUSINESS PROGRAMS

Master of Business Administration (MBA) Full-time, part-time; 64 total credits required; 2 to 4 years to complete program. Concentrations in accounting, finance, marketing, management information systems, organizational behavior/development, operations management.

Master of Science in Accounting (MS) Full-time, part-time; 32 total credits required; 12 months to 4 years to complete program. Concentration in accounting.

Master of Business Administration in Arts Administration (MBA) Full-time; 64 total credits required; 2 to 4 years to complete program. Concentration in arts administration/management.

Executive MBA (EMBA) Part-time; 48 total credits required; up to 2 years to complete program.

ADMISSION

Applications For fall 1997 there were 217 applications for admission. Of those applying, 146 were accepted. Of those accepted, 58 enrolled.

Application Requirements Application form, application fee, bachelor's degree, minimum GPA: 3.0, 2 letters of recommendation, personal statement, college transcript(s).

Recommended for Application GMAT score accepted: minimum 500.

Application Deadline Applications processed on a rolling/continuous basis for both domestic and international students. Application fee: $50.

ACADEMICS

Faculty Full-time 35; part-time 20.

Teaching Methodologies Case study, faculty seminars, group discussion, lecture, research, seminars by members of the business community, team projects.

Technology 250 on-campus computer terminals/PCs are available for student use and are linked by a campus-wide network. The network has full access to the Internet. Students are not required to have their own PC.

Special Opportunities Advanced credit may be earned through transfer of credits from another institution. An internship program is available.

State University of New York at Binghamton (continued)

FINANCES

Costs for 1997–98 Tuition: Full-time: $5100 per year (resident); $8416 per year (nonresident). Part-time: $213 per credit hour (resident); $351 per credit hour (nonresident). Cost varies by number of credits taken. Average 1997–98 room and board costs were $6000 per academic year. Room and board costs vary by occupancy (e.g., single, double, triple), type of accommodation, type of meal plan.

Financial Aid In 1997–98, 19% of students received some institutionally administered aid in the form of fellowships, research assistantships, teaching assistantships, work study, loans. Financial aid is available to part-time students. Application Deadline: 2/15.

Financial Aid Contact Mr. Dennis Lasser, Associate Dean, School of Management, Binghamton, NY 13902-6000. Phone: 607-777-2000; Fax: 607-777-4422.

FACILITIES

Information Resources Glenn G. Bartle Library plus 5 additional on-campus libraries; total holdings of 1,505,000 volumes, 1,402,006 microforms, 9,300 current periodical subscriptions. CD player(s) available for graduate student use. Access provided to online bibliographic retrieval services.

INTERNATIONAL STUDENTS

Demographics 24% of students enrolled are international students [Africa, 3%, Asia, 23%, Europe, 3%, North America, 70%, South America, 1%].

Services and Facilities International student office, international student center, ESL courses, counseling/support services, language tutoring.

Applying TOEFL: minimum score of 550, proof of adequate funds required. Financial aid is available to international students.

International Student Contact Ms. Ellen Badger, Director, International Student and Scholar Services, PO Box 6000, Binghamton, NY 13902-6000. Phone: 607-777-2000; Fax: 607-777-4422.

PLACEMENT

Services include alumni network, career counseling/planning, career fairs, career library, electronic job bank, job interviews arranged, job search course, resume referral to employers, and resume preparation. In 1996–97, 200 organizations participated in on-campus recruiting; 2,000 on-campus interviews were conducted.

Employment Of 1996–97 graduates, 70% were employed within three months of graduation; the average starting salary was $40,000. Types of employment entered: accounting, banking, computer-related, consulting, consumer products, education, energy, finance, financial services, government, health services, high technology, human resources, information systems/technology, insurance, international trade, management, manufacturing, marketing, media, nonprofit, pharmaceutical, retail, service industry, telecommunications, utilities.

Business Program(s) URL: http://som.binghamton.edu/

Program Contact: Frances Littlefield, Coordinator, Graduate Admissions and Advising, PO Box 6000, Binghamton, NY 13902-6000. Phone: 607-777-2316; Fax: 607-777-4422.

See full description on page 998.

State University of New York at Buffalo

School of Management

Buffalo, New York

OVERVIEW

State University of New York at Buffalo is a state-supported, coed university. Enrollment: 23,577 graduate, professional, and undergraduate students; 4,591 full-time matriculated graduate/professional students; 3,286 part-time matriculated graduate/professional students. Founded: 1846. The graduate business unit is in a suburban setting and is on a semester calendar.

HIGHLIGHTS

Enrollment Profile

Full-time: 333
Part-time: 288
Total: 621
Average Age: 28
Fall 1997 Average GPA: 3.1

International: 16%
Women: 33%
Minorities: 7%
Average Class Size: 40
Fall 1997 Average GMAT: 590

Costs

Full-time tuition: $5100 per academic year (resident); $8416 per academic year (nonresident)
Part-time tuition: $213 per credit (resident); $351 per credit (nonresident)

AACSB – The International Association for Management Education accredited

Degree(s) offered in conjunction with SUNY College at Fredonia, SUNY College at Geneseo, St. Bonaventure University

GRADUATE BUSINESS PROGRAMS

Full-time MBA (MBA) Full-time; 60 total credits required; 12 months to 4 years to complete program. Concentrations in accounting, finance, human resources, international business, management, management information systems, manufacturing management, marketing, health care.

Professional MBA (MBA) Part-time; 48 total credits required; minimum of 3 years relevant post-baccalaureate work experience required; 3 years to complete program. Concentration in management.

Executive MBA (MBA) Part-time; 48 total credits required; 22 months to complete program. Concentration in management.

Master of Business Administration/Doctor of Jurisprudence (MBA/JD) Full-time; 96 total credits required; 4 to 6 years to complete program. Concentrations in accounting, finance, human resources, international business, management, management information systems, manufacturing management, marketing, health care.

Master of Business Administration/Master of Architecture (MBA/MArch) Full-time; 96 total credits required; 4 to 6 years to complete program. Concentrations in accounting, finance, human resources, international business, management, management information systems, manufacturing management, marketing, health care.

Master of Business Administration/Master of Science in Geography (MBA/MS) Full-time; 78 total credits required; 3 to 4 years to complete program. Concentrations in accounting, finance, human resources, international business, management, management information systems, manufacturing management, marketing, health care.

Master of Business Administration/Doctor of Medicine (MBA/MD) Full-time; 180 total credits required; 5 years to complete program.

ADMISSION

Applications For fall 1997 there were 727 applications for admission. Of those applying, 360 were accepted. Of those accepted, 206 enrolled.

Application Requirements GMAT score, application form, application fee, bachelor's degree, essay, minimum GPA, 2 letters of recommendation, personal statement, college transcript(s), computer experience: word processing, spreadsheet.

Recommended for Application Resume, work experience.

Application Deadline Applications processed on a rolling/continuous basis for both domestic and international students. Application fee: $50. Deferred entrance is available.

ACADEMICS

Faculty Full-time 57; part-time 6.

Teaching Methodologies Case study, computer-aided instruction, computer analysis, computer simulations, experiential learning, faculty seminars, field projects, group discussion, lecture, research, role playing, seminars by members of the business community, simulations, student presentations, study groups, team projects.

Technology 300 on-campus computer terminals/PCs are available for student use and are linked by a campus-wide network. The network has full access to the Internet. Students are not required to have their own PC.

Special Opportunities International exchange programs in Finland, France, Germany, Korea, Mexico, Republic of Singapore. An internship program is available.

FINANCES

Costs for 1997–98 Tuition: Full-time: $5100 per year (resident); $8416 per year (nonresident). Part-time: $213 per credit (resident); $351 per credit (nonresident). Cost varies by number of credits taken. Fees: Full-time: $662 per academic year (resident); $662 per academic year (nonresident). Part-time: $70 per semester (resident); $70 per semester (nonresident). Fees vary by academic program, number of credits taken. Average 1997–98 room and board costs were $5300 per academic year (on campus) and $5600 per academic year (off campus). Room and board costs vary by campus location, occupancy (e.g., single, double, triple), type of accommodation, type of meal plan.

Financial Aid In 1997–98, 36% of students received some institutionally administered aid in the form of fellowships, research assistantships, teaching assistantships, grants, scholarships, work study, loans. Financial aid is available to part-time students. Application Deadline: 2/15.

Financial Aid Contact Mr. Elias Eldayrie, Director, Student Finances and Records, Hayes C, Buffalo, NY 14214. Phone: 716-829-3724; Fax: 716-829-2022.

FACILITIES

Information Resources Lockwood Library plus 8 additional on-campus libraries; total holdings of 3,047,830 volumes, 4,939,762 microforms, 21,129

current periodical subscriptions. CD player(s) available for graduate student use. Access provided to online bibliographic retrieval services and online databases.

INTERNATIONAL STUDENTS

Demographics 16% of students enrolled are international students [Africa, 2%, Asia, 80%, Europe, 5%, North America, 2%, South America, 2%, other, 9%].

Services and Facilities International student office, international student center, visa services, ESL courses, counseling/support services.

Applying TOEFL: minimum score of 550, TSE: minimum score of 50, proof of adequate funds, proof of health/immunizations required. Financial aid is not available to international students.

International Student Contact Ms. Helen Stevens, Director, International Student Scholar Services, 210 Talbert Hall, Buffalo, NY 14260. Phone: 716-645-2258; Fax: 716-645-6197; E-mail: hstevens@acsu.buffalo.edu

PLACEMENT

Services include alumni network, career counseling/planning, career fairs, career library, career placement, electronic job bank, job interviews arranged, job search course, resume referral to employers, and resume preparation. In 1996–97, 96 organizations participated in on-campus recruiting; 689 on-campus interviews were conducted.

Employment Of 1996–97 graduates, 89% were employed within three months of graduation; the average starting salary was $40,134. Types of employment entered: accounting, banking, communications, computer-related, consulting, consumer products, education, energy, engineering, finance, financial services, government, health services, high technology, human resources, information systems/technology, insurance, international trade, law, management, manufacturing, marketing, media, nonprofit, pharmaceutical, real estate, retail, service industry, telecommunications, transportation, utilities.

Business Program(s) URL: http://www.mgt.buffalo.edu

Program Contact: Katherine M. Gerstle, Assistant Dean and Administrative Director of the MBA Program, 206 Jacobs Management Center, Buffalo, NY 14260. Phone: 716-645-3204; Fax: 716-645-2341; E-mail: sommba@mgt. buffalo.edu

See full description on page 1000.

State University of New York at New Paltz

Department of Business Administration

New Paltz, New York

OVERVIEW

State University of New York at New Paltz is a state-supported, comprehensive institution. Enrollment: 7,500 graduate, professional, and undergraduate students.

HIGHLIGHTS

Enrollment Profile

Full-time: N/R	International: N/R
Part-time: N/R	Women: N/R
Total: 75	Minorities: N/R
Average Age: N/R	Average Class Size: N/R
Fall 1997 Average GPA: N/R	Fall 1997 Average GMAT: N/R

Costs
Full-time tuition: N/R
Part-time tuition: $213 per credit (resident); $351 per credit (nonresident)

GRADUATE BUSINESS PROGRAMS

Master of Science in Accountancy (MS) Full-time, part-time; 33 total credits required; minimum of 18 months to complete program.

Master of Science in Finance (MS) Full-time, part-time; 33 total credits required; minimum of 18 months to complete program.

Master of Science in International Business (MS) Full-time, part-time; 33 total credits required; minimum of 18 months to complete program.

ADMISSION

Application Requirements GMAT score: minimum 400, application form, bachelor's degree, minimum GPA: 3.0, 3 letters of recommendation, college transcript(s).

Recommended for Application Interview, computer experience.

Application Deadline Applications processed on a rolling/continuous basis for both domestic and international students.

ACADEMICS

Teaching Methodologies Group discussion, lecture, student presentations, team projects.

FINANCES

Costs for 1997–98 Tuition: $213 per credit (resident); $351 per credit (nonresident).

Financial Aid Contact Financial Aid Office, New Paltz, NY 12561-2499. Phone: 914-257-3250.

INTERNATIONAL STUDENTS

Demographics N/R

Services and Facilities International student office, international student center, international student housing, visa services, ESL courses, counseling/support services.

Applying TOEFL: minimum score of 550 required.

PLACEMENT

Services include career counseling/planning, job interviews arranged, and resume preparation.

Program Contact: Sue Briggs, New Paltz, NY 12561-2499.

State University of New York at Oswego

School of Business

Oswego, New York

OVERVIEW

State University of New York at Oswego is a state-supported, coed, comprehensive institution. Enrollment: 8,074 graduate, professional, and undergraduate students; 188 full-time matriculated graduate/professional students; 597 part-time matriculated graduate/professional students. Founded: 1861. The graduate business unit is in a small-town setting and is on a semester calendar.

HIGHLIGHTS

Enrollment Profile

Full-time: 42	International: 6%
Part-time: 137	Women: 51%
Total: 179	Minorities: 8%
Average Age: 32	Average Class Size: 16
Fall 1997 Average GPA: 3.1	Fall 1997 Average GMAT: 498

Costs
Full-time tuition: $5100 per academic year (resident); $8416 per academic year (nonresident)
Part-time tuition: N/R

GRADUATE BUSINESS PROGRAMS

Master of Business Administration (MBA) Full-time, part-time; 36-54 total credits required; 12 months to 6 years to complete program.

Master of Business Administration/Accounting (MBA) Full-time, part-time; 36 total credits required; 12 months to 6 years to complete program. Concentration in accounting.

ADMISSION

Applications For fall 1997 there were 75 applications for admission. Of those applying, 70 were accepted. Of those accepted, 62 enrolled.

Application Requirements GMAT score: minimum 400, application form, application fee, bachelor's degree, essay, minimum GPA: 2.5, 3 letters of recommendation, personal statement, college transcript(s).

Application Deadline Applications processed on a rolling/continuous basis for both domestic and international students. Application fee: $50.

ACADEMICS

Faculty Full-time 13; part-time 5.

Teaching Methodologies Case study, computer simulations, faculty seminars, group discussion, lecture, research, seminars by members of the business community, simulations, student presentations, study groups, team projects.

Technology 300 on-campus computer terminals/PCs are available for student use and are linked by a campus-wide network. The network has full access to the Internet. Students are not required to have their own PC.

Special Opportunities Advanced credit may be earned through transfer of credits from another institution.

FINANCES

Costs for 1997–98 Tuition: Full-time: $5100 per year (resident); $8416 per year (nonresident). Cost varies by academic program, number of credits taken. Average 1997–98 room and board costs were $5460 per academic year. Room and board costs vary by occupancy (e.g., single, double, triple), type of meal plan.

Financial Aid In 1997–98, 6% of students received some institutionally administered aid in the form of research assistantships, teaching assistantships. Financial aid is available to part-time students. Application Deadline: 4/1.

State University of New York at Oswego (continued)

FACILITIES

Information Resources Penfield Library; total holdings of 418,772 volumes, 1,718,006 microforms, 2,116 current periodical subscriptions. CD player(s) available for graduate student use. Access provided to online bibliographic retrieval services and online databases.

INTERNATIONAL STUDENTS

Demographics 6% of students enrolled are international students [Asia, 90%, Europe, 10%].

Services and Facilities International student office, international student housing, visa services, ESL courses, counseling/support services.

Applying TOEFL: minimum score of 525, proof of adequate funds, proof of health/immunizations required. Financial aid is not available to international students.

International Student Contact Mr. Gerry Oliver, International Student Advisor, Office of International Studies, Rich Hall, Oswego, NY 13126. Phone: 315-341-5775; Fax: 315-341-2488; E-mail: oliver@oswego.edu

PLACEMENT

Services include career counseling/planning, career fairs, career library, career placement, resume referral to employers, and resume preparation.

Employment Of 1996–97 graduates, 95% were employed within three months of graduation. Types of employment entered: accounting, banking, chemical industry, communications, computer-related, consulting, consumer products, education, energy, finance, financial services, government, health services, high technology, hospitality management, human resources, information systems/technology, insurance, international trade, management, manufacturing, marketing, media, mining, nonprofit, pharmaceutical, real estate, retail, service industry, transportation.

Business Program(s) URL: http://www.oswego.edu/~gradoff/schoolofbusiness.html

Program Contact: Mr. Charles A. Spector, Graduate Director, School of Business, Swetman Hall, Oswego, NY 13126. Phone: 315-341-2911; Fax: 315-341-5440.

State University of New York at Stony Brook

W. Averell Harriman School for Management and Policy

Stony Brook, New York

OVERVIEW

State University of New York at Stony Brook is a state-supported, coed university. Enrollment: 17,665 graduate, professional, and undergraduate students; 3,212 full-time matriculated graduate/professional students; 2,968 part-time matriculated graduate/professional students. Founded: 1957. The graduate business unit is in a suburban setting and is on a semester calendar.

HIGHLIGHTS

Enrollment Profile

Full-time: N/R	International: N/R
Part-time: N/R	Women: N/R
Total: 102	Minorities: N/R
Average Age: 29	Average Class Size: 30
Fall 1997 Average GPA: 3.3	Fall 1997 Average GMAT: 550

Costs

Full-time tuition: $5100 per academic year (resident); $8416 per academic year (nonresident)

Part-time tuition: $213 per credit hour (resident); $351 per credit hour (nonresident)

GRADUATE BUSINESS PROGRAMS

Master of Science in Management and Policy (MS) Full-time, part-time; 60 total credits required; up to 5 years to complete program. Concentrations in entrepreneurship, financial economics, health care, human resources, management information systems, operations management.

Master of Science in Technology Management (MS) Part-time; 35 total credits required; up to 5 years to complete program.

ADMISSION

Applications For fall 1997 there were 155 applications for admission. Of those applying, 103 were accepted. Of those accepted, 58 enrolled.

Application Requirements GMAT score: minimum 500, GRE score, application form, application fee, bachelor's degree, minimum GPA: 3.0, 3 letters of recommendation, personal statement, college transcript(s).

Recommended for Application Resume, computer experience.

Application Deadline 4/15 for fall, 11/1 for spring, 4/15 for fall (international), 11/1 for spring (international). Application fee: $50. Deferred entrance is available.

ACADEMICS

Faculty Full-time 17; part-time 20.

Teaching Methodologies Case study, computer-aided instruction, computer analysis, computer simulations, experiential learning, faculty seminars, field projects, group discussion, lecture, research, role playing, seminars by members of the business community, simulations, student presentations, study groups, team projects.

Technology 28 on-campus computer terminals/PCs are available for student use and are linked by a campus-wide network. The network has full access to the Internet. Students are not required to have their own PC.

Special Opportunities Advanced credit may be earned through transfer of credits from another institution. An internship program is available.

FINANCES

Costs for 1997–98 Tuition: Full-time: $5100 per year (resident); $8416 per year (nonresident). Part-time: $213 per credit hour (resident); $351 per credit hour (nonresident). Cost varies by number of credits taken. Fees: $15 per credit hour (resident); $15 per credit hour (nonresident). Fees vary by academic program, class time (e.g., day/evening), number of credits taken. Average 1997–98 room and board costs were $5350 per academic year. Room and board costs vary by occupancy (e.g., single, double, triple), type of accommodation, type of meal plan.

Financial Aid In 1997–98, 69% of students received some institutionally administered aid in the form of fellowships, research assistantships, teaching assistantships, work study. Application Deadline: 3/1.

Financial Aid Contact Ana Maria Torres, Director, Office of Financial Aid and Student Employment, Stony Brook, NY 11794-0851. Phone: 516-632-6840.

FACILITIES

Information Resources F. Melville Memorial Library plus 7 additional on-campus libraries; total holdings of 1,891,079 volumes, 3,000,000 microforms, 13,000 current periodical subscriptions. CD player(s) available for graduate student use. Access provided to online bibliographic retrieval services.

INTERNATIONAL STUDENTS

Demographics N/R

Services and Facilities International student office, international student housing, visa services, ESL courses, counseling/support services.

Applying TOEFL: minimum score of 550, proof of adequate funds, proof of health/immunizations required. Financial aid is available to international students.

International Student Contact Lynn King Morris, Director of Foreign Student Services, Stony Brook, NY 11794-4433. Phone: 516-632-7040; Fax: 516-632-7243.

PLACEMENT

Services include career counseling/planning, career fairs, career library, career placement, electronic job bank, job interviews arranged, resume referral to employers, and resume preparation.

Employment Of 1996–97 graduates, the average starting salary was $43,000.

Business Program(s) URL: http://www.ceas.sunysb.edu/HAR/

Program Contact: Director of Graduate Studies, W. Averell Harriman School for Management and Policy, Stony Brook, NY 11794-3775. Phone: 516-632-7296; Fax: 516-632-9412; E-mail: lquirk@fac.har.sunysb.edu

See full description on page 1002.

State University of New York College at Oneonta

Department of Economics and Business

Oneonta, New York

OVERVIEW

State University of New York College at Oneonta is a state-supported, coed, comprehensive institution. Enrollment: 5,406 graduate, professional, and undergraduate students; 90 full-time matriculated graduate/professional students; 280 part-time matriculated graduate/professional students. Founded: 1889. The graduate business unit is in a small-town setting and is on a semester calendar.

HIGHLIGHTS

Enrollment Profile
Full-time: 4
Part-time: 9
Total: 13
Average Age: N/R
Fall 1997 Average GPA: 2.92

International: 0%
Women: 46%
Minorities: 8%
Average Class Size: 5
Fall 1997 Average GMAT: 380

Costs
Full-time tuition: $2550 per academic year (resident); $4208 per academic year (nonresident)
Part-time tuition: $213 per credit (resident); $351 per credit (nonresident)

GRADUATE BUSINESS PROGRAMS
MS in Business Economics (MS) Full-time; 30 total credits required; minimum of 2.5 years to complete program.

ADMISSION
Applications For fall 1997 there were 5 applications for admission. Of those applying, 3 were accepted. Of those accepted, 3 enrolled.

Application Requirements Application form, bachelor's degree, minimum GPA: 2.8, 3 letters of recommendation, resume, college transcript(s).

Recommended for Application GMAT score accepted, GRE score accepted.

Application Deadline Applications processed on a rolling/continuous basis for both domestic and international students. Application fee: $50.

ACADEMICS
Faculty Full-time 14; part-time 2.

Teaching Methodologies Case study, computer-aided instruction, experiential learning, field projects, group discussion, lecture, research, seminars by members of the business community, student presentations, study groups, team projects.

Technology 100 on-campus computer terminals/PCs are available for student use and are linked by a campus-wide network. The network has full access to the Internet. Students are not required to have their own PC.

Special Opportunities Advanced credit may be earned through credit by examination, transfer of credits from another institution. An internship program is available.

FINANCES
Costs for 1997–98 Tuition: Full-time: $2550 per semester (resident); $4208 per semester (nonresident). Part-time: $213 per credit (resident); $351 per credit (nonresident). Fees: Full-time: $192 per academic year (resident); $192 per academic year (nonresident). Part-time: $5 per credit (resident); $5 per credit (nonresident). Fees vary by number of credits taken. Average 1997–98 room and board costs were $5456 per academic year (on campus) and $5456 per academic year (off campus).

Financial Aid Grants, scholarships, work study, loans available. Financial aid is available to part-time students.

Financial Aid Contact Bill Goodhue, Director of Financial Aid, 123 Netzer Administration Building, Oneonta, NY 13820-4015. Phone: 607-436-2532; Fax: 607-436-2659; E-mail: goodhuew@oneonta.edu

FACILITIES
Information Resources Milne Library; total holdings of 545,071 volumes, 804,953 microforms, 17,043 current periodical subscriptions.

INTERNATIONAL STUDENTS
Demographics N/R

Services and Facilities International student office, international student housing, ESL courses, counseling/support services.

Applying TOEFL: minimum score of 500, proof of health/immunizations required. Proof of adequate funds recommended. Financial aid is not available to international students.

International Student Contact Susan Jagendorf, International Education Department, Oneonta, NY 13820-4015. Phone: 607-436-2461; Fax: 607-436-2475; E-mail: jagends@oneonta.edu

PLACEMENT
Services include career counseling/planning, career fairs, career library, career placement, job interviews arranged, job search course, and resume preparation. In 1996–97, 20 organizations participated in on-campus recruiting; 35 on-campus interviews were conducted.

Employment Types of employment entered: accounting, banking, communications, computer-related, education, finance, financial services, government, human resources, information systems/technology, insurance, management, marketing, media, nonprofit, real estate, retail, service industry, telecommunications.

Business Program(s) URL: http://www.oneonta.edu/~msbe/

Program Contact: Alfred Lubell, Director of Masters in Business Economics, Netzer Administration Building, Oneonta, NY 13820-4015. Phone: 607-436-2520, 800-SUNY-123; Fax: 607-436-2543; E-mail: lubellam@oneonta.edu

State University of New York Empire State College

Business and Policy Studies Program

Saratoga Springs, New York

OVERVIEW
State University of New York Empire State College is a state-supported, coed, comprehensive institution. Enrollment: 7,122 graduate, professional, and undergraduate students; 22 full-time matriculated graduate/professional students; 323 part-time matriculated graduate/professional students. Founded: 1971. The graduate business unit is in a small-town setting and is on a semester calendar.

HIGHLIGHTS

Enrollment Profile
Full-time: 3
Part-time: 103
Total: 106
Average Age: 41
Fall 1997 Average GPA: N/R

International: 2%
Women: 47%
Minorities: N/R
Average Class Size: N/R
Fall 1997 Average GMAT: N/R

Costs
Full-time tuition: N/R
Part-time tuition: $213 per credit (resident); $351 per credit (nonresident)

GRADUATE BUSINESS PROGRAMS
Master of Arts in Business and Policy Studies (MA) Full-time, part-time, distance learning option; 36 total credits required; 2 to 6 years to complete program.

ADMISSION
Applications For fall 1997 there were 50 applications for admission. Of those applying, 45 were accepted. Of those accepted, 33 enrolled.

Application Requirements Application form, application fee, bachelor's degree, essay, 3 letters of recommendation, personal statement, resume, college transcript(s).

Recommended for Application Work experience, computer experience.

Application Deadline 8/14 for fall, 11/20 for spring, 8/14 for fall (international), 11/20 for spring (international). Application fee: $50. Deferred entrance is available.

ACADEMICS
Faculty Full-time 1; part-time 10.

Teaching Methodologies Case study, computer-aided instruction, computer analysis, faculty seminars, field projects, group discussion, research, student presentations, study groups, team projects.

Technology Computer terminals/PCs are available for student use and are linked by a campus-wide network. The network has full access to the Internet. Students are not required to have their own PC.

Special Opportunities Advanced credit may be earned through credit for military training programs, transfer of credits from another institution. International exchange programs in Austria, Czech Republic, France, Italy, Spain, Switzerland, United Kingdom. An internship program is available.

FINANCES
Costs for 1997–98 Tuition: $213 per credit (resident); $351 per credit (nonresident). Fees: $50 per term (resident); $50 per term (nonresident). Fees vary by number of credits taken.

Financial Aid Fellowships, work study, loans available. Application Deadline: 7/1.

Financial Aid Contact Ms. Eileen Corrigan, Director, Financial Aid, 2 Union Avenue, Saratoga Springs, NY 12866. Phone: 518-587-2100 Ext. 221.

INTERNATIONAL STUDENTS
Demographics 2% of students enrolled are international students.

Services and Facilities International student office.

Applying TOEFL: minimum score of 600, proof of adequate funds, proof of health/immunizations required. Financial aid is not available to international students.

International Student Contact Dr. Kenneth Abrams, Dean for International Programs, 320 Broadway, Saratoga Springs, NY 12866-4390. Phone: 518-587-2100 Ext. 231; Fax: 518-581-8306 ; E-mail: kabrams@sescva.esc.edu

PLACEMENT
Services include alumni network, and electronic job bank.

Business Program(s) URL: http://www.esc.edu

Program Contact: Dr. Dennis DeLong, Dean/Director, Office of Graduate Services, 28 Union Avenue, Saratoga Springs, NY 12866. Phone: 518-587-

State University of New York Empire State College (continued)

2100 Ext. 207, 800-GOTOESC (NY only); Fax: 518-587-4382; E-mail: ddelong@sescva.esc.edu

State University of New York Institute of Technology at Utica/Rome

School of Business

Utica, New York

OVERVIEW
State University of New York Institute of Technology at Utica/Rome is a state-supported, coed, upper-level institution. Enrollment: 1,959 graduate, professional, and undergraduate students; 71 full-time matriculated graduate/professional students; 220 part-time matriculated graduate/professional students. Founded: 1966. The graduate business unit is in a suburban setting and is on a semester calendar.

HIGHLIGHTS

Enrollment Profile

Full-time: 37	International: 1%
Part-time: 83	Women: 52%
Total: 120	Minorities: 7%
Average Age: 35	Average Class Size: 20
Fall 1997 Average GPA: 3.3	Fall 1997 Average GMAT: 490

Costs
Full-time tuition: $5100 per academic year (resident); $8416 per academic year (nonresident)
Part-time tuition: $213 per credit hour (resident); $351 per credit hour (nonresident)

GRADUATE BUSINESS PROGRAMS
Master of Science in Business Management (MS) Full-time, part-time; 33 total credits required; 12 months to 2 years to complete program. Concentrations in accounting, human resources, management science, health care, finance.

Master of Science in Accountancy (MS) Full-time, part-time, distance learning option; 33 total credits required; 12 months to 2 years to complete program.

ADMISSION
Applications For fall 1997 there were 47 applications for admission. Of those applying, 33 were accepted. Of those accepted, 23 enrolled.

Application Requirements Application form, application fee, bachelor's degree, minimum GPA: 3.0, letter of recommendation, college transcript(s), computer experience: basic computer skills course.

Recommended for Application GMAT score accepted, interview.

Application Deadline Applications processed on a rolling/continuous basis for both domestic and international students. Application fee: $50. Deferred entrance is available.

ACADEMICS
Faculty Full-time 13; part-time 4.

Teaching Methodologies Case study, computer analysis, computer simulations, experiential learning, field projects, group discussion, lecture, research, role playing, student presentations, study groups, team projects.

Technology 275 on-campus computer terminals/PCs are available for student use and are linked by a campus-wide network. The network has full access to the Internet. Students are not required to have their own PC.

Special Opportunities Advanced credit may be earned through transfer of credits from another institution. An internship program is available.

FINANCES
Costs for 1997–98 Tuition: Full-time: $5100 per year (resident); $8416 per year (nonresident). Part-time: $213 per credit hour (resident); $351 per credit hour (nonresident). Cost varies by number of credits taken. Fees: Full-time: $419 per academic year (resident); $419 per academic year (nonresident). Part-time: $17 per credit hour (resident); $17 per credit hour (nonresident). Fees vary by campus location, number of credits taken. Average 1997–98 room and board costs were $5880 per academic year (on campus) and $5080 per academic year (off campus). Room and board costs vary by occupancy (e.g., single, double, triple), type of meal plan.

Financial Aid In 1997–98, 23% of students received some institutionally administered aid in the form of fellowships, research assistantships, teaching assistantships, work study, loans. Financial aid is available to part-time students. Application Deadline: 6/15.

Financial Aid Contact Mr. Edward Hutchinson, Director of Financial Aid, PO Box 3050, Utica, NY 13504-3050. Phone: 315-792-7210; Fax: 315-792-7837; E-mail: seah@sunyit.edu

FACILITIES
Information Resources Main library; total holdings of 161,938 volumes, 190,995 microforms, 974 current periodical subscriptions. CD player(s) available for graduate student use. Access provided to online bibliographic retrieval services and online databases.

INTERNATIONAL STUDENTS
Demographics 1% of students enrolled are international students [North America, 100%].

Services and Facilities International student office, visa services, ESL courses, counseling/support services.

Applying TOEFL: minimum score of 550, proof of adequate funds, proof of health/immunizations required. Financial aid is not available to international students.

International Student Contact Ms. Marybeth Lyons, Director of Admissions, PO Box 3050, Utica, NY 13504-3050. Phone: 315-792-7500; Fax: 315-792-7837; E-mail: smbl@sunyit.edu

PLACEMENT
Services include career counseling/planning, career fairs, career library, career placement, electronic job bank, job interviews arranged, resume referral to employers, and resume preparation. In 1996–97, 174 organizations participated in on-campus recruiting; 175 on-campus interviews were conducted.

Employment Of 1996–97 graduates, 85% were employed within three months of graduation; the average starting salary was $32,000. Types of employment entered: accounting, banking, communications, computer-related, consulting, consumer products, energy, engineering, finance, financial services, government, health services, high technology, human resources, information systems/technology, insurance, management, manufacturing, marketing, media, nonprofit, retail, service industry, telecommunications, transportation.

Business Program(s) URL: http://www.sunyit.edu/pubm/

Program Contact: Ms. Marybeth Lyons, Director of Admissions, PO Box 3050, Utica, NY 13504-3050. Phone: 315-792-7500, 800-SUNYTEC; Fax: 315-792-7837; E-mail: smbl@sunyit.edu

State University of New York Maritime College

Graduate Program in Transportation Management

Throgs Neck, New York

OVERVIEW
State University of New York Maritime College is a state-supported, coed, comprehensive institution. Enrollment: 1,060 graduate, professional, and undergraduate students; 25 full-time matriculated graduate/professional students; 145 part-time matriculated graduate/professional students. Founded: 1874. The graduate business unit is in an urban setting and is on a semester calendar.

HIGHLIGHTS

Enrollment Profile

Full-time: 25	International: 35%
Part-time: 145	Women: 10%
Total: 170	Minorities: 9%
Average Age: 30	Average Class Size: 18
Fall 1997 Average GPA: 2.8	Fall 1997 Average GMAT: 420

Costs
Full-time tuition: $2550 per academic year (resident); $4208 per academic year (nonresident)
Part-time tuition: $213 per credit (resident); $351 per credit (nonresident)

GRADUATE BUSINESS PROGRAMS
Master of Science in Transportation Management (MS) Full-time, part-time; 39 total credits required; up to 5 years to complete program. Concentrations in accounting, management systems analysis, system management, logistics, management.

ADMISSION
Applications For fall 1997 there were 60 applications for admission. Of those applying, 50 were accepted. Of those accepted, 45 enrolled.

Application Requirements Application form, application fee, bachelor's degree (must be in field of business), resume, college transcript(s).

Recommended for Application GMAT score accepted, minimum GPA.

Application Deadline Applications processed on a rolling/continuous basis for both domestic and international students. Application fee: $40. Deferred entrance is available.

ACADEMICS
Faculty Full-time 7; part-time 12.

Teaching Methodologies Case study, computer-aided instruction, computer simulations, faculty seminars, group discussion, lecture, research, student presentations.

Technology 20 on-campus computer terminals/PCs are available for student use. The network does not have Internet access. Students are not required to have their own PC.

Special Opportunities Advanced credit may be earned through transfer of credits from another institution. An internship program is available.

FINANCES
Costs for 1997–98 Tuition: Full-time: $2550 per year (resident); $4208 per year (nonresident). Part-time: $213 per credit (resident); $351 per credit (nonresident). Fees: Full-time: $12 per academic year (resident); $12 per academic year (nonresident). Part-time: $1 per credit (resident); $1 per credit (nonresident). Average 1997–98 room and board costs were $5000 per academic year.

Financial Aid In 1997–98, 15% of students received some institutionally administered aid in the form of fellowships, scholarships, work study, loans. Financial aid is available to part-time students. Application Deadline: 5/1.

Financial Aid Contact Marilyn Sullivan, Assistant Financial Aid Advisor, 6 Pennyfield Avenue, Bronx, NY 10465. Phone: 718-409-7267; Fax: 718-409-7392.

FACILITIES
Information Resources Stephen B. Luce Library; total holdings of 70,650 volumes, 20,000 microforms, 550 current periodical subscriptions. Access provided to online bibliographic retrieval services.

INTERNATIONAL STUDENTS
Demographics 35% of students enrolled are international students [Africa, 10%, Asia, 40%, Australia/New Zealand, 4%, Central America, 5%, Europe, 25%, North America, 1%, South America, 5%, other, 10%].

Services and Facilities ESL courses.

Applying TOEFL: minimum score of 500, proof of health/immunizations required. Proof of adequate funds recommended. Financial aid is not available to international students.

International Student Contact Pamela Dettmer, Assistant Administrator, 6 Pennyfield Avenue, Bronx, NY 10465. Phone: 718-409-7285; Fax: 718-409-7359.

PLACEMENT
Services include alumni network, and career placement.

Employment Of 1996–97 graduates, 100% were employed within three months of graduation. Types of employment entered: banking, consulting, education, finance, financial services, government, insurance, international trade, law, management, marketing, service industry, transportation.

Program Contact: Pamela Dettmer, Assistant Administrator, 6 Pennyfield Avenue, Bronx, NY 10465. Phone: 718-409-7285; Fax: 718-409-7359.

Syracuse University

School of Management

Syracuse, New York

OVERVIEW
Syracuse University is an independent-nonprofit, coed university. Enrollment: 15,000 graduate, professional, and undergraduate students; 2,787 full-time matriculated graduate/professional students; 1,643 part-time matriculated graduate/professional students. Founded: 1870. The graduate business unit is in an urban setting and is on a semester calendar.

HIGHLIGHTS

Enrollment Profile
Full-time: 249	International: 17%
Part-time: 438	Women: 32%
Total: 687	Minorities: 10%
Average Age: 28	Average Class Size: 25
Fall 1997 Average GPA: 3.1	Fall 1997 Average GMAT: 550

Costs
Full-time tuition: $16,650 per academic year
Part-time tuition: $555 per credit

AACSB – The International Association for Management Education accredited

Degree(s) offered in conjunction with Shanghai University of Science and Technology

GRADUATE BUSINESS PROGRAMS
Master of Business Administration (MBA) Full-time, part-time, distance learning option; 36-60 total credits required; 11 months to 7 years to complete program. Concentrations in accounting, finance, human resources, management, marketing, new venture management, technology management, logistics, entrepreneurship.

Master of Science in Accounting (MS) Full-time, part-time; 30-63 total credits required; 8 months to 7 years to complete program. Concentration in accounting.

Master of Science in Finance (MS) Full-time, part-time; 30-64 total credits required; 8 months to 7 years to complete program. Concentration in finance.

Master of Business Administration/Doctor of Jurisprudence (MBA/JD) Full-time, part-time; 119 total credits required; 3.7 to 7 years to complete program. Concentrations in accounting, finance, human resources, management, marketing, new venture management, technology management, logistics, entrepreneurship.

Master of Business Administration/Master of Science in Media Management (MBA/MS) Full-time, part-time; 82 total credits required; 2 to 7 years to complete program. Concentrations in accounting, finance, human resources, management, marketing, new venture management, technology management, logistics, entrepreneurship, sports/entertainment management.

Master of Science/Doctor of Jurisprudence (MS/JD) Full-time, part-time; 101-131 total credits required; 2.3 to 7 years to complete program. Concentrations in accounting, finance.

Master of Science in Media Management (MS) Full-time, part-time; 42 total credits required; 12 months to 7 years to complete program. Concentration in sports/entertainment management.

Master of Science/Doctor of Jurisprudence (MS/JD) Full-time, part-time; 91 total credits required; 2 to 7 years to complete program. Concentration in sports/entertainment management.

MBA (EMBA) Part-time; 54 total credits required; 22 months to complete program.

ADMISSION
Applications For fall 1997 there were 659 applications for admission. Of those applying, 238 were accepted. Of those accepted, 137 enrolled.

Application Requirements GMAT score, application form, application fee, bachelor's degree, essay, minimum GPA: 2.0, 2 letters of recommendation, personal statement, resume, college transcript(s), minimum of 1 year of work experience.

Recommended for Application Interview, computer experience.

Application Deadline 5/1 for fall, 5/1 for fall (international). Application fee: $40. Deferred entrance is available.

ACADEMICS
Faculty Full-time 58; part-time 11.

Teaching Methodologies Case study, computer-aided instruction, computer analysis, computer simulations, experiential learning, faculty seminars, field projects, group discussion, lecture, research, role playing, seminars by members of the business community, simulations, student presentations, study groups, team projects.

Technology 500 on-campus computer terminals/PCs are available for student use and are linked by a campus-wide network. The network has full access to the Internet. Students are not required to have their own PC.

Special Opportunities Advanced credit may be earned through credit by examination, transfer of credits from another institution. International exchange programs in France, Hong Kong, Japan, People's Republic of China, Republic of Singapore, South Africa, Spain, United Kingdom. An internship program is available.

FINANCES
Costs for 1997–98 Tuition: Full-time: $16,650 per year. Part-time: $555 per credit. Fees: Full-time: $362 per academic year. Fees vary by academic program, campus location, class time (e.g., day/evening). Average 1997–98 room only costs were $4700 per academic year (on campus) and $8300 per academic year (off campus). Room and board costs vary by campus location, occupancy (e.g., single, double, triple), type of accommodation, type of meal plan.

Financial Aid Fellowships, research assistantships, teaching assistantships, grants, scholarships, work study, loans available. Application Deadline: 3/1.

Financial Aid Contact Ms. Paula Charland, Assistant Dean for MBA and Master's Enrollment, Suite 100, School of Management, Syracuse, NY 13244-2130. Phone: 315-443-9214; Fax: 315-443-9517; E-mail: mbainfo@som.syr.edu

FACILITIES
Information Resources Ernest Stevenson Bird Library plus 6 additional on-campus libraries; total holdings of 2,600,000 volumes, 3,400,000 microforms,

Syracuse University (continued)

11,000 current periodical subscriptions. CD player(s) available for graduate student use. Access provided to online bibliographic retrieval services and online databases.

INTERNATIONAL STUDENTS

Demographics 17% of students enrolled are international students [Africa, 7%, Asia, 77%, Central America, 4%, Europe, 4%, North America, 3%, South America, 4%, other, 1%].

Services and Facilities International student office, international student center, international student housing, visa services, ESL courses, counseling/support services, international orientation week.

Applying TOEFL: minimum score of 580, proof of adequate funds, proof of health/immunizations required. Financial aid is available to international students.

International Student Contact Dr. Patricia A. Burak, Director, Office of International Services, 310 Walnut Place, Syracuse, NY 13244-2380. Phone: 315-443-2457; Fax: 315-443-3091; E-mail: paburak@mailbox.syr.edu

PLACEMENT

Services include alumni network, career counseling/planning, career fairs, career library, career placement, electronic job bank, job interviews arranged, resume referral to employers, and resume preparation. In 1996–97, 130 organizations participated in on-campus recruiting.

Employment Of 1996–97 graduates, 97% were employed within three months of graduation; the average starting salary was $57,000. Types of employment entered: accounting, banking, chemical industry, communications, computer-related, consulting, consumer products, education, energy, engineering, finance, financial services, government, health services, high technology, hospitality management, human resources, information systems/technology, insurance, international trade, law, management, manufacturing, marketing, media, nonprofit, petrochemical, pharmaceutical, real estate, retail, service industry, telecommunications, transportation, utilities.

Business Program(s) URL: http://sominfo.syr.edu

Program Contact: Ms. Paula A. Charland, Assistant Dean for MBA and Master's Enrollment, Suite 100, School of Management, Syracuse, NY 13244-2130. Phone: 315-443-9214; Fax: 315-443-9517; E-mail: mbainfo@som.syr.edu
See full description on page 1008.

Union College

Graduate Management Institute

Schenectady, New York

OVERVIEW

Union College is an independent-nonprofit, coed, comprehensive institution. Enrollment: 2,577 graduate, professional, and undergraduate students; 74 full-time matriculated graduate/professional students; 260 part-time matriculated graduate/professional students. Founded: 1795. The graduate business unit is in an urban setting and is on a trimester calendar.

HIGHLIGHTS

Enrollment Profile
Full-time: 70
Part-time: 150
Total: 220
Average Age: 27
Fall 1997 Average GPA: 3.2

International: 5%
Women: 45%
Minorities: 3%
Average Class Size: 30
Fall 1997 Average GMAT: 580

Costs
Full-time tuition: $12,888 per academic year
Part-time tuition: $1432 per course

Degree(s) offered in conjunction with Albany Law School

GRADUATE BUSINESS PROGRAMS

Master of Business Administration in Accounting (MBA) Full-time, part-time; 60 total credits required; 2 to 6 years to complete program. Concentration in accounting.

Master of Business Administration in Health Systems Administration (MBA) Full-time, part-time; 60 total credits required; 2 to 6 years to complete program.

Master of Business Administration in Management (MBA) Full-time, part-time; 60 total credits required; 2 to 6 years to complete program. Concentration in management.

Master of Business Administration in International Management (MBA) Full-time, part-time; 60 total credits required; 2 to 6 years to complete program. Concentration in international management.

Master of Science in Industrial Administration (MS) Full-time, part-time; 40 total credits required; 12 months to 6 years to complete program. Concentration in industrial administration/management.

Master of Science in Computer Management Systems (MS) Full-time, part-time; 40 total credits required; 12 months to 6 years to complete program. Concentration in information management.

ADMISSION

Applications For fall 1997 there were 63 applications for admission. Of those applying, 58 were accepted. Of those accepted, 38 enrolled.

Application Requirements GMAT score: minimum 500, application form, application fee, bachelor's degree, essay, minimum GPA: 3.0, 3 letters of recommendation, college transcript(s).

Recommended for Application Personal statement, resume, computer experience.

Application Deadline Applications processed on a rolling/continuous basis for both domestic and international students. Application fee: $35. Deferred entrance is available.

ACADEMICS

Faculty Full-time 10; part-time 10.

Teaching Methodologies Case study, computer simulations, field projects, group discussion, lecture, research, seminars by members of the business community, simulations, student presentations, team projects.

Technology 700 on-campus computer terminals/PCs are available for student use and are linked by a campus-wide network. The network has full access to the Internet. Students are not required to have their own PC.

Special Opportunities Advanced credit may be earned through transfer of credits from another institution. An internship program is available.

FINANCES

Costs for 1997–98 Tuition: Full-time: $12,888 per year. Part-time: $1432 per course. Average 1997–98 room only costs were $4500 per academic year (off campus).

Financial Aid In 1997–98, 15% of students received some institutionally administered aid in the form of fellowships, research assistantships, loans. Application Deadline: 3/15.

Financial Aid Contact Ms. Carolyn Micklas, Coordinator of Recruiting and Admissions, Graduate Management Institute, Schenectady, NY 12308. Phone: 518-388-6239; Fax: 518-388-6686; E-mail: micklasc@gar.union.edu

FACILITIES

Information Resources Schaffer Library; total holdings of 496,337 volumes, 586,776 microforms, 1,954 current periodical subscriptions. CD player(s) available for graduate student use. Access provided to online bibliographic retrieval services.

INTERNATIONAL STUDENTS

Demographics 5% of students enrolled are international students [Asia, 50%, Europe, 50%].

Services and Facilities International student office, counseling/support services.

Applying TOEFL: minimum score of 550, proof of adequate funds, proof of health/immunizations required. Financial aid is available to international students.

International Student Contact Ms. Carolyn Micklas, Schenectady, NY 12308. Phone: 518-388-6239; E-mail: micklasc@gar.union.edu

PLACEMENT

Services include alumni network, career counseling/planning, career fairs, career library, career placement, electronic job bank, job interviews arranged, resume referral to employers, and resume preparation.

Employment Of 1996–97 graduates, 100% were employed within three months of graduation; the average starting salary was $45,000. Types of employment entered: accounting, banking, computer-related, consulting, finance, financial services, government, health services, information systems/technology, insurance, law, management, manufacturing, pharmaceutical.

Business Program(s) URL: http://www.union.edu/Academics/Departments/GMI.html

Program Contact: Ms. Carolyn Micklas, Coordinator of Recruiting and Admissions, Graduate Management Institute, Schenectady, NY 12308. Phone: 518-388-6239; Fax: 518-388-6686; E-mail: micklasc@gar.union.edu
See full description on page 1028.

University at Albany, State University of New York *see* State University of New York at Albany

University of Rochester

William E. Simon Graduate School of Business Administration

Rochester, New York

OVERVIEW
The University of Rochester is an independent-nonprofit, coed university. Enrollment: 8,176 graduate, professional, and undergraduate students; 2,851 full-time matriculated graduate/professional students; 824 part-time matriculated graduate/professional students. Founded: 1850. The graduate business unit is in a suburban setting and is on a quarter calendar.

HIGHLIGHTS

Enrollment Profile

Full-time: 570
Part-time: 237
Total: 807
Average Age: 28
Fall 1997 Average GPA: 3.22

International: 32%
Women: 26%
Minorities: 7%
Average Class Size: 36
Fall 1997 Average GMAT: 631

Costs
Full-time tuition: $22,620 per academic year
Part-time tuition: $754 per credit hour

AACSB – The International Association for Management Education accredited

Degree(s) offered in conjunction with University of Bern, Nijenrode University

Consistent with its philosophy of training for the future, the William E. Simon Graduate School of Business Administration at the University of Rochester's internationally integrated M.B.A. program is constantly refining its curricular content to reflect changes in the marketplace. Among new offerings recently introduced are a concentration in health-care management and a brand management specialization within the marketing concentration. This specialization has been developed in cooperation with leading organizations such as the Proctor & Gamble Company. International financial reporting and analysis, managing electronic commerce, and marketing on the Internet are other course additions. An appreciation of similarities and differences across countries' legal systems, market structures, and methods of corporate governance prepare the Simon M.B.A. graduate to enter the global arena. Another crucial element for success in tomorrow's workplace is the demonstrated ability to interact quickly and effectively with coworkers from diverse backgrounds. The fifty different countries represented at Rochester provide an invaluable workshop for developing those skills. Together with annual team training and individual study team evaluation meetings throughout the first year, the School has added specially trained second-year M.B.A. mentors to the team-building infrastructure. As both geographic awareness and rapidly changing technology define changes in business, the Simon School faculty and administration respond with careful curricular adjustments to stay on the cutting edge of business school education.

GRADUATE BUSINESS PROGRAMS
Master of Business Administration (MBA) Full-time, part-time; 67 total credits required; 18 to 22 months to complete program. Concentrations in accounting, economics, entrepreneurship, finance, management information systems, international management, marketing, operations management, public policy and administration, strategic management, health care.

Master of Science in Manufacturing Management (MS) Full-time, part-time; 39 total credits required; 9 to 12 months to complete program. Concentration in manufacturing management.

Master of Science in Information Systems Management (MS) Full-time, part-time; 39 total credits required; 9 to 12 months to complete program. Concentration in management information systems.

Biotech MBA/Master of Science in Microbiology (MBA/MS) Full-time, part-time; 80 total credits required; 2 to 2.3 years to complete program. Concentrations in accounting, economics, entrepreneurship, finance, management information systems, international management, marketing, operations management, public policy and administration, strategic management, health care.

Master of Business Administration/Master of Science in Public Health (MBA/MS) Full-time, part-time; 85 total credits required; 2 to 2.3 years to complete program. Concentrations in accounting, economics, entrepreneurship, finance, management information systems, international management, marketing, operations management, public policy and administration, strategic management, health care.

Master of Business Administration/Master of Science in Nursing (MBA/MS) Full-time, part-time; 85 total credits required; 2.3 to 2.3 years to complete program. Concentrations in accounting, economics, entrepreneurship, finance, management information systems, international management, marketing, opera-

tions management, public policy and administration, strategic management, health care.

Doctor of Philosophy in Business Administration (PhD) Full-time; 90 total credits required; 4.5 to 6 years to complete program.

Executive MBA (MBA) Part-time; 67 total credits required; 20 months to 2 years to complete program.

Master of Science in Finance (MS) Full-time, part-time; 36 total credits required; 9 to 12 months to complete program. Concentration in finance.

MD/MBA Program (MBA/MD) Full-time; minimum of 5 years to complete program.

Master of Science in Service Management (MS) Full-time, part-time; 39 total credits required; 9 to 12 months to complete program.

ADMISSION
Applications For fall 1997 there were 1,419 applications for admission. Of those applying, 452 were accepted. Of those accepted, 165 enrolled.

Application Requirements GMAT score, application form, application fee, bachelor's degree, essay, 2 letters of recommendation, personal statement, resume, college transcript(s).

Recommended for Application Interview, computer experience.

Application Deadline 6/1 for fall, 11/15 for winter, 6/1 for fall (international), 11/15 for winter (international). Application fee: $75. Deferred entrance is available.

ACADEMICS
Faculty Full-time 51; part-time 6.

Teaching Methodologies Case study, computer analysis, field projects, lecture, seminars by members of the business community, student presentations, study groups, team projects.

Technology 66 on-campus computer terminals/PCs are available for student use and are linked by a campus-wide network. The network has full access to the Internet. Students are not required to have their own PC.

Special Opportunities Advanced credit may be earned through transfer of credits from another institution. International exchange programs in Argentina, Australia, Belgium, Finland, Germany, Israel, Japan, Norway. An internship program is available.

FINANCES
Costs for 1997–98 Tuition: Full-time: $22,620 per year. Part-time: $754 per credit hour. Cost varies by number of credits taken. Fees: Full-time: $530 per academic year. Part-time: $450 per year. Average 1997–98 room and board costs were $7160 per academic year (on campus) and $7160 per academic year (off campus). Room and board costs vary by occupancy (e.g., single, double, triple), type of accommodation.

Financial Aid Fellowships, research assistantships, teaching assistantships, scholarships, loans available. Application Deadline: 3/1.

Financial Aid Contact Ms. Pamela Black-Colton, Assistant Dean for MBA Admissions and Administration, William E. Simon Graduate School of Business Administration, Rochester, NY 14627-0107. Phone: 716-275-3533; Fax: 716-271-3907; E-mail: mbaadm@mail.ssb.rochester.edu

FACILITIES
Information Resources Rush Rhees Library plus 7 additional on-campus libraries; total holdings of 2,800,000 volumes, 3,700,000 microforms, 8,650 current periodical subscriptions. CD player(s) available for graduate student use. Access provided to online bibliographic retrieval services and online databases.

INTERNATIONAL STUDENTS
Demographics 32% of students enrolled are international students [Africa, 1%, Asia, 24%, Australia/New Zealand, 1%, Central America, 2%, Europe, 8%, North America, 52%, South America, 10%, other, 2%].

Services and Facilities International student office, international student center, visa services, ESL courses, counseling/support services.

Applying TOEFL: minimum score of 600, proof of adequate funds, proof of health/immunizations required. Financial aid is available to international students.

International Student Contact Ms. Barbara Harris-Smith, Director, International Student Affairs, Morey 209, Rochester, NY 14627-0447. Phone: 716-275-2866; Fax: 716-244-4503; E-mail: bhs@troi.cc.rochester.edu

PLACEMENT
Services include alumni network, career counseling/planning, career fairs, career library, career placement, electronic job bank, job interviews arranged, job search course, resume referral to employers, and resume preparation. In 1996–97, 99 organizations participated in on-campus recruiting; 2,150 on-campus interviews were conducted.

Employment Of 1996–97 graduates, 97% were employed within three months of graduation; the average starting salary was $69,513. Types of employment entered: accounting, banking, chemical industry, communications, computer-related, consulting, consumer products, energy, finance, financial services, health

University of Rochester (continued)

NORTH CAROLINA

services, high technology, hospitality management, information systems/technology, insurance, international trade, management, manufacturing, marketing, nonprofit, petrochemical, pharmaceutical, real estate, retail, service industry, telecommunications, transportation, utilities.

Business Program(s) URL: http://www.ssb.rochester.edu

Program Contact: Ms. Pamela Black-Colton, Assistant Dean for MBA Admissions and Administration, William E. Simon Graduate School of Business Administration, Rochester, NY 14627-0107. Phone: 716-275-3533; Fax: 716-271-3907; E-mail: mbaadm@mail.ssb.rochester.edu

See full description on page 1132.

Wagner College

Department of Economics and Business Administration

Staten Island, New York

OVERVIEW
Wagner College is an independent-nonprofit, coed, comprehensive institution. Enrollment: 2,100 graduate, professional, and undergraduate students. Founded: 1883. The graduate business unit is in a suburban setting and is on a semester calendar.

HIGHLIGHTS

Enrollment Profile

Full-time: N/R	International: N/R
Part-time: N/R	Women: N/R
Total: 122	Minorities: N/R
Average Age: 27	Average Class Size: 10
Fall 1997 Average GPA: N/R	Fall 1997 Average GMAT: N/R

Costs
Full-time tuition: N/R
Part-time tuition: $580 per credit

ACBSP – The American Council of Business Schools and Programs accredited

GRADUATE BUSINESS PROGRAMS
Master of Business Administration (MBA) Full-time, part-time; 36 total credits required; 18 months to 5 years to complete program. Concentrations in finance, marketing, management, international business.

Executive MBA (MBA) Full-time; 36 total credits required; 5 years management experience required; minimum of 18 months to complete program.

ADMISSION
Applications For fall 1997 there were 72 applications for admission.

Application Requirements GMAT score: minimum 550, application form, application fee, bachelor's degree, essay, minimum GPA: 2.7, 2 letters of recommendation, personal statement, college transcript(s), computer experience.

Application Deadline Applications processed on a rolling/continuous basis for both domestic and international students. Application fee: $50, $75 (international).

ACADEMICS
Faculty Full-time 10; part-time 13.

Teaching Methodologies Case study, lecture, student presentations, team projects.

Special Opportunities An internship program is available.

FINANCES
Costs for 1997–98 Tuition: $580 per credit.

Financial Aid Teaching assistantships available.

Financial Aid Contact Edward Keough, Staten Island, NY 10301. Phone: 718-390-3183.

FACILITIES
Information Resources Hormann Library plus 2 additional on-campus libraries; total holdings of 301,771 volumes, 777,712 microforms, 1,546 current periodical subscriptions. Access provided to online bibliographic retrieval services.

INTERNATIONAL STUDENTS
Demographics N/R

Applying TOEFL: minimum score of 550 required.

PLACEMENT
Services include career counseling/planning.

Program Contact: Mr. Angelo Araimo, Director of Admissions, 631 Howard Avenue, Staten Island, NY 10301. Phone: 718-390-3412, 800-221-1010 (NY only)

Appalachian State University

John A. Walker College of Business

Boone, North Carolina

OVERVIEW
Appalachian State University is a state-supported, coed, comprehensive institution. Enrollment: 12,000 graduate, professional, and undergraduate students; 662 full-time matriculated graduate/professional students; 369 part-time matriculated graduate/professional students. Founded: 1899. The graduate business unit is in a small-town setting and is on a semester calendar.

GRADUATE BUSINESS PROGRAMS
Master of Business Administration (MBA)

Master of Science in Accounting (MS)

Master of Arts in Industrial Organizational Psychology and Human Resources (MA)

ACADEMICS
Faculty Full-time 45.

Teaching Methodologies Case study, computer-aided instruction, computer analysis, computer simulations, field projects, group discussion, lecture, role playing, seminars by members of the business community, simulations, student presentations, team projects.

Technology 100 on-campus computer terminals/PCs are available for student use and are linked by a campus-wide network. The network has full access to the Internet. Students are not required to have their own PC.

Special Opportunities Advanced credit may be earned through credit by examination, transfer of credits from another institution.

FACILITIES
Information Resources Carol Grotnes Belk Library plus 2 additional on-campus libraries. CD player(s) available for graduate student use. Access provided to online bibliographic retrieval services.

Program Contact: Assistant Dean of Graduate Studies and External Programs, 4120 Raley Hall, Boone, NC 28608. Phone: 704-262-2922; Fax: 704-262-2925; E-mail: kirkprc@conrad.appstate.edu

Campbell University

Lundy-Fetterman School of Business

Buies Creek, North Carolina

OVERVIEW
Campbell University is an independent-religious, coed university. Enrollment: 6,882 graduate, professional, and undergraduate students; 958 full-time matriculated graduate/professional students; 360 part-time matriculated graduate/professional students. Founded: 1887. The graduate business unit is in a rural setting and is on a semester calendar.

HIGHLIGHTS

Enrollment Profile

Full-time: 11	International: 9%
Part-time: 172	Women: 35%
Total: 183	Minorities: 10%
Average Age: 28	Average Class Size: 30
Fall 1997 Average GPA: 3.1	Fall 1997 Average GMAT: 490

Costs
Full-time tuition: N/R
Part-time tuition: $170 per semester hour

GRADUATE BUSINESS PROGRAMS
Master of Business Administration (MBA) Full-time, part-time; 30 total credits required; 18 months to 5 years to complete program.

ADMISSION
Applications For fall 1997 there were 128 applications for admission. Of those applying, 73 were accepted.

Application Requirements Application form, application fee, bachelor's degree (must be in field of business), minimum GPA: 2.7, 3 letters of recommendation, college transcript(s), computer experience: introductory computer course.

Recommended for Application GMAT score accepted.

Application Deadline Applications processed on a rolling/continuous basis for both domestic and international students. Application fee: $20.

ACADEMICS
Faculty Full-time 8; part-time 5.

Teaching Methodologies Case study, faculty seminars, field projects, group discussion, lecture, research, role playing, seminars by members of the business community, student presentations, study groups, team projects.

Technology Students are not required to have their own PC.

Special Opportunities Advanced credit may be earned through transfer of credits from another institution.

FINANCES
Costs for 1997–98 Tuition: $170 per semester hour. Cost varies by campus location, number of credits taken. Fees vary by campus location, number of credits taken. Average 1997–98 room and board costs were $4000 per academic year. Room and board costs vary by occupancy (e.g., single, double, triple), type of accommodation, type of meal plan.

Financial Aid Contact Ms. Peggy Mason, Director of Financial Aid, PO Box 36, Buies Creek, NC 27506. Phone: 910-893-1310; Fax: 910-893-1288.

FACILITIES
Information Resources Carrie Rich Library plus 2 additional on-campus libraries; total holdings of 346,660 volumes, 675,348 microforms, 3,121 current periodical subscriptions. CD player(s) available for graduate student use. Access provided to online bibliographic retrieval services.

INTERNATIONAL STUDENTS
Demographics 9% of students enrolled are international students.

Services and Facilities International student office, international student center, international student housing, counseling/support services.

Applying TOEFL: minimum score of 550, proof of adequate funds, proof of health/immunizations required. Financial aid is not available to international students.

International Student Contact Mr. George Blanc, Director of International Admissions, PO Box 546, Buies Creek, NC 27506. Phone: 910-893-1415.

PLACEMENT
Services include career placement, job interviews arranged, resume referral to employers, and resume preparation. In 1996–97, 15 organizations participated in on-campus recruiting; 150 on-campus interviews were conducted.

Employment Of 1996–97 graduates, 70% were employed within three months of graduation; the average starting salary was $34,000. Types of employment entered: banking, computer-related, finance, management, marketing, retail.

Program Contact: Mr. Jim Farthing, Jr., Director of Graduate Admissions, PO Box 546, Buies Creek, NC 27506. Phone: 910-893-1200 Ext. 1318; Fax: 910-893-1288.

Duke University

The Fuqua School of Business at Duke University
Durham, North Carolina

OVERVIEW
Duke University is an independent-religious, coed university. Enrollment: 11,881 graduate, professional, and undergraduate students; 4,573 full-time matriculated graduate/professional students; 486 part-time matriculated graduate/professional students. Founded: 1838. The graduate business unit is in a suburban setting and is on a term calendar.

HIGHLIGHTS

Enrollment Profile

Full-time: 680	International: 25%
Part-time: 0	Women: 31%
Total: 680	Minorities: 27%
Average Age: 27	Average Class Size: 50
Fall 1997 Average GPA: 3.34	Fall 1997 Average GMAT: 663

Costs
Full-time tuition: $25,250 per academic year
Part-time tuition: N/R

AACSB – The International Association for Management Education accredited

GRADUATE BUSINESS PROGRAMS
Master of Business Administration (MBA) Full-time; 85 total credits required; 2 years to complete program. Concentrations in management, health care.

Weekend Master of Business Administration (WEMBA) Full-time; 45 total credits required; up to 20 months to complete program. Concentration in management.

Global Executive Master of Business Administration (GEMBA) Full-time, distance learning option; 45 total credits required; up to 19 months to complete program.

ADMISSION
Applications For fall 1997 there were 3,045 applications for admission. Of those applying, 574 were accepted. Of those accepted, 331 enrolled.

Application Requirements GMAT score, application form, application fee, bachelor's degree, essay, minimum GPA: 3.0, 2 letters of recommendation, personal statement, resume, college transcript(s).

Recommended for Application Interview, work experience, computer experience.

Application Deadline 4/28 for fall, 4/28 for fall (international). Application fee: $110. Deferred entrance is available.

ACADEMICS
Faculty Full-time 80; part-time 23.

Teaching Methodologies Case study, computer-aided instruction, computer analysis, computer simulations, experiential learning, faculty seminars, field projects, group discussion, lecture, research, role playing, seminars by members of the business community, simulations, student presentations, study groups, team projects.

Technology 108 on-campus computer terminals/PCs are available for student use and are linked by a campus-wide network. The network has full access to the Internet. Students are required to have their own PC.

Special Opportunities International exchange programs in Australia, Belgium, Costa Rica, Denmark, France, Italy, Mexico, Netherlands, Norway, South Africa, Spain, Sweden, Switzerland, Thailand, United Kingdom.

FINANCES
Costs for 1997–98 Tuition: Full-time: $25,250 per year. Cost varies by academic program. Fees vary by academic program. Average 1997–98 room and board costs were $10,900 per academic year (off campus).

Financial Aid In 1997–98, 76% of students received some institutionally administered aid in the form of scholarships, work study, loans. Application Deadline: 3/1.

Financial Aid Contact Mr. Paul West, Director of Financial Aid, Fuqua School of Business, Box 90128, Durham, NC 27708-0128. Phone: 919-660-7803; Fax: 919-681-6243; E-mail: pdw1@mail.duke.edu

FACILITIES
Information Resources William R. Perkins Library plus 10 additional on-campus libraries; total holdings of 4,330,103 volumes, 3,004,538 microforms, 31,873 current periodical subscriptions. CD player(s) available for graduate student use. Access provided to online bibliographic retrieval services.

INTERNATIONAL STUDENTS
Demographics 25% of students enrolled are international students.

Services and Facilities International student office, international student center, visa services, counseling/support services, summer English program.

Applying TOEFL, proof of adequate funds, proof of health/immunizations required. Financial aid is available to international students.

International Student Contact Katie Joyce, Assistant Director for International Programs, Fuqua School of Business at Duke University, Box 90126, Durham, NC 27708-0126. Phone: 919-660-7807; Fax: 919-681-6243; E-mail: joyce@mail.duke.edu

PLACEMENT
Services include alumni network, career counseling/planning, career fairs, career library, career placement, electronic job bank, job interviews arranged, and resume referral to employers. In 1996–97, 320 organizations participated in on-campus recruiting; 8,918 on-campus interviews were conducted.

Employment Of 1996–97 graduates, 99% were employed within three months of graduation; the average starting salary was $70,884. Types of employment entered: banking, chemical industry, communications, computer-related, consulting, consumer products, energy, engineering, finance, financial services, health services, high technology, human resources, information systems/technology, insurance, international trade, law, management, manufacturing, marketing, media, nonprofit, petrochemical, pharmaceutical, real estate, service industry, telecommunications, transportation, utilities.

Business Program(s) URL: http://www.fuqua.duke.edu

Program Contact: Robert Williams, Director of Admissions, Fuqua School of Business, Box 90104, Durham, NC 27708-0104. Phone: 919-660-7705; Fax: 919-681-8026; E-mail: fuqua-admissions@mail.duke.edu

East Carolina University

School of Business

Greenville, North Carolina

OVERVIEW
East Carolina University is a state-supported, coed university. Enrollment: 18,271 graduate, professional, and undergraduate students; 1,623 full-time matriculated graduate/professional students; 1,868 part-time matriculated graduate/professional students. Founded: 1907. The graduate business unit is in a small-town setting and is on a semester calendar.

HIGHLIGHTS

Enrollment Profile

Full-time: 220	International: 6%
Part-time: 125	Women: 44%
Total: 345	Minorities: 7%
Average Age: 28	Average Class Size: 20
Fall 1997 Average GPA: 3.0	Fall 1997 Average GMAT: 500

Costs
Full-time tuition: $450 per academic year (resident); $4014 per academic year (nonresident)
Part-time tuition: $450 per semester (resident); $2007 per semester (nonresident)

AACSB – The International Association for Management Education accredited

GRADUATE BUSINESS PROGRAMS
Master of Business Administration (MBA) Full-time, part-time; 30-60 total credits required; 8 to 20 months to complete program. Concentrations in health care, travel industry/tourism management.

Master of Science in Accounting (MSA) Full-time, part-time; 30-60 total credits required; 8 to 20 months to complete program. Concentration in accounting.

Doctor of Medicine/Master of Business Administration (MD/MBA) Full-time; 42 total credits required; must be enrolled in an accredited medical school or be a medical resident; 12 months to complete program. Concentration in health care.

ADMISSION
Applications For fall 1997 there were 161 applications for admission. Of those applying, 135 were accepted. Of those accepted, 102 enrolled.

Application Requirements Application form, application fee, bachelor's degree, college transcript(s).

Recommended for Application GMAT score accepted, work experience.

Application Deadline Applications processed on a rolling/continuous basis for both domestic and international students. Application fee: $40. Deferred entrance is available.

ACADEMICS
Faculty Full-time 67.

Teaching Methodologies Case study, computer-aided instruction, computer analysis, computer simulations, experiential learning, field projects, group discussion, lecture, research, role playing, simulations, student presentations, study groups, team projects.

Technology 96 on-campus computer terminals/PCs are available for student use and are linked by a campus-wide network. The network has full access to the Internet. Students are not required to have their own PC.

Special Opportunities Advanced credit may be earned through transfer of credits from another institution. International exchange programs in Australia, France.

FINANCES
Costs for 1997–98 Tuition: Full-time: $450 per semester (resident); $4014 per semester (nonresident). Part-time: $450 per semester (resident); $2007 per semester (nonresident). Cost varies by number of credits taken. Fees: Full-time: $466 per academic year (resident); $466 per academic year (nonresident). Part-time: $233 per semester (resident); $233 per semester (nonresident). Average 1997–98 room and board costs were $4240 per academic year (on campus) and $6000 per academic year (off campus). Room and board costs vary by occupancy (e.g., single, double, triple), type of accommodation, type of meal plan.

Financial Aid In 1997–98, 29% of students received some institutionally administered aid in the form of research assistantships, teaching assistantships, scholarships, work study. Financial aid is available to part-time students. Application Deadline: 6/1.

Financial Aid Contact Dr. Rose Mary Stelma, Director, Student Financial Aid, Greenville, NC 27858-4353. Phone: 252-328-6610; Fax: 252-328-4347.

FACILITIES
Information Resources Joyner Library plus 1 additional on-campus library; total holdings of 1,199,697 volumes, 1,686,538 microforms, 7,788 current periodical subscriptions. CD player(s) available for graduate student use. Access provided to online bibliographic retrieval services and online databases.

INTERNATIONAL STUDENTS
Demographics 6% of students enrolled are international students [Africa, 5%, Asia, 33%, Australia/New Zealand, 5%, Central America, 5%, Europe, 38%, North America, 9%, South America, 5%].

Services and Facilities International student office, international student center, visa services, ESL courses, counseling/support services.

Applying TOEFL: minimum score of 550, proof of adequate funds, proof of health/immunizations required. Financial aid is available to international students.

International Student Contact Dr. Linda McGowan, Overseas Opportunities Coordinator, International Affairs, Greenville, NC 27858-4353. Phone: 252-328-1937; Fax: 252-328-4813; E-mail: mcgowanl@mail.ecu.edu

PLACEMENT
Services include career counseling/planning, career fairs, career library, career placement, electronic job bank, job interviews arranged, and resume preparation. In 1996–97, 257 organizations participated in on-campus recruiting.

Employment Of 1996–97 graduates, 89% were employed within three months of graduation; the average starting salary was $38,000. Types of employment entered: accounting, banking, computer-related, consulting, consumer products, education, finance, financial services, government, health services, high technology, hospitality management, human resources, information systems/technology, insurance, international trade, management, manufacturing, marketing, nonprofit, pharmaceutical, real estate, retail, service industry, telecommunications, transportation, utilities.

Business Program(s) URL: http://www.business.ecu.edu/grad

Program Contact: Mr. Donald B. Boldt, Assistant Dean for Graduate Programs, School of Business, Greenville, NC 27858-4353. Phone: 252-328-6970; Fax: 252-328-2106; E-mail: boldtd@mail.ecu.edu

See full description on page 790.

Elon College

Martha and Spencer Love School of Business

Elon College, North Carolina

OVERVIEW
Elon College is an independent-religious, coed, comprehensive institution. Enrollment: 3,685 graduate, professional, and undergraduate students; 24 full-time matriculated graduate/professional students; 128 part-time matriculated graduate/professional students. Founded: 1889. The graduate business unit is in a suburban setting and is on a 4-1-4 calendar.

HIGHLIGHTS

Enrollment Profile

Full-time: 14	International: 3%
Part-time: 61	Women: 39%
Total: 75	Minorities: 11%
Average Age: 32	Average Class Size: 25
Fall 1997 Average GPA: 3.2	Fall 1997 Average GMAT: 530

Costs
Full-time tuition: N/R
Part-time tuition: $256 per semester hour

GRADUATE BUSINESS PROGRAMS
Master of Business Administration (MBA) Full-time, part-time; 39 total credits required; 18 months to 6 years to complete program. Concentration in leadership.

ADMISSION
Applications For fall 1997 there were 52 applications for admission. Of those applying, 29 were accepted. Of those accepted, 27 enrolled.

Application Requirements GMAT score: minimum 475, application form, application fee, bachelor's degree, minimum GPA, 3 letters of recommendation, personal statement, college transcript(s), minimum of 2 years of work experience, computer experience.

Recommended for Application Resume.

Application Deadline Applications processed on a rolling/continuous basis for both domestic and international students. Application fee: $25.

ACADEMICS
Faculty Full-time 17.

Teaching Methodologies Case study, computer-aided instruction, computer analysis, computer simulations, faculty seminars, field projects, group discussion, lecture, research, seminars by members of the business community, simulations, student presentations, study groups, team projects.

Technology 225 on-campus computer terminals/PCs are available for student use and are linked by a campus-wide network. The network has full access to the Internet. Students are not required to have their own PC.

Special Opportunities Advanced credit may be earned through transfer of credits from another institution.

FINANCES
Costs for 1997–98 Tuition: $256 per semester hour. Average 1997–98 room and board costs were $4300 per academic year (on campus) and $4300 per academic year (off campus).

Financial Aid In 1997–98, 11% of students received some institutionally administered aid in the form of work study, loans. Financial aid is available to part-time students. Application Deadline: 8/1.

Financial Aid Contact Financial Planning Office, Elon College, NC 27244. Phone: 800-334-8448.

FACILITIES
Information Resources McEwen Library; total holdings of 197,000 volumes, 668,925 microforms, 1,700 current periodical subscriptions. CD player(s) available for graduate student use. Access provided to online bibliographic retrieval services and online databases.

INTERNATIONAL STUDENTS
Demographics 3% of students enrolled are international students [Asia, 50%, Europe, 50%].

Services and Facilities International student office, visa services, counseling/support services, writing center, healthcare.

Applying TOEFL: minimum score of 500, proof of adequate funds, proof of health/immunizations required. Financial aid is not available to international students.

International Student Contact Ms. Alice Essen, Elon College, NC 27244. Phone: 800-334-8448; Fax: 336-538-3986.

PLACEMENT
Services include career counseling/planning, career fairs, career library, and resume referral to employers.

Business Program(s) URL: http://www.elon.edu/mba/

Program Contact: Ms. Alice Essen, Director of Graduate Admissions, Office of Graduate Admissions, 2750 Campus Box, Elon College, NC 27244. Phone: 336-584-2474, 800-334-8448; Fax: 336-538-3986; E-mail: gradadm@numen.elon.edu

Fayetteville State University

Program in Business Administration

Fayetteville, North Carolina

OVERVIEW
Fayetteville State University is a state-supported, coed, comprehensive institution. Enrollment: 4,000 graduate, professional, and undergraduate students; 180 full-time matriculated graduate/professional students; 720 part-time matriculated graduate/professional students. Founded: 1867. The graduate business unit is in a suburban setting and is on a semester calendar.

HIGHLIGHTS

Enrollment Profile

Full-time: 10	International: N/R
Part-time: 90	Women: N/R
Total: 100	Minorities: N/R
Average Age: 33	Average Class Size: 15
Fall 1997 Average GPA: 3.3	Fall 1997 Average GMAT: 490

Costs
Full-time tuition: $1334 per academic year (resident); $8176 per academic year (nonresident)
Part-time tuition: $90 per credit (resident); $478 per credit (nonresident)

GRADUATE BUSINESS PROGRAMS
Master of Business Administration (MBA) Full-time, part-time; 36 total credits required; 12 months to 6 years to complete program. Concentrations in finance, international management, management, marketing, accounting, entrepreneurship.

ADMISSION
Applications For fall 1997 there were 100 applications for admission. Of those applying, 35 were accepted. Of those accepted, 25 enrolled.

Application Requirements GMAT score, application form, application fee, bachelor's degree, 2 letters of recommendation, college transcript(s).

Application Deadline 7/30 for fall, 12/15 for spring, 4/30 for summer, 7/15 for fall (international), 12/1 for spring (international), 4/15 for summer (international). Application fee: $20. Deferred entrance is available.

ACADEMICS
Faculty Full-time 29.

Teaching Methodologies Case study, computer-aided instruction, computer analysis, computer simulations, experiential learning, faculty seminars, field projects, group discussion, lecture, research, role playing, student presentations, study groups, team projects.

Technology 50 on-campus computer terminals/PCs are available for student use and are linked by a campus-wide network. The network has full access to the Internet. Students are not required to have their own PC.

Special Opportunities Advanced credit may be earned through transfer of credits from another institution. International exchange programs in Dominican Republic, United Kingdom. An internship program is available.

FINANCES
Costs for 1997–98 Tuition: Full-time: $1334 per year (resident); $8176 per year (nonresident). Part-time: $90 per credit (resident); $478 per credit (nonresident). Cost varies by number of credits taken. Average 1997–98 room only costs were $4000 per academic year (off campus). Room and board costs vary by occupancy (e.g., single, double, triple).

Financial Aid Research assistantships, teaching assistantships, loans available. Financial aid is available to part-time students. Application Deadline: 3/15.

Financial Aid Contact Financial Aid Office, Assistant, 1200 Murchison Road, Fayetteville, NC 28301. Phone: 910-486-1325; Fax: 910-486-1033.

FACILITIES
Information Resources Charles Wadell Chesnutt Library; total holdings of 159,722 volumes, 353,384 microforms, 2,346 current periodical subscriptions. Access provided to online bibliographic retrieval services.

INTERNATIONAL STUDENTS
Demographics N/R

Services and Facilities Visa services, counseling/support services.

Applying TOEFL: minimum score of 550, proof of adequate funds required. Financial aid is not available to international students.

International Student Contact Asad Tavakoli, MBA Director, 1200 Murchison Road, Fayetteville, NC 28301. Phone: 910-486-1197; Fax: 910-486-1033; E-mail: tavakoli@sbe1.uncfsu.edu

PLACEMENT
Services include career counseling/planning, career fairs, career library, career placement, electronic job bank, job interviews arranged, and resume preparation. In 1996–97, 150 organizations participated in on-campus recruiting; 50 on-campus interviews were conducted.

Employment Of 1996–97 graduates, 90% were employed within three months of graduation; the average starting salary was $40,000. Types of employment entered: accounting, banking, communications, computer-related, education, financial services, government, health services, human resources, insurance, management, marketing, real estate, retail.

Business Program(s) URL: http://www.uncfsu.edu/col/bus/index.htm

Program Contact: Asad Tavakoli, MBA Director, 1200 Murchison Road, Fayetteville, NC 28303. Phone: 910-486-1197; Fax: 910-486-1033; E-mail: mba@sbe1.uncfsu.edu

Gardner-Webb University

School of Business

Boiling Springs, North Carolina

OVERVIEW
Gardner-Webb University is an independent-religious, coed, comprehensive institution. Enrollment: 3,038 graduate, professional, and undergraduate students. Founded: 1905. The graduate business unit is in a small-town setting and is on a semester calendar.

HIGHLIGHTS

Enrollment Profile

Full-time: 85	International: 1%
Part-time: 86	Women: 43%
Total: 171	Minorities: 8%
Average Age: 33	Average Class Size: 25
Fall 1997 Average GPA: 3.06	Fall 1997 Average GMAT: 459

Costs
Full-time tuition: N/R
Part-time tuition: $205 per credit hour

Gardner-Webb University (continued)

GRADUATE BUSINESS PROGRAMS

Master of Business Administration (MBA) Full-time, part-time; 36 total credits required; 2 to 6 years to complete program. Concentrations in international business, health care, human resources.

ADMISSION

Applications For fall 1997 there were 72 applications for admission. Of those applying, 60 were accepted. Of those accepted, 60 enrolled.

Application Requirements GMAT score: minimum 400, application form, application fee, bachelor's degree, minimum GPA: 2.25, interview, 3 letters of recommendation, resume, college transcript(s), computer experience: basic computer skills.

Recommended for Application Work experience.

Application Deadline Applications processed on a rolling/continuous basis for both domestic and international students. Application fee: $25.

ACADEMICS

Faculty Full-time 12; part-time 1.

Teaching Methodologies Case study, computer-aided instruction, computer analysis, computer simulations, experiential learning, faculty seminars, field projects, group discussion, lecture, research, role playing, seminars by members of the business community, simulations, student presentations, study groups, team projects.

Technology 100 on-campus computer terminals/PCs are available for student use and are linked by a campus-wide network. The network has full access to the Internet. Students are not required to have their own PC.

Special Opportunities Advanced credit may be earned through transfer of credits from another institution.

FINANCES

Costs for 1997–98 Tuition: $205 per credit hour. Cost varies by number of credits taken. Room and board costs vary by occupancy (e.g., single, double, triple), type of meal plan.

Financial Aid In 1997–98, 15% of students received some institutionally administered aid in the form of loans. Financial aid is available to part-time students.

Financial Aid Contact Mr. Mike Roebuck, Director of Financial Aid, Boiling Springs, NC 28017. Phone: 704-434-4497; Fax: 704-434-6246; E-mail: mroebuck@gardner-webb.edu

FACILITIES

Information Resources John R. Dover Memorial Library; total holdings of 198,000 volumes, 493,000 microforms, 900 current periodical subscriptions. CD player(s) available for graduate student use. Access provided to online bibliographic retrieval services.

INTERNATIONAL STUDENTS

Demographics 1% of students enrolled are international students [Africa, 20%, Asia, 40%, Europe, 20%, other, 20%].

Services and Facilities International student office, international student center, international student housing, counseling/support services, I-20 processing.

Applying TOEFL: minimum score of 500, proof of adequate funds, proof of health/immunizations required. Financial aid is not available to international students.

International Student Contact Mrs. Melissa Swofford, Director of Admissions-MBA, Campus Box 7272, Boiling Springs, NC 28017. Phone: 704-434-4489; Fax: 704-434-4738; E-mail: mswofford@gardner-webb.edu

PLACEMENT

Services include alumni network, career counseling/planning, career placement, electronic job bank, resume referral to employers, and resume preparation.

Business Program(s) URL: http://www.gardner-webb.edu/GWU/main/business/MBA/mbahome.html

Program Contact: Mrs. Melissa Swofford, Director of Admissions-MBA, Campus Box 7272, Boiling Springs, NC 28017. Phone: 704-434-4489, 800-457-4MBA; Fax: 704-434-4738; E-mail: mswofford@gardner-webb.edu

High Point University

Graduate Studies

High Point, North Carolina

OVERVIEW

High Point University is an independent-religious, coed, comprehensive institution. Enrollment: 2,744 graduate, professional, and undergraduate students; 13 full-time matriculated graduate/professional students; 134 part-time matriculated graduate/professional students. Founded: 1924. The graduate business unit is in an urban setting and is on a semester calendar.

HIGHLIGHTS

Enrollment Profile

Full-time: 13	International: 4%
Part-time: 134	Women: 52%
Total: 147	Minorities: 23%
Average Age: 34	Average Class Size: 16
Fall 1997 Average GPA: 3.08	Fall 1997 Average GMAT: 442

Costs
Full-time tuition: $4806 per academic year
Part-time tuition: $267 per credit

GRADUATE BUSINESS PROGRAMS

Master of Business Administration (MBA) Full-time, part-time; 37 total credits required; 2 to 5 years to complete program.

Master of Science in Management (MS) Full-time, part-time; 37 total credits required; 2 to 5 years to complete program.

Master of Science in International Management (MS) Full-time, part-time; 37 total credits required; 2 to 5 years to complete program.

ADMISSION

Applications For fall 1997 there were 62 applications for admission. Of those applying, 57 were accepted. Of those accepted, 41 enrolled.

Application Requirements Application form, application fee, bachelor's degree, minimum GPA: 3.0, 3 letters of recommendation, personal statement, college transcript(s).

Recommended for Application GMAT score accepted.

Application Deadline 4/15 for fall, 10/15 for spring, 3/15 for summer, 4/15 for fall (international), 10/15 for spring (international), 3/15 for summer (international). Application fee: $35, $50 (international). Deferred entrance is available.

ACADEMICS

Faculty Full-time 16.

Teaching Methodologies Case study, computer-aided instruction, computer analysis, computer simulations, field projects, group discussion, lecture, research, simulations, student presentations, team projects.

Technology 150 on-campus computer terminals/PCs are available for student use and are linked by a campus-wide network. The network has full access to the Internet. Students are not required to have their own PC.

Special Opportunities Advanced credit may be earned through transfer of credits from another institution.

FINANCES

Costs for 1997–98 Tuition: Full-time: $4806 per year. Part-time: $267 per credit. Cost varies by number of credits taken. Fees: Full-time: $50 per academic year. Part-time: $50 per semester. Average 1997–98 room and board costs were $5060 per academic year (on campus) and $9000 per academic year (off campus). Room and board costs vary by occupancy (e.g., single, double, triple), type of accommodation, type of meal plan.

Financial Aid In 1997–98, 18% of students received some institutionally administered aid in the form of loans. Financial aid is available to part-time students. Application Deadline: 3/1.

Financial Aid Contact Ms. Dana Kelly, Director of Financial Aid, University Station, Montlieu Avenue, High Point, NC 27262-3598. Phone: 336-841-9128; Fax: 336-841-4599; E-mail: ddooley@acme.highpoint.edu

FACILITIES

Information Resources Herman and Louise Smith Library; total holdings of 152,578 volumes, 63,000 microforms, 1,300 current periodical subscriptions. CD player(s) available for graduate student use. Access provided to online bibliographic retrieval services and online databases.

INTERNATIONAL STUDENTS

Demographics 4% of students enrolled are international students [Africa, 17%, Asia, 33%, Central America, 16%, Europe, 33%, other, 1%].

Applying TOEFL: minimum score of 550, proof of adequate funds required.

International Student Contact Dr. Alberta Herron, Dean of Graduate Studies, University Station, Montlieu Avenue, High Point, NC 27262-3598. Phone: 336-841-9000; Fax: 336-841-4599; E-mail: aherron@acme.highpoint.edu

PLACEMENT

Services include career counseling/planning, career fairs, resume referral to employers, and resume preparation.

Employment Of 1996–97 graduates, 100% were employed within three months of graduation. Types of employment entered: accounting, banking, chemical industry, consulting, health services, insurance, international trade, law, management, real estate, telecommunications, transportation.

Business Program(s) URL: http://acme.highpoint.edu/academic/grad/index. html

Program Contact: Dr. Alberta Herron, Dean of Graduate Studies, University Station, Montlieu Avenue, High Point, NC 27262-3598. Phone: 336-841-9198, 800-345-6993; Fax: 336-841-4599; E-mail: aherrone@acme.highpoint. edu

Lenoir-Rhyne College

Department of Business

Hickory, North Carolina

OVERVIEW
Lenoir-Rhyne College is an independent-religious, comprehensive institution. Enrollment: 15,000 graduate, professional, and undergraduate students.

HIGHLIGHTS

Enrollment Profile
Full-time: 0
Part-time: 39
Total: 39
Average Age: N/R
Fall 1997 Average GPA: 3.13

International: 3%
Women: 41%
Minorities: 5%
Average Class Size: N/R
Fall 1997 Average GMAT: 517

Costs
Full-time tuition: N/R
Part-time tuition: $210 per semester hour

GRADUATE BUSINESS PROGRAMS
Master of Business Administration (MBA) Part-time; 36 total credits required.

ADMISSION
Application Requirements GMAT score, application form, bachelor's degree, essay, minimum GPA: 2.7, 3 letters of recommendation, personal statement, college transcript(s).

Application Deadline Applications processed on a rolling/continuous basis for both domestic and international students.

ACADEMICS
Teaching Methodologies Case study, computer-aided instruction, computer simulations, experiential learning, group discussion, lecture, role playing, simulations, student presentations, team projects.

FINANCES
Costs for 1997–98 Tuition: Part-time: $210 per semester hour.

Financial Aid Contact Dan Klock, Director of Financial Aid, Hickory, NC 28601. Phone: 828-328-7041.

INTERNATIONAL STUDENTS
Demographics 3% of students enrolled are international students.

Services and Facilities International student office, international student housing, visa services, ESL courses, counseling/support services.

PLACEMENT
Services include career counseling/planning.

Program Contact: Graduate Office, PO Box 7420, Hickory, NC 28601. Phone: 828-328-7275.

Meredith College

John W. Weems Graduate School

Raleigh, North Carolina

OVERVIEW
Meredith College is an independent-religious, women only, comprehensive institution. Enrollment: 2,574 graduate, professional, and undergraduate students; 104 full-time matriculated graduate/professional students; 103 part-time matriculated graduate/professional students. Founded: 1891. The graduate business unit is in a suburban setting and is on a semester calendar.

GRADUATE BUSINESS PROGRAMS
Master of Business Administration (MBA)

ACADEMICS
Faculty Full-time 3; part-time 3.

Teaching Methodologies Case study, computer-aided instruction, computer simulations, experiential learning, faculty seminars, field projects, group discussion, lecture, research, role playing, seminars by members of the business community, simulations, student presentations, study groups, team projects.

Technology 100 on-campus computer terminals/PCs are available for student use and are linked by a campus-wide network. The network has full access to the Internet. Students are not required to have their own PC.

Special Opportunities Advanced credit may be earned through transfer of credits from another institution.

FACILITIES
Information Resources Carlyle Campbell Library plus 1 additional on-campus library; total holdings of 138,720 volumes, 36,687 microforms, 771 current periodical subscriptions. CD player(s) available for graduate student use. Access provided to online bibliographic retrieval services.

Program Contact: Administrative Assistant, 3800 Hillsborough Street, Raleigh, NC 27607-5298. Phone: 919-829-8423; Fax: 919-829-2898; E-mail: snodgrassc@meredith.edu

Montreat College

Business Division

Montreat, North Carolina

OVERVIEW
Montreat College is an independent-religious, comprehensive institution. Enrollment: 1,000 graduate, professional, and undergraduate students; 61 full-time matriculated graduate/professional students; part-time matriculated graduate/ professional students. Founded: 1916.

HIGHLIGHTS

Enrollment Profile
Full-time: 61
Part-time: 0
Total: 61
Average Age: N/R
Fall 1997 Average GPA: N/R

International: N/R
Women: N/R
Minorities: N/R
Average Class Size: N/R
Fall 1997 Average GMAT: N/R

Costs
Full-time tuition: $14,000 per academic year
Part-time tuition: $225 per credit

GRADUATE BUSINESS PROGRAMS
Master of Business Administration (MBA) Full-time; 48 total credits required; minimum of 2 years to complete program.

ADMISSION
Application Requirements GMAT score, application form, bachelor's degree, minimum GPA, 3 letters of recommendation, personal statement, resume, college transcript(s), minimum of 2 years of work experience.

Recommended for Application Computer experience.

Application Deadline Applications processed on a rolling/continuous basis for domestic students only.

ACADEMICS
Teaching Methodologies Case study, computer-aided instruction, computer analysis, computer simulations, experiential learning, faculty seminars, field projects, group discussion, lecture, research, role playing, simulations, student presentations, study groups, team projects.

FINANCES
Costs for 1997–98 Tuition: Full-time: $14,000 per year. Part-time: $225 per credit.

Financial Aid Contact Ms. Lisa Lankford, Director of Admissions and Financial Aid, PO Box 1267, Montreat, NC 28757-1267. Phone: 828-669-8012.

INTERNATIONAL STUDENTS
Demographics N/R

Program Contact: Joe Sharp, Director of Marketing, PO Box 1267, Montreat, NC 28757-1267. Phone: 704-669-8012 Ext. 3653, 800-436-2777 (NC only)

North Carolina Central University

School of Business

Durham, North Carolina

OVERVIEW
North Carolina Central University is a state-supported, coed, comprehensive institution. Enrollment: 5,635 graduate, professional, and undergraduate students. Founded: 1910. The graduate business unit is in an urban setting and is on a semester calendar.

North Carolina Central University (continued)

HIGHLIGHTS

Enrollment Profile
Full-time: N/R   International: N/R
Part-time: N/R   Women: N/R
Total: 75   Minorities: N/R
Average Age: 32   Average Class Size: 15
Fall 1997 Average GPA: N/R   Fall 1997 Average GMAT: N/R

Costs
Full-time tuition: $1754 per academic year (resident); $8908 per academic year (nonresident)
Part-time tuition: $430 per 3 semester hours (resident); $2218 per 3 semester hours (nonresident)

ACBSP – The American Council of Business Schools and Programs accredited

GRADUATE BUSINESS PROGRAMS

Master of Business Administration (MBA) Full-time, part-time; 54 total credits required; 2 to 6 years to complete program. Concentrations in accounting, finance, marketing.

ADMISSION

Application Requirements GMAT score, application form, application fee, bachelor's degree, minimum GPA, 2 letters of recommendation, college transcript(s).

Recommended for Application Interview.

Application Deadline Applications processed on a rolling/continuous basis for both domestic and international students. Application fee: $30.

ACADEMICS

Faculty Full-time 36; part-time 5.

Teaching Methodologies Case study, lecture, research, seminars by members of the business community, student presentations, team projects.

FINANCES

Costs for 1997–98 Tuition: Full-time: $1754 per year (resident); $8908 per year (nonresident). Part-time: $430 per 3 semester hours (resident); $2218 per 3 semester hours (nonresident).

Financial Aid Teaching assistantships, work study, loans available. Financial aid is available to part-time students.

Financial Aid Contact Assistant Vice-Chancellor for Scholarships and Student Aid, 1801 Fayetteville Street, Durham, NC 27707-3129. Phone: 919-560-6202.

FACILITIES

Information Resources James E. Shepard Memorial Library plus 3 additional on-campus libraries; total holdings of 614,958 volumes, 860,618 microforms, 4,483 current periodical subscriptions. CD player(s) available for graduate student use. Access provided to online bibliographic retrieval services.

INTERNATIONAL STUDENTS
Demographics N/R

PLACEMENT

Employment Types of employment entered: accounting, banking, computer-related, consulting, education, finance, financial services, government, human resources, information systems/technology, insurance, international trade, management, marketing, nonprofit, real estate, retail, service industry, telecommunications, transportation, utilities.

Business Program(s) URL: http://www.nccu.edu

Program Contact: Associate Dean of Graduate Programs, 1801 Fayetteville Street, Durham, NC 27707-3129. Phone: 919-560-6405.

North Carolina State University

College of Management

Raleigh, North Carolina

OVERVIEW

North Carolina State University is a state-supported, coed university. Enrollment: 27,557 graduate, professional, and undergraduate students; 3,359 full-time matriculated graduate/professional students; 1,791 part-time matriculated graduate/professional students. Founded: 1887. The graduate business unit is in an urban setting and is on a semester calendar.

HIGHLIGHTS

Enrollment Profile
Full-time: 218   International: N/R
Part-time: 192   Women: 37%
Total: 410   Minorities: N/R
Average Age: 30   Average Class Size: 35
Fall 1997 Average GPA: 3.14 Fall 1997 Average GMAT: 594

Costs
Full-time tuition: $2276 per academic year (resident); $11,262 per academic year (nonresident)
Part-time tuition: $819 per semester (resident); $4188 per semester (nonresident)

GRADUATE BUSINESS PROGRAMS

Master of Science in Management (MS) Full-time, part-time; 45 total credits required; 16 months to 6 years to complete program. Concentrations in financial management/planning, management information systems, operations management, technology management.

Master of Accounting (MAcc) Full-time; 30 total credits required; 12 months to 6 years to complete program. Concentration in accounting.

Master of Science in Agricultural Economics (MS) Full-time, part-time; 30 total credits required; 12 months to 6 years to complete program. Concentration in agricultural economics.

Master of Arts in Economics (MA) Full-time, part-time; 30 total credits required; 12 months to 6 years to complete program. Concentration in economics.

PhD in Economics (PhD) Full-time, part-time; up to 6 years to complete program. Concentration in economics.

Master of Economics (MEcon) Full-time, part-time; 30 total credits required; 12 months to 6 years to complete program. Concentration in economics.

ADMISSION

Applications For fall 1997 there were 351 applications for admission.

Application Requirements GMAT score, application form, application fee, bachelor's degree, minimum GPA, 3 letters of recommendation, personal statement, resume, college transcript(s).

Recommended for Application Work experience, computer experience: word processing, spreadsheet, database.

Application Deadline 5/1 for fall, 10/1 for spring, 4/1 for fall (international), 8/15 for spring (international). Application fee: $55. Deferred entrance is available.

ACADEMICS

Faculty Full-time 95; part-time 15.

Teaching Methodologies Case study, computer-aided instruction, computer analysis, computer simulations, field projects, group discussion, lecture, research, simulations, student presentations, team projects.

Technology 100 on-campus computer terminals/PCs are available for student use and are linked by a campus-wide network. The network has full access to the Internet. Students are not required to have their own PC.

Special Opportunities International exchange programs in France, Spain.

FINANCES

Costs for 1997–98 Tuition: Full-time: $2276 per year (resident); $11,262 per year (nonresident). Part-time: $819 per semester (resident); $4188 per semester (nonresident). Cost varies by class time (e.g., day/evening), number of credits taken. Average 1997–98 room and board costs were $8775 per academic year. Room and board costs vary by occupancy (e.g., single, double, triple), type of accommodation, type of meal plan.

Financial Aid Fellowships, research assistantships, teaching assistantships available. Application Deadline: 5/1.

Financial Aid Contact Ms. Julia Rice Mallette, Director, Financial Aid, Box 7302, Raleigh, NC 27695. Phone: 919-515-2334; Fax: 919-515-8422; E-mail: julie_rice@ncsu.edu

FACILITIES

Information Resources D. H. Hill Library plus 5 additional on-campus libraries; total holdings of 2,398,533 volumes, 3,992,559 microforms, 18,526 current periodical subscriptions. CD player(s) available for graduate student use. Access provided to online bibliographic retrieval services.

INTERNATIONAL STUDENTS
Demographics N/R

Services and Facilities International student office, international student center, international student housing, visa services, ESL courses, counseling/support services.

Applying TOEFL: minimum score of 550, proof of adequate funds, proof of health/immunizations required. Financial aid is available to international students.

International Student Contact Mr. Michael Bustle, Director, International Student Office, Box 7306, Raleigh, NC 27695. Phone: 919-515-2961; Fax: 919-515-1402; E-mail: michael_bustle@ncsu.edu

PLACEMENT

Services include career fairs, career library, career placement, electronic job bank, job interviews arranged, and resume referral to employers. In 1996–97, 95 organizations participated in on-campus recruiting.

Employment Of 1996–97 graduates, 95% were employed within three months of graduation; the average starting salary was $54,000. Types of employment entered: accounting, banking, computer-related, consulting, consumer products, engineering, finance, financial services, government, health services, high technology, information systems/technology, management, manufacturing, marketing, pharmaceutical, retail, telecommunications, utilities.

Business Program(s) URL: http://www2.ncsu.edu/ncsu/COM/home.html

Program Contact: Ms. Pamela Bostic, Assistant Director, MSM Program, Box 7229, Raleigh, NC 27695. Phone: 919-515-5584; Fax: 919-515-5073; E-mail: msm@ncsu.edu

See full description on page 902.

Pfeiffer University

Program in Business Administration

Charlotte, North Carolina

OVERVIEW

Pfeiffer University is an independent-religious, coed, comprehensive institution. Enrollment: 1,814 graduate, professional, and undergraduate students. Founded: 1885. The graduate business unit is in a rural setting and is on a semester calendar.

HIGHLIGHTS

Enrollment Profile

Full-time: N/R	International: N/R
Part-time: N/R	Women: 50%
Total: 713	Minorities: N/R
Average Age: N/R	Average Class Size: 20
Fall 1997 Average GPA: N/R	Fall 1997 Average GMAT: N/R

Costs
Full-time tuition: N/R
Part-time tuition: $245 per semester hour

GRADUATE BUSINESS PROGRAMS

Master of Business Administration (MBA) Full-time, part-time; 36 total credits required; 18 months to 5 years to complete program. Concentrations in finance, marketing, international business, entrepreneurship, management.

Master of Business Administration/Master in Health Administration (MBA/MHA) Full-time, part-time; 63 total credits required; 2.5 to 5 years to complete program.

Master of Science in Organizational Management (MSOM) Full-time, part-time; 36 total credits required; 18 months to 5 years to complete program.

ADMISSION

Application Requirements GMAT score: minimum 500, application form, application fee, bachelor's degree, minimum GPA: 3.0, interview, 3 letters of recommendation, college transcript(s).

Recommended for Application GRE score accepted, MAT score accepted, work experience, computer experience.

Application Deadline Applications processed on a rolling/continuous basis for both domestic and international students. Application fee: $50.

ACADEMICS

Faculty Full-time 5; part-time 3.

Teaching Methodologies Case study, research, student presentations, study groups, team projects.

Special Opportunities International exchange programs in France, Germany, United Kingdom.

FINANCES

Costs for 1997–98 Tuition: $245 per semester hour.

Financial Aid Financial aid is available to part-time students.

FACILITIES

Information Resources G. A. Pfeiffer Library; total holdings of 110,000 volumes, 18,000 microforms, 415 current periodical subscriptions.

INTERNATIONAL STUDENTS

Demographics N/R

Program Contact: Admissions Office, 4701 Park Road, Charlotte, NC 28209. Phone: 704-521-9116; Fax: 704-521-8617.

Queens College

McColl School of Business

Charlotte, North Carolina

OVERVIEW

Queens College is an independent-religious, coed, comprehensive institution. Enrollment: 1,652 graduate, professional, and undergraduate students; 119 full-time matriculated graduate/professional students; 260 part-time matriculated graduate/professional students. Founded: 1857. The graduate business unit is in a suburban setting and is on a trimester calendar.

HIGHLIGHTS

Enrollment Profile

Full-time: 78	International: 0%
Part-time: 205	Women: 44%
Total: 283	Minorities: 10%
Average Age: 31	Average Class Size: 30
Fall 1997 Average GPA: N/R	Fall 1997 Average GMAT: 520

Costs
Full-time tuition: $15,000 per academic year
Part-time tuition: $260 per credit hour

ACBSP – The American Council of Business Schools and Programs accredited

GRADUATE BUSINESS PROGRAMS

Master of Business Administration (MBA) Full-time, part-time; 33-45 total credits required; 2 to 5 years to complete program.

Executive MBA (MBA) Full-time; 60 total credits required; 2 years to complete program.

ADMISSION

Applications For fall 1997 there were 84 applications for admission. Of those applying, 76 were accepted. Of those accepted, 60 enrolled.

Application Requirements GMAT score: minimum 450, application form, application fee, bachelor's degree, essay, minimum GPA: 2.5, 2 letters of recommendation, personal statement, resume, college transcript(s), computer experience: computer literacy.

Application Deadline Applications processed on a rolling/continuous basis for both domestic and international students. Application fee: $25. Deferred entrance is available.

ACADEMICS

Faculty Full-time 7; part-time 4.

Teaching Methodologies Case study, computer analysis, group discussion, lecture, research, seminars by members of the business community, student presentations, study groups, team projects.

Technology 40 on-campus computer terminals/PCs are available for student use and are linked by a campus-wide network. The network has partial access to the Internet. Students are not required to have their own PC.

Special Opportunities Advanced credit may be earned through credit for business training programs, transfer of credits from another institution.

FINANCES

Costs for 1997–98 Tuition: Full-time: $15,000 per year. Part-time: $260 per credit hour. Cost varies by academic program, class time (e.g., day/evening). Fees: $20 per term. Fees vary by academic program, class time (e.g., day/evening).

Financial Aid In 1997–98, 43% of students received some institutionally administered aid in the form of fellowships, loans. Financial aid is available to part-time students.

Financial Aid Contact Mr. Tony Carter, Director of Financial Aid, 1900 Selwyn Avenue, Charlotte, NC 28274-0001. Phone: 704-337-2225; Fax: 704-337-2403.

FACILITIES

Information Resources Everett Library; total holdings of 197,000 volumes, 4,200 microforms, 622 current periodical subscriptions. CD player(s) available for graduate student use. Access provided to online bibliographic retrieval services.

INTERNATIONAL STUDENTS

Demographics 0% of students enrolled are international students.

Services and Facilities International student office.

Queens College (continued)

Applying TOEFL: minimum score of 550, proof of adequate funds, proof of health/immunizations required. Financial aid is not available to international students.

International Student Contact Katie Wineman, Director of Admissions, McColl School MBA, 1900 Selwyn Avenue, Charlotte, NC 28274-0002. Phone: 704-337-2224; Fax: 704-337- 2403.

Business Program(s) URL: http://www.queens.edu

Program Contact: Katie Wineman, Director of Admissions. McColl School MBA, McColl School MBA, 1900 Selwyn, Charlotte, NC 28274-0002. Phone: 704-337-2224; Fax: 704-337-2403.

University of North Carolina at Chapel Hill

Kenan-Flagler Business School

Chapel Hill, North Carolina

OVERVIEW
The University of North Carolina at Chapel Hill is a state-supported, coed university. Enrollment: 24,489 graduate, professional, and undergraduate students; 5,463 full-time matriculated graduate/professional students; 3,405 part-time matriculated graduate/professional students. Founded: 1789. The graduate business unit is in a small-town setting and is on a semester calendar.

HIGHLIGHTS

Enrollment Profile

Full-time: 448	International: 20%
Part-time: 0	Women: 31%
Total: 448	Minorities: 14%
Average Age: 28	Average Class Size: 35
Fall 1997 Average GPA: 3.2	Fall 1997 Average GMAT: 640

Costs
Full-time tuition: $1428 per academic year (resident); $13,145 per academic year (nonresident)
Part-time tuition: N/R

AACSB – The International Association for Management Education accredited

GRADUATE BUSINESS PROGRAMS
Master of Business Administration (MBA) Full-time; 59 total credits required; 2 years to complete program. Concentrations in management, marketing, management consulting, manufacturing management, technology management, operations management, banking, real estate, finance, entrepreneurship, human resources, international management.

Master of Business Administration/Doctor of Jurisprudence (MBA/JD) Full-time; 123 total credits required; minimum of 4 years to complete program.

Master of Business Administration/Master of Regional Planning (MBA/MRP) Full-time; 107 total credits required; minimum of 3 years to complete program.

Executive MBA (MBA) Full-time; 57 total credits required; up to 2 years to complete program.

Master of Business Administration/Master of Healthcare Administration (MBA/MHA) Full-time; 110 total credits required; minimum of 3 years to complete program.

Master of Accounting (MAcc) Full-time; 48 total credits required; 12 months to complete program.

ADMISSION
Applications For fall 1997 there were 2,025 applications for admission. Of those applying, 370 were accepted. Of those accepted, 223 enrolled.

Application Requirements Application form, application fee, bachelor's degree, essay, minimum GPA, interview, 3 letters of recommendation, personal statement, resume, college transcript(s), minimum of 2 years of work experience.

Recommended for Application GMAT score accepted, computer experience.

Application Deadline 3/6 for fall, 3/6 for fall (international). Application fee: $60. Deferred entrance is available.

ACADEMICS
Faculty Full-time 39; part-time 19.

Teaching Methodologies Case study, computer-aided instruction, computer analysis, computer simulations, experiential learning, faculty seminars, field projects, group discussion, lecture, research, role playing, seminars by members of the business community, simulations, student presentations, study groups, team projects.

Technology 3,000 on-campus computer terminals/PCs are available for student use and are linked by a campus-wide network. The network has full access to the Internet. Students are required to have their own PC.

Special Opportunities International exchange programs in Australia, Belgium, Brazil, Canada, Denmark, France, Germany, Italy, Netherlands, Norway, Philippines, Spain, Sweden, Switzerland, Thailand, United Kingdom, Venezuela.

FINANCES
Costs for 1997–98 Tuition: Full-time: $1428 per year (resident); $13,145 per year (nonresident). Cost varies by academic program, campus location, class time (e.g., day/evening), number of credits taken. Fees: Full-time: $1937 per academic year (resident); $1937 per academic year (nonresident). Fees vary by academic program, campus location. Average 1997–98 room and board costs were $2315 per academic year (on campus) and $14,000 per academic year (off campus). Room and board costs vary by occupancy (e.g., single, double, triple), type of meal plan.

Financial Aid Fellowships, research assistantships, teaching assistantships, loans available. Financial aid is available to part-time students. Application Deadline: 3/15.

Financial Aid Contact William Cox, Financial Aid Officer, CB 2300 Vance Hall, Chapel Hill, NC 27599. Phone: 919-962-4163; Fax: 919-962-2716; E-mail: cox@unc.edu

FACILITIES
Information Resources Davis Library plus 13 additional on-campus libraries; total holdings of 4,819,186 volumes, 9,009,124 microforms, 43,886 current periodical subscriptions. CD player(s) available for graduate student use. Access provided to online bibliographic retrieval services and online databases.

INTERNATIONAL STUDENTS
Demographics 20% of students enrolled are international students [Asia, 60%, Australia/New Zealand, 1%, Central America, 2%, Europe, 10%, North America, 7%, South America, 14%, other, 7%].

Services and Facilities International student office, international student center, counseling/support services.

Applying TOEFL: minimum score of 600, proof of adequate funds, proof of health/immunizations required. Financial aid is not available to international students.

International Student Contact Lynn Wilson, Associate Director of MBA Admissions, Director, International Recruitment, CB 3490 McCall Building, Chapel Hill, NC 27599. Phone: 919-962-0558; Fax: 919-962-0898; E-mail: lwilson@unc.edu

PLACEMENT
Services include alumni network, career counseling/planning, career fairs, career library, career placement, electronic job bank, job interviews arranged, resume referral to employers, and resume preparation. In 1996–97, 142 organizations participated in on-campus recruiting; 3,311 on-campus interviews were conducted.

Employment Of 1996–97 graduates, 97% were employed within three months of graduation; the average starting salary was $70,568. Types of employment entered: accounting, banking, chemical industry, communications, computer-related, consulting, consumer products, education, energy, engineering, finance, financial services, government, human resources, information systems/technology, insurance, international trade, law, management, manufacturing, marketing, media, nonprofit, petrochemical, pharmaceutical, real estate, retail, service industry, telecommunications, transportation, utilities.

Business Program(s) URL: http://www.bschool.unc.edu/

Program Contact: Jim Danto, Executive Director of the MBA Program, CB 3490 McCall Building, Chapel Hill, NC 27599. Phone: 919-962-3236; Fax: 919-962-0898.

The University of North Carolina at Charlotte

The Belk College of Business Administration

Charlotte, North Carolina

OVERVIEW
The University of North Carolina at Charlotte is a state-supported, coed university. Enrollment: 16,370 graduate, professional, and undergraduate students; 631 full-time matriculated graduate/professional students; 1,997 part-time matriculated graduate/professional students. Founded: 1965. The graduate business unit is in a suburban setting and is on a semester calendar.

HIGHLIGHTS

Enrollment Profile
Full-time: 73
Part-time: 407
Total: 480
Average Age: 30
Fall 1997 Average GPA: 3.1

International: 10%
Women: 37%
Minorities: 11%
Average Class Size: 35
Fall 1997 Average GMAT: 540

Costs
Full-time tuition: $891 per academic year (resident); $4460 per academic year (nonresident)
Part-time tuition: $339 per course (resident); $2121 per course (nonresident)

AACSB – The International Association for Management Education accredited

---

The primary objective of the Belk College of Business Administration's M.B.A. program at the University of North Carolina at Charlotte is to develop leaders for positions in the complex organizations of the future.

The program began in 1970 and is AACSB—The International Association of Management Education accredited. Courses are scheduled in the evening to accomodate part-time students. A part-time student can complete the program in three years. Full-time students can complete the program in two years. The curriculum stresses the universal characteristics of management and their applications in a wide variety of organizations. Management problems and issues are examined from economic, technological, and behavioral perspectives. Concentrations are offered in accounting, business finance, economics, financial institutions/commercial banking, information and technology management, management, and marketing. Students who do not choose a structured concentration may propose a self-structured concentration in a significant area of interest

GRADUATE BUSINESS PROGRAMS

Master of Business Administration (MBA) Full-time, part-time; 42 total credits required; 2 to 6 years to complete program. Concentrations in accounting, economics, finance, management, marketing, information management, technology management, banking.

Master of Accounting (MAcc) Full-time, part-time; 30 total credits required; 12 months to 6 years to complete program. Concentrations in taxation, accounting.

Master of Science in Economics (MS) Full-time, part-time; 30 total credits required; 12 months to 6 years to complete program. Concentrations in economics, finance.

ADMISSION

Applications For fall 1997 there were 247 applications for admission. Of those applying, 178 were accepted. Of those accepted, 109 enrolled.

Application Requirements Application form, application fee, bachelor's degree, minimum GPA: 2.75, 3 letters of recommendation, personal statement, college transcript(s).

Recommended for Application GMAT score accepted: minimum 500, resume, work experience, computer experience.

Application Deadline Applications processed on a rolling/continuous basis for domestic students only. 5/1 for fall (international), 10/1 for spring (international), 4/1 for summer (international). Application fee: $35. Deferred entrance is available.

ACADEMICS

Faculty Full-time 62.

Teaching Methodologies Case study, computer-aided instruction, computer analysis, computer simulations, experiential learning, field projects, group discussion, lecture, research, role playing, seminars by members of the business community, simulations, student presentations, study groups, team projects.

Technology 400 on-campus computer terminals/PCs are available for student use and are linked by a campus-wide network. The network has full access to the Internet. Students are not required to have their own PC.

Special Opportunities Advanced credit may be earned through transfer of credits from another institution.

FINANCES

Costs for 1997–98 Tuition: Full-time: $891 per semester (resident); $4460 per semester (nonresident). Part-time: $339 per course (resident); $2121 per course (nonresident). Cost varies by number of credits taken. Average 1997–98 room and board costs were $4000 per academic year (on campus) and $2700 per academic year (off campus). Room and board costs vary by occupancy (e.g., single, double, triple), type of accommodation, type of meal plan.

Financial Aid In 1997–98, 21% of students received some institutionally administered aid in the form of teaching assistantships, grants, work study, loans. Financial aid is available to part-time students. Application Deadline: 4/1.

Financial Aid Contact Student Financial Aid Office, 9201 University City Boulevard, Charlotte, NC 28223. Phone: 704-547-2461; Fax: 704-547-3132.

FACILITIES

Information Resources J. Murrey Atkins Library; total holdings of 643,024 volumes, 1,250,000 microforms, 4,757 current periodical subscriptions. CD player(s) available for graduate student use. Access provided to online bibliographic retrieval services and online databases.

INTERNATIONAL STUDENTS

Demographics 10% of students enrolled are international students [Africa, 4%, Asia, 66%, Europe, 28%, North America, 2%].

Services and Facilities International student office, international student housing, visa services, ESL courses, counseling/support services.

Applying TOEFL: minimum score of 550, proof of adequate funds, proof of health/immunizations required. Financial aid is not available to international students.

International Student Contact Peggie Reid, International Admissions, Denny Building, Room 211, 9201 University City Boulevard, Charlotte, NC 28223-0001. Phone: 704-547-2694; Fax: 704-510-6340; E-mail: intnladm@email.uncc.edu

PLACEMENT

Services include alumni network, career counseling/planning, career fairs, career library, career placement, job interviews arranged, resume referral to employers, and resume preparation. In 1996–97, 75 organizations participated in on-campus recruiting; 40 on-campus interviews were conducted.

Employment Of 1996–97 graduates, 94% were employed within three months of graduation; the average starting salary was $50,000. Types of employment entered: accounting, banking, computer-related, consulting, consumer products, education, energy, engineering, finance, health services, high technology, human resources, information systems/technology, insurance, management, manufacturing, marketing, retail, service industry.

Business Program(s) URL: http://www.uncc.edu/gradmiss/

Program Contact: Dr. Virginia Geurin, Associate Dean for Graduate Studies and Research, The Belk College of Business Administration, 9201 University Boulevard, Charlotte, NC 28223-0001. Phone: 704-547-2569; Fax: 704-547-4014; E-mail: dtjoyce@email.uncc.edu

University of North Carolina at Greensboro

Joseph M. Bryan School of Business and Economics

Greensboro, North Carolina

OVERVIEW

The University of North Carolina at Greensboro is a state-supported, coed university. Enrollment: 12,500 graduate, professional, and undergraduate students; 1,311 full-time matriculated graduate/professional students; 1,223 part-time matriculated graduate/professional students. Founded: 1891. The graduate business unit is in an urban setting and is on a semester calendar.

HIGHLIGHTS

Enrollment Profile
Full-time: 43
Part-time: 230
Total: 273
Average Age: 31
Fall 1997 Average GPA: 3.1

International: 7%
Women: 36%
Minorities: 18%
Average Class Size: 30
Fall 1997 Average GMAT: 550

Costs
Full-time tuition: $1952 per academic year (resident); $10,270 per academic year (nonresident)
Part-time tuition: $976 per semester (resident); $5135 per semester (nonresident)

AACSB – The International Association for Management Education accredited

GRADUATE BUSINESS PROGRAMS

Evening MBA (MBA) Full-time, part-time; 36-48 total credits required; 2 to 5 years to complete program.

ADMISSION

Applications For fall 1997 there were 140 applications for admission. Of those applying, 70 were accepted. Of those accepted, 48 enrolled.

Application Requirements Application form, application fee, bachelor's degree, essay, 3 letters of recommendation, personal statement, resume, college transcript(s).

Peterson's Guide to MBA Programs 1999

University of North Carolina at Greensboro (continued)

Recommended for Application GMAT score accepted, minimum GPA, interview, minimum of 2 years of work experience, computer experience.

Application Deadline 7/1 for fall, 11/1 for spring, 4/1 for summer, 5/1 for fall (international), 10/1 for spring (international). Application fee: $35. Deferred entrance is available.

ACADEMICS

Faculty Full-time 61; part-time 11.

Teaching Methodologies Case study, computer-aided instruction, computer analysis, computer simulations, experiential learning, field projects, group discussion, lecture, research, simulations, student presentations, study groups, team projects.

Technology 1,200 on-campus computer terminals/PCs are available for student use and are linked by a campus-wide network. The network has full access to the Internet. Students are not required to have their own PC.

Special Opportunities Advanced credit may be earned through transfer of credits from another institution. International exchange programs in Germany, Mexico, United Kingdom.

FINANCES

Costs for 1997–98 Tuition: Full-time: $1952 per year (resident); $10,270 per year (nonresident). Part-time: $976 per semester (resident); $5135 per semester (nonresident). Cost varies by number of credits taken. Fees vary by number of credits taken. Average 1997–98 room and board costs were $4000 per academic year (on campus) and $4500 per academic year (off campus). Room and board costs vary by occupancy (e.g., single, double, triple), type of accommodation, type of meal plan.

Financial Aid Fellowships, research assistantships, teaching assistantships, work study available. Application Deadline: 3/15.

Financial Aid Contact Ms. Deborah Tollefson, Director, Financial Aid, 723 Kenilworth Street, Greensboro, NC 27412-5001. Phone: 336-334-5702; E-mail: tdnagy@friday.uncg.edu

FACILITIES

Information Resources Walter Clinton Jackson Library plus 1 additional on-campus library; total holdings of 850,520 volumes, 810,100 microforms, 5,500 current periodical subscriptions. Access provided to online bibliographic retrieval services.

INTERNATIONAL STUDENTS

Demographics 7% of students enrolled are international students [Africa, 6%, Asia, 37%, Central America, 12%, Europe, 32%, South America, 13%].

Services and Facilities International student office, international student housing, visa services, ESL courses, counseling/support services, international festival.

Applying TOEFL: minimum score of 550, proof of adequate funds, proof of health/immunizations required. Financial aid is not available to international students.

International Student Contact Ms. Martha Trigonis, 55 Elliott University Center, 1000 Spring Garden Street, Greensboro, NC 27412-5001. E-mail: mftrigon@uncg.edu

PLACEMENT

Services include alumni network, career counseling/planning, career fairs, career placement, job interviews arranged, resume referral to employers, and resume preparation. In 1996–97, 110 organizations participated in on-campus recruiting.

Employment Of 1996–97 graduates, 100% were employed within three months of graduation. Types of employment entered: accounting, banking, computer-related, consulting, education, engineering, finance, hospitality management, human resources, management, manufacturing, marketing, service industry, telecommunications.

Business Program(s) URL: http://www.uncg.edu/bae/badm/

Program Contact: Dr. Catherine Holderness, Associate Director for MBA Student Services, Bryan Building, Room 220, 1000 Spring Garden Street, Greensboro, NC 27412-5001. Phone: 336-334-5390; Fax: 336-334-4209; E-mail: c-holder@uncg.edu

See full description on page 1116.

The University of North Carolina at Pembroke

Graduate Studies

Pembroke, North Carolina

OVERVIEW

The University of North Carolina at Pembroke is a state-supported, coed, comprehensive institution. Enrollment: 3,017 graduate, professional, and undergraduate students; 12 full-time matriculated graduate/professional students; 304 part-time matriculated graduate/professional students. Founded: 1887. The graduate business unit is in a rural setting and is on a semester calendar.

HIGHLIGHTS

Enrollment Profile

Full-time: 8	International: 0%
Part-time: 65	Women: 64%
Total: 73	Minorities: 30%
Average Age: 32	Average Class Size: 15
Fall 1997 Average GPA: N/R	Fall 1997 Average GMAT: N/R

Costs
Full-time tuition: $1748 per academic year (resident); $6022 per academic year (nonresident)
Part-time tuition: $219 per 3 hours (resident); $1004 per 3 hours (nonresident)

GRADUATE BUSINESS PROGRAMS

Master of Business Administration (MBA) Full-time, part-time; 36 total credits required; 12 months to 5 years to complete program.

Master of Science in Organizational Leadership Management (MS) Full-time, part-time; 39 total credits required; 2 to 5 years to complete program. Concentrations in public management, public and private management.

ADMISSION

Application Requirements Application form, application fee, bachelor's degree, minimum GPA: 2.5, 3 letters of recommendation, college transcript(s).

Recommended for Application GMAT score accepted, computer experience.

Application Deadline Applications processed on a rolling/continuous basis for domestic students only. 3/1 for fall (international), 9/1 for spring (international). Application fee: $25. Deferred entrance is available.

ACADEMICS

Faculty Full-time 13; part-time 2.

Teaching Methodologies Case study, computer-aided instruction, computer analysis, computer simulations, experiential learning, faculty seminars, field projects, group discussion, lecture, research, role playing, seminars by members of the business community, simulations, student presentations, study groups, team projects.

Technology 250 on-campus computer terminals/PCs are available for student use and are linked by a campus-wide network. The network has full access to the Internet. Students are not required to have their own PC.

Special Opportunities Advanced credit may be earned through credit for military training programs, transfer of credits from another institution. An internship program is available.

FINANCES

Costs for 1997–98 Tuition: Full-time: $1748 per year (resident); $6022 per year (nonresident). Part-time: $219 per 3 hours (resident); $1004 per 3 hours (nonresident). Cost varies by number of credits taken. Fees: Full-time: $508 per academic year (resident); $508 per academic year (nonresident). Part-time: $68 per 3 hours (resident); $68 per 3 hours (nonresident). Fees vary by number of credits taken. Average 1997–98 room and board costs were $3546 per academic year. Room and board costs vary by occupancy (e.g., single, double, triple), type of meal plan.

Financial Aid Research assistantships, loans available. Financial aid is available to part-time students. Application Deadline: 4/15.

Financial Aid Contact Ms. Teresa De Carlo, Director of Financial Aid, 1 University Drive, Pembroke, NC 28372-1510. Phone: 910-521-6000; Fax: 910-521-6497.

FACILITIES

Information Resources Sampson-Livermore Library; total holdings of 194,989 volumes, 143,462 microforms, 1,434 current periodical subscriptions. CD player(s) available for graduate student use. Access provided to online bibliographic retrieval services.

INTERNATIONAL STUDENTS

Demographics N/R

Services and Facilities Counseling/support services.

Applying TOEFL, proof of adequate funds required. Financial aid is not available to international students.

PLACEMENT

Services include career counseling/planning, career fairs, career library, electronic job bank, and job interviews arranged.

Business Program(s) URL: http://www.uncp.edu

Program Contact: Dr. William Gash, Interim Dean of Graduate Studies, 1 University Drive, Pembroke, NC 28372-1510. Phone: 910-521-6271, 800-949-8627 (NC only); Fax: 910-521-6497.

University of North Carolina at Wilmington

Cameron School of Business

Wilmington, North Carolina

OVERVIEW
The University of North Carolina at Wilmington is a state-supported, coed, comprehensive institution. Enrollment: 9,300 graduate, professional, and undergraduate students. Founded: 1947. The graduate business unit is in an urban setting and is on a semester calendar.

HIGHLIGHTS

Enrollment Profile

Full-time: 0	International: 3%
Part-time: 120	Women: 39%
Total: 120	Minorities: 3%
Average Age: 32	Average Class Size: 60
Fall 1997 Average GPA: 3.2	Fall 1997 Average GMAT: 545

Costs
Full-time tuition: N/R
Part-time tuition: $561 per semester (resident); $3244 per semester (nonresident)

AACSB – The International Association for Management Education accredited

GRADUATE BUSINESS PROGRAMS
Master of Business Administration (MBA) Part-time; 48 total credits required; 1 year full-time work experience required; 2 years to complete program. Concentrations in finance, manufacturing management, entrepreneurship, management information systems, marketing, organizational behavior/development.

ADMISSION
Applications For fall 1997 there were 147 applications for admission. Of those applying, 65 were accepted. Of those accepted, 60 enrolled.

Application Requirements Application form, application fee, bachelor's degree, minimum GPA: 3.0, 3 letters of recommendation, college transcript(s), minimum of 1 year of work experience, computer experience: word processing, database, spreadsheet.

Recommended for Application GMAT score accepted, resume.

Application Deadline 3/15 for summer, 3/15 for summer (international). Application fee: $35. Deferred entrance is available.

ACADEMICS
Faculty Full-time 11.

Teaching Methodologies Case study, computer-aided instruction, computer analysis, experiential learning, faculty seminars, field projects, group discussion, lecture, research, role playing, seminars by members of the business community, simulations, student presentations, study groups, team projects.

Technology 200 on-campus computer terminals/PCs are available for student use and are linked by a campus-wide network. The network has full access to the Internet. Students are not required to have their own PC.

Special Opportunities Advanced credit may be earned through transfer of credits from another institution.

FINANCES
Costs for 1997–98 Tuition: Part-time: $561 per semester (resident); $3244 per semester (nonresident). Cost varies by academic program, number of credits taken.

Financial Aid Teaching assistantships, work study available. Financial aid is available to part-time students. Application Deadline: 3/15.

Financial Aid Contact Financial Aid, James Hall, Wilmington, NC 28403. Phone: 910-962-3177.

FACILITIES
Information Resources Randall Library; total holdings of 389,611 volumes, 837,013 microforms, 4,998 current periodical subscriptions. Access provided to online bibliographic retrieval services and online databases.

INTERNATIONAL STUDENTS
Demographics 3% of students enrolled are international students.

Services and Facilities International student office, international student center, ESL courses, counseling/support services.

Applying TOEFL: minimum score of 500, proof of adequate funds, proof of health/immunizations required. Financial aid is available to international students.

International Student Contact Dr. Gary Faulkner, Director, International Programs, University Union, Room 103, 600 South College Drive, Wilmington, NC 28403.

PLACEMENT
Services include alumni network, career counseling/planning, electronic job bank, and resume referral to employers.

Employment Of 1996–97 graduates, 100% were employed within three months of graduation. Types of employment entered: accounting, banking, chemical industry, communications, computer-related, consulting, consumer products, education, energy, finance, financial services, government, health services, high technology, hospitality management, human resources, information systems/technology, insurance, international trade, management, manufacturing, marketing, media, nonprofit, pharmaceutical, real estate, retail, service industry, telecommunications, transportation, utilities.

Business Program(s) URL: http://www.csb.uncwil.edu

Program Contact: Dr. Drew Rosen, MBA Director, 601 South College Road, Wilmington, NC 28403. Phone: 910-962-3677; Fax: 910-962-3815; E-mail: rosenl@uncwil.edu

Wake Forest University

Babcock Graduate School of Management

Winston-Salem, North Carolina

OVERVIEW
Wake Forest University is an independent-nonprofit, coed university. Enrollment: 6,015 graduate, professional, and undergraduate students; 1,835 full-time matriculated graduate/professional students; 407 part-time matriculated graduate/professional students. Founded: 1834. The graduate business unit is in a suburban setting and is on a semester calendar.

HIGHLIGHTS

Enrollment Profile

Full-time: 242	International: 7%
Part-time: 425	Women: 24%
Total: 672	Minorities: 16%
Average Age: 26	Average Class Size: 18
Fall 1997 Average GPA: 3.2	Fall 1997 Average GMAT: 615

Costs
Full-time tuition: $19,200 per academic year
Part-time tuition: $1980 per course

AACSB – The International Association for Management Education accredited

GRADUATE BUSINESS PROGRAMS
Executive MBA (MBA) Part-time; 51 total credits required; 22 months to complete program. Concentrations in finance, marketing, operations management, organizational behavior/development.

Evening MBA (MBA) Part-time; 51 total credits required; 22 months to 5 years to complete program. Concentrations in finance, marketing, operations management, organizational behavior/development.

Evening MBA-Charlotte (MBA) Part-time; 54 total credits required; 2 years to complete program. Concentrations in finance, marketing, operations management, organizational behavior/development.

Doctor of Medicine/Master of Business Administration (MD/MBA) Full-time; 192 total credits required; 5 years to complete program. Concentrations in finance, marketing, operations management, organizational behavior/development.

Doctor of Jurisprudence/Master of Business Administration (JD/MBA) Full-time; 125 total credits required; 3.7 years to complete program. Concentrations in finance, marketing, operations management, organizational behavior/development.

Full-time MBA (MBA) Full-time; 66 total credits required; 22 months to complete program. Concentrations in finance, marketing, operations management, entrepreneurship, management consulting.

ADMISSION
Applications For fall 1997 there were 792 applications for admission. Of those applying, 451 were accepted. Of those accepted, 255 enrolled.

Application Requirements GMAT score, application form, application fee, bachelor's degree, essay, minimum GPA, 2 letters of recommendation, resume, college transcript(s).

Recommended for Application Interview, work experience, computer experience.

Application Deadline Applications processed on a rolling/continuous basis for both domestic and international students. Application fee: $50. Deferred entrance is available.

ACADEMICS
Faculty Full-time 33; part-time 14.

Wake Forest University (continued)

Teaching Methodologies Case study, computer-aided instruction, computer analysis, computer simulations, experiential learning, faculty seminars, field projects, group discussion, lecture, research, role playing, seminars by members of the business community, simulations, student presentations, study groups, team projects.

Technology 32 on-campus computer terminals/PCs are available for student use and are linked by a campus-wide network. The network has full access to the Internet. Students are required to have their own PC.

Special Opportunities International exchange programs in China, France, Germany, Japan, United Kingdom. An internship program is available.

FINANCES
Costs for 1997–98 Tuition: Full-time: $19,200 per year. Part-time: $1980 per course. Fees: Full-time: $100 per academic year. Average 1997–98 room and board costs were $5600 per academic year (off campus).

Financial Aid In 1997–98, 19% of students received some institutionally administered aid in the form of research assistantships, scholarships, loans. Financial aid is available to part-time students. Application Deadline: 3/1.

Financial Aid Contact Ms. Donna Agee, Assistant Director, Admissions and Financial Aid, Reynolda Station, PO Box 7659, Winston-Salem, NC 27109-7659. Phone: 336-758-4424; Fax: 336-758-5830; E-mail: donna-agee@mail.mba.wfu.edu

FACILITIES
Information Resources Z. Smith Reynolds Library plus 3 additional on-campus libraries; total holdings of 1,488,457 volumes, 1,470,932 microforms, 25,975 current periodical subscriptions. CD player(s) available for graduate student use. Access provided to online bibliographic retrieval services and online databases.

INTERNATIONAL STUDENTS
Demographics 7% of students enrolled are international students [Africa, 1%, Asia, 5%, Central America, 1%, Europe, 2%, North America, 90%, South America, 1%].

Services and Facilities International student housing, visa services, counseling/support services, international orientation.

Applying TOEFL: minimum score of 600, proof of adequate funds, proof of health/immunizations required. Financial aid is available to international students.

International Student Contact Ms. Donna Agee, Assistant Director, Admissions and Financial Aid, Reynolda Station, PO Box 7659, Winston-Salem, NC 27109-7659. Phone: 336-758-4424; Fax: 336-758-5830; E-mail: donna_agee@mail.mba.wfu.edu

PLACEMENT
Services include alumni network, career counseling/planning, career fairs, career library, career placement, electronic job bank, job interviews arranged, job search course, resume referral to employers, and resume preparation. In 1996–97, 85 organizations participated in on-campus recruiting; 1,185 on-campus interviews were conducted.

Employment Of 1996–97 graduates, 97% were employed within three months of graduation; the average starting salary was $59,000. Types of employment entered: accounting, banking, communications, computer-related, consulting, consumer products, finance, financial services, health services, insurance, law, management, manufacturing, marketing, service industry, telecommunications, transportation, utilities.

Business Program(s) URL: http://www.mba.wfu.edu

Program Contact: Ms. Dian Smith, Staff Assistant, Reynolda Station, PO Box 7659, Winston-Salem, NC 27109-7659. Phone: 336-758-5422, 800-772-1622 (NC only); Fax: 336-758-5830; E-mail: admissions@mail.mba.wfu.edu
See full description on page 1180.

Western Carolina University

College of Business

Cullowhee, North Carolina

OVERVIEW
Western Carolina University is a state-supported, coed, comprehensive institution. Enrollment: 6,700 graduate, professional, and undergraduate students; 381 full-time matriculated graduate/professional students; 423 part-time matriculated graduate/professional students. Founded: 1889. The graduate business unit is in a rural setting and is on a semester calendar.

HIGHLIGHTS

Enrollment Profile
Full-time: 82
Part-time: 92
Total: 174
Average Age: 28
Fall 1997 Average GPA: 3.25

International: 29%
Women: 42%
Minorities: 5%
Average Class Size: 20
Fall 1997 Average GMAT: 500

Costs
Full-time tuition: $918 per academic year (resident); $8188 per academic year (nonresident)
Part-time tuition: $230 per 3 semester hours (resident); $2047 per 3 semester hours (nonresident)

AACSB – The International Association for Management Education accredited

GRADUATE BUSINESS PROGRAMS
Master of Business Administration (MBA) Full-time, part-time; 60 total credits required; 16 months to 4 years to complete program.

Master of Project Management (MPM) Full-time, part-time, distance learning option; 60 total credits required; 16 months to 3 years to complete program. Concentration in project management.

Master of Accountancy (MAcc) Full-time, part-time; 51 total credits required; 12 months to 3 years to complete program. Concentration in accounting.

ADMISSION
Applications For fall 1997 there were 129 applications for admission. Of those applying, 117 were accepted. Of those accepted, 82 enrolled.

Application Requirements GMAT score, application form, application fee, bachelor's degree, minimum GPA: 2.75, college transcript(s).

Recommended for Application Computer experience.

Application Deadline Applications processed on a rolling/continuous basis for both domestic and international students. Application fee: $35. Deferred entrance is available.

ACADEMICS
Faculty Full-time 38.

Teaching Methodologies Case study, computer analysis, computer simulations, experiential learning, group discussion, lecture, research, role playing, seminars by members of the business community, simulations, student presentations, team projects.

Technology 300 on-campus computer terminals/PCs are available for student use and are linked by a campus-wide network. The network has full access to the Internet. Students are not required to have their own PC.

Special Opportunities Advanced credit may be earned through transfer of credits from another institution. International exchange programs in France, Netherlands, United Kingdom. An internship program is available.

FINANCES
Costs for 1997–98 Tuition: Full-time: $918 per year (resident); $8188 per year (nonresident). Part-time: $230 per 3 semester hours (resident); $2047 per 3 semester hours (nonresident). Cost varies by class time (e.g., day/evening), number of credits taken. Fees: Full-time: $881 per academic year (resident); $881 per academic year (nonresident). Part-time: $86 per 3 semester hours (resident); $86 per 3 semester hours (nonresident). Fees vary by class time (e.g., day/evening), number of credits taken. Average 1997–98 room and board costs were $5000 per academic year (on campus) and $5500 per academic year (off campus). Room and board costs vary by occupancy (e.g., single, double, triple), type of accommodation, type of meal plan.

Financial Aid In 1997–98, 40% of students received some institutionally administered aid in the form of fellowships, research assistantships, teaching assistantships, grants, scholarships, work study, loans. Financial aid is available to part-time students. Application Deadline: 3/31.

Financial Aid Contact Mr. Thomas Grant, Director, Student Financial Aid, Cullowhee, NC 28723. Phone: 704-227-7290; Fax: 704-227-7042.

FACILITIES
Information Resources Hunter Library; total holdings of 500,000 volumes, 1,301,316 microforms, 3,000 current periodical subscriptions. CD player(s) available for graduate student use. Access provided to online bibliographic retrieval services and online databases.

INTERNATIONAL STUDENTS
Demographics 29% of students enrolled are international students [Africa, 2%, Asia, 20%, Europe, 72%, South America, 2%, other, 4%].

Services and Facilities International student office, international student housing, visa services, counseling/support services.

Applying TOEFL: minimum score of 550, proof of adequate funds, proof of health/immunizations required. Financial aid is available to international students.

International Student Contact Mr. Richard Cameron, International Student Advisor, Cullowhee, NC 28723. Phone: 704-227-7234; Fax: 704-227-7036; E-mail: cameron@wcu.edu

PLACEMENT
Services include alumni network, career counseling/planning, career fairs, career library, career placement, electronic job bank, job interviews arranged, job search course, resume referral to employers, and resume preparation.

Employment Of 1996–97 graduates, 90% were employed within three months of graduation. Types of employment entered: accounting, banking, computer-related, finance, financial services, information systems/technology, insurance, management, manufacturing, marketing, retail, service industry, utilities.

Business Program(s) URL: http://www.wcu.edu/cob/index.html

Program Contact: Ms. Faye Deitz, Student Services Assistant, Graduate Programs in Business, Cullowhee, NC 28723. Phone: 704-227-7401; Fax: 704-227-7414; E-mail: fdeitz@wcu.edu

Wingate University

School of Business
Wingate, North Carolina

OVERVIEW
Wingate University is an independent-religious, coed, comprehensive institution. Enrollment: 1,462 graduate, professional, and undergraduate students; full-time matriculated graduate/professional students; 110 part-time matriculated graduate/professional students. Founded: 1896. The graduate business unit is in a suburban setting and is on a semester calendar.

HIGHLIGHTS
Enrollment Profile
Full-time: 0
Part-time: 75
Total: 75
Average Age: 29
Fall 1997 Average GPA: 3.0

International: 3%
Women: 40%
Minorities: 11%
Average Class Size: 19
Fall 1997 Average GMAT: 425

Costs
Full-time tuition: N/R
Part-time tuition: $750 per course

ACBSP – The American Council of Business Schools and Programs accredited

GRADUATE BUSINESS PROGRAMS
Master of Business Administration (MBA) Part-time; 33 total credits required; 2 to 6 years to complete program. Concentration in management.

ADMISSION
Applications For fall 1997 there were 25 applications for admission. Of those applying, 20 were accepted. Of those accepted, 20 enrolled.

Application Requirements Application form, application fee, bachelor's degree, minimum GPA, 2 letters of recommendation, personal statement, college transcript(s), minimum of 1 year of work experience, computer experience: Lotus, word processing.

Recommended for Application GMAT score accepted.

Application Deadline Applications processed on a rolling/continuous basis for both domestic and international students. Application fee: $25, $50 (international). Deferred entrance is available.

ACADEMICS
Faculty Full-time 8; part-time 1.

Teaching Methodologies Case study, computer-aided instruction, field projects, group discussion, lecture, role playing, student presentations, study groups, team projects.

Technology 50 on-campus computer terminals/PCs are available for student use and are linked by a campus-wide network. The network has full access to the Internet. Students are not required to have their own PC.

Special Opportunities Advanced credit may be earned through transfer of credits from another institution.

FINANCES
Costs for 1997–98 Tuition: Part-time: $750 per course.
Financial Aid In 1997–98, 4% of students received some institutionally administered aid in the form of work study. Financial aid is available to part-time students. Application Deadline: 8/1.
Financial Aid Contact Mrs. Betty Whalen, Director, Financial Planning, Wingate, NC 28174. Phone: 704-233-8000; Fax: 704-233-8146.

FACILITIES
Information Resources Ethel K. Smith Library; total holdings of 110,000 volumes, 300,000 microforms, 600 current periodical subscriptions. CD player(s) available for graduate student use. Access provided to online bibliographic retrieval services and online databases.

INTERNATIONAL STUDENTS
Demographics 3% of students enrolled are international students [Asia, 100%].
Applying TOEFL: minimum score of 550, proof of adequate funds, proof of health/immunizations required. Financial aid is not available to international students.

PLACEMENT
Services include career counseling/planning, career fairs, and career placement.
Employment Of 1996–97 graduates, 100% were employed within three months of graduation.

Business Program(s) URL: http://www.wingate.edu

Program Contact: Mrs. Kathryn Rowe, MBA Coordinator, Campus Box 3000, Wingate, NC 28174. Phone: 704-233-8148; Fax: 704-233-8146; E-mail: karowe@wingate.edu

NORTH DAKOTA

Minot State University

College of Business
Minot, North Dakota

OVERVIEW
Minot State University is a state-supported, coed, comprehensive institution. Enrollment: 3,294 graduate, professional, and undergraduate students; 48 full-time matriculated graduate/professional students; 126 part-time matriculated graduate/professional students. Founded: 1913. The graduate business unit is in a small-town setting and is on a semester calendar.

HIGHLIGHTS
Enrollment Profile
Full-time: 5
Part-time: 35
Total: 40
Average Age: 28
Fall 1997 Average GPA: 3.65

International: 3%
Women: 65%
Minorities: N/R
Average Class Size: 14
Fall 1997 Average GMAT: 490

Costs
Full-time tuition: $1223 per academic year (resident); $3264 per academic year (nonresident)
Part-time tuition: $102 per credit (resident); $272 per credit (nonresident)

GRADUATE BUSINESS PROGRAMS
Master of Science in Management (MS) Full-time, part-time, distance learning option; 33 total credits required; 18 months to 6 years to complete program.

ADMISSION
Applications For fall 1997 there were 35 applications for admission. Of those applying, 33 were accepted. Of those accepted, 25 enrolled.

Application Requirements GMAT score, GRE score, application form, bachelor's degree, minimum GPA: 2.75, 3 letters of recommendation, college transcript(s).
Recommended for Application Work experience, computer experience.
Application Deadline Applications processed on a rolling/continuous basis for both domestic and international students. Application fee: $25.

ACADEMICS
Faculty Full-time 14.

Teaching Methodologies Case study, computer-aided instruction, computer analysis, computer simulations, field projects, group discussion, lecture, research, role playing, student presentations, study groups, team projects.

Technology 200 on-campus computer terminals/PCs are available for student use and are linked by a campus-wide network. The network has full access to the Internet. Students are not required to have their own PC.

Special Opportunities Advanced credit may be earned through transfer of credits from another institution.

FINANCES
Costs for 1997–98 Tuition: Full-time: $1223 per year (resident); $3264 per year (nonresident). Part-time: $102 per credit (resident); $272 per credit (nonresident). Cost varies by number of credits taken. Fees: Full-time: $269

Minot State University (continued)

per academic year (resident); $269 per academic year (nonresident). Part-time: $11 per credit (resident); $11 per credit (nonresident). Fees vary by number of credits taken. Average 1997–98 room and board costs were $2565 per academic year (on campus) and $3548 per academic year (off campus). Room and board costs vary by occupancy (e.g., single, double, triple), type of accommodation, type of meal plan.

Financial Aid In 1997–98, 35% of students received some institutionally administered aid in the form of research assistantships, teaching assistantships, scholarships. Financial aid is available to part-time students. Application Deadline: 2/15.

Financial Aid Contact Mr. Dale Gehring, Financial Aid Director, 500 University Avenue West, Minot, ND 58707. Phone: 701-858-3862; Fax: 701-839-6933; E-mail: gehringd@warp6.cs.misu.nodak.edu

FACILITIES
Information Resources Gordon B. Olson Library; total holdings of 360,246 volumes, 590,799 microforms, 1,024 current periodical subscriptions. CD player(s) available for graduate student use. Access provided to online bibliographic retrieval services and online databases.

INTERNATIONAL STUDENTS
Demographics 3% of students enrolled are international students.

Services and Facilities International student office, international student center.

Applying TOEFL: minimum score of 550, proof of adequate funds, proof of health/immunizations required. Financial aid is available to international students.

International Student Contact Ms. Rolaunda Walker, International Student Specialist, 500 University Avenue West, Minot, ND 58707. Phone: 701-858-3348; Fax: 701-858-3386; E-mail: walkerro@warp6.cs.misu.nodak.edu

PLACEMENT
Services include alumni network, career counseling/planning, career fairs, career placement, electronic job bank, job interviews arranged, resume referral to employers, and resume preparation.

Business Program(s) URL: http://www.misu.nodak.edu/business/

Program Contact: Ms. Tammy White, Administrative Assistant-Graduate Programs, 500 University Avenue West, Minot, ND 58707. Phone: 701-858-3250, 800-777-0750; Fax: 701-839-6933; E-mail: whitet@warp6.cs.misu.nodak.edu

North Dakota State University

College of Business Administration

Fargo, North Dakota

OVERVIEW
North Dakota State University is a state-supported, coed university. Enrollment: 9,598 graduate, professional, and undergraduate students; 556 full-time matriculated graduate/professional students; 359 part-time matriculated graduate/professional students. Founded: 1890. The graduate business unit is in a suburban setting and is on a semester calendar.

HIGHLIGHTS
Enrollment Profile
Full-time: 22
Part-time: 44
Total: 66
Average Age: 25
Fall 1997 Average GPA: 3.28

International: 11%
Women: 41%
Minorities: 2%
Average Class Size: 20
Fall 1997 Average GMAT: 535

Costs
Full-time tuition: N/R
Part-time tuition: $116 per credit (resident); $286 per credit (nonresident)

GRADUATE BUSINESS PROGRAMS
Master of Business Administration (MBA) Full-time, part-time, distance learning option; 60 total credits required; 12 months to 7 years to complete program. Concentrations in management, finance, marketing, accounting.

ADMISSION
Applications For fall 1997 there were 46 applications for admission. Of those applying, 26 were accepted. Of those accepted, 20 enrolled.

Application Requirements GMAT score: minimum 450, application form, application fee, bachelor's degree, minimum GPA: 2.8, 3 letters of recommendation, personal statement, college transcript(s).

Application Deadline Applications processed on a rolling/continuous basis for domestic students only. 4/1 for fall (international), 8/1 for spring (international). Application fee: $25. Deferred entrance is available.

ACADEMICS
Faculty Full-time 18.

Teaching Methodologies Case study, computer-aided instruction, computer analysis, experiential learning, faculty seminars, field projects, group discussion, lecture, research, student presentations, study groups, team projects.

Technology 400 on-campus computer terminals/PCs are available for student use and are linked by a campus-wide network. The network has full access to the Internet. Students are not required to have their own PC.

Special Opportunities Advanced credit may be earned through transfer of credits from another institution. International exchange programs in Australia, Mexico, Netherlands. An internship program is available.

FINANCES
Costs for 1997–98 Tuition: $116 per credit (resident); $286 per credit (nonresident). Cost varies by number of credits taken, reciprocity agreements. Fees: $13 per credit (resident); $13 per credit (nonresident). Fees vary by academic program. Average 1997–98 room and board costs were $3034 per academic year (on campus) and $3834 per academic year (off campus). Room and board costs vary by occupancy (e.g., single, double, triple), type of accommodation, type of meal plan.

Financial Aid In 1997–98, 21% of students received some institutionally administered aid in the form of research assistantships, scholarships, work study, loans. Financial aid is available to part-time students. Application Deadline: 3/15.

Financial Aid Contact Ms. Janice Glatt, Senior Lecturer, Box 5137 Putnam Hall, Fargo, ND 58105. Phone: 701-231-8651; Fax: 701-231-7508; E-mail: jglatt@badlands.nodak.edu

FACILITIES
Information Resources Main library plus 3 additional on-campus libraries; total holdings of 486,458 volumes, 242,856 microforms, 5,262 current periodical subscriptions. CD player(s) available for graduate student use. Access provided to online bibliographic retrieval services.

INTERNATIONAL STUDENTS
Demographics 11% of students enrolled are international students [Asia, 100%].

Services and Facilities International student office, ESL courses, counseling/support services.

Applying TOEFL: minimum score of 550, proof of adequate funds, proof of health/immunizations required. Financial aid is available to international students.

International Student Contact Ms. Virginia Packwood, Director of International Programs, Ceres Hall, Fargo, ND 58105. Phone: 701-231-7895; Fax: 701-231-1014.

PLACEMENT
Services include alumni network, career counseling/planning, career fairs, career library, job interviews arranged, resume referral to employers, and resume preparation.

Employment Of 1996–97 graduates, 87% were employed within three months of graduation; the average starting salary was $28,000. Types of employment entered: accounting, banking, computer-related, consulting, education, energy, engineering, finance, financial services, government, health services, hospitality management, human resources, information systems/technology, international trade, management, manufacturing, retail, utilities.

Business Program(s) URL: http://www.ndsu.nodak.edu/ndsu/bgeeslin/cba/

Program Contact: Mr. Paul Brown, MBA Program Director, Box 5137 Putnam Hall, Fargo, ND 58105. Phone: 701-231-7681, 800-488-6378 (ND only); Fax: 701-231-7508; E-mail: pabrown@plains.nodak.edu

University of Mary

Business Division

Bismarck, North Dakota

OVERVIEW
The University of Mary is an independent-religious, coed, comprehensive institution. Enrollment: 2,148 graduate, professional, and undergraduate students; 131 full-time matriculated graduate/professional students; 83 part-time matriculated graduate/professional students. Founded: 1955. The graduate business unit is in a small-town setting and is on a accelerated program of 3 5-month terms calendar.

HIGHLIGHTS

Enrollment Profile
Full-time: 86
Part-time: 45
Total: 131
Average Age: 30
Fall 1997 Average GPA: 3.3

International: 0%
Women: 52%
Minorities: N/R
Average Class Size: 13
Fall 1997 Average GMAT: N/R

Costs
Full-time tuition: N/R
Part-time tuition: $265 per credit

GRADUATE BUSINESS PROGRAMS
Master of Management (MMgt) Full-time, part-time; 30 total credits required; 15 months to 7 years to complete program. Concentrations in health care, human resources.

ADMISSION
Applications For fall 1997 there were 125 applications for admission. Of those applying, 120 were accepted. Of those accepted, 100 enrolled.

Application Requirements Application form, application fee, bachelor's degree, essay, minimum GPA: 2.5, college transcript(s).

Recommended for Application Work experience.

Application Deadline Applications processed on a rolling/continuous basis for both domestic and international students. Application fee: $15. Deferred entrance is available.

ACADEMICS
Faculty Part-time 17.

Teaching Methodologies Case study, computer-aided instruction, computer analysis, experiential learning, faculty seminars, group discussion, lecture, research, seminars by members of the business community, student presentations, study groups, team projects.

Technology 60 on-campus computer terminals/PCs are available for student use and are linked by a campus-wide network. The network has full access to the Internet. Students are not required to have their own PC.

Special Opportunities Advanced credit may be earned through credit by examination, credit for experience, credit for military training programs, credit for business training programs, transfer of credits from another institution. An internship program is available.

FINANCES
Costs for 1997–98 Tuition: $265 per credit. Cost varies by academic program. Average 1997–98 room and board costs were $3500 per academic year (on campus) and $8000 per academic year (off campus). Room and board costs vary by campus location, occupancy (e.g., single, double, triple), type of accommodation, type of meal plan.

Financial Aid In 1997–98, 23% of students received some institutionally administered aid in the form of loans.

Financial Aid Contact Mr. Jeff Jacobs, Director of Financial Aid, 7500 University Drive, Bismarck, ND 58504. Phone: 701-255-7500 Ext. 383; Fax: 701-255-7687.

FACILITIES
Information Resources Main library plus 1 additional on-campus library; total holdings of 55,000 volumes, 2,200 microforms, 500 current periodical subscriptions. CD player(s) available for graduate student use. Access provided to online bibliographic retrieval services.

INTERNATIONAL STUDENTS
Demographics N/R

Services and Facilities Counseling/support services.

Applying TOEFL: minimum score of 550, proof of adequate funds, proof of health/immunizations required. Financial aid is available to international students.

PLACEMENT
Services include career counseling/planning, career fairs, career placement, resume referral to employers, and resume preparation.

Employment Of 1996–97 graduates, 98% were employed within three months of graduation. Types of employment entered: accounting, banking, consulting, energy, health services, high technology, hospitality management, human resources, management, mining, utilities.

Program Contact: Ms. Jeanne Barth, Assistant Director of Admissions, 1500 University Drive, Bismarck, ND 58504-9652. Phone: 701-255-7500 Ext. 370; Fax: 701-255-7687.

University of North Dakota

College of Business and Public Administration
Grand Forks, North Dakota

OVERVIEW
The University of North Dakota is a state-supported, coed university. Enrollment: 11,300 graduate, professional, and undergraduate students; 789 full-time matriculated graduate/professional students; 1,160 part-time matriculated graduate/professional students. Founded: 1883. The graduate business unit is in a small-town setting and is on a semester calendar.

HIGHLIGHTS

Enrollment Profile
Full-time: 15
Part-time: 75
Total: 90
Average Age: 27
Fall 1997 Average GPA: 3.13

International: 7%
Women: 31%
Minorities: 4%
Average Class Size: 26
Fall 1997 Average GMAT: 520

Costs
Full-time tuition: $2738 per academic year (resident); $6612 per academic year (nonresident)
Part-time tuition: $133 per credit (resident); $294 per credit (nonresident)

AACSB – The International Association for Management Education accredited

GRADUATE BUSINESS PROGRAMS
Master of Business Administration (MBA) Full-time, part-time, distance learning option; 60 total credits required; 2 to 7 years to complete program. Concentration in management.

ADMISSION
Applications For fall 1997 there were 70 applications for admission. Of those applying, 66 were accepted. Of those accepted, 43 enrolled.

Application Requirements Application form, application fee, bachelor's degree, essay, minimum GPA: 2.75, 3 letters of recommendation, college transcript(s).

Recommended for Application GMAT score accepted: minimum 450.

Application Deadline Applications processed on a rolling/continuous basis for both domestic and international students. Application fee: $20. Deferred entrance is available.

ACADEMICS
Faculty Full-time 42; part-time 11.

Teaching Methodologies Case study, computer-aided instruction, computer analysis, computer simulations, experiential learning, group discussion, lecture, research, simulations, student presentations, study groups, team projects.

Technology 700 on-campus computer terminals/PCs are available for student use and are linked by a campus-wide network. The network has full access to the Internet. Students are not required to have their own PC.

Special Opportunities Advanced credit may be earned through transfer of credits from another institution. An internship program is available.

FINANCES
Costs for 1997–98 Tuition: Full-time: $2738 per year (resident); $6612 per year (nonresident). Part-time: $133 per credit (resident); $294 per credit (nonresident). Cost varies by number of credits taken, reciprocity agreements. Fees: Full-time: $418 per academic year (resident); $418 per academic year (nonresident). Part-time: $17 per credit (resident); $17 per credit (nonresident). Fees vary by number of credits taken. Average 1997–98 room and board costs were $3000 per academic year (on campus) and $3700 per academic year (off campus). Room and board costs vary by occupancy (e.g., single, double, triple), type of accommodation, type of meal plan.

Financial Aid Fellowships, research assistantships, teaching assistantships, work study, loans available. Application Deadline: 3/15.

Financial Aid Contact Ms. Alice Hoffert, Director of Financial Aid, Box 8371, Grand Forks, ND 58202-8371. Phone: 701-777-3121; Fax: 701-777-4082; E-mail: alice_hoffert@mail.und.nodak.edu

FACILITIES
Information Resources Chester Fritz Library plus 8 additional on-campus libraries; total holdings of 2,000,000 volumes, 7,500 current periodical subscriptions. CD player(s) available for graduate student use. Access provided to online bibliographic retrieval services.

INTERNATIONAL STUDENTS
Demographics 7% of students enrolled are international students [Asia, 33%, Europe, 17%, North America, 50%].

Services and Facilities International student office, international student center, visa services, counseling/support services.

University of North Dakota (continued)

Applying TOEFL: minimum score of 550, proof of adequate funds, proof of health/immunizations required. Financial aid is not available to international students.

International Student Contact Director, International Centre, Box 7109, Grand Forks, ND 58202-7109. Phone: 701-777-4231; Fax: 701-777-4082.

PLACEMENT
Services include alumni network, career counseling/planning, career fairs, career library, electronic job bank, and resume preparation.
Employment Of 1996–97 graduates, 95% were employed within three months of graduation. Types of employment entered: accounting, banking, communications, computer-related, consulting, consumer products, education, energy, engineering, finance, financial services, government, health services, hospitality management, human resources, information systems/technology, insurance, international trade, management, manufacturing, marketing, media, nonprofit, retail, service industry, telecommunications, transportation, utilities.

Business Program(s) URL: http://www.und.nodak.edu

Program Contact: Dr. Jacob Wambsganss, MBA Program Administrator, Box 8098, Grand Forks, ND 58202-8098. Phone: 701-777-2975; Fax: 701-777-5099; E-mail: wambsgan@badlands.nodak.edu

OHIO

Ashland University

School of Business Administration and Economics

Ashland, Ohio

OVERVIEW
Ashland University is an independent-religious, coed, comprehensive institution. Enrollment: 5,737 graduate, professional, and undergraduate students; 517 full-time matriculated graduate/professional students; 2,282 part-time matriculated graduate/professional students. Founded: 1878. The graduate business unit is in a small-town setting and is on a semester calendar.

HIGHLIGHTS

Enrollment Profile
Full-time: 126	International: 7%
Part-time: 404	Women: 40%
Total: 530	Minorities: 5%
Average Age: 34	Average Class Size: 22
Fall 1997 Average GPA: 3.25	Fall 1997 Average GMAT: 500

Costs
Full-time tuition: N/R
Part-time tuition: $350 per credit hour

ACBSP – The American Council of Business Schools and Programs accredited

GRADUATE BUSINESS PROGRAMS
Executive MBA (MBA) Full-time, part-time; 36-53 total credits required; 2 to 5 years to complete program. Concentration in management.

ADMISSION
Applications For fall 1997 there were 162 applications for admission. Of those applying, 151 were accepted. Of those accepted, 143 enrolled.
Application Requirements GMAT score, application form, application fee, bachelor's degree, personal statement, resume, college transcript(s), minimum of 2 years of work experience.
Recommended for Application Minimum GPA: 2.75, interview, letters of recommendation, computer experience.
Application Deadline 7/1 for fall, 11/1 for spring, 3/15 for summer. Application fee: $25. Deferred entrance is available.

ACADEMICS
Faculty Full-time 21; part-time 11.
Teaching Methodologies Case study, computer-aided instruction, computer analysis, computer simulations, faculty seminars, field projects, group discussion, lecture, research, role playing, seminars by members of the business community, simulations, student presentations, study groups, team projects.
Technology 200 on-campus computer terminals/PCs are available for student use and are linked by a campus-wide network. The network has full access to the Internet. Students are not required to have their own PC.

Special Opportunities Advanced credit may be earned through credit by examination, transfer of credits from another institution. International exchange program available.

FINANCES
Costs for 1997–98 Tuition: $350 per credit hour. Average 1997–98 room and board costs were $5200 per academic year (on campus) and $4500 per academic year (off campus). Room and board costs vary by occupancy (e.g., single, double, triple), type of accommodation, type of meal plan.
Financial Aid Contact Mr. Steve Howell, Director, Financial Aid, 401 College Avenue, Ashland, OH 44805-3702. Phone: 419-289-5002; Fax: 419-289-5333; E-mail: showell@ashland.edu

FACILITIES
Information Resources Ashland University Library plus 2 additional on-campus libraries; total holdings of 275,000 volumes, 290,000 microforms, 1,500 current periodical subscriptions. CD player(s) available for graduate student use. Access provided to online bibliographic retrieval services.

INTERNATIONAL STUDENTS
Demographics 7% of students enrolled are international students [Asia, 88%, Central America, 2%, Europe, 2%, North America, 2%, South America, 5%, other, 1%].
Services and Facilities International student office, visa services, ESL courses, counseling/support services.
Applying TOEFL: minimum score of 550, proof of adequate funds, proof of health/immunizations required. Financial aid is not available to international students.
International Student Contact Mr. Thomas Koop, Director, International Student Services, 401 College Avenue, Ashland, OH 44805-3702. Phone: 419-289-5068; Fax: 419-289-5989; E-mail: tkoop@ashland.edu

PLACEMENT
Services include alumni network, career counseling/planning, career fairs, career library, career placement, electronic job bank, job interviews arranged, job search course, resume referral to employers, and resume preparation. In 1996–97, 5 organizations participated in on-campus recruiting.

Business Program(s) URL: http://www.ashland.edu/mba.html

Program Contact: Mr. Stephen W. Krispinsky, Executive Director, MBA Program, 21 Miller Hall, Ashland, OH 44805. Phone: 419-289-5236, 800-882-1548; Fax: 419-289-5910; E-mail: skrispin@ashland.edu

Baldwin-Wallace College

Division of Business Administration

Berea, Ohio

OVERVIEW
Baldwin-Wallace College is an independent-religious, coed, comprehensive institution. Enrollment: 4,635 graduate, professional, and undergraduate students; 41 full-time matriculated graduate/professional students; 573 part-time matriculated graduate/professional students. Founded: 1845. The graduate business unit is in a suburban setting and is on a quarter calendar.

HIGHLIGHTS

Enrollment Profile
Full-time: 41	International: 12%
Part-time: 433	Women: 44%
Total: 474	Minorities: N/R
Average Age: 27	Average Class Size: 25
Fall 1997 Average GPA: 3.0	Fall 1997 Average GMAT: 482

Costs
Full-time tuition: $20,160 per academic year
Part-time tuition: $2016 per course

Baldwin-Wallace College (B-W) offers four distinct programs: the M.B.A. in systems management, the M.B.A. in international management, the M.B.A. in executive management, and the M.B.A. in executive health care management. B-W's M.B.A. programs feature the distinctive systems approach, which focuses on how various business disciplines work together. These programs take a strategic view of management, focusing on decisions that influence long-term business success. The M.B.A. programs at B-W emphasize problem solving, effective communication, group dynamics, team leadership, human resource awareness, and international awareness. Evening and Saturday formats allow working professionals the opportunity to seek a graduate degree without interrupting their careers. All of B-W's graduate programs can be completed part-time in two years. The M.B.A. in international management offers a full-time format, which can be completed in 1½ years. The College also offers advanced graduate certificates in business man-

agement and international management. The M.B.A. programs at B-W provide enrollment opportunities throughout the academic year.

GRADUATE BUSINESS PROGRAMS

Master of Business Administration (MBA) Part-time; 40 total credits required; 2 to 4 years to complete program. Concentration in management.

Executive Master of Business Administration (EMBA) Part-time; 38 total credits required; 2 to 4 years to complete program. Concentrations in management, health care.

International Master of Business Administration (IMBA) Full-time, part-time; 40 total credits required; 12 months to 4 years to complete program. Concentration in international management.

Health Care Executive Master of Business Administration (HCEMBA) Part-time; 38 total credits required; 2 to 4 years to complete program.

ADMISSION

Applications For fall 1997 there were 262 applications for admission. Of those applying, 196 were accepted. Of those accepted, 145 enrolled.

Application Requirements GMAT score: minimum 500, application form, application fee, bachelor's degree, 2 letters of recommendation, resume, college transcript(s), minimum of 2 years of work experience.

Recommended for Application Minimum GPA: 3.0, interview, personal statement, computer experience.

Application Deadline 7/25 for fall, 12/12 for spring, 4/17 for summer, 5/25 for fall (international), 10/12 for spring (international), 2/17 for summer (international). Application fee: $15. Deferred entrance is available.

ACADEMICS

Faculty Full-time 21; part-time 26.

Teaching Methodologies Case study, computer-aided instruction, computer simulations, faculty seminars, field projects, group discussion, lecture, simulations, student presentations, study groups, team projects.

Technology 100 on-campus computer terminals/PCs are available for student use and are linked by a campus-wide network. The network has full access to the Internet. Students are not required to have their own PC.

Special Opportunities Advanced credit may be earned through transfer of credits from another institution. An internship program is available.

FINANCES

Costs for 1997–98 Tuition: Full-time: $20,160 per year. Part-time: $2016 per course. Average 1997–98 room and board costs were $4800 per academic year (off campus).

Financial Aid In 1997–98, 16% of students received some institutionally administered aid in the form of scholarships, work study.

Financial Aid Contact George Rolleston, Director of Financial Aid, 275 Eastland Road, Berea, OH 44017-2088. Phone: 440-826-2108; Fax: 440-826-3868.

FACILITIES

Information Resources Ritter Library plus 1 additional on-campus library; total holdings of 203,000 volumes, 307,000 microforms, 906 current periodical subscriptions. CD player(s) available for graduate student use. Access provided to online bibliographic retrieval services.

INTERNATIONAL STUDENTS

Demographics 12% of students enrolled are international students.

Services and Facilities International student office, ESL courses, counseling/support services.

Applying TOEFL: minimum score of 500, proof of adequate funds required. Financial aid is not available to international students.

International Student Contact Peggy Shepard, Graduate Business Coordinator, 275 Eastland Road, Berea, OH 44017-2088. Phone: 440-826-2196; Fax: 440-826-3868; E-mail: pshepard@bw.edu

PLACEMENT

Services include alumni network, career fairs, career library, and resume preparation.

Business Program(s) URL: http://www.bw.edu

Program Contact: Peggy Shepard, Graduate Business Coordinator, 275 Eastland Road, Berea, OH 44017-2088. Phone: 440-826-2196; Fax: 440-826-3868; E-mail: pshepard@bw.edu
See full description on page 716.

Bowling Green State University

College of Business Administration

Bowling Green, Ohio

OVERVIEW

Bowling Green State University is a state-supported, coed university. Enrollment: 18,622 graduate, professional, and undergraduate students; 1,376 full-time matriculated graduate/professional students; 1,417 part-time matriculated graduate/professional students. Founded: 1910. The graduate business unit is in a small-town setting and is on a semester calendar.

HIGHLIGHTS

Enrollment Profile

Full-time: 94	International: 21%
Part-time: 141	Women: 29%
Total: 235	Minorities: 8%
Average Age: N/R	Average Class Size: 21
Fall 1997 Average GPA: 3.1	Fall 1997 Average GMAT: 556

Costs

Full-time tuition: $5004 per academic year (resident); $10,018 per academic year (nonresident)

Part-time tuition: $232 per credit hour (resident); $471 per credit hour (nonresident)

AACSB – The International Association for Management Education accredited

GRADUATE BUSINESS PROGRAMS

Executive MBA (MBA) Part-time; 36 total credits required; minimum of 2.7 years to complete program.

Master of Organization Development (MOD) Full-time; 34 total credits required; 12 months to 6 years to complete program.

Executive Master of Organization Development (MOD) Part-time; 30 total credits required; 3 to 6 years to complete program.

Master of Business Administration/Master of Organization Development (MBA/MOD) Full-time, part-time; 38 total credits required; 2 to 6 years to complete program.

Master of Accountancy (MAcc) Full-time; 30 total credits required; 12 months to 6 years to complete program.

ADMISSION

Applications For fall 1997 there were 159 applications for admission. Of those applying, 152 were accepted. Of those accepted, 61 enrolled.

Application Requirements Application form, application fee, bachelor's degree, minimum GPA: 2.7, 2 letters of recommendation, personal statement, resume, college transcript(s).

Recommended for Application GMAT score accepted, interview, work experience, computer experience.

Application Deadline 6/1 for fall, 10/15 for spring, 4/15 for fall (international), 9/1 for spring (international). Application fee: $30. Deferred entrance is available.

ACADEMICS

Faculty Full-time 71.

Teaching Methodologies Case study, computer-aided instruction, computer analysis, computer simulations, experiential learning, faculty seminars, field projects, group discussion, lecture, research, seminars by members of the business community, student presentations, study groups, team projects.

Technology 750 on-campus computer terminals/PCs are available for student use and are linked by a campus-wide network. The network has full access to the Internet. Students are not required to have their own PC.

Special Opportunities Advanced credit may be earned through credit by examination, transfer of credits from another institution.

FINANCES

Costs for 1997–98 Tuition: Full-time: $5004 per year (resident); $10,018 per year (nonresident). Part-time: $232 per credit hour (resident); $471 per credit hour (nonresident). Cost varies by academic program, number of credits taken, reciprocity agreements. Fees: Full-time: $758 per academic year (resident); $758 per academic year (nonresident). Part-time: $38 per credit hour (resident); $38 per credit hour (nonresident). Average 1997–98 room and board costs were $5800 per academic year (off campus).

Financial Aid In 1997–98, 21% of students received some institutionally administered aid in the form of research assistantships, teaching assistantships, work study, loans. Application Deadline: 3/1.

Financial Aid Contact Mr. Ronald Hartley, Associate Dean, Graduate Studies in Business Office, College of Business Administration, Room 369 BA, Bowl-

Bowling Green State University (continued)

ing Green, OH 43403. Phone: 419-372-2488; Fax: 419-372-2875; E-mail: mba-info@cba.bgsu.edu

FACILITIES
Information Resources William T. Jerome Library plus 6 additional on-campus libraries; total holdings of 2,125,601 volumes, 2,163,526 microforms, 4,270 current periodical subscriptions. CD player(s) available for graduate student use. Access provided to online bibliographic retrieval services and online databases.

INTERNATIONAL STUDENTS
Demographics 21% of students enrolled are international students.

Services and Facilities International student office, international student center, ESL courses, counseling/support services.

Applying TOEFL: minimum score of 575, proof of adequate funds, proof of health/immunizations required. Financial aid is available to international students.

International Student Contact Mr. Jeff Grilliot, Director of International Programs, Bowling Green, OH 43403. E-mail: jgrilli@bgnet.bgsu.edu

PLACEMENT
Services include alumni network, career counseling/planning, career fairs, career library, electronic job bank, job interviews arranged, resume referral to employers, and resume preparation. In 1996–97, 425 organizations participated in on-campus recruiting; 5,500 on-campus interviews were conducted.

Employment Of 1996–97 graduates, 68% were employed within three months of graduation; the average starting salary was $38,600. Types of employment entered: accounting, banking, chemical industry, computer-related, consulting, consumer products, education, engineering, finance, financial services, government, high technology, hospitality management, human resources, information systems/technology, insurance, international trade, management, manufacturing, marketing, nonprofit, retail.

Business Program(s) URL: http://www.cba.bgsu.edu

Program Contact: Carmen Castro-Rivera, Director, Graduate Studies in Business, College of Business Administration, Room 369 BA, Bowling Green, OH 43403. Phone: 419-372-2488, 800-BGSU-MBA (OH only); Fax: 419-372-2875; E-mail: mba_info@cba.bgsu.edu
See full description on page 730.

Capital University

Graduate School of Administration

Columbus, Ohio

OVERVIEW
Capital University is an independent-religious, coed, comprehensive institution. Enrollment: 3,924 graduate, professional, and undergraduate students. Founded: 1850. The graduate business unit is in a suburban setting and is on a trimester calendar.

HIGHLIGHTS

Enrollment Profile

Full-time: 0	International: 1%
Part-time: 320	Women: N/R
Total: 320	Minorities: 5%
Average Age: 31	Average Class Size: 25
Fall 1997 Average GPA: 3.0	Fall 1997 Average GMAT: 522

Costs
Full-time tuition: $12,000 per academic year
Part-time tuition: $260 per credit

GRADUATE BUSINESS PROGRAMS
Executive MBA (MBA) Part-time; 40 total credits required; 12 months to 5 years to complete program. Concentrations in management, entrepreneurship, finance.

12-month MBA (MBA) Full-time; 40 total credits required; minimum of 12 months to complete program.

ADMISSION
Applications For fall 1997 there were 130 applications for admission. Of those applying, 105 were accepted. Of those accepted, 104 enrolled.

Application Requirements Application form, application fee, bachelor's degree, personal statement, resume, college transcript(s), minimum of 2 years of work experience, computer experience: PC Windows knowledge, spreadsheet.

Recommended for Application GMAT score accepted: minimum 500, essay, minimum GPA: 2.7, interview.

Application Deadline 8/15 for fall, 12/15 for winter, 4/1 for spring, 7/1 for fall (international), 11/1 for winter (international), 3/1 for spring (international). Application fee: $25. Deferred entrance is available.

ACADEMICS
Faculty Full-time 5; part-time 15.

Teaching Methodologies Case study, computer analysis, computer simulations, faculty seminars, group discussion, lecture, seminars by members of the business community, student presentations, study groups, team projects.

Technology 40 on-campus computer terminals/PCs are available for student use and are linked by a campus-wide network. The network has full access to the Internet. Students are not required to have their own PC.

Special Opportunities Advanced credit may be earned through transfer of credits from another institution.

FINANCES
Costs for 1997–98 Tuition: Full-time: $12,000 per program. Part-time: $260 per credit. Average 1997–98 room only costs were $6000 per academic year (off campus).

Financial Aid In 1997–98, 6% of students received some institutionally administered aid in the form of work study, loans. Financial aid is available to part-time students. Application Deadline: 8/1.

Financial Aid Contact June Schlabach, Director of Financial Aid, 2199 East Main Street, Columbus, OH 43209-2394. Phone: 614-236-7113; Fax: 614-236-6820.

FACILITIES
Information Resources Main library plus 1 additional on-campus library; total holdings of 376,003 volumes, 90,617 microforms, 2,816 current periodical subscriptions. CD player(s) available for graduate student use. Access provided to online bibliographic retrieval services.

INTERNATIONAL STUDENTS
Demographics 1% of students enrolled are international students.

Services and Facilities International student office, visa services, ESL courses, counseling/support services.

Applying TOEFL: minimum score of 550, proof of adequate funds, proof of health/immunizations required. Financial aid is not available to international students.

International Student Contact Carolyn Abels, Director of International Education, 2199 East Main Street, Columbus, OH 43209-2394. Phone: 614-236-7102; Fax: 614-236-6171.

PLACEMENT
Services include alumni network, and career counseling/planning.

Employment Of 1996–97 graduates, 100% were employed within three months of graduation. Types of employment entered: banking, computer-related, energy, finance, financial services, health services, high technology, human resources, information systems/technology, insurance, management, marketing, service industry, telecommunications.

Business Program(s) URL: http://www.capital.edu/gsa

Program Contact: Ms. Trudy Rieser, MBA Registrar, 2199 East Main Street, Columbus, OH 43209-2394. Phone: 614-236-6679; Fax: 614-236-6540.

Case Western Reserve University

Weatherhead School of Management

Cleveland, Ohio

OVERVIEW
Case Western Reserve University is an independent-nonprofit, coed university. Enrollment: 9,908 graduate, professional, and undergraduate students; 3,725 full-time matriculated graduate/professional students; 2,574 part-time matriculated graduate/professional students. Founded: 1826. The graduate business unit is in a suburban setting and is on a semester calendar.

HIGHLIGHTS

Enrollment Profile

Full-time: 734	International: 26%
Part-time: 654	Women: 36%
Total: 1,388	Minorities: 10%
Average Age: 28	Average Class Size: 40
Fall 1997 Average GPA: 3.2	Fall 1997 Average GMAT: 605

Costs
Full-time tuition: $20,900 per academic year
Part-time tuition: $873 per credit hour

AACSB – The International Association for Management Education accredited

Degree(s) offered in conjunction with The American Graduate School of International Management, International Management Center

GRADUATE BUSINESS PROGRAMS

64-hour MBA Program (MBA) Full-time; 64 total credits required; 21 months to complete program. Concentrations in accounting, economics, entrepreneurship, finance, human resources, international management, management, management information systems, marketing, nonprofit management, operations management, organizational behavior/development, banking, health care, technology management.

48-hour MBA (MBA) Full-time, part-time; 48 total credits required; 11 months to 3.3 years to complete program. Concentrations in accounting, economics, entrepreneurship, finance, human resources, international management, management, management information systems, marketing, nonprofit management, operations management, organizational behavior/development, banking, health care, technology management.

Executive MBA (MBA) Full-time; 45 total credits required; 2 years to complete program. Concentrations in accounting, taxation.

Master of Accountancy (MAcc) Full-time, part-time; 36-48 total credits required; 11 to 21 months to complete program. Concentrations in accounting, taxation.

Master of Science in Management Information Systems (MSMIS) Full-time, part-time; 42 total credits required; 11 to 21 months to complete program. Concentration in management information systems.

Doctor of Jurisprudence/Master of Business Administration (JD/MBA) Full-time; 115-131 total credits required; 3 to 4 years to complete program. Concentrations in accounting, banking, economics, entrepreneurship, finance, health care, human resources, international management, management, management information systems, marketing, nonprofit management, operations management, organizational behavior/development, technology management.

Master of International Management/ Master of Business Administration (MIM/MBA) Full-time; 66-78 total credits required; 21 months to 2 years to complete program. Concentrations in accounting, banking, economics, entrepreneurship, finance, health care, human resources, international management, management, management information systems, marketing, nonprofit management, operations management, organizational behavior/development, technology management.

Master of Science in Nursing/Master of Business Administration (MSN/MBA) Full-time, part-time; 78-104 total credits required; 2.4 to 4 years to complete program. Concentrations in accounting, banking, economics, entrepreneurship, finance, health care, human resources, international management, management, management information systems, marketing, nonprofit management, operations management, organizational behavior/development, technology management.

Master of Science in Management Science/Master of Business Administration (MSMS/MBA) Full-time, part-time; 78-100 total credits required; 21 months to 5 years to complete program. Concentrations in accounting, banking, economics, entrepreneurship, finance, health care, human resources, international management, management, management information systems, marketing, nonprofit management, operations management, organizational behavior/development, technology management, project management.

Master of Science in Applied Social Sciences/Master of Business Administration (MS/MBA) Full-time, part-time; 93-105 total credits required; 3 to 4 years to complete program. Concentrations in accounting, banking, economics, entrepreneurship, finance, health care, human resources, international management, management, management information systems, marketing, nonprofit management, operations management, organizational behavior/development, technology management, arts administration/management.

Master of Science in Management Information Systems/Master of Business Administration (MSMIS/MBA) Full-time, part-time; 66-76 total credits required; 2.3 to 5 years to complete program. Concentrations in accounting, banking, economics, entrepreneurship, finance, health care, human resources, international management, management, management information systems, marketing, nonprofit management, operations management, organizational behavior/development, technology management.

42-hour MBA Program (MBA) Part-time; 42 total credits required; 3 years to complete program. Concentrations in accounting, banking, economics, entrepreneurship, finance, health care, human resources, international management, management, management information systems, marketing, nonprofit management, operations management, organizational behavior/development, technology management.

51-hour MBA Program (MBA) Part-time; 51 total credits required; 3.3 years to complete program. Concentrations in accounting, banking, economics, entrepreneurship, finance, health care, human resources, international management, management, management information systems, marketing, nonprofit management, operations management, organizational behavior/development, technology management.

ADMISSION

Applications For fall 1997 there were 717 applications for admission. Of those applying, 523 were accepted. Of those accepted, 252 enrolled.

Application Requirements GMAT score, application form, application fee, bachelor's degree, essay, minimum GPA, interview, 2 letters of recommendation, resume, college transcript(s), minimum of 2 years of work experience.

Recommended for Application Computer experience.

Application Deadline 4/10 for fall, 12/5 for spring, 4/10 for summer, 2/15 for fall (international), 2/15 for summer (international). Application fee: $50. Deferred entrance is available.

ACADEMICS

Faculty Full-time 87; part-time 15.

Teaching Methodologies Case study, computer-aided instruction, computer simulations, experiential learning, faculty seminars, field projects, group discussion, lecture, research, role playing, seminars by members of the business community, student presentations, study groups, team projects.

Technology 100 on-campus computer terminals/PCs are available for student use and are linked by a campus-wide network. The network has full access to the Internet. Students are required to have their own PC.

Special Opportunities Advanced credit may be earned through credit by examination, transfer of credits from another institution. International exchange programs in Australia, Denmark, Germany, Hungary, Israel, Mexico, Netherlands, Norway, United Kingdom.

FINANCES

Costs for 1997–98 Tuition: Full-time: $20,900 per year. Part-time: $873 per credit hour. Cost varies by academic program, class time (e.g., day/evening), number of credits taken. Average 1997–98 room and board costs were $9970 per academic year. Room and board costs vary by campus location, occupancy (e.g., single, double, triple), type of accommodation, type of meal plan.

Financial Aid In 1997–98, 70% of students received some institutionally administered aid in the form of fellowships, grants, scholarships, work study, loans. Financial aid is available to part-time students. Application Deadline: 3/15.

Financial Aid Contact Ms. Pam Chamar, Financial Aid Manager , Weatherhead School of Management, 10900 Euclid Avenue, Cleveland, OH 44106-7235. Phone: 216-368-2030; Fax: 216-368-5548; E-mail: pxc3@po.cwru.edu

FACILITIES

Information Resources Kelvin Smith Library plus 5 additional on-campus libraries; total holdings of 1,900,000 volumes, 2,200,000 microforms, 12,973 current periodical subscriptions. CD player(s) available for graduate student use. Access provided to online bibliographic retrieval services and online databases.

INTERNATIONAL STUDENTS

Demographics 26% of students enrolled are international students [Africa, 1%, Asia, 25%, Europe, 3%, North America, 60%, South America, 6%, other, 5%].

Services and Facilities International student office, international student center, visa services, ESL courses, counseling/support services, special pre-MBA language and culture course.

Applying TOEFL: minimum score of 570, proof of adequate funds, proof of health/immunizations required. Financial aid is available to international students.

International Student Contact Ms. Frances Cort, Assistant Dean for Professional Programs , Weatherhead School of Management, 10900 Euclid Avenue, Cleveland, OH 44106-7235. Phone: 216-368-2069; Fax: 216-368-5548; E-mail: fxc@po.cwru.edu

PLACEMENT

Services include alumni network, career counseling/planning, career fairs, career library, career placement, electronic job bank, job interviews arranged, job search course, resume referral to employers, and resume preparation. In 1996–97, 140 organizations participated in on-campus recruiting; 2,018 on-campus interviews were conducted.

Employment Of 1996–97 graduates, 98% were employed within three months of graduation; the average starting salary was $55,500. Types of employment entered: accounting, banking, communications, computer-related, consulting, consumer products, engineering, finance, financial services, health services, high technology, human resources, information systems/technology, insurance, international trade, management, manufacturing, marketing, nonprofit, real estate, service industry, telecommunications.

Business Program(s) URL: http://weatherhead.cwru.edu/

Program Contact: Ms. Linda Gaston, Director of Admissions, 10900 Euclid Avenue, 310 Enterprise Hall, Cleveland, OH 44106-7235. Phone: 216-368-2030, 800-723-0203 (OH only); Fax: 216-368-5548; E-mail: lxg10@po.cwru.edu

See full description on page 742.

Cleveland State University

James J. Nance College of Business Administration

Cleveland, Ohio

OVERVIEW

Cleveland State University is a state-supported, coed university. Enrollment: 15,673 graduate, professional, and undergraduate students; 1,453 full-time matriculated graduate/professional students; 3,291 part-time matriculated graduate/professional students. Founded: 1964. The graduate business unit is in an urban setting and is on a semester calendar.

HIGHLIGHTS

Enrollment Profile

Full-time: 407	International: 23%
Part-time: 803	Women: 40%
Total: 1,210	Minorities: 6%
Average Age: 29	Average Class Size: 31
Fall 1997 Average GPA: 3.0	Fall 1997 Average GMAT: 486

Costs

Full-time tuition: $5050 per academic year (resident); $10,101 per academic year (nonresident)

Part-time tuition: $130 per credit hour (resident); $259 per hour (nonresident)

AACSB – The International Association for Management Education accredited

GRADUATE BUSINESS PROGRAMS

Master of Business Administration (MBA) Full-time, part-time; 31-69 total credits required; 12 months to 6 years to complete program. Concentrations in accounting, advertising, banking, finance, human resources, industrial/labor relations, information management, international and area business studies, management, management information systems, marketing, operations management, organizational behavior/development, quality management, real estate.

Accelerated MBA (MBA) Part-time; 31 total credits required; minimum of 12 months to complete program. Concentrations in finance, human resources, management, marketing, organizational behavior/development.

Executive MBA (MBA) Part-time; 54 total credits required; minimum of 22 months to complete program. Concentration in management.

Master of Business Administration in Health Administration (MBA) Full-time, part-time; 34-66 total credits required; 12 months to 6 years to complete program. Concentrations in organizational behavior/development, organizational management, public and private management, public management.

Master of Accountancy and Financial Information Systems (MAFIS) Full-time, part-time; 33-79 total credits required; 12 months to 6 years to complete program. Concentrations in actuarial science, financial information systems, management information systems.

Master of Computer and Information Science (MCIS) Full-time, part-time; 30-57 total credits required; 12 months to 6 years to complete program. Concentrations in business information science, information management, management information systems, technology management.

Master of Labor Relations and Human Resources (MLRHR) Full-time, part-time; 42-50 total credits required; 12 months to 6 years to complete program. Concentrations in human resources, industrial/labor relations, management, organizational behavior/development, organizational management.

Doctor of Jurisprudence/Master of Business Administration (JD/MBA) Full-time, part-time; 110-139 total credits required; 3.5 to 6 years to complete program. Concentrations in legal administration, management.

ADMISSION

Applications For fall 1997 there were 780 applications for admission. Of those applying, 537 were accepted. Of those accepted, 272 enrolled.

Application Requirements GMAT score, GRE score, application form, application fee, bachelor's degree, minimum GPA, college transcript(s).

Application Deadline 7/15 for fall, 1/1 for spring, 4/12 for summer, 6/15 for fall (international), 12/1 for spring (international), 3/15 for summer (international). Application fee: $25, $50 (international). Deferred entrance is available.

ACADEMICS

Faculty Full-time 74.

Teaching Methodologies Case study, computer-aided instruction, computer analysis, computer simulations, experiential learning, faculty seminars, field projects, group discussion, lecture, research, role playing, seminars by members of the business community, simulations, student presentations, study groups, team projects.

Technology 250 on-campus computer terminals/PCs are available for student use and are linked by a campus-wide network. The network has full access to the Internet. Students are not required to have their own PC.

Special Opportunities Advanced credit may be earned through credit by examination, credit for business training programs, transfer of credits from another institution. International exchange program in United Kingdom. An internship program is available.

FINANCES

Costs for 1997–98 Tuition: Full-time: $5050 per year (resident); $10,101 per year (nonresident). Part-time: $130 per credit hour (resident); $259 per hour (nonresident). Cost varies by number of credits taken. Fees: Full-time: $25 per academic year (resident); $25 per academic year (nonresident). Part-time: $2 per hour (resident); $2 per hour (nonresident). Fees vary by number of credits taken. Average 1997–98 room and board costs were $6300 per academic year (on campus) and $6100 per academic year (off campus). Room and board costs vary by occupancy (e.g., single, double, triple), type of meal plan.

Financial Aid Research assistantships, teaching assistantships, work study available.

Financial Aid Contact Ms. Robbie DeLeur, Director, Financial Aid, 2344 Euclid Avenue, Cleveland, OH 44115. Phone: 216-687-3764; Fax: 216-687-9247; E-mail: r.deleur@popmail.csuohio.edu

FACILITIES

Information Resources Main library plus 1 additional on-campus library; total holdings of 879,000 volumes, 633,684 microforms, 6,548 current periodical subscriptions. CD player(s) available for graduate student use. Access provided to online bibliographic retrieval services.

INTERNATIONAL STUDENTS

Demographics 23% of students enrolled are international students [Africa, 1%, Asia, 24%, Europe, 2%, North America, 72%, South America, 1%].

Services and Facilities International student office, international student center, visa services, ESL courses, counseling/support services.

Applying TOEFL: minimum score of 500, proof of adequate funds, proof of health/immunizations required. TSE, TWE recommended.

International Student Contact Mr. George Burke, Associate Dean, International Students Office, 2344 Euclid Avenue, Room 103, Cleveland, OH 44115. Phone: 216-687-5234; Fax: 216-687-5441.

PLACEMENT

Services include alumni network, career counseling/planning, career fairs, career library, career placement, electronic job bank, job interviews arranged, job search course, resume referral to employers, and resume preparation. In 1996–97, 130 organizations participated in on-campus recruiting.

Employment Of 1996–97 graduates, 88% were employed within three months of graduation; the average starting salary was $49,200. Types of employment entered: accounting, banking, computer-related, consulting, education, finance, financial services, hospitality management, human resources, information systems/technology, insurance, international trade, law, management, manufacturing, marketing, nonprofit, real estate, retail, service industry, telecommunications.

Business Program(s) URL: http://grail.cba.csuohio.edu/cba.html

Program Contact: Mr. Bruce Gottschalk, Administrator, MBA Programs, 1860 East 18th Street, Business Building Room 219, Cleveland, OH 44114. Phone: 216-687-3730; Fax: 216-687-5311; E-mail: p1717%taonode@vmcms.csuohio.edu

See full description on page 758.

Franciscan University of Steubenville

Business Programs

Steubenville, Ohio

OVERVIEW

Franciscan University of Steubenville is an independent-religious, coed, comprehensive institution. Enrollment: 1,950 graduate, professional, and undergraduate students; 176 full-time matriculated graduate/professional students; 216 part-time matriculated graduate/professional students. Founded: 1946. The graduate business unit is in a suburban setting and is on a trimester calendar.

HIGHLIGHTS

Enrollment Profile

Full-time: 9
Part-time: 37
Total: 46
Average Age: N/R
Fall 1997 Average GPA: 3.0

International: 2%
Women: 26%
Minorities: 4%
Average Class Size: 15
Fall 1997 Average GMAT: N/R

Costs

Full-time tuition: N/R
Part-time tuition: $280 per credit

GRADUATE BUSINESS PROGRAMS

Master of Business Administration (MBA) Full-time, part-time; 40 total credits required; minimum of 12 months to complete program. Concentration in accounting.

ADMISSION

Applications For fall 1997 there were 25 applications for admission. Of those applying, 21 were accepted. Of those accepted, 10 enrolled.

Application Requirements Application form, application fee, bachelor's degree, minimum GPA: 2.5, 3 letters of recommendation, personal statement.

Recommended for Application GMAT score accepted: minimum 460, essay, interview, resume.

Application Deadline Applications processed on a rolling/continuous basis for both domestic and international students. Application fee: $20.

ACADEMICS

Faculty Full-time 8; part-time 6.

Teaching Methodologies Case study, computer-aided instruction, computer analysis, faculty seminars, group discussion, lecture, research, role playing, seminars by members of the business community, simulations, student presentations, study groups, team projects.

Technology 83 on-campus computer terminals/PCs are available for student use and are linked by a campus-wide network. The network has full access to the Internet. Students are not required to have their own PC.

Special Opportunities Advanced credit may be earned through transfer of credits from another institution.

FINANCES

Costs for 1997–98 Tuition: $280 per credit. Average 1997–98 room and board costs were $4730 per academic year.

Financial Aid In 1997–98, 43% of students received some institutionally administered aid. Financial aid is available to part-time students.

Financial Aid Contact John Herrmann, Assistant Director, Financial Aid, Financial Aid Department, University Boulevard, Steubenville, OH 43952-6701. Phone: 740-283-6211; Fax: 740-284-5456; E-mail: jherrmann@franuniv.edu

FACILITIES

Information Resources John Paul II Library; total holdings of 220,630 volumes, 154,541 microforms, 1,923 current periodical subscriptions. CD player(s) available for graduate student use. Access provided to online bibliographic retrieval services and online databases.

INTERNATIONAL STUDENTS

Demographics 2% of students enrolled are international students.

Services and Facilities International student office, international student center, counseling/support services.

Applying TOEFL: minimum score of 550, proof of adequate funds required. Financial aid is available to international students.

International Student Contact Mr. Mark McGuire, Associate Director of Graduate Admissions, Admissions Department, University Boulevard, Steubenville, OH 43952-6701. Phone: 740-283-6226; Fax: 740-283-6472; E-mail: mmcguire@franuniv.edu

PLACEMENT

Services include alumni network, and career counseling/planning.

Employment Types of employment entered: accounting, banking, chemical industry, education, engineering, health services, human resources, manufacturing, nonprofit, utilities.

Business Program(s) URL: http://www.franuniv.edu

Program Contact: Mr. Mark McGuire, Associate Director of Graduate Admissions, Admissions Department, University Boulevard, Steubenville, OH 43952-6701. Phone: 740-283-6226, 800-783-6220; Fax: 740-283-6472; E-mail: mmcguire@franuniv.edu

Franklin University

Graduate School of Business

Columbus, Ohio

OVERVIEW

Franklin University is an independent-nonprofit, coed, comprehensive institution. Enrollment: 4,092 graduate, professional, and undergraduate students. Founded: 1902. The graduate business unit is in an urban setting and is on a trimester calendar.

HIGHLIGHTS

Enrollment Profile

Full-time: N/R
Part-time: N/R
Total: 362
Average Age: 33
Fall 1997 Average GPA: N/R

International: N/R
Women: 44%
Minorities: 12%
Average Class Size: 26
Fall 1997 Average GMAT: N/R

Costs

Full-time tuition: $5880 per academic year
Part-time tuition: $270 per credit

GRADUATE BUSINESS PROGRAMS

Master of Business Administration (MBA) Full-time, part-time; 42 total credits required; minimum of 2 years to complete program. Concentrations in health care, international business, organizational management, technology management.

ADMISSION

Applications For fall 1997 there were 217 applications for admission. Of those applying, 200 were accepted. Of those accepted, 177 enrolled.

Application Requirements Application form, application fee, bachelor's degree, essay, letters of recommendation, personal statement, college transcript(s), work experience, computer experience.

Recommended for Application Minimum GPA.

Application Deadline 7/15 for fall, 11/15 for winter, 3/15 for summer. Application fee: $30, $40 (international). Deferred entrance is available.

ACADEMICS

Faculty Full-time 7; part-time 12.

Teaching Methodologies Case study, computer-aided instruction, field projects, group discussion, lecture, research, role playing, seminars by members of the business community, simulations, student presentations, team projects.

Technology 194 on-campus computer terminals/PCs are available for student use and are linked by a campus-wide network. The network has full access to the Internet. Students are not required to have their own PC.

Special Opportunities Advanced credit may be earned through credit for experience, transfer of credits from another institution.

FINANCES

Costs for 1997–98 Tuition: Full-time: $5880 per year. Part-time: $270 per credit. Fees: Full-time: $25 per academic year. Part-time: $25 per trimester.

Financial Aid Scholarships, work study, loans available. Application Deadline: 5/30.

Financial Aid Contact Evelyn Levino, Director of Financial Aid, 201 South Grant Avenue, Columbus, OH 43215-5399. Phone: 614-341-6416; Fax: 614-224-8027; E-mail: levinoe@franklin.edu

FACILITIES

Information Resources Franklin University Library; total holdings of 93,600 volumes, 192,000 microforms, 1,700 current periodical subscriptions. Access provided to online bibliographic retrieval services.

INTERNATIONAL STUDENTS

Demographics N/R

Services and Facilities International student office, ESL courses, counseling/support services.

Applying TOEFL: minimum score of 550, TSE, proof of adequate funds, proof of health/immunizations required.

International Student Contact Patrick Schumer, International Student Services Associate, 201 South Grant Avenue, Columbus, OH 43215. Phone: 614-341-6309; Fax: 614-224-8027; E-mail: schumerp@franklin.edu

PLACEMENT

Services include alumni network, and career counseling/planning.

Business Program(s) URL: http://www.franklin.edu

Program Contact: Kitty Whyte, MBA Student Services Associate, 201 South Grant Avenue, Columbus, OH 43215. Phone: 614-341-6387, 888-341-6237; Fax: 614-221-7723; E-mail: whytek@franklin.edu

Heidelberg College

Tiffin, Ohio

OVERVIEW

Heidelberg College is an independent-religious, coed, comprehensive institution. Enrollment: 1,400 graduate, professional, and undergraduate students. Founded: 1850. The graduate business unit is in a small-town setting and is on a trimester calendar.

HIGHLIGHTS

Enrollment Profile
Full-time: N/R
Part-time: N/R
Total: N/R
Average Age: N/R
Fall 1997 Average GPA: N/R

International: N/R
Women: N/R
Minorities: N/R
Average Class Size: 15
Fall 1997 Average GMAT: N/R

Costs
Full-time tuition: N/R
Part-time tuition: $350 per semester hour

GRADUATE BUSINESS PROGRAMS

Master of Business Administration (MBA) Full-time, part-time; 31 total credits required; 12 months to 6 years to complete program. Concentration in management.

ADMISSION

Application Requirements GMAT score, application form, application fee, bachelor's degree, minimum GPA: 2.7, personal statement, college transcript(s).

Recommended for Application Interview, resume, computer experience.

Application Deadline Applications processed on a rolling/continuous basis for both domestic and international students. Application fee: $35. Deferred entrance is available.

ACADEMICS

Faculty Full-time 10.

Teaching Methodologies Case study, computer analysis, experiential learning, faculty seminars, field projects, group discussion, lecture, research, seminars by members of the business community, simulations, student presentations, study groups, team projects.

Technology Computer terminals/PCs are available for student use and are linked by a campus-wide network. Students are not required to have their own PC.

Special Opportunities Advanced credit may be earned through credit by examination, credit for experience, credit for military training programs, transfer of credits from another institution.

FINANCES

Costs for 1997–98 Tuition: $350 per semester hour.

Financial Aid Financial aid is available to part-time students. Application Deadline: 4/15.

Financial Aid Contact Ms. Juli Weininger, Director of Financial Aid, 310 East Market Street, Tiffin, OH 44883. Phone: 419-448-2293; Fax: 419-448-2124.

FACILITIES

Information Resources Beeghly Library plus 1 additional on-campus library; total holdings of 150,669 volumes, 107,236 microforms, 789 current periodical subscriptions. CD player(s) available for graduate student use. Access provided to online bibliographic retrieval services.

INTERNATIONAL STUDENTS

Demographics N/R

Services and Facilities International student office, international student center, international student housing, ESL courses, counseling/support services.

Applying TOEFL: minimum score of 550, TSE, TWE, proof of adequate funds required.

International Student Contact Mr. Lewis Miller, Director, International Programs, 310 East Market Street, Tiffin, OH 44883. Phone: 419-448-2207; Fax: 419-448-2124; E-mail: lmiller@mail.heidelberg.edu

Business Program(s) URL: http://www.heidelberg.edu

Program Contact: Dr. Henry Rennie, Director, Graduate Studies in Business, 310 East Market Street, Tiffin, OH 44883. Phone: 419-448-2221; Fax: 419-448-2124.

John Carroll University

University Heights, Ohio

OVERVIEW

John Carroll University is an independent-religious, coed, comprehensive institution. Enrollment: 4,326 graduate, professional, and undergraduate students; 170 full-time matriculated graduate/professional students; 637 part-time matriculated graduate/professional students. Founded: 1886. The graduate business unit is in a suburban setting and is on a semester calendar.

HIGHLIGHTS

Enrollment Profile
Full-time: 0
Part-time: 222
Total: 222
Average Age: 28
Fall 1997 Average GPA: 3.13

International: 1%
Women: 40%
Minorities: 3%
Average Class Size: 22
Fall 1997 Average GMAT: 517

Costs
Full-time tuition: N/R
Part-time tuition: $530 per credit hour

AACSB – The International Association for Management Education accredited

GRADUATE BUSINESS PROGRAMS

Master of Business Administration (MBA) Part-time; 60 total credits required; 2 to 6 years to complete program. Concentrations in accounting, economics, finance, management, marketing, international business, logistics.

ADMISSION

Applications For fall 1997 there were 82 applications for admission. Of those applying, 76 were accepted. Of those accepted, 43 enrolled.

Application Requirements GMAT score: minimum 400, application form, application fee, bachelor's degree, minimum GPA: 2.0, 2 letters of recommendation, college transcript(s).

Recommended for Application Work experience.

Application Deadline Applications processed on a rolling/continuous basis for both domestic and international students. Application fee: $25. Deferred entrance is available.

ACADEMICS

Faculty Full-time 32; part-time 3.

Teaching Methodologies Case study, group discussion, lecture, role playing, seminars by members of the business community, student presentations, study groups, team projects.

Technology 95 on-campus computer terminals/PCs are available for student use and are linked by a campus-wide network. The network has full access to the Internet. Students are not required to have their own PC.

Special Opportunities Advanced credit may be earned through transfer of credits from another institution.

FINANCES

Costs for 1997–98 Tuition: Part-time: $530 per credit hour.

Financial Aid In 1997–98, 1% of students received some institutionally administered aid in the form of research assistantships. Financial aid is available to part-time students. Application Deadline: 3/1.

Financial Aid Contact Financial Aid Department, 20700 North Park Boulevard, University Heights, OH 44118-4581. Phone: 216-397-4248.

FACILITIES

Information Resources Grasselli Library; total holdings of 577,051 volumes, 183,142 microforms, 1,860 current periodical subscriptions. CD player(s) available for graduate student use. Access provided to online bibliographic retrieval services.

INTERNATIONAL STUDENTS

Demographics 1% of students enrolled are international students.

Applying Financial aid is not available to international students.

PLACEMENT

Services include alumni network, career counseling/planning, and resume referral to employers.

Employment Of 1996–97 graduates, 100% were employed within three months of graduation; the average starting salary was $47,000.

Business Program(s) URL: http://www1.jcu.edu/schlbus/pages/bsbhome.htm

Program Contact: Dr. James M. Daley, Associate Dean and Director, MBA Program, 20700 North Park Boulevard, University Heights, OH 44118-4581. Phone: 216-397-4507; Fax: 216-397-1728; E-mail: jdaley@jcvaxa.jcu.edu

Kent State University

Graduate School of Management

Kent, Ohio

OVERVIEW
Kent State University is a state-supported, coed university. Enrollment: 20,743 graduate, professional, and undergraduate students; 2,020 full-time matriculated graduate/professional students; 2,735 part-time matriculated graduate/professional students. Founded: 1910. The graduate business unit is in a small-town setting and is on a semester calendar.

HIGHLIGHTS

Enrollment Profile

Full-time: 136	International: 16%
Part-time: 250	Women: 37%
Total: 386	Minorities: 5%
Average Age: 26	Average Class Size: 40
Fall 1997 Average GPA: 3.2	Fall 1997 Average GMAT: 510

Costs
Full-time tuition: $2376 per academic year (resident); $4606 per academic year (nonresident)
Part-time tuition: $216 per credit (resident); $419 per credit (nonresident)

AACSB – The International Association for Management Education accredited

GRADUATE BUSINESS PROGRAMS
Master of Business Administration (MBA) Full-time, part-time; 39-60 total credits required; 12 months to 6 years to complete program. Concentrations in finance, human resources, international and area business studies, leadership, management information systems, marketing, nonprofit management, operations management.

Master of Science in Accounting (MS) Full-time, part-time; 30-53 total credits required; 12 months to 6 years to complete program.

Master of Arts in Economics (MA) Full-time, part-time; 30 total credits required; 12 months to 6 years to complete program.

Master of Business Administration/Master of Science in Nursing (MBA/MS) Full-time, part-time; 70 total credits required; up to 6 years to complete program.

Master of Business Administration/Master of Library Science (MBA/MLS) Full-time, part-time; 70 total credits required; up to 6 years to complete program.

Executive MBA (MBA) Part-time; 45 total credits required; up to 2.2 years to complete program.

ADMISSION
Applications For fall 1997 there were 238 applications for admission. Of those applying, 135 were accepted. Of those accepted, 69 enrolled.

Application Requirements Application form, application fee, bachelor's degree, essay, minimum GPA: 2.75, 3 letters of recommendation, resume, college transcript(s), computer experience: spreadsheet, database.

Recommended for Application GMAT score accepted.

Application Deadline 7/1 for fall, 12/15 for spring, 5/15 for summer, 4/1 for fall (international). Application fee: $30. Deferred entrance is available.

ACADEMICS
Faculty Full-time 43; part-time 3.

Teaching Methodologies Case study, computer-aided instruction, computer analysis, experiential learning, faculty seminars, field projects, group discussion, lecture, research, simulations, student presentations, study groups, team projects.

Technology 400 on-campus computer terminals/PCs are available for student use and are linked by a campus-wide network. The network has full access to the Internet. Students are not required to have their own PC.

Special Opportunities Advanced credit may be earned through transfer of credits from another institution. International exchange program in France. An internship program is available.

FINANCES
Costs for 1997–98 Tuition: Full-time: $2376 per semester (resident); $4606 per semester (nonresident). Part-time: $216 per credit (resident); $419 per credit (nonresident). Cost varies by campus location, number of credits taken. Average 1997–98 room and board costs were $4336 per academic year. Room and board costs vary by occupancy (e.g., single, double, triple), type of accommodation, type of meal plan.

Financial Aid In 1997–98, 13% of students received some institutionally administered aid in the form of fellowships, research assistantships, teaching assistantships, work study, loans. Application Deadline: 4/1.

Financial Aid Contact Student Financial Aid Office, PO Box 5190, Kent, OH 44242-0001. Phone: 330-672-2972; Fax: 330-672-4014.

FACILITIES
Information Resources Main library plus 4 additional on-campus libraries; total holdings of 2,000,000 volumes, 1,000,000 microforms, 8,000 current periodical subscriptions. CD player(s) available for graduate student use. Access provided to online bibliographic retrieval services.

INTERNATIONAL STUDENTS
Demographics 16% of students enrolled are international students [Africa, 9%, Asia, 61%, Europe, 26%, South America, 4%].

Services and Facilities International student office, international student housing, visa services, ESL courses, counseling/support services.

Applying TOEFL: minimum score of 550, proof of adequate funds, proof of health/immunizations required. Financial aid is available to international students.

International Student Contact Assistant Director for International Admissions, Office of Admissions, Kent, OH 44242. Phone: 330-672-2444; Fax: 330-672-4836.

PLACEMENT
Services include alumni network, career counseling/planning, career fairs, career library, career placement, electronic job bank, job interviews arranged, resume referral to employers, and resume preparation. In 1996–97, 500 organizations participated in on-campus recruiting.

Employment Of 1996–97 graduates, 90% were employed within three months of graduation; the average starting salary was $36,200. Types of employment entered: accounting, banking, communications, computer-related, consulting, consumer products, education, finance, financial services, government, health services, hospitality management, human resources, information systems/technology, insurance, management, manufacturing, marketing, media, nonprofit, retail, service industry, utilities.

Business Program(s) URL: http://business.kent.edu

Program Contact: Ms. Louise Ditchey, Associate Director, Graduate School of Management, Kent, OH 44242-0001. Phone: 330-672-2282; Fax: 330-672-7303; E-mail: gradbus@bsa3.kent.edu

Lake Erie College

Division of Management Studies

Painesville, Ohio

OVERVIEW
Lake Erie College is an independent-nonprofit, coed, comprehensive institution. Enrollment: 708 graduate, professional, and undergraduate students; full-time matriculated graduate/professional students; 244 part-time matriculated graduate/professional students. Founded: 1856. The graduate business unit is in a suburban setting and is on a trimester calendar.

HIGHLIGHTS

Enrollment Profile

Full-time: 0	International: N/R
Part-time: 84	Women: 63%
Total: 84	Minorities: 8%
Average Age: 35	Average Class Size: 15
Fall 1997 Average GPA: N/R	Fall 1997 Average GMAT: N/R

Costs
Full-time tuition: N/R
Part-time tuition: $380 per semester hour

GRADUATE BUSINESS PROGRAMS
Master of Business Administration (MBA) Full-time, part-time; 36 total credits required; 16 months to 7 years to complete program. Concentrations in management, health care.

ADMISSION
Applications For fall 1997 there were 30 applications for admission. Of those applying, 25 were accepted. Of those accepted, 16 enrolled.

Application Requirements Application form, application fee, bachelor's degree, essay, minimum GPA: 3.0, interview, personal statement, resume, college transcript(s), minimum of 2 years of work experience.

Application Deadline Applications processed on a rolling/continuous basis for both domestic and international students. Application fee: $20. Deferred entrance is available.

ACADEMICS
Faculty Full-time 6; part-time 4.

Lake Erie College (continued)

Teaching Methodologies Case study, experiential learning, group discussion, lecture, research, student presentations, study groups, team projects.

Technology 72 on-campus computer terminals/PCs are available for student use and are linked by a campus-wide network. The network has full access to the Internet. Students are not required to have their own PC.

Special Opportunities Advanced credit may be earned through transfer of credits from another institution. International exchange programs in Australia, Costa Rica, Czech Republic, France, Ireland, Italy, Poland, Russia, Slovakia, Spain. An internship program is available.

FINANCES
Costs for 1997–98 Tuition: $380 per semester hour. Fees: $20 per semester hour.

Financial Aid Contact Mrs. Leann Kendzerski, Director of Financial Aid, 391 West Washington Street, Painesville, OH 44077-3389. Phone: 440-639-7814.

FACILITIES
Information Resources Lincoln Library; total holdings of 89,232 volumes, 8,091 microforms, 550 current periodical subscriptions. CD player(s) available for graduate student use. Access provided to online bibliographic retrieval services.

INTERNATIONAL STUDENTS
Demographics N/R

Services and Facilities Counseling/support services.

Applying TOEFL: minimum score of 590, proof of adequate funds, proof of health/immunizations required. Financial aid is not available to international students.

International Student Contact Dr. William Blanchard, Associate Dean for Management Studies , 391 West Washington Street, Painesville, OH 44077-3389. Phone: 440-639-7845; Fax: 440-352-3533.

PLACEMENT
Services include career counseling/planning, and career library.

Business Program(s) URL: http://www.lakeerie.edu/admiss/admiss1.htm

Program Contact: Ms. Mary Ann Kalbaugh, Director of Admissions, 391 West Washington Street, Painesville, OH 44077-3389. Phone: 440-352-3361 Ext. 7879, 800-533-4996; Fax: 440-352-3533.

Malone College

Graduate School

Canton, Ohio

OVERVIEW
Malone College is an independent-religious, coed, comprehensive institution. Enrollment: 2,239 graduate, professional, and undergraduate students. Founded: 1892. The graduate business unit is in an urban setting and is on a semester calendar.

HIGHLIGHTS
Enrollment Profile

Full-time: N/R	International: N/R
Part-time: N/R	Women: N/R
Total: 84	Minorities: N/R
Average Age: 37	Average Class Size: 25
Fall 1997 Average GPA: N/R	Fall 1997 Average GMAT: N/R

Costs
Full-time tuition: N/R
Part-time tuition: $334 per semester credit

GRADUATE BUSINESS PROGRAMS
Master of Business Administration (MBA) Part-time; 37 total credits required; minimum of 2 years to complete program.

ADMISSION
Application Requirements Application form, application fee, bachelor's degree, minimum GPA: 2.5, interview, 2 letters of recommendation, college transcript(s).

Recommended for Application GMAT score accepted, work experience, computer experience.

Application Deadline Applications processed on a rolling/continuous basis for both domestic and international students. Application fee: $20. Deferred entrance is available.

ACADEMICS
Faculty Full-time 9; part-time 2.

Teaching Methodologies Case study, computer-aided instruction, computer analysis, computer simulations, field projects, group discussion, lecture, research, role playing, seminars by members of the business community, simulations, student presentations, study groups, team projects.

Technology Students are not required to have their own PC.

Special Opportunities Advanced credit may be earned through transfer of credits from another institution.

FINANCES
Costs for 1997–98 Tuition: Part-time: $334 per semester credit.

Financial Aid Loans available. Financial aid is available to part-time students.

Financial Aid Contact Ms. Laura Heffernan, Financial Aid Office, 515 25th Street, Canton, OH 44709-3897. Phone: 330-471-8160; Fax: 330-471-8343.

FACILITIES
Information Resources Everett L. Cattell Library; total holdings of 129,937 volumes, 375,639 microforms, 1,380 current periodical subscriptions. CD player(s) available for graduate student use. Access provided to online bibliographic retrieval services.

INTERNATIONAL STUDENTS
Demographics N/R

PLACEMENT
Services include career counseling/planning, career fairs, career placement, job interviews arranged, resume referral to employers, and resume preparation.

Business Program(s) URL: http://www.malone.edu/main/mba.htm

Program Contact: Mr. Dan DePasquale, Director of Graduate Student Services, 515 25th Street, Canton, OH 44709-3897. Phone: 800-257-4723; Fax: 330-471-8343; E-mail: gradschool@malone.edu

The McGregor School of Antioch University

Graduate Management Program

Yellow Springs, Ohio

OVERVIEW
The McGregor School of Antioch University is an independent-nonprofit, coed, upper-level institution. Enrollment: 810 graduate, professional, and undergraduate students. Founded: 1988. The graduate business unit is in a small-town setting and is on a quarter calendar.

HIGHLIGHTS
Enrollment Profile

Full-time: 105	International: N/R
Part-time: 0	Women: 48%
Total: 105	Minorities: N/R
Average Age: 33	Average Class Size: 25
Fall 1997 Average GPA: 3.1	Fall 1997 Average GMAT: N/R

Costs
Full-time tuition: $8992 per academic year
Part-time tuition: N/R

GRADUATE BUSINESS PROGRAMS
Master of Arts in Management (MA) Full-time; 64 total credits required; 2 years to complete program.

ADMISSION
Application Requirements Application form, application fee, bachelor's degree, interview, 2 letters of recommendation, personal statement, college transcript(s), work experience.

Application Deadline Applications processed on a rolling/continuous basis for both domestic and international students. Application fee: $35. Deferred entrance is available.

ACADEMICS
Faculty Full-time 4; part-time 18.

Teaching Methodologies Case study, computer analysis, computer simulations, experiential learning, field projects, group discussion, lecture, research, role playing, seminars by members of the business community, simulations, student presentations, study groups, team projects.

Technology The network has full access to the Internet. Students are not required to have their own PC.

Special Opportunities Advanced credit may be earned through transfer of credits from another institution.

FINANCES
Costs for 1997–98 Tuition: Full-time: $8992 per year.

Financial Aid Loans available.

Financial Aid Contact Ms. Kathy John, Financial Aid Director, 800 Livermore Street, Yellow Springs, OH 45387-1609. Fax: 937-767-6461; E-mail: kjohn@mcgregor.antioch.edu

FACILITIES
Information Resources Olive Kettering Library; total holdings of 273,000 volumes, 45,000 microforms, 1,050 current periodical subscriptions. CD player(s) available for graduate student use. Access provided to online bibliographic retrieval services.

INTERNATIONAL STUDENTS
Demographics N/R

PLACEMENT
Employment Of 1996–97 graduates, 98% were employed within three months of graduation. Types of employment entered: banking, computer-related, consulting, consumer products, education, energy, engineering, government, health services, high technology, human resources, information systems/technology, insurance, management, manufacturing, marketing, nonprofit, service industry.

Business Program(s) URL: http://www.mcgregor.edu/man

Program Contact: Ms. Terri Haney, Director of Admissions, 800 Livermore Street, Yellow Springs, OH 45387-1609. Phone: 937-767-6325 Ext. 6275; Fax: 937-767-6461; E-mail: thaney@mcgregor.antioch.edu

Miami University

Richard T. Farmer School of Business Administration

Oxford, Ohio

OVERVIEW
Miami University is a state-related, coed university. Enrollment: 20,517 graduate, professional, and undergraduate students; 931 full-time matriculated graduate/professional students; 790 part-time matriculated graduate/professional students. Founded: 1809. The graduate business unit is in a small-town setting and is on a semester calendar.

HIGHLIGHTS

Enrollment Profile

Full-time: 71	International: 12%
Part-time: 79	Women: 31%
Total: 150	Minorities: 7%
Average Age: 26	Average Class Size: 25
Fall 1997 Average GPA: 3.2	Fall 1997 Average GMAT: 560

Costs
Full-time tuition: $2302 per academic year (resident); $5352 per academic year (nonresident)
Part-time tuition: $192 per hour (resident); $446 per hour (nonresident)

AACSB – The International Association for Management Education accredited

GRADUATE BUSINESS PROGRAMS
Master of Business Administration (MBA) Full-time, part-time; 37-58 total credits required; 12 months to 3 years to complete program. Concentrations in finance, management, decision sciences, marketing, management information systems.

Master of Arts in Economics (MA) Full-time; 30 total credits required; 12 months to complete program. Concentration in economics.

Master of Accountancy (MAcc) Full-time; 30 total credits required; 12 months to complete program. Concentration in accounting.

ADMISSION
Applications For fall 1997 there were 153 applications for admission. Of those applying, 123 were accepted. Of those accepted, 61 enrolled.

Application Requirements GMAT score: minimum 475, application form, application fee, bachelor's degree, essay, minimum GPA: 2.75, interview, 2 letters of recommendation, college transcript(s).

Recommended for Application GRE score accepted, personal statement, resume, work experience, computer experience.

Application Deadline 7/15 for fall, 7/1 for fall (international). Application fee: $35. Deferred entrance is available.

ACADEMICS
Faculty Full-time 118; part-time 5.

Teaching Methodologies Case study, computer-aided instruction, computer analysis, computer simulations, experiential learning, field projects, group discussion, lecture, research, role playing, simulations, student presentations, team projects.

Technology 360 on-campus computer terminals/PCs are available for student use and are linked by a campus-wide network. The network has full access to the Internet. Students are not required to have their own PC.

Special Opportunities Advanced credit may be earned through transfer of credits from another institution. An internship program is available.

FINANCES
Costs for 1997–98 Tuition: Full-time: $2302 per semester (resident); $5352 per semester (nonresident). Part-time: $192 per hour (resident); $446 per hour (nonresident). Cost varies by number of credits taken. Fees: Full-time: $610 per academic year (resident); $610 per academic year (nonresident). Part-time: $65 per hour (resident); $65 per hour (nonresident). Fees vary by number of credits taken. Average 1997–98 room and board costs were $3460 per academic year (on campus) and $3150 per academic year (off campus). Room and board costs vary by campus location, occupancy (e.g., single, double, triple), type of accommodation, type of meal plan.

Financial Aid In 1997–98, 52% of students received some institutionally administered aid in the form of fellowships, research assistantships, loans. Financial aid is available to part-time students. Application Deadline: 3/1.

Financial Aid Contact Mrs. Judy Barille, Director of Graduate Business Programs, Richard T. Farmer School of Business Administration, Oxford, OH 45056. Phone: 513-529-6643; Fax: 513-529-2487; E-mail: barillja@muohio.edu

FACILITIES
Information Resources King Library plus 4 additional on-campus libraries; total holdings of 1,200,000 volumes, 1,800,000 microforms, 6,500 current periodical subscriptions. Access provided to online bibliographic retrieval services.

INTERNATIONAL STUDENTS
Demographics 12% of students enrolled are international students [Africa, 7%, Asia, 62%, Europe, 31%].

Services and Facilities International student office, international student center, international student housing, visa services, counseling/support services, host families.

Applying TOEFL: minimum score of 550, TWE: minimum score of 4, proof of adequate funds, proof of health/immunizations required. Financial aid is available to international students.

International Student Contact Mr. Donald Nelson, Director, International Education Services, Langstroth House, Oxford, OH 45056. Phone: 513-529-2512; Fax: 513-529-7383.

PLACEMENT
Services include alumni network, career counseling/planning, career fairs, career library, career placement, resume referral to employers, and resume preparation. In 1996–97, 428 organizations participated in on-campus recruiting; 10,601 on-campus interviews were conducted.

Employment Of 1996–97 graduates, 86% were employed within three months of graduation; the average starting salary was $43,650. Types of employment entered: accounting, banking, communications, computer-related, consulting, consumer products, education, energy, engineering, finance, financial services, government, health services, human resources, information systems/technology, insurance, management, manufacturing, marketing, pharmaceutical, telecommunications, transportation.

Business Program(s) URL: http://www.muohio.edu

Program Contact: Mrs. Judy Barille, Director of Graduate Business Programs, Richard T. Farmer School of Business Administration, Oxford, OH 45056. Phone: 513-529-6643; Fax: 513-529-2487; E-mail: barillja@muohio.edu

The Ohio State University

Max M. Fisher College of Business

Columbus, Ohio

OVERVIEW
The Ohio State University is a state-supported, coed university. Enrollment: 55,787 graduate, professional, and undergraduate students; 8,963 full-time matriculated graduate/professional students; 4,238 part-time matriculated graduate/professional students. Founded: 1870. The graduate business unit is in an urban setting and is on a quarter calendar.

The Ohio State University (continued)

HIGHLIGHTS

Enrollment Profile
Full-time: 607
Part-time: 137
Total: 744
Average Age: 26
Fall 1997 Average GPA: 3.2

International: 16%
Women: 39%
Minorities: 15%
Average Class Size: 35
Fall 1997 Average GMAT: 621

Costs
Full-time tuition: $5067 per academic year (resident); $12,582 per academic year (nonresident)
Part-time tuition: $4079 per 3 quarters (resident); $10,592 per 3 quarters (nonresident)

AACSB – The International Association for Management Education accredited

GRADUATE BUSINESS PROGRAMS
Full-time MBA (MBA) Full-time; 96 total credits required; 22 months to complete program. Concentrations in accounting, finance, human resources, international business, logistics, management information systems, marketing, operations management, real estate, management consulting.
Evening MBA (MBA) Part-time; 60 total credits required; 22 months to complete program.
Master of Labor and Human Resources (MLHR)

ADMISSION
Applications For fall 1997 there were 1,523 applications for admission. Of those applying, 394 were accepted. Of those accepted, 212 enrolled.
Application Requirements GMAT score: minimum 600, application form, application fee, bachelor's degree, essay, 3 letters of recommendation, personal statement, resume, college transcript(s).
Recommended for Application Minimum GPA: 3.2, interview, minimum of 3 years of work experience, computer experience.
Application Deadline 4/30 for fall, 4/30 for fall (international). Application fee: $30, $40 (international). Deferred entrance is available.

ACADEMICS
Faculty Full-time 80; part-time 1.
Teaching Methodologies Case study, computer-aided instruction, computer analysis, computer simulations, experiential learning, faculty seminars, field projects, group discussion, lecture, role playing, seminars by members of the business community, simulations, student presentations, team projects.
Technology 1,245 on-campus computer terminals/PCs are available for student use and are linked by a campus-wide network. The network has full access to the Internet. Students are not required to have their own PC.
Special Opportunities An internship program is available.

FINANCES
Costs for 1997–98 Tuition: Full-time: $5067 per year (resident); $12,582 per year (nonresident). Part-time: $4079 per 3 quarters (resident); $10,592 per 3 quarters (nonresident). Cost varies by academic program, number of credits taken. Fees: Full-time: $360 per academic year (resident); $360 per academic year (nonresident). Part-time: $360 per 3 quarters (resident); $360 per 3 quarters (nonresident). Average 1997–98 room and board costs were $4482 per academic year (on campus) and $4500 per academic year (off campus). Room and board costs vary by campus location, occupancy (e.g., single, double, triple), type of accommodation, type of meal plan.
Financial Aid In 1997–98, 10% of students received some institutionally administered aid in the form of fellowships, research assistantships, teaching assistantships, scholarships, work study, loans. Application Deadline: 1/15.
Financial Aid Contact Ms. Michelle Jacobson, Manager, Student Services, 2108 Neil Avenue, Gerbach Hall, Columbus, OH 43210. Phone: 614-292-4271; Fax: 614-292-9006; E-mail: jacobson.1@osu.edu

FACILITIES
Information Resources William Oxley Thompson Library plus 20 additional on-campus libraries; total holdings of 4,786,385 volumes, 3,822,981 microforms, 32,812 current periodical subscriptions. CD player(s) available for graduate student use. Access provided to online bibliographic retrieval services and online databases.

INTERNATIONAL STUDENTS
Demographics 16% of students enrolled are international students [Africa, 1%, Asia, 69%, Central America, 3%, Europe, 25%, North America, 1%, South America, 1%].
Services and Facilities International student office, international student center, international student housing, visa services, ESL courses, counseling/support services, international student organization.

Applying TOEFL: minimum score of 600, proof of adequate funds, proof of health/immunizations required. Financial aid is available to international students.
International Student Contact Mr. John Greisberger, Director-International Education, Oxley Hall, 1712 Neil Avenue, Columbus, OH 43210. Phone: 614-292-6101; Fax: 614-292-4725; E-mail: greisberger.1@osu.edu

PLACEMENT
Services include alumni network, career counseling/planning, career fairs, career library, career placement, electronic job bank, job interviews arranged, resume referral to employers, and resume preparation. In 1996–97, 198 organizations participated in on-campus recruiting; 1,025 on-campus interviews were conducted.
Employment Of 1996–97 graduates, 95% were employed within three months of graduation; the average starting salary was $63,565. Types of employment entered: accounting, banking, chemical industry, communications, computer-related, consulting, consumer products, engineering, finance, financial services, government, health services, high technology, human resources, information systems/technology, insurance, international trade, management, manufacturing, marketing, nonprofit, pharmaceutical, real estate, retail, service industry, telecommunications, transportation, utilities.

Business Program(s) URL: http://www.cob.ohio-state.edu

Program Contact: Ms. Pat Strohl, Manager, Recruitment and Admissions, 2108 Neil Avenue, Gerbach Hall, Columbus, OH 43210. Phone: 614-292-8530; Fax: 614-292-9006; E-mail: cobgrd@cob.ohio-state.edu

Ohio University

College of Business

Athens, Ohio

OVERVIEW
Ohio University is a state-supported, coed university. Enrollment: 27,848 graduate, professional, and undergraduate students; 2,143 full-time matriculated graduate/professional students; 877 part-time matriculated graduate/professional students. Founded: 1804. The graduate business unit is in a small-town setting and is on a quarter calendar.

HIGHLIGHTS

Enrollment Profile
Full-time: 49
Part-time: 21
Total: 70
Average Age: 25
Fall 1997 Average GPA: 3.5

International: 34%
Women: 44%
Minorities: 3%
Average Class Size: 30
Fall 1997 Average GMAT: 532

Costs
Full-time tuition: $5492 per academic year (resident); $11,784 per academic year (nonresident)
Part-time tuition: $171 per credit hour (resident); $366 per credit hour (nonresident)

AACSB – The International Association for Management Education accredited

GRADUATE BUSINESS PROGRAMS
Master of Business Administration (MBA) Full-time, part-time, distance learning option; 72 total credits required; 13 months to 2 years to complete program.
Executive MBA (MBA) Part-time; 64 total credits required; 21 months to complete program.
Master of Science in Accountancy (MS) Full-time, part-time; 48 total credits required; 9 months to complete program.
MBA Without Boundaries (MBA) Part-time, distance learning option; 72 total credits required; 2 years to complete program.

ADMISSION
Applications For fall 1997 there were 132 applications for admission. Of those applying, 62 were accepted. Of those accepted, 35 enrolled.
Application Requirements GMAT score: minimum 500, application form, application fee, bachelor's degree, essay, minimum GPA: 3.0, 3 letters of recommendation, college transcript(s).
Recommended for Application Interview, personal statement, resume, minimum of 2 years of work experience, computer experience.
Application Deadline 3/1 for fall, 3/1 for fall (international). Application fee: $30. Deferred entrance is available.

ACADEMICS
Faculty Full-time 58; part-time 10.

Teaching Methodologies Case study, experiential learning, group discussion, lecture, research, seminars by members of the business community, simulations, student presentations, team projects.

Technology Computer terminals/PCs are available for student use and are linked by a campus-wide network. The network has full access to the Internet. Students are required to have their own PC.

Special Opportunities International exchange programs in Brazil, Hungary, Malaysia, South Africa.

FINANCES
Costs for 1997–98 Tuition: Full-time: $5492 per year (resident); $11,784 per year (nonresident). Part-time: $171 per credit hour (resident); $366 per credit hour (nonresident). Cost varies by number of credits taken, reciprocity agreements. Fees: Full-time: $1340 per academic year (resident); $1340 per academic year (nonresident). Part-time: $33 per credit hour (resident); $33 per credit hour (nonresident). Fees vary by campus location, number of credits taken. Average 1997–98 room and board costs were $5680 per academic year (on campus) and $6500 per academic year (off campus). Room and board costs vary by occupancy (e.g., single, double, triple), type of accommodation, type of meal plan.

Financial Aid In 1997–98, 70% of students received some institutionally administered aid in the form of teaching assistantships, scholarships, work study, loans. Application Deadline: 3/1.

Financial Aid Contact Ms. Jan Ross, Graduate Services Coordinator, Copeland Hall 514, Athens, OH 45701-2979. Phone: 614-593-2007; Fax: 614-593-9823; E-mail: rossj@ouvaxa.cats.ohiou.edu

FACILITIES
Information Resources Alden Library plus 1 additional on-campus library; total holdings of 1,398,433 volumes, 2,179,780 microforms, 11,414 current periodical subscriptions. CD player(s) available for graduate student use. Access provided to online bibliographic retrieval services.

INTERNATIONAL STUDENTS
Demographics 34% of students enrolled are international students [Africa, 10%, Asia, 45%, Europe, 10%, North America, 10%, South America, 10%, other, 15%].

Services and Facilities International student office, international student center, ESL courses, counseling/support services.

Applying TOEFL: minimum score of 600, proof of adequate funds required. TWE recommended. Financial aid is available to international students.

International Student Contact Dr. Alan Boyd, Director, International Student and Faculty Services, Scott Quad 172, Athens, OH 45701-2979. Phone: 614-593-4330; Fax: 614-593-4328.

PLACEMENT
Services include career counseling/planning, career fairs, career library, electronic job bank, job interviews arranged, resume referral to employers, and resume preparation.

Employment Of 1996–97 graduates, 92% were employed within three months of graduation. Types of employment entered: accounting, banking, computer-related, consulting, consumer products, education, engineering, finance, financial services, government, information systems/technology, insurance, management, manufacturing, marketing, media, nonprofit.

Business Program(s) URL: http://www.cba.ohiou.edu/www/grad/

Program Contact: Ms. Jan Ross, Graduate Services Coordinator, Copeland Hall 514, Athens, OH 45701-2979. Phone: 614-593-2007; Fax: 614-593-9823; E-mail: rossj@ouvaxa.cats.ohiou.edu
See full description on page 914.

Otterbein College

Department of Business, Accounting and Economics

Westerville, Ohio

OVERVIEW
Otterbein College is an independent-religious, comprehensive institution. The graduate business unit is on a quarter calendar.

HIGHLIGHTS
Enrollment Profile
Full-time: N/R
Part-time: N/R
Total: N/R
Average Age: N/R
Fall 1997 Average GPA: N/R

International: N/R
Women: N/R
Minorities: N/R
Average Class Size: N/R
Fall 1997 Average GMAT: N/R

Costs
Full-time tuition: $5216 per academic year
Part-time tuition: $195 per credit

GRADUATE BUSINESS PROGRAMS
Master of Business Administration (MBA) Full-time, part-time; 64 total credits required; minimum of 2 years to complete program.

ADMISSION
Application Requirements GMAT score, application form, bachelor's degree, minimum GPA, 3 letters of recommendation, personal statement, resume, college transcript(s), work experience, computer experience: general computer proficiency.

Recommended for Application Interview.

Application Deadline Applications processed on a rolling/continuous basis for both domestic and international students.

FINANCES
Costs for 1997–98 Tuition: Full-time: $5216 per quarter. Part-time: $195 per credit.

Financial Aid Contact Financial Aid Office, Westerville, OH 43081. Phone: 614-823-1502.

INTERNATIONAL STUDENTS
Demographics N/R

Services and Facilities International student office.

International Student Contact Chuck Vedder, Director of International Student Programs, Westerville, OH 43081. Phone: 614-823-1312; E-mail: cvedder@otterbein.edu

Business Program(s) URL: http://www.otterbein.edu

Program Contact: Graduate Programs Office, Westerville, OH 43081. Phone: 614-823-3210.

Tiffin University

Program in Business Administration

Tiffin, Ohio

OVERVIEW
Tiffin University is an independent-nonprofit, coed, comprehensive institution. Enrollment: 1,303 graduate, professional, and undergraduate students; 67 full-time matriculated graduate/professional students; 22 part-time matriculated graduate/professional students. Founded: 1888. The graduate business unit is in a small-town setting and is on a semester calendar.

HIGHLIGHTS
Enrollment Profile
Full-time: 67
Part-time: 22
Total: 89
Average Age: 37
Fall 1997 Average GPA: 3.4

International: 4%
Women: 39%
Minorities: 12%
Average Class Size: 28
Fall 1997 Average GMAT: N/R

Costs
Full-time tuition: $6000 per academic year
Part-time tuition: $1500 per module

ACBSP – The American Council of Business Schools and Programs accredited

GRADUATE BUSINESS PROGRAMS
Executive Management MBA (MBA) Full-time, part-time; 33 total credits required; 2 to 6 years to complete program. Concentration in management.

ADMISSION
Applications For fall 1997 there were 42 applications for admission. Of those applying, 39 were accepted. Of those accepted, 38 enrolled.

Application Requirements Application form, application fee, bachelor's degree, essay, minimum GPA: 3.0, interview, 3 letters of recommendation, personal statement, college transcript(s), computer experience: spreadsheets, Microsoft Word.

Recommended for Application Resume, work experience.

Tiffin University (continued)

Application Deadline 8/1 for fall, 12/1 for spring, 7/1 for fall (international). Application fee: $30. Deferred entrance is available.

ACADEMICS
Faculty Full-time 13.

Teaching Methodologies Case study, computer-aided instruction, computer analysis, experiential learning, faculty seminars, field projects, group discussion, lecture, research, role playing, seminars by members of the business community, student presentations, team projects.

Technology 75 on-campus computer terminals/PCs are available for student use and are linked by a campus-wide network. The network has full access to the Internet. Students are not required to have their own PC.

Special Opportunities Advanced credit may be earned through transfer of credits from another institution. International exchange program in United Kingdom.

FINANCES
Costs for 1997–98 Tuition: Full-time: $6000 per year. Part-time: $1500 per module. Cost varies by number of credits taken. Fees: Full-time: $700 per academic year. Part-time: $150 per class. Fees vary by number of credits taken. Average 1997–98 room only costs were $2500 per academic year (off campus). Room and board costs vary by occupancy (e.g., single, double, triple), type of accommodation, type of meal plan.

Financial Aid In 1997–98, 21% of students received some institutionally administered aid in the form of loans. Financial aid is available to part-time students. Application Deadline: 7/31.

Financial Aid Contact Ms. Carol McDonnell, Director of Financial Aid, 155 Miami Street, Tiffin, OH 44883-2161. Phone: 800-968-6446 Ext. 3414.

FACILITIES
Information Resources Pfeiffer Library; total holdings of 22,317 volumes, 43,212 microforms, 147 current periodical subscriptions. CD player(s) available for graduate student use. Access provided to online bibliographic retrieval services.

INTERNATIONAL STUDENTS
Demographics 4% of students enrolled are international students [Asia, 75%, South America, 25%].

Services and Facilities International student office, counseling/support services.

Applying TOEFL: minimum score of 550, proof of adequate funds, proof of health/immunizations required. Financial aid is not available to international students.

International Student Contact Ms. Alice Nichols, Registrar, 155 Miami Street, Tiffin, OH 44883-2161. Phone: 800-968-6446 Ext. 3416.

PLACEMENT
Services include alumni network, career counseling/planning, career fairs, career placement, job interviews arranged, and resume preparation. In 1996–97, 13 organizations participated in on-campus recruiting.

Employment Of 1996–97 graduates, 98% were employed within three months of graduation; the average starting salary was $34,500. Types of employment entered: accounting, banking, communications, computer-related, consulting, education, engineering, finance, financial services, government, health services, hospitality management, human resources, management, manufacturing, marketing, retail, service industry, utilities.

Business Program(s) URL: http://www.tiffin.edu

Program Contact: Mr. Allen Lowery, Director of Graduate Studies, 155 Miami Street, Tiffin, OH 44883-2161. Phone: 419-448-3403, 800-968-6446 (OH only); Fax: 419-443-5002; E-mail: alowery@tiffin.edu

University of Akron

College of Business Administration

Akron, Ohio

OVERVIEW
The University of Akron is a state-supported, coed university. Enrollment: 22,347 graduate, professional, and undergraduate students; 2,167 full-time matriculated graduate/professional students; 1,788 part-time matriculated graduate/professional students. Founded: 1870. The graduate business unit is in an urban setting and is on a semester calendar.

HIGHLIGHTS
Enrollment Profile

Full-time: 184	International: 17%
Part-time: 368	Women: 32%
Total: 552	Minorities: 4%
Average Age: 31	Average Class Size: 22
Fall 1997 Average GPA: 2.823	Fall 1997 Average GMAT: 521

Costs
Full-time tuition: N/R
Part-time tuition: $165 per credit (resident); $308 per credit (nonresident)

AACSB – The International Association for Management Education accredited

GRADUATE BUSINESS PROGRAMS
Master of Business Administration (MBA) Full-time, part-time; 34-58 total credits required; 12 months to 6 years to complete program. Concentrations in accounting, finance, international business, management, marketing, quality management, resources management.

Master of Science in Management (MS) Full-time, part-time; 30-54 total credits required; 12 months to 6 years to complete program. Concentrations in financial management/planning, management information systems.

Master of Taxation (MTax) Full-time, part-time; 30-60 total credits required; 12 months to 6 years to complete program.

Doctor of Jurisprudence/Master of Business Administration (JD/MBA) Full-time, part-time; 103-124 total credits required; 3 to 8 years to complete program. Concentrations in accounting, finance, international business, management, marketing, quality management, resources management.

Doctor of Jurisprudence/Master of Taxation (JD/MTax) Full-time, part-time; 98-116 total credits required; 3 to 8 years to complete program. Concentration in taxation.

Master of Science in Accountancy (MS) Full-time, part-time; 36-60 total credits required; 12 months to 6 years to complete program. Concentration in accounting.

ADMISSION
Applications For fall 1997 there were 133 applications for admission. Of those applying, 112 were accepted. Of those accepted, 42 enrolled.

Application Requirements GMAT score: minimum 450, application form, application fee, bachelor's degree, minimum GPA, college transcript(s).

Recommended for Application Essay, letters of recommendation, personal statement, resume, computer experience.

Application Deadline 8/1 for fall, 12/15 for spring, 6/1 for summer, 6/15 for fall (international), 11/1 for spring (international), 4/1 for summer (international). Application fee: $25, $50 (international). Deferred entrance is available.

ACADEMICS
Faculty Full-time 60; part-time 20.

Teaching Methodologies Case study, computer-aided instruction, computer analysis, computer simulations, experiential learning, field projects, group discussion, lecture, research, role playing, seminars by members of the business community, simulations, student presentations, study groups, team projects.

Technology 173 on-campus computer terminals/PCs are available for student use and are linked by a campus-wide network. The network has full access to the Internet. Students are not required to have their own PC.

Special Opportunities Advanced credit may be earned through transfer of credits from another institution. An internship program is available.

FINANCES
Costs for 1997–98 Tuition: $165 per credit (resident); $308 per credit (nonresident). Cost varies by number of credits taken. Fees: $6 per credit (resident); $6 per credit (nonresident). Fees vary by number of credits taken. Average 1997–98 room and board costs were $7000 per academic year (off campus).

Financial Aid In 1997–98, 14% of students received some institutionally administered aid in the form of fellowships, research assistantships, teaching assistantships, scholarships, work study. Financial aid is available to part-time students. Application Deadline: 1/30.

Financial Aid Contact Miss Myra Weakland, Assistant Director, Graduate Progarms in Business, 259 South Broadway, Room 412, Akron, OH 44325-4805. Phone: 330-972-7043; Fax: 330-972-6588; E-mail: gradadv@uakron.edu

FACILITIES
Information Resources Bierce Library plus 2 additional on-campus libraries; total holdings of 1,078,823 volumes, 1,626,129 microforms, 6,369 current periodical subscriptions. CD player(s) available for graduate student use. Access provided to online bibliographic retrieval services.

INTERNATIONAL STUDENTS

Demographics 17% of students enrolled are international students [Africa, 5%, Asia, 70%, Central America, 5%, Europe, 10%, North America, 3%, South America, 2%, other, 5%].

Services and Facilities International student office, visa services, ESL courses, counseling/support services.

Applying TOEFL: minimum score of 550, proof of adequate funds, proof of health/immunizations required. TSE: minimum score of 50 recommended. Financial aid is available to international students.

International Student Contact Ms. Theresa M. McCune, Admissions Credentials Evaluator, International Programs, 302 Buchtel Common, Akron, OH 44325-4805. Phone: 330-972-6349; Fax: 330-972-8604; E-mail: international@uakron.edu

PLACEMENT

Services include career counseling/planning, career fairs, career library, career placement, electronic job bank, job interviews arranged, resume referral to employers, and resume preparation. In 1996–97, 28 organizations participated in on-campus recruiting.

Employment Types of employment entered: accounting, banking, chemical industry, communications, computer-related, consulting, consumer products, education, engineering, finance, financial services, government, health services, hospitality management, human resources, information systems/technology, insurance, international trade, law, management, manufacturing, marketing, media, nonprofit, petrochemical, pharmaceutical, real estate, retail, service industry, telecommunications, transportation, utilities.

Business Program(s) URL: http://www.uakron.edu/

Program Contact: Miss Myra Weakland, Assistant Director, Graduate Programs in Business, 259 South Broadway, Room 112, Akron, OH 44325-4805. Phone: 330-972-7043; Fax: 330-972-6588; E-mail: gradadv@uakron.edu

University of Cincinnati

Graduate Business Program

Cincinnati, Ohio

OVERVIEW

The University of Cincinnati is a state-supported, coed university. Enrollment: 36,000 graduate, professional, and undergraduate students; 4,759 full-time matriculated graduate/professional students; 3,031 part-time matriculated graduate/professional students. Founded: 1819. The graduate business unit is in an urban setting and is on a quarter calendar.

HIGHLIGHTS

Enrollment Profile

Full-time: 72	International: N/R
Part-time: 279	Women: N/R
Total: 351	Minorities: N/R
Average Age: 31	Average Class Size: 35
Fall 1997 Average GPA: 3.3	Fall 1997 Average GMAT: 597

Costs
Full-time tuition: $5418 per academic year (resident); $10,356 per academic year (nonresident)
Part-time tuition: N/R

AACSB – The International Association for Management Education accredited

GRADUATE BUSINESS PROGRAMS

Master of Business Administration (MBA) Full-time, part-time; 66 total credits required; 12 months to 4.3 years to complete program. Concentrations in finance, marketing, information management, international business, management, operations management, quantitative analysis, construction management, real estate, technology management.

Master of Science in Quantitative Analysis (MS) Full-time, part-time; 45 total credits required; 12 months to 2 years to complete program.

Master of Business Administration/Doctor of Jurisprudence (MBA/JD) Full-time, part-time; 134 total credits required; 3.5 to 7 years to complete program.

Master of Business Administration/Master of Arts in Arts Administration (MBA/MA) Full-time, part-time; 122 total credits required; 3 to 7 years to complete program.

Master of Business Administration/Master of Science in Industrial Engineering (MBA/MS) Full-time, part-time; 87 total credits required; 2 to 7 years to complete program.

ADMISSION

Application Requirements Application form, application fee, bachelor's degree, essay, 2 letters of recommendation, personal statement, resume, college transcript(s), minimum of 2 years of work experience.

Recommended for Application GMAT score accepted: minimum 550, minimum GPA: 3.0, computer experience.

Application Deadline 5/30 for fall, 1/30 for spring, 2/15 for summer. Application fee: $30.

ACADEMICS

Faculty Full-time 42.

Teaching Methodologies Case study, computer-aided instruction, computer analysis, computer simulations, faculty seminars, field projects, group discussion, lecture, role playing, seminars by members of the business community, simulations, student presentations, study groups, team projects.

Technology 200 on-campus computer terminals/PCs are available for student use. Students are not required to have their own PC.

Special Opportunities Advanced credit may be earned through transfer of credits from another institution.

FINANCES

Costs for 1997–98 Tuition: Full-time: $5418 per year (resident); $10,356 per year (nonresident). Cost varies by number of credits taken. Average 1997–98 room and board costs were $8700 per academic year.

Financial Aid Fellowships available. Financial aid is available to part-time students.

Financial Aid Contact Student Financial Aid, 52 Beecher Hall, Cincinnati, OH 45221. Phone: 513-556-6982.

FACILITIES

Information Resources Walter C. Langsam Library plus 18 additional on-campus libraries; total holdings of 1,900,000 volumes, 2,500,000 microforms, 19,500 current periodical subscriptions. CD player(s) available for graduate student use. Access provided to online bibliographic retrieval services.

INTERNATIONAL STUDENTS

Demographics N/R

Services and Facilities International student office, international student center, visa services, counseling/support services.

Applying TOEFL: minimum score of 600, proof of adequate funds, proof of health/immunizations required. Financial aid is available to international students.

International Student Contact Ms. Penny Chapman, Academic Advisor, 103 Lindner Hall, Cincinnati, OH 45221.

PLACEMENT

Services include alumni network, career counseling/planning, career library, career placement, job interviews arranged, job search course, resume referral to employers, and resume preparation. In 1996–97, 70 organizations participated in on-campus recruiting; 70 on-campus interviews were conducted.

Employment Of 1996–97 graduates, 90% were employed within three months of graduation; the average starting salary was $46,200. Types of employment entered: accounting, banking, chemical industry, computer-related, consulting, consumer products, education, energy, engineering, finance, financial services, government, health services, high technology, human resources, information systems/technology, international trade, law, management, manufacturing, marketing, nonprofit, pharmaceutical, real estate, retail, service industry, telecommunications, transportation, utilities.

Business Program(s) URL: http://www.cba.uc.edu

Program Contact: Mr. James H. Bast, Assistant Dean of Graduate Programs, 103 Lindner Hall, Cincinnati, OH 45221. Phone: 513-556-7020 E-mail: graduate@uc.edu

University of Dayton

School of Business Administration

Dayton, Ohio

OVERVIEW

The University of Dayton is an independent-religious, coed university. Enrollment: 10,198 graduate, professional, and undergraduate students; 787 full-time matriculated graduate/professional students; 2,265 part-time matriculated graduate/professional students. Founded: 1850. The graduate business unit is in a suburban setting and is on a trimester calendar.

University of Dayton (continued)

HIGHLIGHTS

Enrollment Profile

Full-time: 83

Part-time: 459

Total: 542

Average Age: 29

Fall 1997 Average GPA: 3.1

International: 8%

Women: 40%

Minorities: 7%

Average Class Size: 30

Fall 1997 Average GMAT: 510

Costs

Full-time tuition: $7362 per academic year

Part-time tuition: $409 per semester hour

AACSB – The International Association for Management Education accredited

GRADUATE BUSINESS PROGRAMS

Master of Business Administration (MBA) Full-time, part-time; 30-52 total credits required; 12 months to 5 years to complete program. Concentrations in finance, international business, management information systems, marketing, operations management, accounting.

Master of Business Administration/Juris Doctor (MBA/JD) Full-time, part-time; 105-127 total credits required; 3.5 to 5 years to complete program. Concentrations in finance, international business, management information systems, marketing, operations management, accounting.

ADMISSION

Applications For fall 1997 there were 179 applications for admission. Of those applying, 161 were accepted. Of those accepted, 129 enrolled.

Application Requirements GMAT score, application form, application fee, bachelor's degree, minimum GPA: 2.5, college transcript(s).

Recommended for Application Essay, interview, letters of recommendation, personal statement, resume, work experience, computer experience.

Application Deadline Applications processed on a rolling/continuous basis for domestic students only. 7/25 for fall (international), 11/25 for winter (international), 4/25 for spring (international), 4/25 for summer (international). Application fee: $30. Deferred entrance is available.

ACADEMICS

Faculty Full-time 54; part-time 21.

Teaching Methodologies Case study, computer-aided instruction, computer analysis, computer simulations, experiential learning, field projects, group discussion, lecture, research, role playing, seminars by members of the business community, simulations, student presentations, study groups, team projects.

Technology 62 on-campus computer terminals/PCs are available for student use and are linked by a campus-wide network. The network has full access to the Internet. Students are not required to have their own PC.

Special Opportunities Advanced credit may be earned through credit by examination, credit for military training programs, credit for business training programs, transfer of credits from another institution. International exchange programs in Finland, Germany, People's Republic of China.

FINANCES

Costs for 1997–98 Tuition: Full-time: $7362 per year. Part-time: $409 per semester hour. Cost varies by number of credits taken. Fees: Full-time: $25 per academic year. Part-time: $25 per semester. Fees vary by campus location. Average 1997–98 room and board costs were $5460 per academic year. Room and board costs vary by occupancy (e.g., single, double, triple), type of accommodation, type of meal plan.

Financial Aid Fellowships, research assistantships, grants, scholarships available. Financial aid is available to part-time students. Application Deadline: 4/15.

Financial Aid Contact Ms. Joyce Wilkins, Director, Office of Financial Aid, 300 College Park Avenue, Dayton, OH 45469-1621. Phone: 937-229-4311; Fax: 937-229-4545; E-mail: wilkins@kahn.admin.udayton.edu

FACILITIES

Information Resources Roesch Library plus 2 additional on-campus libraries; total holdings of 1,403,260 volumes, 708,299 microforms, 7,184 current periodical subscriptions. CD player(s) available for graduate student use. Access provided to online bibliographic retrieval services and online databases.

INTERNATIONAL STUDENTS

Demographics 8% of students enrolled are international students.

Services and Facilities International student office, international student center, international student housing, visa services, ESL courses, counseling/support services.

Applying TOEFL: minimum score of 550, proof of adequate funds, proof of health/immunizations required. Financial aid is not available to international students.

International Student Contact Ms. April Spencer, International Student Advisor, 300 College Park Avenue, Dayton, OH 45469-1481. Phone: 937-229-2748; Fax: 937-229-2766; E-mail: spencer@trinity.udayton.edu

PLACEMENT

Services include alumni network, career counseling/planning, career fairs, career library, career placement, electronic job bank, job interviews arranged, job search course, resume referral to employers, and resume preparation. In 1996–97, 40 organizations participated in on-campus recruiting.

Employment Of 1996–97 graduates, 95% were employed within three months of graduation. Types of employment entered: accounting, banking, communications, computer-related, consulting, consumer products, engineering, finance, financial services, government, health services, high technology, hospitality management, human resources, information systems/technology, insurance, international trade, law, management, manufacturing, marketing, nonprofit, pharmaceutical, real estate, retail, service industry, telecommunications, transportation, utilities.

Business Program(s) URL: http://www.udayton.edu/~mba/

Program Contact: Dr. E. James Dunne, Associate Dean and Director, MBA Program, 300 College Park Avenue, Dayton, OH 45469-2226. Phone: 937-229-3733; Fax: 937-229-3301; E-mail: mba@udayton.edu

The University of Findlay

Business Programs

Findlay, Ohio

OVERVIEW

The University of Findlay is an independent-religious, coed, comprehensive institution. Enrollment: 3,750 graduate, professional, and undergraduate students. Founded: 1882. The graduate business unit is on a semester calendar.

HIGHLIGHTS

Enrollment Profile

Full-time: N/R

Part-time: N/R

Total: 325

Average Age: 30

Fall 1997 Average GPA: 3.1

International: 8%

Women: N/R

Minorities: N/R

Average Class Size: 18

Fall 1997 Average GMAT: 520

Costs

Full-time tuition: N/R

Part-time tuition: $299 per credit hour

GRADUATE BUSINESS PROGRAMS

Master of Business Administration (MBA) Full-time, part-time, distance learning option; 33 total credits required; 12 months to 5 years to complete program. Concentrations in organizational management, health care, public management.

ADMISSION

Applications For fall 1997 there were 57 applications for admission. Of those applying, 56 were accepted. Of those accepted, 50 enrolled.

Application Requirements GMAT score: minimum 300, application form, application fee, bachelor's degree, minimum GPA: 2.5, interview, 3 letters of recommendation, college transcript(s), minimum of 1 year of work experience, computer experience: computer literacy.

Application Deadline Applications processed on a rolling/continuous basis for both domestic and international students. Application fee: $25.

ACADEMICS

Faculty Full-time 10; part-time 5.

Teaching Methodologies Case study, computer-aided instruction, computer analysis, computer simulations, experiential learning, faculty seminars, field projects, group discussion, lecture, research, role playing, seminars by members of the business community, simulations, student presentations, study groups, team projects.

FINANCES

Costs for 1997–98 Tuition: $299 per credit hour.

Financial Aid Research assistantships, work study, loans available. Financial aid is available to part-time students.

Financial Aid Contact Todd Everett, Financial Aid Director, 1000 North Main Street, Findlay, OH 45840-3653. Phone: 419-424-4792.

FACILITIES

Information Resources Shafer Library; total holdings of 122,617 volumes, 90,426 microforms, 896 current periodical subscriptions. CD player(s) available for graduate student use. Access provided to online bibliographic retrieval services.

INTERNATIONAL STUDENTS

Demographics 8% of students enrolled are international students.

Applying TOEFL: minimum score of 525, proof of adequate funds, proof of health/immunizations required. Financial aid is available to international students.

International Student Contact Denise Bunge, International Student Office, 1000 North Main Street, Findlay, OH 45840-3653. Phone: 419-424-4558.

PLACEMENT

Employment Of 1996–97 graduates, 100% were employed within three months of graduation; the average starting salary was $45,000. Types of employment entered: accounting, banking, consulting, finance, health services, international trade, manufacturing, service industry.

Program Contact: Dr. Theodore Alex, MBA Program Director, 1000 North Main Street, Findlay, OH 45840-3653. Phone: 419-424-4676; Fax: 419-424-4822.

University of Toledo

College of Business Administration

Toledo, Ohio

OVERVIEW

The University of Toledo is a state-supported, coed university. Enrollment: 20,307 graduate, professional, and undergraduate students; 1,532 full-time matriculated graduate/professional students; 1,854 part-time matriculated graduate/professional students. Founded: 1872. The graduate business unit is in a suburban setting and is on a semester calendar.

HIGHLIGHTS

Enrollment Profile

Full-time: 75	International: 35%
Part-time: 228	Women: 34%
Total: 303	Minorities: N/R
Average Age: 30	Average Class Size: 35
Fall 1997 Average GPA: 2.97	Fall 1997 Average GMAT: 511

Costs

Full-time tuition: $5505 per academic year (resident); $10,790 per academic year (nonresident)

Part-time tuition: $201 per credit hour (resident); $434 per credit hour (nonresident)

AACSB – The International Association for Management Education accredited

GRADUATE BUSINESS PROGRAMS

Master of Business Administration (MBA) Full-time, part-time; 36-60 total credits required; 12 months to 6 years to complete program. Concentrations in accounting, finance, human resources, international business, management, management information systems, marketing, operations management.

Executive MBA (MBA) Full-time; 42 total credits required; up to 15 months to complete program. Concentrations in entrepreneurship, technology management, management.

Master of Science in Accounting (MS) Full-time, part-time; 30 total credits required; 12 months to 6 years to complete program. Concentration in accounting.

Master of Science in Manufacturing Management (MS) Full-time, part-time; 55 total credits required; 2 to 6 years to complete program. Concentration in manufacturing management.

ADMISSION

Applications For fall 1997 there were 218 applications for admission. Of those applying, 190 were accepted. Of those accepted, 80 enrolled.

Application Requirements Application form, application fee, bachelor's degree, minimum GPA: 2.7, 3 letters of recommendation, personal statement, college transcript(s).

Recommended for Application GMAT score accepted: minimum 450, resume, computer experience.

Application Deadline 8/1 for fall, 11/15 for spring, 4/15 for summer, 5/1 for fall (international), 10/1 for spring (international), 3/1 for summer (international). Application fee: $30. Deferred entrance is available.

ACADEMICS

Faculty Full-time 65; part-time 6.

Teaching Methodologies Case study, computer-aided instruction, computer analysis, computer simulations, experiential learning, faculty seminars, field projects, group discussion, lecture, research, role playing, seminars by members of the business community, simulations, student presentations, study groups, team projects.

Technology 500 on-campus computer terminals/PCs are available for student use and are linked by a campus-wide network. The network has full access to the Internet. Students are not required to have their own PC.

Special Opportunities Advanced credit may be earned through transfer of credits from another institution.

FINANCES

Costs for 1997–98 Tuition: Full-time: $5505 per year (resident); $10,790 per year (nonresident). Part-time: $201 per credit hour (resident); $434 per credit hour (nonresident). Cost varies by academic program, number of credits taken, reciprocity agreements. Fees: Full-time: $781 per academic year (resident); $781 per academic year (nonresident). Part-time: $33 per credit hour (resident); $33 per credit hour (nonresident). Fees vary by academic program, number of credits taken, reciprocity agreements. Average 1997–98 room and board costs were $4194 per academic year (on campus) and $5560 per academic year (off campus). Room and board costs vary by campus location, occupancy (e.g., single, double, triple), type of accommodation, type of meal plan.

Financial Aid Fellowships, research assistantships, teaching assistantships, scholarships available. Financial aid is available to part-time students. Application Deadline: 3/1.

Financial Aid Contact Dr. Edgar Miller, Director of Financial Aid, 2801 West Bancroft, Toledo, OH 43606-3398. Phone: 419-530-7746; Fax: 419-530-7757.

FACILITIES

Information Resources William S. Carlson Library plus 6 additional on-campus libraries; total holdings of 1,600,000 volumes, 1,487,000 microforms, 6,650 current periodical subscriptions. CD player(s) available for graduate student use. Access provided to online bibliographic retrieval services.

INTERNATIONAL STUDENTS

Demographics 35% of students enrolled are international students [Africa, 1%, Asia, 30%, Europe, 2%, North America, 65%, South America, 2%].

Services and Facilities International student office, international student center, international student housing, visa services, ESL courses, counseling/support services.

Applying TOEFL: minimum score of 550, proof of adequate funds, proof of health/immunizations required. Financial aid is available to international students.

International Student Contact Ms. Dawn Malone, Director of International Admissions, Office of International Services, Southwest Academic Center, Room 2000, Toledo, OH 43606-3390. Phone: 419-530-1200; Fax: 419-530-1234; E-mail: intlsvs@utnet.utoledo.edu

PLACEMENT

Services include alumni network, career counseling/planning, career fairs, career library, career placement, electronic job bank, job interviews arranged, resume referral to employers, and resume preparation.

Employment Types of employment entered: accounting, banking, chemical industry, communications, computer-related, consulting, consumer products, education, energy, engineering, finance, financial services, government, health services, hospitality management, human resources, information systems/technology, insurance, international trade, management, manufacturing, marketing, media, nonprofit, petrochemical, pharmaceutical, real estate, retail, service industry, telecommunications, utilities.

Business Program(s) URL: http://www.utoledo.edu/MBA/

Program Contact: Dr. Bruce Kuhlman, MBA Director, Office of Graduate Studies in Business, College of Business Administration, Toledo, OH 43606-3390. Phone: 419-530-2775; Fax: 419-530-7260.
See full description on page 1162.

Walsh University

Program in Management

North Canton, Ohio

OVERVIEW

Walsh University is an independent-religious, coed, comprehensive institution. Enrollment: 1,550 graduate, professional, and undergraduate students; 11 full-time matriculated graduate/professional students; 157 part-time matriculated graduate/professional students. Founded: 1958. The graduate business unit is in a suburban setting and is on a semester calendar.

Walsh University (continued)

HIGHLIGHTS

Enrollment Profile
Full-time: N/R
Part-time: N/R
Total: 65
Average Age: N/R
Fall 1997 Average GPA: 3.032

International: N/R
Women: N/R
Minorities: N/R
Average Class Size: 12
Fall 1997 Average GMAT: 454

Costs
Full-time tuition: N/R
Part-time tuition: $363 per credit hour

GRADUATE BUSINESS PROGRAMS
Master of Arts in Management (MA) Part-time; 42 total credits required; 2 to 5 years to complete program. Concentrations in managerial economics, strategic management, organizational behavior/development, organizational management, project management, quantitative analysis, management information systems, public relations, marketing research, legal administration, business law, financial management/planning, accounting.

ADMISSION
Application Requirements GMAT score, application form, application fee, bachelor's degree, essay, minimum GPA: 2.6, interview, 3 letters of recommendation, college transcript(s), minimum of 1 year of work experience.

Application Deadline Applications processed on a rolling/continuous basis for both domestic and international students. Application fee: $25. Deferred entrance is available.

ACADEMICS
Faculty Full-time 4; part-time 2.

Teaching Methodologies Case study, computer analysis, experiential learning, field projects, group discussion, lecture, research, seminars by members of the business community, student presentations, team projects.

Technology 60 on-campus computer terminals/PCs are available for student use and are linked by a campus-wide network. The network has full access to the Internet. Students are not required to have their own PC.

Special Opportunities Advanced credit may be earned through transfer of credits from another institution. International exchange program in Russia.

FINANCES
Costs for 1997–98 Tuition: Part-time: $363 per credit hour. Fees: Part-time: $10 per credit hour. Average 1997–98 room and board costs were $4500 per academic year.

Financial Aid Contact Ms. Perie Brown, Director of Financial Aid, 2020 Easton Street, NW, North Canton, OH 44720-3396. Phone: 330-490-7147; Fax: 330-490-7165.

FACILITIES
Information Resources Walsh University Library; total holdings of 128,000 volumes, 8,184 microforms, 683 current periodical subscriptions. CD player(s) available for graduate student use. Access provided to online bibliographic retrieval services.

INTERNATIONAL STUDENTS
Demographics N/R

Services and Facilities International student office, ESL courses, counseling/support services.

Applying TOEFL: minimum score of 500, TSE, proof of adequate funds required. Proof of health/immunizations recommended. Financial aid is not available to international students.

International Student Contact Ms. Lori Brindisi, Director of International Student Development, 2020 Easton Street, NW, North Canton, OH 44720-3396. Phone: 330-490-7130; Fax: 330-499-8518; E-mail: brindisi@alex.walsh.edu

PLACEMENT
Services include alumni network, career counseling/planning, career fairs, career library, career placement, job interviews arranged, resume referral to employers, and resume preparation. In 1996–97, 124 organizations participated in on-campus recruiting.

Employment Types of employment entered: management, marketing.

Business Program(s) URL: http://www.walsh.edu

Program Contact: Mr. Brett Freshour, Director of Admissions, 2020 Easton Street, NW, North Canton, OH 44720-3396. Phone: 330-490-7171, 800-362-9846 (OH only); Fax: 330-490-7165; E-mail: admissions@alex.walsh.edu

Wright State University

College of Business and Administration

Dayton, Ohio

OVERVIEW
Wright State University is a state-supported, coed university. Enrollment: 16,033 graduate, professional, and undergraduate students; 1,518 full-time matriculated graduate/professional students; 2,129 part-time matriculated graduate/professional students. Founded: 1964. The graduate business unit is in a suburban setting and is on a quarter calendar.

HIGHLIGHTS

Enrollment Profile
Full-time: 172
Part-time: 413
Total: 585
Average Age: 30
Fall 1997 Average GPA: 3.1

International: 13%
Women: 40%
Minorities: 10%
Average Class Size: 27
Fall 1997 Average GMAT: 531

Costs
Full-time tuition: $1563 per academic year (resident); $2799 per academic year (nonresident)
Part-time tuition: $148 per credit (resident); $263 per credit (nonresident)

AACSB – The International Association for Management Education accredited

GRADUATE BUSINESS PROGRAMS
Master of Business Administration (MBA) Full-time, part-time; 51-74 total credits required; 12 months to 5 years to complete program. Concentrations in economics, finance, international business, logistics, management, management information systems, marketing, operations management, project management, health care.

Master of Science in Social and Applied Economics (MS) Full-time, part-time; 48-60 total credits required; 12 months to 5 years to complete program.

Master of Business Administration/Master of Science in Social and Applied Economics (MBA/MS) Full-time, part-time; 81-104 total credits required; 18 months to 5 years to complete program.

Master of Business Administration/Master of Science in Nursing (MBA/MS) Full-time, part-time; 90-104 total credits required; 2 to 5 years to complete program.

Master of Science in Logistics Management (MS) Full-time, part-time; 51-67 total credits required; 12 months to 5 years to complete program.

ADMISSION
Applications For fall 1997 there were 310 applications for admission. Of those applying, 202 were accepted. Of those accepted, 119 enrolled.

Application Requirements GMAT score, application form, application fee, bachelor's degree, personal statement, college transcript(s).

Application Deadline Applications processed on a rolling/continuous basis for both domestic and international students. Application fee: $25. Deferred entrance is available.

ACADEMICS
Faculty Full-time 64.

Teaching Methodologies Case study, computer analysis, computer simulations, group discussion, lecture, research, role playing, simulations, student presentations, team projects.

Technology 150 on-campus computer terminals/PCs are available for student use and are linked by a campus-wide network. The network has full access to the Internet. Students are not required to have their own PC.

Special Opportunities Advanced credit may be earned through credit by examination, transfer of credits from another institution. International exchange programs in Brazil, Chile, France, Japan, People's Republic of China. An internship program is available.

FINANCES
Costs for 1997–98 Tuition: Full-time: $1563 per quarter (resident); $2799 per quarter (nonresident). Part-time: $148 per credit (resident); $263 per credit (nonresident). Average 1997–98 room and board costs were $4140 per academic year. Room and board costs vary by occupancy (e.g., single, double, triple), type of accommodation, type of meal plan.

Financial Aid Fellowships, research assistantships, teaching assistantships, work study, loans available. Financial aid is available to part-time students.

Financial Aid Contact Mr. David Darr, Director of Financial Aid, Colonel Glenn Highway, Dayton, OH 45435. Phone: 937-873-5721.

FACILITIES
Information Resources Paul Laurence Dunbar Library plus 1 additional on-campus library; total holdings of 643,087 volumes, 1,207,362 microforms, 5,229 current periodical subscriptions. CD player(s) available for graduate student use. Access provided to online bibliographic retrieval services.

INTERNATIONAL STUDENTS
Demographics 13% of students enrolled are international students.

Services and Facilities International student office, ESL courses, counseling/support services.

Applying TOEFL: minimum score of 550, proof of adequate funds required. Financial aid is not available to international students.

International Student Contact Mr. Steve Lyons, Director of International Student Programs, Colonel Glenn Highway, Dayton, OH 45435. Phone: 937-873-5745.

PLACEMENT
Services include alumni network, career counseling/planning, career fairs, career library, career placement, electronic job bank, job interviews arranged, job search course, resume referral to employers, and resume preparation.

Business Program(s) URL: http://www.coba.wright.edu

Program Contact: Mr. James Crawford, Director of Graduate Programs in Business, College of Business and Administration, 110 Rike Hall, Dayton, OH 45435. Phone: 937-873-2437; Fax: 937-873-3545; E-mail: jcrawford@wright.edu
See full description on page 1202.

Xavier University

Williams College of Business Administration
Cincinnati, Ohio

OVERVIEW
Xavier University is an independent-religious, coed, comprehensive institution. Enrollment: 6,226 graduate, professional, and undergraduate students; 681 full-time matriculated graduate/professional students; 1,891 part-time matriculated graduate/professional students. Founded: 1831. The graduate business unit is in an urban setting and is on a semester calendar.

HIGHLIGHTS

Enrollment Profile
Full-time: 256	International: 3%
Part-time: 964	Women: 35%
Total: 1,220	Minorities: N/R
Average Age: 28	Average Class Size: 27
Fall 1997 Average GPA: 3.2	Fall 1997 Average GMAT: 550

Costs
Full-time tuition: $3420 per academic year
Part-time tuition: $380 per credit

AACSB – The International Association for Management Education accredited

GRADUATE BUSINESS PROGRAMS
Master of Business Administration (MBA) Full-time, part-time; 36 total credits required; 12 months to 6 years to complete program. Concentrations in economics, entrepreneurship, finance, human resources, international business, management information systems, marketing, quality management, taxation.

Executive MBA (MBA) Part-time; 48 total credits required; 19 months to complete program.

ADMISSION
Applications For fall 1997 there were 456 applications for admission. Of those applying, 358 were accepted. Of those accepted, 226 enrolled.

Application Requirements Application form, application fee, bachelor's degree, minimum GPA: 2.0, resume, college transcript(s).

Recommended for Application GMAT score accepted, 2 letters of recommendation, minimum of 3 years of work experience, computer experience.

Application Deadline Applications processed on a rolling/continuous basis for both domestic and international students. Application fee: $35. Deferred entrance is available.

ACADEMICS
Faculty Full-time 49; part-time 20.
Teaching Methodologies Case study, computer-aided instruction, computer simulations, field projects, group discussion, lecture, research, role playing, seminars by members of the business community, simulations, student presentations, study groups, team projects.

Technology 200 on-campus computer terminals/PCs are available for student use and are linked by a campus-wide network. The network has full access to the Internet. Students are not required to have their own PC.

Special Opportunities Advanced credit may be earned through credit by examination, credit for experience, transfer of credits from another institution. International exchange programs in Germany, Japan, Republic of Singapore, United Kingdom, United States. An internship program is available.

FINANCES
Costs for 1997–98 Tuition: Full-time: $3420 per semester. Part-time: $380 per credit. Cost varies by number of credits taken. Room and board costs vary by occupancy (e.g., single, double, triple), type of accommodation, type of meal plan.

Financial Aid Research assistantships, loans available. Financial aid is available to part-time students. Application Deadline: 4/1.

Financial Aid Contact Mr. Paul Calme, Director of Financial Aid, 3800 Victory Parkway, Cincinnati, OH 45207-5311. Phone: 513-742-4257; Fax: 513-745-2806; E-mail: calme@admin.xu.edu

FACILITIES
Information Resources McDonald Library plus 1 additional on-campus library; total holdings of 307,702 volumes, 493,594 microforms, 1,500 current periodical subscriptions. CD player(s) available for graduate student use. Access provided to online bibliographic retrieval services and online databases.

INTERNATIONAL STUDENTS
Demographics 3% of students enrolled are international students [Africa, 5%, Asia, 44%, Australia/New Zealand, 1%, Central America, 15%, Europe, 18%, North America, 10%, South America, 5%, other, 2%].

Services and Facilities International student office, international student center, international student housing, visa services, ESL courses, counseling/support services.

Applying TOEFL: minimum score of 550, proof of adequate funds required. Proof of health/immunizations recommended. Financial aid is available to international students.

International Student Contact Katherine Hammett, Director of International Student Services, 3800 Victory Parkway, Cincinnati, OH 45207-2171. Phone: 513-745-2864; Fax: 513-745-3844; E-mail: hammett@admin.xu.edu

PLACEMENT
Services include alumni network, career counseling/planning, career fairs, career library, career placement, electronic job bank, job interviews arranged, job search course, resume referral to employers, and resume preparation. In 1996–97, 100 organizations participated in on-campus recruiting.

Employment Of 1996–97 graduates, 99% were employed within three months of graduation. Types of employment entered: accounting, banking, chemical industry, communications, computer-related, consulting, consumer products, engineering, finance, financial services, government, health services, hospitality management, human resources, information systems/technology, insurance, international trade, law, management, manufacturing, marketing, media, mining, nonprofit, real estate, retail, service industry, telecommunications, utilities.

Business Program(s) URL: http://www.xu.edu/academics/grad.html

Program Contact: Ms. Jennifer Bush, Director of MBA Enrollment Services, 3800 Victory Parkway, Cincinnati, OH 45207-3221. Phone: 513-745-3525; Fax: 513-745-2929; E-mail: xumba@admin.xu.edu
See full description on page 1204.

Youngstown State University

Warren P. Williamson Jr. College of Business Administration
Youngstown, Ohio

OVERVIEW
Youngstown State University is a state-supported, coed, comprehensive institution. Enrollment: 12,324 graduate, professional, and undergraduate students; 311 full-time matriculated graduate/professional students; 867 part-time matriculated graduate/professional students. Founded: 1908. The graduate business unit is in an urban setting and is on a quarter calendar.

HIGHLIGHTS

Enrollment Profile

Full-time: 73

Part-time: 83

Total: 156

Average Age: 29

Fall 1997 Average GPA: 3.12

International: 8%

Women: 37%

Minorities: 4%

Average Class Size: 20

Fall 1997 Average GMAT: 524

Costs

Full-time tuition: N/R

Part-time tuition: $86 per quarter hour (resident); $137 per quarter hour (nonresident)

ACBSP – The American Council of Business Schools and Programs accredited

GRADUATE BUSINESS PROGRAMS

Master of Business Administration (MBA) Full-time, part-time; 52 total credits required; 12 months to 6 years to complete program. Concentrations in accounting, finance, management, marketing.

Executive MBA (MBA) Full-time; 72 total credits required; 5 years professional work experience required; 2 years to complete program.

ADMISSION

Applications For fall 1997 there were 58 applications for admission. Of those applying, 50 were accepted. Of those accepted, 33 enrolled.

Application Requirements GMAT score: minimum 450, application form, application fee, bachelor's degree, personal statement, resume, college transcript(s), computer experience: spreadsheet, word processing.

Recommended for Application Interview.

Application Deadline 8/15 for fall, 11/15 for winter, 2/15 for spring, 5/15 for summer, 1/15 for fall (international), 3/15 for winter (international), 6/15 for spring (international). Application fee: $30, $25 (international). Deferred entrance is available.

ACADEMICS

Faculty Full-time 23; part-time 5.

Teaching Methodologies Case study, computer-aided instruction, computer simulations, experiential learning, group discussion, lecture, research, student presentations, study groups, team projects.

Technology 1,100 on-campus computer terminals/PCs are available for student use and are linked by a campus-wide network. The network has full access to the Internet. Students are not required to have their own PC.

Special Opportunities Advanced credit may be earned through transfer of credits from another institution. International exchange programs in China, Russia, Turkey. An internship program is available.

FINANCES

Costs for 1997–98 Tuition: $86 per quarter hour (resident); $137 per quarter hour (nonresident). Cost varies by reciprocity agreements. Fees: $19 per quarter hour (resident); $19 per quarter hour (nonresident). Average 1997–98 room and board costs were $4000 per academic year (on campus) and $5000 per academic year (off campus). Room and board costs vary by campus location, occupancy (e.g., single, double, triple), type of accommodation, type of meal plan.

Financial Aid In 1997–98, 26% of students received some institutionally administered aid in the form of fellowships, research assistantships, teaching assistantships, grants, scholarships, work study, loans. Financial aid is available to part-time students.

Financial Aid Contact Ms. Beth Bactlett, Administrative Assistant, 410 Wick Avenue, Youngstown, OH 44555-0002. Phone: 330-742-1998.

FACILITIES

Information Resources Maag Library; total holdings of 560,981 volumes, 808,853 microforms, 3,397 current periodical subscriptions. CD player(s) available for graduate student use. Access provided to online bibliographic retrieval services and online databases.

INTERNATIONAL STUDENTS

Demographics 8% of students enrolled are international students [Asia, 30%, Europe, 40%, other, 30%].

Services and Facilities International student office, international student center, ESL courses, counseling/support services.

Applying TOEFL: minimum score of 550, proof of adequate funds required. Financial aid is available to international students.

International Student Contact Dr. Silvia Hyre, Director, Center for International Studies, Phelps Building, Youngstown, OH 44555. Phone: 330-742-1998; E-mail: amspecol@ysub.ysu.edu

PLACEMENT

Services include career counseling/planning, career fairs, career library, career placement, electronic job bank, job interviews arranged, resume referral to employers, and resume preparation. In 1996–97, 15 organizations participated in on-campus recruiting.

Employment Types of employment entered: accounting, banking, communications, computer-related, consulting, consumer products, engineering, finance, financial services, government, health services, human resources, information systems/technology, management, manufacturing, marketing, nonprofit, pharmaceutical, retail, service industry, telecommunications, transportation, utilities.

Business Program(s) URL: http://cc.ysu.edu/~dsrousso/wcba/wcba.htm

Program Contact: Ms. Linda Mohn, MBA Program Coordinator, One University Plaza, Youngstown, OH 44555-0002. Phone: 330-742-3069, 800-336-9978 (OH only); Fax: 330-742-1459; E-mail: asmba001@ysub.ysu.edu

OKLAHOMA

Cameron University

School of Graduate and Professional Studies

Lawton, Oklahoma

OVERVIEW

Cameron University is a state-supported, coed, comprehensive institution. Enrollment: 5,398 graduate, professional, and undergraduate students; 138 full-time matriculated graduate/professional students; 299 part-time matriculated graduate/professional students. Founded: 1909. The graduate business unit is in a small-town setting and is on a semester calendar.

HIGHLIGHTS

Enrollment Profile

Full-time: 13

Part-time: 21

Total: 34

Average Age: 38

Fall 1997 Average GPA: 2.75

International: N/R

Women: 44%

Minorities: 24%

Average Class Size: 17

Fall 1997 Average GMAT: 493

Costs

Full-time tuition: $1750 per academic year (resident); $4050 per academic year (nonresident)

Part-time tuition: $73 per credit (resident); $168 per credit (nonresident)

GRADUATE BUSINESS PROGRAMS

Master of Business Administration (MBA) Full-time, part-time, distance learning option; 33-45 total credits required; 12 months to 6 years to complete program.

ADMISSION

Application Requirements Application form, application fee, bachelor's degree, minimum GPA: 2.0, college transcript(s).

Recommended for Application GMAT score accepted.

Application Deadline Applications processed on a rolling/continuous basis for both domestic and international students. Application fee: $15. Deferred entrance is available.

ACADEMICS

Faculty Full-time 10.

Teaching Methodologies Case study, computer analysis, experiential learning, faculty seminars, field projects, group discussion, lecture, research, seminars by members of the business community, simulations, student presentations, study groups, team projects.

Technology 213 on-campus computer terminals/PCs are available for student use and are linked by a campus-wide network. The network has full access to the Internet. Students are not required to have their own PC.

Special Opportunities Advanced credit may be earned through credit for military training programs, transfer of credits from another institution.

FINANCES

Costs for 1997–98 Tuition: Full-time: $1750 per year (resident); $4050 per year (nonresident). Part-time: $73 per credit (resident); $168 per credit (nonresident). Fees: Full-time: $15 per academic year (resident); $15 per academic year (nonresident). Part-time: $5 per semester (resident); $5 per semester (nonresident). Average 1997–98 room and board costs were $3310 per academic year. Room and board costs vary by occupancy (e.g., single, double, triple).

Financial Aid In 1997–98, 65% of students received some institutionally administered aid in the form of research assistantships, scholarships, work study, loans. Financial aid is available to part-time students. Application Deadline: 4/15.

Financial Aid Contact Ms. Caryn Pacheco, Director of Financial Aid, 2800 West Gore Boulevard, Lawton, OK 73505-6377. Phone: 405-581-2293; Fax: 405-581-5514; E-mail: carynp@cameron.edu

FACILITIES
Information Resources Main library; total holdings of 242,516 volumes, 456,856 microforms, 2,188 current periodical subscriptions. CD player(s) available for graduate student use. Access provided to online bibliographic retrieval services.

INTERNATIONAL STUDENTS
Demographics N/R

Services and Facilities Counseling/support services.

Applying TOEFL: minimum score of 550, proof of adequate funds required. Financial aid is not available to international students.

International Student Contact Dr. David Carl, Dean, School of Graduate and Professional Studies, 2800 West Gore Boulevard, Lawton, OK 73505-6377. Phone: 405-581-2986; Fax: 405-581-5532; E-mail: graduate@cameron.edu

PLACEMENT
Services include career fairs.

Employment Types of employment entered: accounting, banking, finance, government, management.

Business Program(s) URL: http://www.cameron.edu/academic/graduate/business/index.html

Program Contact: Dr. David Carl, Dean, School of Graduate and Professional Studies, 2800 West Gore Boulevard, Lawton, OK 73505-6377. Phone: 405-581-2986; Fax: 405-581-5532; E-mail: graduate@cameron.edu

Northeastern State University

College of Business and Industry

Tahlequah, Oklahoma

OVERVIEW
Northeastern State University is a state-supported, coed, comprehensive institution. Enrollment: 8,710 graduate, professional, and undergraduate students. Founded: 1851. The graduate business unit is in a small-town setting and is on a semester calendar.

HIGHLIGHTS

Enrollment Profile
Full-time: N/R	International: 7%
Part-time: N/R	Women: 37%
Total: 110	Minorities: 24%
Average Age: 34	Average Class Size: 25
Fall 1997 Average GPA: 3.33	Fall 1997 Average GMAT: 430

Costs
Full-time tuition: N/R
Part-time tuition: $327 per 6 hours (resident); $816 per 6 hours (nonresident)

ACBSP – The American Council of Business Schools and Programs accredited

GRADUATE BUSINESS PROGRAMS
Master of Business Administration (MBA) Full-time, part-time; 32 total credits required; 12 to 18 months to complete program. Concentration in management.

ADMISSION
Application Requirements GMAT score: minimum 420, application form, application fee, bachelor's degree, minimum GPA: 2.5, college transcript(s).

Recommended for Application Essay, interview, letters of recommendation, personal statement, resume, work experience, computer experience.

Application Deadline 7/1 for fall, 12/1 for winter, 1/1 for spring, 5/1 for summer, 7/1 for fall (international), 12/1 for winter (international), 1/1 for spring (international), 5/1 for summer (international). Application fee: 25 (international).

ACADEMICS
Faculty Full-time 36; part-time 13.

Teaching Methodologies Case study, computer-aided instruction, computer analysis, computer simulations, experiential learning, field projects, group discus-

sion, lecture, research, role playing, seminars by members of the business community, simulations, student presentations, study groups, team projects.

Technology 24 on-campus computer terminals/PCs are available for student use and are linked by a campus-wide network. The network has full access to the Internet. Students are not required to have their own PC.

Special Opportunities Advanced credit may be earned through transfer of credits from another institution. International exchange programs in Mexico, People's Republic of China.

FINANCES
Costs for 1997–98 Tuition: $327 per 6 hours (resident); $816 per 6 hours (nonresident). Cost varies by academic program, campus location, number of credits taken. Fees: $5 per semester (resident); $5 per semester (nonresident). Fees vary by campus location. Average 1997–98 room and board costs were $2520 per academic year. Room and board costs vary by occupancy (e.g., single, double, triple), type of accommodation, type of meal plan.

Financial Aid Teaching assistantships, work study available. Application Deadline: 3/1.

Financial Aid Contact Peggy Carey, Director, Student Financial Services, 600 North Grand, Tahlequah, OK 74464. Phone: 918-456-5511 Ext. 3456; Fax: 918-458-2015.

FACILITIES
Information Resources John Vaughn Library/Learning Resources Center plus 1 additional on-campus library; total holdings of 482,987 volumes, 535,991 microforms, 2,746 current periodical subscriptions. CD player(s) available for graduate student use. Access provided to online bibliographic retrieval services.

INTERNATIONAL STUDENTS
Demographics 7% of students enrolled are international students.

Services and Facilities International student office, international student housing, counseling/support services.

Applying TOEFL: minimum score of 550, proof of adequate funds required. Financial aid is available to international students.

International Student Contact Kimbra Scott, International Student Coordinator, President's Office, Tahlequah, OK 74464. Phone: 918-458-2000; Fax: 918-458-2015; E-mail: ranallo@cherokee.nsuok.edu

PLACEMENT
Services include alumni network, career counseling/planning, career fairs, career library, career placement, electronic job bank, and resume preparation.

Employment Of 1996–97 graduates, 80% were employed within three months of graduation; the average starting salary was $32,000. Types of employment entered: accounting, banking, communications, computer-related, education, energy, engineering, finance, financial services, government, health services, human resources, insurance, international trade, management, manufacturing, nonprofit, real estate, telecommunications, utilities.

Business Program(s) URL: http://arapaho.nsuok.edu/~cbi/index.html

Program Contact: Dr. Thomas Carment, Coordinator—MBA Program, NSU College of Business and Industry, Tahlequah, OK 74464. Phone: 918-456-5511 Ext. 2905, 800-722-9614 (OK only); Fax: 918-458-2337; E-mail: carment@cherokee.nsuok.edu

Oklahoma City University

Meinders School of Business

Oklahoma City, Oklahoma

OVERVIEW
Oklahoma City University is an independent-religious, coed, comprehensive institution. Enrollment: 4,323 graduate, professional, and undergraduate students; 1,205 full-time matriculated graduate/professional students; 944 part-time matriculated graduate/professional students. The graduate business unit is in a suburban setting and is on a semester calendar.

HIGHLIGHTS

Enrollment Profile
Full-time: 456	International: 50%
Part-time: 761	Women: 36%
Total: 1,217	Minorities: 11%
Average Age: 28	Average Class Size: 30
Fall 1997 Average GPA: N/R	Fall 1997 Average GMAT: N/R

Costs
Full-time tuition: N/R
Part-time tuition: $310 per credit hour

Oklahoma City University (continued)

ACBSP – The American Council of Business Schools and Programs accredited

GRADUATE BUSINESS PROGRAMS

Master of Business Administration (MBA) Full-time, part-time; 45 total credits required; minimum of 20 months to complete program. Concentrations in arts administration/management, international finance, international marketing, finance, marketing, health care, management information systems, management, public management.

Executive MBA (MBA) Full-time, part-time; 45 total credits required; minimum of 20 months to complete program. Concentration in management.

Accounting (MSA) Full-time, part-time; 45 total credits required; minimum of 20 months to complete program. Concentration in accounting.

ADMISSION

Applications For fall 1997 there were 377 applications for admission. Of those applying, 343 were accepted. Of those accepted, 151 enrolled.

Application Requirements Application form, application fee, bachelor's degree, interview, 2 letters of recommendation, personal statement, college transcript(s).

Application Deadline Applications processed on a rolling/continuous basis for both domestic and international students. Application fee: $35, $55 (international).

ACADEMICS

Faculty Full-time 41; part-time 10.

Teaching Methodologies Case study, computer-aided instruction, computer analysis, computer simulations, experiential learning, faculty seminars, field projects, group discussion, lecture, research, role playing, seminars by members of the business community, simulations, student presentations, study groups, team projects.

Technology 130 on-campus computer terminals/PCs are available for student use and are linked by a campus-wide network. The network has full access to the Internet. Students are not required to have their own PC.

Special Opportunities Advanced credit may be earned through transfer of credits from another institution. International exchange programs in Asia, United Kingdom. An internship program is available.

FINANCES

Costs for 1997–98 Tuition: $310 per credit hour. Cost varies by academic program, number of credits taken. Fees vary by academic program. Average 1997–98 room and board costs were $3990 per academic year (on campus) and $5123 per academic year (off campus). Room and board costs vary by occupancy (e.g., single, double, triple), type of accommodation, type of meal plan.

Financial Aid Fellowships, work study, loans available. Financial aid is available to part-time students. Application Deadline: 8/1.

Financial Aid Contact Laura Rahhal, Director of Graduate Admissions, 2501 North Blackwelder, Oklahoma City, OK 73106. Phone: 405-521-5351; Fax: 405-521-5356.

FACILITIES

Information Resources Dulaney-Browne Library plus 1 additional on-campus library; total holdings of 310,749 volumes, 28,136 microforms, 4,644 current periodical subscriptions. CD player(s) available for graduate student use. Access provided to online bibliographic retrieval services and online databases.

INTERNATIONAL STUDENTS

Demographics 50% of students enrolled are international students.

Services and Facilities International student office, international student center, visa services, ESL courses, counseling/support services.

Applying TOEFL: minimum score of 550, proof of health/immunizations required.

International Student Contact Mr. David Yee, Director of International Student Office, 2501 North Blackwelder, Oklahoma City, OK 73106. Phone: 405-521-5358; Fax: 405-521-5946; E-mail: dyee@frodo.okcu.edu

PLACEMENT

Services include alumni network, career counseling/planning, career fairs, career library, career placement, job interviews arranged, job search course, resume referral to employers, and resume preparation. In 1996–97, 65 organizations participated in on-campus recruiting.

Employment Types of employment entered: accounting, banking, chemical industry, communications, computer-related, consulting, education, energy, finance, financial services, government, health services, high technology, hospitality management, human resources, information systems/technology, insurance, international trade, law, management, manufacturing, marketing, media, nonprofit, petrochemical, pharmaceutical, real estate, retail, service industry, telecommunications, transportation, utilities.

Business Program(s) URL: http://www.okcu.edu

Program Contact: Laura Rahhal, Director of Graduate Admissions, 2501 North Blackwelder, Oklahoma City, OK 73106. Phone: 405-521-5351, 800-633-7242 (OK only); Fax: 405-521-5356; E-mail: lrahhal1@frodo.okcu.edu

Oklahoma State University

College of Business Administration

Stillwater, Oklahoma

OVERVIEW

Oklahoma State University is a state-supported, coed university. Enrollment: 25,000 graduate, professional, and undergraduate students. Founded: 1890. The graduate business unit is in a small-town setting and is on a semester calendar.

HIGHLIGHTS

Enrollment Profile

Full-time: 234	International: 15%
Part-time: 340	Women: 36%
Total: 574	Minorities: 8%
Average Age: 26	Average Class Size: 40
Fall 1997 Average GPA: 3.4	Fall 1997 Average GMAT: 570

Costs
Full-time tuition: $1764 per academic year (resident); $5604 per academic year (nonresident)
Part-time tuition: $80 per hour (resident); $240 per hour (nonresident)

AACSB – The International Association for Management Education accredited

Degree(s) offered in conjunction with Rogers University

GRADUATE BUSINESS PROGRAMS

Master of Business Administration (MBA) Full-time, part-time, distance learning option; 38-50 total credits required; 18 months to 2 years to complete program. Concentrations in management, marketing, management information systems, international business, accounting, economics, finance, human resources, operations management, telecommunications management.

Master of Science in Telecommunications Management (MSTM) Full-time, part-time, distance learning option; 33-35 total credits required; 12 months to 5 years to complete program. Concentrations in management, technology management.

Master of Science—Accounting (MS) Full-time, part-time; 24-32 total credits required; 12 months to 5 years to complete program.

Master of Science—Economics (MS) Full-time, part-time; 30-33 total credits required; 12 months to 5 years to complete program.

ADMISSION

Applications For fall 1997 there were 700 applications for admission. Of those applying, 400 were accepted. Of those accepted, 275 enrolled.

Application Requirements GMAT score: minimum 500, application form, application fee, bachelor's degree, essay, minimum GPA: 2.5, 3 letters of recommendation, personal statement, resume, college transcript(s).

Recommended for Application GRE score accepted, work experience, computer experience.

Application Deadline 6/1 for fall, 11/1 for spring, 3/1 for fall (international), 6/1 for spring (international). Application fee: $25. Deferred entrance is available.

ACADEMICS

Faculty Full-time 86.

Teaching Methodologies Case study, computer-aided instruction, computer analysis, computer simulations, experiential learning, faculty seminars, field projects, group discussion, lecture, research, role playing, seminars by members of the business community, simulations, student presentations, study groups, team projects.

Technology 1,000 on-campus computer terminals/PCs are available for student use and are linked by a campus-wide network. The network has full access to the Internet. Students are not required to have their own PC.

Special Opportunities Advanced credit may be earned through transfer of credits from another institution. International exchange program available. An internship program is available.

FINANCES

Costs for 1997–98 Tuition: Full-time: $1764 per year (resident); $5604 per year (nonresident). Part-time: $80 per hour (resident); $240 per hour (nonresident). Fees: Full-time: $397 per academic year (resident); $397 per academic year (nonresident). Part-time: $16 per hour (resident); $16 per hour (nonresident). Fees vary by campus location. Average 1997–98 room and

---

438

board costs were $7700 per academic year (on campus) and $7427 per academic year (off campus). Room and board costs vary by campus location, occupancy (e.g., single, double, triple), type of accommodation, type of meal plan.

Financial Aid Research assistantships, teaching assistantships, scholarships, work study available. Financial aid is available to part-time students. Application Deadline: 6/1.

Financial Aid Contact Financial Aid Office, Hanner Hall, Stillwater, OK 74078. Phone: 405-744-6604; Fax: 405-744-8871.

FACILITIES
Information Resources Edmond Low Library; total holdings of 1,800,000 volumes, 2,100,000 microforms, 15,000 current periodical subscriptions. CD player(s) available for graduate student use. Access provided to online bibliographic retrieval services.

INTERNATIONAL STUDENTS
Demographics 15% of students enrolled are international students.

Services and Facilities International student office, international student center, visa services, ESL courses, counseling/support services.

Applying TOEFL: minimum score of 550, proof of adequate funds, proof of health/immunizations required. Financial aid is available to international students.

International Student Contact Ms. Lou Mara, Senior International Admissions Specialist, Graduate College, 202 Whitehurst, Stillwater, OK 74078-1019. Phone: 800-227-GRAD; Fax: 405-744-8871.

PLACEMENT
Services include alumni network, career counseling/planning, career fairs, career placement, electronic job bank, job interviews arranged, job search course, resume referral to employers, and resume preparation. In 1996–97, 275 organizations participated in on-campus recruiting.

Employment Of 1996–97 graduates, 95% were employed within three months of graduation; the average starting salary was $40,000. Types of employment entered: accounting, banking, chemical industry, communications, computer-related, consulting, consumer products, energy, engineering, finance, financial services, government, health services, high technology, hospitality management, human resources, information systems/technology, insurance, international trade, management, manufacturing, marketing, media, nonprofit, petrochemical, pharmaceutical, real estate, retail, service industry, telecommunications, transportation, utilities.

Business Program(s) URL: http://management.bus.okstate.edu/

Program Contact: Mr. Peter Rosen, Assistant Director, MBA Program, 102 Gundersen Hall, Stillwater, OK 74078-0555. Phone: 405-744-2951; Fax: 405-744-7474; E-mail: mba-osu@okway.okstate.edu

Oral Roberts University

School of Business

Tulsa, Oklahoma

OVERVIEW
Oral Roberts University is an independent-religious, coed university. Enrollment: 4,078 graduate, professional, and undergraduate students; 297 full-time matriculated graduate/professional students; 348 part-time matriculated graduate/professional students. Founded: 1965. The graduate business unit is in a suburban setting and is on a semester calendar.

HIGHLIGHTS

Enrollment Profile

Full-time: 35	International: 43%
Part-time: 30	Women: 40%
Total: 65	Minorities: 6%
Average Age: 30	Average Class Size: 30
Fall 1997 Average GPA: 3.2	Fall 1997 Average GMAT: 489

Costs
Full-time tuition: N/R
Part-time tuition: $259 per hour

GRADUATE BUSINESS PROGRAMS
Master of Business Administration (MBA) Full-time, part-time; 41 total credits required; 18 months to 5 years to complete program. Concentrations in accounting, finance, international business, management, marketing.

ADMISSION
Applications For fall 1997 there were 110 applications for admission. Of those applying, 45 were accepted. Of those accepted, 23 enrolled.

Application Requirements Application form, application fee, bachelor's degree (must be in field of business), essay, minimum GPA: 3.0, interview, letters of recommendation, personal statement, resume, college transcript(s), computer experience.

Recommended for Application GMAT score accepted, work experience.

Application Deadline 7/31 for fall, 12/1 for spring, 5/1 for summer, 7/31 for fall (international), 12/1 for spring (international), 5/1 for summer (international). Application fee: $35. Deferred entrance is available.

ACADEMICS
Faculty Full-time 4; part-time 7.

Teaching Methodologies Case study, computer-aided instruction, computer analysis, computer simulations, faculty seminars, group discussion, lecture, research, role playing, seminars by members of the business community, simulations, student presentations, study groups, team projects.

Technology 25 on-campus computer terminals/PCs are available for student use and are linked by a campus-wide network. The network has full access to the Internet. Students are not required to have their own PC.

Special Opportunities Advanced credit may be earned through transfer of credits from another institution. An internship program is available.

FINANCES
Costs for 1997–98 Tuition: $259 per hour. Average 1997–98 room and board costs were $5000 per academic year (off campus).

Financial Aid Research assistantships, scholarships, loans available. Application Deadline: 6/1.

Financial Aid Contact Mrs. Kathryn Neal, Graduate Financial Counselor, 7777 South Lewis Avenue, Tulsa, OK 74171-0001. Phone: 918-495-6161; Fax: 918-495-6033.

FACILITIES
Information Resources John D. Messick Learning Resources Center; total holdings of 750,000 volumes, 300,000 microforms, 2,150 current periodical subscriptions. Access provided to online bibliographic retrieval services.

INTERNATIONAL STUDENTS
Demographics 43% of students enrolled are international students [Africa, 5%, Asia, 35%, Central America, 20%, Europe, 30%, South America, 10%].

Services and Facilities International student office, ESL courses, counseling/support services.

Applying TOEFL: minimum score of 600, proof of adequate funds, proof of health/immunizations required. Financial aid is available to international students.

International Student Contact Mrs. Mary Cline, International Admissions and Transfers, 7777 South Lewis Avenue, Tulsa, OK 74171-0001. Phone: 918-495-6161; Fax: 918-495-6033; E-mail: admissions@oru.edu

PLACEMENT
Services In 1996–97, 15 organizations participated in on-campus recruiting; 15 on-campus interviews were conducted.

Employment Of 1996–97 graduates, 60% were employed within three months of graduation; the average starting salary was $30,000. Types of employment entered: accounting, banking, computer-related, consulting, education, finance, financial services, insurance, international trade, management, marketing.

Business Program(s) URL: http://www.oru.edu/university/departments/schools/bus/

Program Contact: Mr. Robert Quintana, Recruitment/Admissions Coordinator, 7777 South Lewis Avenue, Tulsa, OK 74171-0001. Phone: 918-495-6161; 800-678-8876; Fax: 918-495-6033; E-mail: grbuadmit@oru.edu

Phillips University

School of Business

Enid, Oklahoma

OVERVIEW
Phillips University is an independent-religious, coed, comprehensive institution. Enrollment: 584 graduate, professional, and undergraduate students; 18 full-time matriculated graduate/professional students; 39 part-time matriculated graduate/professional students. Founded: 1906. The graduate business unit

Phillips University (continued)

is in a small-town setting and is on a semester calendar.

HIGHLIGHTS

Enrollment Profile
Full-time: 4
Part-time: 15
Total: 19
Average Age: 30
Fall 1997 Average GPA: 3.125

International: 5%
Women: 21%
Minorities: N/R
Average Class Size: 12
Fall 1997 Average GMAT: 470

Costs
Full-time tuition: N/R
Part-time tuition: $97 per semester hour

Degree(s) offered in conjunction with Spartan School of Aviation

GRADUATE BUSINESS PROGRAMS
Master of Business Administration (MBA) Full-time, part-time; 36 total credits required; 18 months to 5 years to complete program. Concentration in management.

ADMISSION
Applications For fall 1997 there were 10 applications for admission. Of those applying, 8 were accepted. Of those accepted, 8 enrolled.

Application Requirements GMAT score: minimum 450, application form, application fee, bachelor's degree, essay, college transcript(s).

Recommended for Application Minimum GPA, interview, personal statement.

Application Deadline Applications processed on a rolling/continuous basis for both domestic and international students. Application fee: $20, $75 (international). Deferred entrance is available.

ACADEMICS
Faculty Full-time 5; part-time 7.

Teaching Methodologies Case study, faculty seminars, group discussion, lecture, student presentations, team projects.

Technology 20 on-campus computer terminals/PCs are available for student use. The network has full access to the Internet. Students are not required to have their own PC.

Special Opportunities Advanced credit may be earned through credit for military training programs, transfer of credits from another institution. An internship program is available.

FINANCES
Costs for 1997–98 Tuition: $97 per semester hour. Average 1997–98 room and board costs were $3600 per academic year. Room and board costs vary by occupancy (e.g., single, double, triple), type of accommodation, type of meal plan.

Financial Aid Scholarships, work study, loans available. Financial aid is available to part-time students. Application Deadline: 6/1.

Financial Aid Contact Mrs. Nancy Moats, Director of Financial Aid, 100 South University Avenue, Enid, OK 73701. Phone: 580-548-2280; Fax: 580-237-1607.

FACILITIES
Information Resources Zollars Memorial Library plus 1 additional on-campus library; total holdings of 190,160 volumes, 50,000 microforms, 1,083 current periodical subscriptions. CD player(s) available for graduate student use. Access provided to online bibliographic retrieval services.

INTERNATIONAL STUDENTS
Demographics 5% of students enrolled are international students.

Services and Facilities Visa services, counseling/support services.

Applying TOEFL: minimum score of 550 required. Financial aid is not available to international students.

International Student Contact Tom Lentz, Dean of Students, 100 South University Avenue, Enid, OK 73701-6439. Phone: 580-237-4433 Ext. 298; Fax: 580-237-1607.

PLACEMENT
Services include alumni network, career counseling/planning, career fairs, and career placement.

Employment Of 1996–97 graduates, 90% were employed within three months of graduation. Types of employment entered: accounting, banking, consulting, financial services, government, human resources, insurance, management, marketing, retail.

Business Program(s) URL: http://www.phillips.edu/

Program Contact: Mr. Todd Lucas, Admissions Counselor, 100 South University, Enid, OK 73701-6439. Phone: 580-548-2203 E-mail: admissions@phillips.edu

Southeastern Oklahoma State University

School of Business

Durant, Oklahoma

OVERVIEW
Southeastern Oklahoma State University is a state-supported, coed, comprehensive institution. Enrollment: 3,842 graduate, professional, and undergraduate students. Founded: 1909. The graduate business unit is in a small-town setting and is on a semester calendar.

HIGHLIGHTS

Enrollment Profile
Full-time: N/R
Part-time: N/R
Total: 60
Average Age: 34
Fall 1997 Average GPA: 3.42

International: 17%
Women: 37%
Minorities: N/R
Average Class Size: 20
Fall 1997 Average GMAT: N/R

Costs
Full-time tuition: $1044 per academic year (resident); $2754 per academic year (nonresident)
Part-time tuition: $58 per credit (resident); $153 per credit (nonresident)

GRADUATE BUSINESS PROGRAMS
Master of Business Administration (MBA) Full-time, part-time; 36-57 total credits required; 12 months to 6 years to complete program.

ADMISSION
Applications For fall 1997 there were 40 applications for admission. Of those applying, 30 were accepted. Of those accepted, 20 enrolled.

Application Requirements Application form, bachelor's degree, minimum GPA: 2.75, college transcript(s).

Application Deadline 8/8 for fall, 1/5 for spring, 5/20 for summer. Deferred entrance is available.

ACADEMICS
Faculty Full-time 10.

Teaching Methodologies Case study, experiential learning, group discussion, lecture, research, seminars by members of the business community, student presentations, team projects.

Technology 100 on-campus computer terminals/PCs are available for student use and are linked by a campus-wide network. The network has full access to the Internet. Students are not required to have their own PC.

Special Opportunities Advanced credit may be earned through transfer of credits from another institution.

FINANCES
Costs for 1997–98 Tuition: Full-time: $1044 per year (resident); $2754 per year (nonresident). Part-time: $58 per credit (resident); $153 per credit (nonresident). Cost varies by number of credits taken. Fees: Full-time: $325 per academic year (resident); $325 per academic year (nonresident). Average 1997–98 room and board costs were $1150 per academic year. Room and board costs vary by campus location, occupancy (e.g., single, double, triple), type of accommodation, type of meal plan.

Financial Aid In 1997–98, 38% of students received some institutionally administered aid in the form of work study, loans. Financial aid is available to part-time students. Application Deadline: 6/15.

Financial Aid Contact Director of Student Aid, Box 4113, Durant, OK 74701-0609. Phone: 580-924-0121 Ext. 2406.

FACILITIES
Information Resources Henry G. Bennett Library; total holdings of 178,000 volumes, 398,000 microforms, 1,241 current periodical subscriptions. CD player(s) available for graduate student use. Access provided to online bibliographic retrieval services.

INTERNATIONAL STUDENTS
Demographics 17% of students enrolled are international students.

Applying TOEFL: minimum score of 550 required.

PLACEMENT
Services include alumni network, career counseling/planning, career fairs, career library, career placement, electronic job bank, job interviews arranged, job search course, resume referral to employers, and resume preparation.

Program Contact: Dr. Jack Robinson, Dean, Graduate School, Fifth Avenue, Box 4111, Durant, OK 74701. Phone: 580-924-0121 Ext. 2428, 800-435-1327 (OK only); Fax: 580-920-7472.

Southern Nazarene University

School of Business

Bethany, Oklahoma

OVERVIEW
Southern Nazarene University is an independent-religious, coed, comprehensive institution. Enrollment: 1,799 graduate, professional, and undergraduate students; 270 full-time matriculated graduate/professional students; 35 part-time matriculated graduate/professional students. Founded: 1899. The graduate business unit is in a suburban setting and is on a semester calendar.

HIGHLIGHTS

Enrollment Profile
Full-time: 164
Part-time: 0
Total: 164
Average Age: 35
Fall 1997 Average GPA: 3.1

International: 7%
Women: 45%
Minorities: N/R
Average Class Size: 18
Fall 1997 Average GMAT: 492

Costs
Full-time tuition: $12,000 per academic year
Part-time tuition: N/R

GRADUATE BUSINESS PROGRAMS
Master of Science in Management (MS) Full-time; 32 total credits required; 15 months to complete program. Concentration in management.
Master of Business Administration (MBA) Full-time; 38 total credits required; 18 months to complete program. Concentration in management.

ADMISSION
Application Requirements Application form, application fee, bachelor's degree, essay, minimum GPA, interview, 3 letters of recommendation, personal statement, resume, college transcript(s), minimum of 2 years of work experience, computer experience: computer literacy.
Recommended for Application GMAT score accepted.
Application Deadline Applications processed on a rolling/continuous basis for both domestic and international students. Application fee: $25.

ACADEMICS
Faculty Full-time 5; part-time 11.
Teaching Methodologies Case study, computer-aided instruction, computer analysis, computer simulations, faculty seminars, field projects, group discussion, lecture, research, seminars by members of the business community, student presentations, study groups, team projects.
Technology 100 on-campus computer terminals/PCs are available for student use and are linked by a campus-wide network. The network has full access to the Internet. Students are not required to have their own PC.

FINANCES
Costs for 1997–98 Tuition: Full-time: $12,000 per year. Cost varies by academic program, campus location, number of credits taken. Fees: Full-time: $1300 per academic year. Fees vary by academic program, campus location, number of credits taken.
Financial Aid Contact Mrs. Margaret Rohlmeier, Assistant Financial Aid Director, 6729 Northwest 39th Expressway, Bethany, OK 73008-2694. Phone: 405-491-6685; Fax: 405-491-6302.

FACILITIES
Information Resources R. T. Williams Learning Resources Center; total holdings of 104,069 volumes, 90,626 microforms, 642 current periodical subscriptions. CD player(s) available for graduate student use. Access provided to online bibliographic retrieval services.

INTERNATIONAL STUDENTS
Demographics 7% of students enrolled are international students.
Services and Facilities International student office, visa services.
Applying TOEFL: minimum score of 550 required. Proof of adequate funds, proof of health/immunizations recommended. Financial aid is available to international students.
International Student Contact Ms. Amy Martindale, International Admissions Assistant, 6729 NW 39 Expressway, Bethany, OK 73008. Phone: 405-491-6386; Fax: 405-491-6320.

PLACEMENT
Services include alumni network, and resume preparation. In 1996–97, 10 organizations participated in on-campus recruiting; 10 on-campus interviews were conducted.
Business Program(s) URL: http://www.snu.edu/graduate/departme/business/index.htm

Program Contact: Dr. Wayne Murrow, Acting Director, MSM/MBA, School of Business—Graduate Studies in Management, 6729 Northwest 39th Expressway, Bethany, OK 73008-2694. Phone: 405-491-6316; Fax: 405-491-6302.

Southwestern Oklahoma State University

School of Business

Weatherford, Oklahoma

OVERVIEW
Southwestern Oklahoma State University is a state-supported, coed, comprehensive institution. Enrollment: 4,506 graduate, professional, and undergraduate students; 125 full-time matriculated graduate/professional students; 377 part-time matriculated graduate/professional students. Founded: 1901. The graduate business unit is in a small-town setting and is on a semester calendar.

HIGHLIGHTS

Enrollment Profile
Full-time: 4
Part-time: 26
Total: 30
Average Age: 28
Fall 1997 Average GPA: 3.1

International: 3%
Women: 40%
Minorities: N/R
Average Class Size: 15
Fall 1997 Average GMAT: 550

Costs
Full-time tuition: N/R
Part-time tuition: $75 per hour (resident); $177 per (nonresident)
ACBSP – The American Council of Business Schools and Programs accredited

GRADUATE BUSINESS PROGRAMS
Master of Business Administration (MBA) Full-time, part-time, distance learning option; 33 total credits required; 2 to 5 years to complete program.

ADMISSION
Application Requirements GMAT score, application form, application fee, bachelor's degree, minimum GPA: 2.5, 2 letters of recommendation, college transcript(s).
Recommended for Application Computer experience.
Application Deadline Applications processed on a rolling/continuous basis for both domestic and international students. Application fee: $15. Deferred entrance is available.

ACADEMICS
Faculty Full-time 16.
Teaching Methodologies Case study, field projects, group discussion, lecture, research, student presentations, team projects, interactive television.
Technology 200 on-campus computer terminals/PCs are available for student use and are linked by a campus-wide network. The network has full access to the Internet. Students are not required to have their own PC.
Special Opportunities Advanced credit may be earned through transfer of credits from another institution.

FINANCES
Costs for 1997–98 Tuition: $75 per hour (resident); $177 per (nonresident). Cost varies by academic program. Average 1997–98 room and board costs were $3200 per academic year (on campus) and $3800 per academic year (off campus). Room and board costs vary by occupancy (e.g., single, double, triple), type of meal plan.
Financial Aid In 1997–98, 13% of students received some institutionally administered aid in the form of research assistantships, work study, loans. Application Deadline: 3/1.
Financial Aid Contact Mr. Thomas Ratliff, Director, Financial Aid, 100 Campus Drive, Weatherford, OK 73096. Phone: 580-774-3022; Fax: 580-774-3795.

FACILITIES
Information Resources Al Harris Library; total holdings of 247,038 volumes, 751,460 microforms, 1,369 current periodical subscriptions. CD player(s) available for graduate student use. Access provided to online bibliographic retrieval services.

INTERNATIONAL STUDENTS
Demographics 3% of students enrolled are international students.
Applying TOEFL: minimum score of 550, proof of adequate funds, proof of health/immunizations required. Financial aid is available to international students.

PLACEMENT

Services include alumni network, career counseling/planning, career fairs, electronic job bank, job interviews arranged, resume referral to employers, and resume preparation.

Employment Of 1996–97 graduates, 100% were employed within three months of graduation. Types of employment entered: banking, finance, financial services, health services, insurance, nonprofit.

Program Contact: Dr. Ralph May, Associate Professor, 100 Campus Drive, Weatherford, OK 73096-3098. Phone: 580-774-3279; Fax: 580-774-7067; E-mail: mayr@swosu.edu

University of Central Oklahoma

College of Business Administration

Edmond, Oklahoma

OVERVIEW

The University of Central Oklahoma is a state-supported, coed, comprehensive institution. Enrollment: 14,063 graduate, professional, and undergraduate students; 905 full-time matriculated graduate/professional students; 1,736 part-time matriculated graduate/professional students. Founded: 1890. The graduate business unit is in a suburban setting and is on a semester calendar.

HIGHLIGHTS

Enrollment Profile

Full-time: 291
Part-time: 315
Total: 606
Average Age: 35
Fall 1997 Average GPA: 2.8

International: 19%
Women: 46%
Minorities: 2%
Average Class Size: 20
Fall 1997 Average GMAT: 440

Costs

Full-time tuition: N/R
Part-time tuition: $220 per 3 hours (resident); $501 per 3 hours (nonresident)

ACBSP – The American Council of Business Schools and Programs accredited

GRADUATE BUSINESS PROGRAMS

Master of Business Administration (MBA) Full-time, part-time; 36 total credits required; 3 to 5 years to complete program. Concentrations in accounting, decision sciences, economics, finance, management, management information systems, operations management, international business.

ADMISSION

Applications For fall 1997 there were 135 applications for admission. Of those applying, 135 were accepted. Of those accepted, 135 enrolled.

Application Requirements Application form, application fee, bachelor's degree, minimum GPA: 2.75, college transcript(s), computer experience: computer literacy.

Recommended for Application GMAT score accepted: minimum 450, GRE score accepted: minimum 1,000.

Application Deadline Applications processed on a rolling/continuous basis for both domestic and international students. Application fee: $20. Deferred entrance is available.

ACADEMICS

Faculty Full-time 52; part-time 2.

Teaching Methodologies Case study, computer-aided instruction, computer analysis, computer simulations, faculty seminars, field projects, group discussion, lecture, research, role playing, seminars by members of the business community, simulations, student presentations, study groups, team projects.

Technology 100 on-campus computer terminals/PCs are available for student use and are linked by a campus-wide network. The network has full access to the Internet. Students are not required to have their own PC.

Special Opportunities Advanced credit may be earned through credit for military training programs, transfer of credits from another institution. An internship program is available.

FINANCES

Costs for 1997–98 Tuition: $220 per 3 hours (resident); $501 per 3 hours (nonresident). Cost varies by number of credits taken. Fees: $42 per 3 hours (resident); $42 per 3 hours (nonresident). Fees vary by number of credits taken. Average 1997–98 room and board costs were $2330 per academic year. Room and board costs vary by occupancy (e.g., single, double, triple), type of accommodation, type of meal plan.

Financial Aid Research assistantships, scholarships, work study available. Financial aid is available to part-time students.

Financial Aid Contact Ms. Sheila Fugett, Director, Financial Aid, 100 North University Drive, Edmond, OK 73034-5209. Phone: 405-341-2980 Ext. 3336; Fax: 405-340-7658.

FACILITIES

Information Resources Chambers Library; total holdings of 553,282 volumes, 926,422 microforms, 2,936 current periodical subscriptions. CD player(s) available for graduate student use. Access provided to online bibliographic retrieval services and online databases.

INTERNATIONAL STUDENTS

Demographics 19% of students enrolled are international students.

Services and Facilities International student office, international student center, international student housing, visa services, ESL courses, counseling/support services.

Applying TOEFL, proof of adequate funds, proof of health/immunizations required. Financial aid is not available to international students.

International Student Contact Dr. Ronald Paddack, Director, International Student Services, 100 North University Drive, Edmond, OK 73034. Phone: 405-341-2980 Ext. 2390; Fax: 405-341-4964; E-mail: int-offc@aixl.ucok.edu

PLACEMENT

Services include alumni network, career counseling/planning, career fairs, career library, career placement, electronic job bank, job interviews arranged, job search course, resume referral to employers, and resume preparation. In 1996–97, 169 organizations participated in on-campus recruiting; 1,145 on-campus interviews were conducted.

Employment Of 1996–97 graduates, the average starting salary was $27,967. Types of employment entered: accounting, banking, communications, computer-related, consulting, consumer products, education, finance, financial services, government, high technology, hospitality management, human resources, information systems/technology, insurance, management, manufacturing, marketing, media, mining, nonprofit, retail, service industry, telecommunications.

Program Contact: Ms. Gloria Auth, Director, MBA Program, 100 North University Drive, Edmond, OK 73034-5209. Phone: 405-341-2980 Ext. 3366; Fax: 405-341-4964; E-mail: mba@aixl.ucok.edu

University of Oklahoma

Michael F. Price College of Business

Norman, Oklahoma

OVERVIEW

The University of Oklahoma is a state-supported, coed university. Enrollment: 20,026 graduate, professional, and undergraduate students; 2,197 full-time matriculated graduate/professional students; 2,343 part-time matriculated graduate/professional students. Founded: 1890. The graduate business unit is in a suburban setting and is on a semester calendar.

HIGHLIGHTS

Enrollment Profile

Full-time: 119
Part-time: 136
Total: 255
Average Age: 27
Fall 1997 Average GPA: 3.45

International: 22%
Women: 36%
Minorities: 11%
Average Class Size: 35
Fall 1997 Average GMAT: 570

Costs

Full-time tuition: N/R
Part-time tuition: $92 per credit hour (resident); $266 per credit hour (nonresident)

AACSB – The International Association for Management Education accredited

GRADUATE BUSINESS PROGRAMS

Master of Business Administration (MBA) Full-time, part-time; 55 total credits required; 21 months to 6 years to complete program. Concentrations in finance, marketing, management information systems, management, international business, health care, accounting.

Master of Accountancy (MAcc) Full-time, part-time; 36-49 total credits required; 18 months to 6 years to complete program.

Master of Business Administration/Doctor of Jurisprudence (MBA/JD) Full-time; 126 total credits required; 4 to 6 years to complete program.

PhD in Business (PhD) Full-time. Concentrations in accounting, finance, management, marketing.

OKLAHOMA

ADMISSION

Applications For fall 1997 there were 228 applications for admission. Of those applying, 136 were accepted. Of those accepted, 89 enrolled.

Application Requirements GMAT score, application form, application fee, bachelor's degree, minimum GPA: 3.0, 3 letters of recommendation, personal statement, resume, college transcript(s).

Recommended for Application Interview, computer experience.

Application Deadline Applications processed on a rolling/continuous basis for both domestic and international students. Application fee: $25, $50 (international). Deferred entrance is available.

ACADEMICS

Faculty Full-time 50; part-time 18.

Teaching Methodologies Case study, computer-aided instruction, computer analysis, experiential learning, faculty seminars, field projects, group discussion, lecture, research, seminars by members of the business community, student presentations, study groups, team projects.

Technology Computer terminals/PCs are available for student use and are linked by a campus-wide network. The network has full access to the Internet. Students are not required to have their own PC.

Special Opportunities Advanced credit may be earned through transfer of credits from another institution. International exchange programs in Bulgaria, France, Germany, Sweden.

FINANCES

Costs for 1997–98 Tuition: $92 per credit hour (resident); $266 per credit hour (nonresident). Fees vary by academic program, class time (e.g., day/evening), number of credits taken. Average 1997–98 room and board costs were $7500 per academic year. Room and board costs vary by occupancy (e.g., single, double, triple), type of accommodation, type of meal plan.

Financial Aid In 1997–98, 25% of students received some institutionally administered aid in the form of fellowships, research assistantships, teaching assistantships, scholarships, loans.

Financial Aid Contact Dr. Alice Watkins, Associate Director of Graduate Programs in Business, 307 West Brooks, Room 105K, Norman, OK 73019-0450. Phone: 405-325-4107; Fax: 405-325-1957.

FACILITIES

Information Resources Bizzell Memorial Library plus 8 additional on-campus libraries; total holdings of 2,381,304 volumes, 3,294,140 microforms, 17,400 current periodical subscriptions. CD player(s) available for graduate student use. Access provided to online bibliographic retrieval services.

INTERNATIONAL STUDENTS

Demographics 22% of students enrolled are international students.

Services and Facilities International student office, international student center, international student housing, visa services, ESL courses, counseling/support services, international student organization.

Applying TOEFL: minimum score of 550, TSE, proof of adequate funds, proof of health/immunizations required. Financial aid is available to international students.

International Student Contact Lee Savage, Director of International Student Programs, International Student Services, Norman, OK 73019. Phone: 405-325-3163.

PLACEMENT

Services include alumni network, career counseling/planning, career fairs, career library, career placement, electronic job bank, job interviews arranged, resume referral to employers, and resume preparation. In 1996–97, 280 organizations participated in on-campus recruiting.

Employment Of 1996–97 graduates, 93% were employed within three months of graduation; the average starting salary was $40,000. Types of employment entered: accounting, banking, chemical industry, communications, computer-related, consulting, consumer products, education, energy, engineering, finance, financial services, government, health services, high technology, hospitality management, human resources, information systems/technology, insurance, international trade, law, management, manufacturing, marketing, media, nonprofit, petrochemical, pharmaceutical, retail, service industry, telecommunications, transportation, utilities.

Business Program(s) URL: http://www.ou.edu/mba/

Program Contact: Dr. Alice Watkins, Associate Director of Graduate Programs in Business, 307 West Brooks, Room 105K, Norman, OK 73019-0450. Phone: 405-325-4107; Fax: 405-325-1957; E-mail: awatkins@ou.edu
See full description on page 1120.

University of Tulsa

College of Business Administration
Tulsa, Oklahoma

OVERVIEW
The University of Tulsa is an independent-religious, coed university. Enrollment: 4,573 graduate, professional, and undergraduate students; 981 full-time matriculated graduate/professional students; 407 part-time matriculated graduate/professional students. Founded: 1894. The graduate business unit is in an urban setting and is on a semester calendar.

HIGHLIGHTS

Enrollment Profile
Full-time: 60
Part-time: 180
Total: 240
Average Age: N/R
Fall 1997 Average GPA: 3.23

International: 7%
Women: 50%
Minorities: 10%
Average Class Size: N/R
Fall 1997 Average GMAT: 530

Costs
Full-time tuition: N/R
Part-time tuition: $480 per credit hour

AACSB – The International Association for Management Education accredited

GRADUATE BUSINESS PROGRAMS
Master of Business Administration (MBA) Full-time, part-time; 30-60 total credits required; 15 months to 6 years to complete program. Concentrations in accounting, finance, management.

Master of Science/Master of Accounting and Information Systems (MS/MAIS) Full-time, part-time; 36 total credits required; undergraduate degree in accounting or management information systems preferred; 15 months to 8 years to complete program.

Master of Science/Master of Taxation (MS/MTax) Full-time, part-time; 36 total credits required; 15 months to 8 years to complete program.

ADMISSION
Applications For fall 1997 there were 116 applications for admission. Of those applying, 75 were accepted. Of those accepted, 62 enrolled.

Application Requirements Application form, application fee, bachelor's degree, minimum GPA: 3.0, 3 letters of recommendation, resume, college transcript(s).

Recommended for Application GMAT score accepted: minimum 500, essay, personal statement.

Application Deadline Applications processed on a rolling/continuous basis for both domestic and international students. Application fee: $30. Deferred entrance is available.

ACADEMICS
Faculty Full-time 41; part-time 2.

Teaching Methodologies Case study, computer-aided instruction, computer analysis, computer simulations, experiential learning, faculty seminars, field projects, group discussion, lecture, research, role playing, seminars by members of the business community, student presentations, study groups, team projects.

Technology 40 on-campus computer terminals/PCs are available for student use and are linked by a campus-wide network. The network has full access to the Internet. Students are not required to have their own PC.

Special Opportunities Advanced credit may be earned through credit by examination, transfer of credits from another institution. International exchange programs in Finland, Malaysia, Russia.

FINANCES
Costs for 1997–98 Tuition: $480 per credit hour. Average 1997–98 room and board costs were $2840 per academic year (on campus) and $3150 per academic year (off campus). Room and board costs vary by campus location, occupancy (e.g., single, double, triple), type of accommodation, type of meal plan.

Financial Aid In 1997–98, 15% of students received some institutionally administered aid in the form of fellowships, research assistantships, teaching assistantships, scholarships, work study. Financial aid is available to part-time students. Application Deadline: 2/1.

Financial Aid Contact Office of Financial Aid, 600 South College Avenue, Tulsa, OK 74104-3126. Phone: 918-631-2526; Fax: 918-631-3672.

FACILITIES
Information Resources McFarlin Library plus 1 additional on-campus library; total holdings of 778,417 volumes, 2,381,241 microforms, 7,491 current periodical subscriptions. CD player(s) available for graduate student use. Access provided to online bibliographic retrieval services and online databases.

University of Tulsa (continued)

INTERNATIONAL STUDENTS
Demographics 7% of students enrolled are international students.

Services and Facilities International student office, ESL courses, counseling/support services.

Applying TOEFL: minimum score of 575, proof of adequate funds, proof of health/immunizations required.

International Student Contact Ms. Pam Smith, Dean of International Services and Programs, 600 South College Avenue, Tulsa, OK 74104-3126. Phone: 918-631-2242; Fax: 918-631-3672.

PLACEMENT
Services include career counseling/planning, career fairs, career placement, job interviews arranged, and resume preparation. In 1996–97, 20 organizations participated in on-campus recruiting.

Employment Of 1996–97 graduates, 85% were employed within three months of graduation. Types of employment entered: consulting, finance, government, management, manufacturing, marketing, service industry.

Business Program(s) URL: http://www.cba.utulsa.edu

Program Contact: Graduate Business Studies, 600 South College Avenue, BAH 308, Tulsa, OK 74104-3126. Phone: 918-631-2242, 800-882-4723 (OK only); Fax: 918-631-2142.

OREGON

George Fox University

Department of Business and Economics

Newberg, Oregon

OVERVIEW
George Fox University is an independent-religious, coed university. Enrollment: 2,176 graduate, professional, and undergraduate students; 310 full-time matriculated graduate/professional students; 256 part-time matriculated graduate/professional students. Founded: 1891. The graduate business unit is in an urban setting and is on a trimester calendar.

HIGHLIGHTS

Enrollment Profile

Full-time: 0	International: N/R
Part-time: 84	Women: 37%
Total: 84	Minorities: 14%
Average Age: 37	Average Class Size: 24
Fall 1997 Average GPA: 3.1	Fall 1997 Average GMAT: N/R

Costs
Full-time tuition: N/R
Part-time tuition: $21,240 per degree program

GRADUATE BUSINESS PROGRAMS
Master of Business Administration (MBA) Part-time; 39 total credits required; 2 years work experience required; 2 years to complete program. Concentration in management.

ADMISSION
Applications For fall 1997 there were 80 applications for admission. Of those applying, 61 were accepted. Of those accepted, 48 enrolled.

Application Requirements Application form, application fee, bachelor's degree, essay, minimum GPA: 3.0, interview, 3 letters of recommendation, personal statement, college transcript(s), minimum of 2 years of work experience.

Application Deadline 7/1 for fall. Application fee: $25. Deferred entrance is available.

ACADEMICS
Faculty Full-time 8; part-time 1.

Teaching Methodologies Case study, computer-aided instruction, experiential learning, faculty seminars, field projects, group discussion, lecture, research, role playing, seminars by members of the business community, student presentations, study groups, team projects.

Technology Students are required to have their own PC.

FINANCES
Costs for 1997–98 Tuition: Part-time: $21,240 per degree program.

Financial Aid Loans available. Financial aid is available to part-time students. Application Deadline: 8/1.

Financial Aid Contact Monika Keller, Financial Aid Counselor, 414 North Meridian, Newberg, OR 97132. Phone: 800-765-4369 Ext. 2233; Fax: 503-537-3867; E-mail: mkeller@georgefox.edu

FACILITIES
Information Resources M. J. Murdock Learning Resource Center plus 1 additional on-campus library; total holdings of 170,121 volumes, 149,529 microforms, 1,011 current periodical subscriptions. CD player(s) available for graduate student use. Access provided to online bibliographic retrieval services.

INTERNATIONAL STUDENTS
Demographics N/R

Applying TOEFL: minimum score of 550, proof of adequate funds, proof of health/immunizations required. Financial aid is not available to international students.

PLACEMENT
Services include alumni network, career counseling/planning, career fairs, career library, resume referral to employers, and resume preparation.

Business Program(s) URL: http://www.georgefox.edu

Program Contact: Ms. Jan Cain, Graduate Admissions Counselor, 414 North Meridian, Newberg, OR 97132-2697. Phone: 503-554-2260 Ext. 2263, 800-631-0921 (OR only); Fax: 503-537-3867.

Marylhurst University

Graduate Department of Management

Marylhurst, Oregon

OVERVIEW
Marylhurst University is an independent-religious, coed, comprehensive institution. Enrollment: 1,500 graduate, professional, and undergraduate students. Founded: 1893. The graduate business unit is in a suburban setting and is on a quarter calendar.

HIGHLIGHTS

Enrollment Profile

Full-time: 10	International: 8%
Part-time: 120	Women: 54%
Total: 130	Minorities: 4%
Average Age: 39	Average Class Size: 18
Fall 1997 Average GPA: 3.0	Fall 1997 Average GMAT: 504

Costs
Full-time tuition: N/R
Part-time tuition: $250 per credit hour

GRADUATE BUSINESS PROGRAMS
Master of Business Administration (MBA) Full-time, part-time, distance learning option; 60 total credits required; 12 months to 5 years to complete program. Concentrations in organizational behavior/development, marketing, finance, entrepreneurship.

ADMISSION
Applications For fall 1997 there were 40 applications for admission.

Application Requirements GMAT score: minimum 450, application form, application fee, bachelor's degree, 3 letters of recommendation, personal statement, resume, college transcript(s), minimum of 3 years of work experience.

Recommended for Application Minimum GPA: 2.75, interview, computer experience.

Application Deadline 8/15 for fall, 12/1 for winter, 3/1 for spring, 5/15 for summer, 8/15 for fall (international), 12/1 for winter (international), 3/1 for spring (international), 5/15 for summer (international). Application fee: $80. Deferred entrance is available.

ACADEMICS
Faculty Part-time 20.

Teaching Methodologies Case study, computer-aided instruction, experiential learning, faculty seminars, field projects, group discussion, lecture, research, seminars by members of the business community, simulations, student presentations, study groups, team projects.

Technology 25 on-campus computer terminals/PCs are available for student use and are linked by a campus-wide network. The network has full access to the Internet. Students are not required to have their own PC.

Special Opportunities Advanced credit may be earned through credit by examination, credit for military training programs, transfer of credits from another institution. An internship program is available.

FINANCES
Costs for 1997–98 Tuition: $250 per credit hour. Fees: $17 per quarter. Average 1997–98 room and board costs were $5700 per academic year.

Financial Aid In 1997–98, 33% of students received some institutionally administered aid in the form of work study, loans. Financial aid is available to part-time students.

Financial Aid Contact Mrs. Marlena Mckee-Flores, Director, Financial Aid, 1700 Pacific Highway, PO Box 261, Marylhurst, OR 97036-0261. Phone: 800-634-9982 Ext. 6253; Fax: 503-636-9526; E-mail: finaid@marylhurst.edu

FACILITIES
Information Resources Shoen Library; total holdings of 100,000 volumes, 638 microforms, 450 current periodical subscriptions. CD player(s) available for graduate student use. Access provided to online bibliographic retrieval services and online databases.

INTERNATIONAL STUDENTS
Demographics 8% of students enrolled are international students [Africa, 10%, Asia, 80%, Europe, 10%].

Services and Facilities International student housing, visa services, ESL courses, counseling/support services.

Applying TOEFL: minimum score of 550, TSE, TWE, proof of adequate funds, proof of health/immunizations required. Financial aid is not available to international students.

International Student Contact Susan Kelton, Credentials Evaluator, PO Box 261, Marylhurst, OR 97036-0261. Phone: 503-699-6268; Fax: 503-636-9526; E-mail: skelton@marylhurst.edu

PLACEMENT
Services include alumni network, career fairs, and job interviews arranged.

Employment Types of employment entered: accounting, banking, education, government, health services, high technology, human resources, insurance, manufacturing, marketing, media, nonprofit.

Business Program(s) URL: http://www.marylhurst.edu

Program Contact: Dorothy Deline, Assistant to Graduate Chair, 17600 Pacific Highway, PO Box 261, Marylhurst, OR 97036-0261. Phone: 503-699-6246, 800-634-9982; Fax: 503-636-9526; E-mail: ddeline@marylhurst.edu

Oregon Graduate Institute of Science and Technology

Department of Management in Science and Technology

Portland, Oregon

OVERVIEW
Oregon Graduate Institute of Science and Technology is an independent-nonprofit, graduate institution. Enrollment: 326 graduate, professional, and undergraduate students; 182 full-time matriculated graduate/professional students; 144 part-time matriculated graduate/professional students. The graduate business unit is on a quarter calendar.

HIGHLIGHTS

Enrollment Profile

Full-time: 8	International: 88%
Part-time: 56	Women: N/R
Total: 64	Minorities: N/R
Average Age: N/R	Average Class Size: N/R
Fall 1997 Average GPA: N/R	Fall 1997 Average GMAT: N/R

Costs
Full-time tuition: $4250 per academic year
Part-time tuition: $425 per credit

GRADUATE BUSINESS PROGRAMS
MST in Management (MST) Full-time, part-time; 52 total credits required; minimum of 2 years to complete program. Concentrations in technology management, financial information systems, system management.

ADMISSION
Application Requirements Application form, bachelor's degree, minimum GPA: 3.0, 3 letters of recommendation, personal statement, college transcript(s), minimum of 2 years of work experience.

Recommended for Application GMAT score accepted, GRE score accepted, computer experience.

Application Deadline Applications processed on a rolling/continuous basis for both domestic and international students. Application fee: $50.

ACADEMICS
Teaching Methodologies Case study, computer-aided instruction, computer analysis, computer simulations, experiential learning, faculty seminars, field projects, group discussion, lecture, research, seminars by members of the business community, student presentations, study groups, team projects.

FINANCES
Costs for 1997–98 Tuition: Full-time: $4250 per quarter. Part-time: $425 per credit.

Financial Aid Contact Julie Wilson, Student Services Manager, Portland, OR 97291-1000. Phone: 503-690-1166.

INTERNATIONAL STUDENTS
Demographics 88% of students enrolled are international students.

Applying TOEFL: minimum score of 650 required.

Program Contact: Victoria Tyler, MST Department Administrator, Portland, OR 97291-1000. Phone: 503-748-1335.

Oregon State University

College of Business

Corvallis, Oregon

OVERVIEW
Oregon State University is a state-supported, coed university. Enrollment: 13,975 graduate, professional, and undergraduate students; 2,026 full-time matriculated graduate/professional students; 692 part-time matriculated graduate/professional students. Founded: 1850. The graduate business unit is in a small-town setting and is on a quarter calendar.

HIGHLIGHTS

Enrollment Profile

Full-time: 63	International: 45%
Part-time: 20	Women: 42%
Total: 83	Minorities: 7%
Average Age: 26	Average Class Size: 25
Fall 1997 Average GPA: 3.1	Fall 1997 Average GMAT: 567

Costs
Full-time tuition: $10,020 per academic year (resident); $17,050 per academic year (nonresident)
Part-time tuition: $986 per 4 credits (resident); $1607 per 4 credits (nonresident)

AACSB – The International Association for Management Education accredited

GRADUATE BUSINESS PROGRAMS
Master of Business Administration (MBA) Full-time, part-time; 58-72 total credits required; 12 to 15 months to complete program. Concentration in management.

ADMISSION
Applications For fall 1997 there were 285 applications for admission. Of those applying, 100 were accepted. Of those accepted, 45 enrolled.

Application Requirements GMAT score: minimum 500, application form, application fee, bachelor's degree, minimum GPA: 3.0, 3 letters of recommendation, personal statement, college transcript(s).

Recommended for Application Resume, work experience, computer experience.

Application Deadline 3/1 for fall, 3/1 for fall (international). Application fee: $50. Deferred entrance is available.

ACADEMICS
Faculty Full-time 34; part-time 2.

Teaching Methodologies Case study, computer-aided instruction, computer analysis, computer simulations, experiential learning, faculty seminars, field projects, group discussion, lecture, research, role playing, seminars by members of the business community, simulations, student presentations, study groups, team projects.

Technology 500 on-campus computer terminals/PCs are available for student use and are linked by a campus-wide network. The network has full access to the Internet. Students are not required to have their own PC.

Special Opportunities Advanced credit may be earned through transfer of credits from another institution. International exchange program in Denmark. An internship program is available.

FINANCES
Costs for 1997–98 Tuition: Full-time: $10,020 per program (resident); $17,050 per program (nonresident). Part-time: $986 per 4 credits (resident); $1607 per 4 credits (nonresident). Cost varies by class time (e.g., day/evening), number of credits taken. Fees: Full-time: $130 per academic year (resident); $315 per academic year (nonresident). Fees vary by academic program, number of credits taken. Average 1997–98 room and board costs were $5288 per academic year. Room and board costs vary by occupancy (e.g., single, double, triple), type of accommodation, type of meal plan.

Financial Aid Fellowships, research assistantships, teaching assistantships, scholarships, work study, loans available. Application Deadline: 2/1.

Financial Aid Contact Keith McCreight, Director, Financial Aid Office, OSU Financial Aid Office, AdS A218, Corvallis, OR 97331. Phone: 541-737-2241; Fax: 541-737-4494; E-mail: mccreigk@ccmail.orst.edu

FACILITIES
Information Resources Valley Library; total holdings of 1,300,000 volumes, 1,940,000 microforms, 19,000 current periodical subscriptions. CD player(s) available for graduate student use. Access provided to online bibliographic retrieval services and online databases.

INTERNATIONAL STUDENTS
Demographics 45% of students enrolled are international students [Africa, 3%, Asia, 91%, Europe, 6%].

Services and Facilities International student office, international student center, international student housing, visa services, ESL courses, counseling/support services.

Applying TOEFL: minimum score of 575, proof of adequate funds, proof of health/immunizations required. TSE recommended. Financial aid is available to international students.

International Student Contact Dr. John G. Van de Water, Dean, International Education, 444 Snell, International Education, Corvallis, OR 97331. Phone: 541-737-3006; Fax: 541-737-6482; E-mail: vandewaj@ccmail.orst.edu

PLACEMENT
Services include alumni network, career counseling/planning, career fairs, career library, career placement, electronic job bank, job interviews arranged, job search course, resume referral to employers, and resume preparation. In 1996–97, 200 organizations participated in on-campus recruiting.

Employment Of 1996–97 graduates, 95% were employed within three months of graduation; the average starting salary was $35,000. Types of employment entered: accounting, banking, chemical industry, communications, computer-related, consulting, consumer products, engineering, finance, financial services, government, high technology, human resources, information systems/technology, international trade, manufacturing, marketing, telecommunications.

Business Program(s) URL: http://www.bus.orst.edu/

Program Contact: Fran Saveriano, MBA Program Coordinator, 210 Bexell Hall, Corvallis, OR 97331-2603. Phone: 541-737-3150, 800-228-3187 (OR only); Fax: 541-737-4890; E-mail: saveriano@bus.orst.edu

Portland State University

School of Business Administration

Portland, Oregon

OVERVIEW
Portland State University is a state-supported, coed university. Enrollment: 14,348 graduate, professional, and undergraduate students; 1,680 full-time matriculated graduate/professional students; 2,773 part-time matriculated graduate/professional students. Founded: 1946. The graduate business unit is in an urban setting and is on a quarter calendar.

HIGHLIGHTS

Enrollment Profile

Full-time: 76	International: 13%
Part-time: 309	Women: 41%
Total: 385	Minorities: 10%
Average Age: 30	Average Class Size: 35
Fall 1997 Average GPA: 3.2	Fall 1997 Average GMAT: 556

Costs
Full-time tuition: $6000 per academic year (resident); $10,086 per academic year (nonresident)
Part-time tuition: $1540 per 8 hours (resident); $1540 per 8 hours (nonresident)

AACSB – The International Association for Management Education accredited

GRADUATE BUSINESS PROGRAMS
Master of Business Administration (MBA) Full-time, part-time, distance learning option; 72 total credits required; 12 months to 5 years to complete program. Concentration in technology management.

Engineering Management Program (EMP) Full-time, part-time; 50 total credits required; 12 months to 4 years to complete program.

ADMISSION
Applications For fall 1997 there were 298 applications for admission. Of those applying, 116 were accepted. Of those accepted, 108 enrolled.

Application Requirements Application form, application fee, bachelor's degree, minimum GPA: 2.75, resume, college transcript(s), minimum of 2 years of work experience, computer experience: word processing, spreadsheet.

Recommended for Application GMAT score accepted, letters of recommendation, personal statement.

Application Deadline 4/1 for fall, 8/1 for winter, 3/1 for fall (international), 7/1 for winter (international). Application fee: $50. Deferred entrance is available.

ACADEMICS
Faculty Full-time 47; part-time 21.

Teaching Methodologies Case study, experiential learning, field projects, group discussion, lecture, role playing, seminars by members of the business community, student presentations, study groups, team projects.

Technology 400 on-campus computer terminals/PCs are available for student use and are linked by a campus-wide network. The network has full access to the Internet. Students are not required to have their own PC.

Special Opportunities Advanced credit may be earned through transfer of credits from another institution. International exchange programs in Denmark, Germany. An internship program is available.

FINANCES
Costs for 1997–98 Tuition: Full-time: $6000 per year (resident); $10,086 per year (nonresident). Part-time: $1540 per 8 hours (resident); $1540 per 8 hours (nonresident). Cost varies by number of credits taken, reciprocity agreements. Fees: Full-time: $972 per academic year (resident); $972 per academic year (nonresident). Part-time: $193 per 8 hours (resident); $193 per 8 hours (nonresident). Fees vary by academic program, number of credits taken. Average 1997–98 room only costs were $10,000 per academic year (on campus) and $12,000 per academic year (off campus). Room and board costs vary by campus location, occupancy (e.g., single, double, triple), type of accommodation, type of meal plan.

Financial Aid In 1997–98, 8% of students received some institutionally administered aid in the form of research assistantships, teaching assistantships, work study, loans. Financial aid is available to part-time students. Application Deadline: 3/1.

Financial Aid Contact Ms. Kathy Goff, Assistant Director of Financial Aid, Student Financial Aid Office, PO Box 751, Portland, OR 97207-0751. Phone: 503-725-3461.

FACILITIES
Information Resources Branford Millar Library; total holdings of 1,000,000 volumes, 2,289,009 microforms, 22,001 current periodical subscriptions. CD player(s) available for graduate student use. Access provided to online bibliographic retrieval services and online databases.

INTERNATIONAL STUDENTS
Demographics 13% of students enrolled are international students [Asia, 54%, Central America, 2%, Europe, 42%, North America, 2%].

Services and Facilities International student office, international student center, international student housing, visa services, ESL courses, counseling/support services.

Applying TOEFL: minimum score of 550, proof of adequate funds, proof of health/immunizations required. Financial aid is available to international students.

International Student Contact Dawn White, Director, International Education Services, PO Box 751, Portland, OR 97207. E-mail: whited@pdx.edu

PLACEMENT
Services include alumni network, career counseling/planning, career fairs, career placement, electronic job bank, job interviews arranged, resume referral to employers, and resume preparation. In 1996–97, 30 organizations participated in on-campus recruiting.

Employment Of 1996–97 graduates, 90% were employed within three months of graduation. Types of employment entered: accounting, banking, communications, computer-related, consulting, consumer products, education, engineering, finance, financial services, high technology, human resources, insurance, international trade, management, manufacturing, nonprofit, service industry, telecommunications, transportation, utilities.

Business Program(s) URL: http://www.sba.pdx.edu/

Program Contact: Pam Mitchell, Graduate Programs Administrator, School of Business Administration, PO Box 751, Portland, OR 97207-0751. Phone: 503-725-3712; Fax: 503-725-5850; E-mail: pamm@sba.pdx.edu
See full description on page 932.

University of Oregon

Charles H. Lundquist College of Business

Eugene, Oregon

OVERVIEW
The University of Oregon is a state-supported, coed university. Enrollment: 17,269 graduate, professional, and undergraduate students. Founded: 1872. The graduate business unit is in an urban setting and is on a quarter calendar.

HIGHLIGHTS

Enrollment Profile

Full-time: 198	International: 30%
Part-time: 0	Women: 30%
Total: 198	Minorities: 8%
Average Age: 27	Average Class Size: 25
Fall 1997 Average GPA: 3.3	Fall 1997 Average GMAT: 577

Costs
Full-time tuition: $6150 per academic year (resident); $10,449 per academic year (nonresident)
Part-time tuition: N/R

AACSB – The International Association for Management Education accredited

---

I n 1985, the business schools at Oregon's three largest public universities joined to create a consortium capable of offering one of the highest-quality Executive M.B.A. programs in the country. The Oregon Executive M.B.A. (OEMBA) brings the strengths, resources, and services of the University of Oregon, Oregon State University, and Portland State University together to deliver an outstanding program.

The OEMBA mission is to educate high-potential executives in business theory and practice for strategic decision making in a competitive, global economy. The program grants a Master of Business Administration (M.B.A.) degree from the University of Oregon. The degree program is nationally accredited by AACSB–The International Association for Management Education.

The OEMBA curriculum is designed for working professionals who hold middle- to senior-level management positions and focuses on functional and strategic concepts central to effective leadership and management at the senior level. A minimum of three years of management experience is required. All traditional business disciplines are covered, as are significant emerging management practices, with a balance between theory and practical application.

This executive program is based on the traditional M.B.A. curriculum model but is approached at a higher level due to the extensive experience of the students and the nature of the cohort model.

Classes are offered on alternating Fridays and Saturdays in the Portland area. Students can contact the program office at 503-725-2250 or visit the Web site at http://www.capital.ous.edu/oemba for specific OEMBA application materials.

GRADUATE BUSINESS PROGRAMS
Master of Business Administration (MBA) Full-time; 72 total credits required; 12 months to 2 years to complete program. Concentrations in entrepreneurship, international business, finance, management, marketing, human resources, sports/entertainment management.

ADMISSION
Applications For fall 1997 there were 323 applications for admission. Of those applying, 180 were accepted. Of those accepted, 106 enrolled.

Application Requirements Application form, application fee, bachelor's degree, essay, minimum GPA: 2.8, 2 letters of recommendation, resume, college transcript(s), computer experience: word processing, spreadsheet, graphics.

Recommended for Application GMAT score accepted, work experience.

Application Deadline 3/1 for fall, 3/1 for summer, 2/1 for fall (international), 2/1 for summer (international). Application fee: $50.

ACADEMICS
Faculty Full-time 49; part-time 18.

Teaching Methodologies Case study, computer-aided instruction, computer analysis, computer simulations, experiential learning, faculty seminars, field projects, group discussion, lecture, research, role playing, seminars by members of the business community, simulations, student presentations, study groups, team projects.

Technology 600 on-campus computer terminals/PCs are available for student use and are linked by a campus-wide network. The network has full access to the Internet. Students are not required to have their own PC.

Special Opportunities International exchange programs in Denmark, France, Germany, Japan, Netherlands. An internship program is available.

FINANCES
Costs for 1997–98 Tuition: Full-time: $6150 per year (resident); $10,449 per year (nonresident). Cost varies by class time (e.g., day/evening), number of credits taken. Fees: Full-time: $300 per academic year (resident); $900 per academic year (nonresident). Fees vary by academic program, number of credits taken. Average 1997–98 room and board costs were $4933 per academic year (on campus) and $8550 per academic year (off campus). Room and board costs vary by occupancy (e.g., single, double, triple), type of accommodation, type of meal plan.

Financial Aid In 1997–98, 88% of students received some institutionally administered aid in the form of fellowships, research assistantships, teaching assistantships, scholarships, work study, loans. Financial aid is available to part-time students. Application Deadline: 2/1.

Financial Aid Contact Financial Aid Office, 1278 University of Oregon, 260 Oregon Hall, Eugene, OR 97403-1278. Phone: 541-346-3221.

FACILITIES
Information Resources Knight Library plus 5 additional on-campus libraries; total holdings of 2,024,323 volumes, 1,973,513 microforms, 17,914 current periodical subscriptions. CD player(s) available for graduate student use. Access provided to online bibliographic retrieval services.

INTERNATIONAL STUDENTS
Demographics 30% of students enrolled are international students [Africa, 5%, Asia, 25%, Australia/New Zealand, 5%, Central America, 5%, Europe, 25%, North America, 5%, South America, 15%, other, 15%].

Services and Facilities International student office, international student center, international student housing, visa services, ESL courses, counseling/support services.

Applying TOEFL, proof of adequate funds, proof of health/immunizations required. Financial aid is not available to international students.

International Student Contact Mr. Dan Poston, Director of Master's Programs, Charles H. Lundquist College of Business, Eugene, OR 97403-1208. Phone: 541-346-3306; Fax: 541-346-3347; E-mail: dposton@oregon.uoregon.edu

PLACEMENT
Services include alumni network, career counseling/planning, career fairs, career library, career placement, electronic job bank, job interviews arranged, job search course, resume referral to employers, and resume preparation. In 1996–97, 23 organizations participated in on-campus recruiting; 190 on-campus interviews were conducted.

Employment Of 1996–97 graduates, 97% were employed within three months of graduation; the average starting salary was $46,486. Types of employment entered: accounting, banking, computer-related, consulting, consumer products, education, finance, financial services, government, health services, high technology, hospitality management, human resources, information systems/technology, insurance, law, management, manufacturing, marketing, nonprofit, pharmaceutical, real estate, retail, service industry, telecommunications, utilities.

Business Program(s) URL: http://biz.uoregon.edu

Program Contact: Mr. Dan Poston, Director of Admissions, Charles H. Lundquist College of Business, Eugene, OR 97403-1208. Phone: 541-346-3306; Fax: 541-346-3347; E-mail: dposton@oregon.uoregon.edu

---

University of Portland

School of Business Administration

Portland, Oregon

OVERVIEW
The University of Portland is an independent-religious, coed, comprehensive institution. Enrollment: 2,556 graduate, professional, and undergraduate students; 96 full-time matriculated graduate/professional students; 490 part-time matriculated graduate/professional students. Founded: 1901. The graduate business unit is in an urban setting and is on a semester calendar.

HIGHLIGHTS

Enrollment Profile

Full-time: 23	International: 26%
Part-time: 106	Women: 38%
Total: 129	Minorities: N/R
Average Age: 27	Average Class Size: 20
Fall 1997 Average GPA: 3.14	Fall 1997 Average GMAT: 540

Costs
Full-time tuition: N/R
Part-time tuition: $515 per credit hour

University of Portland (continued)

AACSB – The International Association for Management Education accredited

GRADUATE BUSINESS PROGRAMS

Master of Business Administration (MBA) Full-time, part-time; 30-53 total credits required; 12 months to 6 years to complete program. Concentrations in management, finance, marketing, international business.

ADMISSION

Applications For fall 1997 there were 91 applications for admission. Of those applying, 50 were accepted. Of those accepted, 43 enrolled.

Application Requirements Application form, bachelor's degree, minimum GPA: 2.75, 2 letters of recommendation, personal statement, college transcript(s).

Recommended for Application GMAT score accepted, work experience, computer experience.

Application Deadline 8/1 for fall, 12/1 for spring, 4/1 for summer, 5/1 for fall (international). Application fee: $40.

ACADEMICS

Faculty Full-time 26; part-time 3.

Teaching Methodologies Case study, computer-aided instruction, computer analysis, computer simulations, field projects, group discussion, lecture, research, role playing, simulations, student presentations, study groups, team projects.

Technology 189 on-campus computer terminals/PCs are available for student use and are linked by a campus-wide network. The network has full access to the Internet. Students are not required to have their own PC.

Special Opportunities Advanced credit may be earned through transfer of credits from another institution.

FINANCES

Costs for 1997–98 Tuition: $515 per credit hour. Cost varies by academic program. Average 1997–98 room and board costs were $4710 per academic year. Room and board costs vary by occupancy (e.g., single, double, triple), type of meal plan.

Financial Aid In 1997–98, 5% of students received some institutionally administered aid in the form of scholarships, work study, loans. Financial aid is available to part-time students. Application Deadline: 3/15.

Financial Aid Contact Ms. Rita Lambert, Director of Financial Aid, 5000 North Willamette Boulevard, Portland, OR 97203-5798. Phone: 503-283-7311; Fax: 503-283-7399; E-mail: lambert@uofport.edu

FACILITIES

Information Resources Wilson W. Clark Library; total holdings of 365,000 volumes, 10,500 microforms, 1,300 current periodical subscriptions. CD player(s) available for graduate student use. Access provided to online bibliographic retrieval services.

INTERNATIONAL STUDENTS

Demographics 26% of students enrolled are international students [Africa, 5%, Asia, 85%, Europe, 5%, South America, 5%].

Services and Facilities International student office, ESL courses, counseling/support services, international student association.

Applying TOEFL: minimum score of 570, proof of adequate funds required. Financial aid is available to international students.

International Student Contact Ms. Barbara Segal, Director of International Programs, 5000 North Willamette Boulevard, Portland, OR 97203-5798. Phone: 503-283-7367; Fax: 503-283-7399; E-mail: segal@uofport.edu

PLACEMENT

Services include alumni network, career counseling/planning, career fairs, career library, career placement, electronic job bank, job interviews arranged, job search course, resume referral to employers, and resume preparation.

Employment Types of employment entered: accounting, banking, communications, computer-related, consumer products, education, energy, engineering, finance, financial services, health services, high technology, management, manufacturing, marketing, nonprofit, service industry, telecommunications, transportation.

Business Program(s) URL: http://wally.uofport.edu

Program Contact: Dr. Marti Rhea, Associate Dean/Director, 5000 North Willamette Boulevard, Portland, OR 97203-5798. Phone: 503-283-7225; Fax: 503-978-8041; E-mail: mba-up@up.edu

Willamette University

George H. Atkinson Graduate School of Management

Salem, Oregon

OVERVIEW
Willamette University is an independent-religious, coed, comprehensive institution. Enrollment: 2,548 graduate, professional, and undergraduate students; 587 full-time matriculated graduate/professional students; 50 part-time matriculated graduate/professional students. Founded: 1842. The graduate business unit is in an urban setting and is on a semester calendar.

HIGHLIGHTS

Enrollment Profile

Full-time: 131	International: 24%
Part-time: 33	Women: 33%
Total: 164	Minorities: 12%
Average Age: 26	Average Class Size: 25
Fall 1997 Average GPA: 3.3	Fall 1997 Average GMAT: 550

Costs
Full-time tuition: $14,900 per academic year
Part-time tuition: $497 per credit

AACSB – The International Association for Management Education accredited

GRADUATE BUSINESS PROGRAMS

Master of Management (MMgt) Full-time, part-time; 63 total credits required; 2.2 to 5 years to complete program. Concentrations in accounting, finance, human resources, international management, management, marketing, public management, quantitative analysis, organizational behavior/development, management science.

Master of Management/Doctor of Jurisprudence (MMgt/JD) Full-time; 120 total credits required; 4 years to complete program. Concentrations in accounting, finance, human resources, international management, management, marketing, public management, quantitative analysis, organizational behavior/development, management science.

Accelerated Waiver-Based Program (MMgt) Full-time, part-time; 30-60 total credits required; degree from AACSB-accredited business program, 3.5 cumulative GPA, and 2 years work experience required; 9 months to 2.2 years to complete program. Concentrations in accounting, finance, human resources, international management, management, marketing, public management, quantitative analysis, organizational behavior/development, management science.

ADMISSION

Applications For fall 1997 there were 148 applications for admission. Of those applying, 135 were accepted. Of those accepted, 75 enrolled.

Application Requirements Application form, application fee, bachelor's degree, essay, minimum GPA, 2 letters of recommendation, personal statement, resume, college transcript(s).

Recommended for Application GMAT score accepted, GRE score accepted, interview, work experience, computer experience.

Application Deadline Applications processed on a rolling/continuous basis for both domestic and international students. Application fee: $50. Deferred entrance is available.

ACADEMICS

Faculty Full-time 13; part-time 6.

Teaching Methodologies Case study, computer-aided instruction, computer analysis, computer simulations, experiential learning, faculty seminars, field projects, group discussion, lecture, research, role playing, seminars by members of the business community, simulations, student presentations, study groups, team projects.

Technology 27 on-campus computer terminals/PCs are available for student use and are linked by a campus-wide network. The network has full access to the Internet. Students are not required to have their own PC.

Special Opportunities Advanced credit may be earned through transfer of credits from another institution. International exchange program in People's Republic of China. An internship program is available.

FINANCES

Costs for 1997–98 Tuition: Full-time: $14,900 per year. Part-time: $497 per credit. Cost varies by academic program, number of credits taken. Fees: Full-time: $50 per academic year. Part-time: $50 per year. Average 1997–98 room only costs were $6500 per academic year (on campus) and $5500 per academic year (off campus). Room and board costs vary by occupancy (e.g., single, double, triple), type of accommodation, type of meal plan.

Financial Aid In 1997–98, 70% of students received some institutionally administered aid in the form of research assistantships, scholarships, work study, loans. Financial aid is available to part-time students. Application Deadline: 3/1.

Financial Aid Contact Zofia Miller, Assistant Director of Financial Aid, 900 State Street, Salem, OR 97301. Phone: 503-370-5416; Fax: 503-370-6588; E-mail: zmiller@willamette.edu

FACILITIES
Information Resources Mark O. Hatfield Library plus 1 additional on-campus library; total holdings of 394,730 volumes, 147,399 microforms, 2,791 current periodical subscriptions. CD player(s) available for graduate student use. Access provided to online bibliographic retrieval services and online databases.

INTERNATIONAL STUDENTS
Demographics 24% of students enrolled are international students [Africa, 6%, Asia, 72%, North America, 6%, South America, 6%, other, 10%].

Services and Facilities International student office, visa services, counseling/support services.

Applying TOEFL: minimum score of 550, proof of adequate funds required. Financial aid is available to international students.

International Student Contact Donna McElroy, Director, International Student and Faculty Services, 900 State Street, Salem, OR 97301-3931. Phone: 503-375-5404; Fax: 503-370-6407; E-mail: dmcelroy@willamette.edu

PLACEMENT
Services include alumni network, career counseling/planning, career fairs, career library, career placement, electronic job bank, job interviews arranged, job search course, resume referral to employers, and resume preparation. In 1996–97, 57 organizations participated in on-campus recruiting; 203 on-campus interviews were conducted.

Employment Of 1996–97 graduates, 90% were employed within three months of graduation; the average starting salary was $43,500. Types of employment entered: accounting, banking, communications, computer-related, consulting, consumer products, education, energy, engineering, finance, financial services, government, health services, high technology, hospitality management, human resources, information systems/technology, insurance, international trade, law, management, manufacturing, marketing, media, nonprofit, real estate, retail, service industry, telecommunications, transportation, utilities.

Business Program(s) URL: http://www.willamette.edu/agsm/

Program Contact: Judy O'Neill, Assistant Dean/Director of Admissions, 900 State Street, Salem, OR 97301-3931. Phone: 503-370-6167; Fax: 503-370-3011; E-mail: joneill@willamette.edu

See full description on page 1196.

PENNSYLVANIA

Allentown College of St. Francis de Sales

Business Programs

Center Valley, Pennsylvania

OVERVIEW
Allentown College of St. Francis de Sales is an independent-religious, coed, comprehensive institution. Enrollment: 2,400 graduate, professional, and undergraduate students; full-time matriculated graduate/professional students; 450 part-time matriculated graduate/professional students. Founded: 1964. The graduate business unit is in a rural setting and is on a three 12-week sessions and one 6-week session calendar.

GRADUATE BUSINESS PROGRAMS
Master of Business Administration (MBA)

ACADEMICS
Faculty Full-time 10; part-time 15.

Teaching Methodologies Case study, computer-aided instruction, computer analysis, computer simulations, experiential learning, group discussion, lecture, seminars by members of the business community, simulations, student presentations, study groups, team projects.

Technology 80 on-campus computer terminals/PCs are available for student use and are linked by a campus-wide network. The network has full access to the Internet. Students are not required to have their own PC.

Special Opportunities Advanced credit may be earned through credit by examination, credit for experience, transfer of credits from another institution.

FACILITIES
Information Resources Trexler Library; total holdings of 145,000 volumes, 185,000 microforms, 960 current periodical subscriptions. CD player(s) available for graduate student use. Access provided to online bibliographic retrieval services.

Program Contact: Director, MBA Program, 2755 Station Avenue, Center Valley, PA 18034-9568. Phone: 610-282-4625; Fax: 610-282-2254; E-mail: mba@email.allencol.edu

American College

Richard D. Irwin Graduate School of Management

Bryn Mawr, Pennsylvania

OVERVIEW
American College is an independent-nonprofit, coed, graduate institution. Enrollment: 12,940 graduate, professional, and undergraduate students; full-time matriculated graduate/professional students; 940 part-time matriculated graduate/professional students. Founded: 1927. The graduate business unit is in a suburban setting and is on a quarter calendar.

HIGHLIGHTS

Enrollment Profile
Full-time: 0	International: 3%
Part-time: 940	Women: 33%
Total: 940	Minorities: N/R
Average Age: N/R	Average Class Size: 25
Fall 1997 Average GPA: N/R	Fall 1997 Average GMAT: N/R

Costs
Full-time tuition: N/R
Part-time tuition: $490 per course

GRADUATE BUSINESS PROGRAMS
Master of Science in Financial Services (MS) Full-time, part-time, distance learning option; 36 total credits required; up to 7 years to complete program. Concentration in financial management/planning.

Master of Science in Management (MS) Full-time, part-time, distance learning option; 36 total credits required; up to 7 years to complete program. Concentration in management.

ADMISSION
Application Requirements Application form, application fee, bachelor's degree, essay, personal statement, college transcript(s).

Application Deadline Applications processed on a rolling/continuous basis for both domestic and international students. Application fee: $275.

ACADEMICS
Faculty Full-time 27; part-time 8.

Teaching Methodologies Case study, faculty seminars, group discussion, lecture, research, student presentations, study groups.

Technology 5 on-campus computer terminals/PCs are available for student use. The network has full access to the Internet. Students are not required to have their own PC.

Special Opportunities Advanced credit may be earned through credit by examination.

FINANCES
Costs for 1997–98 Tuition: $490 per course.

Financial Aid Contact Steve McMillan, Director, Graduate Academic Affairs, 270 Bryn Mawr Avenue, Bryn Mawr, PA 19010-2105. E-mail: stevem@amercoll.edu

FACILITIES
Information Resources Lucas Memorial Library plus 1 additional on-campus library; total holdings of 12,500 volumes, 1,000 microforms, 550 current periodical subscriptions. Access provided to online bibliographic retrieval services.

INTERNATIONAL STUDENTS
Demographics 3% of students enrolled are international students.

Applying Financial aid is not available to international students.

PLACEMENT
Services include alumni network.

Employment Of 1996–97 graduates, 100% were employed within three months of graduation.

Business Program(s) URL: http://www.amercoll.edu

Program Contact: Joanne Patterson, Director, Graduate School Administration, 270 Bryn Mawr Avenue, Bryn Mawr, PA 19010-2105. Phone: 610-526-1366; Fax: 610-526-1310; E-mail: joannep@amercoll.edu

Bloomsburg University of Pennsylvania

College of Business

Bloomsburg, Pennsylvania

OVERVIEW
Bloomsburg University of Pennsylvania is a state-supported, coed, comprehensive institution. Founded: 1839. The graduate business unit is in a small-town setting and is on a semester calendar.

HIGHLIGHTS

Enrollment Profile

Full-time: 10	International: 8%
Part-time: 80	Women: 48%
Total: 90	Minorities: 4%
Average Age: 36	Average Class Size: 13
Fall 1997 Average GPA: N/R	Fall 1997 Average GMAT: N/R

Costs

Full-time tuition: $3370 per academic year (resident); $6054 per academic year (nonresident)

Part-time tuition: $187 per credit hour (resident); $336 per credit hour (nonresident)

GRADUATE BUSINESS PROGRAMS

Master of Business Administration (MBA) Full-time, part-time; 36 total credits required; 12 months to 6 years to complete program.

Master of Science in Accountancy (MS) Full-time, part-time; 36 total credits required; up to 6 years to complete program.

Master of Business Education (MBE) Part-time; 36 total credits required; up to 6 years to complete program.

ADMISSION

Application Requirements GMAT score, application form, application fee, bachelor's degree, minimum GPA: 2.5, 3 letters of recommendation, resume, college transcript(s).

Recommended for Application GRE score accepted, MAT score accepted, computer experience.

Application Deadline Applications processed on a rolling/continuous basis for both domestic and international students. Application fee: $25. Deferred entrance is available.

ACADEMICS

Faculty Full-time 40.

Teaching Methodologies Case study, computer-aided instruction, computer simulations, experiential learning, faculty seminars, field projects, group discussion, lecture, research, role playing, seminars by members of the business community, simulations, student presentations, study groups, team projects.

Technology 350 on-campus computer terminals/PCs are available for student use and are linked by a campus-wide network. The network has full access to the Internet. Students are not required to have their own PC.

Special Opportunities Advanced credit may be earned through credit for business training programs, transfer of credits from another institution.

FINANCES

Costs for 1997–98 Tuition: Full-time: $3370 per year (resident); $6054 per year (nonresident). Part-time: $187 per credit hour (resident); $336 per credit hour (nonresident). Cost varies by number of credits taken. Fees: Full-time: $466 per academic year (resident); $466 per academic year (nonresident). Part-time: $73 per semester (resident); $73 per semester (nonresident). Fees vary by number of credits taken.

FACILITIES

Information Resources Harvey A. Andruss Library; total holdings of 335,000 volumes, 1,750,000 microforms, 1,600 current periodical subscriptions. CD player(s) available for graduate student use. Access provided to online bibliographic retrieval services.

INTERNATIONAL STUDENTS

Demographics 8% of students enrolled are international students [Africa, 70%, Asia, 10%, Europe, 20%].

Services and Facilities International student office, international student center, counseling/support services.

Applying TOEFL, proof of adequate funds required.

International Student Contact Dr. Madhau Sharma, Director, International Education, 400 East Second Street, Bloomsburg, PA 17815-1905. Phone: 717-389-4000.

PLACEMENT

Employment Of 1996–97 graduates, 100% were employed within three months of graduation.

Program Contact: Dr. Patrick Schloss, Assistant Vice President and Dean of Graduate Studies and Research, 400 East Second Street, Bloomsburg, PA 17815-1905. Phone: 717-389-4015; Fax: 717-389-3054.

California University of Pennsylvania

School of Graduate Studies and Research

California, Pennsylvania

OVERVIEW
California University of Pennsylvania is a state-supported, coed, comprehensive institution. Enrollment: 5,700 graduate, professional, and undergraduate students; 410 full-time matriculated graduate/professional students; 460 part-time matriculated graduate/professional students. Founded: 1852. The graduate business unit is in a small-town setting and is on a semester calendar.

GRADUATE BUSINESS PROGRAMS
Master of Science in Business Administration (MS)

ACADEMICS
Faculty Part-time 10.

Teaching Methodologies Case study, computer-aided instruction, computer analysis, computer simulations, experiential learning, faculty seminars, field projects, group discussion, lecture, research, role playing, seminars by members of the business community, simulations, student presentations, study groups, team projects.

Technology 200 on-campus computer terminals/PCs are available for student use and are linked by a campus-wide network. The network has full access to the Internet. Students are not required to have their own PC.

Special Opportunities Advanced credit may be earned through transfer of credits from another institution.

FACILITIES
Information Resources Louis L. Manderino Library; total holdings of 330,728 volumes, 1,297,696 microforms, 1,492 current periodical subscriptions. CD player(s) available for graduate student use. Access provided to online bibliographic retrieval services.

Program Contact: Dean of Graduate Studies and Research, 250 University Avenue, California, PA 15419-1394. Phone: 412-938-4187; Fax: 412-938-5712; E-mail: gradschool@cup.edu

Carnegie Mellon University

Graduate School of Industrial Administration

Pittsburgh, Pennsylvania

OVERVIEW
Carnegie Mellon University is an independent-nonprofit, coed university. Enrollment: 7,318 graduate, professional, and undergraduate students; 1,897 full-time matriculated graduate/professional students; 807 part-time matriculated graduate/professional students. Founded: 1900. The graduate business unit is in a suburban setting and is on a six mini-semesters per calendar year.

HIGHLIGHTS

Enrollment Profile

Full-time: 503	International: 40%
Part-time: 175	Women: 19%
Total: 678	Minorities: 9%
Average Age: 28	Average Class Size: 65
Fall 1997 Average GPA: 3.2	Fall 1997 Average GMAT: 640

Costs

Full-time tuition: $24,000 per academic year
Part-time tuition: $250 per unit

AACSB – The International Association for Management Education accredited

GRADUATE BUSINESS PROGRAMS

Master of Science in Industrial Administration (MS) Full-time, part-time; 68 total credits required; 16 months to 2 years to complete program. Concentrations in accounting, economics, entrepreneurship, finance, international business, marketing, management information systems, operations management, quantitative analysis, strategic management, organizational behavior/development.

Master of Science in Industrial Administration/Doctor of Jurisprudence (MS/JD) Full-time; 4 years to complete program.

Master of Science in Computational Finance (MS) Full-time, part-time, distance learning option; 144 total credits required; 12 months to 2 years to complete program. Concentrations in finance, quantitative analysis.

Master of Science in Information Networking (MS) Full-time; 144 total credits required. Concentrations in telecommunications management, information management, management information systems, management systems analysis.

ADMISSION

Applications For fall 1997 there were 1,229 applications for admission. Of those applying, 378 were accepted. Of those accepted, 247 enrolled.

Application Requirements GMAT score, application form, application fee, bachelor's degree, essay, minimum GPA, interview, 3 letters of recommendation, resume, college transcript(s).

Recommended for Application Work experience.

Application Deadline Applications processed on a rolling/continuous basis for both domestic and international students. Application fee: $50. Deferred entrance is available.

ACADEMICS

Faculty Full-time 84; part-time 32.

Teaching Methodologies Case study, computer-aided instruction, computer analysis, computer simulations, experiential learning, faculty seminars, field projects, group discussion, lecture, seminars by members of the business community, simulations, student presentations, study groups, team projects.

Technology 500 on-campus computer terminals/PCs are available for student use and are linked by a campus-wide network. The network has full access to the Internet. Students are required to have their own PC.

Special Opportunities International exchange programs in Austria, France, Germany, Japan, United Kingdom. An internship program is available.

FINANCES

Costs for 1997–98 Tuition: Full-time: $24,000 per year. Part-time: $250 per unit. Fees: Full-time: $100 per academic year. Part-time: $100 per year. Average 1997–98 room and board costs were $6735 per academic year (off campus). Room and board costs vary by campus location, occupancy (e.g., single, double, triple), type of accommodation, type of meal plan.

Financial Aid In 1997–98, 52% of students received some institutionally administered aid in the form of fellowships, teaching assistantships, work study, loans. Application Deadline: 6/1.

Financial Aid Contact Ms. Lauren Tracey, Financial Aid Counselor, Graduate School of Industrial Administration, Pittsburgh, PA 15213-3890. Phone: 412-268-7581; Fax: 412-268-7094.

FACILITIES

Information Resources Hunt Library plus 2 additional on-campus libraries; total holdings of 852,241 volumes, 756,985 microforms, 3,889 current periodical subscriptions. CD player(s) available for graduate student use. Access provided to online bibliographic retrieval services.

INTERNATIONAL STUDENTS

Demographics 40% of students enrolled are international students.

Services and Facilities International student office, international student center, visa services, ESL courses, counseling/support services.

Applying TOEFL: minimum score of 600, proof of adequate funds required. Financial aid is not available to international students.

International Student Contact Dr. Manjula Shyam, Director, International Programs, Graduate School of Industrial Administration, Pittsburgh, PA 15213-3890. Phone: 412-268-7055; Fax: 412-268-6837.

PLACEMENT

Services include alumni network, career counseling/planning, career fairs, career library, career placement, electronic job bank, job interviews arranged, job search course, resume referral to employers, and resume preparation. In 1996–97, 146 organizations participated in on-campus recruiting; 3,782 on-campus interviews were conducted.

Employment Of 1996–97 graduates, 96% were employed within three months of graduation; the average starting salary was $68,372. Types of employment entered: accounting, banking, chemical industry, computer-related, consulting, consumer products, energy, finance, financial services, high technology, information systems/technology, management, manufacturing, marketing, petrochemical, pharmaceutical, telecommunications, transportation, utilities.

Business Program(s) URL: http://www.gsia.cmu.edu

Program Contact: Ms. Laurie Stewart, Director of Admissions, Graduate School of Industrial Administration, Pittsburgh, PA 15213-3890. Phone: 412-268-2272, 800-850-GSIA (PA only); Fax: 412-268-7094; E-mail: gsia-admisions@andrew.cmu.edu
See full description on page 740.

Chatham College

Program in Management

Pittsburgh, Pennsylvania

OVERVIEW

Chatham College is an independent-nonprofit, coed, comprehensive institution. Enrollment: 875 graduate, professional, and undergraduate students. Founded: 1869. The graduate business unit is in an urban setting and is on a semester calendar.

HIGHLIGHTS

Enrollment Profile

Full-time: N/R	International: N/R
Part-time: N/R	Women: N/R
Total: N/R	Minorities: N/R
Average Age: N/R	Average Class Size: 7
Fall 1997 Average GPA: N/R	Fall 1997 Average GMAT: N/R

Costs
Full-time tuition: $7529 per academic year
Part-time tuition: $370 per credit

GRADUATE BUSINESS PROGRAMS

Master of Management (MM) Full-time, part-time; 30-51 total credits required; minimum of 12 months to complete program.

ADMISSION

Application Requirements Application form, bachelor's degree, minimum GPA: 3.0, 2 letters of recommendation, personal statement, college transcript(s), computer experience: word processing, spreadsheet, database, internet.

Recommended for Application Interview, resume, work experience.

Application Deadline Applications processed on a rolling/continuous basis for both domestic and international students. Application fee: $35. Deferred entrance is available.

ACADEMICS

Faculty Full-time 5; part-time 10.

Teaching Methodologies Case study, computer-aided instruction, computer analysis, experiential learning, faculty seminars, field projects, group discussion, lecture, research, role playing, seminars by members of the business community, student presentations, study groups, team projects.

Technology 30 on-campus computer terminals/PCs are available for student use and are linked by a campus-wide network. The network has full access to the Internet. Students are not required to have their own PC.

Special Opportunities Advanced credit may be earned through transfer of credits from another institution. An internship program is available.

FINANCES

Costs for 1997–98 Tuition: Full-time: $7529 per semester. Part-time: $370 per credit. Cost varies by academic program, class time (e.g., day/evening), number of credits taken. Fees: Full-time: $78 per academic year. Part-time: $39 per semester. Average 1997–98 room and board costs were $5940 per academic year. Room and board costs vary by type of meal plan.

Financial Aid Research assistantships, loans available. Financial aid is available to part-time students.

Financial Aid Contact Director of Financial Aid, Pittsburgh, PA 15232. Phone: 412-365-1777; Fax: 412-365-1643.

FACILITIES

Information Resources Jennie King Mellon Library; total holdings of 100,000 volumes, 4,500 microforms, 600 current periodical subscriptions. CD player(s) available for graduate student use. Access provided to online bibliographic retrieval services and online databases.

INTERNATIONAL STUDENTS

Demographics N/R

Services and Facilities International student office, international student housing, ESL courses, counseling/support services.

Applying TOEFL: minimum score of 600 required. Financial aid is not available to international students.

International Student Contact International Admissions Counselor, Pittsburgh, PA 15232. Phone: 412-365-1618.

Chatham College (continued)

PLACEMENT

Services include alumni network, career counseling/planning, career fairs, career library, career placement, electronic job bank, job interviews arranged, resume referral to employers, and resume preparation.

Business Program(s) URL: http://www.chatham.edu/ce

Program Contact: Academic Advisor for Evening and Weekend Studies, Pittsburgh, PA 15232. Phone: 412-365-1858, 800-837-1290 (PA only); Fax: 412-365-1720.

Clarion University of Pennsylvania

College of Business Administration

Clarion, Pennsylvania

OVERVIEW

Clarion University of Pennsylvania is a state-supported, coed, comprehensive institution. Enrollment: 6,209 graduate, professional, and undergraduate students; 238 full-time matriculated graduate/professional students; 155 part-time matriculated graduate/professional students. Founded: 1867. The graduate business unit is in a small-town setting and is on a semester calendar.

HIGHLIGHTS

Enrollment Profile
Full-time: 15
Part-time: 14
Total: 29
Average Age: 31
Fall 1997 Average GPA: 3.38

International: 10%
Women: 31%
Minorities: N/R
Average Class Size: 15
Fall 1997 Average GMAT: 500

Costs
Full-time tuition: $3368 per academic year (resident); $6054 per academic year (nonresident)
Part-time tuition: $187 per credit (resident); $336 per credit (nonresident)

AACSB – The International Association for Management Education accredited

GRADUATE BUSINESS PROGRAMS

Master of Business Administration (MBA) Full-time, part-time; 33 total credits required; 13 months to 2 years to complete program. Concentrations in accounting, economics, finance, management, marketing.

ADMISSION

Applications For fall 1997 there were 53 applications for admission. Of those applying, 46 were accepted. Of those accepted, 15 enrolled.

Application Requirements Application form, application fee, bachelor's degree, minimum GPA: 2.75, 3 letters of recommendation, college transcript(s).

Recommended for Application GMAT score accepted.

Application Deadline 5/1 for fall, 8/1 for spring, 4/1 for fall (international), 7/1 for spring (international). Application fee: $25. Deferred entrance is available.

ACADEMICS

Faculty Part-time 40.

Teaching Methodologies Case study, computer-aided instruction, faculty seminars, field projects, group discussion, lecture, research, student presentations.

Technology 199 on-campus computer terminals/PCs are available for student use and are linked by a campus-wide network. The network has full access to the Internet. Students are not required to have their own PC.

Special Opportunities Advanced credit may be earned through credit for experience, transfer of credits from another institution.

FINANCES

Costs for 1997–98 Tuition: Full-time: $3368 per year (resident); $6054 per year (nonresident). Part-time: $187 per credit (resident); $336 per credit (nonresident). Cost varies by number of credits taken. Average 1997–98 room and board costs were $3074 per academic year. Room and board costs vary by occupancy (e.g., single, double, triple), type of meal plan.

Financial Aid In 1997–98, 34% of students received some institutionally administered aid in the form of research assistantships. Financial aid is available to part-time students. Application Deadline: 5/1.

Financial Aid Contact Mr. Kenneth Grugel, Director of Financial Aid, Egbert Hall, Clarion, PA 16214. Phone: 814-226-2315; Fax: 814-226-2520.

FACILITIES

Information Resources Carlson Library; total holdings of 362,962 volumes, 1,200,000 microforms, 1,689 current periodical subscriptions. Access provided to online bibliographic retrieval services.

INTERNATIONAL STUDENTS

Demographics 10% of students enrolled are international students.

Services and Facilities International student office, international student center, counseling/support services.

Applying TOEFL: minimum score of 550, proof of adequate funds required. Financial aid is not available to international students.

International Student Contact Ms. Linda Heineman, Foreign Student Advisor, International Programs Office, Clarion, PA 16214. Phone: 814-226-2340; Fax: 814-226-2341; E-mail: heineman@mail.clarion.edu

PLACEMENT

Services include alumni network, career counseling/planning, career fairs, career library, career placement, job interviews arranged, job search course, resume referral to employers, and resume preparation. In 1996–97, 100 organizations participated in on-campus recruiting; 29 on-campus interviews were conducted.

Employment Of 1996–97 graduates, 87% were employed within three months of graduation; the average starting salary was $30,500. Types of employment entered: accounting, banking, computer-related, consulting, education, finance, financial services, government, health services, information systems/technology, management, manufacturing, marketing, service industry, transportation.

Business Program(s) URL: http://www.clarion.edu/cob_web1/header.htm

Program Contact: Director of MBA Program, Clarion, PA 16214. Phone: 814-226-2605; Fax: 814-226-1910; E-mail: coba@mail.clarion.edu

See full description on page 750.

Drexel University

College of Business and Administration

Philadelphia, Pennsylvania

OVERVIEW

Drexel University is an independent-nonprofit, coed university. Enrollment: 9,590 graduate, professional, and undergraduate students; 861 full-time matriculated graduate/professional students; 1,924 part-time matriculated graduate/professional students. Founded: 1891. The graduate business unit is in an urban setting and is on a quarter calendar.

HIGHLIGHTS

Enrollment Profile
Full-time: 291
Part-time: 553
Total: 844
Average Age: 26
Fall 1997 Average GPA: 3.28

International: 30%
Women: 38%
Minorities: N/R
Average Class Size: 23
Fall 1997 Average GMAT: 550

Costs
Full-time tuition: N/R
Part-time tuition: $477 per credit

AACSB – The International Association for Management Education accredited

Degree(s) offered in conjunction with École Superieure de Commerce

GRADUATE BUSINESS PROGRAMS

Master of Science in Marketing (MS) Full-time, part-time; 48 total credits required; 12 months to 7 years to complete program. Concentration in marketing.

Master of Science in Accounting (MS) Full-time, part-time; 48 total credits required; 12 months to 7 years to complete program. Concentration in accounting.

Master of Science in Finance (MS) Full-time, part-time; 48 total credits required; 12 months to 7 years to complete program. Concentration in finance.

Master of Science in Taxation (MS) Full-time, part-time; 48 total credits required; 12 months to 7 years to complete program. Concentration in taxation.

Master of Science in Decision Sciences (MS) Full-time, part-time; 48 total credits required; 12 months to 7 years to complete program. Concentration in decision sciences.

Master of Business Administration (MBA) Full-time, part-time; 84 total credits required; 12 months to 7 years to complete program. Concentrations in accounting, banking, economics, financial management/planning, international business, management science, management information systems, marketing, human resources, organizational management, quality management, taxation, finance, management, marketing research, operations management, organizational behavior/development, production management.

ADMISSION

Applications For fall 1997 there were 902 applications for admission. Of those applying, 541 were accepted. Of those accepted, 228 enrolled.

Application Requirements GMAT score, application form, application fee, bachelor's degree, essay, minimum GPA: 3.0, 2 letters of recommendation, personal statement, college transcript(s).

Recommended for Application Resume.

Application Deadline 8/31 for fall, 11/30 for winter, 3/1 for spring, 5/31 for summer, 6/20 for fall (international), 9/25 for winter (international), 1/1 for spring (international), 3/31 for summer (international). Application fee: $35. Deferred entrance is available.

ACADEMICS

Faculty Full-time 70; part-time 38.

Teaching Methodologies Case study, computer analysis, computer simulations, experiential learning, group discussion, research, role playing, seminars by members of the business community, simulations, student presentations, team projects.

Technology Computer terminals/PCs are available for student use and are linked by a campus-wide network. The network has full access to the Internet. Students are not required to have their own PC.

Special Opportunities Advanced credit may be earned through transfer of credits from another institution. International exchange program in France. An internship program is available.

FINANCES

Costs for 1997–98 Tuition: $477 per credit. Cost varies by number of credits taken. Average 1997–98 room and board costs were $7254 per academic year.

Financial Aid In 1997–98, 8% of students received some institutionally administered aid in the form of fellowships, research assistantships, teaching assistantships. Application Deadline: 3/1.

Financial Aid Contact Mr. James Baskett, Director of Financial Aid, 3141 Chestnut Street, Philadelphia, PA 19104-2875. Phone: 215-895-2964; Fax: 215-895-5878; E-mail: baskettj@duvm.ocs.drexel.edu

FACILITIES

Information Resources W. W. Hagerty Library; total holdings of 392,590 volumes, 649,512 microforms, 2,016 current periodical subscriptions. CD player(s) available for graduate student use. Access provided to online bibliographic retrieval services.

INTERNATIONAL STUDENTS

Demographics 30% of students enrolled are international students.

Services and Facilities International student office, international student center, ESL courses.

Applying TOEFL: minimum score of 570, proof of adequate funds required. Financial aid is available to international students.

International Student Contact Director, International Students, Creese Student Center-Room 210, 32nd and Chestnut Streets, Philadelphia, PA 19104. Phone: 215-895-2502.

PLACEMENT

Services include career counseling/planning, career fairs, career library, career placement, electronic job bank, job interviews arranged, and resume preparation.

Business Program(s) URL: http://www.coba.drexel.edu/

Program Contact: Ms. Denise Bigham, Associate Director of Graduate Admissions, College of Business and Administration, 3141 Chestnut Street, Philadelphia, PA 19104-2875. Phone: 215-895-6704, 800-2-DREXEL (PA only); Fax: 215-895-1012; E-mail: bighamdg@duvm.ocs.drexel.edu
See full description on page 786.

Duquesne University

Graduate School of Business Administration

Pittsburgh, Pennsylvania

OVERVIEW

Duquesne University is an independent-religious, coed university. Enrollment: 9,500 graduate, professional, and undergraduate students; 1,484 full-time matriculated graduate/professional students; 2,122 part-time matriculated graduate/professional students. Founded: 1878. The graduate business unit is in an urban setting and is on a semester calendar.

HIGHLIGHTS

Enrollment Profile
Full-time: 139
Part-time: 464
Total: 603
Average Age: 31
Fall 1997 Average GPA: 3.1

International: 7%
Women: 41%
Minorities: 5%
Average Class Size: 22
Fall 1997 Average GMAT: 520

Costs
Full-time tuition: N/R
Part-time tuition: $470 per credit

AACSB – The International Association for Management Education accredited

Duquesne University's Graduate School of Business Administration challenges students to reach their potential in a dynamic, intellectually exciting environment that is driven by a century-long commitment to professional and personal ethics, teaching excellence, continuous improvement, scholarship, and creative academic–business partnerships. The School prepares leaders who can blend technical competence with a broad-based renaissance education.

The distinctive curriculum focuses on total quality, ethics, the integration of disciplines, communications, the management of technology, and an increased global perspective. The application of these issues through the use of real business problems responds to employers' strongly expressed need for graduates who can immediately add value in real-world situations. A comprehensive reading program helps students relate specific business disciplines to the world at large, reflecting a renaissance approach to graduate education. Executive faculty members, executives-in-residence, and advisory boards of business professionals supplement the academic capabilities of a faculty with a roster of outstanding executives who participate in the classroom experience.

The Graduate School of Business Administration provides professional management education of uncompromised quality through instructional excellence in a dynamic environment of change and continuous improvement that offers students excitement, opportunity, and the chance to grow

GRADUATE BUSINESS PROGRAMS

Master of Business Administration (MBA) Full-time, part-time; 56 total credits required; 18 months to 6 years to complete program. Concentrations in accounting, business ethics, economics, finance, human resources, international management, management information systems, marketing, real estate, taxation.

Master of Science in Information Systems Management (MS) Full-time, part-time; 62 total credits required; 18 months to 6 years to complete program.

Master of Business Administration/Master of Science in Information Systems Management (MBA/MS) Full-time, part-time; 80 total credits required; 2 to 6 years to complete program. Concentrations in accounting, business ethics, economics, finance, human resources, international management, management information systems, marketing, real estate, taxation.

Master of Business Administration/Master of Arts in Liberal Studies (MBA/MA) Full-time, part-time; 68 total credits required; 2 to 6 years to complete program. Concentrations in accounting, business ethics, economics, finance, human resources, international management, management information systems, marketing, real estate, taxation.

Master of Business Administration/Doctor of Jurisprudence (MBA/JD) Full-time, part-time; 126 total credits required; 3 to 6 years to complete program. Concentrations in accounting, business ethics, economics, finance, human resources, international management, management information systems, marketing, real estate, taxation.

Master of Business Administration/Master of Science in Environmental Science Management (MBA/MS) Full-time, part-time; 64-68 total credits required; 2 to 6 years to complete program. Concentrations in accounting, business ethics, economics, finance, human resources, international management, management information systems, marketing, real estate, taxation.

Master of Business Administration/Master of Health Management Systems (MBA/MHMS) Full-time, part-time; 67 total credits required; 2 to 6 years to complete program. Concentrations in accounting, business ethics, economics, finance, human resources, international management, management information systems, marketing, real estate, taxation.

Master of Business Administration/Master of Science in Nursing (MBA/MS) Full-time, part-time; 74 total credits required; 2 to 6 years to complete program. Concentrations in accounting, business ethics, economics, finance, human resources, international management, management information systems, marketing, real estate, taxation.

Master of Business Administration/Master of Science in Industrial Pharmacy (MBA/MS) Full-time; 75 total credits required; 2 to 6 years to complete program. Concentrations in accounting, business ethics, economics, finance, human resources, international management, management information systems, marketing, real estate, taxation.

Duquesne University (continued)

Master of Science in Taxation (MS) Full-time, part-time; 30 total credits required; 12 months to 6 years to complete program.

Master of Business Administration/Master of Science in Taxation (MBA/MSTax) Full-time, part-time; 62 total credits required; 2 to 6 years to complete program.

Master of Business Administration/Master of Liberal Studies (MBA/MLS) Full-time, part-time; 69-72 total credits required; 2 to 6 years to complete program.

ADMISSION

Applications For fall 1997 there were 318 applications for admission. Of those applying, 241 were accepted. Of those accepted, 146 enrolled.

Application Requirements GMAT score, application form, application fee, bachelor's degree, minimum GPA, 2 letters of recommendation, personal statement, college transcript(s).

Recommended for Application Resume, work experience, computer experience.

Application Deadline 6/1 for fall, 11/1 for spring, 3/1 for summer, 6/1 for fall (international), 11/1 for spring (international), 3/1 for summer (international). Application fee: $40. Deferred entrance is available.

ACADEMICS

Faculty Full-time 29; part-time 7.

Teaching Methodologies Case study, computer-aided instruction, computer analysis, computer simulations, experiential learning, faculty seminars, field projects, group discussion, lecture, research, role playing, seminars by members of the business community, simulations, student presentations, study groups, team projects.

Technology 200 on-campus computer terminals/PCs are available for student use and are linked by a campus-wide network. The network has full access to the Internet. Students are not required to have their own PC.

Special Opportunities Advanced credit may be earned through credit by examination, credit for experience, credit for business training programs, transfer of credits from another institution. International exchange programs in Colombia, France, Germany, Italy, Japan. An internship program is available.

FINANCES

Costs for 1997–98 Tuition: $470 per credit. Cost varies by campus location, number of credits taken. Fees: $37 per credit. Fees vary by campus location, number of credits taken. Average 1997–98 room and board costs were $5978 per academic year (on campus) and $5978 per academic year (off campus). Room and board costs vary by occupancy (e.g., single, double, triple).

Financial Aid In 1997–98, 5% of students received some institutionally administered aid in the form of research assistantships. Financial aid is available to part-time students. Application Deadline: 7/1.

Financial Aid Contact Mr. Frank Dutkovich, Director, Financial Aid, 600 Forbes Avenue, Pittsburgh, PA 15282. Phone: 412-396-6607.

FACILITIES

Information Resources Gumberg Library plus 1 additional on-campus library; total holdings of 648,357 volumes, 421,136 microforms, 5,587 current periodical subscriptions. CD player(s) available for graduate student use. Access provided to online bibliographic retrieval services.

INTERNATIONAL STUDENTS

Demographics 7% of students enrolled are international students.

Services and Facilities International student office, international student center, visa services, ESL courses, counseling/support services, international student organization.

Applying TOEFL: minimum score of 550, proof of adequate funds, proof of health/immunizations required. TSE, TWE recommended. Financial aid is not available to international students.

International Student Contact Ms. Valentina DeSilva, International Student Advisor , 601 Duquesne Union, Pittsburgh, PA 15282. Phone: 412-396-6113; Fax: 412-396-5178; E-mail: oia@duq2.duq.edu

PLACEMENT

Services include alumni network, career counseling/planning, career fairs, career library, career placement, electronic job bank, job interviews arranged, resume referral to employers, and resume preparation. In 1996–97, 155 organizations participated in on-campus recruiting; 75 on-campus interviews were conducted.

Employment Of 1996–97 graduates, 99% were employed within three months of graduation. Types of employment entered: accounting, banking, communications, computer-related, consulting, consumer products, education, energy, engineering, finance, financial services, government, health services, high technology, human resources, information systems/technology, insurance, international trade, law, management, manufacturing, marketing, media, mining, nonprofit, pharmaceutical, real estate, retail, service industry, telecommunications, transportation, utilities.

Business Program(s) URL: http://www.bus.duq.edu/

Program Contact: Ms. Mary Kay Cunningham, Assistant Director, Graduate Program, Graduate School of Business and Administration, 600 Forbes Avenue, Pittsburgh, PA 15282. Phone: 412-396-6276; Fax: 412-396-5304; E-mail: cunningh@duq2.cc.duq.edu
See full description on page 788.

Eastern College

Graduate Business Programs

St. Davids, Pennsylvania

OVERVIEW

Eastern College is an independent-religious, coed, comprehensive institution. Enrollment: 2,496 graduate, professional, and undergraduate students; 332 full-time matriculated graduate/professional students; 420 part-time matriculated graduate/professional students. The graduate business unit is in a suburban setting and is on a semester calendar.

HIGHLIGHTS

Enrollment Profile

Full-time: 252	International: 8%
Part-time: 121	Women: 43%
Total: 373	Minorities: 24%
Average Age: 37	Average Class Size: 17
Fall 1997 Average GPA: 2.86	Fall 1997 Average GMAT: 500

Costs
Full-time tuition: N/R
Part-time tuition: $368 per credit

Degree(s) offered in conjunction with Eastern Baptist Theological Seminary

GRADUATE BUSINESS PROGRAMS

Traditional MBA (MBA) Full-time, part-time; 36 total credits required; up to 7 years to complete program. Concentrations in finance, marketing, accounting, management, economics.

Master of Business Administration/Master of Science in Non-Profit Management (MBA/MS) Full-time, part-time; 36 total credits required; up to 7 years to complete program. Concentration in nonprofit management.

Fast Track Executive MBA/Master of Science in Health Administration (MBA/MS) Full-time, part-time; 33-39 total credits required; up to 7 years to complete program. Concentration in health care.

Master of Business Administration/Master of Science in Economic Development (MBA/MS) Full-time, part-time; 39 total credits required; up to 7 years to complete program. Concentration in international development management.

Master of Divinity/Master of Business Administration (MDiv/MBA) Full-time, part-time; 116 total credits required; up to 7 years to complete program. Concentrations in international development management, accounting, economics, finance, management.

Fast-track MBA (MBA) Full-time; 39 total credits required; minimum of 22 months to complete program. Concentration in management.

Master of Divinity/Master of Science in Economic Development (MDiv/MS) Full-time, part-time; 116 total credits required; up to 7 years to complete program.

ADMISSION

Application Requirements Application form, application fee, bachelor's degree, essay, minimum GPA: 2.5, 2 letters of recommendation, personal statement, resume, college transcript(s), computer experience: Microsoft Word, database, spreadsheet, presentation.

Recommended for Application GMAT score accepted.

Application Deadline Applications processed on a rolling/continuous basis for both domestic and international students. Application fee: $35. Deferred entrance is available.

ACADEMICS

Faculty Full-time 9; part-time 17.

Teaching Methodologies Computer simulations, faculty seminars, field projects, group discussion, lecture, research, role playing, seminars by members of the business community, student presentations, study groups, team projects.

Technology 40 on-campus computer terminals/PCs are available for student use and are linked by a campus-wide network. The network has full access to the Internet. Students are not required to have their own PC.

Special Opportunities Advanced credit may be earned through credit by examination, transfer of credits from another institution. An internship program is available.

FINANCES
Costs for 1997–98 Tuition: $368 per credit. Cost varies by academic program. Room and board costs vary by occupancy (e.g., single, double, triple), type of accommodation, type of meal plan.

Financial Aid Research assistantships, teaching assistantships, scholarships, work study available. Application Deadline: 8/26.

Financial Aid Contact Janice Hetrick, Director of Financial Aid, 1300 Eagle Road, St. Davids, PA 19087-3696. Phone: 610-341-5842; Fax: 610-341-1723.

FACILITIES
Information Resources Warner Memorial Library plus 1 additional on-campus library; total holdings of 209,361 volumes, 669,906 microforms, 1,205 current periodical subscriptions. CD player(s) available for graduate student use. Access provided to online bibliographic retrieval services.

INTERNATIONAL STUDENTS
Demographics 8% of students enrolled are international students [Africa, 63%, Asia, 17%, Australia/New Zealand, 3%, Central America, 3%, Europe, 7%, North America, 3%, other, 1%].

Services and Facilities International student office, counseling/support services.

Applying TOEFL: minimum score of 550, proof of adequate funds, proof of health/immunizations required. Financial aid is available to international students.

International Student Contact Ms. Lisa Pappas, International Student Advisor, 1300 Eagle Road, St. Davids, PA 19087-3696. Phone: 610-341-1454; Fax: 610-341-1705.

PLACEMENT
Services include career counseling/planning, and career library.

Business Program(s) URL: http://www.eastern.edu/academic/undg/depts/business/index.html

Program Contact: Megan Miscioscia, Graduate Admissions Representative, 1300 Eagle Road, St. Davids, PA 19087-3696. Phone: 610-341-5972; Fax: 610-341-1466; E-mail: gradm@eastern.edu

See full description on page 792.

Gannon University

Dahlkemper School of Business
Erie, Pennsylvania

OVERVIEW
Gannon University is an independent-religious, coed, comprehensive institution. Founded: 1925. The graduate business unit is in a small-town setting and is on a semester calendar.

HIGHLIGHTS

Enrollment Profile
Full-time: N/R
Part-time: N/R
Total: N/R
Average Age: 33
Fall 1997 Average GPA: 3.0

International: N/R
Women: N/R
Minorities: N/R
Average Class Size: 15
Fall 1997 Average GMAT: 467

Costs
Full-time tuition: N/R
Part-time tuition: N/R

GRADUATE BUSINESS PROGRAMS
Master of Business Administration (MBA) Full-time, part-time; 30-48 total credits required; 12 months to 6 years to complete program. Concentrations in accounting, finance, marketing, human resources, public policy and administration.

Master of Science in Nursing/Master of Business Administration (MS/MBA) Full-time, part-time; 69 total credits required; 2 to 6 years to complete program. Concentrations in accounting, finance, marketing, human resources, public policy and administration.

Master of Public Administration (MPA) Full-time, part-time; 36 total credits required; 12 months to 3 years to complete program. Concentrations in public policy and administration, public management, accounting, finance, marketing.

ADMISSION
Application Requirements GMAT score, application form, application fee, bachelor's degree, minimum GPA, 3 letters of recommendation, personal statement, college transcript(s).

Recommended for Application GRE score accepted, interview, work experience, computer experience.

Application Deadline Applications processed on a rolling/continuous basis for both domestic and international students. Application fee: $25. Deferred entrance is available.

ACADEMICS
Teaching Methodologies Case study, field projects, group discussion, lecture, role playing, student presentations, team projects.

Technology 60 on-campus computer terminals/PCs are available for student use and are linked by a campus-wide network. The network has full access to the Internet. Students are not required to have their own PC.

Special Opportunities Advanced credit may be earned through credit by examination, credit for experience, transfer of credits from another institution. An internship program is available.

FINANCES
Costs for 1997–98 Cost varies by academic program, campus location, number of credits taken. Fees vary by campus location. Average 1997–98 room only costs were $2700 per academic year (off campus).

Financial Aid Scholarships available.

Financial Aid Contact Mr. James Treiber, Director of Financial Aid, University Square, Erie, PA 16541. Phone: 814-871-7481.

FACILITIES
Information Resources Nash Library; total holdings of 210,000 volumes, 382,127 microforms, 1,400 current periodical subscriptions. CD player(s) available for graduate student use. Access provided to online bibliographic retrieval services.

INTERNATIONAL STUDENTS
Demographics N/R

Services and Facilities Counseling/support services.

Applying TOEFL: minimum score of 550 required. IELT recommended. Financial aid is not available to international students.

International Student Contact Dr. Marjorie Krebs, Professor, Mental Health/Psychology, University Square, Erie, PA 16541. Phone: 814-871-7721.

PLACEMENT
Services include career counseling/planning, career fairs, career library, career placement, and resume preparation. In 1996–97, 32 organizations participated in on-campus recruiting; 2 on-campus interviews were conducted.

Employment Of 1996–97 graduates, 100% were employed within three months of graduation. Types of employment entered: accounting, engineering, human resources, pharmaceutical.

Business Program(s) URL: http://www.gannon.edu

Program Contact: Dr. David Frew, Director of MBA/MPA Programs, Dahlkemper School of Business, University Square, Erie, PA 16541. Phone: 814-871-7579.

Grove City College

Program in Accounting
Grove City, Pennsylvania

OVERVIEW
Grove City College is an independent-religious, coed, comprehensive institution. Enrollment: 2,293 graduate, professional, and undergraduate students; 4 full-time matriculated graduate/professional students; 21 part-time matriculated graduate/professional students. The graduate business unit is in a small-town setting and is on a semester calendar.

HIGHLIGHTS

Enrollment Profile
Full-time: 4
Part-time: 21
Total: 25
Average Age: N/R
Fall 1997 Average GPA: N/R

International: 0%
Women: 44%
Minorities: 0%
Average Class Size: N/R
Fall 1997 Average GMAT: N/R

Costs
Full-time tuition: N/R
Part-time tuition: $273 per credit

Grove City College (continued)

GRADUATE BUSINESS PROGRAMS
Master of Arts in Accounting (MA) Full-time, part-time; 30 total credits required; 12 months to 2 years to complete program. Concentration in accounting.

ADMISSION
Applications For fall 1997 there were 13 applications for admission. Of those applying, 11 were accepted. Of those accepted, 10 enrolled.

Application Requirements Application form, bachelor's degree, essay, 2 letters of recommendation, college transcript(s).

Recommended for Application Computer experience.

Application Deadline Applications processed on a rolling/continuous basis for both domestic and international students. Application fee: $30.

ACADEMICS
Technology 100 on-campus computer terminals/PCs are available for student use and are linked by a campus-wide network. The network has full access to the Internet. Students are required to have their own PC.

Special Opportunities Advanced credit may be earned through transfer of credits from another institution.

FINANCES
Costs for 1997–98 Tuition: $273 per credit.

Financial Aid Scholarships available.

Financial Aid Contact Mrs. Anne Bowne, Director of Financial Aid, 100 Campus Drive, Grove City, PA 16127-2104. Phone: 724-458-2163; Fax: 724-458-3395.

FACILITIES
Information Resources Henry Buhl Library.

INTERNATIONAL STUDENTS
Demographics N/R

Services and Facilities Counseling/support services.

Applying TOEFL, proof of adequate funds, proof of health/immunizations required. Financial aid is available to international students.

International Student Contact Mr. Jeffrey Mincey, Director of Admissions, 100 Campus Drive, Grove City, PA 16127-2104. Phone: 724-458-2100; Fax: 724-458-3395.

PLACEMENT
Services include alumni network, career counseling/planning, career fairs, career library, career placement, electronic job bank, job interviews arranged, resume referral to employers, and resume preparation. In 1996–97, 120 organizations participated in on-campus recruiting.

Program Contact: Grove City, PA 16127-2104. Phone: 724-458-2000; Fax: 724-458-3395.

GRADUATE BUSINESS PROGRAMS
Master of Business Administration (MBA) Full-time, part-time; 33-51 total credits required; 12 to 18 months to complete program.

Executive MBA (MBA) Part-time; 51 total credits required; 2 years to complete program.

Master of Education in Business (MEd) 30 total credits required.

ADMISSION
Applications For fall 1997 there were 184 applications for admission.

Application Requirements GMAT score: minimum 450, application form, application fee, bachelor's degree, essay, minimum GPA: 2.6, 2 letters of recommendation, personal statement, college transcript(s).

Recommended for Application Resume, work experience, computer experience.

Application Deadline Applications processed on a rolling/continuous basis for both domestic and international students. Application fee: $30.

ACADEMICS
Faculty Full-time 36.

Teaching Methodologies Case study, computer-aided instruction, computer analysis, computer simulations, experiential learning, faculty seminars, field projects, group discussion, lecture, research, seminars by members of the business community, simulations, student presentations, study groups, team projects.

Special Opportunities International exchange programs in Colombia, Finland, France, Germany, Mexico, Spain, United Kingdom. An internship program is available.

FINANCES
Costs for 1997–98 Tuition: $193 per credit (resident); $346 per credit (nonresident). Cost varies by number of credits taken. Fees: $300 per year (resident); $300 per year (nonresident).

Financial Aid Research assistantships, work study available. Financial aid is available to part-time students. Application Deadline: 3/15.

Financial Aid Contact Frederick Joseph, Director, Financial Aid, Indiana, PA 15705. Phone: 724-357-2218.

FACILITIES
Information Resources Stapleton Library; total holdings of 742,873 volumes, 578,371 microforms, 40,755 current periodical subscriptions. CD player(s) available for graduate student use. Access provided to online bibliographic retrieval services.

INTERNATIONAL STUDENTS
Demographics 36% of students enrolled are international students.

Applying TOEFL: minimum score of 500 required.

International Student Contact Ms. Laila Dahan, Director of Office of International Student Services, Sutton Hall, Indiana, PA 15705. Phone: 724-357-2295.

Business Program(s) URL: http://www.iup.edu/busins/

Program Contact: Dr. Krish Krishnan, Director, MBA Program, Eberly College of Business, Indiana, PA 15705. Phone: 724-357-2522; Fax: 724-357-6232.

Indiana University of Pennsylvania

Eberly College of Business

Indiana, Pennsylvania

OVERVIEW
Indiana University of Pennsylvania is a state-supported, coed university. Enrollment: 14,000 graduate, professional, and undergraduate students. Founded: 1875. The graduate business unit is in a small-town setting and is on a semester calendar.

HIGHLIGHTS

Enrollment Profile

Full-time: 118	International: 36%
Part-time: 55	Women: 42%
Total: 173	Minorities: 5%
Average Age: 29	Average Class Size: 20
Fall 1997 Average GPA: N/R	Fall 1997 Average GMAT: N/R

Costs
Full-time tuition: N/R
Part-time tuition: $193 per credit (resident); $346 per credit (nonresident)

King's College

William G. McGowan School of Business

Wilkes-Barre, Pennsylvania

OVERVIEW
King's College is an independent-religious, coed, comprehensive institution. Enrollment: 2,222 graduate, professional, and undergraduate students; full-time matriculated graduate/professional students; 145 part-time matriculated graduate/professional students. Founded: 1946. The graduate business unit is in an urban setting and is on a semester calendar.

HIGHLIGHTS

Enrollment Profile

Full-time: 0	International: 2%
Part-time: 124	Women: 61%
Total: 124	Minorities: 3%
Average Age: 35	Average Class Size: 15
Fall 1997 Average GPA: 3.13	Fall 1997 Average GMAT: N/R

Costs
Full-time tuition: N/R
Part-time tuition: $437 per credit hour

GRADUATE BUSINESS PROGRAMS

Master of Science in Finance (MS) Part-time; 30 total credits required; up to 7 years to complete program. Concentrations in accounting, finance, taxation.

Master of Science in Health Care Administration (MS) Part-time; 42-45 total credits required; up to 7 years to complete program.

ADMISSION

Applications For fall 1997 there were 34 applications for admission. Of those applying, 33 were accepted. Of those accepted, 33 enrolled.

Application Requirements Application form, application fee, bachelor's degree, minimum GPA, 2 letters of recommendation, college transcript(s).

Recommended for Application GMAT score accepted, resume, work experience, computer experience.

Application Deadline Applications processed on a rolling/continuous basis for both domestic and international students. Application fee: $35. Deferred entrance is available.

ACADEMICS

Faculty Full-time 7; part-time 3.

Teaching Methodologies Case study, computer-aided instruction, computer analysis, computer simulations, experiential learning, faculty seminars, group discussion, lecture, research, seminars by members of the business community, simulations, student presentations, study groups, team projects.

Technology Computer terminals/PCs are available for student use and are linked by a campus-wide network. The network has full access to the Internet. Students are not required to have their own PC.

Special Opportunities Advanced credit may be earned through credit by examination, transfer of credits from another institution. An internship program is available.

FINANCES

Costs for 1997–98 Tuition: Part-time: $437 per credit hour. Cost varies by number of credits taken.

FACILITIES

Information Resources D. Leonard Corgan Library; total holdings of 157,000 volumes, 495,500 microforms, 793 current periodical subscriptions. CD player(s) available for graduate student use. Access provided to online bibliographic retrieval services and online databases.

INTERNATIONAL STUDENTS

Demographics 2% of students enrolled are international students [Asia, 100%].

Services and Facilities Visa services, ESL courses.

Applying TOEFL: minimum score of 550, proof of adequate funds required. Proof of health/immunizations recommended. Financial aid is not available to international students.

PLACEMENT

Services include career counseling/planning, career fairs, career library, career placement, and resume preparation.

Employment Types of employment entered: accounting, banking, finance, health services.

Business Program(s) URL: http://www.kings.edu

Program Contact: Dr. Elizabeth S. Lott, Director of Graduate Programs, Graduate Division, 133 North River Street, Wilkes-Barre, PA 18711-0801. Phone: 717-208-5991; Fax: 717-825-9049; E-mail: eslott@rs02.kings.edu

Kutztown University of Pennsylvania

College of Business

Kutztown, Pennsylvania

OVERVIEW

Kutztown University of Pennsylvania is a state-supported, coed, comprehensive institution. Enrollment: 6,836 graduate, professional, and undergraduate students. Founded: 1866. The graduate business unit is in a small-town setting and is on a semester calendar.

HIGHLIGHTS

Enrollment Profile
Full-time: N/R
Part-time: N/R
Total: 200
Average Age: 33
Fall 1997 Average GPA: N/R
International: N/R
Women: N/R
Minorities: N/R
Average Class Size: 15
Fall 1997 Average GMAT: N/R

Costs
Full-time tuition: $3968 per academic year (resident); $6654 per academic year (nonresident)
Part-time tuition: $187 per credit (resident); $336 per credit (nonresident)

GRADUATE BUSINESS PROGRAMS

Master of Business Administration (MBA) Full-time, part-time, distance learning option; 36 total credits required; 12 months to 6 years to complete program. Concentrations in marketing, international business, human resources, finance, health care.

ADMISSION

Application Requirements GMAT score, application form, application fee, bachelor's degree, minimum GPA: 3.0, interview, 3 letters of recommendation, personal statement, resume, college transcript(s), minimum of 5 years of work experience, computer experience.

Application Deadline Applications processed on a rolling/continuous basis for both domestic and international students. Application fee: $25. Deferred entrance is available.

ACADEMICS

Faculty Full-time 7.

Teaching Methodologies Case study, computer-aided instruction, computer analysis, computer simulations, experiential learning, faculty seminars, field projects, group discussion, lecture, research, role playing, seminars by members of the business community, simulations, student presentations, study groups, team projects.

Special Opportunities International exchange programs in Belize, France, Germany, Hungary, Mexico, Russia, Spain, United Kingdom. An internship program is available.

FINANCES

Costs for 1997–98 Tuition: Full-time: $3968 per year (resident); $6654 per year (nonresident). Part-time: $187 per credit (resident); $336 per credit (nonresident). Cost varies by campus location, number of credits taken. Fees: $30 per credit (resident); $44 per credit (nonresident).

Financial Aid Research assistantships, grants, work study, loans available. Financial aid is available to part-time students.

Financial Aid Contact Office of Financial Aid, 218 Stratton Administration Center, Kutztown, PA 19530-0730. Phone: 610-683-4077.

FACILITIES

Information Resources Rohrbach Library; total holdings of 418,839 volumes, 1,118,509 microforms, 1,986 current periodical subscriptions. CD player(s) available for graduate student use. Access provided to online bibliographic retrieval services.

INTERNATIONAL STUDENTS

Demographics N/R

Services and Facilities International student office, counseling/support services.

Applying TOEFL: minimum score of 550, TSE, proof of adequate funds required.

International Student Contact Dr. Joseph Amprey, Kutztown, PA 19530. Phone: 610-683-4215.

PLACEMENT

Services include career counseling/planning, job interviews arranged, resume referral to employers, and resume preparation.

Employment Types of employment entered: accounting, banking, chemical industry, communications, computer-related, consulting, consumer products, finance, financial services, government, health services, high technology, hospitality management, human resources, information systems/technology, insurance, international trade, management, manufacturing, marketing, media, nonprofit, petrochemical, pharmaceutical, real estate, retail, telecommunications, transportation, utilities.

Business Program(s) URL: http://www.kutztown.edu

Program Contact: Mr. Theodore A. Hartz, Dean, College of Business, 225 Beekey Building, Kutztown, PA 19530. Phone: 610-683-4576; Fax: 610-683-4573; E-mail: hartz@kutztown.edu

La Roche College

Graduate Studies Office

Pittsburgh, Pennsylvania

OVERVIEW

La Roche College is an independent-religious, coed, comprehensive institution. Enrollment: 1,568 graduate, professional, and undergraduate students; 73 full-time matriculated graduate/professional students; 212 part-time matriculated graduate/professional students. Founded: 1963. The graduate business unit is in a suburban setting and is on a semester calendar.

HIGHLIGHTS

Enrollment Profile
Full-time: N/R
Part-time: N/R
Total: 125
Average Age: 33
Fall 1997 Average GPA: N/R

International: N/R
Women: N/R
Minorities: N/R
Average Class Size: 20
Fall 1997 Average GMAT: N/R

Costs
Full-time tuition: N/R
Part-time tuition: $385 per credit

GRADUATE BUSINESS PROGRAMS

Master of Science in Human Resources Management (MS) Full-time, part-time; 42 total credits required; 12 months to 6 years to complete program.

ADMISSION

Application Requirements Application form, application fee, bachelor's degree, essay, minimum GPA, 2 letters of recommendation, personal statement, resume, college transcript(s).

Recommended for Application GMAT score accepted, GRE score accepted, MAT score accepted, work experience.

Application Deadline Applications processed on a rolling/continuous basis for both domestic and international students. Application fee: $25. Deferred entrance is available.

ACADEMICS

Faculty Full-time 4; part-time 16.

Teaching Methodologies Case study, experiential learning, faculty seminars, field projects, group discussion, lecture, research, role playing, seminars by members of the business community, simulations, student presentations, study groups, team projects.

Technology 20 on-campus computer terminals/PCs are available for student use and are linked by a campus-wide network. The network has full access to the Internet. Students are not required to have their own PC.

Special Opportunities Advanced credit may be earned through transfer of credits from another institution.

FINANCES

Costs for 1997–98 Tuition: $385 per credit. Cost varies by academic program, number of credits taken.

Financial Aid Loans available. Financial aid is available to part-time students. Application Deadline: 5/1.

Financial Aid Contact Mr. Michael Bertonaschi, 9000 Babcock Boulevard, Pittsburgh, PA 15237-5898. Phone: 412-367-9300; Fax: 412-367-9368; E-mail: bertonm1@laroche.edu

FACILITIES

Information Resources John Wright Library; total holdings of 70,000 volumes, 8,525 microforms, 640 current periodical subscriptions. CD player(s) available for graduate student use. Access provided to online bibliographic retrieval services.

INTERNATIONAL STUDENTS

Demographics N/R

Services and Facilities International student office, international student center, ESL courses, counseling/support services.

Applying TOEFL: minimum score of 550, proof of adequate funds, proof of health/immunizations required. Financial aid is not available to international students.

International Student Contact Dr. Igor Jourin, Assistant to the Dean for Multicultural Education, 9000 Babcock Boulevard, Pittsburgh, PA 15237. Phone: 412-367-9300; Fax: 412-367-9368.

PLACEMENT

Services include alumni network, career counseling/planning, career library, career placement, job interviews arranged, resume referral to employers, and resume preparation.

Employment Types of employment entered: banking, financial services, hospitality management, human resources, management, nonprofit, retail, telecommunications.

Business Program(s) URL: http://www.laroche.edu

Program Contact: Mr. Roland Gane, Director of Admissions for Graduate Studies, 9000 Babcock Boulevard, Pittsburgh, PA 15237. Phone: 412-536-1262; Fax: 412-635-2722; E-mail: gradadm1@laroche.edu

La Salle University

School of Business Administration

Philadelphia, Pennsylvania

OVERVIEW

La Salle University is an independent-religious, coed, comprehensive institution. Enrollment: 5,408 graduate, professional, and undergraduate students. Founded: 1863. The graduate business unit is in a suburban setting and is on a trimester calendar.

HIGHLIGHTS

Enrollment Profile
Full-time: 68
Part-time: 616
Total: 684
Average Age: 32
Fall 1997 Average GPA: 3.1

International: 11%
Women: 44%
Minorities: 12%
Average Class Size: 21
Fall 1997 Average GMAT: 500

Costs
Full-time tuition: N/R
Part-time tuition: $497 per credit

AACSB – The International Association for Management Education accredited

Degree(s) offered in conjunction with Delaware Valley College, Albright College

GRADUATE BUSINESS PROGRAMS

Master of Business Administration (MBA) Full-time, part-time; 33-48 total credits required; 12 months to 5.3 years to complete program. Concentrations in accounting, finance, human resources, management information systems, international business, management, marketing, health care.

ADMISSION

Applications For fall 1997 there were 379 applications for admission. Of those applying, 264 were accepted. Of those accepted, 222 enrolled.

Application Requirements GMAT score, application form, application fee, bachelor's degree, resume, college transcript(s).

Recommended for Application Minimum GPA: 3.0, work experience, computer experience.

Application Deadline 8/14 for fall, 12/15 for spring, 4/15 for summer, 7/15 for fall (international), 11/15 for spring (international), 3/15 for summer (international). Application fee: $30. Deferred entrance is available.

ACADEMICS

Faculty Full-time 38; part-time 10.

Teaching Methodologies Case study, faculty seminars, group discussion, lecture, role playing, seminars by members of the business community, student presentations, study groups, team projects.

Technology 350 on-campus computer terminals/PCs are available for student use and are linked by a campus-wide network. The network has full access to the Internet. Students are not required to have their own PC.

Special Opportunities Advanced credit may be earned through credit by examination, credit for experience, credit for military training programs, credit for business training programs, transfer of credits from another institution.

FINANCES

Costs for 1997–98 Tuition: $497 per credit. Fees: $30 per course. Fees vary by number of credits taken. Average 1997–98 room only costs were $3845 per academic year. Room and board costs vary by campus location, occupancy (e.g., single, double, triple), type of accommodation.

Financial Aid In 1997–98, 2% of students received some institutionally administered aid in the form of research assistantships, scholarships. Application Deadline: 8/15.

Financial Aid Contact Ms. Wendy McLaughlin, Director, Financial Aid, 1900 West Olney Avenue, Philadelphia, PA 19141. Phone: 215-951-1070; E-mail: admiss@lasalle.edu

FACILITIES

Information Resources Connelly Library; total holdings of 340,000 volumes, 50,000 microforms, 1,650 current periodical subscriptions. CD player(s) available for graduate student use. Access provided to online bibliographic retrieval services and online databases.

INTERNATIONAL STUDENTS

Demographics 11% of students enrolled are international students.

Services and Facilities International student office, international student center, visa services, counseling/support services.

Applying TOEFL: minimum score of 550, proof of adequate funds, proof of health/immunizations required. Financial aid is not available to international students.

International Student Contact Ms. Elaine Mshomba, Director, International Student Services, 1900 West Olney Avenue, Philadelphia, PA 19141-1199. Phone: 215-951-1948; E-mail: mshombae@lasalle.edu

PLACEMENT

Services include alumni network, career counseling/planning, career fairs, career library, career placement, electronic job bank, job interviews arranged, job search course, resume referral to employers, and resume preparation.

Employment Of 1996–97 graduates, 99% were employed within three months of graduation.

Business Program(s) URL: http://www.lasalle.edu/academ/sba/sba.htm

Program Contact: Mr. Brian Niles, Director, Marketing and Graduate Enrollment, 1900 West Olney Avenue, Philadelphia, PA 19141. Phone: 215-951-1057; Fax: 215-951-1886; E-mail: niles@lasalle.edu

Lebanon Valley College

Business Programs

Annville, Pennsylvania

OVERVIEW

Lebanon Valley College is an independent-religious, coed, comprehensive institution. Enrollment: full-time matriculated graduate/professional students; 209 part-time matriculated graduate/professional students. Founded: 1866. The graduate business unit is in a small-town setting and is on a semester calendar.

HIGHLIGHTS

Enrollment Profile
Full-time: 0
Part-time: 209
Total: 209
Average Age: 34
Fall 1997 Average GPA: N/R

International: N/R
Women: 38%
Minorities: 8%
Average Class Size: 21
Fall 1997 Average GMAT: 490

Costs
Full-time tuition: N/R
Part-time tuition: $277 per credit

GRADUATE BUSINESS PROGRAMS

Master of Business Administration (MBA) Part-time; 36 total credits required; 2 years work experience required; up to 7 years to complete program.

ADMISSION

Applications For fall 1997 there were 35 applications for admission. Of those applying, 33 were accepted. Of those accepted, 31 enrolled.

Application Requirements GMAT score, application form, application fee, bachelor's degree, interview, resume, college transcript(s), minimum of 2 years of work experience, computer experience: word processing, spreadsheet.

Application Deadline Applications processed on a rolling/continuous basis for both domestic and international students. Application fee: $25.

ACADEMICS

Faculty Full-time 8; part-time 24.

Teaching Methodologies Case study, computer simulations, faculty seminars, group discussion, lecture, role playing, student presentations, team projects.

Technology 77 on-campus computer terminals/PCs are available for student use and are linked by a campus-wide network. The network has full access to the Internet. Students are not required to have their own PC.

Special Opportunities Advanced credit may be earned through transfer of credits from another institution.

FINANCES

Costs for 1997–98 Tuition: Part-time: $277 per credit. Fees: Part-time: $25 per semester.

Financial Aid In 1997–98, 2% of students received some institutionally administered aid.

Financial Aid Contact Mrs. Heather Richardson, Assistant Director of Financial Aid, PO Box R, Annville, PA 17003-0501. Phone: 717-867-6181.

FACILITIES

Information Resources Vernon and Doris Bishop Library; total holdings of 149,894 volumes, 18,005 microforms, 740 current periodical subscriptions.

INTERNATIONAL STUDENTS

Demographics N/R

Services and Facilities International student office, international student center, visa services, ESL courses, counseling/support services.

Applying TOEFL: minimum score of 550 required.

International Student Contact Dr. Arthur Ford, Dean of International Students, PO Box R, Annville, PA 17003-0501. Phone: 717-867-6248.

PLACEMENT

Services include alumni network, career counseling/planning, career library, resume referral to employers, and resume preparation.

Business Program(s) URL: http://www.lvc.edu

Program Contact: Mr. James W. Mentzer, Jr., MBA Director, 101 North College Avenue, Annville, PA 17003-0501. Phone: 717-867-6337 E-mail: mentzer@lvc.edu

Lehigh University

College of Business and Economics

Bethlehem, Pennsylvania

OVERVIEW

Lehigh University is an independent-nonprofit, coed university. Enrollment: 6,316 graduate, professional, and undergraduate students; 803 full-time matriculated graduate/professional students; 1,030 part-time matriculated graduate/professional students. Founded: 1865. The graduate business unit is in a small-town setting and is on a semester calendar.

HIGHLIGHTS

Enrollment Profile
Full-time: 69
Part-time: 345
Total: 414
Average Age: N/R
Fall 1997 Average GPA: 3.2

International: 6%
Women: 33%
Minorities: 3%
Average Class Size: 21
Fall 1997 Average GMAT: 586

Costs
Full-time tuition: $16,200 per academic year
Part-time tuition: $590 per credit hour

AACSB – The International Association for Management Education accredited

GRADUATE BUSINESS PROGRAMS

Master of Business Administration (MBA) Full-time, part-time, distance learning option; 30-48 total credits required; 12 to 18 months to complete program. Concentrations in finance, marketing, international business, technology management, management.

Master of Science in Management of Technology (MS) Part-time; 45 total credits required; 4 years work experience required; 18 months to complete program.

Master of Science in Economics (MS) Part-time; 30 total credits required; 12 months to complete program.

ADMISSION

Applications For fall 1997 there were 353 applications for admission. Of those applying, 209 were accepted. Of those accepted, 166 enrolled.

Application Requirements Application form, application fee, bachelor's degree, essay, minimum GPA, 2 letters of recommendation, personal statement, college transcript(s).

Recommended for Application GMAT score accepted, minimum of 2 years of work experience.

Application Deadline 7/15 for fall, 12/1 for spring, 4/30 for summer, 7/15 for fall (international), 12/1 for spring (international), 4/30 for summer (international). Application fee: $40. Deferred entrance is available.

ACADEMICS

Faculty Full-time 56; part-time 12.

Teaching Methodologies Case study, computer-aided instruction, computer analysis, computer simulations, experiential learning, field projects, group discussion, lecture, research, role playing, seminars by members of the business community, simulations, student presentations, study groups, team projects.

Lehigh University (continued)

Technology 310 on-campus computer terminals/PCs are available for student use and are linked by a campus-wide network. The network has full access to the Internet. Students are not required to have their own PC.

Special Opportunities Advanced credit may be earned through transfer of credits from another institution. An internship program is available.

FINANCES

Costs for 1997-98 Tuition: Full-time: $16,200 per year. Part-time: $590 per credit hour. Cost varies by number of credits taken. Fees: Full-time: $24 per academic year. Part-time: $6 per semester. Fees vary by number of credits taken. Average 1997-98 room only costs were $4380 per academic year (on campus) and $4200 per academic year (off campus).

Financial Aid In 1997-98, 22% of students received some institutionally administered aid in the form of fellowships, research assistantships, teaching assistantships, scholarships, loans. Financial aid is available to part-time students. Application Deadline: 2/1.

Financial Aid Contact Ms. Kathleen Trexler, Associate Dean and Director of the MBA Program, 621 Taylor Street, Bethlehem, PA 18015. Phone: 610-758-3418; Fax: 610-758-5283; E-mail: kat3@lehigh.edu

FACILITIES

Information Resources Fairchild-Martindale Library and Computing Center plus 2 additional on-campus libraries; total holdings of 1,124,000 volumes, 1,900,000 microforms, 10,000 current periodical subscriptions. CD player(s) available for graduate student use. Access provided to online bibliographic retrieval services and online databases.

INTERNATIONAL STUDENTS

Demographics 6% of students enrolled are international students.

Services and Facilities International student office, international student housing, visa services, ESL courses, counseling/support services.

Applying TOEFL: minimum score of 570, proof of adequate funds, proof of health/immunizations required. TSE recommended. Financial aid is available to international students.

International Student Contact International Students and Scholars Office, 5 East Packer Avenue, Whitaker Labs, Bethlehem, PA 18015. Phone: 610-758-4859.

PLACEMENT

Services include alumni network, career counseling/planning, career fairs, career library, job interviews arranged, job search course, resume referral to employers, and resume preparation. In 1996-97, 300 organizations participated in on-campus recruiting; 4,000 on-campus interviews were conducted.

Employment Of 1996-97 graduates, the average starting salary was $45,600. Types of employment entered: accounting, banking, chemical industry, computer-related, consulting, consumer products, education, engineering, finance, financial services, health services, high technology, management, manufacturing, marketing, nonprofit, pharmaceutical, service industry.

Business Program(s) URL: http://www.lehigh.edu/~incbe/incbe.html

Program Contact: Ms. Kathleen A. Trexler, Associate Dean and Director of the MBA Program, College of Business and Economics, 621 Taylor Street, Bethlehem, PA 18015. Phone: 610-758-3418; Fax: 610-758-5283; E-mail: kat3@lehigh.edu

See full description on page 872.

Marywood University

Department of Business and Managerial Science

Scranton, Pennsylvania

OVERVIEW

Marywood University is an independent-religious, coed, comprehensive institution. Enrollment: 3,068 graduate, professional, and undergraduate students; 357 full-time matriculated graduate/professional students; 546 part-time matriculated graduate/professional students. Founded: 1915. The graduate business unit is in a suburban setting and is on a semester calendar.

HIGHLIGHTS

Enrollment Profile
Full-time: 7

Part-time: 85

Total: 92

Average Age: 31

Fall 1997 Average GPA: 2.9

International: 5%

Women: 40%

Minorities: 3%

Average Class Size: 20

Fall 1997 Average GMAT: 480

Costs
Full-time tuition: $7632 per academic year

Part-time tuition: $424 per credit

GRADUATE BUSINESS PROGRAMS

Master of Science in Management Information Systems (MS) Full-time, part-time; 36 total credits required; 2 to 7 years to complete program. Concentration in management information systems.

Master of Business Administration in General Management (MBA) Full-time, part-time; 36 total credits required; 2 to 7 years to complete program. Concentration in management.

Master of Business Administration in Management Information Systems (MBA) Full-time, part-time; 36 total credits required; 2 to 7 years to complete program. Concentration in management information systems.

Master of Business Administration in Finance/Investment (MBA) Full-time, part-time; 36 total credits required; 2 to 7 years to complete program. Concentration in finance.

ADMISSION

Applications For fall 1997 there were 31 applications for admission. Of those applying, 26 were accepted. Of those accepted, 24 enrolled.

Application Requirements Application form, application fee, bachelor's degree, minimum GPA: 3.0, 2 letters of recommendation, college transcript(s), computer experience: Microsoft Office, Microsoft Access, database.

Recommended for Application GMAT score accepted.

Application Deadline Applications processed on a rolling/continuous basis for both domestic and international students. Application fee: $20. Deferred entrance is available.

ACADEMICS

Faculty Full-time 10; part-time 10.

Teaching Methodologies Case study, computer analysis, computer simulations, faculty seminars, group discussion, lecture, research, student presentations, team projects.

Technology 250 on-campus computer terminals/PCs are available for student use and are linked by a campus-wide network. The network has full access to the Internet. Students are not required to have their own PC.

Special Opportunities Advanced credit may be earned through transfer of credits from another institution. An internship program is available.

FINANCES

Costs for 1997-98 Tuition: Full-time: $7632 per year. Part-time: $424 per credit. Cost varies by number of credits taken. Fees: Full-time: $250 per academic year. Part-time: $85 per semester. Average 1997-98 room and board costs were $5700 per academic year. Room and board costs vary by occupancy (e.g., single, double, triple), type of accommodation, type of meal plan.

Financial Aid Research assistantships, scholarships available. Financial aid is available to part-time students. Application Deadline: 3/10.

Financial Aid Contact Stanley F. Skrutski, Director, Financial Aid, 2300 Adams Avenue, Scranton, PA 18509. Phone: 717-348-6211 Ext. 6225; Fax: 717-348-1817.

FACILITIES

Information Resources Learning Resources Center; total holdings of 202,015 volumes, 221,089 microforms, 1,192 current periodical subscriptions. CD player(s) available for graduate student use. Access provided to online bibliographic retrieval services.

INTERNATIONAL STUDENTS

Demographics 5% of students enrolled are international students.

Services and Facilities International student office, international student housing, visa services, ESL courses, counseling/support services.

Applying TOEFL: minimum score of 550, proof of adequate funds, proof of health/immunizations required. Financial aid is not available to international students.

International Student Contact Ms. Ann Boland-Chase, Registrar, 2300 Adams Avenue, Scranton, PA 18504. Phone: 717-348-6211; Fax: 717-961-4762.

PLACEMENT

Services include alumni network, career counseling/planning, career library, career placement, resume referral to employers, and resume preparation.

Employment Of 1996-97 graduates, 97% were employed within three months of graduation; the average starting salary was $40,000.

PENNSYLVANIA

Business Program(s) URL: http://www.marywood.edu/gas/business.htm

Program Contact: Dr. Samir P. Dagher, Executive Director and Chairman, 2300 Adams Avenue, Scranton, PA 18509-1598. Phone: 717-348-6274, 800-338-4207; Fax: 717-961-4762.

Moravian College

Department of Economics and Business

Bethlehem, Pennsylvania

OVERVIEW
Moravian College is an independent-religious, coed, comprehensive institution. Enrollment: 1,856 graduate, professional, and undergraduate students; 4 full-time matriculated graduate/professional students; 114 part-time matriculated graduate/professional students. Founded: 1742. The graduate business unit is in a suburban setting and is on a semester calendar.

HIGHLIGHTS

Enrollment Profile

Full-time: 4

Part-time: 114

Total: 118

Average Age: 34

Fall 1997 Average GPA: 3.0

International: 1%

Women: 35%

Minorities: 4%

Average Class Size: 25

Fall 1997 Average GMAT: 500

Costs
Full-time tuition: N/R
Part-time tuition: $1254 per course

GRADUATE BUSINESS PROGRAMS
Master of Business Administration (MBA) Part-time; 30-62 total credits required; 12 months to 7 years to complete program. Concentration in management.

ADMISSION
Applications For fall 1997 there were 40 applications for admission. Of those applying, 34 were accepted. Of those accepted, 32 enrolled.

Application Requirements GMAT score, application form, application fee, bachelor's degree, 2 letters of recommendation, resume, college transcript(s), computer experience.

Recommended for Application Work experience.

Application Deadline Applications processed on a rolling/continuous basis for both domestic and international students. Application fee: $30. Deferred entrance is available.

ACADEMICS
Faculty Full-time 10; part-time 5.

Teaching Methodologies Case study, experiential learning, field projects, group discussion, lecture, research, role playing, student presentations, team projects.

Technology 50 on-campus computer terminals/PCs are available for student use and are linked by a campus-wide network. The network has full access to the Internet. Students are not required to have their own PC.

Special Opportunities Advanced credit may be earned through credit by examination, transfer of credits from another institution.

FINANCES
Costs for 1997-98 Tuition: Part-time: $1254 per course.

FACILITIES
Information Resources Reeves Library; total holdings of 241,205 volumes, 8,541 microforms, 1,395 current periodical subscriptions. CD player(s) available for graduate student use. Access provided to online bibliographic retrieval services.

INTERNATIONAL STUDENTS
Demographics 1% of students enrolled are international students.

Applying TOEFL: minimum score of 550, proof of adequate funds required. Financial aid is not available to international students.

PLACEMENT
Services include alumni network.

Employment Types of employment entered: engineering, health services, insurance, telecommunications.

Program Contact: Dr. Santo Marabella, Director, The Moravian MBA, 1200 Main Street, Bethlehem, PA 18018. Phone: 610-807-4444; Fax: 610-861-1466; E-mail: mba@moravian.edu

Pennsylvania State University at Erie, The Behrend College

Program in Business Administration

Erie, Pennsylvania

OVERVIEW
Pennsylvania State University at Erie, The Behrend College is a state-related, coed, comprehensive institution. Enrollment: 3,300 graduate, professional, and undergraduate students; 8 full-time matriculated graduate/professional students; 151 part-time matriculated graduate/professional students. Founded: 1948. The graduate business unit is in a suburban setting and is on a semester calendar.

HIGHLIGHTS

Enrollment Profile

Full-time: 8

Part-time: 151

Total: 159

Average Age: 33

Fall 1997 Average GPA: 3.2

International: 1%

Women: 37%

Minorities: 1%

Average Class Size: 30

Fall 1997 Average GMAT: 520

Costs
Full-time tuition: $7320 per academic year (resident); $14,160 per academic year (nonresident)
Part-time tuition: $305 per credit (resident); $590 per credit (nonresident)

GRADUATE BUSINESS PROGRAMS
Master of Business Administration (MBA) Full-time, part-time; 48 total credits required; 18 months to 8 years to complete program.

ADMISSION
Applications For fall 1997 there were 44 applications for admission. Of those applying, 39 were accepted. Of those accepted, 31 enrolled.

Application Requirements GMAT score, application form, application fee, bachelor's degree, essay, minimum GPA, 3 letters of recommendation, personal statement, college transcript(s).

Application Deadline 8/1 for fall, 12/15 for spring, 4/15 for summer, 2/1 for fall (international), 10/1 for spring (international), 2/1 for summer (international). Application fee: $40. Deferred entrance is available.

ACADEMICS
Faculty Full-time 22.

Teaching Methodologies Case study, computer analysis, group discussion, lecture, research, seminars by members of the business community, student presentations, study groups, team projects.

Technology 160 on-campus computer terminals/PCs are available for student use and are linked by a campus-wide network. The network has full access to the Internet. Students are not required to have their own PC.

Special Opportunities Advanced credit may be earned through transfer of credits from another institution. An internship program is available.

FINANCES
Costs for 1997-98 Tuition: Full-time: $7320 per year (resident); $14,160 per year (nonresident). Part-time: $305 per credit (resident); $590 per credit (nonresident). Cost varies by academic program, campus location, number of credits taken. Fees: Full-time: $200 per academic year (resident); $200 per academic year (nonresident). Part-time: $72 per 6 credits (resident); $72 per 6 credits (nonresident). Fees vary by number of credits taken. Average 1997-98 room and board costs were $4950 per academic year (off campus).

Financial Aid In 1997-98, 9% of students received some institutionally administered aid in the form of scholarships, work study, loans. Financial aid is available to part-time students. Application Deadline: 2/15.

Financial Aid Contact Ms. Jane Brady, Assistant Director of Admissions and Financial Aid, Station Road, Erie, PA 16563. Phone: 814-898-6162; Fax: 814-898-6044; E-mail: jub9@psu.edu

FACILITIES
Information Resources Total library holdings of 86,000 volumes, 35,460 microforms, 964 current periodical subscriptions. CD player(s) available for graduate student use. Access provided to online bibliographic retrieval services and online databases.

INTERNATIONAL STUDENTS
Demographics 1% of students enrolled are international students.

Services and Facilities International student office, counseling/support services.

Applying TOEFL: minimum score of 550, proof of adequate funds, proof of health/immunizations required. Financial aid is not available to international students.

Pennsylvania State University at Erie, The Behrend College (continued)

International Student Contact Mr. Ken Miller, Associate Dean of Student Affairs, Station Road, Erie, PA 16563. Phone: 814-898-6111; E-mail: kqm3@psu.edu

PLACEMENT

Services include alumni network, career counseling/planning, career library, career placement, electronic job bank, resume referral to employers, and resume preparation.

Program Contact: Ms. Jane Brady, Assistant Director of Admissions and Financial Aid, Station Road, Erie, PA 16563. Phone: 814-898-6100; Fax: 814-898-6044; E-mail: jub9@psu.edu

Pennsylvania State University Great Valley Graduate Center

School of Graduate Professional Studies

Malvern, Pennsylvania

OVERVIEW

Pennsylvania State University Great Valley Graduate Center is a state-related, coed, graduate institution. Enrollment: 1,590 graduate, professional, and undergraduate students; 71 full-time matriculated graduate/professional students; 1,519 part-time matriculated graduate/professional students. Founded: 1963. The graduate business unit is in an urban setting and is on a 5 seven-week sessions calendar.

HIGHLIGHTS

Enrollment Profile
Full-time: 10
Part-time: 491
Total: 501
Average Age: 34
Fall 1997 Average GPA: 3.11

International: N/R
Women: 48%
Minorities: 10%
Average Class Size: 21
Fall 1997 Average GMAT: 540

Costs
Full-time tuition: N/R
Part-time tuition: $330 per credit (resident); $590 per credit (nonresident)

GRADUATE BUSINESS PROGRAMS

MBA in Management (MBA) Full-time, part-time; 42 total credits required; minimum of 3 years work experience required; 12 months to 6 years to complete program. Concentrations in finance, health care, human resources, management, management information systems, marketing.

MBA in Health Care Policy, Administration, and Management (MBA) Full-time, part-time; 42 total credits required; 12 months to 6 years to complete program.

Concurrent Master's Programs in Business and Information Science (MBA/MSIS) Full-time, part-time; 65 total credits required; 2 to 6 years to complete program. Concentrations in finance, health care, human resources, management, management information systems, marketing.

ADMISSION

Applications For fall 1997 there were 200 applications for admission. Of those applying, 160 were accepted. Of those accepted, 125 enrolled.

Application Requirements GMAT score: minimum 450, application form, application fee, bachelor's degree, minimum GPA: 3.0, 2 letters of recommendation, personal statement, resume, college transcript(s), minimum of 3 years of work experience, computer experience: word processing, spreadsheet, internet.

Application Deadline 7/31 for fall, 11/30 for spring, 4/30 for fall (international), 7/30 for spring (international). Application fee: $40. Deferred entrance is available.

ACADEMICS

Faculty Full-time 16; part-time 23.

Teaching Methodologies Case study, computer-aided instruction, computer analysis, computer simulations, experiential learning, faculty seminars, field projects, group discussion, lecture, research, role playing, seminars by members of the business community, simulations, student presentations, study groups, team projects.

Technology 100 on-campus computer terminals/PCs are available for student use and are linked by a campus-wide network. The network has full access to the Internet. Students are not required to have their own PC.

Special Opportunities Advanced credit may be earned through transfer of credits from another institution. International exchange program in various countries in Europe.

FINANCES

Costs for 1997–98 Tuition: $330 per credit (resident); $590 per credit (nonresident). Cost varies by campus location, number of credits taken. Fees: $50 per semester (resident); $50 per semester (nonresident). Fees vary by campus location, number of credits taken.

Financial Aid Fellowships, research assistantships, grants, scholarships, work study, loans available. Financial aid is available to part-time students.

Financial Aid Contact Ms. Ruth Smiley, Financial Aid Counselor, Penn State Great Valley, 30 East Swedesford Road, Malvern, PA 19355. Phone: 610-648-3248; Fax: 610-889-1334; E-mail: gvmgmt@psu.edu

FACILITIES

Information Resources Pattee Library at University Park plus 1 additional on-campus library; total holdings of 23,000 volumes, 8,263 microforms, 360 current periodical subscriptions. CD player(s) available for graduate student use. Access provided to online bibliographic retrieval services and online databases.

INTERNATIONAL STUDENTS

Demographics N/R

Services and Facilities International student office, admissions counseling.

Applying TOEFL: minimum score of 550, proof of adequate funds required. TSE, TWE recommended. Financial aid is not available to international students.

PLACEMENT

Services include alumni network, career counseling/planning, career fairs, career library, electronic job bank, job search course, resume referral to employers, and resume preparation. In 1996–97, 50 organizations participated in on-campus recruiting; 400 on-campus interviews were conducted.

Employment Of 1996–97 graduates, 99% were employed within three months of graduation. Types of employment entered: accounting, banking, chemical industry, communications, computer-related, consulting, consumer products, education, energy, engineering, finance, financial services, government, health services, high technology, human resources, information systems/technology, management, manufacturing, marketing, nonprofit, pharmaceutical, service industry, telecommunications, transportation, utilities.

Business Program(s) URL: http://www.gv.psu.edu

Program Contact: Ms. Kathy Mingioni, Assistant Director of Admissions, 30 East Swedesford Road, Malvern, PA 19355. Phone: 610-648-3248; Fax: 610-648-3366; E-mail: gvmba@psu.edu
See full description on page 920.

Pennsylvania State University Harrisburg Campus of the Capital College

School of Business Administration

Middletown, Pennsylvania

OVERVIEW

Pennsylvania State University Harrisburg Campus of the Capital College is a state-related, coed, comprehensive institution. Enrollment: 3,466 graduate, professional, and undergraduate students; 140 full-time matriculated graduate/professional students; 1,310 part-time matriculated graduate/professional students. Founded: 1966. The graduate business unit is in a suburban setting and is on a semester calendar.

HIGHLIGHTS

Enrollment Profile
Full-time: 21
Part-time: 279
Total: 300
Average Age: 33
Fall 1997 Average GPA: 3.18

International: N/R
Women: 37%
Minorities: N/R
Average Class Size: 25
Fall 1997 Average GMAT: 570

Costs
Full-time tuition: N/R
Part-time tuition: $305 per credit (resident); $590 per credit (nonresident)

AACSB – The International Association for Management Education accredited

GRADUATE BUSINESS PROGRAMS
Master of Business Administration (MBA) Full-time, part-time; 30 total credits required; 18 months to 6 years to complete program.

Master of Science in Information Systems (MS) Full-time, part-time; 30 total credits required; 18 months to 6 years to complete program. Concentration in management information systems.

ADMISSION
Applications For fall 1997 there were 53 applications for admission. Of those applying, 47 were accepted. Of those accepted, 35 enrolled.

Application Requirements GMAT score, application form, application fee, bachelor's degree, essay, personal statement, college transcript(s), computer experience: microcomputer experience.

Recommended for Application Minimum GPA.

Application Deadline 7/18 for fall, 11/18 for spring, 4/18 for summer, 4/18 for fall (international), 7/18 for spring (international), 11/18 for summer (international). Application fee: $40. Deferred entrance is available.

ACADEMICS
Faculty Full-time 26.

Teaching Methodologies Case study, computer-aided instruction, group discussion, lecture, research, student presentations, team projects.

Technology 131 on-campus computer terminals/PCs are available for student use and are linked by a campus-wide network. The network has full access to the Internet. Students are not required to have their own PC.

Special Opportunities Advanced credit may be earned through transfer of credits from another institution. An internship program is available.

FINANCES
Costs for 1997–98 Tuition: $305 per credit (resident); $590 per credit (nonresident). Cost varies by academic program. Fees vary by number of credits taken. Average 1997–98 room and board costs were $4400 per academic year. Room and board costs vary by campus location, occupancy (e.g., single, double, triple), type of accommodation, type of meal plan.

Financial Aid Research assistantships available.

Financial Aid Contact Ms. Carolyn Julian, Student Aid Advisor, 777 West Harrisburg Pike, Middletown, PA 17057-4898. Phone: 717-948-6307; Fax: 717-948-6008; E-mail: czb3@psu.edu

FACILITIES
Information Resources Richard H. Heindel Library; total holdings of 203,530 volumes, 1,148,635 microforms, 1,557 current periodical subscriptions. CD player(s) available for graduate student use. Access provided to online bibliographic retrieval services and online databases.

INTERNATIONAL STUDENTS
Demographics N/R

Services and Facilities International student office, counseling/support services.

Applying TOEFL: minimum score of 550, proof of adequate funds, proof of health/immunizations required. Financial aid is not available to international students.

International Student Contact Donna Howard, International Student Advisor, 777 West Harrisburg Pike, Middletown, PA 17057-4898. Phone: 717-948-6025; Fax: 717-948-6261; E-mail: djh1@psu.edu

PLACEMENT
Services include alumni network, career counseling/planning, career fairs, career library, career placement, job interviews arranged, resume referral to employers, and resume preparation.

Employment Of 1996–97 graduates, 100% were employed within three months of graduation; the average starting salary was $45,000.

Business Program(s) URL: http://www.hbg.psu.edu/

Program Contact: Admissions, 777 West Harrisburg Pike, Middletown, PA 17057-4898. Phone: 717-948-6250, 800-222-2056; Fax: 717-948-6325; E-mail: rrl1@psu.edu

Pennsylvania State University University Park Campus

Mary Jean and Frank P. Smeal College of Business Administration

University Park, Pennsylvania

OVERVIEW
Pennsylvania State University University Park Campus is a state-related, coed university. Enrollment: 40,471 graduate, professional, and undergraduate students; 4,249 full-time matriculated graduate/professional students; 2,025 part-time matriculated graduate/professional students. Founded: 1855. The graduate business unit is in a small-town setting and is on a semester calendar.

HIGHLIGHTS

Enrollment Profile

Full-time: 257	International: 23%
Part-time: 0	Women: 26%
Total: 257	Minorities: 20%
Average Age: 27	Average Class Size: 45
Fall 1997 Average GPA: 3.2	Fall 1997 Average GMAT: 601

Costs
Full-time tuition: $3608 per academic year (resident); $7070 per academic year (nonresident)
Part-time tuition: N/R

AACSB – The International Association for Management Education accredited

Degree(s) offered in conjunction with Dickinson School of Law

GRADUATE BUSINESS PROGRAMS
Full-time MBA (MBA) Full-time; 48 total credits required; 16 to 21 months to complete program. Concentrations in accounting, finance, international business, logistics, management, management information systems, management science, manufacturing management, marketing, real estate, entrepreneurship, health care, operations management.

Master of Quality and Manufacturing Management (MQM) Full-time; 30 total credits required; 9 months to complete program. Concentrations in manufacturing management, quality management.

Master of Business Administration/Master of Health Administration (MBA/MHA) Full-time; 63 total credits required; 21 months to complete program. Concentration in health care.

Accelerated BS in Science/Master of Business Administration (BS/MBA) Full-time; 140 total credits required; must apply to Eberly College of Science; 5 years to complete program. Concentrations in accounting, finance, international business, logistics, management, management information systems, management science, manufacturing management, marketing, real estate, entrepreneurship, health care, operations management.

ADMISSION
Applications For fall 1997 there were 1,376 applications for admission. Of those applying, 339 were accepted. Of those accepted, 128 enrolled.

Application Requirements GMAT score: minimum 540, application form, application fee, bachelor's degree, essay, minimum GPA: 2.5, interview, letters of recommendation, resume, college transcript(s), minimum of 2 years of work experience.

Recommended for Application Computer experience.

Application Deadline 4/1 for fall, 3/1 for fall (international). Application fee: $40. Deferred entrance is available.

ACADEMICS
Faculty Full-time 102; part-time 41.

Teaching Methodologies Case study, computer-aided instruction, computer analysis, computer simulations, experiential learning, faculty seminars, field projects, group discussion, lecture, research, role playing, seminars by members of the business community, simulations, student presentations, study groups, team projects.

Technology 500 on-campus computer terminals/PCs are available for student use and are linked by a campus-wide network. The network has full access to the Internet. Students are not required to have their own PC.

Special Opportunities Advanced credit may be earned through transfer of credits from another institution. International exchange programs in Australia, Austria, Belgium, Denmark, Finland, France, Germany, New Zealand, Norway, Republic of Singapore, Spain, United Kingdom. An internship program is available.

FINANCES
Costs for 1997–98 Tuition: Full-time: $3608 per semester (resident); $7070 per semester (nonresident). Fees: Full-time: $495 per academic year (resident);

Pennsylvania State University University Park Campus (continued)

$495 per academic year (nonresident). Average 1997–98 room and board costs were $4500 per academic year (on campus) and $4500 per academic year (off campus). Room and board costs vary by campus location, occupancy (e.g., single, double, triple), type of accommodation, type of meal plan.

Financial Aid Fellowships, research assistantships, teaching assistantships, grants, scholarships, work study available. Application Deadline: 2/1.

Financial Aid Contact Office of Student Aid, 314 Shields Building, University Park, PA 16802-1220. Phone: 814-865-6301.

FACILITIES
Information Resources Pattee Library plus 7 additional on-campus libraries; total holdings of 2,540,921 volumes, 2,018,850 microforms, 27,634 current periodical subscriptions. CD player(s) available for graduate student use. Access provided to online bibliographic retrieval services.

INTERNATIONAL STUDENTS
Demographics 23% of students enrolled are international students [Africa, 6%, Asia, 59%, Europe, 29%, South America, 3%, other, 3%].

Services and Facilities International student office, international student center, visa services, ESL courses, counseling/support services.

Applying TOEFL: minimum score of 580, proof of adequate funds, proof of health/immunizations required. Financial aid is available to international students.

International Student Contact Ms. Massume Assaf, Foreign Student Advisor, 222 Boucke Building, University Park, PA 16802-5900. Phone: 814-865-6348; Fax: 814-865-3336; E-mail: mxa3@psu.edu

PLACEMENT
Services include alumni network, career counseling/planning, career fairs, career library, career placement, electronic job bank, job interviews arranged, resume referral to employers, and resume preparation. In 1996–97, 138 organizations participated in on-campus recruiting; 958 on-campus interviews were conducted.

Employment Of 1996–97 graduates, 96% were employed within three months of graduation; the average starting salary was $62,200. Types of employment entered: accounting, banking, chemical industry, communications, computer-related, consulting, consumer products, energy, finance, financial services, health services, high technology, hospitality management, human resources, information systems/technology, insurance, international trade, management, manufacturing, marketing, nonprofit, petrochemical, pharmaceutical, retail, service industry, telecommunications, transportation, utilities.

Business Program(s) URL: http://www.smeal.psu.edu

Program Contact: Mr. Roger Dagen, Director of Marketing, Recruitments and Admissions, MBA Program, The Smeal College of Business Administration, 106 Business Administration Building, University Park, PA 16802-3000. Phone: 814-863-0474, 800-379-6445 (PA only); Fax: 814-863-8072; E-mail: szm6@psu.edu

See full description on page 922.

Philadelphia College of Bible

Organizational Leadership Program

Langhorne, Pennsylvania

OVERVIEW
Philadelphia College of Bible is an independent-religious, comprehensive institution. Enrollment: 1,321 graduate, professional, and undergraduate students. The graduate business unit is on a semester calendar.

HIGHLIGHTS

Enrollment Profile
Full-time: 1
Part-time: 29
Total: 30
Average Age: N/R
Fall 1997 Average GPA: N/R

International: N/R
Women: 30%
Minorities: 33%
Average Class Size: N/R
Fall 1997 Average GMAT: N/R

Costs
Full-time tuition: N/R
Part-time tuition: $275 per credit

GRADUATE BUSINESS PROGRAMS
Master of Science in Organizational Leadership (MS) Full-time, part-time; 44 total credits required; minimum of 2 years to complete program.

ADMISSION
Application Requirements Application form, bachelor's degree, essay, minimum GPA: 2.5, 3 letters of recommendation, personal statement, college transcript(s), work experience.

Recommended for Application Interview, computer experience.

Application Deadline Applications processed on a rolling/continuous basis for both domestic and international students.

ACADEMICS
Teaching Methodologies Case study, computer-aided instruction, computer simulations, experiential learning, faculty seminars, field projects, group discussion, lecture, research, role playing, seminars by members of the business community, simulations, student presentations, study groups, team projects.

FINANCES
Costs for 1997–98 Tuition: $275 per credit.

INTERNATIONAL STUDENTS
Demographics N/R

Program Contact: Jay Desko, Graduate Studies, Langhorne, PA 19047.

Philadelphia College of Textiles and Science

School of Business Administration

Philadelphia, Pennsylvania

OVERVIEW
Philadelphia College of Textiles and Science is an independent-nonprofit, coed, comprehensive institution. Enrollment: 3,423 graduate, professional, and undergraduate students; 262 full-time matriculated graduate/professional students; 405 part-time matriculated graduate/professional students. Founded: 1884. The graduate business unit is in a suburban setting and is on a semester calendar.

HIGHLIGHTS

Enrollment Profile
Full-time: 127
Part-time: 285
Total: 412
Average Age: 28
Fall 1997 Average GPA: 2.94

International: N/R
Women: 47%
Minorities: 20%
Average Class Size: 16
Fall 1997 Average GMAT: 480

Costs
Full-time tuition: N/R
Part-time tuition: $421 per credit

GRADUATE BUSINESS PROGRAMS
Master of Business Administration (MBA) Full-time, part-time; 37 total credits required; 18 months to 7 years to complete program. Concentrations in accounting, finance, international business, marketing, taxation, health care, management.

Master of Business Administration/Master of Science in Instructional Technology (MBA/MS) Full-time, part-time; 58 total credits required; 2.5 to 7 years to complete program. Concentrations in management information systems, technology management.

Master of Business Administration/Master of Science in Textile Marketing (MBA/MS) Full-time, part-time; 58 total credits required; 2.5 to 7 years to complete program.

Master of Business Administration/Master of Science in Taxation (MBA/MS) Full-time, part-time; 55 total credits required; 2.5 to 7 years to complete program. Concentrations in taxation, accounting.

Master of Science in Taxation (MS) Full-time, part-time; 36 total credits required; 18 months to 7 years to complete program. Concentration in taxation.

ADMISSION
Applications For fall 1997 there were 185 applications for admission. Of those applying, 138 were accepted.

Application Requirements Application form, application fee, bachelor's degree, minimum GPA: 2.85, 2 letters of recommendation, personal statement, college transcript(s).

Recommended for Application GMAT score accepted, interview.

Application Deadline Applications processed on a rolling/continuous basis for both domestic and international students. Application fee: $35. Deferred entrance is available.

ACADEMICS
Faculty Full-time 29; part-time 36.

Teaching Methodologies Case study, computer-aided instruction, computer analysis, computer simulations, experiential learning, faculty seminars, field projects, group discussion, lecture, research, role playing, student presentations, team projects.

Technology 240 on-campus computer terminals/PCs are available for student use and are linked by a campus-wide network. The network has full access to the Internet. Students are not required to have their own PC.

Special Opportunities Advanced credit may be earned through credit by examination, transfer of credits from another institution. An internship program is available.

FINANCES
Costs for 1997–98 Tuition: $421 per credit. Cost varies by academic program. Average 1997–98 room and board costs were $6000 per academic year (off campus). Room and board costs vary by type of accommodation, type of meal plan.

Financial Aid Research assistantships, work study available.

Financial Aid Contact Ms. Lisa Cooper, Director of Financial Aid, School House Lane and Henry Avenue, Philadelphia, PA 19144. Phone: 215-951-2940; E-mail: cooperl@philacol.edu

FACILITIES
Information Resources Paul Gutman Library plus 1 additional on-campus library; total holdings of 98,000 volumes, 21,000 microforms, 1,600 current periodical subscriptions. CD player(s) available for graduate student use. Access provided to online bibliographic retrieval services.

INTERNATIONAL STUDENTS
Demographics N/R

Services and Facilities International student office, visa services, ESL courses, counseling/support services.

Applying TOEFL: minimum score of 550, proof of adequate funds, proof of health/immunizations required. Financial aid is not available to international students.

International Student Contact Ms. Yocasta Bras, International Student Advisor, School House Lane and Henry Avenue, Philadelphia, PA 19144. Phone: 215-951-2660.

PLACEMENT
Services include career counseling/planning, career fairs, career library, career placement, job interviews arranged, job search course, resume referral to employers, and resume preparation. In 1996–97, 211 organizations participated in on-campus recruiting.

Employment Types of employment entered: accounting, banking, chemical industry, communications, computer-related, consulting, consumer products, engineering, finance, financial services, government, health services, high technology, human resources, information systems/technology, insurance, international trade, management, manufacturing, marketing, media, nonprofit, pharmaceutical, real estate, retail, service industry, telecommunications, transportation.

Program Contact: Mr. Robert J. Reed, Director of Graduate Admissions, School House Lane and Henry Avenue, Philadelphia, PA 19144. Phone: 215-951-2943; Fax: 215-951-2907; E-mail: reedr@philacol.edu
See full description on page 926.

Point Park College
Business Programs
Pittsburgh, Pennsylvania

OVERVIEW
Point Park College is an independent-nonprofit, coed, comprehensive institution. Enrollment: 2,384 graduate, professional, and undergraduate students; 35 full-time matriculated graduate/professional students; 76 part-time matriculated graduate/professional students. Founded: 1960. The graduate business unit is in an urban setting and is on a semester calendar.

HIGHLIGHTS
Enrollment Profile
Full-time: 25
Part-time: 49
Total: 74
Average Age: 32
Fall 1997 Average GPA: 3.29

International: 54%
Women: 42%
Minorities: 8%
Average Class Size: 15
Fall 1997 Average GMAT: 482

Costs
Full-time tuition: N/R
Part-time tuition: $347 per credit

GRADUATE BUSINESS PROGRAMS
International MBA (MBA) Full-time, part-time; 39-45 total credits required; 16 months to 6 years to complete program. Concentration in international business.

ADMISSION
Applications For fall 1997 there were 131 applications for admission. Of those applying, 46 were accepted. Of those accepted, 37 enrolled.

Application Requirements GMAT score, application form, application fee, bachelor's degree, minimum GPA: 2.75, 2 letters of recommendation, personal statement, college transcript(s).

Recommended for Application Resume, computer experience.

Application Deadline Applications processed on a rolling/continuous basis for both domestic and international students. Application fee: $30. Deferred entrance is available.

ACADEMICS
Faculty Full-time 2; part-time 8.

Teaching Methodologies Case study, computer-aided instruction, computer simulations, experiential learning, field projects, group discussion, lecture, research, seminars by members of the business community, simulations, student presentations, team projects.

Technology 50 on-campus computer terminals/PCs are available for student use. The network has full access to the Internet. Students are not required to have their own PC.

Special Opportunities Advanced credit may be earned through credit by examination, credit for experience, credit for business training programs, transfer of credits from another institution. An internship program is available.

FINANCES
Costs for 1997–98 Tuition: $347 per credit. Average 1997–98 room and board costs were $5174 per academic year. Room and board costs vary by occupancy (e.g., single, double, triple), type of meal plan.

Financial Aid In 1997–98, 15% of students received some institutionally administered aid in the form of research assistantships, grants, scholarships, loans. Financial aid is available to part-time students. Application Deadline: 5/1.

Financial Aid Contact Director, Financial Aid, Financial Aid, 201 Wood Street, Pittsburgh, PA 1522-1984. Phone: 412-392-3935; Fax: 412-391-1980.

FACILITIES
Information Resources The Library Center; total holdings of 250,000 volumes, 28,734 microforms, 549 current periodical subscriptions. CD player(s) available for graduate student use. Access provided to online bibliographic retrieval services.

INTERNATIONAL STUDENTS
Demographics 54% of students enrolled are international students [Africa, 10%, Asia, 55%, Europe, 11%, South America, 12%, other, 12%].

Services and Facilities International student office, international student center, international student housing, visa services, ESL courses, counseling/support services.

Applying TOEFL: minimum score of 500, proof of adequate funds required. Financial aid is available to international students.

International Student Contact Ms. Cynthia Kuo, Coordinator, International Student Development, 201 Wood Street, Pittsburgh, PA 15222-1984. Phone: 412-392-3903; Fax: 412-391-1980.

PLACEMENT
Services include career counseling/planning, career fairs, career library, resume referral to employers, and resume preparation. In 1996–97, 156 organizations participated in on-campus recruiting.

Employment Of 1996–97 graduates, 73% were employed within three months of graduation; the average starting salary was $29,300. Types of employment entered: accounting, banking, chemical industry, communications, computer-related, engineering, government, health services, high technology, information systems/technology, international trade, manufacturing, media, nonprofit, transportation.

Business Program(s) URL: http://www.ppc.edu

Program Contact: Ms. Kathy Ballas, Graduate Admissions Counselor, Graduate Admissions, 201 Wood Street, Pittsburgh, PA 15222-1984. Phone: 412-392-3810, 800-321-0129; Fax: 412-391-1980.

Robert Morris College
Graduate Programs in Business and Related Professional Areas
Moon Township, Pennsylvania

OVERVIEW
Robert Morris College is an independent-nonprofit, coed, comprehensive institution. Enrollment: 4,846 graduate, professional, and undergraduate students;

Robert Morris College (continued)

full-time matriculated graduate/professional students; 899 part-time matriculated graduate/professional students. Founded: 1921. The graduate business unit is in a suburban setting and is on a semester calendar.

HIGHLIGHTS

Enrollment Profile
Full-time: 0
Part-time: 899
Total: 889
Average Age: 33
Fall 1997 Average GPA: 3.09

International: 3%
Women: 44%
Minorities: N/R
Average Class Size: 22
Fall 1997 Average GMAT: 462

Costs
Full-time tuition: N/R
Part-time tuition: $315 per credit

GRADUATE BUSINESS PROGRAMS
Master of Business Administration (MBA) Part-time; 33 total credits required. Concentration in management.

Master of Science (MS) Part-time; 33 total credits required. Concentrations in finance, marketing, sports/entertainment management, health care, taxation, management, accounting, business education, management information systems.

ADMISSION
Applications For fall 1997 there were 268 applications for admission. Of those applying, 250 were accepted. Of those accepted, 201 enrolled.

Application Requirements Application form, application fee, bachelor's degree, essay, interview, 2 letters of recommendation, college transcript(s).

Recommended for Application GMAT score accepted: minimum 500, GRE score accepted, MAT score accepted, minimum GPA: 2.75.

Application Deadline Applications processed on a rolling/continuous basis for both domestic and international students. Application fee: $25. Deferred entrance is available.

ACADEMICS
Faculty Full-time 35; part-time 35.

Teaching Methodologies Case study, computer analysis, computer simulations, experiential learning, group discussion, lecture, simulations, student presentations, study groups, team projects.

Technology 350 on-campus computer terminals/PCs are available for student use and are linked by a campus-wide network. The network has full access to the Internet. Students are not required to have their own PC.

Special Opportunities Advanced credit may be earned through credit for experience, credit for military training programs, credit for business training programs, transfer of credits from another institution. An internship program is available.

FINANCES
Costs for 1997–98 Tuition: Part-time: $315 per credit. Cost varies by academic program. Fees: Part-time: $14 per credit. Average 1997–98 room and board costs were $4744 per academic year. Room and board costs vary by occupancy (e.g., single, double, triple), type of meal plan.

Financial Aid In 1997–98, 22% of students received some institutionally administered aid. Financial aid is available to part-time students. Application Deadline: 5/1.

Financial Aid Contact Mrs. Janet Lawson, Manager of Financial Aid, 881 Narrows Run Road, Moon Township, PA 15108-1189. Phone: 412-262-8267; Fax: 412-262-8601; E-mail: lawson@robert-morris.edu

FACILITIES
Information Resources Moon Campus Library plus 1 additional on-campus library; total holdings of 129,110 volumes, 556 microforms, 938 current periodical subscriptions. CD player(s) available for graduate student use. Access provided to online bibliographic retrieval services and online databases.

INTERNATIONAL STUDENTS
Demographics 3% of students enrolled are international students.

Services and Facilities Counseling/support services.

Applying TOEFL: minimum score of 500, proof of adequate funds required. Financial aid is not available to international students.

International Student Contact Ms. Darcy Tannehill, Associate Dean of Enrollment Management, 881 Narrows Run Road, Moon Township, PA 15108-1189. Phone: 412-227-6808; Fax: 412-281-5539; E-mail: tannehil@robert-morris.edu

Business Program(s) URL: http://www.robert-morris.edu

Program Contact: Mr. Vincent Kane, Recruiting Coordinator, Enrollment Management, 881 Narrows Run Road, Moon Township, PA 15108-1189. Phone: 412-262-8535, 800-762-0097; Fax: 412-299-2425; E-mail: kanev@robert-morris.edu

See full description on page 948.

Rosemont College

Accelerated Program in Management

Rosemont, Pennsylvania

OVERVIEW
Rosemont College is an independent-religious, comprehensive institution. Enrollment: 947 graduate, professional, and undergraduate students; 21 full-time matriculated graduate/professional students; 131 part-time matriculated graduate/professional students.

HIGHLIGHTS

Enrollment Profile
Full-time: 0
Part-time: 75
Total: 75
Average Age: N/R
Fall 1997 Average GPA: N/R

International: N/R
Women: N/R
Minorities: N/R
Average Class Size: N/R
Fall 1997 Average GMAT: N/R

Costs
Full-time tuition: N/R
Part-time tuition: $1275 per 3-credit course

GRADUATE BUSINESS PROGRAMS
Master of Science in Management (MSM) Full-time, part-time; 36 total credits required; minimum of 12 months to complete program.

ADMISSION
Application Requirements Application form, bachelor's degree, essay, interview, 2 letters of recommendation, personal statement, college transcript(s), minimum of 3 years of work experience.

Recommended for Application Minimum GPA.

Application Deadline Applications processed on a rolling/continuous basis for both domestic and international students.

ACADEMICS
Teaching Methodologies Case study, experiential learning, faculty seminars, field projects, group discussion, research, role playing, seminars by members of the business community, simulations, student presentations, study groups, team projects.

FINANCES
Costs for 1997–98 Tuition: $1275 per 3-credit course.

Financial Aid Contact Financial Aid Office, Rosemont, PA 19010-1699. Phone: 610-527-0200 Ext. 2220.

INTERNATIONAL STUDENTS
Demographics N/R

Business Program(s) URL: http://www.rosemont.edu

Program Contact: Rennie Andrews, MSM Coordinator, Rosemont, PA 19010-1699. Phone: 610-527-0200 Ext. 2380.

Saint Francis College

Business Administration Program

Loretto, Pennsylvania

OVERVIEW
Saint Francis College is an independent-religious, coed, comprehensive institution. Enrollment: 1,600 graduate, professional, and undergraduate students. Founded: 1847. The graduate business unit is in a rural setting and is on a semester calendar.

HIGHLIGHTS

Enrollment Profile
Full-time: 8
Part-time: 119
Total: 127
Average Age: 33
Fall 1997 Average GPA: 3.2

International: 0%
Women: 35%
Minorities: N/R
Average Class Size: 16
Fall 1997 Average GMAT: 520

Costs
Full-time tuition: $7272 per academic year
Part-time tuition: $404 per credit

GRADUATE BUSINESS PROGRAMS

Master of Business Administration (MBA) Full-time, part-time; 36-60 total credits required; 12 months to 5 years to complete program. Concentrations in management, finance, human resources, industrial administration/management, industrial/labor relations, marketing, health care, accounting.

ADMISSION

Application Requirements Application form, application fee, bachelor's degree, essay, 3 letters of recommendation, college transcript(s).

Recommended for Application GMAT score accepted, minimum GPA: 2.5, interview, resume.

Application Deadline Applications processed on a rolling/continuous basis for both domestic and international students. Application fee: $30. Deferred entrance is available.

ACADEMICS

Faculty Full-time 7; part-time 8.

Teaching Methodologies Case study, computer-aided instruction, computer analysis, computer simulations, experiential learning, group discussion, lecture, research, role playing, simulations, student presentations, study groups, team projects.

Technology 50 on-campus computer terminals/PCs are available for student use and are linked by a campus-wide network. The network has full access to the Internet. Students are not required to have their own PC.

Special Opportunities Advanced credit may be earned through credit by examination, transfer of credits from another institution. An internship program is available.

FINANCES

Costs for 1997–98 Tuition: Full-time: $7272 per year. Part-time: $404 per credit. Cost varies by academic program. Fees: Full-time: $128 per academic year. Part-time: $64 per semester. Fees vary by academic program. Room and board costs vary by occupancy (e.g., single, double, triple), type of accommodation, type of meal plan.

Financial Aid In 1997–98, 9% of students received some institutionally administered aid in the form of research assistantships, work study.

Financial Aid Contact Mr. Vincent Frank, Financial Aid Director, Padua Hall, Loretto, PA 15940. Phone: 814-472-3010; Fax: 814-472-3044.

FACILITIES

Information Resources Pasquerilla Library; total holdings of 172,160 volumes, 130 microforms, 725 current periodical subscriptions. CD player(s) available for graduate student use. Access provided to online bibliographic retrieval services.

INTERNATIONAL STUDENTS

Demographics N/R

Services and Facilities Counseling/support services.

Applying TOEFL: minimum score of 500, proof of adequate funds, proof of health/immunizations required. Financial aid is available to international students.

PLACEMENT

Services include alumni network, career counseling/planning, career fairs, career library, career placement, job interviews arranged, job search course, resume referral to employers, and resume preparation. In 1996–97, 60 organizations participated in on-campus recruiting; 330 on-campus interviews were conducted.

Employment Of 1996–97 graduates, 95% were employed within three months of graduation; the average starting salary was $35,000. Types of employment entered: accounting, banking, communications, computer-related, consulting, consumer products, education, engineering, finance, financial services, government, health services, high technology, hospitality management, human resources, information systems/technology, insurance, management, manufacturing, marketing, media, mining, nonprofit, real estate, retail, service industry, telecommunications, transportation, utilities.

Program Contact: Dr. Randy L. Frye, Director, MBA Program, 225A Scotus Hall, Loretto, PA 15940. Phone: 814-472-3087, 800-457-6300 (PA only), and/or 800-342-5732 (PA only); Fax: 814-472-3044; E-mail: rfrye@sfcpa.edu

Saint Joseph's University

Erivan K. Haub School of Business

Philadelphia, Pennsylvania

OVERVIEW

Saint Joseph's University is an independent-religious, coed, comprehensive institution. Enrollment: 7,243 graduate, professional, and undergraduate students; 361 full-time matriculated graduate/professional students; 2,577 part-time matriculated graduate/professional students. Founded: 1851. The graduate business unit is in an urban setting and is on a semester calendar.

HIGHLIGHTS

Enrollment Profile

Full-time: 129
Part-time: 1,314
Total: 1,443
Average Age: 29
Fall 1997 Average GPA: 3.0

International: N/R
Women: 38%
Minorities: N/R
Average Class Size: 30
Fall 1997 Average GMAT: 507

Costs
Full-time tuition: $16,610 per academic year
Part-time tuition: $510 per credit

Degree(s) offered in conjunction with Philadelphia College of Osteopathic Medicine

GRADUATE BUSINESS PROGRAMS

Master of Business Administration (MBA) Full-time, part-time, distance learning option; 54 total credits required; 18 months to 5 years to complete program. Concentrations in accounting, finance, management information systems, health care, international business, international marketing, management, marketing.

Executive MBA (EMBA) Full-time; 48 total credits required; up to 21 months to complete program.

Pharmaceutical MBA (MBA) Part-time; 33 total credits required; 8 months to 5 years to complete program.

Master of Science in Program-Food Marketing (MS) Part-time; 32 total credits required; 8 months to 5 years to complete program.

Master of Science in Environmental Protection/Safety Management (MS) Full-time, part-time; 36 total credits required; 18 months to 5 years to complete program.

Master of Science in Public Safety (MS) Full-time, part-time; 36 total credits required; 18 months to 5 years to complete program.

ADMISSION

Applications For fall 1997 there were 276 applications for admission. Of those applying, 210 were accepted. Of those accepted, 165 enrolled.

Application Requirements GMAT score: minimum 450, application form, application fee, bachelor's degree, essay, minimum GPA: 2.8, 2 letters of recommendation, resume, college transcript(s).

Recommended for Application Computer experience.

Application Deadline 7/15 for fall, 11/15 for spring, 4/15 for summer, 7/15 for fall (international), 11/15 for spring (international), 4/15 for summer (international). Application fee: $35. Deferred entrance is available.

ACADEMICS

Faculty Full-time 56; part-time 19.

Teaching Methodologies Case study, group discussion, lecture, role playing, seminars by members of the business community, simulations, student presentations, study groups, team projects.

Technology 130 on-campus computer terminals/PCs are available for student use and are linked by a campus-wide network. The network has full access to the Internet. Students are not required to have their own PC.

Special Opportunities Advanced credit may be earned through transfer of credits from another institution.

FINANCES

Costs for 1997–98 Tuition: Full-time: $16,610 per year. Part-time: $510 per credit. Average 1997–98 room only costs were $6000 per academic year (off campus).

Financial Aid Work study available. Financial aid is available to part-time students.

Financial Aid Contact Mr. Raymond Toole, Financial Aid Counselor, 5600 City Avenue, Philadelphia, PA 19131. Phone: 610-660-1340.

FACILITIES

Information Resources Francis A. Drexel Library plus 1 additional on-campus library; total holdings of 335,000 volumes, 750,000 microforms, 1,850 current periodical subscriptions. CD player(s) available for graduate student use. Access provided to online bibliographic retrieval services.

INTERNATIONAL STUDENTS

Demographics N/R

Services and Facilities International student office, visa services, ESL courses, counseling/support services.

Applying TOEFL: minimum score of 550, proof of adequate funds required. Financial aid is not available to international students.

International Student Contact Dr. Thomas Buckley, Director, Office for International Programs, 5600 City Avenue, Philadelphia, PA 19131. Phone: 610-660-1836.

PLACEMENT

Services include alumni network, career counseling/planning, career library, career placement, resume referral to employers, and resume preparation.

Employment Types of employment entered: accounting, banking, consulting, information systems/technology, marketing.

Business Program(s) URL: http://www.sju.edu

Program Contact: Ms. Adele Foley, Associate Dean/Director, MBA Programs, 5600 City Avenue, Philadelphia, PA 19131. Phone: 610-660-1690; Fax: 610-660-1599.

See full description on page 966.

Slippery Rock University of Pennsylvania

College of Information Science and Business Administration

Slippery Rock, Pennsylvania

OVERVIEW

Slippery Rock University of Pennsylvania is a state-supported, comprehensive institution. Enrollment: 7,500 graduate, professional, and undergraduate students; 280 full-time matriculated graduate/professional students; 420 part-time matriculated graduate/professional students. The graduate business unit is on a semester calendar.

HIGHLIGHTS

Enrollment Profile

Full-time: 15	International: N/R
Part-time: 25	Women: N/R
Total: 40	Minorities: N/R
Average Age: N/R	Average Class Size: N/R
Fall 1997 Average GPA: N/R	Fall 1997 Average GMAT: N/R

Costs
Full-time tuition: N/R
Part-time tuition: N/R

GRADUATE BUSINESS PROGRAMS

Master of Science in Accounting (MS) Full-time, part-time; 30 total credits required; minimum of 2 years to complete program. Concentration in accounting.

Master of Public Administration (MPA) Full-time, part-time; 42 total credits required; minimum of 2 years to complete program.

ADMISSION

Application Requirements Application form, bachelor's degree, minimum GPA: 2.75, college transcript(s).

Recommended for Application GMAT score accepted, GRE score accepted, interview, work experience, computer experience.

Application Deadline Applications processed on a rolling/continuous basis for both domestic and international students.

ACADEMICS

Teaching Methodologies Case study, computer analysis, computer simulations, faculty seminars, field projects, group discussion, lecture, research, role playing, seminars by members of the business community, simulations, student presentations, study groups, team projects.

FINANCES

Financial Aid Contact Financial Aid Office, Slippery Rock, PA 16057. Phone: 724-738-2044.

INTERNATIONAL STUDENTS

Demographics N/R

Services and Facilities International student office, international student center, ESL courses, counseling/support services.

Applying TOEFL required.

Program Contact: Office of Graduate Studies, Slippery Rock, PA 16057. Phone: 724-738-2051; Fax: 724-738-2908.

Temple University

School of Business and Management

Philadelphia, Pennsylvania

OVERVIEW

Temple University is a state-related, coed university. Enrollment: 30,701 graduate, professional, and undergraduate students; 4,304 full-time matriculated graduate/professional students; 3,851 part-time matriculated graduate/professional students. Founded: 1887. The graduate business unit is in an urban setting and is on a semester calendar.

HIGHLIGHTS

Enrollment Profile

Full-time: 229	International: 13%
Part-time: 986	Women: 39%
Total: 1,115	Minorities: 9%
Average Age: 30	Average Class Size: 35
Fall 1997 Average GPA: 3.08	Fall 1997 Average GMAT: 540

Costs
Full-time tuition: $7392 per academic year (resident); $10,296 per academic year (nonresident)
Part-time tuition: $308 per credit (resident); $429 per credit (nonresident)

AACSB – The International Association for Management Education accredited

Degree(s) offered in conjunction with IGS University

Temple University's M.B.A. program provides students with the skills and knowledge identified by business leaders as essential for success. Fully accredited by the AACSB–The International Association for Management Education, the program focuses on team-based, quality-oriented, and cross-functional models of management. Students develop practical expertise through case analyses and presentations, interaction with business practitioners, and team-based projects.

The program comprises eighteen courses (eight core and ten advanced) and offers seventeen areas of concentration. Evening classes and part- or full-time study at Temple University Center City (1616 Walnut Street) and Temple Ambler (in suburban Montgomery County) make the program convenient to the working professionals who comprise 80 percent of the 1,000 M.B.A. students.

A variety of professional development activities—personal counseling, a resume databank, on- and off-campus recruiting, a mentor program, "Executives in the Classroom," and workshops—foster career preparation and opportunities. The School of Business and Management is a major supplier of managerial talent to the Philadelphia region—one of the nation's major business centers. Its extensive network includes 33,000 alumni, most of whom live and work in the region. Regional business leaders, including alumni, are actively involved in the M.B.A. program; they sponsor consulting projects and internships, serve as mentors and guest speakers, offer curriculum input, and more.

GRADUATE BUSINESS PROGRAMS

Master of Business Administration (MBA) Full-time, part-time, distance learning option; 30-54 total credits required; 12 months to 6 years to complete program. Concentrations in accounting, actuarial science, economics, finance, strategic management, human resources, international business, marketing, real estate, risk management, management information systems, health care, operations management.

Master of Science in Business Administration (MS) Full-time, part-time; 30-54 total credits required; 12 months to 6 years to complete program. Concentrations in accounting, management information systems, economics, finance, human resources, marketing, real estate, risk management, health care, operations management.

Master of Business Health Care Management/Master of Science in Health Care Financial Management (MBA/MS) Full-time, part-time; 69 total credits required; 17 months to 6 years to complete program.

Executive MBA (MBA) Part-time; 45 total credits required; 21 months to complete program.

Master of Business Administration in International Business Administration (MBA) Full-time; 30 total credits required; 10 months to complete program.

Master of Science (MS) Full-time, part-time; 30 total credits required; 12 months to 6 years to complete program. Concentration in actuarial science.

ADMISSION

Applications For fall 1997 there were 942 applications for admission. Of those applying, 515 were accepted. Of those accepted, 293 enrolled.

Application Requirements Application form, application fee, bachelor's degree, 2 letters of recommendation, personal statement, college transcript(s).

Recommended for Application GMAT score accepted, minimum GPA, resume, minimum of 2 years of work experience.

Application Deadline 6/1 for fall, 9/30 for spring, 3/15 for summer, 6/1 for fall (international), 9/30 for spring (international), 3/15 for summer (international). Application fee: $40. Deferred entrance is available.

ACADEMICS

Faculty Full-time 121.

Teaching Methodologies Case study, computer-aided instruction, computer analysis, computer simulations, experiential learning, faculty seminars, field projects, group discussion, lecture, research, role playing, seminars by members of the business community, simulations, student presentations, study groups, team projects.

Technology 2,000 on-campus computer terminals/PCs are available for student use and are linked by a campus-wide network. The network has full access to the Internet. Students are not required to have their own PC.

Special Opportunities Advanced credit may be earned through credit by examination, transfer of credits from another institution. International exchange programs in France, Hungary, Italy, Japan. An internship program is available.

FINANCES
Costs for 1997–98 Tuition: Full-time: $7392 per year (resident); $10,296 per year (nonresident). Part-time: $308 per credit (resident); $429 per credit (nonresident). Fees: Full-time: $211 per academic year (resident); $211 per academic year (nonresident). Part-time: $17 per credit hour (resident); $17 per credit hour (nonresident). Average 1997–98 room and board costs were $7800 per academic year. Room and board costs vary by occupancy (e.g., single, double, triple), type of accommodation, type of meal plan.

Financial Aid Fellowships, research assistantships, teaching assistantships, work study, loans available. Application Deadline: 3/15.

Financial Aid Contact Mr. John Morris, Director, 2nd Floor Conwell Hall, Philadelphia, PA 19122. Phone: 215-204-1405; Fax: 215-204-5897.

FACILITIES
Information Resources Paley Library plus 12 additional on-campus libraries; total holdings of 2,189,431 volumes, 2,189,289 microforms, 15,699 current periodical subscriptions. CD player(s) available for graduate student use. Access provided to online bibliographic retrieval services and online databases.

INTERNATIONAL STUDENTS
Demographics 13% of students enrolled are international students.

Services and Facilities International student office, international student housing, visa services, ESL courses, counseling/support services.

Applying TOEFL: minimum score of 575, proof of adequate funds, proof of health/immunizations required. Financial aid is available to international students.

International Student Contact Ms. Delores Arevalo, Director, 203 Vivacqua Hall, PO Box 2843, Philadelphia, PA 19122-6083. Phone: 215-204-7229; Fax: 215-204-6166.

PLACEMENT
Services include alumni network, career counseling/planning, career fairs, career library, career placement, electronic job bank, job interviews arranged, job search course, resume referral to employers, and resume preparation. In 1996–97, 200 organizations participated in on-campus recruiting.

Employment Of 1996–97 graduates, 90% were employed within three months of graduation; the average starting salary was $62,000. Types of employment entered: accounting, banking, chemical industry, communications, computer-related, consulting, education, energy, engineering, finance, financial services, government, health services, high technology, hospitality management, human resources, information systems/technology, insurance, international trade, law, management, manufacturing, marketing, media, nonprofit, pharmaceutical, real estate, retail, service industry, telecommunications, transportation, utilities.

Business Program(s) URL: http://www.sbm.temple.edu/

Program Contact: Ms. Linda Whelan, Director, MBA and MS Programs, 1810 North 13th Street, Speakman Hall, Room 5, Philadelphia, PA 19122. Phone: 215-204-7678; Fax: 215-204-8300 Ext. 215-204-8300; E-mail: linda@sbm.temple.edu
See full description on page 1010.

University of Pennsylvania

Wharton School
Philadelphia, Pennsylvania

OVERVIEW
The University of Pennsylvania is an independent-nonprofit, coed university. Enrollment: 22,469 graduate, professional, and undergraduate students; 8,782 full-time matriculated graduate/professional students; 2,077 part-time matriculated graduate/professional students. Founded: 1740. The graduate business unit is in an urban setting and is on a first year quarter; second year semester calendar.

HIGHLIGHTS
Enrollment Profile
Full-time: 1,533
Part-time: 0
Total: 1,533
Average Age: 27
Fall 1997 Average GPA: 3.4

International: 30%
Women: 28%
Minorities: 16%
Average Class Size: 40
Fall 1997 Average GMAT: 674

Costs
Full-time tuition: $24,990 per academic year
Part-time tuition: N/R

AACSB – The International Association for Management Education accredited

Degree(s) offered in conjunction with Johns Hopkins University

GRADUATE BUSINESS PROGRAMS
Master of Business Administration (MBA) Full-time; 19 total credits required; minimum of 2 years to complete program. Concentrations in accounting, finance, health care, insurance, risk management, management, marketing, operations management, information management, real estate, public policy and administration.

Executive MBA (MBA) Full-time; 2 years to complete program. Concentrations in accounting, finance, health care, insurance, risk management, management, marketing, operations management, information management, real estate, public policy and administration.

ADMISSION
Applications For fall 1997 there were 7,461 applications for admission. Of those applying, 1,085 were accepted. Of those accepted, 792 enrolled.

Application Requirements GMAT score, application form, application fee, bachelor's degree, essay, minimum GPA, 2 letters of recommendation, college transcript(s).

Recommended for Application Interview, work experience.

Application Deadline Applications processed on a rolling/continuous basis for both domestic and international students. Application fee: $125. Deferred entrance is available.

ACADEMICS
Faculty Full-time 184; part-time 85.

Teaching Methodologies Case study, computer-aided instruction, computer analysis, computer simulations, experiential learning, faculty seminars, field projects, group discussion, lecture, research, role playing, seminars by members of the business community, simulations, student presentations, study groups, team projects.

Technology 150 on-campus computer terminals/PCs are available for student use and are linked by a campus-wide network. The network has full access to the Internet. Students are not required to have their own PC.

Special Opportunities Advanced credit may be earned through credit by examination, credit for experience. International exchange programs in Australia, Brazil, France, Italy, Japan, Netherlands, Philippines, Spain, Sweden, United Kingdom.

FINANCES
Costs for 1997–98 Tuition: Full-time: $24,990 per year. Average 1997–98 room and board costs were $8722 per academic year (off campus).

Financial Aid In 1997–98, 60% of students received some institutionally administered aid in the form of fellowships, research assistantships, teaching assistantships, grants, scholarships, work study, loans. Application Deadline: 3/1.

Financial Aid Contact Associate Director of Financial Aid, 102 Vance Hall, Philadelphia, PA 19104-6362. Phone: 215-898-9784.

FACILITIES
Information Resources Van Pelt Library plus 14 additional on-campus libraries; total holdings of 4,200,000 volumes, 1,500,000 microforms, 33,000 current periodical subscriptions. CD player(s) available for graduate student use. Access provided to online bibliographic retrieval services.

INTERNATIONAL STUDENTS
Demographics 30% of students enrolled are international students.

Services and Facilities International student office, international student housing, visa services, ESL courses, counseling/support services.

Applying TOEFL required. Financial aid is available to international students.

International Student Contact Assistant Director of Graduate Student Programs, 216 Vance Hall, Philadelphia, PA 19104-6361. Phone: 215-898-5000.

PLACEMENT
Services include alumni network, career counseling/planning, career library, career placement, job interviews arranged, job search course, resume referral to employers, and resume preparation. In 1996–97, 356 organizations participated in on-campus recruiting.

University of Pennsylvania (continued)

Employment Of 1996–97 graduates, 97% were employed within three months of graduation; the average starting salary was $90,000. Types of employment entered: accounting, banking, chemical industry, communications, computer-related, consulting, consumer products, education, energy, engineering, finance, financial services, government, health services, high technology, hospitality management, human resources, information systems/technology, insurance, international trade, law, management, manufacturing, marketing, media, mining, nonprofit, petrochemical, pharmaceutical, real estate, retail, service industry, telecommunications, transportation, utilities.

Business Program(s) URL: http://www.wharton.upenn.edu/

Program Contact: Mr. Robert J. Alig, Director of MBA Admissions and Financial Aid, 3733 Spruce Street, 102 Vance Hall, Philadelphia, PA 19104-6361. Phone: 215-898-6183; Fax: 215-898-0120; E-mail: mba.admissions@wharton.upenn. edu

See full descriptions on pages 1124 and 1126.

University of Pittsburgh

Joseph M. Katz Graduate School of Business

Pittsburgh, Pennsylvania

OVERVIEW
The University of Pittsburgh is a state-related, coed university. Enrollment: 26,328 graduate, professional, and undergraduate students; 5,896 full-time matriculated graduate/professional students; 3,711 part-time matriculated graduate/professional students. Founded: 1787. The graduate business unit is in an urban setting and is on a trimester calendar.

HIGHLIGHTS

Enrollment Profile

Full-time: 240	International: 11%
Part-time: 638	Women: N/R
Total: 878	Minorities: 3%
Average Age: 26	Average Class Size: 45
Fall 1997 Average GPA: 3.1	Fall 1997 Average GMAT: N/R

Costs
Full-time tuition: $15,375 per academic year (resident); $26,190 per academic year (nonresident)
Part-time tuition: $446 per credit (resident); $834 per credit (nonresident)

AACSB – The International Association for Management Education accredited

GRADUATE BUSINESS PROGRAMS
Full-time MBA (MBA) Full-time, part-time; 50 total credits required; 11 months to 4 years to complete program. Concentrations in accounting, finance, human resources, management, management information systems, marketing, operations management.

Master of Business Administration/Master of Science in Management of Information Systems (MBA/MS) Full-time, part-time; 76 total credits required; 20 months to 6 years to complete program. Concentration in management information systems.

Master of Business Administration/Master of Public and International Affairs (MBA/MPIA) Full-time, part-time; 78 total credits required; 2 to 6 years to complete program.

Master of Business Administration/Master of International Business (MBA/MIB) Full-time, part-time; 76 total credits required; 2 to 6 years to complete program. Concentrations in public management, international business.

Master of Business Administration/Master of Arts (MBA/MA) Full-time, part-time; 82 total credits required; 2 to 6 years to complete program. Concentration in international and area business studies.

Master of Business Administration/Doctor of Jurisprudence (MBA/JD) Full-time, part-time; 119 total credits required; 3.5 to 6 years to complete program.

Master of Business Administration/Master of Science in Nursing (MBA/MS) Full-time, part-time; 81 total credits required; 2 to 6 years to complete program.

Master of Business Administration/Master of Divinity (MBA/MDiv) Full-time, part-time; 108 total credits required; 4 to 6 years to complete program.

ADMISSION
Applications For fall 1997 there were 1,129 applications for admission. Of those applying, 755 were accepted. Of those accepted, 461 enrolled.

Application Requirements Application form, application fee, bachelor's degree, essay, minimum GPA: 2.4, 3 letters of recommendation, personal statement, resume, college transcript(s).

Recommended for Application GMAT score accepted, interview, work experience, computer experience.

Application Deadline Applications processed on a rolling/continuous basis for both domestic and international students. Application fee: $50. Deferred entrance is available.

ACADEMICS
Faculty Full-time 67; part-time 25.

Teaching Methodologies Case study, computer-aided instruction, computer simulations, faculty seminars, field projects, group discussion, lecture, research, role playing, seminars by members of the business community, simulations, student presentations, study groups, team projects.

Technology Computer terminals/PCs are available for student use and are linked by a campus-wide network. The network has full access to the Internet. Students are not required to have their own PC.

Special Opportunities Advanced credit may be earned through transfer of credits from another institution. An internship program is available.

FINANCES
Costs for 1997–98 Tuition: Full-time: $15,375 per 11-month program (resident); $26,190 per 11-month program (nonresident). Part-time: $446 per credit (resident); $834 per credit (nonresident). Cost varies by class time (e.g., day/evening), number of credits taken. Fees: Full-time: $2364 per academic year (resident); $2364 per academic year (nonresident). Part-time: $51 per term (resident); $51 per term (nonresident). Fees vary by class time (e.g., day/evening), number of credits taken. Average 1997–98 room and board costs were $14,000 per academic year (off campus). Room and board costs vary by occupancy (e.g., single, double, triple), type of accommodation, type of meal plan.

Financial Aid Fellowships, teaching assistantships, work study, loans available.

Financial Aid Contact Ms. Kathleen Riehle Valentine, Director of Admissions, 276 Mervis Hall, Pittsburgh, PA 15260. Phone: 412-648-1700; Fax: 412-648-1659; E-mail: mba-admissions@katz.business.pitt.edu

FACILITIES
Information Resources Hillman Library plus 23 additional on-campus libraries; total holdings of 3,201,394 volumes, 3,134,543 microforms, 23,380 current periodical subscriptions. CD player(s) available for graduate student use. Access provided to online bibliographic retrieval services.

INTERNATIONAL STUDENTS
Demographics 11% of students enrolled are international students.

Services and Facilities International student office, international student center, visa services, ESL courses, counseling/support services.

Applying TOEFL: minimum score of 600, proof of adequate funds required. Financial aid is not available to international students.

International Student Contact Mr. Timothy Thompson, Senior Admissions Officer, 725 William Pitt Union, Pittsburgh, PA 15260. Phone: 412-624-7128; Fax: 412-624-7105; E-mail: tst@vms.cis.pitt.edu

PLACEMENT
Services include alumni network, career counseling/planning, career fairs, career library, career placement, electronic job bank, job interviews arranged, resume referral to employers, and resume preparation. In 1996–97, 100 organizations participated in on-campus recruiting; 1,047 on-campus interviews were conducted.

Employment Of 1996–97 graduates, 94% were employed within three months of graduation; the average starting salary was $58,000. Types of employment entered: banking, chemical industry, computer-related, consulting, consumer products, energy, finance, financial services, government, health services, high technology, information systems/technology, insurance, international trade, law, management, manufacturing, marketing, nonprofit, pharmaceutical, retail, service industry, telecommunications, transportation, utilities.

Business Program(s) URL: http://www.pitt.edu/~business/

Program Contact: Ms. Kathleen Riehle Valentine, Director of Admissions, 276 Mervis Hall, Pittsburgh, PA 15260. Phone: 412-648-1700; Fax: 412-648-1659; E-mail: mba-admissions@katz.business.pitt.edu
See full description on page 1128.

University of Scranton

Program in Business Administration

Scranton, Pennsylvania

OVERVIEW
The University of Scranton is an independent-religious, coed, comprehensive institution. Enrollment: 4,816 graduate, professional, and undergraduate students; 210 full-time matriculated graduate/professional students; 475 part-time matriculated graduate/professional students. Founded: 1888. The graduate business unit is in an urban setting and is on a 4-1-4 calendar.

HIGHLIGHTS

Enrollment Profile
Full-time: 43
Part-time: 95
Total: 138
Average Age: 28
Fall 1997 Average GPA: 3.2

International: 21%
Women: 38%
Minorities: N/R
Average Class Size: 11
Fall 1997 Average GMAT: 505

Costs
Full-time tuition: N/R
Part-time tuition: $465 per credit

AACSB – The International Association for Management Education accredited

GRADUATE BUSINESS PROGRAMS
Master of Business Administration (MBA) Full-time, part-time; 36 total credits required; 18 months to 6 years to complete program. Concentrations in accounting, finance, international business, marketing, operations management, management information systems.

ADMISSION
Applications For fall 1997 there were 117 applications for admission. Of those applying, 112 were accepted. Of those accepted, 36 enrolled.

Application Requirements Application form, application fee, bachelor's degree, minimum GPA: 2.75, 3 letters of recommendation, personal statement, college transcript(s).

Recommended for Application GMAT score accepted, resume, computer experience.

Application Deadline Applications processed on a rolling/continuous basis for both domestic and international students. Application fee: $35. Deferred entrance is available.

ACADEMICS
Faculty Full-time 40; part-time 1.

Teaching Methodologies Case study, computer analysis, computer simulations, lecture, research, student presentations, team projects.

Technology 300 on-campus computer terminals/PCs are available for student use and are linked by a campus-wide network. The network has full access to the Internet. Students are not required to have their own PC.

Special Opportunities Advanced credit may be earned through transfer of credits from another institution.

FINANCES
Costs for 1997–98 Tuition: $465 per credit. Cost varies by academic program. Fees: $25 per semester. Average 1997–98 room and board costs were $7500 per academic year (on campus) and $8150 per academic year (off campus). Room and board costs vary by campus location, occupancy (e.g., single, double, triple), type of accommodation, type of meal plan.

Financial Aid Teaching assistantships, work study available. Financial aid is available to part-time students. Application Deadline: 3/1.

Financial Aid Contact Mr. William R. Burke, Director of Financial Aid, The Graduate School, Scranton , PA 18510-4689. Phone: 717-941-7700; Fax: 717-941-6369; E-mail: burkew1@uofs.edu

FACILITIES
Information Resources Harry and Jeanette Weinberg Memorial Library; total holdings of 375,562 volumes, 409,550 microforms, 4,124 current periodical subscriptions. CD player(s) available for graduate student use. Access provided to online bibliographic retrieval services.

INTERNATIONAL STUDENTS
Demographics 21% of students enrolled are international students.

Services and Facilities International student office, international student housing, ESL courses, counseling/support services.

Applying TOEFL: minimum score of 500, proof of adequate funds required. Financial aid is not available to international students.

International Student Contact Mr. Peter J. Blazes, Director of International Student Affairs, Scranton, PA 18510-4632. Phone: 717-941-7575; Fax: 717-941-4252; E-mail: blazesp1@uofs.edu

PLACEMENT
Services include alumni network, career counseling/planning, career fairs, career library, career placement, electronic job bank, job interviews arranged, job search course, resume referral to employers, and resume preparation. In 1996–97, 44 organizations participated in on-campus recruiting.

Business Program(s) URL: http://academic.uofs.edu/department/gradsch/

Program Contact: Mr. James L. Goonan, Director of Graduate Admissions, The Graduate School, Scranton, PA 18510-4632. Phone: 717-941-6304, 800-366-4723; Fax: 717-941-4252; E-mail: goonanj1@uofs.edu

Villanova University

College of Commerce and Finance

Villanova, Pennsylvania

OVERVIEW
Villanova University is an independent-religious, coed, comprehensive institution. Enrollment: 10,561 graduate, professional, and undergraduate students; 1,119 full-time matriculated graduate/professional students; 1,793 part-time matriculated graduate/professional students. Founded: 1842. The graduate business unit is in a suburban setting and is on a semester calendar.

HIGHLIGHTS

Enrollment Profile
Full-time: 55
Part-time: 673
Total: 728
Average Age: 27
Fall 1997 Average GPA: 3.15

International: 2%
Women: 40%
Minorities: 2%
Average Class Size: 27
Fall 1997 Average GMAT: 585

Costs
Full-time tuition: $11,280 per academic year
Part-time tuition: $470 per credit

AACSB – The International Association for Management Education accredited

GRADUATE BUSINESS PROGRAMS
Master of Business Administration (MBA) Full-time, part-time; 33-48 total credits required; 19 months to 7 years to complete program. Concentrations in finance, management information systems, marketing.

Master of Taxation (MTax) Full-time, part-time; 24 total credits required; 12 months to 5 years to complete program.

Doctor of Jurisprudence/Master of Business Administration (JD/MBA) Full-time, part-time; 3 to 10 years to complete program.

ADMISSION
Applications For fall 1997 there were 255 applications for admission. Of those applying, 190 were accepted. Of those accepted, 134 enrolled.

Application Requirements GMAT score, application form, application fee, bachelor's degree, essay, minimum GPA, letters of recommendation, college transcript(s).

Recommended for Application Personal statement, work experience.

Application Deadline 6/30 for fall, 11/15 for spring, 6/30 for fall (international), 11/15 for spring (international). Application fee: $25. Deferred entrance is available.

ACADEMICS
Faculty Full-time 32; part-time 3.

Teaching Methodologies Case study, computer-aided instruction, computer analysis, computer simulations, faculty seminars, group discussion, lecture, research, role playing, seminars by members of the business community, simulations, student presentations, study groups, team projects.

Technology 400 on-campus computer terminals/PCs are available for student use and are linked by a campus-wide network. The network has full access to the Internet. Students are not required to have their own PC.

Special Opportunities Advanced credit may be earned through credit by examination, transfer of credits from another institution.

FINANCES
Costs for 1997–98 Tuition: Full-time: $11,280 per year. Part-time: $470 per credit. Cost varies by academic program. Fees: Full-time: $60 per academic year. Part-time: $30 per semester.

Financial Aid In 1997–98, 2% of students received some institutionally administered aid in the form of research assistantships. Financial aid is available to part-time students.

Financial Aid Contact George Walter, Director of Financial Assistance, Kennedy Hall, 800 Lancaster Avenue, Villanova, PA 19085.

Villanova University (continued)

FACILITIES
Information Resources Falvey Memorial Library plus 1 additional on-campus library; total holdings of 900,000 volumes, 1,694,000 microforms, 4,000 current periodical subscriptions. CD player(s) available for graduate student use. Access provided to online bibliographic retrieval services.

INTERNATIONAL STUDENTS
Demographics 2% of students enrolled are international students [Africa, 10%, Asia, 25%, Europe, 20%, North America, 30%, South America, 10%, other, 5%].

Services and Facilities International student office, international student center, counseling/support services.

Applying TOEFL: minimum score of 600, proof of adequate funds, proof of health/immunizations required. Financial aid is not available to international students.

International Student Contact Stephen McWilliams, Director of International/ Human Services, Corr Hall, 800 Lancaster Avenue, Villanova, PA 19085.

PLACEMENT
Services include career counseling/planning, career fairs, career library, career placement, job interviews arranged, resume referral to employers, and resume preparation.

Business Program(s) URL: http://www.vill.edu

Program Contact: Ms. Melinda German, Director, Graduate Studies in Business, Room 112-Bartley Hall, Villanova, PA 19085-1699. Phone: 610-519-4336; Fax: 610-519-6273.

See full description on page 1176.

Waynesburg College

Graduate Program in Business Administration

Waynesburg, Pennsylvania

OVERVIEW
Waynesburg College is an independent-religious, coed, comprehensive institution. Enrollment: 1,358 graduate, professional, and undergraduate students; 12 full-time matriculated graduate/professional students; 73 part-time matriculated graduate/professional students. Founded: 1849. The graduate business unit is in a small-town setting and is on a semester calendar.

HIGHLIGHTS

Enrollment Profile
Full-time: 12	International: 12%
Part-time: 73	Women: 40%
Total: 85	Minorities: 1%
Average Age: 30	Average Class Size: 20
Fall 1997 Average GPA: N/R	Fall 1997 Average GMAT: 490

Costs
Full-time tuition: N/R
Part-time tuition: $310 per credit hour

GRADUATE BUSINESS PROGRAMS
Master of Business Administration (MBA) Full-time, part-time; 36 total credits required; minimum age requirement: 25; 12 months to 7 years to complete program. Concentration in management.

Executive MBA (MBA) Full-time, part-time; 36 total credits required; minimum age requirement: 25; 12 months to 7 years to complete program. Concentration in leadership.

ADMISSION
Applications For fall 1997 there were 15 applications for admission. Of those applying, 15 were accepted. Of those accepted, 15 enrolled.

Application Requirements GMAT score, application form, bachelor's degree, minimum GPA, interview, 2 letters of recommendation, resume, college transcript(s), minimum of 3 years of work experience.

Application Deadline Applications processed on a rolling/continuous basis for both domestic and international students. Deferred entrance is available.

ACADEMICS
Faculty Part-time 11.

Teaching Methodologies Case study, computer-aided instruction, lecture, student presentations, team projects.

Technology 100 on-campus computer terminals/PCs are available for student use and are linked by a campus-wide network. The network has full access to the Internet. Students are not required to have their own PC.

Special Opportunities Advanced credit may be earned through transfer of credits from another institution. An internship program is available.

FINANCES
Costs for 1997–98 Tuition: $310 per credit hour. Average 1997–98 room and board costs were $4050 per academic year. Room and board costs vary by occupancy (e.g., single, double, triple), type of accommodation, type of meal plan.

Financial Aid In 1997–98, 12% of students received some institutionally administered aid. Financial aid is available to part-time students. Application Deadline: 5/1.

Financial Aid Contact Ms. Karen Pratz, Director, Financial Aid, 51 West College Street, Waynesburg, PA 15370-1222. Phone: 724-852-3227 Ext. 227; Fax: 724-627-6416; E-mail: kpratz@waynesburg.edu

FACILITIES
Information Resources Eberly Library; total holdings of 124,000 volumes, 494 current periodical subscriptions. CD player(s) available for graduate student use. Access provided to online bibliographic retrieval services.

INTERNATIONAL STUDENTS
Demographics 12% of students enrolled are international students [Asia, 100%].

Services and Facilities International student office, international student housing, counseling/support services.

Applying TOEFL required. Financial aid is not available to international students.

International Student Contact Mr. William Hastings, Assistant Director of Admissions, 51 West College Street, Waynesburg, PA 15370-1222. Phone: 724-852-3373 Ext. 373; Fax: 724-627-6416; E-mail: whasting@waynesburg.edu

PLACEMENT
Services include career placement, and resume preparation. In 1996–97, 20 organizations participated in on-campus recruiting; 50 on-campus interviews were conducted.

Employment Of 1996–97 graduates, 95% were employed within three months of graduation. Types of employment entered: accounting, banking, engineering, management, manufacturing, marketing, pharmaceutical.

Business Program(s) URL: http://waynesburg.edu

Program Contact: Mr. Joseph Graff, Dean of Graduate and Professional Studies, 51 West College Street, Waynesburg, PA 15370-1222. Phone: 724-852-3288 Ext. 288, 800-225-7393; Fax: 724-627-6416; E-mail: jgraff@waynesburg.edu

West Chester University of Pennsylvania

School of Business and Public Affairs

West Chester, Pennsylvania

OVERVIEW
West Chester University of Pennsylvania is a state-supported, coed, comprehensive institution. Enrollment: 10,450 graduate, professional, and undergraduate students; 325 full-time matriculated graduate/professional students; 1,549 part-time matriculated graduate/professional students. Founded: 1871. The graduate business unit is in a suburban setting and is on a semester calendar.

HIGHLIGHTS

Enrollment Profile
Full-time: 65	International: 5%
Part-time: 303	Women: 44%
Total: 368	Minorities: 6%
Average Age: 32	Average Class Size: 16
Fall 1997 Average GPA: 2.8	Fall 1997 Average GMAT: 500

Costs
Full-time tuition: N/R
Part-time tuition: $193 per credit (resident); $346 per credit (nonresident)

Degree(s) offered in conjunction with Cabrini College

GRADUATE BUSINESS PROGRAMS
Evening MBA (MBA) Full-time, part-time; 36 total credits required; up to 6 years to complete program. Concentrations in accounting, economics, management.

Executive MBA (MBA) Full-time, part-time; 36 total credits required; 2 to 6 years to complete program. Concentrations in accounting, economics, management.

ADMISSION
Application Requirements GMAT score: minimum 450, application form, bachelor's degree, minimum GPA: 2.75, letters of recommendation, personal statement, resume, college transcript(s).

Recommended for Application Interview, computer experience.

Application Deadline Applications processed on a rolling/continuous basis for both domestic and international students. Deferred entrance is available.

ACADEMICS

Faculty Part-time 17.

Teaching Methodologies Case study, computer-aided instruction, group discussion, lecture, role playing, seminars by members of the business community, student presentations, study groups, team projects.

Technology 2,500 on-campus computer terminals/PCs are available for student use and are linked by a campus-wide network. The network has full access to the Internet. Students are not required to have their own PC.

Special Opportunities Advanced credit may be earned through transfer of credits from another institution.

FINANCES

Costs for 1997–98 Tuition: $193 per credit (resident); $346 per credit (nonresident). Cost varies by academic program, number of credits taken. Fees: $33 per credit (resident); $33 per credit (nonresident). Fees vary by academic program, number of credits taken. Room and board costs vary by campus location, occupancy (e.g., single, double, triple), type of accommodation, type of meal plan.

Financial Aid Research assistantships available. Financial aid is available to part-time students. Application Deadline: 2/15.

Financial Aid Contact Graduate School, University Avenue and High Street, West Chester, PA 19383. Phone: 610-436-2943; Fax: 610-436-2763; E-mail: gradstudy@wcupa.edu

FACILITIES

Information Resources Francis Harvey Green Library plus 1 additional on-campus library; total holdings of 510,349 volumes, 1,033,227 microforms, 3,026 current periodical subscriptions. CD player(s) available for graduate student use. Access provided to online bibliographic retrieval services.

INTERNATIONAL STUDENTS

Demographics 5% of students enrolled are international students.

Services and Facilities International student office, visa services, ESL courses, counseling/support services.

Applying TOEFL: minimum score of 550, proof of adequate funds, proof of health/immunizations required. Financial aid is available to international students.

International Student Contact Berry Degler, Assistant Director, University Avenue and High Street, West Chester, PA 19383. Phone: 610-436-1000; Fax: 610-436-3540; E-mail: bdegler@wcupa.edu

PLACEMENT

Services include alumni network, career counseling/planning, career fairs, career library, career placement, electronic job bank, job search course, and resume preparation.

Employment Types of employment entered: accounting, banking, communications, computer-related, consumer products, education, finance, financial services, government, human resources, insurance, management, manufacturing, marketing, nonprofit, service industry.

Business Program(s) URL: http://www.wcupa.edu

Program Contact: James Hamilton, Director of MBA, University Avenue and High Street, Anderson Hall, West Chester, PA 19383. Phone: 610-436-2608; Fax: 610-436-3458; E-mail: jhamilton@wcupa.edu
See full description on page 1190.

Widener University

School of Business Administration

Chester, Pennsylvania

OVERVIEW

Widener University is an independent-nonprofit, coed, comprehensive institution. Enrollment: 7,624 graduate, professional, and undergraduate students. Founded: 1821. The graduate business unit is in a suburban setting and is on a semester calendar.

HIGHLIGHTS

Enrollment Profile
Full-time: 63
Part-time: 457
Total: 520
Average Age: 31
Fall 1997 Average GPA: 3.2

International: N/R
Women: N/R
Minorities: 11%
Average Class Size: 23
Fall 1997 Average GMAT: 508

Costs
Full-time tuition: N/R
Part-time tuition: $470 per credit

AACSB – The International Association for Management Education accredited

Degree(s) offered in conjunction with Jefferson Medical College

GRADUATE BUSINESS PROGRAMS

Master of Business Administration (MBA) Full-time, part-time; 36-56 total credits required; 15 months to 7 years to complete program. Concentrations in accounting, economics, finance, human resources, international business, management, management information systems, marketing, financial management/planning, environmental economics/management, taxation.

Master of Business Administration in Health and Medical Services Administration (MBA) Full-time, part-time; 37-57 total credits required; 15 months to 7 years to complete program. Concentration in health care.

Master of Science in Health Administration (MS) Full-time, part-time; 34-54 total credits required; 15 months to 7 years to complete program. Concentration in health care.

Master of Science in Accounting (MS) Full-time, part-time; 33-60 total credits required; 15 months to 7 years to complete program.

Master of Science in Human Resources Management (MS) Full-time, part-time; 33-38 total credits required; 15 months to 7 years to complete program.

Master of Science in Taxation (MS) Full-time, part-time; 33-54 total credits required; 15 months to 7 years to complete program.

Master of Health Administration/Doctor of Clinical Psychology (MHA/PsyD) Full-time; 120-160 total credits required.

Master of Business Administration/Juris Doctor (MBA/JD) Full-time, part-time; 4 to 7 years to complete program.

Master of Business Administration/Master of Engineering (MBA/ME) Full-time, part-time; up to 7 years to complete program.

Master of Business Administration/Doctor of Clinical Psychology (MBA/PsyD) Full-time; 120-160 total credits required.

ADMISSION

Applications For fall 1997 there were 202 applications for admission. Of those applying, 170 were accepted.

Application Requirements GMAT score: minimum 450, application form, application fee, bachelor's degree, essay, minimum GPA: 2.5, 2 letters of recommendation, college transcript(s).

Recommended for Application Work experience, computer experience.

Application Deadline 7/1 for fall, 11/1 for spring, 4/1 for summer, 5/1 for fall (international), 9/1 for spring (international), 2/1 for summer (international). Application fee: $25, $325 (international). Deferred entrance is available.

ACADEMICS

Faculty Full-time 39; part-time 13.

Teaching Methodologies Case study, computer-aided instruction, computer analysis, computer simulations, group discussion, lecture, research, student presentations, team projects.

Technology 100 on-campus computer terminals/PCs are available for student use and are linked by a campus-wide network. The network has full access to the Internet. Students are not required to have their own PC.

Special Opportunities Advanced credit may be earned through credit by examination, transfer of credits from another institution. An internship program is available.

FINANCES

Costs for 1997–98 Tuition: $470 per credit. Fees: $15 per semester.

Financial Aid In 1997–98, 19% of students received some institutionally administered aid in the form of research assistantships, work study, loans. Financial aid is available to part-time students. Application Deadline: 4/1.

Financial Aid Contact Ms. Mary Cay Reilly, Associate Director, Financial Aid, One University Place, Chester, PA 19013-5792. Phone: 610-499-4174; Fax: 610-876-9751; E-mail: mary.c.reilly.@widener.edu

FACILITIES

Information Resources Wolfgram Library plus 1 additional on-campus library; total holdings of 500,000 volumes, 15,130 microforms, 1,840 current periodical subscriptions. CD player(s) available for graduate student use. Access provided to online bibliographic retrieval services and online databases.

Widener University (continued)

INTERNATIONAL STUDENTS
Demographics N/R

Services and Facilities International student office, international student center, visa services, ESL courses, counseling/support services.

Applying TOEFL: minimum score of 550, proof of adequate funds, proof of health/immunizations required. TSE, TWE recommended. Financial aid is not available to international students.

International Student Contact Ms. Lois Fuller, Director, International Student Services, One University Place, Chester, PA 19013-5792. Phone: 610-499-4000; Fax: 609-499-4544; E-mail: lois.j.fuller@cyber.widener.edu

PLACEMENT
Services include alumni network, career counseling/planning, career fairs, career library, career placement, job interviews arranged, resume referral to employers, and resume preparation. In 1996–97, 78 organizations participated in on-campus recruiting.

Employment Of 1996–97 graduates, 95% were employed within three months of graduation. Types of employment entered: accounting, banking, chemical industry, consulting, energy, engineering, finance, financial services, government, health services, hospitality management, human resources, information systems/technology, insurance, management, manufacturing, marketing, media, nonprofit, petrochemical, pharmaceutical, retail, service industry, telecommunications, transportation, utilities.

Business Program(s) URL: http://www.sba.widener.edu

Program Contact: Ms. Lisa Bussom, Assistant Dean, Graduate Programs in Business, One University Place, Chester, PA 19013-5792. Phone: 610-499-4305; Fax: 610-499-4615; E-mail: gradbus.advise@widener.edu
See full description on page 1192.

Wilkes University

School of Business, Society, and Public Policy

Wilkes-Barre, Pennsylvania

OVERVIEW
Wilkes University is an independent-nonprofit, coed, comprehensive institution. Enrollment: 2,824 graduate, professional, and undergraduate students. Founded: 1933. The graduate business unit is in a small-town setting and is on a trimester calendar.

HIGHLIGHTS

Enrollment Profile

Full-time: 20	International: N/R
Part-time: 94	Women: N/R
Total: 114	Minorities: N/R
Average Age: 29	Average Class Size: 15
Fall 1997 Average GPA: 3.0	Fall 1997 Average GMAT: 450

Costs
Full-time tuition: N/R
Part-time tuition: $523 per credit

ACBSP – The American Council of Business Schools and Programs accredited

GRADUATE BUSINESS PROGRAMS
Master of Business Administration (MBA) Full-time, part-time; 48 total credits required; 18 months to 3 years to complete program. Concentrations in accounting, finance, human resources, international and area business studies, marketing.

ADMISSION
Applications For fall 1997 there were 80 applications for admission. Of those applying, 60 were accepted. Of those accepted, 50 enrolled.

Application Requirements Application form, application fee, bachelor's degree, minimum GPA: 2.5, 2 letters of recommendation, college transcript(s).

Recommended for Application GMAT score accepted, resume, work experience, computer experience.

Application Deadline Applications processed on a rolling/continuous basis for both domestic and international students. Application fee: $30. Deferred entrance is available.

ACADEMICS
Faculty Full-time 11; part-time 5.

Teaching Methodologies Case study, computer-aided instruction, experiential learning, group discussion, lecture, research, student presentations, study groups, team projects.

Technology 100 on-campus computer terminals/PCs are available for student use and are linked by a campus-wide network. The network has full access to the Internet. Students are not required to have their own PC.

Special Opportunities Advanced credit may be earned through credit by examination, credit for military training programs, credit for business training programs, transfer of credits from another institution.

FINANCES
Costs for 1997–98 Tuition: $523 per credit. Fees: $10 per credit. Average 1997–98 room and board costs were $6830 per academic year.

Financial Aid In 1997–98, 6% of students received some institutionally administered aid in the form of research assistantships. Application Deadline: 2/28.

Financial Aid Contact Mrs. Rachael Lohman, Director, Financial Aid, Student Services Building, Wilkes-Barre, PA 18766. Phone: 717-831-4346.

FACILITIES
Information Resources E. S. Farley Library plus 1 additional on-campus library; total holdings of 220,000 volumes, 700,000 microforms, 1,154 current periodical subscriptions. CD player(s) available for graduate student use. Access provided to online bibliographic retrieval services.

INTERNATIONAL STUDENTS
Demographics N/R

Services and Facilities International student office, international student housing, visa services, ESL courses, counseling/support services.

Applying TOEFL: minimum score of 550, proof of adequate funds, proof of health/immunizations required. Financial aid is not available to international students.

International Student Contact Ms. Barbara King, Coordinator for International Students, Wilkes University, Conyngham Center, Wilkes-Barre, PA 18766. Phone: 717-831-4107; E-mail: king@wilkes1.wilkes.edu

PLACEMENT
Services include career counseling/planning.

Business Program(s) URL: http://www.wilkes.edu/

Program Contact: Dr. Barbara Samuel-Loftus, MBA Program Director, School of Business, Society and Public Policy, Wilkes University, Wilkes-Barre, PA 18766. Phone: 717-408-4703, 800-WILKESU Ext. 4703; E-mail: mbaprog@wilkes1.wilkes.edu

York College of Pennsylvania

Department of Business Administration

York, Pennsylvania

OVERVIEW
York College of Pennsylvania is an independent-nonprofit, coed, comprehensive institution. Enrollment: 5,046 graduate, professional, and undergraduate students; 37 full-time matriculated graduate/professional students; 174 part-time matriculated graduate/professional students. Founded: 1941. The graduate business unit is in a suburban setting and is on a semester calendar.

HIGHLIGHTS

Enrollment Profile

Full-time: 37	International: 7%
Part-time: 174	Women: 45%
Total: 211	Minorities: 8%
Average Age: 32	Average Class Size: 20
Fall 1997 Average GPA: 3.27	Fall 1997 Average GMAT: 494

Costs
Full-time tuition: $5300 per academic year
Part-time tuition: $284 per credit hour

ACBSP – The American Council of Business Schools and Programs accredited

GRADUATE BUSINESS PROGRAMS
Master of Business Administration (MBA) Full-time, part-time; 33 total credits required; 12 months to 7 years to complete program. Concentrations in accounting, human resources, information management, management, marketing, health care.

ADMISSION
Applications For fall 1997 there were 72 applications for admission. Of those applying, 64 were accepted. Of those accepted, 45 enrolled.

Application Requirements Application form, application fee, bachelor's degree, minimum GPA: 2.8, college transcript(s).

Recommended for Application GMAT score accepted: minimum 480.

Application Deadline 7/15 for fall, 12/15 for spring, 4/15 for summer, 7/15 for fall (international), 12/15 for spring (international), 4/15 for summer (international). Application fee: $30.

ACADEMICS

Faculty Full-time 19; part-time 3.

Teaching Methodologies Case study, computer analysis, computer simulations, group discussion, lecture, student presentations, team projects.

Technology 210 on-campus computer terminals/PCs are available for student use and are linked by a campus-wide network. The network has full access to the Internet. Students are not required to have their own PC.

Special Opportunities Advanced credit may be earned through credit by examination, transfer of credits from another institution.

FINANCES

Costs for 1997–98 Tuition: Full-time: $5300 per semester. Part-time: $284 per credit hour. Cost varies by number of credits taken. Fees: Full-time: $100 per academic year. Part-time: $60 per semester. Fees vary by number of credits taken. Average 1997–98 room and board costs were $4500 per academic year (off campus). Room and board costs vary by occupancy (e.g., single, double, triple), type of accommodation, type of meal plan.

Financial Aid Financial aid is available to part-time students. Application Deadline: 4/15.

Financial Aid Contact Mr. Calvin Williams, Director of Financial Aid, York, PA 17405-7199. Phone: 717-846-7788 Ext. 1226; Fax: 717-849-1619.

FACILITIES

Information Resources Schmidt Library; total holdings of 300,000 volumes, 500,000 microforms, 1,400 current periodical subscriptions. CD player(s) available for graduate student use. Access provided to online bibliographic retrieval services.

INTERNATIONAL STUDENTS

Demographics 7% of students enrolled are international students [Asia, 100%].

Services and Facilities International student office, counseling/support services.

Applying TOEFL, proof of adequate funds, proof of health/immunizations required. Financial aid is not available to international students.

International Student Contact Ms. Nancy Spataro, Director of Admissions, York, PA 17405-7199. Phone: 717-846-7788 Ext. 1600; Fax: 717-849-1619.

PLACEMENT

Services include alumni network, career counseling/planning, career fairs, career library, career placement, electronic job bank, job interviews arranged, job search course, resume referral to employers, and resume preparation. In 1996–97, 58 organizations participated in on-campus recruiting; 61 on-campus interviews were conducted.

Employment Of 1996–97 graduates, 89% were employed within three months of graduation; the average starting salary was $28,000. Types of employment entered: accounting, banking, chemical industry, communications, computer-related, consulting, consumer products, education, energy, engineering, finance, financial services, government, health services, high technology, hospitality management, human resources, information systems/technology, insurance, international trade, law, management, manufacturing, marketing, media, nonprofit, pharmaceutical, real estate, retail, service industry, telecommunications, transportation, utilities.

Business Program(s) URL: http://www.ycp.edu/

Program Contact: Mr. John Barbor, Coordinator, MBA Program, York, PA 17405-7199. Phone: 717-815-1491; Fax: 717-849-1619; E-mail: jbarbor@ycp.edu

RHODE ISLAND

Bryant College

Graduate School

Smithfield, Rhode Island

OVERVIEW

Bryant College is an independent-nonprofit, coed, comprehensive institution. Enrollment: 3,266 graduate, professional, and undergraduate students; 53 full-time matriculated graduate/professional students; 487 part-time matriculated graduate/professional students. Founded: 1863. The graduate business unit is in a suburban setting and is on a semester calendar.

HIGHLIGHTS

Enrollment Profile

Full-time: 53	International: 4%
Part-time: 487	Women: 41%
Total: 540	Minorities: 3%
Average Age: 33	Average Class Size: 23
Fall 1997 Average GPA: 3.13	Fall 1997 Average GMAT: 536

Costs
Full-time tuition: N/R
Part-time tuition: $950 per course

AACSB – The International Association for Management Education accredited

Quality, flexibility, and value define the Bryant College M.B.A. courses. They are offered with working professionals in mind, are scheduled throughout the year and meet one evening per week for 2¼ hours at 5 or 7:30 p.m. Most students earn their advanced degrees on a part-time basis while working full-time, and complete degree requirements in three to six years. Full-time study is also available, and students may move from part-time to full-time status at various times throughout the program, as life circumstances change.

Bryant faculty members are accomplished academics and experienced practitioners. Class size averages 23 students, giving students the opportunity to learn with and from other working professionals. The classroom becomes a living case study as students apply their experiences to discussions and group projects.

The Hodgson Memorial Library, considered one of the region's most extensive business libraries, is conveniently located in the College's Unistructure. With an impressive blend of print and electronic resources, the library holds more than 126,000 volumes and also offers LEXIS-NEXIS, DIALOG (offering access to hundreds of databases), and the BRIDGE Information Systems Selective Ticker Service, which provides market data and investment analysis.

GRADUATE BUSINESS PROGRAMS

Master of Business Administration (MBA) Full-time, part-time; 48-54 total credits required; 16 months to 6 years to complete program. Concentrations in accounting, finance, management information systems, international business, management, marketing, operations management, health care.

Master of Science in Accounting (MS) Full-time, part-time; 30-48 total credits required; 12 months to 6 years to complete program. Concentration in accounting.

Master of Science in Taxation (MS) Full-time, part-time; 30 total credits required; 20 months to 6 years to complete program. Concentration in taxation.

ADMISSION

Applications For fall 1997 there were 192 applications for admission. Of those applying, 126 were accepted. Of those accepted, 97 enrolled.

Application Requirements Application form, application fee, bachelor's degree, minimum GPA: 3.0, letter of recommendation, personal statement, resume, college transcript(s).

Recommended for Application GMAT score accepted: minimum 480, work experience.

Application Deadline 7/1 for fall, 11/15 for spring, 4/1 for summer, 4/1 for fall (international), 3/1 for summer (international). Application fee: $55, $70 (international). Deferred entrance is available.

ACADEMICS

Faculty Full-time 45; part-time 43.

Teaching Methodologies Case study, computer-aided instruction, computer analysis, computer simulations, experiential learning, faculty seminars, field projects, group discussion, lecture, research, role playing, seminars by members of the business community, simulations, student presentations, study groups, team projects.

Technology 315 on-campus computer terminals/PCs are available for student use and are linked by a campus-wide network. The network has full access to the Internet. Students are not required to have their own PC.

Special Opportunities Advanced credit may be earned through transfer of credits from another institution.

FINANCES

Costs for 1997–98 Tuition: $950 per course. Cost varies by academic program. Average 1997–98 room and board costs were $7660 per academic year (on campus) and $4950 per academic year (off campus). Room and board costs vary by occupancy (e.g., single, double, triple), type of meal plan.

Financial Aid In 1997–98, 11% of students received some institutionally administered aid in the form of research assistantships. Financial aid is available to part-time students.

Financial Aid Contact Mr. John Canning, Director of Financial Aid, 1150 Douglas Pike, Smithfield, RI 02917-1284. Phone: 401-232-6020; Fax: 401-232-6741; E-mail: jcanning@bryant.edu

Bryant College (continued)

FACILITIES

Information Resources Edith M. Hodgson Memorial Library; total holdings of 119,203 volumes, 12,000 microforms, 1,350 current periodical subscriptions. CD player(s) available for graduate student use. Access provided to online bibliographic retrieval services.

INTERNATIONAL STUDENTS

Demographics 4% of students enrolled are international students [Africa, 4%, Asia, 50%, Europe, 39%, South America, 6%].

Services and Facilities International student office, counseling/support services.

Applying TOEFL: minimum score of 600, proof of adequate funds, proof of health/immunizations required. Financial aid is not available to international students.

International Student Contact Ms. Naurene McDermott, Immigration Processor, 1150 Douglas Pike, Smithfield, RI 02917-1284. Phone: 401-232-6046; Fax: 401-232-6368; E-mail: nmcdermo@bryant.edu

PLACEMENT

Services include alumni network, career counseling/planning, career library, career placement, electronic job bank, job interviews arranged, job search course, resume referral to employers, and resume preparation.

Employment Types of employment entered: pharmaceutical.

Business Program(s) URL: http://www.bryant.edu/graduate/index.html

Program Contact: Ms. Cathy Lalli, Assistant Director of Admissions, 1150 Douglas Pike, Smithfield, RI 02917-1284. Phone: 401-232-6230; Fax: 401-232-6494; E-mail: gradprog@bryant.edu

See full description on page 738.

Johnson & Wales University

Alan Shawn Feinstein Graduate School

Providence, Rhode Island

OVERVIEW

Johnson & Wales University is an independent-nonprofit, coed, comprehensive institution. Enrollment: 10,150 graduate, professional, and undergraduate students; 441 full-time matriculated graduate/professional students; 150 part-time matriculated graduate/professional students. Founded: 1914. The graduate business unit is in an urban setting and is on a quarter calendar.

HIGHLIGHTS

Enrollment Profile

Full-time: 441	International: 38%
Part-time: 150	Women: 49%
Total: 591	Minorities: 10%
Average Age: 28	Average Class Size: 28
Fall 1997 Average GPA: 3.32	Fall 1997 Average GMAT: 495

Costs
Full-time tuition: $1071 per academic year
Part-time tuition: $194 per quarter credit

GRADUATE BUSINESS PROGRAMS

Master of Business Administration in International Business (MBA) Full-time, part-time; 36 total credits required; 12 months to 5 years to complete program. Concentration in international business.

Master of Business Administration in Hospitality Administration (MBA) Full-time, part-time; 36 total credits required; 12 months to 5 years to complete program.

Master of Business Administration in Management (MBA) Full-time, part-time; 36 total credits required; 12 months to 5 years to complete program. Concentration in management.

Master of Business Administration in Accounting (MBA) Full-time, part-time; 36 total credits required; 2 to 5 years to complete program. Concentration in accounting.

ADMISSION

Applications For fall 1997 there were 418 applications for admission. Of those applying, 277 were accepted. Of those accepted, 203 enrolled.

Application Requirements Application form, bachelor's degree, minimum GPA: 2.75, 3 letters of recommendation, college transcript(s).

Recommended for Application GMAT score accepted, GRE score accepted, interview, resume, work experience, computer experience.

Application Deadline Applications processed on a rolling/continuous basis for both domestic and international students. Deferred entrance is available.

ACADEMICS

Faculty Full-time 18; part-time 20.

Teaching Methodologies Case study, computer-aided instruction, computer analysis, experiential learning, faculty seminars, field projects, group discussion, lecture, research, role playing, seminars by members of the business community, student presentations, study groups, team projects.

Technology 414 on-campus computer terminals/PCs are available for student use and are linked by a campus-wide network. The network has full access to the Internet. Students are not required to have their own PC.

Special Opportunities Advanced credit may be earned through transfer of credits from another institution. International exchange program in Sweden. An internship program is available.

FINANCES

Costs for 1997–98 Tuition: Full-time: $1071 per course. Part-time: $194 per quarter credit. Cost varies by class time (e.g., day/evening). Fees: Full-time: $159 per academic year. Average 1997–98 room and board costs were $6027 per academic year (on campus) and $7400 per academic year (off campus). Room and board costs vary by type of accommodation, type of meal plan.

Financial Aid Loans available. Financial aid is available to part-time students. Application Deadline: 5/1.

Financial Aid Contact Ms. Deborah Machowski, Director, Financial Aid, Abbott Park Place, Providence, RI 02903. Phone: 401-598-1405; Fax: 401-598-1040.

FACILITIES

Information Resources Main library plus 2 additional on-campus libraries; total holdings of 76,973 volumes, 11 microforms, 604 current periodical subscriptions. CD player(s) available for graduate student use. Access provided to online bibliographic retrieval services and online databases.

INTERNATIONAL STUDENTS

Demographics 38% of students enrolled are international students.

Services and Facilities International student office, international student center, international student housing, visa services, ESL courses, counseling/support services.

Applying TOEFL: minimum score of 550, proof of adequate funds, proof of health/immunizations required. Financial aid is available to international students.

International Student Contact Ms. Janine DeVellis, International Student Advisor, International Office, Abbott Park Place, Providence, RI 02903. Phone: 401-598-1074; Fax: 401-598-4773.

PLACEMENT

Services include alumni network, career counseling/planning, career fairs, career library, career placement, electronic job bank, job interviews arranged, job search course, resume referral to employers, and resume preparation. In 1996–97, 82 organizations participated in on-campus recruiting; 205 on-campus interviews were conducted.

Employment Types of employment entered: accounting, banking, communications, computer-related, consumer products, education, finance, financial services, government, hospitality management, human resources, information systems/technology, insurance, international trade, management, manufacturing, marketing, nonprofit, retail, service industry, transportation.

Business Program(s) URL: http://www.jwu.edu/

Program Contact: Ms. Karen Cardello, Assistant Director, Graduate Admissions, Abbott Park Place, Providence, RI 02818. Phone: 401-598-1015, 800-343-2565 Ext. 1015 (RI only); Fax: 401-598-4773.

See full description on page 860.

Providence College

Graduate Business Program

Providence, Rhode Island

OVERVIEW

Providence College is an independent-religious, coed, comprehensive institution. Enrollment: 5,922 graduate, professional, and undergraduate students. Founded: 1917. The graduate business unit is in an urban setting and is on a semester calendar.

HIGHLIGHTS

Enrollment Profile

Full-time: 10
Part-time: 267
Total: 277
Average Age: N/R
Fall 1997 Average GPA: 3.0

International: 2%
Women: 27%
Minorities: 1%
Average Class Size: 20
Fall 1997 Average GMAT: 500

Costs

Full-time tuition: $8640 per academic year
Part-time tuition: $729 per 3-credit course

GRADUATE BUSINESS PROGRAMS

Master of Business Administration (MBA) Full-time, part-time; 36 total credits required; 12 months to 5 years to complete program. Concentrations in accounting, economics, finance, international business, marketing, public policy and administration, quantitative analysis.

ADMISSION

Applications For fall 1997 there were 48 applications for admission. Of those applying, 37 were accepted. Of those accepted, 37 enrolled.

Application Requirements GMAT score: minimum 450, application form, application fee, bachelor's degree, minimum GPA: 3.0, 2 letters of recommendation, personal statement, college transcript(s).

Recommended for Application Resume, computer experience.

Application Deadline Applications processed on a rolling/continuous basis for both domestic and international students. Application fee: $40. Deferred entrance is available.

ACADEMICS

Faculty Full-time 19; part-time 10.

Teaching Methodologies Case study, computer-aided instruction, computer analysis, computer simulations, field projects, group discussion, lecture, research, student presentations, team projects.

Technology 150 on-campus computer terminals/PCs are available for student use and are linked by a campus-wide network. The network has full access to the Internet. Students are not required to have their own PC.

Special Opportunities Advanced credit may be earned through transfer of credits from another institution. An internship program is available.

FINANCES

Costs for 1997–98 Tuition: Full-time: $8640 per year. Part-time: $729 per 3-credit course. Cost varies by number of credits taken. Fees: Full-time: $125 per academic year.

Financial Aid In 1997–98, 3% of students received some institutionally administered aid in the form of research assistantships.

Financial Aid Contact Mr. Herbert D'arcy, Jr., Executive Director, Financial Aid Office, River Avenue and Eaton Street, Providence , RI 02918-0001. Phone: 401-865-2602; Fax: 401-865-2057; E-mail: hdarcy@providence.edu

FACILITIES

Information Resources Phillips Memorial Library; total holdings of 261,785 volumes, 27,483 microforms, 55,654 current periodical subscriptions. CD player(s) available for graduate student use. Access provided to online bibliographic retrieval services.

INTERNATIONAL STUDENTS

Demographics 2% of students enrolled are international students [Asia, 83%, Europe, 17%].

Services and Facilities International student office, counseling/support services.

Applying TOEFL: minimum score of 550, proof of adequate funds required. Financial aid is not available to international students.

International Student Contact Dr. John Hogan, International Student Advisor, River Avenue and Eaton Street, Providence, RI 02918-0001. Phone: 401-865-2676; Fax: 401-865-2057; E-mail: jhogan@providence.edu

PLACEMENT

Services include alumni network, career counseling/planning, and career placement.

Employment Types of employment entered: accounting, banking, financial services, management, marketing, pharmaceutical.

Business Program(s) URL: http://www.providence.edu/grad/index.html

Program Contact: Dr. John Shaw, Director, Master of Business Administration Program, River Avenue and Eaton Street, Providence, RI 02918-0001. Phone: 401-865-2333; Fax: 401-865-2978; E-mail: jshaw@providence.edu

Salve Regina University

Graduate School

Newport, Rhode Island

OVERVIEW

Salve Regina University is an independent-religious, coed, comprehensive institution. Enrollment: 2,108 graduate, professional, and undergraduate students; 42 full-time matriculated graduate/professional students; 289 part-time matriculated graduate/professional students. Founded: 1934. The graduate business unit is in a suburban setting and is on a semester calendar.

HIGHLIGHTS

Enrollment Profile

Full-time: 20
Part-time: 140
Total: 160
Average Age: 34
Fall 1997 Average GPA: N/R

International: 1%
Women: 40%
Minorities: 6%
Average Class Size: 10
Fall 1997 Average GMAT: 555

Costs

Full-time tuition: N/R
Part-time tuition: $275 per credit

GRADUATE BUSINESS PROGRAMS

Master of Science in Accounting (MS) Full-time, part-time; 42 total credits required; 2 to 5 years to complete program. Concentration in accounting.

Master of Arts in Human Resource Management (MA) Full-time, part-time; 36 total credits required; 2 to 5 years to complete program. Concentration in human resources.

Master of Science in Information Systems Science (MS) Full-time, part-time; 36 total credits required; 2 to 5 years to complete program. Concentration in management information systems.

Master of Business Administration (MBA) Full-time, part-time; 36 total credits required; 2 to 5 years to complete program. Concentrations in management, accounting, finance, management information systems.

Master of Science in Management (MS) distance learning option; 36 total credits required; 2 to 5 years to complete program. Concentrations in insurance, management.

ADMISSION

Applications For fall 1997 there were 117 applications for admission. Of those applying, 63 were accepted. Of those accepted, 53 enrolled.

Application Requirements Application form, application fee, bachelor's degree, 2 letters of recommendation, personal statement, college transcript(s).

Recommended for Application GMAT score accepted, GRE score accepted, MAT score accepted, resume.

Application Deadline Applications processed on a rolling/continuous basis for both domestic and international students. Application fee: $35. Deferred entrance is available.

ACADEMICS

Faculty Full-time 4; part-time 17.

Teaching Methodologies Case study, computer analysis, computer simulations, group discussion, lecture, research, seminars by members of the business community, student presentations, team projects.

Technology 136 on-campus computer terminals/PCs are available for student use and are linked by a campus-wide network. The network has full access to the Internet. Students are not required to have their own PC.

Special Opportunities Advanced credit may be earned through transfer of credits from another institution.

FINANCES

Costs for 1997–98 Tuition: $275 per credit. Fees: $35 per semester.

Financial Aid In 1997–98, 12% of students received some institutionally administered aid in the form of loans. Financial aid is available to part-time students. Application Deadline: 3/1.

Financial Aid Contact Mrs. Lucile Flanagan, Director of Financial Aid and Veterans Affairs, 100 Ochre Point Avenue, Newport, RI 02840-4192. Phone: 401-847-6650 Ext. 2901; Fax: 401-849-5941.

FACILITIES

Information Resources McKillop Library; total holdings of 116,825 volumes, 6,194 microforms, 1,400 current periodical subscriptions. CD player(s) available for graduate student use. Access provided to online bibliographic retrieval services and online databases.

INTERNATIONAL STUDENTS

Demographics 1% of students enrolled are international students [Europe, 100%].

Services and Facilities ESL courses.

Salve Regina University (continued)

Applying TOEFL: minimum score of 550, proof of adequate funds required. Financial aid is not available to international students.

International Student Contact Ms. Cheryl Serra, Director of Graduate Marketing and Recruiting, 100 Ochre Point Avenue, Newport, RI 02840-4192. Phone: 401-847-6650 Ext. 2105; Fax: 401-848-2823; E-mail: sruadmis@salve.edu

PLACEMENT

Services include alumni network, career counseling/planning, career fairs, career library, and resume preparation.

Business Program(s) URL: http://www.salve.edu

Program Contact: Mr. John Britton, Director of Graduate MBA Program, 100 Ochre Point Avenue, Newport, RI 02840-4192. Phone: 401-847-6650 Ext. 3140, 888-GO-SALVE; Fax: 401-847-0372.

University of Rhode Island

College of Business Administration

Kingston, Rhode Island

OVERVIEW

The University of Rhode Island is a state-supported, coed university. Enrollment: 13,700 graduate, professional, and undergraduate students; 2,325 full-time matriculated graduate/professional students; 1,336 part-time matriculated graduate/professional students. Founded: 1888. The graduate business unit is in a suburban setting and is on a semester calendar.

HIGHLIGHTS

Enrollment Profile

Full-time: 22	International: 3%
Part-time: 161	Women: 30%
Total: 183	Minorities: 4%
Average Age: 29	Average Class Size: 25
Fall 1997 Average GPA: 3.0	Fall 1997 Average GMAT: 582

Costs

Full-time tuition: $6700 per academic year (resident); $17,000 per academic year (nonresident)

Part-time tuition: $187 per credit (resident); $521 per credit (nonresident)

AACSB – The International Association for Management Education accredited

GRADUATE BUSINESS PROGRAMS

Full-time MBA (MBA) Full-time; 54 total credits required; 12 months to complete program. Concentrations in accounting, finance, international business, management, management information systems, marketing.

Part-time MBA (MBA) Part-time; 36-54 total credits required; 2 to 4 years to complete program. Concentrations in accounting, finance, international business, management, management information systems, marketing.

Executive MBA (MBA) Part-time; 54 total credits required; 22 months to complete program. Concentration in management.

Master of Science in Accounting (MS) Full-time, part-time; 30-69 total credits required; 12 months to 4 years to complete program.

ADMISSION

Applications For fall 1997 there were 91 applications for admission. Of those applying, 78 were accepted. Of those accepted, 54 enrolled.

Application Requirements Application form, application fee, bachelor's degree, essay, minimum GPA: 3.0, 2 letters of recommendation, personal statement, college transcript(s).

Recommended for Application GMAT score accepted, resume, computer experience: Microsoft Powerpoint, Microsoft Excel.

Application Deadline 7/15 for fall, 11/15 for spring, 7/15 for fall (international), 11/15 for spring (international). Application fee: $30, $45 (international). Deferred entrance is available.

ACADEMICS

Faculty Full-time 52.

Teaching Methodologies Case study, computer-aided instruction, computer analysis, computer simulations, experiential learning, faculty seminars, field projects, group discussion, lecture, research, role playing, seminars by members of the business community, simulations, student presentations, study groups, team projects.

Technology 200 on-campus computer terminals/PCs are available for student use and are linked by a campus-wide network. The network has full access to the Internet. Students are not required to have their own PC.

Special Opportunities Advanced credit may be earned through credit by examination, transfer of credits from another institution. An internship program is available.

FINANCES

Costs for 1997–98 Tuition: Full-time: $6700 per year (resident); $17,000 per year (nonresident). Part-time: $187 per credit (resident); $521 per credit (nonresident). Cost varies by academic program, number of credits taken. Fees: Full-time: $1300 per academic year (resident); $1300 per academic year (nonresident). Part-time: $30 per semester (resident); $30 per semester (nonresident). Fees vary by academic program, number of credits taken. Average 1997–98 room only costs were $5400 per academic year (on campus) and $6000 per academic year (off campus). Room and board costs vary by occupancy (e.g., single, double, triple), type of accommodation.

Financial Aid Fellowships, research assistantships, scholarships, work study, loans available. Financial aid is available to part-time students. Application Deadline: 2/1.

Financial Aid Contact Financial Aid Office, Roosevelt Hall, Kingston, RI 02881. Phone: 401-874-2314; Fax: 401-874-2002.

FACILITIES

Information Resources University of Rhode Island Library plus 2 additional on-campus libraries; total holdings of 1,090,000 volumes, 1,510,000 microforms, 7,150 current periodical subscriptions. CD player(s) available for graduate student use. Access provided to online bibliographic retrieval services and online databases.

INTERNATIONAL STUDENTS

Demographics 3% of students enrolled are international students [Asia, 33%, Europe, 67%].

Services and Facilities International student office, international student center, international student housing, visa services, counseling/support services.

Applying TOEFL: minimum score of 575, proof of adequate funds, proof of health/immunizations required. Financial aid is not available to international students.

International Student Contact International Students and Scholars Office, 37 Lower College Road, Kingston, RI 02881. Phone: 401-874-2395.

PLACEMENT

Services include alumni network, career counseling/planning, career fairs, career library, career placement, electronic job bank, job interviews arranged, job search course, and resume preparation.

Employment Of 1996–97 graduates, 93% were employed within three months of graduation; the average starting salary was $47,680. Types of employment entered: accounting, banking, computer-related, consulting, consumer products, education, engineering, finance, financial services, government, health services, high technology, human resources, information systems/technology, international trade, management, manufacturing, marketing, nonprofit, pharmaceutical, retail, service industry, telecommunications, utilities.

Business Program(s) URL: http://www.cba.uri.edu

Program Contact: Ms. Lisa Hadzekyriakides, Assistant Director, MBA Programs, 210 Ballentine Hall, 7 Lippitt Road, Kingston, RI 02881-0802. Phone: 401-874-5000; Fax: 401-874-4312; E-mail: hadz@uriacc.uri.edu

SOUTH CAROLINA

Charleston Southern University

Graduate Program in Business

Charleston, South Carolina

OVERVIEW

Charleston Southern University is an independent-religious, coed, comprehensive institution. Enrollment: 2,500 graduate, professional, and undergraduate students; 36 full-time matriculated graduate/professional students; 240 part-time matriculated graduate/professional students. Founded: 1960. The graduate business unit is in a suburban setting and is on a semester calendar.

HIGHLIGHTS

Enrollment Profile

Full-time: 20
Part-time: 180
Total: 200
Average Age: 31
Fall 1997 Average GPA: 2.85

International: 5%
Women: 50%
Minorities: N/R
Average Class Size: 17
Fall 1997 Average GMAT: 450

Costs

Full-time tuition: N/R
Part-time tuition: $204 per semester hour

GRADUATE BUSINESS PROGRAMS

Master of Business Administration (MBA) Full-time, part-time; 30-36 total credits required; 12 months to 6 years to complete program. Concentrations in accounting, finance, health care, organizational behavior/development, management information systems.

ADMISSION

Applications For fall 1997 there were 59 applications for admission.

Application Requirements GMAT score, application form, application fee, bachelor's degree, 2 letters of recommendation, personal statement, college transcript(s), computer experience: word processing, spreadsheet, database.

Application Deadline Applications processed on a rolling/continuous basis for both domestic and international students. Application fee: $25.

ACADEMICS

Faculty Full-time 8; part-time 1.

Teaching Methodologies Case study, computer-aided instruction, computer analysis, computer simulations, group discussion, lecture, research, role playing, seminars by members of the business community, student presentations, study groups, team projects.

Technology 100 on-campus computer terminals/PCs are available for student use and are linked by a campus-wide network. The network has full access to the Internet. Students are not required to have their own PC.

Special Opportunities Advanced credit may be earned through transfer of credits from another institution.

FINANCES

Costs for 1997–98 Tuition: $204 per semester hour. Average 1997–98 room and board costs were $4538 per academic year. Room and board costs vary by occupancy (e.g., single, double, triple).

Financial Aid Research assistantships, loans available. Financial aid is available to part-time students. Application Deadline: 3/1.

Financial Aid Contact Ms. Ellen Green, Director, Financial Aid, PO Box 118087, Charleston, SC 29423-8087. Phone: 843-863-7000; Fax: 843-863-7955.

FACILITIES

Information Resources L. Mendel Rivers Library; total holdings of 122,374 volumes, 115,845 microforms, 1,172 current periodical subscriptions. CD player(s) available for graduate student use. Access provided to online bibliographic retrieval services.

INTERNATIONAL STUDENTS

Demographics 5% of students enrolled are international students [Africa, 24%, Asia, 51%, Europe, 11%, North America, 7%, South America, 7%].

Services and Facilities International student office, counseling/support services.

Applying TOEFL: minimum score of 550, proof of adequate funds, proof of health/immunizations required. Financial aid is available to international students.

International Student Contact Ms. Barbara Mead, Assistant Dean of Students/International Services Director, PO Box 118087, Charleston, SC 29423-8087. Phone: 843-863-8009; Fax: 843-863-7021.

PLACEMENT

Services include career counseling/planning, career fairs, career library, career placement, electronic job bank, job interviews arranged, job search course, resume referral to employers, and resume preparation.

Employment Of 1996–97 graduates, 95% were employed within three months of graduation. Types of employment entered: accounting, banking, chemical industry, communications, computer-related, consulting, education, finance, financial services, government, human resources, insurance, management, manufacturing, marketing.

Program Contact: Mrs. Terri Jordon, MBA Coordinator, PO Box 118087, Charleston, SC 29423-8087. Phone: 843-863-7955; Fax: 843-863-7922.

The Citadel

College of Graduate and Professional Studies

Charleston, South Carolina

OVERVIEW

The Citadel is a state-supported, coed, comprehensive institution. Enrollment: 3,766 graduate, professional, and undergraduate students; 153 full-time matriculated graduate/professional students; 559 part-time matriculated graduate/professional students. Founded: 1842. The graduate business unit is in an urban setting and is on a semester calendar.

HIGHLIGHTS

Enrollment Profile

Full-time: 21
Part-time: 122
Total: 143
Average Age: N/R
Fall 1997 Average GPA: N/R

International: 3%
Women: 30%
Minorities: 7%
Average Class Size: 18
Fall 1997 Average GMAT: 480

Costs

Full-time tuition: N/R
Part-time tuition: $129 per credit hour (resident); $129 per credit hour (nonresident)

AACSB – The International Association for Management Education accredited

GRADUATE BUSINESS PROGRAMS

Master of Business Administration (MBA) Full-time, part-time; 39 total credits required; 2 to 6 years to complete program.

ADMISSION

Application Requirements GMAT score, application form, application fee, bachelor's degree, minimum GPA, 2 letters of recommendation, college transcript(s).

Recommended for Application Essay, work experience, computer experience.

Application Deadline Applications processed on a rolling/continuous basis for both domestic and international students. Application fee: $25. Deferred entrance is available.

ACADEMICS

Faculty Full-time 18.

Teaching Methodologies Case study, computer-aided instruction, computer analysis, experiential learning, field projects, group discussion, lecture, research, role playing, seminars by members of the business community, student presentations, team projects.

Technology 100 on-campus computer terminals/PCs are available for student use and are linked by a campus-wide network. The network has full access to the Internet. Students are not required to have their own PC.

Special Opportunities Advanced credit may be earned through transfer of credits from another institution.

FINANCES

Costs for 1997–98 Tuition: $129 per credit hour (resident); $129 per credit hour (nonresident). Cost varies by number of credits taken.

Financial Aid Financial aid is available to part-time students.

FACILITIES

Information Resources Daniel Memorial Library plus 1 additional on-campus library; total holdings of 193,545 volumes, 935,253 microforms, 1,361 current periodical subscriptions. CD player(s) available for graduate student use. Access provided to online bibliographic retrieval services.

INTERNATIONAL STUDENTS

Demographics 3% of students enrolled are international students.

Applying TOEFL: minimum score of 550 required.

PLACEMENT

Services include alumni network, career fairs, career library, career placement, job interviews arranged, and resume preparation. In 1996–97, 100 organizations participated in on-campus recruiting.

Employment Of 1996–97 graduates, 100% were employed within three months of graduation.

Business Program(s) URL: http://www.citadel.edu/

Program Contact: College of Graduate and Professional Studies, 171 Moultrie Street, Charleston, SC 29409. Phone: 843-953-5188; Fax: 843-953-7630.

Clemson University

College of Business and Public Affairs

Clemson, South Carolina

OVERVIEW
Clemson University is a state-supported, coed university. Enrollment: 16,445 graduate, professional, and undergraduate students; 1,809 full-time matriculated graduate/professional students; 1,936 part-time matriculated graduate/professional students. Founded: 1889. The graduate business unit is in a small-town setting and is on a semester calendar.

HIGHLIGHTS

Enrollment Profile

Full-time: 187	International: 18%
Part-time: 275	Women: 38%
Total: 462	Minorities: 9%
Average Age: 25	Average Class Size: 23
Fall 1997 Average GPA: 3.27	Fall 1997 Average GMAT: 563

Costs
Full-time tuition: $1512 per academic year (resident); $3024 per academic year (nonresident)
Part-time tuition: $194 per credit hour (resident); $384 per credit hour (nonresident)

AACSB – The International Association for Management Education accredited

GRADUATE BUSINESS PROGRAMS
Full-time MBA (MBA) Full-time; 60 total credits required; 21 months to 2 years to complete program.

Part-time MBA (MBA) Part-time; 30 total credits required; 2 years work experience required; 19 months to 6 years to complete program.

International MBA (MBA) Full-time, part-time; 60 total credits required; 12 months to 3 years to complete program.

ADMISSION
Applications For fall 1997 there were 898 applications for admission. Of those applying, 420 were accepted. Of those accepted, 340 enrolled.

Application Requirements Application form, application fee, bachelor's degree, minimum GPA: 2.8, 2 letters of recommendation, resume, college transcript(s), computer experience: university-level computer course.

Recommended for Application GMAT score accepted, minimum of 1 year of work experience.

Application Deadline 6/15 for fall, 4/15 for fall (international). Application fee: $35. Deferred entrance is available.

ACADEMICS
Faculty Full-time 119; part-time 34.

Teaching Methodologies Case study, computer-aided instruction, computer analysis, computer simulations, experiential learning, field projects, group discussion, lecture, research, role playing, seminars by members of the business community, simulations, student presentations, study groups, team projects.

Technology 800 on-campus computer terminals/PCs are available for student use and are linked by a campus-wide network. The network has full access to the Internet. Students are not required to have their own PC.

Special Opportunities Advanced credit may be earned through transfer of credits from another institution.

FINANCES
Costs for 1997–98 Tuition: Full-time: $1512 per semester (resident); $3024 per semester (nonresident). Part-time: $194 per credit hour (resident); $384 per credit hour (nonresident). Cost varies by academic program, campus location, number of credits taken. Fees vary by academic program, campus location. Average 1997–98 room only costs were $2460 per academic year (on campus) and $3150 per academic year (off campus). Room and board costs vary by campus location, occupancy (e.g., single, double, triple), type of accommodation, type of meal plan.

Financial Aid In 1997–98, 42% of students received some institutionally administered aid in the form of fellowships, research assistantships, loans. Financial aid is available to part-time students. Application Deadline: 3/1.

Financial Aid Contact Financial Aid Office, G01 Sikes Hall, Clemson, SC 29634. Phone: 864-656-2423; Fax: 864-656-1831.

FACILITIES
Information Resources Robert Muldrow Cooper Library plus 2 additional on-campus libraries; total holdings of 1,641,340 volumes, 1,052,414 microforms, 11,574 current periodical subscriptions. CD player(s) available for graduate student use. Access provided to online bibliographic retrieval services.

INTERNATIONAL STUDENTS
Demographics 18% of students enrolled are international students [Africa, 2%, Asia, 39%, Central America, 2%, Europe, 49%, North America, 5%, South America, 3%].

Services and Facilities International student office, international student center, visa services, counseling/support services.

Applying TOEFL: minimum score of 550, proof of adequate funds, proof of health/immunizations required. Financial aid is not available to international students.

International Student Contact Office of International Programs and Studies , E 208 Martin Hall, Clemson, SC 29634. Phone: 864-656-2357; Fax: 864-656-4187.

PLACEMENT
Services include career counseling/planning, career fairs, career library, career placement, electronic job bank, job interviews arranged, job search course, resume referral to employers, and resume preparation. In 1996–97, 97 on-campus interviews were conducted.

Employment Of 1996–97 graduates, 90% were employed within three months of graduation; the average starting salary was $42,800. Types of employment entered: accounting, banking, communications, consulting, energy, finance, financial services, government, high technology, human resources, information systems/technology, insurance, management, manufacturing, marketing, nonprofit, service industry, telecommunications, utilities.

Business Program(s) URL: http://business.clemson.edu/

Program Contact: Director of Admissions, MBA Programs, Box 341315, Clemson, SC 29634-1315. Phone: 864-656-3975; Fax: 864-656-0947; E-mail: mba@clemson.edu

See full description on page 756.

Francis Marion University

School of Business

Florence, South Carolina

OVERVIEW
Francis Marion University is a state-supported, coed, comprehensive institution. Enrollment: 3,700 graduate, professional, and undergraduate students; 26 full-time matriculated graduate/professional students; 417 part-time matriculated graduate/professional students. Founded: 1970. The graduate business unit is in a small-town setting and is on a semester calendar.

HIGHLIGHTS

Enrollment Profile

Full-time: 3	International: 5%
Part-time: 60	Women: 49%
Total: 63	Minorities: 16%
Average Age: 29	Average Class Size: 20
Fall 1997 Average GPA: 2.9	Fall 1997 Average GMAT: 485

Costs
Full-time tuition: $3370 per academic year (resident); $6740 per academic year (nonresident)
Part-time tuition: $160 per hour (resident); $321 per hour (nonresident)

AACSB – The International Association for Management Education accredited

Degree(s) offered in conjunction with Medical University of South Carolina

GRADUATE BUSINESS PROGRAMS
Master of Business Administration (MBA) Full-time, part-time, distance learning option; 36 total credits required; 2 to 6 years to complete program.

Master of Business Administration (MBA) Full-time, part-time, distance learning option; 36 total credits required; 2 to 6 years to complete program. Concentration in health care.

ADMISSION
Applications For fall 1997 there were 35 applications for admission. Of those applying, 29 were accepted. Of those accepted, 28 enrolled.

Application Requirements GMAT score, application form, application fee, bachelor's degree, minimum GPA, 2 letters of recommendation, personal statement, college transcript(s), computer experience: computer literacy.

Application Deadline Applications processed on a rolling/continuous basis for both domestic and international students. Application fee: $25. Deferred entrance is available.

ACADEMICS
Faculty Full-time 22.

SOUTH CAROLINA

Teaching Methodologies Case study, computer-aided instruction, computer analysis, group discussion, lecture, student presentations, study groups, team projects.

Technology 100 on-campus computer terminals/PCs are available for student use and are linked by a campus-wide network. The network has full access to the Internet. Students are not required to have their own PC.

Special Opportunities Advanced credit may be earned through transfer of credits from another institution.

FINANCES
Costs for 1997–98 Tuition: Full-time: $3370 per year (resident); $6740 per year (nonresident). Part-time: $160 per hour (resident); $321 per hour (nonresident). Fees: Full-time: $60 per academic year (resident); $60 per academic year (nonresident). Part-time: $30 per semester (resident); $30 per semester (nonresident). Average 1997–98 room and board costs were $3138 per academic year (on campus) and $6000 per academic year (off campus). Room and board costs vary by occupancy (e.g., single, double, triple), type of accommodation, type of meal plan.

Financial Aid In 1997–98, 8% of students received some institutionally administered aid in the form of research assistantships. Financial aid is available to part-time students. Application Deadline: 3/1.

Financial Aid Contact Mr. Scott Brown, Director of Financial Assistance, Box 100547, Florence, SC 29501-0547. Phone: 803-661-1190.

FACILITIES
Information Resources James A. Rogers Library; total holdings of 278,283 volumes, 322,616 microforms, 1,700 current periodical subscriptions. CD player(s) available for graduate student use. Access provided to online bibliographic retrieval services.

INTERNATIONAL STUDENTS
Demographics 5% of students enrolled are international students [Asia, 33%, Europe, 33%, South America, 33%, other, 1%].

Services and Facilities International student office, ESL courses, counseling/support services, international student organization.

Applying TOEFL: minimum score of 550, proof of adequate funds, proof of health/immunizations required. Financial aid is available to international students.

International Student Contact Ms. Catherine Davis, Administrative Assistant to the Provost, Box 100547, Florence, SC 29501-0547. Phone: 803-661-1284.

PLACEMENT
Services include alumni network, career counseling/planning, career fairs, career library, career placement, electronic job bank, job interviews arranged, job search course, resume referral to employers, and resume preparation. In 1996–97, 100 organizations participated in on-campus recruiting; 200 on-campus interviews were conducted.

Employment Of 1996–97 graduates, 95% were employed within three months of graduation. Types of employment entered: accounting, banking, computer-related, consumer products, engineering, finance, government, health services, human resources, information systems/technology, insurance, management, manufacturing, marketing, nonprofit, pharmaceutical, real estate, retail, service industry.

Program Contact: Dr. Robert Barrett, Director, MBA Program, Box 100547, Florence, SC 29501-0547. Phone: 803-661-1419; Fax: 803-661-1432.

South Carolina State University

Department of Agribusiness and Economics
Orangeburg, South Carolina

OVERVIEW
South Carolina State University is a state-supported, coed, comprehensive institution. Enrollment: 4,980 graduate, professional, and undergraduate students; 317 full-time matriculated graduate/professional students; 482 part-time matriculated graduate/professional students. Founded: 1896. The graduate business unit is in a small-town setting and is on a semester calendar.

HIGHLIGHTS

Enrollment Profile
Full-time: 12
Part-time: 9
Total: 21
Average Age: 24
Fall 1997 Average GPA: 2.8

International: 5%
Women: 38%
Minorities: 76%
Average Class Size: 10
Fall 1997 Average GMAT: 400

Costs
Full-time tuition: $2750 per academic year (resident); $2750 per academic year (nonresident)
Part-time tuition: $155 per credit (resident); $155 per credit (nonresident)

GRADUATE BUSINESS PROGRAMS
Master of Science in Agribusiness (MS) Full-time, part-time; 33 total credits required; up to 6 years to complete program. Concentrations in agribusiness, agricultural economics.

ADMISSION
Applications For fall 1997 there were 15 applications for admission. Of those applying, 12 were accepted. Of those accepted, 9 enrolled.

Application Requirements GMAT score, application form, application fee, bachelor's degree, essay, minimum GPA: 2.8, 3 letters of recommendation, college transcript(s).

Recommended for Application GRE score accepted, MAT score accepted.

Application Deadline 7/10 for fall, 11/10 for spring, 5/1 for summer, 7/10 for fall (international), 11/10 for spring (international), 5/1 for summer (international). Application fee: $15.

ACADEMICS
Faculty Full-time 7.

Teaching Methodologies Case study, computer analysis, computer simulations, experiential learning, faculty seminars, group discussion, lecture, research, role playing, seminars by members of the business community, student presentations, team projects.

Technology 100 on-campus computer terminals/PCs are available for student use and are linked by a campus-wide network. The network has full access to the Internet. Students are not required to have their own PC.

Special Opportunities Advanced credit may be earned through transfer of credits from another institution. An internship program is available.

FINANCES
Costs for 1997–98 Tuition: Full-time: $2750 per year (resident); $2750 per year (nonresident). Part-time: $155 per credit (resident); $155 per credit (nonresident). Average 1997–98 room only costs were $2000 per academic year (off campus). Room and board costs vary by occupancy (e.g., single, double, triple), type of accommodation.

Financial Aid In 1997–98, 48% of students received some institutionally administered aid in the form of fellowships, research assistantships, scholarships, work study, loans. Application Deadline: 6/1.

Financial Aid Contact Dr. Nelson Modeste, Chairman, Department of Agribusiness and Economics, Orangeburg, SC 29117. Phone: 803-536-8076.

FACILITIES
Information Resources Miller F. Whittaker Library; total holdings of 273,264 volumes, 686,225 microforms, 1,376 current periodical subscriptions. CD player(s) available for graduate student use. Access provided to online bibliographic retrieval services.

INTERNATIONAL STUDENTS
Demographics 5% of students enrolled are international students [Asia, 100%].

Services and Facilities International student office, visa services, counseling/support services, international student organization.

Applying Proof of adequate funds, proof of health/immunizations required.

International Student Contact Bettylou Terry, Director, Minority and International Programs, PO Box 8123, Orangeburg, SC 29117. Phone: 803-536-8393.

PLACEMENT
Services include alumni network, career counseling/planning, career fairs, career placement, job interviews arranged, and resume preparation.

Employment Of 1996–97 graduates, 100% were employed within three months of graduation; the average starting salary was $28,000. Types of employment entered: accounting, finance, government, management.

Program Contact: Dr. Nelson Modeste, Chairman, Department of Agribusiness and Economics, Orangeburg, SC 29117. Phone: 803-536-8076.

Southern Wesleyan University

Program in Management

Central, South Carolina

OVERVIEW
Southern Wesleyan University is an independent-religious, coed, comprehensive institution. Enrollment: 1,298 graduate, professional, and undergraduate students; 70 full-time matriculated graduate/professional students; part-time matriculated graduate/professional students. Founded: 1906. The graduate business unit is in a small-town setting and is on a continuous calendar.

HIGHLIGHTS

Enrollment Profile
Full-time: 53
Part-time: 0
Total: 53
Average Age: 32
Fall 1997 Average GPA: N/R

International: N/R
Women: 45%
Minorities: 34%
Average Class Size: 16
Fall 1997 Average GMAT: N/R

Costs
Full-time tuition: N/R
Part-time tuition: $240 per credit hour

GRADUATE BUSINESS PROGRAMS
Master of Science in Management (MS) Full-time; 36 total credits required; 18 months to complete program. Concentration in management.

ADMISSION
Application Requirements Application form, application fee, bachelor's degree, minimum GPA: 2.7, 2 letters of recommendation, personal statement, college transcript(s), minimum of 2 years of work experience, computer experience: computer literacy.

Recommended for Application GMAT score accepted, GRE score accepted, MAT score accepted.

Application Deadline Applications processed on a rolling/continuous basis for both domestic and international students. Application fee: $25. Deferred entrance is available.

ACADEMICS
Faculty Full-time 8; part-time 5.

Teaching Methodologies Case study, group discussion, lecture, research, student presentations, study groups, team projects.

Technology Students are required to have their own PC.

Special Opportunities Advanced credit may be earned through transfer of credits from another institution.

FINANCES
Costs for 1997–98 Tuition: $240 per credit hour. Fees: Full-time: $920 per academic year.

Financial Aid In 1997–98, 87% of students received some institutionally administered aid in the form of loans.

Financial Aid Contact Ms. Maria Cathcart, FA Assistant, PO Box 1020 / SWU Box, Central, SC 29630. Phone: 864-639-2453 Ext. 432; Fax: 864-639-1956.

FACILITIES
Information Resources Rickman Library. CD player(s) available for graduate student use. Access provided to online bibliographic retrieval services and online databases.

INTERNATIONAL STUDENTS
Demographics N/R

Applying TOEFL: minimum score of 500 required. Financial aid is not available to international students.

PLACEMENT
Employment Of 1996–97 graduates, 100% were employed within three months of graduation.

Program Contact: Ms. Debra Cummings, Director of Marketing, PO Box 1020/ SWU Box 487, Central, SC 29630. Phone: 864-639-2453, 800-264-5327; Fax: 864-639-4050; E-mail: admissions@swu.edu

University of Charleston, South Carolina

School of Business and Economics, Graduate Studies

Charleston, South Carolina

OVERVIEW
The University of Charleston, South Carolina is a state-supported, coed, graduate institution. Enrollment: 10,978 graduate, professional, and undergraduate students; 248 full-time matriculated graduate/professional students; 253 part-time matriculated graduate/professional students. Founded: 1770. The graduate business unit is in an urban setting and is on a semester calendar.

HIGHLIGHTS

Enrollment Profile
Full-time: 16
Part-time: 17
Total: 33
Average Age: 34
Fall 1997 Average GPA: N/R

International: 3%
Women: 64%
Minorities: 3%
Average Class Size: 10
Fall 1997 Average GMAT: 513

Costs
Full-time tuition: $1251 per academic year (resident); $2565 per academic year (nonresident)
Part-time tuition: $139 per credit hour (resident); $285 per credit hour (nonresident)

GRADUATE BUSINESS PROGRAMS
Master of Science in Accountancy (MS) Full-time, part-time; 30 total credits required; 2 to 5 years to complete program.

ADMISSION
Applications For fall 1997 there were 21 applications for admission. Of those applying, 17 were accepted. Of those accepted, 4 enrolled.

Application Requirements GMAT score, application form, application fee, bachelor's degree, minimum GPA, college transcript(s).

Application Deadline Applications processed on a rolling/continuous basis for both domestic and international students. Application fee: $35. Deferred entrance is available.

ACADEMICS
Faculty Full-time 4.

Teaching Methodologies Case study, group discussion, lecture, research, role playing, seminars by members of the business community, simulations, student presentations, study groups, team projects.

Technology 200 on-campus computer terminals/PCs are available for student use and are linked by a campus-wide network. The network has full access to the Internet. Students are not required to have their own PC.

Special Opportunities Advanced credit may be earned through transfer of credits from another institution.

FINANCES
Costs for 1997–98 Tuition: Full-time: $1251 per semester (resident); $2565 per semester (nonresident). Part-time: $139 per credit hour (resident); $285 per credit hour (nonresident). Fees: Full-time: $33 per academic year (resident); $33 per academic year (nonresident). Part-time: $17 per credit hour (resident); $17 per credit hour (nonresident). Average 1997–98 room and board costs were $7580 per academic year (off campus). Room and board costs vary by type of meal plan.

Financial Aid Fellowships, research assistantships, teaching assistantships, work study available. Financial aid is available to part-time students. Application Deadline: 4/1.

Financial Aid Contact Mr. Donald Griggs, Director, Office of Financial Assistance and Veterans Affairs, 66 George Street, Charleston, SC 29424-0001. Phone: 843-953-5540; Fax: 843-953-7192; E-mail: financialaid@cofc.edu

FACILITIES
Information Resources Robert Scott Small Library; total holdings of 505,000 volumes, 687,203 microforms, 3,032 current periodical subscriptions. CD player(s) available for graduate student use. Access provided to online bibliographic retrieval services.

INTERNATIONAL STUDENTS
Demographics 3% of students enrolled are international students [Asia, 100%].

Services and Facilities International student office, international student center, visa services, ESL courses, counseling/support services.

Applying TOEFL: minimum score of 550, proof of adequate funds, proof of health/immunizations required. Financial aid is not available to international students.

International Student Contact Ms. Laura Hines, Graduate School Coordinator, Suite 310—Randolph Hall, Charleston, SC 29424-0001. Phone: 843-953-5614; Fax: 843-953-1434; E-mail: gradsch@cofc.edu

PLACEMENT

Services include alumni network, career counseling/planning, career fairs, career library, electronic job bank, resume referral to employers, and resume preparation. In 1996–97, 5 organizations participated in on-campus recruiting; 15 on-campus interviews were conducted.

Employment Of 1996–97 graduates, 85% were employed within three months of graduation; the average starting salary was $28,000. Types of employment entered: accounting, banking, financial services, government.

Business Program(s) URL: http://www.cofc.edu/~baecon/

Program Contact: Graduate School Office, Suite 310—Randolph Hall, Charleston, SC 29424-0001. Phone: 843-953-5614; Fax: 843-953-1434; E-mail: gradsch@cofc.edu

University of South Carolina

College of Business Administration

Columbia, South Carolina

OVERVIEW
The University of South Carolina is a state-supported, coed university. Enrollment: 24,971 graduate, professional, and undergraduate students; 5,169 full-time matriculated graduate/professional students; 4,450 part-time matriculated graduate/professional students. Founded: 1801. The graduate business unit is in an urban setting and is on a semester calendar.

HIGHLIGHTS

Enrollment Profile
Full-time: 544
Part-time: 428
Total: 972
Average Age: 27
Fall 1997 Average GPA: 3.3

International: 16%
Women: 29%
Minorities: 6%
Average Class Size: 40
Fall 1997 Average GMAT: 591

Costs
Full-time tuition: $3724 per academic year (resident); $7634 per academic year (nonresident)
Part-time tuition: $185 per credit hour (resident); $380 per credit hour (nonresident)

AACSB – The International Association for Management Education accredited

Degree(s) offered in conjunction with Vienna Business and Economics University

Innovation has been the key to the success of The Darla Moore School of Business at the University of South Carolina. The School has a long history of keeping pace with the ever-changing global economic environment through a blend of academic preparation and real-world experience. Three distinctive degree programs with global opportunities are offered. The Master of International Business Studies (M.I.B.S.) degree program features an integrated business curriculum, formal language training (eight languages), cultural studies, and a six-month overseas internship. The Master of Business Administration (M.B.A.) degree program provides international study opportunities at thirteen locations. The International Master of Business Administration (I.M.B.A.) degree program combines the best of European and American management education in a unique partnership between the University of South Carolina and the Vienna Business and Economics University. By emphasizing foreign languages, cultural studies, overseas internships, and study-abroad programs, The Darla Moore School of Business has earned international recognition. The School believes that global understanding and competency are essential for business students who must operate in a world of few boundaries and constant change.

GRADUATE BUSINESS PROGRAMS
Master of Business Administration (MBA) Full-time; 60 total credits required; 21 months to 2 years to complete program. Concentrations in management, finance, operations management, marketing, management information systems, accounting, entrepreneurship, international business, management, management science, organizational management, strategic management.

Professional MBA Program (MBA) Part-time, distance learning option; 54 total credits required; minimum of 2.6 years to complete program. Concentrations in management, finance, operations management, marketing, management information systems, accounting, entrepreneurship, international business, management, management science, organizational management, strategic management.

Master of Accountancy (MAcc) Full-time; 30 total credits required; 12 to 18 months to complete program. Concentration in accounting.

Master of Taxation (MTax) Full-time; 36 total credits required; 12 to 18 months to complete program. Concentration in taxation.

Master of Human Resources (MHR) Full-time; 42 total credits required; 18 months to 2 years to complete program. Concentrations in human resources, industrial administration/management, industrial/labor relations.

International MBA (IMBA) Full-time; 48 total credits required; minimum of 15 months to complete program. Concentrations in international business, international finance, international management, international marketing, international trade, accounting, finance, management, management information systems, management science, marketing, operations management, organizational management, strategic management, entrepreneurship.

Master of International Business Studies (MIBS) Full-time; 60 total credits required; 2 to 3 years to complete program. Concentrations in international business, international finance, international management, international marketing, international trade, accounting, finance, management, management information systems, management science, marketing, operations management, organizational management, strategic management, entrepreneurship.

Master of Business Administration/Doctor of Jurisprudence (MBA/JD) Full-time; 60 total credits required; minimum of 4 years to complete program. Concentrations in management, business law.

Master of International Business Studies/Doctor of Jurisprudence (MIBS/JD) Full-time; 60 total credits required; minimum of 4 years to complete program. Concentrations in international business, business law.

Master of Science in Business Administration (MS) Full-time; 30-36 total credits required; 12 to 15 months to complete program. Concentrations in management science, operations management, management information systems, marketing.

Master of Arts in Economics (MA) Full-time; 30 total credits required; 12 to 15 months to complete program. Concentration in economics.

Master of Arts in Economics/Doctor of Jurisprudence (MA/JD) Full-time; 48-60 total credits required; 3 to 4 years to complete program. Concentrations in economics, business law.

Master of Science in Business Administration/Doctor of Jurisprudence (MS/JD) Full-time; 48-60 total credits required; 3 to 4 years to complete program. Concentrations in management science, operations management, management information systems, marketing, business law.

Master of Accountancy/Doctor of Jurisprudence (MAcc/JD) Full-time; 48-60 total credits required; 3 to 4 years to complete program. Concentrations in accounting, business law.

Master of Human Resources/Doctor of Jurisprudence (MHR/JD) Full-time; 48-60 total credits required; 3 to 4 years to complete program. Concentrations in human resources, industrial administration/management, industrial/labor relations, business law.

Master of Arts in English/Master of Business Administration (MA/MBA) Full-time; 51 total credits required; 3 to 4 years to complete program. Concentrations in management, management information systems, management science, marketing, operations management.

ADMISSION
Applications For fall 1997 there were 1,368 applications for admission. Of those applying, 858 were accepted. Of those accepted, 507 enrolled.

Application Requirements Application form, application fee, bachelor's degree, essay, minimum GPA: 3.0, 2 letters of recommendation, personal statement, resume, college transcript(s).

Recommended for Application GMAT score accepted: minimum 550, GRE score accepted: minimum 1,140, interview, work experience, computer experience.

Application Deadline 2/1 for fall, 12/1 for spring, 5/1 for summer, 1/1 for fall (international), 11/1 for spring (international), 4/1 for summer (international). Application fee: $35.

ACADEMICS
Faculty Full-time 134; part-time 16.

Teaching Methodologies Case study, computer-aided instruction, computer analysis, computer simulations, experiential learning, faculty seminars, field projects, group discussion, lecture, research, role playing, seminars by members of the business community, simulations, student presentations, study groups, team projects.

Technology 210 on-campus computer terminals/PCs are available for student use and are linked by a campus-wide network. The network has full access to the Internet. Students are not required to have their own PC.

Special Opportunities Advanced credit may be earned through credit by examination, transfer of credits from another institution. International exchange programs in Australia, Belgium, Denmark, Finland, France, Germany, Netherlands, Norway, United Kingdom. An internship program is available.

FINANCES
Costs for 1997–98 Tuition: Full-time: $3724 per year (resident); $7634 per year (nonresident). Part-time: $185 per credit hour (resident); $380 per credit

University of South Carolina (continued)

hour (nonresident). Cost varies by class time (e.g., day/evening), number of credits taken, reciprocity agreements. Fees: Full-time: $2900 per academic year (resident); $4400 per academic year (nonresident). Part-time: $48 per credit hour (resident); $73 per credit hour (nonresident). Fees vary by academic program, class time (e.g., day/evening), number of credits taken, reciprocity agreements. Average 1997–98 room and board costs were $12,000 per academic year (on campus) and $13,000 per academic year (off campus). Room and board costs vary by campus location, occupancy (e.g., single, double, triple), type of accommodation, type of meal plan.

Financial Aid In 1997–98, 32% of students received some institutionally administered aid in the form of fellowships, research assistantships, teaching assistantships, scholarships, work study, loans. Application Deadline: 2/1.

Financial Aid Contact Ms. Libby Shropshier, Director of Graduate Administrative and Financial Affairs, Columbia, SC 29208. Phone: 803-777-6845; Fax: 803-777-0414; E-mail: shropshier@darla.badm.sc.edu

FACILITIES

Information Resources Thomas Cooper Library plus 6 additional on-campus libraries; total holdings of 2,639,171 volumes, 4,075,413 microforms, 20,722 current periodical subscriptions. CD player(s) available for graduate student use. Access provided to online bibliographic retrieval services and online databases.

INTERNATIONAL STUDENTS

Demographics 16% of students enrolled are international students [Africa, 2%, Asia, 30%, Australia/New Zealand, 3%, Europe, 35%, North America, 15%, South America, 10%, other, 5%].

Services and Facilities International student office, international student center, international student housing, visa services, ESL courses, counseling/support services.

Applying TOEFL: minimum score of 600, proof of adequate funds, proof of health/immunizations required. Financial aid is available to international students.

International Student Contact Ms. Patricia Willer, Director of International Programs for Students, James F. Byrne Building, Suite 123, Columbia, SC 29208. Phone: 803-777-7461; Fax: 803-777-0462; E-mail: d800033@vm.sc.edu

PLACEMENT

Services include alumni network, career counseling/planning, career fairs, career library, career placement, electronic job bank, job interviews arranged, resume referral to employers, and resume preparation. In 1996–97, 112 organizations participated in on-campus recruiting; 1,292 on-campus interviews were conducted.

Employment Of 1996–97 graduates, 87% were employed within three months of graduation; the average starting salary was $54,089. Types of employment entered: accounting, banking, chemical industry, communications, computer-related, consulting, consumer products, education, energy, engineering, finance, financial services, government, health services, high technology, hospitality management, human resources, information systems/technology, insurance, international trade, law, management, manufacturing, marketing, nonprofit, petrochemical, pharmaceutical, real estate, retail, service industry, telecommunications, transportation, utilities.

Business Program(s) URL: http://www.business.sc.edu

Program Contact: Ms. Carol Williams, Managing Director of Admissions, Graduate Division, College of Business Administration, Columbia, SC 29208. Phone: 803-777-6749; Fax: 803-777-0414; E-mail: carol@darla.badm.sc.edu
See full description on page 1140.

Winthrop University

College of Business Administration

Rock Hill, South Carolina

OVERVIEW

Winthrop University is a state-supported, coed, comprehensive institution. Enrollment: 5,304 graduate, professional, and undergraduate students. Founded: 1886. The graduate business unit is in a suburban setting and is on a semester calendar.

HIGHLIGHTS

Enrollment Profile
Full-time: 100	International: N/R
Part-time: 150	Women: N/R
Total: 250	Minorities: N/R
Average Age: 34	Average Class Size: 25
Fall 1997 Average GPA: 2.97	Fall 1997 Average GMAT: 500

Costs
Full-time tuition: $1899 per academic year (resident); $3420 per academic year (nonresident)
Part-time tuition: $160 per semester hour (resident); $285 per semester hour (nonresident)

AACSB – The International Association for Management Education accredited

Degree(s) offered in conjunction with Coastal Carolina University

GRADUATE BUSINESS PROGRAMS
Master of Business Administration (MBA) Full-time, part-time, distance learning option; 39 total credits required; minimum of 18 months to complete program.
Master of Business Administration in Accounting (MBA) Full-time, part-time, distance learning option; 33 total credits required; minimum of 18 months to complete program. Concentration in accounting.
Executive MBA (MBA) Full-time; 51 total credits required; minimum of 2 years to complete program.

ADMISSION
Applications For fall 1997 there were 68 applications for admission. Of those applying, 58 were accepted. Of those accepted, 55 enrolled.
Application Requirements GMAT score: minimum 400, application form, application fee, bachelor's degree, minimum GPA, college transcript(s).
Recommended for Application Essay, interview, letters of recommendation, personal statement, work experience, computer experience.
Application Deadline 7/15 for fall, 12/1 for spring, 5/1 for summer, 4/15 for fall (international), 9/15 for spring (international), 5/15 for summer (international). Application fee: $35, $50 (international). Deferred entrance is available.

ACADEMICS
Faculty Full-time 42.
Teaching Methodologies Case study, computer simulations, experiential learning, field projects, group discussion, lecture, research, student presentations, study groups, team projects.
Technology Computer terminals/PCs are available for student use and are linked by a campus-wide network. The network has full access to the Internet. Students are not required to have their own PC.
Special Opportunities Advanced credit may be earned through transfer of credits from another institution. An internship program is available.

FINANCES
Costs for 1997–98 Tuition: Full-time: $1899 per semester (resident); $3420 per semester (nonresident). Part-time: $160 per semester hour (resident); $285 per semester hour (nonresident). Cost varies by number of credits taken, reciprocity agreements. Average 1997–98 room and board costs were $3316 per academic year. Room and board costs vary by occupancy (e.g., single, double, triple), type of accommodation, type of meal plan.
Financial Aid Scholarships, work study available. Financial aid is available to part-time students. Application Deadline: 2/1.
Financial Aid Contact Geneva Drakeford, Director of Financial Resource Center, 117 Tillman, Rock Hill, SC 29733. Phone: 803-323-2189; Fax: 803-323-4528; E-mail: drakefordg@winthrop.edu

FACILITIES
Information Resources Ida Jane Dacus Library; total holdings of 363,606 volumes, 1,060,158 microforms, 2,367 current periodical subscriptions. CD player(s) available for graduate student use. Access provided to online bibliographic retrieval services.

INTERNATIONAL STUDENTS
Demographics N/R
Services and Facilities International student office, international student center, visa services, counseling/support services.
Applying TOEFL: minimum score of 550, proof of adequate funds, proof of health/immunizations required. Financial aid is not available to international students.
International Student Contact Mr. Jeff Jones, International Student Advisor, 204 Tillman, Rock Hill, SC 29733. Phone: 803-323-3440; Fax: 803-323-2340; E-mail: jonesj@winthrop.edu

PLACEMENT

Services include career counseling/planning, career fairs, career library, career placement, electronic job bank, job interviews arranged, resume referral to employers, and resume preparation.

Employment Of 1996–97 graduates, 85% were employed within three months of graduation. Types of employment entered: accounting, banking, engineering.

Program Contact: Ms. Peggy Hager, Director of Graduate School, College of Business Administration, Rock Hill, SC 29733. Phone: 803-323-2409; Fax: 803-323-2539; E-mail: hagerp@mail.winthrop.edu

SOUTH DAKOTA

Huron University

School of Business

Huron, South Dakota

OVERVIEW

Huron University is a proprietary, coed, comprehensive institution. Enrollment: 350 graduate, professional, and undergraduate students; 35 full-time matriculated graduate/professional students; 15 part-time matriculated graduate/professional students. Founded: 1883. The graduate business unit is in a small-town setting and is on a quarter calendar.

HIGHLIGHTS

Enrollment Profile
Full-time: 35
Part-time: 15
Total: 50
Average Age: 25
Fall 1997 Average GPA: 3.31

International: 70%
Women: 50%
Minorities: N/R
Average Class Size: 20
Fall 1997 Average GMAT: 610

Costs
Full-time tuition: $11,440 per academic year
Part-time tuition: $220 per quarter hour

GRADUATE BUSINESS PROGRAMS

Master of Business Administration (MBA) Full-time, part-time.

ADMISSION

Applications For fall 1997 there were 110 applications for admission. Of those applying, 80 were accepted. Of those accepted, 40 enrolled.

Application Requirements Application form, application fee, bachelor's degree, essay, minimum GPA: 3.0, personal statement, resume, college transcript(s).

Recommended for Application GMAT score accepted.

Application Deadline Applications processed on a rolling/continuous basis for both domestic and international students. Application fee: $100, $250 (international). Deferred entrance is available.

ACADEMICS

Faculty Full-time 3; part-time 6.

Teaching Methodologies Case study, computer-aided instruction, computer analysis, computer simulations, experiential learning, faculty seminars, field projects, group discussion, lecture, research, role playing, seminars by members of the business community, simulations, student presentations, study groups, team projects.

Technology 50 on-campus computer terminals/PCs are available for student use and are linked by a campus-wide network. The network has full access to the Internet. Students are not required to have their own PC.

Special Opportunities Advanced credit may be earned through credit for experience, transfer of credits from another institution. International exchange programs in France, Ireland, United Kingdom. An internship program is available.

FINANCES

Costs for 1997–98 Tuition: Full-time: $11,440 per year. Part-time: $220 per quarter hour. Fees: Full-time: $1090 per academic year. Average 1997–98 room and board costs were $8900 per academic year. Room and board costs vary by campus location, type of accommodation, type of meal plan.

Financial Aid In 1997–98, 20% of students received some institutionally administered aid in the form of scholarships. Financial aid is available to part-time students.

Financial Aid Contact Ms. Melissa Hofer, 333 9th Street SW, Huron, SD 57350-2798. Phone: 605-352-8721; Fax: 605-352-7421.

FACILITIES

Information Resources Ella McIntyre Library.

INTERNATIONAL STUDENTS

Demographics 70% of students enrolled are international students [Africa, 5%, Asia, 80%, other, 15%].

Services and Facilities International student office, international student center, international student housing, ESL courses.

Applying TOEFL, proof of adequate funds, proof of health/immunizations required. TSE, TWE recommended. Financial aid is not available to international students.

International Student Contact Ms. Marilyn Hoyt, International Student Director, 333 9th Street SW, Huron, SD 57350-2798. Phone: 605-352-8721; Fax: 605-352-7421.

Business Program(s) URL: http://www.huron.edu

Program Contact: MBA Admissions, 333 9th Street SW, Huron, SD 57350-2798. Phone: 605-352-8721; Fax: 605-352-7421.

University of South Dakota

School of Business

Vermillion, South Dakota

OVERVIEW

The University of South Dakota is a state-supported, coed university. Enrollment: 6,970 graduate, professional, and undergraduate students. Founded: 1862. The graduate business unit is in a small-town setting and is on a semester calendar.

HIGHLIGHTS

Enrollment Profile
Full-time: 82
Part-time: 137
Total: 219
Average Age: N/R
Fall 1997 Average GPA: 3.2

International: 5%
Women: 39%
Minorities: 3%
Average Class Size: 45
Fall 1997 Average GMAT: 518

Costs
Full-time tuition: N/R
Part-time tuition: $82 per credit (resident); $241 per credit (nonresident)

AACSB – The International Association for Management Education accredited

GRADUATE BUSINESS PROGRAMS

Master of Business Administration (MBA) Full-time, part-time; 33 total credits required; 12 months to 7 years to complete program. Concentrations in management, management information systems.

Master of Professional Accountancy (MPA) Full-time, part-time; 30 total credits required; 12 months to 7 years to complete program. Concentration in accounting.

ADMISSION

Application Requirements GMAT score: minimum 400, application form, application fee, bachelor's degree, minimum GPA: 2.7, 2 letters of recommendation, college transcript(s).

Recommended for Application Personal statement.

Application Deadline 7/15 for fall, 11/1 for spring, 3/15 for summer, 7/15 for fall (international), 11/1 for spring (international), 3/15 for summer (international). Application fee: $15. Deferred entrance is available.

ACADEMICS

Faculty Full-time 40.

Teaching Methodologies Case study, computer-aided instruction, computer analysis, computer simulations, faculty seminars, group discussion, lecture.

Technology 60 on-campus computer terminals/PCs are available for student use and are linked by a campus-wide network. The network has partial access to the Internet. Students are not required to have their own PC.

Special Opportunities Advanced credit may be earned through transfer of credits from another institution. An internship program is available.

FINANCES

Costs for 1997–98 Tuition: $82 per credit (resident); $241 per credit (nonresident). Cost varies by campus location, class time (e.g., day/evening), reciprocity agreements. Fees: $41 per credit (resident); $41 per credit (nonresident). Fees vary by campus location, class time (e.g., day/evening), reciprocity agreements. Average 1997–98 room and board costs were $2700 per academic year.

Financial Aid Research assistantships, work study available. Financial aid is available to part-time students.

University of South Dakota (continued)

Financial Aid Contact Clarence Schumacher, Director, 414 East Clark Street, Vermillion, SD 57069-2390. Phone: 605-677-5446; Fax: 605-677-5073.

FACILITIES
Information Resources I. D. Weeks Library plus 2 additional on-campus libraries; total holdings of 667,110 volumes, 645,989 microforms, 8,147 current periodical subscriptions. CD player(s) available for graduate student use. Access provided to online bibliographic retrieval services.

INTERNATIONAL STUDENTS
Demographics 5% of students enrolled are international students.

Services and Facilities International student office, visa services, counseling/support services.

Applying TOEFL: minimum score of 550, proof of adequate funds, proof of health/immunizations required. TWE recommended. Financial aid is not available to international students.

International Student Contact Clarisa Kaiser, International Student Advisor, 414 East Clark Street, Vermillion, SD 57069-2390. Phone: 605-677-6305; Fax: 605-677-5073.

PLACEMENT
Services include alumni network, career counseling/planning, career placement, electronic job bank, job interviews arranged, and resume referral to employers.

Business Program(s) URL: http://www.usd.edu

Program Contact: Diane Hoadley, Director, 414 East Clark Street, Vermillion, SD 57069-2390. Phone: 605-677-5232; Fax: 605-677-5058; E-mail: dhoadley@charlie.usd.edu

TENNESSEE

Belmont University

Jack C. Massey Graduate School of Business

Nashville, Tennessee

OVERVIEW
Belmont University is an independent-religious, coed, comprehensive institution. Enrollment: 2,960 graduate, professional, and undergraduate students. Founded: 1951. The graduate business unit is in an urban setting and is on a trimester calendar.

GRADUATE BUSINESS PROGRAMS
Evening MBA (MBA)

Evening Master of Accountancy (MAcc)

ACADEMICS
Faculty Full-time 11; part-time 13.

Teaching Methodologies Case study, computer-aided instruction, computer simulations, field projects, group discussion, lecture, research, seminars by members of the business community, student presentations, study groups, team projects.

Technology 120 on-campus computer terminals/PCs are available for student use and are linked by a campus-wide network. The network has full access to the Internet. Students are required to have their own PC.

Special Opportunities Advanced credit may be earned through transfer of credits from another institution. International exchange programs in France, Mexico, Russia. An internship program is available.

FACILITIES
Information Resources Lila D. Bunch Library; total holdings of 135,526 volumes, 10,203 microforms, 1,000 current periodical subscriptions. CD player(s) available for graduate student use. Access provided to online bibliographic retrieval services.

Program Contact: Director of Recruitment, 1900 Belmont Boulevard, Nashville, TN 37212-3757. Phone: 615-460-5574; Fax: 615-460-6455; E-mail: mckays@belmont.edu

Christian Brothers University

School of Business

Memphis, Tennessee

OVERVIEW
Christian Brothers University is an independent-religious, coed, comprehensive institution. Enrollment: 1,820 graduate, professional, and undergraduate students; 43 full-time matriculated graduate/professional students; 255 part-time matriculated graduate/professional students. Founded: 1871. The graduate business unit is in an urban setting and is on a semester calendar.

HIGHLIGHTS

Enrollment Profile

Full-time: 43	International: 0%
Part-time: 163	Women: 44%
Total: 206	Minorities: 20%
Average Age: 31	Average Class Size: 17
Fall 1997 Average GPA: 2.98	Fall 1997 Average GMAT: 520

Costs
Full-time tuition: N/R
Part-time tuition: $325 per credit hour

GRADUATE BUSINESS PROGRAMS
Master of Business Administration (MBA) Full-time, part-time; 30 total credits required; 12 months to 5 years to complete program. Concentrations in accounting, finance, management, marketing, information management, strategic management, health care.

Executive MBA (MBA) Full-time; 51 total credits required; 20 months to complete program. Concentrations in information management, strategic management, health care.

ADMISSION
Applications For fall 1997 there were 171 applications for admission. Of those applying, 122 were accepted. Of those accepted, 94 enrolled.

Application Requirements Application form, application fee, bachelor's degree, minimum GPA: 2.0, 2 letters of recommendation.

Recommended for Application GMAT score accepted: minimum 450, computer experience.

Application Deadline Applications processed on a rolling/continuous basis for both domestic and international students. Application fee: $25. Deferred entrance is available.

ACADEMICS
Faculty Full-time 19; part-time 4.

Teaching Methodologies Case study, computer-aided instruction, computer analysis, computer simulations, group discussion, lecture, research, seminars by members of the business community, simulations, student presentations, study groups, team projects.

Technology 150 on-campus computer terminals/PCs are available for student use and are linked by a campus-wide network. The network has full access to the Internet. Students are not required to have their own PC.

Special Opportunities Advanced credit may be earned through transfer of credits from another institution.

FINANCES
Costs for 1997–98 Tuition: $325 per credit hour. Cost varies by academic program. Fees: $30 per semester. Fees vary by academic program. Average 1997–98 room and board costs were $5600 per academic year.

Financial Aid Loans available. Financial aid is available to part-time students.

Financial Aid Contact Mr. Jim Shannon, Student Financial Resources Director, 650 East Parkway South, Memphis, TN 38104-5581. Phone: 901-321-3306; Fax: 901-321-3494; E-mail: ushannon@cbu.edu

FACILITIES
Information Resources Plough Library; total holdings of 95,600 volumes, 1,313 microforms, 590 current periodical subscriptions. CD player(s) available for graduate student use. Access provided to online bibliographic retrieval services.

INTERNATIONAL STUDENTS
Demographics 0% of students enrolled are international students.

Applying TOEFL: minimum score of 550, proof of adequate funds required. Proof of health/immunizations recommended. Financial aid is not available to international students.

PLACEMENT
Services include career counseling/planning, career fairs, career library, career placement, job interviews arranged, resume referral to employers, and resume preparation.

Employment Of 1996–97 graduates, 100% were employed within three months of graduation.

Business Program(s) URL: http://www.cbu.edu/business/

Program Contact: Mr. James Rhodes, Director, MBA Program, 650 East Parkway South, Memphis, TN 38104-5581. Phone: 901-321-3317; Fax: 901-321-3566; E-mail: jtrhodes@cbu.edu

Cumberland University

Business and Economics Division

Lebanon, Tennessee

OVERVIEW
Cumberland University is an independent-nonprofit, coed, comprehensive institution. Enrollment: 1,150 graduate, professional, and undergraduate students; 30 full-time matriculated graduate/professional students; 125 part-time matriculated graduate/professional students. Founded: 1842. The graduate business unit is in a small-town setting and is on a trimester calendar.

HIGHLIGHTS

Enrollment Profile
Full-time: 1
Part-time: 60
Total: 61
Average Age: 33
Fall 1997 Average GPA: 3.1

International: 3%
Women: 33%
Minorities: 7%
Average Class Size: 15
Fall 1997 Average GMAT: 480

Costs
Full-time tuition: N/R
Part-time tuition: $465 per hour

GRADUATE BUSINESS PROGRAMS
Master of Business Administration (MBA) Full-time, part-time; 36 total credits required; 3 to 4 years to complete program.

ADMISSION
Applications For fall 1997 there were 30 applications for admission. Of those applying, 26 were accepted. Of those accepted, 25 enrolled.

Application Requirements Application form, application fee, bachelor's degree, minimum GPA, 3 letters of recommendation, college transcript(s), minimum of 1 year of work experience.

Recommended for Application GMAT score accepted, GRE score accepted, interview, resume.

Application Deadline 8/10 for fall, 1/3 for spring, 5/9 for summer, 8/10 for fall (international), 1/3 for spring (international), 5/9 for summer (international). Application fee: $50. Deferred entrance is available.

ACADEMICS
Faculty Full-time 9; part-time 1.

Teaching Methodologies Case study, computer-aided instruction, computer analysis, computer simulations, experiential learning, field projects, group discussion, lecture, research, role playing, seminars by members of the business community, simulations, student presentations, study groups, team projects.

Technology 65 on-campus computer terminals/PCs are available for student use and are linked by a campus-wide network. The network has full access to the Internet. Students are required to have their own PC.

Special Opportunities Advanced credit may be earned through transfer of credits from another institution.

FINANCES
Costs for 1997–98 Tuition: $465 per hour. Fees: $55 per program. Average 1997–98 room and board costs were $4000 per academic year. Room and board costs vary by occupancy (e.g., single, double, triple), type of meal plan.

Financial Aid In 1997–98, 16% of students received some institutionally administered aid in the form of research assistantships, work study, loans. Financial aid is available to part-time students. Application Deadline: 8/10.

Financial Aid Contact Mr. Larry Vaughan, Financial Aid Office, South Greenwood Street, Lebanon, TN 37087-3554. Phone: 615-444-2562 Ext. 222; Fax: 615-444-2569.

FACILITIES
Information Resources Vise Library; total holdings of 50,000 volumes, 800 microforms, 1,000 current periodical subscriptions. CD player(s) available for graduate student use. Access provided to online bibliographic retrieval services.

INTERNATIONAL STUDENTS
Demographics 3% of students enrolled are international students [Africa, 50%, Asia, 50%].

Services and Facilities Counseling/support services.

Applying Proof of adequate funds, proof of health/immunizations required. Financial aid is not available to international students.

International Student Contact Ms. Pace Pope, South Greenwood Street, Lebanon, TN 37087-3554. Phone: 615-444-2562; Fax: 615-444-2569.

PLACEMENT
Services include career counseling/planning, career fairs, career library, and resume preparation. In 1996–97, 5 organizations participated in on-campus recruiting; 10 on-campus interviews were conducted.

Employment Of 1996–97 graduates, 100% were employed within three months of graduation.

Business Program(s) URL: http://www.cumberland.edu

Program Contact: Dr. Jack Forrest, Coordinator, MBA Program, One Cumberland Square, Lebanon, TN 37087. Phone: 615-444-2562 Ext. 1263, 800-467-0562; Fax: 615-444-2569; E-mail: jeforrest@cumberland.edu

East Tennessee State University

College of Business

Johnson City, Tennessee

OVERVIEW
East Tennessee State University is a state-supported, coed university. Enrollment: 11,347 graduate, professional, and undergraduate students; 292 full-time matriculated graduate/professional students; 1,779 part-time matriculated graduate/professional students. Founded: 1911. The graduate business unit is in an urban setting and is on a semester calendar.

HIGHLIGHTS

Enrollment Profile
Full-time: 55
Part-time: 156
Total: 211
Average Age: 32
Fall 1997 Average GPA: 3.1

International: 9%
Women: 43%
Minorities: 14%
Average Class Size: 17
Fall 1997 Average GMAT: 528

Costs
Full-time tuition: $1183 per academic year (resident); $3351 per academic year (nonresident)
Part-time tuition: $119 per credit hour (resident); $309 per credit hour (nonresident)

AACSB – The International Association for Management Education accredited

GRADUATE BUSINESS PROGRAMS
Master of Business Administration (MBA) Full-time, part-time, distance learning option; 39 total credits required; 16 months to 6 years to complete program.

Master of Accounting (MAcc) Full-time, part-time, distance learning option; 33 total credits required; 12 months to 6 years to complete program. Concentration in accounting.

Master of Public Management (MPM) Full-time, part-time, distance learning option; 45 total credits required; 20 months to 6 years to complete program. Concentrations in city/urban administration, public management, public policy and administration.

ADMISSION
Applications For fall 1997 there were 132 applications for admission. Of those applying, 82 were accepted. Of those accepted, 65 enrolled.

Application Requirements Application form, application fee, bachelor's degree, essay, minimum GPA: 2.5, letters of recommendation, personal statement, college transcript(s), computer experience: word processing, spreadsheet.

Recommended for Application GMAT score accepted: minimum 450, GRE score accepted, minimum of 2 years of work experience.

Application Deadline 6/1 for fall, 11/1 for spring, 5/1 for fall (international), 10/1 for spring (international). Application fee: $25, $35 (international). Deferred entrance is available.

ACADEMICS
Faculty Full-time 37.

Teaching Methodologies Case study, computer-aided instruction, computer analysis, computer simulations, experiential learning, faculty seminars, field projects, group discussion, lecture, research, role playing, seminars by members of the business community, simulations, student presentations, study groups, team projects.

Technology 500 on-campus computer terminals/PCs are available for student use and are linked by a campus-wide network. The network has full access to the Internet. Students are not required to have their own PC.

Special Opportunities Advanced credit may be earned through transfer of credits from another institution.

East Tennessee State University (continued)

FINANCES

Costs for 1997–98 Tuition: Full-time: $1183 per semester (resident); $3351 per semester (nonresident). Part-time: $119 per credit hour (resident); $309 per credit hour (nonresident). Cost varies by number of credits taken. Fees: Full-time: $124 per academic year (resident); $124 per academic year (nonresident). Part-time: $49 per semester (resident); $49 per semester (nonresident). Fees vary by number of credits taken. Average 1997–98 room and board costs were $4100 per academic year. Room and board costs vary by campus location, occupancy (e.g., single, double, triple), type of accommodation.

Financial Aid In 1997–98, 23% of students received some institutionally administered aid in the form of research assistantships, scholarships. Application Deadline: 8/15.

Financial Aid Contact Ms. Margaret Miller, Director of Financial Aid, PO Box 70722, Johnson City, TN 37614. Phone: 423-439-4300; E-mail: finaid@etsu.edu

FACILITIES

Information Resources Sherrod Library plus 2 additional on-campus libraries; total holdings of 617,847 volumes, 1,137,565 microforms, 4,000 current periodical subscriptions. CD player(s) available for graduate student use. Access provided to online bibliographic retrieval services and online databases.

INTERNATIONAL STUDENTS

Demographics 9% of students enrolled are international students [Asia, 80%, Europe, 20%].

Services and Facilities International student office, visa services, ESL courses, counseling/support services.

Applying TOEFL: minimum score of 550, proof of adequate funds, proof of health/immunizations required. Financial aid is available to international students.

International Student Contact Henry Antkiewicz, International Student Director, PO Box 70668, Johnson City, TN 37614. Phone: 423-439-4429; Fax: 423-439-7131.

PLACEMENT

Services include alumni network, career counseling/planning, career placement, electronic job bank, job interviews arranged, resume referral to employers, and resume preparation.

Employment Of 1996–97 graduates, 80% were employed within three months of graduation. Types of employment entered: accounting, banking, chemical industry, communications, consulting, consumer products, education, finance, financial services, government, health services, human resources, insurance, management, marketing, media, nonprofit, pharmaceutical, transportation.

Business Program(s) URL: http://www.business.etsu.edu

Program Contact: Dr. Ronald Green, Director of Graduate Studies for the College of Business, PO Box 70699, Johnson City, TN 37614. Phone: 423-439-5314; Fax: 423-439-5274; E-mail: greenr@etsu.edu

Lincoln Memorial University

DeBusk School of Business

Harrogate, Tennessee

OVERVIEW

Lincoln Memorial University is an independent-nonprofit, coed, comprehensive institution. Enrollment: 2,003 graduate, professional, and undergraduate students; 84 full-time matriculated graduate/professional students; 338 part-time matriculated graduate/professional students. Founded: 1897. The graduate business unit is on a semester calendar.

HIGHLIGHTS

Enrollment Profile
Full-time: 8
Part-time: 41
Total: 49
Average Age: 27
Fall 1997 Average GPA: N/R

International: 4%
Women: 39%
Minorities: N/R
Average Class Size: N/R
Fall 1997 Average GMAT: N/R

Costs
Full-time tuition: N/R
Part-time tuition: $210 per semester hour

GRADUATE BUSINESS PROGRAMS

Master of Business Administration in Management (MBA) Full-time, part-time; 36 total credits required; 18 months to 7 years to complete program.

ADMISSION

Application Requirements GMAT score, application form, application fee, bachelor's degree, essay, minimum GPA, interview, 3 letters of recommendation, college transcript(s).

Application Deadline Applications processed on a rolling/continuous basis for both domestic and international students. Application fee: $25.

ACADEMICS

Faculty Full-time 4.

Teaching Methodologies Case study, computer-aided instruction, faculty seminars, field projects, group discussion, lecture, research, role playing, seminars by members of the business community, simulations, student presentations, study groups, team projects.

FINANCES

Costs for 1997–98 Tuition: $210 per semester hour. Fees: $50 per semester.

Financial Aid In 1997–98, 14% of students received some institutionally administered aid in the form of loans. Financial aid is available to part-time students. Application Deadline: 4/1.

Financial Aid Contact Mrs. Brenda Rector, Financial Aid, Cumberland Gap Parkway, Harrogate, TN 37752. Phone: 800-325-2506.

FACILITIES

Information Resources Bert Vincent Memorial Library; total holdings of 89,168 volumes, 17,202 microforms, 460 current periodical subscriptions. Access provided to online bibliographic retrieval services.

INTERNATIONAL STUDENTS

Demographics 4% of students enrolled are international students.

Applying TOEFL: minimum score of 500, proof of adequate funds, proof of health/immunizations required.

International Student Contact Mr. Conrad Daniels, Dean of Admissions, Cumberland Gap Parkway, Harrogate, TN 37752. Phone: 423-869-6279.

PLACEMENT

Services include career counseling/planning.

Employment Types of employment entered: management.

Program Contact: Dr. Fred Bedelle, Dean, School of Graduate Studies, Cumberland Gap Parkway, Harrogate, TN 37752. 800-325-0900 (TN only), and/or 800-325-2506 (TN only)

Middle Tennessee State University

College of Business

Murfreesboro, Tennessee

OVERVIEW

Middle Tennessee State University is a state-supported, coed university. Enrollment: 17,975 graduate, professional, and undergraduate students; 197 full-time matriculated graduate/professional students; 1,587 part-time matriculated graduate/professional students. Founded: 1911. The graduate business unit is in a small-town setting and is on a semester calendar.

HIGHLIGHTS

Enrollment Profile
Full-time: 63
Part-time: 388
Total: 451
Average Age: 30
Fall 1997 Average GPA: 2.6

International: N/R
Women: 42%
Minorities: 16%
Average Class Size: 27
Fall 1997 Average GMAT: 496

Costs
Full-time tuition: $2560 per academic year (resident); $7386 per academic year (nonresident)
Part-time tuition: $129 per credit hour (resident); $340 per credit hour (nonresident)

AACSB – The International Association for Management Education accredited

GRADUATE BUSINESS PROGRAMS

Master of Business Administration (MBA) Full-time, part-time, distance learning option; 36 total credits required; 12 months to 6 years to complete program.

Master of Science in Accounting and Information Systems (MS) Full-time, part-time, distance learning option; 30 total credits required; 12 months to 6 years to complete program. Concentrations in accounting, management information systems.

Master of Arts in Economics (MA) Full-time, part-time; 33 total credits required; 12 months to 6 years to complete program. Concentrations in economics, industrial/labor relations.

ADMISSION

Application Requirements GMAT score, application form, application fee, bachelor's degree, minimum GPA, college transcript(s).

Application Deadline Applications processed on a rolling/continuous basis for domestic students only. 5/1 for fall (international), 9/1 for spring (international), 2/1 for summer (international). Application fee: $25, $30 (international).

ACADEMICS

Faculty Full-time 62; part-time 1.

Teaching Methodologies Case study, computer-aided instruction, group discussion, lecture, student presentations, team projects.

Technology 98 on-campus computer terminals/PCs are available for student use and are linked by a campus-wide network. The network has full access to the Internet. Students are not required to have their own PC.

Special Opportunities Advanced credit may be earned through transfer of credits from another institution. International exchange programs in Ecuador, France. An internship program is available.

FINANCES

Costs for 1997–98 Tuition: Full-time: $2560 per year (resident); $7386 per year (nonresident). Part-time: $129 per credit hour (resident); $340 per credit hour (nonresident). Fees: Full-time: $308 per academic year (resident); $308 per academic year (nonresident). Part-time: $50 per course (resident); $50 per course (nonresident). Average 1997–98 room only costs were $2600 per academic year (off campus). Room and board costs vary by type of accommodation, type of meal plan.

Financial Aid In 1997–98, 9% of students received some institutionally administered aid in the form of teaching assistantships. Application Deadline: 5/1.

Financial Aid Contact Financial Aid Office, MTSU Box 290, Murfreesboro, TN 37132. Phone: 615-898-2830; Fax: 615-898-4736.

FACILITIES

Information Resources Todd Library; total holdings of 59,676 volumes, 1,064,646 microforms, 3,520 current periodical subscriptions. CD player(s) available for graduate student use. Access provided to online bibliographic retrieval services.

INTERNATIONAL STUDENTS

Demographics N/R

Services and Facilities International student office, counseling/support services.

Applying TOEFL: minimum score of 525, proof of adequate funds, proof of health/immunizations required. Financial aid is available to international students.

International Student Contact Dr. Tech Wubneh, Director, International Programs and Services Office, 202 Cope Administration Building, Murfreesboro, TN 37132. Phone: 615-898-2238; Fax: 615-898-5178.

PLACEMENT

Services include career counseling/planning, career fairs, career library, career placement, job interviews arranged, resume referral to employers, and resume preparation. In 1996–97, 228 organizations participated in on-campus recruiting; 1,000 on-campus interviews were conducted.

Employment Types of employment entered: accounting, banking, finance, financial services.

Program Contact: Dr. Troy Festervand, Director, Graduate Business Studies, MTSU Box 290, Murfreesboro, TN 37132. Phone: 615-898-2964; Fax: 615-898-4736.

Rhodes College

Department of Economics and Business Administration

Memphis, Tennessee

OVERVIEW

Rhodes College is an independent-religious, comprehensive institution. Enrollment: 1,432 graduate, professional, and undergraduate students.

HIGHLIGHTS

Enrollment Profile

Full-time: 12	International: 0%
Part-time: 0	Women: 42%
Total: 12	Minorities: 8%
Average Age: N/R	Average Class Size: N/R
Fall 1997 Average GPA: N/R	Fall 1997 Average GMAT: N/R

Costs
Full-time tuition: $17,363 per academic year
Part-time tuition: N/R

GRADUATE BUSINESS PROGRAMS

Master of Science in Accounting (MS) Full-time, part-time; 30 total credits required; minimum of 12 months to complete program.

ADMISSION

Application Requirements GMAT score, application form, bachelor's degree, minimum GPA, 2 letters of recommendation, college transcript(s).

Recommended for Application Computer experience.

Application Deadline 3/1 for fall, 3/1 for fall (international).

ACADEMICS

Teaching Methodologies Case study, computer-aided instruction, group discussion, lecture, team projects.

FINANCES

Costs for 1997–98 Tuition: Full-time: $17,363 per year.

Financial Aid Contact Financial Aid Office, Memphis, TN 38112-1690. Phone: 901-843-3810.

INTERNATIONAL STUDENTS

Demographics N/R

Services and Facilities International student office, international student housing, visa services, ESL courses, counseling/support services.

Applying TOEFL: minimum score of 550 required.

International Student Contact Katharine Owen-Richardson, Director of International Programs, Memphis, TN 38112-1690. Phone: 901-843-3403.

PLACEMENT

Services include alumni network, career counseling/planning, career fairs, career placement, electronic job bank, job interviews arranged, job search course, resume referral to employers, and resume preparation.

Employment Types of employment entered: accounting.

Program Contact: Pam Church, Director of Accounting, Memphis, TN 38112-1690. Phone: 901-843-3863.

Tennessee State University

College of Business

Nashville, Tennessee

OVERVIEW

Tennessee State University is a state-supported, coed, comprehensive institution. Enrollment: 8,000 graduate, professional, and undergraduate students. Founded: 1912. The graduate business unit is in an urban setting and is on a semester calendar.

HIGHLIGHTS

Enrollment Profile

Full-time: 40	International: 16%
Part-time: 120	Women: 38%
Total: 160	Minorities: 11%
Average Age: 30	Average Class Size: 20
Fall 1997 Average GPA: 2.8	Fall 1997 Average GMAT: 520

Costs
Full-time tuition: N/R
Part-time tuition: $134 per credit (resident); $335 per credit (nonresident)

AACSB – The International Association for Management Education accredited

GRADUATE BUSINESS PROGRAMS

Master of Business Administration (MBA) Full-time, part-time; 34 total credits required; 9 months to 6 years to complete program.

ADMISSION

Applications For fall 1997 there were 130 applications for admission. Of those applying, 70 were accepted.

Application Requirements GMAT score, application form, application fee, bachelor's degree, minimum GPA: 2.0, college transcript(s).

Application Deadline Applications processed on a rolling/continuous basis for both domestic and international students. Application fee: $25. Deferred entrance is available.

ACADEMICS

Faculty Full-time 24; part-time 1.

Teaching Methodologies Case study, computer analysis, group discussion, lecture, seminars by members of the business community, student presentations, team projects.

Technology 48 on-campus computer terminals/PCs are available for student use and are linked by a campus-wide network. The network has full access to the Internet. Students are not required to have their own PC.

Special Opportunities Advanced credit may be earned through transfer of credits from another institution.

FINANCES

Costs for 1997–98 Tuition: $134 per credit (resident); $335 per credit (nonresident). Average 1997–98 room and board costs were $3000 per academic year. Room and board costs vary by occupancy (e.g., single, double, triple), type of meal plan.

Financial Aid In 1997–98, 6% of students received some institutionally administered aid in the form of research assistantships, work study. Financial aid is available to part-time students. Application Deadline: 6/1.

Financial Aid Contact Mr. Wilson Lee, Director of Financial Aid, 3500 John A. Merritt Boulevard, Nashville, TN 37209-1561. Phone: 615-963-5000; Fax: 615-963-7412.

FACILITIES

Information Resources Brown-Daniel Library; total holdings of 407,717 volumes, 14,428 microforms, 1,259 current periodical subscriptions. CD player(s) available for graduate student use. Access provided to online bibliographic retrieval services.

INTERNATIONAL STUDENTS

Demographics 16% of students enrolled are international students [Africa, 5%, Asia, 90%, other, 5%].

Services and Facilities International student office, counseling/support services.

Applying TOEFL: minimum score of 500 required. Financial aid is available to international students.

International Student Contact Mrs. Shirley Wingfield, Student Advisor, 3500 John A. Merritt Boulevard, Nashville, TN 37209-1561. Phone: 615-963-5000; Fax: 615-963-7412.

PLACEMENT

Services include career counseling/planning, career fairs, and job interviews arranged.

Employment Types of employment entered: banking, consumer products, telecommunications.

Program Contact: Dr. George Bruce Hartmann, MBA Coordinator, School of Business, 3500 John A. Merritt Boulevard, Nashville, TN 37209-1561. Phone: 615-963-7146; Fax: 615-963-7139.

Tennessee Technological University

College of Business Administration

Cookeville, Tennessee

OVERVIEW

Tennessee Technological University is a state-supported, coed university. Enrollment: 8,244 graduate, professional, and undergraduate students. Founded: 1915. The graduate business unit is in a small-town setting and is on a semester calendar.

HIGHLIGHTS

Enrollment Profile
Full-time: 68
Part-time: 74
Total: 142
Average Age: 26
Fall 1997 Average GPA: 3.2

International: 9%
Women: 42%
Minorities: 8%
Average Class Size: 25
Fall 1997 Average GMAT: 525

Costs
Full-time tuition: N/R
Part-time tuition: $138 per hour (resident); $211 per hour (nonresident)

AACSB – The International Association for Management Education accredited

GRADUATE BUSINESS PROGRAMS

Master of Business Administration (MBA) Full-time, part-time; 36 total credits required; 12 months to 6 years to complete program. Concentrations in management, accounting, management information systems.

ADMISSION

Application Requirements GMAT score: minimum 500, application form, application fee, bachelor's degree, minimum GPA: 2.5, 3 letters of recommendation, college transcript(s).

Recommended for Application Interview, computer experience.

Application Deadline Applications processed on a rolling/continuous basis for domestic students only. 5/1 for fall (international), 10/1 for spring (international), 3/1 for summer (international). Application fee: $25, $30 (international). Deferred entrance is available.

ACADEMICS

Faculty Full-time 28.

Teaching Methodologies Case study, computer-aided instruction, computer analysis, computer simulations, experiential learning, faculty seminars, field projects, group discussion, lecture, research, role playing, seminars by members of the business community, simulations, student presentations, study groups, team projects.

Technology 201 on-campus computer terminals/PCs are available for student use and are linked by a campus-wide network. The network has full access to the Internet. Students are not required to have their own PC.

Special Opportunities Advanced credit may be earned through transfer of credits from another institution.

FINANCES

Costs for 1997–98 Tuition: $138 per hour (resident); $211 per hour (nonresident). Cost varies by number of credits taken. Fees vary by number of credits taken. Average 1997–98 room and board costs were $4300 per academic year (on campus) and $5000 per academic year (off campus). Room and board costs vary by occupancy (e.g., single, double, triple), type of accommodation, type of meal plan.

Financial Aid In 1997–98, 38% of students received some institutionally administered aid in the form of fellowships, research assistantships, teaching assistantships, scholarships. Financial aid is available to part-time students. Application Deadline: 4/1.

Financial Aid Contact Dr. Virginia Moore, Assistant Dean and Director of MBA Studies, North Dixie Avenue, Cookeville, TN 38505. Phone: 931-372-3600; Fax: 931-372-6249; E-mail: mbastudies@tntech.edu

FACILITIES

Information Resources University Library; total holdings of 1,000,000 volumes. CD player(s) available for graduate student use. Access provided to online bibliographic retrieval services.

INTERNATIONAL STUDENTS

Demographics 9% of students enrolled are international students.

Services and Facilities International student office, visa services, ESL courses.

Applying TOEFL: minimum score of 550, proof of adequate funds, proof of health/immunizations required. Financial aid is available to international students.

International Student Contact Ms. Caroline Dudney, Director of International Student Affairs, North Dixie Avenue, Cookeville, TN 38505. Phone: 931-372-3634; Fax: 931-372-6249.

PLACEMENT

Services include alumni network, career counseling/planning, career fairs, career library, career placement, electronic job bank, job interviews arranged, resume referral to employers, and resume preparation. In 1996–97, 85 organizations participated in on-campus recruiting; 570 on-campus interviews were conducted.

Employment Of 1996–97 graduates, 95% were employed within three months of graduation; the average starting salary was $35,000. Types of employment entered: accounting, banking, chemical industry, communications, computer-related, consulting, consumer products, education, energy, engineering, finance, financial services, government, health services, high technology, hospitality management, human resources, information systems/technology, insurance, international trade, management, manufacturing, marketing, media, mining, nonprofit, petrochemical, pharmaceutical, real estate, retail, service industry, telecommunications, transportation, utilities.

Business Program(s) URL: http://www.tntech.edu/www/acad/cob/

Program Contact: Dr. Virginia Moore, Assistant Dean and Director of MBA Studies, North Dixie Avenue, Cookeville, TN 38505. Phone: 931-372-3600; Fax: 931-372-6249; E-mail: mbastudies@tntech.edu

Trevecca Nazarene University

Major in Organizational Management

Nashville, Tennessee

OVERVIEW
Trevecca Nazarene University is an independent-religious, coed, comprehensive institution. Enrollment: 1,358 graduate, professional, and undergraduate students; 329 full-time matriculated graduate/professional students; 56 part-time matriculated graduate/professional students. Founded: 1901.

HIGHLIGHTS

Enrollment Profile
Full-time: 67
Part-time: 0
Total: 67
Average Age: 34
Fall 1997 Average GPA: 3.03

International: 0%
Women: 45%
Minorities: 25%
Average Class Size: N/R
Fall 1997 Average GMAT: 416

Costs
Full-time tuition: N/R
Part-time tuition: $287 per credit hour

GRADUATE BUSINESS PROGRAMS
Master of Arts in Organizational Management (MA) Full-time; 38 total credits required; up to 20 months to complete program.

ADMISSION
Application Requirements GMAT score, application form, application fee, bachelor's degree, essay, minimum GPA: 2.5, 3 letters of recommendation, resume, college transcript(s).
Recommended for Application Work experience.
Application Deadline Applications processed on a rolling/continuous basis for both domestic and international students. Application fee: $25.

ACADEMICS
Teaching Methodologies Case study, computer-aided instruction, computer analysis, group discussion, lecture, role playing, seminars by members of the business community, student presentations, team projects.

FINANCES
Costs for 1997–98 Tuition: $287 per credit hour.
Financial Aid Contact Bonnie Deese, Financial Aid, 333 Murfreesboro Road, Nashville, TN 37210-2834. Phone: 615-248-1340.

FACILITIES
Information Resources Mackey Library; total holdings of 89,917 volumes, 204,243 microforms, 1,128 current periodical subscriptions. CD player(s) available for graduate student use. Access provided to online bibliographic retrieval services.

INTERNATIONAL STUDENTS
Demographics N/R
Applying TOEFL: minimum score of 500 required.

PLACEMENT
Services include career counseling/planning, career library, career placement, job interviews arranged, job search course, resume referral to employers, and resume preparation.
Employment Types of employment entered: management.

Program Contact: Ms. Charmion Richards, Assistant to the Director, 333 Murfreesboro Road, Nashville, TN 37210-2834. Phone: 615-248-1308; Fax: 615-248-1700; E-mail: crichards@trevecca.edu

Tusculum College

Program in Applied Organizational Management

Greeneville, Tennessee

OVERVIEW
Tusculum College is an independent-religious, coed, comprehensive institution. Enrollment: 1,516 graduate, professional, and undergraduate students; 470 full-time matriculated graduate/professional students; 4 part-time matriculated graduate/professional students. Founded: 1794. The graduate business unit is in a small-town setting and is on a 18-month program calendar.

HIGHLIGHTS

Enrollment Profile
Full-time: 80
Part-time: 1
Total: 81
Average Age: N/R
Fall 1997 Average GPA: N/R

International: 0%
Women: 51%
Minorities: 10%
Average Class Size: 13
Fall 1997 Average GMAT: N/R

Costs
Full-time tuition: N/R
Part-time tuition: $240 per credit hour

GRADUATE BUSINESS PROGRAMS
Master of Arts in Organizational Management (MA) Full-time, part-time; 36 total credits required; 18 months to 5 years to complete program. Concentration in organizational management.

ADMISSION
Applications For fall 1997 there were 107 applications for admission.
Application Requirements GMAT score, GRE score, MAT score, application form, bachelor's degree, essay, minimum GPA: 2.75, 2 letters of recommendation, resume, college transcript(s), minimum of 3 years of work experience.
Recommended for Application Computer experience.
Application Deadline Applications processed on a rolling/continuous basis for both domestic and international students. Deferred entrance is available.

ACADEMICS
Faculty Full-time 4; part-time 14.
Teaching Methodologies Case study, computer-aided instruction, computer simulations, faculty seminars, field projects, group discussion, lecture, research, role playing, seminars by members of the business community, simulations, student presentations, study groups, team projects.
Technology 34 on-campus computer terminals/PCs are available for student use. The network has full access to the Internet. Students are not required to have their own PC.

FINANCES
Costs for 1997–98 Tuition: $240 per credit hour. Cost varies by academic program, class time (e.g., day/evening), number of credits taken.
Financial Aid Loans available.
Financial Aid Contact Pat Shannon, Assistant Director of Financial Aid, PO Box 5049, Greeneville, TN 37743-9997. Phone: 423-636-7300 Ext. 376; Fax: 423-638-7166; E-mail: bpowers@tusculum.edu

FACILITIES
Information Resources Albert Columbus Tate Library; total holdings of 70,500 volumes, 163,266 microforms, 500 current periodical subscriptions. CD player(s) available for graduate student use. Access provided to online bibliographic retrieval services.

INTERNATIONAL STUDENTS
Demographics N/R
Applying TOEFL: minimum score of 550 required.

PLACEMENT
Services include alumni network, career counseling/planning, resume referral to employers, and resume preparation.

Business Program(s) URL: http://www.tusculum.edu

Program Contact: Mr. Don Stout, Executive Director, PO Box 5689, Greeneville, TN 37743-9997. Phone: 423-636-7330; Fax: 423-638-5181; E-mail: dstout@tusculum.edu

Union University

McAfee School of Business Administration

Jackson, Tennessee

OVERVIEW
Union University is an independent-religious, coed, comprehensive institution. Enrollment: 1,995 graduate, professional, and undergraduate students. Founded: 1825. The graduate business unit is in a small-town setting and is on a 8 week courses calendar.

HIGHLIGHTS

Enrollment Profile
Full-time: 62
Part-time: 13
Total: 75
Average Age: N/R
Fall 1997 Average GPA: N/R

International: 1%
Women: 35%
Minorities: N/R
Average Class Size: 22
Fall 1997 Average GMAT: 512

Costs
Full-time tuition: $10,175 per academic year
Part-time tuition: N/R

Located in west Tennessee, Union University is a small, independent Southern Baptist coeducational institution that offers the M.B.A. on both its Jackson and Germantown campuses. Union has a tradition of academic excellence at both the undergraduate and graduate level.

The Union M.B.A. is designed to meet the needs of students who must continue their full-time careers while obtaining the M.B.A. A cohort format is used, whereby students take all the same courses together in lock-step fashion. A new cohort begins each August and February with approximately 20–30 students. The entire program is scheduled in advance. The classes meet one night per week for 4 hours for approximately twenty-four months. There are no prerequisites for students with at least two years of relevant work experience. Students without work experience must take a core of undergraduate business courses.

The M.B.A. courses incorporate case studies, team projects, research, and class discussion as well as lecture for maximum learning potential.

All courses are taught by full-time Union University faculty members. No adjuncts are used, and no video or audio instruction is used in place of full-time faculty members.

GRADUATE BUSINESS PROGRAMS
Master of Business Administration (MBA) Full-time; 37 total credits required; 2 years to complete program. Concentration in management.

ADMISSION
Application Requirements GMAT score: minimum 400, application form, application fee, bachelor's degree, minimum GPA, college transcript(s).

Recommended for Application Minimum of 2 years of work experience, computer experience.

Application Deadline Applications processed on a rolling/continuous basis for both domestic and international students. Application fee: $25, $50 (international). Deferred entrance is available.

ACADEMICS
Faculty Full-time 10.

Teaching Methodologies Case study, group discussion, lecture, research, student presentations, study groups, team projects.

Technology 80 on-campus computer terminals/PCs are available for student use and are linked by a campus-wide network. The network has full access to the Internet. Students are not required to have their own PC.

Special Opportunities Advanced credit may be earned through transfer of credits from another institution.

FINANCES
Costs for 1997–98 Tuition: Full-time: $10,175 per program. Cost varies by number of credits taken. Fees vary by number of credits taken. Average 1997–98 room and board costs were $4180 per academic year. Room and board costs vary by campus location, occupancy (e.g., single, double, triple), type of accommodation, type of meal plan.

Financial Aid Loans available.

Financial Aid Contact Mr. Don Morris, Assistant Vice President and Director of Financial Aid, 1050 Union University Drive, Jackson, TN 38305. Phone: 901-661-5015; Fax: 901-661-5366; E-mail: dmorris@buster.uu.edu

FACILITIES
Information Resources Emma Waters Summar Library; total holdings of 126,361 volumes, 317,376 microforms, 1,106 current periodical subscriptions. CD player(s) available for graduate student use. Access provided to online bibliographic retrieval services and online databases.

INTERNATIONAL STUDENTS
Demographics 1% of students enrolled are international students [South America, 100%].

Services and Facilities ESL courses, counseling/support services.

Applying TOEFL: minimum score of 600, proof of adequate funds, proof of health/immunizations required. Financial aid is not available to international students.

PLACEMENT
Services include career counseling/planning, career fairs, career library, career placement, job interviews arranged, resume referral to employers, and resume preparation.

Business Program(s) URL: http://www.uu.edu/union/academ/GRADUATE/MBA/Index.htm

Program Contact: Mrs. Debbie Newell, MBA Director, 1050 Union University Drive, Jackson, TN 38305. Phone: 901-661-5363; Fax: 901-661-5366; E-mail: dnewell@buster.uu.edu

The University of Memphis

Fogelman College of Business and Economics

Memphis, Tennessee

OVERVIEW
The University of Memphis is a state-supported, coed university. Enrollment: 19,851 graduate, professional, and undergraduate students; 2,339 full-time matriculated graduate/professional students; 2,735 part-time matriculated graduate/professional students. Founded: 1912. The graduate business unit is in a suburban setting and is on a semester calendar.

HIGHLIGHTS

Enrollment Profile
Full-time: 393
Part-time: 368
Total: 761
Average Age: 29
Fall 1997 Average GPA: 3.2

International: N/R
Women: 34%
Minorities: 12%
Average Class Size: 25
Fall 1997 Average GMAT: 535

Costs
Full-time tuition: $2630 per academic year (resident); $6940 per academic year (nonresident)
Part-time tuition: $130 per credit hour (resident); $321 per credit hour (nonresident)

AACSB – The International Association for Management Education accredited

GRADUATE BUSINESS PROGRAMS
Master of Business Administration (MBA) Full-time, part-time; 33-54 total credits required; 12 months to 6 years to complete program. Concentrations in accounting, finance, management information systems, marketing, economics, operations management, management.

Master of Business Administration/Doctor of Jurisprudence (MBA/JD) Full-time, part-time; 54 total credits required; 12 months to 3 years to complete program.

Executive MBA (MBA) Full-time; 48 total credits required; 22 months to complete program.

International MBA (MBA) Full-time; 56 total credits required; 2 years to complete program.

Master of Science in Business Administration (MS) Full-time, part-time; 33 total credits required; 12 months to 6 years to complete program. Concentrations in real estate, finance, management, management information systems, marketing.

Master of Science in Accounting (MS) Full-time, part-time; 30-51 total credits required; 12 months to 6 years to complete program. Concentrations in accounting, taxation, system management.

Master of Arts in Economics (MA) Full-time, part-time; 33 total credits required; 12 months to 6 years to complete program. Concentration in economics.

ADMISSION
Applications For fall 1997 there were 655 applications for admission. Of those applying, 363 were accepted.

Application Requirements GMAT score: minimum 430, application form, application fee, bachelor's degree, college transcript(s).

Recommended for Application GRE score accepted, essay, minimum GPA: 2.0, letters of recommendation, personal statement, computer experience.

492

Peterson's Guide to MBA Programs 1999

Application Deadline 8/1 for fall, 12/1 for spring, 5/1 for summer, 5/1 for fall (international), 9/15 for spring (international), 2/1 for summer (international). Application fee: $25, $50 (international). Deferred entrance is available.

ACADEMICS
Faculty Full-time 96; part-time 6.

Teaching Methodologies Case study, computer-aided instruction, computer analysis, computer simulations, experiential learning, faculty seminars, field projects, group discussion, lecture, research, role playing, seminars by members of the business community, simulations, student presentations, study groups, team projects.

Technology 600 on-campus computer terminals/PCs are available for student use and are linked by a campus-wide network. The network has full access to the Internet. Students are not required to have their own PC.

Special Opportunities Advanced credit may be earned through credit by examination, credit for experience, transfer of credits from another institution. International exchange programs in Brazil, France, Germany, Mexico . An internship program is available.

FINANCES
Costs for 1997–98 Tuition: Full-time: $2630 per year (resident); $6940 per year (nonresident). Part-time: $130 per credit hour (resident); $321 per credit hour (nonresident). Cost varies by number of credits taken, reciprocity agreements. Fees: Full-time: $150 per academic year (resident); $150 per academic year (nonresident). Part-time: $34 per semester (resident); $34 per semester (nonresident). Average 1997–98 room and board costs were $3925 per academic year (on campus) and $3000 per academic year (off campus). Room and board costs vary by campus location, occupancy (e.g., single, double, triple), type of accommodation, type of meal plan.

Financial Aid In 1997–98, 18% of students received some institutionally administered aid in the form of fellowships, research assistantships, teaching assistantships.

Financial Aid Contact Director, Student Financial Aid, Student Financial Aid Office, 312 Scates Hall, Memphis, TN 38152. Phone: 901-678-2303.

FACILITIES
Information Resources Ned R. McWherter Library plus 6 additional on-campus libraries; total holdings of 1,020,842 volumes, 2,634,212 microforms, 4,000 current periodical subscriptions. CD player(s) available for graduate student use. Access provided to online bibliographic retrieval services.

INTERNATIONAL STUDENTS
Demographics N/R

Services and Facilities International student office, visa services, ESL courses, counseling/support services.

Applying TOEFL: minimum score of 550, proof of adequate funds, proof of health/immunizations required. Financial aid is not available to international students.

International Student Contact Emin Babakus, Associate Dean for Academic Programs, Fogelman College of Business and Economics, Room 426, Memphis, TN 38152. Phone: 901-678-3721; Fax: 901-678-4705; E-mail: fcbegp@cc.memphis.edu

PLACEMENT
Services include career counseling/planning, career fairs, career placement, electronic job bank, job interviews arranged, resume referral to employers, and resume preparation. In 1996–97, 100 organizations participated in on-campus recruiting.

Employment Of 1996–97 graduates, 90% were employed within three months of graduation; the average starting salary was $33,000. Types of employment entered: accounting, banking, communications, computer-related, consulting, education, finance, financial services, government, health services, hospitality management, human resources, information systems/technology, insurance, manufacturing, marketing, retail, service industry, transportation, utilities.

Business Program(s) URL: http://business.memphis.edu/

Program Contact: Emin Babakus, Associate Dean for Academic Programs, Fogelman College of Business and Economics, Memphis, TN 38152. Phone: 901-678-3721; Fax: 901-678-4705; E-mail: fcbegp@cc.memphis.edu
See full description on page 1096.

University of Tennessee at Chattanooga

School of Business Administration

Chattanooga, Tennessee

OVERVIEW
The University of Tennessee at Chattanooga is a state-supported, coed, comprehensive institution. Enrollment: 8,296 graduate, professional, and undergraduate students; 331 full-time matriculated graduate/professional students; 985 part-time matriculated graduate/professional students. Founded: 1886. The graduate business unit is in an urban setting and is on a semester calendar.

HIGHLIGHTS

Enrollment Profile

Full-time: 83	International: 7%
Part-time: 320	Women: 46%
Total: 403	Minorities: 8%
Average Age: 32	Average Class Size: 20
Fall 1997 Average GPA: 3.2	Fall 1997 Average GMAT: 525

Costs
Full-time tuition: $2478 per academic year (resident); $6078 per academic year (nonresident)
Part-time tuition: $384 per 3-hour course (resident); $927 per 3-hour course (nonresident)

AACSB – The International Association for Management Education accredited

T he University of Tennessee at Chattanooga Graduate School of Business Administration offers an M.B.A. degree as well as a Master of Accountancy degree. There are ten concentrations in the M.B.A. degree: accounting, economics, entrepreneurship, finance, health services management, human resource management, international, marketing, operations and production management, and organizational management. The M.B.A. is designed for full- and part-time students who wish to acquire a broad educational base for enhancing, changing, or launching a career in business administration. The Graduate School also offers an Executive M.B.A. program designed to accommodate the schedule of business executives who wish to amplify their experience in the workplace with an M.B.A. degree. The M.B.A. program also offers compensatory course work for those without an adequate business background. The compensatory course work is arranged into six foundation classes: Economics for Business Decisions, Introduction to Decision Sciences, Survey of Accounting Principles, Foundations of Financial Management, Essentials of Marketing Management, and Management and Operations Theory. The M.B.A. program can be completed within one year, depending on the student's motivation and need for foundation course work

GRADUATE BUSINESS PROGRAMS
Master of Business Administration (MBA) Part-time, distance learning option; 31-49 total credits required; 2 to 6 years to complete program. Concentrations in accounting, health care, entrepreneurship, international management, finance, information management, operations management, organizational management, economics, human resources, marketing.

Executive Master of Business Administration (EMBA) Full-time, distance learning option; 31-49 total credits required; 12 months to complete program.

Master of Accountancy (MAcc) Part-time; 31-69 total credits required; 2 to 6 years to complete program.

ADMISSION
Applications For fall 1997 there were 213 applications for admission. Of those applying, 157 were accepted. Of those accepted, 74 enrolled.

Application Requirements GMAT score, application form, application fee, bachelor's degree, minimum GPA: 2.5, interview, 2 letters of recommendation, college transcript(s).

Application Deadline Applications processed on a rolling/continuous basis for both domestic and international students. Application fee: $25. Deferred entrance is available.

ACADEMICS
Faculty Full-time 23; part-time 4.

Teaching Methodologies Case study, computer simulations, group discussion, lecture, seminars by members of the business community, student presentations, team projects.

Technology 100 on-campus computer terminals/PCs are available for student use and are linked by a campus-wide network. The network has full access to the Internet. Students are not required to have their own PC.

Special Opportunities Advanced credit may be earned through transfer of credits from another institution. International exchange programs in Australia, People's Republic of China.

FINANCES
Costs for 1997–98 Tuition: Full-time: $2478 per year (resident); $6078 per year (nonresident). Part-time: $384 per 3-hour course (resident); $927 per 3-hour course (nonresident). Cost varies by number of credits taken. Fees vary by number of credits taken. Average 1997–98 room only costs were $2000 per academic year (on campus) and $2500 per academic year (off campus). Room and board costs vary by occupancy (e.g., single, double, triple), type of accommodation.

TENNESSEE

University of Tennessee at Chattanooga (continued)

Financial Aid Fellowships, research assistantships, grants, scholarships, work study, loans available. Financial aid is available to part-time students. Application Deadline: 4/1.

Financial Aid Contact MBA Director, School of Business Administration, 615 McCallie Avenue, Chattanooga, TN 37403-2598. Phone: 423-755-4677.

FACILITIES
Information Resources T. Carter and Margaret Rawlings Lupton Library; total holdings of 433,651 volumes, 1,110,825 microforms, 3,025 current periodical subscriptions. CD player(s) available for graduate student use. Access provided to online bibliographic retrieval services and online databases.

INTERNATIONAL STUDENTS
Demographics 7% of students enrolled are international students [Asia, 10%, North America, 90%].

Services and Facilities International student office, international student housing, visa services, ESL courses, counseling/support services.

Applying TOEFL: minimum score of 500, proof of adequate funds required.

International Student Contact Ms. Nancy Amberson, Graduate International Specialist, 615 McCallie Avenue, Chattanooga, TN 37403-2598. Phone: 423-785-2110.

PLACEMENT
Services include alumni network, career counseling/planning, career fairs, career library, career placement, electronic job bank, job interviews arranged, resume referral to employers, and resume preparation.

Employment Types of employment entered: accounting, banking, computer-related, finance, financial services, government, human resources, management, manufacturing, marketing, nonprofit, service industry.

Business Program(s) URL: http://www.utc.edu/~bschool/

Program Contact: Ms. Leani Drapiza, MBA Office Coordinator, School of Business Administration, 615 McCallie Avenue, Chattanooga, TN 37403-2504. Phone: 423-755-4210, 800-532-3028 (TN only); Fax: 423-785-2329; E-mail: ashley-williams@utc.edu

The University of Tennessee at Martin

School of Business Administration

Martin, Tennessee

OVERVIEW
The University of Tennessee at Martin is a state-supported, coed, comprehensive institution. Enrollment: 6,012 graduate, professional, and undergraduate students. Founded: 1927. The graduate business unit is in a rural setting and is on a semester calendar.

HIGHLIGHTS

Enrollment Profile
Full-time: N/R
Part-time: N/R
Total: 200
Average Age: 28
Fall 1997 Average GPA: 3.19
International: N/R
Women: N/R
Minorities: N/R
Average Class Size: 20
Fall 1997 Average GMAT: 489

Costs
Full-time tuition: $2962 per academic year (resident); $4826 per academic year (nonresident)
Part-time tuition: $165 per credit (resident); $434 per credit (nonresident)

AACSB – The International Association for Management Education accredited

GRADUATE BUSINESS PROGRAMS
Master of Business Administration (MBA) Full-time, part-time, distance learning option; 30 total credits required; 9 months to 5 years to complete program.
Master of Accountancy (MAcc) Full-time, part-time, distance learning option; 30 total credits required; 9 months to 5 years to complete program.

ADMISSION
Application Requirements GMAT score: minimum 400, application form, application fee, bachelor's degree, minimum GPA: 2.5, college transcript(s).
Application Deadline Applications processed on a rolling/continuous basis for both domestic and international students. Application fee: $25, $50 (international). Deferred entrance is available.

ACADEMICS
Faculty Full-time 27.

Teaching Methodologies Case study, computer-aided instruction, computer analysis, group discussion, lecture, research.

Technology 200 on-campus computer terminals/PCs are available for student use and are linked by a campus-wide network. The network has full access to the Internet. Students are not required to have their own PC.

Special Opportunities Advanced credit may be earned through transfer of credits from another institution.

FINANCES
Costs for 1997–98 Tuition: Full-time: $2962 per year (resident); $4826 per year (nonresident). Part-time: $165 per credit (resident); $434 per credit (nonresident). Cost varies by number of credits taken, reciprocity agreements. Fees vary by number of credits taken, reciprocity agreements. Average 1997–98 room and board costs were $3744 per academic year. Room and board costs vary by occupancy (e.g., single, double, triple), type of accommodation, type of meal plan.

Financial Aid In 1997–98, 5% of students received some institutionally administered aid in the form of fellowships, research assistantships. Financial aid is available to part-time students. Application Deadline: 3/1.

Financial Aid Contact Rhandy Hall, Executive Director of Student Financial Assistance, Martin, TN 38238-1000. Phone: 901-587-7040; Fax: 901-587-7019.

FACILITIES
Information Resources Paul Meek Library; total holdings of 309,171 volumes, 504,281 microforms, 1,554 current periodical subscriptions. CD player(s) available for graduate student use. Access provided to online bibliographic retrieval services.

INTERNATIONAL STUDENTS
Demographics N/R

Services and Facilities International student office, international student center, counseling/support services.

Applying TOEFL: minimum score of 525, proof of adequate funds, proof of health/immunizations required.

International Student Contact Dr. John A. Eisterhold, Dean, International Programs, 144 Gooch Hall, Martin, TN 38238-1000. Phone: 901-587-7340; Fax: 901-587-7019.

PLACEMENT
Services include career placement.

Employment Of 1996–97 graduates, 99% were employed within three months of graduation. Types of employment entered: accounting, banking, education, finance, financial services, government, health services, human resources, information systems/technology, management, manufacturing, marketing, nonprofit, retail, service industry, utilities.

Business Program(s) URL: http://www.utm.edu/departments/soba/home.html

Program Contact: Dr. Richard B. Griffin, Coordinator of Graduate Programs in Business Administration, School of Business Administration, Martin, TN 38238-0100. Phone: 901-587-7208; Fax: 901-587-7241; E-mail: bugrad@utm.edu

University of Tennessee, Knoxville

College of Business Administration

Knoxville, Tennessee

OVERVIEW
The University of Tennessee, Knoxville is a state-supported, coed university. Enrollment: 25,086 graduate, professional, and undergraduate students; 3,131 full-time matriculated graduate/professional students; 2,675 part-time matriculated graduate/professional students. Founded: 1794. The graduate business unit is in an urban setting and is on a semester calendar.

HIGHLIGHTS

Enrollment Profile
Full-time: 181
Part-time: 0
Total: 181
Average Age: N/R
Fall 1997 Average GPA: 3.3
International: N/R
Women: N/R
Minorities: N/R
Average Class Size: 45
Fall 1997 Average GMAT: 600

Costs
Full-time tuition: $3142 per academic year (resident); $8210 per academic year (nonresident)
Part-time tuition: N/R

AACSB – The International Association for Management Education accredited

T*he Master of Business Administration program at the University of Tennessee begins with this simple question: "What does every manager need to know?" It is a question that requires two years of long days, longer nights, and countless weekends to answer. The answer lies in action and hands-on, experiential learning and, once mastered, charts a new course for University of Tennessee graduates.*

The School of Business offers an M.B.A. degree with concentrations in economics, environmental management, finance, global business, health-care management, logistics and transportation, management, management of information systems, manufacturing management, marketing, new venture analysis and entrepreneurship, operations management, and statistics. The program is geared toward the full-time student, with admission in the fall semester only. An internship is also required. A B.A./M.B.A., a J.D./M.B.A., and an M.S./M.B.A. in industrial engineering are also offered. In addition, the College offers an Executive M.B.A., a Physician's Executive M.B.A. program, and a part-time Professional M.B.A.

Also offered by the College are master's programs in accounting, economics, management science, and statistics. A Ph.D. program in business administration, with concentrations in accounting, finance, logistics and transportation, management, marketing, or statistics, is offered as well

GRADUATE BUSINESS PROGRAMS

Master of Accounting (MAcc) Full-time; 11 to 15 months to complete program.

Master of Arts in Economics (MA)

Master of Science in Statistics (MS) Full-time; 18 months to 6 years to complete program.

Master of Science in Management Science (MS) Full-time; up to 2 years to complete program.

Master of Science in Industrial Organizational Psychology (MS) Full-time; 3 to 6 years to complete program.

Master of Business Administration (MBA) Full-time; 54 total credits required; 22 months to complete program. Concentrations in economics, finance, international business, management, management science, marketing, entrepreneurship.

Executive MBA (MBA) Full-time; 12 months to complete program.

Physicians Executive Master of Business Administration (PEMBA) Full-time; 45 total credits required; application deadline: 10/1; minimum of 12 months to complete program.

Professional MBA (MBA) Full-time; 45 total credits required; application deadline: 4/10; minimum of 16 months to complete program.

ADMISSION

Application Requirements GMAT score, application form, application fee, bachelor's degree, essay, minimum GPA, 2 letters of recommendation, college transcript(s), computer experience: word processing, spreadsheet.

Recommended for Application Interview, personal statement, resume, work experience.

Application Deadline 3/1 for fall, 3/1 for fall (international). Application fee: $15.

ACADEMICS

Faculty Full-time 100.

Teaching Methodologies Case study, computer analysis, computer simulations, experiential learning, faculty seminars, field projects, group discussion, lecture, research, role playing, seminars by members of the business community, simulations, student presentations, study groups, team projects.

Special Opportunities An internship program is available.

FINANCES

Costs for 1997–98 Tuition: Full-time: $3142 per year (resident); $8210 per year (nonresident).

Financial Aid Fellowships, research assistantships, teaching assistantships, work study, loans available.

Financial Aid Contact Financial Aid Office, Knoxville, TN 37996. Phone: 423-974-3131.

FACILITIES

Information Resources John C. Hodges Library plus 7 additional on-campus libraries; total holdings of 2,000,000 volumes, 2,000,000 microforms, 14,000 current periodical subscriptions. CD player(s) available for graduate student use. Access provided to online bibliographic retrieval services.

INTERNATIONAL STUDENTS

Demographics N/R

Services and Facilities International student office, international student center, international student housing, visa services, ESL courses, counseling/support services.

Applying TOEFL: minimum score of 550 required.

PLACEMENT

Services include alumni network, career counseling/planning, career fairs, career library, career placement, electronic job bank, job interviews arranged, job search course, resume referral to employers, and resume preparation.

Employment Of 1996–97 graduates, the average starting salary was $50,000. Types of employment entered: consulting, finance, financial services, management, transportation.

Business Program(s) URL: http://mba.bus.utk.edu

Program Contact: Ms. Donna Potts, MBA Admissions Director, 527 Stokely Management Center, Knoxville, TN 37996-0552. Phone: 423-974-5033; Fax: 423-974-3826; E-mail: dpotts@utk.edu

See full description on page 1148.

Vanderbilt University

Owen Graduate School of Management

Nashville, Tennessee

OVERVIEW

Vanderbilt University is an independent-nonprofit, coed university. Enrollment: 9,900 graduate, professional, and undergraduate students. Founded: 1873. The graduate business unit is in an urban setting and is on a half semester module calendar.

HIGHLIGHTS

Enrollment Profile

Full-time: 523	International: 20%
Part-time: 0	Women: 26%
Total: 523	Minorities: 7%
Average Age: 27	Average Class Size: 32
Fall 1997 Average GPA: 3.2	Fall 1997 Average GMAT: 625

Costs
Full-time tuition: $22,900 per academic year
Part-time tuition: N/R

AACSB – The International Association for Management Education accredited

Degree(s) offered in conjunction with University of Florida

GRADUATE BUSINESS PROGRAMS

Master of Business Administration (MBA) Full-time; 60 total credits required; 20 months to complete program. Concentrations in accounting, finance, human resources, management information systems, finance, operations management, organizational management.

Master of Business Administration/Doctor of Jurisprudence (MBA/JD) Full-time; 151 total credits required; 3.3 years to complete program. Concentrations in accounting, finance, human resources, management information systems, marketing, operations management, organizational management.

Master of Business Administration/Master of Science in Nursing (MBA/MSN) Full-time; 69 total credits required; 2.1 to 2.5 years to complete program. Concentrations in accounting, finance, human resources, management information systems, marketing, operations management, organizational management, management.

MBA/MA in Latin American Studies Program (MBA/MA) Full-time; 72 total credits required; 2.1 to 2.5 years to complete program. Concentrations in accounting, finance, human resources, management information systems, marketing, operations management, organizational management.

Master of Business Administration/Master of Technology (MBA/MT) Full-time; 72 total credits required; 2.1 to 2.5 years to complete program. Concentrations in management, management information systems, operations management, technology management.

5-year Program (MBA/BA) Full-time; 165 total credits required; 5 years to complete program. Concentrations in asian business studies, finance, human resources, management information systems, operations management, organizational management.

5-year Program (MBA/BS) Full-time; 165 total credits required; 5 years to complete program. Concentrations in asian business studies, finance, human resources, management information systems, operations management, organizational management.

Executive MBA Program (MBA) Full-time; 50 total credits required; minimum of 5 years work experience (including management experience) required; 21 months to complete program. Concentration in management.

International Executive MBA Program (MBA) Full-time, distance learning option; minimum of 5 years work experience (including management experience)

Vanderbilt University (continued)

required; 18 months to complete program. Concentration in international management.

ADMISSION

Applications For fall 1997 there were 1,313 applications for admission. Of those applying, 495 were accepted. Of those accepted, 201 enrolled.

Application Requirements GMAT score, application form, application fee, bachelor's degree, essay, minimum GPA, interview, 2 letters of recommendation, resume, college transcript(s).

Recommended for Application Work experience, computer experience.

Application Deadline 11/15 for fall, 1/15 for winter, 3/15 for spring, 11/15 for fall (international), 1/15 for winter (international), 3/15 for spring (international). Application fee: $50. Deferred entrance is available.

ACADEMICS

Faculty Full-time 47; part-time 16.

Teaching Methodologies Case study, computer-aided instruction, computer analysis, computer simulations, experiential learning, faculty seminars, field projects, group discussion, lecture, research, role playing, seminars by members of the business community, simulations, student presentations, study groups, team projects.

Technology 50 on-campus computer terminals/PCs are available for student use and are linked by a campus-wide network. The network has full access to the Internet. Students are not required to have their own PC.

Special Opportunities Advanced credit may be earned through transfer of credits from another institution. International exchange programs in Austria, Brazil, Chile, Costa Rica, France, Germany, Mexico, Norway, South Africa, United Kingdom, Venezuela.

FINANCES

Costs for 1997–98 Tuition: Full-time: $22,900 per year. Cost varies by academic program. Fees: Full-time: $240 per academic year. Average 1997–98 room only costs were $5500 per academic year (off campus). Room and board costs vary by occupancy (e.g., single, double, triple), type of accommodation, type of meal plan.

Financial Aid In 1997–98, 47% of students received some institutionally administered aid in the form of fellowships, scholarships, work study, loans.

Financial Aid Contact Ms. Laine Fuldauer, Associate Director of Student Services and Admissions, 401 21st Avenue South, Nashville, TN 37203. Phone: 615-322-6469; Fax: 615-343-1175; E-mail: laine.fuldauer@owen.vanderbilt.edu

FACILITIES

Information Resources Jean and Alexander Heard Library plus 8 additional on-campus libraries; total holdings of 2,443,000 volumes, 2,720,000 microforms, 19,800 current periodical subscriptions. CD player(s) available for graduate student use. Access provided to online bibliographic retrieval services and online databases.

INTERNATIONAL STUDENTS

Demographics 20% of students enrolled are international students [Africa, 1%, Asia, 12%, Central America, 1%, Europe, 3%, North America, 77%, South America, 6%].

Services and Facilities International student office, international student center, international student housing, visa services, ESL courses, counseling/support services.

Applying TOEFL, proof of adequate funds, proof of health/immunizations required. Financial aid is available to international students.

International Student Contact Mr. Hayden Estrada, Director of Admissions, Owen Graduate School of Management, 401 21st Avenue South, Nashville, TN 37203. Phone: 615-322-6469; Fax: 615-343-1175; E-mail: admissions@owen.vanderbilt.edu

PLACEMENT

Services include alumni network, career counseling/planning, career fairs, career library, career placement, electronic job bank, job interviews arranged, job search course, resume referral to employers, and resume preparation. In 1996–97, 170 organizations participated in on-campus recruiting; 2,630 on-campus interviews were conducted.

Employment Of 1996–97 graduates, 97% were employed within three months of graduation; the average starting salary was $65,000. Types of employment entered: accounting, banking, chemical industry, communications, computer-related, consulting, consumer products, energy, engineering, finance, financial services, health services, high technology, hospitality management, human resources, information systems/technology, international trade, management, manufacturing, marketing, nonprofit, petrochemical, pharmaceutical, real estate, retail, service industry, telecommunications, transportation.

Business Program(s) URL: http://mba.vanderbilt.edu

Program Contact: Mr. Hayden Estrada, Director of Admissions, 401 21st Avenue South, Owen Graduate School of Management, Nashville, TN 37203. Phone: 615-322-6469, 800-288-OWEN; Fax: 615-343-1175; E-mail: hayden.estrada@owen.vanderbilt.edu

TEXAS

Abilene Christian University

College of Business Administration

Abilene, Texas

OVERVIEW

Abilene Christian University is an independent-religious, coed, comprehensive institution. Enrollment: 4,542 graduate, professional, and undergraduate students; 256 full-time matriculated graduate/professional students; 377 part-time matriculated graduate/professional students. Founded: 1906. The graduate business unit is in a suburban setting and is on a semester calendar.

HIGHLIGHTS

Enrollment Profile

Full-time: 7	International: 14%
Part-time: 7	Women: 43%
Total: 14	Minorities: 14%
Average Age: 28	Average Class Size: N/R
Fall 1997 Average GPA: 3.0	Fall 1997 Average GMAT: 511

Costs

Full-time tuition: $5238 per academic year
Part-time tuition: $291 per credit hour

ACBSP – The American Council of Business Schools and Programs accredited

GRADUATE BUSINESS PROGRAMS

Master of Business Administration (MBA) Full-time, part-time; 40 total credits required; 12 months to 5 years to complete program. Concentrations in management, accounting, information management, nonprofit management.

Master of Accountancy (MAcc) Full-time, part-time; 30 total credits required; 12 months to 5 years to complete program.

ADMISSION

Applications For fall 1997 there were 21 applications for admission. Of those applying, 6 were accepted. Of those accepted, 4 enrolled.

Application Requirements GMAT score: minimum 450, application form, application fee, bachelor's degree, essay, minimum GPA: 2.8, 3 letters of recommendation, personal statement, college transcript(s).

Recommended for Application Minimum of 1 year of work experience, computer experience.

Application Deadline Applications processed on a rolling/continuous basis for both domestic and international students. Application fee: $25, $45 (international). Deferred entrance is available.

ACADEMICS

Faculty Full-time 18; part-time 6.

Teaching Methodologies Case study, computer-aided instruction, computer analysis, computer simulations, experiential learning, field projects, group discussion, lecture, research, role playing, seminars by members of the business community, simulations, student presentations, study groups, team projects.

Technology 500 on-campus computer terminals/PCs are available for student use and are linked by a campus-wide network. The network has full access to the Internet. Students are required to have their own PC.

Special Opportunities Advanced credit may be earned through transfer of credits from another institution. International exchange programs in France, Japan, People's Republic of China, United Kingdom. An internship program is available.

FINANCES

Costs for 1997–98 Tuition: Full-time: $5238 per year. Part-time: $291 per credit hour. Fees: Full-time: $285 per academic year. Part-time: $240 per year. Average 1997–98 room and board costs were $3810 per academic year (on campus) and $3925 per academic year (off campus). Room and board costs vary by occupancy (e.g., single, double, triple), type of accommodation, type of meal plan.

Financial Aid Research assistantships, teaching assistantships, scholarships, work study, loans available. Financial aid is available to part-time students. Application Deadline: 3/1.

Financial Aid Contact Student Financial Services, ACU Box 29007, Abilene, TX 79699-9007. Phone: 915-674-2643; Fax: 915-674-2130.

FACILITIES
Information Resources Margaret and Herman Brown Library; total holdings of 448,574 volumes, 914,474 microforms, 2,276 current periodical subscriptions. CD player(s) available for graduate student use. Access provided to online bibliographic retrieval services and online databases.

INTERNATIONAL STUDENTS
Demographics 14% of students enrolled are international students [Asia, 80%, other, 20%].

Services and Facilities International student office, international student center, visa services, ESL courses, counseling/support services.

Applying TOEFL: minimum score of 550, proof of adequate funds, proof of health/immunizations required. Financial aid is available to international students.

International Student Contact Mr. Ted Presley, Director of International Division, ACU Box 28226, Abilene, TX 79699. Phone: 915-674-2258; Fax: 915-674-2966.

PLACEMENT
Services include alumni network, career counseling/planning, career fairs, career library, career placement, electronic job bank, job interviews arranged, and resume preparation.

Employment Types of employment entered: accounting, banking, communications, computer-related, education, energy, engineering, finance, financial services, government, health services, human resources, information systems/technology, management, manufacturing, marketing, mining, nonprofit, petrochemical, retail, service industry, telecommunications, utilities.

Business Program(s) URL: http://www.acu.edu/academics/mba

Program Contact: Dr. Monty Lynn, Director of the MBA Program, ACU Box 29325, Abilene, TX 79699-9235. Phone: 915-674-2593, 800-395-4723 (TX only); Fax: 915-674-2564; E-mail: monty.lynn@coba.acu.edu

See full description on page 694.

Amber University

Department of Business Administration
Garland, Texas

OVERVIEW
Amber University is an independent-religious, coed, upper-level institution. Enrollment: 1,500 graduate, professional, and undergraduate students; 308 full-time matriculated graduate/professional students; 468 part-time matriculated graduate/professional students. Founded: 1971. The graduate business unit is in a suburban setting and is on a term calendar.

HIGHLIGHTS

Enrollment Profile

Full-time: 40	International: 5%
Part-time: 356	Women: 40%
Total: 396	Minorities: 18%
Average Age: 35	Average Class Size: 25
Fall 1997 Average GPA: 3.0	Fall 1997 Average GMAT: N/R

Costs
Full-time tuition: $3600 per academic year
Part-time tuition: $450 per course

GRADUATE BUSINESS PROGRAMS
General Business MBA (MBA) Full-time, part-time, distance learning option; 36 total credits required.

Master of Business Administration in Management (MBA) Full-time, part-time, distance learning option; 36 total credits required. Concentration in management.

ADMISSION
Applications For fall 1997 there were 325 applications for admission. Of those applying, 320 were accepted. Of those accepted, 300 enrolled.

Application Requirements Application form, application fee, bachelor's degree, minimum GPA: 3.0, college transcript(s).

Recommended for Application Computer experience.

Application Deadline Applications processed on a rolling/continuous basis for domestic students only. 8/1 for fall (international), 11/1 for winter (international), 2/1 for spring (international), 5/1 for summer (international). Application fee: $25.

ACADEMICS
Faculty Full-time 16; part-time 45.

Teaching Methodologies Case study, group discussion, lecture, research, role playing, simulations, student presentations, study groups, team projects.

Technology 25 on-campus computer terminals/PCs are available for student use and are linked by a campus-wide network. The network does not have Internet access. Students are not required to have their own PC.

Special Opportunities Advanced credit may be earned through credit by examination, credit for military training programs, credit for business training programs, transfer of credits from another institution.

FINANCES
Costs for 1997–98 Tuition: Full-time: $3600 per year. Part-time: $450 per course.

Financial Aid Contact Ms. Melinda Reagan, Vice President for Administrative Services, 1700 Eastgate, Garland, TX 75041. Phone: 972-279-6511 Ext. 122; Fax: 972-279-9773.

FACILITIES
Information Resources Amber University Library; total holdings of 21,000 volumes, 1,200 microforms, 75 current periodical subscriptions. Access provided to online bibliographic retrieval services.

INTERNATIONAL STUDENTS
Demographics 5% of students enrolled are international students.

Applying Financial aid is not available to international students.

International Student Contact Dr. Jo Lynn Loyd, Dean For Strategic Planning, 1700 Eastgate Drive, Garland, TX 75041-5595. Phone: 972-279-6511; Fax: 972-279-9773.

PLACEMENT
Employment Of 1996–97 graduates, 90% were employed within three months of graduation. Types of employment entered: accounting, banking, chemical industry, communications, computer-related, finance, government, health services, high technology, hospitality management, human resources, information systems/technology, insurance, management, marketing, nonprofit, retail, service industry, telecommunications.

Business Program(s) URL: http://www.amberu.edu

Program Contact: Ms. Marge Massey, Manager of Admissions, 1700 Eastgate, Garland, TX 75041. Phone: 972-279-6511 Ext. 167; Fax: 972-279-9773.

Angelo State University

Department of Business Administration
San Angelo, Texas

OVERVIEW
Angelo State University is a state-supported, coed, comprehensive institution. Enrollment: 6,279 graduate, professional, and undergraduate students; 132 full-time matriculated graduate/professional students; 274 part-time matriculated graduate/professional students. Founded: 1926. The graduate business unit is in a small-town setting and is on a semester calendar.

HIGHLIGHTS

Enrollment Profile

Full-time: 34	International: 4%
Part-time: 49	Women: 43%
Total: 83	Minorities: 14%
Average Age: 32	Average Class Size: 20
Fall 1997 Average GPA: N/R	Fall 1997 Average GMAT: 503

Costs
Full-time tuition: $1022 per academic year (resident); $7382 per academic year (nonresident)
Part-time tuition: $36 per credit (resident); $246 per credit (nonresident)

ACBSP – The American Council of Business Schools and Programs accredited

GRADUATE BUSINESS PROGRAMS
MBA in Management (MBA) Full-time, part-time; 39 total credits required; 18 months to 6 years to complete program. Concentration in management.

Integrated BBA/MBA in Accounting (BBA/MBA) Full-time, part-time; 154 total credits required; 5 to 6 years to complete program. Concentration in accounting.

Master of Business Administration in Accounting (MBA) Full-time, part-time; 36 total credits required; 18 months to 6 years to complete program. Concentration in accounting.

ADMISSION
Applications For fall 1997 there were 44 applications for admission. Of those applying, 35 were accepted. Of those accepted, 24 enrolled.

Angelo State University (continued)

Application Requirements Application form, application fee, bachelor's degree, minimum GPA: 2.5, college transcript(s).

Recommended for Application GMAT score accepted: minimum 500.

Application Deadline 8/7 for fall, 1/2 for spring, 5/10 for summer, 6/10 for fall (international), 11/1 for spring (international), 3/15 for summer (international). Application fee: $25, $50 (international). Deferred entrance is available.

ACADEMICS

Faculty Full-time 13.

Teaching Methodologies Case study, computer-aided instruction, computer analysis, computer simulations, experiential learning, faculty seminars, field projects, group discussion, lecture, research, role playing, seminars by members of the business community, simulations, student presentations, study groups, team projects.

Technology 305 on-campus computer terminals/PCs are available for student use and are linked by a campus-wide network. The network has full access to the Internet. Students are not required to have their own PC.

Special Opportunities Advanced credit may be earned through transfer of credits from another institution. An internship program is available.

FINANCES

Costs for 1997–98 Tuition: Full-time: $1022 per year (resident); $7382 per year (nonresident). Part-time: $36 per credit (resident); $246 per credit (nonresident). Cost varies by class time (e.g., day/evening), number of credits taken, reciprocity agreements. Fees: Full-time: $1140 per academic year (resident); $1140 per academic year (nonresident). Part-time: $165 per semester (resident); $165 per semester (nonresident). Fees vary by class time (e.g., day/evening), number of credits taken, reciprocity agreements. Average 1997–98 room and board costs were $3968 per academic year. Room and board costs vary by occupancy (e.g., single, double, triple), type of accommodation, type of meal plan.

Financial Aid In 1997–98, 14% of students received some institutionally administered aid in the form of fellowships, research assistantships, teaching assistantships, scholarships, work study. Financial aid is available to part-time students. Application Deadline: 8/1.

Financial Aid Contact Mr. James B. Parker, Financial Aid Director, PO Box 11015, San Angelo, TX 76909. Phone: 915-942-2246; Fax: 915-942-2082; E-mail: j.parker@angelo.edu

FACILITIES

Information Resources Porter Henderson Library; total holdings of 249,349 volumes, 648,373 microforms, 1,937 current periodical subscriptions. CD player(s) available for graduate student use. Access provided to online bibliographic retrieval services.

INTERNATIONAL STUDENTS

Demographics 4% of students enrolled are international students.

Services and Facilities International student office, international student center, counseling/support services.

Applying TOEFL: minimum score of 550, proof of adequate funds, proof of health/immunizations required. Financial aid is available to international students.

International Student Contact Ms. Mitzie Keeling, Admissions Counselor/International Student Advisor, PO Box 11014, San Angelo, TX 76909. Phone: 915-942-2041 Ext. 242; Fax: 915-942-2078; E-mail: mitzie.keeling@mailserv.angelo.edu

PLACEMENT

Services include alumni network, career counseling/planning, career fairs, career library, career placement, job interviews arranged, and resume preparation.

Program Contact: Dr. Carol Diminnie, Graduate Dean, PO Box 10025, San Angelo, TX 76909. Phone: 915-942-2169; Fax: 915-942-2194; E-mail: graduate.school@angelo.edu

Baylor University

Hankamer School of Business

Waco, Texas

OVERVIEW

Baylor University is an independent-religious, coed university. Enrollment: 12,472 graduate, professional, and undergraduate students. Founded: 1845. The graduate business unit is in a suburban setting and is on a semester calendar.

HIGHLIGHTS

Enrollment Profile

Full-time: 163	International: 14%
Part-time: 0	Women: 41%
Total: 163	Minorities: 9%
Average Age: N/R	Average Class Size: 20
Fall 1997 Average GPA: 3.25	Fall 1997 Average GMAT: 581

Costs
Full-time tuition: $11,088 per academic year
Part-time tuition: $308 per hour

AACSB – The International Association for Management Education accredited

GRADUATE BUSINESS PROGRAMS

Master of Business Administration (MBA) Full-time, part-time; 36-60 total credits required; 12 months to 2 years to complete program. Concentrations in accounting, economics, entrepreneurship, finance, international and area business studies, management, management information systems, marketing.

Executive MBA (MBA) Full-time; 47 total credits required; 2 to 5 years to complete program.

Executive MBA in International Management (MBA) Full-time; 48 total credits required; 16 months to 5 years to complete program. Concentration in international business.

Master of International Management (MIM) Full-time, part-time; 36 total credits required; 12 months to 5 years to complete program. Concentration in international business.

Master of Science in Economics (MS) Full-time, part-time; 36 total credits required; 12 months to 5 years to complete program. Concentrations in international economics, economics.

Master of Arts in Economics (MA) Full-time, part-time; 36 total credits required; 12 months to 5 years to complete program. Concentrations in economics, international economics.

Master of Taxation (MTax) Full-time, part-time; 31 total credits required; 12 months to 5 years to complete program. Concentration in taxation.

Master of Accountancy (MAcc) Full-time, part-time; 31 total credits required; 12 months to 5 years to complete program. Concentration in accounting.

Doctor of Jurisprudence/Master of Business Administration (JD/MBA) Full-time, part-time; 132 total credits required; 3 to 5 years to complete program.

Doctor of Jurisprudence/Master of Taxation (JD/MTax) Full-time, part-time; 126 total credits required; 3 to 5 years to complete program.

Master of Science in Information Systems (MS) Full-time, part-time; 36 total credits required; 12 months to 5 years to complete program.

ADMISSION

Applications For fall 1997 there were 212 applications for admission. Of those applying, 155 were accepted. Of those accepted, 73 enrolled.

Application Requirements GMAT score: minimum 500, application form, application fee, bachelor's degree, essay, minimum GPA, 3 letters of recommendation, personal statement, resume, college transcript(s), computer experience: information systems.

Recommended for Application Interview, work experience.

Application Deadline 7/1 for fall, 11/1 for spring, 4/1 for summer. Application fee: $25. Deferred entrance is available.

ACADEMICS

Faculty Full-time 90.

Teaching Methodologies Case study, computer-aided instruction, computer analysis, computer simulations, experiential learning, faculty seminars, field projects, group discussion, lecture, research, seminars by members of the business community, student presentations, study groups, team projects.

Technology 200 on-campus computer terminals/PCs are available for student use and are linked by a campus-wide network. The network has full access to the Internet. Students are not required to have their own PC.

Special Opportunities Advanced credit may be earned through transfer of credits from another institution. International exchange programs in Australia, Canada, Finland, France, Mexico, United Kingdom. An internship program is available.

FINANCES

Costs for 1997–98 Tuition: Full-time: $11,088 per year. Part-time: $308 per hour. Cost varies by academic program, number of credits taken. Fees: Full-time: $1050 per academic year. Part-time: $350 per semester. Fees vary by number of credits taken. Average 1997–98 room and board costs were $5100 per academic year (off campus). Room and board costs vary by occupancy (e.g., single, double, triple), type of accommodation, type of meal plan.

Financial Aid In 1997–98, 44% of students received some institutionally administered aid in the form of research assistantships, work study, loans.

Financial Aid Contact Ms. Jeanette Kucera, Director of Financial Aid, PO Box 7028, Waco, TX 76798-7028. Phone: 254-710-2611; E-mail: jeanette_kucera@ baylor.edu

FACILITIES

Information Resources Moody Memorial Library plus 5 additional on-campus libraries; total holdings of 1,531,771 volumes, 2,000,000 microforms, 10,561 current periodical subscriptions. CD player(s) available for graduate student use. Access provided to online bibliographic retrieval services.

INTERNATIONAL STUDENTS

Demographics 14% of students enrolled are international students.

Services and Facilities International student office, international student center, visa services, ESL courses, counseling/support services.

Applying TOEFL: minimum score of 600, proof of adequate funds, proof of health/immunizations required. Financial aid is available to international students.

International Student Contact Ms. Linda Klatt, Coordinator of International Programs, PO Box 97381, Waco, TX 76798-7381. Phone: 254-710-1461; E-mail: linda_klatt@baylor.edu

PLACEMENT

Services include alumni network, career counseling/planning, career fairs, career library, career placement, electronic job bank, job interviews arranged, resume referral to employers, and resume preparation. In 1996–97, 151 organizations participated in on-campus recruiting; 2,004 on-campus interviews were conducted.

Employment Of 1996–97 graduates, 90% were employed within three months of graduation; the average starting salary was $43,000. Types of employment entered: accounting, banking, communications, computer-related, consulting, education, finance, financial services, high technology, human resources, information systems/technology, insurance, law, management, manufacturing, marketing, real estate, service industry, telecommunications.

Business Program(s) URL: http://hsb.baylor.edu/mba

Program Contact: Ms. Laurie Wilson, Director of Graduate Business Admissions, PO Box 98001, Waco, TX 76798-8001. Phone: 254-710-3718, 800-583-0622; Fax: 254-710-1066; E-mail: laurie_wilson@baylor.edu
See full description on page 720.

Dallas Baptist University

Graduate School of Business

Dallas, Texas

OVERVIEW
Dallas Baptist University is an independent-religious, coed, comprehensive institution. Enrollment: 3,493 graduate, professional, and undergraduate students; 160 full-time matriculated graduate/professional students; 638 part-time matriculated graduate/professional students. Founded: 1965. The graduate business unit is in a suburban setting and is on a semester calendar.

HIGHLIGHTS

Enrollment Profile

Full-time: 82	International: 11%
Part-time: 368	Women: 43%
Total: 450	Minorities: 33%
Average Age: 38	Average Class Size: 12
Fall 1997 Average GPA: N/R	Fall 1997 Average GMAT: 450

Costs
Full-time tuition: $4860 per academic year
Part-time tuition: $270 per semester hour

ACBSP – The American Council of Business Schools and Programs accredited

allas Baptist University's (DBU) Master of Business Administration program is designed to provide the business professional with an education that fulfills the expectations of the business community. The mission of the DBU Graduate School of Business is to develop and graduate individuals who are well prepared to assume positions of leadership and immediately make a positive impact on the organizations of which they are a part. DBU accomplishes this goal by providing a learning environment with leadership, direction, and support through outstanding faculty members who are educationally qualified and experienced in the business environment.

The University's program is unique among most M.B.A. programs. DBU holds the belief that education is best served when it is taught in a Christian context. The DBU College of Business stresses the fundamental aspects of the free enterprise system. The University also recognizes that all students have differ-

ing needs in their pursuit of a graduate education. Therefore, the focus of meeting those needs is on quality and convenience.

The majority of M.B.A. students hold full-time positions of employment. Consequently, most classes are conducted once per week in the evenings and on Saturdays. The main campus is located near the center of the metroplex, and business courses are also offered at various other locations throughout the Dallas/Ft. Worth area.

GRADUATE BUSINESS PROGRAMS

Master of Business Administration (MBA) Full-time, part-time; 36 total credits required; 18 months to 5 years to complete program. Concentrations in accounting, finance, management information systems, management, marketing, international business.

Master of Arts in Organizational Management (MA) Full-time, part-time; 36 total credits required; 18 months to 5 years to complete program. Concentrations in management, human resources.

ADMISSION

Applications For fall 1997 there were 337 applications for admission. Of those applying, 266 were accepted.

Application Requirements Application form, application fee, bachelor's degree, minimum GPA: 3.0, 2 letters of recommendation, personal statement, college transcript(s).

Recommended for Application GMAT score accepted: minimum 425, resume, minimum of 2 years of work experience.

Application Deadline Applications processed on a rolling/continuous basis for both domestic and international students. Application fee: $25. Deferred entrance is available.

ACADEMICS

Faculty Full-time 15; part-time 29.

Teaching Methodologies Case study, computer-aided instruction, computer analysis, computer simulations, field projects, lecture, role playing, seminars by members of the business community, simulations, student presentations, study groups, team projects.

Technology 80 on-campus computer terminals/PCs are available for student use and are linked by a campus-wide network. The network has full access to the Internet. Students are not required to have their own PC.

Special Opportunities Advanced credit may be earned through credit by examination, transfer of credits from another institution. An internship program is available.

FINANCES

Costs for 1997–98 Tuition: Full-time: $4860 per year. Part-time: $270 per semester hour. Cost varies by number of credits taken. Room and board costs vary by occupancy (e.g., single, double, triple), type of meal plan.

Financial Aid In 1997–98, 3% of students received some institutionally administered aid in the form of scholarships, loans. Financial aid is available to part-time students.

Financial Aid Contact Mrs. Mari Notley, Assitant Vice President for Financial Aid, 3000 Mountain Creek Parkway, Dallas, TX 75211-9299. Phone: 214-333-5363; Fax: 214-333-5586; E-mail: rosa@dbu.edu

FACILITIES

Information Resources Vance Memorial Library; total holdings of 192,000 volumes, 373,000 microforms, 590 current periodical subscriptions. Access provided to online bibliographic retrieval services.

INTERNATIONAL STUDENTS

Demographics 11% of students enrolled are international students.

Services and Facilities International student office, international student housing, visa services, ESL courses, counseling/support services.

Applying TOEFL: minimum score of 550, proof of adequate funds, proof of health/immunizations required. Financial aid is not available to international students.

International Student Contact Mrs. Rebecca Brown, Director of International Student Services, 3000 Mountain Creek Parkway, Dallas, TX 75211-9299. Phone: 214-333-5426; Fax: 214-333-5409; E-mail: rebeccab@dbu.edu

PLACEMENT

Services include career fairs, career placement, and electronic job bank.

Business Program(s) URL: http://www.dbu.edu

Program Contact: Mr. Travis Bundrick, Director of Graduate Programs, 3000 Mountain Creek Parkway, Dallas, TX 75211-9299. Phone: 214-333-5243; Fax: 214-333-5579; E-mail: graduate@dbu.edu

East Texas Baptist University

Program in Business Administration

Marshall, Texas

OVERVIEW
East Texas Baptist University is an independent-religious, comprehensive institution. Founded: 1912.

GRADUATE BUSINESS PROGRAMS
Master of Business Administration (MBA)

Program Contact: Office of Graduate Admissions, Fred M. Hale School of Business, Marshall, TX 75670-1498. Phone: 903-935-7963, 800-804-ETBU

Houston Baptist University

College of Business and Economics

Houston, Texas

OVERVIEW
Houston Baptist University is an independent-religious, coed, comprehensive institution. Enrollment: 2,262 graduate, professional, and undergraduate students; 335 full-time matriculated graduate/professional students; 237 part-time matriculated graduate/professional students. Founded: 1960. The graduate business unit is in an urban setting and is on a quarter calendar.

HIGHLIGHTS

Enrollment Profile
Full-time: 225
Part-time: 87
Total: 312
Average Age: N/R
Fall 1997 Average GPA: 2.5

International: 3%
Women: 47%
Minorities: N/R
Average Class Size: 20
Fall 1997 Average GMAT: N/R

Costs
Full-time tuition: N/R
Part-time tuition: $900 per 3-hour course

GRADUATE BUSINESS PROGRAMS
Executive Master of Business Administration (EMBA) Full-time; 60 total credits required; 2 years to complete program. Concentrations in accounting, financial management/planning, marketing.

Master of Business Administration (MBA) Full-time, part-time; 42-51 total credits required; 21 months to 5 years to complete program. Concentrations in management consulting, management systems analysis, marketing research.

Master of Science in Management Computing and Systems (MS) Full-time; 42 total credits required; 21 months to complete program. Concentration in management science.

Master of Science in Human Resource Management (MS) Full-time, part-time; 42 total credits required; 21 months to 5 years to complete program. Concentration in human resources.

Master of Science in Health Administration (MS) Full-time, part-time; 54 total credits required; minimum of 2.3 years to complete program. Concentration in actuarial science.

ADMISSION
Applications For fall 1997 there were 150 applications for admission. Of those applying, 101 were accepted. Of those accepted, 85 enrolled.

Application Requirements GMAT score: minimum 450, application form, application fee, bachelor's degree, minimum GPA: 2.5, interview, 3 letters of recommendation, personal statement, college transcript(s).

Recommended for Application GRE score accepted, work experience, computer experience.

Application Deadline 6/1 for fall, 12/31 for winter, 2/1 for spring, 4/1 for summer. Application fee: $25, $85 (international). Deferred entrance is available.

ACADEMICS
Faculty Full-time 24; part-time 35.

Teaching Methodologies Case study, computer-aided instruction, computer simulations, experiential learning, faculty seminars, field projects, group discussion, lecture, research, role playing, seminars by members of the business community, simulations, student presentations, study groups, team projects.

Technology Computer terminals/PCs are available for student use and are linked by a campus-wide network. The network has full access to the Internet. Students are not required to have their own PC.

Special Opportunities Advanced credit may be earned through transfer of credits from another institution. An internship program is available.

FINANCES
Costs for 1997-98 Tuition: $900 per 3-hour course. Cost varies by academic program, number of credits taken. Average 1997-98 room and board costs were $4049 per academic year (on campus) and $7200 per academic year (off campus). Room and board costs vary by occupancy (e.g., single, double, triple), type of accommodation, type of meal plan.

Financial Aid Grants, loans available. Financial aid is available to part-time students. Application Deadline: 4/1.

Financial Aid Contact Director, Financial Aid, 7502 Fondren Road, Houston, TX 77074. Phone: 281-649-3204; Fax: 281-649-3303.

FACILITIES
Information Resources Moody Library; total holdings of 167,860 volumes, 78,000 microforms, 930 current periodical subscriptions. Access provided to online bibliographic retrieval services.

INTERNATIONAL STUDENTS
Demographics 3% of students enrolled are international students.

Services and Facilities International student office, international student housing, visa services, ESL courses, counseling/support services.

Applying TOEFL: minimum score of 550 required. Financial aid is available to international students.

International Student Contact Ms. Ida Thompson, Director of Admission for Graduate Programs, Graduate Admissions, 7502 Fondren Road, Houston, TX 77074. Phone: 281-649-3302; Fax: 281-649-3011; E-mail: ithompson@hbu.edu

Program Contact: Ms. Ida Thompson, Director of Admission for Graduate Programs, 7502 Fondren Road, Houston, TX 77074-3298. Phone: 281-649-3302; Fax: 281-649-3011; E-mail: ithompson@hbu.edu

Lamar University

College of Business

Beaumont, Texas

OVERVIEW
Lamar University is a state-supported, coed university. Enrollment: 8,100 graduate, professional, and undergraduate students; 294 full-time matriculated graduate/professional students; 331 part-time matriculated graduate/professional students. Founded: 1923. The graduate business unit is in an urban setting and is on a semester calendar.

HIGHLIGHTS

Enrollment Profile
Full-time: 18
Part-time: 46
Total: 64
Average Age: 32
Fall 1997 Average GPA: 3.15

International: 19%
Women: 41%
Minorities: 20%
Average Class Size: 18
Fall 1997 Average GMAT: 530

Costs
Full-time tuition: $576 per academic year (resident); $4428 per academic year (nonresident)
Part-time tuition: $120 per 3-hour course (resident); $738 per 3-hour course (nonresident)

AACSB – The International Association for Management Education accredited

GRADUATE BUSINESS PROGRAMS
Master of Business Administration (MBA) Full-time, part-time; 30-66 total credits required; 12 months to 6 years to complete program. Concentrations in accounting, management.

ADMISSION
Applications For fall 1997 there were 96 applications for admission. Of those applying, 50 were accepted. Of those accepted, 21 enrolled.

Application Requirements Application form, bachelor's degree, minimum GPA: 2.0, college transcript(s).

Recommended for Application GMAT score accepted: minimum 400, interview, letters of recommendation, personal statement, resume, work experience, computer experience.

Application Deadline 5/1 for fall, 10/1 for spring, 3/1 for summer, 3/15 for fall (international), 10/1 for spring (international), 3/1 for summer (international). Deferred entrance is available.

ACADEMICS
Faculty Full-time 35; part-time 5.

Teaching Methodologies Case study, computer-aided instruction, computer analysis, computer simulations, experiential learning, faculty seminars, field projects, group discussion, lecture, research, role playing, seminars by members of the business community, simulations, student presentations, study groups, team projects.

Technology 800 on-campus computer terminals/PCs are available for student use and are linked by a campus-wide network. The network has full access to the Internet. Students are not required to have their own PC.

Special Opportunities Advanced credit may be earned through transfer of credits from another institution. International exchange programs in Estonia, France, Japan, People's Republic of China. An internship program is available.

FINANCES
Costs for 1997–98 Tuition: Full-time: $576 per year (resident); $4428 per year (nonresident). Part-time: $120 per 3-hour course (resident); $738 per 3-hour course (nonresident). Cost varies by number of credits taken. Fees: Full-time: $674 per academic year (resident); $674 per academic year (nonresident). Part-time: $129 per 3-hour course (resident); $129 per 3-hour course (nonresident). Fees vary by number of credits taken. Average 1997–98 room and board costs were $3500 per academic year (on campus) and $3500 per academic year (off campus). Room and board costs vary by occupancy (e.g., single, double, triple), type of accommodation, type of meal plan.

Financial Aid In 1997–98, 31% of students received some institutionally administered aid in the form of fellowships, research assistantships, teaching assistantships, grants, scholarships, work study, loans. Financial aid is available to part-time students. Application Deadline: 4/1.

Financial Aid Contact Ellen Nystrom, Director of Financial Aid, PO Box 10042, Beaumont, TX 77710-0042. Phone: 409-880-2302.

FACILITIES
Information Resources Mary and John Gray Library; total holdings of 628,142 volumes, 1,023,888 microforms, 2,054 current periodical subscriptions. CD player(s) available for graduate student use. Access provided to online bibliographic retrieval services and online databases.

INTERNATIONAL STUDENTS
Demographics 19% of students enrolled are international students [Africa, 10%, Asia, 60%, Central America, 5%, Europe, 5%, South America, 10%, other, 10%].

Services and Facilities International student office, visa services, ESL courses, counseling/support services.

Applying TOEFL: minimum score of 525, proof of adequate funds, proof of health/immunizations required.

International Student Contact Ms. Sandy Drane, International Student Advisor, PO Box 10009, Beaumont, TX 77710-0009. Phone: 409-880-8349.

PLACEMENT
Services include alumni network, career counseling/planning, career fairs, career library, career placement, job interviews arranged, resume referral to employers, and resume preparation.

Employment Of 1996–97 graduates, 80% were employed within three months of graduation; the average starting salary was $42,000. Types of employment entered: accounting, banking, chemical industry, communications, computer-related, consulting, consumer products, education, energy, engineering, finance, financial services, government, health services, high technology, hospitality management, human resources, information systems/technology, insurance, management, manufacturing, marketing, media, mining, nonprofit, petrochemical, pharmaceutical, service industry, telecommunications, transportation, utilities.

Business Program(s) URL: http://www.cob.lamar.edu/

Program Contact: Dr. Robert Swerdlow, Associate Dean, College of Business, PO Box 10059, Beaumont, TX 77710. Phone: 409-880-8604, 800-433-5638 (TX only); Fax: 409-880-8088; E-mail: swerdlowra@hal.lamar.edu

HIGHLIGHTS

Enrollment Profile

Full-time: 323	International: 0%
Part-time: 0	Women: 41%
Total: 323	Minorities: N/R
Average Age: 35	Average Class Size: 16
Fall 1997 Average GPA: 3.0	Fall 1997 Average GMAT: N/R

Costs
Full-time tuition: $7215 per academic year
Part-time tuition: $300 per credit hour

GRADUATE BUSINESS PROGRAMS
Master of Business Administration (MBA) Full-time; 39 total credits required; 3 years work experience required, minimum age requirement: 23; 20 months to 5 years to complete program. Concentration in management.

Master of Science in Management (MS) Full-time; 36 total credits required; 3 years work experience required, minimum age requirement: 23; 20 months to 5 years to complete program. Concentration in management.

ADMISSION
Application Requirements Application form, application fee, bachelor's degree, minimum GPA: 2.8, 2 letters of recommendation, resume, college transcript(s), minimum of 3 years of work experience.

Recommended for Application Computer experience.

Application Deadline Applications processed on a rolling/continuous basis for both domestic and international students. Application fee: $50. Deferred entrance is available.

ACADEMICS
Faculty Full-time 6; part-time 137.

Teaching Methodologies Case study, computer-aided instruction, computer simulations, group discussion, lecture, student presentations, study groups, team projects.

Technology 120 on-campus computer terminals/PCs are available for student use and are linked by a campus-wide network. The network has full access to the Internet. Students are required to have their own PC.

FINANCES
Costs for 1997–98 Tuition: Full-time: $7215 per year. Part-time: $300 per credit hour. Fees: $150 per course.

Financial Aid Contact Ms. Pat Wilson, Assistant Director of Financial Aid, PO Box 7001, Longview, TX 75607. Phone: 800-388-5327 Ext. 3430; Fax: 903-233-3411; E-mail: wilsonp@james.letu.edu

FACILITIES
Information Resources Margaret Estes Library; total holdings of 87,686 volumes, 42,313 microforms, 442 current periodical subscriptions. CD player(s) available for graduate student use. Access provided to online bibliographic retrieval services.

INTERNATIONAL STUDENTS
Demographics N/R

Applying TOEFL: minimum score of 500 required. Financial aid is not available to international students.

PLACEMENT
Services include alumni network, career counseling/planning, career placement, and resume preparation.

Business Program(s) URL: http://www.letu.edu/

Program Contact: Chris Fontaine, Graduate Admissions Counselor, PO Box 7668, Longview, TX 75607. Phone: 903-233-3250 Ext. 3140, 800-388-5327 (TX only); Fax: 903-233-3227.

LeTourneau University

Program in Business Administration

Longview, Texas

OVERVIEW
LeTourneau University is an independent-religious, coed, comprehensive institution. Enrollment: 2,204 graduate, professional, and undergraduate students; 323 full-time matriculated graduate/professional students; part-time matriculated graduate/professional students. Founded: 1946. The graduate business unit is in a suburban setting and is on a non-traditional format calendar.

Midwestern State University

Division of Business Administration

Wichita Falls, Texas

OVERVIEW
Midwestern State University is a state-supported, coed, comprehensive institution. Enrollment: 5,833 graduate, professional, and undergraduate students; 87 full-time matriculated graduate/professional students; 175 part-time matriculated graduate/professional students. Founded: 1922. The graduate business unit is in a small-town setting and is on a semester calendar.

Midwestern State University (continued)

HIGHLIGHTS

Enrollment Profile
Full-time: 16
Part-time: 49
Total: 65
Average Age: 31
Fall 1997 Average GPA: 3.0

International: 5%
Women: 34%
Minorities: 18%
Average Class Size: 20
Fall 1997 Average GMAT: 450

Costs
Full-time tuition: $1000 per academic year (resident); $7464 per academic year (nonresident)
Part-time tuition: $42 per hour (resident); $222 per hour (nonresident)

ACBSP – The American Council of Business Schools and Programs accredited

GRADUATE BUSINESS PROGRAMS
Master of Business Administration (MBA) Full-time, part-time; 36-60 total credits required; 12 months to 6 years to complete program. Concentration in management.

ADMISSION
Applications For fall 1997 there were 20 applications for admission. Of those applying, 18 were accepted. Of those accepted, 15 enrolled.

Application Requirements Application form, application fee, bachelor's degree, college transcript(s).

Recommended for Application GMAT score accepted: minimum 400, minimum GPA: 2.5.

Application Deadline 8/7 for fall, 12/15 for spring, 5/15 for summer, 4/1 for fall (international), 8/1 for spring (international), 1/1 for summer (international). Application fee: 50 (international). Deferred entrance is available.

ACADEMICS
Faculty Full-time 19; part-time 1.

Teaching Methodologies Case study, computer analysis, computer simulations, group discussion, lecture, research, student presentations, team projects.

Technology 100 on-campus computer terminals/PCs are available for student use and are linked by a campus-wide network. The network has full access to the Internet. Students are not required to have their own PC.

Special Opportunities Advanced credit may be earned through transfer of credits from another institution. International exchange programs in Mexico, United Kingdom.

FINANCES
Costs for 1997–98 Tuition: Full-time: $1000 per semester (resident); $7464 per semester (nonresident). Part-time: $42 per hour (resident); $222 per hour (nonresident). Cost varies by number of credits taken, reciprocity agreements. Fees: Full-time: $600 per academic year (resident); $600 per academic year (nonresident). Part-time: $200 per semester (resident); $200 per semester (nonresident). Average 1997–98 room and board costs were $4400 per academic year (on campus) and $4500 per academic year (off campus). Room and board costs vary by type of meal plan.

Financial Aid In 1997–98, 5% of students received some institutionally administered aid in the form of research assistantships, teaching assistantships, scholarships, work study, loans. Financial aid is available to part-time students.

Financial Aid Contact Dr. Henry Van Geem, Jr., Advisor, MBA Program, 3410 Taft Boulevard, Wichita Falls, TX 76308-2096. Phone: 940-397-4367.

FACILITIES
Information Resources Moffett Library; total holdings of 582,276 volumes, 513,062 microforms, 1,024 current periodical subscriptions. Access provided to online bibliographic retrieval services.

INTERNATIONAL STUDENTS
Demographics 5% of students enrolled are international students.

Services and Facilities International student office, ESL courses, counseling/support services.

Applying TOEFL: minimum score of 550, proof of adequate funds, proof of health/immunizations required. Financial aid is not available to international students.

International Student Contact Mr. Uli Bauer, International Student Advisor—International Programs, 3410 Taft Boulevard, Wichita Falls, TX 76308-1096. Phone: 940-397-4208.

PLACEMENT
Services include career counseling/planning, career fairs, and resume preparation. In 1996–97, 5 organizations participated in on-campus recruiting; 5 on-campus interviews were conducted.

Business Program(s) URL: http://www.mwsu.edu

Program Contact: Dr. Henry Van Geem, Jr., Advisor, MBA Program, 3410 Taft Boulevard, Wichita Falls, TX 76308-2096. Phone: 940-397-4367.

Our Lady of the Lake University of San Antonio

School of Business and Public Administration

San Antonio, Texas

OVERVIEW
Our Lady of the Lake University of San Antonio is an independent-religious, coed, comprehensive institution. Enrollment: 3,800 graduate, professional, and undergraduate students; 276 full-time matriculated graduate/professional students; 827 part-time matriculated graduate/professional students. Founded: 1895. The graduate business unit is in an urban setting and is on a trimester calendar.

HIGHLIGHTS

Enrollment Profile
Full-time: 0
Part-time: 558
Total: 558
Average Age: 38
Fall 1997 Average GPA: 3.1

International: 0%
Women: 50%
Minorities: 83%
Average Class Size: 22
Fall 1997 Average GMAT: 430

Costs
Full-time tuition: N/R
Part-time tuition: $353 per credit hour

ACBSP – The American Council of Business Schools and Programs accredited

GRADUATE BUSINESS PROGRAMS
Master of Business Administration (MBA) Part-time; 36 total credits required; 2 to 6 years to complete program. Concentrations in management, finance, international business.

Master of Business Administration in Health Care Management (MBA) Part-time; 36 total credits required; 2 to 6 years to complete program.

ADMISSION
Applications For fall 1997 there were 75 applications for admission. Of those applying, 72 were accepted. Of those accepted, 65 enrolled.

Application Requirements Application form, application fee, bachelor's degree, interview, 2 letters of recommendation, personal statement, resume, college transcript(s), minimum of 3 years of work experience.

Recommended for Application GMAT score accepted, GRE score accepted, MAT score accepted, minimum GPA: 2.5.

Application Deadline 8/21 for fall, 1/2 for spring, 4/25 for summer, 8/21 for fall (international), 1/2 for spring (international), 4/25 for summer (international). Application fee: $15. Deferred entrance is available.

ACADEMICS
Faculty Full-time 25; part-time 47.

Teaching Methodologies Case study, computer analysis, computer simulations, experiential learning, group discussion, lecture, research, role playing, simulations, student presentations, study groups, team projects.

Technology 200 on-campus computer terminals/PCs are available for student use and are linked by a campus-wide network. The network has full access to the Internet. Students are not required to have their own PC.

Special Opportunities Advanced credit may be earned through transfer of credits from another institution.

FINANCES
Costs for 1997–98 Tuition: Part-time: $353 per credit hour. Fees: Part-time: $51 per trimester. Fees vary by number of credits taken.

Financial Aid Fellowships, loans available. Financial aid is available to part-time students. Application Deadline: 4/15.

Financial Aid Contact Mr. Jeff Scofield, 411 Southwest 24th Street, San Antonio, TX 78207-4689. Phone: 210-434-6711 Ext. 319; Fax: 210-434-0824.

FACILITIES
Information Resources St. Florence Library plus 3 additional on-campus libraries; total holdings of 265,874 volumes, 111,129 microforms, 915 current periodical subscriptions. CD player(s) available for graduate student use. Access provided to online bibliographic retrieval services and online databases.

INTERNATIONAL STUDENTS
Demographics 0% of students enrolled are international students [Asia, 100%].

Services and Facilities International student office, international student center, visa services, ESL courses, counseling/support services.

Applying TOEFL: minimum score of 550, proof of adequate funds required. Financial aid is not available to international students.

International Student Contact Ms. Carol Graham, 411 Southwest 24th Street, San Antonio, TX 78207-4689. Phone: 210-434-6711 Ext. 322; Fax: 210-434-0824.

Business Program(s) URL: http://www.ollusa.edu

Program Contact: Mr. Quentin Korte, Assistant Dean, Graduate Programs, 411 Southwest 24th Street, San Antonio, TX 78207-4689. Phone: 210-434-6711 Ext. 412; Fax: 210-434-0821; E-mail: kortb@lake.ollusa.edu

Prairie View A&M University

College of Business

Prairie View, Texas

OVERVIEW
Prairie View A&M University is a state-supported, coed, comprehensive institution. Enrollment: 6,004 graduate, professional, and undergraduate students. Founded: 1876. The graduate business unit is in a rural setting and is on a semester calendar.

HIGHLIGHTS

Enrollment Profile
Full-time: 15
Part-time: 60
Total: 75
Average Age: 28
Fall 1997 Average GPA: 2.85

International: 5%
Women: 53%
Minorities: 69%
Average Class Size: 12
Fall 1997 Average GMAT: 405

Costs
Full-time tuition: N/R
Part-time tuition: $206 per credit (resident); $415 per credit (nonresident)

GRADUATE BUSINESS PROGRAMS
Master of Business Administration (MBA) Full-time, part-time; 36-57 total credits required; 12 months to 4 years to complete program. Concentration in management.

ADMISSION
Applications For fall 1997 there were 26 applications for admission. Of those applying, 19 were accepted. Of those accepted, 16 enrolled.

Application Requirements GMAT score: minimum 350, application form, application fee, bachelor's degree, minimum GPA: 2.75, 3 letters of recommendation, college transcript(s).

Application Deadline Applications processed on a rolling/continuous basis for both domestic and international students. Application fee: $35.

ACADEMICS
Faculty Full-time 12.

Teaching Methodologies Case study, group discussion, lecture, student presentations, team projects.

Technology 25 on-campus computer terminals/PCs are available for student use. Students are not required to have their own PC.

Special Opportunities Advanced credit may be earned through transfer of credits from another institution.

FINANCES
Costs for 1997–98 Tuition: $206 per credit (resident); $415 per credit (nonresident). Cost varies by number of credits taken. Fees: $254 per semester (resident); $254 per semester (nonresident). Average 1997–98 room and board costs were $7242 per academic year (on campus) and $9000 per academic year (off campus).

Financial Aid Work study, loans available. Application Deadline: 6/30.

Financial Aid Contact Mr. D. A. James, Director of Financial Aid, PO Box 188, University Drive, FM 1098, Prairie View, TX 77446. Phone: 409-857-4723.

FACILITIES
Information Resources John B. Coleman Library plus 1 additional on-campus library; total holdings of 284,111 volumes, 372,325 microforms, 1,189 current periodical subscriptions. CD player(s) available for graduate student use. Access provided to online bibliographic retrieval services.

INTERNATIONAL STUDENTS
Demographics 5% of students enrolled are international students [Africa, 50%, Central America, 50%].

Services and Facilities International student office, international student center, counseling/support services.

Applying TOEFL: minimum score of 550, proof of adequate funds, proof of health/immunizations required. Financial aid is not available to international students.

International Student Contact Dr. George Nelson, MBA Program Coordinator, College of Business, Prairie View, TX 77446. Phone: 409-857-4310; Fax: 409-857-2797.

PLACEMENT
Services include career counseling/planning, career fairs, and career placement. In 1996–97, 5 organizations participated in on-campus recruiting; 25 on-campus interviews were conducted.

Employment Types of employment entered: banking, financial services, government, service industry.

Program Contact: Dr. George Nelson, MBA Program Coordinator, College of Business, Prairie View, TX 77446. Phone: 409-857-4310; Fax: 409-857-2797.

Rice University

Jesse H. Jones Graduate School of Management

Houston, Texas

OVERVIEW
Rice University is an independent-nonprofit, coed university. Enrollment: 4,244 graduate, professional, and undergraduate students; 1,431 full-time matriculated graduate/professional students; 118 part-time matriculated graduate/professional students. Founded: 1912. The graduate business unit is in an urban setting and is on a semester calendar.

HIGHLIGHTS

Enrollment Profile
Full-time: 267
Part-time: 0
Total: 267
Average Age: 27
Fall 1997 Average GPA: 3.18

International: 15%
Women: 28%
Minorities: 15%
Average Class Size: 50
Fall 1997 Average GMAT: 632

Costs
Full-time tuition: $15,750 per academic year
Part-time tuition: N/R

AACSB – The International Association for Management Education accredited

GRADUATE BUSINESS PROGRAMS
Master of Business Administration (MBA) Full-time; 64 total credits required; 21 months to complete program. Concentrations in entrepreneurship, finance, international management, management information systems, marketing, strategic management, management.

Master of Business Administration/Master of Engineering (MBA/ME) Full-time; 76 total credits required; 2 years to complete program. Concentration in management.

ADMISSION
Applications For fall 1997 there were 526 applications for admission. Of those applying, 236 were accepted. Of those accepted, 132 enrolled.

Application Requirements Application form, application fee, bachelor's degree, essay, minimum GPA, 3 letters of recommendation, college transcript(s), minimum of 2 years of work experience, computer experience: Microsoft Office.

Recommended for Application GMAT score accepted, interview, personal statement, resume.

Application Deadline 3/1 for fall. Application fee: $25.

ACADEMICS
Faculty Full-time 27; part-time 24.

Teaching Methodologies Case study, computer-aided instruction, computer simulations, experiential learning, faculty seminars, field projects, group discussion, lecture, seminars by members of the business community, simulations, student presentations, study groups, team projects.

Technology 75 on-campus computer terminals/PCs are available for student use and are linked by a campus-wide network. The network has full access to the Internet. Students are required to have their own PC.

Special Opportunities Advanced credit may be earned through transfer of credits from another institution.

FINANCES
Costs for 1997–98 Tuition: Full-time: $15,750 per year. Fees: Full-time: $420 per academic year. Average 1997–98 room and board costs were $8000 per academic year (on campus) and $9000 per academic year (off campus).

TEXAS

Rice University (continued)

Room and board costs vary by occupancy (e.g., single, double, triple), type of accommodation, type of meal plan.

Financial Aid In 1997–98, 69% of students received some institutionally administered aid in the form of scholarships, work study, loans. Application Deadline: 6/1.

Financial Aid Contact Mr. David Hunt, Director of Financial Aid, Office of Financial Aid, MS-12, 6100 Main Street, Houston, TX 77005-1892. Phone: 713-527-4958; Fax: 713-285-5921; E-mail: fina@rice.edu

FACILITIES
Information Resources Fondren Library plus 5 additional on-campus libraries; total holdings of 1,550,098 volumes, 1,950,000 microforms, 14,249 current periodical subscriptions. Access provided to online bibliographic retrieval services.

INTERNATIONAL STUDENTS
Demographics 15% of students enrolled are international students [Africa, 1%, Asia, 69%, Central America, 2%, Europe, 18%, North America, 8%, South America, 2%].

Services and Facilities International student office, international student center, international student housing, visa services, ESL courses, counseling/support services.

Applying TOEFL, proof of adequate funds, proof of health/immunizations required. TWE recommended. Financial aid is not available to international students.

International Student Contact Dr. Adria Baker, Director, International Services, 6100 Main Street, A102, Abercrombie, MS 365, Houston, TX 77005-1892. Phone: 713-527-6095; Fax: 713-285-5199; E-mail: abaker@rice.edu

PLACEMENT
Services include alumni network, career counseling/planning, career fairs, career library, career placement, electronic job bank, job interviews arranged, job search course, resume referral to employers, and resume preparation. In 1996–97, 66 organizations participated in on-campus recruiting; 714 on-campus interviews were conducted.

Employment Of 1996–97 graduates, 90% were employed within three months of graduation; the average starting salary was $61,000. Types of employment entered: accounting, banking, chemical industry, communications, computer-related, consulting, consumer products, energy, engineering, finance, financial services, health services, high technology, human resources, information systems/technology, insurance, international trade, management, manufacturing, marketing, nonprofit, petrochemical, real estate, retail, service industry, telecommunications, transportation, utilities.

Business Program(s) URL: http://www.rice.edu/jgs

Program Contact: Ms. Jill L. Deutser, Director of Admissions and Marketing, Jones Graduate School, MS-531, 6100 Main Street, #270, Houston, TX 77005-1892. Phone: 713-527-4918; Fax: 713-737-5838; E-mail: enterjgs@rice.edu
See full description on page 944.

St. Edward's University

School of Business

Austin, Texas

OVERVIEW
St. Edward's University is an independent-religious, coed, comprehensive institution. Enrollment: 3,101 graduate, professional, and undergraduate students; 76 full-time matriculated graduate/professional students; 498 part-time matriculated graduate/professional students. Founded: 1885. The graduate business unit is in an urban setting and is on a trimester calendar.

HIGHLIGHTS

Enrollment Profile
Full-time: 39
Part-time: 361
Total: 400
Average Age: 32
Fall 1997 Average GPA: 3.0

International: 8%
Women: 38%
Minorities: 21%
Average Class Size: 22
Fall 1997 Average GMAT: 550

Costs
Full-time tuition: N/R
Part-time tuition: $377 per credit hour

Degree(s) offered in conjunction with University of Dallas

GRADUATE BUSINESS PROGRAMS
Master of Business Administration (MBA) Full-time, part-time; 60-66 total credits required; 12 months to 6 years to complete program. Concentrations in management, management information systems, public management, technology management, telecommunications management, public policy and administration, sports/entertainment management.

ADMISSION
Applications For fall 1997 there were 165 applications for admission. Of those applying, 136 were accepted. Of those accepted, 103 enrolled.

Application Requirements Application form, application fee, bachelor's degree, essay, minimum GPA: 2.75, personal statement, resume, college transcript(s).

Recommended for Application GMAT score accepted: minimum 500, GRE score accepted: minimum 1,000, work experience, computer experience.

Application Deadline 7/1 for fall, 12/1 for spring, 4/15 for summer, 7/1 for fall (international), 12/1 for spring (international), 4/15 for summer (international). Application fee: $25. Deferred entrance is available.

ACADEMICS
Faculty Full-time 13; part-time 12.

Teaching Methodologies Case study, computer-aided instruction, computer analysis, computer simulations, faculty seminars, group discussion, lecture, research, role playing, seminars by members of the business community, simulations, student presentations, team projects.

Technology 275 on-campus computer terminals/PCs are available for student use and are linked by a campus-wide network. The network has full access to the Internet. Students are not required to have their own PC.

Special Opportunities Advanced credit may be earned through credit by examination, transfer of credits from another institution.

FINANCES
Costs for 1997–98 Tuition: $377 per credit hour. Average 1997–98 room and board costs were $4700 per academic year. Room and board costs vary by occupancy (e.g., single, double, triple), type of accommodation, type of meal plan.

Financial Aid In 1997–98, 2% of students received some institutionally administered aid in the form of scholarships, loans. Financial aid is available to part-time students. Application Deadline: 3/1.

Financial Aid Contact Ms. Doris Constantine, Director of Financial Aid Services, 3001 South Congress Avenue, Austin, TX 78704-6489. Phone: 512-448-8400; Fax: 512-448-8492; E-mail: doris@admin.stedwards.edu

FACILITIES
Information Resources Scarborough-Phillips Library; total holdings of 106,082 volumes, 85,251 microforms, 960 current periodical subscriptions. CD player(s) available for graduate student use. Access provided to online bibliographic retrieval services.

INTERNATIONAL STUDENTS
Demographics 8% of students enrolled are international students [Africa, 9%, Asia, 73%, Central America, 3%, Europe, 3%, South America, 12%].

Services and Facilities International student office, visa services, counseling/support services.

Applying TOEFL: minimum score of 500, proof of adequate funds required. Financial aid is not available to international students.

International Student Contact Ms. Teri Heimer, International Student Advisor, 3001 South Congress Avenue, Austin, TX 78704-6489. Phone: 512-448-8531; Fax: 512-448-8492; E-mail: terih@admin.stedwards.edu

PLACEMENT
Services include alumni network, career counseling/planning, career fairs, career library, electronic job bank, job interviews arranged, job search course, resume referral to employers, and resume preparation.

Employment Of 1996–97 graduates, 67% were employed within three months of graduation; the average starting salary was $50,000. Types of employment entered: accounting, banking, communications, computer-related, consumer products, education, finance, financial services, government, health services, high technology, information systems/technology, international trade, management, manufacturing, marketing, media, retail, service industry, telecommunications, transportation.

Business Program(s) URL: http://www.stedwards.edu

Program Contact: Mr. Thomas Evans, Director, Graduate Admissions, 3001 South Congress Avenue, Austin, TX 78704-6489. Phone: 512-448-8600; Fax: 512-448-8492; E-mail: tome@admin.stedwards.edu

Peterson's Guide to MBA Programs 1999

St. Mary's University of San Antonio

School of Business and Administration

San Antonio, Texas

OVERVIEW
St. Mary's University of San Antonio is an independent-religious, coed, comprehensive institution. Enrollment: 4,212 graduate, professional, and undergraduate students. Founded: 1852. The graduate business unit is in an urban setting and is on a semester calendar.

HIGHLIGHTS

Enrollment Profile
Full-time: 15
Part-time: 195
Total: 210
Average Age: 29
Fall 1997 Average GPA: N/R

International: 10%
Women: 44%
Minorities: 50%
Average Class Size: 25
Fall 1997 Average GMAT: 475

Costs
Full-time tuition: N/R
Part-time tuition: $383 per credit hour

GRADUATE BUSINESS PROGRAMS
Master of Business Administration (MBA) Full-time, part-time; 33-39 total credits required; 18 months to 5 years to complete program. Concentrations in finance, management, international business.

Master of Accountancy (MAcc) Full-time, part-time; 30 total credits required; 18 months to 5 years to complete program. Concentrations in accounting, taxation.

ADMISSION
Applications For fall 1997 there were 50 applications for admission. Of those applying, 45 were accepted.

Application Requirements GMAT score: minimum 400, application form, application fee, bachelor's degree, minimum GPA: 2.5, 2 letters of recommendation, resume, college transcript(s).

Recommended for Application Essay, interview, personal statement, computer experience.

Application Deadline Applications processed on a rolling/continuous basis for both domestic and international students. Application fee: $15. Deferred entrance is available.

ACADEMICS
Faculty Full-time 17; part-time 7.

Teaching Methodologies Case study, computer-aided instruction, computer analysis, computer simulations, experiential learning, group discussion, lecture, research, role playing, seminars by members of the business community, student presentations, study groups, team projects.

Technology 75 on-campus computer terminals/PCs are available for student use and are linked by a campus-wide network. The network has full access to the Internet. Students are not required to have their own PC.

Special Opportunities Advanced credit may be earned through transfer of credits from another institution. An internship program is available.

FINANCES
Costs for 1997–98 Tuition: $383 per credit hour. Cost varies by number of credits taken. Fees: Full-time: $212 per academic year. Part-time: $53 per semester.

Financial Aid In 1997–98, 2% of students received some institutionally administered aid in the form of research assistantships, work study, loans. Application Deadline: 3/1.

Financial Aid Contact Mr. David Krause, Director, Financial Assistance, 1 Camino Santa Maria, San Antonio, TX 78228-8507. Phone: 210-436-3141.

FACILITIES
Information Resources Academic Library plus 1 additional on-campus library; total holdings of 525,000 volumes, 17,000 microforms, 1,400 current periodical subscriptions. CD player(s) available for graduate student use. Access provided to online bibliographic retrieval services.

INTERNATIONAL STUDENTS
Demographics 10% of students enrolled are international students.

Applying TOEFL: minimum score of 550, proof of adequate funds required. Financial aid is not available to international students.

PLACEMENT
Services include alumni network, career counseling/planning, career fairs, career library, career placement, electronic job bank, job interviews arranged, resume referral to employers, and resume preparation.

Employment Of 1996–97 graduates, 99% were employed within three months of graduation. Types of employment entered: accounting, banking, computer-related, energy, finance, financial services, government, health services, human resources, information systems/technology, insurance, international trade, law, management, manufacturing, marketing, media, nonprofit, retail, service industry, telecommunications, transportation, utilities.

Program Contact: Dr. Thomas Hamilton, MBA Program Director, School of Business and Administration, 1 Camino Santa Maria, San Antonio, TX 78228-8507. Phone: 210-431-2027; Fax: 210-431-2115; E-mail: mba@stmarytx.edu

Sam Houston State University

College of Business Administration

Huntsville, Texas

OVERVIEW
Sam Houston State University is a state-supported, coed, comprehensive institution. Enrollment: 12,568 graduate, professional, and undergraduate students; 373 full-time matriculated graduate/professional students; 926 part-time matriculated graduate/professional students. Founded: 1879. The graduate business unit is in a small-town setting and is on a semester calendar.

HIGHLIGHTS

Enrollment Profile
Full-time: 43
Part-time: 82
Total: 125
Average Age: 27
Fall 1997 Average GPA: 3.04

International: 10%
Women: 44%
Minorities: 14%
Average Class Size: 18
Fall 1997 Average GMAT: 491

Costs
Full-time tuition: $650 per academic year (resident); $3000 per academic year (nonresident)
Part-time tuition: $32 per credit (resident); $171 per credit (nonresident)

AACSB – The International Association for Management Education accredited

GRADUATE BUSINESS PROGRAMS
Master of Business Administration (MBA) Full-time, part-time, distance learning option; 36 total credits required; 12 months to 7 years to complete program.

ADMISSION
Application Requirements GMAT score, application form, application fee, bachelor's degree, minimum GPA, college transcript(s).

Application Deadline Applications processed on a rolling/continuous basis for both domestic and international students. Application fee: $15. Deferred entrance is available.

ACADEMICS
Faculty Full-time 44; part-time 14.

Teaching Methodologies Case study, computer analysis, computer simulations, field projects, group discussion, lecture, research, simulations, student presentations, study groups, team projects.

Technology 150 on-campus computer terminals/PCs are available for student use and are linked by a campus-wide network. The network has full access to the Internet. Students are not required to have their own PC.

Special Opportunities Advanced credit may be earned through transfer of credits from another institution. International exchange program available.

FINANCES
Costs for 1997–98 Tuition: Full-time: $650 per semester (resident); $3000 per semester (nonresident). Part-time: $32 per credit (resident); $171 per credit (nonresident). Cost varies by number of credits taken. Fees: Full-time: $702 per academic year (resident); $702 per academic year (nonresident). Part-time: $51 per semester (resident); $207 per semester (nonresident). Fees vary by number of credits taken. Average 1997–98 room and board costs were $3300 per academic year. Room and board costs vary by occupancy (e.g., single, double, triple), type of accommodation, type of meal plan.

Financial Aid Research assistantships, work study, loans available.

Financial Aid Contact Mr. Douglas Wright, Financial Aid Counselor, PO Box 2328, Huntsville, TX 77341-2328. Phone: 409-294-1724; Fax: 409-294-3668; E-mail: sfa_clww@shsu.edu

FACILITIES
Information Resources Newton Gresham Library; total holdings of 775,642 volumes, 539,363 microforms, 3,028 current periodical subscriptions. CD player(s) available for graduate student use. Access provided to online bibliographic retrieval services.

Sam Houston State University (continued)

INTERNATIONAL STUDENTS

Demographics 10% of students enrolled are international students.

Services and Facilities International student office, visa services, ESL courses, counseling/support services.

Applying TOEFL: minimum score of 550, proof of adequate funds, proof of health/immunizations required. Financial aid is available to international students.

International Student Contact Dean of Graduate Studies, PO Box 2056, Huntsville, TX 77341-2056. Phone: 409-294-1971; Fax: 409-294-3612; E-mail: eco_mjm@shsu.edu

PLACEMENT

Services include alumni network, career counseling/planning, career fairs, career library, career placement, electronic job bank, job interviews arranged, job search course, resume referral to employers, and resume preparation. In 1996–97, 125 organizations participated in on-campus recruiting.

Employment Types of employment entered: accounting, banking, computer-related, consulting, education, engineering, finance, financial services, government, hospitality management, human resources, insurance, management, manufacturing, marketing, nonprofit, pharmaceutical, retail, service industry, utilities.

Business Program(s) URL: http://coba.shsu.edu/mba-home.htm

Program Contact: Dr. Mitchell Muehsam, Dean of Graduate Studies, PO Box 2056, Huntsville, TX 77341-2056. Phone: 409-294-1246; Fax: 409-294-3612; E-mail: eco_mjm@shsu.edu

Southern Methodist University

Edwin L. Cox School of Business

Dallas, Texas

OVERVIEW

Southern Methodist University is an independent-religious, coed university. Enrollment: 9,396 graduate, professional, and undergraduate students; 1,809 full-time matriculated graduate/professional students; 2,273 part-time matriculated graduate/professional students. Founded: 1911. The graduate business unit is in an urban setting and is on a semester calendar.

HIGHLIGHTS

Enrollment Profile
Full-time: 295
Part-time: 453
Total: 748
Average Age: 27
Fall 1997 Average GPA: 3.0

International: 7%
Women: 31%
Minorities: 7%
Average Class Size: 50
Fall 1997 Average GMAT: 611

Costs
Full-time tuition: $21,244 per academic year
Part-time tuition: $645 per hour

AACSB – The International Association for Management Education accredited

GRADUATE BUSINESS PROGRAMS

Master of Business Administration (MBA) Full-time, part-time; 60 total credits required; 2 years to complete program. Concentrations in accounting, business policy/strategy, real estate, management information systems, organizational behavior/development, finance.

Master of Business Administration/Doctor of Jurisprudence (MBA/JD) Full-time; 150 total credits required; 4.5 years to complete program. Concentrations in accounting, business policy/strategy, finance, real estate, management information systems, organizational behavior/development, legal administration.

Master of Business Administration/Master of Arts in Administration (MBA/MA) Full-time; 75 total credits required; 2 years to complete program. Concentrations in accounting, business policy/strategy, finance, real estate, management information systems, organizational behavior/development, arts administration/management.

ADMISSION

Applications For fall 1997 there were 500 applications for admission. Of those applying, 285 were accepted. Of those accepted, 140 enrolled.

Application Requirements Application form, application fee, bachelor's degree, essay, minimum GPA, interview, 2 letters of recommendation, personal statement, resume, college transcript(s), minimum of 2 years of work experience.

Recommended for Application GMAT score accepted, computer experience.

Application Deadline 11/30 for fall, 2/15 for winter, 4/15 for spring, 5/15 for summer, 11/30 for fall (international), 2/15 for winter (international), 4/15 for spring (international), 5/15 for summer (international). Application fee: $50. Deferred entrance is available.

ACADEMICS

Faculty Full-time 76; part-time 28.

Teaching Methodologies Case study, computer analysis, computer simulations, field projects, group discussion, lecture, seminars by members of the business community, simulations, student presentations, study groups, team projects.

Technology 250 on-campus computer terminals/PCs are available for student use and are linked by a campus-wide network. The network has full access to the Internet. Students are not required to have their own PC.

Special Opportunities Advanced credit may be earned through transfer of credits from another institution. International exchange programs in Australia, Belgium, Brazil, France, Japan, Mexico, Republic of Singapore, Spain, United Kingdom, Venezuela.

FINANCES

Costs for 1997–98 Tuition: Full-time: $21,244 per year. Part-time: $645 per hour. Fees: Full-time: $2274 per academic year. Part-time: $80 per hour. Average 1997–98 room and board costs were $6904 per academic year (on campus) and $10,000 per academic year (off campus). Room and board costs vary by occupancy (e.g., single, double, triple), type of accommodation, type of meal plan.

Financial Aid In 1997–98, 31% of students received some institutionally administered aid in the form of research assistantships, scholarships, work study. Financial aid is available to part-time students. Application Deadline: 3/1.

Financial Aid Contact Mr. Mike Novak, Executive Director, Division of Enrollment Services, PO Box 750181, Dallas, TX 75275-0181. Phone: 214-768-3417; Fax: 214-768-0202; E-mail: enrol_serv@mail.smu.edu

FACILITIES

Information Resources Fondren Library plus 6 additional on-campus libraries; total holdings of 2,950,000 volumes, 1,700,000 microforms, 7,000 current periodical subscriptions. CD player(s) available for graduate student use. Access provided to online bibliographic retrieval services and online databases.

INTERNATIONAL STUDENTS

Demographics 7% of students enrolled are international students [Asia, 9%, Central America, 4%, Europe, 2%, North America, 83%, South America, 2%].

Services and Facilities International student office, visa services, counseling/support services.

Applying TOEFL: minimum score of 600, proof of adequate funds, proof of health/immunizations required. Financial aid is available to international students.

International Student Contact Ms. Donna Lau Smith, Director of MBA Admissions, PO Box 750333, Dallas, TX 75275-0333. Phone: 214-768-2630; Fax: 214-768-3956; E-mail: mbainfo@mail.cox.smu.edu

PLACEMENT

Services include alumni network, career counseling/planning, career fairs, career library, career placement, electronic job bank, job interviews arranged, job search course, resume referral to employers, and resume preparation. In 1996–97, 126 organizations participated in on-campus recruiting; 630 on-campus interviews were conducted.

Employment Of 1996–97 graduates, 92% were employed within three months of graduation; the average starting salary was $57,170. Types of employment entered: accounting, banking, chemical industry, communications, computer-related, consulting, consumer products, energy, finance, financial services, government, high technology, human resources, information systems/technology, insurance, international trade, law, management, manufacturing, marketing, nonprofit, petrochemical, pharmaceutical, real estate, service industry, telecommunications, transportation, utilities.

Business Program(s) URL: http://www.cox.smu.edu

Program Contact: Ms. Donna Lau Smith, Director of MBA Admissions, PO Box 750333, Dallas, TX 75275-0333. Phone: 214-768-2630, 800-472-3622; Fax: 214-768-3956; E-mail: mbainfo@mail.cox.smu.edu
See full description on page 994.

Southwest Texas State University

Graduate School of Business

San Marcos, Texas

OVERVIEW

Southwest Texas State University is a state-supported, coed, comprehensive institution. Enrollment: 20,776 graduate, professional, and undergraduate students; 736 full-time matriculated graduate/professional students; 1,605 part-time matriculated graduate/professional students. Founded: 1899. The graduate business unit is in a suburban setting and is, on a semester calendar.

HIGHLIGHTS

Enrollment Profile
Full-time: 89
Part-time: 204
Total: 293
Average Age: 31
Fall 1997 Average GPA: 3.0

International: 4%
Women: 34%
Minorities: 20%
Average Class Size: 25
Fall 1997 Average GMAT: 560

Costs
Full-time tuition: $768 per academic year (resident); $5904 per academic year (nonresident)
Part-time tuition: $192 per 6 hours (resident); $1476 per 6 hours (nonresident)

AACSB – The International Association for Management Education accredited

GRADUATE BUSINESS PROGRAMS
Master of Business Administration (MBA) Full-time, part-time; 60 total credits required; 12 months to 6 years to complete program. Concentration in management.

Master of Accountancy (MAcc) Full-time, part-time; 60 total credits required; 12 months to 6 years to complete program. Concentration in accounting.

ADMISSION
Application Requirements GMAT score: minimum 400, application form, application fee, bachelor's degree, minimum GPA: 2.75, college transcript(s).
Application Deadline 6/15 for fall, 10/15 for spring, 4/15 for summer, 6/15 for fall (international), 10/15 for spring (international), 4/15 for summer (international). Application fee: $25, $75 (international). Deferred entrance is available.

ACADEMICS
Faculty Full-time 43; part-time 7.
Teaching Methodologies Case study, computer analysis, group discussion, lecture, research, student presentations, team projects.
Technology 600 on-campus computer terminals/PCs are available for student use and are linked by a campus-wide network. The network has full access to the Internet. Students are not required to have their own PC.
Special Opportunities Advanced credit may be earned through transfer of credits from another institution. International exchange program in Morocco.

FINANCES
Costs for 1997–98 Tuition: Full-time: $768 per year (resident); $5904 per year (nonresident). Part-time: $192 per 6 hours (resident); $1476 per 6 hours (nonresident). Cost varies by number of credits taken. Fees: Full-time: $1254 per academic year (resident); $1254 per academic year (nonresident). Part-time: $404 per 6 hours (resident); $404 per 6 hours (nonresident). Fees vary by number of credits taken. Average 1997–98 room and board costs were $2730 per academic year (on campus) and $5000 per academic year (off campus). Room and board costs vary by occupancy (e.g., single, double, triple), type of accommodation, type of meal plan.
Financial Aid Research assistantships, teaching assistantships, work study, loans available. Financial aid is available to part-time students. Application Deadline: 4/1.
Financial Aid Contact Ms. Mariko Gomez, Director, Financial Assistance, 601 University Drive, San Marcos, TX 78666. Phone: 512-245-2315; Fax: 512-245-8375.

FACILITIES
Information Resources Alkek Library; total holdings of 966,191 volumes, 1,485,654 microforms, 5,496 current periodical subscriptions. CD player(s) available for graduate student use. Access provided to online bibliographic retrieval services.

INTERNATIONAL STUDENTS
Demographics 4% of students enrolled are international students.
Services and Facilities International student office, international student center, visa services, ESL courses, counseling/support services.
Applying TOEFL: minimum score of 550, TSE: minimum score of 45, proof of adequate funds, proof of health/immunizations required. Financial aid is available to international students.
International Student Contact Dr. Diana Sellers, Director, Office for International Students, 601 University Drive, San Marcos, TX 78666. Phone: 512-245-2507; Fax: 512-245-8375.

PLACEMENT
Services include alumni network, career counseling/planning, career fairs, career library, career placement, and job interviews arranged. In 1996–97, 846 organizations participated in on-campus recruiting.

Employment Of 1996–97 graduates, 96% were employed within three months of graduation. Types of employment entered: accounting, banking, communications, computer-related, consulting, education, engineering, finance, financial services, government, high technology, human resources, information systems/technology, insurance, management, manufacturing, marketing, nonprofit, pharmaceutical, real estate, retail, service industry, telecommunications, transportation, utilities.

Business Program(s) URL: http://www.business.swt.edu

Program Contact: Dr. Robert Olney, Director of Graduate Business Programs, Graduate School of Business, 601 University Drive, San Marcos, TX 78666. Phone: 512-245-3591; Fax: 512-245-8375.

Stephen F. Austin State University

College of Business
Nacogdoches, Texas

OVERVIEW
Stephen F. Austin State University is a state-supported, coed, comprehensive institution. Enrollment: 12,041 graduate, professional, and undergraduate students; 578 full-time matriculated graduate/professional students; 919 part-time matriculated graduate/professional students. The graduate business unit is in a small-town setting and is on a semester calendar.

HIGHLIGHTS

Enrollment Profile
Full-time: 23
Part-time: 56
Total: 79
Average Age: 29
Fall 1997 Average GPA: 3.3

International: 3%
Women: 44%
Minorities: 6%
Average Class Size: 16
Fall 1997 Average GMAT: 486

Costs
Full-time tuition: $408 per academic year (resident); $2976 per academic year (nonresident)
Part-time tuition: $120 per course (resident); $744 per course (nonresident)

AACSB – The International Association for Management Education accredited

GRADUATE BUSINESS PROGRAMS
Master of Business Administration (MBA) Full-time, part-time; 36-57 total credits required; 12 months to 6 years to complete program. Concentration in management.

Master of Professional Accountancy (MPA) Full-time, part-time; 156 total credits required; 5 to 6 years to complete program. Concentration in accounting.

ADMISSION
Applications For fall 1997 there were 53 applications for admission. Of those applying, 43 were accepted. Of those accepted, 34 enrolled.
Application Requirements GMAT score, application form, application fee, bachelor's degree, minimum GPA, college transcript(s).
Recommended for Application Minimum of 2 years of work experience.
Application Deadline 7/20 for fall, 12/10 for spring, 5/1 for summer, 7/20 for fall (international), 12/10 for spring (international), 5/1 for summer (international). Application fee: 25 (international). Deferred entrance is available.

ACADEMICS
Faculty Full-time 48; part-time 1.
Teaching Methodologies Case study, computer analysis, computer simulations, experiential learning, field projects, group discussion, lecture, research, role playing, seminars by members of the business community, simulations, student presentations, team projects.
Technology 214 on-campus computer terminals/PCs are available for student use and are linked by a campus-wide network. The network has full access to the Internet. Students are not required to have their own PC.
Special Opportunities Advanced credit may be earned through credit by examination, credit for experience, credit for military training programs, credit for business training programs, transfer of credits from another institution. An internship program is available.

FINANCES
Costs for 1997–98 Tuition: Full-time: $408 per semester (resident); $2976 per semester (nonresident). Part-time: $120 per course (resident); $744 per course (nonresident). Cost varies by number of credits taken. Fees: Full-time: $469 per academic year (resident); $469 per academic year (nonresident). Part-time: $125 per course (resident); $125 per course (nonresident). Fees vary by number of credits taken. Average 1997–98 room and board costs were

Stephen F. Austin State University (continued)

$4600 per academic year (on campus) and $5000 per academic year (off campus). Room and board costs vary by type of accommodation, type of meal plan.

Financial Aid In 1997–98, 30% of students received some institutionally administered aid in the form of research assistantships, teaching assistantships, scholarships, work study, loans. Financial aid is available to part-time students. Application Deadline: 4/1.

Financial Aid Contact Mr. Michael O'Rear, Director of Financial Aid, PO Box 13052, Nacogdoches, TX 75962. Phone: 409-468-2403; Fax: 409-468-1048.

FACILITIES
Information Resources Ralph W. Steen Library; total holdings of 891,398 volumes, 767,674 microforms, 3,127 current periodical subscriptions. CD player(s) available for graduate student use. Access provided to online bibliographic retrieval services and online databases.

INTERNATIONAL STUDENTS
Demographics 3% of students enrolled are international students [Asia, 100%].

Services and Facilities International student office, counseling/support services.

Applying TOEFL: minimum score of 550, TWE: minimum score of 3, proof of adequate funds, proof of health/immunizations required. Financial aid is not available to international students.

International Student Contact Ms. Stacy Wilson, International Student Advisor, PO Box 13051, Nacogdoches, TX 75962. Phone: 409-468-2504; Fax: 409-468-3849; E-mail: swilson@sfasu.edu

PLACEMENT
Services include career counseling/planning, career fairs, career library, career placement, electronic job bank, job interviews arranged, job search course, resume referral to employers, and resume preparation. In 1996–97, 72 organizations participated in on-campus recruiting; 741 on-campus interviews were conducted.

Employment Types of employment entered: manufacturing, service industry.

Business Program(s) URL: http://www.cob.sfasu.edu/

Program Contact: Dr. Warren W. Fisher, MBA Director, PO Box 13004, Nacogdoches, TX 75962. Phone: 409-468-3101; Fax: 409-468-1560; E-mail: wfisher@sfasu.edu

Sul Ross State University

Department of Business Administration

Alpine, Texas

OVERVIEW
Sul Ross State University is a state-supported, coed, comprehensive institution. Enrollment: 2,600 graduate, professional, and undergraduate students; 176 full-time matriculated graduate/professional students; 499 part-time matriculated graduate/professional students. Founded: 1917. The graduate business unit is in a small-town setting and is on a semester calendar.

HIGHLIGHTS

Enrollment Profile

Full-time: 15	International: 48%
Part-time: 10	Women: 52%
Total: 25	Minorities: 28%
Average Age: 30	Average Class Size: 20
Fall 1997 Average GPA: N/R	Fall 1997 Average GMAT: N/R

Costs
Full-time tuition: N/R
Part-time tuition: $120 per semester hour (resident); $249 per semester hour (nonresident)

ACBSP – The American Council of Business Schools and Programs accredited

GRADUATE BUSINESS PROGRAMS
Master of Business Administration (MBA) Full-time, part-time; 36 total credits required; 12 months to 2 years to complete program. Concentrations in management, international trade.

ADMISSION
Application Requirements GMAT score: minimum 400, application form, bachelor's degree, minimum GPA: 2.75, college transcript(s).

Application Deadline Applications processed on a rolling/continuous basis for both domestic and international students.

ACADEMICS
Faculty Full-time 5.

Teaching Methodologies Case study, lecture, student presentations, team projects.

Technology 40 on-campus computer terminals/PCs are available for student use. Students are not required to have their own PC.

Special Opportunities Advanced credit may be earned through credit by examination, transfer of credits from another institution.

FINANCES
Costs for 1997–98 Tuition: $120 per semester hour (resident); $249 per semester hour (nonresident). Cost varies by number of credits taken. Fees: $35 per semester (resident); $35 per semester (nonresident). Fees vary by number of credits taken.

Financial Aid Teaching assistantships, work study, loans available. Financial aid is available to part-time students. Application Deadline: 5/1.

Financial Aid Contact Juan Garcia, Director of Financial Aid, Alpine, TX 79832. Phone: 915-837-8056; Fax: 915-837-8334.

FACILITIES
Information Resources Bryan Wildenthal Memorial Library; total holdings of 250,266 volumes, 456,492 microforms, 1,951 current periodical subscriptions. CD player(s) available for graduate student use. Access provided to online bibliographic retrieval services.

INTERNATIONAL STUDENTS
Demographics 48% of students enrolled are international students.

Applying TOEFL: minimum score of 520, proof of adequate funds, proof of health/immunizations required.

PLACEMENT
Services include career counseling/planning, career fairs, career library, career placement, electronic job bank, job interviews arranged, job search course, resume referral to employers, and resume preparation. In 1996–97, 75 organizations participated in on-campus recruiting; 30 on-campus interviews were conducted.

Program Contact: Robert Matthews, Graduate Program Advisor, Alpine, TX 79832. Phone: 915-837-8066; Fax: 915-837-8003.
See full description on page 1006.

Tarleton State University

College of Business Administration

Stephenville, Texas

OVERVIEW
Tarleton State University is a state-supported, coed, comprehensive institution. Enrollment: 6,369 graduate, professional, and undergraduate students; 135 full-time matriculated graduate/professional students; 528 part-time matriculated graduate/professional students. Founded: 1899. The graduate business unit is in a small-town setting and is on a semester calendar.

HIGHLIGHTS

Enrollment Profile

Full-time: 37	International: 2%
Part-time: 106	Women: 40%
Total: 143	Minorities: 17%
Average Age: N/R	Average Class Size: 20
Fall 1997 Average GPA: N/R	Fall 1997 Average GMAT: 451

Costs
Full-time tuition: N/R
Part-time tuition: $42 per semester credit hour (resident); $246 per semester credit hour (nonresident)

ACBSP – The American Council of Business Schools and Programs accredited

GRADUATE BUSINESS PROGRAMS
Master of Business Administration (MBA) Full-time, part-time, distance learning option; 36 total credits required; 18 months to 6 years to complete program. Concentrations in accounting, finance, marketing, management, management information systems, agribusiness.

ADMISSION
Applications For fall 1997 there were 40 applications for admission. Of those applying, 37 were accepted. Of those accepted, 32 enrolled.

Application Requirements Application form, application fee, bachelor's degree, minimum GPA: 2.5, college transcript(s).

Recommended for Application GMAT score accepted, GRE score accepted.

Application Deadline Applications processed on a rolling/continuous basis for both domestic and international students. Application fee: $20.

ACADEMICS
Faculty Full-time 11.

Teaching Methodologies Case study, computer-aided instruction, computer analysis, experiential learning, faculty seminars, group discussion, lecture, research, role playing, student presentations, study groups, team projects.

Technology The network has full access to the Internet. Students are not required to have their own PC.

Special Opportunities Advanced credit may be earned through transfer of credits from another institution. An internship program is available.

FINANCES
Costs for 1997–98 Tuition: $42 per semester credit hour (resident); $246 per semester credit hour (nonresident). Cost varies by number of credits taken. Fees: $46 per hour (resident); $46 per hour (nonresident). Fees vary by number of credits taken. Average 1997–98 room and board costs were $3358 per academic year (on campus) and $3358 per academic year (off campus). Room and board costs vary by campus location, type of accommodation, type of meal plan.

Financial Aid Research assistantships, teaching assistantships, grants, scholarships, work study, loans available. Financial aid is available to part-time students. Application Deadline: 6/1.

Financial Aid Contact F. H. Lanis, Financial Aid Director, Box T-0310, Stephenville, TX 76402. Phone: 817-968-9070.

FACILITIES
Information Resources Dick Smith Library; total holdings of 644,452 volumes, 750,000 microforms, 2,000 current periodical subscriptions. CD player(s) available for graduate student use. Access provided to online bibliographic retrieval services.

INTERNATIONAL STUDENTS
Demographics 2% of students enrolled are international students.

Services and Facilities International student office, international student center, international student housing, ESL courses.

Applying TOEFL, proof of adequate funds required.

International Student Contact Dr. Fred Koestler, Director, Box T-0770, Tarleton Station, Stephenville, TX 76402. Phone: 817-968-9632.

PLACEMENT
Services include career counseling/planning, career fairs, and career placement.

Program Contact: Ron Bradberry, Graduate Office/Dean, Box T-0350, Stephenville, TX 76402. Phone: 800-OUR-GRAD.

Texas A&M International University

Graduate School of International Trade and Business Administration

Laredo, Texas

OVERVIEW
Texas A&M International University is a state-supported, coed, comprehensive institution. Enrollment: 2,839 graduate, professional, and undergraduate students; 161 full-time matriculated graduate/professional students; 675 part-time matriculated graduate/professional students. Founded: 1969. The graduate business unit is in an urban setting and is on a semester calendar.

HIGHLIGHTS

Enrollment Profile

Full-time: 124	International: 38%
Part-time: 154	Women: 38%
Total: 278	Minorities: 28%
Average Age: 28	Average Class Size: 15
Fall 1997 Average GPA: 3.24	Fall 1997 Average GMAT: 480

Costs
Full-time tuition: $925 per academic year (resident); $3481 per academic year (nonresident)
Part-time tuition: $120 per 3 credit hours (resident); $744 per 3 credit hours (nonresident)

Degree(s) offered in conjunction with École Superieure de Commerce, Fuchur Technik und Wirtschaft, Instituto Technologico y de Estudios Superiores de Monterrey, Universidad Autonoma de Coahuila

GRADUATE BUSINESS PROGRAMS
Master of Business Administration (MBA) Full-time, part-time; 36 total credits required; 12 months to 5 years to complete program.

Master of Business Administration in International Trade (MBA) Full-time, part-time; 36 total credits required; 12 months to 5 years to complete program. Concentration in international trade.

Master of Science in International Logistics (MS) Full-time, part-time; 36 total credits required; 12 months to 5 years to complete program.

Master of Professional Accountancy (MPA) Full-time, part-time; 36 total credits required; 12 months to 5 years to complete program. Concentration in accounting.

Master of Science in Information Systems (MS) Full-time, part-time; 36 total credits required; 12 months to 5 years to complete program.

Master of Business Administration in International Banking (MBA) Full-time, part-time; 36 total credits required; 12 months to 5 years to complete program. Concentration in international banking.

ADMISSION
Applications For fall 1997 there were 194 applications for admission. Of those applying, 161 were accepted. Of those accepted, 78 enrolled.

Application Requirements GMAT score, GRE score, application form, bachelor's degree, college transcript(s).

Application Deadline 7/1 for fall, 11/1 for spring, 4/1 for summer, 6/1 for fall (international), 10/1 for spring (international), 3/1 for summer (international). Deferred entrance is available.

ACADEMICS
Faculty Full-time 32; part-time 1.

Teaching Methodologies Case study, computer simulations, experiential learning, group discussion, lecture, research, student presentations, study groups, team projects.

Technology 280 on-campus computer terminals/PCs are available for student use and are linked by a campus-wide network. The network has full access to the Internet. Students are not required to have their own PC.

Special Opportunities Advanced credit may be earned through transfer of credits from another institution. International exchange programs in Brazil, Canada, Chile, Costa Rica, France, Germany, Mexico, Morocco, Paraguay, Spain. An internship program is available.

FINANCES
Costs for 1997–98 Tuition: Full-time: $925 per semester (resident); $3481 per semester (nonresident). Part-time: $120 per 3 credit hours (resident); $744 per 3 credit hours (nonresident). Cost varies by number of credits taken, reciprocity agreements. Fees: Full-time: $446 per academic year (resident); $446 per academic year (nonresident). Part-time: $142 per 3 credit hours (resident); $142 per 3 credit hours (nonresident). Fees vary by number of credits taken. Average 1997–98 room only costs were $2850 per academic year (on campus) and $7032 per academic year (off campus). Room and board costs vary by occupancy (e.g., single, double, triple).

Financial Aid Fellowships, scholarships, work study, loans available. Financial aid is available to part-time students. Application Deadline: 11/11.

Financial Aid Contact Mr. Ricardo Ortegón, Director of Graduate Student Services, 5201 University Boulevard, Laredo, TX 78041-1900. Phone: 956-326-2770; Fax: 956-326-2769; E-mail: rortegon@tamiu.edu

FACILITIES
Information Resources Sue and Radcliffe Killam Library; total holdings of 123,802 volumes, 662,151 microforms, 1,994 current periodical subscriptions. CD player(s) available for graduate student use. Access provided to online bibliographic retrieval services and online databases.

INTERNATIONAL STUDENTS
Demographics 38% of students enrolled are international students [Africa, 1%, Asia, 9%, Central America, 1%, Europe, 4%, North America, 82%, South America, 3%].

Services and Facilities International student office, ESL courses, counseling/support services.

Applying TOEFL: minimum score of 550, proof of adequate funds, proof of health/immunizations required. Financial aid is available to international students.

International Student Contact Mr. David VerMilyea, Director of Student Development, 5201 University Boulevard, Laredo, TX 78041-1900. Phone: 956-326-2280; Fax: 956-326-2279; E-mail: deverm@tamiu.edu

PLACEMENT
Services include career counseling/planning, career fairs, career library, job interviews arranged, resume referral to employers, and resume preparation. In

Texas A&M International University (continued)

1996–97, 85 organizations participated in on-campus recruiting; 40 on-campus interviews were conducted.

Employment Types of employment entered: accounting, banking, chemical industry, communications, computer-related, consulting, consumer products, education, energy, finance, financial services, government, health services, high technology, hospitality management, information systems/technology, insurance, international trade, management, manufacturing, marketing, nonprofit, petrochemical, retail, service industry, transportation.

Business Program(s) URL: http://www.tamiu.edu/coba/

Program Contact: Mr. Ricardo Ortegón, Director of Graduate Student Services, 5201 University Boulevard, Laredo, TX 78041-1900. Phone: 956-326-2770; Fax: 956-326-2769; E-mail: rortegon@tamiu.edu

See full description on page 1012.

Texas A&M University

Lowry Mays Graduate School of Business

College Station, Texas

OVERVIEW

Texas A&M University is a state-supported, coed university. Enrollment: 41,461 graduate, professional, and undergraduate students; 5,656 full-time matriculated graduate/professional students; 1,860 part-time matriculated graduate/professional students. Founded: 1876. The graduate business unit is in a small-town setting and is on a semester calendar.

HIGHLIGHTS

Enrollment Profile

Full-time: 640	International: 18%
Part-time: 25	Women: 39%
Total: 665	Minorities: 8%
Average Age: 28	Average Class Size: 35
Fall 1997 Average GPA: 3.27	Fall 1997 Average GMAT: 608

Costs
Full-time tuition: $3500 per academic year (resident); $9200 per academic year (nonresident)
Part-time tuition: $68 per credit hour (resident); $282 per credit hour (nonresident)

AACSB – The International Association for Management Education accredited

GRADUATE BUSINESS PROGRAMS

Master of Business Administration (MBA) Full-time; 53 total credits required; 15 months to 2 years to complete program. Concentrations in accounting, finance, human resources, international business, management information systems, marketing, operations management, international management, entrepreneurship, financial information systems, financial management/planning, information management, international and area business studies, leadership, manufacturing management, new venture management, organizational behavior/development, strategic management, telecommunications management.

Master of Science in Accounting (MS) Full-time, part-time; 36 total credits required; 12 months to 2 years to complete program. Concentrations in accounting, taxation.

Master of Science in Management Information Systems (MS) Full-time, part-time; 36 total credits required; 12 months to 2 years to complete program. Concentrations in management information systems, operations management, technology management.

Master of Science in Finance (MS) Full-time, part-time; 36 total credits required; 12 months to 2 years to complete program. Concentrations in finance, real estate.

Master in Land Economics and Real Estate (MS) Full-time, part-time; 36 total credits required; 12 months to 2.8 years to complete program. Concentration in real estate.

Master of Science in Marketing (MS) Full-time, part-time; 36 total credits required; 12 months to 2 years to complete program. Concentrations in marketing, marketing research.

Master of Science in Management (MS) Full-time, part-time; 36 total credits required; 12 months to 2 years to complete program. Concentrations in human resources, organizational behavior/development.

Master in Life Cycle Engineering and Operations Management (MS) Full-time, part-time, distance learning option; 36 total credits required; 12 months to 2 years to complete program. Concentrations in manufacturing management, production management, operations management.

Executive MBA (MBA) 53 total credits required; 2 years to complete program.

ADMISSION

Applications For fall 1997 there were 1,081 applications for admission. Of those applying, 450 were accepted. Of those accepted, 345 enrolled.

Application Requirements Application form, application fee, bachelor's degree, essay, minimum GPA, 3 letters of recommendation, resume, college transcript(s).

Recommended for Application GMAT score accepted, work experience.

Application Deadline Applications processed on a rolling/continuous basis for both domestic and international students. Application fee: $35, $75 (international). Deferred entrance is available.

ACADEMICS

Faculty Full-time 149; part-time 14.

Teaching Methodologies Case study, computer-aided instruction, computer analysis, computer simulations, field projects, group discussion, lecture, role playing, seminars by members of the business community, simulations, student presentations, team projects.

Technology 200 on-campus computer terminals/PCs are available for student use and are linked by a campus-wide network. The network has full access to the Internet. Students are not required to have their own PC.

Special Opportunities Advanced credit may be earned through transfer of credits from another institution. International exchange programs in Austria, France, Germany, Japan, Mexico. An internship program is available.

FINANCES

Costs for 1997–98 Tuition: Full-time: $3500 per year (resident); $9200 per year (nonresident). Part-time: $68 per credit hour (resident); $282 per credit hour (nonresident). Cost varies by number of credits taken. Fees: Full-time: $1700 per academic year (resident); $1700 per academic year (nonresident). Fees vary by number of credits taken. Average 1997–98 room only costs were $4050 per academic year (off campus). Room and board costs vary by campus location, occupancy (e.g., single, double, triple), type of accommodation, type of meal plan.

Financial Aid In 1997–98, 53% of students received some institutionally administered aid in the form of fellowships, research assistantships, teaching assistantships, work study, loans. Application Deadline: 2/1.

Financial Aid Contact Ms. Anna Hines, Graduate Advisor, Student Financial Aid Office, College Station, TX 77843. Phone: 409-845-3981; Fax: 409-847-9061.

FACILITIES

Information Resources Sterling C. Evans Library plus 1 additional on-campus library; total holdings of 2,300,000 volumes, 4,500,000 microforms, 18,000 current periodical subscriptions. CD player(s) available for graduate student use. Access provided to online bibliographic retrieval services and online databases.

INTERNATIONAL STUDENTS

Demographics 18% of students enrolled are international students [Africa, 1%, Asia, 58%, Central America, 11%, Europe, 20%, North America, 2%, South America, 6%, other, 2%].

Services and Facilities International student office, international student housing, visa services, ESL courses, counseling/support services.

Applying TOEFL: minimum score of 600, proof of adequate funds, proof of health/immunizations required. Financial aid is not available to international students.

International Student Contact Ms. Wendy Boggs, Academic Advisor, Graduate School of Business, 212 Wehner, College Station, TX 77843-4117. Phone: 409-845-4714; Fax: 409-862-2393; E-mail: boggs-w@mba-lab.tamu.edu

PLACEMENT

Services include alumni network, career counseling/planning, career fairs, career library, career placement, electronic job bank, job interviews arranged, resume referral to employers, and resume preparation. In 1996–97, 140 organizations participated in on-campus recruiting; 1,600 on-campus interviews were conducted.

Employment Of 1996–97 graduates, 96% were employed within three months of graduation; the average starting salary was $52,138. Types of employment entered: accounting, banking, chemical industry, communications, computer-related, consulting, energy, engineering, finance, financial services, high technology, human resources, information systems/technology, international trade, management, manufacturing, marketing, petrochemical, pharmaceutical, real estate, retail, service industry, telecommunications, transportation, utilities.

Business Program(s) URL: http://mba.tamu.edu

Program Contact: Ms. Wendy Boggs, Academic Advisor, Graduate School of Business, 212 Wehner, College Station, TX 77843-4117. Phone: 409-845-4714; Fax: 409-862-2393; E-mail: boggs-w@mba-lab.tamu.edu

See full description on page 1014.

Texas A&M University Commerce

College of Business and Technology

Commerce, Texas

OVERVIEW
Texas A&M University Commerce is a state-supported, coed university. Enrollment: 7,661 graduate, professional, and undergraduate students. Founded: 1917. The graduate business unit is in a small-town setting and is on a semester calendar.

HIGHLIGHTS

Enrollment Profile

Full-time: 88
Part-time: 165
Total: 253
Average Age: 31
Fall 1997 Average GPA: 3.2

International: 32%
Women: 43%
Minorities: 23%
Average Class Size: 35
Fall 1997 Average GMAT: 505

Costs

Full-time tuition: $2381 per academic year (resident); $8801 per academic year (nonresident)
Part-time tuition: $612 per 6 hours (resident); $1896 per 6 hours (nonresident)

AACSB – The International Association for Management Education accredited

Degree(s) offered in conjunction with University of North Texas, Texas Woman's University

GRADUATE BUSINESS PROGRAMS
Master of Business Administration (MBA) Full-time, part-time, distance learning option; 36-48 total credits required; 12 months to 6 years to complete program. Concentrations in accounting, economics, finance, human resources, international business, management, management information systems, marketing, technology management.

ADMISSION
Applications For fall 1997 there were 175 applications for admission. Of those applying, 150 were accepted. Of those accepted, 125 enrolled.

Application Requirements GMAT score: minimum 375, application form, application fee, bachelor's degree, minimum GPA: 2.75, college transcript(s).

Recommended for Application Interview, letters of recommendation, personal statement, resume, work experience, computer experience.

Application Deadline 6/1 for fall, 11/1 for spring, 3/15 for summer, 6/1 for fall (international), 11/1 for spring (international), 3/15 for summer (international). Application fee: $25 (international). Deferred entrance is available.

ACADEMICS
Faculty Full-time 22; part-time 1.

Teaching Methodologies Case study, computer-aided instruction, computer analysis, group discussion, lecture, research, student presentations, team projects.

Technology 120 on-campus computer terminals/PCs are available for student use and are linked by a campus-wide network. The network has full access to the Internet. Students are not required to have their own PC.

Special Opportunities Advanced credit may be earned through transfer of credits from another institution. International exchange programs in France, Germany, Italy, Jamaica, Mexico, United Kingdom.

FINANCES
Costs for 1997–98 Tuition: Full-time: $2381 per year (resident); $8801 per year (nonresident). Part-time: $612 per 6 hours (resident); $1896 per 6 hours (nonresident). Cost varies by number of credits taken, reciprocity agreements. Fees vary by number of credits taken. Average 1997–98 room only costs were $2700 per academic year (off campus). Room and board costs vary by occupancy (e.g., single, double, triple), type of accommodation, type of meal plan.

Financial Aid In 1997–98, 4% of students received some institutionally administered aid in the form of research assistantships, scholarships, work study, loans.

Financial Aid Contact Mr. John Patton, Director, Financial Aid, East Texas Station, Commerce, TX 75429-3011. Phone: 903-886-5096; Fax: 903-886-5015; E-mail: john_patton@etsu.edu

FACILITIES
Information Resources James G. Gee Library; total holdings of 1,580,739 volumes, 472,672 microforms, 1,901 current periodical subscriptions. CD player(s) available for graduate student use. Access provided to online bibliographic retrieval services.

INTERNATIONAL STUDENTS
Demographics 32% of students enrolled are international students [Asia, 98%, South America, 1%, other, 1%].

Services and Facilities International student office, international student housing, visa services, counseling/support services.

Applying TOEFL: minimum score of 500, proof of adequate funds required. Financial aid is not available to international students.

International Student Contact Ms. Patsy Pope, International Student Advisor, Commerce, TX 75429-3011. Phone: 903-886-5097; Fax: 903-886-5199; E-mail: paytsy_pope@etsu.edu

PLACEMENT
Employment Of 1996–97 graduates, 82% were employed within three months of graduation; the average starting salary was $42,000. Types of employment entered: banking, finance, financial services, information systems/technology.

Business Program(s) URL: http://www.tamu-commerce.edu/cobt/dean/index.html

Program Contact: Dr. Robert Seay, Assistant Dean, Commerce, TX 75429-3011. Phone: 903-886-5190; Fax: 903-886-5650; E-mail: mba@tamu-commerce.edu

Texas A&M University-Corpus Christi

College of Business Administration

Corpus Christi, Texas

OVERVIEW
Texas A&M University-Corpus Christi is a state-supported, coed, comprehensive institution. Enrollment: 6,025 graduate, professional, and undergraduate students; 385 full-time matriculated graduate/professional students; 1,274 part-time matriculated graduate/professional students. Founded: 1971. The graduate business unit is in an urban setting and is on a semester calendar.

HIGHLIGHTS

Enrollment Profile

Full-time: 41
Part-time: 140
Total: 181
Average Age: 32
Fall 1997 Average GPA: N/R

International: 9%
Women: 43%
Minorities: 44%
Average Class Size: 22
Fall 1997 Average GMAT: N/R

Costs

Full-time tuition: $306 per academic year (resident); $2232 per academic year (nonresident)
Part-time tuition: $120 per 3-hour course (resident); $744 per 3 hour course (nonresident)

GRADUATE BUSINESS PROGRAMS
Master of Business Administration (MBA) Full-time, part-time; 36-60 total credits required; 12 months to 6 years to complete program. Concentrations in health care, international business.

Master of Accountancy (MAcc) Full-time, part-time; 36-60 total credits required; 12 months to 6 years to complete program.

ADMISSION
Applications For fall 1997 there were 72 applications for admission. Of those applying, 66 were accepted. Of those accepted, 64 enrolled.

Application Requirements GMAT score, application form, application fee, bachelor's degree, interview, personal statement, college transcript(s), computer experience: basic computer applications.

Application Deadline 8/15 for fall, 12/15 for spring, 5/15 for summer, 5/1 for fall (international), 9/1 for spring (international), 2/1 for summer (international). Application fee: $10, $30 (international). Deferred entrance is available.

ACADEMICS
Faculty Full-time 32; part-time 6.

Teaching Methodologies Case study, computer-aided instruction, computer analysis, computer simulations, faculty seminars, field projects, group discussion, lecture, research, role playing, seminars by members of the business community, simulations, student presentations, study groups, team projects.

Technology 570 on-campus computer terminals/PCs are available for student use and are linked by a campus-wide network. The network has full access to the Internet. Students are not required to have their own PC.

Special Opportunities Advanced credit may be earned through credit by examination, transfer of credits from another institution. An internship program is available.

Texas A&M University-Corpus Christi (continued)

FINANCES
Costs for 1997–98 Tuition: Full-time: $306 per 9 hours (resident); $2232 per 9 hours (nonresident). Part-time: $120 per 3-hour course (resident); $744 per 3 hour course (nonresident). Cost varies by number of credits taken. Fees: Full-time: $451 per academic year (resident); $451 per academic year (nonresident). Part-time: $187 per 3-hour course (resident); $187 per 3-hour course (nonresident). Fees vary by number of credits taken. Average 1997–98 room and board costs were $5106 per academic year (on campus) and $5265 per academic year (off campus). Room and board costs vary by occupancy (e.g., single, double, triple), type of accommodation.
Financial Aid Grants, scholarships, work study, loans available. Financial aid is available to part-time students. Application Deadline: 4/1.
Financial Aid Contact Ms. Dolly Zeriali, Director, Financial Assistance, 6300 Ocean Drive, Corpus Christi, TX 78412. Phone: 512-994-2417; Fax: 512-994-6095; E-mail: dzeriali@falcon.tamucc.edu

FACILITIES
Information Resources Mary and Jeff Bell Library; total holdings of 322,714 volumes, 484,675 microforms, 1,700 current periodical subscriptions. CD player(s) available for graduate student use. Access provided to online bibliographic retrieval services and online databases.

INTERNATIONAL STUDENTS
Demographics 9% of students enrolled are international students.
Services and Facilities International student office, international student center, international student housing, ESL courses, counseling/support services.
Applying TOEFL: minimum score of 550, proof of adequate funds required. Financial aid is available to international students.
International Student Contact Ms. Maria Fuentes-Martin, Assistant Dean of Students, 6300 Ocean Drive, Corpus Christi, TX 78412. Phone: 512-994-5700; E-mail: marif@falcon.tamucc.edu

PLACEMENT
Services include alumni network, career counseling/planning, career fairs, career library, career placement, electronic job bank, job interviews arranged, job search course, resume referral to employers, and resume preparation. In 1996–97, 250 organizations participated in on-campus recruiting.
Employment Types of employment entered: accounting, banking, communications, computer-related, consulting, finance, financial services, human resources, information systems/technology, management, marketing, petrochemical, retail, service industry.
Business Program(s) URL: http://www.enterprise.tamucc.edu

Program Contact: Ms. Betsy O'Lavin, Director of Master's Programs, College of Business, 6300 Ocean Drive, Corpus Christi, TX 78412-5503. Phone: 512-994-2655, 800-482-6822 (TX only); Fax: 512-994-2725; E-mail: eolavin@falcon.tamucc.edu

Texas A&M University-Kingsville

College of Business Administration

Kingsville, Texas

OVERVIEW
Texas A&M University-Kingsville is a state-supported, coed university. Enrollment: 6,117 graduate, professional, and undergraduate students. Founded: 1917. The graduate business unit is in a small-town setting and is on a semester calendar.

HIGHLIGHTS

Enrollment Profile

Full-time: N/R	International: N/R
Part-time: N/R	Women: N/R
Total: 76	Minorities: N/R
Average Age: 30	Average Class Size: 13
Fall 1997 Average GPA: 2.85	Fall 1997 Average GMAT: 420

Costs
Full-time tuition: $1112 per academic year (resident); $3886 per academic year (nonresident)
Part-time tuition: N/R

ACBSP – The American Council of Business Schools and Programs accredited

GRADUATE BUSINESS PROGRAMS
Master of Business Administration (MBA) Full-time, part-time; 36 total credits required; 12 months to 5 years to complete program. Concentrations in management, marketing, finance, accounting.
Master of Professional Accountancy (MPA) Full-time, part-time; 36 total credits required; 12 months to 5 years to complete program. Concentration in accounting.
Master of Science in Business Administration (MS) Full-time, part-time; 36 total credits required; 12 months to 5 years to complete program.
Master of Professional Accountancy/Bachelor of Business Administration (MPA/BBA) Full-time, part-time; 150 total credits required; 4 to 6 years to complete program.

ADMISSION
Application Requirements GMAT score: minimum 400, application form, application fee, bachelor's degree, minimum GPA: 2.5, college transcript(s).
Recommended for Application Interview.
Application Deadline 4/1 for fall (international), 9/1 for spring (international), 2/1 for summer (international). Application fee: $15, $25 (international).

ACADEMICS
Faculty Full-time 14.
Teaching Methodologies Case study, computer-aided instruction, faculty seminars, field projects, group discussion, lecture, research, student presentations, study groups, team projects.
Technology 100 on-campus computer terminals/PCs are available for student use and are linked by a campus-wide network. The network has full access to the Internet. Students are not required to have their own PC.
Special Opportunities Advanced credit may be earned through transfer of credits from another institution.

FINANCES
Costs for 1997–98 Tuition: Full-time: $1112 per year (resident); $3886 per year (nonresident). Cost varies by number of credits taken, reciprocity agreements. Fees vary by academic program, reciprocity agreements. Room and board costs vary by occupancy (e.g., single, double, triple), type of meal plan.
Financial Aid Work study available. Financial aid is available to part-time students.
Financial Aid Contact Mr. Arturo Pecos, Director, Financial Aid, Campus Box 115, Kingsville, TX 78363. Phone: 512-593-3911; E-mail: kaaposa@taisun1.taiu.edu

FACILITIES
Information Resources James C. Jernigan Library; total holdings of 461,408 volumes, 520,636 microforms, 2,117 current periodical subscriptions. CD player(s) available for graduate student use. Access provided to online bibliographic retrieval services.

INTERNATIONAL STUDENTS
Demographics N/R
Services and Facilities International student office, ESL courses, counseling/support services.
Applying TOEFL: minimum score of 550, proof of adequate funds required. Financial aid is available to international students.
International Student Contact Dr. Donald Hegwood, Professor and Director—Office of International Programs, Campus Box 163, Kingsville, TX 78363. Phone: 512-593-3994; E-mail: kfdahoo@taiu.edu

PLACEMENT
Services include alumni network, career counseling/planning, career fairs, career placement, job interviews arranged, and resume referral to employers.
Business Program(s) URL: http://www.cba.tamuk.edu

Program Contact: Dr. Robert Diersing, Professor and Coordinator of CBA Graduate Programs, Campus Box 182, Kingsville, TX 78363. Phone: 512-593-3802; Fax: 512-593-3708; E-mail: r-diersing@tamuk.edu

Texas A&M University-Texarkana

Division of Business Administration

Texarkana, Texas

OVERVIEW
Texas A&M University-Texarkana is a state-supported, coed, upper-level institution. Enrollment: 1,145 graduate, professional, and undergraduate students; 59 full-time matriculated graduate/professional students; 339 part-time matriculated graduate/professional students. Founded: 1971. The graduate business unit

is in an urban setting and is on a semester calendar.

HIGHLIGHTS

Enrollment Profile
Full-time: 20
Part-time: 103
Total: 123
Average Age: 32
Fall 1997 Average GPA: N/R

International: N/R
Women: 51%
Minorities: 9%
Average Class Size: 20
Fall 1997 Average GMAT: N/R

Costs
Full-time tuition: $1560 per academic year (resident); $7980 per academic year (nonresident)
Part-time tuition: $52 per credit hour (resident); $266 per credit hour (nonresident)

GRADUATE BUSINESS PROGRAMS
Master of Business Administration (MBA) Full-time, part-time; 36 total credits required; up to 5 years to complete program.
Master of Science in Business Administration (MS) Full-time, part-time; 36 total credits required; up to 5 years to complete program.

ADMISSION
Applications For fall 1997 there were 30 applications for admission. Of those applying, 30 were accepted. Of those accepted, 29 enrolled.
Application Requirements Application form, application fee, bachelor's degree, minimum GPA, 3 letters of recommendation, college transcript(s).
Recommended for Application GMAT score accepted.
Application Deadline 7/24 for fall, 12/13 for spring, 4/27 for summer, 6/21 for fall (international), 11/13 for spring (international), 3/27 for summer (international). Application fee: 25 (international). Deferred entrance is available.

ACADEMICS
Faculty Full-time 9.
Teaching Methodologies Case study, computer-aided instruction, computer analysis, computer simulations, experiential learning, field projects, group discussion, lecture, research, simulations, student presentations, study groups, team projects.
Technology 70 on-campus computer terminals/PCs are available for student use and are linked by a campus-wide network. The network has full access to the Internet. Students are not required to have their own PC.
Special Opportunities Advanced credit may be earned through transfer of credits from another institution.

FINANCES
Costs for 1997–98 Tuition: Full-time: $1560 per year (resident); $7980 per year (nonresident). Part-time: $52 per credit hour (resident); $266 per credit hour (nonresident). Cost varies by number of credits taken, reciprocity agreements. Fees: Full-time: $962 per academic year (resident); $962 per academic year (nonresident). Part-time: $32 per credit hour (resident); $32 per credit hour (nonresident). Fees vary by number of credits taken.
Financial Aid In 1997–98, 14% of students received some institutionally administered aid in the form of grants, scholarships. Financial aid is available to part-time students. Application Deadline: 5/1.
Financial Aid Contact Ms. Marilyn Raney, Director of Financial Aid and Veteran Services, 2600 North Robison Road, Texarkana, TX 75501. E-mail: marilyn.raney@tamut.edu

FACILITIES
Information Resources John F. Moss Library plus 1 additional on-campus library; total holdings of 176,358 volumes, 307,619 microforms, 1,072 current periodical subscriptions. CD player(s) available for graduate student use. Access provided to online bibliographic retrieval services.

INTERNATIONAL STUDENTS
Demographics N/R
Applying TOEFL: minimum score of 550, proof of adequate funds required. Financial aid is not available to international students.
International Student Contact Patricia Black, Assistant Director of Admissions and Registrar, PO Box 5518, Texarkana, TX 75503. Phone: 903-223-3068; Fax: 903-832-8890; E-mail: pat.black@tamut.edu

PLACEMENT
Services include alumni network, career counseling/planning, and career fairs.

Program Contact: Dr. David Bejou, Division Head: Business Administration, PO Box 5518, Texarkana, TX 75505-5518. Phone: 903-838-6514; Fax: 903-832-8890.

Texas Christian University

M. J. Neeley School of Business

Fort Worth, Texas

OVERVIEW
Texas Christian University is an independent-religious, coed university. Enrollment: 7,273 graduate, professional, and undergraduate students; 509 full-time matriculated graduate/professional students; 601 part-time matriculated graduate/professional students. Founded: 1873. The graduate business unit is in an urban setting and is on a semester calendar.

HIGHLIGHTS

Enrollment Profile
Full-time: 180
Part-time: 114
Total: 294
Average Age: 28
Fall 1997 Average GPA: 3.1

International: 19%
Women: 30%
Minorities: 5%
Average Class Size: 30
Fall 1997 Average GMAT: 560

Costs
Full-time tuition: $8280 per academic year
Part-time tuition: $345 per semester hour

AACSB – The International Association for Management Education accredited

GRADUATE BUSINESS PROGRAMS
Master of Business Administration (MBA) Full-time, part-time; 48 total credits required; 2 to 3 years to complete program. Concentrations in finance, management, marketing, accounting.
Master of Accounting (MAcc) Full-time; 30 total credits required; 9 months to 2 years to complete program. Concentration in accounting.

ADMISSION
Applications For fall 1997 there were 314 applications for admission. Of those applying, 228 were accepted. Of those accepted, 123 enrolled.
Application Requirements GMAT score, application form, application fee, bachelor's degree, essay, minimum GPA, 3 letters of recommendation, college transcript(s).
Recommended for Application Interview, resume, work experience, computer experience.
Application Deadline Applications processed on a rolling/continuous basis for both domestic and international students. Application fee: $50. Deferred entrance is available.

ACADEMICS
Faculty Full-time 31; part-time 1.
Teaching Methodologies Case study, computer-aided instruction, computer analysis, computer simulations, experiential learning, faculty seminars, field projects, group discussion, lecture, research, role playing, seminars by members of the business community, simulations, student presentations, study groups, team projects.
Technology 200 on-campus computer terminals/PCs are available for student use and are linked by a campus-wide network. The network has full access to the Internet. Students are not required to have their own PC.
Special Opportunities Advanced credit may be earned through transfer of credits from another institution. International exchange programs in France, Germany, Hungary, Mexico. An internship program is available.

FINANCES
Costs for 1997–98 Tuition: Full-time: $8280 per year. Part-time: $345 per semester hour. Cost varies by academic program, number of credits taken. Fees: Full-time: $1200 per academic year. Part-time: $30 per hour. Fees vary by academic program, number of credits taken. Average 1997–98 room and board costs were $9000 per academic year (off campus). Room and board costs vary by campus location, occupancy (e.g., single, double, triple), type of accommodation, type of meal plan.
Financial Aid In 1997–98, 58% of students received some institutionally administered aid in the form of fellowships, research assistantships, grants, scholarships, work study, loans. Financial aid is available to part-time students. Application Deadline: 5/1.
Financial Aid Contact Ms. Debbier Mar, Coordinator, Graduate Financial Aid, PO Box 297012, Fort Worth, TX 76129. Phone: 817-257-7872; Fax: 817-257-7462.

FACILITIES
Information Resources Mary Couts Burnett Library; total holdings of 797,612 volumes, 492,215 microforms, 4,470 current periodical subscriptions. CD player(s) available for graduate student use. Access provided to online bibliographic retrieval services and online databases.

Texas Christian University (continued)

INTERNATIONAL STUDENTS

Demographics 19% of students enrolled are international students [Africa, 2%, Asia, 33%, Australia/New Zealand, 2%, Central America, 5%, Europe, 36%, North America, 15%, South America, 7%].

Services and Facilities International student office, international student center, visa services, ESL courses, counseling/support services.

Applying TOEFL: minimum score of 550, proof of adequate funds, proof of health/immunizations required. Financial aid is available to international students.

International Student Contact Mr. Al Mladenka, Director of International Student Services, PO Box 297003, Fort Worth, TX 76129. Phone: 817-921-7292; Fax: 817-921-7333; E-mail: a.mladenka@tcu.edu

PLACEMENT

Services include alumni network, career counseling/planning, career fairs, career library, career placement, electronic job bank, job interviews arranged, job search course, resume referral to employers, and resume preparation. In 1996–97, 100 organizations participated in on-campus recruiting; 900 on-campus interviews were conducted.

Employment Of 1996–97 graduates, 93% were employed within three months of graduation; the average starting salary was $44,000. Types of employment entered: accounting, banking, chemical industry, communications, computer-related, consulting, consumer products, energy, engineering, finance, financial services, health services, high technology, human resources, information systems/technology, international trade, management, manufacturing, marketing, nonprofit, petrochemical, pharmaceutical, retail, service industry, telecommunications, transportation, utilities.

Business Program(s) URL: http://www.neeley.tcu.edu

Program Contact: Ms. Peggy Conway, Director of MBA Admissions, PO Box 298540, Fort Worth, TX 76129. Phone: 817-257-7531, 800-828-3764 Ext. 7531; Fax: 817-257-6431; E-mail: mbainfo@tcu.edu

See full description on page 1016.

Texas Southern University

Jesse H. Jones School of Business

Houston, Texas

OVERVIEW

Texas Southern University is a state-supported, coed university. Enrollment: 7,318 graduate, professional, and undergraduate students; 1,295 full-time matriculated graduate/professional students; 743 part-time matriculated graduate/professional students. Founded: 1947. The graduate business unit is in an urban setting and is on a semester calendar.

HIGHLIGHTS

Enrollment Profile

Full-time: 40	International: 34%
Part-time: 39	Women: 47%
Total: 79	Minorities: N/R
Average Age: 28	Average Class Size: 20
Fall 1997 Average GPA: 3.07	Fall 1997 Average GMAT: 416

Costs

Full-time tuition: $558 per academic year (resident); $2268 per academic year (nonresident)
Part-time tuition: $372 per 6 hours (resident); $1512 per 6 hours (nonresident)

GRADUATE BUSINESS PROGRAMS

Master of Business Administration (MBA) Full-time, part-time; 33-63 total credits required; up to 6 years to complete program.

Master of Professional Accountancy (MPA) Full-time, part-time; 36 total credits required; 2 to 6 years to complete program.

ADMISSION

Applications For fall 1997 there were 55 applications for admission. Of those applying, 42 were accepted. Of those accepted, 34 enrolled.

Application Requirements GMAT score, application form, application fee, bachelor's degree, minimum GPA: 2.5, college transcript(s).

Application Deadline 7/15 for fall, 11/15 for spring, 5/1 for summer, 7/15 for fall (international), 11/15 for spring (international), 5/1 for summer (international). Application fee: $35, $75 (international). Deferred entrance is available.

ACADEMICS

Faculty Full-time 21; part-time 4.

Teaching Methodologies Case study, computer-aided instruction, computer analysis, computer simulations, experiential learning, faculty seminars, group discussion, lecture, role playing, student presentations, study groups, team projects.

Technology 125 on-campus computer terminals/PCs are available for student use. The network has full access to the Internet. Students are not required to have their own PC.

Special Opportunities Advanced credit may be earned through transfer of credits from another institution.

FINANCES

Costs for 1997–98 Tuition: Full-time: $558 per 9 hours (resident); $2268 per 9 hours (nonresident). Part-time: $372 per 6 hours (resident); $1512 per 6 hours (nonresident). Cost varies by number of credits taken. Fees: Full-time: $350 per academic year (resident); $350 per academic year (nonresident). Part-time: $252 per 6 hours (resident); $252 per 6 hours (nonresident). Average 1997–98 room and board costs were $3400 per academic year (on campus) and $4180 per academic year (off campus). Room and board costs vary by occupancy (e.g., single, double, triple), type of accommodation.

Financial Aid In 1997–98, 5% of students received some institutionally administered aid in the form of research assistantships, teaching assistantships, work study. Application Deadline: 5/1.

Financial Aid Contact Director of Financial Aid, 3100 Cleburne Avenue, Houston, TX 77004.

FACILITIES

Information Resources Robert J. Terry Library plus 2 additional on-campus libraries; total holdings of 457,393 volumes, 363,519 microforms. CD player(s) available for graduate student use. Access provided to online bibliographic retrieval services.

INTERNATIONAL STUDENTS

Demographics 34% of students enrolled are international students [Asia, 14%, other, 86%].

Services and Facilities International student office, ESL courses, counseling/support services.

Applying TOEFL: minimum score of 550, proof of adequate funds, proof of health/immunizations required. Financial aid is available to international students.

International Student Contact Dr. Iris Perkins, Director/International Student Affairs, 3100 Cleburne Avenue, Houston, TX 77004-4584. Phone: 713-313-7894.

PLACEMENT

Services include career fairs, career placement, job interviews arranged, and resume referral to employers. In 1996–97, 95 organizations participated in on-campus recruiting.

Employment Of 1996–97 graduates, 100% were employed within three months of graduation. Types of employment entered: accounting, banking, education, marketing.

Program Contact: Ms. Bobbie Richardson, MBA Coordinator, 3100 Cleburne Avenue, Houston, TX 77004-4584. Phone: 713-313-7309; Fax: 713-313-7705.

Texas Tech University

College of Business Administration

Lubbock, Texas

OVERVIEW

Texas Tech University is a state-supported, coed university. Enrollment: 24,083 graduate, professional, and undergraduate students; 2,766 full-time matriculated graduate/professional students; 1,450 part-time matriculated graduate/professional students. Founded: 1923. The graduate business unit is in an urban setting and is on a semester calendar.

HIGHLIGHTS

Enrollment Profile

Full-time: 338
Part-time: 47
Total: 385
Average Age: N/R
Fall 1997 Average GPA: 3.27

International: 18%
Women: 34%
Minorities: 8%
Average Class Size: 25
Fall 1997 Average GMAT: 540

Costs

Full-time tuition: $2600 per academic year (resident); $8200 per academic year (nonresident)

Part-time tuition: $68 per credit (resident); $282 per credit (nonresident)

AACSB – The International Association for Management Education accredited

Texas Tech University's College of Business Administration offers joint programs in cooperation with other departments on campus. One of the most prominent programs is the M.B.A./Health Organization Management (HOM) offered in conjunction with the School of Medicine. The M.B.A./HOM program is one of eleven in the nation that has been dually accredited by AACSB–The International Association for Management Education and the Accrediting Commission on Education for Health Services Administration (ACEHSA). In the summer of 1998, the College of Business launched the M.B.A./M.D., offering a new joint-degree program that allows students to receive M.B.A. and M.D. degrees concurrently.

The other highly regarded joint-degree programs are the M.B.A./J.D. and the M.S.A./J.D., conducted in cooperation with the School of Law. These programs allow the law students to complete their M.B.A. or M.S.A. degrees concurrently with their law program. The degree plan enables the students to reduce the duration of both programs by 24 credit hours.

In addition, there are two other new joint-degree programs with the College of Business, one of which is the M.B.A./Master of Architecture program with the College of Architecture. The second new program is an M.B.A./Master of Arts in foreign language (French, German, and Spanish). This joint degree is in conjunction with the College of Arts and Sciences.

GRADUATE BUSINESS PROGRAMS

General MBA (MBA) Full-time, part-time; 36 total credits required; 12 months to 6 years to complete program. Concentrations in accounting, agribusiness, entrepreneurship, finance, international business, management, management information systems, marketing.

Master of Science in Business Administration (MS) Full-time, part-time; 36 total credits required; 12 months to 6 years to complete program. Concentrations in banking, finance, management, management information systems, marketing, production management, telecommunications management, quality management.

Master of Science in Accounting (MSA) Full-time, part-time; 36 total credits required; 12 months to 6 years to complete program. Concentration in taxation.

Master of Business Administration in Health Organization Management (MBA) Full-time, part-time; 42 total credits required; 15 months to 6 years to complete program. Concentration in health care.

Master of Business Administration/Doctor of Jurisprudence (MBA/JD) Full-time; 114 total credits required; 3.5 to 6 years to complete program. Concentration in legal administration.

Master of Business Administration/Master of Science in Nursing (MBA/MS) Full-time; 96 total credits required; up to 6 years to complete program. Concentration in health care.

Master of Business Administration/Master of Arts in Architecture (MBA/MA) Full-time; 36 total credits required; up to 6 years to complete program.

Master of Science in Health Organization Management (MS) Full-time, part-time; 36 total credits required; up to 6 years to complete program. Concentrations in health care, management information systems.

MBA/MA in Foreign Language (MBA/MA) Full-time, part-time; 36 total credits required; up to 6 years to complete program.

Master of Business Administration/Doctor of Medicine (MBA/MD) Concentration in health care.

ADMISSION

Applications For fall 1997 there were 289 applications for admission. Of those applying, 191 were accepted. Of those accepted, 91 enrolled.

Application Requirements Application form, application fee, bachelor's degree, minimum GPA: 3.0, 3 letters of recommendation, personal statement, resume, college transcript(s).

Recommended for Application GMAT score accepted: minimum 500, interview, work experience.

Application Deadline Applications processed on a rolling/continuous basis for domestic students only. 4/30 for fall (international), 9/30 for spring (inter-

national), 2/15 for summer (international). Application fee: $25, $50 (international). Deferred entrance is available.

ACADEMICS

Faculty Full-time 54.

Teaching Methodologies Case study, computer-aided instruction, computer simulations, faculty seminars, group discussion, lecture, research, student presentations, study groups, team projects.

Technology 250 on-campus computer terminals/PCs are available for student use and are linked by a campus-wide network. The network has full access to the Internet. Students are not required to have their own PC.

Special Opportunities Advanced credit may be earned through transfer of credits from another institution. International exchange programs in Finland, France, Italy, Mexico, Spain, Turkey, United Kingdom. An internship program is available.

FINANCES

Costs for 1997–98 Tuition: Full-time: $2600 per year (resident); $8200 per year (nonresident). Part-time: $68 per credit (resident); $282 per credit (nonresident). Cost varies by academic program, number of credits taken, reciprocity agreements. Fees: Full-time: $1600 per academic year (resident); $1600 per academic year (nonresident). Part-time: $100 per semester (resident); $100 per semester (nonresident). Fees vary by number of credits taken. Average 1997–98 room and board costs were $3500 per academic year (on campus) and $4800 per academic year (off campus). Room and board costs vary by occupancy (e.g., single, double, triple), type of accommodation.

Financial Aid Fellowships, research assistantships, teaching assistantships, work study available. Financial aid is available to part-time students. Application Deadline: 5/1.

Financial Aid Contact Director of Financial Aid, Box 45011, Lubbock, TX 79409-5011. Phone: 806-742-3681; Fax: 806-742-3958 .

FACILITIES

Information Resources Texas Tech University Library plus 6 additional on-campus libraries; total holdings of 2,298,897 volumes, 2,468,014 microforms, 20,038 current periodical subscriptions. CD player(s) available for graduate student use. Access provided to online bibliographic retrieval services and online databases.

INTERNATIONAL STUDENTS

Demographics 18% of students enrolled are international students [Asia, 80%, Central America, 2%, Europe, 15%, South America, 3%].

Services and Facilities International student office, international student center, ESL courses, counseling/support services.

Applying TOEFL: minimum score of 550, proof of adequate funds, proof of health/immunizations required. Financial aid is not available to international students.

International Student Contact Ms. Nancy Dodge, Director, Graduate Services Center, Box 42101, Lubbock, TX 79409-2101. Phone: 806-742-3184; Fax: 806-742-3958.

PLACEMENT

Services include alumni network, career counseling/planning, career fairs, career library, career placement, electronic job bank, job interviews arranged, job search course, and resume referral to employers. In 1996–97, 400 organizations participated in on-campus recruiting; 5,850 on-campus interviews were conducted.

Employment Of 1996–97 graduates, 59% were employed within three months of graduation; the average starting salary was $39,000. Types of employment entered: accounting, banking, communications, computer-related, consulting, consumer products, education, energy, finance, financial services, government, health services, human resources, information systems/technology, international trade, law, management, manufacturing, marketing, pharmaceutical, retail, service industry, transportation.

Business Program(s) URL: http://www.ba.ttu.edu

Program Contact: Ms. Nancy Dodge, Director, Box 42101, Lubbock, TX 79409-2101. Phone: 806-742-3184, 800-882-6220; Fax: 806-742-3958; E-mail: bagrad@coba2.ttu.edu

See full description on page 1018.

Texas Wesleyan University

School of Business Administration

Fort Worth, Texas

OVERVIEW

Texas Wesleyan University is an independent-religious, coed, comprehensive institution. Enrollment: 3,200 graduate, professional, and undergraduate students; 500 full-time matriculated graduate/professional students; 300 part-time

Texas Wesleyan University (continued)

matriculated graduate/professional students. Founded: 1890. The graduate business unit is in an urban setting and is on a semester calendar.

HIGHLIGHTS

Enrollment Profile
Full-time: 15
Part-time: 77
Total: 92
Average Age: 32
Fall 1997 Average GPA: 3.12

International: 11%
Women: 35%
Minorities: 27%
Average Class Size: 12
Fall 1997 Average GMAT: 455

Costs
Full-time tuition: N/R
Part-time tuition: $275 per credit hour

GRADUATE BUSINESS PROGRAMS
Master of Business Administration (MBA) Full-time, part-time; 36 total credits required; 18 months to 3 years to complete program. Concentrations in accounting, human resources, international business, organizational management.

ADMISSION
Applications For fall 1997 there were 80 applications for admission. Of those applying, 16 were accepted. Of those accepted, 16 enrolled.

Application Requirements Application form, application fee, bachelor's degree, essay, minimum GPA: 2.85, 3 letters of recommendation, personal statement, college transcript(s).

Recommended for Application GMAT score accepted, resume, work experience, computer experience.

Application Deadline Applications processed on a rolling/continuous basis for both domestic and international students. Application fee: $20. Deferred entrance is available.

ACADEMICS
Faculty Full-time 13; part-time 1.

Teaching Methodologies Case study, computer-aided instruction, experiential learning, field projects, group discussion, lecture, research, seminars by members of the business community, student presentations, study groups, team projects.

Technology 150 on-campus computer terminals/PCs are available for student use and are linked by a campus-wide network. The network has full access to the Internet. Students are not required to have their own PC.

Special Opportunities Advanced credit may be earned through credit for experience, credit for military training programs, credit for business training programs, transfer of credits from another institution. An internship program is available.

FINANCES
Costs for 1997–98 Tuition: $275 per credit hour. Cost varies by number of credits taken. Fees: $75 per semester. Fees vary by number of credits taken. Average 1997–98 room and board costs were $8484 per academic year (on campus) and $11,000 per academic year (off campus).

Financial Aid In 1997–98, 3% of students received some institutionally administered aid in the form of research assistantships, scholarships. Financial aid is available to part-time students. Application Deadline: 7/31.

Financial Aid Contact Ms. Karen Krause, Director of Financial Aid, 1201 Wesleyan, Fort Worth, TX 76105-1536. Phone: 817-531-4420; Fax: 817-531-6585.

FACILITIES
Information Resources Middleton Library. CD player(s) available for graduate student use. Access provided to online bibliographic retrieval services and online databases.

INTERNATIONAL STUDENTS
Demographics 11% of students enrolled are international students [Europe, 60%, other, 40%].

Services and Facilities International student office, international student housing, visa services, ESL courses, counseling/support services.

Applying TOEFL: minimum score of 550, proof of adequate funds, proof of health/immunizations required. Financial aid is available to international students.

International Student Contact Ms. Helena Bussell, Assistant to Provost for International Programs, 1201 Wesleyan, Fort Worth, TX 76105-1536. Phone: 817-531-4220; Fax: 817-531-6585.

PLACEMENT
Services include career counseling/planning, career placement, resume referral to employers, and resume preparation. In 1996–97, 100 organizations participated in on-campus recruiting.

Employment Types of employment entered: real estate, retail, service industry, telecommunications.

Business Program(s) URL: http://www.txwesleyan.edu

Program Contact: Mr. Robert McMurrian, Director of Graduate Programs, School of Business, 1201 Wesleyan, Fort Worth, TX 76105-1536. Phone: 817-531-6500; Fax: 817-531-6585; E-mail: robertmc@txwcs.edu

Texas Woman's University

Department of Business and Economics

Denton, Texas

OVERVIEW
Texas Woman's University is a state-supported, primarily women university. Enrollment: 10,000 graduate, professional, and undergraduate students; 1,720 full-time matriculated graduate/professional students; 3,180 part-time matriculated graduate/professional students. Founded: 1901. The graduate business unit is in a suburban setting and is on a semester calendar.

HIGHLIGHTS

Enrollment Profile
Full-time: 5
Part-time: 51
Total: 56
Average Age: 30
Fall 1997 Average GPA: 3.1

International: 21%
Women: 88%
Minorities: 34%
Average Class Size: 25
Fall 1997 Average GMAT: N/R

Costs
Full-time tuition: N/R
Part-time tuition: $75 per credit hour (resident); $288 per credit hour (nonresident)

GRADUATE BUSINESS PROGRAMS
Master of Business Administration (MBA) Full-time, part-time; 36 total credits required; 12 months to 3 years to complete program.

ADMISSION
Applications For fall 1997 there were 37 applications for admission. Of those applying, 30 were accepted. Of those accepted, 20 enrolled.

Application Requirements GMAT score: minimum 400, application form, application fee, bachelor's degree, minimum GPA: 3.0, 3 letters of recommendation, resume, college transcript(s).

Recommended for Application Work experience.

Application Deadline 4/1 for fall, 8/1 for spring, 1/1 for summer, 4/1 for fall (international), 8/1 for spring (international), 1/1 for summer (international). Application fee: $25.

ACADEMICS
Faculty Full-time 13; part-time 9.

Teaching Methodologies Case study, computer-aided instruction, computer analysis, computer simulations, experiential learning, faculty seminars, field projects, group discussion, lecture, research, role playing, seminars by members of the business community, simulations, student presentations, study groups, team projects.

Technology 300 on-campus computer terminals/PCs are available for student use. The network has full access to the Internet. Students are required to have their own PC.

Special Opportunities Advanced credit may be earned through transfer of credits from another institution. International exchange programs in Germany, Japan, Russia. An internship program is available.

FINANCES
Costs for 1997–98 Tuition: $75 per credit hour (resident); $288 per credit hour (nonresident). Cost varies by academic program, number of credits taken, reciprocity agreements. Fees: $33 per credit hour (resident); $33 per credit hour (nonresident). Fees vary by academic program, number of credits taken, reciprocity agreements. Average 1997–98 room and board costs were $6000 per academic year (off campus). Room and board costs vary by occupancy (e.g., single, double, triple), type of accommodation, type of meal plan.

Financial Aid Research assistantships, teaching assistantships available. Application Deadline: 4/1.

Financial Aid Contact Mr. Governor Jackson, Director, Box 425408, Denton, TX 76204. Phone: 940-898-3050; Fax: 940-898-3198.

FACILITIES
Information Resources Mary Evelyn Blagg Huey Library plus 1 additional on-campus library; total holdings of 788,271 volumes, 652,861 microforms, 2,899 current periodical subscriptions. CD player(s) available for graduate student use. Access provided to online bibliographic retrieval services.

INTERNATIONAL STUDENTS
Demographics 21% of students enrolled are international students [Africa, 10%, Asia, 30%, other, 60%].

Services and Facilities International student office, counseling/support services.

Applying TOEFL: minimum score of 550, proof of adequate funds, proof of health/immunizations required. Financial aid is available to international students.

International Student Contact Ms. Leslie Thomas, Coordinator, Box 425738, Denton, TX 76204. Phone: 940-898-3048; Fax: 940-898-3198.

PLACEMENT
Services include alumni network, career counseling/planning, career fairs, career library, career placement, electronic job bank, job interviews arranged, job search course, resume referral to employers, and resume preparation. In 1996–97, 40 organizations participated in on-campus recruiting.

Employment Of 1996–97 graduates, 95% were employed within three months of graduation; the average starting salary was $25,000. Types of employment entered: accounting, banking, computer-related, education, finance, government, health services, hospitality management, human resources, management, marketing, real estate, retail, service industry.

Business Program(s) URL: http://www.twu.edu

Program Contact: Chair, Department of Business and Economics, Box 425738, Denton, TX 76204. Phone: 940-898-2111; Fax: 940-898-2120; E-mail: d_bulls@twu.edu

University of Central Texas

Division of Management, Business and Technology

Killeen, Texas

OVERVIEW
The University of Central Texas is an independent-nonprofit, coed, upper-level institution. Enrollment: 1,039 graduate, professional, and undergraduate students; 116 full-time matriculated graduate/professional students; 253 part-time matriculated graduate/professional students. Founded: 1973. The graduate business unit is in a suburban setting and is on a semester calendar.

HIGHLIGHTS

Enrollment Profile
Full-time: 60
Part-time: 130
Total: 190
Average Age: 34
Fall 1997 Average GPA: 3.0

International: 11%
Women: 58%
Minorities: 45%
Average Class Size: 20
Fall 1997 Average GMAT: N/R

Costs
Full-time tuition: $2664 per academic year
Part-time tuition: $148 per hour

GRADUATE BUSINESS PROGRAMS
Master of Business Administration/Master of Science in Management and Business (MBA/MS) Full-time, part-time; 36 total credits required; 18 months to 5 years to complete program. Concentrations in human resources, leadership, management, management information systems, management science.

Master of Science in Information Systems (MS) Full-time, part-time; 36 total credits required; 18 months to 5 years to complete program. Concentration in management information systems.

Master of Science in Human Resource Management (MS) Full-time, part-time; 36 total credits required; 18 months to 5 years to complete program. Concentration in human resources.

ADMISSION
Application Requirements GMAT score, GRE score, MAT score, application form, application fee, bachelor's degree, minimum GPA: 2.5, college transcript(s).

Recommended for Application Interview.

Application Deadline Applications processed on a rolling/continuous basis for domestic students only. 4/1 for fall (international), 9/1 for spring (international), 1/1 for summer (international). Application fee: $200.

ACADEMICS
Faculty Full-time 9; part-time 14.

Teaching Methodologies Case study, computer-aided instruction, computer analysis, computer simulations, experiential learning, faculty seminars, field projects, group discussion, lecture, research, role playing, seminars by members of the business community, student presentations, study groups, team projects.

Technology 37 on-campus computer terminals/PCs are available for student use. The network does not have Internet access. Students are not required to have their own PC.

Special Opportunities Advanced credit may be earned through transfer of credits from another institution. An internship program is available.

FINANCES
Costs for 1997–98 Tuition: Full-time: $2664 per year. Part-time: $148 per hour. Fees: Full-time: $40 per academic year. Part-time: $10 per course. Average 1997–98 room and board costs were $4839 per academic year (on campus) and $4839 per academic year (off campus).

Financial Aid In 1997–98, 68% of students received some institutionally administered aid in the form of grants, scholarships, work study. Financial aid is available to part-time students.

Financial Aid Contact Ms. Linda Sullivan, Financial Aid Coordinator, PO Box 1416, Killeen, TX 76540. Phone: 254-526-8262 Ext. 242; Fax: 254-526-8403; E-mail: uct31@vvm.com

FACILITIES
Information Resources Ovetta Culp Hobby Library; total holdings of 96,197 volumes, 118,484 microforms, 1,183 current periodical subscriptions. CD player(s) available for graduate student use. Access provided to online bibliographic retrieval services.

INTERNATIONAL STUDENTS
Demographics 11% of students enrolled are international students [Asia, 95%, North America, 5%].

Services and Facilities International student office.

Applying TOEFL: minimum score of 515, proof of adequate funds required. IELT, TSE, TWE recommended. Financial aid is not available to international students.

International Student Contact Ms. Susan Kent, International Student Advisor, PO Box 1416, Killeen, TX 76540. Phone: 254-526-8262 Ext. 260; Fax: 254-526-8403.

PLACEMENT
Services include alumni network, career counseling/planning, career fairs, and career library. In 1996–97, 80 organizations participated in on-campus recruiting.

Employment Types of employment entered: accounting, banking, communications, computer-related, consulting, education, engineering, financial services, government, health services, human resources, information systems/technology, law, management, manufacturing, nonprofit, utilities.

Business Program(s) URL: http://www.vvm.com/uct/

Program Contact: Ms. Pam Asmus, Admissions Advisor, PO Box 1416, Killeen, TX 76540. Phone: 254-526-8262 Ext. 238; Fax: 254-526-8403.

University of Dallas

Graduate School of Management

Irving, Texas

OVERVIEW
The University of Dallas is an independent-religious, coed university. Enrollment: 2,897 graduate, professional, and undergraduate students; 388 full-time matriculated graduate/professional students; 1,378 part-time matriculated graduate/professional students. Founded: 1955. The graduate business unit is in a suburban setting and is on a trimester calendar.

HIGHLIGHTS

Enrollment Profile
Full-time: 317
Part-time: 1,099
Total: 1,416
Average Age: 32
Fall 1997 Average GPA: 3.1

International: 24%
Women: 40%
Minorities: 18%
Average Class Size: 22
Fall 1997 Average GMAT: 520

Costs
Full-time tuition: $9120 per academic year
Part-time tuition: $380 per credit hour

GRADUATE BUSINESS PROGRAMS
Master of Business Administration (MBA) Full-time, part-time; 49 total credits required; 12 months to 6 years to complete program. Concentrations in financial management/planning, human resources, international management, management information systems, marketing, finance, industrial administration/management, management, health care, telecommunications management.

Master of Management (MMgt) Full-time, part-time; 25 total credits required; 12 months to 6 years to complete program. Concentrations in financial management/planning, human resources, international management, management information systems, marketing, finance, industrial administration/management, management, health care, telecommunications management.

TEXAS

University of Dallas (continued)

ADMISSION
Applications For fall 1997 there were 680 applications for admission. Of those applying, 580 were accepted. Of those accepted, 404 enrolled.

Application Requirements GMAT score: minimum 400, application form, application fee, bachelor's degree, minimum GPA: 3.0, 2 letters of recommendation, resume, college transcript(s), computer experience: working knowledge of basic computer concepts.

Recommended for Application Personal statement, minimum of 5 years of work experience.

Application Deadline 7/12 for fall, 11/8 for spring, 7/12 for fall (international), 11/8 for spring (international). Application fee: $30, $50 (international). Deferred entrance is available.

ACADEMICS
Faculty Full-time 20; part-time 59.

Teaching Methodologies Case study, computer-aided instruction, computer analysis, experiential learning, faculty seminars, field projects, group discussion, lecture, research, role playing, seminars by members of the business community, simulations, student presentations, study groups, team projects.

Technology 80 on-campus computer terminals/PCs are available for student use and are linked by a campus-wide network. The network has full access to the Internet. Students are not required to have their own PC.

Special Opportunities Advanced credit may be earned through transfer of credits from another institution. International exchange programs in France, Mexico, Spain. An internship program is available.

FINANCES
Costs for 1997–98 Tuition: Full-time: $9120 per year. Part-time: $380 per credit hour. Cost varies by number of credits taken. Fees: Full-time: $60 per academic year. Part-time: $20 per trimester. Average 1997–98 room and board costs were $5186 per academic year (on campus) and $7500 per academic year (off campus). Room and board costs vary by occupancy (e.g., single, double, triple), type of accommodation, type of meal plan.

Financial Aid In 1997–98, 19% of students received some institutionally administered aid in the form of loans. Financial aid is available to part-time students. Application Deadline: 2/15.

Financial Aid Contact Mr. Peter Bagarozzo, Director, 1845 East Northgate Drive, Irving, TX 75062-4799. Phone: 972-721-5266; Fax: 972-721-5017; E-mail: undadmis@acad.udallas.edu

FACILITIES
Information Resources William A. Blakely Library; total holdings of 295,000 volumes, 75,368 microforms, 1,074 current periodical subscriptions. CD player(s) available for graduate student use. Access provided to online bibliographic retrieval services.

INTERNATIONAL STUDENTS
Demographics 24% of students enrolled are international students [Africa, 3%, Asia, 67%, Central America, 9%, Europe, 9%, North America, 3%, South America, 7%, other, 2%].

Services and Facilities International student office, international student center, ESL courses, counseling/support services.

Applying TOEFL: minimum score of 520, proof of adequate funds required. Proof of health/immunizations recommended. Financial aid is not available to international students.

International Student Contact Ms. Marilyn White, Director of International Student Services, 1845 East Northgate Drive, Irving, TX 75062-4799. Phone: 972-721-5059; Fax: 972-721-4009; E-mail: iep@gsm.udallas.edu

PLACEMENT
Services include alumni network, career counseling/planning, career fairs, career library, career placement, job search course, and resume preparation. In 1996–97, 25 organizations participated in on-campus recruiting.

Employment Types of employment entered: banking, computer-related, energy, financial services, health services, information systems/technology, marketing, telecommunications.

Business Program(s) URL: http://gsm.udallas.edu

Program Contact: Ms. Roxanne Del Rio, Director of Graduate School of Management Admissions, 1845 East Northgate Drive, Irving, TX 75062-4799. Phone: 972-721-5198, 800-832-5622 (TX only); Fax: 972-721-4009.
See full description on page 1060.

University of Houston

College of Business Administration
Houston, Texas

OVERVIEW
The University of Houston is a state-supported, coed university. Enrollment: 31,298 graduate, professional, and undergraduate students; 3,573 full-time matriculated graduate/professional students; 3,675 part-time matriculated graduate/professional students. Founded: 1927. The graduate business unit is in an urban setting and is on a semester calendar.

HIGHLIGHTS

Enrollment Profile

Full-time: 470	International: N/R
Part-time: 571	Women: N/R
Total: 1,041	Minorities: 25%
Average Age: 28	Average Class Size: 40
Fall 1997 Average GPA: 3.21	Fall 1997 Average GMAT: 578

Costs
Full-time tuition: N/R
Part-time tuition: $672 per 6 hours (resident); $2968 per 6 hours (nonresident)

AACSB – The International Association for Management Education accredited

GRADUATE BUSINESS PROGRAMS
Master of Business Administration (MBA) Full-time, part-time; 54 total credits required; 12 months to 5 years to complete program. Concentrations in accounting, finance, international business, management, management information systems, marketing, operations management, entrepreneurship.

Executive MBA/Professional MBA (MBA) Full-time, part-time; 54 total credits required; 2 to 3 years to complete program.

Master of Business Administration/Doctor of Jurisprudence (MBA/JD) Full-time, part-time; 115 total credits required; 3 to 4 years to complete program. Concentrations in accounting, entrepreneurship, finance, international business, management, management information systems, marketing, operations management, quantitative analysis, taxation.

Master of Business Administration/Master of Science (MBA/MS) Full-time, part-time; 78 total credits required; 2 to 3 years to complete program. Concentrations in accounting, entrepreneurship, finance, international business, management, management information systems, marketing, operations management, quantitative analysis, taxation.

Master of Business Administration/Master of Arts in Spanish (MBA/MA) Full-time, part-time; 78 total credits required; 2 to 3 years to complete program. Concentrations in accounting, entrepreneurship, finance, international business, management, management information systems, marketing, operations management, quantitative analysis, taxation.

Master of Science in Accountancy (MS) Full-time, part-time; 60 total credits required; 18 months to 5 years to complete program. Concentrations in accounting, taxation.

ADMISSION
Applications For fall 1997 there were 715 applications for admission. Of those applying, 378 were accepted. Of those accepted, 300 enrolled.

Application Requirements GMAT score: minimum 550, application form, application fee, bachelor's degree, minimum GPA: 3.0, resume, college transcript(s).

Recommended for Application Personal statement, minimum of 2 years of work experience.

Application Deadline 5/1 for fall, 10/1 for spring, 5/1 for fall (international), 10/1 for spring (international). Application fee: $50, $125 (international). Deferred entrance is available.

ACADEMICS
Faculty Full-time 85; part-time 22.

Teaching Methodologies Case study, computer-aided instruction, computer simulations, field projects, group discussion, lecture, research, seminars by members of the business community, student presentations, study groups, team projects.

Technology 120 on-campus computer terminals/PCs are available for student use and are linked by a campus-wide network. The network has full access to the Internet. Students are not required to have their own PC.

Special Opportunities Advanced credit may be earned through transfer of credits from another institution. International exchange programs in Canada, France, Germany, Japan, Mexico.

518

Peterson's Guide to MBA Programs 1999

FINANCES
Costs for 1997–98 Tuition: $672 per 6 hours (resident); $2968 per 6 hours (nonresident). Cost varies by academic program, number of credits taken, reciprocity agreements. Fees: $382 per 6 hours (resident); $382 per 6 hours (nonresident). Fees vary by academic program, class time (e.g., day/evening), number of credits taken, reciprocity agreements. Average 1997–98 room and board costs were $4500 per academic year. Room and board costs vary by campus location, occupancy (e.g., single, double, triple), type of accommodation, type of meal plan.

Financial Aid Fellowships, research assistantships, teaching assistantships, work study, loans available. Financial aid is available to part-time students. Application Deadline: 3/1.

Financial Aid Contact Ms. Linda F. Price, Director, Scholarships and Special Programs, College of Business Administration, 4800 Calhoun, Houston, TX 77204-6283. Phone: 713-743-4620; Fax: 713-743-8837.

FACILITIES
Information Resources M. D. Anderson Library plus 5 additional on-campus libraries; total holdings of 1,804,002 volumes, 3,677,450 microforms, 14,198 current periodical subscriptions. CD player(s) available for graduate student use. Access provided to online bibliographic retrieval services.

INTERNATIONAL STUDENTS
Demographics N/R

Services and Facilities International student office, visa services, ESL courses, counseling/support services.

Applying TOEFL: minimum score of 620, proof of adequate funds required. Financial aid is available to international students.

International Student Contact Anita Gaines, Director, International Student Services and Scholar Services, 4800 Calhoun, Houston, TX 77204. Phone: 713-743-5072; Fax: 713-743-8837.

PLACEMENT
Services include career counseling/planning, career fairs, career library, career placement, electronic job bank, job interviews arranged, job search course, resume referral to employers, and resume preparation. In 1996–97, 90 organizations participated in on-campus recruiting; 1,200 on-campus interviews were conducted.

Employment Of 1996–97 graduates, 85% were employed within three months of graduation; the average starting salary was $42,670. Types of employment entered: accounting, banking, chemical industry, communications, computer-related, consulting, consumer products, education, energy, engineering, finance, financial services, government, health services, high technology, information systems/technology, insurance, management, manufacturing, marketing, nonprofit, petrochemical, pharmaceutical, retail, service industry, telecommunications, utilities.

Business Program(s) URL: http://www.cba.uh.edu

Program Contact: Office of Student Services, College of Business Administration, 4800 Calhoun, Houston, TX 77204-6282. Phone: 713-743-4900; Fax: 713-743-4942; E-mail: uss@cba.uh.edu
See full description on page 1076.

University of Houston-Clear Lake

College of Business and Public Administration

Houston, Texas

OVERVIEW
The University of Houston-Clear Lake is a state-supported, coed, upper-level institution. Enrollment: 6,947 graduate, professional, and undergraduate students; 967 full-time matriculated graduate/professional students; 2,513 part-time matriculated graduate/professional students. Founded: 1974. The graduate business unit is in a suburban setting and is on a semester calendar.

HIGHLIGHTS

Enrollment Profile
Full-time: 348
Part-time: 630
Total: 978
Average Age: 32
Fall 1997 Average GPA: 3.0

International: 13%
Women: 44%
Minorities: 19%
Average Class Size: 35
Fall 1997 Average GMAT: 550

Costs
Full-time tuition: N/R
Part-time tuition: $52 per semester hour (resident); $171 per semester hour (nonresident)

AACSB – The International Association for Management Education accredited

GRADUATE BUSINESS PROGRAMS
Master of Business Administration (MBA) Full-time, part-time; 36-57 total credits required; 2 to 5 years to complete program. Concentrations in entrepreneurship, management information systems, international business, technology management, human resources, environmental economics/management, human resources.

Master of Science in Finance (MS) Full-time, part-time; 36-57 total credits required; 2 to 5 years to complete program. Concentrations in finance, health care.

Master of Science in Accounting (MS) Full-time, part-time; 36-69 total credits required; 2 to 5 years to complete program. Concentration in accounting.

ADMISSION
Applications For fall 1997 there were 435 applications for admission. Of those applying, 332 were accepted. Of those accepted, 302 enrolled.

Application Requirements Application form, application fee, bachelor's degree, minimum GPA: 2.0, college transcript(s).

Recommended for Application GMAT score accepted, GRE score accepted; minimum 950.

Application Deadline 8/1 for fall, 12/1 for spring, 5/1 for summer, 6/1 for fall (international), 10/1 for spring (international), 3/1 for summer (international). Application fee: $30, $70 (international).

ACADEMICS
Faculty Full-time 52; part-time 51.

Teaching Methodologies Case study, computer-aided instruction, computer analysis, computer simulations, experiential learning, faculty seminars, group discussion, lecture, research, role playing, seminars by members of the business community, student presentations, study groups, team projects.

Technology 132 on-campus computer terminals/PCs are available for student use and are linked by a campus-wide network. The network has full access to the Internet. Students are not required to have their own PC.

Special Opportunities Advanced credit may be earned through transfer of credits from another institution. An internship program is available.

FINANCES
Costs for 1997–98 Tuition: $52 per semester hour (resident); $171 per semester hour (nonresident). Cost varies by number of credits taken. Fees vary by academic program, number of credits taken.

Financial Aid Teaching assistantships, scholarships, work study, loans available. Financial aid is available to part-time students. Application Deadline: 5/1.

Financial Aid Contact Ms. JoAnne Greene, Director of Financial Aid and Veterans' Affairs, 270 Bay Area Boulevard, Houston, TX 77058-1098. Phone: 713-283-2485.

FACILITIES
Information Resources Neumann Library; total holdings of 339,254 volumes, 2,455 current periodical subscriptions. CD player(s) available for graduate student use. Access provided to online bibliographic retrieval services.

INTERNATIONAL STUDENTS
Demographics 13% of students enrolled are international students.

Services and Facilities International student office, international student center, international student housing, counseling/support services.

Applying TOEFL: minimum score of 550, proof of adequate funds required. Financial aid is not available to international students.

International Student Contact Ms. Kathryn Dickerson, International Student Advisor, 2700 Bay Area Boulevard, Houston, TX 77058. Phone: 281-283-7600.

Business Program(s) URL: http://www.cl.uh.edu/bpa/index.html

Program Contact: Dr. Sue E. Neeley, Associate Dean, School of Business and Public Administration, Houston, TX 77058-1098. Phone: 713-283-3110.

University of Houston-Victoria

Division of Business Administration

Victoria, Texas

OVERVIEW
The University of Houston-Victoria is a state-supported, coed, upper-level institution. Enrollment: 1,616 graduate, professional, and undergraduate students; 40 full-time matriculated graduate/professional students; 140 part-time matriculated graduate/professional students. Founded: 1973. The graduate business unit is in a small-town setting and is on a semester calendar.

University of Houston-Victoria (continued)

HIGHLIGHTS

Enrollment Profile
Full-time: 30	International: N/R
Part-time: 100	Women: N/R
Total: 130	Minorities: N/R
Average Age: 32	Average Class Size: 15
Fall 1997 Average GPA: 3.2	Fall 1997 Average GMAT: 490

Costs
Full-time tuition: $486 per academic year (resident); $2232 per academic year (nonresident)
Part-time tuition: N/R

GRADUATE BUSINESS PROGRAMS
Master of Business Administration (MBA) Full-time, part-time, distance learning option; 36 total credits required; 12 months to 2 years to complete program. Concentration in management.

Master of Business Administration (MBA) Full-time, part-time, distance learning option; 57 total credits required; 2.5 to 5 years to complete program.

ADMISSION
Application Requirements Application form, bachelor's degree, minimum GPA: 2.5, college transcript(s).

Recommended for Application GMAT score accepted: minimum 400, GRE score accepted: minimum 800, letters of recommendation, computer experience.

Application Deadline Applications processed on a rolling/continuous basis for both domestic and international students. Deferred entrance is available.

ACADEMICS
Faculty Full-time 9; part-time 10.

Teaching Methodologies Case study, computer-aided instruction, computer analysis, computer simulations, experiential learning, faculty seminars, field projects, group discussion, lecture, research, role playing, seminars by members of the business community, simulations, student presentations, study groups, team projects.

Technology 45 on-campus computer terminals/PCs are available for student use and are linked by a campus-wide network. The network has full access to the Internet. Students are not required to have their own PC.

Special Opportunities Advanced credit may be earned through transfer of credits from another institution.

FINANCES
Costs for 1997–98 Tuition: Full-time: $486 per 9 hours (resident); $2232 per 9 hours (nonresident). Cost varies by academic program, number of credits taken. Fees: Full-time: $360 per academic year (resident); $360 per academic year (nonresident). Fees vary by academic program, campus location. Average 1997–98 room only costs were $4500 per academic year (off campus). Room and board costs vary by occupancy (e.g., single, double, triple), type of accommodation.

Financial Aid Research assistantships, teaching assistantships, grants, scholarships, work study available. Financial aid is available to part-time students.

Financial Aid Contact Carolyn Mallory, Director of Financial Aid, 2506 East Red River, Victoria, TX 77901-4450. Phone: 512-788-6303; Fax: 512-572-9377; E-mail: vofacrm@vicux2.vic.uh.edu

FACILITIES
Information Resources Victoria College Library; total holdings of 194,000 volumes, 619,700 microforms, 1,950 current periodical subscriptions. CD player(s) available for graduate student use. Access provided to online bibliographic retrieval services and online databases.

INTERNATIONAL STUDENTS
Demographics N/R

Services and Facilities Visa services, counseling/support services.

Applying TOEFL: minimum score of 500, proof of adequate funds, proof of health/immunizations required. Financial aid is not available to international students.

International Student Contact Richard Phillips, Director of Enrollment, 2506 East Red River, Victoria, TX 77901-4450. Phone: 512-788-6297; Fax: 512-572-9377; E-mail: vermardp@vicvx2.vic.uh.edu

PLACEMENT
Services include alumni network, career fairs, career library, job interviews arranged, job search course, resume referral to employers, and resume preparation. In 1996–97, 20 organizations participated in on-campus recruiting; 80 on-campus interviews were conducted.

Employment Types of employment entered: accounting, banking, computer-related, consumer products, finance, financial services, government, health services, high technology, human resources, information systems/technology, insurance, management, manufacturing, marketing, nonprofit, petrochemical, real estate, retail, utilities.

Business Program(s) URL: http://www.vic.uh.edu/bus/index.htm

Program Contact: Richard Phillips, Director of Enrollment, 2506 East Red River, Victoria, TX 77901-4450. Phone: 512-788-6297; Fax: 512-572-9377; E-mail: vermardp@vicvx2.vic.uh.edu

University of Mary Hardin-Baylor

School of Business

Belton, Texas

OVERVIEW
The University of Mary Hardin-Baylor is an independent-religious, coed, comprehensive institution. Enrollment: 2,244 graduate, professional, and undergraduate students; 33 full-time matriculated graduate/professional students; 195 part-time matriculated graduate/professional students. Founded: 1845. The graduate business unit is in a small-town setting and is on a trimester calendar.

HIGHLIGHTS

Enrollment Profile
Full-time: 7	International: 4%
Part-time: 19	Women: 54%
Total: 26	Minorities: 12%
Average Age: 32	Average Class Size: 16
Fall 1997 Average GPA: 3.2	Fall 1997 Average GMAT: 518

Costs
Full-time tuition: $9720 per academic year
Part-time tuition: $270 per semester hour

GRADUATE BUSINESS PROGRAMS
Master of Business Administration (MBA) Full-time, part-time; 36 total credits required; 12 months to 5 years to complete program. Concentration in management.

ADMISSION
Applications For fall 1997 there were 7 applications for admission. Of those applying, 7 were accepted. Of those accepted, 7 enrolled.

Application Requirements Application form, application fee, bachelor's degree, college transcript(s).

Recommended for Application GMAT score accepted, minimum GPA: 2.5, interview, computer experience.

Application Deadline Applications processed on a rolling/continuous basis for both domestic and international students. Application fee: $35.

ACADEMICS
Faculty Full-time 7; part-time 1.

Teaching Methodologies Case study, faculty seminars, group discussion, lecture, student presentations, team projects.

Technology 70 on-campus computer terminals/PCs are available for student use and are linked by a campus-wide network. The network has full access to the Internet. Students are not required to have their own PC.

Special Opportunities Advanced credit may be earned through transfer of credits from another institution.

FINANCES
Costs for 1997–98 Tuition: Full-time: $9720 per year. Part-time: $270 per semester hour. Cost varies by number of credits taken. Fees: Full-time: $504 per academic year. Part-time: $14 per semester hour. Fees vary by number of credits taken. Average 1997–98 room and board costs were $5610 per academic year. Room and board costs vary by occupancy (e.g., single, double, triple), type of accommodation.

Financial Aid Loans available. Financial aid is available to part-time students.

Financial Aid Contact Mr. Ron Brown, Director of Financial Aid, UMHB Station Box 8004, Belton, TX 76513. Phone: 254-295-4517; Fax: 254-295-4535.

FACILITIES
Information Resources Townsend Library; total holdings of 100,436 volumes, 109,737 microforms, 902 current periodical subscriptions. CD player(s) available for graduate student use. Access provided to online bibliographic retrieval services.

INTERNATIONAL STUDENTS
Demographics 4% of students enrolled are international students [Asia, 100%].

Services and Facilities International student office, visa services, ESL courses, counseling/support services.

Applying TOEFL, proof of adequate funds, proof of health/immunizations required. Financial aid is not available to international students.

International Student Contact Mr. Reed Harris, Director of International Students, UMHB Station Box 8421, Belton, TX 76513. Phone: 254-295-4949; Fax: 254-295-4535.

PLACEMENT
Services include career counseling/planning, career fairs, career placement, job interviews arranged, and resume preparation. In 1996–97, 10 organizations participated in on-campus recruiting.

Employment Of 1996–97 graduates, 100% were employed within three months of graduation. Types of employment entered: accounting, banking, computer-related, consumer products, energy, finance, financial services, information systems/technology, management, manufacturing, marketing, nonprofit, service industry, utilities.

Program Contact: Dr. Lee Baldwin, Dean, School of Business, UMHB Station Box 8018, Belton, TX 76513. Phone: 254-295-4644, 800-727-8642 (TX only); Fax: 254-295-4535.

University of North Texas

College of Business Administration

Denton, Texas

OVERVIEW
The University of North Texas is a state-supported, coed university. Enrollment: 25,605 graduate, professional, and undergraduate students; 2,227 full-time matriculated graduate/professional students; 2,810 part-time matriculated graduate/professional students. Founded: 1890. The graduate business unit is in an urban setting and is on a semester calendar.

HIGHLIGHTS

Enrollment Profile

Full-time: 375	International: 15%
Part-time: 444	Women: 37%
Total: 819	Minorities: 8%
Average Age: 31	Average Class Size: 30
Fall 1997 Average GPA: 2.95	Fall 1997 Average GMAT: 540

Costs
Full-time tuition: N/R
Part-time tuition: $146 per credit hour (resident); $272 per credit hour (nonresident)

AACSB – The International Association for Management Education accredited

GRADUATE BUSINESS PROGRAMS
Master of Business Administration (MBA) Full-time, part-time; 36-48 total credits required; up to 6 years to complete program. Concentrations in human resources, insurance, management science, marketing, production management, real estate, finance, management information systems, management.

Master of Science in Accounting (MS) Full-time, part-time; 36 total credits required; up to 6 years to complete program.

ADMISSION
Applications For fall 1997 there were 380 applications for admission. Of those applying, 245 were accepted. Of those accepted, 7 enrolled.

Application Requirements Application form, application fee, bachelor's degree, minimum GPA: 2.8, college transcript(s), computer experience.

Recommended for Application GMAT score accepted: minimum 450.

Application Deadline Applications processed on a rolling/continuous basis for both domestic and international students. Application fee: $25, $50 (international). Deferred entrance is available.

ACADEMICS
Faculty Full-time 94.

Teaching Methodologies Case study, computer-aided instruction, computer analysis, computer simulations, experiential learning, faculty seminars, field projects, group discussion, lecture, research, role playing, seminars by members of the business community, student presentations, study groups, team projects.

Technology 550 on-campus computer terminals/PCs are available for student use. The network has full access to the Internet. Students are not required to have their own PC.

Special Opportunities Advanced credit may be earned through transfer of credits from another institution. International exchange programs in Mexico, United Kingdom. An internship program is available.

FINANCES
Costs for 1997–98 Tuition: $146 per credit hour (resident); $272 per credit hour (nonresident). Cost varies by number of credits taken. Fees: $100 per credit hour (resident); $100 per credit hour (nonresident). Fees vary by number of credits taken. Average 1997–98 room and board costs were $3664 per academic year.

Financial Aid Fellowships, research assistantships, teaching assistantships, scholarships, work study, loans available.

Financial Aid Contact Financial Aid Office, PO Box 311370, Denton, TX 76203-1370. Phone: 940-565-2302; Fax: 940-565-2738.

FACILITIES
Information Resources A. M. Willis Library plus 2 additional on-campus libraries; total holdings of 1,206,758 volumes, 2,190,831 microforms, 8,775 current periodical subscriptions. CD player(s) available for graduate student use. Access provided to online bibliographic retrieval services.

INTERNATIONAL STUDENTS
Demographics 15% of students enrolled are international students.

Services and Facilities International student office, international student center, international student housing, visa services, ESL courses, counseling/support services.

Applying IELT, TOEFL: minimum score of 550, proof of adequate funds, proof of health/immunizations required.

International Student Contact International Office, PO Box 311067, Denton, TX 76203-1067. Phone: 940-565-2442; Fax: 940-565-4822; E-mail: intl@isp.unt.edu

PLACEMENT
Services include alumni network, career counseling/planning, career fairs, career library, career placement, job interviews arranged, job search course, resume referral to employers, and resume preparation.

Employment Types of employment entered: accounting, banking, communications, computer-related, consulting, education, energy, engineering, finance, financial services, government, health services, high technology, hospitality management, human resources, information systems/technology, insurance, international trade, management, manufacturing, marketing, media, nonprofit, real estate, retail, service industry, telecommunications, transportation.

Business Program(s) URL: http://www-lan.unt.edu/cobabak/www/

Program Contact: Director of Professional Programs, PO Box 311160, Denton, TX 76203-1160. Phone: 940-565-2110; Fax: 940-565-4640; E-mail: galubens@cobaf.unt.edu

University of St. Thomas

Cameron School of Business

Houston, Texas

OVERVIEW
The University of St. Thomas is an independent-religious, coed, comprehensive institution. Enrollment: 2,506 graduate, professional, and undergraduate students; 217 full-time matriculated graduate/professional students; 750 part-time matriculated graduate/professional students. Founded: 1947. The graduate business unit is in an urban setting and is on a semester calendar.

HIGHLIGHTS

Enrollment Profile

Full-time: 123	International: 24%
Part-time: 313	Women: 44%
Total: 436	Minorities: N/R
Average Age: 30	Average Class Size: 17
Fall 1997 Average GPA: N/R	Fall 1997 Average GMAT: N/R

Costs
Full-time tuition: $9840 per academic year
Part-time tuition: $410 per credit

ACBSP – The American Council of Business Schools and Programs accredited

GRADUATE BUSINESS PROGRAMS
Master of Business Administration (MBA) Full-time, part-time; 36 total credits required; up to 6 years to complete program. Concentrations in accounting, finance, international business, management information systems, marketing.

Master of Business Administration/Master of Science in Accounting (MBA/MS) Full-time, part-time; 60 total credits required; up to 6 years to complete program. Concentration in accounting.

Master of Science in Accounting (MSA) Full-time, part-time; 36 total credits required; up to 6 years to complete program. Concentration in accounting.

University of St. Thomas (continued)

Bachelor of Business Administration/Master in Business Administration (BBA/ MBA) Full-time, part-time; 156 total credits required; up to 6 years to complete program. Concentration in accounting.

Master of International Business (MIB) Full-time, part-time; 36 total credits required; up to 6 years to complete program.

ADMISSION

Applications For fall 1997 there were 249 applications for admission. Of those applying, 221 were accepted. Of those accepted, 151 enrolled.

Application Requirements GMAT score, application form, application fee, bachelor's degree, minimum GPA: 2.5, 3 letters of recommendation, personal statement, college transcript(s).

Recommended for Application GRE score accepted, resume, computer experience.

Application Deadline Applications processed on a rolling/continuous basis for both domestic and international students. Application fee: $35. Deferred entrance is available.

ACADEMICS

Faculty Full-time 18; part-time 26.

Teaching Methodologies Case study, group discussion, lecture, research, seminars by members of the business community, student presentations, team projects.

Technology 186 on-campus computer terminals/PCs are available for student use and are linked by a campus-wide network. The network has full access to the Internet. Students are not required to have their own PC.

Special Opportunities Advanced credit may be earned through credit by examination, transfer of credits from another institution.

FINANCES

Costs for 1997-98 Tuition: Full-time: $9840 per year. Part-time: $410 per credit. Cost varies by number of credits taken. Fees: Full-time: $33 per academic year. Part-time: $17 per semester. Fees vary by number of credits taken. Average 1997-98 room and board costs were $4500 per academic year (on campus) and $5400 per academic year (off campus). Room and board costs vary by occupancy (e.g., single, double, triple), type of accommodation, type of meal plan.

Financial Aid Work study, loans available. Financial aid is available to part-time students. Application Deadline: 3/1.

Financial Aid Contact Ms. Linda Ballard, Director of Financial Aid, 3800 Montrose Boulevard, Houston, TX 77006-4694. Phone: 713-525-2170; Fax: 713-525-2142; E-mail: ballard@stthom.edu

FACILITIES

Information Resources Doherty Library plus 2 additional on-campus libraries; total holdings of 202,956 volumes, 447,814 microforms, 1,717 current periodical subscriptions. CD player(s) available for graduate student use. Access provided to online bibliographic retrieval services.

INTERNATIONAL STUDENTS

Demographics 24% of students enrolled are international students.

Services and Facilities International student office, visa services, counseling/ support services.

Applying TOEFL: minimum score of 550, proof of adequate funds required. Financial aid is not available to international students.

International Student Contact Deacon Richard Glor, Registrar/International Student Advisor, 3800 Montrose Boulevard, Houston, TX 77006-4694. Phone: 713-525-2150; Fax: 713-525-3558; E-mail: glor@stthom.edu

PLACEMENT

Services include alumni network, career counseling/planning, career fairs, career library, job interviews arranged, resume referral to employers, and resume preparation.

Business Program(s) URL: http://www.stthom.edu/bschool

Program Contact: Dr. Yhi-Min Ho, Cameron School of Business, 3800 Montrose Boulevard, Houston, TX 77006-4694. Phone: 713-525-2100, 800-460-8878; Fax: 713-525-2110; E-mail: yhiminho@stthom.edu

The University of Texas at Arlington

College of Business Administration

Arlington, Texas

OVERVIEW

The University of Texas at Arlington is a state-supported, coed university. Enrollment: 19,286 graduate, professional, and undergraduate students; 1,717 full-time matriculated graduate/professional students; 2,128 part-time matriculated graduate/professional students. Founded: 1895. The graduate business unit is in a suburban setting and is on a semester calendar.

HIGHLIGHTS

Enrollment Profile

Full-time: 365	International: 25%
Part-time: 498	Women: 38%
Total: 863	Minorities: 10%
Average Age: N/R	Average Class Size: 22
Fall 1997 Average GPA: 3.13	Fall 1997 Average GMAT: 552

Costs

Full-time tuition: $3691 per academic year (resident); $10,411 per academic year (nonresident)

Part-time tuition: $110 per hour (resident); $331 per hour (nonresident)

AACSB – The International Association for Management Education accredited

Degree(s) offered in conjunction with International Institute for Higher Education in Morocco, Thunderbird, The American Graduate School of International Management

GRADUATE BUSINESS PROGRAMS

Master of Business Administration (MBA) Full-time, part-time; 36-48 total credits required; 12 months to 2 years to complete program. Concentrations in accounting, economics, finance, international business, international finance, management, management information systems, management science, management systems analysis, marketing, operations management, system management, technology management, decision sciences.

Master of Professional Accountancy (MPA) Full-time, part-time; 39-60 total credits required; 14 months to 2 years to complete program. Concentration in accounting.

Master of Science in Accounting (MS) Full-time, part-time; 36-75 total credits required; 14 months to 2.3 years to complete program. Concentration in system management.

Master of Science in Taxation (MS) Full-time, part-time; 36-75 total credits required; 14 months to 2.3 years to complete program. Concentration in taxation.

Master of Science in Information Systems (MS) Full-time, part-time; 30-60 total credits required; 14 months to 2 years to complete program. Concentrations in information management, management information systems, management systems analysis, technology management, system management.

Master of Science in Marketing Research (MS) Full-time, part-time; 36-63 total credits required; 12 months to 2 years to complete program. Concentration in marketing research.

Master of Science in Real Estate (MS) Full-time, part-time; 30-57 total credits required; 12 months to 2 years to complete program. Concentration in real estate.

Master of Science in Human Resource Management (MS) Full-time, part-time; 30-63 total credits required; 12 months to 2 years to complete program. Concentrations in human resources, industrial/labor relations.

Master of Arts in Economics (MA) Full-time, part-time; 30-36 total credits required; 12 to 14 months to complete program. Concentration in economics.

ADMISSION

Applications For fall 1997 there were 571 applications for admission. Of those applying, 466 were accepted. Of those accepted, 176 enrolled.

Application Requirements Application form, application fee, bachelor's degree, essay, minimum GPA: 2.7, 3 letters of recommendation, personal statement, college transcript(s), computer experience.

Recommended for Application GMAT score accepted: minimum 480, resume, work experience.

Application Deadline 6/15 for fall, 10/15 for spring, 3/15 for summer, 4/1 for fall (international), 9/1 for spring (international), 1/1 for summer (international). Application fee: $25, $50 (international). Deferred entrance is available.

ACADEMICS

Faculty Full-time 73.

Teaching Methodologies Case study, computer-aided instruction, computer simulations, experiential learning, field projects, group discussion, lecture, research, seminars by members of the business community, simulations, student presentations, study groups, team projects.

Technology 416 on-campus computer terminals/PCs are available for student use and are linked by a campus-wide network. The network has full access to the Internet. Students are not required to have their own PC.

Special Opportunities Advanced credit may be earned through transfer of credits from another institution. International exchange programs in France, Germany,

Mexico, Norway, Republic of Korea, United Kingdom. An internship program is available.

FINANCES

Costs for 1997–98 Tuition: Full-time: $3691 per year (resident); $10,411 per year (nonresident). Part-time: $110 per hour (resident); $331 per hour (nonresident). Cost varies by number of credits taken, reciprocity agreements. Fees: Full-time: $547 per academic year (resident); $697 per academic year (nonresident). Part-time: $16 per hour (resident); $16 per hour (nonresident). Fees vary by number of credits taken, reciprocity agreements. Average 1997–98 room and board costs were $3300 per academic year (on campus) and $4060 per academic year (off campus). Room and board costs vary by occupancy (e.g., single, double, triple), type of accommodation, type of meal plan.

Financial Aid Fellowships, research assistantships, teaching assistantships, scholarships, work study, loans available. Financial aid is available to part-time students.

Financial Aid Contact Ms. Judy Schneider, Director of Financial Aid, UTA Box 19199, Arlington, TX 76019-0199. Phone: 817-272-3561; Fax: 817-272-3555; E-mail: fao@uta.edu

FACILITIES

Information Resources Central Library plus 2 additional on-campus libraries; total holdings of 1,008,751 volumes, 1,509,024 microforms, 5,271 current periodical subscriptions. CD player(s) available for graduate student use. Access provided to online bibliographic retrieval services and online databases.

INTERNATIONAL STUDENTS

Demographics 25% of students enrolled are international students.

Services and Facilities International student office, international student center, ESL courses, counseling/support services.

Applying TOEFL: minimum score of 550, proof of adequate funds, proof of health/immunizations required. Financial aid is available to international students.

International Student Contact Dr. Judy Young, Director of International Office, UTA Box 19028, Arlington, TX 76019. Phone: 817-272-2355; Fax: 817-272-5005; E-mail: international@uta.edu

PLACEMENT

Services include alumni network, career counseling/planning, career fairs, career library, career placement, electronic job bank, job interviews arranged, job search course, resume referral to employers, and resume preparation. In 1996–97, 851 organizations participated in on-campus recruiting; 160 on-campus interviews were conducted.

Employment Of 1996–97 graduates, 84% were employed within three months of graduation; the average starting salary was $40,000. Types of employment entered: accounting, banking, chemical industry, communications, computer-related, consulting, consumer products, education, energy, engineering, finance, financial services, government, health services, high technology, hospitality management, human resources, information systems/technology, insurance, international trade, management, manufacturing, marketing, media, mining, nonprofit, petrochemical, pharmaceutical, real estate, retail, service industry, telecommunications, transportation, utilities.

Program Contact: Ms. Alisa Johnson, Assistant Director of Graduate Programs in Business, UTA Box 19376, Arlington, TX 76019-0376. Phone: 817-272-3004; Fax: 817-272-5799; E-mail: admit@uta.edu
See full description on page 1150.

University of Texas at Austin

Graduate School of Business

Austin, Texas

OVERVIEW

The University of Texas at Austin is a state-supported, coed university. Enrollment: 47,957 graduate, professional, and undergraduate students; 11,641 full-time matriculated graduate/professional students; part-time matriculated graduate/professional students. Founded: 1881. The graduate business unit is in an urban setting and is on a semester calendar.

HIGHLIGHTS

Enrollment Profile

Full-time: 837	International: 15%
Part-time: 0	Women: 25%
Total: 837	Minorities: 11%
Average Age: 28	Average Class Size: 50
Fall 1997 Average GPA: 3.3	Fall 1997 Average GMAT: 645

Costs

Full-time tuition: $3060 per academic year (resident); $12,360 per academic year (nonresident)
Part-time tuition: $102 per semester hour (resident); $412 per semester hour (nonresident)

AACSB – The International Association for Management Education accredited

Degree(s) offered in conjunction with E.M. Lyon, Koblenz School of Corporate Management, Instituto Tecnológico de Estudios Superiores de Monterrey, Fundação Getulio Vargas, Pontificia Universidad Católica

GRADUATE BUSINESS PROGRAMS

Master of Business Administration (MBA) Full-time; 60 total credits required; 2 years to complete program. Concentrations in accounting, entrepreneurship, environmental economics/management, finance, human resources, information management, management, management information systems, marketing, operations management, strategic management.

Executive MBA (MBA) Full-time; 42 total credits required; 22 months to complete program.

Master of Professional Accountancy (MPA) Full-time; 36-60 total credits required; 12 months to 2 years to complete program. Concentrations in accounting, taxation, information management.

Master of Business Administration/Master of Professional Accounting (MBA/MPA) Full-time; 72 total credits required; 3 to 4 years to complete program. Concentrations in accounting, entrepreneurship, environmental economics/management, finance, human resources, information management, management, management information systems, marketing, operations management, strategic management, taxation.

Master of Business Administration/Master of Arts in Communications (MBA/MA) Full-time; 72 total credits required; 3 to 4 years to complete program. Concentrations in accounting, entrepreneurship, environmental economics/management, finance, human resources, information management, management, management information systems, marketing, operations management, strategic management.

Master of Business Administration/Master of Arts in Asian Studies (MBA/MA) Full-time; 66-69 total credits required; 3 to 4 years to complete program. Concentrations in accounting, entrepreneurship, environmental economics/management, finance, human resources, information management, management, management information systems, marketing, operations management, strategic management.

Master of Business Administration/Master of Science in Manufacturing Systems Engineering (MBA/MS) Full-time; 72 total credits required; 3 to 4 years to complete program. Concentrations in accounting, entrepreneurship, environmental economics/management, finance, human resources, information management, management, management information systems, marketing, operations management, strategic management.

Master of Business Administration/Master of Arts in Latin American Studies (MBA/MA) Full-time; 72 total credits required; 3 to 4 years to complete program. Concentrations in accounting, entrepreneurship, environmental economics/management, finance, human resources, information management, management, management information systems, marketing, operations management, strategic management.

Master of Business Administration/Doctor of Jurisprudence (MBA/JD) Full-time; 134 total credits required; 4 to 5 years to complete program. Concentrations in accounting, entrepreneurship, environmental economics/management, finance, human resources, information management, management, management information systems, marketing, operations management, strategic management.

Master of Business Administration/Master of Arts in Middle Eastern Studies (MBA/MA) Full-time; 69 total credits required; 3 to 4 years to complete program. Concentrations in accounting, entrepreneurship, environmental economics/management, decision sciences, human resources, information management, management, management information systems, marketing, operations management, strategic management.

Master of Business Administration/Master of Science in Nursing (MBA/MS) Full-time; 72 total credits required; 3 to 4 years to complete program. Concentrations in accounting, entrepreneurship, environmental economics/management, decision sciences, human resources, information management, management, management information systems, marketing, operations management, strategic management.

Master of Business Administration/Master of Arts in Post-Soviet/Eastern European Studies (MBA/MA) Full-time; 69 total credits required; 3 to 4 years to complete program. Concentrations in accounting, entrepreneurship, environmental economics/management, decision sciences, human resources, information management, management, management information systems, marketing, operations management, strategic management.

Master of Business Administration/Master of Public Affairs (MBA/MPA) Full-time; 75 total credits required; 3 to 4 years to complete program. Concentrations in accounting, entrepreneurship, environmental economics/management, decision sciences, human resources, information management, management, management information systems, marketing, operations management, strategic management, public policy and administration.

ADMISSION
Applications For fall 1997 there were 2,552 applications for admission. Of those applying, 820 were accepted. Of those accepted, 424 enrolled.

Application Requirements GMAT score: minimum 500, application form, application fee, bachelor's degree, essay, minimum GPA: 2.0, 2 letters of recommendation, personal statement, resume, college transcript(s), minimum of 2 years of work experience, computer experience: spreadsheet proficiency.

Application Deadline 1/1 for fall. Applications processed on a rolling/continuous basis for international students only. Application fee: $80, $100 (international). Deferred entrance is available.

ACADEMICS
Faculty Full-time 187.

Teaching Methodologies Case study, computer-aided instruction, computer analysis, computer simulations, experiential learning, faculty seminars, field projects, group discussion, lecture, research, role playing, seminars by members of the business community, simulations, student presentations, study groups, team projects.

Technology 165 on-campus computer terminals/PCs are available for student use and are linked by a campus-wide network. The network has full access to the Internet. Students are required to have their own PC.

Special Opportunities International exchange programs in Australia, Brazil, Canada, Chile, Finland, France, Germany, Hong Kong, Japan, Mexico, Netherlands, Peru, Singapore, Sweden, United Kingdom, Venezuela. An internship program is available.

FINANCES
Costs for 1997–98 Tuition: Full-time: $3060 per year (resident); $12,360 per year (nonresident). Part-time: $102 per semester hour (resident); $412 per semester hour (nonresident). Cost varies by academic program, number of credits taken. Fees: Full-time: $2552 per academic year (resident); $2622 per academic year (nonresident). Average 1997–98 room and board costs were $9450 per academic year (off campus). Room and board costs vary by campus location, occupancy (e.g., single, double, triple), type of accommodation, type of meal plan.

Financial Aid Fellowships, research assistantships, teaching assistantships, grants, scholarships, loans available. Application Deadline: 3/31.

Financial Aid Contact Mrs. Mary Gielstra, Financial Aid Officer, Graduate School of Business, CBA 2.316, Austin, TX 78712. Phone: 512-471-7612; Fax: 512-471-4131; E-mail: famvd@utxdp.dp.utexas.edu

FACILITIES
Information Resources Perry-Castaneda Library plus 20 additional on-campus libraries; total holdings of 7,019,508 volumes, 5,062,330 microforms, 51,171 current periodical subscriptions. CD player(s) available for graduate student use. Access provided to online bibliographic retrieval services and online databases.

INTERNATIONAL STUDENTS
Demographics 15% of students enrolled are international students.

Services and Facilities International student office, international student center, international student housing, visa services, ESL courses, counseling/support services.

Applying TOEFL: minimum score of 600, proof of adequate funds, proof of health/immunizations required. Financial aid is available to international students.

International Student Contact Ms. Linda Butler, International Student Advisor, International Office, PO Drawer A, Austin, TX 78713-7206. Phone: 512-471-1211; Fax: 512-471-8848; E-mail: lindab@mail.utexas.edu

PLACEMENT
Services include alumni network, career counseling/planning, career fairs, career library, career placement, electronic job bank, job interviews arranged, job search course, resume referral to employers, and resume preparation. In 1996–97, 575 organizations participated in on-campus recruiting; 4,423 on-campus interviews were conducted.

Employment Of 1996–97 graduates, 98% were employed within three months of graduation; the average starting salary was $65,637. Types of employment entered: accounting, banking, chemical industry, communications, computer-related, consulting, consumer products, education, energy, engineering, finance, financial services, government, health services, high technology, hospitality management, human resources, information systems/technology, insurance, international trade, law, management, manufacturing, marketing, media, mining, nonprofit, petrochemical, pharmaceutical, real estate, retail, service industry, telecommunications, transportation, utilities.

Business Program(s) URL: http://texasinfo.bus.utexas.edu

Program Contact: Dr. Carl Harris, Director of Admission, MBA Programs, Graduate School of Business, CBA 2.316, Austin, TX 78712-1172. Phone: 512-471-7612; Fax: 512-471-4243; E-mail: texasmba@bus.utexas.edu
See full description on page 1152.

The University of Texas at Brownsville

School of Business
Brownsville, Texas

OVERVIEW
The University of Texas at Brownsville is a state-supported, coed, upper-level institution. Enrollment: 8,800 graduate, professional, and undergraduate students; 43 full-time matriculated graduate/professional students; 419 part-time matriculated graduate/professional students. Founded: 1991. The graduate business unit is in an urban setting and is on a semester calendar.

HIGHLIGHTS

Enrollment Profile

Full-time: 15	International: 34%
Part-time: 145	Women: 44%
Total: 160	Minorities: 78%
Average Age: 28	Average Class Size: 18
Fall 1997 Average GPA: 3.2	Fall 1997 Average GMAT: 450

Costs
Full-time tuition: N/R
Part-time tuition: $229 per course (resident); $889 per course (nonresident)

GRADUATE BUSINESS PROGRAMS
Master of Business Administration (MBA) Full-time, part-time; 30-48 total credits required; 12 months to 7 years to complete program.

ADMISSION
Applications For fall 1997 there were 60 applications for admission. Of those applying, 55 were accepted. Of those accepted, 40 enrolled.

Application Requirements Application form, application fee, bachelor's degree, minimum GPA: 2.8, 2 letters of recommendation, college transcript(s).

Recommended for Application GMAT score accepted: minimum 400.

Application Deadline Applications processed on a rolling/continuous basis for both domestic and international students. Application fee: $15. Deferred entrance is available.

ACADEMICS
Faculty Full-time 18; part-time 1.

Teaching Methodologies Case study, computer-aided instruction, experiential learning, field projects, group discussion, lecture, research, student presentations, study groups, team projects.

Technology 500 on-campus computer terminals/PCs are available for student use and are linked by a campus-wide network. The network has full access to the Internet. Students are not required to have their own PC.

Special Opportunities Advanced credit may be earned through credit for business training programs, transfer of credits from another institution.

FINANCES
Costs for 1997–98 Tuition: $229 per course (resident); $889 per course (nonresident). Cost varies by class time (e.g., day/evening), number of credits taken, reciprocity agreements.

Financial Aid In 1997–98, 19% of students received some institutionally administered aid in the form of scholarships. Financial aid is available to part-time students.

Financial Aid Contact Mr. Albert Barreda, Financial Aid Office, 80 Fort Brown, Brownsville, TX 78520-4991. Phone: 956-544-8277; Fax: 956-544-8229.

FACILITIES
Information Resources Arnulfo L. Oliveira Library; total holdings of 125,254 volumes, 628,882 microforms, 2,219 current periodical subscriptions. CD

player(s) available for graduate student use. Access provided to online bibliographic retrieval services and online databases.

INTERNATIONAL STUDENTS
Demographics 34% of students enrolled are international students [Central America, 1%, Europe, 1%, North America, 97%, South America, 1%].
Services and Facilities International student center, visa services, ESL courses, counseling/support services.
Applying TOEFL: minimum score of 550, proof of health/immunizations required.
International Student Contact Mr. Ernesto Garcia, Director of Enrollment Office, 80 Fort Brown, Brownsville, TX 78520. Phone: 956-544-8254; Fax: 956-544-8832.

PLACEMENT
Services include career counseling/planning, career placement, and resume preparation. In 1996–97, 50 organizations participated in on-campus recruiting.
Employment Of 1996–97 graduates, 90% were employed within three months of graduation. Types of employment entered: accounting, banking, education, engineering, finance, financial services, government, health services, human resources, management, manufacturing, marketing, nonprofit, real estate, retail, transportation.
Business Program(s) URL: http://www.utb.edu/business/

Program Contact: Mr. Ernesto Garcia, Director of Enrollment Office, 80 Fort Brown, Brownsville, TX 78520-4991. Phone: 956-544-8254.

University of Texas at Dallas

School of Management
Richardson, Texas

OVERVIEW
The University of Texas at Dallas is a state-supported, coed university. Enrollment: 9,327 graduate, professional, and undergraduate students; 1,417 full-time matriculated graduate/professional students; 2,643 part-time matriculated graduate/professional students. Founded: 1961. The graduate business unit is in a suburban setting and is on a semester calendar.

HIGHLIGHTS

Enrollment Profile
Full-time: N/R
Part-time: N/R
Total: 1,060
Average Age: 31
Fall 1997 Average GPA: 3.2

International: N/R
Women: 42%
Minorities: 32%
Average Class Size: 35
Fall 1997 Average GMAT: 531

Costs
Full-time tuition: $1379 per academic year (resident); $3305 per academic year (nonresident)
Part-time tuition: $527 per 3 credits (resident); $1169 per course (nonresident)

The University of Texas at Dallas School of Management (SOM) is a metropolitan research and teaching institution that offers master's programs ranging from a Cohort M.B.A. (full-time) to a highly popular part-time M.B.A. curriculum and Master of Science degrees in a variety of concentrations. In addition, the School offers a Master of Science in accountancy with an emphasis on management information systems, a Master of Arts in international management, and extensive executive education programs.

Located in the North Dallas telecom corridor, the School's programs attract young, mid-level managers and upper-level professionals seeking continuing management development. The curriculum focuses on global business issues, change management, and management of technology. SOM's active relationships with corporate partners and the advisory council enhance the student's educational experiences and influence placement opportunities.

GRADUATE BUSINESS PROGRAMS
Master of Arts in International Management (MA) Full-time, part-time, distance learning option; 36 total credits required; 12 months to 5 years to complete program. Concentrations in international management, international development management.
Master of Science in Accounting (MS) Full-time, part-time; 36 total credits required; 12 months to 5 years to complete program. Concentration in accounting.
Master of Science in Business Administration (MS) Full-time, part-time; 36 total credits required; 12 months to 5 years to complete program. Concentrations in operations management, information management, marketing, managerial

economics, organizational behavior/development, public policy and administration, strategic management, finance, management information systems.
Master of Business Administration (MBA) Full-time, part-time, distance learning option; 48 total credits required; 12 months to 5 years to complete program. Concentrations in finance, operations management, information management, marketing, managerial economics, organizational behavior/development, public policy and administration, strategic management, accounting.
Executive MBA (MBA) Part-time; 48 total credits required; 2 years to complete program.
Cohort MBA (MBA) Full-time; 48 total credits required; 16 months to complete program. Concentrations in finance, management information systems, technology management, managerial economics, marketing, organizational behavior/development.

ADMISSION
Applications For fall 1997 there were 443 applications for admission. Of those applying, 390 were accepted. Of those accepted, 280 enrolled.
Application Requirements Application form, application fee, bachelor's degree, minimum GPA, 3 letters of recommendation, personal statement, resume, college transcript(s), computer experience: PC proficiency.
Recommended for Application GMAT score accepted, work experience.
Application Deadline 7/15 for fall, 12/1 for spring, 5/1 for summer, 6/1 for fall (international), 10/1 for spring (international), 4/1 for summer (international). Application fee: $25, $75 (international). Deferred entrance is available.

ACADEMICS
Faculty Full-time 60; part-time 20.
Teaching Methodologies Case study, computer analysis, computer simulations, faculty seminars, field projects, group discussion, lecture, seminars by members of the business community, simulations, student presentations, study groups, team projects.
Technology 310 on-campus computer terminals/PCs are available for student use and are linked by a campus-wide network. The network has full access to the Internet. Students are required to have their own PC.
Special Opportunities Advanced credit may be earned through transfer of credits from another institution. International exchange programs in Mexico, Russia. An internship program is available.

FINANCES
Costs for 1997–98 Tuition: Full-time: $1379 per year (resident); $3305 per year (nonresident). Part-time: $527 per 3 credits (resident); $1169 per course (nonresident). Cost varies by academic program, number of credits taken, reciprocity agreements. Average 1997–98 room only costs were $600 per academic year (off campus). Room and board costs vary by occupancy (e.g., single, double, triple), type of accommodation.
Financial Aid In 1997–98, 6% of students received some institutionally administered aid in the form of fellowships, research assistantships, teaching assistantships, work study. Financial aid is available to part-time students. Application Deadline: 11/1.
Financial Aid Contact Maria Ramos, Director of Financial Aid, MC 12, PO Box 830688, Richardson, TX 75083-0688. Phone: 972-883-2941; Fax: 972-883-2947.

FACILITIES
Information Resources Eugene McDermott Library; total holdings of 524,958 volumes, 1,519,166 microforms, 2,409 current periodical subscriptions. CD player(s) available for graduate student use. Access provided to online bibliographic retrieval services.

INTERNATIONAL STUDENTS
Demographics N/R
Services and Facilities International student office, international student housing, visa services, counseling/support services.
Applying TOEFL: minimum score of 550, proof of adequate funds, proof of health/immunizations required.
International Student Contact Jean Stuart, Director of Admissions and Records, PO Box 830688, MC 11, Richardson, TX 75083-0688. Phone: 972-883-4189; Fax: 972-883-4010.

PLACEMENT
Services include career counseling/planning, career fairs, career library, career placement, electronic job bank, job interviews arranged, resume referral to employers, and resume preparation. In 1996–97, 327 organizations participated in on-campus recruiting; 218 on-campus interviews were conducted.
Employment Of 1996–97 graduates, the average starting salary was $47,000. Types of employment entered: accounting, banking, chemical industry, communications, computer-related, consulting, consumer products, education, energy, engineering, finance, financial services, government, health services, high technology, hospitality management, human resources, information systems/technology, insurance, international trade, law, management, manufacturing,

University of Texas at Dallas (continued)

marketing, media, nonprofit, petrochemical, pharmaceutical, real estate, retail, service industry, telecommunications, transportation, utilities.

Business Program(s) URL: http://www.utdallas.edu/dept/mgmt/

Program Contact: Dr. Gary Horton, Head of Advising, School of Management, Richardson, TX 75083-0688. Phone: 972-883-2701; Fax: 972-883-6425; E-mail: grad-admission@utdallas.edu

See full description on page 1154.

University of Texas at El Paso

College of Business Administration

El Paso, Texas

OVERVIEW
The University of Texas at El Paso is a state-supported, coed university. Enrollment: 14,500 graduate, professional, and undergraduate students. Founded: 1913. The graduate business unit is in an urban setting and is on a semester calendar.

HIGHLIGHTS

Enrollment Profile

Full-time: 60	International: 18%
Part-time: 185	Women: 38%
Total: 245	Minorities: 42%
Average Age: 32	Average Class Size: 40
Fall 1997 Average GPA: N/R	Fall 1997 Average GMAT: N/R

Costs
Full-time tuition: $2350 per academic year (resident); $7294 per academic year (nonresident)
Part-time tuition: $356 per course (resident); $974 per course (nonresident)

AACSB – The International Association for Management Education accredited

GRADUATE BUSINESS PROGRAMS
Master of Business Administration (MBA) Full-time, part-time; 36 total credits required; minimum of 2.3 years to complete program. Concentration in management.

Master of Accountancy (MAcc) 36 total credits required.

Master of Science in Economics (MS) 30-36 total credits required.

Master of Business Administration/Master in Public Administration (MBA/MPA) 60-78 total credits required.

ADMISSION
Applications For fall 1997 there were 127 applications for admission.

Application Requirements GMAT score: minimum 500, application form, bachelor's degree, minimum GPA: 2.75, college transcript(s).

Application Deadline 7/1 for fall, 11/15 for spring, 4/1 for summer, 7/1 for fall (international), 11/15 for spring (international), 4/1 for summer (international).

ACADEMICS
Faculty Full-time 40.

Teaching Methodologies Case study, lecture, student presentations, team projects.

Technology 200 on-campus computer terminals/PCs are available for student use and are linked by a campus-wide network. Students are not required to have their own PC.

Special Opportunities International exchange program available. An internship program is available.

FINANCES
Costs for 1997–98 Tuition: Full-time: $2350 per year (resident); $7294 per year (nonresident). Part-time: $356 per course (resident); $974 per course (nonresident).

Financial Aid Fellowships, research assistantships, teaching assistantships, work study available. Financial aid is available to part-time students. Application Deadline: 3/1.

Financial Aid Contact Ms. Linda Gonzalez-Hensgen, Director of Financial Aid, West Union 202, El Paso, TX 79968. Phone: 915-747-5204.

FACILITIES
Information Resources Main library; total holdings of 812,437 volumes, 1,090,296 microforms, 2,506 current periodical subscriptions. CD player(s) available for graduate student use. Access provided to online bibliographic retrieval services.

INTERNATIONAL STUDENTS
Demographics 18% of students enrolled are international students.

Services and Facilities International student office, visa services, ESL courses, counseling/support services.

Applying TOEFL: minimum score of 600, proof of adequate funds, proof of health/immunizations required. Financial aid is available to international students.

International Student Contact Ms. Debbie Aghte, Director, International Student Office, West Union 211, El Paso, TX 79968. Phone: 915-747-5664.

Business Program(s) URL: http://www.utep.edu/

Program Contact: Graduate Advisor, College of Business, 500 West University Avenue, El Paso, TX 79968. Phone: 915-747-5241; Fax: 915-747-5147.

University of Texas at San Antonio

College of Business

San Antonio, Texas

OVERVIEW
The University of Texas at San Antonio is a state-supported, coed, comprehensive institution. Enrollment: 17,494 graduate, professional, and undergraduate students; 639 full-time matriculated graduate/professional students; 1,976 part-time matriculated graduate/professional students. Founded: 1969. The graduate business unit is in a suburban setting and is on a semester calendar.

HIGHLIGHTS

Enrollment Profile

Full-time: 114	International: 6%
Part-time: 380	Women: 35%
Total: 494	Minorities: 26%
Average Age: 31	Average Class Size: 20
Fall 1997 Average GPA: 3.0	Fall 1997 Average GMAT: 522

Costs
Full-time tuition: $1230 per academic year (resident); $3147 per academic year (nonresident)
Part-time tuition: $99 per semester credit hour (resident); $313 per semester credit hour (nonresident)

AACSB – The International Association for Management Education accredited

GRADUATE BUSINESS PROGRAMS
Master of Business Administration (MBA) Full-time, part-time; 33-57 total credits required; 12 months to 6 years to complete program. Concentrations in accounting, taxation, economics, finance, human resources, technology management, management science, management information systems, health care, marketing.

Master of Business Administration in International Business (MBA) Full-time, part-time; 39-63 total credits required; 12 months to 6 years to complete program.

Master of Science in Accounting (MS) Full-time, part-time; 30-60 total credits required; 12 months to 6 years to complete program.

Master of Taxation (MTax) Full-time, part-time; 30-60 total credits required; 12 months to 6 years to complete program.

Master of Science in Management Technology (MS) Full-time, part-time; 30 total credits required; 12 months to 6 years to complete program.

Executive MBA (MBA) Part-time; 42 total credits required; 21 months to complete program.

Master of Arts in Economics (MA) 33 total credits required; 12 months to 6 years to complete program.

Master of Science in Finance (MS) 33 total credits required; 12 months to 6 years to complete program.

ADMISSION
Applications For fall 1997 there were 202 applications for admission. Of those applying, 138 were accepted. Of those accepted, 92 enrolled.

Application Requirements Application form, application fee, bachelor's degree, minimum GPA: 3.0, personal statement, college transcript(s).

Recommended for Application GMAT score accepted: minimum 500.

Application Deadline 7/1 for fall, 12/1 for spring, 5/1 for summer, 6/1 for fall (international), 10/15 for spring (international), 3/1 for summer (international). Application fee: $20. Deferred entrance is available.

ACADEMICS
Faculty Full-time 78; part-time 25.

Teaching Methodologies Case study, computer-aided instruction, computer analysis, computer simulations, experiential learning, faculty seminars, field projects, group discussion, lecture, research, role playing, seminars by members of the business community, simulations, student presentations, study groups, team projects.

Technology 500 on-campus computer terminals/PCs are available for student use and are linked by a campus-wide network. The network has full access to the Internet. Students are not required to have their own PC.

Special Opportunities Advanced credit may be earned through transfer of credits from another institution. International exchange programs in Canada, England, Mexico. An internship program is available.

FINANCES
Costs for 1997–98 Tuition: Full-time: $1230 per 9 semester hours (resident); $3147 per 9 semester hours (nonresident). Part-time: $99 per semester credit hour (resident); $313 per semester credit hour (nonresident). Cost varies by number of credits taken. Fees: Full-time: $300 per academic year (resident); $300 per academic year (nonresident). Average 1997–98 room only costs were $4000 per academic year (off campus). Room and board costs vary by campus location, occupancy (e.g., single, double, triple), type of accommodation, type of meal plan.

Financial Aid Fellowships, research assistantships, grants, scholarships, work study, loans available. Financial aid is available to part-time students. Application Deadline: 3/31.

Financial Aid Contact Mr. Noe Ortiz, Student Financial Aid , 6900 North Loop 1604 West, San Antonio, TX 78249-0687. Phone: 210-458-4154; Fax: 210-458-4638.

FACILITIES
Information Resources John Peace Library; total holdings of 504,133 volumes, 2,432,752 microforms, 2,329 current periodical subscriptions. CD player(s) available for graduate student use. Access provided to online bibliographic retrieval services and online databases.

INTERNATIONAL STUDENTS
Demographics 6% of students enrolled are international students.

Services and Facilities International student office, international student center, international student housing, visa services, ESL courses, counseling/support services.

Applying TOEFL: minimum score of 500, proof of adequate funds required. Proof of health/immunizations recommended. Financial aid is available to international students.

International Student Contact Ms. Magie Mata, Graduate Admissions Supervisor, 6900 North Loop 1604 West, San Antonio, TX 78249-0603. Phone: 210-458-4330; Fax: 210-458-4332.

PLACEMENT
Services include alumni network, career counseling/planning, career fairs, career library, career placement, electronic job bank, job interviews arranged, job search course, resume referral to employers, and resume preparation. In 1996–97, 50 organizations participated in on-campus recruiting; 200 on-campus interviews were conducted.

Employment Of 1996–97 graduates, the average starting salary was $45,000. Types of employment entered: accounting, banking, communications, computer-related, consulting, consumer products, energy, engineering, finance, financial services, government, health services, high technology, hospitality management, human resources, information systems/technology, insurance, international trade, management, manufacturing, marketing, nonprofit, pharmaceutical, retail, service industry, telecommunications, transportation, utilities.

Business Program(s) URL: http://cobweb.utsa.edu

Program Contact: Ms. Katherine Pope, Graduate Advisor, College of Business, 6900 North Loop 1604 West, San Antonio, TX 78249-0616. Phone: 210-458-4641, 800-669-0919 (TX only); Fax: 210-458-4398; E-mail: MBAinfo@lonestar.utsa.edu

See full description on page 1156.

University of Texas at Tyler

School of Business Administration

Tyler, Texas

OVERVIEW
The University of Texas at Tyler is a state-supported, coed, upper-level institution. Enrollment: 3,459 graduate, professional, and undergraduate students; 177 full-time matriculated graduate/professional students; 910 part-time matriculated graduate/professional students. Founded: 1971. The graduate business unit is in a small-town setting and is on a semester calendar.

HIGHLIGHTS
Enrollment Profile

Full-time: 2	International: 5%
Part-time: 99	Women: 41%
Total: 101	Minorities: 5%
Average Age: 32	Average Class Size: 15
Fall 1997 Average GPA: 3.2	Fall 1997 Average GMAT: 507

Costs
Full-time tuition: N/R
Part-time tuition: $337 per course (resident); $967 per course (nonresident)

AACSB – The International Association for Management Education accredited

GRADUATE BUSINESS PROGRAMS
Master of Business Administration (MBA) Full-time, part-time, distance learning option; 66 total credits required; 12 months to 6 years to complete program. Concentrations in accounting, finance, management, marketing.

Master of Business Administration Health Care Track (MBA) Full-time, part-time, distance learning option; 66 total credits required; 12 months to 6 years to complete program.

ADMISSION
Application Requirements GMAT score, application form, application fee, bachelor's degree, minimum GPA, college transcript(s), computer experience.

Application Deadline Applications processed on a rolling/continuous basis for both domestic and international students. Application fee: 50 (international). Deferred entrance is available.

ACADEMICS
Faculty Full-time 12; part-time 1.

Teaching Methodologies Case study, computer analysis, faculty seminars, field projects, group discussion, lecture, student presentations, team projects.

Technology 40 on-campus computer terminals/PCs are available for student use and are linked by a campus-wide network. The network has full access to the Internet. Students are not required to have their own PC.

Special Opportunities Advanced credit may be earned through transfer of credits from another institution. International exchange program in Mexico. An internship program is available.

FINANCES
Costs for 1997–98 Tuition: $337 per course (resident); $967 per course (nonresident). Cost varies by number of credits taken. Fees vary by number of credits taken. Average 1997–98 room only costs were $2263 per academic year (on campus) and $7200 per academic year (off campus).

Financial Aid Research assistantships, scholarships, work study available. Application Deadline: 7/1.

Financial Aid Contact Financial Aid, 3900 University Boulevard, Tyler, TX 75799-0001. Phone: 903-566-7180.

FACILITIES
Information Resources Robert R. Muntz Library; total holdings of 180,226 volumes, 446,466 microforms, 1,521 current periodical subscriptions. Access provided to online bibliographic retrieval services.

INTERNATIONAL STUDENTS
Demographics 5% of students enrolled are international students.

Services and Facilities Counseling/support services.

Applying TOEFL: minimum score of 550, proof of adequate funds required. Financial aid is not available to international students.

International Student Contact Ms. Elaine Hardiman, Admissions Counselor, 3900 University Boulevard, Tyler, TX 75799-0001. Phone: 903-566-7054.

PLACEMENT
Services include career fairs, and career placement.

Employment Types of employment entered: accounting, engineering, health services.

Business Program(s) URL: http://www.uttyl.edu

Program Contact: Dr. Richard Heiens, Director of Graduate Programs in Business, 3900 University Boulevard, Tyler, TX 75799. Phone: 903-566-7413, 800-UTTYLER; Fax: 903-566-7211; E-mail: rick_heiens@mail.uttyl.edu

University of Texas of the Permian Basin

School of Business

Odessa, Texas

OVERVIEW
The University of Texas of the Permian Basin is a state-supported, coed, comprehensive institution. Founded: 1969. The graduate business unit is in a small-town setting and is on a semester calendar.

HIGHLIGHTS

Enrollment Profile
Full-time: N/R
Part-time: N/R
Total: N/R
Average Age: 33
Fall 1997 Average GPA: N/R

International: N/R
Women: N/R
Minorities: N/R
Average Class Size: 20
Fall 1997 Average GMAT: N/R

Costs
Full-time tuition: N/R
Part-time tuition: $227 per hour (resident); $356 per hour (nonresident)

GRADUATE BUSINESS PROGRAMS
Master of Business Administration in Management (MBA) Full-time, part-time; 60 total credits required; 2 to 8 years to complete program.
Master in Professional Accounting (MPA) Full-time, part-time; 36 total credits required; 12 months to 8 years to complete program.

ADMISSION
Application Requirements GMAT score, application form, bachelor's degree, minimum GPA: 2.5, college transcript(s).
Recommended for Application Computer experience.
Application Deadline Applications processed on a rolling/continuous basis for both domestic and international students. Deferred entrance is available.

ACADEMICS
Faculty Full-time 14; part-time 2.
Teaching Methodologies Case study, computer-aided instruction, computer analysis, experiential learning, field projects, group discussion, lecture, research, seminars by members of the business community, simulations, student presentations, study groups, team projects.
Special Opportunities An internship program is available.

FINANCES
Costs for 1997–98 Tuition: $227 per hour (resident); $356 per hour (nonresident). Cost varies by number of credits taken.
Financial Aid Work study available.
Financial Aid Contact Financial Aid Office, 4901 East University, Odessa, TX 79762-0001. Phone: 915-552-2620.

FACILITIES
Information Resources Main library plus 1 additional on-campus library; total holdings of 27,646 volumes, 1,074,900 microforms, 723 current periodical subscriptions. Access provided to online bibliographic retrieval services.

INTERNATIONAL STUDENTS
Demographics N/R

PLACEMENT
Services include alumni network, career counseling/planning, job search course, and resume preparation.
Employment Types of employment entered: accounting.

Program Contact: Director of Graduate Studies, School of Business, 4901 East University Avenue, Odessa, TX 79762-8301. Phone: 915-552-2530; Fax: 915-552-2174.

University of Texas-Pan American

College of Business Administration

Edinburg, Texas

OVERVIEW
The University of Texas-Pan American is a state-supported, coed, comprehensive institution. Enrollment: 12,692 graduate, professional, and undergraduate students; 180 full-time matriculated graduate/professional students; 885 part-time matriculated graduate/professional students. Founded: 1927. The graduate business unit is in an urban setting and is on a semester calendar.

HIGHLIGHTS

Enrollment Profile
Full-time: 65
Part-time: 62
Total: 127
Average Age: 33
Fall 1997 Average GPA: 3.04

International: 15%
Women: 32%
Minorities: 72%
Average Class Size: 15
Fall 1997 Average GMAT: 486

Costs
Full-time tuition: $1570 per academic year (resident); $6658 per academic year (nonresident)
Part-time tuition: $54 per credit hour (resident); $248 per credit hour (nonresident)

AACSB – The International Association for Management Education accredited

GRADUATE BUSINESS PROGRAMS
Master of Business Administration (MBA) Full-time, part-time; 33 total credits required; 18 months to 7 years to complete program.
Weekend MBA (MBA) Full-time; 33 total credits required; 2 years to complete program.

ADMISSION
Applications For fall 1997 there were 72 applications for admission. Of those applying, 72 were accepted. Of those accepted, 38 enrolled.
Application Requirements Application form, bachelor's degree, essay, minimum GPA, 3 letters of recommendation, college transcript(s).
Recommended for Application GMAT score accepted: minimum 470, interview, personal statement, work experience, computer experience.
Application Deadline 8/1 for fall, 11/1 for spring, 5/1 for summer, 7/1 for fall (international), 10/1 for spring (international), 4/1 for summer (international). Deferred entrance is available.

ACADEMICS
Faculty Full-time 17.
Teaching Methodologies Case study, computer analysis, computer simulations, experiential learning, faculty seminars, field projects, group discussion, lecture, research, role playing, seminars by members of the business community, simulations, student presentations, study groups, team projects.
Technology 600 on-campus computer terminals/PCs are available for student use and are linked by a campus-wide network. The network has full access to the Internet. Students are not required to have their own PC.
Special Opportunities Advanced credit may be earned through transfer of credits from another institution.

FINANCES
Costs for 1997–98 Tuition: Full-time: $1570 per year (resident); $6658 per year (nonresident). Part-time: $54 per credit hour (resident); $248 per credit hour (nonresident). Cost varies by number of credits taken. Fees: Full-time: $886 per academic year (resident); $886 per academic year (nonresident). Fees vary by number of credits taken. Average 1997–98 room and board costs were $2049 per academic year. Room and board costs vary by occupancy (e.g., single, double, triple), type of meal plan.
Financial Aid Fellowships, research assistantships, teaching assistantships, work study available. Financial aid is available to part-time students. Application Deadline: 4/15.
Financial Aid Contact Mr. Arnold Trejo, Director of Financial Aid, 1201 West University Drive, Edinburg, TX 78539. Phone: 956-381-2501.

FACILITIES
Information Resources Library plus 1 additional on-campus library; total holdings of 269,020 volumes, 669,881 microforms, 2,241 current periodical subscriptions. CD player(s) available for graduate student use. Access provided to online bibliographic retrieval services and online databases.

INTERNATIONAL STUDENTS
Demographics 15% of students enrolled are international students.
Services and Facilities International student office, ESL courses, counseling/support services.
Applying TOEFL: minimum score of 500, proof of adequate funds required.
International Student Contact Mr. Ruben Garza, 1201 West University Drive, Edinburg, TX 78539. Phone: 956-381-7005.

PLACEMENT
Services include career counseling/planning, career fairs, and career placement.
Employment Types of employment entered: accounting, banking, computer-related, finance, government, management, manufacturing, petrochemical.

Business Program(s) URL: http://www.coba.panam.edu/mba

Program Contact: Dr. Jane LeMaster, Director of MBA Programs, 1201 West University, Edinburg, TX 78539. Phone: 956-381-3313; Fax: 956-381-3312.

University of the Incarnate Word

College of Professional Studies

San Antonio, Texas

OVERVIEW
The University of the Incarnate Word is an independent-religious, coed, comprehensive institution. Enrollment: 3,312 graduate, professional, and undergraduate students; 48 full-time matriculated graduate/professional students; 605 part-time matriculated graduate/professional students. Founded: 1881. The graduate business unit is in an urban setting and is on a 4-1-4 calendar.

HIGHLIGHTS

Enrollment Profile
Full-time: 37
Part-time: 147
Total: 184
Average Age: 30
Fall 1997 Average GPA: 3.09

International: 7%
Women: 49%
Minorities: 55%
Average Class Size: 12
Fall 1997 Average GMAT: 430

Costs
Full-time tuition: $370 per academic year
Part-time tuition: $370 per semester hour

ACBSP – The American Council of Business Schools and Programs accredited

GRADUATE BUSINESS PROGRAMS
Master of Business Administration (MBA) Full-time, part-time; 36 total credits required; 12 months to 5 years to complete program. Concentrations in sports/entertainment management, international business.

Master of Business Administration (MBA) Full-time, part-time; 36 total credits required; 12 months to 5 years to complete program.

Master of Arts in Administration (MAA) Full-time, part-time; 36 total credits required; 15 months to 5 years to complete program. Concentrations in sports/entertainment management, international business, organizational behavior/development.

Master of Arts in Administration (MAA) Full-time, part-time; 36 total credits required; 15 months to 5 years to complete program.

ADMISSION
Applications For fall 1997 there were 290 applications for admission. Of those applying, 241 were accepted. Of those accepted, 132 enrolled.

Application Requirements Application form, application fee, bachelor's degree, essay, minimum GPA: 2.5, college transcript(s).

Recommended for Application GMAT score accepted: minimum 400, interview, personal statement, resume, work experience.

Application Deadline Applications processed on a rolling/continuous basis for domestic students only. 6/1 for fall (international), 10/1 for spring (international), 2/1 for summer (international). Application fee: $20. Deferred entrance is available.

ACADEMICS
Faculty Full-time 21; part-time 5.

Teaching Methodologies Case study, computer-aided instruction, computer analysis, computer simulations, experiential learning, field projects, group discussion, lecture, research, role playing, seminars by members of the business community, simulations, student presentations, study groups, team projects.

Technology 200 on-campus computer terminals/PCs are available for student use and are linked by a campus-wide network. The network has full access to the Internet. Students are not required to have their own PC.

Special Opportunities Advanced credit may be earned through transfer of credits from another institution. International exchange program available.

FINANCES
Costs for 1997–98 Tuition: Full-time: $370 per semester hour. Part-time: $370 per semester hour. Cost varies by number of credits taken. Average 1997–98 room and board costs were $4738 per academic year (on campus) and $5000 per academic year (off campus). Room and board costs vary by occupancy (e.g., single, double, triple), type of accommodation, type of meal plan.

Financial Aid Work study, loans available. Financial aid is available to part-time students. Application Deadline: 5/31.

Financial Aid Contact Ms. Jan Carey-McDonald, Director of Financial Assistance, 4301 Broadway, Box 308, San Antonio, TX 78209-6397. Phone: 210-829-6008; Fax: 210-283-5053; E-mail: janm@universe.viwtx.edu

FACILITIES
Information Resources J.E. & L.E. Mobee Library; total holdings of 161,131 volumes, 24,599 microforms, 1,464 current periodical subscriptions. CD play-

er(s) available for graduate student use. Access provided to online bibliographic retrieval services.

INTERNATIONAL STUDENTS
Demographics 7% of students enrolled are international students [Asia, 76%, Central America, 20%, South America, 4%].

Services and Facilities International student office, international student housing, visa services, ESL courses, counseling/support services.

Applying TOEFL: minimum score of 550, proof of adequate funds, proof of health/immunizations required. Financial aid is not available to international students.

International Student Contact Mr. Eduardo Torrez, International Student Services, 4301 Broadway, Box 31, San Antonio, TX 78209-6397. Phone: 210-829-3929.

PLACEMENT
Services include alumni network, career counseling/planning, career fairs, career library, career placement, electronic job bank, job interviews arranged, resume referral to employers, and resume preparation.

Business Program(s) URL: http://www.uiw.edu/profstud.html

Program Contact: Mr. Brian Dalton, Dean of Enrollment, Office of Admissions, 4301 Broadway, San Antonio, TX 78209. Phone: 210-829-6005, 800-749-WORD; Fax: 210-829-3921; E-mail: briand@universe.viwtx.edu

Wayland Baptist University

Graduate Studies Office

Plainview, Texas

OVERVIEW
Wayland Baptist University is an independent-religious, coed, comprehensive institution. Enrollment: 4,190 graduate, professional, and undergraduate students; 40 full-time matriculated graduate/professional students; 356 part-time matriculated graduate/professional students. Founded: 1908. The graduate business unit is in a small-town setting and is on a 4-1-4 calendar.

HIGHLIGHTS

Enrollment Profile
Full-time: 20
Part-time: 209
Total: 229
Average Age: 37
Fall 1997 Average GPA: 3.21

International: 1%
Women: 38%
Minorities: 14%
Average Class Size: 8
Fall 1997 Average GMAT: 510

Costs
Full-time tuition: N/R
Part-time tuition: $210 per hour

GRADUATE BUSINESS PROGRAMS
Master of Business Administration (MBA) Full-time, part-time; 36 total credits required; 12 months to 6 years to complete program. Concentrations in management, health care, management information systems, human resources.

ADMISSION
Applications For fall 1997 there were 49 applications for admission. Of those applying, 47 were accepted. Of those accepted, 32 enrolled.

Application Requirements GMAT score, application form, application fee, bachelor's degree, minimum GPA, interview, 3 letters of recommendation, college transcript(s), computer experience: undergraduate computer course.

Recommended for Application GRE score accepted.

Application Deadline Applications processed on a rolling/continuous basis for both domestic and international students. Application fee: $35.

ACADEMICS
Faculty Full-time 11; part-time 27.

Teaching Methodologies Case study, computer-aided instruction, computer simulations, experiential learning, faculty seminars, group discussion, lecture, research, seminars by members of the business community, simulations, student presentations, study groups, team projects.

Technology 179 on-campus computer terminals/PCs are available for student use. The network has full access to the Internet. Students are not required to have their own PC.

Special Opportunities Advanced credit may be earned through transfer of credits from another institution. An internship program is available.

FINANCES
Costs for 1997–98 Tuition: $210 per hour. Cost varies by campus location. Fees: $40 per semester. Fees vary by campus location, number of credits taken. Average 1997–98 room and board costs were $3219 per academic

Wayland Baptist University (continued)

year. Room and board costs vary by occupancy (e.g., single, double, triple), type of accommodation, type of meal plan.

Financial Aid Work study, loans available. Financial aid is available to part-time students. Application Deadline: 5/1.

Financial Aid Contact Ms. Julie Hacker, Director of Financial Aid, 1900 West 7th Street, WBU 597, Plainview, TX 79072-6998. Phone: 806-296-4713; Fax: 806-296-4531.

FACILITIES

Information Resources J. E. and L. E. Mabee Learning Resource Center; total holdings of 105,681 volumes, 166,497 microforms, 495 current periodical subscriptions. CD player(s) available for graduate student use. Access provided to online bibliographic retrieval services.

INTERNATIONAL STUDENTS

Demographics 1% of students enrolled are international students [Asia, 50%, Europe, 50%].

Services and Facilities International student office, ESL courses, counseling/support services.

Applying TOEFL: minimum score of 500, proof of adequate funds, proof of health/immunizations required. Financial aid is available to international students.

International Student Contact Ms. Donna Wiley, Student Services Office Manager, 1900 West Seventh Street, Plainview, TX 79072-6998. Phone: 806-296-4724; Fax: 806-296-4580.

PLACEMENT

Services include career counseling/planning, career library, career placement, job interviews arranged, and resume preparation.

Business Program(s) URL: http://www.wbu.edu

Program Contact: Dr. Bobby Hall, Graduate Studies Director, WBU 575, 1900 West Seventh, Plainview, TX 79072. Phone: 806-296-4574; Fax: 806-296-4538; E-mail: hallb@wbu1.wbu.edu

West Texas A&M University

T. Boone Pickens College of Business

Canyon, Texas

OVERVIEW

West Texas A&M University is a state-supported, coed, comprehensive institution. Enrollment: 6,638 graduate, professional, and undergraduate students; 229 full-time matriculated graduate/professional students; 615 part-time matriculated graduate/professional students. Founded: 1909. The graduate business unit is in a small-town setting and is on a semester calendar.

HIGHLIGHTS

Enrollment Profile

Full-time: 54	International: 27%
Part-time: 134	Women: 35%
Total: 188	Minorities: 9%
Average Age: 30	Average Class Size: 20
Fall 1997 Average GPA: 2.5	Fall 1997 Average GMAT: 510

Costs

Full-time tuition: $2160 per academic year (resident); $7992 per academic year (nonresident)

Part-time tuition: $60 per credit hour (resident); $222 per credit hour (nonresident)

ACBSP – The American Council of Business Schools and Programs accredited

GRADUATE BUSINESS PROGRAMS

Master of Business Administration (MBA) Full-time, part-time; 36 total credits required; 2 to 5 years to complete program. Concentrations in accounting, management, management information systems.

Master of Professional Accountancy (MPA) Full-time, part-time; 36 total credits required; 2 to 5 years to complete program. Concentration in accounting.

Master of Science in Finance and Economics (MS) Full-time, part-time; 36 total credits required; 2 to 5 years to complete program. Concentrations in economics, finance.

Bachelor of Business Administration/Master of Professional Accounting (BBA/MPA) Full-time, part-time; 152 total credits required; up to 5 years to complete program. Concentration in accounting.

ADMISSION

Applications For fall 1997 there were 51 applications for admission. Of those applying, 50 were accepted. Of those accepted, 49 enrolled.

Application Requirements Application form, bachelor's degree, minimum GPA, interview, college transcript(s).

Recommended for Application GMAT score accepted, computer experience.

Application Deadline 8/22 for fall, 1/15 for spring, 6/2 for summer. Deferred entrance is available.

ACADEMICS

Faculty Full-time 10; part-time 8.

Teaching Methodologies Case study, computer-aided instruction, experiential learning, faculty seminars, field projects, group discussion, lecture, research, seminars by members of the business community, student presentations, study groups, team projects.

Technology 300 on-campus computer terminals/PCs are available for student use and are linked by a campus-wide network. The network has full access to the Internet. Students are not required to have their own PC.

Special Opportunities Advanced credit may be earned through credit by examination, transfer of credits from another institution. International exchange program in United Kingdom. An internship program is available.

FINANCES

Costs for 1997–98 Tuition: Full-time: $2160 per year (resident); $7992 per year (nonresident). Part-time: $60 per credit hour (resident); $222 per credit hour (nonresident). Cost varies by number of credits taken, reciprocity agreements. Fees: Full-time: $1476 per academic year (resident); $1476 per academic year (nonresident). Part-time: $41 per credit hour (resident); $41 per credit hour (nonresident). Fees vary by number of credits taken, reciprocity agreements. Average 1997–98 room and board costs were $3500 per academic year (on campus) and $7000 per academic year (off campus). Room and board costs vary by occupancy (e.g., single, double, triple), type of meal plan.

Financial Aid Research assistantships, teaching assistantships, grants, scholarships, work study, loans available. Financial aid is available to part-time students. Application Deadline: 3/1.

Financial Aid Contact Ms. Lynda Tinsley, Director of Student Financial Services, WTAMU Box 999, Canyon, TX 79016-0001. Phone: 806-656-2055; Fax: 806-656-2924.

FACILITIES

Information Resources Cornette Library plus 1 additional on-campus library; total holdings of 349,178 volumes, 125,965 microforms, 1,815 current periodical subscriptions. CD player(s) available for graduate student use. Access provided to online bibliographic retrieval services.

INTERNATIONAL STUDENTS

Demographics 27% of students enrolled are international students [Asia, 97%, Europe, 3%].

Services and Facilities International student office, international student center, international student housing, visa services, ESL courses, counseling/support services.

Applying TOEFL: minimum score of 550, proof of health/immunizations required.

International Student Contact Ms. Kristine Combs, Program Coordinator, International Student Office, WTAMU Box 60999, Canyon, TX 79016-0001. Phone: 806-656-2073; Fax: 806-656-2071.

PLACEMENT

Services include career counseling/planning, career fairs, career library, career placement, job interviews arranged, and resume preparation. In 1996–97, 49 organizations participated in on-campus recruiting; 402 on-campus interviews were conducted.

Employment Types of employment entered: accounting, banking, computer-related, education, finance, financial services, government, human resources, information systems/technology, management, marketing.

Business Program(s) URL: http://www.wtamu.edu/academic/bus/

Program Contact: Dr. Ron Hiner, MBA Coordinator, PO Box 187, Canyon, TX 79016-0001. Phone: 806-656-2517; Fax: 806-656-2514; E-mail: rhiner@ faculty.wtamu.edu

UTAH

Brigham Young University

Marriott School of Management

Provo, Utah

OVERVIEW

Brigham Young University is an independent-religious, coed university. Enrollment: 32,212 graduate, professional, and undergraduate students; 2,050 full-time matriculated graduate/professional students; 1,450 part-time matriculated graduate/professional students. The graduate business unit is in a suburban setting and is on a semester calendar.

HIGHLIGHTS

Enrollment Profile

Full-time: 649	International: 9%
Part-time: 102	Women: 22%
Total: 751	Minorities: 7%
Average Age: 28	Average Class Size: 45
Fall 1997 Average GPA: 3.47	Fall 1997 Average GMAT: 620

Costs
Full-time tuition: N/R
Part-time tuition: N/R

AACSB – The International Association for Management Education accredited

GRADUATE BUSINESS PROGRAMS

Master of Business Administration (MBA) Full-time; 61 total credits required; 2 years to complete program. Concentrations in entrepreneurship, finance, human resources, information management, international business, management, management information systems, marketing, operations management, organizational behavior/development, strategic management, production management, quantitative analysis.

Executive MBA (MBA) Part-time; 51 total credits required; 2 years to complete program. Concentrations in finance, marketing, entrepreneurship, operations management, production management, management information systems, organizational behavior/development, strategic management, quantitative analysis, international business, financial management/planning, real estate, banking, business law, european business studies, international finance.

Master of Accountancy (MAcc) Full-time; 52 total credits required; minimum of 18 months to complete program. Concentrations in accounting, taxation.

Master of Information Systems Management (MISM) Full-time; 84 total credits required; 12 months to 2 years to complete program. Concentrations in accounting, information management, management consulting, management information systems, system management, technology management.

Master of Organizational Behavior (MOB) Full-time, part-time; 53 total credits required; up to 2 years to complete program.

Master of Public Administration (MPA) Full-time; 64 total credits required; 2 years to complete program. Concentrations in city/urban administration, economics, financial management/planning, human resources, information management, legal administration, management information systems, system management, public management.

Executive MPA (MPA) Part-time; 44 total credits required; 3 years to complete program. Concentrations in managerial economics, environmental economics/management, human resources, accounting, quantitative analysis, finance, management, public management.

ADMISSION

Applications For fall 1997 there were 1,021 applications for admission. Of those applying, 559 were accepted. Of those accepted, 378 enrolled.

Application Requirements Application form, application fee, bachelor's degree, minimum GPA: 3.0, 3 letters of recommendation, personal statement, college transcript(s).

Recommended for Application GMAT score accepted: minimum 500, interview, resume, minimum of 2 years of work experience, computer experience.

Application Deadline 3/1 for fall, 1/5 for fall (international). Application fee: $30. Deferred entrance is available.

ACADEMICS

Faculty Full-time 104; part-time 8.

Teaching Methodologies Case study, computer-aided instruction, computer analysis, computer simulations, field projects, group discussion, lecture, research, seminars by members of the business community, simulations, student presentations, study groups, team projects.

Technology 1,800 on-campus computer terminals/PCs are available for student use and are linked by a campus-wide network. The network has full access to the Internet. Students are not required to have their own PC.

Special Opportunities Advanced credit may be earned through transfer of credits from another institution.

FINANCES

Costs for 1997–98 Cost varies by academic program. Average 1997–98 room and board costs were $7200 per academic year (on campus) and $12,380 per academic year (off campus). Room and board costs vary by occupancy (e.g., single, double, triple), type of accommodation, type of meal plan.

Financial Aid In 1997–98, 38% of students received some institutionally administered aid in the form of research assistantships, teaching assistantships, grants, scholarships, loans. Application Deadline: 6/30.

Financial Aid Contact Rixa Oman, Assistant to the Dean, 730 TNRB, Provo, UT 84602-1001. Phone: 801-378-6824; E-mail: rixa_oman@byu.edu

FACILITIES

Information Resources Harold B. Lee Library plus 2 additional on-campus libraries; total holdings of 3,500,000 volumes, 2,100,000 microforms, 17,000 current periodical subscriptions. CD player(s) available for graduate student use. Access provided to online bibliographic retrieval services and online databases.

INTERNATIONAL STUDENTS

Demographics 9% of students enrolled are international students [Africa, 1%, Asia, 13%, Australia/New Zealand, 1%, Europe, 3%, North America, 78%, South America, 4%].

Services and Facilities International student office, international student center, ESL courses, counseling/support services.

Applying TOEFL: minimum score of 570, proof of adequate funds, proof of health/immunizations required. Financial aid is available to international students.

International Student Contact Dr. Lee Radebaugh, Professor, 650 TNRB, Marriott School of Management, Provo, UT 84602-1001. Phone: 801-378-4636; E-mail: lee_radebaugh@byu.edu

PLACEMENT

Services include alumni network, career counseling/planning, career fairs, career library, career placement, job interviews arranged, job search course, resume referral to employers, and resume preparation. In 1996–97, 221 organizations participated in on-campus recruiting; 1,794 on-campus interviews were conducted.

Employment Of 1996–97 graduates, 76% were employed within three months of graduation; the average starting salary was $41,762. Types of employment entered: accounting, banking, chemical industry, communications, computer-related, consulting, consumer products, energy, engineering, finance, financial services, government, health services, high technology, hospitality management, human resources, information systems/technology, insurance, international trade, management, manufacturing, marketing, nonprofit, real estate, retail, service industry, telecommunications, transportation.

Business Program(s) URL: http://msm.byu.edu/programs/grad/mba

Program Contact: Mr. Henry J. Eyring, Professor and MBA Director, 640 Tanner Building, Marriott School of Management, Provo, UT 84602-1001. Phone: 801-378-3500; Fax: 801-378-4808; E-mail: hje@email.byu.edu

See full description on page 736.

Southern Utah University

School of Business

Cedar City, Utah

OVERVIEW

Southern Utah University is a state-supported, coed, comprehensive institution. Enrollment: 6,125 graduate, professional, and undergraduate students; 61 full-time matriculated graduate/professional students; 155 part-time matriculated graduate/professional students. Founded: 1897. The graduate business unit is in a small-town setting and is on a quarter calendar.

Southern Utah University (continued)

HIGHLIGHTS

Enrollment Profile
Full-time: 33
Part-time: 8
Total: 41
Average Age: 25
Fall 1997 Average GPA: 3.5

International: N/R
Women: 37%
Minorities: 5%
Average Class Size: 22
Fall 1997 Average GMAT: 500

Costs
Full-time tuition: $1581 per academic year (resident); $5985 per academic year (nonresident)
Part-time tuition: $47 per hour (resident); $175 per hour (nonresident)

GRADUATE BUSINESS PROGRAMS
Master of Accountancy (MAcc) Full-time, part-time; 46 total credits required; 9 months to 3 years to complete program. Concentration in accounting.

ADMISSION
Applications For fall 1997 there were 27 applications for admission. Of those applying, 22 were accepted. Of those accepted, 22 enrolled.

Application Requirements Application form, application fee, bachelor's degree (must be in field of business), minimum GPA, 3 letters of recommendation, personal statement, college transcript(s), computer experience: spreadsheet, database, word processing.

Recommended for Application GMAT score accepted.

Application Deadline Applications processed on a rolling/continuous basis for both domestic and international students. Application fee: $25. Deferred entrance is available.

ACADEMICS
Faculty Full-time 6.

Teaching Methodologies Case study, computer-aided instruction, computer analysis, computer simulations, field projects, group discussion, lecture, research, seminars by members of the business community, simulations, student presentations, study groups, team projects.

Technology 60 on-campus computer terminals/PCs are available for student use and are linked by a campus-wide network. The network has full access to the Internet. Students are not required to have their own PC.

Special Opportunities An internship program is available.

FINANCES
Costs for 1997–98 Tuition: Full-time: $1581 per year (resident); $5985 per year (nonresident). Part-time: $47 per hour (resident); $175 per hour (nonresident). Cost varies by number of credits taken. Fees: Full-time: $414 per academic year (resident); $414 per academic year (nonresident). Fees vary by number of credits taken. Average 1997–98 room and board costs were $2235 per academic year. Room and board costs vary by occupancy (e.g., single, double, triple), type of accommodation, type of meal plan.

Financial Aid Work study, loans available. Financial aid is available to part-time students.

Financial Aid Contact Mr. Rex Michie, Director of Financial Aid, 357 West Center Street, Cedar City, UT 84720. Phone: 801-586-7735; Fax: 801-586-7736; E-mail: michie@suu.edu

FACILITIES
Information Resources Gerald R. Sherratt Library; total holdings of 197,757 volumes, 615,223 microforms, 2,333 current periodical subscriptions. CD player(s) available for graduate student use. Access provided to online bibliographic retrieval services.

INTERNATIONAL STUDENTS
Demographics N/R

Services and Facilities International student office, visa services, ESL courses, counseling/support services.

Applying TOEFL: minimum score of 500, proof of adequate funds, proof of health/immunizations required. Financial aid is not available to international students.

International Student Contact Ms. Lynne J. Brown, Director of International and Multicultural Services, Shawan Smith Student Center, Cedar City, UT 84720. Phone: 435-586-7700; Fax: 435-865-8223; E-mail: brown-lj@suu.edu

PLACEMENT
Services include alumni network, career counseling/planning, career fairs, career library, career placement, electronic job bank, job interviews arranged, and resume preparation. In 1996–97, 49 organizations participated in on-campus recruiting.

Employment Of 1996–97 graduates, 75% were employed within three months of graduation. Types of employment entered: accounting, banking, consumer products, education, finance, financial services, government, hospitality management, manufacturing.

Business Program(s) URL: http://www.btc.suu.edu/

Program Contact: Ms. Laurie Harris, Secretary, Business Department, Cedar City, UT 84720. Phone: 801-586-5462; Fax: 801-586-5493; E-mail: harris@suu.edu

University of Utah

David Eccles School of Business

Salt Lake City, Utah

OVERVIEW
The University of Utah is a state-supported, coed university. Enrollment: 26,193 graduate, professional, and undergraduate students; 3,942 full-time matriculated graduate/professional students; 966 part-time matriculated graduate/professional students. Founded: 1850. The graduate business unit is in an urban setting and is on a semester calendar.

HIGHLIGHTS

Enrollment Profile
Full-time: 151
Part-time: 183
Total: 334
Average Age: 28
Fall 1997 Average GPA: 3.43

International: 13%
Women: 33%
Minorities: 8%
Average Class Size: 40
Fall 1997 Average GMAT: 579

Costs
Full-time tuition: $3046 per academic year (resident); $9457 per academic year (nonresident)
Part-time tuition: $1891 per year (resident); $5642 per year (nonresident)

AACSB – The International Association for Management Education accredited

GRADUATE BUSINESS PROGRAMS
Accelerated 1-year Program (MBA) Full-time, part-time; 48-56 total credits required; 12 months to 2 years to complete program. Concentrations in health care, international business, technology management.

Master of Business Administration/Doctor of Jurisprudence (MBA/JD) Full-time; 136-144 total credits required; 3 to 4 years to complete program.

Master of Business Administration/Master of Architecture (MBA/MArch) Full-time; 141-149 total credits required; 3 to 4 years to complete program.

Master of Professional Accountancy (MPA) Full-time, part-time; 36-40 total credits required; 9 to 18 months to complete program. Concentration in taxation.

Master of Statistics (MStat) Full-time, part-time; 34-43 total credits required; 12 months to 2 years to complete program. Concentration in management.

Evening MBA (MBA) Part-time; 48 total credits required; 2.3 years to complete program.

Two-year program (MBA) Full-time, part-time; 64-72 total credits required; 18 months to 3 years to complete program. Concentrations in health care, international business, technology management.

Executive MBA (MBA) Part-time; 48 total credits required; 21 months to complete program.

ADMISSION
Applications For fall 1997 there were 434 applications for admission. Of those applying, 276 were accepted. Of those accepted, 168 enrolled.

Application Requirements Application form, application fee, bachelor's degree, essay, minimum GPA: 3.0, 2 letters of recommendation, resume, college transcript(s).

Recommended for Application GMAT score accepted, work experience, computer experience.

Application Deadline 3/1 for fall, 1/15 for summer, 3/1 for fall (international), 1/15 for summer (international). Application fee: $40, $60 (international).

ACADEMICS
Faculty Full-time 60; part-time 24.

Teaching Methodologies Case study, computer analysis, computer simulations, experiential learning, field projects, group discussion, lecture, role playing, seminars by members of the business community, simulations, student presentations, study groups, team projects.

Technology 650 on-campus computer terminals/PCs are available for student use and are linked by a campus-wide network. The network has full access to the Internet. Students are not required to have their own PC.

Special Opportunities International exchange programs in France, Germany, Japan, Mexico, Taiwan, Venezuela.

FINANCES

Costs for 1997–98 Tuition: Full-time: $3046 per year (resident); $9457 per year (nonresident). Part-time: $1891 per year (resident); $5642 per year (nonresident). Cost varies by number of credits taken, reciprocity agreements. Average 1997–98 room and board costs were $6633 per academic year (on campus) and $6633 per academic year (off campus). Room and board costs vary by occupancy (e.g., single, double, triple), type of accommodation, type of meal plan.

Financial Aid Fellowships, teaching assistantships, work study available. Application Deadline: 1/15.

Financial Aid Contact Ms. Wendy Clark, Financial Aid Supervisor—Information Specialist, 201 South 1460 East Room 105, Salt Lake City, UT 84112-9055. Phone: 801-581-6211; Fax: 801-585-6350; E-mail: fawinl@ssb2.saff.utah.edu

FACILITIES

Information Resources Marriott Library plus 2 additional on-campus libraries; total holdings of 3,089,441 volumes, 3,126,567 microforms, 21,807 current periodical subscriptions. CD player(s) available for graduate student use. Access provided to online bibliographic retrieval services and online databases.

INTERNATIONAL STUDENTS

Demographics 13% of students enrolled are international students [Africa, 7%, Asia, 32%, Australia/New Zealand, 2%, Central America, 4%, Europe, 39%, North America, 4%, South America, 7%, other, 5%].

Services and Facilities International student office, international student center, visa services, ESL courses, counseling/support services, international student orientation.

Applying TOEFL: minimum score of 600, TSE: minimum score of 55 required. Financial aid is available to international students.

International Student Contact Ms. Carrie Radmall, Admissions and Scholarship Coordinator, 1645 East Campus Center Drive, Room 101, Salt Lake City, UT 84112-9301. Phone: 801-581-7785; Fax: 801-581-3666; E-mail: masters@business.utah.edu

PLACEMENT

Services include alumni network, career counseling/planning, career fairs, career library, career placement, job interviews arranged, job search course, resume referral to employers, and resume preparation. In 1996–97, 95 organizations participated in on-campus recruiting; 425 on-campus interviews were conducted.

Employment Of 1996–97 graduates, 94% were employed within three months of graduation; the average starting salary was $44,178. Types of employment entered: accounting, banking, computer-related, consulting, energy, engineering, finance, financial services, government, health services, high technology, human resources, information systems/technology, insurance, international trade, law, management, manufacturing, marketing, pharmaceutical, real estate, retail, telecommunications.

Business Program(s) URL: http://www.business.utah.edu/masters

Program Contact: Ms. Carrie Radmall, Admissions and Scholarship Coordinator, 1645 East Campus Center Drive, Room 101, Salt Lake City, UT 84112-9301. Phone: 801-581-7785; Fax: 801-581-3666; E-mail: masters@business.utah.edu
See full description on page 1168.

Utah State University

College of Business

Logan, Utah

OVERVIEW

Utah State University is a state-supported, coed university. Enrollment: 20,808 graduate, professional, and undergraduate students; 919 full-time matriculated graduate/professional students; 1,535 part-time matriculated graduate/professional students. Founded: 1888. The graduate business unit is in an urban setting and is on a semester calendar.

HIGHLIGHTS

Enrollment Profile

Full-time: 145	International: 20%
Part-time: 225	Women: 27%
Total: 370	Minorities: 4%
Average Age: 30	Average Class Size: 30
Fall 1997 Average GPA: 3.35	Fall 1997 Average GMAT: 560

Costs
Full-time tuition: $2426 per academic year (resident); $7438 per academic year (nonresident)
Part-time tuition: $754 per quarter (resident); $2314 per quarter (nonresident)

AACSB – The International Association for Management Education accredited

Degree(s) offered in conjunction with Utah Valley State College, Dixie College

GRADUATE BUSINESS PROGRAMS

Master of Accountancy (MAcc) Full-time, part-time; 30 total credits required; minimum of 9 months to complete program. Concentration in taxation.

Master of Science in Business Information Systems and Education (MS) Full-time, part-time, distance learning option; 33 total credits required; minimum of 12 months to complete program. Concentrations in business education, business information science, information management.

Master of Science in Economics (MS) Full-time, part-time; 30 total credits required; minimum of 9 months to complete program. Concentrations in agricultural economics, managerial economics, developmental economics.

Master of Business Administration (MBA) Full-time, part-time, distance learning option; 30 total credits required; minimum of 9 months to complete program. Concentrations in accounting, business information science, management science, quantitative analysis, manufacturing management, entrepreneurship, international economics.

Master of Social Science in Human Resource Management (MSS) Full-time, part-time, distance learning option; 36 total credits required; minimum of 12 months to complete program.

ADMISSION

Application Requirements Application form, application fee, bachelor's degree, minimum GPA: 3.0, 3 letters of recommendation, personal statement, college transcript(s).

Recommended for Application GMAT score accepted: minimum 500, GRE score accepted, work experience.

Application Deadline Applications processed on a rolling/continuous basis for both domestic and international students. Application fee: $30, $35 (international). Deferred entrance is available.

ACADEMICS

Faculty Full-time 81; part-time 5.

Teaching Methodologies Case study, computer analysis, computer simulations, experiential learning, faculty seminars, group discussion, lecture, research, role playing, seminars by members of the business community, student presentations, study groups, team projects.

Technology Computer terminals/PCs are available for student use and are linked by a campus-wide network. The network has full access to the Internet. Students are not required to have their own PC.

Special Opportunities Advanced credit may be earned through transfer of credits from another institution. International exchange programs in Australia, Mexico, United Kingdom. An internship program is available.

FINANCES

Costs for 1997–98 Tuition: Full-time: $2426 per year (resident); $7438 per year (nonresident). Part-time: $754 per quarter (resident); $2314 per quarter (nonresident). Cost varies by campus location, class time (e.g., day/evening), number of credits taken, reciprocity agreements. Average 1997–98 room and board costs were $4852 per academic year. Room and board costs vary by occupancy (e.g., single, double, triple), type of accommodation, type of meal plan.

Financial Aid In 1997–98, 20% of students received some institutionally administered aid in the form of fellowships, research assistantships, teaching assistantships, work study, loans. Application Deadline: 4/1.

Financial Aid Contact Director of Financial Aid, University Hill, Logan, UT 84322. Phone: 435-797-0174.

FACILITIES

Information Resources Merrill Library and Learning Resource Center plus 5 additional on-campus libraries; total holdings of 1,217,218 volumes, 2,031,556 microforms, 14,035 current periodical subscriptions. CD player(s) available for graduate student use. Access provided to online bibliographic retrieval services.

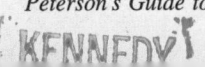

Utah State University (continued)

INTERNATIONAL STUDENTS

Demographics 20% of students enrolled are international students.

Services and Facilities International student office, international student center, ESL courses, counseling/support services.

Applying TOEFL: minimum score of 550, proof of adequate funds required. Proof of health/immunizations recommended. Financial aid is available to international students.

International Student Contact Ms. Afton Tew, Director, International Students/ Scholars, University Hill, Logan, UT 84322. Phone: 435-797-1124; Fax: 435-797-3522; E-mail: global@cc.usu.edu

PLACEMENT

Services include alumni network, career counseling/planning, career fairs, career library, career placement, electronic job bank, job interviews arranged, resume referral to employers, and resume preparation. In 1996–97, 80 organizations participated in on-campus recruiting.

Employment Of 1996–97 graduates, 80% were employed within three months of graduation. Types of employment entered: accounting, banking, chemical industry, communications, computer-related, education, finance, financial services, government, health services, high technology, hospitality management, information systems/technology, insurance, management, marketing, nonprofit, pharmaceutical, real estate, retail, transportation, utilities.

Business Program(s) URL: http://www.bus.usu.edu

Program Contact: School of Graduate Studies, University Hill, Logan, UT 84322. Phone: 435-797-1189.

Weber State University

College of Business and Economics

Ogden, Utah

OVERVIEW

Weber State University is a state-supported, coed, comprehensive institution. Enrollment: 14,613 graduate, professional, and undergraduate students; 44 full-time matriculated graduate/professional students; 104 part-time matriculated graduate/professional students. Founded: 1889. The graduate business unit is in a suburban setting and is on a semester calendar.

HIGHLIGHTS

Enrollment Profile

Full-time: 40	International: 8%
Part-time: 20	Women: 48%
Total: 60	Minorities: 5%
Average Age: 31	Average Class Size: 18
Fall 1997 Average GPA: 3.4	Fall 1997 Average GMAT: 570

Costs
Full-time tuition: $1716 per academic year (resident); $6006 per academic year (nonresident)
Part-time tuition: $1036 per year (resident); $3628 per year (nonresident)

AACSB – The International Association for Management Education accredited

GRADUATE BUSINESS PROGRAMS

Master of Professional Accountancy (MPAcc) Full-time, part-time, distance learning option; 40 total credits required; 12 months to 6 years to complete program. Concentrations in accounting, financial management/planning, taxation.

ADMISSION

Applications For fall 1997 there were 50 applications for admission. Of those applying, 31 were accepted. Of those accepted, 28 enrolled.

Application Requirements GMAT score, application form, bachelor's degree, minimum GPA, college transcript(s).

Recommended for Application Interview, letters of recommendation, work experience, computer experience.

Application Deadline 7/1 for fall, 10/1 for spring, 7/1 for fall (international), 10/1 for spring (international). Application fee: $30, $35 (international). Deferred entrance is available.

ACADEMICS

Faculty Full-time 5; part-time 2.

Teaching Methodologies Case study, computer-aided instruction, computer analysis, computer simulations, experiential learning, faculty seminars, field projects, group discussion, lecture, research, role playing, seminars by members of the business community, simulations, student presentations, study groups, team projects.

Technology 600 on-campus computer terminals/PCs are available for student use and are linked by a campus-wide network. The network has full access to the Internet. Students are not required to have their own PC.

Special Opportunities Advanced credit may be earned through transfer of credits from another institution. An internship program is available.

FINANCES

Costs for 1997–98 Tuition: Full-time: $1716 per year (resident); $6006 per year (nonresident). Part-time: $1036 per year (resident); $3628 per year (nonresident). Fees: Full-time: $426 per academic year (resident); $426 per academic year (nonresident). Part-time: $280 per year (resident); $280 per year (nonresident). Average 1997–98 room and board costs were $3605 per academic year (on campus) and $5670 per academic year (off campus). Room and board costs vary by occupancy (e.g., single, double, triple), type of accommodation, type of meal plan.

Financial Aid Research assistantships, scholarships available. Financial aid is available to part-time students. Application Deadline: 2/1.

Financial Aid Contact Dr. James Swearingen, Graduate Coordinator, 3803 University Circle, Ogden, UT 84408-3803. Phone: 801-626-6000; Fax: 801-626-7423; E-mail: jswearingen@weber.edu

FACILITIES

Information Resources Stewart Library; total holdings of 407,956 volumes, 453,388 microforms, 2,196 current periodical subscriptions. CD player(s) available for graduate student use. Access provided to online bibliographic retrieval services and online databases.

INTERNATIONAL STUDENTS

Demographics 8% of students enrolled are international students [Asia, 80%, other, 20%].

Services and Facilities International student office, international student center, international student housing, visa services, ESL courses, counseling/support services.

Applying Proof of adequate funds, proof of health/immunizations required. TOEFL recommended. Financial aid is available to international students.

International Student Contact Dr. James Swearingen, Graduate Coordinator, 3803 University Circle, Ogden, UT 84408-3803. Phone: 801-626-6897 Ext. 6897; Fax: 801-626-7423 Ext. 7423; E-mail: jswearingen@weber.edu

PLACEMENT

Services include alumni network, career counseling/planning, career fairs, career library, career placement, electronic job bank, job interviews arranged, resume referral to employers, and resume preparation. In 1996–97, 326 organizations participated in on-campus recruiting; 2,772 on-campus interviews were conducted.

Employment Of 1996–97 graduates, 93% were employed within three months of graduation; the average starting salary was $32,500.

Business Program(s) URL: http://www.weber.edu/COBE/htmls/Cobe.htm

Program Contact: Dr. James Swearingen, Graduate Coordinator, 3803 University Circle, Ogden, UT 84408-3803. Phone: 801-626-6897; Fax: 801-626-7423; E-mail: jswearingen@weber.edu

Westminster College of Salt Lake City

Bill and Vieve Gore School of Business

Salt Lake City, Utah

OVERVIEW

Westminster College of Salt Lake City is an independent-nonprofit, coed, comprehensive institution. Enrollment: 2,140 graduate, professional, and undergraduate students; 149 full-time matriculated graduate/professional students; 370 part-time matriculated graduate/professional students. Founded: 1875. The graduate business unit is in a suburban setting and is on a semester calendar.

HIGHLIGHTS

Enrollment Profile

Full-time: 101	International: 3%
Part-time: 274	Women: 36%
Total: 375	Minorities: 8%
Average Age: 33	Average Class Size: 19
Fall 1997 Average GPA: 3.118	Fall 1997 Average GMAT: 511

Costs
Full-time tuition: $5740 per academic year
Part-time tuition: $410 per hour

GRADUATE BUSINESS PROGRAMS
Master of Business Administration (MBA) Full-time, part-time; 42 total credits required; up to 6 years to complete program. Concentrations in accounting, finance, human resources, international business, marketing, health care, economics, organizational behavior/development, information management, resources management.

ADMISSION
Applications For fall 1997 there were 173 applications for admission. Of those applying, 154 were accepted. Of those accepted, 108 enrolled.

Application Requirements GMAT score: minimum 500, application form, application fee, bachelor's degree, minimum GPA: 3.0, resume, college transcript(s).

Recommended for Application GRE score accepted, minimum of 3 years of work experience.

Application Deadline Applications processed on a rolling/continuous basis for domestic students only. 7/1 for fall (international), 10/1 for spring (international), 3/1 for summer (international). Application fee: $25. Deferred entrance is available.

ACADEMICS
Faculty Full-time 15; part-time 8.

Teaching Methodologies Case study, computer-aided instruction, computer analysis, computer simulations, experiential learning, faculty seminars, field projects, group discussion, lecture, research, role playing, seminars by members of the business community, simulations, student presentations, study groups, team projects.

Technology 175 on-campus computer terminals/PCs are available for student use and are linked by a campus-wide network. The network has full access to the Internet. Students are not required to have their own PC.

Special Opportunities Advanced credit may be earned through transfer of credits from another institution. An internship program is available.

FINANCES
Costs for 1997–98 Tuition: Full-time: $5740 per semester. Part-time: $410 per hour. Fees: Full-time: $100 per academic year. Part-time: $65 per hour. Fees vary by number of credits taken. Average 1997–98 room and board costs were $5900 per academic year (off campus).

Financial Aid In 1997–98, 67% of students received some institutionally administered aid. Financial aid is available to part-time students.

Financial Aid Contact Ms. Ruth Henneman, Director of Financial Aid, 1840 South 1300 East, Salt Lake City, UT 84105-3697. Phone: 801-488-4105; Fax: 801-485-1989; E-mail: faidpub@wcslc.edu

FACILITIES
Information Resources Ginger Gore Giovale Library; total holdings of 83,620 volumes, 492 microforms, 1,272 current periodical subscriptions. CD player(s) available for graduate student use. Access provided to online bibliographic retrieval services.

INTERNATIONAL STUDENTS
Demographics 3% of students enrolled are international students [Asia, 46%, Europe, 31%, North America, 15%, South America, 8%].

Services and Facilities Counseling/support services.

Applying TOEFL: minimum score of 550, proof of adequate funds required. Financial aid is not available to international students.

International Student Contact Ms. Stephanie Sherman, Assistant Director of Admissions, 1840 South 1300 East, Salt Lake City, UT 84105-3697. Phone: 801-488-4200; Fax: 801-484-3252; E-mail: admispub@wcslc.edu

PLACEMENT
Services include alumni network, career counseling/planning, career fairs, career library, electronic job bank, job search course, and resume preparation. In 1996–97, 10 organizations participated in on-campus recruiting; 5 on-campus interviews were conducted.

Employment Types of employment entered: accounting, finance, information systems/technology.

Business Program(s) URL: http://www.wcslc.edu

Program Contact: Mr. Phillip J. Alletto, Vice President for Student Development and Enrollment Management, 1840 South 1300 East, Salt Lake City, UT 84105-3697. Phone: 801-488-4200, 800-748-4753; Fax: 801-484-3252; E-mail: admispub@wcslc.edu

VERMONT

Saint Michael's College

Prevel School Graduate Program in Administration and Management
Colchester, Vermont

OVERVIEW
Saint Michael's College is an independent-religious, comprehensive institution. Enrollment: 1,700 graduate, professional, and undergraduate students.

HIGHLIGHTS
Enrollment Profile
Full-time: N/R
Part-time: N/R
Total: 300
Average Age: N/R
Fall 1997 Average GPA: N/R

International: N/R
Women: N/R
Minorities: N/R
Average Class Size: N/R
Fall 1997 Average GMAT: N/R

Costs
Full-time tuition: N/R
Part-time tuition: $290 per credit hour

GRADUATE BUSINESS PROGRAMS
Master of Science in Administration (MSA) Full-time, part-time; 37 total credits required; minimum of 2 years to complete program. Concentrations in organizational behavior/development, organizational management, human resources, information management, marketing, management information systems, nonprofit management, business policy/strategy.

ADMISSION
Application Requirements Application form, bachelor's degree, essay, minimum GPA: 2.8, 2 letters of recommendation, resume, college transcript(s), minimum of 3 years of work experience.

Application Deadline Applications processed on a rolling/continuous basis for both domestic and international students. Application fee: $25.

ACADEMICS
Teaching Methodologies Case study, experiential learning, faculty seminars, field projects, group discussion, lecture, research, role playing, simulations, student presentations, study groups, team projects.

FINANCES
Costs for 1997–98 Tuition: $290 per credit hour.

Financial Aid Contact Financial Aid Office, Colchester, VT 05439. Phone: 802-654-3243.

INTERNATIONAL STUDENTS
Demographics N/R

Applying TOEFL: minimum score of 550 required.

Business Program(s) URL: http://www.smcvt.edu/prevelsch/grad_catalog/msacoverpage.htm

Program Contact: JoAnne Gloria, Administrative Assistant for Graduate Programs, Colchester, VT 05439. Phone: 802-654-2369.

School for International Training

Program in International and Intercultural Management
Brattleboro, Vermont

OVERVIEW
School for International Training is an independent-nonprofit, coed, upper-level institution. Enrollment: 1,604 graduate, professional, and undergraduate students; 177 full-time matriculated graduate/professional students; 206 part-time matriculated graduate/professional students. Founded: 1964. The graduate business unit is in a rural setting and is on a semester calendar.

School for International Training (continued)

HIGHLIGHTS

Enrollment Profile
Full-time: 95
Part-time: 91
Total: 186
Average Age: 28
Fall 1997 Average GPA: N/R

International: N/R
Women: 74%
Minorities: N/R
Average Class Size: 30
Fall 1997 Average GMAT: N/R

Costs
Full-time tuition: $18,500 per academic year
Part-time tuition: N/R

GRADUATE BUSINESS PROGRAMS
Master of International and Intercultural Management (MIIM) Full-time, part-time; 36 total credits required; 2 to 5 years to complete program. Concentrations in international development management, international management, management, nonprofit management.

ADMISSION
Applications For fall 1997 there were 258 applications for admission. Of those applying, 206 were accepted. Of those accepted, 186 enrolled.

Application Requirements Application form, application fee, bachelor's degree, essay, 4 letters of recommendation, personal statement, resume, college transcript(s), minimum of 1 year of work experience.

Recommended for Application Interview.

Application Deadline Applications processed on a rolling/continuous basis for both domestic and international students. Application fee: $45. Deferred entrance is available.

ACADEMICS
Faculty Full-time 8; part-time 12.

Teaching Methodologies Case study, experiential learning, field projects, group discussion, lecture, research, role playing, seminars by members of the business community, simulations, student presentations, study groups, team projects.

Technology 24 on-campus computer terminals/PCs are available for student use and are linked by a campus-wide network. The network has full access to the Internet. Students are not required to have their own PC.

Special Opportunities Advanced credit may be earned through transfer of credits from another institution.

FINANCES
Costs for 1997–98 Tuition: Full-time: $18,500 per degree. Cost varies by academic program. Fees: Full-time: $1283 per academic year. Average 1997–98 room and board costs were $6416 per academic year (on campus) and $10,200 per academic year (off campus). Room and board costs vary by occupancy (e.g., single, double, triple), type of accommodation, type of meal plan.

Financial Aid In 1997–98, 31% of students received some institutionally administered aid in the form of grants, scholarships, work study, loans. Application Deadline: 4/1.

Financial Aid Contact Mary Henderson, Financial Aid Officer, Kipling Road, Brattleboro, VT 05302-0676. Phone: 800-336-1616 Ext. 328; Fax: 802-258-3500; E-mail: finaid@sit.edu

FACILITIES
Information Resources Donald B. Watt Library; total holdings of 30,000 volumes, 7,900 microforms, 450 current periodical subscriptions.

INTERNATIONAL STUDENTS
Demographics N/R

Services and Facilities International student office, visa services, ESL courses, counseling/support services.

Applying TOEFL: minimum score of 550, proof of adequate funds, proof of health/immunizations required.

International Student Contact Janet Hulnick, International Student Advisor, Kipling Road, PO Box 676, Brattleboro, VT 05302. Fax: 802-258-8248.

PLACEMENT
Services include alumni network, career counseling/planning, career library, job interviews arranged, job search course, and resume preparation.

Employment Types of employment entered: consulting, education, government, human resources, management, marketing, nonprofit.

Business Program(s) URL: http://www.worldlearning.org/sit.hmtl

Program Contact: Kim Noble, Admission Assistant, Kipling Road, PO Box 676, Brattleboro, VT 05302. Phone: 800-336-1616 Ext. 3267; Fax: 802-258-3500; E-mail: admissions@sit.edu

University of Vermont

School of Business Administration
Burlington, Vermont

OVERVIEW
The University of Vermont is a state-supported, coed university. Enrollment: 9,341 graduate, professional, and undergraduate students. Founded: 1791. The graduate business unit is in a suburban setting and is on a semester calendar.

HIGHLIGHTS

Enrollment Profile
Full-time: 13
Part-time: 58
Total: 71
Average Age: 27
Fall 1997 Average GPA: 3.2

International: 10%
Women: 39%
Minorities: 7%
Average Class Size: 17
Fall 1997 Average GMAT: 568

Costs
Full-time tuition: $7032 per academic year (resident); $17,580 per academic year (nonresident)
Part-time tuition: $293 per credit (resident); $733 per credit (nonresident)

AACSB – The International Association for Management Education accredited

T he School of Business at the University of Vermont is distinguished by its continuing effort to provide a superior educational experience for its students. The M.B.A. program prepares a select group of high-quality students for effective management practice in businesses, public sector agencies, and not-for-profit institutions. Courses emphasize the understanding and critical evaluation of conceptual and theoretical principles relevant to the decision-making process. The program, which is accredited by AACSB–The International Association for Management Education, builds a foundation of enduring business knowledge that helps students solve problems and adapt to changing environments. Students receive individualized guidance from a world-class faculty in applying knowledge to develop practical strategies for implementing change in actual organizations.

The University prides itself on maintaining a small, high-quality program. With approximately 85 enrolled students, the School is able to maintain a high level of personalization and integrity in the educational process. The average class size is 17 students. Classes in the School of Business are not taught by graduate students. Rather, classroom teachers are faculty members who possess doctoral degrees and who conduct significant scholarly research in their respective fields.

The University is located in Burlington, a community of approximately 110,000 nestled between the Green Mountains and Lake Champlain.

GRADUATE BUSINESS PROGRAMS
Master of Business Administration (MBA) Full-time, part-time; 48 total credits required; 12 months to 5 years to complete program.

ADMISSION
Applications For fall 1997 there were 76 applications for admission. Of those applying, 55 were accepted. Of those accepted, 31 enrolled.

Application Requirements Application form, application fee, bachelor's degree, 3 letters of recommendation, personal statement, college transcript(s), computer experience.

Recommended for Application GMAT score accepted.

Application Deadline Applications processed on a rolling/continuous basis for both domestic and international students. Application fee: $25. Deferred entrance is available.

ACADEMICS
Faculty Full-time 21.

Teaching Methodologies Case study, computer-aided instruction, computer analysis, computer simulations, experiential learning, field projects, group discussion, lecture, research, seminars by members of the business community, simulations, student presentations, study groups, team projects.

Technology 100 on-campus computer terminals/PCs are available for student use and are linked by a campus-wide network. The network has full access to the Internet. Students are not required to have their own PC.

Special Opportunities Advanced credit may be earned through transfer of credits from another institution.

FINANCES
Costs for 1997–98 Tuition: Full-time: $7032 per year (resident); $17,580 per year (nonresident). Part-time: $293 per credit (resident); $733 per credit (nonresident). Cost varies by number of credits taken. Fees: Full-time: $316 per academic year (resident); $316 per academic year (nonresident). Part-

time: $172 per semester (resident); $172 per semester (nonresident). Average 1997–98 room only costs were $3348 per academic year (on campus) and $6300 per academic year (off campus). Room and board costs vary by occupancy (e.g., single, double, triple), type of accommodation, type of meal plan.

Financial Aid Research assistantships, teaching assistantships available. Application Deadline: 3/1.

Financial Aid Contact Mr. Don Honeman, Director of Financial Aid, 330 Waterman Building, Burlington, VT 05405. Phone: 802-656-3156; Fax: 802-656-4076.

FACILITIES
Information Resources Bailey-Howe Library plus 2 additional on-campus libraries; total holdings of 1,185,252 volumes, 851,895 microforms, 8,000 current periodical subscriptions. CD player(s) available for graduate student use. Access provided to online bibliographic retrieval services and online databases.

INTERNATIONAL STUDENTS
Demographics 10% of students enrolled are international students [Asia, 13%, Europe, 87%].

Services and Facilities International student office, international student center, visa services, counseling/support services.

Applying TOEFL: minimum score of 550 required. Financial aid is not available to international students.

International Student Contact Ms. Jackie Siebert, International Student Advisor, B161 Living/Learning Center, Faculty Box 8, Burlington, VT 05405. Phone: 802-656-4296; Fax: 802-656-8553.

PLACEMENT
Services include career library, and resume preparation.

Business Program(s) URL: http://www.bsad.emba.uvm.edu

Program Contact: Ms. Nancy Parmalee, MBA Program Administrator, 319 Kalkin Hall, Burlington, VT 05405. Phone: 802-656-0655; Fax: 802-656-8279; E-mail: mba@bsadpo.emba.uvm.edu

VIRGINIA

Averett College

Program in Business Administration

Danville, Virginia

OVERVIEW
Averett College is an independent-religious, coed, comprehensive institution. Enrollment: 2,400 graduate, professional, and undergraduate students. Founded: 1859. The graduate business unit is in an urban setting and is on a trimester calendar.

GRADUATE BUSINESS PROGRAMS
Master of Business Administration (MBA)

ACADEMICS
Faculty Full-time 11; part-time 60.

Teaching Methodologies Case study, computer-aided instruction, computer simulations, experiential learning, faculty seminars, group discussion, research, role playing, simulations, student presentations, study groups, team projects.

Technology The network has full access to the Internet. Students are not required to have their own PC.

Special Opportunities Advanced credit may be earned through transfer of credits from another institution.

FACILITIES
Information Resources Mary B. Blount Library; total holdings of 98,530 volumes, 26,626 microforms, 481 current periodical subscriptions. CD player(s) available for graduate student use. Access provided to online bibliographic retrieval services.

Program Contact: Marketing Manager, PO Box 2670, Danville, VA 24541. Phone: 804-791-5851, 800-448-5233 (VA only); Fax: 804-791-5850; E-mail: averett1.oramail@appollogrp.edu

College of William and Mary

Graduate School of Business Administration

Williamsburg, Virginia

OVERVIEW
College of William and Mary is a state-supported, coed university. Enrollment: 7,547 graduate, professional, and undergraduate students; 1,385 full-time matriculated graduate/professional students; 575 part-time matriculated graduate/professional students. Founded: 1693. The graduate business unit is in a small-town setting and is on a semester calendar.

HIGHLIGHTS

Enrollment Profile

Full-time: 215	International: 12%
Part-time: 135	Women: 30%
Total: 350	Minorities: 10%
Average Age: 29	Average Class Size: 50
Fall 1997 Average GPA: 3.25	Fall 1997 Average GMAT: 620

Costs
Full-time tuition: $6500 per academic year (resident); $16,500 per academic year (nonresident)
Part-time tuition: $220 per credit hour (resident); $515 per credit hour (nonresident)

AACSB – The International Association for Management Education accredited

GRADUATE BUSINESS PROGRAMS
Full-time MBA (MBA) Full-time; 65 total credits required; 2 years to complete program. Concentrations in accounting, finance, marketing, information management, operations management, management.

Evening MBA (MBA) Part-time; 48 total credits required; 3 to 6 years to complete program. Concentrations in accounting, finance, marketing, information management, operations management, management.

Executive MBA (MBA) Part-time; 45 total credits required; 20 months to complete program. Concentrations in accounting, finance, marketing, information management, operations management, management.

ADMISSION
Applications For fall 1997 there were 460 applications for admission. Of those applying, 165 were accepted. Of those accepted, 105 enrolled.

Application Requirements Application form, application fee, bachelor's degree, essay, interview, 2 letters of recommendation, personal statement, resume, college transcript(s), minimum of 2 years of work experience, computer experience: Microsoft Windows, Microsoft Office, Microsoft Excel.

Recommended for Application GMAT score accepted: minimum 550.

Application Deadline Applications processed on a rolling/continuous basis for both domestic and international students. Application fee: $50. Deferred entrance is available.

ACADEMICS
Faculty Full-time 48; part-time 5.

Teaching Methodologies Case study, computer-aided instruction, computer analysis, computer simulations, experiential learning, faculty seminars, field projects, group discussion, lecture, research, role playing, seminars by members of the business community, simulations, student presentations, study groups, team projects.

Technology 50 on-campus computer terminals/PCs are available for student use and are linked by a campus-wide network. The network has full access to the Internet.

Special Opportunities International exchange programs in Costa Rica, Norway. An internship program is available.

FINANCES
Costs for 1997–98 Tuition: Full-time: $6500 per year (resident); $16,500 per year (nonresident). Part-time: $220 per credit hour (resident); $515 per credit hour (nonresident). Average 1997–98 room and board costs were $4500 per academic year (on campus) and $4500 per academic year (off campus). Room and board costs vary by occupancy (e.g., single, double, triple), type of accommodation, type of meal plan.

Financial Aid In 1997–98, 83% of students received some institutionally administered aid in the form of fellowships, research assistantships, scholarships, work study, loans. Application Deadline: 3/1.

Financial Aid Contact Ms. Susan Rivera, Director of MBA Admissions/Student Services, PO Box 8795, Williamsburg, VA 23187-8795. Phone: 757-221-2898; Fax: 757-221-2958; E-mail: sgrive@dogwood.tyler.wm.edu

FACILITIES
Information Resources Swem Library plus 8 additional on-campus libraries; total holdings of 1,245,179 volumes, 1,800,207 microforms, 10,414 cur-

rent periodical subscriptions. CD player(s) available for graduate student use. Access provided to online bibliographic retrieval services and online databases.

INTERNATIONAL STUDENTS

Demographics 12% of students enrolled are international students [Asia, 8%, Central America, 2%, Europe, 2%, North America, 88%].

Services and Facilities International student office, international student center, international student housing, visa services, counseling/support services.

Applying TOEFL: minimum score of 600, proof of adequate funds, proof of health/immunizations required. Financial aid is not available to international students.

International Student Contact Ms. Susan Rivera, Director of MBA Admissions/ Student Services, Blow Memorial Hall—Room 255, Williamsburg, VA 23187. Phone: 757-221-2898; Fax: 757-221-2958; E-mail: sgrive@dogwood.tyler. wm.edu

PLACEMENT

Services include alumni network, career counseling/planning, career fairs, career library, career placement, electronic job bank, job interviews arranged, job search course, resume referral to employers, and resume preparation. In 1996–97, 105 organizations participated in on-campus recruiting; 135 on-campus interviews were conducted.

Employment Of 1996–97 graduates, 100% were employed within three months of graduation; the average starting salary was $59,500. Types of employment entered: accounting, banking, chemical industry, communications, computer-related, consulting, consumer products, education, energy, engineering, finance, financial services, government, health services, high technology, human resources, insurance, international trade, law, management, manufacturing, marketing, media, mining, nonprofit, pharmaceutical, real estate, retail, service industry, telecommunications, transportation, utilities.

Business Program(s) URL: http://business.tyler.wm.edu

Program Contact: Ms. Susan Rivera, Director of MBA Admissions/Student Services, PO Box 8795, Williamsburg, VA 23187-8795. Phone: 757-221-2898, 888-203-6994; Fax: 757-221-2958; E-mail: sgrive@dogwood.tyler.wm.edu

See full description on page 762.

George Mason University

School of Management

Fairfax, Virginia

OVERVIEW

George Mason University is a state-supported, coed university. Enrollment: 24,172 graduate, professional, and undergraduate students; 1,720 full-time matriculated graduate/professional students; 5,358 part-time matriculated graduate/professional students. Founded: 1957. The graduate business unit is in a suburban setting and is on a semester calendar.

HIGHLIGHTS

Enrollment Profile

Full-time: 231	International: 10%
Part-time: 543	Women: 39%
Total: 774	Minorities: 13%
Average Age: 31	Average Class Size: 30
Fall 1997 Average GPA: 3.1	Fall 1997 Average GMAT: 590

Costs

Full-time tuition: $6168 per academic year (resident); $12,240 per academic year (nonresident)

Part-time tuition: $257 per credit hour (resident); $510 per credit hour (nonresident)

AACSB – The International Association for Management Education accredited

GRADUATE BUSINESS PROGRAMS

Executive MBA (EMBA) Full-time; 55 total credits required; up to 22 months to complete program.

Two-year MBA (MBA) Full-time, distance learning option; 48 total credits required; 21 months to 6 years to complete program. Concentrations in accounting, decision sciences, entrepreneurship, finance, international business, management, management information systems, marketing, organizational behavior/ development.

Fast Track MBA (MBA) Part-time; 48 total credits required; 2.8 years to complete program. Concentrations in entrepreneurship, international business, inter-

national finance, accounting, management, decision sciences, finance, international business, management information systems, marketing, organizational behavior/development.

Master of Science in Nursing/Master of Business Administration (MS/MBA) Full-time, part-time; 57 total credits required; 21 months to 6 years to complete program. Concentration in health care.

ADMISSION

Applications For fall 1997 there were 538 applications for admission. Of those applying, 335 were accepted. Of those accepted, 161 enrolled.

Application Requirements GMAT score, application form, application fee, bachelor's degree, essay, minimum GPA: 3.0, 2 letters of recommendation, resume, college transcript(s), minimum of 2 years of work experience.

Recommended for Application Interview, computer experience: PC software.

Application Deadline 4/1 for fall, 10/1 for spring, 3/1 for fall (international), 9/1 for spring (international). Application fee: $50.

ACADEMICS

Faculty Full-time 73; part-time 23.

Teaching Methodologies Case study, computer-aided instruction, computer analysis, experiential learning, faculty seminars, field projects, group discussion, lecture, research, seminars by members of the business community, simulations, student presentations, study groups, team projects.

Technology 986 on-campus computer terminals/PCs are available for student use and are linked by a campus-wide network. The network has full access to the Internet. Students are not required to have their own PC.

Special Opportunities Advanced credit may be earned through transfer of credits from another institution. International exchange programs in China, Costa Rica, France, Germany, Israel, Mexico, Switzerland, United Kingdom. An internship program is available.

FINANCES

Costs for 1997–98 Tuition: Full-time: $6168 per year (resident); $12,240 per year (nonresident). Part-time: $257 per credit hour (resident); $510 per credit hour (nonresident). Cost varies by academic program, number of credits taken. Average 1997–98 room and board costs were $6000 per academic year. Room and board costs vary by campus location, occupancy (e.g., single, double, triple), type of accommodation, type of meal plan.

Financial Aid In 1997–98, 19% of students received some institutionally administered aid in the form of fellowships, research assistantships. Financial aid is available to part-time students. Application Deadline: 3/1.

Financial Aid Contact Ms. Jennifer Douglas, Director, Financial Aid, 4400 University Drive, Mail Stop 3B5, Fairfax, VA 22030. Phone: 703-993-2353; Fax: 703-993-2350.

FACILITIES

Information Resources Fenwick Library plus 1 additional on-campus library; total holdings of 635,284 volumes, 1,683,847 microforms, 9,191 current periodical subscriptions. CD player(s) available for graduate student use. Access provided to online bibliographic retrieval services.

INTERNATIONAL STUDENTS

Demographics 10% of students enrolled are international students [Africa, 8%, Asia, 49%, Central America, 9%, Europe, 31%, North America, 3%].

Services and Facilities International student office, international student center, visa services, ESL courses, counseling/support services.

Applying TOEFL: minimum score of 600, proof of adequate funds, proof of health/immunizations required. Financial aid is not available to international students.

International Student Contact Ms. Julia Friedheim, Director, International Programs and Services, 4400 University Drive, Mail Stop 4C3, Fairfax, VA 22030. Phone: 703-993-2970; Fax: 703-993-2966; E-mail: gradadms@som.gmu. edu

PLACEMENT

Services include alumni network, career counseling/planning, career fairs, career library, career placement, electronic job bank, job interviews arranged, job search course, resume referral to employers, and resume preparation. In 1996–97, 21 organizations participated in on-campus recruiting; 155 on-campus interviews were conducted.

Employment Of 1996–97 graduates, 90% were employed within three months of graduation; the average starting salary was $56,642. Types of employment entered: accounting, banking, communications, computer-related, consulting, consumer products, finance, financial services, government, health services, high technology, information systems/technology, management, manufacturing, marketing, nonprofit, real estate, service industry, telecommunications.

Business Program(s) URL: http://www.som.gmu.edu/gbi/

Program Contact: Ms. Vicki Day, Coordinator, Admissions, 4400 University Drive, Mail Stop 5A2, Fairfax, VA 22030. Phone: 703-993-2136; Fax: 703-993-1886; E-mail: gradadms@som.gmu.edu

See full description on page 824.

Hampton University

School of Business

Hampton, Virginia

OVERVIEW
Hampton University is an independent-nonprofit, coed, comprehensive institution. Enrollment: 5,705 graduate, professional, and undergraduate students; 200 full-time matriculated graduate/professional students; 180 part-time matriculated graduate/professional students. Founded: 1868. The graduate business unit is in a suburban setting and is on a semester calendar.

HIGHLIGHTS

Enrollment Profile
Full-time: 5
Part-time: 13
Total: 18
Average Age: 30
Fall 1997 Average GPA: 2.9

International: 6%
Women: 67%
Minorities: 94%
Average Class Size: 15
Fall 1997 Average GMAT: 410

Costs
Full-time tuition: $4038 per academic year
Part-time tuition: $220 per credit hour

GRADUATE BUSINESS PROGRAMS
Master of Business Administration (MBA) Full-time, part-time; 60 total credits required; 16 months to 7 years to complete program.

ADMISSION
Application Requirements GMAT score, application form, application fee, bachelor's degree, minimum GPA: 2.5, 2 letters of recommendation, college transcript(s).

Application Deadline Applications processed on a rolling/continuous basis for both domestic and international students. Application fee: $25. Deferred entrance is available.

ACADEMICS
Faculty Full-time 7; part-time 3.

Teaching Methodologies Case study, computer-aided instruction, computer analysis, computer simulations, group discussion, lecture, research, student presentations, team projects.

Technology 55 on-campus computer terminals/PCs are available for student use. The network does not have Internet access. Students are not required to have their own PC.

Special Opportunities Advanced credit may be earned through credit by examination, credit for experience, credit for military training programs, transfer of credits from another institution. An internship program is available.

FINANCES
Costs for 1997–98 Tuition: Full-time: $4038 per year. Part-time: $220 per credit hour. Fees: $25 per semester.

Financial Aid In 1997–98, 61% of students received some institutionally administered aid in the form of teaching assistantships. Financial aid is available to part-time students. Application Deadline: 5/1.

Financial Aid Contact Financial Aid Office, Hampton, VA 23668. Phone: 757-727-5332; Fax: 757-727-5746.

FACILITIES
Information Resources William R. and Norma B. Harvey Library plus 4 additional on-campus libraries; total holdings of 400,000 volumes, 350,000 microforms, 1,500 current periodical subscriptions. CD player(s) available for graduate student use. Access provided to online bibliographic retrieval services.

INTERNATIONAL STUDENTS
Demographics 6% of students enrolled are international students [Africa, 100%].

Services and Facilities International student office, counseling/support services.

Applying TOEFL, proof of adequate funds, proof of health/immunizations required. Financial aid is not available to international students.

International Student Contact Mr. Burl Bowens, Assistant Dean of Men, Office of the Dean of Men, Hampton, VA 23668-0001. Phone: 757-727-5503; Fax: 757-727-5746.

PLACEMENT
Services include career counseling/planning, career fairs, career library, career placement, and resume referral to employers. In 1996–97, 400 organizations participated in on-campus recruiting.

Employment Of 1996–97 graduates, 95% were employed within three months of graduation; the average starting salary was $38,000. Types of employment entered: accounting, banking, computer-related, consulting, consumer products, education, finance, financial services, government, health services, hospitality management, human resources, information systems/technology, man-

agement, manufacturing, marketing, media, nonprofit, pharmaceutical, retail, service industry, utilities.

Business Program(s) URL: http://www.hamptonu.edu/

Program Contact: Dr. Sharon Hope, Director, MBA Program, School of Business, Hampton, VA 23668-0001. Phone: 757-727-5863; Fax: 757-727-5048.

James Madison University

College of Business

Harrisonburg, Virginia

OVERVIEW
James Madison University is a state-supported, coed, comprehensive institution. Enrollment: 12,000 graduate, professional, and undergraduate students. Founded: 1908. The graduate business unit is in a small-town setting and is on a semester calendar.

HIGHLIGHTS

Enrollment Profile
Full-time: 30
Part-time: 120
Total: 150
Average Age: 29
Fall 1997 Average GPA: 2.85

International: 7%
Women: N/R
Minorities: N/R
Average Class Size: 15
Fall 1997 Average GMAT: N/R

Costs
Full-time tuition: N/R
Part-time tuition: $134 per credit hour (resident); $404 per credit hour (nonresident)

AACSB – The International Association for Management Education accredited

Degree(s) offered in conjunction with Thunderbird, The American Graduate School of International Management

GRADUATE BUSINESS PROGRAMS
Master of Business Administration (MBA) Full-time, part-time, distance learning option; 33 total credits required; 15 months to 6 years to complete program. Concentrations in health care, entrepreneurship, technology management.

ADMISSION
Applications For fall 1997 there were 30 applications for admission. Of those applying, 27 were accepted. Of those accepted, 23 enrolled.

Application Requirements GMAT score: minimum 500, application form, application fee, bachelor's degree, essay, minimum GPA: 2.75, 2 letters of recommendation, resume, college transcript(s), minimum of 2 years of work experience.

Application Deadline Applications processed on a rolling/continuous basis for both domestic and international students. Application fee: $50.

ACADEMICS
Faculty Full-time 40.

Teaching Methodologies Case study, experiential learning, field projects, group discussion, lecture, research, student presentations, study groups, team projects.

Technology Computer terminals/PCs are available for student use and are linked by a campus-wide network. The network has full access to the Internet. Students are not required to have their own PC.

Special Opportunities Advanced credit may be earned through transfer of credits from another institution. International exchange programs in Germany, Hong Kong, Japan, Switzerland.

FINANCES
Costs for 1997–98 Tuition: $134 per credit hour (resident); $404 per credit hour (nonresident).

Financial Aid Fellowships, teaching assistantships, grants, scholarships, work study available. Financial aid is available to part-time students. Application Deadline: 2/15.

Financial Aid Contact Financial Aid Office, Harrisonburg, VA 22807. Phone: 540-568-7820.

FACILITIES
Information Resources Carrier Library plus 1 additional on-campus library; total holdings of 352,160 volumes, 1,273,176 microforms, 2,312 current periodical subscriptions. CD player(s) available for graduate student use. Access provided to online bibliographic retrieval services.

INTERNATIONAL STUDENTS
Demographics 7% of students enrolled are international students.

Services and Facilities International student office, international student center, visa services, counseling/support services.

James Madison University (continued)

Applying TOEFL: minimum score of 500, proof of adequate funds required.
International Student Contact Graduate School, Harrisonburg, VA 22807. Phone: 540-568-6131.

Business Program(s) URL: http://www.jmu.edu

Program Contact: MBA Program Office, James Madison University, Harrisonburg, VA 22807. Phone: 540-568-3253.

Lynchburg College

School of Business and Economics

Lynchburg, Virginia

OVERVIEW
Lynchburg College is an independent-religious, coed, comprehensive institution. Enrollment: 21 full-time matriculated graduate/professional students; 66 part-time matriculated graduate/professional students. Founded: 1903. The graduate business unit is in an urban setting and is on a semester calendar.

HIGHLIGHTS

Enrollment Profile

Full-time: 21

Part-time: 66

Total: 87

Average Age: N/R

Fall 1997 Average GPA: 3.1

International: 2%

Women: 40%

Minorities: 5%

Average Class Size: 14

Fall 1997 Average GMAT: 510

Costs

Full-time tuition: N/R

Part-time tuition: $255 per hour

GRADUATE BUSINESS PROGRAMS
Two-year MBA (MBA) Full-time, part-time; 48 total credits required; 2 to 5 years to complete program.

One-year MBA (MBA) Full-time, part-time; 30 total credits required; must have undergraduate business degree; 12 months to 5 years to complete program.

Corporate MBA (MBA) Part-time, distance learning option; 48 total credits required; 2 years to complete program. Concentration in management.

ADMISSION
Applications For fall 1997 there were 29 applications for admission. Of those applying, 21 were accepted. Of those accepted, 21 enrolled.

Application Requirements Application form, application fee, bachelor's degree, minimum GPA: 2.5, 3 letters of recommendation, personal statement, college transcript(s).

Recommended for Application GMAT score accepted: minimum 400, interview, work experience, computer experience.

Application Deadline 6/1 for summer, 5/1 for summer (international). Application fee: $30.

ACADEMICS
Faculty Full-time 14; part-time 6.

Teaching Methodologies Case study, computer analysis, computer simulations, experiential learning, faculty seminars, field projects, group discussion, lecture, research, role playing, seminars by members of the business community, simulations, student presentations, study groups, team projects.

Technology 218 on-campus computer terminals/PCs are available for student use and are linked by a campus-wide network. The network has full access to the Internet. Students are not required to have their own PC.

Special Opportunities Advanced credit may be earned through credit by examination, transfer of credits from another institution. International exchange programs in Canada, England, Japan, Republic of Korea. An internship program is available.

FINANCES
Costs for 1997–98 Tuition: $255 per hour. Fees: $1000 per program. Average 1997–98 room and board costs were $4400 per academic year. Room and board costs vary by campus location, occupancy (e.g., single, double, triple), type of accommodation, type of meal plan.

Financial Aid In 1997–98, 11% of students received some institutionally administered aid in the form of research assistantships, teaching assistantships, grants, loans. Application Deadline: 5/1.

Financial Aid Contact Ms. Sarah Snow, Director of Financial Aid, 1501 Lakeside Drive, Lynchburg, VA 24501. Phone: 804-544-8228; Fax: 804-544-8653; E-mail: snow@lynchburg.edu

FACILITIES
Information Resources Knight-Capron Library; total holdings of 161,920 volumes, 200,000 microforms, 711 current periodical subscriptions. CD player(s) available for graduate student use. Access provided to online bibliographic retrieval services and online databases.

INTERNATIONAL STUDENTS
Demographics 2% of students enrolled are international students [South America, 100%].

Services and Facilities International student office, visa services, counseling/support services.

Applying TOEFL: minimum score of 550, proof of adequate funds required. TWE, proof of health/immunizations recommended. Financial aid is not available to international students.

International Student Contact Ms. Annette Stadtherr, Enrollment Counselor, Enrollment Services, 150 Lakeside Drive, Lynchburg, VA 24501. Phone: 800-426-8101; Fax: 804-544-8653; E-mail: stadtherr@lynchburg.edu

PLACEMENT
Services include alumni network, career counseling/planning, career fairs, career library, career placement, electronic job bank, job interviews arranged, job search course, and resume preparation.

Employment Of 1996–97 graduates, 97% were employed within three months of graduation. Types of employment entered: accounting, banking, education, engineering, finance, financial services, high technology, human resources, information systems/technology, insurance, management, manufacturing, marketing, nonprofit.

Business Program(s) URL: http://www.lynchburg.edu/business/

Program Contact: Dr. David Behrs, Vice President of Enrollment, 1501 Lakeside Drive, Lynchburg, VA 24501-3199. Phone: 804-544-8300, 800-426-8101; Fax: 804-544-8653; E-mail: behrs@lynchburg.edu

Marymount University

School of Business Administration

Arlington, Virginia

OVERVIEW
Marymount University is an independent-religious, coed, comprehensive institution. Enrollment: 3,695 graduate, professional, and undergraduate students; 367 full-time matriculated graduate/professional students; 1,354 part-time matriculated graduate/professional students. Founded: 1950. The graduate business unit is in a suburban setting and is on a semester calendar.

HIGHLIGHTS

Enrollment Profile

Full-time: 84

Part-time: 824

Total: 908

Average Age: 35

Fall 1997 Average GPA: 3.0

International: 4%

Women: 61%

Minorities: 19%

Average Class Size: 16

Fall 1997 Average GMAT: 500

Costs

Full-time tuition: N/R

Part-time tuition: $465 per credit hour

ACBSP – The American Council of Business Schools and Programs accredited

GRADUATE BUSINESS PROGRAMS
Master of Business Administration (MBA) Full-time, part-time; 36-63 total credits required; 12 months to 5 years to complete program. Concentration in management.

Master of Science in Information Management (MS) Full-time, part-time; 36 total credits required; 12 months to 5 years to complete program. Concentration in information management.

Master of Arts in Legal Administration (MA) Full-time, part-time; 36 total credits required; 12 months to 5 years to complete program. Concentration in legal administration.

Master of Science in Health Care Management (MS) Full-time, part-time; 36 total credits required; 12 months to 5 years to complete program. Concentration in health care.

Master of Arts in Human Resource Management (MA) Full-time, part-time; 36 total credits required; 12 months to 5 years to complete program. Concentration in human resources.

Master of Arts in Human Performance Systems (MA) Full-time, part-time; 36 total credits required; 12 months to 5 years to complete program. Concentration in human resources.

Master of Arts in Organization Development (MA) Full-time, part-time; 36 total credits required; 12 months to 5 years to complete program. Concentration in organizational behavior/development.

Master of Science in Organizational Leadership and Innovation (MS) Full-time, part-time; 36 total credits required; 12 months to 5 years to complete program. Concentration in leadership.

ADMISSION

Applications For fall 1997 there were 377 applications for admission. Of those applying, 291 were accepted. Of those accepted, 222 enrolled.

Application Requirements Application form, application fee, bachelor's degree, essay, minimum GPA, interview, 2 letters of recommendation, personal statement, college transcript(s).

Recommended for Application GMAT score accepted, GRE score accepted, resume, work experience, computer experience.

Application Deadline Applications processed on a rolling/continuous basis for both domestic and international students. Application fee: $35. Deferred entrance is available.

ACADEMICS

Faculty Full-time 35; part-time 50.

Teaching Methodologies Case study, computer-aided instruction, computer analysis, computer simulations, experiential learning, field projects, group discussion, lecture, research, role playing, seminars by members of the business community, simulations, student presentations, study groups, team projects.

Technology 550 on-campus computer terminals/PCs are available for student use and are linked by a campus-wide network. The network has full access to the Internet. Students are not required to have their own PC.

Special Opportunities Advanced credit may be earned through transfer of credits from another institution.

FINANCES

Costs for 1997–98 Tuition: $465 per credit hour. Cost varies by number of credits taken. Fees: $5 per credit hour. Fees vary by number of credits taken. Average 1997–98 room and board costs were $5980 per academic year. Room and board costs vary by occupancy (e.g., single, double, triple).

Financial Aid In 1997–98, 15% of students received some institutionally administered aid in the form of fellowships, grants, loans. Financial aid is available to part-time students.

Financial Aid Contact Ms. Debbie Raines, Director of Financial Aid, 2807 North Glebe Road, Arlington, VA 22207-4299. Phone: 703-284-1530; Fax: 703-516-4771; E-mail: draines@marymount.edu

FACILITIES

Information Resources Reinsch Library plus 1 additional on-campus library; total holdings of 176,213 volumes, 255,755 microforms, 1,072 current periodical subscriptions. CD player(s) available for graduate student use. Access provided to online bibliographic retrieval services and online databases.

INTERNATIONAL STUDENTS

Demographics 4% of students enrolled are international students [Africa, 8%, Asia, 41%, Central America, 6%, Europe, 18%, South America, 21%, other, 6%].

Services and Facilities International student office, international student housing, ESL courses, counseling/support services.

Applying TOEFL: minimum score of 600 required. Financial aid is not available to international students.

International Student Contact Sr. Irene Cody, International Admissions Counselor, 2807 North Glebe Road, Arlington, VA 22207-4299. Phone: 703-522-5600; Fax: 703-522-0349; E-mail: admissions@marymount.edu

PLACEMENT

Services include alumni network, career counseling/planning, career fairs, career library, job interviews arranged, resume referral to employers, and resume preparation. In 1996–97, 86 organizations participated in on-campus recruiting.

Employment Types of employment entered: accounting, computer-related, consulting, financial services, government, health services, high technology, human resources, information systems/technology, law, management, telecommunications.

Business Program(s) URL: http://www.marymount.edu

Program Contact: Dr. Timothy McCrudden, Coordinator of Graduate Business Admissions, Ballston Campus, School of Business Administration, 2807 North Glebe Road, Arlington, VA 22207-4299. Phone: 703-284-5901, 800-548-7638; Fax: 703-527-3815; E-mail: admissions@marymount.edu

Old Dominion University

College of Business and Public Administration

Norfolk, Virginia

OVERVIEW

Old Dominion University is a state-supported, coed university. Enrollment: 16,490 graduate, professional, and undergraduate students; 1,415 full-time matriculated graduate/professional students; 2,135 part-time matriculated graduate/professional students. Founded: 1930. The graduate business unit is in an urban setting and is on a semester calendar.

HIGHLIGHTS

Enrollment Profile

Full-time: 155	International: 20%
Part-time: 415	Women: 40%
Total: 570	Minorities: 12%
Average Age: 31	Average Class Size: 25
Fall 1997 Average GPA: 3.0	Fall 1997 Average GMAT: 530

Costs
Full-time tuition: N/R
Part-time tuition: $180 per credit (resident); $477 per credit (nonresident)

AACSB – The International Association for Management Education accredited

GRADUATE BUSINESS PROGRAMS

Master of Business Administration (MBA) Full-time, part-time, distance learning option; 49 total credits required; 16 months to 4.1 years to complete program. Concentrations in accounting, finance, international business, management, management information systems, marketing, public policy and administration, health care, information management.

Master of Taxation (MTax) Full-time, part-time, distance learning option; minimum of 2 years to complete program.

Master of Science in Accounting (MSA) Full-time, part-time; minimum of 2 years to complete program.

Master of Arts (MA) Full-time, part-time; minimum of 20 months to complete program. Concentration in economics.

ADMISSION

Applications For fall 1997 there were 309 applications for admission. Of those applying, 256 were accepted. Of those accepted, 197 enrolled.

Application Requirements GMAT score, application form, application fee, bachelor's degree, essay, minimum GPA: 2.5, letter of recommendation, personal statement, college transcript(s).

Recommended for Application Work experience.

Application Deadline 7/1 for fall, 11/1 for spring, 4/1 for summer, 4/1 for fall (international), 10/1 for spring (international), 2/1 for summer (international). Application fee: $30. Deferred entrance is available.

ACADEMICS

Faculty Full-time 105; part-time 4.

Teaching Methodologies Case study, computer analysis, experiential learning, field projects, group discussion, lecture, research, seminars by members of the business community, student presentations, study groups, team projects.

Technology 100 on-campus computer terminals/PCs are available for student use and are linked by a campus-wide network. The network has full access to the Internet. Students are not required to have their own PC.

Special Opportunities Advanced credit may be earned through credit by examination, credit for experience, transfer of credits from another institution. International exchange programs in Australia, Costa Rica, Denmark, Japan, Mexico, Republic of Korea, United Kingdom. An internship program is available.

FINANCES

Costs for 1997–98 Tuition: $180 per credit (resident); $477 per credit (nonresident). Cost varies by campus location. Fees: $48 per semester (resident); $48 per semester (nonresident). Fees vary by number of credits taken. Average 1997–98 room and board costs were $5000 per academic year (on campus) and $5000 per academic year (off campus). Room and board costs vary by occupancy (e.g., single, double, triple), type of accommodation, type of meal plan.

Financial Aid In 1997–98, 8% of students received some institutionally administered aid in the form of fellowships, research assistantships, work study, loans. Financial aid is available to part-time students. Application Deadline: 2/15.

Financial Aid Contact Dr. Bruce Rubin, Jr., Director, MBA Program, 111 Constant Hall, Norfolk, VA 23529. Phone: 757-683-3585; Fax: 757-683-5750.

FACILITIES

Information Resources University Library plus 1 additional on-campus library; total holdings of 842,328 volumes, 1,110,477 microforms, 6,835 current periodical subscriptions. CD player(s) available for graduate student use. Access provided to online bibliographic retrieval services.

INTERNATIONAL STUDENTS

Demographics 20% of students enrolled are international students [Asia, 29%, Central America, 2%, Europe, 40%, South America, 2%, other, 27%].

Services and Facilities International student office, international student center, international student housing, visa services, ESL courses, counseling/support services.

Applying TOEFL: minimum score of 550, proof of adequate funds, proof of health/immunizations required. Financial aid is not available to international students.

International Student Contact Ms. Jan Aycock, Director, International Admissions, Dragas International Center, Norfolk, VA 23529. Phone: 757-683-3701; Fax: 757-683-5196; E-mail: jaycock@odu.edu

PLACEMENT

Services include alumni network, career counseling/planning, career fairs, career library, career placement, electronic job bank, job interviews arranged, job search course, resume referral to employers, and resume preparation. In 1996–97, 60 organizations participated in on-campus recruiting; 475 on-campus interviews were conducted.

Employment Types of employment entered: accounting, banking, communications, computer-related, consumer products, engineering, finance, financial services, government, health services, high technology, information systems/technology, insurance, international trade, management, manufacturing, marketing, media, nonprofit, real estate, retail, service industry, telecommunications, transportation, utilities.

Business Program(s) URL: http://www.odu.edu

Program Contact: Dr. Bruce Rubin, Director, MBA Program, 111 Constant Hall, Norfolk, VA 23529. Phone: 757-683-3585; Fax: 757-683-5750; E-mail: brubin@odu.edu

Radford University

College of Business and Economics

Radford, Virginia

OVERVIEW

Radford University is a state-supported, coed, comprehensive institution. Enrollment: 8,534 graduate, professional, and undergraduate students; 521 full-time matriculated graduate/professional students; 679 part-time matriculated graduate/professional students. Founded: 1910. The graduate business unit is in a small-town setting and is on a semester calendar.

HIGHLIGHTS

Enrollment Profile

Full-time: 39	International: 22%
Part-time: 57	Women: 42%
Total: 96	Minorities: 29%
Average Age: 30	Average Class Size: 15
Fall 1997 Average GPA: 2.93	Fall 1997 Average GMAT: 500

Costs
Full-time tuition: $2240 per academic year (resident); $5518 per academic year (nonresident)
Part-time tuition: $142 per credit hour (resident); $278 per credit hour (nonresident)

AACSB – The International Association for Management Education accredited

GRADUATE BUSINESS PROGRAMS

Master of Business Administration (MBA) Full-time, part-time; 30 total credits required; 12 months to 5 years to complete program. Concentrations in accounting, finance, management, marketing, information management.

Master of Science in International Economics (MS) Full-time, part-time; 30 total credits required; 12 months to 5 years to complete program. Concentrations in international economics, international finance, international trade.

ADMISSION

Applications For fall 1997 there were 111 applications for admission. Of those applying, 70 were accepted. Of those accepted, 44 enrolled.

Application Requirements GMAT score: minimum 450, application form, application fee, bachelor's degree, minimum GPA: 2.7, 2 letters of recommendation, college transcript(s).

Recommended for Application GRE score accepted: minimum 1,000, MAT score accepted: minimum 50, personal statement, resume, computer experience.

Application Deadline Applications processed on a rolling/continuous basis for both domestic and international students. Application fee: $25. Deferred entrance is available.

ACADEMICS

Faculty Full-time 28; part-time 6.

Teaching Methodologies Case study, computer-aided instruction, computer analysis, computer simulations, experiential learning, field projects, group discussion, lecture, research, role playing, simulations, student presentations, study groups, team projects.

Technology 700 on-campus computer terminals/PCs are available for student use and are linked by a campus-wide network. The network has full access to the Internet. Students are not required to have their own PC.

Special Opportunities Advanced credit may be earned through transfer of credits from another institution. International exchange program in Belgium. An internship program is available.

FINANCES

Costs for 1997–98 Tuition: Full-time: $2240 per year (resident); $5518 per year (nonresident). Part-time: $142 per credit hour (resident); $278 per credit hour (nonresident). Cost varies by number of credits taken. Fees: Full-time: $1164 per academic year (resident); $1164 per academic year (nonresident). Fees vary by number of credits taken. Average 1997–98 room and board costs were $4416 per academic year (on campus) and $5500 per academic year (off campus). Room and board costs vary by occupancy (e.g., single, double, triple), type of meal plan.

Financial Aid In 1997–98, 52% of students received some institutionally administered aid in the form of fellowships, teaching assistantships, grants, scholarships, work study. Application Deadline: 4/1.

Financial Aid Contact Mr. Herbert H. Johnston, Director, Financial Aid, Box 6905, Radford, VA 24142. Phone: 540-831-5408; Fax: 540-831-5138; E-mail: bjohnston@runet.edu

FACILITIES

Information Resources McConnell Library; total holdings of 312,131 volumes, 1,414,198 microforms, 3,292 current periodical subscriptions. CD player(s) available for graduate student use. Access provided to online bibliographic retrieval services and online databases.

INTERNATIONAL STUDENTS

Demographics 22% of students enrolled are international students [Africa, 71%, Europe, 19%, South America, 10%].

Services and Facilities International student office, international student center, visa services, ESL courses, counseling/support services.

Applying TOEFL: minimum score of 550 required. Financial aid is not available to international students.

International Student Contact Ms. Jane Wemhoener, Director, International Programs, Box 7002, Radford, VA 24142. Phone: 540-831-6200; Fax: 540-831-6619; E-mail: jwemhoen@runet.edu

PLACEMENT

Services include alumni network, career counseling/planning, career fairs, career placement, job interviews arranged, job search course, resume referral to employers, and resume preparation. In 1996–97, 75 organizations participated in on-campus recruiting; 50 on-campus interviews were conducted.

Employment Of 1996–97 graduates, 92% were employed within three months of graduation; the average starting salary was $36,000. Types of employment entered: accounting, banking, communications, computer-related, consulting, consumer products, education, engineering, finance, financial services, government, health services, high technology, hospitality management, human resources, information systems/technology, insurance, international trade, management, manufacturing, marketing, media, nonprofit, petrochemical, real estate, retail, service industry, telecommunications, transportation, utilities.

Business Program(s) URL: http://www.runet.edu

Program Contact: Dr. Wayne Saubert, Director, MBA Program, Box 6956, Radford, VA 24142. Phone: 540-831-5258, 800-890-4265; Fax: 540-831-6655; E-mail: rumba@runet.edu

Regent University

School of Business

Virginia Beach, Virginia

OVERVIEW

Regent University is an independent-nonprofit, coed, graduate institution. Enrollment: 1,389 graduate, professional, and undergraduate students; 1,042 full-time matriculated graduate/professional students; 347 part-time matriculated graduate/professional students. Founded: 1977. The graduate business unit is in a suburban setting and is on a trimester calendar.

HIGHLIGHTS

Enrollment Profile

Full-time: 134
Part-time: 104
Total: 238
Average Age: 35
Fall 1997 Average GPA: 3.0

International: 6%
Women: 28%
Minorities: 17%
Average Class Size: 20
Fall 1997 Average GMAT: N/R

Costs

Full-time tuition: $11,700 per academic year
Part-time tuition: $325 per credit hour

Regent University School of Business takes a unique approach in graduate business education, one that has its foundation in Judeo-Christian ethics. Regent graduates possess the values, integrity, and business skills that are just what today's top executives look for in the managers they hire and the partners they select.

Servant leadership can be seen in organizations whose leaders serve their employees—employees who in turn serve the customer. Such organizations consistently outperform their competitors. For example, Sam Walton, by empowering his employees to serve the customer, built the Wal-Mart chain from a single store to the largest retail company world. Similarly, the Toro Corporation used principles of servant management to turn a dying company into a robust and vigorous enterprise.

To help integrate these principles in a relevant and meaningful way, the Regent School of Business offers a rare balance of faith and business expertise in accredited graduate school programs. While all courses are taught from a Judeo-Christian perspective, Regent is not a Bible school. It simply approaches its academic offerings from the postulate that there is a right way and a wrong way to do business. These ethical standards of honesty, fairness, and service produce graduates who are both personally and financially successful.

Regent School of Business gives its students more than the competitive benefit of a graduate degree. It offers spiritual applications for life and career.

GRADUATE BUSINESS PROGRAMS

Master of Business Administration (MBA) Full-time, part-time, distance learning option; 57 total credits required; 12 months to 5 years to complete program. Concentrations in financial management/planning, international business, marketing, entrepreneurship, nonprofit management.

Master of Arts in Management (MA) Full-time, part-time, distance learning option; 39 total credits required; 12 months to 5 years to complete program. Concentrations in financial management/planning, international business, marketing, entrepreneurship, nonprofit management.

ADMISSION

Applications For fall 1997 there were 139 applications for admission. Of those applying, 120 were accepted. Of those accepted, 70 enrolled.

Application Requirements Application form, application fee, bachelor's degree, minimum GPA: 2.75, interview, 2 letters of recommendation, personal statement, resume, college transcript(s), computer experience: e-mail, internet, word processing.

Application Deadline Applications processed on a rolling/continuous basis for both domestic and international students. Application fee: $40. Deferred entrance is available.

ACADEMICS

Faculty Full-time 6; part-time 2.

Teaching Methodologies Case study, experiential learning, faculty seminars, field projects, group discussion, lecture, research, role playing, seminars by members of the business community, student presentations, study groups, team projects.

Technology 100 on-campus computer terminals/PCs are available for student use and are linked by a campus-wide network. The network has full access to the Internet. Students are required to have their own PC.

Special Opportunities Advanced credit may be earned through credit by examination, transfer of credits from another institution. An internship program is available.

FINANCES

Costs for 1997–98 Tuition: Full-time: $11,700 per year. Part-time: $325 per credit hour. Fees vary by academic program. Average 1997–98 room and board costs were $8000 per academic year (off campus). Room and board costs vary by occupancy (e.g., single, double, triple), type of accommodation.

Financial Aid In 1997–98, 24% of students received some institutionally administered aid in the form of grants, scholarships. Financial aid is available to part-time students. Application Deadline: 7/15.

Financial Aid Contact Tom Stansbury, Director of Marketing, Recruitment and Admissions, 1000 Regent University Drive, Virginia Beach, VA 23464-9800. Phone: 757-226-4356; Fax: 757-226-4369; E-mail: tomstan@regent.edu

FACILITIES

Information Resources University Library plus 1 additional on-campus library; total holdings of 269,491 volumes, 1,279,034 microforms, 3,900 current periodical subscriptions. CD player(s) available for graduate student use. Access provided to online bibliographic retrieval services.

INTERNATIONAL STUDENTS

Demographics 6% of students enrolled are international students.

Services and Facilities International student office, ESL courses, counseling/support services.

Applying TOEFL: minimum score of 550, proof of adequate funds, proof of health/immunizations required. Financial aid is available to international students.

International Student Contact Michael Gray, Enrollment Manager, 1000 Regent University Drive, Virginia Beach, VA 23464-9800. Phone: 757-226-4096; Fax: 757-226-4369; E-mail: michgra@regent.edu

PLACEMENT

Services include alumni network, career counseling/planning, career fairs, career library, career placement, electronic job bank, job search course, resume referral to employers, and resume preparation. In 1996–97, 30 organizations participated in on-campus recruiting; 15 on-campus interviews were conducted.

Employment Of 1996–97 graduates, 90% were employed within three months of graduation; the average starting salary was $30,000. Types of employment entered: accounting, banking, communications, computer-related, consulting, energy, financial services, hospitality management, human resources, information systems/technology, insurance, law, management, manufacturing, marketing, media, nonprofit, pharmaceutical, telecommunications.

Business Program(s) URL: http://www.regent.edu/acad/schbus/

Program Contact: Tom Stansbury, Director of Marketing, Recruitment and Admissions, 1000 Regent University Drive, Virginia Beach, VA 23464-9800. Phone: 757-226-4356, 800-477-3642; Fax: 757-226-4369; E-mail: tomstan@regent.edu
See full description on page 940.

Shenandoah University

Harry F. Byrd, Jr. School of Business

Winchester, Virginia

OVERVIEW

Shenandoah University is an independent-religious, coed, comprehensive institution. Enrollment: 1,933 graduate, professional, and undergraduate students; 433 full-time matriculated graduate/professional students; 234 part-time matriculated graduate/professional students. Founded: 1875. The graduate business unit is in a small-town setting and is on a trimester calendar.

HIGHLIGHTS

Enrollment Profile

Full-time: 23
Part-time: 58
Total: 81
Average Age: 33
Fall 1997 Average GPA: 3.1

International: 26%
Women: 38%
Minorities: 5%
Average Class Size: 15
Fall 1997 Average GMAT: 500

Costs

Full-time tuition: N/R
Part-time tuition: $450 per hour

Shenandoah University (continued)

GRADUATE BUSINESS PROGRAMS

Master of Business Administration (MBA) Full-time, part-time; 36 total credits required; 12 months to 2 years to complete program. Concentrations in accounting, banking, international business, management, marketing, health care, management information systems, public management.

ADMISSION

Applications For fall 1997 there were 35 applications for admission. Of those applying, 28 were accepted.

Application Requirements GMAT score, application form, application fee, bachelor's degree, essay, interview, 2 letters of recommendation, personal statement, resume, college transcript(s), computer experience: computer literacy.

Recommended for Application GRE score accepted, MAT score accepted, minimum GPA: 2.5.

Application Deadline Applications processed on a rolling/continuous basis for both domestic and international students. Application fee: $30. Deferred entrance is available.

ACADEMICS

Faculty Full-time 12; part-time 20.

Teaching Methodologies Case study, experiential learning, field projects, group discussion, lecture, role playing, student presentations, study groups, team projects.

Technology 50 on-campus computer terminals/PCs are available for student use and are linked by a campus-wide network. The network has full access to the Internet. Students are not required to have their own PC.

Special Opportunities Advanced credit may be earned through transfer of credits from another institution. International exchange programs in People's Republic of China, United Kingdom. An internship program is available.

FINANCES

Costs for 1997–98 Tuition: $450 per hour. Cost varies by academic program, number of credits taken. Average 1997–98 room and board costs were $7500 per academic year (on campus) and $5400 per academic year (off campus). Room and board costs vary by occupancy (e.g., single, double, triple), type of accommodation, type of meal plan.

Financial Aid In 1997–98, 25% of students received some institutionally administered aid in the form of fellowships, scholarships. Financial aid is available to part-time students. Application Deadline: 2/15.

Financial Aid Contact Ms. Nancy Bragg, Director, Financial Aid, 1460 University Drive, Winchester, VA 22601-5195. Phone: 540-665-4538; Fax: 540-665-5433; E-mail: nbragg@su.edu

FACILITIES

Information Resources Alson H. Smith Jr. Library plus 1 additional on-campus library; total holdings of 105,092 volumes, 59,744 microforms, 665 current periodical subscriptions. CD player(s) available for graduate student use. Access provided to online bibliographic retrieval services.

INTERNATIONAL STUDENTS

Demographics 26% of students enrolled are international students [Africa, 10%, Asia, 90%].

Services and Facilities International student office, international student center, ESL courses, counseling/support services.

Applying TOEFL: minimum score of 550, proof of adequate funds, proof of health/immunizations required. Financial aid is available to international students.

International Student Contact Dr. William Berghaus, Associate Vice President—Academic Programs, 1460 University Drive, Winchester, VA 22601-5195. Phone: 540-665-4520; Fax: 540-665-5433; E-mail: bberghau@su.edu

PLACEMENT

Services include alumni network, career counseling/planning, resume referral to employers, and resume preparation.

Employment Of 1996–97 graduates, 85% were employed within three months of graduation. Types of employment entered: accounting, banking, computer-related, education, finance, financial services, government, health services, management, marketing, telecommunications.

Business Program(s) URL: http://www.su.edu/bsb/

Program Contact: Mr. Michael Carpenter, Director of Admissions, 1460 University Drive, Winchester, VA 22601-5195. Phone: 540-665-4581; Fax: 540-665-4627; E-mail: mcarpent@su.edu

University of Richmond

The Richard S. Reynolds Graduate School

Richmond, Virginia

OVERVIEW

The University of Richmond is an independent-nonprofit, coed, comprehensive institution. Enrollment: 4,425 graduate, professional, and undergraduate students; 522 full-time matriculated graduate/professional students; 266 part-time matriculated graduate/professional students. Founded: 1830. The graduate business unit is in a suburban setting and is on a semester calendar.

HIGHLIGHTS

Enrollment Profile

Full-time: 7	International: 2%
Part-time: 260	Women: 37%
Total: 267	Minorities: 3%
Average Age: 29	Average Class Size: 21
Fall 1997 Average GPA: 3.0	Fall 1997 Average GMAT: 623

Costs

Full-time tuition: $17,670 per academic year
Part-time tuition: $870 per course

AACSB – The International Association for Management Education accredited

GRADUATE BUSINESS PROGRAMS

Master of Business Administration (MBA) Full-time, part-time; 51 total credits required; 10 months to 5 years to complete program.

Master of Business Administration/Doctor of Jurisprudence (MBA/JD) Full-time; 110-125 total credits required; 3 to 4 years to complete program.

ADMISSION

Applications For fall 1997 there were 52 applications for admission. Of those applying, 25 were accepted. Of those accepted, 22 enrolled.

Application Requirements Application form, application fee, bachelor's degree, minimum GPA, college transcript(s), minimum of 2 years of work experience.

Recommended for Application GMAT score accepted: minimum 540.

Application Deadline 7/1 for fall, 11/1 for spring, 3/1 for summer, 5/1 for fall (international), 9/1 for spring (international), 1/1 for summer (international). Application fee: $25. Deferred entrance is available.

ACADEMICS

Faculty Full-time 42; part-time 9.

Teaching Methodologies Case study, computer-aided instruction, computer analysis, computer simulations, field projects, group discussion, lecture, research, role playing, seminars by members of the business community, simulations, student presentations, study groups, team projects.

Technology 149 on-campus computer terminals/PCs are available for student use and are linked by a campus-wide network. The network has full access to the Internet. Students are not required to have their own PC.

Special Opportunities Advanced credit may be earned through transfer of credits from another institution.

FINANCES

Costs for 1997–98 Tuition: Full-time: $17,670 per year. Part-time: $870 per course. Cost varies by academic program, number of credits taken.

Financial Aid In 1997–98, 8% of students received some institutionally administered aid in the form of research assistantships, loans. Financial aid is available to part-time students. Application Deadline: 7/1.

Financial Aid Contact Ms. Cynthia Bolger, Director, Financial Aid Office, Sarah Brunet Hall, Richmond, VA 23173. Phone: 804-289-8438; Fax: 804-289-6003; E-mail: cbolger@richmond.edu

FACILITIES

Information Resources Boatwright Memorial Library plus 4 additional on-campus libraries; total holdings of 500,000 volumes, 120,000 microforms, 6,000 current periodical subscriptions. CD player(s) available for graduate student use. Access provided to online bibliographic retrieval services and online databases.

INTERNATIONAL STUDENTS

Demographics 2% of students enrolled are international students [Asia, 75%, Europe, 25%].

Services and Facilities International student office, visa services, counseling/support services.

Applying TOEFL: minimum score of 550, proof of adequate funds, proof of health/immunizations required. Financial aid is available to international students.

International Student Contact Dr. Robert Phillips, Director, Richmond, VA 23173. Phone: 804-289-8000; Fax: 804-289-8943.

PLACEMENT
Services include alumni network, career counseling/planning, career fairs, career library, career placement, electronic job bank, job interviews arranged, resume referral to employers, and resume preparation. In 1996–97, 200 organizations participated in on-campus recruiting; 1,800 on-campus interviews were conducted.

Employment Types of employment entered: accounting, banking, computer-related, consulting, consumer products, finance, financial services, human resources, information systems/technology, insurance, management, manufacturing, marketing, pharmaceutical, service industry, utilities.

Business Program(s) URL: http://www.richmond.edu/business/mba/

Program Contact: Ms. Arlene Davis, Administrative Assistant, The E. Claiborne Robins School of Business, Richmond, VA 23173. Phone: 804-289-8553; Fax: 804-287-6544; E-mail: davis@richmond.edu

University of Virginia

Darden Graduate School of Business Administration

Charlottesville, Virginia

OVERVIEW
The University of Virginia is a state-supported, coed university. Enrollment: 18,417 graduate, professional, and undergraduate students; 5,427 full-time matriculated graduate/professional students; 408 part-time matriculated graduate/professional students. Founded: 1819. The graduate business unit is in a small-town setting and is on a semester calendar.

HIGHLIGHTS

Enrollment Profile

Full-time: 497	International: 16%
Part-time: 0	Women: 30%
Total: 497	Minorities: 25%
Average Age: 28	Average Class Size: 40
Fall 1997 Average GPA: 3.3	Fall 1997 Average GMAT: 660

Costs
Full-time tuition: $13,835 per academic year (resident); $20,429 per academic year (nonresident)
Part-time tuition: N/R

AACSB – The International Association for Management Education accredited

Degree(s) offered in conjunction with Hong Kong University of Science and Technology, Solvay Business School in Brussels, International University of Japan

GRADUATE BUSINESS PROGRAMS
Master of Business Administration (MBA) Full-time; 78 total credits required; up to 2 years to complete program.

Master of Business Administration/Master of Arts (MBA/MA) Full-time; up to 3 years to complete program.

Master of Business Administration/Doctor of Jurisprudence (MBA/JD) Full-time; up to 4 years to complete program.

Master of Business Administration/Master of Engineering (MBA/ME) Full-time; 93 total credits required; up to 3 years to complete program.

Master of Business Administration/Master of Science in Nursing (MBA/MS) Full-time; 93 total credits required; up to 3 years to complete program.

Master of Business Administration/Doctor of Philosophy (MBA/PhD) Full-time; up to 4 years to complete program.

ADMISSION
Applications For fall 1997 there were 3,111 applications for admission. Of those applying, 489 were accepted. Of those accepted, 248 enrolled.

Application Requirements GMAT score, application form, application fee, essay, minimum GPA, letters of recommendation, personal statement, college transcript(s), work experience.

Recommended for Application Bachelor's degree, interview, computer experience.

Application Deadline 4/1 for fall, 4/1 for fall (international). Application fee: $100. Deferred entrance is available.

ACADEMICS
Faculty Full-time 53; part-time 34.

Teaching Methodologies Case study, computer-aided instruction, computer analysis, computer simulations, experiential learning, field projects, group discus-

sion, lecture, research, role playing, seminars by members of the business community, simulations, student presentations, study groups, team projects.

Technology 56 on-campus computer terminals/PCs are available for student use and are linked by a campus-wide network. The network has full access to the Internet. Students are required to have their own PC.

Special Opportunities International exchange programs in Belgium, Hong Kong, Japan.

FINANCES
Costs for 1997–98 Tuition: Full-time: $13,835 per year (resident); $20,429 per year (nonresident). Average 1997–98 room and board costs were $11,560 per academic year (off campus).

Financial Aid In 1997–98, 81% of students received some institutionally administered aid in the form of fellowships, scholarships, loans. Application Deadline: 5/1.

Financial Aid Contact Mr. Laurence Mueller, PO Box 6550, Charlottesville, VA 22906. Phone: 804-924-7559; Fax: 804-924-4859; E-mail: griffine@darden.gbus.virginia.edu

FACILITIES
Information Resources Alderman Library plus 16 additional on-campus libraries; total holdings of 4,059,252 volumes, 4,224,549 microforms, 38,192 current periodical subscriptions. Access provided to online bibliographic retrieval services and online databases.

INTERNATIONAL STUDENTS
Demographics 16% of students enrolled are international students.

Services and Facilities International student office, international student center, counseling/support services.

Applying TOEFL, proof of adequate funds, proof of health/immunizations required. Financial aid is available to international students.

International Student Contact Ms. Suzanne Louis, Associate Director, Exchange Visitor Program Office, Minor Hall 209, Charlottesville, VA 22903. Phone: 804-982-3015; Fax: 804-982-3011; E-mail: sl@virginia.edu

PLACEMENT
Services include alumni network, career counseling/planning, career fairs, career library, career placement, electronic job bank, job interviews arranged, job search course, resume referral to employers, and resume preparation. In 1996–97, 191 organizations participated in on-campus recruiting; 4,763 on-campus interviews were conducted.

Employment Of 1996–97 graduates, 100% were employed within three months of graduation; the average starting salary was $74,000. Types of employment entered: accounting, banking, chemical industry, communications, computer-related, consulting, consumer products, education, engineering, finance, financial services, government, health services, high technology, hospitality management, human resources, information systems/technology, insurance, international trade, law, management, manufacturing, marketing, media, mining, nonprofit, petrochemical, pharmaceutical, real estate, retail, service industry, telecommunications, transportation, utilities.

Business Program(s) URL: http://www.darden.virginia.edu

Program Contact: Mr. A. Jon Megibow, Director of Admissions, PO Box 6550, Charlottesville, VA 22906. Phone: 804-924-7281, 800-UVA-MBA-1; Fax: 804-924-4859; E-mail: darden@virginia.edu

Virginia Commonwealth University

School of Business

Richmond, Virginia

OVERVIEW
Virginia Commonwealth University is a state-supported, coed university. Enrollment: 22,702 graduate, professional, and undergraduate students; 3,680 full-time matriculated graduate/professional students; 1,963 part-time matriculated graduate/professional students. Founded: 1837. The graduate business unit is in an urban setting and is on a semester calendar.

VIRGINIA

Virginia Commonwealth University (continued)

HIGHLIGHTS

Enrollment Profile
Full-time: 108
Part-time: 355
Total: 463
Average Age: 32
Fall 1997 Average GPA: 3.0

International: 8%
Women: 41%
Minorities: 9%
Average Class Size: 25
Fall 1997 Average GMAT: 560

Costs
Full-time tuition: $3810 per academic year (resident); $12,265 per academic year (nonresident)
Part-time tuition: $212 per credit (resident); $627 per credit (nonresident)

AACSB – The International Association for Management Education accredited

GRADUATE BUSINESS PROGRAMS
Master of Business Administration (MBA) Full-time, part-time, distance learning option; 30 total credits required; 12 months to 5 years to complete program. Concentrations in accounting, decision sciences, economics, finance, human resources, marketing, real estate, risk management.
Fast Track MBA (MBA) Part-time; 39 total credits required; up to 18 months to complete program.
Master of Arts in Economics (MA) Full-time, part-time, distance learning option; 30 total credits required; 12 months to 5 years to complete program. Concentrations in economics, financial economics.
Master of Science in Business (MS) Full-time, part-time, distance learning option; 30 total credits required; 12 months to 5 years to complete program. Concentrations in decision sciences, economics, finance, human resources, marketing, real estate, risk management.
Master of Taxation (MTax) Full-time, part-time, distance learning option; 30 total credits required; 12 months to 5 years to complete program. Concentration in taxation.

ADMISSION
Applications For fall 1997 there were 362 applications for admission. Of those applying, 206 were accepted. Of those accepted, 96 enrolled.
Application Requirements GMAT score: minimum 550, application form, application fee, bachelor's degree, minimum GPA: 2.7, interview, 3 letters of recommendation, personal statement, college transcript(s).
Recommended for Application Resume, minimum of 3 years of work experience.
Application Deadline 7/1 for fall, 12/1 for spring, 4/1 for summer, 4/1 for fall (international), 10/1 for spring (international), 2/1 for summer (international). Application fee: $30. Deferred entrance is available.

ACADEMICS
Faculty Full-time 90.
Teaching Methodologies Case study, computer-aided instruction, computer analysis, computer simulations, faculty seminars, field projects, group discussion, lecture, seminars by members of the business community, student presentations, study groups, team projects.
Technology 200 on-campus computer terminals/PCs are available for student use and are linked by a campus-wide network. The network has full access to the Internet. Students are not required to have their own PC.
Special Opportunities Advanced credit may be earned through transfer of credits from another institution. International exchange program in France. An internship program is available.

FINANCES
Costs for 1997–98 Tuition: Full-time: $3810 per year (resident); $12,265 per year (nonresident). Part-time: $212 per credit (resident); $627 per credit (nonresident). Cost varies by number of credits taken, reciprocity agreements. Fees: Full-time: $949 per academic year (resident); $949 per academic year (nonresident). Part-time: $36 per credit (resident); $36 per credit (nonresident). Fees vary by academic program, class time (e.g., day/evening), number of credits taken. Average 1997–98 room and board costs were $3000 per academic year (on campus) and $4500 per academic year (off campus). Room and board costs vary by occupancy (e.g., single, double, triple), type of accommodation, type of meal plan.
Financial Aid Fellowships, research assistantships, teaching assistantships, work study, loans available. Financial aid is available to part-time students. Application Deadline: 3/15.
Financial Aid Contact Sallie Reese, Program Support Tech, Box 844000, 1015 Floyd Avenue, Richmond, VA 23284-4000. Phone: 804-828-1741; Fax: 804-828-7174; E-mail: sreese@busnet.bus.vcu.edu

FACILITIES
Information Resources Cabell/Tompkins-McCaw Libraries; total holdings of 935,000 volumes, 8,300 current periodical subscriptions. CD player(s) available for graduate student use. Access provided to online bibliographic retrieval services and online databases.

INTERNATIONAL STUDENTS
Demographics 8% of students enrolled are international students [Asia, 78%, Australia/New Zealand, 3%, Europe, 5%, North America, 3%, other, 11%].
Services and Facilities International student office, international student center, ESL courses, counseling/support services.
Applying TOEFL: minimum score of 600, TSE, TWE, proof of adequate funds, proof of health/immunizations required. Financial aid is not available to international students.
International Student Contact Center for International Programs, 916 West Franklin Street, Box 843043, Richmond, VA 23284. Phone: 804-828-6016; Fax: 804-828-2552.

PLACEMENT
Services include alumni network, career counseling/planning, career fairs, career library, career placement, electronic job bank, job interviews arranged, and resume preparation.
Employment Of 1996–97 graduates, 95% were employed within three months of graduation; the average starting salary was $30,000.
Business Program(s) URL: http://www.vcu.edu/busweb/
Program Contact: Janice Covington, Senior Secretary, Box 844000, 1015 Floyd Avenue, Richmond, VA 23284-4000. Phone: 804-828-1741; Fax: 804-828-7174; E-mail: jcovington@busnet.bus.vcu.edu

Virginia Polytechnic Institute and State University

Pamplin College of Business
Blacksburg, Virginia

OVERVIEW
Virginia Polytechnic Institute and State University is a state-supported, coed university. Enrollment: 24,812 graduate, professional, and undergraduate students. Founded: 1872. The graduate business unit is in a small-town setting and is on a semester calendar.

HIGHLIGHTS

Enrollment Profile
Full-time: 300
Part-time: 450
Total: 750
Average Age: 25
Fall 1997 Average GPA: 3.21

International: N/R
Women: N/R
Minorities: N/R
Average Class Size: 30
Fall 1997 Average GMAT: 574

Costs
Full-time tuition: N/R
Part-time tuition: $229 per hour (resident); $374 per hour (nonresident)

AACSB – The International Association for Management Education accredited

GRADUATE BUSINESS PROGRAMS
Master of Business Administration (MBA) Full-time, part-time, distance learning option; 48 total credits required; 18 months to 2 years to complete program. Concentrations in management, management science, marketing, finance, human resources, leadership, international business, financial management/planning.
Master of Accountancy (MAcc) Full-time, part-time.

ADMISSION
Application Requirements GMAT score, application form, application fee, bachelor's degree, minimum GPA, 2 letters of recommendation, resume, college transcript(s), computer experience: word processing, statistics.
Application Deadline Applications processed on a rolling/continuous basis for both domestic and international students. Application fee: $25. Deferred entrance is available.

ACADEMICS
Teaching Methodologies Case study, computer-aided instruction, computer analysis, computer simulations, experiential learning, faculty seminars, field projects, group discussion, lecture, research, seminars by members of the business community, simulations, student presentations, study groups, team projects.
Special Opportunities International exchange program in Republic of Singapore.

FINANCES

Costs for 1997–98 Tuition: $229 per hour (resident); $374 per hour (nonresident). Cost varies by number of credits taken.

Financial Aid Fellowships, research assistantships, teaching assistantships, loans available.

Financial Aid Contact Ms. Joyce Bohr, Blacksburg, VA 24061-0202. Phone: 540-321-6152.

FACILITIES

Information Resources Carol M. Newman Library plus 3 additional on-campus libraries; total holdings of 1,545,000 volumes, 3,927,000 microforms, 17,200 current periodical subscriptions. Access provided to online bibliographic retrieval services.

INTERNATIONAL STUDENTS

Demographics N/R

Services and Facilities International student office, counseling/support services.

Applying TOEFL required.

International Student Contact Ms. Joyce Bohr, Blacksburg, VA 24061-0202. Phone: 540-231-6152.

PLACEMENT

Services include alumni network, resume referral to employers, and resume preparation.

Employment Types of employment entered: accounting, banking, chemical industry, communications, computer-related, consulting, consumer products, education, energy, engineering, finance, financial services, government, health services, high technology, hospitality management, human resources, information systems/technology, insurance, international trade, law, management, manufacturing, marketing, media, mining, nonprofit, petrochemical, pharmaceutical, real estate, retail, service industry, telecommunications, transportation, utilities.

Business Program(s) URL: http://www.cob.vt.edu/busweb/gradpag.htm

Program Contact: Ms. Joyce Bohr, Admissions Coordinator, 1044 Pamplin Hall, Blacksburg, VA 24061-0209. Phone: 540-231-6152; Fax: 540-231-4487; E-mail: mbainfo@vt.edu
See full description on page 1178.

Virginia State University

School of Business

Petersburg, Virginia

OVERVIEW

Virginia State University is a state-supported, coed, comprehensive institution. Enrollment: 4,007 graduate, professional, and undergraduate students; 74 full-time matriculated graduate/professional students; 406 part-time matriculated graduate/professional students. Founded: 1882.

HIGHLIGHTS

Enrollment Profile
Full-time: 3
Part-time: 9
Total: 12
Average Age: 25
Fall 1997 Average GPA: N/R

International: 0%
Women: 25%
Minorities: 67%
Average Class Size: N/R
Fall 1997 Average GMAT: N/R

Costs
Full-time tuition: N/R
Part-time tuition: $133 per credit hour (resident); $364 per credit hour (nonresident)

GRADUATE BUSINESS PROGRAMS

Master of Arts in Economics (MA) Full-time, part-time; 30-36 total credits required; 18 months to 6 years to complete program.

ADMISSION

Application Requirements Application form, application fee, bachelor's degree, college transcript(s).

Recommended for Application GRE score accepted, minimum GPA: 2.0.

Application Deadline Applications processed on a rolling/continuous basis for both domestic and international students. Application fee: $25.

ACADEMICS

Faculty Full-time 7.

Teaching Methodologies Group discussion, lecture, student presentations, study groups, team projects.

FINANCES

Costs for 1997–98 Tuition: $133 per credit hour (resident); $364 per credit hour (nonresident).

Financial Aid Fellowships, work study available.

Financial Aid Contact Financial Aid Office, Petersburg, VA 23806-0001. Phone: 804-524-5990.

FACILITIES

Information Resources Johnston Memorial Library; total holdings of 253,153 volumes, 551,139 microforms, 1,083 current periodical subscriptions. CD player(s) available for graduate student use. Access provided to online bibliographic retrieval services.

INTERNATIONAL STUDENTS

Demographics N/R

Services and Facilities International student office, counseling/support services.

Applying TOEFL: minimum score of 500 required.

Program Contact: Graduate School Admissions, Box 9080, Petersburg, VA 23806-0001. Phone: 804-524-5984; Fax: 804-524-5401.

WASHINGTON

Antioch University Seattle

Graduate Management Program

Seattle, Washington

OVERVIEW

Antioch University Seattle is an independent-nonprofit, coed, upper-level institution. Enrollment: 750 graduate, professional, and undergraduate students. The graduate business unit is in an urban setting and is on a quarter calendar.

HIGHLIGHTS

Enrollment Profile
Full-time: 45
Part-time: 0
Total: 45
Average Age: 39
Fall 1997 Average GPA: N/R

International: 2%
Women: 44%
Minorities: N/R
Average Class Size: 25
Fall 1997 Average GMAT: N/R

Costs
Full-time tuition: $12,500 per academic year
Part-time tuition: $380 per credit

GRADUATE BUSINESS PROGRAMS

Master of Science in Management (MS) Full-time; 66 total credits required; up to 20 months to complete program. Concentrations in business ethics, economics, finance, human resources, international business, leadership, management, operations management, organizational behavior/development, organizational management, quality management, strategic management, marketing.

ADMISSION

Applications For fall 1997 there were 28 applications for admission. Of those applying, 27 were accepted. Of those accepted, 20 enrolled.

Application Requirements Application form, application fee, bachelor's degree, essay, interview, 2 letters of recommendation, personal statement, resume, college transcript(s).

Recommended for Application Work experience.

Application Deadline 6/1 for fall, 6/1 for fall (international). Application fee: $50. Deferred entrance is available.

ACADEMICS

Faculty Full-time 3; part-time 2.

Teaching Methodologies Case study, computer simulations, experiential learning, faculty seminars, field projects, group discussion, lecture, research, seminars by members of the business community, simulations, student presentations, study groups, team projects.

Technology 9 on-campus computer terminals/PCs are available for student use and are linked by a campus-wide network. The network has partial access to the Internet. Students are required to have their own PC.

FINANCES

Costs for 1997–98 Tuition: Full-time: $12,500 per year. Part-time: $380 per credit. Fees: Full-time: $110 per academic year.

Financial Aid In 1997–98, 18% of students received some institutionally administered aid in the form of work study, loans. Application Deadline: 7/15.

Antioch University Seattle (continued)

Financial Aid Contact Financial Aid Officer, 2607 Second Avenue, Seattle, WA 98121-1211. Phone: 206-441-5352 Ext. 5003; Fax: 206-441-3307.

FACILITIES
Information Resources Antioch University Library; total holdings of 5,130 volumes, 20 current periodical subscriptions. CD player(s) available for graduate student use. Access provided to online bibliographic retrieval services.

INTERNATIONAL STUDENTS
Demographics 2% of students enrolled are international students.

Applying TOEFL: minimum score of 600, proof of adequate funds required. Financial aid is not available to international students.

International Student Contact Ms. Melessa Rogers, Office Manager, 2607 Second Avenue, Seattle, WA 98121-1211. Phone: 206-441-5352 Ext. 5701; Fax: 206-441-3307.

PLACEMENT
Services include alumni network, career counseling/planning, and job search course.

Employment Of 1996–97 graduates, 95% were employed within three months of graduation. Types of employment entered: accounting, banking, communications, computer-related, consulting, energy, financial services, government, health services, high technology, hospitality management, human resources, insurance, management, marketing, telecommunications, utilities.

Business Program(s) URL: http://www.seattleantioch.edu/GMP/default.html

Program Contact: Ms. Melessa Rogers, Office Manager, 2607 Second Avenue, Seattle, WA 98121-1211. Phone: 206-441-5352 Ext. 5701; Fax: 206-441-3307.

City University

Graduate School of Business and Management Professions

Bellevue, Washington

OVERVIEW
City University is an independent-nonprofit, coed, comprehensive institution. Enrollment: 13,970 graduate, professional, and undergraduate students; 1,211 full-time matriculated graduate/professional students; 4,709 part-time matriculated graduate/professional students. Founded: 1973. The graduate business unit is in a suburban setting and is on a quarter calendar.

HIGHLIGHTS

Enrollment Profile
Full-time: 450
Part-time: 2,819
Total: 3,269
Average Age: 37
Fall 1997 Average GPA: N/R

International: 36%
Women: 36%
Minorities: N/R
Average Class Size: N/R
Fall 1997 Average GMAT: N/R

Costs
Full-time tuition: $6720 per academic year
Part-time tuition: $280 per credit hour

GRADUATE BUSINESS PROGRAMS
Master of Business Administration (MBA) Full-time, part-time, distance learning option; 45 total credits required. Concentrations in financial management/planning, leadership, management information systems, marketing.

Master of Arts in Management (MA) Full-time, part-time, distance learning option; 45 total credits required. Concentration in management.

Master of Public Administration (MPA) Full-time, part-time, distance learning option; 45 total credits required. Concentrations in public policy and administration, legal administration.

Executive Master of Arts in Leadership (EMA) Full-time, part-time, distance learning option; 45 total credits required. Concentrations in leadership, organizational behavior/development.

Master of Business Administration/Master of Public Administration (MBA/MPA) Full-time, part-time, distance learning option; 60 total credits required.

Master of Science (MS) 45 total credits required.

ADMISSION
Applications For fall 1997 there were 1,451 applications for admission. Of those applying, 1,451 were accepted. Of those accepted, 582 enrolled.

Application Requirements Application form, application fee, bachelor's degree, college transcript(s).

Recommended for Application Computer experience.

Application Deadline Applications processed on a rolling/continuous basis for both domestic and international students. Application fee: $75, $175 (international). Deferred entrance is available.

ACADEMICS
Faculty Full-time 14; part-time 689.

Teaching Methodologies Case study, computer-aided instruction, computer analysis, computer simulations, faculty seminars, group discussion, lecture, research, role playing, seminars by members of the business community, simulations, student presentations, study groups, team projects.

Technology 100 on-campus computer terminals/PCs are available for student use. The network has full access to the Internet. Students are not required to have their own PC.

Special Opportunities Advanced credit may be earned through credit by examination, credit for military training programs, transfer of credits from another institution.

FINANCES
Costs for 1997–98 Tuition: Full-time: $6720 per year. Part-time: $280 per credit hour.

Financial Aid In 1997–98, 5% of students received some institutionally administered aid in the form of scholarships, loans. Financial aid is available to part-time students.

Financial Aid Contact Financial Aid Counselor, 335-116th Avenue SE, Bellevue, WA 98004. Phone: 425-637-1010; Fax: 425-637-9689; E-mail: jroberts@cityu.edu

FACILITIES
Information Resources Main library; total holdings of 30,450 volumes, 405,227 microforms, 1,100 current periodical subscriptions. CD player(s) available for graduate student use. Access provided to online bibliographic retrieval services.

INTERNATIONAL STUDENTS
Demographics 36% of students enrolled are international students.

Services and Facilities International student office, ESL courses, counseling/support services, international student orientation, housing referral.

Applying TOEFL: minimum score of 540, proof of adequate funds required. Financial aid is not available to international students.

International Student Contact Ms. Mei Yang, International Advising Director, 919 SW Grady Way, 2nd Floor, Renton, WA 98055. Phone: 425-637-1010 Ext. 3819; Fax: 425-204-3929; E-mail: info@cityu.edu

PLACEMENT
Services include alumni network, career counseling/planning, career library, electronic job bank, resume referral to employers, and resume preparation.

Business Program(s) URL: http://www.cityu.edu

Program Contact: Admissions Advisor, 919 SW Grady Way, 2nd Floor, Renton, WA 98055. Phone: 425-637-1010, 800-426-5596 (WA only); Fax: 425-277-2437; E-mail: info@cityu.edu

Eastern Washington University

College of Business Administration and Public Administration

Cheney, Washington

OVERVIEW
Eastern Washington University is a state-supported, coed, comprehensive institution. Enrollment: 7,860 graduate, professional, and undergraduate students; 439 full-time matriculated graduate/professional students; 349 part-time matriculated graduate/professional students. Founded: 1882. The graduate business unit is in an urban setting and is on a quarter calendar.

GRADUATE BUSINESS PROGRAMS
Master of Business Administration (MBA)

Master of Business Administration/Master of Public Administration (MBA/MPA)

ACADEMICS
Faculty Full-time 21.

Teaching Methodologies Case study, computer-aided instruction, computer analysis, computer simulations, group discussion, lecture, research, simulations, student presentations, study groups, team projects.

Technology 56 on-campus computer terminals/PCs are available for student use and are linked by a campus-wide network. The network has full access to the Internet. Students are not required to have their own PC.

Special Opportunities Advanced credit may be earned through transfer of credits from another institution. An internship program is available.

FACILITIES

Information Resources John F. Kennedy Library plus 3 additional on-campus libraries; total holdings of 441,562 volumes, 1,121,239 microforms, 5,231 current periodical subscriptions. CD player(s) available for graduate student use. Access provided to online bibliographic retrieval services.

Program Contact: Director, MBA Program and International Programs, 668 North Riverpoint Boulevard, Suite A, Spokane, WA 99202. Phone: 509-358-2270; Fax: 509-358-2267.

Gonzaga University

School of Business Administration

Spokane, Washington

OVERVIEW

Gonzaga University is an independent-religious, coed, comprehensive institution. Enrollment: 3,938 graduate, professional, and undergraduate students; 649 full-time matriculated graduate/professional students; 238 part-time matriculated graduate/professional students. Founded: 1887. The graduate business unit is in an urban setting and is on a semester calendar.

HIGHLIGHTS

Enrollment Profile

Full-time: 119	International: 16%
Part-time: 51	Women: 35%
Total: 170	Minorities: 9%
Average Age: 27	Average Class Size: 15
Fall 1997 Average GPA: 3.3	Fall 1997 Average GMAT: 532

Costs
Full-time tuition: N/R
Part-time tuition: $395 per credit hour

AACSB – The International Association for Management Education accredited

GRADUATE BUSINESS PROGRAMS

Master of Business Administration (MBA) Full-time, part-time; 33 total credits required; 12 months to 5 years to complete program.

Master of Accountancy (MAcc) Full-time, part-time; 30 total credits required; 12 months to 5 years to complete program.

Master of Business Administration/Doctor of Jurisprudence (MBA/JD) Full-time; 114 total credits required; 4 to 5 years to complete program.

Master of Accountancy/Doctor of Jurisprudence (MAcc/JD) Full-time; 111 total credits required; 4 to 5 years to complete program.

ADMISSION

Applications For fall 1997 there were 206 applications for admission. Of those applying, 121 were accepted. Of those accepted, 73 enrolled.

Application Requirements GMAT score: minimum 500, application form, application fee, bachelor's degree, minimum GPA, 2 letters of recommendation, college transcript(s).

Application Deadline Applications processed on a rolling/continuous basis for both domestic and international students. Application fee: $40. Deferred entrance is available.

ACADEMICS

Faculty Full-time 26; part-time 4.

Teaching Methodologies Case study, computer-aided instruction, computer analysis, faculty seminars, field projects, group discussion, lecture, research, role playing, student presentations, study groups, team projects.

Technology 115 on-campus computer terminals/PCs are available for student use and are linked by a campus-wide network. The network has full access to the Internet. Students are not required to have their own PC.

Special Opportunities Advanced credit may be earned through transfer of credits from another institution. International exchange programs in China, Italy. An internship program is available.

FINANCES

Costs for 1997–98 Tuition: $395 per credit hour. Average 1997–98 room and board costs were $6000 per academic year (on campus) and $7500 per academic year (off campus). Room and board costs vary by occupancy (e.g., single, double, triple), type of accommodation, type of meal plan.

Financial Aid In 1997–98, 21% of students received some institutionally administered aid in the form of research assistantships, scholarships, work study, loans. Financial aid is available to part-time students. Application Deadline: 2/1.

Financial Aid Contact Mr. Tim Henning, Associate Director of Financial Aid, Spokane, WA 99258. Phone: 509-328-4220 Ext. 3182; Fax: 509-324-5718; E-mail: henning@gu.gonzagu.edu

FACILITIES

Information Resources Foley Center plus 2 additional on-campus libraries; total holdings of 550,000 volumes, 290,000 microforms, 4,200 current periodical subscriptions. CD player(s) available for graduate student use. Access provided to online bibliographic retrieval services.

INTERNATIONAL STUDENTS

Demographics 16% of students enrolled are international students [Africa, 10%, Asia, 50%, Europe, 10%, North America, 25%, South America, 5%].

Services and Facilities International student office, international student center, ESL courses, counseling/support services, language tutoring.

Applying TOEFL: minimum score of 550, proof of adequate funds, proof of health/immunizations required. Financial aid is not available to international students.

International Student Contact Mr. Raymond Fadeley, Director, International Students Program, Spokane, WA 99258. Phone: 509-328-4220 Ext. 6284; Fax: 509-324-5814; E-mail: fadeley@gonzaga.edu

PLACEMENT

Services include alumni network, career counseling/planning, career fairs, career library, career placement, electronic job bank, job interviews arranged, job search course, resume referral to employers, and resume preparation. In 1996–97, 187 organizations participated in on-campus recruiting; 450 on-campus interviews were conducted.

Employment Of 1996–97 graduates, 90% were employed within three months of graduation; the average starting salary was $50,000. Types of employment entered: accounting, banking, chemical industry, communications, computer-related, consulting, consumer products, education, energy, engineering, finance, financial services, government, health services, high technology, hospitality management, human resources, information systems/technology, insurance, international trade, law, management, manufacturing, marketing, media, mining, nonprofit, petrochemical, pharmaceutical, real estate, retail, service industry, telecommunications, transportation, utilities.

Business Program(s) URL: http://www.gonzaga.edu/mba-macc

Program Contact: Dr. Larry Lewis, Associate Dean, School of Business Administration, Spokane, WA 99258. Phone: 509-328-4220 Ext. 3430, 800-572-9658 (WA only), and/or 800-523-9712 (WA only); Fax: 509-324-5811; E-mail: lewis@jepson.gonzaga.edu

Pacific Lutheran University

School of Business

Tacoma, Washington

OVERVIEW

Pacific Lutheran University is an independent-religious, coed, comprehensive institution. Enrollment: 3,555 graduate, professional, and undergraduate students; 125 full-time matriculated graduate/professional students; 101 part-time matriculated graduate/professional students. Founded: 1890. The graduate business unit is in a suburban setting and is on a 4-1-4 calendar.

HIGHLIGHTS

Enrollment Profile

Full-time: 51	International: 16%
Part-time: 38	Women: 36%
Total: 89	Minorities: 6%
Average Age: 35	Average Class Size: 16
Fall 1997 Average GPA: 3.2	Fall 1997 Average GMAT: 540

Costs
Full-time tuition: $11,352 per academic year
Part-time tuition: $473 per semester hour

AACSB – The International Association for Management Education accredited

GRADUATE BUSINESS PROGRAMS

Master of Business Administration (MBA) Full-time, part-time; 40-48 total credits required; application deadline: 6/1for Saturday program; 18 months to 7 years to complete program. Concentration in technology management.

ADMISSION

Applications For fall 1997 there were 61 applications for admission. Of those applying, 47 were accepted. Of those accepted, 32 enrolled.

Application Requirements GMAT score: minimum 470, application form, application fee, bachelor's degree, minimum GPA: 2.75, 2 letters of recommendation, personal statement, resume, college transcript(s).

Pacific Lutheran University (continued)

Application Deadline Applications processed on a rolling/continuous basis for both domestic and international students. Application fee: $35. Deferred entrance is available.

ACADEMICS
Faculty Full-time 9; part-time 3.

Teaching Methodologies Case study, computer analysis, computer simulations, experiential learning, field projects, group discussion, lecture, research, simulations, student presentations, team projects.

Technology 50 on-campus computer terminals/PCs are available for student use and are linked by a campus-wide network. The network has full access to the Internet. Students are not required to have their own PC.

Special Opportunities Advanced credit may be earned through credit by examination, transfer of credits from another institution. An internship program is available.

FINANCES
Costs for 1997–98 Tuition: Full-time: $11,352 per year. Part-time: $473 per semester hour. Cost varies by number of credits taken. Average 1997–98 room and board costs were $4690 per academic year (on campus) and $6000 per academic year (off campus). Room and board costs vary by occupancy (e.g., single, double, triple), type of meal plan.

Financial Aid Fellowships, research assistantships, scholarships, work study available. Financial aid is available to part-time students. Application Deadline: 3/1.

Financial Aid Contact Kay Soltis, Director of Financial Aid, Pacific Lutheran University, Tacoma, WA 98447. Phone: 253-535-7161; Fax: 253-535-8320; E-mail: finaid@plu.edu

FACILITIES
Information Resources Robert Mortvedt Library; total holdings of 241,161 volumes, 75,603 microforms, 2,000 current periodical subscriptions. CD player(s) available for graduate student use. Access provided to online bibliographic retrieval services and online databases.

INTERNATIONAL STUDENTS
Demographics 16% of students enrolled are international students [Asia, 71%, Central America, 7%, Europe, 21%].

Services and Facilities International student office, international student center, international student housing, visa services, ESL courses, counseling/support services.

Applying TOEFL: minimum score of 550, proof of adequate funds, proof of health/immunizations required. Financial aid is available to international students.

International Student Contact David Gerry, Coordinator, International Student Services, Pacific Lutheran University, Tacoma, WA 98447. Phone: 253-535-7194; Fax: 253-535-8752; E-mail: gerrydp@plu.edu

PLACEMENT
Services include alumni network, career counseling/planning, career library, resume referral to employers, and resume preparation.

Business Program(s) URL: http://www.plu.edu/~busa/mba.html

Program Contact: Jan Dempsey, Director of Graduate Programs, School of Business, Pacific Lutheran University, Tacoma, WA 98447. Phone: 253-535-7250, 800-274-6758; Fax: 253-535-8723; E-mail: business@plu.edu
See full description on page 918.

Saint Martin's College

Business and Economics Division

Lacey, Washington

OVERVIEW
Saint Martin's College is an independent-religious, coed, comprehensive institution. Enrollment: 1,651 graduate, professional, and undergraduate students. Founded: 1895. The graduate business unit is in a small-town setting and is on a term calendar.

HIGHLIGHTS

Enrollment Profile

Full-time: N/R	International: 5%
Part-time: N/R	Women: N/R
Total: 130	Minorities: 12%
Average Age: 34	Average Class Size: 15
Fall 1997 Average GPA: N/R	Fall 1997 Average GMAT: 480

Costs
Full-time tuition: N/R
Part-time tuition: $450 per credit hour

GRADUATE BUSINESS PROGRAMS
Master of Business Administration (MBA) Full-time, part-time; 33 total credits required; 12 months to 7 years to complete program.

ADMISSION
Application Requirements GMAT score, application form, application fee, bachelor's degree, minimum GPA, college transcript(s).

Recommended for Application GRE score accepted, interview, computer experience.

Application Deadline Applications processed on a rolling/continuous basis for both domestic and international students. Application fee: $35. Deferred entrance is available.

ACADEMICS
Faculty Full-time 6; part-time 8.

Teaching Methodologies Case study, computer-aided instruction, computer analysis, computer simulations, faculty seminars, group discussion, lecture, research, seminars by members of the business community, student presentations, study groups, team projects.

Technology Computer terminals/PCs are available for student use and are linked by a campus-wide network. The network has full access to the Internet. Students are not required to have their own PC.

Special Opportunities Advanced credit may be earned through credit for military training programs, transfer of credits from another institution.

FINANCES
Costs for 1997–98 Tuition: $450 per credit hour.

Financial Aid Grants, scholarships, work study, loans available. Financial aid is available to part-time students. Application Deadline: 3/1.

Financial Aid Contact Mr. Ron Noborikawa, Director, Offices of Admissions and Financial Aid, 5300 Pacific Avenue, SE, Lacey, WA 98503-7500. Phone: 360-438-4463; Fax: 360-459-4124; E-mail: admissions@stmartin.edu

FACILITIES
Information Resources Saint Martin's College Library; total holdings of 87,500 volumes, 19,500 microforms, 550 current periodical subscriptions. CD player(s) available for graduate student use. Access provided to online bibliographic retrieval services.

INTERNATIONAL STUDENTS
Demographics 5% of students enrolled are international students [Asia, 100%].

Services and Facilities International student office, visa services, ESL courses, counseling/support services.

Applying TOEFL: minimum score of 525, proof of adequate funds required. Financial aid is not available to international students.

International Student Contact Ms. Josephine Yung, Director of International Student Services, 5300 Pacific Avenue, SE, Lacey, WA 98502. Phone: 360-438-4375; Fax: 360-459-4124.

PLACEMENT
Services include alumni network, career counseling/planning, career fairs, career library, career placement, electronic job bank, job interviews arranged, resume referral to employers, and resume preparation.

Employment Of 1996–97 graduates, 95% were employed within three months of graduation.

Business Program(s) URL: http://www.stmartin.edu

Program Contact: Mr. Haldon Wilson, Jr., MBA Director, 5300 Pacific Avenue, SE, Lacey, WA 98503. Phone: 360-438-4326, 800-368-8803; Fax: 360-438-4522; E-mail: hwilson@stmartin.edu

Seattle Pacific University

School of Business and Economics

Seattle, Washington

OVERVIEW
Seattle Pacific University is an independent-religious, coed, comprehensive institution. Enrollment: 3,321 graduate, professional, and undergraduate students;

WASHINGTON

79 full-time matriculated graduate/professional students; 707 part-time matriculated graduate/professional students. Founded: 1891. The graduate business unit is in an urban setting and is on a quarter calendar.

HIGHLIGHTS

Enrollment Profile

Full-time: 24

Part-time: 139

Total: 163

Average Age: 31

Fall 1997 Average GPA: 3.12

International: 15%

Women: 40%

Minorities: 10%

Average Class Size: 17

Fall 1997 Average GMAT: 523

Costs

Full-time tuition: $11,124 per academic year

Part-time tuition: $412 per quarter credit hour

GRADUATE BUSINESS PROGRAMS

Master of Business Administration (MBA) Full-time, part-time; 45-72 total credits required; 12 months to 6 years to complete program. Concentrations in management, management information systems, human resources.

Master of Science in Information Systems Management (MS) Full-time, part-time; 45-60 total credits required; 12 months to 6 years to complete program. Concentration in management information systems.

ADMISSION

Applications For fall 1997 there were 50 applications for admission. Of those applying, 38 were accepted. Of those accepted, 26 enrolled.

Application Requirements GMAT score: minimum 460, application form, application fee, bachelor's degree, essay, 2 letters of recommendation, resume, college transcript(s), minimum of 1 year of work experience.

Recommended for Application Minimum GPA, computer experience.

Application Deadline 8/1 for fall, 11/1 for winter, 2/1 for spring, 5/1 for summer, 8/1 for fall (international), 11/1 for winter (international), 2/1 for spring (international), 5/1 for summer (international). Application fee: $35. Deferred entrance is available.

ACADEMICS

Faculty Full-time 19; part-time 6.

Teaching Methodologies Case study, computer analysis, computer simulations, experiential learning, field projects, group discussion, lecture, research, role playing, seminars by members of the business community, student presentations, study groups, team projects.

Technology 118 on-campus computer terminals/PCs are available for student use and are linked by a campus-wide network. The network has full access to the Internet. Students are not required to have their own PC.

Special Opportunities Advanced credit may be earned through credit by examination, transfer of credits from another institution.

FINANCES

Costs for 1997–98 Tuition: Full-time: $11,124 per year. Part-time: $412 per quarter credit hour. Fees: Full-time: $50 per academic year. Part-time: $50 per program. Average 1997–98 room and board costs were $5550 per academic year (on campus) and $6500 per academic year (off campus). Room and board costs vary by occupancy (e.g., single, double, triple), type of accommodation, type of meal plan.

Financial Aid In 1997–98, 7% of students received some institutionally administered aid in the form of research assistantships. Financial aid is available to part-time students.

Financial Aid Contact Office of Financial Aid, 3307 Third Avenue West, Seattle, WA 98119-1997. Phone: 206-281-2046.

FACILITIES

Information Resources Main library; total holdings of 176,500 volumes, 417,800 microforms, 1,572 current periodical subscriptions. CD player(s) available for graduate student use. Access provided to online bibliographic retrieval services.

INTERNATIONAL STUDENTS

Demographics 15% of students enrolled are international students.

Services and Facilities International student office, ESL courses, counseling/support services.

Applying TOEFL: minimum score of 565, proof of adequate funds required. Financial aid is not available to international students.

International Student Contact Mr. Kevin McMahan, International Program Coordinator, 3307 Third Avenue West, Seattle, WA 98119. Phone: 206-281-2486; Fax: 206-281-2730.

PLACEMENT

Services include career counseling/planning, career fairs, career library, career placement, electronic job bank, job interviews arranged, job search course, and resume preparation.

Employment Of 1996–97 graduates, 96% were employed within three months of graduation. Types of employment entered: communications, computer-

related, consulting, consumer products, education, engineering, finance, financial services, government, health services, high technology, human resources, information systems/technology, insurance, international trade, management, manufacturing, marketing, nonprofit, retail, service industry, telecommunications.

Business Program(s) URL: http://www.spu.edu/depts/sbe

Program Contact: Ms. Debra Wysomierski, Assistant Graduate Director, 3307 Third Avenue West, Seattle, WA 98119. Phone: 206-281-2753; Fax: 206-281-2733; E-mail: djwysom@spu.edu

See full description on page 982.

Seattle University

Albers School of Business and Economics

Seattle, Washington

OVERVIEW

Seattle University is an independent-religious, coed, comprehensive institution. Enrollment: 5,739 graduate, professional, and undergraduate students; 1,042 full-time matriculated graduate/professional students; 1,537 part-time matriculated graduate/professional students. Founded: 1891. The graduate business unit is in an urban setting and is on a quarter calendar.

HIGHLIGHTS

Enrollment Profile

Full-time: 135

Part-time: 589

Total: 724

Average Age: 32

Fall 1997 Average GPA: 3.2

International: 13%

Women: 40%

Minorities: 10%

Average Class Size: 30

Fall 1997 Average GMAT: 560

Costs

Full-time tuition: N/R

Part-time tuition: $440 per quarter hour

AACSB – The International Association for Management Education accredited

GRADUATE BUSINESS PROGRAMS

Master of Business Administration (MBA) Full-time, part-time; 55-73 total credits required; 12 months to 6 years to complete program. Concentrations in accounting, business law, economics, finance, human resources, management information systems, international business, management, marketing, operations management.

Master of Science in Finance (MS) Full-time, part-time; 45-63 total credits required; 12 months to 6 years to complete program.

Master of International Business (MIB) Full-time, part-time; 45-64 total credits required; 12 months to 6 years to complete program.

Master of Applied Economics (MAE) Full-time, part-time; 45-63 total credits required; 12 months to 6 years to complete program.

ADMISSION

Applications For fall 1997 there were 284 applications for admission. Of those applying, 208 were accepted. Of those accepted, 134 enrolled.

Application Requirements GMAT score: minimum 500, application form, application fee, bachelor's degree, minimum GPA: 3.0, resume, college transcript(s), minimum of 1 year of work experience.

Application Deadline 8/20 for fall, 11/20 for winter, 2/20 for spring, 5/20 for summer, 6/1 for fall (international), 9/1 for winter (international), 1/1 for spring (international), 3/1 for summer (international). Application fee: $55. Deferred entrance is available.

ACADEMICS

Faculty Full-time 42; part-time 14.

Teaching Methodologies Case study, computer-aided instruction, computer analysis, computer simulations, experiential learning, field projects, group discussion, lecture, research, seminars by members of the business community, simulations, student presentations, study groups, team projects.

Technology 401 on-campus computer terminals/PCs are available for student use and are linked by a campus-wide network. The network has full access to the Internet. Students are not required to have their own PC.

Special Opportunities Advanced credit may be earned through transfer of credits from another institution. An internship program is available.

FINANCES

Costs for 1997–98 Tuition: $440 per quarter hour. Cost varies by number of credits taken. Average 1997–98 room and board costs were $5493 per academic year (on campus) and $5637 per academic year (off campus). Room and board costs vary by occupancy (e.g., single, double, triple), type of meal plan.

Seattle University (continued)

Financial Aid Research assistantships, scholarships, work study, loans available. Financial aid is available to part-time students. Application Deadline: 2/1.

Financial Aid Contact Jim White, Director, Financial Aid and Student Employment, 900 Broadway, Seattle, WA 98122. Phone: 206-296-5480; E-mail: whitejim@seattleu.edu

FACILITIES

Information Resources A. A. Lemieux Library; total holdings of 261,046 volumes, 91,946 microforms, 6,396 current periodical subscriptions. CD player(s) available for graduate student use. Access provided to online bibliographic retrieval services and online databases.

INTERNATIONAL STUDENTS

Demographics 13% of students enrolled are international students [Asia, 86%, Europe, 5%, North America, 2%, other, 7%].

Services and Facilities International student office, international student center, visa services, ESL courses, counseling/support services, international student clubs.

Applying TOEFL: minimum score of 580, proof of adequate funds required. Financial aid is not available to international students.

International Student Contact Faizi Ghodsi, Director, International Student Center, 900 Broadway, Seattle, WA 98122. Phone: 206-296-6000; E-mail: ghodsif@seattleu.edu

PLACEMENT

Services include alumni network, career counseling/planning, career fairs, career library, career placement, job interviews arranged, job search course, resume referral to employers, and resume preparation. In 1996–97, 98 organizations participated in on-campus recruiting.

Employment Types of employment entered: accounting, banking, communications, computer-related, consulting, finance, financial services, human resources, information systems/technology, insurance, management, manufacturing, marketing, pharmaceutical, telecommunications.

Business Program(s) URL: http://www.seattleu.edu/asbe

Program Contact: Michael McKeon, Dean of Admissions, Graduate Admissions, 900 Broadway, Seattle, WA 98122. Phone: 206-296-5900, 800-542-0833 (WA only), and/or 800-426-7123 (WA only); Fax: 206-296-5902; E-mail: grad-admissions@seattleu.edu

See full description on page 984.

University of Washington

School of Business Administration

Seattle, Washington

OVERVIEW

The University of Washington is a state-supported, coed university. Enrollment: 33,719 graduate, professional, and undergraduate students; 7,488 full-time matriculated graduate/professional students; 1,639 part-time matriculated graduate/professional students. Founded: 1861. The graduate business unit is in an urban setting and is on a quarter calendar.

HIGHLIGHTS

Enrollment Profile

Full-time: 339	International: 15%
Part-time: 94	Women: 36%
Total: 433	Minorities: 13%
Average Age: 28	Average Class Size: 35
Fall 1997 Average GPA: 3.28	Fall 1997 Average GMAT: 632

Costs

Full-time tuition: $5232 per academic year (resident); $12,966 per academic year (nonresident)

Part-time tuition: $1682 per quarter (resident); $4158 per quarter (nonresident)

AACSB – The International Association for Management Education accredited

GRADUATE BUSINESS PROGRAMS

Master of Business Administration (MBA) Full-time; 96 total credits required; 2 to 6 years to complete program. Concentrations in management, accounting, decision sciences, economics, entrepreneurship, finance, human resources, information management, management information systems, managerial economics, marketing, operations management, organizational behavior/development, quantitative analysis, strategic management.

Evening MBA (MBA) Part-time; 88 total credits required; 2.8 to 3.8 years to complete program. Concentration in management.

Executive MBA (MBA) Part-time; 66 total credits required; 2 years to complete program. Concentration in management.

Master of Business Administration/Master of Health Administration (MBA/MHA) Full-time; 112 total credits required; 2 to 6 years to complete program. Concentration in management.

Master of Business Administration/Master of Arts in International Studies (MBA/MA) Full-time; 132 total credits required; 3 to 6 years to complete program. Concentrations in international and area business studies, international business, international economics, international finance, international logistics, international management, international marketing, international trade.

PEMM-Program in Engineering and Manufacturing Management (MBA/MS) Full-time; 188 total credits required; 2 to 6 years to complete program. Concentrations in manufacturing management, production management.

Master of Business Administration/Doctor of Jurisprudence (MBA/JD) Full-time; 212 total credits required; 4 to 6 years to complete program. Concentrations in business law, legal administration.

Master of Professional Accounting in Taxation (MPA) Full-time, part-time; 48 total credits required; 12 months to 6 years to complete program. Concentration in taxation.

ADMISSION

Applications For fall 1997 there were 1,107 applications for admission. Of those applying, 337 were accepted. Of those accepted, 142 enrolled.

Application Requirements Application form, application fee, bachelor's degree, essay, minimum GPA: 3.0, 2 letters of recommendation, personal statement, resume, college transcript(s), computer experience: computer literacy.

Recommended for Application GMAT score accepted, interview, minimum of 2 years of work experience.

Application Deadline 3/15 for fall, 3/15 for fall (international). Application fee: $45.

ACADEMICS

Faculty Full-time 107; part-time 31.

Teaching Methodologies Case study, computer analysis, group discussion, lecture, research, seminars by members of the business community, student presentations, study groups, team projects.

Technology 130 on-campus computer terminals/PCs are available for student use and are linked by a campus-wide network. The network has full access to the Internet. Students are not required to have their own PC.

Special Opportunities International exchange programs in Chile, Denmark, Finland, France, Germany, Hong Kong, India, Japan, Mexico, People's Republic of China, Spain, Switzerland, United Kingdom.

FINANCES

Costs for 1997–98 Tuition: Full-time: $5232 per year (resident); $12,966 per year (nonresident). Part-time: $1682 per quarter (resident); $4158 per quarter (nonresident). Cost varies by class time (e.g., day/evening), number of credits taken. Fees: Full-time: $300 per academic year (resident); $300 per academic year (nonresident). Part-time: $150 per year (resident); $150 per year (nonresident). Average 1997–98 room and board costs were $7674 per academic year (on campus) and $8200 per academic year (off campus). Room and board costs vary by campus location, occupancy (e.g., single, double, triple), type of accommodation, type of meal plan.

Financial Aid In 1997–98, 43% of students received some institutionally administered aid in the form of fellowships, research assistantships, teaching assistantships, grants, scholarships, work study, loans. Application Deadline: 3/15.

Financial Aid Contact Barbara Pearson, Assistant Director, Box 353200, Seattle, WA 98195-3200. Phone: 206-685-8916; Fax: 206-616-7351.

FACILITIES

Information Resources Suzzallo Library plus 18 additional on-campus libraries; total holdings of 5,355,140 volumes, 6,070,069 microforms, 56,535 current periodical subscriptions. CD player(s) available for graduate student use. Access provided to online bibliographic retrieval services.

INTERNATIONAL STUDENTS

Demographics 15% of students enrolled are international students [Asia, 80%, Australia/New Zealand, 1%, Europe, 16%, North America, 1%, South America, 1%, other, 1%].

Services and Facilities International student office, international student center, international student housing, visa services, ESL courses, counseling/support services.

Applying TOEFL: minimum score of 600, proof of adequate funds, proof of health/immunizations required. TSE recommended. Financial aid is not available to international students.

International Student Contact Ms. Francine Shafer, Associate Director, Box 353200, Seattle, WA 98195-3200. Phone: 206-543-4661; Fax: 206-616-7351; E-mail: seneca@u.washington.edu

PLACEMENT

Services include alumni network, career counseling/planning, career fairs, career library, electronic job bank, job interviews arranged, job search course, resume referral to employers, and resume preparation. In 1996–97, 61 organizations participated in on-campus recruiting; 760 on-campus interviews were conducted.

Employment Of 1996–97 graduates, 84% were employed within three months of graduation; the average starting salary was $53,556. Types of employment entered: accounting, banking, communications, computer-related, consulting, finance, financial services, government, health services, high technology, human resources, information systems/technology, international trade, management, manufacturing, marketing, nonprofit, pharmaceutical, real estate, service industry, telecommunications, transportation.

Business Program(s) URL: http://weber.u.washington.edu/~bschool

Program Contact: MBA Program Office, Box 353200, 110 Mackenzie Hall, Seattle, WA 98195-3200. Phone: 206-543-4661; Fax: 206-616-7351; E-mail: mba@u.washington.edu
See full description on page 1170.

Washington State University

College of Business and Economics

Pullman, Washington

OVERVIEW

Washington State University is a state-supported, coed university. Enrollment: 17,000 graduate, professional, and undergraduate students; 1,920 full-time matriculated graduate/professional students; 380 part-time matriculated graduate/professional students. Founded: 1890. The graduate business unit is in a small-town setting and is on a semester calendar.

HIGHLIGHTS

Enrollment Profile
Full-time: 150
Part-time: 0
Total: 150
Average Age: 28
Fall 1997 Average GPA: 3.4

International: 36%
Women: 37%
Minorities: 12%
Average Class Size: 20
Fall 1997 Average GMAT: 550

Costs
Full-time tuition: $5334 per academic year (resident); $13,380 per academic year (nonresident)
Part-time tuition: $267 per credit (resident); $669 per credit (nonresident)

AACSB – The International Association for Management Education accredited

GRADUATE BUSINESS PROGRAMS

Master of Business Administration (MBA) Full-time; 32-64 total credits required; 12 months to 2 years to complete program. Concentrations in accounting, decision sciences, finance, international business, management information systems, marketing, real estate, travel industry/tourism management.

Master of Accounting (MAcc) Full-time; 34 total credits required; 12 months to 2 years to complete program. Concentrations in accounting, taxation.

ADMISSION

Applications For fall 1997 there were 432 applications for admission. Of those applying, 122 were accepted. Of those accepted, 48 enrolled.

Application Requirements GMAT score: minimum 550, application form, application fee, bachelor's degree, minimum GPA: 3.0, 3 letters of recommendation, resume, college transcript(s).

Recommended for Application Personal statement, work experience, computer experience.

Application Deadline Applications processed on a rolling/continuous basis for domestic students only. 3/1 for fall (international), 7/1 for spring (international), 3/1 for summer (international). Application fee: $35. Deferred entrance is available.

ACADEMICS

Faculty Full-time 52; part-time 8.

Teaching Methodologies Case study, computer-aided instruction, computer analysis, computer simulations, experiential learning, faculty seminars, field projects, group discussion, seminars by members of the business community, student presentations, study groups, team projects.

Technology 130 on-campus computer terminals/PCs are available for student use and are linked by a campus-wide network. The network has full access to the Internet. Students are not required to have their own PC.

Special Opportunities Advanced credit may be earned through transfer of credits from another institution. International exchange programs in Germany, Norway, People's Republic of China, Russia, Switzerland, Thailand, Ukraine. An internship program is available.

FINANCES

Costs for 1997–98 Tuition: Full-time: $5334 per year (resident); $13,380 per year (nonresident). Part-time: $267 per credit (resident); $669 per credit (nonresident). Average 1997–98 room and board costs were $7166 per academic year (on campus) and $7166 per academic year (off campus). Room and board costs vary by campus location, occupancy (e.g., single, double, triple), type of accommodation, type of meal plan.

Financial Aid Research assistantships, teaching assistantships, scholarships, work study, loans available. Application Deadline: 4/1.

Financial Aid Contact Wayne Sparks, Director, Financial Aid Office, Lighty Student Services Building, Room 380, Pullman, WA 99164-1068. Phone: 509-335-9711; Fax: 509-335-3421.

FACILITIES

Information Resources Holland Library plus 6 additional on-campus libraries; total holdings of 1,757,256 volumes, 2,959,044 microforms, 24,356 current periodical subscriptions. CD player(s) available for graduate student use. Access provided to online bibliographic retrieval services and online databases.

INTERNATIONAL STUDENTS

Demographics 36% of students enrolled are international students [Africa, 6%, Asia, 78%, Europe, 12%, South America, 1%, other, 3%].

Services and Facilities International student office, international student center, international student housing, visa services, ESL courses, counseling/support services.

Applying TOEFL: minimum score of 580, proof of adequate funds, proof of health/immunizations required. Financial aid is available to international students.

International Student Contact Susan Wohld, Associate Director, International Programs, Pullman, WA 99164-5110. Phone: 509-335-4508; Fax: 509-335-2373.

PLACEMENT

Services include alumni network, career counseling/planning, career fairs, career library, career placement, job search course, resume referral to employers, and resume preparation. In 1996–97, 55 organizations participated in on-campus recruiting.

Employment Of 1996–97 graduates, 94% were employed within three months of graduation; the average starting salary was $40,500. Types of employment entered: accounting, banking, communications, computer-related, consulting, consumer products, education, energy, engineering, finance, financial services, government, health services, high technology, hospitality management, human resources, information systems/technology, insurance, international trade, law, management, manufacturing, marketing, nonprofit, real estate, retail, service industry, telecommunications, transportation.

Business Program(s) URL: http://www.cbe.wsu.edu/

Program Contact: Dr. Val Miskin, Director, College of Business and Economics, Pullman, WA 99164-4744. Phone: 509-335-7617; Fax: 509-335-4735; E-mail: mba@wsu.edu

Western Washington University

College of Business and Economics

Bellingham, Washington

OVERVIEW

Western Washington University is a state-supported, coed, comprehensive institution. Enrollment: 11,000 graduate, professional, and undergraduate students. Founded: 1893. The graduate business unit is in a small-town setting and is on a quarter calendar.

Western Washington University (continued)

HIGHLIGHTS

Enrollment Profile
Full-time: 22
Part-time: 31
Total: 53
Average Age: 29
Fall 1997 Average GPA: 3.15

International: 19%
Women: 51%
Minorities: 9%
Average Class Size: 30
Fall 1997 Average GMAT: 545

Costs
Full-time tuition: $1400 per academic year (resident); $4260 per academic year (nonresident)
Part-time tuition: $140 per credit (resident); $426 per credit (nonresident)

AACSB – The International Association for Management Education accredited

GRADUATE BUSINESS PROGRAMS
Master of Business Administration (MBA) Full-time, part-time; 88 total credits required; 18 months to 2.8 years to complete program.

ADMISSION
Applications For fall 1997 there were 39 applications for admission. Of those applying, 33 were accepted. Of those accepted, 24 enrolled.

Application Requirements GMAT score, application form, application fee, bachelor's degree, minimum GPA: 3.0, resume, college transcript(s), computer experience: computer literacy.

Application Deadline 5/1 for summer, 1/1 for summer (international). Application fee: $35.

ACADEMICS
Faculty Full-time 46; part-time 6.

Teaching Methodologies Case study, computer analysis, computer simulations, experiential learning, faculty seminars, field projects, group discussion, lecture, research, role playing, seminars by members of the business community, simulations, student presentations, study groups, team projects.

Technology 50 on-campus computer terminals/PCs are available for student use and are linked by a campus-wide network. The network has full access to the Internet. Students are not required to have their own PC.

Special Opportunities Advanced credit may be earned through transfer of credits from another institution.

FINANCES
Costs for 1997–98 Tuition: Full-time: $1400 per quarter (resident); $4260 per quarter (nonresident). Part-time: $140 per credit (resident); $426 per credit (nonresident). Fees: $60 per quarter (resident); $60 per quarter (nonresident). Room and board costs vary by campus location, occupancy (e.g., single, double, triple), type of accommodation, type of meal plan.

Financial Aid Teaching assistantships, scholarships, work study, loans available. Financial aid is available to part-time students. Application Deadline: 3/31.

Financial Aid Contact Student Financial Resources, MS 9006, 516 High Street, Bellingham, WA 98225-9900. Phone: 360-650-3470.

FACILITIES
Information Resources Mabel Zoe Wilson Library; total holdings of 650,000 volumes, 2,000,000 microforms, 5,500 current periodical subscriptions. CD player(s) available for graduate student use. Access provided to online bibliographic retrieval services and online databases.

INTERNATIONAL STUDENTS
Demographics 19% of students enrolled are international students [Africa, 10%, Asia, 60%, North America, 30%].

Services and Facilities International student office, visa services, counseling/support services.

Applying TOEFL: minimum score of 565, proof of adequate funds, proof of health/immunizations required. Financial aid is not available to international students.

International Student Contact Multicultural Services Center, 516 High Street, Bellingham, WA 98225-5996. Phone: 360-650-3843.

PLACEMENT
Services include career counseling/planning, career fairs, career library, career placement, job interviews arranged, job search course, resume referral to employers, and resume preparation.

Business Program(s) URL: http://www.cbe.wwu.edu/mba

Program Contact: Program Coordinator, MBA Program, MS 9072, Bellingham, WA 98225-9900. Phone: 360-650-3898; Fax: 360-650-4844.

Whitworth College

Whitworth Graduate School of International Management

Spokane, Washington

OVERVIEW
Whitworth College is an independent-religious, coed, comprehensive institution. Enrollment: 2,043 graduate, professional, and undergraduate students; 157 full-time matriculated graduate/professional students; 85 part-time matriculated graduate/professional students. Founded: 1890. The graduate business unit is in a suburban setting and is on a 6-week semester with two 6-week blocks calendar.

HIGHLIGHTS

Enrollment Profile
Full-time: 48
Part-time: 0
Total: 48
Average Age: 32
Fall 1997 Average GPA: 3.3

International: 38%
Women: 38%
Minorities: N/R
Average Class Size: 20
Fall 1997 Average GMAT: 530

Costs
Full-time tuition: $6400 per academic year
Part-time tuition: $320 per credit

GRADUATE BUSINESS PROGRAMS
Master of International Management (MIM) Full-time, part-time; 37 total credits required; 12 months to 6 years to complete program. Concentration in international management.

ADMISSION
Applications For fall 1997 there were 39 applications for admission. Of those applying, 28 were accepted. Of those accepted, 22 enrolled.

Application Requirements Application form, application fee, bachelor's degree, essay, minimum GPA: 3.0, 2 letters of recommendation, personal statement, resume, college transcript(s).

Recommended for Application GMAT score accepted, GRE score accepted, minimum of 5 years of work experience, computer experience.

Application Deadline 3/1 for fall, 11/1 for spring, 3/1 for fall (international), 11/1 for spring (international). Application fee: $35. Deferred entrance is available.

ACADEMICS
Faculty Full-time 4; part-time 14.

Teaching Methodologies Case study, computer-aided instruction, field projects, group discussion, lecture, research, role playing, seminars by members of the business community, simulations, student presentations, study groups, team projects.

Technology 88 on-campus computer terminals/PCs are available for student use and are linked by a campus-wide network. The network has full access to the Internet. Students are not required to have their own PC.

Special Opportunities Advanced credit may be earned through credit for military training programs, transfer of credits from another institution. International exchange programs in Netherlands, Korea. An internship program is available.

FINANCES
Costs for 1997–98 Tuition: Full-time: $6400 per 20 credits. Part-time: $320 per credit. Cost varies by number of credits taken. Average 1997–98 room and board costs were $5400 per academic year (on campus) and $5400 per academic year (off campus). Room and board costs vary by occupancy (e.g., single, double, triple), type of accommodation, type of meal plan.

Financial Aid In 1997–98, 52% of students received some institutionally administered aid in the form of grants, scholarships, work study, loans. Application Deadline: 4/1.

Financial Aid Contact Mrs. Wendy Olson, Director of Financial Aid, West 300 Hawthorne Road, MS-2704, Spokane, WA 99251-0001. Phone: 509-777-1000 Ext. 4306; Fax: 509-777-3725; E-mail: wolson@whitworth.edu

FACILITIES
Information Resources Harriet Cheney Cowles Memorial Library plus 1 additional on-campus library; total holdings of 151,000 volumes, 48,000 microforms, 775 current periodical subscriptions. CD player(s) available for graduate student use. Access provided to online bibliographic retrieval services and online databases.

INTERNATIONAL STUDENTS
Demographics 38% of students enrolled are international students [Africa, 5%, Asia, 70%, Central America, 5%, Europe, 15%, South America, 5%].

Services and Facilities International student office, international student housing, visa services, ESL courses, counseling/support services, International Club.

Applying TOEFL: minimum score of 550, TWE: minimum score of 4, proof of adequate funds, proof of health/immunizations required. Financial aid is available to international students.

International Student Contact Mrs. Michelle-Lynne Morimoto, Assistant Director, 300 West Hawthorne Road, MS-2704, Spokane, WA 99251-0001. Phone: 509-777-3742; Fax: 509-777-3723; E-mail: mmorimoto@whitworth.edu

PLACEMENT

Services include alumni network, career counseling/planning, career fairs, career library, electronic job bank, job search course, resume referral to employers, and resume preparation.

Employment Of 1996–97 graduates, 95% were employed within three months of graduation. Types of employment entered: banking, communications, computer-related, education, energy, financial services, human resources, information systems/technology, international trade, management, marketing, nonprofit, telecommunications, utilities.

Business Program(s) URL: http://www.whitworth.edu/dept/mim/mim_home.htm

Program Contact: Mrs. Michelle-Lynne Morimoto, Assistant Director, West 300 Hawthorne Road, Spokane, WA 99251-0001. Phone: 509-777-3742, 800-929-6981 (WA only), and/or 800-929-6891 (WA only); Fax: 509-777-3723; E-mail: mmorimoto@whitworth.edu

WEST VIRGINIA

Marshall University

College of Business

Huntington, West Virginia

OVERVIEW

Marshall University is a state-supported, coed, comprehensive institution. Enrollment: 11,106 graduate, professional, and undergraduate students. Founded: 1837. The graduate business unit is in a small-town setting and is on a semester calendar.

HIGHLIGHTS

Enrollment Profile

Full-time: N/R
Part-time: N/R
Total: 170
Average Age: N/R
Fall 1997 Average GPA: 3.0

International: 12%
Women: N/R
Minorities: 15%
Average Class Size: 20
Fall 1997 Average GMAT: 530

Costs

Full-time tuition: $1158 per academic year (resident); $3325 per academic year (nonresident)
Part-time tuition: $121 per credit hour (resident); $361 per credit hour (nonresident)

AACSB – The International Association for Management Education accredited

GRADUATE BUSINESS PROGRAMS

Master of Business Administration (MBA) Full-time, part-time; 36 total credits required; 12 months to 5 years to complete program.

Saturdays Only MBA (MBA) Part-time; 36 total credits required; 18 months to 2 years to complete program.

ADMISSION

Applications For fall 1997 there were 72 applications for admission. Of those applying, 65 were accepted. Of those accepted, 57 enrolled.

Application Requirements GMAT score: minimum 500, application form, application fee, bachelor's degree, minimum GPA: 2.5, college transcript(s), computer experience: Lotus 123, WordPerfect, Internet.

Recommended for Application Interview, letters of recommendation, resume.

Application Deadline Applications processed on a rolling/continuous basis for both domestic and international students. Application fee: $15, $25 (international). Deferred entrance is available.

ACADEMICS

Faculty Full-time 31.

Teaching Methodologies Case study, computer-aided instruction, computer analysis, group discussion, lecture, research, role playing, seminars by members of the business community, student presentations, study groups, team projects.

Technology 210 on-campus computer terminals/PCs are available for student use and are linked by a campus-wide network. The network has full access to the Internet. Students are not required to have their own PC.

Special Opportunities Advanced credit may be earned through transfer of credits from another institution. International exchange programs in People's Republic of China, Spain, United Kingdom. An internship program is available.

FINANCES

Costs for 1997–98 Tuition: Full-time: $1158 per semester (resident); $3325 per semester (nonresident). Part-time: $121 per credit hour (resident); $361 per credit hour (nonresident). Average 1997–98 room and board costs were $4280 per academic year. Room and board costs vary by occupancy (e.g., single, double, triple), type of meal plan.

Financial Aid In 1997–98, 30% of students received some institutionally administered aid in the form of research assistantships, teaching assistantships, work study, loans. Financial aid is available to part-time students. Application Deadline: 6/1.

Financial Aid Contact Mr. Jack Toney, Director of Financial Aid, 400 Hal Greer Boulevard, Huntington, WV 25755-2020. Phone: 304-696-3162; Fax: 304-696-3242; E-mail: toney@marshall.edu

FACILITIES

Information Resources James E. Morrow Library; total holdings of 422,025 volumes, 186,065 microforms, 2,748 current periodical subscriptions. CD player(s) available for graduate student use. Access provided to online bibliographic retrieval services.

INTERNATIONAL STUDENTS

Demographics 12% of students enrolled are international students [Asia, 75%, Europe, 25%].

Services and Facilities International student office, international student center, visa services, ESL courses, counseling/support services.

Applying TOEFL: minimum score of 525, proof of adequate funds, proof of health/immunizations required. Financial aid is not available to international students.

International Student Contact International Programs Office, 400 Hal Greer Boulevard, Huntington, WV 25755-2020. Phone: 304-696-2379; Fax: 304-696-6353; E-mail: edwards@marshall.edu

PLACEMENT

Services include alumni network, career counseling/planning, career fairs, career library, career placement, electronic job bank, job interviews arranged, job search course, resume referral to employers, and resume preparation. In 1996–97, 150 organizations participated in on-campus recruiting; 75 on-campus interviews were conducted.

Employment Types of employment entered: accounting, banking, chemical industry, computer-related, education, engineering, finance, financial services, health services, hospitality management, human resources, insurance, management, marketing.

Business Program(s) URL: http://www.marshall.edu/cob/

Program Contact: Dr. Chandra Akkihal, Director of Graduate Studies, 400 Hal Greer Boulevard, Corbly Hall 217, Huntington, WV 25755-2305. Phone: 304-696-2315; Fax: 304-696-3116; E-mail: akkihal@marshall.edu

Marshall University Graduate College

College of Business and Economics

South Charleston, West Virginia

OVERVIEW

Marshall University Graduate College is a state-supported, coed, graduate institution. Enrollment: 1,890 graduate, professional, and undergraduate students; 61 full-time matriculated graduate/professional students; 1,829 part-time matriculated graduate/professional students. Founded: 1972. The graduate business unit is in a small-town setting and is on a semester calendar.

HIGHLIGHTS

Enrollment Profile

Full-time: 150
Part-time: 230
Total: 380
Average Age: 35
Fall 1997 Average GPA: N/R

International: N/R
Women: N/R
Minorities: N/R
Average Class Size: 35
Fall 1997 Average GMAT: N/R

Costs

Full-time tuition: N/R
Part-time tuition: $158 per credit hour (resident); $449 per credit hour (nonresident)

Marshall University Graduate College (continued)

GRADUATE BUSINESS PROGRAMS

Master of Business Administration (MBA) Full-time; 48 total credits required; 14 months to complete program.

Executive Master of Business Administration (EMBA) Part-time, distance learning option; 48 total credits required; 2.5 years to complete program.

Master of Science in Industrial Relations (MS) Full-time, part-time; 47 total credits required; 12 months to 7 years to complete program.

Master of Professional Accountancy (MPA) Full-time, part-time; 39 total credits required; 12 months to 7 years to complete program.

Master of Arts in Economics (MA) Full-time, part-time; 37 total credits required; 2 to 7 years to complete program.

ADMISSION

Application Requirements GMAT score, GRE score, application form, application fee, bachelor's degree, minimum GPA, resume, college transcript(s).

Recommended for Application Essay, interview, letters of recommendation, personal statement, computer experience.

Application Deadline Applications processed on a rolling/continuous basis for both domestic and international students. Application fee: $45. Deferred entrance is available.

ACADEMICS

Faculty Full-time 10; part-time 3.

Teaching Methodologies Case study, computer-aided instruction, computer analysis, computer simulations, experiential learning, faculty seminars, field projects, group discussion, lecture, research, seminars by members of the business community, simulations, student presentations, study groups, team projects.

Special Opportunities An internship program is available.

FINANCES

Costs for 1997–98 Tuition: $158 per credit hour (resident); $449 per credit hour (nonresident). Cost varies by academic program. Fees: $33 per credit hour (resident); $33 per credit hour (nonresident). Fees vary by academic program, number of credits taken.

Financial Aid Work study available. Financial aid is available to part-time students.

Financial Aid Contact Financial Aid Office, 100 Angus E Peyton Drive, South Charleston, WV 25303-1600. Phone: 304-293-5242.

FACILITIES

Information Resources Drain-Jordan Library; total holdings of 47,027 volumes, 476,041 microforms, 490 current periodical subscriptions. CD player(s) available for graduate student use. Access provided to online bibliographic retrieval services.

INTERNATIONAL STUDENTS

Demographics N/R

Services and Facilities International student office, international student center.

Applying TOEFL: minimum score of 550 required.

PLACEMENT

Services include alumni network, career counseling/planning, career fairs, career library, career placement, electronic job bank, job interviews arranged, job search course, resume referral to employers, and resume preparation.

Employment Types of employment entered: accounting, banking, chemical industry, communications, computer-related, consulting, consumer products, education, energy, engineering, finance, financial services, government, health services, high technology, hospitality management, information systems/technology, insurance, law, management, manufacturing, marketing, mining, nonprofit, petrochemical, pharmaceutical, retail, service industry, telecommunications, utilities.

Program Contact: Ms. Mary R. Thomas, Assistant Director, Graduate Programs, College of Business and Economics, PO Box 6025, Morgantown, WV 26506-6025. Phone: 304-293-7811; Fax: 304-293-7061; E-mail: thomas@wvube1.bc.wvu.edu

The University of Charleston

Jones-Benedum Division of Business

Charleston, West Virginia

OVERVIEW

The University of Charleston is an independent-nonprofit, coed, comprehensive institution. Enrollment: 1,500 graduate, professional, and undergraduate students. Founded: 1888. The graduate business unit is in an urban setting and is on a semester calendar.

HIGHLIGHTS

Enrollment Profile

Full-time: N/R	International: N/R
Part-time: N/R	Women: N/R
Total: N/R	Minorities: N/R
Average Age: N/R	Average Class Size: 15
Fall 1997 Average GPA: N/R	Fall 1997 Average GMAT: N/R

Costs
Full-time tuition: N/R
Part-time tuition: $515 per credit hour

GRADUATE BUSINESS PROGRAMS

Executive MBA (MBA) Part-time; 40 total credits required; 2 years to complete program.

Master of Human Resource Management (MHRM) Part-time; 36 total credits required; 2 to 7 years to complete program.

ADMISSION

Application Requirements GMAT score, application form, application fee, bachelor's degree, minimum GPA, 3 letters of recommendation, college transcript(s), work experience.

Recommended for Application GRE score accepted, MAT score accepted.

Application Deadline Applications processed on a rolling/continuous basis for both domestic and international students. Application fee: $40. Deferred entrance is available.

ACADEMICS

Faculty Full-time 5; part-time 16.

Teaching Methodologies Case study, computer-aided instruction, computer analysis, computer simulations, experiential learning, group discussion, lecture, research, student presentations, study groups, team projects.

FINANCES

Costs for 1997–98 Tuition: Part-time: $515 per credit hour. Cost varies by academic program, number of credits taken.

Financial Aid Financial aid is available to part-time students.

FACILITIES

Information Resources Andrew S. Thomas Library; total holdings of 110,000 volumes, 130,000 microforms, 800 current periodical subscriptions. CD player(s) available for graduate student use. Access provided to online bibliographic retrieval services.

INTERNATIONAL STUDENTS

Demographics N/R

Applying TOEFL: minimum score of 600 required.

Business Program(s) URL: http://intranet.uchaswv.edu/academic/graduate.html

Program Contact: Mr. Dennis McMillen, Chairperson, Division of Business, Jones-Binedum Division of Business, 2300 MacCorkle Avenue SE, Charleston, WV 25304. Phone: 304-357-4863; Fax: 304-357-4872.

West Virginia University

College of Business and Economics

Morgantown, West Virginia

OVERVIEW

West Virginia University is a state-supported, coed university. Enrollment: 22,238 graduate, professional, and undergraduate students; 3,268 full-time matriculated graduate/professional students; 1,908 part-time matriculated graduate/professional students. Founded: 1867. The graduate business unit is in a small-town setting and is on a semester calendar.

HIGHLIGHTS

Enrollment Profile

Full-time: 178	International: 10%
Part-time: 220	Women: 42%
Total: 398	Minorities: 4%
Average Age: 28	Average Class Size: 30
Fall 1997 Average GPA: 3.4	Fall 1997 Average GMAT: 580

Costs
Full-time tuition: $2805 per academic year (resident); $8056 per academic year (nonresident)
Part-time tuition: $158 per credit hour (resident); $449 per credit hour (nonresident)

AACSB – The International Association for Management Education accredited

GRADUATE BUSINESS PROGRAMS

Master of Business Administration (MBA) Full-time; 48 total credits required; 14 months to complete program.

Executive MBA (MBA) Full-time, distance learning option; 48 total credits required; 2.5 years to complete program.

Master of Science in Industrial Relations (MS) Full-time, part-time; 47 total credits required; 12 months to 7 years to complete program.

Master of Professional Accountancy (MPA) Full-time, part-time; 30 total credits required; 12 months to 7 years to complete program.

ADMISSION

Applications For fall 1997 there were 93 applications for admission. Of those applying, 34 were accepted. Of those accepted, 32 enrolled.

Application Requirements Application form, application fee, bachelor's degree, minimum GPA: 3.0, resume, college transcript(s).

Recommended for Application GMAT score accepted: minimum 500, GRE score accepted, essay, interview, letters of recommendation, personal statement, computer experience.

Application Deadline Applications processed on a rolling/continuous basis for both domestic and international students. Application fee: $45. Deferred entrance is available.

ACADEMICS

Faculty Full-time 64; part-time 1.

Teaching Methodologies Case study, computer-aided instruction, computer analysis, computer simulations, experiential learning, faculty seminars, field projects, group discussion, lecture, research, role playing, seminars by members of the business community, simulations, student presentations, study groups, team projects.

Technology 60 on-campus computer terminals/PCs are available for student use and are linked by a campus-wide network. The network has full access to the Internet. Students are not required to have their own PC.

Special Opportunities An internship program is available.

FINANCES

Costs for 1997–98 Tuition: Full-time: $2805 per semester (resident); $8056 per semester (nonresident). Part-time: $158 per credit hour (resident); $449 per credit hour (nonresident). Cost varies by number of credits taken. Fees: $51 per semester hour (resident); $58 per semester hour (nonresident). Fees vary by number of credits taken.

Financial Aid Fellowships, research assistantships, teaching assistantships, work study, loans available. Application Deadline: 2/1.

Financial Aid Contact Financial Aid Office, Morgantown, WV 26506. Phone: 304-293-5242.

FACILITIES

Information Resources Charles C. Wise, Jr. Library plus 8 additional on-campus libraries; total holdings of 1,877,320 volumes, 2,612,148 microforms, 13,137 current periodical subscriptions. CD player(s) available for graduate student use. Access provided to online bibliographic retrieval services.

INTERNATIONAL STUDENTS

Demographics 10% of students enrolled are international students.

Services and Facilities International student office.

Applying TOEFL: minimum score of 550 required.

International Student Contact Don Delgado, Director of International Admissions, PO Box 6009, Morgantown, WV 26506. Phone: 304-293-2121.

PLACEMENT

Services include alumni network, career fairs, job interviews arranged, job search course, resume referral to employers, and resume preparation.

Employment Types of employment entered: accounting, banking, consulting, finance, financial services, high technology, human resources, information systems/technology, insurance, international trade, management, marketing, service industry.

Business Program(s) URL: http://www.wvu.edu/~colbe/

Program Contact: Dr. Paul J. Speaker, Director, Graduate Programs, PO Box 6025, Morgantown, WV 26506. Phone: 304-293-5408; Fax: 304-293-2385; E-mail: cramsey2@wvu.edu

West Virginia Wesleyan College

Faculty of Business

Buckhannon, West Virginia

OVERVIEW

West Virginia Wesleyan College is an independent-religious, coed, comprehensive institution. Enrollment: 1,600 graduate, professional, and undergraduate students. Founded: 1890. The graduate business unit is in a small-town setting and is on a semester calendar.

HIGHLIGHTS

Enrollment Profile
Full-time: N/R
Part-time: N/R
Total: 100
Average Age: 32
Fall 1997 Average GPA: N/R

International: 9%
Women: 36%
Minorities: N/R
Average Class Size: 15
Fall 1997 Average GMAT: N/R

Costs
Full-time tuition: N/R
Part-time tuition: $290 per credit hour

GRADUATE BUSINESS PROGRAMS

Master of Business Administration (MBA) Full-time, part-time; 36 total credits required; 12 months to 7 years to complete program.

ADMISSION

Application Requirements GMAT score, application form, application fee, bachelor's degree, interview, personal statement, college transcript(s).

Application Deadline Applications processed on a rolling/continuous basis for both domestic and international students. Application fee: $15.

ACADEMICS

Faculty Part-time 9.

Teaching Methodologies Case study, computer-aided instruction, computer analysis, computer simulations, experiential learning, field projects, group discussion, lecture, research, role playing, seminars by members of the business community, simulations, student presentations, study groups, team projects.

Technology 200 on-campus computer terminals/PCs are available for student use and are linked by a campus-wide network. The network has full access to the Internet. Students are not required to have their own PC.

Special Opportunities Advanced credit may be earned through transfer of credits from another institution.

FINANCES

Costs for 1997–98 Tuition: $290 per credit hour.

Financial Aid In 1997–98, 15% of students received some institutionally administered aid in the form of teaching assistantships, work study. Financial aid is available to part-time students.

Financial Aid Contact Lana Golden, Director of Student Affairs, 59 College Avenue, Buckhannon, WV 26201. Phone: 304-473-8080; Fax: 304-472-2571.

FACILITIES

Information Resources A. M. Pfeiffer Library plus 1 additional on-campus library; total holdings of 145,000 volumes, 9,702 microforms, 677 current periodical subscriptions. CD player(s) available for graduate student use. Access provided to online bibliographic retrieval services.

INTERNATIONAL STUDENTS

Demographics 9% of students enrolled are international students [Asia, 100%].

Services and Facilities International student office.

Applying TOEFL: minimum score of 500 required.

International Student Contact Alice Leigh, Assistant Dean, 59 College Avenue, Buckhannon, WV 26201. Phone: 304-473-8440; Fax: 304-472-2571.

Business Program(s) URL: http://www.wvwc.edu/aca/bus/busfront.htm

Program Contact: Dr. David McCauley, Director of MBA Program, 59 College Avenue, Buckhannon, WV 26201. Phone: 304-473-8MBA; Fax: 304-473-8479.

Wheeling Jesuit University

Graduate Business Program

Wheeling, West Virginia

OVERVIEW

Wheeling Jesuit University is an independent-religious, coed, comprehensive institution. Enrollment: 1,527 graduate, professional, and undergraduate students;

Wheeling Jesuit University (continued)

85 full-time matriculated graduate/professional students; 129 part-time matriculated graduate/professional students. Founded: 1954. The graduate business unit is in a small-town setting and is on a semester calendar.

HIGHLIGHTS

Enrollment Profile
Full-time: 11
Part-time: 113
Total: 124
Average Age: 31
Fall 1997 Average GPA: 2.92

International: 3%
Women: 44%
Minorities: 2%
Average Class Size: 20
Fall 1997 Average GMAT: 490

Costs
Full-time tuition: N/R
Part-time tuition: $1130 per 3 credits

GRADUATE BUSINESS PROGRAMS
Master of Business Administration (MBA) Full-time, part-time; 54 total credits required; 12 months to 7 years to complete program.

Master of Science in Accountancy (MS) Full-time, part-time; 36 total credits required; 12 months to 7 years to complete program.

ADMISSION
Applications For fall 1997 there were 31 applications for admission. Of those applying, 29 were accepted. Of those accepted, 20 enrolled.

Application Requirements GMAT score: minimum 475, application form, application fee, bachelor's degree, minimum GPA: 2.75, 3 letters of recommendation, college transcript(s).

Recommended for Application Interview.

Application Deadline Applications processed on a rolling/continuous basis for domestic students only. 8/1 for fall (international), 12/15 for spring (international), 4/15 for summer (international). Application fee: $25. Deferred entrance is available.

ACADEMICS
Faculty Full-time 7; part-time 5.

Teaching Methodologies Case study, computer-aided instruction, computer analysis, computer simulations, experiential learning, faculty seminars, field projects, group discussion, lecture, research, role playing, seminars by members of the business community, simulations, student presentations, study groups, team projects.

Technology 50 on-campus computer terminals/PCs are available for student use and are linked by a campus-wide network. The network has full access to the Internet. Students are not required to have their own PC.

Special Opportunities Advanced credit may be earned through credit by examination, transfer of credits from another institution. An internship program is available.

FINANCES
Costs for 1997–98 Tuition: $1130 per 3 credits. Fees: $50 per semester. Average 1997–98 room and board costs were $4870 per academic year. Room and board costs vary by occupancy (e.g., single, double, triple), type of accommodation.

Financial Aid Research assistantships, loans available. Application Deadline: 5/1.

Financial Aid Contact Su Saunders, Director of Student Financial Planning, 316 Washington Avenue, Wheeling, WV 26003-6295. Phone: 304-243-2304; Fax: 304-243-2500; E-mail: saunders@wju.edu

FACILITIES
Information Resources Bishop Hodges Library plus 2 additional on-campus libraries; total holdings of 142,009 volumes, 103,179 microforms. CD player(s) available for graduate student use. Access provided to online bibliographic retrieval services.

INTERNATIONAL STUDENTS
Demographics 3% of students enrolled are international students [Asia, 75%, Central America, 25%].

Services and Facilities International student office, international student center, visa services, ESL courses, counseling/support services, international student organization.

Applying TOEFL: minimum score of 550, proof of adequate funds required. Financial aid is available to international students.

International Student Contact Eileen Viglietta, International Student Advisor, 316 Washington Avenue, Wheeling, WV 26003-6295. Phone: 304-243-2235; Fax: 304-243-2243; E-mail: eileenv@wju.edu

PLACEMENT
Services include alumni network, career counseling/planning, career fairs, career library, career placement, job interviews arranged, and resume preparation. In 1996–97, 50 organizations participated in on-campus recruiting.

Employment Types of employment entered: accounting, banking, chemical industry, communications, computer-related, consumer products, education, engineering, finance, government, health services, high technology, hospitality management, human resources, information systems/technology, insurance, law, management, manufacturing, marketing, media, mining, nonprofit, petrochemical, pharmaceutical, real estate, retail, service industry, telecommunications, transportation.

Business Program(s) URL: http://www.wjc.edu

Program Contact: Dr. Edward Younkins, Director of Graduate Business Programs, 316 Washington Avenue, Wheeling, WV 26003-6295. Phone: 304-243-2255; Fax: 304-243-4441.

WISCONSIN

Cardinal Stritch University

College of Business and Management

Milwaukee, Wisconsin

OVERVIEW
Cardinal Stritch University is an independent-religious, coed, comprehensive institution. Enrollment: 5,526 graduate, professional, and undergraduate students; 699 full-time matriculated graduate/professional students; 1,932 part-time matriculated graduate/professional students. Founded: 1937. The graduate business unit is in a suburban setting and is on a 6-8 week sessions calendar.

HIGHLIGHTS

Enrollment Profile
Full-time: 595
Part-time: 0
Total: 595
Average Age: 35
Fall 1997 Average GPA: N/R

International: N/R
Women: 50%
Minorities: 17%
Average Class Size: 16
Fall 1997 Average GMAT: N/R

Costs
Full-time tuition: N/R
Part-time tuition: $365 per credit

GRADUATE BUSINESS PROGRAMS
Master of Business Administration (MBA) Full-time; 36 total credits required; 2.5 to 7 years to complete program.

Master of Science in Management (MS) Full-time; 33 total credits required; 2 to 7 years to complete program.

Master of Science in Health Services Administration (MS) Full-time; 34 total credits required; 2 to 7 years to complete program.

ADMISSION
Application Requirements Application form, application fee, bachelor's degree, minimum GPA: 2.5, resume, college transcript(s), minimum of 3 years of work experience.

Recommended for Application Computer experience.

Application Deadline Applications processed on a rolling/continuous basis for both domestic and international students. Application fee: $25. Deferred entrance is available.

ACADEMICS
Faculty Full-time 7; part-time 213.

Teaching Methodologies Case study, computer-aided instruction, computer analysis, computer simulations, experiential learning, field projects, group discussion, research, role playing, seminars by members of the business community, student presentations, study groups, team projects.

Technology The network has full access to the Internet. Students are required to have their own PC.

Special Opportunities Advanced credit may be earned through transfer of credits from another institution.

FINANCES
Costs for 1997–98 Tuition: $365 per credit. Cost varies by academic program, number of credits taken.

Financial Aid Work study, loans available.

Financial Aid Contact Financial Aid Office, 6801 North Yates Road, Milwaukee, WI 53217-3985. Phone: 414-410-4046; Fax: 414-351-7516.

FACILITIES
Information Resources Main library plus 1 additional on-campus library; total holdings of 773,355 volumes, 108,278 microforms, 1,223 current periodi-

cal subscriptions. CD player(s) available for graduate student use. Access provided to online bibliographic retrieval services.

INTERNATIONAL STUDENTS
Demographics N/R

Services and Facilities International student office.

Applying TOEFL: minimum score of 600 required.

International Student Contact Program Representative, College of Business and Management, 6801 North Yates Road, Milwaukee, WI 53217. Phone: 800-347-8822 Ext. 435; Fax: 414-351-7516.

PLACEMENT
Services include career counseling/planning, career fairs, career library, career placement, electronic job bank, resume referral to employers, and resume preparation.

Program Contact: Program Representative, College of Business and Management, 6801 North Yates Road, Milwaukee, WI 53217. Phone: 414-410-4000, 800-347-8822 Ext. 4317 (WI only); Fax: 414-351-7516.

Concordia University Wisconsin

Business Programs
Mequon, Wisconsin

OVERVIEW
Concordia University Wisconsin is an independent-religious, coed, comprehensive institution. Enrollment: 4,137 graduate, professional, and undergraduate students; 24 full-time matriculated graduate/professional students; 363 part-time matriculated graduate/professional students. Founded: 1881. The graduate business unit is in a suburban setting and is on a accelerated calendar.

HIGHLIGHTS

Enrollment Profile
Full-time: 80
Part-time: 40
Total: 120
Average Age: N/R
Fall 1997 Average GPA: 3.23

International: 20%
Women: 58%
Minorities: N/R
Average Class Size: 15
Fall 1997 Average GMAT: N/R

Costs
Full-time tuition: $11,700 per academic year
Part-time tuition: $300 per credit

GRADUATE BUSINESS PROGRAMS
Master of Business Administration (MBA) Full-time, part-time, distance learning option; 39-45 total credits required; 12 months to 5 years to complete program. Concentrations in finance, human resources, management, marketing, international business, nonprofit organization, business education, management information systems, public policy and administration, risk management.

Master of International Business (MIB) Full-time, part-time, distance learning option; 36 total credits required; 22 months to 5 years to complete program. Concentration in international business.

ADMISSION
Application Requirements Application form, application fee, bachelor's degree, essay, minimum GPA: 3.0, 2 letters of recommendation, personal statement, resume, college transcript(s).

Recommended for Application Interview, minimum of 2 years of work experience, computer experience.

Application Deadline Applications processed on a rolling/continuous basis for both domestic and international students. Application fee: $25. Deferred entrance is available.

ACADEMICS
Faculty Part-time 32.

Teaching Methodologies Case study, computer-aided instruction, computer analysis, computer simulations, experiential learning, field projects, group discussion, lecture, research, role playing, seminars by members of the business community, simulations, student presentations, study groups, team projects.

Technology 120 on-campus computer terminals/PCs are available for student use and are linked by a campus-wide network. The network has full access to the Internet. Students are not required to have their own PC.

Special Opportunities Advanced credit may be earned through transfer of credits from another institution. An internship program is available.

FINANCES
Costs for 1997–98 Tuition: Full-time: $11,700 per program. Part-time: $300 per credit.

Financial Aid Work study, loans available. Application Deadline: 5/1.

Financial Aid Contact Mr. Ed Schroeder, Director, Financial Aid, 12800 North Lake Shore Drive, Mequon, WI 53097-2402. Phone: 414-243-4348; Fax: 414-243-4428.

FACILITIES
Information Resources Rincker Library plus 1 additional on-campus library; total holdings of 90,000 volumes, 128,000 microforms, 750 current periodical subscriptions. CD player(s) available for graduate student use. Access provided to online bibliographic retrieval services.

INTERNATIONAL STUDENTS
Demographics 20% of students enrolled are international students [Africa, 15%, Asia, 36%, Central America, 8%, Europe, 24%, South America, 8%].

Services and Facilities International student office, international student center, ESL courses, counseling/support services.

Applying TOEFL: minimum score of 550, proof of adequate funds required. Financial aid is not available to international students.

International Student Contact Ms. Wendy Grapatin, Director of International Center, 12800 North Lake Shore Drive, Mequon, WI 53097. Phone: 414-243-5700 Ext. 366; Fax: 414-243-4459.

PLACEMENT
Services include career counseling/planning, career fairs, career placement, resume referral to employers, and resume preparation.

Employment Of 1996–97 graduates, 100% were employed within three months of graduation. Types of employment entered: banking, computer-related, consulting, education, finance, financial services, government, health services, information systems/technology, management, marketing, nonprofit, service industry.

Business Program(s) URL: http://www.cuw.edu/mba.html#top

Program Contact: Mr. David Borst, Director, Graduate Business Programs, 12800 North Lake Shore Drive, Mequon, WI 53097-2402. Phone: 414-243-4298, 800-665-6564 (WI only); Fax: 414-243-4428; E-mail: dborst@bach.cuw.edu

Edgewood College

Program in Business
Madison, Wisconsin

OVERVIEW
Edgewood College is an independent-religious, coed, comprehensive institution. Enrollment: 2,600 graduate, professional, and undergraduate students; 60 full-time matriculated graduate/professional students; 540 part-time matriculated graduate/professional students. Founded: 1927.

GRADUATE BUSINESS PROGRAMS
Master of Business Administration (MBA)

ACADEMICS
Teaching Methodologies Case study, experiential learning, field projects, lecture, simulations, team projects.

FACILITIES
Information Resources Oscar Rennebohm Library; total holdings of 57,355 volumes, 10,172 microforms, 400 current periodical subscriptions. CD player(s) available for graduate student use. Access provided to online bibliographic retrieval services.

Program Contact: Graduate Office, 855 Woodrow Street, Madison, WI 53711-1998. Phone: 608-257-4861 Ext. 2282; Fax: 608-257-1455.

Lakeland College

Graduate Studies Division
Sheboygan, Wisconsin

OVERVIEW
Lakeland College is an independent-religious, coed, comprehensive institution. Enrollment: 3,391 graduate, professional, and undergraduate students; full-time matriculated graduate/professional students; 114 part-time matriculated graduate/professional students. Founded: 1862. The graduate business unit is in a rural setting and is on a semester calendar.

Lakeland College (continued)

HIGHLIGHTS

Enrollment Profile

Full-time: 0
Part-time: 114
Total: 114
Average Age: 30
Fall 1997 Average GPA: N/R

International: 2%
Women: 61%
Minorities: 4%
Average Class Size: 20
Fall 1997 Average GMAT: 480

Costs

Full-time tuition: N/R
Part-time tuition: $215 per credit

GRADUATE BUSINESS PROGRAMS

Master of Business Administration (MBA) Part-time; 36 total credits required; 3 to 7 years to complete program. Concentrations in accounting, international and area business studies, marketing.

ADMISSION

Applications For fall 1997 there were 17 applications for admission. Of those applying, 15 were accepted. Of those accepted, 15 enrolled.

Application Requirements GMAT score: minimum 450, application form, application fee, bachelor's degree, minimum GPA: 2.75, 2 letters of recommendation, resume, college transcript(s), computer experience: undergraduate course in information processing.

Application Deadline Applications processed on a rolling/continuous basis for both domestic and international students. Application fee: $25. Deferred entrance is available.

ACADEMICS

Faculty Part-time 13.

Teaching Methodologies Case study, computer-aided instruction, computer simulations, field projects, group discussion, lecture, student presentations, study groups, team projects.

Technology 48 on-campus computer terminals/PCs are available for student use and are linked by a campus-wide network. The network has full access to the Internet. Students are not required to have their own PC.

Special Opportunities Advanced credit may be earned through transfer of credits from another institution.

FINANCES

Costs for 1997–98 Tuition: Part-time: $215 per credit. Cost varies by academic program, number of credits taken.

Financial Aid Loans available. Financial aid is available to part-time students.

Financial Aid Contact Don Seymour, PO Box 359, Sheboygan, WI 53082-0359. Phone: 920-565-1297; Fax: 920-565-1206.

FACILITIES

Information Resources John Esch Library; total holdings of 64,000 volumes, 25,283 microforms, 293 current periodical subscriptions. CD player(s) available for graduate student use.

INTERNATIONAL STUDENTS

Demographics 2% of students enrolled are international students [Asia, 100%].

Services and Facilities International student office, international student center, ESL courses, counseling/support services.

Applying TOEFL: minimum score of 550, proof of adequate funds required. Financial aid is available to international students.

International Student Contact International Students Advisor, PO Box 359, Sheboygan, WI 53082-0359. Phone: 920-565-1502; Fax: 920-565-1206.

PLACEMENT

Services include alumni network, career counseling/planning, career fairs, career library, electronic job bank, job search course, resume referral to employers, and resume preparation.

Employment Types of employment entered: banking, finance, financial services, management.

Business Program(s) URL: http://www.lakeland.edu

Program Contact: Ms. Shawn Holzman, Graduate Program Coordinator, PO Box 359, Sheboygan, WI 53082-0359. Phone: 920-565-1256, 800-569-2166 (WI only); Fax: 920-565-1206.

Marian College of Fond du Lac

Business Division

Fond du Lac, Wisconsin

OVERVIEW

Marian College of Fond du Lac is an independent-religious, coed, comprehensive institution. Enrollment: 2,600 graduate, professional, and undergraduate students; full-time matriculated graduate/professional students; 980 part-time matriculated graduate/professional students. Founded: 1936. The graduate business unit is in a small-town setting and is on a semester calendar.

HIGHLIGHTS

Enrollment Profile

Full-time: 0
Part-time: 81
Total: 81
Average Age: 35
Fall 1997 Average GPA: N/R

International: 4%
Women: 51%
Minorities: 2%
Average Class Size: 11
Fall 1997 Average GMAT: N/R

Costs

Full-time tuition: N/R
Part-time tuition: $275 per credit

GRADUATE BUSINESS PROGRAMS

Master of Science in Organizational Leadership and Quality (MS) Part-time; 36 total credits required; 21 months to 2 years to complete program. Concentrations in leadership, quality management.

ADMISSION

Application Requirements Application form, application fee, bachelor's degree, essay, minimum GPA: 2.5, 2 letters of recommendation, personal statement, college transcript(s), minimum of 3 years of work experience.

Recommended for Application Interview, resume, computer experience.

Application Deadline Applications processed on a rolling/continuous basis for both domestic and international students. Application fee: $25. Deferred entrance is available.

ACADEMICS

Faculty Full-time 3; part-time 7.

Teaching Methodologies Case study, computer-aided instruction, computer analysis, computer simulations, experiential learning, field projects, group discussion, lecture, research, role playing, simulations, student presentations, study groups, team projects.

Technology 54 on-campus computer terminals/PCs are available for student use. The network has partial access to the Internet. Students are not required to have their own PC.

Special Opportunities Advanced credit may be earned through transfer of credits from another institution.

FINANCES

Costs for 1997–98 Tuition: Part-time: $275 per credit.

Financial Aid In 1997–98, 12% of students received some institutionally administered aid in the form of work study. Financial aid is available to part-time students. Application Deadline: 3/1.

Financial Aid Contact Ms. Debbie McKinney, Director of Financial Aid, 45 South National Avenue, Fond du Lac, WI 54935-4699. Phone: 920-923-7614; Fax: 920-923-7154.

FACILITIES

Information Resources Cardinal Meyer Library; total holdings of 94,000 volumes, 10,000 microforms, 725 current periodical subscriptions. CD player(s) available for graduate student use. Access provided to online bibliographic retrieval services.

INTERNATIONAL STUDENTS

Demographics 4% of students enrolled are international students.

Applying TOEFL required. Financial aid is not available to international students.

PLACEMENT

Services include alumni network. In 1996–97, 5 organizations participated in on-campus recruiting; 3 on-campus interviews were conducted.

Employment Of 1996–97 graduates, 100% were employed within three months of graduation; the average starting salary was $40,000. Types of employment entered: consulting, engineering, health services, manufacturing.

Program Contact: Ms. Bev Compton, Program Coordinator, Business Division, 45 South National Avenue, Fond du Lac, WI 54935-4699. Phone: 920-923-7651; Fax: 920-923-7154.

Marquette University

College of Business Administration

Milwaukee, Wisconsin

OVERVIEW
Marquette University is an independent-religious, coed university. Enrollment: 10,610 graduate, professional, and undergraduate students; 887 full-time matriculated graduate/professional students; 1,468 part-time matriculated graduate/professional students. Founded: 1864. The graduate business unit is in an urban setting and is on a semester calendar.

HIGHLIGHTS

Enrollment Profile
Full-time: 75
Part-time: 651
Total: 726
Average Age: 30
Fall 1997 Average GPA: 3.22

International: 5%
Women: 34%
Minorities: 7%
Average Class Size: 28
Fall 1997 Average GMAT: 575

Costs
Full-time tuition: N/R
Part-time tuition: $510 per credit hour

AACSB – The International Association for Management Education accredited

GRADUATE BUSINESS PROGRAMS
Master of Business Administration (MBA) Full-time, part-time; 33-48 total credits required; 12 months to 6 years to complete program. Concentrations in marketing, economics, accounting, leadership, quality management, finance, international business.

Executive MBA (EMBA) Full-time, part-time; 51 total credits required; minimum of 5 years managerial experience required; 17 months to complete program.

Master of Science in Human Resources (MS) Full-time, part-time; 36-48 total credits required; 12 months to 6 years to complete program.

Master of Science in Accounting (MS) Full-time, part-time; 30-45 total credits required; 12 months to 6 years to complete program.

Master of Science in Applied Economics (MS) Full-time, part-time; 30-42 total credits required; 12 months to 6 years to complete program. Concentrations in international economics, financial economics, public policy and administration.

Master of Science in Engineering Management (MS) Full-time, part-time; 36 total credits required; 12 months to 6 years to complete program.

ADMISSION
Applications For fall 1997 there were 303 applications for admission. Of those applying, 225 were accepted. Of those accepted, 185 enrolled.

Application Requirements GMAT score, application form, application fee, bachelor's degree, essay, personal statement, resume, college transcript(s).

Recommended for Application Letters of recommendation, work experience, computer experience.

Application Deadline Applications processed on a rolling/continuous basis for both domestic and international students. Application fee: $40. Deferred entrance is available.

ACADEMICS
Faculty Full-time 55; part-time 5.

Teaching Methodologies Case study, computer-aided instruction, computer analysis, computer simulations, experiential learning, faculty seminars, field projects, group discussion, lecture, research, role playing, seminars by members of the business community, student presentations, study groups, team projects.

Technology Computer terminals/PCs are available for student use and are linked by a campus-wide network. The network has full access to the Internet. Students are not required to have their own PC.

Special Opportunities Advanced credit may be earned through transfer of credits from another institution. International exchange programs in Australia, Austria, Belgium, Denmark, Spain, United Kingdom. An internship program is available.

FINANCES
Costs for 1997-98 Tuition: $510 per credit hour. Cost varies by academic program. Average 1997–98 room only costs were $4788 per academic year. Room and board costs vary by occupancy (e.g., single, double, triple), type of accommodation.

Financial Aid Research assistantships, teaching assistantships, grants, scholarships, work study available. Financial aid is available to part-time students. Application Deadline: 2/15.

Financial Aid Contact Thomas Marek, Financial Aid Coordinator, Graduate School, PO Box 1881, Milwaukee, WI 53201-1881. Phone: 414-288-5325; Fax: 414-288-1902; E-mail: marekt@ums.mu.edu

FACILITIES
Information Resources Memorial Library plus 2 additional on-campus libraries; total holdings of 1,000,000 volumes, 268,607 microforms, 10,000 current periodical subscriptions. CD player(s) available for graduate student use. Access provided to online bibliographic retrieval services and online databases.

INTERNATIONAL STUDENTS
Demographics 5% of students enrolled are international students [Africa, 5%, Asia, 40%, Australia/New Zealand, 5%, Central America, 5%, Europe, 25%, North America, 15%, South America, 5%].

Services and Facilities International student office, international student center, visa services, ESL courses, counseling/support services.

Applying TOEFL: minimum score of 550, proof of adequate funds, proof of health/immunizations required. Financial aid is available to international students.

International Student Contact Joseph Fox, Assistant Dean, Director of Graduate Programs, PO Box 1811, Milwaukee, WI 53201-1881. Phone: 414-288-7145; Fax: 414-288-1660; E-mail: foxj@biz.mu.edu

PLACEMENT
Services include alumni network, career counseling/planning, career fairs, career library, career placement, electronic job bank, job interviews arranged, resume referral to employers, and resume preparation.

Employment Of 1996–97 graduates, 100% were employed within three months of graduation. Types of employment entered: financial services, manufacturing.

Business Program(s) URL: http://www.busadm.mu.edu

Program Contact: Joseph Fox, Assistant Dean, Director of Graduate Programs, PO Box 1881, Milwaukee, WI 53201-1881. Phone: 414-288-7145; Fax: 414-288-1660; E-mail: foxj@biz.mu.edu

Milwaukee School of Engineering

Program in Engineering Management

Milwaukee, Wisconsin

OVERVIEW
Milwaukee School of Engineering is an independent-nonprofit, coed, comprehensive institution. Enrollment: 3,028 graduate, professional, and undergraduate students; 74 full-time matriculated graduate/professional students; 412 part-time matriculated graduate/professional students. Founded: 1903.

HIGHLIGHTS

Enrollment Profile
Full-time: 0
Part-time: 294
Total: 294
Average Age: 28
Fall 1997 Average GPA: 2.9

International: 6%
Women: 11%
Minorities: 3%
Average Class Size: N/R
Fall 1997 Average GMAT: N/R

Costs
Full-time tuition: N/R
Part-time tuition: $365 per credit

GRADUATE BUSINESS PROGRAMS
Master of Science in Engineering Management (MS) Part-time, distance learning option; 48-51 total credits required; 3 to 7 years to complete program. Concentrations in quality management, marketing, operations management, project management.

ADMISSION
Application Requirements Application form, application fee, bachelor's degree, minimum GPA: 2.8, 2 letters of recommendation, personal statement, college transcript(s), minimum of 3 years of work experience, computer experience: Microsoft Word.

Recommended for Application GMAT score accepted.

Application Deadline Applications processed on a rolling/continuous basis for both domestic and international students. Application fee: $30.

ACADEMICS
Teaching Methodologies Case study, computer-aided instruction, experiential learning, faculty seminars, group discussion, lecture, research, role playing, seminars by members of the business community, simulations, student presentations, study groups, team projects.

FINANCES
Costs for 1997-98 Tuition: Part-time: $365 per credit.

Financial Aid Contact Ms. Sue Hebert, Director of Financial Aid, 1025 North Broadway, Milwaukee, WI 53202-3109. Phone: 414-277-7223.

Milwaukee School of Engineering (continued)

FACILITIES

Information Resources Walter Schroeder Memorial Library; total holdings of 53,000 volumes, 48,000 microforms, 623 current periodical subscriptions. CD player(s) available for graduate student use. Access provided to online bibliographic retrieval services.

INTERNATIONAL STUDENTS

Demographics 6% of students enrolled are international students.

Applying TOEFL: minimum score of 550, proof of adequate funds, proof of health/immunizations required.

International Student Contact Patrick Coffey, Dean of Student Life, 1025 North Broadway, Milwaukee, WI 53202-3109. Phone: 414-277-7226.

Program Contact: Ms. Cheryl Donnelly, Director, Continuing Education, 1025 North Broadway, Milwaukee, WI 53202-3109. Phone: 414-277-7156 E-mail: donnelly@admin.msoe.edu

Silver Lake College

Program in Management and Organizational Behavior

Manitowoc, Wisconsin

OVERVIEW

Silver Lake College is an independent-religious, coed, comprehensive institution. Enrollment: 1,050 graduate, professional, and undergraduate students; 61 full-time matriculated graduate/professional students; 129 part-time matriculated graduate/professional students. Founded: 1935. The graduate business unit is in a small-town setting and is on a 8-week sessions calendar.

HIGHLIGHTS

Enrollment Profile

Full-time: 61	International: N/R
Part-time: 129	Women: 54%
Total: 190	Minorities: 3%
Average Age: 36	Average Class Size: 20
Fall 1997 Average GPA: 3.0	Fall 1997 Average GMAT: N/R

Costs
Full-time tuition: N/R
Part-time tuition: $230 per credit

GRADUATE BUSINESS PROGRAMS

Master of Science in Management and Organizational Behavior (MS) Full-time, part-time; 40 total credits required; 2 to 7 years to complete program. Concentrations in management, health care, human resources, international business.

ADMISSION

Application Requirements Application form, bachelor's degree, minimum GPA: 3.0, letters of recommendation, personal statement, resume, college transcript(s).

Recommended for Application Computer experience.

Application Deadline Applications processed on a rolling/continuous basis for domestic students only. Application fee: $30.

ACADEMICS

Faculty Part-time 15.

Teaching Methodologies Case study, computer-aided instruction, computer analysis, faculty seminars, field projects, group discussion, lecture, research, role playing, seminars by members of the business community, student presentations, study groups, team projects.

Technology 50 on-campus computer terminals/PCs are available for student use and are linked by a campus-wide network. The network has full access to the Internet. Students are not required to have their own PC.

Special Opportunities Advanced credit may be earned through credit for business training programs, transfer of credits from another institution.

FINANCES

Costs for 1997–98 Tuition: $230 per credit.

Financial Aid In 1997–98, 14% of students received some institutionally administered aid in the form of grants, scholarships, loans.

Financial Aid Contact Sr. Mary Beth Kornely, Director, Student Financial Aid, Manitowoc, WI 54220-9340. Phone: 920-684-6691; Fax: 920-684-7082.

FACILITIES

Information Resources Silver Lake College Library plus 1 additional on-campus library; total holdings of 65,056 volumes, 20,214 microforms, 215 current periodical subscriptions. CD player(s) available for graduate student use. Access provided to online bibliographic retrieval services and online databases.

INTERNATIONAL STUDENTS
Demographics N/R

PLACEMENT

Services include alumni network, career counseling/planning, career fairs, career placement, and resume preparation.

Employment Of 1996–97 graduates, 100% were employed within three months of graduation.

Business Program(s) URL: http://www.sl.edu/slc.html

Program Contact: Mr. Alan Heffner, Director, Graduate Business Programs, Manitowoc, WI 54220-9340. Phone: 920-686-6189; Fax: 920-684-7082; E-mail: aheffner@sl.edu

University of Wisconsin-Eau Claire

School of Business

Eau Claire, Wisconsin

OVERVIEW

The University of Wisconsin-Eau Claire is a state-supported, coed, comprehensive institution. Enrollment: 10,331 graduate, professional, and undergraduate students; 154 full-time matriculated graduate/professional students; 308 part-time matriculated graduate/professional students. Founded: 1916. The graduate business unit is in a small-town setting and is on a semester calendar.

HIGHLIGHTS

Enrollment Profile

Full-time: 4	International: N/R
Part-time: 57	Women: 34%
Total: 61	Minorities: 10%
Average Age: 33	Average Class Size: 20
Fall 1997 Average GPA: 3.2	Fall 1997 Average GMAT: 530

Costs
Full-time tuition: N/R
Part-time tuition: $204 per credit (resident); $581 per credit (nonresident)

AACSB – The International Association for Management Education accredited

GRADUATE BUSINESS PROGRAMS

Master of Business Administration (MBA) Full-time, part-time, distance learning option; 30 total credits required; 17 months to 2.5 years to complete program.

ADMISSION

Application Requirements GMAT score: minimum 475, application form, application fee, bachelor's degree, minimum GPA: 2.75, resume, college transcript(s).

Recommended for Application Letters of recommendation, personal statement, computer experience.

Application Deadline Applications processed on a rolling/continuous basis for both domestic and international students. Application fee: $45. Deferred entrance is available.

ACADEMICS

Faculty Full-time 24.

Teaching Methodologies Case study, computer-aided instruction, computer analysis, computer simulations, field projects, group discussion, lecture, research, role playing, seminars by members of the business community, simulations, student presentations, study groups, team projects.

Technology 1,000 on-campus computer terminals/PCs are available for student use and are linked by a campus-wide network. The network has full access to the Internet. Students are not required to have their own PC.

Special Opportunities Advanced credit may be earned through transfer of credits from another institution.

FINANCES

Costs for 1997–98 Tuition: $204 per credit (resident); $581 per credit (nonresident). Cost varies by number of credits taken, reciprocity agreements. Fees: $200 per year (resident); $581 per year (nonresident). Average 1997–98 room and board costs were $2850 per academic year. Room and board costs vary by occupancy (e.g., single, double, triple), type of accommodation, type of meal plan.

Financial Aid Fellowships, research assistantships, work study, loans available. Financial aid is available to part-time students.

Financial Aid Contact Department of Financial Aid, PO Box 4004, Eau Claire, WI 54702-4004. Phone: 715-836-3373; Fax: 715-836-2380.

FACILITIES
Information Resources William D. McIntyre Library; total holdings of 514,650 volumes, 1,444,264 microforms, 1,998 current periodical subscriptions. CD player(s) available for graduate student use. Access provided to online bibliographic retrieval services.

INTERNATIONAL STUDENTS
Demographics N/R

Services and Facilities International student office, international student housing, ESL courses, counseling/support services.

Applying TOEFL: minimum score of 550, proof of adequate funds required. Proof of health/immunizations recommended. Financial aid is available to international students.

International Student Contact Director of International Education, PO Box 4004, Eau Claire, WI 54702-4004. Phone: 715-836-4411; Fax: 715-836-2380.

PLACEMENT
Services include career counseling/planning, career fairs, career library, career placement, electronic job bank, job interviews arranged, resume referral to employers, and resume preparation. In 1996–97, 230 organizations participated in on-campus recruiting.

Employment Of 1996–97 graduates, 90% were employed within three months of graduation. Types of employment entered: accounting, banking, computer-related, consumer products, education, engineering, finance, financial services, government, health services, human resources, information systems/technology, management, manufacturing, marketing, real estate, service industry.

Business Program(s) URL: http://www.uwec.edu

Program Contact: Dr. Robert Erffmeyer, MBA Program Coordinator, PO Box 4004, Eau Claire, WI 54702-4004. Phone: 715-836-5473; Fax: 715-836-2944; E-mail: erffmerc@uwec.edu

University of Wisconsin-Green Bay

Program in Administrative Sciences
Green Bay, Wisconsin

OVERVIEW
The University of Wisconsin-Green Bay is a state-supported, coed, comprehensive institution. Enrollment: 5,509 graduate, professional, and undergraduate students; 81 full-time matriculated graduate/professional students; 58 part-time matriculated graduate/professional students. Founded: 1965.

HIGHLIGHTS

Enrollment Profile
Full-time: N/R
Part-time: N/R
Total: 28
Average Age: 31
Fall 1997 Average GPA: N/R
International: N/R
Women: N/R
Minorities: N/R
Average Class Size: N/R
Fall 1997 Average GMAT: N/R

Costs
Full-time tuition: $3130 per academic year (resident); $10,358 per academic year (nonresident)
Part-time tuition: N/R

GRADUATE BUSINESS PROGRAMS
MS in Administrative Science (MS) Full-time, part-time; 36 total credits required.

ADMISSION
Applications For fall 1997 there were 16 applications for admission.
Application Requirements GMAT score, GRE score, application form, bachelor's degree, minimum GPA, letters of recommendation, college transcript(s).
Application Deadline Applications processed on a rolling/continuous basis for both domestic and international students.

ACADEMICS
Faculty Full-time 11.
Teaching Methodologies Case study, group discussion.

FINANCES
Costs for 1997–98 Tuition: Full-time: $3130 per year (resident); $10,358 per year (nonresident).
Financial Aid In 1997–98, 11% of students received some institutionally administered aid in the form of research assistantships, teaching assistantships, work study, loans. Application Deadline: 7/15.
Financial Aid Contact Ron Ronnenberg, 2420 Nicolet Drive, Green Bay, WI 54311-7001. Phone: 920-465-2075.

FACILITIES
Information Resources Cofrin Library plus 1 additional on-campus library; total holdings of 287,365 volumes, 804,741 microforms, 1,420 current periodical subscriptions. CD player(s) available for graduate student use. Access provided to online bibliographic retrieval services.

INTERNATIONAL STUDENTS
Demographics N/R

Services and Facilities International student office, international student center.
International Student Contact International Office, 2420 Nicolet Drive, Green Bay, WI 54311-7001. Phone: 920-465-2413.

PLACEMENT
Services include career counseling/planning, job interviews arranged, job search course, and resume preparation.

Program Contact: David Littig, 2420 Nicolet Drive, Green Bay, WI 54311-7001. Phone: 920-465-2081.

University of Wisconsin-La Crosse

College of Business Administration
La Crosse, Wisconsin

OVERVIEW
The University of Wisconsin-La Crosse is a state-supported, coed, comprehensive institution. Enrollment: 8,600 graduate, professional, and undergraduate students; 238 full-time matriculated graduate/professional students; 264 part-time matriculated graduate/professional students. Founded: 1909. The graduate business unit is in a small-town setting and is on a semester calendar.

HIGHLIGHTS

Enrollment Profile
Full-time: 21
Part-time: 71
Total: 92
Average Age: 27
Fall 1997 Average GPA: 3.3
International: 21%
Women: 30%
Minorities: 4%
Average Class Size: 30
Fall 1997 Average GMAT: 530

Costs
Full-time tuition: $3670 per academic year (resident); $10,300 per academic year (nonresident)
Part-time tuition: $227 per semester credit (resident); $628 per semester credit (nonresident)

AACSB – The International Association for Management Education accredited

GRADUATE BUSINESS PROGRAMS
Master of Business Administration (MBA) Full-time, part-time, distance learning option; 30-60 total credits required; 18 months to 3 years to complete program.

ADMISSION
Applications For fall 1997 there were 34 applications for admission. Of those applying, 32 were accepted. Of those accepted, 17 enrolled.
Application Requirements GMAT score, application form, application fee, bachelor's degree, minimum GPA: 2.85, college transcript(s).
Recommended for Application Letters of recommendation, work experience.
Application Deadline Applications processed on a rolling/continuous basis for both domestic and international students. Application fee: $38. Deferred entrance is available.

ACADEMICS
Faculty Full-time 43.
Teaching Methodologies Case study, computer-aided instruction, group discussion, lecture, research, role playing, simulations, student presentations, team projects.
Technology 700 on-campus computer terminals/PCs are available for student use and are linked by a campus-wide network. The network has full access to the Internet. Students are not required to have their own PC.
Special Opportunities Advanced credit may be earned through transfer of credits from another institution.

FINANCES
Costs for 1997–98 Tuition: Full-time: $3670 per year (resident); $10,300 per year (nonresident). Part-time: $227 per semester credit (resident); $628 per semester credit (nonresident). Cost varies by reciprocity agreements. Average 1997–98 room and board costs were $6000 per academic year (off campus). Room and board costs vary by type of meal plan.
Financial Aid In 1997–98, 13% of students received some institutionally administered aid in the form of research assistantships, work study. Financial aid is available to part-time students. Application Deadline: 3/1.

University of Wisconsin-La Crosse (continued)

Financial Aid Contact Mr. A.C. Stadthaus, Director of Financial Aid, 1725 State Street, La Crosse, WI 54601-3742. Phone: 608-785-8604.

FACILITIES

Information Resources Murphy Library plus 3 additional on-campus libraries; total holdings of 414,922 volumes, 990,244 microforms, 1,896 current periodical subscriptions. CD player(s) available for graduate student use. Access provided to online bibliographic retrieval services.

INTERNATIONAL STUDENTS

Demographics 21% of students enrolled are international students.

Services and Facilities International student office, international student center, ESL courses, counseling/support services.

Applying TOEFL: minimum score of 550, proof of adequate funds, proof of health/immunizations required.

International Student Contact Mr. Jay Lokken, Director, Office of International Education, 1725 State Street, La Crosse, WI 54601-3742. Phone: 608-785-8016.

PLACEMENT

Services include career counseling/planning, career fairs, career library, electronic job bank, resume referral to employers, and resume preparation.

Business Program(s) URL: http://www.uwlax.edu/

Program Contact: Ms. Amelia Dittman, Coordinator, MBA Program, 1725 State Street, La Crosse, WI 54601-3742. Phone: 608-785-8092; Fax: 608-785-6700; E-mail: dittman@mail.uwlax.edu

University of Wisconsin-Madison

School of Business

Madison, Wisconsin

OVERVIEW

The University of Wisconsin-Madison is a state-supported, coed university. Enrollment: 40,305 graduate, professional, and undergraduate students; 10,172 full-time matriculated graduate/professional students; 2,008 part-time matriculated graduate/professional students. Founded: 1849. The graduate business unit is in an urban setting and is on a semester calendar.

HIGHLIGHTS

Enrollment Profile

Full-time: 457	International: N/R
Part-time: 0	Women: N/R
Total: 457	Minorities: N/R
Average Age: 27	Average Class Size: 30
Fall 1997 Average GPA: 3.36	Fall 1997 Average GMAT: 595

Costs
Full-time tuition: $5666 per academic year (resident); $15,380 per academic year (nonresident)
Part-time tuition: N/R

AACSB – The International Association for Management Education accredited

GRADUATE BUSINESS PROGRAMS

Master of Business Administration (MBA) Full-time; 35-54 total credits required; 12 months to 3 years to complete program. Concentrations in accounting, entrepreneurship, finance, human resources, information management, international business, management information systems, marketing, logistics, operations management, quality management, real estate, risk management, insurance, management, banking.

Master of Science in Business (MS) Full-time, part-time; 30-48 total credits required; 12 months to 4 years to complete program. Concentrations in actuarial science, entrepreneurship, finance, human resources, insurance, international business, logistics, management, management information systems, manufacturing management, marketing research, operations management, quality management, real estate, risk management, technology management, banking.

Master of Arts in Business (MA) Full-time; 40-46 total credits required; 12 months to 4 years to complete program. Concentration in arts administration/management.

Executive MBA (EMBA) Full-time; 2 years to complete program. Concentration in management.

Master of Accountancy (MAcc) Full-time; 30-66 total credits required; 12 months to 4 years to complete program. Concentrations in accounting, taxation.

Evening MBA (MBA) Part-time; 55 total credits required; minimum of 3 years to complete program.

ADMISSION

Applications For fall 1997 there were 1,018 applications for admission. Of those applying, 302 were accepted. Of those accepted, 159 enrolled.

Application Requirements GMAT score, application form, application fee, bachelor's degree, essay, minimum GPA: 3.0, 3 letters of recommendation, resume, college transcript(s), computer experience: computer literacy.

Recommended for Application Minimum of 2 years of work experience.

Application Deadline 5/1 for fall, 10/1 for spring, 5/1 for fall (international), 10/1 for spring (international). Application fee: $38.

ACADEMICS

Faculty Full-time 82; part-time 1.

Teaching Methodologies Case study, computer-aided instruction, computer analysis, computer simulations, experiential learning, faculty seminars, field projects, group discussion, lecture, research, role playing, seminars by members of the business community, simulations, student presentations, study groups, team projects.

Technology Computer terminals/PCs are available for student use and are linked by a campus-wide network. The network has full access to the Internet. Students are required to have their own PC.

Special Opportunities Advanced credit may be earned through transfer of credits from another institution. International exchange programs in Austria, Chile, Denmark, France, Germany, Mexico, People's Republic of China, Thailand, United Kingdom. An internship program is available.

FINANCES

Costs for 1997–98 Tuition: Full-time: $5666 per year (resident); $15,380 per year (nonresident). Cost varies by number of credits taken, reciprocity agreements. Average 1997–98 room and board costs were $5256 per academic year (on campus) and $6756 per academic year (off campus). Room and board costs vary by occupancy (e.g., single, double, triple), type of accommodation, type of meal plan.

Financial Aid In 1997–98, 34% of students received some institutionally administered aid in the form of fellowships, research assistantships, teaching assistantships, grants, scholarships, work study, loans. Application Deadline: 2/15.

Financial Aid Contact Graduate Programs Office, 2266 Grainger Hall, 975 University Avenue, Madison, WI 53706-1323. Phone: 608-262-1555; Fax: 608-265-4192; E-mail: uwmadmba@bus.wisc.edu

FACILITIES

Information Resources Memorial Library plus 44 additional on-campus libraries; total holdings of 5,535,592 volumes, 4,139,554 microforms, 46,130 current periodical subscriptions. CD player(s) available for graduate student use. Access provided to online bibliographic retrieval services.

INTERNATIONAL STUDENTS

Demographics N/R

Services and Facilities International student office, international student center, international student housing, visa services, ESL courses, counseling/support services.

Applying TOEFL: minimum score of 600, proof of adequate funds, proof of health/immunizations required. TSE recommended. Financial aid is not available to international students.

International Student Contact Director, International Students and Scholar Services, 975 University Avenue, Madison, WI 53706-1380. Phone: 608-262-2044.

PLACEMENT

Services include alumni network, career counseling/planning, career fairs, career library, career placement, electronic job bank, job interviews arranged, job search course, resume referral to employers, and resume preparation. In 1996–97, 212 organizations participated in on-campus recruiting; 798 on-campus interviews were conducted.

Employment Of 1996–97 graduates, 92% were employed within three months of graduation; the average starting salary was $54,396. Types of employment entered: accounting, banking, chemical industry, communications, computer-related, consulting, consumer products, education, engineering, finance, financial services, government, health services, high technology, human resources, information systems/technology, insurance, law, management, manufacturing, marketing, media, nonprofit, pharmaceutical, real estate, retail, service industry, telecommunications, transportation, utilities.

Business Program(s) URL: http://www.wisc.edu/bschool

Program Contact: Graduate Programs Office, 2266 Grainger Hall, 975 University Avenue, Madison, WI 53706. Phone: 608-262-1555; Fax: 608-265-4192; E-mail: uwmadmba@bus.wisc.edu
See full description on page 1174.

University of Wisconsin-Milwaukee

School of Business Administration

Milwaukee, Wisconsin

OVERVIEW
The University of Wisconsin-Milwaukee is a state-supported, coed university. Enrollment: 22,251 graduate, professional, and undergraduate students; 1,272 full-time matriculated graduate/professional students; 3,294 part-time matriculated graduate/professional students. Founded: 1955. The graduate business unit is in an urban setting and is on a semester calendar.

HIGHLIGHTS

Enrollment Profile

Full-time: 169	International: 12%
Part-time: 657	Women: 40%
Total: 826	Minorities: 7%
Average Age: 31	Average Class Size: 30
Fall 1997 Average GPA: 3.1	Fall 1997 Average GMAT: 540

Costs
Full-time tuition: $2642 per academic year (resident); $7478 per academic year (nonresident)
Part-time tuition: $350 per credit (resident); $934 per credit (nonresident)

AACSB – The International Association for Management Education accredited

GRADUATE BUSINESS PROGRAMS
Master of Business Administration (MBA) Full-time, part-time; 32 total credits required; 2 to 7 years to complete program.

Executive MBA (MBA) Full-time; 32 total credits required; 22 months to complete program.

Master of Science in Management (MS) Full-time, part-time; 30-32 total credits required; 2 to 7 years to complete program. Concentrations in accounting, finance, management information systems, marketing, taxation, international business, health care, organizational management, quality management.

ADMISSION
Applications For fall 1997 there were 337 applications for admission. Of those applying, 219 were accepted. Of those accepted, 163 enrolled.

Application Requirements Application form, application fee, bachelor's degree, minimum GPA: 2.75, personal statement, college transcript(s).

Recommended for Application GMAT score accepted, GRE score accepted.

Application Deadline Applications processed on a rolling/continuous basis for both domestic and international students. Application fee: $45, $75 (international). Deferred entrance is available.

ACADEMICS
Faculty Full-time 61.

Teaching Methodologies Case study, computer analysis, computer simulations, faculty seminars, field projects, group discussion, lecture, research, role playing, seminars by members of the business community, student presentations, study groups, team projects.

Technology 350 on-campus computer terminals/PCs are available for student use and are linked by a campus-wide network. The network has full access to the Internet. Students are not required to have their own PC.

Special Opportunities Advanced credit may be earned through transfer of credits from another institution. An internship program is available.

FINANCES
Costs for 1997–98 Tuition: Full-time: $2642 per semester (resident); $7478 per semester (nonresident). Part-time: $350 per credit (resident); $934 per credit (nonresident). Cost varies by number of credits taken, reciprocity agreements. Fees: Full-time: $240 per academic year (resident); $240 per academic year (nonresident). Part-time: $149 per credit (resident); $149 per credit (nonresident). Fees vary by number of credits taken. Average 1997–98 room only costs were $2457 per academic year. Room and board costs vary by occupancy (e.g., single, double, triple), type of accommodation, type of meal plan.

Financial Aid Fellowships, research assistantships, teaching assistantships, grants, scholarships, work study available. Financial aid is available to part-time students. Application Deadline: 4/15.

Financial Aid Contact Sharon Simons, Assistant Director, Financial Aid and Student Employment, PO Box 469, Milwaukee, WI 53201. Phone: 414-229-5392; E-mail: simons@csd.uwm.edu

FACILITIES
Information Resources Golda Meir Library; total holdings of 1,718,988 volumes, 1,614,514 microforms, 5,586 current periodical subscriptions. CD player(s) available for graduate student use. Access provided to online bibliographic retrieval services and online databases.

INTERNATIONAL STUDENTS
Demographics 12% of students enrolled are international students.

Services and Facilities International student office, international student center, visa services, ESL courses, counseling/support services.

Applying TOEFL: minimum score of 550, proof of adequate funds required. Financial aid is not available to international students.

International Student Contact Sharon Seager, Graduate Evaluator, International Studies and Programs, PO Box 340, Milwaukee, WI 53201. Phone: 414-229-4845; Fax: 414-229-3750; E-mail: international@csd.uwm.edu

PLACEMENT
Services include alumni network, career counseling/planning, career fairs, career library, career placement, electronic job bank, job interviews arranged, resume referral to employers, and resume preparation.

Business Program(s) URL: http://www.uwm.edu/Dept/Business/SBA/

Program Contact: Sarah M. Sandin, MBA/MS Program Manager, School of Business Administration, PO Box 742, Milwaukee, WI 53201-0742. Phone: 414-229-5403; Fax: 414-229-2372; E-mail: uwmbusmasters@csd.uwm.edu

University of Wisconsin-Oshkosh

College of Business Administration

Oshkosh, Wisconsin

OVERVIEW
The University of Wisconsin-Oshkosh is a state-supported, coed, comprehensive institution. Enrollment: 10,528 graduate, professional, and undergraduate students; 198 full-time matriculated graduate/professional students; 1,104 part-time matriculated graduate/professional students. Founded: 1871. The graduate business unit is in a small-town setting and is on a semester calendar.

HIGHLIGHTS

Enrollment Profile

Full-time: 29	International: 3%
Part-time: 496	Women: 60%
Total: 525	Minorities: 2%
Average Age: 31	Average Class Size: 30
Fall 1997 Average GPA: 3.1	Fall 1997 Average GMAT: 540

Costs
Full-time tuition: $1900 per academic year (resident); $5600 per academic year (nonresident)
Part-time tuition: $200 per credit (resident); $600 per credit (nonresident)

AACSB – The International Association for Management Education accredited

Degree(s) offered in conjunction with University of Wisconsin-Green Bay, University of Wisconsin-Stevens Point

GRADUATE BUSINESS PROGRAMS
Master of Business Administration (MBA) Full-time, part-time, distance learning option; 30-51 total credits required; 12 months to 7 years to complete program. Concentrations in finance, human resources, management information systems, management, marketing.

ADMISSION
Applications For fall 1997 there were 220 applications for admission. Of those applying, 200 were accepted. Of those accepted, 100 enrolled.

Application Requirements GMAT score: minimum 450, application form, application fee, bachelor's degree, minimum GPA: 2.75, personal statement, college transcript(s).

Recommended for Application Work experience, computer experience.

Application Deadline 7/1 for fall, 12/1 for spring, 4/1 for summer, 7/1 for fall (international), 12/1 for spring (international), 4/1 for summer (international). Application fee: $45. Deferred entrance is available.

ACADEMICS
Faculty Full-time 45.

Teaching Methodologies Case study, computer simulations, experiential learning, field projects, group discussion, lecture, research, role playing, simulations, student presentations, team projects.

Technology 500 on-campus computer terminals/PCs are available for student use and are linked by a campus-wide network. The network has full access to the Internet. Students are not required to have their own PC.

University of Wisconsin-Oshkosh (continued)

Special Opportunities Advanced credit may be earned through transfer of credits from another institution.

FINANCES

Costs for 1997–98 Tuition: Full-time: $1900 per semester (resident); $5600 per semester (nonresident). Part-time: $200 per credit (resident); $600 per credit (nonresident). Fees: Full-time: $200 per academic year (resident); $200 per academic year (nonresident). Part-time: $23 per credit (resident); $23 per credit (nonresident). Average 1997–98 room and board costs were $3500 per academic year (on campus) and $4700 per academic year (off campus).

Financial Aid In 1997–98, 5% of students received some institutionally administered aid in the form of research assistantships, work study, loans. Financial aid is available to part-time students. Application Deadline: 3/15.

Financial Aid Contact Mr. Ken Cook, Director of Financial Aid, Financial Aid Office, Oshkosh, WI 54901. Phone: 414-424-3377; Fax: 414-424-0284; E-mail: meyers@uwosh.edu

FACILITIES

Information Resources Polk Library; total holdings of 439,614 volumes, 127,305 microforms, 1,787 current periodical subscriptions. CD player(s) available for graduate student use. Access provided to online bibliographic retrieval services and online databases.

INTERNATIONAL STUDENTS

Demographics 3% of students enrolled are international students [Africa, 10%, Asia, 50%, Europe, 25%, North America, 15%].

Services and Facilities International student office, international student center, international student housing, counseling/support services.

Applying TOEFL: minimum score of 550, proof of adequate funds, proof of health/immunizations required. Financial aid is available to international students.

International Student Contact Ms. Judy Jaeger, International Student Advisor, Dean of Students Office, Oshkosh, WI 54901. Phone: 414-424-3100; Fax: 414-424-7317; E-mail: jaeger@uwosh.edu

PLACEMENT

Services include alumni network, career counseling/planning, career fairs, career library, career placement, electronic job bank, job interviews arranged, job search course, resume referral to employers, and resume preparation. In 1996–97, 40 organizations participated in on-campus recruiting; 25 on-campus interviews were conducted.

Employment Of 1996–97 graduates, 98% were employed within three months of graduation. Types of employment entered: accounting, banking, consulting, consumer products, finance, financial services, government, human resources, information systems/technology, management, manufacturing, marketing, nonprofit, retail, service industry, telecommunications, utilities.

Business Program(s) URL: http://www.uwosh.edu/colleges/coba/mba.htm

Program Contact: Ms. Lynn Grancorbitz, MBA Program Assistant Director and Advisor, 800 Algoma Boulevard, Oshkosh, WI 54901-3551. Phone: 414-424-1436, 800-633-1430 (WI only); Fax: 414-424-7413; E-mail: mba@pobox.uwosh.edu

University of Wisconsin-Parkside

School of Business and Administrative Science

Kenosha, Wisconsin

OVERVIEW

The University of Wisconsin-Parkside is a state-supported, coed, comprehensive institution. Enrollment: 4,500 graduate, professional, and undergraduate students. Founded: 1965. The graduate business unit is in an urban setting and is on a semester calendar.

HIGHLIGHTS

Enrollment Profile

Full-time: 0	International: 2%
Part-time: 113	Women: 43%
Total: 113	Minorities: 10%
Average Age: 29	Average Class Size: 25
Fall 1997 Average GPA: 3.2	Fall 1997 Average GMAT: 500

Costs
Full-time tuition: N/R
Part-time tuition: $521 per course (resident); $1559 per course (nonresident)

AACSB – The International Association for Management Education accredited

GRADUATE BUSINESS PROGRAMS
Master of Business Administration (MBA) Part-time; 33 total credits required; 2.5 to 7 years to complete program.

ADMISSION

Applications For fall 1997 there were 43 applications for admission. Of those applying, 29 were accepted.

Application Requirements GMAT score: minimum 450, application form, application fee, bachelor's degree, minimum GPA: 2.75, 2 letters of recommendation, personal statement, resume, college transcript(s).

Recommended for Application Work experience.

Application Deadline 8/1 for fall, 12/15 for spring, 4/15 for summer. Application fee: $45. Deferred entrance is available.

ACADEMICS

Faculty Full-time 19.

Teaching Methodologies Case study, computer analysis, computer simulations, group discussion, role playing, simulations, student presentations, team projects.

Technology 100 on-campus computer terminals/PCs are available for student use and are linked by a campus-wide network. The network has full access to the Internet. Students are not required to have their own PC.

Special Opportunities Advanced credit may be earned through transfer of credits from another institution.

FINANCES

Costs for 1997–98 Tuition: Part-time: $521 per course (resident); $1559 per course (nonresident). Cost varies by class time (e.g., day/evening), number of credits taken, reciprocity agreements. Fees: Part-time: $23 per credit (resident); $23 per credit (nonresident).

Financial Aid Contact Mr. Carl Buck, Director of Financial Aid, 900 Wood Road, Box 2000, Kenosha, WI 53141-2000. Phone: 414-595-2577.

FACILITIES

Information Resources Wyllie Library-Learning Center; total holdings of 326,000 volumes, 684,000 microforms, 1,550 current periodical subscriptions. Access provided to online bibliographic retrieval services.

INTERNATIONAL STUDENTS

Demographics 2% of students enrolled are international students.

Services and Facilities International student office, visa services, counseling/support services.

Applying Financial aid is not available to international students.

International Student Contact International Student Services, 900 Wood Road, Box 2000, Kenosha, WI 53141-2000. Phone: 414-595-2600.

PLACEMENT

Services include career counseling/planning, career library, and career placement.

Employment Of 1996–97 graduates, 98% were employed within three months of graduation. Types of employment entered: accounting, banking, computer-related, engineering, finance, human resources, information systems/technology, insurance, management, marketing, pharmaceutical, real estate, telecommunications, utilities.

Business Program(s) URL: http://www.uwp.edu/academic/business/

Program Contact: Mr. Brad Piazza, Assistant to the Dean, School of Business and Technology, 900 Wood Road, Box 2000, Kenosha, WI 53141-2000. Phone: 414-595-2046; Fax: 414-595-2680; E-mail: bradley.piazza@uwp.edu

University of Wisconsin-Stout

Program in Training and Development and Program in Management Technology

Menomonie, Wisconsin

OVERVIEW

The University of Wisconsin-Stout is a state-supported, coed, comprehensive institution. Enrollment: 7,545 graduate, professional, and undergraduate students; 299 full-time matriculated graduate/professional students; 458 part-time matriculated graduate/professional students. Founded: 1891. The graduate business unit is in a small-town setting and is on a semester calendar.

HIGHLIGHTS

Enrollment Profile
Full-time: 39
Part-time: 56
Total: 95
Average Age: 32
Fall 1997 Average GPA: N/R

International: 13%
Women: 48%
Minorities: 9%
Average Class Size: 25
Fall 1997 Average GMAT: N/R

Costs
Full-time tuition: $3129 per academic year (resident); $7229 per academic year (nonresident)
Part-time tuition: $174 per credit (resident); $402 per credit (nonresident)

GRADUATE BUSINESS PROGRAMS
Training and Development (MS) Full-time, part-time; 30 total credits required; up to 7 years to complete program.

Management Technology (MS) Full-time, part-time; 30 total credits required; 2 years work experience required; up to 7 years to complete program. Concentrations in industrial administration/management, construction management, arts administration/management, risk management, system management, industrial/labor relations.

ADMISSION
Applications For fall 1997 there were 42 applications for admission. Of those applying, 34 were accepted. Of those accepted, 23 enrolled.

Application Requirements Application form, bachelor's degree, minimum GPA: 2.75, letters of recommendation, personal statement, college transcript(s), work experience, computer experience: introductory computer course or equivalent computer experience.

Recommended for Application Resume.

Application Deadline Applications processed on a rolling/continuous basis for both domestic and international students. Application fee: $38.

ACADEMICS
Faculty Full-time 20; part-time 5.

Teaching Methodologies Case study, computer-aided instruction, computer simulations, experiential learning, faculty seminars, field projects, group discussion, lecture, research, role playing, seminars by members of the business community, simulations, student presentations, study groups, team projects.

Technology 500 on-campus computer terminals/PCs are available for student use and are linked by a campus-wide network. The network has full access to the Internet. Students are not required to have their own PC.

Special Opportunities Advanced credit may be earned through credit by examination, transfer of credits from another institution. International exchange programs in Australia, England, France, Germany, Mexico, Scotland, Sweden, Wales. An internship program is available.

FINANCES
Costs for 1997–98 Tuition: Full-time: $3129 per year (resident); $7229 per year (nonresident). Part-time: $174 per credit (resident); $402 per credit (nonresident). Cost varies by reciprocity agreements. Fees: Full-time: $468 per academic year (resident); $468 per academic year (nonresident). Part-time: $26 per credit (resident); $26 per credit (nonresident). Average 1997–98 room and board costs were $3062 per academic year. Room and board costs vary by occupancy (e.g., single, double, triple), type of meal plan.

Financial Aid Fellowships, research assistantships, teaching assistantships, grants, scholarships, work study available. Financial aid is available to part-time students. Application Deadline: 4/1.

Financial Aid Contact Suzanne Carlson, Director of Financial Aid, Menomonie, WI 54751. Phone: 715-232-1363; Fax: 715-232-5246; E-mail: carlsonsu@uwstout.edu

FACILITIES
Information Resources Library Learning Center; total holdings of 225,503 volumes, 1,086,703 microforms, 1,310 current periodical subscriptions. CD player(s) available for graduate student use. Access provided to online bibliographic retrieval services and online databases.

INTERNATIONAL STUDENTS
Demographics 13% of students enrolled are international students [Asia, 29%, North America, 71%].

Services and Facilities International student office, international student center, international student housing, visa services, ESL courses, counseling/support services.

Applying TOEFL: minimum score of 500, proof of adequate funds required. Financial aid is available to international students.

International Student Contact Vickie Kuester, Administrative Program Specialist, Menomonie, WI 54751. Phone: 715-232-2132; Fax: 715-232-2500; E-mail: kuesterv@uwstout.edu

PLACEMENT
Services include alumni network, career counseling/planning, career fairs, career library, career placement, electronic job bank, job interviews arranged, job search course, resume referral to employers, and resume preparation.

Employment Of 1996–97 graduates, 99% were employed within three months of graduation; the average starting salary was $26,000. Types of employment entered: accounting, communications, computer-related, consulting, consumer products, education, energy, engineering, government, health services, high technology, human resources, information systems/technology, insurance, international trade, management, manufacturing, marketing, media, nonprofit, real estate, retail, service industry, telecommunications, utilities.

Business Program(s) URL: http://www.uwstout.edu

Program Contact: Menomonie, WI 54751. Phone: 715-232-1431; Fax: 715-232-1667.

University of Wisconsin-Whitewater

College of Business and Economics
Whitewater, Wisconsin

OVERVIEW
The University of Wisconsin-Whitewater is a state-supported, coed, comprehensive institution. Enrollment: 14,017 graduate, professional, and undergraduate students; 508 full-time matriculated graduate/professional students; 813 part-time matriculated graduate/professional students. Founded: 1868. The graduate business unit is in a small-town setting and is on a semester calendar.

HIGHLIGHTS

Enrollment Profile
Full-time: 159
Part-time: 173
Total: 332
Average Age: N/R
Fall 1997 Average GPA: 3.17

International: 20%
Women: 42%
Minorities: N/R
Average Class Size: 18
Fall 1997 Average GMAT: 515

Costs
Full-time tuition: $656 per academic year (resident)
Part-time tuition: $656 per 3-credit class (resident); $1856 per 3-credit class (nonresident)

AACSB – The International Association for Management Education accredited

GRADUATE BUSINESS PROGRAMS
Graduate Business Program (MBA) Full-time, part-time, distance learning option; 36-72 total credits required; GMAT score: minimum 570 required; 2 to 7 years to complete program. Concentrations in accounting, finance, international business, management, marketing, production management, decision sciences, health care, technology management.

Graduate Business program (MPA) Full-time, part-time; 30 total credits required; GMAT score: minimum 570 required; 2 to 7 years to complete program. Concentration in accounting.

Master of Science in Management Computer Systems (MS) Part-time; 36 total credits required; 3 years to complete program. Concentration in management information systems.

ADMISSION
Applications For fall 1997 there were 93 applications for admission. Of those applying, 89 were accepted. Of those accepted, 53 enrolled.

Application Requirements Application form, application fee, bachelor's degree, minimum GPA: 2.75, college transcript(s).

Recommended for Application GMAT score accepted.

Application Deadline 7/15 for fall, 12/1 for spring, 5/1 for summer, 6/15 for fall (international), 10/1 for spring (international), 3/1 for summer (international). Application fee: $45. Deferred entrance is available.

ACADEMICS
Faculty Full-time 75; part-time 5.

Teaching Methodologies Case study, computer-aided instruction, computer analysis, computer simulations, field projects, group discussion, lecture, research, seminars by members of the business community, simulations, student presentations, study groups, team projects.

Technology 500 on-campus computer terminals/PCs are available for student use and are linked by a campus-wide network. The network has full access to the Internet. Students are not required to have their own PC.

Special Opportunities Advanced credit may be earned through transfer of credits from another institution. International exchange programs in Czech Republic, France, Japan, Mexico, Netherlands, Russia, Sweden.

University of Wisconsin–Whitewater (continued)

FINANCES

Costs for 1997–98 Tuition: Full-time: $656 per 3-credit class (resident). Part-time: $656 per 3-credit class (resident); $1856 per 3-credit class (nonresident). Cost varies by number of credits taken. Average 1997–98 room and board costs were $3770 per academic year (on campus) and $2900 per academic year (off campus). Room and board costs vary by occupancy (e.g., single, double, triple), type of meal plan.

Financial Aid In 1997–98, 16% of students received some institutionally administered aid in the form of research assistantships, work study. Financial aid is available to part-time students. Application Deadline: 4/15.

Financial Aid Contact Financial Aid Office, Library, 800 West Main Street, Whitewater, WI 53190. Phone: 414-472-1130; Fax: 414-472-5655.

FACILITIES

Information Resources Andersen Library; total holdings of 393,300 volumes, 1,015,700 microforms, 2,702 current periodical subscriptions. CD player(s) available for graduate student use. Access provided to online bibliographic retrieval services and online databases.

INTERNATIONAL STUDENTS

Demographics 20% of students enrolled are international students [Africa, 8%, Asia, 76%, Europe, 8%, South America, 8%].

Services and Facilities International student office, international student center, international student housing, ESL courses, counseling/support services.

Applying TOEFL: minimum score of 550, proof of adequate funds required. Financial aid is not available to international students.

International Student Contact Mr. Stephen Kazar, Director, International Programs, Roseman Hall, Whitewater, WI 53190. Phone: 414-472-4992; Fax: 414-472-1515; E-mail: kazars@uwwvax.uww.edu

PLACEMENT

Services include career counseling/planning, career fairs, electronic job bank, job interviews arranged, and resume referral to employers. In 1996–97, 192 organizations participated in on-campus recruiting; 2,285 on-campus interviews were conducted.

Employment Of 1996–97 graduates, 95% were employed within three months of graduation. Types of employment entered: accounting, banking, chemical industry, communications, computer-related, consulting, consumer products, education, energy, engineering, finance, financial services, government, health services, high technology, hospitality management, human resources, information systems/technology, insurance, management, manufacturing, marketing, media, nonprofit, pharmaceutical, retail, service industry, telecommunications, transportation, utilities.

Business Program(s) URL: http://www.uww.edu/business/

Program Contact: Dr. Donald Zahn, Associate Dean, College of Business and Economics, Carlson Hall, Whitewater, WI 53190. Phone: 414-472-1945, 888-622-5506; Fax: 414-472-4863; E-mail: zahnd@uwwvax.uww.edu

WYOMING

University of Wyoming

College of Business

Laramie, Wyoming

OVERVIEW

The University of Wyoming is a state-supported, coed university. Enrollment: 9,877 graduate, professional, and undergraduate students; 1,062 full-time matriculated graduate/professional students; 1,369 part-time matriculated graduate/professional students. Founded: 1886. The graduate business unit is in an urban setting and is on a semester calendar.

HIGHLIGHTS

Enrollment Profile

Full-time: 27	International: 7%
Part-time: 44	Women: 54%
Total: 71	Minorities: 4%
Average Age: 34	Average Class Size: 15
Fall 1997 Average GPA: 3.2	Fall 1997 Average GMAT: 570

Costs
Full-time tuition: $2812 per academic year (resident); $7518 per academic year (nonresident)
Part-time tuition: $135 per credit hour (resident); $418 per credit hour (nonresident)

AACSB – The International Association for Management Education accredited

GRADUATE BUSINESS PROGRAMS

Master of Business Administration (MBA) Full-time, part-time, distance learning option; 54 total credits required; 11 months to 6 years to complete program.

ADMISSION

Applications For fall 1997 there were 126 applications for admission. Of those applying, 33 were accepted.

Application Requirements GMAT score: minimum 500, application form, application fee, bachelor's degree, essay, minimum GPA: 3.0, 3 letters of recommendation, personal statement, college transcript(s).

Recommended for Application Resume, minimum of 2 years of work experience.

Application Deadline 3/31 for fall. Application fee: $40. Deferred entrance is available.

ACADEMICS

Teaching Methodologies Case study, computer simulations, experiential learning, field projects, group discussion, lecture, research, role playing, simulations, student presentations, team projects.

Technology 229 on-campus computer terminals/PCs are available for student use and are linked by a campus-wide network. The network has full access to the Internet. Students are not required to have their own PC.

Special Opportunities Advanced credit may be earned through transfer of credits from another institution. International exchange program in France. An internship program is available.

FINANCES

Costs for 1997–98 Tuition: Full-time: $2812 per year (resident); $7518 per year (nonresident). Part-time: $135 per credit hour (resident); $418 per credit hour (nonresident). Cost varies by academic program, campus location, class time (e.g., day/evening), number of credits taken, reciprocity agreements. Fees: Full-time: $382 per academic year (resident); $382 per academic year (nonresident). Part-time: $7 per credit hour (resident); $7 per credit hour (nonresident). Fees vary by class time (e.g., day/evening), number of credits taken, reciprocity agreements. Average 1997–98 room and board costs were $4244 per academic year. Room and board costs vary by campus location, occupancy (e.g., single, double, triple), type of accommodation, type of meal plan.

Financial Aid In 1997–98, 58% of students received some institutionally administered aid in the form of fellowships, research assistantships, scholarships, work study, loans. Financial aid is available to part-time students. Application Deadline: 3/1.

Financial Aid Contact Student Financial Aid, PO Box 3335, Laramie, WY 82070. Phone: 307-766-2116; Fax: 307-766-3800.

FACILITIES

Information Resources Coe Library plus 5 additional on-campus libraries; total holdings of 1,200,000 volumes, 2,375,560 microforms, 11,000 current periodical subscriptions. CD player(s) available for graduate student use. Access provided to online bibliographic retrieval services and online databases.

INTERNATIONAL STUDENTS

Demographics 7% of students enrolled are international students [Asia, 87%, Europe, 13%].

Services and Facilities International student office, international student center, visa services, ESL courses, counseling/support services, newsletter, student exchange program, international student organization.

Applying TOEFL: minimum score of 540, proof of adequate funds, proof of health/immunizations required. Financial aid is available to international students.

International Student Contact Mr. Dennis Dreher, Director, International Student Services, PO Box 3228, Laramie, WY 82071. Phone: 307-766-5193; Fax: 307-766-4053; E-mail: wecnhelp@uwyo.edu

PLACEMENT

Services include alumni network, career counseling/planning, career fairs, career library, career placement, job interviews arranged, resume referral to employers, and resume preparation.

Employment Of 1996–97 graduates, 90% were employed within three months of graduation; the average starting salary was $42,000. Types of employment entered: banking, communications, computer-related, consulting, education, energy, finance, financial services, government, health services, hospitality management, human resources, international trade, management, manufacturing, marketing, media, mining, retail, service industry, telecommunications, transportation.

Business Program(s) URL: http://www.uwyo.edu/bu/mgt/cobhp1.htm

Program Contact: Director, MBA Program, College of Business, PO Box 3275, Laramie, WY 82071. Phone: 307-766-2449; Fax: 307-766-4028; E-mail: mba@uwyo.edu

GUAM

University of Guam

College of Business and Public Administration

Mangilao, Guam

OVERVIEW
The University of Guam is a territory-supported, coed, comprehensive institution. Founded: 1952.

GRADUATE BUSINESS PROGRAMS
Master of Business Administration (MBA)
Master of Public Administration (MPA)

ACADEMICS
Faculty Full-time 7.

FACILITIES
Information Resources Robert F. Kennedy Memorial Library; total holdings of 66,352 volumes, 703,306 microforms, 3,060 current periodical subscriptions. CD player(s) available for graduate student use. Access provided to online bibliographic retrieval services.

Program Contact: Dean, College of Business and Public Administration, Mangilao, GU 96923. Phone: 671-735-2550.

PUERTO RICO

Inter American University of Puerto Rico, Metropolitan Campus

Division of Economics and Business Administration

San Juan, Puerto Rico

OVERVIEW
Inter American University of Puerto Rico, Metropolitan Campus is an independent-nonprofit, coed, comprehensive institution. Enrollment: 11,000 graduate, professional, and undergraduate students. Founded: 1960. The graduate business unit is on a trimester calendar.

HIGHLIGHTS

Enrollment Profile
Full-time: N/R	International: N/R
Part-time: N/R	Women: N/R
Total: 250	Minorities: N/R
Average Age: 23	Average Class Size: N/R
Fall 1997 Average GPA: N/R	Fall 1997 Average GMAT: N/R

Costs
Full-time tuition: N/R
Part-time tuition: N/R

GRADUATE BUSINESS PROGRAMS
Master of Business Administration (MBA) Full-time, part-time; 42 total credits required; 2 to 5 years to complete program. Concentrations in accounting, finance, marketing, human resources, industrial administration/management.

ADMISSION
Application Requirements GMAT score, application form, bachelor's degree, minimum GPA: 2.75, interview, college transcript(s).
Recommended for Application Computer experience.
Application Deadline 5/15 for fall, 5/15 for fall (international).

ACADEMICS
Faculty Full-time 19; part-time 30.
Teaching Methodologies Case study, computer-aided instruction, computer analysis, computer simulations, experiential learning, field projects, group discussion, role playing, simulations, student presentations, team projects.

FINANCES
Financial Aid Contact Financial Aid Office, PO Box 1293, San Juan, PR 00919-1293. Phone: 787-758-2891.

FACILITIES
Information Resources Main library; total holdings of 101,907 volumes, 446,414 microforms, 1,990 current periodical subscriptions. CD player(s) available for graduate student use. Access provided to online bibliographic retrieval services.

INTERNATIONAL STUDENTS
Demographics N/R
Services and Facilities International student office, international student center, international student housing, counseling/support services.
International Student Contact English Trimester Program, PO Box 1293, San Juan, PR 00919-1293. Phone: 787-758-0837.

PLACEMENT
Services include career counseling/planning, job interviews arranged, and resume referral to employers.

Program Contact: English Trimester Program, PO Box 1293, San Juan, PR 00919-1293. Phone: 787-758-0837.

Inter American University of Puerto Rico, San Germán Campus

Department of Business Administration

San Germán, Puerto Rico

OVERVIEW
Inter American University of Puerto Rico, San Germán Campus is an independent-nonprofit, coed, comprehensive institution. Enrollment: 6,022 graduate, professional, and undergraduate students; 233 full-time matriculated graduate/professional students; 722 part-time matriculated graduate/professional students. Founded: 1912. The graduate business unit is in a small-town setting and is on a semester calendar.

HIGHLIGHTS

Enrollment Profile
Full-time: 79	International: N/R
Part-time: 294	Women: 60%
Total: 373	Minorities: N/R
Average Age: 29	Average Class Size: 20
Fall 1997 Average GPA: 2.5	Fall 1997 Average GMAT: N/R

Costs
Full-time tuition: $2610 per academic year
Part-time tuition: $145 per credit

GRADUATE BUSINESS PROGRAMS
Master of Business Administration (MBA) Full-time, part-time; 42 total credits required; 2.5 to 7 years to complete program. Concentrations in accounting, finance, human resources, industrial administration/management, marketing, business education.

ADMISSION
Applications For fall 1997 there were 202 applications for admission. Of those applying, 181 were accepted. Of those accepted, 121 enrolled.
Application Requirements GMAT score, application form, application fee, bachelor's degree, minimum GPA: 2.5, 2 letters of recommendation, college transcript(s).
Recommended for Application Resume, computer experience.

Application Deadline Applications processed on a rolling/continuous basis for both domestic and international students. Application fee: $31.

ACADEMICS
Faculty Full-time 11; part-time 15.

Teaching Methodologies Case study, lecture, student presentations, team projects.

Technology 200 on-campus computer terminals/PCs are available for student use and are linked by a campus-wide network. The network has full access to the Internet. Students are not required to have their own PC.

FINANCES
Costs for 1997–98 Tuition: Full-time: $2610 per year. Part-time: $145 per credit. Fees: Full-time: $354 per academic year. Part-time: $354 per year. Average 1997–98 room and board costs were $2200 per academic year.

Financial Aid Fellowships, teaching assistantships, scholarships, work study, loans available. Application Deadline: 5/15.

Financial Aid Contact Ms. Maria Lugo, Director of Financial Aid, PO Box 5100, San German, PR 00683. Phone: 787-264-1912 Ext. 7252; Fax: 787-892-6350.

FACILITIES
Information Resources Juan Cancio Ortiz Library; total holdings of 155,109 volumes, 502,361 microforms, 1,815 current periodical subscriptions. CD player(s) available for graduate student use. Access provided to online bibliographic retrieval services.

INTERNATIONAL STUDENTS
Demographics 1% of students enrolled are international students [Central America, 100%].

Services and Facilities International student office, international student center, ESL courses, counseling/support services.

Applying Proof of health/immunizations required. Financial aid is available to international students.

International Student Contact Ms. Dolly Claudio, International Student Program Director, PO Box 5100, San German, PR 00683. Phone: 787-264-1912 Ext. 7298; Fax: 787-892-6350.

PLACEMENT
Services include alumni network, career placement, and resume preparation.

Employment Types of employment entered: education, hospitality management, human resources, retail, service industry.

Program Contact: Ms. Mildred Camacho, Admissions Director, PO Box 5100, San German, PR 00683. Phone: 787-892-3090; Fax: 787-892-6350.

Pontifical Catholic University of Puerto Rico

College of Business Administration
Ponce, Puerto Rico

OVERVIEW
Pontifical Catholic University of Puerto Rico is an independent-religious, coed, comprehensive institution. Enrollment: 11,480 graduate, professional, and undergraduate students; 620 full-time matriculated graduate/professional students; 701 part-time matriculated graduate/professional students. Founded: 1948. The graduate business unit is in an urban setting and is on a semester calendar.

GRADUATE BUSINESS PROGRAMS
Master of Business Administration (MBA)
Master of Business Administration/Doctor of Jurisprudence (MBA/JD)

ACADEMICS
Faculty Full-time 4; part-time 10.

Teaching Methodologies Case study, computer-aided instruction, faculty seminars, group discussion, lecture, research, seminars by members of the business community, student presentations, team projects.

Technology 100 on-campus computer terminals/PCs are available for student use and are linked by a campus-wide network. The network has full access to the Internet. Students are not required to have their own PC.

Special Opportunities Advanced credit may be earned through transfer of credits from another institution.

FACILITIES
Information Resources Encarnación Valdés Library plus 1 additional on-campus library; total holdings of 227,464 volumes, 378,917 microforms, 43,789 current periodical subscriptions. CD player(s) available for graduate student use. Access provided to online bibliographic retrieval services.

Program Contact: Director of Admissions, 2250 Las Americas Avenue, Suite 584, Ponce, PR 00731-4295. Phone: 787-841-2000 Ext. 424, 800-981-5040; Fax: 787-840-4295.

Universidad del Turabo

Programs in Business Administration
Gurabo, Puerto Rico

OVERVIEW
The Universidad del Turabo is an independent-nonprofit, coed, comprehensive institution. Founded: 1972. The graduate business unit is in a suburban setting and is on a semester calendar.

GRADUATE BUSINESS PROGRAMS
Master of Business Administration (MBA)

ACADEMICS
Teaching Methodologies Computer-aided instruction, experiential learning, faculty seminars, field projects, group discussion, lecture, research, seminars by members of the business community, student presentations, study groups.

Technology 144 on-campus computer terminals/PCs are available for student use and are linked by a campus-wide network. The network has full access to the Internet. Students are not required to have their own PC.

Special Opportunities Advanced credit may be earned through transfer of credits from another institution.

FACILITIES
Information Resources Recursos De Aprendizaje; total holdings of 66,342 volumes, 364 microforms, 764 current periodical subscriptions. Access provided to online bibliographic retrieval services.

Program Contact: Director of Admissions, PO Box 3030, Gurabo, PR 00778-3030. Phone: 809-743-7979 Ext. 4350.

University of Puerto Rico, Mayagüez Campus

College of Business Administration
Mayaguez, Puerto Rico

OVERVIEW
The University of Puerto Rico, Mayagüez Campus is a commonwealth-supported, coed university. Enrollment: 12,846 graduate, professional, and undergraduate students. Founded: 1911.

HIGHLIGHTS
Enrollment Profile

Full-time: N/R	International: N/R
Part-time: N/R	Women: N/R
Total: 89	Minorities: N/R
Average Age: N/R	Average Class Size: N/R
Fall 1997 Average GPA: N/R	Fall 1997 Average GMAT: N/R

Costs
Full-time tuition: N/R
Part-time tuition: $75 per credit (resident); $1750 per semester (nonresident)

GRADUATE BUSINESS PROGRAMS
Master of Business Administration (MBA)

ADMISSION
Application Requirements GMAT score, application form, application fee, bachelor's degree, minimum GPA, 3 letters of recommendation.

Recommended for Application Work experience, computer experience.

Application Deadline 2/28 for fall, 9/15 for spring, 2/28 for fall (international), 9/15 for spring (international). Application fee: $15.

ACADEMICS
Faculty Full-time 10; part-time 8.

FINANCES
Costs for 1997–98 Tuition: Part-time: $75 per credit (resident); $1750 per semester (nonresident). Cost varies by reciprocity agreements. Average 1997–98 room only costs were $3000 per academic year (on campus) and $3000 per academic year (off campus). Room and board costs vary by type of accommodation.

Financial Aid Fellowships, research assistantships, teaching assistantships available.

FACILITIES
Information Resources General library; total holdings of 849,113 volumes, 544,150 microforms, 2,967 current periodical subscriptions. Access provided to online bibliographic retrieval services.

INTERNATIONAL STUDENTS
Demographics N/R

Services and Facilities International student office, visa services, ESL courses, counseling/support services.

International Student Contact Gildreth González, Director, International Students Office, Mayagüez, PR 00681-5000. Phone: 787-265-2896.

Business Program(s) URL: http://www-rum.upr.clu.edu

Program Contact: College of Business Administration, PO Box 5000, Mayagüez, PR 00681-5000. Phone: 787-832-4040 Ext. 2067.

University of Puerto Rico, Río Piedras

Graduate School of Business Administration

San Juan, Puerto Rico

OVERVIEW
The University of Puerto Rico, Río Piedras is a commonwealth-supported, coed university. Founded: 1903. The graduate business unit is in an urban setting and is on a semester calendar.

HIGHLIGHTS

Enrollment Profile
Full-time: N/R
Part-time: N/R
Total: N/R
Average Age: N/R
Fall 1997 Average GPA: 3.4

International: N/R
Women: N/R
Minorities: N/R
Average Class Size: 20
Fall 1997 Average GMAT: 460

Costs
Full-time tuition: N/R
Part-time tuition: N/R

GRADUATE BUSINESS PROGRAMS
Master of Business Administration (MBA) Full-time, part-time; 52 total credits required; 2 to 6 years to complete program. Concentrations in accounting, finance, international business, managerial economics, marketing, operations management, quantitative analysis.

ADMISSION
Application Requirements Application form, application fee, bachelor's degree, essay, minimum GPA: 3.0, 2 letters of recommendation, college transcript(s).
Recommended for Application GMAT score accepted: minimum 450, computer experience.
Application Deadline 2/28 for fall, 9/1 for spring. Application fee: $15.

ACADEMICS
Faculty Full-time 7; part-time 13.
Teaching Methodologies Case study, computer-aided instruction, computer analysis, computer simulations, faculty seminars, field projects, group discussion, lecture, research, seminars by members of the business community, simulations, student presentations.
Technology 60 on-campus computer terminals/PCs are available for student use. The network has full access to the Internet. Students are not required to have their own PC.
Special Opportunities Advanced credit may be earned through credit by examination, transfer of credits from another institution. International exchange programs in Dominican Republic, Mexico. An internship program is available.

FINANCES
Costs for 1997–98 Cost varies by number of credits taken. Average 1997–98 room only costs were $650 per academic year (on campus) and $3000 per academic year (off campus).
Financial Aid Fellowships, research assistantships, teaching assistantships, work study, loans available. Application Deadline: 5/31.
Financial Aid Contact Miss Luz M. Santiago, Director, Financial Aid Programs, PO Box 23336, San Juan, PR 00931-3336. Phone: 787-764-0000 Ext. 3055, 5601; Fax: 787-763-5733.

FACILITIES
Information Resources Jose M. Lazaro Library plus 19 additional on-campus libraries; total holdings of 4,091,981 volumes, 1,637,866 microforms, 4,966 current periodical subscriptions. CD player(s) available for graduate student use. Access provided to online bibliographic retrieval services.

INTERNATIONAL STUDENTS
Demographics N/R
Services and Facilities International student office, visa services, counseling/support services, language tutoring.
Applying Proof of adequate funds, proof of health/immunizations required. Financial aid is not available to international students.
International Student Contact Ms. Luz M. Diaz, Director, PO Box 23336, San Juan, PR 00931-3336. Phone: 787-764-0000 Ext. 3055, 5601; Fax: 787-763-5733.

PLACEMENT
Services include career fairs, and job interviews arranged.
Employment Types of employment entered: accounting, banking, chemical industry, communications, computer-related, consulting, consumer products, education, engineering, finance, financial services, government, health services, high technology, human resources, information systems/technology, insurance, law, management, manufacturing, marketing, media, nonprofit, pharmaceutical, real estate, retail, service industry, telecommunications, transportation, utilities.

Program Contact: Ms. Carmen Gonzalez, Student Affairs Official, PO Box 23325, San Juan, PR 00931-3325. Phone: 787-764-0000 Ext. 4128, 2083; Fax: 787-763-6911.

University of the Sacred Heart

Business School

San Juan, Puerto Rico

OVERVIEW
The University of the Sacred Heart is an independent-religious, coed, comprehensive institution. Enrollment: 5,202 graduate, professional, and undergraduate students; 53 full-time matriculated graduate/professional students; 315 part-time matriculated graduate/professional students. Founded: 1935. The graduate business unit is in an urban setting and is on a semester calendar.

HIGHLIGHTS

Enrollment Profile
Full-time: 6
Part-time: 204
Total: 210
Average Age: 30
Fall 1997 Average GPA: 2.75

International: N/R
Women: 45%
Minorities: N/R
Average Class Size: 12
Fall 1997 Average GMAT: 500

Costs
Full-time tuition: N/R
Part-time tuition: $150 per credit

GRADUATE BUSINESS PROGRAMS
Master of Business Administration in Management Information Systems (MBA) Full-time, part-time; 48 total credits required; 3 to 6 years to complete program. Concentration in management information systems.
Master of Business Administration in Human Resource Management (MBA) Full-time, part-time; 47 total credits required; 3 to 6 years to complete program. Concentration in human resources.
Master of Business Administration in Marketing (MBA) Full-time, part-time; 47 total credits required; 3 to 6 years to complete program. Concentration in marketing.
Master of Business Administration in Taxation (MBA) Full-time, part-time; 47 total credits required; 3 to 6 years to complete program. Concentration in taxation.

ADMISSION
Applications For fall 1997 there were 93 applications for admission. Of those applying, 50 were accepted. Of those accepted, 38 enrolled.
Application Requirements Application form, application fee, bachelor's degree, essay, minimum GPA: 2.75, interview, 2 letters of recommendation, resume, college transcript(s).
Recommended for Application GMAT score accepted: minimum 500, computer experience.
Application Deadline Applications processed on a rolling/continuous basis for both domestic and international students. Application fee: $25.

ACADEMICS
Faculty Full-time 6; part-time 11.
Teaching Methodologies Case study, computer-aided instruction, computer analysis, faculty seminars, field projects, group discussion, lecture, research, seminars by members of the business community, simulations, student presentations, study groups, team projects.

University of the Sacred Heart (continued)

Technology 300 on-campus computer terminals/PCs are available for student use and are linked by a campus-wide network. The network has full access to the Internet. Students are not required to have their own PC.

Special Opportunities Advanced credit may be earned through transfer of credits from another institution. International exchange program available.

FINANCES

Costs for 1997–98 Tuition: $150 per credit. Cost varies by academic program, number of credits taken, reciprocity agreements. Fees: $120 per semester. Fees vary by reciprocity agreements. Average 1997–98 room and board costs were $4218 per academic year (off campus).

Financial Aid Scholarships, work study, loans available. Application Deadline: 5/31.

Financial Aid Contact Mrs. Maria A. Torres, Financial Aid Office Director, P. O. Bos 12383, San Juan, PR 00914-0383. Phone: 787-728-1515 Ext. 3605; Fax: 787-728-1515 Ext. 3609; E-mail: am_torres@uscsi.usc.clu.edu

FACILITIES

Information Resources Madre María Teresa Guevara Library; total holdings of 192,265 volumes, 39,315 microforms, 1,398 current periodical subscriptions. CD player(s) available for graduate student use. Access provided to online bibliographic retrieval services.

INTERNATIONAL STUDENTS

Demographics 1% of students enrolled are international students [South America, 100%].

Applying Proof of adequate funds, proof of health/immunizations required. Financial aid is not available to international students.

International Student Contact Mrs. Ivette Lugo-Fabre, Co-op and Student Exchange Program Coordinator, P. O. Box 12383, San Juan, PR 00914-0383. Phone: 787-728-1515 Ext. 1218; Fax: 787-727-7880; E-mail: i_lugo@uscac1.usc.clu.edu

PLACEMENT

Services include alumni network, career counseling/planning, career fairs, career library, career placement, electronic job bank, job interviews arranged, job search course, resume referral to employers, and resume preparation. In 1996–97, 6 organizations participated in on-campus recruiting.

Employment Types of employment entered: information systems/technology, management.

Business Program(s) URL: http://www.usc.clu.edu

Program Contact: Dr. Blanca Villamil, Interim Director of Promotion and Admissions Office, Box 12383, San Juan, PR 00914-0383. Phone: 787-728-1515 Ext. 3595; Fax: 787-727-5890; E-mail: anieves@uscsi.usc.clu.edu

VIRGIN ISLANDS

University of the Virgin Islands

Division of Business Administration

Charlotte Amalie, St. Thomas, Virgin Islands

OVERVIEW

The University of the Virgin Islands is a territory-supported, coed, comprehensive institution. Enrollment: 2,898 graduate, professional, and undergraduate students; 27 full-time matriculated graduate/professional students, 205 part-time matriculated graduate/professional students. Founded: 1962. The graduate business unit is in a small-town setting and is on a semester calendar.

GRADUATE BUSINESS PROGRAMS

Master of Business Administration (MBA)

ACADEMICS

Faculty Full-time 7.

Teaching Methodologies Case study, computer-aided instruction, field projects, group discussion, lecture, research, student presentations, study groups.

Technology 100 on-campus computer terminals/PCs are available for student use and are linked by a campus-wide network. The network has full access to the Internet. Students are not required to have their own PC.

FACILITIES

Information Resources Ralph Paiewonsky Library plus 1 additional on-campus library; total holdings of 103,253 volumes, 822,058 microforms, 1,020 current periodical subscriptions. Access provided to online bibliographic retrieval services.

Program Contact: Office of Management, 2 John Brewers Bay, Charlotte Amalie, St. Thomas, VI 00802-9990. Phone: 809-693-1151.

AUSTRALIA

Australian National University

Managing Business in Asia Program

Canberra, Australia

OVERVIEW

Australian National University is a federally supported, coed institution. Enrollment: 9,936 graduate, professional, and undergraduate students; 1,454 full-time matriculated graduate/professional students; 926 part-time matriculated graduate/professional students. Founded: 1946. The graduate business unit is in a small-town setting and is on a trimester calendar.

HIGHLIGHTS

Enrollment Profile

Full-time: N/R	International: N/R
Part-time: N/R	Women: N/R
Total: N/R	Minorities: N/R
Average Age: 31	Average Class Size: 26
Fall 1997 Average GPA: N/R	Fall 1997 Average GMAT: N/R

Costs
Full-time tuition: Aus$27,500 per academic year (resident); Aus$27,500 per academic year (nonresident)
Part-time tuition: N/R

GRADUATE BUSINESS PROGRAMS

Master of Business Administration (MBA) Full-time; 25 total credits required; 13 to 15 months to complete program. Concentrations in asian business studies, strategic management.

ADMISSION

Application Requirements Application form, bachelor's degree, letters of recommendation, personal statement, resume, college transcript(s), minimum of 3 years of work experience.

Recommended for Application GMAT score accepted, computer experience.

Application Deadline Applications processed on a rolling/continuous basis for domestic students only. 3/31 for winter (international).

ACADEMICS

Faculty Full-time 2; part-time 25.

Teaching Methodologies Case study, computer-aided instruction, computer analysis, faculty seminars, group discussion, lecture, student presentations, study groups, team projects.

Technology 40 on-campus computer terminals/PCs are available for student use. The network has full access to the Internet. Students are not required to have their own PC.

Special Opportunities Advanced credit may be earned through transfer of credits from another institution. International exchange program in China. An internship program is available.

FINANCES

Costs for 1997–98 Tuition: Full-time: Aus$27,500 per program (resident); Aus$27,500 per program (nonresident). Average 1997–98 room and board costs were Aus$9000 per academic year. Room and board costs vary by type of accommodation, type of meal plan.

Financial Aid Scholarships available. Application Deadline: 3/31.

Financial Aid Contact Mark Dodgson, MBA Program, Australia Asia Management Centre, Old Canberra House Lennox Crossing, Canberra. Phone: 61-2-249-4890; Fax: 61-2-249-4895; E-mail: mgr.mba.program@anu.edu.au

FACILITIES

Information Resources Menzies Library plus 8 additional on-campus libraries; total holdings of 1,800,000 volumes, 13,000 current periodical subscriptions. CD player(s) available for graduate student use. Access provided to online bibliographic retrieval services and online databases.

INTERNATIONAL STUDENTS
Demographics N/R

Services and Facilities International student office, international student housing, ESL courses, counseling/support services.

Applying IELT: minimum score of 6.5, TOEFL: minimum score of 570, TWE: minimum score of 4.5 required. Financial aid is available to international students.

International Student Contact Mr. Ian Harris, Director, International Education Office, Canberra. Phone: 61-2-249-3682; Fax: 61-2-249-4806.

PLACEMENT
Services include career counseling/planning, and resume preparation.

Employment Of 1996–97 graduates, 90% were employed within three months of graduation. Types of employment entered: banking, consulting, hospitality management, human resources, international trade, marketing, real estate, service industry.

Business Program(s) URL: http://www.anu.edu.au/academia/graduate/programs/b2/

Program Contact: Mark Dodgson, MBA Program, Australia Asia Management Centre, Old Canberra House Lennox Crossing, Canberra ACT 0200, Australia. Phone: 61-2-249-4890; Fax: 61-2-249-4895; E-mail: mgr.mba.program@anu.edu.au

Bond University

School of Business

Gold Coast, Australia

OVERVIEW
Bond University is an independent-nonprofit, coed institution. Founded: 1989. The graduate business unit is in a suburban setting and is on a trimester calendar.

HIGHLIGHTS

Enrollment Profile

Full-time: N/R	International: N/R
Part-time: N/R	Women: N/R
Total: N/R	Minorities: N/R
Average Age: 30	Average Class Size: 25
Fall 1997 Average GPA: N/R	Fall 1997 Average GMAT: N/R

Costs
Full-time tuition: Aus$25,800 per academic year
Part-time tuition: Aus$2150 per unit

GRADUATE BUSINESS PROGRAMS
Master of Business Administration (MBA) Full-time, part-time; 12 total credits required; 12 months to 9 years to complete program. Concentrations in accounting, entrepreneurship, finance, human resources, international business, leadership, marketing, strategic management, business law, business policy/strategy, management, new venture management, technology management, asian business studies.

Executive MBA (MBA) Part-time; 12 total credits required; 13 months to 9 years to complete program. Concentrations in asian business studies, international business, management, marketing, entrepreneurship.

Master of International Management (MIM) Full-time, part-time; 12 total credits required; 12 months to 9 years to complete program. Concentrations in entrepreneurship, finance, human resources, international business, international management, leadership, management, marketing, accounting, asian business studies, new venture management.

Master of Technology Management (MTM) Full-time, part-time; 12 total credits required; 12 months to 9 years to complete program. Concentrations in information management, technology management.

Master of Accounting (MAcc) Full-time, part-time; 15 total credits required; 15 months to 9 years to complete program. Concentration in accounting.

Master of Business Administration/Master of International Management (MBA/MIM) Full-time, part-time; 18 total credits required; 20 months to 9 years to complete program. Concentrations in accounting, entrepreneurship, finance, international business, marketing, strategic management, management.

Master of Business Administration/Master of Accountancy (MBA/MAcc) Full-time, part-time; 20 total credits required; 2 to 9 years to complete program. Concentrations in accounting, entrepreneurship, finance, international business, marketing, management.

Master of Business Administration/Master of Technology Management (MBA/MTM) Full-time, part-time; 18 total credits required; 20 months to 9 years to complete program. Concentrations in accounting, entrepreneurship, finance, international business, marketing, strategic management, management, technology management.

Master of Business Administration/Master of Information Analysis Management (MBA/MIA) Full-time, part-time; 18 total credits required; 20 months to 9 years to complete program. Concentrations in accounting, entrepreneurship, finance, marketing, strategic management, management, technology management.

Master of Business Administration/Master of Information Technology (MBA/MIT) Full-time, part-time; 18 total credits required; 20 months to 9 years to complete program. Concentrations in accounting, entrepreneurship, finance, management, marketing, strategic management, technology management.

Master of Business Administration/Master of Jurisprudence (MBA/MLJ) Full-time, part-time; 18 total credits required; 20 months to 9 years to complete program. Concentrations in accounting, entrepreneurship, finance, business law, management, marketing, strategic management.

Master of Business Administration/Master of Law (MBA/MBL) Full-time, part-time; 18 total credits required; 20 months to 9 years to complete program. Concentrations in accounting, entrepreneurship, finance, business law, management, marketing, strategic management.

Master of Business Administration/Master of Business Law (MBA/MLB) Full-time, part-time; 18 total credits required; 20 months to 9 years to complete program. Concentrations in accounting, entrepreneurship, finance, business law, management, marketing, strategic management.

Master of International Business (MIB) Full-time, part-time; 12 total credits required; 12 months to 9 years to complete program. Concentrations in entrepreneurship, finance, human resources, international business, international management, leadership, manufacturing management, marketing, asian business studies, new venture management.

ADMISSION
Application Requirements Application form, 2 letters of recommendation, personal statement, resume, college transcript(s), minimum of 2 years of work experience.

Recommended for Application GMAT score accepted: minimum 550, bachelor's degree.

Application Deadline Applications processed on a rolling/continuous basis for both domestic and international students. Deferred entrance is available.

ACADEMICS
Faculty Full-time 28; part-time 2.

Teaching Methodologies Case study, computer-aided instruction, computer analysis, computer simulations, experiential learning, faculty seminars, field projects, group discussion, lecture, research, role playing, seminars by members of the business community, simulations, student presentations, study groups, team projects.

Technology 160 on-campus computer terminals/PCs are available for student use and are linked by a campus-wide network. The network has full access to the Internet. Students are required to have their own PC.

Special Opportunities Advanced credit may be earned through transfer of credits from another institution. International exchange programs in Canada, France.

FINANCES
Costs for 1997–98 Tuition: Full-time: Aus$25,800 per program. Part-time: Aus$2150 per unit. Cost varies by number of credits taken. Average 1997–98 room and board costs were Aus$10,500 per academic year (on campus) and Aus$10,500 per academic year (off campus). Room and board costs vary by occupancy (e.g., single, double, triple), type of accommodation.

Financial Aid Application Deadline: 11/1.

Financial Aid Contact Ms. Kim Rowley, Admissions Officer, University Drive, Robina, Queensland 4229, Australia. Phone: 61-7-5595-1035; Fax: 61-7-5595-1015; E-mail: kim_rowley@bond.edu.au

FACILITIES
Information Resources Bond Library plus 1 additional on-campus library; total holdings of 18,000 volumes, 502 current periodical subscriptions. CD player(s) available for graduate student use. Access provided to online bibliographic retrieval services.

INTERNATIONAL STUDENTS
Demographics N/R

Services and Facilities International student office, international student center, visa services, ESL courses, counseling/support services.

Applying IELT: minimum score of 6.5, TOEFL: minimum score of 560, TWE: minimum score of 5, proof of adequate funds required.

International Student Contact Ms. Jodie Maguire, Student Service Officer, Student Services, Robina, Queensland 4229, Australia. Phone: 61-7-5595-4001; Fax: 61-7-5595-1160; E-mail: jodie_maguire@bond.edu.au

PLACEMENT
Services include alumni network, career counseling/planning, career fairs, career library, career placement, electronic job bank, resume referral to employers, and resume preparation. In 1996–97, 10 organizations participated in on-campus recruiting.

Employment Types of employment entered: accounting, banking, communications, computer-related, consulting, consumer products, education, energy, engineering, finance, financial services, government, health services, hospitality management, human resources, information systems/technology, insurance, international trade, law, management, marketing, media, mining, nonprofit,

Bond University (continued)

pharmaceutical, real estate, retail, service industry, telecommunications, transportation.

Business Program(s) URL: http://bond.edu.au/Bond/Schools/Bus/Welcome. html

Program Contact: Mrs. Kathie Parkinson, Manager, Academic Programs, School of Business, University Drive, Robina, Gold Coast, Queensland 4229, Australia. Phone: 61-7-5595-2254; Fax: 61-7-5595-1160; E-mail: kathie_parkinson@ bond.edu.au

Curtin University of Technology

Graduate School of Business

Perth, Western Australia, Australia

OVERVIEW
Curtin University of Technology coed institution. Enrollment: 24,551 graduate, professional, and undergraduate students. The graduate business unit is in an urban setting and is on a trimester calendar.

HIGHLIGHTS

Enrollment Profile

Full-time: 37	International: 35%
Part-time: 166	Women: 24%
Total: 203	Minorities: N/R
Average Age: 29	Average Class Size: 30
Fall 1997 Average GPA: N/R	Fall 1997 Average GMAT: 570

Costs
Full-time tuition: N/R
Part-time tuition: Aus$16,800 per course (resident); Aus$26,400 per course (nonresident)

Degree(s) offered in conjunction with various institutions in Asia

GRADUATE BUSINESS PROGRAMS
Master of Leadership Management (MLM) Full-time, part-time; 18 months to 3 years to complete program. Concentrations in leadership, organizational behavior/development, human resources, entrepreneurship, decision sciences, international and area business studies, management, marketing, quality management, strategic management, organizational management, accounting, international development management, operations management, legal administration.

Doctor of Business Administration (DBA) Full-time, part-time; 2 to 6 years to complete program. Concentrations in research and development administration, marketing research, project management, strategic management, international management, decision sciences.

Master of Business Administration (MBA) Full-time, part-time, distance learning option; 16 months to 3 years to complete program. Concentrations in accounting, asian business studies, banking, business law, business policy/strategy, financial economics, human resources, industrial/labor relations, information management, international business, international management, leadership, marketing, organizational behavior/development, quality management, quantitative analysis, project management, international marketing.

ADMISSION
Applications For fall 1997 there were 109 applications for admission. Of those applying, 40 were accepted. Of those accepted, 40 enrolled.

Application Requirements Application form, application fee, bachelor's degree, interview, 2 letters of recommendation, personal statement, college transcript(s), minimum of 3 years of work experience.

Recommended for Application GMAT score accepted, essay, resume, computer experience: computer literacy.

Application Deadline Applications processed on a rolling/continuous basis for both domestic and international students. Application fee: 100 (international). Deferred entrance is available.

ACADEMICS
Faculty Full-time 11; part-time 20.

Teaching Methodologies Case study, computer-aided instruction, computer analysis, computer simulations, faculty seminars, field projects, group discussion, lecture, research, role playing, seminars by members of the business community, student presentations, study groups, team projects.

Technology 36 on-campus computer terminals/PCs are available for student use and are linked by a campus-wide network. The network has full access to the Internet. Students are not required to have their own PC.

Special Opportunities Advanced credit may be earned through credit by examination, credit for business training programs, transfer of credits from

another institution. International exchange programs in Canada, Europe, Japan, Korea, Malaysia, United Kingdom, United States.

FINANCES
Costs for 1997–98 Tuition: Aus$16,800 per course (resident); Aus$26,400 per course (nonresident). Cost varies by number of credits taken. Average 1997–98 room and board costs were Aus$7280 per academic year (on campus) and Aus$7800 per academic year (off campus).

Financial Aid In 1997–98, 4% of students received some institutionally administered aid in the form of research assistantships, teaching assistantships, scholarships, work study. Application Deadline: 9/1.

Financial Aid Contact Delia Rogers, Scholarships Manager, PO Box U1987, Perth, Western Australia 6102, Australia. Phone: 61-8-9266-3119; Fax: 61-8-9266-3793; E-mail: delia.rogers@curtin.edu.au

FACILITIES
Information Resources T.L. Robertson Library plus 3 additional on-campus libraries; total holdings of 575,762 volumes, 469,618 microforms, 5,300 current periodical subscriptions. CD player(s) available for graduate student use. Access provided to online bibliographic retrieval services and online databases.

INTERNATIONAL STUDENTS
Demographics 35% of students enrolled are international students [Africa, 3%, Asia, 88%, Central America, 1%, Europe, 5%, North America, 3%].

Services and Facilities International student office, international student center, international student housing, ESL courses, counseling/support services.

Applying IELT: minimum score of 7, TOEFL: minimum score of 580, proof of adequate funds, proof of health/immunizations required. Financial aid is available to international students.

International Student Contact Dr. Sylvester Boudville, Dean of International Programs, International Office, GPO Box U1987, Perth, Western Australia 6102, Australia. Phone: 61-8-9266-3064; Fax: 61-8-9266-3960; E-mail: ar@gsb.curtin.edu.au

PLACEMENT
Services include alumni network, career counseling/planning, electronic job bank, resume referral to employers, and resume preparation.

Employment Of 1996–97 graduates, 95% were employed within three months of graduation; the average starting salary was Aus$70,000. Types of employment entered: accounting, banking, chemical industry, communications, computer-related, consulting, consumer products, education, energy, engineering, finance, financial services, government, health services, human resources, information systems/technology, international trade, management, manufacturing, marketing, media, mining, nonprofit, petrochemical, pharmaceutical, real estate, retail, service industry, telecommunications, transportation, utilities.

Business Program(s) URL: http://www.cbs.curtin.edu.au/

Program Contact: Ms. Lee Malone, Enrollment Officer, Graduate School of Business, QVI, 250 St. Georges Terrace, Perth, Western Australia 6001, Australia. Phone: 61-8-9266-3460; Fax: 61-8-9266-3368; E-mail: l.malone@ gsb.curtin.edu.au

Deakin University

Faculty of Business and Law

Geelong, Australia

OVERVIEW
Deakin University coed institution. Founded: 1974. The graduate business unit is on a semester calendar.

HIGHLIGHTS

Enrollment Profile

Full-time: N/R	International: N/R
Part-time: N/R	Women: N/R
Total: N/R	Minorities: N/R
Average Age: 34	Average Class Size: N/R
Fall 1997 Average GPA: N/R	Fall 1997 Average GMAT: N/R

Costs
Full-time tuition: N/R
Part-time tuition: N/R

GRADUATE BUSINESS PROGRAMS
Distance Learning MBA (MBA) Part-time, distance learning option; 3 to 9 years to complete program.

ADMISSION
Application Requirements Application form, bachelor's degree, essay, 2 letters of recommendation, personal statement, resume, college transcript(s), minimum of 2 years of work experience.

Recommended for Application GMAT score accepted: minimum 600.

ACADEMICS
Faculty Full-time 26.

Teaching Methodologies Case study, computer-aided instruction, computer simulations.

Technology Computer terminals/PCs are available for student use and are linked by a campus-wide network. Students are required to have their own PC.

Special Opportunities International exchange program available.

FACILITIES
Information Resources Deakin University Library; total holdings of 1,115,550 volumes, 8,587 current periodical subscriptions. CD player(s) available for graduate student use. Access provided to online bibliographic retrieval services.

INTERNATIONAL STUDENTS
Demographics N/R

Services and Facilities International student office.

Applying IELT: minimum score of 6, TOEFL: minimum score of 580, TWE: minimum score of 5 required. Financial aid is not available to international students.

PLACEMENT
Services include alumni network, and career counseling/planning.

Employment Types of employment entered: banking, consulting, finance, financial services, government, health services, law, management, manufacturing, telecommunications.

Business Program(s) URL: http://www.deakin.edu.au

Program Contact: MBA Program Director, Faculty of Business and Law, Geelong 3217, Australia. Phone: 61-52-271-192; Fax: 61-52-272-655; E-mail: mbaeng@deakin.edu

Edith Cowan University

Faculty of Business

Churchlands, Australia

OVERVIEW
Edith Cowan University is a federally supported, coed institution. Enrollment: 20,275 graduate, professional, and undergraduate students; 238 full-time matriculated graduate/professional students; 720 part-time matriculated graduate/professional students. Founded: 1972. The graduate business unit is in a suburban setting and is on a semester calendar.

HIGHLIGHTS

Enrollment Profile

Full-time: 137	International: 43%
Part-time: 263	Women: 38%
Total: 400	Minorities: N/R
Average Age: 30	Average Class Size: 15
Fall 1997 Average GPA: N/R	Fall 1997 Average GMAT: N/R

Costs
Full-time tuition: Aus$950 per academic year (resident); Aus$12,600 per academic year (nonresident)
Part-time tuition: N/R

GRADUATE BUSINESS PROGRAMS
Master of Professional Accountancy (MPA) Full-time, part-time; 2 to 4 years to complete program. Concentrations in accounting, taxation.

Master of Professional Information Systems (MPIS) Full-time, part-time; 2 to 4 years to complete program. Concentrations in contract management, financial information systems, information management, management science, operations management, technology management.

Master of Business (MB) Full-time, part-time; 2 to 4 years to complete program. Concentrations in accounting, economics, finance, information management, marketing, management, human resources.

Master of Business Administration (MBA) Full-time, part-time, distance learning option; 16 total credits required; 2 to 4 years to complete program. Concentrations in accounting, human resources, information management, international

business, management, marketing, asian business studies, advertising, economics, finance, financial information systems, marketing research, organizational behavior/development, travel industry/tourism management.

ADMISSION
Applications For fall 1997 there were 430 applications for admission. Of those applying, 290 were accepted. Of those accepted, 228 enrolled.

Application Requirements Application form, bachelor's degree, letters of recommendation, personal statement, resume.

Recommended for Application Minimum GPA: 2.6, interview, college transcript(s), minimum of 2 years of work experience, computer experience.

Application Deadline Applications processed on a rolling/continuous basis for both domestic and international students. Deferred entrance is available.

ACADEMICS
Faculty Full-time 70; part-time 40.

Teaching Methodologies Case study, computer-aided instruction, computer analysis, computer simulations, experiential learning, faculty seminars, field projects, group discussion, lecture, research, role playing, seminars by members of the business community, simulations, student presentations, study groups, team projects.

Technology Computer terminals/PCs are available for student use and are linked by a campus-wide network. The network has full access to the Internet. Students are not required to have their own PC.

Special Opportunities Advanced credit may be earned through credit by examination, credit for business training programs, transfer of credits from another institution. International exchange programs in Indonesia, Malaysia, United Kingdom, United States.

FINANCES
Costs for 1997–98 Tuition: Full-time: Aus$950 per unit (resident); Aus$12,600 per year (nonresident). Cost varies by number of credits taken. Room and board costs vary by type of accommodation.

Financial Aid Research assistantships, teaching assistantships, grants, scholarships available. Financial aid is available to part-time students.

Financial Aid Contact Financial Aid Office, Pearson Street, Churchlands, Western Australia 6018, Australia. Phone: 61-9-273-8333; Fax: 61-9-273-8754.

FACILITIES
Information Resources Edith Cowan University Library plus 5 additional on-campus libraries. CD player(s) available for graduate student use. Access provided to online bibliographic retrieval services and online databases.

INTERNATIONAL STUDENTS
Demographics 43% of students enrolled are international students [Africa, 8%, Asia, 87%, Europe, 5%].

Services and Facilities International student office, international student center, international student housing, ESL courses, counseling/support services.

Applying IELT: minimum score of 6, TOEFL: minimum score of 650 required. Financial aid is not available to international students.

International Student Contact International Students Office, Pearson Street, Churchlands, Western Australia 6018, Australia. Phone: 61-9-273-8499; Fax: 61-9-273-8732.

PLACEMENT
Services include alumni network, and career counseling/planning. In 1996–97, 20 organizations participated in on-campus recruiting.

Employment Of 1996–97 graduates, 98% were employed within three months of graduation. Types of employment entered: accounting, banking, communications, computer-related, consumer products, education, energy, finance, financial services, government, health services, high technology, hospitality management, human resources, information systems/technology, insurance, international trade, management, manufacturing, marketing, mining, nonprofit, real estate, retail, service industry, telecommunications, utilities.

Business Program(s) URL: http://www.bs.ac.cowan.edu.au/

Program Contact: Mr. Barry Chapman, Director, Higher Degrees, Faculty of Business, Pearson Street, Churchlands, Western Australia 6018, Australia. Phone: 61-9-273-8427; Fax: 61-9-273-8754; E-mail: bchapman@cowan.edu.au

La Trobe University

Faculty of Law and Management

Bundoora, Australia

OVERVIEW
La Trobe University coed institution. Founded: 1967. The graduate business unit is in a suburban setting and is on a quarter calendar.

La Trobe University (continued)

HIGHLIGHTS

Enrollment Profile
Full-time: N/R
Part-time: N/R
Total: N/R
Average Age: 25
Fall 1997 Average GPA: N/R

International: N/R
Women: N/R
Minorities: N/R
Average Class Size: N/R
Fall 1997 Average GMAT: N/R

Costs
Full-time tuition: N/R
Part-time tuition: N/R

GRADUATE BUSINESS PROGRAMS
Master of Business Administration (MBA) Full-time, part-time; 12 months to 4 years to complete program. Concentration in management.

ADMISSION
Application Requirements Application fee, 2 letters of recommendation, college transcript(s), minimum of 2 years of work experience.

Recommended for Application Resume.

Application Deadline 9/27 for spring. Application fee: 50 (international).

ACADEMICS
Teaching Methodologies Case study, faculty seminars, field projects, lecture, seminars by members of the business community, team projects.

Technology The network has full access to the Internet. Students are not required to have their own PC.

FINANCES
Costs for 1997–98 Room and board costs vary by occupancy (e.g., single, double, triple).

Financial Aid Contact Mr. Brett Slade, Deputy Director, MBA Program, Bundoora, Victoria 3083, Australia. Phone: 61-39-458-2755; Fax: 61-39-458-2575; E-mail: mba@latrobe.edu.au

FACILITIES
Information Resources Bundoora Library plus 2 additional on-campus libraries.

INTERNATIONAL STUDENTS
Demographics N/R

Applying IELT: minimum score of 6.5, TOEFL: minimum score of 575 required.

International Student Contact Mr. John McPartland, Deputy Director of International Programs, Budoora, Victoria 3083, Australia. Phone: 61-39-458-2755; Fax: 61-39-458-2575.

PLACEMENT
Services include alumni network, and career placement.

Employment Types of employment entered: consulting, finance, government, service industry.

Business Program(s) URL: http://www.latrobe.edu.au

Program Contact: MBA Program, Faculty of Law and Management, Bundoora, Victoria 3083, Australia. Phone: 61-39-479-1979; Fax: 61-39-474-1484; E-mail: mba@latrobe.edu.au

Macquarie University

Macquarie Graduate School of Management

Sydney, New South Wales, Australia

OVERVIEW
Macquarie University coed institution. Enrollment: 18,523 graduate, professional, and undergraduate students; 1,472 full-time matriculated graduate/professional students; 3,513 part-time matriculated graduate/professional students. Founded: 1969. The graduate business unit is in a suburban setting and is on a term calendar.

HIGHLIGHTS

Enrollment Profile
Full-time: N/R
Part-time: N/R
Total: 1,490
Average Age: 34
Fall 1997 Average GPA: N/R

International: 31%
Women: 38%
Minorities: N/R
Average Class Size: 40
Fall 1997 Average GMAT: N/R

Costs
Full-time tuition: N/R
Part-time tuition: N/R

GRADUATE BUSINESS PROGRAMS
Master of Business Administration (MBA) Full-time, part-time; 64 total credits required; 12 months to 3 years to complete program. Concentrations in economics, financial management/planning, human resources, information management, management, management information systems, marketing, operations management, organizational behavior/development, strategic management, international management, technology management.

Master of Management (MMgt) Full-time, part-time; 40 total credits required; 12 to 18 months to complete program. Concentrations in financial management/planning, human resources, information management, marketing, organizational behavior/development, strategic management, management, management information systems, operations management, international management, technology management.

ADMISSION
Applications For fall 1997 there were 994 applications for admission. Of those applying, 786 were accepted. Of those accepted, 597 enrolled.

Application Requirements Application form, bachelor's degree, minimum GPA: 3.0, 3 letters of recommendation, personal statement, college transcript(s), minimum of 5 years of work experience.

Recommended for Application Computer experience.

Application Deadline 10/30 for winter. Applications processed on a rolling/continuous basis for international students only.

ACADEMICS
Faculty Full-time 35; part-time 30.

Teaching Methodologies Case study, computer-aided instruction, computer analysis, computer simulations, experiential learning, faculty seminars, field projects, group discussion, lecture, research, seminars by members of the business community, simulations, student presentations, study groups, team projects.

Technology 30 on-campus computer terminals/PCs are available for student use and are linked by a campus-wide network. The network has full access to the Internet. Students are not required to have their own PC.

Special Opportunities Advanced credit may be earned through credit by examination, transfer of credits from another institution. International exchange programs in France, People's Republic of China, Sweden, United Kingdom.

FINANCES
Costs for 1997–98 Cost varies by campus location. Fees vary by campus location. Average 1997–98 room and board costs were Aus$9500 per academic year (on campus) and Aus$10,000 per academic year (off campus). Room and board costs vary by occupancy (e.g., single, double, triple), type of accommodation.

Financial Aid Contact Mrs. Melenna Krenmayr, Admissions and Scholarships Officer, Sydney, New South Wales 2109, Australia. Phone: 61-2-9850-7346; Fax: 61-2-9850-7733; E-mail: iso@mq.edu.au

FACILITIES
Information Resources Macquarie University Library; total holdings of 726,114 volumes, 885,000 microforms, 304,237 current periodical subscriptions. CD player(s) available for graduate student use. Access provided to online bibliographic retrieval services and online databases.

INTERNATIONAL STUDENTS
Demographics 31% of students enrolled are international students [Asia, 97%, Europe, 2%, North America, 1%].

Services and Facilities International student office, international student center, international student housing, visa services, ESL courses, counseling/support services.

Applying IELT: minimum score of 6, TOEFL: minimum score of 550, proof of adequate funds required. Financial aid is not available to international students.

International Student Contact Mrs. Melenna Krenmayr, Admissions and Scholarships Officer, Sydney, New South Wales 2109, Australia. Phone: 61-2-9850-7346; Fax: 61-2-9850-7733; E-mail: isd@mq.edu.au

PLACEMENT
Services include alumni network, career counseling/planning, career placement, job interviews arranged, resume referral to employers, and resume preparation.

Employment Of 1996–97 graduates, 100% were employed within three months of graduation; the average starting salary was Aus$80,000.

Business Program(s) URL: http://www.gsm.mq.edu.au/

Program Contact: Ms. Kim Wright, Marketing Coordinator, Graduate School of Management, Sydney, New South Wales 2109, Australia. Phone: 61-2-9850-9944; Fax: 61-2-9850-9022; E-mail: kim.wright@mq.edu.au

Monash University

Monash Mt. Eliza Business School

Caulfield East, Victoria, Australia

OVERVIEW
Monash University is a federally supported, coed institution. Enrollment: 42,044 graduate, professional, and undergraduate students; 6,174 full-time matriculated graduate/professional students; 3,806 part-time matriculated graduate/professional students. Founded: 1960. The graduate business unit is in a suburban setting and is on a trimester calendar.

HIGHLIGHTS

Enrollment Profile
Full-time: 180
Part-time: 363
Total: 543
Average Age: 30
Fall 1997 Average GPA: N/R

International: 26%
Women: 34%
Minorities: N/R
Average Class Size: 30
Fall 1997 Average GMAT: N/R

Costs
Full-time tuition: N/R
Part-time tuition: N/R

Degree(s) offered in conjunction with The Chinese University of Hong Kong, Institut Pengembangan Manajemen (Indonesia)

GRADUATE BUSINESS PROGRAMS
Master of Business Administration (MBA) Full-time, part-time; 16 months to 6 years to complete program. Concentrations in accounting, economics, finance, international management, human resources, international business, management, management information systems, marketing, quality management, organizational behavior/development, public policy and administration, quantitative analysis, strategic management, asian business studies, business ethics, business policy/strategy, international and area business studies.

Graduate Diploma of Business Administration (GDBA) Full-time, part-time; 12 months to 3 years to complete program. Concentrations in accounting, economics, finance, international management, human resources, international business, management, management information systems, marketing, quality management, organizational behavior/development, public policy and administration, quantitative analysis, strategic management, asian business studies, business ethics, business policy/strategy, international and area business studies.

Graduate Certificate of Business Administration (GCBA) Full-time, part-time; 6 to 16 months to complete program. Concentrations in accounting, quantitative analysis, international business, organizational behavior/development.

ADMISSION
Applications For fall 1997 there were 750 applications for admission. Of those applying, 375 were accepted. Of those accepted, 265 enrolled.

Application Requirements Application form, application fee, bachelor's degree, minimum GPA: 3.0, 2 letters of recommendation, personal statement, college transcript(s), minimum of 2 years of work experience.

Recommended for Application GMAT score accepted: minimum 575.

Application Deadline 4/30 for winter, 10/31 for summer, 5/30 for winter (international), 11/30 for summer (international). Application fee: 50 (international). Deferred entrance is available.

ACADEMICS
Faculty Full-time 55; part-time 14.

Teaching Methodologies Case study, computer-aided instruction, computer simulations, group discussion, lecture, research, seminars by members of the business community, simulations, student presentations, study groups, team projects.

Technology 540 on-campus computer terminals/PCs are available for student use and are linked by a campus-wide network. The network has full access to the Internet. Students are not required to have their own PC.

Special Opportunities Advanced credit may be earned through transfer of credits from another institution. International exchange programs in France, Germany, Hong Kong, Indonesia, Japan, Thailand, United Kingdom, United States.

FINANCES
Costs for 1997–98 Cost varies by number of credits taken. Average 1997–98 room and board costs were Aus$85,000 per academic year. Room and board costs vary by campus location, occupancy (e.g., single, double, triple), type of accommodation, type of meal plan.

FACILITIES
Information Resources Monash University Library plus 9 additional on-campus libraries; total holdings of 1,545,964 volumes, 209,020 microforms, 531,808 current periodical subscriptions. CD player(s) available for graduate student use. Access provided to online bibliographic retrieval services and online databases.

INTERNATIONAL STUDENTS
Demographics 26% of students enrolled are international students [Asia, 94%, Europe, 5%, North America, 1%].

Services and Facilities International student office, international student center, international student housing, visa services, ESL courses, counseling/support services.

Applying IELT: minimum score of 6.5, TOEFL: minimum score of 580, TWE: minimum score of 5, proof of health/immunizations required. Financial aid is not available to international students.

International Student Contact Ms. Christine Montgomery, MBA International Liaison Officer, PO Box 2224, Caulfield Junction, Victoria 3161, Australia. Phone: 61-39-215-1850; Fax: 61-39-215-1821; E-mail: genmba@mteliza.edu.au

PLACEMENT
Services include alumni network, career counseling/planning, career fairs, career library, career placement, job interviews arranged, job search course, and resume preparation. In 1996–97, 25 organizations participated in on-campus recruiting.

Employment Of 1996–97 graduates, 98% were employed within three months of graduation; the average starting salary was Aus$60,000. Types of employment entered: accounting, banking, communications, consulting, consumer products, finance, financial services, government, health services, hospitality management, human resources, international trade, management, marketing, pharmaceutical, service industry, telecommunications, utilities.

Business Program(s) URL: http://www.mteliza.edu.au

Program Contact: Ms. Christine Montgomery, MBA Admissions Officer, MBA Admissions, PO Box 2224, Caulfield Junction, Victoria 3161, Australia. Phone: 61-39-215-1850; Fax: 61-39-215-1821; E-mail: genmba@mteliza.edu.au

Murdoch University

School of Business

Perth, Australia

OVERVIEW
Murdoch University is a federally supported, coed institution. Founded: 1975. The graduate business unit is in a suburban setting and is on a trimester calendar.

HIGHLIGHTS

Enrollment Profile
Full-time: N/R
Part-time: N/R
Total: N/R
Average Age: 24
Fall 1997 Average GPA: N/R

International: N/R
Women: N/R
Minorities: N/R
Average Class Size: 35
Fall 1997 Average GMAT: 525

Costs
Full-time tuition: Aus$14,100 per academic year (resident); Aus$22,000 per academic year (nonresident)
Part-time tuition: Aus$4700 per trimester (resident); Aus$6900 per trimester (nonresident)

GRADUATE BUSINESS PROGRAMS
Master of International Business (MIB) Full-time, part-time; 48 total credits required; 12 months to 2 years to complete program. Concentrations in accounting, organizational management, system management, strategic management, finance, economics, human resources, organizational behavior/development, marketing research, taxation, marketing, financial information systems, legal administration.

One-year MBA (MBA) Full-time, part-time; 12 months to 4 years to complete program. Concentrations in management, international business.

One-year MIB (MIB) Full-time, part-time; 12 months to 4 years to complete program. Concentrations in international marketing, asian business studies, international business, international finance, accounting, strategic management, international economics, japanese business studies.

Doctor of Business Administration (DBA) Full-time, part-time; 72 total credits required; 2 to 5 years to complete program. Concentration in resources management.

ADMISSION
Application Requirements GMAT score: minimum 500, application form, letters of recommendation, personal statement, resume, college transcript(s), minimum of 2 years of work experience.

Application Deadline 11/30 for fall, 10/31 for fall (international). Deferred entrance is available.

ACADEMICS
Faculty Full-time 60; part-time 20.

Murdoch University (continued)

Teaching Methodologies Case study, computer analysis, computer simulations, faculty seminars, lecture, research, role playing, seminars by members of the business community, student presentations, team projects.

Technology 100 on-campus computer terminals/PCs are available for student use and are linked by a campus-wide network. The network has full access to the Internet. Students are not required to have their own PC.

Special Opportunities Advanced credit may be earned through credit by examination, transfer of credits from another institution. International exchange program in United States.

FINANCES

Costs for 1997–98 Tuition: Full-time: Aus$14,100 per year (resident); Aus$22,000 per year (nonresident). Part-time: Aus$4700 per trimester (resident); Aus$6900 per trimester (nonresident). Cost varies by number of credits taken. Average 1997–98 room and board costs were Aus$8150 per academic year (off campus).

Financial Aid Grants, scholarships available. Application Deadline: 10/31.

Financial Aid Contact Mrs. Anne Randall, Research Degrees and Scholarships Officer, Research Department, South Street, Murdoch. Phone: 61-9-360-2179; Fax: 61-9-360-6503; E-mail: arandall@central.murdoch.edu.au

FACILITIES

Information Resources Murdoch Library; total holdings of 28,105 volumes, 5 microforms, 975 current periodical subscriptions. CD player(s) available for graduate student use. Access provided to online bibliographic retrieval services.

INTERNATIONAL STUDENTS

Demographics N/R

Services and Facilities International student office, international student center, international student housing, ESL courses, counseling/support services.

Applying TOEFL: minimum score of 550 required. IELT: minimum score of 6 recommended. Financial aid is available to international students.

International Student Contact Mr. Peter Tan, Director of International Office, 6150 Murdoch, Murdoch. Phone: 61-9-360-6000; Fax: 61-9-360-6001; E-mail: ptan@central.murdoch.edu.au

PLACEMENT

Services include alumni network, and career placement. In 1996–97, 7 on-campus interviews were conducted.

Employment Of 1996–97 graduates, 70% were employed within three months of graduation; the average starting salary was Aus$50,000. Types of employment entered: accounting, banking, communications, computer-related, consulting, consumer products, education, engineering, finance, financial services, government, health services, hospitality management, human resources, information systems/technology, insurance, international trade, law, management, manufacturing, marketing, media, mining, nonprofit, petrochemical, real estate, retail, service industry, telecommunications, transportation, utilities.

Business Program(s) URL: http://www.murdoch.edu.au

Program Contact: Mrs. Helen Wiggins, Programme Secretary, MBA, MIB, and DBA, School of Business, Murdoch 6150, Australia. Phone: 61-893-60-6046; Fax: 61-893-60-6776; E-mail: wiggins@commerce.murdoch.edu.au

Royal Melbourne Institute of Technology

Graduate School of Business

Melbourne, Australia

OVERVIEW
Royal Melbourne Institute of Technology coed institution. Founded: 1889. The graduate business unit is in an urban setting and is on a semester calendar.

HIGHLIGHTS

Enrollment Profile
Full-time: N/R
Part-time: N/R
Total: N/R
Average Age: 30
Fall 1997 Average GPA: N/R

International: N/R
Women: N/R
Minorities: N/R
Average Class Size: 30
Fall 1997 Average GMAT: N/R

Costs
Full-time tuition: N/R
Part-time tuition: N/R

Degree(s) offered in conjunction with Malaysian Institute of Management, Singapore Institute of Management

GRADUATE BUSINESS PROGRAMS
Master of Business Administration (MBA) Full-time, part-time; 18 months to 5 years to complete program. Concentration in management.

Master of Business Administration in International Management (MBA) Part-time; 2 to 5 years to complete program. Concentration in international management.

Doctor of Business Administration (DBA) Part-time; 3 to 7 years to complete program. Concentrations in strategic management, business policy/strategy.

Master of Business in Corporate Governance (MB) Part-time; 18 months to 5 years to complete program. Concentrations in business ethics, business law, business policy/strategy.

Master of Business in Accountancy (MB) Full-time, part-time; 18 months to 5 years to complete program. Concentration in accounting.

Master of Business in Information Technology (MB) Full-time, part-time; 12 months to 5 years to complete program. Concentrations in business information science, technology management.

Master of Corporate Law (MCL) Full-time, part-time; 18 months to 5 years to complete program. Concentration in business law.

Master of Taxation (MTax) Part-time; 18 months to 5 years to complete program. Concentration in taxation.

Master of Finance (MF) Full-time, part-time; 14 months to 5 years to complete program. Concentrations in international finance, finance, economics.

Master of Business in Logistics Management (MB) Full-time, part-time, distance learning option; 12 months to 5 years to complete program. Concentrations in logistics, international logistics.

Master of Business in Integrated Logistics Management (MB) Full-time, part-time, distance learning option; 12 months to 5 years to complete program. Concentrations in logistics, international logistics.

Master of Business in Property (MB) Full-time, part-time; 18 months to 5 years to complete program. Concentration in real estate.

Masters of Business in Industrial Relations/Human Resource Management (MB) Part-time; 12 months to 5 years to complete program. Concentrations in human resources, industrial administration/management.

Masters of Business in Municipal Management and Health Administration (MB) Part-time; 12 months to 5 years to complete program. Concentrations in health care, public policy and administration.

ADMISSION
Application Requirements Application form, application fee, bachelor's degree, interview, personal statement, resume, college transcript(s), work experience, computer experience: spreadsheet.

Application Deadline 2/1 for fall. Application fee: 100 (international).

ACADEMICS
Faculty Full-time 40; part-time 60.

Teaching Methodologies Case study, computer-aided instruction, computer analysis, experiential learning, faculty seminars, field projects, group discussion, lecture, research, role playing, seminars by members of the business community, simulations, student presentations, study groups, team projects.

Technology 30 on-campus computer terminals/PCs are available for student use and are linked by a campus-wide network. The network has full access to the Internet. Students are required to have their own PC.

Special Opportunities Advanced credit may be earned through credit by examination, transfer of credits from another institution. International exchange programs in Denmark, France, Sweden, United Kingdom, United States.

FINANCES
Costs for 1997–98 Cost varies by academic program.

Financial Aid Scholarships, loans available. Financial aid is available to part-time students.

Financial Aid Contact International Services Financial Aid Officer, GPO Box 2476V, Melbourne, Victoria 3001, Australia. Phone: 61-39-660-5156; Fax: 61-39-663-6925; E-mail: isu@rmit.edu.au

INTERNATIONAL STUDENTS
Demographics N/R

Services and Facilities International student center, international student housing, visa services, ESL courses, counseling/support services.

Applying IELT: minimum score of 6.5, TOEFL: minimum score of 580 required. Financial aid is available to international students.

International Student Contact Ms. Karen Dunwoodie, Manager-International Students Program (MBA), Graduate School, 239 Bourke Street, Melbourne, Victoria 3000, Australia. Phone: 61-39-660-5577.

PLACEMENT
Services include alumni network, career placement, and resume preparation.

Employment Of 1996–97 graduates, 95% were employed within three months of graduation; the average starting salary was Aus$60,000. Types of employment entered: consulting, finance, management, service industry.

Business Program(s) URL: http://www.bf.rmit.edu.au/

Program Contact: Peter Sheldrake, Director of Graduate Studies, GPO Box 2476V, Melbourne, Victoria 3001, Australia. Phone: 61-39-660-5601; Fax: 61-39-660-5599.

The University of Adelaide

Graduate School of Management

Adelaide, South Australia, Australia

OVERVIEW
The University of Adelaide coed institution. Enrollment: 14,021 graduate, professional, and undergraduate students; 1,533 full-time matriculated graduate/professional students; 319 part-time matriculated graduate/professional students. Founded: 1874. The graduate business unit is in an urban setting and is on a trimester calendar.

HIGHLIGHTS

Enrollment Profile

Full-time: 20	International: 4%
Part-time: 355	Women: 27%
Total: 375	Minorities: N/R
Average Age: 30	Average Class Size: 40
Fall 1997 Average GPA: N/R	Fall 1997 Average GMAT: 600

Costs
Full-time tuition: Aus$22,400 per academic year (resident); Aus$31,500 per academic year (nonresident)
Part-time tuition: Aus$1400 per subject (resident); Aus$1969 per subject (nonresident)

Degree(s) offered in conjunction with The University of Queensland, The University of Sydney, Deakin University, University of Tasmania, The University of Western Australia

GRADUATE BUSINESS PROGRAMS
Master of Business Administration (MBA) Full-time, part-time; 48 total credits required; 2 years relevant work experience required; 12 months to 6 years to complete program. Concentrations in finance, asian business studies, marketing, international management.

ADMISSION
Applications For fall 1997 there were 45 applications for admission. Of those applying, 37 were accepted. Of those accepted, 33 enrolled.

Application Requirements GMAT score, application form, application fee, bachelor's degree, 2 letters of recommendation, personal statement, resume, college transcript(s), minimum of 2 years of work experience, computer experience: Word for Windows, Microsoft Excel, Microsoft Powerpoint.

Application Deadline 6/15 for fall, 11/15 for spring, 6/15 for fall (international), 11/15 for spring (international). Application fee: 50 (international). Deferred entrance is available.

ACADEMICS
Faculty Full-time 7; part-time 11.

Teaching Methodologies Case study, group discussion, lecture, research, seminars by members of the business community, student presentations, team projects.

Technology 15 on-campus computer terminals/PCs are available for student use and are linked by a campus-wide network. The network has full access to the Internet. Students are not required to have their own PC.

Special Opportunities Advanced credit may be earned through transfer of credits from another institution. International exchange program in Finland.

FINANCES
Costs for 1997–98 Tuition: Full-time: Aus$22,400 per program (resident); Aus$31,500 per program (nonresident). Part-time: Aus$1400 per subject (resident); Aus$1969 per subject (nonresident). Cost varies by academic program, number of credits taken. Fees: Full-time: Aus$260 per academic year. Fees vary by number of credits taken. Average 1997–98 room and board costs were Aus$7072 per academic year (on campus) and Aus$6760 per academic year (off campus). Room and board costs vary by campus location, occupancy (e.g., single, double, triple), type of accommodation, type of meal plan.

Financial Aid Scholarships available.

Financial Aid Contact Ms. Lisa Brown, International Programs Office, Adelaide, South Australia 5005, Australia. Phone: 61-8-8303-4069; Fax: 61-8-8232-3741; E-mail: lbrown@registry.adelaide.edu.au

FACILITIES
Information Resources Barr Smith Library plus 2 additional on-campus libraries; total holdings of 1,533,402 volumes, 241,037 microforms, 12,565 current periodical subscriptions. CD player(s) available for graduate student use. Access provided to online bibliographic retrieval services and online databases.

INTERNATIONAL STUDENTS
Demographics 4% of students enrolled are international students [Africa, 5%, Asia, 15%, Australia/New Zealand, 81%, Europe, 3%, other, 5%].

Services and Facilities International student office, international student housing, visa services, ESL courses, counseling/support services.

Applying IELT: minimum score of 6, TOEFL: minimum score of 580, TWE: minimum score of 6, proof of adequate funds required.

International Student Contact Mr. Dennis Murray, Director of International Programs, Adelaide, South Australia 5005, Australia. Phone: 61-8-8303-5252; Fax: 61-8-8223-3741; E-mail: dmurray@registry.adelaide.edu.au

PLACEMENT
Services include alumni network.

Employment Of 1996–97 graduates, 99% were employed within three months of graduation; the average starting salary was Aus$70,000. Types of employment entered: accounting, banking, consulting, education, engineering, finance, government, international trade, management, manufacturing, marketing, mining, service industry.

Business Program(s) URL: http://www.gsm.adelaide.edu.au

Program Contact: Ms. Carol McHugh, School Registrar, Graduate School of Management, Adelaide, South Australia 5005, Australia. Phone: 61-8-8303-5525; Fax: 61-8-8223-4782; E-mail: cmchugh@gsm.adelaide.edu.au

University of Melbourne

Melbourne Business School

Melbourne, Victoria, Australia

OVERVIEW
The University of Melbourne is an independent-nonprofit, coed institution. Enrollment: 33,935 graduate, professional, and undergraduate students; 2,900 full-time matriculated graduate/professional students; 5,600 part-time matriculated graduate/professional students. Founded: 1853. The graduate business unit is in an urban setting and is on a trimester calendar.

HIGHLIGHTS

Enrollment Profile

Full-time: 236	International: 14%
Part-time: 524	Women: 29%
Total: 760	Minorities: N/R
Average Age: 29	Average Class Size: 55
Fall 1997 Average GPA: N/R	Fall 1997 Average GMAT: 640

Costs
Full-time tuition: Aus$40,000 per academic year
Part-time tuition: Aus$1650 per subject

GRADUATE BUSINESS PROGRAMS
Master of Business Administration (MBA) Full-time, part-time; 20 total credits required; 16 months to 4 years to complete program. Concentrations in finance, international management, management information systems, marketing, organizational management.

Master of Management Technology (MMT) Full-time, part-time; 16 total credits required; 16 months to 4 years to complete program. Concentrations in information management, management information systems, operations management, project management.

Master of Marketing (MM) Full-time, part-time; 12 total credits required; 12 months to 3 years to complete program. Concentration in marketing.

ADMISSION
Application Requirements GMAT score, application form, bachelor's degree, personal statement, resume, college transcript(s), minimum of 2 years of work experience.

Recommended for Application Letters of recommendation.

Application Deadline 10/31 for winter, 10/31 for winter (international). Deferred entrance is available.

ACADEMICS
Faculty Full-time 31; part-time 20.

University of Melbourne (continued)

Teaching Methodologies Case study, computer simulations, experiential learning, field projects, lecture, seminars by members of the business community, student presentations, team projects.

Technology 42 on-campus computer terminals/PCs are available for student use and are linked by a campus-wide network. The network has full access to the Internet. Students are not required to have their own PC.

Special Opportunities Advanced credit may be earned through transfer of credits from another institution. International exchange programs in Austria, Canada, Denmark, France, Germany, Hong Kong, India, Israel, Italy, Philippines, Republic of Singapore, Republic of South Africa, Spain, Switzerland, United Kingdom, United States.

FINANCES
Costs for 1997–98 Tuition: Full-time: Aus$40,000 per program. Part-time: Aus$1650 per subject. Cost varies by academic program. Average 1997–98 room only costs were Aus$7500 per academic year (on campus) and Aus$12,000 per academic year (off campus). Room and board costs vary by occupancy (e.g., single, double, triple), type of accommodation.

Financial Aid In 1997–98, 5% of students received some institutionally administered aid in the form of research assistantships, teaching assistantships, scholarships.

Financial Aid Contact Financial Aid, Ground Floor, Baldwin Spencer Building, Melbourne, Victoria 3052, Australia. Phone: 61-3-9344-6053; Fax: 61-3-9344-5624.

FACILITIES
Information Resources Baillieu Library plus 18 additional on-campus libraries; total holdings of 3,000,000 volumes. CD player(s) available for graduate student use. Access provided to online bibliographic retrieval services.

INTERNATIONAL STUDENTS
Demographics 14% of students enrolled are international students [Asia, 56%, Australia/New Zealand, 8%, Europe, 16%, North America, 8%, other, 12%].

Services and Facilities International student office, international student center, international student housing, visa services, ESL courses, counseling/support services.

Applying IELT: minimum score of 6.5, proof of adequate funds, proof of health/immunizations required. Financial aid is not available to international students.

International Student Contact Ms. Ann Sankey, Executive Officer, 200 Leicester Street, Melbourne, Victoria 3052, Australia. Phone: 61-3-9349-8122; Fax: 61-3-9349-8133; E-mail: a.sankey@mbs.unimelb.edu.au

PLACEMENT
Services include alumni network, career counseling/planning, career fairs, career placement, job interviews arranged, resume referral to employers, and resume preparation. In 1996–97, 36 organizations participated in on-campus recruiting.

Employment Of 1996–97 graduates, 93% were employed within three months of graduation; the average starting salary was Aus$95,000. Types of employment entered: accounting, banking, chemical industry, communications, computer-related, consulting, consumer products, education, energy, engineering, finance, financial services, government, health services, information systems/technology, management, manufacturing, marketing, nonprofit, service industry, telecommunications.

Business Program(s) URL: http://www.mbs.unimelb.edu.au

Program Contact: Ms. Ann Sankey, Executive Officer, 200 Leicester Street, Melbourne, Victoria 3052, Australia. Phone: 61-3-9349-8122; Fax: 61-3-9349-8133; E-mail: a.sankey@mbs.unimelb.edu.au

University of Newcastle

Graduate School of Business

Newcastle, Australia

OVERVIEW
The University of Newcastle is a federally supported, coed institution. Enrollment: 17,000 graduate, professional, and undergraduate students. Founded: 1968. The graduate business unit is in a suburban setting and is on a semester calendar.

HIGHLIGHTS

Enrollment Profile
Full-time: N/R	International: N/R
Part-time: N/R	Women: N/R
Total: 350	Minorities: N/R
Average Age: 34	Average Class Size: 30
Fall 1997 Average GPA: N/R	Fall 1997 Average GMAT: N/R

Costs
Full-time tuition: Aus$12,000 per academic year (resident); Aus$17,400 per academic year (nonresident)
Part-time tuition: N/R

GRADUATE BUSINESS PROGRAMS
Master of Business Administration (MBA) Full-time, part-time; 18 months to 3 years to complete program. Concentrations in accounting, business information science, business law, commerce, economics, financial economics, human resources, international marketing, management information systems, marketing, marketing research, quantitative analysis.

ADMISSION
Application Requirements Application fee, bachelor's degree, personal statement, resume, college transcript(s), minimum of 3 years of work experience.

Recommended for Application GMAT score accepted: minimum 500.

Application Deadline 6/20 for winter, 12/12 for summer.

ACADEMICS
Faculty Full-time 25; part-time 5.

Teaching Methodologies Case study, computer-aided instruction, group discussion, lecture, seminars by members of the business community, student presentations, team projects.

Technology 60 on-campus computer terminals/PCs are available for student use and are linked by a campus-wide network. The network has full access to the Internet. Students are not required to have their own PC.

Special Opportunities Advanced credit may be earned through transfer of credits from another institution.

FINANCES
Costs for 1997–98 Tuition: Full-time: Aus$12,000 per year (resident); Aus$17,400 per year (nonresident). Cost varies by number of credits taken. Average 1997–98 room and board costs were Aus$8320 per academic year.

Financial Aid Scholarships, loans available. Financial aid is available to part-time students. Application Deadline: 1/1.

Financial Aid Contact Student Support Office, New Castle, New South Wales 2308, Australia. Phone: 61-2-49 21 6466; Fax: 61-49-217-398.

FACILITIES
Information Resources Auchmuty Library plus 1 additional on-campus library. CD player(s) available for graduate student use. Access provided to online bibliographic retrieval services.

INTERNATIONAL STUDENTS
Demographics N/R

Services and Facilities International student office, international student center, international student housing, visa services, ESL courses, counseling/support services.

Applying IELT: minimum score of 6.5, TOEFL: minimum score of 550, TWE: minimum score of 4.5 required. Proof of adequate funds, proof of health/immunizations recommended. Financial aid is not available to international students.

International Student Contact Janet Aisbett, Professor of Information Systems, Newcastle, New South Wales 2308, Australia. Phone: 61-2-49 21 7248; Fax: 61-49-217-398.

PLACEMENT
Services include alumni network, and resume preparation.

Employment Types of employment entered: accounting, banking, finance, financial services, government, human resources, information systems/technology, law, management, marketing.

Business Program(s) URL: http://www.newcastle.edu.au/studying/studying.htm

Program Contact: Ms. Patricia Chipchase, Administrative Officer, Graduate School of Business, Callaghan, New South Wales 2308, Australia. Phone: 61-2-49 21 8749; Fax: 61-2-49 21 7398; E-mail: gsbinfo@cc.newcastle.edu.au

University of New South Wales

Australian Graduate School of Management

Sydney, Australia

OVERVIEW
The University of New South Wales coed institution. Enrollment: 29,920 graduate, professional, and undergraduate students; 2,968 full-time matriculated graduate/professional students; 6,146 part-time matriculated graduate/professional students. Founded: 1949. The graduate business unit is in an urban setting and is on a trimester calendar.

HIGHLIGHTS

Enrollment Profile

Full-time: 229	International: 5%
Part-time: 1,100	Women: 29%
Total: 1,329	Minorities: N/R
Average Age: 35	Average Class Size: 23
Fall 1997 Average GPA: N/R	Fall 1997 Average GMAT: 630

Costs
Full-time tuition: N/R
Part-time tuition: N/R

GRADUATE BUSINESS PROGRAMS
Master of Business Administration (MBA) Full-time; 18 to 21 months to complete program. Concentrations in management, finance, entrepreneurship, accounting, marketing, industrial/labor relations, operations management, organizational behavior/development, economics, quality mancgement, quantitative analysis.

Executive Master of Business Administration (EMBA) Part-time, distance learning option; up to 3 years to complete program. Concentrations in management, finance, international management, accounting, actuarial science, economics, management systems analysis, marketing, organizational behavior/development, organizational management, quality management, strategic management.

ADMISSION
Application Requirements Application form, bachelor's degree, essay, minimum GPA: 3.0, 2 letters of recommendation, personal statement, college transcript(s), minimum of 2 years of work experience.

Recommended for Application GMAT score accepted: minimum 550, computer experience.

Application Deadline 6/6 for winter, 11/27 for summer, 11/30 for summer (international). Deferred entrance is available.

ACADEMICS
Faculty Full-time 45; part-time 103.

Teaching Methodologies Case study, computer-aided instruction, computer simulations, faculty seminars, field projects, group discussion, lecture, role playing, seminars by members of the business community, simulations, student presentations, study groups, team projects.

Technology 42 on-campus computer terminals/PCs are available for student use and are linked by a campus-wide network. The network has full access to the Internet. Students are not required to have their own PC.

FINANCES
Costs for 1997–98 Cost varies by academic program. Average 1997–98 room and board costs were Aus$9360 per academic year (on campus) and Aus$10,000 per academic year (off campus). Room and board costs vary by campus location, occupancy (e.g., single, double, triple), type of accommodation, type of meal plan.

Financial Aid Scholarships available. Application Deadline: 11/30.

Financial Aid Contact Financial Aid Office, Sydney, New South Wales 2052, Australia. Phone: 61-2-9385 1000; Fax: 61-2-9385 2000.

FACILITIES
Information Resources University of New South Wales Library plus 4 additional on-campus libraries; total holdings of 1,800,000 volumes, 207,750 microforms, 20,000 current periodical subscriptions. CD player(s) available for graduate student use. Access provided to online bibliographic retrieval services.

INTERNATIONAL STUDENTS
Demographics 5% of students enrolled are international students [Africa, 4%, Asia, 39%, Australia/New Zealand, 39%, Europe, 12%, North America, 6%].

Services and Facilities International student office, international student center, international student housing, visa services, ESL courses, counseling/support services.

International Student Contact Ms. Rosamond Christie, Manager, Academic Affairs, Australian Graduate School of Management, Sydney, New South Wales 2052, Australia. Phone: 61-2-9931-9220; Fax: 61-2-9931-9231.

PLACEMENT
Services include alumni network, career counseling/planning, career placement, job search course, resume referral to employers, and resume preparation. In 1996–97, 32 organizations participated in on-campus recruiting.

Employment Of 1996–97 graduates, 96% were employed within three months of graduation; the average starting salary was Aus$88,000. Types of employment entered: accounting, banking, communications, computer-related, consulting, engineering, finance, financial services, human resources, law, management, manufacturing, marketing, pharmaceutical, service industry, telecommunications.

Business Program(s) URL: http://www.agsm.unsw.edu.au

Program Contact: Australian Graduate School of Management, Sydney, New South Wales 2052, Australia. Phone: 61-2-9931-9220; Fax: 61-2-9931-9231.

University of Southern Queensland

Faculty of Business

Toowoomba, Queensland, Australia

OVERVIEW
The University of Southern Queensland is a publicly supported, coed institution. Enrollment: 18,462 graduate, professional, and undergraduate students. Founded: 1967. The graduate business unit is in a rural setting and is on a trimester calendar.

HIGHLIGHTS

Enrollment Profile

Full-time: 17	International: 32%
Part-time: 1,187	Women: 99%
Total: 1,204	Minorities: N/R
Average Age: 35	Average Class Size: N/R
Fall 1997 Average GPA: N/R	Fall 1997 Average GMAT: N/R

Costs
Full-time tuition: N/R
Part-time tuition: Aus$800 per unit (resident); Aus$1050 per unit (nonresident)

GRADUATE BUSINESS PROGRAMS
Master of Business (MB) Full-time, part-time; 4 to 5 years to complete program.

Master of Information Technology (MIT) Full-time, part-time, distance learning option; 2 to 4 years to complete program.

Distance Learning MBA (MBA) Part-time, distance learning option; 18 months to 4 years to complete program.

ADMISSION
Applications For fall 1997 there were 662 applications for admission. Of those applying, 560 were accepted. Of those accepted, 425 enrolled.

Application Requirements Application form, bachelor's degree, letters of recommendation, personal statement, resume, college transcript(s), minimum of 2 years of work experience.

Application Deadline 5/31 for winter, 10/31 for summer, 6/20 for winter (international), 1/17 for summer (international). Deferred entrance is available.

ACADEMICS
Faculty Full-time 30.

Teaching Methodologies Case study, computer-aided instruction, experiential learning, group discussion, lecture, research, role playing, student presentations, study groups.

Technology The network has full access to the Internet. Students are required to have their own PC.

Special Opportunities Advanced credit may be earned through credit for business training programs, transfer of credits from another institution.

FINANCES
Costs for 1997–98 Tuition: Aus$800 per unit (resident); Aus$1050 per unit (nonresident). Average 1997–98 room and board costs were Aus$5056 per academic year (on campus) and Aus$5120 per academic year (off campus).

Financial Aid Contact Ms. Colleen Hartmann, Administration Officer, Faculty of Business, Toowoomba, Queensland 4350, Australia. Phone: 61-7-46311881; Fax: 61-7-46312811; E-mail: bizness@usq.edu.au

FACILITIES
Information Resources University of Southern Queensland Library; total holdings of 236,000 volumes, 5,500 current periodical subscriptions. CD player(s) available for graduate student use. Access provided to online bibliographic retrieval services.

University of Southern Queensland (continued)

INTERNATIONAL STUDENTS
Demographics 32% of students enrolled are international students.

Services and Facilities International student office, international student center, international student housing, ESL courses, counseling/support services.

Applying IELT: minimum score of 6.5, TOEFL: minimum score of 550 required. Financial aid is not available to international students.

International Student Contact International Education Centre, Private Mail Bag #1, PO Darling Heights, Toowoomba, Queensland 4350, Australia. Phone: 61-7-46312362; Fax: 61-7-46362211.

PLACEMENT
Services include alumni network, and career placement.

Employment Types of employment entered: banking, education, engineering, finance, management, service industry.

Business Program(s) URL: http://www.usq.edu.au

Program Contact: Ms. Colleen Hartmann, Administration Officer, Faculty of Business, Toowoomba, Queensland 4350, Australia. Phone: 61-7-46311881; Fax: 61-7-46312811; E-mail: bizness@usq.edu.au

The University of Sydney

Graduate School of Business

Sydney, New South Wales, Australia

OVERVIEW
The University of Sydney is a federally supported, coed institution. Enrollment: 31,000 graduate, professional, and undergraduate students. Founded: 1850. The graduate business unit is in an urban setting and is on a semester calendar.

HIGHLIGHTS

Enrollment Profile

Full-time: 150	International: 25%
Part-time: 300	Women: 45%
Total: 450	Minorities: N/R
Average Age: 29	Average Class Size: 35
Fall 1997 Average GPA: N/R	Fall 1997 Average GMAT: 660

Costs
Full-time tuition: Aus$10,600 per academic year (nonresident)
Part-time tuition: Aus$6000 per semester (resident)

Degree(s) offered in conjunction with Leipzig Graduate School of Management (Germany), University of Science and Technology of China

GRADUATE BUSINESS PROGRAMS
Master of Business Administration (MBA) Full-time, part-time; 48 total credits required; 2 years full-time work experience and high GMAT score required; 18 months to 3 years to complete program. Concentration in management.

Master of Management (MMgt) Full-time, part-time; 36 total credits required; 18 months to 2.5 years to complete program. Concentration in management.

ADMISSION
Applications For fall 1997 there were 183 applications for admission. Of those applying, 94 were accepted. Of those accepted, 78 enrolled.

Application Requirements Application form, bachelor's degree, 2 letters of recommendation, personal statement, resume, college transcript(s), minimum of 2 years of work experience.

Recommended for Application GMAT score accepted, computer experience.

Application Deadline 10/30 for winter, 4/30 for summer, 10/30 for winter (international), 4/30 for summer (international). Deferred entrance is available.

ACADEMICS
Faculty Full-time 13; part-time 25.

Teaching Methodologies Case study, lecture, student presentations, team projects.

Technology 30 on-campus computer terminals/PCs are available for student use and are linked by a campus-wide network. The network has full access to the Internet. Students are not required to have their own PC.

Special Opportunities Advanced credit may be earned through transfer of credits from another institution. International exchange programs in France, Germany, Japan, Malaysia, People's Republic of China.

FINANCES
Costs for 1997–98 Tuition: Full-time: Aus$10,600 per semester (nonresident). Part-time: Aus$6000 per semester (resident). Cost varies by number of credits taken. Fees: Aus$300 per year. Average 1997–98 room and board costs were Aus$17,000 per academic year (on campus) and Aus$15,000 per academic year (off campus). Room and board costs vary by campus location, occupancy (e.g., single, double, triple), type of accommodation.

Financial Aid In 1997–98, 2% of students received some institutionally administered aid in the form of scholarships. Application Deadline: 9/30.

Financial Aid Contact Ms. Ayling Rubin, Scholarships, University of Sydney, Newtown, New South Wales 2006, Australia. Phone: 61-2-9351-2778; E-mail: a.rubin@usyd.edu.au

FACILITIES
Information Resources Fisher Library.

INTERNATIONAL STUDENTS
Demographics 25% of students enrolled are international students [Africa, 10%, Asia, 80%, Europe, 10%].

Services and Facilities International student office, international student center, international student housing, visa services, ESL courses, counseling/support services.

Applying IELT: minimum score of 6.5, TOEFL: minimum score of 575, TWE: minimum score of 4.5 required. Financial aid is available to international students.

International Student Contact Mr. Aashish Ali, Manager, International Office, Sydney, New South Wales 2006, Australia. Phone: 61-2-9351-5846.

PLACEMENT
Services include alumni network, career counseling/planning, career fairs, job search course, resume referral to employers, and resume preparation.

Employment Of 1996–97 graduates, 95% were employed within three months of graduation. Types of employment entered: accounting, banking, consulting, insurance, manufacturing.

Business Program(s) URL: http://www.usyd.edu.au/su/gsb/

Program Contact: Ms. Jenny Woodward, Student Liaison Officer, The Graduate School of Business, Locked Bag 20, Newtown, New South Wales 2042, Australia. Phone: 61-2-9351-0037; Fax: 61-2-9351-0099; E-mail: jennyw@gsb.usyd.edu.au

University of Technology, Sydney

Graduate School of Business

Sydney, New South Wales, Australia

OVERVIEW
The University of Technology, Sydney coed institution. Enrollment: 23,952 graduate, professional, and undergraduate students. Founded: 1965. The graduate business unit is in an urban setting and is on a semester calendar.

HIGHLIGHTS

Enrollment Profile

Full-time: 463	International: 11%
Part-time: 2,110	Women: 35%
Total: 2,573	Minorities: N/R
Average Age: 32	Average Class Size: 30
Fall 1997 Average GPA: N/R	Fall 1997 Average GMAT: N/R

Costs
Full-time tuition: N/R
Part-time tuition: N/R

GRADUATE BUSINESS PROGRAMS
Master of Business Administration (MBA) Full-time, part-time; 96 total credits required; 18 months to 6 years to complete program. Concentrations in management, leadership, strategic management, organizational behavior/development, project management, marketing, finance.

Master of Business (MB) Full-time, part-time; 72 total credits required; 18 months to 4.5 years to complete program. Concentrations in accounting, finance, operations management, marketing, international marketing, international business, industrial/labor relations.

Master of Management (MMgt) Full-time, part-time; 72 total credits required; 18 months to 4.5 years to complete program. Concentrations in management, public management, nonprofit management, arts administration/management, sports/entertainment management, travel industry/tourism management, health care.

ADMISSION
Applications For fall 1997 there were 2,154 applications for admission. Of those applying, 1,517 were accepted. Of those accepted, 974 enrolled.

Application Requirements Application form, application fee, bachelor's degree, letter of recommendation, resume, college transcript(s), minimum of 2 years of work experience.

Recommended for Application Personal statement.

Application Deadline 10/15 for fall, 5/31 for spring, 10/31 for fall (international), 5/31 for spring (international). Application fee: 50 (international).

ACADEMICS
Faculty Full-time 130; part-time 100.

Teaching Methodologies Case study, computer simulations, experiential learning, group discussion, lecture, research, role playing, student presentations, study groups, team projects.

Technology 360 on-campus computer terminals/PCs are available for student use and are linked by a campus-wide network. The network has full access to the Internet. Students are not required to have their own PC.

Special Opportunities Advanced credit may be earned through credit by examination, transfer of credits from another institution. International exchange programs in Canada, Denmark, France, Japan.

FINANCES
Costs for 1997–98 Cost varies by academic program, number of credits taken.

Financial Aid In 1997–98, 8% of students received some institutionally administered aid. Financial aid is available to part-time students. Application Deadline: 1/20.

Financial Aid Contact Student Services, PO Box 123, Broadway, Sydney, New South Wales 2007, Australia. Phone: 61-2-9514-1177; Fax: 61-2-9514-3554.

FACILITIES
Information Resources City Campus Library plus 1 additional on-campus library; total holdings of 650,952 volumes. CD player(s) available for graduate student use. Access provided to online bibliographic retrieval services.

INTERNATIONAL STUDENTS
Demographics 11% of students enrolled are international students [Africa, 1%, Asia, 95%, Europe, 1%, North America, 1%, other, 2%].

Services and Facilities International student office, international student center, international student housing, ESL courses, counseling/support services.

Applying IELT: minimum score of 6.5, TOEFL: minimum score of 575, TWE: minimum score of 4.5, proof of adequate funds, proof of health/immunizations required. Financial aid is not available to international students.

International Student Contact Ms. Sarah King, Information Officer, International Programs, UTS, PO Box 123, Broadway, New South Wales 2007, Australia. Phone: 61-2-9514-1531; Fax: 61-2-9514-1530; E-mail: sarah.king@uts.edu.au

PLACEMENT
Services include alumni network, career counseling/planning, career fairs, and career library.

Employment Types of employment entered: education, government, management.

Business Program(s) URL: http://www.bus.uts.edu.au/gsb

Program Contact: Ms. Lucia Liggieri, Graduate Student Advisor, PO Box 123, Broadway, Sydney, New South Wales 2007, Australia. Phone: 61-2-9514-3660; Fax: 61-2-9514-3554; E-mail: lucia.liggieri@uts.edu.au

The University of Western Australia

Graduate School of Management

Nedlands, Western Australia, Australia

OVERVIEW
The University of Western Australia coed institution. Enrollment: 14,114 graduate, professional, and undergraduate students; 1,166 full-time matriculated graduate/professional students; 1,157 part-time matriculated graduate/professional students. Founded: 1911. The graduate business unit is in a suburban setting and is on a trimester calendar.

HIGHLIGHTS

Enrollment Profile
Full-time: 140	International: 25%
Part-time: 260	Women: 33%
Total: 400	Minorities: N/R
Average Age: 28	Average Class Size: 30
Fall 1997 Average GPA: N/R	Fall 1997 Average GMAT: 590

Costs
Full-time tuition: Aus$4400 per academic year (resident); Aus$8000 per academic year (nonresident)
Part-time tuition: Aus$1100 per unit (resident); Aus$2000 per unit (nonresident)

Degree(s) offered in conjunction with Consortium of Australian Business and Management Schools

GRADUATE BUSINESS PROGRAMS
Master of Business Administration (MBA) Full-time, part-time; 16 months to 6 years to complete program. Concentrations in finance, human resources, information management, international business, marketing, operations management, management.

ADMISSION
Applications For fall 1997 there were 245 applications for admission. Of those applying, 216 were accepted. Of those accepted, 114 enrolled.

Application Requirements Application form, bachelor's degree, minimum GPA: 2.75, 2 letters of recommendation, personal statement, college transcript(s), minimum of 2 years of work experience.

Recommended for Application GMAT score accepted, interview, resume, computer experience.

Application Deadline 11/30 for fall, 7/31 for spring, 10/31 for fall (international), 6/30 for spring (international). Deferred entrance is available.

ACADEMICS
Faculty Full-time 20; part-time 10.

Teaching Methodologies Case study, computer analysis, computer simulations, experiential learning, faculty seminars, group discussion, lecture, research, role playing, seminars by members of the business community, simulations, student presentations, study groups, team projects.

Technology 100 on-campus computer terminals/PCs are available for student use and are linked by a campus-wide network. The network has full access to the Internet. Students are not required to have their own PC.

Special Opportunities Advanced credit may be earned through credit by examination, credit for business training programs, transfer of credits from another institution. International exchange programs in Canada, Denmark, Germany, Hong Kong, Japan, Republic of Singapore, United States.

FINANCES
Costs for 1997–98 Tuition: Full-time: Aus$4400 per trimester (resident); Aus$8000 per trimester (nonresident). Part-time: Aus$1100 per unit (resident); Aus$2000 per unit (nonresident). Fees: Full-time: Aus$200 per academic year (resident); Aus$300 per academic year (nonresident). Part-time: Aus$200 per year (resident); Aus$300 per year (nonresident). Average 1997–98 room and board costs were Aus$13,000 per academic year.

FACILITIES
Information Resources Reid Library plus 4 additional on-campus libraries; total holdings of 2,000,000 volumes, 10,000 current periodical subscriptions. CD player(s) available for graduate student use. Access provided to online bibliographic retrieval services.

INTERNATIONAL STUDENTS
Demographics 25% of students enrolled are international students [Asia, 95%, Europe, 5%].

Services and Facilities International student office, international student center, international student housing, visa services, ESL courses, counseling/support services.

Applying IELT: minimum score of 6.5, TOEFL: minimum score of 550 required. Financial aid is not available to international students.

International Student Contact Dr. Roger Smith, GSM International Studies Coordinator, Graduate School of Management, Stirling Highway, Nedlands, Western Australia 6907, Australia. Phone: 61-9-380-1441; Fax: 61-9-380-1072; E-mail: rsmith@ecel.uwa.edu.au

PLACEMENT
Services include alumni network, and career counseling/planning.

Employment Of 1996–97 graduates, 95% were employed within three months of graduation; the average starting salary was Aus$55,000. Types of employment entered: accounting, banking, communications, computer-related, consulting, consumer products, education, energy, engineering, finance, financial services, government, health services, hospitality management, human resources, information systems/technology, international trade, management, manufacturing, marketing, media, mining, pharmaceutical, retail, service industry, telecommunications, transportation, utilities.

Business Program(s) URL: http://www.ecel.uwa.edu.au/

Program Contact: Dr. Roger Smith, GSM International Studies Coordinator, Graduate School of Management, Stirling Highway, Nedlands, Western Australia 6907, Australia. Phone: 61-9-380-1441; Fax: 61-9-380-1072; E-mail: rsmith@ecel.uwa.edu.au

University of Western Sydney, Macarthur

Faculty of Business and Technology

Campbelltown, Australia

OVERVIEW

The University of Western Sydney, Macarthur coed institution. Enrollment: 25,000 graduate, professional, and undergraduate students. Founded: 1989. The graduate business unit is in a suburban setting and is on a quarter calendar.

HIGHLIGHTS

Enrollment Profile

Full-time: 70

Part-time: 10

Total: 80

Average Age: 27

Fall 1997 Average GPA: N/R

International: N/R

Women: N/R

Minorities: N/R

Average Class Size: 20

Fall 1997 Average GMAT: N/R

Costs

Full-time tuition: N/R

Part-time tuition: N/R

GRADUATE BUSINESS PROGRAMS

Master of Business Administration in International Business (MBA) Full-time, part-time; 12 months to 4 years to complete program. Concentrations in accounting, economics, entrepreneurship, finance, international business, management, marketing, organizational behavior/development, strategic management, quality management, organizational management, managerial economics.

Master of Business Administration in Tourism Management (MBA) Full-time, part-time; 12 months to 4 years to complete program. Concentrations in travel industry/tourism management, accounting, economics, entrepreneurship, finance, international business, management, managerial economics, organizational management, quality management, strategic management.

Master of Business Administration in Hotel Management (MBA) Full-time, part-time; 12 months to 4 years to complete program. Concentrations in travel industry/tourism management, accounting, economics, entrepreneurship, finance, international business, management, managerial economics, organizational management, quality management, strategic management.

Master of International Economics (MIE) Full-time, part-time; 12 months to 4 years to complete program. Concentrations in international economics, international finance, finance, environmental economics/management.

Master of Commerce in Accounting (MComm) Full-time, part-time; 12 months to 4 years to complete program. Concentrations in accounting, organizational behavior/development.

ADMISSION

Application Requirements Application form, bachelor's degree, 2 letters of recommendation, college transcript(s), minimum of 2 years of work experience.

Recommended for Application Computer experience.

Application Deadline 7/31 for fall, 11/1 for winter, 2/31 for spring, 5/30 for summer, 7/31 for fall (international), 11/1 for winter (international), 2/31 for spring (international), 5/30 for summer (international). Deferred entrance is available.

ACADEMICS

Faculty Full-time 30.

Teaching Methodologies Case study, lecture, research, seminars by members of the business community, student presentations, team projects.

Technology 60 on-campus computer terminals/PCs are available for student use and are linked by a campus-wide network. The network has full access to the Internet. Students are not required to have their own PC.

Special Opportunities Advanced credit may be earned through transfer of credits from another institution. International exchange program available.

FINANCES

Costs for 1997–98 Average 1997–98 room only costs were Aus$10,000 per academic year. Room and board costs vary by type of accommodation.

Financial Aid Contact Mr. Ross Taylor, Director of International Programs, PO Box 555, Campbelltown, New South Wales 2560, Australia. Phone: 61-246-203-313; Fax: 61-246-266-677.

FACILITIES

Information Resources Total library holdings of 275,000 volumes, 3,700 current periodical subscriptions. CD player(s) available for graduate student use. Access provided to online bibliographic retrieval services and online databases.

INTERNATIONAL STUDENTS

Demographics N/R

Services and Facilities International student office, international student center, international student housing, visa services, ESL courses, counseling/support services.

Applying IELT: minimum score of 6, TOEFL: minimum score of 570, proof of adequate funds required.

International Student Contact Ms. Ingrid Elliston, Executive Officer, Office of International Programs, PO Box 555, Campbelltown, New South Wales 2560, Australia. Phone: 61-246-203-313; Fax: 61-246-266-677; E-mail: i.elliston@uws.edu.au

PLACEMENT

Services include alumni network, career counseling/planning, and career fairs.

Employment Types of employment entered: accounting, banking, consulting, engineering, finance, government, health services, hospitality management, human resources, information systems/technology, international trade, management, manufacturing, service industry, telecommunications.

Business Program(s) URL: http://www.macarthur.uws.edu.au

Program Contact: Mr. Ross Taylor, Director of International Programs, PO Box 555, Campbelltown, New South Wales 2560, Australia. Phone: 61-246-203-313; Fax: 61-246-266-677.

AUSTRIA

Vienna University of Economics and Business Administration

Business Program/International MBA

Vienna, Austria

OVERVIEW

Vienna University of Economics and Business Administration is a publicly supported, coed institution. Enrollment: 27,800 graduate, professional, and undergraduate students. Founded: 1898. The graduate business unit is in an urban setting and is on a quarter calendar.

HIGHLIGHTS

Enrollment Profile

Full-time: 50

Part-time: 0

Total: 50

Average Age: 28

Fall 1997 Average GPA: N/R

International: 98%

Women: 34%

Minorities: N/R

Average Class Size: 47

Fall 1997 Average GMAT: 590

Costs

Full-time tuition: $25,000 per academic year (resident); $25,000 per academic year (nonresident)

Part-time tuition: $25,000 per program (resident); $25,000 per program (nonresident)

Degree(s) offered in conjunction with University of South Carolina

GRADUATE BUSINESS PROGRAMS

International MBA (MBA) Full-time; 48 total credits required; 15 months to complete program. Concentrations in international business, international management.

ADMISSION

Applications For fall 1997 there were 225 applications for admission. Of those applying, 81 were accepted. Of those accepted, 50 enrolled.

Application Requirements Application form, application fee, bachelor's degree, essay, 2 letters of recommendation, personal statement, resume, college transcript(s).

Recommended for Application GMAT score accepted, minimum GPA, interview, minimum of 2 years of work experience, computer experience.

Application Deadline 2/1 for summer, 2/1 for summer (international). Application fee: $35. Deferred entrance is available.

ACADEMICS

Faculty Full-time 25.

Teaching Methodologies Case study, computer-aided instruction, field projects, group discussion, seminars by members of the business community, student presentations, study groups, team projects.

Technology 600 on-campus computer terminals/PCs are available for student use and are linked by a campus-wide network. The network has full access to the Internet. Students are required to have their own PC.

Special Opportunities International exchange program in United States.

FINANCES
Costs for 1997–98 Tuition: Full-time: $25,000 per program (resident); $25,000 per program (nonresident). Part-time: $25,000 per program (resident); $25,000 per program (nonresident). Average 1997–98 room and board costs were $10,000 per academic year (off campus). Room and board costs vary by occupancy (e.g., single, double, triple), type of accommodation, type of meal plan.

Financial Aid Fellowships, teaching assistantships, scholarships, loans available. Application Deadline: 4/1.

Financial Aid Contact Cindy Peachey, Financial Aid Officer, Financial Aid Office, Columbia. Phone: 43-1-31336; Fax: 803-777-0941; E-mail: peachy-cindy@scarolina.edu

FACILITIES
Information Resources Wien Library plus 20 additional on-campus libraries; total holdings of 602,338 volumes, 275 microforms, 2,272 current periodical subscriptions. CD player(s) available for graduate student use.

INTERNATIONAL STUDENTS
Demographics 98% of students enrolled are international students [Asia, 4%, Central America, 2%, Europe, 20%, North America, 71%, South America, 3%].

Services and Facilities International student office, international student center, visa services, ESL courses, counseling/support services.

Applying TOEFL: minimum score of 550, proof of adequate funds, proof of health/immunizations required. Financial aid is available to international students.

International Student Contact Alexander Hofmann, Student Affairs Manager, IMBA Augasse 2-6, Vienna. Phone: 43-1-31336 Ext. 5312; Fax: 43-1-31336 Ext. 768; E-mail: imba@isis.wu-wien.ac.at

PLACEMENT
Services include alumni network, career counseling/planning, career fairs, career library, electronic job bank, job interviews arranged, job search course, resume referral to employers, and resume preparation. In 1996–97, 200 organizations participated in on-campus recruiting.

Employment Of 1996–97 graduates, 92% were employed within three months of graduation; the average starting salary was $60,000. Types of employment entered: accounting, banking, chemical industry, computer-related, consulting, consumer products, finance, financial services, information systems/technology, insurance, international trade, management, marketing, nonprofit, telecommunications.

Business Program(s) URL: http://www.wu-wien.ac.at/inst/imba

Program Contact: Francien Maerz, Assistant to Director, IMBA Augasse 2-6 A, Vienna A-1090, Austria. Phone: 43-1-31336 Ext. 4327; Fax: 43-1-31336 Ext. 768.

BANGLADESH

International University of Business Agriculture and Technology (IUBAT)

College of Business Administration

Dhaka, Bangladesh

OVERVIEW
International University of Business Agriculture and Technology (IUBAT) is an independent-nonprofit, coed institution. Enrollment: 969 graduate, professional, and undergraduate students. Founded: 1991. The graduate business unit is in an urban setting and is on a semester calendar.

HIGHLIGHTS

Enrollment Profile
Full-time: N/R	International: 1%
Part-time: N/R	Women: N/R
Total: 82	Minorities: N/R
Average Age: 24	Average Class Size: 30
Fall 1997 Average GPA: N/R	Fall 1997 Average GMAT: N/R

Costs
Full-time tuition: $4884 per academic year
Part-time tuition: N/R

Peterson's Guide to MBA Programs 1999

Degree(s) offered in conjunction with various institutions in North America, Europe, Australia, and Asia

GRADUATE BUSINESS PROGRAMS
Master of Business Administration (MBA) Full-time; 36 total credits required; minimum of 20 months to complete program. Concentrations in financial management/planning, management, management science, marketing, operations management, production management.

ADMISSION
Applications For fall 1997 there were 56 applications for admission. Of those applying, 29 were accepted. Of those accepted, 19 enrolled.

Application Requirements Application form, application fee, bachelor's degree, 3 letters of recommendation, personal statement, resume, college transcript(s).

Recommended for Application Interview.

Application Deadline Applications processed on a rolling/continuous basis for both domestic and international students. Application fee: 150 Taka. Deferred entrance is available.

ACADEMICS
Faculty Full-time 5; part-time 24.

Teaching Methodologies Case study, computer-aided instruction, computer analysis, computer simulations, experiential learning, faculty seminars, field projects, group discussion, lecture, research, role playing, seminars by members of the business community, simulations, student presentations, study groups, team projects.

Technology 15 on-campus computer terminals/PCs are available for student use. The network does not have Internet access. Students are not required to have their own PC.

Special Opportunities Advanced credit may be earned through credit by examination, transfer of credits from another institution. International exchange programs in Canada, Netherlands, United States.

FINANCES
Costs for 1997–98 Tuition: Full-time: $4884 per program. Cost varies by academic program, class time (e.g., day/evening), number of credits taken. Fees: Full-time: $2250 per academic year. Average 1997–98 room and board costs were $500 per academic year (off campus). Room and board costs vary by occupancy (e.g., single, double, triple), type of accommodation, type of meal plan.

Financial Aid In 1997–98, 11% of students received some institutionally administered aid in the form of research assistantships, teaching assistantships, scholarships, work study, loans.

FACILITIES
Information Resources IUBAT Library and Information Services; total holdings of 6,800 volumes, 70 microforms, 32 current periodical subscriptions.

INTERNATIONAL STUDENTS
Demographics 1% of students enrolled are international students [Asia, 100%].

Applying Proof of adequate funds, proof of health/immunizations required. TOEFL, TSE, TWE recommended. Financial aid is available to international students.

PLACEMENT
Services include alumni network, career counseling/planning, career placement, job interviews arranged, and resume referral to employers.

Employment Of 1996–97 graduates, 100% were employed within three months of graduation; the average starting salary was 120,000 Taka. Types of employment entered: health services, marketing.

Business Program(s) URL: http://www.bangla.net/iubat

Program Contact: Dr. M. Alimullah Miyan, Vice Chancellor, IUBAT, House 135, Road 9A, Dhanmondi, Dhaka 1000, Bangladesh. Phone: 880-2-81-60-64; Fax: 880-2-81-04-94; E-mail: am@iubat.bdmail.net

University of Dhaka

Institute of Business Administration

Dhaka, Bangladesh

OVERVIEW
The University of Dhaka coed institution. Founded: 1921. The graduate business unit is in an urban setting and is on a semester calendar.

HIGHLIGHTS

Enrollment Profile
Full-time: N/R
Part-time: N/R
Total: N/R
Average Age: 25
Fall 1997 Average GPA: N/R

International: N/R
Women: N/R
Minorities: N/R
Average Class Size: 60
Fall 1997 Average GMAT: 500

Costs
Full-time tuition: N/R
Part-time tuition: N/R

GRADUATE BUSINESS PROGRAMS

Master of Business Administration (MBA) Full-time, part-time; 60 total credits required; 2.5 to 8 years to complete program. Concentrations in finance, human resources, marketing, production management, information management.

Master of Philosophy (MPhil) Full-time; 2 to 4 years to complete program. Concentrations in entrepreneurship, human resources, public policy and administration.

Doctor of Philosophy (PhD) Part-time; 3 to 8 years to complete program. Concentration in business policy/strategy.

ADMISSION

Applications For fall 1997 there were 3,200 applications for admission.

Application Requirements Bachelor's degree, essay, interview, letters of recommendation, resume, college transcript(s).

Recommended for Application GMAT score accepted.

ACADEMICS

Faculty Full-time 41; part-time 6.

Teaching Methodologies Case study, computer-aided instruction, computer analysis, computer simulations, experiential learning, faculty seminars, field projects, group discussion, lecture, student presentations, study groups, team projects.

Technology 3 on-campus computer terminals/PCs are available for student use. The network has partial access to the Internet. Students are not required to have their own PC.

Special Opportunities Advanced credit may be earned through transfer of credits from another institution. An internship program is available.

FINANCES

Costs for 1997–98 Room and board costs vary by campus location, occupancy (e.g., single, double, triple).

Financial Aid Application Deadline: 3/31.

Financial Aid Contact Dr. Abdur Rab, Director, Institute of Business Administration, Dhaka. Phone: 880-2-867-815; Fax: 880-2-865-583; E-mail: rab@bangla.net

FACILITIES

Information Resources Dhaka University Library plus 12 additional on-campus libraries; total holdings of 1,050,000 volumes, 500 current periodical subscriptions.

INTERNATIONAL STUDENTS

Demographics N/R

Services and Facilities Counseling/support services.

Applying TOEFL recommended. Financial aid is not available to international students.

PLACEMENT

Services include alumni network, career counseling/planning, career placement, job interviews arranged, resume referral to employers, and resume preparation.

Employment Types of employment entered: banking, computer-related, consumer products, finance, management, marketing, pharmaceutical, service industry.

Program Contact: Director, Institute of Business Administration, Dhaka 1000, Bangladesh. Phone: 880-2-50-57-22.

BELGIUM

European University

International Center for Management Studies

Antwerp, Belgium

OVERVIEW

European University is a proprietary, coed institution. Enrollment: 4,600 graduate, professional, and undergraduate students. Founded: 1973. The graduate business unit is in an urban setting and is on a trimester calendar.

HIGHLIGHTS

Enrollment Profile
Full-time: 40
Part-time: 33
Total: 73
Average Age: 27
Fall 1997 Average GPA: 3.0

International: 88%
Women: 32%
Minorities: N/R
Average Class Size: N/R
Fall 1997 Average GMAT: 500

Costs
Full-time tuition: $12,000 per academic year
Part-time tuition: N/R

GRADUATE BUSINESS PROGRAMS

Master of Business Administration (MBA) Full-time, part-time; 12 months to 3 years to complete program. Concentrations in management, marketing, strategic management, travel industry/tourism management, finance.

Executive MBA (MBA) Full-time; 12 months to complete program. Concentrations in management, marketing, strategic management, travel industry/tourism management, finance.

Master of Science in Information Systems (MS) Full-time, part-time; 12 months to 3 years to complete program.

Master of Transportation and Logistics (MTL) Full-time, part-time; 12 months to 3 years to complete program.

Master of Arts in Business Communications and Public Relations (MA) Full-time, part-time; 12 months to 3 years to complete program.

Master of Science in International Hospitality and Tourism Management (MS) Full-time, part-time; 12 months to 3 years to complete program.

ADMISSION

Applications For fall 1997 there were 107 applications for admission. Of those applying, 50 were accepted. Of those accepted, 40 enrolled.

Application Requirements Application form, application fee, bachelor's degree (must be in field of business), interview, 2 letters of recommendation, personal statement, resume, college transcript(s).

Recommended for Application GMAT score accepted: minimum 450.

Application Deadline Applications processed on a rolling/continuous basis for both domestic and international students. Application fee: $100.

ACADEMICS

Teaching Methodologies Case study, computer analysis, group discussion, lecture, research, student presentations, team projects.

Special Opportunities International exchange program available.

FINANCES

Costs for 1997–98 Tuition: Full-time: $12,000 per program. Cost varies by campus location. Room and board costs vary by campus location, occupancy (e.g., single, double, triple), type of accommodation.

INTERNATIONAL STUDENTS

Demographics 88% of students enrolled are international students [Africa, 8%, Asia, 24%, Europe, 30%, North America, 15%, South America, 12%, other, 11%].

Services and Facilities International student office, international student center, international student housing, visa services, ESL courses, counseling/support services.

Applying TOEFL: minimum score of 450 required.

International Student Contact Mr. Luc Van Mele, Dean (Director of MBA Admissions), Jacob Jordenstraat 77, Antwerp. Phone: 32-3-218-5431.

PLACEMENT

Services include alumni network, career counseling/planning, career fairs, career placement, job interviews arranged, and resume preparation.

Employment Types of employment entered: accounting, banking, consulting, finance, financial services, hospitality management, information systems/technology, insurance, international trade, law, management, marketing, real estate, service industry, telecommunications, transportation.

Business Program(s) URL: http://www.euruni.be/

Program Contact: Mr. Luc Van Mele, Director of MBA Admissions, Jacob Jordaensstraat 77, Antwerp 2018, Belgium. Phone: 32-3-218-5431; Fax: 32-3-218-5868.

See full description on page 810.

Katholieke Universiteit Leuven

Department of Applied Economic Sciences

Leuven, Belgium

OVERVIEW
Katholieke Universiteit Leuven is a federally supported, primarily male institution. Enrollment: 24,000 graduate, professional, and undergraduate students. Founded: 1425. The graduate business unit is in a small-town setting and is on a semester calendar.

HIGHLIGHTS

Enrollment Profile
Full-time: 60
Part-time: 60
Total: 120
Average Age: 28
Fall 1997 Average GPA: N/R

International: 50%
Women: N/R
Minorities: N/R
Average Class Size: 100
Fall 1997 Average GMAT: 610

Costs
Full-time tuition: 18,000 Belgian francs per academic year (resident); 18,000 Belgian francs per academic year (nonresident)
Part-time tuition: 10,000 Belgian francs per year (resident); 10,000 Belgian francs per year (nonresident)

GRADUATE BUSINESS PROGRAMS
Master of Business Administration (MBA) Full-time, part-time; 10 to 22 months to complete program. Concentrations in accounting, business information science, european business studies, finance, human resources, international business, international finance, management, marketing, operations management, organizational behavior/development, quantitative analysis, strategic management.
Master of Science in Marketing (MS) Full-time; minimum of 10 months to complete program.
Master Of Science in Applied Economics (MS) Full-time; minimum of 10 months to complete program.

ADMISSION
Applications For fall 1997 there were 250 applications for admission. Of those applying, 130 were accepted. Of those accepted, 120 enrolled.
Application Requirements GMAT score: minimum 550, application form, application fee, bachelor's degree, minimum GPA, 2 letters of recommendation, personal statement.
Recommended for Application Resume, work experience, computer experience.
Application Deadline 7/31 for fall, 5/1 for fall (international). Application fee: 2000 Belgian francs. Deferred entrance is available.

ACADEMICS
Faculty Full-time 44.
Teaching Methodologies Case study, computer-aided instruction, computer analysis, computer simulations, faculty seminars, field projects, group discussion, lecture, research, role playing, seminars by members of the business community, simulations, student presentations, study groups, team projects.
Technology 100 on-campus computer terminals/PCs are available for student use and are linked by a campus-wide network. The network has full access to the Internet. Students are not required to have their own PC.
Special Opportunities International exchange programs in Spain, United States.

FINANCES
Costs for 1997–98 Tuition: Full-time: 18,000 Belgian francs per year (resident); 18,000 Belgian francs per year (nonresident). Part-time: 10,000 Belgian francs per year (resident); 10,000 Belgian francs per year (nonresident).

FACILITIES
Information Resources K.U. Leuven Central Library plus 30 additional on-campus libraries; total holdings of 60,000 volumes. CD player(s) available for graduate student use. Access provided to online bibliographic retrieval services.

INTERNATIONAL STUDENTS
Demographics 50% of students enrolled are international students [Africa, 2%, Asia, 31%, Europe, 48%, North America, 12%, South America, 7%].
Services and Facilities International student office, international student center, international student housing, counseling/support services.

Applying Proof of adequate funds required. Financial aid is not available to international students.
International Student Contact Mrs. Gonda Huybens, Program Coordinator, Naamsestrat 69, Leuven. Phone: 32-16-326-619; Fax: 32-16-326-620; E-mail: gonda.huybens@econ.kuleuven.ac.be

PLACEMENT
Services include alumni network, career fairs, and job interviews arranged. In 1996–97, 12 organizations participated in on-campus recruiting.
Business Program(s) URL: http://www.econ.kuleuven.ac.be/
Program Contact: Mrs. Gonda Huybens, Program Coordinator, Naamsestraat 69, Leuven B-3000, Belgium. Phone: 32-16-663-219; Fax: 32-16-663-220.

St. Ignatius University Faculty of Antwerp (UFSIA)

Center for Business Administration

Antwerp, Belgium

OVERVIEW
St. Ignatius University Faculty of Antwerp (UFSIA) coed institution. Enrollment: 3,600 graduate, professional, and undergraduate students; 120 full-time matriculated graduate/professional students; 30 part-time matriculated graduate/professional students. Founded: 1852. The graduate business unit is in an urban setting and is on a trimester calendar.

HIGHLIGHTS

Enrollment Profile
Full-time: 65
Part-time: 5
Total: 70
Average Age: 25
Fall 1997 Average GPA: N/R

International: 29%
Women: 43%
Minorities: N/R
Average Class Size: 45
Fall 1997 Average GMAT: 550

Costs
Full-time tuition: N/R
Part-time tuition: N/R

GRADUATE BUSINESS PROGRAMS
Master of Business Administration (MBA) Full-time, part-time; 60 total credits required; 10 months to complete program. Concentration in management.

ADMISSION
Applications For fall 1997 there were 120 applications for admission. Of those applying, 70 were accepted. Of those accepted, 65 enrolled.
Application Requirements Application form, bachelor's degree (must be in field of business), 2 letters of recommendation, college transcript(s).
Recommended for Application GMAT score accepted: minimum 550, interview, personal statement, resume, computer experience.
Application Deadline 8/1 for fall, 4/1 for fall (international).

ACADEMICS
Faculty Full-time 5; part-time 20.
Teaching Methodologies Case study, computer-aided instruction, computer analysis, computer simulations, field projects, group discussion, lecture, role playing, simulations, student presentations, team projects.
Technology 100 on-campus computer terminals/PCs are available for student use and are linked by a campus-wide network. The network has full access to the Internet. Students are not required to have their own PC.
Special Opportunities Advanced credit may be earned through credit by examination, transfer of credits from another institution. International exchange programs in Canada, Japan, Mexico, Republic of Singapore, Republic of South Africa, United Kingdom, United States. An internship program is available.

FINANCES
Costs for 1997–98 Average 1997–98 room only costs were 80,000 Belgian francs per academic year (on campus) and 100,000 Belgian francs per academic year (off campus). Room and board costs vary by type of accommodation.

FACILITIES
Information Resources Central Library plus 6 additional on-campus libraries; total holdings of 700,000 volumes, 3,000 current periodical subscriptions. CD player(s) available for graduate student use. Access provided to online bibliographic retrieval services.

INTERNATIONAL STUDENTS
Demographics 29% of students enrolled are international students [Africa, 5%, Asia, 30%, Central America, 5%, Europe, 30%, North America, 25%, South America, 5%].

St. Ignatius University Faculty of Antwerp (UFSIA) (continued)

Services and Facilities International student office, international student center, international student housing, counseling/support services.

Applying Proof of adequate funds required. Financial aid is not available to international students.

International Student Contact Ms. Katrien Dickele, Administrative Coordinator, Prinsstraat 13, Antwerp. Phone: 32-3-220-4035; Fax: 32-3-220-4079; E-mail: cba.dickele.k@alpha.ufsia.ac.be

PLACEMENT
Services include alumni network, career fairs, career placement, and electronic job bank. In 1996–97, 30 organizations participated in on-campus recruiting; 100 on-campus interviews were conducted.

Employment Of 1996–97 graduates, 90% were employed within three months of graduation; the average starting salary was 85,000 Belgian francs. Types of employment entered: accounting, banking, consulting, education, engineering, finance, government, insurance, international trade, management, marketing, service industry.

Business Program(s) URL: http://www.ufsia.ac.be/MBA

Program Contact: Ms. Katrien Dickele, Administrative Coordinator, Prinsstraat 13, Antwerp 2000, Belgium. Phone: 32-3-220-4035; Fax: 32-3-220-4079.

CANADA

Athabasca University

Centre for Innovative Management

Athabasca, Canada

OVERVIEW
Athabasca University is a province-supported, coed institution. Enrollment: 14,000 graduate, professional, and undergraduate students; full-time matriculated graduate/professional students; 472 part-time matriculated graduate/professional students. Founded: 1970. The graduate business unit is in an urban setting and is on a phase calendar.

HIGHLIGHTS

Enrollment Profile
Full-time: 0
Part-time: 472
Total: 472
Average Age: 40
Fall 1997 Average GPA: N/R

International: 1%
Women: 29%
Minorities: N/R
Average Class Size: 45
Fall 1997 Average GMAT: 536

Costs
Full-time tuition: N/R
Part-time tuition: Can$19,550 per program (resident); Can$19,550 per program (nonresident)

Degree(s) offered in conjunction with University of Guelph

Athabasca University's Executive M.B.A. program is conducted through a unique distance learning model that enables students to combine their studies with their careers. As an electronically delivered program, students have the ability to complete their studies from the comfort and convenience of home, from work, or while on the road. This allows them to work according to their own schedules, without losing valuable time through commutes and preset classes.

The program aims to give its students the skills they need to succeed in the multifaceted role of modern managers, which includes being a leader, team player, decision maker, and coach. Students focus on key tasks on management— managing strategy, information, people, resources, markets, and operations— from a decision-making perspective. Throughout the program, students apply the theories they are learning to real situations in their own organizations.

The Athabasca M.B.A. utilizes Lotus Notes, a groupware product that enables students to access course information and materials, conduct group discussions, complete teamwork projects, and submit course work electronically. Students and faculty and staff members are all connected, creating a rich, interactive learning environment, while giving students the support and services they require to succeed.

Students must complete ten required courses, two electives, two comprehensive exams, and one applied project for a total of 48 credits. In addition, students must attend one weeklong summer school and two weekend schools

GRADUATE BUSINESS PROGRAMS
Executive MBA (MBA) Part-time, distance learning option; 48 total credits required; 2.5 to 6 years to complete program. Concentrations in accounting, entrepreneurship, human resources, information management, international marketing, management, management information systems, marketing, operations management, project management, public management, strategic management, leadership, business law, decision sciences, organizational behavior/development.

ADMISSION
Applications For fall 1997 there were 177 applications for admission. Of those applying, 137 were accepted. Of those accepted, 102 enrolled.

Application Requirements Application form, application fee, bachelor's degree, personal statement, resume, college transcript(s), minimum of 3 years of work experience, computer experience: Microsoft Word, Microsoft Excel.

Application Deadline 6/28 for fall, 10/31 for winter, 2/28 for spring, 6/28 for fall (international), 10/31 for winter (international), 2/28 for spring (international). Application fee: Can$100. Deferred entrance is available.

ACADEMICS
Faculty Full-time 5; part-time 47.

Teaching Methodologies Case study, computer-aided instruction, computer analysis, computer simulations, experiential learning, faculty seminars, field projects, group discussion, research, simulations, student presentations, study groups, team projects.

Technology The network has full access to the Internet. Students are required to have their own PC.

Special Opportunities Advanced credit may be earned through credit by examination, transfer of credits from another institution.

FINANCES
Costs for 1997–98 Tuition: Part-time: Can$19,550 per program (resident); Can$19,550 per program (nonresident).

FACILITIES
Information Resources Athabasca University Library; total holdings of 126,000 volumes, 115 microforms, 650 current periodical subscriptions. Access provided to online bibliographic retrieval services and online databases.

INTERNATIONAL STUDENTS
Demographics 1% of students enrolled are international students.

Applying Financial aid is not available to international students.

Business Program(s) URL: http://www.athabascau.ca

Program Contact: Ms. Shelley Lynes, Manager, Registration, Records, and Graduate Student Affairs, 301, 22 Sir Winston Churchill Avenue, St. Albert T8N 1B4, Canada. Phone: 403-459-1144, 800-561-4650 (AB only); Fax: 403-459-2093.

Carleton University

School of Business

Ottawa, Canada

OVERVIEW
Carleton University is a province-supported, coed institution. Enrollment: 17,541 graduate, professional, and undergraduate students; 1,641 full-time matriculated graduate/professional students; 715 part-time matriculated graduate/professional students. Founded: 1942. The graduate business unit is in an urban setting and is on a Canadian standard year calendar.

HIGHLIGHTS

Enrollment Profile
Full-time: N/R
Part-time: N/R
Total: N/R
Average Age: 25
Fall 1997 Average GPA: 9.0

International: N/R
Women: N/R
Minorities: N/R
Average Class Size: 12
Fall 1997 Average GMAT: 550

Costs
Full-time tuition: Can$3886 per academic year (resident); Can$8786 per academic year (nonresident)
Part-time tuition: N/R

The School of Business is an exciting and innovative unit, situated amidst one of the best learning environments in the world. Its location in the nation's capital provides easy access to technology-oriented firms in Ottawa's "Silicon Valley North" and to corporate headquarters, libraries, research centres, major Canadian and international government agencies, embassies, and other organizations.

Enrollment in the Masters of Management Studies (M.M.S.), is limited, so every student benefits from the individual attention and support of faculty members with a wide variety of research interests and experiences. M.M.S. students have access to a cutting-edge microcomputing environment and the University's comprehensive computer resources. Eight organized research units offer vital learning support and provide well-established links with businesss, government, and academic organizations throughout Canada and the world. These links enable students to research topics that are critical to success in the evolving global environment.

The M.M.S. provides an innovative alternative to traditional M.B.A. programs by focusing on developing specialized applied research and analytical skills for resolving complex business problems in an intensive and personalized education environment. A combination of attributes revolving around the student-faculty-curriculum business practice nexus, along with guidance from faculty members in specific functional areas of interest, allows students to design a custom-tailored curriculum that fits their needs

GRADUATE BUSINESS PROGRAMS
Master of Management Studies (MMS) Full-time, part-time; 12 months to 3 years to complete program. Concentrations in business information science, finance, international business, management, marketing, production management, research and development administration.

ADMISSION
Application Requirements GMAT score, application form, application fee, bachelor's degree, GPA: minimum 7.0 on a 12 scale, 2 letters of recommendation, personal statement, college transcript(s).

Application Deadline Applications processed on a rolling/continuous basis for both domestic and international students. Application fee: Can$35. Deferred entrance is available.

ACADEMICS
Faculty Full-time 32; part-time 38.

Teaching Methodologies Case study, computer analysis, computer simulations, faculty seminars, field projects, group discussion, lecture, research, seminars by members of the business community, simulations, student presentations, study groups, team projects.

Technology Computer terminals/PCs are available for student use and are linked by a campus-wide network. The network has full access to the Internet. Students are not required to have their own PC.

Special Opportunities Advanced credit may be earned through transfer of credits from another institution.

FINANCES
Costs for 1997–98 Tuition: Full-time: Can$3886 per year (resident); Can$8786 per year (nonresident). Cost varies by reciprocity agreements. Average 1997–98 room and board costs were Can$5000 per academic year (on campus) and Can$6600 per academic year (off campus). Room and board costs vary by occupancy (e.g., single, double, triple).

Financial Aid Research assistantships, teaching assistantships, scholarships available. Application Deadline: 3/1.

Financial Aid Contact Jean Blair, Graduate Secretary, School of Business, 1125 Colonel By Drive, Ottawa. Phone: 613-520-2600 Ext. 8077; E-mail: j_blair@carleton.ca

FACILITIES
Information Resources Maxwell MacOdrum Library; total holdings of 2,000,000 volumes, 916,973 microforms, 12,903 current periodical subscriptions. CD player(s) available for graduate student use. Access provided to online bibliographic retrieval services.

INTERNATIONAL STUDENTS
Demographics N/R

Services and Facilities International student office, international student center, visa services, ESL courses, counseling/support services.

Applying TOEFL: minimum score of 550, proof of adequate funds required.

International Student Contact Jean Blair, Graduate Secretary, School of Business, 1125 Colonel By Drive, Ottawa. Phone: 613-520-2600 Ext. 8077; E-mail: j_blair@carleton.ca

PLACEMENT
Services include career counseling/planning, career fairs, career placement, electronic job bank, job interviews arranged, resume referral to employers, and resume preparation. In 1996–97, 110 organizations participated in on-campus recruiting; 416 on-campus interviews were conducted.

Employment Of 1996–97 graduates, 100% were employed within three months of graduation; the average starting salary was Can$40,000. Types of employment entered: accounting, banking, communications, computer-related, consulting, finance, financial services, government, high technology, information systems/technology, international trade, manufacturing, marketing, media, telecommunications.

Business Program(s) URL: http://www.business.carleton.ca

Program Contact: Dr. Ashwani Srivastava, Associate Professor and Supervisor of Graduate Programs, School of Business, 1125 Colonel By Drive, Ottawa K1S 5B6, Canada. Phone: 613-520-2600 Ext. 2514; Fax: 613-520-2532.

Concordia University

Faculty of Commerce and Administration
Montreal, Canada

OVERVIEW
Concordia University is a province-supported, coed institution. Enrollment: 24,266 graduate, professional, and undergraduate students; 2,440 full-time matriculated graduate/professional students; 833 part-time matriculated graduate/professional students. The graduate business unit is in an urban setting and is on a trimester calendar.

HIGHLIGHTS

Enrollment Profile

Full-time: 111	International: 5%
Part-time: 264	Women: 49%
Total: 375	Minorities: N/R
Average Age: 30	Average Class Size: 40
Fall 1997 Average GPA: 3.15	Fall 1997 Average GMAT: 570

Costs
Full-time tuition: Can$1622 per academic year (resident); Can$8262 per academic year (nonresident)
Part-time tuition: Can$155 per credit (resident); Can$275 per credit (nonresident)

AACSB – The International Association for Management Education accredited

GRADUATE BUSINESS PROGRAMS
Master of Business Administration (MBA) Full-time, part-time; 63 total credits required; 2.5 to 7 years to complete program.

Executive MBA (MBA) Full-time; 54 total credits required; up to 2 years to complete program.

ADMISSION
Applications For fall 1997 there were 438 applications for admission. Of those applying, 176 were accepted. Of those accepted, 97 enrolled.

Application Requirements Application form, application fee, bachelor's degree, minimum GPA: 3.0, 3 letters of recommendation, personal statement, college transcript(s), minimum of 2 years of work experience.

Recommended for Application GMAT score accepted, computer experience.

Application Deadline 6/30 for fall, 10/30 for winter, 2/28 for summer, 2/15 for fall (international), 6/15 for winter (international), 10/15 for summer (international). Application fee: Can$30. Deferred entrance is available.

ACADEMICS
Faculty Full-time 23; part-time 7.

Teaching Methodologies Case study, computer-aided instruction, experiential learning, field projects, group discussion, lecture, research, role playing, student presentations, study groups, team projects.

Technology Computer terminals/PCs are available for student use and are linked by a campus-wide network. The network has full access to the Internet. Students are not required to have their own PC.

Special Opportunities Advanced credit may be earned through transfer of credits from another institution. International exchange programs in France, Germany, Sweden, United Kingdom, United States.

FINANCES
Costs for 1997–98 Tuition: Full-time: Can$1622 per year (resident); Can$8262 per year (nonresident). Part-time: Can$155 per credit (resident); Can$275 per credit (nonresident). Cost varies by reciprocity agreements. Fees: Full-time: Can$579 per academic year (resident); Can$1054 per academic year (nonresident). Part-time: Can$10 per credit (resident); Can$10 per credit (nonresident). Average 1997–98 room only costs were Can$2202 per academic year (on campus) and Can$3500 per academic year (off campus). Room and board costs vary by occupancy (e.g., single, double, triple).

Financial Aid Fellowships available. Application Deadline: 4/30.

Concordia University (continued)

Financial Aid Contact Phung Tu, Coordinator, Financial Aid, 1455 de Maisonneuve Boulevard West, LB085-5, Montreal. Phone: 514-848-3521; Fax: 514-848-3508.

FACILITIES
Information Resources Webster Library plus 1 additional on-campus library; total holdings of 120,000 volumes, 387,465 microforms, 6,070 current periodical subscriptions. CD player(s) available for graduate student use. Access provided to online bibliographic retrieval services.

INTERNATIONAL STUDENTS
Demographics 5% of students enrolled are international students [Asia, 5%, Europe, 1%, South America, 1%, other, 93%].

Services and Facilities International student office, international student center, ESL courses, counseling/support services, health insurance program, international student orientation.

Applying TOEFL: minimum score of 600 required. Financial aid is not available to international students.

International Student Contact Claudette Fortier, Coordinator, 1455 de Maisonneuve Boulevard West, Montreal. Phone: 514-848-3514; Fax: 514-848-3599; E-mail: fortier@topaz.condordia.ca

PLACEMENT
Services include career counseling/planning, career fairs, career library, career placement, job interviews arranged, job search course, resume referral to employers, and resume preparation. In 1996–97, 100 organizations participated in on-campus recruiting.

Employment Of 1996–97 graduates, 80% were employed within three months of graduation. Types of employment entered: accounting, banking, communications, computer-related, consulting, consumer products, education, engineering, finance, financial services, government, health services, high technology, information systems/technology, insurance, management, manufacturing, marketing, mining, pharmaceutical, retail, service industry, telecommunications, transportation.

Business Program(s) URL: http://www-commerce.concordia.ca/fca/mba.htm

Program Contact: Rebecca Midgeley, Admissions Officer, 1455 de Maisonneuve Boulevard West, Montreal H3G 1M8, Canada. Phone: 514-848-2717; Fax: 514-848-2816; E-mail: profmba@vax2.concordia.ca

See full description on page 768.

Dalhousie University

Faculty of Management
Halifax, Canada

OVERVIEW
Dalhousie University is a province-supported, coed institution. Enrollment: 13,000 graduate, professional, and undergraduate students; 197 full-time matriculated graduate/professional students; 43 part-time matriculated graduate/professional students. Founded: 1818. The graduate business unit is in a small-town setting and is on a semester calendar.

HIGHLIGHTS

Enrollment Profile

Full-time: 100	International: 8%
Part-time: 6	Women: 37%
Total: 106	Minorities: N/R
Average Age: 26	Average Class Size: 25
Fall 1997 Average GPA: 3.35	Fall 1997 Average GMAT: 595

Costs
Full-time tuition: Can$4975 per academic year (resident); Can$7925 per academic year (nonresident)
Part-time tuition: Can$1613 per year (resident); Can$4675 per year (nonresident)

GRADUATE BUSINESS PROGRAMS
Master of Business Administration (MBA) Full-time, part-time; 60 total credits required; 20 months to 5 years to complete program. Concentrations in accounting, management systems analysis, system management, environmental economics/management, international business, marketing, public policy and administration, developmental economics, health care, human resources, finance, economics, management information systems, operations management.

Accelerated MBA for Business Graduates (MBA) Full-time, part-time; 39 total credits required; 10 months to 2.5 years to complete program. Concentra-

tions in accounting, management systems analysis, system management, environmental economics/management, international business, marketing, public policy and administration, developmental economics, health care, human resources, finance, economics, management information systems, operations management.

Financial Services MBA (MBA) Full-time, part-time, distance learning option; 27 total credits required; up to 5 years to complete program. Concentration in banking.

ADMISSION
Applications For fall 1997 there were 495 applications for admission. Of those applying, 210 were accepted. Of those accepted, 109 enrolled.

Application Requirements Application form, application fee, bachelor's degree, essay, minimum GPA: 3.0, 2 letters of recommendation, personal statement, resume, college transcript(s).

Recommended for Application GMAT score accepted: minimum 550, GRE score accepted, work experience, computer experience.

Application Deadline 6/1 for fall, 11/1 for winter, 4/1 for fall (international), 9/1 for winter (international). Application fee: Can$55.

ACADEMICS
Faculty Full-time 32; part-time 20.

Teaching Methodologies Case study, experiential learning, field projects, group discussion, lecture, research, role playing, seminars by members of the business community, student presentations, team projects.

Technology 300 on-campus computer terminals/PCs are available for student use and are linked by a campus-wide network. The network has full access to the Internet. Students are not required to have their own PC.

Special Opportunities Advanced credit may be earned through credit for business training programs, transfer of credits from another institution. International exchange programs in Denmark, Finland, France, Mexico, Netherlands, Republic of Korea, Sweden, United Kingdom. An internship program is available.

FINANCES
Costs for 1997–98 Tuition: Full-time: Can$4975 per year (resident); Can$7925 per year (nonresident). Part-time: Can$1613 per year (resident); Can$4675 per year (nonresident). Cost varies by academic program. Average 1997–98 room and board costs were Can$4800 per academic year (on campus) and Can$4800 per academic year (off campus). Room and board costs vary by occupancy (e.g., single, double, triple), type of accommodation, type of meal plan.

Financial Aid In 1997–98, 20% of students received some institutionally administered aid in the form of fellowships, research assistantships, teaching assistantships, scholarships. Application Deadline: 3/1.

Financial Aid Contact Mr. Philip Rees, MBA Program Coordinator, School of Business Administration, 6152 Coburg Road, Halifax. Phone: 902-494-7080; Fax: 902-494-1107.

FACILITIES
Information Resources Killiam Library plus 2 additional on-campus libraries; total holdings of 1,200,000 volumes, 340,000 microforms, 8,182 current periodical subscriptions. CD player(s) available for graduate student use. Access provided to online bibliographic retrieval services and online databases.

INTERNATIONAL STUDENTS
Demographics 8% of students enrolled are international students [Africa, 36%, Asia, 50%, Europe, 14%].

Services and Facilities International student office, international student center, counseling/support services.

Applying TOEFL: minimum score of 580, proof of adequate funds required. Proof of health/immunizations recommended. Financial aid is not available to international students.

International Student Contact Ms. Caroline Sequeira, Advisor, International Student Centre, 6136 University Avenue, Halifax. Phone: 902-494-7077; Fax: 902-494-2042; E-mail: caroline.sequeira@dal.ca

PLACEMENT
Services include alumni network, career counseling/planning, career library, career placement, job search course, resume referral to employers, and resume preparation. In 1996–97, 35 organizations participated in on-campus recruiting; 60 on-campus interviews were conducted.

Employment Of 1996–97 graduates, 85% were employed within three months of graduation; the average starting salary was Can$47,500. Types of employment entered: accounting, banking, communications, computer-related, consulting, engineering, finance, financial services, government, health services, high technology, human resources, information systems/technology, international trade, management, marketing, nonprofit, pharmaceutical, telecommunications, transportation, utilities.

Business Program(s) URL: http://www.mgmt.dal.ca/

Program Contact: Mr. Philip Rees, MBA Program Coordinator, School of Business Administration, 6152 Coburg Road, Halifax B3H 3J5, Canada. Phone:

902-494-2846, 888-432-5622 (NS only); Fax: 902-494-1107; E-mail: mba.admissions@dal.ca

See full description on page 774.

École des Hautes Études Commerciales

Montreal, Canada

OVERVIEW
École des Hautes Études Commerciales is a province-supported, coed institution. Enrollment: 9,070 graduate, professional, and undergraduate students; 793 full-time matriculated graduate/professional students; 1,158 part-time matriculated graduate/professional students. Founded: 1907. The graduate business unit is in an urban setting and is on a trimester calendar.

HIGHLIGHTS

Enrollment Profile

Full-time: 143
Part-time: 500
Total: 643
Average Age: 33
Fall 1997 Average GPA: N/R

International: 12%
Women: 40%
Minorities: N/R
Average Class Size: 30
Fall 1997 Average GMAT: N/R

Costs

Full-time tuition: Can$3211 per academic year (resident); Can$14,651 per academic year (nonresident)
Part-time tuition: Can$62 per credit (resident); Can$282 per credit (nonresident)

GRADUATE BUSINESS PROGRAMS
Master of Business Administration (MBA) Full-time, part-time; 52 total credits required; 12 months to 3 years to complete program. Concentrations in financial management/planning, entrepreneurship, international management, technology management, marketing, human resources.

ADMISSION
Applications For fall 1997 there were 516 applications for admission. Of those applying, 322 were accepted. Of those accepted, 232 enrolled.

Application Requirements GMAT score, application form, application fee, bachelor's degree, GPA: minimum 70.0 on a 100 scale, 3 letters of recommendation, personal statement, resume, college transcript(s), minimum of 2 years of work experience.

Application Deadline 4/1 for fall, 10/1 for winter, 4/1 for fall (international), 10/1 for winter (international). Application fee: Can$40.

ACADEMICS
Faculty Full-time 166; part-time 6.

Teaching Methodologies Case study, computer simulations, experiential learning, field projects, group discussion, lecture, role playing, seminars by members of the business community, simulations, student presentations, study groups, team projects.

Technology 204 on-campus computer terminals/PCs are available for student use and are linked by a campus-wide network. The network has full access to the Internet. Students are required to have their own PC.

Special Opportunities International exchange programs in France, Switzerland, United Kingdom, Spain, Mexico, Finland.

FINANCES
Costs for 1997–98 Tuition: Full-time: Can$3211 per year (resident); Can$14,651 per year (nonresident). Part-time: Can$62 per credit (resident); Can$282 per credit (nonresident). Cost varies by academic program, reciprocity agreements. Fees: Full-time: Can$304 per academic year (resident); Can$304 per academic year (nonresident). Fees vary by academic program. Average 1997–98 room and board costs were Can$8200 per academic year (on campus) and Can$10,000 per academic year (off campus).

Financial Aid In 1997–98, 8% of students received some institutionally administered aid.

Financial Aid Contact International Exchange Program Coordinator, 3000, Chemin de la Côte-Sainte-Catherine, Montreal. Phone: 514-340-6840; Fax: 514-340-6761; E-mail: jean-michel.stam@hec.ca

FACILITIES
Information Resources Bibliotheque Myriam & J. Robert Ouimet; total holdings of 325,000 volumes, 5,100 microforms, 6,541 current periodical subscriptions. CD player(s) available for graduate student use. Access provided to online bibliographic retrieval services and online databases.

INTERNATIONAL STUDENTS
Demographics 12% of students enrolled are international students [Africa, 34%, Asia, 4%, Central America, 1%, Europe, 47%, South America, 7%, other, 7%].

Services and Facilities International student office, international student center, counseling/support services, housing support.

Applying Financial aid is not available to international students.

International Student Contact International Exchange Program Coordinator, 3000, Chemin de la Côte-Sainte-Catherine, Montreal. Phone: 514-340-6840; Fax: 514-340-6761; E-mail: jean-michel.stam@hec.ca

PLACEMENT
Services include alumni network, career counseling/planning, career fairs, career placement, job interviews arranged, job search course, resume referral to employers, and resume preparation.

Employment Of 1996–97 graduates, 95% were employed within three months of graduation; the average starting salary was Can$56,000. Types of employment entered: accounting, banking, communications, computer-related, consulting, consumer products, energy, finance, financial services, government, health services, high technology, human resources, information systems/technology, insurance, international trade, management, manufacturing, marketing, nonprofit, petrochemical, pharmaceutical, real estate, retail, service industry, telecommunications, transportation, utilities.

Business Program(s) URL: http://www.hec.ca/mba/

Program Contact: Mrs. Diane St.-Pierre, MBA Program Student Advisor, 3000, Chemin de la Côte-Sainte-Catherine, Montreal H3T 2A7, Canada. Phone: 514-340-6136; Fax: 514-340-6411; E-mail: mba@hec.ca

See full description on page 796.

Laurentian University

Sudbury, Canada

OVERVIEW
Laurentian University is a province-supported, coed institution. Enrollment: 7,659 graduate, professional, and undergraduate students; 187 full-time matriculated graduate/professional students; 159 part-time matriculated graduate/professional students. Founded: 1960. The graduate business unit is in an urban setting and is on a Canadian standard year calendar.

HIGHLIGHTS

Enrollment Profile

Full-time: 10
Part-time: 41
Total: 51
Average Age: N/R
Fall 1997 Average GPA: N/R

International: 4%
Women: 41%
Minorities: N/R
Average Class Size: 10
Fall 1997 Average GMAT: 568

Costs

Full-time tuition: Can$4975 per academic year (resident); Can$9072 per academic year (nonresident)
Part-time tuition: Can$995 per 6-credit course (resident); Can$1814 per 6 credit course (nonresident)

GRADUATE BUSINESS PROGRAMS
Master of Business Administration (MBA) Full-time, part-time, distance learning option; 60 total credits required; 2 to 8 years to complete program. Concentrations in finance, human resources, marketing.

ADMISSION
Applications For fall 1997 there were 34 applications for admission. Of those applying, 9 were accepted. Of those accepted, 5 enrolled.

Application Requirements GMAT score: minimum 500, application form, application fee, bachelor's degree, GPA: minimum 70.0 on a 100 scale, 2 letters of recommendation, personal statement, college transcript(s), minimum of 2 years of work experience, computer experience: word processing, spreadsheet, database.

Application Deadline 5/31 for fall, 5/31 for fall (international). Application fee: Can$50.

ACADEMICS
Teaching Methodologies Case study, computer-aided instruction, computer analysis, computer simulations, experiential learning, faculty seminars, field projects, group discussion, lecture, research, role playing, seminars by members of the business community, simulations, student presentations, study groups, team projects.

Technology 40 on-campus computer terminals/PCs are available for student use and are linked by a campus-wide network. The network has full access to the Internet. Students are not required to have their own PC.

Special Opportunities Advanced credit may be earned through transfer of credits from another institution.

Laurentian University (continued)

FINANCES

Costs for 1997–98 Tuition: Full-time: Can$4975 per year (resident); Can$9072 per year (nonresident). Part-time: Can$995 per 6-credit course (resident); Can$1814 per 6 credit course (nonresident). Cost varies by academic program, number of credits taken. Fees: Full-time: Can$194 per academic year (resident); Can$194 per academic year (nonresident). Part-time: Can$15 per year (resident); Can$15 per year (nonresident). Average 1997–98 room only costs were Can$5640 per academic year (on campus) and Can$12,000 per academic year (off campus). Room and board costs vary by occupancy (e.g., single, double, triple), type of accommodation, type of meal plan.

Financial Aid In 1997–98, 10% of students received some institutionally administered aid in the form of teaching assistantships.

Financial Aid Contact Dr. Ozhand Ganjavi, Chair, MBA Program, Ramsey Lake Road, Sudbury. Phone: 705-675-1151 Ext. 2138; Fax: 705-673-6518; E-mail: oganjavi@nickel.laurentian.ca

FACILITIES

Information Resources J. N. Desmarias Library plus 2 additional on-campus libraries; total holdings of 610,100 volumes, 306,500 microforms, 3,100 current periodical subscriptions. CD player(s) available for graduate student use. Access provided to online bibliographic retrieval services.

INTERNATIONAL STUDENTS

Demographics 4% of students enrolled are international students.

Services and Facilities International student office, ESL courses, counseling/support services.

Applying TOEFL: minimum score of 550 required. Financial aid is not available to international students.

International Student Contact Wendy Gerhard, Director, Laurentian International, Ramsey Lake Road, Sudbury. Phone: 705-675-1151 Ext. 1556; Fax: 705-673-6518.

PLACEMENT

Services include alumni network, electronic job bank, and job interviews arranged.

Employment Of 1996–97 graduates, 100% were employed within three months of graduation.

Business Program(s) URL: http://www.laurentian.ca/www/index.html

Program Contact: Dr. Ozhand Ganjavi, Chair, MBA Program, Ramsey Lake Road, Sudbury P3E 2C6, Canada. Phone: 705-675-1151 Ext. 2138; Fax: 705-673-6518; E-mail: oganjavi@nickel.laurentian.ca

McGill University

Faculty of Management

Montreal, Canada

OVERVIEW

McGill University is a province-supported, coed institution. Enrollment: 30,945 graduate, professional, and undergraduate students; 305 full-time matriculated graduate/professional students; 290 part-time matriculated graduate/professional students. Founded: 1821. The graduate business unit is in an urban setting and is on a trimester in first year; semester in second year calendar.

HIGHLIGHTS

Enrollment Profile

Full-time: 292	International: 56%
Part-time: 0	Women: 28%
Total: 292	Minorities: N/R
Average Age: 26	Average Class Size: 50
Fall 1997 Average GPA: 3.32	Fall 1997 Average GMAT: 610

Costs

Full-time tuition: Can$2497 per academic year (resident); Can$16,000 per academic year (nonresident)
Part-time tuition: N/R

GRADUATE BUSINESS PROGRAMS

Master of Business Administration (MBA) Full-time, part-time; 60 total credits required; 20 months to complete program. Concentrations in finance, international and area business studies, international business, international development management, international finance, international management, international marketing, management, marketing, strategic management, operations management, entrepreneurship.

Master of Business Administration/Doctor of Jurisprudence (MBA/JD) Full-time; 138 total credits required; 4 to 5 years to complete program.

Master of Business Administration/Diploma in Asian Studies (MBA/DIP) Full-time; 75 total credits required; 2 to 2.3 years to complete program. Concentration in asian business studies.

Master of Management Manufacturing (MMM) Full-time, part-time; 45 total credits required; 20 months to complete program. Concentration in manufacturing management.

Agriculture Master of Business Administration (MS/MBA) Full-time; 60 total credits required; 2.7 years to complete program. Concentration in agribusiness.

ADMISSION

Applications For fall 1997 there were 666 applications for admission. Of those applying, 325 were accepted. Of those accepted, 139 enrolled.

Application Requirements GMAT score: minimum 550, application form, application fee, bachelor's degree, essay, minimum GPA: 3.0, 2 letters of recommendation, personal statement, resume, college transcript(s), minimum of 1 year of work experience.

Recommended for Application Computer experience.

Application Deadline 5/15 for fall, 4/1 for fall (international). Application fee: Can$100.

ACADEMICS

Faculty Full-time 40; part-time 43.

Teaching Methodologies Case study, computer-aided instruction, computer simulations, group discussion, lecture, role playing, seminars by members of the business community, student presentations, study groups, team projects.

Technology 85 on-campus computer terminals/PCs are available for student use and are linked by a campus-wide network. The network has full access to the Internet. Students are not required to have their own PC.

Special Opportunities Advanced credit may be earned through transfer of credits from another institution. International exchange programs in Belgium, France, Germany, Holland, Italy, Philippines, Republic of Korea, Spain, Sweden, Thailand, United Kingdom, United States. An internship program is available.

FINANCES

Costs for 1997–98 Tuition: Full-time: Can$2497 per year (resident); Can$16,000 per year (nonresident). Cost varies by number of credits taken, reciprocity agreements. Fees vary by number of credits taken. Average 1997–98 room and board costs were Can$8500 per academic year (off campus).

Financial Aid In 1997–98, 42% of students received some institutionally administered aid in the form of fellowships, teaching assistantships, scholarships.

Financial Aid Contact MBA Admissions Office, 1001 Sherbrooke Street West, Montreal. Phone: 514-398-4066; Fax: 514-398-2499.

FACILITIES

Information Resources Howard Ross Library plus 18 additional on-campus libraries; total holdings of 270,000 volumes, 1,039,889 microforms, 17,516 current periodical subscriptions. CD player(s) available for graduate student use. Access provided to online bibliographic retrieval services and online databases.

INTERNATIONAL STUDENTS

Demographics 56% of students enrolled are international students [Africa, 2%, Asia, 26%, Australia/New Zealand, 1%, Central America, 1%, Europe, 14%, North America, 48%, South America, 4%, other, 4%].

Services and Facilities International student office, international student center, ESL courses, counseling/support services.

Applying TOEFL: minimum score of 600, proof of adequate funds required. Proof of health/immunizations recommended. Financial aid is available to international students.

International Student Contact International Student Advisor, 3637 Peel Street, Montreal. Phone: 514-398-6015.

PLACEMENT

Services include alumni network, career counseling/planning, career fairs, career library, career placement, job interviews arranged, resume referral to employers, and resume preparation. In 1996–97, 112 organizations participated in on-campus recruiting; 483 on-campus interviews were conducted.

Employment Of 1996–97 graduates, 95% were employed within three months of graduation; the average starting salary was Can$61,000. Types of employment entered: accounting, banking, communications, computer-related, consulting, consumer products, finance, financial services, government, health services, high technology, human resources, information systems/technology, insurance, international trade, law, management, manufacturing, marketing, media, mining, nonprofit, petrochemical, pharmaceutical, real estate, retail, service industry, telecommunications, transportation, utilities.

Business Program(s) URL: http://www.management.mcgill.ca

Program Contact: MBA Admissions Officer, 1001 Sherbrooke Street West, Montreal H3A 1G5, Canada. Phone: 514-398-4066; Fax: 514-398-2499; E-mail: mba@management.mcgill.ca

See full description on page 884.

McMaster University

Michael G. DeGroote School of Business

Hamilton, Canada

OVERVIEW

McMaster University is a province-supported, coed institution. Enrollment: 16,000 graduate, professional, and undergraduate students; 2,000 full-time matriculated graduate/professional students; 500 part-time matriculated graduate/professional students. Founded: 1887. The graduate business unit is in a suburban setting and is on a trimester calendar.

HIGHLIGHTS

Enrollment Profile

Full-time: 245	International: 1%
Part-time: 206	Women: 30%
Total: 451	Minorities: N/R
Average Age: 26	Average Class Size: 28
Fall 1997 Average GPA: 3.5	Fall 1997 Average GMAT: 610

Costs

Full-time tuition: Can$4748 per academic year (resident); Can$12,000 per academic year (nonresident)

Part-time tuition: Can$431 per course (resident); Can$1500 per course (nonresident)

GRADUATE BUSINESS PROGRAMS

Master of Business Administration (MBA) Full-time, part-time; 20 total credits required; 20 months to 8 years to complete program. Concentrations in accounting, finance, health care, human resources, management, management science, management information systems, marketing, operations management, technology management.

ADMISSION

Applications For fall 1997 there were 582 applications for admission. Of those applying, 318 were accepted. Of those accepted, 191 enrolled.

Application Requirements GMAT score: minimum 580, application form, application fee, bachelor's degree, minimum GPA: 3.0, interview, 2 letters of recommendation, personal statement, resume, college transcript(s).

Recommended for Application Work experience, computer experience.

Application Deadline 6/1 for fall, 6/1 for fall (international). Application fee: Can$100.

ACADEMICS

Faculty Full-time 51; part-time 18.

Teaching Methodologies Case study, computer-aided instruction, computer analysis, computer simulations, experiential learning, faculty seminars, field projects, group discussion, lecture, research, seminars by members of the business community, simulations, student presentations, team projects, workshops.

Technology 90 on-campus computer terminals/PCs are available for student use and are linked by a campus-wide network. The network has full access to the Internet. Students are not required to have their own PC.

Special Opportunities International exchange programs in Denmark, Germany, Mexico, Norway, United Kingdom. An internship program is available.

FINANCES

Costs for 1997–98 Tuition: Full-time: Can$4748 per year (resident); Can$12,000 per year (nonresident). Part-time: Can$431 per course (resident); Can$1500 per course (nonresident). Fees: Full-time: Can$296 per academic year (resident); Can$296 per academic year (nonresident). Part-time: Can$12 per term (resident); Can$12 per term (nonresident). Average 1997–98 room and board costs were Can$5400 per academic year (on campus) and Can$5800 per academic year (off campus). Room and board costs vary by type of meal plan.

Financial Aid In 1997–98, 22% of students received some institutionally administered aid in the form of teaching assistantships, scholarships, work study, loans. Application Deadline: 6/1.

Financial Aid Contact Ms. Denise Ellis, Manager, Student Financial Aid, Hamilton Hall, Room 404, Hamilton. Phone: 905-525-9140 Ext. 24319; Fax: 905-521-8632.

FACILITIES

Information Resources Mills Memorial Library plus 3 additional on-campus libraries; total holdings of 1,600,000 volumes, 1,400,000 microforms, 13,859 current periodical subscriptions. CD player(s) available for graduate student use. Access provided to online bibliographic retrieval services and online databases.

INTERNATIONAL STUDENTS

Demographics 1% of students enrolled are international students.

Services and Facilities International student office, international student center, visa services, ESL courses, counseling/support services, language tutoring.

Applying TOEFL recommended. Financial aid is not available to international students.

International Student Contact Miss Cheryl Jackson, International Students Advisor, Hamilton Hall, Room 405, Hamilton. Phone: 905-525-9140 Ext. 24748; Fax: 905-521-8632.

PLACEMENT

Services include alumni network, career counseling/planning, career fairs, career library, career placement, electronic job bank, job interviews arranged, job search course, resume referral to employers, and resume preparation. In 1996–97, 160 organizations participated in on-campus recruiting.

Employment Of 1996–97 graduates, 98% were employed within three months of graduation; the average starting salary was Can$42,700. Types of employment entered: accounting, banking, communications, computer-related, consulting, consumer products, energy, finance, financial services, government, health services, high technology, human resources, information systems/technology, management, manufacturing, marketing, mining, nonprofit, petrochemical, pharmaceutical, retail, service industry, telecommunications, utilities.

Business Program(s) URL: http://www.business.mcmaster.ca

Program Contact: Mrs. Denise Anderson, Manager, Recruiting and Admissions, Michael DeGroote Building, Room 104 (MGD 104), Hamilton L8S 4M4, Canada. Phone: 905-525-9140 Ext. 24433; Fax: 905-521-8632; E-mail: mbainfo@mcmaster.ca

Memorial University of Newfoundland

Faculty of Business Administration

St. John's, Canada

OVERVIEW

Memorial University of Newfoundland is a province-supported, coed institution. Enrollment: 16,000 graduate, professional, and undergraduate students; 639 full-time matriculated graduate/professional students; 499 part-time matriculated graduate/professional students. Founded: 1925. The graduate business unit is in an urban setting and is on a semester calendar.

HIGHLIGHTS

Enrollment Profile

Full-time: 60	International: 3%
Part-time: 145	Women: 47%
Total: 205	Minorities: N/R
Average Age: 31	Average Class Size: 24
Fall 1997 Average GPA: 2.5	Fall 1997 Average GMAT: 580

Costs

Full-time tuition: N/R

Part-time tuition: Can$5800 per program (resident); Can$5800 per program (nonresident)

GRADUATE BUSINESS PROGRAMS

Master of Business Administration in General Management (MBA) Full-time, part-time; 20 total credits required; 8 months to 7 years to complete program.

ADMISSION

Applications For fall 1997 there were 99 applications for admission. Of those applying, 70 were accepted. Of those accepted, 56 enrolled.

Application Requirements Application form, application fee, GPA: minimum 2.0 on a 3 scale, 3 letters of recommendation, personal statement, college transcript(s).

Recommended for Application GMAT score accepted: minimum 520, bachelor's degree, resume, work experience.

Application Deadline Applications processed on a rolling/continuous basis for both domestic and international students. Application fee: Can$30. Deferred entrance is available.

ACADEMICS

Faculty Full-time 28; part-time 1.

Teaching Methodologies Case study, computer-aided instruction, computer analysis, computer simulations, experiential learning, faculty seminars, field projects, group discussion, lecture, research, role playing, seminars by members of the business community, simulations, student presentations, study groups, team projects.

Technology 55 on-campus computer terminals/PCs are available for student use. The network has full access to the Internet. Students are not required to have their own PC.

CANADA

Memorial University of Newfoundland (continued)

Special Opportunities Advanced credit may be earned through credit by examination, transfer of credits from another institution. International exchange programs in France, Germany, Netherlands, Norway, Sweden, United Kingdom.

FINANCES
Costs for 1997–98 Tuition: Can$5800 per program (resident); Can$5800 per program (nonresident). Fees: Can$15 per semester (resident); Can$15 per semester (nonresident). Average 1997–98 room and board costs were Can$7920 per academic year (on campus) and Can$5700 per academic year (off campus). Room and board costs vary by occupancy (e.g., single, double, triple), type of accommodation, type of meal plan.
Financial Aid In 1997–98, 7% of students received some institutionally administered aid in the form of fellowships, research assistantships, scholarships.
Financial Aid Contact Dr. Herbert F. MacKenzie, Associate Dean, Graduate Program and Research, Faculty of Business Administration, St. John's. Phone: 709-737-8522; Fax: 709-737-2467; E-mail: hmackenz@plato.ucs.mun.ca

FACILITIES
Information Resources Queen Elizabeth II Library plus 4 additional on-campus libraries; total holdings of 2,500,000 volumes, 1,000,000 microforms, 8,000 current periodical subscriptions. CD player(s) available for graduate student use. Access provided to online bibliographic retrieval services.

INTERNATIONAL STUDENTS
Demographics 3% of students enrolled are international students [Africa, 50%, Asia, 50%].
Services and Facilities ESL courses, counseling/support services.
Applying TOEFL: minimum score of 580 required. Financial aid is not available to international students.
International Student Contact Mr. Blair Winsor, Director, Centre for International Business Studies, Faculty of Business Administration, St. John's. Phone: 709-737-4504; Fax: 709-737-7999; E-mail: bwinsor@morgan.ucs.mun.ca

PLACEMENT
Services include career counseling/planning, career library, career placement, and resume referral to employers. In 1996–97, 10 organizations participated in on-campus recruiting.
Employment Of 1996–97 graduates, 95% were employed within three months of graduation. Types of employment entered: accounting, banking, communications, computer-related, consulting, consumer products, education, energy, engineering, finance, financial services, government, health services, high technology, hospitality management, human resources, information systems/technology, international trade, management, manufacturing, marketing, media, nonprofit, service industry, telecommunications, transportation, utilities.

Business Program(s) URL: http://www.mun.ca/business/

Program Contact: Dr. Herbert F. MacKenzie, Associate Dean, Graduate Program and Research, Faculty of Business Administration, St. John's A1B 3X5, Canada. Phone: 709-737-8522; Fax: 709-737-2467; E-mail: hmackenz@plato.ucs.mun.ca

Queen's University at Kingston

School of Business

Kingston, Canada

OVERVIEW
Queen's University at Kingston is a province-supported, coed institution. Enrollment: 17,138 graduate, professional, and undergraduate students; 2,059 full-time matriculated graduate/professional students; 572 part-time matriculated graduate/professional students. Founded: 1841. The graduate business unit is in an urban setting and is on a 12-month program calendar.

HIGHLIGHTS

Enrollment Profile
Full-time: 60
Part-time: 0
Total: 60
Average Age: 30
Fall 1997 Average GPA: 3.3

International: 13%
Women: 18%
Minorities: N/R
Average Class Size: 60
Fall 1997 Average GMAT: 648

Costs
Full-time tuition: N/R
Part-time tuition: N/R

GRADUATE BUSINESS PROGRAMS
MBA for Science and Technology (MBA) Full-time; 23 total credits required; minimum of 12 months to complete program. Concentrations in finance, marketing.
Executive MBA (EMBA) Full-time, distance learning option; 23 total credits required; minimum of 2 years to complete program.
National Executive Master of Business Administration (NEMBA) Full-time, distance learning option; 23 total credits required; minimum of 2 years to complete program.

ADMISSION
Applications For fall 1997 there were 250 applications for admission. Of those applying, 80 were accepted. Of those accepted, 60 enrolled.
Application Requirements GMAT score: minimum 580, application form, application fee, bachelor's degree, essay, minimum GPA: 3.0, interview, 2 letters of recommendation, personal statement, resume, college transcript(s), minimum of 2 years of work experience, computer experience: word processing, spreadsheet, database.
Application Deadline 12/1 for winter, 12/1 for winter (international). Application fee: Can$100.

ACADEMICS
Faculty Full-time 24.
Teaching Methodologies Case study, computer-aided instruction, experiential learning, faculty seminars, field projects, group discussion, lecture, seminars by members of the business community, simulations, student presentations, study groups, team projects.
Technology Computer terminals/PCs are available for student use and are linked by a campus-wide network. The network has full access to the Internet. Students are not required to have their own PC.

FINANCES
Costs for 1997–98 Average 1997–98 room and board costs were Can$7500 per academic year (on campus) and Can$12,500 per academic year (off campus). Room and board costs vary by campus location, occupancy (e.g., single, double, triple), type of accommodation, type of meal plan.
Financial Aid In 1997–98, 83% of students received some institutionally administered aid in the form of loans. Application Deadline: 3/1.
Financial Aid Contact Ms. Donna Lounsbury, Director, MBA for Science and Technology, Mackintosh-Corry Hall, Kingston. Phone: 613-545-2302; Fax: 613-545-6281; E-mail: lounsbur@qsilver.queensu.ca

FACILITIES
Information Resources Stauffer Library plus 20 additional on-campus libraries. CD player(s) available for graduate student use. Access provided to online bibliographic retrieval services.

INTERNATIONAL STUDENTS
Demographics 13% of students enrolled are international students.
Services and Facilities International student office, international student center, ESL courses, counseling/support services.
Applying TOEFL: minimum score of 600, proof of adequate funds, proof of health/immunizations required. Financial aid is not available to international students.
International Student Contact Ms. Susan Anderson, International Student Advisor, International Centre, John Deutsch University Centre, Kingston. Phone: 613-545-2604; Fax: 613-545-6190.

PLACEMENT
Services include alumni network, career counseling/planning, career fairs, career library, career placement, job interviews arranged, job search course, resume referral to employers, and resume preparation. In 1996–97, 126 organizations participated in on-campus recruiting.
Employment Of 1996–97 graduates, 90% were employed within three months of graduation; the average starting salary was Can$69,000. Types of employment entered: banking, chemical industry, communications, computer-related, consulting, energy, engineering, finance, financial services, health services, high technology, information systems/technology, management, manufacturing, marketing, mining, petrochemical, pharmaceutical, service industry, telecommunications.

Business Program(s) URL: http://qsilver.queensu.ca/MBAst

Program Contact: Ms. Donna Lounsbury, Director, MBA for Science and Technology, MacKintosh-Corry Hall, Kingston K7L 3N6, Canada. Phone: 613-545-2302; Fax: 613-545-6281; E-mail: lounsbur@qsilver.queensu.ca
See full description on page 936.

Saint Mary's University

Frank H. Sobey Faculty of Commerce

Halifax, Canada

OVERVIEW

Saint Mary's University is a province-supported, coed institution. Enrollment: 7,251 graduate, professional, and undergraduate students; 178 full-time matriculated graduate/professional students; 180 part-time matriculated graduate/professional students. Founded: 1802. The graduate business unit is in an urban setting and is on a semester calendar.

HIGHLIGHTS

Enrollment Profile

Full-time: 147
Part-time: 121
Total: 268
Average Age: 32
Fall 1997 Average GPA: 3.2

International: 11%
Women: 35%
Minorities: N/R
Average Class Size: 21
Fall 1997 Average GMAT: 575

Costs

Full-time tuition: N/R
Part-time tuition: Can$750 per credit (resident); Can$1380 per credit (nonresident)

GRADUATE BUSINESS PROGRAMS

Master of Business Administration (MBA) Full-time, part-time; 12 months to 2 years to complete program. Concentrations in international management, entrepreneurship, financial economics, human resources.

Executive MBA (MBA) Part-time; up to 2 years to complete program. Concentration in management.

ADMISSION

Applications For fall 1997 there were 278 applications for admission. Of those applying, 179 were accepted. Of those accepted, 112 enrolled.

Application Requirements GMAT score: minimum 500, application form, application fee, 3 letters of recommendation, personal statement, college transcript(s).

Recommended for Application Bachelor's degree, resume, work experience.

Application Deadline Applications processed on a rolling/continuous basis for both domestic and international students. Application fee: Can$30. Deferred entrance is available.

ACADEMICS

Faculty Full-time 63; part-time 104.

Teaching Methodologies Case study, lecture, seminars by members of the business community, student presentations, team projects.

Technology 335 on-campus computer terminals/PCs are available for student use and are linked by a campus-wide network. The network has full access to the Internet. Students are not required to have their own PC.

Special Opportunities Advanced credit may be earned through credit by examination, credit for experience, credit for military training programs, credit for business training programs, transfer of credits from another institution. International exchange program in various countries.

FINANCES

Costs for 1997–98 Tuition: Can$750 per credit (resident); Can$1380 per credit (nonresident). Cost varies by academic program, number of credits taken. Fees: Can$19 per year (resident); Can$19 per year (nonresident). Fees vary by number of credits taken. Average 1997–98 room and board costs were Can$4600 per academic year. Room and board costs vary by occupancy (e.g., single, double, triple), type of accommodation, type of meal plan.

Financial Aid Scholarships available.

Financial Aid Contact Ms. Jennifer Johnson, Program Manager, Loyola Building, Robie Street, Halifax. Phone: 902-420-5729; Fax: 902-420-5119; E-mail: jennifer.johnson@stmarys.ca

FACILITIES

Information Resources Patrick Power Library; total holdings of 385,310 volumes, 628,180 microforms, 1,973 current periodical subscriptions. CD player(s) available for graduate student use. Access provided to online bibliographic retrieval services and online databases.

INTERNATIONAL STUDENTS

Demographics 11% of students enrolled are international students [Africa, 17%, Asia, 41%, Europe, 15%, North America, 9%, South America, 9%, other, 9%].

Services and Facilities International student office, international student center, ESL courses, counseling/support services.

Applying TOEFL: minimum score of 600 required. Financial aid is available to international students.

International Student Contact Ms. Alana Robb, International Student Advisor, International Centre, Room 115, Burke Building, Halifax. Phone: 902-420-5436; Fax: 902-420-5288; E-mail: arobb@shark.stmarys.ca

PLACEMENT

Services include alumni network, job search course, and resume preparation. In 1996–97, 1,000 organizations participated in on-campus recruiting; 30 on-campus interviews were conducted.

Employment Types of employment entered: accounting, banking, finance, financial services, service industry.

Business Program(s) URL: http://www.stmarys.ca/academic/commerce/

Program Contact: Ms. Jennifer Johnson, Program Manager, Loyola Building, Robie Street, Halifax B3H 3C3, Canada. Phone: 902-420-5729; Fax: 902-420-5119; E-mail: jennifer.johnson@stmarys.ca

Simon Fraser University

Faculty of Business Administration

Burnaby, Canada

OVERVIEW

Simon Fraser University is a province-supported, coed institution. Enrollment: 18,759 graduate, professional, and undergraduate students; 2,041 full-time matriculated graduate/professional students; 360 part-time matriculated graduate/professional students. Founded: 1965. The graduate business unit is in a suburban setting and is on a trimester calendar.

HIGHLIGHTS

Enrollment Profile

Full-time: 147
Part-time: 0
Total: 147
Average Age: 27
Fall 1997 Average GPA: 3.3

International: 17%
Women: 39%
Minorities: N/R
Average Class Size: 20
Fall 1997 Average GMAT: 620

Costs

Full-time tuition: Can$2400 per academic year (resident); Can$2400 per academic year (nonresident)
Part-time tuition: N/R

GRADUATE BUSINESS PROGRAMS

Master of Business Administration (MBA) Full-time; 36 total credits required; 12 months to 2.5 years to complete program. Concentrations in finance, human resources, management information systems, management science, marketing, business policy/strategy.

Master of Business Administration/Master of Resource Management (MBA/MRM) Full-time; 98 total credits required; 3 to 4 years to complete program. Concentration in resources management.

ADMISSION

Applications For fall 1997 there were 298 applications for admission. Of those applying, 118 were accepted. Of those accepted, 51 enrolled.

Application Requirements GMAT score: minimum 550, application form, application fee, bachelor's degree, minimum GPA: 3.0, 3 letters of recommendation, personal statement, resume, college transcript(s), minimum of 2 years of work experience, computer experience: undergraduate computer course.

Application Deadline 4/1 for fall, 10/1 for spring, 2/1 for summer, 4/1 for fall (international), 10/1 for spring (international), 2/1 for summer (international). Application fee: Can$55. Deferred entrance is available.

ACADEMICS

Faculty Full-time 52; part-time 18.

Teaching Methodologies Case study, computer-aided instruction, computer analysis, computer simulations, experiential learning, faculty seminars, field projects, group discussion, lecture, research, seminars by members of the business community, simulations, student presentations, study groups, team projects.

Technology 1,000 on-campus computer terminals/PCs are available for student use and are linked by a campus-wide network. The network has full access to the Internet. Students are not required to have their own PC.

Special Opportunities Advanced credit may be earned through transfer of credits from another institution. International exchange programs in Germany, United Kingdom.

FINANCES

Costs for 1997–98 Tuition: Full-time: Can$2400 per year (resident); Can$2400 per year (nonresident). Fees: Full-time: Can$100 per academic year (resident); Can$100 per academic year (nonresident). Average 1997–98 room only costs were Can$4629 per academic year (on campus) and Can$5400 per

Simon Fraser University (continued)

academic year (off campus). Room and board costs vary by occupancy (e.g., single, double, triple), type of accommodation.

Financial Aid In 1997–98, 68% of students received some institutionally administered aid in the form of fellowships, research assistantships, teaching assistantships, grants, scholarships, work study, loans. Application Deadline: 3/15.

Financial Aid Contact Ms. Charlotte French, Director, Financial Assistance, Office of the Registrar, Burnaby. Phone: 604-291-4356; Fax: 604-291-4722; E-mail: fiassist@sfu.ca

FACILITIES

Information Resources W. A. C. Bennett Library; total holdings of 1,254,530,000 volumes, 962,918 microforms, 9,819 current periodical subscriptions. CD player(s) available for graduate student use. Access provided to online bibliographic retrieval services.

INTERNATIONAL STUDENTS

Demographics 17% of students enrolled are international students [Asia, 60%, Australia/New Zealand, 5%, Europe, 20%, North America, 10%, South America, 5%].

Services and Facilities International student office, international student center, visa services, counseling/support services.

Applying TOEFL: minimum score of 570, TWE: minimum score of 5, proof of adequate funds, proof of health/immunizations required. Financial aid is available to international students.

International Student Contact Mr. Randall Martin, Director, International Student and Exchange Services (IESS), Office of the Registrar, Burnaby. Phone: 604-291-5840; Fax: 604-291-5880; E-mail: randall_martin@sfu.ca

PLACEMENT

Services include career counseling/planning, career fairs, electronic job bank, and resume referral to employers. In 1996–97, 2 organizations participated in on-campus recruiting.

Employment Of 1996–97 graduates, the average starting salary was Can$50,000. Types of employment entered: accounting, banking, computer-related, consulting, finance, government, health services, high technology, human resources, information systems/technology, law, management, marketing, utilities.

Business Program(s) URL: http://www.bus.sfu.ca./

Program Contact: Mrs. Noory Lalji, Coordinator, MBA Program, Faculty of Business Administration, Burnaby V5A 1S6, Canada. Phone: 604-291-3639; Fax: 604-291-3404; E-mail: noory_lalji@sfu.ca

Université de Moncton

Faculty d' Administration

Moncton, Canada

OVERVIEW

The Université de Moncton is a province-supported, coed institution. Enrollment: 10,000 graduate, professional, and undergraduate students. Founded: 1963. The graduate business unit is in an urban setting and is on a semester calendar.

HIGHLIGHTS

Enrollment Profile

Full-time: 55	International: 13%
Part-time: 120	Women: 35%
Total: 175	Minorities: N/R
Average Age: 34	Average Class Size: 30
Fall 1997 Average GPA: N/R	Fall 1997 Average GMAT: N/R

Costs
Full-time tuition: N/R
Part-time tuition: Can$132 per credit (resident); Can$176 per credit (nonresident)

GRADUATE BUSINESS PROGRAMS

Master of Business Administration (MBA) Full-time, part-time; 45 total credits required; 2 to 2.3 years to complete program.

Multi-media MBA (MBA) Part-time, distance learning option; 45 total credits required; 3 to 5 years to complete program.

Master of Business Administration/Bachelor of Laws (MBA/LLB) 122 total credits required; 4 to 5 years to complete program.

ADMISSION

Applications For fall 1997 there were 150 applications for admission. Of those applying, 60 were accepted. Of those accepted, 30 enrolled.

Application Requirements Application form, application fee, bachelor's degree, minimum GPA: 3.0, 2 letters of recommendation, personal statement, resume, college transcript(s).

Recommended for Application Interview, computer experience.

Application Deadline 6/15 for fall, 2/1 for fall (international). Application fee: Can$50. Deferred entrance is available.

ACADEMICS

Faculty Full-time 26; part-time 20.

Teaching Methodologies Case study, computer-aided instruction, computer analysis, computer simulations, faculty seminars, group discussion, lecture, research, simulations, student presentations, team projects.

Technology 120 on-campus computer terminals/PCs are available for student use and are linked by a campus-wide network. The network has full access to the Internet. Students are required to have their own PC.

Special Opportunities International exchange programs in Belgium, France. An internship program is available.

FINANCES

Costs for 1997–98 Tuition: Can$132 per credit (resident); Can$176 per credit (nonresident). Average 1997–98 room and board costs were Can$4300 per academic year.

Financial Aid In 1997–98, 3% of students received some institutionally administered aid in the form of fellowships, scholarships. Application Deadline: 3/15.

Financial Aid Contact Mrs. Louise McIntyre, Service des Bourses et de L'Aide Financiere, Moncton. Phone: 506-858-3731; Fax: 506-858-4492; E-mail: mcintyl@umoncton.ca

FACILITIES

Information Resources Champlain Library; total holdings of 800,000 volumes, 60,000 microforms, 2,800 current periodical subscriptions. CD player(s) available for graduate student use. Access provided to online bibliographic retrieval services.

INTERNATIONAL STUDENTS

Demographics 13% of students enrolled are international students [Africa, 70%, other, 30%].

Services and Facilities International student office, international student center, counseling/support services.

Applying Proof of adequate funds, proof of health/immunizations required. Financial aid is not available to international students.

International Student Contact Mr. Hermel Deschenes, Service aux Etudiants Etrangers, Moneton. Phone: 506-858-3713; Fax: 506-858-4492; E-mail: descheh@umoncton.ca

PLACEMENT

Services include alumni network, career counseling/planning, career placement, electronic job bank, job interviews arranged, job search course, resume referral to employers, and resume preparation. In 1996–97, 10 organizations participated in on-campus recruiting; 100 on-campus interviews were conducted.

Employment Of 1996–97 graduates, 100% were employed within three months of graduation. Types of employment entered: banking, consulting, education, energy, financial services, government, health services, insurance, marketing, service industry, telecommunications.

Business Program(s) URL: http://www.umoncton.ca

Program Contact: Dr. Nha Nguyen, MBA Program Director, Université de Moncton, Moncton E1A 3E9, Canada. Phone: 506-858-4231; Fax: 506-858-4093; E-mail: nguyenn@umoncton.ca

Université de Sherbrooke

Faculty of Administration

Sherbrooke, Canada

OVERVIEW

The Université de Sherbrooke is an independent-nonprofit, coed institution. Founded: 1954. The graduate business unit is in an urban setting and is on a semester calendar.

GRADUATE BUSINESS PROGRAMS

Master in Administration (MS)

Master of Business Administration (MBA)

Master of Finance (MF)

FACILITIES
Information Resources Total library holdings of 1,200,000 volumes, 5,937 current periodical subscriptions. Access provided to online bibliographic retrieval services.

Program Contact: Director of MBA, 1150 University Boulevard, Sherbrooke U1K 2R1, Canada. Phone: 819-821-7333.

Université du Québec à Montréal

École des Sciences de la Gestion

Montreal, Canada

OVERVIEW
The Université du Québec à Montréal is a province-supported, coed institution. Founded: 1969. The graduate business unit is in an urban setting and is on a trimester calendar.

GRADUATE BUSINESS PROGRAMS
Master of Business Administration (MBA)

ACADEMICS
Teaching Methodologies Case study, lecture, student presentations, team projects.

FACILITIES
Information Resources Total library holdings of 1,456,324 volumes, 10,296 current periodical subscriptions. Access provided to online bibliographic retrieval services.

Program Contact: MBA Director, Universite' du Quebec a Montreal, CP8888 Succarsale Centre-Ville, Montreal H3C 3PB, Canada. Phone: 514-987-4448; Fax: 514-987-7728.

Université Laval

Faculty des Sciences de l'Administration

Sainte-Foy, Canada

OVERVIEW
The Université Laval is an independent-nonprofit, coed institution. Enrollment: 34,000 graduate, professional, and undergraduate students. Founded: 1852. The graduate business unit is in a suburban setting and is on a semester calendar.

HIGHLIGHTS

Enrollment Profile

Full-time: 360	International: 16%
Part-time: 327	Women: 40%
Total: 687	Minorities: N/R
Average Age: 30	Average Class Size: 25
Fall 1997 Average GPA: N/R	Fall 1997 Average GMAT: N/R

Costs
Full-time tuition: N/R
Part-time tuition: N/R

AACSB – The International Association for Management Education accredited

Degree(s) offered in conjunction with York University

GRADUATE BUSINESS PROGRAMS
Master of Business Administration (MBA) Full-time, part-time; 45 total credits required; 16 months to 4 years to complete program. Concentrations in accounting, finance, health care, international business, management, management information systems, marketing, operations management, quantitative analysis.

ADMISSION
Applications For fall 1997 there were 450 applications for admission. Of those applying, 250 were accepted. Of those accepted, 125 enrolled.

Application Requirements Application form, application fee, bachelor's degree, minimum GPA: 3.2, 3 letters of recommendation, resume, college transcript(s).

Recommended for Application Computer experience.

Application Deadline 8/14 for fall, 11/30 for winter, 8/14 for fall (international), 11/30 for winter (international). Application fee: Can$30. Deferred entrance is available.

ACADEMICS
Faculty Full-time 60; part-time 5.

Teaching Methodologies Case study, lecture, research, seminars by members of the business community, student presentations, team projects.

Technology 150 on-campus computer terminals/PCs are available for student use and are linked by a campus-wide network. The network has full access to the Internet. Students are not required to have their own PC.

Special Opportunities International exchange programs in Belgium, France, Sweden, United Kingdom, United States.

FINANCES
Financial Aid In 1997–98, 7% of students received some institutionally administered aid in the form of research assistantships. Financial aid is available to part-time students.

Financial Aid Contact Service des Bourses L'Aide Financiere, Cité Universitaire, Quebec. Phone: 418-656-2131 Ext. 3332; Fax: 418-656-2624.

FACILITIES
Information Resources Main institution library plus 1 additional on-campus library; total holdings of 1,900,000 volumes, 49,400 microforms, 17,900 current periodical subscriptions. CD player(s) available for graduate student use. Access provided to online bibliographic retrieval services.

INTERNATIONAL STUDENTS
Demographics 16% of students enrolled are international students.

Services and Facilities International student office, language tutoring.

Applying Proof of adequate funds, proof of health/immunizations required.

International Student Contact Mrs. Marie Lemay, Cité Universitaire, Quebec. Phone: 418-656-7325; Fax: 418-656-2624.

PLACEMENT
Services include career placement.

Business Program(s) URL: http://www.fsa.ulaval.ca/formation/maitrise/mba/mbalaval.html

Program Contact: Mr. Andre Gascon, Director of the MBA Program, Cité Universitaire, Quebec G1K 7P4, Canada. Phone: 418-656-3091; Fax: 418-656-2624.

University of Alberta

Faculty of Business

Edmonton, Canada

OVERVIEW
The University of Alberta is a province-supported, coed institution. Enrollment: 29,859 graduate, professional, and undergraduate students; 2,935 full-time matriculated graduate/professional students; 1,333 part-time matriculated graduate/professional students. Founded: 1906. The graduate business unit is in an urban setting and is on a Canadian standard year calendar.

HIGHLIGHTS

Enrollment Profile

Full-time: 128	International: 9%
Part-time: 157	Women: 40%
Total: 285	Minorities: N/R
Average Age: 27	Average Class Size: 50
Fall 1997 Average GPA: 7.1	Fall 1997 Average GMAT: 610

Costs
Full-time tuition: Can$3710 per academic year (resident); Can$6980 per academic year (nonresident)
Part-time tuition: Can$327 per 3 credits (resident); Can$654 per 3 credits (nonresident)

AACSB – The International Association for Management Education accredited

Degree(s) offered in conjunction with University of Calgary

GRADUATE BUSINESS PROGRAMS
Master of Business Administration (MBA) Full-time, part-time; 57 total credits required; 15 to 19 months to complete program. Concentrations in international and area business studies, public management, health care, sports/entertainment management.

Master of Business Administration/Master of Engineering (MBA/MEng) Full-time, part-time; 66 total credits required; 19 months to 2 years to complete program.

Master of Business Administration/Master of Agriculture (MBA/MAg) Full-time, part-time; 66 total credits required; 19 months to 2 years to complete program.

Master of Business Administration/Master of Forestry (MBA/MF) Full-time, part-time; 66 total credits required; 19 months to 2 years to complete program.

Master of Business AdministrationTechnology Transfer (MBA) Full-time, part-time; 57 total credits required; 15 to 19 months to complete program.

University of Alberta (continued)

Energy MBA (MBA) Full-time, part-time; 57 total credits required; 15 to 19 months to complete program.

Leisure and Sport Management (MBA) Full-time, part-time; 57 total credits required; minimum of 20 months to complete program.

International Business (MBA) 57 total credits required.

ADMISSION

Applications For fall 1997 there were 277 applications for admission. Of those applying, 172 were accepted. Of those accepted, 105 enrolled.

Application Requirements Application form, application fee, bachelor's degree, minimum GPA: 3.0, 3 letters of recommendation, personal statement, resume, college transcript(s).

Recommended for Application GMAT score accepted, work experience, computer experience.

Application Deadline Applications processed on a rolling/continuous basis for domestic students only. 2/1 for fall (international). Application fee: Can$60.

ACADEMICS

Faculty Full-time 70; part-time 30.

Teaching Methodologies Case study, computer-aided instruction, computer analysis, computer simulations, faculty seminars, field projects, group discussion, lecture, seminars by members of the business community, simulations, student presentations, study groups, team projects.

Technology 682 on-campus computer terminals/PCs are available for student use and are linked by a campus-wide network. The network has full access to the Internet. Students are not required to have their own PC.

Special Opportunities International exchange programs in Australia, Austria, Finland, France, Germany, Japan, Mexico, United States.

FINANCES

Costs for 1997–98 Tuition: Full-time: Can$3710 per year (resident); Can$6980 per year (nonresident). Part-time: Can$327 per 3 credits (resident); Can$654 per 3 credits (nonresident). Average 1997–98 room and board costs were Can$2236 per academic year (on campus) and Can$3480 per academic year (off campus). Room and board costs vary by campus location, occupancy (e.g., single, double, triple), type of accommodation, type of meal plan.

Financial Aid Application Deadline: 1/31.

Financial Aid Contact Dr. Kay Devine, Associate Dean, MBA Program, Faculty of Business, Edmonton. Phone: 403-492-3946; Fax: 403-492-7825.

FACILITIES

Information Resources Rutherford Library; total holdings of 2,500,000 volumes, 1,700,000 microforms, 15,000 current periodical subscriptions. CD player(s) available for graduate student use. Access provided to online bibliographic retrieval services and online databases.

INTERNATIONAL STUDENTS

Demographics 9% of students enrolled are international students [Asia, 45%, Europe, 10%, North America, 40%, South America, 5%].

Services and Facilities International student office, international student center, international student housing, counseling/support services.

Applying TOEFL: minimum score of 600 required. Financial aid is not available to international students.

International Student Contact Dr. Kay Devine, Associate Dean, Faculty of Business, Edmonton. Phone: 403-492-3946; Fax: 403-492-7825; E-mail: kstratto@gpu.srv.ualberta.ca

PLACEMENT

Services include career counseling/planning, career library, career placement, job interviews arranged, job search course, and resume preparation. In 1996–97, 20 organizations participated in on-campus recruiting; 100 on-campus interviews were conducted.

Employment Of 1996–97 graduates, 80% were employed within three months of graduation; the average starting salary was Can$51,382. Types of employment entered: banking, chemical industry, communications, computer-related, consulting, consumer products, education, energy, engineering, finance, financial services, health services, high technology, human resources, information systems/technology, insurance, international trade, law, management, nonprofit, petrochemical, pharmaceutical, service industry, telecommunications, transportation, utilities.

Business Program(s) URL: http://www.ualberta.ca/~mba

Program Contact: Dr. Kay Devine, Associate Dean, Faculty of Business, Edmonton T6G 2R6, Canada. Phone: 403-492-3946; Fax: 403-492-7825; E-mail: kstratto@gpu.srv.ualberta.ca

University of British Columbia

Faculty of Commerce and Business Administration

Vancouver, Canada

OVERVIEW

The University of British Columbia is a province-supported, coed institution. Enrollment: 32,464 graduate, professional, and undergraduate students; 6,182 full-time matriculated graduate/professional students; part-time matriculated graduate/professional students. Founded: 1908. The graduate business unit is in a suburban setting and is on a semester calendar.

HIGHLIGHTS

Enrollment Profile

Full-time: 218	International: 20%
Part-time: 24	Women: 29%
Total: 242	Minorities: N/R
Average Age: 27	Average Class Size: 30
Fall 1997 Average GPA: 3.3	Fall 1997 Average GMAT: 620

Costs
Full-time tuition: Can$15,000 per academic year (resident);
   Can$20,000 per academic year (nonresident)
Part-time tuition: N/R

*T*he University of British Columbia (UBC) launched a new M.B.A. program in September 1995. The program is a challenging, integrated educational experience redesigned to reflect the rapidly changing business climate. The program is full-time only and is completed in fifteen continuous months. Students are led by experienced faculty members who have a strong commitment to excellence in teaching and research.

The principal components of the program include an integrated core, specializations, internships, and projects. The integrated core component is designed to provide students with a foundation in finance, marketing, human resources, accounting, economics, statistics, and information systems. Following the core, M.B.A. students are required to select a specialization. Students choose among six specializations, including entrepreneurship, finance, information technology management, strategic management, supply chain management, and marketing. In addition, international business is offered as an adjunct to any of the specializations. Internships and projects are directly related to the area of specialization and are an integral part of the program.

Many exciting opportunities exist to gain a global perspective. Students may select specialized international courses; interact with UBC's multicultural student body, faculty, and visiting scholars; and participate in one of the faculty's twenty-eight exchange programs worldwide.

UBC's M.B.A. program continues to provide students with an innovative approach to management education.

GRADUATE BUSINESS PROGRAMS

Master of Business Administration (MBA) Full-time; 51 total credits required; 15 months to complete program. Concentrations in entrepreneurship, finance, management information systems, operations management, marketing, .

Master of Science in Business Administration (MS) Full-time; 30 total credits required; 12 months to 3 years to complete program. Concentrations in finance, management information systems, management science, logistics, real estate, public and private management.

Baccalaureate of Law/Master of Business Administration (LLB/MBA) Full-time; 136 total credits required; 4 to 5 years to complete program. Concentrations in entrepreneurship, finance, logistics, management information systems, marketing, operations management.

ADMISSION

Applications For fall 1997 there were 665 applications for admission. Of those applying, 266 were accepted. Of those accepted, 112 enrolled.

Application Requirements Application form, application fee, bachelor's degree, essay, minimum GPA: 3.2, 3 letters of recommendation, personal statement, resume, college transcript(s), computer experience: word processing, spreadsheets.

Recommended for Application GMAT score accepted, minimum of 2 years of work experience.

Application Deadline 4/30 for fall, 3/31 for fall (international). Application fee: Can$125.

ACADEMICS

Faculty Full-time 85; part-time 10.

Teaching Methodologies Case study, computer-aided instruction, computer analysis, computer simulations, experiential learning, faculty seminars, field projects, group discussion, lecture, research, seminars by members of the business community, simulations, student presentations, study groups, team projects.

Technology 84 on-campus computer terminals/PCs are available for student use and are linked by a campus-wide network. The network has full access to the Internet. Students are required to have their own PC.

Special Opportunities International exchange programs in Australia, Austria, Brazil, Denmark, France, Germany, Hong Kong, Israel, Italy, Japan, Korea, Malaysia, Mexico, Netherlands, Norway, Republic of Singapore, Spain, Sweden, Switzerland, United Kingdom. An internship program is available.

FINANCES
Costs for 1997–98 Tuition: Full-time: Can$15,000 per program (resident); Can$20,000 per program (nonresident). Cost varies by academic program. Average 1997–98 room and board costs were Can$7200 per academic year (on campus) and Can$10,800 per academic year (off campus). Room and board costs vary by occupancy (e.g., single, double, triple), type of accommodation, type of meal plan.

Financial Aid In 1997–98, 6% of students received some institutionally administered aid in the form of fellowships, research assistantships, teaching assistantships, grants, scholarships, work study, loans.

FACILITIES
Information Resources Main library plus 21 additional on-campus libraries; total holdings of 3,113,500 volumes, 4,014,000 microforms, 23,000 current periodical subscriptions. CD player(s) available for graduate student use. Access provided to online bibliographic retrieval services and online databases.

INTERNATIONAL STUDENTS
Demographics 20% of students enrolled are international students.

Services and Facilities International student office, international student center, international student housing, ESL courses, counseling/support services.

Applying TOEFL: minimum score of 600, proof of adequate funds required. Financial aid is available to international students.

International Student Contact Ms. Winnie Cheung, Director of International Student Services, International House, 1783 West Mall, Vancouver. Phone: 604-822-5021; Fax: 604-822-5099; E-mail: isc@unixg.ubc.ca

PLACEMENT
Services include alumni network, career counseling/planning, career fairs, career library, career placement, electronic job bank, job interviews arranged, job search course, resume referral to employers, and resume preparation. In 1996–97, 200 organizations participated in on-campus recruiting.

Employment Of 1996–97 graduates, 65% were employed within three months of graduation; the average starting salary was Can$59,000. Types of employment entered: banking, communications, computer-related, consulting, consumer products, energy, engineering, finance, financial services, government, high technology, human resources, information systems/technology, international trade, management, manufacturing, marketing, mining, nonprofit, petrochemical, pharmaceutical, real estate, service industry, telecommunications, transportation, utilities.

Business Program(s) URL: http://www.commerce.ubc.ca

Program Contact: Ms. Ethel Davis, Assistant Dean and Director, 102-2053 Main Mall, Vancouver V6T 1Z2, Canada. Phone: 604-822-8422; Fax: 604-822-9030; E-mail: masters.programs@commerce.ubc.ca
See full description on page 1042.

The University of Calgary

Faculty of Management

Calgary, Canada

OVERVIEW
The University of Calgary is a province-supported, coed institution. Enrollment: 22,843 graduate, professional, and undergraduate students; 2,468 full-time matriculated graduate/professional students; 903 part-time matriculated graduate/professional students. Founded: 1960. The graduate business unit is in a suburban setting and is on a semester calendar.

HIGHLIGHTS

Enrollment Profile
Full-time: 106	International: 3%
Part-time: 249	Women: 39%
Total: 355	Minorities: N/R
Average Age: 31	Average Class Size: 30
Fall 1997 Average GPA: 3.2	Fall 1997 Average GMAT: 585

Costs
Full-time tuition: Can$10,000 per academic year (resident);
  Can$20,000 per academic year (nonresident)
Part-time tuition: Can$454 per credit (resident); Can$908 per credit
  (nonresident)

AACSB – The International Association for Management Education accredited

GRADUATE BUSINESS PROGRAMS
Master of Business Administration in Enterprise Development (MBA) Full-time; 20 total credits required; up to 2 years to complete program. Concentrations in accounting, entrepreneurship, finance, international business, management information systems, marketing, operations management, organizational behavior/development, project management.

Master of Business Administration (MBA) Part-time; 20 total credits required; 4 to 6 years to complete program. Concentrations in accounting, entrepreneurship, finance, international business, management information systems, marketing, operations management, organizational behavior/development, project management.

Executive MBA (MBA) Part-time; 20 total credits required; up to 2 years to complete program.

ADMISSION
Applications For fall 1997 there were 295 applications for admission. Of those applying, 182 were accepted. Of those accepted, 118 enrolled.

Application Requirements Application form, application fee, bachelor's degree, minimum GPA: 3.0, 3 letters of recommendation, personal statement, resume, college transcript(s), minimum of 3 years of work experience.

Recommended for Application GMAT score accepted: minimum 500, computer experience.

Application Deadline 5/1 for fall, 9/1 for winter, 5/1 for fall (international), 9/1 for winter (international). Application fee: Can$60.

ACADEMICS
Faculty Full-time 84; part-time 30.

Teaching Methodologies Case study, group discussion, lecture, student presentations, study groups, team projects.

Technology Computer terminals/PCs are available for student use and are linked by a campus-wide network. The network has full access to the Internet. Students are required to have their own PC.

Special Opportunities Advanced credit may be earned through transfer of credits from another institution. International exchange programs in Ireland, Mexico, United States.

FINANCES
Costs for 1997–98 Tuition: Full-time: Can$10,000 per program (resident); Can$20,000 per program (nonresident). Part-time: Can$454 per credit (resident); Can$908 per credit (nonresident). Cost varies by academic program, class time (e.g., day/evening). Fees: Full-time: Can$350 per academic year. Part-time: Can$200 per year. Fees vary by academic program. Average 1997–98 room and board costs were Can$5000 per academic year. Room and board costs vary by occupancy (e.g., single, double, triple), type of accommodation, type of meal plan.

Financial Aid Fellowships, research assistantships, scholarships, loans available. Application Deadline: 2/1.

FACILITIES
Information Resources McKimmie Library plus 4 additional on-campus libraries; total holdings of 1,670,218 volumes, 3,381,452 microforms, 13,400 current periodical subscriptions. CD player(s) available for graduate student use.

INTERNATIONAL STUDENTS
Demographics 3% of students enrolled are international students.

Services and Facilities International student office, international student center, counseling/support services.

Applying TOEFL: minimum score of 550, proof of adequate funds required. Financial aid is not available to international students.

International Student Contact Glynn Hunter, Coordinator, International Students, 2500 University Drive, NW, Calgary. Phone: 403-220-7532; Fax: 403-282-7298.

PLACEMENT
Services include alumni network, career counseling/planning, career fairs, career library, career placement, electronic job bank, job interviews arranged, job search course, resume referral to employers, and resume preparation. In 1996–97, 118 organizations participated in on-campus recruiting; 182 on-campus interviews were conducted.

Employment Of 1996–97 graduates, 87% were employed within three months of graduation; the average starting salary was Can$59,111. Types of employment entered: banking, communications, computer-related, consulting, consumer products, education, energy, engineering, finance, financial services, health services, human resources, information systems/technology, management, manufacturing, marketing, petrochemical, pharmaceutical, real estate, service industry, telecommunications, transportation, utilities.

Business Program(s) URL: http://www.ucalgary.ca/mg/mba/

The University of Calgary (continued)

Program Contact: MBA Program Office, Faculty of Management, 2500 University Drive, NW, Calgary T2N 1N4, Canada. Phone: 403-220-3808; Fax: 403-282-0095; E-mail: dcbeeler@mgmt.ucalgary.ca

University of Guelph

Business Programs

Guelph, Canada

OVERVIEW
The University of Guelph is a province-supported, coed institution. Enrollment: 13,911 graduate, professional, and undergraduate students; 1,489 full-time matriculated graduate/professional students; 131 part-time matriculated graduate/professional students. Founded: 1964. The graduate business unit is in a small-town setting and is on a trimester calendar.

HIGHLIGHTS

Enrollment Profile

Full-time: 28	International: 47%
Part-time: 2	Women: 37%
Total: 30	Minorities: N/R
Average Age: 29	Average Class Size: 20
Fall 1997 Average GPA: 3.0	Fall 1997 Average GMAT: N/R

Costs
Full-time tuition: Can$6000 per academic year (resident); Can$6000 per academic year (nonresident)
Part-time tuition: N/R

GRADUATE BUSINESS PROGRAMS
Master of Business Administration in Agriculture (MBA) Full-time; up to 16 months to complete program. Concentrations in agribusiness, agricultural economics.

ADMISSION
Applications For fall 1997 there were 21 applications for admission. Of those applying, 15 were accepted. Of those accepted, 14 enrolled.

Application Requirements GMAT score, application form, application fee, bachelor's degree, 2 letters of recommendation, personal statement, resume, college transcript(s).

Recommended for Application Interview, work experience, computer experience.

Application Deadline 6/1 for fall (international). Application fee: Can$60.

ACADEMICS
Faculty Full-time 13; part-time 2.

Teaching Methodologies Case study, computer-aided instruction, computer analysis, computer simulations, experiential learning, faculty seminars, field projects, group discussion, lecture, research, role playing, seminars by members of the business community, simulations, student presentations, study groups, team projects.

Technology 100 on-campus computer terminals/PCs are available for student use and are linked by a campus-wide network. The network has full access to the Internet. Students are required to have their own PC.

Special Opportunities International exchange programs in France, Italy.

FINANCES
Costs for 1997–98 Tuition: Full-time: Can$6000 per year (resident); Can$6000 per year (nonresident). Average 1997–98 room and board costs were Can$5472 per academic year. Room and board costs vary by campus location, occupancy (e.g., single, double, triple), type of accommodation, type of meal plan.

Financial Aid In 1997–98, 77% of students received some institutionally administered aid in the form of scholarships.

Financial Aid Contact Dr. Erna Van Duren, MBA Coordinator, Department of Agricultural Economics and Business, Guelph. Phone: 519-824-4120 Ext. 2100; Fax: 519-767-1510; E-mail: vanduren@agec.uoguelph.ca

FACILITIES
Information Resources McLaughlin Library plus 1 additional on-campus library; total holdings of 2,500,000 volumes, 5,000 current periodical subscriptions. CD player(s) available for graduate student use. Access provided to online bibliographic retrieval services.

INTERNATIONAL STUDENTS
Demographics 47% of students enrolled are international students [Africa, 3%, Asia, 7%, Central America, 3%, Europe, 7%, North America, 47%, South America, 7%, other, 26%].

Services and Facilities International student office, international student center, international student housing, visa services, counseling/support services.

Applying TOEFL: minimum score of 550, proof of adequate funds required. Financial aid is not available to international students.

PLACEMENT
Services include alumni network, career counseling/planning, career library, career placement, electronic job bank, job interviews arranged, job search course, resume referral to employers, and resume preparation. In 1996–97, 50 organizations participated in on-campus recruiting; 60 on-campus interviews were conducted.

Employment Of 1996–97 graduates, 100% were employed within three months of graduation. Types of employment entered: banking, communications, computer-related, consulting, financial services, government, information systems/technology.

Business Program(s) URL: http://www.uoguelph.ca

Program Contact: Dr. Erna Van Duren, MBA Coordinator, Department of Agricultural Economics and Business, Guelph N1G 2W1, Canada. Phone: 519-824-4120 Ext. 2100; Fax: 519-767-1510; E-mail: vanduren@agec.uoguelph.ca

University of Manitoba

Faculty of Management

Winnipeg, Canada

OVERVIEW
The University of Manitoba is a province-supported, coed institution. Enrollment: 23,000 graduate, professional, and undergraduate students; 2,265 full-time matriculated graduate/professional students; 1,000 part-time matriculated graduate/professional students. Founded: 1877. The graduate business unit is in a suburban setting and is on a 11 consecutive months calendar.

HIGHLIGHTS

Enrollment Profile

Full-time: 24	International: 2%
Part-time: 105	Women: 29%
Total: 129	Minorities: N/R
Average Age: 32	Average Class Size: 24
Fall 1997 Average GPA: 3.35	Fall 1997 Average GMAT: 590

Costs
Full-time tuition: Can$17,600 per academic year (resident); Can$17,600 per academic year (nonresident)
Part-time tuition: N/R

GRADUATE BUSINESS PROGRAMS
Full-time MBA (MBA) Full-time; 66 total credits required; 11 months to complete program. Concentration in management.

Part-time MBA (MBA) Part-time; 60 total credits required; 3 to 6 years to complete program. Concentrations in management science, agribusiness, finance, industrial/labor relations, management, marketing.

ADMISSION
Applications For fall 1997 there were 120 applications for admission. Of those applying, 32 were accepted. Of those accepted, 16 enrolled.

Application Requirements GMAT score: minimum 450, application form, application fee, bachelor's degree, minimum GPA: 3.0, interview, 3 letters of recommendation, personal statement, resume, college transcript(s), minimum of 3 years of work experience.

Recommended for Application Computer experience: word processing, spreadsheet.

Application Deadline 5/1 for fall, 1/15 for fall (international). Application fee: Can$50. Deferred entrance is available.

ACADEMICS
Faculty Full-time 60; part-time 10.

Teaching Methodologies Case study, computer-aided instruction, computer analysis, computer simulations, experiential learning, faculty seminars, field projects, group discussion, lecture, research, role playing, seminars by members of the business community, simulations, student presentations, study groups, team projects.

Technology 125 on-campus computer terminals/PCs are available for student use and are linked by a campus-wide network. The network has full access to the Internet. Students are not required to have their own PC.

FINANCES
Costs for 1997–98 Tuition: Full-time: Can$17,600 per program (resident); Can$17,600 per program (nonresident). Fees: Full-time: Can$6000 per academic year (resident); Can$6000 per academic year (nonresident). Part-

time: Can$100 per year (resident); Can$100 per year (nonresident). Average 1997–98 room and board costs were Can$6000 per academic year (on campus) and Can$5500 per academic year (off campus). Room and board costs vary by occupancy (e.g., single, double, triple), type of meal plan.

Financial Aid In 1997–98, 5% of students received some institutionally administered aid in the form of fellowships, scholarships. Application Deadline: 1/15.

Financial Aid Contact Mr. Peter Dueck, Director, Financial Aid and Awards, Room 421, University Centre Building, Winnipeg. Phone: 204-474-6382; E-mail: peter_dueck@umanitoba.ca

FACILITIES
Information Resources Elizabeth Dafoe Library plus 9 additional on-campus libraries; total holdings of 1,740,025 volumes, 2,694,609 microforms, 8,991 current periodical subscriptions. CD player(s) available for graduate student use. Access provided to online bibliographic retrieval services.

INTERNATIONAL STUDENTS
Demographics 2% of students enrolled are international students [North America, 90%, other, 10%].

Services and Facilities International student office, international student center, international student housing, visa services, ESL courses, counseling/support services.

Applying TOEFL: minimum score of 550, proof of adequate funds, proof of health/immunizations required. Financial aid is not available to international students.

International Student Contact Dr. Lyle Eide, Director, International Centre for Students, 541 University Center, Winnipeg. Phone: 204-474-8501; E-mail: lyle_eide@umanitoba.ca

PLACEMENT
Services include alumni network, career counseling/planning, career fairs, career library, career placement, electronic job bank, job interviews arranged, job search course, resume referral to employers, and resume preparation. In 1996–97, 100 organizations participated in on-campus recruiting; 50 on-campus interviews were conducted.

Employment Of 1996–97 graduates, 100% were employed within three months of graduation; the average starting salary was Can$65,000. Types of employment entered: banking, communications, computer-related, consulting, consumer products, engineering, finance, financial services, government, health services, human resources, information systems/technology, international trade, management, manufacturing, marketing, nonprofit, service industry, telecommunications, utilities.

Business Program(s) URL: http://www.umanitoba.ca/management/mbapage.html

Program Contact: Ms. Susan Eide, MBA Program Manager, 273 Drake Centre, Winnipeg R3T 5V4, Canada. Phone: 204-474-8448, 800-622-6296 (MB only); Fax: 204-474-7529; E-mail: eides@ms.umanitoba.ca
See full description on page 1092.

University of New Brunswick

Faculty of Business

Saint John, Canada

OVERVIEW
The University of New Brunswick is a province-supported, coed institution. Enrollment: 2,800 graduate, professional, and undergraduate students; 50 full-time matriculated graduate/professional students; 67 part-time matriculated graduate/professional students. Founded: 1800. The graduate business unit is in an urban setting and is on a module calendar.

HIGHLIGHTS

Enrollment Profile

Full-time: 20	International: 13%
Part-time: 44	Women: 34%
Total: 64	Minorities: N/R
Average Age: 30	Average Class Size: 20
Fall 1997 Average GPA: 3.3	Fall 1997 Average GMAT: 600

Costs
Full-time tuition: Can$18,000 per academic year (resident); Can$18,000 per academic year (nonresident)
Part-time tuition: Can$500 per semester (resident); Can$500 per semester (nonresident)

GRADUATE BUSINESS PROGRAMS
Master of Business Administration (MBA) Full-time, part-time; 65 total credits required; 11 months to 6 years to complete program. Concentrations in international and area business studies, international business.

ADMISSION
Applications For fall 1997 there were 70 applications for admission. Of those applying, 35 were accepted. Of those accepted, 25 enrolled.

Application Requirements GMAT score: minimum 550, application form, application fee, bachelor's degree, minimum GPA: 3.0, 3 letters of recommendation, personal statement, resume, college transcript(s), minimum of 2 years of work experience.

Recommended for Application Computer experience.

Application Deadline Applications processed on a rolling/continuous basis for both domestic and international students. Application fee: Can$100. Deferred entrance is available.

ACADEMICS
Faculty Full-time 18; part-time 10.

Teaching Methodologies Case study, computer-aided instruction, computer analysis, experiential learning, faculty seminars, field projects, group discussion, lecture, research, role playing, seminars by members of the business community, simulations, student presentations, study groups, team projects.

Technology 100 on-campus computer terminals/PCs are available for student use and are linked by a campus-wide network. The network has full access to the Internet. Students are not required to have their own PC.

Special Opportunities Advanced credit may be earned through credit by examination, transfer of credits from another institution. International exchange program in various countries in Asia and Europe. An internship program is available.

FINANCES
Costs for 1997–98 Tuition: Full-time: Can$18,000 per year (resident); Can$18,000 per year (nonresident). Part-time: Can$500 per semester (resident); Can$500 per semester (nonresident). Cost varies by academic program, campus location. Fees: Full-time: Can$337 per academic year. Part-time: Can$700 per year. Fees vary by academic program. Average 1997–98 room and board costs were Can$6000 per academic year (on campus) and Can$2800 per academic year (off campus). Room and board costs vary by occupancy (e.g., single, double, triple), type of accommodation, type of meal plan.

Financial Aid In 1997–98, 31% of students received some institutionally administered aid in the form of scholarships, work study. Application Deadline: 3/15.

Financial Aid Contact Ms. Connie Stafford, MBA Coordinator, PO Box 5050, Saint John. Phone: 506-648-5735; Fax: 506-648-5574; E-mail: mba@unbsj.ca

FACILITIES
Information Resources Ward Chipman Library; total holdings of 177,000 volumes, 60,000 microforms. CD player(s) available for graduate student use. Access provided to online bibliographic retrieval services.

INTERNATIONAL STUDENTS
Demographics 13% of students enrolled are international students [Asia, 87%, Europe, 13%].

Services and Facilities International student office, international student center, visa services, ESL courses, counseling/support services, international student organization.

Applying TOEFL: minimum score of 550 required. TSE, TWE recommended. Financial aid is available to international students.

International Student Contact Mr. Peter Donahue, Assistant Director, Student Services, PO Box 5050, Saint John. Phone: 506-648-5680; Fax: 506-648-5528; E-mail: donahue@unbsj.ca

PLACEMENT
Services include career counseling/planning, career fairs, job search course, and resume preparation.

Employment Of 1996–97 graduates, 100% were employed within three months of graduation. Types of employment entered: computer-related, consumer products, financial services, government, telecommunications.

Business Program(s) URL: http://www.unbsj.ca/academic/mba.htm

Program Contact: Ms. Connie Stafford, MBA Coordinator, PO Box 5050, Saint John E2L 4L5, Canada. Phone: 506-648-5735, 800-508-6275; Fax: 506-648-5574; E-mail: mba@unbsj.ca

University of New Brunswick

Faculty of Administration

Fredericton, Canada

OVERVIEW

The University of New Brunswick is a province-supported, coed institution. Enrollment: 12,346 graduate, professional, and undergraduate students; 788 full-time matriculated graduate/professional students; 465 part-time matriculated graduate/professional students. Founded: 1785. The graduate business unit is in an urban setting and is on a Canadian standard year calendar.

HIGHLIGHTS

Enrollment Profile
Full-time: 45
Part-time: 53
Total: 98
Average Age: 27
Fall 1997 Average GPA: 3.3

International: N/R
Women: N/R
Minorities: N/R
Average Class Size: 25
Fall 1997 Average GMAT: 550

Costs
Full-time tuition: Can$3330 per academic year (resident); Can$5630 per academic year (nonresident)
Part-time tuition: N/R

GRADUATE BUSINESS PROGRAMS

Master of Business Administration (MBA) Full-time, part-time; 60 total credits required; up to 2 years to complete program.

ADMISSION

Application Requirements GMAT score: minimum 550, application form, application fee, bachelor's degree, minimum GPA: 3.0, 3 letters of recommendation, personal statement, college transcript(s).

Recommended for Application Resume, work experience, computer experience.

Application Deadline 5/30 for fall, 5/30 for fall (international). Application fee: Can$50.

ACADEMICS

Faculty Full-time 39; part-time 10.

Teaching Methodologies Case study, experiential learning, field projects, lecture, seminars by members of the business community, student presentations, team projects.

Technology 15 on-campus computer terminals/PCs are available for student use and are linked by a campus-wide network. The network has full access to the Internet. Students are not required to have their own PC.

Special Opportunities International exchange programs in France, Sweden. An internship program is available.

FINANCES

Costs for 1997–98 Tuition: Full-time: Can$3330 per year (resident); Can$5630 per year (nonresident). Cost varies by number of credits taken.

Financial Aid Teaching assistantships, scholarships available.

Financial Aid Contact Karen Ivey, MBA Secretary, Tilley Hall 332, Fredricton. Phone: 506-453-4766; Fax: 506-453-3561.

FACILITIES

Information Resources Harriet Irving Library plus 6 additional on-campus libraries; total holdings of 1,000,000 volumes, 1,900,000 microforms, 6,200 current periodical subscriptions. CD player(s) available for graduate student use. Access provided to online bibliographic retrieval services.

INTERNATIONAL STUDENTS

Demographics N/R

Services and Facilities International student office, international student housing, counseling/support services.

Applying TOEFL: minimum score of 550, proof of adequate funds, proof of health/immunizations required. Financial aid is not available to international students.

PLACEMENT

Services include alumni network, career fairs, and electronic job bank.

Employment Types of employment entered: banking, consulting, finance, retail, service industry.

Business Program(s) URL: http://www.unb.ca

Program Contact: Karen Ivey, MBA Secretary, Tilley Hall 332, Fredricton E3B 5A3, Canada. Phone: 506-453-4766; Fax: 506-453-3561.

University of Ottawa

Faculty of Administration

Ottawa, Canada

OVERVIEW

The University of Ottawa is a province-supported, coed institution. Enrollment: 18,000 graduate, professional, and undergraduate students. Founded: 1848. The graduate business unit is in an urban setting and is on a trimester calendar.

HIGHLIGHTS

Enrollment Profile
Full-time: 157
Part-time: 328
Total: 485
Average Age: 29
Fall 1997 Average GPA: 3.0

International: 15%
Women: 39%
Minorities: N/R
Average Class Size: 40
Fall 1997 Average GMAT: 580

Costs
Full-time tuition: Can$1912 per academic year (resident); Can$3630 per academic year (nonresident)
Part-time tuition: Can$150 per credit (resident); Can$300 per credit (nonresident)

Degree(s) offered in conjunction with Nipissing University

GRADUATE BUSINESS PROGRAMS

Master of Business Administration (MBA) Full-time, part-time; 60 total credits required; 16 months to 4 years to complete program. Concentrations in finance, public management, technology management, international management, marketing, management.

International Master of Business Administration (IMBA) Full-time, part-time; 30 total credits required; 12 months to 6 years to complete program. Concentration in international management.

Executive Master of Business Administration (EMBA) Full-time; 60 total credits required; up to 2 years to complete program. Concentration in management.

ADMISSION

Applications For fall 1997 there were 550 applications for admission. Of those applying, 302 were accepted. Of those accepted, 166 enrolled.

Application Requirements GMAT score, application form, application fee, bachelor's degree, essay, minimum GPA: 2.8, 2 letters of recommendation, personal statement, resume, college transcript(s), minimum of 2 years of work experience.

Recommended for Application GRE score accepted, computer experience.

Application Deadline 3/1 for fall. Application fee: Can$60.

ACADEMICS

Faculty Full-time 67; part-time 31.

Teaching Methodologies Case study, computer-aided instruction, computer analysis, faculty seminars, field projects, group discussion, lecture, research, role playing, seminars by members of the business community, student presentations, study groups, team projects.

Technology 150 on-campus computer terminals/PCs are available for student use and are linked by a campus-wide network. The network has full access to the Internet. Students are not required to have their own PC.

Special Opportunities Advanced credit may be earned through transfer of credits from another institution. International exchange programs in Belgium, France, Germany, Spain, Switzerland, Thailand, United Kingdom, United States. An internship program is available.

FINANCES

Costs for 1997–98 Tuition: Full-time: Can$1912 per session (resident); Can$3630 per session (nonresident). Part-time: Can$150 per credit (resident); Can$300 per credit (nonresident). Fees: Full-time: Can$82 per academic year (resident); Can$82 per academic year (nonresident). Part-time: Can$37 per session (resident); Can$37 per session (nonresident). Average 1997–98 room and board costs were Can$7600 per academic year (on campus) and Can$10,800 per academic year (off campus). Room and board costs vary by occupancy (e.g., single, double, triple), type of accommodation, type of meal plan.

Financial Aid In 1997–98, 34% of students received some institutionally administered aid in the form of research assistantships, teaching assistantships, scholarships.

Financial Aid Contact Mr. Timothy Russwurm, Administrator, Financial Aid Office, PO Box 450, Station A, Ottawa . Phone: 613-562-5800 Ext. 1239.

FACILITIES

Information Resources Morisset Library plus 7 additional on-campus libraries; total holdings of 1,381,300 volumes, 1,175,700 microforms, 11,200 current periodical subscriptions. CD player(s) available for graduate student use. Access provided to online bibliographic retrieval services.

INTERNATIONAL STUDENTS
Demographics 15% of students enrolled are international students [Asia, 40%, Europe, 50%].

Services and Facilities International student office, international student center, ESL courses, counseling/support services.

Applying TOEFL: minimum score of 550, proof of adequate funds, proof of health/immunizations required. Financial aid is available to international students.

International Student Contact Ms. Sylvie Seguin-Jak, Administrator, IMBA Program, PO Box 450, Station A, Ottawa. Phone: 613-562-5821; Fax: 613-562-5167.

PLACEMENT
Services include alumni network, career counseling/planning, career fairs, career library, career placement, electronic job bank, job interviews arranged, job search course, resume referral to employers, and resume preparation. In 1996–97, 300 organizations participated in on-campus recruiting.

Employment Types of employment entered: accounting, banking, consulting, finance, insurance, service industry.

Business Program(s) URL: http://www.admin.uottawa.ca

Program Contact: Ms. Diane Sarrazin, Administrator, PO Box 450, Station A, Ottawa K1N 6N5, Canada. Phone: 613-562-5884, 800-965-5512; Fax: 613-562-5912; E-mail: sarrazin@admin.uottawa.ca

University of Regina

Faculty of Administration

Regina, Canada

OVERVIEW
The University of Regina is a province-supported, coed institution. Enrollment: 11,572 graduate, professional, and undergraduate students; 255 full-time matriculated graduate/professional students; 674 part-time matriculated graduate/professional students. Founded: 1974. The graduate business unit is in an urban setting and is on a Canadian standard year calendar.

HIGHLIGHTS

Enrollment Profile

Full-time: 5	International: 3%
Part-time: 63	Women: 41%
Total: 68	Minorities: N/R
Average Age: 32	Average Class Size: 25
Fall 1997 Average GPA: 3.2	Fall 1997 Average GMAT: N/R

Costs
Full-time tuition: N/R
Part-time tuition: Can$563 per course (resident); Can$563 per course (nonresident)

GRADUATE BUSINESS PROGRAMS
Master of Business Administration (MBA) Full-time, part-time; 57 total credits required; 2.5 to 5 years to complete program. Concentration in management.

Master of Public Administration (MPA) Full-time, part-time; 57 total credits required; 2.5 to 5 years to complete program. Concentration in public policy and administration.

ADMISSION
Applications For fall 1997 there were 44 applications for admission. Of those applying, 32 were accepted. Of those accepted, 24 enrolled.

Application Requirements GMAT score: minimum 550, application form, bachelor's degree, minimum GPA: 3.0, interview, 2 letters of recommendation, personal statement, resume, college transcript(s), minimum of 2 years of work experience.

Application Deadline Applications processed on a rolling/continuous basis for both domestic and international students. Deferred entrance is available.

ACADEMICS
Faculty Full-time 20; part-time 15.

Teaching Methodologies Case study, computer analysis, experiential learning, field projects, group discussion, lecture, research, role playing, seminars by members of the business community, simulations, student presentations, team projects.

Technology 40 on-campus computer terminals/PCs are available for student use and are linked by a campus-wide network. The network has full access to the Internet. Students are not required to have their own PC.

Special Opportunities Advanced credit may be earned through transfer of credits from another institution. An internship program is available.

FINANCES
Costs for 1997–98 Tuition: Can$563 per course (resident); Can$563 per course (nonresident). Cost varies by academic program, number of credits taken. Fees: Can$65 per course (resident); Can$65 per course (nonresident). Fees vary by academic program. Average 1997–98 room only costs were Can$2180 per academic year (on campus) and Can$3600 per academic year (off campus). Room and board costs vary by campus location, occupancy (e.g., single, double, triple), type of accommodation, type of meal plan.

Financial Aid In 1997–98, 3% of students received some institutionally administered aid in the form of research assistantships, teaching assistantships, scholarships, work study, loans.

Financial Aid Contact Mr. Jack Ito, Chair of Graduate Program, Faculty of Administration, Regina. Phone: 306-585-4724; Fax: 306-585-4805.

FACILITIES
Information Resources Main library plus 5 additional on-campus libraries; total holdings of 808,854 volumes, 1,158,374 microforms, 3,017 current periodical subscriptions. CD player(s) available for graduate student use. Access provided to online bibliographic retrieval services and online databases.

INTERNATIONAL STUDENTS
Demographics 3% of students enrolled are international students [Asia, 100%].

Services and Facilities International student office, international student center, visa services, ESL courses, counseling/support services.

Applying TOEFL: minimum score of 580 required. Financial aid is not available to international students.

International Student Contact Mr. Sel Murray, Manager of Student Affairs/International Student Services, Regina. Phone: 306-585-4017 ; Fax: 306-585-4957.

PLACEMENT
Services include career counseling/planning, career fairs, career placement, electronic job bank, job interviews arranged, job search course, and resume preparation.

Employment Of 1996–97 graduates, 80% were employed within three months of graduation. Types of employment entered: banking, chemical industry, energy, government, petrochemical, telecommunications.

Business Program(s) URL: http://www.uregina.ca

Program Contact: Mr. Jack Ito, Chair of Graduate Program, Faculty of Administration, Regina S4S 0A2, Canada. Phone: 306-585-4724; Fax: 306-585-4805; E-mail: jack.ito@leroy.cc.uregina.ca

University of Saskatchewan

College of Commerce

Saskatoon, Canada

OVERVIEW
The University of Saskatchewan is a province-supported, coed institution. Enrollment: 18,411 graduate, professional, and undergraduate students; 1,295 full-time matriculated graduate/professional students; 465 part-time matriculated graduate/professional students. Founded: 1907. The graduate business unit is in an urban setting and is on a semester calendar.

HIGHLIGHTS

Enrollment Profile

Full-time: 50	International: 22%
Part-time: 92	Women: 39%
Total: 142	Minorities: N/R
Average Age: 30	Average Class Size: 30
Fall 1997 Average GPA: N/R	Fall 1997 Average GMAT: 560

Costs
Full-time tuition: N/R
Part-time tuition: Can$357 per 3-credit course (resident); Can$357 per 3-credit course (nonresident)

GRADUATE BUSINESS PROGRAMS
Master of Business Administration (MBA) Full-time, part-time; 30-60 total credits required; 8 months to 5 years to complete program. Concentration in commerce.

Master of Science in Accounting (Thesis program) (MSc) Full-time, part-time; 8 months to 5 years to complete program. Concentration in accounting.

ADMISSION
Applications For fall 1997 there were 153 applications for admission. Of those applying, 94 were accepted. Of those accepted, 59 enrolled.

University of Saskatchewan (continued)

Application Requirements Application form, application fee, bachelor's degree, GPA: minimum 70.0 on a 100 scale, 3 letters of recommendation, college transcript(s).

Recommended for Application GMAT score accepted: minimum 500, resume, minimum of 5 years of work experience, computer experience.

Application Deadline 6/30 for fall, 10/31 for winter, 4/30 for fall (international), 8/30 for winter (international). Application fee: Can$50. Deferred entrance is available.

ACADEMICS
Faculty Full-time 35; part-time 16.

Teaching Methodologies Case study, computer-aided instruction, computer simulations, experiential learning, faculty seminars, field projects, group discussion, lecture, research, seminars by members of the business community, simulations, student presentations, study groups, team projects.

Technology 89 on-campus computer terminals/PCs are available for student use and are linked by a campus-wide network. The network has full access to the Internet. Students are not required to have their own PC.

Special Opportunities Advanced credit may be earned through credit for business training programs, transfer of credits from another institution. An internship program is available.

FINANCES
Costs for 1997–98 Tuition: Can$357 per 3-credit course (resident); Can$357 per 3-credit course (nonresident). Cost varies by academic program, number of credits taken. Fees vary by academic program, number of credits taken. Average 1997–98 room and board costs were Can$3976 per academic year (on campus) and Can$4000 per academic year (off campus). Room and board costs vary by occupancy (e.g., single, double, triple), type of accommodation, type of meal plan.

Financial Aid In 1997–98, 4% of students received some institutionally administered aid in the form of fellowships, research assistantships, teaching assistantships, scholarships. Application Deadline: 2/15.

Financial Aid Contact Assistant Dean (Programs), College of Commerce, 25 Campus Drive, Saskatoon. Phone: 306-966-4785; Fax: 306-966-8709.

FACILITIES
Information Resources Main library plus 7 additional on-campus libraries; total holdings of 1,675,644 volumes, 2,300,000 microforms, 10,092 current periodical subscriptions. CD player(s) available for graduate student use. Access provided to online bibliographic retrieval services.

INTERNATIONAL STUDENTS
Demographics 22% of students enrolled are international students [Africa, 7%, Asia, 51%, Central America, 4%, Europe, 19%, North America, 19%].

Services and Facilities International student office, international student center, ESL courses, counseling/support services.

Applying TOEFL: minimum score of 550 required. Financial aid is available to international students.

International Student Contact Mr. Kurt Tischler, Advisor, 1 Campus Drive, Room 60, Place Riel, Saskatoon. Phone: 306-966-4923; Fax: 306-966-5081; E-mail: tischler@admin.usask.ca

PLACEMENT
Services include alumni network, career library, career placement, electronic job bank, job interviews arranged, job search course, resume referral to employers, and resume preparation. In 1996–97, 15 organizations participated in on-campus recruiting.

Employment Of 1996–97 graduates, 71% were employed within three months of graduation; the average starting salary was Can$30,000. Types of employment entered: consulting, energy, government, insurance, pharmaceutical, transportation.

Business Program(s) URL: http://www.commerce.usask.ca/mba/mbahome.htm

Program Contact: Ms. Chandra Kretzer, Administrative Assistant, College of Commerce, 25 Campus Drive, Saskatoon S7N 5A7, Canada. Phone: 306-966-4785; Fax: 306-966-8709; E-mail: kretzer@commerce.usask.ca

University of Toronto

Joseph L. Rotman School of Management
Toronto, Canada

OVERVIEW
The University of Toronto is a province-supported, coed institution. Enrollment: 50,292 graduate, professional, and undergraduate students; 6,170 full-time matriculated graduate/professional students; 1,714 part-time matriculated graduate/professional students. Founded: 1827. The graduate business unit is in an urban setting and is on a Canadian standard year calendar.

HIGHLIGHTS

Enrollment Profile

Full-time: 240	International: 27%
Part-time: 165	Women: 33%
Total: 405	Minorities: N/R
Average Age: 27	Average Class Size: 60
Fall 1997 Average GPA: 3.2	Fall 1997 Average GMAT: 648

Costs
Full-time tuition: Can$7390 per academic year (resident); Can$13,610 per academic year (nonresident)
Part-time tuition: Can$1890 per year (resident); Can$4327 per year (nonresident)

GRADUATE BUSINESS PROGRAMS
Full-time MBA (MBA) Full-time; 60 total credits required; 20 months to 3.5 years to complete program. Concentrations in management, finance, strategic management, marketing, economics, operations management, organizational behavior/development.

Executive MBA (EMBA) Part-time; 60 total credits required; up to 2 years to complete program. Concentration in management.

Part-time MBA (MBA) Part-time; 60 total credits required; 3.3 to 6 years to complete program. Concentrations in management, finance, strategic management, marketing, economics, operations management, organizational behavior/development.

Master of Management and Professional Accounting (MMPA) Full-time; 70 total credits required; 16 months to 2.3 years to complete program. Concentrations in accounting, management.

Baccalaureate of Law/Master of Business Administration (LLB/MBA) Full-time; 60 total credits required; 3.7 years to complete program. Concentrations in management, finance, research and development administration, marketing, economics, operations management, organizational behavior/development.

ADMISSION
Applications For fall 1997 there were 853 applications for admission. Of those applying, 200 were accepted. Of those accepted, 122 enrolled.

Application Requirements GMAT score: minimum 550, application form, application fee, bachelor's degree, essay, minimum GPA: 3.0, 3 letters of recommendation, personal statement, resume, college transcript(s), minimum of 2 years of work experience.

Recommended for Application Interview, computer experience.

Application Deadline 4/30 for fall, 9/30 for winter, 4/30 for fall (international), 9/30 for winter (international). Application fee: Can$100. Deferred entrance is available.

ACADEMICS
Faculty Full-time 72; part-time 34.

Teaching Methodologies Case study, computer-aided instruction, computer analysis, experiential learning, field projects, group discussion, lecture, role playing, seminars by members of the business community, simulations, student presentations, study groups, team projects.

Technology 50 on-campus computer terminals/PCs are available for student use and are linked by a campus-wide network. The network has full access to the Internet. Students are not required to have their own PC.

Special Opportunities International exchange programs in France, Germany, Hong Kong, Italy, Republic of Singapore. An internship program is available.

FINANCES
Costs for 1997–98 Tuition: Full-time: Can$7390 per year (resident); Can$13,610 per year (nonresident). Part-time: Can$1890 per year (resident); Can$4327 per year (nonresident). Cost varies by academic program. Fees: Full-time: Can$1250 per academic year (resident); Can$1250 per academic year (nonresident). Part-time: Can$400 per year (resident); Can$400 per year (nonresident). Fees vary by academic program. Average 1997–98 room and board costs were Can$10,000 per academic year (on campus) and Can$13,000 per academic year (off campus). Room and board costs vary by campus location, occupancy (e.g., single, double, triple), type of accommodation, type of meal plan.

Financial Aid In 1997–98, 6% of students received some institutionally administered aid in the form of fellowships, research assistantships, teaching assistantships, scholarships. Application Deadline: 4/30.

Financial Aid Contact Ms. Margaret Bauer, MBA Program Assistant, 105 St. George Street, Toronto. Phone: 416-978-1983; Fax: 416-978-5812; E-mail: bauer@mgmt.utoronto.ca

FACILITIES
Information Resources Robarts Library plus 57 additional on-campus libraries; total holdings of 7,400,000 volumes, 3,400,000 microforms, 28,000 cur-

rent periodical subscriptions. CD player(s) available for graduate student use. Access provided to online bibliographic retrieval services.

INTERNATIONAL STUDENTS
Demographics 27% of students enrolled are international students.

Services and Facilities International student office, international student center.

Applying IELT: minimum score of 7, TOEFL: minimum score of 600, TWE: minimum score of 5 required. Financial aid is available to international students.

International Student Contact Ms. Catherine Lewis, Associate Director, MBA Program, 105 St. George Street, ., Toronto. Phone: 416-978-5108; Fax: 416-978-5812; E-mail: lewis@mgmt.utoronto.ca

PLACEMENT
Services include alumni network, career counseling/planning, career fairs, career library, career placement, electronic job bank, job interviews arranged, job search course, resume referral to employers, and resume preparation. In 1996–97, 550 organizations participated in on-campus recruiting.

Employment Of 1996–97 graduates, 98% were employed within three months of graduation; the average starting salary was Can$70,300. Types of employment entered: accounting, banking, communications, computer-related, consulting, consumer products, energy, engineering, finance, financial services, health services, high technology, human resources, information systems/technology, insurance, international trade, law, management, manufacturing, marketing, mining, petrochemical, retail, telecommunications, utilities.

Business Program(s) URL: http://www.mgmt.utoronto.ca

Program Contact: Ms. Almira Mun, Assistant Director, Recruiting and Admissions, MBA Program, 105 St. George Street, Toronto M5S 3E6, Canada. Phone: 416-978-3499; Fax: 416-978-5812; E-mail: mbaprog@mgmt.utoronto.ca
See full description on page 1164.

University of Victoria

Faculty of Business

Victoria, Canada

OVERVIEW
The University of Victoria is a province-supported, coed institution. Enrollment: 15,000 graduate, professional, and undergraduate students. Founded: 1963. The graduate business unit is in a suburban setting and is on a Canadian standard year calendar.

HIGHLIGHTS

Enrollment Profile

Full-time: 70	International: N/R
Part-time: 70	Women: N/R
Total: 140	Minorities: N/R
Average Age: 33	Average Class Size: 30
Fall 1997 Average GPA: 3.35	Fall 1997 Average GMAT: 601

Costs
Full-time tuition: Can$8000 per academic year (resident); Can$8000 per academic year (nonresident)
Part-time tuition: N/R

GRADUATE BUSINESS PROGRAMS
Master of Business Administration (MBA) Full-time, part-time; 56 total credits required; 21 months to 3.1 years to complete program. Concentrations in international business, entrepreneurship, travel industry/tourism management.

ADMISSION
Application Requirements GMAT score, application form, application fee, bachelor's degree, essay, minimum GPA: 3.0, interview, 2 letters of recommendation, resume, college transcript(s).

Recommended for Application Work experience, computer experience.

Application Deadline 5/31 for fall, 5/31 for fall (international). Application fee: Can$45.

ACADEMICS
Faculty Full-time 32; part-time 6.

Teaching Methodologies Case study, field projects, lecture, seminars by members of the business community, study groups, team projects.

Technology 75 on-campus computer terminals/PCs are available for student use and are linked by a campus-wide network. The network has full access to the Internet. Students are not required to have their own PC.

Special Opportunities International exchange programs in France, Indonesia, Japan, Malaysia, Mexico, Republic of Singapore, Taiwan. An internship program is available.

FINANCES
Costs for 1997–98 Tuition: Full-time: Can$8000 per program (resident); Can$8000 per program (nonresident). Average 1997–98 room only costs were Can$6000 per academic year (off campus). Room and board costs vary by campus location, occupancy (e.g., single, double, triple), type of accommodation, type of meal plan.

Financial Aid In 1997–98, 5% of students received some institutionally administered aid in the form of fellowships, research assistantships, scholarships. Application Deadline: 2/15.

Financial Aid Contact Mr. Nicholas James, MBA Admissions Officer, PO Box 1700, Victoria. Phone: 250-721-6050; Fax: 250-721-6067; E-mail: njames@business.uvic.ca

FACILITIES
Information Resources McPherson Library plus 3 additional on-campus libraries; total holdings of 1,200,000 volumes, 1,500,000 microforms, 500 current periodical subscriptions. CD player(s) available for graduate student use. Access provided to online bibliographic retrieval services.

INTERNATIONAL STUDENTS
Demographics N/R

Services and Facilities Counseling/support services.

Applying TOEFL: minimum score of 575 required. Financial aid is available to international students.

International Student Contact Mr. Nicholas James, MBA Admissions Officer, PO Box 1700, Victoria. Phone: 250-721-6058; Fax: 250-721-6067; E-mail: njames@business.uvic.ca

PLACEMENT
Services include alumni network, career counseling/planning, career placement, job search course, resume referral to employers, and resume preparation.

Employment Types of employment entered: accounting, banking, computer-related, consulting, consumer products, education, finance, government, health services, high technology, hospitality management, human resources, information systems/technology, international trade, management, marketing, retail, service industry, telecommunications.

Business Program(s) URL: http://www.business.uvic.ca/mba/

Program Contact: Mr. Nicholas James, MBA Admissions Officer, PO Box 1700, Victoria V8W 2Y2, Canada. Phone: 250-721-6058; Fax: 250-721-6067; E-mail: njames@business.uvic.ca

University of Waterloo

School of Accountancy

Waterloo, Canada

OVERVIEW
The University of Waterloo is a province-supported, coed institution. Enrollment: 2,067 graduate, professional, and undergraduate students; 1,714 full-time matriculated graduate/professional students; 353 part-time matriculated graduate/professional students.

HIGHLIGHTS

Enrollment Profile

Full-time: N/R	International: N/R
Part-time: N/R	Women: N/R
Total: N/R	Minorities: N/R
Average Age: N/R	Average Class Size: N/R
Fall 1997 Average GPA: N/R	Fall 1997 Average GMAT: N/R

Costs
Full-time tuition: N/R
Part-time tuition: N/R

GRADUATE BUSINESS PROGRAMS
Master of Accounting (MAcc) Full-time, part-time.

MOT in Management Sciences (MOT) Full-time, part-time, distance learning option.

Master of Taxation (MTax) Full-time, part-time.

Masters of Finance in Accounting (MF) Full-time, part-time.

Master of Finance in Statistics (MF) Full-time, part-time.

Master of Finance in Economics (MF) Full-time, part-time.

ADMISSION
Application Requirements Application form, bachelor's degree (must be in field of business), 3 letters of recommendation, college transcript(s).

Recommended for Application GMAT score accepted, work experience.

University of Waterloo (continued)

Application Deadline Applications processed on a rolling/continuous basis for both domestic and international students.

ACADEMICS
Faculty Full-time 23; part-time 4.
Teaching Methodologies Case study, group discussion, lecture.

FINANCES
Costs for 1997–98 Cost varies by academic program.
Financial Aid Contact Student Awards, 200 University Avenue West, Waterloo. Phone: 519-888-3583.

FACILITIES
Information Resources Main library plus 2 additional on-campus libraries; total holdings of 2,800,000 volumes, 1,000,000 microforms, 11,349 current periodical subscriptions. CD player(s) available for graduate student use. Access provided to online bibliographic retrieval services.

INTERNATIONAL STUDENTS
Demographics N/R
Services and Facilities International student office, international student center, international student housing, visa services, ESL courses, counseling/support services.
Applying TOEFL required.
International Student Contact Darlene Bryans, 200 University Avenue West, Waterloo. Phone: 519-888-4567.

PLACEMENT
Services include job interviews arranged, job search course, and resume preparation.

Program Contact: 200 University Avenue West, Waterloo N2L 3G1, Canada. Phone: 519-888-4567.

The University of Western Ontario

Richard Ivey School of Business

London, Canada

OVERVIEW
The University of Western Ontario is a province-supported, coed institution. Enrollment: 27,000 graduate, professional, and undergraduate students; 2,500 full-time matriculated graduate/professional students; 2,500 part-time matriculated graduate/professional students. Founded: 1878. The graduate business unit is in a suburban setting and is on a Canadian standard year calendar.

HIGHLIGHTS

Enrollment Profile

Full-time: 450	International: 10%
Part-time: 0	Women: 25%
Total: 450	Minorities: N/R
Average Age: 28	Average Class Size: 70
Fall 1997 Average GPA: 3.0	Fall 1997 Average GMAT: 630

Costs
Full-time tuition: Can$12,000 per academic year (resident);
  Can$14,000 per academic year (nonresident)
Part-time tuition: N/R

The Ivey Business School has been repeatedly recognized as the best management school in Canada by *Canadian Business* and among the best in the world by *Asia Inc., Asian Business, Business Week, U.S. News & World Report,* and *The Journal of International Management.*

Students are trained by outstanding faculty members in a real-world case-method environment and have the most practical and effective business skills. Students acquire experience solving—as individuals, as team members, and as team leaders—challenges and problems of actual businesses around the world. Ivey faculty members and case writers travel worldwide to research actual enterprises whose situations are unique because of the inherent cultural and political climates.

The program is full-time only and is completed in two years. Using cases, role-playing, simulations, and negotiation exercises, it provides a two-year general management program with a global perspective. Opportunities for international experiences are available through student academic exchanges, overseas projects, and international case competitions. Ivey also offers undergraduate business, Executive M.B.A. (in Canada and Hong Kong), Videoconferencing Executive M.B.A., LL.B./M.B.A., and Ph.D. programs.

GRADUATE BUSINESS PROGRAMS
Master of Business Administration (MBA) Full-time; 18 total credits required; 20 months to complete program. Concentrations in accounting, asian business studies, banking, business information science, economics, entrepreneurship, european business studies, finance, human resources, management science, marketing, operations management, organizational behavior/development, production management, strategic management, taxation, international and area business studies.

ADMISSION
Applications For fall 1997 there were 900 applications for admission.
Application Requirements Application form, application fee, bachelor's degree, essay, minimum GPA: 2.7, personal statement, resume, college transcript(s), minimum of 2 years of work experience.
Recommended for Application GMAT score accepted: minimum 560, interview, letters of recommendation, computer experience.
Application Deadline Applications processed on a rolling/continuous basis for both domestic and international students. Application fee: Can$100. Deferred entrance is available.

ACADEMICS
Faculty Full-time 80.
Teaching Methodologies Case study, computer-aided instruction, computer simulations, experiential learning, faculty seminars, field projects, group discussion, lecture, research, role playing, seminars by members of the business community, simulations, student presentations, study groups, team projects.
Technology 30 on-campus computer terminals/PCs are available for student use and are linked by a campus-wide network. The network has full access to the Internet. Students are required to have their own PC.
Special Opportunities International exchange programs in Austria, Belgium, Denmark, France, Germany, Hong Kong, Italy, Mexico, Netherlands, Philippines, Republic of Korea, Republic of Singapore, Spain, Sweden, Switzerland. An internship program is available.

FINANCES
Costs for 1997–98 Tuition: Full-time: Can$12,000 per year (resident); Can$14,000 per year (nonresident). Average 1997–98 room and board costs were Can$6000 per academic year (on campus) and Can$6000 per academic year (off campus). Room and board costs vary by campus location, occupancy (e.g., single, double, triple), type of accommodation, type of meal plan.
Financial Aid In 1997–98, 22% of students received some institutionally administered aid in the form of scholarships, work study.
Financial Aid Contact Ms. Larysa Gamula, Admissions Office Director, 1151 Richmond Street North, London. Phone: 519-661-3212; Fax: 519-661-3431; E-mail: admiss@ivey.uwo.ca

FACILITIES
Information Resources Weldon Library plus 7 additional on-campus libraries; total holdings of 2,060,800 volumes, 2,860,000 microforms, 17,300 current periodical subscriptions. CD player(s) available for graduate student use. Access provided to online bibliographic retrieval services and online databases.

INTERNATIONAL STUDENTS
Demographics 10% of students enrolled are international students [Africa, 1%, Asia, 7%, Central America, 1%, Europe, 3%, North America, 85%, South America, 2%, other, 1%].
Services and Facilities International student office, international student center, visa services, ESL courses, counseling/support services.
Applying TOEFL: minimum score of 600, proof of adequate funds required. TSE, proof of health/immunizations recommended. Financial aid is available to international students.
International Student Contact Ms. Larysa Gamula, Admissions Director, 1151 Richmond Street North, Richard Ivey School of Business, London. Phone: 519-661-3212; Fax: 519-661-3431.

PLACEMENT
Services include alumni network, career counseling/planning, career fairs, career library, career placement, electronic job bank, job interviews arranged, job search course, resume referral to employers, and resume preparation. In 1996–97, 200 organizations participated in on-campus recruiting.
Employment Of 1996–97 graduates, 91% were employed within three months of graduation; the average starting salary was Can$70,910. Types of employment entered: accounting, banking, communications, computer-related, consulting, consumer products, education, energy, engineering, finance, financial services, government, health services, high technology, hospitality management, human resources, information systems/technology, insurance, international trade, law, management, manufacturing, marketing, media, nonprofit, petrochemical, pharmaceutical, service industry, telecommunications, transportation, utilities.

Business Program(s) URL: http://www.ivey.uwo.ca

Program Contact: Ms. Larysa Gamula, Admissions Director, Richard Ivey School of Business, 1151 Richmond Street North, London N6A 3K7, Canada. Phone: 519-661-3212; Fax: 519-661-3431.
See full description on page 1172.

University of Windsor

Faculty of Business Administration

Windsor, Canada

OVERVIEW
The University of Windsor is a province-supported, coed institution. Enrollment: 1,300 graduate, professional, and undergraduate students; 647 full-time matriculated graduate/professional students; 212 part-time matriculated graduate/professional students. Founded: 1964. The graduate business unit is in an urban setting and is on a trimester calendar.

HIGHLIGHTS

Enrollment Profile

Full-time: 123	International: 10%
Part-time: 61	Women: N/R
Total: 184	Minorities: N/R
Average Age: 25	Average Class Size: 35
Fall 1997 Average GPA: 3.3	Fall 1997 Average GMAT: 570

Costs
Full-time tuition: Can$4250 per academic year (resident); Can$8250 per academic year (nonresident)
Part-time tuition: Can$707 per term (resident); Can$1375 per term (nonresident)

GRADUATE BUSINESS PROGRAMS
Master of Business Administration (MBA) Full-time, part-time; 12 months to 6 years to complete program.
Master of Business Administration Co-op (MBA) Full-time; 2 years to complete program.
Master of Business Administration/Bachelor of Laws (MBA/LLB) Full-time; 4 years to complete program.

ADMISSION
Applications For fall 1997 there were 550 applications for admission.
Application Requirements Application form, application fee, bachelor's degree, minimum GPA: 3.0, letter of recommendation, resume, college transcript(s).
Recommended for Application GMAT score accepted: minimum 500, essay, interview, work experience.
Application Deadline Applications processed on a rolling/continuous basis for both domestic and international students. Application fee: $50. Deferred entrance is available.

ACADEMICS
Faculty Full-time 36.
Teaching Methodologies Case study, computer-aided instruction, computer analysis, computer simulations, experiential learning, faculty seminars, group discussion, lecture, research, seminars by members of the business community, simulations, student presentations, study groups, team projects.
Technology 250 on-campus computer terminals/PCs are available for student use and are linked by a campus-wide network. The network has full access to the Internet. Students are not required to have their own PC.
Special Opportunities Advanced credit may be earned through transfer of credits from another institution. International exchange programs in France, Germany, Italy, Japan, Spain, United Kingdom. An internship program is available.

FINANCES
Costs for 1997–98 Tuition: Full-time: Can$4250 per year (resident); Can$8250 per year (nonresident). Part-time: Can$707 per term (resident); Can$1375 per term (nonresident). Cost varies by academic program, number of credits taken. Fees: Full-time: Can$125 per academic year (resident); Can$220 per academic year (nonresident). Part-time: Can$30 per term (resident); Can$75 per term (nonresident). Average 1997–98 room and board costs were Can$4500 per academic year (on campus) and Can$3500 per academic year (off campus). Room and board costs vary by occupancy (e.g., single, double, triple), type of accommodation, type of meal plan.
Financial Aid Teaching assistantships, work study available. Application Deadline: 2/15.
Financial Aid Contact Mr. Orv Houser, Director of Awards, Awards and Financial Aid, 401 Sunset Avenue, Windsor. Phone: 519-253-4232 Ext. 3311; Fax: 519-973-7046; E-mail: oscar@uwindsor.ca

FACILITIES
Information Resources Leddy Library plus 1 additional on-campus library; total holdings of 2,340,251 volumes, 1,100,000 microforms, 8,900 current periodical subscriptions. CD player(s) available for graduate student use. Access provided to online bibliographic retrieval services.

INTERNATIONAL STUDENTS
Demographics 10% of students enrolled are international students.
Services and Facilities International student office, international student center, international student housing, visa services, counseling/support services.
Applying TOEFL: minimum score of 600, proof of adequate funds, proof of health/immunizations required. Financial aid is not available to international students.
International Student Contact Mr. Richard Lanspeary, International Students Advisor, 401 Sunset Avenue, Windsor. Phone: 519-253-4232 Ext. 3901; Fax: 519-973-7046; E-mail: lanspea@uwindsor.ca

PLACEMENT
Services include alumni network, career counseling/planning, career fairs, career library, career placement, electronic job bank, job interviews arranged, job search course, resume referral to employers, and resume preparation. In 1996–97, 19 organizations participated in on-campus recruiting; 19 on-campus interviews were conducted.
Employment Of 1996–97 graduates, 65% were employed within three months of graduation; the average starting salary was Can$38,500. Types of employment entered: banking, chemical industry, communications, computer-related, consulting, consumer products, energy, finance, financial services, government, health services, high technology, hospitality management, human resources, information systems/technology, insurance, law, management, manufacturing, marketing, media, mining, nonprofit, pharmaceutical, real estate, service industry, telecommunications, transportation, utilities.
Business Program(s) URL: http://www.uwindsor.ca/faculty/busad/newbusgrad.html

Program Contact: Mr. Michael Houston, Assistant to Dean, Faculty of Business Administration, 401 Sunset Avenue, Windsor N9B 3P4, Canada. Phone: 519-253-4232 Ext. 3097; Fax: 519-973-7073; E-mail: mikeh@uwindsor.ca

Wilfrid Laurier University

School of Business and Economics

Waterloo, Canada

OVERVIEW
Wilfrid Laurier University is a province-supported, coed institution. Enrollment: 5,800 graduate, professional, and undergraduate students; 475 full-time matriculated graduate/professional students; 395 part-time matriculated graduate/professional students. Founded: 1911. The graduate business unit is in an urban setting and is on a semester calendar.

HIGHLIGHTS

Enrollment Profile

Full-time: 76	International: 2%
Part-time: 212	Women: 41%
Total: 288	Minorities: N/R
Average Age: 33	Average Class Size: 45
Fall 1997 Average GPA: 9.0	Fall 1997 Average GMAT: 590

Costs
Full-time tuition: Can$4860 per academic year (resident); Can$10,500 per academic year (nonresident)
Part-time tuition: Can$876 per term (resident)

GRADUATE BUSINESS PROGRAMS
Master of Business Administration (MBA) Full-time, part-time; 12 months to 5 years to complete program.
Master of Arts in Business Economics (MA) Full-time; 12 to 18 months to complete program.
Community-Based MBA (MBA) Part-time; 3.3 to 4 years to complete program.

ADMISSION
Applications For fall 1997 there were 515 applications for admission. Of those applying, 250 were accepted. Of those accepted, 226 enrolled.
Application Requirements Application form, application fee, bachelor's degree, GPA: minimum 8.0 on a 12 scale, 3 letters of recommendation, personal statement, resume, college transcript(s), minimum of 2 years of work experience.
Recommended for Application GMAT score accepted: minimum 550, essay, computer experience.

Wilfrid Laurier University (continued)

Application Deadline 5/1 for fall, 5/1 for fall (international). Application fee: Can$100.

ACADEMICS

Faculty Full-time 15.

Teaching Methodologies Case study, computer-aided instruction, computer analysis, computer simulations, experiential learning, faculty seminars, field projects, group discussion, lecture, research, role playing, seminars by members of the business community, simulations, student presentations, study groups, team projects.

Technology 245 on-campus computer terminals/PCs are available for student use and are linked by a campus-wide network. The network has full access to the Internet. Students are not required to have their own PC.

Special Opportunities Advanced credit may be earned through transfer of credits from another institution. International exchange program in all continents.

FINANCES

Costs for 1997–98 Tuition: Full-time: Can$4860 per year (resident); Can$10,500 per year (nonresident). Part-time: Can$876 per term (resident). Cost varies by academic program, campus location, number of credits taken. Fees: Full-time: Can$580 per academic year (resident); Can$580 per academic year (nonresident). Part-time: Can$500 per term. Fees vary by academic program, campus location, number of credits taken. Average 1997–98 room and board costs were Can$8100 per academic year (on campus) and Can$8400 per academic year (off campus). Room and board costs vary by occupancy (e.g., single, double, triple), type of accommodation, type of meal plan.

Financial Aid In 1997–98, 35% of students received some institutionally administered aid in the form of fellowships, research assistantships, teaching assistantships, scholarships, loans. Financial aid is available to part-time students. Application Deadline: 11/1.

Financial Aid Contact Pauline Delion, Director of Student Awards, 75 University Avenue West, Waterloo. Phone: 519-884-0710 Ext. 4256; Fax: 519-886-6978; E-mail: pdelion@mach2.wlu.ca

FACILITIES

Information Resources Wilfrid Laurier Library; total holdings of 435,000 volumes, 425,000 microforms. CD player(s) available for graduate student use. Access provided to online bibliographic retrieval services and online databases.

INTERNATIONAL STUDENTS

Demographics 2% of students enrolled are international students [Asia, 7%, Central America, 1%, North America, 92%].

Services and Facilities International student office, international student center, international student housing, visa services, counseling/support services.

Applying TOEFL: minimum score of 550 required. Financial aid is available to international students.

International Student Contact Dr. Alex Murray, Acting Director of Laurier International, 75 University Avenue West, Waterloo. Phone: 519-884-0710 Ext. 6704; Fax: 519-884-8853; E-mail: amurray@mach1.wlu.ca

PLACEMENT

Services include alumni network, career counseling/planning, career fairs, career library, career placement, electronic job bank, job interviews arranged, job search course, resume referral to employers, and resume preparation. In 1996–97, 49 organizations participated in on-campus recruiting.

Employment Of 1996–97 graduates, 90% were employed within three months of graduation; the average starting salary was Can$58,800. Types of employment entered: accounting, banking, chemical industry, communications, computer-related, consulting, consumer products, education, energy, engineering, finance, financial services, government, health services, high technology, hospitality management, human resources, information systems/technology, insurance, international trade, law, management, manufacturing, marketing, media, mining, nonprofit, petrochemical, pharmaceutical, real estate, retail, service industry, telecommunications, transportation, utilities.

Business Program(s) URL: http://www.wlu.ca/~wwwsbe

Program Contact: Dianne Hotson, Administrator, 75 University Avenue West, Waterloo N2L 3C5, Canada. Phone: 519-884-0710 Ext. 2544; Fax: 519-886-6978; E-mail: wlumba@wlu.ca

See full description on page 1194.

York University

Schulich School of Business

Toronto, Canada

OVERVIEW

York University is a province-supported, coed institution. Enrollment: 40,000 graduate, professional, and undergraduate students; 2,201 full-time matriculated graduate/professional students; 1,333 part-time matriculated graduate/professional students. Founded: 1959. The graduate business unit is in a suburban setting and is on a trimester calendar.

HIGHLIGHTS

Enrollment Profile

Full-time: N/R	International: N/R
Part-time: N/R	Women: N/R
Total: 1,500	Minorities: N/R
Average Age: 29	Average Class Size: 38
Fall 1997 Average GPA: 3.2	Fall 1997 Average GMAT: 615

Costs

Full-time tuition: Can$2150 per academic year (resident); Can$8650 per academic year (nonresident)

Part-time tuition: Can$1100 per term (resident); Can$4300 per term (nonresident)

Degree(s) offered in conjunction with Université Laval, E. M. Lyon

GRADUATE BUSINESS PROGRAMS

Master of Business Administration (MBA) Full-time, part-time; 60 total credits required; 8 months to 6 years to complete program. Concentrations in accounting, arts administration/management, strategic management, business ethics, real estate, economics, entrepreneurship, finance, financial management/planning, organizational behavior/development, information management, international and area business studies, international business, public management, management information systems, management science, marketing, nonprofit management.

Master of Business Administration/Bachelor of Laws (MBA/LLB) Full-time; 122 total credits required; 6 years to complete program. Concentrations in accounting, arts administration/management, strategic management, business ethics, real estate, economics, entrepreneurship, finance, financial management/planning, organizational behavior/development, information management, international and area business studies, international business, public management, management science, marketing, nonprofit management, management information systems.

International Master of Business Administration (IMBA) Full-time; 72 total credits required; 2 years to complete program. Concentrations in accounting, arts administration/management, strategic management, business ethics, real estate, economics, entrepreneurship, finance, financial management/planning, organizational behavior/development, information management, international and area business studies, international business, public management, management science, marketing, nonprofit management, japanese business studies, international trade, international management, international finance, international banking, management information systems.

Master of Public Administration (MPA) Full-time, part-time; 60 total credits required; 12 months to 6 years to complete program. Concentrations in public and private management, public management, public policy and administration, accounting, strategic management, business ethics, real estate, economics, entrepreneurship, finance, financial management/planning, organizational behavior/development, information management, international business, marketing research, management information systems, marketing, nonprofit management, management science, strategic management.

ADMISSION

Application Requirements GMAT score, application form, application fee, bachelor's degree, essay, minimum GPA: 3.0, 2 letters of recommendation, personal statement, resume, college transcript(s).

Recommended for Application Minimum of 2 years of work experience, computer experience.

Application Deadline 5/1 for fall, 10/15 for winter, 5/1 for fall (international), 10/15 for winter (international). Application fee: Can$300. Deferred entrance is available.

ACADEMICS

Faculty Full-time 78; part-time 90.

Teaching Methodologies Case study, computer-aided instruction, computer analysis, computer simulations, experiential learning, faculty seminars, field projects, group discussion, lecture, research, role playing, seminars by members of the business community, simulations, student presentations, study groups, team projects.

Technology 50 on-campus computer terminals/PCs are available for student use. The network has full access to the Internet. Students are required to have their own PC.

Special Opportunities Advanced credit may be earned through credit by examination, transfer of credits from another institution. International exchange programs in Australia and various countries in Asia, Europe, and South America. An internship program is available.

FINANCES
Costs for 1997–98 Tuition: Full-time: Can$2150 per term (resident); Can$8650 per term (nonresident). Part-time: Can$1100 per term (resident); Can$4300 per term (nonresident). Fees: Can$186 per term (resident); Can$186 per term (nonresident). Fees vary by number of credits taken. Average 1997–98 room only costs were Can$5200 per academic year. Room and board costs vary by occupancy (e.g., single, double, triple), type of accommodation.

Financial Aid Fellowships, research assistantships, teaching assistantships, grants, scholarships, loans available. Application Deadline: 6/1.

Financial Aid Contact Ms. Charmaine Courtis, Director, Student Affairs and International Relations, Schulich School of Business, 4700 Keele Street, North York. Phone: 416-736-5059; Fax: 416-736-5687; E-mail: ccourtis@bus. yorku.ca

FACILITIES
Information Resources Scott Library plus 4 additional on-campus libraries; total holdings of 2,129,555 volumes, 2,800,000 microforms, 1,100 current periodical subscriptions. CD player(s) available for graduate student use. Access provided to online bibliographic retrieval services.

INTERNATIONAL STUDENTS
Demographics N/R

Services and Facilities International student office, international student center, international student housing, visa services, ESL courses, counseling/support services.

Applying IELT, TOEFL: minimum score of 600 required. Proof of adequate funds recommended. Financial aid is not available to international students.

International Student Contact Ms. Charmaine Courtis, Director, Student Affairs and International Relations, Schulich School of Business, 4700 Keele Street, North York. Phone: 416-736-5059; Fax: 416-736-5762; E-mail: ccourtis@ bus.yorku.ca

PLACEMENT
Services include alumni network, career counseling/planning, career fairs, career library, career placement, electronic job bank, job interviews arranged, job search course, resume referral to employers, and resume preparation. In 1996–97, 2,000 organizations participated in on-campus recruiting.

Employment Of 1996–97 graduates, 90% were employed within three months of graduation; the average starting salary was Can$69,000. Types of employment entered: accounting, banking, communications, computer-related, consulting, consumer products, finance, financial services, government, high technology, human resources, information systems/technology, insurance, international trade, management, manufacturing, marketing, media, mining, nonprofit, pharmaceutical, real estate, retail, service industry, telecommunications, transportation, utilities.

Business Program(s) URL: http://www.bus.yorku.ca

Program Contact: Ms. Carol Pattenden, Assistant Director, Admissions, Schulich School of Business, 4700 Keele Street, North York M3J 1P3, Canada. Phone: 416-736-5060; Fax: 416-736-5687; E-mail: cpattend@bus.yorku.ca
See full description on page 1206.

CAYMAN ISLANDS

International College of the Cayman Islands

Graduate Studies Program

Newlands, Grand Cayman, Cayman Islands

OVERVIEW
International College of the Cayman Islands is an independent-nonprofit, coed institution. Enrollment: 428 graduate, professional, and undergraduate students; 26 full-time matriculated graduate/professional students; 13 part-time matriculated graduate/professional students. Founded: 1970. The graduate business unit is in a small-town setting and is on a quarter calendar.

HIGHLIGHTS

Enrollment Profile
Full-time: 26
Part-time: 13
Total: 39
Average Age: 34
Fall 1997 Average GPA: N/R

International: 72%
Women: 56%
Minorities: N/R
Average Class Size: 15
Fall 1997 Average GMAT: N/R

Costs
Full-time tuition: $3000 per academic year
Part-time tuition: $100 per quarter credit

GRADUATE BUSINESS PROGRAMS
Master of Business Administration (MBA) Full-time, part-time; 60 total credits required; minimum of 18 months to complete program.

Master of Science in Management (MS) Full-time, part-time; 60 total credits required; minimum of 18 months to complete program. Concentrations in human resources, business education.

ADMISSION
Application Requirements Application form, application fee, bachelor's degree, 3 letters of recommendation, college transcript(s).

Recommended for Application GMAT score accepted, work experience.

Application Deadline Applications processed on a rolling/continuous basis for domestic students only. 6/15 for fall (international), 10/1 for winter (international), 1/1 for spring (international), 3/15 for summer (international). Application fee: $38. Deferred entrance is available.

ACADEMICS
Faculty Full-time 6; part-time 3.

Teaching Methodologies Case study, experiential learning, faculty seminars, field projects, group discussion, lecture, research, role playing, seminars by members of the business community, student presentations, study groups, team projects.

Technology 15 on-campus computer terminals/PCs are available for student use. The network has full access to the Internet. Students are not required to have their own PC.

Special Opportunities Advanced credit may be earned through credit by examination, transfer of credits from another institution. An internship program is available.

FINANCES
Costs for 1997–98 Tuition: Full-time: $3000 per year. Part-time: $100 per quarter credit. Cost varies by number of credits taken. Fees: Full-time: $450 per academic year. Average 1997–98 room only costs were $2438 per academic year. Room and board costs vary by occupancy (e.g., single, double, triple).

Financial Aid In 1997–98, 3% of students received some institutionally administered aid in the form of work study.

Financial Aid Contact Mrs. Maria Leggatt, Admissions Representative, PO Box 136 , Savannah Post Office, Newlands, Grand Cayman, Cayman Islands. Phone: 809-947-1100; Fax: 809-947-1210.

FACILITIES
Information Resources Main library; total holdings of 16,000 volumes, 1,200 microforms, 115 current periodical subscriptions. CD player(s) available for graduate student use.

INTERNATIONAL STUDENTS
Demographics 72% of students enrolled are international students [Asia, 3%, Central America, 3%, Europe, 8%, North America, 23%, South America, 10%, other, 53%].

Services and Facilities International student housing, ESL courses, counseling/support services.

Applying TOEFL required. Financial aid is available to international students.

PLACEMENT
Services include alumni network, career counseling/planning, career library, and resume referral to employers.

Program Contact: Dr. Eileen Dounce, Director of Graduate Studies, PO Box 136, Savannah Post Office, Newlands, Grand Cayman, Cayman Islands. Phone: 345-947-1100; Fax: 345-947-1210.

CHINA

COSTA RICA

Fudan University

School of Management

Shanghai, China

OVERVIEW
Fudan University is a publicly supported, primarily male institution. Enrollment: full-time matriculated graduate/professional students; 620 part-time matriculated graduate/professional students. Founded: 1905. The graduate business unit is in an urban setting and is on a semester calendar.

HIGHLIGHTS

Enrollment Profile

Full-time: 0	International: N/R
Part-time: 620	Women: 27%
Total: 620	Minorities: N/R
Average Age: 32	Average Class Size: 50
Fall 1997 Average GPA: N/R	Fall 1997 Average GMAT: N/R

Costs
Full-time tuition: N/R
Part-time tuition: N/R

GRADUATE BUSINESS PROGRAMS
Master of Business Administration (MBA)

ADMISSION
Applications For fall 1997 there were 1,479 applications for admission. Of those applying, 210 were accepted. Of those accepted, 210 enrolled.
Application Requirements Application form, bachelor's degree, interview, 2 letters of recommendation, work experience.
Recommended for Application Essay.

ACADEMICS
Faculty Full-time 111.
Teaching Methodologies Case study, computer-aided instruction, experiential learning, faculty seminars, field projects, group discussion, lecture, research, role playing, student presentations, study groups, team projects.
Technology 100 on-campus computer terminals/PCs are available for student use and are linked by a campus-wide network. The network has partial access to the Internet. Students are not required to have their own PC.
Special Opportunities Advanced credit may be earned through credit by examination. An internship program is available.

FACILITIES
Information Resources Fudan University Library; total holdings of 3,500,000 volumes, 5,200 current periodical subscriptions.

INTERNATIONAL STUDENTS
Demographics N/R

PLACEMENT
Services include alumni network, and career fairs.
Employment Of 1996–97 graduates, 100% were employed within three months of graduation; the average starting salary was 30,000 Chinese yen. Types of employment entered: accounting, banking, chemical industry, communications, computer-related, consulting, consumer products, education, energy, engineering, finance, financial services, government, health services, high technology, hospitality management, human resources, information systems/technology, insurance, international trade, law, management, manufacturing, media, petrochemical, pharmaceutical, real estate, retail, service industry, telecommunications, transportation, utilities.

Business Program(s) URL: http://www.fudan.sh.cn/manage/et1.html

Program Contact: 220 Handan Road, Shanghai 200433, China. Phone: 86-21-549 2222; Fax: 86-21-549 1875.

INCAE (Instituto Centroamericano de Administración de Empresas)

Graduate Program

La Garita, Alajuela, Costa Rica

OVERVIEW
INCAE (Instituto Centroamericano de Administración de Empresas) is an independent-nonprofit, coed institution. Enrollment: 441 graduate, professional, and undergraduate students; 355 full-time matriculated graduate/professional students; 86 part-time matriculated graduate/professional students. Founded: 1964. The graduate business unit is in a suburban setting and is on a trimester calendar.

HIGHLIGHTS

Enrollment Profile

Full-time: 355	International: N/R
Part-time: 86	Women: 30%
Total: 441	Minorities: N/R
Average Age: 28	Average Class Size: 15
Fall 1997 Average GPA: N/R	Fall 1997 Average GMAT: 550

Costs
Full-time tuition: $11,500 per academic year
Part-time tuition: N/R

GRADUATE BUSINESS PROGRAMS
Master of Business Administration (MBA) Full-time, part-time; up to 2 years to complete program. Concentrations in economics, management, technology management, resources management.
Master of Business Economics (MBE) Full-time, part-time; up to 2 years to complete program. Concentrations in economics, management.

ADMISSION
Applications For fall 1997 there were 530 applications for admission. Of those applying, 319 were accepted. Of those accepted, 117 enrolled.
Application Requirements GMAT score: minimum 550, GRE score, application form, application fee, bachelor's degree, essay, 3 letters of recommendation, personal statement, resume, college transcript(s), minimum of 2 years of work experience.
Recommended for Application Interview.
Application Deadline 7/15 for fall, 7/15 for fall (international). Application fee: $50. Deferred entrance is available.

ACADEMICS
Faculty Full-time 31.
Teaching Methodologies Case study, computer-aided instruction, computer simulations, faculty seminars, field projects, group discussion, lecture, simulations, student presentations, study groups, team projects.
Technology 16 on-campus computer terminals/PCs are available for student use and are linked by a campus-wide network. The network has full access to the Internet. Students are not required to have their own PC.
Special Opportunities International exchange programs in Germany, Spain, United States.

FINANCES
Costs for 1997–98 Tuition: Full-time: $11,500 per year. Cost varies by academic program, campus location. Average 1997–98 room and board costs were $2937 per academic year.
Financial Aid In 1997–98, 3% of students received some institutionally administered aid in the form of grants, scholarships, loans. Application Deadline: 6/16.
Financial Aid Contact Dr. Roberto Artavia, Dean, Apartado Postal 960-4050, La Garita, Alajuela, Costa Rica. Phone: 50-6-443-0506; E-mail: mercadeo@mail.incae.ac.cr

FACILITIES
Information Resources Campus Library plus 2 additional on-campus libraries; total holdings of 40,000 volumes, 900 current periodical subscriptions. CD player(s) available for graduate student use. Access provided to online bibliographic retrieval services.

INTERNATIONAL STUDENTS
Demographics N/R
Applying Financial aid is available to international students.

PLACEMENT

Services include alumni network, career counseling/planning, career fairs, career placement, electronic job bank, job interviews arranged, job search course, resume referral to employers, and resume preparation. In 1996–97, 400 organizations participated in on-campus recruiting.

Employment Of 1996–97 graduates, 60% were employed within three months of graduation; the average starting salary was $53,000. Types of employment entered: accounting, banking, communications, computer-related, consulting, consumer products, engineering, finance, financial services, high technology, human resources, information systems/technology, international trade, management, manufacturing, marketing, nonprofit, pharmaceutical, service industry, telecommunications, transportation.

Business Program(s) URL: http://www.incae.ac.cr

Program Contact: Dr. Roberto Artavia, Dean, Apartado Postal 960-4050, La Garita, Alajuela, Costa Rica. Phone: 50-6-443-0506; Fax: 50-6-433-9555; E-mail: mercadeo@mail.incae.ac.cr

CZECH REPUBLIC

Czech Management Center

Graduate School of Business

Celákovice, Czech Republic

OVERVIEW

Czech Management Center coed institution. Founded: 1990. The graduate business unit is in a small-town setting and is on a semester calendar.

HIGHLIGHTS

Enrollment Profile

Full-time: N/R	International: N/R
Part-time: N/R	Women: 27%
Total: 30	Minorities: N/R
Average Age: 28	Average Class Size: 25
Fall 1997 Average GPA: N/R	Fall 1997 Average GMAT: 544

Costs
Full-time tuition: N/R
Part-time tuition: N/R

Degree(s) offered in conjunction with University of Arizona, Tulane University, Université Laval, University of Manitoba, University of Pittsburgh, University of Toronto, University of Windsor, Wilfrid Laurier University

GRADUATE BUSINESS PROGRAMS

Full-time MBA (MBA) Full-time, part-time; 51 total credits required; 12 months to 2 years to complete program. Concentrations in management, international and area business studies, finance.

Executive MBA (EMBA) Part-time; 51 total credits required; minimum of 2.5 years to complete program. Concentrations in management, international and area business studies, finance.

ADMISSION

Application Requirements GMAT score: minimum 500, application form, application fee, bachelor's degree, essay, minimum GPA: 3.0, letter of recommendation, resume, college transcript(s), minimum of 2 years of work experience.

Recommended for Application Interview, computer experience.

Application Deadline 12/1 for winter, 11/1 for winter (international). Application fee: 500 Czech koruna, 35 Czech koruna (international). Deferred entrance is available.

ACADEMICS

Faculty Full-time 10; part-time 15.

Teaching Methodologies Case study, computer-aided instruction, computer simulations, faculty seminars, field projects, group discussion, lecture, role playing, seminars by members of the business community, simulations, student presentations, study groups, team projects.

Technology 30 on-campus computer terminals/PCs are available for student use and are linked by a campus-wide network. The network has full access to the Internet. Students are not required to have their own PC.

Special Opportunities Advanced credit may be earned through credit by examination, transfer of credits from another institution. International exchange programs in Canada, Denmark, Italy, United Kingdom, United States. An internship program is available.

FINANCES

Costs for 1997–98 Cost varies by academic program, class time (e.g., day/evening), number of credits taken, reciprocity agreements. Average 1997–98 room and board costs were $1700 per academic year.

Financial Aid In 1997–98, 57% of students received some institutionally administered aid in the form of scholarships, loans. Financial aid is available to part-time students. Application Deadline: 10/31.

Financial Aid Contact Mr. Stephen Schackwitz, Manager, Graduate Programs, Czech Management Center, MBA Office, námestí 5, kvetna 2, Celákovice. Phone: 420-202-89 21 51; Fax: 420-202-89 19 97; E-mail: schack@cmc.cz

FACILITIES

Information Resources CMC Management Library; total holdings of 7,000 volumes, 70 current periodical subscriptions. CD player(s) available for graduate student use. Access provided to online bibliographic retrieval services and online databases.

INTERNATIONAL STUDENTS

Demographics N/R

Services and Facilities International student office, international student housing, visa services, ESL courses.

Applying TOEFL required. Financial aid is available to international students.

International Student Contact MBA Office, námestí 5, kvetna 2, Celákovice. Phone: 420-202-89 21 51; Fax: 420-202-89 21 50.

PLACEMENT

Services include alumni network, career counseling/planning, career fairs, career placement, job interviews arranged, resume referral to employers, and resume preparation. In 1996–97, 46 organizations participated in on-campus recruiting; 420 on-campus interviews were conducted.

Employment Of 1996–97 graduates, 90% were employed within three months of graduation; the average starting salary was 564,000 Czech koruna. Types of employment entered: accounting, banking, communications, computer-related, consulting, consumer products, education, engineering, finance, financial services, government, human resources, information systems/technology, international trade, management, manufacturing, marketing, petrochemical, pharmaceutical, real estate, retail, service industry, telecommunications.

Business Program(s) URL: http://www.cmc.cz/

Program Contact: MBA Office, námestí 5, kvetna 2, Celákovice 250 88, Czech Republic. Phone: 420-202-89 21 51; Fax: 420-202-89 21 50; E-mail: info@cmc.cz

DENMARK

Copenhagen Business School

Faculty of Economics and Business Administration

Copenhagen N, Denmark

OVERVIEW

Copenhagen Business School is a publicly supported, coed institution. Enrollment: 13,651 graduate, professional, and undergraduate students. Founded: 1917. The graduate business unit is in an urban setting and is on a semester calendar.

HIGHLIGHTS

Enrollment Profile

Full-time: N/R	International: N/R
Part-time: N/R	Women: N/R
Total: 3,164	Minorities: N/R
Average Age: N/R	Average Class Size: 30
Fall 1997 Average GPA: N/R	Fall 1997 Average GMAT: N/R

Costs
Full-time tuition: N/R
Part-time tuition: N/R

Copenhagen Business School (continued)

Degree(s) offered in conjunction with Denmark School of Design

GRADUATE BUSINESS PROGRAMS

Master of Science in Economics and Business Administration (MS) Full-time; 2 to 5.8 years to complete program. Concentrations in economics, finance, human resources, international business, international management, international marketing, organizational behavior/development, technology management, strategic management, international logistics.

Master of Science in Business Economics and Auditing (MS) Full-time; proficiency in Danish required; 2 to 5.8 years to complete program. Concentrations in taxation, accounting, business law.

Master of Science in Business Administration and Computer Science (MS) Full-time; proficiency in Danish required; 2 to 5.8 years to complete program. Concentrations in information management, organizational behavior/development, project management, economics, management information systems.

Master of Science in Business Administration and Commercial Law (MS) Full-time; proficiency in Danish required; 2 to 5.8 years to complete program. Concentrations in business law, economics, finance, taxation, organizational behavior/development.

Master of Science in Business Administration and Management Science (MS) Full-time; proficiency in Danish required; 2 to 5.8 years to complete program. Concentrations in management science, economics, finance, management systems analysis, quantitative analysis, marketing research.

Master of Science in Business Administration and Modern Language (MS) Full-time; proficiency in Danish and German or French or Spanish or Russian required; 2 to 5.8 years to complete program. Concentrations in international business, international and area business studies, international management, developmental economics.

Master of Science in Business Administration and Japanese Language and Culture (MS) Full-time; proficiency in Danish and Japanese required; 2 to 5.8 years to complete program. Concentrations in asian business studies, japanese business studies, international business, international management.

Master of Business Administration (MBA) Part-time; minimum of 3 years relevant full-time work experience and proficiency in Danish required; 2 years to complete program. Concentrations in management, international business, finance, strategic management, international management, logistics, organizational management, marketing.

Master of Public Administration (MPA) Part-time; minimum of 5 years relevant full-time work experience and proficiency in Danish required; 2 years to complete program. Concentrations in economics, public management, public policy and administration, management, strategic management, organizational behavior/development.

ADMISSION

Application Requirements Application form, bachelor's degree, resume, college transcript(s).

Recommended for Application Computer experience.

Application Deadline 6/1 for fall, 12/1 for spring, 6/1 for fall (international), 6/1 for spring (international). Deferred entrance is available.

ACADEMICS

Faculty Full-time 221; part-time 920.

Teaching Methodologies Case study, computer-aided instruction, computer analysis, computer simulations, experiential learning, faculty seminars, field projects, group discussion, lecture, research, role playing, seminars by members of the business community, simulations, student presentations, study groups, team projects.

Technology 500 on-campus computer terminals/PCs are available for student use and are linked by a campus-wide network. The network has full access to the Internet. Students are not required to have their own PC.

Special Opportunities Advanced credit may be earned through transfer of credits from another institution. International exchange program in approximately 250 business schools and universities worldwide. An internship program is available.

FINANCES

Costs for 1997–98 Average 1997–98 room only costs were 45,000 Danish kroner per academic year (off campus). Room and board costs vary by type of accommodation, type of meal plan.

Financial Aid Grants available.

FACILITIES

Information Resources Copenhagen Business School Library plus 1 additional on-campus library; total holdings of 183,800 volumes, 20,755 current periodical subscriptions. CD player(s) available for graduate student use. Access provided to online bibliographic retrieval services and online databases.

INTERNATIONAL STUDENTS

Demographics N/R

Services and Facilities International student office, international student center, international student housing, counseling/support services.

Applying TOEFL: minimum score of 575 required. Financial aid is available to international students.

International Student Contact Ms. Robin Jensen, Head of International Office, Dalgas Have 15, DK 2000, Fredericksburg. Phone: 45-3815-3006; Fax: 45-3815-3825; E-mail: reception.intoff@cbs.dk

PLACEMENT

Services include electronic job bank, and job search course.

Employment Of 1996–97 graduates, 100% were employed within three months of graduation. Types of employment entered: accounting, banking, communications, computer-related, consulting, consumer products, education, finance, financial services, government, high technology, human resources, information systems/technology, insurance, international trade, law, management, manufacturing, marketing, media, nonprofit, real estate, retail, service industry, telecommunications, transportation.

Business Program(s) URL: http://www.cbs.dk

Program Contact: Admissions Office, 7-9 Struenseegade, DK 2200, Copenhagen N, Denmark. Phone: 45-3815-2710; Fax: 45-3815-3825; E-mail: cm.oefak@cbs.dk

EGYPT

American University in Cairo

School of Business, Economics and Communication

Cairo, Egypt

OVERVIEW

American University in Cairo is an independent-nonprofit, coed institution. Enrollment: 4,500 graduate, professional, and undergraduate students. Founded: 1919. The graduate business unit is in an urban setting and is on a trimester calendar.

HIGHLIGHTS

Enrollment Profile

Full-time: N/R	International: N/R
Part-time: N/R	Women: N/R
Total: N/R	Minorities: N/R
Average Age: 33	Average Class Size: 22
Fall 1997 Average GPA: N/R	Fall 1997 Average GMAT: 600

Costs
Full-time tuition: N/R
Part-time tuition: N/R

GRADUATE BUSINESS PROGRAMS

Master of Business Administration (MBA) Full-time, part-time; 48 total credits required; 2 to 7 years to complete program. Concentrations in management, business law, strategic management, international banking, international trade.

Master of Public Administration (MPA) Full-time, part-time; 48 total credits required; 18 months to 7 years to complete program.

Program in Economics (MA) 27 total credits required; minimum of 18 months to complete program.

ADMISSION

Application Requirements Application form, application fee, bachelor's degree, minimum GPA: 3.0, 2 letters of recommendation, personal statement, resume, college transcript(s), minimum of 2 years of work experience.

Recommended for Application GMAT score accepted: minimum 600, GRE score accepted, computer experience.

Application Deadline 3/31 for fall, 11/1 for spring. Application fee: $35.

ACADEMICS

Faculty Full-time 21; part-time 20.

Teaching Methodologies Case study, lecture, role playing, seminars by members of the business community, simulations, team projects.

FINANCES

Costs for 1997–98 Cost varies by number of credits taken. Average 1997–98 room only costs were $2000 per academic year (on campus) and $1200 per academic year (off campus). Room and board costs vary by occupancy (e.g., single, double, triple).

Financial Aid Fellowships, research assistantships, teaching assistantships, scholarships, work study available.

FACILITIES
Information Resources AUC Library plus 1 additional on-campus library; total holdings of 266,000 volumes, 24,000 microforms, 2,400 current periodical subscriptions. CD player(s) available for graduate student use.

INTERNATIONAL STUDENTS
Demographics N/R

Applying TOEFL: minimum score of 550, proof of adequate funds, proof of health/immunizations required.

PLACEMENT
Services include alumni network, career counseling/planning, career library, resume referral to employers, and resume preparation.

Business Program(s) URL: http://auc-acs.eun.eg/

Program Contact: Office of Student Affairs, 420 Fifth Avenue, Third Floor, New York 10018-2729, Egypt. Phone: 212-730-8800; Fax: 212-730-1600; E-mail: aucegypt@aucnyo.edu

FINLAND

Helsinki School of Economics and Business Administration

International Center

Helsinki, Finland

OVERVIEW
Helsinki School of Economics and Business Administration is a publicly supported, coed institution. Enrollment: 4,500 graduate, professional, and undergraduate students; 1,200 full-time matriculated graduate/professional students; 500 part-time matriculated graduate/professional students. Founded: 1904. The graduate business unit is in an urban setting and is on a year calendar.

HIGHLIGHTS

Enrollment Profile

Full-time: N/R	International: N/R
Part-time: N/R	Women: N/R
Total: 170	Minorities: N/R
Average Age: 29	Average Class Size: 30
Fall 1997 Average GPA: N/R	Fall 1997 Average GMAT: 570

Costs
Full-time tuition: N/R
Part-time tuition: $18,500 per program (resident); $18,500 per program (nonresident)

GRADUATE BUSINESS PROGRAMS
International MBA (MBA) Full-time; 75 total credits required; 18 months to 4 years to complete program. Concentrations in international business, international management, finance, technology management.

Executive MBA (EMBA) Part-time; 42 total credits required; 12 months to 4 years to complete program. Concentrations in international business, management.

ADMISSION
Application Requirements GMAT score: minimum 500, application form, bachelor's degree, essay, personal statement, college transcript(s), minimum of 2 years of work experience.

Recommended for Application Minimum GPA, interview, letters of recommendation, resume, computer experience.

Application Deadline 9/15 for winter, 9/15 for winter (international). Deferred entrance is available.

ACADEMICS
Faculty Part-time 85.

Teaching Methodologies Case study, computer-aided instruction, computer analysis, computer simulations, experiential learning, field projects, group discussion, lecture, research, role playing, seminars by members of the business community, simulations, student presentations, study groups, team projects.

Technology 30 on-campus computer terminals/PCs are available for student use and are linked by a campus-wide network. The network has full access to the Internet. Students are not required to have their own PC.

Special Opportunities Advanced credit may be earned through credit by examination, transfer of credits from another institution. International exchange programs in Australia, Canada, India, Japan, Norway, Pakistan, Republic of Korea, Switzerland, Thailand, United Kingdom, United States.

FINANCES
Costs for 1997–98 Tuition: $18,500 per program (resident); $18,500 per program (nonresident). Cost varies by academic program. Average 1997–98 room only costs were $3150 per academic year (on campus) and $5000 per academic year (off campus). Room and board costs vary by campus location, occupancy (e.g., single, double, triple), type of accommodation.

FACILITIES
Information Resources HSEBA Library plus 7 additional on-campus libraries; total holdings of 280,000 volumes, 1,600 current periodical subscriptions. CD player(s) available for graduate student use. Access provided to online bibliographic retrieval services.

INTERNATIONAL STUDENTS
Demographics N/R

Services and Facilities International student office, international student housing, visa services, counseling/support services.

Applying TOEFL: minimum score of 500, proof of adequate funds required. Financial aid is not available to international students.

International Student Contact Ms. Soile Saloranta, Assistant Director, Foreign Relations (MBA Student Exchange), Hietaniemenkatu 7A, 3rd Floor, Helsinki. Phone: 358-9-4313641; Fax: 358-9-4313641; E-mail: salorant@hkkk.fi

PLACEMENT
Services include alumni network, career counseling/planning, career fairs, career library, career placement, job interviews arranged, job search course, resume referral to employers, and resume preparation. In 1996–97, 200 organizations participated in on-campus recruiting; 10 on-campus interviews were conducted.

Employment Of 1996–97 graduates, 70% were employed within three months of graduation. Types of employment entered: banking, communications, consulting, consumer products, education, finance, financial services, government, high technology, human resources, international trade, management, manufacturing, marketing, media, nonprofit, retail, service industry, telecommunications, transportation.

Business Program(s) URL: http://www.hkkk.fi/

Program Contact: Niina Haaslahei, External Relations Assistant, Hietaniemenkatu 7A, 3rd Floor, Helsinki 00100, Finland. Phone: 358-9-4313224; Fax: 358-9-4313613; E-mail: mbafi@hkkk.fi

FRANCE

EAP-European School of Management

School of Management

Paris Cedex 17, France

OVERVIEW
EAP-European School of Management is a publicly supported, coed institution. Enrollment: 25 graduate, professional, and undergraduate students; 25 full-time matriculated graduate/professional students; part-time matriculated graduate/professional students. The graduate business unit is in an urban setting and is on a 7-phase calendar.

HIGHLIGHTS

Enrollment Profile

Full-time: 25	International: 84%
Part-time: 0	Women: 16%
Total: 25	Minorities: N/R
Average Age: 30	Average Class Size: N/R
Fall 1997 Average GPA: N/R	Fall 1997 Average GMAT: 610

Costs
Full-time tuition: 125,000 French francs per academic year (resident); 125,000 French francs per academic year (nonresident)
Part-time tuition: N/R

GRADUATE BUSINESS PROGRAMS
Executive Master of Business Administration (EMBA) Full-time; up to 12 months to complete program. Concentrations in accounting, economics, finance, human resources, international business, management, marketing, operations management, public policy and administration, strategic management, technology management.

International MBA (MBA) Full-time; minimum of 12 months to complete program. Concentrations in international management, management.

EAP-European School of Management (continued)

International Executive MBA (MBA) Part-time; 16 months to 2.7 years to complete program. Concentrations in international business, european business studies.

ADMISSION

Applications For fall 1997 there were 59 applications for admission. Of those applying; 26 were accepted. Of those accepted, 25 enrolled.

Application Requirements GMAT score: minimum 550, application form, application fee, bachelor's degree, essay, interview, 2 letters of recommendation, personal statement, resume, college transcript(s), minimum of 5 years of work experience.

Recommended for Application Computer experience.

Application Deadline 10/15 for fall, 10/15 for fall (international). Application fee: 600 French francs. Deferred entrance is available.

ACADEMICS

Faculty Full-time 35; part-time 15.

Teaching Methodologies Case study, computer-aided instruction, computer simulations, faculty seminars, field projects, group discussion, lecture, seminars by members of the business community, student presentations, study groups, team projects.

Technology 12 on-campus computer terminals/PCs are available for student use and are linked by a campus-wide network. The network has full access to the Internet. Students are required to have their own PC.

Special Opportunities An internship program is available.

FINANCES

Costs for 1997–98 Tuition: Full-time: 125,000 French francs per year (resident); 125,000 French francs per year (nonresident). Average 1997–98 room and board costs were 120,000 French francs per academic year (off campus). Room and board costs vary by occupancy (e.g., single, double, triple), type of accommodation, type of meal plan.

Financial Aid Research assistantships available.

FACILITIES

Information Resources Centre de Documentation; total holdings of 16,500 volumes, 2,200 microforms, 375 current periodical subscriptions. CD player(s) available for graduate student use. Access provided to online bibliographic retrieval services.

INTERNATIONAL STUDENTS

Demographics 84% of students enrolled are international students [Asia, 16%, Europe, 64%, North America, 12%, South America, 8%].

Services and Facilities International student office, international student center, counseling/support services.

Applying TOEFL: minimum score of 600 required. Financial aid is not available to international students.

International Student Contact Farhad Rad-Serecht, Dean, MBA Programs, EAP, European School of Management, 6 avenue de la Porte de Champerret, Paris Cedex 17. Phone: 33-1-4409-3332; Fax: 33-1-4409-3335; E-mail: fradserecht@eap.schamp.ccip.fr

PLACEMENT

Services include alumni network, career counseling/planning, career library, electronic job bank, job interviews arranged, job search course, resume referral to employers, and resume preparation. In 1996–97, 12 organizations participated in on-campus recruiting; 12 on-campus interviews were conducted.

Employment Of 1996–97 graduates, 95% were employed within three months of graduation; the average starting salary was $110,000. Types of employment entered: banking, consulting, consumer products, finance, financial services, government, human resources, international trade, manufacturing, marketing, service industry, telecommunications.

Business Program(s) URL: http://www.eap.net

Program Contact: Ms. Brigitte Blandin, MBA Program Coordinator, 6 avenue de la Porte de Champerret, Paris Cedex 17 75838, France. Phone: 33-1-4409-3331; Fax: 33-1-4409-3335.

École Nationale des Ponts et Chaussées

ENPC Graduate School of International Business

Paris 75343 Cedex 07, France

OVERVIEW

École Nationale des Ponts et Chaussées is an independent-nonprofit, coed institution. Enrollment: 967 graduate, professional, and undergraduate students. Founded: 1747. The graduate business unit is in an urban setting and is on a trimester calendar.

HIGHLIGHTS

Enrollment Profile

Full-time: 55	International: 85%
Part-time: 0	Women: 42%
Total: 55	Minorities: N/R
Average Age: 29	Average Class Size: N/R
Fall 1997 Average GPA: N/R	Fall 1997 Average GMAT: 570

Costs

Full-time tuition: 110,000 French francs per academic year
Part-time tuition: N/R

Degree(s) offered in conjunction with University of Bristol, University of Belgrano, The National University of Cuyo, The IIS Institute of Management

GRADUATE BUSINESS PROGRAMS

Master of Business Administration in International Business (MBA) Full-time, part-time; 19 total credits required; 13 to 15 months to complete program. Concentrations in entrepreneurship, financial management/planning, international and area business studies, international business, international finance, international management, japanese business studies, leadership, logistics, management information systems, marketing, operations management, strategic management, technology management, international economics, international marketing, organizational management, asian business studies, european business studies.

ADMISSION

Applications For fall 1997 there were 200 applications for admission. Of those applying, 71 were accepted. Of those accepted, 55 enrolled.

Application Requirements GMAT score, application form, application fee, bachelor's degree, essay, minimum GPA, interview, 3 letters of recommendation, personal statement, resume, college transcript(s), work experience, computer experience.

Application Deadline Applications processed on a rolling/continuous basis for both domestic and international students. Application fee: 500 French francs. Deferred entrance is available.

ACADEMICS

Faculty Full-time 6; part-time 60.

Teaching Methodologies Case study, computer-aided instruction, computer simulations, experiential learning, faculty seminars, field projects, group discussion, lecture, research, role playing, seminars by members of the business community, simulations, student presentations, study groups, team projects.

Technology 30 on-campus computer terminals/PCs are available for student use and are linked by a campus-wide network. The network has full access to the Internet. Students are required to have their own PC.

Special Opportunities Advanced credit may be earned through transfer of credits from another institution. International exchange programs in Argentina, Czech Republic, Hong Kong, India, Japan, Morocco, Poland, Slovenia, United Kingdom, United States. An internship program is available.

FINANCES

Costs for 1997–98 Tuition: Full-time: 110,000 French francs per year. Fees: Full-time: 7600 French francs per academic year. Average 1997–98 room and board costs were 70,000 French francs per academic year (off campus). Room and board costs vary by occupancy (e.g., single, double, triple), type of accommodation, type of meal plan.

Financial Aid In 1997–98, 18% of students received some institutionally administered aid in the form of grants, scholarships, work study.

Financial Aid Contact Ms. Mayalene Crossley, Admissions Director, MIB-ENPC, 28, rue des Saints-Pères, Paris Cedex 07. Phone: 33-1-4458-2854; Fax: 33-1-4015-9347; E-mail: jensen@paris.enpc.fr

FACILITIES

Information Resources Centre de Documentation Contemperaine et Historique; total holdings of 150,000 volumes, 200 microforms, 700 current periodical subscriptions. CD player(s) available for graduate student use.

INTERNATIONAL STUDENTS

Demographics 85% of students enrolled are international students [Africa, 12%, Asia, 23%, Europe, 38%, North America, 19%, South America, 8%].

Services and Facilities Counseling/support services, development services, career services.

Applying TOEFL: minimum score of 550, proof of adequate funds required. Proof of health/immunizations recommended. Financial aid is available to international students.

International Student Contact Mrs. Mayalene Crossley, Admissions Director, MIB-ENPC, 28, rue des Saints-Pères, Paris Cedex 07. Phone: 33-1-4458-2855; Fax: 33-1-4015-9347; E-mail: mib.admit@paris.enpc.fr

PLACEMENT

Services include alumni network, career counseling/planning, career fairs, career placement, electronic job bank, job search course, resume referral to employers, and resume preparation. In 1996–97, 20 organizations participated in on-campus recruiting; 34 on-campus interviews were conducted.

Employment Of 1996–97 graduates, 85% were employed within three months of graduation. Types of employment entered: accounting, banking, chemical industry, communications, computer-related, consulting, consumer products, education, engineering, finance, financial services, high technology, human resources, information systems/technology, insurance, international trade, management, manufacturing, marketing, media, nonprofit, pharmaceutical, retail, service industry, telecommunications, transportation, utilities.

Business Program(s) URL: http://www.enpc.fr/mib/pres.htm

Program Contact: Ms. Karina Jensen, International Communication and Development Manager, MIB-ENPC, 28, rue des Saints-Pères, Paris 75343 Cedex 07 75343, France. Phone: 33-1-4458-2854; Fax: 33-1-4015-9347; E-mail: jensen@paris.enpc.fr

École Supérieure de Commerce de Rouen

Business Programs

Mount Saint Aignan Cedex, France

OVERVIEW
École Supérieure de Commerce de Rouen is an independent-nonprofit, coed institution. Enrollment: 950 graduate, professional, and undergraduate students. Founded: 1871. The graduate business unit is in a small-town setting and is on a semester calendar.

GRADUATE BUSINESS PROGRAMS
Executive MBA/Master of Science in Management (MBA/MS)

ACADEMICS
Teaching Methodologies Case study, faculty seminars, lecture, seminars by members of the business community, student presentations, team projects.

Technology Computer terminals/PCs are available for student use and are linked by a campus-wide network. The network has full access to the Internet. Students are required to have their own PC.

Special Opportunities International exchange program available.

FACILITIES
Information Resources Total library holdings of 10,000 volumes, 370 current periodical subscriptions. CD player(s) available for graduate student use.

Program Contact: EMBA Associate Director, BP 188, Mount Sain Aignan 76136, France. Phone: 33-232-827-402; Fax: 33-232-760-662; E-mail: nicole. brinsdon@esc-1.rouen.fr

École Supérieure des Sciences Économiques et Commerciales

ESSEC School of Management

Cergy-Pontoise, France

OVERVIEW
École Supérieure des Sciences Économiques et Commerciales is an independent-nonprofit, coed institution. Enrollment: 2,899 graduate, professional, and undergraduate students; 2,160 full-time matriculated graduate/professional students; 90 part-time matriculated graduate/professional students. Founded: 1907. The graduate business unit is in a suburban setting and is on a trimester calendar.

HIGHLIGHTS

Enrollment Profile

Full-time: 2,160	International: 12%
Part-time: 90	Women: 39%
Total: 2,250	Minorities: N/R
Average Age: 21	Average Class Size: N/R
Fall 1997 Average GPA: N/R	Fall 1997 Average GMAT: N/R

Costs
Full-time tuition: 127,500 French francs per academic year
Part-time tuition: N/R

AACSB – The International Association for Management Education accredited

Degree(s) offered in conjunction with Cornell University, University of Salamanca, Budapest University of Economic Sciences and Budapest Technical University, Warsaw Agricultural University

GRADUATE BUSINESS PROGRAMS
Executive MBA (MBA) Part-time; 60 total credits required; 5 years work experience required; minimum of 22 months to complete program. Concentrations in international business, management.

Master of Management (MM) Full-time; 28 total credits required; 2 years of preparatory schooling required; minimum of 15 months to complete program. Concentrations in international business, management, accounting, economics, finance, human resources, marketing, operations management.

MBA in Luxury Brand Management (MBA) Full-time; 3 years work experience required; minimum of 11 months to complete program.

MBA in International Agrifood Management (MBA) Full-time; 3 years work experience required; minimum of 11 months to complete program.

MS in International Hotel Management (MS) Full-time; 34 total credits required; 1 year work experience in sector required; minimum of 22 months to complete program.

MS in Marketing Management (MS) Full-time; 13 months to complete program. Concentration in international marketing.

MS in Financial Techniques (MS) Full-time; 13 months to complete program. Concentration in international finance.

MS in Insurance Finance (MS) Full-time; 13 months to complete program.

MS in Logistics Management and Engineering (MS) Full-time; 13 months to complete program.

MS in International Supply Management (MS) Full-time; 13 months to complete program. Concentrations in industrial administration/management, international logistics, international trade, materials management.

MS in International Legal Affairs and Management (MS) Full-time; 13 months to complete program. Concentrations in business law, legal administration, management.

MS in Urban and Environmental Management and Services (MS) Full-time; 13 months to complete program. Concentrations in city/urban administration, public and private management, public management, public policy and administration, management.

MS in Food Industry Management (MS) Full-time; 13 months to complete program. Concentrations in agribusiness, agricultural economics, management.

MS in Strategy and Management (MS) Full-time; 13 months to complete program.

MS in Management of Information Systems and Telecommunications Networks (MS) Part-time; 2 years to complete program. Concentrations in system management, management systems analysis, management information systems.

ADMISSION
Application Requirements Application form, application fee, bachelor's degree, essay, interview, 2 letters of recommendation, college transcript(s), minimum of 5 years of work experience.

Recommended for Application GMAT score accepted.

Application Deadline 6/5 for fall. Application fee: 980 French francs. Deferred entrance is available.

ACADEMICS
Faculty Full-time 70; part-time 300.

Teaching Methodologies Case study, computer simulations, faculty seminars, field projects, group discussion, lecture, research, seminars by members of the business community, simulations, student presentations, team projects.

Technology 150 on-campus computer terminals/PCs are available for student use and are linked by a campus-wide network. The network has full access to the Internet. Students are not required to have their own PC.

Special Opportunities Advanced credit may be earned through credit by examination. International exchange programs in Argentina, Australia, Austria, Brazil, Belgium, Canada, China, Finland, India, Italy, Israel, Japan, Korea, Mexico, Norway, The Netherlands, Russia, Singapore, Sweden, Thailand, United Kingdom. An internship program is available.

FINANCES
Costs for 1997–98 Tuition: Full-time: 127,500 French francs per program. Cost varies by academic program. Average 1997–98 room and board costs were 10,000 French francs per academic year (on campus) and 10,000 French francs per academic year (off campus). Room and board costs vary by occupancy (e.g., single, double, triple), type of accommodation.

Financial Aid Contact Mrs. Cecile Gerard, Head of Student Social Services, BP 230 2 Place de la Defense, Cergy-Pontoise. Phone: 33-1-3443-3107; Fax: 33-1-3443-3001.

École Supérieure des Sciences Économiques et Commerciales (continued)

FACILITIES

Information Resources Total library holdings of 100,000 volumes, 300 current periodical subscriptions. CD player(s) available for graduate student use. Access provided to online bibliographic retrieval services and online databases.

INTERNATIONAL STUDENTS

Demographics 12% of students enrolled are international students [Africa, 22%, Asia, 18%, Central America, 1%, Europe, 36%, North America, 7%, South America, 2%, other, 14%].

Services and Facilities International student office, international student housing, visa services, ESL courses, counseling/support services.

Applying TOEFL: minimum score of 500, proof of adequate funds, proof of health/immunizations required. Financial aid is not available to international students.

International Student Contact Mrs Gisele Dessagne, International Student Relations Officer, Avenue B Hirsch, BP 105, Cergy-Pontoise. Phone: 33-1-3443-3144; Fax: 33-1-3443-3111; E-mail: dessagne@edu.essec.fr

PLACEMENT

Services include alumni network, career counseling/planning, career fairs, resume referral to employers, and resume preparation. In 1996–97, 125 organizations participated in on-campus recruiting; 580 on-campus interviews were conducted.

Employment Of 1996–97 graduates, 90% were employed within three months of graduation; the average starting salary was 220,000 French francs. Types of employment entered: accounting, banking, chemical industry, communications, computer-related, consulting, consumer products, education, engineering, finance, financial services, government, health services, high technology, hospitality management, information systems/technology, insurance, international trade, law, management, manufacturing, marketing, media, retail, telecommunications.

Business Program(s) URL: http://www.essec.fr

Program Contact: Mrs Michele Lempereur, Associate Director for International Relations, Avenue Bernard Hirsch, Cergy-Pontoise 95021, France. Phone: 33-1-3443-3000; Fax: 33-1-3443-3001.

E. M. Lyon

Cesma MBA

Ecully Cedex, France

OVERVIEW

E. M. Lyon is an independent-nonprofit, coed institution. Enrollment: 5,615 graduate, professional, and undergraduate students; 5,510 full-time matriculated graduate/professional students; 105 part-time matriculated graduate/professional students. Founded: 1872. The graduate business unit is in a suburban setting and is on a trimester calendar.

HIGHLIGHTS

Enrollment Profile

Full-time: 46	International: N/R
Part-time: 24	Women: 17%
Total: 70	Minorities: N/R
Average Age: 31	Average Class Size: 35
Fall 1997 Average GPA: N/R	Fall 1997 Average GMAT: 600

Costs
Full-time tuition: 97,000 French francs per academic year
Part-time tuition: 30,000 French francs per year

Degree(s) offered in conjunction with Cranfield School of Management, University of Belgrano

GRADUATE BUSINESS PROGRAMS

Cesma MBA (MBA) Full-time, part-time; 12 months to 2 years to complete program. Concentration in management.

Master of Management (MM) Full-time; 2 to 3 years to complete program. Concentration in management.

Master of Science in Service Company Management (MS) Full-time; minimum of 12 months to complete program. Concentration in management.

Master of Science in Corporate Finance (MS) Full-time; minimum of 12 months to complete program. Concentration in finance.

Master of Science in Technology Management (MS) Full-time; minimum of 12 months to complete program. Concentration in technology management.

Master of Science in Industrial Marketing (MS) Full-time; minimum of 12 months to complete program. Concentration in marketing.

ADMISSION

Applications For fall 1997 there were 210 applications for admission. Of those applying, 120 were accepted. Of those accepted, 70 enrolled.

Application Requirements Application form, application fee, bachelor's degree, interview, 2 letters of recommendation, resume, minimum of 4 years of work experience.

Recommended for Application GMAT score accepted: minimum 550.

Application Deadline 6/15 for fall. Application fee: 650 French francs. Deferred entrance is available.

ACADEMICS

Faculty Full-time 85; part-time 412.

Teaching Methodologies Case study, computer-aided instruction, computer simulations, experiential learning, faculty seminars, field projects, group discussion, lecture, research, role playing, seminars by members of the business community, simulations, student presentations, study groups, team projects.

Technology 130 on-campus computer terminals/PCs are available for student use and are linked by a campus-wide network. The network has full access to the Internet. Students are required to have their own PC.

Special Opportunities Advanced credit may be earned through credit by examination, transfer of credits from another institution. International exchange programs in Argentina, Canada, Spain, United Kingdom, United States. An internship program is available.

FINANCES

Costs for 1997–98 Tuition: Full-time: 97,000 French francs per year. Part-time: 30,000 French francs per year. Average 1997–98 room and board costs were 50,000 French francs per academic year (on campus) and 50,000 French francs per academic year (off campus). Room and board costs vary by campus location, occupancy (e.g., single, double, triple).

Financial Aid In 1997–98, 36% of students received some institutionally administered aid in the form of scholarships, loans. Financial aid is available to part-time students. Application Deadline: 10/31.

Financial Aid Contact Ms. Jacqueline DelBello, Assistant of Information and Exchange Program, 23, Avenue Guy de Collongue, BP 174, Ecully Cedex. Phone: 33-478-337-865; Fax: 33-478-336-169; E-mail: cesmamba@em_lyon.com

FACILITIES

Information Resources Infomédiathéque; total holdings of 15,000 volumes, 400 current periodical subscriptions. CD player(s) available for graduate student use. Access provided to online bibliographic retrieval services.

INTERNATIONAL STUDENTS

Demographics N/R

Services and Facilities International student office, international student center, ESL courses, counseling/support services.

Applying TOEFL: minimum score of 600 required. Financial aid is available to international students.

International Student Contact Ms. Jacqueline Del Bello, Assistant of Information and Enchange Program, 23, Avenue Guy de Collongue, BP 174, Ecully Cedex. Phone: 33-478-337-865; Fax: 33-478-336-169; E-mail: cesmamba@em_lyon.com

PLACEMENT

Services include alumni network, career counseling/planning, career fairs, career library, career placement, electronic job bank, job interviews arranged, job search course, resume referral to employers, and resume preparation. In 1996–97, 100 organizations participated in on-campus recruiting.

Employment Of 1996–97 graduates, 85% were employed within three months of graduation; the average starting salary was 380,000 French francs. Types of employment entered: accounting, banking, chemical industry, communications, consulting, consumer products, energy, engineering, finance, financial services, high technology, human resources, information systems/technology, insurance, international trade, management, manufacturing, marketing, media, nonprofit, petrochemical, pharmaceutical, real estate, retail, service industry, telecommunications, transportation, utilities.

Business Program(s) URL: http://www.em-lyon.com

Program Contact: Ms. Jacqueline DelBello, Assistant of Information and Exchange Program, 23, Avenue Guy de Collongue, BP 174, Ecully Cedex 69132, France. Phone: 33-478-337-865; Fax: 33-478-336-169; E-mail: cesmamba@em-lyon.com
See full description on page 802.

Groupe CERAM

Ceram ESC Nice School of Management

Sophia Antipolis Cedex, France

OVERVIEW
Groupe CERAM is a publicly supported, coed institution. Enrollment: 1,100 graduate, professional, and undergraduate students. The graduate business unit is in a suburban setting and is on a trimester calendar.

HIGHLIGHTS

Enrollment Profile

Full-time: 40	International: N/R
Part-time: 0	Women: N/R
Total: 40	Minorities: N/R
Average Age: 29	Average Class Size: 25
Fall 1997 Average GPA: N/R	Fall 1997 Average GMAT: N/R

Costs
Full-time tuition: 96,600 French francs per academic year (resident); 96,600 French francs per academic year (nonresident)
Part-time tuition: N/R

Degree(s) offered in conjunction with University of Phoenix, Shanghai Institute of Foreign Trade

GRADUATE BUSINESS PROGRAMS
International MBA (MBA) Full-time, part-time, distance learning option; 51 total credits required; 10 months to 2 years to complete program. Concentrations in accounting, economics, entrepreneurship, international business, management, management information systems, marketing, operations management, organizational behavior/development, strategic management.

ADMISSION
Application Requirements Application form, application fee, bachelor's degree, minimum GPA, interview, 2 letters of recommendation, personal statement, resume, college transcript(s), minimum of 3 years of work experience, computer experience.

Recommended for Application GMAT score accepted.

Application Deadline Applications processed on a rolling/continuous basis for both domestic and international students. Application fee: 900 French francs. Deferred entrance is available.

ACADEMICS
Faculty Full-time 35; part-time 150.

Teaching Methodologies Case study, computer-aided instruction, computer simulations, field projects, group discussion, lecture, seminars by members of the business community, simulations, student presentations, study groups, team projects.

Technology 36 on-campus computer terminals/PCs are available for student use and are linked by a campus-wide network. The network has full access to the Internet. Students are required to have their own PC.

FINANCES
Costs for 1997–98 Tuition: Full-time: 96,600 French francs per year (resident); 96,600 French francs per year (nonresident). Fees: Full-time: 2500 French francs per academic year (resident); 2500 French francs per academic year (nonresident). Average 1997–98 room only costs were 20,000 French francs per academic year (off campus).

Financial Aid Contact Lars Smith, Director of MBA Programs, BP 085, Sophia Antipolis Cedex. Phone: 33-493-954-520; Fax: 33-493-954-540.

INTERNATIONAL STUDENTS
Demographics N/R

Services and Facilities International student office, international student center, international student housing, visa services, counseling/support services.

Applying TOEFL recommended.

International Student Contact Mrs. Isabel Guiol, Coordinator of International Programs, BP 085, Sophia Antipolis Cedex. Phone: 33-493-954-545; Fax: 33-493-954-524.

PLACEMENT
Services include alumni network, career placement, job interviews arranged, and resume preparation. In 1996–97, 200 organizations participated in on-campus recruiting.

Employment Of 1996–97 graduates, 90% were employed within three months of graduation; the average starting salary was 320,000 French francs. Types of employment entered: banking, communications, computer-related, consulting, engineering, finance, financial services, government, human resources, management, marketing.

Program Contact: BP 085, Sophia Antipolis Cedex 06902, France. Phone: 33-493-954-520; Fax: 33-493-954-540.

Groupe ESC Clermont

Clermont Graduate School of Management

Clermont-Ferrand, France

OVERVIEW
Groupe ESC Clermont coed institution. Founded: 1919. The graduate business unit is in an urban setting.

GRADUATE BUSINESS PROGRAMS
Master of Business Administration (MBA)

ACADEMICS
Faculty Full-time 4.

Teaching Methodologies Case study, faculty seminars, lecture, research, seminars by members of the business community, team projects.

Technology 137 on-campus computer terminals/PCs are available for student use and are linked by a campus-wide network. Students are not required to have their own PC.

Special Opportunities International exchange programs in Peru, Russia, United States.

FACILITIES
Information Resources Total library holdings of 6,000 volumes.

Program Contact: Head of Recruitment, 2 boulevard Trudaine, Clermont-Ferrand 63037, France. Phone: 33-73-989-494; Fax: 33-73-982-449.

Groupe ESC Nantes Atlantique

Groupe ESC Nantes Atlantique Business Programs

Nantes Cedex 3, France

OVERVIEW
Groupe ESC Nantes Atlantique is an independent-nonprofit, coed institution. Enrollment: 1,127 full-time matriculated graduate/professional students; 29 part-time matriculated graduate/professional students. Founded: 1900. The graduate business unit is in an urban setting and is on a quarter calendar.

HIGHLIGHTS

Enrollment Profile

Full-time: 1,127	International: 6%
Part-time: 0	Women: N/R
Total: 1,127	Minorities: N/R
Average Age: 20	Average Class Size: 25
Fall 1997 Average GPA: N/R	Fall 1997 Average GMAT: N/R

Costs
Full-time tuition: 90,000 French francs per academic year
Part-time tuition: N/R

Degree(s) offered in conjunction with Universidad Comercial de Deusto-Brilbao, University of Bradford

GRADUATE BUSINESS PROGRAMS
MBA in European Management (MBA) Full-time; 60 total credits required; 13 months to complete program.

Euro-MBA (MBA) Full-time, distance learning option; 18 total credits required; 2 years to complete program.

Master in Management (MM) Full-time, part-time; 120 total credits required; 2 years to complete program.

ADMISSION
Applications For fall 1997 there were 4,980 applications for admission. Of those applying, 1,459 were accepted. Of those accepted, 250 enrolled.

Application Requirements Application form, application fee, bachelor's degree, interview, 2 letters of recommendation, personal statement, resume, college transcript(s).

Recommended for Application Work experience.

Application Deadline Applications processed on a rolling/continuous basis for both domestic and international students. Application fee: 600 French francs. Deferred entrance is available.

ACADEMICS
Faculty Full-time 43; part-time 250.

Teaching Methodologies Case study, computer-aided instruction, computer simulations, experiential learning, field projects, group discussion, lecture, role playing, seminars by members of the business community, simulations, student presentations, study groups, team projects.

Groupe ESC Nantes Atlantique (continued)

Technology 100 on-campus computer terminals/PCs are available for student use and are linked by a campus-wide network. The network has full access to the Internet. Students are not required to have their own PC.

Special Opportunities Advanced credit may be earned through credit by examination. International exchange programs in Asia, Canada, United States, various Western European countries. An internship program is available.

FINANCES
Costs for 1997–98 Tuition: Full-time: 90,000 French francs per program. Fees: Full-time: 600 French francs per academic year. Average 1997–98 room only costs were 18,000 French francs per academic year (off campus). Room and board costs vary by occupancy (e.g., single, double, triple), type of accommodation.

FACILITIES
Information Resources Mediatheque ESCNA; total holdings of 13,000 volumes, 480 current periodical subscriptions. CD player(s) available for graduate student use. Access provided to online bibliographic retrieval services.

INTERNATIONAL STUDENTS
Demographics 6% of students enrolled are international students [Europe, 95%, North America, 5%].

Services and Facilities International student office, counseling/support services.

Applying Proof of adequate funds required. Proof of health/immunizations recommended. Financial aid is not available to international students.

International Student Contact David Read, Associate Director of International Relations, 8, route de la Joneliére, Nantes Cedex 3. Phone: 33-2-4037-3434; Fax: 33-2-4037-4530.

PLACEMENT
Services include alumni network, career counseling/planning, career fairs, career library, career placement, electronic job bank, job interviews arranged, job search course, resume referral to employers, and resume preparation. In 1996–97, 60 organizations participated in on-campus recruiting; 392 on-campus interviews were conducted.

Employment Of 1996–97 graduates, 94% were employed within three months of graduation; the average starting salary was 180,000 French francs. Types of employment entered: accounting, banking, chemical industry, communications, computer-related, consulting, consumer products, education, finance, financial services, government, human resources, information systems/technology, insurance, international trade, management, marketing, media, nonprofit, pharmaceutical, retail, service industry, telecommunications.

Business Program(s) URL: http://www.escna.fr

Program Contact: David Read, Associate Director of International Relations, 8, route de la Joneliére, Nantes Cedex 3 44312, France. Phone: 33-2-4037-3434; Fax: 33-2-4037-4530; E-mail: dread@escna.fr

Groupe ESC Toulouse

ESC Toulouse Graduate School of Management
Toulouse Cedex 7, France

OVERVIEW
Groupe ESC Toulouse coed institution. Enrollment: 1,021 graduate, professional, and undergraduate students; 650 full-time matriculated graduate/professional students; part-time matriculated graduate/professional students. Founded: 1903. The graduate business unit is in an urban setting and is on a trimester calendar.

HIGHLIGHTS

Enrollment Profile

Full-time: 650	International: 14%
Part-time: 0	Women: 48%
Total: 650	Minorities: N/R
Average Age: 23	Average Class Size: N/R
Fall 1997 Average GPA: N/R	Fall 1997 Average GMAT: N/R

Costs
Full-time tuition: N/R
Part-time tuition: N/R

Degree(s) offered in conjunction with University of Strathclyde

GRADUATE BUSINESS PROGRAMS
ESC Cycle Superieur (DESM) Full-time; 2 to 3 years to complete program. Concentrations in business law, entrepreneurship, finance, industrial administration/management, information management, international development management, marketing research, public management, human resources.

MS Audit Interne et Controle de Gestion (MS) Full-time; 12 to 18 months to complete program. Concentration in management systems analysis.

MS Banque et Ingenierie Financiere (MS) Full-time; 12 to 18 months to complete program. Concentrations in banking, financial management/planning.

MS Marketing et Communication Commerciale (MS) Full-time; 12 to 18 months to complete program. Concentrations in marketing, marketing research.

MS Management de l'Innovation et de la Technologie (MS) Full-time; 12 to 18 months to complete program. Concentrations in technology management, project management.

MS Management de la Sante (MS) Full-time; 12 to 18 months to complete program. Concentration in health care.

MS Management et Ingenierie des Otganisations (MS) Full-time; 12 to 18 months to complete program. Concentration in management information systems.

MS Manager Public (MS) Full-time; 12 to 18 months to complete program. Concentration in public management.

MS Marketing et Technologie Argro-Alimentaires (MS) Full-time; 12 to 18 months to complete program. Concentrations in agribusiness, technology management.

European MBA (MBA) Full-time; 80 total credits required; 12 months to complete program. Concentration in european business studies.

ADMISSION
Applications For fall 1997 there were 2,111 applications for admission. Of those applying, 426 were accepted. Of those accepted, 374 enrolled.

Application Requirements Application form, bachelor's degree, 2 letters of recommendation, personal statement, resume, college transcript(s), computer experience: computer literacy.

Recommended for Application Minimum GPA, interview, work experience.

Application Deadline 7/30 for fall, 6/30 for fall (international). Deferred entrance is available.

ACADEMICS
Faculty Full-time 41; part-time 70.

Teaching Methodologies Case study, computer-aided instruction, computer simulations, experiential learning, faculty seminars, field projects, group discussion, lecture, research, seminars by members of the business community, simulations, student presentations, study groups, team projects.

Technology 40 on-campus computer terminals/PCs are available for student use. Students are required to have their own PC.

Special Opportunities Advanced credit may be earned through credit by examination, credit for business training programs, transfer of credits from another institution. International exchange programs in Canada, Colombia, Finland, Germany, Ireland, Israel, Mexico, Spain, United Kingdom, United States. An internship program is available.

FINANCES
Costs for 1997–98 Cost varies by academic program. Fees vary by academic program. Average 1997–98 room only costs were 25,000 French francs per academic year (on campus) and 32,000 French francs per academic year (off campus). Room and board costs vary by occupancy (e.g., single, double, triple), type of accommodation.

FACILITIES
Information Resources Mediatheque ESCT; total holdings of 12,000 volumes, 310 current periodical subscriptions. CD player(s) available for graduate student use. Access provided to online bibliographic retrieval services.

INTERNATIONAL STUDENTS
Demographics 14% of students enrolled are international students.

Services and Facilities International student office, counseling/support services.

Applying Proof of adequate funds, proof of health/immunizations required. Financial aid is not available to international students.

International Student Contact Mr. William McNulty, Director, International Relations, 20 Boulevard Lascrosses, BP1070, Toulouse Cedex 7. Phone: 33-561-294-918; Fax: 33-5 61-294994.

PLACEMENT
Services include alumni network, career counseling/planning, career fairs, career placement, and resume preparation. In 1996–97, 35 organizations participated in on-campus recruiting; 70 on-campus interviews were conducted.

Employment Of 1996–97 graduates, 85% were employed within three months of graduation; the average starting salary was 175,000 French francs. Types of employment entered: accounting, banking, chemical industry, communications, computer-related, consulting, consumer products, energy, engineering, finance, financial services, high technology, human resources, information systems/technology, insurance, international trade, management, manufacturing, marketing, media, nonprofit, petrochemical, pharmaceutical, retail, service industry, telecommunications, transportation.

Business Program(s) URL: http://www.esc-toulouse.fr

Program Contact: Dr. Andres Atenza, Directeur ESC Toulouse, 20 Boulevard Lascrosses, BP1070, Toulouse Cedex 7 31068, France. Phone: 33-561-294-992; Fax: 33-561-294-994; E-mail: esc@esc-toulouse.fr

HEC Graduate School of Management

Institute Supérieur des Affaires

Jouy-en-Josas Cedex, France

OVERVIEW
HEC Graduate School of Management is a publicly supported, coed institution. Enrollment: 1,700 graduate, professional, and undergraduate students; 132 full-time matriculated graduate/professional students; part-time matriculated graduate/professional students. Founded: 1881. The graduate business unit is in a suburban setting and is on a quarter calendar.

HIGHLIGHTS

Enrollment Profile

Full-time: 132	International: 45%
Part-time: 0	Women: 20%
Total: 132	Minorities: N/R
Average Age: 29	Average Class Size: N/R
Fall 1997 Average GPA: 2.5	Fall 1997 Average GMAT: 560

Costs
Full-time tuition: N/R
Part-time tuition: 125,000 French francs per program (resident); 125,000 French francs per program (nonresident)

Degree(s) offered in conjunction with Tufts University

GRADUATE BUSINESS PROGRAMS
Bilingual MBA Programme (MBA) Full-time; 70 total credits required; 16 months to complete program. Concentrations in accounting, entrepreneurship, finance, human resources, international business, international finance, international management, international marketing, management, marketing, production management, public and private management, strategic management, management consulting, financial management/planning.

ADMISSION
Applications For fall 1997 there were 600 applications for admission.

Application Requirements GMAT score, application form, application fee, bachelor's degree, essay, minimum GPA: 2.5, interview, 2 letters of recommendation, personal statement, resume, college transcript(s).

Recommended for Application Minimum of 2 years of work experience, computer experience.

Application Deadline Applications processed on a rolling/continuous basis for both domestic and international students. Application fee: 450 French francs. Deferred entrance is available.

ACADEMICS
Faculty Full-time 106; part-time 70.

Teaching Methodologies Case study, computer-aided instruction, computer analysis, computer simulations, experiential learning, faculty seminars, field projects, group discussion, lecture, research, role playing, seminars by members of the business community, simulations, student presentations, study groups, team projects, field audits.

Technology 120 on-campus computer terminals/PCs are available for student use and are linked by a campus-wide network. The network has full access to the Internet. Students are not required to have their own PC.

Special Opportunities International exchange programs in Brazil, Canada, Hong Kong, Italy, Japan, Mexico, Netherlands, Spain, United Kingdom, United States.

FINANCES
Costs for 1997–98 Tuition: 125,000 French francs per program (resident); 125,000 French francs per program (nonresident). Average 1997–98 room and board costs were 40,000 French francs per academic year (on campus) and 65,000 French francs per academic year (off campus). Room and board costs vary by type of accommodation.

Financial Aid In 1997–98, 42% of students received some institutionally administered aid in the form of grants, scholarships, loans. Application Deadline: 6/2.

Financial Aid Contact Mme. Françoise Guyo, Financial Aid Officer, 1, rue de la Libération, Jouy-en-Josas Cedex. Phone: 33-1-3967-7380; Fax: 33-1-3967-7465.

FACILITIES
Information Resources Groupe HEC Library; total holdings of 65,000 volumes, 650 current periodical subscriptions. CD player(s) available for graduate student use. Access provided to online bibliographic retrieval services.

INTERNATIONAL STUDENTS
Demographics 45% of students enrolled are international students [Africa, 5%, Asia, 15%, Central America, 7%, Europe, 36%, North America, 30%, South America, 7%].

Services and Facilities International student office, international student housing, visa services, counseling/support services.

Applying TOEFL: minimum score of 600, TSE, TWE, proof of adequate funds, proof of health/immunizations required. Financial aid is available to international students.

International Student Contact Ms. Pantea Denoyelle, Director of Development, 1, rue de la Libération, Jouy-en-Jasas Cedex. Phone: 33-1-3967-7376; Fax: 33-1-3967-7465.

PLACEMENT
Services include alumni network, career counseling/planning, career fairs, career library, job interviews arranged, job search course, resume referral to employers, and resume preparation. In 1996–97, 130 organizations participated in on-campus recruiting.

Employment Of 1996–97 graduates, 92% were employed within three months of graduation; the average starting salary was 407,184 French francs. Types of employment entered: accounting, banking, chemical industry, communications, computer-related, consulting, consumer products, energy, engineering, finance, financial services, health services, high technology, human resources, information systems/technology, insurance, international trade, law, management, manufacturing, marketing, media, petrochemical, pharmaceutical, service industry, telecommunications, utilities.

Business Program(s) URL: http://www.hec.fr

Program Contact: Mr. Antoine Vidal, Admissions Officer, 1, rue de la Libération, Jouy-en-Josas 78351, France. Phone: 33-1-3967-7379; Fax: 33-1-3967-7465; E-mail: isadmission@gwsmtp.hec.fr

INSEAD (The European Institute of Business Administration)

Business Programs

Fontainebleau Cedex, France

OVERVIEW
INSEAD (The European Institute of Business Administration) is an independent-nonprofit, coed institution. Enrollment: 563 graduate, professional, and undergraduate students; 563 full-time matriculated graduate/professional students; part-time matriculated graduate/professional students. Founded: 1959. The graduate business unit is in a small-town setting and is on a 5 periods of 8 weeks calendar.

HIGHLIGHTS

Enrollment Profile

Full-time: 563	International: 87%
Part-time: 0	Women: 19%
Total: 563	Minorities: N/R
Average Age: 28	Average Class Size: 32
Fall 1997 Average GPA: N/R	Fall 1997 Average GMAT: 670

Costs
Full-time tuition: 159,000 French francs per academic year
Part-time tuition: N/R

GRADUATE BUSINESS PROGRAMS
Master of Business Administration (MBA) Full-time; minimum of 11 months to complete program. Concentrations in international management, leadership.

PhD in Management (PhD) Full-time; minimum of 4 years to complete program.

ADMISSION
Application Requirements Application form, application fee, essay, interview, 2 letters of recommendation, personal statement, resume, college transcript(s), minimum of 1 year of work experience.

Recommended for Application GMAT score accepted, bachelor's degree.

Application Deadline Applications processed on a rolling/continuous basis for both domestic and international students. Application fee: 700 French francs. Deferred entrance is available.

ACADEMICS
Faculty Full-time 102; part-time 35.

FRANCE

INSEAD (The European Institute of Business Administration) (continued)

Teaching Methodologies Case study, computer-aided instruction, computer simulations, experiential learning, faculty seminars, field projects, group discussion, lecture, research, role playing, seminars by members of the business community, simulations, student presentations, study groups, team projects.

Technology 150 on-campus computer terminals/PCs are available for student use and are linked by a campus-wide network. The network has full access to the Internet. Students are not required to have their own PC.

FINANCES
Costs for 1997–98 Tuition: Full-time: 159,000 French francs per year. Average 1997–98 room and board costs were 100,000 French francs per academic year (off campus). Room and board costs vary by occupancy (e.g., single, double, triple), type of accommodation, type of meal plan.

Financial Aid Research assistantships, scholarships, loans available.

Financial Aid Contact MBA Admissions Office, Boulevard de Constance, Fontainebleau. Phone: 33-01-6072-4273; Fax: 33-01-6074-5530; E-mail: admissions@insead.fr

FACILITIES
Information Resources Doriot Library plus 1 additional on-campus library; total holdings of 53,000 volumes, 1,350 current periodical subscriptions. CD player(s) available for graduate student use. Access provided to online bibliographic retrieval services and online databases.

INTERNATIONAL STUDENTS
Demographics 87% of students enrolled are international students [Asia, 7%, Australia/New Zealand, 3%, Central America, 2%, Europe, 66%, North America, 15%, South America, 2%, other, 6%].

Services and Facilities International student office, international student center, international student housing, visa services, ESL courses, counseling/support services, career management services.

Applying TOEFL: minimum score of 620, proof of health/immunizations required. Financial aid is available to international students.

International Student Contact MBA Admissions Office, Boulevard de Constance, Fountainbleau. Phone: 33-1-6072-4273; Fax: 33-1-6074-5530; E-mail: admissions@insead.fr

PLACEMENT
Services include alumni network, career counseling/planning, career fairs, career library, career placement, electronic job bank, job interviews arranged, job search course, resume referral to employers, and resume preparation. In 1996–97, 201 organizations participated in on-campus recruiting; 4,950 on-campus interviews were conducted.

Employment Of 1996–97 graduates, 90% were employed within three months of graduation; the average starting salary was 400,000 French francs. Types of employment entered: accounting, banking, chemical industry, communications, computer-related, consulting, consumer products, education, energy, engineering, finance, financial services, government, health services, high technology, hospitality management, human resources, information systems/technology, insurance, international trade, law, management, manufacturing, marketing, media, mining, nonprofit, petrochemical, pharmaceutical, real estate, retail, service industry, telecommunications, transportation, utilities.

Business Program(s) URL: http://www.insead.fr/mba

Program Contact: MBA Admissions Office, Boulevard de Constance, Fontainbleau 77305, France. Phone: 33-1-60-72-4273; Fax: 33-1-60-74-5530; E-mail: admissions@insead.fr
See full description on page 848.

Institut Superieur de Gestion

ISG International School of Business
Paris, France

OVERVIEW
Institut Superieur de Gestion coed institution. Enrollment: 1,310 graduate, professional, and undergraduate students; 54 full-time matriculated graduate/professional students; 27 part-time matriculated graduate/professional students. Founded: 1967. The graduate business unit is in an urban setting and is on a trimester calendar.

HIGHLIGHTS

Enrollment Profile
Full-time: 18
Part-time: 27
Total: 45
Average Age: 29
Fall 1997 Average GPA: 3.4

International: 69%
Women: 44%
Minorities: N/R
Average Class Size: 20
Fall 1997 Average GMAT: 570

Costs
Full-time tuition: N/R
Part-time tuition: N/R

GRADUATE BUSINESS PROGRAMS
International MBA (MBA) Full-time; 15 months to complete program. Concentrations in accounting, business law, european business studies, finance, international and area business studies, international business, international management, international marketing, japanese business studies, managerial economics, risk management, business policy/strategy, economics.

Executive MBA (MBA) Part-time; 21 months to complete program. Concentrations in accounting, marketing, technology management, finance, managerial economics, business ethics, management, european business studies, international and area business studies, business law, logistics, business policy/strategy, economics.

ADMISSION
Applications For fall 1997 there were 100 applications for admission. Of those applying, 50 were accepted. Of those accepted, 45 enrolled.

Application Requirements GMAT score: minimum 550, application form, application fee, bachelor's degree, essay, minimum GPA: 3.0, interview, 2 letters of recommendation, personal statement, resume, college transcript(s).

Recommended for Application Work experience, computer experience.

Application Deadline 7/31 for fall, 7/31 for fall (international). Application fee: 500 French francs. Deferred entrance is available.

ACADEMICS
Faculty Full-time 12; part-time 28.

Teaching Methodologies Case study, computer-aided instruction, computer simulations, field projects, group discussion, lecture, research, role playing, seminars by members of the business community, simulations, student presentations, study groups, team projects.

Technology 50 on-campus computer terminals/PCs are available for student use and are linked by a campus-wide network. The network has full access to the Internet. Students are required to have their own PC.

FINANCES
Costs for 1997–98 Cost varies by academic program. Average 1997–98 room only costs were 3000 French francs per academic year (off campus). Room and board costs vary by campus location, occupancy (e.g., single, double, triple), type of accommodation.

FACILITIES
Information Resources American Library in Paris plus 1 additional on-campus library. CD player(s) available for graduate student use.

INTERNATIONAL STUDENTS
Demographics 69% of students enrolled are international students.

Services and Facilities International student office, international student center, international student housing, visa services, ESL courses, counseling/support services.

Applying TOEFL: minimum score of 550 required. Financial aid is not available to international students.

International Student Contact Mr. Amir Kermani, Admissions Director/Associate Dean, 6, 8 rue de Lota, Paris. Phone: 33-1-5626 1107; Fax: 33-1-5626 1106; E-mail: isb@isg.fr

PLACEMENT
Services include alumni network, career counseling/planning, career fairs, career library, career placement, and resume preparation. In 1996–97, 30 organizations participated in on-campus recruiting; 200 on-campus interviews were conducted.

Employment Of 1996–97 graduates, 80% were employed within three months of graduation; the average starting salary was $45,000. Types of employment entered: banking, chemical industry, communications, computer-related, consulting, consumer products, engineering, finance, financial services, human resources, information systems/technology, international trade, manufacturing, marketing, pharmaceutical, telecommunications.

Business Program(s) URL: http://www.isg.fr

Program Contact: Mr. Amir Kermani, Admissions Director/Associate Dean, 6, 8 rue de Lota, Paris 75116, France. Phone: 33-1-5626 1107; Fax: 33-1-5626 1106; E-mail: isb@isg.fr

Reims Graduate Business School

Reims Business School

Reims Cedex, France

OVERVIEW
Reims Graduate Business School is a federally supported, coed institution. Founded: 1928. The graduate business unit is in a suburban setting and is on a trimester calendar.

GRADUATE BUSINESS PROGRAMS
Master of Business Administration (MBA)

ACADEMICS
Faculty Full-time 7; part-time 3.

Teaching Methodologies Case study, faculty seminars, research, seminars by members of the business community, student presentations, team projects.

Technology 30 on-campus computer terminals/PCs are available for student use and are linked by a campus-wide network. Students are not required to have their own PC.

Special Opportunities International exchange programs in Czech Republic, Hungary, United Kingdom. An internship program is available.

FACILITIES
Information Resources Total library holdings of 10,000 volumes, 300 current periodical subscriptions.

Program Contact: Program Director, BP 302, Reims Cedex 51061, France. Phone: 33-26-774-604; Fax: 33-26-774-604.

Schiller International University

Business Programs

Strasbourg, France

OVERVIEW
Schiller International University is an independent-nonprofit, coed institution. Founded: 1964. The graduate business unit is in an urban setting and is on a semester calendar.

HIGHLIGHTS

Enrollment Profile

Full-time: N/R	International: N/R
Part-time: N/R	Women: N/R
Total: N/R	Minorities: N/R
Average Age: 28	Average Class Size: 11
Fall 1997 Average GPA: N/R	Fall 1997 Average GMAT: N/R

Costs
Full-time tuition: N/R
Part-time tuition: N/R

Degree(s) offered in conjunction with Schiller Germany, Schiller Spain, Schiller Switzerland, Schiller United Kingdom, Schiller United States

GRADUATE BUSINESS PROGRAMS
Master of Business Administration in International Business (MBA) Part-time; 62 total credits required; 12 months to 3 years to complete program.

ADMISSION
Application Requirements Application form, application fee, bachelor's degree (must be in field of business), personal statement, college transcript(s).

Recommended for Application GMAT score accepted, minimum GPA: 3.0, work experience, computer experience.

Application Deadline Applications processed on a rolling/continuous basis for both domestic and international students. Application fee: $35. Deferred entrance is available.

ACADEMICS
Faculty Part-time 9.

Teaching Methodologies Case study, experiential learning, faculty seminars, field projects, group discussion, lecture, research, role playing, student presentations, study groups, team projects.

Technology Students are not required to have their own PC.

Special Opportunities Advanced credit may be earned through credit by examination, transfer of credits from another institution. International exchange programs in Germany, Spain, Switzerland, United Kingdom, United States. An internship program is available.

FINANCES
Costs for 1997–98 Cost varies by academic program, campus location, number of credits taken. Fees vary by academic program, campus location. Average 1997–98 room and board costs were 30,800 French francs per academic year. Room and board costs vary by campus location, occupancy (e.g., single, double, triple).

Financial Aid Grants, scholarships, loans available. Application Deadline: 3/30.

Financial Aid Contact Mr. James Sutherland, Financial Aid Officer, 453 Edgewater Drive, Dunedin. Phone: 813-736-5082; Fax: 813-734-0359.

FACILITIES
Information Resources Main library, 5,885 microforms.

INTERNATIONAL STUDENTS
Demographics N/R

Services and Facilities International student office, international student center, international student housing, ESL courses, counseling/support services.

Applying TOEFL: minimum score of 550 recommended. Financial aid is available to international students.

International Student Contact Director of Admissions, Chateau Pourtales, 161 rue Melanie, Strasbourg. Phone: 33-3-8845-8464; Fax: 33-3-8845-8460.

PLACEMENT
Services include alumni network, career counseling/planning, career placement, job interviews arranged, and resume preparation.

Employment Types of employment entered: accounting, banking, chemical industry, communications, computer-related, consulting, consumer products, education, engineering, finance, financial services, government, health services, hospitality management, human resources, information systems/technology, international trade, law, management, manufacturing, marketing, retail, service industry, telecommunications, transportation, utilities.

Business Program(s) URL: http://www.schiller.edu/

Program Contact: Dr. Christoph Leibrecht, Director of Admissions, 453 Edgewater Drive, Dunedin 34698-7532, France. Phone: 813-736-5082; Fax: 813-734-0359; E-mail: study@campus.schiller.edu

Schiller International University

Business Programs

Paris, France

OVERVIEW
Schiller International University is an independent-nonprofit, coed institution. Enrollment: 132 graduate, professional, and undergraduate students; 36 full-time matriculated graduate/professional students; 23 part-time matriculated graduate/professional students. Founded: 1964. The graduate business unit is in an urban setting and is on a semester calendar.

HIGHLIGHTS

Enrollment Profile

Full-time: 36	International: N/R
Part-time: 23	Women: N/R
Total: 59	Minorities: N/R
Average Age: N/R	Average Class Size: 15
Fall 1997 Average GPA: N/R	Fall 1997 Average GMAT: N/R

Costs
Full-time tuition: N/R
Part-time tuition: 6600 French francs per course

Degree(s) offered in conjunction with Schiller Germany, Schiller Spain, Schiller Switzerland, Schiller United Kingdom, Schiller United States

GRADUATE BUSINESS PROGRAMS
Master of Business Administration in International Business (MBA) Full-time, part-time; 62 total credits required; 12 months to 3 years to complete program.

Master of Arts in International Relations and Diplomacy (MA) Full-time, part-time; 62 total credits required; 12 months to 3 years to complete program.

ADMISSION
Application Requirements GMAT score, application form, application fee, bachelor's degree (must be in field of business), personal statement, college transcript(s).

Recommended for Application Minimum GPA: 3.0, work experience, computer experience.

Application Deadline Applications processed on a rolling/continuous basis for both domestic and international students. Application fee: $35. Deferred entrance is available.

Schiller International University (continued)

ACADEMICS

Faculty Full-time 5; part-time 10.

Teaching Methodologies Case study, computer-aided instruction, experiential learning, faculty seminars, field projects, group discussion, lecture, research, seminars by members of the business community, student presentations, study groups, team projects.

Technology Students are not required to have their own PC.

Special Opportunities Advanced credit may be earned through credit by examination, transfer of credits from another institution. International exchange programs in France, Spain, Switzerland, United Kingdom, United States. An internship program is available.

FINANCES

Costs for 1997–98 Tuition: 6600 French francs per course. Cost varies by academic program, campus location, number of credits taken. Fees: 1360 French francs per semester. Fees vary by academic program, campus location.

Financial Aid Grants, scholarships, loans available. Application Deadline: 3/30.

Financial Aid Contact Mr. James Sutherland, Financial Aid Officer, 453 Edgewater Drive, Dunedin. Phone: 813-736-5082; Fax: 813-734-0359.

FACILITIES

Information Resources American Library; total holdings of 6,905 volumes, 41 current periodical subscriptions.

INTERNATIONAL STUDENTS

Demographics N/R

Services and Facilities International student office, international student center, international student housing, ESL courses, counseling/support services.

Applying TOEFL: minimum score of 550 recommended. Financial aid is available to international students.

International Student Contact Director of Information and Alumni Affairs, 453 Edgewater Drive, Dunedin. Phone: 813-736-5082; Fax: 33-01-4538 5430.

PLACEMENT

Services include alumni network, career placement, job search course, and resume preparation.

Employment Types of employment entered: accounting, banking, communications, computer-related, consulting, consumer products, education, engineering, finance, financial services, government, health services, hospitality management, human resources, information systems/technology, insurance, international trade, law, management, marketing, retail, service industry, telecommunications, transportation.

Business Program(s) URL: http://www.schiller.edu/

Program Contact: Dr. Christoph Leibrecht, Director of Admissions, 453 Edgewater Drive, Dunedin 34698-7532, France. Phone: 813-736-5082; Fax: 813-734-0359; E-mail: study@campus.schiller.edu

THESEUS Institute

International Management Institute

Sophia Antipolis Cedex, France

OVERVIEW

THESEUS Institute is an independent-nonprofit, primarily male institution. Enrollment: 25 graduate, professional, and undergraduate students. Founded: 1989. The graduate business unit is in a suburban setting and is on a September-July calendar.

HIGHLIGHTS

Enrollment Profile

Full-time: 25	International: N/R
Part-time: 0	Women: N/R
Total: 25	Minorities: N/R
Average Age: 30	Average Class Size: N/R
Fall 1997 Average GPA: N/R	Fall 1997 Average GMAT: 600

Costs
Full-time tuition: 140,000 French francs per academic year
Part-time tuition: N/R

*S*ince 1989, when the M.B.A. program was set up in the south of France by the Institute's founders, including one of France's most prestigious Grande Ecoles, Télécom Paris, THESEUS has created an image of leading-edge teaching for the information age. It has come as somewhat of a surprise to see the number of alumni in recent years who have set up their own companies, particularly in the high-technology areas but also in more traditional areas such as import-export and distribution.

Baba Mamedov, a graduate of THESEUS's fourth M.B.A. class, has set up his own highly successful enterprise in Azerbaidjan and now operates a fleet of aircraft that carries his company's goods across the world. Ed Soon from Singapore has his own fine wines start-up. Tim O'Connor, an Australian graduate, spends his time between Silicon Valley and Paris, the two offices of a semi–start-up information technology company that specializes in video indexing and extraction for which he acts as Executive Vice President. Martin Glaettli, a Swiss-Canadian graduate, took over an industrial firm in Switzerland, and he is now Chairman of a Swiss holding company. Sander Van der Blonk, a Dutch graduate, has set up his own successful Web design and consulting firm in the Netherlands. John Edwards, a recent British graduate, formerly at Oracle, is the leading force behind the set of the European operations of an expanding U.S. software developer aimed at the retail business

GRADUATE BUSINESS PROGRAMS

MBA in Innovation, Strategy Information, and Technology (MBA) Full-time; 10 months to complete program. Concentration in strategic management.

ADMISSION

Applications For fall 1997 there were 86 applications for admission. Of those applying, 27 were accepted. Of those accepted, 25 enrolled.

Application Requirements GMAT score: minimum 550, application form, application fee, bachelor's degree, essay, interview, 2 letters of recommendation, college transcript(s), minimum of 5 years of work experience.

Recommended for Application Minimum GPA, personal statement, computer experience.

Application Deadline 6/30 for fall, 6/30 for fall (international). Application fee: 350 French francs. Deferred entrance is available.

ACADEMICS

Faculty Full-time 6; part-time 40.

Teaching Methodologies Case study, computer-aided instruction, computer analysis, computer simulations, experiential learning, field projects, group discussion, lecture, role playing, seminars by members of the business community, simulations, student presentations, study groups, team projects.

Technology 35 on-campus computer terminals/PCs are available for student use and are linked by a campus-wide network. The network has full access to the Internet. Students are not required to have their own PC.

Special Opportunities Advanced credit may be earned through transfer of credits from another institution. An internship program is available.

FINANCES

Costs for 1997–98 Tuition: Full-time: 140,000 French francs per program. Fees: Full-time: 350 French francs per academic year. Average 1997–98 room only costs were 30,000 French francs per academic year (off campus).

FACILITIES

Information Resources Information Center; total holdings of 3,500 volumes, 105 current periodical subscriptions. CD player(s) available for graduate student use. Access provided to online bibliographic retrieval services.

INTERNATIONAL STUDENTS

Demographics N/R

Services and Facilities International student office, international student housing, visa services, ESL courses, counseling/support services.

Applying Proof of adequate funds, proof of health/immunizations recommended. Financial aid is not available to international students.

International Student Contact Ms. Andree Ferre, MBA Program Coordinator, BP 169, Rue Albert Einstein, Sophia Antipolis Cedex. Phone: 33-4-9294-5174; Fax: 33-4-9365-3837; E-mail: ferre@theseus.fr

PLACEMENT

Services include alumni network, career counseling/planning, career fairs, career library, electronic job bank, job interviews arranged, job search course, resume referral to employers, and resume preparation.

Employment Of 1996–97 graduates, 100% were employed within three months of graduation. Types of employment entered: accounting, communications, computer-related, consulting, education, engineering, government, high technology, hospitality management, information systems/technology, management, marketing, pharmaceutical, service industry, telecommunications.

Business Program(s) URL: http://www.theseus.fr

Program Contact: Mr. Eddy Travia, Head of MBA Admissions, BP 169, Rue Albert Einstein, Sophia Antipolis Cedex 06903, France. Phone: 33-4-9294-5107; Fax: 33-4-9365-3837; E-mail: admissions@theseus.fr
See full description on page 1020.

GERMANY

Schiller International University

Business Programs

Heidelberg, Germany

OVERVIEW
Schiller International University is an independent-nonprofit, coed institution. Founded: 1964. The graduate business unit is in an urban setting and is on a semester calendar.

HIGHLIGHTS

Enrollment Profile
Full-time: N/R
Part-time: N/R
Total: N/R
Average Age: N/R
Fall 1997 Average GPA: N/R

International: N/R
Women: N/R
Minorities: N/R
Average Class Size: 15
Fall 1997 Average GMAT: N/R

Costs
Full-time tuition: N/R
Part-time tuition: N/R

Degree(s) offered in conjunction with Schiller France, Schiller Spain, Schiller Switzerland, Schiller United Kingdom, Schiller United States

GRADUATE BUSINESS PROGRAMS
Master of Business Administration in International Business (MBA) Full-time, part-time; 62 total credits required; 12 months to 3 years to complete program.
Master of International Management in International Business (MIM) Full-time, part-time; 62 total credits required; 12 months to 3 years to complete program.
Executive MBA (MBA) Part-time; minimum of 2 years to complete program.

ADMISSION
Application Requirements GMAT score, application form, application fee, bachelor's degree, personal statement, college transcript(s).
Recommended for Application Minimum GPA: 3.0, work experience, computer experience.
Application Deadline Applications processed on a rolling/continuous basis for both domestic and international students. Application fee: $35. Deferred entrance is available.

ACADEMICS
Faculty Part-time 10.
Teaching Methodologies Case study, computer-aided instruction, computer analysis, experiential learning, faculty seminars, field projects, group discussion, lecture, research, seminars by members of the business community, student presentations, study groups, team projects.
Technology Students are not required to have their own PC.
Special Opportunities Advanced credit may be earned through credit by examination, transfer of credits from another institution. International exchange programs in France, Spain, Switzerland, United Kingdom, United States. An internship program is available.

FINANCES
Costs for 1997–98 Cost varies by academic program, campus location, number of credits taken. Fees vary by academic program, campus location.
Financial Aid Grants, scholarships, loans available. Application Deadline: 3/30.
Financial Aid Contact Mr. James Sutherland, Financial Aid Officer, 453 Edgewater Drive, Dunedin. Phone: 813-736-5082; Fax: 813-734-0359.

FACILITIES
Information Resources Main library; total holdings of 8,000 volumes, 94 current periodical subscriptions.

INTERNATIONAL STUDENTS
Demographics N/R
Services and Facilities International student office, international student center, international student housing, ESL courses, counseling/support services.
Applying TOEFL: minimum score of 550 recommended. Financial aid is available to international students.
International Student Contact Director of Admissions, Bergstrasse 106, Heidelberg. Phone: 49-6221-45810; Fax: 49-6221-402703.

PLACEMENT
Services include alumni network, career placement, job search course, and resume preparation.

Employment Types of employment entered: accounting, banking, communications, computer-related, consulting, consumer products, education, engineering, finance, financial services, government, health services, hospitality management, human resources, information systems/technology, insurance, international trade, law, management, manufacturing, marketing, media, mining, nonprofit, real estate, retail, service industry, telecommunications, transportation, utilities.
Business Program(s) URL: http://www.schiller.edu/
Program Contact: Dr. Christoph Leibrecht, Director of Admissions, 453 Edgewater Drive, Dunedin 34698-7532, Germany. Phone: 813-736-5082; Fax: 813-734-0359; E-mail: christof@campus.schiller.edu

WHU Koblenz

Otto-Beisheim Graduate School of Management

Vallendar, Germany

OVERVIEW
WHU Koblenz is an independent-nonprofit, coed institution. Enrollment: 318 graduate, professional, and undergraduate students; 270 full-time matriculated graduate/professional students; 48 part-time matriculated graduate/professional students. Founded: 1984. The graduate business unit is in a suburban setting and is on a semester calendar.

HIGHLIGHTS

Enrollment Profile
Full-time: 270
Part-time: 48
Total: 318
Average Age: 26
Fall 1997 Average GPA: N/R

International: 6%
Women: N/R
Minorities: N/R
Average Class Size: 65
Fall 1997 Average GMAT: 631

Costs
Full-time tuition: 12,000 German marks per academic year
Part-time tuition: 48,000 German marks per program

Degree(s) offered in conjunction with University of Texas at Austin, Lyon Graduate School of Business, Lancaster University

GRADUATE BUSINESS PROGRAMS
Executive MBA (MBA) Part-time; 3 years work experience required; minimum of 2 years to complete program.
Double Degree Program (MBA) Full-time; up to 12 months to complete program.

ADMISSION
Applications For fall 1997 there were 463 applications for admission. Of those applying, 70 were accepted. Of those accepted, 70 enrolled.
Application Requirements Application form, application fee, bachelor's degree, interview, resume, minimum of 2 years of work experience.
Recommended for Application GMAT score accepted: minimum 530.
Application Deadline 4/15 for fall, 4/15 for fall (international). Application fee: $60.

ACADEMICS
Faculty Full-time 16; part-time 30.
Teaching Methodologies Case study, computer-aided instruction, faculty seminars, field projects, group discussion, lecture, research, seminars by members of the business community, student presentations, study groups, team projects.
Technology 50 on-campus computer terminals/PCs are available for student use. The network has full access to the Internet. Students are not required to have their own PC.
Special Opportunities Advanced credit may be earned through credit by examination, transfer of credits from another institution. International exchange programs in Australia, Belgium, Brazil, Canada, Chile, Costa Rica, Denmark, Finland, France, Ireland, Italy, Japan, Mexico, Netherlands, Norway, Peoples Republic of China, Portugal, Republic of South Africa, Russia. An internship program is available.

FINANCES
Costs for 1997–98 Tuition: Full-time: 12,000 German marks per year. Part-time: 48,000 German marks per program. Average 1997–98 room and board costs were 1300 German marks per academic year (off campus). Room and board costs vary by occupancy (e.g., single, double, triple), type of accommodation, type of meal plan.
Financial Aid Fellowships, research assistantships, grants available.
Financial Aid Contact Anke Bruehl-Tschuck, Admissions Officer, Burgplatz 2, 56179 Vallender, Vallendar. Phone: 49-261-6509122; Fax: 49-261-6509111.

WHU Koblenz (continued)

FACILITIES
Information Resources Hochschulbibliothek; total holdings of 30,000 volumes, 300 current periodical subscriptions. CD player(s) available for graduate student use. Access provided to online bibliographic retrieval services.

INTERNATIONAL STUDENTS
Demographics 6% of students enrolled are international students [Europe, 80%, North America, 20%].

Services and Facilities International student office, international student center, international student housing, counseling/support services, German language courses.

Applying TOEFL: minimum score of 530 required. Financial aid is available to international students.

International Student Contact Axel Schumacher-Schroter, Director, International Programmes, Burgplatz 2, Vallender. Phone: 49-261-6509141; Fax: 49-261-6509111; E-mail: ip@whu-koblenz.de

PLACEMENT
Services include alumni network, career counseling/planning, career fairs, career placement, job interviews arranged, and resume referral to employers. In 1996–97, 35 organizations participated in on-campus recruiting; 150 on-campus interviews were conducted.

Employment Of 1996–97 graduates, 100% were employed within three months of graduation; the average starting salary was $35,000. Types of employment entered: accounting, banking, chemical industry, communications, computer-related, consulting, consumer products, energy, finance, financial services, government, human resources, insurance, international trade, management, marketing, media, service industry.

Business Program(s) URL: http://www.whu-koblenz.de/eindex.htm

Program Contact: Anke Bruehl-Tschuck, Admissions Officer, Burgplatz 2, Vallendar 56179, Germany. Phone: 49-261-6509122; Fax: 49-261-6509111; E-mail: abruehl@whu-koblenz.de

GREECE

Athens University of Economics and Business

Department of Business Administration

Athens, Greece

OVERVIEW
Athens University of Economics and Business is a private institution. Enrollment: 45 full-time matriculated graduate/professional students; 5 part-time matriculated graduate/professional students. Founded: 1920. The graduate business unit is in an urban setting and is on a semester calendar.

HIGHLIGHTS

Enrollment Profile

Full-time: 45	International: N/R
Part-time: 5	Women: N/R
Total: 50	Minorities: N/R
Average Age: 25	Average Class Size: 20
Fall 1997 Average GPA: N/R	Fall 1997 Average GMAT: 540

Costs
Full-time tuition: 250,000 Greek drachmas per academic year (resident)
Part-time tuition: N/R

GRADUATE BUSINESS PROGRAMS
Master of Business Administration (MBA) Full-time; 2 to 2.3 years to complete program.

ADMISSION
Applications For fall 1997 there were 70 applications for admission. Of those applying, 20 were accepted. Of those accepted, 20 enrolled.

Application Requirements GMAT score: minimum 550, application form, bachelor's degree, minimum GPA, interview, resume, college transcript(s), computer experience.

Application Deadline Deferred entrance is available.

ACADEMICS
Faculty Full-time 15.

Teaching Methodologies Case study, computer analysis, faculty seminars, field projects, group discussion, lecture, research, seminars by members of the business community, student presentations, team projects.

Technology 150 on-campus computer terminals/PCs are available for student use and are linked by a campus-wide network. The network has full access to the Internet. Students are required to have their own PC.

Special Opportunities International exchange program in various countries.

FINANCES
Costs for 1997–98 Tuition: Full-time: 250,000 Greek drachmas per semester (resident).

Financial Aid In 1997–98, 24% of students received some institutionally administered aid in the form of fellowships, research assistantships. Application Deadline: 10/1.

Financial Aid Contact Ms. Maria Haidemenaki, Registrar of Graduate Studies, 76 Patission Street, Athens.

FACILITIES
Information Resources Main library; total holdings of 70,000 volumes, 1,500 microforms, 1,000 current periodical subscriptions. CD player(s) available for graduate student use. Access provided to online bibliographic retrieval services and online databases.

INTERNATIONAL STUDENTS
Demographics N/R

Applying Financial aid is not available to international students.

International Student Contact Ms. Maria Haidemenaki, Registrar of Graduate Programs, 76 Patission Street, Athens. Phone: 322-823-7361 Ext. 322; Fax: 822-6204.

PLACEMENT
Services include career counseling/planning, career library, job interviews arranged, and resume referral to employers.

Business Program(s) URL: http://www.aueb.gr

Program Contact: Ms. Maria Haidemenaki, Registrar of Graduate Programs, 76 Patission Street, Athens 10434, Greece.

HONG KONG

The Chinese University of Hong Kong

Faculty of Business Administration

Shatin, NT, Hong Kong

OVERVIEW
The Chinese University of Hong Kong is a federally supported, coed institution. Enrollment: 13,061 graduate, professional, and undergraduate students; 1,116 full-time matriculated graduate/professional students; 2,059 part-time matriculated graduate/professional students. Founded: 1963. The graduate business unit is in a suburban setting and is on a semester, trimester, quarter calendar.

HIGHLIGHTS

Enrollment Profile

Full-time: 107	International: 3%
Part-time: 407	Women: 36%
Total: 514	Minorities: N/R
Average Age: 29	Average Class Size: 45
Fall 1997 Average GPA: N/R	Fall 1997 Average GMAT: 620

Costs
Full-time tuition: 42,100 Hong Kong dollars per academic year (resident); 42,100 Hong Kong dollars per academic year (nonresident)
Part-time tuition: N/R

GRADUATE BUSINESS PROGRAMS
Two-Year MBA Program (MBA) Full-time; 54 total credits required; 20 months to 5 years to complete program. Concentrations in accounting, decision sciences, finance, international business, management, marketing, managerial economics.

Executive MBA (EMBA) Part-time; 54 total credits required; 2 to 4 years to complete program. Concentrations in management, decision sciences, finance, managerial economics, marketing, leadership, strategic management.

Master of Science in Finance (MSc) Part-time; 30 total credits required; up to 2 years to complete program. Concentration in finance.

Master of Philosophy in Business Administration (MPhil) Full-time, part-time; 24 total credits required; 2 to 5 years to complete program. Concentrations in accounting, decision sciences, finance, marketing, management, international business, managerial economics.

Doctor of Philosophy in Business Administration (PhD) Full-time, part-time; 3 to 8 years to complete program. Concentrations in accounting, decision sciences, finance, management, marketing, international business, managerial economics.

Three-Year MBA Program (MBA) Part-time; 54 total credits required; minimum of 3 years post-qualification work experience required; 2 to 5 years to complete program. Concentrations in accounting, decision sciences, finance, international business, management, marketing, managerial economics.

Master of Accountancy (MAcc) Part-time; 30 total credits required; 2 to 3 years to complete program. Concentration in accounting.

Master of Science in International Business Program (MSc) Part-time; 30 total credits required; up to 2 years to complete program. Concentration in international business.

Master of Science in Information and Technology Management Program (MSc) Part-time; 27-33 total credits required; up to 19 months to complete program. Concentration in management information systems.

Master of Science in Business Economics Program (MSc) Part-time; 27-33 total credits required; up to 19 months to complete program. Concentration in managerial economics.

ADMISSION
Applications For fall 1997 there were 1,250 applications for admission.

Application Requirements Application form, application fee, bachelor's degree, minimum GPA: 3.0, interview, 2 letters of recommendation, personal statement, college transcript(s), work experience.

Recommended for Application GMAT score accepted.

Application Deadline 2/28 for fall. Application fee: 180 Hong Kong dollars. Deferred entrance is available.

ACADEMICS
Faculty Full-time 110; part-time 4.

Teaching Methodologies Case study, faculty seminars, field projects, group discussion, lecture, research, seminars by members of the business community, student presentations, study groups, team projects.

Technology Computer terminals/PCs are available for student use and are linked by a campus-wide network. The network has full access to the Internet. Students are not required to have their own PC.

Special Opportunities Advanced credit may be earned through credit by examination. International exchange programs in Australia, Canada, Japan, United Kingdom, United States. An internship program is available.

FINANCES
Costs for 1997–98 Tuition: Full-time: 42,100 Hong Kong dollars per year (resident); 42,100 Hong Kong dollars per year (nonresident). Cost varies by academic program, number of credits taken. Average 1997–98 room only costs were 10,000 Hong Kong dollars per academic year. Room and board costs vary by occupancy (e.g., single, double, triple).

Financial Aid In 1997–98, 7% of students received some institutionally administered aid in the form of research assistantships, teaching assistantships, scholarships, loans.

Financial Aid Contact Ms. Lauren Lee, Admissions Coordinator, Shatin, NT. Phone: 852-2-609-7786; Fax: 852-2-603-2689; E-mail: laurenlee@cuhk.edu.hk

FACILITIES
Information Resources University Library plus 8 additional on-campus libraries; total holdings of 1,370,000 volumes, 9,410 current periodical subscriptions. CD player(s) available for graduate student use. Access provided to online databases.

INTERNATIONAL STUDENTS
Demographics 3% of students enrolled are international students.

Services and Facilities International student office, international student center, international student housing, visa services, counseling/support services.

Applying Proof of adequate funds required. Proof of health/immunizations recommended. Financial aid is not available to international students.

International Student Contact Ms. Lauren Lee, Exchange Programmes Coordinator, Shatin, NT. Phone: 852-2-609-7786; Fax: 852-2-603-6289; E-mail: laurenlee@cuhk.edu.hk

PLACEMENT
Services include alumni network, career counseling/planning, career library, career placement, electronic job bank, job interviews arranged, job search course, resume referral to employers, and resume preparation.

Employment Of 1996–97 graduates, 95% were employed within three months of graduation; the average starting salary was 240,000 Hong Kong dollars. Types of employment entered: accounting, banking, communications, consult-

ing, consumer products, education, engineering, finance, financial services, human resources, management, marketing, media, petrochemical, real estate, retail, service industry, telecommunications.

Business Program(s) URL: http://www.cuhk.edu.hk/baf/graduate.html

Program Contact: Ms. Lauren Lee, Admissions Coordinator, Shatin, NT, Hong Kong. Phone: 852-2-609-7786; Fax: 852-2-603-2689; E-mail: laurenlee@cuhk.edu.hk

Hong Kong Baptist University

School of Business
Kowloon Tong, Hong Kong

OVERVIEW
Hong Kong Baptist University is a federally supported, coed institution. Enrollment: 4,753 graduate, professional, and undergraduate students; 91 full-time matriculated graduate/professional students; 520 part-time matriculated graduate/professional students. Founded: 1956. The graduate business unit is in an urban setting and is on a trimester calendar.

HIGHLIGHTS

Enrollment Profile

Full-time: 0	International: N/R
Part-time: 88	Women: 34%
Total: 88	Minorities: N/R
Average Age: 34	Average Class Size: 45
Fall 1997 Average GPA: N/R	Fall 1997 Average GMAT: 528

Costs
Full-time tuition: N/R
Part-time tuition: 57,600 Hong Kong dollars per year (resident); 57,600 Hong Kong dollars per year (nonresident)

GRADUATE BUSINESS PROGRAMS
Master of Business Administration (MBA) Part-time; 36 total credits required; up to 2 years to complete program. Concentrations in accounting, economics, entrepreneurship, finance, human resources, international business, management, management information systems, marketing, operations management, organizational behavior/development, quantitative analysis, strategic management.

ADMISSION
Applications For fall 1997 there were 141 applications for admission. Of those applying, 89 were accepted. Of those accepted, 50 enrolled.

Application Requirements Application form, application fee, bachelor's degree, interview, 2 letters of recommendation, resume, college transcript(s), minimum of 2 years of work experience.

Recommended for Application GMAT score accepted: minimum 500, computer experience.

Application Deadline 3/15 for fall, 3/15 for fall (international). Application fee: 150 Hong Kong dollars.

ACADEMICS
Faculty Full-time 14.

Teaching Methodologies Case study, faculty seminars, field projects, group discussion, lecture, research, seminars by members of the business community, student presentations, team projects.

Technology 200 on-campus computer terminals/PCs are available for student use and are linked by a campus-wide network. The network has full access to the Internet. Students are not required to have their own PC.

Special Opportunities Advanced credit may be earned through credit by examination.

FINANCES
Costs for 1997–98 Tuition: Part-time: 57,600 Hong Kong dollars per year (resident); 57,600 Hong Kong dollars per year (nonresident).

Financial Aid Scholarships available.

Financial Aid Contact Scholarship and Financial Aid Section, Academic Registry, Kowloon-Tong. Phone: 852-2-339-7936; Fax: 852-2-339-7373.

FACILITIES
Information Resources Au Shue Hung Memorial Library plus 2 additional on-campus libraries; total holdings of 522,646 volumes, 14,516 microforms, 4,373 current periodical subscriptions. CD player(s) available for graduate student use. Access provided to online databases.

INTERNATIONAL STUDENTS
Demographics N/R

Services and Facilities International student office, international student housing, counseling/support services.

Hong Kong Baptist University (continued)

Applying Financial aid is not available to international students.

International Student Contact Mr. Benny Petty, Assistant Professor, Department of English, Hong Kong Baptist University, Kowloon Tong. Phone: 852-2-339-7308; Fax: 852-2-338-0374; E-mail: blpetty@hkbu.edu.hk

PLACEMENT

Services include career placement.

Employment Types of employment entered: accounting, banking, engineering, finance, financial services, government, human resources, information systems/technology, international trade, management, marketing, service industry.

Business Program(s) URL: http://www.hkbu.edu.hk/~bus/mba.htm

Program Contact: Ms. Cecelia Tsui, Executive Officer—Research and Postgraduate Studies Section, Academic Registry, Kowloon-Tong, Hong Kong. Phone: 852-2-339-7929; Fax: 852-2-339-7373; E-mail: postgrad@hkbu.edu.hk

The Hong Kong University of Science and Technology

School of Business and Management

Kowloon, Hong Kong

OVERVIEW

The Hong Kong University of Science and Technology is a locally supported, coed institution. Enrollment: 7,176 graduate, professional, and undergraduate students; 805 full-time matriculated graduate/professional students; 722 part-time matriculated graduate/professional students. Founded: 1991. The graduate business unit is in a suburban setting and is on a semester calendar.

HIGHLIGHTS

Enrollment Profile

Full-time: 99	International: 9%
Part-time: 331	Women: 32%
Total: 430	Minorities: N/R
Average Age: 29	Average Class Size: 65
Fall 1997 Average GPA: N/R	Fall 1997 Average GMAT: 613

Costs
Full-time tuition: N/R
Part-time tuition: N/R

Degree(s) offered in conjunction with Northwestern University

GRADUATE BUSINESS PROGRAMS

Master of Business Administration (MBA) Full-time, part-time; 46-56 total credits required; 2 to 5 years to complete program. Concentrations in finance, information management.

Master of Science in Economics (MS) Full-time, part-time; 36 total credits required; 18 months to 5 years to complete program.

Master of Philosophy (MPhil) Full-time, part-time; 18 total credits required; 2 to 5 years to complete program. Concentrations in accounting, economics, finance, marketing, management, system management, information management.

Master of Science in Investment Management (MS) Part-time; 33 total credits required; 2 to 5 years to complete program.

Master of Science in Information Systems Management (MS) Part-time; 30 total credits required; 2 to 5 years to complete program.

Executive Master of Business Administration (EMBA) Part-time; 30 total credits required; 16 months to complete program.

ADMISSION

Applications For fall 1997 there were 1,029 applications for admission. Of those applying, 275 were accepted. Of those accepted, 174 enrolled.

Application Requirements GMAT score, application form, application fee, bachelor's degree, essay, minimum GPA: 3.0, interview, 2 letters of recommendation, personal statement, college transcript(s), minimum of 1 year of work experience.

Recommended for Application GRE score accepted.

Application Deadline 4/15 for fall, 2/28 for fall (international). Application fee: $16. Deferred entrance is available.

ACADEMICS

Faculty Full-time 145.

Teaching Methodologies Case study, computer-aided instruction, computer simulations, faculty seminars, field projects, group discussion, lecture, research, role playing, seminars by members of the business community, simulations, student presentations, study groups, team projects.

Technology 525 on-campus computer terminals/PCs are available for student use and are linked by a campus-wide network. The network has full access to the Internet. Students are not required to have their own PC.

Special Opportunities Advanced credit may be earned through credit by examination. International exchange programs in Australia, Canada, France, Germany, Japan, People's Republic of China, Spain, United Kingdom, United States. An internship program is available.

FINANCES

Costs for 1997–98 Cost varies by academic program. Fees vary by academic program. Average 1997–98 room only costs were $1806 per academic year (on campus) and $4400 per academic year (off campus). Room and board costs vary by occupancy (e.g., single, double, triple), type of accommodation.

Financial Aid In 1997–98, 20% of students received some institutionally administered aid in the form of research assistantships, teaching assistantships, scholarships. Application Deadline: 9/1.

Financial Aid Contact Ms. Pui Hung Mak, Executive Officer, School of Business and Management, Clear Water Bay, Kowloon. Phone: 852-2-358-7537; Fax: 852-2-705-9596; E-mail: hkustmba@ust.hk

FACILITIES

Information Resources University Library; total holdings of 403,157 volumes, 68,764 microforms, 6,797 current periodical subscriptions. CD player(s) available for graduate student use. Access provided to online bibliographic retrieval services and online databases.

INTERNATIONAL STUDENTS

Demographics 9% of students enrolled are international students [Asia, 68%, Europe, 5%, North America, 27%].

Services and Facilities Visa services, counseling/support services.

Applying IELT, TOEFL required. Financial aid is available to international students.

International Student Contact Ms. Doris Chan, Placement Officer, School of Business and Management, Clear Water Bay, Kowloon. Phone: 852-2-358-7534; Fax: 852-2-705-9596; E-mail: bmsdoris@ust.hk

PLACEMENT

Services include alumni network, career library, career placement, job interviews arranged, resume referral to employers, and resume preparation. In 1996–97, 55 organizations participated in on-campus recruiting.

Employment Of 1996–97 graduates, 91% were employed within three months of graduation; the average starting salary was $38,380. Types of employment entered: accounting, banking, consulting, consumer products, engineering, finance, financial services, information systems/technology, marketing, telecommunications.

Business Program(s) URL: http://www.bm.ust.hk/

Program Contact: Ms. Pui Hung Mak, Executive Officer, School of Business and Management, Clear Water Bay, Kowloon, Hong Kong. Phone: 852-2-358-7537; Fax: 852-2-705-9596; E-mail: hkustmba@ust.hk

University of Hong Kong

University of Hong Kong School of BusinessHong Kong

OVERVIEW

The University of Hong Kong coed institution. Enrollment: 13,500 graduate, professional, and undergraduate students. The graduate business unit is in an urban setting and is on a semester calendar.

HIGHLIGHTS

Enrollment Profile

Full-time: 0	International: N/R
Part-time: 190	Women: 24%
Total: 190	Minorities: N/R
Average Age: 28	Average Class Size: 40
Fall 1997 Average GPA: N/R	Fall 1997 Average GMAT: N/R

Costs
Full-time tuition: N/R
Part-time tuition: 57,150 Hong Kong dollars per year (resident); 57,150 Hong Kong dollars per year (nonresident)

GRADUATE BUSINESS PROGRAMS
Master of Business Administration (MBA) Part-time; 2 to 4 years to complete program. Concentrations in accounting, economics, entrepreneurship, finance, human resources, international business, management, management systems analysis, marketing, organizational behavior/development, strategic management, managerial economics, technology management, business law, international marketing.

ADMISSION
Applications For fall 1997 there were 350 applications for admission. Of those applying, 67 were accepted.
Application Requirements Application form, bachelor's degree, essay, interview, letters of recommendation, personal statement, college transcript(s), minimum of 3 years of work experience.
Recommended for Application GMAT score accepted: minimum 550.
Application Deadline 4/3 for fall, 4/3 for fall (international). Application fee: 150 Hong Kong dollars. Deferred entrance is available.

ACADEMICS
Faculty Full-time 25; part-time 6.
Teaching Methodologies Case study, lecture, team projects.
Technology Computer terminals/PCs are available for student use and are linked by a campus-wide network. The network has full access to the Internet. Students are not required to have their own PC.

FINANCES
Costs for 1997–98 Tuition: Part-time: 57,150 Hong Kong dollars per year (resident); 57,150 Hong Kong dollars per year (nonresident).
Financial Aid Contact Dr. Su Han Chan, Program Director, University of Hong Kong School of Business. Phone: 852-2-859-1021; Fax: 852-2-858-5614; E-mail: hkumba@hkucc.hku.hk

INTERNATIONAL STUDENTS
Demographics N/R
Applying TOEFL: minimum score of 550 required. Financial aid is not available to international students.

PLACEMENT
Services include career placement.
Employment Types of employment entered: accounting, banking, communications, computer-related, consulting, engineering, finance, financial services, government, human resources, information systems/technology, insurance, international trade, management, marketing, media, real estate, service industry, telecommunications.
Business Program(s) URL: http://www.hku.hk/business/

Program Contact: Dr. Su Han Chan, Program Director, University of Hong Kong School of Business, Hong Kong. Phone: 852-2-859-1021; Fax: 852-2-858-5614; E-mail: hkumba@hkucc.hku.hk

INDONESIA

Institut Pengembangan Manajemen Indonesia

Business Programs
Jakarta, Indonesia

OVERVIEW
Institut Pengembangan Manajemen Indonesia is an independent-nonprofit, coed institution. Founded: 1982. The graduate business unit is in an urban setting and is on a trimester calendar.

HIGHLIGHTS

Enrollment Profile
Full-time: N/R
Part-time: N/R
Total: N/R
Average Age: 29
Fall 1997 Average GPA: N/R

International: N/R
Women: N/R
Minorities: N/R
Average Class Size: 40
Fall 1997 Average GMAT: 475

Costs
Full-time tuition: N/R
Part-time tuition: N/R

Degree(s) offered in conjunction with Monash University

GRADUATE BUSINESS PROGRAMS
Master of Business Administration (MBA) Full-time; 2 years work experience required; up to 12 months to complete program. Concentration in international business.
Executive Master of Business Administration (EMBA) Part-time; 5 years work experience required; up to 2.1 years to complete program. Concentration in international business.

ADMISSION
Application Requirements GMAT score: minimum 475, application form, application fee, bachelor's degree, interview, 2 letters of recommendation, personal statement, resume, college transcript(s).
Application Deadline 10/1 for summer. Application fee: $25.

ACADEMICS
Faculty Full-time 8; part-time 3.
Teaching Methodologies Case study, group discussion, lecture, student presentations, team projects.
Technology 15 on-campus computer terminals/PCs are available for student use and are linked by a campus-wide network. The network does not have Internet access. Students are not required to have their own PC.

FINANCES
Financial Aid Contact Dr. Antarikso Abdulrahman, Program Director, JL Rajajati Timur I/1, Jakarta. Phone: 62-21-797-0419 Ext. 228; Fax: 62-21-797-0374.

FACILITIES
Information Resources Institut Pengembangan Manajemen Indonesia Library; total holdings of 5,000 volumes, 65 current periodical subscriptions. CD player(s) available for graduate student use.

INTERNATIONAL STUDENTS
Demographics N/R
Applying TOEFL: minimum score of 575 required. Financial aid is not available to international students.
International Student Contact Dr. Antarikso Abdulrahman, Program Director, JL Rawajati Timur I/1, Jakarta. Phone: 62-21-797-0419 Ext. 228; Fax: 62-21-797-0374.

PLACEMENT
Services include alumni network, career fairs, career library, career placement, resume referral to employers, and resume preparation. In 1996–97, 50 organizations participated in on-campus recruiting.
Employment Types of employment entered: banking, consumer products, engineering, finance, government, information systems/technology, international trade, law, management, manufacturing, retail, service industry.

Program Contact: Program Director, IMPI Campus, Jl. Rawajati Timur I/1, Kalibata, Jakarta 12750, Indonesia. Phone: 62-21-797-0419; Fax: 62-21-797-0509; E-mail: ipmimba@rad.net.id

IRELAND

University College Cork

Faculty of Commerce
Cork, Ireland

OVERVIEW
The University College Cork is a federally supported, coed institution. Enrollment: 10,158 graduate, professional, and undergraduate students; 1,668 full-time matriculated graduate/professional students; 373 part-time matriculated graduate/professional students. Founded: 1849. The graduate business unit is in an urban setting and is on a semester calendar.

627

IRELAND

University College Cork (continued)

HIGHLIGHTS

Enrollment Profile
Full-time: N/R
Part-time: N/R
Total: N/R
Average Age: 23
Fall 1997 Average GPA: N/R

International: N/R
Women: N/R
Minorities: N/R
Average Class Size: 32
Fall 1997 Average GMAT: 475

Costs
Full-time tuition: N/R
Part-time tuition: 4840 Irish pounds per year (resident); 4400 Irish pounds per year (nonresident)

GRADUATE BUSINESS PROGRAMS

Executive MBA (MBA) Part-time; minimum of 2 years to complete program. Concentrations in accounting, management systems analysis, system management, business ethics, economics, entrepreneurship, financial management/planning, human resources, leadership, management information systems, managerial economics, marketing, new venture management, operations management, strategic management.

Master of Commerce (MComm) Part-time.

Master of Business Studies in Business Economics (MBS) Full-time.

Master of Business Studies in Entrepreneurialism (MBS) Full-time, part-time.

Master of Business Studies in European Accounting (MBS)

Master of Business Studies in Managerial Information and Managerial Accounting Systems (MBS) Full-time.

Master of Science in Public Administration (MS) Part-time.

Master of Science in Accounting, Finance, and Management Information Systems (MS) Full-time, part-time.

Master of Science in Strategic Management (MS) Full-time, part-time.

Master of Economic Science (MEcon) Full-time, part-time.

ADMISSION

Application Requirements GMAT score, application form, application fee.

Recommended for Application Bachelor's degree, 2 letters of recommendation, personal statement, resume, college transcript(s), minimum of 2 years of work experience.

Application Deadline 9/11 for fall, 9/11 for fall (international). Application fee: 31 Irish pounds.

ACADEMICS

Faculty Full-time 96.

Teaching Methodologies Case study, computer-aided instruction, computer analysis, faculty seminars, group discussion, lecture, research, seminars by members of the business community, student presentations, study groups, team projects.

Technology The network has full access to the Internet.

FINANCES

Costs for 1997–98 Tuition: 4840 Irish pounds per year (resident); 4400 Irish pounds per year (nonresident). Cost varies by academic program.

FACILITIES

Information Resources Boole Library.

INTERNATIONAL STUDENTS

Demographics N/R

Services and Facilities International student office, counseling/support services.

Program Contact: Ms. Marie McSwiney, MBA Administrative Support, Faculty of Commerce, Western Road, Cork, Ireland. Phone: 353-21-902-394; Fax: 353-21-271-092; E-mail: staf8006@ucc.ie

University College Dublin

The Michael Smurfit Graduate School of Business

Blackrock, County Dublin, Ireland

OVERVIEW

The University College Dublin is a federally supported, coed institution. Enrollment: 17,000 graduate, professional, and undergraduate students; 660 full-time matriculated graduate/professional students; 375 part-time matriculated graduate/professional students. Founded: 1854. The graduate business unit is in a suburban setting and is on a semester calendar.

HIGHLIGHTS

Enrollment Profile
Full-time: 31
Part-time: 79
Total: 110
Average Age: 29
Fall 1997 Average GPA: N/R

International: 7%
Women: N/R
Minorities: N/R
Average Class Size: 35
Fall 1997 Average GMAT: 610

Costs
Full-time tuition: 7500 Irish pounds per academic year (resident); 10,000 Irish pounds per academic year (nonresident)
Part-time tuition: N/R

GRADUATE BUSINESS PROGRAMS

Master of Business Administration (MBA) Full-time; 21 total credits required; up to 12 months to complete program. Concentrations in marketing, finance, human resources, entrepreneurship, accounting, management information systems, business law, economics, insurance, international marketing, international and area business studies, manufacturing management, organizational behavior/development, strategic management.

Executive Master of Business Administration (EMBA) Part-time; 21 total credits required; up to 2 years to complete program. Concentrations in marketing, finance, human resources, entrepreneurship, accounting, management information systems.

Master of Business Studies (MBS) Full-time, part-time; undergraduate business degree or a degree in a cognate discipline required; 12 months to 2 years to complete program. Concentrations in finance, human resources, international and area business studies, international marketing, management information systems, marketing, marketing research, organizational behavior/development, strategic management, travel industry/tourism management, actuarial science, international business, manufacturing management.

Master of Management Science (MMS) Full-time; undergraduate business, math, or computing degree required; 12 months to complete program. Concentration in management science.

Disability Management (MS) Full-time; minimum of 12 months to complete program. Concentration in management.

Master of Science Marketing Practice (MSMP) Full-time; undergraduate degree in business marketing required; 12 months to complete program. Concentrations in marketing, marketing research.

Master of Commerce (MComm)

Doctor of Philosophy (PhD) Full-time, part-time.

ADMISSION

Applications For fall 1997 there were 140 applications for admission. Of those applying, 69 were accepted. Of those accepted, 69 enrolled.

Application Requirements GRE score, application form, application fee, bachelor's degree, 2 letters of recommendation, resume, college transcript(s), minimum of 3 years of work experience.

Recommended for Application GMAT score accepted, interview.

Application Deadline 3/31 for fall, 3/31 for fall (international). Application fee: 20 Irish pounds.

ACADEMICS

Faculty Full-time 35; part-time 52.

Teaching Methodologies Case study, computer-aided instruction, computer analysis, computer simulations, experiential learning, faculty seminars, field projects, group discussion, lecture, research, role playing, seminars by members of the business community, simulations, student presentations, study groups, team projects.

Technology 144 on-campus computer terminals/PCs are available for student use and are linked by a campus-wide network. The network has full access to the Internet. Students are not required to have their own PC.

Special Opportunities International exchange programs in Austria, Belgium, Denmark, France, Germany, Greece, Holland, Italy, Norway, Portugal, Scotland, Spain, Sweden, United Kingdom, United States.

FINANCES

Costs for 1997–98 Tuition: Full-time: 7500 Irish pounds per year (resident); 10,000 Irish pounds per year (nonresident). Cost varies by academic program, class time (e.g., day/evening). Fees vary by academic program, class time (e.g., day/evening). Average 1997–98 room only costs were 1559 Irish pounds per academic year (on campus) and 2025 Irish pounds per academic year (off campus).

FACILITIES

Information Resources University College Dublin Library. CD player(s) available for graduate student use. Access provided to online bibliographic retrieval services and online databases.

INTERNATIONAL STUDENTS

Demographics 7% of students enrolled are international students.

Services and Facilities International student office, international student center, international student housing, counseling/support services.
Applying TOEFL required.
International Student Contact Mr. Colm Small, International Affairs Officer, Carysfort Avenue, Blackrock, County Dublin, Ireland. Phone: 353-1-706-8337; Fax: 353-1-283-1911; E-mail: csmall@blackrock.ucd.ie

PLACEMENT
Services include alumni network, career placement, job interviews arranged, and resume referral to employers.
Employment Types of employment entered: accounting, banking, government, management, retail.
Business Program(s) URL: http://www.ucd.ie/gsb/welcome.html

Program Contact: Ms. Margaret Bannon, MBA Program Manager, Carysfort Avenue, Blackrock, County Dublin, Ireland. Phone: 353-1-706-8860; Fax: 353-1-283-1911; E-mail: mbannon @blackrock.ucd.ie

University College, Galway

Faculty of Commerce
Galway, Ireland

OVERVIEW
The University College, Galway is a federally supported institution. Enrollment: 10,000 graduate, professional, and undergraduate students. Founded: 1845. The graduate business unit is in an urban setting and is on a term calendar.

HIGHLIGHTS

Enrollment Profile
Full-time: 0
Part-time: 25
Total: 25
Average Age: 30
Fall 1997 Average GPA: N/R

International: N/R
Women: 36%
Minorities: N/R
Average Class Size: N/R
Fall 1997 Average GMAT: N/R

Costs
Full-time tuition: 3745 Irish pounds per academic year (resident)
Part-time tuition: N/R

GRADUATE BUSINESS PROGRAMS
Executive MBA (MBA) Full-time, part-time; 12 months to 2 years to complete program. Concentrations in accounting, economics, entrepreneurship, finance, human resources, management, management information systems, marketing, operations management, organizational behavior/development, quantitative analysis, strategic management, business law, quality management.

ADMISSION
Application Requirements Application form, bachelor's degree, interview, college transcript(s), minimum of 3 years of work experience.
Recommended for Application GMAT score accepted: minimum 450.
Application Deadline Applications processed on a rolling/continuous basis for both domestic and international students.

ACADEMICS
Teaching Methodologies Case study, lecture, research, seminars by members of the business community, student presentations.
Technology 40 on-campus computer terminals/PCs are available for student use and are linked by a campus-wide network. The network has full access to the Internet. Students are required to have their own PC.

FINANCES
Costs for 1997–98 Tuition: Full-time: 3745 Irish pounds per year (resident).

INTERNATIONAL STUDENTS
Demographics N/R
Services and Facilities International student office.
Applying Proof of adequate funds, proof of health/immunizations required. Financial aid is not available to international students.
International Student Contact Mr. Seamus O'Grady, International Affairs Office, University Road, Galway. Phone: 353-91-524-411 Ext. 2144; Fax: 353-91-525-051; E-mail: intloffice@mis.ucg.ie

Program Contact: Mr. Joseph McAllister, Department of Management, Galway, Ireland. Phone: 353-91-524-411 Ext. 3079; Fax: 353-91-524-130; E-mail: joe.mcallister@ucg.ie

University of Limerick

College of Business
Limerick, Ireland

OVERVIEW
The University of Limerick is a federally supported, coed institution. Enrollment: 8,464 graduate, professional, and undergraduate students; 695 full-time matriculated graduate/professional students; 256 part-time matriculated graduate/professional students. Founded: 1972. The graduate business unit is in a suburban setting and is on a semester calendar.

HIGHLIGHTS

Enrollment Profile
Full-time: 174
Part-time: 57
Total: 231
Average Age: N/R
Fall 1997 Average GPA: N/R

International: 3%
Women: 48%
Minorities: N/R
Average Class Size: 20
Fall 1997 Average GMAT: 560

Costs
Full-time tuition: 4375 Irish pounds per academic year (resident); 8750 Irish pounds per academic year (nonresident)
Part-time tuition: N/R

GRADUATE BUSINESS PROGRAMS
Corporate MBA (MBA) Part-time; 60 total credits required; up to 2 years to complete program. Concentrations in entrepreneurship, human resources, international management.
Executive MBA (MBA) Part-time; 60 total credits required; up to 2 years to complete program. Concentrations in entrepreneurship, human resources, international management.
Master of Business Studies in European Human Resources Management (MBS) Part-time; 60 total credits required; up to 2 years to complete program. Concentrations in human resources, industrial/labor relations.
Master of Project Management (MPM) Part-time; 90 total credits required; up to 2 years to complete program. Concentrations in organizational behavior/development, project management.
Master of Business Studies (MBS) Full-time, part-time; 12 months to 2 years to complete program.
Master of Business Studies in Entrepreneurial Studies (MBS) Full-time; 60 total credits required; up to 2 years to complete program.

ADMISSION
Applications For fall 1997 there were 470 applications for admission.
Application Requirements Application form, bachelor's degree, minimum GPA: 3.0, interview, college transcript(s).
Recommended for Application GMAT score accepted.
Application Deadline Applications processed on a rolling/continuous basis for both domestic and international students.

ACADEMICS
Faculty Full-time 61.
Teaching Methodologies Case study, computer-aided instruction, computer analysis, computer simulations, experiential learning, faculty seminars, field projects, group discussion, lecture, research, role playing, seminars by members of the business community, simulations, student presentations, study groups, team projects.
Technology 1,200 on-campus computer terminals/PCs are available for student use and are linked by a campus-wide network. The network has full access to the Internet. Students are not required to have their own PC.
Special Opportunities Advanced credit may be earned through credit by examination, transfer of credits from another institution.

FINANCES
Costs for 1997–98 Tuition: Full-time: 4375 Irish pounds per year (resident); 8750 Irish pounds per year (nonresident). Average 1997–98 room only costs were 1693 Irish pounds per academic year. Room and board costs vary by occupancy (e.g., single, double, triple).
Financial Aid Grants, scholarships available.
Financial Aid Contact Ms. Ann Lyons, Administrative Assistant, Admissions Office, Limerick. Phone: 353-61-202-366; Fax: 353-61-334-859.

FACILITIES
Information Resources University of Limerick Library plus 1 additional on-campus library; total holdings of 140,000 volumes, 7,300 microforms, 2,000 current periodical subscriptions. CD player(s) available for graduate student use. Access provided to online bibliographic retrieval services.

University of Limerick (continued)

INTERNATIONAL STUDENTS
Demographics 3% of students enrolled are international students [Europe, 71%, North America, 29%].

Services and Facilities International student office, international student center, international student housing, ESL courses, counseling/support services.

Applying TOEFL: minimum score of 550, proof of adequate funds required. Financial aid is not available to international students.

International Student Contact Ms. Ann Lyons, Administrative Assistant, Admissions Office, Limerick. Phone: 353-61-202-366; Fax: 353-61-334-859.

PLACEMENT
Services include alumni network, career counseling/planning, career fairs, career library, job interviews arranged, and resume referral to employers.

Business Program(s) URL: http://www.ul.ie/~business/

Program Contact: Ms. Ann Lyons, Administrative Assistant, Admissions Office, Limerick, Ireland. Phone: 353-61-202-366; Fax: 353-61-334-859.

ISRAEL

Bar-Ilan University

S. Daniel Abraham Center of Economics and Business, The Graduate School of Business

Ramat Gan, Israel

OVERVIEW
Bar-Ilan University is a private, coed institution. Enrollment: 22,000 graduate, professional, and undergraduate students; 1,000 full-time matriculated graduate/professional students; 1,000 part-time matriculated graduate/professional students. Founded: 1955. The graduate business unit is in a suburban setting and is on a seven week course cycle calendar.

HIGHLIGHTS

Enrollment Profile

Full-time: 20	International: 90%
Part-time: 0	Women: 40%
Total: 20	Minorities: N/R
Average Age: 23	Average Class Size: 20
Fall 1997 Average GPA: N/R	Fall 1997 Average GMAT: N/R

Costs
Full-time tuition: N/R
Part-time tuition: N/R

GRADUATE BUSINESS PROGRAMS
International MBA (MBA) Full-time, part-time; 25 total credits required; minimum of 14 months to complete program. Concentrations in international and area business studies, economics, finance, management, marketing, management information systems.

ADMISSION
Application Requirements GMAT score, application form, application fee, bachelor's degree, essay, 2 letters of recommendation, college transcript(s).

Recommended for Application Interview, computer experience.

Application Deadline 3/30 for summer, 3/30 for summer (international). Application fee: $50. Deferred entrance is available.

ACADEMICS
Faculty Full-time 22.

Teaching Methodologies Computer simulations, faculty seminars, field projects, lecture, research, seminars by members of the business community, simulations.

Technology 25 on-campus computer terminals/PCs are available for student use and are linked by a campus-wide network. The network has full access to the Internet. Students are not required to have their own PC.

Special Opportunities An internship program is available.

FINANCES
Costs for 1997–98 Average 1997–98 room and board costs were $6000 per academic year (off campus). Room and board costs vary by occupancy (e.g., single, double, triple).

FACILITIES
Information Resources Wurzweiler Library plus 5 additional on-campus libraries; total holdings of 800,000 volumes, 2,000 current periodical subscriptions.

CD player(s) available for graduate student use. Access provided to online bibliographic retrieval services.

INTERNATIONAL STUDENTS
Demographics 90% of students enrolled are international students [Asia, 10%, Europe, 10%, North America, 80%].

Services and Facilities International student office, international student center, international student housing, counseling/support services.

Applying Financial aid is not available to international students.

International Student Contact Ms. Cindy Sinvani, Coordinator, International MBA, Ramat Gan. Phone: 972-3-531-7914; Fax: 972-3-535-3182; E-mail: imba@mail.biu.ac.il

PLACEMENT
Services include career placement.

Employment Types of employment entered: accounting, banking, computer-related, consulting, finance, high technology, human resources, information systems/technology, law, management, marketing, nonprofit, retail, service industry, telecommunications.

Business Program(s) URL: http://www.biu.ac.il/soc/sb/imba

Program Contact: Ms. Cindy Sinvani, Coordinator, International MBA, Ramat Gan 52900, Israel. Phone: 972-3-531-7914; Fax: 972-3-535-3182; E-mail: imba@mail.biu.ac.il

Hebrew University of Jerusalem

Jerusalem School of Business Administration

Jerusalem, Israel

OVERVIEW
Hebrew University of Jerusalem is an independent-nonprofit institution. Founded: 1918.

GRADUATE BUSINESS PROGRAMS
Master of Business Administration (MBA)
Executive MBA (MBA)

ACADEMICS
Faculty Full-time 32.

FACILITIES
Information Resources The Jewish National and University Library.

Program Contact: Administrative Coordinator, Jerusalem School of Business Administration, Mt. Scopus, Jerusalem 91905, Israel. Phone: 972-2-883-236; Fax: 972-2-881-341.

Tel Aviv University

Leon Recanati Graduate School of Business Administration

Tel Aviv, Israel

OVERVIEW
Tel Aviv University coed institution. Enrollment: 25,409 graduate, professional, and undergraduate students. Founded: 1956. The graduate business unit is in an urban setting and is on a semester calendar.

HIGHLIGHTS

Enrollment Profile

Full-time: N/R	International: N/R
Part-time: N/R	Women: N/R
Total: 1,958	Minorities: N/R
Average Age: 29	Average Class Size: 45
Fall 1997 Average GPA: N/R	Fall 1997 Average GMAT: 600

Costs
Full-time tuition: N/R
Part-time tuition: N/R

Degree(s) offered in conjunction with Northwestern University

GRADUATE BUSINESS PROGRAMS
Master of Business Administration (MBA) Full-time, part-time; 30 total credits required; 2 to 5 years to complete program. Concentrations in accounting, finance, insurance, management information systems, marketing, operations management, organizational behavior/development, decision sciences, financial information systems, information management, risk management, international management, project management, technology management, human resources, management.

Executive MBA (EMBA) Full-time, part-time; 30 total credits required; 16 months to complete program.

Kellogg-Recanati International Executive MBA (EMBA) Full-time, part-time; 30 total credits required; minimum of 2 years to complete program.

Master of Health Administration (MHA) Full-time, part-time; 30 total credits required; 2 to 5 years to complete program.

Master of Science in Management Sciences—Operations Research (MSc) Full-time, part-time; 22 total credits required; thesis required; 2 to 5 years to complete program.

Master of Science in Management Sciences—Information Systems (MSc) Full-time, part-time; 22 total credits required; thesis required; 2 to 5 years to complete program.

Master of Science in Management Sciences—Organizational Behavior (MSc) Full-time, part-time; 22 total credits required; thesis required; 2 to 5 years to complete program.

Master of Science in Management Sciences—Finance (MSc) Full-time, part-time; 22 total credits required; thesis required; 2 to 5 years to complete program. Concentration in accounting.

ADMISSION
Applications For fall 1997 there were 1,096 applications for admission. Of those applying, 455 were accepted. Of those accepted, 421 enrolled.

Application Requirements Application form, application fee, bachelor's degree, GPA: minimum 70.0 on a 100 scale, college transcript(s).

Recommended for Application GMAT score accepted.

Application Deadline 2/1 for fall, 11/1 for spring, 5/1 for fall (international). Application fee: $160.

ACADEMICS
Faculty Full-time 80; part-time 165.

Teaching Methodologies Case study, lecture, research, seminars by members of the business community, student presentations, team projects.

Technology 100 on-campus computer terminals/PCs are available for student use and are linked by a campus-wide network. The network has full access to the Internet. Students are not required to have their own PC.

Special Opportunities Advanced credit may be earned through credit by examination, transfer of credits from another institution. International exchange programs in Canada, Finland, France, United States.

FINANCES
Costs for 1997–98 Average 1997–98 room and board costs were $800 per academic year (on campus) and $900 per academic year (off campus). Room and board costs vary by occupancy (e.g., single, double, triple), type of accommodation.

Financial Aid Research assistantships, teaching assistantships, grants, scholarships available. Financial aid is available to part-time students.

Financial Aid Contact Financial Aid Office, Tel Aviv University, Tel Aviv. Phone: 972-3-640-8067.

FACILITIES
Information Resources The Elias Sourasky Library plus 3 additional on-campus libraries; total holdings of 2,000,000 volumes, 8,800 current periodical subscriptions. CD player(s) available for graduate student use. Access provided to online bibliographic retrieval services and online databases.

INTERNATIONAL STUDENTS
Demographics N/R

Services and Facilities Counseling/support services, language tutoring.

Applying Financial aid is not available to international students.

International Student Contact Mrs. Gali Berzak, Faculty of Management, Tel Aviv University, Tel Aviv. Phone: 972-3-640-8069; Fax: 972-3-640-9560; E-mail: galibz@post.tau.ac.il

PLACEMENT
Services include career counseling/planning, career fairs, career library, job interviews arranged, job search course, and resume preparation. In 1996–97, 120 organizations participated in on-campus recruiting; 30 on-campus interviews were conducted.

Employment Types of employment entered: accounting, banking, communications, computer-related, consulting, consumer products, education, engineering, finance, financial services, government, high technology, human resources, insurance, international trade, management, manufacturing, marketing, media, nonprofit, utilities.

Business Program(s) URL: http://www.tau.ac.il/gsba/

Program Contact: Mrs. Orit Prihed, Secretary, Admission Affairs, Faculty of Management, Tel Aviv 69978, Israel. Phone: 972-3-640-8069; Fax: 972-3-640-9560; E-mail: prihed@post.tau.ac.il

ITALY

Bocconi University

SDA Bocconi

Milan, Italy

OVERVIEW
Bocconi University is a proprietary, coed institution. Enrollment: 22,430 graduate, professional, and undergraduate students; 205 full-time matriculated graduate/professional students; 10,225 part-time matriculated graduate/professional students. Founded: 1902. The graduate business unit is in an urban setting and is on a 16-month program (September-December) and 12-month program (January-December) calendar.

HIGHLIGHTS

Enrollment Profile

Full-time: 198	International: 31%
Part-time: 117	Women: 52%
Total: 315	Minorities: N/R
Average Age: 30	Average Class Size: 60
Fall 1997 Average GPA: N/R	Fall 1997 Average GMAT: 590

Costs
Full-time tuition: 32,000,000 Italian lire per academic year
Part-time tuition: N/R

Degree(s) offered in conjunction with Johns Hopkins University

GRADUATE BUSINESS PROGRAMS
Bilingual MBA (MBA) Full-time; up to 16 months to complete program. Concentrations in management, project management, international management, international and area business studies, financial information systems, management information systems.

Master of International Economics and Management (MIEM) Full-time; up to 12 months to complete program. Concentrations in international management, international economics.

ADMISSION
Applications For fall 1997 there were 1,200 applications for admission. Of those applying, 370 were accepted. Of those accepted, 315 enrolled.

Application Requirements Application form, application fee, bachelor's degree, essay, minimum GPA, interview, 2 letters of recommendation, personal statement, resume, college transcript(s), minimum of 1 year of work experience.

Recommended for Application GMAT score accepted, GRE score accepted.

Application Deadline 4/30 for fall, 4/30 for fall (international). Application fee: 150,000 Italian lire. Deferred entrance is available.

ACADEMICS
Faculty Full-time 150; part-time 50.

Teaching Methodologies Case study, computer-aided instruction, computer analysis, computer simulations, faculty seminars, field projects, group discussion, lecture, research, role playing, seminars by members of the business community, simulations, student presentations, study groups, team projects.

Technology 100 on-campus computer terminals/PCs are available for student use and are linked by a campus-wide network. The network has full access to the Internet. Students are not required to have their own PC.

Special Opportunities International exchange programs in Australia, France, Japan, Netherlands, United Kingdom, United States. An internship program is available.

FINANCES
Costs for 1997–98 Tuition: Full-time: 32,000,000 Italian lire per year. Cost varies by academic program. Fees vary by academic program. Average 1997–98 room and board costs were 18,000,000 Italian lire per academic year (off campus).

Financial Aid In 1997–98, 8% of students received some institutionally administered aid in the form of scholarships. Application Deadline: 4/30.

Financial Aid Contact Ms. Rossana Camera, Admissions and Financial Aid Officer, Via Balilla 16/18, Milano. Phone: 39-2-5836 3286; Fax: 39-2-5836 3275; E-mail: rossana.camera@sda.uni-bocconi.it

FACILITIES
Information Resources Bocconi University Library; total holdings of 610,000 volumes, 100 microforms, 3,000 current periodical subscriptions. CD player(s) available for graduate student use. Access provided to online bibliographic retrieval services and online databases.

Bocconi University (continued)

INTERNATIONAL STUDENTS
Demographics 31% of students enrolled are international students [Asia, 10%, Central America, 5%, Europe, 52%, North America, 18%, South America, 15%].

Services and Facilities International student office, international student center, international student housing, visa services, counseling/support services, language tutoring.

Applying TOEFL, proof of adequate funds, proof of health/immunizations required. Financial aid is available to international students.

International Student Contact Ms. Daniela Miglioli, Student and Internal Relations, Via Balilla 16/18, Milano. Phone: 39-2-5836 3273; Fax: 39-2-5836 3282; E-mail: daniela.miglioli@sda.uni-bocconi.it

PLACEMENT
Services include alumni network, career counseling/planning, career library, career placement, electronic job bank, job interviews arranged, job search course, resume referral to employers, and resume preparation. In 1996–97, 144 organizations participated in on-campus recruiting; 994 on-campus interviews were conducted.

Employment Of 1996–97 graduates, 90% were employed within three months of graduation; the average starting salary was 80,000,000 Italian lire. Types of employment entered: banking, chemical industry, computer-related, consulting, consumer products, education, engineering, finance, financial services, high technology, human resources, information systems/technology, international trade, management, manufacturing, marketing, media, nonprofit, pharmaceutical, service industry, telecommunications.

Business Program(s) URL: http://www.sda.uni-bocconi.it

Program Contact: Ms. Luisa Negri, Admissions Officer, Via Balilla 16/18, Milano 20136, Italy. Phone: 39-2-5836 3286; Fax: 39-2-5836 3275; E-mail: luisa.negri@sda.uni-bocconi.it

JAPAN

International University of Japan

Graduate School of International Management

Minami Uonuma-gun, Niigata, Japan

OVERVIEW
International University of Japan is an independent-nonprofit, primarily male institution. Enrollment: 245 graduate, professional, and undergraduate students; 245 full-time matriculated graduate/professional students; part-time matriculated graduate/professional students. Founded: 1982. The graduate business unit is in a rural setting and is on a quarter calendar.

HIGHLIGHTS

Enrollment Profile

Full-time: 126	International: 63%
Part-time: 0	Women: 18%
Total: 126	Minorities: N/R
Average Age: 28	Average Class Size: 10
Fall 1997 Average GPA: N/R	Fall 1997 Average GMAT: 615

Costs
Full-time tuition: ¥1,900,000 per academic year
Part-time tuition: N/R

A s a private graduate institution founded by Japan's leading corporations, International University of Japan (IUJ) has unique access to top executives who speak at the University, to future job opportunities, and to summer internships.

The student body includes Japanese students from top corporations as well as future business leaders from the top firms in the APEC region. This means that IUJ students graduate with a built-in network of contacts throughout the region that is personally and professionally rewarding for a lifetime.

IUJ's focus is on the Asia-Pacific marketplace. IUJ's faculty is already well versed in management practices in this region—an advantage that other business schools around the world are only beginning to recognize.

The IUJ students are drawn from the U.S., Europe, Africa, and the Middle East—from all parts of the world—and they live and work together in a beauti-

ful rural campus equipped with the best hardware and software in Japan. It is an ideal venue in which to study, learn, and make friends.

Without question, the Asia-Pacific region will witness the world's most dynamic economic growth well into the twenty-first century. IUJ encourages its students and graduates to shape their professional skills to meet this challenge

GRADUATE BUSINESS PROGRAMS
International Management Program (MBA) Full-time; 54 total credits required; interview for domestic applicants required; 22 months to 4 years to complete program. Concentrations in asian business studies, business law, finance, information management, international business, international finance, international management, japanese business studies, management information systems.

ADMISSION
Applications For fall 1997 there were 214 applications for admission. Of those applying, 111 were accepted. Of those accepted, 72 enrolled.

Application Requirements Application form, application fee, bachelor's degree, essay, interview, 2 letters of recommendation, personal statement, college transcript(s).

Recommended for Application GMAT score accepted, work experience.

Application Deadline 3/27 for fall, 4/3 for fall (international). Application fee: ¥30,000, ¥5000 (international). Deferred entrance is available.

ACADEMICS
Faculty Full-time 16; part-time 20.

Teaching Methodologies Case study, computer-aided instruction, computer analysis, computer simulations, experiential learning, faculty seminars, field projects, group discussion, lecture, research, role playing, seminars by members of the business community, simulations, student presentations, study groups, team projects.

Technology 50 on-campus computer terminals/PCs are available for student use and are linked by a campus-wide network. The network has full access to the Internet. Students are not required to have their own PC.

Special Opportunities Advanced credit may be earned through transfer of credits from another institution. International exchange programs in Belgium, Canada, China, Finland, France, Italy, Republic of Singapore, Thailand, United Kingdom, United States, Spain.

FINANCES
Costs for 1997–98 Tuition: Full-time: ¥1,900,000 per year. Fees: Full-time: ¥300,000 per academic year. Average 1997–98 room and board costs were ¥984,000 per academic year (on campus) and ¥1,140,000 per academic year (off campus). Room and board costs vary by occupancy (e.g., single, double, triple), type of accommodation, type of meal plan.

Financial Aid In 1997–98, 18% of students received some institutionally administered aid in the form of research assistantships, teaching assistantships, scholarships. Application Deadline: 3/7.

Financial Aid Contact Ms. Miyoko Wada, Office of Graduate School of International Management (MBA Program Office), Yamato-machi, Minami Uonuma-gun, Niigata 949-7277, Japan. Phone: 81-257-79-1500; Fax: 81-257-79-4443; E-mail: admgsim@iuj.ac.jp

FACILITIES
Information Resources Matsushita Library and Information Center; total holdings of 120,000 volumes, 1,410 microforms, 750 current periodical subscriptions. CD player(s) available for graduate student use. Access provided to online bibliographic retrieval services and online databases.

INTERNATIONAL STUDENTS
Demographics 63% of students enrolled are international students [Africa, 2%, Asia, 85%, Europe, 7%, North America, 5%, South America, 1%].

Services and Facilities International student office, visa services, ESL courses, counseling/support services, Japanese language courses.

Applying TOEFL: minimum score of 550, proof of adequate funds, proof of health/immunizations required. Financial aid is available to international students.

International Student Contact Ms. Miyoko Wada, Office of Graduate School of International Management (MBA Program Office), Yamato-machi, Minami Uonuma-gun, Niigata 949-7277, Japan. Phone: 81-257-79-1500; Fax: 81-257-79-4443; E-mail: admgsim@iuj.ac.jp

PLACEMENT
Services include alumni network, career counseling/planning, career library, career placement, job interviews arranged, job search course, resume referral to employers, and resume preparation. In 1996–97, 17 organizations participated in on-campus recruiting.

Employment Types of employment entered: accounting, banking, chemical industry, communications, computer-related, consulting, consumer products, education, engineering, finance, financial services, government, high technology, human resources, information systems/technology, insurance, international trade, management, manufacturing, marketing, nonprofit, petrochemical, pharmaceutical, retail, service industry, telecommunications, transportation, utilities.

Business Program(s) URL: http://www.iuj.ac.jp

Program Contact: Ms. Miyoko Wada, Office of Graduate School of International Management (MBA Program Office), Yamato-machi, Minami Uonuma-gun, Niigata 949-7277, Japan. Phone: 81-257-79-1500; Fax: 81-257-79-4443; E-mail: admgsim@iuj.ac.jp

See full description on page 852.

Waseda University

Graduate School of Asia-Pacific Studies

Tokyo 169-50, Japan

OVERVIEW
Waseda University is a private, coed institution. Enrollment: 46,418 graduate, professional, and undergraduate students. Founded: 1882. The graduate business unit is in an urban setting and is on a quarter calendar.

HIGHLIGHTS

Enrollment Profile

Full-time: 101	International: 37%
Part-time: 4	Women: 15%
Total: 105	Minorities: N/R
Average Age: N/R	Average Class Size: 20
Fall 1997 Average GPA: N/R	Fall 1997 Average GMAT: N/R

Costs
Full-time tuition: N/R
Part-time tuition: N/R

GRADUATE BUSINESS PROGRAMS
Master of Business Administration (MBA) Full-time, part-time; 30 total credits required; 18 months to 2 years to complete program. Concentrations in accounting, asian business studies, business information science, business policy/strategy, entrepreneurship, finance, information management, international finance, international management, japanese business studies, logistics, management systems analysis, marketing, operations management, production management, strategic management, system management.

ADMISSION
Applications For fall 1997 there were 134 applications for admission. Of those applying, 112 were accepted. Of those accepted, 105 enrolled.

Application Requirements Application form, bachelor's degree, essay, interview, letters of recommendation, personal statement, resume, college transcript(s), minimum of 3 years of work experience.

Application Deadline 3/31 for fall, 2/6 for spring, 3/31 for fall (international), 1/16 for spring (international). Application fee: ¥35,000, ¥37,500 (international).

ACADEMICS
Faculty Full-time 20; part-time 28.

Teaching Methodologies Case study, computer-aided instruction, experiential learning, faculty seminars, field projects, group discussion, lecture, research, role playing, seminars by members of the business community, student presentations, study groups, team projects.

Technology 310 on-campus computer terminals/PCs are available for student use and are linked by a campus-wide network. The network has full access to the Internet. Students are required to have their own PC.

Special Opportunities Advanced credit may be earned through credit by examination, transfer of credits from another institution. International exchange programs in various Asian, European, and North American countries. An internship program is available.

FINANCES
Financial Aid Fellowships, scholarships available. Application Deadline: 3/31.

Financial Aid Contact Mr. Kenji Shibata, Admissions Officer, Nishi-Waseda Bldg. 7F, 1-21-1 Nishi-Waseda Shinjuku-ku, Tokyo. Phone: 81-3-5286-3877; Fax: 81-3-3232-7075; E-mail: gsaps@mn.waseda.ac.jp

FACILITIES
Information Resources Central Library plus 4 additional on-campus libraries; total holdings of 2,772,808 volumes.

INTERNATIONAL STUDENTS
Demographics 37% of students enrolled are international students [Asia, 85%, Europe, 5%, North America, 10%].

Services and Facilities International student office, international student center, international student housing, visa services, ESL courses.

Applying TOEFL, proof of adequate funds, proof of health/immunizations required. Financial aid is available to international students.

International Student Contact Mr. Kenji Shibata, Admissions Officer, Nishi-Waseda Building 7F, 1-21-1 Nishi-Waseda Shinjuku-ku, Tokyo. Phone: 81-3-5286-3877; Fax: 81-3-3232-7075; E-mail: gsaps@mn.waseda.ac.jp

PLACEMENT
Services include career counseling/planning, career library, and career placement.

Business Program(s) URL: http://www.waseda.ac.jp/schl/w-com/w-comm/comm-e.html

Program Contact: Mr. Kenji Shibata, Graduate School of Asia-Pacific Studies, Nishiwaseda Bldg. 7F, 1-21-1 Nishiwaseda, Shinjuku-ku, Tokyo 169-0051, Japan. Phone: 81-3-52-86-3877; Fax: 81-3-32-32-7075; E-mail: gsaps@mn.waseda.ac.jp

See full description on page 1184.

MEXICO

Duxx Graduate School of Business Leadership

Business Programs

Garza Garcia NL, Mexico

OVERVIEW
Duxx Graduate School of Business Leadership is a private, coed institution. Enrollment: 30 graduate, professional, and undergraduate students. The graduate business unit is on a modules calendar.

HIGHLIGHTS

Enrollment Profile

Full-time: 30	International: N/R
Part-time: 0	Women: 10%
Total: 30	Minorities: N/R
Average Age: 28	Average Class Size: N/R
Fall 1997 Average GPA: N/R	Fall 1997 Average GMAT: N/R

Costs
Full-time tuition: N/R
Part-time tuition: N/R

GRADUATE BUSINESS PROGRAMS
Master of Business Leadership (MBL) Full-time; minimum of 12 months to complete program.

ADMISSION
Application Requirements GMAT score, application form, bachelor's degree, essay, interview, 2 letters of recommendation, resume, college transcript(s), minimum of 2 years of work experience.

Application Deadline 4/30 for fall, 11/14 for spring. Application fee: $100.

ACADEMICS
Teaching Methodologies Group discussion, lecture, seminars by members of the business community.

FINANCES
Costs for 1997–98 Average 1997–98 room and board costs were $6500 per academic year.

FACILITIES
Information Resources The Information Center; total holdings of 4,891 volumes. CD player(s) available for graduate student use. Access provided to online bibliographic retrieval services and online databases.

INTERNATIONAL STUDENTS
Demographics N/R

Applying TOEFL required.

PLACEMENT
Services include career placement.

Employment Types of employment entered: accounting, banking, chemical industry, communications, computer-related, consulting, consumer products, education, finance, financial services, management, marketing, nonprofit, service industry, telecommunications.

Business Program(s) URL: http://www.duxx.mx

Program Contact: Martha L. Garcia, Admissions, Calzada del Valle 106 Ote., Col. Del Valle, Garza Garcia, NL 66220, México. Phone: 52-8-356-1313; Fax: 52-8-356-1326; E-mail: mail@duxx.mx

Instituto Tecnológico y de Estudios Superiores de Monterrey

Monterrey, Nuevo León, Mexico

OVERVIEW
Instituto Tecnológico y de Estudios Superiores de Monterrey is an independent-nonprofit, primarily male institution. Enrollment: 14,062 graduate, professional, and undergraduate students; 606 full-time matriculated graduate/professional students; 1,410 part-time matriculated graduate/professional students. Founded: 1943. The graduate business unit is in an urban setting and is on a trimester calendar.

GRADUATE BUSINESS PROGRAMS
Master of Science in Finance (MS)

Master of Science in Marketing (MS)

Master of Science in International Management for Latin America (MIMLA) (MS)

Master of Business Administration (MBA)

ACADEMICS
Faculty Full-time 74; part-time 42.

Teaching Methodologies Case study, computer analysis, computer simulations, faculty seminars, field projects, group discussion, lecture, research, seminars by members of the business community, simulations, student presentations, team projects.

Technology 1,060 on-campus computer terminals/PCs are available for student use and are linked by a campus-wide network. The network has full access to the Internet. Students are not required to have their own PC.

Special Opportunities Advanced credit may be earned through credit by examination, transfer of credits from another institution. International exchange programs in Brazil, Canada, Chile, Ecuador, France, Germany, Norway, Spain, Sweden, United Kingdom, United States, Venezuela. An internship program is available.

FACILITIES
Information Resources Biblioteca-Centro de Informacion (BCI) plus 3 additional on-campus libraries; total holdings of 283,019 volumes, 30 microforms, 2,440 current periodical subscriptions. CD player(s) available for graduate student use. Access provided to online bibliographic retrieval services.

Program Contact: Communications and Promotion Coordinator, Sucursal de Correos J, Monterrey, Nuevo Leon 64849, Mexico. Phone: 52-08-358-2000 Ext. 6200; Fax: 52-08-358-9802; E-mail: mguajard@campus.mty.itesm.mx

Instituto Tecnológico y de Estudios Superiores de Monterrey, Campus Estado de México

Atizapan de Zaragoza, Mexico

OVERVIEW
Instituto Tecnológico y de Estudios Superiores de Monterrey, Campus Estado de México is an independent-nonprofit, coed institution. Founded: 1978.

GRADUATE BUSINESS PROGRAMS
Master of Administration (MA)

Master in Administration of Technological Information (MA)

Master of Finance (MF)

Master of Marketing (MM)

ACADEMICS
Faculty Full-time 97; part-time 73.

FACILITIES
Information Resources Total library holdings of 40,293 volumes, 34 microforms, 517 current periodical subscriptions. CD player(s) available for graduate student use. Access provided to online bibliographic retrieval services.

Program Contact: Camino al Lago de Guadalupe Km 4, Atizapan de Zaragoza 52500, Mexico. Phone: 915-326-5594.

Instituto Tecnológico y de Estudios Superiores de Monterrey, Campus Guadalajara

Zapopan, Jalisco, Mexico

OVERVIEW
Instituto Tecnológico y de Estudios Superiores de Monterrey, Campus Guadalajara is an independent-nonprofit, primarily male institution. Enrollment: 2,440 graduate, professional, and undergraduate students. Founded: 1943. The graduate business unit is in a suburban setting and is on a trimester calendar.

HIGHLIGHTS

Enrollment Profile

Full-time: N/R	International: 2%
Part-time: N/R	Women: N/R
Total: 225	Minorities: N/R
Average Age: 27	Average Class Size: 18
Fall 1997 Average GPA: N/R	Fall 1997 Average GMAT: N/R

Costs
Full-time tuition: 24,600 Mexican pesos per academic year
Part-time tuition: 16,996 Mexican pesos per trimester

Degree(s) offered in conjunction with Thunderbird, The American Graduate School of International Management

GRADUATE BUSINESS PROGRAMS
Executive MBA (MBA) Full-time, part-time; 15 months to 4.2 years to complete program. Concentrations in finance, marketing, international business, leadership.

Master of Finance (MF) Full-time, part-time; 15 months to 4.2 years to complete program.

Master of Marketing (MM) Full-time, part-time.

ADMISSION
Applications For fall 1997 there were 42 applications for admission. Of those applying, 38 were accepted. Of those accepted, 38 enrolled.

Application Requirements Application form, application fee, bachelor's degree, GPA: minimum 8.0 on a 10 scale, interview, letter of recommendation, resume, college transcript(s).

Recommended for Application Minimum of 2 years of work experience, computer experience.

Application Deadline 9/5 for fall, 1/11 for winter, 4/15 for spring, 7/10 for summer. Application fee: 315 Mexican pesos. Deferred entrance is available.

ACADEMICS
Faculty Full-time 9; part-time 32.

Teaching Methodologies Case study, computer-aided instruction, computer simulations, faculty seminars, field projects, group discussion, lecture, research, role playing, simulations, student presentations, study groups, team projects.

Technology 215 on-campus computer terminals/PCs are available for student use and are linked by a campus-wide network. The network has full access to the Internet. Students are not required to have their own PC.

Special Opportunities Advanced credit may be earned through credit by examination, transfer of credits from another institution. International exchange programs in Canada, France, Germany, Norway, Spain, Sweden, United States, Venezuela.

FINANCES
Costs for 1997–98 Tuition: Full-time: 24,600 Mexican pesos per trimester. Part-time: 16,996 Mexican pesos per trimester. Cost varies by academic program, number of credits taken.

Financial Aid Fellowships, grants, scholarships, loans available. Financial aid is available to part-time students. Application Deadline: 9/1.

Financial Aid Contact Pedro Munoz, Director de Becas, Avenida General Ramón Corona 2514, Zapopan, Jalisco. Phone: 52-3-669-3044 Ext. 244.

FACILITIES
Information Resources Main library plus 1 additional on-campus library; total holdings of 18,000 volumes, 1,278 microforms, 188 current periodical subscriptions. CD player(s) available for graduate student use. Access provided to online bibliographic retrieval services.

INTERNATIONAL STUDENTS
Demographics 2% of students enrolled are international students [Europe, 60%, North America, 20%, South America, 20%].

Services and Facilities International student office, international student center, counseling/support services.

Applying Proof of health/immunizations recommended. Financial aid is not available to international students.

International Student Contact Lic. Roberto Orozco, International Programs Director, Avenida General Ramón Corona 2514, Zapopan, Jalisco. Phone: 52-3-669-3000 Ext. 283; Fax: 52-3-699-3093; E-mail: rorozco@rectoria.rzp.itesm.mx

PLACEMENT
Services include alumni network, career library, career placement, electronic job bank, job interviews arranged, job search course, and resume preparation. In 1996–97, 20 on-campus interviews were conducted.

Employment Types of employment entered: banking, computer-related, finance, human resources, international trade, management, manufacturing.

Business Program(s) URL: http://www.gda.itesm.mx

Program Contact: Ana M. Lomeli, Directora de Escolar, Avenida General Ramón Corona 2514, Zapopan, Jalisco 45140, Mexico. Phone: 52-3-669-3000 Ext. 230 E-mail: alomeli@campus.gda.itesm.mx

Instituto Tecnológico y de Estudios Superiores de Monterrey, Campus Laguna

Graduate School

Torreon, Coahuila, Mexico

OVERVIEW
Instituto Tecnológico y de Estudios Superiores de Monterrey, Campus Laguna is an independent-nonprofit, coed institution. Founded: 1976.

GRADUATE BUSINESS PROGRAMS
Master of Administration (MA)
Master of Finance (MF)
Master of Marketing (MM)

ACADEMICS
Faculty Full-time 7; part-time 12.

FACILITIES
Information Resources Main library; total holdings of 15,000 volumes, 2,200 microforms, 300 current periodical subscriptions. CD player(s) available for graduate student use. Access provided to online bibliographic retrieval services.

Program Contact: Apartado Postal 506, Torreon, Coahuila 32583, Mexico. Phone: 52-17-206-363 Ext. 204 E-mail: jgutierr@campus.lag.itesm.mx

Instituto Tecnológico y de Estudios Superiores de Monterrey, Campus León

Program in Business Administration

Leon, Guanajuato, Mexico

OVERVIEW
Instituto Tecnológico y de Estudios Superiores de Monterrey, Campus León is an independent-nonprofit, coed institution. Founded: 1978.

GRADUATE BUSINESS PROGRAMS
Master of Administration (MA)
Master of Finance (MF)
Master of Marketing (MM)

ACADEMICS
Faculty Full-time 19; part-time 6.

FACILITIES
Information Resources Main library; total holdings of 16,475 volumes, 191 current periodical subscriptions.

Program Contact: Director, Master's Department, E. Garza Sada s/n Col. Cerro Gordo, Leon, Guanajuato 37190, Mexico. Phone: 52-47-171-080; Fax: 52-47-184-529; E-mail: epuente@campus.leo.itesm.mx

Instituto Tecnológico y de Estudios Superiores de Monterrey, Campus México City

Programs in Business

Mexico City, D.F., Mexico

OVERVIEW
Instituto Tecnológico y de Estudios Superiores de Monterrey, Campus México City is an independent-nonprofit, coed institution. Enrollment: 5,180 graduate, professional, and undergraduate students. The graduate business unit is in an urban setting and is on a trimester calendar.

HIGHLIGHTS

Enrollment Profile
Full-time: N/R
Part-time: N/R
Total: N/R
Average Age: 29
Fall 1997 Average GPA: 8.7

International: N/R
Women: N/R
Minorities: N/R
Average Class Size: 20
Fall 1997 Average GMAT: N/R

Costs
Full-time tuition: 75,000 Mexican pesos per academic year
Part-time tuition: 6960 Mexican pesos per subject

Degree(s) offered in conjunction with University of Texas at Austin

GRADUATE BUSINESS PROGRAMS
Master of Business Administration (MBA) Full-time, part-time; 18 months to 2.5 years to complete program. Concentrations in marketing, financial economics, international business, human resources, organizational management.

Master of Economics (MEcon) Full-time, part-time; 18 months to 2.5 years to complete program. Concentrations in marketing, strategic management, international business, developmental economics.

Master of Finance (MF) Full-time, part-time; 18 months to 2.5 years to complete program. Concentrations in marketing, international business, international finance.

Master of Administration in Information Technology (MA) Full-time, part-time, distance learning option; 18 months to 2.5 years to complete program. Concentrations in information management, management, management information systems.

Master of Science in Computer Science (MS) Full-time, part-time, distance learning option; 18 months to 2.5 years to complete program. Concentrations in technology management, management information systems.

Master of Science in Quality Systems (MS) Full-time, part-time, distance learning option; 18 months to 2.5 years to complete program. Concentrations in quality management, management, management science.

Master of Education (MEd) 18 months to 2.5 years to complete program. Concentration in management science.

Master of Developmental Engineering (MDE) Part-time, distance learning option; 18 months to 2.5 years to complete program. Concentration in developmental economics.

Master of Industrial Engineering (MIE) Part-time, distance learning option; 18 months to 2.5 years to complete program. Concentrations in industrial administration/management, production management, project management, quality management.

EMBA in Mexico City (EMBA) minimum of 5 years work experience and GMAT score required; minimum of 2 years to complete program.

ADMISSION
Application Requirements Application form, application fee, bachelor's degree, essay, GPA: minimum 8.0 on a 10 scale, interview, personal statement, resume.
Recommended for Application Work experience, computer experience.
Application Deadline 8/13 for fall, 6/25 for summer. Application fee: 375 Mexican pesos. Deferred entrance is available.

ACADEMICS
Faculty Full-time 10; part-time 37.
Teaching Methodologies Case study, computer-aided instruction, computer simulations, experiential learning, field projects, group discussion, lecture, research, student presentations, study groups, team projects.
Technology 126 on-campus computer terminals/PCs are available for student use and are linked by a campus-wide network. The network has full access to the Internet. Students are not required to have their own PC.
Special Opportunities Advanced credit may be earned through credit for business training programs. International exchange program in United States.

Instituto Tecnológico y de Estudios Superiores de Monterrey, Campus México City (continued)

FINANCES
Costs for 1997–98 Tuition: Full-time: 75,000 Mexican pesos per year. Part-time: 6960 Mexican pesos per subject. Cost varies by academic program, number of credits taken.

Financial Aid Research assistantships, teaching assistantships, scholarships, loans available. Financial aid is available to part-time students.

Financial Aid Contact Vianey Alfaro, Scholarships Coordinator, Calle del Puente 222, Mexico City, D.F.. Phone: 52-5-723-2136; Fax: 52-5-673-2500; E-mail: valfaro@campus.ccm.itesm.mx

FACILITIES
Information Resources Main library plus 1 additional on-campus library; total holdings of 57,863 volumes, 260 microforms, 248 current periodical subscriptions. CD player(s) available for graduate student use. Access provided to online bibliographic retrieval services.

INTERNATIONAL STUDENTS
Demographics N/R

Services and Facilities Counseling/support services.

International Student Contact Lourdes Ortiz Gonzalez, Scholar Services Coordinator, Calle del Puente 222, Mexico City, D.F.. Phone: 52-5-723-2067; Fax: 52-5-673-2500; E-mail: mortiz@campus.ccm.itesm.mx

PLACEMENT
Services include alumni network, career counseling/planning, career fairs, career library, and electronic job bank. In 1996–97, 36 organizations participated in on-campus recruiting.

Employment Of 1996–97 graduates, 98% were employed within three months of graduation; the average starting salary was 108,000 Mexican pesos. Types of employment entered: accounting, banking, communications, computer-related, consulting, education, finance, financial services, government, human resources, information systems/technology, international trade, management, manufacturing, marketing, nonprofit, service industry, telecommunications.

Program Contact: Maria de Lourdes Ortiz Gonzalez, Scholar Services Coordinator, Calle del Puente 222, Mexico City, D.F. 14380, Mexico. Phone: 52-5-723-2067; Fax: 52-5-673-2500; E-mail: mortiz@campus.ccm.itesm.mx

Instituto Tecnológico y de Estudios Superiores de Monterrey, Campus Querétaro

EGADE School of Business

Querétaro, Mexico

OVERVIEW
Instituto Tecnológico y de Estudios Superiores de Monterrey, Campus Querétaro is an independent-nonprofit, coed institution. Enrollment: 3,000 graduate, professional, and undergraduate students; full-time matriculated graduate/professional students; 155 part-time matriculated graduate/professional students. The graduate business unit is in an urban setting and is on a trimester calendar.

HIGHLIGHTS

Enrollment Profile

Full-time: 0	International: N/R
Part-time: 140	Women: 40%
Total: 140	Minorities: N/R
Average Age: 38	Average Class Size: 15
Fall 1997 Average GPA: N/R	Fall 1997 Average GMAT: N/R

Costs
Full-time tuition: N/R
Part-time tuition: $1000 per course

Degree(s) offered in conjunction with Thunderbird, The American Graduate School of International Management

GRADUATE BUSINESS PROGRAMS
Master of Business Administration (MBA) Part-time; 192 total credits required; 15 months to 4 years to complete program. Concentrations in marketing, finance, international management.

ADMISSION
Applications For fall 1997 there were 100 applications for admission. Of those applying, 80 were accepted. Of those accepted, 60 enrolled.

Application Requirements GMAT score: minimum 500, application form, bachelor's degree, minimum GPA: 3.0, 2 letters of recommendation, minimum of 2 years of work experience.

Recommended for Application Interview.

Application Deadline 8/15 for fall, 12/5 for winter, 8/1 for fall (international), 11/20 for winter (international). Deferred entrance is available.

ACADEMICS
Faculty Full-time 9; part-time 4.

Teaching Methodologies Case study, computer-aided instruction, computer simulations, field projects, group discussion, lecture, research, simulations, student presentations, study groups, team projects.

Technology 350 on-campus computer terminals/PCs are available for student use and are linked by a campus-wide network. The network has full access to the Internet. Students are not required to have their own PC.

Special Opportunities Advanced credit may be earned through credit by examination, transfer of credits from another institution. International exchange programs in Canada, France, Germany, Norway, Spain, United States. An internship program is available.

FINANCES
Costs for 1997–98 Tuition: Part-time: $1000 per course. Cost varies by number of credits taken. Fees: Part-time: $210 per year. Fees vary by number of credits taken, reciprocity agreements. Average 1997–98 room and board costs were $4000 per academic year (off campus). Room and board costs vary by campus location, occupancy (e.g., single, double, triple), type of accommodation, type of meal plan.

FACILITIES
Information Resources Robert Ruiz Obregon Library plus 1 additional on-campus library; total holdings of 31,832 volumes, 620 current periodical subscriptions. CD player(s) available for graduate student use. Access provided to online bibliographic retrieval services.

INTERNATIONAL STUDENTS
Demographics N/R

Services and Facilities International student office, international student center, counseling/support services.

Applying TOEFL: minimum score of 570 required.

International Student Contact Alberto Dorantes, Sr., Principal Registrar, Avenida J. Oviedo lo Parques Industriales, Querétaro. Phone: 52-42-118-158; Fax: 52-42-173-828; E-mail: jnoriega@campus.qro.itesm.mx

PLACEMENT
Employment Of 1996–97 graduates, 95% were employed within three months of graduation. Types of employment entered: banking, manufacturing, marketing, service industry.

Business Program(s) URL: http://www.sistema.itesm.mx

Program Contact: Raul Cardenas, Dean, MBA Program, Avenida J. Oviedo 10 Parques Industriales, Querétaro 76000, Mexico. Phone: 52-42-118-192; Fax: 52-42-118-193; E-mail: rcardena@campus.qro.itesm.mx

Instituto Tecnológico y de Estudios Superiores de Monterrey, Campus Toluca

Graduate Programs

Toluca, Estado de Mexico, Mexico

OVERVIEW
Instituto Tecnológico y de Estudios Superiores de Monterrey, Campus Toluca is an independent-nonprofit, coed institution. Founded: 1982.

GRADUATE BUSINESS PROGRAMS
Master of Business Administration (MBA)
Master in Finance (MS)
Master in Marketing (MS)
Master in International Management (MS)
Master in Information Technology Management (MS)

ACADEMICS
Faculty Full-time 5; part-time 5.

FACILITIES
Information Resources Garza Sada Library plus 2 additional on-campus libraries; total holdings of 50,000 volumes, 320 current periodical subscriptions. CD player(s) available for graduate student use. Access provided to online bibliographic retrieval services.

Program Contact: Assistant Director, Ex-Hacienda La Pila, Toluca, Estado de Mexico 50000, Mexico. Phone: 52-83-740-999 Ext. 2740; Fax: 52-83-741-178; E-mail: eherrera@campus.tol.itesm.mx

Universidad de las Américas- Puebla

Business and Management School

Puebla, Mexico

OVERVIEW
The Universidad de las Américas- Puebla is an independent-nonprofit, coed institution. Enrollment: 5,900 graduate, professional, and undergraduate students.

HIGHLIGHTS

Enrollment Profile
Full-time: 50
Part-time: 50
Total: 100
Average Age: N/R
Fall 1997 Average GPA: N/R

International: N/R
Women: 50%
Minorities: N/R
Average Class Size: N/R
Fall 1997 Average GMAT: N/R

Costs
Full-time tuition: N/R
Part-time tuition: 920 Mexican pesos per credit

GRADUATE BUSINESS PROGRAMS
Master of Business Administration (MBA) Full-time, part-time; 40-45 total credits required; 18 months to 4 years to complete program. Concentrations in international business, human resources.

ADMISSION
Application Requirements Application form, application fee, bachelor's degree, minimum GPA, 2 letters of recommendation, college transcript(s).
Application Deadline 6/1 for fall, 2/1 for spring, 6/1 for fall (international), 2/1 for spring (international). Application fee: 320 Mexican pesos.

ACADEMICS
Faculty Full-time 22; part-time 14.
Teaching Methodologies Case study, group discussion, lecture, research, student presentations.

FINANCES
Costs for 1997–98 Tuition: 920 Mexican pesos per credit.
Financial Aid Contact Financial Aid Office, Apartado 100, Sta Catarina Martir, Puebla. Phone: 52-22 292-013.

FACILITIES
Information Resources Biblioteca Central plus 3 additional on-campus libraries; total holdings of 150,000 volumes, 1,000 current periodical subscriptions. Access provided to online bibliographic retrieval services.

INTERNATIONAL STUDENTS
Demographics N/R
Services and Facilities International student office.
Applying TOEFL: minimum score of 500 required.
International Student Contact International Students Office, Apartado 100, Sta Catarina Martir, Puebla. Phone: 52-22-293-160.

PLACEMENT
Services include job interviews arranged, and resume referral to employers.
Employment Types of employment entered: international trade, management, marketing, service industry.

Program Contact: Dr. Jose Luis Roval, MBA Admissions Office, Apartado 100, Sta Catarina Martir, Puebla 72820, Mexico. Phone: 52-22-292-112.

MONACO

University of Southern Europe

Monaco Graduate School

Monte Carlo, Monaco

OVERVIEW
The University of Southern Europe is an independent-nonprofit, coed institution. Enrollment: 150 graduate, professional, and undergraduate students; 23 full-time matriculated graduate/professional students; 2 part-time matriculated graduate/professional students. Founded: 1986. The graduate business unit is in an urban setting and is on a trimester calendar.

HIGHLIGHTS

Enrollment Profile
Full-time: 23
Part-time: 2
Total: 25
Average Age: 28
Fall 1997 Average GPA: N/R

International: 100%
Women: 28%
Minorities: N/R
Average Class Size: 25
Fall 1997 Average GMAT: 560

Costs
Full-time tuition: 96,500 French francs per academic year
Part-time tuition: N/R

Degree(s) offered in conjunction with SAA University of Torino, New York University

GRADUATE BUSINESS PROGRAMS
Master of Business Administration (MBA) Full-time, part-time; 60 total credits required; 10 to 20 months to complete program. Concentrations in finance, international marketing.
Master of Science in Financial Management (MS) Full-time; 45-60 total credits required; 10 to 12 months to complete program.

ADMISSION
Applications For fall 1997 there were 95 applications for admission. Of those applying, 32 were accepted. Of those accepted, 25 enrolled.
Application Requirements Application form, application fee, bachelor's degree, interview, 2 letters of recommendation, personal statement, college transcript(s).
Recommended for Application GMAT score accepted, GRE score accepted, minimum GPA: 3.0, resume, minimum of 2 years of work experience, computer experience.
Application Deadline 6/30 for fall. Applications processed on a rolling/continuous basis for international students only. Application fee: 800 French francs. Deferred entrance is available.

ACADEMICS
Faculty Full-time 15; part-time 25.
Teaching Methodologies Case study, computer-aided instruction, computer analysis, computer simulations, experiential learning, field projects, group discussion, lecture, research, role playing, seminars by members of the business community, simulations, student presentations, team projects.
Technology 20 on-campus computer terminals/PCs are available for student use and are linked by a campus-wide network. The network has full access to the Internet. Students are required to have their own PC.
Special Opportunities Advanced credit may be earned through credit for experience, transfer of credits from another institution.

FINANCES
Costs for 1997–98 Tuition: Full-time: 96,500 French francs per year. Cost varies by academic program, number of credits taken. Fees: Full-time: 5500 French francs per academic year. Average 1997–98 room only costs were 40,000 French francs per academic year (off campus). Room and board costs vary by occupancy (e.g., single, double, triple), type of accommodation.
Financial Aid In 1997–98, 8% of students received some institutionally administered aid in the form of teaching assistantships, scholarships, work study. Application Deadline: 5/31.
Financial Aid Contact Mr. Olivier Marfaing, Director of Finance, 2, avenue Prince Héréditaire Albert, Monte Carlo. Phone: 377-97-986995; Fax: 377-92-052830; E-mail: use@monaco.mc

FACILITIES
Information Resources University of Southern Europe Library; total holdings of 3,000 volumes, 45 current periodical subscriptions. CD player(s) available for graduate student use. Access provided to online bibliographic retrieval services and online databases.

INTERNATIONAL STUDENTS
Demographics 100% of students enrolled are international students [Asia, 8%, Europe, 52%, North America, 24%, South America, 8%, other, 8%].
Services and Facilities International student office, international student center, international student housing, visa services, ESL courses, counseling/support services.
Applying TOEFL: minimum score of 550 required.
International Student Contact Ms. Anne Mickey, Director of International Programs , 2, avenue Prince Héréditaire Albert, Monte Carlo. Phone: 377-97-986986; Fax: 377-92-052830.

PLACEMENT
Services include alumni network, career counseling/planning, career placement, job interviews arranged, job search course, and resume preparation.
Employment Of 1996–97 graduates, 87% were employed within three months of graduation; the average starting salary was $65,000. Types of employment entered: accounting, banking, communications, computer-related, consulting, consumer products, finance, financial services, government, hospitality man-

University of Southern Europe (continued)

agement, insurance, international trade, management, marketing, media, real estate, retail, service industry.

Program Contact: Ms. Nathalie Le Curieux-Belfond, Director of Admissions, 2, avenue Prince Héréditaire Albert, Monte Carlo MC 98000, Monaco. Phone: 377-97-986990; Fax: 377-92-052830; E-mail: nlecurieuxbelfond@univmonaco.edu

NETHERLANDS

Erasmus University Rotterdam

Rotterdam School of Management

Rotterdam, Netherlands

OVERVIEW
Erasmus University Rotterdam is a proprietary, coed institution. Enrollment: 16,000 graduate, professional, and undergraduate students; 700 full-time matriculated graduate/professional students; 900 part-time matriculated graduate/professional students. Founded: 1970. The graduate business unit is in an urban setting and is on a semester calendar.

HIGHLIGHTS

Enrollment Profile

Full-time: 240	International: 88%
Part-time: 0	Women: 23%
Total: 240	Minorities: N/R
Average Age: 29	Average Class Size: 55
Fall 1997 Average GPA: 3.2	Fall 1997 Average GMAT: 600

Costs
Full-time tuition: 42,500 Dutch guilders per academic year
Part-time tuition: N/R

AACSB – The International Association for Management Education accredited

GRADUATE BUSINESS PROGRAMS
Full-time International MBA Program (MBA) Full-time; 23 total credits required; 18 months to complete program. Concentrations in entrepreneurship, international business, international finance, international marketing, management information systems, strategic management, human resources.

Full-time International MBA/Master of Business Informatics (MBA/MBI) Full-time; 27 total credits required; 18 months to complete program. Concentrations in entrepreneurship, international business, international finance, international marketing, management information systems, strategic management.

ADMISSION
Applications For fall 1997 there were 700 applications for admission.

Application Requirements GMAT score, application form, application fee, bachelor's degree, essay, interview, 2 letters of recommendation, personal statement, minimum of 2 years of work experience, computer experience: Windows applications.

Recommended for Application Minimum GPA, college transcript(s).

Application Deadline 6/15 for fall, 6/15 for fall (international). Application fee: 100 Dutch guilders. Deferred entrance is available.

ACADEMICS
Faculty Full-time 70; part-time 60.

Teaching Methodologies Case study, computer simulations, faculty seminars, field projects, group discussion, lecture, role playing, simulations, student presentations, study groups, team projects.

Technology 200 on-campus computer terminals/PCs are available for student use and are linked by a campus-wide network. The network has full access to the Internet. Students are required to have their own PC.

Special Opportunities Advanced credit may be earned through credit by examination. International exchange programs in Australia, Canada, France, Germany, Italy, Japan, Mexico, Philipines, Republic of South Africa, Spain, United Kingdom, United States. An internship program is available.

FINANCES
Costs for 1997–98 Tuition: Full-time: 42,500 Dutch guilders per program. Cost varies by academic program. Average 1997–98 room only costs were 9600 Dutch guilders per academic year (on campus) and 12,000 Dutch guilders

per academic year (off campus). Room and board costs vary by occupancy (e.g., single, double, triple), type of accommodation.

Financial Aid Loans available.

Financial Aid Contact Ms. Connie Tai, Admissions Office, Rotterdam School of Management, PO Box 1738, Rotterdam. Phone: 31-10-408-2222; Fax: 31-10-452-9509; E-mail: rsm@fac.rsm.eur.nl

FACILITIES
Information Resources University Library plus 1 additional on-campus library; total holdings of 800,000 volumes, 8,000 current periodical subscriptions. CD player(s) available for graduate student use. Access provided to online bibliographic retrieval services.

INTERNATIONAL STUDENTS
Demographics 88% of students enrolled are international students [Asia, 20%, Australia/New Zealand, 2%, Europe, 55%, North America, 15%, South America, 5%, other, 3%].

Services and Facilities International student office, international student center, international student housing, visa services, counseling/support services.

Applying TOEFL recommended. Financial aid is not available to international students.

International Student Contact Ms. Connie Tai, Admissions Office, Rotterdam School of Management, PO Box 1738, Rotterdam. Phone: 31-10-408-2222; Fax: 31-10-452-9509; E-mail: rsm@fac.rsm.eur.nl

PLACEMENT
Services include alumni network, career counseling/planning, career fairs, career library, career placement, electronic job bank, job interviews arranged, job search course, resume referral to employers, and resume preparation. In 1996–97, 100 organizations participated in on-campus recruiting; 300 on-campus interviews were conducted.

Employment Of 1996–97 graduates, 80% were employed within three months of graduation; the average starting salary was 125,000 Dutch guilders. Types of employment entered: banking, chemical industry, communications, computer-related, consulting, consumer products, energy, engineering, finance, government, health services, information systems/technology, international trade, management, manufacturing, marketing, media, nonprofit, pharmaceutical, service industry, telecommunications, transportation.

Business Program(s) URL: http://www.rsm.eur.nl/rsm

Program Contact: Ms. Connie Tai, MBA Admissions Director, Rotterdam School of Management, PO Box 1738, Rotterdam 3000 DR, Netherlands. Phone: 31-10-408-1936; Fax: 31-10-452-9509; E-mail: rsm@fac.rsm.eur.nl
See full description on page 808.

Nijenrode University

Netherlands Business School

Breukelen, Netherlands

OVERVIEW
Nijenrode University is an independent-nonprofit, coed institution. Enrollment: 600 graduate, professional, and undergraduate students. Founded: 1946. The graduate business unit is in a small-town setting and is on a 13-month program calendar.

HIGHLIGHTS

Enrollment Profile

Full-time: 60	International: 60%
Part-time: 35	Women: 19%
Total: 95	Minorities: N/R
Average Age: 29	Average Class Size: 60
Fall 1997 Average GPA: 3.5	Fall 1997 Average GMAT: 600

Costs
Full-time tuition: 38,000 Dutch guilders per academic year
Part-time tuition: 95,000 Dutch guilders per 18-month program

Degree(s) offered in conjunction with Rochester University, De Vlerick voor Management at University of Ghent (Belgium), University St. Gallen (Switzerland), William E. Simon Graduate School of Business Administration

GRADUATE BUSINESS PROGRAMS
International MBA (MBA) Full-time; 80 total credits required; up to 13 months to complete program. Concentrations in management, international management, entrepreneurship.

Executive MBA (MBA) Part-time; 75 total credits required; up to 18 months to complete program. Concentrations in management, international management, entrepreneurship.

MBA in Financial Services and Insurance (MBA) Part-time, distance learning option; 60 total credits required; up to 18 months to complete program. Concentrations in banking, finance, financial economics, financial information systems, financial management/planning, international banking, international finance, management.

Modular MBA (MBA) Part-time, distance learning option; 60 total credits required; up to 18 months to complete program. Concentrations in management, international management, entrepreneurship.

ADMISSION

Applications For fall 1997 there were 350 applications for admission. Of those applying, 90 were accepted. Of those accepted, 60 enrolled.

Application Requirements Application form, application fee, bachelor's degree, essay, minimum GPA: 3.2, interview, 2 letters of recommendation, resume, college transcript(s), minimum of 2 years of work experience.

Recommended for Application GMAT score accepted: minimum 550, personal statement, computer experience.

Application Deadline 5/15 for fall, 5/15 for fall (international). Application fee: 150 Dutch guilders. Deferred entrance is available.

ACADEMICS

Faculty Full-time 40; part-time 15.

Teaching Methodologies Case study, computer-aided instruction, computer analysis, computer simulations, experiential learning, field projects, group discussion, lecture, research, role playing, seminars by members of the business community, simulations, student presentations, study groups, team projects.

Technology 90 on-campus computer terminals/PCs are available for student use and are linked by a campus-wide network. The network has full access to the Internet. Students are not required to have their own PC.

Special Opportunities An internship program is available.

FINANCES

Costs for 1997–98 Tuition: Full-time: 38,000 Dutch guilders per program. Part-time: 95,000 Dutch guilders per 18-month program. Average 1997–98 room and board costs were 12,000 Dutch guilders per academic year (on campus) and 1500 Dutch guilders per academic year (off campus). Room and board costs vary by type of accommodation, type of meal plan.

Financial Aid In 1997–98, 5% of students received some institutionally administered aid in the form of loans. Application Deadline: 5/15.

Financial Aid Contact Ms. Natasha Van Dalen, Admissions Officer, Straatwey 25, Breukelen. Phone: 31-346-291-607; Fax: 31-346-250-595; E-mail: dalen@nijerode.nl

FACILITIES

Information Resources Nijenrode University Library; total holdings of 27,000 volumes, 350 microforms, 800 current periodical subscriptions. CD player(s) available for graduate student use. Access provided to online bibliographic retrieval services.

INTERNATIONAL STUDENTS

Demographics 60% of students enrolled are international students [Africa, 7%, Asia, 23%, Europe, 44%, North America, 19%, South America, 7%].

Services and Facilities International student office, international student housing, visa services, counseling/support services.

Applying TOEFL: minimum score of 600, proof of adequate funds, proof of health/immunizations required. Financial aid is not available to international students.

International Student Contact Ms. Natasha Van Dalen, MBA Admissions Officer, MBA Office, Straatweg 25, Breukelen. Phone: 31-346-291-607; Fax: 31-346-250-295; E-mail: dalen@nijenrode.nl

PLACEMENT

Services include alumni network, career counseling/planning, career fairs, career placement, job interviews arranged, resume referral to employers, and resume preparation. In 1996–97, 80 organizations participated in on-campus recruiting; 180 on-campus interviews were conducted.

Employment Of 1996–97 graduates, 93% were employed within three months of graduation; the average starting salary was 108,000 Dutch guilders. Types of employment entered: banking, consulting, consumer products, finance, financial services, manufacturing, petrochemical, service industry, transportation.

Business Program(s) URL: http://www.nijenrode.nl

Program Contact: Ms. Natasha Van Dalen, Admissions Officer, MBA Office, Straatweg 25, Breukelen 3621 BG, Netherlands. Phone: 31-346-291-607; Fax: 31-346-250-595; E-mail: dalen@nijenrode.nl
See full description on page 900.

Open University of the Netherlands

Business Programs

Heerlen, Netherlands

OVERVIEW
Open University of the Netherlands is a publicly supported, coed institution. Enrollment: 23,524 graduate, professional, and undergraduate students. Founded: 1984. The graduate business unit is in a suburban setting and is on a trimester calendar.

HIGHLIGHTS

Enrollment Profile

Full-time: 0	International: 71%
Part-time: 28	Women: 54%
Total: 28	Minorities: N/R
Average Age: 34	Average Class Size: N/R
Fall 1997 Average GPA: N/R	Fall 1997 Average GMAT: N/R

Costs
Full-time tuition: 7500 European currency units per academic year (resident); 7500 European currency units per academic year (nonresident)
Part-time tuition: N/R

Degree(s) offered in conjunction with IAE Aix-en-Provence, ESC Nantes Atlantique

GRADUATE BUSINESS PROGRAMS
Euro*MBA Programme (MBA) Part-time, distance learning option; 3 years work experience required, proficiency in English required; minimum of 2 years to complete program. Concentrations in international marketing, international finance, international management, public policy and administration, human resources, business law, european business studies.

ADMISSION
Applications For fall 1997 there were 40 applications for admission. Of those applying, 35 were accepted. Of those accepted, 28 enrolled.

Application Requirements Application form, application fee, bachelor's degree, 2 letters of recommendation, resume, college transcript(s), minimum of 3 years of work experience, computer experience: Lotus 1-2-3, Lotus Notes, Microsoft Word.

Recommended for Application Interview, personal statement.

Application Deadline 7/1 for fall, 11/15 for winter, 3/15 for spring, 7/1 for fall (international), 11/15 for winter (international), 3/15 for spring (international). Application fee: 250 European currency units.

ACADEMICS
Teaching Methodologies Case study, computer-aided instruction, computer analysis, computer simulations, experiential learning, group discussion, lecture, seminars by members of the business community, simulations, study groups, team projects.

Technology Computer terminals/PCs are available for student use and are linked by a campus-wide network. The network has full access to the Internet. Students are required to have their own PC.

Special Opportunities International exchange programs in Finland, France, Germany, Ireland, Spain.

FINANCES
Costs for 1997–98 Tuition: Full-time: 7500 European currency units per year (resident); 7500 European currency units per year (nonresident).

INTERNATIONAL STUDENTS
Demographics 71% of students enrolled are international students [Asia, 6%, Australia/New Zealand, 6%, Europe, 76%, North America, 6%, South America, 6%].

Applying TOEFL, TSE, TWE recommended. Financial aid is not available to international students.

International Student Contact Dr. Ronald S.J. Tuninga, Director Euro* MBA Programme, Vallenburgerweg 167, PO Box 2960, Heerlen. Phone: 31-45-5762507; Fax: 31-45-5762103; E-mail: ron.tuninga@ouh.nl

PLACEMENT
Services include alumni network, job interviews arranged, and resume preparation.

Employment Types of employment entered: financial services, international trade, service industry.

Business Program(s) URL: http://www.ou.nl

Program Contact: Dr. Ronald S.J. Tuninga, Director, Euro*MBA Programme, Euro*MBA Desk, Valkenburgerweg 167, Heerlen 6149AT, Netherlands. Phone: 31-45-576-2587; Fax: 31-45-576-2103; E-mail: euro.mba-desk@ouh.nl

University of Twente

TSM Business School

Enschede, Netherlands

OVERVIEW

The University of Twente coed institution. Enrollment: 6,000 graduate, professional, and undergraduate students; 5,000 full-time matriculated graduate/professional students; 1,000 part-time matriculated graduate/professional students. Founded: 1961. The graduate business unit is in a rural setting and is on a trimester calendar.

HIGHLIGHTS

Enrollment Profile

Full-time: 28	International: 53%
Part-time: 21	Women: 12%
Total: 49	Minorities: N/R
Average Age: 30	Average Class Size: 24
Fall 1997 Average GPA: N/R	Fall 1997 Average GMAT: 550

Costs
Full-time tuition: N/R
Part-time tuition: N/R

Degree(s) offered in conjunction with University of Groningen, University of Eindhoven

GRADUATE BUSINESS PROGRAMS

Full-time MBA (MBA) Full-time; 18 months to complete program. Concentrations in technology management, entrepreneurship, leadership.

Executive Part-time MBA (MBA) Part-time; 22 months to complete program. Concentrations in technology management, entrepreneurship, leadership.

ADMISSION

Applications For fall 1997 there were 117 applications for admission. Of those applying, 52 were accepted. Of those accepted, 49 enrolled.

Application Requirements Application form, bachelor's degree, essay, interview, resume, minimum of 3 years of work experience.

Recommended for Application GMAT score accepted: minimum 500, minimum GPA: 3.5, letters of recommendation, personal statement, college transcript(s), computer experience.

Application Deadline Applications processed on a rolling/continuous basis for both domestic and international students. Application fee: 1000 Dutch guilders.

ACADEMICS

Faculty Full-time 40; part-time 70.

Teaching Methodologies Case study, computer-aided instruction, computer analysis, computer simulations, experiential learning, faculty seminars, field projects, group discussion, lecture, research, role playing, seminars by members of the business community, simulations, student presentations, study groups, team projects.

Technology 200 on-campus computer terminals/PCs are available for student use and are linked by a campus-wide network. The network has full access to the Internet. Students are required to have their own PC.

Special Opportunities International exchange programs in France, United States.

FINANCES

Costs for 1997–98 Cost varies by academic program, class time (e.g., day/evening). Average 1997–98 room only costs were 300 Dutch guilders per academic year (on campus) and 350 Dutch guilders per academic year (off campus). Room and board costs vary by occupancy (e.g., single, double, triple), type of accommodation.

Financial Aid In 1997–98, 24% of students received some institutionally administered aid in the form of grants, work study, loans. Application Deadline: 8/1.

Financial Aid Contact Mr. Leo J. Salazar, Marketing Manager, TSM Business School, PO Box 217, Enschede. Phone: 31-53-489-8009; Fax: 31-53-489-4848; E-mail: ljsalazar@tsm.utwente.nl

FACILITIES

Information Resources General library plus 6 additional on-campus libraries; total holdings of 350,000 volumes, 2,850 current periodical subscriptions. CD player(s) available for graduate student use. Access provided to online bibliographic retrieval services.

INTERNATIONAL STUDENTS

Demographics 53% of students enrolled are international students [Africa, 4%, Asia, 33%, Europe, 59%, South America, 4%].

Services and Facilities International student office, international student housing, visa services, ESL courses, counseling/support services.

Applying Proof of adequate funds required. TOEFL recommended. Financial aid is available to international students.

International Student Contact Mr. Leo J. Salazar, Marketing Manager, TSM Business School, PO Box 217, Enschede. Phone: 31-53-489-8009; Fax: 31-53-489-4848; E-mail: ljsalazar@tsm.utwente.nl

PLACEMENT

Services include alumni network, career counseling/planning, career fairs, resume referral to employers, and resume preparation. In 1996–97, 50 organizations participated in on-campus recruiting.

Employment Of 1996–97 graduates, 80% were employed within three months of graduation. Types of employment entered: accounting, banking, chemical industry, communications, computer-related, consulting, consumer products, education, energy, engineering, finance, financial services, high technology, information systems/technology, insurance, international trade, manufacturing, marketing, media, nonprofit, petrochemical, pharmaceutical, service industry, telecommunications, transportation, utilities.

Business Program(s) URL: http://www.tsm.nl

Program Contact: Mr. Leo J. Salazar, Marketing Manager, TSM Business School, PO Box 217, Enschede 7500AE, Netherlands. Phone: 31-53-489-8009; Fax: 31-53-489-4848; E-mail: ljsalazar@tsm.utwente.nl
See full description on page 1166.

NEW ZEALAND

University of Auckland

Executive Programs

Auckland, New Zealand

OVERVIEW

The University of Auckland is a federally supported, coed institution. Enrollment: 24,300 graduate, professional, and undergraduate students; 2,375 full-time matriculated graduate/professional students; 2,106 part-time matriculated graduate/professional students. Founded: 1883. The graduate business unit is in an urban setting and is on a semester calendar.

HIGHLIGHTS

Enrollment Profile

Full-time: 256	International: 9%
Part-time: 1,100	Women: 33%
Total: 1,356	Minorities: N/R
Average Age: 41	Average Class Size: 39
Fall 1997 Average GPA: 7.2	Fall 1997 Average GMAT: 508

Costs
Full-time tuition: NZ$8156 per academic year (resident); NZ$19,238 per academic year (nonresident)
Part-time tuition: N/R

GRADUATE BUSINESS PROGRAMS

Master of Business Administration (MBA) Full-time, part-time; 28 total credits required; interview required; 18 months to 2 years to complete program. Concentration in organizational behavior/development.

Master of International Business (MIB) Full-time; 28 total credits required; 2 years to complete program. Concentrations in international marketing, international trade, international management, international and area business studies.

Master of Management (MMgt) Full-time, part-time; 28 total credits required; 2 years to complete program. Concentrations in organizational behavior/development, strategic management.

Master of Health Management (MHM) Full-time, part-time; 28 total credits required; 3 years work experience in health sector required; 2 to 4 years to complete program. Concentrations in health care, organizational behavior/development, management.

ADMISSION

Applications For fall 1997 there were 2,913 applications for admission. Of those applying, 1,481 were accepted. Of those accepted, 1,321 enrolled.

Application Requirements GMAT score: minimum 500, application form, application fee, bachelor's degree, 3 letters of recommendation, personal statement, college transcript(s).

Recommended for Application Minimum GPA, interview, resume, computer experience.

Application Deadline 10/15 for spring. Application fee: NZ$50. Deferred entrance is available.

ACADEMICS
Faculty Full-time 37; part-time 37.

Teaching Methodologies Case study, computer simulations, experiential learning, field projects, lecture, seminars by members of the business community, student presentations, study groups, team projects.

Technology 600 on-campus computer terminals/PCs are available for student use and are linked by a campus-wide network. The network has full access to the Internet. Students are required to have their own PC.

Special Opportunities International exchange programs in Australia, Canada, Finland. An internship program is available.

FINANCES
Costs for 1997–98 Tuition: Full-time: NZ$8156 per year (resident); NZ$19,238 per year (nonresident). Cost varies by academic program, number of credits taken. Fees vary by academic program, number of credits taken.

Financial Aid Financial aid is available to part-time students.

Financial Aid Contact Marie Wilson, Associate Dean, Private Bag 92019, Auckland 1. Phone: 64-9-373-7999; Fax: 64-9-373-7437; E-mail: mba@auckland.ac.nz

FACILITIES
Information Resources General library plus 9 additional on-campus libraries; total holdings of 1,800,000 volumes. CD player(s) available for graduate student use. Access provided to online bibliographic retrieval services.

INTERNATIONAL STUDENTS
Demographics 9% of students enrolled are international students [Asia, 90%, Europe, 10%].

Services and Facilities International student office, international student center, ESL courses.

Applying IELT: minimum score of 6 required. Financial aid is not available to international students.

International Student Contact Mr. Lindsay Spedding, Administrative Officer—Postgraduate Admissions International, International Students Office, Private Bag 92019, Auckland. Phone: 64-9-373-7599; Fax: 64-9-373-7405.

PLACEMENT
Services include alumni network, career counseling/planning, career fairs, and resume preparation.

Employment Of 1996–97 graduates, 99% were employed within three months of graduation. Types of employment entered: accounting, banking, chemical industry, computer-related, consulting, consumer products, education, energy, engineering, finance, financial services, government, health services, high technology, hospitality management, human resources, information systems/technology, insurance, international trade, law, management, manufacturing, marketing, media, mining, nonprofit, pharmaceutical, real estate, retail, service industry, telecommunications, transportation, utilities.

Business Program(s) URL: http://www.business.auckland.ac.nz/

Program Contact: Hilary Alcorn, Master of International Business Program, Private Bag 92019, Auckland 1, New Zealand. Phone: 64-9-373-7539; Fax: 64-9-373-7437; E-mail: h.alcorn@auckland.ac.nz

University of Canterbury

Department of Management

Christchurch, New Zealand

OVERVIEW
The University of Canterbury is a publicly supported, coed institution. Enrollment: 12,000 graduate, professional, and undergraduate students. Founded: 1873. The graduate business unit is in a suburban setting and is on a term calendar.

HIGHLIGHTS

Enrollment Profile

Full-time: N/R	International: N/R
Part-time: N/R	Women: N/R
Total: N/R	Minorities: N/R
Average Age: N/R	Average Class Size: 37
Fall 1997 Average GPA: N/R	Fall 1997 Average GMAT: N/R

Costs
Full-time tuition: N/R
Part-time tuition: N/R

GRADUATE BUSINESS PROGRAMS
Master of Business Administration (MBA) Full-time, part-time; 15 months to 2.5 years to complete program. Concentrations in management, strategic management, finance, marketing, management information systems, accounting, quantitative analysis, economics, human resources, production management, organizational behavior/development.

ADMISSION
Application Requirements Application form, application fee, bachelor's degree, letters of recommendation, personal statement, college transcript(s), minimum of 2 years of work experience, computer experience: Microsoft Excel, Microsoft Windows.

Recommended for Application GMAT score accepted: minimum 560.

Application Deadline 11/15 for winter, 9/15 for winter (international). Application fee: NZ$60.

ACADEMICS
Teaching Methodologies Case study, computer-aided instruction, computer simulations, group discussion, lecture, seminars by members of the business community, simulations, student presentations, study groups, team projects.

Technology 20 on-campus computer terminals/PCs are available for student use and are linked by a campus-wide network. The network has full access to the Internet. Students are not required to have their own PC.

FINANCES
Financial Aid Grants, scholarships, loans available.

Financial Aid Contact Shelley Caines, MBA Secretary, Private Bag 4800, Christchurch. Phone: 64-3-364-2657; Fax: 64-3-364-2020.

FACILITIES
Information Resources Central Library plus 5 additional on-campus libraries. CD player(s) available for graduate student use. Access provided to online bibliographic retrieval services and online databases.

INTERNATIONAL STUDENTS
Demographics N/R

Services and Facilities International student center.

Applying IELT, TOEFL: minimum score of 600, TWE required. Financial aid is available to international students.

International Student Contact International Student Centre, Private Bag 4800, Christchurch. Phone: 64-3-364 2391; Fax: 64-3-364 2603.

PLACEMENT
Services include career counseling/planning, and career placement.

Employment Types of employment entered: consulting, finance, government, service industry.

Business Program(s) URL: http://www.canterbury.ac.nz

Program Contact: Shelley Caines, MBA Secretary, Private Bag 4800, Christchurch 8020, New Zealand. Phone: 64-3-364-2657; Fax: 64-3-364-2020.

University of Otago

Advanced Business Programme

Dunedin, New Zealand

OVERVIEW
The University of Otago is a federally supported, coed institution. Founded: 1869. The graduate business unit is in a small-town setting and is on a quarter calendar.

HIGHLIGHTS

Enrollment Profile

Full-time: N/R	International: N/R
Part-time: N/R	Women: N/R
Total: N/R	Minorities: N/R
Average Age: 31	Average Class Size: 25
Fall 1997 Average GPA: N/R	Fall 1997 Average GMAT: 600

Costs
Full-time tuition: NZ$20,000 per academic year (resident); NZ$33,000 per academic year (nonresident)
Part-time tuition: N/R

University of Otago (continued)

GRADUATE BUSINESS PROGRAMS
Master of Business Administration (MBA) Full-time; 18 total credits required; minimum of 16 months to complete program. Concentrations in international business, strategic management.
Master of Tourism (MT) Full-time; up to 2 years to complete program.

ADMISSION
Application Requirements GMAT score: minimum 550, application form, application fee, essay, interview, 2 letters of recommendation, personal statement, resume, college transcript(s), minimum of 3 years of work experience.
Recommended for Application Bachelor's degree.
Application Deadline 12/1 for winter. Application fee: NZ$100.

ACADEMICS
Faculty Full-time 17.
Teaching Methodologies Case study, lecture, student presentations, team projects.
Technology 20 on-campus computer terminals/PCs are available for student use and are linked by a campus-wide network. The network has full access to the Internet. Students are required to have their own PC.
Special Opportunities An internship program is available.

FINANCES
Costs for 1997–98 Tuition: Full-time: NZ$20,000 per year (resident); NZ$33,000 per year (nonresident). Average 1997–98 room and board costs were NZ$28,993 per academic year (off campus).
Financial Aid Loans available.
Financial Aid Contact Geoffrey Lorigan, Director of Programme, PO Box 56, Dunedin. Phone: 64-3-479-8046; Fax: 64-3-479-8045; E-mail: mbainfo@commerce.otago.ac.nz

FACILITIES
Information Resources University of Otago Central Library plus 6 additional on-campus libraries. CD player(s) available for graduate student use. Access provided to online bibliographic retrieval services.

INTERNATIONAL STUDENTS
Demographics N/R
Applying IELT: minimum score of 6.5, TOEFL: minimum score of 575, TWE: minimum score of 4.5 required. Financial aid is available to international students.
International Student Contact Geoffrey Lorigan, Director of Programme, PO Box 56, Dunedin. Phone: 64-3-479-8046; Fax: 64-3-479-8046; E-mail: mbainfo@commerce.otago.ac.nz

PLACEMENT
Services include alumni network, career counseling/planning, resume referral to employers, and resume preparation.
Employment Of 1996–97 graduates, 95% were employed within three months of graduation. Types of employment entered: consulting, international trade, management.
Business Program(s) URL: http://divcom.otago.ac.nz:800/mba

Program Contact: Geoffrey Lorigan, Director of Programme, PO Box 56, Dunedin, New Zealand. Phone: 64-3-479-8046; Fax: 64-3-479-8045; E-mail: mbainfo@commerce.otago.ac.nz
See full description on page 1122.

HIGHLIGHTS
Enrollment Profile

Full-time: N/R	International: N/R
Part-time: N/R	Women: N/R
Total: N/R	Minorities: N/R
Average Age: 31	Average Class Size: N/R
Fall 1997 Average GPA: N/R	Fall 1997 Average GMAT: N/R

Costs
Full-time tuition: N/R
Part-time tuition: N/R

GRADUATE BUSINESS PROGRAMS
Master of Business Administration (MBA) Full-time; up to 12 months to complete program. Concentration in management.
Master of Business Administration (MBA) Part-time; up to 2 years to complete program. Concentration in management.

ADMISSION
Application Requirements Application form, application fee, bachelor's degree, interview, 3 letters of recommendation, resume, college transcript(s), minimum of 3 years of work experience.
Recommended for Application GMAT score accepted.
Application Deadline Applications processed on a rolling/continuous basis for both domestic and international students. Application fee: NZ$100.

ACADEMICS
Faculty Part-time 25.
Teaching Methodologies Case study, computer simulations, group discussion, lecture, research, student presentations, study groups, team projects.
Technology 400 on-campus computer terminals/PCs are available for student use and are linked by a campus-wide network. The network has full access to the Internet. Students are not required to have their own PC.

FINANCES
Financial Aid Scholarships available.
Financial Aid Contact Dr. Ed Weymes, Director of Executive Education, Private Bag 3105, Hamilton. Phone: 64-7-838-4198; Fax: 64-7-838-4675; E-mail: weymesed@waikato.ac.nz

FACILITIES
Information Resources Central Library plus 2 additional on-campus libraries; total holdings of 763,150 volumes.

INTERNATIONAL STUDENTS
Demographics N/R
Services and Facilities International student center, international student housing, counseling/support services.
Applying TOEFL: minimum score of 630 required. Financial aid is available to international students.
International Student Contact Ms. Lynette Muter, International Manager, Private Bag 3105, Hamilton. Phone: 64-7-838-4727; Fax: 64-7-838-4269.

PLACEMENT
Services include alumni network, career counseling/planning, and career placement.
Employment Types of employment entered: finance, hospitality management, human resources, management, marketing, media, pharmaceutical, service industry.
Business Program(s) URL: http://www.waikato.ac.nz

Program Contact: Dr. Ed Weymes, Director of Executive Education, Waikato Management School, Private Bag 3105, Hamilton, New Zealand. Phone: 64-7-838-4220; Fax: 64-7-838-4675; E-mail: weymesed@waikato.ac.nz

University of Waikato

School of Management Studies

Hamilton, New Zealand

OVERVIEW
The University of Waikato is a publicly supported, coed institution. Enrollment: 11,000 graduate, professional, and undergraduate students. Founded: 1964. The graduate business unit is in a suburban setting and is on a module calendar.

Victoria University of Wellington

Graduate School of Business and Government Management

Wellington, New Zealand

OVERVIEW
Victoria University of Wellington is a federally supported, coed institution. Enrollment: 13,752 graduate, professional, and undergraduate students; 1,007 full-time matriculated graduate/professional students; 1,466 part-time matriculated graduate/professional students. The graduate business unit is in an urban setting and is on a trimester calendar.

HIGHLIGHTS

Enrollment Profile

Full-time: 81

Part-time: 537

Total: 618

Average Age: 35

Fall 1997 Average GPA: N/R

International: N/R

Women: 46%

Minorities: N/R

Average Class Size: 25

Fall 1997 Average GMAT: 551

Costs

Full-time tuition: NZ$4680 per academic year (resident); NZ$6375 per academic year (nonresident)

Part-time tuition: NZ$1040 per course (resident); NZ$25,500 per degree (nonresident)

GRADUATE BUSINESS PROGRAMS

Master of Business Administration (MBA) Full-time, part-time; 16 months to 4 years to complete program. Concentrations in accounting, international business.

Master of Management (MMgt) Part-time; 21 months to 4 years to complete program.

ADMISSION

Applications For fall 1997 there were 350 applications for admission.

Application Requirements GMAT score, application form, application fee, interview, 2 letters of recommendation, personal statement, resume, college transcript(s), minimum of 5 years of work experience.

Recommended for Application Bachelor's degree, computer experience.

Application Deadline Applications processed on a rolling/continuous basis for both domestic and international students. Application fee: 110 (international).

ACADEMICS

Faculty Full-time 115; part-time 5.

Teaching Methodologies Case study, computer analysis, computer simulations, experiential learning, faculty seminars, field projects, group discussion, lecture, research, role playing, seminars by members of the business community, student presentations, study groups, team projects.

Technology Computer terminals/PCs are available for student use and are linked by a campus-wide network. The network has full access to the Internet. Students are not required to have their own PC.

Special Opportunities Advanced credit may be earned through credit by examination. International exchange programs in Australia, Italy, Republic of Korea, Sweden, Thailand, United States.

FINANCES

Costs for 1997–98 Tuition: Full-time: NZ$4680 per trimester (resident); NZ$6375 per trimester (nonresident). Part-time: NZ$1040 per course (resident); NZ$25,500 per degree (nonresident). Cost varies by academic program, number of credits taken, reciprocity agreements. Fees: Full-time: NZ$179 per academic year (resident); NZ$179 per academic year (nonresident). Part-time: NZ$90 per trimester (resident); NZ$90 per trimester (nonresident). Fees vary by academic program, number of credits taken. Average 1997–98 room and board costs were NZ$4900 per academic year (on campus) and NZ$2700 per academic year (off campus). Room and board costs vary by occupancy (e.g., single, double, triple), type of accommodation, type of meal plan.

Financial Aid Teaching assistantships, grants, loans available.

Financial Aid Contact Student Finance Office, PO Box 600, Wellington. Phone: 64-4-495-5111; Fax: 64-4-496-5400; E-mail: student-finance@vuw.ac.nz

FACILITIES

Information Resources Main institution library plus 3 additional on-campus libraries; total holdings of 700,000 volumes, 57,000 microforms, 8,000 current periodical subscriptions. CD player(s) available for graduate student use. Access provided to online bibliographic retrieval services and online databases.

INTERNATIONAL STUDENTS

Demographics N/R

Services and Facilities International student office, international student housing, visa services, ESL courses, counseling/support services.

Applying IELT: minimum score of 6, TOEFL: minimum score of 600, proof of adequate funds required. Proof of health/immunizations recommended. Financial aid is not available to international students.

International Student Contact Eleni Geris, International Liaison Officer, PO Box 600, Wellington. Phone: 64-4-471-5350; Fax: 64-4-495-5056; E-mail: international-students@vuw.ac.nz

PLACEMENT

Services include alumni network, career counseling/planning, career library, job interviews arranged, job search course, resume referral to employers, and resume preparation. In 1996–97, 70 organizations participated in on-campus recruiting.

Employment Of 1996–97 graduates, the average starting salary was NZ$63,000. Types of employment entered: accounting, banking, communications, computer-related, consulting, education, energy, engineering, finance,

financial services, government, health services, human resources, information systems/technology, insurance, international trade, law, management, manufacturing, marketing, nonprofit, pharmaceutical, service industry, telecommunications.

Business Program(s) URL: http://www.vuw.ac.nz/gsbgm/

Program Contact: Monica Chow, MBA Programme Administrator, PO Box 600, Wellington, New Zealand. Phone: 64-4-471-5367; Fax: 64-4-496-5435; E-mail: mba@vuw.ac.nz

NORWAY

Norwegian School of Management

Graduate School

Sandvika, Norway

OVERVIEW

Norwegian School of Management is an independent-nonprofit, coed institution. Enrollment: 16,000 graduate, professional, and undergraduate students; 180 full-time matriculated graduate/professional students; 20 part-time matriculated graduate/professional students. Founded: 1943. The graduate business unit is in a small-town setting and is on a quarter and trimester calendar.

HIGHLIGHTS

Enrollment Profile

Full-time: 180

Part-time: 20

Total: 200

Average Age: 30

Fall 1997 Average GPA: N/R

International: 45%

Women: 40%

Minorities: N/R

Average Class Size: 30

Fall 1997 Average GMAT: 560

Costs

Full-time tuition: 122,000 Norwegian kroner per academic year

Part-time tuition: 180,000 Norwegian kroner per program

GRADUATE BUSINESS PROGRAMS

Full-time MBA (MBA) Full-time; 40 total credits required; 12 months to complete program. Concentrations in leadership, strategic management.

Part-time MBA (MBA) Part-time; 40 total credits required; 2 years to complete program. Concentrations in leadership, strategic management.

Master of Science (MS) Full-time; 40 total credits required; 12 months to 3 years to complete program. Concentrations in international business, financial economics, marketing, strategic management, environmental economics/management.

ADMISSION

Applications For fall 1997 there were 600 applications for admission. Of those applying, 265 were accepted. Of those accepted, 200 enrolled.

Application Requirements GMAT score: minimum 500, application form, bachelor's degree, minimum GPA, interview, 3 letters of recommendation, personal statement, college transcript(s), minimum of 3 years of work experience.

Recommended for Application Resume, computer experience.

Application Deadline 3/15 for fall, 3/15 for fall (international). Deferred entrance is available.

ACADEMICS

Faculty Full-time 55; part-time 5.

Teaching Methodologies Case study, computer-aided instruction, computer simulations, faculty seminars, field projects, group discussion, lecture, research, role playing, seminars by members of the business community, simulations, student presentations, study groups, team projects.

Technology 50 on-campus computer terminals/PCs are available for student use and are linked by a campus-wide network. The network has full access to the Internet. Students are not required to have their own PC.

Special Opportunities International exchange program in various countries.

FINANCES

Costs for 1997–98 Tuition: Full-time: 122,000 Norwegian kroner per program. Part-time: 180,000 Norwegian kroner per program. Cost varies by academic program. Average 1997–98 room only costs were 2750 Norwegian kroner per academic year (on campus) and 3000 Norwegian kroner per academic year (off campus). Room and board costs vary by occupancy (e.g., single, double, triple), type of accommodation.

Financial Aid Research assistantships, teaching assistantships, grants, scholarships, loans available. Financial aid is available to part-time students. Application Deadline: 3/15.

Norwegian School of Management (continued)

Financial Aid Contact Ms. Gillian Kennedy, Coordinator of MBA Program, PO Box 580, Sandvika. Phone: 47-67570595; Fax: 47-67570541; E-mail: adm95024@bi.no

FACILITIES
Information Resources Norwegian School of Management Library; total holdings of 50,000 volumes, 700 current periodical subscriptions. CD player(s) available for graduate student use. Access provided to online bibliographic retrieval services and online databases.

INTERNATIONAL STUDENTS
Demographics 45% of students enrolled are international students [Africa, 5%, Asia, 15%, Australia/New Zealand, 5%, Central America, 1%, Europe, 40%, North America, 10%, South America, 1%, other, 23%].

Services and Facilities International student office, international student center, international student housing, visa services, counseling/support services, language tutoring, airport collection service for exchange students.

Applying Proof of adequate funds required. Financial aid is available to international students.

International Student Contact Mrs. Kjersti Stokke, International Coordinator, PO Box 580, Sandvika. Phone: 47-67570835; Fax: 47-67570541; E-mail: kjersti.e.stokke@bi.no

PLACEMENT
Services include alumni network, career counseling/planning, career library, career placement, job interviews arranged, job search course, resume referral to employers, and resume preparation.

Employment Of 1996–97 graduates, 88% were employed within three months of graduation; the average starting salary was $61,500. Types of employment entered: accounting, banking, chemical industry, communications, computer-related, consulting, consumer products, energy, engineering, finance, financial services, government, health services, high technology, hospitality management, human resources, information systems/technology, insurance, international trade, management, manufacturing, marketing, media, nonprofit, petrochemical, pharmaceutical, service industry, telecommunications, utilities.

Business Program(s) URL: http://www.bi.no

Program Contact: Ms. Gillian Kennedy, Coordinator of MBA Program, PO Box 580, Sandvika N-1301, Norway. Phone: 47-67570559; Fax: 47-67570541; E-mail: adm95024@bi.no

University of Oslo

Department of Economics

Oslo, Norway

OVERVIEW
The University of Oslo coed institution. Enrollment: 38,000 graduate, professional, and undergraduate students; 315 full-time matriculated graduate/professional students; 60 part-time matriculated graduate/professional students. Founded: 1811. The graduate business unit is in an urban setting and is on a semester calendar.

HIGHLIGHTS

Enrollment Profile
Full-time: 315	International: 9%
Part-time: 60	Women: 33%
Total: 375	Minorities: N/R
Average Age: 24	Average Class Size: 20
Fall 1997 Average GPA: N/R	Fall 1997 Average GMAT: N/R

Costs
Full-time tuition: N/R
Part-time tuition: 330 Norwegian kroner per semester (resident); 330 Norwegian kroner per semester (nonresident)

GRADUATE BUSINESS PROGRAMS
Masters Degree in Economics (CO) Full-time; up to 2 years to complete program. Concentrations in management, strategic management, economics, international trade, logistics, human resources.

ADMISSION
Applications For fall 1997 there were 58 applications for admission. Of those applying, 58 were accepted. Of those accepted, 46 enrolled.

Application Requirements Application form, personal statement, resume, college transcript(s).

Recommended for Application Letters of recommendation.

Application Deadline 6/1 for fall, 12/1 for spring.

ACADEMICS
Faculty Full-time 42.

Teaching Methodologies Case study, faculty seminars, lecture, team projects.

Technology Computer terminals/PCs are available for student use and are linked by a campus-wide network. Students are not required to have their own PC.

Special Opportunities International exchange program in France.

FINANCES
Costs for 1997–98 Tuition: 330 Norwegian kroner per semester (resident); 330 Norwegian kroner per semester (nonresident). Average 1997–98 room only costs were 1750 Norwegian kroner per academic year. Room and board costs vary by occupancy (e.g., single, double, triple), type of accommodation.

Financial Aid Contact Mrs. Rosita Bergh Lundstoel, Senior Executive Officer, PO Box 1095, Blindern, Oslo. Phone: 47-22-854-353; Fax: 47-22-855-035; E-mail: rosita.bergh@econ.uio.no

FACILITIES
Information Resources The University Library.

INTERNATIONAL STUDENTS
Demographics 9% of students enrolled are international students [Africa, 50%, Europe, 50%].

Applying TSE, TWE required. Financial aid is not available to international students.

International Student Contact Mrs. Rosita Bergh Lundstoel, Senior Executive Officer, Department of Economics, PO Box 1095, Blindern, Oslo. Phone: 47-22-855-127; Fax: 47-22-855-035.

PLACEMENT
Services include alumni network, career placement, job search course, and resume preparation.

Employment Types of employment entered: banking, finance, international trade, service industry.

Business Program(s) URL: http://www.uio.no

Program Contact: Mrs. Rosita Bergh Lundstoel, Senior Executive Officer, PO Box 1095, Blindern, Oslo N-0317, Norway. Phone: 47-22-854-353; Fax: 47-22-855-035; E-mail: rosita.bergh@econ.uio.no

PAKISTAN

Lahore University of Management Sciences

Graduate School of Business Administration

Lahore Cantt, Pakistan

OVERVIEW
Lahore University of Management Sciences is an independent-nonprofit, coed institution. Founded: 1984. The graduate business unit is in a suburban setting and is on a quarter calendar.

HIGHLIGHTS

Enrollment Profile
Full-time: 183	International: 4%
Part-time: 0	Women: 23%
Total: 183	Minorities: N/R
Average Age: 24	Average Class Size: 100
Fall 1997 Average GPA: N/R	Fall 1997 Average GMAT: 560

Costs
Full-time tuition: 147,000 Pakistani rupees per academic year
Part-time tuition: N/R

GRADUATE BUSINESS PROGRAMS
Master of Business Administration (MBA) Full-time; 21 months to 2 years to complete program. Concentrations in finance, management, marketing.

ADMISSION
Applications For fall 1997 there were 600 applications for admission. Of those applying, 137 were accepted. Of those accepted, 107 enrolled.

Application Requirements Application form, bachelor's degree, essay, interview, 2 letters of recommendation, personal statement, college transcript(s).

Recommended for Application GMAT score accepted: minimum 450.

Application Deadline 3/2 for fall, 3/2 for fall (international). Application fee: 700 Pakistani rupees, 50 Pakistani rupees (international). Deferred entrance is available.

ACADEMICS

Faculty Full-time 28; part-time 23.

Teaching Methodologies Case study, seminars by members of the business community, student presentations, team projects.

Technology 120 on-campus computer terminals/PCs are available for student use and are linked by a campus-wide network. The network has full access to the Internet. Students are not required to have their own PC.

Special Opportunities Advanced credit may be earned through credit by examination. International exchange program available. An internship program is available.

FINANCES

Costs for 1997–98 Tuition: Full-time: 147,000 Pakistani rupees per year. Fees: Full-time: 15,000 Pakistani rupees per academic year. Average 1997–98 room only costs were 30,000 Pakistani rupees per academic year.

Financial Aid Scholarships, loans available. Application Deadline: 3/2.

Financial Aid Contact Ms. Shazi Malik, Manager, Student Affairs, Opposite Sector U, Phase II LCCHS, Lahore Cantt, Punjab 54792, Pakistan. Phone: 92-42-572 2440 Ext. 2171; Fax: 92-42-572-2591.

FACILITIES

Information Resources Lahore University of Management Sciences Library; total holdings of 17,000 volumes, 240 current periodical subscriptions. CD player(s) available for graduate student use. Access provided to online bibliographic retrieval services and online databases.

INTERNATIONAL STUDENTS

Demographics 4% of students enrolled are international students [Asia, 100%].

Services and Facilities International student office, international student center, visa services, ESL courses, counseling/support services.

Applying Financial aid is available to international students.

International Student Contact Ms. Shazi Malik, Manager, Student Affairs, Opposite Sector U, Phase II LCCHS, Lahore Cantt, Punjab 54792, Pakistan. Phone: 92-42-572-2140 Ext. 2171; Fax: 92-42-572-2591; E-mail: shazi@lums.edu.pk

PLACEMENT

Services include alumni network, career counseling/planning, career fairs, career library, career placement, job interviews arranged, resume referral to employers, and resume preparation. In 1996–97, 10 organizations participated in on-campus recruiting; 30 on-campus interviews were conducted.

Employment Of 1996–97 graduates, 70% were employed within three months of graduation; the average starting salary was 240,000 Pakistani rupees. Types of employment entered: accounting, banking, communications, computer-related, consulting, consumer products, education, energy, engineering, finance, government, human resources, information systems/technology, insurance, management, manufacturing, marketing, media, nonprofit, pharmaceutical, telecommunications.

Business Program(s) URL: http://www.lums.edu.pk/

Program Contact: Ms. Shazi Malik, Manager, Student Affairs, Opposite Sector U, Phase II LCCHS, Lahore Cantt, Punjab 54792, Pakistan. Phone: 92-42-572-2440 Ext. 2171; Fax: 92-42-572-2592; E-mail: admissions@lums.edu.pk

PERU

Escuela de Administracion de Negocios para Graduados

Programa Magister

Lima, Peru

OVERVIEW

Escuela de Administracion de Negocios para Graduados is an independent-nonprofit, coed institution. Enrollment: 3,752 graduate, professional, and undergraduate students; 120 full-time matriculated graduate/professional students; 190 part-time matriculated graduate/professional students. Founded: 1963. The graduate business unit is in an urban setting and is on a semester and quarter calendar.

HIGHLIGHTS

Enrollment Profile

Full-time: 117	International: N/R
Part-time: 176	Women: 13%
Total: 293	Minorities: N/R
Average Age: 30	Average Class Size: 40
Fall 1997 Average GPA: N/R	Fall 1997 Average GMAT: N/R

Costs
Full-time tuition: $15,500 per academic year
Part-time tuition: $16,000 per program

GRADUATE BUSINESS PROGRAMS

Programa Magister Full-time (MBA) Full-time; up to 13 months to complete program. Concentrations in entrepreneurship, finance, marketing, operations management.

Programa Magister Part-time (MBA) Part-time; 3 years work experience required; 2.5 to 3 years to complete program.

ADMISSION

Applications For fall 1997 there were 610 applications for admission.

Application Requirements Application form, bachelor's degree, interview, personal statement, resume, college transcript(s), minimum of 1 year of work experience.

Application Deadline Applications processed on a rolling/continuous basis for both domestic and international students. Deferred entrance is available.

ACADEMICS

Faculty Full-time 32.

Teaching Methodologies Case study, computer-aided instruction, computer analysis, computer simulations, group discussion, lecture, seminars by members of the business community, student presentations, study groups, team projects.

Technology 60 on-campus computer terminals/PCs are available for student use and are linked by a campus-wide network. The network has full access to the Internet. Students are not required to have their own PC.

Special Opportunities International exchange programs in Belgium, Brazil, Chile, United States.

FINANCES

Costs for 1997–98 Tuition: Full-time: $15,500 per year. Part-time: $16,000 per program. Average 1997–98 room and board costs were $4800 per academic year (off campus). Room and board costs vary by occupancy (e.g., single, double, triple), type of accommodation, type of meal plan.

Financial Aid In 1997–98, 2% of students received some institutionally administered aid.

Financial Aid Contact Mr. Fernando Jurado, Admissions Office Manager, Apdo 1846, Lima. E-mail: fjurado@lan1.esan.edu.pe

FACILITIES

Information Resources Total library holdings of 32,000 volumes, 200 current periodical subscriptions. CD player(s) available for graduate student use. Access provided to online bibliographic retrieval services.

INTERNATIONAL STUDENTS

Demographics N/R

Services and Facilities International student housing, counseling/support services.

Applying Proof of health/immunizations required. Financial aid is not available to international students.

International Student Contact Ms. Ana Maria Villanueva, Director of Institutional Relations, Apdo 1846, Lima. E-mail: avilla@lan1.esan.edu.pe

PLACEMENT

Services include alumni network, career counseling/planning, electronic job bank, job interviews arranged, resume referral to employers, and resume preparation. In 1996–97, 50 organizations participated in on-campus recruiting; 379 on-campus interviews were conducted.

Employment Of 1996–97 graduates, 60% were employed within three months of graduation; the average starting salary was $25,000. Types of employment entered: banking, chemical industry, communications, computer-related, consulting, consumer products, education, energy, engineering, finance, government, health services, high technology, human resources, information systems/technology, management, marketing, mining, nonprofit, service industry, telecommunications, utilities.

Business Program(s) URL: http://www.esan.edu.pe

Program Contact: Mr. Carlos Leon-Milla, Marketing and Admissions Manager, Apdo 1846, Lima 100, Peru. E-mail: cleon@lan1.esan.edu.pe

PORTUGAL

Instituto Empresarial Portuense

Business School

Matosinhos, Portugal

OVERVIEW
Instituto Empresarial Portuense is an independent-nonprofit, coed institution. Founded: 1992. The graduate business unit is in a suburban setting and is on a trimester calendar.

HIGHLIGHTS

Enrollment Profile
Full-time: N/R
Part-time: N/R
Total: N/R
Average Age: N/R
Fall 1997 Average GPA: N/R

International: N/R
Women: N/R
Minorities: N/R
Average Class Size: N/R
Fall 1997 Average GMAT: N/R

Costs
Full-time tuition: N/R
Part-time tuition: N/R

GRADUATE BUSINESS PROGRAMS
MBA in Enterprise Management (MBA)
MBA in Commercialization and Marketing (MBA)

ADMISSION
Application Requirements Application form, bachelor's degree, minimum of 3 years of work experience.
Recommended for Application GMAT score accepted.

ACADEMICS
Teaching Methodologies Case study, faculty seminars, lecture, research, seminars by members of the business community, student presentations, team projects.
Special Opportunities International exchange program in Spain.

FINANCES
Financial Aid Grants, scholarships, loans available. Financial aid is available to part-time students.

INTERNATIONAL STUDENTS
Demographics N/R
Applying Financial aid is available to international students.

PLACEMENT
Services include alumni network, and resume referral to employers.
Employment Types of employment entered: consulting, finance, international trade, service industry.

Program Contact: Exponor- Le Ça da Palmeria, Matosinhos 4450, Portugal. Phone: 351-2-998-1716; Fax: 351-2-995-6984.

Universidade do Porto

Graduate School of Business

Porto, Portugal

OVERVIEW
The Universidade do Porto coed institution. Enrollment: 22,000 graduate, professional, and undergraduate students. Founded: 1911. The graduate business unit is in an urban setting and is on a trimester calendar.

HIGHLIGHTS

Enrollment Profile
Full-time: N/R
Part-time: N/R
Total: 57
Average Age: 30
Fall 1997 Average GPA: N/R

International: N/R
Women: N/R
Minorities: N/R
Average Class Size: 25
Fall 1997 Average GMAT: N/R

Costs
Full-time tuition: N/R
Part-time tuition: N/R

GRADUATE BUSINESS PROGRAMS
Master of Business Administration (MBA) Full-time, part-time; 12 months to 2 years to complete program. Concentrations in management, finance, strategic management, human resources, international finance, marketing, organizational behavior/development, accounting, economics.
MS in Quantitative Methods in Management (MS) Full-time, part-time.

ADMISSION
Application Requirements Application form, application fee, bachelor's degree, interview, 2 letters of recommendation, college transcript(s).
Recommended for Application GMAT score accepted, work experience, computer experience.
Application Deadline 6/30 for fall, 6/30 for fall (international). Application fee: 10,000 Portugese escudos.

ACADEMICS
Teaching Methodologies Computer-aided instruction, lecture, role playing, seminars by members of the business community, simulations, team projects.
Technology 13 on-campus computer terminals/PCs are available for student use and are linked by a campus-wide network. The network has full access to the Internet. Students are not required to have their own PC.

FINANCES
Costs for 1997–98 Cost varies by academic program.
Financial Aid Scholarships, loans available. Financial aid is available to part-time students. Application Deadline: 6/1.
Financial Aid Contact Mr. Rui Guimaraes, MBA Program Director, Rua de Salazares 842, Porto. Phone: 351-2-618-8699; Fax: 351-2-610-0861.

INTERNATIONAL STUDENTS
Demographics N/R
Applying TSE, TWE required. Financial aid is not available to international students.
International Student Contact Rui Guimaraes, Dean, Rua D. Manuel II, Porto. Phone: 351-2-207-3650; Fax: 351-2-610-0861.

PLACEMENT
Services include alumni network, career placement, and resume preparation.
Employment Types of employment entered: banking, finance, management, service industry.
Business Program(s) URL: http://www.up.pt

Program Contact: Mr. Rui Guimaraes, MBA Program Director, Rua De Salazaies 842, Porto 4100, Portugal. Phone: 351-2-618-8699; Fax: 351-2-610-0861.

Universidade Nova de Lisboa

Faculdade de Economia-Gestao

Lisbon, Portugal

OVERVIEW
The Universidade Nova de Lisboa is a federally supported, coed institution. Enrollment: 1,875 graduate, professional, and undergraduate students; 606 full-time matriculated graduate/professional students; 34 part-time matriculated graduate/professional students. The graduate business unit is in an urban setting and is on a trimester calendar.

HIGHLIGHTS

Enrollment Profile
Full-time: 16
Part-time: 34
Total: 50
Average Age: 28
Fall 1997 Average GPA: N/R

International: N/R
Women: 18%
Minorities: N/R
Average Class Size: 40
Fall 1997 Average GMAT: 600

Costs
Full-time tuition: 1,400,000 Portugese escudos per academic year (resident); 1,400,000 Portugese escudos per academic year (nonresident)
Part-time tuition: N/R

GRADUATE BUSINESS PROGRAMS

Master of Business Administration (MBA) Full-time, part-time; 37 total credits required; 12 months to 2 years to complete program. Concentrations in finance, human resources, management, marketing.

ADMISSION

Applications For fall 1997 there were 76 applications for admission. Of those applying, 42 were accepted. Of those accepted, 34 enrolled.

Application Requirements GMAT score, application form, application fee, bachelor's degree, essay, GPA: minimum 14.0 on a 20 scale, interview, 3 letters of recommendation, personal statement, resume, college transcript(s), minimum of 2 years of work experience.

Application Deadline 5/30 for winter, 5/30 for winter (international). Application fee: 26,000 Portugese escudos.

ACADEMICS

Faculty Part-time 22.

Teaching Methodologies Case study, lecture, seminars by members of the business community, simulations, team projects.

Technology 10 on-campus computer terminals/PCs are available for student use and are linked by a campus-wide network.

FINANCES

Costs for 1997–98 Tuition: Full-time: 1,400,000 Portugese escudos per year (resident); 1,400,000 Portugese escudos per year (nonresident).

FACILITIES

Information Resources Almada Negreiros Library plus 1 additional on-campus library; total holdings of 23,000 volumes, 12,470 current periodical subscriptions. CD player(s) available for graduate student use. Access provided to online databases.

INTERNATIONAL STUDENTS

Demographics N/R

Services and Facilities International student office, counseling/support services.

Applying TOEFL: minimum score of 500 required.

International Student Contact Ms. Fatima Jesus, Rua Marquês de Fronteira, 20, Lisbon. Phone: 351-1-3833624; Fax: 351-1-3874229; E-mail: fjesus@feunix.fe.unl.pt

PLACEMENT

Services include career placement. In 1996–97, 72 organizations participated in on-campus recruiting; 5 on-campus interviews were conducted.

Employment Of 1996–97 graduates, 89% were employed within three months of graduation. Types of employment entered: banking, chemical industry, computer-related, consulting, consumer products, education, financial services, telecommunications.

Business Program(s) URL: http://www.fe.unl.pt

Program Contact: Manuel Baganha, Program Director, Rua Marques de Fronteira, 20, Lisbon 1070, Portugal. Phone: 351-1-382-6111; Fax: 351-1-387-3973.

REPUBLIC OF SINGAPORE

Nanyang Technological University

Nanyang Business School

Singapore, Republic of Singapore

OVERVIEW

Nanyang Technological University is a federally supported, coed institution. Enrollment: 15,661 graduate, professional, and undergraduate students. Founded: 1981. The graduate business unit is in a suburban setting and is on a trimester calendar.

HIGHLIGHTS

Enrollment Profile

Full-time: 60	International: 29%
Part-time: 357	Women: 26%
Total: 417	Minorities: N/R
Average Age: 32	Average Class Size: 25
Fall 1997 Average GPA: 3.2	Fall 1997 Average GMAT: 600

Costs

Full-time tuition: $1875 per academic year (resident); $1875 per academic year (nonresident)
Part-time tuition: $1250 per trimester (resident); $1250 per trimester (nonresident)

GRADUATE BUSINESS PROGRAMS

Master of Business Administration (MBA) Full-time, part-time; 54 total credits required; 16 months to 4 years to complete program. Concentrations in accounting, banking, business law, finance, international business, management information systems, technology management, travel industry/tourism management, strategic management, insurance.

ADMISSION

Applications For fall 1997 there were 800 applications for admission. Of those applying, 220 were accepted. Of those accepted, 180 enrolled.

Application Requirements GMAT score: minimum 550, application form, bachelor's degree, minimum GPA: 3.0, interview, 2 letters of recommendation, personal statement, resume, college transcript(s), minimum of 2 years of work experience.

Recommended for Application GRE score accepted.

Application Deadline Applications processed on a rolling/continuous basis for both domestic and international students. Application fee: $25. Deferred entrance is available.

ACADEMICS

Faculty Full-time 85; part-time 21.

Teaching Methodologies Case study, computer-aided instruction, computer analysis, experiential learning, faculty seminars, field projects, group discussion, lecture, research, seminars by members of the business community, student presentations, study groups, team projects.

Technology 1,400 on-campus computer terminals/PCs are available for student use and are linked by a campus-wide network. The network has full access to the Internet. Students are not required to have their own PC.

Special Opportunities Advanced credit may be earned through credit by examination, transfer of credits from another institution. International exchange programs in Australia, Belgium, Canada, France, Mexico, New Zealand, Norway, Spain, Switzerland, United Kingdom, United States.

FINANCES

Costs for 1997–98 Tuition: Full-time: $1875 per trimester (resident); $1875 per trimester (nonresident). Part-time: $1250 per trimester (resident); $1250 per trimester (nonresident). Average 1997–98 room only costs were $1818 per academic year (on campus) and $2545 per academic year (off campus). Room and board costs vary by occupancy (e.g., single, double, triple), type of accommodation.

Financial Aid In 1997–98, 2% of students received some institutionally administered aid in the form of teaching assistantships, scholarships.

Financial Aid Contact Mrs. Wee Lee Yam, Deputy Administrative Director, Nanyang Avenue, Singapore. Phone: 65-791-1744 Ext. 5001; Fax: 65-791-3561; E-mail: awlyam@ntu.edu.sg

FACILITIES

Information Resources Library 1 plus 1 additional on-campus library; total holdings of 450,000 volumes, 4,000 current periodical subscriptions. CD player(s) available for graduate student use. Access provided to online bibliographic retrieval services.

INTERNATIONAL STUDENTS

Demographics 29% of students enrolled are international students [Asia, 70%, Australia/New Zealand, 5%, Central America, 5%, Europe, 15%, North America, 5%].

Services and Facilities International student housing, ESL courses, counseling/support services.

Applying TOEFL: minimum score of 600, proof of adequate funds, proof of health/immunizations recommended. Financial aid is available to international students.

International Student Contact Ms. Pearlie Koh, Director, International Exchange Programme, Nanyang Avenue, Singapore. Phone: 65-791-1744 Ext. 6145; Fax: 65-791-3561.

PLACEMENT

Services include alumni network, career counseling/planning, career fairs, and career placement.

Nanyang Technological University (continued)

Employment Of 1996–97 graduates, 95% were employed within three months of graduation. Types of employment entered: accounting, banking, chemical industry, communications, computer-related, consulting, consumer products, education, engineering, finance, financial services, government, health services, high technology, hospitality management, human resources, information systems/technology, law, management, manufacturing, marketing, nonprofit, petrochemical, real estate, service industry, telecommunications, transportation, utilities.

Business Program(s) URL: http://www.nanyangmba.ntu.edu.sg

Program Contact: Mrs. Wee Lee Yam, Deputy Administrative Director, Nanyang Avenue, Singapore 639798, Republic of Singapor. Phone: 65-791-1744 Ext. 5001; Fax: 65-791-3561; E-mail: awlyam@ntu.edu.sg

National University of Singapore

Graduate School of Business

Singapore, Republic of Singapore

OVERVIEW
National University of Singapore coed institution. Founded: 1980. The graduate business unit is in a suburban setting and is on a trimester calendar.

HIGHLIGHTS

Enrollment Profile

Full-time: N/R	International: N/R
Part-time: N/R	Women: N/R
Total: N/R	Minorities: N/R
Average Age: 30	Average Class Size: 24
Fall 1997 Average GPA: N/R	Fall 1997 Average GMAT: 616

Costs
Full-time tuition: 7170 Singapore dollars per academic year (resident); 14,340 Singapore dollars per academic year (nonresident)
Part-time tuition: 12,190 Singapore dollars per year (resident); 24,380 Singapore dollars per year (nonresident)

GRADUATE BUSINESS PROGRAMS
Master of Business Administration (MBA) Full-time, part-time; 12 months to 6 years to complete program. Concentrations in finance, banking, accounting, marketing, management, organizational behavior/development, international business, operations management, management information systems, strategic management.

Master of Science in Management of Technology (MS) Full-time, part-time; 9 months to 5 years to complete program. Concentrations in managerial economics, technology management, accounting, management information systems, operations management.

Asia Pacific Executive Master of Business Administration (MBA) Part-time; 48 total credits required; 18 months to 4 years to complete program.

ADMISSION
Application Requirements GMAT score: minimum 550, GRE score, application form, application fee, bachelor's degree, essay, interview, 2 letters of recommendation, personal statement, resume, college transcript(s), minimum of 2 years of work experience.

Recommended for Application Computer experience: word processing, spreadsheet.

Application Deadline 10/31 for winter, 1/31 for summer. Application fee: 20 Singapore dollars. Deferred entrance is available.

ACADEMICS
Faculty Full-time 49; part-time 5.

Teaching Methodologies Case study, computer-aided instruction, computer analysis, computer simulations, experiential learning, field projects, group discussion, lecture, research, role playing, seminars by members of the business community, simulations, student presentations, study groups, team projects.

Technology 3,500 on-campus computer terminals/PCs are available for student use and are linked by a campus-wide network. The network has full access to the Internet. Students are not required to have their own PC.

Special Opportunities Advanced credit may be earned through credit by examination, transfer of credits from another institution. International exchange programs in Canada, Denmark, France, Japan, Sweden, Switzerland, United States.

FINANCES
Costs for 1997–98 Tuition: Full-time: 7170 Singapore dollars per year (resident); 14,340 Singapore dollars per year (nonresident). Part-time: 12,190 Singapore dollars per year (resident); 24,380 Singapore dollars per year (nonresident).

Cost varies by academic program, class time (e.g., day/evening), reciprocity agreements. Average 1997–98 room and board costs were 7250 Singapore dollars per academic year (off campus). Room and board costs vary by occupancy (e.g., single, double, triple), type of accommodation, type of meal plan.

Financial Aid Scholarships, loans available. Application Deadline: 6/30.

Financial Aid Contact Mr. Teck-Kiang Tan, Senior Administrative Officer, 10 Kent Ridge Crescent, Singapore. E-mail: gsbtantk@nus.edu.sg

FACILITIES
Information Resources Central Library plus 5 additional on-campus libraries; total holdings of 2,050,000 volumes, 361,000 microforms. CD player(s) available for graduate student use. Access provided to online bibliographic retrieval services.

INTERNATIONAL STUDENTS
Demographics N/R

Services and Facilities International student office, international student housing.

Applying TOEFL: minimum score of 580, proof of adequate funds required. Financial aid is available to international students.

International Student Contact Mr. Teck-Kiang Tan, Senior Administrative Officer, 10 Kent Ridge Crescent, Singapore. Phone: 65-772-3427; Fax: 65-778-2681; E-mail: gsbtantk@nus.edu.sg

Business Program(s) URL: http://www.fba.nus.edu.sg/

Program Contact: Teck Kiang Tan, Graduate School of Business, 10 Kent Ridge Crescent, Singapore 119260, Republic of Singapor. Phone: 65-772-2068; Fax: 65-778-2681; E-mail: gsbadml@nus.sg

RUSSIAN FEDERATION

The International Management Institute of St. Petersburg

Marketing Department

St. Petersburg, Russian Federation

OVERVIEW
The International Management Institute of St. Petersburg is a private institution. Enrollment: 850 graduate, professional, and undergraduate students. Founded: 1989. The graduate business unit is in an urban setting and is on a semester calendar.

HIGHLIGHTS

Enrollment Profile

Full-time: 0	International: 4%
Part-time: 55	Women: 38%
Total: 55	Minorities: N/R
Average Age: 34	Average Class Size: 33
Fall 1997 Average GPA: N/R	Fall 1997 Average GMAT: 610

Costs
Full-time tuition: N/R
Part-time tuition: N/R

Degree(s) offered in conjunction with École de Management Lyon (France), ESADE (Spain), Henley Management College (United Kingdom), SDA Bocconi (Italy)

GRADUATE BUSINESS PROGRAMS
Executive MBA (MBA) Part-time; 50-70 total credits required; 18 to 22 months to complete program. Concentration in management consulting.

ADMISSION
Application Requirements Application form, bachelor's degree, interview, 2 letters of recommendation, minimum of 3 years of work experience, computer experience: Microsoft Word, Microsoft Excel.

Recommended for Application GMAT score accepted.

Application Deadline Applications processed on a rolling/continuous basis for both domestic and international students.

ACADEMICS
Teaching Methodologies Case study, computer analysis, computer simulations, faculty seminars, field projects, group discussion, lecture, research, role playing, seminars by members of the business community, simulations, student presentations, team projects.

Technology 38 on-campus computer terminals/PCs are available for student use and are linked by a campus-wide network. The network has full access to the Internet. Students are not required to have their own PC.

FACILITIES
Information Resources Total library holdings of 8,000 volumes.

INTERNATIONAL STUDENTS
Demographics 4% of students enrolled are international students [Europe, 100%].

Applying TOEFL: minimum score of 500 required. Financial aid is not available to international students.

Program Contact: Entrance 9, Smolny, St. Petersburg 193060, Russian Federation. Phone: 7-812-278-5650; Fax: 7-812-271-0717.

SLOVENIA

International Executive Development Center

School of Business Administration

Kranj, Slovenia

OVERVIEW
International Executive Development Center coed institution. Enrollment: 1,500 graduate, professional, and undergraduate students. Founded: 1986. The graduate business unit is in a rural setting and is on a module calendar.

HIGHLIGHTS

Enrollment Profile

Full-time: 0	International: 50%
Part-time: 50	Women: 26%
Total: 50	Minorities: N/R
Average Age: 33	Average Class Size: 40
Fall 1997 Average GPA: N/R	Fall 1997 Average GMAT: N/R

Costs
Full-time tuition: N/R
Part-time tuition: N/R

GRADUATE BUSINESS PROGRAMS
Master of Business Administration (MBA) Part-time; up to 17 months to complete program. Concentrations in management, finance, accounting, organizational management, human resources, strategic management.

Executive Master of Business Administration (EMBA) Part-time; 5-10 years work experience (3 years managerial experience) preferred; 12 months to complete program. Concentrations in accounting, business ethics, finance, marketing, strategic management, human resources, international business, international finance, international marketing, leadership, operations management, organizational behavior/development, travel industry/tourism management, project management, management.

President's Master of Business Administration (PMBA) Part-time; must hold top position within company; 12 months to 3 years to complete program. Concentrations in management, finance, accounting, marketing, strategic management, business ethics, human resources, international business, international finance, international marketing, leadership, operations management, organizational behavior/development, travel industry/tourism management, project management.

ADMISSION
Application Requirements GMAT score, application form, bachelor's degree, interview, 3 letters of recommendation, personal statement, resume, minimum of 3 years of work experience.

Application Deadline 10/31 for winter, 10/31 for winter (international). Deferred entrance is available.

ACADEMICS
Faculty Full-time 3; part-time 40.

Teaching Methodologies Case study, field projects, group discussion, lecture, role playing, seminars by members of the business community, simulations, student presentations, study groups, team projects.

Technology 12 on-campus computer terminals/PCs are available for student use and are linked by a campus-wide network. The network has full access to the Internet. Students are not required to have their own PC.

FINANCES
Costs for 1997–98 Cost varies by academic program. Average 1997–98 room and board costs were 10,000 German marks per academic year (on campus) and 5000 German marks per academic year (off campus). Room and board costs vary by occupancy (e.g., single, double, triple), type of accommodation, type of meal plan.

Financial Aid Scholarships, loans available. Application Deadline: 10/31.

Financial Aid Contact Ms. Brigita Krsnik, MBA Coordinator, Brdo Pri Kranju, Kranj. Phone: 386-64-221-761; Fax: 386-64-222-070; E-mail: metoda@iedc/brdo.sl

FACILITIES
Information Resources IEDC Resource Center; total holdings of 2,807 volumes, 33 current periodical subscriptions. CD player(s) available for graduate student use. Access provided to online databases.

INTERNATIONAL STUDENTS
Demographics 50% of students enrolled are international students [Asia, 3%, Europe, 97%].

Services and Facilities International student housing, visa services, counseling/support services.

Applying Financial aid is available to international students.

International Student Contact Dr. Judith Van Walsum-Stachowicz, MBA Director, Brdo pri Kranju, Kranj. Phone: 386-64-221-761; Fax: 386-64-222-070; E-mail: judith@iedc.brdo.si

PLACEMENT
Services include alumni network, career counseling/planning, career library, resume referral to employers, and resume preparation.

Employment Of 1996–97 graduates, 100% were employed within three months of graduation. Types of employment entered: accounting, banking, engineering, insurance, international trade, management.

Business Program(s) URL: http://www.iedc-brdo.si/brddo.si

Program Contact: Mrs. Brigita Krsnik, MBA Coordinator, BRDO pri Kranju, Kranj 4000, Slovenia. Phone: 386-64-221-761; Fax: 386-64-222-070.

SOUTH AFRICA

Rhodes University

Management Department

Grahamstown, South Africa

OVERVIEW
Rhodes University is an independent-nonprofit institution. Enrollment: 4,000 graduate, professional, and undergraduate students.

HIGHLIGHTS

Enrollment Profile

Full-time: 88	International: N/R
Part-time: 10	Women: N/R
Total: 98	Minorities: N/R
Average Age: N/R	Average Class Size: N/R
Fall 1997 Average GPA: N/R	Fall 1997 Average GMAT: N/R

Costs
Full-time tuition: 4500 South African rand per academic year
Part-time tuition: N/R

GRADUATE BUSINESS PROGRAMS
Master of Commerce (MComm) Full-time; minimum of 2 years to complete program. Concentrations in accounting, economics, management, information management, management information systems.

Master of Economics (MEcon) Full-time; minimum of 2 years to complete program. Concentrations in economics, finance.

Doctor of Economics (DEcon) Full-time; minimum of 3 years to complete program. Concentrations in economics, finance.

ADMISSION
Application Requirements Application form, bachelor's degree, minimum GPA, letters of recommendation, college transcript(s).

Recommended for Application Essay, interview, personal statement, resume, work experience, computer experience.

Application Deadline Applications processed on a rolling/continuous basis for both domestic and international students.

ACADEMICS
Teaching Methodologies Case study, computer-aided instruction, computer analysis, computer simulations, experiential learning, faculty seminars, field projects, group discussion, lecture, research, seminars by members of the business community, student presentations, study groups, team projects.

FINANCES
Costs for 1997–98 Tuition: Full-time: 4500 South African rand per year.

Rhodes University (continued)

Financial Aid Contact Helen Pienaar, Senior Administrative Assistant, POB 94, Grahamstown. Phone: 27-46-603-8111.

INTERNATIONAL STUDENTS
Demographics N/R
Services and Facilities International student office, international student center, international student housing, visa services, ESL courses, counseling/support services.
Applying TOEFL required.
International Student Contact Helen Pienaar, Senior Administrative Assistant, POB 94, Grahamstown. Phone: 27-46-603-8111.

Program Contact: Steve Fourie, Admissions Counselor, POB 94, Grahamstown, South Africa. Phone: 27-46-603-8111.

University of Cape Town

Graduate School of Business

Cape Town, Cape, South Africa

OVERVIEW
The University of Cape Town is a federally supported, coed institution. Enrollment: 92 full-time matriculated graduate/professional students; 54 part-time matriculated graduate/professional students. Founded: 1964. The graduate business unit is in an urban setting and is on a quarter calendar.

HIGHLIGHTS

Enrollment Profile

Full-time: 92	International: 22%
Part-time: 54	Women: 20%
Total: 146	Minorities: N/R
Average Age: 30	Average Class Size: 46
Fall 1997 Average GPA: N/R	Fall 1997 Average GMAT: 610

Costs
Full-time tuition: 33,000 South African rand per academic year (resident); 33,000 South African rand per academic year (nonresident)
Part-time tuition: N/R

GRADUATE BUSINESS PROGRAMS
Master of Business Administration (MBA) Full-time, part-time; 12 months to 2 years to complete program.

ADMISSION
Applications For fall 1997 there were 222 applications for admission. Of those applying, 146 were accepted. Of those accepted, 146 enrolled.
Application Requirements Application form, application fee, bachelor's degree, interview, 2 letters of recommendation, resume, college transcript(s), minimum of 3 years of work experience.
Recommended for Application GMAT score accepted.
Application Deadline Applications processed on a rolling/continuous basis for both domestic and international students. Application fee: 200 South African rand, 100 South African rand (international). Deferred entrance is available.

ACADEMICS
Faculty Full-time 16; part-time 15.
Teaching Methodologies Case study, computer-aided instruction, computer simulations, experiential learning, field projects, group discussion, lecture, research, seminars by members of the business community, student presentations, study groups, team projects.
Technology 20 on-campus computer terminals/PCs are available for student use and are linked by a campus-wide network. The network has full access to the Internet. Students are not required to have their own PC.
Special Opportunities International exchange programs in Norway, United Kingdom, United States.

FINANCES
Costs for 1997–98 Tuition: Full-time: 33,000 South African rand per year (resident); 33,000 South African rand per year (nonresident). Average 1997–98 room and board costs were 24,900 South African rand per academic year (on campus) and 17,600 South African rand per academic year (off campus). Room and board costs vary by type of accommodation.
Financial Aid Contact Ms. Janet Kirkwood, Head of MBA Administration, Private Bag Rondebosch, Cape Town, Cape 7701, South Africa. Phone: 27-21-406-1317; Fax: 27-21-215-693; E-mail: janetk@gsb2.uct.ac.za

FACILITIES
Information Resources Library and Business Information Centre; total holdings of 10,000 volumes. Access provided to online databases.

INTERNATIONAL STUDENTS
Demographics 22% of students enrolled are international students [Africa, 83%, Asia, 1%, Europe, 13%, North America, 2%, South America, 1%].
Services and Facilities International student center, counseling/support services.
Applying TOEFL: minimum score of 600 required. Financial aid is not available to international students.
International Student Contact Ms. Janet Kirkwood, Head of MBA Administration, The Graduate School of Business, Private Bag Rondebosch, Cape Town, Cape 7701, South Africa. Phone: 27-21-406-1317; Fax: 27-21-215-693; E-mail: janetk@gsb2.uct.ac.za

PLACEMENT
Services include alumni network, career counseling/planning, career library, career placement, job search course, resume referral to employers, and resume preparation. In 1996–97, 20 organizations participated in on-campus recruiting.
Employment Of 1996–97 graduates, 90% were employed within three months of graduation. Types of employment entered: accounting, banking, chemical industry, communications, computer-related, consulting, consumer products, engineering, finance, financial services, health services, high technology, human resources, information systems/technology, insurance, international trade, management, manufacturing, marketing, media, mining, petrochemical, pharmaceutical, retail, telecommunications, transportation, utilities.

Business Program(s) URL: http://www.gsb.uct.ac.za/

Program Contact: Ms. Nickey Phillips, Recruitment Office, Private Bag Rondebosch, Cape Town, Cape 7701, South Africa. Phone: 27-21-406-1339; Fax: 27-21-215-693; E-mail: nickyphi@gsb2.uct.ac.za

University of the Witwatersrand

Graduate School of Business Administration

Johannesburg, South Africa

OVERVIEW
The University of the Witwatersrand is a federally supported, coed institution. Enrollment: 19,000 graduate, professional, and undergraduate students. Founded: 1922. The graduate business unit is in an urban setting and is on a quarter calendar.

HIGHLIGHTS

Enrollment Profile

Full-time: 48	International: 3%
Part-time: 241	Women: 24%
Total: 289	Minorities: N/R
Average Age: 29	Average Class Size: 60
Fall 1997 Average GPA: N/R	Fall 1997 Average GMAT: 580

Costs
Full-time tuition: 35,000 South African rand per academic year (resident); 36,000 South African rand per academic year (nonresident)
Part-time tuition: N/R

GRADUATE BUSINESS PROGRAMS
Master of Business Administration (MBA) Full-time, part-time; 12 months to 3 years to complete program. Concentrations in accounting, economics, finance, international management, management information systems, marketing, materials management, production management, quantitative analysis, public management, strategic management, entrepreneurship, industrial/labor relations, international business, operations management.

ADMISSION
Applications For fall 1997 there were 910 applications for admission. Of those applying, 173 were accepted. Of those accepted, 155 enrolled.
Application Requirements Application form, bachelor's degree, letters of recommendation, personal statement, college transcript(s), minimum of 4 years of work experience.
Recommended for Application GMAT score accepted, essay, resume, computer experience.
Application Deadline 7/31 for fall, 2/28 for winter, 8/30 for winter (international), 1/30 for spring (international). Application fee: 200 (international).

ACADEMICS
Faculty Full-time 23; part-time 10.
Teaching Methodologies Case study, experiential learning, group discussion, lecture, research, student presentations, team projects.

Technology 40 on-campus computer terminals/PCs are available for student use and are linked by a campus-wide network. The network has full access to the Internet. Students are not required to have their own PC.

Special Opportunities International exchange programs in Australia, Netherlands, United Kingdom, United States.

FINANCES
Costs for 1997–98 Tuition: Full-time: 35,000 South African rand per program (resident); 36,000 South African rand per program (nonresident).

Financial Aid Scholarships, loans available.

Financial Aid Contact Ms. Liz Fick, Senior Assistant Registrar, Private Bag X3, Wits, Witwatersrand. Phone: 27-11-716-3256; Fax: 27-11-643-2336.

FACILITIES
Information Resources John Schlesinger Library; total holdings of 15,000 volumes, 200 current periodical subscriptions. Access provided to online bibliographic retrieval services.

INTERNATIONAL STUDENTS
Demographics 3% of students enrolled are international students [Africa, 100%].

Services and Facilities International student office, international student center, international student housing.

Applying Proof of adequate funds, proof of health/immunizations required. IELT recommended. Financial aid is not available to international students.

International Student Contact Mrs. Anne Fraser, International Student Coordinator, Box 98, Witwatersrand. Phone: 27-11-488-5627; Fax: 27-11-643-2336; E-mail: frasera@zeus.mgmt.wits.ac.za

PLACEMENT
Services include alumni network, career placement, job interviews arranged, and resume preparation. In 1996–97, 12 organizations participated in on-campus recruiting; 40 on-campus interviews were conducted.

Employment Of 1996–97 graduates, 80% were employed within three months of graduation. Types of employment entered: accounting, banking, communications, consulting, consumer products, finance, financial services, government, information systems/technology, insurance, international trade, management, manufacturing, real estate, retail, service industry.

Business Program(s) URL: http://www.wits.ac.ZA/wbs

Program Contact: Mrs. Lesley Salter, Assistant Registrar, PO Box 98, Witwatersrand 2050, South Africa. Phone: 27-11-488-5661; Fax: 27-11-643-2336; E-mail: 130fbi@witsumb.wits.ac.za

See full description on page 1160.

SPAIN

EAP-European School of Management

Business School
Madrid, Spain

OVERVIEW
EAP-European School of Management is a federally supported, coed institution. Enrollment: 88 graduate, professional, and undergraduate students; 74 full-time matriculated graduate/professional students; 14 part-time matriculated graduate/professional students. Founded: 1973. The graduate business unit is in a suburban setting.

HIGHLIGHTS
Enrollment Profile
Full-time: 74
Part-time: 14
Total: 88
Average Age: 29
Fall 1997 Average GPA: N/R

International: N/R
Women: N/R
Minorities: N/R
Average Class Size: N/R
Fall 1997 Average GMAT: N/R

Costs
Full-time tuition: N/R
Part-time tuition: N/R

GRADUATE BUSINESS PROGRAMS
European Master of International Management (EMIM) Full-time; proficiency in Spanish and English required; up to 3 years to complete program.

Full-time MBA (MBA) Full-time; 7 years professional work experience required; up to 12 months to complete program. Concentrations in accounting, finance, human resources, business information science, marketing, organizational behavior/development, taxation.

International Executive Master of Business Administration (IEMBA) Part-time; up to 16 months to complete program. Concentrations in accounting, finance, human resources, business information science, marketing, organizational behavior/development, taxation.

ADMISSION
Application Requirements GMAT score: minimum 550, application form, application fee, bachelor's degree, interview, resume, minimum of 4 years of work experience.

Recommended for Application MAT score accepted, college transcript(s).

Application Deadline 9/30 for winter. Application fee: 10,000 pesetas.

ACADEMICS
Faculty Full-time 50.

Teaching Methodologies Case study, computer-aided instruction, group discussion, lecture, team projects.

Special Opportunities International exchange programs in France, Germany, United Kingdom.

FINANCES
Financial Aid Contact Mr. Ramon Rodriquez, Director of External Relations, Arroyofirsno Street, 1, Madrid. Phone: 34-91-386-2511; Fax: 34-91-373-9229.

INTERNATIONAL STUDENTS
Demographics N/R

Applying TOEFL: minimum score of 600, TSE, TWE required.

PLACEMENT
Services include alumni network, job interviews arranged, and resume preparation.

Employment Types of employment entered: accounting, banking, government, management, retail.

Business Program(s) URL: http://www.eap.net/english/index.html

Program Contact: Mr. Julian Peinador, Director, Arroyofirsno Street, 1, Madrid 28035, Spain. Phone: 34-91-386-2511; Fax: 34-91-373-9229.

Escola d'Alta Direcció i Administració (EADA)

Business Programs
Barcelona, Spain

OVERVIEW
Escola d'Alta Direcció i Administració (EADA) is a proprietary, coed institution. Enrollment: 3,000 graduate, professional, and undergraduate students. Founded: 1957. The graduate business unit is in an urban setting and is on a trimester calendar.

HIGHLIGHTS
Enrollment Profile
Full-time: 30
Part-time: 30
Total: 60
Average Age: 30
Fall 1997 Average GPA: N/R

International: N/R
Women: N/R
Minorities: N/R
Average Class Size: 25
Fall 1997 Average GMAT: N/R

Costs
Full-time tuition: 1,400,000 Spanish pesetas per academic year
Part-time tuition: 1,090,000 Spanish pesetas per year

GRADUATE BUSINESS PROGRAMS
Executive MBA (MBA) Part-time; 2 years to complete program. Concentration in management.

Master of Business Administration (MBA) Full-time; 12 months to complete program. Concentration in management.

ADMISSION
Applications For fall 1997 there were 94 applications for admission. Of those applying, 48 were accepted. Of those accepted, 33 enrolled.

Application Requirements GMAT score, application form, bachelor's degree, essay, interview, personal statement, resume, college transcript(s).

Recommended for Application Letters of recommendation, work experience.

Escola d'Alta Direcció i Administració (EADA) (continued)

Application Deadline Applications processed on a rolling/continuous basis for both domestic and international students. Deferred entrance is available.

ACADEMICS
Faculty Full-time 15; part-time 10.

Teaching Methodologies Case study, computer-aided instruction, computer simulations, experiential learning, faculty seminars, field projects, group discussion, lecture, role playing, seminars by members of the business community, simulations, student presentations, study groups, team projects.

Technology 50 on-campus computer terminals/PCs are available for student use. Students are not required to have their own PC.

Special Opportunities International exchange program in United Kingdom.

FINANCES
Costs for 1997–98 Tuition: Full-time: 1,400,000 Spanish pesetas per year. Part-time: 1,090,000 Spanish pesetas per year.

Financial Aid In 1997–98, 2% of students received some institutionally administered aid in the form of loans. Financial aid is available to part-time students. Application Deadline: 6/1.

Financial Aid Contact Mrs. Brita Hektoen, MBA Director, Aragó 204, Barcelona. Phone: 34-93-323-1208; Fax: 34-93-323-7317.

FACILITIES
Information Resources EADA Main Library plus 1 additional on-campus library; total holdings of 30,000 volumes, 250 current periodical subscriptions. Access provided to online bibliographic retrieval services.

INTERNATIONAL STUDENTS
Demographics N/R

Services and Facilities Counseling/support services.

Applying Financial aid is not available to international students.

International Student Contact Mrs. Brita Hektoen, MBA Director, Aragó 204, Barcelona. Phone: 34-93-323-1208; Fax: 34-93-323-7317; E-mail: eada@cinet.jcr.es.

PLACEMENT
Services include alumni network, career counseling/planning, career library, career placement, electronic job bank, job search course, and resume preparation.

Employment Of 1996–97 graduates, 80% were employed within three months of graduation. Types of employment entered: banking, chemical industry, communications, computer-related, consulting, consumer products, energy, engineering, finance, financial services, government, health services, high technology, human resources, insurance, international trade, management, manufacturing, marketing, nonprofit, petrochemical, pharmaceutical, retail, service industry, telecommunications, transportation.

Business Program(s) URL: http://www.eada.es

Program Contact: Mrs. Brita Hektoen, MBA Director, Aragó 204, Barcelona 08011, Spain. Phone: 34-93-323-1208; Fax: 34-93-323-7317.

Escuela Superior de Administración y Dirección de Empresas (ESADE)

Business School

Barcelona, Spain

OVERVIEW
Escuela Superior de Administración y Dirección de Empresas (ESADE) coed institution. Enrollment: 5,475 graduate, professional, and undergraduate students; 358 full-time matriculated graduate/professional students; 3,632 part-time matriculated graduate/professional students. Founded: 1958. The graduate business unit is in an urban setting and is on a trimester calendar.

HIGHLIGHTS

Enrollment Profile

Full-time: 283	International: 16%
Part-time: 302	Women: 29%
Total: 585	Minorities: N/R
Average Age: 27	Average Class Size: 30
Fall 1997 Average GPA: N/R	Fall 1997 Average GMAT: 600

Costs
Full-time tuition: N/R
Part-time tuition: N/R

GRADUATE BUSINESS PROGRAMS
Full-time MBA (MBA) Full-time; 100 total credits required; minimum of 21 months to complete program. Concentrations in finance, human resources, international management, operations management, public management, taxation, marketing, management information systems, health care, business policy/strategy.

Part-time MBA (MBA) Part-time; 85 total credits required; minimum of 23 months to complete program. Concentrations in finance, human resources, marketing, operations management, public management, taxation, management information systems, international management, health care, business policy/strategy.

ADMISSION
Applications For fall 1997 there were 615 applications for admission. Of those applying, 370 were accepted. Of those accepted, 259 enrolled.

Application Requirements Application form, application fee, bachelor's degree, interview, resume, college transcript(s).

Recommended for Application GMAT score accepted: minimum 550, minimum of 1 year of work experience.

Application Deadline 6/28 for fall, 6/28 for fall (international). Application fee: 10,000 pesetas, 100 pesetas (international).

ACADEMICS
Faculty Full-time 169; part-time 248.

Teaching Methodologies Case study, computer analysis, computer simulations, faculty seminars, field projects, group discussion, lecture, role playing, seminars by members of the business community, simulations, student presentations, study groups, team projects.

Technology 180 on-campus computer terminals/PCs are available for student use and are linked by a campus-wide network. The network has full access to the Internet. Students are not required to have their own PC.

Special Opportunities Advanced credit may be earned through credit by examination, credit for experience, credit for business training programs. International exchange programs in Australia, Belgium, Brazil, Canada, France, Germany, Hong Kong, India, Israel, Italy, Japan, Korea, Malaysia, Mexico, Netherlands, Norway, Philippines, Republic of Singapore, Republic of South Africa, United Kingdom, United States, Venezuela. An internship program is available.

FINANCES
Costs for 1997–98 Average 1997–98 room and board costs were 800,000 pesetas per academic year (off campus). Room and board costs vary by occupancy (e.g., single, double, triple), type of accommodation.

Financial Aid Scholarships, work study available. Financial aid is available to part-time students.

Financial Aid Contact Ms. Catalina Pons, Director of Admissions, Avenida de Pedralbes 60-62, Barcelona. Phone: 34-93-280 29 95; Fax: 34-93-204 81 05; E-mail: info@esade.es

FACILITIES
Information Resources Biblioteca ESADE; total holdings of 52,000 volumes, 10 microforms, 700 current periodical subscriptions. CD player(s) available for graduate student use. Access provided to online bibliographic retrieval services.

INTERNATIONAL STUDENTS
Demographics 16% of students enrolled are international students [Asia, 2%, Central America, 4%, Europe, 85%, North America, 5%, South America, 4%].

Services and Facilities International student office, international student center, international student housing, ESL courses, counseling/support services.

Applying TOEFL required. Financial aid is available to international students.

International Student Contact Ms. Antonia Maria Serra, Exchange Coordinator, Avenida de Pedralbes 60-62, Barcelona. Phone: 34-93-280 61 62 Ext. 241; Fax: 34-93-204 81 05; E-mail: serram@m.esade.es

PLACEMENT
Services include alumni network, career counseling/planning, career fairs, career library, career placement, electronic job bank, job interviews arranged, job search course, resume referral to employers, and resume preparation. In 1996–97, 350 organizations participated in on-campus recruiting.

Employment Of 1996–97 graduates, 100% were employed within three months of graduation. Types of employment entered: accounting, banking, chemical industry, communications, computer-related, consulting, consumer products, finance, financial services, human resources, information systems/technology, international trade, law, management, manufacturing, marketing, petrochemical, pharmaceutical, real estate, retail, service industry, telecommunications.

Business Program(s) URL: http://www.esade.es/indexi.htm

Program Contact: Ms. Catalina Pons, Director of Admissions, Avenida de Pedralbes 60-62, Barcelona 08034, Spain. Phone: 34-93-280 29 95; Fax: 34-93-204 81 05; E-mail: info@esade.es

IADE

Instituto Universitario de Administracion de Empresas

Madrid, Spain

OVERVIEW

IADE coed institution. Enrollment: 30,000 graduate, professional, and undergraduate students. Founded: 1981. The graduate business unit is in a suburban setting and is on a trimester calendar.

HIGHLIGHTS

Enrollment Profile

Full-time: 90	International: 35%
Part-time: 60	Women: 50%
Total: 150	Minorities: N/R
Average Age: 24	Average Class Size: 35
Fall 1997 Average GPA: N/R	Fall 1997 Average GMAT: N/R

Costs

Full-time tuition: N/R	Part-time tuition: N/R

GRADUATE BUSINESS PROGRAMS

Master of Business Administration (MBA) Full-time; 100 total credits required; work experience required; 9 to 18 months to complete program. Concentrations in accounting, business education, business information science, business law, business policy/strategy, decision sciences, economics, finance, human resources, international economics, international finance, management information systems, marketing, quality management, quantitative analysis, strategic management, industrial/labor relations, financial economics.

Executive Master in Banking Management (MBM) Part-time; 80 total credits required; work experience required; 6 months to complete program. Concentrations in financial management/planning, financial information systems, marketing, actuarial science, banking, business law, commerce, finance, human resources, international business, international economics, organizational management, quality management, strategic management.

Executive MBA (MBA) Part-time; 65 total credits required; 4 months to complete program. Concentrations in strategic management, production management, financial management/planning, new venture management, quality management, information management, organizational management, international economics, strategic management, international finance, international marketing, international management, organizational behavior/development, new venture management, human resources.

Master of Science, Technology and Society (MS) Part-time; 11 months to complete program. Concentrations in business policy/strategy, developmental economics, management science, organizational behavior/development, public management, public policy and administration, research and development administration, technology management, telecommunications management.

ADMISSION

Applications For fall 1997 there were 350 applications for admission. Of those applying, 175 were accepted. Of those accepted, 150 enrolled.

Application Requirements GMAT score: minimum 580, application form, application fee, bachelor's degree, interview, 2 letters of recommendation, resume, college transcript(s).

Application Deadline 6/15 for spring, 9/15 for summer, 6/15 for spring (international), 9/15 for summer (international). Application fee: 5000 pesetas.

ACADEMICS

Faculty Full-time 40; part-time 45.

Teaching Methodologies Case study, computer-aided instruction, computer analysis, computer simulations, experiential learning, faculty seminars, field projects, group discussion, seminars by members of the business community, simulations, student presentations, study groups, team projects.

Technology 30 on-campus computer terminals/PCs are available for student use. The network has full access to the Internet. Students are required to have their own PC.

Special Opportunities Advanced credit may be earned through credit by examination, credit for experience, credit for business training programs. International exchange programs in France, Germany, Italy, United Kingdom. An internship program is available.

FINANCES

Costs for 1997–98 Average 1997–98 room and board costs were 900,000 pesetas per academic year (off campus).

Financial Aid In 1997–98, 3% of students received some institutionally administered aid in the form of scholarships. Application Deadline: 9/15.

FACILITIES

Information Resources Biblioteca Central de la UAM plus 6 additional on-campus libraries; total holdings of 400,000 volumes, 800 current periodical subscriptions. CD player(s) available for graduate student use. Access provided to online bibliographic retrieval services and online databases.

INTERNATIONAL STUDENTS

Demographics 35% of students enrolled are international students [Central America, 20%, Europe, 40%, South America, 30%, other, 10%].

Services and Facilities International student office, international student center, international student housing, counseling/support services.

Applying Financial aid is not available to international students.

International Student Contact Angeles Luque de la Torre, International Affairs, Ciudad Universitaria de Cantablanco, Madrid. Phone: 34 -1-397-4269; Fax: 34-1-397-4218.

PLACEMENT

Employment Of 1996–97 graduates, 80% were employed within three months of graduation; the average starting salary was 1,800,000 pesetas. Types of employment entered: banking, consulting, finance, human resources.

Program Contact: Begona Santos Urda, MBA Coordinator, Ciudad Universitaria de Cantablanco, Madrid 28049, Spain. Phone: 34-1-397-4161; Fax: 34-1-397-4218.

IESE International Graduate School of Management *see* University of Navarra

Instituto de Empresa

Business School

Madrid, Spain

OVERVIEW

Instituto de Empresa is an independent-nonprofit, coed institution. Founded: 1973. The graduate business unit is in an urban setting and is on a trimester calendar.

HIGHLIGHTS

Enrollment Profile

Full-time: N/R	International: N/R
Part-time: N/R	Women: N/R
Total: N/R	Minorities: N/R
Average Age: 26	Average Class Size: 50
Fall 1997 Average GPA: N/R	Fall 1997 Average GMAT: 620

Costs

Full-time tuition: N/R	Part-time tuition: N/R

GRADUATE BUSINESS PROGRAMS

Master of Business Administration (MBA) Full-time, part-time; 10 to 12 months to complete program. Concentrations in accounting, economics, entrepreneurship, finance, human resources, international business, management, management information systems, marketing, operations management, organizational behavior/development, public policy and administration, quantitative analysis, strategic management.

International MBA (IMBA) Full-time; up to 15 months to complete program. Concentrations in accounting, economics, entrepreneurship, finance, human resources, international business, management, management information systems, marketing, operations management, organizational behavior/development, public policy and administration, quantitative analysis, strategic management.

Master of Corporate Legal Counseling (MAJ) Full-time.

Master of Corporate Tax Counseling (MAF) Full-time.

ADMISSION

Application Requirements Application form, bachelor's degree, interview, 3 letters of recommendation, college transcript(s).

Recommended for Application GMAT score accepted: minimum 550.

Application Deadline Applications processed on a rolling/continuous basis for both domestic and international students.

ACADEMICS

Faculty Full-time 50; part-time 125.

Teaching Methodologies Case study, faculty seminars, lecture, role playing, seminars by members of the business community, student presentations, team projects.

Technology 100 on-campus computer terminals/PCs are available for student use and are linked by a campus-wide network. The network has full access to the Internet. Students are not required to have their own PC.

Special Opportunities International exchange programs in Mexico, United States. An internship program is available.

FINANCES

Financial Aid Scholarships available. Financial aid is available to part-time students. Application Deadline: 6/30.

Instituto de Empresa (continued)

Financial Aid Contact Margarita Alonso, Admissions and Marketing Direction, c/ Maria de Molina 11, 13y 15, Madrid. Phone: 34-1-562-8100; Fax: 34-1-411-5503.

INTERNATIONAL STUDENTS
Demographics N/R

Applying TOEFL recommended. Financial aid is available to international students.

PLACEMENT
Services include alumni network, career counseling/planning, career placement, job interviews arranged, and job search course. In 1996–97, 1,259 organizations participated in on-campus recruiting.

Employment Of 1996–97 graduates, the average starting salary was 3,750,000 pesetas. Types of employment entered: banking, consulting, finance, government, information systems/technology, law, management, manufacturing, marketing, media, nonprofit, pharmaceutical, service industry, telecommunications.

Business Program(s) URL: http://www.ie.ucm.es

Program Contact: Margarita Alonso, Admissions and Marketing Direction, c/ Maria de Molina 11, 13y 15, Madrid 28006, Spain. Phone: 34-1-562-8100; Fax: 34-1-411-5503.

Schiller International University

Business Programs

Madrid, Spain

OVERVIEW
Schiller International University is an independent-nonprofit, coed institution. Founded: 1988. The graduate business unit is in an urban setting and is on a semester calendar.

HIGHLIGHTS

Enrollment Profile

Full-time: N/R	International: N/R
Part-time: N/R	Women: N/R
Total: N/R	Minorities: N/R
Average Age: N/R	Average Class Size: 15
Fall 1997 Average GPA: N/R	Fall 1997 Average GMAT: N/R

Costs
Full-time tuition: N/R
Part-time tuition: N/R

Degree(s) offered in conjunction with Schiller France, Schiller Germany, Schiller Switzerland, Schiller United Kingdom, Schiller United States

GRADUATE BUSINESS PROGRAMS
Master of Business Administration in International Business (MBA) Full-time, part-time; 62 total credits required; 12 months to 3 years to complete program.

Master of Business Administration in Hotel Management (MBA) Full-time, part-time; 62 total credits required; 12 months to 3 years to complete program.

ADMISSION
Application Requirements Application form, application fee, bachelor's degree (must be in field of business), personal statement, college transcript(s).

Recommended for Application GMAT score accepted, minimum GPA: 3.0, work experience, computer experience.

Application Deadline Applications processed on a rolling/continuous basis for both domestic and international students. Application fee: $35.

ACADEMICS
Teaching Methodologies Case study, experiential learning, faculty seminars, field projects, group discussion, lecture, research, student presentations, study groups, team projects.

Technology Students are not required to have their own PC.

Special Opportunities Advanced credit may be earned through credit by examination, transfer of credits from another institution. International exchange programs in France, Germany, Switzerland, United Kingdom, United States. An internship program is available.

FINANCES
Costs for 1997–98 Cost varies by academic program, campus location, number of credits taken. Fees vary by academic program, campus location. Room and board costs vary by campus location, occupancy (e.g., single, double, triple), type of accommodation.

Financial Aid Grants, scholarships, loans available. Application Deadline: 3/30.

Financial Aid Contact Mr. James Sutherland, Financial Aid Officer, 453 Edgewater Drive, Dunedin. Phone: 813-736-5082; Fax: 813-734-0359.

FACILITIES
Information Resources Biblioteca Nacional; total holdings of 8,296 volumes, 66 microforms, 58 current periodical subscriptions.

INTERNATIONAL STUDENTS
Demographics N/R

Services and Facilities International student office, international student center, international student housing, ESL courses, counseling/support services.

Applying TOEFL: minimum score of 550 recommended. Financial aid is available to international students.

International Student Contact Director of Admissions, Calle de Rodriguez San Pedro, 10, Madrid. Phone: 34-1-446-2349; Fax: 34-1-593-4446.

PLACEMENT
Services include alumni network, career placement, and resume preparation.

Employment Types of employment entered: accounting, banking, communications, computer-related, consulting, education, engineering, finance, financial services, government, health services, hospitality management, human resources, information systems/technology, insurance, international trade, law, management, marketing, retail, service industry, telecommunications, transportation.

Business Program(s) URL: http://www.schiller.edu/

Program Contact: Dr. Christoph Leibrecht, Director of Admissions, 453 Edgewater Drive, Dunedin 34698-7532, Spain. Phone: 813-736-5082; Fax: 813-734-0359; E-mail: study@campus.schiller.edu

University of Navarra

IESE International Graduate School of Management

Barcelona, Spain

OVERVIEW
The University of Navarra is an independent-nonprofit, coed institution. Enrollment: 456 graduate, professional, and undergraduate students; 456 full-time matriculated graduate/professional students; part-time matriculated graduate/professional students. Founded: 1958. The graduate business unit is in an urban setting and is on a trimester calendar.

HIGHLIGHTS

Enrollment Profile

Full-time: N/R	International: N/R
Part-time: N/R	Women: N/R
Total: 425	Minorities: N/R
Average Age: 27	Average Class Size: 50
Fall 1997 Average GPA: N/R	Fall 1997 Average GMAT: 615

Costs
Full-time tuition: 2,300,000 pesetas per academic year
Part-time tuition: N/R

Founded in 1958, IESE International Graduate School of Management, with campuses in Barcelona and Madrid, is one of Europe's leading business schools and highly regarded in Spain. Having established the first bilingual M.B.A. program in the world, IESE not only provides students with a unique and challenging M.B.A. education but also prepares managers in two of the most important languages of commerce in today's increasingly global environment.

Truly international in nature, IESE's faculty and student body represent more than forty countries, thus enriching the M.B.A. experience. Students are encouraged to participate in the International Exchange Program with thirteen of the top business schools on four continents. The International Advisory Board, composed of chairmen and presidents of some of the world's most important multinational companies, advises IESE's Board of Governors on the state of the international economy and developments in management. In collaboration with the Harvard Business School, Stanford, and the University of Michigan, IESE offers management development courses for senior executives. In addition, IESE has assisted in establishing business schools in Asia, Eastern Europe, Latin America, and Africa and has provided training for professors of business administration from universities in Central and Eastern Europe.

GRADUATE BUSINESS PROGRAMS
MBA (MBA) Full-time; up to 21 months to complete program.

ADMISSION
Applications For fall 1997 there were 1,000 applications for admission. Of those applying, 343 were accepted. Of those accepted, 216 enrolled.

Application Requirements Application form, bachelor's degree, essay, minimum GPA, interview, 2 letters of recommendation, personal statement, resume, college transcript(s).

Recommended for Application GMAT score accepted, work experience.

Application Deadline 5/1 for fall, 5/1 for fall (international). Deferred entrance is available.

ACADEMICS
Faculty Full-time 77; part-time 36.

Teaching Methodologies Case study, computer-aided instruction, computer analysis, computer simulations, experiential learning, faculty seminars, field projects, group discussion, lecture, research, role playing, seminars by members of the business community, simulations, student presentations, study groups, team projects.

Technology 80 on-campus computer terminals/PCs are available for student use and are linked by a campus-wide network. The network has full access to the Internet. Students are not required to have their own PC.

Special Opportunities International exchange programs in Canada, Costa Rica, Hong Kong, Japan, Mexico, Netherlands, People's Republic of China, United Kingdom, United States. An internship program is available.

FINANCES
Costs for 1997–98 Tuition: Full-time: 2,300,000 pesetas per year. Average 1997–98 room only costs were 660,000 pesetas per academic year (off campus). Room and board costs vary by occupancy (e.g., single, double, triple), type of accommodation, type of meal plan.

Financial Aid Grants, scholarships, loans available. Application Deadline: 4/1.

Financial Aid Contact MBA Admissions Department, Avenida Pearson, 21, Barcelona. Phone: 34-93-253-4229; Fax: 34-93-253-4343.

FACILITIES
Information Resources IESE Library; total holdings of 36,000 volumes, 745 current periodical subscriptions. CD player(s) available for graduate student use. Access provided to online bibliographic retrieval services and online databases.

INTERNATIONAL STUDENTS
Demographics N/R

Applying TOEFL: minimum score of 600 required. Financial aid is available to international students.

PLACEMENT
Services include alumni network, career counseling/planning, career fairs, career library, career placement, electronic job bank, job interviews arranged, resume referral to employers, and resume preparation. In 1996–97, 367 organizations participated in on-campus recruiting; 1,600 on-campus interviews were conducted.

Employment Of 1996–97 graduates, 95% were employed within three months of graduation; the average starting salary was 10,100,000 pesetas. Types of employment entered: accounting, banking, chemical industry, communications, computer-related, consulting, consumer products, education, energy, engineering, finance, financial services, health services, high technology, hospitality management, human resources, information systems/technology, insurance, international trade, management, manufacturing, marketing, media, nonprofit, petrochemical, pharmaceutical, real estate, retail, service industry, telecommunications, transportation.

Business Program(s) URL: http://www.iese.edu

Program Contact: MBA Admissions Department, Avenida Pearson, 21, Barcelona 08034, Spain. Phone: 34-93-253-4229; Fax: 34-93-253-4343; E-mail: mbainfo@iese.edu

See full description on page 1106.

SWEDEN

Göteborg University

School of Economics and Commercial Laws
Goteborg, Sweden

OVERVIEW
Göteborg University coed institution. Founded: 1896. The graduate business unit is in an urban setting and is on a semester calendar.

GRADUATE BUSINESS PROGRAMS
International MBA (MBA)

Business Management (MS)

International Business Program (MS)

ACADEMICS
Faculty Part-time 14.

Teaching Methodologies Case study, lecture, student presentations, team projects.

FACILITIES
Information Resources Goteborg University Library plus 6 additional on-campus libraries.

Program Contact: Department of Business Administration, School of Economics and Commercial Law, S-411 80 Göteborg 41401, Sweden. Phone: 46-31-773 1467; Fax: 46-31-773 1847; E-mail: stefan.schiller@mgmt.gu.se

Stockholm School of Economics

Department of Business Administration
Stockholm, Sweden

OVERVIEW
Stockholm School of Economics is an independent-nonprofit, coed institution. Founded: 1909. The graduate business unit is on a semester calendar.

GRADUATE BUSINESS PROGRAMS
Master of Science (MS)

Master of Science in International Economics and Business (MS)

Executive Master of Business Administration (EMBA)

ACADEMICS
Teaching Methodologies Case study, lecture, research, seminars by members of the business community.

Technology 60 on-campus computer terminals/PCs are available for student use and are linked by a campus-wide network. The network has full access to the Internet.

Special Opportunities International exchange programs in Australia, Austria, Belgium, Brazil, Canada, Denmark, Finland, France, Germany, Italy, Japan, Mexico, Norway, Spain, United Kingdom, United States of America. An internship program is available.

FACILITIES
Information Resources Stockholm School of Economics Library.

Program Contact: International Graduate Program, Box 6501, S-113 83 Stockholm, Sweden. Phone: 46-8-7369520; Fax: 46-8-319927; E-mail: iibdo@hhs.sc

SWITZERLAND

American Graduate School of Business

Master of International Business Administration Program
La Tour-de-Peilz, Switzerland

OVERVIEW
American Graduate School of Business is an independent-nonprofit, coed institution. Enrollment: 40 graduate, professional, and undergraduate students; 40 full-time matriculated graduate/professional students; part-time matriculated graduate/professional students. Founded: 1991. The graduate business unit is in a small-town setting and is on a semester calendar.

HIGHLIGHTS

Enrollment Profile

Full-time: 40	International: 98%
Part-time: 0	Women: 38%
Total: 40	Minorities: N/R
Average Age: 27	Average Class Size: 12
Fall 1997 Average GPA: N/R	Fall 1997 Average GMAT: 520

Costs
Full-time tuition: 30,000 Swiss francs per academic year
Part-time tuition: 2700 Swiss francs per course

American Graduate School of Business (continued)

GRADUATE BUSINESS PROGRAMS

Master of International Business Administration (MIBA) Full-time, part-time; 39 total credits required; 12 months to 2 years to complete program. Concentration in international business.

ADMISSION

Applications For fall 1997 there were 50 applications for admission. Of those applying, 25 were accepted.

Application Requirements GMAT score, application form, application fee, bachelor's degree, essay, minimum GPA: 2.7, 2 letters of recommendation, personal statement, resume, college transcript(s).

Recommended for Application GRE score accepted, work experience, computer experience.

Application Deadline Applications processed on a rolling/continuous basis for both domestic and international students. Application fee: 100 Swiss francs. Deferred entrance is available.

ACADEMICS

Faculty Full-time 4; part-time 8.

Teaching Methodologies Case study, computer-aided instruction, faculty seminars, group discussion, lecture, research, seminars by members of the business community, student presentations, study groups, team projects.

Technology 8 on-campus computer terminals/PCs are available for student use. The network has full access to the Internet. Students are not required to have their own PC.

Special Opportunities Advanced credit may be earned through transfer of credits from another institution. An internship program is available.

FINANCES

Costs for 1997–98 Tuition: Full-time: 30,000 Swiss francs per year. Part-time: 2700 Swiss francs per course. Cost varies by number of credits taken. Average 1997–98 room and board costs were 9000 Swiss francs per academic year (off campus).

Financial Aid In 1997–98, 18% of students received some institutionally administered aid in the form of scholarships, work study. Application Deadline: 6/15.

Financial Aid Contact Mrs. Marcela Ellerbrock, Registrar, Place des Anciéns-Fossés, La Tour-de-Peilz. Phone: 41-21-944-9501; Fax: 41-21-944-9504; E-mail: agsb@vtx.ch

FACILITIES

Information Resources University of Lausanne Library plus 1 additional on-campus library; total holdings of 1,200,000 volumes, 11 current periodical subscriptions. Access provided to online bibliographic retrieval services.

INTERNATIONAL STUDENTS

Demographics 98% of students enrolled are international students [Asia, 45%, Europe, 40%, North America, 15%].

Services and Facilities International student office, international student housing, visa services, ESL courses.

Applying TOEFL: minimum score of 550, proof of adequate funds required. Proof of health/immunizations recommended. Financial aid is available to international students.

International Student Contact Mme. Carmen Corchon-Pernet, Director of Student Affairs/President Steering Committee, Place des Anciéns Fossés, LaTour-de-Peilz. Phone: 41-21-944-9501; Fax: 41-21-944-9504; E-mail: agsb@vtx.ch

PLACEMENT

Services include alumni network, job interviews arranged, and resume preparation.

Employment Of 1996–97 graduates, 85% were employed within three months of graduation; the average starting salary was 5000 Swiss francs. Types of employment entered: accounting, banking, consulting, education, health services, hospitality management, international trade, management, marketing, nonprofit, transportation.

Program Contact: Director of Admissions, AGSB, Place des Anciéns-Fossés, La Tour-de-Peilz 1814, Switzerland. Phone: 41-21-944-9501; Fax: 41-21-944-9504; E-mail: agsb@vtx.ch
See full description on page 700.

Graduate School of Business Administration Zürich

Business Programs

Zürich, Switzerland

OVERVIEW
Graduate School of Business Administration Zürich is an independent-nonprofit, primarily male institution. Enrollment: full-time matriculated graduate/professional students; 1,250 part-time matriculated graduate/professional students. The graduate business unit is in an urban setting and is on a 2-week block courses calendar.

HIGHLIGHTS

Enrollment Profile

Full-time: 0	International: N/R
Part-time: 1,250	Women: 12%
Total: 1,250	Minorities: N/R
Average Age: 36	Average Class Size: 32
Fall 1997 Average GPA: N/R	Fall 1997 Average GMAT: 560

Costs
Full-time tuition: N/R
Part-time tuition: N/R

Degree(s) offered in conjunction with State University of New York at Albany

GRADUATE BUSINESS PROGRAMS

Executive MBA (MBA) Full-time, part-time, distance learning option; 60-120 total credits required; 12 months to 4 years to complete program. Concentrations in accounting, human resources, financial management/planning, management information systems, marketing, operations management, strategic management, organizational behavior/development, logistics, international business, international development management, international economics, international finance, international logistics, international management, international marketing, management systems analysis.

Master of Business Administration/Master of Science (MBA/MS) Full-time, part-time, distance learning option; 60-100 total credits required; 12 months to 2 years to complete program. Concentrations in accounting, business law, economics, logistics, management, marketing, management systems analysis.

ADMISSION

Applications For fall 1997 there were 2,400 applications for admission. Of those applying, 650 were accepted. Of those accepted, 450 enrolled.

Application Requirements Application form, application fee, interview, personal statement, resume, minimum of 5 years of work experience.

Recommended for Application GMAT score accepted: minimum 550, bachelor's degree, minimum GPA: 3.5, letters of recommendation, college transcript(s), computer experience.

Application Deadline Applications processed on a rolling/continuous basis for both domestic and international students. Application fee: 150 Swiss francs. Deferred entrance is available.

ACADEMICS

Faculty Full-time 42; part-time 10.

Teaching Methodologies Case study, computer-aided instruction, field projects, group discussion, lecture, research, seminars by members of the business community, simulations, student presentations, team projects.

Technology 50 on-campus computer terminals/PCs are available for student use and are linked by a campus-wide network. The network has full access to the Internet. Students are required to have their own PC.

Special Opportunities Advanced credit may be earned through credit by examination, credit for experience, credit for business training programs, transfer of credits from another institution. International exchange program in United States.

FINANCES

Financial Aid Loans available. Financial aid is available to part-time students.

Financial Aid Contact Dr. Albert Stähli, Dean , Schützengasse 4, Zürich. Phone: 41-1-211-6068; Fax: 41-1-221-0984.

FACILITIES

Information Resources Central Library of Zurich; total holdings of 10,000,000 volumes, 2,000 current periodical subscriptions. Access provided to online bibliographic retrieval services and online databases.

INTERNATIONAL STUDENTS

Demographics N/R

Services and Facilities International student office, international student center, visa services, counseling/support services.

Applying TOEFL: minimum score of 550 required. Financial aid is not available to international students.

International Student Contact Heinrich Brugger, Admissions Officer, Schützengasse 4, Zürich. Phone: 41-1-211-6068; Fax: 41-1-221-0984.

PLACEMENT
Services include alumni network, career counseling/planning, career library, and resume referral to employers. In 1996–97, 50 organizations participated in on-campus recruiting.

Employment Of 1996–97 graduates, 100% were employed within three months of graduation; the average starting salary was 200,000 Swiss francs. Types of employment entered: banking, chemical industry, communications, computer-related, consulting, consumer products, engineering, finance, health services, hospitality management, human resources, information systems/technology, insurance, management, manufacturing, marketing, media, pharmaceutical, telecommunications.

Business Program(s) URL: http://www.gsba.ch

Program Contact: Heinrich Brugger, Admissions Officer, Schützengasse 4, Zürich 8023, Switzerland. Phone: 41-1-211-6068; Fax: 41-1-221-0984.

International Institute for Management Development (IMD)

Business Programs

Lausanne, Switzerland

OVERVIEW
International Institute for Management Development (IMD) is an independent-nonprofit, coed institution. Founded: 1957. The graduate business unit is in a small-town setting and is on a module calendar.

HIGHLIGHTS

Enrollment Profile
Full-time: 83	International: 94%
Part-time: 0	Women: 16%
Total: 83	Minorities: N/R
Average Age: 31	Average Class Size: 83
Fall 1997 Average GPA: N/R	Fall 1997 Average GMAT: 620

Costs
Full-time tuition: 41,000 Swiss francs per academic year
Part-time tuition: N/R

GRADUATE BUSINESS PROGRAMS
Master of Business Administration (MBA) Full-time; up to 11 months to complete program. Concentration in management.

ADMISSION
Applications For fall 1997 there were 750 applications for admission. Of those applying, 90 were accepted. Of those accepted, 83 enrolled.

Application Requirements Application form, bachelor's degree, essay, interview, 3 letters of recommendation, personal statement, resume, college transcript(s), minimum of 3 years of work experience.

Recommended for Application GMAT score accepted, computer experience.

Application Deadline Applications processed on a rolling/continuous basis for both domestic and international students. Application fee: 250 Swiss francs.

ACADEMICS
Faculty Full-time 43.

Teaching Methodologies Case study, experiential learning, field projects, group discussion, lecture, role playing, seminars by members of the business community, study groups, team projects.

Technology 35 on-campus computer terminals/PCs are available for student use and are linked by a campus-wide network. The network has full access to the Internet. Students are required to have their own PC.

FINANCES
Costs for 1997–98 Tuition: Full-time: 41,000 Swiss francs per program.

Financial Aid Scholarships, loans available. Application Deadline: 8/1.

FACILITIES
Information Resources IMD Library; total holdings of 12,000 volumes, 600 current periodical subscriptions. CD player(s) available for graduate student use. Access provided to online bibliographic retrieval services.

INTERNATIONAL STUDENTS
Demographics 94% of students enrolled are international students [Africa, 3%, Asia, 19%, Australia/New Zealand, 3%, Europe, 59%, North America, 5%, South America, 10%, other, 1%].

Services and Facilities Assistance in finding housing.
Applying Financial aid is available to international students.

PLACEMENT
Services include alumni network, career counseling/planning, career placement, job interviews arranged, job search course, and resume preparation. In 1996–97, 62 organizations participated in on-campus recruiting; 890 on-campus interviews were conducted.

Employment Of 1996–97 graduates, 100% were employed within three months of graduation; the average starting salary was $93,000. Types of employment entered: consulting, consumer products, finance, high technology, management, marketing, pharmaceutical, telecommunications.

Business Program(s) URL: http://www.imd.ch

Program Contact: Ms. Marianne Wheeler, MBA Admissions and Information Officer, Chemin de Bellerive 23, PO Box 915, Lausanne CH-1001, Switzerland. Phone: 41-21-618-0298; Fax: 41-21-618-0615; E-mail: mbainfo@imd.ch
See full description on page 850.

Schiller International University, American College of Switzerland

Business Programs

CH-1854 Leysin, Switzerland

OVERVIEW
Schiller International University, American College of Switzerland is an independent-nonprofit, coed institution. Enrollment: 88 graduate, professional, and undergraduate students. Founded: 1964. The graduate business unit is in an urban setting and is on a semester calendar.

GRADUATE BUSINESS PROGRAMS
MBA in International Business (MBA)

ACADEMICS
Faculty Part-time 7.

Teaching Methodologies Case study, lecture, research, student presentations.

Technology Students are not required to have their own PC.

Special Opportunities Advanced credit may be earned through credit by examination, transfer of credits from another institution. International exchange programs in France, Germany, Spain, Switzerland, United Kingdom, United States.

FACILITIES
Information Resources La Pyrole Library; total holdings of 48,000 volumes, 700 microforms, 100 current periodical subscriptions.

Program Contact: Director of Admissions, 453 Edgewater Drive, Dunedin 34698-7532, Switzerland. Phone: 813-736-5082; Fax: 813-734-0359; E-mail: study@campus.schiller.edu

Université de Lausanne

École des Hautes Etudes Commerciales

Lausanne, Switzerland

OVERVIEW
The Université de Lausanne is a publicly supported, coed institution. Enrollment: 8,700 graduate, professional, and undergraduate students. Founded: 1537. The graduate business unit is in a suburban setting and is on a semester calendar.

HIGHLIGHTS

Enrollment Profile
Full-time: 100	International: 38%
Part-time: 30	Women: 31%
Total: 130	Minorities: N/R
Average Age: 32	Average Class Size: 30
Fall 1997 Average GPA: N/R	Fall 1997 Average GMAT: 570

Costs
Full-time tuition: 10,000 Swiss francs per academic year (resident); 10,000 Swiss francs per academic year (nonresident)
Part-time tuition: 17,000 Swiss francs per 2 years (resident); 17,000 Swiss francs per 2 years (nonresident)

Université de Lausanne (continued)

Degree(s) offered in conjunction with École Polytechnique Federale de Lausanne

GRADUATE BUSINESS PROGRAMS

Master of Business Administration (MBA) Full-time, part-time; 12 months to 2 years to complete program. Concentration in management.

Master of International Management (MIM) Full-time; up to 15 months to complete program. Concentration in international management.

Master of Business Finance (MBF) Full-time, part-time; 12 months to 2 years to complete program. Concentration in finance.

Master in Business Informatics (MBI) Full-time, part-time; 12 months to 2 years to complete program. Concentration in information management.

Master of Science (MS) Full-time, part-time; 12 months to 2 years to complete program. Concentration in economics.

Master in Management of Technology (MOT) Full-time; up to 12 months to complete program. Concentration in technology management.

ADMISSION

Applications For fall 1997 there were 600 applications for admission. Of those applying, 145 were accepted. Of those accepted, 130 enrolled.

Application Requirements GMAT score: minimum 550, application form, application fee, bachelor's degree, interview, personal statement, resume, college transcript(s), minimum of 2 years of work experience.

Recommended for Application Minimum GPA, 2 letters of recommendation, computer experience.

Application Deadline 6/30 for fall, 9/15 for fall (international). Application fee: 200 Swiss francs.

ACADEMICS

Faculty Full-time 40; part-time 20.

Teaching Methodologies Case study, computer-aided instruction, computer simulations, experiential learning, faculty seminars, field projects, group discussion, lecture, seminars by members of the business community, student presentations, study groups, team projects.

Technology 200 on-campus computer terminals/PCs are available for student use and are linked by a campus-wide network. The network has full access to the Internet. Students are required to have their own PC.

Special Opportunities International exchange programs in Belgium, Canada, Hong Kong, Singapore, United Kingdom, United States. An internship program is available.

FINANCES

Costs for 1997–98 Tuition: Full-time: 10,000 Swiss francs per year (resident); 10,000 Swiss francs per year (nonresident). Part-time: 17,000 Swiss francs per 2 years (resident); 17,000 Swiss francs per 2 years (nonresident). Cost varies by academic program. Fees: Full-time: 2000 Swiss francs per academic year (resident); 2000 Swiss francs per academic year (nonresident). Part-time: 3000 Swiss francs per 2 years (resident); 3000 Swiss francs per 2 years (nonresident). Fees vary by academic program. Average 1997–98 room and board costs were 18,000 Swiss francs per academic year (off campus). Room and board costs vary by occupancy (e.g., single, double, triple), type of accommodation, type of meal plan.

FACILITIES

Information Resources Bibliotheque Cantonale et Universitaire; total holdings of 1,660,000 volumes, 71,200 microforms, 7,500 current periodical subscriptions. CD player(s) available for graduate student use. Access provided to online bibliographic retrieval services and online databases.

INTERNATIONAL STUDENTS

Demographics 38% of students enrolled are international students.

Services and Facilities Counseling/support services.

Applying TOEFL recommended. Financial aid is not available to international students.

International Student Contact Ms. Nicole Farcinade, Program Administrator, BFSH1, École des HEC, MBA Program, Lausanne. Phone: 41-21-692-3390; Fax: 41-21-692-3395; E-mail: nicole.farcinade@hec.unil.ch

PLACEMENT

Services include alumni network, career library, electronic job bank, resume referral to employers, and resume preparation.

Employment Of 1996–97 graduates, 90% were employed within three months of graduation. Types of employment entered: accounting, banking, consulting, consumer products, energy, finance, financial services, international trade, management, marketing.

Business Program(s) URL: http://www.hec.unil.ch/INSTITUT/IUMI/INDEX.HTM

Program Contact: Ms. Nicole Farcinade, Program Administrator, BFSH 1, École des HEC, MBA Program, Lausanne CH-1015, Switzerland. Phone: 41-21-692-3390; Fax: 41-21-692-3395; E-mail: nicole.farcinade@hec.unil.ch

University of St. Gallen

Business School

St. Gallen, Switzerland

OVERVIEW

The University of St. Gallen coed institution. Enrollment: 4,045 graduate, professional, and undergraduate students. Founded: 1898. The graduate business unit is in a small-town setting and is on a module calendar.

HIGHLIGHTS

Enrollment Profile

Full-time: 2,500	International: N/R
Part-time: 700	Women: N/R
Total: 3,200	Minorities: N/R
Average Age: 37	Average Class Size: 45
Fall 1997 Average GPA: N/R	Fall 1997 Average GMAT: N/R

Costs
Full-time tuition: N/R
Part-time tuition: N/R

GRADUATE BUSINESS PROGRAMS

Executive Master of Business Administration (EMBA) Part-time; up to 2 years to complete program. Concentrations in management, finance, international banking, international trade, banking.

ADMISSION

Application Requirements Application form, bachelor's degree, 3 letters of recommendation, personal statement, minimum of 3 years of work experience.

Application Deadline Applications processed on a rolling/continuous basis for both domestic and international students.

ACADEMICS

Faculty Part-time 120.

Teaching Methodologies Case study, computer-aided instruction, computer analysis, field projects, lecture, seminars by members of the business community, simulations, student presentations, team projects.

Technology 150 on-campus computer terminals/PCs are available for student use and are linked by a campus-wide network. The network has full access to the Internet. Students are not required to have their own PC.

FINANCES

Costs for 1997–98 Cost varies by academic program.

Financial Aid Contact Mr. Gion Pallecchi, Program Administrator, Holzweid, St. Gallen. Phone: 41-71-224-2701; Fax: 41-71-224-2700; E-mail: gion-andre.pallecci@nud.unisg.ch

FACILITIES

Information Resources Main library; total holdings of 280,000 volumes, 1,200 current periodical subscriptions. CD player(s) available for graduate student use. Access provided to online bibliographic retrieval services.

INTERNATIONAL STUDENTS

Demographics N/R

International Student Contact Claudia Rossei, Student Exchange Coordinator, Dufourstr. 50, CH-9000, St. Gallen. Phone: 41-71-224-2339.

PLACEMENT

Services include alumni network, career counseling/planning, career placement, and electronic job bank.

Employment Types of employment entered: banking, consulting, engineering, finance, international trade.

Business Program(s) URL: http://www.unisg.ch/~ndu

Program Contact: Mr. Gion Pallecchi, Program Administrator, Holzweid, St. Gallen CH-9010, Switzerland. Phone: 41-71-224-2701; Fax: 41-71-224-2700; E-mail: gion-andre.pallecci@nud.unisg.ch

THAILAND

Bangkok University

Graduate School

Bangkok, Thailand

OVERVIEW
Bangkok University coed institution. Enrollment: 21,000 graduate, professional, and undergraduate students; 300 full-time matriculated graduate/professional students; part-time matriculated graduate/professional students. The graduate business unit is in an urban setting and is on a semester calendar.

HIGHLIGHTS

Enrollment Profile
Full-time: 300
Part-time: 0
Total: 300
Average Age: N/R
Fall 1997 Average GPA: 3.3

International: 8%
Women: N/R
Minorities: N/R
Average Class Size: 30
Fall 1997 Average GMAT: 500

Costs
Full-time tuition: N/R
Part-time tuition: N/R

GRADUATE BUSINESS PROGRAMS
Master of Business Administration (MBA) Full-time; 48 total credits required; 2 to 8 years to complete program. Concentrations in entrepreneurship, finance, human resources, international business, management, management information systems, marketing, operations management, organizational behavior/development, quantitative analysis.

ADMISSION
Applications For fall 1997 there were 1,100 applications for admission. Of those applying, 150 were accepted. Of those accepted, 135 enrolled.
Application Requirements Application form, application fee, bachelor's degree, minimum GPA: 2.5, interview, 3 letters of recommendation, college transcript(s).
Recommended for Application GMAT score accepted: minimum 450.
Application Deadline 3/1 for fall, 4/7 for fall (international). Application fee: 300 Thai baht.

ACADEMICS
Faculty Full-time 15; part-time 25.
Teaching Methodologies Computer-aided instruction, experiential learning, faculty seminars, group discussion, lecture, research, seminars by members of the business community, student presentations, study groups, team projects.
Technology Computer terminals/PCs are available for student use and are linked by a campus-wide network. The network has full access to the Internet. Students are required to have their own PC.
Special Opportunities Advanced credit may be earned through transfer of credits from another institution. International exchange programs in Australia, Japan, United States.

FINANCES
Costs for 1997–98 Average 1997–98 room only costs were 3000 Thai baht per academic year (off campus). Room and board costs vary by occupancy (e.g., single, double, triple), type of accommodation.
Financial Aid Contact Admissions Office, 40/4 Rama IV Road, Bangkok. Phone: 66-2-671-7508-9; Fax: 66-2-240-1516; E-mail: gloria@lily.bu.ac.th

FACILITIES
Information Resources Central Library; total holdings of 200,000 volumes, 927 current periodical subscriptions.

INTERNATIONAL STUDENTS
Demographics 8% of students enrolled are international students.
Services and Facilities International student office, international student center, visa services, counseling/support services.
Applying TOEFL: minimum score of 550, proof of adequate funds, proof of health/immunizations required. Financial aid is available to international students.
International Student Contact Dr. Siriwan Rattanakarn, Director, International Program Center, 40/4 Rama IV Road, Bangkok. Phone: 66-2-671-7508-9; Fax: 66-2-240-1516.

Program Contact: Dr. Gloria Vidheecharoen, Director, Graduate School, 40/4 Rama IV Road, Bangkok 10110, Thailand. Phone: 66-2-671-7507; Fax: 66-2-240-1516; E-mail: gloria@lily.bu.ac.th

Chulalongkorn University

Sasin Graduate Institute of Business Administration

Bangkok, Thailand

OVERVIEW
Chulalongkorn University is an independent-nonprofit, coed institution. Enrollment: 16,121 graduate, professional, and undergraduate students. Founded: 1902. The graduate business unit is in an urban setting and is on a quarter calendar.

HIGHLIGHTS

Enrollment Profile
Full-time: 250
Part-time: 150
Total: 400
Average Age: 25
Fall 1997 Average GPA: 3.07

International: 9%
Women: 49%
Minorities: N/R
Average Class Size: 100
Fall 1997 Average GMAT: 510

Costs
Full-time tuition: $13,875 per academic year
Part-time tuition: N/R

Degree(s) offered in conjunction with Northwestern University, University of Pennsylvania

GRADUATE BUSINESS PROGRAMS
Master of Business Administration (MBA) Full-time; 75 total credits required; 2 to 4 years to complete program. Concentrations in finance, management, marketing, organizational behavior/development.
Executive Master of Management (MMgt) Part-time; 72 total credits required; 2 to 4 years to complete program. Concentration in management.

ADMISSION
Applications For fall 1997 there were 353 applications for admission. Of those applying, 170 were accepted. Of those accepted, 150 enrolled.
Application Requirements GMAT score, application form, application fee, bachelor's degree, essay, minimum GPA, interview, 2 letters of recommendation, personal statement, college transcript(s), work experience.
Recommended for Application Computer experience.
Application Deadline 1/15 for spring, 1/15 for spring (international). Application fee: $32. Deferred entrance is available.

ACADEMICS
Faculty Full-time 7; part-time 27.
Teaching Methodologies Case study, computer-aided instruction, field projects, group discussion, lecture, seminars by members of the business community, simulations, student presentations, study groups, team projects.
Technology 120 on-campus computer terminals/PCs are available for student use and are linked by a campus-wide network. The network has full access to the Internet. Students are not required to have their own PC.
Special Opportunities Advanced credit may be earned through credit by examination, transfer of credits from another institution. International exchange programs in Canada, France, Germany, Japan, United States. An internship program is available.

FINANCES
Costs for 1997–98 Tuition: Full-time: $13,875 per program. Cost varies by academic program, number of credits taken. Fees: Full-time: $120 per academic year. Average 1997–98 room only costs were $4500 per academic year (on campus) and $6500 per academic year (off campus). Room and board costs vary by occupancy (e.g., single, double, triple).
Financial Aid Contact Mrs. Lalida Ruangtrakool, Chief of Admission and Financial Aid Section, Sasa Patasala Building, Soi Chulalongkorn 12, Phyathai Road, Bangkok. Phone: 66-2-216-8833 Ext. 3856; Fax: 66-2-216-1312; E-mail: rlalida@chula.ac.th

FACILITIES
Information Resources Center for Academic Resources plus 24 additional on-campus libraries; total holdings of 8,000 volumes, 120 microforms. CD player(s) available for graduate student use. Access provided to online bibliographic retrieval services.

INTERNATIONAL STUDENTS
Demographics 9% of students enrolled are international students [Asia, 54%, Europe, 20%, North America, 26%].
Services and Facilities International student office, international student housing, visa services.
Applying TOEFL, proof of health/immunizations required.
International Student Contact Mrs. Oranong Tiradechavataya, Chief of Student Affairs Section, Sasin Graduate Institute of Business Administration, Chulalongkorn

Chulalongkorn University (continued)

University, Sasa Patasala Building, Soi Chula 12 (2) Phyathai, Bangkok. Phone: 66-2-216-8833 Ext. 3862; Fax: 66-2-216-1312; E-mail: ssasotr@chula. ac.th

PLACEMENT
Services include alumni network, career counseling/planning, career placement, job interviews arranged, resume referral to employers, and resume preparation. In 1996–97, 28 organizations participated in on-campus recruiting; 3 on-campus interviews were conducted.

Employment Of 1996–97 graduates, 99% were employed within three months of graduation. Types of employment entered: accounting, banking, chemical industry, communications, computer-related, consulting, consumer products, education, energy, engineering, finance, financial services, government, health services, high technology, hospitality management, human resources, information systems/technology, management, manufacturing, marketing, media, nonprofit, petrochemical, pharmaceutical, real estate, retail, service industry, telecommunications.

Business Program(s) URL: http://www.chula.ac.th/international/sasin

Program Contact: Mrs. Lalida Ruangtrakool, Chief of Admission and Financial Aid Section, Sasa Patasala Building, Soi Chulalongkorn 12, Phyathai Road, Bangkok 10330, Thailand. Phone: 66-2-216-8833 Ext. 3856; Fax: 66-2-216-1312; E-mail: rlalida@chula.ac.th

See full description on page 746.

TURKEY

Bilkent University

School of Business Administration

Ankara, Turkey

OVERVIEW
Bilkent University is an independent-nonprofit, coed institution. Enrollment: 10,000 graduate, professional, and undergraduate students. Founded: 1984. The graduate business unit is in a rural setting and is on a semester calendar.

HIGHLIGHTS

Enrollment Profile
Full-time: 94
Part-time: 0
Total: 94
Average Age: 26
Fall 1997 Average GPA: N/R

International: N/R
Women: 37%
Minorities: N/R
Average Class Size: 35
Fall 1997 Average GMAT: 550

Costs
Full-time tuition: $4350 per academic year
Part-time tuition: N/R

GRADUATE BUSINESS PROGRAMS
Master of Business Administration (MBA) Full-time; 60 total credits required; 20 months to 3 years to complete program. Concentrations in finance, management, marketing, organizational behavior/development, quantitative analysis, international business.

ADMISSION
Applications For fall 1997 there were 120 applications for admission.
Application Requirements GMAT score: minimum 500, application form, bachelor's degree, interview, 2 letters of recommendation, personal statement, college transcript(s).
Recommended for Application GRE score accepted.
Application Deadline 8/21 for fall, 6/16 for fall (international).

ACADEMICS
Faculty Full-time 29; part-time 14.
Teaching Methodologies Case study, faculty seminars, lecture, seminars by members of the business community, student presentations, team projects.
Technology 900 on-campus computer terminals/PCs are available for student use and are linked by a campus-wide network. The network has full access to the Internet. Students are not required to have their own PC.
Special Opportunities International exchange programs in Denmark, Israel, United States.

FINANCES
Costs for 1997–98 Tuition: Full-time: $4350 per year. Room and board costs vary by campus location, occupancy (e.g., single, double, triple), type of accommodation.
Financial Aid Scholarships available. Application Deadline: 6/16.
Financial Aid Contact Mr. Erdal Erel, Associate Dean, Ankara. Phone: 90-312-266-4164; Fax: 90-312-266-4950; E-mail: fba@bilkent.edu.tr

FACILITIES
Information Resources Bilkent University Library; total holdings of 250,000 volumes. CD player(s) available for graduate student use. Access provided to online bibliographic retrieval services and online databases.

INTERNATIONAL STUDENTS
Demographics N/R
Services and Facilities International student office, international student center, counseling/support services, international student orientation, Turkish language lessons.
Applying TOEFL: minimum score of 550 required. Financial aid is available to international students.
International Student Contact Ms. Sule Berilgen, International Center Coordinator, Bilkent University, International Center, Ankara. Phone: 90-312-266-4000 Ext. 1636; Fax: 90-312-266-4958.

PLACEMENT
Services include alumni network, career counseling/planning, career fairs, career library, career placement, job interviews arranged, resume referral to employers, and resume preparation.
Employment Types of employment entered: accounting, banking, consulting, finance, government, service industry.
Business Program(s) URL: http://www.art.bilkent.edu.tr/graduate/mba/index.html

Program Contact: Mr. Erdal Erel, Associate Dean, Bilkent University, Ankara 06533, Turkey. Phone: 90-312-266-4164; Fax: 90-312-266-4958; E-mail: fba@bilkent.edu.tr

UKRAINE

Kyiv State University of Economics

MBA Program

Kyiv, Ukraine

OVERVIEW
Kyiv State University of Economics is a private, coed institution. Founded: 1912.

HIGHLIGHTS

Enrollment Profile
Full-time: N/R
Part-time: N/R
Total: N/R
Average Age: 25
Fall 1997 Average GPA: N/R

International: N/R
Women: N/R
Minorities: N/R
Average Class Size: N/R
Fall 1997 Average GMAT: N/R

Costs
Full-time tuition: N/R
Part-time tuition: N/R

GRADUATE BUSINESS PROGRAMS
Master of Business Administration (MBA) Full-time, distance learning option; 12 months to 2 years to complete program. Concentrations in banking, insurance, marketing, project management, international management.

ADMISSION
Application Requirements Bachelor's degree, interview, 2 letters of recommendation.
Recommended for Application Work experience.

INTERNATIONAL STUDENTS
Demographics N/R

Program Contact: Mr. Anatoly M. Poruchnik, MBA Administrator, Pere, Kyiv 252057, Ukraine. Phone: 380-44-446-5055; Fax: 380-44-226-2573; E-mail: ssv@ksue.carrier.kiev.ua

UNITED KINGDOM

The American InterContinental University

School of Business

London, England, United Kingdom

OVERVIEW

The American InterContinental University is a proprietary, coed institution. Enrollment: 1,000 graduate, professional, and undergraduate students; 40 full-time matriculated graduate/professional students; 10 part-time matriculated graduate/professional students. Founded: 1970. The graduate business unit is in an urban setting and is on a quarter calendar.

HIGHLIGHTS

Enrollment Profile

Full-time: 40	International: N/R
Part-time: 10	Women: 20%
Total: 50	Minorities: N/R
Average Age: 27	Average Class Size: 6
Fall 1997 Average GPA: 3.1	Fall 1997 Average GMAT: N/R

Costs
Full-time tuition: $5407 per academic year
Part-time tuition: $1803 per 5 quarter hours

GRADUATE BUSINESS PROGRAMS

Master of Business Administration in International Business (MBA) Full-time, part-time; 60 total credits required; 10 months to 2 years to complete program. Concentration in international business.

Master of Information Technology (MIT) Full-time, part-time, distance learning option; 60 total credits required; CPAB examination required; 12 months to 2 years to complete program. Concentration in system management.

ADMISSION

Applications For fall 1997 there were 50 applications for admission. Of those applying, 30 were accepted. Of those accepted, 27 enrolled.

Application Requirements GMAT score, application form, application fee, bachelor's degree, minimum GPA: 2.5, interview, 2 letters of recommendation, personal statement, resume, college transcript(s).

Recommended for Application GRE score accepted, MAT score accepted, essay, work experience, computer experience.

Application Deadline Applications processed on a rolling/continuous basis for both domestic and international students. Application fee: $35. Deferred entrance is available.

ACADEMICS

Faculty Full-time 17.

Teaching Methodologies Case study, computer-aided instruction, experiential learning, faculty seminars, field projects, group discussion, lecture, research, seminars by members of the business community, student presentations, study groups, team projects.

Technology 50 on-campus computer terminals/PCs are available for student use and are linked by a campus-wide network. The network has full access to the Internet. Students are not required to have their own PC.

Special Opportunities Advanced credit may be earned through transfer of credits from another institution. International exchange program in United Arab Emirates. An internship program is available.

FINANCES

Costs for 1997–98 Tuition: Full-time: $5407 per year. Part-time: $1803 per 5 quarter hours. Cost varies by campus location, number of credits taken. Fees vary by campus location, number of credits taken. Average 1997–98 room only costs were $2240 per academic year. Room and board costs vary by campus location, occupancy (e.g., single, double, triple).

Financial Aid In 1997–98, 14% of students received some institutionally administered aid in the form of scholarships, loans. Financial aid is available to part-time students.

Financial Aid Contact Ms. Connie King, Director of Financial Aid, 330 Peachtree Road NE, Atlanta, England 30326-1016, United Kingdom. Phone: 800-255-6839 Ext. 4120; Fax: 404-812-4179; E-mail: cking@aiuniv.edu

FACILITIES

Information Resources Niklaus Weibel Library; total holdings of 25,000 volumes, 305 current periodical subscriptions. CD player(s) available for graduate student use. Access provided to online bibliographic retrieval services.

INTERNATIONAL STUDENTS

Demographics N/R

Services and Facilities International student housing, ESL courses, counseling/support services.

Applying TOEFL: minimum score of 550, proof of adequate funds, proof of health/immunizations required. Financial aid is not available to international students.

International Student Contact Dr. Drew Hageman, Dean of Business, 110 Marylebone High Street, London, England W1M 3DB, United Kingdom. Phone: 44-171-486-1772; Fax: 44-171-935-8144; E-mail: ahageman@aiuniv.edu

PLACEMENT

Services include alumni network, career counseling/planning, job interviews arranged, resume referral to employers, and resume preparation.

Employment Types of employment entered: accounting, banking, communications, computer-related, finance, financial services, government, human resources, international trade, management, marketing, retail.

Business Program(s) URL: http://www.aiuniv.edu

Program Contact: Mr. Michael Swift, International Programs/Study Abroad, 3340 Peachtree Road NE, Suite 2000, Atlanta, England 30326, United Kingdom. Phone: 800-255-6839; Fax: 404-364-6611; E-mail: mswift@aiuniv.edu

Ashridge Management College

Ashridge Executive MBA Program

Berkhamsted, Hertfordshire, United Kingdom

OVERVIEW

Ashridge Management College is an independent-nonprofit, coed institution. Enrollment: 180 graduate, professional, and undergraduate students; 25 full-time matriculated graduate/professional students; 72 part-time matriculated graduate/professional students. Founded: 1959. The graduate business unit is in a rural setting and is on a modular calendar.

HIGHLIGHTS

Enrollment Profile

Full-time: 25	International: 46%
Part-time: 72	Women: 24%
Total: 97	Minorities: N/R
Average Age: 34	Average Class Size: 25
Fall 1997 Average GPA: N/R	Fall 1997 Average GMAT: 590

Costs
Full-time tuition: N/R
Part-time tuition: £17,000 per program

Degree(s) offered in conjunction with City University

GRADUATE BUSINESS PROGRAMS

Master of Business Administration (MBA) Full-time, part-time; 12 months to 2 years to complete program. Concentrations in accounting, economics, finance, human resources, international business, management, management information systems, marketing, operations management, organizational behavior/development, quantitative analysis.

Ashridge Executive MBA (MBA) Full-time, part-time; 12 months to 2 years to complete program. Concentrations in finance, human resources, leadership, marketing, organizational behavior/development, operations management, business ethics, international and area business studies, international finance, logistics, management consulting, project management, strategic management, technology management, international marketing.

ADMISSION

Applications For fall 1997 there were 83 applications for admission. Of those applying, 73 were accepted. Of those accepted, 72 enrolled.

Application Requirements GMAT score, application form, interview, 2 letters of recommendation, resume, college transcript(s), minimum of 5 years of work experience.

Recommended for Application Bachelor's degree.

Application Deadline Applications processed on a rolling/continuous basis for both domestic and international students.

ACADEMICS

Faculty Full-time 15; part-time 26.

Teaching Methodologies Case study, computer-aided instruction, computer simulations, faculty seminars, group discussion, lecture, role playing, seminars by members of the business community, simulations, student presentations, study groups.

Technology 85 on-campus computer terminals/PCs are available for student use and are linked by a campus-wide network. The network has full access to the Internet. Students are required to have their own PC.

Ashridge Management College (continued)

Special Opportunities International exchange programs in Austria, Hungary. An internship program is available.

FINANCES
Costs for 1997–98 Tuition: £17,000 per program. Average 1997–98 room and board costs were £6000 per academic year.

FACILITIES
Information Resources Learning Resource Center; total holdings of 8,000 volumes, 600 current periodical subscriptions. CD player(s) available for graduate student use.

INTERNATIONAL STUDENTS
Demographics 46% of students enrolled are international students [Africa, 2%, Asia, 5%, Europe, 91%, other, 2%].

Services and Facilities Language tutoring.

Applying Proof of adequate funds, proof of health/immunizations required. Financial aid is not available to international students.

International Student Contact Mrs. Doris Boyle, Admissions Officer, Berkhamsted, Hertfordshire HP4 1NS, United Kingdom. Phone: 44-1442-841-143; Fax: 44-1442-841-144; E-mail: doris.boyle@ashridge.org.uk

PLACEMENT
Services include alumni network, career counseling/planning, electronic job bank, resume referral to employers, and resume preparation.

Employment Of 1996–97 graduates, 100% were employed within three months of graduation. Types of employment entered: consulting, financial services, management, manufacturing, marketing, retail.

Program Contact: Mrs. Doris Boyle, Admissions Officer, Berkhamsted, Hertfordshire HP4 1NS, United Kingdom. Phone: 44-1442-841-143; Fax: 44-1442-841-144; E-mail: doris.boyle@ashridge.org.uk

Aston University

Aston Business School

Birmingham, England, United Kingdom

OVERVIEW
Aston University is a federally supported, coed institution. Founded: 1966. The graduate business unit is in an urban setting and is on a trimester calendar.

HIGHLIGHTS

Enrollment Profile

Full-time: N/R	International: N/R
Part-time: N/R	Women: N/R
Total: N/R	Minorities: N/R
Average Age: 27	Average Class Size: 30
Fall 1997 Average GPA: N/R	Fall 1997 Average GMAT: N/R

Costs
Full-time tuition: N/R
Part-time tuition: N/R

GRADUATE BUSINESS PROGRAMS
Master of Business Administration (MBA) Full-time, part-time, distance learning option; 12 months to 5 years to complete program. Concentrations in quality management, industrial administration/management, accounting, economics, finance, health care, human resources, international business, management, marketing, operations management, organizational behavior/development, public policy and administration, quantitative analysis, strategic management, european business studies.

Master of Business Administration in Public Services Management (MBA) Full-time, part-time, distance learning option; 12 months to 5 years to complete program. Concentrations in health care, public management, public policy and administration, nonprofit management, strategic management.

Master of Business Administration in Education Management (MBA) Full-time, part-time, distance learning option; 12 months to 5 years to complete program. Concentrations in public policy and administration, public management, business education.

Master of Science in Marketing Management (MS) Full-time, distance learning option; minimum of 12 months to complete program. Concentrations in management, marketing, marketing research, strategic management.

Master of Science in Business Studies (MS) Full-time, distance learning option; minimum of 12 months to complete program. Concentrations in accounting, human resources, finance, management, operations management, strategic management.

Master of Science in Personnel Management (MS) Full-time, part-time, distance learning option; minimum of 12 months to complete program. Concentrations in human resources, industrial/labor relations, management, strategic management.

Master of Science in Financial Management and Control (MS) Full-time, part-time, distance learning option; minimum of 12 months to complete program. Concentrations in finance, accounting, financial management/planning, management, strategic management.

Master of Science in International Business (MS) Full-time, part-time, distance learning option; minimum of 12 months to complete program. Concentrations in international business, international management, international marketing, management, strategic management.

Master of Science in Public Services Management (MS) Full-time, part-time, distance learning option; 12 months to 5 years to complete program. Concentrations in health care, public management, public policy and administration, nonprofit management.

ADMISSION
Application Requirements GMAT score: minimum 550, application form, bachelor's degree, 2 letters of recommendation, minimum of 3 years of work experience.

Application Deadline Applications processed on a rolling/continuous basis for both domestic and international students.

ACADEMICS
Faculty Full-time 40; part-time 10.

Teaching Methodologies Case study, computer simulations, experiential learning, group discussion, lecture, research, seminars by members of the business community, simulations, student presentations, study groups, team projects.

Technology 300 on-campus computer terminals/PCs are available for student use and are linked by a campus-wide network. The network has full access to the Internet. Students are not required to have their own PC.

Special Opportunities International exchange programs in France, Hungary, Netherlands, Spain. An internship program is available.

FINANCES
Costs for 1997–98 Cost varies by academic program.

INTERNATIONAL STUDENTS
Demographics N/R

Services and Facilities International student office, international student housing, counseling/support services, English language courses.

Applying IELT: minimum score of 6.5, TOEFL: minimum score of 600, proof of adequate funds required. Financial aid is not available to international students.

International Student Contact Ms. Jenny Moore, Course Administrator, Postgraduate Office, Aston Business School, Birmingham, England B4 7ET, United Kingdom. Phone: 44-121-359-3011 Ext. 4936; Fax: 44-121-333-4731; E-mail: j.m.moore@aston.ac.uk

PLACEMENT
Services include alumni network, career counseling/planning, career fairs, career library, job search course, resume referral to employers, and resume preparation.

Employment Of 1996–97 graduates, 98% were employed within three months of graduation. Types of employment entered: accounting, banking, communications, computer-related, consulting, consumer products, education, energy, engineering, finance, financial services, health services, high technology, human resources, information systems/technology, international trade, management, manufacturing, marketing, media, nonprofit, petrochemical, pharmaceutical, service industry, telecommunications, transportation, utilities.

Business Program(s) URL: http://www.abs.aston.ac.uk/

Program Contact: Ms. Jenny Moore, Course Administrator, Postgraduate Office, Aston Business School, Birmingham, England B4 7ET, United Kingdom. Phone: 44-121-359-3011 Ext. 4936; Fax: 44-121-333-4731; E-mail: j.m.moore@aston.ac.uk

City University

Business School

London, England, United Kingdom

OVERVIEW
City University is a federally supported, coed institution. Enrollment: 8,255 graduate, professional, and undergraduate students; 1,692 full-time matriculated graduate/professional students; 1,799 part-time matriculated graduate/professional students. Founded: 1894. The graduate business unit is in an urban setting and is on a trimester calendar.

HIGHLIGHTS

Enrollment Profile

Full-time: N/R

Part-time: N/R

Total: 1,928

Average Age: N/R

Fall 1997 Average GPA: N/R

International: 43%

Women: 33%

Minorities: N/R

Average Class Size: 30

Fall 1997 Average GMAT: 570

Costs

Full-time tuition: £13,000 per academic year (resident); £13,000 per academic year (nonresident)

Part-time tuition: £18,000 per program (resident); £18,000 per program (nonresident)

GRADUATE BUSINESS PROGRAMS

Master of Science in Finance (MS) Full-time; 12 months to complete program. Concentration in finance.

Master of Science in Insurance and Risk Management (MS) Full-time, part-time; 12 months to 2 years to complete program. Concentrations in insurance, risk management.

Master of Science in Mathematical Trading and Finance (MS) Full-time, part-time; 12 months to 2 years to complete program. Concentrations in finance, financial economics, international finance, quantitative analysis.

Master Science in Investment Management (MS) Full-time; 12 months to complete program. Concentrations in finance, risk management, financial management/planning.

Master of Science in Corporate Property Management (MS) Full-time, part-time; 12 months to 2 years to complete program. Concentrations in finance, real estate, construction management.

Master of Science in Property Investment (MS) Full-time, part-time; 12 months to 2 years to complete program. Concentrations in finance, real estate, construction management.

Master of Arts in Property Valuation and Law (MA) Full-time, part-time; 12 months to 2 years to complete program. Concentrations in real estate, construction management.

Master of Science in Internal Auditing and Management (MS) Full-time, part-time; 12 months to 2 years to complete program. Concentrations in actuarial science, finance, management.

Day MBA (MBA) Full-time; 3 years work experience required; 12 months to complete program. Concentrations in entrepreneurship, finance, human resources, international business, marketing, technology management, telecommunications management.

Evening MBA (MBA) Part-time; 2 years decision making experience required; 2 to 5.7 years to complete program. Concentration in management.

Management (Consortium) MBA (MBA) Part-time; 5 years work experience required; 2 to 5 years to complete program. Concentration in management.

Shipping and Finance (MS) Full-time, part-time; 2 years work experience required; 12 months to 2 years to complete program. Concentrations in finance, international trade, economics.

Transport Trade and Finance (MS) Full-time, part-time; 2 years work experience required; 12 months to 2 years to complete program. Concentrations in finance, international trade, logistics, economics, international logistics.

ADMISSION

Applications For fall 1997 there were 8,000 applications for admission. Of those applying, 1,928 were accepted. Of those accepted, 1,928 enrolled.

Application Requirements Application form, application fee, bachelor's degree, minimum GPA: 3.5, 2 letters of recommendation, personal statement.

Recommended for Application GMAT score accepted: minimum 550, resume, computer experience.

Application Deadline 5/31 for fall, 5/31 for fall (international). Application fee: £35. Deferred entrance is available.

ACADEMICS

Faculty Full-time 82; part-time 120.

Teaching Methodologies Case study, computer-aided instruction, computer analysis, computer simulations, faculty seminars, field projects, group discussion, lecture, research, role playing, seminars by members of the business community, student presentations, study groups, team projects.

Technology 30 on-campus computer terminals/PCs are available for student use and are linked by a campus-wide network. The network has full access to the Internet. Students are not required to have their own PC.

Special Opportunities International exchange programs in Austria, Belgium, France, Germany, Italy, Norway, Spain. An internship program is available.

FINANCES

Costs for 1997–98 Tuition: Full-time: £13,000 per year (resident); £13,000 per year (nonresident). Part-time: £18,000 per program (resident); £18,000 per program (nonresident). Cost varies by academic program, number of credits

taken, reciprocity agreements. Average 1997–98 room and board costs were £3200 per academic year (on campus) and £3500 per academic year (off campus). Room and board costs vary by campus location, type of meal plan.

Financial Aid In 1997–98, 1% of students received some institutionally administered aid in the form of research assistantships, scholarships. Application Deadline: 5/31.

Financial Aid Contact Ms. Liz Taylor, Post Graduate Admissions Officer, Frobisher Crescent, Barbican Center, London, England EC2Y 8HB, United Kingdom. Phone: 44-171-477-8606; Fax: 44-171-477-8593; E-mail: cubs-postgrad@city.ac.uk

FACILITIES

Information Resources City University Library plus 5 additional on-campus libraries; total holdings of 330,000 volumes, 400 current periodical subscriptions. CD player(s) available for graduate student use. Access provided to online bibliographic retrieval services and online databases.

INTERNATIONAL STUDENTS

Demographics 43% of students enrolled are international students.

Services and Facilities International student office, visa services, ESL courses, counseling/support services.

Applying IELT: minimum score of 7, TOEFL: minimum score of 650, proof of adequate funds required. Financial aid is available to international students.

International Student Contact Ms. Liz Taylor, Post Graduate Admissions Officer, Frobisher Crescent, Barbican Center, London, England EC2Y 8HB, United Kingdom. Phone: 44-171-477-8606; Fax: 44-171-477-8593; E-mail: cubs-postgrad@city.ac.uk

PLACEMENT

Services include alumni network, career counseling/planning, career fairs, career library, career placement, electronic job bank, job interviews arranged, job search course, resume referral to employers, and resume preparation. In 1996–97, 60 organizations participated in on-campus recruiting.

Employment Of 1996–97 graduates, 65% were employed within three months of graduation; the average starting salary was £37,000. Types of employment entered: accounting, banking, communications, computer-related, consulting, education, energy, engineering, finance, financial services, high technology, human resources, information systems/technology, insurance, international trade, marketing, media, nonprofit, pharmaceutical, real estate, retail, service industry, telecommunications, transportation.

Business Program(s) URL: http://www.city.ac.uk/cubs

Program Contact: Ms. Liz Taylor, Post Graduate Admissions Officer, Frobisher Crescent, Barbican Center, London, England EC2Y 8HB, United Kingdom. Phone: 44-171-477-8606; Fax: 44-171-477-8593; E-mail: cubs-postgrad@city.ac.uk

Cranfield University

Cranfield School of Management

Cranfield, Bedford, United Kingdom

OVERVIEW

Cranfield University is a federally supported, primarily male institution. Enrollment: 1,467 graduate, professional, and undergraduate students; 1,026 full-time matriculated graduate/professional students; 441 part-time matriculated graduate/professional students. Founded: 1946. The graduate business unit is in a rural setting and is on a quarter calendar.

HIGHLIGHTS

Enrollment Profile

Full-time: 166

Part-time: 134

Total: 300

Average Age: 32

Fall 1997 Average GPA: N/R

International: 27%

Women: 22%

Minorities: N/R

Average Class Size: 45

Fall 1997 Average GMAT: 615

Costs

Full-time tuition: £15,000 per academic year (resident); £15,000 per academic year (nonresident)

Part-time tuition: £10,000 per year (resident); £10,000 per year (nonresident)

Cranfield University (continued)

GRADUATE BUSINESS PROGRAMS

Master of Business Administration (MBA) Full-time; 43 total credits required; 12 months to complete program. Concentrations in management, human resources, public management.

Executive MBA (MBA) Part-time; 44 total credits required; 2 years to complete program. Concentrations in management, public management.

Master of Science in Project Management (MSc) Full-time; 43 total credits required; 12 months to complete program. Concentrations in management, project management.

Executive Master of Science in Project Management (MSc) Part-time; 44 total credits required; 2 years to complete program. Concentrations in management, project management.

ADMISSION

Applications For fall 1997 there were 501 applications for admission. Of those applying, 256 were accepted. Of those accepted, 166 enrolled.

Application Requirements GMAT score: minimum 550, application form, interview, 2 letters of recommendation, college transcript(s), minimum of 3 years of work experience.

Recommended for Application Bachelor's degree.

Application Deadline Applications processed on a rolling/continuous basis for both domestic and international students. Deferred entrance is available.

ACADEMICS

Faculty Full-time 85; part-time 40.

Teaching Methodologies Case study, computer-aided instruction, experiential learning, field projects, group discussion, lecture, research, role playing, seminars by members of the business community, simulations, student presentations, study groups, team projects.

Technology 65 on-campus computer terminals/PCs are available for student use and are linked by a campus-wide network. The network has full access to the Internet. Students are not required to have their own PC.

Special Opportunities International exchange programs in Australia, Brazil, France, Republic of Singapore, Republic of South Africa, Spain, United States.

FINANCES

Costs for 1997–98 Tuition: Full-time: £15,000 per year (resident); £15,000 per year (nonresident). Part-time: £10,000 per year (resident); £10,000 per year (nonresident). Average 1997–98 room and board costs were £4000 per academic year (on campus) and £4000 per academic year (off campus). Room and board costs vary by occupancy (e.g., single, double, triple), type of accommodation, type of meal plan.

Financial Aid In 1997–98, 5% of students received some institutionally administered aid in the form of scholarships. Application Deadline: 4/1.

Financial Aid Contact Mrs. Pat Hayes, Admissions Officer, Cranfield School of Management, Cranfield, Bedford, Bedford MK43 OAL, United Kingdom. Phone: 44-1234-754-431; Fax: 44-1234-752-439; E-mail: p.hayes@cranfield.ac.uk

FACILITIES

Information Resources Cranfield Information and Library Service plus 1 additional on-campus library; total holdings of 60,000 volumes, 100,000 microforms, 500 current periodical subscriptions. CD player(s) available for graduate student use. Access provided to online bibliographic retrieval services and online databases.

INTERNATIONAL STUDENTS

Demographics 27% of students enrolled are international students [Africa, 10%, Asia, 37%, Australia/New Zealand, 4%, Europe, 38%, North America, 4%, South America, 7%].

Services and Facilities International student office, counseling/support services.

Applying IELT: minimum score of 7, TOEFL: minimum score of 600, proof of adequate funds required. Financial aid is available to international students.

International Student Contact Mrs. Maureen Williams, Graduate Programmes Marketing Executive, Cranfield, Bedford, Bedford MK43 OAL, United Kingdom. Phone: 44-1234-751-122; Fax: 44-1234-752-439; E-mail: m.williams@cranfield.ac.uk

PLACEMENT

Services include alumni network, career counseling/planning, career library, job interviews arranged, job search course, and resume preparation. In 1996–97, 141 organizations participated in on-campus recruiting; 1,217 on-campus interviews were conducted.

Employment Of 1996–97 graduates, 95% were employed within three months of graduation. Types of employment entered: accounting, banking, chemical industry, communications, computer-related, consulting, consumer products, energy, finance, financial services, health services, high technology, human resources, information systems/technology, insurance, management, manufactur-

ing, marketing, media, nonprofit, petrochemical, pharmaceutical, service industry, telecommunications.

Business Program(s) URL: http://www.cranfield.ac.uk/som/

Program Contact: Mrs. Pat Hayes, Admissions Officer, Cranfield School of Management, Cranfield, Bedford, Bedford MK43 OAL, United Kingdom. Phone: 44-1234-754-431; Fax: 44-1234-752-439; E-mail: p.hayes@cranfield.ac.uk

See full description on page 772.

De Montfort University

Leicester Business School

Leicester, England, United Kingdom

OVERVIEW

De Montfort University is a federally supported, coed institution. Founded: 1989. The graduate business unit is in a suburban setting and is on a trimester calendar.

GRADUATE BUSINESS PROGRAMS

Master of Business Administration (MBA)

ACADEMICS

Faculty Full-time 120; part-time 20.

Teaching Methodologies Case study, lecture, research, seminars by members of the business community, student presentations, team projects.

Technology Computer terminals/PCs are available for student use and are linked by a campus-wide network. The network has full access to the Internet. Students are not required to have their own PC.

Special Opportunities International exchange programs in France, Indonesia, South Africa.

FACILITIES

Information Resources Kimberlin Library. CD player(s) available for graduate student use. Access provided to online bibliographic retrieval services.

Program Contact: MBA Program Administrator, The Gateway, Leicester, England LE1 9BH, United Kingdom. Phone: 44-116-257-7230; Fax: 44-116-251-7548.

EAP-European School of Management

Business Programs

Oxford, United Kingdom

OVERVIEW

EAP-European School of Management coed institution. Founded: 1973. The graduate business unit is in an urban setting and is on a trimester calendar.

HIGHLIGHTS

Enrollment Profile

Full-time: N/R	International: N/R
Part-time: N/R	Women: N/R
Total: N/R	Minorities: N/R
Average Age: 25	Average Class Size: 40
Fall 1997 Average GPA: N/R	Fall 1997 Average GMAT: 570

Costs
Full-time tuition: N/R
Part-time tuition: N/R

GRADUATE BUSINESS PROGRAMS

European Master of Management (MM) Full-time; European Management Admissions Test (EMAT) and fluency in first two languages of program required; 3 to 4 years to complete program. Concentrations in international management, international business, european business studies.

European MBA in International Business (MBA) Full-time; GMAT score: minimum 550, TOEFL score: minimum 600, and 4 years relevant work experience required; 12 months to 2 years to complete program. Concentrations in international business, international management, strategic management.

ADMISSION

Application Requirements Application form, application fee, bachelor's degree, essay, minimum GPA, interview, 2 letters of recommendation, personal statement, resume, college transcript(s), work experience.

Application Deadline 4/15 for fall, 9/15 for winter. Application fee: 300 French francs. Deferred entrance is available.

ACADEMICS

Faculty Full-time 45; part-time 50.

Teaching Methodologies Case study, computer-aided instruction, computer simulations, experiential learning, field projects, group discussion, lecture, research, seminars by members of the business community, simulations, student presentations, study groups, team projects.

Technology 100 on-campus computer terminals/PCs are available for student use and are linked by a campus-wide network. The network has full access to the Internet. Students are not required to have their own PC.

Special Opportunities International exchange programs in France, Germany, Poland, Spain, United Kingdom. An internship program is available.

FINANCES
Costs for 1997–98 Cost varies by academic program. Room and board costs vary by campus location.
Financial Aid Scholarships available.

INTERNATIONAL STUDENTS
Demographics N/R

Services and Facilities International student office, counseling/support services.

Applying TOEFL, proof of adequate funds required. Financial aid is available to international students.

International Student Contact Mr. Kitson Smith, International Dean of Students, 12 Merton Street, Oxford. Phone: 44-1865–26 32 00; Fax: 44-1865–25 19 60.

PLACEMENT
Services include alumni network, career counseling/planning, career fairs, electronic job bank, and job search course. In 1996–97, 20 organizations participated in on-campus recruiting.

Employment Of 1996–97 graduates, 90% were employed within three months of graduation. Types of employment entered: accounting, banking, communications, computer-related, consulting, consumer products, finance, human resources, information systems/technology, international trade, management, marketing, media, petrochemical, pharmaceutical, retail, service industry, telecommunications.

Business Program(s) URL: http://www.eap.net

Program Contact: Christine Taylor, External Relations, 12 Merton Street, Oxford, England OX1 4JH, United Kingdom. Phone: 44-1865-263-201; Fax: 44-1865-251960; E-mail: ctaylor@eap.net

Henley Management College

Business Programs

Oxfordshire, England, United Kingdom

OVERVIEW
Henley Management College is an independent-nonprofit, coed institution. Enrollment: 50 full-time matriculated graduate/professional students; 109 part-time matriculated graduate/professional students. Founded: 1945. The graduate business unit is in a rural setting and is on a trimester calendar.

HIGHLIGHTS

Enrollment Profile

Full-time: 50	International: N/R
Part-time: 109	Women: N/R
Total: 159	Minorities: N/R
Average Age: 30	Average Class Size: 50
Fall 1997 Average GPA: N/R	Fall 1997 Average GMAT: N/R

Costs
Full-time tuition: £14,000 per academic year
Part-time tuition: £15,550 per 2-year program

Degree(s) offered in conjunction with Brunel University, Regent's College

GRADUATE BUSINESS PROGRAMS
Master of Business Administration (MBA) Full-time, part-time, distance learning option; 12 months to 3 years to complete program. Concentrations in management, strategic management.

Master of Business Administration/Master of Science in Project Management (MBA/MS) Part-time, distance learning option; 2 to 3 years to complete program. Concentration in project management.

Doctor of Business Administration (DBA) distance learning option; minimum of 4 years to complete program. Concentrations in human resources, research and development administration.

ADMISSION
Applications For fall 1997 there were 210 applications for admission. Of those applying, 184 were accepted. Of those accepted, 159 enrolled.

Application Requirements Application form, application fee, bachelor's degree, minimum GPA: 2.75, interview, 2 letters of recommendation, work experience.

Application Deadline Applications processed on a rolling/continuous basis for both domestic and international students.

ACADEMICS
Faculty Full-time 52; part-time 59.

Teaching Methodologies Case study, computer simulations, faculty seminars, group discussion, lecture, research, simulations, student presentations, team projects.

Technology 50 on-campus computer terminals/PCs are available for student use and are linked by a campus-wide network. The network has full access to the Internet. Students are not required to have their own PC.

Special Opportunities International exchange programs in Belgium, Czech Republic, France, Germany, Netherlands, Spain, Sweden, United States.

FINANCES
Costs for 1997–98 Tuition: Full-time: £14,000 per year. Part-time: £15,550 per 2-year program. Cost varies by academic program, reciprocity agreements. Fees vary by academic program. Average 1997–98 room only costs were £1650 per academic year. Room and board costs vary by campus location, occupancy (e.g., single, double, triple), type of accommodation.

FACILITIES
Information Resources Henley Management College Library; total holdings of 15,000 volumes, 375 current periodical subscriptions. CD player(s) available for graduate student use. Access provided to online bibliographic retrieval services.

INTERNATIONAL STUDENTS
Demographics N/R

Services and Facilities International student office, international student housing, ESL courses, counseling/support services.

Applying IELT, TOEFL required. Financial aid is not available to international students.

International Student Contact Mr. Oliver Herrold, Admissions Officer (Full-Time MBA), Henley Regent's College, Regent's Park, Inner Circle, London, England NW1 4NS, United Kingdom. Phone: 44-171-487-7452 ; Fax: 44-171-487-7425.

PLACEMENT
Services include alumni network, career counseling/planning, career fairs, career library, career placement, resume referral to employers, and resume preparation.

Business Program(s) URL: http://www.henleymc.ac.uk

Program Contact: Information, Greenlands, Henley-on-Thames, Oxfordshire, England RG9 3AU, United Kingdom. Phone: 44-1491-571-454; Fax: 44-1491-410-184; E-mail: jillf@henleymc.ac.uk

Heriot-Watt University

Edinburgh Business School

Edinburgh, Scotland, United Kingdom

OVERVIEW
Heriot-Watt University coed institution. Enrollment: 4,500 graduate, professional, and undergraduate students. Founded: 1966. The graduate business unit is in a rural setting and is on a quarter calendar.

HIGHLIGHTS

Enrollment Profile

Full-time: 30	International: 21%
Part-time: 90	Women: 33%
Total: 120	Minorities: N/R
Average Age: 36	Average Class Size: N/R
Fall 1997 Average GPA: N/R	Fall 1997 Average GMAT: N/R

Costs
Full-time tuition: N/R
Part-time tuition: N/R

Degree(s) offered in conjunction with Technical University of Budapest

GRADUATE BUSINESS PROGRAMS
Master of Business Administration (MBA) Full-time, part-time, distance learning option; 60 total credits required; 12 months to 7 years to complete program.

Master of Science in International Accounting and Financial Studies (MS) Full-time; 12 months to complete program.

Master of Science in International Banking and Financial Studies (MS) Full-time; 12 months to complete program.

Consortium MBA (MBA) 60 total credits required; 2.3 to 7 years to complete program.

Heriot-Watt University (continued)

ADMISSION

Applications For fall 1997 there were 205 applications for admission. Of those applying, 130 were accepted. Of those accepted, 60 enrolled.

Application Requirements Application form, minimum of 2 years of work experience.

Recommended for Application GMAT score accepted, bachelor's degree, resume.

Application Deadline Applications processed on a rolling/continuous basis for both domestic and international students. Deferred entrance is available.

ACADEMICS

Faculty Full-time 25; part-time 20.

Teaching Methodologies Case study, computer-aided instruction, computer simulations, experiential learning, field projects, group discussion, lecture, seminars by members of the business community, simulations, student presentations, team projects.

Technology 300 on-campus computer terminals/PCs are available for student use and are linked by a campus-wide network. The network has full access to the Internet. Students are required to have their own PC.

Special Opportunities Advanced credit may be earned through credit by examination, credit for business training programs, transfer of credits from another institution.

FINANCES

Costs for 1997–98 Cost varies by number of credits taken. Average 1997–98 room and board costs were £2592 per academic year. Room and board costs vary by campus location, occupancy (e.g., single, double, triple), type of accommodation, type of meal plan.

FACILITIES

Information Resources Heriot-Watt University Library plus 10 additional on-campus libraries; total holdings of 200,000 volumes. CD player(s) available for graduate student use. Access provided to online bibliographic retrieval services and online databases.

INTERNATIONAL STUDENTS

Demographics 21% of students enrolled are international students [Africa, 10%, Asia, 31%, Australia/New Zealand, 5%, Europe, 21%, North America, 17%, other, 16%].

Services and Facilities International student office, international student center, visa services, ESL courses, counseling/support services.

Applying TOEFL: minimum score of 550 required. Financial aid is not available to international students.

International Student Contact Dr. David Boak, Director, International Division, Riccarton, Edinburgh, Scotland EH14 4AS, United Kingdom.

PLACEMENT

Services include alumni network, career counseling/planning, career fairs, career library, job search course, resume referral to employers, and resume preparation.

Employment Types of employment entered: accounting, communications, computer-related, consulting, engineering, finance, health services, marketing.

Business Program(s) URL: http://www.ebs.hw.ac.uk

Program Contact: Ms. Gillian Steele, Director of MBA Programmes, Edinburgh Business School, Edinburgh, Scotland EH14 4AS, United Kingdom. Phone: 44-131-449-5111; Fax: 44-131-451-3190; E-mail: enquiries@ebs.hw.ac.uk

Huron University USA in London

MBA Program

London, England, United Kingdom

OVERVIEW

Huron University USA in London is a proprietary, coed institution. Enrollment: 350 graduate, professional, and undergraduate students; 53 full-time matriculated graduate/professional students; 27 part-time matriculated graduate/professional students. Founded: 1883. The graduate business unit is in an urban setting and is on a semester calendar.

HIGHLIGHTS

Enrollment Profile

Full-time: 53	International: 100%
Part-time: 27	Women: 40%
Total: 80	Minorities: N/R
Average Age: 26	Average Class Size: 15
Fall 1997 Average GPA: 3.0	Fall 1997 Average GMAT: 480

Costs
Full-time tuition: £8700 per academic year
Part-time tuition: £750 per class

Huron University USA in London strives to continuously reinvent itself in order to offer academic programs and professional development opportunities that are in pace with the ever-changing global marketplace. Although a free-standing, American-style institution on European soil, Huron University USA in London has recently established a close strategic alliance with Marlboro College, Vermont. John Kenneth Galbraith, a distinguished Harvard economist and former U.S. Ambassador to India, has described Marlboro as "one of the small jewels of American education." The alliance is seen by both institutions as a beneficial situation that will serve students well in the global environment of the twenty-first century. The focus is on fostering the skills that are essential for those who aspire to senior executive positions. Thus, developing leadership potential by encouraging analytical thinking, problem solving, and the exercise of sound judgement are emphasized. Young men and women from more than sixty nations study at Huron University USA in London. Its extensive global network of alumni and professional contacts offers opportunities for work placements during the course of the program and/or business activities following graduation. At Huron University USA in London, a strong emphasis is placed on individual needs, and it is understood that the world of business is wide reaching. Opportunities exist both in traditional areas such as banking, finance, and marketing and in less traditional areas such as environmental consultancy, community development, tourism, sports promotion, specialist media, think-tanks, NGO's, and fund-raising foundations both in the United Kingdom and abroad

GRADUATE BUSINESS PROGRAMS

Master of Business Administration (MBA) Full-time, part-time; 36-63 total credits required; 12 months to 2 years to complete program. Concentrations in entrepreneurship, international finance, management information systems, marketing.

ADMISSION

Applications For fall 1997 there were 63 applications for admission. Of those applying, 55 were accepted. Of those accepted, 40 enrolled.

Application Requirements Application form, application fee, essay, minimum GPA: 2.75, 2 letters of recommendation, resume, college transcript(s).

Recommended for Application GMAT score accepted: minimum 450, bachelor's degree, interview, personal statement, computer experience.

Application Deadline Applications processed on a rolling/continuous basis for both domestic and international students. Application fee: £25. Deferred entrance is available.

ACADEMICS

Faculty Full-time 11.

Teaching Methodologies Case study, computer-aided instruction, computer simulations, experiential learning, faculty seminars, field projects, group discussion, lecture, research, role playing, seminars by members of the business community, student presentations, team projects.

Technology 70 on-campus computer terminals/PCs are available for student use and are linked by a campus-wide network. The network has full access to the Internet. Students are not required to have their own PC.

Special Opportunities Advanced credit may be earned through credit for experience, credit for business training programs, transfer of credits from another institution. An internship program is available.

FINANCES

Costs for 1997–98 Tuition: Full-time: £8700 per academic year. Part-time: £750 per class. Cost varies by number of credits taken. Average 1997–98 room only costs were £4000 per academic year (on campus) and £4500 per academic year (off campus). Room and board costs vary by occupancy (e.g., single, double, triple), type of accommodation.

Financial Aid In 1997–98, 19% of students received some institutionally administered aid in the form of scholarships, work study.

Financial Aid Contact Mr. Marco Gorin, Director of Admissions, 58 Princes Gate, London, England SW7 2PG, United Kingdom. Phone: 44-171-581-4899 Ext. 23; Fax: 44-171-589-9406; E-mail: marco@huron.ac.uk

FACILITIES

Information Resources CD player(s) available for graduate student use. Access provided to online bibliographic retrieval services.

INTERNATIONAL STUDENTS

Demographics 100% of students enrolled are international students [Africa, 16%, Asia, 39%, Europe, 29%, other, 16%].

Services and Facilities International student office, international student housing, visa services, ESL courses, counseling/support services.

Applying TOEFL: minimum score of 550, proof of adequate funds required. Financial aid is available to international students.

International Student Contact Mrs. Michele Keville, Director of Student Affairs, 58 Princes Gate, London, England SW7 2PG, United Kingdom. Phone: 44-171-581-4899 Ext. 33; Fax: 44-171-589-9406; E-mail: michele@huron.ac.uk

PLACEMENT

Services include alumni network, career counseling/planning, career fairs, job interviews arranged, job search course, resume referral to employers, and resume preparation.

Employment Of 1996–97 graduates, 75% were employed within three months of graduation; the average starting salary was £16,000. Types of employment entered: accounting, banking, communications, computer-related, consulting, consumer products, education, finance, financial services, government, hospitality management, human resources, international trade, management, manufacturing, marketing, media, nonprofit, retail.

Business Program(s) URL: http://www.huron.ac.uk

Program Contact: Mr. Marco Gorin, Director of Admissions, 58 Princes Gate, London, England SW7 2PG, United Kingdom. Phone: 44-171-581-4899 Ext. 23; Fax: 44-171-589-9406; E-mail: marco@huron.ac.uk
See full description on page 840.

Imperial College

Management School

London, England, United Kingdom

OVERVIEW

Imperial College coed institution. Enrollment: 7,500 graduate, professional, and undergraduate students. Founded: 1901. The graduate business unit is in an urban setting and is on a trimester calendar.

HIGHLIGHTS

Enrollment Profile

Full-time: 160	International: N/R
Part-time: 80	Women: 29%
Total: 240	Minorities: N/R
Average Age: 28	Average Class Size: 35
Fall 1997 Average GPA: N/R	Fall 1997 Average GMAT: 550

Costs
Full-time tuition: N/R
Part-time tuition: N/R

GRADUATE BUSINESS PROGRAMS

Full-time MBA (MBA) Full-time; 2 years work experience required; 12 months to complete program. Concentrations in entrepreneurship, new venture management, marketing, finance, project management, public management.

Part-time MBA (MBA) Part-time; 3 years work experience required; 2.3 years to complete program. Concentrations in public management, project management, new venture management, marketing, finance, entrepreneurship, health care.

MSc in Finance (MSc) Full-time; 12 months to complete program. Concentrations in finance, international finance.

ADMISSION

Applications For fall 1997 there were 1,000 applications for admission. Of those applying, 200 were accepted. Of those accepted, 160 enrolled.

Application Requirements GMAT score: minimum 600, application form, bachelor's degree, minimum GPA, interview, 2 letters of recommendation, resume, college transcript(s), minimum of 2 years of work experience.

Recommended for Application Essay, personal statement, computer experience.

Application Deadline 7/31 for fall, 7/31 for fall (international). Deferred entrance is available.

ACADEMICS

Faculty Full-time 38; part-time 12.

Teaching Methodologies Case study, field projects, lecture, seminars by members of the business community, student presentations, team projects.

Technology 50 on-campus computer terminals/PCs are available for student use and are linked by a campus-wide network. The network has full access to the Internet. Students are not required to have their own PC.

FINANCES

Costs for 1997–98 Average 1997–98 room and board costs were £3750 per academic year (off campus). Room and board costs vary by campus location, occupancy (e.g., single, double, triple), type of accommodation, type of meal plan.

Financial Aid Contact Ms. Debbie Johnson, MBA Admissions Officer, 53 Princes Gate, London, England SW7 2PG, United Kingdom. Phone: 44-171-594-9149; Fax: 44-171-823-7685; E-mail: m.school@ic.ac.uk

FACILITIES

Information Resources Management Collection plus 10 additional on-campus libraries. CD player(s) available for graduate student use. Access provided to online bibliographic retrieval services and online databases.

INTERNATIONAL STUDENTS
Demographics N/R

Applying IELT: minimum score of 6, TOEFL: minimum score of 600, proof of adequate funds required. Financial aid is not available to international students.

PLACEMENT

Services include alumni network, career counseling/planning, career fairs, career library, career placement, job interviews arranged, resume referral to employers, and resume preparation. In 1996–97, 50 organizations participated in on-campus recruiting; 40 on-campus interviews were conducted.

Employment Of 1996–97 graduates, 90% were employed within three months of graduation; the average starting salary was £35,000. Types of employment entered: accounting, banking, chemical industry, communications, computer-related, consulting, consumer products, education, energy, engineering, finance, financial services, government, health services, high technology, human resources, information systems/technology, management, manufacturing, marketing, media, nonprofit, petrochemical, pharmaceutical, retail, service industry, telecommunications, transportation.

Business Program(s) URL: http://mscmga.ms.ic.ac.uk/

Program Contact: Ms. Debbie Johnson, MBA Admissions Officer, 53 Princes Gate, London, England SW7 2PG, United Kingdom. Phone: 44-171-594-9149; Fax: 44-171-823-7685; E-mail: m.school@ic.ac.uk

Kingston University

Kingston Business School

Kingston upon Thames, Surrey, United Kingdom

OVERVIEW

Kingston University coed institution. Enrollment: 5,000 graduate, professional, and undergraduate students. Founded: 1970. The graduate business unit is in a suburban setting and is on a trimester calendar.

HIGHLIGHTS

Enrollment Profile

Full-time: N/R	International: N/R
Part-time: N/R	Women: N/R
Total: N/R	Minorities: N/R
Average Age: 34	Average Class Size: 30
Fall 1997 Average GPA: N/R	Fall 1997 Average GMAT: N/R

Costs
Full-time tuition: N/R
Part-time tuition: N/R

GRADUATE BUSINESS PROGRAMS

Master of Business Administration (MBA) Part-time; minimum of 2 years to complete program.

Master of Arts in Accounting and Finance (MA) Full-time; minimum of 2 years to complete program.

Master of Arts in Employment Relations and Law (MA) Part-time; minimum of 2 years to complete program.

Master of Arts in Managing Human Resources (MA) Part-time; minimum of 2 years to complete program.

Master of Arts in Marketing (MA) Full-time, part-time; 12 months to 2 years to complete program.

Master of Arts in Personnel Management (MA) Full-time, part-time; 12 months to 2 years to complete program.

Master of Arts in Strategic Financial Management (MA) Part-time; minimum of 2 years to complete program.

Master of Arts in Business Management (MA) Full-time; 12 months to 2.5 years to complete program.

Kingston University (continued)

ADMISSION

Application Requirements Application form, bachelor's degree, letters of recommendation, personal statement, college transcript(s), minimum of 5 years of work experience.

Recommended for Application Interview, computer experience.

Application Deadline 8/30 for fall, 8/30 for fall (international). Application fee: £25.

ACADEMICS

Faculty Full-time 90; part-time 20.

Teaching Methodologies Case study, computer-aided instruction, computer analysis, experiential learning, faculty seminars, field projects, group discussion, lecture, research, seminars by members of the business community, student presentations, study groups, team projects.

Technology 200 on-campus computer terminals/PCs are available for student use and are linked by a campus-wide network. The network has full access to the Internet. Students are not required to have their own PC.

Special Opportunities Advanced credit may be earned through credit by examination, credit for experience, credit for business training programs, transfer of credits from another institution.

FINANCES

Costs for 1997–98 Cost varies by academic program, reciprocity agreements. Average 1997–98 room only costs were £3000 per academic year. Room and board costs vary by campus location, type of accommodation, type of meal plan.

FACILITIES

Information Resources Kingston Hill Library plus 3 additional on-campus libraries. CD player(s) available for graduate student use. Access provided to online bibliographic retrieval services and online databases.

INTERNATIONAL STUDENTS

Demographics N/R

Services and Facilities International student office, ESL courses.

Applying IELT: minimum score of 7.5, TOEFL: minimum score of 600 required. Proof of adequate funds recommended.

International Student Contact International Officer-Students, Millennium House, 21 Eden Street, Kingston upon Thames, Surrey KT1 1BL, United Kingdom. Phone: 44-181-547-7755; Fax: 44-181-547-7789.

PLACEMENT

Services include alumni network, career counseling/planning, and career library.

Employment Types of employment entered: accounting, banking, chemical industry, communications, computer-related, consulting, consumer products, education, energy, engineering, finance, financial services, government, health services, high technology, human resources, information systems/technology, insurance, international trade, law, management, manufacturing, marketing, media, nonprofit, petrochemical, pharmaceutical, retail, service industry, telecommunications, transportation, utilities.

Business Program(s) URL: http://polaris.kingston.ac.uk:8080/

Program Contact: MBA Administrator, Kingston Hill, Kingston upon Thames, Surrey KT2 7LB, United Kingdom. Phone: 44-181-547-7120; Fax: 44-181-547-7452.

Lancaster University

Management School

Lancaster, United Kingdom

OVERVIEW

Lancaster University is a publicly supported, coed institution. Enrollment: 10,333 graduate, professional, and undergraduate students. Founded: 1964. The graduate business unit is in a small-town setting and is on a trimester calendar.

HIGHLIGHTS

Enrollment Profile

Full-time: N/R	International: N/R
Part-time: N/R	Women: N/R
Total: 273	Minorities: N/R
Average Age: 29	Average Class Size: N/R
Fall 1997 Average GPA: N/R	Fall 1997 Average GMAT: 600

Costs
Full-time tuition: N/R
Part-time tuition: £10,500 per program (resident); £10,500 per program (nonresident)

GRADUATE BUSINESS PROGRAMS

Master of Business Administration (MBA) Full-time; 12 to 18 months to complete program. Concentration in management.

Master of Science in Information Management (MS) Full-time; 12 months to complete program. Concentration in information management.

Master of Science in Finance (MS) Full-time; 12 months to complete program. Concentration in finance.

Master of Arts in Accounting and Finance (MA) Full-time; 12 months to complete program. Concentrations in accounting, finance.

Master of Science in Operational Research (MS) Full-time; 12 months to complete program. Concentrations in logistics, management science, operations management.

Master of Science in International Trade and Finance (MS) Full-time; 12 months to complete program. Concentrations in international economics, logistics.

Master of Arts in Management and Organizational Learning (MA) Full-time; 12 months to complete program. Concentration in organizational management.

Master of Arts in Organizational Analysis (MA) Full-time, part-time; 12 months to 2 years to complete program. Concentration in organizational behavior/development.

Master of Philosophy in Critical Management (MPhil) Concentration in logistics.

Master of Arts in Management Learning (MA) Part-time, distance learning option; 2 to 2.2 years to complete program. Concentration in organizational management.

ADMISSION

Application Requirements GMAT score: minimum 600, application form, bachelor's degree, 2 letters of recommendation, college transcript(s), minimum of 3 years of work experience.

Recommended for Application Interview, resume, computer experience.

Application Deadline 6/30 for fall, 6/30 for fall (international). Deferred entrance is available.

ACADEMICS

Faculty Full-time 85; part-time 10.

Teaching Methodologies Case study, experiential learning, faculty seminars, group discussion, lecture, seminars by members of the business community, simulations, student presentations, team projects.

Technology 80 on-campus computer terminals/PCs are available for student use and are linked by a campus-wide network. The network has full access to the Internet. Students are not required to have their own PC.

Special Opportunities International exchange programs in Austria, Denmark, France, Germany, Italy, Netherlands, Norway, Spain, Switzerland. An internship program is available.

FINANCES

Costs for 1997–98 Tuition: £10,500 per program (resident); £10,500 per program (nonresident). Cost varies by reciprocity agreements.

Financial Aid Scholarships available. Application Deadline: 6/30.

Financial Aid Contact Course Director, University House, Lancaster. Phone: 44-1524-594-068; Fax: 44-1524-592-417; E-mail: mba@lancs.ac.uk

FACILITIES

Information Resources CD player(s) available for graduate student use. Access provided to online bibliographic retrieval services.

INTERNATIONAL STUDENTS

Demographics N/R

Services and Facilities International student office, international student center, ESL courses, counseling/support services, language tutoring, religious facilities.

Applying IELT: minimum score of 6.5, TOEFL: minimum score of 580, proof of adequate funds required. Financial aid is available to international students.

International Student Contact Dr. John Withrington, International Officer, University House, Lancaster. Phone: 44-1524-592-037; E-mail: jwithrington@lancaster.ac.uk

PLACEMENT

Services include alumni network, career counseling/planning, career library, job search course, and resume preparation.

Business Program(s) URL: http://www.lancs.ac.uk/users/manschool/index. htm

Program Contact: Management School, University House, Lancaster LA1 4YX, United Kingdom. Phone: 44-1524-543-628; Fax: 44-1524-847-321.

London School of Economics and Political Science

The Graduate School

London, England, United Kingdom

OVERVIEW
London School of Economics and Political Science coed institution. Enrollment: 6,518 graduate, professional, and undergraduate students. Founded: 1895. The graduate business unit is in an urban setting and is on a trimester calendar.

HIGHLIGHTS

Enrollment Profile
Full-time: N/R
Part-time: N/R
Total: N/R
Average Age: N/R
Fall 1997 Average GPA: N/R

International: N/R
Women: N/R
Minorities: N/R
Average Class Size: N/R
Fall 1997 Average GMAT: N/R

Costs
Full-time tuition: N/R
Part-time tuition: N/R

Degree(s) offered in conjunction with Community of European Management Schools (CEMS)

GRADUATE BUSINESS PROGRAMS
Master of Science in Accounting and Finance (MSc) Full-time; 9 months to complete program.
Master of Science in International Accounting and Finance (MSc) Full-time; 9 months to complete program.
Master of Science in Finance and Economics (MSc) Full-time; minimum of 10 months to complete program.
Master of Science in Economics (MSc) Full-time; minimum of 10 months to complete program.
Master of Science in Econometrics and Mathematical Economics (MSc) Full-time; minimum of 9 months to complete program.
Master of Science in Industrial Relations and Personnel Management (MSc) Full-time; minimum of 12 months to complete program.
Master of Science in Management (MSc) Full-time; minimum of 12 months to complete program. Concentration in public management.
Master of Science in Management of Non-Governmental Organizations (MSc) Full-time; minimum of 12 months to complete program.
Master of Science in Voluntary Sector Organizations (MSc) Full-time; minimum of 12 months to complete program.
Master of Science in Public Administration and Public Policy (MSc) Full-time; minimum of 12 months to complete program.
Master of Science in Analysis, Design, and Management of Information Systems (MSc) Full-time; minimum of 12 months to complete program.
Master of Science in Decision Sciences (MSc) Full-time; minimum of 12 months to complete program.
Diploma in Business Studies (Dip) Full-time; minimum of 9 months to complete program.

ADMISSION
Application Requirements Application form, application fee, bachelor's degree, minimum GPA: 3.5, 2 letters of recommendation, personal statement, college transcript(s).
Recommended for Application GMAT score accepted, GRE score accepted.
Application Deadline 4/1 for fall, 4/1 for fall (international). Application fee: £25.

ACADEMICS
Teaching Methodologies Case study, computer-aided instruction, computer analysis, computer simulations, group discussion, lecture, research, seminars by members of the business community, student presentations, study groups, team projects.
Technology 500 on-campus computer terminals/PCs are available for student use and are linked by a campus-wide network. The network has full access to the Internet. Students are not required to have their own PC.

Special Opportunities International exchange programs in Belgium, Czech Republic, France, Germany, Hungary, Italy, Netherlands, Norway, Spain, Sweden, Switzerland,.

FINANCES
Costs for 1997–98 Cost varies by academic program. Average 1997–98 room and board costs were £7004 per academic year (on campus) and £8951 per academic year (off campus). Room and board costs vary by campus location, occupancy (e.g., single, double, triple), type of accommodation, type of meal plan.
Financial Aid Grants, scholarships, loans available.
Financial Aid Contact Graduate Admissions Office, Houghton Street, London, England WC2A 2AE, United Kingdom. Phone: 44-171-4057686.

FACILITIES
Information Resources British Library of Political and Economic Science. CD player(s) available for graduate student use. Access provided to online bibliographic retrieval services.

INTERNATIONAL STUDENTS
Demographics N/R
Services and Facilities ESL courses.
Applying IELT: minimum score of 6.5, TOEFL: minimum score of 600 required. Financial aid is available to international students.

PLACEMENT
Services include alumni network, career counseling/planning, career fairs, career library, career placement, job search course, and resume preparation.
Employment Of 1996–97 graduates, 98% were employed within three months of graduation. Types of employment entered: accounting, banking, communications, computer-related, consulting, education, energy, finance, financial services, government, health services, human resources, information systems/technology, insurance, law, management, manufacturing, marketing, media, nonprofit, petrochemical, real estate, retail, service industry, telecommunications, transportation, utilities.

Business Program(s) URL: http://www.lse.ac.uk/

Program Contact: The Graduate Admissions Office, Houghton Street, London, England WC2A 2AE, United Kingdom. Phone: 44-171-955-7160; Fax: 44-171-955-6137; E-mail: graduate-school@lse.ac.uk

Loughborough University

Management Development Centre

Loughborough, Leicestershire, United Kingdom

OVERVIEW
Loughborough University coed institution. Enrollment: 9,963 graduate, professional, and undergraduate students; 653 full-time matriculated graduate/professional students; 722 part-time matriculated graduate/professional students. Founded: 1968. The graduate business unit is in a small-town setting and is on a term calendar.

HIGHLIGHTS

Enrollment Profile
Full-time: 0
Part-time: 155
Total: 155
Average Age: 30
Fall 1997 Average GPA: N/R

International: N/R
Women: N/R
Minorities: N/R
Average Class Size: 30
Fall 1997 Average GMAT: N/R

Costs
Full-time tuition: N/R
Part-time tuition: N/R

GRADUATE BUSINESS PROGRAMS
Executive Master of Business Administration (EMBA) Part-time; 180 total credits required; 3 to 7 years to complete program. Concentrations in management, human resources, finance, international business, strategic management, economics, marketing, decision sciences.
Master of Science in Management (MSc) Full-time; 150 total credits required; minimum of 12 months to complete program.

ADMISSION
Applications For fall 1997 there were 55 applications for admission. Of those applying, 50 were accepted.
Application Requirements Application form, bachelor's degree, minimum GPA, 2 letters of recommendation, resume, minimum of 3 years of work experience.
Recommended for Application GMAT score accepted, essay, interview.
Application Deadline 8/25 for fall, 8/25 for fall (international).

Loughborough University (continued)

ACADEMICS

Faculty Part-time 60.

Teaching Methodologies Case study, computer analysis, lecture, role playing, seminars by members of the business community, student presentations.

Technology Computer terminals/PCs are available for student use and are linked by a campus-wide network. The network has full access to the Internet. Students are not required to have their own PC.

Special Opportunities Advanced credit may be earned through credit by examination.

FINANCES

Costs for 1997–98 Cost varies by academic program, number of credits taken.

Financial Aid Contact Ms. Gabriella Stenson, MBA Administrator, Loughborough, Leicestershire LE11 3TU, United Kingdom. Phone: 44-150-922-3398; Fax: 44-150-922-3963.

INTERNATIONAL STUDENTS

Demographics N/R

Applying TOEFL: minimum score of 550 required. Financial aid is not available to international students.

International Student Contact MSc Management Administration, Loughborough, Leicestershire LE11 3TU, United Kingdom. Phone: 44-150-922-3291; Fax: 44-1509-223-963.

PLACEMENT

Services include alumni network.

Employment Types of employment entered: banking.

Business Program(s) URL: http://info.lut.ac.uk/departments/bs/

Program Contact: Ms. Gabriella Stenson, MBA Administrator, Loughborough, Leicestershire LE11 3TU, United Kingdom. Phone: 44-150-922-3398; Fax: 44-150-922-3963.

Manchester Metropolitan University

Faculty of Management and Business, Department of Management

Manchester, England, United Kingdom

OVERVIEW

Manchester Metropolitan University coed institution. Enrollment: 30,000 graduate, professional, and undergraduate students. Founded: 1970. The graduate business unit is in an urban setting and is on a module calendar.

HIGHLIGHTS

Enrollment Profile

Full-time: 0	International: N/R
Part-time: 110	Women: 33%
Total: 110	Minorities: N/R
Average Age: 33	Average Class Size: 35
Fall 1997 Average GPA: N/R	Fall 1997 Average GMAT: N/R

Costs
Full-time tuition: N/R
Part-time tuition: N/R

GRADUATE BUSINESS PROGRAMS

Master of Business Administration (MBA) Part-time; 2.5 to 5 years to complete program. Concentrations in accounting, finance, international business, management, operations management, organizational behavior/development, public policy and administration, quality management, health care, marketing, business ethics, strategic management, human resources.

ADMISSION

Application Requirements Application form, bachelor's degree, interview, 2 letters of recommendation, resume, minimum of 5 years of work experience.

Application Deadline Applications processed on a rolling/continuous basis for domestic students only.

ACADEMICS

Faculty Full-time 20; part-time 30.

Teaching Methodologies Case study, computer-aided instruction, faculty seminars, group discussion, lecture, research, student presentations, study groups, team projects.

Technology Computer terminals/PCs are available for student use and are linked by a campus-wide network. The network has full access to the Internet. Students are not required to have their own PC.

Special Opportunities International exchange programs in Czech Republic, Hungary, Spain.

FINANCES

Financial Aid Contact Finance Department, Manchester, England M1 3GH, United Kingdom. Phone: 44-161-247-1833.

FACILITIES

Information Resources Aytoun Library; total holdings of 35,000 volumes, 300 current periodical subscriptions.

INTERNATIONAL STUDENTS

Demographics N/R

Business Program(s) URL: http://www.fmb.mmu.ac.uk

Program Contact: Mr. Jon Crebbin, MBA Course Administrator, Manchester, England M1 3GH, United Kingdom. Phone: 44-161-247-3717; Fax: 44-161-247-6319; E-mail: j.crebbin@mmu.ac.uk

Middlesex University

Business School

London, England, United Kingdom

OVERVIEW

Middlesex University coed institution. Enrollment: 21,000 graduate, professional, and undergraduate students. The graduate business unit is in a suburban setting and is on a semester calendar.

HIGHLIGHTS

Enrollment Profile

Full-time: 50	International: 41%
Part-time: 35	Women: 35%
Total: 85	Minorities: N/R
Average Age: 27	Average Class Size: 60
Fall 1997 Average GPA: N/R	Fall 1997 Average GMAT: N/R

Costs
Full-time tuition: N/R
Part-time tuition: N/R

GRADUATE BUSINESS PROGRAMS

Master of Business Administration (MBA) Full-time, part-time; 200 total credits required; 15 months to 2.3 years to complete program. Concentrations in accounting, finance, human resources, international business, management, marketing, operations management.

ADMISSION

Application Requirements GMAT score, application form, bachelor's degree, interview, 2 letters of recommendation, personal statement, college transcript(s), minimum of 3 years of work experience.

Recommended for Application Computer experience.

Application Deadline Applications processed on a rolling/continuous basis for both domestic and international students.

ACADEMICS

Faculty Full-time 110.

Teaching Methodologies Case study, computer-aided instruction, computer simulations, lecture, seminars by members of the business community, student presentations, team projects.

FINANCES

Financial Aid Contact Ms. Martine Clarke, MBA Admissions Administrator, The Burroughs, Hendon, London, England NW4 4BT, United Kingdom. Phone: 44-181-362-5986; Fax: 44-181-362-6069; E-mail: m.clarke@mdx.ac.uk

INTERNATIONAL STUDENTS

Demographics 41% of students enrolled are international students [Africa, 14%, Asia, 40%, Australia/New Zealand, 6%, Central America, 3%, Europe, 31%, North America, 3%, South America, 3%].

Applying IELT: minimum score of 6.5, TOEFL: minimum score of 550 required. Financial aid is not available to international students.

PLACEMENT

Services include alumni network, career counseling/planning, career library, and resume preparation.

Employment Types of employment entered: financial services, retail, service industry.

Business Program(s) URL: http://www.mdx.ac.uk

Program Contact: Ms. Martine Clarke, MBA Admissions Administrator, The Burroughs, Hendon, London, England NW4 4BT, United Kingdom. Phone: 44-181-362-5090; Fax: 44-181-362-6069; E-mail: m.clarke@mdx.ac.uk

Napier University

Napier Business School

Edinburgh, Scotland, United Kingdom

OVERVIEW
Napier University coed institution. Enrollment: 11,467 graduate, professional, and undergraduate students. Founded: 1964. The graduate business unit is in a suburban setting and is on a semester calendar.

HIGHLIGHTS

Enrollment Profile

Full-time: 0	International: N/R
Part-time: 460	Women: 42%
Total: 460	Minorities: N/R
Average Age: 35	Average Class Size: 38
Fall 1997 Average GPA: N/R	Fall 1997 Average GMAT: N/R

Costs
Full-time tuition: N/R
Part-time tuition: N/R

Degree(s) offered in conjunction with Kingston Business School

GRADUATE BUSINESS PROGRAMS
Part-time MBA (MBA) Part-time; 3 to 5 years to complete program.
Open-learning MBA Program (MBA) Part-time, distance learning option; 2 to 4 years to complete program.
Distance Learning MBA (MBA) Part-time, distance learning option; 3 to 5 years to complete program.

ADMISSION
Application Requirements GRE score, application form, 2 letters of recommendation, personal statement, resume, college transcript(s).
Recommended for Application Bachelor's degree (must be in field of business), interview, work experience, computer experience.
Application Deadline Applications processed on a rolling/continuous basis for domestic students only. 8/1 for fall (international). Deferred entrance is available.

ACADEMICS
Faculty Full-time 130; part-time 55.
Teaching Methodologies Case study, computer-aided instruction, computer simulations.
Technology Computer terminals/PCs are available for student use and are linked by a campus-wide network. The network has partial access to the Internet. Students are not required to have their own PC.
Special Opportunities Advanced credit may be earned through credit by examination, credit for experience, credit for military training programs, credit for business training programs, transfer of credits from another institution. International exchange program in Netherlands.

FINANCES
Costs for 1997–98 Cost varies by academic program. Fees vary by academic program.

FACILITIES
Information Resources Sighthill Library plus 3 additional on-campus libraries; total holdings of 270,000 volumes, 650 microforms, 2,200 current periodical subscriptions. CD player(s) available for graduate student use. Access provided to online bibliographic retrieval services.

INTERNATIONAL STUDENTS
Demographics N/R
Services and Facilities International student office, international student center, counseling/support services.
Applying Proof of adequate funds required. TOEFL, proof of health/immunizations recommended. Financial aid is not available to international students.

PLACEMENT
Services include alumni network, career counseling/planning, career fairs, career library, and resume preparation.
Employment Types of employment entered: accounting, banking, communications, computer-related, consulting, consumer products, education, energy, engineering, finance, financial services, government, health services, high technology, hospitality management, human resources, information systems/technology, insurance, international trade, management, manufacturing, marketing, media, nonprofit, retail, service industry, telecommunications, transportation, utilities.

Program Contact: Mrs. Sheila Ferrier, South Craig, Craighouse Campus, Craighouse Road, Edinburgh, Scotland EH10 5LG, United Kingdom. Phone: 44-131-455-5016; Fax: 44-131-455-5040; E-mail: s.ferrier@napier.ac.uk

Open University

Business School

Milton Keynes, England, United Kingdom

OVERVIEW
Open University coed institution. Founded: 1965. The graduate business unit is on a term calendar.

HIGHLIGHTS

Enrollment Profile

Full-time: 0	International: N/R
Part-time: 1,000	Women: N/R
Total: 1,000	Minorities: N/R
Average Age: 35	Average Class Size: N/R
Fall 1997 Average GPA: N/R	Fall 1997 Average GMAT: N/R

Costs
Full-time tuition: N/R
Part-time tuition: N/R

GRADUATE BUSINESS PROGRAMS
Master of Business Administration (MBA) distance learning option; 120 total credits required; 3 to 10 years to complete program. Concentrations in management, strategic management, human resources, environmental economics/management, business education, public policy and administration, organizational behavior/development.

ADMISSION
Application Requirements Application form, college transcript(s), minimum of 5 years of work experience.
Application Deadline Applications processed on a rolling/continuous basis for both domestic and international students.

ACADEMICS
Faculty Full-time 36.
Teaching Methodologies Computer-aided instruction, computer analysis, computer simulations, study groups, team projects.
Technology Computer terminals/PCs are available for student use and are linked by a campus-wide network. The network has full access to the Internet. Students are not required to have their own PC.

FINANCES
Financial Aid Contact Mr. Richard Wheatcroft, Program Director, PO Box 481, Walton Hall, Milton Keynes, Buckinghaimshire MK7 657, United Kingdom. Phone: 44-1908-655-851.

INTERNATIONAL STUDENTS
Demographics N/R
Applying Financial aid is not available to international students.

PLACEMENT
Services include alumni network, career placement, and resume preparation.
Employment Types of employment entered: consulting, finance, government, law, management, retail, service industry.
Business Program(s) URL: http://oubs.open.ac.uk/

Program Contact: Ms. Christine McIlroy, Customer Services Department, PO Box 481, Walton Hall, Milton Keynes, England MK7 6B7, United Kingdom. Phone: 44-1908-652-143; Fax: 44-1908-655-898.

Oxford Brookes University

School of Business

Oxford, United Kingdom

OVERVIEW
Oxford Brookes University is a publicly supported, coed institution. Founded: 1930. The graduate business unit is in a suburban setting and is on a term calendar.

Oxford Brookes University (continued)

HIGHLIGHTS

Enrollment Profile
Full-time: 50
Part-time: 300
Total: 350
Average Age: 28
Fall 1997 Average GPA: N/R

International: N/R
Women: N/R
Minorities: N/R
Average Class Size: 25
Fall 1997 Average GMAT: 500

Costs
Full-time tuition: £7650 per academic year (resident); £7650 per academic year (nonresident)
Part-time tuition: N/R

GRADUATE BUSINESS PROGRAMS
Master of Business Administration (MBA) Full-time, part-time, distance learning option; 183 total credits required; 12 months to 2 years to complete program. Concentrations in management, operations management, organizational management, human resources, marketing.

ADMISSION
Applications For fall 1997 there were 700 applications for admission. Of those applying, 350 were accepted.

Application Requirements GMAT score: minimum 550, application form, bachelor's degree, 2 letters of recommendation, personal statement, college transcript(s), minimum of 2 years of work experience.

Recommended for Application Interview, resume.

Application Deadline Applications processed on a rolling/continuous basis for both domestic and international students. Deferred entrance is available.

ACADEMICS
Faculty Full-time 45.

Teaching Methodologies Case study, computer simulations, group discussion, lecture, role playing, seminars by members of the business community, simulations, student presentations, team projects.

Technology 700 on-campus computer terminals/PCs are available for student use and are linked by a campus-wide network. The network has full access to the Internet. Students are not required to have their own PC.

Special Opportunities Advanced credit may be earned through transfer of credits from another institution.

FINANCES
Costs for 1997–98 Tuition: Full-time: £7650 per year (resident); £7650 per year (nonresident).

Financial Aid Contact Mrs. Jackie Carter, MBA Course Administrator, School of Business, Wheatley Campus, Oxford, Oxfordshire OX33 1HX, United Kingdom. Phone: 44-186-548-5920; Fax: 44-186-548-5905; E-mail: mba@brooks.ac.uk

FACILITIES
Information Resources University Library. CD player(s) available for graduate student use.

INTERNATIONAL STUDENTS
Demographics N/R

Services and Facilities International student office, international student center, international student housing, counseling/support services.

Applying IELT: minimum score of 6, TOEFL: minimum score of 550 required.

International Student Contact Dr. Mark Ames, International Students Advisor, Gipsy Lane Campus, Headington, Oxford. Phone: 44-186-548-4680.

PLACEMENT
Services include alumni network, career counseling/planning, and career placement.

Employment Types of employment entered: accounting, banking, consulting, finance, government.

Business Program(s) URL: http://www.brookes.ac.uk/business/

Program Contact: Mrs. Jackie Carter, MBA Course Administrator, School of Business, Wheatley Campus, Oxford, Oxfordshire OX33 1HX, United Kingdom. Phone: 44-186-548-5920; Fax: 44-186-548-5905; E-mail: mba@brooks.ac.uk

Richmond, The American International University in London

School of Business

Richmond, Surrey, England, United Kingdom

OVERVIEW
Richmond, The American International University in London is an independent-nonprofit, coed institution. Enrollment: 1,232 graduate, professional, and undergraduate students; 85 full-time matriculated graduate/professional students; 44 part-time matriculated graduate/professional students. Founded: 1972. The graduate business unit is in an urban setting and is on a semester calendar.

HIGHLIGHTS

Enrollment Profile
Full-time: 50
Part-time: 38
Total: 88
Average Age: 26
Fall 1997 Average GPA: 3.3

International: N/R
Women: 52%
Minorities: N/R
Average Class Size: 24
Fall 1997 Average GMAT: 540

Costs
Full-time tuition: £5050 per academic year
Part-time tuition: £995 per course

GRADUATE BUSINESS PROGRAMS
Evening, Part-time, Full-time MBA-Master of Business Administration in General Management (MBA) Full-time, part-time; 45 total credits required; 12 months to 2 years to complete program. Concentrations in international business, international finance, international marketing.

Master of Science in Systems Engineering (MS) Full-time, part-time; 45 total credits required; 12 months to 2 years to complete program. Concentration in system management.

Master of Business Administration in International Marketing (MBA) Full-time, part-time; 45 total credits required; 12 months to 2 years to complete program.

Master of Business Administration in International Finance (MBA) Full-time, part-time; 45 total credits required; 12 months to 2 years to complete program.

ADMISSION
Applications For fall 1997 there were 116 applications for admission. Of those applying, 86 were accepted. Of those accepted, 39 enrolled.

Application Requirements Application form, application fee, bachelor's degree, essay, minimum GPA: 3.0, 2 letters of recommendation, personal statement, resume, college transcript(s), minimum of 2 years of work experience.

Recommended for Application Interview, computer experience.

Application Deadline Applications processed on a rolling/continuous basis for both domestic and international students. Application fee: £35. Deferred entrance is available.

ACADEMICS
Faculty Full-time 7; part-time 10.

Teaching Methodologies Case study, computer-aided instruction, computer analysis, computer simulations, experiential learning, faculty seminars, field projects, group discussion, lecture, research, role playing, seminars by members of the business community, simulations, student presentations, study groups, team projects.

Technology 54 on-campus computer terminals/PCs are available for student use and are linked by a campus-wide network. The network has full access to the Internet. Students are not required to have their own PC.

Special Opportunities Advanced credit may be earned through credit by examination, credit for experience, credit for military training programs, credit for business training programs, transfer of credits from another institution. An internship program is available.

FINANCES
Costs for 1997–98 Tuition: Full-time: £5050 per semester. Part-time: £995 per course. Cost varies by academic program, number of credits taken. Fees: Full-time: £210 per academic year. Part-time: £55 per semester. Fees vary by academic program, class time (e.g., day/evening). Average 1997–98 room and board costs were £4300 per academic year. Room and board costs vary by occupancy (e.g., single, double, triple).

Financial Aid In 1997–98, 11% of students received some institutionally administered aid in the form of scholarships.

Financial Aid Contact Ms. Anne Weedon, Financial Aid Administrator , Queens Road, Richmond, Surrey, England TW10 6JP, United Kingdom. Phone: 44-181-332-8244; Fax: 44-181-332-1596.

FACILITIES
Information Resources Richmond Hill Library plus 2 additional on-campus libraries; total holdings of 80,000 volumes, 7 microforms, 270 current periodical

subscriptions. CD player(s) available for graduate student use. Access provided to online bibliographic retrieval services.

INTERNATIONAL STUDENTS
Demographics N/R

Services and Facilities International student office, international student housing, counseling/support services.

Applying TOEFL: minimum score of 550, proof of adequate funds required. Proof of health/immunizations recommended. Financial aid is available to international students.

International Student Contact Ms. Catherine Byrne, Assistant Dean of Graduate Admissions, 16 Young Street, London, England W8 5EH, United Kingdom. Phone: 44-171-368-8475; Fax: 44-171-376-0836; E-mail: grad@richmond.ac.uk

PLACEMENT
Services include alumni network, career counseling/planning, career fairs, career placement, resume referral to employers, and resume preparation.

Employment Of 1996–97 graduates, 100% were employed within three months of graduation. Types of employment entered: accounting, banking, chemical industry, communications, computer-related, consulting, consumer products, education, engineering, finance, financial services, government, health services, high technology, human resources, information systems/technology, international trade, law, management, manufacturing, marketing, media, nonprofit, pharmaceutical, real estate, retail, service industry, telecommunications, transportation, utilities.

Business Program(s) URL: http://www.richmond.ac.uk

Program Contact: Ms. Catherine Byrne, Assistant Dean of Graduate Admissions, 16 Young Street, London, England W8 5EH, United Kingdom. Phone: 44-171-368-8475; Fax: 44-171-376-0836; E-mail: grad@richmond.ac.uk
See full description on page 946.

Schiller International University

Business Programs

London, England, United Kingdom

OVERVIEW
Schiller International University is an independent-nonprofit, coed institution. Founded: 1964. The graduate business unit is in an urban setting and is on a semester calendar.

HIGHLIGHTS

Enrollment Profile
Full-time: N/R
Part-time: N/R
Total: N/R
Average Age: N/R
Fall 1997 Average GPA: N/R

International: N/R
Women: N/R
Minorities: N/R
Average Class Size: 15
Fall 1997 Average GMAT: N/R

Costs
Full-time tuition: N/R
Part-time tuition: N/R

Degree(s) offered in conjunction with Schiller France, Schiller Germany, Schiller Spain, Schiller Switzerland, Schiller United States

GRADUATE BUSINESS PROGRAMS
Master of Business Administration in International Business (MBA) Full-time, part-time; 62 total credits required; 12 months to 3 years to complete program.

Master of Business Administration in Hotel Management (MBA) Full-time, part-time; 62 total credits required; 12 months to 3 years to complete program.

Master of Arts in International Hotel and Tourism Management (MA) Full-time; 45 total credits required; 12 months to 3 years to complete program.

Master of Arts in International Relations and Diplomacy (MA) Full-time, part-time; 62 total credits required; 12 months to 3 years to complete program.

ADMISSION
Application Requirements GMAT score, application form, application fee, bachelor's degree (must be in field of business), personal statement, college transcript(s).

Recommended for Application Minimum GPA: 3.0, work experience, computer experience.

Application Deadline Applications processed on a rolling/continuous basis for both domestic and international students. Application fee: $35. Deferred entrance is available.

ACADEMICS
Faculty Full-time 12; part-time 48.

Teaching Methodologies Case study, computer-aided instruction, computer analysis, experiential learning, faculty seminars, field projects, group discussion, lecture, research, seminars by members of the business community, student presentations, study groups, team projects.

Technology 10 on-campus computer terminals/PCs are available for student use. The network has partial access to the Internet. Students are not required to have their own PC.

Special Opportunities Advanced credit may be earned through credit by examination, transfer of credits from another institution. International exchange programs in France, Germany, Spain, Switzerland, United States. An internship program is available.

FINANCES
Costs for 1997–98 Cost varies by academic program, campus location, number of credits taken. Fees vary by academic program, campus location. Room and board costs vary by campus location, occupancy (e.g., single, double, triple).

Financial Aid Grants, scholarships, loans available. Application Deadline: 3/30.

Financial Aid Contact Mr. James Sutherland, Financial Aid Officer, 453 Edgewater Drive, Dunedin, England 34698, United Kingdom. Phone: 813-736-5082; Fax: 813-734-0359.

FACILITIES
Information Resources Main library; total holdings of 10,403 volumes, 105 current periodical subscriptions.

INTERNATIONAL STUDENTS
Demographics N/R

Services and Facilities International student office, international student center, international student housing, ESL courses, counseling/support services.

Applying TOEFL: minimum score of 550 recommended. Financial aid is available to international students.

International Student Contact Ms. Karynn Selman, Associate Director of Admissions, 51-55 Waterloo Road, London, England SE1 8TX, United Kingdom. Phone: 44-171-928-8484; Fax: 44-171-620-1226.

PLACEMENT
Services include alumni network, career placement, and resume preparation.

Employment Types of employment entered: accounting, banking, communications, computer-related, consulting, education, engineering, finance, financial services, government, health services, hospitality management, human resources, information systems/technology, insurance, international trade, law, management, marketing, retail, service industry, telecommunications, transportation, utilities.

Business Program(s) URL: http://www.schiller.edu/

Program Contact: Dr. Christoph Leibrecht, Director of Admissions, 453 Edgewater Drive, Dunedin, England 34698-7532, United Kingdom. Phone: 813-736-5082; Fax: 813-734-0359; E-mail: study@campus.schiller.edu

Sheffield Hallam University

Business School

Sheffield, England, United Kingdom

OVERVIEW
Sheffield Hallam University is a publicly supported, coed institution. Enrollment: 18,000 graduate, professional, and undergraduate students; 1,000 full-time matriculated graduate/professional students; 3,000 part-time matriculated graduate/professional students. Founded: 1969. The graduate business unit is in an urban setting and is on a semester calendar.

HIGHLIGHTS

Enrollment Profile
Full-time: 200
Part-time: 1,000
Total: 1,200
Average Age: 27
Fall 1997 Average GPA: N/R

International: 54%
Women: 38%
Minorities: N/R
Average Class Size: 20
Fall 1997 Average GMAT: 550

Costs
Full-time tuition: £7750 per academic year (resident); £7750 per academic year (nonresident)
Part-time tuition: £1300 per semester (resident); £1300 per semester (nonresident)

Sheffield Hallam University (continued)

Degree(s) offered in conjunction with Technical University (Prague), Tampee Institute (Finland), Fachhochschule (Germany)

GRADUATE BUSINESS PROGRAMS

International MBA (MBA) Full-time, part-time; 180 total credits required; 12 months to 3 years to complete program. Concentrations in management, international business.

Master of Business Administration (MBA) Part-time, distance learning option; 180 total credits required; 2 to 4 years to complete program. Concentration in management.

Master of Science in International Business (MS) Full-time, part-time; 180 total credits required; 12 months to 3 years to complete program. Concentration in international business.

Master of Science in International Marketing (MS) Full-time, part-time; 180 total credits required; 12 months to 3 years to complete program. Concentration in international marketing.

Master of Science in Organization Development (MS) Full-time, part-time; 180 total credits required; 12 months to 3 years to complete program. Concentration in organizational behavior/development.

Master of Science in Human Resource Management (MS) Full-time, part-time; 180 total credits required; 12 months to 3 years to complete program. Concentration in human resources.

Master of Science in Strategic Information Systems Management (MS) Full-time, part-time; 180 total credits required; 12 months to 3 years to complete program. Concentration in management information systems.

MBA (for Professional Services) (MBA) Part-time; 180 total credits required; 2 to 4 years to complete program. Concentrations in management, public management.

Master of Science in Human Resource Development (MS) Full-time, part-time; 180 total credits required; 12 months to 3 years to complete program. Concentration in human resources.

Master of Science in Management Studies (MS) Full-time, part-time; 180 total credits required; 12 months to 3 years to complete program. Concentration in management.

MS in Total Quality Management (MS) distance learning option; 2 to 4 years to complete program. Concentration in quality management.

MS in Business Process Development (MS) distance learning option; 2 to 4 years to complete program. Concentration in system management.

MS in Operational Research (MS) distance learning option; 2 to 4 years to complete program. Concentration in management science.

MA in Finance and Banking (MA) Part-time; 2 to 4 years to complete program. Concentrations in banking, financial management/planning, accounting.

European MBA (MBA) Full-time; 12 months to 3 years to complete program.

MS in Operational Research for Health Services (MS) distance learning option; 180 total credits required; 2 to 4 years to complete program. Concentrations in banking, financial management/planning, accounting.

MS in Operational Research for Health Services (MS) distance learning option; 2 to 4 years to complete program. Concentration in management science.

Master of Business Administration in Information Technology Management (MBA) distance learning option; 3 to 5 years to complete program. Concentrations in management, management information systems, system management, information management.

Master of Business Administration in Financial Management (MBA) Part-time, distance learning option; 3 to 5 years to complete program. Concentrations in management, financial management/planning, international finance.

Master of Business Administration in Financial Services (MBA) Part-time; 3 to 5 years to complete program. Concentrations in management, banking, insurance, international banking.

MBA in Consultancy (MBA) Full-time; 3 to 5 years to complete program. Concentrations in management, european business studies.

ADMISSION

Applications For fall 1997 there were 2,000 applications for admission. Of those applying, 1,200 were accepted. Of those accepted, 800 enrolled.

Application Requirements GMAT score: minimum 500, application form, bachelor's degree, 2 letters of recommendation, personal statement, resume, college transcript(s), minimum of 2 years of work experience.

Application Deadline 7/31 for fall, 11/30 for winter, 7/31 for fall (international), 11/30 for winter (international). Deferred entrance is available.

ACADEMICS

Faculty Full-time 100; part-time 30.

Teaching Methodologies Case study, computer simulations, experiential learning, field projects, group discussion, lecture, research, seminars by members of the business community, simulations, student presentations, team projects.

Technology 1,000 on-campus computer terminals/PCs are available for student use and are linked by a campus-wide network. The network has full access to the Internet. Students are not required to have their own PC.

Special Opportunities Advanced credit may be earned through credit by examination, credit for experience, transfer of credits from another institution. International exchange programs in Australia, Canada, France, Germany, United States.

FINANCES

Costs for 1997–98 Tuition: Full-time: £7750 per program (resident); £7750 per program (nonresident). Part-time: £1300 per semester (resident); £1300 per semester (nonresident). Cost varies by number of credits taken, reciprocity agreements. Average 1997–98 room and board costs were £2000 per academic year (on campus) and £2000 per academic year (off campus). Room and board costs vary by campus location, occupancy (e.g., single, double, triple), type of accommodation, type of meal plan.

Financial Aid Research assistantships available.

Financial Aid Contact Ms. Jayne Barker, Business School Postgraduate Programme Coordinator (MBA), BITC Building, Howard Street, Sheffield, England S1 1WB, United Kingdom. Phone: 44-114-253-2820; Fax: 44-114-225-5268; E-mail: sbs.pgdinfo@shu.ac.uk

FACILITIES

Information Resources Library and Learning Centre (Adsetts Centre) plus 4 additional on-campus libraries; total holdings of 500,000 volumes, 16,000 microforms, 3,700 current periodical subscriptions. CD player(s) available for graduate student use. Access provided to online bibliographic retrieval services and online databases.

INTERNATIONAL STUDENTS

Demographics 54% of students enrolled are international students [Africa, 5%, Asia, 20%, Europe, 60%, North America, 5%, other, 10%].

Services and Facilities International student office, international student housing, visa services, ESL courses, counseling/support services.

Applying IELT: minimum score of 5.5, TOEFL: minimum score of 500 required. Proof of adequate funds recommended. Financial aid is not available to international students.

International Student Contact John Kirk, Business Development Officer (International Officer), International Office, Pond Street, Sheffield, England S1 1WB, United Kingdom. Phone: 44-114-253-3930; Fax: 44-114-253-2046; E-mail: j.kirk@shu.ac.uk

PLACEMENT

Services include alumni network, career library, career placement, and resume preparation. In 1996–97, 200 organizations participated in on-campus recruiting; 200 on-campus interviews were conducted.

Employment Of 1996–97 graduates, 100% were employed within three months of graduation. Types of employment entered: banking, chemical industry, computer-related, education, energy, engineering, finance, financial services, health services, high technology, human resources, information systems/technology, international trade, management, manufacturing, marketing, nonprofit, retail, service industry, telecommunications, transportation, utilities.

Business Program(s) URL: http://www.shu.ac.uk/

Program Contact: Ms. Joanne Houghton, Business School Postgraduate Programme Admissions Officer, B.I.T.C. Building, Howard Street, Sheffield, England S1 1WB, United Kingdom. Phone: 44-114-253-2820; Fax: 44-114-225-5268; E-mail: sbs.pgdinfo@shu.ac.uk

South Bank University

Business School

London, England, United Kingdom

OVERVIEW

South Bank University is a publicly supported, coed institution. Enrollment: 18,000 graduate, professional, and undergraduate students. Founded: 1894. The graduate business unit is in an urban setting and is on a semester calendar.

HIGHLIGHTS

Enrollment Profile

Full-time: 300
Part-time: 700
Total: 1,000
Average Age: 29
Fall 1997 Average GPA: N/R

International: N/R
Women: 50%
Minorities: N/R
Average Class Size: 20
Fall 1997 Average GMAT: N/R

Costs

Full-time tuition: £6250 per academic year (resident); £7900 per academic year (nonresident)
Part-time tuition: N/R

GRADUATE BUSINESS PROGRAMS

Master of Business Administration (MBA) Part-time; 18 months to 2.5 years to complete program. Concentrations in management, marketing, organizational behavior/development, organizational management, strategic management, financial management/planning, accounting, business policy/strategy, human resources.

Master of Science (MS) Full-time, part-time; 18 months to 2 years to complete program. Concentrations in public policy and administration, human resources, international business, technology management.

Master of Business Administration in International Management (MBA) Full-time; minimum of 18 months to complete program.

European MBA (MBA) Full-time; minimum of 18 months to complete program.

ADMISSION

Application Requirements Application form, bachelor's degree, interview, 2 letters of recommendation, resume, college transcript(s), minimum of 2 years of work experience.

Recommended for Application Computer experience.

Application Deadline 9/15 for fall, 9/15 for fall (international). Application fee: £100. Deferred entrance is available.

ACADEMICS

Faculty Full-time 200; part-time 200.

Teaching Methodologies Case study, field projects, group discussion, lecture, role playing, seminars by members of the business community, simulations, student presentations, study groups, team projects.

Technology 1,000 on-campus computer terminals/PCs are available for student use and are linked by a campus-wide network. The network has full access to the Internet. Students are not required to have their own PC.

Special Opportunities Advanced credit may be earned through credit by examination, transfer of credits from another institution. International exchange programs in Finland, France, Germany, Spain.

FINANCES

Costs for 1997–98 Tuition: Full-time: £6250 per program (resident); £7900 per program (nonresident). Cost varies by campus location. Average 1997–98 room only costs were £1800 per academic year. Room and board costs vary by type of accommodation.

Financial Aid Contact Mr. Charles Fenech, MBA Program Director, 103 Borough Road, London, England SE1 0AA, United Kingdom. Phone: 44-171-815-7783; Fax: 44-171-815-8280.

INTERNATIONAL STUDENTS

Demographics N/R

Services and Facilities International student office, international student housing, ESL courses, counseling/support services.

Applying IELT: minimum score of 6, TOEFL: minimum score of 600 required. Financial aid is not available to international students.

International Student Contact Ms. Maggie Hammond, Student Support Office, 103 Borough Road, London, England SE1 0AA, United Kingdom. Phone: 44-171-815-6401.

PLACEMENT

Services include alumni network, career counseling/planning, career placement, and resume preparation.

Employment Types of employment entered: consulting, finance, government, information systems/technology, management, service industry.

Program Contact: Mr. Charles Fenech, MBA Program Director, 103 Borough Road, London, England SE1 0AA, United Kingdom. Phone: 44-171-815-7783; Fax: 44-171-815-8280.

University of Bath

School of Management

Bath, England, United Kingdom

OVERVIEW

The University of Bath is a federally supported, coed institution. Enrollment: 8,171 graduate, professional, and undergraduate students; 1,097 full-time matriculated graduate/professional students; 1,966 part-time matriculated graduate/professional students. Founded: 1966. The graduate business unit is in a suburban setting and is on a term (MSC in Management: semesters) calendar.

HIGHLIGHTS

Enrollment Profile

Full-time: 163
Part-time: 306
Total: 469
Average Age: 33
Fall 1997 Average GPA: N/R

International: 38%
Women: 35%
Minorities: N/R
Average Class Size: 35
Fall 1997 Average GMAT: 550

Costs

Full-time tuition: £11,000 per academic year (resident); £11,000 per academic year (nonresident)
Part-time tuition: £7000 per year (resident); £7000 per year (nonresident)

Degree(s) offered in conjunction with Malaysian Institute of Management

GRADUATE BUSINESS PROGRAMS

Full-time MBA (MBA) Full-time; 75 total credits required; 3 years full-time business experience and GMAT score: minimum 550 required; 12 to 18 months to complete program. Concentrations in management, entrepreneurship, strategic management, business policy/strategy.

Executive MBA (MBA) Part-time; 75 total credits required; 5 years full-time business experience and GMAT score: minimum 550 required; 2 to 2.5 years to complete program. Concentrations in management, strategic management, international business, business policy/strategy.

Master of Science in Management (MSc) Full-time; 60 total credits required; open only to non-business graduates, with minimum 2nd class honours degree; 12 to 15 months to complete program. Concentration in management.

Master of Science in Management and Strategic Information Systems (MSc) Full-time; 60 total credits required; minimum 2nd class honours degree required; 12 to 15 months to complete program. Concentrations in management, management information systems.

Modular MBA (MBA) Part-time; 75 total credits required; minimum of 3 years full-time business experience and GMAT score: minimum 550 required; 3 to 8 years to complete program. Concentrations in management, strategic management, business policy/strategy.

MIM-Bath Executive MBA (MBA) Part-time; 75 total credits required; minimum of 5 years full-time business experience and GMAT score: minimum 550 required; 2 to 2.5 years to complete program. Concentrations in management, strategic management, international business, business policy/strategy.

MSc in Responsibility and Business Practice (MSc) Part-time; 75 total credits required; 2 to 2.5 years to complete program. Concentrations in business ethics, environmental economics/management.

Master of Philosophy in Purchasing and Supply (MPhil) Part-time; 75 total credits required; 2 to 2.5 years to complete program. Concentration in materials management.

Research MPhil/PhD (MPhil/PhD) Full-time, part-time; 2 to 5 years to complete program. Concentrations in management, management information systems, environmental economics/management, international business, marketing, human resources, organizational behavior/development, international marketing, construction management, industrial/labor relations, operations management, materials management, production management, technology management.

MSc in Management with Marketing (MSc) Full-time; 60 total credits required; open only to non-business graduates, with minimum 2nd class honours degree; 12 to 15 months to complete program. Concentrations in management, marketing.

Master of Science in Management with Human Resource Management (MSc) Full-time; 60 total credits required; 12 to 15 months to complete program. Concentrations in management, human resources.

Master of Science in Management with Financial Management (MSc) Full-time; 60 total credits required; 12 to 15 months to complete program. Concentrations in management, finance.

University of Bath (continued)

Master of Science in Management with Accounting and Information Systems (MSc) Full-time; 60 total credits required; 12 to 15 months to complete program. Concentrations in management, accounting, management information systems.

ADMISSION
Applications For fall 1997 there were 574 applications for admission. Of those applying, 303 were accepted. Of those accepted, 134 enrolled.

Application Requirements GMAT score, application form, bachelor's degree, 2 letters of recommendation, personal statement, resume, college transcript(s), minimum of 3 years of work experience.

Recommended for Application Interview, computer experience.

Application Deadline 8/31 for fall, 8/31 for fall (international). Deferred entrance is available.

ACADEMICS
Faculty Full-time 50; part-time 35.

Teaching Methodologies Case study, computer analysis, experiential learning, faculty seminars, field projects, group discussion, lecture, research, role playing, seminars by members of the business community, simulations, student presentations, study groups, team projects.

Technology 400 on-campus computer terminals/PCs are available for student use and are linked by a campus-wide network. The network has full access to the Internet. Students are not required to have their own PC.

Special Opportunities Advanced credit may be earned through credit by examination.

FINANCES
Costs for 1997–98 Tuition: Full-time: £11,000 per year (resident); £11,000 per year (nonresident). Part-time: £7000 per year (resident); £7000 per year (nonresident). Cost varies by academic program, class time (e.g., day/evening), number of credits taken. Average 1997–98 room only costs were £2500 per academic year (on campus) and £2500 per academic year (off campus). Room and board costs vary by campus location, occupancy (e.g., single, double, triple), type of accommodation.

Financial Aid In 1997–98, 2% of students received some institutionally administered aid in the form of research assistantships, scholarships. Application Deadline: 6/30.

Financial Aid Contact Director of Research/Course Administrator, Claverton Down, Bath, England BA2 7AY, United Kingdom. Phone: 44-1225-826742; Fax: 44-1225-826473.

FACILITIES
Information Resources University of Bath Library; total holdings of 450,000 volumes, 5,000 microforms, 2,500 current periodical subscriptions. CD player(s) available for graduate student use. Access provided to online bibliographic retrieval services and online databases.

INTERNATIONAL STUDENTS
Demographics 38% of students enrolled are international students [Africa, 2%, Asia, 42%, Australia/New Zealand, 5%, Central America, 1%, Europe, 25%, North America, 12%, South America, 4%, other, 9%].

Services and Facilities International student office, international student housing, ESL courses, counseling/support services, international student organization.

Applying IELT: minimum score of 6.5, TOEFL: minimum score of 600, proof of adequate funds, proof of health/immunizations required. TSE, TWE recommended. Financial aid is available to international students.

International Student Contact Ms. Carla Dewhurst, International Officer, Clavertown Down, Bath, England BA2 7AY, United Kingdom. Phone: 44-1225-826832; Fax: 44-1225-826366; E-mail: international_office@bath.ac.uk

PLACEMENT
Services include alumni network, career counseling/planning, career fairs, career library, job interviews arranged, job search course, resume referral to employers, and resume preparation. In 1996–97, 98 organizations participated in on-campus recruiting; 550 on-campus interviews were conducted.

Employment Of 1996–97 graduates, 70% were employed within three months of graduation; the average starting salary was £33,000. Types of employment entered: accounting, banking, chemical industry, communications, computer-related, consulting, consumer products, energy, engineering, finance, financial services, health services, high technology, human resources, information systems/technology, international trade, management, manufacturing, marketing, nonprofit, petrochemical, pharmaceutical, retail, service industry, telecommunications, utilities.

Business Program(s) URL: http://www.bath.ac.uk/Departments/Management

Program Contact: MBA Administrator, Claverton Down, Bath, England BA2 7AY, United Kingdom. Phone: 44-122-826-152; Fax: 44-1225-826-210; E-mail: mba-info@management.bath.ac.uk

University of Birmingham

Birmingham Business School
Birmingham, England, United Kingdom

OVERVIEW
The University of Birmingham coed institution. Enrollment: 19,204 graduate, professional, and undergraduate students; 3,299 full-time matriculated graduate/professional students; 2,220 part-time matriculated graduate/professional students. Founded: 1899. The graduate business unit is in a suburban setting and is on a semester calendar.

HIGHLIGHTS

Enrollment Profile

Full-time: 127	International: N/R
Part-time: 230	Women: N/R
Total: 357	Minorities: N/R
Average Age: 31	Average Class Size: N/R
Fall 1997 Average GPA: N/R	Fall 1997 Average GMAT: 590

Costs
Full-time tuition: N/R
Part-time tuition: N/R

Degree(s) offered in conjunction with École Superieure de Commerce

GRADUATE BUSINESS PROGRAMS
International Master of Business Administration (IMBA) Full-time, part-time; 12 months to 2 years to complete program. Concentration in management.

Master of Business Administration in European Business (MBA) Full-time; 12 months to 2 years to complete program.

Master of Business Administration in International Banking and Finance (MBA) Full-time; 12 months to 2 years to complete program.

Executive MBA (MBA) Part-time.

ADMISSION
Applications For fall 1997 there were 2,200 applications for admission. Of those applying, 480 were accepted. Of those accepted, 332 enrolled.

Application Requirements Application form, 2 letters of recommendation, minimum of 5 years of work experience.

Recommended for Application GMAT score accepted.

Application Deadline Applications processed on a rolling/continuous basis for both domestic and international students.

ACADEMICS
Faculty Full-time 45; part-time 8.

Teaching Methodologies Case study, lecture, student presentations, team projects.

Technology 300 on-campus computer terminals/PCs are available for student use and are linked by a campus-wide network. The network has full access to the Internet. Students are not required to have their own PC.

FINANCES
Costs for 1997–98 Cost varies by academic program. Average 1997–98 room and board costs were £4500 per academic year. Room and board costs vary by campus location, occupancy (e.g., single, double, triple), type of accommodation, type of meal plan.

Financial Aid Contact Mr. David Perman, Program Director, Priorsfield 46, Edgbaston, England B15 2RU, United Kingdom. Phone: 44-121-414-6693; Fax: 44-121-414-3553; E-mail: mba@bham.ac.uk

FACILITIES
Information Resources Main library plus 5 additional on-campus libraries; total holdings of 2,500,000 volumes. CD player(s) available for graduate student use. Access provided to online bibliographic retrieval services.

INTERNATIONAL STUDENTS
Demographics N/R

Services and Facilities International student center, international student housing, visa services, ESL courses, counseling/support services.

Applying IELT: minimum score of 5.5, TOEFL: minimum score of 550 required. Financial aid is available to international students.

International Student Contact Mr. David Perman, Program Director, Priorsfield 46 Edgbaston Park Road, Birmingham, England B15 2RU, United Kingdom. Phone: 44-121-414-6693; Fax: 44-121-414-3553.

PLACEMENT
Services include alumni network, career placement, job search course, resume referral to employers, and resume preparation.

Employment Types of employment entered: accounting, banking, manufacturing, service industry.

Business Program(s) URL: http://www.bham.ac.uk/business/

Program Contact: Mr. David Perman, Program Director, Priorsfield 46, Edgbaston Park Road, Birmingham, England B15 2RU, United Kingdom. Phone: 44-121-414-6693; Fax: 44-121-414-3553; E-mail: mba@bham.ac.uk

University of Bradford

Bradford Management Center

Bradford, West Yorkshire, United Kingdom

OVERVIEW
The University of Bradford is a federally supported, coed institution. The graduate business unit is in a suburban setting and is on a term calendar.

HIGHLIGHTS

Enrollment Profile

Full-time: 80	International: 30%
Part-time: 70	Women: 33%
Total: 150	Minorities: N/R
Average Age: 31	Average Class Size: N/R
Fall 1997 Average GPA: N/R	Fall 1997 Average GMAT: 590

Costs
Full-time tuition: £9250 per academic year (resident); £9750 per academic year (nonresident)
Part-time tuition: N/R

Degree(s) offered in conjunction with NIMBAS Graduate School of Management (Netherlands)

GRADUATE BUSINESS PROGRAMS
Master of Business Administration (MBA) Full-time, part-time, distance learning option; 12 months to 6 years to complete program. Concentrations in accounting, economics, financial management/planning, human resources, international business, management science, marketing, operations management, production management, quality management, strategic management.

ADMISSION
Applications For fall 1997 there were 600 applications for admission. Of those applying, 250 were accepted. Of those accepted, 150 enrolled.

Application Requirements Application form, application fee, bachelor's degree, 2 letters of recommendation, minimum of 3 years of work experience.

Recommended for Application GMAT score accepted: minimum 550, interview, resume, college transcript(s), computer experience: computer literacy, Microsoft Windows 95.

Application Deadline 8/15 for fall, 8/15 for fall (international). Deferred entrance is available.

ACADEMICS
Faculty Full-time 60; part-time 40.

Teaching Methodologies Case study, computer-aided instruction, computer analysis, computer simulations, experiential learning, faculty seminars, group discussion, lecture, research, role playing, seminars by members of the business community, simulations, student presentations, study groups, team projects.

Technology 150 on-campus computer terminals/PCs are available for student use and are linked by a campus-wide network. The network has full access to the Internet. Students are not required to have their own PC.

Special Opportunities Advanced credit may be earned through credit by examination. International exchange programs in France, Netherlands.

FINANCES
Costs for 1997–98 Tuition: Full-time: £9250 per year (resident); £9750 per year (nonresident). Cost varies by academic program. Average 1997–98 room only costs were £2600 per academic year (on campus) and £2500 per academic year (off campus).

FACILITIES
Information Resources J. B. Priestley Library plus 2 additional on-campus libraries; total holdings of 550,000 volumes. CD player(s) available for graduate student use. Access provided to online bibliographic retrieval services and online databases.

INTERNATIONAL STUDENTS
Demographics 30% of students enrolled are international students [Africa, 8%, Asia, 30%, Australia/New Zealand, 5%, Europe, 44%, North America, 8%, South America, 5%].

Services and Facilities International student housing, counseling/support services.

Applying IELT: minimum score of 7, TOEFL: minimum score of 550, proof of adequate funds required. Financial aid is not available to international students.

International Student Contact Mrs. Gail Barbour, MBA Administrative Secretary, Bradford Management Centre, Emm Lake, Bradford, West Yorkshire BD9 4JL,

United Kingdom. Phone: 44-1274-234-373; Fax: 44-1274-232-311; E-mail: g.h.barbour@bradford.ac.uk

PLACEMENT
Services include alumni network, career counseling/planning, career fairs, career library, career placement, job search course, resume referral to employers, and resume preparation.

Employment Of 1996–97 graduates, 85% were employed within three months of graduation; the average starting salary was £39,000. Types of employment entered: accounting, banking, chemical industry, communications, computer-related, consulting, consumer products, education, energy, engineering, finance, financial services, government, health services, high technology, hospitality management, human resources, information systems/technology, insurance, international trade, law, management, manufacturing, marketing, media, nonprofit, petrochemical, pharmaceutical, real estate, retail, service industry, telecommunications, transportation, utilities.

Business Program(s) URL: http://www.brad.ac.uk/acad/mancen/

Program Contact: Mrs. Gail Barbour, MBA Administrative Secretary, Bradford Management Centre, Emm Lane, Bradford, West Yorkshire BD9 4JL, United Kingdom. Phone: 44-127-234-373; Fax: 44-1274-232-311; E-mail: g.h.barbour@bradford.ac.uk

University of Brighton

Center for Management Development

Brighton, Sussex, United Kingdom

OVERVIEW
The University of Brighton is a federally supported, coed institution. Enrollment: 11,000 graduate, professional, and undergraduate students; 504 full-time matriculated graduate/professional students; 1,719 part-time matriculated graduate/professional students. Founded: 1970. The graduate business unit is in a small-town setting and is on a semester calendar.

HIGHLIGHTS

Enrollment Profile

Full-time: 30	International: 67%
Part-time: 250	Women: 68%
Total: 280	Minorities: N/R
Average Age: 27	Average Class Size: 25
Fall 1997 Average GPA: N/R	Fall 1997 Average GMAT: 550

Costs
Full-time tuition: £6360 per academic year (resident); £7350 per academic year (nonresident)
Part-time tuition: N/R

Degree(s) offered in conjunction with various institutions in Europe

GRADUATE BUSINESS PROGRAMS
Master of Business Administration/Master of Science in Technology Management (MBA/MS) Concentrations in accounting, finance, technology management, system management, manufacturing management, materials management, management information systems, quality management, quantitative analysis, project management.

Executive MBA (MBA) Part-time; 140 total credits required; 3 to 5 years to complete program. Concentrations in accounting, european business studies, economics, finance, human resources, international business, management, management information systems, marketing, operations management, organizational behavior/development, strategic management, travel industry/tourism management.

Master of Business Administration (MBA) Full-time; 120 total credits required; 12 to 16 months to complete program. Concentrations in accounting, european business studies, economics, finance, human resources, international banking, management, management information systems, marketing research, operations management, organizational behavior/development, strategic management, travel industry/tourism management, entrepreneurship, international marketing, public policy and administration, management consulting, technology management.

ADMISSION
Applications For fall 1997 there were 112 applications for admission. Of those applying, 26 were accepted. Of those accepted, 26 enrolled.

Application Requirements Application form, application fee, bachelor's degree, interview, 2 letters of recommendation, personal statement, resume, college transcript(s), minimum of 3 years of work experience.

Recommended for Application GMAT score accepted.

Application Deadline 8/30 for fall, 1/30 for spring, 8/30 for fall (international), 1/30 for spring (international). Application fee: £10. Deferred entrance is available.

University of Brighton (continued)

ACADEMICS

Faculty Full-time 45; part-time 10.

Teaching Methodologies Case study, lecture, research, seminars by members of the business community, student presentations, study groups, team projects.

Technology 130 on-campus computer terminals/PCs are available for student use and are linked by a campus-wide network. The network has full access to the Internet. Students are not required to have their own PC.

Special Opportunities International exchange programs in France, Germany, Italy, Spain, United States.

FINANCES

Costs for 1997–98 Tuition: Full-time: £6360 per year (resident); £7350 per year (nonresident). Cost varies by academic program, reciprocity agreements. Average 1997–98 room only costs were £1900 per academic year (on campus) and £1900 per academic year (off campus). Room and board costs vary by occupancy (e.g., single, double, triple).

Financial Aid In 1997–98, 1% of students received some institutionally administered aid in the form of scholarships. Application Deadline: 6/30.

Financial Aid Contact Ms. Julie Grahem, Administrator, Academic Registry, Mithras House, Lewes Road, Brighton, East Sussex BN2 4AT, United Kingdom. Phone: 44-1273-642-821; Fax: 44-1273-642-825.

FACILITIES

Information Resources Aldrich Library plus 2 additional on-campus libraries. CD player(s) available for graduate student use. Access provided to online bibliographic retrieval services.

INTERNATIONAL STUDENTS

Demographics 67% of students enrolled are international students [Africa, 1%, Asia, 24%, Australia/New Zealand, 1%, Central America, 5%, Europe, 40%, North America, 2%, South America, 5%, other, 22%].

Services and Facilities International student office, international student center, ESL courses, counseling/support services, language tutoring.

Applying IELT: minimum score of 6.5, TOEFL: minimum score of 590 required. Financial aid is available to international students.

International Student Contact Mr. Sean Tonkin, Senior Program Administrator, MBA Program, Mithras House, Lewes Road, Brighton, Sussex BN2 4AT, United Kingdom. Phone: 44-1273-642-794; Fax: 44-1273-642-980.

PLACEMENT

Services include alumni network, career counseling/planning, career library, resume referral to employers, and resume preparation.

Employment Of 1996–97 graduates, 80% were employed within three months of graduation. Types of employment entered: accounting, banking, communications, computer-related, consulting, consumer products, education, engineering, finance, financial services, government, health services, high technology, hospitality management, international trade, management, manufacturing, nonprofit, pharmaceutical, retail, service industry, telecommunications.

Business Program(s) URL: http://www.bus.bton.ac.uk/FTNT/BusSchool/Depts/CMD/CMD.html

Program Contact: Mr. Sean Tonkin, Senior Program Administrator, MBA Program, Mithras House, Lewes Road, Brighton, Sussex BN2 4AT, United Kingdom. Phone: 44-1273-642-794; Fax: 44-1273-642-980.

University of Bristol

Graduate School of International Business

Bristol, England, United Kingdom

OVERVIEW

The University of Bristol is a federally supported, coed institution. Enrollment: 11,000 graduate, professional, and undergraduate students. Founded: 1867. The graduate business unit is in an urban setting and is on a semester calendar.

HIGHLIGHTS

Enrollment Profile

Full-time: 60	International: N/R
Part-time: 10	Women: N/R
Total: 70	Minorities: N/R
Average Age: 28	Average Class Size: 30
Fall 1997 Average GPA: N/R	Fall 1997 Average GMAT: 500

Costs

Full-time tuition: N/R
Part-time tuition: £13,500 per program (resident); £13,500 per program (nonresident)

Degree(s) offered in conjunction with École Nationale des Ponts et Chaussées, University of Ljubljana, University of Hong Kong, University of Katowice

GRADUATE BUSINESS PROGRAMS

MBA in International Business (MBA) Full-time, part-time; 15 total credits required; up to 15 months to complete program. Concentrations in accounting, economics, entrepreneurship, finance, human resources, international business, management, marketing, organizational behavior/development, quantitative analysis, strategic management, banking, business ethics, business law, european business studies, information management, international finance, international economics, international marketing, japanese business studies, leadership, international management, project management, technology management.

Executive MBA (MBA) Part-time; up to 2 years to complete program. Concentrations in accounting, economics, entrepreneurship, finance, human resources, international business, management, marketing, organizational behavior/development, quantitative analysis, strategic management, banking, business ethics, business law, european business studies, information management, international finance, international economics, international marketing, japanese business studies, leadership, international management, project management, technology management.

ADMISSION

Applications For fall 1997 there were 300 applications for admission. Of those applying, 90 were accepted. Of those accepted, 60 enrolled.

Application Requirements Application form, application fee, bachelor's degree, interview, 3 letters of recommendation, personal statement, resume, minimum of 2 years of work experience.

Recommended for Application Computer experience.

Application Deadline 8/15 for fall, 8/15 for fall (international). Application fee: £25. Deferred entrance is available.

ACADEMICS

Faculty Full-time 10; part-time 38.

Teaching Methodologies Case study, computer-aided instruction, computer simulations, experiential learning, faculty seminars, field projects, group discussion, lecture, research, seminars by members of the business community, student presentations, study groups, team projects.

Technology 100 on-campus computer terminals/PCs are available for student use and are linked by a campus-wide network. The network has full access to the Internet. Students are required to have their own PC.

Special Opportunities International exchange program available. An internship program is available.

FINANCES

Costs for 1997–98 Tuition: £13,500 per program (resident); £13,500 per program (nonresident).

Financial Aid In 1997–98, 1% of students received some institutionally administered aid in the form of scholarships. Application Deadline: 6/30.

Financial Aid Contact Ms. Judy Denham, Administrative Director, 10 Woodland Road, Bristol, England BS8 1UQ, United Kingdom. Phone: 44-117-973-7683; Fax: 44-117-973-7687; E-mail: gsintbus@bristol.ac.uk

FACILITIES

Information Resources Arts and Social Sciences Library plus 6 additional on-campus libraries. CD player(s) available for graduate student use. Access provided to online bibliographic retrieval services.

INTERNATIONAL STUDENTS

Demographics N/R

Services and Facilities International student office, international student center, ESL courses.

Applying IELT: minimum score of 7, TOEFL: minimum score of 600, proof of adequate funds required. Financial aid is available to international students.

International Student Contact Ms. Judy Denham, Administrative Director, 10 Woodland Road, Bristol, England BS8 1UQ, United Kingdom. Phone: 44-117-973-7683; Fax: 44-117-973-7687.

PLACEMENT

Services include alumni network, career counseling/planning, career fairs, career library, career placement, electronic job bank, job interviews arranged, job search course, resume referral to employers, and resume preparation.

Employment Of 1996–97 graduates, 95% were employed within three months of graduation. Types of employment entered: banking, communications, consulting, consumer products, energy, engineering, finance, financial services, high technology, information systems/technology, insurance, international trade, management, manufacturing, marketing, retail, service industry, telecommunications.

Business Program(s) URL: http://www.bris.ac.uk/Depts/MBA/

Program Contact: Ms. Judy Denham, Administrative Director, Graduate School of International Business, 10 Woodland Road, Bristol, England BS8 1UQ, United

Kingdom. Phone: 44-117-973-7683; Fax: 44-117-973-7687; E-mail: gsintbus@ bristol.ac.uk

See full description on page 1040.

University of Durham

Durham, England, United Kingdom

OVERVIEW
The University of Durham coed institution. Enrollment: 11,700 graduate, professional, and undergraduate students. Founded: 1832. The graduate business unit is in a small-town setting and is on a trimester calendar.

HIGHLIGHTS

Enrollment Profile

Full-time: 100	International: 20%
Part-time: 200	Women: 22%
Total: 300	Minorities: N/R
Average Age: 31	Average Class Size: 50
Fall 1997 Average GPA: N/R	Fall 1997 Average GMAT: N/R

Costs
Full-time tuition: N/R
Part-time tuition: N/R

GRADUATE BUSINESS PROGRAMS
Master of Business Administration (MBA) Full-time, part-time, distance learning option; 12 months to 4 years to complete program.

ADMISSION
Applications For fall 1997 there were 400 applications for admission. Of those applying, 140 were accepted. Of those accepted, 103 enrolled.
Application Requirements Application form, bachelor's degree, 2 letters of recommendation, personal statement, minimum of 2 years of work experience.
Recommended for Application GRE score accepted.
Application Deadline 8/30 for fall, 8/30 for fall (international). Deferred entrance is available.

ACADEMICS
Faculty Full-time 50; part-time 20.
Teaching Methodologies Case study, computer-aided instruction, computer simulations, experiential learning, faculty seminars, field projects, group discussion, lecture, research, role playing, seminars by members of the business community, simulations, student presentations, study groups, team projects.
Technology 150 on-campus computer terminals/PCs are available for student use and are linked by a campus-wide network. The network has full access to the Internet. Students are not required to have their own PC.

FINANCES
Costs for 1997–98 Cost varies by reciprocity agreements. Average 1997–98 room and board costs were £5500 per academic year. Room and board costs vary by campus location, occupancy (e.g., single, double, triple), type of accommodation, type of meal plan.
Financial Aid Contact Miss Anne-Marie Nevin, MBA Program Manager, Business School , Mill Hill Lane, Durham, England DH1 3LB, United Kingdom. Phone: 44-191-374-2203; Fax: 44-191-374-3748.

FACILITIES
Information Resources Durham University Library plus 1,000,000 additional on-campus libraries, 3,000 current periodical subscriptions. CD player(s) available for graduate student use. Access provided to online bibliographic retrieval services and online databases.

INTERNATIONAL STUDENTS
Demographics 20% of students enrolled are international students [Africa, 9%, Asia, 17%, Europe, 65%, other, 9%].
Services and Facilities International student office, international student center, ESL courses, counseling/support services.
Applying IELT: minimum score of 6.5, TOEFL: minimum score of 550, proof of adequate funds required. Financial aid is not available to international students.
International Student Contact Ms. Joanne Purves, International Student Coordinator, International Office, Old Shire Hall, Durham, England DM1 3HP, United Kingdom. Phone: 44-191-374-7219; Fax: 44-191-374-7216; E-mail: j.n. purves@durham.ac.uk

PLACEMENT
Services include alumni network, career counseling/planning, career fairs, career library, electronic job bank, job search course, resume referral to employers, and resume preparation.

Employment Types of employment entered: consulting, engineering, finance, financial services, information systems/technology, telecommunications.

Business Program(s) URL: http://www.dur.ac.uk/dubs/

Program Contact: Miss Anne-Marie Nevin, MBA Program Manager, Business School, Mill Hill Lane, Durham, England DH1 3LB, United Kingdom. Phone: 44-191-374-2203; Fax: 44-191-374-3748; E-mail: ms.dubs@durham.ac.uk

University of Edinburgh

Edinburgh, Scotland, United Kingdom

OVERVIEW
The University of Edinburgh is a federally supported, coed institution. Enrollment: 15,208 graduate, professional, and undergraduate students; 2,221 full-time matriculated graduate/professional students; 1,515 part-time matriculated graduate/professional students. Founded: 1583. The graduate business unit is in an urban setting and is on a trimester calendar.

HIGHLIGHTS

Enrollment Profile

Full-time: 100	International: 20%
Part-time: 250	Women: 29%
Total: 350	Minorities: N/R
Average Age: 31	Average Class Size: 40
Fall 1997 Average GPA: N/R	Fall 1997 Average GMAT: 590

Costs
Full-time tuition: £9300 per academic year (resident); £9900 per academic year (nonresident)
Part-time tuition: £8500 per program (resident); £8500 per program (nonresident)

GRADUATE BUSINESS PROGRAMS
Full-time MBA (MBA) Full-time; 12 months to complete program. Concentrations in management, entrepreneurship, finance, marketing, international business, nonprofit management, organizational behavior/development, nonprofit organization, operations management, strategic management.
Master of Science in Logistics (MS) Full-time; 12 months to complete program. Concentrations in logistics, technology management, business policy/strategy, international logistics.
Part-time MBA (MBA) Part-time; 2.5 to 3 years to complete program. Concentrations in management, entrepreneurship, finance, marketing, international business, nonprofit management, organizational behavior/development, technology management, operations management, strategic management.
Master of Science in Management Science and Operations Research (MS) Full-time; 12 months to complete program. Concentrations in international logistics, logistics, management, quantitative analysis, international business, management science.
Financial Mathematics (MS) Full-time; 12 months to complete program. Concentrations in finance, financial information systems, banking, risk management.

ADMISSION
Applications For fall 1997 there were 690 applications for admission. Of those applying, 170 were accepted. Of those accepted, 100 enrolled.
Application Requirements GMAT score: minimum 600, application form, essay, 2 letters of recommendation, personal statement, resume, college transcript(s), minimum of 2 years of work experience.
Recommended for Application Bachelor's degree, interview, computer experience.
Application Deadline Applications processed on a rolling/continuous basis for both domestic and international students. Deferred entrance is available.

ACADEMICS
Faculty Full-time 70; part-time 13.
Teaching Methodologies Case study, computer-aided instruction, computer simulations, experiential learning, faculty seminars, field projects, group discussion, lecture, research, seminars by members of the business community, simulations, student presentations, study groups, team projects.
Technology 60 on-campus computer terminals/PCs are available for student use and are linked by a campus-wide network. The network has full access to the Internet. Students are not required to have their own PC.
Special Opportunities Advanced credit may be earned through transfer of credits from another institution. An internship program is available.

FINANCES
Costs for 1997–98 Tuition: Full-time: £9300 per year (resident); £9900 per year (nonresident). Part-time: £8500 per program (resident); £8500 per program (nonresident). Cost varies by reciprocity agreements. Average 1997–98

University of Edinburgh (continued)

room and board costs were £5500 per academic year (on campus) and £7000 per academic year (off campus). Room and board costs vary by occupancy (e.g., single, double, triple), type of accommodation, type of meal plan.

Financial Aid In 1997–98, 7% of students received some institutionally administered aid in the form of scholarships.

Financial Aid Contact Mrs. Patricia Fraser, Full-time MBA Administrator, 7 Bristo Square, Edinburgh, Scotland EH8 9AL, United Kingdom. Phone: 44-131-650-8066; Fax: 44-131-650-6501; E-mail: trishf@ed.ac.uk

FACILITIES

Information Resources Edinburgh University Library plus 4 additional on-campus libraries; total holdings of 1,919,000 volumes, 150,000 microforms, 11,000 current periodical subscriptions. CD player(s) available for graduate student use. Access provided to online bibliographic retrieval services and online databases.

INTERNATIONAL STUDENTS

Demographics 20% of students enrolled are international students [Africa, 8%, Asia, 20%, Australia/New Zealand, 5%, Central America, 4%, Europe, 42%, North America, 15%, South America, 6%].

Services and Facilities International student office, international student center, international student housing, ESL courses, counseling/support services.

Applying IELT: minimum score of 6.5, TOEFL: minimum score of 580, TWE: minimum score of 5, proof of adequate funds, proof of health/immunizations required. Financial aid is not available to international students.

International Student Contact Mr. Richard Kerley, Director, 7 Bristo Square, Edinburgh, Scotland EH8 9AL, United Kingdom. Phone: 44-131-650-8068; Fax: 44-131-650-8077; E-mail: r.kerley@ed.ac.uk

PLACEMENT

Services include alumni network, career counseling/planning, career fairs, career library, electronic job bank, job search course, resume referral to employers, and resume preparation. In 1996–97, 100 organizations participated in on-campus recruiting; 50 on-campus interviews were conducted.

Employment Of 1996–97 graduates, 80% were employed within three months of graduation. Types of employment entered: accounting, banking, communications, computer-related, consulting, consumer products, education, energy, engineering, finance, financial services, government, health services, high technology, hospitality management, human resources, information systems/technology, insurance, international trade, law, management, manufacturing, marketing, media, nonprofit, pharmaceutical, real estate, retail, service industry, telecommunications, transportation, utilities.

Business Program(s) URL: http://www.ems.ed.ac.uk/

Program Contact: Ms. Patricia Fraser, Full-time MBA Administrator, 7 Bristo Square, Edinburgh, Scotland EH8 9AL, United Kingdom. Phone: 44-131-650-8066; Fax: 44-131-650-6501; E-mail: management.school@ed.ac.uk
See full description on page 1068.

University of Glasgow

University of Glasgow Business School

Glasgow, Scotland, United Kingdom

OVERVIEW

The University of Glasgow coed institution. Enrollment: 19,000 graduate, professional, and undergraduate students; 1,964 full-time matriculated graduate/professional students; 1,296 part-time matriculated graduate/professional students. Founded: 1451. The graduate business unit is in an urban setting and is on a trimester calendar.

HIGHLIGHTS

Enrollment Profile

Full-time: 28	International: 16%
Part-time: 155	Women: 34%
Total: 183	Minorities: N/R
Average Age: 32	Average Class Size: 45
Fall 1997 Average GPA: N/R	Fall 1997 Average GMAT: 600

Costs
Full-time tuition: N/R
Part-time tuition: N/R

GRADUATE BUSINESS PROGRAMS

Executive MBA (MBA) Part-time; 3 years to complete program. Concentrations in accounting, economics, entrepreneurship, finance, human resources, information management, international management, leadership, management, marketing, operations management, organizational behavior/development, organizational management, project management, strategic management, technology management.

International MBA (MBA) Full-time; 12 months to complete program. Concentrations in accounting, business law, economics, entrepreneurship, european business studies, finance, human resources, information management, international business, international finance, international trade, marketing, operations management, organizational behavior/development, organizational management, strategic management, technology management.

ADMISSION

Applications For fall 1997 there were 300 applications for admission. Of those applying, 80 were accepted.

Application Requirements GMAT score, application form, application fee, bachelor's degree, 2 letters of recommendation, college transcript(s), work experience.

Recommended for Application Minimum GPA, computer experience.

Application Deadline 9/1 for fall, 8/1 for fall (international). Application fee: 150 (international). Deferred entrance is available.

ACADEMICS

Faculty Full-time 73; part-time 9.

Teaching Methodologies Case study, computer-aided instruction, computer analysis, computer simulations, experiential learning, faculty seminars, field projects, group discussion, lecture, research, role playing, seminars by members of the business community, simulations, student presentations, study groups, team projects.

Technology 125 on-campus computer terminals/PCs are available for student use and are linked by a campus-wide network. The network has full access to the Internet. Students are not required to have their own PC.

Special Opportunities International exchange programs in Asia, Denmark, Finland, France, Ireland, Malaysia, Netherlands, Portugal. An internship program is available.

FINANCES

Costs for 1997–98 Average 1997–98 room and board costs were £3900 per academic year. Room and board costs vary by campus location, occupancy (e.g., single, double, triple), type of accommodation, type of meal plan.

Financial Aid Loans available.

Financial Aid Contact Dr. Geoffrey Southern, Director, International MBA Programme, 59 South Park Avenue, Glasgow, Scotland G12 8LF, United Kingdom. Phone: 44-141-330-3993; Fax: 44-141-330-4939; E-mail: g.southern@mgt.gla.ac.uk

FACILITIES

Information Resources University Library plus 4 additional on-campus libraries; total holdings of 1,700,000 volumes, 370,000 microforms, 8,400 current periodical subscriptions. CD player(s) available for graduate student use. Access provided to online bibliographic retrieval services and online databases.

INTERNATIONAL STUDENTS

Demographics 16% of students enrolled are international students [Africa, 8%, Asia, 50%, Europe, 27%, South America, 4%, other, 11%].

Services and Facilities International student office, international student center, international student housing, ESL courses, counseling/support services.

Applying Proof of adequate funds, proof of health/immunizations required. IELT, TOEFL recommended. Financial aid is not available to international students.

International Student Contact Dr. Robert Paton, Director, Marketing and Programme Development, 53 South Park Avenue, Glasgow, Scotland G12 8LF, United Kingdom. Phone: 44-141-330-3993 Ext. 5037; Fax: 44-141-330-4939; E-mail: r.paton@mgt.gla.ac.uk

PLACEMENT

Services include career counseling/planning, career fairs, and career library.

Employment Of 1996–97 graduates, 90% were employed within three months of graduation. Types of employment entered: accounting, banking, consulting, education, engineering, finance, government, health services, information systems/technology, insurance, international trade, management, manufacturing, service industry, transportation.

Program Contact: Dr. Robert Paton, Director, Marketing and Programme Development, 53 South Park Avenue, Glasgow, Scotland G12 8LF, United Kingdom. Phone: 44-141-330-3993 Ext. 5037; Fax: 44-141-330-4939; E-mail: r.paton@mgt.gla.ac.uk

University of Hull

School of Management

Hull, East Yorkshire, United Kingdom

OVERVIEW
The University of Hull coed institution. Enrollment: 11,500 graduate, professional, and undergraduate students. Founded: 1927. The graduate business unit is in a suburban setting and is on a semester calendar.

HIGHLIGHTS ━━━━━━━

Enrollment Profile
Full-time: N/R
Part-time: N/R
Total: 120
Average Age: 25
Fall 1997 Average GPA: N/R

International: N/R
Women: 40%
Minorities: N/R
Average Class Size: 40
Fall 1997 Average GMAT: N/R

Costs
Full-time tuition: N/R
Part-time tuition: N/R

GRADUATE BUSINESS PROGRAMS
Master of Business Administration in Financial Management (MBA) Full-time; up to 12 months to complete program.
Master of Business Administration in Information Management (MBA) Full-time; up to 12 months to complete program.
Master of Arts in Management Systems (MA) Full-time; up to 12 months to complete program.
General MBA (MBA) Full-time, part-time; 12 months to 2 years to complete program.

ADMISSION
Application Requirements Application form, application fee, bachelor's degree, 2 letters of recommendation, resume, college transcript(s), minimum of 3 years of work experience.
Recommended for Application Computer experience.
Application Deadline 8/15 for fall, 8/1 for fall (international). Application fee: £50.

ACADEMICS
Faculty Full-time 45; part-time 8.
Teaching Methodologies Case study, faculty seminars, lecture, research, student presentations.
Technology 65 on-campus computer terminals/PCs are available for student use and are linked by a campus-wide network. The network has full access to the Internet. Students are not required to have their own PC.

FINANCES
Costs for 1997–98 Cost varies by academic program, reciprocity agreements. Average 1997–98 room only costs were £1820 per academic year. Room and board costs vary by campus location, type of accommodation.
Financial Aid Scholarships available.
Financial Aid Contact Mr. Louis Fong, Deputy Director, Cottingham Road, Hull, East Yorkshire HU6 7RX, United Kingdom. E-mail: l.horrocks@msd.hull.ac.uk

FACILITIES
Information Resources Brynor Jones Library; total holdings of 1,100,000 volumes. CD player(s) available for graduate student use. Access provided to online bibliographic retrieval services.

INTERNATIONAL STUDENTS
Demographics N/R
Services and Facilities International student office, international student center, international student housing, visa services, ESL courses, counseling/support services.
Applying IELT: minimum score of 6, TOEFL: minimum score of 550 required. Financial aid is available to international students.
International Student Contact Derek Newham, Head, International Office, Cottingham Road, Hull, East Yorkshire HU6 7RX, United Kingdom. Phone: 44-1482-466-579.

PLACEMENT
Services include alumni network, career fairs, career placement, electronic job bank, job interviews arranged, job search course, and resume preparation.
Employment Types of employment entered: accounting, financial services, government, management, retail, service industry.
Business Program(s) URL: http://www.hull.ac.uk

Program Contact: Mr. Louis Fong, Deputy Director, Cottingham Road, Hull, East Yorkshire HV6 7RX, United Kingdom. E-mail: l.horrocks@msd.hull.ac.uk

University of London

London Business School

London, England, United Kingdom

OVERVIEW
The University of London is an independent-nonprofit, coed institution. Enrollment: 1,074 graduate, professional, and undergraduate students; 684 full-time matriculated graduate/professional students; 390 part-time matriculated graduate/professional students. Founded: 1965. The graduate business unit is in an urban setting and is on a term calendar.

HIGHLIGHTS ━━━━━━━

Enrollment Profile
Full-time: 466
Part-time: 266
Total: 732
Average Age: 29
Fall 1997 Average GPA: N/R

International: 62%
Women: 22%
Minorities: N/R
Average Class Size: 60
Fall 1997 Average GMAT: 650

Costs
Full-time tuition: £26,000 per academic year
Part-time tuition: N/R

GRADUATE BUSINESS PROGRAMS
Full-time MBA (MBA) Full-time; 28 total credits required; 21 months to complete program.
Executive MBA (MBA) Part-time; 28 total credits required; 2 years to complete program.
Master of Science in Management (MS) Full-time; 13 total credits required; 10 months to complete program.
Master of Science in Finance (MS) Full-time, part-time; 10 total credits required; 9 months to 2 years to complete program.
PhD in Management (PhD) Full-time; 3.5 to 5 years to complete program. Concentrations in decision sciences, economics, accounting, finance, marketing, operations management, strategic management, international management.

ADMISSION
Application Requirements GMAT score, application form, application fee, bachelor's degree, essay, interview, 2 letters of recommendation, personal statement, college transcript(s), minimum of 3 years of work experience.
Recommended for Application Minimum GPA, resume, computer experience.
Application Deadline 5/1 for fall, 5/1 for fall (international). Application fee: $100.

ACADEMICS
Faculty Full-time 109; part-time 20.
Teaching Methodologies Case study, computer-aided instruction, computer analysis, computer simulations, experiential learning, faculty seminars, field projects, group discussion, lecture, research, role playing, seminars by members of the business community, simulations, student presentations, study groups, team projects.
Technology 165 on-campus computer terminals/PCs are available for student use and are linked by a campus-wide network. The network has full access to the Internet. Students are required to have their own PC.
Special Opportunities International exchange programs in Argentina, Australia, Brazil, Canada, Germany, Hong Kong, Italy, Japan, Mexico, Republic of Korea, Spain, United States, Venezuela. An internship program is available.

FINANCES
Costs for 1997–98 Tuition: Full-time: £26,000 per program.
Financial Aid In 1997–98, 6% of students received some institutionally administered aid in the form of scholarships. Financial aid is available to part-time students. Application Deadline: 3/1.
Financial Aid Contact Mr. Gareth Howells, Programme Manager, Full-time MBA Programme, Sussex Place, Regent's Park, London, England NW1 4SA, United Kingdom. Phone: 44-171-706-6863; Fax: 44-171-724-7875; E-mail: ghowells@lbs.ac.uk

FACILITIES
Information Resources London Business School Library plus 1 additional on-campus library; total holdings of 20,000 volumes, 1,000 current periodical subscriptions. CD player(s) available for graduate student use. Access provided to online bibliographic retrieval services.

INTERNATIONAL STUDENTS
Demographics 62% of students enrolled are international students.
Services and Facilities International student office, international student center, counseling/support services.

University of London (continued)

Applying IELT, TOEFL, proof of adequate funds recommended. Financial aid is available to international students.

International Student Contact Ms. Catherine Gibbs, Programme Manager, Full-time MBA Programme, Sussex Place, Regent's Park, London, England NW1 4SA, United Kingdom. Phone: 44-171-262-5050; Fax: 44-171-724-7875.

PLACEMENT

Services include alumni network, career counseling/planning, career fairs, career library, career placement, electronic job bank, job interviews arranged, job search course, resume referral to employers, and resume preparation. In 1996–97, 450 organizations participated in on-campus recruiting; 1,223 on-campus interviews were conducted.

Employment Of 1996–97 graduates, 91% were employed within three months of graduation; the average starting salary was £47,000. Types of employment entered: accounting, banking, chemical industry, communications, computer-related, consulting, consumer products, education, energy, engineering, finance, financial services, government, health services, high technology, hospitality management, human resources, information systems/technology, insurance, international trade, law, management, manufacturing, marketing, media, mining, nonprofit, petrochemical, pharmaceutical, retail, service industry, telecommunications, transportation, utilities.

Business Program(s) URL: http://www.lbs.ac.uk

Program Contact: Mr. Sean Dillon, MBA Information Officer, MBA Programme Office, Sussex Place, Regent's Park, London, England NW1 4SA, United Kingdom. Phone: 44-171-706-6861; Fax: 44-171-724-7875; E-mail: mba-info@lbs.ac.uk

The University of Manchester

Manchester Business School

Manchester, England, United Kingdom

OVERVIEW

The University of Manchester is a publicly supported, coed institution. Enrollment: 400 graduate, professional, and undergraduate students; 250 full-time matriculated graduate/professional students; 150 part-time matriculated graduate/professional students. Founded: 1965. The graduate business unit is in an urban setting and is on a term calendar.

HIGHLIGHTS

Enrollment Profile

Full-time: 250	International: 35%
Part-time: 150	Women: 38%
Total: 400	Minorities: N/R
Average Age: 28	Average Class Size: 14
Fall 1997 Average GPA: N/R	Fall 1997 Average GMAT: 597

Costs
Full-time tuition: £19,000 per academic year (resident); £16,000 per academic year (nonresident)
Part-time tuition: N/R

GRADUATE BUSINESS PROGRAMS

Master of Business Administration (MBA) Full-time, part-time; 18 months to 5 years to complete program. Concentrations in international business, accounting, entrepreneurship, financial management/planning, management consulting, marketing, organizational behavior/development, strategic management.

ADMISSION

Applications For fall 1997 there were 650 applications for admission. Of those applying, 250 were accepted. Of those accepted, 165 enrolled.

Application Requirements GMAT score, application form, bachelor's degree, essay, 2 letters of recommendation, college transcript(s), minimum of 3 years of work experience.

Recommended for Application Interview, resume, computer experience.

Application Deadline 6/30 for fall, 6/30 for fall (international). Application fee: £50. Deferred entrance is available.

ACADEMICS

Faculty Full-time 50; part-time 40.

Teaching Methodologies Case study, computer analysis, experiential learning, field projects, lecture, seminars by members of the business community, simulations, student presentations, team projects.

Technology 50 on-campus computer terminals/PCs are available for student use and are linked by a campus-wide network. The network has full access to the Internet. Students are not required to have their own PC.

Special Opportunities Advanced credit may be earned through transfer of credits from another institution. International exchange programs in Australia, Brazil, Canada, Finland, France, Germany, Italy, Japan, Mexico, Netherlands, Norway, People's Republic of China, Republic of Singapore, Spain, Sweden, United States. An internship program is available.

FINANCES

Costs for 1997–98 Tuition: Full-time: £19,000 per year (resident); £16,000 per year (nonresident). Cost varies by academic program. Average 1997–98 room only costs were £1500 per academic year. Room and board costs vary by campus location, type of accommodation, type of meal plan.

Financial Aid Contact Ms. Helen Dowd, Admissions Officer, Booth Street West, Manchester, England M15 6PB, United Kingdom. Phone: 44-161-275-6311; Fax: 44-161-275-6489; E-mail: h.dowd@fs2.mbs.ac.uk

FACILITIES

Information Resources Manchester Business School Library; total holdings of 45,000 volumes, 3,000 microforms, 750 current periodical subscriptions. CD player(s) available for graduate student use. Access provided to online bibliographic retrieval services and online databases.

INTERNATIONAL STUDENTS

Demographics 35% of students enrolled are international students [Africa, 15%, Asia, 20%, Central America, 5%, Europe, 30%, North America, 15%, South America, 15%].

Services and Facilities ESL courses, counseling/support services.

Applying IELT: minimum score of 6, TOEFL: minimum score of 580, proof of adequate funds required. Financial aid is not available to international students.

International Student Contact Ms. Helen Dowd, Admissions Officer, Booth Street West, Manchester, England M15 6PB, United Kingdom. Phone: 44-161-275-6311; Fax: 44-161-275-6489.

PLACEMENT

Services include alumni network, career counseling/planning, career fairs, career library, career placement, electronic job bank, job interviews arranged, job search course, resume referral to employers, and resume preparation. In 1996–97, 50 organizations participated in on-campus recruiting; 50 on-campus interviews were conducted.

Employment Of 1996–97 graduates, 95% were employed within three months of graduation; the average starting salary was £39,000. Types of employment entered: accounting, banking, consulting, finance, manufacturing, marketing, service industry.

Business Program(s) URL: http://www.mbs.ac.uk

Program Contact: Ms. Helen Dowd, Admissions Officer, Booth Street West, Manchester, England M15 6PB, United Kingdom. Phone: 44-161-275-6311; Fax: 44-161-275-6489; E-mail: h.dowd@fs2.mbs.ac.uk

University of Newcastle upon Tyne

School of Management

Newcastle, United Kingdom

OVERVIEW

The University of Newcastle upon Tyne is a federally supported, coed institution. Enrollment: 13,000 graduate, professional, and undergraduate students; 1,500 full-time matriculated graduate/professional students; 1,500 part-time matriculated graduate/professional students. Founded: 1963. The graduate business unit is in an urban setting and is on a semester calendar.

HIGHLIGHTS

Enrollment Profile

Full-time: 228	International: 30%
Part-time: 69	Women: 47%
Total: 297	Minorities: N/R
Average Age: 27	Average Class Size: 20
Fall 1997 Average GPA: N/R	Fall 1997 Average GMAT: 530

Costs
Full-time tuition: £7500 per academic year (resident); £9500 per academic year (nonresident)
Part-time tuition: N/R

GRADUATE BUSINESS PROGRAMS

Master of Business Administration (MBA) Full-time, part-time; 12 months to 2.5 years to complete program. Concentrations in organizational behavior/development, accounting, operations management, marketing, human resources, banking, economics, nonprofit management, entrepreneurship, international marketing.

ADMISSION

Applications For fall 1997 there were 1,800 applications for admission. Of those applying, 400 were accepted. Of those accepted, 297 enrolled.

Application Requirements GMAT score: minimum 500, application form, 2 letters of recommendation, college transcript(s), minimum of 3 years of work experience.

Application Deadline 8/1 for fall, 8/1 for fall (international). Deferred entrance is available.

ACADEMICS

Faculty Full-time 25.

Teaching Methodologies Faculty seminars, seminars by members of the business community.

Technology Computer terminals/PCs are available for student use and are linked by a campus-wide network. Students are not required to have their own PC.

FINANCES

Costs for 1997–98 Tuition: Full-time: £7500 per year (resident); £9500 per year (nonresident). Cost varies by reciprocity agreements. Average 1997–98 room and board costs were £2400 per academic year.

Financial Aid Contact Student Office, Office of Registrar, Kensington Terrace, Newcastle upon Tyne. Phone: 44-191-222-8672.

FACILITIES

Information Resources Robinson Library.

INTERNATIONAL STUDENTS

Demographics 30% of students enrolled are international students.

Services and Facilities International student office, international student housing, ESL courses, counseling/support services.

Applying IELT: minimum score of 6.5, TOEFL: minimum score of 580 required. Financial aid is not available to international students.

International Student Contact Admissions/International Office, Kensington Terrace, Newcastle upon Tyne. Phone: 44-191-222-8672.

PLACEMENT

Services include career fairs.

Employment Types of employment entered: consulting, finance, management, manufacturing.

Business Program(s) URL: http://www.ncl.ac.uk/postgraduate/mgt.studies/

Program Contact: MBA Administrator, Armstrong Building, Queen Victoria Road, Newcastle upon Tyne NE1 7RU, United Kingdom. Phone: 44-191-222-7440; Fax: 44-191-222-8131; E-mail: mba-courses@ncl.ac.uk

University of Northumbria

Newcastle Business School

Newcastle upon Tyne, England, United Kingdom

OVERVIEW

The University of Northumbria coed institution. Enrollment: 20,000 graduate, professional, and undergraduate students. Founded: 1992. The graduate business unit is in a rural setting and is on a semester calendar.

HIGHLIGHTS

Enrollment Profile

Full-time: N/R	International: N/R
Part-time: N/R	Women: N/R
Total: 100	Minorities: N/R
Average Age: 31	Average Class Size: 15
Fall 1997 Average GPA: N/R	Fall 1997 Average GMAT: N/R

Costs
Full-time tuition: N/R
Part-time tuition: N/R

GRADUATE BUSINESS PROGRAMS

Master of Business Administration (MBA) Full-time, part-time, distance learning option; 80 total credits required; 12 months to 3 years to complete program. Concentrations in finance, marketing, organizational behavior/development, management information systems, management science, strategic management.

Master of European Business Administration (MEBA) Full-time; 80 total credits required; up to 12 months to complete program. Concentrations in finance, marketing, organizational behavior/development, management information systems, strategic management, human resources, economics, international banking, international business, international trade.

Master of Arts in International Business Administration (MA) Full-time, part-time; 80 total credits required; no work experience necessary.

ADMISSION

Application Requirements Application form, bachelor's degree, personal statement, college transcript(s), minimum of 3 years of work experience.

Recommended for Application GMAT score accepted: minimum 550, letter of recommendation, resume, computer experience.

Application Deadline Applications processed on a rolling/continuous basis for both domestic and international students.

ACADEMICS

Faculty Full-time 9.

Teaching Methodologies Case study, computer simulations, lecture, role playing, seminars by members of the business community, student presentations, study groups, team projects.

Technology 60 on-campus computer terminals/PCs are available for student use and are linked by a campus-wide network. The network has full access to the Internet. Students are not required to have their own PC.

Special Opportunities International exchange program in United States. An internship program is available.

FINANCES

Costs for 1997–98 Average 1997–98 room only costs were £1575 per academic year. Room and board costs vary by type of accommodation.

Financial Aid Contact Mr. Ceridwyn Bessant, MBA Program Director, Longhirst Campus, Longhirst Hall, Morpeth, Northumberland NE 613 LL, United Kingdom. Phone: 44-1670-795-000; Fax: 44-1670-795-021; E-mail: turner.lynn@unn.ac.uk

INTERNATIONAL STUDENTS

Demographics N/R

Services and Facilities International student office, international student housing, ESL courses, counseling/support services.

Applying IELT: minimum score of 5.5, TOEFL: minimum score of 550 required. Financial aid is not available to international students.

International Student Contact Morris Tymock, Ellison Building, Ellison Place, Newcastle upon Tyne, England NE1 8ST, United Kingdom. Phone: 44-191-232-6002; E-mail: 44 191 232 6002

PLACEMENT

Services include alumni network, career counseling/planning, career placement, and resume preparation.

Employment Types of employment entered: banking, finance, international trade, law, management, service industry.

Program Contact: Mr. Ceridwyn Bessant, MBA Program Director, Longhirst Campus, Longhirst Hall, Morpeth, Northumberland NE613LL, United Kingdom. Phone: 44-167-79-5000; Fax: 44-1670-795-021.

University of Nottingham

School of Management and Finance

Nottingham, United Kingdom

OVERVIEW

The University of Nottingham is a federally supported, coed institution. Enrollment: 21,600 graduate, professional, and undergraduate students; 6,600 full-time matriculated graduate/professional students; 1,350 part-time matriculated graduate/professional students. Founded: 1881. The graduate business unit is in a suburban setting and is on a semester calendar.

University of Nottingham (continued)

HIGHLIGHTS

Enrollment Profile

Full-time: 70
Part-time: 249
Total: 319
Average Age: 32
Fall 1997 Average GPA: N/R

International: 16%
Women: 37%
Minorities: N/R
Average Class Size: 35
Fall 1997 Average GMAT: 570

Costs

Full-time tuition: £7980 per academic year (resident); £9000 per academic year (nonresident)
Part-time tuition: £665 per course (resident); £750 per course (nonresident)

GRADUATE BUSINESS PROGRAMS

General MBA (MBA) Full-time, part-time; 180 total credits required; 12 months to 4 years to complete program. Concentrations in management, organizational management, international business, marketing, business ethics, entrepreneurship, human resources, strategic management, international management.

MBA in Financial Studies (MBA) Full-time, part-time; 180 total credits required; 12 months to 4 years to complete program. Concentrations in finance, management, banking, international finance, insurance, strategic management, management information systems, accounting.

MBA in Education (MBA) Full-time, part-time; 180 total credits required; 2 to 4 years to complete program. Concentrations in management, public management, public policy and administration, strategic management, nonprofit management, nonprofit organization.

MBA in Health (MBA) Full-time, part-time; 180 total credits required; 2 to 4 years to complete program. Concentrations in management, public management, public policy and administration, strategic management, nonprofit management, nonprofit organization.

Executive MBA (MBA) Part-time; 180 total credits required; 2 to 4 years to complete program. Concentrations in management, organizational management, international business, marketing, business ethics, entrepreneurship, human resources, strategic management, international management.

Modular MBA (MBA) Part-time; 180 total credits required; 2 to 4 years to complete program. Concentrations in management, profit management, international business, marketing, business ethics, entrepreneurship, human resources, strategic management, international management, public management.

International MBA (MBA) Full-time; 180 total credits required; 12 months to complete program. Concentrations in management, international management, international business, international marketing, business ethics, entrepreneurship, public management.

Criminal Justice MBA (MBA) Full-time, part-time; 180 total credits required; 12 months to 4 years to complete program. Concentrations in management, public management, public policy and administration, strategic management, nonprofit management, nonprofit organization.

Local Government MBA (MBA) Full-time, part-time; 180 total credits required; 12 months to 4 years to complete program. Concentrations in management, public management, public policy and administration, strategic management, nonprofit management, nonprofit organization.

Voluntary Sector MBA (MBA) Full-time, part-time; 180 total credits required; 12 months to 4 years to complete program. Concentrations in management, public management, public policy and administration, strategic management, nonprofit management, nonprofit organization.

ADMISSION

Applications For fall 1997 there were 860 applications for admission. Of those applying, 274 were accepted. Of those accepted, 145 enrolled.

Application Requirements GMAT score: minimum 550, application form, bachelor's degree, 2 letters of recommendation, personal statement, resume, college transcript(s), minimum of 3 years of work experience.

Recommended for Application Essay, interview, computer experience.

Application Deadline Applications processed on a rolling/continuous basis for both domestic and international students. Deferred entrance is available.

ACADEMICS

Faculty Full-time 49; part-time 10.

Teaching Methodologies Case study, computer-aided instruction, computer analysis, computer simulations, experiential learning, faculty seminars, field projects, group discussion, lecture, research, role playing, seminars by members of the business community, simulations, student presentations, study groups, team projects.

Technology 1,000 on-campus computer terminals/PCs are available for student use and are linked by a campus-wide network. The network has full access to the Internet. Students are not required to have their own PC.

Special Opportunities Advanced credit may be earned through transfer of credits from another institution. International exchange programs in Canada, France, Germany, United States.

FINANCES

Costs for 1997–98 Tuition: Full-time: £7980 per program (resident); £9000 per program (nonresident). Part-time: £665 per course (resident); £750 per course (nonresident). Cost varies by academic program. Average 1997–98 room only costs were £1850 per academic year (on campus) and £2200 per academic year (off campus). Room and board costs vary by occupancy (e.g., single, double, triple), type of accommodation, type of meal plan.

Financial Aid In 1997–98, 3% of students received some institutionally administered aid in the form of loans. Financial aid is available to part-time students.

Financial Aid Contact Margaret Hamilton, MBA Administrator, Portland Building, University Park, Nottingham. Phone: 44-115-555-0001; Fax: 44-115-951-5503; E-mail: smf.mba@linl.smf.nottingham.ac.uk

FACILITIES

Information Resources Hallward Library plus 4 additional on-campus libraries; total holdings of 600,000 volumes. CD player(s) available for graduate student use. Access provided to online bibliographic retrieval services and online databases.

INTERNATIONAL STUDENTS

Demographics 16% of students enrolled are international students [Africa, 13%, Asia, 35%, Europe, 44%, North America, 2%, South America, 1%, other, 5%].

Services and Facilities International student office, international student center, international student housing, ESL courses, counseling/support services.

Applying IELT: minimum score of 6.5, TOEFL: minimum score of 600, TWE: minimum score of 4, proof of adequate funds, proof of health/immunizations required. Financial aid is not available to international students.

International Student Contact Dr. Christine Humphrey, Director, International Office, Portland Building, University of Nottingham, University Park, Nottingham. Phone: 44-115-951-5243; Fax: 44-115-951-5503.

PLACEMENT

Services include alumni network, career counseling/planning, career fairs, career library, career placement, job interviews arranged, resume referral to employers, and resume preparation. In 1996–97, 80 organizations participated in on-campus recruiting.

Employment Of 1996–97 graduates, 95% were employed within three months of graduation. Types of employment entered: accounting, banking, communications, computer-related, consulting, consumer products, education, energy, engineering, finance, financial services, government, health services, high technology, hospitality management, human resources, information systems/technology, insurance, international trade, management, manufacturing, marketing, media, nonprofit, petrochemical, pharmaceutical, retail, service industry, telecommunications, transportation, utilities.

Business Program(s) URL: http://www.nottingham.ac.uk/unbs/

Program Contact: Mr. Ron Hodges, Admissions Director, Portland Building, University Park, Nottingham NG7 2RD, United Kingdom. Phone: 44-115-951-5500; Fax: 44-115-951-5503.

University of Oxford

School of Management Studies

Oxford, United Kingdom

OVERVIEW

The University of Oxford is a federally supported, coed institution. Enrollment: 11,282 graduate, professional, and undergraduate students. Founded: 1200. The graduate business unit is in an urban setting and is on a term calendar.

HIGHLIGHTS

Enrollment Profile

Full-time: 116
Part-time: 0
Total: 116
Average Age: 28
Fall 1997 Average GPA: N/R

International: 71%
Women: 17%
Minorities: N/R
Average Class Size: N/R
Fall 1997 Average GMAT: 650

Costs

Full-time tuition: £15,000 per academic year (resident); £15,000 per academic year (nonresident)
Part-time tuition: N/R

GRADUATE BUSINESS PROGRAMS

Master of Business Administration (MBA) Full-time; minimum of 12 months to complete program. Concentrations in accounting, strategic management, information management, leadership, marketing.

Master of Science in Management Research (MS) Full-time; minimum of 12 months to complete program.

Master of Science in Industrial Relations and Human Resource Management (MS) Full-time; minimum of 12 months to complete program. Concentrations in industrial/labor relations, human resources.

PhD in Management Studies (PhD) Full-time; 2 to 3 years to complete program.

ADMISSION

Applications For fall 1997 there were 220 applications for admission. Of those applying, 71 were accepted. Of those accepted, 49 enrolled.

Application Requirements GMAT score: minimum 620, application form, application fee, essay, minimum GPA: 3.5, 3 letters of recommendation, personal statement, resume.

Recommended for Application Work experience.

Application Deadline Applications processed on a rolling/continuous basis for both domestic and international students. Application fee: £60. Deferred entrance is available.

ACADEMICS

Faculty Full-time 30.

Teaching Methodologies Case study, faculty seminars, group discussion, lecture, seminars by members of the business community, student presentations, study groups, team projects.

Technology Computer terminals/PCs are available for student use and are linked by a campus-wide network. The network has full access to the Internet. Students are required to have their own PC.

Special Opportunities International exchange program available.

FINANCES

Costs for 1997–98 Tuition: Full-time: £15,000 per year (resident); £15,000 per year (nonresident). Average 1997–98 room and board costs were £6000 per academic year.

Financial Aid Scholarships available.

Financial Aid Contact International Office, Wellington Square, Oxford. Phone: 44-1865-270-105; Fax: 44-1865-270-708.

FACILITIES

Information Resources Main institution library plus 111 additional on-campus libraries.

INTERNATIONAL STUDENTS

Demographics 71% of students enrolled are international students.

Services and Facilities International student office, international student center, international student housing, counseling/support services.

Applying TOEFL: minimum score of 600, proof of adequate funds required. Financial aid is available to international students.

International Student Contact Ms. Beverly Potts, International Office, University Offices, Wellington Square, Oxford. Phone: 44-1865-270-189; Fax: 44-1865-228-471.

PLACEMENT

Services include alumni network, career counseling/planning, career fairs, career library, career placement, job interviews arranged, and resume preparation.

Business Program(s) URL: http://units.ox.ac.uk/departments/obs/

Program Contact: Mrs. Alison Mills, MBA Administrator, The Radcliffe Infirmary Woodstock Road, Oxford, Oxon OX2 6HE, United Kingdom. Phone: 44-186-228-477; Fax: 44-1865-228-471; E-mail: enquiries@obs.ox.ac.uk

University of Plymouth

Business School

Plymouth, England, United Kingdom

OVERVIEW

The University of Plymouth coed institution. Enrollment: 22,200 graduate, professional, and undergraduate students. The graduate business unit is in an urban setting and is on a semester calendar.

HIGHLIGHTS

Enrollment Profile

Full-time: 45	International: 17%
Part-time: 244	Women: 52%
Total: 289	Minorities: N/R
Average Age: N/R	Average Class Size: 30
Fall 1997 Average GPA: N/R	Fall 1997 Average GMAT: N/R

Costs
Full-time tuition: N/R
Part-time tuition: N/R

GRADUATE BUSINESS PROGRAMS

Master of Business Administration (MBA) Full-time, part-time; 120 total credits required; 12 months to 3 years to complete program. Concentration in management.

Master of International Business (MIB) Full-time; 120 total credits required; 12 months to 2 years to complete program. Concentrations in international management, international marketing, international finance, international development management.

Master of Management Studies (MMS) Full-time, part-time; 120 total credits required; 12 months to 2 years to complete program. Concentration in management.

Master of Human Resource Management (MHRM) Part-time; 120 total credits required; 12 months to complete program. Concentrations in management, human resources.

Master of Marketing (MM) Full-time, part-time; 120 total credits required; 12 months to complete program. Concentrations in management, marketing, marketing research.

Master of Science in Management of Technology (MS) Part-time; 120 total credits required; 2 to 3 years to complete program. Concentrations in manufacturing management, technology management.

Master of Arts in Health Care Management (MA) Full-time, part-time; 120 total credits required; 12 months to 2 years to complete program. Concentrations in health care, management.

Master of Business Administration in Finance (MBA) Full-time, part-time; 120 total credits required; 12 months to 2 years to complete program. Concentrations in management, finance.

ADMISSION

Application Requirements GMAT score: minimum 550, application form, application fee, bachelor's degree.

Recommended for Application Interview, letters of recommendation, personal statement, resume, work experience, computer experience.

Application Deadline Applications processed on a rolling/continuous basis for both domestic and international students. Application fee: £6250.

ACADEMICS

Faculty Full-time 75.

Teaching Methodologies Case study, computer-aided instruction, computer simulations, experiential learning, faculty seminars, group discussion, lecture, research, role playing, seminars by members of the business community, simulations, student presentations, study groups, team projects.

Technology 1,250 on-campus computer terminals/PCs are available for student use and are linked by a campus-wide network. The network has full access to the Internet. Students are not required to have their own PC.

Special Opportunities Advanced credit may be earned through credit for experience, transfer of credits from another institution. International exchange programs in France, Germany, Netherlands.

FINANCES

Costs for 1997–98 Cost varies by academic program. Average 1997–98 room only costs were £2500 per academic year (on campus) and £3000 per academic year (off campus). Room and board costs vary by campus location, occupancy (e.g., single, double, triple), type of accommodation.

Financial Aid Grants, scholarships, loans available.

Financial Aid Contact Mr. Paul Williamson, Postgraduate Administrator, Drake Circus, Plymouth, England PL4 8AA, United Kingdom. Phone: 44-1752-232-859; Fax: 44-1752-232-853; E-mail: postgrad@pbs.plym.ac.uk

FACILITIES

Information Resources The Library plus 5 additional on-campus libraries; total holdings of 413,420 volumes, 3,000 current periodical subscriptions. CD player(s) available for graduate student use. Access provided to online bibliographic retrieval services.

INTERNATIONAL STUDENTS

Demographics 17% of students enrolled are international students [Africa, 5%, Asia, 15%, Europe, 80%].

Services and Facilities International student office, international student center, counseling/support services.

University of Plymouth (continued)

Applying IELT: minimum score of 6.5, TOEFL: minimum score of 550 required. Financial aid is available to international students.

International Student Contact Ms. Carol Roden, Director, International Office, Drake Circus, Plymouth, England PL4 8AA, United Kingdom. Phone: 44-1752-232-013; Fax: 44-1752-232-014; E-mail: intoff@plymouth.ac.uk

PLACEMENT

Services include alumni network, career fairs, career library, career placement, and job interviews arranged.

Employment Types of employment entered: banking, computer-related, consulting, education, finance, financial services, health services, human resources, management, marketing, nonprofit, retail, service industry.

Business Program(s) URL: http://www.pbs.plym.ac.uk/

Program Contact: Mr. Paul Williamson, Postgraduate Administrator, Drake Circus, Plymouth, England PL4 8AA, United Kingdom. Phone: 44-1752-232-499; Fax: 44-1752-232-853; E-mail: postgrad@pbs.plym.ac.uk

University of Reading

ISMA Centre

Reading, England, United Kingdom

OVERVIEW

The University of Reading is a private, coed institution. Enrollment: 12,500 graduate, professional, and undergraduate students. Founded: 1892. The graduate business unit is in a suburban setting and is on a three ten week terms calendar.

HIGHLIGHTS

Enrollment Profile

Full-time: 118	International: 83%
Part-time: 0	Women: 19%
Total: 118	Minorities: N/R
Average Age: 25	Average Class Size: 118
Fall 1997 Average GPA: 3.3	Fall 1997 Average GMAT: 604

Costs
Full-time tuition: N/R
Part-time tuition: N/R

GRADUATE BUSINESS PROGRAMS

Master of Science in International Securities, Investment, and Banking (MS) Full-time; high level of numeracy required; 9 months to complete program. Concentrations in finance, international banking.

Master of Science in Finance, Regulation, and Risk Management (MS) Full-time; 9 months to complete program. Concentrations in finance, risk management.

ADMISSION

Applications For fall 1997 there were 629 applications for admission. Of those applying, 180 were accepted. Of those accepted, 120 enrolled.

Application Requirements Application form, bachelor's degree, minimum GPA: 3.3, 2 letters of recommendation, personal statement, college transcript(s).

Recommended for Application GMAT score accepted: minimum 600.

Application Deadline Applications processed on a rolling/continuous basis for both domestic and international students. Application fee: £24. Deferred entrance is available.

ACADEMICS

Faculty Full-time 11; part-time 11.

Teaching Methodologies Case study, computer-aided instruction, computer analysis, computer simulations, experiential learning, faculty seminars, field projects, group discussion, lecture, research, role playing, seminars by members of the business community, simulations, student presentations, study groups, team projects.

Technology 50 on-campus computer terminals/PCs are available for student use and are linked by a campus-wide network. The network has full access to the Internet. Students are not required to have their own PC.

FINANCES

Costs for 1997–98 Average 1997–98 room and board costs were £2550 per academic year (on campus) and £600 per academic year (off campus).

FACILITIES

Information Resources University Library. CD player(s) available for graduate student use. Access provided to online bibliographic retrieval services.

INTERNATIONAL STUDENTS

Demographics 83% of students enrolled are international students [Africa, 12%, Asia, 18%, Australia/New Zealand, 5%, Central America, 2%, Europe, 45%, North America, 13%, South America, 5%].

Services and Facilities International student office, international student housing, counseling/support services.

Applying IELT: minimum score of 7, TOEFL: minimum score of 590, TWE: minimum score of 4.5, proof of adequate funds required. Financial aid is not available to international students.

International Student Contact Ms. Zoe Lewsley, Admissions Coordinator, ISMA Centre, Whiteknights Park, Reading, England R96 6BA, United Kingdom. Phone: 44-118-931-6675; Fax: 44-118-931-4741; E-mail: admin@ismacentre. rdg.ac.uk

PLACEMENT

Services include alumni network, career counseling/planning, career fairs, career library, job search course, resume referral to employers, and resume preparation. In 1996–97, 15 organizations participated in on-campus recruiting.

Employment Of 1996–97 graduates, 70% were employed within three months of graduation; the average starting salary was £28,000. Types of employment entered: accounting, banking, computer-related, consulting, finance, information systems/technology, management.

Business Program(s) URL: http://www.ismacentre.reading.ac.uk

Program Contact: Ms. Zoë Lewsley, Admissions Coordinator, Whiteknights Park, PO Box 242, Reading, England RG6 6BA, United Kingdom. Phone: 44-118-931-6675; Fax: 44-118-931-4741; E-mail: admin@ismacentre.reading.ac.uk
See full description on page 1130.

University of Salford

Management School

Salford, Greater Manchester, United Kingdom

OVERVIEW

The University of Salford coed institution. Enrollment: 16,000 graduate, professional, and undergraduate students; 1,000 full-time matriculated graduate/professional students; 1,500 part-time matriculated graduate/professional students. Founded: 1967. The graduate business unit is in an urban setting and is on a term calendar.

HIGHLIGHTS

Enrollment Profile

Full-time: 150	International: 32%
Part-time: 270	Women: 40%
Total: 420	Minorities: N/R
Average Age: 29	Average Class Size: 20
Fall 1997 Average GPA: N/R	Fall 1997 Average GMAT: N/R

Costs
Full-time tuition: N/R
Part-time tuition: N/R

GRADUATE BUSINESS PROGRAMS

Master of Business Administration (MBA) Full-time, part-time; 12 months to 5 years to complete program. Concentration in management.

Master of Science (MS) Full-time, part-time; 12 months to 5 years to complete program. Concentrations in human resources, finance, marketing, international business, management information systems, logistics, quality management, international trade, international banking, technology management, developmental economics.

ADMISSION

Applications For fall 1997 there were 1,750 applications for admission. Of those applying, 740 were accepted. Of those accepted, 420 enrolled.

Application Requirements Application form, bachelor's degree, 2 letters of recommendation, personal statement, college transcript(s), minimum of 2 years of work experience.

Recommended for Application Minimum GPA, resume, computer experience.

Application Deadline Applications processed on a rolling/continuous basis for both domestic and international students. Deferred entrance is available.

ACADEMICS

Faculty Full-time 35.

Teaching Methodologies Case study, computer-aided instruction, computer analysis, computer simulations, faculty seminars, group discussion, lecture, role playing, seminars by members of the business community, simulations, student presentations, team projects.

Technology 1,000 on-campus computer terminals/PCs are available for student use and are linked by a campus-wide network. The network has full access to the Internet. Students are not required to have their own PC.

FINANCES
Costs for 1997–98 Cost varies by academic program. Average 1997–98 room only costs were £2500 per academic year (on campus) and £3300 per academic year (off campus). Room and board costs vary by campus location, occupancy (e.g., single, double, triple), type of accommodation.
Financial Aid Contact Mr. David C. Lavender, Director of Admissions, The Management School, Salford, Greater Manchester M5 4WT, United Kingdom. Phone: 44-161-295-5530 Ext. 5071; Fax: 44-161-295-5022; E-mail: d.c. lavender@man-sch.salford.ac.uk

FACILITIES
Information Resources Clifford-Whitworth Library plus 4 additional on-campus libraries; total holdings of 540,000 volumes, 2,000 current periodical subscriptions. CD player(s) available for graduate student use. Access provided to online bibliographic retrieval services and online databases.

INTERNATIONAL STUDENTS
Demographics 32% of students enrolled are international students [Africa, 8%, Asia, 25%, Australia/New Zealand, 8%, Central America, 5%, Europe, 25%, North America, 3%, South America, 5%, other, 21%].
Services and Facilities International student office, international student center, international student housing, counseling/support services.
Applying IELT: minimum score of 6, TOEFL: minimum score of 550 required. Proof of adequate funds recommended. Financial aid is not available to international students.
International Student Contact Mr. David C. Lavender, Director of Admissions, The Management School, Salford, Greater Manchester M5 4WT, United Kingdom. Phone: 44-161-295-5530 Ext. 5071; Fax: 44-161-295-5022; E-mail: d.c.lavender@man-sch.salford.ac.uk

PLACEMENT
Services include alumni network, career counseling/planning, career library, career placement, job search course, and resume preparation.
Employment Of 1996–97 graduates, 85% were employed within three months of graduation; the average starting salary was £20,000. Types of employment entered: accounting, banking, computer-related, consumer products, education, finance, financial services, government, human resources, international trade, management, manufacturing, marketing, media, pharmaceutical, service industry, transportation.
Business Program(s) URL: http://www.salford.ac.uk/man-sch/homepage. html

Program Contact: Mr. David C. Lavender, Director of Admissions, The Management School, Salford, Greater Manchester M5 4WT, United Kingdom. Phone: 44-161-295-5530 Ext. 5071; Fax: 44-161-295-5022; E-mail: d.c. lavender@man-sch.salford.ac.uk

University of Sheffield

Management School

Sheffield, England, United Kingdom

OVERVIEW
The University of Sheffield coed institution. Enrollment: 20,555 graduate, professional, and undergraduate students; 2,512 full-time matriculated graduate/professional students; 2,002 part-time matriculated graduate/professional students. Founded: 1897. The graduate business unit is in an urban setting and is on a semester calendar.

HIGHLIGHTS

Enrollment Profile
Full-time: 45
Part-time: 30
Total: 75
Average Age: 29
Fall 1997 Average GPA: N/R

International: 69%
Women: 33%
Minorities: N/R
Average Class Size: 45
Fall 1997 Average GMAT: 575

Costs
Full-time tuition: N/R
Part-time tuition: N/R

GRADUATE BUSINESS PROGRAMS
Master of Business Administration (MBA) Full-time; 15 months to 2 years to complete program. Concentrations in management, accounting, international business, marketing, finance.

ADMISSION
Applications For fall 1997 there were 470 applications for admission. Of those applying, 165 were accepted. Of those accepted, 84 enrolled.
Application Requirements Application form, application fee, bachelor's degree, minimum GPA: 3.5, 2 letters of recommendation, college transcript(s), minimum of 2 years of work experience.
Recommended for Application GMAT score accepted: minimum 550, personal statement, resume.
Application Deadline Applications processed on a rolling/continuous basis for both domestic and international students. Application fee: £25.

ACADEMICS
Faculty Full-time 35; part-time 6.
Teaching Methodologies Case study, computer-aided instruction, experiential learning, field projects, group discussion, lecture, research, seminars by members of the business community, student presentations, team projects.
Technology 90 on-campus computer terminals/PCs are available for student use and are linked by a campus-wide network. The network has full access to the Internet. Students are not required to have their own PC.
Special Opportunities Advanced credit may be earned through credit by examination, credit for experience. International exchange programs in Denmark, France, Sweden.

FINANCES
Costs for 1997–98 Average 1997–98 room only costs were £1768 per academic year (off campus). Room and board costs vary by occupancy (e.g., single, double, triple), type of accommodation.
Financial Aid In 1997–98, 5% of students received some institutionally administered aid. Application Deadline: 9/15.

FACILITIES
Information Resources Sheffield Library plus 12 additional on-campus libraries. CD player(s) available for graduate student use. Access provided to online bibliographic retrieval services.

INTERNATIONAL STUDENTS
Demographics 69% of students enrolled are international students [Africa, 5%, Asia, 25%, Australia/New Zealand, 3%, Europe, 65%, North America, 2%].
Services and Facilities International student office, international student center, international student housing, ESL courses, counseling/support services, language tutoring.
Applying IELT: minimum score of 6.5, TOEFL: minimum score of 575, TWE: minimum score of 4.5, proof of adequate funds required. Financial aid is not available to international students.
International Student Contact Ms. Debora Green, International Student Officer, Academic Registrar's Office, Firte Court, Western Bank, Sheffield, England S10 2TN, United Kingdom. Phone: 44-114-282-4916; Fax: 44-114-222-3348.

PLACEMENT
Services include alumni network, career counseling/planning, career fairs, and career library.
Employment Of 1996–97 graduates, 80% were employed within three months of graduation. Types of employment entered: accounting, banking, communications, computer-related, consulting, consumer products, education, finance, financial services, government, health services, hospitality management, human resources, information systems/technology, insurance, management, manufacturing, marketing, media, real estate, retail, service industry, telecommunications, transportation, utilities.
Business Program(s) URL: http://www.shef.ac.uk

Program Contact: Ms. Debra Maxwell, MBA Program Manager, Management School, 9 Mappin Street, Sheffield, England S1 4DT, United Kingdom. Phone: 44-114-282-5297; Fax: 44-114-272-5103; E-mail: d.maxwell@sheffield. ac.uk

University of Stirling

School of Management

Stirling, United Kingdom

OVERVIEW
The University of Stirling coed institution. Enrollment: 7,500 graduate, professional, and undergraduate students; 760 full-time matriculated graduate/professional students; 500 part-time matriculated graduate/professional students.

University of Stirling (continued)

Founded: 1967. The graduate business unit is in a rural setting and is on a semester calendar.

HIGHLIGHTS

Enrollment Profile

Full-time: 28	International: 71%
Part-time: 0	Women: 50%
Total: 28	Minorities: N/R
Average Age: N/R	Average Class Size: N/R
Fall 1997 Average GPA: N/R	Fall 1997 Average GMAT: N/R

Costs
Full-time tuition: N/R
Part-time tuition: N/R

GRADUATE BUSINESS PROGRAMS

Master of Business Administration (MBA) Full-time; 15 total credits required; 12 months to complete program. Concentrations in finance, management information systems, marketing, entrepreneurship, international business, human resources.

ADMISSION

Applications For fall 1997 there were 304 applications for admission. Of those applying, 48 were accepted. Of those accepted, 28 enrolled.

Application Requirements Application form, bachelor's degree, minimum GPA: 2.7, 2 letters of recommendation, personal statement, college transcript(s), minimum of 2 years of work experience.

Application Deadline Applications processed on a rolling/continuous basis for both domestic and international students. Deferred entrance is available.

ACADEMICS

Faculty Full-time 30; part-time 2.

Teaching Methodologies Case study, field projects, group discussion, lecture, seminars by members of the business community, simulations, student presentations, study groups, team projects.

Technology 350 on-campus computer terminals/PCs are available for student use and are linked by a campus-wide network. The network has full access to the Internet. Students are not required to have their own PC.

FINANCES

Costs for 1997–98 Cost varies by reciprocity agreements. Average 1997–98 room only costs were £2100 per academic year.

Financial Aid Contact Mrs. June Johnston, MBA Administrator, Faculty of Management, Stirling. Phone: 44-1786-467-415; Fax: 44-1786-450-776.

FACILITIES

Information Resources University Library; total holdings of 500,000 volumes, 2,500 current periodical subscriptions. CD player(s) available for graduate student use. Access provided to online bibliographic retrieval services.

INTERNATIONAL STUDENTS

Demographics 71% of students enrolled are international students [Africa, 13%, Asia, 15%, Central America, 4%, Europe, 68%, other, 2%].

Services and Facilities International student office, counseling/support services.

Applying IELT: minimum score of 6.5, TOEFL: minimum score of 550, proof of adequate funds required. Financial aid is not available to international students.

International Student Contact Mrs. June Johnston, MBA Administrator, Faculty of Management, Stirling. Phone: 44-1786-467-415; Fax: 44-1786-450-776.

PLACEMENT

Services include career counseling/planning, and career library.

Employment Types of employment entered: banking, finance, financial services, information systems/technology, international trade, marketing.

Program Contact: Mrs. June Johnston, MBA Administrator, Faculty of Management, Stirling FK9 4LA, United Kingdom. Phone: 44-1786-467-415; Fax: 44-1786-450-776.

University of Strathclyde

Strathclyde Graduate Business School

Glasgow, Scotland, United Kingdom

OVERVIEW

The University of Strathclyde is a federally supported, coed institution. Enrollment: 14,000 graduate, professional, and undergraduate students. Founded: 1796. The graduate business unit is in an urban setting and is on a semester calendar.

HIGHLIGHTS

Enrollment Profile

Full-time: 95	International: 17%
Part-time: 250	Women: 29%
Total: 345	Minorities: N/R
Average Age: 31	Average Class Size: 40
Fall 1997 Average GPA: N/R	Fall 1997 Average GMAT: N/R

Costs
Full-time tuition: £10,750 per academic year (resident); £10,750 per academic year (nonresident)
Part-time tuition: £8925 per program (resident); £8925 per program (nonresident)

GRADUATE BUSINESS PROGRAMS

Master of Business Administration (MBA) Full-time, part-time, distance learning option; 60 total credits required; 3 years work experience required, minimum age requirement: 24; 12 months to 6 years to complete program. Concentration in strategic management.

International Master of Business Administration (IMBA) Part-time, distance learning option; 60 total credits required; 3 years work experience required, minimum age requirement: 24; 2.5 to 3.5 years to complete program.

Master of Science in Business and Management (MSc) Full-time; 60 total credits required; minimum of 12 months to complete program.

Master of Science in Faculties Management (MSc) Full-time, part-time; 60 total credits required; 12 months to 3 years to complete program.

Master of Science in Procurement Management (MSc) distance learning option; 60 total credits required; minimum of 3 years to complete program.

Master of Science in Business Information Systems (MSc) Full-time; minimum of 12 months to complete program.

ADMISSION

Applications For fall 1997 there were 670 applications for admission. Of those applying, 200 were accepted.

Application Requirements Application form, 2 letters of recommendation, personal statement, college transcript(s), minimum of 3 years of work experience.

Recommended for Application GMAT score accepted.

Application Deadline 9/1 for fall, 3/1 for spring, 9/1 for fall (international), 3/1 for spring (international). Deferred entrance is available.

ACADEMICS

Faculty Full-time 175; part-time 25.

Teaching Methodologies Case study, faculty seminars, group discussion, lecture, research, seminars by members of the business community, student presentations, study groups, team projects.

Technology 40 on-campus computer terminals/PCs are available for student use and are linked by a campus-wide network. The network has full access to the Internet. Students are not required to have their own PC.

Special Opportunities International exchange program in France. An internship program is available.

FINANCES

Costs for 1997–98 Tuition: Full-time: £10,750 per program (resident); £10,750 per program (nonresident). Part-time: £8925 per program (resident); £8925 per program (nonresident). Average 1997–98 room only costs were £2500 per academic year (on campus) and £2500 per academic year (off campus). Room and board costs vary by occupancy (e.g., single, double, triple), type of accommodation, type of meal plan.

Financial Aid Contact Ms. Margaret Lavery, Admissions Officer, 199 Cathedral Street, Glasgow, Scotland G4 0QU, United Kingdom. Phone: 44-141-553-6118; Fax: 44-141-552-8851; E-mail: admissions@sgbs.strath.ac.uk

FACILITIES

Information Resources Andersonian Library plus 5 additional on-campus libraries. Access provided to online databases.

INTERNATIONAL STUDENTS

Demographics 17% of students enrolled are international students [Africa, 7%, Asia, 34%, Australia/New Zealand, 3%, Central America, 3%, Europe, 49%, North America, 1%, other, 3%].

Services and Facilities International student office, international student center, counseling/support services.

Applying IELT: minimum score of 6.5, TOEFL: minimum score of 600, proof of adequate funds, proof of health/immunizations required. Financial aid is not available to international students.

International Student Contact Mrs. Fiona Mitchell, Full-time MBA Program Administrator, 199 Cathedral Street, Glasgow, Scotland G4 0QU, United Kingdom. Phone: 44-141-553-6005; Fax: 44-141-552-2501.

PLACEMENT
Services include alumni network, career counseling/planning, career library, career placement, job interviews arranged, resume referral to employers, and resume preparation.

Employment Of 1996–97 graduates, 98% were employed within three months of graduation. Types of employment entered: banking, computer-related, consulting, education, engineering, finance, financial services, health services, information systems/technology, insurance, management, manufacturing, marketing, service industry, utilities.

Business Program(s) URL: http://www.strath.ac.uk/Departments/SGBS

Program Contact: Ms. Meg Lavery, Admissions Manager, 199 Cathedral Street, Glasgow, Scotland G4 0QU, United Kingdom. Phone: 44-141-553-6056; Fax: 44-141-552-8351; E-mail: admissions@sgbs.strath.ac.uk

University of the West of England, Bristol

Bristol Business School

Bristol, England, United Kingdom

OVERVIEW
The University of the West of England, Bristol is a federally supported, coed institution. Enrollment: 15,000 graduate, professional, and undergraduate students. Founded: 1885. The graduate business unit is in a suburban setting and is on a trimester calendar.

HIGHLIGHTS

Enrollment Profile
Full-time: 104
Part-time: 1,215
Total: 1,319
Average Age: 34
Fall 1997 Average GPA: N/R

International: 1%
Women: 51%
Minorities: N/R
Average Class Size: 30
Fall 1997 Average GMAT: N/R

Costs
Full-time tuition: N/R
Part-time tuition: £7600 per program (resident); £7600 per program (nonresident)

Degree(s) offered in conjunction with Georg-Simon-Ohm Fachochschule

GRADUATE BUSINESS PROGRAMS
Master of Business Administration (MBA) Part-time; 2 years management experience required; 18 months to 2.5 years to complete program. Concentrations in accounting, economics, finance, management, management information systems, marketing, operations management, organizational behavior/development, quantitative analysis, strategic management, human resources, business policy/strategy, public policy and administration, taxation.

UK Route (MBA) Full-time; 2 years management experience required; 12 months to complete program. Concentrations in accounting, economics, entrepreneurship, finance, management, management information systems, marketing, operations management, organizational behavior/development, quantitative analysis, strategic management, human resources, business policy/strategy, public policy and administration, taxation, international finance, project management, international marketing.

European Route (MBA) Full-time; 2 years management experience required; 12 months to complete program. Concentrations in accounting, economics, entrepreneurship, finance, management, management information systems, marketing, operations management, organizational behavior/development, quantitative analysis, strategic management, human resources, business policy/strategy, public policy and administration, taxation, international finance, project management, international marketing, european business studies.

MA in Marketing (MA) Full-time, part-time; 12 months to 2.5 years to complete program. Concentrations in management information systems, marketing, strategic management, marketing research, business education, international marketing.

MA in Finance (MA) Full-time, part-time; 12 months to 2.5 years to complete program. Concentrations in taxation, finance, financial information systems, financial management/planning, accounting, risk management, international finance, accounting.

MA in Personnel Management (MA) Full-time, part-time; minimum of 12 months to complete program. Concentrations in human resources, business ethics, business law, industrial/labor relations, manpower administration.

ADMISSION
Application Requirements GMAT score: minimum 500, application form, bachelor's degree, interview, minimum of 2 years of work experience.

Recommended for Application Computer experience.

Application Deadline Applications processed on a rolling/continuous basis for both domestic and international students. Deferred entrance is available.

ACADEMICS
Faculty Full-time 28.

Teaching Methodologies Case study, computer-aided instruction, computer analysis, computer simulations, experiential learning, faculty seminars, group discussion, lecture, research, role playing, seminars by members of the business community, simulations, student presentations, study groups, team projects.

Technology 3,500 on-campus computer terminals/PCs are available for student use and are linked by a campus-wide network. The network has full access to the Internet. Students are not required to have their own PC.

FINANCES
Costs for 1997–98 Tuition: £7600 per program (resident); £7600 per program (nonresident). Cost varies by academic program, campus location.

Financial Aid Contact Centre for Student Affairs, University of the West of England, Frenchay Campus, Bristol, England BS16 1QY, United Kingdom. Phone: 44-117-965-6261; Fax: 44-117-976-3851.

FACILITIES
Information Resources Bolland Library; total holdings of 500,000 volumes, 3,700 current periodical subscriptions. CD player(s) available for graduate student use. Access provided to online bibliographic retrieval services and online databases.

INTERNATIONAL STUDENTS
Demographics 1% of students enrolled are international students.

Services and Facilities International student office, international student center, international student housing, ESL courses, counseling/support services.

Applying IELT: minimum score of 6, TOEFL: minimum score of 570 required. Financial aid is not available to international students.

International Student Contact Ms. Sharon Bohin, MBA Admissions Officer, Bristol Business School, Frenchay Campus, Bristol, England BS16 1QY, United Kingdom. Phone: 44-117-965-6261 Ext. 2857; Fax: 44-117-976-2718 ; E-mail: business@uwe.ac.uk

PLACEMENT
Services include career counseling/planning, and career library.

Employment Types of employment entered: accounting, banking, chemical industry, communications, computer-related, consulting, consumer products, education, energy, engineering, finance, financial services, government, health services, high technology, hospitality management, human resources, information systems/technology, insurance, international trade, law, management, manufacturing, marketing, media, nonprofit, petrochemical, pharmaceutical, real estate, retail, service industry, telecommunications, transportation, utilities.

Business Program(s) URL: http://www.uwe.ac.uk

Program Contact: Ms. Sharon Bohin, Admissions Officer, Bristol Business School, Frenchay Campus, Bristol, England BS16 1QY, United Kingdom. Phone: 44-117-976-3848 Ext. 2857; Fax: 44-117-976-2718; E-mail: business@uwe.ac.uk

University of Ulster at Jordanstown

Ulster Business School

Newtownabbey, Northern Ireland, United Kingdom

OVERVIEW
The University of Ulster at Jordanstown is a federally supported, coed institution. Founded: 1985. The graduate business unit is in a suburban setting and is on a semester calendar.

HIGHLIGHTS

Enrollment Profile
Full-time: 50
Part-time: 460
Total: 510
Average Age: 33
Fall 1997 Average GPA: N/R

International: 2%
Women: 31%
Minorities: N/R
Average Class Size: 90
Fall 1997 Average GMAT: 500

Costs
Full-time tuition: £3150 per academic year (resident); £7700 per academic year (nonresident)
Part-time tuition: N/R

Peterson's Guide to MBA Programs 1999

689

University of Ulster at Jordanstown (continued)

GRADUATE BUSINESS PROGRAMS

Master of Business Administration (MBA) Full-time, part-time; minimum of 3 years work experience required; 12 months to 3 years to complete program. Concentrations in accounting, economics, entrepreneurship, finance, management information systems, management, marketing. ·

MBA in International Business (MBA) Full-time, part-time; minimum of 3 years work experience required; 12 months to 3 years to complete program. Concentrations in accounting, economics, entrepreneurship, finance, management information systems, management, marketing.

Executive MBA (MBA) Part-time; minimum of 3 years work experience required; 2 to 3 years to complete program.

Postgraduate Diploma/MSc in Business Improvement (MSc) Part-time; minimum of 3 years work experience in a management position required; 16 months to 2 years to complete program. Concentrations in business policy/strategy, finance, financial management/planning, leadership, management, risk management, strategic management.

Executive Programme/MSc in Executive Leadership (MSc) Part-time; minimum of 7 years management experience at a senior level required; 16 months to 2 years to complete program. Concentrations in business policy/strategy, entrepreneurship, information management, leadership, management, strategic management.

ADMISSION

Application Requirements Application form, bachelor's degree, 2 letters of recommendation, minimum of 3 years of work experience.

Recommended for Application GMAT score accepted: minimum 450, personal statement, resume, college transcript(s).

Application Deadline 5/31 for fall.

ACADEMICS

Faculty Full-time 25.

Teaching Methodologies Lecture, seminars by members of the business community, team projects.

Technology The network has full access to the Internet. Students are not required to have their own PC.

FINANCES

Costs for 1997–98 Tuition: Full-time: £3150 per program (resident); £7700 per program (nonresident).

INTERNATIONAL STUDENTS

Demographics 2% of students enrolled are international students [Asia, 75%, Europe, 25%].

Services and Facilities International student office, international student housing, counseling/support services.

Applying TOEFL: minimum score of 550 required. Financial aid is not available to international students.

International Student Contact Stephen Parkinson, Dean, Shore Road, Newtownabbey, County Antrim BT37 0QB, Northern Ireland. Phone: 44-1232-368-087; Fax: 44-1232-366-843; E-mail: s.parkinson@ulst.ac.uk

PLACEMENT

Services include career counseling/planning, career fairs, career library, career placement, electronic job bank, and resume preparation.

Employment Types of employment entered: accounting, banking, communications, engineering, finance, financial services, government, human resources, management, manufacturing, marketing, nonprofit, pharmaceutical, retail, telecommunications, transportation.

Program Contact: Stephen Parkinson, Dean, Shore Road, Newtownabbey, County Antrim BT37 0QB, Northern Ireland. Phone: 44-1232-368-087; Fax: 44-1232-366-843; E-mail: s.parkinson@ulst.ac.uk

University of Wales

Business School

Cardiff, Wales, United Kingdom

OVERVIEW

The University of Wales coed institution. Enrollment: 14,262 graduate, professional, and undergraduate students. Founded: 1883. The graduate business unit is in an urban setting and is on a semester calendar.

HIGHLIGHTS

Enrollment Profile

Full-time: N/R	International: N/R
Part-time: N/R	Women: N/R
Total: 400	Minorities: N/R
Average Age: 22	Average Class Size: N/R
Fall 1997 Average GPA: N/R	Fall 1997 Average GMAT: N/R

Costs
Full-time tuition: N/R
Part-time tuition: N/R

GRADUATE BUSINESS PROGRAMS

Master of Business Administration (MBA) Full-time, part-time; 12 months to 2 years to complete program. Concentrations in management, public and private management, organizational management, environmental economics/management, international and area business studies.

Master of Science, International Banking and Finance (MSc) Full-time, part-time.

Master of Science, Human Resource Management (MSc) Full-time, part-time.

Master of Science, Financial Economics (MSc) Full-time, part-time.

ADMISSION

Application Requirements Application form, bachelor's degree, 2 letters of recommendation, college transcript(s).

Recommended for Application Minimum GPA, personal statement, resume, work experience, computer experience.

Application Deadline 7/31 for fall, 7/31 for fall (international). Deferred entrance is available.

ACADEMICS

Faculty Full-time 120.

Teaching Methodologies Case study, experiential learning, field projects, group discussion, lecture.

Technology Computer terminals/PCs are available for student use and are linked by a campus-wide network. The network has full access to the Internet. Students are not required to have their own PC.

FINANCES

Costs for 1997–98 Average 1997–98 room only costs were £6080 per academic year. Room and board costs vary by campus location, occupancy (e.g., single, double, triple), type of accommodation, type of meal plan.

Financial Aid Contact Ms. Rosemarie Dillon, Senior Assistant Registrar, PO Box 495, Cardiff, Wales CF1 3XD, United Kingdom. Phone: 44-1222-874-413; Fax: 44-1222-874-130.

INTERNATIONAL STUDENTS

Demographics N/R

Applying IELT: minimum score of 6.5, TOEFL: minimum score of 570 required. Financial aid is not available to international students.

International Student Contact Dr. Timothy Westlake, Head of International Office, PO Box 921, Cardiff, Wales CF1 3XQ, United Kingdom. Phone: 44-1222-874-432; Fax: 44-1222-827-622; E-mail: internat@ac.uk

PLACEMENT

Services include alumni network, career counseling/planning, and career placement.

Employment Types of employment entered: banking, consulting, finance, management, service industry.

Business Program(s) URL: http://www.cf.ac.uk/uwcc/carbs/carbs.html

Program Contact: Ms. Rosemarie Dillon, Senior Assistant Registrar, PO Box 495, Cardiff, Wales CF1 3XO, United Kingdom. Phone: 44-1222-874-413; Fax: 44-1222-874-130.

University of Warwick

Warwick Business School

Coventry, England, United Kingdom

OVERVIEW

The University of Warwick is a federally supported, coed institution. Enrollment: 15,600 graduate, professional, and undergraduate students; 2,300 full-time matriculated graduate/professional students; 3,600 part-time matriculated graduate/professional students. The graduate business unit is in a suburban setting and is on a trimester calendar.

HIGHLIGHTS

Enrollment Profile
Full-time: 1,106
Part-time: 2,054
Total: 3,160
Average Age: 32
Fall 1997 Average GPA: N/R

International: 50%
Women: 30%
Minorities: N/R
Average Class Size: 75
Fall 1997 Average GMAT: 610

Costs
Full-time tuition: £14,000 per academic year (resident); £14,000 per academic year (nonresident)
Part-time tuition: £4416 per program (resident); £4416 per program (nonresident)

GRADUATE BUSINESS PROGRAMS
Full-time MBA (MBA) Full-time; 12 months to complete program.

Evening MBA (MBA) Part-time; 3 years to complete program.

Modular MBA (MBA) Part-time; 4 years work experience required; 3 years to complete program.

Master of Science in Economics and Finance (MS) Full-time; 12 months to complete program.

Master of Science in Management Science and Operational Research (MS) Full-time, part-time; 12 months to 2 years to complete program.

Master of Arts in Industrial Relations (MA) Full-time, part-time; 12 months to 2 years to complete program.

Master of Arts in European Industrial Relations (MA) Full-time, part-time; 12 months to 2 years to complete program.

Master of Arts in Organization Studies (MA) Full-time, part-time; 12 months to 2 years to complete program.

Distance Learning MBA (MBA) distance learning option; 3 to 8 years to complete program.

ADMISSION
Applications For fall 1997 there were 5,700 applications for admission.

Application Requirements GMAT score: minimum 570, application form, application fee, bachelor's degree, interview, 2 letters of recommendation, resume, minimum of 3 years of work experience.

Recommended for Application Essay, personal statement, college transcript(s), computer experience.

Application Deadline Applications processed on a rolling/continuous basis for both domestic and international students. Application fee: £40. Deferred entrance is available.

ACADEMICS
Faculty Full-time 106; part-time 2.

Teaching Methodologies Case study, computer simulations, faculty seminars, field projects, group discussion, lecture, research, role playing, seminars by members of the business community, simulations, student presentations, study groups, team projects.

Technology Computer terminals/PCs are available for student use and are linked by a campus-wide network. The network has full access to the Internet. Students are not required to have their own PC.

Special Opportunities International exchange programs in Austria, Belgium, Canada, Denmark, Finland, France, Germany, Holland, Italy, South Africa, Sweden, United States. An internship program is available.

FINANCES
Costs for 1997–98 Tuition: Full-time: £14,000 per program (resident); £14,000 per program (nonresident). Part-time: £4416 per program (resident); £4416 per program (nonresident). Cost varies by academic program, class time (e.g., day/evening). Average 1997–98 room only costs were £2500 per academic year (on campus) and £2800 per academic year (off campus). Room and board costs vary by campus location, type of accommodation, type of meal plan.

Financial Aid Teaching assistantships, scholarships available.

Financial Aid Contact Ms. Karen Bull, Admissions Secretary, Warwick Business School, Coventry, England CV4 7AL, United Kingdom. Phone: 44-1203-524-485; Fax: 44-1203-524-643.

FACILITIES
Information Resources The University Library plus 4 additional on-campus libraries; total holdings of 900,000 volumes, 5,500 current periodical subscriptions. CD player(s) available for graduate student use. Access provided to online bibliographic retrieval services and online databases.

INTERNATIONAL STUDENTS
Demographics 50% of students enrolled are international students [Africa, 2%, Asia, 8%, Australia/New Zealand, 1%, Central America, 1%, Europe, 70%, North America, 2%, South America, 2%, other, 14%].

Services and Facilities International student office, international student center, international student housing, counseling/support services, international student orientation, language center.

Applying TOEFL: minimum score of 600, proof of adequate funds, proof of health/immunizations recommended. Financial aid is not available to international students.

International Student Contact Mrs. Diana Holton, Communications Officer, Warwick Business School, Coventry, England CV4 7AL, United Kingdom . Phone: 44-1203-534-306; Fax: 44-1203-523-719; E-mail: inquiries@wbs.warwick.ac.uk

PLACEMENT
Services include alumni network, career counseling/planning, career fairs, career library, career placement, job interviews arranged, job search course, resume referral to employers, and resume preparation. In 1996–97, 15 organizations participated in on-campus recruiting; 210 on-campus interviews were conducted.

Employment Of 1996–97 graduates, 90% were employed within three months of graduation; the average starting salary was £45,000. Types of employment entered: accounting, banking, communications, computer-related, consulting, consumer products, education, finance, financial services, government, health services, high technology, human resources, information systems/technology, insurance, law, management, manufacturing, marketing, nonprofit, retail, service industry.

Business Program(s) URL: http://www.wbs.warwick.ac.uk

Program Contact: Ms. Karen Bull, Programme Secretary, Warwick Business School, Coventry, England CV4 7AL, United Kingdom. Phone: 44-1203-524-485; Fax: 44-1203-524-643.

University of Westminster

Business School

London, England, United Kingdom

OVERVIEW
The University of Westminster coed institution. Enrollment: 10,000 graduate, professional, and undergraduate students. Founded: 1838. The graduate business unit is in an urban setting and is on a semester calendar.

HIGHLIGHTS

Enrollment Profile
Full-time: 70
Part-time: 190
Total: 260
Average Age: 32
Fall 1997 Average GPA: N/R

International: 23%
Women: 48%
Minorities: N/R
Average Class Size: 25
Fall 1997 Average GMAT: N/R

Costs
Full-time tuition: N/R
Part-time tuition: N/R

GRADUATE BUSINESS PROGRAMS
Master of Business Administration (MBA) Full-time, part-time; minimum age requirement: 25; 12 months to 2 years to complete program. Concentration in management.

Master of Business Administration in Design Management (MBA) Part-time, distance learning option; minimum age requirement: 25; up to 2 years to complete program.

ADMISSION
Application Requirements Application form, bachelor's degree, 2 letters of recommendation, personal statement, resume, college transcript(s), minimum of 3 years of work experience.

Recommended for Application GMAT score accepted, essay, interview.

Application Deadline Applications processed on a rolling/continuous basis for both domestic and international students.

ACADEMICS
Faculty Full-time 40; part-time 10.

Teaching Methodologies Case study, lecture, seminars by members of the business community, team projects.

INTERNATIONAL STUDENTS
Demographics 23% of students enrolled are international students [Africa, 10%, Asia, 10%, Central America, 10%, Europe, 50%, North America, 10%, South America, 10%].

Services and Facilities International student office, international student center, international student housing.

University of Westminster (continued)

Applying IELT: minimum score of 6, TOEFL: minimum score of 650 required. Financial aid is not available to international students.

International Student Contact Ms. Kerry Sullivan, MBA Course Coordinator, 35 Malibone Road, London, England NW1 5LS, United Kingdom. Phone: 44-171-911-5000 Ext. 3087; Fax: 44-171-911-5059; E-mail: sullivk@westminster.ac.uk

PLACEMENT
Services include alumni network, career placement, and resume preparation.
Employment Types of employment entered: accounting, finance, financial services, international trade, service industry.

Program Contact: Ms. Kerry Sullivan, MBA Course Coordinator, 35 Malibone Road, London, England NW1 5LS, United Kingdom. Phone: 44-171-911-5000 Ext. 3087; Fax: 44-171-911-5059; E-mail: sullivk@westminster.ac.uk

In-Depth Descriptions of MBA Programs

The following In-Depth Descriptions were prepared for this book by the dean or director of the MBA program or business school. Each description is designed to give the student a sense of the individuality of the school.

The absence from this section of any institution does not constitute an editorial decision on the part of Peterson's. In essence, this section is an open forum for institutions, on a voluntary basis, to communicate their particular messages to prospective students. The descriptions are arranged alphabetically by the official name of the institution.

Abilene Christian University

PREPARING FOR SERVICE AND LEADERSHIP

The distinction of ACU's M.B.A. program is that it offers a high-quality business education in a values-oriented environment. Abilene Christian University maintains a forty-year history of offering graduate business education to students from around the globe. We are proud to announce a new M.B.A. program for 1998—one that integrates cutting-edge business methods and technology with time-proven ideas. Whether they are beginning in business or seasoned executives, our alumni attest to the time spent at ACU as being a worthy investment.

—Jack A. Griggs, Dean

Programs and Curricular Focus

The ACU M.B.A. requires 40 hours of course work and can be completed in twelve to sixteen months. The first year includes an integrated business core that deepens skills, knowledge, and values for managerial careers. A May term internship or international field study follows the first year. Smaller projects that enrich managerial knowledge and skills are integrated throughout the curriculum. The third and final semester consists of in-depth specialization courses. Concentrations are currently offered in accounting, human resources and management, knowledge management, not-for-profit leadership, and ministry and mission.

The M.B.A. curriculum allows mentorships to develop between students and faculty members. It is rigorous yet supportive, leverages technology, and emphasizes a learning-by-doing orientation. Faculty members teach using the case method, classroom and electronic discussion, computer simulation, lecturettes, team projects, and field work. Some classes include videoconferencing links to experts in industry. ACU also offers a 30-hour Master of Accountancy (M.Acc.). The College of Business Administration is fully accredited by ACBSP and is in precandidacy for accreditation by AACSB–The International Association for Management Education.

Students and the M.B.A. Experience

M.B.A. students come from a variety of backgrounds. Approximately two thirds of them are working professionals representing manufacturing, banking, health care, utilities, public service, and other fields. The other third are full-time U.S. and international students. Joining employed and full-time students in classes enriches cross-industry and cross-cultural perspectives. The average age of the M.B.A. students is 28. Seventy-five percent have two or more years of work experience.

The Faculty

Nineteen full-time business professors combine strong academic, research, and business experience with Christian values, a dedication to teaching, and ongoing professional development. Combined, the faculty members have more than 360 years of business and consulting experience with firms such as Exxon, Conoco, EDS, Bank of America, Rockwell, and Texas Instruments. They hold outstanding academic credentials, with degrees from universities such as Boston, Texas, Texas A&M, Indiana, Arizona State, Southern Methodist, South Carolina, Illinois, Tulane, and Cornell. Half have lived or worked for an extended period outside the U.S. Several adjunct faculty members are experts who teach elective courses related to their professions.

The Business School Network

The ACU College of Business Administration maintains close ties to businesses in Texas and globally through its alumni, internship programs, videoconferences, and various support and review councils.

Prominent Alumni

ACU's College of Business Administration alumni include Royce Caldwell (B.S., 1961), President/CEO of Southwestern Bell Operations; C. E. "Doc" Cornutt (B.S., 1970), President, Hunt Capital; Bruce Huff (B.S., 1972), CFO,

Harken Energy Corporation; Robert D. Hunter (B.S., 1952; M.B.A., 1976), House of Representatives, State of Texas Legislature; Don C. Jackson (B.S., 1953), former Deputy Director of the National Security Agency; Du Hyen "Duke" Jung (M.S., 1964), President of Chunma World Corporation (Korea); S. Douglas Smith (B.S., 1960), former President of Hospital Corporation of America Consulting; and J. McDonald Williams (B.S., 1963), Chairman of the Board of the Trammell Crow Company. The College is proud of all its alumni who are working and living meaningfully in a variety of roles.

The College and Environs

Abilene Christian University emphasizes high-quality academics in a distinctively Christian environment. *U.S. News & World Report* recently named ACU as a "Best Value" in higher education based on academic quality, cost, and financial aid awarded. It also listed ACU in its *Best Colleges Guide,* ranking it in the highest quarter for academic quality among schools in its category. Founded in 1906, ACU is a private, comprehensive university with an enrollment of about 4,400. ACU is affiliated with Churches of Christ and is one of the largest private universities in the Southwest.

Located about 180 miles west of Dallas, Abilene is a city of 108,000 people, offering a safe community for living and study. It was rated by *Money* magazine as one of the best places to live in the U.S. The city has a philharmonic and opera, museums, two large medical complexes, three universities, a small airport, a zoo, city parks, excellent schools, and a lot of Southwestern culture. Dyess Air Force Base is also located in Abilene.

Facilities

The Mabee Business Building is a beautiful facility built in 1986 and equipped with case-type classrooms, a computer lab, student lounge, faculty offices, and tree-planted atrium.

The ACU Library holds more than 1 million books, microforms, audiovisual materials, government documents, and periodicals. LEXIS-NEXIS and other

Abilene Christian University's campus is home to students from fifty states and forty to sixty countries each year.

TOEFL scores. Selection also depends upon an applicant's achievements, talents, and motivation for graduate business education. Professional and international experience, foreign languages, writing ability, interpersonal and leadership skills, entrepreneurship, and personal integrity are some favored qualifications.

Finances

Tuition, books, transportation, and living expenses for the 1998–99 academic year are approximately $13,105. Tuition alone is $308 per semester hour. Partial tuition scholarships and graduate assistantships are awarded on the basis of academic merit and financial need to U.S. citizens and foreign nationals. The Student Financial Services Office assists financially eligible applicants who are U.S. citizens to meet their educational and living expenses.

International Students

ACU is a welcoming setting for international students. International diversity is valued, with 20 to 30 percent of the M.B.A. students coming from countries such as Belarus, Botswana, Chile, China, El Salvador, Hong Kong, Japan, Singapore, Taiwan, Thailand, Uganda, and Uzbekistan. An orientation familiarizes students with the campus, library and computer network, American culture and business education, and the city of Abilene. An intensive English program is offered for students wishing to improve TOEFL or TSE scores.

Application Facts and Dates

Students may apply at any time during the year but are encouraged to apply at least three months prior to the semester in which they plan to begin course work. Full-time students begin in August, although some arrive early to take summer leveling or language course work. Part-time students may begin in June, August, or January. Applicants receive notification shortly after receipt of the complete application. For further information or application materials, students should contact:

The Graduate School
ACU Box 29140
Abilene Christian University
Abilene, Texas 79699-9140
Telephone: 800-395-4723 (toll-free)
915-674-2354 (outside the U.S. and Canada)
Fax: 915-674-6717
E-mail: mbainfo@pe.acu.edu
World Wide Web: http://www.acu.edu/academics/mba

online computer periodical indexes are available. The catalog is fully automated and linked to five local university and public libraries.

Technology Environment

The College of Business Administration computer lab is equipped with more than ninety desktop computers with word processing, database, spreadsheet, and presentation software and laser printers. Students have free access to e-mail and the Internet through ACU's fiber-optic network.

Placement

The Career Services Office helps students develop the skills needed to make sound career decisions and conduct effective job searches. Recruitment usually takes place off campus. Nearly all ACU M.B.A. graduates have employment opportunities identified and selected within two months of graduation. Recent employers of full-time students include GTE, Otis Elevator, the U.S. Department of Justice, General Electric, Samsung, Ernst & Young, and Coopers & Lybrand.

Admission

Students are admitted to the program based on a careful evaluation of academic records, professional qualifications, GMAT scores, and personal attributes. Most applicants whose first language is not English are requested to submit

Adelphi University

School of Management and Business

Garden City, New York

DEVELOPING BUSINESS LEADERS FOR THE TWENTY-FIRST CENTURY

▶ *Today, business needs leaders with the analytic sophistication and entrepreneurial judgment to effectively deal with the forces that are transforming our "global village." Rather than attempting to train individuals for jobs that may not even exist two or three years hence, our progressive interdisciplinary approach to management education is designed to produce individuals with a broad education who have the managerial competence, curiosity, and creativity needed for success in the twenty-first century.*

In this era of enormous challenges and radical possibilities, we are guided by a firm commitment that ensures our graduates will be thinkers with a broad perspective as well as proficient in the skills necessary for professional excellence and success.

—Rakesh C. Gupta, Dean

Programs and Curricular Focus

In keeping with Adelphi University's tradition of a liberal education, all of the School's graduate degree programs provide for a general management orientation along with solid training in all the functional areas of business. This general management orientation is achieved through a highly integrated group of professional foundation core courses. Through the foundation core, students acquire the analytic and quantitative decision-making skills needed for success by learning how to view and resolve management problems from all functional perspectives.

The program's breadth component examines twenty-first-century management issues, such as leadership, future trends, entrepreneurship, technology management, and total quality management on the global level and is designed to further enrich the students' professional and learning experience.

Themes such as the global perspective, creativity, change and innovation, team building, ethics, and cultural diversity are important components of the programs of study. These are not individual courses but unifying themes that are infused into the entire curricula.

Elective and specialization courses are also integral to the programs, affording students the opportunity to tailor their program of study to their own professional interests and career needs.

In addition to the M.B.A. with its eight areas of specialization, the School offers an M.B.A./CPA degree program; M.S. degrees in accounting and in finance and banking; and graduate certificates in banking, human resources management, and management. The number of credits required to earn a degree and the length of time it takes to complete a degree program vary and are dependent upon the student's previous academic background and on whether he or she chooses to study on a full-time or part-time basis.

Students and the M.B.A. Experience

Students come from across the United States and many other countries, bringing with them a wide variety of undergraduate majors and professional backgrounds. They form a dynamic community whose diversity enriches the educational experience. Professional clubs and organizations, such as the Accounting Society, the Marketing and Finance clubs, and the Business Council, bring together students with common interests.

Guest speakers, internship opportunities, and the Distinguished Lecture Series further serve to enhance and enrich the learning environment.

There is a Student Board that serves as an advisory council, and interaction between the faculty, staff, and students is strong, even outside the classroom. Faculty and staff support and participate in events run by students, and students also get the opportunity to network with alumni, advisory board members, and other corporate executives at other special events.

Special Features

Course schedules are designed to accommodate the schedules of men and women engaged in full-time careers. In addition to the main Garden City campus, courses are also offered at the Huntington Center, making graduate business education more accessible to those who reside on eastern Long Island. Courses at both locations are scheduled Monday through Thursday evenings and on Saturdays. Each course meets once a week.

A weekend M.B.A. program option is also available at the University's Garden City campus, Huntington Center, and Manhattan Center (located in Soho). Classes meet on Friday evenings and Saturday mornings. Trisemester programming enables qualified business majors to earn an M.B.A. in about eighteen months.

Switching between campuses is a student's option. Students may take courses at Garden City one semester and go to Huntington the next, or they may take courses at all three campuses during the same semester.

The Faculty

The School's faculty members have strong academic and professional backgrounds. Many have held top-level positions in business, engage in research and publication activities, and have been educated at many of the best academic institutions around the world.

Excellence in, and equal emphasis on, both teaching and research is the hallmark of the School. The faculty's research is considered to be pioneering and on the cutting edge and consistently wins critical acclaim and praise from both the academic and business worlds. The faculty members' wide range of expertise makes them sought after as consultants to major companies, entrepreneurial firms, and not-for-profit agencies.

The students profit from the faculty's academic and professional backgrounds, as well as from their commitment to the advancement of knowledge in their area of specialization. All of the research and consulting the professors do enriches every course they teach, and this, in combination with their dynamic and superb teaching skills, enables them to effectively communicate the principles and practices of management as it is actually conducted.

The Business School Network

An advisory board helps ensure that the programs meet the needs of the corporate community and provide and assist with internships and job placements. The School's advisory board consists of prominent alumni, CEOs, presidents, CFOs, and other senior executives from major corporations.

The College and Environs

Adelphi University is located in Garden City, Long Island, New York, a beautiful suburban community that is approximately 18 miles east of midtown Manhattan. It is the oldest private university on Long Island. Today, a full-time faculty of nearly 200 serves a student body of about 6,000 undergraduate and graduate degree candidates.

The location affords easy access both to the beaches, waters, and quiet living of Long Island and to the commercial and cultural capital of the world, New York City.

Facilities

The average class size in the School of Management and Business is only 20, and many of the classrooms are outfitted with the very latest in multimedia technology.

The library is completely computerized. It houses approximately 470,000 volumes and an ever-growing collection of electronic resources based on CD-ROM technology.

Adelphi boasts one of the largest mainframe computer installations on Long Island, and, in addition, there are more than 450 IBM and Macintosh personal computers that are available for student use. Access to the Internet and a large variety of CD-ROM databases is also available.

Placement

Placement is coordinated through the University's Center for Career Planning and Placement. More than 200 top corporations, major banks, and international accounting firms recruit on campus.

Experienced counselors take the time to assess the student's interests and skills and to help the student effectively market himself or herself and make the right career decisions whether he or she is a young graduate, an experienced professional seeking a career change, or someone returning to the work force.

Admission

Candidates applying for admission must submit a completed application form with an essay, official transcripts, two letters of recommendation, and their score on the Graduate Management Admission Test (GMAT) to the Office of Graduate Admissions. The GMAT score for students enrolling at Adelphi has recently ranged between 450 and 500. The average undergraduate GPA has been 3.0.

International applicants must also submit a TOEFL score of at least 550, as well as a declaration and certificate of finances.

Finances

For 1997–98, the comprehensive tuition and fee rate for 12 or more credits was $14,850. The rate for 1-11 credits was $465 per credit plus a $150 nonrefundable University fee. Additional fees and charges may be assessed. Students should consult with the Office of Student Financial Services for the latest tuition rate and fee information, as well as the latest information concerning financial aid.

Students should consult with the Office of Residential Life and Housing for information about the availability and costs for graduate housing.

Application Facts and Dates

Applicants should file their application and supporting credentials by the following dates: fall semester, August 15; spring semester, December 15; and summer sessions, May 15. For more information, applicants should contact:

Jennifer Spiegel
Associate Director of Graduate
    Admissions
Adelphi University
Garden City, New York 11530
Telephone: 800-ADELPHI (toll-free)
Fax: 516-877-3039
E-mail: admissions@adelphi.edu
World Wide Web: http://www.adelphi.
    edu

Alfred University

College of Business

Alfred, New York

> ### RESPONDING TO CRITICAL DEMANDS
>
> *Alfred University's M.B.A. responds to three critical demands from the marketplace. First, it offers an interdisciplinary approach to management education. Second, it is practice oriented, focusing on application and skill development. Third, it is compact and accessible, providing students an efficient opportunity for completing graduate work in a reasonable time period. This work is completed on a personal scale, with small classes and close interaction with faculty members and peers. These features provide an intense and dynamic learning environment.*
>
> —Dr. David Szczerbacki, Dean

Programs and Curricular Focus

The Alfred University M.B.A. is a general management degree that emphasizes the development of leadership. The program can be completed in a minimum of 30 semester credit hours or a maximum of 54 semester credit hours. Individuals possessing an undergraduate degree in business or the equivalent are, in most cases, able to complete the program with 30 credit hours. Individuals with little or no business education first complete the foundation classes, then move into the core and electives. This can total a maximum of 54 credits.

The time frame for the M.B.A. is two semesters and one summer session for those requiring 30 credits. Those requiring up to 54 credits may require an additional two semesters. The program is available on a full-time and part-time basis.

Foundation classes are in the functional areas of business: accounting, economics, financial management, information systems, statistics, quantitative methods, organizational behavior, and marketing. This body of knowledge totals 24 semester credit hours. Students complete this sequence before entering the M.B.A. core classes.

The core focuses on leadership development in a global, highly competitive business environment. The work is case-based and involves team analysis and problem solving. The classes are leadership dynamics; financial decision making; legal, political, and social environment of business; global dimensions of management; quality information systems; and a capstone strategic management simulation. This M.B.A. core is 18 semester credit hours.

Elective courses may be selected from the areas of accounting, economics, finance, information systems, management, marketing, and quantitative methods. Students are also able to integrate graduate course work from other colleges within Alfred University. These include ceramic engineering, community services administration, and education. All electives are tailored to meet the career objectives of M.B.A. students.

Students and the M.B.A. Experience

The M.B.A. program enrolls approximately 10 full-time students and 30 part-time students. The average age of full-time students is 25, and they average two to three years of work experience before entering the M.B.A. program. Approximately 25 percent are female, and the majority of the full-time students have a business undergraduate degree. Part-time students average 32 years of age and are equally divided among business, engineering, and liberal arts educational backgrounds.

Classwork in the M.B.A. core is teamwork in nature. This creates a high degree of camaraderie among students, which is enhanced by the fact that full-time students move through these classes as a group.

The Faculty

M.B.A. students benefit from faculty members who have significant practical experiences in their field of interest. They are constantly engaged in research, which enriches the classroom learning process and in which students may participate. All College of Business graduate faculty members hold doctorates in their field. The ratio of faculty members to students is 1:16.

The Business School Network

The M.B.A. program at Alfred University is supported by an advisory board comprising senior managers from companies such as Corning Inc., Dresser-Rand, and GE. These corporate leaders provide significant input as to the relevance of the curriculum and trends in management practice. They also enrich the program by critiquing case presentations and speaking on recent developments in management practice.

The College maintains an Executive in Residence program that brings important corporate and government leaders to campus for extended periods. These executives serve as resources for M.B.A. classes and participate in various seminars and colloquia of the College.

The College and Environs

Alfred University, founded in 1836, comprises the privately endowed Colleges of Business, Engineering and Professional Studies, and Liberal Arts and Sciences as well as the publicly funded New York State College of Ceramics. The oldest coeducational institution in New York State, the University grants degrees at the bachelor's, master's, and doctoral levels. The fifty-eight building, 232-acre hillside campus adjoins the village of Alfred, located in an attractive natural setting between the foothills of the Allegheny Mountains and the Finger Lakes Region of upstate New York.

Alfred University is consistently ranked among the top comprehensive universities in the Northeast.

Facilities

The College of Business is housed in the recently completed F. W. Olin Building. This $5.6-million facility offers outstanding classroom, lecture, conferencing, and laboratory facilities. The M.B.A. program is supported by multiple mainframe and personal computer systems. These include a networked classroom as well as an open computing area for student use. The

College has a separate Decision Support Center, which is used for electronic group decision making, as well as an advanced computer laboratory for projects such as neural networking and expert systems.

Most of the classrooms are equipped for in-class computer utilization. The networks are connected to the DEC Vax, which enables access to the Internet.

The University maintains two libraries, Scholes Library of Ceramics, which supports engineering and the College of Ceramics, as well as Herrick Library, which supports liberal arts and sciences, professional studies, and the College of Business. Herrick Library holds nearly a quarter of a million volumes and more than 1,000 periodicals. Library holdings include CD-ROM workstations for reference and corporate information. National and international sources are available through the Internet. It also maintains an automated online public access system.

Placement

The University Career Development Center works closely with M.B.A. students. All M.B.A. students are required to complete a two-session Career Development Seminar as part of their professional development. This program covers areas such as resume and cover letter writing, electronic job searching, effective interviewing, and how to survive the first year of one's first job.

Admission

Admission to the M.B.A. program is based on undergraduate performance, letters of recommendation, and GMAT scores. Recommendations are typically submitted by a former employer and professor. Using the formula GMAT plus undergraduate GPA times 200, the College requires a minimum total score of 1025.

Finances

Tuition for the 1998–99 academic year is $20,376. Room and board are $6790 per year. Books and supplies are approximately $380 per semester. The College of Business is able to offer all qualified full-time students a graduate assistantship, which reduces tuition by half. The assistantship requires students to work 7.5 hours per week, typically with a graduate faculty member in their area of interest. These assistantships are renewable.

Financial aid, typically in the form of loans, is available. Information can be obtained from the Office of Student Financial Aid at 607-871-2159.

Application Facts and Dates

Applications are accepted until early June. For more information, students should contact:

Dr. David Szczerbacki, Dean
College of Business
Alfred University
Alfred, New York 14802
Telephone: 607-871-2646
Fax: 607-871-2114
E-mail: fszczerbacki@bigvax.alfred.edu

For applications, students should contact:

Office of Graduate Admissions
Alfred University
Saxon Drive
Alfred, New York 14802-1232
Telephone: 607-871-2141
            800-541-9229 (toll-free)

American Graduate School of Business

La Tour-de-Peilz (Montreux), Switzerland

> ## DEVELOPING BUSINESS LEADERS FOR THE TWENTY-FIRST CENTURY
>
> *AGSB, the American Graduate School of Business, is a nonprofit private institution of higher education, offering the Master of International Business Administration, the specialized M.B.A. AGSB has the unique ability to claim a dedicated and caring faculty, a small but select student body composed of eighteen nationalities, and a sound academic program designed to prepare students to lead the world and meet the challenges of the future. By providing a basis for competent and responsible leadership in business and politics, AGSB aims to develop in each student a respect and understanding of individuals of different cultures and a desire for continued intellectual growth.*
>
> *—Carmen Corchon Pernet, President, Steering Committee*

Programs and Curricular Focus

The Master of International Business Administration (M.I.B.A.) program offered by AGSB is based on a philosophy that the world's future leaders must operate in a multicultural environment and be able to adapt to changing social, political, legal, and economic conditions. The M.I.B.A. is a one-year intensive program for university graduates who hold a bachelor's degree with a major in business administration. For university graduates who do not hold such a degree, the M.I.B.A. is a two-year program, with the first year consisting of business foundation courses.

To earn the M.I.B.A. degree, the student must successfully complete a program consisting of eight internationally oriented core courses (24 semester credit hours), one two-term seminar course (3 semester credit hours), two advanced foreign language courses (6 semester credit hours), and an internship with project (6 semester credit hours). At least 30 semester credit hours of work (excluding foundation courses) must be completed in residence. For students whose foreign language competence is below the level required for the M.I.B.A. program, AGSB will arrange for special language courses outside the regular curriculum.

Courses for the M.I.B.A. degree include International Business Economics, International Accounting Practices, The International Legal and Ethical Environment, International Management, International Marketing, Decision Theory, Information Systems Concepts, International Finance, the Special Topics

Seminar, Advanced Foreign Language, Business Foreign Language, and the Project Internship.

All of the programs offered by AGSB are authorized by the Department of Education of the Canton of Vaud, Switzerland, and by the Commission of Higher Education of the State of Georgia, United States, under the Nonpublic Postsecondary Educational Institutions Act.

Students and the M.I.B.A. Experience

The student body at AGSB is truly international in scope. While 38 percent of the participants are American, the rest are from Europe (31 percent), the Pacific Rim (23 percent), and other regions (8 percent). The average student at AGSB is 26 years old with roughly five years of work experience. Forty-five percent of the student body are women, and most of the students have a previous background in business, engineering, or related technologies.

Special Features

An integral and distinguishing part of the M.I.B.A. program is the three- to six-month internship, in which the student is involved in the normal business operations of an organization. The nature of the internship is defined prior to a student's placement with a company. This internship must be taken under the sponsorship of the M.I.B.A. program and may be carried out in any country. Over the course of the internship, the student submits periodic reports and a final internship project, covering an in-depth

company and industry analysis relating to the internship. With the directed internship experience and related projects, the substantial language training provided by the M.I.B.A. program, and the international education given through the academic courses, AGSB's M.I.B.A. graduates are well-equipped to enter the international business arena.

The Faculty

The M.I.B.A. program provides a basis for competent and responsible leadership in international business, government, and nonprofit organizations. The language of instruction is English, with courses taught by dedicated, highly-trained, multilingual faculty members with extensive international experience. Methods of teaching include lectures, case analyses, student presentations, seminars with leaders from business and government, and directed internships with national and international organizations. Students benefit from the numerous field trips to such internationally recognized establishments as Nestlé, Caterpillar, and the Zurich Stock Exchange, to name a few.

The Business School Network

All of the AGSB programs are designed to develop an understanding of human behavior, cultural sensitivity, and a global perspective in business and politics. AGSB's location in Switzerland helps accomplish these objectives. The Montreux-Vevey region affords easy access to the culturally rich and internationally active cities of Geneva, Zurich, and Bern. Geneva, with its many international organizations such as the United Nations, the World Trade Organization, the International Labor Organization, and the World Health Organization, is an ideal setting for students to observe and become involved in the world of international relations. In addition, the university city of Lausanne is only 20 minutes away by car or rail. Switzerland's central location in Europe makes Paris, Milan, Munich, and other business and political centers quickly and easily accessible by rail, air, or private transportation.

"AGSB is more than a valuable education; it is an experience of a lifetime."—student quotation

The College and Environs

Located on the shores of Lac Léman (Lake Geneva) in the heart of the Swiss Riviera, La Tour-de-Peilz offers a relatively mild climate. Long known for its tourist appeal, the Montreux-Vevey region, of which La Tour-de-Peilz is a part, has also built a cultural reputation through events such as the Montreux Jazz Festival. Annual international conferences and symposiums, in communication and direct marketing for example, indicate the region's vibrancy and commitment to the world of business.

Students may take advantage of many extracurricular activities such as cycling, hiking, sailing, and skiing in the internationally known resorts of the Swiss Alps. The ski areas of Gstaad, Verbier, and Crans-Montana are easily accessible for a day's outing. For an evening's excursion, theaters, museums, and cinemas abound.

Facilities

AGSB is one of the few private schools in Switzerland with modern facilities specially designed to serve the needs of its students. The facilities include modern classrooms, faculty and administrative offices, a computer laboratory, specially-equipped language classrooms, a student lounge, and a library reference room. A special modem link to the University of Lausanne Library complex allows for easy reference to over 1.2 million volumes, and next-day book delivery service affords quick access within the AGSB facilities.

Placement

All of the programs at AGSB emphasize the importance of oral presentations as a means to enrich interpersonal communi-

cation skills. In the end, students are well-prepared for the interview process. Students are assisted in their resume writing, often into several languages, by experienced professionals. AGSB works directly with M.I.B.A. candidates in their search for an internship that is both stimulating to the student and beneficial to the corporate sponsor. In many cases, the relationship between the intern and the sponsor is so mutually rewarding that the student is requested to remain with the organization following graduation.

Admission

Applicants for the M.I.B.A. program must possess a bachelor's degree from a recognized college or university and demonstrate an academic record indicating potential for success in the M.I.B.A. program. To apply for admission, students must complete application procedures and submit scores for the Graduate Management Admission Test (GMAT) as well as the Test of English as a Foreign Language (TOEFL) for nonnative English speakers.

Finances

For 1997–98, tuition and fees were SwFr 15,000 per semester. Living expenses, including housing, food, and transportation, are estimated at SwFr 1000 per month, depending on the living standard to which the student is accustomed. AGSB is one of the few European business schools whose students are eligible to receive financial assistance through the Graduate Management Admission Council's comprehensive M.B.A. loan program. Scholarships, based on merit and financial need, are available to U.S. and international students.

Application Facts and Dates

AGSB has a policy of rolling admissions, with students admitted on a space-available basis. Notification of acceptance or rejection will be made in writing as soon as possible after an applicant has completed admissions procedures. For more information, applicants should contact:

Director of Admissions
AGSB
The American Graduate School of
     Business
Place des Anciens-Fossés
1814 La Tour-de-Peilz (P)
Switzerland
Telephone: 0041-21-944-95–01
Fax: 0041-21-944-95–04
E-mail: agsb@vtx.ch

American University

Kogod College of Business Administration

Washington, D.C.

KOGOD'S ADVANTAGE IN THE GLOBAL ECONOMY

The Kogod M.B.A. Program prepares students to meet the challenges they are sure to encounter as managers in the global marketplace of the twenty-first century. While preserving our 45-year-old tradition of outstanding business education—including small classes, professors who are recognized authorities in their fields, state-of-the-art computer facilities, concern for ethical and social responsibility, and outstanding career placement—we have created dynamic, innovative curricula to give students a competitive edge.

Kogod students train to become complete managers. They learn to see business as a system with interdependent parts, to master at least one functional area of business, and to think creatively, lead, motivate, and inspire. Our location in the nation's capital gives students the unique opportunity to observe the crucial relationship between business and government and the globalization of their field of study.

—Myron J. Roomkin, Dean

Programs and Curricular Focus

Kogod's M.B.A. program focuses on the realities of the global economy using cross-functional coordination, teamwork, internships, field studies, and ties with the business community. Students gain a broad base of practical skills and a theoretical understanding of the issues in today's global business environment.

The program consists of 54 credit hours of study, with 39 in core courses, 9 in an area of concentration, and 6 in electives. It is offered in both full- and part-time formats. Students who have completed the equivalent of the first semester of the M.B.A. program in their undergraduate curriculum with a B or better may qualify for a block waiver of the first 13 credits in the full-time program or individual course waivers in the part-time program.

The core curriculum provides a broad foundation in the functional areas of business. Course work in the first year includes accounting, economics, organizational behavior, statistics, operations research, marketing, finance, information systems, international business, and managerial skills. Second-year students gain knowledge in ethical standards, quality management, and legal issues confronting the global business manager. Full-time students participate in a field study, working in small teams on a consulting assignment for a firm in the business community. Students can also choose an area of concentration from one of ten different fields or design

their own, with faculty approval, choosing courses from Kogod and other American University (AU) schools and colleges.

Full-time students entering in the fall can complete the program in twenty-one months; with block waivers for the first semester, the program can be completed sooner. Entering in January allows completion in seventeen months. A flexible evening program is also offered.

Joint-degree programs, with some courses counting toward both programs, are also offered with other AU colleges. Among these are the J.D./M.B.A., the M.B.A./M.A. in international affairs, and the M.S. in personnel and human resource management. In addition, Kogod offers Master of Science degrees in accounting, taxation, and finance, requiring 30 to 63 credit hours of study.

Students and the M.B.A. Experience

Students at the University come from all fifty states and 150 countries and represent nearly all age groups and interests. Many business students are already successful executives and bring relevant experience with them into the classroom.

Students in the M.B.A. program have undergraduate degrees from all the disciplines. In a recent entering class, the average age was 26, with five as the average number of years of work experience. Forty percent of the class were women; 20 percent were members of minority groups.

Teamwork shapes a student's studies at Kogod. In the first year, students develop a strong sense of camaraderie as they take all their classes with the same 35 students, or cohort, who are further divided into study teams of 5 students.

Domestic and international internships give students real-world, hands-on experience.

❖ Global Focus

The Kogod program promotes a global orientation through diversity training, links with international institutions, and international exchange programs. In the M.B.A. program, students can work for one of the many international organizations based in Washington or intern abroad with a multinational organization. They can also choose to become exchange students at a distinguished foreign university.

A global perspective permeates the entire curriculum. More than 40 percent of Kogod graduate students are from one of fifty-five nations. In their classes, students learn to do business with people from Latin America, the Middle East, the Pacific Rim, and Europe by learning about business with them.

The Faculty

Kogod's reputation is distinguished by a faculty of internationally recognized scholars who, like Kogod students, come from every corner of the world. Through their consultancies with all sectors of government and business and their own research, the 59 full-time faculty members have an immense body of knowledge to share with students. Kogod faculty members involve students in developing state-of-the-art solutions to real problems facing industry today.

The Business School Network

Kogod's ties with national and international businesses ensure that students make solid professional contacts and get a thorough grounding in the realities of the global economy. Executives in residence give students insight into day-to-day problem solving in current business practice. Prominent men and women, high-echelon officials from

The future home of the Kogod College of Business Administration.

industry, government, and nonprofit organizations, answer students' queries in a leadership speaker series. Business leaders, union leaders, and government officials keep students abreast of current trends and strategy at the dean's annual leadership conference. In addition, the Board of Visitors ensures that the program stays in step with the global business environment.

Field projects and internships with firms in the thriving private sector of Washington (in communications, biotechnology, and software development, to name a few areas) offer outstanding opportunities for making corporate contacts. Through AU's connections to organizations throughout the world, students expand their professional networks abroad.

The College and Environs

American University is an independent, coeducational university in Washington, D.C., chartered by an Act of Congress in 1893. The Kogod College of Business Administration was the first such college in the nation's capital; its M.B.A. program has been offered since 1949. The University's 76-acre main campus, site of Kogod's offices and classrooms, and an 8-acre satellite campus are located in northwest Washington. In quiet, residential neighborhoods surrounded by embassies and historic buildings, both campuses are minutes from the wealth of historical and cultural resources of the city. Home to political leaders, diplomats, and businesspeople, Washington is vibrant, diverse, and stimulating.

Placement

Kogod's Graduate Business Career Services Office is available exclusively to graduate business students. From orientation through graduation and beyond, this office offers career workshops, one-on-one

career advising, resume and cover letter critiquing services, and job and internship postings sent directly to student e-mail accounts. The office also promotes networking with alumni and other professionals through an alumni database, networking receptions, career fairs, and other professional events throughout the year.

Kogod is a founding member of the Capital M.B.A. Consortium, an annual fall event that brings national and international employers to the Washington area to interview M.B.A. students from fifteen accredited graduate business programs. In addition, Kogod's Career Services Office hosts employers in the fall and spring semesters for on-campus interviewing and company information sessions.

Students have full access to the University's Co-op Office, which assists students in finding credit-bearing work experiences during the graduate program. Domestic and international co-ops are available.

Admission

To apply to the Kogod graduate business programs, students must have a baccalaureate degree from a regionally accredited institution, a satisfactory score on the Graduate Management Admission Test (GMAT), and a satisfactory grade point average for the last 60 hours of academic work. If English is not an applicant's native language, he or she must present a satisfactory score on the Test of English as a Foreign Language (TOEFL). The M.B.A. program and the M.S. programs in accounting and finance do not require an undergraduate degree in a particular discipline; the graduate taxation program requires an undergraduate degree in business administration.

The Kogod graduate admissions committee pays close attention to how applicants present themselves in the application's Personal Statements. The committee looks for well-written and carefully crafted statements that indicate an applicant's commitment both to graduate study and to his or her particular field of study. Above all, American University seeks graduate students who are committed to excellence. Prior work experience is encouraged but not required.

Finances

Tuition for the Kogod M.B.A. Program is $687 per credit hour for part-time students and $9540 per semester for full-time students. This fee also covers the costs for the orientation and all workshops. The cost of the Master of Science degree programs is $687 per credit hour. Additional costs for full-time students include room and board, books, and other miscellaneous fees and expenses.

Financial awards based on merit are available for full-time students, who are automatically considered for this type of aid when they apply for admission. Need-based financial assistance, in the form of federally or commercially sponsored loans, is available for full- and part-time students. To apply, students need to submit the Free Application for Federal Student Aid by March 1. The loan programs have a variety of qualifications and eligibility requirements, which are maintained in the University's collection of information. Only U.S. citizens and permanent residents are eligible for federal need-based aid.

Notification of financial assistance is March 15 through June.

Application Facts and Dates

Applications are accepted for fall and spring enrollment on a rolling admissions basis. For priority consideration for merit awards, applications should be on file by June 1 for fall enrollment and by November 1 for spring enrollment. For more information, students should contact:

Director of Admissions
Kogod College of Business
    Administration
American University
4400 Massachusetts Avenue, NW
Washington, D.C. 20016
Telephone: 202-885-1913
            800-AN-AU-MBA
            (toll-free)
Fax: 202-885-1078
E-mail: aumbams@american.edu

ASU Arizona State University

College of Business

Tempe, Arizona

REALISTIC KNOWLEDGE—THE ASU MBA PROGRAM

These are exciting times for business professionals. Global markets are expanding rapidly and opening new doors. Fast-paced technological advances are rendering established products and services obsolete and changing the way business is conducted. The ASU MBA Program is committed to providing an M.B.A. experience that will prepare students for management positions in this dynamic business climate. The program is characterized by two main features. The first is an emphasis on the carefully selected, critical skills of leadership, teamwork, communications, global and multicultural awareness, and realistic knowledge of business practice. The second is a faculty cognizant of the business knowledge and skills necessary to meet the demands of the twenty-first century.

I am proud to introduce you to this vital, creative, future-oriented institution and its outstanding programs and faculty. I invite you to visit us and meet faculty, staff, and students. See for yourself the campus environment, with its semitropical beauty, outstanding computer facilities, nationally ranked research library, and unparalleled recreational facilities.

—Larry Edward Penley, Dean

Programs and Curricular Focus

The objective of the ASU MBA Program at is to provide an enriching educational experience that has lifelong value. The central theme is to build and strengthen students' knowledge, basic skills, and managerial abilities by means of technical, analytical, and case materials associated with the functional areas of business.

The first-year core provides students with a broad exposure to functional areas of business applicable to many types of businesses. Special emphasis is given to team skills, analytical skills, ethical decision-making skills, and written and oral communication. Options for the second year include career tracks in service marketing and management, supply chain management, financial management and markets, dual degrees in Master of Accountancy, Taxation, Information Management, Health Services Administration, and Economics. An MIM with Thunderbird (AGSIM) may also be completed in the second year. Other master's programs may be considered for concurrent degrees (e.g., M.S. in engineering).

Dual degrees that take more than two years are the M.B.A./J.D. and M.B.A./ M.S. in architecture. Application must be made separately to each program for acceptance. The ASU MBA for Executives program and the Ph.D. degree in business administration and in economics are also available.

Students and the M.B.A. Experience

Students at ASU have diverse academic and geographic backgrounds. In the fall 1997 entering class, the average age was 28, with five years of work experience. Eighteen percent of the students are ethnic minorities, 20 percent are international students, and 34 percent are women. Forty-two percent of the students are from the Southwest and West, but more students are applying from other parts of the country as ASU rises in national prominence. Business and engineering bachelor's degrees are held by the largest percentage of incoming students.

Students automatically become members of the ASU MBA Association and may participate in community service through the Collegiate Volunteer Council, contribute to the ASU MBA Newsletter, work on field projects, do summer internships, or join the Graduate Women in Business organization, Hispanic MBA Student Association, Black Student MBA Association, ASU MBAsia, or the Masters Consulting Group.

Arizona State is one of seventeen universities nationwide that participates in the Washington Campus program. This one-month opportunity is available for credit between the first and second year.

❖ Global Focus

A summer program is available in Toulouse, France. English is the language of instruction for this program and other international summer programs. Other exchange programs include Group ESC Toulouse—Toulouse, France, and Universidad Carlos III de Madrid— Madrid, Spain.

The Faculty

The nationally renowned faculty at Arizona State is cognizant of the business knowledge and skills necessary for a changing business environment. All courses are taught by full-time faculty members with established records in business, consulting, leading-edge research, and professional education. The School of Accountancy and Information Management has one of the largest accounting faculties in the United States. The College has 165 full-time faculty members, 62 of whom teach in the ASU MBA Program.

The Business School Network

Corporate Partnerships

The ASU College of Business, one of the largest comprehensive business schools in the nation, is emerging as a leader in management research and education. Contributing to the College's success is its close relationship with the business community through organizations like the Dean's Council of 100. Faculty members and senior managers recently collaborated in the Business Partners program to develop a challenging vision and responsive strategic plan for the College of Business. A key part of that strategy involves increasing relationships with local and international companies.

Most career tracks in the ASU MBA Program offer a practicum or an applied project. These hands-on activities allow students to develop problem-solving skills, enhance communication skills, and gain valuable insight into current issues involving the business community. These projects put students in touch with innovations in technology and practical uses of research.

Prominent Alumni

Distinguished alumni include Craig Weatherup, CEO, PepsiCo; Tom Evans, Publisher, *U.S. News & World Report*; Steve Marriot, Vice President of Corporate Marketing, Marriot Hotels; John Darragh, President and CEO, Standard Register; Scott Wald, President, ASAP Software Company; Jim Baum, Senior Vice President and Assistant General Manager, Motorola-SSTG; and Steve Evans, Partner, Evans-Withy-combe.

The College and Environs

ASU, founded in 1885, is the sixth-largest university in the United States, with more than 44,500 students on its 700-acre main campus. Spacious walkways and modern architecture define the picturesque campus setting. ASU's campus evolved into an arbore-tum of national status in 1990—one of six in Arizona. The sunny and semitropi-cal climate contributes to a Southwestern lifestyle with mild winter temperatures that enable students to enjoy the outdoors year-round.

Facilities

The University's Charles Trumbull Hayden Library is one of the largest research libraries in North America. It contains more than 2.9 million volumes, including many in business and econom-ics, and the specialized Arthur C. Young Tax Collection.

The College of Business is housed in two adjacent buildings that contain an auditorium; lecture halls; seminar rooms; faculty, administrative, and graduate offices; and several computer resource centers. The M.B.A. Program Suite includes the M.B.A. Student Center, the Project Room, conference rooms, student organization offices, and classrooms. A media services center and University registration site are also located in the College. The College is home to the L. William Seidman Research Institute, whose affiliated centers and programs conduct specialized research on business topics such as entrepreneurship, econom-ics, finance, ethics, and quality.

Technology Environment

ASU has one of the largest and most comprehensive computing facilities of all U.S. universities. The Computing Commons provides access to Macintosh and IBM PCs. All printers are laser printers. A variety of Internet software packages provide students with access to e-mail and Internet news groups and opportunities to browse the Internet. There are numerous other computer sites on campus, including a fully equipped project room in the ASU MBA Suite of the College of Business.

Placement

Ninety-eight percent of the May 1997 ASU MBA graduating class was placed within three months after graduation, more than 83 percent within the first month. The Career Management Center assists M.B.A. students to determine their career interest areas and informs potential employers how ASU MBA students will meet their needs. The MBA Director of Career Management works with a wide variety of firms to bring interviewers to ASU.

Admission

Application to the ASU MBA Program is open to individuals holding a bachelor's degree or its equivalent in any discipline from an accredited college or university. During evaluation of candidates, the Ad-missions Committee looks for well-rounded individuals with strong academic credentials, managerial experience or po-tential, and the ability to contribute to the diversity of the class. Transcripts, GMAT scores, TOEFL and TSE scores when re-quired, work history, a personal statement, and letters of recommendation all influ-ence the decision. The entering class of fall 1997 had an average GPA of 3.3 on a 4.0 scale, an average GMAT score of 609, an average TOEFL score of 620, and average postbaccalaureate work experience of four and a half years. Due to the high volume of applications and the limited size of the entering class, students are strongly en-couraged to apply as early as possible.

Finances

Estimated tuition costs for 1998–99 are $4158 for Arizona residents and $11,110 for nonresidents. Books and supplies average $1200 per year. Most ASU MBA students live off campus in nearby apartment complexes where the rent ranges from $450 to $600 (one to two bedrooms) per month. On-campus residential facilities are available on a limited basis and cost approximately $7500 (room, board, and personal expenses).

A limited number of tuition scholar-ships and assistantships are available on a competitive basis. These awards are based strictly on merit and are awarded for one year only. State and federal funds should be pursued through the ASU Financial Assistance Office.

International Students

International diversity is highly valued at ASU, and nearly 20 percent of its M.B.A. students come from outside the U.S., from large countries as well as some of the smallest. During orientation and throughout the year, sponsored activities help international students adjust to the U.S. business and social climate.

Application Facts and Dates

Application deadlines are December 15, March 1, and May 1. Decision letters are usually mailed thirty to forty-five days after each deadline. A file must be complete before it will be evaluated. Annual admission to the full-time and part-time M.B.A. programs is for the fall term only. Graduate college applications are available on the World Wide Web (http://www.asu.edu/graduate/forms/ adm.html) For more information, students should contact:

Ms. Judith Heilala
Director of ASU MBA Admissions
   and Recruiting
ASU MBA Program
College of Business
Arizona State University
Box 874906
Tempe, Arizona 85287-4906
Telephone: 602-965-3332
Fax: 602-965-8569
World Wide Web:
   http://www.cob.asu.edu/mba/ (for
      ASU MBA)
   http://www.cob.asu.edu/acct (for
      School of Accountancy and
      Information Management)
   http://www.cob.asu.edu/hap/index.
      html (for Health Administration)

Armstrong University

TRAINING WORLD BUSINESS LEADERS FOR THE TWENTY-FIRST CENTURY

Continuously enhancing what it has done for many years, Armstrong University trains domestic and international students to assume global business management and leadership roles. Our faculty members bring theory and practical experience together to provide students with specific, practical management skills they can use on the job immediately, anywhere in the world. Our curricula were revised recently to increase emphasis on internationalism and leadership. Curricula are built around problem-solving approaches that stress analytical proficiency, creativity, and teamwork, enabling students to work across cultures, manage change, and seize opportunities with entrepreneurial vision.

Programs and Curricular Focus

All successful organizations—whether public or private, national or international, profit or nonprofit—require mastery of business principles. The Armstrong M.B.A. curriculum relates theories to practices, with the goal of turning students into professionals.

Twelve courses are required for the M.B.A. degree: eight core and four concentration courses. All courses include contemporary computer applications whenever possible. The core courses teach the most indispensable business fundamentals. To develop a sharper focus on specific aspects of business, students take four courses within one of the following concentration areas: finance and accounting, international business, international business law, or marketing management.

Armstrong University's Doctor of Business Administration Program is in process and awaiting approval by the Bureau for Private Post-secondary and Vocational Education.

Since the latest techniques may well be obsolete in a short period, problems are approached with intellectual flexibility, analytical skill, and creativity. Students are prepared to deal with the dynamism of business and not simply locked into techniques that may soon be passé.

Students and the M.B.A. Experience

Business is an international subject whose principles are applicable universally. The student profile supports the M.B.A. program's cross-cultural emphasis. Individuals from thirty-two countries attend Armstrong University. The average student is 26 years old, with approximately two years of work experience in various fields, including engineering, education, and banking. Women comprise 40 percent of the class.

Education at the University is a very personal matter. Student-teacher interaction is encouraged through small classes and easy access to faculty members. Faculty and administrative staff members are eager to help each student achieve his or her academic goals. Peer relationships are also central to the educational experience. Many assignments require students to put theory into practice and model real-world situations by integrating teamwork and case studies into the learning process. Conducting case analyses, research, and presentations in teams is central to the M.B.A. curriculum.

❖ Global Focus

The M.B.A. program focuses on the growing global economy. Realizing the importance of providing students with the necessary tools to excel in today's international marketplace, globalism is a structural part of the program, not merely an intellectual focus. The culturally diverse student body, staff, faculty, and alumni are a reflection of the international community. At Armstrong, students have the opportunity to interact in a multinational environment that equips them with the skills to become respon-

sible business leaders in the emerging interdependent world economy.

The Faculty

The professors at Armstrong University are distinguished academics who have significant experience in business practice and education. Each possesses a doctoral degree or other terminal degree, such as the Master of Business Administration. Classes are small in order to give students high-quality contact with instructors. Faculty members are experienced in working with students from diverse backgrounds.

The Business School Network
Corporate Partnerships

Armstrong's Business Advisory Council helps the University develop and maintain a curriculum that is current, realistic, and relevant to the needs of the business community. In regular meetings with University officials, the council reviews and evaluates the mission, the objectives, and the programs of the University. It also identifies ways in which the external community can support the University. Council members guest lecture in classes and speak to groups of students on topics of current interest. The council includes representatives from banking, consulting, insurance, technology, education, and politics (U.S. and abroad).

Armstrong's Board of Directors includes prominent representatives from the fields of law, finance, international business, politics, publishing, and education who provide leadership and guidance based on their areas of expertise.

Armstrong also hosts a lecture series in which executives and international business experts offer insights and perspectives that enhance the students' learning experience.

The College and Environs

Armstrong is a small, independent university. Its diverse student population reflects that of the city in which it is located. Oakland is noted for its tolerant attitude and cosmopolitan atmosphere.

Opportunities to explore cultural arts are varied and countless. Small, inexpensive restaurants, clubs, and stores abound. The institution's urban setting in the San Francisco Bay Area, a major business center, and its proximity to Silicon Valley, the high-technology center of the United States, make it an ideal place to study business.

Technology Environment

Armstrong University's computer lab houses state-of-the-art personal computers running on the Novell 3.12 network. Microcomputer systems are networked so that they can act as workstations to access a variety of mail, bulletin boards, and a high-speed network connecting universities and research centers worldwide.

The Library has 10,000 volumes and receives about 100 periodical titles. Students have access to several CD-ROM databases that index and abstract business and general subject periodicals. One database provides full-text articles from regional business journals. Students enjoy open-stack privileges at the University of California and public library systems and remote access to those systems via modem. Students are also encouraged to explore the vast research and reference opportunities offered via the Internet.

Placement

Job placement services are available in the Career Management Services (CMS) Department. The CMS Director assists students in their job search both before and after graduation. It maintains current listings of part-time and full-time positions. In addition, the staff members are available to advise students about career planning, job placement, resume preparation, and interview skills.

Admission

Applicants are admitted based on demonstrated academic abilities. Personal qualities, such as maturity and motivation, are also considered. Applicants to the Graduate School must have earned a bachelor's degree from an approved college or university with at least a 2.5 GPA. All applicants are required to submit an application for admission and have official transcripts sent to the Office of Admissions from every college and university attended. TOEFL scores of 500 or above are required of all applicants whose native language is not English and who graduated from an institution where English was not used as the only language of instruction. Students without a TOEFL score may be admitted conditionally contingent upon completion of English Level 4.

Finances

The 1997–98 tuition and fees were $4200 per semester. Books and supplies are estimated at $350 per academic year. The average cost for room and board is $7500 per academic year.

Application Facts and Dates

Applications for admission are accepted throughout the year, and students may enter in the fall or spring semester or summer session. For more information, students should contact:

Office of Admissions
Armstrong University
1608 Webster Street
Oakland, California 94612
Telephone: 510-835-7900 Ext. 10
        800-222-9297 (toll-free)
Fax: 510-835-8935
E-mail: admin@armstrong-u.edu
World Wide Web: http://www.
  armstrong-u.edu

Arthur D. Little School of Management

One-Year Master of Science in Management Program

Chestnut Hill and Cambridge, Massachusetts

THE CORPORATE ADVANTAGE

If you are an experienced professional ready to assume greater managerial responsibility and are looking for a minimal disruption of your career and income, the Master of Science in Management (M.S.M.) program at the Arthur D. Little School of Management (ADLSOM) may be for you. Arthur D. Little, Inc., a leading international consulting firm, is the only corporation to create an accredited graduate business program. We provide the unequaled opportunity to combine leading academic theory and the best consulting practices, all in an international context.

Arthur D. Little concentrates on helping major economic entities and businesses improve their operations, products, and processes by providing pragmatic solutions and visible involvement in the implementation of those solutions. Similarly, the M.S.M. is designed to provide a practical, experience-based curriculum with an emphasis on global issues, cross-cultural awareness, and team building. Courses are taught by practicing Boston-area business school professors and Arthur D. Little consultants who bring their knowledge to the classroom. We engage our participants in an intensive, year-long dialogue to develop and strengthen their management skills, which allows them to become more effective within their organizations.

We encourage to you to visit our program. We think you will see what makes our program truly unique in the international business school marketplace.

—William G. Makris, Director of Marketing and Chairman, Admission Committee

Programs and Curricular Focus

The Arthur D. Little School of Management offers a one-year Master of Science in Management degree designed for experienced professionals moving into positions of increased managerial responsibility. The program is distinguished from most other traditional M.B.A. programs by its practical, experience-based, problem-solving orientation and by its global learning environment. Many of the professors are Arthur D. Little consultants. The M.S.M. program offers a curriculum similar to that of a two-year M.B.A. program in an intensive eleven-month period. The academic year, which begins in August and ends in July, is carefully organized into three interrelated phases, each lasting from thirteen to seventeen weeks.

The curriculum blends courses in basic managerial skills, including accounting, economics, organizational behavior, and management communication, with the functional areas of management, including finance, marketing, operations management, and information systems. Participants are provided with a comprehensive understanding of international economic growth and change, including national strategies and the global economy. Finally, students are introduced to a strategic framework of the management of business in a globally competitive economy, including industry analysis and strategic planning, policy implementation, and management of technology. Electives include international financial management, marketing research, business process redesign, leadership, and total quality management.

Students and the M.B.A. Experience

One of the leading attributes of the program is the depth of the professional experience of the class participants. Enrollment in the M.S.M. program represents the diversity of most work environments, bringing together professionals with different educational backgrounds such as finance, law, and engineering. Although the profile of a typical ADLSOM student varies, most participants have between four and eight years of work experience and are in their early or middle thirties. Many are sponsored by their employers or by international agencies and return to their organizations after graduation. ADLSOM students are among the most experienced in the business school marketplace.

❖ Global Focus

The diversity of the class provides a unique opportunity to learn and practice the skills of international business management by working closely with colleagues from approximately twenty-two countries. The students represent a broad diversity of cultures and a wide range of industry and functional expertise. Each year, 65 participants, more than 90 percent of whom are international students, are enrolled in the M.S.M. program. Courses and projects are designed to incorporate teamwork and team building as an approach to developing managerial skills. Class discussions, study groups, and projects completed in teams provide intense cross-cultural experiences and the opportunity to gain a global perspective in nearly every course.

Special Features

The M.S.M. offers action learning—solving actual business problems—as an integral component of the curriculum. Through the Industry Research Project, M.S.M. students are partnered with Arthur D. Little consultants to assist in the completion of an ongoing problem facing one of Arthur D. Little's clients. Each team, consisting of 6 to 8 members, conducts extensive library-based research, culminating in a draft report and plans for the field research portion of the project. Each group then spends time conducting field research by visiting firms in its chosen industry. The groups complete their projects by submitting a final research report and making an oral presentation of their findings. In addition, several simulation exercises reinforce the practical nature of the curriculum.

ADLSOM offers several Executive Education and Custom Programs each year. They are a part of the School's commitment to learning and change. These practical, experience-based courses draw heavily on the extensive experience of Arthur D. Little's international consulting staff to help managers gain the necessary skills to meet the challenges that are the key to success in today's business environment.

The Faculty

Professors in the M.S.M. program are Arthur D. Little consultants and visiting faculty from leading Boston-area business schools. The consultants bring their client orientation to the classroom to guarantee a curriculum based more on a practical application than on theory.

The Business School Network

As a result of its strategic alliance with Boston College's (BC) Carroll School of Management, the program is housed on BC's 148-acre Chestnut Hill campus and at ADLSOM headquarters in Cambridge. While at Boston College, M.S.M. participants have complete access to all the academic and athletic facilities of Boston College. During the elective portion of the M.S.M., students are able to cross-register for courses with BC's Carroll School of Management graduate offerings.

M.S.M. students also learn about Arthur D. Little through special presentations arranged throughout the year.

The College and Environs

Since 1964, more than 3,300 professionals from more than 115 countries have participated in ADLSOM's programs. Founded as a subsidiary of Arthur D. Little, ADLSOM was chartered in 1971 and received its accreditation in 1976 from the New England Association of Schools and Colleges, Inc.

The School of Management is currently a precandidate for accreditation from AACSB-The International Association for Management Education.

Arthur D. Little and Boston College are located in the metropolitan Boston area. Boston is home to more than fifty universities, institutes, and colleges. Boston provides outstanding cultural, social, athletic, and academic resources.

Facilities

ADLSOM participants have access to all of the facilities at Boston College and Arthur D. Little headquarters in Cambridge.

Classes are held in a state-of-the-art classroom within the Wallace E. Carroll School of Management's Fulton Hall. The Carroll School recently received $15 million in renovations and offers students several resources, including team study rooms, a career resources room, and a quiet-study library. The building facilitates interaction among the different student groups in the business school and is a central location on BC's campus for presentations from various members of the business community.

In addition to the space in the Fulton Hall, the School's offices are located at 194 Beacon Street in a beautiful Georgian brick house. The 194 Beacon Street location, a few minutes' walk from the classroom, provides a central meeting place for program participants. The house has a student lounge, a communication area for messages and announcements, and a kitchen with a refrigerator and a microwave. All administrative and faculty offices are also in the building.

The Boston College library system provides a wide array of resources for research and learning. The BC collections consist of more than 1.5 million volumes, plus microfilm, serials, government documents, and media. In addition, there is an outstanding computing facility within the library complex. Access to ADLSOM's Global Information Resources and a vast interlibrary loan network is also available.

All facilities are convenient to library, computing, and parking facilities, as well as shuttle bus service to public transportation and residential neighborhoods.

Placement

The School works individually with each participant to develop a career strategy. The Career Management Curriculum (CMC) is a 12-hour course designed to enhance skill development regarding the job-search process. CMC is complemented by workshops to further enhance job-search skills and provide opportunities to practice these new techniques. CMC provides individual career counseling, presentations of industry panels, and access to networking events in con-

junction with Boston College's Carroll School of Management.

Finances

Tuition for the one-year M.S.M. program is $32,000. The fee covers the cost of all instruction and includes transportation for the travel required for the Industry Research Project. Participants should plan to spend $1900 to cover books and instructional materials and $2600 for a laptop computer. There is an additional fee of $2500 for the Summer Preparatory Program. The estimated annual living expenses, including rent, utilities, food, medical insurance, local transportation, and laptop computer, are $20,500. Participants who are U.S. citizens or permanent residents may be eligible for federally insured Stafford loans, which are available through banks and other lending institutions. Limited partial tuition scholarships are also available.

International Students

More than 90 percent of the M.S.M. student body comes from outside the United States. In 1997–98, 34 percent of the class was from Asia; 36 percent, Latin America; 2 percent, Africa, 3 percent, the Middle East; and 17 percent, Europe.

Admission

The application deadlines for August enrollment are January 15, March 1, and May 1. Late applications are reviewed on a space-available basis. Applicants for the M.S.M. program are considered on the basis of a qualitative evaluation of the relevance of work experience and career objectives, the applicant's undergraduate records, strength of recommendations, personal motivation, and analytical ability. Submission of a GMAT score is required, and a TOEFL score must be submitted where appropriate. Interviews are recommended and are often required.

Application Facts and Dates

Applicants are reviewed when all documents have been received. Early application is suggested, as enrollment is limited. Correspondence and information should be directed to:

William G. Makris
Director of Marketing
Arthur D. Little School of
  Management
194 Beacon Street
Chestnut Hill, Massachusetts 02467-3853
Telephone: 617-552-2877
Fax: 617-552-2051
E-mail: adlschool.mgmt@adlittle.com
World Wide Web: http://www.
  arthurdlittle.com/som/som.html

Auburn University

Auburn University, Alabama

EDUCATION FOR SUCCESS IN THE TWENTY-FIRST CENTURY

Increased competition, reengineering, social responsibilities, and borderless corporations affect American business and American business schools. Business schools must create, through classroom learning, real-life situations, team-building, and leadership exercises, students who are more versatile and globally aware. Students still require the knowledge and analytical skills of the traditional graduate, but also should be more skilled in understanding organizations and the needs of colleagues and employees. Students should be more entrepreneurial, more confident in assuming leadership roles, and more sophisticated in the use of technology. Graduates of the Auburn M.B.A. program will acquire these qualities as well as a firm grounding in the traditional business disciplines.

I urge you to weigh the merits of our program, compare it with others, hold it to the highest of standards. I believe you will agree that the Auburn M.B.A. program offers exceptional value for our students and provides the education necessary to succeed in the business world of the twenty-first century.

—C. Wayne Alderman, Dean

Programs and Curricular Focus

Auburn University's Master of Business Administration program is fully accredited by the AACSB–The International Association for Management Education. The M.B.A. program is designed to prepare students for positions of leadership in public and private enterprise. The program, which consists of 60 to 88 quarter hours of course work, is flexible enough to accommodate students from any undergraduate program. At Auburn, the focus is on the core analytical and communication skills that best prepare students for an uncertain future. The program incorporates a mix of theory with practical applications and supplements traditional lectures with case analyses. While the program keeps abreast of the latest trends, it is not trendy. The curriculum has staying power; it reflects the broad, fundamental knowledge upon which students can build a successful career, while allowing students to specialize and develop further expertise in a particular area of concentration. Students take eleven core courses in the program and four electives. Foundation courses are also offered in all five business areas to prepare students from any background to take the core courses in the M.B.A. curriculum. Students choose their electives to earn a concentration in a variety of functional areas, which can include finance, human resource management, marketing,

operations management, management information systems, economics, management of technology, agribusiness, and natural resources management. A team case analysis is the capstone requirement for the degree. Classes typically have from 10 to 50 students in them. Most students can complete the program in five to seven quarters of full-time work. Students are required to have had undergraduate courses in calculus and statistics prior to entering the program.

Since 1990, the Auburn M.B.A. has also been available off campus through the video-based Graduate Outreach Program. Well over 100 students have completed their degrees through this flexible, innovative program. This program offers professionals the opportunity to continue their education while maintaining full-time employment, wherever they may be located. Video-based M.B.A. students receive the same instruction as on-campus students and complete all class assignments and tests. Students from across the United States in Fortune 500 companies, small firms, and all branches of the military are currently earning an Auburn M.B.A. through the Graduate Outreach Program.

Students and the M.B.A. Experience

There are approximately 270 students in Auburn's M.B.A. program, with equal

percentages on and off campus. The average GMAT for the entering class in the fall of 1996 was 595, with an average GPA of 3.1. Thirty-seven percent of the students are female, and 9 percent are international students. Degree backgrounds include business (32 percent), engineering (42 percent), liberal arts (15 percent), with the remainder a mix of other disciplines. While work experience is not a requirement for admission, it is encouraged. Many on-campus students have significant business experience to bring to the classroom. For those students that do not, an internship while in the program is strongly encouraged. While teamwork is a strong focus within the curriculum, individual responsibility and accountability is stressed, as well. There are a number of professional student associations on campus, including an active M.B.A. student association that sponsors many activities.

The Faculty

The M.B.A. faculty members of Auburn University's College of Business excel as instructors and researchers. All faculty members have doctoral degrees and all are actively involved in research and consulting, keeping at the forefront of their disciplines. Good teaching is taken seriously and that is reflected in the quality of classroom instruction. By keeping the classes small, professors can take the time to work with the students individually. By making themselves available outside of the classroom, the faculty members provide a supportive atmosphere for learning, while at the same time they challenge the students to succeed.

The Business School Network

Interactions with the business community, through guest lecturers, company visits, and case analyses, are as important a component of an M.B.A. as the classroom lecture. That interaction strengthens the context in which students develop their understanding of theory. The Auburn program is constantly developing new networks and linkages for the students.

Corporate Partnerships

The Auburn M.B.A. Alumni Advisory Board, comprising 25 prominent business leaders throughout the country, works closely with the M.B.A. program to provide both programmatic advice and financial support. In addition, they actively work to identify and expand placement and internship opportunities, provide guest lecturers for the classroom, recruit companies to host site visits, or participate in team strategic analyses. They also cosponsor social events throughout the year, including football tailgate parties, picnics, and other informal gatherings that give the students a chance to discuss various business issues one-on-one with experienced professionals.

Prominent Alumni

Auburn M.B.A. graduates hold senior positions in local, national, and international companies, including BellSouth, Nationsbank, Chevron, Eastman Chemical, Andersen Consulting, Ernst and Young, IBM, Hewlett-Packard, McDonnell Douglas, Sprint, Southern Company, Michelin, Texas Instruments, UDS Motorola, and many others. An Auburn M.B.A. was listed in the June 1996 issue of *Entrepreneur* magazine as one of the top 100 new business entrepreneurs in the United States.

The College and Environs

Auburn University, ranked by *1995 Guide to 101 of the Best Values in America's Colleges and Universities* as a national flagship university, is a land-grant institution dedicated to serving Alabama and the nation through instruction, research, and extension.

Chartered in 1856, the University is located in the friendly, small-town environment of Auburn, Alabama. The University's beautiful 1,900-acre campus is home to 21,505 students (including 2,772 graduate students), 1,100 faculty members, a library with more than 2.4 million volumes, and more than fifty major academic buildings.

Auburn is approximately a 2-hour drive from the metropolitan areas of Atlanta, Georgia, and Birmingham, Alabama, and a 3½-hour drive from the Gulf Coast beaches.

Facilities

Classes are held in a new $15-million facility that is one of the most modern structures of its type in the nation. The building includes curved and tiered classrooms, a conference room designed as a formal reception area to entertain business guests and host small meetings, a video M.B.A. classroom, and six audiovisual classrooms linked to the Auburn University satellite system. The quality of the educational environment provided by the new building is among the finest in the country.

Placement

The Auburn University placement office provides students with personal help on developing interview skills, resume preparation, alumni networking, and access to on-campus corporate recruiting. In addition, placement efforts within the M.B.A. program include direct contacts with businesses, the distribution of a resume book, and position notifications through an e-mail network. The 1997 average starting salary for on-campus students without significant prior work experience was $42,000 (range of $28,000 to $62,000), with a 97 percent placement rate within three months of graduation.

Admission

The Auburn M.B.A. program accepts applicants for all four quarters of the academic year. Applicants must submit transcripts of all previous college work, recent GMAT and TOEFL scores, completed Graduate School and M.B.A. applications, and three letters of recommendation with a $25 application fee ($50 for international students). Prior work experience is a plus, and personal interviews are encouraged.

Finances

Tuition per quarter for the 1997–98 academic year was $785 for in-state students and $2355 for out-of-state students. Students enrolled in the video-based M.B.A. program pay $225 per credit hour. Most of the M.B.A. classes are 5 credit hours.

Application Facts and Dates

Applications are accepted for fall (deadline, 8/15), winter (deadline, 11/15), spring (deadline, 2/15), and summer (deadline, 5/15) quarters, though students are encouraged to submit completed applications well in advance of these deadlines.

Completed applications are reviewed by the M.B.A. Admission Committee and students are generally informed within two weeks of the receipt of all elements of the application. For more information, students should contact:

Dr. Daniel M. Gropper
M.B.A. Program Director
Suite 503
College of Business
Auburn University
Auburn, Alabama 36849
Telephone: 334-844-4060
Fax: 334-844-4861
E-mail: dgropper@business.auburn.edu
World Wide Web: www.mba.business.auburn.edu

Babson College

EDUCATING THE WORLD'S FUTURE ENTREPRENEURIAL LEADERS

The Franklin W. Olin Graduate School of Business at Babson College is committed to educating entrepreneurial leaders. Entrepreneurial leadership is a way of thinking and acting to create opportunities. Recognized as the world leader in entrepreneurial education and as a leader in integrated curriculum design, Babson is a very special place to study. Students are noted for their creativity, teamwork, and ability to see business problems from a holistic perspective. I know that as you read more about Babson, you will want to become a part of this unique educational community.

—Robert E. Holmes, The Murata Dean

Programs and Curricular Focus

All programs emphasize the global aspects of business and the value of the entrepreneurial spirit.

The Two-Year M.B.A. program is a coordinated curriculum based on the theme of entrepreneurial leadership in a changing global environment. First-year discussions and course work trace the business development cycle from the invention of a product or service, through assessing the business opportunity, into creating the marketing and delivery systems, and onto further development of products in the cycle. The highlight of the first year is participation in the mentor program, which assigns student teams to year-long projects with local businesses. Students complete two projects for the mentor company: one that analyzes the company's industry externally and another that evaluates an internal system. Teams provide written reports for both projects and present findings to top management. In the second year of the two-year M.B.A. program, students complete a schedule that is equivalent to ten courses (30 credit hours) and that builds on the first-year experience, which allows students to focus on elective study.

The One-Year M.B.A. is an accelerated program that allows students with an undergraduate business degree to complete their M.B.A. in three full-time semesters. Beginning each May, students enroll in a series of integrated modules over the first semester and then join the second-year M.B.A. students to complete the equivalent of fifteen courses in one calendar year.

The Evening M.B.A. program begins each fall and spring. Initial steps as part of a larger redesign of the Evening M.B.A. curriculum bring more intensive and integrated course work. Team-taught integrated courses cross at least two subject areas.

Students and the M.B.A. Experience

Students in the Two-Year M.B.A. program are, on average, 29 years old and have about six years of work experience. GMAT scores range from 510 to 800. Women comprise one third of the class. Students come from such diverse industries as banking and investment institutions to advertising, biotechnology, publishing, and telecommunications.

❖ Global Focus

Global business perspectives are not new at Babson. An international concentration is available and requires bilinguality, participation in an International Management Internship Program (IMIP), and completion of required and elective international courses. The IMIP places students in structured field consulting projects with corporations in Asia, Australia, Europe, and South America. International electives combine intensive classroom experience with industry-based projects in ten international cities. Students may study abroad at one of Babson's partner schools in Ecuador, England, France, Japan, Norway, Spain, and Venezuela. International internships, electives, and study-abroad opportunities satisfy the Two-Year M.B.A. program cross-cultural requirement and are open to students in all Babson programs.

Special Features

Babson fosters the entrepreneurial spirit through a variety of activities and opportunities, including electives, endowed chairs in entrepreneurship, induction of innovative business people into the Academy of Distinguished Entrepreneurs on Founder's Day, the Douglass Foundation Entrepreneurial Prizes, and the Babson Entrepreneurial Exchange, a student-run network of current and future entrepreneurs who exchange information about business development and venture opportunities.

The Faculty

Babson's faculty is an internationally and professionally diverse group, representing nations in Asia, Australia, Europe, and North and South America and with backgrounds in pharmaceutical, banking, high-technology, retailing, and other industries. They are practitioners and scholars, executives and teachers, and researchers and consultants who have lived and worked in international settings.

The Business School Network

Corporate Partnership

Successful business partnerships have always been a major component of Babson's programs. First-year student teams consult with Boston-area organizations through the year-long mentor program. The Management Consulting Field Experience Office offers about twenty-three second-year consulting projects. In 1998, 60 M.B.A. students went abroad to complete projects for small, local companies and large, multinational corporations.

The Graduate Advisory Board offers feedback on curriculum initiatives and facilitates ongoing relationships with the business community. The international advisory boards draw worldwide membership from senior executives with demonstrated expertise in global management.

The College and Environs

Babson College, founded in 1919 by financier and entrepreneur Roger W.

Building on the strength of seventy-five years of excellence in management education, Babson College embraces new challenges and opportunities and furthers successes.

Babson, is located on a 450-acre wooded site in Wellesley, Massachusetts, just 12 miles from Boston. Boston and the surrounding region offer a pleasing and exciting environment with a rich artistic, historic, and intellectual life.

Facilities
The Horn Library houses 120,000 volumes, 1,400 periodicals, and a collection of business and financial statements from 10,000 corporations. Online search services provide access to more than 250 databases, covering bibliographical and statistical information, thirty-five newspapers, and 100 maga-zines. Students and faculty can access the online systems of LEXIS-NEXIS, Dialog, FirstSearch, Prodigy, Bridge, Dow Jones, DataStar, and Investext.

Graduate housing offers living units of various sizes in eleven buildings, with surrounding recreation and picnic areas.

Technology Environment
The Horn Computer Center is equipped with 150 computer workstations that run a diversified library of business-oriented programs in a Windows environment. A separate lab houses twenty-five Macintosh SE computers. The center operates a 24-hour computer lab. Most classrooms are equipped with computer projection hard-ware. Babson expects that entering stu-dents are comfortable with basic spread-sheet and word-processing operations.

Placement
Made up of a staff of 4 professionals, the Center for Career Development offers a career management curriculum that is

integrated into the first-year course work and is required for all full-time students; an online professional development survey of work experience and interests, allowing the staff to direct students to internship and employment opportunities; internships offering either stipends or course credit; job fairs; and online alumni and employer databases.

Admission
Students are admitted to the program based on a careful evaluation of academic records, professional qualifications, GMAT scores, and personal attributes. Interviews are required. Current class GMAT scores are in the 510 to 800 range, and the average undergraduate GPA is 3.1. International students must submit TOEFL results and official English translations of all academic documents. All candidates should have strong mathematics, computer, economics, and business writing skills.

Finances
Nine-month academic year cost estimates for 1998–99 for the Two-Year M.B.A. pro-gram are $22,600 for tuition, $1300 for books and supplies, $6930 for housing, and $2880 for food. Tuition for the One-Year M.B.A. program is $30,960. Per-course tuition is $2046. The pre-M.B.A. for international students costs $1000.

Merit programs that award scholarships include Babson Fellows, Olin Fellows, Babson Fellowships for Students of Color, Olin Scholarships, and Babson Scholars.

International Students
International students representing twenty-four different countries comprise 27 per-

cent of M.B.A. enrollment. The pre-M.B.A. orientation for international students begins two weeks before Module I classes. This intensive program consists of familiarization with the campus, library, computer center, and other services and workshops. Also, Babson faculty members present a basic introduction to economics, marketing, and the case method. Recre-ational and social events are scheduled. International students may apply for a U.S. internship, as well as being eligible for the International Management Internship Pro-gram (IMIP).

Application Facts and Dates
Application deadlines for the Two-Year M.B.A. program are January 15, March 1, and April 15; for the One-Year M.B.A. program, December 15 and January 15; and for the Evening M.B.A. program, November 1 and December 1 for spring admission and May 15 and June 15 for fall admission. Decisions are mailed four to six weeks after each deadline. For more information, applicants should contact:

Office of Graduate Admission
F. W. Olin Graduate School of
    Business
Babson Park, Massachusetts 02157-
    0310
Telephone: 781-239-4317
                800-488-4512 (toll-free
                    within the U.S.)
Fax: 781-239-4194
E-mail: mbaadmission@babson.edu
World Wide Web: http://www.babson.
    edu/mba

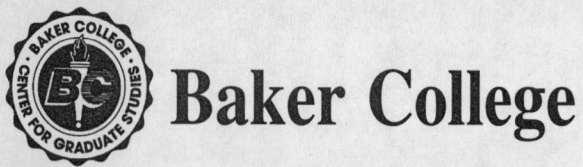

Baker College

Center for Graduate Studies

Flint, Michigan

DEVELOPING LEADERS FOR THE TWENTY-FIRST CENTURY

"Executives are problem solvers; at best, they are visionaries, developing and implementing strategies for the twenty-first century." I read that definition in someone's catalog in the past year. I thought then that it was a marvelous way of introducing a graduate program in business. I still do! In fact, these words are so important to the accurate description of what we do at Baker College that we have formulated our vision statement along the same lines: "Developing leaders, thinkers, visionaries, and problem solvers who can effectively empower both self and others in a dynamic and global economic environment."

The business programs at Baker College are the product of years of planning. We asked our students, faculty and staff members, and the employers in our communities to tell us what they wanted. Then we set out to make sure we gave them the very best possible programs to support all those constituencies. We've even added a computer component to make the M.B.A. experience a memorable one. Most importantly, we continue to support and implement the marvelous mission and purpose statements of this organization. The M.B.A. programs at Baker College have been specifically designed with your experience, goals, and aspirations in mind.

Whether you are a manager, a professional, or an entrepreneur seeking to improve your business or leadership skills, Baker College offers you adult-oriented, practical, convenient, and efficient programs tailored for your lifestyle and needs.

—Dr. Stephen L. Williams

Programs and Curricular Focus

Baker College's program seeks to combine the best of conventional academic training with the best of field-based learning. Most typical business disciplines are represented in the curriculum because the College believes that a successful manager must be conversant with different aspects of running any of today's organizations or companies. Thus, the standard curriculum addresses accounting, computers, finance, communications, ethics, marketing, and management. This M.B.A. program is organized into six areas of concentration: communications and information systems, research and analytical support, economic and financial applications, issues within and outside the organization, leadership and the management process, and emphasis in the chosen concentration area. Students may elect to focus their studies in one of the following areas: computer information systems, health-care management, human resource management, industrial management, integrated health care, international business, leadership studies, or marketing.

The curriculum at Baker College is offered in two different models, which are designed to accommodate the schedules of almost all working adults. The executive model requires a total of 50 quarter hours, and all students in this program can complete their academic program in eighteen months by enrolling in two concurrent classes each term. Students are expected to produce a portfolio, which is designed as both a research tool during the program and a good reference tool once the student completes the degree.

The traditional model requires a total of 60 quarter hours. There is an extensive research project required in conjunction with this approach. Students in this approach can expect to graduate in two years by enrolling in two courses each quarter.

M.B.A. programs are offered on campuses in Flint, Owosso, Muskegon, Port Huron, Cadillac, Auburn Hills, Mount Clemens, and Jackson, Michigan. The program is also available in corporate facilities and through Baker College On-line.

Students and the M.B.A. Experience

Baker College students bring a wide range of experience and backgrounds to the classroom. Typically, experiences represented are in areas such as business, education, psychology, engineering, and medicine. These diverse backgrounds and experiences are valued highly by Baker and are incorporated into the curriculum of the M.B.A. program.

Fifty-two percent of graduate students at Baker are women, 20 percent are members of minority groups, and about 4 percent are international students.

Special Features

Baker College, a recognized leader in the development of market-worthy educational and training opportunities, stands in the unique position of being able to meet the special needs of working adults. The tradition of quality with flexibility has enabled Baker to establish accredited degree programs in a variety of nontraditional settings.

In meeting with this tradition, courses are offered in three formats: weekend, week-night, and on line. Students are able to attend courses on campus one weekend a month or one night a week for nine weeks. Students also have the option to take courses on line in six-week sessions with no on-ground classroom requirements.

The Faculty

Baker College faculty members know their business. Faculty members are selected for both their business experience and their academic credentials and bring great breadth and depth to the program. The flexibility of course offerings allows Baker to expose graduate students to instructors from all over the United States. This cadre of professionals, known as Baker's National Faculty, brings experience from their industries and is committed to the best education program possible.

The focus of Baker's faculty is somewhat different from traditional universities. Instead of placing an emphasis on empirical research, Baker values practitioner-oriented education.

Faculty members remain continually active in their professions by consulting, conducting seminars, running their own businesses, writing, volunteering in their communities, and even working for other organizations.

The Business School Network

Corporate Partnerships

An advisory board of community leaders is established for every discipline at Baker College. These advisory boards give advice on current and future curricula, program needs or changes, employment opportunities for students, and other general advice on college activities. Students have the ability to interact with community leaders outside the classroom through the Baker College Leadership Institute.

The College and Environs

The Baker College System has evolved from schools that have been providing high-quality and practitioner-oriented degree programs in Michigan for more than a century.

The oldest of the system schools was founded in 1888 by Woodbridge Ferris in Muskegon. In 1911, Eldon Baker established Baker Business University in Flint. These two institutions merged to form the Baker College System in 1986; it is now the largest private not-for-profit independent college in the state of Michigan. Total enrollment figures, including outreach operations, for the system exceeds 13,000 students. The Center for Graduate Studies has approximately 600 students located throughout the system.

Facilities

The Baker College Library System is part of the Flint Area Library Consortium (FALCON), a consortium of libraries based in Flint that supports an online catalog database of more than 500,000 holdings of the Baker College System Libraries, the GMI Engineering and Management Institute, Mott Community College, and the eighteen branches of the Genesee County libraries. Baker also participates in the Online Computer Library Center interlibrary loan subsystem. The library facility also features INFOTRAC periodical indexing databases, the UMI/ProQuest General Periodicals On-Disc and Business Periodicals On-Disc full-article imaging station, and Books-in-Print with Reviews. Fiche and microfilm collections provide additional document retrieval resources.

Technology Environment

Every Baker College student is assigned an e-mail account on the BakerNet system. Through this system, students are able to communicate with each other and their instructors as well as members of the graduate school staff. Students may also use their accounts to access the World Wide Web. There are more than 1,100 microcomputers in student labs available for student use.

Placement

Baker College prides itself on the fact that 98 percent of all graduates are employed. A successfully employed graduate is the result of the College's continuous contact with hundreds of employers throughout the year as well as the annual Job Fair. Approximately seventy employers participate in the Job Fair every year. The employment service of the College is a lifetime arrangement for all graduates.

Admission

To qualify for admission to Baker College's M.B.A. program, a student must have a bachelor's degree from a regionally accredited institution, have a 2.5 or better GPA in their undergraduate work, be able to display appropriate oral and written communication skills, submit three letters of reference, submit a current resume, and have completed no less than three years of full-time work. A TOEFL score is required for all applicants for whom English is not the native language. Once submitted, the applicant's record will be evaluated by an Admissions Committee.

Finances

Tuition for the 1998–99 school year is $215 per quarter hour. The total program cost is approximately $12,500. The cost of books ranges from $150 to $200 each quarter.

Application Facts and Dates

Baker College uses a rolling admissions process, so there are no deadlines for applications, and students are able to begin at any quarter. Once the Admissions Committee receives an application, applicants usually receive a decision in approximately four weeks.

Chuck Gurden
Director of Graduate Admissions
Center for Graduate Studies
Baker College
1050 West Bristol Road
Flint, Michigan 48507
Telephone: 810-766-4397
         800-469-3165 (toll-free)
Fax: 810-766-4399
E-mail: gradschl@baker.edu or
    gurden_c@corpfl.baker.edu

Baldwin-Wallace College

Berea, Ohio

THE M.B.A. THAT PREPARES INTERNATIONAL MANAGERS FOR SUCCESS

Many of America's most highly respected M.B.A. programs have recently begun to incorporate "new" concepts like teamwork, hands-on experience, and multidisciplinary curricula. At Baldwin-Wallace College, our M.B.A. programs were founded on these fundamental philosophies—in 1972.

Every manager knows that corporations have become increasingly global in their operations and that their work forces have become increasingly diverse. To effectively lead these corporations, the ideal executive of the future needs to be global in outlook, able to capitalize on diversity, and a master of teamwork. The Baldwin-Wallace College M.B.A. in International Management program challenges students to foster these qualities.

—Tom Riemenschneider, Director, International M.B.A. Programs

Programs and Curricular Focus

The M.B.A. in International Management (I.M.B.A.) is offered through both full-time and part-time programs. The full-time program is designed to meet the needs of individuals seeking significant career advancement or the education necessary to become managers in a global setting. It has a sixteen-month sequential format requiring class attendance 9 hours per week during each of four 15-week terms. Students have the opportunity to study with part-time students who, in most cases, are currently employed in international management positions.

The part-time evening program is designed to meet the needs of individuals who are working in such areas as accounting, data processing, engineering, marketing, and management and are seriously seeking significant career advancement as managers in a global corporate setting. The program has a sequential two-year format requiring class attendance 3 hours per evening, two evenings per week.

Students have the opportunity to take foundation courses with other graduate students. These foundation courses make it possible for students with little or no undergraduate business education to successfully participate in the program.

Baldwin-Wallace also offers M.B.A and Executive M.B.A. programs through its Division of Business Administration. These two-year, part-time programs are based on teamwork, hands-on experience, and multidisciplinary curricula. The M.B.A. program is designed for individu-

als with at least two years of business experience. Approximately 270 students are currently enrolled in the evening and weekend classes. The Executive M.B.A. program is designed for individuals with at least seven years of managerial experience. Approximately 100 students are currently enrolled in this program, with classes that meet every other weekend for two years.

Students and the M.B.A. Experience

The M.B.A. in International Management welcomes nearly 50 percent of its students from outside the United States. I.M.B.A. students represent six continents and more than nineteen countries including Argentina, China, Germany, Greece, Indonesia, Japan, Korea, Thailand, and Turkey. Of the more than 100 students enrolled in the program, approximately three fourths have prior work experience, one fourth are women, and one half are enrolled full-time.

❖ Global Focus

Students really learn from each other at Baldwin-Wallace. As they are put into mixed groups, they explore differing logic patterns and approaches to solving problems from their various countries. The Internet is used to link students from several countries. Working together and communicating by computer network, this diverse group analyzes all phases of an actual multinational company. Through this project, students gain a better

understanding of the business, communication, and organizational skills needed to work with international teams.

Special Features

A series of faculty-led management study tours is available to students in the M.B.A. programs. Past tours have visited China, Japan, Nicaragua, and Thailand.

There is an American Language Academy (ALA) program on the Baldwin-Wallace campus. ALA offers English as a foreign language preparation designed specifically for I.M.B.A. applicants and candidates. Many I.M.B.A. students successfully meet the TOEFL requirement while studying at the ALA. In addition, these students receive an orientation to academic life at Baldwin-Wallace as well as to the facilities and resources of the I.M.B.A. program.

The Faculty

Committed to teaching rather than research, the full-time and adjunct faculty share the College's commitment to "Quality Education with a Personal Touch." The faculty members bring a unique combination of educational and professional experiences to their teaching responsibilities. Within the student-centered, teaching-oriented environment, education is the number one priority.

The Business School Network

Through on-site and in-class projects, business partnerships enable students to put their knowledge to work. Field studies, internships, and supervised in-company research projects place students in regional businesses where they work with corporate leaders to identify problems and develop solutions.

The College and Environs

Baldwin-Wallace is a liberal arts college, founded in 1845. The campus features forty buildings on 56 tree-shaded acres. The College serves approximately 4,700 students, of whom 4,100 are undergraduate students and 600 are graduate students.

The campus is located in Berea, a picturesque suburban area 14 miles southwest of Cleveland. It is easily accessible from Cleveland Hopkins International Airport (2 miles) and from interstate highways I-71, I-80, and I-480.

Many cultural and recreational activities are held on the Baldwin-Wallace College campus. Students can attend athletic events, concerts, theater productions, movies, and lectures by speakers who come from throughout the United States to address a variety of topics. For most events, admission is free.

Cleveland is the headquarters city for eighty-three major corporations with annual sales exceeding $100 million, a concentration larger than that of Los Angeles, Boston, or Atlanta. Cleveland is also the twelfth-largest consumer market, the eighth-largest industrial market, and the twelfth-largest retail market in the United States.

The Cleveland area offers a range of cultural, recreational, and entertainment opportunities. Outstanding museums and galleries, professional sports events, exciting nightlife, and a citywide park system are a short distance from campus.

Placement

The College Office of Career Services works aggressively to help students with career placement, career counseling and planning, resume referral to employers, and resume preparation. The Office of Career Services also has a career library and sponsors career fairs.

Admission

Required for admission into the I.M.B.A. program are a bachelor's degree from an accredited institution, two letters of recommendation, a resume, and a satisfactory score on the Graduate Management Admission Test (GMAT). The average GMAT score for entering students is 476.

For students whose native language is not English, a minimum of 500 is required on the Test of English as a Foreign Language (TOEFL). Applicants who have not taken the TOEFL or those with TOEFL scores of less than 500 are eligible for conditional acceptance. Course work in Business English as a Second Language is required of students with a TOEFL score less than 523. International students must present proof of adequate funds to cover the cost of study.

Finances

Tuition for 1998–99 is $1512 for each of the program's twelve courses and $504 for each seminar elective course. In addition to the tuition, a book cost of approximately $85 per course is to be expected.

Off-campus housing is available in the immediate area. The Office of Residential Life maintains a list of off-campus rooms, apartments, and houses that may be rented by students. Apartment rents start at $350 per month. An on-campus board plan is offered at approximately $800 per quarter. On-campus housing is available to graduate students.

Application Facts and Dates

Students may begin the I.M.B.A. program at three times throughout the year: September, January, and late April. Students should apply well ahead of the desired starting date, as it takes approximately three months to complete the application process. For more information, students should contact:

International M.B.A. Programs
275 Eastland Road
Berea, Ohio 44017-2088
Telephone: 440-826-2196
Fax: 440-826-3868
E-mail: pshepard@bw.edu

Baruch College of the City University of New York

Baruch College

Zicklin School of Business

New York, New York

> ### AN M.B.A. IN A GLOBAL ENVIRONMENT
>
> *Baruch College is proud of its place in New York City, the world's most dynamic financial and cultural center. We are uniquely positioned to provide students with an excellent education at a very reasonable cost in a global environment. Our outstanding faculty, flexible full- and part-time programs, and convenient location offer students unequaled access to opportunities for both learning and professional advancement.*
>
> —Sidney Lirtzman, Dean

Programs and Curricular Focus

Baruch has recently completed a two-year revision of its M.B.A. program. The M.B.A. now requires a total of 54 credits: 27 credits of core courses, 9 elective credits, and 18 credits in an area of specialization. One of the strengths of the program lies in its combination of a solid business core with a wide array of specialized courses. The core curriculum is designed to provide students with an understanding of the basic principles of both management and the environment in which managerial decisions are made. Courses include accountancy, economics, finance, behavioral sciences, quantitative methods, information systems, production, and marketing.

Supplementing the core are 9 credits of elective courses, including one international elective, one quantitative elective, and one general elective. Beyond the core, students can specialize in accountancy, computer information systems, economics, entrepreneurship, finance and investments, health-care administration, industrial/organizational psychology, international business, management, marketing, operations research, statistics, or taxation.

Those who wish to design their own M.B.A. programs can select unique, cross-disciplinary combinations of courses to fulfill the 18-credit specialization requirement. These combinations are useful for students interested in careers in such fields as marketing in financial institutions or banking operations. A few examples of the many specialization courses available to students are Futures and Forwards Markets, Options Markets, Mergers and Acquisitions, International Trade and Investment Law, International Commodity Trading, International Corporate Finance, Computer Simulation for Solving Business Problems, Product Planning and Development, and Entrepreneurial Ventures.

Students and the M.B.A. Experience

Baruch's reputation for excellence extends to all parts of the world, attracting students from New York, neighboring states, and abroad. The cohort-style M.B.A. program offers students the option of full-time or part-time study. Full-time students complete the degree program in two years, part-time students in four. The diverse group of men and women doing graduate work at Baruch hold undergraduate degrees from more than 200 colleges and universities. There are more than 400 international graduate students, who represent approximately fifty countries.

The average graduate student at Baruch is 28 years old. Although students generally have an average of five years of work experience, applicants with little or no work experience are occasionally admitted. Many M.B.A. students at Baruch have undergraduate degrees in business, but the majority have majored in engineering, the liberal arts, or the social sciences. Professional experience varies widely. Forty percent of the students are women, while members of minority groups represent almost 30 percent of the student body. International students make up 25 percent of the M.B.A. student population.

The Faculty

The faculty at Baruch is top-notch, with strong academic credentials and ties to New York's business and financial communities. All share a commitment to teaching. Baruch's recently retired Harry Markowitz held the Marvin M. Speiser Professorship when he earned the Nobel Prize in Economics in 1990. Other faculty members recognized for outstanding honors include June O'Neill, the director of the Congressional Budget Office; E. S. Savas, an expert on privatization of public enterprises; and Yoshihiro Tsurumi, an authority on cultural and economic relations between the United States and Japan.

The Business School Network
Prominent Alumni

The Baruch degree is highly valued. Graduates may be found at all levels in business, industry, and public life. Notable graduates include Laura Altschuler, President, New York City League of Women Voters; the Honorable Abraham D. Beame, former Mayor of the City of New York; Dov C. Schlein, President and Chief Operating Officer, Republic Bank of New York; Bert Wasserman, Executive Vice President, Time Warner, Inc.; and Jules L. Winter, Chief Operating Officer, American Stock Exchange.

The College and Environs

Baruch's urban campus is ideally located near the picturesque Gramercy Park area and immediately to the east of the historic Flatiron District. It extends from East 18th Street to East 26th Street and is surrounded by a variety of ethnic restaurants and stores of all kinds. All of New York City's museums, theaters, concert halls, clubs, sports arenas, and beaches are easily accessible by public transportation.

Technology Environment

In addition to the seven other buildings comprising Baruch's campus, the first building of the north campus opened on East 25th Street in 1994. This completely renovated 1890s classic houses The William and Anita Newman Library, the Baruch Computing and Technology Center (which includes 400 computer workstations in an open-access lab),

One of Baruch College's main buildings, located in the center of activity at 23rd Street and Lexington Avenue in Manhattan.

student and administrative offices, and a state-of-the-art multimedia center.

More than three times the size of its predecessor, the 1,450-seat library has local area networks that provide access to a wide variety of electronic information resources. The Dow Jones News/ Retrieval, LEXIS-NEXIS, and Dialog services are among the online databases available, and students and faculty members can access the Internet, gateway to the libraries and databases of the world. The Newman Library's traditional collections consist of 270,000 volumes, 2,100 current periodical subscriptions, 1.6 million microforms, and 500 audiovisual materials, including films, videos, audio recordings, and CD-ROMs. The Media Resources Lab houses 107 Apple Power PCs, all equipped with CD-ROM for multimedia capability. Twelve of these PCs have interactive videodisc capability and are available for research and information gathering.

Placement

An office dedicated to M.B.A. placement opened in 1996. Career counseling is available in person or by telephone. Students can receive information on job opportunities and advice on resume writing, job search strategies, interviewing techniques, and individual concerns. Videos that cover such topics as interviewing and career planning are available in the office, as is company literature for students who wish to research prospective employers.

Career fairs, on-campus recruiting, graduate roundtables, symposia, and other networking opportunities are held throughout the year.

Admission

Applicants for any M.B.A. program must take the Graduate Management Admission Test (GMAT). The average student entering the program has a GMAT score of 580 and an undergraduate grade point average of 3.2. International students whose native language is not English must take the Test of English as a Foreign Language (TOEFL) and the Test of Written English (TWE). In addition to test scores, applicants must submit application forms, an essay, a resume, official transcripts from every college or university attended, two letters of recommendation, and a nonrefundable application fee of $40.

Finances

Tuition for New York State residents is $2175 per semester for full-time and $185 per credit for part-time study. For out-of-state residents and international students, tuition is $3800 for full-time and $320 per credit for part-time study. Tuition is subject to change without notice. Average estimated annual costs for books, supplies, transportation, and personal expenses for students living with their parents are about $6000. Students who do not live with their parents should anticipate approximately $10,000 in expenses per year.

There are a limited number of graduate research assistantships, which are awarded solely on the basis of merit to qualified full-time graduate students. The assistantships carry an annual stipend of $5000 and are renewable for one year; they do not include a tuition waiver.

In the fall, the Mitsui USA Foundation awards two annual scholarships of $5000 each to newly admitted full-time students pursuing an M.B.A. degree in international business. Applicants for the Mitsui Scholarships must be United States citizens or permanent residents. The Carl Spielvogel Scholarship offers an annual award of $5000 in the fall to newly admitted full-time students pursuing an M.B.A. degree in international marketing.

Financial aid is also available to graduate students through a wide variety of sources, including various state, federal, and College programs. Other than graduate research assistantships, which do not include tuition waivers, there is no significant financial aid for international students.

Application Facts and Dates

Application deadlines for fall admission are May 1 for international students and June 15 for domestic students; for spring, the deadlines are November 1 for international students and December 1 for domestic students. Applicants are encouraged to submit their applications as early as possible, particularly if they wish to be considered for a graduate research assistantship or scholarship.

To request application materials or to make an appointment to speak with an admissions counselor, applicants should contact:

Office of Graduate Admissions
Baruch College of the City
  University of New York
17 Lexington Avenue, Box H-0880
New York, New York 10010-5585
Telephone: 212-802-2330

Baylor University

Hankamer School of Business

Waco, Texas

▶ DISCOVER THE OPPORTUNITIES

Immerse yourself in hands-on applications of classroom theory through direct interaction with an actively functioning company. Each semester, one publicly held company serves as the "focus firm," and its core issues become the centerpiece for the M.B.A. curriculum. At the conclusion of one year in Baylor's M.B.A. program, you will have experienced complex issues facing two different focus firms.

Come see for yourself. The best way to learn about Baylor's graduate business programs is to visit our campus, tour the facilities, and sit in on classes. Meet current students and see how you can join the Baylor graduates who are emerging as tomorrow's business leaders.

—Linda Livingstone, Associate Dean for Graduate Programs

Programs and Curricular Focus

The Hankamer School of Business at Baylor offers a variety of graduate degrees designed to meet different career goals. These are the Master of Business Administration (M.B.A.), Master of Business Administration in International Management (M.B.A.-I.M.), Master of International Management (M.I.M.), Master of Business Administration in Information Systems (M.B.A.-I.S.M.), Master of Science in Information Systems (M.S.I.S.), Master of Taxation (M.Tax.), Master of Accountancy (M.Acc.), and Master of Science in Economics (M.S.Eco.). Two additional degrees offered in cooperation with Baylor School of Law are the Doctor of Jurisprudence/Master of Business Administration (J.D./M.B.A.) and the Doctor of Jurisprudence/Master of Taxation (J.D./M.Tax.).

Baylor also offers a joint degree in business and information systems, the Master of Business Administration/Master of Science in Information Systems (M.B.A./M.S.I.S.).

The M.B.A. is an applied program designed to thoroughly educate participants in the fundamental areas of business. Each semester, one publicly held company volunteers to serve as the M.B.A. "focus firm." The focus firm approach to learning provides real-time delivery of theoretical applications, technological advances, global awareness, functional integration, and team-centered learning. The focus firm offers a more authentic business experience than simulation exercises, case studies, or field trips. Not only do students learn about current business trends, they also apply their skills to solve ongoing business problems.

In addition to the focus firm, corporate executives frequently serve as guest speakers on campus. Professors also arrange on-site visits with many Texas firms, during which students apply principles learned in the classroom.

Because it is an accelerated program, most students complete the Baylor M.B.A. in three, four, or five semesters. Students with an undergraduate degree in business can enter the M.B.A. program directly. For those without a business background, a unique one-semester Integrated Management Seminar is offered that satisfies all business prerequisites.

Distance learning and videoconferencing are integral parts of classroom activities. Videoconferencing sessions with corporate executives are held each semester in conjunction with the focus firm project. In addition, many classrooms are equipped with the latest innovations in multimedia presentation devices.

Students and the M.B.A. Experience

Each year, the Hankamer School of Business attracts hundreds of talented graduate students who want to discover the opportunities of graduate education. Their origins are diverse—from backgrounds in business and engineering to music and from a variety of states and countries—and at Baylor they come

together in a team-centered learning environment. What they find is a level of excellence and commitment to high-quality graduate education.

The Faculty

Nationally recognized faculty members who are dedicated to their students' intellectual growth take teaching seriously. They encourage active discussions and debate both in and out of the classroom. Recognized as a personalized program, students cite the expertise and accessibility of faculty members as one of the strengths of the Baylor M.B.A. program. Core classes are intentionally limited to an average of 25 students, while electives average about 10 students, allowing for a more personalized teaching environment. All graduate courses are taught by faculty members who hold doctoral degrees.

Baylor faculty members serve on corporate advisory boards and hold leadership positions in professional organizations in order to maintain active ties with the business community.

The Hankamer School of Business houses the Graduate Center, a newly renovated area designed for graduate business programs.

Students cite the expertise and accessibility of faculty members as one of the strengths of the Baylor M.B.A. program.

The College and Environs

Founded in 1845, Baylor University is Texas's oldest institution of higher learning in continuous existence since its founding. The 432-acre campus is located on the banks of the Brazos River in Waco, Texas, a metropolitan area of 200,000 people. Baylor is located just 90 miles south of Dallas and 90 miles north of Austin. The enrollment at Baylor is more than 12,000 students, of whom approximately 2,000 are graduate students. Enrollment for graduate business programs is limited to about 160 students.

Facilities

To advance the separate identity of the graduate business programs, a specific area of the business school's facilities is being converted into a Graduate Center. It will house core faculty offices, a videoconferencing area, graduate administration offices, and a graduate student study area.

The Central Libraries, Special Libraries, and Resource Centers of Baylor house more than 1.5 million bound volumes, more than 2 million microforms and government document pieces, and thousands of audiovisual items, maps, charts, and photographs. Information is stored on microfilm, microfiche, CD-ROM, computer disks, videotape, compact discs, and cassette tapes in addition to traditional print books and journals.

Technology Environment

The Casey Computer Center contains more than seventy IBM and twenty Macintosh computers as well as scanning equipment and color printers. Graduate students have free access to the Internet and e-mail service. Baylor was recently named the twenty-second "best wired" school by *Yahoo! Internet Life*.

Placement

A special resource to currently enrolled students and alumni, Baylor Career Services Center assists students in formulating and implementing career planning techniques, in providing career resource and job listings, and directing resumes to interested companies. An M.B.A. Coordinator in the Career Services Center works only with graduate business students to coordinate on- and off-campus interviews with some of the nation's largest firms, government agencies, and other organizations. Within three months of graduation, 93 percent of Baylor M.B.A. graduates are employed. Graduates are routinely sought by larger firms in the Southwest region of the United States.

Admission

Admission is based on an applicant's professional experience, successful academic history, GMAT scores, resume, letters of recommendation, and, for international students, TOEFL scores. In 1997–98, average GMAT scores were 580 and the average GPA was 3.23 (on a 4.0 scale). For international students, TOEFL scores must be at least 600. Professional work experience is strongly encouraged. Students admitted with less than two full years of work experience are required to complete a semester-long internship in addition to the 36 hours of course work. Interviews are required for applicants without two full years of work experience, and interviews are recommended but not required for all other applicants.

Finances

One of the most affordable private institutions in the country, Baylor's tuition is $308 per semester hour. At the graduate level, full-time study consists of 12 semester hours. Graduate assistantships are available on a competitive basis for students wishing to reduce the cost of their graduate education. A graduate assistantship provides 50 to 100 percent tuition remission plus a stipend of $315 per month. Graduate assistants work 10 to 15 hours per week as research assistants for faculty members. For additional questions regarding financial aid, students can contact the Student Financial Aid Office at 254-710-2611.

International Students

International students from countries such as the Czech Republic, China, India, Russia, Mexico, Canada, and Pakistan make up about 15 percent of the enrollment in Baylor graduate business programs. International students provide a global perspective, representing a unique component to the programs. For additional questions regarding visa and immigration requirements, students can contact the International Programs Office at 254-710-1461.

Application Facts and Dates

The deadline for applications for admission for fall entrance is July 1; for spring entrance, November 1; and for summer entrance, April 1. Applications are processed on a rolling basis. For international students to be considered for the highly competitive graduate assistantships, they should observe the following application deadlines: for consideration for fall entry, April 1; for spring entry, September 1; and for summer entry, February 1. For more information, students should contact:

Director of Graduate Admissions
Hankamer School of Business
Baylor University
P.O. Box 98001
Waco, Texas 76798-8001
Telephone: 254-710-3718
          800-583-0622 (toll-free)
Fax: 254-710-1066
E-mail: mba@hsb.baylor.edu
World Wide Web: http://hsb.baylor.edu/mba

Bentley College

Graduate School of Business

Waltham, Massachusetts

BUSINESS SPECIALISTS AT BENTLEY GRADUATE SCHOOL OF BUSINESS

One of Bentley's greatest strengths is meeting the needs of business specialists and generalists alike. Along with providing general breadth in business, our programs speak to the fact that, in the labor market, specialties are valued. The integrated Full-Time M.B.A. program, a Self-Paced M.B.A. with fifteen different concentrations, and highly focused Master of Science degrees are flexible and attentive to the needs of individual students. An extensive curriculum, teaching excellence, field-based learning opportunities, and Bentley's close proximity to the educational and cultural resources of Boston all contribute to a powerful academic framework that stimulates professionalism, the development of business acumen, and social responsibility.

—Patricia M. Flynn, Dean

Programs and Curricular Focus

In order to prepare managers for today's challenges in business, Bentley offers two distinct M.B.A. programs: the Full-Time M.B.A. (a unique two-year program) and the Self-Paced M.B.A. (a flexible part-time or full-time program).

The Full-Time M.B.A. program is an intensive, two-year program that gives students an integrated understanding of the business organization. It focuses on building competitive advantage by designing effective business processes and adopting a customer orientation. Key business concepts such as accounting, economics, finance, information technology, marketing, management, and operations are interrelated and build upon each other in a multiperspective format. Elective courses, internships, and field-based learning experiences allow students to customize the program to meet their individual interests and career goals. Second-year electives can be used to create a concentration (such as accounting, finance, management information systems, or marketing) or to explore different areas of business.

The Self-Paced M.B.A. provides the flexibility and choice that allows each student to create a program that best complements his or her academic background and career interests. It can be completed in as little as one year with full advanced standing credit. The program allows students to specialize their broad-based management degree by selecting a concentration in one of fifteen areas: accountancy, advanced accoun-

tancy, business communications, business data analysis, business economics, business ethics, entrepreneurial studies, finance, international business, management, management information systems, management of technology, marketing, operations management, and taxation. Depth is added to the Self-Paced M.B.A. curriculum by shared electives from Bentley's seven business specialty programs, which include Master of Science degrees in accountancy, accounting information systems, business economics, computer information systems, finance, personal financial planning, and taxation.

Students and the M.B.A. Experience

Bentley, the largest graduate school of business in New England, brings together approximately 1,800 students representing fifty-four countries. This includes 250 full-time and 1,550 part-time students; 44 percent are women. While work experience is preferred, students with no prior work experience may apply.

❖ Global Focus

A focus on the global economy permeates the Bentley curriculum. Specific subjects and courses that explore international themes in all graduate programs are offered. Students interested in studying abroad can enroll in seven- to ten-day study tour courses in which they spend seven to ten days in countries that include Australia, Austria, China, Estonia, France,

Japan, and the Netherlands. Intermediate business language courses are offered in French, Spanish, and Italian.

The Graduate School's international perspective is enhanced through collaboration agreements with Groupe ESC Clermont in Clermont, France, and with Export Akademie Baden-Wurtemberg in Reutingen, Germany.

The Faculty

Experience, expertise, and accessibility are the trademarks of Bentley's faculty. Dedicated teaching professionals highly regarded in their respective fields, they are available to students and bring the most current and critical concepts and experiences to the classroom. Consulting keeps them current with business trends and technological advances. As a result, curriculum and course content remain up-to-date and oriented in the real world.

The Business School Network

The business community supports both curriculum design and student networking at Bentley. The Graduate School Advisory Council and MBA Advisory Board, made up of key executives from the Boston area's multinational, national, and regional firms, provides ongoing corporate input for program development. Bentley brings a real-world approach to the educational process through activities that promote interaction among graduate students and business professionals. Students can connect with guest speakers who participate in the Graduate School's Executive Speaker Series, INSIGHTS From Successful Business Women, and events sponsored by student organizations. In addition, Bentley's popular Mentor Program pairs students with business professionals, who serve as resources on job-related issues and concerns.

Through the Alumni Career Exploration (ACE) Network, more than 1,000 alumni are available to meet with students to discuss their career development, share information about work experience, assist with interviewing skills, and connect students with other corporate resource people.

The College and Environs

Founded in 1917, the College is an independent, coeducational institution recognized internationally for its excellence in professional business education. In addition to the students at the Graduate School, more than 3,000 undergraduates are enrolled in business and liberal arts. Bentley is accredited by AACSB–The International Association for Management Education and regionally accredited by the New England Association of Schools and Colleges (NEASC).

Located in Waltham, Massachusetts, at the heart of the region's high-technology sector, the 110-acre suburban campus is minutes from Boston's business, financial, and cultural resources; 30 minutes from Logan International Airport; and a 3-hour drive from New York City.

Facilities

The library houses more than 200,000 volumes, receives more than 1,700 periodicals, and has 155,000 microform titles. Study rooms, computer terminals, and various databases (e.g., LEXIS-NEXIS, Dow Jones News Retrieval Service, and InfoTrac) are available for student use. The media services department provides television facilities, conferencing telephones, video conferencing, and recordings for both instruction and group-work support.

Bentley has a limited number of furnished one- and two-bedroom apartments and single dormitory rooms that are equipped with a personal computer connection to the campus network. Interested applicants should request a housing application.

The Dana Physical Education Center houses an Olympic-size swimming pool, exercise rooms, an indoor track, basketball courts, racquetball courts, and a dance studio.

Technology Environment

Bentley is committed to continually upgrading its technological resources to ensure that graduate students understand how business processes can be enhanced through the strategic application of information technology. It is one of only six academic institutions in the nation to have an on-site financial Trading Room. The multimillion-dollar facility simulates actual stock exchange experience and serves as a practical vehicle for learning across a range of academic disciplines.

The integration of business and technology further supports graduate student study through the school's Graduate Computer Learning Center, CIS CASE Lab, CE Lab, on- and off-campus access to individual accounts, e-mail, and various sophisticated research database systems that are used for research. Communication and group interaction are enhanced by the use of videotape, course Web sites, faculty and student home pages, and group work.

Placement

Bentley's separate Graduate Career Center assists students with networking and provides an impressive array of career planning resources. Workshops help students obtain information, refine job search strategies, develop effective personal marketing materials, and prepare for employment interviews. More than 200 local, national, and international employers visit the campus annually to recruit graduate students. Ninety-seven percent of all 1997 graduates had jobs within six months after commencement.

Admission

Students in the M.S. and Self-Paced M.B.A. programs begin their studies in the fall, spring, or summer terms. Students in the Full-Time M.B.A. program begin in September and move through their two-year program together.

Applicants should submit a completed application form, a $50 application fee, official transcripts of all academic work beyond high school, GMAT scores, and two letters of recommendation. An evaluative interview and updated resume are required for Full-Time M.B.A. applicants.

Finances

The 1998–99 academic-year tuition is $2050 per 3-credit course. Books, supplies, health insurance, living expenses, and personal expenses for a nine-month academic year are approximately $11,935. Summer living expenses are approximately $2565. Costs are subject to change.

Graduate Assistantships (GA) are available for highly qualified applicants and consist of a tuition waiver and possibly a stipend in exchange for work as a research assistant.

International Students

Bentley supports international students through a seminar series on the academic, cultural, and social aspects of the U.S. graduate school experience. Individual tutoring in language skills is available. In addition, the Joseph M. Cronin International Center has a full-time information student adviser and staff to meet the social and academic needs of international students. The Graduate Career Center also conducts seminars on immigration regulations and U.S. employment and labor certification and provides information on overseas job postings.

Application Facts and Dates

For fall start in September, the preferred deadline for GA applicants, international candidates, or those wishing an early decision to ensure options for housing and financial assistance is March 1; the regular application deadline is June 1. For spring start in January, the preferred deadline for GA applicants, international candidates, or those wishing an early decision is October 1; the regular application deadline is November 1. For summer start in May, the regular application deadline is March 1.

For more information, applicants should make inquiries to:

Graduate School of Business
Bentley College
175 Forest Street
Waltham, Massachusetts 02154-4705
Telephone: 781-891-2108
Fax: 781-891-2464
E-mail: gradadm@bentley.edu
World Wide Web: http://www.bentley.edu/admissions/graduate

bʃu Boise State University

Boise, Idaho

ON THE ROAD TO KNOWLEDGE AND CHANGE

Our program's goal is to equip you, our future leaders, with the skills necessary to manage in the present environment and the learning skills needed to respond to change.

Through the tremendous support of our business advisory council, our program is able to achieve a high level of quality as well as provide excellent opportunities for our students to interact with businesses as part of their educational experience.

Boise State is surrounded by an exciting city that offers a variety of social, educational, cultural, and recreational opportunities. This setting will encourage you to discover more about yourself and the world around you.

When you come to Boise State University, I can promise you a demanding and academic intellectual environment along with an extremely enjoyable social environment. At Boise State University, you will find traditions of pride, determination, and, above all, academic excellence. It will be a road full of challenge, new knowledge, and great change.

—William N. Ruud, Dean

Program and Curricular Focus

The Master of Business Administration degree program at Boise State University is designed to prepare future business leaders to handle the challenges of change in a global economy. Emphasizing the needs of fully employed students, the program strives to provide students with a thorough grounding in each of the functional business areas. Integration of students' knowledge across these functional disciplines is one of the program's key objectives.

The Boise State M.B.A. program provides a general perspective of business management that requires students to consider the social, environmental, and ethical context of managerial actions. It is a high-quality academic program that assists in the development of tomorrow's business leaders. It provides a general management perspective that enables students to target problems, select viable alternatives, and take appropriate action. Boise State makes the international perspective a priority throughout the curriculum.

The Boise State M.B.A. requires a minimum of 33 semester credit hours and a maximum of 54 semester credit hours. The exact number of credits required depends upon the student's prior academic experience. While there is no major available in the M.B.A. program, once students satisfy the functional core

of courses, they emphasize an area of concentration with their elective credits. This specialization can expand beyond business to such areas as public administration or health administration.

Students and the M.B.A. Experience

Students in Boise State University's M.B.A. program bring a wide variety of work experiences and geographic and academic diversity to their M.B.A. experience. Many Boise State M.B.A. students are professional people, continuing their education while working full-time. This mix of backgrounds promotes the beneficial exchange of experience and ideas among peers, a significant factor in the quality and excitement of the program.

A recent student profile shows that the average student is 32 years old, with an average of over six years of full-time work experience. Women comprise 42 percent of the student population, and students who are members of minority groups make up 15 percent of the M.B.A. student body.

Most Boise State M.B.A. students have undergraduate degrees in business, engineering, science, or social science.

Special Features

Boise State University's M.B.A. program is small enough to enable students to

work in groups on classwork and projects. Many projects are required that develop small group, negotiation, and presentation skills—the same skills demanded of successful managers.

The Faculty

The College of Business and Economics faculty brings a high standard of excellence to Boise State's M.B.A. program. The M.B.A. faculty members hold doctoral degrees from universities across the nation. Most have extensive experience in business, industry, or consulting. This actual business experience enables the faculty to bring a realistic and pragmatic orientation to the classroom.

Boise State University's faculty members are dedicated to excellence in teaching. The faculty consults with, and researches for, top businesses to constantly update materials and to bring the most practical and current business information and problems/solutions into the classroom. This day-to-day contact allows Boise State's faculty members to gain knowledge of the skills businesses find valuable as well as the tools and information students need to allow insight into tomorrow's business needs. The M.B.A. curriculum incorporates these insights to ensure that the program addresses the demands professional managers confront.

The Business School Network
Corporate Partnerships
Boise is the commercial, financial, health-care, and government center of Idaho, allowing students to reach beyond the classroom for experiences not available elsewhere in the state. Boise State University has the advantage of being situated in a city where major firms are headquartered, including Albertson's, Boise Cascade, Idaho Power, Morrison-Knudsen, Ore-Ida, Simplot, Trus Joist, and the state's leading banks and insurance companies. Major manufacturing locations for Hewlett-Packard and Micron Technology are also located in Boise.

Prominent Alumni
The College of Business and Economics counts among its alumni a number of

notable business leaders, including William C. Glynn, CEO of Intermountain Gas; George A. Haneke, CFO of Micron Computer; Douglas G. Hansen, Controller, US Bancorp; Daniel J. Kunz, President and CEO, MK Corp.; Alan J. Moore, Vice President and CFO, MK Corp.; Sony M. Perry, Vice President, Telecommunications, NCI Information Systems, Inc.; Lyle R. Price, Bechtel; Mary J. Schofield, Controller of Hewlett-Packard's Boise Division; Jan B. Packwood, Executive Vice President, Idaho Power; Randy J. Lawrence, CFO, Western Power Sports, Inc.; Allen Lavelle, President, Pacific Property Consultants; Lorelli Hackler, Controller, Micron Technology; Russell Fulcher, National Sales Manager, Micron Technology; Dean A. Froehlich, Financial Vice President, Lewis-Clark State College; Deborah L. Flandro, Manager of Planning, Hewlett-Packard; Christian J. Anton, CEO, St. Alphonsus Regional Medical Center; John Jack Veale, Vice President of Finance and Administration, Spicer Gas/USA Fuel; Ronald D. Sargent, Senior Vice President, Bank of America; and Claudia G. Peterson, CFO, Golden Valley Health Centers.

The College and Environs

Boise State University is located in Boise, Idaho's capital and largest city and one of America's most enjoyable places to live and learn, featuring big city opportunities and small town friendliness. Set against a backdrop of mountains where the Boise River flows out of its lava canyons into a fertile valley, Boise is one of the most appealing metropolitan areas in the West. Named for the Boise River, present-day Boise is a green tribute to the magic of irrigation, with its parks, greenbelt, tree-lined neighborhood streets, golf courses, and University campus. Boise has a pleasant four-season climate; it is one of the premier locations in the country for those who like the outdoors.

Founded in 1932 as a private community college, today Boise State University has the largest enrollment in Idaho with about 17,000 students, more than 200 of

whom are in the M.B.A. program. Students come from all parts of the world and from diverse academic and professional backgrounds.

Technology Environment

Through the Office of Information Technology, Boise State University provides student access to the University's computer resources. Many of Boise State's offices and computer labs are connected to the campus fiber-optic network, allowing users to tap into the Campus-Wide Information System or gain access to the Internet, BITNET, and other networks.

The College of Business and Economics has its own computing facilities, consisting of two microcomputing laboratories with approximately seventy terminals. Facilities are open seven days a week during convenient hours. The College of Business and Economics also houses three electronic classrooms furnished with the latest multimedia systems.

Placement

Boise State University's Career Center provides career guidance and information through computerized career guidance/information systems and from professional staff members. Information and advice on résumé and cover letter writing, application procedures, interviewing, and other job-hunting skills are available. A library of career and employer information is also available. Notification of employment opportunities, participation in on-campus interviews, and optional establishment of a file of professional references are available to M.B.A. students during the academic year in which they complete their degree.

Admission

Applicants must possess a bachelor's degree from an accredited institution. Completed applications must include official transcripts from all institutions previously attended, a GMAT report, two letters of recommendation, a current

professional resume, and an essay. In addition, two years of significant work experience is required but can be waived based on a superior GMAT score. The average GMAT score of enrolling students is 545; the average undergraduate GPA is 3.2.

A score of at least 550 on the TOEFL is required of all students for whom English is not the native language. International students must also present proof of adequate funding and certified English translations of transcripts.

There are no prerequisite courses for admission, but students must have a basic level of proficiency in college-level algebra and with word processing, database, and spreadsheet programs.

Finances

Tuition and fees for 1997–98 were $3500 for Idaho residents and $11,000 for nonresidents. On-campus and off-campus housing is available. Most graduate students choose to live off campus in nearby apartments. Many live within walking distance. On-campus room and board are estimated to cost $5600 for the academic year. Off-campus housing and food costs average $11,000 a year.

A number of graduate assistantships are available. To be eligible, students must be admitted to the M.B.A. program and attend as full-time students during the academic year(s) of the awards. The application deadline is March 1.

Application Facts and Dates

Application deadlines are October 1 and March 1.

For more information, students should contact:

Renee Anchustegui
Business Graduate Studies
College of Business and Economics
  B610
Boise State University
1910 University Drive
Boise, Idaho 83725
Telephone: 208-385-1126
Fax: 208-385-4989
E-mail: abuanchu@bsu.idbsu.edu

Boston College

Wallace E. Carroll Graduate School of Management

Chestnut Hill, Massachusetts

PREPARING STRATEGIC LEADERS

▶ *Today's successful executives are distinguished by their ability to manage teams, develop technology-based solutions to complex problems, and provide strategic leadership in constantly evolving organizations. Looking toward the twenty-first century, it is our ability to develop these qualities that differentiates the M.B.A. Program of the Carroll Graduate School of Management (CGSOM) from other graduate management programs.*

As a result of our innovative curriculum, distinguished faculty, and exceptional facilities, CGSOM is an emerging leader among M.B.A. programs. Our Management Practice curriculum has created a dynamic learning environment that is surpassed only by the quality of our globally diverse student body. Increasingly recognized as a place to find strategically intuitive and action-oriented managers, the Boston College M.B.A. is a logical choice if you desire a global perspective, unsurpassed analytical skills, and an understanding of strategic leadership in a global society.

—Hassell H. McClellan, Graduate Dean

Programs and Curricular Focus

The M.B.A. program at Boston College's Wallace E. Carroll Graduate School of Management provides students with the skills and perspectives necessary for success in today's global and technology-based business environment. In addition to receiving a thorough education in the functional areas of business, students have numerous opportunities to apply their knowledge in real-world settings. Students grapple with actual management problems through innovative classroom exercises, consulting projects, and new venture planning activities. This unique combination of classroom and applied learning gives Boston College M.B.A. students a distinct career advantage.

The curriculum is designed not only to provide an understanding of the fundamentals of management, but also to offer abundant opportunities to tailor the program to meet specific needs and career goals. After completing the core study, students have many opportunities to explore possible career paths through electives, concentrations, industry-specific programs, independent studies, and other options. These options include concentrations in the traditional functional areas as well as interdisciplinary "specialty concentrations" in such topics as entrepreneurship, consulting, international management, and the management of financial institutions.

The School also offers a number of dual-degree programs: the M.B.A./J.D.,

the M.B.A./M.S.W., the M.B.A./Ph.D. in sociology, the M.B.A./M.A. in mathematics, and the M.B.A./M.S. in biology, nursing, or geology/geophysics. Offered on a full- or part-time (evening) basis, the M.B.A. program at Boston College's Carroll Graduate School of Management is part of a portfolio of programs that includes a Master of Science in finance and a Ph.D. in management, with concentrations in finance and organization studies.

Students and the M.B.A. Experience

There are approximately 220 full-time and 550 evening M.B.A. students. Approximately thirty percent of students in the M.B.A. program are women. Full-time M.B.A. students have an average of 3.5 years of full-time work experience; evening M.B.A. students have an average of 5.3 years.

❖ Global Focus

Boston College's M.B.A. curriculum is global in its outlook. Global management issues are woven throughout the curriculum so that course work across the spectrum of functional areas routinely addresses the international dimensions of business. Moreover, with approximately one third of the entering full-time class typically made up of international students, a global perspective comes naturally to the program. Students develop world-wide

perspectives in a kind of learning laboratory that is much like the business environment into which they will graduate.

In response to the growing importance placed by corporate employers on a broad range of global management experiences, the Carroll Graduate School maintains an extensive program of international study opportunities. One such opportunity is the International Management Experience (IME). Offered annually at the end of the spring semester, this elective allows M.B.A. students to study a region of the world and see first-hand how business is conducted. During the three weeks of travel, students visit corporations, major commercial centers, and government agencies. The 1998 IMEs will include Asia and Western Europe.

Special Features

Due to the increasing demand for technology-savvy executives, the M.B.A. program is launching a management of information technology concentration in fall 1998. In conjunction with other graduate programs at Boston College, the M.B.A. program is offering dual degrees that enable students to receive an M.B.A. degree and a master's degree in math, geology/geophysics, or biology. Students accepted to the M.B.A. program with graduate degrees in law, mathematics, nursing, social work, or a natural science discipline from accredited U.S. institutions may be eligible for up to 12 credit hours of advanced standing.

The Faculty

The members of the Carroll Graduate School of Management faculty represent a vibrant mix of knowledge, experience, and professional dedication. Many of them bring extensive industry backgrounds and contacts directly into the classroom, which adds to the "real-world" aspect of the learning experience. Common to all the faculty members is a commitment to balancing scholarship and teaching excellence.

The Business School Network
Corporate Partnerships

Top executives regularly visit the Carroll Graduate School of Management. The

M.B.A. Executive Lecture Series and the new Executive in Residence Program are just two examples of programs that give students the chance to interact directly with leaders in the business and nonprofit worlds.

The Carroll Graduate School of Management has also formed a first-of-its-kind strategic alliance with the Arthur D. Little School of Management to explore new directions in the delivery of management education. The Arthur D. Little School of Management provides worldwide training for Arthur D. Little, Inc., an international consulting firm.

The Board of Advisors, a group of senior executives from leading companies, consults regularly with the Carroll Graduate School on program and curricular issues. The School also sponsors the Chief Executives Club of Boston, a prestigious business speaking forum.

CGSOM supports students in exploring career options through internships. Moreover, the school has developed an Executive Fellows Program in partnership with State Street Global Advisors, the nation's third-largest investment manager. Through this program, students participate in internships in investment management research and financial services marketing. The school is committed to expanding these opportunities through partnerships with other leading corporations.

The College and Environs

Located on 185 acres on the Boston line, Boston College is just a short ride by car or subway from downtown Boston, a world-renowned center of culture, learning, and industry.

Boston College is a coeducational, two-campus university with four undergraduate schools and six graduate and professional schools. The University offers fourteen degree programs and two certificate programs and enrolls 8,900 full-time undergraduates and 4,600 graduate students. Established in 1863, Boston College is the largest Jesuit-affiliated university in the country.

Facilities

Fulton Hall, which houses the Carroll Graduate School of Management, is a state-of-the-art center for management education. Among Fulton's advantages: many classrooms outfitted with advanced computer and audiovisual technologies, including direct Internet access; abundant space for meetings, study groups, and gatherings, including a dramatic five-story atrium that functions as the School's "town square"; and the location in the heart of Boston College's Chestnut Hill campus, close to the libraries, the recreation complex, and the student union.

Computer facilities are available to M.B.A. students in the graduate computer lab in Fulton Hall and in the O'Neill Computing Facility, which provide access to a wide variety of hardware, software, and peripherals.

The University's libraries offer a wealth of resources to support research, teaching, and learning. The book collections exceed 1.6 million volumes and approximately 17,000 serial titles are currently received. The library holds 2.5 million microforms. In addition, Boston College libraries provide access to more than 500 databases, including many in business and economics.

Graduate housing is not provided on campus; however, the Office of University Housing provides off-campus listings and suggestions for interested students.

Placement

Boston College's Carroll Graduate School of Management is committed to helping students achieve the best possible career outcomes. The Office of Career Services provides M.B.A. students with the means to achieve their career goals through placement initiatives, career coaching, and other services. The office also serves as a bridge to corporations through its outreach activities and links to Boston College's worldwide alumni network.

Services include on- and off-campus recruiting programs, resume books for first- and second-year students, a job-posting system, and two career fairs. The office also maintains a database of alumni career advisers and offers career advising, interviewing and resume-writing workshops, information sessions, and a library of career resources.

Admission

The Carroll Graduate School of Management welcomes applications from graduates of accredited colleges and universities. For the M.B.A. program, the Admissions Committee considers applicants with academic backgrounds from virtually all areas of study.

Courses in business administration or management are not required for admission to the Carroll Graduate School of Management M.B.A. program. However, students are expected to be proficient in English and mathematics. In addition, all applicants are expected to take the GMAT. International students must have the equivalent of a U.S. bachelor's degree and a minimum score of 600 on the TOEFL exam.

The Admissions Committee looks for evidence of academic and management potential. Work experience and prior academic performance are significant criteria in their evaluation. In general, students enter the program after at least two years of full-time work experience. Leadership and community involvement are also important factors in admissions decisions.

Finances

Tuition for the 1998–99 academic year is $714 per credit hour. Books, fees, and supplies average $966 per year and medical insurance is $455. Living expenses currently average $5662 per semester.

The Carroll School offers a significant program of graduate assistantships or scholarships to full-time M.B.A. classes. Awardees usually have two or more years of full-time work experience, a score of 630 or above on the GMAT, a grade point average of 3.2 or above, and a strong set of application materials. Graduate assistantships involve research or administrative duties in exchange for tuition remission. A portion of assistantship awards is subject to tax.

In addition to the assistantships and scholarships offered through the Carroll School, the University Financial Aid Office offers a variety of programs to help students finance their education.

Application Facts and Dates

The evening M.B.A. program admits students in September and January; the full-time M.B.A. program begins only in September. Admission deadlines are April 1 for the full-time M.B.A., November 15 for January admission to the evening program, and July 1 for September admission. International students must submit a complete application and TOEFL score by March 1. Deadlines for assistantships are outlined in the application. Prospective students may apply online through the M.B.A. Web site or at http://www.MBA.CollegeEdge. com. For more information, applicants should contact:

Simone P. Marthers,
Director of M.B.A. Admissions
Wallace E. Carroll Graduate School of
    Management
Fulton Hall, Room 315
Boston College
140 Commonwealth Avenue
Chestnut Hill, Massachusetts 02167-
    3808
Telephone: 617-552-3920
Fax: 617-552-8078
World Wide Web: http://www.bc.edu/
    mba

Boston University

School of Management

Boston, Massachusetts

THE BOSTON UNIVERSITY M.B.A.: A FOCUS ON THE SYSTEM

The Boston University M.B.A. curriculum is a pioneering program designed to concentrate on management processes instead of functions alone. In this M.B.A. program, you will learn management as a system—a horizontal continuum of interdependent departments or functions. Many graduate schools structure their curriculum to develop general managers. But they tend to take a segmented route, where accounting is isolated from marketing, operations from finance, and so on. In such classes, case studies are usually approached for an accounting (or marketing or operations) solution only. That is not how the real world operates. At Boston University, we develop general managers with a view that extends across multiple departments to encompass the whole organization.

—Louis E. Lataif, Dean

Programs and Curricular Focus

Boston University offers the M.B.A. in general management, with specializations in entrepreneurship, finance, international management, marketing, operations, organizational behavior, and strategy. The University also offers the M.B.A. in health-care management, the M.B.A. in public and nonprofit management, the executive M.B.A., the M.S. in management information systems, and the Doctor of Business Administration.

The M.B.A. program provides graduates with the full range of foundation skills required to be an outstanding and adaptable performer immediately upon graduation, the competencies required for long-term career development, and the perspectives necessary to understand the complex social and ethical dimensions of management. The program provides real-world action learning coupled with a rigorous, research-based conceptual education. Each of the first three semesters of the full-time program is anchored by team-taught courses: The Global Manager, The Global Environment, and The Global Organization. Each offers a cross-disciplinary understanding of organizations and their broader environments.

The optimum way to understand management processes and systems is by pooling the expertise from various disciplines. The faculty members team-teach several courses, interactively dissecting each topic or case study of the day from their own respective viewpoint. Under their guidance, students learn to develop holistic, relevant solutions, rather than one-dimensional, academic ones.

Teamwork is an essential part of today's workplace, and thus it is a major component of the M.B.A. education. In most Boston University M.B.A. courses, students work in consistent cohorts, simulating the way actual organizations work. Students join in study teams, project teams, and consulting teams to outside industry. Each of these experiences helps the student learn how to facilitate the teamwork process in every phase of his or her M.B.A. education and career.

Students and the M.B.A. Experience

Boston University has the most internationally diverse student body in the nation (as reported by the Institute of International Education), and this is reflected in the M.B.A. program. Thirty-nine percent of the students are international. The students, who come from six continents, benefit from a rich and varied interchange of views. The M.B.A. curriculum capitalizes on this diversity in its emphasis on the global business environment. The students are highly intelligent, diverse, ambitious, and determined to make a positive difference in society. Their active participation in the evaluations of the programs and activities ensures a continuing vibrancy and responsiveness in the School.

There are approximately 1,500 students enrolled in the M.B.A. programs.

Applications are traditionally received from approximately sixty-five countries. The average student is 27 years old, has three to five years of work experience, and entered the program with an average TOEFL score of 611 and GMAT score of 608.

❖ Global Focus

Students can begin their M.B.A. program by joining a ten-week management program in Kobe, Japan. The program draws students from the Pacific Rim and countries around the world for a rich intercultural experience. Courses taught by Boston University professors combine classroom work with field visits and guest lecturers to help students develop an understanding of the social, political, and economic aspects of global business. During their second year, students may live and study abroad through the student exchange programs between Boston University and the University of Manchester, England, or the University of Lyon, France.

Special Features

The School of Management has developed a three-week orientation program to help international students adjust to the dynamic atmosphere of the American M.B.A. classroom and to prepare for the rigorous demands of case discussions. This distinctive program provides both English instruction and an introduction to the M.B.A. curriculum. Attendance may be required for students whose native language is not English and whose prior academic work has not been in English or has not fully prepared them for the case study method.

Students have the opportunity to read, analyze, and discuss actual case studies. The orientation program also introduces students to the American economic system, including the operation of private firms and the role the American government plays in the business environment. Students also receive training in preparation for class presentations and an introduction to the M.B.A. classroom culture. There is a fee for the program.

The Faculty

The faculty is the School of Management's major resource. Committed to advancing management knowledge, through both theoretical and applied research, and to improving the quality of teaching and learning, faculty members bring the benefits of their vast professional experience to the classroom. The faculty members have earned worldwide recognition and respect for their applied research. They bring a refreshing approach to teaching within interdisciplinary frameworks and also bring wide-ranging experience with local, national, and global organizations.

The Business School Network

The Boston University School of Management has a wealth of research centers and institutes, each of which addresses issues that extend beyond the boundaries of traditional disciplines. These organizations have become magnets for faculty members from disciplines around Boston University and for top-level managers from around the world, who come together and share their understanding of contemporary management challenges.

The research centers and institutes and the School's executive training programs offer significant advantages to students seeking leadership roles in major organizations. Through an industrial network that extends around the globe, faculty members maintain contact and exchange data with colleagues in universities and business firms. This real-world involvement brings exciting results into the classroom—timely and topical material for case studies and a steady stream of high-level managers from a variety of firms.

The College and Environs

The fourth-largest private university in the nation, Boston University is consolidated at the 86-acre Charles River Campus and Boston University's Medical Center in the city's South End. The School of Management was established as the College of Business Administration in 1913 and is located on the Charles River Campus. Boston offers a wealth of cultural, educational, sports, and social resources. Combining a proud history with a contemporary lifestyle, it is a cosmopolitan center for the financial and insurance industries, the heart of the high-technology industry, an extensive medical and educational center, and the capital of Massachusetts. As the hub of one of the nation's largest metropolitan areas, Boston offers numerous opportunities for strong practical experience in business, government, health, technology, and public management.

Facilities

The Boston University School of Management opened the nation's most technologically advanced building for management education in 1997. Designed specifically for teaching management as an integrated system, and built to accommodate team learning and team teaching, the new building integrates leading-edge technology throughout. The building features classrooms with computer ports and plugs for all students, instructional workstations with Internet access, and advanced audiovisual capabilities for slide, videotape, and computer-generated presentations. In addition, the management library houses more than 90,000 books, periodicals, and journals, as well as the latest technology for information retrieval.

Placement

The School of Management's state-of-the-art Career Center assists students in making informed career and life decisions. Through comprehensive career education programming, job development services, and individualized career counseling, the center collaborates with students in developing and managing careers at both the entry and experienced level. The number of firms recruiting on campus in 1997–98 increased nearly 40 percent over the previous year.

Admission

The requirements for applying are a completed application form with a nonrefundable $50 application fee, official transcripts of the academic record from each college or university attended, three letters of evaluation, and results of the Graduate Management Admission Test (GMAT).

International applicants must also submit English translations of transcripts (the undergraduate degree must be equivalent to a U.S. bachelor's degree), results of the Test of English as a Foreign Language (TOEFL) (if the student's native language is English or if the student received an undergraduate degree from an institution where English is the language of instruction, the TOEFL is not required), and the International Student Data Form and financial documents. Since scholarship funds are not generally available to international students, applicants must submit a financial declaration showing adequate funding for both tuition and living expenses for the duration of the M.B.A. program.

Finances

Tuition for the 1998–99 academic year is $22,830, and fees are approximately $215. Single students living off campus should anticipate living costs for nine months of approximately $18,000; the costs for married students are estimated at $22,000. Most students live in apartments in nearby neighborhoods, easily accessible from the School by public transportation. The program offers scholarships, work-study awards, and endowment funding to full-time students. Awards are made based on academic merit. All students are required to have medical insurance, estimated at $520.

Application Facts and Dates

Students seeking financial aid should apply by March 15. The deadlines for September admission are April 15 for full-time study (domestic students) and June 15 for part-time study. The deadline for January admission is November 15 (part-time study only).

International students are admitted to the M.B.A. program for full-time study in September only. All international applications must be received by the Graduate Admissions Office by March 1.

Applications are reviewed on a rolling basis. Review begins in February for September admission. Students are encouraged to submit applications early to ensure adequate processing time. An online application is available through the Web site. For more information, applicants should contact:

Boston University School of
    Management
Graduate Admissions Office
595 Commonwealth Avenue
Boston, Massachusetts 02215
Telephone: 617-353-2670
Fax: 617-353-7368
E-mail: mba@bu.edu
World Wide Web: http://management.
    bu.edu

Bowling Green State University

Bowling Green, Ohio

CREATING LEADERS FOR A CHANGING WORLD

The mission of the Bowling Green State University (BGSU) M.B.A. program is to qualify individuals to be effective managers, innovative leaders, and team builders in private- or public-sector organizations. Although we believe our curriculum is current and rigorous, we are the first to stress that lectures, case studies, simulations, and group projects relative to business fundamentals are not enough. The market demands leaders who can work collaboratively with a diverse team of peers, identify and solve unstructured business problems, and recognize, anticipate, and manage uncertainty and change while making decisions that are both ethical and profitable for the organization. To prepare our students for life beyond the classroom, we complement the traditional course offerings with professional development seminars that are designed to provide skill developmental opportunities in the areas demanded by the market. You are invited to look at the Bowling Green State University M.B.A. program. Our business is helping you succeed!

—Carmen Castro-Rivera, Director

Programs and Curricular Focus

The curriculum of the Bowling Green State University M.B.A. program reflects a basic belief that M.B.A. graduates should be generalists with a fundamental knowledge of business functions and an ability to integrate those functions within a constantly changing environment. Because this emphasis is applicable to any type of organization, the Bowling Green M.B.A. is increasingly viewed as excellent preparation for careers in traditionally non-M.B.A. fields.

The M.B.A. program's broad curriculum provides candidates with an understanding of the major facets of business operations. It includes work in the social, theoretical, and historical foundations of business, quantitative controls, research methodology, and decision making through the development of advanced functional skills. Although core courses develop the traditional knowledge of business fundamentals (accounting, economics, finance, operations, marketing, organizational behavior, and strategy) throughout the program, M.B.A. candidates are challenged to go beyond a general understanding of the fundamentals to appraise the political, social, and economic implications of business decisions. Students also have the opportunity to declare formal specializations in management information systems, operations research, and supply chain management.

The M.B.A. degree requires a minimum of 34 hours of graduate-level course work. The full-time program can be completed within one calendar year by students with appropriate undergraduate preparation in business. Generally, students without undergraduate preparation in business complete their programs within eighteen to twenty-four months. A business degree is not required as a prerequisite for study in the BGSU M.B.A. program.

The Executive M.B.A. program is a rigorous and concentrated program that results in the M.B.A. degree after completion of six 2-week sessions over a three-year period. Candidates must be nominated by their employer and should hold substantial responsibility in their organizations.

Incoming students into any of the M.B.A. program options (part-time, full-time, or executive) are expected to have satisfactorily completed course work in calculus, personal computer skills, and introductory economics.

Students and the M.B.A. Experience

The Bowling Green M.B.A. program, accredited by AACSB–The International Association for Management Education, is recognized nationally for the quality of its students and faculty. With a full-time enrollment of just over 100 students, the M.B.A. at Bowling Green offers many of the advantages of a small school atmosphere (class size is no more than 25 students) but also the resources of a top-notch research university. The current student population includes students from twenty-three countries and nineteen states. In a typical class, students range in age from 23 to 50. At least 50 percent of those enrolled have a minimum of three years' work experience; however, years of work experience range from zero to thirty. Approximately 25 percent of each entering class is international in composition. Undergraduate majors range from biology to political science to engineering, and work experience varies from investment banking to pharmacy.

Students involved in any graduate program in the College of Business Administration are invited to join the Graduate Business Student Association (GBSA). The GBSA promotes opportunities for learning, personal development, networking, and socializing via plant tours, alumni receptions, monthly speakers, and numerous other activities.

Special Features

In addition to in-class learning, full-time students take part in a cocurricular Professional Development Series (PDS). The PDS is offered through the office of Graduate Studies in Business at Bowling Green State University and helps prepare graduate business students for the demands of a changing world. The primary goal of the PDS is to expand the graduate business students' experiences beyond the classroom into today's world of business, commerce, and nonprofit organizations and to further bridge the gap between valuable theoretical knowledge and the practical competitive requirements of the workplace.

The PDS is designed to complement and supplement the graduate business academic program by presenting working seminars highlighting essential leadership skills and the hottest business issues. Many of the seminars are presented by business executives or organizations from the regional and international business communities. These individuals bring their breadth of experience directly to the graduate business student on campus. Topics have included Personal Effectiveness; the Polished Professional; the Job Search: Interviewing and Networking; Creating a Resume that Gets Results; Negotiations: Getting to Yes Every Time; Coaching Skills; and Effective Communication and the Real World.

The Faculty

Because the faculty greatly influences the quality of learning in any formal education program, all graduate faculty members are selected on the basis of superior scholarship in both teaching and research. Many of the faculty members at BGSU are nationally and internationally renowned. Distinguished faculty members include a National Association of Purchasing Managers' Professor and two University Distinguished Teaching Award recipients.

Many members of the faculty are actively involved in consulting in both the public and private sectors and have brought the results of their observations, experiences, and research into the classroom. A high priority for the faculty is to prepare students for the roles of leadership they will assume. Faculty members accomplish this not only by excellent teaching but also by advising students on their business research and consulting projects.

The Business School Network

Students in the M.B.A. program connect with the Ohio business community via field studies, consulting projects, internship opportunities, symposiums, and conferences sponsored by departments in the College. Corporate leaders are featured speakers at the annual student banquet and at the biweekly professional development seminars.

Bowling Green State University also has a corporate M.B.A. partnership with Dana Corporation and recruits extensively at numerous organizations in northwest Ohio for a part-time program of more than 200 students.

The College and Environs

Bowling Green State University was founded in 1910. The 1,338-acre campus houses more than 100 buildings in a small-town setting. BGSU serves approximately 14,535 undergraduate students and 2,793 graduate students. The College of Business Administration serves approximately 2,000 undergraduates and 400 graduate students.

BGSU is located 23 miles south of Toledo, just off Interstate Highway 75.

Airport transportation is provided by the Toledo Express Airport or the Detroit Metropolitan Airport, which is approximately an hour's drive north from Bowling Green. Metropolitan areas within comfortable driving distance include Indianapolis, Chicago, Cincinnati, Columbus, Dayton, and Windsor, Ontario.

The nine-story Jerome Library (the largest campus library) houses more than 4 million items. Through OhioLINK, BGSU students have access to an additional 17 million volumes held in Ohio's other state university libraries. The comprehensive network of academic computing resources, including DEC/VAX and IBM major systems, along with IBM and Apple microcomputers, includes a Business Administration Computer Lab with sixty personal computers and terminals located in the Business Administration building.

The student recreation center features indoor tennis and track, several basketball and volleyball courts, more than fifteen racquetball courts, and an Olympic-size swimming pool.

Placement

The Career Services Office provides students with personal help on developing interviewing skills, resume preparation, alumni and professional networking skills and opportunities, and access to on-campus corporate recruiters. These services are provided using state-of-the-art Web-based computer systems that have received national recognition.

BGSU M.B.A. graduates find themselves employed worldwide in a variety of both large and small corporations. A sampling of employers of recent graduates includes such companies as Allied Signal, BP Oil Company, Cap Gemini of America, Honda Manufacturing of America, Intel, the Kellogg Company, Andersen Consulting, Owens-Corning, and Procter & Gamble.

Admission

The Bowling Green Graduate Studies in Business Office welcomes applications from individuals regardless of undergraduate majors. Applicants must submit an application, transcripts of all previous college work, GMAT scores (and TOEFL when applicable), two letters of recommendation, a personal statement, a current resume, and a $30 application fee. Prior work experience is also reviewed when making assistantship decisions. Interviews are encouraged when possible. Students

may begin the application process by submitting an electronic application (http://www.bgsu.edu/colleges/gradcol/).

Finances

Tuition and fees in 1997–98 for 12 semester hours (full-time) per semester for Ohio residents was $2881. Nonresidents paid $5388 per semester. Additional costs of books and supplies varied from $375 to $750 for the academic year.

The primary form of financial aid is the graduate assistantship (GA). Highly qualified full-time students may be eligible for a GA position providing a stipend and scholarship covering all tuition and fees for the semesters of the appointment. A student serving the fall and spring semesters also receives a scholarship covering all tuition for the summer semester. In the 1997–98 academic year, the stipends ranged from $3450 to $6900. GA positions are available through the College of Business Administration. They are also available through the Instructional Media Center and the Office of Greek Life. Approximately 85 percent of full-time M.B.A. students receive graduate assistantships.

Application Facts and Dates

Applications for admission to the full-time M.B.A. program from international applicants should be received by April 15 for a fall start date and September 1 for a spring start date. Domestic applicants to the full-time program should submit their completed applications by June 1 for a fall start date and October 15 for the spring. Applicants receive an admission decision approximately six weeks after Graduate Studies in Business receives a completed application.

Any student desiring a graduate assistantship should have all application materials submitted by February 1. First-round GA candidates are notified by April 15.

For more information, applicants should contact:

Carmen Castro-Rivera, Director
Graduate Studies in Business
Bowling Green State University
Bowling Green, Ohio 43403
Telephone: 419-372-2488
              800-BGSU-MBA
Fax: 419-372-2875
E-mail: mba_info@cba.bgsu.edu
World Wide Web: http://www.cba.
    bgsu.edu

Brandeis University

Waltham, Massachusetts

PREPARING PROFESSIONALS FOR THE GLOBAL ECONOMY

The Graduate School of International Economics and Finance is the first school at a major U.S. university to focus on global markets, the best possible preparation for professional careers in the global economy. Our degree programs, with their strong analytical and financial orientations, will equip you with the practical and conceptual skills that are necessary to be successful in doing business across borders. Classes are small—we accept about 55 students per year—but very diverse, as more than forty countries are represented. The internationally known faculty comprises a dynamic teaching and research team that works closely with MBAi students in course work as well as on projects outside the classroom. Our approach is thoroughly international and includes a semester of study overseas with one of our twenty partner exchange schools.

—Peter A. Petri, Carl J. Shapiro Professor of International Finance and Dean

Programs and Curricular Focus

The MBA/International Program (MBAi) is a full-time degree program intended for students with prior work experience and offers a focused practical education in international business administration built upon a strong foundation of analysis and applied technical skills. The program provides excellent preparation for positions in multinational companies, international financial institutions, and government agencies. The program requires completion of sixteen courses over a two-year period, including one semester overseas at one of the School's prestigious partner universities.

For students who are in the early stages of their careers or who have just earned an undergraduate degree, the Graduate School offers the Lemberg M.A. in International Economics and Finance (MAief), which has an interdisciplinary curriculum in international business, finance, or economics and shares many core courses with the MBAi Program. Like the MBAi, the Lemberg Program requires two years of full-time study, including a semester abroad at one of four partner institutions. For professionals with significant work experience, the M.A. in International Economics and Finance Program features a one-year, three-semester, fast-track midcareer option that runs through a fall and spring semester and includes two summer courses and a major research project. Company sponsorship is not required for midcareer students.

Finally, the part-time M.S. in Finance Program is an evening program for working professionals seeking to develop skills in financial theory and analysis with an international focus. The M.S. is offered year-round and requires completion of ten courses: five required courses and five electives. Electives include one-week field studies in major international financial markets. Although the usual progress through the program is two courses per semester, students on a fast track may complete the degree in fifteen months.

Students and the M.B.A. Experience

The MBA/International Program at the Graduate School of International Economics and Finance at Brandeis University develops expertise in doing business across borders. The Graduate School provides a cosmopolitan yet intimate environment that supports students in developing and reaching their goals. Each entering class is limited to 55 master's students (MBAi and MAief), affording every individual the opportunity to get to know and interact with classmates, faculty members, and administrators through a variety of academic and extracurricular activities. The student body is diverse, with about 60 percent of the students from outside the United States; typically, more than forty nations are represented at the School. About 40 percent of the students are women and about 15 percent are members of minority groups.

❖ Global Focus

Since the entire curriculum is focused on developing skills for use in the global marketplace and since the students are from such diverse international backgrounds, each class becomes an international learning experience. Students often work in multicultural teams with a faculty of internationally known experts, and differences in perspectives and cultural norms are actively discussed.

Special Features

The MBAi and Lemberg MAief Programs are the only professional programs in the U.S. that require a semester of graduate study overseas. Students choose to study at one of twenty partner schools and in so doing develop a firsthand understanding of the business and economic systems of a major foreign country. Many students take course work in the local language, attaining the foreign language proficiency required for graduation. This semester abroad also allows participants to develop friendships and networks that usually intensify and expand after graduation.

The Faculty

The faculty includes several internationally known authorities on business management, exchange rates and trade policy, patents and technology transfer, and Asian economies and business. Other members conduct research with a focus on international finance. In addition, several high-level executives from Boston's business, finance, and legal communities offer their expertise in applied technical areas as adjunct professors.

Many of the faculty members conduct research in the School's Asia Pacific Center for Economics and Business using grant funding provided by prestigious international agencies, such as the Center for Global Partnership, the Luce Foundation, the United Nations, and the World Bank. The Graduate School has also been designated as one of thirteen official Asia Pacific Economic Cooperation (APEC) Study Centers in the U.S. and is the only such center in New England.

The Business School Network

The Graduate School has developed an extensive network of partnerships with financial and multinational corporations and with professionals in the finance and economics professions. Corporate partners include BankAmerica, Citicorp, Coopers & Lybrand, Imperial Chemical Industries (ICI), Macandrews and Forbes, Revlon, and the Sony Corporation. The multinational Board of Overseers of the School includes executives from Arthur Andersen & Co., the Bank of Tokyo-Mitsubishi Ltd., Erving Industries, Fuji Xerox Co., Goldman Sachs, ICI, Mellon Bank, the Monitor Company, the Ssangyong Business Group of Korea, and the World Bank. Visitors from these companies and many others provide opportunities to address important issues through informal lectures, conferences, and seminars. The School also runs an Executive Education Program in alliance strategy.

The College and Environs

Founded in 1948, Brandeis is one of the leading private research universities in the United States, with approximately 3,000 undergraduates and 1,100 graduate students. The University is situated on a parklike campus 10 miles west of Boston and Cambridge, while the Graduate School is located in a wooded corner of the campus in the Sachar International Center. The University has superb sports and theater facilities and brings a series of distinguished lecturers, artists, and performance groups to campus. Public transportation provides quick access to Boston's cultural and educational amenities and to nearby ocean and New England rural attractions.

Facilities

Master's students frequently participate in faculty research and in seminars and discussions with visiting scholars and practitioners. As an APEC Study Center, there are special opportunities for those interested in Asian economics and business.

The School operates its own IBM-compatible computer network with access to current software, databases, LEXIS-NEXIS, and the World Wide Web. Students have access to university libraries and to other resources through the Boston Library Consortium and through exchange agreements with other leading colleges and universities in the area.

Placement

Virtually all graduates of the program are employed in positions utilizing their economic, financial, and international training. Leading employers include Citibank, KPMG Peat Marwick, Morgan Stanley, and the U.S. Federal Reserve Banks. Graduates from recent classes have received offers from consulting firms such as the Boston Consulting Group and McKinsey & Co. and from corporations such as Adidas America, AT&T, and Microsoft. Students work closely with the Associate Dean and with the Hiatt Career Development Center staff to learn about career alternatives and to implement an effective career development strategy during their time at Brandeis.

Admission

Applicants for all master's programs are required to have an American bachelor's degree or the equivalent foreign degree. Prior training in a modern foreign language is highly desirable. All applications should include official copies of transcripts and three letters of recommendations. All international applicants must submit TOEFL scores.

Applicants to the MBAi and M.S. in Finance Programs should have some prior work experience and must submit scores from the GMAT (not the GRE).

For the Lemberg MAief Program, prior course work should include at least two semesters of economics and one semester of international relations or politics. MAief applicants must also submit scores from either the general GRE or the GMAT. Mid-Career MAief applicants must fulfill the above requirements but will normally not be considered for admission with less than five years of full-time work experience, including at least six months of living experience outside their home country.

Finances

Tuition charges for full-time students for 1998–99 are $23,360 per year for MBAi and M.A. students. Tuition for the twelve-month Mid-Career M.A. Program is $35,040. Tuition rates for the part-time M.S. in Finance program are $2100 per course. Ten-month living expenses in the area are estimated to range from $8,500 to $10,000 for a single student. Limited on-campus housing is available; most students live within a short commute of campus.

Candidates may apply for tuition scholarships, assistantships, and loans, which are available to American and international students. Special American Leadership Awards are available to U.S. citizens or permanent resident applicants who exhibit outstanding potential for international careers.

International Students

Approximately 60 percent of the graduate students are international, typically coming from more than forty nations. Well-represented areas include the Far East, Latin America, and Central and Eastern Europe. The University also has a large international population and provides support through the International Students Office and via an active International Student Association.

Application Facts and Dates

Application deadlines are February 15 for an April 1 notification and April 15 for notification in May. Candidates applying for financial aid are urged to meet the February 15 deadline. For further information, students should contact:

Marsha Ginn
Associate Dean for Admissions
Graduate School of International
    Economics and Finance
Brandeis University, MS-032
P.O. Box 9110
Waltham, Massachusetts 02454-9110
Telephone: 781-736-2252
Fax: 781-736-2263
E-mail: admissions@lemberg.brandeis.
    edu
World Wide Web: http://www.
    brandeis.edu/ief/

Brandeis University

A CUTTING-EDGE MANAGEMENT EDUCATION

This is an exciting time in the Heller Graduate School's history. This is because our country is in the midst of a service revolution. The human services—health care, elder services, child, youth, and family services, and so on—all represent fast-growing economic sectors. New trends are affecting the delivery of social services—social patterns are changing, health services needs are intensifying, and the population is aging. These trends are challenging, yet they are creating opportunities for a talented cadre of managers who understand the policy issues that affect the provision of services and who are capable of leading organizations and delivery systems into the future. Few general management M.B.A. programs focus on the policies, programs, and underlying values that drive the human services sector. Heller's unique blend of cutting-edge management education combined with a deeper understanding of the social policy context of health and human services gives our graduates a comparative advantage.

—Jon Chilingerian, Director, Master's Program

Programs and Curricular Focus

Brandeis University's Master of Management (M.M.) and Master of Business Administration (M.B.A.) degrees in health and human services at the Heller Graduate School prepare individuals for leadership positions in the complex and changing environments of public and private for-profit and not-for-profit health and human services organizations. The context-specific curriculum at the core of both degrees is at the intersection of cutting-edge management and policy, educating effective leaders who will take organizations into the twenty-first century. Both degrees promote an awareness of how politics and markets work in the context of social policy. Students acquire a quantitative proficiency that is used in problem finding, modeling, implementation, and evaluation; a mastery of organizational structures and processes; skills in handling and communicating information; a comprehension of and respect for strategy; and a working knowledge of financial and managerial accounting and control, all aspects of which are adapted to meet the goals of the particular degree.

The M.M. degree is designed to meet the needs of individuals planning careers in small, community-based provider organizations; government agencies; think tanks; or foundations and prepare tomorrow's leaders to manage multiple aspects of an organization, from operations to marketing to financial control. The new M.B.A. (human services) degree

prepares individuals to become managers in large, multisite health and human services corporate structures, developing future leaders who are trained to utilize large information systems and solve complex problems in an increasingly global environment. Master's students can declare management concentrations in health care, human services, or child, youth, and family services. Full-time day study is completed in fifteen months, starting in June. There is an evening program for the M.M. degree only. Heller has joint-degree programs with Brandeis's Hornstein Program in Jewish communal services and with Tufts University's School of Medicine and Northeastern University's College of Business Administration for an M.D./M.B.A. in health-care management.

Students and the M.B.A. Experience

Heller students are drawn from many places geographically and professionally. Many have worked in health and human services organizations, while others have decided to change careers. Of the June 1997 Master of Management class, the average student was 27 years old; students' ages ranged from 21 to 55. Fifty-nine percent were from Massachusetts, and 79 percent were women. All were enrolled full-time, and 20 percent were enrolled in the dual-degree program in Jewish communal services with the Hornstein Program.

Heller's master's program, composed of both the M.M. and M.B.A. degree programs, will enroll approximately 35–40 full-time students in the upcoming year.

Special Features

In addition to a focus on health and human services, Heller provides its master's students the rich history and offerings of its doctoral program in social policy. Students augment their management training with policy courses in the areas of child, youth, and family services; health care; developmental disabilities; elder services; substance abuse; poverty; workforce and community development; violence; and social change and inequality.

Master's study culminates with a Team Consulting Project, which allows students to apply their management and analytical skills to solve real organizational problems. Teams of 3 to 7 students provide management consulting services to community-based health or human services agencies during a 2½- to 3-month period. By working on a real-world problem with its human resources, technical, financial, strategic, or other management challenges, students are better prepared to function as managers in their chosen health and human services field after they graduate.

The Heller Alumni Network is more than 1,000 strong and spans forty-three states and nineteen countries. Alumni keep the Heller Graduate School abreast of career trends, job opportunities, and networking leads.

The Faculty

Heller's faculty includes a mix of outstanding scholars and practitioners trained in fundamental management sciences, traditional social science disciplines, and multidisciplinary policy sciences. Of those teaching required courses in the master's program, 82 percent have doctorates. The faculty is committed to integration of social policy and management in the curriculum, as demonstrated, for example, by the health and human services context module that takes place in classroom sessions of management courses during the first summer of the program.

The Business School Network

Since its founding in 1959, the Heller Graduate School has built ties to local, regional, national, and international health and human services organizations. Through the School's Team Consulting Project requirement, many local agencies have worked with Heller School master's students and have high regard for their work. Many Heller alumni—employed by such organizations as Pew Charitable Trusts, U.S. Department of Health and Human Services, Johnson & Johnson, Massachusetts Society for the Prevention of Cruelty to Children, and Harvard Pilgrim Health Care—maintain active interactions with the School. The School's Board of Overseers includes individuals based in diverse organizations such as A-D-S Group/The Multicare Companies, Partners HealthCare Systems, W. K. Kellogg Foundation, and Blue Cross and Blue Shield of Massachusetts.

The College and Environs

Founded in 1948, Brandeis University has become one of the leading small private research universities in the United States, having earned recognition by Phi Beta Kappa only thirteen years after its founding; Brandeis is the youngest institution to be so honored in more than 100 years. In a national review, Brandeis was named the top emerging research institution in the United States.

The University has a student population of 3,800, almost 1,000 of whom are graduate students. Brandeis offers students a broad diversity of events: The University attracts noted speakers and artists, there are weekly classical music concerts, and the Spingold Theater Arts Center stages a varied program of dramatic entertainment. The Rose Art Museum offers a full range of paintings and sculpture by prominent artists. Student groups and clubs exist for a wide variety of academic and leisure activities. The Gosman Sports Center is a new facility with an indoor track, multipurpose courts, a swimming pool, and weight/fitness rooms. The Boston Celtics train in the Brandeis facilities.

Minutes from Boston, the Heller Graduate School is on Brandeis's picturesque 235-acre suburban campus in Waltham. Shuttle buses and the commuter train link the campus to the state capital, which is rich in history and offers many attractions and cultural resources, and provide easy access to beaches and mountains.

Facilities

Management students interested in social policy benefit from association with an expert research staff in six policy centers conducting nationally significant projects in a wide range of areas. Heller course offerings reflect the work of the Institute for Health Policy, the Policy Center on Aging, the Center for Human Resources, the Family and Children's Policy Center, the Center for Social Change, and the Nathan and Toby Starr Center for Mental Retardation. In addition to the work at the six centers, active research is conducted in mental health, substance abuse, work and inequality, and long-term care.

The School also has a state-of-the-art student computer lab containing Windows NT workstations capable of the word processing, spreadsheet development, statistical analysis, and Internet access required for the academic demands of the master's program and anticipated for future employment.

Placement

The educational goal of the master's program is to develop outstanding leaders who are well-prepared for managerial roles in health and human services organizations and responsible citizenship in the community. To assist students in their transition back into the workforce, the Associate Dean for Academic Services and the Career Services Coordinator at the Heller Graduate School provide counseling to students regarding job searches and networking, coordinate listings of job opportunities, and manage the Heller Career Mentor Program, which involves alumni who have volunteered to be coaches and advisers to students reentering the workforce.

Graduates of the master's program have gone on to hold a variety of challenging positions in the not-for-profit, public, and for-profit sectors. According to a recent survey, 71 percent are in management/administration, and 29 percent are in research/policy analysis. For the new M.B.A. (human services) program, career placement is expected to be equally successful.

Admission

Recruitment of students to the Heller Graduate School is focused on those individuals who plan to become managers and leaders in health and human services. M.M. students must have an undergraduate degree and two or more years of work experience, although some applicants who have excellent academic records and evidence of leadership potential are accepted directly from undergraduate programs. M.B.A. students must have an undergraduate degree and two or more years of work experience in health or human services (or two years of work experience in another field and extensive volunteer experience in health or human services). Admission is competitive and based on a completed application, Graduate Management Admission Test (GMAT) scores (GRE scores are acceptable for those applying to the M.M. program), undergraduate academic performance, two letters of recommendation, and a writing sample.

Finances

For 1997–98, the cost of study for the full-time, fifteen-month program was $5320 per semester (four-semester program). Part-time and evening study was $1850 per course.

The Heller School attempts to assist as many students as possible in securing financial aid. Candidates for admission are expected to explore a variety of outside funding sources, such as private scholarships, G.I. bill benefits, and government loan programs. The School has a limited number of need-based scholarships as well as administrative assistantships. In order to be eligible for financial aid of any kind, a candidate must have both the Free Application for Federal Student Aid (FAFSA) and the CSS PROFILE on file at the School. Forms may be obtained from the Office of Admissions. Aid decisions are made on the combined basis of financial need and academic merit. Evening program students can apply for student loans by filing the FAFSA.

In 1998–99, the cost of living for a single student is about $1300 a month. University housing at Brandeis University is limited; most students rent nearby apartments. Rents for a studio apartment are $500 to $650 a month; a one-bedroom apartment rents for $600 to $700 a month.

Application Facts and Dates

Application forms and financial aid information can be obtained from the Office of Admissions. M.M. and M.B.A. day program applicants must submit their materials by March 15 to begin the program in June, though review of applications begins in November and early application is encouraged. Applications to the M.M. evening program must be submitted by August 1 for fall admission and December 1 for spring admission. Prospective applicants are invited to attend information sessions.

For more information, students should contact:

Office of Admissions
The Heller Graduate School, MS 035
Brandeis University
Waltham, Massachusetts 02454-9110
Telephone: 781-736-3820
Fax: 781-736-3881
E-mail: najarian@binah.cc.brandeis.
   edu
World Wide Web: http://www.
   brandeis.edu/heller

Brigham Young University

Marriott School of Management

Provo, Utah

DEVELOPING LEADERS FOR THE 21ST CENTURY

At the Marriott School of Management we have high expectations. We expect to educate students who exhibit a particular set of values, professional expertise, and commitment to leadership. These young men and women will become catalysts for good within their families, organizations, churches, and communities.

Second, we expect Marriott School faculty to conduct research that will have an impact on management in a very pragmatic way—not just esoteric research, although that's important—but research that will be meaningful to the management community and to management education.

Next, we want to help motivate students to understand the need for service and volunteerism. Many of the problems we have in our world will only be solved if individuals help other individuals; hence, the opportunities for service in a management context are very real and important.

Finally, we expect that support groups associated with the Marriott School will provide the necessary financial and professional resources and support needed to accomplish our destiny.

—Ned C. Hill, Dean

Programs and Curricular Focus

The Master of Business Administration Program at Brigham Young University (BYU) prepares men and women for leadership positions in organizations throughout the world. The program emphasizes both general knowledge and leadership skills based on a solid ethical foundation.

The first year of the M.B.A. program provides solid grounding in the functional areas of business and an interdisciplinary perspective through integrative case teaching. During the second year, students meet with faculty specialists to design a course of study that meets their individual goals and prepares them to function in the areas of business in which they have interest.

In the early 1990s, major changes were introduced into the first-year M.B.A. curriculum offering. New courses were added in business strategy, information systems, data analysis, and business and government as they relate to the international economy. Classwork emphasizes the case method, and professors from various disciplines team teach. In this way, a case is evaluated from many perspectives.

Steps have been taken to integrate the M.B.A. students with other graduate students in the Marriott School. Students from the five graduate programs are involved in computer simulations, research consulting projects, and special research projects.

Students and the M.B.A. Experience

The M.B.A. program uses combinations of case study, conference, lecture, computer simulation, group presentation, and field research methods, all designed to develop managerial skills and to assist in the acquisition of knowledge. As a result, a high level of student participation is required. The classroom becomes a forum for considering management problems, testing analytical skill and judgment, exercising oral and written expression, and increasing knowledge. Students work extensively in groups. The average GMAT score for the class of 1999 was 620 and 3.47 was the average GPA.

❖ Global Focus

The Marriott School values the broad understanding and perspective that students from minorities and many countries bring to its classrooms. Twenty percent of the students come from outside the U.S., more than 57 percent of the faculty and 80 percent of the students are bilingual, and some 30 percent speak a third language. This diversity enhances the education of Marriott School students and prepares them to work in today's global market.

Special Features

The Marriott School includes three Centers of Excellence. The Center for the Study of Values in Organizations emphasizes ethical behavior and value systems in management and in life as a whole, and an ethics class is a required part of the M.B.A. program. The Center for Entrepreneurship brings in renowned executives for a weekly lecture series and helps provide research projects, internships, and classes that focus on creativity and real-world management skills. The Center of International Business Education and Research (CIBER) focuses on an international curriculum (business classes are taught in a number of foreign languages), faculty research programs, international conferences, and visiting international faculty.

The Faculty

The Marriott School has excellent faculty members who are productive scholars with a commitment to students and to teaching.

Brigham Young University is nestled in the heart of the beautiful Wasatch Mountains.

Students in the Marriott School enjoy a close association with the faculty.

In this role, they become mentors as well as teachers. Marriott School faculty members are willing and able to teach, direct, and inspire students. Senior faculty members also mentor younger, less seasoned teachers as they learn how to provide the motivation necessary for students to achieve excellence in their academic pursuits. The Marriott School's goal is to retain faculty members who are committed to excellence in all their activities, including teaching, research and writing, professional development, and academic service.

The Business School Network

One of the strengths of the Marriott School of Management is its support from national professional groups, including the Marriott School National Advisory Council, Entrepreneur Founders, Marriott School Alumni Board, and national and international chapters of the BYU Management Society. These select groups of experienced men and women have become leaders in business and government. They return to BYU to help direct and support the Marriott School by meeting regularly with administration and faculty, speaking to students in several weekly lecture series, and committing their time, abilities, and resources to the students and School.

Prominent Alumni

Prominent alumni and supporters include the Chair/CEO of Black & Decker; Chair of Geneva Steel; President and CEO of *Times Mirror*; Senior VP of CSX Transportation; Chair of Host Marriott; Founder/CEO of Covey Leadership Center; Executive VP/CEO of the National Association of Home Builders; President and CEO of Fisher-Price, Inc.; partner of Price Waterhouse; and Vice President of American Airlines.

The College and Environs

BYU is the largest privately owned, church-sponsored university in the United States. It was established by the Church of Jesus Christ of Latter-day Saints in 1875.

BYU's beautiful 600-acre campus is located in Provo, Utah, at the foot of the Wasatch Mountains. The University has excellent cultural programs and is near numerous outdoor recreational areas for skiing (water and snow), hiking, and camping. Salt Lake City, 45 miles north, offers the Utah Symphony, Ballet West, and Pioneer Theater, as well as professional basketball, baseball, and hockey.

Brigham Young has approximately 29,000 full-time students, including 900 in the Marriott School.

Facilities

The School is located in the N. Eldon Tanner Building. This facility provides a management library, computer facilities, research areas, technology enhanced learning environment (TELE) classrooms, and special graduate study rooms. The Harold B. Lee Library houses more than 3 million bound volumes and an extensive collection of pamphlets and titles on microfilm.

Technology Environment

The Marriott School provides two computer labs as well as off-campus access to computing resources via modem. Incoming students receive computer training, and the use of computers is integrated directly with course material. Students receive extensive training in the use of business-related computer applications.

Placement

The Career Services Office serves as the liaison between recruiting organizations and Marriott School graduate students and faculty. Career Services is committed to helping graduates begin a rewarding career and to assisting local and national companies in hiring outstanding graduates. The director and professional staff are available throughout the year to facilitate both on- and off-campus recruitment efforts.

Students and alumni are invited to utilize contact databases, research careers and companies covered in the library, and receive career counseling. Students may also include their resumes in the annual Graduate Student CD-ROM, which goes out to hundreds of companies.

Admission

The M.B.A. admissions committee considers a student's overall GPA, particularly a student's grades for the last two years of undergraduate education; the GMAT score, paying particular attention to the quantitative score; and evidence of leadership skills from the letter of intent, the letters of recommendation and response on the application form, and work experience. Students who have not graduated from a U.S. university must also receive a minimum score of at least 570 on the TOEFL.

Finances

Tuition for 1998–99 is $2560 per semester for members of the Church of Jesus Christ of Latter-day Saints and $3975 per semester for nonmembers. Books and supplies average $700 per semester.

The School provides financial assistance to qualified students through scholarship grants, teaching and research assistantships, and internships, as well as through loans (including Stafford Loans) handled by the University's Financial Aid Department. Approximately 60 to 70 percent of Marriott School students receive some financial assistance.

International Students

Approximately 20 percent of M.B.A. students are international and BYU provides numerous support programs through the International Students Program office. Fifty-seven percent of the faculty and 80 percent of the students are bilingual.

Application Facts and Dates

The priority and international student application deadline is January 15. The final application deadline is March 1. Students should take the GMAT no later than January of the year in which they are applying. It is recommended that students apply early as applications are evaluated in order of their receipt and completion.

The Marriott School of Management
M.B.A. Program
640 Tanner Building
Brigham Young University
Provo, Utah 84602
Telephone: 801-378-3500
Fax: 801-378-4808
E-mail: mba@byu.edu
World Wide Web: http://msm.byu.edu/
    programs/grad/mba

Bryant College

Graduate School

Smithfield, Rhode Island

PROFESSIONAL DEVELOPMENT THROUGH A STUDENT-CENTERED PROGRAM

The Graduate School at Bryant College is dedicated to providing students a rich and rewarding professional development experience. All of our efforts, from admission to commencement, are student centered. We aspire, in particular, to ensure that graduate programs and instructional methods are tailored to meet the distinctive needs of the professional population we serve.

I am delighted to invite students to participate in the Bryant M.B.A. I am confident that it will prove to be among the most rewarding experiences of their professional lives.

—Dayle Nattress, Dean

Programs and Curricular Focus

The Bryant M.B.A. program uses a hands-on approach to learning that links theory to real life and prepares business-people to manage change, build and lead cohesive teams, and make sound decisions based upon incisive analysis. M.B.A. students may choose to concentrate in accounting, computer information systems, finance, health-care management, international business, management, operations management, marketing, or general business. The Bryant M.B.A. program is accredited by the prestigious AACSB–The International Association for Management Education.

Program courses are offered in the evening. Most students complete the program on a part-time basis while working full-time, and earn their degrees in three to six years. Students carrying a full-time course load who have undergraduate degrees in business may achieve their degrees in as little as one year. International students must maintain full-time status.

The M.B.A. program consists of 48 semester hours of courses. Required core courses provide 33 credits of a broad business foundation. The program is completed with 15 credits of electives, most in a chosen field of concentration.

Professionals in the field of accounting may be interested in Bryant's Master of Science in Taxation or Master of Science in Accounting programs. Experienced managers who already have a master's degree but are interested in developing their knowledge in a particular field may be interested in a Certificate of Advanced Graduate Study (C.A.G.S.).

Students and the M.B.A. Experience

Bryant graduate students possess diverse academic and professional backgrounds. Students have completed undergraduate degrees in business, social sciences, and engineering. Entering students are an average age of 28, with five or more years of professional work experience, primarily in service industries or manufacturing. Women represent 41 percent of the total graduate student population, and international students comprise approximately 32 percent of full-time graduate enrollment.

The M.B.A. curriculum is infused with the challenges of professional practice. Courses are designed to connect to each other and to relate to the real world, adding relevance, coherence, and immediacy to the curriculum. In all classes, the focus is on active, participative learning, using a variety of methods and media, including in-class exercises, role playing, case studies, debates, group projects, and lecture. Bryant's graduate programs provide rigorous immersion into the nuts and bolts of business in such areas as accounting, finance, marketing, and management. There is also an in-depth examination of the all-important intangibles that can make or break a career. Bryant's programs do not just balance the books; they help students to become balanced professionally by developing skills such as leadership, communication, and team building.

The Faculty

Bryant's graduate faculty members are distinguished authors, researchers, consultants, and professional leaders in national and international business, industry, and government. They are full-time professors recognized for their research contributions published in academic and practitioner journals. In addition, faculty members have experience in the areas of public accounting, private accounting, and consulting. They use their practical experience to illustrate and supplement business theories learned in class. Class size averages 23 students, allowing for valuable interaction between the students and professor.

The Business School Network

Bryant College is more than a leader in business education, it is also renowned for practicing the principles it teaches. Through the College's outreach efforts, Bryant students and faculty and staff members form an important resource for the state's economic growth. Students have opportunities to become involved in international trade, telecommunications, management development, technology transfer, and small-business development.

The College and Environs

Bryant College was founded in Providence in 1863. Today it continues in its mission to educate successful business-people.

The campus is located on 387 acres in suburban Smithfield, Rhode Island. Modern facilities include a comprehensive business library, computer center, language/learning laboratory, student center, classrooms, and a fitness/sports complex. Students interested in living on campus may choose between traditional double rooms and suites or award-winning town houses.

Placement

The Career Services Office offers a variety of services, including counseling and assessment of career decision making. Assistance is also available for résumé writing, interviewing, and job search strategies. Students can access a resource library to research careers or companies. A weekly publication lists current job openings. Students can participate in Bryant's corporate recruiting program.

Admission

Because Bryant's program integrates real-world experience with concepts, it is preferred that applicants have a minimum of two years of work experience. Entry requirements include a bachelor's degree from an accredited institution. A strong score on the Graduate Management Admission Test (GMAT) is required. For students for whom English is not their primary language, a satisfactory score on the Test of English as a Foreign Language (TOEFL) is required. Prospective students must also submit an official transcript, one letter of recommendation, and a 500-word statement of objectives.

Finances

Tuition for the 1998–99 academic year is $1025 per 3-credit course. The fee for a single room in the town houses during the 1998–99 school year is $4910; for a double, $4820. A $100 deposit is required to reserve a room. A nineteen-meal-per-week plan costs $2750.

Students may compete for graduate assistantships, working with an academic department related to their concentration area or with the Center for International Business (CIB). Responsibilities may include faculty support, academic research, or preparation of class materials. Up to four courses may be offset with an assistantship, at which a student may work a maximum of 16 hours per week.

International Students

Thirty-two percent of the full-time graduate students come from outside of the United States. The Multicultural Student Services Office provides orientation directed to acclimating international students to American classroom conduct and culture. This office provides ongoing support and counsel.

Application Facts and Dates

Application deadlines are July 1 for the fall semester, November 15 for the spring semester, and April 1 for the summer session. There is a $55 application fee that must be submitted with the completed application form. International students' admission applications and full-time students' graduate assistant applications are due April 1 for the fall term, November 15 for the spring term, and March 1 for the summer term. For more information, students should contact:

Graduate Admission
Bryant College
1150 Douglas Pike
Smithfield, Rhode Island 02917
Telephone: 401-232-6230
Fax: 401-232-6494
E-mail: gradprog@bryant.edu

Carnegie Mellon University

Graduate School of Industrial Administration

Pittsburgh, Pennsylvania

▶ BUILDING A SUCCESSFUL CAREER TOGETHER

What makes Carnegie Mellon University's Graduate School of Industrial Administration (GSIA) savvy enough to always be in touch with the latest dynamic global economy, industries, currencies, and multimedia intelligence? Superb management processes tie the students, faculty, and school to the business community of tomorrow. We recognize that the challenge for our graduates will be to anticipate, adapt, and lead in this dynamic economy. We educate professionals who can analyze data quickly and apply quantitative methods easily. Our students learn to capture the best technology and bring it to markets successfully. Armed with consensus-building skills, our students form lifelong partnerships with our business school—partnerships that help them harness the management technologies of today's new economy.

—Douglas M. Dunn, Dean

Programs and Curricular Focus

By the terms of its original charter, GSIA offers a two-year full-time Master of Science in Industrial Administration (M.S.I.A.) degree, which is similar to the M.B.A. degree. To fulfill the requirements for the M.S.I.A. degree, students must satisfactorily complete, with a grade of C- or better, all of the required courses, totaling 96 units, and a minimum of 108 units of elective courses. To encourage collaboration and to encourage students to choose courses that challenge them, student grades and class rank are not disclosed. Almost all students leave GSIA at the end of their first year for a summer internship.

GSIA emphasizes interdisciplinary thinking. There are no departments at GSIA, and there are no required majors in the M.S.I.A. program, although students must fulfill certain breadth and depth requirements. A rich collection of electives allows students the flexibility to focus on areas of special interest.

GSIA also offers a three-year M.S.I.A. option, which provides students with a chance to earn a graduate degree while continuing their careers; an early graduation option; an intensive, twelve month M.S. in Computational Finance (M.S.C.F.) program; a twenty month Master's in Business Management and Software Engineering (M.B.M.S.E.) program; a two-year Master of Science in Civil Engineering and Management (M.S.C.E.M.) program; a two-year Master of Science in Environmental Engineering and Management program; a fourteen month Master of Science in Informa-

tion Networking program (M.S.I.N.); a J.D./M.S.I.A. dual-degree program offered in conjunction with the University of Pittsburgh School of Law; and a collaborative program in private and public management and policy in conjunction with Carnegie Mellon's Heinz School of Public Policy and Management.

Students and the M.B.A. Experience

The GSIA student body exhibits diverse backgrounds, with undergraduate degrees split almost evenly between technical and nontechnical majors. All parts of the United States and more than thirty countries are represented in the average entering class, which normally numbers 220. About 99 percent of GSIA students have full-time post-graduate work experience, with an average of four years each. This mix of students invigorates the educational experience at GSIA, where teamwork and student interaction play a larger role than at virtually any other top business school. Because GSIA recognizes that most managers' business lives revolve around critical small group meetings, students work on projects in small groups for many of their courses. GSIA's emphasis on group work encourages the development of interpersonal skills while fostering a cooperative, rather than competitive, educational experience.

❖ Global Focus

M.S.I.A. candidates can spend a semester abroad attending one of GSIA's many partner universities, including Koblenz School of Corporate Management in

Germany, Lyon Graduate School of Business in France, Manchester Business School in the United Kingdom, The Wirtschaftsuniversitat Wien in Austria, Aoyama Gaukin University in Japan, and the Monterrey Institute of Technology in Mexico. GSIA also has formed numerous alliances with other universities worldwide, including the University of Bradford in the United Kingdom, the Academy of National Economy in Russia, the University of Nancy in France, Universitat Pompeu Fabra in Spain, Hong Kong University of Science and Technology, City Polytechnic of Hong Kong, and Umea University in Sweden. GSIA is also the home of the Carnegie Bosch Institute for Applied Studies in International Management.

While most courses offer a global perspective, GSIA offers several specific courses in international business, as well as language courses in French, German, Japanese, and Spanish that are specifically tailored for business students. The School also features project courses with global corporations and opportunities for students to visit other countries and learn from those countries' cultures and business practices.

Special Features

The School's mini-semester system—a GSIA innovation now copied by other top business schools—splits the typical semester in half, creating four mini-semesters per academic year. This enables students to gain exposure to a wide range of topics and unique courses (18 electives in all) such as FAST—the program in Financial Analysis and Security Trading, which gives students access to the latest trading hardware, software, and data feeds—and the Entrepreneurship Project—which teaches students to create and evaluate ideas for new businesses.

The capstone course, Management Game, taken during the spring of the first year and fall of the second year, uses complex computer simulations of a consumer products industry to engage students in teamwork, decision making, negotiation, and communication. Teams of 5 to 7 students act as senior managers and make strategic decisions involving marketing, financing, production, and research and development. Each team meets with a board of directors, often drawn from major corporations, and works out labor contracts with representatives from local unions. Area bankers arrange financing, and teams seek out legal advice from third-year law students at the University of Pittsburgh Law School.

The Faculty

GSIA faculty members have won worldwide acclaim—as well as three Nobel Prizes—for their groundbreaking research in organizational theory, artificial intelligence, operations research, and corporate finance. Faculty members from various fields work together on projects, as it is GSIA's conviction that important new ideas come from interdisciplinary research. The small size of the student body results in a student-faculty ratio that is among the best of top-tier graduate business programs.

The Business School Network

GSIA students gain hands-on experience by helping client companies with real-life problems.

Carnegie Mellon was recently selected from a group of elite colleges and universities to participate with industry partners in the Total Quality Management (TQM) University Challenge. The Challenge matches educational institutions with corporate sponsors, who stimulate the introduction of TQM principles and concepts into curriculum and educational administration. With the strong support of Carnegie Mellon's partner, Xerox, GSIA has made a commitment to introducing TQM methods that have proven successful across many different businesses and industries.

Prominent Alumni

Because of its commitment to progressive, interdisciplinary education, Carnegie Mellon alumni rapidly become leaders. Among its 49,000 alumni, the University counts nearly 3,400 company chairpersons, chief executive officers, presidents, and vice presidents, including Paul A. Allaire (class of 1966), Chairman and CEO, Xerox Corporation; Michael J. Bertasso (class of 1976), Senior Vice President, H.J. Heinz Company; David A. Coulter (class of 1971), CEO, Bank America Corporation; Cyrus F. Freidheim Jr. (class of 1963), Vice Chairman, Booz•Allen & Hamilton, Inc.; T. Jerome Holleran (class of 1969), President, Precision Medical Products, Inc.; T. Patrick Kelly (class of 1984), CFO, The SABRE Group; James H. Levy (class of 1966), Chairman and CEO, Park Lane Group; Paul W. Lewis (class of 1973), Assistant Treasurer, Ford Motor Company; Therese E. Myers (class of 1968), CEO, Bouquet Multimedia; Anne-Marie Petach (class of 1984), Assistant Treasurer, Ford Motor Company; J. Thomas Presby (class of 1963), COO, Deloitte

and Touche; and Frank A. Risch (class of 1966), Assistant Treasurer, Exxon Corporation.

The College and Environs

Carnegie Mellon is a small university of approximately 7,000 students; more than one third are graduate students. Nearly 560 faculty members hold full-time teaching positions, and another 250 are scientists on research staffs.

Pittsburgh is a big-league city with small-town assets—low crime rates, tree-lined streets, and one of the cleanest and healthiest environments of any major city. Cozy neighborhoods, Fortune 500 headquarters, major league sports teams, and world-class symphony, opera, ballet, and theater all reside in this friendly city. Pittsburgh is one of the top ten largest corporate headquarters cities in the United States, and Pittsburgh International Airport is one of the largest in the nation.

Technology Environment

Nearly 500 personal computers, 150 printers, and 200 advanced workstations, as well as connections to the world's most important networks, enable students to download software, utilize databases, conduct research, or keep in touch via e-mail. Many classrooms are equipped with power and network hookups allowing students to plug in portable computers. There are also satellite downlinks to all classrooms, and the school has installed interactive video equipment to take advantage of videoconferencing, using this technology for job interviews and discussions with corporate project partners. Nearly all GSIA students enroll in voluntary, noncredit training courses in which they learn to use the University's sophisticated computer networks—the backbone of current and future computing.

Placement

The Career Opportunities Center provides excellent resources for every GSIA student's job search. Individual counseling and job search workshops help students plot their job search strategies and polish resume writing, interviewing, and salary negotiation skills. Career forums bring panels of corporate representatives from various fields to campus, and students are encouraged to contact alumni who have succeeded in their area of interest. Recruiting forums provide students with opportunities to talk to firms in various parts of the U.S. and the world. Students have access to numerous other resources including a World Wide Web recruiting system, alumni database, and interactive searches. Alumni are active in providing mock interviews, resume reviews, and mentoring relationships.

Admission

GSIA seeks a diverse student body and welcomes applications from those who have worked and studied in many fields; previous study in business-related areas is not required. Because the M.S.I.A. program is quantitatively and analytically oriented, previous course work and a demonstrated capacity for mathematics are essential for successful performance; therefore, GSIA requires that applicants complete two full semesters of calculus before enrolling as first-year students. Students must possess good interpersonal and communications skills and must be highly motivated, self-directed, energetic, and innovative. GSIA looks at the applicant's entire academic record: grade trends, major areas of study, school of graduation, extracurricular activities, and part-time and full-time work. GMAT scores, letters of recommendation, essays, and a personal interview are also vital to the evaluation process. Above all, GSIA's central concern in admissions is the applicant's academic potential and promise for a productive management career.

Finances

Estimated 1998–99 tuition and fees costs are: tuition, $24,000; activity fee, $100; room and board, $9400; and books, $1000. Carnegie Mellon provides a variety of scholarships and financial aid possibilities designed to equalize educational opportunities. Financial aid awards are based on need as determined by filing the U.S. Department of Education's Free Application for Federal Student Aid (FAFSA) and the NEED ACCESS Application. Scholarship awards are based solely on merit. GSIA General Fellowships are awarded to students in good academic standing who demonstrate financial need. Federal Perkins Loans, Federal Stafford Loans, privately insured loans, and work-study are also available.

Application Facts and Dates

Students who apply by November 15 are notified by December 15; those who apply by January 15 are notified by February 15; those who apply by March 15 are notified by April 15. After March 15 admissions are on a rolling basis. Interested students should contact:

Graduate School of Industrial Administration
Carnegie Mellon University
Schenley Park
Pittsburgh, Pennsylvania 15213
Telephone: 412-268-2272
        800-850-GSIA (toll-free, U.S. only)
Fax: 412-268-4209
E-mail: gsia-admissions@andrew.cmu.edu
World Wide Web: http://www.gsia.cmu.edu

Case Western Reserve University

Weatherhead School of Management

Cleveland, Ohio

A DISTINCTIVE M.B.A. EXPERIENCE

The Weatherhead School offers an M.B.A. experience unlike other programs. With its focus on creating human, economic, and intellectual value, the Weatherhead M.B.A. program provides the knowledge as well as the skills necessary for effective leadership.

Each Weatherhead student receives a personal assessment and designs an individual learning plan. Classes are small, and our faculty are easily accessible. Weatherhead's Mentor Program was the first to provide one-on-one career guidance from executive mentors. Our students gain practical experience through field projects and internships and international perspective through study abroad.

We invite you to discover the distinctive Weatherhead M.B.A. experience.

—Scott S. Cowen, Dean

Programs and Curricular Focus

The Weatherhead M.B.A. curriculum emphasizes the assessment and development of management skills along with knowledge of the functional areas of business and offers a liberalizing experience through exploration of the diverse contexts of management.

Begun in 1997, the Weatherhead School offers an integrative M.B.A. core curriculum that enhances the potential of each student to create value by drawing from different perspectives to identify, analyze, and resolve complex problems; develop and enhance organizational leadership; make a personal commitment to lifelong learning; add value in a special area of expertise; and contribute to the betterment of communities and society.

Spanning the first year of the M.B.A. program is the Strategic Issues and Applications course, which introduces M.B.A. students to the complexity of issues confronting the manager and the organization.

The Management Assessment and Development course fosters educational partnerships that offer students an active role in developing the shape and character of their learning experience.

Using information gained through individual abilities assessments, M.B.A. students enroll in appropriate Managerial and Career Skills modules. Working in small groups, students learn to master skills in presentation, written and oral communications, group management, team building, negotiation, persuasion, and collaboration. Second-year M.B.A.

students engage in biweekly dialogues with leaders of regional and multinational organizations in Executive Leadership Dialogues.

The Weatherhead M.B.A. program offers a unique functional core that integrates the management disciplines while also providing students with the tools necessary to identify and analyze issues. The eight core courses are integrated with the Strategic Issues and Applications course to form a solid foundation for management and decision making.

Students complete interdisciplinary thematic electives to examine the ways in which external influences and issues affect organizations and their managers.

The Weatherhead School offers both a four-semester M.B.A. curriculum and an accelerated program for undergraduate business majors beginning in June and ending in May of the following year. Both programs are available on a full-time and part-time basis. Joint-degree programs with the schools of law, nursing, and engineering are available along with master's programs in accountancy and nonprofit organizations, the Master of Science in Management Information Systems, and the Executive Master of Business Administration degree program.

Students and the M.B.A. Experience

The Weatherhead program is composed of highly qualified individuals representing a diversity of academic, professional, and cultural backgrounds and experi-

ences. The average student is 27 years old, with four years of work experience. Women comprise 32 percent of the class. The campus culture is enriched by international students, who represent 40 percent of the class and forty-eight countries. A typical class represents twenty-five states and twenty countries.

Weatherhead students have undergraduate degrees in a wide variety of disciplines.

❖ Global Focus

M.B.A. students may choose a concentration in international management or complete a joint M.B.A./Master of International Management degree program with the Thunderbird School in Glendale, Arizona. Internship opportunities for M.B.A. students are available in several countries during the summer term. The Weatherhead School participates in third-semester M.B.A. exchange programs with schools of management on four continents. Weatherhead students may participate as Agency for International Development (AID) business advisers in developing countries at the end of their first year in the program and in the M.B.A. Enterprise Corps in one- to two-year post–M.B.A. positions in firms in the former Eastern Bloc nations.

Students can complete their first year of the M.B.A. program at the International Management Center (IMC) in Budapest, Hungary, the most prestigious management school in Central/Eastern Europe.

Special Features

During the first year of the program, the Weatherhead Office of Career Planning and Placement matches students with Cleveland-area executives and managers who help to focus students' academic and career interests. Along with the traditional business concentrations, Weatherhead offers concentrations in the areas of health-care management, technology management, nonprofit management, and entrepreneurial studies.

The Faculty

There are 87 full-time faculty members, all of whom have a doctorate in their

field. Many of the faculty members have earned international reputations for teaching and research. The faculty is housed in seven different departments: accountancy, banking and finance, economics, MIDS, marketing and policy studies, operations research, and organizational behavior. Students benefit from a student-faculty ratio of 14:1.

The Business School Network

The Weatherhead School has forged a strong network of corporate partners in the northeast Ohio area (headquarters of thirty of the Fortune 500 corporations). Students engage in a variety of field projects under the guidance of experienced area executives. The curriculum is enhanced by guest lecturers and speakers from the corporate community.

The Visiting Committee of the Weatherhead School of Management is composed of leaders in the international community who have a continuing concern for the quality of management education. The committee provides counsel and assistance to the School throughout the year.

The College and Environs

The Weatherhead School of Management resides in a parklike campus setting in Cleveland's University Circle. Campus neighbors include Severance Hall, home of the Cleveland Orchestra, and the Cleveland Art and History museums. The Weatherhead campus places students within what is probably the most

extensive concentration of educational, scientific, medical, and cultural institutions in the United States.

Technology Environment

The Weatherhead computer network makes available a wide variety of software, languages, and peripheral equipment. Qualified support personnel are on duty daily, and computer instruction and seminars are offered. Computer-supported conference rooms are available. The School maintains computer-supported classrooms for computer literacy and M.B.A. class instruction. The University computing resources include a unique fiber-optic network linking more than eighty-five campus buildings. Users have access to a range of information resources and networks. Other resources include an integrated online library system and access to off-campus resources, including the Internet.

Placement

The Weatherhead School's Office of Career Planning and Placement provides a placement program for each student. It assists students in focusing career interests and invites recruiters to campus to participate in information sessions, receptions, career forums, seminars, workshops, and mock interviews. A full schedule of placement interviews for both summer and permanent positions is conducted in the fall and spring semesters. In the CareerNet program, alumni

from across the country provide advice and placement assistance to students and graduates. Students can access the entire M.B.A. alumni database through the School computer lab. The Weatherhead School is a founding member of the National M.B.A. Consortium in Chicago, a cooperative corporate interview day for M.B.A. students, with eighty separate corporate schedules.

Admission

Applicants are admitted on the basis of academic and professional accomplishments, performance on the GMAT, individual career goals, written recommendations, and responses to interview and application essay questions. The median GMAT score is 605. The average undergraduate GPA is 3.2. Class size is limited to 150 students.

The Test of English as a Foreign Language is required of all applicants whose native language is not English and who graduated from an educational institution where the language of instruction was not English. A special four-week MBA Language Skills Program is available.

Finances

The 1998–99 tuition and fees are $10,450 per semester. Books and supplies are estimated at $750 per semester. The estimate for room and board is $4985 per semester.

A limited number of merit scholarships are available for individuals with exceptional academic, professional, and life experiences. The School offers an Express Financial Aid Service to expedite determination of the financing options that are available.

International Students

The School offers international students a tuition stabilization plan, internships, and multicultural experiences through the multicultural task force and International Business Club.

Application Facts and Dates

The final application deadline for all applicants is usually in early April. For international candidates living outside the United States, the early decision deadline is usually in mid-February. For more information, students should contact:

Linda Gaston
Director of Admissions
The Weatherhead School of
    Management
Case Western Reserve University
Cleveland, Ohio 44106-7235
Telephone: 800-723-0203
Fax: 216-368-5548
E-mail: lxg10@po.cwru.edu

Chapman University

Orange, California

STRONG FACULTY, SMALL PROGRAM = STUDENT SUCCESS

The Chapman M.B.A. benefits from efforts to build a strong faculty with a commitment to excellent teaching and research, linked to the entrepreneurial heritage of our Orange County location and building on the strong analytical framework of our economics faculty.

This small program offers students good working relationships with a competitive faculty that is committed to student success. The focus on information technology forms the basis for strategic advantage both now and in the future.

The Chapman M.B.A. and our School of Business and Economics represent important resources for competitive U.S. and global learning. We welcome your consideration of our program.

—Richard McDowell, Dean

Programs and Curricular Focus

The Chapman M.B.A. offers students the concepts and tools necessary to formulate sound strategic decisions as well as the leadership skills needed to implement those plans. The program provides rigorous training in the analytical and communication skills needed for success in the contemporary global and entrepreneurial business environment. Specifically, the program is designed to provide a solid economic foundation for making business decisions; develop skills in applying financial, marketing, management, information technology, and statistical techniques to complex management problems; and improve skills in effectively presenting and implementing solutions to business problems.

The M.B.A. curriculum is divided into four groups of courses: 1) cornerstone courses that provide the skills necessary to complete the core courses and are waivable based on demonstrated competence; 2) core courses covering all functional areas of business; 3) capstone courses, which are integrative in nature and; 4) electives through which students may customize the program.

Chapman offers an Executive M.B.A. program for working professionals with organizational experience. The two-year program includes three residentials—one regional, one national, and one international trip designed to provide three important perspectives on business issues and practices.

Students and the M.B.A. Experience

Chapman's School of Business and Economics has a diverse M.B.A. population that totals 175 full- and part-time students and 50 executive M.B.A.'s. The average age at entrance to the M.B.A. program is 27, with four years of work experience. Women comprise 38 percent of the M.B.A. student population, and minority students make up 30 percent. Foreign nationals comprise 19 percent of the student body, with 20 percent coming from Europe, 75 percent from Asia, and the remaining 5 percent from throughout the world.

❖ Global Focus

Chapman's Walter Schmid Center for International Business was founded in 1992. Its goal is to establish a high-quality international database and to provide facilities and support for students and faculty engaged in international business and economics research. The center also disseminates results of its research to the business community and consults both U.S. and international companies on all data required to make decisions for international trade, i.e. markets, business conditions, and the legal and regulatory environments. The Fletcher Jones Chair in International Business plays a leadership role in the Center and in the integration of an international dimension in the School's research and curriculum.

Special Features

The Ralph W. Leatherby Center for Entrepreneurship and Business Ethics was es-

tablished to promote the study of entrepreneurship within a framework of ethical business practices. The center provides a sequence of entrepreneurial courses, creates opportunities for students to work closely with entrepreneurs, arranges seminars, and provides general reference information relevant to entrepreneurs. The founding of this center demonstrates the University's dedication to the nurturing and promotion of entrepreneurialism.

The Faculty

Faculty members at the School of Business and Economics have as their first priority the enhancement of the learning experience. Chapman has a long tradition of emphasizing outstanding teaching. Faculty members have chosen to teach in a small school, with an emphasis on personalized education. They are accessible and approachable. At the same time, the Chapman faculty members are from major universities, are committed to research and scholarly endeavors, and are well-published in major academic journals.

The Business School Network

The A. Gary Anderson Center for Economic Research provides the cornerstone for Chapman's strong relationship with the southern California business community. The center, with the involvement of students, has developed and continually improves a complex econometric model used to forecast economic trends for southern California. One thousand business leaders participate annually in the School of Business and Economics forecast events. The Ralph W. Leatherby Center for Entrepreneurship and Business Ethics sponsors conferences and guest speakers on small business. There are numerous additional opportunities for students to interface with business leaders through guest lectures and speaker series.

The College and Environs

Founded in 1861, Chapman University is situated on a 42-acre parklike campus in Orange, California. The mission of the University is to provide a personalized education of distinction that leads to

inquiring, ethical, and productive lives as global citizens. Chapman is located 35 miles southeast of Los Angeles and 90 miles from San Diego and Mexico. Ocean beaches are less than 10 miles away; mountains and deserts are within an hour's drive. Within minutes are such attractions as Disneyland, Knott's Berry Farm, Orange County Performing Arts Center, Pacific Amphitheater, and Anaheim Stadium.

Facilities

The Thurmond Clark Library contains 200,000 volumes and subscribes to 1,200 periodical titles, 257 of which are business periodicals. *Moody's Company Data on CD-ROM* provides access to company information on more than 10,000 U.S. companies. Business literature can be researched by using the compact disc ABI/Inform. All items on the Business Periodical Index are available either on the shelves, on disc, or through interlibrary loan.

The use of computer technology is an integral part of the M.B.A. program. The School of Business and Economics has an IBM-based computer lab, with staff available for individual assistance. In addition, workshops are given for those who need to learn or refresh their skills. For those students who prefer to use Macintosh systems, there is a Macintosh lab on campus. The University is part of the Internet system, and each student receives an Internet account number.

Placement

The Career Development Center offers a number of services and programs that assist students with their professional

development. The dual focus includes both assisting students in identifying their career goals and preparing them for an effective job search. On-campus recruiting takes place in the fall (for accounting firms) and spring semesters. National as well as local companies come to campus to recruit students. Networking is encouraged through alumni mentor programs and alumni career days.

Admission

Admission to the M.B.A. program requires a bachelor's degree from an accredited college or university, a completed application for admission, transcripts of all previous course work, an acceptable score on the GMAT, and two letters of recommendation. International students must submit a TOEFL score of 550 or above and a statement of financial resources.

Finances

The 1998–99 tuition for the M.B.A. program is $545 per credit for either part- or full-time study. Tuition for the Executive M.B.A. is $42,000 for the two-year program. Financial aid opportunities are offered to graduate students through tuition grants, graduate fellowships, and loans. The loan programs include the federally sponsored Stafford subsidized and unsubsidized student loans and privately sponsored loans.

International Students

Nineteen percent of Chapman's M.B.A. population comes from outside the United States. The International Students Services office acts as a source of information and assistance, with the goal of making the international experience a comfortable and productive one. The office sponsors an orientation program; counseling on academic, financial and personal matters; assistance in class registration; information on immigration requirements; and information on social and cultural events. Various informational and social events are organized throughout the year.

Application Facts and Dates

Applications for the fall, spring, and summer sessions should be received by June 15, November 15, and April 15, respectively. The deadline for consideration for financial aid is March 2. For information and application materials, students should contact:

Office of Graduate Admissions
Chapman University
333 North Glassell Street
Orange, California 92866
Telephone: 714-997-6786

Chulalongkorn University

Bangkok, Thailand

THE SOUTHEAST ASIAN ECONOMY

In today's highly interdependent global economy, a cough in New York suddenly becomes a bad cold in Tokyo and vice versa. Thailand is no exception as it faces many great challenges in overcoming the current economic malaise in Asia. In order to facilitate Thailand's recovery, the Sasin Graduate Institute of Business Administration seeks to meld proven Western business theories and practices with Asian sensibilities by offering a two-year M.B.A. program second to none in this region. A unique academic venture among Chulalongkorn University, the J. L. Kellogg Graduate School of Management of Northwestern University, and the Wharton School of the University of Pennsylvania, Sasin aims at producing graduates comparable in knowledge and skills with those trained at leading business schools abroad.

—Toemsakdi Krishnamra, Director

Programs and Curricular Focus

The management subjects taught in Sasin's M.B.A. program are of vital importance to Asian countries. Teaching is by case study balanced with lectures, seminars, and group work, with emphasis placed on the relationship between theory and practice. The curriculum stresses the application of the theoretical training to the practical problems managers face today and are likely to face in the future. Student activities, too, address current management issues through direct interaction with the business community in numerous events relevant to Asian needs.

The curriculum is a tightly integrated program, resembling those taught at both Kellogg and Wharton. Some adaptations have been made to suit the Asian environment. The overall program consists of twelve core and thirteen supportive courses. Although intended to emphasize general management education, concentrations in any functional field of management—finance, marketing, operations management, or human resources management—are possible.

By design, M.B.A. classes are small, thus offering students the rare educational experience of personal relationships with faculty members and other students. Approximately 110 students are admitted to the program each year.

Sasin also offers a Master of Management degree program for midcareer executives, senior executives, and entrepreneurs. It is a two-year general management program, with classes meeting every Saturday and some Wednesday evenings. The Master of Science and Graduate Diploma in Human Resource Management programs are specially designed for managers with responsibilities for personnel and human resources. The Senior Executive Program, an intensive three-week residential program, is designed for senior executives holding key management positions in business or government who wish to broaden their knowledge in management.

Students and the M.B.A. Experience

It is no cliché to say that enrolling at Sasin gives students the chance to study with Thailand's future leaders. Comprising the crème-de-la-crème of a dynamic middle- to upper-class cross section of the Thai population as well as a strong international representation, the student body is a self-motivating, doggedly loyal web of trust and friendship. The average Sasin student is 25 years old and has three years of work experience; a third of these students already have had considerable experience overseas. The student body is also split evenly along gender lines. Students are diverse in their educational backgrounds and work experiences.

Both inside and outside the classroom, cooperation among students is strongly encouraged. Problems frequently are assigned to groups of students rather than to individuals, thus giving students experience in working as part of a team to achieve a common solution. This teamwork is reinforced in extracurricular activities that enrich the students' academic lives through interactions with the business community in Thailand as well as through organization of charity events centered around traditional Thai celebrations.

❖ Global Focus

Sasin offers the opportunity for second-year students to broaden their international business knowledge by studying abroad. M.B.A. students with superior academic records may participate in the Student Exchange Program by spending a quarter or semester at one of Sasin's cooperating institutions in the United States, Canada, England, France, Germany, Italy, Japan, and the Netherlands: J. L. Kellogg Graduate School of Management of Northwestern University, the Wharton School of the University of Pennsylvania, the Fuqua School of Business of Duke University, the Marshall School of Business of the University of Southern California, the Johnson Graduate School of Management of Cornell University, the Schulich School of Business of York University, the Manchester Business School of the University of Manchester, Ecole Superieure des Sciences Economiques et Commerciales, Hautes Etudes Commerciales, Wissenschaftliche Hochschule fur Unternehmensfuhrung, Bocconi University, Graduate School of International Management of International University of Japan, and Rotterdam School of Management of Erasmus Graduate School of Business. Exchange students may take up to four quarter courses or three semester courses.

Special Features

The first year begins with the four-day orientation program called Conceptual Issues in Management Week. The program is set up to orient students in various fields of management. Prior to the start of the M.B.A. program, Sasin also provides tutorial courses in mathematics, accounting, and economics for students who do not have sufficient background in those areas.

Sasin Graduate Institute of Business Administration at Chulalongkorn University.

Another feature is the M.B.A. Conference, which is aimed at strengthening the relationships among the students and providing the unique opportunity for them to meet and have informal discussion with Sasin alumni who have succeeded in various fields of business. The conference is a three-day residential seminar held during the break between the first and second modules.

The Faculty

The faculty members for the program are drawn exclusively from Kellogg and Wharton as well as Sasin and its staff of adjunct professors. They offer a rich combination of experience in professional management problems and practices, having often served as consultants in industry, government, health care, education, and transportation throughout the United States. Textbooks and casebooks written by these faculty members are used in management schools both in the United States and in other countries.

The College and Environs

Sasin is located on the campus of Chulalongkorn University, the oldest and best-known university in Thailand. The campus covers an area of 500 acres in the Patumwan District. The University consists of seventeen faculties, three graduate schools, eleven institutes, and other administrative offices. Sasin is situated in downtown Bangkok, within easy reach of an infinite variety of businesses, civil service offices, and shopping centers.

Bangkok, the capital city, has a population of 6 million and is extremely urbanized. It caters to diverse interests. There are temples, museums, and other historic sites for those interested in traditional Thai culture.

Facilities

Sasin students have access to all the University's recreation and sports facilities. Other facilities include a centrally air-conditioned study center, a special business and management library, and access to Chulalongkorn University's highly advanced computer center and international electronic communication networks and microcomputer laboratory.

Placement

Sasin graduates work for most of the best corporations or organizations in Thailand. Major industries often chosen by Sasin graduates are finance and securities, banking, and manufacturing. Many firms hold informal receptions for M.B.A. students to enable them to meet with corporate representatives and to learn about the companies before the interviews. In addition, many employers recruit through the Placement Office, which arranges for formal job interviews on campus. Many employers are familiar with Sasin because they take part in providing internships, corporate scholarships, or otherwise assist the M.B.A. program.

Admission

Sasin looks for students with outstanding potential for leadership as well as the intellectual and interpersonal skills needed to make a meaningful contribution to the academic and extracurricular life of Sasin. Rather than rely on an admissions formula that stipulates a minimum test score, grade point average, or years of work experience, the Admissions Committee prefers to evaluate the combined effect of an applicant's prior academic achievements and personal accomplishments for use as the basis of its decision. In order to make such an evaluation, applicants should take the GMAT, submit official transcripts from all universities previously attended, submit two recommendations, and meet with a Kellogg or Sasin representative for an interview. All nonnative English-speaking applicants must take the TOEFL.

Finances

Estimated expenses for the 1998–99 academic year are as follows: in the first year, tuition is $7215; in the second year, tuition is $6660. These tuitions include all textbooks and course materials. There are student activities fees and an electronic data processing fee of $145 per year. Living accommodations are $4500, and meals and personal expenses total $4800; these two figures are estimated for students who live on campus. Miscellaneous expenses are $200. The comprehensive cost comes to $16,860 for the first year and $16,305 for the second.

Application Facts and Dates

The application for May admission must be received by January 15. M.B.A. interviews in Bangkok are normally scheduled for two weeks in February. Notification of the admission decision is normally mailed to the applicants by March 8. For more information, contact:

Admissions Office
Sasin Graduate Institute of Business
   Administration of Chulalongkorn
   University
Sasa Patasala Building
Soi Chulalongkorn 12, Phyathai Road
Bangkok 10330
Thailand
Telephone: 662-216-8833 Ext. 3850-1
   or 3856-7
Fax: 662-216-1312
E-mail: lalida@sasa.sasin.chula.ac.th

Claremont Graduate University

A FUSION OF LEADERSHIP, STRATEGY, AND MANAGEMENT

The Drucker School is committed to providing a world-class education by delivering academic programs of the highest caliber. Our Drucker M.B.A. accentuates two priorities—to equip our students for their next career assignment and to prepare them for future executive responsibility. We emphasize the application of management knowledge in the service of practice, and we prepare our students to meet the challenges of developing and integrating specialized units. We are capable of delivering such an education because our faculty members are outstanding scholars and share a deep understanding of the challenges that face practicing managers.

—Synthia Wachtel-Marquez, Director, Management Program/Drucker M.B.A.

Programs and Curricular Focus

The Peter F. Drucker Graduate School of Management has been delivering top-quality executive and management education for more than twenty-five years. From its earliest days, the School has emphasized the importance of outstanding scholarship and its relevance to practicing managers. One of the two degree programs, the Master of Business Administration (the Drucker M.B.A.), is geared toward those students who join the School with two to five years of prior work experience. The Executive Management Program educates managers who work in the upper echelon of their organizations.

The early-career M.B.A. provides leadership and strategy training for the advancement of individuals and organizations, and it is widely recognized for academic rigor, exceptional teaching, and a highly personalized and supportive environment. The Drucker M.B.A. embodies the philosophies of management pioneer Peter F. Drucker, a longtime faculty member and prolific writer and lecturer on management. The program's success is based on several key concepts, including the convergence of theory and practice, aligning core competencies and market needs, and succeeding as an exemplary executive. Students learn to apply cutting-edge theory and the best practices from multiple disciplines, functions, and cultures to pivotal management and leadership challenges to derive and implement innovative solutions that address short-term needs and position the students and their organizations for long-term success. Students are also trained to integrate

the talents of individuals, departments, organizations, industries, societies, and nations to achieve rapid progress. Drucker graduates benefit from course work designed to provide them with vision, critical insight, know-how, skills, and tools to become exemplary strategic leaders.

Students and the M.B.A. Experience

The Drucker M.B.A. comprises 60 academic units (with 4 units allotted to a typical course). The program takes between twenty-four and thirty-six months to complete, depending on whether a student attends full- or part-time and has prior business course work and experience. Classroom experience is enriched through student participation and faculty blending of the theory and practice of strategy, leadership, and management.

The Drucker M.B.A. recognizes that leadership potential comes in a variety of forms. The program provides students with substantial value to complement their unique talents, undergraduate course work, and work experience. The curriculum instills a powerful knowledge base with a minimum number of required courses.

Special Features

The Drucker M.B.A. features internship options, including honors consulting projects and mentoring programs.

The honors consulting projects provide students with the opportunity to master strategic management and consulting. The mentoring program offers students access to a powerful network of senior managers

within the Drucker community and younger applicants who need guidance.

Full-time students pursue internships between the spring term of their first year and the fall term of their second with the assistance of Claremont Graduate University's Office of Career Services and Corporate Relations.

The Faculty

Faculty members of the Peter F. Drucker Graduate School of Management study strategically important managerial issues and advance the theory and practice of management through teaching and field-based research. The faculty's emphasis on strategically important issues stresses the strategic dimension of each functional area and the role of executive leadership in outstanding organizational performance.

The Drucker School's faculty members are selected for the high quality of their academic training and research, their knowledge of management and leadership practice, and their superior teaching skills. Most of the full-time faculty members are experienced consultants or have significant managerial experience.

The Business School Network

Through Drucker School institutes, faculty research, and consulting alliances, the Drucker School maintains key relationships in the business community. The School's Board of Visitors includes CEOs and other eminent businesspeople who provide guidance and financial resources to further the Drucker School's programs. The Dean's Executive-in-Residence Program provides small-group and one-on-one interaction between Drucker M.B.A. students and senior executives. Corporate partners, such as Deloitte & Touche, sponsor research, collaborate with Drucker School faculty members, and regularly recruit Drucker M.B.A. interns and graduates.

The College and Environs

The Claremont Colleges are a group of small and distinguished liberal arts colleges. Claremont Graduate University, founded in 1925, was the second member of The Claremont Colleges. It provides graduate education in the liberal arts,

The new home of the Drucker School at Claremont.

information technology, and management. The University enrolls approximately 1,600 students, about 225 of them in the Early Career Management Program (Drucker M.B.A.) and another 225 in the Executive Management Program.

The mission of Claremont Graduate University is to prepare a diverse group of outstanding individuals to assume leadership roles in the worldwide community through research, teaching, and practice in selected fields. Claremont Graduate University believes superb instruction, innovative research, and practical experience are the keys to an excellent graduate education; educational institutions have an obligation to become civically engaged in order to enrich and to better serve society; institutions of higher education must be ethically vigilant, consciously exploring normative and moral issues; knowledge consists of more than facts and has more than merely utilitarian ends; knowledge pursues and reflects values; education is immeasurably enriched by the experience and insights of those outside the educational community; human diversity is indispensable for improving the quality and texture of the educational experience; ongoing education is a lifelong responsibility of the global community's leaders; and advanced education is essential for the well-being and future of an increasingly complex society.

Claremont is a beautiful residential community of 34,000 located 35 miles east of Los Angeles, close to skiing, the beach, the desert, and other recreational areas. This pleasant college town with an Ivy League atmosphere is situated in the foothills of the San Gabriel Mountains.

Technology Environment
Claremont Graduate University has an academic computing center reserved for stu-

dent use. IBM, Apple, and Digital Equipment computers are provided in this area. Most software packages utilized in instruction are Microsoft products, but many other software packages are available.

The Claremont Colleges' Honnold-Mudd Library is advanced in electronic access and CD-ROM capability.

Placement
The Office of Career Services and Corporate Relations helps students and alumni effectively manage their career paths to ensure long-term success in their chosen fields. Career Services and leaders within the Drucker School conduct a consistent marketing and corporate communications program to solicit additional placement opportunities in areas of interest to CGU students and alumni. Career Services maintains an aggressive program of flexible and tailored response to potential employers based on a state-of-the-art resume database. Career Services also offers a variety of services, including one-on-one counseling, resume and cover letter critiquing, networking opportunities, individual job listings, on- and off-campus recruiting, a career resources library, and a number of career skills workshops. CGU is a member of the West Coast M.B.A. Consortium, which offers a very successful three-day recruiting event each winter.

In 1997, 94 percent of Drucker M.B.A. graduates were placed within six months. The average starting salary was $63,808. These graduates took diverse positions in consulting, general management, marketing, finance, information sciences, and operations.

Admission
Applicants to the Drucker M.B.A. program must submit a completed application, a GMAT score, undergraduate and graduate school transcripts, three letters of reference, a resume, a personal statement, and an application fee to the Admissions Office of Claremont Graduate University.

Finances
Full-time tuition for the 1998–99 academic year is $23,437. Part-time tuition is $913 per unit in the Early Career Management Program and $1020 per unit in the Executive Management Program. Living expenses are about $12,000 for on-campus residence and $15,500 for off-campus residence for the academic year.

Approximately 50 percent of Drucker M.B.A. students receive fellowships, assistantships, or other grants, with the average award amounting to about $2500. Institutional aid programs based on both academic merit and financial need are available, as are loans and work-study programs.

International Students
To support a global learning environment in the Drucker School, approximately one half of incoming Drucker M.B.A. students are international. The Claremont Colleges excel in helping these students feel welcome and receive maximum benefit from their degrees. In the intimate and collegial environment, domestic and international students share their experiences and perspectives for a truly global graduate education.

Application Facts and Dates
The Drucker School utilizes a rolling admissions process for fall, spring, and summer admissions. February 15 is the priority deadline for financial aid consideration. Late applications are accepted. Applicants are notified of the admission decision within six weeks of applying.

For further information or to request an application, students should contact:

The Office of Educational Counseling and Recruiting
The Peter F. Drucker Graduate School of Management
Claremont Graduate University
The Claremont Colleges
1021 North Dartmouth
Claremont, California 91711-6184
Telephone: 800-944-4312 (toll-free)
Fax: 909-621-8543
E-mail: mba@cgu.edu
World Wide Web: http://www.cgu.edu/drucker

CLARION UNIVERSITY

Clarion University of Pennsylvania

College of Business Administration

Clarion, Pennsylvania

SUCCESS BEGINS WITH KNOWLEDGE

The M.B.A. at Clarion University is an ideal blend of theoretical knowledge and practical application that develops managers for responsible positions in business, industry, and government. The faculty members teaching in this program are outstanding national scholars, yet they possess significant managerial experience upon which graduate students may draw. Full accreditation by AACSB–The International Association for Management Education ensures the highest-quality academic program, and Clarion's attractive tuition puts graduate business education within reach for nearly everyone.

—Dr. Joseph Grunewald, Dean

Programs and Curricular Focus

The major objective of graduate study in the College of Business Administration is to provide those enrolled with the opportunity to develop a basic core of knowledge concerning the theory, techniques, and practices of administering business activities. In addition to studying the basic core of knowledge, candidates for the M.B.A. degree have the opportunity for in-depth study in a particular area of interest.

The program is designed to accommodate candidates with an undergraduate degree in business administration as well as graduates from other degree programs. Candidates with undergraduate degrees other than business administration must take foundation courses that make up the undergraduate common body of knowledge in business administration. Foundation requirements may be removed by course work at Clarion or other approved institutions.

This nonthesis program leading to the M.B.A. is based on a total requirement of 33 credits beyond the foundation courses, which are determined at the time of admission. Twenty-four of these 33 credits are specifically required courses. All students must take courses in organizational structure and behavior, quantitative analysis for business decisions, management accounting, managerial economics, financial management, production management, marketing decision making, and a capstone course in business policy. The remaining 9 credits in the program are elective, permitting the student to design the program to particular objectives with the approval of the M.B.A. Director.

The normal length of study for students attending full-time is two years. An accelerated three-semester program without summer study is also available. Students can also enroll in the program on a part-time basis.

Students and the M.B.A. Experience

Students enrolled in the M.B.A. program have greatly varied experiences. Undergraduate academic backgrounds include not only business administration but also social sciences, engineering, and computer technology. The M.B.A. program brings together students who are recent graduates with others who have as much as twenty years of professional experience. Approximately 20 percent of students are enrolled part-time bringing valuable current perspectives to the classroom. Fourteen percent of those enrolled are international students and 27 percent are women.

Special Features

Clarion's M.B.A. offers special features that enhance student learning. They include exposure to national scholars and editors of major American professional journals; "live case" business consulting opportunities; opportunity for international study and travel; up-to-date, in-classroom learning technology, opportunity for student/faculty research, and small class size supporting extensive interaction.

Students pursuing the M.B.A. degree may enroll in the professional accountancy course of study. The sequence of 36 semester hours of graduate course work is designed to prepare students for entry into the practice of professional accountancy as prescribed by the American Institute of Certified Public Accountants.

The Faculty

Courses in the M.B.A. program are taught exclusively by qualified faculty members who are active in scholarship and business consultation. Faculty members represent diverse backgrounds academically, professionally, and culturally. Twenty percent of the faculty members are women, 17 percent are international, and 13 percent are from minority groups. Faculty members hold degrees in accounting, economics, finance, law, marketing, administrative sciences, and engineering. Students in the program find that faculty members bring a unique blend of professional, academic, and international perspectives that enhance the classroom experience.

The Business School Network

Having "real-world" experiences that are woven into the fabric of graduate business education assures that an M.B.A. degree provides the kind of educational experience that is highly desired by employers. Clarion brings this perspective to its graduate program through its Business Advisory Council, which is comprised of top-level business executives from corporations across America. M.B.A. course work provides the opportunity for graduate students to work

FACULTY LIST

Department Heads:
Robert S. Balough, Director, M.B.A. Program and Chair, Department of Economics
Soga O. Ewedemi, Chair, Department of Finance
Joseph P. Grunenwald, Dean, College of Business Administration
Paul Y. Kim, Chair, Department of Marketing
Mary Lou Pae, Assistant Dean
James G. Pesek, Chair, Department of Administrative Sciences
Charles J. Pineno, Chair, Department of Accountancy

directly with corporations and other organizations in solving real business problems through research, consultation, and participative decision making. Choosing a program like Clarion's, in which business applications are a primary focus, is the first step toward an effective managerial career.

The College and Environs

Clarion University of Pennsylvania was established in 1867. It is one of the fourteen institutions in the state system of higher education of Pennsylvania. The University has an enrollment of approximately 6,000 students, 19 percent of whom are students in the College of Business Administration. In a typical year, approximately 50 students are enrolled in the Master of Business Administration (M.B.A.) program, with approximately 35 attending full-time. The University has grown significantly during the past twenty years. Most of the physical plant consists of newer buildings.

Located high on the Allegheny Plateau overlooking the Clarion River, the University is surrounded by some of Pennsylvania's most scenic resort areas. The rolling, wooded countryside affords some of the best hunting, fishing, camping, and hiking in northwestern Pennsylvania. The Clarion River and its tributaries provide an ideal setting for summer boating, swimming, and aquatic sports.

Facilities

The College of Business Administration is located in Still Hall, the newest classroom building on campus. In addition to classrooms and a 225-seat auditorium, this modern facility includes an up-to-date microcomputer lab and reading/study center.

Technology Environment

Students are provided terminal access to the University's DEC VAX 6440 networked mainframe. All students receive an account that allows them to access all VSM-8550 VAX programming languages, the library system, and the Internet, from the Still Hall computer lab.

Many electronic databases are available including WestLaw Tax Library, Citibase macro data tapes, CRSP tapes, IMF trade data, Panel Study of Income Dynamics, Consumer Expenditure Surveys, County Business Patterns, and other databases. Additionally, faculty members have access to and support for computer software such as SAS, TSP, Soritec, Statistic-A, Viza, RATS, Compenstat, LINDO, GINO, Markstrat, Epistat, StatAnalyst, and other PC and mainframe packages.

Placement

The University maintains an Office of Placement Services. This office is visited annually by representatives of leading companies. The M.B.A. program has had an excellent job placement record over the past several years.

Admission

Admission to the M.B.A. program is open to qualified graduates of recognized colleges or universities accredited by a regional or general accrediting agency. The Graduate Management Admissions Test (GMAT) score report, official transcripts from all previous colleges and universities attended, and three letters of reference must be submitted. A combination of satisfactory GMAT score and undergraduate GPA is required. International students presenting transcripts from institutions outside the U.S. must submit an official Test of English as a Foreign Language (TOEFL) score of 550 or higher.

Finances

The total cost for out-of-state students enrolled in the M.B.A. program for the 1998–99 academic year, not including the summer term, is estimated at $12,978. This includes basic tuition and fees, housing, meals, books, and insurance. The cost for Pennsylvania resident students is lower reflecting the lower tuition rate. Graduate assistantships are available to qualified students and cover all or part of the basic tuition and fees expenses and provide a stipend. All international students admitted to the M.B.A. program who are not awarded a graduate assistantship qualify to receive an international assistantship award in the form of tuition reductions of $3000 to $5000.

Application Facts and Dates

Domestic student applications are considered on a continuous basis without application deadline. The international student application deadlines are July 1 for the fall term and November 1 for the spring term. For further information, students should contact:

Director of the M.B.A. Program
Clarion University of Pennsylvania
Clarion, Pennsylvania 16214
Telephone: 814-226-2605
Fax: 814-226-1910
E-mail: mba@clarion.edu
World Wide Web: http://www.clarion.edu
http://www.clarion.edu/cob_webl/header.htm

Clarkson University

Potsdam, New York

> ### ENCOURAGING THE ENTREPRENEURIAL SPIRIT
>
> *Clarkson University's School of Business creates the leaders of today and tomorrow who are energized by the entrepreneurial spirit. At the heart of the curricula are three essential building blocks: technology and information management, personal and leadership development, and cross-functional business thinking. We encourage professional experiences with local, national, and international organizations to develop students' entrepreneurial abilities and to provide pedagogical advantages outside the traditional classroom setting. Our Center for Leadership and Entrepreneurial Development provides resources and opportunities for students to gain valuable experience. With Canada on our doorstep, the opportunity for international business experience is eagerly engaged through our Canadian-U.S. Business Center.*
>
> —Victor P. Pease, Dean

Programs and Curricular Focus

Accredited by the AACSB–The International Association for Management Education, Clarkson University offers M.B.A. and Master of Science in Management Systems (M.S.M.S.) degree programs that prepare students for professional positions within an increasingly global and dynamic environment. The focus of the Clarkson M.B.A. is on developing students' leadership and managerial abilities and in developing their abilities to analyze problems and make effective decisions. The ability to work effectively in teams is critically important in today's business environment. Teamwork, effective communication skills, experiential learning, and leadership development are central to the Clarkson M.B.A. program.

The majority of Clarkson M.B.A. students complete the program requirements in one academic year. The fast-paced and highly integrated curriculum includes 10 core modules and 12 academic credits devoted to the development of functional and experiential learning (see right).

To participate in Clarkson's One-Year M.B.A. program, students must have completed courses deemed equivalent to first-year foundation requirements—accounting, business law, computer applications, economics, finance, management, marketing, production, and statistics—prior to entering the program. Undergraduate business majors are typically able to complete the M.B.A. in one year. Nonbusiness majors can also receive transfer credit for foundation courses taken during their undergraduate studies and can complete any

remaining foundation requirements at Clarkson, prior to entering the One-Year M.B.A. program.

The M.S. in Management Systems (M.S.M.S.) program can also be completed in one to two years and allows for the development of highly focused expertise in one of four dynamic areas: information systems, human resources, marketing, and manufacturing management.

Students and the M.B.A. Experience

At each year's commencement exercises, students gather to say their good-byes, and, without question, the M.B.A. class produces the loudest cheers and the sincerest tears. This degree of closeness stems from the team emphasis, the co-experiences, and the intensity of the Clarkson M.B.A. program.

This annual outcome is even more significant when one considers the diversity

of each class's membership. Typically one third are women and one fifth represent international students and members of minority groups. Academically, two fifths are from undergraduate programs in engineering, science, or liberal arts. Students returning from industry, who typically account for one quarter of the class, bring professional experience into the class discussions, team activities, and experiential projects. Clarkson attracts energetic individuals who possess the ambition and leadership skills necessary to accept challenges and reach for high achievements.

❖ Global Focus

Modern industries in all countries need managers and business leaders who understand the complexities and opportunities associated with international competition. Clarkson's ties with Canadian industry and its proximity to Montreal and Ottawa allow Clarkson M.B.A. and M.S.M.S. students to deal firsthand with international business issues. While Canada is America's largest trading partner, conducting business with Canada still embodies the complexities of foreign trade.

The Center for Canadian-U.S. Business Studies is unique among graduate programs and a major component of the Clarkson M.B.A. and M.S.M.S. programs. The Canadian-U.S. Business Consulting Service provides Clarkson students with a unique opportunity to gain practical business experience through the study of cross-border trade and economic opportunities. Professionally staffed and managed by Clarkson M.B.A. and M.S.M.S. students, the program provides client engagements

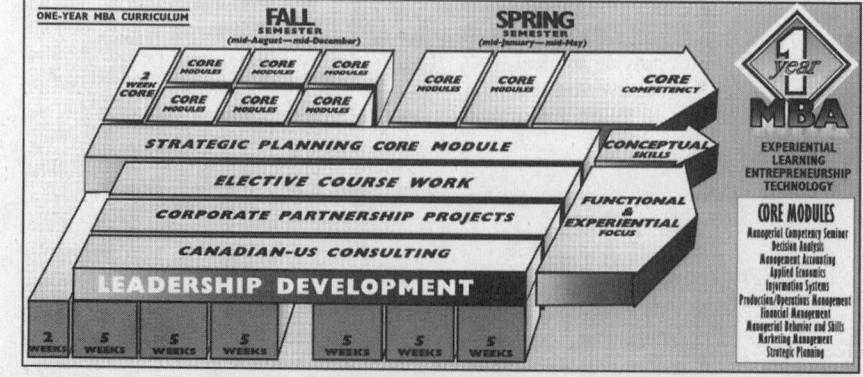

that can lead to permanent career opportunities after graduation.

In addition to Clarkson's focus on Canadian—U.S. business issues, a joint program is offered with the Maastricht School of Management (Netherlands) and the University of Ottawa (Canada). This program provides firsthand exposure to international business issues.

Special Features

Clarkson's M.B.A. Leadership Program begins with a two-week Managerial Competency Seminar starting in mid-August. During this core module, students are individually assessed. From this assessment, individual developmental plans are created. Individualized feedback is received from a professional assessment organization, Clarkson faculty members, and fellow M.B.A. students. Throughout the remainder of their program, students engage in course work and experiential activities to further develop these skills. A follow-up assessment in the spring semester acts as an outcome measure for this central focus of the program.

The Faculty

More than 90 percent of the faculty members possess a doctorate. Faculty members bring creative ideas and introduce exciting experiential components into their courses. At the same time, faculty members conduct research and publish their findings in top scholarly journals.

The Business School Network

Clarkson's graduate business programs reflect the advisory input from an executive council staffed by such firms as Goldman-Sachs, CIGNA, Coopers & Lybrand, Digital Equipment, Chase Manhattan Bank, and Imperial Oil.

In addition, the University's Executive-In-Residence program brings corporate executives and other organizational leaders to campus to share the managerial and leadership philosophies of today's business leaders. Prominent alumni, such as John McLennan, President and CEO of Bell Canada, regularly participate in these activities.

All graduate students have opportunities to participate in projects and intern experiences with corporations such as Alcoa, Corning, Niagara Mohawk, Nynex, and Xerox.

The College and Environs

An intellectual and cultural oasis nestled within a rural setting, Clarkson University enrolls approximately 2,200 undergraduate and 400 graduate students in the disciplines of business, engineering, and science. One-Year M.B.A. students typically number between 80 and 100. Potsdam, New York (population 10,200), is a short drive from the scenic Adirondack Park; 80 miles from Ottawa, Ontario; and 90 miles from Montreal, Quebec. In addition to Clarkson's 640-acre campus, the region is home to three other institutions: Potsdam College of the State University of New York, St. Lawrence University, and SUNY College of Technology at Canton, all within a 10-mile radius.

Technology Environment

Clarkson M.B.A. and M.S.M.S. students have a wide range of computer technology available to them: fifty 386/486/RS6000 workstations linked by three Novell servers with access to the Internet. Publishing capabilities exist in the desktop publishing lab, complete with color scanning and printing devices.

As a Novell Educational Partner, Clarkson offers several Novell Certification Courses to M.B.A. and M.S.M.S. students.

Placement

Placement services include on-line resume referral, alumni referral networks, and a variety of workshops throughout the year. In addition, the career center sponsors an industrial fair and participates in the NYS M.B.A. Consortium, an organization focused on placing M.B.A. students. On-campus interviews by more than 150 organizations round out Clarkson's placement services. In 1997, more than 80 percent of graduates were employed within three months of graduation.

Admission

Admission decisions are based on upper-division GPA, the highest attained GMAT score, and relevant professional experience. The average GPA is 3.3 and the average GMAT score is 540. Students for whom English is not their native language must submit scores of at least 600 on the TOEFL and 50 on the Test of Spoken English (TSE). International students must present proof of adequate funds to cover all program costs. All students must have health insurance, either through Clarkson or another provider.

Finances

The 1998–99 tuition costs for the M.B.A. program are $20,352; costs are $19,080 for the M.S.M.S. Fees are $175. Additional fees may be necessary for those students required to take the mandatory English as a Second Language (ESL) placement exam. Books, living expenses, and other costs are estimated to be $7700 per year. Each year, roughly three fourths of incoming M.B.A. students receive merit-based tuition remission awards ranging from 20 to 100 percent. All applicants are considered for these awards, which are based solely on the aforementioned admissions criteria. In addition, candidates can apply for residence life positions that usually include room and board and, in some cases, a stipend.

International Students

Culture nights, diversity festivals, and the International Reading Room are all examples of Clarkson's efforts to enhance the acclimation of international students into Clarkson life. Students needing to improve TOEFL or TSE scores can enroll in intensive English language programs at regional institutions with which Clarkson has close working relationships.

Application Facts and Dates

Clarkson accepts applications on a rolling basis. Students who have been accepted and have received credit for all foundation requirements may begin the One-Year M.B.A. program in mid-August only. Students enrolling for the M.S.M.S. or to fulfill foundation requirements may enter in either the fall or spring semester. For more information, students should contact:

Office of Graduate Business Programs
Clarkson University
P.O. Box 5770
Potsdam, New York 13699
Telephone: 315-268-6613
Fax: 315-268-3810
E-mail: gradprog@icarus.som.
  clarkson.edu
World Wide Web: http://phoenix.som.
  clarkson.edu/

Clark University

Graduate School of Management

Worcester, Massachusetts

THE NEW M.B.A. IN THE GLOBAL ECONOMY

Clark University is a research-oriented institution that believes the basis of good teaching is research. Our faculty, through the facility of small classes, discuss cutting-edge concepts of both practical and theoretical natures to provide students with the necessary foundation for addressing critical issues in the global economy. The extraordinary accessibility of our faculty builds a rapport with students that enhances the learning environment. Our globally focused curriculum and multicultural student body prepares graduates for the complexity of international business.

—Maurry Tamarkin, Dean

Programs and Curricular Focus

As part of a university offering an M.B.A. degree nationally accredited by AACSB–The International Association for Management Education, Clark University's Graduate School of Management offers a personal setting for a multinational management education and attracts students from more than thirty countries.

Clark's integrated M.B.A. curriculum goes far beyond offering the fundamentals. Through projects and internships, the program provides students with rich opportunities to work on multidisciplinary teams with people from all over the world. Students solve complex business problems designed to develop an understanding of global marketplace trends, sharpen leadership skills, and acquire essential practical experience.

Clark's M.B.A. curriculum is designed to provide students with strong analytical foundations and critical management judgment. What sets Clark apart is its emphasis designing courses that reflect the way the world does business: in teams of managers bringing together diverse cultures, skills, and experiences to meet the toughest business challenges.

Other curricular features include a one-year M.B.A. for business undergraduates, an M.B.A. in health services offered jointly with the University of Massachusetts Medical School, a Master of Science in Finance (M.S.F.) degree program, an expanded accounting concentration that qualifies students to sit for the CPA exam, study-abroad programs, a one-week international management course in Europe, and the opportunity to audit one course per semester in other divisions of the University.

Students and the M.B.A. Experience

Clark's M.B.A. program attracts a diverse student body. Hailing from many states and countries around the world, students come together to form a microcosm of the international business arena. They work together in teams in many courses, notably the Projects in Management course. This course offers students the opportunity to work as a member of a consulting team on actual management problems facing corporations that have contracted with Clark for consulting services.

The average full-time student has one to two years of full-time professional work experience, along with a record of strong undergraduate achievement. Fewer than 30 percent of students have an undergraduate business background. Women comprise 46 percent of the class,

and approximately half of the students come from overseas. Because of the program's small size, students readily form lasting friendships with their classmates and professors; friendships that stand them in good stead as they enter the business world in both the U.S. and abroad.

❖ Global Focus

Students' understanding of the world's way of doing business is not limited to just a few courses at Clark. Clark has intentionally created a curriculum that reflects the world's rapidly changing business environment, and international issues are discussed in every class. Students also develop a personal understanding of global topics by getting to know students from all over the world.

Special Features

Clark's Center for the Management of New Ventures offers graduate instruction in the creation and management of new companies or of new ventures in existing firms. M.B.A. students participate in the New Ventures Seminar, a weekly meeting with successful entrepreneurs and executives in venture capital firms.

The Faculty

The Graduate School of Management emphasizes excellence in both teaching and research. The School's reputation in

754

Peterson's Guide to MBA Programs 1999

the United States and abroad is maintained, in large measure, through respect for the intellectual contributions of its faculty members. The School is a community, and it fosters collegiality and close relationships between students and faculty members.

The Business School Network

Faculty consulting and research activities ensure Clark's link to the business community. Semester after semester, corporations, Fortune 500 firms among them, turn to Clark for assistance in addressing management issues. A visiting committee, comprising prominent CEOs and other top executives, ensures that the M.B.A. curriculum is continually refined to reflect the dynamic nature of business.

The College and Environs

A teaching and research institution founded in 1887, Clark University is the second-oldest graduate institution in the nation. Clark is one of only three New England universities, with Harvard and Yale, to be a founding member of the Association of American Universities. Clark is the only U.S. institution of its size to have its M.B.A., M.S.F., and undergraduate management program nationally accredited. The University's tree-shaded residential

campus is located in Worcester, New England's second-largest city and a center of high technology, biotechnology, and financial services industries. Boston is just a short drive away.

Placement

Because of the program's small size, students have unparalleled access to career-related services for a university of Clark's quality. From the first day of orientation, career services staff members are ready to help students assess their skills, research career options, develop experience, prepare their resumes, and meet employers. Alumni mentoring, individual advising, mock interviews, and on-campus recruiting are just a few of the many career services offerings. The staff members never forget that students' primary motivating factor in seeking an M.B.A. is to improve employment prospects.

Admission

Clark seeks students who will add to the vitality of the interactions between faculty members and students. Applications from men and women with diverse educational and professional backgrounds are encouraged. The average GMAT for the most recently enrolled class was 575 (80

percent of students scored between 480 and 660). A minimum TOEFL score of 550 is required for international students. In addition to these factors, students' records of undergraduate academic achievement along with letters of recommendation and a personal statement are considered. Although no formal academic or professional business background is required for admission, a solid preparation in English, mathematics, and economics is beneficial.

Finances

Tuition is calculated on a per course basis, rather than per semester. For the 1998–99 academic year, tuition per course is $1925. Mandatory activity and insurance fees are estimated at $626. Living and personal expenses, including books, are estimated at $9000.

The Graduate School of Management offers scholarship assistance, based exclusively on merit, to both U.S. and international students. Awards range up to 100 percent of tuition. All applicants are considered for these merit-based awards.

International Students

Clark University is an exceptionally hospitable place for international students. With students from more than seventy countries and with an M.B.A. class composed of approximately 50 percent international students, the University prides itself on the range of support services available to these students. The University maintains a department dedicated to the service of students from overseas, assisting them with the social, cultural, and academic adjustments to life at an American University.

Application Facts and Dates

For the fall semester, the admission deadline is June 1, and, for the spring semester, the admission deadline is December 1. For more information, students should contact:

Mr. John Brandon
Director of Admissions
Graduate School of Management
Clark University
950 Main Street
Worcester, Massachusetts 01610-1477
Telephone: 508-793-7406
Fax: 508-793-8822
E-mail: clarkmba@vax.clarku.edu
World Wide Web: http://www.mba.
    clarku.edu

Clemson University

College of Business and Public Affairs

Clemson, South Carolina

DISTINCTIVE AND DIVERSE OPPORTUNITIES—A CLEMSON TRADITION

Clemson has a proud history of educating leaders in many fields. Our M.B.A. programs are dedicated to creating leaders in the field of business and preparing them for success in an ever-changing and dynamic global economy. Our unique combination of M.B.A. programs attracts talented, highly motivated young professionals with diverse cultural heritages, academic backgrounds, and business experiences.

Since our clientele have such varied backgrounds and needs, we offer a variety of M.B.A. programs. Whether your requirements are international, needing a multicultural experience and demanding work environment; supplementary, requiring a flexible evening program located in an urban setting; or expanding, looking for a dedicated, intensive but personal program set in a small, scenic collegiate town, Clemson can offer you a challenging and rewarding experience.

—Jerry Trapnell, Dean

Programs and Curricular Focus

Clemson University's M.B.A. programs, which are AACSB accredited, enable individuals to study advanced, integrated concepts of business, industry, and government. Students include active managers as well as recent graduates interested in expanding their analytical, business, and interpersonal skills.

Full-time participants take a sequence of twenty courses (sixteen core and four electives), including financial accounting, business ethics, quantitative decision making, organizational behavior, managerial competencies, and marketing strategies. The four elective courses, taken in the spring and summer of the second year, allow students to tailor the program for specific interests. Diverse learning environments offer approaches that include role playing, simulations, internships, consulting, teamwork, and case studies.

Clemson offers a highly concentrated international program, taught in English, in Italy and Slovenia. Participants, selected worldwide, take sixteen courses and, optionally, one or two internships in Italy and Slovenia during the fall and spring and complete the twelve-month curriculum with four more courses, including two electives, on Clemson's campus. While course content and learning approaches are similar to the full-time program, the faculty members use the students' diverse international and cultural backgrounds to enrich the learning environment. In addition to the full-time program, there are also weekend executive programs in Italy and Slovenia.

Clemson's part-time, evening program allows business professionals who have at least two years of work experience to pursue a degree in Greenville, South Carolina, at the University Center or in Greenwood, South Carolina, on Lander University's campus. Students with no undergraduate business courses can expect to complete the nine prerequisite, eight core, and two elective courses in approximately 3½ years. Course content and delivery are similar to the full-time program but provide more flexibility for the nontraditional student. Students actively enrich class learning by contributing and integrating business experiences.

Students and the M.B.A. Experience

Clemson's M.B.A. students are drawn worldwide, providing a rich infusion of cultural and business backgrounds. The average student is 26, with three years of work experience. Half have business degrees, 37 percent engineering and pure sciences, and 13 percent social sciences and humanities. A third are women. Thirty-one percent of the students are international, representing more than twenty countries. The domestic students come from the South (55 percent), Northeast (23 percent), Midwest (13 percent), and West (9 percent).

❖ Global Focus

Clemson offers students many opportunities to broaden their international perspectives. During the summer between their first and second year, full-time students can take four courses abroad, participate in an internship, or pursue a foreign language on the Clemson campus. Frequent guest lecturers from multinational firms provide a unique international perspective. In addition, Clemson's international program in Italy provides visits to and internships with international firms, opportunity for language and cultural immersion, and optional international travel.

The Faculty

Clemson's faculty members all carry a Ph.D. in their teaching discipline. They are highly qualified to bring students outstanding learning opportunities by offering superb teaching skills, applied business research and professional experience, and high-quality student interaction.

The Business School Network

Corporate Partnerships

As part of a land-grant university with strong traditional ties to the business community, the College of Business and Public Affairs maintains dynamic partnerships with area corporate leaders. The College Advancement Board, composed of prominent business executives from South Carolina industry including IBM, Sonoco, and Price Waterhouse, provides critical business guidance, expertise, and participation for College programs. Internships, field trips, hands-on consulting, and executive guest speakers provide additional real-world exposure for the M.B.A. student.

The College and Environs

Clemson is a state-assisted university located in South Carolina's lake and mountain region. The campus itself consists of more than 1,400 wooded acres on the former plantation of John C. Calhoun. Founded in 1889, the University has a student population of approximately 16,000 and offers more than 100 graduate degrees in almost seventy areas.

The town of Clemson is a small college community of 15,000 located on the shores of Lake Hartwell. Large population centers are conveniently located within 30 to 45 minutes of the area.

Technology Environment

The University computing facilities include a campuswide network linking all labs and University departments, network links to the Internet, microcomputer labs containing almost 400 computers, a large mainframe computer, and five VAX machines. The computer labs are strategically located throughout the campus. The library's more than 1.6 million items, including books, periodicals, microforms, databases, CDs, and government publications, are accessible for index and catalog search via on-line computer access.

Placement

Clemson's Career Services Center provides assistance to students in identifying and obtaining professional positions through on-campus interviews, research resources, and student-developed network contacts. In addition, the center offers a full range of services, including career counseling, career assessment testing, resume preparation workshops, online job listings, resume referrals, video interviewing, and career fairs.

Admission

Acceptance is based on careful appraisal of each candidate's academic record, performance on the Graduate Management Admission Test (GMAT), letters of recommendation, and work experience. The admission process is highly personalized, with emphasis on each applicant's accomplishments. A score of at least 550 on the TOEFL is required for all students whose native language is not English.

Calculus and fundamentals of computers are prerequisites for the full-time program on the Clemson campus. The evening programs require basic prerequisite courses in calculus, statistics, management, marketing, economics, finance, accounting, business law, and management information systems.

Finances

In 1998–99, tuition and fees for the Clemson campus full-time program are $1745 per semester for South Carolina residents and $3394 per semester for nonresidents. Books and supplies cost approximately $800 per year. On-campus housing ranges from $930 per semester for a residence hall to $1280 for a 4-person apartment. Off-campus apartments typically cost around $400 per month. A limited number of graduate assistantships are available. Awards are based on personal interviews and candidates' qualifications.

Tuition for the evening programs in 1998–99 is $200 per semester hour for South Carolina residents and $408 per hour for nonresidents. Tuition and fees for the international M.B.A. program in Italy are approximately $16,000 for the 1998–99 program.

All tuition and fees are subject to change as conditions warrant.

Application Facts and Dates

Application deadlines for the full-time program are April 15 for international students and June 15 for domestic students. For the part-time program, deadlines are April 15, July 15, and November 30. For more information, students should contact:

Director of Admissions
M.B.A. Programs
Clemson University
Box 341315
Clemson, South Carolina 29634-1315
Telephone: 864-656-3975
Fax: 864-656-0947
E-mail: mba@clemson.edu
World Wide Web: http://www.clemson.edu/business/MBA

CSU Cleveland State University

NEW CURRICULUM AND FLEXIBLE PROGRAMS

▶ *Cleveland State University offers the opportunity to earn an M.B.A. degree in the heart of one of America's most exciting cities. The new M.B.A. curriculum features full integration of the business disciplines, an expanded emphasis on global business practices, team dynamics, and management of innovation and technology. Programs are scheduled for full-time or part-time students and meet on weekdays or weekends, daytime or evening, on campus and at business locations outside the downtown area. Flexibility of options enables students to tailor a program to meet their specific needs. The new building contains state-of-the-art classroom space, computer labs, faculty offices, conference rooms, and distance learning technology.*

—Robert L. Minter, Dean

Programs and Curricular Focus

CSU offers a variety of M.B.A. programs. There are full-time and part-time programs, given both in the daytime and evening. There is also a one-year, accelerated program; classes meet all day Saturday and every other Friday evening, starting in August. The Executive M.B.A. is a twenty-two-month program with classes primarily on Saturdays, featuring international and governmental seminars; the program is limited to candidates with business experience. The M.B.A. in Health Care Administration is a special program that features an internship and course work with a health-care emphasis. The J.D./M.B.A. is a joint program with the Cleveland Marshall College of Law that permits students to work on both degrees simultaneously.

The curriculum exposes students to the full range of business disciplines in both skill-building and integrative courses. It consists of three levels of course work: skill development, basic business knowledge, and core courses.

Skill development courses are offered in spoken and written communications, computer literacy, mathematics, and statistics; these courses may be waived through prior course work or departmental examination.

Basic business knowledge courses are offered in business environment, economics, financial accounting, financial management, management, marketing, organizational behavior, and production management. These courses are prerequisite to the M.B.A. core courses and may be waived through prior course work.

Core courses consist of environment of international business, finance, human resource management and labor relations, management of innovation and technology, managerial accounting, marketing, and team dynamics. Other program requirements are a capstone seminar focusing on the interrelationships between the major business disciplines and three elective courses, one of which may be either a research project or a business internship.

Students and the M.B.A. Experience

CSU has a student population of 16,000, drawn from the city of Cleveland, its suburbs, and many countries of Europe, Central and South America, Africa, and Asia. The 1,100 graduate students are drawn from each of these areas, range in age from their early 20s to 50s, and provide a broad racial and cultural mix. Many have established business careers. The classroom experience gives each student a chance to work alongside persons of different backgrounds and heritages.

❖ Global Focus

International trade is one of Cleveland's and northeastern Ohio's most active business segments. The import-export community has provided CSU with a rich resource of materials for building a global emphasis into the core courses of the M.B.A. program and enables CSU to present the course Environment of International Business as part of the M.B.A. core.

The Faculty

Each member of the graduate faculty of the James J. Nance College of Business Administration has an earned doctorate in his or her academic discipline. The total full-time faculty numbers 75, with extensive industry experience and international background.

The Business School Network

CSU's proximity to the central business district affords regular interchange with the rich commercial and industrial activities of the area. Programs emphasize the practical application of business principles, affording students the opportunity to learn from the area's leading practitioners. Members of the College of Business Administration's Visiting Committee represent major corporations in the area, providing students opportunities to interact at the top level of decision making. Frequent guest speakers expose students to a variety of styles and corporate cultures.

The College and Environs

The James J. Nance College of Business Administration is one of seven colleges of Cleveland State University. The campus is located within a short walk of the central business district; Playhouse Square, a major theater and entertainment area; and Gateway, a new major sports complex. Cleveland offers a world-class symphony orchestra, opera and ballet companies, theater companies, three major-league sports teams, and one of the most extensive networks of public parks in the United States. A new building for the College of Business Administration opened in January 1998.

Facilities

The resources of CSU's main library and Law Library and those of the Cleveland Public Library system are available to M.B.A. students. The Computer Center provides student access to mainframe computing, several personal computer laboratories, online interactive processing, and use of OhioLINK and Dialog information retrieval systems.

Placement

CSU's Career Services Center offers advice on career direction and the career development process. It operates a placement service to match student skills with job opportunities from more than 500 companies.

Admission

Applicants for M.B.A. programs must possess a baccalaureate degree from an accredited college or university and must take the Graduate Management Admission Test (GMAT). Admission is based on undergraduate grade point average and GMAT score. International applicants must also take the Test of English as a Foreign Language (TOEFL) and achieve a score of at least 525.

Finances

For 1998–99, graduate tuition is $194.25 per credit hour for Ohio residents and

$388.50 per credit hour for nonresidents, plus a $2.25 per-credit-hour technology fee. Books and supplies average $60 to $95 per course. Financial aid in the form of tuition grants is available to a limited number of highly qualified first-year graduate students. Dormitory space ranging from $1505 to $2508 per semester (excluding meals) is available on a limited basis. Relatively low-cost rental housing is available in Cleveland and nearby suburbs; monthly rates range from $300 to $500.

International Students

CSU's International Student Services Office provides counseling in matters dealing with visas, housing, and academic affairs and conducts an orientation program prior to a student's initial quarter of classes.

The International Student M.B.A. Bridge Program is available to students with three-year bachelor's degrees who meet the regular admission standards. They are required to complete 24 credit hours of bridge courses. Successful

completion of the bridge program enables the student to complete the entire M.B.A. program in two years on a full-time basis. Students are evaluated and are given specific course assignments based on their individual background and preparation.

Application Facts and Dates

Applicants should submit an application at least two months prior to the quarter of desired entrance. Official copies of transcripts must be forwarded to CSU directly from all institutions previously attended. Test scores (GMAT and TOEFL) must be reported directly by the Educational Testing Service. Copies of program descriptions and application forms may be obtained from:

James J. Nance College of Business
   Administration
Cleveland State University
1860 East 18th Street
Cleveland, Ohio 44114
Telephone: 216-687-3730
Fax: 216-687-5311

The College of Saint Rose

TOOLS FOR SUCCESS IN THE TWENTY-FIRST CENTURY

Today's increasingly competitive business environment requires that an M.B.A. program provide students with opportunities to acquire cutting edge knowledge, analytical abilities, and practical application skills to prepare business managers for productive and efficient leadership. The Saint Rose M.B.A. curriculum is designed to meet these requirements. The Saint Rose M.B.A. program includes course work that addresses subjects such as leadership, communication, production and quality management, finance, technology, human resource management, and marketing. The Saint Rose M.B.A curriculum and instruction synthesize contemporary realities with theoretical analyses of those realities.

The business world of the twenty-first century will present managers with even more challenges than they face today. Graduates of our M.B.A. program are equipped today with the tools to meet the demands of tomorrow successfully.

—Margaret Kirwin, Associate Vice President for Academic Affairs

Programs and Curricular Focus

The School of Business offers two M.B.A. program options: the part-time M.B.A. and the one-year M.B.A. Both options share the goal of preparing M.B.A. students to be effective, innovative managers. The Saint Rose M.B.A. program is accredited by the Association of Collegiate Business Schools and Programs.

The courses of the M.B.A. program are designed to teach students how to lead and communicate, on the job and in the community. Faculty members utilize a variety of teaching tools, such as class discussion, case analyses, simulations, seminars, technology sessions, and individual and group projects. Students are expected to graduate with the ability to define, analyze, and solve problems; apply legal and ethical considerations in the decision-making process; communicate effectively; and develop competitively driven strategic plans that integrate economic optimization, cost of capital, market opportunities, production, technology, and human resources. All program options require the completion of a minimum of 36 graduate credit hours. Students may transfer up to 12 degree-applicable graduate credits from another accredited institution.

The part-time M.B.A. option allows students to schedule flexibly; most opt to take one or two courses per semester or an accelerated option that is designed to be completed in two years, including a summer semester. Both of these program op-

tions require students to complete nine core courses, two elective courses, and one capstone course.

The one-year M.B.A. option combines intensive course work with career development opportunities, including a mentorship with a local business executive and a 6-credit internship.

Saint Rose offers a Juris Doctor/ Master of Business Administration (J.D./M.B.A.) program jointly with Albany Law School that can be completed in four years of full-time study. In addition, the College's satellite location in Glens Falls, New York, an hour north of Albany, provides students with a convenient alternative site at which they can complete some of the 36 required credits of the M.B.A. program.

Students and the M.B.A. Experience

Saint Rose M.B.A. students are competitive while collegial; faculty members are accessible and student-oriented. The average age of M.B.A. students is 33, and the majority live within a 50-mile radius of Saint Rose. Thirty-six percent of the M.B.A. students are women; 29 percent are international students.

The M.B.A. program is structured to accommodate the needs of a wide range of students, including those with substantial knowledge of business, students without an undergraduate business degree or previous business experience, and students returning to advanced study after an absence.

Classes for the M.B.A. are conveniently scheduled in the evenings and on weekends to fit into the schedules of students who work full-time or have other commitments during the day. Students enrolled in the intensive one-year M.B.A. option attend classes primarily during the day. Class size is kept to an average of 20 students in order to facilitate interaction in the classroom.

Special Features

Saint Rose offers a one-year M.B.A. program option to students who have successfully completed a set of ten prerequisite, undergraduate, business-related courses. This option provides students with the outstanding opportunities of a mentorship program and a graduate internship. When students enter the program, they are paired with business executives in their fields of interest who help them explore career options and network in the local business community throughout the academic year. The one-year option culminates with a 6-credit internship that places students as interns in business organizations. Several businesses have offered M.B.A. interns full-time employment as a result of their outstanding work.

The Faculty

Graduate business faculty members are professionals with significant experience who have built strong relationships with members of the business community and remain involved with companies, nonprofit organizations, and government agencies in a variety of capacities. All M.B.A. courses are taught by full-time faculty members or business, professional, or government experts. Ninety percent of the faculty members in the School of Business hold a doctorate or the highest degree in their area of expertise, and 40 percent of the faculty members are women.

The Business School Network
Corporate Partnerships

The College of Saint Rose Peter M. Tully Endowed Lecture on Financial Services and Economic Development strengthens ties with Capital Region businesses and provides a forum to explore financial sector developments. The institute's Advisory Board includes members from Key Corp; AT&T; Chase Manhattan Bank, NA; Fleet Bank; ALBANK; Independent Bankers Association of New York State; and the New York State Department of Economic Development.

Prominent Alumni

Prominent alumni of the School of Business include Betty Barnette, Treasurer of the City of Albany; Josephine Farinella, a partner in the firm Farinella Construction Co. Inc.; Charles A. Reinemann, Vice President of Investments and Financial Consultant for Smith Barney, a member of Travelers Group; and Kelly Mansfield Waechter, former Vice President for Key PrivateBank.

The College and Environs

Founded in 1920 by the Sisters of Saint Joseph of Carondelet, Saint Rose is a private, independent, coeducational institution located on a 25-acre urban residential campus in Albany, New York, the state capital. The College serves approximately 4,000 graduate and undergraduate students. Albany offers a wide variety of entertainment and cultural events. The Adirondack and Catskill Mountains of New York and the Green Mountains of Vermont are within easy driving distance. In addition, New York City, Montreal, and Boston are each less than 4 hour's drive away.

Facilities

The campus of sixty-two historic and contemporary buildings features the Neil Hellman Library, Science Center, Learning Center, Pauline K. Winkler Speech-Language and Hearing Center, music building, Picotte Hall art center, Campus Activities Center, athletic facilities, and renovated Victorian homes.

Two classrooms designed to facilitate faculty-student interaction are reserved for use by M.B.A. classes. Both classrooms feature state-of-the-art technology that allows faculty members to utilize computer-based instructional support.

The open-stack Neil Hellman Library contains more than 195,000 volumes, 1,050 periodical subscriptions, 215,000 titles on microform, and a collection of rare books. The library's resources include an online catalog, CD-ROM databases, librarian-assisted database searching, Internet access, and interlibrary loan services.

On-campus housing for graduate students consists of five residence halls and eleven apartments. Off-campus housing also is readily available in the vicinity of Saint Rose.

Technology Environment

The use of computers is integral to the course work of M.B.A. students; many assignments require proficiency with word processing, spreadsheet, and presentation software applications. The College's campuswide network provides access to PC and Macintosh computer laboratories and library facilities as well as the Internet, World Wide Web, cable television, and telephone. User assistance and laser printing are available in all computer laboratories, and some also offer scanning and color printing capabilities.

Placement

The College's Center for Career Development and Services provides students and alumni with career assessment and counseling, computerized placement and resume services, a computer-assisted career guidance system and job searching, a career resource center, job banks, resume development information, resume referral, credential files, on-campus interviews, videotaped mock interviews, job fairs, and workshops.

Admission

Admission to any of the three M.B.A. program options is dependent upon the completion of an undergraduate degree program at an accredited college or university. An applicant with a background in any undergraduate major is qualified to apply; however, students must meet M.B.A. program prerequisites prior to beginning their studies.

Applicants must file a completed application form, official transcripts from all colleges and universities attended, a personal essay, and two letters of recommendation for graduate study. There is a nonrefundable application fee of $25. International students should request the international application. Only individuals with an undergraduate GPA of less than 3.0 must submit Graduate Management Admission Test (GMAT) scores. Applicants whose native language is not English must submit TOEFL scores.

Finances

Tuition for the 1998–99 academic year is $338 per semester hour of credit. Saint

Rose serves graduate students through a comprehensive program of federal, state, and institutional financial aid, which may include Federal Stafford Student Loans (subsidized and unsubsidized), the New York State Tuition Assistance Program (TAP), graduate assistantships, graduate multicultural scholarships, or graduate merit scholarships, if the applicant is qualified. Applicants are required to submit the Free Application for Federal Student Aid (FAFSA), the New York State Tuition Assistance application, and signed copies of federal and state income tax documents and W-2 wage statements. To be considered for assistance, students must file for aid by March 1 for the fall and summer semesters and by November 1 for the spring semester.

International Students

The College's Office of International Programs is located in the Center for Cultural Diversity. Also located on campus are the International Student Organization and an English Language Study Center (ELSC). A full-time adviser coordinates activities and programs for international students studying at Saint Rose, including orientation, immigration and personal advisement, language assessment and assistance, and the coordination of on- and off-campus community programs.

Application Facts and Dates

Application deadlines are December 1 for the spring semester, April 1 for the summer semester, and July 15 for the fall semester.

M.B.A. Program Director
School of Business
The College of Saint Rose
Albany, New York 12203-1490
Telephone: 518-454-5272
Fax: 518-458-5449
E-mail: mba@rosnet.strose.edu
World Wide Web: http://www.strose.
   edu

or

Dean of Graduate and Adult and
   Continuing Education Admissions
The College of Saint Rose
432 Western Avenue
Albany, New York 12203-1490
Telephone: 518-454-5143
Fax: 518-458-5479
E-mail: ace@rosnet.strose.edu

College of William and Mary

> ## OUR MISSION: REFLECTING WILLIAM AND MARY VALUES
>
> *The mission of the M.B.A. program at the College of William and Mary is to serve the commonwealth, the nation, and the international community by offering high-quality educational programs. Reflecting its tradition of excellence, the M.B.A. program accomplishes this mission by application of five basic principles: (1) reflecting William and Mary values; (2) teamwork and building leadership skills; (3) functional skill building; (4) interaction with the external community; and (5) learning through doing (internships and mandatory field studies).*
>
> *—Larry Pulley, Dean*

Programs and Curricular Focus

During the first year of the M.B.A. program, students are assigned to teams of 6 people with whom they work very closely. The members of these teams are very diverse in terms of gender, age, academic background, work experience, and areas of interest. The incoming class is made up of approximately 100 new students, divided into two sections of 50. Students take a mixture of courses in financial and managerial accounting, quantitative methods, operations management, organizational behavior, marketing, economics, finance, management communications, information systems, and business policy.

All entering students are required to bring a computer with them into the program. They are used consistently throughout their course work.

In the second year, students return from their highly successful internships ready to focus on their areas of concentration (accounting, finance, marketing, operations/information technology, or human resource management). Students also have the option of remaining on a generalist track, taking a combination of electives from different areas. All students participate in a field studies project, providing them with first-hand experience and the opportunity of making immediate contributions to the companies that participate.

Students and the M.B.A. Experience

William and Mary students bring with them a wide range and depth of experiences. Undergraduate majors range from anthropology to engineering, and work experiences extend from architectural engineering to nonprofit management to corporate finance.

About 40 percent of incoming students have liberal arts and science degrees and approximately 15 percent have engineering backgrounds. More than 95 percent of each entering class has at least two years of significant full-time work experience. Of each entering class (approximately 100 new students), 32 percent are women, 15 percent are students of color, and 12 percent are foreign nationals.

Special Features

Study-abroad opportunities are available during the first semester of the second year with Norges Handelshoyskole (Norwegian School of Economics) or the INCAE M.B.A. program in Costa Rica. Joint-degree programs are also available with the Marshall Wythe School of Law and the Thomas Jefferson Program in Public Policy.

William and Mary students are strongly encouraged to participate in one of the fifteen active committees within the MBAA (the student government organization).

Every William and Mary student participates in a field studies project during the second year. Students are given the opportunity to work with a team of students at a company (according to their area of interest) and complete a real hands-on project.

The Faculty

With more than 53 full-time faculty members on board, William and Mary offers an outstanding 4:1 ratio of students to professors. Not only do the professors possess a wide range of skills and backgrounds, they are widely known and are noted researchers and outstanding teachers. Students are encouraged to seek out professors for individual counseling and assistance; students are always welcome to discuss issues with their professors.

Graduate research assistants have excellent opportunities to participate in assisting faculty members with their active and diverse research projects during the second year of the program.

The Business School Network

Members of the Advisory Board at William and Mary take an active interest in the students. Twice a year they visit the campus and students give team presentations to them. Members of the Advisory Board and the alumni have ties to all the major industrial centers in the nation as those in select international cities.

Prominent Alumni

Prominent alumni are invited to address students and serve as active participants in the annual "Mock Interview Relay," which is always a successful event for

Crim Dell.

Wren Building.

both the students and alumni. They also serve as guest panelists and lecturers throughout the year.

The College and Environs

The College of William and Mary is the second-oldest institution of higher learning in the United States. It was founded in 1693 by King William III and Queen Mary II of England. Its alumni include 4 signers of the Declaration of Independence, 3 U.S. presidents, 4 justices of the Supreme Court, more than 30 U.S. senators, and more than 60 members of the House of Representatives.

Colonial Williamsburg is in close proximity to the school. In 1995 it was named one of the top six vacation spots for families in the U.S. Each year, students on field trips from all over the country visit this historic area. The

William and Mary campus is part of the Colonial Williamsburg tour and it boasts the oldest classroom in America (the original classroom from 1693 is still in operation).

Close to Williamsburg are the cities of Richmond, Newport News, Hampton, and Virginia Beach, homes to every type of business from international manufacturing facilities to Fortune 500 corporate headquarters.

Facilities

William and Mary has excellent resources available at Swem Library and has its own Professional Resource Center in Tyler Hall. In Blow Hall (where all William and Mary M.B.A. classes are held) is its computer lab, available for all M.B.A. students to use. All students bring their own computers with them into the program, and computer technology is used widely throughout the curriculum. All students are connected to and utilize the Internet on a constant basis.

Placement

William and Mary's Career and Employer Development Office, which works exclusively for the M.B.A. program, has an active staff of 3 full-time employees who work closely with each individual student in the program. The "Big Seven" of placement activities available within the M.B.A. program include The M.B.A. Connection; M.B.A. Career Coaches and Mentors; M.B.A. Career Conversations; M.B.A. Career Seminars; M.B.A. Mock Interview Relay; M.B.A. networking events in Washington, D.C.; New York, and Richmond; and M.B.A. internships.

Approximately 98 percent of all M.B.A. students take part in a summer internship program. At the time of graduation (early May each year), 90 percent of the class has been placed. Within three months of graduation, approximately 95 to

100 percent are placed. The average starting salary for 1998 graduates was approximately $60,000.

Admission

Requirements for admission include a minimum of two years of work experience, GMAT scores (the range of scores is usually 550–740, and a minimum of 580 is recommended), official transcripts from all colleges and universities attended, current resumes, and personal interviews (students unable to visit the campus personally due to time/distance constraints may arrange a telephone interview with the Director of Admissions). International students must also submit TOEFL scores (minimum recommended score 600). Admissions are made on a rolling basis beginning October 1 each year and ending May 1. Decisions are made within 2 weeks of a file being completed and students are notified immediately of their status.

Finances

Tuition for Virginia residents for 1998–99 is $6820; for out-of-state students it is $16,138. Average living expenses are estimated at approximately $16,000 per year.

Application Facts and Dates

For application materials, students should contact:

Ms. Susan Rivera
Director of M.B.A. Admissions/
   Student Services
College of William and Mary
P.O. Box 8795
Williamsburg, Virginia 23187-8795
Telephone: 757-221-2900
            757-221-2898
            888-203-6994 (toll-free)
Fax: 757-221-2958
E-mail: sgrive@dogwood.tyler.wm.edu
World Wide Web: http://business.tyler.
   wm.edu

Colorado State University

Fort Collins, Colorado

TRADITION, TECHNOLOGY, TRANSFORMATION

These words are at the heart of the College of Business at Colorado State University. Here a tradition of academic excellence merges with a contemporary focus on technology to bring transformation to students and businesses. The College is leading the way in the push to graduate decision makers who have the managerial knowledge and functional skills necessary for success in a technology-driven, global business environment.

—Daniel E. Costello, Dean

Programs and Curricular Focus

Diversity is a key word in the College of Business—diversity in programs as well as the student body. The College, accredited by AACSB–The International Association for Management Education, employs a full range of programs to address the needs of the entire spectrum of students: domestic and international, part-time and full-time, on-campus and off-campus distance learning. Students can obtain a general M.B.A. degree or an M.S. degree in business administration with a specific concentration. Students may complete the M.B.A. degree in one of four different programs: an accelerated eleven-month program, an Evening M.B.A. program, a Distance M.B.A. program, or an Executive M.B.A. program (Denver). The content of each program is integrative and has a strong emphasis on information technology, global issues, and teamwork.

The Accelerated M.B.A. program provides an opportunity to quickly supplement an undergraduate degree with a graduate business degree. This 36-credit program requires a full-time commitment and meets during the day, Monday through Friday.

The Evening M.B.A. program is designed to serve the needs of working professionals. This 36-credit program takes twenty-two months to complete, including one summer session. All classes meet in the evening, Monday through Thursday.

The College is very proud to be a nationally recognized leader in distance M.B.A. education. *Forbes* magazine ranks Colorado State University's Network for Learning (CSUN) program among the nation's top twenty distance degree programs. Through the CSUN program, the classroom is brought directly to the student via the Internet and videotape. The CSUN Distance M.B.A. program is designed to serve work-

ing professionals who need flexibility in schedule and location. There is no on-campus requirement; course work is completed entirely at a distance. This 36-credit program takes two or four years to complete and includes some summer classes.

The Executive M.B.A. program is an accelerated program designed for students who wish to complete their M.B.A. degree in twenty-one months. The schedule is sensitive to the needs of working professionals. The executive site is in Colorado State University's Denver Center, located in downtown Denver, Colorado. The facility, including a computer center with multimedia instructional equipment, is specifically designed to support a state-of-the-art M.B.A. curriculum.

Students and the M.B.A. Experience

Diversity and balance characterize the on-campus graduate student body, resulting in an interactive, stimulating learning environment. More than half of Colorado State's M.B.A. students establish their careers be-

fore enrolling in graduate school. The College admits a select number of highly qualified international students each year to maintain the international enrollment at approximately 30 percent of its graduate population.

The Faculty

Research conducted by the College of Business faculty has led to published articles in respected journals such as *The Journal of Marketing, The Academy of Management Review,* and *The Journal of Retailing.* Equally impressive is the extensive applied business experience of the faculty members. More than 50 percent have significant business experience in their professional portfolios. Faculty members integrate their applied business experience and their research experience to bring a balanced approach to classroom instruction, creating a learning environment that exemplifies the best in modern management education.

The Business School Network

The College of Business Advisory Council is a vital element in maintaining a productive relationship between the College of Business and the business and professional community. Membership includes upper-level managers from public and private institutions, government, and international firms. In a typical year, College of Business students have frequent opportunities to interact with corporate executives from major firms in all areas of business.

Rockwell Hall

The College and Environs
Colorado State University, located at the foot of the picturesque Rocky Mountains, is recognized worldwide for its contributions to technology and science, quality of instruction, and discoveries that improve the world's quality of life, health, environment, and economy. A Carnegie Foundation Class I research university, Colorado State represents the best of the land-grant traditions—education, research, and service. The College of Business contributes to the University's growth, prestige, and national acclaim through its emphasis on excellence in instruction and research.

The city of Fort Collins offers a relaxed lifestyle and an abundance of cultural and social activities. Skiing, hiking, backpacking, and water sports areas are all adjacent to Fort Collins. More than 53 miles of bikeways wind along the Cache la Poudre River. Fort Collins has a clear, dry climate with more than 300 days of sunshine and a generally pleasant temperature throughout the year.

Technology Environment
The future of business is inextricably linked to technology. The underlying philosophy at the College of Business is an integration of technology into the academic program. This integration prepares students for the future in two ways: first, by providing them with a tool bag that includes the ability to use technology in their chosen fields, and second, by helping them gain an understanding of the way technology will affect them and the business world in the future. Every graduate course is held in the College's new technology wing. Each state-of-the-art classroom in the new wing has an instruction station equipped with a computer with Internet access and the latest computerized presentation equipment. The College of Business supports two fully accessible computer labs for the exclusive use of business students. The Hewlett-Packard Student Computer Laboratory is equipped with seventy-four Pentium-class computers, including Windows 95–based PCs and Macintoshes, seven networked laser printers, two color printers, a scanner, and more than sixty soft-

ware packages. The computer teaching lab houses another thirty-three computers.

Placement
The University Career Center and the College of Business career counselors work closely with faculty members to offer a wide range of placement opportunities to master's candidates in business. Many local, national, and international firms have developed a recruiting relationship with Colorado State University. For example, Hewlett-Packard Company considers the College of Business one of their top ten recruiting schools. In 1997, Hewlett-Packard hired more graduates from Colorado State's College of Business than from any other business school in the country. In addition, the College of Business participates in the Rocky Mountain M.B.A. Consortium.

Admission
An applicant for admission must have earned a bachelor's degree in any field from an accredited college or university. Admission is dependent primarily on an integrated analysis of an applicant's undergraduate grade point average, score on the Graduate Management Admission Test (GMAT), and letters of recommendation. The Evening M.B.A. and CSUN Distance M.B.A. programs require a minimum of four years of work experience. The Denver Executive M.B.A. program requires a minimum of eight years of work experience.

If the applicant's native language is not English, the Test of English as a Foreign Language (TOEFL), with a minimum score of 565, is also required. International students are required to submit proof of adequate funding for support for the length of time necessary to obtain their degree, and they must have health insurance.

To request an information packet, students should visit the College on the World Wide Web at http://www.csu-business.net or contact the College admissions office (telephone: 970-491-6471).

Finances
The College offers several teaching and research assistantships in every business

discipline. In addition, tuition scholarships may be awarded. An application for a teaching or research assistantship is included in the application packet. Assistantships are not available for distance education students.

Tuition for a Colorado resident for the eleven-month Accelerated M.B.A. program is $1638 per semester, plus $516 for summer session. Resident tuition for the Evening M.B.A. program is $1202 per semester, plus $516 for summer session. Nonresident tuition for the Accelerated M.B.A. program is $5283 per semester, plus $1732 for summer session. Nonresident tuition for the Evening M.B.A. program is $3634 per semester, plus $1732 for summer session. Tuition for the CSUN Distance M.B.A. program is assessed per credit hour and written as a student credit hour (SCH). Tuition includes delivery of the tapes to the student or to the site but does not include the cost to return the tapes. Current rates are $328 per SCH to Colorado sites, $368 per SCH to non-Colorado sites, and $384 per SCH to individuals. These figures are based on the current published schedules and are subject to change without notice.

Prices for housing vary, depending on the type of housing, amenities, and proximity to campus. For detailed information on current housing costs and availability, students should contact the Office of Housing and Food Services (telephone: 970-491-6511).

Application Facts and Dates
Colorado State admits students to the Accelerated M.B.A. and Evening M.B.A. programs for the fall semester only. For information on application deadlines, students should visit the College's Web site at the address listed below. For information on the application deadlines for the Executive M.B.A. program, students should contact the EMBA Director at 303-534-3194. There is a limited number of seats available for each M.B.A. program, so students are encouraged to apply early. The graduate admission application requires a nonrefundable fee of $30. For further information, students should contact:

Dr. Jon Clark, Associate Dean
College of Business
Colorado State University
Fort Collins, Colorado 80523-1270
Telephone: 970-491-6471
Fax: 970-491-0596

Distance Education Center
College of Business
Colorado State University
Fort Collins, Colorado 80523-1270
Telephone: 800-491-4MBA (4622)
    Ext. 1 (toll-free)
Fax: 970-491-2348
World Wide Web: http://www.csu-business.net

COLUMBIA
BUSINESS
SCHOOL

Columbia University

Columbia Business School

New York, New York

THE GLOBAL M.B.A.

Given the constant changes in the global business environment, today's M.B.A. must equip students with practical, adaptable skills that give them a competitive edge and prepare them to be leaders in the international marketplace. Columbia Business School meets this challenge by combining an outstanding faculty with the unmatched resources of an Ivy League university in a living laboratory—New York City.

The School's location and strong relationships enable it to draw more than 300 business leaders to campus every year—as teachers, speakers, adjunct lecturers, and advisers. Whether they are headquartered in New York or just passing through, the opportunity to learn from those who have made an impact on the global business community adds to the School's unique academic and hands-on atmosphere.

The Columbia M.B.A. provides students with unparalleled opportunities and options for mobility across fields and industries in leadership roles and meeting the demands of the dynamic, international marketplace of the twenty-first century.

—Professor Meyer Feldberg, Dean

Programs and Curricular Focus

Hailed as one of the most innovative M.B.A. curricula, Columbia Business School's structure and course offerings prepare students to take leadership roles in tomorrow's fastest-growing industries, from media and entertainment to real estate finance, while giving them fundamental skills across all disciplines. Virtually every course, seminar, and conference approaches business as a global undertaking.

The first two terms of study consist of the core curriculum. Addressing four main themes—globalization, total quality management, ethics, and human resource management—the core is taught in clusters of approximately 60 students, which not only fosters cooperative and teamwork skills but also provides students with the opportunity to learn from the striking diversity of their peers and to form lasting bonds.

More than 180 elective courses in thirteen fields of concentration provide opportunities for second-year M.B.A. students to focus their studies. Combining strong offerings in the disciplines of accounting, finance, marketing, and management with cutting-edge concentrations such as entrepreneurship; media, entertainment, and communications; and real estate, students graduate with a breadth of basic skills and a depth of knowledge in their chosen field.

Students may opt to pursue one of the eleven dual-degree programs offered jointly by the Business School and other schools at Columbia University or may select electives at any of those schools. The Executive M.B.A. program allows executives, who are sponsored by their employers, to earn M.B.A.s without interrupting their careers in a flexible degree program that meets on Friday or every other Friday and Saturday.

Students and the M.B.A. Experience

Diversity and individuality are the hallmarks of the Columbia Business School student body. Approximately 38 percent of the students are women, and nearly one quarter are members of minority groups, making the School consistently the most diverse of the nation's top business schools. The School's global reputation and location in New York City attract large numbers of students from different cultures and backgrounds. A typical class includes lawyers, physicians, consultants, musicians, writers, professional athletes, and entrepreneurs. Their diverse interests are reflected in the more than ninety professional, social, and academic student-run organizations at the School. These clubs often sponsor programs and lectures that enhance classroom work and contribute to the community.

❖ Global Focus

Students, faculty, and members of the Columbia Business School community come from all parts of the nation and the globe, creating a vibrant international community. Hailing from nearly sixty countries, forty states, and 140 undergraduate institutions, the student body is highly talented and culturally diverse. One out of every 3 students was born outside of the U.S., and more than half of the students from the U.S. have lived or worked outside of the country. The majority of Columbia Business School students speak at least two languages fluently.

The Jerome A. Chazen Institute of International Business is the focal point for international programs at the School. The Institute sponsors overseas study tours to six continents, lecture series, conferences, and student-exchange programs in addition to business-oriented language programs.

The Faculty

Columbia Business School has a full-time faculty of 105. The faculty members combine excellence in teaching with rigorous research that adds to the core of academic scholarship and addresses issues of practical importance to the business-place. Their pioneering research, widespread consultation, and commitment to the creation of new knowledge produce an energy that carries into the classroom. More than 85 adjunct faculty members, professionals culled from the Fortune 500, bring their expertise and experience into the classroom in areas ranging from investment banking to new media and from venture capital to real estate. An outstanding resource, the faculty prepares students to solve real problems by blending theory with practice.

The Business School Network

Corporate Partnerships

The Business School's location and relationships with New York's largest firms and industry leaders create unique opportunities for students. During a typical day, students can attend a lecture featuring guest speakers from AT&T, Xerox, Avis, J. P. Morgan, the National

---

Professor Rajeev Kohli's class.

Basketball Association, or Donaldson, Lufkin & Jenrette; visit a major corporation's headquarters as part of a group project; or meet on campus with or in the downtown office of a recruiter for a discussion regarding employment opportunities. Many students take advantage of informational interviews with one of the Business School's 10,000 alumni who live in and around New York or of networking opportunities through forty alumni clubs around the world.

Contributing to the academic experience, the School draws adjunct professors from their offices to the classroom to add real-world application to course work. Courses such as Inner City Consulting, Initial Public Offerings, and Emerging Financial Markets are developed and co-taught by Business School faculty members and senior managers at selected corporations. A key competitive advantage is that students learn the pace, perspective, and culture of the business community from the inside out and can hit the ground running upon graduation.

Prominent Alumni
Alumni remain actively involved with the School, participating in student-run events, conducting admission interviews, and advising students through the Alumni Counseling Board. Many prominent alumni, including Warren Buffett (M.S. '51), Chairman, Berkshire Hathaway, Inc.; Michael Gould (M.B.A. '68), Chairman and CEO, Bloomingdale's; Henry R. Kravis (M.B.A. '69), founding partner, Kohlberg Kravis Roberts & Company; Rochelle Lazarus (M.B.A. '70), President and CEO, Ogilvy & Mather Worldwide; and Benjamin Rosen (M.B.A. '61), Chairman, Compaq Computer Corporation and Rosen Motors Corporation, contribute demonstrated leadership and management expertise as in-class lecturers, members of the School's governing board, and guest speakers at Business School events.

The College and Environs
Columbia University was founded in 1754 as King's College by a royal charter of King George II of England. It is the oldest institution of higher learning in the state of New York and the fifth oldest in the United States. Columbia University's campus, located on the Upper West Side of Manhattan in a hilly neighborhood called Morningside Heights, is bordered by Riverside Park and Morningside Park. The 36 acres include tree-shaded lawns and brick paths connecting stately buildings and the University's fifteen colleges and graduate schools.

Facilities
As part of the School's comprehensive facility development strategy, a new Business School classroom building, to be shared with the Law School, is scheduled to open in January 1999. It will provide state-of-the-art classrooms and group and team study and project space as well as reception and event space. Facility development plans include the renovation and reallocation of space in Uris Hall—the eight-story Business School building that houses the School's classrooms, faculty and administrative offices, the Thomas J. Watson Library of Business and Economics, Computing and Information Services, and a café. Other plans include the possible development of a new residence facility.

Placement
Columbia Business School maintains one of the strongest corporate recruiting programs, consistently ranking among the top five favorite hunting grounds of corporate recruiters. The School's proximity to Wall Street and to leading firms in all industries provides unparalleled opportunities for students. More than 400 companies recruited on-campus last year, and the School received more than 2,700 job postings from firms worldwide.

The recruiting environment is on-line, allowing more than 10,500 first- and second-year interviews to be scheduled annually. The Office of Career Services provides more than sixty workshops, seminars, and panels that cover topics ranging from conducting effective job searches and networking to career changes and from presentation skills to writing cover letters. Students can also take advantage of individualized career counseling and one-on-one resume reviews with Career Services officers.

Admission
Applicants are evaluated in three categories: professional promise, personal characteristics, and academic credentials. The School looks for well-rounded people from diverse economic, social, ethnic, geographic, and professional backgrounds. Ideal applicants have demonstrated leadership, have the ability to work as members of a team, and can contribute to the academic experience of their peers. Admission prerequisites include a bachelor's degree, a minimum of two years of work experience, GMAT scores, and, for international students, TOEFL scores. The School selects those applicants who have the focus and drive to become tomorrow's business leaders.

Finances
The cost of tuition per term at Columbia Business School for the 1998–99 academic year is $13,260. There are three kinds of financial aid available: fellowships, based on academic, professional, and personal merit; scholarships, based on financial need; and loans. Questions may be directed to the Office of Financial Aid, Room 218, Uris Hall (telephone: 212-854-4057).

Application Facts and Dates

Domestic application deadlines are April 20 for the fall semester, October 1 for the winter semester, and February 1 for the summer semester. International application deadlines are March 1 for the fall semester, October 1 for the winter semester, and February 1 for the summer semester. Decisions are sent out on a rolling basis.

For more information, students should contact:

Office of Admissions
Columbia Business School
Room 105, Uris Hall
Columbia University
3022 Broadway
New York, New York 10027
Telephone: 212-854-1961
Fax: 212-662-6754
E-mail: gohermes@claven.gsb.
    columbia.edu
World Wide Web: http://www.
    columbia.edu/cu/business/

 Concordia
UNIVERSITY

Concordia University

CONCORDIA UNIVERSITY EXCELLENCE CONFIRMED BY ACCREDITATION

Why should you choose Concordia University for your M.B.A.? The reason that has the greatest significance for most students is the University's accreditation by AACSB–The International Association for Management Education. This special designation is given to select schools that fulfill the rigorous standards in their teaching and research profiles, and Concordia is proud to be one of these. For you, the student, this means that you will receive excellent teaching, small classes, and direct personal contact with professors who are at the cutting edge of research in their fields. It also means that the high quality of your degree will be recognized by employers when you graduate, and it gives meaning to what we say about Concordia: "real education for the real world."

Concordia University is more than just academic excellence. We are also known for the approachability and friendliness of our faculty and staff members, and our students are the number one priority at the business school. In fact, our students are what make Concordia special. We have an outstanding group of individuals with a wealth of professional experience. Our students often say that after their classroom experience, they learn a great deal from their peers.

We believe that there is no other program that offers this combination of academic excellence, student diversity, and accessibility to the faculty and the staff.

—Lea Prevel Katsanis, Ph.D., Director, M.B.A. Program

Program and Curricular Focus

As the nature of business becomes more complex and new technologies speed up the tempo of change, the management of companies and institutions becomes increasingly a task for professionals. It is precisely with this fact in mind that the Concordia M.B.A. Program has been designed. Whether one's interests lie in achieving a high-level management position in industry or government, an entrepreneurial career, or simply extending one's education to increase the scope of opportunities, an M.B.A. from Concordia provides the necessary ingredients. These include an emphasis on teamwork, motivating others, and interpersonal skills in an applied learning environment.

In addition, Concordia University has been confirmed as one of the leading business schools by AACSB–The International Association for Management Education. Out of approximately 1,200 institutions that offer business programs, only 305 U.S. and four Canadian schools have accreditation. This designation is a seal of approval for the high quality of programs offered by Concordia University's Faculty of Commerce and Administration.

The Concordia M.B.A. Program emphasizes an interdisciplinary general management perspective. This orientation provides

students with the expertise they need to become effective business professionals. The program's overall goal focuses on the achievement of managerial success in an increasingly complex and competitive business environment. The objective of the program is to enable students to integrate the knowledge and skills they have acquired in the principal functional areas of business to achieve overall corporate goals; make decisions that reflect sensitivity to the relationships between the firm and the social, ethical, economic, and political environments in which it operates, both locally and internationally; apply the analytical, interpersonal, and communication skills necessary for the effective management of human capital, technical, and information resources; and refine their career goals to develop the confidence to confront an ever-changing business environment.

Students and the M.B.A. Experience

The Concordia M.B.A. student body consists of 375 individuals with varied academic, cultural, and professional backgrounds. This creates a dynamic learning environment in which students learn from each other. On average, students are 30 years of age with six years of full-time work experience. Women

comprise approximately 40 percent of the class. The ratio of full-time to part-time students is 60:40.

Concordia takes pride in providing its students with approachable and friendly faculty and staff members who treat them with respect. This makes the learning experience more effective and more enjoyable.

❖ Global Focus

The Concordia University curriculum is designed to take a global focus in all courses. In addition, a multicultural student body and faculty allows for diverse viewpoints and business philosophies. In keeping with this focus, exchange programs are available at Gothenburg School of Economics and Commercial Law in Sweden, the Schiller Institute at the University of Heidelberg in Germany, and the Centre d'Enseignement et de Recherche Applique au Management in France.

Special Features

The International Case Competition is an annual event that was created and is directed by students at Concordia University. M.B.A. programs from around the world participate in what has grown into a prestigious, highly recognized, five-day thirty-team competition. The event provides access to industry leaders and excellent opportunities for networking.

Another important feature of the M.B.A. program is the option of taking the practicum or business research paper. The practicum project provides students with an opportunity to carry out an in-depth investigation of an actual business problem within an organization. The business research paper is a one-on-one research project with a professor in a specialized area of interest to the student.

The Faculty

Concordia's faculty is one of the largest and most respected in Canada because of its experience and international background. Many professors are consultants in industry and government, and others are internationally known for their research. Faculty members are selected by a separate committee to be members of the core M.B.A. faculty, and appointments are made every three years. These faculty members have a special interest in the M.B.A. program and are a valuable resource to students. In addition, Concordia has faculty members who have attained spe-

cial recognition. For example, Professor Michel Laroche is a Fellow of the Royal Society of Canada; Professor Steven Appelbaum was recently selected for the *Financial Post's* Leaders in Management Award; and Associate Professor Bryan Barbieri was selected by the alumni to receive the Alumni Award for Excellence in Teaching.

The Business School Network

Corporate Partnership
The M.B.A. program is closely linked to the pharmaceutical industry in Canada. The Pharmaceutical Management Centre offers a seminar in pharmaceutical marketing, which is open to M.B.A. students. In addition, the University has linkages with the Canadian aviation industry.

Prominent Alumni
Concordia alumni hold many prominent industry positions around the world, and the University is proud to count the following individuals as its graduates: Holger Kluge, President of Personal and Commercial Banking, CIBC; Brian Steck, Chairman and CEO, Nesbitt Burns; Donald Wright, President and COO, Toronto Dominion Securities; Andre Desmarais, President and co-CEO, Power Corporation of Canada; and Robert Mac-Donald, President, Bell Helicopter Textron.

The College and Environs
Concordia University is an English-language university located in the city of Montreal, the second-largest French-speaking city in the world. Montreal is located on an island in the heart of the St. Lawrence Valley. It dates back to the seventeenth century and is built around a mountain known as Mont-Royal in the centre of the island. The city is within an hour's drive of New York and Vermont in the U.S. and a myriad of lakes and ski resorts in the Laurentian mountains and the Eastern Townships.

Few cities are as exciting and multidimensional as Montreal. As one of the great cities of the world, it has an Olympic Stadium, a famous hockey team, a National League baseball team, world-class art galleries, an excellent metro system, and some of the finest shops this side of the Atlantic. Montreal is a major financial, business, and industrial centre.

Facilities
The confident, modern stance of Concordia's downtown campus, where all the M.B.A. classes are held, is symbolic of the energy and forward thinking that have made this institution into one of the largest universities in Canada. The University has two campuses: the Sir George Williams Campus in the heart of the city and the Loyola Campus, nestled in a tranquil setting near Montreal West. The two campuses are connected by the door-to-door shuttle bus service operated by the University and by the bus and metro system of the city of Montreal.

Concordia offers a rich university experience to its community of more than 25,000 full- and part-time students. In its faculties—Arts and Science, Commerce and Administration, Engineering and Computer Science, and Fine Arts—there are more than 150 academic programs leading to bachelor's, master's, and doctoral degrees.

The Faculty of Commerce and Administration is located in the Guy Metro Building on the Sir George Williams campus. In addition to lecture halls and seminar rooms, it houses the Webster Library, which contains reference and research material selected to meet the specific needs of commerce and administration graduate students.

Technology Environment
The Faculty has its own computer lab with Pentium computers and a wide variety of

business software. Students are connected by e-mail to faculty and staff members and to each other for ease of communication.

Placement
Student job searches are supported by the Faculty of Commerce and Administration Placement Centre, which is instrumental in marketing Concordia graduates to major national and international corporations. Each year, on-campus information and recruiting sessions are held on an ongoing basis.

Admission
Acceptance into the Concordia M.B.A. Program is based on academic qualifications and work experience and is highly competitive. Applicants must have completed a bachelor's degree with high standing at a recognized institution and achieved a satisfactory score on the GMAT. A minimum of two years of full-time work experience is also required.

Finances
Annual program fees for 1998–99 for a full-time student registered in 30 credits per year are Can$2750 for Quebec residents, Can$3775 for residents of other Canadian provinces, and Can$9350 for international students. Costs for books and materials are approximately Can$800 per year. Beyond program costs, students should budget for living expenses of at least Can$11,000 per year. This figure is based on the standard needs of a single person and includes accommodation, groceries, clothing, public transportation, and miscellaneous expenditures.

For U.S. students, the favorable 40 percent exchange rate provides a significant benefit for both tuition and living expenses.

Application Facts and Dates

The program provides three entry dates per year: September, January, and May. The application deadlines for September entry are June 1 for Canadian residents and February 15 for international students; for January entry, they are October 30 for Canadian residents and June 15 for international students; and for May, February 28 for Canadian residents and October 15 for international students. Applications for full-time study should be submitted to the Faculty of Commerce and Administration at the address below, along with a Can$50 application fee. International students are eligible for full-time study only.

M.B.A. Program
Faculty of Commerce and
    Administration
Concordia University
1455 de Maisonneuve Boulevard
    West, GM-710
Montreal, Quebec H3G 1M8
Canada

Cornell University

Ithaca, New York

> ### SMALL . . . RIGOROUS . . . INNOVATIVE . . . INTERNATIONAL . . . CAREER RELEVANT
>
> *At Cornell's Johnson School, we have turned our classrooms into high-speed, interactive environments that are every bit as intense as life in the business world. The curriculum is built around career-relevant learning: real-time data analysis, live cases, immersion learning, and specialized leadership development. Our relatively small size encourages greater interaction among students than is typically found in larger schools. Our faculty members pride themselves on their accessibility as well as their superior teaching; their office doors—and not infrequently, their homes—are open to students. Our diverse international community ensures that developing a global perspective becomes a personal process rather than an academic exercise. Together, it adds up to a simultaneously challenging and supportive environment that is conducive to building the foundation for personal and professional success.*
>
> —Robert J. Swieringa, Dean

Program and Curricular Focus

The Johnson School program combines rigor and flexibility. A revamped first-year core includes greater integration between functional areas and a heavier emphasis on case analysis, strategy, and leadership, team-building, and communication skills.

Core courses are scheduled so that students may take electives during their first year and gain advanced training prior to the summer internship. Many students participate in the acclaimed immersion courses (currently offered in marketing, manufacturing management, finance, and investment banking). Immersion courses offer an integrated, real-world focus, which has made them vastly popular with students and recruiters alike.

The Parker Center's Wall Street–quality trading room (equipped with $1.5 million of commercial analyst software) and student-run investment fund offer hands-on experience in securities analysis and the opportunity to assist faculty members and the center's corporate partners in the development of money-management strategies.

The popular entrepreneurship program focuses on high-growth businesses and enables students to interact closely with successful entrepreneurs and to work as consultants for start-up and small businesses. The leadership program is one of the few to combine self-assessment, academic theory, and leadership projects to ensure the broadest impact.

Johnson students are also encouraged to make full use of Cornell's other internationally renowned programs, such as industrial and labor relations, biotechnology, law, engineering, health-care management, public policy, international development, hotel administration, Asian languages, and advanced computing. One quarter of the M.B.A. program, and sometimes more, may be fulfilled with any graduate-level course at Cornell.

Students and the M.B.A. Experience

The Johnson School tradition of both working and socializing together leads to an unusually strong sense of community and collegiality. The average age of students is 28, and the average work experience is five years. Women comprise 30 percent of the class; members of minority groups, 11 percent; and international students, 28 percent. About one third of the students are married.

❖ Global Focus

Exchange programs with sixteen overseas universities, intersession study tours (recent destinations include China, India, Romania, and Venezuela), and internships through the School's Central and Eastern European Development (CEED) Program allow students to experience international business firsthand. On campus, international business concerns are fully integrated into the curriculum. The joint M.B.A./M.A. in Asian studies and

Cornell's varied offerings in regional and language studies supplement the Johnson School program. The large number of students from outside the U.S. ensures a global perspective and forms the foundation for a future international business network. The Johnson School is one of the only business schools to allow academic credit for foreign language study.

Special Features

The highly competitive two-year, full-tuition-plus-stipend Park Leadership Fellowships, open only to U.S. citizens, are awarded to 30 entering M.B.A. students each year. Park Fellows receive enriched leadership opportunities and are expected to complete a leadership project.

The Twelve-Month M.B.A. Option allows individuals with graduate degrees in scientific or technical fields to complete an accelerated core curriculum during the summer (June to August) and join the second-year class in the fall.

Joint-degree programs exist in human resources management, engineering, law, and Asian studies. A certificate in financial engineering is also available.

The Faculty

Johnson School faculty members consistently receive high marks for the quality of their teaching and research. Because of their links with the business world, they are also a good resource for sound career advice. Reflecting the School's strong commitment to promoting women in business, one quarter of the faculty members are women.

The Business School Network
Corporate Partnerships

The Visiting Executives Program, immersion courses, the Park Leadership Fellows Program, the Managerial Skills Program, and the Johnson Mentor Program, as well as the large number of conferences, symposia, and networking events organized by the student professional organizations, provide a wide variety of formal and informal opportunities to interact with successful business leaders. Corporate advisory boards, and often corporate sponsorship, exist for a number of programs, including the Parker

The renovation of Sage Hall, the Johnson School's new home, has turned one of Cornell's most dramatic buildings into one of the most technologically advanced management education centers in the world.

Center, the entrepreneurship program, and the immersion courses. Corporate leaders also sit on the Johnson School Advisory Board.

The College and Environs

Cornell is an Ivy League university, and its 19,000 students hail from more than 100 countries. Ithaca, with its combination of cosmopolitan sophistication and small-town accessibility, offers residents the best of both worlds—diverse cultural offerings and recreational activities in a beautiful setting of lakes, waterfalls, forests, and countryside. Students with families find it a hospitable place for balancing family and career; the public school system is excellent.

Facilities

Sage Hall, the Johnson School's new home, is located in the center of the Cornell campus. The $38.2-million

historic renovation project, completed in 1998, has turned one of Cornell's original and most dramatic buildings into one of the most technologically advanced management education centers in the world.

Technology Environment

Sage Hall's state-of-the-art technology infrastructure includes fiber-optic cable throughout the building, 1,400 computer ports, distance learning and teleconferencing capabilities, three student computing labs, a multimedia lab, and access to live electronic data feeds from the top financial information services, including Bridge, Bloomberg, and First Call. The Parker Center's "trading room" is equipped with more than $1.5 million of the most sophisticated analyst software. Beginning in 1998, entering students are required to own a personal computer.

Placement

More than 175 companies recruit on campus, and students average ten on-campus interviews for permanent jobs. Ninety-six percent of students had job offers by graduation, and satisfaction with those jobs averaged 9.2 on a 10-point scale. Through Career Network, 800 alumni in the U.S. and overseas offer information and mock interviews, resume critiques, job search advice, and correspondence opportunities. Individual counseling sessions support targeted job searches.

The new Johnson Mentor Program matches M.B.A. students with successful Cornell alumni for advice and support in their fields of interest. In addition to School-sponsored networking programs, the School participates in a variety of career forums and corporate recruiting events across the U.S. and Europe. A special fund supplements salaries for summer internships at small entrepreneurial and midsize companies. The School also offers a variety of lifetime career services for alumni.

Admission

The Admissions Committee considers an applicant's prior academic performance,

GMAT scores, range and depth of work experience, demonstrated leadership, interpersonal and writing skills, interviewing ability, extracurricular and community involvement, career aspirations, recommendations, and previous achievements. For the class of 1997, the average GMAT score was 636; the average undergraduate GPA, 3.3; and the average TOEFL score, 643. Interviews are set at the discretion of the Office of Admissions, and both staff member and alumni interviews are given equal weight. All applicants are encouraged to visit the campus; the Office of Admissions arranges for a student host.

Finances

In 1998–99, tuition is $24,400. Books cost $890, and housing and food costs approximately $7300 (based on the cost of sharing a moderately priced apartment). The School awards more than $1.5 million in merit-based scholarships each year in addition to need-based loans and work-study funds. International applicants receive similar consideration as U.S. citizens for merit-based awards.

Application Facts and Dates

Application deadlines are November 15, January 15 (final deadline for the Twelve-Month M.B.A. Option and Park Fellowships), March 1 (final deadline for international students), and April 15. Decision letters are mailed January 31, April 1, May 15, and June 15. For more information, students should contact:

Office of Admissions
Sage Hall
Cornell University
Ithaca, New York 14853-6201
Telephone: 607-255-4526
    800-847-2082 (toll-free in
    the U.S. and Canada)
Fax: 607-255-0065
E-mail: mba@johnson.cornell.edu
World Wide Web: http://www.johnson.
   cornell.edu/

Cranfield University

THE CRANFIELD PROCESS

I was attracted to Cranfield originally as a recruiter of M.B.A. graduates for an international consultancy. Cranfield was my first choice because of the high quality of the graduates not only in terms of their ability and experience but also of the perceptible difference the Cranfield experience had made to them.

The sheer high quality and diversity of our student body remain the cornerstone of the program. The highly participative and intensive process seeks to leverage upon that asset and to ensure not only the acquisition of general management knowledge and skills but also, centrally, the development of the personal managerial effectiveness of the participants.

The program is continuously developed and innovated to ensure that it meets the ever-changing needs of the world of management now and in the future. The Cranfield M.B.A. has proved to be an important springboard to success.

—Professor Leo Murray, Director

Programs and Curricular Focus

The Cranfield experience is the result of a combination of the personal learning process, the context in which the learning takes place, and the specific content of the program. This total experience is unique to Cranfield.

Central to the learning process are the emphasis on personal development that runs through the whole program, the sharing of experience and skills through the learning teams, and the practical case study approach.

At Cranfield, participants learn in the context of a stimulating environment and a mature and diverse student body. Faculty members have management experience and maintain strong links with organizations from the private and public sectors.

The content of the program is both practical and international. It is constantly updated and reviewed to ensure that what is learned at Cranfield will enable participants to cope with the speed of change and meet the challenges of a dynamic, global business environment.

The one-year program is very intensive, covering much of the same ground in the four taught terms as the traditional two-year American programs. During the first two terms, participants increase their knowledge of the basic elements of business management. The course structure stresses the integral nature of key functional areas and the interrelationships between them. Terms three and four provide the opportunity to customize the program by selecting a group of courses from more than seventy electives, including European languages.

Cranfield also offers a two-year, part-time Executive M.B.A. program, enabling participants to remain in full-time employment. They attend Cranfield on sixteen weekends (all day Friday and Saturday) and for four 1-week residential periods each year.

Students and the M.B.A. Experience

With an age range from 25 to 45 (average age 31) and approximately eight years of work experience behind them, participants come from a wide variety of industry backgrounds and job functions: from all aspects of business through the armed forces and the public sector to the professions. The Cranfield approach to learning, with its emphasis on learning teams and the use of case studies, draws on the experience and skills of these participants. The student body is becoming increasingly international, with 40 percent of the current students coming from overseas, representing twenty-eight countries. Women make up about 24 percent of the total. The annual intake of around 160 students is divided into four streams, ensuring class sizes of less than 50. The program is large enough to provide a diversity of experience, and yet small enough for all the students to get to know each other, creating a cooperative but dynamic environment for study.

Cranfield's horseshoe-shaped lecture theaters encourage high-level classroom discussions.

Cranfield's M.B.A. students come from all over the world.

❖ Global Focus

Cranfield's core programs all have an international perspective, and there are specific core courses in corporate and international strategy and global business environment. Elective courses give the opportunity to study business and management in the Far East, the Americas, Europe, and developing countries. Exchange programs exist with schools in the Far East, the U.S.A., South Africa, and continental Europe, and there is a double-degree program with EM Lyon in France. Increasingly, students are undertaking overseas, short consultancy-type projects as part of the program.

Special Features

A four-week preprogram English language and business culture course is offered to students speaking English as a second language and may be a condition of the offer of placement in the program. The course prepares students for the intensive workload and participative style of teaching at Cranfield by means of interactive lectures, group discussions, individual presentations, mini-projects, role play, and report writing.

The Faculty

The program is taught by people who understand the problems of putting theory into practice. The majority of Cranfield faculty members have managerial experience, a strength reinforced by close links with outside organizations through consultancy, sponsored research, and teaching on executive development programs with practicing managers. Most of the faculty members are preeminent in their field, with a significant number of

books, publications, and articles to their names. With some 90 members in the full-time teaching staff, 18 visiting professors, and 36 research staff members, the School of Management faculty is one of the largest in Europe.

The Business School Network

In addition to the permanent faculty, Cranfield has more than 40 visiting fellows, including a number of high-profile leaders of industry.

Several of the core and elective courses involve students in working on projects with outside organizations. These include a business check-up course, during which teams of students carry out a complete business audit.

M.B.A. participants also have structured access to the 6,000 senior managers who attend the School's executive development programs each year.

The College and Environs

Founded in 1967, the School is a faculty of Cranfield University, and the campus is entirely postgraduate, serving some 1,500 master's and doctoral students. Set in a peaceful area of the Bedfordshire countryside, Cranfield is midway between Oxford and Cambridge, only an hour's drive from London and a similar distance from Stratford-upon-Avon, birthplace of William Shakespeare. Although the setting is rural, Cranfield is only 5 miles from the fastest-growing business and industrial center in Britain, Milton Keynes, with all its sporting and cultural amenities. The location, away from the distractions of city life, fosters a positive community spirit amongst the students.

Placement

The caliber of the student body and the efficiency of the Career Development Service give participants the edge in their job search. The School has its own Career Development Office dedicated to the unsponsored M.B.A. students. Services include personal planning and stocktaking workshops; lectures on various aspects of job searching; individual career counseling sessions; seminars with alumni on networking, careers, and CV writing; advice and assistance on interview techniques and researching companies; and corporate presentations. A "liftoff" elective course at the end of the program prepares students for integration back into the workforce. The School's alumni association also operates an Executive Recruitment Service.

Admission

Entry requirements include a good degree from a U.K. university or its equivalent from a similar overseas institution, at least three years of post-qualification work experience, and a good GMAT score. An IELTS or TOEFL score is required from candidates for whom English is a second language.

Finances

Tuition fees for all students for the 1998–99 academic year are £15,000 sterling. Candidates should allow approximately £7000 sterling for accommodation, living costs, and books for the one-year program. Fees for the 1999–2000 part-time M.B.A. program will be £10,000 per annum.

Application Facts and Dates

Places are offered on a continuing basis from January onward. Although there is no cutoff date, early application is strongly recommended. Processing applications and arranging interviews for overseas candidates takes about four weeks, and a decision can normally be expected within a week of the interview. The application forms can be found on the School's Web address (http://www.cranfield.ac.uk/som/applicfo.htm) and downloaded onto a PC for completion.

Mrs. Pat Hayes
Admissions Officer
Cranfield School of Management
Cranfield, Bedford, England MK43 0AL
Telephone: 44(0)1234 754431
Fax: 44(0)1234 752439
E-mail: p.hayes@cranfield.ac.uk
World Wide Web: http://www.cranfield.ac.uk/som/

Dalhousie University

Halifax, Nova Scotia, Canada

PREPARING STUDENTS FOR A COMPLEX SOCIETY

We provide students with an excellent general management education, a true appreciation of effective people skills, and a high level of technical abilities. The M.B.A. degree is designed to meet the needs of active professionals from the private, public, and nonprofit sectors. Students work closely together and with faculty members in a small urban environment that provides for excellent quality of life. The program assists students in developing and enhancing the critical values and talents necessary to solve the problems of a complex society, gives them an edge in a highly competitive job market, and better prepares them for life in a rapidly changing, technological society.

—Philip J. Rosson, Ph.D., Dean, Faculty of Management

Programs and Curricular Focus

The Dalhousie University M.B.A. Program brings together intelligent and highly motivated men and women from Canada and other nations. They are involved in a demanding, globally focused curriculum by an internationally respected faculty. The program makes frequent use of the Atlantic Canadian business community to enrich the M.B.A. learning experience through practical application of skills and abilities.

The Dalhousie M.B.A. degree is recognized internationally for its excellence. Top Canadian firms actively recruit Dalhousie M.B.A. graduates, who are supported in their job search by the Career Resource Centre. Whether a student wants to work for a multinational corporation, a small start-up company, or start one of his or her own, the curriculum provides the knowledge, skills, and abilities to succeed. Highly motivated classmates significantly enhance the learning environment and provide a lifetime international network of friends.

Dalhousie's Faculty of Management offers two options for graduate business education: the Two-Year M.B.A. Program, which is twenty months (two 8-month academic periods) or an Accelerated Ten-Month M.B.A. Program for applicants with an undergraduate degree in business. Both programs are offered part-time and are usually completed within three to six years.

The M.B.A./LL.B. Program is a four-year joint-degree program offered by the Faculty of Management and Dalhou-

sie Law School. It begins only in September and requires full-time attendance.

Students and the M.B.A. Experience

Dalhousie's culture encourages students to grow with, rather than at the expense of, their peers. About 50 percent of the students in each class are native to central and western Canada. The international and domestic students come from varied ethnic and socioeconomic backgrounds. International students represent more than 10 percent of the student body. Women constitute about one third of each class. Seventy-five percent of the students have worked two years or more before enrollment, with an average of 4½ years of work experience. Students average 28 years of age. The students come from diverse academic backgrounds ranging from the arts to the sciences.

❖ Global Focus

The Dalhousie M.B.A. Program emphasizes international content throughout the M.B.A. curriculum. Students are continually exposed to a global perspective of management through the first-year curriculum. Students gain additional exposure and experience through the Centre for International Business Studies. The Centre offers a variety of second-year elective courses focused specifically on international business, the Foreign Study Mission, and international internships.

Dalhousie M.B.A. students can also participate in exchange programs with a

number of top business schools in Europe, Latin America, and Asia. Exchanges add an even greater international dimension to the M.B.A. education. Students can elect to study abroad for one term after completion of the first year of the M.B.A. Program. The School's Centre for International Business Studies, in addition to developing the international business curriculum, coordinates an annual Foreign Study Mission and international internships.

Special Features

Dalhousie offers students a unique experience among Canadian M.B.A. programs because of its small size of fewer than 200 students. The size allows more academic and social involvement between faculty members and students and among students themselves. It allows faculty members to maintain an open-door policy and administer more team projects and directed studies, including a major consulting project for business clients in the second year. In these projects, student teams work with local businesses on key issues and problems, presenting solutions to the clients at year's end.

A variety of teaching approaches are used, including lectures/discussions, case studies, team projects, simulation exercises, and independent study. With a student-faculty ratio of 8:1, each student is ensured individual attention.

The Faculty

Professors and researchers include nationally and internationally renowned experts in core business areas and in information sciences, international business, finance, and marketing. Together they provide an open, supportive, and balanced approach, enabling the student to bring theory and real-world experience together.

The Business School Network
Corporate Partnerships

Dalhousie's M.B.A. Program, located in downtown Halifax, takes full advantage of its proximity by drawing on Atlantic Canadian business leaders as instructors

in classrooms and as speakers at numerous special events. Group projects in the M.B.A. program use local businesses as the focal point for their activities. The School's Advisory Board comprises the top business leaders in Canada, who regularly meet at the school to offer their advice and assistance.

Prominent Alumni

Dalhousie's M.B.A. Program has produced more than 2,000 graduates who occupy significant leadership positions in business and organizations throughout Canada and internationally. They comprise part of the growing Dalhousie University alumni network of business contacts and friends, which includes graduates of the University of Toronto Bachelor of Commerce Program and other management programs.

The College and Environs

Dalhousie University is set in a picturesque urban campus with appealing ivy-covered schools, libraries, resource centres, recreational facilities, and dormitories. The University is centrally located in historic Halifax, Nova Scotia's capital city and Atlantic Canada's premier centre for business, international trade, the arts, and entertainment.

In addition to being the regional center for finance, government, health care, and education, the city enjoys an entrepreneurial spirit and an information technology community growing in international success and reputation. Greater Halifax has a population of about 350,000, which makes it big enough to have many of the good things of a larger city—such as cultural activities, sports,

nightlife, public transportation, and an international airport—as well as many of the best aspects of a smaller city.

Technology Environment

Students have access to some of the best communication technology available on university campuses today. They communicate with each other, with outside businesses, and with the world's research resources at the touch of a button. State-of-the-art multimedia stations, color printers, presentation and layout software, and analytical programs are just a few of the technology resources readily available in the School's computer facilities.

Placement

The M.B.A. Career Resource Centre actively helps students prepare themselves for the job search and recruitment process. The Career Resource Centre provides a job-listing service, an on-campus recruiting program, and assistance to the M.B.A. alumni. Last year, more than seventy companies were in contact with the Career Resource Centre to recruit Dalhousie M.B.A. graduates. Dalhousie's Career and Counseling Centre helps students prepare and manage their careers. The Career and Counseling Centre offers individual career counseling, resume clinics, mock interview sessions, and a career resource library.

Admission

Candidates for admission are evaluated on a total portfolio of previous performance, personal characteristics, life experiences, and professional and academic references. Candidates must

have a recognized undergraduate degree with a minimum B average in their final two years of study (70 percent, a 3.0 GPA, or Second Class Standing with Honours); GMAT results (scores above 550 preferred); full-time work experience (two years or its equivalent preferred); demonstrated evidence of leadership, initiative, and a superior capacity for high-level work productivity; and two professional or academic reference letters. A very good command of both written and spoken English is essential for all incoming graduate students. International students must submit results of the TOEFL exam (normally 580 or greater).

Finances

Tuition for the 1998–99 academic year is Can$4975 for Canadian full-time M.B.A. students and Can$1725 for part-time students. International students pay Can$7925 for the full-time program and Can$4675 for the part-time program. In addition to tuition fees, a full-time student spends approximately Can$1500 per year on other fees, books, case materials, and supplies. Living expenses, food, lodging, and personal expenses are minimally estimated to be Can$8000 for the academic year. Some financial assistance is available to qualified applicants.

International Students

Diversity in Dalhousie's M.B.A. Program includes a rich mix of cultural and ethnic backgrounds of students. The M.B.A. Program enrolls about 15 percent of each class from many different countries outside of Canada, including Japan, Bosnia, Russia, China, Sweden, and the United States.

Application Facts and Dates

Applicants to the full-time program are admitted only in September of each year. Canadian applicants must forward complete application documents by June 1. International students must complete their application process by April 1 at the latest. Applicants to the part-time program are subject to the deadlines noted above.

Mr. Phillip Rees
M.B.A. Program Director
School of Business Administration
Dalhousie University
6152 Coburg Road
Halifax, Nova Scotia
Canada B3H 3J5
Telephone: 902-494-2846
            888-432-5622 (toll-free)
Fax: 902-494-1107
E-mail: philip.rees@dal.ca
World Wide Web: http://www.mgmt.
    dal.ca/

Dartmouth College

The Amos Tuck School of Business

Hanover, New Hampshire

A CHALLENGE YOU FACE TOGETHER

A student once said that when you graduate from Tuck, you've gained your education, your diploma, and friends for life. That statement captures something very special about Tuck that goes beyond statistics. Without a doubt, Tuck is one of the most selective and academically challenging M.B.A. programs. We provide students with an excellent general management education, a true appreciation of effective people skills, and a high level of technical abilities. Although the Tuck experience is rigorous, it is also supportive. Students work closely together, and with faculty, in a small-town, rural New England environment that provides for excellent quality of life. If you are interested in Tuck, I suggest that you contact some of our alumni. They are the best evidence of the value of the Tuck M.B.A..

—Paul Danos, Dean

Programs and Curricular Focus

Founded in 1900, Tuck was the first graduate school of management in the world, and it is the only top U.S. business school that offers the M.B.A. degree exclusively.

During the first year of study, all students take a set of fourteen required, equal-credit courses. Integrative, interactive, and international aspects of management weave through the curriculum. During every term of the first year, students participate in an integrative learning exercise. Interactive abilities are enhanced through management communication and organizational behavior courses, frequent team projects, oral presentations, and written assignments. International dimensions of management are emphasized in global economic environment and international leadership courses and in most other courses as well. Over one third of all course content is international. Half of all Tuck faculty members have lived and taught overseas.

Building on their first-year background, second-year students select courses according to their interests and career aspirations. They choose from over fifty elective courses without requiring a specific major. Students may undertake independent study projects that earn credit as second-year electives.

New exchange programs are available with the HEC in France; Templeton College in Oxford, England; and IMD in Switzerland. These programs are in addition to Tuck's exchange programs with the London School of Business; the Instituto de Estudios Superiores in Barcelona, Spain; and the International University of Japan. Joint-degree programs are available in international affairs (with Tufts University's Fletcher School of Law and Diplomacy), medicine (with Dartmouth Medical School), and engineering (with Dartmouth's Thayer School of Engineering).

In May 1997, Tuck formed a global alliance with Oxford University's Templeton College (UK) and the HEC School of Management (France) to pursue innovative high-technology collaboration. The alliance is an opportunity for students, faculty members, and alumni from each school to come together in the virtual classroom and share knowledge, expertise, and ideas.

Students and the M.B.A. Experience

Tuck's culture encourages students to grow with, rather than at the expense of, their peers. International students make up 19 percent of Tuck's overall student population. International and domestic students come from varied ethnic and socioeconomic backgrounds. Members of minority groups represent more than 35 percent of the student body. Women constitute about one third of each class, and married students represent approximately one quarter of the student population. All students at Tuck have worked prior to coming to campus. The average student has five years of work experience. Students average 27 years of age. About 40 percent majored in business or economics before coming to Tuck. Twenty-three percent studied engineering, and many have graduate degrees.

Special Features

Tuck is unique among M.B.A. programs because of its small size of fewer than 400 students. The size allows more intellectual and social involvement between faculty members and students and among students themselves. It allows faculty members to administer more team projects, including a consulting project for business clients in the first term. In these projects, student teams work with local businesses on predefined problems, presenting solutions to the clients at term's end. Another enriching student project is the TYCOON business simulation game. Devised and implemented by a Tuck graduate, TYCOON is a computerized simulation where teams of students compete with other teams to successfully launch a project.

The Faculty

Tuck faculty members are renowned for their teaching and scholarly excellence. A variety of teaching approaches are used, including lecture/discussions, case studies, team projects, simulation exercises, and independent studies. With a student-faculty ratio of 10:1, each student is assured ample interaction and individual attention.

The Business School Network

Corporate Partnerships

Nearly 200 top executives, many of whom are Tuck alumni, come to Hanover every year to participate in the Visiting Executive Program. Among the visiting executives Tuck has hosted recently are Robert Galvin, Chairman, Executive Committee of the Board of Directors, Motorola Inc.; Michael Eisner, Chairman and CEO, The Walt Disney Company; John E. Pepper, CEO, the Procter & Gamble Company; John Amerman, Chairman and CEO, Mattel, Inc; and Janet Robinson, President and General Manager, *The New York Times*.

Prominent Alumni

Among the best known of Tuck's business graduates are John W. Amerman, Chairman and CEO of Mattel, Incorporated (Class of 1954); Andrew C. Sigler, Chairman of the Board of Champion International (Class of 1956); John H. Foster, Chairman and CEO of NovaCare (Class of 1967); Frank C. Herringer, President of Transamerica Corporation (Class of 1965); Christopher A. Sinclair, President and CEO of PepsiCo Foods and Beverages

Tuck Hall—the first building on campus.

International (Class of 1973); Paul N. Clark, President of the Pharmaceutical Division and Senior Vice President, Abbott Laboratories (Class of 1971); Lisa A. Conte, President and CEO of Shaman Pharmaceuticals Inc. (Class of 1985); Noreen Doyle, Head of Syndications and Credit, Banking Unit, European Bank for Reconstruction and Development (Class of 1974); Edmond F. Noel Jr., President and CEO of Colorado Sports Council (Class of 1969); Didier R. Pineau-Valencienne, Le President-Directeur Général, Groupe Schneider (Paris) (Class of 1957); and L. William Seidman, Chief Commentator, CNBC (formerly Chairman of FDIC) (Class of 1944).

The College and Environs

Tuck is located on the campus of Dartmouth College in picturesque Hanover. Students enjoy full use of Dartmouth's academic and cultural facilities. The libraries comprise one of the finest collections in New England. The Hopkins Center for the Performing Arts offers a broad range of locally and internationally produced theater, music, dance, and film. The Hood Museum of Art presents exhibitions from all cultures and periods. Outdoor activities are a favorite of Tuck students and the Dartmouth community at large. Dartmouth's athletic facilities include several gymnasiums, pools, skating rinks, and weight-training equipment. There is also a boat house, golf course, and ski area.

Technology Environment

Dartmouth College and the Tuck School have always been at the forefront of new technology. Tuck's cutting-edge computing environment entered a new era in 1996 with the complete renovation of its student computer lab and the addition of the Whittemore Wing for Information Technology. This new facility offers the latest in desktop and mobile computing along with facilities for videoconferencing, multimedia production, data visualization, and group collaboration. All classrooms and study rooms at Tuck are equipped with computers and network jacks, which provide access to library databases, online information services, e-mail and bulletin boards, file service, high-speed laser printers, and the World Wide Web. Projectors in all classrooms support the use of computers and video for instruction and student presentations. Network jacks in all student dormitory rooms and dial-up support for students off campus guarantee that all these services can be accessed from student computers as well. In addition, all students are required to own a laptop computer.

Placement

Beginning early in the fall, first-year students may attend career panels and company briefings. Assistance is offered in resume writing and interviewing skills. The career resource library contains extensive and frequently updated company information, files on growth industries, and handout materials to help students prepare for their job search. Each year more than 140 leading companies send representatives to interview graduating students on campus, and more than 100 companies come to select summer interns. In addition, more than 700 companies contact Tuck with job listings.

Admission

The application consists of a personal application form, essay questions, official transcripts from every college or university ever attended, at least two letters of recommendation, scores from the GMAT taken within five years, and a nonrefundable application fee of $100. Applicants for whom English is not their native language or who have not attended an undergraduate institution in which English is the language of instruction must take the Test of English as a Foreign Language (TOEFL). Interviews are not required for admission but are encouraged. Off-campus interviewing is often available.

Finances

Tuition for the 1997–98 school year was $24,900. This charge covered instruction, instructional facilities, and infirmary care services. For tuition, food, room, books and supplies, and personal expenses, a single student should budget approximately $40,000; a married student, approximately $4000 to $4500 more. The School provides financial assistance to qualified applicants through deferred-payment loans and a limited number of scholarships and fellowships.

International Students

Tuck welcomes international students. In the Classes of 1998 and 1999, there are students from Argentina, Australia, Belgium, Brazil, Canada, China, England, Germany, Ghana, Haiti, Hong Kong, India, Ireland, Italy, Japan, Korea, Mexico, the Netherlands, New Zealand, Peru, Philippines, Russia, Scotland, Sri Lanka, Switzerland, Thailand, Turkey, and Ukraine.

Application Facts and Dates

A rolling decision process is used, so applicants are urged to complete their applications as early as possible. Students whose applications are received by mid-December are notified by mid-January, mid-January by mid-February, mid-February by mid-March, and mid-April by mid-May. Applicants may call for exact dates. For more information, students should contact:

Ms. Sally O. Jaeger
Director of Admissions
The Amos Tuck School
100 Tuck Hall
Dartmouth College
Hanover, New Hampshire 03755
Telephone: 603-646-3162
Fax: 603-646-1308

DePaul University

Charles H. Kellstadt Graduate School of Business

Chicago, Illinois

CHANGE IS THE ONLY CONSTANT—KELLSTADT PREPARES BUSINESS MANAGERS FOR THE LONG TERM

This much we know about the future of business: Change is the only constant. What this means for people seeking graduate business education is that they must prepare for change. At Kellstadt, we are committed to providing our students with the arsenal of skills needed to be successful managers in today's business climate and throughout their careers.

Our philosophy, our curriculum, and our history reflect that commitment. Our bold and entrepreneurial style, our long-standing relationship with Chicago's most powerful business leaders, our experienced faculty's hard-hitting practical approach to teaching . . . these are the foundation of a Kellstadt education. As a result, our graduates are in demand because they have the knowledge and skills it takes to contribute to the success of their organizations.

Kellstadt has one of the largest graduate business enrollments in the country. Our size supports extraordinary depth among our faculty and the largest number of courses offered anywhere in the Chicago area.

It is, however, our national reputation in which we take the most pride. We are ranked among the top ten part-time M.B.A. programs nationally by U.S. News & World Report and among the top ten according to "Bowman's Accounting Report" for the number of graduates who are currently partners in the "Big Six"; in addition Success magazine has ranked our entrepreneurship program in the top twenty-five; and the Gourman Report ranks us among the top 10 percent of graduate business programs nationally. These rankings reflect the strength of our faculty and the quality of our graduates.

—Ronald J. Patten, Dean

Programs and Curricular Focus

All Kellstadt programs carry the prestigious AACSB–The International Association for Management Education accreditation, and Kellstadt is one of the 10 percent of graduate business schools with membership in the General Management Admission Council (GMAC). The M.B.A. program provides a foundation of broad business functions with nine specialized concentrations: business economics, entrepreneurship, finance, human resource management, international business, management accounting, management information systems, marketing management, and operations management. The emphasis of the M.B.A. program is on decision making and the integration of the functional areas of business. With the exception of the intensive M.B.A. in International Marketing and Finance (MBA/IMF) program, all courses are taught in the evening and on weekends, allowing students to pursue careers during the day. A complete "Weekend M.B.A." is another Kellstadt option that responds to the needs of business professionals.

The School's contemporary focus is reflected in the international flavor of its offerings, its expanding ties to the world business community, and in the scope of course offerings. The curriculum consists of four coordinated components: the internal environment of business, the external environment, managerial decision making, and a functional area of concentration. Mathematics, statistics, and computer literacy are integral components of the curriculum. All students take a course in effective communication, team taught by faculty members in the Departments of Marketing and Management, which is designed to develop the necessary skills to influence the decision-making process.

Students and the M.B.A. Experience

Kellstadt's students are unique in their experience and diversity. Most are working professionals who bring experience from every business area, in large corporations, small firms, and the nonprofit sector. They are known for their

work ethic and are interested in real issues and real-world applications.

Kellstadt's students completed their undergraduate studies in institutions throughout the United States and in many other countries. Approximately 60 percent earned undergraduate degrees in business or economics, while the remaining 40 percent have degrees in nonbusiness disciplines.

❖ Global Focus

The intensive eighteen-month M.B.A. in International Marketing and Finance (MBA/IMF) is Kellstadt's most notable example of its global focus. This program evolved in response to extensive discussions with business leaders who expressed the need for managers who have new skills and innovative approaches to what is now a business evolution.

In just eighteen months, this one-of-a-kind program prepares students for rapid changes in the international marketplace. The integration of financial and marketing decision making with a pragmatic international business orientation is the hallmark of the MBA/IMF. Unique features include an international practicum, a network of international contacts that is second to none, and Kellstadt's full-time teaching faculty joined by its business partners and corporate executives.

Special Features

Students are attracted to the very important practicum component of the MBA/IMF program. Internship opportunities have included such organizations as Abbott Laboratories in Paris, Saatchi & Saatchi in Dublin, Arthur Andersen in Vienna, and Leo Burnett in Hong Kong, to name just a few. DePaul's business partners all over the world make these experiences possible.

Of particular interest are courses that address current, new, or emerging business issues. A few examples of these special topics courses include Topics in International Money and Banking, Global Environmental Economy, Marketing to the Pacific Rim, and Case Studies in TQM.

The required capstone course, Strategic Analysis for Competing Globally, views the impact of contemporary issues on organizational strategy. Its

DePaul Center, at the Center of Chicago.

team interaction, problem solving, and group decision making mirror the way strategic planning occurs in the best of real-world business environments.

The Faculty

One hundred fourteen full-time teaching professionals represent the core of the faculty. All are committed to teaching and scholarship, and many have received national recognition. Most important, the faculty members illustrate Kellstadt's hard-hitting practical orientation in that many of them are consistently called upon by the business community for their expertise.

Supplementing the full-time faculty is a pool of approximately 200 business professionals currently active in all aspects of business. It is precisely this blend of experts that accounts for the ideal mix of theory and practice that identifies a Kellstadt education.

The Business School Network

A powerful alumni network of more than 13,000 Kellstadt graduates provides students with the door opener that can make the difference in career advancement. Leo Burnett, United Airlines, Arthur Andersen, Motorola, Abbott Laboratories, Baxter International, and Amoco are just a few examples of businesses that employ DePaul graduates.

Corporate Partnerships

The 49-member Advisory Council represents a veritable "Who's Who" in American business and keeps the School on the edge of today's business needs. The Senior Executive Lectures Series brings CEOs and senior managers to campus to share

their views of current business issues. The Executive-in-Residence program utilizes business leaders as faculty members for one to three years. Cooperative agreements with countries in Europe, Asia, and Central America have created additional relationships with multinational companies abroad.

The College and Environs

Kellstadt's home in the heart of Chicago's commercial and cultural center and its two suburban campuses in corporate corridors provide abundant career choices and contacts. Chicago indelibly stamps the curriculum and philosophy of the School. The city boasts one of the world's foremost symphony orchestras and art museums and some of the nation's best theater and is home to numerous Fortune 500 companies. Just as Chicago is a resource for the University, so is DePaul a resource for the city.

Technology Environment

DePaul Center, home to the Kellstadt Graduate School of Business, is a twenty-first-century facility. Its features include six U-shaped "case" classrooms; state-of-the-art video, computer simulation, and CD-ROM displays; tiered classrooms wired for PCs at each desk; and a marketing research facility equipped for the most advanced technology necessary to make complex marketing decisions. In short, DePaul Center is one of the most state-of-the-art educational environments in the country.

Placement

DePaul University's Center for Career Development works as a powerful link between the business community and Kellstadt's students and alumni. A computerized database provides a matching service for the most efficient job search. Comprehensive job fairs, workshops, and alumni networking are a few of the services available to students. Last year the center received 1,728 job leads for M.B.A. students, and 122 companies conducted 732 on-campus interviews.

Admission

Applications for the evening program are considered for entrance in any of four quarters: fall, winter, spring, or summer. Applications for the Weekend M.B.A. are considered for the fall only. Decisions are based on prior academic performance, which must include a bachelor's degree, scores on the GMAT, and work experience.

Admission to the eighteen-month MBA/IMF occurs only for the fall quarter. In addition to the above credentials, students must submit a written

statement, and an interview is required. Special consideration is given to students with international backgrounds.

In addition to the above credentials, international students and students educated outside the United States must submit scores on the TOEFL. For specific information about other requirements for international students, applicants should contact DePaul University's International Student Advisor.

Finances

Evening student tuition for 1997–98 was $1920 per course. Tuition for the eighteen-month MBA/IMF was $2124 per course. On-campus housing is not available. Off-campus room and board are estimated to cost $1500 per month.

In addition to financial aid opportunities that include loans, Federal Work-Study, and part-time employment, the Kellstadt Graduate School of Business offers a number of graduate assistantships that comprise a stipend of $4000 to $4500 and tuition scholarships for a maximum of nine courses per year.

Application Facts and Dates

Application deadlines for the M.B.A. program are August 1 for fall quarter, November 1 for winter quarter, March 1 for spring quarter, and May 1 for summer quarter. The application deadline for the M.B.A. in International Marketing and Finance program is May 1 for students interested in receiving consideration for graduate scholarships or graduate assistantships; applications received after March 1 will be considered on a space-available basis. The application fee is $40. For information about the M.B.A. program, students should contact:

Christine Munoz
Director of Admission
Kellstadt Graduate School of Business
DePaul University
1 East Jackson Boulevard
Chicago, Illinois 60604
Telephone: 312-362-8810
Fax: 312-362-6677
E-mail: mbainfo@wppost.depaul.edu
World Wide Web: http://www.depaul.
edu

For information about the MBA/IMF program, students should contact:

Dee Dee Wolff
Kellstadt Graduate School of Business
DePaul University
1 East Jackson Boulevard
Chicago, Illinois 60604
Telephone: 312-362-8811
Fax: 312-362-8828
E-mail: mbaimf@wppost.depaul.edu
World Wide Web: http://www.depaul.
edu/~mbaimf

Dominican College of San Rafael

> ### THE NEW M.B.A. IN THE GLOBAL ECONOMY
>
> *Four terms characterize the dramatic changes that are taking place in the world today: technology, globalization, collaboration, and competitive advantage. Dominican College's Graduate Program in Pacific Basin Studies reflects these realities through its interdisciplinary curriculum, international faculty and students, and extensive community outreach programs.*
>
> *Alumni and students describe the program as challenging, up-to-date, and one that gives students valuable business contacts. The program is supportive and flexible, serving students from diverse cultural and professional backgrounds. A rare academic experience, the Graduate Program in Pacific Basin Studies provides a thorough education about the world's most dynamic region in an intimate learning atmosphere. I invite you to learn more about our exciting program.*
>
> —Françoise O. Lepage, Dean

Programs and Curricular Focus

The Graduate Program in Pacific Basin Studies, a department of the School of Business and International Studies, offers interdisciplinary M.B.A. degrees to students preparing for careers in international finance, economics, or business with a focus on the Asia-Pacific region. Students learn and benefit from the dynamic curriculum and practical training through internship and corporate research programs in the international environment of the San Francisco Bay Area.

The M.B.A. program typically takes two years to complete and includes 55 academic units, an internship, language study, and direct involvement in corporate research projects for companies such as Bank of America, Ernst & Young, Bechtel Group, Tandem Computers, and Sun Microsystems. Courses are taught in the late afternoon, evening, and weekends, allowing students to work during traditional business hours.

Students and the M.B.A. Experience

Dominican's M.B.A. students are academically, professionally, and ethnically diverse. Students have an average of 4½ years of work experience, and their average age is 27. The student profile is diverse; 44 percent are international students from Asia, Europe, Latin America, the Middle East, and Australia. Women comprise 38 percent of the student body. The diversity of the student body has a positive impact on students'

experiences, as what happens inside and outside of the classroom is an accurate reflection of modern business realities.

Sixty-nine percent of students have an undergraduate degree in the social sciences and the humanities and 31 percent have an undergraduate degree in business and economics.

Collaborative work is emphasized, and students frequently work together in teams and study groups. Given the diverse student body, class interaction and group work are daily, real-life exercises in cross-cultural communication.

Special Features

Internships are a required component of the M.B.A. program and are matched as closely as possible to the student's area of interest. Internships are available at various companies worldwide and are often an important factor in securing employment after graduation.

Professional Development Seminars are held throughout the academic year. Top-level business and nonprofit executives give informal presentations about their industries and firms to students.

The Faculty

The distinguished multinational faculty, headed by Dr. Françoise Lepage, is continually active in the international arena, bringing fresh concepts and network contacts to the program. Beyond their contributions as Dominican College lecturers and facilitators, faculty members are business owners and executives,

management consultants, political and economic rights advocates, and members of major corporate and civic boards.

The Business School Network

Corporate Partnerships

The Pacific Basin Council assists in the development and promotion of the graduate program, ensuring the program's quality and relevance while developing job placement and internship opportunities for students. Its members, who represent international business, nonprofit organizations and government, provide strong links to those sectors throughout the world. Council members represent

organizations such as the Asia Foundation, Arthur Andersen & Co., Bank of America, Bechtel Group Inc., Georgetown University, Harvard University, and Sun Microsystems.

As a way of increasing cooperation with the business community, encouraging corporate involvement, and giving students direct experience in business research methods, the graduate program arranges for students to undertake specific research projects for major corporations located in the San Francisco Bay Area. Students benefit from direct involvement in research projects for firms such as BHP-Utah International, Bechtel Group, Ernst & Young, and Pacific Gas & Electric.

The College and Environs
The beautiful 80-acre wooded campus is centrally located at America's gateway to the Pacific, just 11 miles north of San Francisco. The campus is also within a short distance of Berkeley and the Silicon Valley. Nestled among tree-covered hills overlooking San Francisco Bay, San Rafael and the surrounding area offer an exciting array of cultural and recreational activities.

Facilities
The Alemany Library contains 97,000 volumes and microfilm reels and receives 500 periodicals. The Fletcher Jones Computer Center features IBM-PCs, Macintoshes, Sun Microsystem workstations, Internet access, and database searches.

A limited number of residence hall rooms are available for single graduate students. Housing for single and married students is available in the immediate area at varying costs.

Placement
Students receive individualized placement assistance from faculty members. Alumni have been hired or made offers by such organizations as Andersen Consulting Group, Autodesk, Bechtel Group, Beringer Wine Estates, Berlitz, Charles Schwab, Chubb & Sons, Ciba-Geigy, Creative Artists Agency, Ernst & Young, The Gap, Hewlett Packard, Hitachi Ltd., Host Marriott, Institute of Southeast Asian Studies, Johnson & Johnson, Levi Strauss & Co., Merrill Lynch, Montgomery Securities, Oracle Corporation, Pacific Gas & Electric, Republic National Bank, Sprint, United Airlines, U.S. Department of Energy, University of Maryland, Warner Brothers, and Westdeutsches Landesbank.

Admission
To be admitted unconditionally to the M.B.A. program, the applicant must meet all requirements of the School of Business. Successful applicants must hold a bachelor's degree or the equivalent and submit a complete application along with three letters of reference, a general essay, and transcripts. In addition, M.B.A. applicants should have already taken macroeconomics, microeconomics, statistics, managerial finance, managerial accounting, and college algebra. Any deficiencies in this background must be made up before the beginning of the third semester of graduate study.

Finances
Graduate tuition for full-time study in the 1998–99 academic year is $12,816, and the estimated total expenses for the same year are $22,234. This amount includes tuition, fees, books, supplies, room, board, transportation, and personal expenses.

A limited number of departmental fellowships are awarded each year. Students may apply for federal and state financial aid, including loans from the Federal Stafford Student Loan Program.

International Students
Forty-seven percent of the student body is American; 36 percent are from Asia, with the balance coming from Europe, the Middle East, and Latin America. Orientations for international students are held each August to acclimate students to the U.S. and the San Francisco Bay Area.

Application Facts and Dates
Priority deadlines are March 2 for fall and December 1 for spring. Qualified candidates will be considered as long as vacancies exist. For complete information, students should contact:

School of Business and International Studies
Dominican College of San Rafael
50 Acacia Avenue
San Rafael, California 94901
Telephone: 415-257-1359
Fax: 415-459-3206
E-mail: pbsadm@dominican.edu
World Wide Web: http://www. dominican.edu/Schools/BIS/PBS/

Dominican University

SHAPING THE FUTURE TAKES A VISION

Nearly 100 years ago, the Sinsinawa Dominicans had the vision to found Rosary College, an institution of higher education dedicated to excellence in teaching and learning. In 1977, the College added a new dimension to its vision by starting the Graduate School of Business (GSB), the Chicagoland area's first collegiate graduate business school. Now, in 1998, the vision and tradition of Rosary College live on, as our institution has become Dominican University.

Despite these continual changes, the one constant in our history is a dedication to preparing graduates to meet the challenges of a changing world. Today, our commitment to superior teaching and learning provides students with the education they need to work in a global economy, to cope with immense technological change, and to succeed in constantly changing organizational structures.

As we near the twenty-first century, Dominican University provides its students with a vision of what their careers can be and the means to turn that vision into reality. Like the original founders, the faculty members of the Graduate School of Business are able to look beyond the short-term horizon to forecast the needs of tomorrow's business community and then prepare graduates to meet those needs. That's why Dominican University alumni currently hold high-ranking positions in a wide array of America's largest corporations, as well as in midsize and entrepreneurial business and financial institutions.

Shaping your future takes a vision. Your professional future depends upon gaining superior business skills, not just acquiring a credential. That's why top-notch professionals continue to choose our programs. At Dominican University, our future looks bright and so can yours.

—Dr. Molly Burke, Dean, School of Business

Programs and Curricular Focus

The primary goals of the Graduate School of Business are to achieve excellence in teaching and to promote excellence in learning. The course of study is intended for students who are either entering the business and management professions or who are preparing for advancement within their professions. The program also serves the continuing education needs of practicing managers through its Center for Effective Organizations.

A candidate for the M.B.A. normally needs seventeen courses to complete the degree. The seventeen-course curriculum consists of seven foundation courses, five core courses, and five electives. Depending upon the candidate's undergraduate preparation, one to all of the foundation courses may be waived. A minimum of ten courses is required for the degree. The M.B.A. program offers a choice of nine areas of concentration: accounting, entrepreneurship, finance, general management, health-care administration, management information systems, marketing, human resource management, and international business. Do-

minican University also offers master's degrees in organization management (M.S. O.M.), accounting (M.S.A.), and management information systems (M.S./M.I.S.).

In order to serve the needs of students whose professional commitments require extensive travel, the Graduate School of Business offers a weekend M.B.A. program. Depending upon the candidate's academic background, a part-time student can complete this program in two calendar years, including one summer session. The Graduate School of Business also offers several joint-degree programs. The M.B.A./J.D. program is awarded in cooperation with The John Marshall Law School of Chicago. The M.B.A./M.L.I.S. is awarded in cooperation with the Dominican University Graduate School of Library and Information Science. The five-year B.A./M.B.A. is offered to qualified Dominican University juniors and seniors.

Students and the M.B.A. Experience

Students enrolled in the Graduate School of Business bring a wide range of professional

and academic experiences into the classroom. The graduate business program is 60 percent men and 40 percent women, with an average age of 29. Students entering the M.B.A. program have approximately seven years of work experience.

Cultural diversity enriches the Graduate School of Business. International students represent 12 percent of the graduate business student body and come from more than twenty countries.

Special Features

Student interaction with the faculty at Dominican University is not limited to the classroom. Traditionally, Dominican University offers a variety of activities designed to develop and enhance student-faculty relationships.

Incoming students are given the opportunity to meet one another, current students, alumni, and faculty members through new-student orientation.

The Graduate School of Business offers on site international business courses for those students with an interest in studying abroad. The European and Asian business programs are extensive two-week courses offered to graduate business students every other summer.

Graduate business students looking to pursue their personal interests closer to home are encouraged to become involved with the Graduate School of Business Student Government Association. This organization sponsors a host of social and networking events for graduate business students throughout the year. Eligible students are encouraged to join Sigma Iota Epsilon, the National Honor Society of the Academy of Management. This past year, the Dominican University chapter was recognized at the Annual Academy of Management meeting as the Outstanding Chapter of the Year.

The Faculty

Dominican University has a commitment to excellence in teaching and the Graduate School of Business faculty is made up of highly experienced practitioners in their respective fields. Faculty interests are diverse. Some faculty members are involved in topical research projects and are widely published, while other faculty members are

called upon by many of Chicago's top businesses for consultation.

More than 75 percent of the courses are taught by professors who have completed their doctorate. Part-time faculty members are selectively chosen based upon their education, specialized skills, and accomplishments within the business community. Together, these full- and part-time faculty members offer Dominican students a rich and diverse business education that integrates theory and research into practical experience.

The Business School Network

Corporate Partnerships

The majority of Dominican's alumni live within the greater Chicago area. Consequently, students have access to an enormous network of business professionals working in diverse fields. The GSB Alumni Association and the Alumni Career Network offer a variety of events designed to keep students in constant contact with Dominican alumni from all around Chicago and beyond.

The Graduate School of Business serves the needs of local, national, and international businesses through the Center for Effective Organizations (CEO). The CEO provides practical training for working managers in a variety of industries and fields.

Prominent Alumni

The Graduate School of Business is proud to count among its distinguished alumni senior executives from America's largest corporations, such as Ameritech, Motorola, and Zenith, as well as business leaders from some of Chicago's most well-known mid-size companies. Alumni are particularly prominent in the field of banking, where many Graduate School of Business graduates are senior executives at such organizations as First Chicago NBD, Citibank, Harris Bank, and LaSalle National.

The College and Environs

Dominican University traces its origin to the charter granted in 1848 by the state of Wisconsin to St. Clara Academy. The academy was formally incorporated as St. Clara College in 1901. In 1918, the school was moved to River Forest, incorporated in Illinois, and renamed Rosary College. In 1997, Rosary College became Dominican University.

Dominican University is home to more than 2,000 graduate and undergraduate students. It is conveniently located just 20 minutes west of downtown Chicago. Dominican offers its students an excellent opportunity to take advantage of all the Chicago business community has to offer while also enjoying Dominican's lovely, quiet River Forest campus.

The Graduate School of Business also offers classes at several sites throughout Chicago, including Northbrook, which is conveniently located just 25 minutes north of downtown Chicago.

Technology Environment

Dominican offers two computer laboratories and four computer classrooms for students' use. In these facilities, students can use Dominican's software, send and receive e-mail, and search the information superhighway via the Internet. All students are entitled to receive a network account that permits use of the Internet free of charge.

Students also have access to a collection of more than 210,000 volumes, 1,100 current periodical and newspaper titles, CD-ROMs, and 100,000 federal documents in the Rebecca Crown Library. For students involved in large research projects, Crown's professional librarians are available to assist students with a variety of tasks, including Dialog database searches.

Placement

Working closely with Dominican University's Placement Office, the Graduate School of Business provides students with a number of opportunities and services designed to facilitate a productive job search. Because the majority of Dominican's alumni live and work in the greater Chicago area, graduating students have an enormous network of business professionals in many fields who are willing to assist with the job placement process. The Graduate School of Business Career Consortium posts career opportunities in the School of Business office on a weekly basis.

Admission

Admission to the Graduate School of Business is open to those who hold a bachelor's degree in any field from an accredited institution. No prior business courses are required. The Committee on Graduate Admissions bases its decision on the applicant's total academic record, satisfactory scores on the Graduate Management Admission Test, three letters of reference from the applicant's professors and/or supervisors, and pertinent information from the student's application. Students may enter the program at the beginning of the fall, spring, or summer terms.

The Graduate School of Business welcomes applications from international students. For those who were educated outside the United States and/or require an F-1 visa and an I-20 form, an official TOEFL score of 550 or above is also required. All international students are required to show proof of financial support for one year.

Finances

Tuition for the 1998–99 term is $1380 per 3-credit-hour course. Room and board for the 1998–99 term range from $4760 to $5900, depending on the meal plan chosen. Books and supplies are approximately $75 per course, and there is a student fee of $10 per course.

International Students

The classroom experience is strengthened by a strong international student community. An international student adviser assists all international students with the application and admission process.

Application Facts and Dates

Applications are accepted on a rolling basis. While there is no application deadline, it is recommended that all application materials be submitted to the Graduate School of Business at least one month before the beginning of the semester in which the student desires admission. Notification of admission is usually provided within two weeks of the time all information is received. For additional information, students should contact:

Dan Condon, Ph.D.
Director of Admissions and Advising
Dominican University
Graduate School of Business
7900 West Division Street
River Forest, Illinois 60305-1066
Telephone: 708-524-6233
Fax: 708-366-5360
E-mail: gradbus@email.dom.edu

Dowling College

Oakdale, Long Island, New York

Programs and Curricular Focus

Dowling offers students five M.B.A. degree programs to choose from. These include general management, aviation management, banking and finance, public management, and total quality management.

The degree in general management provides students with a comprehensive foundation in various managerial disciplines. It is the ideal degree for students who did not specialize in business at the undergraduate level. It is also suited for managers in small to midsize firms responsible for more than one managerial function during the course of a working day.

The M.B.A. in aviation management is designated for aviation management professionals as well as individuals who aspire to land positions in the industry. Managers will learn to run their divisions more efficiently and keep pace with the kinetic elements impacting the aviation industry today. This degree is applicable to professionals affiliated with air carriers, airport facilities, aerospace companies, and industry sectors such as manufacturing and government.

Banking and finance are among the most dynamic industries in the global economy. Due to the changing of financial markets worldwide and the greater variety of financial instruments evolving, the information needed to thrive in this environment is expanding rapidly.

Acquiring the skills necessary to manage not-for-profit institutions or government is at the core of Dowling's

public management M.B.A. program. Courses such as Quantitative Methods for Public Sector Decision Making, Not-for-Profit Marketing, and Public Sector Economics help focus the 36-credit program on the specifics of this diverse field.

The M.B.A. in Total Quality Management (TQM) challenges students to meet customer needs in addition to traditional business operations. Students are instructed in TQM theories by faculty members who are leaders in quality management education.

Dowling also offers busy executives the opportunity to earn their M.B.A. in general management or banking and finance in a distinctive Saturdays-only structure. Students can complete their degree in as little as sixteen months.

Students and the M.B.A. Experience

Dowling's M.B.A. student population is a diverse one, ranging from recent baccalaureate degree graduates to established business men and women to physicians, Ph.D.'s, and other professionals. The average age is 32 and graduate students comprise 37 percent of the student body. Dowling's international scope continues to grow with the addition of its new National Aviation and Transportation Center®, a unique facility dedicated to the study and research of global transportation issues.

Dowling's management simulation capstone requirement places students in

real-world situations. Students work in teams and must demonstrate the successful start-up of a business venture and direct its capital distribution, purchasing efforts, marketing campaigns, cash flow logistics, and related responsibilities. In addition, students enrolled in Dowling's innovative Accelerated Saturday M.B.A. program work in assigned groups to facilitate the concept of teamwork and move in unison as the program progresses.

Special Features

The Accelerated Saturday M.B.A. program enables students to complete their degree in only three semesters by attending classes all day on Saturdays. It offers an innovative luncheon speakers series; a state-of-the-art notebook computer with word processing, spreadsheet, and presentation software; and all required textbooks. The speakers series features prominent local, national, and international business professionals and has included George Gallup of Gallup Poll International; Jerry Goodman of Adam Smith's Money World; Ben Cohen, cofounder of Ben & Jerry's Homemade Ice Cream; and Michael Moore, director of the documentary *Roger & Me*.

The Faculty

Conducted within the personalized atmosphere of a small college, the graduate business program at Dowling has a faculty of highly qualified experienced business professionals. Faculty members are noted for their presentations, scholarly works, expert testimony, professional standing, and national conference participation.

The Business School Network

Across Long Island, throughout the nation, and around the globe, Dowling's innovative partnerships with businesses have spawned numerous benefits for M.B.A. students, including lectures, internships, and specific networking opportunities. Dowling's Board of Trustees and Advisory Council members, whose business expertise is vital in the College's exemplary leadership, serve as successful corporate examples. The members are often on campus, creating opportunities for students to meet with them.

The College and Environs

Originated in 1955 as Suffolk County's first four-year college, Dowling is nestled on a 52-acre campus along the picturesque banks of the Connetquot River on Long Island's south shore. Approximately 50 miles east of midtown Manhattan, it is within easy reach of New York's theaters and museums and just minutes from Long Island's beautiful beaches, parks,

recreational facilities, and other cultural attractions. Students at Dowling have the best of both worlds: city and country.

Fortunoff Hall is the focal point of the Oakdale campus. Built at the turn of the century by industrial magnate William K. Vanderbilt, this exquisitely preserved mansion houses administrative and faculty offices, as well as ornately designed ceremonial rooms that are now used for meetings and lectures.

Facilities

The Nicholas and Constance Racanelli Center for Learning Resources houses Dowling's library. Its collections include 182,661 volumes, 1,100 current periodicals, 577,097 microforms, and 10,577 government documents.

Another valuable research tool is the Online Computer Library Center (OCLC) used by Dowling's librarians to access the collections of thousands of libraries, universities, and research centers worldwide.

The Academic Computing Center, which has three multimedia classrooms, three labs for individual use, and a faculty resource center, is available to students during extended day and evening hours. The College's membership in the New York State Education and Research Network (NYSERNet) serves as a gateway to the Internet, a global network providing access to thousands of computers for research and communication.

Placement

The Office of Cooperative Education, Career Counseling, and Internship maintains a network of partnerships with businesses on Long Island, in New York, and across the nation. On-campus recruiters from respected companies are regularly scheduled, and Dowling's M.B.A. graduates maintain a high visibility quotient. Students can also attend special lectures on resume writing, interviewing, and careerpathing. Students are encouraged to attend the varied networking activities that Dowling's alumni organization provides throughout the year.

Admission

Each candidate's academic record, scores on the required Graduate Management

Admission Test (GMAT), and work experience are considered in the admission process. A GMAT score of 475 or more and a minimum 2.8 GPA in undergraduate work are preferred.

In addition to the minimum 36 credits of graduate work, each qualified applicant with a limited background in business administration must successfully complete certain preparatory courses. These areas of study might include accounting, economics, quantitative methods, computer science, and management. For students using English as a second language, a TOEFL score of 550 or better is required.

Finances

Tuition is $440 per graduate credit, and certain student fees are applicable. On-campus housing is available in apartment-style suites for $3600 per semester and there are ample off-campus apartments within easy travel distance of the College.

While numerous scholarship programs are available, various financing methods can be explored with a personal financial aid counselor. The College offers students individual guidance on flexible payment options available such as a tuition and fee deferred payment plan for each semester. Credit cards may also be used to pay tuition and fees. Additionally, for two academic years, new students may have their tuition charges frozen at their entering semester rate.

International Students

Individualized tutorial programs are available to students who need special help with the English language.

Application Facts and Dates

For more information, students should contact:

Dr. Anthony Libertella, Dean
School of Business
Dowling College
Idle Hour Boulevard
Oakdale, Long Island, New York
   11769-1999
Telephone: 516-244-3355
           800-DOWLING (toll-free)
Fax: 516-589-6644
   516-244-5098
World Wide Web: http://www.dowling.edu

Drexel University

College of Business and Administration

Philadelphia, Pennsylvania

> **AN INTEGRATED, HOLISTIC APPROACH**
>
> *Drexel stands at the forefront of a national movement to revitalize the M.B.A. degree. An integrative, holistic approach lies at the core of the Drexel curriculum. This approach responds to the demands of the business world that M.B.A. graduates have a "big picture" view. The educational objective of the Drexel M.B.A. is to prepare each student for lifelong professional development. The experience encompasses not only specific professional skills, but also a general intellectual framework for approaching business opportunities. This framework provides the M.B.A. graduate with the ability to respond creatively to future trends.*
>
> *—Tom Hindelang, Associate Dean*

Programs and Curricular Focus

The M.B.A. program at Drexel is designed to meet a wide range of student needs. It can provide a broad, balanced curriculum or one that's more focused. The M.B.A. program offers the conceptual tools to back up previously acquired experience, or it can provide professional experience as part of the M.B.A. studies. In fact, the program can be tailored to match a wide variety of student preferences. Many of the courses have been enhanced through an added emphasis on people skills, pragmatic exercises, communication skills, global perspectives, technology, and ethical dimensions of business.

The M.B.A. program has concentrations in fifteen areas and may be pursued on a full-time or part-time basis, day or evening. There is also a general M.B.A. program that is offered on Saturdays. Drexel's academic calendar of four 10-week terms gives students the option to enter most of the College's programs at any time of the year.

The M.B.A. degree program requires completion of 84 credits, consisting of twelve 3-credit foundation courses and sixteen 3-credit advanced courses. It is organized as a two-year program, but the actual time required to complete the degree depends on the number of credits that a student transfers into the program and the number of courses he or she chooses to register for each term.

The foundation courses represent the basic knowledge required by AACSB– The International Association for Management Education, which has fully accredited the College's M.B.A. program. In general, the foundation courses should

be completed before the advanced courses are undertaken. Some or all foundation courses can be waived if a student has completed equivalent courses as an undergraduate.

The advanced level includes five required core courses, five professional electives (one course from each of five business disciplines), four courses in the student's field of concentration, and two business electives.

Students and the M.B.A. Experience

Drexel's M.B.A. program enrolls approximately 1,000 students, one fourth of whom are enrolled full-time. These students represent widely diverse backgrounds: those entering directly from undergraduate programs and businesspeople with years of experience; those who completed undergraduate degrees at Drexel as well as alumni of universities in Europe and Asia; and those with degrees in business subjects along with engineers, scientists, physicians, liberal arts graduates, and military officers. Not only is Drexel's program flexible enough to accommodate these many individuals, it is also enriched by the variety of their perspectives. Approximately 60 percent of the full-time students are international.

Special Features

The Drexel Career Integrated Education option (CIE) provides a wealth of real-world hands-on career experience. The CIE option allows students to enrich their master's studies in business by earning credit for supervised employment experience related to their academic and

career goals. This option provides an outstanding opportunity for recent college graduates to begin building their base of experience as well as their resumes, for international students to gain experience in the American workplace and Americans to gain international experience working abroad, and for established professionals to prepare for a transition from one career field to another. For those students seeking to gain global experience, Drexel's M.B.A. program offers the opportunity to take some courses at L'Ecole Supérieure de Commerce de Paris (ESCP). Drexel students and French students take many of their courses abroad, and both can earn their M.B.A. degrees from Drexel.

The Faculty

Drexel's College of Business and Administration has an outstanding faculty. More than 95 percent hold the doctoral degree, and they have earned distinction for their published research as well as for the many journals and textbooks they have edited or authored. In keeping with the College's practical orientation, faculty members also enjoy strong ties with the business community, dramatically enhancing the educational environment at the College. Drexel faculty members have served as consultants for a range of corporations, government agencies, and other organizations. Corporate and entrepreneurial leaders augment the full-time faculty by coming to campus as guest lecturers or part-time teachers.

The Business School Network

Drexel's College of Business and Administration maintains extensive relationships with the business community through an advisory board consisting of senior executives from major corporations and nonprofit organizations. The advisory board meets with the dean and faculty on a regular basis to provide input for curriculum and program revision and development.

The College's relationship with the local business community is further enhanced by the prestigious Business Leader of the Year Award, which grew out of one student's suggestion that the

College cite a business leader as an example of success, service, citizenship, and leadership. The student who made that suggestion, George M. Ross, Class of '55, is now a resident partner with Goldman, Sachs, and Co. and a past Business Leader of the Year Award recipient.

The College and Environs

Philadelphia is an appealing place to earn a graduate degree. As a leading center for commerce, industry, government, and the arts, the city also offers museums, libraries, and other resources that support learning. The metropolitan area provides ample employment opportunities for students and graduates alike, in such growing fields as banking, finance, pharmaceuticals, insurance, and telecommunications.

Philadelphia features countless opportunities for cultural and recreational activities, as well. Historic sites, such as Independence Hall and the Liberty Bell; major league teams in baseball, basketball, football, and ice hockey; the world-famous Philadelphia Orchestra; and the Philadelphia Museum of Art are only a few of the attractions that students enjoy. Fairmount Park, the nation's largest city park; the Philadelphia Zoo; and Penn's Landing, the city's riverfront development, provide additional options for spare-time activities. Ethnically diverse Philadelphia is often called "the city of neighborhoods," with such colorful communities to visit as Chinatown and South Philadelphia's Italian Market.

Drexel is ideally located for students to take advantage of public transportation. Just two blocks away is 30th Street Station—Philadelphia's major railroad station and a stop for Amtrak trains from New York City and Washington, D.C., local commuter trains, and a shuttle to the airport. New Jersey's beaches and Pennsylvania's Pocono Mountains are each within a 2-hour drive of the city. The University also provides ample parking.

Facilities

The College of Business and Administration is housed in two buildings on campus. The buildings contain modern lecture halls, conference rooms, and the Center for Executive Education. University computer facilities include several mainframes and the campus is networked. Students have access to the Internet with their own account. In addition, the University microcomputer support facility contains more than 500 Macintosh microcomputers and supports a full range of consulting and training workshop services. Business students also have access to the College of Business and Administration's own IBM PC and Macintosh Power PC computer labs.

Placement

Placement services are provided through the Career Services Center (CSC) free of charge up to one year past date of graduation. Graduates can also obtain job listings and use other resources at any time. For those students who wish to refine their interviewing skills, Drexel offers the General Electric Video Interview Program (GEVIP). This service allows students to practice their interviewing skills on videotape to learn where they can make improvements. Drexel's CSC has its own Career Library. It contains extensive files and videotapes of general career and specific employer information from which students can develop a list of potential employers. Drexel offers an on-campus interview program. Each fall, winter, and spring, employer representatives visit campus to interview the current graduating class for upcoming employment opportunities. Candidates are selected for interviews by the employer organizations.

Admission

All applicants must have received a four-year bachelor's degree from an accredited college or university. Degrees earned abroad must be deemed equivalent. The College of Business and Administration's admissions committee reviews applicants based on undergraduate accomplishments, performance on the GMAT, previous professional accomplishments, career goals, references, and the personal essay.

Students whose native language is not English and who do not hold degrees from U.S. institutions are required to submit a score on the Test of English as a Foreign Language (TOEFL).

Finances

Tuition for master's courses is billed by the credit hour. As of the 1997–98 academic year, the cost was $477 per credit hour; all graduate business courses are 3 credits. Tuition is the same for full-time and part-time students.

Graduate assistantships are available to full-time master's business students. An assistantship requires the student to work for 20 hours per week for a department or professor in return for tuition remission for three courses per term plus a monthly stipend. Applications for assistantships are available in the Graduate Business Office. Federal Stafford Student Loans and other loans are available for part-time and full-time students through the University's Financial Aid Office.

International Students

International students are an important component of Drexel's graduate student body and are actively recruited. International students come from all over the world and more than forty countries, including Asia, the Pacific Rim, Europe, South America, and Canada. The International Students Office conducts an orientation program to assist international students in becoming acclimated to the American social and educational culture.

Application Facts and Dates

Drexel's College of Business and Administration admits students for each of its four quarters. For the fall quarter, the final application deadline is August 31 for U.S. citizens and June 20 for non–U.S. citizens. For the winter quarter, the deadline is November 30 for U.S. citizens and September 25 for noncitizens. For the spring quarter, it is March 1 for citizens and January 3 for noncitizens, and for the summer, it is May 31 for citizens and March 31 for noncitizens. For more information, students should contact:

Office of Graduate Admissions
Drexel University, Box P
Philadelphia, Pennsylvania 19104
Telephone: 215-895-6700
E-mail: admissions-grad@
    post.drexel.edu

Duquesne University

Pittsburgh, Pennsylvania

PREPARING FOR THE TWENTY-FIRST CENTURY

Graduate schools of business have a special obligation to help prepare their students for the challenges and opportunities of the twenty-first century. We at Duquesne are especially mindful of that obligation to all of our stakeholders—our students, our supporters, the business community, and the greater society of which we are a part. Our Graduate School of Business at Duquesne University is committed to excellence in a dynamic environment of change and continuous improvement. We hope the information that we provide below helps you to make an informed decision about your future education—and, of course, we hope that you select our Graduate School of Business.

—Thomas J. Murrin, Dean

Programs and Curricular Focus

Fully accredited by AACSB–The International Association for Management Education, Duquesne University's Graduate School of Business provides a program of study that is consistent with its mission of "preparing leaders who appreciate the importance of blending technical competence with a broad-based education that positions them to add value in a highly competitive global business environment." The curriculum is structured to provide fundamental skills in quantitative and qualitative analysis, a solid foundation in key functional areas of business, and an opportunity for students to apply their skills and knowledge to real-world business problems. Students also have an opportunity to choose a specialization in several disciplines, including accounting, environmental management, ethics, finance, human resource management, health-care management, international business, information systems management, marketing, and taxation. The Graduate School of Business also offers Master of Science degrees in information systems management and taxation. A dual M.B.A./M.S. in information systems management is also available.

The M.B.A. curriculum stresses the relationships among business disciplines. A three-course business problems sequence provides students with the opportunity to integrate their knowledge of functional disciplines and develop recommendations for dealing with real business problems presented by the faculty, business practitioners, and the executive faculty.

The contemporary business issues of globalization, ethics, total quality, and the management of technology are integrated in all core courses as is a reading program that is designed to relate the specific disciplines to the world at large.

Based on the belief that students are best able to position themselves competitively if they can present samples of work completed in their graduate studies and professional positions, students are required to organize a portfolio of substantive, professionally presented work accomplished during their program of study.

Students and the M.B.A. Experience

The student body of approximately 580 students is diverse. Full-time students, who make up approximately 25 percent of the enrollment, get an enriching experience by sharing classes with full-time business professionals who are working toward their degrees on a part-time basis. Part-time students bring an average of five years of professional work experience to the classroom, providing a rich source of real-world issues that add value to the educational experience.

The student body also represents countries from around the world, including those in Africa, Asia, Europe, and Latin America, who bring an important international dimension to the program.

Special Features

The Graduate School of Business believes that it makes good sense for a university

to leverage its resources for the maximum benefit of its students. Therefore, it has developed important partnerships with other schools on the campus to offer dual-degree programs. The M.B.A. degree and degrees in environmental science and management, health management systems, industrial pharmacy, liberal studies, law, and nursing are offered.

The Faculty

The faculty members of the Graduate School of Business are committed to teaching excellence, scholarship that focuses on real business problems, and developing creative academic-business partnerships. The academic and professional experiences of the faculty members are complemented by the executive faculty who, teamed with the full-time faculty, regularly address classes in their areas of expertise, directly relating their daily experiences to the material covered in the courses. Graduate students benefit from the exposure to a roster of executives, including chief executive officers, presidents, vice-presidents, and top administrators.

The Business School Network

The Graduate School of Business has built a significant network with the business community that helps to promote its commitment to business-academic partnerships. Approximately 150 business professionals are members of the School's ten advisory boards. They offer their expertise and guidance on curricular matters and internship and professional placement opportunities to the students.

The College and Environs

Duquesne University first opened its doors as the Pittsburgh Catholic College of the Holy Ghost in October 1878. With its beautifully self-contained 39-acre campus of tree-lined walks, fountains, and a blend of modern and historic buildings, Duquesne provides a hilltop vista overlooking one of the nation's most attractive cities for its 9,000 students.

Long-noted as one of the world's great business centers, Pittsburgh combines the features of big-city living with many of the charms and personal characteristics of a much smaller town. Pittsburgh is one of the largest corporate headquarters centers in the United States and has developed a strong civic identity and sense of pride in its rebirth as a modern urban community. Students from Duquesne and other colleges and universities in the city can choose from a wide variety of cultural, social, and sporting events and programs.

Facilities

The Graduate School of Business is located in Rockwell Hall, at the downtown Pittsburgh edge of the University's campus. Facilities in the building include special seminar and conference rooms, a lecture hall/theater complex, and the University's Communications and Information Technology Center, which features two Digital Equipment Corporation mainframe computers and a new computer resource center for student use.

The Graduate School of Business operates three computer laboratories dedicated to personal computers and their use across the business curriculum, online access to software and applications associated with the University's mainframe system, and multimedia development.

The University's Gumberg Library houses nearly 500,000 volumes, more than 3,700 journal titles, and an extensive microprint and audiovisual center. Other library facilities include an online card catalog and a CD-ROM center that permits users to access the library's data files. The CD-ROM system gives students access to hundreds of additional periodicals not physically housed in the library.

Placement

Career planning and placement services are provided through the University's Office of Career Services. In addition, the M.B.A. Office of Career Development, located in the Graduate School of Business, works closely with the University's Office of Career Services to develop placement opportunities for its students. Workshops on resume writing, mock interview sessions, and career fairs that attract major employers to campus are some of the services available to students. Students may also take advantage of the Duquesne University Career Advisory Network, an organization made up of alumni of the Graduate School of Business to provide professional networking opportunities for students and alumni.

Admission

Candidates who have earned an undergraduate degree from an accredited four-year college or university (or its equivalent in another country) are eligible for admission. Admissions criteria include the undergraduate grade point average; the quality of undergraduate course work completed; scores on the Graduate Management Admissions Test; at least two letters of recommendation from those who can make reasonable judgments on the candidate's potential for graduate study, including professors and/or business associates; a personal essay; and the quality and duration of work experience. International students are required to provide proof of adequate financial support and, if their native language is not English, take the Test of English as a Foreign Language (TOEFL).

Finances

Tuition for the 1998–99 academic year is $481 per credit. There is also a $39 University fee charged for each credit. Room and board are $3079 per semester, based on double occupancy. Housing is also available off campus. The University's Office of Residence Life can assist students in locating off-campus housing. A limited number of graduate assistantships, which provide up to 9 credits of tuition remission each semester and a monthly cash stipend, are available to students. The application fee is $40.

International Students

Students come to Duquesne University's campus from ninety countries throughout the world. Approximately 11 percent of the M.B.A. students come from countries in Africa, Asia, Europe, and Latin America. The University offers substantial support for international students through its International Affairs Office. ESL programs are available to help students improve their skills in English. An active International Student Organization provides networking support and social and educational activities for international students.

Application Facts and Dates

Application deadlines are June 1 for fall admission, November 1 for spring admission, and March 1 for summer admission. Students applying for the fall who are scheduled to take the GMAT in June should submit the completed application by June 1 indicating that they are taking the GMAT in June. The review process for their applications will be completed after GMAT scores are received. For more information, students should contact:

The Graduate School of Business
704 Rockwell Hall
Duquesne University
Pittsburgh, Pennsylvania 15282
Telephone: 412-396-6276
Fax: 412-396-5304
E-mail: grad-bus@next.duq.edu
World Wide Web: http://www.bus.duq.edu/SBA.html

East Carolina University

Greenville, North Carolina

AN M.B.A. WITH ADVANTAGES

In today's competitive environment, it pays to investigate all of your M.B.A. options. At East Carolina University (ECU), we offer an M.B.A. program with four distinct advantages: professional preparation, recognized quality, program flexibility, and exceptional value.

—Ernest B. Uhr, Dean

Programs and Curricular Focus

The M.B.A. program at East Carolina University is one of approximately 300 graduate business programs accredited by the AACSB–The International Association for Management Education and was the second program accredited in North Carolina. It is one of approximately 130 M.B.A. programs that belong to the Graduate Management Admissions Council.

The goal of the M.B.A. program is to prepare men and women for managerial leadership in profit and nonprofit organizations. Required and elective courses are taught from the managerial perspective. A blend of teaching methods, including lectures, discussions, computer simulations, team projects, cases, and independent study, is used to develop critical thinking and human relations skills. The average class size is nineteen.

The ECU M.B.A. program is flexible and can be individually tailored to the student's background and needs. For example, students who have previously taken business administration courses at the undergraduate level and received high grades may be exempted from some or all of the first-year M.B.A. classes. Such waivers could reduce the program to a minimum of 30 semester hours, or one year full-time. The maximum program length is 60 semester hours or two years.

Students may begin the M.B.A. program in any term—fall, spring, or summer. Spring or summer entrance presents no scheduling problems, since courses required of new students are offered in all terms. The availability of two terms each summer allows students to accelerate the completion of the program.

Students working full-time can complete the M.B.A. by taking evening classes, since all courses have an evening section. Part-time students set their own pace, depending on their work requirements, and most finish in two to five years.

The ECU Schools of Medicine and Business offer a joint M.D./M.B.A. program, which takes five years to complete. The M.D./M.B.A. program is also available to students who are accepted to or enrolled in another accredited medical school. Medical residents whose training program allows one year away from clinical responsibilities may enroll in the M.D./M.B.A. program. Students enter in late June and complete the M.B.A. program twelve months later. The GMAT requirement is waived for applicants with M.D. degrees or students from accredited medical schools.

Students and the M.B.A. Experience

East Carolina's M.B.A. students are drawn from a wide variety of educational and business backgrounds. Approximately 170 attend full-time, and 130 work full-time and attend part-time. The typical student is 28 years old and has six years of work experience. The 1997–98 student body included 41 percent women and 8 percent minorities. Approximately 50 percent have undergraduate business degrees and about 20 percent studied engineering or science. The social sciences and health professions were also strongly represented, including 6 M.D.'s. Approximately 85 different undergraduate institutions were represented in the student body.

Special Features

In addition to elective courses in the traditional business subjects, East Carolina's M.B.A. program offers five options in related fields. About 15 percent of the students take their electives in another ECU professional school and receive a certificate from that school. Options are available in health-care management, hospitality management, apparel and textile management, development and environmental planning, and school business management.

The Faculty

ECU is committed to high-quality teaching. Faculty members' backgrounds are diverse and cosmopolitan and include extensive business, consulting, teaching, and research experience. The School of Business faculty members hold graduate degrees from institutions such as Duke, Georgetown, Harvard, Indiana, North Carolina, Virginia, Wharton, Arizona State, Florida, Georgia, Illinois, Michigan State, Tennessee, Texas, Texas A&M, and Wisconsin. Professors are dedicated to providing meaningful, challenging experiences for ECU's M.B.A. students and are readily available for discussion and assistance outside the classroom.

The Business School Network

Many M.B.A.'s work full-time for major organizations and attend graduate school part-time. Full- and part-time students are in class together and work on projects that enhance learning and networking opportunities. Eastern North Carolina is home to scores of major corporations, including DuPont, Firestone, Frigidaire, Procter and Gamble, Sara Lee, and TRW.

Through the Small Business Institute, students can get hands-on experience consulting with local developing businesses.

The School of Business is served by a distinguished Business Advisory Council of 35 senior executives who advise the dean on a broad range of issues. These executives participate as guest lecturers in many courses each year.

The College and Environs

East Carolina University, founded in 1907, is the third-largest campus of the University of North Carolina. Enrollment is about 17,800 students, which includes

Home of the ECU School of Busines.

2,800 graduate students and 300 medical students. The ECU School of Medicine is one of the top producers of primary-care physicians in the nation.

Quality of life during the M.B.A. experience is an important consideration. Greenville is a comfortable city of 53,000 with a reasonable cost of living, a temperate climate, and a relaxed outdoor lifestyle. It is an educational, commercial, industrial, medical, and cultural center.

The North Carolina beaches are 90 minutes away, and it's a half-day drive to the mountains and skiing. Greenville is a 1-hour drive from I-95 and is served by regional airports.

Facilities

The M.B.A. program is housed in a modern facility, completed in 1988, which includes a large, comfortable M.B.A. lounge and study area. ECU's Joyner Library holds 1.2 million bound volumes plus microforms and periodicals.

Technology Environment

M.B.A. computing is available in a lab with thirty-two Macintosh computers and sixty-four computers with Windows 95 that are connected to a 155-Mbps campus network with a 10-Mbps link to the Internet. A variety of software packages and databases are available, including Microsoft Office 97 Professional.

Placement

East Carolina University Career Services provides career and placement services to M.B.A. students and recent alumni. Resume preparation and interviewing skills workshops and computerized databases are part of the services offered to M.B.A.'s. A career fair and on-campus recruiting are augmented by business contacts through the School of Business as well as Career Services.

The Office of Cooperative Education assists M.B.A. students in preparing for and securing career-related temporary employment, usually of a semester's duration. This is particularly valuable for students who do not have extensive full-time work experience. With ECU's flexible M.B.A. program, co-op jobs do not create scheduling problems because students can easily interrupt and then resume their programs.

Admission

The ECU M.B.A. program is open to applicants with baccalaureate degrees from accredited institutions in business and nonbusiness fields. Work experience is recommended but not required. Ability is evaluated on the basis of the applicant's prior undergraduate record and performance on the Graduate Management Admission Test (GMAT). The average GMAT score is approximately 500. A GMAT review course is available twice a year through the School of Business's Division of Professional Programs.

Applications from non-English-speaking countries must submit results of the Test of English as a Foreign Language (TOEFL). The minimum acceptable TOEFL score is 550.

Finances

Value is a function of quality and cost. East Carolina provides a substantial accredited M.B.A. program at a reasonable cost. Full-time tuition and fees are $1800 per academic year for North Carolina residents and $9000 per year for nonresidents, with additional charges for optional summer sessions. Tuition and fees for part-time students are lower.

Waivers of business core classes may provide additional value by eliminating one or more semester's tuition, fees, and living expenses.

Off-campus housing, estimated at $6000 per year, is readily available and is used by most graduate students. University housing is also available.

The School of Business offers approximately seventy-five graduate assistantships awarded on academic merit. Students may earn between $2750 and $5500 per year working 10 to 20 hours each week assisting professors in research or working with undergraduates in the computer labs.

International Students

The ECU M.B.A. program welcomes international students. During 1997–98, there were students from Brazil, Canada, China, France, Germany, Guyana, Hungary, India, Japan, Kazakhstan, Mexico, Panama, Sierra Leone, Switzerland, Turkmenistan, the United Kingdom, and Uzbekistan.

Application Facts and Dates

Applications are accepted for any term. Early applications are strongly encouraged because of the rolling admission process. For more information and an application, students should contact:

Donald B. Boldt
Assistant Dean for Graduate Programs
School of Business
East Carolina University
Greenville, North Carolina 27858-4353
Telephone: 252-328-6970
Fax: 252-328-2106
E-mail: boldtd@mail.ecu.edu
World Wide Web: http://www.business.ecu.edu/grad

Eastern College

St. Davids, Pennsylvania

> ### DEVELOPING BUSINESS LEADERS FOR THE TWENTY-FIRST CENTURY
>
> *Eastern's programs are responsive to the specialized needs of students, offering a variety of concentrations (nonprofit management, health administration, economic development, and accounting), timeframes for completion of the degree (evening M.B.A. and fast-track M.B.A.), and featuring in-class use of laptop computer technology by students and faculty members.*
>
> —Vivian Nix-Early, Dean

Programs and Curricular Focus

The traditional M.B.A. program consists of a general program and six concentrations: accounting, economics, finance, management, marketing, and general studies. The core curriculum for the traditional program consists of courses in accounting, economics, finance, organizational behavior, marketing management, quantitative decision-making, and business ethics. In addition, Eastern offers the M.B.A. and M.S. in economic development and the M.B.A. and M.S. in nonprofit management. The innovative concentration in nonprofit organizations includes courses in fundraising, legal mandates, public relations, strategic planning, and management of volunteers.

Courses are organized into three groups: foundation courses, core (required) courses, and specific elective courses for the concentrations. To earn a degree in the traditional M.B.A. or the nonprofit management M.B.A. program, students must complete 36 semester/credit hours of graduate courses. To earn an M.S. in nonprofit management, students are requried to complete 33 semester/credit hours. Similarly, 42 semester/credit hours are required for the M.B.A. in economic development program and 36 semester/credit hours are required for the M.S. in economic development program. Students may also be required to take foundation courses, contingent on a review of previous course work.

Eastern College offers three dual-degree programs with Eastern Baptist Theological Seminary. The joint degrees of 116 total credit hours are M.Div./M.S. economic development, M.Div./M.B.A. economic development, and M.Div./

M.B.A. traditional. Eastern also offers a twenty-two-month intensive M.B.A. program.

Students and the M.B.A. Experience

Students at Eastern College bring diverse resumes as well as culturally varied backgrounds to their M.B.A. experience. The average student is a 30-year-old with seven years of work experience. Women comprise one third of the student population, and minority students make up 16 percent.

The Northeast sends 65 percent of Eastern College M.B.A. students, while 5 percent come from the Midwest. Six percent come from the West Coast, and international students make up the final 24 percent.

Eastern College students not only learn from the professors, they learn from each other. The diverse cultural and business backgrounds of the professors and students offer each student the opportunity to explore other countries and careers without leaving the classroom.

Special Features

The economic development program offers many opportunities to develop a broader understanding of cross-cultural issues. The capstones to this program involve Two-Thirds World summer field courses in an international setting, as well as a two-semester internship in a community development center located in the city of Philadelphia. The internship enables the student to develop professional experience in an urban setting. The primary emphasis is placed on the creation and growth of microscale and small-scale enterprises.

More than half of the total courses, including all the foundation courses of the M.B.A. program, are available on video distance learning. At least two thirds of economic development students receive financial aid. Internships are available in the nonprofit management and economic development programs.

The Faculty

The business programs have attracted and employed the talents of an experienced and dynamic faculty. Faculty members have researched, visited, lived, and performed professionally all over the world. They have established and managed businesses and development organizations. They have also served as consultants to international and urban organizations.

The Business School Network

Since the inception of the M.B.A. program, there have been strong partnerships with corporations and organizations in the Philadelphia metro and suburban areas. Students in the nonprofit M.B.A. program have the opportunity to introduce fundraising strategic plans to foundations for professional review and critique. This as well as other networking experiences are available in the business program.

The College and Environs

In 1982, Eastern College launched the first Master of Business Administration program in the western suburbs of Philadelphia. Located in St. Davids on the main line of Philadelphia, Eastern College is a beautiful suburban campus within 3 miles of Interstate 476. Only 20 minutes by train or car from the city, the heart of the campus is the Charles S. Walton estate, built in 1913. Eastern has grown beyond the original estate to include twenty-six buildings and more than 100 acres of woods, ponds, creeks, and lawns. The total population at Eastern College has grown to more than 2,600 students.

Technology Environment

Eastern College has its own computing lab facilities, consisting of over fifty

Kershaw Burbank Jr., M.P.S., Assistant Professor.

Anthony Campolo, Ph.D., Professor of Sociology.

Margaret Clark, Ph.D., Associate Professor of Finance.

Thomas Dahlstrom, M.B.A., Associate Professor of Business.

James Engel, Ph.D., Distinguished Professor of Marketing.

J. Samuel Escobar, Ph.D., Thornley B. Wood Professor of Missiology (EBTS).

Linwood T. Geiger, Ph.D., Distinguished Professor of International Economics.

Mark C. Halsey, M.B.A., Assistant Professor of Management.

A. Gilbert Heebner, Ph.D., Distinguished Professor of Economics.

Harold C. Howard, Ph.D., Professor of Leadership Development.

Eloise Hiebert Meneses, Ph.D., Assistant Professor of Anthropology.

Elizabeth Morgan, Ph.D., Professor of Literature and Social Renewal.

Patricia Nelson, Ed.D., Coordinator of Health Administration Program and Professor of Health Administration.

Ronald J. Sider, Ph.D., Professor of Theology and Culture (EBTS).

John Stapleford, Ph.D., Director of Business Programs.

Alan Tharp, Ph.D., Dean of Undergraduate Studies and Associate Professor of International Relations.

David Unander, Ph.D., Associate Professor of Biology.

Van Weigel, Ph.D., Associate Professor of Ethics and Economic Development.

terminals. There is a separate computer lab for graduate students. The computer lab is open from 9 a.m. to 11 p.m., Monday through Friday. It is also open on the weekends. The intensive M.B.A. program (Fast-Track M.B.A.) at Eastern College provides each of the business students with a laptop computer. The Warner Library is an attractive and comfortable facility housing more than 13,000 volumes. The library is a part of the OCLC information network, opening 22 million volumes to students as resources.

Placement

The career center at Eastern College enables graduate students the opportunity to develop networks in the Philadelphia area. The career center has contacts with many of the national and international companies based in the eastern Pennsylvania region.

Admission

Admission to an M.B.A. or an M.S. program is open to all qualified college graduates, regardless of field of undergraduate study. Those wishing to apply for admissions to any of the M.B.A. or M.S. programs should submit the following: a complete application form; a nonrefundable application fee of $35; official undergraduate transcripts indicating a minimum undergraduate GPA of 2.5; two letters of professional recommendation; official results of the GMAT (not required for the M.S. programs); and for international students, the official results of the TOEFL, with a minimum total score of 550 on the paper-based test or 213 on the computer-based test. Students who wish to take a limited number of courses at the graduate level may enroll as nondegree, provisional students.

Finances

Tuition for graduate courses is $380 per semester credit hour, and for foundation courses, the tuition is $315 per semester credit hour. Estimated fees for the 1998–99 year are $650 for all students.

Books and miscellaneous expenses are approximately $3200 per year. Estimated living expenses for a single student are approximately $4400 for housing and $2700 for food per year. Married couples typically spend $6900 for housing and $3400 for food.

Assistantships and scholarships are available for certain M.B.A. programs. Students must apply for assistance to be eligible for either an assistantship or for a scholarship.

International Students

One fourth of the graduate students at Eastern College come from outside the United States. The on-campus international student adviser provides international students assistance in becoming acclimated to their new environment as well as to American culture and practices.

Application Facts and Dates

Once an application is complete, it is evaluated, and a response is given in a timely manner. Eastern's commitment is to keep students well informed through all stages of this process. Admissions are handled on a rolling basis, and there is no application deadline. However, students are urged to apply well in advance of the semester they plan to enter. For more information, students should contact:

Leonard N. Jamison
Director of Graduate Admissions
Mark Wagner
Graduate Admissions Representative

Eastern College
Graduate Admissions
1300 Eagle Road
St. Davids, Pennsylvania 19087
Telephone: 610-341-5972
Fax: 610-341-1466
E-mail: gradm@eastern.edu

Eastern Michigan University

Ypsilanti, Michigan

PROGRESSIVE AND PRACTICAL

Eastern Michigan University's College of Business combines a progressive curriculum with a diverse student body to create a graduate program that is designed to help transform corporate America. Our graduate programs offer students impressive management tools and practical business experience and develops valuable interpersonal and communication skills. We offer an M.B.A. program and master's programs in accounting, computer-based information systems, and human resource and organizational development.

We are proud of the accomplishments of our graduates. They symbolize the quality of our programs. Our outstanding facilities, experienced faculty, and connections with corporate leaders make Eastern Michigan's College of Business an exceptional learning environment.

—Stewart L. Tubbs, Dean

Programs and Curricular Focus

The M.B.A. program gives students a broad understanding of business functions, including the relationship of business to society as a whole, the impact of legal forces on business, and the internationalization of today's business climate. The program is designed to provide a general M.B.A. or a specialized M.B.A. in finance, financial accounting, human resource management, information systems management, international business, marketing, organizational development, production/operations management, strategic quality management, or tax accounting. This program requires 57 to 63 semester hours of graduate-level courses; however, students with undergraduate business degrees may need as few as 33 semester hours of graduate-level course work to complete the program. The educational emphasis is on a combination of state-of-the-art tools, concepts, and theory for practical application. An international perspective is provided throughout. Courses are offered in the evenings and on weekends. All graduate programs are accredited by the AACSB—The International Association for Management Education.

Students and the M.B.A. Experience

The College of Business has 535 students in the M.B.A. program, representing a wide variety of academic degrees, nationalities, and work experiences. The average student is 30 years old and has

an undergraduate GPA of 3.01, a GMAT score of 520, and seven years of work experience. Forty-eight percent of the students are women, and 3 percent are members of minority groups. International students, representing thirty-two countries, comprise 31 percent of the student population. Approximately half of the students have undergraduate degrees in business, while the other half have undergraduate degrees in arts and sciences, education, engineering, nursing, and the humanities.

❖ Global Focus

The College of Business offers many opportunities that enhance and strengthen students' perspectives on the global business environment. Double master's degree programs with the Export-Akademie Baden-Wuerttemberg in Reutlinger, Germany, and with Escuela Superior de Gestion Comercial (ESIC) in Madrid, Spain, affords students the opportunity to earn an M.B.A. in international business from EMU and a master's degree in business from the international institution. Currently, the College of Business is exploring a joint-degree program through EMU's World College in France. EMU is one of six U.S. schools in the nineteen-member Institute of International Education Regional Area Mobility Program working with exchange students from Canada and Mexico. Eastern offers an extensive cooperative education program and was one of nine institutions listed in *International Business* magazine's "Who's Who in International Co-op Programs."

The Faculty

Faculty members of the College of Business are among the finest teachers and researchers in the country. There are 73 full-time tenured faculty members.

The Business School Network

Corporate Partnerships

The College of Business has established a number of strong partnerships with corporations in southeastern Michigan, affording students a variety of opportunities for fieldwork and networking with business leaders. Students interact directly with prominent businesspersons through courses in survey and organizational diagnosis, human resource development, communication and organizational development and executive seminars and a management practicum. The 28-member College of Business Development Board includes CEOs and high-ranking officers from companies such as Ameritech, Gerber Products Company, Comerica Bank, Chrysler Motor Company, Ford Motor Company, and General Motors.

Prominent Alumni

Graduates of the College of Business include business leaders such as Timothy Adams, President of Chrysler-Europe; Marcia Allen, Partner with Coopers and Lybrand; Ron Campbell, Chief Financial Officer for the Detroit Pistons; and Bruce Halle, owner of Discount Tires.

The College and Environs

Eastern Michigan University, founded in 1849, is a coeducational institution located in the heart of the industrial and culturally rich region of southeastern Michigan. The University is a focal point of the historic city of Ypsilanti, located near the Detroit metropolitan area. With a student population of more than 23,000, the University offers instruction through five academic colleges. The University's 200 acres of lawn and wooded areas and 18 miles of walkways and jogging trails make the campus a beautiful learning environment. A 188,000-square-foot recreation/intramu-

Eastern Michigan's College of Business is one of only 305 business schools in the country accredited by the AACSB—The International Association for Management Education.

ral facility, newly renovated student union, University-owned Corporate Education Center, championship golf course, and the soon-to-be-completed University Library are among the many impressive University facilities.

Facilities

Among the University's 105 campus facilities is the Gary M. Owen College of Business building. This 122,000-square-foot state-of-the-art facility was completed in 1990. It includes classrooms, computer labs, seminar rooms, departmental offices, and behavioral labs that simulate a typical business environment.

Technology Environment

To ensure the success of its graduates, the College of Business has equipped its microcomputer laboratory with fifty microcomputers (Pentium 75-mhz and 90-mhz) and ten Macintosh computers connected through an Ethernet interface. The lab also has thirty Alpha terminals for accessing the University's mainframe. Computer and video equipment in the behavioral labs allows both presentation of controlled information and accurate recording of subjects' responses.

Placement

EMU's Career Services Office has established strong relationships with

on-campus recruiters and offers a number of services, workshops, and programs to aid students in their job searches. Among other strong relationships with Fortune 500 and multinational companies, Eastern Michigan has more than 1,300 graduate business alumni working at Ford Motor Company and is one of the fifteen key universities for Chrysler.

A representative of the Career Services Office works on-site at the College of Business to help students secure job interviews, co-op positions, and internships. Graduates of the M.B.A. program have the highest starting salaries among those who have completed any graduate program in the University, with a reported average salary of more than $48,000.

Admission

Admission is granted to those graduates of accredited institutions whose undergraduate GPA and GMAT scores indicate a high promise of success in graduate business studies. The average GMAT score for enrolling College of Business graduate students is 520. The average undergraduate GPA is 3.01.

International students must also provide proof of a degree from an accredited college overseas and official transcripts or mark sheets, results of the

Test of English as a Foreign Language (TOEFL) or Michigan Test ELI, a statement of financial responsibility, and two letters of recommendation. The I-20 form for the F-1 Visa cannot be issued until the student has been admitted to a degree program.

Finances

Estimated full-time tuition and fees for 1997–98 were $4800 per year for Michigan residents and $10,800 per year for nonresidents. Books and supplies cost approximately $1200 per year. Rent for on-campus apartments ranges from $380 to $500 per month; off-campus rents range from $400 to $700 per month.

A limited number of graduate assistantships are available for full-time graduate students. Assistantships require 20 hours of work per week and carry a stipend of $5614 to $5850 for two semesters. Inquiries regarding these programs should be addressed to the head of the department in which the student intends to specialize.

International Students

International students, representing thirty-two different countries, comprise 31 percent of the total graduate business student population at EMU. Programs and services offered through the Foreign Student Affairs office and support from a number of international student organizations help international students acclimate to the University environment.

Application Facts and Dates

Normal application deadlines for domestic students are November 15 for winter semester, March 15 for spring semester, and June 15 for fall semester. The deadlines for international students are November 1, March 1, and June 1 respectively. For late application processing, students should contact the coordinator of graduate programs.

For more information, students should contact:

William E. Whitmire
Graduate Business Programs
    Coordinator
401 Gary M. Owen Building
Eastern Michigan University
Ypsilanti, Michigan 48197
Telephone: 734-487-4444
Fax: 734-480-0618
E-mail: bill.whitmire@emich.edu
World Wide Web: http://www.emich.
    edu

École des Hautes Études Commerciales

Montreal, Canada

> **THE WORLD IS CHANGING—OUR M.B.A. AS WELL**
>
> *Completely redesigned, our M.B.A. program has undergone major changes that enables it to remain one of the front-runners in business education, as it has for the past twenty-five years. Implemented in the fall of 1996, the program has been extremely well received by students and businesspeople alike. This endorsement confirms the École des HEC's ability to understand the needs of the market and take appropriate action.*
>
> *—Jean-Marie Toulouse, Director*

Program and Curricular Focus

Since its creation more than twenty-five years ago, the HEC M.B.A. has undergone a variety of adjustments designed to keep the program constantly a step ahead. The curriculum structure, teaching approach, and course content ensure that the HEC M.B.A. accurately reflects the cross-functionality of management. Teaching is multidisciplinary and follows an approach that is more theme-oriented than functional, so that students develop a broad and accurate vision of managerial roles as well as strong problem-solving skills.

For full-time students, the intensive M.B.A. extends over fifty-four weeks. A part-time option is also available for students who want to remain "in action" at their places of work.

The HEC M.B.A. degree program is composed of four phases. During the first phase, students learn about business fundamentals, the skills required in today's business world, and the inherent complexity of management. In the second phase, they learn to master the basic techniques of the management trade and gain insight into how various functions interrelate.

With its exceptional range of more than 100 courses, the third phase—the core of the program—allows students to tailor the program to fit their needs by choosing a personalized major and acquiring leading-edge management techniques. Students can also opt for one of the cross-functional majors: entrepreneurship, management of technological innovation, management of service companies, and international management. HEC also offers such traditional majors as corporate finance, marketing, investment and portfolio management, general management, business economics, human resources management, and information technologies.

The fourth and final phase focuses on managing all aspects of change: technology, structures and processes, human resources management, personal attitudes, and strategy. In addition to the courses in change management, students take part in a supervised field project in an organization, within a small team, under the supervision of professors.

Students and the M.B.A. Experience

Although all of them have met the same criteria, candidates admitted to the HEC M.B.A. program are nevertheless an extremely diverse group. In nearly 70 percent of cases, they have a bachelor's degree in a field other than business administration. They have acquired their work experience in a wide variety of economic sectors. Their ranks include engineers, lawyers, psychologists, biologists, communications consultants, accountants, information system specialists, and administrators, each of whom brings his or her own wealth of knowledge and experience to the program. The School expects to increase its intake of international M.B.A. students, which should reach 50 percent of the M.B.A. student body in the medium term, compared to close to 30 percent at present.

The average student is 32 years old, with eight years of full-time work experience. Thirty-eight percent of the student population is female.

❖ Global Focus

"We want to enable students to become managers who act as responsible agents of change, ethical and respectful of others. Students will therefore be made highly aware of society's problems and of the local and international issues facing business. Our program strongly empha-
sizes qualities such as openness to the world, adaptability to change, curiosity and inventiveness, team spirit, and proficiency in foreign languages."
—Alain Noël, Director, M.B.A. program

More than ever, HEC's M.B.A. provides a strong international perspective throughout its curriculum as well as through its major in international management. During the third phase of the program, honor students can even add an international experience to their education by traveling to another country as part of the School's exchange program. Moreover, to encourage students to become proficient in foreign languages, up to one quarter of courses may be given in English within five years; some may be taught in Spanish.

Finally, another feature of the HEC M.B.A. is the emphasis it places on individual attention. Throughout the program, students receive academic counseling and personal support from professors who guide them in their choice of courses and field project.

The Faculty

École des Hautes Études Commerciales is renowned for its qualified and multidisciplinary teaching staff, the largest business administration faculty in Canada. It includes 175 career professors, all graduates of major universities in North America and Europe, supported by 225 lecturers who are also full-time managers.

HEC professors are experts in their fields who are much in demand as consultants to companies. A great many of them have backgrounds in management or as corporate executives. Several sit on the boards of large and medium-sized businesses, professional associations, or community organizations.

The Business School Network

Businesspeople are aware that their career advancement—and even the success of some of their projects—depends partly on the quality of their networks. HEC M.B.A. alumni form just such a network. The close ties they formed with their fellow students during their years of study continue to bear fruit throughout

HEC's ultramodern facilities provide students with an exceptional environment for living and learning.

their professional careers. The HEC M.B.A. network includes some 3,050 managers who have graduated from the program since its creation more than twenty-five years ago.

The M.B.A. program counts among its alumni a number of notable leaders, including Guy Bisaillon, First Vice President, Quebec, Scotia Bank; Pauline Marois, Minister, Education, Government of Quebec; Serge Bragdon, President and CEO, Uniboard Canada; Denis Côté, Vice President, Worldwide Marketing and Sales, Harris Corporation, Farinon Division (U.S.A.); and Daisy Aubry-Golaz, President, Georg Fischer Disa Group International (Switzerland).

The College and Environs

Montreal's unique blend of intellectual, economic, and cultural characteristics makes it a popular destination for international students.

In Montreal, students find a harmonious blend of North American efficiency and European refinement.

Greater Montreal began assuming a technological vocation several years ago, and today, half of Canada's pharmaceutical companies are clustered there. Nearly one third of Canada's industrial research is conducted in the city. Several Montreal companies are world leaders in high-

technology sectors, including telecommunications, aeronautics, aerospace, and biotechnology.

Situated on Mount Royal, an immense park in the heart of Montreal, HEC just minutes from the downtown core and is served by several bus lines and by a subway station.

Facilities

Since the fall of 1996, HEC has been housed in a brand-new building on Côte-Sainte-Catherine Road, on the edge of the Université de Montréal campus. With multimedia rooms, study carrels, and comfortable lounges, the School's open and spacious new facilities provide students with an exceptional environment for living and learning.

HEC's library is recognized as one of the world's largest business administration libraries. People come from far and wide to consult its unique collection of 315,000 documents, including 7,200 periodicals from a variety of countries, covering all management-related fields. Research is facilitated by the library's computerized reference system.

The library has an imposing collection of annual reports from large and medium-sized businesses, an essential source of information for preparing field studies and corporate projects. Also available are several Canadian, American, and European databanks on CD-ROM. Students also have access to major business and general information newspapers and magazines, including several years of back issues available on microfilm.

Technology Environment

Equipped with state-of-the-art computer and telecommunications facilities, the new HEC building enables students and staff members to make the most of advanced information technologies. New students are required to purchase a portable computer, which will give them the opportunity to hone their computer skills as well as gain access to greater resources.

Placement

The School's Placement Office provides valuable long-term support to HEC M.B.A. graduates, who have access to this service throughout their careers.

The department provides a wide variety of counseling services to assist students in

their search for employment and attainment of their career goals; these services include individual career profile evaluations, proactive job-search techniques, job interview simulations, curriculum vitae writing techniques, descriptions of trends in the job market, and information on companies and career planning.

Admission

Every application for admission to the HEC M.B.A. program is carefully evaluated by a committee composed of professors and members of the program administration. The requirements for admission are a bachelor's degree with a minimum average grade of 70; at least two years of relevant work experience; satisfactory results on the HEC M.B.A. admission tests or in the GMAT (Graduate Management Admission Test), which must be written within prescribed time limits; and a good knowledge of oral and written French (lectures are given in French), as well as sufficient knowledge of written English.

Finances

For the 1998–99 school year, tuition fees for international students are Can$15,500 for the entire fifty-four-week, intensive M.B.A. program. However, students from certain countries and those whose status meets certain criteria are exempted from these tuition fees and pay the same amount as Quebec residents, which is Can$3500 for the entire intensive M.B.A. in 1998–99.

Application Facts and Dates

Candidates who wish to be admitted for a specific term must submit their applications before the following deadlines: fall term, April 1, and winter term, October 1.

For more information on procedures for applying for residency in Canada, tuition fees, or admission to the HEC M.B.A. program, applicants should contact:

Registrar's Office
École des Hautes Études
    Commerciales
3000, Chemin de la Côte-Sainte-
    Catherine
Montréal, Québec H3T 2A7
Canada
Telephone: 514-340-6151
Fax: 514-340-6411
E-mail: mba@hec.ca
World Wide Web: http://www.hec.ca

Embry-Riddle Aeronautical University

Business Administration Department

Daytona Beach, Florida

AN M.B.A. AIMED AT THE FUTURE

Business graduate programs that best prepare a student for a successful career are those that supply a broad-based foundation in the basics and then provide special training and experience in a particular area. The M.B.A. program at Embry-Riddle follows this model, with a special emphasis on aviation. The program is particularly relevant today because aviation promises a future of exciting growth.

There are some industries that have always required a truly global approach, many of which change at high speed due to rapidly advancing technology and many that are unusually capital dependent. But of all the industries in the world, it is difficult to imagine one that embodies all of these characteristics to the same extent as the aviation/aerospace industry.

The Business Department and its programs are set up to specifically target all the unique characteristics of this industry and provide its participants exceptional knowledge and skills for management.

—Andres Zellweger, Dean

Programs and Curricular Focus

The Master of Business Administration (M.B.A.) degree program is designed to develop aviation managers who can apply the concepts of modern management techniques to the challenges of the aviation industry. There are two M.B.A. options: the Master of Business Administration in Aviation (M.B.A./A.) and the Executive Master of Business Administration (Executive M.B.A.). The M.B.A./A. is offered as a full-time resident program on the Daytona Beach campus and as a classroom program at more than 100 resident centers throughout the United States and in Europe through the Extended Campus' College of Career Education. The Executive Master of Business Administration requires a part-time residency on the Daytona Beach campus. The M.B.A. curriculum combines a strong traditional business core with specialization electives in aerospace production and operations management, international management and aviation policy, airline operations and management, airport operations and management, aviation law and insurance, aviation labor relations, and aviation economics. The development of versatility and analytical resourcefulness are two of the key aims of the M.B.A. program. The program is fashioned to stress pragmatic solutions to the managerial, technical, and operational problems likely to arise in the aviation industry as a result of the frequent and sweeping changes that occur in technol-

ogy as well as in the domestic and international regulations with which the industry must abide.

M.B.A./A. candidates must complete a minimum of 39 credit hours of course work consisting of 27 hours of core curriculum, thesis or graduate research project options, and specified electives. The M.B.A./A. degree program can usually be completed in eighteen months.

Executive M.B.A. candidates are generally sponsored by their employer. The program is delivered over eighteen months in a series of six 2-week residency sessions, approximately one session per calendar quarter, with assigned work between the residency sessions. The capstone activity, the Executive Project, is designed to benefit both the participant and the sponsoring organization by giving the participant the opportunity to apply the knowledge and diagnostic competencies learned throughout the program to a specific business issue of the sponsor.

Students and the M.B.A. Experience

The graduate programs currently enroll approximately 235 graduate students on the Daytona Beach campus. The College of Career Education enrolls about 3,000 students in graduate degree programs off campus at more than 100 locations throughout the United States and Europe. Of the graduate students on the Daytona

campus, 30 percent are from other countries, 20 percent are women, and 11 percent are members of minority groups. Approximately 12 percent of the campus-based graduate students are employed full-time; many hold professional positions in the aviation industry. In the M.B.A. degree program, students with diverse academic backgrounds but with common scholastic abilities enrich the program. The majority of incoming students have business degrees. The average age of incoming students is 28, and 25 percent are women.

The Faculty

The business administration faculty takes pride in bringing relevant, real-world problems, issues, and experiences into the classrooms. A high priority for the faculty is to prepare students for the roles of leadership they will assume. Faculty members accomplish this not only by excellent teaching but also by advising students on their business research and consulting projects. Many members of the faculty serve as consultants to a variety of industries. The diverse backgrounds of the faculty members provide a multi-cultural teaching field, with an emphasis on global standards and practices.

The Business School Network

The Embry-Riddle Business Program Advisory Committee (Daytona Beach campus) provides key input to the M.B.A. program by helping to develop the program curricula on a continuous basis to meet the current demands of the industry. Through this process, Embry-Riddle is able to shape the curriculum as necessary to provide students with the skills and educational background that suit the current needs of the aviation/aerospace industry. The Embry-Riddle Business Program Advisory Committee, which is composed of various distinguished representatives from throughout the industry, participates directly with the M.B.A./A. program by providing key guest speakers and lecturers for industry colloquiums and specialized classroom lectures. Through these events, students are able to further nurture their talents and develop contacts within the industry itself.

The College and Environs

The University comprises the eastern campus at Daytona Beach; a western campus in Prescott, Arizona; and the Extended Campus, with off-campus programs. Within the field of aviation, Embry-Riddle Aeronautical University has built a reputation for high-quality instruction in its programs since its founding in 1926.

The Daytona Beach campus is located next to the Daytona Beach International Airport and 10 minutes from the Daytona beaches. Within an hour's drive are Disney World and EPCOT, Kennedy Space Center, SeaWorld, Universal Studios, and St. Augustine. The Extended Campus resident centers are located in thirty-seven states and seven other nations. (See http://www.ec.erau.edu for a location map.)

Technology Environment

A cluster of mainframes (UNIX and IBM) and PCs supported by a telecommunications network provide the faculty and students with the latest advances in information management and computing facilities. These are augmented by academic student labs, the Airway Science Simulation Lab, and the Aviation Human Factors Research Lab. Extensive modern computer facilities and Internet access are available to all students.

Placement

In addition to contacts gained from internships, the M.B.A./A. degree program conducts a very aggressive placement program for its graduates. Years of research and consulting have allowed the faculty to cultivate un- matched contacts within the aviation industry, and its network provides job opportunities for graduates. The Career Services Office sponsors an annual industry Career Expo, which attracts more than 100 major companies such as Boeing, Federal Express, Delta, and United Airlines. In addition, the Career Resource Center offers corporate profiles, job postings, and development information. The office also assists with resume development and interview preparation.

Admission

The desired minimum undergraduate cumulative GPA is 2.5 on a 4.0 scale, with a minimum 3.0 in the junior and senior years. The GMAT is a requirement of the M.B.A./A. program. Extensive work experience, some at the management/supervisory level, is required of Executive M.B.A. candidates.

Finances

In 1998–99, tuition costs are $425 per semester hour on the Daytona Beach campus and $220 per semester hour at the Extended Campus resident centers. The cost of books and supplies are estimated at $300 per semester. Some on-campus housing is available to graduate students on the Daytona Beach campus. A standard double-occupancy room is $1350 per semester; a privacy or efficiency apartment is $1550 per semester. Single students sharing rental and utility expenses can expect yearly off-campus room and board expenses of $3800. Scholarship aid and graduate assistantships are available but limited. Students may apply for financial aid by calling 800-943-6279 (toll-free). All graduate programs are approved for Veterans Administration education benefits. The fee for the Executive M.B.A. option is $45,000, which includes University tuition, activity fees, all books, class materials, and lodging.

Application Facts and Dates

Applications are accepted on a revolving basis and should be completed thirty days prior to the start of a semester for U.S. citizens and resident aliens and ninety days prior for international students.

Applicants should contact the admissions office that corresponds to their preferred mode of study:

Graduate Admissions
Daytona Beach Campus
Telephone: 904-226-6115
          800-388-3728 (toll-free)
Fax: 904-226-7050
E-mail: taitg@cts.db.erau.edu
World Wide Web: http://www.db.erau.edu

Business Administration Office
Executive Management Institute
Telephone: 904-225-7946
Fax: 904-226-7984
E-mail: kelleyk@cts.db.erau.edu

College of Career Education
Admissions, Records and Registration
Extended Campus
Telephone: 904-226-6910
Fax: 904-226-6984
World Wide Web: http://www.ec.erau.edu

The mailing address is the same for all of the above:
Embry-Riddle Aeronautical University
600 S. Clyde Morris Boulevard
Daytona Beach, Florida 32114-3900

FACULTY LIST

The following are faculty members at the Daytona Beach campus:

Bruce D. Chadbourne, Ed.D., Florida Atlantic. Insurance and risk management.

Abe Harraf, Ph.D., Utah. Air transportation and economics.

Robert N. McGrath, Ph.D., LSU. Maintenance and logistics management.

Easwar Nyshadham, Ph.D., Mississippi. Management information systems and operations management.

John L. Pope, Ph.D., Berkeley. Organizational behavior, human resource management and leadership.

Vadhindran K. Rao, Ph.D., Mississippi. Finance.

Dawna L. Rhoades, Ph.D., Houston. Strategic planning and international management.

James R. Swanson, Ph.D., Florida. Management information systems.

Thomas Tacker, Ph.D., North Carolina. Political economics.

Boris Trnavskis, Ph.D., Calgary. Air transportation planning.

Bijan Vasigh, Ph.D., NYU. Finance and economics.

Blaise P. Waguespak Jr., Ph.D., North Texas. Marketing and management.

Philip A. Weatherford, Ed.D., Florida Atlantic. Transportation, organizational behavior, human resource management.

Seth Young, Ph.D., Berkeley. Airline and airport management.

The following are faculty members at the Extended Campus:

Thomas S. Barker, Ph.D., North Texas. Business policy and economics.

Robert A. Bertsch, Ed.D., Tulsa. Research methods, strategic marketing.

Chester Crosby, Ph.D., St. Louis. Production management and labor relations.

Paul K. Dygert, Ph.D., Michigan. Economics.

Edward E. Gordhammer, Ph.D., Oregon. Airport operations, strategic marketing.

William F. Herlehy, Ph.D., Kent State. Business policy, labor relations.

Kent J. Horne, Ph.D., North Dakota. Organizational behavior, global information management.

William H. Kraus, Ph.D., USC. Human resource development, business policy.

William L. March, Ed.D., Indiana. Operations research, business policy.

Frederick E. McNally, Ed.D., San Francisco. Organizational behavior.

David A. Miramonti, Ed.D., Western Michigan. Organizational behavior.

Vance F. Mitchell, Ph.D., Berkeley. Business policy, organizational behavior.

Thomas Moe, J.D., North Dakota. Aviation law, insurance.

John L. Neff, Ed.D., Indiana. Human resource development, business policy.

Donald M. Nixon, Ph.D., Colorado State. Strategic marketing, economics.

Franz G. Rosenhammer, D.B.A., Tennessee. Research methods.

Bruce A. Rothwell, Ph.D., Alabama. Labor relations.

Richard G. Schlapman, Ed.D., North Dakota. Research methods.

James T. Schultz, Ed.D., USC. Labor relations, organizational behavior.

Sidney E. Wheeler, Ph.D., Florida. Business policy, labor relations.

Emerson College

Boston, Massachusetts

PIONEERING BUSINESS EDUCATION THROUGH COMMUNICATION

All business functions are fundamentally activities of communication. Establishing an image for a corporation, positioning goods and services in the marketplace, responding to external circumstances such as legislative regulations and environmental disasters, and organizing and leading the members of a work team all require knowledge of the communication process. The study of communication within the business context concerns the strategic design, deployment, and assessment of messages and message campaigns.

Through two of its master's programs, Integrated Marketing Communication and Global Marketing Communication and Advertising, Emerson College has pioneered business education with a communication focus. Our distinguished faculty of academics and professionals prepares students for careers in marketing communication, advertising, management, and public relations for both domestic and global industries.

—Stuart Sigman, Dean

Programs and Curricular Focus

Emerson College offers programs of study leading to the M.A. in Integrated Marketing Communication and the M.A. in Global Marketing Communication and Advertising.

A newly defined professional degree program, the M.A. in Integrated Marketing Communication at Emerson unites the marketing functions of advertising, public relations, direct marketing, sales promotion, and interactive marketing under a comprehensive strategic approach. Emerson's programs provide degree candidates with a big-picture perspective, unifying all marketing functions toward a single goal: Better enabling business, not-for-profit, social causes, and individuals—such as politicians, actors, and athletes—to communicate with customers and publics. This focus gives students a wider breadth of course offerings across the marketing function as well as depth within specialty areas, such as marketing for the arts and entertainment industries or marketing within a global context.

The M.A. in Global Marketing Communication and Advertising is an intensive one-year, full-time program that prepares students to meet the diverse requirements of a rapidly growing global economy. Through courses such as Cultural Foundations of Buyer Behavior and New Technologies in Global Markets, the program prepares global marketers who understand the distinctive challenges

of targeting multicultural audiences. Each course offers a cutting-edge approach that blends theory with hands-on application. The program's tightly integrated academic structure includes internships in a broad range of enterprises both in the United States and abroad. Graduates go on to positions in international brand management, account management at international ad agencies, marketing management at international firms or U.S. firms seeking expansion, and international consulting, among others.

Students and the Program Experience

Global Marketing Communication and Advertising students are a diverse group. Nearly one third have come from outside the U.S., and almost half were in the workforce for periods ranging from two to fourteen years before enrolling in the program. Their ages have ranged from 22 to 42 years, with an average age of 27.

Emerson draws full-time Integrated Marketing Communication students from more than thirty-eight countries, with backgrounds in law, business, and the liberal arts and sciences. With more than a 20 percent international population, the classroom experience offers the global perspective necessary for educating future business leaders. Emerson's part-time students consist of working professionals from Boston's advertising and corporate community.

❖ Global Focus

Today's increasingly dynamic global marketplace, and its predicted surge in the next decade, demands specialized skills from marketing communication professionals. In an intensive one-year, full-time program, Global Marketing Communication and Advertising prepares students to meet the diverse requirements of a rapidly growing global economy. Its tightly integrated academic structure includes specialized courses and an internship. Past international internships have included the World Wildlife Fund, Grey Advertising, CNN, the Foreign Trade Academy, McCann-Erickson Worldwide, Honeywell, Hungarian Tourist Bureau, and ITT.

Special Features

EmComm, Emerson's in-house advertising agency, is dedicated to providing a training ground for tomorrow's marketing communication professionals. EmComm gives students practical experience in strategic marketing and advertising with both on- and off-campus accounts. Students work with real clients, professional graphic production companies, and sound studios, equipping them with valuable hands-on experience.

Graduate students in the School of Communication, Management and Public Policy may also spend a semester at Emerson's Los Angeles campus. The L.A. program is a fast-paced semester in which students work at internships by day and take classes with Emerson professors and industry professionals in the late afternoon and evening. Furnished housing is adjacent to the Los Angeles Center and just minutes from Universal Studios, Warner Brothers, and NBC Studios.

The Faculty

The School of Communication, Management and Public Policy faculty members are well-respected scholars and professionals drawn from all over the world. Through an integrated approach to business education, Emerson faculty members commit themselves to a curriculum of both theory and hands-on experience and foster a friendly openness with students both in and out of the classroom. Many faculty members have achieved national and worldwide recognition through their research and professional achievements.

The Business School Network

With more than 16,000 Emerson alumni working worldwide, Emerson's vast network of alumni professionals provide a great resource for guidance on seeking leadership in a particular career field. Alumni members of the Emerson Career Connection are available for informational interviews and may be contacted through the Office of Career Services. Recent employers of graduates include Arnold Communication, Bell Atlantic, The Gillette Company, Hill Holiday Atschiller, Norwegian Cruise Line, Prudential Securities, and Reebok.

The College and Environs

Emerson College is an independent, privately supported, coeducational, specialized college. Founded in Boston in 1880, it is the only college in the nation entirely devoted to the communication arts and sciences. It has been a pioneer in all aspects of communication and, together with a broad base of studies in the humanities and the sciences, they constitute the unique function of the institution. The increasingly vital role of communication in today's world gives added relevance and significance to an Emerson education.

Located in the heart of Boston near Beacon Hill and the Boston Common, Emerson College lies in the midst of one of the nation's largest media and publishing markets and corporate centers. Culturally, Boston is a cosmopolitan city at the highest level. It is home to an active theater district, the world-famous Boston Symphony Orchestra, the legendary Celtics and Red Sox, and the Museum of Fine Arts, open without charge to Emerson students. Emerson's urban campus, itself a Boston landmark, is within walking distance of eclectic neighborhood bistros, the Public Garden, Newbury Street's shopping district, the Charles River Esplanade, and the Freedom Trail, along which are some of the most important landmarks in U.S. history.

Facilities

The Emerson College Library houses more than 185,000 print and nonprint items that focus on the communication arts and sciences. Through membership in the Fenway Consortium, graduate students have access to more than 2 million volumes. Computer-assisted reference services provide bibliographic databases through Dialog, BRS, and other online services. The On-line Computer Library Center is used for student research support. Other facilities include a focus group interview room complete with observation room and two-way mirror, computers equipped with SPSS for Windows, Version 7.5, and Internet access for validated scales.

Placement

The Career Services Office has been established to provide internship and job placement as well as lifetime career assistance. Listing more than 1,500 positions in Boston, the United States, and Europe, Emerson's internship program is the largest of its kind. Internships are available in every variety of media, corporate, nonprofit, theatrical, medical, and political organization.

Admission

Admission to the graduate programs is based on a combination of factors, including academic performance, GRE or GMAT scores, letters of recommendation, personal and professional experience, portfolios, and potential contributions to the proposed major field of study.

An application and fee must be submitted along with an official transcript and three letters of recommendation. International students must submit results of the Test of English as a Foreign Language (TOEFL).

Emerson College encourages applications from graduating college seniors and from individuals who wish to reenter the labor market, seek a career change, or strengthen their credentials. Part-time evening degree programs are available in several of the major program areas.

Finances

Tuition for the 1998–99 academic year is $566 per credit. Though Emerson does not offer on-campus housing to graduate students, the College's Office of Off-Campus Housing assists graduate students in arranging for private accommodations in the Boston area. Costs of living in Boston are comparable to those in any large metropolitan city.

Several types of financial aid are available to graduate students, including need-based loans and awards based on academic merit. Merit awards consist of teaching, research, and administrative assistantships. The deadline for applicants interested in merit-based awards is March 1.

The Cecil and Helen Rose Ethics in Communication Scholarship is awarded to a graduate student who demonstrates a career interest that furthers the importance of ethics in effective and responsible communication.

International Students

Emerson College offers a unique six-week intensive language program for international graduate students. This preparatory program is designed to strengthen and develop necessary communication skills in order to succeed both in and out of the classroom. In a supportive environment, the program integrates academic work, English language preparation, and social and cultural activities. There is an additional fee for the program.

Application Facts and Dates

July 15 is the application deadline for fall enrollment; December 1, for spring. For further information, students should contact:

Director of Graduate Admission
Emerson College
100 Beacon Street
Boston, Massachusetts 02116
Telephone: 617-824-8610
Fax: 617-824-8614
E-mail: gradapp@emerson.edu
World Wide Web: http://www.
   emerson.edu

E. M. Lyon

Ecully, France

ENHANCING YOUR MANAGEMENT CAREER WITH AN INNOVATIVE EUROPEAN M.B.A.

For more than 25 years, the Cesma M.B.A. has provided excellence in graduate management education. At Cesma M.B.A., we dedicate ourselves to providing you with the tools and the opportunities you need for the challenges of the international business environment. Our pedagogy encourages you to share your experience while learning from your classmates and our renowned faculty. Even before you graduate, the esprit de corps of the Cesma M.B.A. alumni and our placement service will help you to set your sights on your new career. We look forward to welcoming you to Cesma M.B.A. and to helping you to acquire that winning edge.

—Bernard Belletante, Dean for Academic Programs

Programs and Curricular Focus

The Cesma M.B.A. program is a bilingual, European-style M.B.A., accredited by AMBA (Association of M.B.A.'s) and is ranked among the leading M.B.A. programs in Europe.

Since 1997, a single program designed to make an impact on both an organizational and an individual level is offered in two different versions: a one-year full-time format or a two-year part-time format for executives.

Three interrelated themes characterize the Cesma M.B.A. program and guide its teaching approach: the development of personal managerial competencies, entrepreneurship, and comparative and intercultural management.

These, together with opportunities to acquire knowledge and understanding in the basic management disciplines, are in response to the needs of companies in today's complex and changing business world.

Via core courses, international courses, and electives; personal development workshops; and a series of interdisciplinary seminars, participants are encouraged to learn starting from concrete cases and from their own personal and professional experience. There is a strong emphasis on group work, which, given the diversity of the Cesma M.B.A. year-group, provides a rich laboratory of intercultural exchanges. In addition to company placements, a range of independent projects is proposed—both in France and elsewhere—to enable participants to develop their capacity to analyze

situations, imagine solutions, make recommendations, and then take responsibility for action.

Students and the M.B.A. Experience

A typical Cesma M.B.A. year-group is composed of 20 percent women. One third of the participants are from countries other than France, representing 15 different nationalities from around the world. The average age is 30 years. Ninety percent are practicing managers with an average of seven years of experience and the remaining 10 percent are recent graduates. A substantial proportion of those with management experience have worked in an international context before joining the program. The part-time program is composed entirely of practicing managers.

In terms of academic background, approximately 30 percent are engineers, 20 percent are scientists, and 50 percent have arts, languages, social sciences, or other types of degrees.

The diversity of the year-group is one of the real strengths of the Cesma M.B.A. As in any project team, participants find themselves constantly confronted with the challenges of working in intercultural and interprofessional groups. They are encouraged to support and to learn as much from each other as they do from the program.

❖ Global Focus

International and comparative management issues are at the heart of the Cesma

M.B.A. curriculum and are inescapably present in the work of the different tutorial and study groups. Certain courses, such as Globalisation, Cultural Diversity and Management Practice, International Commerce, and International Strategy and Globalization, focus specifically on these questions. Others, like the workshops on Geopolitics and Human Resource Management in Intercultural Contexts, explore cultural differences in depth.

Specific missions, normally conducted in small groups, give participants an opportunity to work on the creation of business start-up plans, consulting projects, or other types of action research in companies, both in France and in other countries. Two customized tracks are proposed at the end of the year, permitting those participants who so wish to specialize either in European human resource management or in entrepreneurship.

There are also opportunities for shorter or longer periods of exchange with Cesma's partner schools. They include Cranfield School of Management, U.K., with whom there is a double-degree arrangement; the Management School at Lancaster University, U.K.; ESADE in Barcelona, Spain; Carnegie Mellon in Pittsburgh, U.S.A.; HEC in Montreal, Canada; Waseda University in Tokyo, Japan; and Belgrano University in Argentina.

The Faculty

Eighty permanent members make up the teaching and research faculty at E. M. Lyon. They are recruited not only on the basis of academic qualifications but also according to their business experience and international exposure.

Numerous visiting international professors and experts participate in the Cesma M.B.A. program every year. Twenty percent of the permanent faculty are from other countries and 25 percent are women. By encouraging research and collaboration with institutions in other countries, as well as consulting in companies, E. M. Lyon has allowed its faculty members to attain high degrees of competence and to produce numerous publications.

The Business School Network

The traditionally close links with the Lyon Chamber of Commerce and Industry and the funding of educational and research projects as well as international scholarships by companies have made E. M. Lyon exceptionally responsive to the needs of business.

Cesma M.B.A. offers operational training based on pragmatism and encourages participants to develop their group strength, team spirit, and their abilities to anticipate and adapt to change.

Representatives and professionals from various sectors and functions in companies often participate in the many seminars that punctuate the program.

Company representatives and managers also take part in a series of discussions and conferences within the courses. On campus, numerous events are organized in order to provide the most favorable conditions for in-depth exchange between students and companies. More than 100 European firms and European subsidiaries of international companies visit E. M. Lyon each year to give presentations and to prospect for potential employees among the students.

The College and Environs

E. M. Lyon was created in 1872. Initially established in Lyon, the school experienced strong growth, which in 1972 led it to move to an ultramodern campus in Ecully, a residential suburb minutes from the center of Lyon. The campus is spread within a teaching and research zone that includes higher educational institutions, a small business incubator, and a number of high-tech firms.

It is located near Lyon's city center, France's second largest city. Lyon has an unrivaled geographical situation, and it takes only a two- to three-hour drive to get to Alpine skiing resorts or the beaches of the French Riviera.

Facilities

Educational resources includes a documentation center (12,500 bound volumes, 380 periodicals, CD-ROMs), a database and computer center, audiovisual facilities (television studios), and language laboratory facilities. A gymnasium and several tennis courts complete the infrastructure of the school. The campus offers the Cesma M.B.A. participants accommodations and restaurant facilities (two residence complexes, a cafeteria, and a restaurant).

Placement

Counselors from the E. M. Lyon Careers and Orientation Department offer individualized support and advice to participants in planning their career and in their search for employment. Each year, the E. M. Lyon Career office receives notices for more than 4,000 job openings.

Cesma M.B.A. graduates have responsibilities all over the world, mainly in medium-sized companies owned by large multinationals. One third work as managing directors or directors of subsidiaries and 44 percent work in commercial or marketing functions. The most represented sector is industry (56 percent), with the remainder working in finance or as consultants. In the last

twenty-five years, 20 percent of graduates have created their own companies.

Admission

Applicants are at least 24 years of age, highly motivated, have great intellectual ability, and are committed. Ideal applicants are managers holding a first degree and possessing significant work experience. The admission process is in two stages.

First, the completed application form must be submitted and, if approved, the applicant is then invited to the second stage—the admissions tests and the selection interview. GMAT or TAGE-MAGE (French equivalent of GMAT) as well as the TOEFL or the Cesma M.B.A. French test scores are required. It is possible to arrange to take the admissions tests and to participate in a selection interview in specified countries other than in France.

Finances

For 1998–99, the application fee is Fr 650, the tuition fee for the full-time program is Fr 97,000 (payable in installments). Living expenses are estimated to be approximately Fr 50,000.

International Students

One third of Cesma M.B.A. participants are from countries other than France and 15 nationalities are represented. Ninety percent are from Europe, 1.5 percent are from Central America, 7 percent are from North America, and 1.5 percent are from other areas. At the participants' disposal are an information and advisory service, career counseling, and bilingual French and English language tuition.

Application Facts and Dates

There is only one intake per year, in September, and applications must be submitted by June 15. Interested students should contact:

Cesma M.B.A.
E. M. Lyon
23 Avenue Guy de Collongue
BP 174, 69132
Ecully Cedex
France
Telephone: 33 4 78 33 78 65
Fax: 33 4 78 33 77 55
E-mail: cesmamba@em-lyon.com
World Wide Web: http://www.em-lyon. com

Emory University

Roberto C. Goizueta Business School

Atlanta, Georgia

> ### BUILDING MOMENTUM AT A WORLD-CLASS INSTITUTION
> *As I join Goizueta Business School as Dean, several remarkable events have charged 1998 with renewed momentum. Recent gifts of $40 million enable the School to expand its recruitment of world-class faculty members and to increase student fellowships and scholarships. With these resources as well as a new state-of-the-art building, cutting-edge technology, and an innovative curriculum, the School will quickly move forward in its progress toward preeminence.*
> —Thomas S. Robertson, Dean

Programs and Curricular Focus
The Goizueta Business School M.B.A. program offers students the opportunity to pursue an M.B.A. in a flexible, innovative environment. Students are encouraged to work closely with professors, to individualize a course of study, and to customize career goals. The core curriculum has been redesigned, creating the "flex core," allowing students to take electives earlier in the program. In addition, a weeklong introduction to each semester consists of a simulation game in the fall term, and in the spring, a focus module addressing contemporary industry or region-specific issues is taught. Faculty members use teaching methods best suited to the course material, including cases, lectures, class discussions, student presentations, team and field projects, and computer simulations with a balanced emphasis on quantitative and qualitative approaches.

During the first year, students complete a core curriculum that stresses the fundamental building blocks of business and the basic principles in each of the primary functional areas. During the second year, students have the opportunity to develop an area of concentration in areas that include finance, marketing, management, accounting, or decision and information analysis.

In addition to the full-time, two-year M.B.A. program, other programs leading to the M.B.A. degree are offered. Graduates of undergraduate business schools accredited by AACSB–The International Association for Management Education may start the program in the summer semester and complete the program in one calendar year. The Goizueta Business School also offers a part-time, three-year evening M.B.A. program for working professionals and a sixteen-month Executive M.B.A. program for candidates with significant managerial experience. Joint-degree programs are available with the law school, J.D./M.B.A. (four years); the School of Public Health, M.P.H./M.B.A. (five semesters); the Candler School of Theology, M.B.A./M.Div. (four years), and the School of Nursing, M.B.A./M.N. (six semesters), as well as certificate programs through an area studies track.

Students and the M.B.A. Experience
The Goizueta Business School consists of 270 full-time and 170 part-time M.B.A. students, who come from a wide variety of academic disciplines, geographic regions, and professions. For the full-time program, the average length of postgraduate work is more than four years, with 99 percent of the students having more than one year of work experience. Thirty percent of the students are women, 12 percent are members of minority groups, and almost 30 percent are international students who represent twenty countries. The range of GMAT scores is 530–710 for the middle 80 percent.

❖ Global Focus
Students at the Goizueta Business School experience global issues on many levels within the M.B.A. program. The Global Perspectives course, taught in the second semester, serves as an introduction using a multidisciplinary, integrated approach. By bringing all the functional disciplines together, the course helps students learn to operate in a global environment and develop political, cultural, ethical, and geographic perspectives. There are also course electives in finance, accounting, management, and marketing.

Students have the opportunity to study abroad in exchange programs currently offered with more than twelve universities in such countries as China, Costa Rica, England, Finland, France, Germany, Italy, Mexico, Singapore, and Venezuela. Specialized programs with Soviet, Post-Soviet, and East European Studies and Latin American Area Studies at Emory University enable students to gain further experience in a geographic area.

Special Features
Students at the Goizueta Business School are very involved in the Atlanta community. A case competition organized by the Emory Marketing Club gives students the opportunity to apply marketing research skills to real business challenges for such companies as the Coca-Cola Company, the Ritz-Carlton Hotel, the American Red Cross, Georgia-Pacific Corporation, Suntory, and BellSouth. Community involvement also occurs with such projects as volunteer days and fund-raising events for dealing with societal problems of Atlanta's underprivileged residents.

The Faculty
Emory places teaching first among equals with respect to scholarly research and service to the business community. Faculty members have joined the Business School from such institutions as Chicago, Harvard, Michigan, MIT, Northwestern, Pennsylvania (Wharton), Stanford, and Yale.

The Business School Network
Corporate Partnerships
The Customer Business Development Track involves such companies as Procter & Gamble, Coca-Cola, Kodak, and Chubb in a program that incorporates integration of classroom learning and clinical fieldwork experiences for students.

The College and Environs
The city of Atlanta is the business, cultural, and international center of the

southeastern United States and, according to *Fortune* magazine, is considered by business leaders to be one of the top five cities in which to do business. It is the sixteenth-largest metropolitan area in the nation and the largest in the Southeast. The moderate climate and reasonable cost of living, in addition to an impressive array of cultural and recreational offerings, attract people from all over the world. More than 450 of the Fortune 500 companies have headquarters or offices in Atlanta.

Emory University is located 6 miles from downtown Atlanta on the northeast side of the city. The campus consists of 550 heavily wooded acres in a nice residential neighborhood. Emory offers students access to the resources of a cosmopolitan university community with more than 9,000 students. The diverse learning environment is enhanced by specialized centers and affiliates such as the Carter Center, the Yerkes Primate Center, the Law and Economics Center, Scholars Press, and the Centers for Disease Control and Prevention (CDC).

Facilities

The Goizueta Business School moved into its new home on Emory's campus in July 1997. The building is 119,000 square feet, with state-of-the-art technology throughout the facility. The five-story structure has a strategic design that facilitates an interactive teaching and research environment.

Technology Environment

Computing at the Goizueta Business School is comprehensive with modern

facilities, a professional staff, and extensive documentation. Extensive library resources are available to students with online databases such as ABI Inform business magazine index, LEXIS-NEXIS, and Dow Jones News/Retrieval Service.

Placement

The mission of the Office of Career Services is centered around assisting students in pragmatically focusing particular abilities, experiences, and interests toward a career goal and helping the student develop an individual strategy for marketing himself or herself in order to conduct an effective job search. Workshops, speakers, internships, mentors, and alumni are some of the resources available to students.

Admission

Admission to the M.B.A. program is highly selective. Each candidate is evaluated on the basis of his or her ability to perform in an academically rigorous environment as well as contribute to classroom discussions based on work and/or life experiences. Diversity and international perspectives are valued in the admission process. To apply to the Goizueta Business School, a student must submit the results of the Graduate Management Admission Test (GMAT); official transcripts from all previous undergraduate, graduate, and professional work; three letters of recommendation; and the completed application form including statistical data, work history, and essays. Applicants from non-English-speaking countries also must submit scores from the Test of English as a

Foreign Language (TOEFL) and a statement of financial resources.

Finances

Tuition for the 1998–99 academic year at Goizueta Business School is $24,200. The estimated annual living expenses and fees for a student living off campus total $15,030. Students who complete an application by February 15 are automatically considered for merit-based scholarships. Need-based aid in the form of loans is available to M.B.A. students. Applicants should file the FAFSA and Financial Aid PROFILE for loan consideration. To contact Emory University's Financial Aid Office, students should call 404-727-1141 or write to Financial Aid Office, Emory University, Atlanta, Georgia 30322.

International Students

International students are encouraged to apply. Good communication skills are essential to the program. Applicants whose native language is not English must score a minimum of 600 on the TOEFL. A limited amount of merit-based financial assistance is available for international students.

Application Facts and Dates

The deadline for applying to the two-year, full-time M.B.A. program is March 31. For full scholarship consideration, the application deadline is February 15. Applications for the one-year M.B.A. program are due February 15; for the evening M.B.A. program, March 1. Applications are available via the School's Web site (address below). Students may also obtain applications and admissions information from:

Julie R. Barefoot
Assistant Dean of Admissions and
   Career Services
Goizueta Business School
Emory University
Atlanta, Georgia 30322-2712
Telephone: 404-727-6311
Fax: 404-727-4612
World Wide Web: http://www.emory.
   edu/BUS/

Emporia State University

School of Business/M.B.A. Program

Emporia, Kansas

PREPARING STUDENTS FOR TOMORROW

Emporia State University's (ESU) School of Business prepares students to excel in an increasingly global business environment. We are small enough to practice a truly student-oriented philosophy but large enough to provide a high-quality educational experience.

Our M.B.A. faculty members maintain close relations with business practitioners and integrate business experiences into classroom presentations. The School of Business Council of Advisors, comprised of prominent business and government leaders, represents a key link in keeping abreast of current and emerging trends.

We care about our students and focus our efforts on providing a meaningful educational experience to prepare them for tomorrow's business world.

—S. A. Hashmi, Dean

Programs and Curricular Focus

The standard M.B.A. program is a sequence of courses (36 credit hours) designed to assure competency in the functional areas of business and also to enable a student to acquire content breadth by choosing elective courses. Required courses include study in the areas of accounting, finance, management, information systems for management, managerial economics, marketing, and quantitative methods. Elective courses may be taken in a wide range of subject-matter areas. Increasingly, many students choose elective courses in international finance, international management, and international marketing.

The School also offers a specialized M.B.A. degree (36 credit hours), with a concentration in accounting. This curriculum prepares students for high-level accounting positions and enables them to meet requirements for admission to the uniform CPA examination. In addition to taking required courses in areas such as finance, marketing, and management, students must take a required accounting course and choose two additional elective courses in accounting.

In both M.B.A. curriculums, completion of a core of undergraduate prerequisite business courses is necessary before full admission status is granted. These courses may have been taken to fulfill undergraduate degree requirements or may be taken at Emporia State University. The reason for requiring prerequisite study is to provide a basic understanding of business that can be further developed by study at the graduate level.

Students and the M.B.A. Experience

M.B.A. students have diverse academic and experiential backgrounds. While some have a limited amount of work experience, others have extensive experience in various managerial positions. A typical M.B.A. student is 30 years old, has four or five years of work experience, and completes degree requirements primarily for professional career development. Seventy percent of the students are men, and between 30 and 35 percent are students who come to the United States to pursue an M.B.A. degree.

As part of their instructional methodology, many professors stress teamwork. Also, students have opportunities to complete internships or to work in cooperation with a professor to complete independent study covering a specialized topic of mutual interest. Although the majority of students have completed undergraduate business degrees, an undergraduate major in business is not a requirement for admission.

The Faculty

Professors who teach M.B.A. courses are members of the graduate faculty. Approximately one fourth of the faculty are women. In addition to instructional responsibilities, many faculty members work as consultants to businesses, government agencies, and educational organizations. They conduct research, publish papers, and are leaders in professional organizations. Several faculty members have authored or coauthored textbooks printed by major publishing companies. These professional activities bring a high level of intellectual excitement and realism to the classroom.

The Business School Network

Corporate Partnerships

The School maintains strong relationships with business and industry. In addition to the availability of cooperative study and internship opportunities, some professors work directly with companies to involve students in real-world projects as a component of the classroom educational experience. The business community serves as an important resource to provide valuable expertise and guidance. Each year, the M.B.A. Student Association sponsors educational programs and hosts business leaders who give lectures and participate in seminars.

Prominent Alumni

Numerous alumni have made noteworthy accomplishments during their professional careers. These graduates include Dennis Casarona, president of Graphic Promotions; Kay Gerdes, vice president of operations for Farm Credit Services; Salief Keita, director of agencies for Banque Malienne de Credit et de Depots (Mali); Ken Lerman, a widely known business consultant who formerly served as marketing director for Pizza Hut and Taco Tico; and Yasunori Watanabe, country general manager for TNT Worldwide (Japan).

The College and Environs

"A place where people care about you" is how students describe Emporia State University. With an enrollment of approximately 6,000 students, ESU offers twenty-four graduate degree programs. The University is small enough for students to develop friendships, yet large enough to offer a variety of educational programs.

With a population of nearly 30,000, Emporia is an educational, industrial,

The School of Business is housed in Cremer Hall, a modern five-story building.

trade, and medical center serving east-central Kansas. It is situated on the eastern edge of the Bluestem region of the Flint Hills and is surrounded by numerous lakes and recreational facilities. The city is located on the Kansas Turnpike, Interstate 35, and the main line of the Santa Fe Railroad. Three major metropolitan areas of Kansas (Topeka, Kansas City, and Wichita) can easily be reached from Emporia.

Placement

The Office of Career Development, Cooperative Education, and Placement

Services coordinates arrangements for corporate recruiters to visit the campus. Students and alumni have access to weekly listings of position vacancies. Each year, the School sponsors a career fair, which gives students opportunities to become acquainted with potential employers. The M.B.A. Student Association encourages networking with corporate executives and sponsors programs to help develop effective interviewing skills.

Admission

Applicants need a minimum grade point average of 2.5 (A=4.0) for the last 60

credit hours of undergraduate study. In addition, an acceptable score on the Graduate Management Admission Test (GMAT) is required for unconditional admission. The score on the GMAT and the academic transcript are used to determine admission status. Those granted probationary status must submit an acceptable GMAT score before or during their first semester of graduate study.

Finances

For the 1998–99 academic year, fees for a full course load are $3006 per semester for nonresidents. For the 1998 summer session, nonresident fees are $250 per credit hour. Fees are established by the Kansas Board of Regents and are subject to change. Estimated cost of room and board is $3600 per academic year. The cost of books and supplies is approximately $250 per semester. The University Housing Office maintains a list of off-campus rooms, apartments, and houses that may be rented by students. Also, housing is available at the University-owned Emporia State Apartments.

Each year, the School offers a number of graduate assistantships to qualified students. Graduate assistants also may be eligible for reduced fees.

International Students

International students represent approximately one third of the M.B.A. enrollment. The majority of these students come from African, Asian, and South American countries. The University sponsors a number of activities and organizations to accommodate the needs of international students. Also, specialized intensive English language training is available on campus.

Application Facts and Dates

Students are admitted for terms beginning in August, January, and June, with corresponding deadlines of June 1, November 1, and April 1. Applications are processed on a continuous basis. For additional information concerning the application process, admission requirements, or graduate assistantships, students should contact:

Dr. Donald S. Miller
Director, M.B.A. Program
School of Business
Campus Box 4059
Emporia State University
Emporia, Kansas 66801-5087
Telephone: 316-341-5456
Fax: 316-341-6346
E-mail: millerdo@emporia.edu
World Wide Web: http://www.emporia.
edu/business

Active interaction between students and professors characterizes classroom sessions.

RSM *Erasms* Erasmus University Rotterdam

Rotterdam School of Management

Rotterdam, the Netherlands

> ### BUILDING UPON SUCCESS
>
> *The ability to innovate and to remain at the leading edge of developments in management theory and practice are critical for the success of M.B.A. participants and of M.B.A. programs. The Rotterdam School of Management continuously strives to build upon the success we have achieved through a continuous focus on issues of international business, information technology, and soft management skills. These features complement an in-depth, integrated M.B.A. curriculum aimed at creating managers capable of leading global companies.*
>
> —J. Wil Foppen, Dean

Programs and Curricular Focus

The Rotterdam School of Management (RSM) offers two full-time M.B.A. programs: the International M.B.A. Program in General Management and the International M.B.A./M.B.I. (Master of Business Administration/Master of Business Informatics) Program. These eighteen-month programs start each September and are taught entirely in English.

The curriculum of the International M.B.A. Program in General Management covers all major aspects of general management. The first year consists of mandatory courses in management basics and functional areas and includes communication workshops.

The International M.B.A./M.B.I. program is designed for students who, in addition to a general management education, wish to receive theoretical and practical training in the managerial aspects of information technology (IT). M.B.A./M.B.I. graduates help bridge the gap between specialists in information technology and managers who are the main users of information systems. It is clearly not a technical program, but a management program. The M.B.A./M.B.I. program is largely identical to the M.B.A. program but includes M.B.I.-exclusive class blocks later in the program.

The first-year course period for both M.B.A. and M.B.A./M.B.I. students ends with a project management and consulting workshop. During the summer, students are required to undertake an in-company project. M.B.A./M.B.I. students take a required M.B.I. block of courses before performing an IT in-company project.

The second year allows students to tailor their studies to areas of their interest. Through electives and mini-courses, they can focus on areas such as corporate finance, marketing, or IT. Students also have the opportunity to participate in an exchange program with top business schools worldwide in their second year.

Students and the M.B.A. Experience

The Rotterdam School of Management is a business school that attracts students from all over the world. Some forty-eight different nationalities are represented in the current student population of 120 students per year. Only 15 percent of students are Dutch; the remaining 85 percent are international. Students come from a wide variety of academic backgrounds. An average breakdown is 30 percent engineering, 30 percent business, 15 percent science and medicine, 10 percent economics, 10 percent humanities and social sciences, and 5 percent law. The average age of students is 29, and the average number of years of work experience is five.

Working in groups is an essential element of the M.B.A. programs. The emphasis on teamwork provides a realistic model for the way in which management issues are handled in the business world. Students learn the vital significance of teamwork and the value of cooperation when they are confronted with a wide range of approaches to a single problem. By forming teams of students with different cultural and educational backgrounds, various problem-solving techniques are recognized and appreciated. This enriches the learning experience of all students.

Special Features

The Rotterdam School of Management is consistently ranked as one of Europe's top five business schools. *The Economist*'s "Which M.B.A.?" describes the School as innovative, interesting, and friendly.

In addition to the functionally based courses, the M.B.A. programs include extensive workshops, seminars, and mini-courses aimed at building practical skills. Furthermore, students undertake consultancy projects for companies and nonprofit organizations.

In the third semester of the M.B.A. programs, students can apply to go on exchange to a business school in the U.S. (e.g., Wharton, Kellogg, Chicago, Columbia, Berkeley), Europe (e.g., Bocconi-Italy, IESE-Spain, MBS-U.K.), South Africa, Japan, or Mexico.

The Faculty

The academic faculty represents a mix of professors from the Rotterdam School of Management and Erasmus University, visiting faculty members of prestigious international universities, and consultants and managers active in different industries. Faculty members are international professionals who bring up-to-date management techniques and practices into the classroom. They are committed to a wide range of teaching methods such as lectures, case studies, field trips, group work, management games, and real-life projects.

The Business School Network

The Rotterdam School of Management was founded with the support of major Dutch multinationals and has since developed close ties with the international business community. Companies like Citibank, Arthur D. Little, and ABN AMRO Bank actively take part in the curriculum of the M.B.A. program.

The RSM Alumni Association is a very international network of all RSM graduates. Alumni are closely involved in the School's activities and are always

pleased to meet potential students and discuss their experiences at the RSM with them.

The College and Environs

The Rotterdam School of Management is a foundation of Erasmus University Rotterdam, which is renowned for its business orientation. The University was founded in 1913 by Rotterdam entrepreneurs and named after Erasmus Desiderius Roterodamus. Erasmus was born in Rotterdam in the late fifteenth century. He was a leader of the liberal reform movement in Europe and dreamed of democracy of the intellect and correct use of free will. It is this humanist tradition that still lives on in the University, which today has more than 16,000 students, of whom some 1,600 are enrolled in postgraduate studies.

Facilities

The Rotterdam School of Management is located on the Woudestein Campus of the Erasmus University. The University campus is situated close to the center of Rotterdam. The RSM offers housing services for all international students near the University campus. The language laboratory at Erasmus University is available to RSM students. The RSM has a school restaurant/bar. The Business Library provides business information and supports M.B.A. students' and alumni's

search for information on management and business. The resources of the library are specifically selected to support the M.B.A. and M.B.A./M.B.I. curricula. Students can also make use of the sports center, the main library, and information services from Erasmus University.

Technology Environment

The RSM has excellent computer facilities with dedicated computer labs. The PC network from Novell contains a wide range of software packages, such as database programs, presentation graphics, spreadsheets, statistics, word processing, online information services, and others. RSM students can also make use of electronic mail worldwide and Internet access.

Placement

The Career Planning Office is dedicated fully to the career development needs of all M.B.A. students while serving the recruitment necessities of companies internationally. The Career Planning Office organizes workshops in resume and cover letter writing, self-assessment, and interviewing techniques. The resume (curriculum vitae) book provides a valuable database for both on- and off-campus recruiters. Students are encouraged to include their resumes on the Internet pages of the RSM.

For many RSM students, the yearly on-campus company presentations and selection interviews turn out to be the starting point of their careers. The RSM is a target school for recruitment among leading national and international companies.

Admission

The RSM welcomes applications from outstanding men and women whose intellectual ability, management potential, and personal qualities indicate that they will benefit from and contribute to the learning environment. Eligibility requirements include a recognized university degree, GMAT scores, two letters of recommendation (academic and/or professional), work experience, proficiency in English, and a personal interview with one of RSM's alumni in the applicant's country of residence.

Finances

The tuition fees for the 1998–2000 programs are DFL 42,500 ($21,500) for the entire M.B.A. program and DFL 46,000 ($23,000) for the entire M.B.A./M.B.I. program.

Other expenses, such as room rent, books, and living expenses, are estimated to be around $17,500 for the entire program duration of eighteen months.

International Students

All RSM activities are international by definition, as the student body represents so many nationalities. Students can receive assistance with applications for visa and housing matters.

Application Facts and Dates

The application deadline is June 15. Applications are processed on a continuous basis in order of receipt. Late applicants will be placed on a waiting list. Applicants should contact:

Ms. Connie Tai, M.B.A.
Admissions Director
Rotterdam School of Management
Erasmus Graduate School of Business
P.O. Box 1738
3000 DR ROTTERDAM
The Netherlands
Telephone: 31-10-4081936/2768
Fax: 31-10-4529509
E-mail: rsm@fac.rsm.eur.nl
World Wide Web: http://www.rsm.eur.nl/rsm

European University

WHAT WILL IT TAKE TO LEAD IN THE TWENTY-FIRST CENTURY?

As the pace of global changes accelerates, managers must become increasingly adaptable. Since its origin, European University (EU) has been educating the manager of tomorrow. Constantly adapting its highly participative, comprehensive, and intensive M.B.A. program to the changing world is our commitment.

Our M.B.A. program is designed to teach students, the future leaders, to become well-versed in international business and to speak foreign languages, but most importantly, they must convey an understanding of other societies and encourage students to think globally and strategically beyond their own national borders.

The new generation of managers must be hands-on, action driven, and able to think globally and understand the intercultural aspects of management. They must act ethically, be masters of leadership skills and be technologically up-to-date.

We no longer shape our world from the academic's theoretical starting point nor from the industrialist's mechanistic viewpoint. At best, it is a complex interrelation of the two and their resulting offshoots. The programs offered by EU meet this challenge.

—Dr. Roger DeBruycker, Dean

Programs and Curricular Focus

The European University's M.B.A. program consists of fifteen courses divided over three terms of ten weeks each. The full-time student can complete the program in one academic year. The lectures are given each weekday, from Monday through Friday, from 6 p.m. to 9 p.m. The program can be extended up to three years for part-time study.

The University encourages students to improve their language skills by choosing among the language courses offered in Dutch, English, French, German, Italian, Japanese, and Spanish.

Besides the Master of Business Administration program, European University offers also the Master of Science in Information Systems, Master in Transportation and Logistics, Master of Arts in Business Communication and Public Relations, and Master of Science in International Hospitality and Tourism Management.

Students and the M.B.A. Experience

To prevent business theory from remaining abstract and inapplicable, students at European University are taught, in part, by the case study method.

They also learn to think strategically when making decisions, to empathize with the other person's situation, to inspire others to contribute to the success of a project, and to think independently by questioning rather than blindly accepting subject material. Throughout the academic year, students are given a number of assignments and tests so that their progress can be gauged.

Graduate students are between 22 and 45 years of age with university degrees in business economics, engineering, law, or social sciences. Approximately 48 percent of each campus student body comes from abroad.

Special Features

After completing the M.B.A. program at European University students have the opportunity to enter complementary graduate programs in India, Indonesia, Korea, Mexico, Thailand, and the United States.

European University's Montreux campus offers a program in business that seeks to increase internal executive performance and motivation.

The Executive M.B.A. program has been carefully structured to equip executives with the integrated, strategic, pragmatic, and professional knowledge necessary to assume the responsibilities of leadership in the international business community.

Besides these master's programs, European University offers exchange programs and dual degree programs.

The Faculty

Virtually all professors have other occupations in addition to their faculty positions at European University. This ensures the practical nature of the curricula and makes it possible for students to benefit from the experience these professors have accumulated throughout their business careers.

A selection of the organizations represented by faculty members are Alcatell-Bell Telephone, Union de Banque Suisses, Nestle, Citibank, United Nations Geneva, Swissair, and Olivetti.

In addition, several faculty members are professional lawyers, accountants, or consultants.

The faculty members of European University provide consulting services to organizations and companies. This service is often linked to in-company training programs.

The Business School Network

Corporate Partnerships

Students of European University benefit from regularly scheduled lectures from nationally and internationally renowned professionals and academics.

To expose M.B.A. students to a variety of career options, each campus organizes a series of company visits. This allows students to obtain firsthand information on various types of industries. In addition to regularly scheduled classes, European University organizes seminars directed by professionals with outstanding reputations in the business community at large. These seminars are organized on campus or on an in-company basis and deal with a variety of current business topics.

The College and Environs

The European University was founded in 1973 in Antwerp, Belgium. The institution has been growing ever since and now includes fifteen campuses in eight European countries: Antwerp and Brussels in Belgium; Paris and Toulouse in France; Montreux, Geneva, and Zug in Switzerland; Barcelona and Madrid in Spain; Maastricht and The Hague in the Netherlands; Athens in Greece; Lisbon and Porto in Portugal; Warsaw in Poland; and Munich in Germany.

The campuses are centrally located in each city and are easily accessible by public transportation.

Facilities

Students live off-campus in one of the many rooms, studios, or apartments available in the neighborhood of each study center. In Antwerp and Brussels however, the campus provides attractive dormitories and popular student clubs. At all campuses, the University's housing office is happy to assist students in finding accommodations.

Technology Environment

Realizing the importance of information processing, each campus has its own data processing center equipped with state-of-the-art computers (IBM, Unisys, and others). These centers are intended not only for computer science courses, but also for the students' daily use. European University students also have access to a variety of business information databases.

Placement

European University's Placement Office provides consultation and assistance in career services for all graduates. It maintains close contact with numerous companies throughout Europe and provides information on internship and permanent job opportunities. Almost 100 percent of graduates find a satisfactory position soon after graduation.

Admission

When applying for admission to European University, applicants must submit a completed application form with supporting documents, such as financial guarantees in the form of letters from sponsors and bank certificates for non-European applicants; have completed an undergraduate degree; and submit official GMAT scores. A TOEFL score is required of applicants for whom English is not their native language.

Finances

Tuition is due at the beginning of each academic term according to the schedule. The educational budget depends on the choice of campus. The 1997–98 budget for graduate students in Antwerp and Brussels, Belgium was $12,000, which included tuition, fees, and books.

International Students

One of the great cultural advantages of European University is its diverse student body. The students represent nearly fifty nationalities from all over the world.

Each campus has its own student associations with officers elected by the student body. The officers are in charge of organizing social, cultural, athletic, and educational events.

Application Facts and Dates

Students register during a prescribed period at the beginning of each academic term. Registration must be completed in accordance with the procedures as determined by the administration. Interested students should contact:

Mr. L. Van Mele
Director of Admissions
European University
International Management Institute
Jacob Jordaensstraat 77
2018 Antwerp
Belgium
Telephone: 32 3 218 54 31
Fax: 32 3 218 58 68
E-mail: info@euruni.be
WWW: http://www.euruni.be

Fairfield University

IN THE HEART OF BUSINESS

The Fairfield University School of Business is in the heart of one of the most exciting business learning environments in the world. Only 50 miles northeast of New York City, we are surrounded by more than 100 Fortune 500 headquarters, and Fairfield County alone hosts the largest concentration of U.S. headquarters of foreign multinationals. We enjoy close partnerships with these great companies—organizations that also employ our M.B.A. students and enhance our learning laboratory.

The Fairfield M.B.A. is also distinctive because our business school is a leader in business curriculum innovation, and we capitalize on our faculty members' expertise and their business experience. Our M.B.A. is accredited by AACSB–The International Association for Management Education.

If you want to meet the challenges of the twenty-first century, come study with us in the heart of business.

—Walter G. Ryba, Dean

Programs and Curricular Focus

An M.B.A. program is meant to be a generalist degree that covers all the relevant topical areas and gives a student the opportunity to specialize, but not major, in a functional area of business. The M.B.A. program has three components: core courses, breadth courses, and specialization or concentration courses.

The core courses are not required courses; they are designed to provide fundamental tools and functional area competencies for students who either did not major in a business specialty as undergraduates, did not perform well academically as undergraduates, or took only a portion of the functional and tool courses that comprise the M.B.A. core. Therefore, the core courses are prerequisites to the "true" M.B.A. program.

The "true" M.B.A. program comprises the breadth courses and the specialization courses. The new AACSB–The International Association for Management Education accreditation standards require at least 30 semester hours of study beyond the core. Fairfield limits the number of options offered in both the breadth and specialization courses to strengthen the program pedagogically with a strong set of breadth courses that everyone must take and a limited number of specialization electives to provide a focus for each concentration.

Most students admitted to the program are able to waive selected core courses on the basis of previous course work, upon

successful completion of a written qualifying examination, or based on relevant work experience when combined with related course work, qualifying examinations, program of graduate study, and other factors.

All students are expected to demonstrate and/or attain proficiency in the use of microcomputers and the mainframe computer during their program of study. Computer use is integrated throughout the curriculum, and it is expected in each course. The School provides fully equipped microcomputer labs for student use, and each student may obtain a computer account for access to the University's mainframe systems.

The specialization options include courses in accounting, finance, human resource management, information technology, international business, and marketing.

The overall program requirements include a basic statistics course, 30 credit hours in core courses, 18 credit hours in breadth courses, and 12 credit hours in specialization courses, for a total of 62 credit hours. A minimum of 36 credit hours must be taken at Fairfield.

Students and the M.B.A. Experience

Students in Fairfield's M.B.A. program have a wide variety of academic and work experience. Although some students in the program are recent college graduates, the average age of students is 27 years, with four years of full-time work experience.

❖ Global Focus

Fairfield's M.B.A. program emphasizes the recognition that business is international by nature. One of the key specialization areas for students is in international business. In addition, virtually all courses discuss international implications of their discipline. The student body represents many nations, with connections to many major international corporations. Student exchange opportunities are available in several countries.

Special Features

The newly revised curriculum includes practical applications of critical business skills, including negotiation and dispute resolution and market valuation and analysis. Many courses emphasize the role of technology in the competitive position of the firm in a global economy.

The Faculty

The Fairfield faculty have always emphasized outstanding teaching. Ninety percent of the 37 full-time graduate faculty members have extensive experience in the business world, and all have their appropriate terminal degrees. There is great diversity among the members of the faculty.

The Business School Network

Corporate Partnerships

The School has been the recipient of several major corporate grants for support of curriculum and faculty development. A close relationship exists with dozens of major corporations in Fairfield County, which is the third-largest center of corporate headquarters in the nation. The School also has an outstanding Advisory Council of business leaders from the nation's largest corporations. Corporate executives participate extensively as guests and lecturers in many courses every semester.

The College and Environs

Fairfield University is a coeducational institution of higher learning founded by the Society of Jesus in 1942 and proudly aspires to the Jesuit tradition of developing the whole intellectual potential of its students and creating the true sense of ethical and social responsibility within them.

The 200-acre campus is among the most beautiful in the country. The buildings are modern and well suited to the needs of the students.

U.S. News & World Report in 1994 and 1995 rated Fairfield one of the top two comprehensive universities in the Northeast in the regional category.

Fairfield University is situated in a suburban area on the Connecticut shore of Long Island Sound about 1 hour from New York City and 3 hours from Boston. The University is in America's "academic corridor," which contains the largest concentration of colleges and universities in the United States along with many cultural, recreational, and intellectual activities.

Facilities

The Nyselius Library contains more than 325,000 volumes, 500,000 microforms, and 1,849 journals and newspapers, with extensive business collections. There is access to library facilities throughout the area. Buildings on campus are fiber-optic-equipped. The Computer Center includes a DEC VAX 8600 with terminals throughout the campus; there is also a campuswide network of microcomputers.

Placement

The University offers a placement office with a full-time professional staff to assist students. There are on-campus recruiting visits by representatives of many of the top corporations in the nation. On-site visits also are possible with area corporate headquarters and those in nearby New York City.

Admission

Students who hold a bachelor's degree in any field or major from an accredited college or university and who have demonstrated their ability or potential to do high-quality academic work are encouraged to apply. The criteria for admission to the M.B.A. and the M.S. programs are a strong undergraduate grade point average and an appropriate score on the Graduate Management Admission Test (GMAT). A formula score of at least 1100, derived by multiplying the grade point average by 200 and adding the GMAT score, is usually required for admission. Complete official transcripts of all undergraduate and graduate work, two letters of recommendation, and a letter of self-evaluation or an enumeration of work experience must all be submitted. Students from non-English-speaking countries are required to submit a Test of English as a Foreign Language (TOEFL) score of 550 or better. Applicants to the certificate program are not required to submit GMAT scores.

Finances

In 1998–99, tuition is $450 per credit hour for part-time students and $7500 per semester for full-time students. The registration fee is $20 per semester.

The large majority of graduate students live off campus in the surrounding communities. Housing costs in the area vary widely. There is a limited supply of on-campus housing available; single rooms with board are approximately $3600 per semester.

Scholarship aid is available but limited. Most students are employed and receive substantial financial support from their employers. Graduate research assistantships are also available in limited supply. Students may apply for financial assistance after having been accepted into a program. Assistance is usually limited to U.S. citizens.

International Students

The International Programs and Student Services Offices offer special services for international students, including arrangements for housing, board, transportation, and amenities. Currently, there are 10 students from Europe and 2 from Canada enrolled. In addition, another 80 international students are studying on campus in other programs.

Application Facts and Dates

Applications are accepted on a revolving basis and should be completed prior to August 15 for those who wish to begin in the fall semester, prior to December 15 to begin in the spring semester, and prior to May 15 to begin in the summer semester. The application fee is $40.

Students should address all questions or requests for information and application materials to:

Graduate Admissions
School of Business
Fairfield University
Fairfield, Connecticut 06430
Telephone: 203-254-4180
Fax: 203-254-4105

FACULTY LIST

Jeffrey B. Arthur, Assistant Professor of Management; Ph.D., Cornell.

Bharat B. Bhalla, Professor of Finance; Ph.D., Cornell.

Russell P. Boisjoly, Professor of Finance; D.B.A., Indiana.

Bruce Bradford, Assistant Professor of Accounting; Ph.D., Memphis; CPA.

Paul Caster, Associate Professor of Accounting; Ph.D., North Texas.

Gerald O. Cavallo, Associate Professor of Marketing; Ph.D., CUNY Graduate Center.

J. Michael Cavanaugh, Associate Professor of Management; Ph.D., Massachusetts.

Arjun Chaudhuri, Associate Professor of Marketing; Ph.D., Connecticut.

Elia V. Chepaitis, Associate Professor of Information Systems; Ph.D., Connecticut.

Thomas E. Conine Jr., Professor of Finance; Ph.D., NYU.

Robert L. DeMichiell, Professor of Information Systems; Ph.D., Connecticut.

Sandra J. Ducoffe, Associate Professor of Marketing; Ph.D., Michigan State.

Walter F. Hlawitschka, Associate Professor of Finance; Ph.D., Virginia.

Christopher L. Huntley, Assistant Professor of Information Systems; Ph.D., Virginia.

Oscar W. Jensen, Professor of Quantitative Analysis; Ph.D., Connecticut.

Helene W. Johns, Assistant Professor of Accounting; LL.M., Florida; CPA.

Lucy V. Katz, Professor of Business Law; J.D., NYU.

Gregory D. Koutmos, Professor of Finance; Ph.D., CUNY Graduate Center.

Philip J. Lane, Associate Professor of Economics; Ph.D., Tufts.

Mark S. LeClair, Associate Professor of Economics; Ph.D., Rutgers.

Patrick Lee, Assistant Professor of Operations Management; Ph.D., Carnegie Mellon.

Lisa A. Mainiero, Professor of Management; Ph.D., Yale.

Anna Martin, Assistant Professor of Finance; Ph.D., Florida Atlantic University.

R. Keith Martin, Professor of Information Systems; Ph.D., Washington (Seattle).

Dawn W. Massey, Assistant Professor of Accounting; Ph.D., Connecticut; CPA.

Sharlene McEvoy, Professor of Business Law; J.D., Connecticut; Ph.D., UCLA.

Krishna Mohan, Associate Professor of Marketing; Ph.D., Wisconsin–Madison.

Milo W. Peck Jr., Assistant Professor of Accounting and Associate Dean; LL.M., Boston University; CPA.

Patricia M. Poli, Assistant Professor of Accounting; Ph.D., NYU; CPA.

Walter G. Ryba Jr., Professor of Business Law and Dean; J.D., Connecticut.

Carl A. Scheraga, Associate Professor of International Business; Ph.D., Connecticut.

David P. Schmidt, Associate Professor of Business Ethics; Ph.D., Chicago.

Anna Tavis, Visiting PepsiCo Scholar; Ph.D., Princeton.

Cheryl L. Tromley, Associate Professor of Management; Ph.D., Yale.

Michael T. Tucker, Professor of Finance; D.B.A., Boston University.

Michael A. Zigarelli, Assistant Professor of Management; Ph.D., Rutgers.

Fairleigh Dickinson University

Florham–Madison, New Jersey ❖ *Teaneck–Hackensack, New Jersey*

THE M.B.A. AND THE INDIVIDUAL

The Samuel J. Silberman M.B.A. has been crafted to recognize the new reality of a career in business. Today's business school graduate cannot look to organizations for career security but rather must look to his or her own employability. Whether an individual is employed by a large organization or in his or her own business, he or she must think like an entrepreneur, constantly searching for new opportunities. The Silberman M.B.A. provides students with the skills to identify and capitalize on these opportunities. The work of the faculty in developing a curriculum that meets the needs of the individual who has chosen business as a career received national attention in the September 1994 issue of Success magazine where the Silberman College was named as being among the twenty-five best business schools in the nation for entrepreneurs.

The College has a high-quality teaching faculty using an innovative curriculum developed for the contemporary business environment. This combination is designed to give each Silberman M.B.A. graduate the competitive edge necessary to maintain his or her employability and to succeed in a global business community that is characterized by rapid technological and social change.

—Paul Lerman, Dean

Programs and Curricular Focus

The Samuel J. Silberman College of Business Administration has been dedicated to providing high-quality innovative programs for more than thirty years. The College strives to develop graduates who are prepared to compete in a rapidly changing business environment. A completely revised Master of Business Administration curriculum, introduced in 1995, reflects the integrated, cross-functional manner in which contemporary business operates.

The program is designed to address the complex demands placed on organizations and the individuals who manage them. Global perspectives and ethical concerns of business are integrated into all courses. The development and refinement of student communication skills is an important component of the integrative courses that form the program core. Topics critical to the value creation process, such as entrepreneurship, creativity, and strategic thinking, are introduced early in the program. The influences of politics, the law, the environment, technology, society, and demographic diversity are integrated throughout the program.

Students begin the program by participating in the M.B.A. Preparation Seminar, a modular course that introduces

ethical perspectives for business and evaluates student oral communication skills. Program requirements include successful completion of between 34½ and 60 credits, depending on waiver of core courses. Core courses comprise four tiers: The External and Internal Environment of Business, The Manager's Skill Set, Functional Areas and Technical Core, and Capstone. Students major in one of eleven fields of study and complete breadth courses outside of the field of specialization. Students may choose to fulfill their breadth requirements with courses outside of the College in areas such as corporate communication or foreign language and culture.

Other program offerings include an Executive M.B.A., an Executive M.B.A. in health systems management (H.E.M.B.A.), an M.S. in Taxation, and a one-year full-time M.B.A. in global management. The College also offers a five-course post-M.B.A. certificate program in eleven subject areas for individuals already holding an M.B.A.

Students and the M.B.A. Experience

❖ Global Focus

In addition to international business courses offered on the New Jersey

campuses, M.B.A. students have the opportunity to attend a two-week summer seminar at the University's historic Wroxton College campus in Oxfordshire, England. During the seminar, students meet with key academic, business, and political leaders and tour major corporate locations. This program immerses students in British culture and invites them to view international business from a different perspective.

Special Features

In addition to traditional majors, the College offers an M.B.A. in pharmaceutical-chemical studies, the only one of its kind in the nation. The program is conducted on the campuses as well as at corporate locations of Bristol-Myers Squibb, Johnson & Johnson, and Miles Pharmaceuticals. CEOs and other top executives of industry companies meet with students on a weekly basis during each semester. The College's Executive M.B.A. in health systems management, launched in September 1998, is New Jersey's only executive-level program focusing on the management of health systems.

All students enrolled in the College's graduate business programs participate in at least one course on entrepreneurship offered by the Center for Entrepreneurial Studies. Students may choose to select a sequence of courses in this area. Internship opportunities with new ventures are available.

The Faculty

The 80 faculty members bring a combination of industry experience and academic training to the classroom. The faculty is committed to excellence in teaching. Faculty research interests concentrate on application of theory to business practice and are supported by research centers that include the Center for the New Jersey Economy, the Center for Human Resource Management, the Center for Entrepreneurship, the Center for Advanced Marketing Studies, and the Center for Pharmaceutical-Chemical Studies.

The Business School Network

Corporate Partnerships

Each of the academic departments is guided by a corporate advisory board that works with the faculty in developing the curriculum. Members of the advisory boards are often guest lecturers.

Prominent Alumni

The College counts among its alumni a number of leading corporate executives, including Patrick Zenner, President and CEO, Hoffman-LaRoche, Inc.; Stephen Sudovar, Senior Vice President, Pharmaceuticals Division, Hoffman-LaRoche, Inc.; Ron Dorfler, Senior Vice President and Chief Financial Officer, Capital Cities/ABC Inc.; Dennis Strigl, President and Chief Executive Officer, Bell Atlantic NYNEX Mobile; Richard Swift, Chairman, President, and Chief Executive Officer, Foster Wheeler Corp.; and Ronald Brill, Executive Vice President and Chief Administrative Officer, Home Depot.

The College and Environs

The 115-acre Teaneck–Hackensack Campus stretches along the east and west banks of the Hackensack River. Robison Hall, the Weiner Library, and Alumni Hall sit on the river's east edge, while the College of Business Administration, located in Dickinson Hall, sits on the west edge. The Florham–Madison Campus is a beautifully landscaped park of 187 acres. Its Georgian-style buildings have been adapted to the educational needs of the University. Both the Teaneck–Hackensack and Florham–Madison campuses are located in attractive residential suburbs close to local theaters, restaurants, and sports arenas. Students can easily reach the business, cultural, and social offerings of New York City by private or public transportation.

Wroxton College, the overseas campus of the University, was originally built as an abbey and later became the home of Lord North in the 1700s. It is centrally located in England between Oxford and Stratford-upon-Avon.

Facilities

The University has recently made a major investment in facilities. On the Teaneck–Hackensack Campus, the College resides in a building that recently underwent a $12-million renovation. College facilities include executive classrooms, three computer laboratories, and an up-to-date business research library. On the Florham–Madison Campus, the College occupies a major part of a 100-room mansion designed by Stanford White. A new recreation center was completed in 1995.

Technology Environment

Graduate students have access to a Prime 5370, VAX 4000/5000, Sun 490, and DEC Alpha Sable 2100 and a wide variety of software for use independent of campus or location. There are several PC laboratories on each campus. All PCs are connected to a central file server through a local area network with access to the University-wide network and the worldwide Internet.

Placement

The Office of Career Development and Placement offers career and placement services to all M.B.A. students and alumni. On-campus recruiting programs and career fairs are augmented by a large network of corporate contacts. Computerized databases and resume and interviewing workshops are a regular part of the services offered to M.B.A. students.

Admission

The College considers each candidate's academic record, GMAT score, and professional experience in the admission process. International students whose native language is not English are required to submit a TOEFL score. It is recommended that students have a basic knowledge of statistics; computer usage, including spreadsheets and word processing; and mathematics, including calculus.

Finances

Tuition for most graduate programs in 1998–99 is $522 per credit hour. Books and supplies are approximately $1200 per year. Approximately twenty-five graduate assistantships are available to qualified candidates, offering tuition remission and a stipend.

International Students

International students from twenty-three countries represent 8 percent of the M.B.A. students. Extensive English language preparation and assistance programs are available.

Application Facts and Dates

Application deadlines are August 25 for fall admission and January 12 for spring admission. For additional information, students should contact:

Office of Adult and Graduate
   Admissions
Fairleigh Dickinson University
1000 River Road
Teaneck, New Jersey 07666
Telephone: 800-338-8803 (toll-free)

FERRIS STATE UNIVERSITY

Ferris State University

College of Business

Big Rapids, Michigan

> ### PREPARING FOR A BRIGHT BUSINESS FUTURE
>
> *The mission of the Information Systems Management (ISM) program at Ferris State University is to provide high-quality graduate instruction in current technologies and continuous improvement management philosophies in an innovative, stimulating, and globally diverse learning environment. Our ISM program is a superb choice for the manager who wants to understand how complex systems are integrated toward resolution of specific business problems. Learning is continuous in a campus environment that blends leading-edge technology, an experienced faculty, and a globally diverse graduate student body. The ISM program graduates professionals with the skills and understanding to excel into the next century.*
>
> —Dr. Joseph C. Rallo, Dean

Programs and Curricular Focus

The Master of Science in information systems management (M.S. ISM) in the College of Business at Ferris State University is a multidiscipline, applied management program that focuses on technical, human, operational, strategic, and information resource management. The M.S. ISM is composed of a core sequence of four courses (13 semester credit hours), a 12-credit hour, four-course discipline-specific emphasis, and a thesis, a capstone project, or a three-course option (6–9 credit hours).

The core sequence focuses on management issues and techniques in an information-age organization; strategic operation, business, ethical, legal, and competitive considerations for management in an information-age organization; financial planning, acquisition, and decision making to achieve defined organizational objectives; and how to design, conduct, and interpret empirical research and project-focused activities. The thesis, capstone project, or three-course option is required of all M.S. ISM candidates.

M.S. ISM courses are scheduled to facilitate full-time completion of the program in fifteen months.

Students and the M.S. Experience

The entering class for the academic year in the full-time program is about 40 students; about 40 students also enter on a part-time basis each year. The classes vary in size, from one-on-one independent study with an instructor to a more classical classroom environment with about 20 students.

The program has been termed a technical M.B.A. or applied M.B.A. because of its blend of business management issues relating to information systems.

Recently, Ferris State University signed an agreement with the Hogeschool Enschede in the Netherlands, which allows the M.S. ISM program to be offered partly in Europe, offering students the opportunity to gain international experience. The third group of 7 students are currently enrolled in the program.

Special Features

Special courses are offered via the Internet and on weekends each semester. It is not possible to complete the program entirely in these formats. The program allows for the transfer of two graduate classes that are equivalent to required classes in the program from recognized, accredited colleges, schools, and universities. Part-time study is available at several off-campus sites, including Flint and Grand Rapids, Michigan.

The Faculty

Ferris State University has a full-time faculty of nearly 500 instructors teaching in nearly 100 programs. The ISM program is led by senior faculty members of the College of Business who have special interest in the areas of continuous quality improvement, virtual communities, the application of Internet technologies, and the use of telecommunications in business.

The Business School Network

The University has been a pioneer in information systems education since 1963. The extensive business experience of the faculty, a close working relationship with an advisory committee of people in industry, and Ferris' long experience in career-related education make this a top option for students looking to pursue the M.S. ISM.

The College and Environs

Founded in 1884, Ferris State University is Michigan's foremost professional and technical university and is located on a 600-acre campus on the banks of the Muskegon River in Mecosta County, midway between Grand Rapids and Cadillac and the northern and southern ends of Michigan's Lower Peninsula. Big Rapids, with a population of 12,600, is in an area rich in recreational activity, with 100 lakes; thousands of acres of open, rolling terrain; woodlands; creeks; and rivers in the vicinity. Nearly 10,000 students are enrolled in the University.

Technology Environment

ISM students are provided access to the Internet via the program's server (http://pada.ferris.edu), which is part of the overall University network. Both e-mail addresses and home pages for ISM students are provided by the program. While University labs are widely available to ISM students, it is recommended that students have their own personal computers.

The Abigail S. Timme Library serves as a gateway to a variety of information resources available both on-site and remotely in print and digital formats. Through licensed access to remote Internet sites, library users may view and print full-text articles from more than

816

1,400 magazine and journal titles. Article abstracts are available for more than 2,000 additional titles. An on-site collection of more than twenty networked CD-ROMs provides further specialization information for library users. Electronic document delivery and interlibrary loan services significantly supplement the library's array of knowledge resources.

Placement

The placement rate is 100 percent in both the United States and the international job market. The University's students have experienced high job placement rates because its programs are tailored to the needs of employers.

Admission

Entrance requirements for the M.S. ISM program are a baccalaureate degree, a minimum GPA of 2.75, a minimum GPA of 3.0 in prerequisite courses (statistics, management, accounting or finance,

computer literacy, and contract law), and a writing sample. The applicants' preparatory background is reviewed to ensure that each individual has the education or experience to succeed in emphasis studies. All applicants must also submit official undergraduate and graduate course transcripts, a one-page typed essay explaining reasons for seeking admission, and a resume. Candidates interested in enrolling in selected M.S. ISM courses may be granted guest admission. Guest application information is available in the graduate program department office (616-592-2168). Students whose native language is not English must have a minimum TOEFL score of 550.

Finances

Students should contact the M.S. ISM program office for information regarding graduate assistantships. For information concerning loans and work-study awards, students should contact the FSU Office of

Financial Aid, 420 Oak Street, Big Rapids, Michigan 49307-2020 (telephone: 616-592-2110).

International Students

The program is composed of approximately 50 percent international students.

Application Facts and Dates

Applications for M.S. ISM admission should be received by July 1 for the fall semester, November 1 for the winter semester, and April 1 for the summer semester.

For more information, students should contact:

Coordinator M.S. ISM
S-C 101
1420 Knollview Drive
Big Rapids, Michigan 49307-2289
Telephone: 616-592-2168
Fax: 616-592-2973
E-mail: perrinj@ism.ferris.edu
World Wide Web: http://ism.ferris.edu

Fitchburg State College

Fitchburg, Massachusetts

A COMMITMENT TO EXCELLENCE

For more than 100 years, Fitchburg State College has provided quality educational opportunities that enhance the lives of individual students and enrich the larger community. Our mission is clear: to offer career and professional programs responsive to students' and to the nation's need for economic and cultural expansion. You will find our programs intellectually challenging and professionally rewarding. Our commitment to excellence is reflected in the Master of Business Administration degree program. We are proud of our faculty, our program, our facilities, and our students. All who join us receive the individual attention and professional and personal development that have come to be a hallmark of Fitchburg State College.

—Michele Moran Zide, Dean

Program and Curricular Focus

The program of study for the Master of Business Administration (M.B.A.) degree includes a foundation-level core of 24 credits and 30 credits of advanced study. It is designed to provide students with the skills and knowledge necessary to become leaders in business and in administration. The program seeks to develop decision makers with strong analytic skills who are socially responsible, sensitive to cultural diversity, and aware of the broadening world market.

Three course clusters are included: A foundation level core of 8 courses (24 credits) intended to provide essential background knowledge regarding accounting, economics, management, marketing, finance, quantitative analysis, business law, and data processing. (It is assumed that most students entering the program with an undergraduate degree in business administration will be able to waive these foundation courses. Life experience credit may be used for waiver of some of the foundation courses based on evaluation and recommendation of a faculty committee).

An advanced core requirements/applications level of 6 courses (18 credits) providing students with advanced skills and knowledge regarding current business and management practice and methodology.

In addition to the foundation and advanced required courses, each student selects accounting, human resources management, or management as an area of specialization. Each of these 12 semester hour tracks includes a free

elective. To satisfy the requirement, the student may choose a course from any of the M.B.A. course offerings or, with the permission of the Graduate Program Chair, a course from another graduate discipline. Students electing the accounting track must either be graduates of approved undergraduate accounting programs or have at least 24 undergraduate credit hours beyond basic accounting, with the approval of the Program Director.

Students and the M.B.A. Experience

The students of the Fitchburg State College graduate program contribute a diversity of cultural, professional, and educational experiences to the campus environment. The average age of the student body is 28. Demographically, 45 percent of the students are women and 6 percent are minorities. International students from several different world regions comprise 10 percent of the class. Graduate students have undergraduate degrees and professional experience in a variety of disciplines including business administration, economics, engineering, education, behavioral sciences, humanities, and the pure sciences.

The Faculty

Simply put, the faculty is one of the finest available at a college of this size. Members are a diverse group whose backgrounds provide a balance of professional, research, and classroom skills. However, the classroom always

comes first, and while some classes may be conducted in lecture format, a collaborative learning environment is emphasized, which includes case analysis, group discussions, and special projects. Each course is designed to integrate real-world application with a theoretical foundation.

The Business School Network

The Business Administration Department has established a strong partnership with the regional business community through the department's Montachusett Economic Center (MEC). The MEC provides

FACULTY LIST

students and faculty with the opportunity to collaborate on diverse business projects with area professionals. These projects include economic research, management and marketing consultation, small business assistance, and various demographic studies. The MEC hosts several seminars each year which provide high quality presentations on a variety of business topics to students, faculty, and area professionals.

A Graduate Business Studies Advisory Board contributes counsel and assistance to the College in its goal of providing a high-quality graduate experience to its students. The diversity of the business community is well represented by the leaders who serve as members of this committee.

The College also offers the M.B.A. program in conjunction with the Vivekenanda School of Post-Graduate Studies in Hyderabad, India. Upon successful completion of foundation-level course work in India, students opt to continue their M.B.A. studies in India at the Vivekenanda School or in the United States at Fitchburg State College. Eligible candidates who complete the program are awarded the M.B.A. degree from Fitchburg State College.

The College and Environs

The College is located in a residential section of Fitchburg, a few blocks from Main Street. The 35-acre main campus includes about 30 buildings, and just down the street are 35-acres of athletic fields. The Mt. Wachusett ski area is nearby, with some of the finest skiing in the east. Minutes from some of the state's best hiking, fishing, rock climbing, and canoeing, the college is also just an hour from Boston and its vast cultural offerings, a half-hour from Worcester's Centrum, and an hour from Hampton and other beaches that dot the Massachusetts–New Hampshire shoreline.

Facilities

The College's excellent computer facilities include e-mail and Internet access capabilities in every classroom, office, and residence hall as well as dial-up capabilities that utilize an Alpha Server 2100 and a Proliant DHCP server that hosts TCP/IP to the entire campus at high-speed T-1 connectivity.

While the College has five general-purpose computer labs and five residence hall computer labs, the Business Administration Department has a dedicated lab

with thirty Pentium computers. Applications available to students include MS Office97 Pro, SPSS, Web-page development tools, project management, multimedia authoring suites, and the Internet.

The College Library provides 96 hours of weekly service, online access to the library's catalog, and more than sixty databases via the library's home page. A CD-ROM local area network provides ready access to heavily utilized subscription services. There are approximately 263,000 volumes and 1,467 current periodicals, which are supplemented by the 404,000-item Education Resources Information Center (ERIC). Additional services include interlibrary loans and reciprocal borrowing privileges.

Placement

In any given year, more than 600 employers hire Fitchburg State College graduates. Roughly 90 percent are employed full-time within six months of graduation—a tribute primarily to the quality of the education they received, but also to the help they got with career planning.

Throughout the year, Career Services offers workshops on such topics as resume writing, job interviewing, further graduate schooling, choosing a career, and finding a job. There are specific programs for specific majors, networking nights with alumni, and on-campus interviews with recruiters.

Fitchburg State College believes that career planning is a long-term—indeed a lifelong—exercise. It's part of an overall process of self-assessment that is fostered in all aspects of campus life.

Admission

Fitchburg State College Admissions criteria meet the standards of the two national accrediting agencies (AACSB–The International Association of Management Education and ACBSP). In addition to the College's standard admission requirements for the master's degree programs, all applicants are expected to have an undergraduate GPA not less than 2.8, a GMAT score of not less than 400 and a formula score of not less than 1000. The formula is 200 times the overall undergraduate grade point average, based on the standard 4.0 scale, plus the total GMAT score.

Finances

A typical budget for a graduate student carrying 6 credits each semester for the

school year is: tuition $1680, fees $194, room (off-campus) $1800, board (off-campus) $1700, books/supplies $300, transportation $500, personal/miscellaneous $1500, total $7590. Not all students will spend exactly this amount. Some will spend more, others less. Budgets for graduate students taking other than 6 credits per semester will vary. Students are awarded financial aid based on total budget. Some graduate scholarships in varying amounts are available in the form of tuition and fee waivers. Student loans include Federal Perkins Loans and William D. Ford Federal Direct Student Loans. Some graduate student employment is available through the Federal Work Study program, Fitchburg State College Employment, and employment through the Off-Campus Employment Center. For application deadlines, process, and procedures the student should contact the Graduate Office.

Application Facts and Dates

Under the College's rolling admissions policy, applications may be submitted at any time. An applicant for enrollment in the Master of Business Administration program is required to submit an application (obtainable from the Graduate Office), an official transcript of his/her bachelor's degree, an official report of the Graduate Management Admissions Test (GMAT), a professional resume, and three letters of recommendation. Recommendations are welcome from individuals under whom the applicant has studied and/or under whose immediate supervision he/she has worked in a professional capacity. Recommendations are also welcome from others who are in a position to offer a pertinent appraisal of applicant's academic and interpersonal skills, ability, and potential. In addition to the GMAT, natives of non-English speaking countries will be required to submit satisfactory TOEFL scores.

The Graduate Office accepts a maximum of 6 semester hours in transfer from regionally accredited graduate schools. Transfer credit requests are processed upon application for admission. Applications must be submitted to:

The Admissions Office
Fitchburg State College
160 Pearl Street
Fitchburg, Massachusetts 01420-2697
Telephone: 978-665-3144
Fax: 978-665-3658
World Wide Web: http://www.fsc.edu

Florida International University

> ## BUSINESS LEADERS IN THE NEXT MILLENNIUM
>
> *The M.B.A. at Florida International University (FIU) is characterized by its focus on academic excellence and its use of innovative approaches to enhance learning. The overall setting is a global environment that nourishes a balanced mix of creativity, academic foundations, and interaction with today's real-world business practices.*
>
> *The program is the hallmark of the College of Business Administration and has been a notable success since its inception. Over the last fifteen years, the program has steadily educated a remarkable number of south Floridians. Most of its graduates are among today's leaders, professionals, and business entrepreneurs in Florida.*

Programs and Curricular Focus

FIU's College of Business Administration (CBA) offers degree programs leading to the Master of Business Administration (M.B.A.), the Master of Accounting (M.Acc.), the Master in International Business (M.I.B.), the Master of Science in Finance (M.S.F.), and the Master of Science in Taxation (M.S.T.). It also offers doctoral programs in business administration that lead to the Doctor of Philosophy (Ph.D.) degree, with tracks in accounting, decision sciences, finance, information systems, international business, management, and marketing. These programs are all accredited by AACSB–The International Association for Management Education.

The M.B.A. program at FIU caters to both full-time and career professionals and is flexible enough to accommodate candidates from most disciplines. The program offers a coherent body of knowledge and practice that is in line with the anticipated future trends and developments. Classes are offered during the day and in the evening. Furthermore, the program offers specialization options in several functional areas.

The M.B.A. program has two tracks: a track of 40 credit hours and a track of 61 credit hours. The former is for students who have an undergraduate degree in business that was awarded five years or less prior to acceptance in the program from a school accredited by AACSB–The International Association for Management Education. This track consists of nine nonwaivable core courses and four courses of approved electives, which may

be taken toward a concentration in one subject area. The longer track is for students who have a nonbusiness undergraduate degree, a business undergraduate degree from a school not accredited by AACSB–The International Association for Management Education, or a business undergraduate degree awarded more than five years prior to acceptance into this program. This track is similar to the 40-credit-hour track except for seven waivable precore courses.

FIU's College of Business Administration also offers alternative business programs, including the E.M.B.A. and a series of postgraduate studies and certificates in banking, insurance, international finance, international business, international marketing, savings and loans, management of quality health-care systems, human resource administration, and training and human resource development.

Students and the M.B.A. Experience

A wide range of student activities and organizations complement and enhance

the educational goals of FIU's extensive programs. Notable among these organizations are the MBA Society and the Alumni Association. The MBA Society, which is organized by students, maintains an active role in curriculum affairs, networking with outside businesses, and facilitating placement of the M.B.A. graduates. Seminars and social events are held throughout the year to complement the students' core curriculum and provide an enriching environment beyond the daily activities.

Students with diverse academic and personal backgrounds but with common scholastic abilities enrich the program. The majority of the incoming students have business degrees, with at least two years of work experience with private or public organizations. The average age of the incoming students is 26, and the men-women student ratio is about even. Most of the students are from south Florida, are bilingual, and have personal or business linkages with one or more Latin-American countries. Less than 10 percent of the students are international.

Special Features

The program offers real value and has been recognized several times by *U.S.News & World Report* as one of the best buys in higher education. The program nourishes corporate linkages and is viewed with respect in the business community. It has managed to stay ahead of the technical know-how because information technologies and computers are integrated into the program.

FIU's location in Miami offers students the academic advantage of attending a university in a major urban environment with a rich diversity of people, languages, and cultures. The city is in the forefront of international trade, finance, and banking. Strategically located at the crossroads of the Americas, Miami is headquarters to hundreds of international companies. Its impressive downtown skyline is a reflection of the soaring business and financial industry, which translates into a wealth of opportunities for FIU students and graduates.

The Faculty

The program enjoys a highly qualified faculty; more than 95 percent of the M.B.A. faculty members possess Ph.D.'s, and most have several years of practical and consulting business experience. They are committed to excel in both teaching and research and bring a diversity of perspectives and a variety of teaching techniques into the classroom environment. The breadth and scope of their research are also diverse and encompass practical and theoretical topics in today's increasingly global and dynamic business environment.

The Business School Network

Five distinctive CBA centers supplement the program through their diverse activities of research, roundtables, speaker series, and other professional linkages and forums with the business community. In addition, the program is guided by a policy review board that consists of 7 ranked faculty members who continuously monitor the program and establish policy guidelines in order to fine-tune it and keep it abreast of the current and future developments in the field. A number of advisory boards that consist of civic leaders, corporate executives, and alumni advise the College and its centers on the future developments in the field. The MBA Society also maintains an active role in networking with outside businesses and placement of the M.B.A. graduates.

The College and Environs

Florida International University, a comprehensive, multicampus, urban research institution located in Miami, is committed to providing both excellence and access to all qualified students who desire to pursue higher education. The University, a member institution of the State University System of Florida, offers a variety of academic programs and courses at the bachelor's, master's, and doctoral degree levels, which are designed to respond to today's rapidly changing environment.

The University enjoys two major campuses in Dade County and two academic centers in Broward County. The main campus, University Park, is located about 5 miles west of the financial centers of

Miami, a city famous for its four S's: sun, sea, sand, and skyline. South Florida is a crossroads of the Americas, a trend-setting region for banking, business, and international finance.

The College of Business Administration is housed in an elegant building, located in a prime site that overlooks the main entrance to the University. The building, designed and constructed for the CBA from 1989 to 1992, is equipped with modern lecture halls, case-study rooms, advanced communication network facilities, and the latest state-of-the-art EDP and other computer facilities.

Technology Environment

A cluster of mainframes (VAX, UNIX, IBM, Alpha) and PCs supported with a regional network of telecommunications provide the faculty and students with the latest advances in information management and computing facilities. These are augmented by several student labs and a number of general/special purpose databases that may be accessed by modems.

Placement

The University Career Services' automated systems provide employers and M.B.A.'s with placement activities and networking opportunities. M.B.A.'s register for on-campus recruiting and resume referrals through the Resume Expert diskette and may choose to have Career Services place their resumes on the Internet for easy access by national and international employers.

Career Services also sponsors the M.B.A. Forum, which allows M.B.A.'s to hear employers describe career information in the areas of marketing, consulting, and financial/international business. In addition, career fairs are sponsored twice a year, and various job-search workshops teach M.B.A.'s soft skills such as etiquette, networking, and interviewing.

Admission

Admission to the M.B.A. program requires the fulfillment of the general University requirements for admission to graduate programs, a bachelor's degree from a regionally accredited college or university, dem-

onstration of a high promise of success in graduate studies as determined by the faculty, and a minimum combination of the Graduate Management Admission Test (GMAT) and the upper-division grade point average. Students whose native language is not English must also obtain a minimum score of 500 on the TOEFL or an equivalent score on a comparable examination.

Finances

The 1998–99 approved graduate credit-hour tuition per semester is $129.57 for Florida residents and $434.96 for non-Florida residents. Other student fees are about $55 per semester. Tuition and fees are subject to change without notice.

The University adheres to the philosophy that a student is entitled to a college education regardless of his or her financial condition. The financial aid program at the University includes limited scholarships, grants, loans, and campus employment. Financial aid is limited, and a student's need is determined on an individual basis by using evaluation criteria provided by national agencies.

Application Facts and Dates

Application forms for admission are mailed from the admissions office upon request. CBA employs a rolling admission process, and students are admitted each year for the fall, spring, and summer sessions. The admission process may require as long as two months after the receipt of the application, official transcripts, and test scores. It is the student's responsibility to have copies of the official transcripts of all previously earned college or university credits sent directly from the institution to the admissions office. Copies of transcripts submitted by applicants are not acceptable for admission purposes.

For admission application:

Office of Admissions
PC 140, University Park Campus
Florida International University
Miami, Florida 33199
Telephone: 305-348-2363
Fax: 305-348-3648

For program information:

M.B.A. Office
College of Business Administration
BA 220
University Park Campus
Florida International University
Miami, Florida 33199
Telephone: 305-348-3256
Fax : 305-348-3278
E-mail: mba@fiu.edu
World Wide Web: http://www.fiu.edu/
~mba

Fordham University

> ### URBI ET ORBI—FOR THE CITY AND THE WORLD
>
> *This headline is one of the first tangible examples of the total redesign of our school. We are committed to making Fordham's Graduate School of Business Administration a leading, world-class business school and are moving toward that goal.*
>
> *Our close ties to New York companies help position us as New York City's business ambassador to the world.*
>
> *As for our students, we know each of them, care about each one's future, and are devoted to doing all we can to insure their success in business, at every level, in any country of the world.*
>
> —Ernest J. Scalberg, Dean

Programs and Curricular Focus

Concern for quality drives Fordham's M.B.A. program. Through the required courses of the program, students acquire the knowledge and basic skills necessary to become leaders in business. In the classroom, faculty members teach fundamental theory and current research tied to pragmatic solutions, so students master both abstract and applied methods of thinking.

Students also develop expertise in a specific field by taking a concentration in one of six areas: accounting, communications and media management, finance, information and communications systems, management systems, and marketing. An International Business Designation is also available as a complement to a student's selected area of concentration. Fordham's course of study is organized on a trimester system (three terms per year) commencing in September, January, and April. Each student can decide how quickly he or she earns the Fordham M.B.A. A full-time student may complete the program in fifteen to eighteen months.

The 60-credit M.B.A. degree program has eight courses (24 credits) in the core business curriculum, including fundamentals of accounting, financial environment, information systems, business law, marketing management, operations management, and business policy. Upper-level courses in a student's selected concentration, together with electives both in and out of that concentration, fill out the M.B.A. program.

Fordham offers an eighteen-month Deming Scholars M.B.A. Program in Quality Management, a joint J.D./M.B.A. program with Fordham Law School, and an M.S. in taxation. A 90-credit M.B.A. in

Taxation and Accounting Program combines the M.B.A. in professional accounting with the M.S. in taxation to prepare students to be taxation professionals.

The 1998–99 academic year heralds the third year of Fordham's Global Professional Master of Business Administration (GP-MBA). Enrollment in the GP-MBA has tripled since its inception in the fall of 1996, attesting to the program's success. This 69-credit program is designed for individuals planning a career in international business and responds to the growing demand for M.B.A.'s in the global marketplace.

An exciting new executive-style program that Fordham offers is geared toward advanced professionals and managers. The Transnational M.B.A. (T.M.B.A.) is for students who will either have ten or more years of business experience or are on a fast track to upper-level managerial positions. This program features forms of distance learning, with classes held one weekend per month in an executive retreat setting.

The soon-to-be-offered M.B.A. Upgrade is part of the business school's commitment to lifelong learning. This program is designed to provide the most current and forward-thinking business education to individuals who completed their M.B.A. degrees ten or more years ago. Like other programs at Fordham, the M.B.A. Upgrade will have a significant emphasis on global business and technology.

A final new offering is the Beijing M.B.A. Fordham's Graduate School of Business Administration is serving as the lead school in a consortium of twenty-four U.S. Jesuit universities that will offer an M.B.A. program in Beijing, China.

Fordham will be the degree-granting institution in this program.

Students and the M.B.A. Experience

The total student population of Fordham's graduate business school is approximately 1,600, with 250 attending on a full-time basis and 1,350 attending on a part-time basis. The average age is 28; 41 percent are women. Students representing more than thirty countries comprise nearly 40 percent of the full-time student body.

On average, Fordham business students have had four years of work experience. As a consequence, many classroom discussions are enriched by students contributing their own on-the-job experiences.

The Faculty

Fordham has 85 full-time faculty members, 96 percent of whom hold a Ph.D. or a similar terminal degree. Women comprise 27 percent of the group. Approximately one third of the faculty members have origins in Western Europe, South America, and Asia. The adjunct faculty pool totals 132, with approximately 50 teaching in a given trimester.

Many members of the faculty serve as consultants to a variety of industries as well as to foreign governments and institutions. The diverse backgrounds of the faculty members provide a multicultural teaching field, with an emphasis on global standards and practices.

The Business School Network

Because of Fordham's graduate business school's location in New York City, which many consider the business capital of the world, students have easy access to a "who's who" of corporate leaders and Wall Street executives who visit the campus regularly.

Corporate Partnerships

In addition to guest speakers in classes, at seminars, and in panel discussions, students are able to take advantage of several formal programs that provide business contacts: the Mentoring Program, which sponsors one-on-one relationships between individual students and executives; the Field Study Program, in which teams of students solve

The Lincoln Center campus, looking south to the World Trade Center.

problems for real corporate assignments; the Master in Taxation and Accounting (M.T.A.) program, funded largely by the accounting and tax industries that then hire the program's graduates; and the Global Fellowship program, which provides students with fellowships where students work for foreign companies in developing nations on a pro-bono basis.

Prominent Alumni

Standard and Poor's most recent Executive/College Survey ranked Fordham in the top forty U.S. colleges and universities and number one in Jesuit institutions with the largest alumni representation in leading executive positions. *U.S. News & World Report*'s 1998 overall rankings placed Fordham's Graduate School of Business Administration among the top quarter in the country and ranked Fordham GBA's part-time program fourteenth nationally.

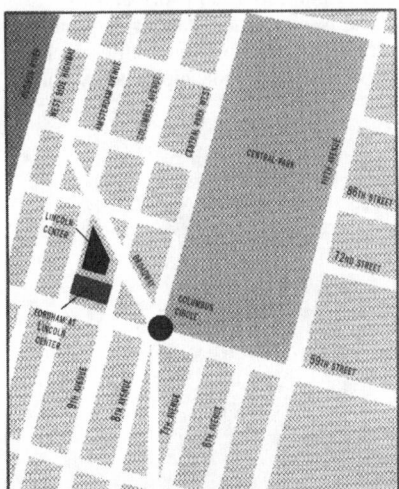

Fordham at Lincoln Center, with Columbus Circle and Central Park.

The College and Environs

Fordham's Graduate School of Business Administration was established in 1969 and is founded on the Jesuit tradition of high-quality education. Fordham's business school is located at Lincoln Center on a campus that marks the southern border of the cultural heart of New York City.

The Lincoln Center campus consists of the academic building, the residence hall, and the School of Law, all of which are connected by a central plaza that serves as an island of calm in a city of skyscrapers. It is one block from Central Park and Columbus Circle, a major transportation hub in midtown Manhattan.

Placement

Fordham's Career Development Office offers individual counseling, workshops, and mock interview sessions to guide students in the subtleties of networking, information gathering, and interviewing. Eligible candidates also submit resumes for inclusion in the GBA Resume Book, which is sent to more than 500 companies.

Panel discussions by industry representatives provide the chance to learn about career opportunities and trends in particular areas of academic concentration. In the Mentor Program, students talk to top business executives, one-on-one, to obtain career advice and guidance.

Admission

The principal elements that define a Fordham student are academic and professional accomplishments, clearly defined career objectives, motivation, and personal integrity. Each candidate must possess the U.S. equivalent of a four-year baccalaureate degree and must have taken the Graduate Management Admission

Test (GMAT). The candidate's academic record, GMAT scores, personal statements, professional recommendations, and work experience are considered in the admission process. The average GMAT score of those admitted in 1998 was 570.

Applicants from non-English-speaking countries must submit the results of the Test of English as a Foreign Language (TOEFL). The minimum TOEFL score accepted is 600.

Finances

The annual tuition for a full-time student in 1998–99 is $25,200 for 45 credit hours of study. The average part-time student completes 18 credits per year, which costs $10,080 in 1998–99. The estimated cost of fees, insurance, books, and supplies is $1550 per year. Off-campus housing, although greatly varied, is estimated to cost $11,000.

Fordham uses the Free Application for Federal Student Aid (FAFSA) to determine the need of each student for any scholarship, graduate assistantship, or loan, thus the FAFSA should be filed as soon as possible. Deadlines and requirements differ based on the specific aid program.

International Students

Forty percent of Fordham's full-time M.B.A. student population comes from other countries; more than thirty countries are represented in the School. The International Student Society, which is self-governing, hosts multicultural events and takes advantage of New York City's international character for its many social and business activities.

Application Facts and Dates

Application deadlines are June 1 for the September trimester, November 1 for the January trimester, and March 1 for the April trimester for part-time applicants only. Decisions are made on a rolling basis. Notification is usually within one month after application is completed.

International students are asked to submit their application one month prior to the regular deadlines, and they must also provide documentation that they have the resources to pay for their studies prior to receiving their visa. For more information, students should contact:

Dean of Admissions
Graduate School of Business
    Administration
Fordham University
113 West 60th Street, Suite 619
New York, New York 10023
Telephone: 212-636-6200
Fax: 212-636-7076
E-mail: admission@bschool.bnet.
    fordham.edu
World Wide Web: http://www.bnet.
    fordham.edu

George Mason University

Fairfax, Virginia

A UNIVERSITY FOR TOMORROW

Our programs provide a solid business core curriculum with strong emphasis on communication and information technologies, entrepreneurial thinking, and the social and cultural aspects of global business.

—Dr. Teresa Domzal, Dean

Programs and Curricular Focus

Students in the Fast-Track M.B.A. program at George Mason University's School of Management are challenged to develop the strategic thinking skills necessary to take advantage of the opportunities created by information technology and an increasingly global marketplace. The Fast-Track M.B.A. program stresses creativity, analytical proficiency, and effective communication combined with a team-oriented learning environment to prepare graduates for today's dynamic business community. The experience is enhanced through alliances GMU has forged with one of the nation's most prosperous and fastest growing economic regions.

The 48-credit-hour curriculum includes eleven core courses designed to solidify students' understanding of a broad range of business principles and practices. These courses cover the spectrum of business functions, from accounting, finance, and operations through marketing, organizational behavior, and strategy. From this foundation, students move on to master an area of interest through five elective courses. Specializations are offered in the areas of accounting, decision sciences, finance, management of information systems, management, marketing, and strategy. Students also have the opportunity to take courses on other topics, such as entrepreneurship, small business consulting, and international business.

Interwoven throughout every course is an emphasis on the impact of information technology, global sensitivity, and entrepreneurial enterprise. A cohort class structure promotes interaction between students and faculty members. No single teaching style dominates. Professors use instructional techniques best suited to the subject matter and needs of the students.

Typical classes use small groups and cases to support theoretical learning.

Students complete the program in three years on a part-time basis.

Students and the M.B.A. Experience

Approximately 200 Fast-Track M.B.A. students bring strong academic and professional backgrounds to the GMU M.B.A. program. Students have undergraduate degrees in a broad range of disciplines. Typical classes have consisted of majors in humanities and social science (22 percent), business (25 percent), engineering and science (25 percent), and other (28 percent). The typical student is 28 years old and has more than five years of professional work experience. The program's diversity and team-oriented environment provide for a dynamic learning experience.

The Faculty

The location and entrepreneurial philosophy of George Mason University have attracted a diverse and accomplished business faculty. The men and women are active researchers and stimulating teachers who are eager to share their knowledge and professional accomplishments with students. Easy access to professors is the norm in the M.B.A. program.

The Business School Network

The School of Management and the business community have forged strong ties and created a number of opportunities for students to enhance their education with real-world application. The Century Club is a program that pairs students with local business executives. These executives, many of whom are GMU graduates, provide students with a mentor as they progress through their studies. The club also sponsors guest lectures and networking opportunities for students.

The College and Environs

George Mason University's serene, 583-acre wooded campus is located 16 miles west of Washington D.C., in the booming high-technology suburbs of northern Virginia. Washington, D.C. is only a 20-minute drive away and provides students with a multitude of cultural, social, culinary, and entertainment options. Northern Virginia is home to a booming business and technology center and is only a short drive to many points of interest. The history and physical beauty of the state of Virginia are readily accessible. Major cities such as New York and Philadelphia are within

A glass atrium links two sections of Enterprise Hall, which houses the School of Management.

The $30-million Johnson Learning Center combines state-of-the-art open space library with retail, recreational, and food service space.

a few hours of the campus. The beautiful coastal communities of Maryland and North Carolina are close by, as are the mountains and ski resorts of West Virginia and Pennsylvania. For other destinations, GMU is only 20 minutes away from Washington's two major airports.

George Mason University enrolls almost 24,000 students in 104 degree programs. The University has emerged as one of the most innovative and visionary institutions in the state and the nation.

Technology Environment

The University's modern and multiple computer facilities are augmented by the School of Management's exclusive LAN. This network links students with the University, faculty members, each other, and the outside world through the Internet. Students use Lotus Notes for e-mail and for creating databases for classes and group projects. Most students use the network to complete large portions of class projects on line, minimizing the need for multiple face-to-face meetings. The School's virtual environment extends into the classroom, with many professors setting up databases to post class notes, current articles, and readings. These databases are also used to continue classroom discussions in between sessions.

Students also have access to proprietary databases such as Compustat PC Plus, Bloomberg, and LEXIS-NEXIS. The University and the School of Management use the Microsoft Office 97 Suite, including Word, Excel, Access, and PowerPoint.

Placement

The Career Services Office (CSO) is a proactive partner in a graduate student's career development. The CSO provides information sessions, resume critiques, individual career counseling, a resource room/video library, and an array of career workshops. Twice a year, the CSO coordinates on-campus recruiting, which includes mock interviews, corporate briefing sessions, and on-campus interviews. Graduate students also have access to an online jobs/internships database, an online Resume Referral Service, a regional employer symposium, a fifteen-university M.B.A. recruiting

consortium, and ongoing internship opportunities with local companies.

Admission

The program seeks applicants with diverse academic, professional, ethnic, and national backgrounds. The academic record, GMAT/TOEFL scores, communication skills, and work experience are evaluated for admission to the program. The mean GMAT and TOEFL scores of enrolled students are 620 and 635, respectively. Applicants must hold a degree equivalent to an American bachelor's degree that requires at least four years of study at the university level. Applicants whose native language is not English must submit a TOEFL score. International applicants must provide proof of financial resources for approximately $20,000 in living and educational expenses. Detailed instructions for international applicants are found in the application.

Finances

Tuition for the 1998–99 academic year is $257 per credit hour for Virginia residents and $521 per credit hour for nonresidents. Books and insurance cost approximately $1500 per year. A campus apartment and meal plan cost approximately $6000 for two semesters. Off-campus housing, estimated at $8000 per year, is abundant and a popular choice of graduate business students. Assistance in finding housing is available.

International Students

George Mason prides itself on the diversity of its student population. Typically, more than twenty-five different nations are represented in the M.B.A. population. The University's English Language Institute, Office of International Programs and Services, and International Exchange Programs are valuable resources for all students.

Application Facts and Dates

Early applications are strongly encouraged due to the rolling admissions process. The application deadline is April 1 for fall and November 1 for spring. For more information, students should contact:

School of Management Admissions
Mailstop 5A2
George Mason University
Fairfax, Virginia 22030-4444
Telephone: 703-993-2136
Fax: 703-993-1886
E-mail: gradadms@som.gmu.edu
World Wide Web: http://www.gmu.edu

Georgetown University

Washington, D.C.

THE M.B.A. FOR THE GLOBAL MARKETPLACE

Business seeks leaders who have the tools to perform critical analysis, the vision to plan and implement strategically, and the global awareness to compete in tomorrow's marketplace. The new Georgetown M.B.A. curriculum meets the needs of business and prepares students for professional success. The Georgetown Program provides a rigorous education for the future, a future in which every industry is international, every economic issue is global, and every major corporation is multinational. Through six team-based, integrative experiences; thread courses in international business as well as technology and knowledge management; an extensive selection of six-week and twelve-week elective courses; career track options; and a "Global Experience" that combines one week of international field-based learning with twelve weeks of related course work, Georgetown delivers an M.B.A. for the global marketplace.

Programs and Curricular Focus

The Georgetown M.B.A. Program is a 60-credit, full-time, nonthesis program. Students complete all requirements for the degree in two academic years. Required courses, with the exception of electives, are taught during the first year to give Georgetown M.B.A. students the best academic preparation for their summer internships. Electives are offered as six-week module courses or twelve-week semester courses. Almost half of the program is made up of elective course work. The Georgetown M.B.A. focuses on business knowledge applied in an international context through its integrative experiences, the non-U.S. field-based learning exercise, the international business thread course, the Washington, D.C., location, and the diversity of both its students and faculty.

In addition to electives offered by the School of Business, students often enroll in other University courses that focus on international or business issues. To enhance opportunities to pursue regional interests in global business, qualified M.B.A. students are able to receive graduate elective credit for courses offered in various area studies programs or in the International Business Diplomacy Certificate Program. Opportunities to study abroad during the summer or semester are sponsored by the School.

In conjunction with the Georgetown University Law Center and the School of Foreign Service, there are a four-year program leading to the J.D./M.B.A. degree and a three-year program leading

to the M.B.A./M.S.F.S. degree, respectively. A three-year M.B.A./M.P.P. degree and a five-year M.D./M.B.A. are also offered. The International Executive M.B.A. Program is an eighteen-month M.B.A. program for students with a minimum of eight years of work experience. The Georgetown M.B.A. Program is accredited by AACSB–The International Association for Management Education.

Students and the M.B.A. Experience

Georgetown M.B.A. students bring diverse academic, professional, and personal backgrounds to the program. The fall 1997 entering class numbered 249 and represented every region of the U.S. as well as thirty-four countries. Thirty-five percent of the students are non-U.S. citizens, and 86 percent have nonnative language proficiency and/or have lived or studied abroad. Women comprise 32 percent of the class, and minorities represent 14 percent. The average age of the students is 28, and 97 percent of the class has had one year or more of professional, full-time, postbaccalaureate experience, averaging 4.7 years. The diverse backgrounds of Georgetown M.B.A. students contribute greatly to the curricular and cocurricular aspects of the program through class participation, group work, and student activities.

Small class sizes encourage student participation and interaction. Teaching methodology includes case study and

lecture style. Group projects are an integral part of the curriculum.

The Faculty

The School of Business faculty members have strong academic and professional backgrounds. Many have held positions in business or government; lived, worked, or studied abroad; and been educated at many of the best academic institutions around the world. Faculty members concentrate on both research and teaching.

Georgetown University traditionally emphasizes strong student-faculty interaction. School of Business faculty members are available to students, working together with them on research projects and career decision making. Faculty members also serve as advisers to student clubs in the M.B.A. program, where their expertise in functional areas serves as a great resource for students planning events of professional interest.

The Business School Network

The Georgetown School of Business has developed strong ties with local, national, and international business leaders. The School's location in Washington, D.C., is an asset for the M.B.A. program. The program's relationship with business and government provides students with opportunities for on-site projects, internships, and guest speakers.

The School of Business is served by three distinguished boards: the Board of Visitors, the Graduate Advisory Board, and the Parents Council. The boards advise the Dean on a broad range of issues related to strategy, program enhancement, faculty, curriculum, resource development, and student career opportunities.

The Center for Business-Government Relations, the Center for International Business, the Connelly Program in Business Ethics, and the Global Entrepreneurship Program also serve as research and program arms of the business school. The Credit Research Center and the *Journal of International Business Studies* moved to Georgetown in 1997.

The College and Environs

Georgetown's main campus is located in the heart of the historic Georgetown area of Washington, D.C., alongside the Potomac River. The home of the School of Business, Old North, was constructed in 1795 and is the oldest surviving University building. It is a designated historic landmark. By January 1999, M.B.A. administrative offices, the student lounge, and expanded classroom space and meeting areas will move to the newly renovated School of Business Annex. Washington is a world crossroads for political and corporate leaders. As the seat of the federal government, Washington is the headquarters of many international organizations and major corporations. It provides an ideal laboratory for the study of global management issues and business-government relations.

Facilities

The Washington, D.C., area offers excellent research facilities, including the Library of Congress, trade and professional organizations, agencies and departments of the federal government, foreign embassies, and many businesses. Georgetown M.B.A. students have access to six University libraries, including the Lauinger Library, which houses the School of Business collection. Lauinger has more than 2 million volumes, 2.6 million microforms, 435,400 government documents, 26,000 current serials, and seats 1,350. The School of Business Technology Center contains the Boland Information Systems Laboratory (BISL) and the Decision Support Center (DSC). These computer labs are for use by the students and faculty members of the business school and have approximately 100 IBM-compatible computers. Every unit is connected to a local area network with a broad range of application software and access to the University's minicomputer and mainframe. Internet access and other external information services such as Dow Jones News/Retrieval Service, LEXIS-NEXIS, and Bloomberg are also available. Students can also access the School network by laptop computer in the newest case-study classrooms and the M.B.A. lounge.

Placement

M.B.A. career management professionals are available to assist and advise students in developing and attaining their career goals. Through individual and group sessions as well as special programs and events, first- and second-year M.B.A. students develop the skills needed to make sound career decisions and conduct effective job searches. Career management services available to M.B.A. students include consortium events, the alumni database, career advising, career information, workshops, on-campus recruiting, the Hoya-Link electronic resume database, the M.B.A. Career Extravaganza, resume books, and summer internships.

Ninety-five percent of the 1997 Georgetown M.B.A. graduates had employment offers by September 30, 1997. The median annual salary, exclusive of sign-on bonuses, commissions, and other benefits, was $64,500 for the class of 1997. More than 100 companies recruited on campus during 1997–98.

While career services are available to all students, international students should be aware that job opportunities in the United States are limited by the type of visa they hold.

Admission

Men and women holding baccalaureate degrees from accredited colleges or universities are eligible for consideration for admission. Georgetown seeks a diverse student body and encourages applications from students with a wide variety of academic backgrounds including the liberal arts and sciences and business.

Academic qualifications are determined by the previous higher education record as indicated by transcripts, letters of recommendation, and results of the Graduate Management Admission Test (GMAT). In addition, international applicants are required to submit results from the TOEFL unless they have obtained an academic degree from a university in a country where English is the native language.

Selection also depends upon an applicant's distinctive achievements, ideas, talents, and motivation for graduate business education. Professional experience, while not required, strengthens an application. International experience, foreign languages, writing ability, interpersonal skills, leadership ability, and entrepreneurship are some favored qualifications. The Admissions Committee seeks to admit students representing various geographic, economic, racial, religious, and minority groups.

Finances

Tuition, fees, books, supplies, transportation, and living expenses for the 1998–99 academic year are approximately $36,000.

The Graduate School and the School of Business award partial- and full-tuition scholarships. Scholarship awards are made on the basis of merit. Recipients of scholarships and stipends are M.B.A. Scholars who provide research assistance to the faculty. All applicants who are offered admission are considered for scholarship awards; no additional application materials are necessary. Both U.S. citizens and international students are considered for scholarships.

The Georgetown University Office of Student Financial Services attempts to assist financially eligible applicants who are U.S. citizens and permanent residents of the U.S. to meet their educational and living costs. Financial eligibility is met by a combination of loans and employment and is awarded on the basis of financial need.

International Students

Services and organizations available to international students include the Office of International Programs, English as a foreign language classes, Off-Campus Housing Office, and the Graduate Business Programs Office. The M.B.A. program office sponsors an Orientation Residency and preparatory workshops prior to the start of the program for all students.

The fall 1997 M.B.A. entering class included students from the following countries: Argentina; Armenia; Australia; Brazil; Canada; Colombia; Ecuador; El Salvador; France; Germany; India; Indonesia; Italy; Japan; Malaysia; Mexico; the People's Republic of China and Hong Kong; Peru; Philippines; Russia; South Korea; Spain; Taiwan, R.O.C.; Thailand; Trinidad; Turkey; Ukraine; United Kingdom; United States; Uruguay; Venezuela; and Yugoslavia.

Application Facts and Dates

Admission is for the fall semester only; there are no midyear admissions. Applications are considered on a rolling basis. The final deadline for submission of application materials is April 15. International students, students seeking financial assistance, and joint-degree candidates are encouraged to apply before February 1.

For additional information and questions about the Georgetown M.B.A. Program, students should contact:

M.B.A. Admissions Office
School of Business
105 Old North
Box 571148
Georgetown University
Washington, D.C. 20057-1148
Telephone: 202-687-4200
Fax: 202-687-7809
E-mail: mba@gunet.georgetown.edu
World Wide Web: http://www.gsb.georgetown.edu

The George Washington University

School of Business and Public Management

Washington, D.C.

AN M.B.A. BUILT ON STRENGTHS

▶ *It has been aptly referred to as "permanent whitewater"—today's business climate of rapid change, obstacles, and opportunities. With business flowing ever more freely across international boundaries, the times call for a new way of educating leaders. At The George Washington University (GW) we've responded by redesigning our M.B.A.: strengthening the core curriculum, adding the option of taking all first-year courses with the same group of students, building more flexibility into concentration options, and putting an even greater emphasis on the quality of teaching.*

Fortunately, the strengths we had to build on were formidable. Our diverse and accomplished faculty has far more practical business experience than most, and Washington is the ideal learning laboratory for exploring international business and the interface between the private and public sectors.

Now we have created initiatives that enable our students to have even more enriching experiences. For instance, through the Greater Washington Board of Trade, our international students work with global businesses headquartered here. We are also creating a center for dealing with economic development problems, and to help students develop entrepreneurial skills, we have established the Center for the Advancement of Small Business.

We expect students to be able to find information, analyze it effectively, communicate their ideas convincingly, and work both in teams and independently to find innovative solutions as they become true professionals who can navigate the course of business successfully, with grace and integrity.

—Robert F. Dyer, Associate Dean, Graduate Programs

Programs and Curricular Focus

The George Washington University Master of Business Administration is designed to deliver a strong general management education through core and integrative courses while maintaining an array of options and opportunities that can be packaged differently for each student.

The full-time M.B.A. program (50–54 credit hours) is designed with a first-year cohort experience structured to promote teamwork; it provides opportunities to approach problems and issues across the curriculum and is enhanced by a series of cocurricular activities that are constructed to support and expand upon classroom concepts. A practicum and a capstone course, designed to integrate the M.B.A. courses, are also required. Students may pursue any of fifteen concentrations (accounting; finance and investments; health services administration; human resources management; information systems management; international business; logistics, operations, and materials management; management decision making; management of science, technology, and innovation; marketing;

organizational behavior and development; real estate and urban development; small business and entrepreneurship; strategic management and public policy; and tourism and hospitality management) or craft an individualized concentration. Electives provide flexibility and opportunities for additional depth and breadth.

There are a number of options for students whose lives do not permit full-time study. The accelerated M.B.A. program provides a fast-paced cohort option for employed students. Students attend this 40–48 credit program on a year-round basis, and this option includes residencies as well as applied and integrated projects. The self-paced M.B.A. program (also 40–48 credits) is the most flexible, permitting enrollment in any combination of semesters and at any credit load, as long as the program is completed in five years. Because working professionals have a myriad of needs, a concentration is not required. Electives, which constitute half of the program, help students position themselves for immediate and long-range opportunities. The Executive M.B.A. program, currently a

60-hour, two-year cohort program, is designed for middle- and senior-level managers who seek an intensive program to enhance their career development. The program consists of courses taught on alternate Fridays and Saturdays, plus four residencies, including one overseas. It emphasizes management of technology and innovation, management of a culturally diverse work force, and international business.

Through a special credit-hour transfer arrangement between the School of Business and Public Management and GW's School of Law, students can complete both the M.B.A. and J.D. degrees within four years. (Part-time students must do it in five.) Also, students may pursue degrees in the School of Business and Public Management and GW's Elliott School of International Affairs simultaneously, receiving the M.B.A. and M.A. in two to three years.

In addition to the MBA degree, the GW School of Business and Public Management offers the Master of Accountancy, the Master of Public Administration, the Master of Science in acquisition management, finance, information systems management, or project management, and the Master of Tourism Administration. The Ph.D. is offered in accountancy, business administration, health services administration, human resources management, information and decision systems, management and organization, and public administration.

Students and the M.B.A. Experience

GW M.B.A. students are intellectually mature people who have exhibited a strong potential for management and leadership. The average student is 26 years old. Thirty-eight percent of M.B.A. students are women, and 11 percent are members of U.S. minority groups. International students comprise 43 percent of the student body.

More than 75 percent of GW M.B.A. students possess substantial business experience before beginning their graduate work. They come from domestic and foreign corporations, family-owned companies, nonprofit organizations, private practices, and the arts. Many work on Capitol Hill or in one of the businesses headquartered in the Washington area.

❖ Global Focus

With students from sixty-nine countries, GW offers a culturally diverse environment for learning about life and business around the world. In addition to the core course, The World Economy, students are required to take at least one additional elective that adds international background. For students who choose to study abroad, exchange programs have been established in Europe, Asia, and South America.

The School of Business and Public Management is located within a few blocks of the World Bank, the International Monetary Fund, and embassies from around the world, offering GW M.B.A. students a unique opportunity to gain a global perspective. In addition to internships with international agencies in the Washington area, students may develop opportunities for internships in other countries. For example, a student recently interned at an advertising agency in Ecuador and another in South Africa with USAID in small business and economic development.

The Faculty

The program faculty members form a diverse group of highly respected experts, many of whom have achieved national and international prominence for their research, writing, and professional accomplishments. These experienced executives, managers, and consultants bring an incisive knowledge of current issues to the classroom. In addition to working closely with students, faculty members work together to address themes that cut across all aspects of business, such as management communication, business ethics, cross-cultural management, and career development. This collaborative effort makes it easier for students to integrate their knowledge.

The Business School Network

Students of the School of Business and Public Management develop an extraordinary loyalty to their alma mater, as evidenced by more than 30,000 alumni in the fifty states and seventy countries. This extensive network is the key to helping graduating students establish contacts in the area in which they plan to settle. Through the mentor program, alumni offer guidance in their various areas of expertise, serve on panels to help students make intelligent career decisions, and evaluate students' performance in workshops and case studies.

The Dean's Associates Council includes leaders from both the private and public sectors. These partnerships provide direction for the School of Business and Public Management and opportunities for students to meet and learn from today's business leaders.

The College and Environs

Unquestionably one of the most exciting cities in the world, Washington, D.C., is a global center of power and influence. Courses and faculty members provide opportunities for access to, and the development of, insider perspectives. Living in Washington means enjoying the beauty of four glorious seasons and being in the midst of a region filled with historic sites and natural beauty. Attracting interesting people from all over the world, Washington boasts the highest percentage of college graduates of any metropolitan area in the country. In addition to a wide array of Fortune 500 companies and technology-based industries, the area provides a wealth of cultural and recreational attractions that few cities can match.

Located five blocks from the White House in the historic Foggy Bottom area of northwest Washington, The George Washington University is an integral part of the city. Modern and efficient public transportation makes it easy to participate in the exciting life of the capital city.

Placement

Career services are available to GW M.B.A. students from a variety of resources. The School's Graduate Career Center offers comprehensive career planning and placement services. The M.B.A. Association and the Alumni Association regularly sponsor networking activities and career panels. Cooperative education opportunities and internships become an excellent network for future career opportunities. M.B.A. students find faculty members ready and willing to provide career advice and networking opportunities. These resources allow each student to develop an aggressive strategy for finding the best opportunities after graduation.

Admission

The School of Business and Public Management seeks candidates who have demonstrated potential for management and who have the intellectual ability, maturity, initiative, and creativity to fully participate in the challenging interdisciplinary environment. Applicants must have a bachelor's degree from a regionally accredited college or university. Selection is based upon the applicant's academic record, work experience, statement of

purpose, recommendations, and scores on the required Graduate Management Admission Test (GMAT).

Applications from international students are welcome. Proficiency in reading, writing, and speaking English must be demonstrated by all students from countries where English is not an official language. International students, in addition to the above listed requirements, must submit certified English translations of all academic records of course work corresponding to a bachelor's degree in the United States; scores for the Test of English as a Foreign Language (TOEFL), with a total score of 550 or higher; and a financial certificate, which is required of any applicant who plans to enter or remain in the United States to study and whose immigration status will be either F-1 (student) or J-1 (exchange visitor).

Finances

Tuition for the academic year 1998–99 is $680 per credit hour plus a University fee of $34.50 per credit hour. Full-time students normally take 12 to 15 credits per semester. Books, supplies, and health insurance cost approximately $1700 per year. Estimated costs for room, board, and miscellaneous personal expenses total about $10,000 per academic year. The majority of graduate students live off campus.

A number of graduate assistantships and fellowships are available based on academic merit. To be considered, applicants must complete the admissions application process no later than February 1. Additional aid sources are available on the World Wide Web.

Application Facts and Dates

Full consideration for the fall semester is given to applications that are submitted no later than April 1 and for the spring semester by October 1. Applications are considered after the indicated dates on a space-available basis. Students who wish to be considered for fellowships must complete the application process no later than February 1. For more information, students should contact the Office of Graduate Admissions and indicate which M.B.A. options they are interested in.

Office of Graduate Admissions
School of Business and Public
   Management
The George Washington University
710 21st Street, NW
Washington, D.C. 20052
Telephone: 202-994-6584
Fax: 202-994-6382
E-mail: sbpmapp@gwu.edu
World Wide Web: http://www.sbpm.gwu.edu

Georgia Institute of Technology

DuPree College of Management

Atlanta, Georgia

CHANGES IN THE NINETIES

▶ *The decade of the 1990s has brought national recognition to the DuPree College of Management and has enabled us to broaden our areas of outreach and expertise. The Center for International Business Education and Research, which was created in 1993, is one of twenty-six national resource centers of excellence funded by the Department of Education to promote competitiveness in global markets through educational initiatives. In 1994, Tom DuPree, a 1974 alumnus, donated $5 million to establish the DuPree Center for Entrepreneurship. A grant from IBM in 1995 created the International Quality Center for Change Leadership. In 1996, Mr. DuPree made an additional gift of $20 million. In recognition of his generosity, the College has been named for him.*

—Lloyd Byars, Interim Dean

Programs and Curricular Focus

Georgia Tech's DuPree College of Management offers accredited programs leading to the Master of Science in Management (M.S.M.) and Ph.D. degrees. Both programs have a strong analytical and quantitative emphasis. Classes in these programs are offered only during the day and are limited to full-time students. The M.S.M. curriculum contains 60 semester hours that are divided into core requirements and elective concentrations. This permits completion of the program in four semesters, spread over two academic years. The ten core courses include accounting, finance, human resources, information technology, international business, marketing, microeconomics, operations management, organizational behavior, and strategic management.

The core curriculum provides the essential understanding of the disciplines underlying modern management education, the functional areas of management, and the environments in which modern organizations function. Ten electives provide an opportunity for in-depth study in one or more of the concentration areas. The curriculum requires no business prerequisites or specific undergraduate preparation other than one calculus course. Students with specific interests or career goals can also arrange concentration areas in other Georgia Tech graduate programs. The M.S.M. program is ideally suited for students whose interest in professional management practice is coupled with strong analytical ability. The Ph.D. program is small, research oriented,

and highly selective. For the most part, Ph.D. course work and research requirements are determined on an individual basis, and close associations with faculty members as well as early research involvement are standard.

Students and the M.B.A. Experience

Typically, the management student body is made up of students who, as undergraduates, majored in engineering (40 percent), business (35 percent), and the sciences and humanities (25 percent). Most students have had four or more years of full-time work experience. The median age is 27. Approximately 35 percent of the students are from the Southeast, and 30 percent are women. The diverse backgrounds of the students strengthen and enrich class discussions. There are generally 200 graduate students in the College of Management, with class sizes averaging 50 students in the first year and 25 students per class in second-year electives. Graduates of the M.S.M. program have gone on to hold management consulting positions with national accounting and management consulting firms; line management and plant operations positions with manufacturing organizations; marketing and general staff positions with consumer goods, computer, and manufacturing firms; and corporate finance and investment management positions with financial organizations in various industries.

The Faculty

The DuPree College of Management is distinguished by a faculty that is dedicated to providing an optimal learning environment for students. Faculty members have consistently been recognized for their superior availability and responsiveness to students and effectively mesh research, case analysis, and business theory into real-world problem solutions. The management faculty prepares students with superb academic backgrounds to positively influence business operations in a variety of industries and enterprises.

Students value the opportunity to have a group of specialists available for advice in career, curricular, and research interests. Beyond instruction, the management faculty is an ideal resource for corporate managers.

The Business School Network

Georgia Tech's location in Atlanta provides easy access to the business community and the classroom. Corporate executives frequently attend graduate classes to share their experiences and to describe changes and growth in their organizations and industry. The College of Management's Board of Advisors and the Board of the DuPree Center for Entrepreneurship provide feedback, information, and advice to students on an ongoing basis. In addition, Georgia Tech's Advanced Technology Development Center (ATDC) advises small entrepreneurial firms about business planning and strategy.

The Graduate Students in Management (GSM) student club arranges networking events with alumni, promotes a guest speaker series, and works closely with the faculty and administration to upgrade the programs and facilities. In addition, many M.S.M. students are actively involved in community service events. They believe that volunteering in the community is an important part of their lives. Their participation in the varied volunteer activities coordinated by the M.S.M. community service organizations enriches them as well as the groups or individuals assisted.

The College and Environs

Georgia Tech was founded in 1885 to bring technological education to the Southeast. Since 1945, the College of Management has provided graduate management education that complements a technical undergraduate background. Georgia's Tech's 330-acre wooded campus borders midtown Atlanta. As a global center of commerce, Atlanta is home to more than 1,200 international businesses. Seventy-three countries maintain consulates and chambers of commerce in the city. More than 730 of the Fortune 1000 businesses have offices in the Atlanta area. Atlanta's metropolitan area, which spreads over twenty counties and includes more than 3.4 million people, is the twelfth largest in the country.

Facilities

The M.S.M. program provides a synergy between technology and management. Students have access to the Georgia Research Alliance, a centerpiece of the state's economic development strategy. In 1996, the Alliance completed construction of the Georgia Center for Advanced Telecommunications Technology (GCATT) building, which houses high-tech business incubators, research centers, and established telecommunications businesses. The Georgia Tech Library and Information Center houses one of the nation's largest collections of scientific and technical information, with more than 2.7 million volumes. The catalog record of the library is on line, as part of the Georgia Tech Electronic Library (GTEL), and is available through the campus computer network.

Technology Environment

Georgia Tech's Office of Information Technology (OIT) provides campuswide technology support. OIT issues computer accounts for Internet access, e-mail, and homework and class assignments. The campus network connects more than 130 campus buildings via fiber-optic cable. The DuPree College has several 24-hour computer labs with PCs and Macintoshes, scanners, and printers.

Placement

DuPree College's Office of Graduate Management Career Services is the liaison between the business community and DuPree College. Its primary mission is to support M.S.M. students in their career development and job search. In fulfilling this mission, Career Services provides M.S.M. students with opportunities to interview with corporate recruiters, and students are advised in career planning and job search techniques.

Corporate support activities are designed to expand and strengthen the business community's involvement with DuPree College. Frequent contact with hundreds of companies provides an open line of communication between employers and the School's students and faculty members.

Admission

The master's program may be entered in the fall quarter only; doctoral students may enter in any quarter. Application forms may be obtained from the College of Management. GMAT scores, transcripts of all previous college work, two essays, and two letters of evaluation are required from master's program applicants. Doctoral program applicants should contact the Director of Graduate Admissions for specific application requirements. Applicants from non-English-speaking countries must submit TOEFL scores and a certified statement of financial resources.

Finances

In 1998–99, annual tuition and fees are $3627 for Georgia residents and $12,465 for out-of-state students. On-campus housing costs are approximately $450 per quarter. Off-campus housing ranges between $300 and $450 per month.

Master's-level graduate research or teaching assistantships receive an annual stipend of $6000, with tuition reduced to $252 per quarter. Ph.D.-level graduate assistants receive $9000 per year, with tuition reduced to $252 per quarter. The President's Fellowships and the Regent's Opportunity Scholarships provide additional financial awards up to $5000 and remission of all tuition costs. These awards are offered based on an applicant's ability, potential contribution to the program, and background. Assistance is also available through federal and state loan programs.

Application Facts and Dates

February 15 is the deadline for consideration for graduate assistantships and financial aid. Applications and credentials from international students must also be received by February 15. Applications from U.S. citizens and permanent residents must be received by April 15.

Questions and requests for additional information should be directed to:

Graduate Admissions Office
DuPree College of Management
Georgia Institute of Technology
Atlanta, Georgia 30332-0520
Telephone: 404-894-8722
Fax: 404-894-4199
E-mail: msm@mgt.gatech.edu
World Wide Web: http://www.iac.
    gatech.edu/dupree

Georgia State University

GeorgiaState
University

College of Business Administration

Atlanta, Georgia

SERIOUS STUDENTS DEMAND SERIOUS TEACHING

The College of Business Administration has developed nationally recognized specialties in many areas to help our mature and serious students realize their ambitions. Whether your goal is to land a job with an Atlanta-based company, to work abroad, or to better your position within your current company, Georgia State can equip you with the knowledge and tools you need. The College is known not only for the breadth and flexibility of the graduate programs but also for its reputation as an eminent research institution that offers outstanding teaching. Our commitment to excellence earned our part-time M.B.A. program a fourth-place ranking in this year's U.S. News & World Report.

—Dr. Sidney Harris, Dean

Programs and Curricular Focus

Business schools are not known for flexibility and allowing students personal choice. However, Georgia State is not like most business schools. The College is not so specialized that students can't find classes to match their interests. At the same time, the College is a recognized leader in such fields as accounting, computer information systems, and risk management.

The College offers the M.B.A. degree in three formats, as well as sixteen specialized master's programs. Students can earn an M.B.A. with a major or concentration from one of eleven areas. Classes are offered during the daytime, evenings, and on Saturdays. Georgia State's part-time M.B.A. program was ranked fourth in *U.S. News & World Report*'s 1998 listing of the nation's best graduate schools.

The Flexible M.B.A. (FMBA) offers the greatest choice of day, evening, and Saturday courses for both full- and part-time students. Students plan course schedules to fit their needs and can start in any semester. The Concentrated M.B.A. (CMBA) program, starting in the summer only, is a one-year, full-time, team-oriented program for professionals with at least two years of work experience, regardless of undergraduate major. The Executive M.B.A. (EMBA) is a lockstep, two-year program designed for managers with ten or more years of career experience, with classes on alternating Fridays and Saturdays.

Any M.B.A. student can earn a concentration (four courses) or a major (seven courses) in the following areas:

accounting, decision sciences, economics, finance, general business, information systems, international business, management, marketing, personnel and employment relations, real estate, and risk management and insurance.

While the M.B.A. is a general management degree, the College's specialized master's degrees allow students to focus on one functional business area. The Master of Science is offered with majors in business economics, computer information systems, decision sciences, finance, management, marketing, personal financial planning, personnel and employment relations, and risk management and insurance.

Other degrees include the Master of International Business, which requires that students become proficient in another language and intern overseas; Master of Actuarial Science; Master of Professional Accountancy; Master of Science in Health Administration; Master of Science in Real Estate; and Master of Taxation as well as joint programs such as the M.B.A./Master of Health Administration and M.B.A./J.D.

Students and the M.B.A. Experience

Business students at Georgia State learn not only from the faculty but also from each other. That's because the average master's student is 28 years old with five years of full-time work experience. Students discover that this work experience, and that of their colleagues, is a vital component of the Georgia State program. There are almost 1,500 M.B.A.

students and 750 specialized master's students. Of all master's students, 37 percent are women, 17 percent are members of minority groups, and 14 percent are international. The program is large and offers numerous classes in specialized fields not found at other schools. This allows students the opportunity to explore their areas of interest and meet their career goals.

The Faculty

The College's 190 full-time faculty members are teachers, researchers, authors, and leaders. Georgia State business faculty members take pride in bringing relevant, real-world problems, issues, and experiences into the classroom. With degrees from Harvard, MIT, Wharton, and Northwestern, Georgia State faculty members also attract students to one of the largest doctoral programs in the nation.

The Business School Network

As the largest business program in the Atlanta area, Georgia State's 39,000 business alumni serve as a great network. The College's own Board of Advisors includes more than 40 of the city's top CEOs, presidents, partners, and entrepreneurs, attesting to the strong community support.

Prominent Alumni

Some of the nation's top executives are among the College's alumni. They include: Bill Dahlberg, CEO of The Southern Co.; Jerry Dempsey, CEO of PPG Industries; Ken Lewis, President of NationsBank, Corp.; Parker Petit, Chairman of Matria Healthcare, Inc.; David Stonecipher, CEO of Jefferson-Pilot Corp.; and James Copeland, Managing Partner of Deloitte & Touche.

The College and Environs

Located in the heart of downtown Atlanta's business and financial district, Georgia State University is home to 24,000 students, making it one of the two largest of the state's universities. The 28-acre main campus includes the Pullen Library, which houses more than 1.5 million volumes. In addition to the main

---

832

In the heart of downtown Atlanta, Georgia State University fosters close ties with the business community. Atlanta produced 88,400 new jobs in 1996, and experts predict the city will lead the country in job growth through the year 2000.

campus, graduate evening and weekend classes are also offered at the University's North Metro Center in Dunwoody.

Facilities

Just across the street from the city's rapid rail hub, the College of Business Administration is located in the historic Citizens and Southern National Bank Building, which was donated to the College by NationsBank. The building houses all College faculty and administrative offices, including the Office of Academic Assistance and Master's Admissions and the Graduate Business Placement Office.

Placement

The Graduate Business Placement Office offers comprehensive placement services, including an employer library and lists of job and internship opportunities as well as computer terminals for online and database job searches. The office offers workshops to help students in their job search and also hosts the annual Business Career Expo, which attracts more than 125 employers and almost 1,000 students. Career counselors are also available to provide individual assessments of students' career goals and opportunities. More placement information can be found at the College of Business Administration's Web site (http://www-cba.gsu/wwwgpo).

Admission

Admission into the College's graduate programs is competitive, with each applicant being evaluated individually in relation to the current group of candidates. The Master's Admissions Committee considers previous academic performance and educational background, work experience, and GMAT scores. The College's average GMAT for all graduate programs is 570, with an average undergraduate GPA of 3.0. Previous academic work in business is not required.

Finances

Graduate tuition for the 1998–99 academic year is $318 per 3-hour course for residents and $1272 for nonresidents. Students must also pay $228 per semester for student activity, recreation, transportation, health, and athletics fees. Tuition rates are subject to change.

The University awards a limited number of merit and need-based scholarships to eligible students and sponsors various institutional and government loan programs. Full-time students are eligible for research assistantships and a limited number of nonresident fee waivers, which are awarded based on academic performance in graduate course work. For information on scholarship and loan opportunities, students should contact the Office of Student Financial Aid at 404-651-2227. For information on graduate assistantships, students should contact the Office of Academic Assistance and Master's Admissions at the number below.

Application Facts and Dates

Individuals who have earned undergraduate degrees from a regionally accredited institution may apply for graduate admission for any semester (except for the EMBA, which begins only in the fall, and the CMBA, which begins only in the summer). For an application and admission information, students should contact:

Office of Academic Assistance and
    Master's Admissions
College of Business Administration
Georgia State University
University Plaza
Atlanta, Georgia 30303-3083
Telephone: 404-651-1913
Fax: 404-651-0219
World Wide Web: http://www.cba.gsu.
    edu

Golden Gate University

School of Business

San Francisco, California

> **A REAL-WORLD APPROACH TO EDUCATION**
>
> *The M.B.A. program at Golden Gate University is designed to help working professionals gain the knowledge, skills, and confidence they need to assume broader corporate responsibilities. Ambitious, professional adult students find a real-world approach to education here and benefit from the experience and knowledge of their classmates as well as from their instructors—full- and part-time scholar-practitioners. We are proud to say that more San Francisco Bay Area business executives have earned their M.B.A. from Golden Gate than from any other university in northern California.*
>
> —Hamid Shomali, Dean

Programs and Curricular Focus

The M.B.A. program at Golden Gate University provides a solid grounding in the core areas of business management as well as the opportunity to specialize in one of fourteen separate areas. The program consists of three components: the general business program, or foundation courses; the advanced program, or core courses; and an area of concentration. Four general business courses provide an essential foundation for the more advanced core and concentration courses. These general business courses may be waived if students have completed comparable courses elsewhere. Eight core courses in areas such as financial management, human resources, managerial analysis and communication, business policy and strategy, marketing, and operations ensure that all M.B.A. program graduates have a comprehensive knowledge of the core areas of business, regardless of their area of concentration. The final four courses are taken in an area of specialization, allowing students to develop expertise in a specific area of business.

An Executive M.B.A. program is offered for managers and professionals who want to integrate a full-time sixteen-month M.B.A. program with their current work schedules. A joint M.B.A./ J.D. degree program is also available in conjunction with the Golden Gate School of Law.

Students and the M.B.A. Experience

Students in the Golden Gate M.B.A. program bring a wide variety of work experiences and academic diversity to the classroom. About 80 percent of the students attend part-time while working either full- or part-time. Fifty percent of M.B.A. students are women.

❖ Global Focus

Among the core courses is The Manager in the International Economy, which provides exposure to the role of multinationals in the global economy; legal, cultural, and financial environments facing multinational corporations; host/home country relationships with multinationals; and policy, strategy, and management challenges faced by multinational corporations. An international perspective also is included throughout the M.B.A. program, as appropriate.

Special Features

One of the special features of the M.B.A. program at Golden Gate is the opportunity to choose one of fourteen areas of concentration, in addition to the foundation and core courses required. Students take four courses to develop expertise in one of the following areas: accounting, finance, human resource management, information systems, international business, management, marketing, operations management, organizational behavior and development, or telecommunications management.

A general course of study is also available. Instead of choosing a concentration, students select four courses from different areas to give them a broad look at management issues.

The Faculty

The faculty is composed of scholar-practitioner full- and part-time educators. Many are career professionals who also have advanced degrees and extensive classroom experience. They bring real-world problems and events to the classroom. The faculty is also specially trained to make sure that classes are relevant, challenging, and meet the needs of adult students.

The Business School Network

Since 1953, feedback from M.B.A. students, alumni, and the business community has been used to continuously improve the M.B.A. program. Advisory boards comprising corporate and industry executives provide valuable input in each management discipline that helps keep the curriculum current.

Prominent Alumni

More San Francisco Bay Area business executives have earned their M.B.A. degrees from Golden Gate University than from any other university in northern California. Some, like Bank of America CEO Richard Rosenberg (M.B.A. class of 1963, J.D. class of 1966), rose to the very pinnacle of their professions. Others, like Eleanor Yu (M.B.A. class of 1986), president and CEO of AdLand Advertising and one of the most powerful Asian women in the American advertising industry, became highly successful entrepreneurs.

The College and Environs

Golden Gate University traces its origins to the founding of the San Francisco YMCA in 1853, the oldest founding date in the city for an institution of higher learning.

A pioneer in the case-study method of instruction, Golden Gate is recognized for applied education for the professions. The University provides instruction for more than 7,000 students at the associate, baccalaureate, master's, and doctoral levels on nine campuses along the West Coast of the United States and abroad.

Classrooms, the general and law libraries, and the principal offices of Golden Gate University are located in

San Francisco's financial district. Other University campuses are in San Francisco's East and North Bay, Monterey, Sacramento, southern California, Silicon Valley, Seattle, and Southeast Asia.

Placement

The skilled staff in the Career Services Center works closely with students and employers. Students benefit from professional career counseling, job-search workshops and programs, computerized skills assessment, placement services, networking opportunities through the STAR (Student Alumni Referral) network, and the annual career fairs that feature on-campus recruiting by major corporations. These free services provide M.B.A. students with the competitive edge in launching and in furthering their careers.

Admission

Applicants to the M.B.A. program must have an earned bachelor's degree from a regionally accredited college or university in the United States or the equivalent from a recognized foreign institution. Students must also satisfy basic mathematics, writing, and computer proficiencies.

Applicants to the M.B.A. program must submit an official score report from the GMAT (Graduate Management Admission Test), official transcripts from all schools previously attended, a 200- to 300-word statement of purpose, and a completed graduate application form along with the appropriate application fee. (Some applicants are not required to provide a GMAT score.)

Applicants whose native language is not English are required to meet the English language proficiency requirement by having achieved a TOEFL score of at least 550 or by completing (or showing evidence of having completed) courses equivalent to Golden Gate's English 1A and 1B.

Finances

Golden Gate University is one of the most affordable private universities in northern California. Tuition and fees are the same for California residents and nonresidents. Golden Gate University charges tuition by the course, and costs vary by department and location. For 1998–99, graduate tuition ranges from $1380 to $1455 per course. Books and supplies cost $250–$325 per trimester for full-time students.

Application Facts and Dates

The University accepts applications on a rolling admissions basis beginning up to one year prior to enrollment, and applications are reviewed as they become complete. International students should apply by the following dates: July 1 for fall trimester, November 1 for spring trimester, and March 1 for summer trimester. For more information, students should contact:

Enrollment Services
Golden Gate University
536 Mission Street
San Francisco, California 94105-2968
Telephone: 415-442-7800
　　　　　800-448-4968 (toll-free)
Fax: 415-442-7807
E-mail: info@ggu.edu
World Wide Web: http://www.ggu.edu

Hawaii Pacific University

Honolulu, Hawaii

MEETING TODAY'S GLOBAL CHALLENGE

Hawaii Pacific University's (HPU) M.B.A. enhances the career development of today's business professional. The HPU student body is culturally diverse, with representatives from Hawaii, the U.S. mainland, and more than eighty countries. HPU offers the skills, knowledge, and training required in today's highly competitive global business environment.

Academic programs combine practice, theory, and the skills needed in modern career fields. Students learn to implement the latest developments in computer technology, business simulations, communications theory, and strategic planning. Our graduates are well prepared for success in today's rapidly changing marketplace.

—Richard T. Ward, Dean of Graduate Management Studies

Programs and Curricular Focus

The Hawaii Pacific University M.B.A. program requires 45 semester hours of graduate work (fifteen courses). Core requirements (27 semester hours) include accounting, economics, information systems, finance, law, international business management, human resource management, marketing, and quantitative methods. Elective courses (12 semester hours) may be taken in nine different areas. The last area is the capstone series (6 semester hours), which includes Management Policy and Strategy Formulation and completion of the Professional Paper.

Joint-degree programs (66 semester hours) include the M.B.A./Master of Arts in Human Resource Management, M.B.A./Master of Arts in Organizational Change, M.B.A./Master of Arts in Management, and the M.B.A./Master of Science in Information Systems (M.S.I.S.).

Full-time students can complete the program in eighteen months. Part-time students can complete the program in twenty-four months. Students must complete their professional paper within seven years of initial enrollment in graduate courses and within one year from first enrollment in the Professional Paper course.

Hawaii Pacific University is an independent, not-for-profit, coeducational, nonsectarian, career-oriented postsecondary institution founded in 1965. It is accredited by the Accrediting Commission for Senior Colleges and Universities of the Western Association of Schools and Colleges. The University is a member of the American Assembly of Collegiate Schools of Business. HPU is recognized by the Hawaii Commission of Post-Secondary Education, approved for veteran's benefits, and authorized to issue I-20 documents to international students.

Students and the M.B.A. Experience

The average age of graduate students at Hawaii Pacific University is between 25 and 29 years of age. Students represent more than eighty countries. Teamwork is an essential ingredient of the M.B.A. program. In various courses throughout the program, students are formed into teams to solve problems collectively and to achieve a better understanding of group dynamics and challenges while producing specific desired results. Hands-on experience is gained through internships with leading Honolulu corporations. For example, students work in accounting, human resource management, and marketing internships, to name but a few.

The Faculty

The M.B.A. program at Hawaii Pacific University permits students to study with some of the most distinguished professors in the Pacific region. Faculty members have contemporary experience with leading corporations, outstanding academic credentials, and a dedication to teaching. The graduate faculty includes 42 (7 women) full-time and 18 (7 women) part-time teachers. Seventy-five percent of the faculty hold the doctorate or its equivalent. Average class size is 24. Two full-time academic advisers are available to assist students.

The Business School Network

The Honolulu business community plays an integral role in the Hawaii Pacific University M.B.A. program. Many of Honolulu's leading corporations sponsor students for internships, many of which eventually result in offers of full-time employment. Senior executives of local investment firms, health-care systems, banks, schools, law firms, and trust companies serve on the University Board of Trustees, providing vision and direction for the future. Other HPU M.B.A. graduates serve on the Alumni Board, helping maintain a base of future employment contacts for new graduates as well as supporting the University. HPU also integrates the business community into the curriculum through the use of guest speakers with individual areas of expertise in appropriate academic disciplines, exposing students to current issues and emerging trends.

The College and Environs

Hawaii Pacific combines the excitement of an urban downtown campus with the serenity of a residential campus set in the foothills of the Koolau mountains. The main campus is located in downtown Honolulu, business and financial center of the Pacific. There are also eight satellite campuses located at Pearl Harbor, Barbers Point, Hickam Air Force Base, Schofield Barracks, Fort Shafter, Tripler Army Medical Center, Kaneohe Marine Corps Air Station, and Camp Smith.

Facilities

Meader Library and two additional on-campus libraries are available to students. Total holdings include 159,000 volumes, 200,000 microforms, and 1,740 current periodical subscriptions. There are thirty-five personal computers in all libraries. CD-ROM players are available for graduate student use. Access is provided to online bibliographic retrieval services.

Rooms and/or apartments are available to single students (180 units) at an average cost of $7000 per year, including board; on-campus housing is not available to married students. The typical monthly cost of living in off-campus housing not owned by the University is $600. For further graduate housing information, students should contact Student Housing at 808-233-3184.

Technology Environment

Computer networks run on DOS Novell, UNIX, and Macintosh. All students have free access to the Internet. Computer labs are available from 8 a.m. to 9 p.m. daily and from 8 a.m. to 5 p.m. weekends.

Placement

Hawaii Pacific University's Career Planning and Placement Center provides, free of charge, two sponsored job fairs per year, job search preparation, seminars, on-campus recruiters, employer visits, workshops, job placement, national computerized resume referral services, a career resource library, internships, and campus employment opportunities. International student advisers are available to provide current information regarding visas, passports, F-1 regulations, work permits, and other concerns critical to international students.

Admission

Admission requirements include a completed application, official transcripts from each postsecondary school attended (sent directly to HPU), a document showing conferral of the bachelor's degree, and two letters of reference. International students should submit certified copies of "A" level (or similar postsecondary) examinations directly to HPU. The Test of English as a Foreign Language (TOEFL) is recommended unless students have completed a bachelor's degree from an accredited American college or university with a grade point average of 2.7 or above.

Hawaii Pacific University seeks students with academic promise, outstanding career potential, and high motivation.

Finances

For the 1998–99 academic year, graduate tuition is $7920, living expenses are $7750, and other expenses (books and insurance) are $1430; the total cost is $17,100. Part-time cost is $330 per credit hour.

Aid is available to part-time students. The University participates in all federal financial aid programs designated for graduate students. These programs provide aid in the form of subsidized (need-based) and unsubsidized (non-need-based) Federal Stafford Student Loans. Through these loans, funds may be available to cover a student's entire cost of education. To apply for aid, students must submit the Free Application for Federal Student Aid (FAFSA) after January 1. Mailing of student award letters usually begins in April. For further financial aid information, students should contact Mr. Walter Fleming at 808-544-0253.

International Students

The International Student Office provides a variety of services to international students, including advising on personal, interpersonal, cultural, and academic matters; assisting on immigration matters, especially F-1 requirements, I-20 extensions, and work authorization; advising on money management and housing needs; conducting orientation programs to facilitate academic and social adjustment; and providing medical insurance information. An International Day is held each year to highlight the contributions of HPU's diverse student population. There are fourteen different country-specific organizations on campus.

Application Facts and Dates

Admission decisions for the M.B.A. program are made on a rolling basis, and applicants are notified between one and two weeks after all documents have been submitted. Completed applications should be sent to:

Graduate Admissions
1164 Bishop Street, Suite 1510
Honolulu, Hawaii 96813
Telephone: 808-544-0279
            800-669-4724 (toll-free)
Fax: 808-544-0280
E-mail: gradservctr@hpu.edu

Hofstra University

Frank G. Zarb School of Business

Hempstead, New York

THE NEW ZARB M.B.A.

The Zarb School of Business is engaged in a variety of exciting initiatives that directly complement the traditionally strong graduate program offered to students interested in the global dimensions of business and the innumerable advantages of studying within a campus-based program in proximity to New York City. Among the most exciting developments in some time are our new curriculum, implementation of the McGraw-Hill Technology Lab for the use of our students, and the construction of the University's new high-technology building, which will be dedicated primarily to business school use and will open in 1999.

—Ralph S. Polimeni, Ph.D., Dean

Programs and Curricular Focus

The newly revised M.B.A. program at the Zarb School reflects the actual environment in which contemporary managers must make decisions, often under conditions of uncertainty. Course work exposes students to innovative strategies, group interaction, and simulated business situations. The curriculum emphasizes a course-functional approach to teaching. It also provides an experiential learning component within which students engage in business consulting and corporate internships as a means of refining their managerial skills. Students gain hands-on experience with technology, acquire a perspective on international business practices, and study environmental and ethical factors as they pertain to business, government, and not-for-profit organizations.

The M.B.A. program is comprised of six tiers. The first is residency requirements, which establish facility with computer technology, information resources, and calculus. The second is the core competencies, which establish a basic functional understanding of business. The third is an advanced core, which provides students with a more sophisticated understanding of the functional areas of business and how they are applied across the organization. The fourth component is a cluster of courses called The Contemporary Business Environment, which is a fully interdisciplinary component of the program and includes coverage of communications skills, leadership, and an appreciation for and understanding of a truly diverse and global marketplace. The fifth component of the program enables students to focus

on one of seven areas of specialization, including accounting, business computer information systems, banking and finance, marketing, management, international business, or taxation. The sixth and final component is a project-based course, which may take the form of a consulting engagement, internship, research project, or management game.

A one-year, 42-credit program is available for students who hold a baccalaureate degree in business. The regular program is two years and 66 credits. Both part-time and full-time programs are available, as is a J.D./M.B.A., which is offered in conjunction with the Hofstra School of Law.

Students and the M.B.A. Experience

Most students entering the Zarb M.B.A. program have at least two years of full-time work experience. Ten states and twenty-eight other countries are represented among the student body. About 10 percent of the full-time students are members of minority groups, 38 percent are international, and 30 percent are women. Numerous organizations are open to M.B.A. students, including the M.B.A. Association, the Graduate Women in Business Organization, the Minority Student Organization, AISEC, and the Organization of International Students. One of the most popular student organizations is the Hofstra Business Consulting Group. Membership in the Group is by application and "hire"-only, and the organization is run similarly to external consulting practices. The Group provides

students with hands-on consulting experience and remuneration for their services.

Team projects and the application of technology to conducting business in a dynamically changing world are all critical to the Zarb M.B.A. program, as is the program of internships and study-abroad opportunities. The location of the University on Long Island and within a 40-minute commute from Manhattan provides extraordinary opportunities for employment, internships, and social and cultural activities.

❖ Global Focus

In revising the M.B.A. curriculum, the Zarb School renewed its long-standing commitment to the importance of exposing students to the business of doing business in an international marketplace. The curriculum content focuses heavily on globalization and emphasizes an international focus in virtually every course. These classroom experiences are complemented by the Zarb School's conference series on U.S.-International Trade, by the very diverse faculty, and by the School's Merrill Lynch Center for the Study of International Financial Services and Markets. Each of these provides students with unique opportunities to interact with senior business leaders as well as visiting academicians who are focused on trade and finance issues that affect the U.S. and its trading partners.

Special Features

A full complement of services is available for international students enrolled in the Zarb M.B.A. Program. For those requiring course work in the English language, a full program of instruction is available through the English Language Program.

The Faculty

More than 100 faculty members, representing a combination of academicians and business practitioners, teach in the M.B.A. program. It is significant to note that, while many business schools devote senior faculty energies primarily to research, the mission of the Zarb School faculty has always been to be, above all, excellent teachers. This philosophy results in a faculty that possesses both extensive business experience and excellent academic credentials, allowing for a balanced approach to theory and practice in the curriculum, as well as a balance of active scholarship, interaction with students, and involvement in the business community. A complete profile of the faculty is available from the Graduate Programs Office.

The Business School Network

Networking with the local, regional, and international business communities has traditionally been an important part of the Zarb School M.B.A. experience, and that tradition continues. Linkages with these communities are manifested through a variety of means, including the Dean's Executive Council, which is composed of business leaders; an active alumni network, which includes senior officers at a number of multinational corporations; and the Dean's Lecture Series on topics of timely importance to the business community and to students. In addition, Hofstra's Business Development Center, which houses the Merrill Lynch Center for the Study of International Financial Services and Markets, the Family Business Forum, the Long Island Venture Group, the Small Business Institute, and other entities, provides an additional platform for enhanced networking opportunities. A series of conferences that address United States trade issues in the context of other countries throughout the world offers M.B.A. students and alumni access to senior managers and faculty members from a host of organizations. Recent conferences organized to examine American trade relationships were cosponsored by Erasmus/The Rotterdam School of Management (the Netherlands) and SDA Bocconi (Italy).

Distinguished alumni of the School include its namesake, Frank G. Zarb, Chairman, Chief Executive Officer, and President of the National Association of Securities Dealers.

The College and Environs

Hofstra is located on a parklike 238-acre campus in a suburban, residential area of Long Island, New York. The campus has been designated as an arboretum by the American Association of Botanical Gardens and Arboreta. It is within a 40-minute train ride of Manhattan. In addition to the enormous opportunities for cultural, professional, and social activities offered by virtue of Hofstra's location

near New York City, the University hosts more than 500 cultural events of its own each year. Athletic facilities include the only indoor Olympic-size pool on Long Island, the fully equipped Physical Fitness and Recreation Centers, and a stadium that seats 15,000.

Facilities

The Axinn Library serves the Zarb School of Business through a fully computerized system featuring LEXICAT, an online listing that includes more than 500,000 records of books, periodicals, microfilms, and media. Other services offered are Business Periodicals on Disk, ABI/Inform, Newspaper Abstracts on Disk, and the Dow Jones News Retrieval Service. Extensive computer lab facilities that support a variety of software applications are available. Microsoft Windows is the operating platform utilized most extensively by the Zarb School. Every M.B.A. student is immediately assigned an e-mail account, which may be utilized for Internet access, upon enrollment. No additional charge is assessed for this service. The McGraw-Hill Technology Laboratory in the Axinn Library consolidates all of McGraw-Hill's proprietary software and databases into one facility available to students and faculty members for research and educational purposes.

The School subscribes to Standard & Poor's Compustat database, which contains company reports and market information for more than 8,000 companies as well as PDE Bank, Full Coverage, and Global Vantage Files. The Center for Research in Security Prices (CRSP) database, which includes daily and monthly price and volume information for more than 8,000 firms, is also available to M.B.A. students.

The main classroom building for the Zarb School is Breslin Hall, which contains rooms equipped for full computer demonstration and instruction. On-campus housing is readily available to M.B.A. students in the form of apartments and dormitories.

Placement

A full complement of career development services is available to M.B.A. students. These services include on- and off-campus recruiting, general job-search information (e.g., interviewing, resume preparation), a comprehensive interview and placement library, videotaping of interview simulations, computerized job banks, career planning seminars, and assistance with internships and part-time employment.

Admission

Admission is selective. Candidates are required to complete the graduate application and all supporting forms and to submit two letters of recommendation, a resume, a statement of professional objectives, official transcripts from every college or university attended, and scores obtained on the Graduate Management Admission Test (GMAT). International students are also required to submit scores obtained on the TOEFL.

For the most recently admitted class, the middle 80 percent range of GMAT scores was from 430 to 610; the average undergraduate grade point average was 3.2 on a 4.0 scale. All credentials submitted in support of the application for admission are carefully considered in making the admission decision.

Finances

Tuition is assessed on a per credit basis, and was $442 for each credit in 1997–98, with courses carrying 3 credits each. Hofstra is a private institution, so tuition is the same for residents and nonresidents of New York State. Room, board, books, and supplies bring the annual cost of an M.B.A. education to approximately $24,000. Financial aid is available in the form of fellowships that provide partial tuition credit and graduate assistantship positions. There is no aid available for international students.

Application Facts and Dates

Hofstra subscribes to a rolling admissions policy, with suggested filing deadlines of May 1 for fall admission and November 1 for spring admission. Students planning to apply for financial aid should file both admission and financial aid forms no later than March 1 for fall and October 1 for spring. Candidates are generally advised of admission decisions no later than six weeks after the application is completed. Students may obtain additional information and application materials from:

Office of Admissions
100 Hofstra University
Hempstead, New York 11549
Telephone: 516-463-6700
Fax: 516-560-7660
E-mail: hofstra@hofstra.edu

Office of Graduate Programs
Frank G. Zarb School of Business
134 Hofstra University
Hempstead, New York 11549
Telephone: 516-463-5683
Fax: 516-463-5268
E-mail: humba@hofstra.edu

Huron University USA in London

M.B.A. Program

London, England

FOSTERING THE SKILLS ESSENTIAL FOR LEADERSHIP

It is a special pleasure to introduce the Huron-London M.B.A. because it is a very special program, as you will discover. Ours is first and foremost a classic American M.B.A. The courses are designed to expose participants to all the major functional areas of responsibility in business and other types of organizations and to develop an appreciation of the environment in which modern business is conducted.

Our focus is on fostering the skills essential for those who aspire to senior executive positions. Thus, we emphasize developing leadership potential by encouraging analytical thinking, problem solving, and the exercise of sound judgment. The case study approach remains important for achievement of these objectives, and we also work through simulation and role-playing exercises.

We are here to serve your needs and to ensure that you leave us enriched not only by the programs but also by the enduring friendships that are the hallmark of our international community. I look forward to welcoming you personally to the world of opportunities that Huron University USA in London can help create.

—Ray Hilditch, Provost

Programs and Curricular Focus

The Huron-London M.B.A. is designed to give students a solid, comprehensive foundation in business. The core consists of eighteen courses (up to six courses can be waived depending on the student's prior business education), which explore the key areas of business. A student can deepen this broad-based M.B.A. education by adding a concentration in entrepreneurship, international finance, marketing, or management information systems. Each concentration requires three additional courses. To make the concentrations practical and "hands-on," an internship, networking project, consultancy, field study project, or directed study project is part of every concentration.

Huron University USA in London offers a special opportunity to recent graduates with less than two years of appropriate work experience. The Recent Graduate Program enables those students to take an immediate step toward a high-level management career, whatever degree they currently hold.

Students and the M.B.A. Experience

At Huron University USA in London, students experience the international community of the future, sharing their lectures, seminars, and social life with students from more than fifty nations. Students find a genuine feeling of internationalism that inspires them, the faculty, and the curriculum.

The Huron-London M.B.A. prepares each student to be an effective manager of people through a program of practical, hands-on training. In small, interactive groups, students develop managerial techniques and their own personal and team skills in realistic business situations. By the end of the program, students have evolved a highly effective management style that allows them to react positively and constructively to new situations. The Huron-London MBA helps develop the skills and knowledge appropriate to senior management, including understanding the global business environment; enhancing practical knowledge of core business functional areas of responsibility; refining techniques of analysis, problem solving, and decision making; managing change; cooperating with and learning from peers; improving written and verbal communication skills; and enhancing awareness of students' strengths and weaknesses.

The Huron-London M.B.A. is for participants moving rapidly into senior management positions, and the traditional structure of the program reflects this. It prepares students to take a leading role overseeing all business functions without specializing in one particular area. The emphasis is on a generalist perspective, which is appropriate for those aspiring to senior roles. In addition, there is an opportunity to build on this generalist emphasis by taking additional courses that can lead to a functional specialisation.

❖ Global Focus

The business world of the twenty-first century will be both fast-changing and truly international. In this highly competitive environment, successful business leaders will require an M.B.A. that gives them the skill and knowledge to turn the new threats of the global market into valuable opportunities for their organizations. With many years of experience in education for business and links with campuses in some of the leading business centers of the world, Huron University USA in London is well placed to offer an M.B.A. of this calibre.

The M.B.A. is recognised across the world as the gold standard of graduate management education. Already established for many years in the United States, an M.B.A. is increasingly becoming the passport to high-level management in the United Kingdom and in other countries. Huron University USA in London knows that tomorrow's business community will be a global one, and its M.B.A. program will equip students to operate successfully in that new world order. Tomorrow's leaders from around the world come together at Huron in a unique educational environment that is not only stimulating and supportive but also professional and friendly.

The Faculty

Huron University USA in London offers students the opportunity to interact with experienced academic personnel with first-hand insight in the professional world. These professionals provide personalised academic and career guidance.

The Business School Network

Students undertake an international M.B.A. degree for many different reasons. They may wish to start their own business or join a multinational corporation. They may be seeking more rapid advancement in their career or may see the M.B.A. as a transitional device to open up new and different opportunities. One concept is common to these varied personal aspirations—professional development. The Ambassador Program is unique to Huron-London in that it provides students with a variety of ways in which they can begin to fulfill their ambitions while they are still in the last semester of the program. Careful scheduling ensures that students can devote at least two full days a week to the Ambassador Program. Committed students may concentrate exclusively on this experiential learning process for a full semester.

In the penultimate semester of the M.B.A. program, students meet with their academic adviser to discuss the way they wish to use the Ambassador Program. Faculty and staff members are responsive to individual ambitions and aspirations. There is no administrative limit to the possible types of projects and assignments that might be accommodated under the Ambassador Program. The limitations lie purely in the student's ability to conceptualise an idea and put it into practice with the help of the professional staff. Above all, it should be an exercise geared to the student's own plans beyond graduation—a platform for the inevitable transition back into the world of work.

The College and Environs

Huron University USA in London has its premises in leafy South Kensington, a few minutes' walk from the tube station and near the museum area. The former embassy building is directly opposite Imperial College, a constituent college of London University. Huron-London students have full access to Imperial College's catering, sports, and recreational facilities, including bars, restaurants, an indoor swimming pool, and a gymnasium complex.

The Huron-London building complements the University's growing reputation as a small, caring liberal arts institution that pays close attention to the needs of students and their families. The premises provide appropriate facilities for the exciting and challenging range of programs and courses. Dedicated classroom space and an elegant boardroom are available. The library houses more than 3,000 volumes and subscribes to more than sixty general and specialised journals. A networked CD-ROM facility enables access to a wide range of reference and bibliographical materials. Huron-London students have full research access to the Imperial College Library.

All items indexed on CD-ROM may be borrowed by arrangement with the University librarian, who can also arrange access to other important business reference collections in London, such as the City Business Library.

Technology Environment

The University building has been extensively modernised to provide excellent academic facilities. As part of this modernisation, a backbone local area network (LAN) that connects all academic computing facilities in the University onto a single network was installed. Student workstations are located in two general-purpose computer laboratories. The majority of student workstations are Pentium processor-based machines, and all have an industry-

standard office suite installed. Each mini-LAN also has local printing facilities and appropriate special-purpose software. The library's networked CD-ROM stacker is accessible from any academic workstation. Scanning facilities are also available. In addition, the College also offers Internet and World Wide Web access, also accessible from any student workstation. As part of the general computing services, the College also provides each student with a password-protected e-mail account and personal space on the main academic system's file server. A secure dial-in service that allows students access to Huron's computing resources from off-site locations is being installed.

Placement

Huron University USA in London has an extensive network of work placement opportunities that students can utilise in London. Occasionally, internships can be undertaken in other geographical locations, provided that suitable supervisory arrangements can be made. In addition to the University's contacts, students may refer contacts of their own to the Internship Director for possible use in the program.

Work placements are almost always project-based. They require at least 150 hours of supervised work experience and culminate in reports filed with the Internship Director by the student and workplace supervisor. The *Internship Handbook* contains details. United Kingdom employment law does not permit non-EU citizens to receive payment for internship placements. However, successful placements enhance resumes and can lead to permanent work.

Students with established plans beyond graduation may wish to develop a project that would allow them to utilise Huron-London business contacts to network with possible clients and employers in preparation for work beyond the M.B.A. This generally takes the form of a series of prearranged meetings and interviews with senior managers in such diverse fields as banking and finance, international trade, marketing, information systems, or other areas of specialisation of specific interest to the individual. During the project, the student undertakes field research using the external contacts as a resource. The research is typically based around a questionnaire. Beyond the intrinsic value of the research, the contacts made in the process often prove to be invaluable for future professional advancement. These projects are individually tailored to the needs of students.

The flexibility of the Ambassador Program allows Huron-London to respond to other specific projects that students wish to develop. Experienced students may wish to undertake a consultancy project. Overseas students may wish to undertake field re-

search in another country. Those who aspire to start their own business may wish to develop a business plan. Students may also undertake a project that is more desk research (library) based.

This can be accommodated under the umbrella of the Ambassador Program after consultation with the M.B.A. Director, his staff, and the student's adviser. Huron-London has an impressive Business Mentor Group—businesspeople sympathetic to the needs of young aspiring professionals—to help with advice and information. It is an important function of the University to put final-semester students in touch with these practitioners. This is also achieved through regular networking evenings that attract senior people from business, the community, and embassies who visit the campus and provide support and opportunities.

Suitably qualified students may register for the Ambassador Program as a full-time, stand-alone project separate from the M.B.A. program. It may also be used as part of a portfolio of qualifications for nontraditional students to gain entry into the M.B.A. (subject to fulfillment of other criteria). Details are available from the Admissions Office.

Admission

The standard requirement for admission is a first degree. The GMAT test is a graduation requirement. Students may take the test before they start the program or during their first semester. If possible, students should meet with or contact the M.B.A. Director for advice on their studies. A TOEFL score of at least 550 is required of all applicants for whom English is not their native language. Applicants are evaluated on their individual qualities, academic background, and professional experience.

Finances

The 1998–99 educational budget is $22,000. This includes tuition fees, room and board, books, and miscellaneous fees.

Application Facts and Dates

Huron University USA in London operates a rolling admission policy, with semesters starting in September, January, and May. To receive further information on the program and admission procedures, students should contact:

Marco Gorin, M.B.A.
Director of Admissions
Huron University USA in London
58 Princes Gate
London SW7 2PG
England
Telephone: 44-171-584 9696
Fax: 44-171-589 9406
E-mail: admissions@huron.ac.uk
World Wide Web: http://www.huron.ac.uk

Illinois Institute of Technology

Chicago, Illinois

> ### PREPARATION FOR A SUCCESSFUL CAREER
>
> *A Stuart education is designed to prepare students for a successful and satisfying career. The curriculum provides depth in specific areas of interest within a holistic, comprehensive business and management perspective, along with the technological and quantitative literacy needed in today's business world. Stuart faculty members can offer the benefits of experiences in and with the business world, as well as the results of scholarly endeavors. Fellow students—working professionals, recent college graduates, and international students—also enhance the educational experience with fresh ideas, practical experience, and global perspectives.*
>
> *—M. Zia Hassan, Dean*

Programs and Curricular Focus

Today's global economy, the segmentation of national markets, changing technologies, and opportunities created by new entrepreneurial structures require an M.B.A. education that is global, comprehensive, and technologically oriented. At the same time, the much-publicized elimination of middle management is a clear sign that businesses today require managers who have depth in one specialized area or who have a flexible range of skills in many areas.

The Stuart M.B.A. degree program provides a thorough grounding in the functional areas of business, an understanding of the business applications of technology and analytic methods, and eleven specialized areas of study, within a holistic, global-management perspective.

The curriculum is made up of twenty courses. Eight core courses cover the body of knowledge common to the M.B.A. degree: finance, financial and managerial accounting, international business, marketing, managerial economics, operations management, organizational behavior, and statistical methods. Students also take eleven electives and may choose to specialize in one or two of eleven areas: finance, financial risk management, information management, international business, management science, marketing, operations management, organization and management, quality management, strategic management, and telecommunications management. All students complete their degree by taking Business Policy, a capstone course that integrates the development and implementation of strategy.

Small, interactive classes stimulate students to develop creative solutions, often using case studies. All classes are conducted in English. Classes, which are held in the evening, follow a schedule of four 11-week quarters a year. Students take from fourteen to twenty courses, depending on their academic background. Some full-time students can complete the program in one year.

The Stuart School also offers an M.S. in Financial Markets and Trading (M.S.F.M.T.); an M.S. in operations and technology management, environmental management, or marketing communication; and a Ph.D. in operations management or in financial management. Several joint degrees are available: M.B.A./M.S.F.M.T., M.B.A./M.E.M., M.B.A./M.P.A., and, with sister institution Chicago-Kent Law School, J.D./M.B.A. and J.D./M.S.F.M.T.

Students and the M.B.A. Experience

The M.B.A. student body of approximately 400 individuals comprises eighteen nationalities, with 17 percent international students; people with a wide range of academic, cultural, national, and business backgrounds; ages ranging from students who have just received their bachelor's degrees to professionals who have spent years in the work force; 20 percent full-time students; and students who hold managerial positions in Chicago corporations and elsewhere. Degree backgrounds include economics, science or technology, and law, with the remainder a mix of other disciplines.

The mix of students and professionals from a wide range of academic, cultural, national, and business backgrounds enriches class interaction. At Stuart, students learn from classmates as well as from professors. Typically, students pool their strengths and work in teams to solve problems. Most students and professors possess hands-on experience that they share in class discussion. Classmates include students who hold managerial positions in Chicago corporations and students from other countries. This diversity enables the creation of professional networks to prepare for teamwork in the global economy.

The Faculty

Stuart's faculty includes scholars in the areas of technology management, marketing, information technology, telecommunications standards, organizational design and behavior, quality management, computer modeling, computer-integrated manufacturing, flexible manufacturing systems, demand forecasting, economic forecasting and risk management, and derivatives and foreign exchange. Because its members serve as consultants with corporations, government agencies, and research firms throughout the world, the faculty brings a practical point of view to management issues.

More than one quarter of the faculty hold undergraduate or graduate degrees from academic institutions outside the United States, giving the Stuart faculty a distinctly international character.

The Business School Network

The Stuart School Overseers/Student Support Program links students with senior-level executives from a range of industries. These executives hold positions at such companies as Abbott Laboratories; AT&T; Celtic Life Insurance Company; Eastman Kodak Company; First Chicago Corporation; Kamco Plastics, Inc.; Kelco Industries, Inc.; Motorola, Inc.; and Smith Barney and serve as mentors and career advisers. Students also network with fellow students, many of whom are working professionals, and with Stuart alumni and thousands of other IIT alumni with contacts in many areas of business, industry, and government.

The College and Environs
Founded in 1890, the Illinois Institute of Technology (IIT), a private university with an enrollment of 7,000, is internationally recognized for advanced work in engineering, business, law, architecture, design, and science. IIT offers fourteen bachelor's, thirty-eight master's, fourteen doctoral, and three law degrees. The Stuart School's main campus is located near the financial district in downtown Chicago. Suburban locations are in Wheaton, 45 minutes west of the Chicago loop, and at Motorola's Galvin Center in Schaumburg, 45 minutes northwest. In 1995, Chicago was home to more Forbes 500 companies than any other city in the U.S., except for New York City. Among the companies headquartered in the Chicago area are McDonald's, Ameritech, Motorola, Archer Daniels Midland, Amoco, United Airlines, Sears, and Baxter International. The city offers many business opportunities for Stuart M.B.A. students, from internships and part-time employment to full-time careers. The city also offers a wealth of recreational and cultural opportunities, ranging from professional sports teams to avant-garde theater, along with beaches and parks. The area's cosmopolitan population offers an interesting and varied choice of cuisines and activities.

Facilities
The Stuart Business Library is located in the Information Center on floors six through ten of the Downtown Campus. The Information Center is an open-stack collection of more than 525,000 volumes, including the business holdings of the Stuart Business Library, the Chicago-Kent Law Library, and the Library of International Relations, which contains international materials in history, economics, political science, and law. The Center houses important collections of the European Union, the United Nations, the International Monetary Fund, International Labor Organization, and the World Health Organization.

The Information Center has a seating capacity of more than six hundred and contains several computer classrooms, duplicating rooms, microfilm facilities, and small-group study rooms. Seating throughout the center provides access to all of the networked computer facilities, including online research systems both local and remote, such as LEXIS-NEXIS, Illinet Online, and Business Periodicals Global, and a number of CD-ROM databases. The tenth-floor reading room is a modern reproduction of a traditional nineteenth-century reading room, with a 33-foot vaulted ceiling and a stunning view of the Chicago skyline.

Stuart students also have access to IIT's full library system, including the Paul V. Galvin Library on the Main Campus with its collections in engineering, science, social sciences, humanities and arts, and the Biegler Library at IIT's Rice Campus. In addition, using the Illinet Online library catalog, students can search for and obtain access to books in hundreds of other Illinois libraries.

Technology Environment
The Downtown Campus Computer Lab provides access to a wide range of business tools and resources through a Windows interface. Computers in the lab are linked by a campuswide computer network to the library and other campus computer labs. Software includes several of the major spreadsheet and word processing programs and database and presentation managers used in business today. Ten CD-ROM databases include Standard & Poor's Corporations, Thomas Register, Knight-Ridder, US Business Reporter, Investexts, and F&S Index. Students can explore the Internet on any of the lab's computers using a number of popular browsers, including Netscape.

The Quantitative Research Lab (QRL) provides an interactive computer-based learning environment featuring simulated trading, investment analysis, and industry databases. This network receives real-time data on cash and futures prices from around the world. The computer programs that are used are also used in the financial industry and the simulated trading environment allows students to trade with other students at Stuart or at other universities. Historical data is also available through two CD-ROM databases.

Placement
Chicago is a dynamic international center of finance, business, and industry whose economic world includes Fortune 500 companies, many midwestern United States major industries, thriving entrepreneurial ventures, and the world's largest futures and options exchanges. The Stuart Career Planning Center, with strong ties to the business community, offers counseling about career planning, goals, and job search strategies, as well as services in developing students' interviewing and resume-writing skills. Companies that have recruited Stuart School students include AT&T; Arthur Andersen; Cargill; Chicago Board of Trade; Citicorp; Commonwealth Edison; Ernst & Young; First Chicago; Fuji Securities, Inc.; Morgan Stanley & Company; Reuters; Shell Oil; and Walgreens.

Admission
Admission to the Stuart M.B.A. program requires submission of a completed application form, two letters of recommendation, official transcripts, GMAT scores, and a summary of work experience. International applicants must also have a TOEFL score of 600 (for scores between 550 and 599, IIT's English Proficiency Review is also required) and a financial affidavit in the amount of $29,140 for the academic year 1998–99.

Finances
Tuition for 1998–99 is $1620 per course. Full-time students must register for at least three courses a quarter. International students attending on a J-1 visa must enroll for $50,000 health insurance coverage; the fee for the basic policy is $57.25 per quarter. Students should anticipate an expense of approximately $100 for books and supplies for each course taken. Room and board on the Main Campus, 3 miles south of the Downtown Center, ranges from $4720 to $8900 for the academic year. An hourly shuttle bus connects the two campuses. Discounted apartment rentals are available, within a block of the downtown campus, to Stuart School students.

International Students
The Stuart School student body has a diverse makeup of cultures and nationalities, including 15 percent who are international students. The International Cultural Center at IIT offers a variety of services relating to personal, visa, and immigration concerns; advises students about career planning and internship options; and holds social, cultural, and educational events. IIT also offers counseling and health services, cultural and religious programs, disability resources, and multicultural services.

Application Facts and Dates
Applications are due two months before classes start. Admission decisions typically are sent within three weeks of receipt of all credentials. For more information, students should contact:

Lynn Miller, Ph.D., Assistant Dean of Admission and M.B.A. Program
Stuart School of Business
Illinois Institute of Technology
565 West Adams Street
Chicago, Illinois 60661-3691
Telephone: 312-906-6544
Fax: 312-906-6549
E-mail: lmiller@stuart.iit.edu
World Wide Web: http://www.stuart.iit.edu

Illinois State University

Normal, Illinois

THE ILLINOIS STATE M.B.A. PROGRAM—ADDING VALUE TO A DIVERSE STUDENT BODY

We at Illinois State know our M.B.A. students are investing their most valuable resources—time, energy, and dollars—to earn their advanced degrees. With that in mind, we are committed to adding value to the career of every student pursuing the M.B.A. The Illinois State University College of Business has as its mission providing student-centered lifelong learning and ensuring students the ability to reach their full potential. Our faculty members are accessible and dedicated to making every course an excellent learning experience for M.B.A. students. We have added value by updating the curriculum, and our courses combine serious scholarship with practical approaches. Indeed, in a survey of our graduates, the faculty earned highest praise. Personalized advising also adds value by helping M.B.A. candidates choose the right courses to fulfill their personal and professional goals.

—Dixie Mills, Dean

Programs and Curricular Focus

Illinois State accepts both full- and part-time students. Full-time students typically take three or four classes, and part-time students two, per academic semester. All classes are offered in the evening; thus, full- and part-time students benefit from one another's experiences during class discussions and group activities.

The program curriculum has three interrelated parts: foundation, core, and elective courses. Graduate-level foundation courses are designed for the student with no previous business university course work in order to prepare the student for graduate-level core courses. Students who have earned an undergraduate business degree typically take few, if any, of the seven foundation courses.

The core and elective course requirements for the program consist of 36 semester hours of study (twelve courses). The nine core courses are designed to build analytical, decision-making, and communication skills across the functional areas of business, culminating with an integrative capstone course on organizational strategy and planning.

Students may choose to concentrate or diversify the three elective courses in the areas of accounting, finance, marketing, international business, human resources, law, insurance, agribusiness, business communication, applied computer science, and industrial technology.

Full-time students are encouraged to complete an internship experience as one elective.

The College also offers a graduate program leading to the Master of Science in Accountancy.

Students and the M.B.A. Experience

Illinois State M.B.A. alumni give the program a 95 percent satisfaction rating. A supportive environment encourages students to reach their potential during and beyond their program. The College is committed to providing the best student-centered education in business, serving the needs of business and society by giving students the time and support needed as they progress toward their degrees and by preparing students for lifelong learning. Concern for students is illustrated by small class sizes (averaging fewer than 25 students), the abundance of elective courses, faculty members who are accessible to students and who challenge them to broaden their business perspectives, and active alumni and student organizations designed to enhance networking and professional skills.

A diverse student body adds to the quality of the M.B.A. experience. More than 200 part-time and full-time students, whose professional and academic backgrounds vary widely, take classes together. Small classes and M.B.A. Association activities allow students to learn from each other as they exchange perspectives reflecting different cultures, professions, and industries.

The M.B.A. Association also allows students to develop leadership and organizational skills through serving as officers or M.B.A. ambassadors. The association sponsors professional, philanthropic, and social activities.

The Faculty

The graduate faculty members hold degrees from major universities throughout the nation. The faculty members combine a strong student-centered orientation with their personal involvement in managerial relevant research. These faculty dimensions foster a stimulating learning environment within which to study contemporary business topics. During exit interviews, graduating M.B.A. students consistently list student-professor relationships, accessibility of professors, and high quality of the courses offered as areas of particular strength for the Illinois State M.B.A. program.

The Business School Network
Corporate Partnerships

Grants from major corporate partners such as State Farm Insurance, Caterpillar, and MassMutual Insurance have enabled the College to complete major updates in the computer lab and in classroom technology. The M.B.A. program has been offered on a contractual basis to employees of Illinova, a major Illinois utility company, and is currently offered on-site to employees of Archer Daniels Midland Company, Bridgestone-Firestone, and Caterpillar, Inc. The College also developed and teaches a two-week overseas study program for the Lloyd's of London APEX Programme. In addition, the College is home to the Katie Insurance School. With funding in excess of $3 million from insurance companies, the Katie Insurance School is devoted to providing the finest undergraduate and graduate insurance programs in the country and sponsors a number of continuing education and professional development programs.

Prominent Alumni

The Illinois State University M.B.A. program counts among its alumni a number of notable business leaders, including Ann Baughan, Assistant Vice President, State Farm Insurance; Robert English, President, English & Associates; John Franklin, Owner, Innotech Communications; Karl Heien, Vice President, Smith Barney Inc.; Phil Maughan, Vice President, The Northern Trust Company; Duane Miller, CEO, Country Companies; Warren Schmidgall, Executive Vice President, Hill's Pet Nutrition Inc.; James C. Tyree, Chairman and CEO, Mesirow Financial Group; and James Van Houten, President/CEO, MSI Insurance.

The College and Environs

Founded in 1857 as the first public institution of higher education in the state, Illinois State has developed into a major university. It prides itself on providing personalized instruction of high quality, developing student potential through superior teaching.

Bloomington-Normal was recognized by *Money* magazine as one of the nation's most livable communities. Five major highways intersect in the Twin Cities, which are in McLean County midway between St. Louis and Chicago. An Amtrak train station is just two blocks from the Illinois State campus, and major airlines serve the local airport.

The community is one of the state's fastest growing, with a population of 95,000. Firms with national headquarters in central Illinois include State Farm Insurance Companies, Caterpillar Inc., Mitsubishi Motor Manufacturing, The Eureka Company, and Country Companies. Other major employers in the twin cities include BroMenn Healthcare, St. Joseph Medical Center, Bridgestone/Firestone OTR, and General Electric.

Facilities

Milner Library contains more than 1.8 million items, including in excess of 5,700 journals and 85,000 titles in business and economics. Business publications are located on a single floor in the library. Students can access the library system remotely for online searching of fifty-two databases in business and economics, full-text databases covering more than 300 journals, the *Business Periodicals Index,* and other indexes on CD-ROM. The Library Computer System online catalog provides access to the collections of forty other university and college libraries in Illinois.

Technology Environment

The College of Business maintains computer labs with hundreds of personal computers (486 or Pentium processors), featuring the current software programs students are likely to encounter in the business world. Other labs are available 24 hours a day. The computer center offers numerous seminars, open to graduate students, on software packages and current computing topics.

Placement

The University's Counseling and Career Services Center assists students with career decisions, resumes, and finding positions after graduation. In addition, the M.B.A. office sponsors seminars on using networking to improve job opportunities. M.B.A. Alumni Network members assist students in a variety of ways, including mentoring. Ninety-four percent of Illinois State M.B.A.'s are employed when they complete their degrees, with a majority earning more than $35,000 in those jobs at graduation. Sixty-one percent of graduates now earn $30,000–$60,000; 8 percent earn more than $100,000.

Admission

Admission is limited to holders of baccalaureate degrees who demonstrate high promise of success in graduate business study. All undergraduate majors are acceptable. Criteria considered in the evaluation of applicants are Graduate Management Admission Test (GMAT) score, GPA earned during the last 60 credit hours of undergraduate work, letters of recommendation, and personal essays.

Applicants need to submit an M.B.A. application, essays, a resume, and two letters of recommendation to the M.B.A. office. In addition, official GMAT scores, Test of English as a Foreign Language (TOEFL) scores (if applicable), the graduate school application, and official transcripts must be submitted to the graduate school.

Recently admitted students have an average GPA of 3.37 and GMAT score of 550 (target minimum 450). The minimum TOEFL score (required of students whose native language is not English) is 600 (average 620).

Finances

In-state tuition and fees for 1998–99 are $1335 per semester for students taking three courses. Out-of-state tuition is approximately 2½ times the in-state tuition.

Graduate assistantships, tuition waivers, scholarships, student loans, and veterans assistance programs are available. Applications are reviewed in late April for fall graduate assistantship appointments, tuition waivers, and other financial aid and in October for spring semester.

International Students

Twelve percent of current M.B.A.'s are international students, hailing from Africa, Asia, Canada, Europe, Mexico, and South America. The University provides a week-long orientation for international students, an International House dormitory, and married student housing. The Intensive English Language Institute offers programming for family members who are building their language skills.

Application Facts and Dates

Students may begin their programs during any of the three semesters. Full consideration for financial aid and for advance class registration will be given to those submitting completed applications by March 15 for fall admission, October 15 for spring admission, and April 1 for summer admission.

For further information, students should contact:

The M.B.A. Program
College of Business
Campus Box 5500
Illinois State University
Normal, Illinois 61790-5500
Telephone: 309-438-8388
Fax: 309-438-5510
E-mail: isumba@ilstu.edu
World Wide Web: http://gilbreth.cob.ilstu.edu/mba

Indiana University Bloomington

EDUCATING FOR THE TWENTY-FIRST CENTURY

▶ *Indiana's faculty members are committed to teaching and research—a combination that demands intellect, energy, and a willingness to put some of the best hours of their lives into the classroom. We have created an academic environment in which change occurs as a matter of course—in the curriculum, in ways of teaching and learning, in just about everything. No one should have the slightest doubt that our graduates are technically competent. Years ago, we would have taken that as high praise. Now it is merely an expectation. So we ask ourselves what it is that distinguishes the truly exceptional student. I'd say it is leadership, teamwork, persuasion, communications, and critical thinking. The Indiana graduate with those skills and abilitites is the M.B.A. of the twenty-first century.*

—Dan Dalton, Dean

Programs and Curricular Focus

The first year of the M.B.A. curriculum is designed to provide students with basic business principles and management tools. Students complete foundation courses and functional core sequences that include integrative teaching methods, group work, and consideration of the global economy. Critical issues of cultural diversity, ethics, and communication are integrated across the curriculum. The second year of the program is flexible. Students usually choose at least one major, but double majors and minors are available, as well as a range of electives and a self-design major option. Entrepreneurship, finance, general management, human resource management, information systems, international business, marketing, and production and operations are the primary majors offered.

In the second year, students also take part in the 'policy core', an integrated curriculum that includes business and government, international issues, law, macroeconomics, and strategy.

Students and the M.B.A. Experience

Each year, Indiana enrolls an entering class of approximately 275 students. International students make up 20 percent, women 28 percent, and minority students 15 percent of the student population. The average age for students is 28 years, with an age range of approximately 21 to 40. The average number of years of work experience is four, and students come from a broad range of professional backgrounds. Twenty-nine percent of students are married. Thirty-six percent of the students are from the Midwest, 17 percent from the West and Southwest, 18 percent from the Northeast and Mid-Atlantic, and 9 percent from the South. The program puts heavy emphasis on teamwork, community involvement, and an integrated understanding of business functions and issues.

❖ Global Focus

The Indiana M.B.A. program features several study abroad options, foreign language tutoring and instruction, and integrated exposure to international issues. Students may earn a Certificate of Global Achievement through a combination of course work, cultural exposure, and language accomplishments.

The Faculty

M.B.A. faculty members are some of the most accomplished in the School of Business. Those who volunteer to be part of the core faculty have intensive contact with M.B.A. students in class and outside the classroom, serving as mentors to student teams and participating in orientation activities. Core faculty members work together to prepare an integrated curriculum that eliminates redundancy and emphasizes areas of connection among specific disciplines.

The Business School Network

Corporate Partnerships

Students have access to corporate leaders beginning during orientation, where they meet professionals in a roundtable format to learn about different functions and industries. Case competitions sponsored by corporations such as Deloitte & Touche and Kraft are a regular feature. Student clubs such as the Finance Guild and Marketing Club regularly sponsor seminars and host speakers from the corporate community.

The College and Environs

Indiana University at Bloomington has 35,000 students on an 18,000-acre campus located in a midwestern "college town" of about 63,000. The town is set among the rolling hills of southern Indiana, and the campus has been rated among the five most beautiful in the U.S. The University boasts one of the finest music schools in the world. Bloomington and the University have efficient, economical public transportation available, and the city and campus are very safe for students and families.

Facilities

On-campus student housing is available for both single and married students. Indiana University maintains an extensive computer network that provides access to mainframe computers, databases, and the Internet. M.B.A. students routinely use the electronic mail system, the Internet, the Dow Jones News/Retrieval Service, and other electronic resources. The School of Business library has more than 150,000 volumes of research materials. The main library, across the street from the School of Business, is internationally recognized as one of the best university libraries.

Technology Environment

All students are required to own personal computers and use them to complete their academic work. Computer clusters in the School of Business and around campus provide access to software, electronic services, and printers. Faculty members regularly use computer technology in the classroom.

Placement

The School's nationally recognized Business Placement Office has comprehensive resources and programs to help students secure internships and full-time employment. More than 230 companies visit the campus each year to recruit M.B.A. students for positions around the country. The Placement Office also produces resume books and provides students access to an alumni database.

Admission

Indiana University admits M.B.A. students for the fall semester only. A minimum TOEFL score of 580 is required for non-native English speakers. The average GMAT score is approximately 630. The Indiana M.B.A. Program seeks applicants who are motivated, interested in working in diverse groups, and have a strong professional focus.

Finances

Tuition and fees for the 1998–99 academic year are $8775 for in-state students and $17,013 for out-of-state students. Room and board are approximately $6014, books and supplies $1350, personal expenses $3900, and the computer allowance is $3000, for a total budget of $31,269 for out-of-state students. Approximately 35 percent of Indiana's M.B.A. students receive financial aid from the School of Business. Graduate assistantships are available; these provide a partial fee remission and stipend in return for a minimal work obligation with faculty members or within administrative departments in the School of Business. In addition, more than $200,000 in scholarship funds is awarded each year to M.B.A. students. The business school awards are based on merit, not need. The IU Office of Student Financial Assistance administers federal financial aid based on student need. (The cost of a personal computer is calculated into the student's financial aid budget.) Indiana University participates in the Consortium for Graduate Study in Management, which offers substantial support for candidates from minority groups.

International Students

Twenty percent of Indiana's M.B.A. students are non-U.S. citizens. An active International Business Society within the M.B.A. program provides important professional and personal support. The University has a large graduate student and international student population as well. International students enjoy the supportive atmosphere of the M.B.A. program, and the high level of student services helps them acclimate to their new environment.

Application Facts and Dates

The Indiana University M.B.A. program offers several application deadlines. Applicants who meet the early deadlines are considered first. Application deadlines for domestic students and permanent residents are December 1, January 15, and March 1. Application deadlines for international students are December 1 and February 1. Decisions on complete applications can be expected approximately eight weeks from each deadline. Applicants are encouraged to meet the early deadlines. For application materials and information, students should contact:

Kelley Graduate School of Business
M.B.A. Program
1309 East Tenth Street, Room 254
Indiana University
Bloomington, Indiana 47405-1701
Telephone: 812-855-8006
           800-994-8622 (toll-free
           within the U.S.)
Fax: 812-855-9039
E-mail: mbaoffice@indiana.edu
World Wide Web: http://www.bus.
    indiana.edu/MBA

INSEAD (The European Institute of Business Administration)

Business Programs

Fontainebleau, France

► **LEARNING FOR LEADERSHIP**

With so many good M.B.A. programmes to choose from, why take ten months in France for an M.B.A. from INSEAD? INSEAD is the largest and best-known of the truly international business schools—the schools with no dominant culture. There are 600 of the best and brightest M.B.A.'s at INSEAD from fifty different countries. With the workweek regularly reaching 70 hours, INSEAD is not for the faint-hearted. A participant described her experience here as "drinking from a fire hydrant." INSEAD also can be fun, judging from the intense social life that accompanies the intense academics. Finally, students have the full educational benefit, recognition, and career potential of a prestigious M.B.A. in less than a year. We look forward to welcoming students to campus who want an international management education, thrive on hard work and intense pressure, and seek intellectual stimulation.

—H. Landis Gabel, Associate Dean

Programs and Curricular Focus

INSEAD's M.B.A. programme ensures a solid general management education, while allowing participants to tailor the programme to individual requirements. To achieve this goal, the programme begins with a series of core courses that cover the fundamentals of business. These ensure that participants obtain a common level of knowledge in the fundamentals of business, irrespective of their backgrounds. The second phase of the programme introduces participants to broader management issues and to the wider economic and political environment that influences both corporate strategies and national industrial policies. The programme's final phase allows participants to select courses to match their career needs and interests. Electives allow participants to focus on a field of particular interest or to further investigate general management issues.

INSEAD's pedagogical approach is pragmatic. It seeks to prepare participants by simulating business reality in a low-risk environment. This means that the M.B.A. programme is based on problem solving in small groups, active participation in class, and individual preparation and research.

There are two 10½-month programmes each year. One programme starts in late August and ends in early July; the other runs from January to December, with a six-week summer recess. Although always evolving, the two programmes are virtually identical in structure and content. Both programmes are organised into five periods of eight weeks, each period ending with exams followed by a short break. Each period consists of a minimum number of courses for which a participant must register. In order to qualify for the INSEAD M.B.A. degree, participants must obtain credits in at least twenty-two courses. Courses are taught almost entirely in English.

Students and the M.B.A. Experience

The INSEAD M.B.A. programme is a year of opportunity to make lasting friendships that span the world, to be inspired by professors, and to meet and listen to leading international business figures on campus. Despite the amount of time devoted to studying, INSEAD is a constant hub of varied activities. The level and intensity of the M.B.A. programme demand highly qualified participants. In an atmosphere of camaraderie and competition, participants are pushed to discover their limits, as well as their potential.

The M.B.A. participants represent nearly fifty different nationalities. Not only is the group as a whole international, but each individual has an international outlook, with more than two thirds of INSEAD's M.B.A. participants speaking three or more languages and more than half the class having studied or worked abroad. The average age of participants is 28, and the majority of participants have between three and five years of professional experience.

Special Features

The INSEAD M.B.A. programme is an intensive one that demands that participants commit themselves from day one. A year spent on campus provides a sound generalist management education, broadens horizons, and prepares participants for an international career, without the two-year interruption common to many other programmes. The high quality of faculty and participants, the alumni and corporate network, and a truly international environment have combined to make INSEAD one of the top management schools in the world.

The Faculty

INSEAD prides itself on the many talents of its faculty members and their close ties with both the academic and business communities. The 102 permanent professors, with qualifications from distinguished institutions around the world, represent more than twenty different nationalities. The relevance of their teaching and the innovation in their research are guaranteed by close partnerships with industry, nourished by the constant interaction with about 4,000 business executives who attend programmes at INSEAD each year. INSEAD's faculty regularly receive international awards for cases, books, and articles and for their contribution to the academic community in management.

The Business School Network

While many of the advantages of an INSEAD M.B.A. degree are obvious during the course of the programme, some become more visible with time. The importance of the International Alumni Association is one. There are 18,500 INSEAD alumni, of whom more than 10,000 have graduated from the M.B.A. programme and 8,500 from executive programmes of at least four weeks in length. As corporations push for global integration, the value of international contacts is increasing. The ability to pick up the telephone to question a former classmate is increasingly useful in the context of global competition.

A growing network of leading corporations endorses INSEAD's commitment to education in an international context, expressing confidence in INSEAD's teaching and research through generous and highly valued contributions. Through combined research projects, executive education programmes, and M.B.A. and executive alumni, INSEAD has constructed a unique global network of contacts in influential positions. Over time and across distances, the INSEAD network is proving to be a critical tie in bringing successful people and businesses together.

The College and Environs

Created in 1959, INSEAD is located in Fontainebleau, France, which is 65 kilometers southeast of Paris. The wooded campus is situated on the edge of the Fontainebleau Forest, which has an area of roughly 50,000 acres, providing opportunity for hikes, rock-climbing, mountain biking, and horseback riding. At the same time, Paris is less than an hour away, easily accessible by train or highway.

Technology Environment

There are 150 microcomputers available for student use as well as network connections for laptop users. Participants have access to the Internet and Intranet, internal e-mail, and a variety of online CD-ROM databases.

Placement

INSEAD's Career Management Service (CMS) is an advisory and information resource for M.B.A. participants preparing for their career after graduation. CMS organises a wide range of activities to assist M.B.A. participants in their job searches and career plans, including career counselling, seminars, workshops, and an extensive company resource centre. Special assistance and information sources are available to facilitate independent job search in parallel with on-campus recruitment.

The CMS acts as a liaison between M.B.A. participants and companies, organising the logistics for all on-campus recruitment. More than 100 companies recruit on INSEAD's campus twice a year. In 1997, approximately 460 different companies sought INSEAD M.B.A.'s for career employment, and participants received an average of more than three job offers.

Admission

INSEAD aims to attract talented young professionals from a wide range of cultural, academic, and professional backgrounds with high potential for effective leadership in complex international business environments. Sharp intellectual curiosity, with a desire to learn and stretch oneself in a rigorous academic programme, is expected, as well as personal qualities to contribute meaningfully to the many academic and extracurricular activities at INSEAD.

In addition to completing the application, which includes biographical data, essays, and a job description, applicants must take the GMAT. If preselected, the candidate will be invited to attend at least two evaluative interviews. The TOEFL may also be required for nonnative English-speaking candidates.

All candidates must be fluent in English and have a working knowledge of a second language before starting the programme. Upon completion of the programme, all participants must demonstrate knowledge of a third language.

Finances

Tuition for the academic year 1998–99 is Fr159,000, and it is estimated that a single participant should budget a total of Fr259,000.

International Students

The international nature of INSEAD makes it unique. No single nationality typically exceeds 17 percent of the student body; it is the INSEAD culture that dominates. Diversity helps ensure that participants see the world through new perspectives and learn how to benefit from both the conflicts and synergies that arise. Ten months spent studying, working, and living among culturally diverse influences means adapting to new approaches, accepting that listening is also learning, and cooperating to achieve results.

Application Facts and Dates

INSEAD has two intakes, one in August and one in January. Admission is on a rolling basis, but it is strongly recommended that candidates submit their application as soon as it is complete.

For further information, students should visit INSEAD's Web site at the address listed below. A full brochure and application may be requested via the Web site or by sending an e-mail or a fax to the M.B.A. Admissions Office. Inquiries should include the student's name, address, telephone number, date of birth, nationality, and e-mail address.

Students may also write to:

INSEAD
M.B.A. Admissions Office
Boulevard de Constance
77305 Fontainebleau Cedex
France
Fax: 011 33 1 60 72 55 30
E-mail: admissions@insead.fr
World Wide Web: http://www.insead.fr/MBA

International Institute for Management Development

Lausanne, Switzerland

IMD—THE LEADER IN INTERNATIONAL MANAGEMENT EDUCATION

The IMD M.B.A. program is designed to enable a very selective number of highly qualified, young professionals, who have demonstrated significant achievement early in their careers, to reach responsible positions in international management. Our very intensive program aims at the top end of the spectrum in terms of the calibre of the participants and program rigor. The small class size of 80 participants, representing thirty-five different countries, fosters our belief that world-class business leaders are not mass produced; they are developed with a large degree of personalized attention in a practical, action-oriented environment. This is the only way they can master the craft of leadership in an international arena.

—Dominique Turpin, Director

Programs and Curricular Focus

The IMD M.B.A. program is an intense eleven-month program (January through December) designed to develop students' strong general management skills with an international focus. The combined total of 900 classroom and study-group contact hours are equivalent to a two-year full-time program.

The IMD M.B.A. program prepares the student to manage and lead in the increasingly global business environment. In addition to the program content, which is international in its geographic coverage, the multinationality of participants and faculty promotes a truly international perspective. More than thirty-five nationalities are represented in a single class of 80 participants, and nearly twenty nationalities are represented among the faculty. Learning to manage effectively in an international setting, where no single nationality dominates, is an integral part of the IMD experience.

The eight modules of the M.B.A. program provide the context for integrated learning. In each module, averaging four to five weeks in length, a number of different, yet complementary, fields of management are combined into a unified learning experience. As a result, participants gain a complete understanding of each field, as well as how they work together. Moreover, the learning process is cumulative; skills learned in one module are reinforced and built upon in subsequent modules.

The IMD program is inspired more by management practice than academic theory. First, the learning material is focused on current and emerging issues in management practice. Second, the M.B.A. faculty also teaches business leaders in the IMD executive education programs, which allows them to stay in constant touch with management reality. Third, working in teams ensures that the participants tap into the large reservoir of experience among their classmates.

A typical learning activity at IMD is made up of three phases. First, participants study assigned cases individually, identifying issues that require further depth of understanding. They then work in small groups, broadening their outlook by testing their opinions and drawing on the experiences of group members from different cultural and business backgrounds. Participants spend one third of their time working in teams, which develops their skills in problem solving, communication, and leadership in an international environment. Finally, in the classroom, guided by faculty members, participants explore new concepts, share experiences, and are challenged to present their opinions and solutions.

IMD limits the class size to 80 participants, reinforcing the belief that the small class size allows innovation, flexibility, and a personal interplay between students and faculty that few schools can match. No single nationality exceeds 10 percent of the student body.

Students and the M.B.A. Experience

IMD strongly believes that each participant is a key source of learning for other participants in the program. Accordingly, every effort is made to ensure that the right balance occurs among the 80 participants, in terms of work experience, nationality, and academic background, to maximize the learning experience. The students have an average of seven years of work experience, with a range of three to twelve years. Seventy percent of the participants have their experience in industry, 12 percent in financial services, 15 percent in consulting, and 3 percent in other areas. All participants have shown fast career progression, and many have international work experience. The program has a standard of requiring significant career accomplishments; therefore, the average age of participants is 31, with a range of 26 to 35 years.

IMD is a truly international environment; no single nationality dominates the classroom. Thirty-five countries are represented in a single class, with 58 percent of the participants coming from Europe, 20 percent from Asia, 8 percent from North America, 6 percent from Latin America, 4 percent from Australia, and 4 percent from Africa and the Middle East. The educational background of the M.B.A. participants is also quite varied. For the class of 1998, the breakdown is as follows: engineering, 32 percent; business and commerce, 30 percent; social sciences, 15 percent; natural sciences, 12 percent; and humanities, 11 percent.

Special Features

International Consulting Projects are an integral part of the M.B.A. program. Participants serve as consultants to the top management of client companies and advise them on critical, far-reaching management issues. It is the perfect opportunity to apply their classroom learning to developing creative, results-oriented solutions to real management problems. The projects address issues from strategy formulation to operational problems. The International Consulting Projects follow a systematic four-phase approach: the industry analysis phase, the company analysis phase, the issue analysis phase, and the implementation and feedback phase.

Participants work in teams of 5 to 6, under the guidance of a faculty adviser. Client companies are located all over the world and include a variety of industries and sectors.

The Team Initiated Enterprise (TIE) projects were developed as a direct response to company comments that M.B.A. graduates are good at analyzing but not very talented at initiating and implementing. The participants are simply told to create an initiative that provides value for someone else and see it through to implementation. The only stipulation is that it be a worthwhile learning experience for the team. The teams are self-selected, and the projects take place across the first half of the program. In the past, participants put a team on top of Mont Blanc; opened a day-care center for students' children; raised $169,000 for a children's hospital in Budapest, Hungary; and taught business education to entrepreneurs in Eastern Europe.

The Faculty

M.B.A. participants receive a high degree of personal attention at IMD with a student-faculty ratio of 3:1. The faculty also reflects IMD's internationality, with almost twenty different nationalities represented. The M.B.A. faculty members are extensively involved in teaching in IMD's executive education programs and, therefore, maintain a close relationship with real-world management issues. The faculty members contribute to the M.B.A. program through teaching and leading discussions in class, as well as serving as advisers for the International Consulting Projects.

The Business School Network

More than 120 companies worldwide have formed a special relationship with IMD through the Partner Program and Business Associate Network. They are IMD's partners in industry and constitute a unique network based on the common goal of improving performance in international management. These companies help ensure that IMD's M.B.A. program addresses the real needs of business via their input on program design and review. In addition, M.B.A. participants have access to hundreds of executives who participate in IMD's executive education program on the same campus.

IMD's partner companies include Andersen Consulting, Astra AB, AT&T, Baxter International, Caterpillar, Citicorp, Exxon, IBM Europe, Mercedes Benz, Nestlé S.A., and Sony Europe. Business associates include Ajinomoto Co., Inc.; Booz Allen & Hamilton; British Steel; Fiat S.p.A.; General Motors Corporation; Heineken N.V.; Hewlett-Packard S.A.; Philip Morris; Shell International; Taiwan Semiconductor Manufacturing Co. Ltd.; and AB Volvo.

The College and Environs

The history of IMD goes back to 1946 when Alcan created IMI in Geneva, Europe's first business school, and 1957 when Nestlé founded IMEDE, Lausanne, with the active involvement of the Harvard Business School. The merger of the resources and the wide experience of the two institutions gave birth to IMD in 1989.

IMD is located in Lausanne, a French-speaking region where there is a strong tradition of international exchange. Lausanne is also home to the International Olympic Committee. The campus is just 40 minutes from Geneva, home to several European corporate headquarters, the United Nations, and several international organizations. The IMD community is small and friendly, allowing participants and faculty to mix freely on a first-name basis. The atmosphere strikes the right balance between very intensive study and informality. More importantly, IMD's international character brings participants into daily contact with people from many different cultures and traditions.

Placement

IMD M.B.A. graduates are internationally recognized as a very select group of professionally trained managers, and they are recruited by leading companies to take on challenging roles in international management. The Career Services Office coordinates activities with experienced professionals for counselling participants on resumes, interviewing, and effective job search. In addition, an IMD M.B.A. Resume Portfolio, containing participant resumes, is produced and distributed globally. During the second half of the program, companies are invited to interview participants on campus.

For the class of 1997, 97 percent of the participants received at least one job offer by graduation, with an average of three offers per participant. Graduates went around the globe, including 78 percent to Europe and 16 percent to Asia and Australia. Sixty percent went into industry (in a variety of sectors and functions), 24 percent into consulting, and 16 percent into financial services. The average starting salary was $93,000, and the median starting salary was $92,000 (both figures do not include bonuses). This represented a 65 percent increase over pre-M.B.A. salaries

Admission

Admission requirements stress career progression, management potential, and intellectual ability. Only a small number of applicants are selected for admission, and the admissions committee looks for a good balance among the following criteria: career progression, management potential, education, GMAT performance, the interview, and English language ability. Candidates must have a minimum of three years of full-time work experience, during which they have displayed a steady increase in responsibilities. They must demonstrate potential for holding a management position and be motivated toward building a career in international management. Candidates normally possess the equivalent of a bachelor's degree from a university, polytechnic, or a similar institute of higher learning. They must demonstrate strong verbal and quantitative reasoning abilities in their GMAT scores. Candidates whose applications pass the initial assessment of the Admissions Committee are invited to interview at IMD. English is the only working language, and candidates must have a full command of spoken and written English. On average, participants speak two or three languages fluently, including English.

Finances

The fees for a self-sponsored participant are set at a subsidized level of SwFr 41,000, which is equivalent to approximately $28,000. Company-sponsored candidates are charged the full cost of their education, SwFr 61,000, which is equivalent to approximately $42,000. Fees cover tuition, use of the library and computer facilities, office supplies, and lunch at IMD during the week.

Rent and other living expenses vary depending on participants' family situation and personal lifestyle. IMD estimates the boarding costs for the full year, including travelling to and from Switzerland, to be approximately SwFr 21,000 ($14,500).

IMD offers several scholarships and accepted participants who have difficulty financing their education will be referred to the IMD M.B.A. Alumni Association, which may be able to offer help in the form of a low-interest rate loan.

Application Facts and Dates

Application deadlines are January 15, March 1, April 1, May 1, June 1, August 1, and September 1. Candidates receive notification of the admissions committee's decision approximately six weeks after the deadline date. For more information, applicants should contact:

Ms. Marianne Wheeler
M.B.A. Information Officer
IMD
Chemin de Bellerive 23
P.O. Box 915
CH-1001
Lausanne, Switzerland
Telephone: 41-21-618-0298
            41-21-618-0111
Fax: 41-21-618-0615
E-mail: mbainfo@imd.ch
World Wide Web: http://www.imd.ch/

International University of Japan

Yamato-machi, Niigata, Japan

THE NEW M.B.A. IN THE GLOBAL ECONOMY

The challenge we face in today's dramatically changing world economy is to effectively manage complex webs of linkages of business transactions across different nations. An understanding is needed of the political, economic, and cultural characteristics of the world marketplace, especially that of Asia as a production platform and its market potential for the twenty-first century. The International University of Japan (IUJ) M.B.A. program meets the challenges of globalization by establishing joint external projects with the Asian business community and by training international managers to apply cross-functional knowledge and integrated problem-solving skills to make effective decisions within complex multinational business contexts.

—Ushio Sumita, Dean

Programs and Curricular Focus

The IUJ M.B.A. program admits approximately 70 highly qualified students per year from a large number of countries, including Japan, the U.S., and Asian and European countries.

The program focuses on a comparative analysis of Japan, the U.S., and Asia; assessment of the impact of advanced information technologies on global business practice; cross-functional knowledge and integrated problem-solving skills; assessment of legal issues for global business involving Japan, the U.S., China, and other Asian countries; and use of the Internet and state-of-the-art multimedia presentation software/hardware.

The global orientation is evident throughout the curriculum. A culturally diverse faculty teaching an equally diverse student body brings comparative perspectives to many of the individual courses. This encourages the application of theory and concepts to different national contexts and the recognition of institutional differences among various countries, particularly those of Japan, the U.S., and Asian countries. The program also offers students an opportunity to learn more about Japanese management and industrial systems and gain a perspective on Japan's international competitiveness in leading-edge, high-technology industries. It also emphasizes development of cross-cultural communication and management skills. The program is carefully sequenced to maximize the efficiency of the learning process.

The first year consists of fifteen required courses, plus appropriate language courses. During the second year, students take one required course and select an appropriate number of courses from among the two dozen or so elective courses offered each year. In addition, students choose an area of special interest to investigate in depth for their research project.

The curriculum is enhanced by opportunities to meet with visiting executives and scholars, to participate in summer activities (internships with Japanese corporations or attendance at a U.S. summer program), to spend one term on exchange in an M.B.A. program in another country, and to interact daily with people from many different countries and professional backgrounds.

Students and the M.B.A. Experience

The IUJ M.B.A. program's student body consists of a selected group of experienced managers of whom roughly 40 percent are Japanese. The others come from Africa, Europe, North and South America, the Indian subcontinent, and other parts of Asia. Only 1 of every 3–4 applicants meets the standards set for admission and each brings a unique perspective and background to the program. As the number of students per graduating class has grown, so has the diversity of students in terms of the number of women and the number of different national, industrial, educational, and cultural backgrounds represented in the student body.

The class of 2000 has an average age of 28 with an average of four years of business experience. Most of these students obtained their undergraduate degrees in economics, engineering, or social science; most speak two or three languages, some as many as five.

❖ Global Focus

The original mission and purpose of IUJ as conceived by its founders is as valid and vital today as it was then. The mission is to train young men and women for professional careers in global business for the twenty-first century. The times call for a new breed of professionals both in Japan and around the world who can function successfully anywhere in the world. IUJ strives to develop such new talents.

Special Features

The Local Business Community Involvement Program is a required course running throughout the first year. Students are divided into small groups and have a chance to work on activity analyses of the local business community. This course is designed not only to integrate all functional areas to identify and solve business problems, but also to build among multinational students high competency in cross-cultural communication and team management.

Consistent with IUJ's curriculum and research emphasis, students are encouraged to conduct joint research with faculty on Japan and Asia while satisfying the second-year research project requirement. Cumulative research results of students and faculty members should propose an innovative vision of Japan's role in Asia in the global era.

The Faculty

To teach culturally diverse students with a new management perspective, IUJ has recruited an internationally oriented, multicultural and highly qualified faculty. The core group of permanent faculty members is augmented by visiting faculty members from North America, Europe, and other institutions in Asia. While the vast majority of faculty members have Ph.D. degrees, the research at IUJ focuses on highly relevant international business issues and the research and consulting activities of the

faculty naturally flow back into the class-room and the overall curriculum.

The Business School Network

IUJ works cooperatively to actively engage the international business community. Examples of such connections include courses taught by business practitioners from major corporations in Japan, guest executive speakers in class and through the IUJ Senior Executive Seminars, student course work involving corporate-sponsored projects, faculty research and consulting relationships, and class visits to plant sites.

In addition to opportunities to meet with international executives and officials, the IUJ M.B.A. program also provides students with the opportunity to interact with local corporations in the area. The Local Business Community Involvement Program is promoted through regular academic courses throughout the year and students have a chance to work on real-life projects at local corporations and to closely analyze Japanese management approaches from the viewpoint of parts suppliers to major manufacturing companies.

The College and Environs

The International University of Japan, a private graduate-level institution, was founded in 1982 with extensive support from Japan's industrial, financial, and educational circles. The Graduate School of International Management M.B.A. Program at IUJ was established in 1988 with the support of the Amos Tuck School of Business Administration, Dartmouth College, and is the only program of its kind accredited by Japan's Ministry of Education. Only a 100-minute

train ride from central Tokyo, the IUJ campus is located in a beautiful valley surrounded by magnificent mountains.

Facilities

The IUJ campus houses classrooms, offices, and the Matsushita Library and Information Center, with a constantly expanding collection of books, periodicals, and databases, as well as student access to IBM and Macintosh computers with international networking capabilities. Other facilities include dormitories for single and married students, a gymnasium, a school cafeteria, and a campus store.

Placement

A substantial portion of the student body is corporate-sponsored. These students continue as employees while attending the program and form one of their primary connections to Japanese companies. Corporate connections to the IUJ M.B.A. program are enhanced and expanded each year through the graduates who obtain full-time employment with various business organizations. The Office of Student Services and faculty members provide valuable assistance and information to aid graduating students in finding permanent employment at multinational companies within Japan. Proficiency in the Japanese language plays a great role in placing nonnative Japanese speakers.

Admission

Admission requirements include an undergraduate degree, GMAT (average among scholarship recipients for the class of 2000: 632), TOEFL (average for the class of 2000: 586), two references, and

preferred work experience of two years (average is four years for the class of 2000).

Furthermore, applicants are carefully reviewed on the basis of a combination of several criteria including well defined motivation to pursue graduate study in business and the potential to achieve leadership positions in management; the maturity and sense of purpose essential to a demanding educational experience, including a concept of the value of an international M.B.A. program to the applicant's career plans and expectation; and a personal sense of values consistent with the standards and purposes of the IUJ M.B.A. program.

There are no prerequisite courses for admission, but students must have a strong working knowledge of accounting, statistics, and economics.

Finances

A breakdown of tution, fees, and expenses include admission fee ¥300,000, program tuition fee per academic year ¥1,900,000, summer program in the U.S. (optional) ¥700,000, monthly expenses: books and supplies, ¥20,000, single room with a bath¥32,000, utilities ¥5,000, meals on campus ¥40,000, total minimum expense per month ¥97,000.

A great number of scholarships and tuition waivers in varying amounts are available to qualified non-sponsored students.

International Students

Approximately 60 percent of the student body is international. Furthermore, exchange students from twenty-one prominent business schools impart multifaceted and invaluable perspectives into class discussions. Exchange partners include Chinese University of Hong Kong, National University of Singapore, Chulalongkorn University, New York University, Dartmouth College, London Business School, and others.

Application Facts and Dates

Application deadlines for overseas applicants for 1999 September enrollment are February 5 and April 2. For more information, students should contact:

Office of Student Recruitment
International University of Japan
Yamato-machi, Niigata 949-7277
Japan
Telephone: 81 257 79-1104
Fax:81 257 79-1188
E-mail: admis@iuj.ac.jp

Iona College

New Rochelle, New York

LEADERSHIP—THE HAGAN M.B.A. PROGRAM

▶ *In the face of the swift and complex developments of today's rapidly changing global marketplace, leaders must act quickly and competitively—adding value to their organizations. The most effective leaders will be able to mobilize teams of employees to solve problems creatively.*

—Nicholas J. Beutell, Dean

Programs and Curricular Focus

The goal of the Hagan School of Business M.B.A. program is to produce graduates and future leaders who understand business and its challenges as the twenty-first century approaches. It seeks to graduate women and men who have the skills to work productively in a high-technology society, demonstrate sensitivity to the global and multicultural character of business, provide strategic leadership in a competitive environment, and subscribe to high ethical standards in the practice of their profession.

The new M.B.A. curriculum consists of core courses in the functional areas of business perspectives (an integrated overview), followed by a major concentration allowing for specialized study, advanced electives that provide students an opportunity to custom design the breadth component of the curriculum, and a capstone course.

Computer applications are integrated into the program, as are the development of presentation and communication skills. Case studies, team projects, computer simulation games, experiential exercises, and lectures are the commonly used methods of teaching.

The calendar follows a trimester schedule of twelve weeks each, with two summer sessions, allowing students to earn more credits within the year. Classes meet once a week in the evening, Monday through Thursday from 6:30 to 9:30, with some Saturday morning classes.

The number of credits required for the degree is 57 before waivers and transfer credits are applied. There is a six-year limit to finish the program. A typical M.B.A. student takes 45 credits and completes the program in four years on a part-time basis or two years full-time.

Students and the M.B.A. Experience

Almost all of the students in the program hold full-time jobs at Fortune 500 companies, major brokerage houses, large commercial banks, and insurance companies. Midsize and small companies are also well represented. Many students hold middle-management positions in blue-chip firms such as IBM, Bell Atlantic, Chase Manhattan Bank, Kraft-General Foods, and Lederle Laboratories, to cite a few.

The average age of the students is 29. They have, on the average, about seven years of full-time work experience in various industries. It is this maturity, diverse corporate background, and significant work experience that they bring to the program and contribute to the overall quality of the learning process.

The student body is represented by approximately the same number of women and men. Most come from the tristate area of New York, New Jersey, and Connecticut. International students represent all continents.

❖ Global Focus

The institutional thrust toward global education and the international character of the faculty members strengthen the goal dimension of the M.B.A. curriculum. Students are encouraged to participate in the summer courses offered abroad.

The Faculty

The Hagan School of Business faculty members are dedicated teachers and professionals. As teacher-scholars, they keep current in their fields of expertise, doing research, publishing, and giving presentations at academic conferences. As professionals, they blend theory and practice, drawing upon their own and

their students' business experience. Among them are internationally recognized experts in such diverse fields as artificial intelligence, case writing, corporate values, and business ethics.

With very few exceptions, those who teach in the M.B.A. program are full-time, with appropriate terminal degrees earned at America's top universities. Students recognize them for their teaching excellence and seek their advice on career matters.

The Business School Network

Corporate Partnerships

Through the Dean's Business Advisory Council, made up of business executives from corporations that send students to the program, the Hagan School has created a partnership venue with business. Through the council, business has a real opportunity to influence the strategic direction of the School. It is mechanisms of this kind that allow the School to be responsive to the needs of the business community and offer a relevant curriculum. The Hagan Business Forum brings successful alumni as well as prominent local business executives to the campus to give lectures on current issues to the student body. The Hagan Report keeps alumni and students informed.

Prominent Alumni

The Hagan School is proud to count among its distinguished alumni senior executives and business leaders from America's largest and best corporations, such as Philip Morris, Citicorp, IBM, Kraft Foods, Bell Atlantic, and Merrill Lynch.

The College and Environs

Iona College was founded in 1940 by the Congregation of Christian Brothers. Its main campus is located in New Rochelle, a small city on the Long Island Sound in Westchester County, about 20 miles north of the heart of Manhattan. The M.B.A. program is also offered in Rockland County, a few miles west of the Hudson River.

With its strategic locations and proximity to New York City, the Hagan School of Business enables students to

Hagan Hall.

benefit from the rich, diversified environment that is attuned to the advances and innovations of the global market. The New York metropolitan area is the home of many major national and multinational corporations, such as IBM, Texaco, and PepsiCo, as well as many of the nation's largest banks, brokerage houses, and insurance firms.

Technology Environment

The academic programs of the Hagan School are strongly supported by state-of-the-art computer equipment and software. Two multimedia Pentium labs are available in Hagan Hall. More than 500 PCs are available for student use in public facilities, with some of them open around the clock seven days a week. The Helen T. Arrigoni Library and Technology Center houses multimedia systems with access to the Internet and other popular on-line databases, including ABI/INFORM.

Many course requirements involve the use of computers, and every student is provided with a computer account, an e-mail address, and access to the system.

State-of-the-art interactive video and multimedia systems are available for teaching and student learning. TVs and VCRs with cable access and satellite downlinks are found in Hagan classrooms.

Placement

The Office of Career Services of Iona College provides students with career counseling and job search assistance. It alerts students to job openings and positions in companies and to the organizations that seek graduates of the College. Resume referral, mock interviews, and counseling for alumni are among the services available to students.

Admission

Admission is selective and based on an evaluation of the student's academic record, scores on the Graduate Management Admission Test (GMAT), references, and work experience. Applications and credentials should be sent to the Graduate Admissions Office of the Hagan School of Business.

Rolling admissions allow students to begin studies in any trimester: fall, winter, spring, or summer. TOEFL scores are required for all students whose native language is not English. International students must provide evidence of adequate funds to cover all expenses.

Finances

Tuition per credit in 1998–99 is $473. Books and supplies cost approximately $1500 per year. There are no boarding facilities on campus for graduate students. Living expense estimates range from $10,000 to $12,000 for ten months, not including vacation periods.

A limited number of graduate assistantships are available to full-time students.

Application Facts and Dates

Rolling admissions allow students to submit their application any time. However, completed applications should be received no later than two weeks prior to the start of the trimester for which the student plans to enroll. For more information, students should contact:

Ms. Carol Shea
Director of M.B.A. Admissions
Hagan School of Business
Iona College
715 North Avenue
New Rochelle, New York 10801-1890
Telephone: 914-633-2288
Fax: 914-633-2012
E-mail: cshea@iona.edu

Iowa State University

Ames, Iowa

EXCELLENCE IN AMERICA'S HEARTLAND

The Iowa State University (ISU) M.B.A. program is staffed with educators who love what they do. We do it well, attracting students from all over the world. Iowa State works to serve you, the education consumer, by providing a flexible and competitive learning environment.

Iowa State understands the value you place on your education. Ours is a culture dedicated to excellence in graduate business education and whose faculty is active in research, committed to innovative teaching, and accessible to students.

Students are not just numbers here. Iowa State offers a wide array of educational resources in an environment sensitive to individual student needs. We provide an environment where students can stretch and grow as professionals and as people, making Iowa State a warm and inviting place to be.

—Benjamin J. Allen, Dean

Programs and Curricular Focus

The Iowa State University M.B.A. program offers a friendly, personal environment that emphasizes flexibility and teamwork. As our world gets smaller, and its demographics change, the ability to work effectively with a diverse population is vital to the foundation of global success. First-year M.B.A. students are preassigned to small work groups that are chosen to maximize each member's contribution to diversity, personal strengths, and academic and work backgrounds. Students are then challenged with innovative projects and a curriculum that dovetails with global management issues.

M.B.A. candidates may pursue their course work through a full-time program or, to accommodate employed students, through the part-time Saturday M.B.A. program. The two-year 48-credit-hour M.B.A. program consists of an integrated core curriculum and 24 credit hours of electives. Teamwork is an integral part of the first-year M.B.A. experience. Second-year students tailor their course work to meet individual academic and career goals. By placing a premium on flexibility and accessibility, the program guides candidates through interactive projects that recreate a corporate environment.

M.B.A. students may opt to concentrate their studies in a particular area. Areas of specialization include accounting, agribusiness, finance, management information systems, manufacturing and quality, and marketing.

Students and the M.B.A. Experience

The 220 graduate business students at Iowa State reflect a diversity of educational, cultural, and professional backgrounds. Drawing upon the University's international stature, the Iowa State M.B.A. program attracts students worldwide, representing eighteen countries. Thirty percent of the students are women. Thirty-five percent of Iowa State M.B.A. students bring an undergraduate degree in business to their graduate experience, and 25 percent reflect a background in engineering. Science undergraduates make up 20 percent, and social sciences, humanities, and other degrees illustrate the other varying backgrounds of undergraduates who seek the College of Business for graduate work. Iowa State's Saturday M.B.A. candidates represent industry sectors throughout the state of Iowa, including agriculture, education, financial services, health and human services, manufacturing, and small business.

Students are encouraged to be active participants in the M.B.A. Association. This organization promotes career development activities, plans social events, and serves as a representative body for M.B.A. students in the College.

❖ Global Focus

To add an international dimension, Iowa State M.B.A. students who wish to study abroad can find many programs and countries to which their graduate program can be tailored. The Study Abroad Center has extensive information on both the ISU Exchange Program and the International Internship Program. The Iowa State College of Business also offers an ongoing exchange program with the University of Glasgow in Scotland to allow M.B.A. students to earn credit toward their graduate management degree by studying abroad.

Special Features

M.B.A. students may enhance their educational experience through the College's close association with various centers. The Pappajohn Center for Entrepreneurship offers educational and outreach programs aimed at developing the entrepreneurial interests and capabilities of M.B.A. students. An annual M.B.A. Student Competition in New Venture Planning awards start-up funding to aspiring entrepreneurs who are judged to have developed and presented the best business plan for their enterprises. M.B.A. students may be given the opportunity to provide research support and consulting services to Iowa small businesses through the Iowa Small Business Development Center. M.B.A. students interested in transportation and logistics management may select course work offered by the College's Department of Logistics, Operations, and Management Information Systems. Research opportunities are available to M.B.A. students through the Center for Transportation Research and Education. M.B.A. students may participate in an annual conference sponsored by the Murray G. Bacon Center for Ethics in Business.

The Faculty

The College of Business counts among its faculty members some of the best scholars in the profession, including several Fulbright recipients. Faculty members participate in international faculty exchange programs and have become respected providers of education and research in the international arena. Recent exchanges have involved Portugal, Ireland, and Belgium. In addition, the College of Business has hosted faculty members from Croatia, Egypt, Russia, the Czech Republic, and Slovakia. In turn,

Iowa State faculty members have also taught in these countries.

The Business School Network
Corporate Partnerships
Iowa State University places immense importance on the exchange of ideas between academic and corporate environments. The College of Business Dean's Advisory Council meets regularly to share its members' expertise and ideas for the M.B.A. program. Speakers from corporations, including Pioneer Hi-Bred International, Texas Instruments, and General Mills, lecture regularly, and M.B.A. students visit local and regional facilities to observe businesses in action. Through the College's Executive-in-Residence program, M.B.A. students interact with prominent business leaders who visit the Iowa State University campus twice yearly.

Prominent Alumni
Iowa State University counts among its 14,000 business alumni many business leaders, including Bill Adams, Chairman and CEO, Armstrong World Industries (retired); Lynn Vorbrich, President, Iowa Power and Light; Charles S. Johnson, Executive Vice President, Pioneer Hi-Bred International Inc.; Glenn R. Blake, Director, Corporate Personnel, General Mills, Inc.; Cheryl Gruetzmacher Gordon, Senior Managing Director, Rothschild North America; Scott Johnson, President, Norwest Bank Iowa; Cara Heiden, Executive Vice President, Norwest Mortgage, Inc.; Steve Bergstrom, President, Natural Gas Clearinghouse; and Richard Stark, President, Iowa Commodities, Ltd.

The College and Environs
The 1,000-acre campus features a quiet lake and a parklike setting. As part of Ames, a community of 50,000, the University is set in the geographic center of the United States, in an area that offers a pleasing mixture of urban and rural life. Founded in 1858, Iowa State is the first land-grant university to have been established under the Morrill Land-Grant Act. The institution was charged with promoting "liberal and practical education . . . in the several pursuits and professions of college life." Today, with close to 25,000 students, Iowa State University is fulfilling that mission: educating students and delivering research discoveries and service to the public.

Facilities
Two recently remodeled computer labs in the College of Business provide the latest in computer hardware and software technology to M.B.A. students. A new distance learning classroom offers instantaneous audiovisual capability to remote sites throughout the state of Iowa. The Durham Computation Center houses 24-hour computer labs and offers related support services for students.

The Parks Library offers a comfortable, friendly environment with more than 4 million holdings, including maps, films, government publications, and archival and audiovisual materials. Also, the library's online information system, SCHOLAR, provides access to the local online catalog.

Technology Environment
The College of Business, with the help of generous corporate support, offers state-of-the-art computer technology, including Project Vincent, a network of high-performance workstations. This network allows access to supercomputing, visualization, and numeric computation both on and off campus, setting Project Vincent apart from other like endeavors and placing Iowa State among the U.S. leaders in networking workstations and computers.

Placement
The College of Business offers comprehensive career development and placement programs and services, including job search workshops, career counseling, a career resources center, internship coordination, and campus interviews. A full-time director provides individual career services support to M.B.A. students.

Admission
Each applicant is carefully assessed in terms of his or her intellectual potential, academic achievement, work and professional involvement, interpersonal communication skills, career goals, and motivation. Educational records are reviewed from official transcripts, as well as scores from the Graduate Management Admission Test (GMAT). Three letters of recommendation, a resume, and the candidate's responses to the essay portion of the application are also required.

Finances
The College of Business and its affiliated centers offer a number of graduate assistantships to qualified M.B.A. students. Graduate assistants pay resident fees and receive a monthly stipend. Graduate assistants in good academic standing are also awarded a scholarship covering a portion of the resident fee. M.B.A. students wishing to be considered for a graduate assistantship may indicate so on the ISU Graduate College application form. Information on scholarships and fellowships is available from the Graduate College, the Office of Minority Student Affairs, and the College of Business. Outstanding students may be qualified to receive a monetary award through the Premium for Academic Excellence (PACE) program in the Graduate College. PACE recipients generally have an undergraduate GPA of 3.5 or better or a GPA of 3.8 in previous graduate work. The Office of Student Financial Aid offers financial assistance through low-interest loans of various types and employment assistance.

International Students
The Office of International Students and Scholars (OISS) provides orientation and advising to new international students. The OISS acts as a route through which international students can utilize local community services. It also serves as a liaison with the U.S. Information Agency and the Immigration and Naturalization Service to bring visiting scholars and students to Iowa State University.

Application Facts and Dates
For the M.B.A. program, admission is granted for the fall semester only. Students should submit the Graduate College application form, application fee, official transcripts, and TOEFL scores (if applicable) to the Office of Admissions, 100 Alumni Hall, Iowa State University, Ames, Iowa 50011. Students should submit GMAT scores, letters of reference, a resume, and the personal essays to the Graduate Programs Office at the address below. The deadline for submission of all application materials is May 1 (March 1 for international students). For more information, students should contact:

Director of Graduate Admissions
College of Business
218 Carver Hall
Iowa State University
Ames, Iowa 50011-2063
Telephone: 515-294-8118
 800-433-3452 (toll-free)
Fax: 515-294-2446
E-mail: busgrad@iastate.edu
World Wide Web: http://www.iastate.edu/~isubuscoll/homepage.html

JOHNS HOPKINS
U N I V E R S I T Y
School of Continuing Studies

Johns Hopkins University

School of Continuing Studies, Division of Business and Management

Baltimore, Maryland

BUSINESS AT HOPKINS: LEARNING THROUGH LEADERSHIP

At the Johns Hopkins University Division of Business and Management, students find an academic environment geared to both adult part-time learning and the business marketplace.

The largest part-time graduate business program in the Baltimore-Washington area, the University's curricula and support services are expressly designed for adult learning. Small classes feature Hopkins professors and leading executives from the region's outstanding corporate, government, and nonprofit sectors. Innovative master's degrees and specialized concentrations allow students to tailor programs of study to specific goals and interests. Capstone courses and special projects pair students with local companies to address real business challenges. Extensive support services include individual academic advising and career development through the University's extensive Career and Life Planning Center, which assists students in career evaluation and job search strategies.

Hopkins offers business courses at five convenient sites in the Baltimore-Washington region. Evening and weekend classes also help meet the demanding needs of today's working professionals.

The following program description outlines the University's dual mission of providing both a superior academic environment and a lifelong resource for personal and professional growth.

—Robert Nachtmann, Director and Associate Dean

Programs and Curricular Focus

Business programs at Hopkins focus on adult students seeking new levels of success as full-time professionals through part-time study. Students choose from a full range of master's and certificate programs, all tailored to provide the business skills and knowledge necessary to compete in an increasingly evolving and competitive marketplace. The curriculum combines practical learning experiences with academic excellence, an outstanding faculty, and flexible formats and scheduling at convenient class locations throughout the Baltimore-Washington metropolitan area.

The most extensive degree program is the Master of Science in business. It builds on a solid, rigorous foundation of business competencies as recommended by AACSB–The International Association for Management Education. In addition, the M.S. in business offers students a specialized and competitive edge through concentration options in finance, international business, management, information systems, marketing, and human resource management. An accelerated M.S. in business degree program, which enables students to complete course work in an expedited fashion without sacrificing content or

quality, is an option for those holding an undergraduate degree in business.

A central advantage of the Hopkins business program is the number of specialized degrees in addition to the M.S. in business and its concentrations. These programs include the Master of Science in marketing, the Master of Science in real estate (one of the few real estate master's programs in the country), the Master of Science in information and telecommunication systems for business, and the new Master of Science in organization development and human resources. The Police Executive Leadership Program, the first graduate program of its kind in the country, prepares law enforcement executives for the changing role and structure of police departments in the community and region. The Hopkins Schools of Continuing Studies (SCS) and Nursing offer a dual-degree program, the Master of Science in Nursing/Master of Science in business.

While curriculum, sequence, degree requirements, and program length may differ for each program, students usually complete their degree requirements within three to six years.

Hopkins also offers a wide range of certificate programs in business, providing intensive, short-term study in cohort groups. In many instances, credits earned can be transferred to an appropriate master's degree program. Programs include the new Graduate Certificate in Investments, certificates in information and telecommunication systems, the new Skilled Facilitator's Certificate, the Leadership Development Program for Minority Managers, Fellows in Change Management, and Women, Leadership, and Change. Two certificates, the Business of Medicine (in cooperation with the Hopkins School of Medicine) and the Business of Nursing (offered with the Hopkins School of Nursing), blend business and health-care disciplines. Through a partnership with the Caliber Learning Network, the Hopkins Business of Medicine is also offered via distance learning at more than thirty locations throughout the country.

Students and the Master's Experience

Students enrolled in all master's programs benefit from leadership and learning advantages that are unique to Hopkins. The outstanding faculty is composed of some of the region's foremost academicians and business world practitioners. Hopkins teachers involve students in actual business practices through case studies, special projects, and culminating capstone courses, which apply newfound skills and understanding to a diverse range of business challenges currently facing area organizations. Working in teams, students select a regional company, studying all aspects of its business, including market, operations, finance, and distribution. They next prepare strategic plans for their companies, presenting these plans to company officials and other business leaders, who ask students to defend their recommendations. Organizations who have recently engaged capstone students include Baltimore Gas and Electric Company; Giant Food, Inc.; the American Red Cross; Bell Atlantic; and Legg Mason, Incorporated.

The Faculty

The Division of Business and Management blends an experienced full-time faculty with some of the region's foremost business leaders, administrators, and entrepreneurs in the public, private, and nonprofit sectors to create an exciting, innovative teaching dynamic. Hopkins faculty members are not merely experts in their fields; they involve their students in hands-on projects that address current challenges facing real businesses.

Faculty members encourage a partnership approach to learning, which involves students in role playing, debates, case studies, simulations, research, guest speakers, and strategy sessions, among other activities. Capstone courses and special projects focus learning on real business challenges faced by area corporations. Many of these organizations have gone on to adopt the strategies and recommendations of their student "partners."

The Business School Network

Some of the Baltimore-Washington area's most prominent and progressive businesses and institutions are represented on the Hopkins faculty, including The Rouse Company, First National Bank of Maryland, Alex. Brown Kleinwort Benson, CSX Intermodal, Bell Atlantic, UNISYS Corporation, and the United States Department of the Treasury.

Local business leaders also serve on a number of SCS's academic and community advisory boards.

The College and Environs

Johns Hopkins University was founded in Baltimore in 1876 and was the first American university dedicated to both advanced study and scientific research. There are eight academic divisions within the University, including the School of Continuing Studies.

Hopkins began teaching part-time students in 1909. Engineering and business programs were added to the curriculum in 1916. The first graduate degree in business was offered in 1971, and within three years the Division branched out into the Baltimore-Washington corridor with the Columbia, Maryland, Center. Renamed the School of Continuing Studies in 1984, the Division has continued its rapid growth with three additional off-campus centers.

Fifth in the country in population and strategically located on the mid-Atlantic coast, the Baltimore-Washington metropolitan area offers an unmatched array of business and cultural resources and attractions as well as some of the nation's leading institutions of higher learning.

Facilities

The central Hopkins campus, Homewood, is situated on 140 acres in residential north Baltimore. In this traditional academic atmosphere, SCS maintains its administrative offices and the offices of its two other academic units, the Division of Education and the Division of Liberal Arts. The Schools of Arts and Sciences and Engineering and the University's administration also are located at Homewood. The renowned Milton S. Eisenhower Library, as well as a full-service bookstore, post office, cafeteria, and extensive computing and distance learning facilities, are available to students at this location.

In addition to Homewood, Hopkins features four satellite campuses in the Baltimore-Washington metropolitan area. The Downtown Center, located in the heart of Baltimore's business district, houses the offices of the Division of Business and Management. The Columbia Center is centrally located between Baltimore and Washington. The Montgomery County Center is located in Rockville, Maryland, along I-270, just north of the nation's capital. The Washington, D.C., Center is located in the District, near Dupont Circle. All sites feature classrooms, computer labs, conventional and online library resources, a bookstore, academic advising services, and other amenities.

Technology Environment

Hopkins has formed a partnership with the Caliber Learning Network, Inc.^{SM}, to deliver distributed education programs. Caliber classrooms integrate three communication technologies to provide an effective, interactive learning environment. Digital satellite broadcasting delivers the instructor's lecture live to each Caliber classroom. Two-way room-based videoconferencing, with large-screen monitors, enables live, real-time discussions between instructors and students. PCs with local- and wide-area networking enable students to ask further questions of instructors, subject-matter experts, and other students and to view the instructor's course material. Using a center's Internet-enabled workstation or an Internet connection at home or at work, students can log onto Caliber's secure server between class sessions to review notes, ask questions, download required readings, discuss issues with peers, or access the University's Milton S. Eisenhower Library.

Placement

Professional career counselors in the SCS Career and Life Planning Center guide students through the career decision-making process and assist them in the job search. Students have access to services such as computerized guidance and information systems, career planning workshops and panel presentations, a multimedia resource library, job search consultations, networking receptions, a job bank, job fairs, an electronic placement file service, and an electronic resume referral service. Students also are matched with alumni and SCS advisory board members for networking and interviewing.

Admission

To be considered for admission to any degree or certificate program, individuals must submit a formal application (including an essay), official transcripts from all postsecondary institutions attended, and an application fee. Because specific admissions requirements vary by program, applicants should contact the admissions office or appropriate academic division to determine specific admissions criteria, suitability of prior degrees, or certification requirements. Applicants for graduate degrees and certificate programs must hold a bachelor's degree from a regionally accredited college or university.

Finances

Tuition varies from program to program, and within programs themselves, depending upon individual course costs and other specific expenses. Students should contact the admissions office for full information on program and course fees and other costs, including application and registration fees. All tuition and fees must be paid in full at the time of registration; registrations cannot be processed unless accompanied by appropriate payment. Students with employer tuition remission benefits must provide appropriate documentation at the time of registration.

Application Facts and Dates

SCS has a rolling admissions policy, meaning there is no application deadline except for cohort group programs. Individuals should allow from six to eight weeks for completion of the entire admissions process (from submission of the application to admissions decision).

Students should address all correspondence to:

Office of Admissions
School of Continuing Studies
Johns Hopkins University
6740 Alexander Bell Drive
Columbia, Maryland 21046
Telephone: 410-309-1270
Fax: 410-209-0007
E-mail: scsinfo@jhu.edu
World Wide Web: http://www.scs.jhu.edu

Johnson & Wales University

> ### CHALLENGES OF THE YEAR 2000 AND BEYOND
>
> *The Graduate School's commitment to a high-quality advanced career education is the central theme of our vision for the twenty-first century at Johnson & Wales University. It is the forefront of our ongoing investment of time and energy in maintaining the highest standards for our faculty members and curricula in a students-come-first environment.*
>
> —Clif Boyle, Dean

Programs and Curricular Focus

The Graduate School at Johnson & Wales University offers M.B.A.'s in the following areas:

Accounting: The M.B.A. with a concentration in accounting is designed to allow for advanced study in accounting as well as in management. Successful completion of this flexible program will assist individuals who wish to advance into management positions within accounting firms and departments.

Hospitality Administration: The hospitality industry is a rapid-growth segment of the global economy. The M.B.A. degree prepares students for challenging management careers in hotels and hotel-related businesses.

International Business: The M.B.A. in international business program is designed for students who are preparing for careers in multinational firms, internationally oriented financial institutions, and national and international agencies.

Management: The M.B.A. in management allows students to develop managerial competencies with concentrations in the areas of business organizations, financial management, human resource management, and marketing.

The Graduate School also offers an M.S. degree in accounting and instructional technology as well as an M.A. degree in teacher education.

Students and the M.B.A. Experience

The graduate students at Johnson & Wales represent diverse cultural, professional, and academic backgrounds. The average student is 27 years old, with four years of work-related experience. The enrollment mix includes students from fifty-five countries, with women representing 43 percent of the enrollment population. The majority of American students come from the Northeast (52 percent). Another 41 percent of graduate enrollment are international students. Most of the students have undergraduate degrees in business, with many others having backgrounds in education or liberal arts. Employers provide tuition reimbursement for 23 percent of American students, and 68 percent of American students are working while pursuing their graduate studies.

Special Features

There are convenient day and evening classes to accommodate any schedule; accelerated programs that allow a student to graduate in one year; and three terms instead of semesters, allowing the student to complete more courses in less time. There is a diverse student population, representing fifty-five countries; a student-focused faculty with esteemed academic and professional experience; creative tuition-payment arrangements; specialized programs with career opportunities; and an outstanding career-placement department that offers lifetime placement services.

The Faculty

The Graduate School faculty consists of individuals with excellent teaching skills who focus on professional development and provide a learning environment that encourages student participation. The faculty members are selected based on their academic achievements and professional experiences. They are devoted to preparing students for success in the workplace and go through extensive training on working with a diverse student population and staying informed on the latest technology. The graduate faculty members either hold terminal or professional degrees or are working toward these degrees.

The Business School Network
Corporate Partnerships

Johnson & Wales University is continuously expanding its relationship with corporate America. As University guests, local business leaders meet with students to discuss current business trends and developments. Brainstorming and problem-solving skills are sharpened as real-life situations are addressed. As the alumni base grows, many return and discuss how their course work applies to their daily routine.

Prominent Alumni

Johnson & Wales University prides itself on preparing men and women for leadership roles, often as entrepreneurs in business, industry, and education. Alumni hold top positions in a variety of businesses that range from finance to food. Some prominent alumni are Ira Kaplan, President, Servolift Eastern Corporation; Leonard Pinault, President, Foxboro National Bank; Joseph Damore, President, Food Systems IDBA, Inc.; Tracey Trosko, President, First National Network, Inc.; and William Francis, President, Marbil Enterprises, Inc.

The College and Environs

Johnson & Wales University's main campus is located in Providence, Rhode Island. Providence is New England's second-largest city, but it retains its historic charm in combination with the resources of a cultural, business, and industrial center. An hour from the city of Boston, Massachusetts, and less than 4 hours from New York City, Providence is also within easy reach of such well-known vacation spots as Newport, Rhode Island, and Cape Cod, Massachusetts.

A true city campus, Johnson & Wales's facilities are located throughout Providence, a city that provides students with a wide variety of cultural, educational, recreational, and social activities. Students enjoy the local restaurants and shops and are able to take advantage of a

myriad of theater, music, and performance opportunities. From museums to sports events and Broadway shows to shopping, the city offers something for everyone.

Interstate buses and trains are near Johnson & Wales's downtown campus, and the T. F. Green Airport, served by most major U.S. airlines, is adjacent to the J&W's Radisson Airport Hotel in nearby Warwick, Rhode Island.

Technology Environment

The Academic Computer Center in the Xavier Complex features extensive equipment available for student use. Each IBM PS/2 computer features a minimum of 30 megabytes of internal memory. These machines have extensive color graphics capabilities.

The Harborside Computer Lab is made up of two rooms, housing a total of forty-five IBM-compatible machines, fifteen dot-matrix printers, and an NEC Silent Writer 95 laser printer.

Placement

The Career Development Office (CDO) of Johnson & Wales University provides assistance to graduate students as soon as they enroll. The CDO sponsors workshops on resume writing, company

research, and interviewing, as well as guest speakers. A job hotline also provides postings of full- and part-time jobs on and off campus. Ninety-eight percent of Johnson & Wales students find work after college in their chosen field. Global companies such as Walt Disney; hotel chains such as Four Seasons, Marriott, and Hyatt; resorts such as Canyon Ranch; casinos such as Caesars Palace; and well-known companies such as Abraham & Straus have all hired Johnson & Wales students.

Admission

All applicants must submit a signed application, official college transcripts, and three letters of recommendation to the Graduate Admissions Office. In addition, all international students must submit a TOEFL score (unless they wish to be placed in the University's ESL program), a declaration of financial support, and a financial statement that supports the information given in the declaration of financial support.

Finances

Tuition for 1998–99 for day school is $238 per quarter credit hour; for the evening school, it is $194 per quarter credit hour. Foundation courses are $96 per quarter

credit hour. Tuition is subject to change. All master's programs are 54 quarter credits; each course is 4.5 quarter credits. Books and supplies cost approximately $800 per year.

Although most graduate students choose to live in independent housing near the campus, room and board are available for graduate students at the University. The University estimates that living expenses for an academic year for a student living off campus are $7500. For more information about room and board, students should contact the Office of Residential Life (401-598-1132). For assistance and information regarding independent housing, students should contact the Graduate Admissions Office (401-598-1015).

International Students

The uniqueness of Johnson & Wales's Graduate School attracts professionals and students from across the country and around the globe. Forty-one percent of the students attending the Graduate School are international students, representing fifty-five countries. The University offers international students courses in English as a second language, academic counseling, advice on Immigration and Naturalization Service rules, and assistance with off-campus housing. In addition, the University organizes international ambassador and host-family programs and supports international associations.

Application Facts and Dates

Applications are reviewed on a rolling admission basis. Once all application requirements are met, the Graduate Admissions staff takes pride in processing the application materials in a timely manner. Enrollment is very limited, and applicants are encouraged to submit required documents as early as possible for each of the fall, winter, spring, and summer terms. All one-year day school programs start in the fall term only. For more information, students should contact:

Allan G. Freedman
Director, Graduate Admissions
8 Abbott Park Place
Providence, Rhode Island 02903
Telephone: 401-598-1015
Fax: 401-598-4773

Kansas State University

Manhattan, Kansas

NEWLY RESTRUCTURED, NOW INCORPORATING A CAPSTONE BUSINESS PRACTICUM

I eagerly invite you to explore the newly restructured and refocused M.B.A. program offered by Kansas State's (K-State's) College of Business Administration. K-State's M.B.A. degree will provide you with the management skills and business knowledge you need to excel in today's global business environment. Our curriculum combines conceptual, analytical, and experiential approaches to learning both in and out of the classroom. You will face challenges ranging from individual projects and case studies to group projects and practicums, all designed to stretch you to your maximum potential and to prepare you well for the career field you have chosen.

The key to our excellence is our understanding, highly approachable faculty members who pride themselves on working with you as you pursue your course work, tackle your practicum project, engage in your career planning, and manage your job search. All of our graduate faculty members bring their business experiences into the classroom, conduct research, and participate in faculty internships so that you will have access to cutting-edge business theories and processes. As testimony to the outstanding caliber of our M.B.A. program, our College is among the 20 percent of business schools and colleges in the nation that are accredited by AACSB–The International Association for Management Education.

An M.B.A. degree from K-State's College of Business Administration is an investment that will yield high returns for talented, ambitious, and dedicated students. The lifelong benefits of a high-quality education are priceless. We invite you to fully explore our Web site and/or visit us in person.

—Yar M. Ebadi, Dean

Programs and Curricular Focus

The K-State M.B.A. program is 52 credit hours in length and is designed to be completed in two years of full-time study or four years of part-time evening study. The theme of the program is "intrapreneurship," which is defined as "an entrepreneurial attitude and approach to management and problem solving within any organization, large or small." Oral and written communication skills are sharpened throughout the curriculum. The program culminates with a required capstone practicum. Four components comprise the curriculum: the business core (24 credit hours, up to 12 hours of which are waiveable depending on undergraduate course work, that cover basic accounting, economics, statistics, management, marketing, finance, and information systems), the advanced core (12 credit hours that cover the interdisciplinary areas of international business; problem solving; legal, social, and public policy issues; and advanced finance), the integration core (7 credit hours of

strategy with the capstone practicum), and a set of electives/concentration (9 credit hours of any course work of interest or a prespecified set of courses that form a concentration focused on agribusiness, finance, international business, marketing, or management).

The Business Practicum requires teams of students to become consultants and provide recommendations for solving an actual business problem. The course is facilitated by a team of 4 faculty members, one from each department, to ensure that all functional areas of the problem are addressed and analyzed.

A variety of summer internships are available each year for second-year students to gain additional practical experience before graduation.

Students and the M.B.A. Experience

The K-State M.B.A. program is intentionally small to foster close relationships with faculty members and classmates.

Enrollment is capped at 100 full-time equivalent students; up to 50 new students are admitted per year (admission is allowed in the fall and spring semesters). Core class sizes are approximately 35 to 50 students, and elective classes range in size from 10 to 20 students. Approximately 25 percent of M.B.A. students hail from countries other than the United States. In the recent past, students from Canada, Colombia, France, Germany, India, Korea, Nigeria, Panama, South Africa, Taiwan, and Thailand have graduated from the program. About 10 percent of students are members of minority groups, 45 percent are women, and 33 percent are part-time evening students. The average age of students is 27. Approximately 45 percent of students have an undergraduate degree in business, whether from a domestic or international school; the balance of students have backgrounds in engineering, social sciences, agriculture, natural sciences, or the humanities. Several exchange students from Europe, Central America, or South America start the program each year. This breadth of the student body enhances classroom and practicum experiences, as students relate their personal work and/or native country experiences to their fellow students.

The Faculty

The 38 graduate faculty members in the College of Business Administration are committed to high-quality instruction and maintenance of their aggressive research agendas. Because of this research, students receive a cutting-edge business education. Faculty members incorporate the latest advances in classroom technology, from Internet plant tours to simulation competitions. Most importantly, all graduate classes are taught by certified graduate faculty members. Uncertified adjunct professors never teach.

The Business School Network

The College of Business Administration at K-State firmly believes in keeping in constant contact with business constituents to ensure that courses and curricula stay on the cutting edge. The Dean has a well-rounded Advisory Council of top

862

executives from regional firms. In addition, the College has entered into formal partnerships with Payless Shoe-Source, Edward Jones, and Security Benefit, which provide student scholarships and internships, faculty minisabbaticals, executives-in-residence, and regular facility tours. These companies, along with many other area firms, provide opportunities for practicums.

The College and Environs

Kansas State University is located in the city of Manhattan in north-central Kansas, situated in the northern end of the beautiful Flint Hills. It is located 100 miles west of Kansas City on Interstate 70. The city was founded in the first days of Kansas settlement and currently has a population of 44,000 in the city and 100,000 in the immediate region. The nearby Konza Prairie, always available for an exhilarating evening or weekend hike, is the only research tallgrass prairie in existence in North America. Major employers include the Fort Riley Military Reservation, Troy Design and Manufacturing (producers of electric cars), Kansas Farm Bureau, Parker-Hannefin, and Quaker Oats.

Life in Manhattan incorporates a rich variety of cultural experiences. Theatrical performances are sponsored by the McCain Series. The Beach Art Museum houses an extensive collection of Kansas artists' works and hosts traveling collections. The Landon Lecture Series brings world-renowned leaders, such as former presidents Jimmy Carter and Ronald Reagan, the Reverend Jesse Jackson, and General Wojciech Jaruzelski, to campus.

Facilities

The College is located in the newly refurbished Calvin Hall. While the historic native limestone structure is more than 100 years old, it houses state-of-the-art faculty offices, multimedia classrooms, private group-study rooms, comfortable study and snack areas, a boardroom-style conference room, and a computer lab reserved exclusively for College of Business Administration students. A shady, peaceful outdoor courtyard is a popular place for students to meet and relax.

Technology Environment

All faculty and staff offices, five multimedia classrooms, all group-study rooms, and all lab computers are networked via the College's local area network (LAN). Many faculty members place their course notes on the Web. K-State is a member of the Internet 2 Consortium and provides dial-up Internet services to students with a portable or home computer. Direct access is available to the Bloomberg, Compustat, and CRSP financial databases. In collaboration with Hale Library, the College LAN provides access to LEXIS-NEXIS, ABI/INFORM, IAC Business and Company ASAP, and FirstSearch.

Placement

K-State has an outstanding Career and Employment Services Center. It sponsors the area's largest Career Fair every September. At least 300 employers come to campus annually to recruit K-State graduates. With this extensive network of employer links, approximately 85 percent to 90 percent of M.B.A. graduates qualified to work in the United States secure positions before they graduate.

Admission

Applications are welcomed from highly qualified domestic and international students. A minimum 3.0 GPA, 500 GMAT score, and 1150 index score are the academic criteria required for regular admission. The index score is calculated as (200 X GPA) + GMAT. A very limited number of probationary admissions are made if not all three of the minimum criteria are met. International students who meet these academic qualifications but who do not meet the 590 minimum TOEFL score are recommended for admittance to the English Language Program (ELP) on a part- or full-time basis before regular admission is granted.

Finances

Tuition for the 1998–99 academic year is $101 per credit hour for Kansas residents and $329 per credit hour for nonresidents. The estimated total annual costs for tuition, fees, books, housing, health insurance, and personal expenses are $13,000 for Kansas residents and $20,000 for nonresidents.

Merit-based financial assistance is available through scholarships and assistantships. Domestic and international students may apply for the fall semester awards. Deadlines are noted below.

Application Facts and Dates

Fall semester application packets are due March 1 for international applicants and domestic applicants with requests for financial assistance or August 1 for domestic applicants without requests for financial assistance. Spring semester application packets are due September 1 for international applicants and domestic applicants with requests for financial assistance or January 1 for domestic applicants without requests for financial assistance. Summer semester requests for admission are not accepted. The online application is available at http://www.grad.ksu.edu/grad/.

Admission is on a rolling basis, and applicants learn their admission status within three weeks of receipt of their complete application packet. Applicants should send their materials to:

Dr. Cynthia S. McCahon, Director of
    Graduate Studies
110 Calvin Hall
Kansas State University
Manhattan, Kansas 66506-0501
World Wide Web: http://www.cba.ksu.
    edu/grad/grad.htm

Those with questions should contact:
Telephone: 785-532-7190
Fax: 785-532-7216
E-mail: flynn@ksu.edu

KELLER
GRADUATE SCHOOL
OF MANAGEMENT

Keller Graduate School of Management

Master of Business Administration Program

Oakbrook Terrace, Illinois

DEVELOPING BUSINESS LEADERS FOR THE TWENTY-FIRST CENTURY

► *In today's rapidly changing business environment, a manager's responsibilities are becoming increasingly complex. Technological advances, increasing demographic diversity, and global competition have prompted an ever-growing need for professionally trained managers in all fields.*

A Keller M.B.A. equips you with everything you need to meet those business challenges, including dynamic instruction by a faculty of professionals with proven success in the business world. A national leader in postgraduate education designed for working professionals, Keller teaches you to apply management theories and concepts to the realities of everyday business operations. The result? Better managers and more profitable businesses.

—Timothy H. Ricordati, Dean

Programs and Curricular Focus

Geared toward working adults, Keller teaches students to master the special skills and concepts businesses demand from today's management professionals. Students, and their employers, can rest assured that those who have graduated from Keller's M.B.A. program are able to blend management theory with real-world applications in a multitude of business settings.

Each Keller M.B.A. student receives a solid background in every important business discipline. Keller also builds flexibility into that sturdy foundation by offering a wide range of electives. That way, students can customize their degree to suit personal and professional interests.

The Keller M.B.A. program requires students to complete sixteen courses of 4 quarter credit hours each. There are five management core courses: Principles of Accounting and Finance, Applied Managerial Statistics and Quality, Leadership and Organizational Behavior, Managerial Applications of Information Technology, and Marketing Management. Five program-specific courses are Managerial Accounting; Managerial Finance; Legal, Political and Ethical Dimensions of Business; Economics; and the Business Planning Seminar. Finally, students may choose from six electives in any functional area, including accounting, human resources management, finance, information systems, general management, marketing, health services management, and project management.

Keller also offers the Master of Accounting and Financial Management,

the Master of Human Resource Management, the Master of Project Management, and the Master of Telecommunications Management degrees.

Class hours are designed to accommodate work and family responsibilities. Keller offers five 10-week terms each year. Classes meet once a week for 3½ hours, either on weekday evenings or Saturdays.

Keller's twenty-four nationwide locations enable students to continue their education after job transfers, temporary assignments, or other relocations with the least possible disruption to their academic schedules.

Students and the M.B.A. Experience

Keller students are working adults who bring their diverse experiences to the classroom. They want, and insist on, useful and relevant instruction. At Keller, knowledge is meant to be practiced in real-world situations, and that "practitioner orientation" colors everything that is done at the School. Whatever their ultimate career goals, students come to Keller for flexible, personalized instruction that equips them for the challenges of a complex, competitive, and rapidly changing working environment.

Nearly 6,000 professionals nationwide have turned to Keller for their advanced business education. A bachelor's degree in business is not required to enter the program; more than half of all Keller students hold undergraduate degrees in nonbusiness fields.

The Faculty

Keller faculty members practice what they teach. They are working professionals who deal with cutting-edge business and management issues both inside and outside the classroom. They bring their expertise to the classroom, emphasizing theories, practices, and issues that most benefit students in the working world. At Keller, it is believed that when students learn from instructors who work in the field in which they teach, they get as close to real-world learning as possible.

The Business School Network

Keller's faculty consists of practicing business professionals—leaders in the corporate community as well as in the classroom. These professionals bring business contacts as well as hands-on knowledge and experience to Keller's students.

Keller's faculty includes both part- and full-time instructors who are effective communicators, coaches, and mentors as well as practitioners with extensive management experience. Those who teach full-time commit most of their working hours to teaching and curricula development while remaining actively involved in business as consultants and participants in professional organizations. Part-time instructors are full-time managers whose teaching provides adult students with vital professional enrichment and perspectives. All faculty members have developed contacts and relationships with a variety of academic and professional fields and geographic locations. The relationships students develop with these instructors often lead to mentoring arrangements, professional contacts, and even job offers.

The College and Environs

Keller was founded in 1973 on the idea that the most important components of management education are effective teaching and student mastery of practical management skills. Keller's twenty-four educational centers in eight states are home to a diverse faculty and student body with a variety of backgrounds and experience. Because of students' multiple real-world demands, Keller centers are in major metropolitan areas and near

accessible transportation routes, keeping commuting time to a minimum. These centers' locations include Mesa and Phoenix, Arizona; Irvine, Long Beach, San Diego, and Pomona, California; Alpharetta, Atlanta, and Decatur, Georgia; Chicago Loop, Lisle, Orland Park, Schaumburg, Elgin, Lincolnshire, and Oakbrook in Illinois; Kansas City downtown, Kansas City south, St. Louis west, and St. Louis downtown in Missouri; Milwaukee and Waukesha, Wisconsin; and Tysons Corner, Virginia.

Facilities

Keller's multiple locations offer a variety of accommodations, and they all provide comfortable areas in which to study, relax, and learn. Most centers include spacious classrooms in handy locations, vending areas, student lounges, and convenient hours for computer labs and

information centers. The information centers offer Internet access to 300 databases, alternative texts, student study guides, career service materials, and periodicals.

Placement

Keller Career Services Department helps management-level students and graduates find jobs in accounting, finance, general management, health services, human resources, information systems, manufacturing, marketing, project management, and sales.

Admission

For regular admission, applicants must hold a baccalaureate degree from a U.S. institution accredited by, or in candidacy status with, a regional accrediting agency recognized by the U.S. Department of

Education (international applicants must hold a degree equivalent to a U.S. baccalaureate degree); pass the Graduate Management Admission Test or the Graduate Record Examinations or Keller's alternative admission test; complete a personal interview with an admissions representative; and complete a written application.

Applicants with postbaccalaureate degrees from accredited graduate schools must complete an application and an interview as well as document their degree. However, they do not need to take an admissions test.

Keller's application process is streamlined, so students learn quickly whether they've been accepted.

Finances

Tuition per course (4 quarter credit hours) differs by state, ranging from $955 to $1170. After acceptance into Keller, new students pay a $100 tuition deposit, which is credited toward the first term's tuition. Tuition is payable in full at registration or in installments of two or three payments (with small handling fees for the latter two choices). Books and materials average $75 per course.

Application Facts and Dates

Keller holds five 10-week terms each year. They begin in September, November, February, April, and June. Students may begin their program with any term. There is no application fee. For more information, students should contact:

Keller Graduate School of
    Management
One Tower Lane, 9th Floor
Oakbrook Terrace, Illinois 60181
Telephone: 630-571-1818

Kennesaw State University

Kennesaw, Georgia

MAXIMIZE THE RETURN ON YOUR INVESTMENT

Obtaining an M.B.A. that is accredited by AACSB–The International Association for Management Education is a challenging, invigorating, and rewarding endeavor. People who invest their time and money to attend such programs are increasingly asking about "bottom-line benefits." "What am I going to gain by attending this program?" Sponsoring companies are asking similar questions. "What are the benefits of sending someone to such a program?" At Kennesaw State University (KSU) we have directed our efforts toward ensuring that associates in the M.B.A. program maximize the return on their investment.

The Coles College M.B.A. is an innovative, interactive, integrated program that incorporates real-life experiences into every component. The program is process-oriented rather than functionally oriented and taught in a team environment that simulates the workplace. Individuals completing the program become complete managers and leaders with new ideas, broad perspectives, international business savvy, technology awareness, and an expanded international business network.

We look forward to sharing a learning experience with you and to helping you prepare for an ever-changing, global, competitive future.

—Timothy S. Mescon, Dean

Programs and Curricular Focus

Participants in the Coles College M.B.A. Program don't expect results, they demand them. That's why many have chosen to attend this program. They are looking for fresh new ideas and the opportunity to build skills that can be applied directly to their organizations. Kennesaw State meets these demands by structuring its program to facilitate and encourage the exchange of ideas and problem-solving techniques—real-world, real-business, real-results. Participants leave every class, every meeting, and every function with information, insights, and abilities they can use to make a difference in their own—and their companies'—performance. In this rapidly changing global environment, those using old techniques and old ways will be left behind. Only fresh new approaches and ideas can provide the power and leverage needed to meet the challenges facing businesses today.

Teamwork is a vital component of the learning process at the Coles College of Business. Indeed, one challenge that the College accepts is to most closely emulate the challenges and opportunities that students face in the world of work in the private and public sectors. To this end, it has structured a highly concentrated 36-semester-hour, twelve-course program that enables students to master the core body of graduate business education as well as to select from one of ten leading-edge program concentrations.

The core competency sequence includes course work in managerial accounting, managerial economics, financial analysis and decision making, operations management, management and organizational behavior, marketing management, and corporate strategy. In addition, all students select at least one international core course from a number that are available.

In the latter half of the program, students select a major concentration from one of ten areas. Students immerse themselves in one of these majors by completing four courses, 12 semester hours, in a disciplined area of study. M.B.A. major options available to Coles College students include accounting, business administration, business economics, information systems, entrepreneurship, finance, human resources management and development, and marketing. A range of just-in-time course options are available to provide Coles College students with the latest theory and practice in all of the aforementioned optional courses of study.

The Coles College M.B.A. program is offered in the evenings and on weekends; therefore, it particularly appeals to

working professionals or full-time students committed to utilizing their days for internships or research and study. All graduate and undergraduate business programs at the Coles College of Business are fully accredited by AACSB–The International Association for Management Education.

Students and the M.B.A. Experience

The approximately 1,100 graduate students at the Coles College bring a variety of backgrounds and experiences, and academic and cultural diversity, to the M.B.A. program. The average student is a 30-year-old with six years of full-time professional work experience. Women comprise approximately one half of the graduate student population, and members of minority groups represent about 10 percent. Approximately 60 percent of Coles College M.B.A. students have baccalaureate degrees in business, but a number have completed undergraduate studies in engineering, liberal arts, and the sciences. About 10 percent of KSU's students are international, coming from more than 102 nations.

❖ Global Focus

The faculty members in the Coles College of Business are committed to internationalizing the curriculum through ongoing research, development, and travel. In the past few years alone, faculty members have served as guest lecturers or conducted sophisticated research projects in Australia, Canada, China, India, Korea, Mexico, Poland, Romania, Russia, and South Africa. In addition, students always have the option to complete up to three courses for credit at international universities or term-long exchange or travel programs.

Special Features

The Tetley Distinguished Leader Lecture Series brings an array of chief executive officers to campus throughout the academic year. During their visit to the Coles College, these leaders and entrepreneurs formally address students and the faculty and then interact with students in a more casual setting. Endowed by Tetley Tea, this

series has attracted distinguished leaders from business, industry, and the nonprofit sector, including, among others, Bernard Marcus and Arthur Blank, cofounders of The Home Depot; Jerry Dempsey, Chairman, PPG Industries; Thomas Wheeler, President and CEO, Mass Mutual; and A. D. Correll, Chairman, Georgia-Pacific.

The Faculty

The Coles College of Business is proud of the fact that its 85 full-time, tenure-track faculty members are committed to a balance of teaching, scholarship, and service. Across each of the Coles College's four academic departments, the faculty members represent a unique blend of gifted instructors who successfully meld issues in the world of work with leading-edge theory and practice. The College has been cited for its commitment to diversity and has a distinctive number of faculty members across all disciplines, providing a truly global focus. Women represent more than 30 percent of the faculty in the Coles College of Business.

The College and Environs

Kennesaw State University is nestled on 200 acres in suburban Atlanta, just 25 minutes north of downtown. Because access to the campus is directly off Interstate 75 north, students have the opportunity to live in a variety of convenient locations throughout the Atlanta area. The University is part of the University System of Georgia and was founded in 1963. With a student population in excess of 13,000, KSU offers instruction through five colleges and schools in more than fifty fields.

The metropolitan Atlanta area is headquarters to a number of Fortune 500

companies and is North American and regional headquarters to a number of other leading multinational organizations.

Facilities

The Coles College is housed in the 110,000-square-foot state-of-the-art A. L. Burruss Building, with tiered lecture halls, networked computer labs, and all faculty and administrative offices. The College's Sturgis Library is considered by many to be among the finest in the nation for online access to periodicals, databases, and network services. A charter member of SOLINET and a member of the Online Computer Library Center, Sturgis Library is part of an international network of libraries. Faculty members and students have access to Galileo, a Web-based system that ensures access to a core of research materials. Sturgis Library houses 550,000 volumes of books and government documents, 3,300 serial publications, and a million pieces of microform.

Technology Environment

The Coles College faculty is committed to leveraging technology. To this end, students find numerous computer applications utilized throughout the curriculum. In addition, networked labs are available in the College for M.B.A. student use. In collaboration with the Sturgis Library, students have online access to LEXIS-NEXIS and NAARS as well as dozens of other online services.

Placement

Kennesaw State and the Coles College of Business are proud of the services offered through Career Services, which works diligently to secure strong linkages with on-campus recruiters and to assist students in developing other professional contacts and resources. Career Services regularly secures interview schedules with leading local, regional, national, and multinational employers. Regular seminars and workshops are offered to students to refine interviewing and presentation skills. Career Services is a national leader in the utilization of technology to assist M.B.A. students in recognizing their career goals. A few technology-based programs that are available to M.B.A. students include resume expert; KSU JOBS, a job networking system of positions specifically available to Kennesaw State students; and National Employment Wire Service, NEWS, which lists current job opportunities and positions throughout the United States.

Admission

To be admitted unconditionally to the M.B.A. program, an applicant must satisfy standards involving the following predictors of success: the adjusted GPA, GMAT or GRE scores, and work experience. An

applicant is required to have an adjusted undergraduate GPA (UGPA) of at least 2.75 on a 4.0 scale plus a total score of at least 450 on the GMAT or a total score of at least 1350 on the General Test of the GRE. Also, the applicant should have a minimum of two years of work experience for unconditional admission to the M.B.A. program. In reviewing the academic work of applicants, the Admissions Committee evaluates the junior/senior adjusted GPA for all applicants. In cases where the applicant has done additional accredited undergraduate work beyond the bachelor's degree or has done accredited graduate work, the most recent two-year adjusted GPA is used in the admissions consideration. Applicants to the M.B.A. program who are deficient in one or more of the required criteria may be admitted with provisional standing. To be eligible for provisional standing, a student must have either a minimum undergraduate cumulative GPA of 3.0 or a minimum score of 500 on the GMAT or 1500 on the GRE. A score of at least 550 on the TOEFL is required for all students for whom English is not the native language.

Finances

In 1998–99, tuition and fees for students taking fewer than 12 credit hours are $78 per credit hour for Georgia residents and $207 per credit hour for nonresidents. Georgia residents who take more than 12 hours pay $928 in tuition and fees per semester; nonresidents, $2460 per semester. There are two semesters during the standard academic year and a third, summer session.

Loans and scholarships are available on both a merit- and a need-based analysis through the Office of Financial Aid. Various alternatives are available to international students as well.

Application Facts and Dates

The Coles College of Business admits qualified students to the M.B.A. program for study in the fall, spring, or summer terms. Approximate application deadlines are July 15, November 15, and April 7, respectively, in any given year. For more information, students should contact:

Michael J. Coles College of Business
Graduate Business Programs
Kennesaw State University
1000 Chastain Road
Kennesaw, Georgia 30144-5591
Telephone: 770-423-6050
Fax: 770-423-6141
E-mail: gselden@ksumail.kennesaw.
  edu
World Wide Web: http://coles.
  kennesaw.edu

Lake Forest Graduate School of Management

Chicago, Lake Forest, and Schaumburg, Illinois

LEARNING FOR LEADERSHIP

At the Lake Forest Graduate School of Management, we believe that the business leaders of the future need skills that are relevant and immediately applicable to today's evolving business environment. With leading executives in industry and the nonprofit world serving as our faculty, our Executive MBA Program offers professional, motivated adult students a solid grounding in business theory, with a strong focus on business application.

All of our courses feature a supportive learning environment—one in which resources, guidance, and classroom activities are conducive to students' developing the competence and confidence with which they can make significant contributions to their organizations. LFGSM's unique offerings in the area of international management attract many Chicago-area professionals who have seen others in their organizations grow and succeed as a result of their participation in our program, in the international courses in particular. The learning environment, along with the focus on real business issues and skills, are key elements of our pragmatic, results-oriented approach to business education known as "Leadership Learning^sm."

Students grow professionally and personally in this dynamic, interactive learning environment where the business leaders of today are mentors to the business leaders of tomorrow.

—John N. Popoli, Vice President and Academic Dean

Programs and Curricular Focus

The Executive Master's in Business Administration Program consists of a standard sequence of sixteen courses (including three electives). Each course in the sequence draws upon and integrates skills and knowledge from the courses that precede it. Each course meets for ten weeks. The program can be completed in either two or four years. Classes meet on weekday evenings or on Saturdays.

Courses are taught by professionals who bring the realities of business from the boardroom to the classroom. The School employs a diverse seminar approach that includes case studies and simulations, lectures, videotape analyses, and team projects, exposing each candidate to a full spectrum of viewpoints and methodologies. The blending of solid business theory with practical experience makes what students learn in the classroom applicable the very next day.

The Lake Forest Graduate School of Management (LFGSM) is accredited by the North Central Association of Colleges and Schools at the graduate level and is authorized to grant master's degrees by the Illinois Board of Higher Education.

Students and the M.B.A. Experience

LFGSM students are a diverse group of experienced, working adults who have made career advancement a priority. Thirty-five percent are female. The average student is 33 years old and has been employed for eleven years in a management or management-track position by a Chicago-area corporation.

Students share experiences and business problems that often serve as topics of discussion in classes. Study teams meet informally as needed for collaborative learning purposes and networking.

❖ Global Focus

The LFGSM curriculum assumes every manager needs a broad knowledge of international management issues to succeed. The core course International Management is a requirement for all students and addresses the impact of cultural, economic, political, and other variables on global and domestic businesses.

In addition, each year current students and alumni have the opportunity for an

in-depth look at international management practices and international cultures through the elective study-abroad courses. Students gain insight into the challenges facing international business and develop a different perspective on business in the United States. Each study-abroad course features group assignments that examine issues particular to the region.

International Management—A Western European Perspective is offered during the summer and includes business visits in Paris and London, culminating with classes at Fitzwilliam College at Cambridge University in England, with introductory sessions in Paris, France.

International Management—An Eastern European Perspective is offered during the fall and provides students with first-hand information on doing business in the emerging, free-market economy of Eastern Europe. The course includes classes at the Czech Management Center and business visits in Vilnius, Lithuania; Warsaw, Poland; and Prague, Czech Republic.

International Management—An Asian-Pacific Perspective is offered during the spring and includes classes at Nanyang Technological University as

Students and instructors in the *International Management: An Asian-Pacific Perspective* program pose before the Temple of the Emerald Buddha at the Emperor's Grand Palace in Bangkok, Thailand.

well as business and cultural visits in Singapore and Bangkok, Thailand. The challenges of Southeast Asia as an emerging free-market region are addressed in terms of development, economy, and growth.

The Faculty

Faculty members are active participants in the business world who bring their daily experiences and know-how to the classroom. At LFGSM, professionals teach professionals. Students experience a microcosm of the business world in every class. The faculty members create a supportive learning environment that gives students the opportunity to work with new ideas and skills under conditions that provoke thought and experimentation.

More than half of the faculty members hold or have held titles of CEO, President, CFO, Vice President, Partner, Treasurer, Controller, or General Counsel in their companies. Others are successful directors, business consultants, and functional specialists. Each has a minimum of a master's degree and fifteen years of professional work experience.

The Business School Network

LFGSM was founded in 1946 as a partnership between business and education and has maintained close ties with the business community. More than 4,500 alumni, 875 students, and 150 faculty members work for some of Chicago's finest companies, such as Abbott Laboratories; Motorola, Inc.; W. W. Grainger, Inc.; Baxter International; Fel-Pro, Inc.; Kraft Foods, Inc.; and many others. An active board of directors comprising 26 Chicago-area executives actively spearheads new programs and development in addition to strategic planning and policy making.

LFGSM is active in the business community, providing needs assessment and leadership training for corporate managers through the School's Leadership Education Advancing Performance Program (LEAP).

The College and Environs

LFGSM maintains three full-service campus locations, with computers available at each location. The Lake Forest campus provides a modern atmosphere on the traditional grounds of Lake Forest College.

Vice President and Academic Dean, John N. Popoli.

The Chicago campus is located in the Federal Reserve Bank Building, especially convenient for those students who work downtown.

The Schaumburg campus is housed on the campus of Motorola, Inc., at the Galvin Center.

Placement

LFGSM students are actively employed at the time of acceptance. The School offers a placement network only for students and alumni who become unemployed. This network helps students and alumni write resumes and work on interviewing skills and acts as a support group.

Admission

Applicants are considered for admission in three quarters: fall, winter, and spring. LFGSM requires a bachelor's degree and undergraduate transcripts, GMAT or GRE scores, a letter of recommendation from the immediate supervisor, and an interview with an admissions representative.

While undergraduate grades and entrance exam scores are a factor, LFGSM places an even greater emphasis

on the student's current achievements and future prospects. Applicants must demonstrate communication and leadership skills and the ability to work productively in an organization and in a team environment in addition to having at least four years of work experience.

Applicants who do not hold an advanced degree (minimum bachelor's or equivalent) from a U.S. or other English-speaking college or university will be required to either take the GMAT with writing section or produce an equivalent writing sample privately proctored at LFGSM.

Finances

Tuition for the 1998–99 academic year is $1575 per course, which includes books and computer software. A majority of LFGSM students receive tuition reimbursement from their employers.

LFGSM provides some private scholarship assistance to qualified individuals. LFGSM is also a participant in the Federal Family Educational Loan Program, which provides students with subsidized and unsubsidized Federal Stafford Student Loans. The School is approved for educational aid to eligible veterans by the state approving agency. Details about scholarships and other independent educational loan programs are available from the Business Office (847-234-5005).

Application Facts and Dates

Application deadlines for the M.B.A. program are August 7 for the fall start, January 8 for the winter start, and March 26 for the spring start. The application fee is $35. For further information about the M.B.A. program, students should contact:

Ms. Kristin Kraai-Keely
Director of Admissions, Chicago Campus
The Lake Forest Graduate School of Management
176 West Jackson Boulevard
Chicago, Illinois 60604
Telephone: 312-435-5330
Fax: 312-435-5333
E-mail: admiss@lfgsm.edu
World Wide Web: http://www.lfgsm.edu

Lake Superior State University

Sault Sainte Marie, Michigan

LEADING BUSINESS INTO THE TWENTY-FIRST CENTURY

▶ *Maintaining the competitive edge—that's what business needs to do if it is to succeed and flourish in the twenty-first century. Global competition, efficient operation, and cost-effective management are keys to a successful transition into the next millennium. Students in Lake Superior State University's M.B.A. program are immersed in sound theory and practice for successful business administration. Graduates take their place among the leaders in business, manufacturing, and education.*

—Ray Adams, Dean, College of Engineering, Mathematics and Business

Programs and Curricular Focus

The Master of Business Administration program at Lake Superior State University (LSSU) offers general business education to students from diverse academic backgrounds. The program develops and enhances leadership skills for early and midcareer managers. Cultural and international diversity characterizes the students.

The M.B.A. program at LSSU reflects a realistic approach to graduate management education. Courses tend to be more applied and practical, for the practicing manager. The evening and weekend format of course offerings is tailored for the employed person.

The curriculum includes 24 semester credits of preparatory courses in economics, statistics, law, accounting, finance, management, and marketing. All or part of these requirements may be waived on the basis of successful completion of equivalent undergraduate courses. Students also have the opportunity to earn credit by examination in these preparatory courses.

Upon completion of the preparatory courses, 36 additional semester credits are required. Of these 36 credits, 21 consist of the required Professional Component and 15 credits are elective courses. The Professional Component courses include managerial economics, research techniques, managerial accounting and control, financial management, administrative policy, organizational behavior, and marketing management. A wide variety of electives is available to suit the individual needs of M.B.A. students.

Students and the M.B.A. Experience

Students in Lake Superior State's M.B.A. program bring with them a diverse background in academics and work experience. Approximately half of the incoming students have undergraduate preparation in the liberal arts, science, or technology and the other half have business and economics backgrounds. They range in age from 22 to 50 years, with an average age of 35. The ratio of male to female is 1:1. Virtually all of LSSU's M.B.A. students are employed while they pursue their studies. They average five years of work experience in business, government, education, the nonprofit sector, and Native American tribal administration.

The Faculty

The M.B.A. faculty is responsible for the governance and curriculum of the M.B.A. program. The faculty in the M.B.A. program includes full-time faculty members from the School of Business as well as graduate faculty members from other institutions and qualified business practitioners. They bring a diverse perspective, both theoretical and practical, to the classroom.

The Business School Network

An M.B.A. Advisory Council assists the University in curriculum development and serves as a liaison between the M.B.A. program and the area it serves. The council is composed of business executives, corporate recruiters, and alumni who help M.B.A. faculty and staff members to be sensitive to current trends in business and to the evolving needs of professional development.

The College and Environs

Lake Superior State is the newest of Michigan's fifteen state universities. The site of the University was originally Fort Brady, an army outpost first established in 1822. In 1946, the fort was deactivated and the facilities became the home of the Sault Ste. Marie branch of the Michigan College of Mining and Technology (now Michigan Technological University). The Michigan legislature granted "Sault Tech" autonomy in 1966, creating Lake Superior State College. Its first baccalaureate degrees were offered in 1969, and in 1987 the Legislature changed the name to Lake Superior State University. Today, more than 3,500 undergraduate and graduate students pursue their studies at LSSU.

Lake Superior State University's beautiful 125-acre campus overlooks the Michigan and Ontario twin cities of Sault Ste. Marie, the second-oldest settlement in North America, founded in 1668; the St. Mary's River, which forms the border between the U.S. and Canada; and the world famous Soo Locks, which link Lake Huron and the mighty Lake Superior.

Facilities

The University Library provides a wide variety of resources and services for students and the faculty. It contains more than 126,000 volumes, 16,000 bound volumes of periodicals, 75,000 microforms, and more than 40,000 paper government documents. The current subscription list exceeds 1,000 individual titles. To assist faculty members and students in obtaining materials from other libraries, LSSU maintains an interlibrary loan service through OCLC, a computer service linked to libraries throughout the United States with access to more than 19 million books and periodicals.

The James Norris Physical Education Center features an ice arena, three gymnasiums, swimming and diving pools, handball-racquetball courts, a dance studio, a shooting range, wrestling and weight training rooms, eight outdoor tennis courts, a softball diamond, a soccer field, and a six-lane, all-weather quarter-mile track.

Technology Environment

Students at Lake Superior State University utilize a wide variety of computer services. Computer laboratories with more than 200 personal computers are available in several locations, most with Internet access. Network access to a DEC MicroVax 3400 mainframe, various departmental computer labs, a computerized library reference system, and informational databases on CD-ROM are also available.

Placement

Lake Superior State University maintains a centralized career planning and placement service for alumni and graduates. The function of the Office of Career Planning and Placement is to assist students in locating suitable and desirable employment. This is accomplished by arranging interviews with representatives of schools, business, industry, and government agencies; by mailing employment credentials to prospective employers; and by notifying graduates of employment opportunities. Regular contact is maintained with employers both on and off campus in an effort to promote their interest in employing Lake Superior State University students.

Admission

Admission to the M.B.A. Program is based on possession of a recognized baccalaureate degree, comprising a minimum of 120 semester credits, from an accredited college or university; two letters of recommendation, with one preferably from an academic source and one required from an employer or supervisor; completion of the application form; official transcripts of all previous postsecondary work, with certified translations for non-English transcripts, from which an undergraduate grade point average can be computed (to be considered official, transcripts must be sent directly from the former institution(s) to LSSU); and scores for the Graduate Management Admissions Test (GMAT) taken within the past five years. Applicants must also have a minimum of 1000 points using Formula 1 (200 x GPA + GMAT score ≥ 1000) based on their GPA (4.0 scale) from the last 60 semester credits of undergraduate work or they must have a minimum of 950 points using Formula 2 (200 x GPA + GMAT score ≥ 950) based on their GPA (4.0 scale) for all undergraduate work. For full admission, a minimum score of 28 for the quantitative GMAT score and 25 for the verbal GMAT score are required. Applicants who do not receive the minimum quantitative or verbal scores will be required to complete additional preparatory work for full admission. Students whose first language is not English must submit an official Test of English as a Foreign Language (TOEFL) report or its equivalent. This report will be used solely for diagnostic purposes and is not a factor affecting admissibility to the program.

Finances

The graduate tuition rate for the 1998–99 academic year is $171.75 per credit hour. The same rate applies to in-state or out-of-state students. Approximate costs for room and board are $2500 per semester.

Most M.B.A. students are employed full-time and attending the University on a part-time basis. Consequently, most M.B.A. students do not receive financial aid. Graduate assistantships are not offered; however, the University does offer a wide variety of financial aid programs based on financial need.

International Students

Because of Lake Superior State's location on the international border between Sault Ste. Marie, Michigan, and Sault Ste. Marie, Ontario, Canada, a large number of M.B.A. students are Canadian. This provides an excellent opportunity for students to compare differing economic and business environments and to appreciate the diversity that such proximity provides. In addition to the large Canadian contingent, LSSU has also hosted students from other countries. These students further contribute to the international flavor of LSSU's M.B.A. program.

Application Facts and Dates

Applications for the M.B.A. Program are accepted any time throughout the year for admission in the fall, spring, or summer semesters. Those seeking admission into the M.B.A. program must submit all required application materials along with a $25 (U.S.) nonrefundable application fee. Applications and other materials should be sent to:

Lake Superior State University
Office of Admissions
650 West Easterday
Sault Ste. Marie, Michigan 49783
Telephone: 906-635-2231
       888-800-LSSU Ext. 2231
       (toll-free in the U.S. and
       Canada)
Fax: 906-635-6669
World Wide Web: http://www.lssu.edu

Lehigh University

THE PERFECT FIT FOR STUDENTS WHO MEAN BUSINESS

This is an exciting time to begin pursuing your M.B.A. at Lehigh University. Our new, innovative M.B.A. core allows students to integrate not only their course work but their professional experiences as well. Classes are designed to focus on the effects of business problems and opportunities from the perspective of the firm as a whole. All core classes are interdisciplinary and are taught by a faculty team committed to excellence in the M.B.A. Program. Our highly experienced students share their knowledge through class discussions and team assignments, which provide exposure to a wide variety of business practices.

Students who mean business—about their careers, about learning, and about contributing to the education of their classmates—will find Lehigh's M.B.A. the perfect fit.

—Patti Ota, Dean

Programs and Curricular Focus

Lehigh's M.B.A. Program focuses on the impact of business problems and solutions on all areas of the company. Business issues are viewed and taught from the perspective of the firm as a whole rather than along departmental lines, and each course is team taught by faculty members from several different disciplines. The 36-credit-hour M.B.A. Program begins with a two-day weekend orientation. The core consists of four interdisciplinary modules and ends with a capstone industry project. Students are encouraged to design industry projects within their own firms or with a corporate partner. This approach provides the opportunity to apply the body of knowledge acquired in the core and provides added exposure for the students within their own firms, possibly in business areas outside their current positions.

Due to the compact and integrated core, students have increased flexibility to tailor the program to their individual needs. Students may select a concentration in finance, international business, management, management of technology, or marketing or pursue a broader experience by selecting courses from a variety of disciplines.

Effective oral and written communication skills and leadership ability have become important keys to success in business. Using case studies, group projects, and a team approach to learning, Lehigh's curriculum helps students experience the dynamics of group

behavior in organizations and teaches methods used to motivate workers and resolve conflicts.

Lehigh students bring a rich depth of experience in a variety of industries and disciplines into the classroom. Students have an average of eight years of work experience, and 20 percent have master's degrees or doctorates in areas other than business. Class discussions encourage students to share these experiences, which broadens their knowledge base by exposure to a variety of practices within business and industry.

Lehigh's M.B.A. Program has been accredited by AACSB–The International Association for Management Education for more than thirty years and provides the cornerstone for career advancement.

Students and the M.B.A. Experience

Lehigh's 375 M.B.A. students come from a variety of academic and professional backgrounds, have achieved distinction academically and/or professionally, are highly committed, and bring a wide range of qualities to the program.

Thirty-five percent of M.B.A. students come from undergraduate backgrounds in business and economics, 55 percent from engineering and applied science, and 10 percent from liberal arts. Women comprise about 30 percent of the M.B.A. population, and 95 percent have full-time professional work experience.

Eighty-five percent of Lehigh M.B.A. students attend classes part-time and are

an important part of the learning environment. Their business experience and sense of purpose enhance the educational experience of all students.

Special Features

The MBA*Plus* program gives Lehigh's M.B.A. graduates the opportunity to enroll in current courses at less than one third of the regular cost. Graduates gain ongoing, cost-effective access to courses that can enhance their professional development and advance their careers; they are able to keep current in their fields and acquire new skills.

The Faculty

Excellent teaching is a hallmark of business education at Lehigh, with 98 percent of the College of Business and Economics' 57 full-time faculty members holding doctoral degrees. Faculty members play an important role in the educational and research activities of interdisciplinary centers and institutes both inside and outside of Lehigh, which ensures that students receive exposure to the latest information. Students are also exposed to the applications experience of carefully chosen business practitioners.

The Iacocca Institute and the College's six centers complement the activities of its academic departments. They host conferences and visiting experts, sponsor faculty and student research, and provide services to business firms and the educational community.

The Business School Network

Corporate Partnerships

Lehigh maintains extensive relationships with the corporate community. The Business Advisory Council is made up of highly accomplished business leaders who are active in committees on curriculum, alumni relations, and distance learning. The Council provides a direct link between the College of Business and Economics and the business world. Members are among the visiting executives who interact with students in conferences, major lectures, classroom sessions, and informal discussions.

Rauch Business Center.

Lehigh's distance learning initiative enables employees of its partners to complete a Lehigh M.B.A. while taking their classes at the corporate site. These students interact with the class on campus through voice communication, a computer message center, fax, and interactive white boards.

The Small Business Development Center (SBDC) provides opportunities for students to serve as business analysts, providing consulting services for small- and medium-sized businesses in northeast Pennsylvania. M.B.A. students also may complete field projects with SBDC's clients and the International Trade Development Program.

The College and Environs

Lehigh University, founded in 1865, consists of three distinctive, contiguous areas totaling more than 1,600 acres. Located 90 miles southwest of New York City and 50 miles north of Philadelphia, the Lehigh Valley is Pennsylvania's fourth-largest metropolitan area. Bethlehem, one of the three principal cities of the Lehigh Valley, is a center of industry, high technology, culture, and education.

Facilities

The Rauch Business Center, headquarters of the College of Business and Economics, is a modern, dynamic, professional environment for learning and teaching. There are forty well-equipped classrooms, computer labs, an auditorium, and conference rooms with advanced computing and audio-visual capabilities.

The Clayton Conference Center wing has excellent facilities for executive education programs, conferences, seminars, and other special programs.

Technology Environment

Along with books and journals, Lehigh's library system includes electronic data bases and microfilm, computer software, and media collections. Via the campus-wide integrated voice and data communication network, users can access the Internet, the World Wide Web, the libraries' online catalog, and hundreds of national and international electronic databases and can submit reference inquiries, place orders, request media services, and request delivery of documents electronically.

The campus network provides access to mainframe computers, the Integrated Library System, and other computers on campus. The Computing Center houses several mainframes and maintains hundreds of microcomputers in sites across campus.

Placement

Lehigh has a long tradition of producing successful business leaders and supports an active recruiting effort. A wide variety of corporations and government agencies recruit M.B.A.'s through on-campus interviews, which are conducted in the fall and spring. Career prospects for graduates of Lehigh's graduate management programs are excellent.

The Office of Career Services offers a full range of services to support students' career search efforts. Professional career counselors are available to help students define career goals and initiate the job search process.

Admission

Candidates must have completed an undergraduate program at an accredited U.S. college or university. International students must have sixteen years of formal education, including four years at the university level. A TOEFL score is required of all applicants for whom English is not the native language. The credentials evaluated by the faculty admission committee include the candidate's undergraduate background, GMAT scores, personal essay, letters of recommendation, and relevant professional work experience.

Finances

Tuition charges for the 1998–99 academic year are $600 per credit hour. Apartment costs range from $365 per month for an efficiency apartment to $500 per month for a three-bedroom apartment.

Several types of financial aid are available, including M.B.A. Scholarships, teaching assistantships (which cover tuition and pay a stipend of $10,000 for the academic year), and business analyst posts in the Small Business Development Center and in Competitive Technologies. Those wishing to be considered for financial aid should submit all application materials, including GMAT scores, by February 1 for aid in the following academic year.

Application Facts and Dates

Lehigh evaluates applications on a rolling basis and usually notifies applicants of admission decisions within three weeks of receiving a completed application. Deadlines for regular students are July 15 for fall semester, December 1 for spring semester, April 30 for summer session I, and June 15 for summer session II. Associate students may apply up to two weeks before the beginning of classes in any semester or summer session.

For more information, students should contact:

Kathleen A. Trexler
Associate Dean and Director–M.B.A.
  Program
Lehigh University
College of Business and Economics
621 Taylor Street
Bethlehem, Pennsylvania 18015
Telephone: 610-758-3418
Fax: 610-758-5283
E-mail: kat3@lehigh.edu
World Wide Web: http://www.lehigh.
  edu

Loyola College

DEVELOPING BUSINESS LEADERS FOR THE TWENTY-FIRST CENTURY

Loyola College is first and foremost a Jesuit institution. Our small, caring environment and Ignatian traditions prepare our students for the workplace, where they are integrative thinkers, creative problem solvers, active team players, and, especially, leaders aware of their impact on coworkers, the organization, the community, and the world.

There is a Jesuit philosophy at Loyola that affects every student's experience, and that is personal care—care of the person. We are proud of the way our faculty, staff, and administration make Loyola students their greatest priority, helping them to graduate better businesspeople and individuals.

—Peter Lorenzi, Dean

Programs and Curricular Focus

The Sellinger School M.B.A. program challenges the student to acquire a practical and highly integrated understanding of today's business organizations. Separate functional area courses will be replaced by an advanced, integrated course set called The Value-Added Organization, which reflects the dynamic nature of today's business organizations. Students study the essential components of the modern business enterprise: the operations, marketing, and finance functions that are common to any entity, be it a service provider or manufacturer.

In The Value-Added Organization, a set of cases will be repeated in each course within the set, but from a different functional perspective. The student gains a cross-functional understanding and an ability to see the impact of decision making at different levels within an organization.

The Sellinger School M.B.A. program totals 51 credits and is open to business and nonbusiness undergraduates. The program includes 21 credits of core courses that are waiveable for recent undergraduates of business and business-related disciplines and 30 credits of advanced course work (or ten courses). Of the ten advanced courses, all students must take five required courses; the remaining five courses are electives. The five required courses feature The Value-Added Organization (three courses), a leadership and social responsibility course, and a final course that serves as a capstone, transforming

functional expertise into mission and strategy. The five elective courses may include a concentration—up to three courses in one functional area.

Also available are two Executive M.B.A. programs and a Master of Science in Finance program.

Students and the M.B.A. Experience

Students at the Sellinger School come from a wide variety of professional and academic backgrounds. The average student is 29 years old, works full-time, resides in the state of Maryland, and attends classes part-time in the evening. Full-time students comprise 5 percent of the traditional evening M.B.A. program. Women comprise 40 percent of the student population, and members of minority groups make up 5 percent. There are international students attending the Sellinger School from such countries as France, Germany, Holland, Indonesia, and Thailand.

The majority of Sellinger School M.B.A. candidates have undergraduate degrees in business administration or the social sciences, with 18 percent coming from an engineering or science background.

The Faculty

The Sellinger School faculty numbers 47 full-time teachers, with 96 percent holding doctoral-level degrees. Only a small portion of an M.B.A. student's experience includes adjunct faculty, due to the Sellinger School's commitment to a professional teaching environment.

A large majority of the faculty worked at high levels within their area of expertise before they became teachers, and many continue to practice in their field through work in corporations, their own companies, or consulting.

Many professors had distinguished careers running business operations in the United States, Europe, and the Orient, adding to their effectiveness in the classroom.

The Business School Network

Corporate Partnerships

The Sellinger School promotes the belief that the M.B.A. student is only one of the program's customers; the other is the student's employer. It is part of the School's mission to train new leaders for today's changing organizations, and there is no better way for a school to impart the knowledge of leadership than by asking its corporate customers what is needed in M.B.A. graduates to make them effective leaders in their respective organizations.

To that end, there are fifteen active advisory boards made up of local and regional business leaders and graduates of Sellinger programs who regularly meet to counsel and advise the faculty on curricular issues and needed skill sets. Some companies with whom Sellinger has particularly close relationships occasionally provide live situations for students to use as case studies in their M.B.A. program, a feature that students find particularly stimulating.

The College and Environs

Loyola College in Maryland is located in a beautiful residential section of northern Baltimore city. The 86-acre campus is known as Evergreen campus, a testament to the many green lawns, evergreen trees, flower-lined walkways, and floral gardens that dot the campus.

Founded in 1852, Loyola College is a small, private, Catholic, Jesuit liberal arts college that enrolls approximately 3,000 full-time undergraduates in thirty-three majors and 3,000 graduate students studying nine professional disciplines.

The city of Baltimore is located within an hour's drive of Washington, D.C., and within an easy train ride of many East Coast cities, including New York City and Philadelphia.

Facilities

The main campus in Baltimore holds four classroom buildings, a 300,000-volume library, a college center housing state-of-the-art athletic and fine arts facilities, tennis courts, athletic fields, and a beautifully restored Tudor mansion, Evergreen's centerpiece. Undergraduate residence halls and apartments are located on the eastern and western sides of the main campus.

Classes for traditional M.B.A. students are also held at two graduate centers in Timonium and Columbia, Maryland.

Computer labs are located in virtually all buildings on the main and satellite campuses, and students have access 24 hours a day at most sites.

Technology Environment

The College has a computer and telephone network that connects classroom facilities, offices, the library, and laboratories to a digital and video network of global and local data and communication systems. The Sellinger School has an excellent MIS laboratory,

and the College has IBM, Macintosh, and DEC midframe computing laboratories.

Placement

Loyola College's Career Development and Placement Center provides a variety of services to students seeking employment. Once an applicant to the Sellinger School, a student has immediate access to workshops, testing, and private counseling services designed to assist students in such endeavors as career selection, resume writing, and interviewing skills.

A year-round, on-campus recruitment program hosts more than 200 companies, which interview graduating students for positions. Of those, more than 120 companies seek graduating M.B.A. students for jobs. The center also maintains active job referral and alumni advisory networks, which provide leads to graduating students and alumni.

Admission

Admission is based on undergraduate performance (GPA), scores on the Graduate Management Admission Test (GMAT), and career progress. Each program puts a different emphasis on these criteria. International students must also have transcripts evaluated by a recognized service and must submit TOEFL scores if their degree is from a

non-English-speaking university. Traditional programs admit students for each term, and the Executive M.B.A. programs admit only for the fall.

The average enrolled M.B.A. student holds a GMAT score of 530, an undergraduate GPA of 3.2, and has been working professionally for four to five years. International students who are required to take the TOEFL are expected to achieve a minimum score of 550.

Finances

M.B.A. program tuition is charged on a per-credit basis and is $365 per credit in 1998–99. Most classes are 3 credits each. There is a $25 registration fee every semester in which a student takes courses, and books are purchased separately. M.B.A. students may attend classes year-round on a full-time (9 credits) or part-time (3–6 credits) basis. Students in the Executive M.B.A. programs pay a flat tuition charge per academic year, with the summers off.

Assistance is available through the Federal Stafford Student Loan programs to qualified students.

International Students

The Sellinger School embraces a diverse student population and therefore welcomes applications from students outside the United States. International students should have a command of the English language and some work experience. Due to limited institutional assistance, proof is required of sufficient financial resources to fully meet educational costs while attending Loyola College. An orientation session and assistance in locating housing are provided.

Application Facts and Dates

Application deadlines for the M.B.A. program are July 20 for the fall term (May 15 for international students), November 20 for the spring term (August 15 for international students), and April 20 for the summer term (January 15 for international students). Once an application file is complete with all required and official documents, a student is usually notified in writing within two weeks. For more information, applicants should contact:

Director of Graduate Business
   Programs
Loyola College
4501 North Charles Street
Baltimore, Maryland 21210-2699
Telephone: 410-617-5067
E-mail: mba@loyola.edu

Loyola Marymount University

Los Angeles, California

PREPARING FOR THE TWENTY-FIRST CENTURY

The key word for the last half of the 1990s is transition. These uncertain times create unbelievable opportunities for those who are prepared to make things happen. This is why I call our LMU program M.B.A.+. In addition to functional knowledge, human dynamics skills, global competition, and cultural diversity, our M.B.A. program focuses on the needs of individuals and organizations in transition.

Our faculty is eager to help you reach beyond the demands of the classroom. They are noted for outstanding teaching, widely published research, and experience in a variety of industries.

The M.B.A.+ program stresses the ethical dimensions of decisions. Our annual Business Ethics Week conference helps students learn how business leaders in various fields address ethical issues.

As you prepare for the challenges of the twenty-first century, you will definitely want to put the LMU M.B.A.+ program into your career development equation.

—John T. Wholihan, Dean

Programs and Curricular Focus

The Loyola Marymount M.B.A. Program develops ethical leaders who possess the knowledge and skills to effectively manage organizations in a diverse and global economy. Students are taught how to create value, handle risk, and manage change.

The core curriculum consists of nine courses, some or all of which may be waived by students with recent bachelor's degrees in business. Competence may also be determined by examination.

Upon completion of the core, students select domestic or international electives to gain breadth of knowledge as well as expertise in a particular area. The domestic track requires three courses in an area of emphasis as well as five additional courses from other areas. Students elect either comparative management systems, strategy courses, or an integrative project to complete the program.

Students selecting the international track receive the M.B.A. degree plus a Graduate Certificate in International Business after completing the same number of courses as are required for the domestic track. In addition to international breadth courses, participation in comparative management systems is required. This provides the opportunity to study the area of emphasis within a given industry outside the United States.

Comparative management systems is also available to domestic-track students.

Depending on waivers and the integrative option selected, ten to twenty courses are required. Full-time students with undergraduate degrees in business often complete the M.B.A. program within one year.

Loyola Marymount offers a J.D./ M.B.A. program, enabling a student to earn both degrees in four years.

Students and the M.B.A. Experience

Eighty percent of students in the Loyola Marymount M.B.A. Program are fully employed professionals from a wide variety of industries in southern California. Twenty percent of the students attend on a full-time basis. While some students enter the program directly after undergraduate school, most do have work experience. The average student is 28 years old, with four years of work experience. Women account for 44 percent of the student body, and 13 percent are members of minority groups.

Eleven percent of the population are international students from all over the world. International students often provide alternative analyses of the global dimension of business problems, which are extremely valuable in the classroom.

Half of the students have undergraduate degrees in business, 30 percent in the social sciences, and 20 percent in engineering.

❖ Global Focus

The M.B.A. program offers a wide variety of courses that examine the global nature of business. In addition, students have the opportunity to participate in an exchange program in France.

For sixteen years, the M.B.A. program has sponsored comparative management systems, a two-semester international-strategy sequence. Students form functional-area groups and spend a year analyzing a particular industry and regional area. At the conclusion of the year, students spend three weeks meeting with industry executives in the region selected for study. Most recently, the course examined the bottling industry in southern Africa. In 1998–99, the students focus on ecotourism in the South Pacific.

The Faculty

Loyola Marymount's faculty members are exceptional teachers who actively participate in research in their fields. Approximately 94 percent of all courses are taught by faculty members who have doctoral degrees. Classes are intentionally small, to provide faculty members with opportunities to interact with individual students on a regular basis.

Women comprise 16 percent of the faculty, and 14 percent of the faculty are members of minority groups. Loyola Marymount's strong international emphasis is supported by faculty members from India, Korea, Ghana, Hong Kong, Great Britain, and Russia.

The Business School Network

The Business Advisory Council, comprising corporate leaders from a variety of industries, is actively involved in the M.B.A. program. Some of the members serve as speakers for M.B.A. classes or conferences. Others are involved in the recruiting and placement efforts of the M.B.A. program. One of the members coordinates a group of students who meet monthly with prominent entrepreneurs.

The College and Environs

Loyola University, a Jesuit institution incorporated in 1928, merged with

Marymount College in 1973 to form Loyola Marymount University. The M.B.A. program was instituted in 1974. The Westchester campus has a student population of more than 4,500. The Loyola Law School is located in downtown Los Angeles.

Loyola Marymount University is located in a lovely residential neighborhood on a bluff offering magnificent views of Marina del Rey and the Pacific Ocean. Excellent weather plus proximity to local beaches provides the perfect setting for outdoor sports. Los Angeles offers an extraordinary variety of theaters, museums, and professional sports teams, all a short distance from the University.

Technology Environment

M.B.A. students have access via networks to an attractive array of computer and related technologies. Word processing and spreadsheets are available through the campuswide network. Specific applications, such as simulation and statistical packages, are accessible via departmental networks.

With the opening of the Conrad N. Hilton Center for Business in 1995, two hands-on computer classrooms were added. The Hilton facility is intended to provide access to a new generation of technologies. Traditional videoconferencing will permit students and faculty members to participate in classes from remote locations. Desktop videoconferencing will enable group projects and collaborative research efforts from remote locations.

Placement

Loyola Marymount's Career Development and Placement Office provides a variety of services. Students get advice on resume preparation and interviewing skills. Online databases, career fairs, and on-campus interviews are also available. The M.B.A. Office provides additional placement services, including the distribution of resume books to local employers each semester as well as daily maintenance of a list of jobs and internship opportunities.

Admission

Each applicant's undergraduate record, GMAT scores, and recommendation letters form the basis for evaluation. Although not required, relevant work experience is considered. The minimum GMAT score is 400, with the average score approximately 550. The average undergraduate GPA is 3.2.

International students must achieve a TOEFL score of at least 600 and must present proof of sufficient funds to cover tuition and living expenses for the full period of study.

All entering students are assumed to be proficient in English composition, business mathematics, and computer applications.

Finances

Tuition for 1998–99 is $620 per unit. Each course is 3 units. Annual fees for full-time students are estimated to be $421. Fees for part-time students are estimated to be $268. In addition, all students must have health insurance. The cost of books and supplies varies from approximately $60 to $100 per course.

Merit-based research assistantships are available, as are a limited number of need-based grants. In addition, the Financial Aid Office can provide information on loan programs available to M.B.A. students.

Application Facts and Dates

Applications are accepted for the fall, spring, and summer semesters. There are no specific deadlines; the M.B.A. Office has a policy of rolling admissions. Once the University has received all application materials, the application package is reviewed and the applicant notified within two weeks. For more information, students should contact:

Ms. Charisse Woods, Coordinator
M.B.A. Office
Loyola Marymount University
Los Angeles, California 90045–8387
Telephone: 310-338-2848
Fax: 310-338-2899
E-mail: cwoods@popmail.lmu.edu

Loyola University Chicago

BUILDING SKILLS FOR LIFE

For more than 450 years, Jesuits have been educating men and women for positions of leadership in business, government, and the professions. We at Loyola University Chicago are proud to be a part of this tradition. It has provided four main themes that form the foundation of our M.B.A. program: teaching excellence, skills for life, global vision, and socially responsible leadership. These themes are the solid foundation on which you can build an individual program of study tailored to your needs. We invite you to explore how the Loyola University Chicago approach can benefit you as you pursue your career goals.

—William Bryan, Dean

Programs and Curricular Focus

The Loyola M.B.A. program ranges from fourteen to eighteen courses, depending on the student's undergraduate background. This includes between two and ten required courses and eight to twelve electives. Electives can be used to earn fields of specialization in thirteen areas, such as finance and health-care administration, financial derivatives, or international business.

All classes contain a mix of part-time and full-time students. It is the belief at Loyola that this design is intellectually healthy since it permits all M.B.A. students to interact in the same classroom setting.

The Graduate School of Business offers students the opportunity to pursue an M.B.A. degree, a dual M.B.A./J.D. degree, or a dual M.B.A./M.S.N. degree. Each of the dual-degree programs allows the student to earn the degrees in a shorter period of time than if they were pursued independently.

Students and the M.B.A. Experience

The students have undergraduate degrees from more than 200 universities across the globe. The typical Loyola University Chicago M.B.A. student is 27 years old, with 4 years of full-time work experience; 36 percent of the students are women, 9.5 percent are members of minority groups, and 17 percent are international. Approximately half of Loyola's students earned their undergraduate degree in business, 30 percent in arts and science, and 10 percent in economics.

❖ Global Focus

Loyola helps prepare students for the international demands of business by routinely including international considerations in all of the courses and by offering courses that focus solely on the international dimensions of a topic. All M.B.A. students must take at least one international course. A student can also earn an international specialization as part of the overall M.B.A. by building three to four international courses into his or her program.

Students whose career goals demand an intensive grounding in international business can take advantage of innovative programs in Athens, Bangkok, Istanbul, and Rome. Under these programs, intensive two-week summer courses are offered that focus on topical international issues and are taught by the best of Loyola's Chicago faculty. Since each session is compressed into a two-week block, both part-time and full-time students have the opportunity to attend. Past courses have focused on such issues as strategic marketing in Europe, international management, the European Union, and emerging markets. Students may also study at Loyola exchanges in Beijing, China, and Seoul, Korea.

Special Features

Loyola provides Individual Development Seminars for M.B.A. students throughout the year. These seminars are free and address topics such as communication skills, personal quality management, entrepreneurship, negotiating skills, and career strategies. In addition, the Graduate School of Business Distinguished

Speaker Series hosts prominent academic, business, and government leaders to speak on current issues. The four research centers embody Loyola University Chicago's philosophy of blending the theoretical with the practical by linking real-world business needs with the University's ongoing research. Research conducted by the centers is incorporated into many classroom programs.

The Faculty

The Loyola University Chicago faculty is strongly committed to teaching as well as research. Because 97 percent of the faculty is full-time, classes are taught by experienced, highly trained leaders in their fields. Part-time faculty members are used on a very selective basis and only when they offer specialized skills. Class size is purposely kept small in order to ensure that the faculty is accessible to students—both inside and outside the classroom.

As leaders in their fields, most faculty members have important industry and community ties in such areas as family business, total quality management, and financial and policy studies. So, in teaching, they offer a scholarly approach gained through research as well as practical business experience.

The faculty's dedication to research invigorates the M.B.A. experience by developing new ideas that can be applied in the classroom. The faculty is involved in an impressive range of research projects in all major areas of business and is also widely published.

The Business School Network

Corporate Partnerships

Seventy-five percent of Loyola's alumni live within the greater Chicago area. Already established and successful in the business world, these alumni provide significant networking opportunities for students. As a result, major businesses in the Chicago area and from around the country are frequently on campus to speak to students and alumni, to advise faculty and administrators on current management education issues, and to recruit Loyola's graduates.

Prominent Alumni

Among Loyola's prominent M.B.A. alumni are Michael Quinlan, Chairman of the Board, McDonald's Corporation; Philip Deon, Chairman of the Board and CEO, Dell Webb Corporation; John Menzer, Executive Vice President and CFO, Wal-Mart Stores, Inc.; Robert Parkinson, Executive Vice President, Abbott Labs, Inc.; and Joseph Scully, Chairman of the Board and CEO, St. Paul Federal Bank for Savings.

The College and Environs

The Graduate School of Business campus is located adjacent to Chicago's Magnificent Mile. LaSalle Street is home to the Chicago Board of Trade, Chicago Board Options Exchange, and Chicago Mercantile Exchange, making the city one of the largest financial trading centers in the world. Many national and multinational companies in a broad range of industries are headquartered in Chicago. As a result, job opportunities at major firms abound throughout the Chicago area, in fields as diverse as manufacturing, health care, and consulting.

Technology Environment

The Graduate School of Business is housed in the new Graduate Business Center. Loyola's M.B.A. students have state-of-the-art computers and software for instructional and individual use. The Loyola library system offers numerous computerized resources including the Internet, LEXIS-NEXIS, Legal Index, FirstSearch, and LUIS (the Loyola library computerized catalog). Databases on CD-ROM include Business Periodicals on Disc, General Business File, and others.

Placement

The M.B.A. Placement Service advisers are available to help students with resumes, cover letters, career counseling and planning, and job search strategies. Videotaped mock interview sessions, conducted by business professionals who also provide oral and written feedback, are held twice each year. In addition, training workshops on the nuts and bolts of job hunting (such as resume writing, interviewing techniques, targeting potential employers, salary negotiation, and networking) are scheduled throughout the year.

In addition to the many on-campus recruiting opportunities with an array of employers, Loyola sponsors the Midwest M.B.A. Consortium with four other universities. Opportunities for networking and skill building are also provided through Loyola's Career Consultants Network, the M.B.A. alumni organization dedicated to assisting students in their job search activities. Students can also join alumni in the Chicago area several times each year when they meet on campus for professional and social occasions.

Admission

Students are admitted to the School as candidates for the M.B.A. degree on the bases of interest, aptitude, and capacity for business study as indicated by their previous academic record; achievement scores on the Graduate Management Admission Test (GMAT); recommendations from 3 faculty members or employers; and pertinent information from their applications.

The average student's undergraduate GPA is 3.1, with a range from 2.5 to 4.0. The average GMAT score is 520, with a range from 400 to 720. Average work experience of the entering students is 4 years.

Loyola welcomes applications from international students who have completed a four-year bachelor's degree or its equivalent. A minimum TOEFL score of 550 and proof of financial support for one year are required.

Finances

Tuition for 1998–99 is $1985 per course for both full- and part-time students. A wide variety of housing is available both on and off campus. Many full-time students live in the Gold Coast area of Chicago, which is within walking distance of the Graduate School of Business. Other graduate students choose to live in graduate housing facilities that are located 10 miles north of the Water Tower Campus at Loyola's Lake Shore Campus. The estimated cost of room and board for twelve months is between $8000 and $12,000. The Graduate Business Scholars Program provides more than twenty merit-based assistantships per year to full-time students.

International Students

Loyola's M.B.A. program is greatly enhanced by more than 170 international students from more than forty different countries. Several countries represented include Brazil, Canada, China, Colombia, Denmark, France, Germany, Greece, India, Indonesia, Italy, Japan, Korea, Mexico, the Philippines, Spain, Taiwan, Thailand, Turkey, and Venezuela. Loyola's Students of the World chapter provides an immediate link for international students, while the Office of International Services and Programs helps international students adjust to living and studying in the United States. Chicago's ethnic and culinary diversity make this "city of neighborhoods" a comfortable and exciting home for citizens from around the world.

Application Facts and Dates

A student may enter the program at the beginning of any of the four quarters. To ensure admission in the quarter of choice, the student should apply well in advance. Loyola functions on a rolling admission basis, however, applications are accepted until these deadlines: for the fall quarter, August 1; the winter quarter, October 1; the spring quarter, January 1; and the summer quarter, April 1. For additional information, students should contact:

Admissions Coordinator
Graduate School of Business
Loyola University Chicago
820 North Michigan Avenue
Chicago, Illinois 60611
Telephone: 312-915-6120
Fax: 312-915-7207
E-mail: mba-loyola@luc.edu
World Wide Web:
    http://www.luc.edu/depts/mba

Manhattan College

Riverdale, New York

A LEARNING COMMUNITY FOR WORKING PROFESSIONALS

Our M.B.A. students are working professionals who attend classes Saturday mornings and weekday evenings. We work hard to provide a sense of community. Our students know each other, the faculty members, and administrators even though they are part-time students. Classes are small—the average size is 17 students—so student involvement is expected. Our policies and procedures are streamlined to fit the needs of working people. We are responsive to individual needs.

—Charles E. Brunner, Director of M.B.A. Program

Programs and Curricular Focus

The M.B.A. Program is 39 graduate credits (thirteen courses) plus six foundation prerequisite areas in accounting, economics, computer systems, corporate finance, marketing, and statistics. The prerequisite areas can be waived for some students. There are nine required graduate core courses. The remaining four graduate courses can be used to concentrate in finance, international business, management, and marketing and to take electives. Students may customize their own set of courses for a concentration with the approval of the director.

Courses are offered year-round. There are courses offered during the fall and spring semesters as well as an intensive three-week January session and two 6-week summer sessions. Students complete the program in about two years by taking one or two courses per term.

Students and the M.B.A. Experience

The Manhattan College M.B.A. students reflect New York's diversity. More than 95 percent of the 200 students have full-time jobs and are residents of the metropolitan area. The average age is 27 years old. Almost 40 percent of students are women. About 25 percent of students are members of minority groups. Students have a wide variety of undergraduate majors in addition to business, including engineering, history, psychology, languages, and literature. International students make up about 5 percent of the student body.

Students frequently work together on team projects. The elective experiential

leadership and team-building course is very popular. Students and faculty members frequently communicate through e-mail.

The Faculty

Nearly 100 percent of full-time faculty members have Ph.D. degrees, but several specialized courses each term are instructed by adjunct professors from industry. Many of the full-time faculty members have industry experience.

The Business School Network

Manhattan College alumni are well represented in prominent positions of managerial success in organizations such as Chase Manhattan, Citibank, Con Ed,

Depository Trust, IBM, J. Walter Thompson, Morgan Guaranty Trust, NYNEX, and many more. The College's location, about 10 miles from midtown Manhattan, facilitates networking. In addition to an active Board of Advisors, the network is enhanced through activities of the M.B.A. Program. The major part

of one Saturday each fall and each spring is devoted to a lunch and discussion forum for an important business issue. Manhattan College alumni attend the forums and are frequently presenters and discussants.

The College and Environs

Manhattan College overlooks Van Cortlandt Park in the Riverdale section of the Bronx. The immediate neighborhood is bounded by the beautiful Fieldston residential neighborhood on the west and a small business district to the east. Access is easy via the Henry Hudson Parkway and the New York Thruway (I-87) for automobiles and the IRT 1/9 subway line, a short 5-minute walk from campus. Parking is free during the evenings and on Saturdays and is just a few steps from class.

Technology Environment

All M.B.A. students have accounts on the Manhattan College computer network. The network provides Internet access and a wide range of application software. There are two computer labs in DeLa-Salle Hall, where the School of Business is located. M.B.A. students also have access to the Learning and Resource Center on the lower campus for additional computers and technical assistance. It is highly recommended that students have access to their own computer and Internet service if they cannot easily use campus facilities. Many courses utilize computer exercises and research, and the computer information system is a primary means of communication.

Placement

The Career Services Center at Manhattan College serves both the graduate and undergraduate programs. In addition to providing students opportunities to interview with companies, the Career Services Center offers career counseling services and various workshops in resume writing and interviewing. There are also a limited number of internship opportunities available to M.B.A. students.

Admission

Undergraduate grade index, Graduate Management Admission Test (GMAT) scores, reference letters, and personal and business experience are all considered in the selection process. The average undergraduate grade index is about 3.0. Work experience and demonstrated career achievements of applicants are significant selection factors. A minimum of three years' work experience is recommended. Applicants are evaluated on a rolling basis so they may begin taking courses soon after acceptance.

Finances

Tuition for 1998–99 for the M.B.A. Program is $440 per credit, or $1320 per 3-credit course. The application fee is $50, and there is a charge of $50 for registration each term. The estimated total for tuition and fees for the 39-credit graduate program is $17,560 over about two years. There is a tuition deferral program for approved employers, and students may pay through an installment program. Financial aid is limited to loans for qualified students.

Application Facts and Dates

Completed applications must be received by August 10 for fall semester and January 7 for spring semester. Prospective students are welcome to visit with M.B.A. students and faculty members on Saturday mornings. Students should call the M.B.A. office for visiting information.

For information students should contact:

Charles E. Brunner, Director of
     M.B.A. Program
School of Business
Manhattan College
Riverdale, New York 10471
Telephone: 718-862-7222 or 7290
Fax: 718-862-8023
E-mail: cbrunner@manhattan.edu

Marist College

School of Management

Poughkeepsie, New York

GRADUATES ABLE TO IDENTIFY OPPORTUNITIES AND ASSESS RISKS

Companies need managers who can navigate an increasingly complex business environment. Managers who understand the competitive demands of our global economy are better able to identify opportunities and assess risks. As a result, they are poised to become the corporate leaders of tomorrow.

The objective of Marist's M.B.A. program is to cultivate managers capable of effective decision making. In addition to addressing the nuances of a global economy, Marist's program focuses on developing the analytical, communication, and leadership skills essential for success. Special emphasis is placed on total quality management and the behavioral influences that impact the well-being of modern organizations.

The outcome: Marist graduates possess the strategic perspective necessary to help lead their organizations into the next century.

—Gordon Badovick, Ph.D., Dean

Program and Curricular Focus

The M.B.A. at Marist College is a challenging program designed for highly motivated individuals. The full program entails 54 credit hours of study. However, certain courses may be waived, reducing degree requirements to as few as 30 credit hours.

Twenty-four credit hours of M.B.A. foundation courses provide students with a working knowledge of the functional areas of business administration and the requisite quantitative skills. These courses may be waived on the basis of recent undergraduate/graduate course work or course work in combination with relevant professional experience.

Eighteen credit hours of M.B.A. core courses, required of all students, afford a more in-depth look at management issues and provide the necessary perspective for effective decision making. Topics covered include management accounting, managerial economics, global environment of business, industrial/international marketing, management science, quality management in operations, and corporate financial theory.

Students can customize Marist's program to meet their own professional and career needs via 9 credits of elective course work. Elective courses are available in accounting, finance, health services administration, human resources management, information systems, and marketing. The M.B.A. culminates with

the Business Policy Seminar, which integrates concepts studied throughout the program.

Classes are held weekday evenings and on Saturday. Each class entails a commitment of no more than one session per week. Part-time students can accelerate their studies by taking more than one class per semester. Full-time students generally attend classes Monday–Thursday evening or may exercise the option of taking courses on line. The time required to complete the program depends on the number of credits required for the degree and the number of courses a student elects to complete each term.

Students and the M.B.A. Experience

In the classroom, Marist's M.B.A. faculty members do more than deliver a lecture. An average class size of 15 students ensures ample opportunities for student-faculty exchange. As a result, faculty members actively involve students in the learning experience. In-class exercises, case studies, computer simulations, group projects, and presentations all play an integral role in the process. By use of this multidimensional teaching model, learning occurs not only from the faculty but from fellow students who bring an array of perspectives into the classroom.

Marist's M.B.A. students come from a broad spectrum of career and undergraduate academic backgrounds. The majority

are residents of the Hudson Valley region pursuing their studies on a part-time basis. However, Marist has an increasing population of full-time students from throughout the U.S., Europe, and Asia. Their average age is 32, and there is an approximately equal number of men and women.

Special Features

Those who find it difficult to attend class during the week can pursue the same high-quality graduate education with online M.B.A. courses. Online M.B.A. courses are offered in eight-week sections, allowing for maximum flexibility and time utilization.

The Faculty

More than 30 predominantly full-time faculty members bring an abundance of management experience into the classroom. Many are skilled corporate professionals and almost all have a Ph.D.

Marist's M.B.A. faculty members are actively involved in research, publishing, and consulting and are frequently called upon to give professional presentations. However, the College has a long-standing commitment to excellence in teaching, and it is here that the faculty excels.

The Business School Network

The increasingly complex nature of the global business environment necessitates that the School of Management routinely review and enhance the M.B.A. program. An Advisory Board, consisting of senior executives from national corporations and entrepreneurs from the Hudson Valley Region, meets regularly to review the responsiveness of Marist's program to the needs of the business community.

Members of the Advisory Board and M.B.A. alumni offer guest lectures and provide students with the opportunity to establish a network of highly regarded business professionals. The School of Management also sponsors the Marist Bureau of Economic Research and an Executive Seminar Series.

The College and Environs

Marist is an independent coeducational college of the liberal arts and sciences,

founded in 1929. The College's 120-acre suburban campus sits on the banks of the scenic Hudson River, in Poughkeepsie, New York, 75 miles north of New York City. More than 4,400 undergraduate and 530 graduate students are currently pursuing their degrees at Marist.

Marist is chartered by the Board of Regents of the University of the State of New York and accredited by the State Department of Education and the Middle States Association of Colleges and Schools. The College holds memberships in AACSB–The International Association for Management Education and the Middle Atlantic Association Colleges of Business Administration.

Technology Environment

A $16-million joint study with IBM has placed Marist among the most technologically sophisticated liberal arts colleges in the country. An IBM Enterprise Systems 9121 mainframe computer provides the College with computer power ordinarily associated with large research universities. In addition, Marist's integrated voice and data telecommunications system provides students with around-the-clock access to the mainframe computer, the library, and a variety of services, including phone mail, electronic mail, and access to the World Wide Web. M.B.A.

students have ample access to terminals and personal computers in College labs. Those who have computers with modems may also access Marist's system from their home or office.

Placement

The Center for Career Development and Field Experience offers a variety of services to assist M.B.A. students. Career information, individual assessment, job search preparation, and employment services, including an annual Employer Expo and on-campus interviews, are available to students and alumni.

Admission

Marist's M.B.A. is designed for individuals from a wide variety of academic and professional backgrounds. However, graduate study in business does require a reasonable level of mathematical and computer competence.

Admission to Marist's program is selective. Students admitted to the program generally have an above-average undergraduate academic record. However, other factors, such as course work beyond the baccalaureate, relevant professional experience, and achievement on the GMAT, are also taken into consideration. Students enrolling in Marist's M.B.A.

program have an average undergraduate GPA of 3.1 and an average GMAT score of 520.

Students whose native language is not English are required to submit official results of the TOEFL and TWE. Marist requires minimum scores of 550 and 4.0 respectively.

Finances

Tuition for the 1998–99 academic year is $419 per credit hour. While Marist College does not provide graduate student housing, ample housing is available in the surrounding community. Costs vary widely; however, students willing to share an apartment generally find that housing and board can cost between $600 and $800 per month. Books, fees, supplies, and insurance cost approximately $1600 per academic year.

Need-based financial assistance is available for full- and part-time study. Marist participates in the Federal Stafford Student Loan and Federal Work-Study programs, and grant funding is available through the College. Matriculated students seeking financial assistance should file the Free Application for Federal Student Aid as well as Marist's own Application for Financial Aid for Graduate Students.

A deferred tuition plan is available for those receiving tuition reimbursement from their employers.

International Students

International students are welcome members of the College community. Marist has an international student adviser who assists students with cultural, academic, and visa issues. There is also an orientation program that familiarizes students with the College and surrounding community. Unfortunately, the College is unable to offer financial assistance to international students.

Application Facts and Dates

Applications for admission are reviewed on a rolling basis for admission in any term.

For more information, students should contact:

Eileen Bull
Assistant Dean, Graduate and
    Continuing Education
Marist College
290 North Road
Poughkeepsie, New York 12601-1387
Telephone: 914-575-3800
Fax: 914-575-3640
E-mail: graduate@marist.edu
World Wide Web: http://www.marist.edu

McGill University

Montreal, Quebec, Canada

CREATING VALUE—A PRACTICAL, INTEGRATIVE APPROACH

To prepare students for truly rewarding careers in a continually changing global business environment, the McGill M.B.A. program provides a unique pedagogical experience. Not only are all the core-year courses fully interconnected, they are team-taught. The rapport that develops between students and professors enhances the flexibility, adaptability, and people-oriented skills the curriculum develops. With an understanding of how to create value for the greatest benefit of an organization as a whole, students get more out of their chosen area of concentration in the second year. As a result, the McGill M.B.A. program produces specialists who can integrate across functional areas—and offer employers a responsible competitive edge.

—Wallace Crowston, Dean

Programs and Curricular Focus

The McGill M.B.A. is an internationally renowned graduate business program designed to provide students with a comprehensive understanding of the concepts of business, specialized knowledge in their chosen field, and the international perspective needed to meet the challenges of today's complex business environment.

Building on traditional strengths in functional areas, the McGill M.B.A. program takes the learning experience one step further. Not only are students provided with a strong grounding in the basic business disciplines, they are also provided with the intangible skills explicitly sought by employers today—the ability to apply their knowledge for the greatest benefit to the organization, to make effective decisions, to both work in teams and lead others, and to adapt to nonstructured situations.

The McGill M.B.A. program is a twenty-month program. In the core year, students follow a sequence of courses taught in three separate nine-week modules. The second year is free of required courses. Students tailor their studies to meet their specific career goals and interests. Choosing from more than fifty elective courses, students pursue in-depth study in one of the following fields: entrepreneurship, finance, international business, management for developing economies, marketing, operations management, or strategic management. If they prefer, studnts can create their own general management concentration.

Students may also complete the program on a part-time basis.

Students and the M.B.A. Experience

Students typically hail from every corner of the globe, come from a wide variety of cultures and backgrounds, and possess highly diversified educational and work-related experience. Students also share a number of common characteristics—intelligence, inquisitiveness, an openness to learning and embracing new ideas, and a high degree of motivation.

Of the 150 full-time students in the 1997–98 class, the ratio of women to men was 1:3, the average age was 26, and they represented fourteen countries; 40 percent spoke two languages and 42 percent spoke three or more. They came from a cross-section of universities: 13 percent American, 44 percent other international, 23 percent Canadian outside Quebec, and the balance from Quebec; 34 percent held a B.A., 29 percent a B.Sc., 15 percent a B.Eng., and 22 percent a B.Com./B.B.A.

A number of M.B.A. activities, such as the weekly Speakers Series and the M.B.A. Business Luncheon, put students in direct contact with leading businesspeople. For those who enjoy the thrill of competition, Case Competitions are held, which match McGill's case-analysis skills against those of other M.B.A. programs. Students can also participate in the annual M.B.A. Games and the Investment Fund Game.

Special Features

McGill is world renowned as a leader in international management education. All students acquire an inherent understanding of international commerce and an appreciation for other cultures in McGill's multicultural learning environment, and those interested in international business enjoy exceptional opportunities to network and acquire experience.

McGill M.B.A. students can further expand on the international experiences provided through the program by participating in the Faculty's international student exchange program. Students earn academic credit while studying at one of twenty-one world-class universities located in Europe, North America, Latin America, or the Far East.

M.B.A. I: THE BASICS OF MANAGEMENT

MODULE I:	MODULE II:	MODULE III:
Financial Accounting	Finance or Elements of Modern Finance I	Information Systems
Organizational Behaviour	Marketing	International Environment
Managerial Economics	Operations Management	Organizational Strategy
Management Statistics	Human Resource Management	Management Accounting or
Integrative Core Course	Research, Development and Engineering	Elements of Modern Finance II
(full-year course)		

Through the many cross-disciplinary and joint-degree programs offered with the M.B.A. program, students not only have the opportunity to gain specialized knowledge in today's leading fields, they also benefit greatly from the contact and interaction with the unique students attracted to these programs. Programs offered include the Master in Manufacturing Management (M.M.M.), M.B.A./ Diploma in Management (Asian studies), medicine and management (M.D.– M.B.A.), management and law (M.B.A./ Law), M.Sc. (agricultural economics)/ M.B.A., and the master's program in economic policy management (EPM).

The Faculty

McGill Management is composed of an eclectic team of faculty members who enjoy the challenges that the M.B.A. program affords them, particularly the core year's integrative course, which they jointly plan, teach, and grade.

They represent fifteen nationalities and have all lived, studied, and worked in countries around the world. They bring direct experience of business practices in other countries to the classroom, and many have proven themselves to be in the forefront of research in cross-cultural and multinational business issues. Two interesting faculty-supported initiatives are the McGill Business Consulting Group and its international counterpart, the McGill International Consulting Group (MICG), which offer students professional opportunities.

The Business School Network

Corporate Partnerships

McGill's learning environment includes involvement with businesses of every size in every industry sector, as well as government agencies and departments.

Through various projects, events, and a range of faculty and student initiatives, students interact with CEOs, entrepreneurs, consultants, managers, government officials, conference delegates, and visiting faculty from around the world. They benefit from exceptional opportunities to learn, contribute, network, and explore career directions.

The Faculty continually benefits from valuable counsel from its Faculty of Management International Advisory Board, composed of 11 prominent businesspeople.

The College and Environs

McGill is recognized around the world for its high standards in teaching and research, and it has achieved international renown for its Faculties of Agriculture, Dentistry, Engineering, Law, Management, and Medicine.

Founded in 1821, the University now comprises fifty institutional buildings for eleven faculties on 75 acres in downtown Montreal. Montreal, North America's most multicultural business center and one of its leading centers for high-tech RD&E, is considered to be one of its most cultured and cosmopolitan cities.

McGill has an undergraduate enrollment of more than 25,000 and a graduate enrollment of 6,000.

Facilities

McGill Management occupies a building specifically designed for its needs. Classrooms have been refurbished with built-in, state-of-the-art computers; video cameras; and 3M data display units that allow professors to select from a variety of teaching mediums. Each classroom features laptop computer connections and is wired for Internet access. Facilities available to M.B.A. students include a lounge and study area, the Acer M.B.A. Computer Lab, and an impressive library featuring electronic database searching services and a number of networked databases. Students also have access to more than 3 million volumes housed in the University's comprehensive system of libraries and specialized collections.

Students enjoy excellent sports facilities, efficient housing services, a graduate house, and a health service.

Placement

Placement starts in Orientation Week when the Management Career Centre holds the first of many networking occasions. Students seeking both permanent and summer employment benefit from workshops, videotaped mock interviews, one-on-one career counselling, a resource library, and an alumni reference database.

The center provides job listings; holds an annual M.B.A. Career Day; publishes a graduating class book, which is distributed to prospective employers in Canada and abroad; and follows up on interviews with both students and employers.

Continual interaction with companies has made McGill's Management Career Centre a valued resource for employers and students alike.

Admission

Admission is competitive. Decisions are based on many factors: solid academic credentials (minimum 3.0 CGPA, average 3.3); a strong GMAT score (minimum 550, average 610); a TOEFL score of 600 if English was not the language of university education; at least one year of relevant work experience; professional and extracurricular achievements; and letters of reference.

Finances

Tuition fees for the 1998–99 academic year are Can$2497 for Quebec residents, Can$3697 for other Canadian citizens, and Can$16,000 for international students. Bilateral agreements exist with several nations to obtain an international fee waiver.

All accepted candidates are automatically considered for financial aid and fellowships.

A minimal figure for living expenses per academic year is Can$8000 for single students and Can$10,000 for married students.

International Students

International students are warmly received and supported in the Faculty's multicultural environment. In addition, the University runs a combined Student Aid/International Advisor's office to handle all nonacademic matters of concern, such as visa status, immigration procedures, health insurance requirements, and cost estimates for Foreign Exchange boards.

Application Facts and Dates

Applications for the full-time program are accepted for September only. Application deadlines are May 15 for Canadian students and April 1 for international students. The application fee is Can$100.

For more information, applicants should contact:

The McGill M.B.A.
Faculty of Management
McGill University
1001 Sherbrooke Street West
Montreal, Quebec H3A 1G5
Canada
Telephone: 514-398-4066
Fax: 514-398-2499
E-mail: mba@management.mcgill.ca
World Wide Web: http://www.
   management.mcgill.ca

Mississippi State University

Starkville, Mississippi

DRIVEN BY EXCELLENCE

The mission and purpose of the College of Business and Industry is to develop business and professional leaders for the twenty-first century who will positively influence organizations through ethical standards, their management skills, and their ability to manage change in a global society. The College is further dedicated to increasing knowledge through scholarly research and fostering economic development through the application of applied research and services to increase the effectiveness, efficiency, and productivity of business and industry. The M.B.A. program is an integral part, and its graduates a manifestation, of this mission and purpose. The evolutionary nature of business and industry is reflected in the M.B.A. program through the process of continuous improvement. In a phrase, the M.B.A. program is "Driven by Excellence."

—Harvey S. Lewis, Dean

Programs and Curricular Focus

The objective of the M.B.A. program is to provide a broad background for business leadership through an emphasis on practical administrative problems. Candidates for the M.B.A. program must complete 30 hours of course work at the graduate level, including a core of 24 hours in the areas of accounting, economics, finance, management, marketing, and statistics, plus a capstone course in business strategy. The remaining 6 hours of graduate courses are elective and may be selected from either within or outside of business.

For M.B.A. candidates who do not hold undergraduate degrees in business, a set of prerequisite courses must be completed. These include courses in accounting, business information systems, economics, finance, legal environment of business, management, marketing, and statistics.

Full-time students with an undergraduate business degree can complete the M.B.A. program in three semesters or one year, and part-time students with an undergraduate business degree can complete the program in five semesters or slightly less than two years. In the absence of previous academic training in business, full-time students can complete the program within two years, and part-time students can usually complete the program within four. The maximum time frame within which the degree may be completed is six years.

Students and the M.B.A. Experience

While ages may range from early twenties to late forties, the average age of

students in the M.B.A. program at Mississippi State University (MSU) is 27. The average amount of full-time work experience, since receiving their undergraduate degree, is between two and three years. The student body is generally composed of approximately 60 percent men and 40 percent women. African-American students constitute approximately 10 percent and international students approximately 20 percent of the student body. While undergraduate backgrounds vary from animal husbandry to zoology, the majority of the students hold undergraduate degrees in business, with engineering being the second most prevalent undergraduate background.

The Faculty

The graduate faculty in the College of Business and Industry, a subset of the general faculty, consists of approximately 55 members. Members are reviewed every five years for reappointment to the graduate faculty. Members of the graduate faculty all hold advanced degrees in their respective areas of expertise. Approximately 15 percent of the faculty members are women. Foreign nationals compose about 20 percent of the faculty.

The Business School Network

The corporate community cooperates with the University in several ways to provide students with opportunities for hands-on business contact. The annual M.B.A. Welcome and Orientation Program allows students to interact with corporate leaders and ask questions in a casual atmosphere.

Brown bag lunches are frequently held, highlighting corporate executives who discuss their company policies and opportunities for employment.

The College and Environs

The College of Business and Industry is located in McCool Hall at the center of MSU's campus. The University forms a part of a cohesive town-university community with the growing agricultural-commercial-industrial town of Starkville. Located in the eastern part of north-central Mississippi, it is 125 miles northeast of Jackson and 23 miles west of Columbus. Away from urban complexities, the community enjoys many intellectual, cultural, and recreational advantages: the MSU–Starkville Civic Symphony and Chorus; the Starkville Community Theater; the University Lyceum series, which presents performances by popular musical groups of regional and national celebrity; frequent intercollegiate athletic events in modern facilities; and a variety of recreational opportunities on playing fields, courts, lakes, and the nearby Tennessee-Tombigbee Waterway.

Technology Environment

The College of Business and Industry has installed and made available for faculty and student use a large-scale local area network. This network contains more than 200 PC stations and is MS-DOS based using Sperry/Novell Netware. Four student labs with state-of-the-art software applications are available for College of Business and Industry student assignments. There is also an electronic classroom that provides interactive instruction opportunities for faculty members and students to deal with more sophisticated data and analytical techniques. Assistance is available to provide students with computer-assisted instruction topics as well as personal problem solving. A Sun 4/280 UNIX system allows access to UNIX software packages as well as to the Internet.

Placement

Assisting its graduates in finding jobs is a primary concern of Mississippi State University. In order to give its students the best pos-

McCool Hall.

sible opportunities, the University operates the Career Services Center and the Cooperative Education Program.

The Career Services Center (CSC) brings approximately eighty-five businesses to campus each semester to interview students for full-time jobs and professional-level summer employment. In preparation for these interviews, the CSC offers resume critiques and seminars that focus on writing effective resumes, honing interviewing skills, and looking for jobs.

The CSC also maintains an alumni career network and critiques videotaped mock interviews. In addition, the CSC sponsors Career Day, a program that brings more than 100 businesses to campus each September to let students make future job contacts and gain more information on potential career paths.

Admission

An applicant for admission to graduate study should hold a bachelor's degree, have an undergraduate GPA of at least 3.0 in the last 60 hours of baccalaureate work, and have a minimum GMAT score of 500. A student whose GPA or GMAT is insufficient may be considered for admission if he or she exceeds the minimum required in the other criterion and has a well-written statement of purpose and strong reference letters.

An international applicant who does not hold an undergraduate degree from a U.S. institution must submit a TOEFL report reflecting a score of 575 or higher, with the application. Students who score below 575 will not be considered for admission into the program.

Finances

For students taking 9 to 13 graduate credit hours in the fall or spring term, estimated tuition and fees are $1237 for Mississippi residents and $2216 for nonresidents. Students enrolling in more than 13 hours must pay according to the rate established per credit hour, which is currently $111 per credit hour, and an activity fee per credit hour, now $31.39. Residence halls cost approximately $600; books and supplies cost approximately $240; meals, $915; and personal expenses, $740. Fees are subject to change without notice.

A number of assistantships are awarded to students working toward their master's degree. These awards, which include a monthly stipend, also include tuition waivers. The awards are based on the student's GMAT score and GPA, with consideration of the student's skills and the needs of the College. Students must be enrolled full-time to be eligible for an assistantship.

Application Facts and Dates

To ensure full consideration for admission to the M.B.A. program, all application materials must be received according to the following deadlines: fall semester, July 1; spring semester, November 1; first summer term, April 1; and second summer term, May 1. For an application and additional information on the M.B.A. program, or on other graduate programs of study in the College of Business and Industry, students should call or write:

Graduate Studies in Business
College of Business and Industry
Mississippi State University
P.O. Drawer 5288
Mississippi State, Mississippi 39762
Telephone: 601-325-1891
Fax: 601-325-2410
E-mail: gsb@cobilan.msstate.edu

Monterey Institute of International Studies

Fisher Graduate School of International Business

Monterey, California

GOING GLOBAL WITH THE MONTEREY M.B.A.

The M.B.A. program at the Monterey Institute provides a passport to entrepreneurship in international business. M.B.A. students find they can "meet the world in Monterey." Up to 50 percent of M.B.A. students come from outside the United States. Most students have studied or worked abroad, and all students can communicate in at least one language in addition to English. The emphasis on multicultural teamwork further enhances the atmosphere of a global village.

The Monterey M.B.A. combines this international orientation with an entrepreneurial focus. Our goal is to educate innovative leaders who can function effectively in many cultural environments and in global business. At Monterey, students complement their course work with active learning in real-life business settings. We believe these abilities underlie success in international management. To foster their growth, we have created an intimate, collegial M.B.A. program where students and faculty work together in a supportive learning environment.

—William R. Pendergast, Dean

Programs and Curricular Focus

The Monterey M.B.A. prepares students for leadership in international business by developing competence in basic business disciplines, communication skills in at least one foreign language, and interpersonal skills including problem solving and cross-cultural teamwork. The Monterey Institute offers a two-year M.B.A. program, a one-year advanced-entry M.B.A. program, and a weekend Executive M.B.A. program. It also offers a Master's International M.B.A. program as a joint venture with the Peace Corps.

The two-year M.B.A. program enrolls students with prior study in diverse academic fields, work experience, and a minimum of two years of university-level foreign language courses. Students enter this program in August or January.

The one-year advanced-entry program enrolls students with previous formal undergraduate business education, significant work experience, and a minimum of three years of university-level foreign language courses. Students enter this program in August or January.

Concentrations within both M.B.A. programs are offered in international trade management, entrepreneurial management, international marketing, international economics and finance, regional business environments, international human resources management, and global business.

Students and the M.B.A. Experience

The Monterey M.B.A. emphasizes the development of skills for effective teamwork in multicultural settings, both in individual courses and particularly in the International Business Plan (IBP).

The IBP integrates the functional disciplines of management through the development of a detailed international business plan for a sponsoring company. It exposes students to the unique aspects of international business environments, hones communication and presentation skills, and develops a strong entrepreneurial orientation. Plans are accomplished in close consultation with a team of experienced faculty members. Students also develop strong relationships with experienced executives at sponsoring companies.

Forty percent of the M.B.A. students are citizens of countries outside the United States. Fifty percent of the students are women, and approximately 11 percent of American students are members of minority groups.

❖ Global Focus

The Monterey M.B.A. has a distinctive emphasis on cross-cultural communication and effectiveness. During the M.B.A. program, students combine business courses with language study in Arabic, Chinese, English, French, German, Japanese, Russian, or Spanish. Although fluency in English is required of all students, one of the Institute's unique opportunities is the availability of business courses taught in languages other than English.

Special Features

Students discover numerous extracurricular opportunities, including the annual International Business and Trade Conference. Internships and participation in international market research and case studies are available through the Business and Economic Development Center, the Small Business Institute, and the International Trade Research Center. The new Center for Trade and Commercial Diplomacy provides a context for conferences and other research activities. Internships and advanced language study are also available through the Institute's summer programs in France, Mexico, China, and Germany.

The Faculty

Teaching is the paramount mission of the M.B.A. faculty, who are not distracted by the demands of undergraduates or of a research-oriented doctoral program. The small size of the Monterey M.B.A. program creates a sense of intimacy and cohesion between students and faculty members, who encourage lively classroom interaction. The faculty members maintain an active intellectual and professional agenda and a close involvement with corporate contacts.

The Business School Network

Corporate Partnerships

Dynamic, innovative companies form partnerships with the Monterey Institute to manage expansion, explore foreign markets, and experiment with new business concepts. Corporate partnerships include business plan sponsorship, internships, job placement, and guest speakers. Students, in consultation with faculty, also conduct research through the business assistance centers. Business executives provide feedback that is part of the continuous improvement of the Monterey M.B.A.

Prominent Alumni

Monterey M.B.A. alumni live and work around the world. They provide a network that is available for business and social contacts. Alumni often return to Monterey and maintain supportive relationships with faculty and administration. Access to this alumni network is an enduring asset for Monterey graduates.

The College and Environs

The Monterey Institute of International Studies has been a leader since 1955 in integrating advanced foreign language education into professional graduate programs in international business, international policy studies, and international public administration. The Monterey Institute also offers M.A. degrees in teaching English to speakers of other languages (TESOL), teaching foreign language, and in translation and interpretation. About half of the 750 students represent more than fifty countries outside the United States. Students share a multidisciplinary experience in course work and social activities.

The Monterey Institute is situated in one of the most spectacular natural environments in the world. The Monterey Peninsula is 120 miles south of San Francisco on California's central coast, surrounded by ocean and mountains; it has a population of 100,000. Students benefit from exposure to the nearby high-tech companies of the Silicon Valley, hospitality industries, and a concentration of agribusiness enterprises.

Facilities

The Monterey Institute's specialized international library has a collection of 68,000 carefully selected volumes and 550 periodical titles, about one third in languages other than English. Its state-of-the-art integrated computer system handles all major library functions. In addition, the CD-ROM workstations offer indexing, abstracts, or full text of periodical articles. On-line database access to a vast array of information is also available through reference services.

Technology Environment

All M.B.A. candidates are expected to achieve literacy in the use of the standard computer software used in today's business environments. Windows-based and Macintosh microcomputer laboratories are available for course-related computing in accounting, finance, quantitative methods, and decision sciences. They also offer workshops, individual assistance, and free Internet access. Computer instruction is further integrated in the preparation of the International Business Plans.

Placement

The School's programs and counseling facilitate job and internship searches, both in the United States and abroad. It provides career counseling, workshops and videotapes on job search skills, coaching for job and internship searches, and a library of internationally oriented career information. Students have access to databases on internship opportunities and to the Institute's 1,400 M.B.A. alumni, who are available to discuss students' career interests and job hunting in their fields and geographic areas.

Admission

Applicants to the M.B.A. programs must have a bachelor's degree from an approved college or university in the United States or the equivalent, with a minimum grade point average of 3.0 on a 4.0 scale. All M.B.A. applicants must submit the GMAT score report and demonstrate foreign language proficiency, or else extend their program with summer language study. Nonnative English speakers must submit a minimum TOEFL score of 550 for the two-year program and a minimum score of 600 for the advanced-entry program. Preference is given to applicants with prior business experience.

Finances

The 1998–99 tuition and fees are $18,200 per year for the two-year M.B.A. program and $24,400 for the advanced-entry M.B.A. program. Personal expenses for housing, food, books and supplies, and other incidentals are estimated at an additional $7500 per year.

Competitive half-tuition scholarships are available to students who combine academic merit with international experience. Scholarship applicants must meet eligibility requirements and complete their admission and scholarship application procedures by the date specified on the scholarship application form.

In addition, some forms of need-based financial aid, available only to U.S. citizens and eligible noncitizens, have application deadlines.

International Students

In recent years, the largest numbers of international M.B.A. students have come from Norway, Japan, France, Thailand, Germany, Belgium, Finland, Denmark, and Austria.

Nonnative speakers of English must use English as their language of study to fulfill the language component. Students who demonstrate exceptionally high levels of written and oral English may take other elective courses in English or study a third language if they qualify at the appropriate level.

In addition to the required orientation for all new students, there is a supplementary orientation for international students and other workshops during the academic year.

Application Facts and Dates

Application may be made at any time, provided it is received at least one month prior to the applicant's proposed semester of enrollment or three months in advance for international students residing in their home countries. Applicants are notified of their admission status within four weeks after the application file is complete.

To request literature about the Monterey M.B.A. or if there are questions regarding application procedures, students should contact:

Monterey Institute of International Studies
Admissions Office
425 Van Buren Street
Monterey, California 93940
Telephone: 408-647-4123
Fax: 408-647-6405
E-mail: admit@miis.edu
World Wide Web: http://www.miis.edu

National University

La Jolla, California

AN M.B.A. PROGRAM THAT ENCOMPASSES THEORETICAL CONCEPTS AND PRACTICAL APPLICATIONS

▶ *The Master of Business Administration (M.B.A.) program provides adult learners with a comprehensive foundation for business decision making and prepares them to be more effective leaders in a rapidly changing business environment. As businesses struggle to cope with a changing work force, new technologies, and more complex government regulations, the need becomes more acute for leaders who possess the knowledge and skills that ensure future success.*

National University has been producing business leaders for more than twenty-five years, and its rigorous, market-driven business programs clearly mark the path to success. We are pleased to help applicants determine how our programs might contribute to their future success.

—Dr. S. M. Azordegan, Dean

Programs and Curricular Focus

The M.B.A. programs at National University have several areas of curricular focus. National offers a general M.B.A. as well as areas of specialization in global management, law, technology management, international business, public administration, entrepreneurship, marketing, environmental management, financial management, human resources management, health-care administration, and telecommunications systems management.

Core requirements consist of ten 5-quarter unit courses designed to provide a solid academic foundation for adult students preparing themselves for the business environment. Courses include accounting and financial management, business research, global management, human resources, international marketing, and strategic planning. The curriculum culminates to help students in a final M.B.A. project.

Students who do not have an undergraduate business degree must satisfactorily complete foundation courses. Successful completion of a foundation skills aptitude exam will exempt students from individual foundation courses. Foundation courses include accounting, algebra, finance, macroeconomics, microeconomics, and statistics.

Students and the M.B.A. Experience

National's School of Management and Technology programs encompass both theoretical concepts and practical

applications. They place special emphasis on the role of management in the formulation and administration of policy and strategic plans.

More than 1,700 students are currently enrolled in graduate business programs at National. Approximately 75 percent of the students are enrolled in the M.B.A. program. The average age of enrolled students is 34, and about half are women. Most students are employed full-time as middle- or upper-level management professionals in business, technology, or government. Class discussions in graduate seminars are enhanced by the maturity, motivation, and varied backgrounds and work experiences of the students.

National draws transfer students from more than 200 universities, with varied interests in careers in accounting, environmental management, finance, health care, human resources, international business, and telecommunications systems.

❖ Global Focus

The M.B.A. degree program culminates in an original, comprehensive project based on a current problem at a deliberately selected site. After completion of statistics and business research methodology and 30 additional quarter units, students are enrolled in the "M.B.A. Project." Students are formed into teams of three or four students who have a common interest or area of specialization and whose schedules enable them to work together. Teams and individuals present their completed project to the Uni-

versity community; the subject organization, if applicable; or at a scheduled presentation event.

Special Features

The Master of Business Administration provides adult learners with a comprehensive foundation for business decision making that prepares them to lead effectively in a rapidly changing business environment. The program enables graduates to manage the challenges of today, including globalization, diversity, social and ethical responsibility, and technology, and to anticipate and adapt to the challenges of tomorrow. The degree encompasses the theoretical concepts and practical applications for business practitioners. Special emphasis is placed on the role of management in the formulation and administration of corporate policy and strategic plans.

The Faculty

The professors selected to teach in National University's M.B.A. program are among the finest in their chosen fields. They combine academic expertise with real-life experience in the professional world. All faculty members are personally committed to students in the program and are readily available to discuss the course work and any other questions to ensure greater student understanding and success.

All faculty members not only hold advanced degrees in their areas of expertise but are respected professionals with many years of career experience. Learning is facilitated through lectures, outside reading, class discussions, case studies, and research projects relating to problems within the students' interests. The expansive knowledge of the students and the diversity of their backgrounds add richness to the group learning experience.

The Business School Network

Alumni, leaders in business, technology, and military, play an integral part in National's statewide business school network. National draws on the expertise and knowledge from local advisory boards, professors in the field in which

---

Muhammad Amin, Assistant Professor;
  Ph.D. Electrical and computer engineer-
  ing.
Hassan Badkoobehi, Assistant Professor;
  Ph.D. Engineering.
John Byrne Jr., Associate Professor; J.D.
  Law.
George Drops, Associate Professor; Ph.D.
  Psychology.
Muhammad El-Mefleh, Assistant Professor;
  Ph.D. Economics.
Reza Fadaei, Associate Professor; Ph.D.
  Economics.
Consolacion L. Fajardo, Assistant Professor;
  D.P.A. Accounting.
Thomas Green, Assistant Professor; Ph.D.
  Sociology.
Deborah LeBlanc, Associate Professor;
  D.P.A. Public administration.
Darryl J. Mitry, Associate Professor; Ph.D.
  Economics.
Jerry Ngati, Assistant Professor; Ph.D.
  Accounting.
Leonid B. Preiser, Professor and Chair;
  Ph.D. Communications technology.
Donald A. Schwartz, Associate Professor;
  J.D., Accounting.
Gary J. Zucca, Assistant Professor; Ph.D.
  Sociology.

they teach, and representatives from local industries who often volunteer to speak in the classroom. On-site programs in business and government entities also serve as a key networking component

The College and Environs

Chartered in 1971, National University is a nonprofit, nonsectarian, independent institution accredited by the Western Association of Schools and Colleges. The University's academic goal is to provide educational opportunities in a meaningful format that prepares students for leadership roles while increasing their competence in specific academic areas. Students are encouraged to register only once for an entire degree program, taking courses in one-month modules of intensive study. A wide variety of core, specialization, and elective courses are offered each month. Both day and evening classes are available.

Facilities

National University's library has been developed with attention to the overall educational purpose of serving career-oriented adults. The University's library includes more than 155,000 volumes and about 2,700 periodicals. Students have free access to the Library Resources Online System (LIBROS), which is on an IBM-platform computer and is available at more than 850 mainframe terminals throughout the University. In addition, students can access the Online Public Access Catalog (OPAC), which contains the bibliographic records for all materials owned by the library.

Writing Across the Curriculum is a University-wide program that enriches students in all areas of learning through the development of writing skills and critical thinking. The University is dedicated to providing students and faculty members with the full range of conceptual, material, and instructional resources and support systems necessary to meet the goals of making writing and research the primary vehicle of education at the University and to distinguish graduates of National University in the eyes of employers and the general public.

Classes are offered at twenty centers in metropolitan areas throughout California, providing increased flexibility. The University also has computer labs, which are open seven days a week to allow students access to the technology required for the programs.

Placement

National has a strong network of more than 55,000 alumni who are employed in business, industry, or government careers. Students who are seeking employment in their career can meet individually with faculty members for career guidance.

Admission

Applicants for master's programs must hold a bachelor's degree or higher from an accredited college or university and have a minimum GPA of 2.5. Under certain conditions, admission on probation may be granted to applicants whose average is 2.0–2.49. All applicants must file a University application, pay a nonrefundable $60 application fee, ($100 for international applicants), and have official transcripts sent to the records office from every college or university previously attended. The University sets no deadlines for receipt of applications for admission and operates under a continuous admission policy. Students may begin their studies any month of the year and pursue their program without delay, following the special one-course-per-month format.

Finances

Many students receive tuition assistance from their employers in the United States or abroad. Students may be eligible for various types of financial assistance such as grants, loans, work-study opportunities, and scholarships, as provided by federal, state, and University programs. Application forms are available in the financial aid office. The University is approved for the training of veterans and maintains a full-service veterans' affairs office.

International Students

National University has students from more than 75 countries enrolled in business programs. Approximately 25 percent of the students in the M.B.A. program are international. Students must provide academic transcripts, a statement of finances, and a TOEFL score of at least 550 or proof of English proficiency.

Application Facts and Dates

For domestic inquiries, students should contact:

M.B.A. Program
National University
11255 North Torrey Pines Road
La Jolla, California 92037
Telephone: 800-NAT-UNIV
        (628-8648, toll-free)
Fax: 619-642-8709
World Wide Web: http://www.nu.edu

For international inquiries, students should contact:

M.B.A. Program
National University
4121 Camino del Rio South
San Diego, California 92108
Telephone: 619-563-7200

New Hampshire College

Manchester, New Hampshire

REAL WORLD MANAGEMENT—THE M.B.A. AT NEW HAMPSHIRE COLLEGE

The M.B.A. degree at New Hampshire College has always been strongly linked to real-world management. From the very beginning we developed a degree with a practical orientation to the business world. And our focus is far more than business in the region or in the United States: we have as well an international orientation to the business world.

Our multinational culture at the Graduate School and our international programs that students may combine with the M.B.A. have long established us as an environment of choice for students directed toward careers in international business.

The response we receive from business leaders, from those who hire and employ our students, is that we are sending them the kind of leader that today's world demands.

—Jacqueline F. Mara, Dean

Programs and Curricular Focus

The New Hampshire College M.B.A. program offers students a range of program options and learning experiences to accommodate the needs of the diverse student body. Both full-time and part-time options are available. Full-time study requires between twelve and eighteen months of work, depending upon both prerequisite work and the pace at which the student chooses to move through the program. Part-time students are generally able to complete the program within 2½ to 3½ years.

New Hampshire College is accredited by the Association of Collegiate Business Schools and Programs (ACBSP). The emphasis of the College is on excellence in teaching, reflected in the combined academic and professional application approach of the M.B.A. program. The case-study method, teamwork, lecture, and practical experience are combined to prepare students for the expectations of complex business environments.

The M.B.A. program also offers courses via distance learning. Using the Internet, students have the option of completing selected M.B.A. courses electronically.

All students are required to take eleven core courses. Students thereafter have the option of pursuing a choice of more than seventy electives either to satisfy their M.B.A. electives or by

combining the M.B.A. with one or more of thirteen certificate programs and six M.S. programs.

The certificate programs include the disciplines of accounting, artificial intelligence, computer information systems, finance, government finance, health administration, human relations management, international business, marketing, operations management, school business administration, taxation, and training and development.

Combined-degree programs are available with the M.S. degree in international business, finance, computer information systems, business education, accounting, or community economic development.

Students and the M.B.A. Experience

The Graduate School's diverse student body creates a dynamic atmosphere for learning. While some of the students enter the program directly out of college, most have two or more years of work experience to share in the classroom. The College realizes the need for students to gain a world view of business and has been successful in recruiting students from more than twenty-five countries.

Students range in age from 21 to 55 and represent a broad spectrum of academic backgrounds and disciplines. Women comprise 40 percent of the graduate enrollment, and international students represent 12 percent.

Forty percent of students have undergraduate degrees in business administration. Other academic backgrounds include engineering, social sciences, education, and the humanities.

❖ Global Focus

New Hampshire College's M.B.A. program includes students from around the world—Canada, Colombia, Egypt, India, Japan, Kenya, Mexico, Russia, South Africa, South Korea, Spain, Sweden, Taiwan, and Turkey are among the countries represented in the program.

In small-class settings, students are exposed to one another's cultural backgrounds and business practices, significantly enhancing their M.B.A. experience.

The M.B.A. curriculum is developed to incorporate the program's international perspective. Case studies and practical applications in required course work provide students with a critical understanding of global business issues.

In addition, elective options in such topics as multinational finance, international negotiations, and international trade and competitiveness can be taken with the M.B.A. degree.

Students wishing to develop a more intensive focus may pursue a certificate in international business or the M.S. in international business in combination with the M.B.A. degree.

New Hampshire College now offers its M.B.A. program in Dubai, United Arab Emirates, and in Athens, Greece. The program is taught primarily by graduate school faculty members who travel from Manchester, New Hampshire, to Dubai for a one-term teaching assignment.

The Faculty

New Hampshire College's faculty members are strongly oriented toward interactive teaching approaches. The focus is on direct involvement in the realities of business management. In addition to their superior academic credentials, the faculty members have extensive experience in business—many of them in international settings.

The Business School Network

Corporate Partnerships

The Institute for Management Research, Development and Assistance is a program of the Graduate School of Business. Its purpose is to conduct and provide business consulting and assistance services to private and nonprofit companies, both nationally and internationally.

The institute uses graduate students to support its activities in business research, training, and management assistance. Of special interest is its Center for International Business, which focuses on all facets of business in relation to international clients or U.S. clients with international requirements.

In addition, advisory boards composed of corporate leaders consistently assist the Graduate School in developing programs that best match the needs of the business community.

The College and Environs

New Hampshire College offers uncrowded, attractive surroundings and easy access to the cultural and other advantages of metropolitan centers. The campus is an hour's drive from Boston and within easy traveling distance of the state's seacoast, lakes, and mountain areas.

Facilities

The Graduate School of Business recently moved to a new state-of-the-art facility on the main campus in Manchester. The building contains modern lecture halls, classrooms, and seminar and conference rooms. The building houses a computer center, classroom PCs are networked, and students have access to the Internet with their own accounts.

Technology Environment

Graduate students have access to a range of modern computing capabilities through the College laboratories. Personal computers, with applications such as Windows-based Lotus SmartSuite, are provided for instructional and student use at all locations. Access to a Digital MicroVax and an IBM mainframe is also available. All student computing laboratories are linked to the Internet.

Placement

New Hampshire College's Career Development Center provides extensive on-campus recruitment opportunities. In addition, internships for credit are available to full-time degree candidates approved by the faculty. Additional services include career advising and assistance in résumé preparation.

Admission

Students with bachelor's degrees from accredited institutions are invited to apply to New Hampshire College's M.B.A. program. Although many applicants have work experience in business or other professional settings, students who are just completing their undergraduate careers are also encouraged to apply.

Unconditional admission to the M.B.A. program requires that the student have previously completed specific business-related courses. Students lacking the courses may be required to take Graduate School of Business foundation courses. International students whose native language is not English must submit TOEFL results.

Finances

Tuition and fees for 1998–99 for full-time students are $17,044, with additional fees of approximately $530. Books and supplies are about $1000 a year.

Application Facts and Dates

Admissions decisions are made on a rolling basis, with a letter normally sent to an applicant within two weeks after the file is complete. International students may obtain applications from the Center for International Education at New Hampshire College (telephone: 603-645-9629, fax: 603-645-9603). For more information, students should contact:

Dean, Graduate School of Business
New Hampshire College
2500 North River Road
Manchester, New Hampshire
    03106-1044
Telephone: 603-644-3102
Fax: 603-644-3144
E-mail: gradad@nhc.edu
World Wide Web: http://www.nhc.edu

New School for Social Research

Robert J. Milano Graduate School of Management and Urban Policy

New York, New York

Programs and Curricular Focus

The Milano Graduate School's curriculum enables each student to acquire an in-depth understanding of the management and policy analysis skills necessary to be an effective professional. The required School-wide core of four courses, policy analysis, economic analysis, quantitative methods, and management and organizational behavior, is designed to provide a firm foundation for work in the student's program. Each degree program also requires its students to complete a five-course program core that focuses on essential material that professionals in that field must master. These courses build on the generic management and policy analysis theories and skills developed in the School-wide core. To round out their degree requirements, students complete five elective courses chosen from the array of options in their specific program or from appropriate courses offered elsewhere in the Milano Graduate School. The opportunity exists for students to specialize further by clustering their electives in a concentration or certificate area within their professional discipline.

Attempted on a full-time basis, the curriculum typically takes two years to complete; on a part-time basis, the typical length of time to complete the program is three years. Full-time students are strongly encouraged to undertake a summer internship between their first and second years of study. These internships, in appropriate agencies and organizations, enable students to become involved in actual work settings with professionals and the issues they confront, which helps students enhance the knowledge and skills developed in the classroom.

Students and the M.S. Experience

One of the major strengths of the Milano Graduate School is the diversity of its faculty members, students, and administrators. Students come from across the United States and a number of other countries. More than one third of the student body is African American, Latino, and Asian American, and more than half are women. Entering students' ages range from 21 to 50, and the range in years of work experience is comparable. This diversity in ethnicity, age, experience, and geography enhances the quality of discourse in the classroom and provides students with a global outlook.

Special Features

The Milano Graduate School of Management and Urban Policy hosts the Leadership Center, which provides an innovative, intellectually stimulating environment within which organizations can learn and practice more effective techniques needed to face current workplace challenges. The center's goals are to develop and present innovative programs to organizational leaders who must manage change in the workplace, to enhance the skills of human resources professionals so they can form strategic partnerships with corporate decision makers, to conduct focused research to explore human resources issues especially relevant in today's diverse and complex environment, and to offer internship opportunities to enhance student development through involvement in these activities.

The Faculty

The Milano Graduate School's faculty represents a diverse cross-section in terms of ethnicity and fields of interest. Approximately one third of the full-time faculty members are female; approximately one quarter of the full-time faculty members are members of historically underrepresented groups. Supplementing the full-time faculty is the adjunct faculty pool. Adjunct faculty members include corporation executives, current and former government officials, and executives of nonprofit enterprises. Most are currently practicing their professions and are able to bring to their teaching firsthand experience and insights that make theory come alive.

The Business School Network

The Milano Graduate School provides numerous opportunities for students to network with members of the business and professional communities. The adjunct faculty members provide a real link to the professional world and are adept at merging theory with practice. Through internships, students are placed in real-world situations and are confronted with developing solutions to the types of problems professionals face on a regular basis. Each of the School's four programs has an advisory board, comprising practitioners who provide insights on curricular issues. Mentoring opportunities are developed in conjunction with the Office of Career Development and Placement.

Prominent Alumni

Examples of positions attained by graduates of the master's degree programs include Director of Human Resources, Central New Jersey Medical Group; Research Associate, Human Resource/Organizational Effectiveness, The Conference Board; Vice President, Citibank; Supervisor, Pension, Health and Unemployment, New York City Department of Environmental Protection; Director, Personnel Operations, Coopers & Lybrand; Program Officer, Housing and Economic Development, Ford Foundation; Chief Financial Officer, Bellevue Hospital; Associate Commissioner for Administration, NYC Department of Probation; National Director of Major and Planned Gifts, AmFAR; Executive Director of College Advancement, Concordia College; Director of Project Management, Vera Institute of Justice; Program Officer, New York City Department for the Aging; and Chief Operating Officer, Promesa, Inc.

The College and Environs

Established in 1919, the New School for Social Research has exemplified a rare tradition of educational innovation. It offers a variety of day, evening, and weekend programs of undergraduate, graduate, and adult education. The university, located in Greenwich Village, is readily accessible from all parts of New York City. Students in the Robert J. Milano Graduate School of Management and Urban Policy are welcome to participate in the many courses and cultural events sponsored by the Graduate Faculty of Political and Social Science and by the Adult Division of the New School.

Placement

The Office of Career Development and Placement assists students in locating internships and provides a full range of counseling and referral services.

Admission

Admission requirements include the completed application form, official transcripts from each postsecondary institution attended, two letters of reference, a 300-word essay, and an interview with a member of the program staff.

Finances

Tuition in 1998–99 for the Robert J. Milano Graduate School of Management and Urban Policy is $622 per credit, payable at registration. A list of fees is included in the brochure describing the various programs. The Milano Graduate School participates in all federal financial aid programs, including the Federal Work-Study program and the Federal Perkins Loan program. Fellowships, assistantships, merit scholarships, and need-based tuition remission are also available.

Application Facts and Dates

The admission decisions are made on a rolling basis after a careful examination of transcripts and letters of recommendation. There is no formal application deadline, but applicants requesting financial aid should apply by April 15 for the fall semester.

Office of Admissions and Financial Aid
Robert J. Milano Graduate School of Management and Urban Policy
66 Fifth Avenue, 7th Floor
New York, New York 10011
Telephone: 212-229-5462
Fax: 212-229-8935
E-mail: mgsinfo@newschool.edu

New York Institute of Technology

PROVIDING AN EDGE TO SUCCESSFULLY COMPETE IN THE WORLD OF BUSINESS

New York Institute of Technology (NYIT) has been in the forefront of career education for four decades, facilitating contemporary challenging careers for thousands of men and women from all walks of life. The graduate business schools's offerings in particular have been designed to enhance personal and professional growth of men and women who are already in business or plan to enter the business world. A responsive faculty of gifted men and women who have distinguished themselves in teaching, research, and the business world bring their unique expertise to NYIT students through curriculum offerings that focus on today's increasingly global and technological orientation. As a result, the graduate offerings provide an edge to our student body to compete successfully in the world of business.

—Dr. J.-C. Spender, Dean

Programs and Curricular Focus

The M.B.A. program at NYIT is designed to provide the student with a working knowledge of the world of business. This includes the ability to analyze and forecast environmental trends, formulate business strategies, and manage functional programs; utilize modern theoretical frameworks in the solution of practical business problems; and synchronize the diversity of the workplace with the requirements of ever-changing markets and societal constituencies.

The curriculum consists of nine core courses aimed to equip the student with a managerial "toolkit" in the basic functional areas of business. The core curriculum culminates in an integrative, multidisciplinary business policy seminar.

Further concentration is available in the areas of accounting, energy management, finance, general management, health-care administration, international business, management of information systems, marketing, human resources management, and labor relations.

To complete the M.B.A. degree, candidates in either the 36-credit general management concentration or in any of the other 42-credit concentrations are required to select from among a master thesis project, an oral examination, or completion of additional course work.

Candidates without prior satisfactory business course work are required to complete up to four additional prerequisite courses in addition to the other degree requirements. Therefore, depending upon the need for prerequisites and selected concen-

tration, total credit requirements vary from thirty-six to fifty-four.

A joint M.B.A./D.O. degree is offered in conjunction with the New York College of Osteopathic Medicine (NYCOM) of NYIT.

Students and the M.B.A. Experience

The student body is diverse in terms of ethnicity, gender, socioeconomic characteristics, and professional status, allowing for synergistic educational interactions. The educational process is further enhanced by small class size, interactions with professors, and student-oriented administration.

NYIT students generally fall into one or more of three categories. Many are practicing professionals in such fields as engineering, police and security, accounting, marketing, and research and are preparing to become managers in their specialized areas. A second group, already in management positions at a variety of levels, are in the process of improving administrative skills in order to achieve better performance in their present jobs or gain promotions. The final category is composed of students who enroll directly after completing college.

The great majority of the M.B.A. students are pursuing their degrees on a part-time basis while maintaining full-time employment. In order to accommodate the scheduling needs of this group of students, classes are offered on evenings and weekends on the three New York campuses (Manhattan; Old West-

bury, Long Island; and Islip, Long Island) and in a Saturday-only format at the Boca Raton, Florida, site.

In addition, the M.B.A. program is also offered on line to provide all students, regardless of location or time constraints, an opportunity to complete their degree. Students should see NYIT's Web site (http://www.nyit.edu/olc) for more information about the online program.

❖ Global Focus

Recognizing that today's successful business leader requires a global perspective, all courses incorporate global content. Furthermore, NYIT's M.B.A. program offers an international business concentration that provides students with an opportunity to enroll in courses covering such areas as international finance, international marketing, cross-cultural promotion, import-export operations, and comparative economic systems. In addition, M.B.A. students benefit from the opportunity to study and communicate with students from other countries, who comprise approximately 30 percent of the total annual enrollment, as well as faculty members who have international backgrounds and roots.

The Faculty

All courses are taught and administered by faculty members. No teaching assistants are used for any facet of the educational experience. Full-time faculty members hold terminal degrees from leading U.S. and international institutions. Furthermore, they represent a broad spectrum of business and consulting experience. Adjunct faculty members are utilized to supplement the program's needs in the areas of their unique experience. All in all, faculty members are selected for their academic background, practical experience, and their love for teaching.

The Business School Network

NYIT's Graduate School of Management maintains ongoing relationships with local tri-state business communities through its more than 3,500 alumni and an Advisory Council, whose members represent such well-known organizations as Olsten Corporation; Chemical/Chase Banking Corporation; Harrows, Inc.; and Coopers & Ly-

brand. In addition, several successful on-site M.B.A. programs have been designed and offered to corporate employees.

The College and Environs

Few states offer students more in the way of culture, history, entertainment, or opportunity than New York. The New York Stock Exchange, major financial institutions, broadcast and communication firms, and clothing designers and manufacturers represent just a sampling of the industry that makes New York so dynamic.

NYIT's Manhattan campus is ideally located in the heart of New York City. On Broadway and 61st Street, the campus is adjacent to Lincoln Center and only a short walk from the world-renowned Carnegie Hall. Major museums such as the American Museum of Natural History and the Metropolitan Museum of Art are easily accessible, as are the many other museums located throughout the five boroughs.

With a choice from more than 200 museums and historic sites, students attending either the Old Westbury or Islip campus also find many interesting things to do and places to visit. Long Island is also known worldwide for its beaches and waterways, including the Hamptons and Montauk Point.

International students find a visit to the United Nations of special interest and sports fans find it difficult to choose from among the many professional and collegiate basketball, hockey, soccer, football, and baseball games that are available throughout the year.

Facilities

NYIT libraries are maintained at all campuses, and all students have access to total collections through intralibrary loan service. As a member of the Long Island Resources Council and the New York Metropolitan Reference and Research Library Agency, NYIT provides access to holdings of other academic libraries in the area. Bibliographic searches on computer databases are available through the Wisser Library on the Old Westbury Campus.

Computer lab facilities are available on each campus. All three New York campuses are connected via an interactive state-of-the-art system of distance learning laboratory rooms, which permits a course to be simultaneously taught to students at two or more sites. This feature provides students with an opportunity to gain valuable experience in using the latest technology being used by many corporations for meetings and other forms of communication.

Placement

NYIT maintains a Career Development and Placement Office with a full-time professional staff who assists graduate students in making informed choices. Career counseling, including job search, resume preparation, and interviewing techniques, is provided. On-campus recruiting visits are scheduled with many of the nation's top corporations. The active Business School alumni also provide mentoring and networking opportunities.

Admission

All applicants are required to hold a bachelor's degree or its equivalent from an accredited college or university and must submit the completed application form, application fee, official transcript from each institution previously attended, and scores obtained on the Graduate Management Admissions Test (GMAT). Each application and accompanying materials receive a personal review from the M.B.A. director or M.B.A. administrator. Admission is predicated on the achievement of a satisfactory composite score, as established by the M.B.A. faculty. The composite score consists of a weighted combination of the applicant's undergraduate quality point average and the score achieved on the GMAT. Applicants may be admitted to either fully or provisionally matriculated status, depending on the composite score.

Finances

Tuition for 1998–99 is $413 per graduate credit, along with a one-time application

fee of $50. Tuition charges are the same for both residents and nonresidents of New York State. Most students live off-campus in adjacent residential communities. However, NYIT does provide graduate housing on the Islip campus. Costs for on-campus housing for 1998–99 range from $1600 to $1800 per semester, and meal plan costs range from $1400 to $1550 per semester. Limited financial aid in the form of tuition credit is available through graduate assistantships and graduate student aide positions. Candidates may also qualify for one of three types of graduate scholarships, which will reduce tuition by one third. The Office of Financial Aid assists applicants who are seeking loans or other available forms of assistance.

International Students

New York Institute of Technology has a long, rich tradition of enrolling qualified graduate students who have completed undergraduate degrees in other countries. International candidates to the M.B.A. program must meet all conditions previously listed and submit a TOEFL of at least 500 for consideration. Prospective international students should note that NYIT tests applicants with less than a 550 on TOEFL. Those students may be required to enroll in additional English courses.

The M.B.A. department also considers applications from students who have successfully completed three- or four-year postsecondary programs at accredited international institutions that are equivalent to at least three years of undergraduate study in the United States. If accepted, such students enroll in a special "bridge" program, which, among other conditions, requires completion of an additional 30 credits of undergraduate/graduate course work.

Application Facts and Dates

NYIT maintains a policy of rolling admissions without cut-off dates but recommends submission of application materials by June for the fall semester and by October for the spring semester. Typically, applicants receive an admissions decision within four to six weeks after receipt of application.

Requests for application materials or additional information should be addressed to:

Glenn S. Berman
Executive Director of Admissions
New York Institute of Technology
P.O. Box 8000
Old Westbury, New York 11568-8000
Telephone: 516-686-7871
        800-345-NYIT (toll-free)
Fax: 516-626-0419
E-mail: gberman@iris.nyit.edu

New York University

Leonard N. Stern School of Business

New York, New York

THE STERN SCHOOL: A WORLD LEADER IN GLOBAL BUSINESS EDUCATION

► *The Stern School of Business offers an M.B.A. program that infuses every course with the principles of globalism, teamwork, and strong communication skills. Stern graduates are leaders in virtually every sector of the world's economy.*

Our superb Management Education Center is located at the epicenter of the world's business decision making, a stone's throw away from the corporate suites of Wall Street and midtown Manhattan. We're visited by leaders of industry and finance on a regular basis. We have a strong sense of community, with more than half of our distinguished faculty living within a few blocks of the School.

As a training ground for people equipping themselves to lead business into the next century, Stern is more than the sum of its students, faculty, and curriculum. It's a laboratory where everyday ideas get tested and creative solutions are applied to complex business problems.

—George G. Daly, Dean

Programs and Curricular Focus

The Stern M.B.A. program provides an integrated curriculum that establishes a solid foundation for success in business. The excellent faculty, strong global focus, and relationship with the professional community create opportunities for students to gain expertise.

Stern's curriculum is divided into three parts: the core courses, major courses, and electives. The core program, which students take in "blocks" or cohort groups, provides analytical and conceptual foundations and hones the functional skills required to solve complex business problems. Students specialize in the second semester by taking elective courses that prepare them for summer internships. The program offers numerous electives taught by leading scholars. Independent surveys rank many of Stern's functional areas among the world's best. Most notable are international business, finance, information systems, marketing, and entrepreneurial studies.

Stern's novel Multidisciplinary Exercise in Teambuilding (MET) complements the first-year experience. Designed to replicate an actual business setting, small teams of students spend five weeks examining a leading company. The exercise develops management communication and strategic business insights through studying the case history of a company facing real challenges. The culmination of the MET finds teams presenting their corporate strategy to a Board of Directors composed of faculty members and business executives. Students concentrate on major and elective course work during the second year, while the "block" structure continues in the required capstone courses.

Students and the M.B.A. Experience

Stern's integrative approach to management education requires teams of teachers to present a comprehensive view of a common problem. For example, Stern's analysis of General Motors' purchase of Electronic Data Systems incorporated several disciplines. The management professor outlined the strengths and weaknesses of corporate diversification. The information systems faculty member detailed the technological imperatives of the deal. The accounting professor pinpointed a financial concept that caused disputes between parent and subsidiary. Finally, the statistics professor charted the quantitative performance of corporate diversification strategies. This integrative approach brings subjects to life.

Stern students come from all over the world; one third of the students are from more than fifty countries, and the domestic students come from across the country. They form a lively community whose diversity enriches Stern. Students have ambitious and unique career goals. Many hope to work on Wall Street; others want to work for multinational consumer product companies, start new businesses, work with nonprofit organizations, and more.

Students have an average of four years of work experience coming from many industries. Women comprise 35 percent of the population, and minority students make up 18 percent. As undergraduates, Stern students have studied social sciences (32 percent), business administration (32 percent), mathematics/science (22 percent), and humanities (9 percent).

❖ Global Focus

The Stern School is uniquely qualified to provide one of the world's most internationally oriented M.B.A. programs. Few business schools have such a diverse range of nationalities, cultures, and backgrounds in its student body. Stern's international business department offers many electives and the opportunity to co-major with another functional area.

As a founding member of the International Management Program, Stern has been providing students with the opportunity to gain further education at one of more than thirty other top business schools around the world. Stern is one of a select group of U.S. graduate business schools to offer certification in European–North American Studies in Management.

For less formal education, student groups conduct trips to other countries. Previous trips have included visits to the Far East, Eastern Europe, South America, Africa, Europe, and the Middle East. Through the M.B.A. Enterprise Corps, Stern graduates have acquired jobs in emerging international markets.

Special Features

The Entrepreneurs' Exchange, Graduate Finance Association, Graduate Marketing Association, and Emerging Markets Association enable students to discuss career options. Student-run professional consulting groups, such as the Urban Business Assistance Corporation (UBAC), help members of minority groups and women start businesses. The European-American Consulting Forum enables students to consult for multinational firms.

The Office of Student Activities is committed to enhancing the lives of students and providing close interaction among faculty members, administrators, and students. There are several Dean's Hours, which enable students to meet

The Management Education Center at the Stern School of Business.

informally to discuss pressing issues. Students meet alumni and other corporate executives at special events, such as Stern's Annual Alumni Business Conference, and through speaking engagements like the "Meet America's CEO's" series.

The Faculty

Stern's faculty presently includes Nobel laureates, members of the National Academy of Science, prize-winning authors, and dozens of scholars whose research interests and teaching skills have been recognized worldwide. They often rank highest for published work and are regularly sought as consultants by major corporations. The 200 full-time and 100 adjunct faculty members bring a wealth of international experience to the classroom.

The Business School Network

Prominent business leaders teach in the classroom and also speak frequently at student-organized events.

Prominent Alumni

More than 50,000 Stern alumni hold positions in every major industry worldwide. Stern counts among its alumni a number of notable business leaders, including Alan Greenspan, Chairman of the Federal Reserve; Jeffrey Koo, Chairman and CEO of ChinaTrust Commercial Bank; Leonard N. Stern, Chairman and CEO of The Hartz Group, Inc.; Tatsuro Toyoda, President of Toyota Motor Company; Harvey Golub, Chairman and CEO of American Express; Henry Kaufman, President of Henry Kaufman & Co.; Richard S. Fuld Jr., Chairman and CEO of Lehman Brothers; Mary Farrell, Managing Director of Paine Webber; and Thomas Labrecque, President and COO of The Chase Manhattan Bank, N.A.

The College and Environs

New York University, established in 1831, has thirteen schools, colleges, and divisions at five major centers in Manhattan. The graduate business school was opened in 1916.

Stern has more than thirty student organizations that enhance extracurricular life at the School. Students have free use of the Coles Sports and Recreation Center, one of NYC's best-equipped fitness facilities. The cultural wealth of New York City enriches students. Numerous off-Broadway theaters, concert halls, jazz clubs, and cafés are within steps of campus.

Facilities

In the 1980s, several internationally renowned research centers were established at the University. They are the Center for Japan-U.S. Business and Economic Studies, the Salomon Center, the Glucksman Institute for Research in Securities Markets, and the Berkley Center for Entrepreneurial Studies. In 1992, the Stern School opened the Management Education Center (MEC). The MEC offers spacious, modern classrooms as well as advanced computing and communications technology.

Placement

Students who use the services of the Office of Career Development (OCD) find their desired jobs through on-campus interviews, job postings, and other proactive search activities. More than 200 companies come to Stern during the year to interview students for full-time and summer employment. Many of the recruiting companies also host corporate presentations before interviewing on campus. These events are useful for helping students obtain a sharper career focus and gain knowledge about the industry; they also provide networking opportunities.

To ensure that key corporate recruiters evaluate the resumes of Stern students, OCD publishes resume books, indexed by areas of interest, language skills, international working authorization, professional licenses, and other categories. They are circulated to more than 300 leading employers and also posted on the World Wide Web. Through OCD's Corporate Outreach Program, additional resumes are sent to companies that advertise job opportunities. A spring career fair provides students with information about growing companies and networking opportunities in alternative fields. The top industries chosen by graduates are investment banking, commercial banking, management consulting, and consumer products.

Admission

The M.B.A. program is open to any qualified person who holds a bachelor's degree from an accredited undergraduate institution. When reviewing applications, Stern evaluates the candidate's previous academic work, GMAT score, nature and extent of previous work experience, personal essays, and letters of recommendation. All applicants whose native language is not English must take the TOEFL. Interviews are conducted by Admission Committee invitation only.

Finances

Full-time tuition and fees for the 1997–98 academic year were $25,486. Merit-based scholarships are available.

International Students

More than one third of Stern's class comes from outside of the United States. The Management Communication Program offers a seven-day seminar, "Communicating in American Business." The workshop offers an opportunity to work with faculty members and businesspeople. Several student groups promote international partnerships throughout Stern.

Application Facts and Dates

The full-time M.B.A. program begins in the fall only (March 15 deadline). January 15 is the deadline for scholarship consideration. For more information, students should contact:

Director, M.B.A. Admissions
Office of M.B.A. Admissions and
    Financial Aid
Leonard N. Stern School of Business
New York University
44 West Fourth Street, Suite 10-160
New York, New York 10012-1126
Telephone: 212-998-0600
Fax: 212-995-4231
E-mail: sternmba@stern.nyu.edu
World Wide Web: http://www.stern.
    nyu.edu/

Nijenrode University

Breukelen, The Netherlands

IN DUALITATE FORTITUDO

Nijenrode is an exciting place. It is where you can complete the traditional elements of an M.B.A. and, at the same time, not only study but also "live" internationality and experience cross-cultural life in a professional business setting. Today, the Nijenrode credo, In Dualitate Fortitudo, means that success in business requires diversity in terms of the tools, skills, and behaviours you uphold. In addition, we recognise that we have an obligation to train future managers to lead organisations and the communities of which they are part into a new era. This requires lateral thinkers who can adjust, adapt, and innovate. It is through this ability that our graduates show, time and time again, that they have the strength of character to take the lead.

—Karel Samsom, Associate Dean of M.B.A. Programmes and Professor of Entrepreneurship

Program and Curricular Focus

Nijenrode University strives to ensure that its M.B.A. graduates develop a global mindset. Managers of the twenty-first century must learn to appreciate the behavior, beliefs, values, and business practices of individuals and organizations from different parts of the world. As a result, the programme's focus is on international business and the creation of a multicultural environment in which the development of interpersonal as well as conceptual skills is nurtured. The focus of the International M.B.A. Programme is general management in an international context. This intensive, full-time, thirteen-month programme is conducted in English and has candidates who represent nationalities from around the world. A strong emphasis is placed on broadening the perspective of young managers in all areas of business. The programme includes five terms of course work and a challenging three-month company-sponsored project or optional finance specialisation. In addition to providing students with a thorough grounding in marketing, finance, accounting, and operations management, the programme also focuses on developing the ability to communicate, motivate, and lead. It is an intensive programme that combines a variety of teaching methods with different learning styles. The objective for the International M.B.A. is not only to inform but also to inspire.

Students and the M.B.A. Experience

The Nijenrode M.B.A. class is characterised by its diversity. Candidates come from a rich variety of backgrounds and professions. The participants have an average of about four years of professional experience in a variety of business backgrounds.

The Business School Network

Nijenrode University, with its long-established tradition of providing business education, is supported by leading names in the corporate world. Half a century ago, KLM Royal Dutch Airlines, Unilever, Shell, and Philips, among others, agreed on a common internationally oriented goal and combined forces to establish the first business school in the Netherlands—Nijenrode. Today, these companies remain among the world leaders and enjoy international recognition and the respect of the business community worldwide. Students who choose to earn an M.B.A. at Nijenrode University become part of its heritage and enjoy a connection to some of the biggest names in business.

One of Nijenrode's strengths has traditionally been its close links with business, which is reflected in the participation of executives in all facets of the School's activities. Recognising the importance of this component, Nijenrode University has made the Executive Forum an integral part of the International M.B.A. Programme. Prominent guest speakers from business and governmental and international institutions are invited to take part in the Executive Forum, a meeting place for the exchange of ideas and the discussion of salient issues that effect successful functioning of companies in the global marketplace.

The College and Environs

Nijenrode University lies between the River Vecht and the Amsterdam-Rhine Canal in the heart of Holland. Amsterdam, a city renowned for its vibrancy and culture, and Schipol Airport (voted the world's number one airport on numerous occasions) are only 20 kilometers (12 miles) away. Nijenrode is conveniently located on one of Holland's main highways, which provides easy access to international airports, ferry terminals, the rest of the country, and the whole of Europe.

A history rich in culture, commerce, and creativity has earned the Netherlands international recognition. Today, the country's technological skills and entrepreneurship are globally admired. Recently, the Economist Intelligence Unit put the Netherlands at the top of its rankings of the most desirable global business environments over the next five years.

Facilities

The Nijenrode campus, covering 140 acres of rich parkland, is bordered by a nature reserve with ample wildlife. The thirteenth-century castle and picturesque coach house provide a stunning contrast to the modern student accommodations. Residence on campus is optional but recommended because it enables students to fully benefit from the Nijenrode community and to talk and work with colleagues outside office hours. Living on campus also reduces travel costs and time. The accommodation is just a short walk from the classrooms and is close to the restaurant, launderette, and leisure facilities. All standard rooms have a private bathroom, bed, wardrobe, desk, bookcase, and refrigerator. Fully furnished rooms, some with a kitchenette, are also available. Extra services, such as telephone, cable, TV, and linen and room cleaning are provided at extra cost.

At the heart of the campus is Nijenrode's library, an indispensable source of information for students and researchers in international management. The quality of the library is underlined by the number of corporate clients and alumni who continue to use its services on a regular basis. More information about the Nijenrode Library and its services is available via the Internet at http://www.nijenrode.nl/library.

ing in a short amount of time. Clearly, it takes a certain type of individual to cope with the pace of this approach. The one-year International M.B.A. Programme at Nijenrode University is for men and women who have demonstrated the potential for greater advancement. Nijenrode seeks individuals who have the vision to seize opportunities, the intellectual ability to grasp complex concepts, the motivation to learn in a team-oriented environment, the interpersonal skills to communicate effectively, the integrity to act according to high ethical standards, the emotional intelligence to appreciate multi-cultural surroundings, the potential to lead and win the respect of others, and the drive to succeed. Candidates must possess a university degree (or equivalent) with an excellent academic record and have a thorough command of written and spoken English as well as two years of full-time professional work experience (preferred). Candidates must also submit results of the Graduate Management Admission Test (GMAT) and the Test of English as a Foreign Language (for nonnative English speakers only) in addition to an application package that includes written essays and letters of recommendation. A selection interview takes place after the complete application package has been reviewed by the Admissions Committee.

Technology Environment

Innovation characterises Nijenrode's approach to information services. The best and latest equipment is available 24 hours per day for student use. Two computer rooms are equipped with eighty networked personal computers that run Windows 95 and Microsoft Office 97. Other programmes, including graphics suites, various Internet applications, and software to create personalized Web pages are also available. On arrival, students are assigned computer accounts and have access to e-mail and databases worldwide via the Internet. Computers are also installed in the small conference rooms that are available for group meetings and discussions.

Full multimedia facilities in all classrooms support a wide range of teaching techniques, which enables professors and students to use personal computers that are linked to professional presentation media, audiovisual equipment, and computer-simulation facilities. Recognising the value of exposing students to the latest technology, Toshiba recently donated seven top-of-the-line multimedia laptop computers, which have been installed in all De Rooij classrooms. During the course of the programme, students master a range of presentation techniques, from simple whiteboard demonstrations to sophisticated PowerPoint shows. In addition, guest speakers can interact with students via videoconferencing. Students who are unable to attend one of the Universi-

ty's important occasions, such as the ceremony at which Bill Gates was awarded an honorary Nijenrode doctorate degree, are able to watch it live on the Internet.

Placement

With so many people undertaking an M.B.A. programme in order to augment or shift their careers, career services is always an important component. At Nijenrode, M.B.A. Career Services is part of fulfilling the promise of education and developing career opportunities. Career Services plays an integral role in students' job searches by helping them to clarify career objectives and by matching their talents with the right companies. More broadly, through its many recruiting activities, the Office of Career Services provides an important point of contact with the corporate world.

The other main clients of the Office of Career Services are the employing and recruiting companies. Each year, top multinational companies come to Nijenrode to present their firms to the class and to conduct recruiting sessions. The Office of Career Services positions itself as a business partner for these organisations and continuously seeks new ways in which to support them in their recruiting efforts.

Admission

Over the years, Nijenrode has developed a way of teaching that allows maximum learn-

Finances

The thirteen-month 1998–99 International M.B.A. Programme costs DFL 38,000 (excluding books). Use of the business school library and 24-hour access to computer and Internet facilities are also included. Although costs vary according to individual expectations and lifestyle, monthly rent and living expenses are between DFL 1500 and DFL 2000 for a single student. Most students choose to live on campus.

Application Facts and Dates

Applications are processed on a continuous basis in order of receipt and should be submitted as early as possible. The Admissions Committee begins reviewing applications in December. The final application deadline for the M.B.A. Programme is May 15. The Admissions Committee makes every effort to provide students with their final decisions within four weeks after the completed application is received. For more information, students should contact:

M.B.A. Admissions Office
Nijenrode University
Straatweg 25
3621 BG Breukelen
The Netherlands
Telephone: 011 31 346 29 1607
Fax: 011 31 346 25 05 95
E-mail: mba@nijenrode.nl

North Carolina State University

College of Management

Raleigh, North Carolina

USING TECHNOLOGY FOR COMPETITIVE ADVANTAGE

In 1993 I became the founding dean of North Carolina State University's (NC State) new College of Management after nineteen years as dean at Michigan State. We are building a program from the ground up—hiring the faculty and designing a curriculum that meets the needs of tomorrow's managers. The Master of Science in Management program at NC State emphasizes the management of information, operations, and technology, areas that have been traditionally neglected in M.B.A. programs. Our technology focus leverages the strengths of NC State in engineering, science, and design and prepares our graduates for leadership roles in high-tech companies, many of which operate here in the Research Triangle.

—Richard J. Lewis, Dean

Programs and Curricular Focus

The Master of Science in Management (M.S.M.) program is a specialized degree emphasizing the management of technology. An integrative curriculum introduced in the fall of 1995 emphasizes business processes, such as new product development, rather than traditional organizational functions, such as marketing or finance. Students begin the program with a course that provides an overview of critical business processes, an introduction to business strategy, and initial training in individual and group effectiveness. Core material related to traditional business functions, such as finance and marketing, is covered in half-semester modules that emphasize those topics that every manager needs to know and that are especially relevant to technology management. In their last semester, all students complete a practicum in which they work on a management issue in a real organization. Full-time students can complete the program in three to four semesters; part-time students can finish in 2½ to 3 years, including summer terms.

The technology focus of the program comes from two sources. First, all students take core courses in operations management, management information systems, leadership, and management of technology. Then, all students complete a concentration related to management of technology, such as operations, information systems, technology transfer, or product development. Students also have the option to take advanced courses in engineering or science. In any semester M.S.M. students may take courses in industrial engineering, electrical engineering, statistics, and computer science to gain skills and knowledge that are not generally available in most business schools. Many students in other colleges at NC State receive minors in management and are enrolled in the same management courses as M.S.M. students, creating a more diverse learning environment.

Students and the M.S.M. Experience

Almost all M.S.M. students have professional work experience, many with high-technology industries such as telecommunications or software and others in industries such as health care or financial services, where technology is the key to competitive advantage. A technical background is not essential for the M.S.M., but all students must be willing to learn about technology and the management challenges it creates. More than 60 percent of M.S.M. students have undergraduate degrees in science, computer science, or engineering. Another 24 percent were business majors. The rest come from a variety of fields, including the social sciences and humanities.

The average M.S.M. student has 5.8 years of work experience. The age range of students is between 22 and 45. Women comprise approximately 30 percent of each entering class; members of minority groups, approximately 8 percent; and international students, 15 percent.

Special Features

The Technology, Education, and Commercialization (TEC) program within the M.S.M. is designed to promote both educational and technology transfer objectives. Supported by the National Science Foundation, graduate students and faculty members in the College of Management work closely in teams with their counterparts in the science and engineering disciplines to identify, evaluate, and commercialize promising technologies.

The TEC curriculum follows the complete product development cycle. Students gain evaluation skills for commercializing new technologies along with an understanding of what it takes to start and run a high-technology business. By working together, management and engineering students learn to understand each other and to share broader perspectives. Students also interact with business experts and entrepreneurs from outside the University.

The Faculty

The 88 graduate faculty members affiliated with the College of Management bring a diversity of perspectives to the classroom. Faculty members in the College's graduate programs have been selected for the Board of Governors' Award, Alumni Distinguished Professorships, and the Academy of Outstanding Teachers. They match their teaching methods to the subject material, using case discussions, group projects, lectures, class discussions, and guest speakers, as appropriate.

The faculty is committed to breaking down organizational barriers to teaching and research. More than a dozen of the graduate faculty members have joint appointments with other departments and graduate programs. The faculty is internationally renowned for research, with several members serving on editorial boards of journals in various fields. Many faculty members have had careers in management before receiving their doctoral degrees and stay in touch with today's business world through consulting and executive education.

The Business School Network

M.S.M. students have multiple opportunities to network with businesses. Some of these opportunities are built into the courses. Students in the TEC program interact extensively with venture capitalists, entrepreneurs, and lawyers to learn how to launch a high-technology enterprise. Many TEC projects involve technologies under consideration at local companies. Based on his experience with TEC, Jeffrey Glass, Director of Research and Development at Kobe Steel USA in Research Triangle Park, said, "I think the concept is fantastic. There is a real void in teaching product development in high-tech. So I think this program will be great for industry." The practicum requirement also gives students opportunities to interact with local companies.

Outside of the classroom, many full-time students help finance their graduate study and gain valuable work experience in co-op positions at the leading companies in the Research Triangle area, such as IBM, Northern Telecom, Glaxo Wellcome, and Ericsson. These positions can be obtained either through the University or by networking with classmates. Another key part of the M.S.M. network is the College of Management's Board of Advisors, which includes representatives from the leading companies in the region, including IBM, Northern Telecom, Wachovia, and Carolina Power and Light.

The College and Environs

NC State was founded in 1889 as a land-grant institution that, within 100 years, has become one of the nation's leading research universities. Located in the Research Triangle, a world-renowned center of research, industry, technology, and education, the College of Management is housed on the 623-acre main campus of NC State, which lies just west of downtown Raleigh, the state capital. NC State comprises eleven colleges and schools serving a total student population of 27,000. More than 5,000 of those students are in graduate programs.

Facilities

The College of Management is headquartered in Nelson Hall, which houses classrooms, computer labs, and the offices of the faculty members and students. The College of Management's computer lab houses 100 microcomputers connected to a campuswide Unix-based network. Students have access to a wide range of spreadsheet, word processing, database, statistical, and econometric software along with several large databases. D. H. Hill Library, located near the center of campus, offers access to millions of volumes of books and journals and an extensive and growing collection of CD-ROM and electronic databases. Graduate students also have borrowing privileges at Duke, UNC–Chapel Hill, and NC Central.

Placement

An M.S.M. degree gives students skills that are highly valued by employers. The College's students have access to a wide range of programs and services to enhance their marketability. Self-assessment exercises are built into the courses, and professional career counseling is available at the Career Planning and Placement Center (CPPC). CPPC provides workshops on resume writing and cover letters, interviewing skills, and job search strategies. In addition to on-campus recruiting for permanent jobs and internships, CPPC maintains an on-line resume referral service, job listing notebooks, job fairs, and a library of information about career opportunities with specific companies. In addition, students may post their resumes on the M.S.M. home page on the World Wide Web.

Admission

M.S.M. students must have a baccalaureate degree from an accredited college or university and are strongly encouraged to have had courses in calculus, statistics, and economics. Admissions decisions are based on previous academic performance, GMAT scores (590 average, no minimum cutoff score), an essay, letters of reference, and previous work and volunteer experience. Applicants whose native language is other than English, regardless of citizenship, must also submit TOEFL scores of at least 550. Interviews are not required.

Finances

The 1997–98 budget for M.S.M. students depended on the number of credit hours the student took and the student's residency status. For full-time students who were North Carolina residents, the tuition and fees cost $1138 per semester; the estimated total for living expenses, including tuition and fees, books, medical insurance, housing, food, clothing, transportation, and other miscellaneous items, was $6423 per semester. Tuition and fees for full-time nonresidents were $5631 per semester, with estimated total living expenses at $10,916 per semester. Part-time students who were North Carolina residents paid $819 per semester for tuition and fees only; nonresidents paid $4188. Graduate assistantships are available to full-time students through the College of Management. Grants and loan programs are available through the Graduate School and the University's Financial Aid Office.

Application Facts and Dates

The NC State M.S.M. program accepts applications for both the fall and spring semesters, with application deadlines of May 1 and October 1, respectively. Once an application has been received and is complete, it is reviewed for admission. This rolling admission process allows an applicant to receive an admission decision within two weeks of receipt of a completed application.

Ms. Pam Bostic
Assistant Director
M.S.M. Program
North Carolina State University
Box 7229
Raleigh, North Carolina 27695
Telephone: 919-515-5584
Fax: 919-515-5073
E-mail: msm@ncsu.edu

Northeastern University

Boston, Massachusetts

M.B.A.S DESIGNED FOR THE REAL WORLD

For nearly fifty years, Northeastern University's Graduate School of Business Administration has provided students all over the world with what many feel is the best practice-oriented business curriculum in the nation. The focus is on practical learning that uses relevant, real-world experience to hone marketable skills. Five M.B.A. programs and a Master of Science in Finance are offered, with flexible full- and part-time scheduling available to fit individual objectives, work schedules, and lifestyles. The Graduate School of Business Administration is accredited by the AACSB–The International Association for Management Education.

—Mary Elise Wirtz, Director

Programs and Curricular Focus

Rich in the tradition of experience-based education, the Graduate School of Business Administration is known for excellence in application and integration of theory and practice. The twenty-one-month Cooperative Education M.B.A. Program combines six months of integrative course work with a six-month paid professional business experience. A final nine months completes the degree. Cooperative Education M.B.A. students begin the program in January and June of each year.

In the two-year Full-Time M.B.A. Program, students stay connected to the workforce through relationships with their executive mentors, tailored electives, internships, independent study, and team consulting projects. A typical entering class consists of students from a myriad of professional, cultural, and academic backgrounds. Career goals can be equally diverse. Students begin this program each September.

In both programs, students master a general management curriculum and choose from a broad range of elective courses. These electives allow students to tailor their degree to match their own needs and interests. Electives can be taken within any of Northeastern's nine graduate and professional schools. Independent study projects can be designed for in-depth pursuit of a subject of special interest.

The J.D./M.B.A. is an accelerated forty-five-month program. Candidates must apply and be accepted to both programs.

The Faculty

More than 100 full-time professors, organized in six groups and eighteen functional areas, teach M.B.A. students in the Graduate School of Business Administration. Their credentials, experience, research interests, and publications are profiled in a booklet that is mailed on request. Many are active as consultants to businesses around the world. All are accustomed to being challenged on the practical applications of their research.

Placement

M.B.A. students at Northeastern have their own dedicated Career Center next to their

classrooms and lounges. Recognizing the challenging nature of the workforce, Northeastern actively trains students in a broad range of skills for job search and career advancement. Workshops are tailored each year to student needs. The M.B.A. Career Center serves the employers by matching resumes for employment openings and provides students with advanced technology for targeting job search campaigns. Panels of graduates and mentors provide stimulus and support. Alumni are welcome to use the M.B.A. Career Center to refresh their skills.

Admission

Successful applicants demonstrate academic competence through their undergraduate records and a GMAT score; motivation and maturity are demonstrated through essays and recommendations. Personal interviews are required for admission to the Cooperative M.B.A. Program. Prospective students are invited to visit the campus and meet with current students who conduct tours, arrange class visits, and answer questions.

Finances

Total tuition costs for the Full-Time or Cooperative M.B.A. Programs in

1998–99 are $42,000 ($500 per quarter hour for a total of 84 quarter hours of course work). Average earnings of about $15,000 during the six-month Cooperative Education employment period help students defray these costs. Tuition rates, fees, rules, regulations, and curricula are subject to revision by the president and the Board of Trustees at any time.

International Students

The University's International Student Office helps with the issues associated with living in a foreign country. It offers counseling on immigration regulations, as well as with academic, financial, and personal concerns. The office also acts as a liaison between the departments, colleges, and agencies concerned with foreign nationals in the academic community.

Application Facts and Dates

The application deadline for the Full-Time M.B.A. Program is April 1 (February 15 for early decision). The admissions committee will review applications after April 1 if space is still available. The deadline for the January Cooperative Education M.B.A. class is November 1; for the June class, the deadline is April 15. Students are admitted on a rolling basis. For more information, students should contact:

Graduate School of Business
350 Dodge Hall
360 Huntington Avenue
Northeastern University
Boston, Massachusetts 02115
Telephone: 617-373-2714
Fax: 617-373-8564
E-mail: gsba@cba.neu.edu
World Wide Web: http://www.cba.neu.edu/gsba

Northern Illinois University

DeKalb, Illinois

PREPARING FOR THE CHALLENGES OF THE NEXT MILLENNIUM

With the opening of Northern Illinois University's (NIU) second regional education center in the fall of 1995, a national model for programmatic delivery, our M.B.A. program complements the University's commitment to the nontraditional, working professional seeking high-quality master's-level education in business administration through affordable, conveniently located learning centers.

Following extensive input from our stakeholders, our recently revised M.B.A. curriculum will provide students with greater opportunities than ever before to hone their communication and technical skills as they prepare for "Workplace 2000." We at NIU are dedicated to making the College of Business the "School of Choice" in our region, as our nation and world face the daunting academic and professional challenges of the next millennium.

—David K. Graf, Dean

Programs and Curricular Focus

NIU's M.B.A. program provides challenging opportunities for the mastery of traditional, current, and emerging business knowledge and produces high-quality graduates with the competencies and abilities necessary to participate effectively in a rapidly changing, increasingly diverse, global business environment. Throughout the program, students integrate the themes of a global view of business, leadership, ethics, and communication into term papers, case presentations, and classroom discussions. Along with information systems support and elective courses, program objectives are achieved through a required communications block, sequencing of business functions, and an integrative capstone experience. The College also offers an Executive M.B.A. program in a twenty-one-month delivery format at the Hoffman Estates campus and four specialized master's programs: the Master of Accounting Science (M.A.S.), the Master of Science in Taxation (M.S.T.), the Master of Science degree in finance (M.S.), and the Master of Science degree in management information systems (M.S.). All of the graduate business programs at NIU are accredited by AACSB–The International Association for Management Education. Total graduate enrollment in the College of Business is approximately 800.

For those students with nonbusiness undergraduate degrees, the 18-hour/nine-course Foundations track includes the functional business courses requisite to success in the M.B.A. program. At the time of application, credentials analysis determines those Foundations courses required by each candidate. Depending upon that review, students may be waived from all, some, or none of the Foundations requirements.

Once beyond the Foundations block, all students follow the communications-business function-integrative capstone track. Electives and information support systems fill out the 31-hour/eleven-course program (excluding the Foundations block). Topics not routinely covered under traditional business curricula, such as emerging technologies, are addressed through an innovative "Colloquium Series," and students interested in doing an area of study can pursue the fields of finance, international business, management information systems, marketing, or strategic management. Students select the pace at which they progress in the M.B.A. program, with most students taking one or two courses at a time. With an evening/part-time/off-campus focus, NIU's M.B.A. program has been designed and courses scheduled at its sites in Hoffman Estates, Rockford, and Naperville to accommodate the needs of the working professional.

Students and the M.B.A. Experience

The Chicago area is a major center for technological, financial, retail, and manufacturing organizations, and NIU's students reflect the diversity of their workplaces. As a result, discussions, team projects, and papers are enriched by the students' business experience. The "typical" student entering NIU's program in 1997–98 had an undergraduate GPA of 3.16 on a 4.0 scale and a 547 GMAT score and was 32 years old, with nine years of work experience. Ninety-five percent of the 1997–98 entering class were employed full-time while enrolled in the M.B.A. program.

The Faculty

NIU is proud to note that the Department of Accountancy is often ranked in the top ten in the Public Accounting Report's survey of undergraduate accounting programs and consistently places among the top institutions nationally on the CPA pass rate. In December 1995, *Computerworld* magazine ranked NIU's M.S. in management information systems program among the top twenty-five "Techno MBAs" in the nation. In December 1995, the *Journal of Finance* placed NIU's Department of Finance among the top 30 percent of all schools nationally in terms of total articles published in the top sixteen finance journals. In addition to research endeavors, faculty members engage broadly in corporate relationships and have extensive real-world business experience.

The Business School Network
Corporate Partnerships

The College of Business learning experience is enhanced a great deal by partnerships with business. The Board of Executive Advisors, consisting of business and community leaders, provides a forum for partnership and dialogue between the College and the business community. The Executive Club, a group of prominent business alumni, assists the College in the implementation of its strategic plan to become the "School of Choice." Executive-in-residence programs, internship programs, continuous program improvement, strategic planning, and public speaking forums, as well as many opportunities for interaction with business executives, are some of the initiatives provided by these partnerships with business.

Prominent Alumni

The College of Business is proud of the large number of senior executive alumni who are major players in the corporate community in a wide variety of industries. Michael Corrao, President and Chief Operating Officer of Gingiss International; Eileen Scudder, Partner-in-Charge of Litigation Services Group at Deloitte & Touche LLP; Dennis Sester, Corporate Vice President at Motorola, Inc.; and Charles Ruder, President of United Way–Chicago, represent just a few of NIU's prominent alumni.

The College and Environs

Northern Illinois University is a comprehensive university established in 1895 by an act of the Illinois General Assembly. In fulfilling its mission to the northern Illinois region by recognizing the changing demands of the nontraditional student, NIU has opened education centers in Hoffman Estates and Rockford within the past four years. Both centers provide services or access to services comparable to those found on the main campus. The total student population at the University is 22,082.

The students engaged in M.B.A. course work at NIU's Hoffman Estates and Naperville campuses live and work almost exclusively in Chicago and its suburban areas—one of the most dynamic regions in the world for commerce and industry. Both campuses are within a 40-mile radius of Chicago's "Loop." Students at the Rockford and DeKalb campuses live and work primarily in those locales. DeKalb is a quiet, semirural town located 65 miles west of Chicago, while Rockford is the second-largest city in the state of Illinois and is well known for its industrial manufacturing base.

Facilities

The University libraries contain nearly 1.5 million volumes, 16,000 current periodical titles, 2.6 million microform units, more than 215,000 maps, and more than 1.2 million government publications and hold membership in the Center for Research Libraries and the Illinet Online (IO) System.

Technology Environment

The M.B.A. programs at the Hoffman Estates and Rockford Education Centers offer modern computer labs for teaching and individual student use. All computers are networked and linked to NIU's main communication backbone on campus in DeKalb. Students have access to a wide variety of general-purpose software, specialized business applications, and databases, and faculty members and students have send/receive capability via e-mail as well as full access to the Internet. Students may also access the campus mainframe and minicomputers remotely from home through high-speed communication servers. Every business student is given unlimited access to College of Business' computer resources on the main DeKalb campus and may use the computing facilities at the site at which their courses are offered.

Placement

Since students usually are already employed on a full-time basis when they enter the M.B.A. program, graduates generally are managers and directors at many of the Fortune 500 companies whose offices are located in the Chicago area and around the world within a year of their graduation. The average salary for NIU's 1996 M.B.A. graduates was $66,069.

Admission

Admission is competitive and limited to those candidates who can demonstrate high promise of success. The College of Business considers several indicators of potential, including undergraduate GPA, GMAT score, work experience, leadership and communication skills (as described in the goals statement and resume), and two letters of recommendation. A minimum TOEFL score of 550 is required for all applicants whose native language is not English. Candidates may also be asked to come in for an interview or to submit additional materials deemed important in assessing their potential for success in the M.B.A. program.

Finances

Course charges off campus are approximately $266 per semester hour. Tuition and fees for DeKalb courses are approximately $145 per semester hour. These amounts are subject to change without notice.

Students in the M.B.A. program generally live in the Chicago suburban areas or in Rockford. For on-campus students, the University offers several residence hall options.

A limited number of partial scholarships are available for M.B.A. students. Need-based financial aid is administered by the University's Financial Aid Office. Full-time students are eligible to apply for graduate assistantships.

Application Facts and Dates

There is a $30 nonrefundable application fee payable by money order or check drawn on a U.S. bank. For U.S. citizens, the completed application form and fee must be received by the graduate school by June 1 for fall semester, November 1 for spring semester, and April 1 for summer session. All remaining application materials must be received by August 1 for fall semester, January 1 for spring semester, and June 1 for summer session. International students must submit all application materials prior to May 1 for consideration for admission for fall semester or by October 1 for spring semester. For more information, students should contact:

Director, Graduate Studies in Business
　　and Research
College of Business
Wirtz Hall 146
Northern Illinois University
DeKalb, Illinois 60115-2897
Telephone: 815-753-1245
　　　　　　800-323-8714 (Illinois
　　　　　　　　toll-free)
E-mail: ljacobs@niu.edu
World Wide Web: http://www.cob.niu.
　　edu/grad/grad.html

NORTH PARK UNIVERSITY North Park University

The Center for Management Education

Chicago, Illinois

> ### ETHICAL ISSUES IN BUSINESS
>
> *The course work in the Center for Management Education is reflective of what you would expect in any good graduate business program. One notable difference at North Park, however, is the unusually high degree of attention given to ethical issues. Becoming accquainted with and being committed to bringing into one's management practice ethical perspectives does not happen easily. The necessity and importance of doing so, however, is essential, as much of what our students face on a daily basis is dependent upon moral and ethical behavior. Our faculty are experienced in discussing ethical issues and are committed to helping our students acquire a strong ethical framework for decision making.*
>
> —Dean A. Lundgren, Director

Programs and Curricular Focus

The M.B.A. program at North Park University is designed primarily to meet the advanced educational needs of business professionals and to respond to the preferences expressed by the corporate community for management personnel who possess the ability to write and speak effectively, have a capacity for critical and quantitative analysis, and the ability to function as a member of a team and provide leadership within an organization. Consistent with North Park's Christian heritage, the M.B.A. program seeks to instill in its students a sense of moral responsibility that is expressed in personal integrity and social concern and is responsive to the ethical dimensions of decision making.

The North Park University M.B.A. program offers students the ultimate in scheduling flexibility and convenience. As a part-time program, the M.B.A. program offers classes on weeknights and Saturdays and students may complete the degree entirely on Saturdays if they desire. The academic year consists of five 8-week quads commencing in September, October, January, March, and June. The M.B.A. requires from sixteen to twenty courses, depending upon a student's undergraduate preparation. Full-time students take two courses per quad and can complete the degree in two years (summer classes may or may not be required). Part-time students take one course per quad. Students with appropriate liberal arts backgrounds may complete the M.B.A. program in one calendar year, taking three courses per term for four quarters. The North Park M.B.A. is a general management degree, and students do have

the option of specializing in entrepreneurship, human resource management, and organizational development.

The Center for Management Education and the North Park Seminary offer two joint-degree programs that allow students to obtain an M.B.A./M.Div or M.B.A./M.A.T.S. For health-care professionals, the Center for Management Education and North Park's School of Nursing offer an M.B.A./M.S.N.

Students and the M.B.A. Experience

North Park M.B.A. students come from a range of cultural, academic, and managerial backgrounds. Forty percent of incoming students have undergraduate business degrees and their average age at entrance is 33. There are currently 250 students in the M.B.A. program, of which 45 percent are women and 25 percent are minorities. M.B.A. students come from a variety of work environments, with large representations from the service, healthcare, and nonprofit sectors.

Special Features

Consistent with North Park's commitment to the individual, each M.B.A. student will have a faculty member as their program and career adviser. Such an arrangement demonstrates the personal nature of the M.B.A. program and gives students an opportunity to interact with faculty members outside the classroom setting. International students find North Park an excellent place to pursue their graduate

education. Its location in the city provides numerous opportunities for part-time internships.

The Faculty

North Park faculty members come from rich and diverse academic and management backgrounds. With professional degrees from institutions such as Harvard, Stanford, and the University of Chicago, North Park faculty members are uniquely qualified for management instruction.

The Business School Network

The Center for Management Education regularly hosts corporate and community leaders to the classroom. In addition, appearances by corporate recruiters and trainers help assist students with career planning and placement.

The College and Environs

Founded in 1891, North Park is a private University that has a more than 100 year tradition of educating students for service and leadership. North Park is located in a park-like campus setting on the northwest side of Chicago, just minutes from downtown Chicago and easily accessible from most expressways and public transportation. Repeatedly selected by *U.S. News & World Report* as one of the top ten Midwest regional liberal arts colleges, North Park enjoys a wide reputation for academic excellence. With a current enrollment of more than 2,100 students, North Park offers a full compliment of academic programs at the undergraduate level and currently offers programs in business, community develpoment, education, nursing, and theology at the graduate level.

Facilities

North Park's Wallgren and Mellander libraries have access to more than 3 million books, periodicals, and microfilms. In addition, students have access to the University's three computing centers.

Technology Environment

Computing facilities for M.B.A. students includes more than 300 microcomputers in three student labs. In addition, the University computing network is accessible by modem.

Placement

As a part-time program, nearly all M.B.A. students currently hold full-time positions. The Center for Management Education does offer, in conjunction with the University, career placement services for students.

Admission

Admission to the M.B.A. program requires an undergraduate degree (or its foreign equivalent) from an accredited institution; GMAT, GRE, or MAT score (no minimum required); completion of the M.B.A. application; and two letters of recommendation. A minimum TOEFL score of 550 is required of all applicants for whom English is not their native language.

Finances

Tuition for the North Park M.B.A. program is $970 per course for the 1998–99 academic year. Tuition includes all fees and user costs, including parking. It does not include costs for books and materials. The M.B.A. program offers two scholarships for both full- and part-time students. Students with an undergraduate GPA of 3.25 (based on a 4.0 scale) or above or a GMAT score of 600 or above will automatically receive a Presidential Scholarship, which covers 30 percent of tuition costs. Students with an undergraduate GPA of 3.0 or above (based upon a 4.0 scale) or GMAT score of 550 or above will automatically receive a Dean's Scholarship, which covers 15 percent of tuition costs. Loans are available through the Federal Stafford Student Loan Program and several other loan programs.

International Students

Campus housing for international students is not provided. In addition, the Center for Management Education does not provide assistantships of any kind for international students.

Application Facts and Dates

The Center for Management Education accepts applications on a rolling admissions process for any of the five academic quads. Prospective applicants are encouraged to apply well in advance of the quad in which they plan to enter. Upon receipt of all materials, applicants will be notified of the admission decision within four weeks. For application materials, students should contact:

Christopher Nicholson
Associate Director of Admission,
    Graduate and Adult Programs
The Center for Management Education
North Park University
3225 West Foster Avenue
Chicago, Illinois 60625
Telephone: 773-244-5518
    800-888-6728 (toll-free)
Fax: 773-244-4953
E-mail: cln@northpark.edu

 # Northwood University

Midland, Michigan

DISCOVER MANAGEMENT

Understanding the art of management is difficult. Mastery is impossible. Business success often is fleeting, more a function of the circumstances than the skill of the executive. Sustained corporate success, thus sustained management excellence, is rare. Yet, business schools continue to promise, "if you would just get our M.B.A., you too will be prepared to achieve management excellence." Unfortunately, it is just not that easy. If the practice of management is difficult, the learning and acquiring of the necessary skills so too must be difficult and a lifelong undertaking.

At the DeVos Graduate School of Management, we have designed our programs to provide the opportunity for students to begin the acquisition of skills. Our approach is grounded in the following five guidelines: management is about finding and fixing problems, not as an individual doing tasks, but through others as part of an organization; management is about thinking and reasoning, not buzzwords, fads, formulas, panaceas, beliefs, or simplistic answers. The only right answer is "it depends." Management actions must be based on reality, not just the application of answers. No answer works under all situations, thus management must understand the circumstances; management must deal not only with the "what" that needs to be accomplished, but also the "how" of leading an organization to change; management education must deal with not only intellectual development but also attitudinal and emotional development; and experiential learning (case method, simulation) is more effective and lasting than cognitive learning.

In summary, the acquisition of management skills becomes about change in you—understanding your limiting factors and working to eliminate them.

—Dr. William T. Busby, Dean

Programs and Curricular Focus

The Richard DeVos Graduate School of Management offers the M.B.A. in two distinct formats: the Executive M.B.A. and the Full-Time M.B.A.

Rather than functional concentrations or majors, the focus of the DeVos M.B.A. program centers on developing students' leadership, problem-solving, and integration skills.

The fifteen-month, Full-Time M.B.A. program is designed for students from any undergraduate major who have little or no work experience. Small cohort sections of approximately 30 students participate in weekday, daytime courses beginning in late September and continuing year-round for fifteen months.

"Learning by doing" is the cornerstone of this innovative program. The curriculum is highly experiential and immerses students in an atmosphere of continually practicing, assessing, and refining their management skills in dynamic, realistic environments. These interactions occur through a combination of cognitive learning (thinking, reasoning, and acquiring knowledge) and experiential training through case analysis, role play exercises, business and management simulations, and other interactive experiences.

The Executive M.B.A. (EMBA) program is designed to significantly enhance the performance capability and executive potential of experienced business professionals. The program focuses on enhancing skills by engaging the intellectual, attitudinal, and emotional development required for students to reach their full executive potential. The EMBA is conducted one night a week for a thirty-month period. The curriculum is organized to ensure maximum development, team building, and support for the aspiring executive.

Students and the M.B.A. Experience

The success of the students' experience is a result of assuming an active "partner" role in their education rather than remaining the passive "consumer." Coming from a wide variety of undergraduate majors, students have demonstrated an ability to excel in the classroom and a strong drive to develop their managerial potential.

Both M.B.A. programs compel students to recognize and eliminate their limiting factors, to honestly face change, and to build upon their strengths and experiences as they strive to learn together.

Full-Time and Executive M.B.A. students come from diverse educational training and backgrounds. Their individual experiences bring reality and breadth to the classroom. The focus of the program moves beyond the functional problems and perspectives and into enduring, performance-enhancing action for the organization as a whole.

❖ Global Focus

As there is no longer a distinction between global and domestic business, the DeVos curriculum is designed to develop the cosmopolitan manager. All courses and activities are designed with a global perspective, and the students hail from around the globe. In addition, the University offers English as a second language programs and foreign language classes year-round.

The Faculty

The faculty members of the DeVos Graduate School of Management aspire to the highest standards of personal and professional growth for their students. They combine academic credentials with significant business experience to bring a mix of reality and practicality to the classroom. The University, a professional school of management, is a teaching institution committed to providing its students with the skills required for graduates to add immediate value to the firms in which they are hired and to the global business community.

The Business School Network

Corporate Partnerships

Outstanding business leaders, professors with executive experience, and M.B.A.

alumni assist in the development and implementation of the M.B.A. curriculum. The Full-Time M.B.A. program also utilizes the unique Pathways, Leadership, Unity, and Service (PLUS) program to enhance students' career development. The PLUS program is comprised of a series of career-assistance modules throughout the entire fifteen-month period. Modules cover such subjects as professional attire, etiquette, and networking and includes the Executive Lecture Series.

The College and Environs

Nestled in a natural woodland setting, the campus was designed by Alden B. Dow and stands as a tribute to its founders, who were concerned with endowing others with freedom and an obligation to think carefully of the future. Set on 268 acres, the University hosts an impressive array of facilities.

The city of Midland is located in the "palm of the mitten-shaped lower peninsula of Michigan." A diverse, dynamic, and culturally rich community, Midland is home to the corporate headquarters of the Dow Chemical Company and the Dow Corning Corporation. The city is on the cutting edge of scientific research and development and draws residents from around the globe.

Facilities

The Richard DeVos Graduate School of Management at Northwood University is housed in a state-of-the-art facility on the Midland, Michigan campus. This complex contains multimedia classroom facilities, break-out rooms, computer facilities, a career resource library, and faculty and administrative offices designed specifically to suit the interactive nature of the M.B.A. programs.

Placement

The Graduate School and Office of Career Assistance and Job Placement are committed to helping students prepare for the challenges of the M.B.A. program and to enhancing their job skills.

Orientation enables students to interact with members of their study groups and participate in team-building events, campus activities, and academic exercises. Students participate in a comprehensive individual assessment (CIA) that inventories their skills, strengths, weaknesses, and career objectives and allows them to pinpoint the skills they need to develop for their personal and managerial growth. Students periodically revisit their CIAs with staff members throughout the fifteen months.

Career assistance staff members also provide guidance on resume writing and persuasive job search correspondence and videotape students in mock interview situations.

A variety of corporate and alumni contact databases are available to assist students in individual job search strategies. The resources of the Office of Career Assistance and Job Placement are available to alumni at any time during their careers.

Admission

The Richard DeVos Graduate School of Management offers challenging and rigorous academic programs. Admission is selective and is based on academic acumen and a high motivation to attain challenging personal, professional, and educational goals.

To be eligible for admission, a student must have earned the equivalent of a four-year baccalaureate degree from an accredited institution. No specific undergraduate major is considered preferable; however, nonbusiness degree recipients must fulfill the four prerequisite courses of principles of accounting, principles of microeconomics, principles of macroeconomics, and college algebra or calculus.

GMAT results are considered along with all other application materials, but there is no score that precludes a candidate from receiving serious consideration by the Graduate Admission Committee and there is no score that guarantees admission. Applicants for whom English is not their native language are required to submit a TOEFL score.

Executive M.B.A. candidates are required to have an evaluative personal interview.

Finances

Total program costs for 1999–2000 for the Full-Time M.B.A. will be $18,000. This amount covers all tuition, fees, and books for the fifteen-month program. Total program costs for 1999–2000 for the Executive M.B.A. will be $20,000. This amount covers all tuition, fees, and books for the thirty-month program.

Off-campus living expenses for a single individual are estimated at approximately $600 per month. Financial assistance is available in the form of fellowships, scholarships, various government-supported aid and loan programs, and the M.B.A. loan program.

International Students

The Graduate School welcomes applications from qualified international students. All international students are expected to carry a normal course load and to complete the program in the allotted time period.

Application Facts and Dates

Applications for admission are accepted on a rolling basis throughout the year. The Graduate School Admission Committee begins reviewing applications by mid-fall. Applicants are notified of committee decisions within six weeks of receipt of all application materials and supporting documents. For more information, students should contact:

Richard DeVos Graduate School of
    Management
Northwood University
3225 Cook Road
Midland, Michigan 48640
Telephone: 517-837-4488
            800-MBA-9000 (toll-free)
Fax: 517-832-7744
E-mail: mba@northwood.edu
World Wide Web: http://www.
    northwood.edu/mba

Nova Southeastern University

School of Business and Entrepreneurship

Fort Lauderdale, Florida

EMPHASIZING A REAL-WORLD EXPERIENCE

Nova Southeastern University's (NSU) carefully designed and sequenced full-time M.B.A. and M.I.B.A. degree programs emphasize application of business concepts to the real world. The programs' curricula provide students with a solid foundation in functional areas of business and equip them with the necessary leadership and managerial skills.

—Dr. Randolph A. Pohlman, Dean

Programs and Curricular Focus

Nova Southeastern University's School of Business and Entrepreneurship offers innovative and highly flexible full-time Master of Business Administration (M.B.A.) and Master of International Business Administration (M.I.B.A.) degree programs designed for students with an undergraduate degree who have little or no work experience. The format and schedule enable students to enroll full-time and complete all degree requirements in one calendar year. The program format consists of four terms per year, commencing in January, April, July, and October. Students may enter the programs in the October or January terms and enroll in classes scheduled on Monday through Thursday. Although not recommended, students may also choose to enroll for classes in the weekend program. The weekend classes include adult, postentry professional students who are pursuing graduate degrees on a part-time basis.

The School also offers a joint program leading to a simultaneous awarding of the J.D. and the M.B.A. or M.I.B.A. degrees. Students admitted to the joint program must complete the first-year program at the law center (28 hours). They are not permitted to enroll in courses at the School of Business and Entrepreneurship during that period.

Students and the M.B.A. Experience

The typical student enrolled in the full-time M.B.A. program is 27 years of age, with less than two years of full-time work experience. Fifty-four percent of the students are men, and minority students make up 28 percent of the population. Fifty-three percent of the School of

Business and Entrepreneurship students come from Southeastern states, while 31.5 percent of the student body comes from Northeastern states.

Students in the full-time M.I.B.A. program bring a wide variety of geographic and academic diversity to the classroom. The average age is equivalent to that of the M.B.A. student; however, the ethnic distribution is quite broad. Twenty-four percent of M.I.B.A. students are Hispanic, 22 percent are Asian or Pacific Islander, and 13 percent are African American. The majority of M.B.A. and M.I.B.A. students possess undergraduate degrees in business administration; however, such a degree is not a requirement.

Special Features

Full-time M.B.A. and M.I.B.A. students are required to fulfill the internship requirement before graduation. The internship consists of 240 work hours in a private or public institution. The ultimate goal of the internship requirement is to help the student gain further insight into the practical nature of business. Block-Buster Video, the Florida Marlins, Smith-Barney-Shearson, and Holy Cross Hospital are but a few of the high-quality organizations that have trained and supported NSU's M.B.A. and M.I.B.A. students.

Another special feature is the ability to complete undergraduate prerequisite courses on line. All prerequisite courses for the M.B.A. and a portion of the prerequisites for the M.I.B.A. program went on line as of January 1998. In addition, M.B.A. students wishing to pursue their graduate studies on line may do so commencing with the 1998 summer term.

The Faculty

All full-time faculty members at the School of Business and Entrepreneurship have earned doctorates in their respective fields and have either owned their own business or worked in business or are engaged in consulting. A national core of adjunct faculty complements NSU's full-time professional staff. The diverse backgrounds and years of experience of the faculty facilitate in-depth discussion across a broad spectrum. A special effort is made to integrate practical with theoretical points of view.

The College and Environs

Nova Southeastern University is located on 232 acres in the town of Davie, Florida, just southwest of Fort Lauderdale. While the students enjoy a quiet, safe, suburban campus, NSU is easy to reach by public and private transportation. The graduate School of Business and Entrepreneurship is located on a separate 10-acre campus near downtown Fort Lauderdale.

The area is a principal coastal region in South Florida. The climate is subtropical and has an average year-round temperature of 75 degrees. The nearby cities of Fort Lauderdale and Miami offer many activities, including the Fort Lauderdale Museum of Art, the Museum of Science and Discovery, the Center for Performing Arts, the Miami Dolphins training camp, Bayside Marketplace, and Cocowalk.

Facilities

To provide a high-quality educational experience, the School has invested time and resources to improve the students' technological and research training. One of the University's major computer resources, the MicroLab, offers hardware and software resources for course work and workshops based on applied microcomputer technology. The lab has the most popular microcomputers—IBM, Zenith, Gateway, and Apple—and online facilities are available for access to the UNIX operating system.

The Albert and Birdie Einstein Library houses the University's major collection of books and journals in the humanities and sciences. Its more than 75,000 volumes can be searched through the library's computer catalog. In addition, more than twenty specialized indexes in CD-ROM format are available, as is dial-up access to the online catalog.

Placement

The purpose of NSU's Career Resource Center is to assist students in all aspects of the decision-making, planning, and placement process. Its mission is to support students and alumni and enhance their development through a variety of career-related services. The center strongly encourages active participation in students' development throughout their college years and beyond.

Admission

Admission to NSU's full-time M.B.A. and M.I.B.A. programs is competitive and is based on a number of important factors, including a student's undergraduate GPA or Graduate Management Admission Test scores.

Finances

Financial support is usually provided in the form of loans, with eligibility based on financial need. Individuals wishing to apply for financial assistance must fill out the NSU financial aid application and a Free Application for Federal Student Aid form (FAFSA). Financial aid transcripts must be submitted from each institution that the student previously attended, regardless of whether or not financial aid was received. Estimated costs for the one-year M.B.A. or M.I.B.A. degree, including room and board, range from $26,000 to $28,000. Students who have questions concerning financial assistance are encouraged to contact the Office of Student Financial Aid at 800-522-3243 (toll-free).

International Students

International applicants must submit a TOEFL score of 550 or higher, accompanied by a copy of their undergraduate transcripts printed in or translated to English. Transcripts must show specific subjects taken and the grade earned in each. If grades are expressed other than in an American system, a statement from the school must accompany the transcript showing conversion to an American scale. Diplomas, certificates, or general letters indicating attendance at a school do not substitute for transcripts. In addition, all international student applicants must submit transcripts and documents from international institutions to World Education Services, Inc., for a multipurpose evaluation of the undergraduate degree earned and the institution granting it.

To further develop the student, graduate assistantships are available to students who have completed the first level of courses in the M.B.A. or M.I.B.A. programs. The assistantships pay the equivalent of the course tuition in exchange for negotiated student services.

Application Facts and Dates

Application deadlines are March 1, May 31, August 30, and November 30. For more information, students should contact:

Ms. Cherie Baker, Marketing Manager
Nova Southeastern University
3100 SW Ninth Avenue
Fort Lauderdale, Florida 33315
Telephone: 800-672-7223 Ext. 5100
 (toll-free)
Fax: 954-262-3822

Ohio University

College of Business

Athens, Ohio

> **EXPERIENCE THE DIFFERENCE**
>
> *Our mission in the College of Business at Ohio University is to provide a learning environment that enables individuals to develop the knowledge, skills, and capabilities needed for success in the complex, global business community of the twenty-first century.*
>
> —Glenn Corlett, Dean

Programs and Curricular Focus

An intense thirteen-month learning experience, the full-time M.B.A. program uses an action-learning format that places the learner into exactly the type of projects and work situations that he or she will face as a leader of information-age organizations in the twenty-first century. The students learn basic business concepts but learn them in the context of their use, maximizing the students' ability to both recall and apply those concepts as they move back into the work world. The students develop the skills (communication, collaboration, teamwork) and the personal characteristics (initiative, creativity, personal responsibility) that are becoming so necessary to succeed. The understanding of the complexities of international business is enhanced through participation in the Joint Student Study Project Abroad. Comfort with information technology increases dramatically as the students regularly access information through the resources of the Internet, collaborate electronically over time and space, and develop and make professional-level computer-driven presentations.

Classes are lock-stepped beginning August 1 and ending September 1. The central learning core of the program is a series of projects. Students approach and solve the problems, in groups and individually. As students approach the problem, content is presented to them in modules, with each module presented at the time when it is useful to the students for solution of the current learning problem. Modules are delivered by a core faculty team.

Because of the learning environment, students learn to work utilizing the latest information technology, and they learn how to work together collaboratively, managing ill-structured problems with a minimum of direction.

High-potential, working individuals with a minimum of two to four years' experience may benefit from Ohio University's part-time program. Combining a series of short, high-intensity residencies with on-line education based on the OUMBA Intranet, a virtual learning community, the program effectively integrates work and learning. Detailed information is available via the World Wide Web (http://oumba.cob. ohiou.edu/~oumba/).

The M.B.A. programs are accredited by the AACSB–The International Association for Management Education.

Students and the M.B.A. Experience

There are about 40 students in the full-time M.B.A. program; all parts of the United States and many other countries are represented. About half of the students have liberal arts or technical backgrounds. Diversity of class makeup is a priority. The typical class is about 50 percent women; age ranges from 21 to 45, experience ranges from summer internships to 20 years, members of minority groups range from 5 to 10 percent, and about 40 percent of the student body is international (from such countries as Belgium, China, France, Germany, Ghana, Hong Kong, Hungary, India, Malaysia, Taiwan, and Thailand). There are a number of graduate student associations on campus, including an active M.B.A. student association that sponsors many activities.

❖ Global Focus

In addition to an overall global perspective, there is a mandatory requirement for each student to participate in the Joint Student Study Project Abroad. This project is a two-week experience in which students are placed in teams with students from the host country; each team is assigned to one company, analyzes a problem of the company's choosing, and then presents the results to management.

The Faculty

Program modules are delivered by faculty members who hold doctoral degrees and have relevant experience. For a class of 40 full-time M.B.A. students, 6 faculty members are assigned to the class; as an integrated team they are responsible for the selection of projects and the modules to be delivered. The team relies on other faculty members within the College to deliver modules depending on the expertise needed for the problem at hand. Typically, the core team is composed of men and women faculty members with domestic and international experience and provides expertise in accounting, business law, finance, human resource management, management, management information systems, marketing, operations, and quantitative business analysis.

The Business School Network

Corporate Partnerships

Corporate leaders from Athens and other communities are asked to be part of continuous improvement teams that reside within the College of Business. These continuous improvement teams deal with student development and curriculum development, among other things.

The Executive Advisory Board and the Society of Alumni and Friends are composed of business managers who provide advice and direction to the program. Often members of these organizations become mentors to students; meetings are formally set up in fall and spring quarters to introduce these businesspeople to M.B.A. students.

The College and Environs

Founded in 1804, Ohio University has grown from a single building to 108 principal buildings covering 623 acres. Full-time enrollment was about 19,000 in 1997–98, including about 3,000 in the Graduate College, University-wide. Student facilities include the aquatic center, an indoor ice-skating rink, a golf course, and basketball, tennis, and racquetball courts.

Facilities

Ohio University's Alden Library, a modern seven-story air-conditioned building, has well more than a million bound volumes, including more than 50,000 documents on business topics. Alden is a repository for U.S. government documents.

Technology Environment

The College of Business is wired for information technology well into the twenty-first century. The physical and technological environments are designed to support the team-oriented, project-based nature of the learning process.

The College of Business Administration maintains four microcomputer labs containing a mixture of Macintosh and IBM-compatible computers. Numerous word processing, spreadsheet, database, graphics, and statistical software packages are available in these labs. In addition, the College of Business maintains a Digital Equipment Corporation VAX 6210 connected to an instructional terminal lab. All facilities are fully networked together and to the Ohio University wide-area network, which includes IBM mainframes, online library systems, electronic mail, and Internet access.

Placement

There are two major recruiting fairs at Ohio University for meeting employers, as well as a constant flow of campus visits by recruiting organizations. A listing of companies who wish to interview is posted weekly on the campuswide electronic network, and students are encouraged to sign up for interviews with companies of their choice.

Admission

Factors considered for admission include undergraduate grade point average, scores on the GMAT (Graduate Management Admission Test), work experience, a personal essay, an interview (in person or by phone), and recommendations. Successful applicants typically have at least a 3.0 undergraduate cumulative average (on a 4.0 scale) and a score of 500 or better on the GMAT. In addition, international applicants typically have a TOEFL score of 600 or better. All applicants for admission must submit two official transcripts of undergraduate work and three letters of recommendation.

Finances

For 1998–99, the comprehensive fee for a normal quarter's load (9–18 hours inclusive) is $1373 for Ohio residents and $2946 for nonresidents. The fee for the Joint Student Study Project Abroad is estimated at $4000. In addition, there is a general fee of $335 per quarter. Scholarships with tuition waivers and stipends up to $8100 are available to qualified applicants based on merit. A number of scholarships have been designated for members of qualified minority groups. Awards of aid are generally announced in April.

Both University and private housing are available for single and married students. Housing costs vary from $400 to $600 per month, depending upon accommodations and furnishings. Room and board costs in University housing were $1500 per quarter in 1997–98.

International Students

About 40 percent of the candidates are international students who represent such countries as Belgium, China, France, Germany, Ghana, Hong Kong, Hungary, India, Malaysia, Taiwan, and Thailand, among others.

Application Facts and Dates

Applications, with a $30 fee and all supporting credentials, must be received no later than March 1. Students are encouraged to forward application materials well in advance of the deadline. Students are notified no later than May 1 about acceptance into the program. For additional information, students should contact:

M.B.A. Program
Copeland Hall 514
College of Business Administration
Ohio University
Athens, Ohio 45701
Telephone: 614-593-2007
World Wide Web: http://www.cba.
   ohiou.edu/www/grad/

FACULTY LIST

School of Accountancy
Yining Chen, Ph.D., Assistant Professor.
Ted Compton, Ph.D., Professor.
James Cox, Ph.D., Associate Professor.
Carol Anne Hilton, Ph.D., Assistant Professor.
Joseph N. Hilton, Ph.D., Assistant Professor.
Leon Hoshower, Ph.D., Associate Professor.
Robert Jamison, Ph.D., Professor.
David Kirch, Ph.D., Associate Professor.
E. James Meddaugh, Ph.D., Professor.
David Senteney, Ph.D., Assistant Professor.
Florence Sharp, Ph.D., O'Bleness Professor of Accounting.
Robert Sharp, Ph.D., Associate Professor and Director.

Department of Finance
Bruce Berlin, Ph.D., Assistant Professor.
Natalie Chieffe, Ph.D. candidate, Assistant Professor.
Jeffrey A. Manzi, Ph.D., Assistant Professor.
Azmi Mikhail, Ph.D., Professor.
Dwight Pugh, Ph.D., Associate Professor.
Ganas K. Rakes, Ph.D., O'Bleness Professor of Banking and Chair.
Nanda Rangan, Ph.D., Professor.
John Reynolds, M.B.A., Lecturer.

Department of Management Systems
Frank Barone, Ph.D., Associate Professor and Associate Dean.
Thomas W. Bolland, Ph.D., Professor of Quantitative Business Analysis.
Gerard Carvalho, Ph.D., Associate Professor.
David S. Chappell, Ph.D., Assistant Professor.
Garth Coombs, Ph.D., Assistant Professor.
Kenneth Cutright, Ph.D., Associate Professor.
C. Michael Gray, J.D., Lecturer in Law.
Patricia C. Gunn, J.D., Associate Professor of Law.
John Keifer, Ph.D. candidate, Lecturer.
Mary Carter Keifer, J.D., Associate Professor of Law.
Manjulika Koshal, Ph.D., Professor of Business Administration.
Arthur Marinelli, Ph.D., Professor of Law and Chair.
Clarence Martin, Ph.D., Associate Professor.
Peggy Miller, Ph.D., Lecturer.
Richard Milter, Ph.D., Associate Professor.
Valerie Perotti, Ph.D., Professor.
Bonnie Roach, Ph.D., Associate Professor of Human Resource Management.
Jessie C. Roberson Jr., J.D., Associate Professor of Law.

Richard C. Scamehorn, M.B.A., Executive in Residence.
John Schermerhorn, Ph.D., O'Bleness Professor of Management.
Hugh Sherman, Ph.D., Assistant Professor.
Lucian Spataro, Ph.D., Professor.
John E. Stinson, Ph.D., Professor.
Rebecca Thacker, Ph.D., Assistant Professor of Human Resource Management.
Ed Yost, Ph.D., Associate Professor.

Department of Marketing
Catherine N. Axinn, Ph.D., Associate Professor.
Elizabeth Blair, Ph.D., Associate Professor.
Barbara Dyer, Ph.D., Assistant Professor.
Ashok Gupta, Ph.D., Professor and Chair.
Timothy P. Hartman, Ph.D., Associate Professor.
Daniel Innis, Ph.D., Assistant Professor.
Kahandas Nandola, Ph.D., Professor.
Jane Sojka, Ph.D., Assistant Professor.

Department of Management Information Systems
John Day, Ph.D., Professor and Chair.
Ellsworth Holden, M.A., Assistant Professor.
Hao Lou, Ph.D., Assistant Professor.
Thomas G. Luce, Ph.D., Professor.
Anne H. McClanahan, Ph.D., Professor.
James Perotti, Ph.D., Professor.
David Sutherland, Ph.D., Assistant Professor.

 # Pace University

A DYNAMIC M.B.A.—DEVELOPING GLOBAL MANAGERS FOR THE TWENTY-FIRST CENTURY

In a rapidly changing business environment, major corporations depend on Pace University's Lubin School of Business to provide global business managers to lead them into the twenty-first century. Lubin's M.B.A. program, recently revised and continually being improved, carefully integrates theory and practical applications and offers exciting opportunities for experiential and team learning. Our campus locations, in downtown New York City, minutes away from Wall Street, and at the White Plains Graduate Center, convenient to the headquarters of Fortune 500 companies, provide particularly vibrant environments for professional development. Importantly, Lubin's distinguished faculty members are committed to excellence in teaching and are dedicated to producing successful graduates. Attesting to that success, Lubin alumni are and will continue to be leaders in all fields of business.

—Arthur L. Centonze, Dean

Programs and Curricular Focus

The M.B.A. degree program at the Lubin School of Business is characterized by a curriculum that stresses professional skills while offering students the opportunity to specialize in accounting, business economics, financial management, health systems management, information systems, international business, management, management science, marketing, or taxation. M.B.A. courses reflect the integrated, cross-functional way business operates. Global considerations appear in all appropriate courses, as do critical issues such as technology, ethics, workforce diversity, quality management, and entrepreneurship. Depending upon prior academic course work, between 36 and 61 degree credits are required for most specializations. All Lubin students must demonstrate proficiency in computing, business writing, and quantitative methods.

A core of foundation courses covers fundamental managerial and analytical skills. At the next level, the integrative core builds on the foundation courses to provide the managerial breadth of the curriculum. Cohort classes for the managerial skills courses place the same students together during their first year of study, creating a platform for mastering teamwork and setting up opportunities for networking throughout the M.B.A. experience and beyond. The critical business skills developed translate into greater job success and new opportunities long before graduation.

Lubin also offers a number of special programs for students seeking advanced professional business education. The One-Year M.B.A. in Financial Management program offers qualified business professionals and recent college graduates an accelerated M.B.A. program. The twenty-one-month Executive M.B.A. program affords middle- and upper-level managers the opportunity to enhance and sharpen their business knowledge and skills. Also available are the J.D./M.B.A. program (in conjunction with the Pace University School of Law); Master of Science degree programs in accounting, economics, investment management, and taxation; post-master's Advanced Professional Certificate programs; and a doctoral program in business.

Students and the M.B.A. Experience

Lubin students are busy, highly motivated individuals who seek graduate business education to advance their careers or to enter the business world. The average M.B.A. student at Pace University has seven years of work experience and is 29 years old. Women comprise nearly 48 percent of the current enrollment, minority students 20 percent, and international students 20 percent. Approximately 75 percent of the student population is from the northeast region of the United States.

Students enter the Lubin M.B.A. program with a broad range of academic and professional backgrounds, including business, engineering and technology, humanities, social sciences, physical sciences, mathematics, nursing, and education.

❖ Global Focus

Lubin's strong international focus and reputation for excellence attract many international students to its New York City and Westchester County campuses. These students' diverse cultural perspectives and backgrounds contribute significantly to the global focus and flavor of business education at Lubin. The Lubin School participates in a variety of student and faculty relationships with universities and business schools around the world. Since 1989, the School has been engaged in an exchange of faculty members and students with Tokyo Keizai University, including joint research projects in marketing and advertising. It has an exchange program with Heidelberg University in Heidelberg, Germany and various business schools in Paris and Grenoble, France.

Special Features

New Lubin M.B.A. students participate in a special orientation program that includes a series of workshops and presentations designed to familiarize them with the curriculum, faculty, and student services. Full-time and part-time students take the same courses, taught by the same faculty members, throughout the M.B.A. program. During the first year of study, cohort groups of students participate in a 6-credit managerial theory and skills course. The faculty facilitates classwork through experiential and interactive team exercises, enabling students to increase their cognitive and effective capacity to build constructive relationships with individuals and groups.

The Faculty

Virtually all full-time faculty members are doctorally prepared, and 75 percent of the part-time faculty members hold doctoral degrees. The faculty members of the Lubin School are committed to excellence in teaching and the professional growth of students. Classes are small (average class size is 22 students), and professors are firmly committed to being accessible to students. Outside of the classroom, opportunities are provided for students to conduct research with faculty members, publish findings jointly, and take active roles in coordinating conferences and special programs.

The Business School Network
Corporate Partnerships
Top executives from major corporations participate in Lubin's Executive-in-Residence Program every year, providing opportunities for Lubin graduate students to interact with prominent business leaders from around the world. In addition, an advisory board of business executives and the School's extensive corporate network ensure that the curriculum reflects the changing needs of business.

The College and Environs
Founded in 1906, Pace University is a comprehensive, diversified, coeducational institution with campuses in New York City and Westchester County. Degrees are offered through the Dyson College of Arts and Sciences, the School of Computer Science and Information Systems, the Lubin School of Business, the School of Education, the Lienhard School of Nursing, and the School of Law. Pace University is chartered by the Regents of the State of New York and accredited by the Middle States Association of Colleges and Schools. The Lubin School of Business is accredited by the AACSB–The International Association for Management Education. The M.B.A. program may be pursued at the New York City Campus, which is a self-contained educational complex in lower Manhattan serving the adjacent Wall Street financial community, or the Lubin Graduate Center in White Plains, Westchester County, New York. The Graduate Center is located in the heart of the White Plains business district. Both locations provide easy access to the nation's most significant cultural resources, including major theaters, museums, and concert halls.

Facilities
Pace University's completely integrated online library system holds approximately 825,000 volumes and subscribes to nearly 4,000 serial publications. Electronic access to internal and external information and knowledge sources, including locally mounted CD-ROM databases, online retrieval systems, and the Internet is available. The Pace libraries annually contract with DIALOG, BRS, LEXIS/NEXIS, and Dow Jones/News Retrieval to access statistical, bibliographic, directory, and full-text databases that cover all major subjects. The University computing network provides access to a range of both mainframe and microcomputing hardware and

software. More than 250 computers are currently located in academic computing facilities. Pace University's wide-area network (Pace Net) can be accessed from labs, dormitory rooms, and offices. Computing facilities housed in the Chase Computer Center are for the exclusive use of Lubin students and faculty members. The Lubin School of Business's Center for Applied Research, Center for Global Financial Markets, Center for International Business Studies, and Center for Innovation and Entrepreneurship offer students diverse research opportunities.

Placement
The University Career Development and Placement Services help graduate business students make informed choices. Pace's Cooperative Education Program places Lubin graduate students in paid, career-related working experiences while they pursue their degrees. Because of its close ties to business, the Pace Cooperative Education Program is one of the largest in the United States. Career counseling, which includes job search preparation, resume writing, and interviewing skills, is provided. Leading corporations, banks, accounting firms, insurance companies, retailers, brokerage houses and nonprofit and government organizations regularly recruit Pace M.B.A. students and utilize Pace's Resume Referral Program. The Alumni Mentor Program gives students an opportunity to speak with Pace alumni about their individual occupations, and the Pace Network offers a medium through which to obtain career information and develop personal contacts with Lubin graduates and other students.

Admission
Admission is open to qualified recipients of bachelor's degrees in any field from accredited undergraduate institutions. All applicants for the M.B.A., M.S., and doctoral programs are required to submit official Graduate Management Admission Test score reports. The Lubin School of Business welcomes applications from graduates of colleges and universities in other countries. International students are expected to have sufficient finances available to cover all expenses for the entire period of graduate study. Applicants whose native language is not English are required to submit official TOEFL scores. The evaluation of applicants is based upon capacity for scholarship as indicated by the undergraduate record, GMAT scores, class rank, previous graduate study (if any), letters of reference, career objectives, and other available information.

Finances
Tuition in 1998–99 is $545 per credit. A variety of loan and deferred-payment options are available.

A number of graduate scholarships and assistantships are offered. Scholarships are awarded on the basis of outstanding academic performance as indicated by the applicant's previous college record and standardized test scores. Assistantships are available for full- and part-time students. Graduate assistants received stipends of up to $5300 per year for 1997–98 and tuition remission for up to 24 credits. Students interested in applying for a graduate assistantship are advised to apply early because in-person interviews are required.

Room and board in 1998–99 cost approximately $7200 for the academic year. Books, supplies, health insurance, and personal expenses are estimated to cost an additional $5500. Students planning to pursue summer study should anticipate an additional cost of approximately $3000, excluding tuition and fees.

International Students
International students at the Lubin School make up about 20 percent of the enrollment. Home countries include, among others, Canada, China, Columbia, France, Germany, India, Japan, Mexico, Pakistan, Russia, Taiwan, and Turkey.

Pace University and the Lubin School of Business are dedicated to providing a supportive environment for international students. Special services are provided through the International Student and Scholars Offices and the English Language Institute.

Application Facts and Dates
The application fee is $60. Preferred application deadlines are August 1 for fall, December 1 for spring, May 1 for summer session I, and June 1 for summer session II. International applicants are requested to submit credentials approximately one month earlier than the aforementioned dates. For more information, students should contact:

New York City Campus:
Office of Graduate Admission
Pace University
1 Pace Plaza
New York, New York 10038-1598
Telephone: 212-346-1531
Fax: 212-346-1585
E-mail: gradny@pace.edu

White Plains Campus:
Office of Graduate Admission
Pace University
1 Martine Avenue
White Plains, New York 10606-1909
Telephone: 914-422-4283
Fax: 914-422-4287
E-mail: gradwp@pace.edu

Pacific Lutheran University

Tacoma, Washington

INNOVATIVE, HIGH-QUALITY, STUDENT-CENTERED, AND PERSONAL

These are some of the words that define the M.B.A. program at Pacific Lutheran University (PLU). The educational environment here is personal in scale, supportive in nature, and responsive to individual and student needs and provides opportunities for students and faculty members to be partners in learning. Our M.B.A. program is widely respected in the region for its high quality and has been professionally accredited by AACSB–The International Association for Management Education for more than twenty years. Our new technology and innovation management (TIM) concentration places the curriculum at the cutting edge of preparation for the new millennium. The breadth of our electives responds directly to student-expressed needs. PLU's M.B.A. program brings the relevant topics for today's and tomorrow's realities to students in creative ways.

—Donald R. Bell, Dean

Programs and Curricular Focus

The M.B.A. program is renowned for its strong business training that engages innovative concepts of course integration with interactive teaching and a focus on relevance. It reinforces strong values, ethics, and service and acknowledges the multicultural influences driving today's market. Students learn sound management through exposure to functional areas of business. Theory and practice are balanced through classroom lectures, case studies, and projects.

Pacific Lutheran University offers two options for completing an M.B.A. degree. Students may choose between an M.B.A. degree and an M.B.A. degree with a concentration in technology and innovation management. The M.B.A. program focuses on the development of critical skills in teamwork, communication, technology, problem solving, leadership, multicultural management, and change management. The M.B.A. with a TIM concentration incorporates these critical skills with a focus on technical management issues and is more relevant to the careers of individuals who work in technology-oriented companies and industries.

Either program option consists of 48 semester credit hours. Students in the M.B.A. program take a core of 34 credit hours and 14 credit hours of electives. Students in the M.B.A. program with a TIM concentration take a core of 30 credit hours and 18 credit hours in technology and innovation management.

Courses are taught in the evening to accommodate both working professionals and full-time students. The M.B.A. program with a TIM concentration is also offered in a two-year, Saturday-only format.

Students and the M.B.A. Experience

Students in the M.B.A. program benefit from small class sizes (average 16 students), which allow for a dynamic and personalized M.B.A. program. The students enrolled in the M.B.A. program in 1997–98 averaged age 34 and had an average of eight years' work experience at entrance. Forty-four percent had undergraduate degrees in business, and 24 percent had degrees in science/engineering. Thirty-seven percent of the students were women. International students comprised 15 percent of the students. Their average GMAT score was 528, and the average entering GPA was 3.2.

Students are from varied academic and professional backgrounds. Ninety-five percent of M.B.A. students have work experience before entering the M.B.A. program, and the majority of M.B.A. students earn a degree while continuing their careers. Students who are not employed full-time have the option of participating in internships or graduate assistantships concurrent with their M.B.A. studies. Through membership in PLUS Business, the student-alumni association, M.B.A. students may

participate in the Career Mentorship Program. This program links students with business alumni in the professional community to investigate different careers and receive personal guidance in exploring career options. Students also enjoy the benefits of participating in alumni networking events, where they can interact with business alumni in an informal setting.

The Faculty

PLU's M.B.A. faculty members bring both academic credentials and private-sector experience to the classroom. They teach business fundamentals as well as the most current issues and trends. The faculty members are dedicated to teaching, research, and community service; are active members of professional associations; and are recipients of numerous awards and other forms of recognition. Twelve full-time and part-time faculty members currently teach in the M.B.A. program.

The Business School Network

Corporate Partnerships

More than 25 leaders from private, public, and not-for-profit organizations are represented on the School's Executive Advisory Board—from Arthur Andersen and Boeing to the Tacoma Art Museum and the World Trade Center, Tacoma. The School supports an active alumni organization, a corporate mentoring network for students, an advisory board of leading entrepreneurs for its entrepreneurship program, and the nation's only student chapter of the Society for Information Management (SIM). Several recent partnerships with companies such as Boeing and the Frank Russell Company have been formed to serve Russian, Chinese, Korean, and Saudi executives.

The College and Environs

Pacific Lutheran University is an independent university with enrollment of 3,600 students. Its beautiful tree-lined campus is located on 126 acres immediately adjacent to the city of Tacoma (population 162,100). The campus is 40 miles south of Seattle and 20 miles south of Sea-Tac International Airport. Located in the midst of the Puget Sound region, the campus is within a short drive of a wide variety of natural attractions, including Mt. Rainier, the Olympic and Cascade mountain ranges, Puget Sound, the Pacific Ocean, and numerous lakes and rivers.

Facilities

M.B.A. students have access to a full range of University services and resources. The Robert A. L. Mortvedt Library, serving the University community with more than 500,000 books, periodicals, and microfilm and audiovisual materials, receives more than 2,000 current magazines, journals, and newspapers and offers online information access technologies. The University Center offers the convenience of a coffee shop, computer user room, bookstore, and commuter lounge. Athletic facilities include a swimming pool, golf course, fitness center, racquetball courts, tennis courts, basketball courts, track, and gymnasium. Single-room on-campus housing is available for graduate students in Kriedler Hall, a facility dedicated to serving graduate students.

Technology Environment

M.B.A. course work is closely linked to technology throughout the program. M.B.A. students need access to a PC with compatible software. University computer user rooms provide students with access to the latest in information technology. The School of Business also manages a computer laboratory equipped with Micron Pentiums, CD-ROM drives, and a VGA projection system. All students are provided access to the Internet through their individual PLU accounts.

Placement

M.B.A. students may take advantage of the many career development resources offered by Pacific Lutheran University and the School of Business. The Center for Careers and Employment serves the campus community and provides counseling, workshops, and a complete library of employment opportunities. Students benefit from School of Business career-oriented programs, including the career mentorship program, which links students with business alumni in the professional community, networking events, and internships.

Graduates of the M.B.A. program are employed worldwide in organizations ranging from small entrepreneurial ventures to Fortune 500 companies. Boeing, Andersen Consulting, Microsoft, Frank Russell Company, and Starbucks Coffee are examples of organizations that employ Pacific Lutheran University M.B.A. graduates.

Admission

Students who have completed a bachelor's degree (in any field) from an accredited college or university are eligible to apply to the M.B.A. program. Minimum requirements for admission are a 2.75 GPA, a 470 GMAT score, and a 1050 formula score (GPA × 200 + GMAT). A minimum 550 TOEFL score is required of applicants whose native language is not English. Exceptions will be evaluated individually, based on a presentation of factors indicating an equivalence to admission standards, potential for success in the graduate school, and other contributing factors. To apply, a completed Application for Graduate Study, a $35 fee, two letters of recommendation, a current resume, official transcripts of all prior academic work, an official GMAT score, and a TOEFL score (if applicable) are required.

Finances

Tuition for the 1998–99 academic year is $490 per semester hour. Full-time

students can expect to take up to 24 semester hours in one year ($11,760). Estimated yearly expenses for full-time students include room and board ($4890), books and supplies ($800), and personal expenses ($2000). Part-time students should expect expenses of $125 per 4 semester hour course for books and supplies.

Financial aid for M.B.A. students is available in the form of Federal Perkins Loans, Federal Stafford Student Loans, graduate assistantships (up to $5000), and scholarships. The priority deadline for assistantship and scholarship applications is April 1. The University also offers scholarships in the amount of $2000 to eligible international students.

Application Facts and Dates

The evening M.B.A. program and the evening M.B.A. TIM program offer year-round admission, so students may apply at any time. Applications for these programs are evaluated as soon as they are complete, and students may enroll in fall, January, spring, or either one of the two summer sessions. Applicants receive notification approximately one to two weeks after the completed application is received. The two-year Saturday M.B.A. TIM program begins each fall semester, and the application deadline is June 1. Applications received after the June 1 deadline are evaluated, and qualified applicants may be admitted on a space-available basis. For more information or an application, students should contact:

Jan Dempsey
Director of Graduate Programs
School of Business
Pacific Lutheran University
Tacoma, Washington 98447
Telephone: 253-535-7250
Fax: 253-535-8723
E-mail: business@plu.edu
World Wide Web: http://www.plu.edu/
~busa/mba.html

Pennsylvania State University

AN EDUCATION IN LEADERSHIP

More than a conventional M.B.A. program, the Penn State Great Valley School of Management prepares leaders for today's marketplace by providing hard-edged business skills in addition to the broad intellectual framework and practical application skills necessary to manage in an ever-changing global economy.

Through the School's unique course of study, students look at every issue from a management perspective, exchange ideas in a highly dramatic and interactive setting, and graduate as rigorously trained and highly desirable job candidates. We have a solid tradition of building leaders who can effectively manage resources. Our graduates are provided with the intellectual tools to run organizations; to articulate a vision; to motivate colleagues and employees; to integrate finance, accounting, marketing, information systems, organizational behavior, and human resources; and to think "out of the box."

What makes a Penn State Great Valley M.B.A. different from the rest? Curriculum, faculty, educational philosophy, and environment. The curriculum is broad-based and cross-functional, emphasizing horizontal thinking, team learning, and understanding of management systems. Penn State Great Valley is a national prototype—the nation's first permanent educational facility built in a corporate park, marking an historic merger between higher education and business and industry. The School stands shoulder to shoulder with world-class businesses, which lends a fast-paced, cutting-edge flavor to the learning process. Top faculty are attracted to the strategic location and have extensive real-world experience in every area of the global economy.

If you aspire to a rigorous and stimulating professional education designed to prepare you for leadership positions in the years ahead, I invite you to consider Penn State Great Valley's School of Management.

—Carla A. Holway, Director of Graduate Program Administration

Programs and Curricular Focus

Each year, about 225 new students enter the program as a group and take the first-year courses in sequence, a structure meant to encourage them to feel at ease and to share knowledge and experiences freely. All students complete a core sequence of five courses during that first year, covering the theoretical, methodological, and technological components of business and management. This core provides the knowledge and skills essential to all private and public management and establishes a foundation for subsequent course work and specialized study. Beginning in the second year, courses augment the core, offering a focused package of required and elective courses. Students may choose from options in business administration or health-care administration.

Students and the Program Experience

Today the M.B.A. program is the largest of Penn State's 140 graduate programs,

attracting a diverse group of students, from corporate executives and entrepreneurs to physicians and other professionals employed in business, engineering, health and human services, and scientific fields. As busy professionals who regularly juggle responsibilities ranging from details to global issues, they have joined the management program to expand their knowledge and increase their options. They enjoy small classes alive with discussion and debate, accessible faculty members, and a rigorous curriculum.

Classes are small—typically limited to 25 students—and are forums for ideas and experiences. Professors use a variety of instructional techniques, including group discussions, interactive lectures, case analysis, team exercises, computer work, simulations, and guest speakers. Often classes divide into small groups that focus on hands-on activities to illustrate theoretical learning and the

value of working closely with others who have diverse viewpoints.

Most classes meet in seven-week sessions, allowing students to take one course at a time and complete two courses each semester. Five courses (15 graduate credits) may be completed each year. Evening or Saturday classes enable students to participate in the program while maintaining full-time professional positions.

Special Features

Second-year courses allow students to shape the program to meet their individual career needs in either the private or public sectors. The business administration option focuses on traditional management domains—accounting, finance, marketing, and economics and their role in developing and executing business strategy—and develops students' understanding of today's global economy and the competitive forces that shape it. A rich offering of electives provides depth and breadth in a variety of areas, including finance, marketing, MIS, strategy, entrepreneurship, and management (both operations and human resource).

The health-care administration option is for professionals pursuing management careers in health-care or health-related professions. It combines courses specific to the health-care industry with study in business and management. A typical class includes practicing physicians; managers of clinical and operational areas; nurse supervisors, clinicians, and allied health professionals; and reimbursement, finance, accounting, and information specialists. Students represent payers and providers as well as organizations that supply products and services to health-care providers such as the pharmaceutical industry, information systems companies, the managed-care industry, government, and professional organizations.

The Faculty

Faculty members combine top academic credentials with a firm grasp of the real-world issues challenging organizations today. They value both high-quality teaching and cutting-edge research; many are well known in their respective areas of expertise and were attracted by the campus's strategic location and entrepreneurial spirit.

They represent a mix of academic scholars and business professionals, an intentional configuration that offers students a theoretical foundation supplemented by an ample dose of practical knowledge. A distinguished list of full-time professors, all of whom hold a doctoral degree, are the core of this diverse group. In addition to teaching and research functions, these faculty members serve as advisers, assisting students in selecting courses and planning their programs. Off campus, they are in demand as consultants to a myriad of organizations.

Adding to this vital resource is a cadre of adjunct professors, most of whom hold full-time corporate positions or manage their own businesses. As working professionals, they draw on limitless practical wisdom, showing students how fundamental theories relate to real-world issues.

Faculty members and students work closely together. Through formal courses, seminars, after-class discussions, and professional and social functions, faculty members share knowledge and experience, challenging students to become independent thinkers, build on their experiences, and explore their capabilities.

The Business School Network

The campus has been a leader in forging relationships with the business community throughout eastern Pennsylvania. Business and industry, as well as government, education, and health-care organizations have been active supporters of the management program because they know the value of being able to count on a cadre of well-prepared employees. They see the management program reflecting the University at its best, reaching out to educate leaders, not just to train workers. Prominent executives join in classes as a way to share their valuable experience and perspectives. Area businesses have provided financial support to enhance scholarship funds and develop co-curricular activities. Most faculty members have professional experience in major corporations, in nonprofit organizations, or as entrepreneurs, bringing a spectrum of insight to the classroom. An advisory board composed of prominent business leaders provides guidance on strategic, curricular, and career issues.

The College and Environs

Penn State Great Valley School of Professional Graduate Studies is one of twenty-five campuses of the Pennsylvania State University, an internationally known teaching and research university. Located in suburban Philadelphia, just minutes from King of Prussia and West Chester, the campus is a national prototype and marks an historic merger of higher education with business and industry. The campus's location, sitting shoulder to shoulder with world-class businesses, lends a fast-paced, cutting-edge flavor to the learning process. Distinctive among the more than eighty colleges and universities in the Philadelphia area, this market-responsive institution is the region's only all-graduate center designed and operated specifically for working adults.

Technology Environment

Research facilities at Penn State Great Valley include extensive computing resources and a research library.

The Computer Center provides laboratories and classroom networks of more than 150 Pentium-class and Macintosh microcomputer workstations for student use. These workstations are connected to the campus's Local Area Network (LAN) and to the University's Wide Area Network (WAN). The latter allows students access to the Internet and the World Wide Web. Students are provided e-mail accounts and dial-up access to facilitate remote use of University-wide computer resources, libraries, and the World Wide Web.

The research library at Penn State Great Valley houses more than 24,000 books; 360 current professional, trade, and popular periodicals; and a collection of government publications, microfiche, CD-ROM, and books on audiotape. Drawing on the resources of the entire University, the library at Great Valley is part of Penn State's University Libraries system, one of the leading academic research library organizations in the nation. Students have access to more than 4 million cataloged volumes, 1.4 million government publications, and 32,000 current journals and serials plus a number of informational materials in various formats—from maps to microforms. Other accessible resources include materials at all Big Ten university libraries, other national research centers, and the Tri-State College Library Cooperative, an organization that provides members with access to the library resources of more than thirty colleges in the Philadelphia area.

Placement

Faculty and staff members understand that in today's world, changing jobs, even industries, is fairly typical. To support students who are evaluating their career options, the Career Advancement Center services include self-assessment instruments, networking with businesses, job-search support, workshops, and a resource library. A career counselor works one-on-one with students to plot career strategy.

Admission

Most students enter in the fall semester; some begin in January. To apply, students are required to submit an application, a $40 application fee, two official transcripts from each school previously attended, a current resume, two recommendation forms, a statement of career objective, GMAT scores, and a completed computer survey report. A TOEFL score is required of international applicants whose native language is not English or whose undergraduate instruction was not in English.

The program seeks applicants whose academic background, work experience, demonstrated leadership, and communication skills meet the program's challenges. Candidates must hold a baccalaureate degree and should have a minimum of several years of work experience. Individuals with a broad undergraduate background (science, engineering, the liberal arts, health sciences, education, and the humanities) as well as those holding a degree in business may apply for admission.

Finances

Many part-time adult graduate students benefit from tuition reimbursement plans offered by their employers or draw on personal savings. A student aid counselor can provide information about a range of financial aid options to supplement those resources, including loans, grants, work-study, fellowships, graduate assistantships, and scholarships. For more information, students should contact the Office of Student Aid at 610-648-3212.

Application Facts and Dates

Applications for fall admission may be submitted beginning in January and will be accepted through early August or until all spaces in the program have been committed. Applications for January admission may be submitted through late November. For more information, students should contact:

Penn State Great Valley Admissions Office
30 East Swedesford Road
Malvern, Pennsylvania 19355
Telephone: 610-648-3248
Fax: 610-889-1334
E-mail: gvmgmt@psugv.psu.edu

PENNSTATE

The Pennsylvania State University

The Smeal College of Business Administration

University Park, Pennsylvania

> ### THE SMEAL COLLEGE ADVANTAGE
>
> *Penn State's Smeal College offers a superb learning environment. Our university is a leading national research institution with a culture of research-driven instruction and a campus atmosphere that facilitates education. Faculty members pursue studies of sophisticated relevance, drawing keen interest from the private sector and assuring that classroom instruction is new, fresh, and grounded on enduring principles. Global management, diversity, and total quality concepts are fully integrated into our curriculum and our small classes assure personal interaction between faculty and students.*
>
> *Please visit our campus, meet our faculty, and sit in on a class. You will be warmly welcomed.*
>
> —J. D. Hammond, Dean and William Elliott Chairholder

Programs and Curricular Focus

The Smeal College M.B.A. program challenges the student with a comprehensive balance between theory and application and provides a solid foundation for conceptual and strategic decision-making skills.

This full-time program consists of a two-year, 48-credit curriculum. Integrated modules emphasize fundamental management skills and activities with twelve required core courses. As students progress, they are required to apply their knowledge to the solution of increasingly complex business problems. While not totally case-oriented, the Smeal M.B.A. program uses this method as an important instructional device in a significant percentage of its classes. The second year of the program provides students the freedom to focus on an area of emphasis among the business disciplines or the many other subjects offered at Penn State's University Park Campus.

Other opportunities at The Smeal College are wide ranging and include combined degree programs, such as the M.B.A./M.H.A. This program brings together work in business management with health administration, a growing field with burgeoning career possibilities. With the Penn State College of Engineering, Smeal has launched the Quality and Manufacturing Management (QMM) program, a one-year course of graduate study focusing on product development, quality, and manufacturing. Developed with a high degree of industry involvement, the QMM program features a professional internship, field trips, and visits from practicing managers.

Additional new programs are on the horizon at Smeal, such as the J.D./M.B.A.

Students and the M.B.A. Experience

Penn State M.B.A. students bring rich and diverse academic and cultural backgrounds to the program, creating a dynamic and exciting learning environment. A typical entering class numbers 140 students of which 25 percent are women, 15 percent are members of minority groups, and 25 percent are international students representing over twenty-five nations on six continents. The average student is 27 years of age. Over 85 percent of the class has at least one year of full-time professional experience.

Limited class size and an emphasis on group projects encourage a team spirit, a respect for human values, and a strong work ethic. Teaching methodologies include lectures, case studies, problems, readings, management simulations, games, and role playing.

❖ Global Focus

Smeal's M.B.A. students learn to conduct business in an interrelated global environment. In each of the M.B.A. core classes, students not only will view business from this global perspective, but also share experiences with students from any of twenty-five nations. To expand this concept of a global classroom, The Smeal College also has assembled a wide network of exchange programs with institutions abroad. Currently, students may pursue studies at graduate institutions in Australia, Belgium,

Denmark, England, Finland, France, Germany, Mexico, New Zealand, Norway, Singapore, and Spain.

Special Features

M.B.A. Action jump-starts a graduate education at Penn State through an intense one-day series of outdoor experiences emphasizing trust and teamwork. M.B.A. Action helps students to value strengths and leadership in others while learning more about those qualities in themselves.

A year-long managerial communications course has been an integral part of the core curriculum for twenty years. This course was the first of its kind in the country to have been made a required component of an M.B.A. program. The course has evolved into one that emphasizes a managerial approach to communications and helps integrate concepts from all the core courses.

The Faculty

The Smeal College M.B.A. faculty offers world-class teaching ability, applied business research, global consulting experience, and a dedication to excellence in delivery of the M.B.A. academic program. All 100 members of the graduate faculty hold doctoral degrees and those selected to instruct in the M.B.A. program are known for their experience and skill in enhancing the learning environment. The M.B.A. faculty members interact with students both inside and outside the classroom, providing a personal educational experience unique to a small M.B.A. program.

The Business School Network

The Smeal College retains close ties to business leaders in both the public and private sector. Two boards—the Board of Visitors and the Alumni Society Board of Directors—provide a critical source of national and international business expertise and keep the college and its students abreast of the needs of the business community. These ties allow students to participate in mentoring programs with leading alumni, develop powerful networks, and meet with executives who participate in the Executive Interaction Series.

The College and Environs

The University Park/State College community is connected, vibrant, comfortable, and unique. Located within 250 miles of major nerve centers like New York, Philadelphia, Washington, Pittsburgh, and Detroit, this central Pennsylvania area combines the intellectual and artistic energy of an internationally known university with the amenities of a small, growing city. The cosmopolitan campus is only a bike ride away from open fields and wooded ridges. The standard of living is high, the crime rate is low, and the lifestyle is among the nation's most stress free. "Happy Valley," as the region is known, is an ideal place to study and live.

Facilities

Smeal M.B.A. classrooms and administrative offices are concentrated in three buildings at University Park. Classroom interaction is promoted by state-of-the-art instructional facilities for core and elective courses.

The University libraries are superb for study and research, containing over 3.2 million volumes. Recognized for its library automation, Penn State offers computerized search capabilities and access to numerous CD-ROM and Internet databases. A resource sharing network with the Big Ten university libraries opens access to any information not available at Penn State.

On-campus and off-campus housing is available for both single students and students with families.

Technology Environment

The Smeal College offers M.B.A. students computer laboratories equipped with 150 latest technology IBM systems and a comprehensive suite of software. All labs are connected to the local Penn State network and the Internet. Each M.B.A. student is provided an account for e-mail and access to the World Wide Web.

Placement

The Smeal College M.B.A. program's professional development staff works aggressively to help students chart a clear career path, develop effective job-search skills, and build a corporate and alumni network. Career management services available to M.B.A. students include consortium events, professional development seminars, resume writing workshops, recruitment resume book, alumni networking, simulated interview programs, and summer internships.

To prepare students for career interviewing, the M.B.A. Association sponsors a Simulated Interview Program prior to the recruiting season. Students meet with corporate representatives in a videotaped interview situation to obtain constructive feedback from the interviewer.

Admission

Penn State seeks a diverse student body and encourages applications from students with a wide variety of academic backgrounds. Men and women with baccalaureate degrees from accredited colleges or universities are eligible for consideration.

Previous academic records, test scores, previous work experience, recommendations, leadership experiences, and other evidence of maturity and motivation are considered in the admission process. The Graduate Management Admission Test (GMAT) is required and competitive TOEFL scores are required of applicants from non-English-speaking countries. Personal interviews are strongly recommended but not required.

Finances

Tuition for the 1998–99 year is $3608 per semester for in-state residents and $7070 per semester for nonresidents. Books and supplies cost approximately $1200 per year. University residence hall rooms and apartments are available for single students from $1090 to $1455 per semester (1998–99). University apartments also are available for students with families and single students for $325 to $485 per month (1998–99). Meal plans ranging from $1065 to $1330 per semester (1998–99) are offered to all students. Off-campus living expenses for single students are estimated to be $650 per month.

Merit-based fellowships and scholarships and a limited number of graduate assistantships are awarded to qualified students. Need-based grants, loans, and work-study programs may be pursued through the University's Office of Student Aid.

International Students

International students arrive one week prior to M.B.A. orientation to engage in a week of activities designed to get them settled into the University environment. A student-run committee provides a valuable link for international students, who want to get the most out of their time at the University by hosting a wide variety of events designed to help all students share their cultural heritage.

Application Facts and Dates

Admissions are conducted on a rolling basis. The deadline for receipt of applications is March 1 for international students and April 1 for U.S. students. All application materials must be submitted in one packet, with the exception of GMAT or TOEFL scores. For more information, students should contact:

M.B.A. Program
The Smeal College of Business Administration
The Pennsylvania State University
106 Business Administration Building
University Park, Pennsylvania 16802-3000
Telephone: 814-863-0474
Fax: 814-863-8072
E-mail: szm6@psu.edu
World Wide Web: http://www.smeal. psu.edu/mba/

Pepperdine University

Malibu, California

LEADERSHIP FOR THE GLOBAL MARKETPLACE

The Graziadio School is ideally suited to prepare you for a leadership role in this rapidly expanding global marketplace. We understand the reality of the internationalization of business and have established business linkages around the world. The ability to understand the role of constantly advancing technology in business decisions is a primary objective of the programs we teach. The Pepperdine experience is different in another way—our strong commitment to values. In the business world, ethical conduct starts with individuals, not with government or corporations. Preparing you to pursue a career founded on ethical values is a fundamental mission of Pepperdine.

—Dr. Otis Baskin, Dean

Programs and Curricular Focus

Designed to prepare students for managerial leadership roles, the Master of Business Administration (M.B.A.) and Master of International Business (M.I.B.) degrees are offered in an environment that fosters an understanding of the behavioral aspects of management. The program organizes faculty and students to interact in a learning community. The curriculum emphasizes a global perspective of international business, ethics, communication, and decision-making skills.

The M.B.A. provides students with a working knowledge of business administration and management. The one-year, 48-unit program is geared toward students who have completed the necessary business prerequisites and have a minimum of two years of professional work experience. The two-year, 60-unit program includes an opportunity for a summer internship, which is strongly encouraged, and the option to study abroad for a trimester. Both M.B.A. programs offer concentrations in marketing and finance. A joint J.D./M.B.A. program is also offered in conjunction with the School of Law.

Students in the M.I.B. program enter either the French, German, or Spanish track. The M.I.B. degree equips students with the management tools, cultural and global understanding, and language skills necessary for a successful international business career. The first year consists of an international business curriculum and intensive language study at the Malibu campus. During the second year, students travel to Frankfurt, Montpellier, or Monterrey to complete their course work and an internship. An intermediate-level language proficiency is required at the start of the program. Students also have the flexibilty to complete their full-time internship in any French-, German-, or Spanish-speaking country.

Students and the M.B.A. Experience

The business school students represent a diverse range of professional and educational backgrounds. Such diversity contributes to a culture of collaboration. This culture enhances the practical, hands-on learning process. New students are quickly initiated into the M.B.A. program through the communication workshop. The three-day event develops the trust and camaraderie that characterize the entire program. The School values teamwork as an integral part of business education. Professors structure a collaborative learning environment in every class, which helps cultivate well-balanced personal and professional development in each student. The small class sizes (approximately 25 students in a class) foster community-type relationships between faculty members and students.

❖ Global Focus

The two-year M.B.A. programs offer an excellent opportunity to literally expand one's horizons and obtain a broader global perspective, while gaining an appreciation and general background in international business. Students may choose to study abroad for a trimester during their second year. Students apply for this trimester-abroad program based on the academic performance of their first trimester. This unique experience is offered at partner institutions located in one of the following countries: Belgium, China, France, Germany, Hong Kong, Mexico, the Netherlands, the Philippines, Spain, and Thailand.

Special Features

Pepperdine is distinguished by programs designed to enhance the student's practical learning experience. During the first semester, students participate in the Civic Leadership Program, a nonprofit consulting project, which is an excellent opportunity for students to observe organizations and to recommend changes while supporting the community.

Ethical and legal issues are also reinforced through the Seminar in Business Ethics at the Nellis Federal Prison Camp outside Las Vegas. Students interview a panel of white-collar criminals about the potential impact of business decisions.

The Faculty

All faculty members are selected for their vast range of research and management experience in the business world as well as their strong academic qualifications and values-centered focus in teaching. More than 90 percent of the faculty members hold Ph.D. degrees and continue to remain very active in the business community, including consulting relationships and involvement with advisory boards. Students appreciate the accessibility of their professors, the individual attention they receive, and the personal faculty-student relationships that are built as a direct result of these.

The Business School Network

With more than 23,000 graduates, the Graziadio School has one of the largest business school alumni networks in the United States.

Corporate Partnerships

The business school is active in the community, with close ties to corporations and industry through its professional and executive programs. The full-time M.B.A. and M.I.B. programs in Malibu

The Graziadio School is located on the main campus of Pepperdine University in the coastal community of Malibu, amid a beautiful mountain landscape overlooking the Pacific Ocean.

benefit from the School's vast network of alumni and corporate relationships. Students have the opportunity to complete a practicum with an executive, to perform executive interviews, and to consult with nonprofit organizations.

Prominent Alumni

The Graziadio School has many alumni who are top executives of major corporations and leaders in the community. The Presidential/Key Executive M.B.A. program alone boasts a long list of impressive names in the business community representing such industries as aerospace, biotechnology, entertainment, health care, and manufacturing. The close-knit alumni association brings together graduates from all programs through professional and social activities to help develop individual networks and interaction with alumni from various industries and companies throughout the world.

The College and Environs

Founded in 1937, Pepperdine University presents a unique combination of academic excellence and a strong commitment to values. The University is an independent institution that enrolls about 9,500 students in five colleges. The Malibu campus is located about 35 miles from downtown Los Angeles.

The School of Business and Management was established in 1969 and was a pioneer in executive M.B.A. education, developing its hallmark by its practical approach to teaching students ethical business concepts that are applicable in the real world. While the full-time programs only enroll about 200 students, the School is still one of the largest in the country, including all of its programs. It was endowed as The George L. Graziadio School of Business and Management in 1996.

Facilities

The 830-acre campus includes athletic facilities such as an Olympic-size swimming pool; gymnasium; baseball, track, and soccer fields; a fitness center; and tennis courts.

Research facilities that are easily accessible to business students include the Payson Library and the School of Law library. At The Graziadio School's academic computing center, both IBM-compatible and Apple computers are available with up-to-date software and research and Internet tools.

Placement

Recognizing the complexity of the career-planning process and the variety of options available to Pepperdine graduates, the Career Development Center (CDC) provides extensive services to meet the professional development needs of the students. The center partners with students in the process of career management, from self-assessment to placement in a career that meets individual goals. The following are among the many services offered: career consultations, seminars, recruitment consortiums, on-line job postings, internship support, student resume Web pages, a resource library, a career exploration breakfast (networking), industry forums, and on- and off-campus interview events. As a result, graduates from these Pepperdine programs are sought by a variety of domestic and international firms.

Admission

Consideration is based on many factors in the application process. The average GPA is 3.1, and the average GMAT scores are between 590 and 600. While work experience is not required for the two-year M.B.A. program and the M.I.B. program, it is preferred and can greatly enhance an individual's application. The one-year M.B.A. program requires a minimum of two years of work experience. Students' work experience averages 3–4 years prior to entering the program.

Leadership qualities and personal characteristics are considered along with the written essays and recommendations. The admission committee seeks individuals who display academic strength and show promise to make a positive contribution to the small-group and interactive classroom environment.

Finances

Tuition is $11,025 per trimester for the 1998–99 academic year. The one-year M.B.A. program consists of a total of three consecutive trimesters. Both the two-year M.B.A. and the M.I.B. consist of two trimesters per year; the M.I.B. also includes a minitrimester at the end of the first year.

Merit-based scholarships and graduate assistantships are available to full-time students. The admission packet contains the information necessary to apply for a scholarship.

On-campus graduate housing is available for $2500 to $3600 per trimester. Typically, 4 students share a two-bedroom apartment. Many students choose to live off campus, with costs averaging $600 per month.

International Students

International students represent about 45 percent of the enrollment in the full-time programs. The Office of International Student Services provides credential evaluations, language tutoring, visa services, and ESL courses.

A minimum TOEFL score of 550 is required for students whose native language is not English.

Application Facts and Dates

Application deadlines are May 1 for two-year M.B.A. and M.I.B. programs (September admissions) and February 15 for the one-year M.B.A. program (April admissions). After this time, applications are reviewed on a space-available basis. There is a $45 application fee. For more information, students should contact:

Admissions Department
The Graziadio School of Business and Management
Pepperdine University
24255 Pacific Coast Highway
Malibu, California 90263-4858
Telephone: 800-726-9283 (toll-free)
310-456-4858 (outside the U.S.)
Fax: 310-456-4876
E-mail: gsbmadm@pepperdine.edu
World Wide Web: http://bschool.pepperdine.edu

Philadelphia College of Textiles & Science

Philadelphia, Pennsylvania

GRADUATE STUDY—AN ECLECTIC APPROACH

► *The culture of our small, coeducational campus is such that significant faculty-student interaction is a virtual certainty. While ongoing research is critical for our faculty members, their primary focus remains teaching. The curriculum and all learning experiences are directed toward developing the skills and contacts needed to succeed in modern global commerce.*

We are very proud of our faculty members, students, and alumni. We invite you to participate in our exploration of the dynamic forces which will shape the coming decades in entrepreneurial endeavors, trade, banking, finance, and corporate management.

—Raymond R. Poteau, Dean

Programs and Curricular Focus

The M.B.A. program at Philadelphia College of Textiles & Science is designed to provide students with the skills and abilities that employers are looking for to lead corporate America into the twenty-first century—a global perspective, competence in leading-edge technology, and innovative and entrepreneurial thinking. The curriculum responds to global and managerial skills needed to be successful in the years to come. Students analyze important and challenging issues in an action-learning and team-building environment, while sharpening decision-making, managerial, and entrepreneurial skills. Furthermore, students develop the ability to interact and communicate with diverse groups, so that they can function effectively in a competitive business environment.

The program comprises eight core courses (22 credits), three option area courses (9 credits), a capstone course in strategic planning (3 credits), and one free elective (3 credits) that may be selected from the M.B.A. program or other graduate program. The eight core courses include Management Communications, the Art of Negotiations, and Managing in the 21st Century, along with courses in the functional areas of business. Students may select from one of the seven option areas: accounting, business administration, finance, health-care management, international business, marketing, or taxation. It is also possible to construct a custom option based on special interests and goals. All students are required to fulfill foundation require-

ments that may be waived based on undergraduate curriculum and/or work experience.

Other opportunities at Philadelphia College include joint-degree programs. The joint degrees offered are an M.B.A./ M.S. in Taxation (55 credits), an M.B.A./ M.S. in Textile Marketing (58 credits), and an M.B.A./M.S. in Instructional Technology (55 credits). In addition, the College offers an M.S. in Taxation.

Students and the M.B.A. Experience

Students come from the Northeast region of the country and abroad to study in the M.B.A. program at Philadelphia College of Textiles & Science. The average student is 28 years old and has six years of work experience. Nearly one half of the students are women, and approximately 12 percent are international students.

❖ Global Focus

International dimensions are incorporated into all courses. In addition, students have the opportunity to participate in an overseas trip that exposes them to a number of foreign cultures and businesses. Over the last five years, the class has traveled to France, Belgium, and England, where students met with business leaders, labor leaders, and political leaders in the European Union.

The Faculty

Philadelphia College of Textiles & Science is a teaching institution where the

primary focus is the students. Classes are small (average size is 16), which allows for extensive faculty-student interaction. The M.B.A. faculty combines both full-time professors and business leaders from the Philadelphia area. This unique combination provides an interesting mix of real-world experiences and applied research in the classroom.

The College and Environs

Founded in 1884, the Philadelphia College of Textiles & Science is an independent, career-oriented institution that offers both graduate and undergraduate programs of study. Currently, Philadelphia College offers eight professionally oriented graduate programs, each providing a blend of academic theory and real-world applications.

On a small, coeducational college campus, Philadelphia College fosters close relationships between faculty members and students and enrolls a student body that is academically and culturally diverse. The College is primarily a teaching institution that also encourages research as a service to industry and as a vehicle for faculty and student development. The 100-acre campus is situated 15 minutes from Center City Philadelphia, the fifth-largest city in the nation.

Facilities

The new Paul J. Gutman Library is a state-of-the-art facility. A fully computerized book catalog allows access via computer both in the library and from remote locations. The main book collection consists of more than 84,000 volumes, with special emphasis in the areas of architecture, business, design, and textile arts. Networked electronic databases provide access to more than 1,850 journals, publications, and newspapers, including Infotrac, General Business Index, and SEC 10K Filings. The library has more than 550 journal titles available in full-text retrieval format.

Placement

Graduates of Philadelphia College of Textiles & Science are guaranteed lifetime assistance with career counseling. Last year, nearly 200 companies visited the campus, well above the national average of 23 recruiters per year. Full-time graduate students may take advantage of the extensive on-campus recruiting schedule. Evening hours are also available twice a week, and workshops in resume writing, interview skills, and job search tips are scheduled regularly throughout the semester.

Admission

Candidates who seek admission are reviewed based on the merit of their academic record, work experience, and the required Graduate Management Admission Test (GMAT). Depending on the applicant's academic background, foundation courses may be required.

International students may begin in either the spring or fall semester. A minimum TOEFL score of 550 is required for students for whom English is not their native language. International students must provide proof of adequate funds to cover the cost of tuition, room and board, and expenses.

Finances

The estimated cost for full-time enrollment in 1998–99 is $5376 ($448 per credit). Books and supplies cost approximately $500.

International Students

Twelve percent of M.B.A. students at Philadelphia College of Textiles & Science come from outside the United States. International students must take the English language placement exam prior to registering for classes. The International Society is one of the largest groups on campus. It provides students with a network of support for problem solving, social activities, and general advising.

Application Facts and Dates

Applications are accepted for fall, spring, and summer semesters and are reviewed on a rolling basis. International applicants should send complete applications by June 1 for fall semester and October 1 for spring semester. For more information, applicants should contact:

Mr. Robert J. Reed
Director of Graduate Admissions
Philadelphia College of Textiles &
    Science
School House Lane and Henry Avenue
Philadelphia, Pennsylvania 19144
Telephone: 215-951-2943
Fax: 215-951-2907
E-mail: reedr@philacol.edu

Plymouth State College

M.B.A. Program

Plymouth, New Hampshire

LEARN WITH WORKING PROFESSIONALS

The Plymouth State College (PSC) M.B.A. program is an evening program designed to meet the needs of working professionals as well as full-time students. Our classes are taught by full-time PSC faculty members, most of whom have their doctorates and extensive experience in business or government. Faculty members remain at the leading edge of their fields through continuing study and publishing in their areas of expertise. M.B.A. students have the opportunity to help New Hampshire small businesses and gain consulting experience through participation in a Small Business Institute (SBI) team. Over the twenty-two years of the SBI's existence, student teams working under the guidance of faculty members have made important contributions to more than 300 client companies while earning thirty-one state, regional, and/or national awards. Come to the beautiful Lakes Region at the foothills of the White Mountains of New Hampshire and learn with working professionals.

—Colleen C. Brickley, Director, Graduate Studies in Business

Programs and Curricular Focus

Plymouth State College is nationally accredited by the Association of Collegiate Business Schools and Programs (ACBSP). As a regional state college of the University System of New Hampshire, Plymouth State College is dedicated to bringing high-quality business education to regional and international students who join the journey to excellence. A major goal is to provide this educational experience at an extremely attractive cost to the student.

Because the students come from the most diverse of academic backgrounds, PSC has adopted a distinctive two-part curriculum. The first part consists of taking undergraduate courses or demonstrating competence in financial accounting, macroeconomics, microeconomics, statistics, psychology, and microcomputers. Students with a bachelor's degree in business would, ordinarily, have fulfilled these undergraduate requirements before beginning their graduate courses at PSC. Those students who have not already taken these undergraduate courses may complete them at any accredited college or university of their choice before coming to PSC or may complete this first part of the curriculum at PSC. Alternatively, the student may satisfy these first-part undergraduate requirements by examination, i.e., the College Level Entrance Proficiency (CLEP) or PSC competency examination(s). The PSC competency examinations are prepared, administered, and evaluated by PSC.

The second part of the curriculum consists of ten core and two elective graduate courses, for a total of twelve courses of 3 credits each (36 graduate credits). As an option, the student may complete a Master's Research Project (MRP) of 6 credits in lieu of the two electives. The MRP can vary from traditional research to examination of a contemporary business problem. Also, there is the opportunity for individual enrollments and/or independent studies. The faculty has been quite eager to work with students on such projects. The ten core courses are modeled after the strongest academic curricula. These courses are the Legal Environment of Business, Accounting for Managers, Marketing Techniques, Quantitative Analysis, Managing Organizational Behavior, Managerial Economics, Financial Analysis and Decision Making, Information Technology in Organizations, Operations Management, and Seminar in Executive Management.

As a benefit of the two-part curriculum approach, students who have completed the program's undergraduate competency requirements before their arrival at PSC can complete the M.B.A. program in nine months by taking four M.B.A. courses in each of three 12-week terms. This scheduling approach has the dual benefit of dramatic reductions in both tuition costs and the time to earn the M.B.A. degree.

The schedule allows for completion in different time periods as well. Many full-time students complete the program in anywhere from twelve to twenty-one months or more, depending on the number of course requirements that must be satisfied at the start of their program. Flexibility is a keynote of the program.

Students and the M.B.A. Experience

Students average 35 years of age, with more than ten years of work experience. They come from banking, medical, retailing, manufacturing, government, and educational organizations, to name only a few. About 45 percent are women, 8 percent are members of minority groups, and 92 percent are from New Hampshire, Maine, Massachusetts, and Vermont. Each year, there are between 5 and 12 international students.

Students work in teams, develop joint papers, and make team presentations. The program averages between 15 and 20 full-time students and more than 500 part-time working professionals, which enables the full-time students to gain much from the interaction with their working colleagues. As a result, many of the full-time students gain employment in the organizations of their part-time colleagues. This symbiotic relationship has flourished over the twenty-three-year history of the program.

Special Features

Because international students have diverse interests and come from many different countries, the faculty generously devotes time to individual enrollments and independent studies. These opportunities help the international student explore topics of interest. Typical topics are comparative studies in economics and/or law, marketing issues, and organizational behavior.

For international students desiring postgraduate training, the program has been successful in finding suitable placement. About one third of the international students take advantage of this postgraduate training.

The Faculty

The Department of Business at PSC has 22 full-time faculty members, all of whom teach in both the graduate and undergraduate programs. Three of the faculty members are women, and 3 are members of minority groups. More than half have extensive experience in business or management. Teaching and advising are strong components of the faculty culture and a great source of satisfaction to the faculty.

The Business School Network

The Board of Trustees of the University System includes several prominent business leaders who develop guidance for the M.B.A. program. In addition, the Small Business Institute program places the faculty in continual contact with regional business leaders who give advice and valuable feedback to the program.

Prominent Alumni

Some prominent graduates of the M.B.A. program are Jane Babin, Assistant Professor, PSC; Stanley Arnold, Director of Revenue, State of New Hampshire; Christina Ferris, Associate Professor, Johnson State College, Johnson, VT; Jeffrey Coombs, President, Ossipee Mountain Land Company, Tamworth, NH; Frank Johns, Vice President of Operations, Locktite Luminescent Systems, Lebanon, NH; Nancy Stewart, President, North Country Management Systems, North Conway, NH; Dr. Gary Hagens, Oral Surgeon; and Linda Normandin, Vice President, Laconia Savings Bank, Laconia, NH.

The College and Environs

Plymouth State College is a unit of the University System of New Hampshire. Founded in 1871, the College has undergone many changes and has shifted its role from that of a normal school, and later (1970) a state teachers college, to that of a multipurpose institution. It offers the Master of Education and the Master of Business Administration, as well as associate and bachelor's degrees.

Plymouth is situated in the Lakes and White Mountain region of New Hampshire. The scenic beauty of the area is breathtaking, and the surrounding countryside is a center for extensive recreational activities, available year-round. Students have access to skiing, boating, fishing opportunities, and lovely camps with a wealth of amenities. The town of Plymouth has a year-round population of 6,000, with a seasonal increase of twice that number. Plymouth is approximately 2 hours from both Boston, Massachusetts, and Portland, Maine. Hartford, Connecticut, is 3½ hours away. The capital city of Concord is only 40 minutes south on Interstate 93. A jetport is located in Manchester, about 1 hour south on Interstate 93.

Facilities

Classes are taught in Hyde Hall, which also contains the Department of Business

computer cluster with more than forty IBM microcomputers. There are several other clusters about the campus shared by all students.

On-campus apartments are available for full-time students, and there are also apartments available in the town of Plymouth. These apartments are all within walking distance of the academic buildings on campus.

Research in the field of business management is facilitated by the rapidly expanding holdings of the Lamson Library. In addition to 250,000 volumes and 475,000 units of filmed and recorded materials, the library houses a remote-access system for retrieval of appropriate audiovisual programs. Formal library support services are supplemented by a Department of Business collection and by interlibrary agreements with other institutions. Computer resources available allow communication with other institutions throughout the country. In addition, there are microcomputers, which include IBM and Macintosh PCs, available in public clusters.

Technology Environment

PSC uses Digital VAX minicomputers for both administrative and academic computing. There are more than 100 terminals distributed throughout the campus and dormitories, as well as more than twenty port selectors for students who live off campus and have their own computers. Services include e-mail and access to the Internet. Although students are encouraged to bring a computer to PSC, there are seven microcomputer clusters in addition to the terminals.

Placement

The Career Development Office serves both undergraduate and graduate students. Because many of the graduate students are working professionals, the services are utilized most frequently by full-time students. The office has been highly successful in helping international students find opportunities for postgraduate training. Internships are also arranged when appropriate.

Admission

Applicants must submit proof of a bachelor's degree (official transcripts), a GPA of 2.5 or higher, three letters of recommendation (on the forms provided), and acceptable GMAT scores. International applicants must also submit acceptable TOEFL scores and notarized certification of financial resources to cover the costs of education and living expenses.

The admissions board considers the total aspect of the application; therefore,

there are no cut-off scores, except for a desired minimum TOEFL score of 550.

The average GMAT score is about 490, with a range of 400 to 760. The average undergraduate GPA is about 3.1 on a 4.0 scale. The GPA of the student is often more reliable than the GMAT score as a predictor than the GMAT score, so more weight is given to the GPA of the applicant. About 50 percent of the students have bachelor's degrees in fields other than business.

Finances

The 1998–99 tuition rate is $273 per credit for state residents and $299 per credit for all others. Therefore, the 36-credit graduate program costs are $9828 for state residents and $10,764 for all others. All fees are included in the above rates, including graduation fees.

In addition to tuition, books may cost between $75 and $160 per course, for a total of about $1700. An additional $5000 for other living expenses should be anticipated.

Graduate students may live in single and double rooms in College residence halls, with meal service included. The costs for room and board for the 1997–98 year were $2460 per semester for a single and $2282 per semester per person for a double. Apartments for married and single students are available on campus. Off-campus living arrangements can also be made; these vary greatly in cost.

International Students

International students have a unique opportunity to learn with working professionals in a small regional state college environment. The academic experience includes current practice in real business organizations as learned from fellow students.

Polytechnic University

Brooklyn, New York

GO BEYOND THE GENERIC M.B.A.—KNOWLEDGE, ECONOMY

Mastering broadly defined technology management for operational and strategic advantages is increasingly the key difference between success and failure for businesses competing in this knowledge-intensive global economy. By combining the best of a mainstream M.B.A. program with carefully tailored courses critical to technologically driven manufacturing and a wide range of service-sector industries, including electronic business, Polytechnic prepares a wide range of professionals to succeed in the areas of greatest growth in the emerging economy.

—Mel Horwitch, Chair, Department of Management

Programs and Curricular Focus

As the nation's second-oldest science and technology university, Polytechnic is committed to high-level and advanced development, research, and diverse learning programs that deal with technology management on a broad front, including the strategic use of information technology, electronic business, and innovation strategy.

Polytechnic University is the major technology-based higher education institute in the New York City/tristate region, which is the world center for innovation of all aspects of technology/management decision making. Emphasizing technology management, Polytechnic offers the Master of Science in Management (M.S.M.), which, along with the M.B.A., is recognized by the Graduate Management Admission Council as a graduate professional management degree. In addition, Polytechnic offers the Master of Science in organizational behavior, the Master of Science in financial engineering, the Master of Science in telecommunications and information management, and the Master of Science in management of technology. The Master of Science in telecommunications and information management and Master of Science in management of technology are offered in an executive format, meeting full Fridays and Saturdays of alternating weeks, totaling twenty-eight weekends over two years, at the New York Information Technology Center in Manhattan. Other programs are offered for full- or part-time students, with classes meeting after normal business hours. Each program, except the

executive format programs, offers a group of core courses and choices of concentrations and electives that allow students to specialize in areas that are important to their careers. Concentrations for the M.S.M. include construction management, technology management, human resource management, information management, telecommunications management, and operations management. Concentrations for the M.S. in organizational behavior include training and development, human resource management, and management of change.

The evening M.S.M. requires 42 credits (fourteen courses). The executive programs require 36 credits (twelve courses).

Students and the M.B.A. Experience

In 1997–98, more than 425 students were enrolled in graduate management programs, including more than 140 in executive format programs. About 90 percent of these students attended Polytechnic part-time while pursuing their careers. The range of industries represented included financial; computing; information technology and telecommunications; chemicals and pharmaceuticals; oil, gas, and electric power generation and distribution; entertainment; defense and aerospace; retailing; imaging; medical; government; transportation; and large-scale construction.

Reflecting the vibrant, international New York City community, students from many countries provide the programs with an international, multicultural

perspective that enhances a real-world understanding of global technology management issues. Students' undergraduate educations are mainly engineering or scientific; however, reflecting a need for a broad understanding of all aspects of technology management decision making, a wide variety of educational backgrounds and corporate responsibilities are welcome into the programs. A technology background is not required.

Most classes at Polytechnic are small, averaging 15–20 students. Access to professors, individual attention, and class participation are strengths not often found in larger institutions.

The Faculty

The management faculty is composed of highly respected scholars in innovation, operations, information technology, marketing, human resources and organizational behavior, finance and accounting, and strategic management. In addition, adjunct professors from a wide range of industries bring their expertise and vast experience to the classroom, where both theory and practice lead to a balanced, complete, and well-structured management education.

As pioneering developers in the field of technology management, Polytechnic's management department faculty stands at the cutting edge of critical, practical issues that face companies and managers in the rapidly changing, knowledge-based global business environment. Moreover, the department is increasingly developing curriculum materials in both paper and digital forms that deal with a wide range of technology management issues, particularly in the rapidly developing electronic business arena.

The Management Department Network

With its New York City location, Polytechnic's Department of Management is able to draw support from leaders in critical industries. The Industry Advisory Committee includes the Senior Vice President in charge of Technology Strategy at Merrill Lynch, the head of the high-technology practice with the Boston

Consulting Group, a leading-edge entrepreneur in the sophisticated use of information, the Chief Knowledge Officer at Monitor Company, a senior partner in consulting services for Price Waterhouse, and a well-known Chief Technology Officer.

The network of Polytechnic University graduates extends around the world and includes many senior executives in management, engineering, and science in nearly every service and manufacturing industry where technology plays an important role, which increasingly includes all sectors of the economy.

The College and Environs

Polytechnic's main campus is located near the East River in downtown Brooklyn. The financial engineering, management of technology, and telecommunications and information management programs are held in Manhattan. A second campus at the center of Long Island and a Graduate Center in Westchester County provide easy access. The Department of Management recently established its Institute for Technology and Enterprise in the heart of "Silicon Alley" in Manhattan.

Founded in 1854 and still known fondly as "Brooklyn Poly," the University is home to more than 4,000 graduate and undergraduate students in science, technology, and management. The unrivaled capacity of New York City to entertain, inform, and stimulate provides students with an experience unmatched in the world. But New York is also unrivaled as a business capital, providing graduates with access to the leading companies in every industry, including a new, booming multimedia center where start-ups and conglomerates compete for the technological talents that the city draws.

Facilities

The Bern Dibner Library of Science and Technology contains more than 200,000 volumes and has extensive database, multimedia, and Internet capabilities. Students at the Long Island and Westchester campuses have their own, smaller libraries and can request that any materials be sent to their campus from the Dibner Library in Brooklyn.

The University maintains large computer facilities for students and faculty with Internet and modem access. The Distance Learning Facility allows students at different campuses to attend lectures and classes together, enriching potential student interactivity.

The world-famous New York Public Library system, including the main research library and the new Library of Science, Industry, and Business, are available to students.

Placement

While nearly all management students are already employed, the University has career placement specialists for those interested in new opportunities. Industry recruiters visit regularly because of the high reputation Polytechnic has enjoyed for many years. In addition, the networks that exist between students and between students and faculty frequently open corporate doors that are not available to others.

Admission

Criteria for admission include having a bachelor's degree with at least a B average from an accredited college or university and demonstrated evidence of motivation, maturity, and the ability to benefit from and contribute to professional graduate studies. An applicant who does not meet all the criteria may be admitted as a nondegree student with the opportunity subsequently to become a degree candidate. Satisfactory scores on the Graduate Management Admission Test (GMAT) or an acceptable equivalent test such as the Graduate Record Examinations (GRE) may be used as support for admission to degree studies.

Finances

Tuition for the 1997–98 academic year was $645 per credit hour. All graduate management courses are 3 credits. The application fee is $45, but students may take up to three courses as special students without paying the application fee. Credit for special students is applied toward the degree requirements upon matriculation. The University fee was $230 per semester for full-time students and $85 per semester for part-time students.

Application Facts and Dates

Applications for graduate study are accepted at any time. Students may begin their programs of study in the spring, summer, or fall semesters, except for executive programs, where admission is for fall only. Application information is available from:

Evelyn Lombardo
Management Department
Polytechnic University
6 Metrotech Center
Brooklyn, New York 11201
Telephone: 718-260-3254
Fax: 718-260-3874
E-mail: elombard@duke.poly.edu
World Wide Web: http://www.poly.edu
http://www.mot-tim.poly.edu

Portland State University

Portland, Oregon

EXPLORING BUSINESS IN AN URBAN ENVIRONMENT

At Portland State University's (PSU) School of Business Administration, we are setting a pace for the twenty-first century by moving above and beyond the boundaries of conventional business education. Our graduate programs combine academic integrity with an applied, practical orientation, including involvement with business partners, to produce leaders and professionals to meet the challenges of the global marketplace.

The urban setting of Portland State University provides the best possible learning environment to prepare our graduates for the increasingly competitive world of business. We are committed to providing an outstanding learning experience that prepares our graduates to enter the workplace with needed knowledge, skills, understanding, and drive to be successful for themselves and their employers.

—Roger S. Ahlbrandt, Dean

Programs and Curricular Focus

In the M.B.A. curriculum, emphasis is given to an integrated and systemic perspective of how business competitiveness is achieved. The themes of decision making, problem solving, managing innovation and change, quality management practices, and global competitiveness cut across the program. Careful attention is given to communication, leadership, teamwork skills, and close involvement with the business community. The two-year, 72-quarter-credit M.B.A. program is composed of five distinct elements designed to produce a systematic and integrated understanding of business operations. These elements are business perspective and foundation skills, business disciplines, integrated applications, a business project, and a specialization. Learning is facilitated by use of team and project-based learning, information and information technology, and continued exposure to the thinking and practices of world-class business firms and their leaders. The Master of International Management (M.I.M.) is an innovative twelve-month full-time program (six 8-week terms) or a two-year part-time program that is specifically tailored to address the business challenges created by the world's shifting political, economic, and technological developments. The curriculum (17 core courses; 65 mandatory quarter-credit hours) combines an in-depth exploration of innovative business practices and their relationship to contemporary world affairs

and includes mandatory language study, executive seminars, corporate visits and a three-week field study trip to China and Japan. The School of Business Administration participates in the systems science Ph.D. program, which combines the study of systems with the study of business. Students work closely with faculty members to design an individualized program of study that gives each student the needed foundation in systems, research, and two fields of business.

Students and the M.B.A. Experience

Students in the PSU graduate business programs are a major resource for enhancing the total learning experience. More than 80 percent of the M.B.A. students are employed at the time of admission, with an average of six years of business experience. The average age is 29, and 39 percent are women. Approximately 15 percent are minority and international students. The classroom environment, which includes teams and active student interaction, is rich in diversity of experience, gender, and culture. Sharing and learning from each other is a hallmark of PSU graduate business education. Students in the M.I.M. program have approximately seven years of work and international experience. The average age of the students in the M.I.M. program is 32. The academic experience is augmented by the cultural diversity represented in a student body in which international students represent 51 percent of the total enrollment.

❖ Global Focus

In addition to the M.B.A. program's focus on competing in a global environment, the School of Business, in association with the Oregon Joint Professional Schools of Business, offers the M.I.M. degree. This program concentrates on application-oriented knowledge and practical skills that can be applied globally. The M.I.M. emphasizes the essentials of international business and includes a focus on the evolving cultural mores, transforming social systems, and new politics that impact international business daily. The M.I.M. program prepares the talented and highly motivated professional to meet the future of a competitive global business environment.

Special Features

Students in the M.B.A. program are members of a cohort group and complete two 8-hour integrated courses, with each team taught by several faculty members. Students also participate, individually or in teams, in an applied business project. Additional activities are available to help in career planning and development of computer skills. There is a pre-M.I.M. program designed to ensure academic success for students who have a limited academic business background. The eight-week program begins in late June and covers the fundamentals of business statistics, financial accounting, business finance, microeconomics, and macroeconomics. M.I.M. students also study a second language and participate in a field study trip to Japan and China.

The Faculty

The faculty is a significant strength of the School of Business Administration, bringing to the classroom a strong educational foundation, practical business experience, and dedication to student learning. Faculty members have traveled and taught in the Pacific Rim, the Middle East, Europe, Russia, and the Commonwealth of Independent States. In addition, the best talents within the business community are brought to the classroom as lecturers and guest speakers. A unique feature of the M.I.M. program is that the faculty is drawn from the internationally oriented faculty members at Portland State University, the University of Oregon, and Oregon State University. Furthermore, the M.I.M. program

Students can enjoy Portland's beautiful waterfront.

invites internationally recognized professors and business and government leaders from around the world to participate as faculty members.

The Business School Network

Corporate Partnerships
The School of Business Administration has forged close ties with the business community of the Pacific Northwest and the Pacific Rim. Partnership relationships are used to facilitate applied research, student projects, internships, faculty development, classroom participation by business executives and for networking opportunities for employment for graduates. The M.I.M. program utilizes international business executives to lead executive seminars. In addition, students travel to corporations to interact with business executives to gain firsthand knowledge about doing business internationally.

The College and Environs
Portland State University is ideally situated only 90 minutes from beaches and mountain slopes. As Oregon's economic and population center and a gateway to the Pacific Rim, Portland offers unique opportunities for business, industry, government, and the University to enhance partnerships that promote economic, social, cultural, and international development. Founded in 1946, the campus of nearly 15,000 students occupies forty buildings in a 36-acre area. The University is built around the Park Blocks, a greenway area reserved for pedestrians and bicyclists.

Facilities
The School of Business is located just a few minutes' walk from the downtown Portland business district. Students have access to the University's main library, which houses nearly 1 million volumes, including approximately 10,000 serial publications, a growing number of CD-ROM and online computer databases, and an extensive collection of government documents. Portland State University has nu-

merous housing facilities and options in providing desirable and affordable housing to students of the University. The M.I.M. program is located at the CAPITAL Center about 20 minutes from the main campus in the midst of the "Silicon Forest." Surrounded by numerous high-technology firms and other graduate programs, students study in a modern facility equipped with a high-technology presentation classroom, an executive-style conference room, and a comfortable student reading room.

Technology Environment
The School of Business Administration has a special computer lab for graduate students, equipped with high-speed laser printers and over twenty-five workstations. From here, students have access to the University's main computer, the Portland Area Library System (PORTALS), the Internet, and numerous other databases. The M.I.M. program provides a new, state-of-the-art language and computer lab. Students can do their language study or computer work in one of thirty workstations.

Placement
Career development and networking opportunities, coordinated through Corporate, Student, and Alumni Relations, are provided through seminars, workshops, and information meetings. Other resources include an internship program, the Portland State University Career Center, the PSU Business Association (PSUBA), the MBA Student Association (MBASA), and the M.I.M. Student Association (MIMSA).

Admission
Each candidate's academic record, scores on the required Graduate Management Admission Test (GMAT), and work experience are considered in the M.B.A. admission process. The averages for recently admitted students are a GMAT score of 589 and an undergraduate GPA of 3.3. Students may elect to participate in the full-time day program (fall admittance only) or

in the evening program (fall and winter admittance). The evening program is primarily for part-time students. The M.I.M. program prefers students who have at least two years of professional work experience, a GMAT score of at least 500 or an acceptable GRE score, and outstanding letters of recommendation and personal essay. Students who have no or a limited academic business background are required to participate in the eight-week summer pre-M.I.M. program. All international students who did not graduate from a U.S. institution must participate in the pre-M.I.M. program. International students whose native language is not English must score at least 550 on the TOEFL and must present proof of their financial resources.

Finances
Estimated full-time tuition for the M.B.A. program in 1998–99 is $6000 for in-state residents and $10,068 for nonresidents. A limited number of scholarships and graduate assistantships are available. Tuition for students enrolling in the 1999–2000 Master of International Management program is $18,500 plus a $3500 travel fee for the field study to China and Japan. Students enrolled in the pre-M.I.M. program pay an additional fee based on the number of pre-M.I.M. courses required.

International Students
A number of international students from countries in South America, Asia, and Europe participate in the graduate programs at Portland State University. The M.I.M. program has a 51 percent international student population.

Application Facts and Dates
Application deadlines for the M.B.A. program for international students are March 1 for fall admission and July 1 for winter admission; for domestic students, the dates are April 1 for fall admission and August 1 for winter admission. The Master of International Management program has a February 1 deadline for international students and an April 1 deadline for domestic students. For more information, applicants should contact:

Director of Student Services
School of Business Administration
Portland State University
P.O. Box 751
Portland, Oregon 97207-0751
Telephone: 503-725-3712
Fax: 503-725-5850

For the M.I.M. program, contact:

Oregon Joint Professional Schools of
    Business
18640 Northwest Walker Road, #1066
Beaverton, Oregon 97006-1975
Telephone: 800-879-5088 (toll-free)
Fax: 503-725-2290
E-mail: mim@capital.ous.edu

Purdue University

Krannert Graduate School of Management

West Lafayette, Indiana

> ### THE SCIENCE AND THE ART OF MANAGEMENT
>
> *The Krannert programs combine the "science"—management information systems, finance, operations—with the "art"—creative problem solving, presentation skills, team building—of business management. Our focus is hands-on and high-tech. Krannert is consistently recognized as one of the best educational values among top business schools.*
>
> —Dennis J. Weidenaar, Dean

Programs and Curricular Focus

The Master of Science in Management (M.S.M.) is a two-year residential program. Students select from options in accounting, finance, human resource management, management information systems, marketing, operations, strategic management, and three interdisciplinary options: general, international, or manufacturing management. The Master of Science in Human Resource Management (M.S.H.R.M.) is a two-year residential program that combines the best of human resource management with a strong business focus. The Master of Science in Industrial Administration (M.S.I.A.) is an eleven-month residential program that allows students to earn a management degree in a condensed time span. All three programs benefit from the global reputation of Purdue University.

The programs emphasize fundamental management theory, case studies, teamwork, and experiential learning opportunities, including computer simulations and consulting projects. The small program size (fewer than 500 students) allows frequent interaction with and personal attention from faculty members. Students also learn from each other in diverse, cross-disciplinary study teams. Complementing course work, student-run organizations provide leadership opportunities, networking with executives and recruiters, and personal and professional development.

Students and the Program Experience

Recruiters seek Krannert graduates because of their reputation for making smart, data-driven business decisions and their leadership skills and strong work ethic. Krannert students come from a wide range of undergraduate disciplines, with engineering, science, and mathematics well represented. The average age at entry is 27. Twenty-seven percent of the students are women, 9 percent are members of minority groups, and 30 percent are international. Four years of work experience is the average, but motivated students without on-the-job experience should still apply. In addition to Krannert's traditional strengths in production/operations management, students enjoy strong placement in corporate finance and consulting.

Special Features

Krannert uses specialized labs, computer simulations, and off-campus projects to enhance the study of specific management issues such as globalization and the information technology revolution. As an SAP Partner School, Krannert offers many advantages. The Enterprise Integration Lab, for example, runs SAP R/3 software using real company data. Students can analyze information from all areas of a company simultaneously and see how management decisions impact the various business functions of the enterprise. The International Multidisciplinary Management Project sends students abroad for a consulting project with an international company. The Student Managed Investment Fund gives students a hands-on opportunity to learn asset management and security analysis through investing real financial capital.

The Faculty

Krannert has 80 full-time management and economics faculty members. Due to the small program size, students view Krannert faculty members as professional peers as well as professors. Faculty members are responsive to student input concerning everything from course topics and speakers to class administration. Faculty evaluations are published each module to ensure high-quality teaching. Courses are reviewed regularly, often with input from alumni and recruiters, to reflect the changing business world. Purdue's reputation as a research university means Krannert faculty members make a point to include relevant, current applications of cutting-edge research in their courses.

The Business School Network

Krannert alumni and the corporations they work for are important contributors to the master's programs. Corporations and their representatives fund graduate awards, sponsor students, provide computer hardware and software, make presentations in courses and at special events, host interns, and actively recruit on and off campus. Some of the School's major corporate partners include Caterpillar, Eastman Kodak, Eli Lilly, Ernst & Young, Ford, General Motors, Hewlett-Packard, Ingersoll-Rand, USF&G, GE, GTE, Pricewaterhouse Coopers, Procter & Gamble, and United Technologies.

Information technology, such as SAP R/3 enterprise integration software, is a key component of Krannert's curricula.

Krannert graduates are sought by top corporations, especially in the consulting, computer, and automotive industries.

Students meet and interact with top executives through the Krannert Executive Forum presentation series, the Dean's Advisory Council, and the Krannert School Alumni Association Board. The Alumni Mentor Program links first-year students with active alumni as a source of advice about management studies and careers.

The College and Environs

Purdue University, a world-class research and teaching institution, has 35,000 students and 2,200 faculty members at West Lafayette, Indiana. In addition to management, Purdue is known for its strengths in engineering, computer science, and agriculture. Krannert takes pride in its affiliation with these University programs as well as its corporate partnerships in providing nationally ranked and accredited master's in management programs.

Krannert is located in a friendly college town in the midst of America's thriving heartland. The area economy is strong, and there are many job opportunities for spouses. Local schools are top-rated, and neighborhoods are safe and pleasant. Summers are warm and sunny, with some snow in winter. Chicago and Indianapolis are easily accessible by Interstate 65 for day trips, professional sporting events, and big-city culture.

Technology Environment

Students benefit from Krannert's exceptional information technology infrastructure. The computer laboratories have been developed in conjunction with corporate partners such as Ameritech, AT&T, Hewlett-Packard, IBM, Microsoft, PictureTel, and SAP America. The Krannert Library, with extensive online resources, is conveniently located in the same complex students attend for classes. Students and faculty members are fully wired with Internet access and e-mail, which encourages them to communicate, exchange data, and conduct research.

Placement

Graduates of Krannert's three master's programs are sought by recruiters in the fields of corporate finance, operations, consulting, information systems, human resource management, and marketing. Major recruiters include Allied Signal, Ernst & Young, FedEx, Ford, General Motors, Hewlett-Packard, IBM, Intel, International Paper, Pricewaterhouse, Procter & Gamble, and United Technologies. Finance, operations, and consulting are the top functions; consulting, computers and electronics, and automotive are the top industries. Preliminary data for June 1998 shows that $67,975 was the average base salary and $84,590 was the average first-year compensation. In addition to a full range of traditional placement services, all student resumes are searchable online at the School's World Wide Web address.

Admission

Test scores, grade point averages, work experience, and leadership potential are assessed during the admissions process.

Applicants must submit academic records, GMAT scores, essays, recommendations, and resumes. GMAT scores typically range from 590–710; the average GPA is 3.2. Campus interviews are available after applications are submitted. TOEFL scores are required of applicants from non-English speaking countries. Admissions are conducted on a rolling basis. Prospective students should contact the admissions office about spring preview weekend or tour arrangements throughout the year. Purdue University is an equal access/equal opportunity university.

Finances

Krannert provides a world-class educational value at competitive tuition rates. Estimated 1998–99 academic year tuition for the M.S.M. and M.S.H.R.M. programs is $7176 for Indiana residents and $15,424 for nonresidents. Estimated 1998–99 tuition for the eleven-month M.S.I.A. program is $9116 for Indiana residents and $19,679 for nonresidents.

Graduate awards are based on academic merit and other criteria and typically range from $2000 to $8000. Graduate awards are restricted to U.S. citizens and permanent residents. Assistantships, typically awarded during the second year of study, provide a monthly stipend and a partial tuition and fee remission ranging from $8600 to $18,000 a year. Residence hall counselorships provide room and board, a stipend for books, and a partial tuition and fee remission. All students are eligible to apply for residence hall counselorships. Federal Stafford Student Loans are available to U.S. citizens and eligible noncitizens.

Application Facts and Dates

Students should apply by November 1 to receive a decision by December 15. The international application deadline is February 1. Late applications may be accepted through May.

For more information, students should contact:

Ward Snearly, Director of Admissions
1310 Krannert Center, Room 104
Krannert Graduate School of
    Management
Purdue University
West Lafayette, Indiana 47907-1310
Telephone: 765-494-4365
Fax: 765-494-9841
E-mail: krannert_ms@mgmt.purdue.
    edu
World Wide Web: http://www.mgmt.
    purdue.edu

Queen's University at Kingston

M.B.A. for Science & Technology

Kingston, Ontario, Canada

MAKING A DIFFERENCE

The decision to pursue an M.B.A. says a great deal about you. It says you want to achieve career success. It says you want to develop the knowledge, skills, and perspectives required to be an effective manager. It says you are prepared to make a major investment in your future. Above all, it says you want to make a difference in this world.

The Queen's M.B.A. for Science & Technology will prepare you to make that difference. The program augments traditional M.B.A. programming with a special emphasis on the distinctive challenges facing science- and technology-focused organizations and the professional needs of those who lead them. The result is a one-year, comprehensive program that embodies a bold new approach to graduate management education.

—Jim McKeen, Chair

Program and Curricular Focus

The twelve-month Queen's M.B.A. for Science and Technology curriculum gives students the knowledge, management skills, and perspective they need to succeed in today's globally oriented, technology-rich organizations. It takes full advantage of the strong science and technology backgrounds of its students, leveraging their abilities into sophisticated applications.

The Queen's curriculum has four progressive stages. Students first develop a solid base in the disciplines and core concepts of management (stage one), then progress to the key functional fields of business—marketing, finance, and operations/information technology (stage two). With this strong foundation, they are ready to integrate knowledge from a strategic perspective (stage three). Students conclude the program with an intensive period of study in their chosen concentration and a monthlong field project that gives them hands-on experience in business management (stage four). In addition, the academic curriculum is complemented by several weeklong professional development modules that provide students with an array of tools and skills to enhance their managerial effectiveness.

Students and the M.B.A. Experience

Students enrolled in the Queen's M.B.A. for Science and Technology have undergraduate degrees in engineering, science, computer science, health science, or mathematics. They bring a wide variety of work experiences and geographic diversity. The average age is 30, and students have an average of six years' work experience.

Lectures, case studies, and individual and team exercises are used in varying proportions depending on the subject matter. Field projects, in particular the mandatory four-week major project, provide a hands-on learning experience in which students apply course materials in real-world, real-time applications.

Students are assigned to a team. Each team is provided with a faculty mentor. Team members operate in an atmosphere of mutual support that mirrors the kinds of professional relationships found in the workplace.

Special Features

One special feature of the Queen's M.B.A. for Science & Technology is its focus on science and technology. The professors, students, textbooks, and cases are all focused on understanding, analyzing, and overcoming the unique challenges faced by science and technology executives.

The program emphasizes the skills for success that graduates need. It not only covers all of the core elements of a traditional M.B.A., but it also helps students hone and develop special skills through five professional development modules. The students are immersed in high-performance team training, presenta-tion skills workshops, project management seminars, and much more.

Most schools help with job placement, but few offer the comprehensive career management students get at Queen's. Led by a full-time M.B.A. Career Manager, Queen's gives its students professional job search training and spares no effort in bringing industry leaders to campus. In short, advancing students' careers is a top priority at Queen's.

The Faculty

Faculty members for the M.B.A. for Science and Technology program are handpicked from more than 50 full-time faculty members in the School of Business. The faculty members are rich in business experience and offer excellence in teaching, research, and consulting.

The faculty at Queen's has long prided itself on accessibility to students and commitment to teaching excellence. Beyond the classroom, Queen's faculty has a history of widespread involvement in student programs.

Faculty members from other universities around the world also participate in the M.B.A. for Science and Technology through videoconferencing or as visiting lecturers. Guest speakers from industry and government participate actively in classes and in the professional development programs.

The College and Environs

Since its first day of classes in 1842, Queen's University has embodied a standard of excellence in education that makes it one of Canada's leading universities. Queen's distinctiveness is illustrated in the "Queen's Spirit," which has developed from the combination of a close-knit campus community, educational excellence, and beautiful surroundings.

Queen's University is located in the heart of Kingston, Ontario, Canada. Kingston is set within a labyrinth of lakes and waterways. With a population of 120,000, Kingston offers an outstanding quality of life to both families and singles. Kingston enjoys an abundance of cultural and recreational activities. From its rich historical heritage to its outstand-

ing fishing and sailing waters, Kingston provides a wide variety of attractions. Kingston also provides easy access to major centers of business, technology development, and government, as it is situated within easy reach of Ottawa, Toronto, Montreal, and Syracuse.

Facilities

The M.B.A. for Science & Technology program has a world-class facility built specifically to accommodate and facilitate the curriculum and learning process. It provides participants with exclusive use of a state-of-the-art teaching theatre, seminar rooms, and student and administrative offices.

Beyond the dedicated facility, students have access to Queen's wide array of athletic, academic, and student service facilities. These include the $43-million Stauffer Library and Electronic Information Centre, a $25-million Bioscience Complex, and the $20-million Walter Light Technology Centre.

Technology Environment

An extensive collection of audiovisual and information technologies extends the boundaries and capabilities of the physical facility. Through partnerships with IBM and Microsoft, each student gains low-cost access to a powerful

notebook computer and leading-edge software. When coupled with the computer groupware and other communication tools that connect every room and office, the result is a "virtual facility" that electronically links the program to the world.

Placement

The program serves as an active partner in the career development and placement efforts of students. Students benefit from both a dedicated M.B.A. career manager and an affiliation with the University-wide Career Services.

Special workshops focusing on career development skills, resume writing, and interviewing are held regularly. The M.B.A. Resume Book for the graduating class is very well regarded by the business community and is circulated widely to potential employers.

In their twelve months at Queen's, students attend career days, trade shows, and industry conferences set up exclusively for their participation.

Admission

The Queen's M.B.A. for Science & Technology is designed for graduates in the science and engineering fields who have significant professional experience and the potential for continued career

growth in management. Engineers, scientists, computer specialists, health-care professionals, and entrepreneurs, among others, represent the professions of candidates chosen to participate.

Candidates for admission are required to have at least two years of full-time work experience; an undergraduate degree in health science, science, engineering, mathematics, or computer science; a minimum score of 580 on the Graduate Management Admission Test (GMAT); two personal evaluations; and a willing-ness and desire to actively participate in highly intensive interactive classes. After an initial review of all materials, an interview with an officer of the program is scheduled. A final evaluation is made by the admissions committee based on a wide range of criteria, including the candidate's experience and performance and potential to contribute to the group learning experience.

Finances

Fees for the 1999–2000 year have been set at Can$29,500. In order to maintain the broadest possible level of accessibil-ity, the M.B.A. Program for Science & Technology has entered into an agreement with the Royal Bank of Canada to provide an attractive financing package for individuals who are Canadian citizens or landed immigrants.

This Income Contingent Loan Plan allows students to borrow their full tuition fee and an extra Can$10,000 to cover personal living expenses. Queen's University covers the interest costs on the entire loan while the student is in the program and the interest on the tuition portion until the individual is back in the workforce and earning at least Can$50,000 per year.

Application Facts and Dates

Applicants are encouraged to apply early, as enrollment is limited to a maximum of 60. Applications are reviewed on a rolling admissions basis. The deadline for submitting applications is December 1, 1998, for the session beginning in May 1999.

For more information, students should contact:

M.B.A. for Science & Technology
School of Business
Queen's University
Kingston, Ontario K7L 3N6
Canada
Telephone: 613-545-2302
Fax: 613-545-2013
E-mail: mbast@qsilver.queensu.ca
World Wide Web: http://qsilver.
    queensu.ca/mbast

Q Quinnipiac College

QUINNIPIAC COLLEGE

School of Business

Hamden, Connecticut

INNOVATIVE BUSINESS EDUCATION

The challenges that face business today are to remain viable and competitive in a global economy. This is no simple task since we are all dealing with evolving technology and increasing diversification in the workforce. To meet these challenges one must be able to plan strategic management effectively and adapt efficiently in a changing business environment. The Quinnipiac College Master of Business Administration program will provide you with the tools required for successful business leadership in the twenty-first century.

The Master of Business Administration program at Quinnipiac College provides an innovative business education. Doctorally and professionally qualified faculty members interact with students in small classes and through student team projects. This educational process is provided in our state-of-the-art Lender School of Business Center.

The Quinnipiac M.B.A. program provides a superior learning opportunity through its responsive faculty members, talented students, and a dynamic state-of-the-art learning facility adjacent to a vital business community.

—Phillip B. Frese, Dean

Programs and Curricular Focus

The Master of Business Administration program at Quinnipiac College is designed to give students a practical, useful education that helps them achieve success in the business world. Students gain insight into business systems and theory and develop skills in independent thinking and problem solving. The ethics of business, strategic planning, policy development, and interpersonal communications are part of a student's curriculum. Graduates of Quinnipiac's M.B.A. program are equipped with the skills necessary to be action-oriented, hands-on managers in the twenty-first century.

All M.B.A. students must complete a 30-hour core curriculum that includes such classes as financial management, organizational theory, and quantitative decision analysis. A capstone course, the Integrative Management Seminar, is also part of the core. Students who enter the program without formal business training or academic experience may need to complete a series of introductory courses that provide the basic business educational foundation needed to complete the M.B.A. core curriculum.

Following completion of the core curriculum, students may opt for a 6-credit thesis program, involving research with a faculty adviser. This option requires 36 credits for graduation. Those pursuing thesis research develop a concentration in

accounting/taxation, computer information systems, economics, finance, health administration, international business, management, or marketing.

In lieu of a thesis, students may choose to take three additional courses that build on core subjects. These courses may focus on a specific concentration or cover multiple disciplines. This option requires 39 credit hours for graduation.

Students may apply for acceptance to both the Law School and the M.B.A. program and, upon completion of both programs, receive a J.D./M.B.A. degree. This specialized joint program shortens the length of time necessary to receive the degrees. There is an 18-credit overlap—9 credits in each program—that counts toward both degrees. M.B.A. students have a concentration in law. A thesis option is not available to participants in the joint program.

Qualified Quinnipiac undergraduate students planning to continue with graduate study immediately after completing their undergraduate studies are eligible to apply for a five-year B.S./M.B.A. This program is designed for outstanding undergraduates with an overall GPA of at least 3.0 who are majoring in business administration.

Part-time students can complete the M.B.A. program in three years, depending on the number of classes taken each semester and the length of the thesis project.

A full-time degree program can be completed in as little as fifteen months.

Students and the M.B.A. Experience

Quinnipiac's diverse full- and part-time student body represents a rich mix of background and experience, ranging from mid- and top-level managers, beginning and veteran entrepreneurs, family and small-business owner-operators, and accomplished professionals seeking to develop business leadership competencies to recent baccalaureate recipients preparing to enter the business world. There are approximately 200 students enrolled in the M.B.A. program; 40 percent are women. The average age of students is 30 years. A small but significant number of international students are enrolled in the M.B.A. program, and the College has made a firm commitment to increase the diversity of the student body.

❖ Global Focus

Every curriculum area addresses the problems and challenges of doing business globally. An optional three-week summer session has taken M.B.A. students to Europe, Latin America, and Asia. This intensive experience includes seminars, comprehensive studies, lectures from corporate executives, and meetings with government officials.

The Faculty

Guiding Quinnipiac's M.B.A. program is a faculty with exceptional academic credentials and proven business experience. The College's 46 instructors hold doctorates or equivalent degrees from such prestigious institutions as Berkeley, Brown, Columbia, Harvard, New York University, Yale, and other leading institutions. Many have professional as well as academic backgrounds.

Although their first commitment is to teaching, Quinnipiac's faculty members are also active professionals, knowledgeable about the latest developments in their fields through consulting, leading executive seminars, research, publication, and attendance at conferences and workshops. Among their many areas of expertise are information systems,

entrepreneurship, organizational development, fiscal policy, marketing, and
competitive strategy.

The Business School Network
Quinnipiac College's School of Business
has been one of the traditional strengths
of the College for more than sixty years
and has strong relationships with
businesses and industry throughout the
Northeast. Through Quinnipiac's professors and internship programs, the College
maintains its network of connections with
the business world. The School of
Business has studied new markets in
Japan for Connecticut companies and the
economic impact of a regional airport,
and consulted on health management
programs in Central America and the
Caribbean. The M.B.A. program also
features a lecture series, which brings in
prominent corporate executives who
shape today's business issues.

Prominent Alumni
The 8,000 alumni of the School of Business
have made their mark in a wide range of
businesses. Graduates of Quinnipiac in-
clude Murray Lender, H. Lender & Sons
Restaurants and M&M Investments; Paula
Tomasetti, Vice President of Goldman Sa-
chs & Company; Robert J. Hauser, CEO of
Commonwealth Land Title Company; and
Gabriel Ferrucci, President and CEO of
Keystone Engineering Company.

The College and Environs
Founded in 1929, Quinnipiac is a private,
nonsectarian, coeducational institution
located in Hamden, Connecticut. The College offers a full range of undergraduate
and graduate programs through the School
of Health Sciences, the College for Adults,
the School of Business, the School of Liberal Arts, and the School of Law.

The mission of Quinnipiac College is
the integration of liberal and professional
studies. Quinnipiac guides its students
toward the acquisition of knowledge both
in the classroom and in all areas of
student life, emphasizing critical and
creative thinking, effective communication skills, and the ability to make
informed value judgments. The special
mission of the graduate programs is to
provide professionals with the advanced
competencies needed to assume leadership positions in their chosen fields.

Quinnipiac College's beautiful and
safe central location in southern Connecticut, between New Haven and
Hartford, is convenient to New York and
Boston. It also gives students access to
numerous major corporations and science,
health-care, and research facilities in the
area. The campus itself—180 acres—
features thirty-two modern buildings and
eighteen impressive residence halls.

Adjoining the campus is Sleeping Giant
Mountain and State Park, with 20 miles
of scenic hiking trails.

Facilities
The heart and home of the M.B.A. program is Quinnipiac's Lender School of
Business Center, designed to accommodate
the particular needs of graduate students.
Local area network classrooms include
monitors and keyboards at each desk plus
line-of-sight contact with the discussion
leader. Case rooms allow groups to work
on business problems in lecture-discus-
sions. Team study rooms provide a technologically advanced, learning-conducive
environment in which to develop problem-
solving strategies with classmates. A reading room features periodicals, access to
databases, and CD-ROM stations.

Technology Environment
The Research Library provides M.B.A. students with access to such databases as ABI/
INFORM, LEXIS-NEXIS, and the Business Periodicals Index on CD-ROM. A
large library of the latest versions of software used by business and industry is available for student use. Online access to the
Dialog database, as well as a comprehensive collection of business holdings in hard
copy, is also available for all students.

Placement
Quinnipiac M.B.A. graduates currently
hold top positions in such companies as
United Technologies, Bayer Corporation,
Aetna, and General Electric. On-campus
recruiters visit Quinnipiac each year in
search of prospective employees.
Recruiters include four of the "big six"
accounting firms, a division of NBC in
New York, Pratt & Whitney, and other
regional manufacturing firms, insurance
companies, banks, pharmaceutical
companies, health-care organizations, and
state and federal government agencies.
The College arranges job interviews for
students, assists with preparation of
resumes, and maintains an alumni
network of potential job contacts for
graduate students. Other placement
services and resources available to
students include career counseling/
planning, career fairs on campus, and a
career library. Most School of Business
graduates find positions in their fields
within three months of graduation.

Admission
Admission to the M.B.A. program at Quinnipiac College is competitive. Students
seeking admission must have earned a baccalaureate degree in either a business or a
nonbusiness field, have a minimum GPA of
2.5, and submit Graduate Management Admission Test (GMAT) scores to the College.

Candidates who wish to interview prior to
admission may arrange for an appointment
with the director of the M.B.A. program.

The College utilizes a formula-based
admission system as a primary application
screening tool. This system, called "1000-
combined," is helps admissions counselors
determine a candidate's eligibility by multiplying a candidate's GPA by 200 and
adding total GMAT scores to this sum to
reach a minimum acceptable score of
1000. For example, a candidate with a 2.5
GPA would need a minimum GMAT score
of 500 to be considered qualified for admission. The M.B.A. admissions committee does not consider GMAT scores of less
than 400 acceptable for admission to the
program. It should be noted that meeting
these minimum standards does not guarantee admission. Work experience and recommendations are also strongly considered
in the process.

Finances
For 1998–99, the tuition rate for all M.B.A.
students is $395 per credit hour. Part-time
students pay a $20 registration fee each
semester. Full-time students are charged a
student fee of $185 for access to the student
health center and athletic facilities.

The College offers several types of financial aid to help both full- and part-time
students fund their education. Most are
supplementary to personal resources and
include savings, employer tuition benefits,
and other forms of assistance. Graduate
assistantships are available on a limited
basis to both full- and part-time students.
M.B.A. candidates are eligible to apply for
subsidized and unsubsidized Federal
Stafford Student Loans. Students may also
apply for privately sponsored commercial
loan programs such as GradEXCEL, TERI,
or Family Educational Loan Program
(FELP).

Application Facts and Dates
Applications for the M.B.A. program are
accepted throughout the year for both
full- and part-time study. Candidates are
encouraged to submit applications as
early as possible to ensure consideration
for the semester desired. A complete
application consists of the following: an
application form, a $45 application fee,
GMAT scores, two recommendations, a
recent resume, and transcripts of all
undergraduate and graduate work
completed. For more information,
applicants should contact:

Mr. Scott Farber
Director of Graduate Admissions
Quinnipiac College
275 Mount Carmel Avenue
Hamden, Connecticut 06518-9936
Telephone: 203-281-8795
Fax: 203-281-8906
E-mail: qcgradadmi@quinnipiac.edu

Regent University

Virginia Beach, Virginia

SERVICE: THE BEST STRATEGY FOR SUCCESS

Business touches everyone's life every day—through the products and services they consume and in their work relationships. Business leaders, through their personal values and decisions, shape that business experience for millions of people throughout the world. What an opportunity to demonstrate integrity in the marketplace and to bless people with rewarding jobs and useful products!

The Regent University School of Business, through its Christian worldview and its focus on people, is graduating M.B.A.'s ready to fulfill that opportunity. These leaders are combining technical business skills with biblically based management principles, blending faith with excellence in a time-proven philosophy we call Servant Leadership. It is proving to be the best strategy for success and the best assurance of personal career satisfaction.

—John Mulford, Ph.D., Dean

Programs and Curricular Focus

The School of Business offers the Master of Business Administration (M.B.A.) degree and the Master of Arts (M.A.) in management degree. Students may earn either degree on campus, by distance learning, or through a combination of both.

Both degree programs are designed to accommodate the diverse backgrounds and life circumstances of students. Extensive prerequisites are offered to prepare the student who may not have accrued management/business experience or relevant course work over the last ten years.

Specialization tracks include *entrepreneurship, entrepreneurial tentmaking, *financial planning, international business, *management, *managerial control, marketing, media management, missions management, and *nonprofit management (*offered through distance education).

Students and the M.B.A. Experience

Regent business students are diverse in religious, national, and ethnic origins and number approximately 245. Seventy-three are women; 67 are members of minority groups. The average student age is 35.

Special Features

Regent University offers the Accelerated Scholars and Professionals Program (ASAP) that allows some students to enter their master's program without

having received a bachelor's degree. Successful applicants to this program have accrued a minimum of 90 credits toward their undergraduate degree and have five years of business experience.

The School of Business offers a cognate for the Ph.D. in organizational leadership that may be earned through the Regent Center for Leadership Studies. This degree is offered via the Internet only. Business courses in this program are taught by the same full-time faculty members who teach on campus.

Joint degrees are available, including the Juris Doctor (J.D.), Master of Education (M.Ed.), and Master of Divinity (M.Div.).

The Faculty

Regent School of Business has a distinguished faculty of published scholars who represent a variety of professional backgrounds, from small-business entrepreneurs to top-level employees in Fortune 500 companies.

The Business School Network

Regent School of Business hosts the Executive Leadership Series—a string of vibrant conferences featuring nationally and internationally known business leaders who are proponents of "servant leadership" in their business operations. Dynamic guests have included such notables as Zig Ziglar, Philip B. Crosby, Ken Melrose, Foster Friess, and Truett Cathy. Students are afforded opportunities

to interact directly with these individuals to gain firsthand business information.

Prominent Alumni

Regent alumni are enjoying a variety of satisfying and successful careers. Examples of Regent's notable alumni include Arun Daniel, Manager, Resort Development, Walt Disney Company, Orlando, Florida; Edward Scott Rigell, Owner/President, Freedom Ford, Norfolk and Hampton, Virginia; Thomas G. Mandl, Product Design Engineer, Ford Motor Company, Dearborn, Michigan; Robert Allen Rohrer, Industrial Analyst, The Boeing Company, Seattle, Washington; Vivian Lee Adams, National Account Manager–Military Sales, L'Eggs Hosiery; Tom W. H. Yeh, Product Manager, Campbell Soup Asia Ltd./Taiwan Branch, Taipei, Taiwan; Ronald Murray Farrar, National Business Manager, Mercedes Benz Club of America; Roger K. Rawley, Senior Engineer–Teleconferencing, WANG/I-NET, Billerica, Massachusetts; James D. Litherland, Head of Environmental Services, JFK Hartwyck; Pamela Cartwright, Director of Cancer Services, Senatara Health Systems, Norfolk, Virginia; Brian V. Magnone, Director, Treasury and Cash Management, Christian Broadcasting Network, Virginia Beach, Virginia; Stephen L. McPherson, Attorney, Virginia Court of Appeals, Norfolk, Virginia; and Leslie A. Parker, Magistrate, State of Virginia.

The College and Environs

Regent University is a graduate institution offering twenty-one master's and doctoral degrees from a Judeo-Christian worldview. Regent's eight colleges and schools include Business, Communication, Counseling, Divinity, Education, Government, Law, and Organizational Leadership.

Located on a 700-acre complex in Virginia Beach, Virginia, the Regent University campus is a fascinating study of Georgian architecture accented with arched windows and hand-hewn brick. Since its founding in 1977 by Dr. M. G. "Pat" Robertson, Regent has grown to an enrollment of 1,700 students. In addition to main campus programs in Virginia

Beach, Regent offers several degree programs in its northern Virginia/Washington, D.C.–area extension. More than ten graduate degree programs are available via the Internet and distance learning. Regent University is accredited by the Commission on Colleges of the Southern Association of Colleges and Schools (1866 Southern Lane, Decatur, Georgia 30033-4097; telephone: 404-679-4500) to award master's and doctoral degrees. The Regent University School of Law is fully accredited by the American Bar Association (ABA).

Facilities

Regent University offers its students a technologically advanced educational environment. As a pioneer in distance/online education, Regent offers more than ten degree programs on the Internet, including the M.B.A. and the M.A. in management. The learning environment is enhanced internally and externally through resources such as Dynacom video distribution, teleconferencing, and RealMedia. Computers, with online research capabilities, are available to students across the campus.

Placement

The School of Business maintains a strong Alumni Network that supports the career search efforts of Regent students. In addition, the mentoring nature of the School provides individualized placement assistance and counseling throughout the student's program.

Admission

With the exception of ASAP students (see Special Features), admission to Regent University requires a completed four-year bachelor's degree from a state and regionally accredited postsecondary institution. Applicants possessing earned degrees from nonaccredited institutions are considered on an individual basis. Other criteria for admission are a cumulative undergraduate GPA of at least 2.75 verified by official transcripts, a resume, two recommendations, one interview in person or by telephone, maturity in spiritual and/or character qualities, and personal goals consistent with the mission and goals of Regent. All students (not only distance learners) are required to have the computer literacy to install and configure common software, use a computer modem, access an online service, send and receive messages with attachments via e-mail, and upload and download computer files. The School of Business will not teach or train applicants in computer use.

Finances

Tuition for the School of Business is $325 per semester–credit hour. Students accepted for enrollment may apply for Federal Stafford Student Loans and a variety of School-specific scholarships and grants. Veterans' benefits also apply. Active military participants receive an automatic 25 percent discount. The School of Business is DANTES approved.

Application Facts and Dates

Application deadlines are two weeks before the start of any given term. There is a $40 application fee. Forms may be downloaded from the Web site or obtained by mail. For more information, students should contact:

Regent University School of Business
1000 Regent University Drive
Virginia Beach, Virginia 23464-9800
Telephone: 800-477-3642 (toll-free)
Fax: 757-226-4369
E-mail: busschool@regent.edu
World Wide Web: http://www.regent.edu/acad/schbus

Rensselaer Polytechnic Institute

Lally School of Management and Technology

Troy, New York

MANAGEMENT AND TECHNOLOGY M.B.A. AT RENSSELAER

◆The Lally School of Management and Technology at Rensselaer is focused on the intersection of management and technology, and everything we do begins with the conviction that for all firms in all future markets, sustainable competitive advantage will be built upon a technological foundation. Our mission is to educate a new breed of managers who are prepared to lead their companies in the effective and strategic use of technology.

—Joseph G. Ecker, Dean

Programs and Curricular Focus

The Lally School's master's programs focus on three areas of management and technology: "value creation," "management systems," and "financial technology."

Value creation refers to the process of developing and sustaining new products and businesses. This process is at the core of the conversion of technology to competitive advantage, and all our students are expected to develop an understanding of it and to have gained at least some exposure to its practice. For example, a required two-semester sequence in product development is one of the centerpieces of the M.B.A. program. An emphasis on business plan development and team-based field projects with start-up companies cuts across all graduate programs. Students who choose to specialize in this area of focus choose among course offerings in product development and management, manufacturing, environmental management, and technological entrepreneurship. The Lally School was ranked seventeenth by *Success* magazine among business school programs in entrepreneurship and first in overall program score; in technological entrepreneurship, Lally believes it has the strongest program in the world. The new business incubator, which houses thirty-five technology-based start-ups on campus and has become a living laboratory for students, was recently named by the National Business Incubation Association as the best of 500 new business incubators in the country. Professors Mark Rice and Pier Abetti are generally among the world's leading experts in business incubation and have traveled around the world advising governments on new business develop-

ment. As many as 10 faculty members, ranging from experts in marketing to manufacturing to accounting, are collaborating on an $800,000 Sloan Foundation-funded study of the management of "discontinuous" new product and business development in established Fortune 500 companies.

Management systems refers to the integration of the disciplines of management with information systems and technology and quantitative techniques and skills. This area of focus grows out of the School's historical strengths in operations research and statistics. Many graduate students, for example, pursue a dual degree combining an M.B.A. with an M.S. in industrial engineering. Like the emphasis on value creation, the School's emphasis on management systems is reflected in both the core curricula and the concentrations. In the core, all students are required to take an integrated two-semester sequence on quantitative techniques and a one-semester course on information systems and technology. In the concentrations, students pursue depth in information systems and, with increasing frequency, dual degrees combining an M.B.A. and an M.S. in industrial engineering. The School's focus on systems is well recognized by industry, particularly consulting firms like Andersen, American Management Systems, and Ernst & Young. Reflecting this recognition by industry, in the most recent rankings of "techno-M.B.A." information systems programs by *Computer World*, the program was ranked eighteenth in the country.

Financial technology is, in many respects, a subset of management

systems. It refers to the intersection of finance, information technology, and quantitative techniques. Students are able to build expertise in financial engineering, financial information systems, and venture financing. This is an emerging area of growth for the School, based on a belief that there are huge career opportunities at this point of intersection. The world of finance is being transformed by information and communications technology and by the dramatic associated increases in computing capacity. This transformation is making the traditional finance major somewhat obsolete and is creating demand for graduates who combine the depth of the traditional finance major (in such fields as investments, options and futures, and risk management) with the technical savvy and modeling capabilities of the more traditional technology oriented students that are typically attracted to the Lally School.

Students and the M.B.A. Experience

In the first year, courses are composed of modules, which are grouped into different "streams" or clusters of management and technology disciplines. For example, one stream focuses on the new product development process by integrating modules on marketing, design, manufacturing, managerial accounting, pricing and distribution, and performance measurement. Students are organized in teams, and each team develops a new product idea as it experiences each of these modules. Other streams include statistics and operations management, designing, and developing and staffing high-performance organizations, as well as accounting, economics, and financial management.

The second year is composed of five required courses and five electives. Two of the required courses form a strategy sequence on trends in science and technology that are likely to lead to new classes of products and businesses in decades ahead. The practicum experience, a course in business ethics, and a course in international business fulfill the required courses. The remainder of the program can be tailored to the student's interest and may include a concentration. Concentrations include management information systems, technological entrepreneurship, research and development management, manufacturing systems, manufacturing management, product development, environmental management and policy, and financial technology. During the second year, students have the option of participating in our International Management Exchange Program by spending a semester abroad in one of eight leading universities in Western Europe and Asia.

The Business School Network
Rensselaer has always had exceptionally strong ties with business and industry. Many of Rensselaer's graduates have chosen to apply their talents and ingenuity to founding, growing, and leading successful high-tech firms. Building on this tradition, Rensselaer has developed a systematic program for preparing students for entrepreneurship, both within established corporations and in new start-up ventures.

Entrepreneurship is a mainstream activity of the School, reflecting a deeply-held conviction that all technology driven firms must continuously pursue new business creation for long-term survival and success. The Lally School of Management and Technology is not only one of a handful of institutions that offers a curriculum in entrepreneurship, it is also one of the best. The value creation process in general, and technological entrepreneurship in particular, is our singular area of strength.

The Faculty
Faculty members at the Lally School of Management and Technology are characterized by vigor, dynamism, and a strong commitment to the business application of technology. Courses provide historical context, classical applications, and current perspectives—but the emphasis is on the future: providing M.B.A.'s with the innovative tools needed for success in the high-technology business environment of the twenty-first century.

Faculty members include experts in finance, computer applications, artificial intelligence, manufacturing, statistics, policy and strategy, international business, organizational design, product development, and marketing. Almost all of the full-time faculty members have substantial managerial experience in business or government.

The College and Environs
Troy, Albany, and Schenectady form an upstate metro area—New York's Capitol Region—with a population of nearly 750,000. The area is a major center for government, industrial, research, and academic activity. The headquarters or research centers for some of the world's largest technology-based firms are within easy driving

distance of the Capitol Region. A second campus in Hartford, Connecticut, now offers M.S. and M.B.A. degrees.

Technology Environment
Rensselaer is a technology-rich environment, and the Lally School takes full advantage of this fact. M.B.A. classes make extensive use of PC-based software for course work. Teams of students are assigned the use of a laptop computer for the first year of the program. A wide variety of high-end computing facilities are located throughout the campus, including a network of more than 600 UNIX-based workstations and many PC, Macintosh, and multimedia labs.

In addition to computing facilities, Rensselaer M.B.A.'s have the ability to draw on the abilities and knowledge of world-class researchers and research centers located on the campus. As one example, when a team of M.B.A.'s in the product development course needed to design a plastic housing for their product, they consulted materials experts in the Rensselaer Design and Manufacturing Institute to assist them.

Placement
The School views placement of its students as its ultimate measure of success. To that end, M.B.A.'s are provided with assistance in their job search efforts by both the campuswide Career Development Center and by the Lally School's Career Resources Office. Companies that have hired Rensselaer M.B.A.'s recently include Allied Signal, Andersen Consulting, American Management Systems, AT&T, Boeing, BT/Alex Brown, Citicorp, Ernst & Young, General Electric, IBM, Johnson & Johnson, Lucent Technologies, Oracle, Pitney Bowes, Procter & Gamble, Salomon Brothers, United Technologies, and a host of others. Nearly 40 percent of the graduates each year choose positions in the financial services or management consulting fields, another 20 percent go to jobs in MIS, and the remainder choose marketing or operations management positions.

Admission
With the focus of the Lally School on the intersection of management and technology, most applicants have undergraduate and/or master's degrees in engineering and science. However, applicants with degrees in other fields who have strong quantitative skills and interests in technology are also welcome. Most applicants have significant work experience, though each year a small number of recent college graduates from programs in engineering and science are considered for admission.

Applicants must take the Graduate Management Admissions Test (GMAT). Applicants whose native language is not English must also take the TOEFL. All credentials

(official transcripts, test score reports, etc.) must be submitted to the Office of M.B.A. Admissions.

Finances
Tuition is $630 per credit hour. Full-time students pay tuition and fees of $18,900 per year. Living expenses are estimated at $9500 per year. Approximately 20 percent of entering full-time M.B.A. students will receive a partial, merit-based scholarship. This scholarship consists of 6 tuition credits per semester for four semesters, which is presently valued at $15,120 or 40 percent of overall tuition costs. Other types of scholarships are available for highly qualified students, including full tuition fellowships for 1 student per year in manufacturing and for 1 female entrepreneur. A limited number of graduate assistantships are awarded to select M.B.A. students entering their second year of study. These assistantships provide a stipend of $2400 per semester in return for 10 hours of work per week. The work entails such activities as grading and research. Approximately fifteen assistantships are offered on a competitive basis each year.

International Students
Nearly 40 percent of all full-time M.B.A.'s in the program come from outside the United States. This strong international representation helps to create a dynamic and globally aware environment for class discussions, team projects, and the overall Lally School community.

Application Facts and Dates
The standard academic year for the full-time M.B.A. program begins in late August and ends in mid-May of the following year. The schedule for the part-time program is flexible and can be tailored to the student's needs. Matriculation for either program can begin in January as well as in August. A selection of courses are also offered in the summer for students who wish to accelerate or who prefer to take fewer courses during the academic year. The application deadline for fall semester is May 1; for spring semester, the deadline is November 1.

Early submission of applications is strongly encouraged. Applications are considered on a first-come, first-served basis. An online application is available at the Web site listed below.

To request an informational brochure and application, contact:

Director, M&T M.B.A. Program
Lally School of Management and
    Technology
Rensselaer Polytechnic Institute
Troy, New York 12180-3590
Telephone: 518-276-4800
Fax: 518-276-8661
E-mail: management@rpi.edu
World Wide Web: http://lallyschool.rpi.
    edu

Rice University

Jesse H. Jones Graduate School of Management

Houston, Texas

RICE M.B.A.: TURNING KNOWLEDGE INTO ACTION TO CREATE LEADERS

There was a time when earning an M.B.A. meant you had mastered the theories of finance and accounting. Today, classroom learning is only one aspect of a complete business education, and the scope of subjects has broadened immensely. In the era of rapid globalization, change is the only constant, and companies want more than good managers; they want great leaders who can resolve issues with a multidisciplinary approach.

At the Jones School, we have always considered judgment, leadership, and communication skills as important as leading-edge knowledge. But now, we are taking the learning experience one step further. After seeking input from faculty, students, and industry leaders—including top management at major corporations to determine which skills they consider most valuable—we have developed an innovative curriculum that builds on theory with an experiential learning process we call Action Learning. At Rice, you'll cultivate the tools you need to excel regardless of your chosen specialty, graduating with knowledge and confidence. We hope you'll join us!

—Gilbert R. Whitaker Jr., Dean

Programs and Curricular Focus

The Jones Graduate School has implemented a new Action Learning Curriculum that is one of the few programs of its kind in the nation. The M.B.A. program combines three essential elements: a comprehensive and challenging core curriculum providing students with a solid foundation of basic business disciplines; a required Action Learning Project, a summer internship, and numerous field project–oriented electives offering ample opportunities for real-world practice; and a host of specialized electives allowing students to further integrate their knowledge and empower them to achieve their career objectives. All courses in the two-year full-time program are streamlined into flexible modules of five, ten, or fifteen weeks each. Managerial communication is integrated across the curriculum, with instruction in strategic communications and both team and individual coaching in oral and written communication.

Depending on the subject matter, faculty members utilize multiple instructional methods to enhance the learning process— case-method study, analytical and quantitative approaches, lectures and discussions, oral and written reports, theoretical studies, management simulation games, individual study, and teamwork.

The first-year core courses address a wide range of management subjects, including finance, accounting, data analysis, marketing, the global business environment, information technology, and organizational behavior. A sequence of modules on leadership and managerial skills includes influence tactics, navigating the political landscape, negotiating effectively, building partnerships, communicating with hostile audiences, when to partner, and when to compete.

Early in the spring semester, students complement their core courses with an elective designed to help them develop a specialty. During the final ten weeks, teams of students integrate the business disciplines they have studied into an Action Learning Project for a host company.

The second year includes core courses in entrepreneurship and strategy formulation and implementation. Students customize the remainder of their schedule with 25 credit hours of specialized electives from the Jones School's course offerings and/or upper-level courses from other Rice University departments.

The School offers three joint-degree options: an M.B.A./Master of Engineering with the Brown School of Engineering, an M.B.A./M.D. with Baylor College of Medicine, and an M.B.A./Ph.D. with Baylor.

Students and the M.B.A. Experience

A total of 270 M.B.A. students from all regions of the United States and twenty-three other countries were enrolled in 1997–98. Forty percent had engineering or science backgrounds; 41 percent majored in business or economics. The mid-50 percent of the students had between 2½ and 7 years of work experience before entering the program. The average age was 27. Women comprise 25 percent of the student body; international students, 12 percent; and members of minority groups, 12 percent.

Courses are sectioned to keep the class size to no more than 50 students, thus promoting greater classroom participation and contact with faculty members.

The Faculty

The faculty maintains an important balance between teaching and research, believing that current industry knowledge is as critical as textbooks to education. All of the School's instructors are either academics with significant business or consulting experience or business executives with significant classroom experience who teach specialized elective courses. With a student-faculty ratio of 9:1, students have opportunities to work closely with their instructors. Faculty members are interested in the students' career goals as well as their academic abilities and are willing to spend extra time helping students develop knowledge and skills.

The Business School Network

The Jones School maintains close ties with the business community through its Council of Overseers, a group of distinguished executives who advise the School on its focus and direction, and the Dean's Lecture series, in which business leaders discuss topics of their choice with students. All students spend the last five weeks of their first year working full-time on site to solve a specific problem for a Houston-area company. Many elective courses also include field projects that give students real-world experience with area businesses. In addition, alumni return to the School to advise students on career choices, serve on stand-

Lovett Hall, Rice University's administration building and one of its original structures.

ing committees, and recruit students for summer internships and permanent positions.

The College and Environs

Rice University, a private, nonsectarian, coeducational institution, admitted its first students in 1912. The Jones School is one of seven academic units offering undergraduate and graduate studies in management, architecture, natural science, engineering, social science, music, and humanities. Rice, which has the tenth-largest endowment of any university in the country, deliberately keeps its enrollment relatively small; the student body of 4,100 includes 1,400 graduate students. The low student-faculty ratio ensures that students receive individual attention from their professors.

The University is situated on a beautiful 300-acre tree-lined campus in one of Houston's finest residential districts yet is only 3 miles from the city center and is adjacent to the world-renowned Texas Medical Center. The nation's fourth-largest city, Houston has the third-largest concentration of Fortune 500 corporate headquarters and is also an operating center for more than half of the world's largest non-U.S.-based corporations. Among the growth industries in the city's well-diversified economy are finance, high technology, engineering/design services, energy, and health-care services. Houston's symphony, ballet, grand opera, and repertory theater are nationally known performing arts organizations. Sports fans enjoy a variety of professional and collegiate teams.

Facilities

The Business Information Center has online capabilities and subscribes to

various compact-disc services that provide financial and bibliographic information. Students also have access to the University research and depository library, which contains 1.9 million volumes, 2.4 million microforms, 12,000 current serials and periodicals, and 83,000 titles on audio and video tapes and compact discs. Students can access the Internet, exchange files, and send and receive e-mail from home or from various locations within the School. Several classrooms contain state-of-the-art projection systems equipped with personal computers and VCRs.

Placement

The Career Planning Center provides instruction in resume and cover letter writing, job interviewing techniques, and use of the School's online, compact disc, and paper sources of company and industry information. Alumni help students sharpen their skills by participating in mock interviews and career panels. Students are actively assisted in finding summer internships between the first and second years. In addition to a full schedule of on-campus recruiting, graduating students also have access to companies that attend the M.B.A. Consortium event in Atlanta and, for international students, similar events in Miami and Orlando. An additional source of contacts for summer internships is the New York M.B.A. Consortium event, which attracts students interested in finance and consulting.

Admission

Admitted for the fall semester only, applicants must submit essays, three

recommendations, and transcripts from all universities attended. GMAT scores are required of all M.B.A. applicants, and TOEFL scores are required of applicants whose native language is not English unless an applicant received an undergraduate degree from a U.S. university. Applicants to the joint M.B.A./Master of Engineering program must submit scores from the GRE rather than the GMAT; applicants to the joint M.B.A./M.D. or M.B.A./Ph.D. programs must submit scores from the MCAT. Candidates are evaluated on their academic records, leadership potential, motivation to succeed, and professional work experience. Personal interviews are strongly recommended.

Finances

Annual tuition for 1998–99 is $15,750. Other estimated annual costs include living expenses, $10,000 (single); books, $1000; fees, $420; computer and software (first year only), $4000; and health insurance, about $600. A limited number of scholarships (partial remission of tuition) are available; loan funds are available to those who demonstrate need. Only U.S. citizens are eligible for scholarships and loans. The deadline for loan applications is June 1.

Application Facts and Dates

The deadlines for completed applications are December 1, January 15, March 1, and April 15; prospective students are advised to submit their applications by March 1 at the latest, since most admissions decisions are made in the first three rounds. Admissions decisions are mailed within the six weeks following each deadline. For further information, students should contact:

Ms. Jill L. Deutser
Director of Admissions and Marketing
Jesse H. Jones Graduate School of
    Management - MS 531
Rice University
6100 Main Street
Houston, Texas 77005-1892
Telephone: 888-844-4773 (toll-free)
Fax: 713-737-6147
E-mail: enterjgs@rice.edu
World Wide Web: http://www.rice.edu/
    jgs

Richmond, The American International University in London

London, United Kingdom

THE RICHMOND M.B.A. PROGRAM EXPERIENCE

In the Richmond M.B.A. Program, you will exchange ideas and experience a lively community with colleagues from many countries. Discussions and case studies will build upon this natural laboratory of experience and ideas. You will also have the opportunity to use up-to-date information technology to analyze complex problems and communicate effectively. Students make use of the remarkable business and cultural resources of London, one of the most exciting cities in the world.

Completing the Richmond M.B.A. will make you a better manager. The most distinctive feature of our program that ensures this result is our faculty, representing academic excellence and business experience. Both faculty members and students are drawn from an international background, with our 100 students representing more than thirty-five countries in a balanced mix of cultures, creating a highly interactive environment.

Welcome to the most formative period in your business life.

—Clive Bateson, Dean

Programs and Curricular Focus

The Richmond M.B.A. program is an intensive eleven- to fifteen-month program designed to develop strong general management skills with an international focus. Richmond is the oldest and largest American university in Britain. The curricular system is based on the U.S. or modular approach of individual courses, and students are required to complete fifteen courses, taken over three semesters, to complete their degree. Each semester has an approximate duration of fifteen weeks. Students meeting the qualifications are eligible for a maximum of five course exemptions, bringing the completion of the course to two semesters. There are three admissions intakes per year: January, May, and September.

The Richmond M.B.A. has all the hallmarks of best practice in management education: experiential learning, modularity, credit for prior achievement, and the flexibility of full-time, part-time, and evening programs. Among the leaders in this endeavor, Richmond provides a broad American-style university education. The flexible program allows students to specialize in a particular field. Following two semesters of core courses, graduates may choose to specialize in general management, international marketing, international finance, or systems engineering.

Students and the M.B.A. Experience

Richmond strongly believes that each participant is a key source of learning for other participants in the program. The student body consists of approximately 100 students, with an average age of 26, who represent more than thirty-five countries. Each student brings a unique perspective and background to the program with their work experience in accounting, business, commerce, economics, engineering, humanities, law, mathematics, and science. Students have an average of more than four years of work experience.

Special Features

The Richmond International Internship is designed to provide participants with project-oriented management experience in a culture other than their own. Interns take this opportunity to apply their classroom learning to develop creative, results-oriented solutions to real management issues. Interns also develop projects within their workplace, addressing issues from strategy formulation to operational bottlenecks. Participants work under the guidance of the International Internship Office and a faculty adviser. Client companies are located all over the world and include a variety of industries and sectors.

The Richmond Alumni Association is also a valuable asset to present and future

members. Globally minded professionals are aware that their career advancement and success in project coordination depend heavily on the quality of their networks. Richmond maintains close ties with alumni across the globe. As students go out to compete in the international arena, these relationships are a key advantage.

Whether getting started right after graduation or making a midcareer transition, who graduates know may be as important as what they know. Through alumni connections, the University maintains a major networking facility into the latest practical developments in management.

The Faculty

M.B.A. participants receive a high degree of personal attention at Richmond, with an average class size of 20. To teach culturally diverse students with a new and ever-changing management perspective, Richmond has recruited an internationally oriented, multicultural, and highly qualified faculty. Students benefit from the involvement of senior practicing managers with full-time and visiting fellows from Africa, Asia, Europe, and North America. The faculty members encourage students through the application of extensive case study analysis, proactive discussions, and constant group and teamwork activities.

The Business School Network

Local and international business leaders also take part in this network as University guests to discuss current business trends and developments with students. In training new leaders for today's changing organizations, Richmond feels there is no better way for a school to impart the knowledge of leadership than by asking corporate customers what they look for in M.B.A. graduates that will make them effective leaders.

The College and Environs

One of the management, financial, and marketing centers of the world, London is clearly the right place to be. Richmond is a center of academic excellence that provides postgraduate and undergraduate studies in a broad range of disciplines to

more than 1,000 students. Richmond's two campuses are located in Richmond and the central London area of Kensington. The M.B.A. program, housed at the Kensington site, combines a metropolitan location with its library and computer laboratories, as well as student and faculty facilities, to provide an excellent base for M.B.A. studies.

Students' leisure time is enriched by activities of local theater, shared athletic facilities, and the entertainment opportunities provided by one of the world's leading cities. Kensington is within easy walking distance of the Royal Albert Hall, Hyde Park, the Royal Colleges of Music and Art, the Victoria and Albert Museum, Imperial College of Science and Technology, the Museum of Natural History, and many theaters, restaurants, and department stores.

Placement

The Internship Office provides assistance to students in clarifying their career goals for appropriate placement for the internship and seeks to match students' skills with company needs for the internship placement. Richmond M.B.A. graduates

are internationally recognized as a select group of professional managers, and they are recruited by leading companies to take on challenging roles on a global level.

Richmond has established relationships with a number of industry leaders, including British Airways, CitiBank, CNN International, Coca-Cola, International General Electric, Lehman Brothers, Merrill Lynch, Standard Chartered Bank, Texaco, Turner Broadcasting, Visa International, and many other smaller companies.

Admission

Admission requirements stress career progression, management potential, and intellectual ability. The Graduate Admissions Committee looks for a balance among the following criteria: career progression, management potential, employment, GMAT performance (540 or higher), and English language ability (TOEFL examinations, with a score of 600 or higher). Candidates should have previous work experience that displays a steady increase in responsibilities. Candidates are required to have the equivalent of a bachelor's degree from a university, polytechnic, or similar institute of higher learning. They must also demon-

strate strong verbal and quantitative reasoning abilities. English is the working language, and candidates must have a full command of spoken and written English.

Finances

The fees for a self-sponsored participant are set at £995 per course or £5050 per semester, including insurance and student activities fees, tuition, and use of library and computer facilities with personal Internet and online database access. Room and board is also provided at £2295 per semester. Accommodations include three meals per day, laundry facilities, room cleaning service, and library and computer lab access. In addition to single rooms, shared rooms are also available.

Application Facts and Dates

Application deadlines are December 15 for spring semester enrollment, May 5 for summer, and August 22 for the fall semester. Candidates receive notification of the Admissions Committee's decision approximately three weeks after the deadline date. For more information, applicants should contact:

Assistant Dean of Admissions for Graduate Programs
Richmond, The American International University in London
16 Young Street
London W8 5EH
England
Telephone: 44 171 368 8475
Fax: 44 171 376 0836
E-mail: grad@richmond.ac.uk
World Wide Web: http://www. richmond.ac.uk

Applicants in the United States or Canada may contact the Boston Admissions Office:

U.S.A. Office of Admissions
Richmond, The American International University in London
19 Bay State Road
Boston, Massachusetts 02215
Telephone: 617-954-9942
Fax: 617-236-4703
World Wide Web: http://www. richmond.ac.uk

Robert Morris College

Pittsburgh, Pennsylvania

PROFESSIONAL EDUCATION THAT LISTENS TO THE WORLD'S BUSINESSES

Robert Morris College's graduate programs are known for their focus on the mainstream business areas of accounting, finance, management, and marketing through the M.B.A. and M.S. in business degree programs. Niche businesses, such as health services management, sport management, communications and information systems, and computer and information systems, are taught through the M.B.A. Pluses and M.S. degree programs. Related to but outside the business areas are four other M.S. degrees in business education, communications and information systems, instructional leadership, and taxation (legally based, business oriented, and thoroughly integrated).

—Jo-Ann Sipple, Vice President for Academic and Student Affairs

Programs and Curricular Focus

Robert Morris College's graduate degree programs, built on the foundation of undergraduate professionally focused programs, distinguish the College by keeping close to employers' needs and high standards of business and professional education. Like the undergraduate programs at Robert Morris College, all M.B.A. and M.S. degree programs emphasize communications, the hallmark of a Robert Morris College education. Each of the College's three professional schools has built its graduate degree programs in keeping with the College's mission and vision statements of integrating liberal arts with professional and applied programs in the mainstream and niche businesses as well as in communications, education, government, informatics, mathematics, social sciences, and health-related fields.

All M.B.A. and M.S. degrees require 30–36 credits, depending on the field of interest. M.B.A. Pluses provide 30 credits of shared M.B.A. work and 12 more hours in a niche professional field. Traditionally, these degrees were developed for two different populations of graduate students: the M.B.A. for students who hold degrees in fields other than business and need a management degree at the graduate level and the M.S. in business concentrations for students who hold undergraduate business degrees and need a specialty in one of the business concentrations.

Specifically, the College offers an M.B.A. with a management emphasis; M.B.A. Pluses; M.S. degrees in account-ing, communications and information systems, computer information systems, finance, health services management, marketing, and sport management; and an M.S. degree in business education, communications and information systems, and instructional leadership and taxation. The College's programs are formatted for part-time study by working professionals and may be adapted for full-time students.

Students and the M.B.A. Experience

Of its student body of more than 5,000 people, 1,000 are enrolled in professional graduate degree programs. Five hundred of those are specifically enrolled in the M.B.A. or M.B.A. Plus programs. The average age of graduate students is 32, with an age range of 22 to 70. Most are full-time employees with at least three to five years of work experience. Women comprise almost half of the graduate student body. Students come from diverse professional backgrounds, such as accounting firms, banking firms, computer and information industries, communications industries, health industries, law firms, and marketing agencies as well as professional and recreational sports.

❖ Global Focus

In addition to integrating global issues into the regular M.B.A. and M.S. in business programs, Robert Morris will offer an International M.B.A. on a full-time basis for qualified students. They will study three months at a time at Universidad Interamericana, Costa Rica (January–March); Robert Morris College (May–July); and University of Southern Europe, Monaco (September–November) each year. For students from around the world who may not have appropriate undergraduate preparation, each institution will offer a year's M.B.A. preparation program, including proficiency in one other language besides English, the language of instruction.

Special Features

The College offers accelerated M.S. degrees in accounting, marketing, and instructional leadership at off-campus sites. The accounting, marketing, and instructional leadership degrees are offered at the College's Cranberry, Pennsylvania site, and the accounting degree is offered at the College's South Hills site. These degrees can be completed in two years.

The One-Day-A-Week M.B.A. allows students to attend classes on Saturday to earn their M.B.A. Students follow a class sequence that guarantees their graduation date in two years.

The Faculty

Robert Morris College's full-time and adjunct faculty members have strong academic and professional industry-based experience and training in the areas of business, education, communications and information systems, and taxation. Faculty members are committed to teaching and advising students individually and collectively by program goals, student interest, and student aptitude. The faculty encourages field projects and cooperative education (internships) based on student experience and aptitude.

The Business School Network

Close ties to the business and corporate communities have always been at the heart of the Robert Morris College enterprise. In the words of the College's President, Edward A. Nicholson, Ph.D., "Robert Morris is a strong institution because it has a concern for students and a concern for employers' needs. It is that connection, we think, that must be always

kept in the forefront of what we do. My vision is that we even strengthen that connection." Faculty members in the graduate programs help students realize that vision by relating the theoretical and practical aspects of their courses directly to business needs.

The College and Environs
Robert Morris College was founded in 1921 as the Pittsburgh School of Accountancy. It is a four-year, private, coeducational, independent institution. The College has two locations, the Moon Township Campus and the Downtown Pittsburgh Campus. The 230-acre main campus is located in suburban Moon Township, located 17 miles from downtown Pittsburgh. The Downtown Pittsburgh Campus is located in the heart of Pittsburgh's "Golden Triangle," the city's metropolitan area and site of the nation's eleventh-largest concentration of Fortune 500 company corporate head-quarters.

Facilities
The Learning Resource Center provides a variety of learning facilities, including a traditional library with 129,110 bound volumes, 327,670 items on microfilm, and 937 current periodical subscriptions.

The library houses an extensive tax library and specializes in business information and materials. The Academic Media Center, with full production facilities, provides students with opportunities to collaborate on projects in all areas of media, including television production, audio production, and photography.

Technology Environment
All students are encouraged to own personal computers with Internet access to perform academic tasks. However, computer clusters are located on both campus locations for students, providing access to appropriate software, electronic services, and printers.

Placement
The College's Office of Career Services offers career advising, a comprehensive on-campus recruiting program, resume referral service, and resources to support the job search.

Admission
Each graduate degree program typically requires the Graduate Management Admission Test (GMAT) for business degrees or the Graduate Record Examina-

tion (GRE) or Miller Analogies Test (MAT) for other degrees. International students are required to submit the results of the Test of English as a Foreign Language (TOEFL). Students should contact the Graduate Admissions Office for further information.

It is the policy of Robert Morris College to provide equal opportunity in all educational programs and activities, admission of students, and conditions of employment for all qualified individuals regardless of race, color, sex, religion, age, disability, and national origin.

Finances
Tuition ranges from $298 to $343 per credit, depending on the program of study chosen, in addition to the $15 College fee per credit. Resident facilities are available only at the Moon Township Campus.

Financial aid is available for graduate students in the form of student loans and graduate assistantships.

International Students
The College has a growing international student community. The International Student Organization and International Student Office is designed to integrate new students, assist in internship and employment placement, locate housing, advise in course selection, and assist in immigration and international student issues.

Application Facts and Dates
It is the belief of the faculty of the College that any individual who is highly motivated to learn should be given the opportunity to begin study.

A $25 application fee is required.
For additional information and requirements for application, students should contact:

Vincent Kane, Recruiting Coordinator
Enrollment Management
881 Narrows Run Road
Moon Township, Pennsylvania
   15108-1189
Telephone: 412-262-8535
            800-762-0097 (toll-free)
Fax: 412-299-2425
E-mail: kanev@robert-morris.edu

R·I·T Rochester Institute of Technology

College of Business

Rochester, New York

> ## SHARPENING OUR FOCUS
>
> *Information is the lifeblood of any organization, and technology pumps that information through the system. RIT's College of Business is committed to providing its M.B.A. students with a firm grounding in the technological tools and skills they will need to manage information in today's modern organization. Our graduates are valued by employers because they combine leadership skills with technological expertise.*
>
> *On behalf of the RIT College of Business, I am proud to offer you an opportunity to broaden your perspective and prepare for the larger responsibilities that lie ahead.*
>
> —Lyn D. Pankoff, Dean

Programs and Curricular Focus

The Master of Business Administration (M.B.A.) program provides students with a rigorous, interdisciplinary education preparing them for the challenges of the global environment. An emphasis on technology, a commitment to quality, and a global perspective are the foundations upon which the program is built.

Industry leaders look for employees with comprehensive backgrounds who can integrate an area of specialization with other functional areas of business. Rochester Institute of Technology (RIT) emphasizes that approach. The curriculum begins with a solid, mainstream grounding in all the functional areas of business and combines that foundation with the flexibility that allows students to specialize in one or two areas of expertise. In the classroom, students find a balanced approach between the theoretical and the applied, with an emphasis on concepts, skills, and techniques that are immediately applicable to the workplace.

The M.B.A. curriculum consists of eighteen courses, with eight devoted to core functional areas and ten available for concentration areas and electives. All courses carry 4 credit hours. The academic year is divided into four quarters of eleven weeks each. Students create a concentration field of study by selecting a four-course sequence in a particular area. Students have the option of a second field of concentration, leaving two open electives.

Traditional business concentrations include public and corporate accounting, finance, health systems administration, human resource management, interna-

tional business, management and leadership, marketing and sales management, marketing research, and quality and organizational improvement.

A major benefit of earning an M.B.A. at RIT is the number of resources and courses in highly specialized technologies. Technical concentrations include management information systems, manufacturing management, quality and applied statistics, technology management, computer-integrated technology, engineering management, quantitative decision making, software development, and telecommunications.

The College of Business also offers two other master's degree programs. The M.S. in finance degree program is designed to create financial professionals who can adapt to the dynamic changes and growth in financial industry. The M.S. in manufacturing management and leadership is a degree program offered jointly by the Colleges of Business and Engineering. The program is designed to educate graduates to lead manufacturing teams and organizations in a global economy.

Students and the M.B.A. Experience

Students in the College of Business come from diverse backgrounds and a variety of work experiences. The average student is 29 years old with four years of full-time professional work experience. Students without work experience are encouraged to participate in RIT's cooperative education program. International students comprise one quarter of the student population, and women make up 40 percent of the M.B.A population.

Approximately one third of RIT's M.B.A students have technical undergraduate degrees, 40 percent have degrees in business administration, and the remaining have degrees in social science, the arts, and humanities.

❖ Global Focus

The international business program addresses the growing demand for global managers who understand the international business environment. The program emphasizes the interrelationships among such business functions as marketing, management, and finance in a worldwide economic environment. The interdisciplinary curriculum combines international business theory and practice using academic courses and employer-focused research projects that address global corporate strategies.

In 1989, RIT established the U.S. Business School in Prague. Every year, RIT grants M.B.A degrees to approximately 40 students from the Czech Republic and other Eastern European countries.

The Faculty

The College of Business faculty members have integrated a high-quality approach to education, combining business theory with hands-on application in the classroom. The faculty members are totally committed to scholarship, teaching, and service to the community. They continually update their knowledge of the business environment by outside consulting for multinational corporations and government agencies, bringing a unique perspective into the classroom. More than 95 percent have doctoral degrees in their field of study.

The Business School Network

The College of Business maintains extensive relationships with industry. In additional to faculty business and government consulting, the College sponsors the Council on the College of Business, which is composed of prominent industry leaders from around the country who advise the College on strategic issues. The College of Business

Peterson's Guide to MBA Programs 1999

The Max Lowenthal Building houses the College of Business.

was among a few elite schools chosen to receive the Motorola University Challenge Award and the IBM Total Quality Management Competition, receiving a $1.28-million grant to integrate quality into the curriculum.

The College and Environs
Founded in 1829, RIT is a privately endowed university situated on 1,400 acres of beautiful rolling suburban land. RIT enrolls more than 13,000 students in its seven colleges. The College of Business has been serving the community for more than seventy years and currently has 14,500 alumni located in all fifty states and in thirty-eight countries throughout the world.

Rochester, New York, is a stimulating and inventive metropolitan community of over 1 million people. The community is known as "The World's Image Centre" ® due to its unique imaging history and the vast number of businesses engaged in some aspect of imaging technology, service, or products.

Located on Lake Ontario, Rochester offers numerous employment, cultural, and recreational resources for RIT graduate business students and their families. Home to professional hockey, soccer, and baseball teams, the city also has attractive parks, exciting museums, and an array of institutions for the performing arts.

Technology Environment
Rochester Institute of Technology is a national leader in incorporating computer

technology into the classroom. Students have access to extensive computer resources throughout the campus. The College of Business has recently updated its computer lab with forty new state-of-the-art stand-alone computers, giving students access to the latest business and productivity software used at leading international companies.

Wallace Memorial Library provides users with access to external databases from more than 100 terminals and workstations. These databases include CARL Uncover, Dow Jones News Retrieval Service, LEXIS-NEXIS, ABI/Inform, First Search, Internet Securities, and CCH Tax Researcher. Remote access from all College of Business classrooms and lounge areas is available.

Placement
The Office of Cooperative Education and Career Services offers an array of services for graduate business students, including resume preparation, interviewing techniques, job-search strategies, and individual counseling. They provide critical job leads in addition to coordinating the campus recruiting visits of hundreds of employers each year.

RIT's educational philosophy emphasizes not only theory but also the practical application of theories. This dual emphasis is prized by employers and offers graduates upward career mobility and the flexibility for changes in career direction.

Admission
Admission to the M.B.A. program is granted to promising graduates of accredited baccalaureate degree programs. Transcripts, a Graduate Management Admission Test (GMAT) score, relevant professional experience, a personal statement, and recommendations are evaluated by the Graduate Admissions Committee. International applicants must submit the results of the Test of English as a Foreign Language (TOEFL) as part of the application process. The TOEFL requirement is waived for native speakers of English and for those submitting transcripts and diplomas from American undergraduate schools.

Finances
Tuition and fees for the 1998–99 academic year are $18,765 plus $135 for the student activity fee. Books and supplies cost approximately $1500 per year.

Scholarships and assistantships are available. These awards are based on academic merit.

International Students
Twenty-four percent of the graduate students are international, coming from countries in Asia, the Pacific Rim, Eastern and Western Europe, Africa, and Central and South America. These students bring a unique perspective to the classroom, thereby enhancing the understanding of various worldwide cultures.

Application Facts and Dates
Operating on the quarter system, RIT utilizes a rolling admission process. Students are accepted for entry into the M.B.A. program in the fall, winter, spring, and summer. Application for admission should be on file at least five weeks prior to the start of the quarter. For more information, students should contact:

Graduate Business Programs Office
College of Business
Rochester Institute of Technology
105 Lomb Memorial Drive
Rochester, New York 14623-5608
Telephone: 716-475-6221
E-mail: gradbus@rit.edu
World Wide Web: http://www.cob.rit.edu

Rollins College

Crummer Graduate School of Business

Winter Park/Orlando, Florida

> ### TAKING THE LEAD
>
> *Students seek an M.B.A. not only to increase their base of knowledge but also to enhance their career opportunities. By pursuing an M.B.A. degree, they are taking the lead in managing their own futures. Similarly, the Crummer School has taken the lead in graduate management study by developing its curriculum into four M.B.A. programs that meet the needs of today's students. Depending on your academic and professional background, the Crummer School has an M.B.A. program that suits you, and I encourage you to learn more about these innovative opportunities.*
>
> —Edward A. Moses, Dean and Barnett Banks Professor of Finance

Programs and Curricular Focus

The Crummer School offers four M.B.A. programs. Each is designed to provide a general management education with the opportunity to earn a concentration in a chosen business discipline through selection of the elective courses.

The Accelerated M.B.A. (AMBA) Program is a full-time, one-year program for students with at least three years of significant work experience. It is an intensive 54-credit-hour curriculum.

The Early Advantage M.B.A. (EAMBA) Program is a traditional full-time, two-year program for recent college graduates. This 59.5-credit-hour program places special emphasis on career development and includes an international study trip.

The Professional M.B.A. (PMBA) Program is a thirty-two-month evening program designed for working professionals. The 50-credit-hour lock-step curriculum offers two classes each week.

The Executive M.B.A. (EMBA) Program is a twenty-month program for experienced managers. Classes meet on alternating Fridays and Saturdays, all day, and the 50-credit-hour curriculum includes an international study trip.

Students and the M.B.A. Experience

The Crummer School enrolls 50 AMBA students, 60 EAMBA students, 70 PMBA students, and 30 EMBA students each year. As a result of the lock-step format, more than 90 percent of the matriculated students graduate each year.

Crummer classes average 25 percent international students (full-time only) and 35 percent women. Approximately one third of Crummer students have business undergraduate degrees; other disciplines include engineering, humanities, computer science, and the social sciences.

❖ Global Focus

Each Crummer student completes a required international business course as part of the core curriculum. In addition, all EAMBA and EMBA students complete an international study trip as part of their core sequence.

The Crummer School offers all students the opportunity to choose a Global Business Practicum elective. Students work with an actual company with operations overseas to solve a business problem. After conducting research on campus, students travel overseas to meet with business executives and employees to study the problem in person. The students then present their analyses, recommendations, and suggestions for implementation to the company and the professor.

Special Features

The Crummer School provides each student with a notebook computer upon enrollment. The computer is used extensively both in and out of the classroom for spreadsheet and database development, presentation graphics, and online research. Students also use the Internet extensively for research and communication via e-mail.

In addition, the Crummer School is one of only twenty-one schools accredited by the AACSB—The International Association for Management Education at the graduate level only. This means that all of the School's facilities, career development series, and faculty members are devoted exclusively to M.B.A. students.

The Faculty

The Crummer School hires only experienced faculty members with proven track records and doctorate degrees. Because of the integrative nature of the Crummer curriculum, faculty members work closely together to ensure that each class builds upon the others, thereby avoiding a redundancy of material and creating an interdisciplinary approach to education.

Class sizes are kept intentionally small so that faculty-student interaction is high. Because all faculty members are housed in the Crummer building and are readily accessible by e-mail, communication with them is convenient and frequent.

In addition to their teaching experience, faculty members maintain close ties with the business community through consulting work and research. This brings the theoretical material to life in the classroom and encourages immediate application of the course material.

The Business School Network

Corporate Partnerships

Because of its location in one of the nation's fastest-growing business communities, the Crummer School has forged ties with business leaders from a variety of industries. These relationships result not only in financial support in the form of scholarships and resources but also provide Crummer students with role models in the Crummer Mentor Program and in the career development process. These relationships also provide members of the Crummer faculty and administration with crucial insight into the skills that companies seek from M.B.A. graduates.

Prominent Alumni

Crummer alumni have risen to the top in a variety of industries throughout the world. Companies such as Johnson & Johnson, Walt Disney World, and BellSouth have Crummer graduates at the helm.

The College and Environs

As the oldest university in the state of Florida, Rollins College carries a long history of providing excellent liberal arts education. Located in the charming city of Winter Park, the small, private college is just 5 miles from downtown Orlando, a booming business community. In addition to the well-known theme park attractions, the Orlando area is home to many international headquarters, including Harris Corporation, AAA, Tupperware, and Lockheed Martin.

Facilities

Crummer Hall houses all Crummer classrooms as well as all faculty and administrative offices. The executive-style classrooms feature state-of-the-art projection equipment and LAN access. The career development area is an elegant location for recruiters to interview Crummer students. The building also features a student lounge, study rooms, and two computer labs. Within the next year, a planned expansion of the Crummer building will offer students further resources.

Technology Environment

Each student receives a notebook computer that runs Windows and the Microsoft Office suite. Students have off-campus access to their e-mail accounts, enabling 24-hour communications among students and faculty and staff members.

Placement

The career development services at the Crummer School are devoted exclusively to graduate students. All full-time students complete a career development course as part of their curriculum. In addition, one-on-one counseling, business seminars, corporate information sessions, videotaped mock interviews, and extensive on- and off-campus interviewing schedules are available.

As a founding member of the M.B.A. Consortium of fifteen top business schools, the Crummer School offers students the opportunity to travel to New York and Atlanta each year to interview with numerous corporate recruiters.

Admission

The Crummer School evaluates each candidate on an individual basis, seeking a balance among the various application criteria. Each applicant to the Crummer School is required to submit a formal application, an application fee, a score on the Graduate Management Admission Test (GMAT), all undergraduate and graduate transcripts, and two to three letters of recommendation. Work experience is evaluated for all but the EAMBA Program.

The average full-time student enters the program with a 3.2 undergraduate GPA and a 590 on the GMAT. Average work experience for the AMBA Program is seven years.

The Crummer School invites international applicants with a completed bachelor's degree, a score on the TOEFL, and proof of financial support.

Finances

Total tuition is $32,000 ($10,660 a term) for the Accelerated M.B.A. Program; $40,800 ($10,200 a term) for the Early Advantage M.B.A. Program; $31,360 ($3920 a term) for the Professional M.B.A. Program; and $39,900 ($9975 a term) for the Executive M.B.A. Program. All tuition costs include the notebook computer, and tuition for the EAMBA and EMBA Programs includes an international study trip. Not included are living expenses or books (except for EMBA students).

There is no on-campus housing for M.B.A. students, but apartments near the school are abundant and reasonably priced. The estimated cost of living for one year is $13,500 for full-time students.

Merit-based scholarships and graduate assistantships are available to full-time students. Each application is automatically reviewed for these awards.

Application Facts and Dates

Admission is granted on a rolling basis for each program, and early application is encouraged. The AMBA Program starts each June, the EAMBA and EMBA Programs start each August, and the PMBA Program starts in both September and January. For additional information, please direct correspondence to the appropriate program director at the following address:

Director of Admission
Crummer Graduate School of Business
Rollins College
1000 Holt Avenue 2722
Winter Park, Florida 32789-4499
Telephone: 407-646-2405
        800-866-2405 (toll-free)
Fax: 407-646-2402
E-mail: jfinfrock@rollins.edu
World Wide Web: http://www.
  crummer.rollins.edu

Roosevelt University

> ### AN M.B.A. PROGRAM FOR BUSINESS PROFESSIONALS
>
> *Roosevelt University's M.B.A. has been designed for the working business professional—so you really learn from your classmates as much as your professors. We have a healthy respect for the experiences our students bring into the classroom, and we provide flexible options and a commitment to student service. In the fall of 1998, we began offering two new innovative programs: an M.B.A. in arts management at our downtown Chicago campus and an Executive Master of Business Administration (EMBA) in strategic management at our Schaumburg campus.*
>
> —James Cicarelli, Dean

Programs and Curricular Focus

The faculty members at Roosevelt University believe they are offering the most innovative M.B.A. in the Chicago area. Roosevelt's M.B.A. represents a complete rethinking of what is taught and how it is taught. The focus of the learning process is the shared responsibility of the student and the instructor. Classes are small, the contact personal. Teamwork and group projects are stressed, with many case analyses that include written and oral presentations. Above all, each student is expected to contribute to the education of his or her colleagues, because adult learners have considerable expertise to share with classmates.

The emphasis of the program is to integrate business core competencies with specialized education to create genuine expertise in one of the functional areas of business or in a concentration from other graduate programs within the University. Some of these areas include hospitality management, integrated marketing communication, and training and development.

Students entering the M.B.A. program with a liberal arts or other nonbusiness baccalaureate degree take all eight core courses. Each course is a self-contained analysis of the stated topic; no prior exposure to the topic is expected or required. Students whose academic preparation or work experience has given them a high degree of expertise in a specific subject may petition to take a more advanced course in lieu of the required course. In addition to the core classes, each M.B.A. student completes a concentration of three courses and one elective for a total of twelve courses (36 credits) to complete their degree.

Students and the M.B.A. Experience

Approximately 560 graduate business students attend classes at Roosevelt. Students of varied backgrounds and ages, from many states and more than fifty countries, pursue graduate studies at the University. Most work part- or full-time and find evening and weekend classes well suited to their schedules.

Special Features

Roosevelt University is among the few universities to offer an M.B.A. in arts management. With reduced government support and shifting corporate foundation priorities, the need is greater than ever for skilled business-trained professional and arts administrators. In addition to the core courses, students also take cultural, managerial, and economic environment of the arts; marketing and development of the arts; labor-management relations in the arts; and legal environment of the arts.

Another special feature of the Roosevelt University graduate business college is an Executive Master of Business Administration program. This highly advanced program features executive field experiences on local, national, and international levels as well as a variety of Strategic Leadership Seminars.

The Faculty

Roosevelt University has a diverse faculty representing the culture and the vibrancy of the city. The business faculty includes 25 full-time and more than 40 part-time members.

The Business School Network
Corporate Partnerships

Roosevelt University's corporate clients include an impressive roster of Chicago-area businesses and corporations. By inviting Roosevelt to bring its academic programs to their work sites, they have helped open new doors for their employees and made a strong investment in human potential. Through the Partners in Corporate Education (PCE) program, Roosevelt currently offers graduate classes and degree programs on-site at more than thirty companies and organizations, including AT&T, Kemper, Motorola, and Sears.

The College and Environs

From its founding as a private university in 1945, Roosevelt pioneered the education of adults and nontraditional students, creating a diverse learning environment for all students. Today, its

educational programs are recognized nationwide, and students throughout metropolitan Chicago and from around the world pursue degrees at its two campuses. Roosevelt's characteristics provide a number of graduate educational benefits: small classes that encourage an open exchange of ideas, an outstanding faculty, excellent academic programs, scheduling flexibility to accommodate working students, and counseling and career planning services.

Facilities

The University offers academic support services and academic computer facilities at both campuses. Student labs feature IBM-compatible PCs and Macintosh equipment, all with the latest software. Research materials are available from just about anywhere in the world, due to interlibrary loans, online computer networks, and electronic databases. Chicago's Murray-Green Library houses more than 300,000 volumes, a music collection with more than 40,000 books and scores, and more than 10,000 sound recordings. Featuring similar services, the Schaumburg Campus Library is also a link between students and the Murray-Green Library. Books and copies of articles are delivered daily from the Chicago campus to the Schaumburg campus.

Placement

Roosevelt University maintains an active placement service for graduates of all of its professional programs. In addition to the fact that business firms from all over the country recruit at Roosevelt, placement opportunities for graduates are enhanced by the University's location in Chicago, where employment opportunities are many and varied.

The Career Counseling and Placement Office assists students in finding part-time, full-time, and second-career positions. Its services remain available to Roosevelt graduates, who may take advantage of a full range of career counseling, planning, and placement opportunities.

Admission

Admission to the M.B.A. program depends on previous academic success and work experience. Domestic students have three options. If they have a bachelor's degree from a regionally accredited college or university and have a grade point average of 3.25 or higher (4.0 scale) or a graduate degree in any discipline, they are granted direct admission. Applicants whose grade point average is 2.8 to 3.24 must submit a detailed work history, a letter of career objectives and goals, or the results of the Graduate Management Admission Test (GMAT). Admission is determined after review of the submitted documents. The third option is for applicants whose grade point average is below 2.8. They must submit a work history, a letter of career objectives and goals, and a GMAT score. Admission is determined after review of these documents.

International students seeking admission to the M.B.A. program must submit a transcript of college-level work, a GMAT score, and results of both the Test of English as a Foreign Language

(TOEFL) and the Test of Written English (TWE). Visa services, TOEFL scores of at least 550, and a TWE of 3.5 or higher are required for application. Admission is based on a weighted combination of these measures of ability and aptitude.

The GMAT is not required for the EMBA program but, if results are submitted, is used for additional input.

Finances

Tuition for 1998–99 is $8010 per year for full-time students and $445 per credit for part-time students. There is a mandatory fee of $100 for all students. Scholarships are available that provide grants to cover a partial cost of tuition. Some graduate assistantships are offered by the University that cover tuition and provide a stipend in the range of $4500 for the academic year. Applications for scholarships and assistantships must be submitted by February 15. The University has limited loan funds. Federal Perkins Loans (formerly National Direct Student Loan Program) are also available. A number of business firms in the Chicago area have employee tuition-reimbursement programs, and many of Roosevelt University's students matriculate under these arrangements.

International Students

International students constitute 7 percent of the student body. Support services include an office/center that provides language tutoring in ESL courses.

Application Facts and Dates

Students should write to the Office of Admissions indicating their field of interest. The deadlines for admission are August 1 for the fall semester, December 1 for the spring semester, and April 15 for the summer terms. The application fee is $25. International students pay an application fee of $35. For more information, students should contact:

Chicago Campus
Roosevelt University
430 South Michigan Avenue
Chicago, Illinois 60605
Telephone: 312-341-3612
Fax: 312-341-3523
    Schaumburg Campus
    Albert A. Robin Campus
    Roosevelt University
    1651 McConnor Parkway
Schaumburg, Illinois 60173
Telephone: 847-619-8600
Fax: 847-619-8636
E-mail: mbadvise@acfsysv.roosevelt.edu
E-mail: admitcc@admrs6k.roosevelt.edu
World Wide Web: http://www.roosevelt.edu

Rutgers, The State University of New Jersey

School of Management and Labor Relations

New Brunswick, New Jersey

DEVELOPING LEADERS IN EMPLOYMENT RELATIONS AND MANAGEMENT

The way that work is performed, where it is performed, and how it is performed have changed substantially over the past decade. The master's programs offered by the School of Management and Labor Relations at Rutgers University prepare professionals to manage in this transformed work environment, to anticipate its continued changes, and to help their organizations to operate effectively in an increasingly competitive environment. The Master of Human Resource Management degree program prepares professionals to function either as generalists or specialists (and increasingly as line managers) in business and nonprofit organizations. The Master of Labor and Industrial Relations degree program prepares professionals to serve either as union leaders or as managers of industrial relations for organizations whose employees are unionized. Both programs are enhanced by an internationally respected faculty, whose members' research and professional activities bring to the curriculum a blend of theoretical and practical knowledge to prepare our students for careers in employment relations and management.

—John F. Burton Jr., Dean

Programs and Curricular Focus

The School of Management and Labor Relations (SMLR) offers a Master of Human Resource Management (M.H.R.M.) degree and a Master of Labor and Industrial Relations (M.L.I.R.) degree.

The M.H.R.M. degree program, which requires 48 credits of course work, concentrates on the social science theoretical foundations as well as the functional areas of HRM. It combines work design, measurement, staffing, development, rewards, and governance systems into an integrated HRM system strategically linked to an organization's business plan. Students are accepted into the program on a full-time or part-time basis, and courses are scheduled in the late afternoon and evening for the convenience of working adults.

The M.L.I.R. degree program, which requires 39 credits of course work, affords students the opportunity to explore the causes and consequences of changes in labor relations as well as to develop the professional skills necessary to function in their chosen fields. The program combines professional education in the discipline of labor relations with a broader approach to the study of work and work-related issues. Students prepare to pursue careers in the labor movement, in labor relations for private and public sector employers, or in government agencies that regulate employment.

Students and the Program Experience

Approximately 200 students are enrolled in the two SMLR master's degree programs, offered in New Brunswick, of which 50 are full-time. Two-thirds are women, 13 percent are international, and 14 percent are members of minority groups. The average age is 30. A majority have social science bachelor's degrees, particularly psychology, business, economics, and political science, but any major is considered. The large proportion of student work in human resources and labor relations enriches the classroom discussions and is a source of networking for all students. There are approximately 100 students taking M.H.R.M. courses off campus at corporate sites in New Jersey and in Asia. New Brunswick students are offered scholarships to attend courses in Singapore and Indonesia, and students in the Singapore and Indonesia programs may take courses in New Brunswick.

Special Features

The primary special feature is an emphasis on getting practical experience for students through internships. The proximity of a wide variety of the nation's leading businesses and unions provides excellent opportunities for internships, research, and eventual job placement.

The program is also offered in Singapore, Indonesia, and China and off-site in New Jersey at firms such as AT&T and Prudential.

A two-day orientation begins the M.H.R.M. program, when new students learn about current trends in the human resource profession and about the emerging field of international human resource management. They engage in a simulation that develops team-building skills, and they learn how to use the University library's electronic retrieval system.

The Faculty

SMLR has an outstanding, internationally known faculty, whose members are among the leaders of their respective fields. The 28 faculty members are drawn from several disciplines, including business, economics, history, industrial relations, law, psychology, and sociology. One third are women and 7 percent are members of minority groups.

The Business School Network

A State Advisory Council comprising labor, management, and public officials advises the School's Dean and staff on policy regarding the educational and research operations of SMLR. In addition, corporate and union leaders are called upon on numerous occasions to advise the faculty on curriculum needs. SMLR has a steady relationship with several business leaders in which there is an exchange of expertise, recruitment of students for jobs and internships, and financial support from the firms to SMLR.

The College and Environs

Chartered in 1766, Rutgers is now one of the nation's largest state university systems; enrollment at the New Brunswick, Newark, and Camden campuses is approximately 48,000 students. New Brunswick, with a population of about 42,000, is located in central New Jersey at Exit 9 of the New Jersey Turnpike and along the New York–Philadelphia railroad line. The many educational, cultural, and recreational resources of the New York–Philadelphia region are easily accessible to the interested student, and Rutgers attracts many distinguished visitors, lecturers, and performing artists not always available to less favorably situated institutions.

Technology Environment

Students have access to a thirty-five-station, state-of-the-art computer laboratory, with access to the Internet, and Rutgers' Center for Computer and Information Services, which contains some of the most powerful and innovative computer equipment in the country. Students are encouraged to develop computer skills through courses that rely heavily on the computer and its application to human resource issues. Computers are used for most course assignments.

Placement

Because the programs provide students with a broad theoretical foundation and an impressive array of professional skills, graduates have consistently obtained excellent positions in a variety of organizations. Recent placements of SMLR students include IBM, AT&T, Merck, Ingersoll Rand, GE, Merrill Lynch, Allied Signal, and FMC.

Admission

The Graduate Record Examinations General Test or the Graduate Management Admissions Test is required. Admission decisions are made by judgment, not formula, but successful applicants are expected to achieve competitive grades and scores and provide letters of recommendation that indicate potential for graduate study.

Finances

State residents pursuing full-time graduate study without financial assistance from the University paid tuition and student fees that totaled $6700 for the 1997–98 academic year. Nonresidents and international students paid $9528. Books and supplies cost another $800. Dormitory housing for the 1997–98 academic year was $4102 to $4682. A full meal plan for the academic year costs $2202. Additional living expenses were $3000. Off-campus housing is generally more costly.

Application Facts and Dates

The M.H.R.M. and M.L.I.R. program application deadlines are March 1 for the summer session, May 1 (M.H.R.M.) and July 1 (M.L.I.R.) for the fall semester, and November 1 (M.H.R.M.) and December 1 (M.L.I.R.) for the fall semester, and November 1 (M.H.R.M.) and December 1 (M.L.I.R.) for the spring semester. The programs have a rolling admissions policy.

Director
Graduate Program in Human Resource
    Management
Janice H. Levin Building
Rutgers, The State University of New
    Jersey
94 Rockafeller Road
Piscataway, New Jersey 08854-8054
Telephone: 732-445-5973
Fax: 732-445-2830
E-mail: mhrm@rci.rutgers.edu

Director
Graduate Program in Labor and
    Industrial Relations
Labor Education Center
Rutgers, The State University of New
    Jersey
Ryders Lane, P.O. Box 231
New Brunswick, New Jersey 08903
Telephone: 732-932-8559
Fax: 732-932-8677
E-mail: mlir@rci.rutgers.edu

Sacred Heart University

Fairfield, Connecticut

THE M.B.A. EXPERIENCE AT SACRED HEART UNIVERSITY

Our M.B.A. curriculum offers an excellent exposure to the practical applications of business theory. Interactive classroom sessions frequently incorporate team-based learning experiences that challenge each student's intellectual resource. Such exposures are facilitated by faculty members with a vast array of professional business accomplishments that complement their academic credentials. A Sacred Heart University M.B.A. graduate possesses a well-balanced portfolio of skills required for the challenging business environment of the next century.

—Scott R. Colvin, Program Director

Programs and Curricular Focus

Sacred Heart University's M.B.A. program places a strong emphasis on the application of business theory to the realities of the business world. The program offers eight areas of concentration: accounting, economics, finance, health care, human resources management, international business, marketing, and management information systems. Completion of the M.B.A. requires 33 credit hours of core requirements as well as 15 credit hours of electives. The University also offers a dual M.S.N./ M.B.A. degree for registered nurses who seek administrative positions in health-care facilities. Students are required to meet the criteria for admission in both programs in order to enroll in the M.S.N./M.B.A. program.

Throughout their program of study, students actively engage themselves in team projects, simulations, and case studies. Program faculty members take pride in their dedication to teaching, and they work closely with students to formulate creative solutions and new ideas. The program and its curriculum are designed to emphasize the development of management skills, ethical standards, problem-solving skills, computer skills, and an awareness of the global marketplace. Students will also find internship opportunities with corporations large and small. These internships provide an abundance of practical experience, and will enable students to bring these experiences back to the classroom.

The academic calendar for the M.B.A. program is divided into three 12-week modules as well as a six-week summer session. Courses are held during weekday evenings as well as on Saturday morn-

ings. A majority of the courses are offered on the main campus located in Fairfield. In addition, courses are offered in Danbury and Stamford, Connecticut. The M.B.A. program is also offered on a campus located in the Grand Duchy of Luxembourg.

Students and the M.B.A. Experience

Sacred Heart's M.B.A. program is the largest graduate degree program at the University, with more than 600 students. The program consists of graduate students from diverse backgrounds and other countries. Most are part-time students from Connecticut and New York. Students bring an average of five years of work experience in areas such as manufacturing, consumer products, and financial services.

Not only do students have the opportunity to learn through their course work and internships, they gain insights into the current trends in management through research and publication. Students are encouraged to write articles and serve on the Editorial Board of *Vanguard,* a business journal published by the Faculty of Management.

❖ Global Focus

Students have the unique opportunity to study at the Sacred Heart University campus located in the Grand Duchy of Luxembourg. It is the only academically accredited M.B.A. program in Luxembourg. Courses are taught in English in six-week modules each year. Luxembourg serves as an international finance center in Western Europe where more than 200 banks and 6,000 holding companies are

registered. Students from virtually every European country have participated in studies there. M.B.A. program participants from Connecticut may attend courses in Luxembourg, and gain from the cultural experience of taking classes with European business people.

The Faculty

Twenty-three full-time faculty members bring a wealth of academic training and business experience into the classroom. Their primary focus is teaching. In addition, they serve as consultants to major corporations and government agencies such as the International Monetary Fund, International Paper, and the U.S. Department of Commerce. Faculty members also serve on the boards of directors of a number of companies. The program is a candidate for accreditation by AACSB–The International Association for Management Education.

The Business School Network

An advisory committee composed of program alumni and corporate leaders assist the faculty in updating the curriculum offerings to meet today's business needs. In addition, executives often serve as guest lecturers and make presentations on developing trends to students in the program. The program has established partnerships with several companies like General Electric, American Skandia, and Uno Restaurant Corporation.

The College and Environs

Founded in 1963, Sacred Heart University is a coeducational, independent, comprehensive institution of higher learning in the Catholic intellectual tradition. The Fairfield campus is located on 56 acres adjacent to the Merritt Parkway. In recent years, the University has experienced phenomenal growth in enrollment, the faculty, and facilities. Current enrollment exceeds 5,500 students, of whom 1,500 are graduate students, which makes it the third largest Catholic university in New England.

Fairfield is an attractive suburban community located one hour north of New York City and two hours south of

Boston. Established in 1639, the community and the surrounding area have been considered one of the nation's more dynamic business and economic regions and is home to numerous Fortune 500 companies. The campus is located near regional attractions and recreational areas.

Placement

Personnel in the Career Development office are available to plan and organize extracurricular activities for students in the program. They also arrange for interviews with companies visiting the campus to recruit students. Employment opportunities and internships are publicized on the M.B.A. Career Services bulletin board.

Admission

A bachelor's degree is required, along with a minimum grade point average of 2.8 and a GMAT score of at least 450. International applicants must have TOEFL score of 550 or better. The most important factors regarding admission into the program are maturity, work experience, motivation, and quality of undergraduate work. An interview is not required, but it is recommended.

Finances

Tuition for M.B.A. students for the 1998–99 academic year is $395 per credit hour. A limited number of assistantships are available to graduate students on a competitive basis. GradEXCEL Loans, Federal Student Loan Programs, and deferred payment plans are available through the Office of Financial Assistance. Most graduate students commute to campus. Off-campus housing costs in neighboring communities range from $400 to $800 per month for rent. University housing is available to graduate students at an approximate cost of $3419 per semester.

International Students

Sacred Heart University has made a strong commitment to increasing the number of international graduate students who enter the University community. Currently, there are more than 120 undergraduate and graduate students representing sixty-six countries enrolled in full-time study.

Application Facts and Dates

Students must submit an application with a $40 nonrefundable fee ($100 for international applicants), GMAT test scores, two letters of recommendation, transcripts of all prior college course work, and a resume. International applications will need to demonstrate their ability to finance their education in order to be eligible for a F-1 Visa. Applications are considered on a rolling basis. Applicants will be notified as soon as possible any decision regarding applications.

Scott R. Colvin, Director
M.B.A. Program
Sacred Heart University
5151 Park Avenue
Fairfield, Connecticut 06432-1000
Telephone: 203-371-7850
Fax: 203-365-7538
E-mail: colvins@sacredheart.edu
World Wide Web: http://www.
sacredheart.edu/

Office of Graduate Admissions
Sacred Heart University
5151 Park Avenue
Fairfield, Connecticut 06432-1000
Telephone: 203-371-7880
Fax: 203-365-4732
E-mail: gradstudies@sacredheart.edu
World Wide Web: http://www.
sacredheart.edu/

Saginaw Valley State University

College of Business and Management

University Center, Michigan

DEVELOPING BUSINESS LEADERS FOR THE TWENTY-FIRST CENTURY

VALUE ADDED is the most important concept for evaluating how to use your time effectively. The faculty of Saginaw Valley State University's (SVSU) College of Business and Management provides a curriculum and environment that enables students to lead productive and rewarding lives as we enter the twenty-first century. The M.B.A. focuses on the development of critical-thinking skills that can be applied to our rapidly changing global economic environment. The M.B.A. moves beyond the traditional concept of disseminating knowledge and discussing theory by developing problem-solving skills, communication skills, and teamwork skills. M.B.A. graduates are able to work across the traditional functional areas of business and add real value to their organizations.

As you consider pursuing an M.B.A., remember that we stress "flexibility" in our program. While our more traditional student works full-time and attends SVSU as a part-time student, we have a growing number of full-time students in our program. While it is possible to earn a more general M.B.A., it also is possible to select a concentration in several functional areas, with management and finance currently the most popular. In addition, in conjunction with the M.B.A., we offer a Certificate of International Business.

In closing, it is important that you understand that providing an active learning environment requires a significant investment in human and physical capital. SVSU has invested in human capital by offering a quality M.B.A. curriculum emphasizing small classes and individualized attention from full-time faculty members. As for physical investment, the recent construction of Curtiss Hall provides a home for the M.B.A. program with state-of-the-art technology. It is considered by many to be the premier instructional resource in the region.

—Severin C. Carlson, Dean, College of Business and Management

Programs and Curricular Focus

The purpose of the M.B.A. program at SVSU is to create and disseminate knowledge necessary for the students to become leaders in profit and nonprofit organizations operating in a complex global economy. The objective of the program is to produce graduates who have a comprehensive view of the firm, are able to use complex methodologies and tools for analyzing data to support managerial decisions, have the creative and critical-thinking skills necessary for decision making and problem solving, have effective written and oral skills and the ability to work in a team, and understand the impact of demographic diversity and the influence of ethical, political, social, legal, environmental, and global issues on organizations.

The M.B.A. program is available to holders of a four-year bachelor's degree in any subject. The program consists of a core of nine courses plus three graduate-level business elective courses. The length of the program ranges from 31 to 47 credit hours, depending upon undergraduate preparation. Students may choose not to concentrate or may concentrate in a variety of areas, namely, accounting, finance, economics, management, marketing, and international business.

In conjunction with an SVSU M.B.A., a Certificate in International Business is awarded to students upon satisfactory completion of selected graduate electives in international business. These courses may be used simultaneously to satisfy the electives required for the M.B.A. Students who have already obtained an M.B.A. and who desire to obtain a Certificate in International Business may do so by completing additional required courses that are not part of their official transcripts.

Students and the M.B.A. Experience

Telephone and fax registration combined with convenient evening classes make the program attractive to employed students. Courses are offered during fall, winter, and spring/summer semesters. The program is designed for students who would like individual attention. Classes are small, usually less than 25 students.

A cross-functional and increased international emphasis has been incorporated into the recently revised M.B.A. curriculum. Students enrolled in SVSU's M.B.A. program receive a variety of educational experiences including, but not limited to, computer simulations, real-world projects, group projects, presentations, cases, lectures, and computer projects.

Approximately 120 students are enrolled in the M.B.A. program. The average age at matriculation is 29. Approximately 47 percent have undergraduate degrees in business, 31 percent are from the sciences and engineering, and the remaining students are from social sciences, humanities, and other areas. The students are generally employed full-time and have worked four to six years prior to entering the M.B.A. program. The student population is approximately 10 percent international, 10 percent members of minority groups, and 42 percent female.

The Faculty

The faculty consists of excellent scholars and teachers. More than 95 percent of the full-time faculty members are doctorally or terminally qualified, and many have international teaching experience. Due to the small size of the program, faculty members regularly meet with students outside of class to assist them with their learning.

The Business School Network

There are more than 500 M.B.A. alumni to be found worldwide in a variety of profit and nonprofit organizations. Alumni are invited to upgrade their skills in the M.B.A. Plus program. Alumni work with faculty members to discuss current business issues that are later incorporated into course work or research. The College of Business and Management maintains close ties with the regional business community and uses

M.B.A. classes generally meet in Curtiss Hall, part of a 224,137-square-foot complex containing classrooms, meeting and conference facilities, and a theater and recital hall. The building was opened in January 1997.

those ties to develop educational direction for the future. The College has a Dean's Advisory Board consisting of prominent regional business leaders who are instrumental in suggesting new directions for the College. A second partnership was created between the College of Business and Management and the Saginaw Valley Manufacturers Association for the purpose of developing programs involving international trade.

The College and Environs

SVSU is a state-supported university located just north of Saginaw, Michigan, within a triangle formed by Bay City, Saginaw, and Midland. It was chartered in 1963 and enrolls approximately 7,800 students. The University is located in a semirural environment just south of Lake Huron. Dow Chemical Company and General Motors Corporation are dominant firms in the area. SVSU's location within the tri-county area offers excellent cultural, medical, recreational, and professional facilities.

Facilities

M.B.A. classes generally meet in Curtiss Hall, part of a 224,137-square-foot complex containing classrooms, meeting and conference facilities, and a theater and recital hall. The building was opened in January 1997.

The University operates eleven computer labs for students. The computer labs have state-of-the-art IBM-compatible or Apple computers.

The library contains more than 200,000 bound volumes and is growing continually. The library also houses generous collections of periodicals, audiovisual materials, and government documents as well as the University archives and 250,000 microforms. CD-ROM workstations provide access to a number of databases. STAT-USA and Global Trade Information are international databases that are available.

For students choosing to live on campus, Pine Grove Apartments provide an attractive and convenient on-campus environment. All units are furnished and have their own kitchen, living room, and dining and porch/patio areas.

Placement

SVSU has a central placement office dedicated to working with students for the purpose of developing resumes, instruction on interviewing techniques, career advising, and referrals. Recruiters regularly visit the campus to interview students. Other services include, but are not limited to, campus job fairs, job search workshops, credential resume referral, job postings, alumni access to job listings, and a career resource library.

Admission

Applications for admission are reviewed on a rolling basis. Full or provisional admission is available. The required admission portfolio includes a completed application form, application fee, a written statement of purpose, a four-year

bachelor's degree from a regionally accredited educational institution, GMAT scores, TOEFL scores (from international students whose native language is not English), two letters of recommendation, and a statement of work experience and professional achievements (if any). Prospective students are encouraged to schedule an evaluative interview.

Finances

Tuition for 1998–99 is $158.50 (resident) and $311.30 (nonresident) per credit hour. An $8.70 general service fee is assessed per credit hour. Total additional costs for books, off-campus room and board, transportation, and other expenses are approximately $6280 per year.

Graduate assistantships and fellowships as well as subsidized and unsubsidized Federal Stafford Student Loans are available to qualified students. The Michigan Graduate Work-Study Program is available to students with established financial need and proven Michigan residency. The Gladys and Samuel Marble Graduate Business Scholarship is available to assist deserving M.B.A. students who previously attended Delta College.

International Students

The Office of International Programs provides a comprehensive orientation for international students. A 21-hour-per-week intensive English as a second language (ESL) program is available for students who need additional language study before beginning academic programs. The TOEFL exam is not required for admission to the ESL program.

Application Facts and Dates

Applicants for admission are reviewed on a rolling basis. Admission decisions are made and applicants notified as soon as the application portfolio is completed. Inquiries about degree or certificate programs should be directed to:

Office of Graduate Admissions
Saginaw Valley State University
7400 Bay Road
University Center, Michigan 48710-0001
Telephone: 517-249-1696
Fax: 517-790-0180
E-mail: gradadm@svsu.edu
World Wide Web: http://www.svsu.edu

St. Ambrose University

Davenport, Iowa

DEVELOPING VISIONARY LEADERS FOR A GLOBAL BUSINESS COMMUNITY

We invite you to join our dynamic students from around the world committed to achieving a Master of Business Administration (M.B.A.) degree in the St. Ambrose University H.L. McLaughlin One-Year M.B.A. Program. The program is dedicated to building well-rounded leaders for an increasingly competitive global economy by enhancing managerial skills and professional competency. Since 1977, our part-time M.B.A. program has prepared working individuals for advancement in private, public, and nonprofit sectors of the business world. Now our visionary, nationally accredited one-year program offers students a superior, accelerated opportunity to increase their earning potential and advance their careers. You'll receive a world-class education while experiencing the heartland of America, where people are friendly, down to earth, and have the finest work ethic in the country. We pride ourselves on educational excellence, family values, and safe living conditions in our beautiful community on the Mississippi River.

—Dr. John W. Collis, Dean

Programs and Curricular Focus

This twelve-month, full-time M.B.A. program is open to those holding a bachelor's degree in any major. Classes are taught during the day, or students may choose a combination of day, night, or Saturday course offerings.

The academic year is August 1–July 31. Degree requirements include fifteen 3-credit courses for a total of 45 semester hours of credit. Students are encouraged to keep outside employment to a minimum, given the rigorous schedule.

The program is nationally accredited by the Association of Collegiate Business Schools and Programs.

Courses include case studies, lectures, discussions, and projects, with emphasis on group work, team orientation, and practical application.

Two weeks of pre-semester courses focus on leadership building and labor/management skills.

Fall semester courses each meet once a week, 3 hours a day for twelve weeks. Fall courses focus on statistical methods for decision making, financial accounting, macroeconomics, and organizational theory, behavior, and communication.

During a two-week winter interim, students study business ethics for nine days, 6 hours each day.

Spring semester courses meet once a week, 3 hours a day for twelve weeks. Spring courses examine managerial accounting, managerial economics, the legal and social environment of business, and human resource management.

During the summer, two courses meet once a week, 3 hours a day for twelve weeks, and two courses are split into six-week sessions, each meeting twice a week for 3 hours a day.

Students scoring below the 35th percentile on the quantitative portion of the GMAT are required to take mathematics for management and economics during the third week of August.

A part-time M.B.A. program is also available. Course work and requirements are identical to the one-year program. Classes are offered evenings in seven locations and also on Saturdays on campus.

Students and the M.B.A. Experience

The St. Ambrose One-Year M.B.A. Program currently draws 85 percent of its students from the United States and 15 percent from other countries. Students range in age from 23 to 55; the median age is 32. Sixty percent hold bachelor's degrees in business or economics, 20 percent have degrees in science or technology, and 20 percent hold a variety of other bachelor's degrees. The ratio of men to women is 3:2. Forty-eight percent of students enter the program with more than five years of work experience, while eight percent have less than one year of experience.

Students gain a real-world learning experience that combines hands-on industry knowledge with academics. The diversity of the St. Ambrose One-Year M.B.A. student body enriches the learning experience.

Special Features

Small classes (30 maximum) allow excellent opportunities to share knowledge and ideas with classmates and faculty members. The university draws on rich community resources, and students participate in projects at area businesses focusing on local, national, and international issues. Opportunities for course work abroad are also available.

The Faculty

The University's faculty members bring extensive industrial and academic knowledge into the classroom. More than 80 percent of St. Ambrose M.B.A. professors hold doctorates and all have master's degrees. Students enjoy significant access and interaction with faculty members. The faculty places emphasis on case studies of real-world situations. This blend of academic credentials with practical experience enhances the application of an M.B.A. education in the workplace.

The Business School Network

Answering the needs of area companies who wanted stronger, more competent leaders, St. Ambrose University created a contemporary approach to its M.B.A. program. The University is located within a region of eastern Iowa/western Illinois that is home to many internationally known organizations such as Alcoa, Blue Cross/Blue Shield, Deere and Company, General Electric, Goodyear Tire and Rubber, Hon Industries, Motorola, and Rockwell International. Today, many of these corporations partner with the university in the professional development of employees. Company representatives serve as adjunct faculty members

In the heart of the Midwest, on the great Mississippi River, lies Davenport, Iowa, home of St. Ambrose University.

and guest speakers and provide tours, internships, and employment opportunities.

The College and Environs

Founded in 1882, St. Ambrose University is a progressive, private university campus. Studies provide world-class education through undergraduate and graduate studies. Nestled among beautiful oak trees in the center of the community, St. Ambrose provides convenient and modern campus resources close to restaurants, stores, and activities. More than 2,800 students, including undergraduates, M.B.A. students, and other graduate-program students, provide a diverse mix of culture, interests, and personalities. Davenport, Iowa, is the largest of fifteen Iowa and Illinois communities that make up the Quad Cities area. Together, the area's population exceeds 400,000. Flowing right through the middle of the communities is the mighty Mississippi River, one of this country's grandest landmarks.

Facilities

A new, state-of-the-art library offers the latest computer technology and serves as the campus hub for technological communication with the world. Other facilities offer a full range of academic and career counseling, health care, athletics, culture, and extracurricular opportunities. On- and off-campus living accommodations can be arranged by the Office of Student Services.

Technology Environment

Campus labs are equipped with personal computer and Macintosh formats. Students have access to the Internet and the most recent software on the market.

Placement

The University's Academic Support Center and Career Counseling Center offer educational and career assistance. Programs, job fairs, and campus recruiting help students identify career areas, develop job search strategies, hone interviewing skills, and find competitive employment opportunities.

Admission

Ideal candidates for the St. Ambrose University One-Year M.B.A. Program include recent college graduates electing to complete an M.B.A. before starting their careers, professionals granted a one-year sabbatical or leave of absence to seek an M.B.A., and professionals in career transition. Prerequisites for admission include submission of official undergraduate degree transcripts and GMAT scores, and completion of an application for admission. Applicants are evaluated based on their undergraduate GPA and GMAT score. A minimum TOEFL score of 550 (paper-based) or 213 (computer-based) is required for international students whose native language or

undergraduate experience is not in English. Through the Quad-Cities International Learning Project, students who score between 500 and 550 (paper-based) or 173 and 213 (computer-based) on the TOEFL can be admitted into the M.B.A. program after successfully completing one month to one year of ESL programming at a local community college. A comprehensive orientation program, academic advising, and numerous support services are available to international students.

Finances

The program costs $402 per credit hour. This rate is subject to change each spring semester. The total cost to complete 45 credit hours and receive an M.B.A. degree is approximately $18,500. Additional costs include a $25 application fee and $10 first registration fee. Typical off-campus housing costs between $4,800 and $7,200 per year. On-campus housing is $995 per semester. Meal plans are optional.

Low-interest government loans and some research assistantships are available for U.S. citizens. Many domestic students participate in tuition-reimbursement programs with their employers.

St. Ambrose does not provide financial aid to international students. A three-course tuition deposit of $3,465 is required of international students one month prior to the beginning of the first semester.

Application Facts and Dates

The application deadline is April 15 for students wishing to begin classes on August 1. However, applicants will be considered up to the start of M.B.A. Orientation. Students receive acceptance notices approximately two weeks after receipt of the completed application. For more information, students should contact:

John W. Collis, Ph.D.
Director, H.L. McLaughlin M.B.A. Program and Dean, College of Business
St. Ambrose University
518 W. Locust Street
Davenport, Iowa 52803
Telephone: 319-333-6270
          888-MBA-1-SAU (toll-free within the U.S.)
Fax: 319-333-6268
E-mail: mba@saunix.sau.edu
World Wide Web: http://www.sau.edu

St. John's University

Jamaica, New York

GLOBAL PERSPECTIVE TO BUSINESS: THE ST. JOHN'S M.B.A. ADVANTAGE

St. John's objective is to produce M.B.A. graduates who will be successful in business. We strive to give our students a long-term advantage by enabling them to acquire a broad base of skills in the major business disciplines to adapt to changing job requirements.

The program is fully accredited by AACSB–The International Association for Management Education and emphasizes critical thinking in analytical decision making. Students are prepared for an entrepreneurial future in a global economy, while receiving a strong indoctrination in ethical values. It is these elements of the M.B.A. program that enable our graduates to successfully exercise their leadership skills in business.

—Peter J. Tobin, Dean

Programs and Curricular Focus

The College of Business Administration offers programs of study leading to the M.B.A. degree, with concentrations in accounting and taxation, decision science, economics, finance, financial services, international finance, management, marketing, marketing management, and computer information systems for managers. The program requires the completion of a minimum of 39 credits taken on either a part-time or full-time basis. These credits are divided into three parts: the M.B.A. curriculum (seven courses), the field of specialization (four courses), and the electives (two courses). In addition, a student who has not taken undergraduate business and economics courses may be required to complete additional credits in the core area, which is determined on an individual basis. The master's thesis option provides the opportunity to plan and execute research study while responding creatively to an intellectual challenge determined by the student's own interests.

The College of Business Administration is accredited by AACSB–The International Association for Management Education, the sole accrediting agency for M.B.A. degree programs.

A joint M.B.A./J.D. degree program is offered. Completion requires three years of full-time study.

Students and the M.B.A. Experience

St. John's student population comprises a large number of individuals with diverse work experience. Most are employed full-time in career-track jobs while pursuing their M.B.A. All candidates are groomed to effectively communicate with executives in all fields.

Students are exposed to the dynamics of group interaction by simulated business situations. They learn negotiation and persuasion skills, how to motivate people, and how to excel in a team environment.

Classes focus on the application of business theory to real-world situations. Students learn to analyze information and make informed decisions in a variety of realistic business situations.

The M.B.A. program is international in scope to provide the student with knowledge of international operations and corporations. Two study-abroad courses are offered: the London Economics/Finance Seminar and the International Marketing Seminar.

The graduate center in Rome is St. John's University's first graduate program overseas. It is located at the Pontificio Oratorio San Pietro, Via Santa Maria Mediatrice, 24, Roma 00165, Italy. The areas of concentration for the M.B.A. degree program are international finance and marketing. This program is designed to enhance St. John's reputation as a leader in business education in the global marketplace. The M.B.A. program in Rome is the same as the existing Master of Business Administration program in New York City. Students registered at each campus may take courses at the other campuses of St. John's.

Special Features

The St. John's Executive-in-Residence Program provides a select group of students with a practical exposure to business as a preparation for entering the business world. Students meet with high-level business executives who candidly discuss the nature of their firms, corporate problems, and possible solutions. Sessions use a case study method, drawing examples from actual business situations, a format that helps students react responsibly to the complexities of upper-level decision making. Strategic plans are also developed by students and evaluated by upper management.

The Advanced Professional Certificate Program (APC) enables M.B.A. students to gain additional knowledge in a new field, providing the competitive edge necessary to move forward into the next millennium. The APC is earned by the satisfactory completion of at least 18 credits with an index of 3.0 in all courses.

The Faculty

St. John's faculty members possess strong academic credentials as well as professional business experience; more than 90 percent hold a doctorate. Professors are selected on the basis of their moral and ethical strengths, since they must serve as role models for the next generation of business leaders.

The overriding goal is to have St. John's graduates be considered complete professionals, promoted through the working partnership of a skilled and caring faculty that instills intellectual curiosity in students and helps them grow personally and academically.

The Business School Network

The College forges a strong partnership with corporations and focuses on the issues that are of concern in today's global economy. The annual Business Conference headlines distinguished guest speakers, including CEOs and other senior executives of major corporations. In addition, the Henry George Lecture Series is a semiannual event that features a prominent expert in the field of economics who speaks to the students on current topics.

The Business Research Institute promotes research in the field of business administration and publishes the *Review of Business,* a refereed publication with a national review board consisting of distinguished business leaders.

The College and Environs

The Queens and Staten Island campuses provide easy access to the vast resources of the world's foremost metropolis. The Queens campus has 100 rolling acres in residential Hillcrest, with broad lawns, modern buildings, and a spectacular view of the New York skyline. It is a mere 11 miles from midtown Manhattan, providing easy access to all boroughs of New York City and Long Island.

The Staten Island campus is on 16.5 acres on Grimes Hill, overlooking New York Harbor. It offers the full facilities, activities, and resources of the University in a "small college" setting, while being easily accessible from Brooklyn and New Jersey.

Facilities

University libraries consist of three facilities: the Main University Library and the Law School Library on the Queens campus and the Loretto Memorial Library on the Staten Island campus. In addition to more than 1.5 million volumes of books, bound periodicals, and microfilm/microfiche materials, extensive government research reference materials are housed in the main library, a significant repository for U.S. government documents. Specific support for the study of business is provided by a collection of more than 63,422 book titles and 648 business periodical subscriptions. There is also an extensive collection of abstracts and a comprehensive interloan program. The library houses specialized services from Commerce Clearing House, Research Institute of America, Standard and Poor's, Moody's, Dun & Bradstreet, and Value Line.

Technology Environment

Students and faculty members have access to microcomputer laboratories, which contain more than 200 Intel workstations and more than 30 high-end Macintosh computers. Two of these labs are located at the Queens campus, one in Staten Island, and the fourth in Rome, Italy. As a result of recently completed major hardware/software upgrades, St. John's has Pentium 166 platforms with 32 MB of RAM, matched by high-end SONY stereo-ready monitors; NT 4.0 operating system (OS), the most powerful MS Windows-based OS; the MS Office 97 Professional suite; and many other Windows 95/NT-based applications. All the computers are connected to the campus network, UNIX servers, and Windows NT file servers. Macintosh computing resources consist primarily of 85/8600 series Power PCs, with internal zip drives, 48 MB of RAM, and running MAC 8.x OS. Printing facilities consist of shared high-speed laser printers and color printers.

Of the ninety-four multimedia classrooms, seventy-six are located on the Queens campus, and eighteen are located on the Staten Island campus. There are twelve microcomputer classrooms on the Queens campus and four on the Staten Island campus, which house both Intel Pentium and Macintosh computers. The Rome campus has one combination computer classroom/lab with IBM-compatible equipment.

Placement

The Career Center's professional placement programs offer a wide variety of services designed to give each graduate student and alumnus the competitive edge. Services and resources include career advisement, on-campus interviews, full-time and part-time employment opportunities, a career resource library, resume preparation and interview techniques, a videotape library, and mock interview sessions.

Admission

All applicants must possess a baccalaureate degree from an accredited undergraduate institution. The candidate should submit, in addition to the $40 nonrefundable application fee, official transcripts from all undergraduate, graduate, and professional schools attended and the results of the GMAT. Applicants whose native language is not English must submit the results of the TOEFL. In addition, an English as a second language placement test is administered to all international students holding an F-1 or J-1 visa.

Finances

Tuition in 1998–99 is $600 per credit. An additional $75 general fee per term is due at the time of registration. A limited number of graduate assistantships are awarded, based on academic merit.

Living expenses in the New York metropolitan area vary widely, depending on housing and lifestyle. The University does not provide residences for students. Private rentals in Queens begin at approximately $800 per month.

Application Facts and Dates

Applications are accepted on a rolling basis. For more information, students should contact:

Mr. Gregory D. Pizzigno
Assistant Dean/Director of Graduate Programs
College of Business Administration
St. John's University
8000 Utopia Parkway
Jamaica, New York 11439
Telephone: 718-990-6417
Fax: 718-990-5727

Dr. Donna M. Narducci
Assistant Dean/Director of Business Programs, Staten Island
College of Business Administration
St. John's University
300 Howard Avenue
Staten Island, New York 10301
Telephone: 718-390-4509
Fax: 718-390-4291

Mr. Thomas McQuillan
Assistant Dean/Director of Rome Campus
St. John's University
Rome Campus
Via Santa Maria Mediatrice, 24
Rome 00165
Italy
Telephone: 011-396-636-937
Fax: 011-396-636-901
E-mail: mcquillt@stjohns.edu

Saint Joseph's University

Erivan K. Haub School of Business

Philadelphia, Pennsylvania

EXCELLENCE IN GRADUATE BUSINESS EDUCATION

The M.B.A. program at Saint Joseph's University has a rich history of providing excellent graduate business education. We continuously strive to offer a dynamic combination of cutting-edge theory and practice to those who will be the business leaders of the twenty-first century. Our experienced faculty members are active partners in the learning process. Through their ongoing involvement and research in their respective business disciplines, the faculty creates stimulating environments whereby students can develop the knowledge and skills needed to prosper in highly competitive global business environments.

—Gregory G. Dell'Omo, Dean

DEPARTMENT CHAIRS

Accounting: Joseph M. Ragan, Associate Professor; M.B.A.; CPA.
Finance: Harold F. Rahmlow, Assistant Professor; Ph.D.
Management & Information Systems: Elizabeth B. Davis, Associate Professor; Ph.D.
Marketing: John B. Lord, Professor; Ph.D.

Program and Curricular Focus

Saint Joseph's M.B.A., designed for working professionals, is a part-time evening and Saturday program that provides a practical, real-world-based curriculum. It has been developed to give every student the breadth of knowledge necessary in all areas of business as well as the depth of knowledge required to become a specialist in one particular area of study. This winning combination of course offerings provides Saint Joseph's M.B.A. students with the appropriate knowledge to succeed in their chosen fields. The M.B.A. curriculum consists of nineteen courses. The first eight foundation core courses introduce students to basic business theories and applications. These eight courses have been developed for students who do not have an undergraduate background in business. Students who have earned an undergraduate degree in business may receive waivers for the foundation core. Students who establish competency through work experience or in-house training may also receive a waiver of a foundation course by passing a challenge examination for the applicable course. The advanced core contains seven courses that provide additional breadth of coverage of the common body of knowledge. Additionally, students are also required to take three courses in an area of specialization. These three courses allow the development of expertise in a specific area of interest. The specialization areas offered at Saint Joseph's University include accounting, finance, health and medical services administration, information systems, international business, international marketing, management, marketing, and a general M.B.A. Saint Joseph's M.B.A. program culminates in the ultimate team project: the required integrative course, Business Policy, which utilizes all of the knowledge gained in the program to develop a business plan. Integral to success in this course are the skills to work in the "team" framework, developed throughout the program.

Students and the M.B.A. Experience

One of the measures of an effective M.B.A. program is the number of students who choose that particular program because it meets their needs and professional goals. Today, about 1,300 working professionals from 400 corporate and not-for-profit organizations pursue their M.B.A. at Saint Joseph's University. Students are employed as managers, bankers, engineers, programmers, accountants, lawyers, and other professionals who contribute to Saint Joseph's unique M.B.A. environment. The student mix provides a challenging forum where principles are discussed in light of practical applications and real contexts. This setting also furnishes an atmosphere where students can develop leadership qualities and learn dynamics for team presentations.

Students specializing in accounting, finance, international business, international marketing, marketing, or management may participate in the study tours. These study tours allow students to meet with top corporate executives while exploring another part of the world.

The Faculty

In Saint Joseph's M.B.A. program, students are taught by well-qualified full- and part-time professors whose combination of academic credentials and business experience provides for dynamic classroom interaction. Program professors hold doctoral degrees from well-known universities. Just as important, they possess hands-on business expertise coupled with a commitment to work with students on creative solutions to tough business problems.

The Business School Network
Corporate Partnerships

Saint Joseph's M.B.A. program strives to establish partnerships with area corporations by affording these corporations the opportunity to develop their employees professionally by supporting their bid for graduate studies in the evening. Working students contribute greatly to dynamic classroom interaction and in return can apply these new business principles to their current workplace.

The College and Environs

Founded in 1851, Saint Joseph's University is one of twenty-eight Jesuit colleges and universities in the United States. The total University enrollment is 7,100 students, about 1,300 of whom are M.B.A. students. The University is conveniently located on the western boundary of the city of Philadelphia on wooded and landscaped grounds and combines urban accessibility with the traditional charm of the city's well-known Main Line. The environment provides an aura of seclusion, yet the educational, cultural, and entertainment resources of metropolitan Philadelphia are easily accessible.

An off-campus site at Ursinus College in Collegeville, Pennsylvania, is available for Saint Joseph's M.B.A. students

Mandeville Hall.

residing or employed in the northern part of the Greater Delaware Valley.

Facilities
Saint Joseph's University opens its newest building, Mandeville Hall, in fall 1998. This technologically advanced $25-million building is a three-story, 89,000-square-foot facility that houses the Erivan K. Haub School of Business, the Center for Food Marketing Research, and the Academy of Food Marketing. Included in the building are new classrooms, a lecture hall, seminar rooms, research facilities, computer labs, a 180-seat teletorium equipped for teleconferencing and with a translation booth for international presentations, faculty and administrative offices, and informational gathering spaces. Many of the teaching areas are highly innovative in concept and are equipped with interactive communication multimedia technology, which greatly enhances pedagogical possibilities.

One of the most innovative concepts consists of a suite of classrooms that includes two moot board rooms, a preparation seminar room, a video room, and meeting break-out rooms. These rooms are modeled after the moot court concept in law schools. They accommodate the teachings of real-world situations through dramatizations and analysis of interactive business negotiations. They are equipped with stepped, semicircular seating that surrounds a board room table. Video cameras are available to record sessions for later replay or for simultaneous projection to the teletorium or off-site locations around the globe.

The Francis A. Drexel Library contains a business collection of approximately 335,000 bound volumes, 1,800 periodical subscriptions, 750,000 microforms, more than 2,750 videos, and Fortune 500 annual reports. The business print collection also contains a high percentage of the Harvard Core, a list of more than 3,500 books recommended by the Harvard Business School, and it serves as a selective depository for U.S. government documents. The library has an online public access catalog for searching its holdings and the holdings of other university libraries. The catalog is accessible from remote locations via the University's academic computer. There are 100 computer terminals available to Saint Joseph's students, and the following online services are available to M.B.A. students: Dialog, LEXIS-NEXIS, the Internet, the World Wide Web, FirstSearch, and Uncover. The Instructional Media Center (IMC) at Saint Joseph's University offers students assistance with presentation materials. The IMC has more than 900 videotapes, which can be viewed in the center or signed out if needed as part of a presentation.

Placement
Services at the Career Services Center include individual career counseling, job search advising, access to alumni contact lists, and the career resource library, which contains occupational information, employer literature/directories, and current employment listings. Workshops are offered on resume writing, interviewing, and job search techniques. Graduating students can also participate in on-campus recruiting. In addition, job search assistance is available in the form of a resume referral program.

Admission
Applicants for admission must possess a baccalaureate degree from an accredited college or university. The applicant must submit the following documentation: a completed application form accompanied by the application fee and an essay, official transcripts indicating receipt of a baccalaureate degree, official scores on the Graduate Management Admission Test (GMAT), two letters of recommendation, and an updated resume. International applicants whose native language is not English are required to take the Test of English as a Foreign Language (TOEFL) and submit proof of adequate financial resources. The decision for accepting applicants into the program is made by the admissions committee after it has reviewed the completed application package.

Finances
Tuition and fees for the 1998–99 academic year are $510 per credit hour or $1530 per course. On-campus housing for graduate students is available, subject to space limitations. Since the majority of the graduate students are fully employed, they live in the local geographic area. Living costs in the greater Delaware Valley area are reasonable when compared to costs in other large urban centers. Additionally, a limited number of graduate assistantships are available for full-time graduate students.

Application Facts and Dates
Students are admitted for enrollment in September, January, or May of each year. Application should be submitted as far in advance as possible for the following deadlines: July 15 for the fall semester; November 15 for the spring semester; and April 15 for the summer semester. For more information, applicants should contact:

Ms. Adele C. Foley
Associate Dean/Director, M.B.A.
  Programs
Saint Joseph's University
5600 City Avenue
Philadelphia, Pennsylvania 19131-1395
Telephone: 610-660-1690
Fax: 610-660-1599
E-mail: sjumba@sju.edu
World Wide Web: http://www.sju.edu

Saint Louis University

> ### THE PARTNERSHIP
>
> *Selecting an M.B.A. program binds both the student and the institution to an education partnership. While students devote great energy and time to academic studies, we dedicate ourselves to preparing them not only to meet, but to exceed the challenges of today's dynamic business world. This is accomplished by providing an M.B.A. program that responds to the demands of the marketplace.*
>
> *We look forward to the opportunity to welcome you into an education partnership and to work together toward your professional and personal success. I hope you will contact me or Dr. Steven W. Miller, Director of Graduate and Professional Programs, to learn more about the M.B.A. at Saint Louis University's School of Business and Administration.*
>
> —Neil E. Seitz, Dean

Programs and Curricular Focus

A revised M.B.A. program, developed after extensive research comparing current requirements with business realities and expectations, began in 1995. This revised program not only furnishes the basic business foundation but also advances subject matter into areas indicated as essential by top corporate professionals. The rigors of academic learning are blended with opportunities to increase proficiency in oral and written communications, in leadership and teamwork skills, and in understanding group dynamics and the importance of a global perspective.

The M.B.A. program is 57 credit hours in length. Competency in calculus is required. Students begin with 18 credit hours of core requirements that provide an overview of the key business disciplines. Nine 2-credit-hour courses are completed in accounting, economics, finance, management, business statistics, information technology, marketing, legal environment of business, and managerial communications. Some of these courses are waived for students who have demonstrated sufficient academic background.

The advanced requirements (27 credit hours) consist of seven 3-credit-hour courses that more deeply examine the business fields. Students must also complete a 2-credit-hour business ethics course and two integrated modules. The modules are each 2 credit hours and are team taught case and simulation courses that approach learning from an interdisci-

plinary focus, allowing students to employ problem-solving techniques.

Twelve hours of electives are then chosen by the student to build areas of emphasis or broaden overall business knowledge.

The M.B.A. can be completed alone or as part of a joint-degree program. The University offers the Juris Doctor/M.B.A., the Master of Science in Nursing/M.B.A., and the Master of Health Administration/M.B.A.

Students and the M.B.A. Experience

During 1997, nearly 600 students were completing graduate business degrees at the School. Approximately 60 percent of those students were men, and 35 percent of the students were studying on a full-time basis.

Students bring a variety of educational and professional backgrounds to the program. While the majority are from undergraduate business disciplines, students often combine an M.B.A. with engineering, nursing, social services, law, and medical careers, to name a few. Many of the students are returning to school—on either a part-time or full-time basis—after years of professional employment, while some enroll directly from an undergraduate program.

❖ Global Focus

To strengthen efforts toward globalizing the M.B.A. experience, the School actively recruits students from abroad. Domestic M.B.A. students are also

encouraged to study abroad by enrolling in courses offered by the School itself or other institutions. The School has sponsored intersession M.B.A. classes in Madrid, Spain, and at the City University of Hong Kong. Fifteen years ago, the School recognized the growing importance of the globalization of business and created a special Institute of International Business. The first of its kind a decade and a half ago, the institute continues to sponsor a number of conferences throughout the year and has created the executive master's degree in international business studies as well as a full-time Master of International Business degree.

The Faculty

Faculty members in the School of Business and Administration are key elements in the education partnership. Sixty full-time, tenure-track faculty members support the School's six business departments. Within these academic units, 98 percent of the faculty members are doctorally qualified.

As scholars in their fields, faculty members are invited to engage actively in research and professional activities. Nearly 96 percent have published or presented their research in the past five years. Their accomplishments include regional, national, and international efforts with books, journal articles, proceedings, and professional presentations.

In furthering efforts to blend a global focus into all aspects of the M.B.A. program, business faculty members have embraced the challenge to participate in programs abroad, traveling to a number of countries in roles such as visiting scholars, guest lecturers, and conference attendees.

The Business School Network

Corporate Partnerships

St. Louis ranks fifth nationwide as headquarters for Fortune 100 companies, providing a wealth of business opportunities. Strong bonds have already been forged with many companies. For example, the Mercantile Foundation recently funded Business Leadership: The

The School of Business and Administration is housed in Davis-Shaughnessy Hall, which has been renovated to provide modern facilities, including two fully equipped computer labs and a student lounge for relaxing.

Mercantile Program for Women. This innovative program, the first of its kind nationwide, will provide female M.B.A. students with special opportunities and programs. Emerson Electric supports a Center for Business Ethics, and the Jefferson Smurfit Corporation funded a Center for Entrepreneurial Studies.

Prominent Alumni

Many alumni remain in St. Louis, while others return to their homes in the United States and in countries abroad, extending the School's ties throughout the world. Part of the success of the corporate partnerships is the strong contingent of loyal and committed local alumni who hold titles such as president, CEO, chairman of the board, and partner for large local, national, and international firms.

The College and Environs

Saint Louis University, a private, Jesuit institution offering undergraduate, graduate, and professional degrees in more than eighty programs of study, has grown into an academic institution with a reputation for excellence in education and attentiveness to the individual student. Last year enrollment neared 11,500 students from all over the United States and seventy-seven other countries. Located in an urban area, the campus provides a parklike setting with attractive surroundings, including fountains, grassy quads, and a clock-tower. Student housing options include on-campus dormitories or off-campus apartments within walking distance of the School.

As for recreation, the city of St. Louis offers many cultural and recreational activities, while Saint Louis University's nationally ranked Billiken basketball and soccer teams provide sports entertainment. Students can also use the University's recreation center, gym, and sport field.

Technology Environment

The extensive University facilities include a library network equipped with CD-ROM catalog service and electronic databases (ABI/INFORM, LEXIS/NEXIS, and Business Periodicals ONDISC). Technology is ever expanding, with two fully equipped computer labs in the School of Business and Administration.

Placement

The University's Career Center and the School of Business and Administration collaborate to provide a convenient satellite Career Center office in the business school. The site also houses the staff of the School's internship program, who are building a network of opportunities for M.B.A. students.

Admission

Each candidate for admission to the M.B.A. program in the School of Business and Administration is evaluated based on the information submitted during the application process: an application with a nonrefundable $40 fee, two letters of recommendation, transcripts from prior institutions, and the GMAT score report.

International students are asked to apply at least six months in advance of desired entry. International applicants are also required to take the TOEFL and, if a student visa is desired, to submit certification of financial support for the full period of study.

Finances

In 1998–99, tuition is $602 per credit hour. Housing rates for facilities on campus average $2600 per year, depending on the dorm selected and the number of occupants per room. A full meal plan costs approximately $2700 per year.

Off-campus housing close to the campus averages $500 per month (including utilities), with food expenses approximating $75 per week.

Textbooks cost approximately $50 to $100 per class, and, for those students who prefer to park in campus lots, parking permits range from $60 to $100 per semester.

Full-time M.B.A. students beginning in a fall semester who wish to be considered for scholarships and research assistantships must apply by April 1. Federal aid and a special budget plan are also available through the University's Office of Financial Aid.

International Students

Thirty percent of current M.B.A. students come from outside the United States. Special programs for international students include English courses upon arrival and a progressive orientation throughout the first several weeks of school. International student organizations are also available for socializing and as an added support network.

Application Facts and Dates

Application deadlines are July 15 for fall entry, December 1 for spring entry, and April 15 for summer entry. International students are asked to apply six months in advance. For more information, students should contact:

M.B.A. Admissions
The School of Business and
    Administration
Saint Louis University
3674 Lindell Boulevard
St. Louis, Missouri 63108
Telephone: 314-977-3800
Fax: 314-977-3897
E-mail: busadmin@slu.edu
World Wide Web: http://www.slu.edu

Saint Mary's College of California

INTEGRITY—A NECESSITY FOR SUCCESS

We seek to educate mature adults for challenging and productive management careers in the dynamic global marketplace of the 1990s and into the twenty-first century. The programs are designed to prepare students who have a strong knowledge base, analytical skills, intellectual openness and flexibility, a capacity for life-long learning, and an instinct for inquiry; will operate creatively, with vision and imagination, in a complex domestic and international business environment; can apply theory-based knowledge and analytical approaches to diverse, "real-life" management problems; and understand that business management is a profession and not simply a vocation. The School's highly regarded faculty includes teacher/scholars with earned doctorates from leading universities and substantial professional experience, as well as senior-level business practitioners. An underlying premise of education at Saint Mary's is that integrity is not a nicety but a necessity for a successful and satisfying life. Accordingly, a consideration of the ethical implications of business policies and operations is an integral aspect of our curricula.

—Edwin M. Epstein, Dean

Programs and Curricular Focus

Graduate study in business administration began at Saint Mary's in 1975 with the establishment of the well-respected executive M.B.A. program. It was followed by the evening M.B.A. program in 1984 and the M.B.A. in international business program in 1990. Most graduate business students at Saint Mary's College are working business professionals who have chosen to earn their M.B.A. degrees on a part-time basis. Students of the M.B.A. in international business program have left the workplace for one year to complete their degrees on a full-time basis.

The executive M.B.A. program is offered in three formats, weeknight, alternate weekends, or Saturday, for twenty-one months. The flexibility of the evening M.B.A. program allows students to enroll in one, two, or three courses per quarter. Most students complete this program in 2½ years. The M.B.A. in international business program is taught in an intensive 13½-month schedule, with four courses per quarter. Courses are held in the afternoons and evenings.

The executive M.B.A. program offers a general management perspective. Classes are scheduled in a lock-step pattern, with two classes per quarter, including three electives. The evening M.B.A. program comprises foundation courses, core courses, and electives in

finance, marketing, and international business. Class times are determined two years in advance, so students may plan their own schedules when they begin the program. The M.B.A. in international business program provides students with core M.B.A. skills while immersing them in the international environment of business. Courses cover business competition in the regional markets, international economics, and political and social differences that affect transnational and multinational businesses.

Students and the M.B.A. Experience

Students in the graduate business programs have earned undergraduate degrees in engineering, science, and the liberal arts, as well as in business and economics. This diversity of backgrounds contributes to the learning that takes place in study groups, an integral part of the curriculum. Students represent virtually all industries, including telecommunications, financial services, engineering, health care, scientific research, consumer product sales, and nonprofit organizations. A strength of the graduate business programs most often cited by students is the professors' emphasis on practical, everyday application of the theory taught in the classroom. Students in the executive M.B.A. program have

worked an average of fifteen years before beginning their studies, while students in the evening M.B.A. and international business programs have worked approximately five years. The average age of students in the executive M.B.A. program is 38, while in the evening M.B.A. and international business programs, the average age is 28. Students in the evening M.B.A. and the executive M.B.A. programs live and work in counties surrounding San Francisco and Oakland. Students in the M.B.A. in international business program come from a variety of other countries as well as the United States.

Special Features

Short-term study-abroad opportunities are available to M.B.A. students. Saint Mary's offers a two-week international study tour in conjunction with Sheffield University in the United Kingdom for students of the evening M.B.A. and M.B.A. in international business programs. Students in the evening M.B.A. program may also spend a semester as an exchange student at the University of Rennes, France. Students from the University of Rennes may study at Saint Mary's.

Management development seminars are offered on a quarterly basis to students in the evening M.B.A. program. These seminars cover practical aspects of business, such as negotiation, time management, and career development. Evening M.B.A. students must participate in four seminars to complete graduation requirements.

The Faculty

The graduate business faculty includes both Ph.D.-trained scholars and experienced business professionals, a combination that reinforces the balance between theory and practice and is a distinguishing characteristic of M.B.A. education at Saint Mary's. Both groups of teachers share a deep commitment to provide academically sound training for professional managers. Because the College places emphasis on teaching rather than research, the primary measure of faculty success is teaching effectiveness, with student evaluation of professors' performance taken very seriously. Professor accessibility is a key element of student satisfaction with the graduate business programs.

The Business School Network

The ties between the San Francisco Bay corporate community and the graduate business programs are varied. Professors invite local business leaders to be guest lecturers. Students interact with local firms, developing strategic business plans that serve as final class projects for the students and as future direction for the companies. Local employers, who believe that a Saint Mary's M.B.A. education adds value to their organizations, sponsor students in the graduate business programs. Alumni association members serve as resources for graduate business students seeking new professional opportunities.

The College and Environs

Saint Mary's College, established in 1863, is one of the oldest institutions of higher learning in California. It is owned and directed by the Christian Brothers, a Catholic teaching congregation. The student population totals about 4,000. The 420-acre campus in Moraga, 20 miles east of San Francisco, lies in a valley surrounded by the hills of a former ranch, which is now parkland open to recreation. It is considered one of the most beautiful and safest colleges in California. The College possesses a rural serenity yet is located in Contra Costa County, a rapidly developing commercial center specializing in financial services, telecommunications, manufacturing, and retail operations.

Placement

The Career Development Center at Saint Mary's College offers self-assessment and career counseling services to graduate students and alumni. A career newsletter with job postings is circulated to all M.B.A. students. The Graduate Business Program facilitates student and graduate networking with the alumni association.

Admission

Applicants with an undergraduate degree in any area are welcome. For students applying to the evening M.B.A. and the M.B.A. in international business programs, the undergraduate GPA, score on the required Graduate Management Admission Test (GMAT), and two letters of recommendation are considered. Applicants to the executive M.B.A. program must currently be employed and have a minimum of five years of business experience, as well as a baccalaureate degree and two recommendations. These candidates are interviewed once their applications are complete; the extent of management experience is given special consideration. The GMAT is not required of executive M.B.A. applicants. A TOEFL score of 550 is required of all candidates whose undergraduate study was not in English.

Students are admitted to the executive M.B.A. program in October, January, and April; to the evening M.B.A. program in October, January, April, and July; and to the M.B.A. in international business program in October.

International applicants must show proof of sufficient funds to cover tuition, fees, and living expenses for the duration of the entire program to which they are applying.

Finances

Tuition for the evening M.B.A. and M.B.A. in international business programs is calculated per course, estimated at $1425 for the 1998–99 academic year. Each M.B.A. course is worth 4 quarter units. In the evening M.B.A. and the M.B.A. in international business programs there are eighteen courses each. Executive M.B.A. students are guaranteed a fixed quarterly fee for the duration of the program. In 1998–99, this is approximately $3339–$3996. Living and personal expenses vary according to where students live in the community; on-campus housing is not available for graduate students. Books and supplies average $200 per quarter. Financial aid for graduate study at Saint Mary's is limited to student loans. No teaching fellowships are available.

International Students

Conditional admission is possible for graduates of Saint Mary's Intensive English Program. These applicants must meet the minimum admission requirements for either the evening M.B.A. or the M.B.A. in international business programs. Students from Asia comprise 70 percent of the international student population; European students make up 13 percent.

Application Facts and Dates

There are no application deadlines; it is recommended that applicants send admission materials eight weeks prior to the quarter in which they wish to begin M.B.A. studies. Admission is made on a rolling basis, and decision letters are mailed within two weeks of the date applicants' files are complete. For more information, applicants should contact:

Director of Admissions
Graduate Business Programs
Saint Mary's College
P.O. Box 4240
Moraga, California 94575-4240
Telephone: 925-631-4500
Fax: 925-376-6521
E-mail: smcmba@stmarys-ca.edu

Saint Peter's College

M.B.A. Programs

Jersey City, New Jersey

THIS WORLD IS GOING DIGITAL. BUSINESS IS GOING GLOBAL. WHERE ARE YOU GOING?

With an M.B.A. from Saint Peter's College, you can go anywhere you choose. A recent Standard & Poor's survey of 56,000 business leaders ranked Saint Peter's College in the top twenty liberal arts colleges graduating America's leading corporate officers.

Our 48-credit M.B.A. is taught on a flexible trimester schedule, which means you can complete the program faster than students on a traditional semester calendar. By taking summer session courses, you can earn your degree in two years.

—Director of M.B.A. Programs

Program and Curricular Focus

The M.B.A. program at Saint Peter's College offers three concentrations: management, management information systems, and international business. The M.B.A. is a 48-credit program, including a common core of 24 credits. The concentration in management focuses on teaching students organizational structures and management control to create flexible, adaptive, and effective organizations. The management information systems concentration teaches students to understand how to use information technologies to build information-age organizations. The international business concentration teaches students the strategies needed for taking a worldwide perspective of a firm's business.

Saint Peter's College utilizes the trimester calendar so students can earn their degrees quickly. This unique scheduling pattern offers students three 10-week sessions in one academic year—fall, winter, and spring. The M.B.A. program can be completed strictly in the evenings or on the weekends. Students can also mix and match their class schedule by taking evening and weekend courses. By choosing the weekend schedule, students benefit by having three weekends off in each ten-week trimester. Evening classes meet one night per week.

Students and the M.B.A. Experience

Total enrollment at Saint Peter's is 3,515. Of this number, 215 are graduate business students. Eighty percent of the students enrolled in graduate business programs attend part-time; 35 percent are women; 13 percent are international students; and 19 percent are members of minority groups. The average age of students in the business program is 28.

The Faculty

In addition to being dedicated teachers, the faculty members at Saint Peter's College hold Ph.D.'s from leading universities and are scholars and researchers in their fields. The faculty utilizes a variety of teaching approaches, including lectures, classroom discussions, case studies, team projects, simulation exercises, and independent study.

The College and Environs

Saint Peter's College, founded in 1872, is a Jesuit, Catholic, coeducational, liberal arts college in an urban setting that seeks to develop the whole person in preparation for a lifetime of learning, leadership, and service in a diverse and global society. Committed to academic excellence and individual attention, Saint Peter's College provides education informed by values.

Saint Peter's College offers two campuses with convenient locations. The main campus has long been a landmark on Kennedy Boulevard in Jersey City, New Jersey. The College's atmosphere, architecture, and activity reflect a dynamic, vital, urban institution that offers important intellectual resources to the community. The New York City skyline, visible from Jersey City, is a constant reminder of the College's proximity to a major cultural and financial center. The branch campus at Englewood Cliffs in Bergen County, New Jersey, was established as a college for adults. The campus is perched on a bluff overlooking northern Manhattan and the Hudson River, located on the Palisades, one mile north of the George Washington Bridge.

Facilities

The libraries of Saint Peter's College provide extensive services and research facilities to the College community at both campuses. The Theresa and Edward O'Toole Library in Jersey City is fully automated, and the catalog is accessible via the campus network. The Jersey City and Englewood Cliffs libraries hold more than 300,000 volumes. Both libraries provide access to databases in business, nursing, and the humanities. The O'Toole Library also provides a computer lab for word processing and Internet access. The College's computer facilities offer a unique opportunity for students to have hands-on access to several state-of-the-art computer systems as well as a variety of microcomputers. The center has an open-door policy, which means that all

students are granted access to the computer facilities. The College's computers are linked to worldwide computer networks such as the Internet and Usenet. The networks provide a method for students to communicate with other students and researchers. All students, upon registration, have free access to these networks.

Placement

Saint Peter's College guides students toward a successful career, a career change, or advancement in their current professions. Services range from career counseling and resume review to current job listings.

A Standard & Poor's survey of 56,000 business leaders ranked Saint Peter's College in the top twenty liberal arts colleges that have graduated America's leading corporate officers. Saint Peter's College has an alumni network of 20,000 active members across the country and abroad.

Admission

A complete graduate admission application to the M.B.A. program includes the $20 application fee, official undergraduate transcripts, official graduate transcripts, official GMAT score report, and three completed recommendation forms from professional or academic references.

International applicants need to submit all of the above plus an official international credential evaluation of undergraduate and graduate degrees and official TOEFL scores. An initial review of the complete application for admission is conducted by the Office of Graduate Admission. The file is then forwarded to the M.B.A. Program Director for an admission decision. All correspondence should be conducted with the Office of Graduate Admission.

Finances

To make financing an education possible, Saint Peter's financial aid advisers help students explore the best means of affording their degree. Options include tuition deferment and installment plans, employer-sponsored tuition reimbursement plans, and student loans. Interested students should call a financial aid adviser at 201-915-9308.

The cost of tuition for graduate study in 1998–99 is $516 per credit.

Application Facts and Dates

For more information, students should contact:

Barbara A. Bertsch
Graduate Admissions Coordinator
Saint Peter's College
2641 Kennedy Boulevard
Jersey City, New Jersey 07306
Telephone: 201-915-9216
Fax: 201-432-5860
E-mail: admissions@spcvxa.spc.edu
World Wide Web: http://www.spc.edu

St. Thomas University

Department of Business Administration

Miami, Florida

FOSTERING MORAL AND ETHICAL VALUES

A small university with a personal interest in every student, St. Thomas University has evolved from its humble beginnings as Biscayne College, enrolling some 35 students, to our present enrollment of 2,270 students, representing twenty-five states and forty-seven different countries. While our growth has been dramatic, we have not lost sight of our focal point—the individual student. As a Catholic university welcoming students from all faiths, we remain dedicated to fostering moral and ethical values in the Judeo-Christian tradition. Our students graduate with a sound base from which to build successful careers and productive lives. Our undergraduate programs, graduate programs, and school of law combine to create an educational environment providing students with sound academic preparation for the twenty-first century. The multicultural makeup of our student body offers students a community rich in diversity, preparing them well for their part in the ever changing global community in which we live. The catalogue will provide you with information you will need to shape an academic program for your years ahead. However, there is another aspect of St. Thomas the catalogue cannot express—the personal side of the education experience. Quite simply, we are a small university with a personal interest in every student.

—Rev. Monsignor Franklyn M. Casale, President

Programs and Curricular Focus

The St. Thomas University Master of Business Administration degree is designed for students who are currently in, or plan to enter, responsible positions in management, health management, international business, or sports management as well as professional positions in accounting. The M.B.A. program provides a balance between the quantitative and qualitative aspects of management and focuses on the needs of part time students who may have special concerns because of their employment responsibilities. The M.B.A. also provides an opportunity for full-time students to complete the degree program in four semesters.

The M.B.A. curriculum provides a basic knowledge in the primary core areas of business (24 semester hours) and intensive preparation in one of the five specializations (18 semester hours), except for the accounting specialization, which requires 21 hours of business core and 21 hours of accounting, and is only available to students with an undergraduate degree in accounting or its equivalent. A series of three preparatory courses (9 credits total) provide the needed base skills for those students who have not majored in business or related areas in their undergraduate degree. Concepts and

theory are combined with application. The program's objective is to develop potential managers who not only have the knowledge necessary for today's rapidly changing business environment, but have the skills to apply and utilize this knowledge on an appropriate basis.

St. Thomas University is accredited by the Commission on Colleges of the Southern Association of Colleges and Schools to award bachelor's, master's, and Juris Doctor degrees. The Law School received full accreditation from the American Bar Association in 1994.

Students and the M.B.A. Experience

The total enrollment for the 1997–98 academic year was approximately 2,270 students. The graduate student population is approximately 600. St. Thomas University provides a learning environment that is intellectually challenging, yet supportive. Classes are kept small to foster maximum interaction between students and faculty members. Many students are working professionals who, along with faculty members, help place theoretical approaches in the context of real-life practical experience. All M.B.A. courses are during nonbusiness hours.

The Faculty

The St. Thomas University Master of Business Administration program has full-time and adjunct faculty members representing a broad background in management, health management, international business, sports administration, and accounting. The graduate faculty has a working relationship with a variety of governmental agencies and businesses, which in turn provide graduate professionals from business, industry, government, education, counseling centers, law enforcement, health care, professional sport management, and the ministry to serve as adjunct faculty members or guest lecturers. The dynamic mixture of academicians and practitioners provides an exciting learning environment.

The College and Environs

St. Thomas University is a small, private, coeducational institution of higher learning sponsored by the Roman Catholic Archdiocese of Miami. St. Thomas offers undergraduate, graduate, professional, and continuing-education programs joining a rich liberal arts curriculum with practical skills that create and enhance career opportunities. Its community of scholars welcomes men and women of all ages, races, nationalities, religious traditions, and beliefs. The University is located midway between Fort Lauderdale and downtown Miami. The University was founded by the Order of Augustinian Friars in 1961 as Biscayne College. It traces its roots to the Universidad de Santo Tomas de Villanueva in Havana, Cuba. In recognition of expanding graduate programs and the founding of the Law School, University status was attained in 1984. Sponsorship was passed to the Archdiocese of Miami in 1988.

South Florida is an international business center. As a major metropolitan center and focus of international business, south Florida offers a wide range of employment opportunities, professional development activities, and cultural leisure events. The general south Florida area offers an unlimited number of attractions and activities which have helped to add to its growth and continuing appeal to tourists. The climate allows for enjoyment of year-round activities that are not possible in many other parts of the United States. St. Thomas' 140-acre campus provides the setting for a variety of sports and leisure activities.

Technology Environment

The main library and law library contain more than 330,000 volumes and volume equivalences. In addition, the main library is a federal depository library and thus has many federal documents available for study. The libraries subscribe to almost 1,000 periodicals and microfilms. The library is a member of Southeast Florida Library Information Network (SEFLIN), which provides for the sharing of resources among south Florida libraries. Online computer searching systems and media center are also available for student use. Moreover, two microcomputer centers are available to supplement the University data processing center. Media facilities include two large screening rooms, a language laboratory, an instructional television recording studio, a film and videotape collection room, and a radio station.

Placement

The Career Center specializes in combining one-on-one advising with the latest in career technology, including an electronic resume writing package/database, a 24-hour Jobline, and a computerized career planning program. Workshops are offered on resume writing, interviewing skills, and business etiquette. Semiannual Career Expos host nearly seventy-five employers who converge on campus to offer full-time professional opportunities, internships, and part-time jobs. On-campus interviews include opportunities with Fortune 500 and small companies and government and service agencies. Students have access to career library holdings and an up-to-date computer lab connected to the Internet.

Admission

Prospective M.B.A. students must have a bachelor's degree from an accredited college or university with at least a 3.0 grade point average. If not, students must submit GRE or GMAT scores. International students must demonstrate adequate proficiency in English by submitting scores from the Test of English as a Foreign Language (TOEFL), with the Test of Written English (TWE).

Finances

Tuition for M.B.A. students during the 1997–98 academic year was $390 per credit. Financial assistance is available to M.B.A. students in the form of graduate assistantships, academic scholarships, and federal aid programs. Time payment plans are also available. Some students receive some type of tuition reimbursement for approved job-related M.B.A. courses. Individuals employed in the south Florida area, or by a national or statewide firm based in the area, should contact their human resources department to determine eligibility.

On-campus room and board are available to M.B.A. students through the Office of Student Life. Costs start at $5670 per year. Housing applications should be submitted by July 1. Family housing is not available on campus, but rental apartments abound in the surrounding area. Reasonably priced meals and sandwiches are available on campus.

Application Facts and Dates

St. Thomas University has a rolling admissions policy for students interested in receiving an early decision status letter. Other applicants are encouraged to adhere to the following application deadlines: for applicants to the sports administration program, May 1 for the fall semester, October 1 for the spring semester, and March 1 for the summer term; for domestic applicants to all other programs, June 15 for the fall semester, November 15 for the spring semester, and March 15 for the summer term; and for international applicants, March 1 for the fall semester, September 1 for the spring semester, and January 1 for the summer term.

All requests for information and application forms or admission status should be directed to:

Office of Graduate Admissions
St. Thomas University
16400 NW 32nd Avenue
Miami, Florida 33054

Telephone: 305-628-6714
305-628-6610
800-367-9006 (toll-free in Florida)
800-367-9010 (toll-free outside Florida)
Fax: 305-628-6591
World Wide Web: http://www.stu.edu

San Jose State University

San Jose, California

AN INVITATION FROM THE DEAN

If you are looking for an exciting, challenging, and comprehensive M.B.A. program to prepare you for career advancement, I invite you into an education partnership in which we'll work together toward your professional and personal success. The mission of the College of Business is to be the institution of opportunity, providing innovative business education and applied research for the Silicon Valley region. San Jose State University (SJSU) has one of the best accredited graduate business programs for employed adults, an outstanding faculty, and more than seventy different graduate courses from which to choose. Moreover, our excellent contacts in the dynamic Silicon Valley business community enrich both our faculty members and students. We look forward to receipt of your application to our M.B.A. program and will be delighted at the opportunity to welcome you. I hope you will contact us, especially at our Web site, to learn more about our M.B.A. program. The opportunities in Silicon Valley for professional advancement as well as cultural and recreational activities are outstanding. Our graduates find such great opportunities here that they never want to leave.

—Marshall Burak, Dean

Programs and Curricular Focus

The SJSU College of Business Graduate Programs combine applied techniques and academic rigor to provide innovative management education. The programs are innovative in design and delivery, tailored to the needs of full-time working professionals seeking part-time graduate business education in the evenings or on weekends. The College's aim is to help students become professionally accomplished, socially and fiscally responsible, and personally enriched.

The M.B.A. programs provide advanced management education for generalists and for those who want to specialize in finance, marketing, organizational development, global business, entrepreneurship and ventures, information and operations management, manufacturing management, health-care management, and transportation management. The M.B.A. degree program is available in either an on-campus or off-campus format, with identical admission requirements, course work, faculty members, and student backgrounds. The primary difference between the two programs is the delivery mode. Both programs require sixteen courses of 3-semester units each; three courses may be waivable.

The On-Campus M.B.A. Program is offered in a sixteen-week semester

format. Students typically take one or two courses each semester. A full-time student may complete the degree in eighteen months; a part-time student may complete it in two to four years.

The Accelerated Off-Campus M.B.A. Program is an exciting innovation in delivery. The program is offered in convenient locations throughout Silicon Valley on a year-round basis in consecutive eight-week sessions. Course work is very compressed and intensive, so students take only one course per session. A part-time student may complete the degree in two to three years. Tuition is significantly higher than it is for the on-campus program.

The Corporate M.B.A. Program is available for major Silicon Valley companies. These companies may engage SJSU to provide a convenient and academically challenging M.B.A. education on-site to a cohort of their employees. The students and the company benefit from company-specific class projects and assignments. This program may be completed in twenty-nine months by taking one class at a time in the evenings and on weekends.

The M.S. Tax Program offers students technical knowledge, understanding of tax policy, and research and analytical skills

development. Schedules of classes are designed to accommodate tax professionals.

The M.S. Accountancy Program is an accelerated full-time program that admits a limited number of nonbusiness undergraduate majors who desire to change their career path to professional accounting.

Students and the M.B.A. Experience

Total student enrollment in all graduate business programs is approximately 715. Ninety-five percent of the M.B.A. students work full-time and bring their valuable backgrounds into class discussions. Forty percent are women, approximately 15 percent are international students, and the average age is 32. About 15 percent already have nonbusiness advanced degrees. The average GMAT score is 565, and the average undergraduate GPA is 3.42 (4.0 scale).

❖ Global Focus

To strengthen efforts toward globalizing the M.B.A. experience, the College actively recruits international students, has reciprocal student exchange agreements with foreign universities, and infuses global issues into most courses.

Special Features

Of special note is the first class required of new students: Developing and Managing People. This class builds a sense of esprit de corps among entering students and builds a foundation for, and skills in, teamwork and leadership. It also provides the individual student with clarity of vision and plans for his or her personal and professional future.

The Faculty

The College of Business faculty numbers more than 120 professionally trained and experienced individuals. Nearly all of the 55 faculty members delivering graduate courses hold doctoral degrees. Most have extensive experience in business and industry as well, thus bringing realism and practicality to the classroom experience as well as linking class material to current applied practices in business. Active use is made of guest lecturers, field studies, in-firm projects, internships, and special events/field trips. The faculty's objective is to make the students' M.B.A. education relevant and applied in the context of today's rapidly changing business environment.

The Business School Network
The Dean's Advisory Board, consisting of distinguished CEOs and business leaders, provides substantive input and direction reflecting the high level of excellence of the M.B.A. programs. The Alumni Association maintains a vital link among the College, its alumni, and current students by sponsoring a series of programs and events.

The College and Environs
SJSU, founded in 1857, is the oldest public university on the West Coast and one of the largest of the twenty-two institutions in the California State University System. The College of Business, 5,000 students strong, has continuously met the requirements for national accreditation by the prestigious AACSB–The International Association for Management Education. SJSU is in the elite set of approximately 250, or 8 percent, of business schools nationwide that hold the AACSB accreditation at both the graduate and undergraduate levels. The University is accredited by the Western Association of Schools and Colleges (WASC).

SJSU has a world-class Student Activities Center, including an Olympic-size swimming pool, basketball arena, gymnasiums, and fitness centers all with ongoing activities for individuals or groups. Outdoor activities at the beach or mountains as well as the symphony, ballet, theater, museums, and professional sports enrich life in San Jose. San Jose is about 45 miles south of the city of San Francisco.

Facilities
The SJSU library is part of the extensive California State University library system, a resource with more than 25 million volumes electronically indexed and accessed. Of special note is the College of Business Computer Lab, dedicated entirely to business students. It is qualitatively and quantitatively one of the best in the system, including both software and hardware.

Technology Environment
SJSU is located in an urban setting in the heart of the famed, high-technology Silicon Valley of California. Silicon Valley is noted as being the incubator of most of the world's electronic hardware and software. This location provides a rich, stimulating, exponentially growing economic community for hundreds of businesses in markets as diverse as electronics, software, biotechnology, banking, aerospace, genetic engineering, consumer products, and agriculture as well as governmental organizations. The excitement of business growth is infused throughout the College's classes and curriculum.

Placement
Recruiting by more than 250 firms annually via the SJSU Career Planning & Placement Office results in business students being offered numerous job opportunities.

Admission
Applying requires submission of the official California State University Graduate Admission Forms and a $59 fee via U.S. Mail or Web site; official, sealed transcripts from all universities attended; and scores for the GMAT. No letters of reference are required. If preparatory education was in a language other than English, a score of 550 is necessary on the Test of English as a Foreign Language (TOEFL).

Admission is granted to any applicant who submits the completed application, shows via official transcripts a GPA of at least 3.0 on a 4.0 scale in the most recent 60 semester units (average GPA, 3.42) and the award of an accredited bachelor's degree, and shows an overall GMAT score of at least 500 (average GMAT score, 565), with sub-scores of at least the 50th percentile in both quantitative and verbal portions. Admission is noncompetitive; all qualified applicants are admitted.

Finances
Fees in 1997–98 for the state-supported On-Campus M.B.A. Program were $1008.50 per semester full-time and $675.50 per semester part-time. Nonresidents and international students have additional fees. Fees for the Accelerated Off-Campus M.B.A. Program were $885 per course. Books and supplies cost approximately $125 per course. A variety of loans, grants, work-study credits, fee deferments, and scholarships, for both domestic and international students, are available through the Financial Aid Office of the University.

Most graduate students, already employed, live in their own homes or apartments. There is a variety of both on- and off-campus housing, at many cost levels, to suit student needs.

Application Facts and Dates
Applicants for the M.B.A. programs may apply year-round. Deadlines are June 1 for fall semester admission and September 15 for spring admission. International students have earlier deadlines as indicated on the University's Web site. Other business graduate programs admit once per year. For application packets or more information, students should contact:

Ms. Amy Kassing, Director of
    Admissions
Business Graduate Programs Office,
    BT-250
College of Business
San Jose State University
One Washington Square
San Jose, California 95192-0162
Tel: 408-924-3425
Fax: 408-924-3426
E-mail: mba@cob.sjsu.edu
World Wide Web: http://www.cob.sjsu.
    edu/graduate

Santa Clara University

Thomas and Dorothy Leavey School of Business and Administration

Santa Clara, California

SANTA CLARA—THE PREMIER M.B.A. PROGRAM

Santa Clara offers the premier M.B.A. program for working professionals in Silicon Valley, and is currently ranked among the nation's top fifteen part-time programs. Our extraordinarily beautiful campus is located in the midst of the world's greatest concentration of technological and scientific talent and most dynamic economic marketplaces. This environment fuels our classrooms and inspires our student body, resonates within our faculty, permeates our curriculum, shapes our graduates, and underscores our commitment to quality instruction, rigorous inquiry, and high-performance expectations.

Santa Clara is proud to be a Jesuit business school. It means we take seriously the education of the whole person. Beyond building competence, at Santa Clara we foster conscience and compassion so that students have the ability to consider what is right rather than just doing things right and can appreciate the creation of purpose as well as capital. Still, ours is a practical approach to educating future business leaders, as embodied within these words of St. Ignatius: "To know and not to do, is not to know."

Santa Clara's faculty do original research and contribute firsthand to knowledge generation, as opposed to merely reporting about the research of others. They also write for thinking managers and executives in a wide variety of practitioner-oriented publications. Their impressive accomplishments in scholarship, impacting both theory and practice, are balanced by a strong commitment to continuous improvement in teaching and service to students.

We seek men and women who are willing to work hard and who want to make a difference in their organizations and in the lives of others.

—Barry Z. Posner, Dean

Programs and Curricular Focus

Santa Clara University's M.B.A. program was in the original group of programs accredited by AACSB–The International Association for Management Education in 1961. Reaccredited in 1996, the program has consistently met the AACSB's high standards on applicant admissions, curriculum design and content, faculty scholarship, and instructional acumen. The curriculum blends instruction in theory with practical applications, enriched by faculty members engaged in state-of-the-art research and students who deal daily with real-life organizational concerns. The program is ideally suited for people who want to pursue their education while continuing in their current job positions. However, many students attend on a full-time basis, taking advantage of the flexible evening class scheduling and the opportunity to meet and study with employees from more than 500 Silicon Valley companies.

The course of study at Santa Clara University takes a generalist perspective, preparing students to be decision makers across the various functional fields. A full range of electives does, however, allow in-depth concentration in selected areas. Students may choose their own pattern of electives or follow one of the suggested study plans leading to a concentration in finance, information systems, international business, managing technology and innovation, quantitative approaches to business problems, marketing management, market research, or operations.

Depending on prior academic background, students take between fifteen and twenty-four courses to obtain their degrees. Two courses bracket the program: Managerial Competencies and Team Effectiveness, taken within the first two quarters of residence, and the capstone course, Business Policy, taken within the last two quarters of residence.

The Leavey School of Business also offers a joint J.D./M.B.A. program with the School of Law. This combined-degree program allows students to obtain both the J.D. and the M.B.A. degree in less time than if the degrees were earned independently. Students must meet the admissions requirements of both the School of Law and the School of Business.

The Institute of Agribusiness at Santa Clara University, in conjunction with the Leavey School of Business, offers an M.B.A. in agribusiness. The Institute, founded in 1973, is an internationally recognized center for agribusiness management education. The curriculum incorporates both general management courses and agribusiness management courses, and many students complement their course work by participating in the institute's internship, mentor, and site visit programs.

The Institute of Agribusiness and the Peace Corps offer a special opportunity for students interested in becoming Peace Corps volunteers after they complete an agribusiness M.B.A. The Masters International Program (MIP) is designed to develop volunteers who have agribusiness management skills.

Students and the M.B.A. Experience

Approximately 85 percent of the 1,100 M.B.A. students at Santa Clara study part-time as they pursue their careers. Attending part-time, students generally take 3½ years to complete the program, while full-time students complete the program in 2 years. The average student is 27 years old upon entering the program and has more than five years of work experience. Thirty-six percent of M.B.A. students are women, and 8 percent of the student body is composed of international students.

Current M.B.A. students come from more than 400 undergraduate colleges and universities across the United States, as well as from international institutions. Undergraduate majors represented are humanities and social sciences, including economics (29 percent); engineering (43 percent); business (26 percent); and other disciplines (2 percent). Ten percent of entering students already hold an advanced degree. This blend of academic backgrounds and work experience provides opportunities for enhanced learning inside and outside of the classroom.

The Faculty

The faculty of the Leavey School possesses national stature in each of its six

major departments—Economics, Organizational Analysis and Management, Marketing, Finance, Operations Management and Information Systems, and Accounting as well as the Institute of Agribusiness. In each department, faculty members play leading roles in their professional associations and in editorial capacities for the top scholarly journals in their fields. This excellence in scholarship is balanced by a strong commitment to teaching and continuous improvement in service to students. The faculty also represents the global world of business today, representing twelve different countries.

The Business School Network
Alumni of the M.B.A. program at Santa Clara University hold executive positions in more than 800 innovative and rapidly growing businesses. The M.B.A. Alumni Association plays an active role in supporting personal and career development of both fellow alumni and current students. As a vital link between the business school and its alumni, the association sponsors a series of educational programs and alumni networking opportunities.

Corporate Partnerships
The Leavey School of Business and Administration Advisory Board consists of 40 distinguished CEOs and business leaders. This active board provides a vehicle for the business community to provide input and communicate concerns directly to top administrators and faculty at Santa Clara. The composition of this board and the willingness of top executives to serve on it reflect and reinforce awareness of the Leavey School and its M.B.A. program at the highest levels in local and national organizations. The high regard for the Santa Clara M.B.A. is also demonstrated by the number of companies that provide tuition reimbursement plans to encourage their employees to continue their professional development at Santa Clara.

Prominent Alumni
Since 1961, more than 8,500 men and women have received their M.B.A. degrees and have achieved eminence in one of the country's most dynamic regions. Among the University alumni are 435 company presidents and 625 senior corporate executives. In addition, many alumni have started successful entrepreneurial ventures.

The College and Environs
Santa Clara University, founded in 1851, was the first institution of higher learning on the West Coast. The University was established on the Mission Santa Clara de Asis, and the Mission remains at the center of the University. Santa Clara University currently enrolls more than 7,500 students in its graduate and undergraduate programs.

Santa Clara is located 46 miles south of San Francisco, in Silicon Valley, an area rich in opportunities. The cultural and entertainment center of San Francisco and the magnificent vistas of Marin County are within 1 hour's travel. Also close by are the beaches of Santa Cruz and the Napa Valley wine country, and even closer are the cultural and sports opportunities available in San Jose.

Placement
Career Services offers complete career services for students and alumni, including counseling, on-campus recruiting, seminars, and workshops. Recruiting is ongoing due to Santa Clara's year-round admission and graduation schedule for M.B.A. students. Workshops help students focus on self-assessment, resume writing, and job-search strategies. Career Services maintains the M.B.A. Alumni Network, a database of more than 500 alumni who provide informational interviews. They are also an active participant in the West Coast M.B.A. Consortium, which hosts an annual recruiting event with fifty companies and twelve M.B.A. programs in attendance.

Admission
Applicants are required to submit their GMAT results, transcripts from all schools previously attended, two essays, two recommendations, and the Santa Clara application form and fee. All of these factors are taken into account by the Admissions Committee when evaluating an application. The average GMAT score of entering M.B.A. students is 630, and the average GPA is 3.25. Although there is no academic business background required before entering the program, applicants must be proficient in algebra and possess basic computer skills.

For any applicant whose first language is not English, the TOEFL and TWE are also required. The minimum acceptable TOEFL score is 600, and the minimum TWE score is 4.0. Effective with the new computer-based test, the minimum acceptable TOEFL score is 250.

Finances
Tuition for 1998–99 is $458 per quarter unit, and all classes are 3 units. Tuition for the Institute of Agribusiness is $483 per quarter unit. Each quarter, there is a $12 registration fee and a $10 Student Association fee. Books and supplies cost approximately $100 per course.

Financial assistance is generally available to M.B.A. students who have good academic records and can show financial need. Most financial aid covers partial tuition only and is in the form of M.B.A. Project Assistantships, which require working on administrative and/or research tasks. The Institute of Agribusiness offers separate grants and awards for students enrolled in their program. Limited resources do not allow the School to offer financial aid to international students. The deadlines to apply for financial aid are one month after the application deadline for each quarter.

Application Facts and Dates
Application deadlines are March 1 for the fall quarter early decision, June 1 for the fall quarter, September 1 for the winter quarter, and December 1 for the spring quarter. Decision letters are mailed out six to eight weeks after the application deadline. For more information, contact:

Ms. Elizabeth Ford, Assistant Dean
M.B.A. Admissions
Leavey School of Business and
    Administration
Santa Clara University
500 El Camino Real
Santa Clara, California 95053
Telephone: 408-554-4500
Fax: 408-554-4571
E-mail: mbaadmissions@scu.edu
World Wide Web: http://lsb.scu.edu

Schiller International University

Business Programs

Dunedin, Florida ❖ *London, United Kingdom* ❖ *Paris, France* ❖ *Strasbourg, France* ❖
Engelberg, Switzerland ❖ *Leysin, Switzerland* ❖ *Heidelberg, Germany* ❖ *Madrid, Spain* ❖

> ### BUILDING THE INTERNATIONAL THEME AT SIU
> *The Schiller (SIU) M.B.A. is more than the sum of its component courses. The M.B.A. in international business builds upon the student's previous studies in international marketing, management, finance, and economics and relates these studies to real-world international management situations via case studies, business games, computer simulations, research projects, and class discussion of current global issues. The international business theme is inherent in every facet of the program; the international focus on curriculum, the multinational background of the faculty and the students, and the nature of the projects.*
>
> —Dr. Walter Leibrecht, President

Programs and Curricular Focus

Program courses involve theoretical and practical applications, strategic decision-making, teamwork and group mobilization, understanding diverse interdependent environmental forces, and incorporating ethical standards into business decisions.

The 45-semester-credit program may be completed during two semesters and a summer session on a full-time basis, or in two years on a part-time basis. Students must complete fifteen M.B.A. courses including seven core courses; one of each in the areas of advanced accounting, finance, information technology, international management, international marketing, managerial statistics, and methods of research and analysis. The remaining course requirements include eight electives from approved M.B.A. courses and a final comprehensive examination. The overall GPA for all graduate courses completed must be at least 3.0.

The M.B.A. in International Hotel and Tourism Management is directed to students in the fields of business, hotel/restaurant management, and tourism and related areas who wish to earn an advanced business degree. The course work, comprising five international hotel and tourism management courses, in addition to ten M.B.A. courses, provides the credentials to enter the industry at management level. The degree is offered at the London-Waterloo campus and also at the Florida Campus of SIU. It can be completed in two semesters and a summer session of full-time study, and working professionals can earn this degree on a part-time basis in two to four years. The program consists of fifteen

3-credit courses, plus a final comprehensive examination. The overall GPA must be at least 3.0.

M.B.A. programs are offered at SIU's Dunedin, Florida; London, England; Paris, France; Madrid, Spain; and Heidelberg, Germany campuses.

Students and the M.B.A. Experience

Schiller is a university where each student counts, is taken seriously, and where faculty members know students by name. The close attention paid to each individual student is one of the hallmarks of an SIU education.

The Schiller philosophy is based on the conviction that the give and take between students and their teachers is the very essence of education and can never be replaced, not even by the best technical equipment. It is from this personal relationship that students receive inspiration.

The Faculty

The real assets of Schiller are the high quality of its students and their dedication to serious study, as well as the excellence of its instructors. Schiller faculty members are carefully selected not only for the quality of their educational background but also for their practical experience in their fields of expertise.

The educational process puts particular emphasis on developing international and cross-cultural competencies through foreign language skills, facility, intercampus transfer, and other international

academic opportunities, as well as an intense interaction among people with diverse backgrounds.

The Business School Network

The Office of Alumni Affairs coordinates the University's relationships with former SIU students around the world. Using a computerized list, which is continuously updated, the Alumni Affairs Office issues a University Newsletter to all former students and organizes an alumni network to assist potential SIU students. This office is also responsible for collecting evaluations of its own effectiveness. SIU maintains Alumni Affairs staff in the United States to help students and parents in assessing and selecting study abroad opportunities as well as assisting alumni in maintaining their sharing and alumni networking options. An alumni directory is available at each campus.

The College and Environs

Schiller International University was established in 1964, laying the foundation of what was to become a small, independent university offering its students an education of high quality. During the 1960s, when many large universities emerged as mass institutions in which the individual student often felt lost in a crowd, the founding of Schiller was a conscious departure from the growing anonymity of such institutions. With alumni from more than 130 countries and with men and women from more than 100 nations currently enrolled, SIU offers students the unique opportunity to gain an American education in an international setting. English is the language of instruction at all of SIU's ten campuses in six countries where students are prepared for careers in academic institutions, business and management, governmental agencies, multinational organizations, and social services or for further education in their chosen field. Through enrollment in both practical and theoretical courses and through discussions in small classes with instructors and classmates of multicultural backgrounds, students gain firsthand knowledge of business and cultural relations among the peoples of the world. SIU students have the unique opportunity to transfer among SIU's campuses without losing any credits while continuing their chosen program of study. SIU's campuses are in Dunedin, Florida, U.S.; central London, England; Paris and Strasbourg, France; Heidelberg, Germany; Engelberg and Leysin, Switzerland; and Madrid, Spain.

Admission

Admissions requirements include completion of a bachelor's degree with a business specialization (i.e., accounting, economics, finance and management, law, marketing, statistics) or a bachelor's degree in a nonbusiness field followed by business studies at diploma-level or a preparatory program. The average GPA for all graduate courses completed must be at least 3.0, and all students must submit GMAT scores.

Finances

Schiller International University is an independent institution with limited funds for financial aid. Students are encouraged to seek assistance through private or governmental loans and scholarship programs before applying to the University.

Students wishing to apply for financial assistance from SIU should request a scholarship application form when applying for admission.

Graduate fees for the one-year program (two semesters and the summer session) of fifteen courses are $14,850, the activity fee is $360, and the liability deposit is $120 (the liability deposit is refundable).

International Students

From its founding, the University has dedicated itself to the encouragement and active development of international understanding. Schiller study programs have a distinct international focus. Its student body, which is presently from more than 100 nations, has the invaluable experience of studying together with students from many different national and cultural backgrounds and the opportunity to form lifelong relationships. Personal initiative is encouraged throughout. The development of an entrepreneurial spirit is another hallmark of a Schiller education.

Application Facts and Dates

Applications are processed on a rolling basis. For further information, students should contact:

Christoph Leibrecht
Director of Admissions
Schiller International University
453 Edgewater Drive
Dunedin, Florida 34698-7532
Telephone: 813-736-5082
          800-336-4133 (toll-free)
Fax: 813-734-0359
World Wide Web: http://www.schiller.
   edu

Seattle Pacific University

Seattle, Washington

SERVICE AND LEADERSHIP IN BUSINESS AND SOCIETY

We take pride in the fact that our M.B.A. degree offers the highest quality management education. We seek students who want to make a positive difference in their workplaces and in their communities. We are a learning community focused on a commitment to Christian faith, experiential learning, and collaborative learning. Our M.B.A. graduates are prepared to provide values-based leadership in any organization, think and act strategically, manage knowledge-based organizations that emphasize the intellectual capital of their members, and apply in-depth knowledge in an emphasis area.

—Alexander D. Hill, Dean

Programs and Curricular Focus

The M.B.A. program at Seattle Pacific University (SPU) offers the highest quality graduate management education informed by Christian faith and values. Beyond the advanced instruction in management covered by all students, the degree can be tailored by one's choice of electives to provide depth in specific areas. Current areas of emphasis include general management, human resource management, and information systems management. A separate Master of Science in Information Systems Management (M.S.I.S.M.) degree is also offered.

The M.B.A. curriculum consists of twenty-four courses divided among nine core, ten advanced, and five elective subjects. The ten core courses are waivable based upon prior college course work. Each course is 3 quarter credits and meets for one 3-hour session each week. A flexible schedule of summer classes is also offered. The related M.S.I.S.M. degree consists of a total of twenty courses. This more specialized degree may be pursued individually or can be earned by completing 27 credits (nine courses) beyond the M.B.A.

Courses are taught at two Seattle-area locations in a convenient evening format. Some Saturday morning classes are also available. The program may be pursued on either a full-time or part-time basis.

Students and the M.B.A. Experience

With an average age of 32, Seattle Pacific graduate students bring a wealth of experiences with them to the classroom. Small classes allow dynamic interaction between professors and students, individually or in teams. Students come with diverse employment backgrounds ranging from manufacturing and high-technology industries, for which the Puget Sound region is noted, to service and small-business sectors.

International students comprise about 15 percent of the M.B.A. student body; women account for about 47 percent of the students. Three-quarters of the M.B.A. students are employed full-time.

Special Features

Students may choose to develop their own business plans or conduct independent research in the Practice of Business course. Electives may be chosen from a variety of disciplines. Popular electives have included such courses as Advanced Negotiations, Entrepreneurial Management, Pacific-Rim Enterprise, and Telecommunications and Networking.

The Faculty

The faculty is known for its high quality of instruction and broad experience in the marketplace. Additional faculty members in the M.S.I.S.M. program are drawn from industry. An executive-in-residence and a small number of adjunct instructors complete the teaching faculty.

The Business School Network

Composed of more than 30 senior executives from Puget Sound–area companies, SPU's Executive Advisory Council (EAC) is a valuable networking resource for the School of Business and Economics. Through example and professional guidance, these executives interact with faculty and students to assist in providing a high-quality M.B.A. program based on Christian ethical principles. EAC members meet with faculty members at quarterly luncheons to discuss academic programs and the needs of the Pacific Northwest business community. Many of these executives also participate in a special breakfast program in which M.B.A. students also participate.

The College and Environs

Founded in 1891 as an outreach of the Free Methodist Church of North America, Seattle Pacific University has served the Seattle community through Christian higher education for more than 100 years. On-campus enrollment includes 2,400 undergraduate students and 1,200 graduate students, of whom approximately 200 are pursuing M.B.A. or M.S.I.S.M. degrees. The School of Business and Economics is one of three professional schools that, along with the College of Arts and Sciences, administer the academic programs of the University.

Seattle Pacific University is located on the north side of Queen Anne Hill, just north of downtown Seattle, Washington. The attractive campus borders the Lake Washington Ship Canal, which joins Lake Union with Puget Sound. Seattle is the premier business and trade center of the Pacific Northwest and is the U.S. gateway to the Pacific Rim. Bounded by the Cascade Mountains to the east, by the Olympic Mountains and Puget Sound to the west, and by Mount Rainier to the south, the region is a haven for all forms of outdoor recreation. The city and region also have a wide variety of cultural and sporting attractions.

Facilities

The School of Business and Economics is housed in McKenna Hall, built in 1981. Second-floor faculty and administrative offices and conference rooms, together with first-floor classrooms and a computer lab, provide a convenient, safe, and attractive educational setting.

Graduate business courses are also taught at a South King County classroom location. Students may elect to take classes at either site.

Seattle Pacific University has served the Pacific Northwest through Christian higher education for more than 100 years.

Construction of the new campus library was completed in 1994. This spacious, state-of-the-art facility offers online access to a wide range of publications and research materials, as well as traditional periodical and text sources. High-technology classroom learning environments are being used.

Placement

Career services and resources are available from the University's Career Development Center. These include job openings notebooks (for full-time jobs), internship openings notebooks, career library (career, job search, and company information), career workshops, and career fairs.

Admission

Admission to the M.B.A. program requires successful completion of the GMAT; the GRE is required for admission to the M.S.I.S.M. program. A minimum TOEFL score of 565 is required of all applicants whose native language is not English. An essay and two recommendations are also required for admission. Significant work experience and clearly expressed career goals are very important factors in the admission decision process. Applications are encouraged from students holding accredited bachelor's degrees from all disciplines. M.S.I.S.M. applicants should also be able to document experience with at least two programming languages.

Finances

A limited number of graduate assistantship positions are offered each year, and student loans are available for U.S. students taking at least two courses each term. Tuition for the 1998–99 academic year is $412 per quarter credit hour ($1236 per course). One-time application ($35) and matriculation ($50) fees and a $200 advance tuition payment are charged. Typical textbook and miscellaneous costs average $110 per course. Room and board costs for three quarters of study range from approximately $4600 in campus residence halls or University-owned, nontraditional housing up to $6200 for off-campus residence.

International Students

Seattle Pacific welcomes the enrollment of international students. Special educational and social programs are designed to enhance students' cross-cultural experiences. Counseling assistance is also provided for academic achievement, cultural adaptations, and financial and legal concerns at the Center for Special Populations.

Application Facts and Dates

Applications are accepted for all quarters, including summer. Admission deadlines generally precede the quarter of admission by two months. Applicants should contact the graduate program coordinator for additional information and an admission packet.

Ms. Debra Wysomierski
Assistant Graduate Director
School of Business and Economics
Seattle Pacific University
3307 Third Avenue West
Seattle, Washington 98119
Telephone: 206-281-2753
Fax: 206-281-2733
E-mail: djwysom@spu.edu
World Wide Web: http://www.spu.edu/depts/sbe

Seattle University

> **DEVELOPING CRITICAL SKILLS FOR SUCCESSFUL CAREERS**
>
> *This is an exciting time to pursue a graduate degree in business, especially in a commercial center as vibrant as Seattle. In the Albers School M.B.A. program, you will acquire more than just the relevant tools to cope with the rapid pace of change in the business environment. You will develop the critical thinking, learning, and communication skills necessary to create and manage your own successful career. But beyond those critical elements of management education, an Albers program will advance your potential to improve organizations that depend upon your leadership. Consistent with the 500-year tradition of Jesuit education, the program inspires you to serve your community by advancing your understanding of your role as a manager in a global society.*
>
> —Jan Warren Duggar, Dean

Programs and Curricular Focus

Seattle University's graduate business programs offer a winning combination of two distinctive competencies—top-quality academic programs in business and economics and exceptional flexibility and accessibility for both part-time and full-time students. Students enjoy the environment and service of a small private school and the benefits of a large graduate student population.

The Albers School's niche has been, and will continue to be, educating managers from around the world to be leaders in their industries and in their communities. The goals are to stimulate students with the latest global business practices, provoke analytical thinking and discussion among the best and the brightest, and develop an ethical foundation for sound business decisions. The curriculum immerses students in the latest business practices, helps them integrate different functions within the firm, teaches them how to work more effectively in teams, and develops their understanding of what it takes to be a leader in these rapidly changing times.

The M.B.A. program has three components. First, there are six fundamental business preparatory classes. These courses give students the basic foundation on which to build advanced studies. Students who have completed comparable course work with a grade of B (3.0) or better have the option of waiving these classes based on self-assessment materials. Students without previous course work are required to take these classes. The next ten courses are core courses and are required for all students. These courses are the heart of the M.B.A. program. Most are case based and require considerable integration and application to the business world. Electives are the third component. Students choose eight electives that meet their needs and interests. The Albers School offers more than fifty electives in ten different concentrations at the leading edge of business and economics. Students may also choose one elective from other graduate programs at Seattle University, such as the Master of Public Administration or Master of Software Engineering.

All of the graduate classes in business and economics are offered Monday through Thursday in the late afternoon and evening as well as on Saturday mornings and afternoons. Students pick and choose convenient class times, quarter to quarter. Most classes meet once a week for approximately 3 hours. Most part-time students take two classes per quarter and attend four quarters per year. Full-time students generally take three or four classes each quarter. Students can move between part-time and full-time status and, if needed, step out for a quarter or two and easily return to continue the degree.

Seattle University belongs to a consortium of Jesuit M.B.A. programs across the country that allow nearly full transfer of credit between programs. For students concerned about a possible relocation during their M.B.A. program, this agreement can protect their investment.

Students and the M.B.A. Experience

The Albers School of Business and Economics serves approximately 725 graduate students from across the U.S. and North America, Asia, Europe, Latin America, and Africa. The reputation for rigorous and challenging academics, teaching excellence, and emphasis on integrity in business draws some of the best students in the world. Students work and learn with others from large corporate backgrounds as well as small entrepreneurial organizations. Students come from leading technology and aerospace firms, premier financial institutions, manufacturing and health-care organizations, and multinational corporations in a multitude of industries. Students have the chance to build relationships with students from around the world, some of whom will someday manage companies that play a dominant role in world commerce and economics.

The Albers School is very proud of its exceptional and diverse student body. Eighty-five percent of the graduate students attend part-time and work for many large and small organizations in the region. It also has a number of full-time students, many of whom are international. The international students bring their unique cultures and perspectives to the classroom. Students have the opportunity to work with others from North American countries as well as from Asia, Europe, and South America.

Approximately 38 percent of the students have an undergraduate major in engineering or science, 36 percent have a Bachelor of Arts in business degree, and the remaining students have degrees in fields ranging from economics to the humanities. The Albers School looks for students who are bright, motivated, and capable of succeeding in a challenging academic program and who bring their own unique experience to the classroom.

❖ Global Focus

Albers School graduate students may choose to take classes abroad in the very popular international study tours. Seattle University faculty members take small groups of students to Europe, Asia, and

Latin America to experience global business practices firsthand. These international trips last from nine days to two weeks, accommodating the part-time as well as the full-time students. They are excellent opportunities to learn about international business with faculty members who know the ropes.

Special Features

The Entrepreneurship Center champions the entrepreneurial spirit and talents of the students and local emerging businesses through free consulting and outreach. Under the direction of faculty and/or industry mentors, teams of students in the center's Small Business Institute work with new business owners to develop strategic plans based upon overall analysis of the firm and external conditions. More than 1,500 small businesses have participated in this successful program over the past twenty years. The Entrepreneurship Center also offers student consulting for commercial and not-for-profit organizations and takes a special interest in targeting unemployed, low-income, and inner-city individuals who want to start or are in the process of starting microenterprise ventures.

The Faculty

Jesuit schools are well known for excellence in teaching. The Albers School recruits and rewards faculty members who love to teach and are good at it. Faculty members are at the leading edge of their fields through their research and publishing but are also exceptionally capable of integrating business disciplines, communicating knowledge to students, and applying what is learned in the classroom to the real world. Above all, the faculty members care. They are accessible, knowledgeable, and interested in the students' success.

The Business School Network

Corporate Partnerships

A mentor program—one of the first implemented for an evening program and now in its fifth year—helps students network with senior executives as well as get a clearer perspective on their careers. The M.B.A. program relies heavily on the guidance of business leaders from companies that lead the region and the world in their industries.

The College and Environs

Seattle University was founded in 1891 and is one of the twenty-eight Jesuit Schools. Now serving 6,000 undergraduate, graduate, and law students representing forty-two states and territories and seventy-one nations as well as a plethora of religious and ideological viewpoints, the University has a diverse and culturally rich learning environment. The Albers School, established in 1945, has grown significantly over the past few decades and now has the largest M.B.A. program in the Northwest accredited by AACSB–The International Association for Management Education. The proximity to the Pacific Rim, along with local thriving technology, manufacturing, and aerospace industries, creates an ideal environment for learning about the global realities and practices of business.

Facilities

Completely renovated in 1995, the Pigott Building is home to the Albers School. Its welcoming atrium serves as a meeting place for students and a site for special events, such as the Executive Mentor kick-off each fall. First-floor classrooms are designed for case method courses, with tiered comfortable seating and multimedia capabilities. The building also houses computer labs, Albers faculty and staff offices, and, of course, an espresso stand.

Placement

The Albers graduate population is diverse in its experience base and career needs. In response, the Albers Placement Center services are highly individualized and available to working professionals with busy schedules. The center offers a number of services and programs: Graduate Career Management Program, Career Expo, Internships, Executive Mentorship Program, Executives in Residence, and weekly job listings.

Admission

Prerequisites for admission include completion of an undergraduate degree in any subject at an accredited U.S. college or its equivalent in another country, a GMAT test score above 500, a minimum of one year of work experience, and completion of an Albers School graduate application.

Applicants from non-English-speaking countries must also submit TOEFL scores of 580 or above. Students who score below the minimum are required to complete Seattle University's Culture and Language Bridge Program, offered in the fall. International students must also submit a Seattle University international application, which includes official financial statements.

Finances

Tuition in 1998–99 is $440 per credit hour. There is also a tuition application fee of $55 and a matriculation fee of $70.

Graduate students must be enrolled at least part-time (3 credits) to be considered for financial assistance. There are three financial aid options available— student loans, scholarships, and graduate assistantships.

Application Facts and Dates

Students may apply for any quarter. Once admitted, a student can begin the M.B.A. program in fall, winter, spring, summer, or intersession (mid-August to mid-September). Applicants receive a decision approximately four weeks after receipt of completed application materials. For further information, students should contact:

Graduate Admissions
Seattle University
900 Broadway
Seattle, Washington 98122
Telephone: 206-296-5900
E-mail: grad-admissions@seattleu.edu
World Wide Web: http://www.seattleu.
  edu/asbe

Seton Hall University

GRADUATE EDUCATION FOCUSED ON BUSINESS INNOVATION

> *In today's highly complex environment, you, as a decision maker, must act quickly and with great resolve. You must learn how to manage yourself, work effectively in teams, grasp the complexities of the organizational environment, and appreciate the broad-based factors driving the future. You must understand information systems and the complex interactions of political realities of effective leadership. Seton Hall University's (SHU) W. Paul Stillman School of Business faculty, administration, and alumni are dedicated to facilitating your development toward lifelong professional learning.*
>
> —John H. Shannon, Dean

Programs and Curricular Focus

The M.B.A. curriculum is designed to provide a strong graduate-level business foundation and encourage specialization in timely areas of employer need and personal interest in today's global and technological workforce. Through an increasingly active, integrative, experiential, adult-learning environment, the School is in the business of providing students with the information, skills, and competencies integral to career advancement.

The evening program provides professionals with a five-tier curriculum built on core courses, concentration electives, free electives, and the capstone experience (business policy). Eligible students can waive up to 30 credits of this 60-credit M.B.A. program through previously completed, approved course work and challenge exams. M.B.A. concentrations in the evening program are accounting, economics, finance, human resource management, management, management information systems, marketing, quantitative analysis, and sports management.

The 1998–99 Day M.B.A. Program provides a full-time program to select applicants interested in earning an M.B.A. in sixteen months. This innovative cohort program revolves around seminars, "live" and simulated case studies, teamwork, and an externship/consulting project.

Master of Science programs in accounting, human resource management, information systems, international business, professional accounting, and taxation as well as joint degrees, includ-ing the M.B.A./J.D. and the M.B.A./M.S. in international business, are also offered. A certificate in international business is available in conjunction with the M.B.A.

Students and the M.B.A. Experience

The Seton Hall M.B.A. experience is best described as an amalgamation of program development and delivery system innovations and the strong foundation upon which the School has built its name. Its reputation earned national recognition when the School became the first private business school in the state to be accredited by AACSB–The International Association for Management Education and has gained momentum with the implementation of its Day M.B.A. Program.

❖ Global Focus

The globalization of business has been integrated into the School's graduate business education even before it became fashionable. Through the Institute for International Business, established in 1964, the School has cooperative agreements with sister institutions in China, the Dominican Republic, France, and Russia; sponsored academic scholars; implemented Master of Science, joint M.B.A./M.S., and certificate in international business programs; and expanded M.B.A. electives. In 1994, the Institute received a $1-million endowment grant from the W. Paul Stillman Terminating Trust.

Special Features

Three recent developments that have a great effect on the quality and responsiveness of the School's graduate business programs are the M.B.A. Reengineering Team initiative (which culminated in the sixteen-month, full-time Day M.B.A. Program), the School of Business' Mobile Computing Project/University Information Technology Plan, and the implementation of six new Master of Science programs.

The Faculty

The Stillman School of Business' 55 faculty members facilitate professional business education through a variety of teaching methods, including lecture, seminars, "live" and simulated business cases, and the integration of technology. The School's low faculty-student ratio and small class size encourage opportunities for one-on-one interaction. Its faculty members have expertise in all areas of business and are published in nationally and internationally recognized business journals.

The Business School Network

Seton Hall's network of corporate partners and alumni is extensive and

FACULTY LIST

Department Chairs:
Accounting and Taxation: James W. Greenspan, Ph.D., Texas A&M.
Computing and Decision Sciences: David Rosenthal (Acting), Ph.D., Pennsylvania.
Economics: John J. Dall Jr., (Acting) Ph.D., Pennsylvania (Wharton).
Finance and Legal Studies: Philip R. Phillips, Ph.D., NYU.
Management: Leigh Stelzer, Ph.D., Michigan.
Marketing: Joseph Z. Wisenblit, Ph.D., CUNY.

Center/Institute Directors:
Center for Leadership Studies: Karen E. Boroff, Ph.D., Columbia.
Center for Sports Management: Ann Mayo, Ph.D., Ohio State.
Center for Tax Research: Brian Greenstein, Ph.D., Houston.
Division of Research: Sheldon Epstein, Ph.D., NYU.
Institute for International Business: Agnes Olszewski, Ph.D., Warsaw.

active. Examples of industry relationships include IBM's Mobile Computing Initiative, AT&T's off-campus program, and the Arthur Andersen Planning Skills Center. Alumni commitment is ongoing through active participation in School of Business Alumni Council–sponsored networking and social events such as periodic "Meet the Dean" receptions and golf and tennis outings. When the School has needed the input of business leaders in program development, alumni have contributed their time and shared their expertise in such initiatives as the M.B.A. Reengineering Team, which met for hundreds of hours this past year.

The College and Environs

Seton Hall's heritage has provided the School with the foundation for its success. Founded in 1856, SHU is the largest and oldest diocesan university in the nation and maintains regional accreditation through the Middle States Association of Colleges and Schools. Located on 58 acres in the suburban village of South Orange, New Jersey, it is 14 miles from New York City and less than ½ mile from the Midtown Direct train. The School of Business, founded in 1950, was the first private school in New Jersey to earn accreditation by AACSB– The International Association for Management Education. With approximately 850 graduate students, close to 50 percent of the School's enrollment, the University's commitment to graduate study in business is evident.

Facilities

The new state-of-the-art academic facility at the School of Business has corporate-style breakout and multimedia rooms, a student lounge, a computer lab, and an amphitheater.

Another facility that confirms Seton Hall's commitment to innovation is the Walsh Library. Opened in 1994, the

155,000-square-foot Walsh Library seats more than 1,100 students. Technology available includes CD-ROM databases (both index and full-text), multimedia computer labs, audiovisual installations, an electronic visual aid (scanner-reader), and Setoncat, the online catalog of holdings accessible both on site and via the campus network.

Technology Environment

In addition to University-wide computer and information services, the School of Business's Andersen Planning Skills Center provides technical support services solely to business students. The School of Business is committed to its long-range strategic plan for computing and information technology.

Placement

The University's Career Services Department provides a team of professionals designated to work solely with School of Business students. A comprehensive program of career development, cooperative education, employment recruiting, and training is offered.

Admission

For consideration, applicants must hold a baccalaureate degree from a regionally accredited college. Although all requests will be considered on their merit, a minimum GPA of 3.0, a GMAT score of 500, and 550 on the TOEFL (for international students), are generally required. Decisions are based on the following submitted evidence of relevant professional and academic potential: work experience and credentials, personal statement, grade point average, letters of academic and professional recommendation, and score on the GMAT and TOEFL. A limited number of Master of Science (not M.B.A.) applicants with extensive, relevant professional experi-

ence and exemplary academic records are granted GMAT waivers. Additional information is required of international applicants. Members of minority groups are encouraged to apply.

Finances

Tuition for the 1998–99 academic year is $530 per credit. There is a fall and spring registration fee of $85 for part-time students and $105 for full-time students per semester ($45 per summer and winter). For information on School-funded aid, which is in the form of graduate assistantships for selected full-time students, admitted students should contact SHU's Graduate Services Office by mail or at 973-275-2036. For federal financial aid and loan information, students should contact the University Financial Aid Office by mail or at 973-761-9350.

International Students

Applications from international students interested in full-time studies are encouraged. The University's Office of International Programs provides and organizes a wide variety of supportive services.

The School of Business's Institute for International Business works closely with visiting dignitaries and scholars.

Application Facts and Dates

Graduate applications are considered year-round on a rolling basis. For further information, students should contact:

Student Information Office
W. Paul Stillman School of Business
Seton Hall University
400 South Orange Avenue
South Orange, New Jersey 07079-2692
Telephone: 973-761-9222
Fax: 973-761-9217
E-mail: busgrad@shu.edu

Simmons College

EDUCATING WOMEN FOR POSITIONS OF POWER AND LEADERSHIP

▶ *A quarter of a century ago, the Simmons Graduate School of Management (GSM) was among the first to educate women for positions of power and leadership. Today, we remain the only business school in the world designed exclusively for women. Our challenge is the same: to help women succeed in business and to move from middle management into the most senior positions in organizations of every kind. Wherever senior managers meet, Simmons is determined to position skilled and confident women among them, competing equally, with insight and a real understanding of the business environment.*

—Patricia O'Brien, Dean

Programs and Curricular Focus

In its emphasis on functional knowledge and quantitative skills, the Simmons M.B.A. program is identical to those offered at other business schools. What sets Simmons apart is its distinctive behavioral focus. This is available nowhere else, and it is available to full-time and part-time students alike.

Simmons offers three M.B.A. program options. The full-time option provides the content of a traditional two-year, four-semester M.B.A. curriculum in an intensive three-semester program. Women who want to parallel work and earnings with education can earn their M.B.A. part-time in either a two-year or a three-year sequence.

The M.B.A. curriculum is a structured sequence of courses, carefully integrated to build upon and reinforce one another. Students take courses in economics, quantitative analysis, accounting, finance, marketing, operations, and strategic planning with a special focus on national and international markets and competition; in the management of organizations—with courses in team strategies, organizational structure, human resources management, communication, and negotiations; and in individual career development. There are electives in advanced accounting, entrepreneurship, corporate and international finance, healthcare management, and product management. Students may also opt for an internship in lieu of an elective.

Students and the M.B.A. Experience

With work experience averaging eight to ten years, students come to Simmons knowing a great deal about themselves and what they want from their education. They include women in the process of career change, women who have reached a career plateau, and women with substantial management experience who want to move up.

In the current class, minority enrollment is 9 percent and international enrollment is 20 percent. Sixty percent of the students majored in the humanities or social sciences, while 40 percent majored in math, economics, or the sciences.

Study groups and structured group projects encourage team development, as leaders and as followers.

The Faculty

Twenty faculty members teach in the M.B.A. program; 15 are women. They are graduates of leading doctoral and M.B.A. programs.

The Business School Network

Corporate Partnerships

Simmons students connect with the New England business community through semester-long consulting projects and internships. Corporate leaders are frequent guest lecturers, and the School partners with corporations, such as pioneering a move to bring current students into the Gillette Corporation's international management trainee program.

The College and Environs

The School is centrally located in Boston's vibrant academic and cultural community just across the Charles River from Cambridge and is within walking distance of the world-renowned Boston Symphony Orchestra and the Museum of Fine Arts.

Relatively compact among major cities, Boston is a walkable city with an old seaport that is now a completely revitalized waterfront with marinas, shops, theaters, island ferries, seafood restaurants, miniparks, and walkways.

Facilities

The School is housed in a historic complex of turn-of-the-century townhouses. Classrooms, administrative and faculty offices, the computer laboratory, and the library are situated within one city block.

The GSM library contains the latest volumes and periodicals in business and business-related fields as well as a media center with videotaping facilities. Students also have access to the Simmons College main campus library as well as several major libraries in the immediate area, including the famous Kirstein Business Library in Boston's financial district.

The College's new Sports Center offers a running track, swimming pool, squash and racquetball court, and exercise equipment.

All the facilities of Simmons College, including the new sports center, are available to GSM students at the main campus, a short distance away.

Technology Environment

The School is equipped with its own microcomputer lab. The computer lab also offers terminals exclusively for work on the Internet and e-mail. Additional microcomputing terminals are available in the undergraduate computing facility.

Through the library's online computer terminals, students can access more than fifty Boston-area university and public library catalogs and forty subject-divided databases, including the Business Periodical Index, Business News Abstracts, Wilson Business Abstracts, and Paperchase (medical information). ABI/Inform, Business Dateline, Morningstar Mutual Funds, SEC/Disclosure, and the National Trade Data Bank are all available on CD-ROM computer workstations. Simmons is a member of the Fenway Library Consortium.

Placement

The Office of Career Development, dedicated to the M.B.A. program, provides personalized and comprehensive career planning and placement services. Advice on appropriate career direction, resume writing, interview preparation, and salary negotiation is integrated with a required Career Strategies course. The office provides students with access to job opportunities through its on-campus recruiting program, functions and industry panels, correspondence recruiting services, job bank, and two job fairs that are attended by a wide range of companies. Approximately 1,000 employers receive the resumes of all graduating students.

Admission

Admission is competitive. The Admissions Committee measures potential for both academic success in the program and professional success thereafter. The committee looks closely at the candidate's preparation for a highly quantitative course of study. It does not follow a formula in making its decisions; rather it evaluates the candidate's ability, aptitude, and promise by examining the whole as revealed in the application materials. An applicant must have at least two years of full-time work experience.

The following materials are needed to fulfill application requirements: a completed application form, an application fee, three letters of recommendation, official transcripts of all academic study beyond high school, and a score report from the GMAT. International students whose native language is not English must submit a TOEFL score. Interviews are strongly encouraged.

Finances

The cost of tuition for the 1998–99 academic year is $596 per credit hour. Forty-five credits are required for the degree. The estimated cost for fees, books, and supplies is $3000.

Financial assistance consists of scholarships, grants, and federal loans, which may be offered separately or in combination. Deans' Scholarships and International Deans' Scholarships are available, and candidates applying to the program are automatically considered. These awards are based on merit. The deadline for scholarship consideration is March 30.

To be considered for aid, a student should file the necessary aid forms by March 1, if possible.

International Students

Fifteen percent of Simmons' full-time M.B.A. students come from outside the United States, with representation this year from Europe, Asia, Africa, and the Caribbean.

Alumnae or current students assist international students on their arrival in the United States, and alumnae have often hosted students until they secure permanent housing.

Application Facts and Dates

The School has a rolling admission policy designed to let students choose their admission decision date. Students are admitted for part-time study in both the fall and spring. Deadlines for part-time study are June 30 for the fall and November 15 for spring. The deadline for full-time study is April 30. For more information, students should contact:

Admission Office
Simmons Graduate School of
  Management
409 Commonwealth Avenue
Boston, Massachusetts 02215
Telephone: 617-521-3840
            800-597-1MBA (toll-free)
Fax: 617-521-3880
E-mail: gsmadm@simmons.edu

SIU Southern Illinois University at Carbondale

College of Business and Administration

Carbondale, Illinois

DEVELOPING BUSINESS LEADERS FOR THE 21ST CENTURY

▶ *The focus of the M.B.A. program at Southern Illinois University at Carbondale (SIUC) is toward preparing students for managerial positions in business and government. To facilitate the learning process, the faculty uses a variety of teaching methods, including case discussions, lectures, guest speakers, computer simulations, and student consulting projects with area businesses. In today's global marketplace, it is important that students learn how to conduct business with people from all parts of the world. At SIUC, students have the opportunity to do that while completing the requirements for the SIUC M.B.A. degree. We are proud that our program attracts international students from a wide variety of countries. It is my pleasure to invite you to consider the M.B.A. program at SIUC.*

—Siva Balasubramanian, Acting Dean

Programs and Curricular Focus

The M.B.A. program at Southern Illinois University at Carbondale is a 33-credit nonthesis program oriented toward preparing students for managerial positions in business and government. Beginning in 1998, the College of Business and Administration is pleased to offer incoming Master of Business Administration (M.B.A.) students three new options. Students may choose among the M.B.A. in international business (IB), the M.B.A. in management of information (MOI), or the M.B.A. in general studies. Students in the general studies M.B.A. program may choose to specialize in a wide variety of areas within the College, including finance, management, and marketing, or outside the College, including agribusiness economics, industrial technology, workforce education, and computer science. The M.B.A. curriculum consists of 33 credit hours of core course work, with additional foundation course requirements for students with nonbusiness undergraduate degrees. The revised M.B.A. program has expanded the elective options, allowing students greater latitude in customizing their learning experience. Students are encouraged to take advantage of the accessibility of graduate faculty members to complete an independent study or thesis in their chosen area of concentration. The M.B.A. program is accredited by AACSB–The International Association for Management Education.

The College of Business and Administration offers three concurrent degree programs. The School of Law (M.B.A./

J.D.), the School of Mass Communication (M.B.A./M.A. in telecommunications), and the School of Agribusiness Economics (M.B.A./M.S. in agribusiness economics) work with the College to provide these unique educational choices. The College offers students the opportunity to study in France through exchange agreements with GROUP ESC Grenoble and GROUPE Sup de Co Montpellier.

Students and the M.B.A. Experience

The M.B.A. program enrolls approximately 120 students. Nearly 50 percent of the students are international and represent approximately twenty different countries. There is an equal number of men and women. Most students have had previous work experience and attend the program full-time. Small class sizes encourage student participation and interaction. Teaching methodology includes case-study and lecture style. Group projects are an integral part of the curriculum.

The Faculty

The M.B.A. faculty, consisting of members of the School of Accountancy and the Departments of Finance, Management, and Marketing, has a true perspective of business. Many faculty members have both traveled extensively and taught in Asia and Europe. Students benefit from studying under professors who have current knowledge about what is happening in the business world. Many of the M.B.A. faculty members have worked in

business and continue to be active as consultants to business firms.

The Business School Network

Top executives from businesses across the nation serve on the College of Business External Advisory Board. The board, which meets twice a year, serves as a group of consultants and advisers to the Dean. The board provides an effective link between business education within the College and business practice within the community. It also serves as a sounding board for programs and activities of the College in areas such as curriculum development, strategic planning, long-range development, and international management.

Many members of the External Advisory Board are alumni of the College of Business and Administration as well as members of the College's Hall of Fame. These senior-level executives represent companies such as Ameritech; A. T. Kearney, Inc.; Caterpillar, Inc.; Cisco Systems; Coopers & Lybrand; Hyatt Corporation; John Deere Foundation; KeyCorp; Northwestern Mutual Life; Peabody Holding Company; The Toro Company; Toshiba; and World Color Press.

The College and Environs

The University is located in Carbondale, Illinois, approximately 100 miles southeast of St. Louis, Missouri. Immediately south of Carbondale are the Illinois Ozarks, some of the most beautiful and rugged terrain in the state. Within 10 miles of campus are two state parks, four recreational lakes, and the 240,000-acre Shawnee National Forest. Camping, caving, rock climbing, boating, hunting, and fishing are just a few of the diversions that are easily accessible. The University was chartered in 1869 and is fully accredited by the North Central Association of Colleges and Schools. There are approximately 22,000 students enrolled.

Facilities

Morris Library, located in the center of the campus and near the College of

Business, contains some 2.2 million volumes, more than 3.2 million units of microforms, and about 12,500 current serial subscriptions. Library users have access to nearly 900 electronic data files and CD-ROM products via multiple workstations located throughout the building and through the Internet (World Wide Web). Up-to-date information about library services is available via the Library Information Networks (LINKS) component of the campuswide computer network or through the library's Web page (http://www.lib.SIU.edu).

Students have access to the University's computing facilities. Network-based resources are provided to desktops by UNIX-based RISC servers and an IBM mainframe (ES/9021-500, with vector processor) and four Computer Learning Centers, with computer classrooms and general access areas equipped with a variety of microcomputers. Housed in the same building as the College is a computer laboratory with IBM-compatible PCs and linkage to the University's computer facilities.

Placement

Career development and placement services are provided by University Career Services and the College's H. Scott Hines Placement Center. Recent graduates have accepted positions with companies such as A. G. Edwards, ABN-AMRO, Allstate, Arthur Andersen Consulting, Caterpillar, Deloitte and Touche LP, KPMG Peat Marwick, McNeill Pharmaceuticals, Pacific Bell Mobile Services, and Southwestern Bell Mobile Systems. Some graduates choose to continue their education toward doctoral as well as other degrees, such as the J.D.

Admission

To be eligible for admissions, applicants must hold a baccalaureate degree from an accredited college or university. Applicants with backgrounds that include the liberal arts and sciences are encouraged to apply. Admission to the program is based on the applicant's undergraduate record, a satisfactory score on the Graduate Management Admission Test (GMAT), and other evidence pertaining to ability to perform well in graduate work

in business administration. Special circumstances and work experience may be considered if presented. No minimum GMAT score is required. All applicants whose primary spoken language is not English must obtain a score of 550 or better on the Test of English as a Foreign Language (TOEFL). The TOEFL must have been taken twenty-four months prior to the semester for which the applicant is seeking admission. If an international applicant has completed at least 100 semester hours of graded course work at an accredited institution in the U.S., the applicant is given the same consideration for admission to the M.B.A. program as a U.S. citizen in regard to the use of English as a foreign language.

Finances

Tuition and fees are established by the Board of Trustees and are subject to change without prior notification. In 1998–99, the per-semester tuition and fees for a student enrolled for 12 credit hours are $1703 (Illinois resident) and $4074 (nonresident). This includes $221 per semester for student medical benefits, which can be waived for students carrying comparable coverage. Southern Illinois University at Carbondale offers residence hall double- and single-occupancy housing for graduate students on a first-come, first-served basis. Efficiency apartments for single graduate students are also available. Family housing is available at two apartment complexes operated by SIUC. Many off-campus rental units are available within walking distance of the campus, including apartments, boarding houses, and mobile homes. Costs for these lodgings vary. In 1998–99, residence hall rates are $1880 for double occupancy and $2427 for single occupancy per semester, including room and board. University apartments rent for $333 per month for an efficiency and $361 per month for a one-bedroom, utilities included.

Graduate assistantships and fellowships provide a monthly salary plus a tuition waiver (fees are not waived). Approximately 25 percent of students receive graduate assistantships through the College. Many more obtain tuition scholarships or find assistantships elsewhere on campus once they are enrolled. Low-interest, federally backed

loans are available through the SIUC Financial Aid Office. Fellowships are awarded on a competitive basis. There are few sources of assistance available to entering international students at the master's level. International students are required to show that they have made satisfactory arrangements to meet their financial obligations at SIUC before admission.

International Students

The International Students and Scholars Office provides a wide range of services and programs for international students. The office is located at Northwest Annex, 860 Lincoln Drive, Building 5, Mail Code 6514, Southern Illinois University at Carbondale, Carbondale, Illinois 62901 (telephone: 618-453-5774; e-mail: iss@siuc.edu). The office may be contacted about housing, financial, and other general questions. Campuswide, international students and scholars total nearly 2,300 and represent 110 countries.

Application Facts and Dates

Admission is permitted for the fall (August), spring (January) and summer (May/June) terms. A nonrefundable application fee of $20 is required. Applications are considered on a rolling basis. The suggested application deadlines are as follows: assistantship applicants, March 15 (fall), September 15 (spring), and February 15 (summer); fellowship applicants, November 15 of the year prior to attendance (fall awards only); other U.S. applicants, June 15 (fall), November 15 (spring), and April 15 (summer); and other international applicants, April 15 (fall), September 15 (spring), and February 15 (summer).

For additional information and questions about the SIUC M.B.A. program, students should contact:

Graduate Programs Office
College of Business and
   Administration
Rehn Hall 133
Mail Code 4625
Southern Illinois University at
   Carbondale
Carbondale, Illinois 62901-4625
Telephone: 618-453-3030
Fax: 618-453-7961
E-mail: mbagp@siuc.edu

SIU Southern Illinois University at Edwardsville

Edwardsville, Illinois

THE SIUE M.B.A.: EDUCATIONAL ENHANCEMENT FOR THE WORKING PROFESSIONAL

▶ *The M.B.A. program offers practicing professionals the opportunity to build an educational foundation for career growth while remaining employed. Classes are taught in the evening and on weekends, using full-time faculty at two locations. Classes are also offered by interactive video to locations on community college campuses in Southern Illinois.*

The faculty is noted for teaching that is current, with respect to theory and practice. Instruction emphasizes the application of concepts and principles to business issues and the development of interpersonal and team-building skills.

Students must develop the oral, written, and critical-thinking skills demanded by the business community to complete the M.B.A. successfully. The program promotes the ability to integrate disciplinary concepts.

—M. Robert Carver Jr., Dean

Programs and Curricular Focus

The M.B.A. curriculum aims at preparing individuals for managerial careers leading to advancement through middle- and upper-level positions in business and not-for-profit organizations.

The M.B.A. degree requires a minimum of 30 hours of graduate-level course work consisting of four required courses (12 hours) plus six elective courses (18 hours). The number of hours to be taken in core and pre-entry courses is determined after an analysis of the candidate's previous academic background. Students complete four required courses: MBA 531, External Environment of Business; MBA 532, International Business Environment; MBA 533, Leadership, Influence, and Managerial Effectiveness; and MBA 534, Strategic Management.

Elective courses provide the opportunity for concentration in one or more of the business disciplines.

Students can earn a specialization in management information systems. The M.B.A./M.I.S. specialization combines management skills with the study of information systems and design.

The M.B.A. program has been accredited by AACSB–The International Association for Management Education since 1975.

Students and the M.B.A. Experience

The typical M.B.A. student is employed on a full-time basis while working on the degree. As such, most students have significant business experience. The average student is 31 years old with eight years of full-time work experience. Women represent 35 percent of the student population.

More than two thirds of the students are professionals such as architects, engineers, lawyers, nurses, or doctors or have management positions as accountants, management analysts, education administrators, financial managers, or marketing managers.

❖ Global Focus

The School of Business has developed student and faculty exchange programs with business schools and universities in France, Great Britain, Mexico, and the Netherlands.

Special Features

In addition to graduate fellowships and department-based graduate assistantships, the program provides students with the possibility of corporate-sponsored assistantships/internships.

The Faculty

The faculty of the School of Business is dedicated to providing high-quality instruction and to the personal and professional development of the students enrolled in the M.B.A. program. The skills and backgrounds of the faculty span nearly the entire range of the research-practical experience continuum.

The Business School Network

Corporate Partnerships

The School's Advisory Board includes business executives from a wide range of fields, and students have several opportunities to meet with these corporate leaders.

Prominent Alumni

Notable business leaders who are alumni of the School of Business include Robert Baer, President and Chief Executive Officer, United Van Lines; Wilton Heylinger, Dean, School of Business, Morris Brown College; Ralph Korte, President, Korte Construction Company; Mitch Meyers, President, Zipatoni Company; and James Milligan, President (retired), Spaulding Sports Centers.

The College and Environs

The Edwardsville campus of Southern Illinois University is located on 2,600 acres of gently rolling hills and timberland near the Mississippi River, 17 miles northeast of St. Louis, Missouri. Current enrollment is approximately 11,000 students, of whom nearly 2,800 are graduate students. Master's-level programs are offered in more than thirty fields.

Facilities

The Elijah P. Lovejoy Library is a member of ILLNET Online, a statewide automated resource-sharing network. Through it, 20 million items at thirty-five academic libraries as well as 800 other Illinois libraries can be identified and borrowed. The library also belongs to the Online Computer Library Center (OCLC), which provides access to collections at more than 13,000 libraries in the United States and forty-five other countries. Special arrangements also permit graduate students access to many of the academic, special, and public libraries in the metropolitan St. Louis area.

Technology Environment

The School of Business has its own microcomputer laboratory with about forty computers for student use. In addition, there are two computerized classrooms with a total of more than sixty microcomputers that are networked to a video-projection system and to the campus backbone fiber-optic network.

Placement

Top international companies regularly conduct on-campus interviews at the Career Development Center. The office also presents numerous workshops covering such topics as job search strategies, interviewing, resume writing, and goal setting. In addition, the office works closely with students to formulate specific career plans.

Admission

The following formula is used by the School of Business to evaluate applicants for the M.B.A. degree program: admission score equals 200 times the undergraduate grade-point average (A=4.0), plus the GMAT score. For unconditional admission, unless otherwise noted, applicants must have a minimum admission score of 950, using the four-year cumulative undergraduate grade-point average, or 1000, using the grade-point average of the last two years of undergraduate courses. Applicants must earn a minimum total score of 400 on the GMAT, with raw scores of at least 20 on both the verbal and quantitative portions of the test, and an Analytical Writing Score of at least 4.0. International students must also earn a score of 550 on the TOEFL examination and submit a test score on the Test of Spoken English (TSE).

Finances

Tuition and fees in 1998–99 for 9 semester hours (three courses) are $1090 for Illinois residents and $2806 for nonresidents. Part-time tuition (6 hours) is $803 for Illinois and St. Louis residents and $1948 for nonresidents. The additional cost of books and supplies varies from $500 to $1000 per year.

Single-student living expenses at the campus Cougar Village apartments are $994 per semester (including utilities), and there is an optional meal plan that costs $100–$500. Family housing is approximately $600 per semester. Housing at the Residence Hall is $1270 per semester plus a required meal plan that costs $665. Off-campus housing is estimated to cost $2000 per semester.

International Students

Special exchange programs are available with schools in England and Mexico. The St. Louis area has many opportunities for international business interests, and the M.B.A. program offers an array of international business courses.

Application Facts and Dates

Students should apply for admission no fewer than five weeks prior to the start of the semester in which they want to begin taking classes. Once the University has received official transcripts and GMAT scores, applicants will be notified as to admission within two weeks. For more information, applicants should contact:

Office of Student Services
School of Business
Box 1086
Southern Illinois University at
    Edwardsville
Edwardsville, Illinois 62026-1086
Telephone: 618-650-3840
Fax: 618-650-3979

FACULTY LIST

Accounting

M. Robert Carver Jr., Professor and Dean; Ph.D. Financial accounting, taxation.
Michael Costigan, Associate Professor and Chairperson; Ph.D. Managerial accounting.
Maurice L. Hirsch Jr., Professor and Associate Dean; Ph.D. Managerial accounting.
Thomas E. King, Professor; Ph.D. Financial accounting, theory.
Linda Lovata, Associate Professor; Ph.D. Accounting systems, managerial accounting.
Alan K. Ortegren, Associate Professor; Ph.D. Financial accounting, theory.
Marsha Puro, Associate Professor; Ph.D. Financial accounting.
Brad Reed, Assistant Professor; Ph.D. Financial accounting, auditing.

Computer Management and Information Systems

Douglas Bock, Professor and Chairperson; Ph.D. Management information systems and design.
Robert W. Klepper, Professor; Ph.D. Management information systems.
Jo Ellen Moore, Assistant Professor; Ph.D. Decision support systems.
John F. Schrage, Associate Professor; Ph.D. Management information systems theory and design.
Mary R. Sumner, Professor; Ed.D. Educational administration, end-user computing, information systems for business-structured systems analysis and design, CASEtools, decision support systems.

David J. Werner, Professor and Chancellor; Ph.D. Management information systems theory and design, simulation.

Economics

David E. Ault, Professor; Ph.D. International economics, labor economics.
Radcliffe G. Edmonds Jr., Associate Professor; Ph.D. Econometrics, international economics.
Donald S. Elliott Jr., Professor and Chairperson; Ph.D. State and local finance.
Rik W. Hafer, Professor; Ph.D. Monetary theory and policy, macroeconomics.
Ali Kutan, Associate Professor; Ph.D. International economics, macroeconomics.
Stanford L. Levin, Professor; Ph.D. Public utility regulation, industrial organization.
An-Yhi Lin, Professor; Ph.D. Econometrics, mathematical economics, economic development.
John B. Meisel, Professor; Ph.D. Industrial organization, antitrust policy.
John C. Navin, Associate Professor; Ph.D. Public finance, labor economics.
Gilbert L. Rutman, Professor; Ph.D. Labor economics, African economic development.

Finance

Rakesh Bharati, Associate Professor; Ph.D. Investment, information economics.
Susan Crain, Assistant Professor; Ph.D. Corporate finance.
Jacky C. So, Professor and Chairperson; Ph.D. International and corporate finance.
Ken Stanton, Assistant Professor; Ph.D. Financial institutions.

Management

Janice R. Joplin, Assistant Professor; Ph.D. Organizational behavior.
Kathryn Martell, Associate Professor; Ph.D. Strategy, international.
Joseph F. Michlitsch, Associate Professor; Ph.D. Organizational theory, strategy, and policy.
Gertrude Pannirselvam, Assistant Professor; Ph.D. Production and operations management.
Timothy S. Schoenecker, Assistant Professor; Ph.D. Strategy.
Donald E. Strickland, Professor and Chairperson; Ph.D. Organizational behavior.
George M. Sullivan, Professor; J.D. Regulation, business law, organizational design, business and society.
Laura Swanson, Assistant Professor; Ph.D., candidate. Production and operations management.
John M. Virgo, Professor; Ph.D. Manpower planning, business and society.

Marketing

Ralph W. Giacobbe, Associate Professor; Ph.D. Marketing research, consumer behavior, personal selling, services marketing, product marketing.
Jack Kaikati, Professor and Chairperson; D.B.A. International marketing, marketing management.
Raymond F. LaGarce, Professor; Ph.D. Marketing strategy, management, promotion management.
James M. Lynch, Associate Professor; J.D., Ph.D. Advertising and promotion, marketing research.
Madhav Segal, Professor; Ph.D. Marketing research and information management, product/services marketing management.

Edwin L. Cox School of Business

Dallas, Texas

REAL BUSINESS EDUCATION FOR REAL BUSINESS LEADERS

Getting an M.B.A. education certainly broadens your understanding of fundamental business theories, but the Cox M.B.A. does more. Our special programs and connections to the business community can make all the difference in your career.

Through our unique Business Leadership Center, you receive training in leadership and management skills—subjects not taught at most business schools. Our Associate Board Executive Mentor Program complements your classroom learning by matching you with a senior business executive who can provide additional career coaching and networking relationships throughout your career. We are here not just to launch careers but to enrich the lives of our students. At the Cox School, we create real business leaders by providing a real business experience.

—Albert J. Niemi Jr., Dean

Programs and Curricular Focus

The Cox M.B.A. program provides an integrated curriculum that helps students establish a solid foundation for success in business. The small class size encourages students to work closely with the faculty and individualize their M.B.A. experience. Located in Dallas, a national and international business center, the Cox School M.B.A. program offers nationally recognized faculty members, a global focus, and close ties with the business community. At Cox, M.B.A.'s gain much more than a business education—they gain a personalized business experience.

The two-year M.B.A. curriculum is composed of 60 credit hours, or twenty courses. In the first year, students complete eight core courses and have an opportunity to take two electives. Second-year students take two core courses and may select eight electives. Electives allow students to develop an emphasis in areas such as finance, business policy, marketing, entrepreneurship, accounting, organizational behavior, business administration, management information systems, and real estate.

Cox's unique Business Leadership Center (BLC) complements the classroom curriculum throughout the two-year period. Designed to help students develop effective management skills, the BLC's innovative program hones leadership and team skills through seminars centered on interpersonal and communication skills, team building, and negotiation skills. Courses are organized by business leaders

and taught by outside consultants from some of today's most progressive corporations.

In addition to the full-time two-year M.B.A. program, Cox offers a part-time, three-year professional M.B.A. program developed for working professionals and a twenty-one-month executive M.B.A. program for candidates with significant managerial experience.

Joint-degree programs are offered in conjunction with the law school for a Juris Doctor/M.B.A. (four years) and with the Meadows School of Arts for a Master of Arts in administration/M.B.A. (six semesters).

Students and the M.B.A. Experience

Cox students come from all regions of the United States and the world. The M.B.A. program consists of more than 250 full-time students, with approximately 25 percent hailing from countries other than the U.S. Students have a wide variety of academic disciplines and professional experiences. The average amount of work experience prior to entering the M.B.A. program is slightly more than four years, and the average age is approximately 27. Women comprise nearly 30 percent of the population, and minorities account for approximately 8 percent of the student body.

Because Cox enrolls one of the smallest classes among the top twenty-five U.S. business schools, a rapport not found in larger programs exists among students and between students and staff

and faculty members. The small size also gives students opportunities to take on more extensive leadership roles in M.B.A. organizations such as the Finance Club, the Investment Club, the Marketing Association, Women in Business, the Energy Club, and the Entrepreneur and Venture Capital Club.

❖ Global Focus

Today's business leaders must be global thinkers. Cox M.B.A. courses integrate international perspectives throughout the two-year program. Global classroom learning is also enhanced by the nearly 25 percent of students who come from countries other than the U.S. The School's location at the gateway to NAFTA and Latin America is well-positioned for enhancing international perspectives.

An international study program allows select students to experience their international business education firsthand by studying abroad. Cox has relationships with schools in Australia, Belgium, Brazil, Denmark, England, France, Japan, Mexico, Singapore, Spain, and Venezuela. Students study at one of these institutions for one semester, leveraging the opportunity to strengthen regional focus or enhance a particular area of study.

Special Features

In addition to the Business Leadership Center, the Cox School's specialized institutes supplement the traditional classroom experience. The Caruth Institute of Owner-Managed Business focuses on entrepreneurship, the Maguire Oil & Gas Institute promotes the study of oil and gas markets and issues, and the SMU Finance Institute promotes interaction between financial practitioners and the SMU finance community. Like the Business Leadership Center, all Cox institutes provide a forum for students, faculty members, and the business community to participate in interactive programs and research.

The Faculty

Cox students benefit from a nationally recognized faculty that is approachable and accessible and is as dedicated to teaching as it is to research. Classes are taught using a variety of teaching methods that are best suited for the course material, including cases, lectures, class discussions, student presentations, team and field projects, and computer simulations. The Cox M.B.A. curriculum is developed to equally emphasize quantitative and qualitative skills.

The Business School Network

Executive Mentor Program

At Cox, interaction with the business community is encouraged and formalized for students. Because Cox believes that an M.B.A. education should serve as a catalyst for career development, the School established the Associate Board Executive Mentor Program with more than 150 top business executives who actively serve as mentors to Cox M.B.A. students.

The structure of the student/mentor relationship is as diverse as the individuals participating in the program. In addition to being a valuable source of industry-specific business contacts, a mentor relationship can provide students with insightful career advice, an inside track on current business trends, and a valuable perspective from an experienced business person.

Prominent Alumni

Prominent Cox alumni include Howard M. Dean, CEO and Director, Dean Foods; Martin Flanagan, Senior Vice President and CFO, Franklin Resources; Charles Hansen Jr., Chairman and CEO, Pillowtex Corporation; James MacNaughton, Managing Director, Salomon Smith Barney; Ken Morris, Senior Vice President and Chief Technology Officer, PeopleSoft; John J. Murphy, former Chairman, President, and CEO, Dresser Industries; William O'Neill, Chairman, Investor's Business Daily; Eckhard Pfeiffer, CEO, Compaq Computers; and John Tolleson, former Chairman and CEO, First USA.

The College and Environs

SMU, established in 1911, has six different schools and graduate programs in addition to its undergraduate program. The total undergraduate and graduate population is approximately 9,100 students.

The University's location in one of the world's major centers of commerce gives students an excellent advantage. The city of Dallas ranks third in the United States as a site of major corporate headquarters and sixth in the world for multinational corporate headquarters. The city offers a wide variety of cultural events and opportunities, from national league sports to the nationally renowned Myerson Symphony Center and the Dallas Museum of Art.

Technology Environment

From state-of-the-art classrooms to the newly renovated Business Information Center, the Cox School offers the latest in business technologies. Students utilize an in-house network (accessible from home) to communicate with other students and faculty members, connect with the Internet to conduct classroom assignments, and access numerous business databases and research tools.

Placement

The M.B.A. Career Management Office (CMO) seeks to equip students with the skills and opportunities to develop and implement successful career strategies. Students participate in the Career

Management Training Program, a series of required and optional workshops designed to enhance a student's success in the competitive job search process. M.B.A. students receive individualized career counseling sessions year-round and have access to significant opportunities for recruiting on campus and through resume referrals.

Admission

Admission to the M.B.A. programs at the Edwin L. Cox School of Business is highly selective. The Cox School seeks a diverse student body and encourages applications from students with a wide variety of academic backgrounds and work experiences. The Admissions Committee seeks to admit students who represent various geographic, economic, religious, and ethnic groups.

Successful applicants are well-rounded individuals who have clearly demonstrated academic achievement in addition to a commitment and capacity for leadership in today's dynamic business world. Candidates should demonstrate such qualities as leadership ability, initiative, management potential, written communication skills, interpersonal skills, and an entrepreneurial spirit.

Finances

The cost of tuition and fees for 1998–99 is estimated at $22,298; books and supplies are approximately $1200. Off-campus housing generally costs between $550 and $1100 per month. Scholarships are available and are awarded strictly on merit.

Application Facts and Dates

Students enter the full-time program in the fall semester only (orientation is held mid-August). Application deadlines for all applicants to the full-time M.B.A. program are as follows: early decision, November 30; first read, February 15; and second read, April 15. Applications received after April 15 are evaluated on a space-available basis only.

Students enter the part-time program in the fall and spring (orientation is held mid-January). The application deadline for fall admission is May 15; for spring admission, November 1.

Donna Lau Smith
Director of M.B.A. Admissions
Edwin L. Cox School of Business
Southern Methodist University
P.O. Box 750333
Dallas, Texas 75275-0333
Telephone: 214-768-2630
          800-472-3622 (toll-free)
Fax: 214-768-3956
E-mail: mbainfo@mail.cox.smu.edu
World Wide Web: http://www.cox.smu.edu

State University of New York at Albany

BUSINESS TODAY: INFORMATION SYSTEMS AT THE CORE

We at the University at Albany believe that the creative application of information systems to business functions is the key to business growth. Therefore, the design and application of information systems for business and industry are at the core of our master's programs. Our goal is to develop leaders who have both the managerial and technical competence to navigate wisely through the world of information and the ethical and moral compass to use it for improving the human condition. A master's degree from the University at Albany School of Business can be your key to success in the age of information.

The University at Albany is also one of the best values in education today. Whether you're a New York resident or are from out of state, you'll find the School of Business to be one of the most affordable graduate programs in the Northeast. Couple that affordability with our commitment to the highest educational standards, and University at Albany graduate business programs are ones you won't want to overlook.

—Donald D. Bourque, Dean

Programs and Curricular Focus

Albany's graduate programs are focused on the information age, weaving information systems and state-of-the-art technology into the entire curriculum. The School offers an M.B.A. with concentrations in finance, human resource/information systems, management information systems, and marketing and M.S. degrees in accounting and taxation. In keeping with the dynamic quality of modern business, the education provided at Albany emphasizes problem-solving techniques and analysis rather than memorization.

Albany's first-year M.B.A. curriculum includes instruction in financial reporting, analysis, and markets; domestic and global economic environments; creation and distribution of goods and services; and human behavior in organizations. The global issues that form the context for business are integrated into courses throughout the curriculum and are specifically covered in global management, which integrates key management functions with the social, legal, and political implications of conducting business in an international environment.

In the second year, small classes (10 to 30 students) ensure a higher degree of interaction with faculty members. Areas of concentration are closely connected to real-world needs of important markets, and faculty-supervised consulting projects (field projects) offer students the opportunity to apply concepts and principles taught in the classroom to real-world problems.

Albany has one of the only human resource/information systems concentrations of its kind in the country, enhanced by two of today's premier HR information systems software packages (PeopleSoft and Humanic Design) so that students learn by using the actual software they are likely to use in their careers.

Albany's accounting programs accommodate students with or without an undergraduate accounting degree. Graduates of any bachelor's degree program can study for two years, receive an M.S. in accounting, and qualify to take the CPA examination. Students with undergraduate degrees in accounting can earn their master's degree in one year, specializing in taxation or information systems. Both of these programs qualify to reduce the experience requirement for the CPA. Pass rates on the CPA examination of graduates of these programs are in the top 10 percent in the nation.

In addition to the full-time M.B.A. program, the School offers several part-time programs, including an evening M.B.A. program, a weekend program, and a joint M.B.A. program with the Graduate School of Business Administration in Zurich, Switzerland.

Students and the M.B.A. Experience

An interactive team-building orientation at the beginning of the first year, many group projects, and small classes in the second year all contribute to the Albany M.B.A. experience. A diverse student body helps students learn firsthand about working with people of different ages, cultures, ethnic origins, and professional backgrounds. Student organizations also help to promote collegiality. Students typically come from ten to twelve countries, which, in an entering class of 80 to 85, gives a relatively high proportion of international students and increases the opportunities for gaining insights into business customs and practices around the globe.

Special Features

Two distinguishing elements of the University at Albany full-time M.B.A. programs are the first-year global management course and the second-year field project. Global management, a 4-credit-hour course taken in the second semester, gives the student an intensive overview of international business practices.

The field project is the centerpiece of several of the School's concentrations. This nine-month consulting project for a major company or state agency provides students concrete, hands-on experience that prepares them for positions with dynamic organizations and gives them a competitive advantage in the job market.

The Faculty

Albany's faculty includes nationally and internationally known specialists in areas such as management information systems, change management, taxation, consumer behavior, leadership, finance, and marketing. It includes a well-known authority on fixed-income securities, several internationally renowned scholars in the field of data quality, internationally known specialists in decision support systems, and a best-selling author. Many faculty members are sought after internationally as consultants, researchers, and teachers. They bring research and academic knowledge, practical experi-

ence, and a real interest in teaching to the classroom to enrich the students' learning experience. Without exception, they are dedicated to their profession and to ensuring that students receive a high-quality education and are prepared to enter the world of business.

The Business School Network

Corporate Partnerships

The School has developed strong ties in the corporate world through field projects and through its alumni, who return to Albany recruiting for their companies. In the capital region, the School's relationships and presence in the business community afford students opportunities to work on real business projects.

Prominent Alumni

The School's alumni have made their marks far and wide. They include high-ranking executives at Arthur Andersen & Co., Andersen Consulting, Goldman Sachs, American Management Systems, Chase Manhattan Bank, the Travelers Group, Deloitte & Touche, Price Waterhouse, Deutsch Morgan Greenfield Bank, KFC Division of Pepsico, Sony Corporation of America, Bristol-Myers Squibb, Lehman Brothers, Pfizer Pharmaceuticals, Ernst & Young, and Merrill Lynch Municipal Bond Research, to name just a few.

The College and Environs

The University at Albany is one of four graduate research University Centers in the State University of New York System. Enrolling 16,000 students, the University is noted for academic excellence and a commitment to access and diversity. The capital region offers students a host of internship and work opportunities in government, finance, education, business, and the arts. The campus is easily accessible by air, rail, auto, and bus.

Facilities

The University's libraries house more than 1.8 million volumes and take full advantage of emerging information technologies. Through a combination of computer-based user interfaces, electronic archives, and links to local and global computer networks, the University libraries offer a broad range of powerful search and retrieval tools. The Interactive Media Center contains an impressive array of commercially produced software and media. Students also have access to the New York State Library, which houses more than 19 million books, documents, maps, and other resources. The School of Business maintains several computer labs for the use of business students, including a new facility, opened in fall 1997, exclusively for the use of first-year graduate students. Each of the five areas of concentration has a computer lab designated for its second-year students. In addition, the University maintains four public user rooms that are available to School of Business students. All classrooms are wired for Internet access, and five mobile presentation systems are available for classroom use by faculty members and students.

Placement

The School of Business is especially successful in placing graduates. The School has a highly interactive Office of Career Services that teaches students how to market themselves in order to give them the edge they need to land good jobs. The School's faculty members are committed to seeing students placed in good jobs and devote much time and energy to the placement process. In addition, an extensive network of alumni in key positions in the business world helps open important doors for Albany graduates. The University also maintains a comprehensive Career Development Center that is available for all students.

Admission

To apply to the School of Business, students must submit a completed and signed application, official transcripts of all previous graduate and undergraduate course work, the official report of the Graduate Management Admission Test (GMAT), three letters of recommendation, and the application fee. Admission is based on all components of the application, with particular emphasis on GMAT scores and undergraduate grade point average. Work experience and a demonstrated ability to be successful in the program are also taken into consideration. The average GMAT score is approximately 565 (computed using the scores of all admitted students); the average undergraduate GPA is approximately 3.2.

Finances

For 1998–99, full-time tuition for New York residents is $2550 per semester; for out-of-state and international students, full-time tuition is $4208 per semester. For part-time students (those taking fewer than 12 credits per semester), tuition is $213 per credit for New York residents and $351 per credit for nonresidents. Graduate assistantships are awarded on the basis of prior academic record and previous work experience. Assistantship stipends range from $2750 to $6000 per year plus a tuition scholarship commensurate with the award. The Barry L. Gold Scholarship was established in memory of an Albany M.B.A. alumnus and is given to individuals who demonstrate both academic excellence and financial need and who are entering full-time graduate study in the School of Business. Loans, grants, and work-study aid are awarded by the University based on financial need. Approximately 25 percent of all students receive some form of financial aid from the School of Business. Students interested in applying for financial aid should submit their applications and requests for aid by March 1.

Application Facts and Dates

The University at Albany uses a rolling admission process, evaluating applications in order of receipt and completion. Applicants receive a decision approximately four weeks after the School receives a completed application. Applications should be submitted and complete by July 1. To obtain an application or for additional information, students should contact:

Office of Graduate Admissions,
   AD 112
SUNY at Albany
Albany, New York 12222
Telephone: 800-UALBANY (toll-free)
   (mention code PET)
World Wide Web: http://www.albany.
   edu/business

State University of New York at Binghamton

School of Management

Binghamton, New York

EDUCATING MEN AND WOMEN FOR LEADERSHIP POSITIONS

The School of Management's programs reflect our commitment to educating men and women for leadership positions in a variety of career fields. Our graduates are leaders in entrepreneurship, university teaching and research, and management of small businesses, major corporations, government and social agencies, and arts organizations. Underlying each of our programs is the conviction that a well-developed sense of social responsibility and an ethical approach are essential characteristics of leadership in all fields of endeavor. We make a serious commitment to those students selected for our programs, and the relationship between the School and every student lasts the whole of each one's career. As a Binghamton University graduate, you will become one of the outstanding individuals who have earned and are expanding the international reputation for excellence enjoyed by the University and the School of Management.

—Glenn A. Pitman, Dean

Programs and Curricular Focus

The School of Management has designed a curriculum to prepare students with the essential skill set needed to be competitive in today's rapidly changing corporate, nonprofit, or public sectors. The next generation of leaders will be expected to combine technical competence with a keen sense of the skills necessary for effective persuasion and negotiation. Consequently, Binghamton instills a generalist's perspective, integrating business fundamentals to bring about creative solutions that are new, different, and better.

The Four Semester program is designed for students who wish to combine their liberal arts, fine arts, science, or engineering background with business to create a dynamic career track. While no prerequisite business course work is required, a working knowledge of calculus and well-developed English and computer skills are expected. Spring and fall enrollment are available. The first year consists of core courses that provide the base for more individualized study in the second year. In addition, the first year emphasizes the role of managers in today's society by integrating social responsibility, leadership, and cultural sensitivity. The second year includes advanced course work in each field while offering an opportunity to focus on a career specialization. Faculty members work as teams in the classroom, integrat-

ing selected course material to illustrate the links across disciplines.

The Fast Track program offers an accelerated nine-month M.B.A. for students carefully selected based upon their solid foundation in business essentials. Only students who have graduated within three years from a school accredited by AACSB–The International Association for Management Education or the equivalent are accepted. Courses basically consist of the third and fourth semester of the Four Semester program. Only fall admission is available.

Binghamton also offers an M.B.A. with a specialization in arts management. The program consists of core and advanced business courses with specialized arts management electives. Most students come to this program with an undergraduate degree in the visual or performing arts along with work experience in their field.

Students and the M.B.A. Experience

A growing number of students come to the University with several years of varied work experience. Most are from the northeastern United States, but, increasingly, students are drawn from other parts of the country and from abroad. This diversity enriches the fabric of life at the School of Management. About 40 percent of incoming students have a liberal arts and sciences degree,

and 10 percent have training in engineering. More than 50 percent of incoming students are women, and the average age is 27 years. Fifteen percent are members of minority groups, and 33 percent are international students from more than eight countries.

The Faculty

The School of Management's 48 faculty members bring expertise in a wide range of theoretical, cultural, and practical perspectives. Faculty members come from top universities throughout the world and have published articles and books in the most prestigious journals in their respective fields. Teaching is highly valued; several faculty members have been honored with the University's top teaching awards.

The Business School Network

Binghamton encourages all students to participate in an internship as part of their M.B.A. experience. The Corporate Associates Program provides one such opportunity by allowing students to intern with top-level managers at local companies, such as Lockheed-Martin and New York State Electric and Gas. Top-level managers from throughout the country are also invited to Binghamton to meet with students in the Executive-in-Residence program.

The School has also developed a mentor program to sharpen student skills through working one-on-one with a business professional. Students meet with their mentors several times over the course of the year to discuss how to apply classroom learning to real business situations.

The College and Environs

Binghamton's campus is compactly designed, well maintained, and noted for its scenic setting on a wooded hillside near the Susquehanna River. The University has a 1.5-million volume multibranch research library, a state-of-the-art computer center, and exceptional facilities for the fine and performing arts, including several theaters, music listening and practice rooms, and dance, art,

sculpture, and graphics studios. Exhibitions and performances by University groups and internationally known artists add to the cultural richness of the campus. Extensive recreational and physical education facilities are also available. The Nature Preserve, a 117-acre forest and wetland area with a 6-acre pond, forms the southern boundary of the campus.

Placement

Students benefit from the many services and resources offered by the Career Development Office. The office staff assists students with meeting immediate career goals as well as with lifelong career planning. Specially trained counselors are available to work with students one-on-one as requested; however, the vast resources of the office make it easy to self-direct a job search.

Services offered by the Binghamton Career Development Office include resume development, a candidate referral system, campus interviews, a job hotline, individual counseling, career workshops, a career resource library, an alumni career network, and a career development Web page.

Admission

General requirements are a baccalaureate degree from a college or university of recognized standing, two official transcripts of all previous college work, two letters of recommendation from persons acquainted with the applicant's academic achievements (for recent graduates) or with work-related performance (for those currently employed), official Graduate Management Admission Test (GMAT) scores, and a personal statement. Careful consideration is given to each of these

items during the admission process. The Test of English as a Foreign Language (TOEFL) is required of most applicants whose native language is not English; a minimum score of 570 is generally required for admission.

Finances

Estimated costs for full-time study for the 1998–99 academic year are as follows: annual tuition and fees for state residents, $5591, and, for nonresidents, $8907; housing and meals, $6144; and health insurance (twelve months), $248. These costs are subject to change and vary with a student's standard of living and costs for books, supplies, travel, and miscellaneous items. Preterm fees apply only in the first year and vary depending on the program.

Application Facts and Dates

Admission to the Fast Track program takes place only for the fall semester. The Four Semester program allows admission during the fall or spring, with a required summer term for spring admissions. Applications are reviewed on a rolling basis and should be submitted no later than sixty days before the start of the semester in which a student plans to enroll. Applicants receive a decision within one month from the time that the completed application is received.

Graduate Admissions
School of Management
Binghamton University
P.O. Box 6015
Binghamton, New York 13902-6015
Telephone: 607-777-2316
E-mail: mba@binghamton.edu
World Wide Web:
    http://som.binghamton.edu

State University of New York at Buffalo

Buffalo, New York

BUILDING SUCCESS; IMPACTING THE FUTURE

At the State University of New York at Buffalo we have developed an M.B.A. program that combines the thinking of today's best scholars and managers with a solid background in management fundamentals. We thoroughly prepare our students for career success through a curriculum that brings the real world into the classroom for discussion and analysis of management practices across every major business discipline. In recent years, our M.B.A. program has been infused with a dynamic customer service approach to management education that enables us to quickly respond to the needs of students and to the emerging trends of business. Our goal is to produce M.B.A. graduates qualified to make an immediate impact within any business environment, anywhere in the world. This philosophy has earned our M.B.A. program a reputation for excellence nationwide and across international boundaries; a reputation that continues to grow with the successes of our students.

—Lewis Mandell, Dean

Programs and Curricular Focus

According to *The Gourman Report* ranking, the School of Management is considered to be the leading business school in the State University of New York (SUNY) system. The M.B.A. program is defined by a combination of attributes that are rare among business schools today: outstanding value and exceptional educational quality. Accredited by the American Assembly of Collegiate Schools of Business, the M.B.A. provides students with a thorough understanding of management fundamentals, complemented by specialized instruction in state-of-the-art business theory and an introduction to new developments in management practices. Students progress through their studies as members of cohort groups, a feature that encourages team building and group projects, which are foundations of the program.

The two-year, 60-credit, full-time program is built around a new 30-hour core and flex-core curriculum that require students to complete nine courses in their first year, which prepares them to select one of the ten majors offered in the program. Upon completion of the core, students begin to target their career direction and customize their program by choosing electives within their major. Students are also required to participate in the School's highly regarded internship program, considered to be one of the largest and best in the country according

to national statistics and student satisfaction surveys. The School of Management receives more than 1,000 requests for interns per year from businesses, so students can select opportunities most valuable to their career goals. Upon completion of the curriculum, students will have developed the critical-thinking, problem-solving, and career skills necessary for success in a global business environment.

Dual degree programs are available in law (J.D./M.B.A.), medicine (M.D./M.B.A.), architecture (M. Arch./M.B.A.), and geography (M.A./M.B.A.). The School of Management also offers joint undergraduate/M.B.A. degree programs in computer science, economics, engineering, geography, management, pharmacy, and sociology, which generally allow for completion of both degrees in five years instead of six. A three-year, part-time Professional M.B.A. program, a 22-month Executive M.B.A. program, and a Ph.D. in management program are also offered. A one-year Master of Science in Accounting program was recently launched at the School of Management.

Students and the M.B.A. Experience

The full-time student population of the M.B.A. program is composed of 300 talented individuals who come from a variety of backgrounds and possess a variety of prior work experiences. The

average age of students is 26 years. Twenty-five percent of the M.B.A. student population is international, and 38 percent are women. Students readily become acquainted with each other and draw from one another's experiences and expertise as a result of the program's emphasis on team building and group projects. Many students receive tuition stipends through assistantship and fellowship programs.

❖ Global Focus

The M.B.A. program offers students the opportunity to gain invaluable international business experience and acquire an understanding of cultural differences that have an impact on business operations in a global marketplace through participation in the international internship program. Students who have participated in the program in the past have worked summers for multinational companies in Argentina, Belgium, Brazil, China, and Indonesia. The School also has student exchange programs with institutions in Finland, France, Germany, Mexico, and Singapore.

Faculty members at the School of Management bring an international perspective to all M.B.A. courses as a result of their participation in the School's Executive M.B.A. Program in Singapore, the first U.S.-accredited M.B.A. program in that country. The School also operated the first U.S. M.B.A. program in China and draws on the expertise of alumni from that program to benefit students who wish to pursue international business careers.

Special Features

The innovative M.B.A. Advantage program greatly enhances the educational experience of its students by providing them with opportunities to develop professional, personal, and career skills that will give them a competitive edge in the job market. During a series of fun and informative activities and seminars, which begin during student orientation and continue throughout students' M.B.A. careers, students receive valuable instruction in team skills, problem solving, networking, and even business

University at Buffalo M.B.A. students regularly meet with corporate executives to discuss job opportunities and trends in various business fields.

etiquette, among other topics. M.B.A. Advantage is also an excellent way to get to know fellow students.

The Faculty

The M.B.A. faculty includes internationally renowned scholars in the fields of accounting, finance, management science and systems, marketing, and organization and human resources. Many faculty members have had articles published in top-tier academic journals, and their expertise and research is often cited by national business publications that cover important trends in business. Six faculty members have received the prestigious SUNY Chancellor's Award for Excellence in Teaching.

The Business School Network

Buffalo is home to several large, multinational companies and numerous successful small and mid-size businesses that offer important resources for the M.B.A curriculum. For instance, nine national companies have adopted courses in the School's core M.B.A. curriculum as part of an unique program in which corporate executives give students an insider's look at company operations and strategies. Called Adopt-A-Course, this nationally cited program gives classroom theory a real-world atmosphere and is very popular with students and faculty.

Students also have access to the expertise of business leaders through the M.B.A. program's executive luncheon series, during which small groups of students meet with executives to discuss business operations and job opportunities in specific business fields.

Prominent alumni of the School of Management include Mickey Drexler,

CEO of The Gap; Linda Wachner, CEO of Warnaco; Tanri Abeng, president of Wisma Bakrie; Robert Rich Sr., chairman and founder of Rich Products; and David Gasiewicz, general manager of worldwide infrastructure operations for Microsoft.

The College and Environs

The School of Management is part of SUNY at Buffalo, New York's premier public center for graduate and professional education and the state's largest and most comprehensive public university. As the only public member of the prestigious Association of American Universities in New York and New England, the University at Buffalo ranks high among the nation's leading universities.

The second-largest city in New York State, Buffalo offers big-city attractions and convenience, while still being safe, livable, and easygoing. Buffalo has a first-rate orchestra; one of the leading modern art collections in the world, located in the Albright-Knox Art Gallery; a downtown theater district; professional sports teams; and a lively nightlife.

Placement

The Award of Excellence recently presented to the School's Career Resource Center by the National Association of Colleges and Employers (NACE), is a testament to the outstanding service students receive from the center's talented staff. The Career Resource Center works with a wide variety of national firms to bring interviewers to the campus. It also participates in annual national M.B.A. consortia in Washington, D.C. and Chicago, exclusive corporate interviewing events for M.B.A. students from the

nation's top business schools. The center also provides career counseling and job-search workshops and links students to successful alumni through its innovative telementor program. Average starting salaries of the School's M.B.A graduates have risen 17 percent in the past year due mainly to the efforts of the center's staff members.

Admission

Individuals holding a bachelor's degree or an equivalent degree from an accredited college or university are welcome to apply to the M.B.A. program. Submission of a GMAT score is required. International students must submit a minimum score of 550 on the TOEFL and provide proof of adequate funds.

Average GMAT scores for accepted students typically range from 580 to 600, and full-time students possess an average of 2.5 years of prior work experience. The nature and length of prior work experience, leadership attributes, and undergraduate GPA also factor into the admission process.

Finances

Tuition for 1998–99 is $5100 per year for in-state students and $8416 per year for out-of-state students. A limited number of assistantships, fellowships, and scholarships for qualified students are offered. Prospective students should plan to take the GMAT as early as possible and should ideally complete their application by March 1 to be eligible for financial support. In general, graduate assistants receive a full or partial tuition waiver and stipend in return for a specified amount of work for a professor or administrator. Scholarships can take the form of one-time cash awards or on-going financial assistance.

Application Facts and Dates

The application deadline for the full-time M.B.A. program is July 1. Students are admitted for the fall semester only. Once an application file is complete with all required official documents, a prospective student is usually notified within one month. For more information, applicants should contact:

Katherine M. Gerstle
Assistant Dean and Administrative
    Director of the M.B.A. Program
State University of New York at
    Buffalo
206 Jacobs Management Center
Buffalo, New York 14260-4000
Telephone: 716-645-3204
Fax: 716-645-2341
E-mail: sommba@mgt.buffalo.edu
World Wide Web: www.mgt.buffalo.
    edu

State University of New York at Stony Brook

Stony Brook, New York

MANAGING IN THE TWENTY-FIRST CENTURY

Businesses now operate penitentiaries and school districts. Nonprofit organizations compete with businesses in health-care delivery. Governments both regulate and encourage trade. One lesson is clear: business managers need to understand and be prepared to deal with nonprofit organizations and government agencies.

At Harriman, we take this to heart. Our curriculum integrates knowledge about the three sectors into almost every course. Our Internship Program and Group Project course provide students with hands-on experience in all three sectors. Our faculty members perform research on the questions that arise as the sectors relate with one another.

This is how the Harriman School stands out among its peers. Come join the excitement!

—Dr. Thomas R. Sexton, Director

Programs and Curricular Focus

The W. Averell Harriman School for Management and Policy offers programs of study leading to the Master of Science degree in management and policy and the Master of Science degree in technology management. The curriculum for the M.S. in management and policy consists of eighteen courses totaling 60 credits, of which thirteen courses constitute the core. The remaining courses are electives that can be packaged to provide specialization in areas such as finance and economics, health-care management, human resource management, information systems management, and operations management. Three of the master's degree elective options lead to a New York State Advanced Certificate: human resource management, health-care management, and information systems management.

The M.S. degrees from the Harriman School are virtually identical to the M.B.A. degree. The School's curriculum devotes the same attention to managerial functions, such as accounting, finance, human resources, marketing, and operations, as do standard M.B.A. programs. Similarly, the Harriman School program, like leading M.B.A. programs, includes course work in economics, information systems, decision models, statistics, and strategy. Yet, the Harriman School program goes beyond most M.B.A. programs by exploring ways in which business, government, and nonprofit organizations interact. This is in keeping with the School's philosophy that

managers in the twenty-first century must be well versed in all three sectors to be truly effective.

For students interested in government, the Harriman School M.S. in management and policy is similar to an M.P.A. (Master of Public Administration). The principal difference is that the Harriman School program places more emphasis on computer information systems, quantitative decision analysis, and the interactions of government with business and nonprofit organizations. These are the areas that make the difference between a Harriman School graduate and one from a typical M.P.A. program. For students interested in nonprofit management, the Harriman program provides a rare educational experience. Students who are exposed to broad management issues are especially well prepared for careers in nonprofit management.

The Harriman School offers two additional programs to students who qualify: the Advanced Credit Program and the Technology Management Program. The Advanced Credit Program is designed to supplement previous graduate education with management and policy analysis. The program consists of ten courses and an internship. The program normally leads to the M.S. in management and policy in one year.

The Technology Management Program is a part-time program for midcareer professionals and executives. A specially designed series of modules, offered one night per week and every other Saturday,

leads to the M.S. degree in technology management in two academic years. The program focuses on utilizing technology to better manage human and physical resources in industries characterized by rapid technological change. Applicants are expected to have at least four years of relevant experience; many have educational backgrounds in science, technology, or engineering.

Students and the Program Experience

Harriman's master's students are a diverse group. Students from all over the world bring their unique personal and career-related experiences to the program. Many students come to Harriman following their undergraduate work, while others are established members of the business community seeking to broaden their career opportunities. The Harriman program exposes all students to theoretical and practical aspects of management.

Students gain practical experience through participation in the eight- to twelve-week paid internship program. Full-time students typically complete the internship requirement during the summer between their first and second years. Students benefit from the program by gaining career-related experience. Students also establish contacts in business, government, or nonprofit organizations, depending on their interests.

Harriman students gain additional experience through participation in a group project course in which students, in conjunction with faculty members, serve as consultants to clients who request assistance for various projects. Students acquire hands-on experience and provide a valuable service to business, government, and nonprofit organizations.

The Faculty

Faculty members of the Harriman School are strongly committed to teaching and fostering working relationships with students inside and outside the classroom, while maintaining their involvement in research. In their research, Harriman professors examine complex issues and problems confronting today's managers and decision makers in high-technology businesses, nonprofit organizations, and government agencies. They analyze businesses and other institutions as well as the economic, regulatory, and technological forces underlying decision-making processes and ongoing changes within these organizations. They keep close contact not only with other researchers in the United States and abroad, but also with regional, national, and international businesses by conducting applied research projects and working as consultants.

Harriman School students benefit from this high-caliber research in several ways. Faculty members often revise and develop new course materials to incorporate current research into their teaching and instruction. They strongly believe that exposing students to the latest knowledge and management skills best prepares them for future challenges while making the classroom experience dynamic and stimulating. Harriman students work closely with professors, and all students are invited to participate in seminars conducted by the School's researchers.

The Business School Network

The location of the Harriman School within the College of Engineering and Applied Sciences provides the Harriman School with a unique link to regional industry. The Harriman School participates in the Strategic Partnership for Industrial Resurgence (SPIR), which provides funds from New York State to promote relationships between the School and the business community. Students are encouraged to work with faculty members on SPIR projects. The Harriman School also invites business leaders to speak in an executive lecture series, allowing students the opportunity to interact with individuals who are shaping the managerial environment of tomorrow.

The College and Environs

SUNY at Stony Brook is located on the North Shore of Long Island, 50 miles east of New York City, with easy access to the unparalleled resources of the metropolitan area. For those seeking alternatives to the urban scene, the area surrounding the University and points east offer several public beaches, thousands of acres of national forest, quaint villages, wineries, numerous historical sites, the Hamptons, and ferries to southern New England.

Technology Environment

The Harriman School maintains a thoroughly modern computing facility for its students. PCs equipped with the latest software are linked to the library, faculty members, the Internet, and the World Wide Web. The campus's computer complex consists of an IBM system with hundreds of remote devices on the campus. The Frank Melville Jr. Memorial Library houses more than 2 million volumes bound and in microformat and receives more than 14,000 serial publications annually.

Placement

The University Career Placement Center helps students explore their career objectives, identify career opportunities, and conduct successful job searches. Placement services include individual consulting sessions, workshops on essential job search skills, and coordination of internship and job interviews.

Admission

The Harriman School invites applications from individuals regardless of undergraduate major. Students who excel in the program typically have previous experience, academic or otherwise, with computers and quantitative methods. Prior to admission, students are required to have completed at least one semester of calculus with a grade of C or better and to submit a completed application for admission form with official transcripts from all universities and colleges attended, recent GMAT or GRE scores, three letters of reference, and a nonrefundable $50 application fee. International students whose native language is not English must submit a TOEFL score of 550 or above. Almost all admitted students have a GPA of 3.0 or better.

Finances

Tuition for the 1997–98 academic year was $2550 per semester for residents of New York and $4208 per semester for nonresidents. Books and fees can be expected to add another $500 to $700 to the cost of study. Applicants are encouraged to apply for financial support, which the department awards based on merit. Need-based financial aid programs are also available and include New York State and federally guaranteed student loans as well as the Federal Work-Study Program. Dormitories and garden apartments are available on campus. Rates for 1997–98 range from $243 a month to $790 a month for apartments, while residence halls start at $1647 per semester, excluding meals.

Application Facts and Dates

Completed applications for students seeking financial aid must be received no later than March 1 for admission in the fall. For those students not seeking financial aid, the deadline is April 15. Spring admission is possible; the application deadline is November 1. Financial awards are made in early April for the following academic year. For an application package, students should contact:

Office of Student Services
W. Averell Harriman School for
    Management and Policy
University at Stony Brook
Stony Brook, New York 11794-3775
Telephone: 516-632-7296
Fax: 516-632-9412
E-mail: oss@fac.har.sunysb.edu
World Wide Web: http://www.ceas.
    sunysb.edu/har.html/

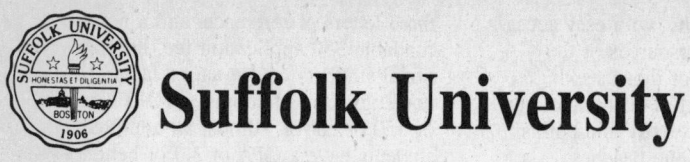

Suffolk University

Boston, Massachusetts

IT ALL COMES DOWN TO TEACHING

At Suffolk University, students are our most important customers. We provide you with an exceptionally qualified faculty, a flexible, carefully crafted curriculum that prepares you to anticipate—not merely respond to—the political, social, and economic transformations of the coming decades. You graduate as a skilled, ethical manager—a leader as well as a team player—who blends theoretical and technical expertise with practical work experience in your field.

But we do not stop there. Every professor we hire must care passionately about teaching. I am proud of the faculty we have built: they are teachers who incorporate considerable scholarly research and professional experience into the classroom. Many are nationally and internationally known for their work and must juggle lecture, consulting, and research demands, but nothing interferes with their teaching and office hour schedules. Students are the highest priority.

Thousands of success stories have emerged from our classrooms. Come join us at Suffolk University Frank Sawyer School of Management. Let us help you create your own success story.

—John F. Brennan, Dean

Programs and Curricular Focus

The Suffolk University Sawyer School of Management enrolls 2,300 students, of whom 1,250 are graduate students. All degree programs are offered on a full- or part-time basis so that students can complete their graduate programs while still working in their chosen professions. The School offers fifteen degree programs, which include an executive program, degrees in public management (M.P.A.), and joint programs with the Law School. Class schedules are flexible, with courses offered in the daytime, late afternoon, and evenings and Saturdays so that students can keep full- or part-time positions or begin an internship or co-op job as part of a full-time course of study.

Suffolk's full-time faculty members have excellent academic training and credentials. Everything a student learns is grounded in the realities of professional experience. One professor might be a former vice president of Gillette, another a senior executive from a Big Six accounting firm or a consultant to a government or international agency. Students might include a portfolio manager from a brokerage firm or a nurse manager from a local hospital.

The M.B.A. curriculum includes a required integrative course, "Tomorrow's Manager;" ten core courses; an experientially based capstone course; and six electives. The core courses cover the major functional areas of management, including accounting, computer systems, marketing, management, finance, economics, statistics, business law, communication, and organizational behavior. With strong undergraduate preparation in business, a student can utilize the waiver policy and complete the M.B.A. program in as few as ten courses in a year or less of full-time study. Courses are waived through proficiency exams or equivalent academic work that was taken at the undergraduate or graduate level. Students may also choose to specialize by taking three advanced electives in areas such as international business, CIS, finance, accounting, marketing, and entrepreneurial studies. An accelerated M.B.A. for attorneys is also available.

The Sawyer School offers graduate degree programs in specialty areas, as well as several joint-degree programs. The Master of Science in Accounting (M.S.A.), Master of Science in Taxation (M.S.T.), Master of Science in Finance (M.S.F.), Master of Science in Financial Services/Banking (M.S.F.S.B.), and Master of Science in Entrepreneurial Studies (M.S.E.S.) are offered. There are also several health-related programs. These include an M.B.A. with a concentration in health administration; an M.P.A. with a concentration in health administration; an M.P.A. with a concentration in disability studies; and a Master of Health Administration for those students already possessing a master's degree in another field. Joint degrees include the M.B.A./J.D., M.S.F./J.D., M.P.A./J.D., and a Master of Science in International Economics (M.S.I.E.)/J.D. in the College of Liberal Arts and Sciences. There are Executive M.B.A. and accelerated M.P.A. programs, with classes taught only on Saturdays. A combined M.B.A./G.D.P.A. (Graduate Diploma in Professional Accounting) and a combined M.P.A./M.S. in mental health counseling are also available.

Students and the M.B.A. Experience

Diversity and flexibility are the keys to the M.B.A. programs at Suffolk University. Students in the M.B.A. degree programs have an average of three to five years of work experience, while students in the Executive M.B.A. program may have ten or more years of experience. Full-time M.B.A. students are not required to have work experience. Last year the average work experience for full-time students was 3.8 years. The average age is 27 in the M.B.A. programs and 34 in the Executive M.B.A. program. Women comprise approximately 40 percent of each program. Approximately 12 percent of the graduate students are international students from more than twenty countries. In the full-time M.B.A. program, at least one third of the students are international.

❖ Global Focus

Each year more than 350 international students from sixty-two countries come to Boston to attend Suffolk University. A global perspective is an integral part of the Sawyer School at every level—curriculum, faculty, student body, and linkages to the international business community. In addition, the Sawyer School offers a selection of international business courses, including short seminars and site visits to businesses, universities, and government agencies in the Czech Republic, England, France, Ireland, Italy, and Spain. Not all sites are visited every year.

The University also maintains the Center for International Education, which supports the English Language for Internationals (ELI) program, sponsors short-term executive programs for internationals, and provides full-time assistance to international students for immigration advising, housing placement, and travel purposes. The center also sponsors orientation and other short-term cultural programs for international students.

The Faculty

Suffolk faculty members are well known for their expertise in such diverse fields as international management, investment analysis and financial policy, direct marketing, personal selling, buyer behavior, health-care marketing, public accounting, total quality management, and professional ethics. There are more than 60 full-time faculty members, 93 percent of whom hold Ph.D. degrees, giving the Sawyer School one of the highest faculty-Ph.D. ratios in the country.

The Business School Network

Corporate Partnerships

Suffolk's Sawyer School of Management maintains close ties with senior managers in both the public and private sectors through active advisory boards that meet regularly with the faculty of each department. Advisory board members include representatives from the Big Six accounting firms, banks, and insurance companies, in addition to executives from large and small businesses, health administrators, government officials, and managers in not-for-profit organizations. Students in the full-time M.B.A. program have an opportunity to complete internships or co-op experiences with such firms as Gillette, Polaroid, Fidelity, John Hancock, and the Federal Reserve Bank in Boston.

Prominent Alumni

The Sawyer School of Management is proud of its more than 6,000 graduate alumni. Among these are Edward McDonnell, former President of Seagram International, and Richard Rosenberg, former CEO of Bank of America. Both have been actively involved in speaking with the alumni and with current students.

The College and Environs

Boston, a dynamic center of education, culture, and commerce for centuries and a truly liveable city, is home to the Sawyer School. Located on historic Beacon Hill in the heart of Boston, Suffolk University was founded in 1937 and comprises the Sawyer School of Management, the College of Liberal Arts and Sciences, and the Law School, with a total enrollment of 6,200 students. The Sawyer School is the only school of management in New England to be accredited by both AACSB–The International Association for Management Education and the National Association of Schools of Public Affairs and Administration (NASPAA).

The urban location of the University, next door to the Massachusetts State House, is a special advantage. Students are within walking distance of Boston's financial and world trade districts, the center of government, renowned medical centers, and major cultural institutions. The location and reputation of the School of Management make it possible to draw upon the resources and expertise of these institutions to complement and enrich its approach to global business.

Technology Environment

Students have access to the University's PRIME 6350 superminicomputer seven days a week from computer stations on campus or by phone. Electronic access is available to the worldwide Internet system and the LEXIS–NEXIS service. There are a University-wide electronic mail system and user access to online library services such as ABI/INFORM. Microcomputer resources are centered in a modern computing facility, which includes a large student computer laboratory, two computer laboratory classrooms, computerized case classrooms, and a computer station in the graduate student lounge. A separate facility is dedicated to word processing. Multimedia amphitheater classrooms with videoconferencing capabilities enhance learning.

Placement

Career services available to graduate students include the Alumni/ae Career Resources Network, which is an active association of more than 275 recent graduates in every area of management. Network members serve as an important source of information and contacts for job search strategies and placement.

Other career services include career assessment and individual career counseling; extensive listings of full- and part-time jobs, co-op opportunities, and internships; workshops on resumes and interview and job search strategies; a comprehensive career library; regularly scheduled career fairs and an Executive Speaker Seminar Series; and on- and off-campus recruitment programs.

Admission

The Sawyer School of Management seeks qualified, capable applicants with distinguished undergraduate degrees from diverse educational and professional backgrounds. To apply, students must submit an application, transcripts of all academic work, GMAT scores, two letters of recommendation, a current resume, and a statement of professional goals. The average GMAT score for M.B.A. students is approximately 520. M.P.A. students are not required to submit any test scores. Applicants to the J.D./M.B.A. program and the accelerated M.B.A. for attorneys program may substitute the LSAT for the GMAT.

International applicants must submit a TOEFL score of at least 550 and a statement of financial resources.

Finances

The Sawyer School of Management offers several innovative financial aid programs. Last year, graduate management students were awarded more than $3 million in aid in the form of grants, loans, employment programs, fellowships, and assistantships. Tuition varies by program. The annual costs are $17,490 full-time or $1749 per course for the M.B.A., $16,122 full-time or $1611 per course for the M.P.A. and the M.H.A., and $19,212 full-time or $1920 per course for the M.S.F. and the M.S.F.S.B. The costs are $18,300 full-time or $1830 per course for the M.S.A. and the M.S.T., $17,490 full-time or $1749 per course for the M.S.E.S., $2169 per course for the Executive M.B.A., and $20,250 per year for the M.B.A./J.D. and the M.P.A./J.D. Additional costs are estimated at $10,000 per year.

Application Facts and Dates

Suffolk University accepts applications for fall (September), spring (January), or summer (May). The M.S.F. and Executive M.B.A. programs admit students in the fall and spring only. Application deadlines are June 15 for fall, November 15 for spring, and April 15 for summer. For the M.S.F. program, application dates are June 15 and November 15. For the Executive M.B.A. program, the deadlines are August 15 and February 15. Students applying for financial aid for the fall semester must submit their admission application by March 15. For more information, students should contact:

Judith L. Reynolds
Director of Graduate Admission
Suffolk University
8 Ashburton Place
Boston, Massachusetts 02108
Telephone: 617-573-8302
Fax: 617-523-0116
E-mail: grad.admission@admin. suffolk.edu

Sul Ross State University

Department of Business Administration

Alpine, Texas

> ### THE NEW M.B.A. IN THE GLOBAL ECONOMY
>
> *At Sul Ross, the M.B.A. experience not only prepares you in areas expected of traditional M.B.A. programs, it places added emphasis on preparing you for the demands of the global economy. This combined emphasis will help make you more capable and confident as practitioners in the new global economy.*
>
> —Chester E. Sample, Dean

Programs and Curricular Focus

The M.B.A. at Sul Ross is a hands-on program that develops scholarship and leadership by combining classroom instruction with projects, in addition to encounters with outstanding business professionals.

The program consists of 36 semester hours, of which 27 hours are core requirements completed by all majors and 9 hours are electives. The core requirements cover the basic functional areas of business, including concepts and applications of accounting, financial management, management practices, marketing, and quantitative analysis. The electives provide concentrated emphasis in one of two areas: international trade or management.

Specifically, international trade provides considerable exposure and program content related to the international business environment. Option two, management, prepares managers for positions of increasing responsibility and focuses more on domestic business practices.

At Sul Ross, students are prepared for business careers that will offer challenges, rewards, and opportunities for leadership. The overriding goal is to provide a high-quality education in the best possible environment while helping students meet social, academic, and professional needs.

Students and the M.B.A. Experience

Sul Ross M.B.A. students include people from many different areas of the world. The students have different social, cultural, economic, and work experience backgrounds. This level of diversity provides an M.B.A. student core that is unique. International students make up the majority of students in the program.

In addition to traditional classroom activities, students have the added bonus of working on hands-on projects—developing team reports, solving real-life case situations, and traveling in groups to Mexico for trade seminars.

The educational programs offered by the Department of Business Administration develop scholarship and leadership by combining classroom instruction with projects, in addition to encounters with outstanding business professionals. These activities provide students with a more complete educational package.

The Faculty

The business department provides a strong foundation in both theory and practice across the functions of business. All business department faculty members have industry experience, which adds to the practical side of instruction, and have degrees from major universities, which adds to the theoretical side. The business department faculty members make continuous efforts in staying abreast of changes in business practices, which help students learn the latest developments in industry practices and trends.

The Business School Network

The M.B.A. program brings businesses and students together to address issues of mutual interest, providing actual, hands-on experience. There are many opportunities available in the international business areas, due in part to the University's proximity to Mexico.

There are advantages in providing practical experiences to the students, and the program strongly encourages individual development in these areas based on interest and background. There is also an increasingly effective M.B.A. alumni association that provides students with lifelong contacts and increases networking opportunities.

The College and Environs

The Sul Ross campus, on nearly 640 acres, sits on the side of Hancock Mountain overlooking Alpine. Sul Ross has been serving the educational needs of the Southwest since opening its doors in 1920.

Sul Ross is a university for today's student who has the future in mind. It is a place where students can receive a high-quality education and still receive the personal attention they deserve. The campus is located in Alpine in the Davis Mountains and Big Bend country of west Texas far from the hustle and bustle and pollution of metropolitan areas. The areas around Alpine provide a center for students who enjoy camping, hiking, and rafting.

Placement

The Career Services and Testing Center offers complete placement services to the student. There are workshops on career choices, interviewing skill development, and job search strategies. In addition, the center is a member of the West Central Career Consortium, which holds an annual job fair. On-campus visits by employers are scheduled at various times throughout the year. The center also maintains listings of job announcements, credential mailing services, and Internet access to career information and job search links.

Admission

Admission to the Sul Ross State University M.B.A. program is based on many factors, including academic preparation, GMAT scores, completion of an undergraduate degree, and promise for graduate work. For unconditional admission, a student must show a minimum score of 400 on the GMAT and, where applicable or necessary, a minimum TOEFL score of 520. Probationary admission is allowed under unusual circumstances. Industry experience is encouraged but not required.

Finances

Tuition and fees for two full semesters are approximately $1600 for residents and $6900 for nonresidents. A nonresident student who receives a scholarship equal to or more than $1000 per year or a graduate assistantship qualifies for resident tuition.

Total expenses for two full semesters are approximately $5750 for a Texas resident and approximately $11,060 for a nonresident. These amounts include tuition and fees, textbooks, supplies, transportation, room and board, and other incidental living expenses. All scholarships, fellowships, and graduate assistantships are awarded on a competitive basis. There are a variety of programs to help students financially, including departmental scholarships, University scholarships, grants, loans, and on-campus jobs.

For help in planning their financial future with Sul Ross State University and for additional questions regarding financial aid (grants and loans), students should contact the Student Financial Aid Office, Sul Ross State University, Box C-113, Alpine, Texas 79832 (telephone: 915-837-8055).

International Students

Approximately half of the active M.B.A. student body at any particular time is international. There are students from many different countries; historically, the countries most represented have been Mexico and those of the Pacific Rim. The international student at Sul Ross is vitally important to the continued success of the program, as the international trade option is especially suited to these students. In addition, the international students provide a necessary perspective that encourages diverse thinking and a global perspective that permeates all areas of the program.

Application Facts and Dates

Applications for the M.B.A. program are accepted year-round. Official documents must be on file in the admissions office before students register for classes. International students must have official paperwork on file in the admissions office one month before registering.

Students interested in an application should contact the Sul Ross State University Graduate Office, Box C-2, Alpine, Texas 79832 (telephone: 915-837-8050) or contact the address below.

Mr. Robert Matthews
Graduate Program Advisor
Department of Business
    Administration
Sul Ross State University
Box C-35
Alpine, Texas 79832
Telephone: 915-837-8066
Fax: 915-837-8003
E-mail: business@sulross.edu
World Wide Web: http://www.sulross.
    edu

Syracuse University

THE M.B.A. FOR THE ROAD AHEAD

Long before most business schools, we embarked on a journey to redefine the M.B.A. We challenged the assumptions of traditional theory-based programs. We recognized the need to equip our students to compete in the global economy. We investigated opportunities presented by increasing diversity. We examined the role of ethics in business practice and the need for responsible use of natural resources. Our retooled curriculum met with resounding acclaim. Our strategic shift in approach to educating the next generation of leaders set a national trend among other schools. And more than ever, our graduates are achieving remarkable success in an extraordinary range of industries. With a Syracuse M.B.A., you'll be uniquely positioned to take your career across borders and time zones as a key corporate player or global entrepreneur. Wherever you want to go, if you have the drive, you can get there from here.

—George R. Burman, Dean

Programs and Curricular Focus

The M.B.A. curriculum is based on the premise that all managers need broad knowledge and skills, as well as functional expertise. The seven pervasive theme courses are the signature of the new curriculum. The themes—diversity, globalization, quality, ethics, the environment, critical thinking, and paradigms of management—represent the challenges that pervade every function of management today.

The heart of the curriculum is its integrated group of professional core courses that introduce the concepts of the functional areas of business and the relationships that exist among them. Seven elective courses are also integral to the program, offering students the opportunity to tailor the program to their own professional and career interests.

Concentrations are offered in nine areas: accounting, finance, general management, global entrepreneurship, innovation management, management of technology, marketing management, strategic management of human resources, and supply chain management. Elective courses may also be selected from any other graduate program at Syracuse University; engineering, communications, law, computer science, and economics are such examples. Joint-degree programs may also be designed that combine a master's degree in any other graduate program with an M.B.A.

The M.B.A. program includes a 60-credit curriculum that comprises 39 credits of required courses and 21 credits of electives. During the first year, students follow

a prescribed sequence that includes pervasive theme courses, personal skills courses, and most professional core courses. During the second year, students complete their required core courses, as well as seven electives. There is an accelerated M.B.A. program for those who hold an undergraduate degree in management and have significant work experience.

Additional graduate degree programs include the Master of Science (M.S.) in accounting; the Master of Science (M.S.) in finance; the Juris Doctor (J.D./M.B.A. and J.D./M.S. in accounting) in cooperation with the College of Law; a Master of Professional Studies (M.P.S.) in media administration, offered jointly with the S.I. Newhouse School of Public Communications; and an independent study program.

Students and the M.B.A. Experience

The Syracuse M.B.A. program has a diverse, talented, and interactive student body. More than one third of the 225 full-time M.B.A. students are women, 16 percent are minorities, and 38 percent are from other countries. Approximately 80 percent of the M.B.A. students have worked full-time for at least one year prior to enrolling; the average is five years.

Undergraduate majors include such diverse areas as history, engineering, nursing, accounting, and economics. Students are placed in teamwork groups of 4 to 5 individuals of various educa-

tional/professional experiences and backgrounds; these groups, in addition to small classes averaging 30 students, help create a feeling of intimacy within a large collegiate environment of 14,000 students and prepare graduates for today's team-oriented organizational environment.

❖ Global Focus

There are both required and elective courses in international business. In the summer, courses are offered in Shangai and internship programs are offered in Hong Kong, London, and Singapore. As a member of the Thunderbird consortium of business schools, students can spend a semester of study at The American Graduate School of International Management in Arizona or at any of their campuses abroad. Another important aspect of the program is that students from other countries contribute to a global classroom experience.

Special Features

New students begin the fall semester with Leadership Week, a five-day orientation program; participants include the faculty and distinguished business leaders. Leadership Week offers new students opportunities for building teams and support groups and an introduction to other personal skills areas, including managing conflict, communication, ethics in management, and teamwork and groups.

The Faculty

The members of the faculty of the Syracuse School of Management are distinguished by their accomplishments in research and consulting, their effectiveness in the classroom, and their genuine concern for students. Teaching methods vary from subject to subject, as appropriate. Methods of instruction include lectures, student presentations, class discussions, case studies, small-group projects, computer and management simulations, and other techniques. Instructional methods take full advantage of the program's small group structure and unique experience base represented by the students in the program.

The Business School Network

"In considering new hires," says Peter M. Sturtevant, a vice president of Xerox Corporation, "one of the qualities we look for is the ability to be a quick study—to get a good understanding of the company quickly."

Syracuse M.B.A. program graduates are quick studies because they can draw on broad exposure to business and business practitioners. Corporate ties are woven throughout the fabric of the program, affording contact with managers in every relevant field and speciality. This explains why graduates find themselves at home in today's complex corporate environment.

The College and Environs

Founded in 1870, Syracuse University—a private, nonsectarian liberal arts institution—is one of the largest and most comprehensive independent universities in the nation. The School of Management, in existence since 1919, has offered graduate programs since 1947. The fiftieth anniversary of the Syracuse M.B.A. is being observed and celebrated in the 1998–99 academic year.

Syracuse is a moderately sized, friendly city located in upstate New York. New York City, Boston, Philadelphia, Toronto, and Montreal are all less than a one-half-day drive away. Most importantly, being so close to these major metropolitan centers provides ease of access for graduates to the vast northeastern U.S. M.B.A. job market.

Facilities

The University libraries serve the informational and research needs of the entire Syracuse University community. The library system is one of the largest in the country and ranks in the top 2 percent of university libraries nationally. It contains more than 6 million books, periodicals, and pieces of microform information housed in the main Ernest Stevenson Bird Library and five branch libraries. Also available are sixteen microcomputer clusters of twenty to fifty IBM and Macintosh personal computers, which are found at several campus locations, including the School of Management.

Placement

The Career Center provides M.B.A. students with personal help on developing interview skills, resume preparation, alumni networking, and access to on-campus corporate recruiting. In 1997, graduates averaged $57,000 in starting salary, considerably above the national average for M.B.A. graduates. Employers of the class of 1997 included such diverse organizations as Andersen Consulting, Ford, IBM, LG International, UTC/Carrier, and Xerox.

Admission

Applicants must submit transcripts of all previous college work, their GMAT and TOEFL scores, a completed application for admission, and letters of recommendation, together with a $40 application fee. Prior work experience is strongly preferred, and personal interviews are encouraged. An online application can be found at http://mba.collegeedge.com.

Finances

Tuition in 1998–99 is $555 per credit ($16,650 for an academic year of 30 credits). Books and other course materials are estimated at $1200 per academic year.

Approximately 30 percent of the M.B.A. students receive merit-based assistance in the form of fellowships, assistantships, or scholarships. Fellowships include full remittance of tuition plus a generous stipend. For 1998–99, scholarships include 10–30 credits of remitted tuition, and assistantships include a stipend of $1800 to $7200. Most assistantships also include a scholarship.

Application Facts and Dates

Applications for admission to the full-time M.B.A. program should be submitted by May 1 for fall admission.

For more information, applicants should contact:

For the master's programs:
Paula A. Charland, Director
M.B.A. and Master's Admission and
    Financial Aid Office
Suite 100
School of Management
Syracuse University
Syracuse, New York 13244-2130
Telephone: 315-443-9214
Fax: 315-443-9517
E-mail: mbainfo@som.syr.edu

For the Ph.D. program:
Associate Dean S. P. Raj, Director
Ph.D. Program
Suite 200/Dean's Office
School of Management
Syracuse University
Syracuse, New York 13244-2130
Telephone: 315-443-1001
Fax: 315-443-5389
World Wide Web: http://sominfo.syr.edu/

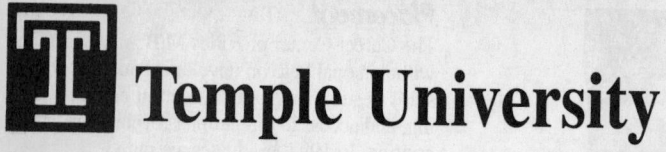

Temple University

Philadelphia, Pennsylvania

> **DEVELOPING BUSINESS LEADERS FOR THE TWENTY-FIRST CENTURY**
>
> *M.B.A. students acquire the skills and knowledge identified by business leaders as essential for success. They graduate with the ability to succeed in small, mid-sized, and large organizations—and the capacity to become one of tomorrow's business leaders.*
>
> —Linda J. Whelan, Director

Programs and Curricular Focus

The M.B.A. curriculum focuses on team-based, quality-oriented, and cross-functional models of management. Students develop practical expertise through case analyses and presentations, interaction with business practitioners, and team-based projects. Interdisciplinary courses demonstrate how integrated business functions drive organizations and enable students to view organizations from the perspective of the total enterprise, while developing expertise in one area.

The program has eight core and ten advanced courses. Students choose from seventeen concentrations, including accounting, actuarial science, business administration, chemistry, computer and information sciences, economics, finance, general and strategic management, health administration, human resource administration, international business, management science/operations management, marketing, physical distribution, real estate and urban land studies, risk management and insurance, and statistics. Full- and part-time M.B.A. study is available. Approximately 80 percent of the 1,000 M.B.A. students attend part-time in the evening. Classes are held at Temple University Center City (1616 Walnut Street), Temple Amber (20 miles north of the city), and Temple Harrisburg campuses.

A twenty-two-month Executive M.B.A. program prepares experienced managers (ten or more years of experience, including five in management) for top-level positions. Classes meet on alternate Fridays and Saturdays, allowing participants to complete their studies without career interruption

The International M.B.A. Program, with study in France, the United States, and Japan, is offered in collaboration with the IS University in France. The one-year IBM Program is designed for students with undergraduate business degrees from schools accredited by AACSB–The International Association for Management Education (other students must take the core courses first).

Joint programs include the M.B.A./J.D. in law and management with the School of Law, the M.B.A./D.M.D. in dentistry and management with the School of Dentistry, the M.B.A./M.S. in environmental health with the College of Engineering, and the M.B.A./M.S. in health administration/health-care financial management. All programs are fully accredited by AACSB–The International Association for Management Education.

The Master of Science in Business Administration (M.S.B.A.) programs (ten courses) provide in-depth knowledge of one discipline: accounting, finance, health-care financial management, human resource administration, information technology, marketing, real estate, risk management, or insurance. They are designed for students with undergraduate business degrees from schools accredited by AACSB–The International Association for Management Education. The Master of Science in actuarial science and statistics are graduate research degrees; each has ten courses plus a comprehensive examination.

Students and the M.B.A. Experience

Eighty percent of Temple M.B.A. students establish their careers before enrolling in graduate school; the average student has four years of work experience and is 28 years old. Eighty percent work full-time and attend Temple part-time. More than 40 percent have undergraduate degrees in business. Most students are from the Mid-Atlantic region; 9 percent are from Canada, Europe, and the Middle East. The minority enrollment is approximately 10 percent.

The M.B.A. Student Association enables students to build a network through guest speakers, professional development programs, and social events.

Special Features

M.B.A. education doesn't stop at the classroom door. The M.B.A. Professional Development Seminars (on leadership, presentations, and career planning) help students develop managerial skills and prepare for the job market. A Mentor Program featuring successful alumni and friends of the school helps students sharpen their career focus and make contacts.

The Faculty

The graduate faculty challenges students to analyze, anticipate, and innovate. Committed to teaching excellence, many of the school's 125 full-time faculty members are nationally and internationally recognized in their fields. Faculty members pursue a wide range of research activities. Faculty contacts with businesses established through research and consulting enhances the learning experience.

The Business School Network

Temple University is a major supplier of managerial talent to the Philadelphia region business community, one of the nation's major business centers. Area business leaders serve as "Executives in the Classroom," sponsor consulting projects and internships, serve as mentors, offer curriculum input, and more.

The Business School has more than 33,000 graduates, most of whom live and work in the region. Prominent alumni include Lacy Hunt (Ph.D. class of 1969), Chief Economist, USA, HSBC Holdings; Gail F. Lieberman (M.B.A. class of 1977), Vice President-Managing Director and CFO, Moody's Investors Service; Margaret M. McGoldrick (M.B.A. class

of 1976), Executive Director and CEO, Medical College of Pennsylvania and Hahnemann University Hospital System; Samuel H. Steinberg (M.B.A. class of 1977), Chief Executive Officer, the Graduate Hospital; and Nicholas A. Rago (B.S. class of 1974), Senior Vice President, Service Companies, The Dial Corporation.

The College and Environs

Founded in 1884, Temple University is a senior comprehensive research institution that awards bachelor's degrees in 100 disciplines, master's degrees in eighty, and doctorates in sixty. More than 29,000 students are enrolled in the University's sixteen schools and colleges.

Philadelphia, the fifth-largest city in the United States, is an international center of commerce, culture, and history. Strategically located in the dynamic industrial region between New York and Washington, D.C., the region is home to thousands of small, mid-sized, and large businesses.

Facilities

Graduate students have access to state-of-the-art library and computer

facilities at the Amber, Center City, and Main campuses. Each campus has an extensive computer network and a Scholar's Information Center, a network of research databases. Students can borrow books from Paley Library, the University's main research library.

Placement

The M.B.A. and M.S. Placement Office develops job leads for M.B.A. and M.S. students and alumni. Services include individual career assistance, on- and off-campus recruiting, corporate presentations, a resume databank, workshops, mentoring, and a resume book. During the 1997–98 academic year, more than ninety companies interviewed Temple M.B.A. students.

Admission

Students may start the M.B.A. program in the fall, spring, or summer. The acceptance rate is approximately 50 percent. The average GMAT score is 540, and the average undergraduate grade point average is 3.1. Work experience is encouraged.

Finances

Graduate tuition at Temple University is among the lowest of any university in Pennsylvania. Tuition for the academic year 1997–98 was $308 per credit hour for Pennsylvania residents and $429 for others. Most part-time students take 3 to 6 credits per semester; most full-time students take 12 to 15.

Students who work full-time may find that their employers have a tuition reimbursement program. Temple offers a few assistantships and scholarships for full-time, matriculated M.B.A. students. For more information on financial aid, those interested should contact the Financial Aid Office (215-204-1492), Temple University, Conwell Hall, 2nd Floor, Philadelphia, Pennsylvania, 19122. Affordable housing is available both on and off campus. Room and board costs $8000 in on-campus housing for the 1998–99 academic year.

Application Facts and Dates

The application deadlines are June 1 for the fall semester, September 30 for the spring semester, and March 15 for the summer semester. Students should address application inquiries to:

School of Business and Management
Speakman Hall, Room 5
Temple University
Philadelphia, Pennsylvania 19122
Telephone: 215-204-7678
Fax: 215-204-8300
E-mail: linda@sbm.temple.edu

Texas A&M International University

A MICROCOSM OF INTERNATIONAL BUSINESS

We take pride in the tradition of providing specialized graduate business education to our small but very dynamic cadre of students. During the last two decades, we have trained over 500 M.B.A.'s with specialization in international trade. Recently we have added the M.S. in international banking and the M.S. in international logistics to the list of pioneering programs.

Students in the Graduate School of International Trade and Business Administration have lived and studied in a microcosm of international business. In addition to having gone through an eminently specialized curriculum, they have benefitted from interaction with a highly diversified faculty and student body. The faculty in the College of Business represents ten countries, and the alumni, sixty-three countries and forty states.

—Dr. Khosrow Fatemi, Dean

Programs and Curricular Focus

In foreseeing the ever-accelerating changes in the global economy and international commerce, the Graduate School of International Trade and Business Administration has pioneered specialized graduate business programs responsive to the world's dynamic business environment. These specialized programs include an M.B.A. in International Trade; M.B.A. in International Banking; and an M.S. in International Logistics. In addition to these specialized programs, a general M.B.A. (taught either in English or Spanish), an M.S. in Information Systems, and a Master of Professional Accountancy (M.P.Acc.) are also offered.

The M.B.A. in International Trade prepares students from a broad spectrum of experiences, cultures, and academic disciplines with the skills necessary to assume leadership roles in the international business community. The M.B.A. in International Banking prepares a cadre of international business leaders with a mastery of the various activities of international banking and a thorough knowledge of different functions performed by international banks. The M.S. in International Logistics prepares students with the skills to assume leadership roles in this vital portion of the international transportation community. This program, although traditional in approach, emphasizes Electronic Data Interchange (EDI) and international transportation. The program introduces students to basic transportation research methods combined with an overview of the tradi-

tional logistics disciplines in addition to an introduction to computer science.

All the graduate programs are composed of twelve courses (the M.S. programs have the choice of substituting two courses for a thesis). To ensure that students are prepared to pursue a business curriculum, as many as seven prerequisite business courses may be required. Students having completed prior business courses may apply for course waivers.

Students and the M.B.A. Experience

Students bring to the classroom a wide variety of academic backgrounds, such as international relations, area studies, various business disciplines, foreign languages, and other degree fields. They emanate from all regions of the world. Since 1979, sixty-three countries and forty states have been represented in these specialized international business programs. The average age of the graduate business student is 27.

❖ Global Focus

The strength of the programs is exemplified by a curriculum that consists of forty graduate international business courses; a faculty with extensive practical international business experience; international exposure through study or exchange programs throughout the world; research opportunities and activities that include publication of *The International Trade*

Journal, Border Business Indicators, and the *NAFTA Digest;* and an internationally diverse student body.

The geographic location of the University is in Laredo, Texas, one of the United States' largest inland ports of trade and the only city on the juncture of Interstate 35 and the Pan American Highway. This provides an ideal "laboratory" to observe international business activities on a daily basis.

The Faculty

The faculty members have a very diverse and international background. Approximately 84 percent of the faculty members have extensive international business experience or are foreign nationals. Faculty members collectively possess functional literacy in twenty different languages and have living and/or working experience in Africa, Europe, the Middle East, South and Central America, and Asia.

The College and Environs

Texas A&M International University is one of the newest university campuses in the United States. Founded in 1969 as Texas A&I at Laredo, the University was located on the historic site of old Fort McIntosh. In the fall of 1995, the University experienced major innovative changes such as becoming a comprehensive University offering a wide variety and level of degrees and majors, many of which have an international component. The most dynamic change has been moving into a brand-new, state-of-the-art campus situated in northeast Laredo.

Located in south Texas, the city of Laredo is approximately 150 miles from San Antonio, Corpus Christi, and Monterrey, Mexico. Established at an important gateway between the United States and Latin America, Laredo is one of the fastest growing cities in the United States.

Facilities

In the fall of 1995, Texas A&M International University moved into a brand-new, state-of-the-art campus in northeast Laredo. Phases I and II of construction include a joint library and administration building; business administration, science, arts and humanities, and all-purpose classroom buildings; and a kinesiology building. There are also on-campus garden-style apartments, featuring card-access fencing; one-, two-, and four-bedroom units; a small computer lab; a pool; a clubhouse; sand volleyball courts; and laundry facilities.

Technology Environment

There are eight student-access computing laboratories with more than 260 IBM Pentiums and/or Power Macintoshes for instructional purposes. These facilities are open 90 hours per week. In addition, all classrooms have audio/visual capabilities and some have sophisticated multimedia capabilities. There is also a Trans Texas Video Network in place which provides two way interactive video conference capabilities between 60 locations statewide.

Placement

The Office of Career Planning and Placement provides a spectrum of services to students and graduates in the areas of career development and professional employment. Professional staff members advise students on all aspects of career preparation and the job search.

Recruiters visit the University each March for annual career fairs. Other services include a career resources library, posting of current job vacancies, a candidate referral service, on-campus recruitment, and student employment.

Admission

Students can enter the University in any semester. Full graduate standing is

granted to applicants whose undergraduate GPA on all upper-division course work is at least 3.2 (on a 4.0 scale). Applicants who do not meet this requirement must submit GMAT or GRE scores.

Students who do not have at least one year of full-time academic studies at an accredited U.S. college or university or who come from a country where English is not the official language must earn a minimum score of 550 on the TOEFL. Students who do not have a satisfactory TOEFL score may enroll in Texas A&M International University's International Language Institute, which offers intensive English language courses, TOEFL preparation courses, and an institutional TOEFL. Students must also present proof of adequate funds for educational expenses.

Finances

Tuition and fees for 1998–99 are $925.16 for a 12-semester-hour load for Texas residents and $3481.16 for non-Texas residents and international students. Full-time students generally take 12 hours per long term, summer being optional. Books and supplies average $75 per class.

All students enrolled in one of the graduate business programs are eligible to apply for fellowships. The fellowships are competitive and awarded according to

merit criteria. The fellowship permits out-of-state and international students to pay in-state tuition and gives them a stipend.

International Students

Fifty percent of the full-time students are foreign nationals. In any given semester, 25 percent are from Asia, 25 percent are from Latin America, and 20 percent are from Europe, Africa, and the Middle East, with the remaining 30 percent emanating from both near and far states. Students needing to strengthen their English may do so at the University's International Language Institute.

Application Facts and Dates

Applications are accepted for any semester. Students are encouraged to begin the admissions process as far in advance as possible. For more information, applicants should contact:

Mr. Ray Ortegón
Director of Graduate Student Services
Texas A&M International University
5201 University Boulevard
Laredo, Texas 78041-1900
Telephone: 956-326-2270
Fax: 956-326-2769
E-mail: coba@tamiu.edu
World Wide Web: http://www.tamiu.
edu

FACULTY LIST

William Larry Boyd, Professor of Finance and Provost and Vice President for Academic Affairs; Ph.D. Corporate finance.

Martin Broin, Assistant Professor of Operations Management; Ph.D. Location theory.

Willie Newton Cargill, Associate Professor of Accounting; Ph.D. Accounting.

Barry Carr, Assistant Professor of Economics; Ph.D. Agricultural economics.

Jim Qingjun Chen, Assistant Professor of Computer Information Systems; Ph.D. System design, computer-aided software engineering.

Kamal Fatehi, Professor of Management and Chair, Department of Management and Marketing; Ph.D. International management.

Khosrow Fatemi, Professor of International Business and Dean of the College of Business Administration; Ph.D.

Alain D. Genestre, Assistant Professor of Marketing; D.B.A., Ph.D. French, marketing management, distribution, international marketing.

James Giermanski, Professor of International Trade; D.A.

Cindy Houser, Assistant Professor of Economics; Ph.D. International economics, economic development.

Pedro S. Hurtado, Associate Professor of Business Administration; Ph.D. Transportation.

Muhammad Mazharul Islam, Associate Professor of International Trade; Ph.D. Domestic

and international finance, investment banking, financial institutions.

Kurt R. Jesswein, Associate Professor of International Banking; Ph.D. International banking and finance, exchange risk management, new banking products and techniques.

Leland G. Jordan, Associate Professor of Accounting; D.B.A. Managerial accounting, financial accounting.

George Kostopoulos, Visiting Professor of Information Systems; Ph.D. Information systems, computer engineering.

Michael Landeck, Professor of Marketing and International Business; Ph.D. International marketing, North American Free Trade Agreement.

Stephen Lunce, Associate Professor of Computer Information Systems; Ph.D. Systems analysis and design, decision support systems, knowledge-based systems.

Jacqueline Rowley Mayfield, Assistant Professor of Management and Business Communications; Ph.D. Management, communications.

Milton Mayfield, Assistant Professor of Management and Research Methodology; Ph.D. Management, statistics.

Thomas McGhee, Associate Professor of Accounting; Ph.D. International accounting.

Stephen McNett, Associate Professor of Accounting and Chair for the Department of Accounting and Information Systems; Ph.D. Accounting.

Sridhar P. Nerur, Assistant Professor of Information Systems; Ph.D. Database, artificial intelligence application.

Kamal D. Parhizgar, Professor of Business Administration; Ph.D. Strategic management.

J. Michael Patrick, Professor of Economics and Chair, Department of Economics and Finance; Ph.D.

Jacqueline Lou Power, Assistant Professor of Accounting; Ph.D. International accounting standards, accounting systems for small businesses, capital markets, professional ethics.

David Norton Roberts, Assistant Professor of Accounting/Business Law; J.D. Commercial law.

Antonio J. Rodriguez, Associate Professor of Business Administration/Economics; Ph.D. Treasury bills, futures trading.

Betty Rogers, Assistant Professor of Business; Ph.D. Computer applications, communications.

Henry Smith, Assistant Professor of Accounting; Ph.D. candidate. Managerial accounting.

Stephanie Smith, Assistant Professor of Finance; Ph.D. Corporate finance.

Edward N. Willman, Associate Professor of Business; Ph.D. Computer programming, decision sciences.

Rama Yelkur, Assistant Professor of Marketing; Ph.D. International marketing, strategic alliance.

Texas A&M University

> **FLEXIBILITY IN ACHIEVING YOUR CAREER GOALS**
>
> *The Mays M.B.A. Program at Texas A&M offers students flexibility in tailoring their education to maximize their career potential. In addition to flexibility in the composition of concentration areas and in the length of the program, the Mays M.B.A. provides students with an excellent return on their educational investment. Tuition costs are among the lowest in the nation, and competitive starting salaries combine with a high placement rate. Our small size allows for personalized attention in the classroom and in student services. At the Mays M.B.A., we continuously improve our program to better prepare you for career success.*
>
> *—A. Benton Cocanougher, Dean*

Programs and Curricular Focus

Texas A&M's M.B.A. program is a carefully crafted approach to advanced business education. This highly integrated, 53-semester-hour program includes 32 hours of required courses and 21 hours of electives. The program can be completed in sixteen or twenty-one months. The first year consists of a lockstep curriculum in which all M.B.A. students take the same courses. These core courses emphasize the development and mastery of competencies essential for successful managers. Courses cover all the basic business disciplines, including concepts and applications of accounting, financial management, economics, management, marketing, quantitative analysis, and business computing. Business communication skills are developed throughout the year.

The integrated curriculum actively involves students in learning by doing as they tackle real-world business cases, simulations, and many other true-to-business situations. Teamwork is a hallmark of the M.B.A. program. Mays M.B.A. teams and team projects reflect the real world of business in which professionals with a range of knowledge and experience join together to achieve goals and solve problems.

Students work with, and learn from, global leaders in business, industry, and government. Students analyze, strategize, and develop short- and long-term business plans. They have use of today's most advanced technology for learning, for communicating, and for preparing and delivering presentations. Students implement their plans through organization, motivation, teamwork, and leadership. In effect, they experience being a manager while in the program. In the process, they build a portfolio of competencies that equips them for the business challenges in their future.

Students and the M.B.A. Experience

With a total enrollment of 180, Mays M.B.A. students represent a diversity of professional, educational, and cultural backgrounds from across the United States and around the world. More than 97 percent of Mays M.B.A.'s have two or more years' full-time work experience, with the average being about four years. The average age is 28. International students comprise 20 percent of the M.B.A. population and represent more than 15 different countries. More than 30 percent of all M.B.A.'s are female, while approximately 10 percent are members of minority groups. The program's small, select enrollment encourages a sense of a community among M.B.A. students and provides many leadership opportunities for M.B.A.'s.

At the start of the Mays M.B.A. Program, students become part of a 5- to 6-member team. Team members bring to the team a diverse mix of cultural, academic, and work backgrounds. M.B.A.'s participate in team projects in each class, and semester-long team projects are presented at the end of each term. In addition to accomplishing academic goals through team experiences, M.B.A.'s study team effectiveness and put their studies to use in the team environment.

❖ Global Focus

Mays M.B.A.'s are encouraged to participate in international study-abroad and exchange programs. A variety of these are offered in Austria, Germany, France, Japan, and Mexico. Many study-abroad opportunities are designed to take place in the breaks between semesters, so students can gain international experience while using summer months for taking classes or participating in internships. Students can also receive a Certificate in International Business by completing 15 semester hours in international business and culture and a summer/semester study-abroad experience and achieving foreign language proficiency.

In addition, with a 20 percent international population, an international perspective is incorporated into all classroom activities. Each student team has at least one international team member.

The Faculty

Texas A&M's M.B.A. faculty is a distinguished body of scholars, extensively published and nationally recognized for their accomplishments. The faculty members are noted for their openness, their willingness to counsel and guide students outside the classroom, and their sincere commitment to the development and success of the students.

Texas A&M's faculty members are actively linked to the corporate world. They make valuable contributions to business through consulting and executive development programs and by holding leadership positions in professional organizations and serving on corporate advisory boards.

The Business School Network

Students and former students of Texas A&M have perhaps the largest network in the world. Once students attend Texas A&M, they become a part of the powerful Aggie Network, which can assist students in research, internships, and placement. M.B.A. alumni are active throughout the Mays M.B.A. Program, participating in mentoring activities, the Graduate Business Career Conference, and annual alumni golf outings. In addition, the M.B.A. Corporate Advisory Board, comprised of corporate and industry leaders, consults regularly to provide guidance on program and curricular issues.

The College and Environs

Established in 1876 as the first public college in the state, Texas A&M University today has become a world leader in teaching, research, and public service, with an enrollment of nearly 43,000 students. Located in College Station in the heart of Texas, the University is strategically located in the Texas Triangle, a dynamic and diverse region formed by the Dallas, Houston, and Austin metroplexes. Home to numerous global corporate headquarters, this region offers some of the nation's largest corporate environments—thus allowing M.B.A.'s easy access to corporate partners and recruiting opportunities.

Texas A&M's Graduate School of Business is located in the ultramodern E. L. Wehner Building. All classrooms are equipped with the latest in computing and communications technology, providing an exceptional learning environment.

Technology Environment

The Wehner Media Center and Masters Computer Lab are equipped with dozens of Pentium-powered PCs with CD-ROM drives and the latest operating systems and applications. M.B.A.'s may use the computers 24 hours a day. Color scanners, laser printers, video camera, scan converters, and projection equipment are available at no charge. Dial-up access to the network and the Internet is readily available. Classrooms are equipped with multimedia computers, VCRs, and desktop video/data color projectors. The West Campus Library offers electronic resources, including a CD-ROM library with articles and images on a full range of business and management topics and online services such as LEXIS-NEXIS.

Placement

The Graduate Business Career Services Office aggressively promotes the employment of A&M M.B.A.'s. The office has a 95 percent placement rate, with placements throughout the nation.

For each M.B.A., the office offers highly personalized services, including career counseling, employer development, personal skills workshops, video interviews, and internship assistance. Interaction and relationship development between students and corporate recruiters is encouraged through recruiting events such as the Graduate Business Career Conference held each fall.

Admission

Admission to the Mays M.B.A. Program at Texas A&M is based on several factors, including demonstrated leadership and academic potential, completion of a four-year bachelor's degree, GMAT scores (average 610, verbal and quantitative score must be above the 50th percentile), TOEFL scores for international students whose native language is not English (minimum score: 600 paper-based, 250 computer-based), the last 60 hours of undergraduate course work (average GPA is 3.4 on a 4.0 scale), references, a phone or personal interview, and work experience. Texas A&M requires the equivalent of two years' full-time work experience. In rare instances, admission is offered to persons with less work experience who present truly outstanding evidence of leadership experience as well as superior academic credentials.

Finances

Among the lowest in the country, tuition and fees are approximately $3500 for residents and $9200 for nonresidents for two full semesters. A nonresident student who receives a scholarship from the Mays M.B.A. Program qualifies for resident tuition. Total two-semester expenses for a Texas resident are approximately $14,000 and, for a nonresident, approximately $19,700—this includes tuition and fees, books, supplies, transportation, room and board, and incidental and living expenses.

Numerous scholarships are available to assist students. For highly qualified students who apply before February 15, a competitive $12,000 fellowship is available. Additional significant scholarships, fellowships, and graduate assistantships are awarded on a competitive basis. First-round scholarship decisions are made for those applications received by

February 15. Early application is highly encouraged for maximum award consideration. Subsequent rounds of awards are made until all funds are exhausted.

For additional questions regarding financial aid, students should contact the Student Financial Aid Office, Texas A&M University, College Station, Texas 77843-1252; telephone: 409-845-3981; Web site: http://faid.tamu.edu.

International Students

Approximately 20 percent of the Mays M.B.A. student body is international, representing countries from around the world. International students are a very important component of the Mays M.B.A. Program, as they encourage diversity and a global perspective in the classroom and in team activities.

All questions regarding visa and immigration requirements should be addressed to International Student Services at 409-845-1824 or e-mail: iss@iss.tamu.edu.

Application Facts and Dates

Admission to the Mays M.B.A. Program is for the fall semester only. Applications are considered on a rolling basis, with an application deadline of May 1. International students should apply prior to March 1. All applications are considered on a competitive basis for scholarship awards, with the first round of award made to those applications received prior to February 15. Early application is essential for maximum award consideration. All applicants must submit a completed graduate application with a nonrefundable application fee ($35, domestic; $75, international), a student information sheet and essay questions, college transcripts, official GMAT scores, three reference letters, and a resume.

Students interested in an application or additional information should contact:

Mays M.B.A. Program Office
Mays Graduate School of Business
Texas A&M University
College Station, Texas 77843-4117
Telephone: 409-845-4714
Fax: 409-862-2393
E-mail: maysmba@tamu.edu
World Wide Web: http://mba.tamu.edu
(application form is available on the
    home page)

Texas Christian University

> ### THE NEELEY ADVANTAGE
>
> *In the Neeley School, we understand that it takes more than technical expertise to succeed in today's dynamic business environment. Working with our faculty members and corporate partners, we have developed a curriculum that integrates sound business fundamentals with multiple opportunities to round out the academic experience. Communication skills, technology, and hands-on learning are equally emphasized at the Neeley School—both inside and outside of the classroom.*
>
> *Neeley School faculty and staff members are committed to providing students with opportunities to achieve their academic as well as professional potential. Knowledgeable. Confident. Prepared. Neeley graduates are ready to face the challenges and contribute to the success of today's organizations.*
>
> —H. Kirk Downey, Dean

Programs and Curricular Focus

Because managers seldom face clearly defined problems or opportunities, the Neeley School designed a curriculum to give its graduates a strategic, integrated perspective of business. Eleven required core courses cover a myriad of business principles. Five elective courses allow for more detailed study in one or more areas. The 48-semester-hour program is completed in two academic years by full-time students.

Neeley School faculty members work closely across functional departments to integrate core classes through special case studies and group projects. Classroom instruction is tied to the business world through guest presentations by visiting executives and corporate-based field projects. Faculty members employ a variety of teaching methods in the classroom. The environment is highly interactive and team-oriented.

In addition to a strong conceptual framework, the program emphasizes the development of essential managerial skills, such as effective communication. The innovative Center for Productive Communication provides dedicated professional staff and state-of-the-art facilities as a resource to M.B.A. students.

Students and the M.B.A. Experience

The Neeley School M.B.A. program attracts a diverse group of students. As a private university, Texas Christian University (TCU) does not serve a

defined geographic area. The objective is to bring talented students from many countries and regions to share experiences and learn from each other. Approximately one fourth of the full-time M.B.A. class comes from outside the United States. Of the remaining students, about half are from Texas and half are from other parts of the United States. Neeley School M.B.A. students also come from a broad range of academic and professional backgrounds. About half hold undergraduate degrees in business. The others have majored in liberal arts, science, technology/engineering, and the fine arts. On average, full-time students have completed two years of professional experience after earning their undergraduate degrees.

Although diverse, all Neeley School M.B.A. students do share certain characteristics. They are academically talented individuals with demonstrated leadership skills. They are highly motivated and possess a history of success. A typical entering full-time M.B.A. class at TCU includes about 100 students.

❖ Global Focus

Second-year M.B.A. students may participate in semester-long exchange programs with universities in Dijon, France; Freiburg, Germany; and Chihuahua or Puebla, Mexico. In addition, TCU faculty members lead a summer study program in Germany featuring visits to leading business firms, homestays with

German families, and sessions sponsored by German alumni of the Neeley School.

Special Features

Throughout the curriculum and in several innovative programs, Neeley School M.B.A. students put business theory into practice. Students in the Educational Investment Fund (EIF), the largest student-run investment portfolio in the United States, manage more than $1 million. Through the Student Enterprise Program, teams of M.B.A. student consultants are hired by companies to solve real business problems. Through the Summer Internship Program, approximately 95 percent of the M.B.A. students secure professional-level positions in a variety of industries.

The Faculty

The Neeley School's graduate faculty includes 30 individuals widely recognized as leaders in their academic fields. The dedicated faculty members are respected researchers and frequent consultants to industry. All M.B.A. faculty members hold a Ph.D. or a terminal degree in their field. All classes are taught by faculty members; there are no teaching assistants.

The Business School Network

Corporate Partnerships

The Neeley School works closely with business leaders in developing the M.B.A. curriculum and special programs. The International Board of Visitors, a corporate advisory board of senior-level executives from the U.S. and abroad, serves as a sounding board for the dean and faculty.

The Neeley School's extensive corporate ties directly impact the M.B.A. student's experience. Through the Executive-in-Residence Program, 15 to 20 executives are brought to campus each year for guest lectures and small group discussions with students. The required Industry Perspectives Series of seminars led by seasoned professionals offers students detailed exploration of important issues, such as diversity in the workplace, managing change and technology, and ethical and global issues. The M.B.A. Alumni Association's mentor program matches students with alumni from their chosen career field.

Prominent Alumni

Many TCU alumni have established themselves as business leaders, including John Roach, Chairman and CEO, Tandy Corporation; Roger King, Senior Vice President of Human Resources, PepsiCo; and Webb Joiner, President, Bell Helicopter-Textron, Inc.

The College and Environs

Founded in 1873, Texas Christian University is a private university located in Fort Worth, Texas. TCU limits its total undergraduate and graduate enrollment to approximately 7,000 students so that all may benefit from personalized programs and services. TCU has a long-standing reputation for excellence in teaching and research and is accredited by all major accreditation associations.

Although founded by a Christian denomination, TCU is today an independent institution attracting students from many different cultures and faiths. Religious instruction is not a component of the M.B.A. curriculum.

TCU's location provides access to the Dallas–Fort Worth metroplex, a thriving metropolitan area of approximately 4 million people and home to a broad range of industries. Because of the area's central U.S. location, pleasant climate, and relatively low cost of living, many major firms have headquarters or branch offices based in Dallas–Fort Worth. The area is also home to world-class museums, major professional sports, and numerous other recreational opportunities.

Technology Environment

M.B.A. students have access to more than ninety microcomputers in on-site computer labs. The labs are open daily from 8 a.m. to midnight. All computers are linked to a campus network with access to the Internet and the World Wide Web. Many of TCU's library resources are available through the computer network, including the card catalog, CD-ROM databases, and online information services such as Dow Jones News/ Retrieval Service.

Placement

In addition to the full range of programs offered by TCU's Career Planning and Placement Center, the Neeley School dedicates professional staff and developmental resources to career activities. The relatively small program size allows for an individualized approach to career planning and placement. Student career goals and planning skills are evaluated early in the program. Emphasis is placed on helping students build meaningful professional networks during their years as a student.

Admission

The nature of the Neeley School M.B.A. program requires that a holistic approach be used in the admissions process. No single criterion, such as a test score, can determine eligibility for admission. The applicant must demonstrate not only academic ability but also the desire and ability to perform in a highly interactive, team-based environment. The previous academic record, relevant test scores, experience, motivation, maturity, and leadership ability are all considered in the admissions process. Professional work experience is preferred but not required.

Applicants are asked to submit a completed application, personal essays, official transcripts from each university attended, three letters of reference, official GMAT scores, and official TOEFL scores for international applicants (minimum score of 550 required).

Finances

As a private university, TCU does not charge higher tuition for out-of-state or international students. For full-time M.B.A. students at TCU for the 1998–99 academic year, tuition is $8280 ($345 per semester hour), fees are $1200, and the estimated cost of books and supplies is $700. The cost of room and board varies depending on the lifestyle of the individual student. The estimated cost for rent, meals, and living expenses for students is about $8000 per academic year.

Through the Neeley School's aggressive scholarship program, approximately half of full-time M.B.A. students receive merit-based awards. Financial assistance based on academic merit is available to students of all nationalities. A number of special corporate-sponsored scholarships include a guaranteed summer internship and a generous living stipend.

International Students

Approximately 35 percent of TCU's full-time M.B.A. students come from outside the United States. Typically, international students come to TCU from Europe, Mexico, South America, and Asia. The Neeley School's small class sizes and emphasis on personal attention can be especially important to students from other cultures. Dedicated faculty members are committed to working closely with students, in and out of the classroom.

Application Facts and Dates

Application deadlines are March 15 for scholarship consideration and April 31 is the general deadline. Following the deadlines, applications are accepted on a space-available basis only. Due to the limited class size, students are encouraged to apply early. Applications are received as early as a year prior to admission.

Admission decisions are made on a rolling basis. Decisions are usually communicated three to four weeks after the completed application is received. For more information, applicants should contact:

Ms. Peggy Conway
Director of M.B.A. Admissions
M. J. Neeley School of Business
Texas Christian University
P.O. Box 298540
Fort Worth, Texas 76129
Telephone: 817-257-7531
          800-828-3764 Ext. 7531
          (toll-free within the U.S.)
Fax: 817-257-6431
E-mail: mbainfo@tcu.edu
World Wide Web: http://www.neeley. tcu.edu

Texas Tech University

AN INVITATION FROM THE DEAN

The College of Business Administration at Texas Tech University is an exciting place to be working toward a master's degree in these genuinely challenging times of rapid change. Your experience in college will be the sum of many learning experiences you will have with the faculty and fellow students.

You'll develop leadership and management skills by engaging in skill-building exercises and teamwork. You'll be a part of project teams that will work in the "real world" with businesses, hospitals, community organizations, and government agencies. You'll use the latest information technology tools.

A master's degree in business from Texas Tech will start you on the path of lifelong professional development and learning that will be an integral part of your career.

—Roy D. Howell, Dean

Programs and Curricular Focus

The College offers ten fully accredited graduate degree programs. The M.B.A. program is designed to provide a broad background in business complemented by a well-developed managerial perspective and strong analytical skills. Core courses cover the financial, managerial, economical, marketing, and analytical functions of the firm. The Strategic and Global Management course provides a comprehensive overview of all these functions. Concentrations and electives offer the opportunity to develop the specialized knowledge and skills needed for various managerial careers. Concentrations include entrepreneurial studies, finance, foreign language, health organization management, international business, management, management information systems (MIS), and marketing.

The Master of Science in business administration (M.S./BA) degree program is designed to produce specialists in one of the following functions of business: business statistics, finance, management, marketing, MIS, operations management, or telecommunication technology.

The Master of Science in Accounting (M.S.A.) degree is offered for students who wish to specialize in the areas of auditing/financial reporting, controllership, and taxation.

The M.B.A. and M.S./BA programs may be completed in one to two years, depending on the student's background. The M.S.A. program can take 1 to 2½ years.

The College of Business Administration also offers joint programs in association with the School of Law, the School of Nursing, the School of Medicine, the College of Architecture, and the College of Arts and Sciences. M.B.A./J.D. and M.S.A./J.D. programs can be completed in three to four years; the M.B.A./M.S.N. takes 69 credit hours to complete. M.B.A./Health Organization Management (HOM) certification is offered through a joint program with Texas Tech Health Sciences Center. M.B.A./M.D. is also offered jointly with the School of Medicine. M.B.A./M.A. in architecture and the M.B.A./M.A. in foreign language degree programs allow students to complete two degrees while reducing the duration of both programs by 24 credit hours.

The Ph.D. degree prepares students for careers in teaching, scholarly research, and publication. Doctoral students achieve high levels of expertise in their area of specialization.

Students and the M.B.A. Experience

The College of Business Administration enrolls about 350 master's and 90 doctoral students. Approximately 60 percent of the students are from the Southwest; the remaining 40 percent come from other areas of the United States and many other countries. They bring to their graduate studies diverse backgrounds in the liberal arts, the sciences, engineering, and business administration. More than two thirds have previous work experience.

The average age of the students in the program is 26. Of the incoming students, 34 percent are women, 10 percent are members of minority groups, and 32 percent are international students representing twenty-seven countries.

Students regularly work in teams, take on consulting or marketing research projects from local businesses, do field studies and site visits, and gain firsthand experience through internships and part-time positions. Presentations and group projects build students' confidence and ability to make public speeches.

❖ Global Focus

Students from other countries contribute to the understanding of diverse cultures, traditions, and political frameworks. In addition, a concentration in international business and study-abroad programs in leading business schools in England, Finland, France, Germany, Italy, Mexico, and Spain are available.

Texas Tech is totally committed to globalism, promotes the understanding of global cultures, and enriches the learning environment in and out of the classroom.

The Faculty

With more than 50 graduate faculty members, Texas Tech has one of the lowest graduate student-faculty ratios among business schools accredited by AACSB–The International Association for Management Education. One of the most talented resource bases in the country, the College's faculty members have a long tradition of successfully integrating teaching and research interests. College of Business Administration faculty members have been recognized for their efforts by industry and academia, receiving numerous awards and grants, including American Marketing Association/Irwin Distinguished Marketing Educator, Academy of Marketing Science, Academy of Management, and Data Processing Management Association's Distinguished Information Sciences Awards.

The Business School Network

The relationship between the College and the business community is a strong bond that offers benefits in both directions. The Chief Executives' Roundtable (CER) provides a forum for top professionals in the area that builds a close link between the College, the students, and the local business community. CER members serve as guest lecturers in graduate classes and provide student teams the opportunity to work on challenging problems or special initiatives in their businesses. In networking with these entrepreneurs and leaders, students gain insights that are invaluable to their career development.

Advisory councils are made up of members who are drawn from a variety of organizations and firms across the country. In addition, the College of Business Administration has established alliances with leading companies in the nation that are constantly recruiting its graduates. Ernst and Young, Arthur Andersen, Andersen Consulting Co., IBM, Exxon, Bank One, Texas Commerce Bank, Compaq, Texas Instruments, Methodist Hospital, St. Mary of the Plains Hospital, Coopers and Lybrand, Deloitte and Touche, and SBC Communications are a few of these corporate partners.

The College and Environs

Founded in 1923, Texas Tech University is a major state-supported coeducational institution with an enrollment of 24,000 students. The University complex includes seven colleges; highly regarded schools of law, medicine, and health sciences; and the graduate school. Professional and graduate degrees are offered in ninety disciplines. Along with accreditation by AACSB–The International Association for Management Education for the College of Business Administration's programs, health organization management master's and certification programs are accredited by the Accrediting Commission on Education for Health Services Administration (ACEHSA).

With a population of 250,000, Lubbock has the amenities of a major metropolitan area, yet it maintains its small-town charm. Lubbock is a principal financial, trade, medical, and industrial center and a growing agricultural, petroleum, and ranching region. The city has a thriving cultural life, featuring a symphony orchestra, three internationally acclaimed wineries, and an annual three-day art festival. As a new member of the Big 12, Texas Tech hosts a variety of intercollegiate sports events. Situated

on the high plains of west Texas, Lubbock has a pleasant climate year-round, with about 265 days of sunshine annually and low humidity.

Facilities

Graduate study in business at Texas Tech is supported by excellent library and computer resources. The University library collections include approximately 1.9 million volumes and 16,000 current serial titles. Scholarly and general business articles are readily referenced through the Business Index, a comprehensive, up-to-date microfilm service. An efficient interlibrary loan service provides materials not available on campus. The Advanced Technology Learning Center (ATLC) provides state-of-the-art capabilities for computing and communications. Computer resources in the College include an internal VAX-11/750 system, microcomputer labs, and a remote-access center linked to the University's central computing facilities. More than seventy computer terminals access the large systems, and an extensive library of software packages is available.

Placement

The College supports an active placement effort. Interview rooms in the Graduate Services Center are reserved for employers seeking graduate business students. Students may also utilize the University-wide career planning and placement center. In addition to Texas Tech's annual career fairs, Marketplace 2000, the College of Business Administration's individualized career fair, is held every spring for graduate students' placement.

The Graduate Services Center provides students with career evaluation, counseling, a career library, and workshops on resume writing, job search strategies, business correspondence, and interviewing techniques. The latest technology in hiring, recruiting, and placement is utilized to assist students with their job search.

Admission

Admission is based upon the academic records and the GMAT score. International applicants whose native language is not English must have a minimum 550 TOEFL score. A minimum GMAT score of 500 and minimum undergraduate GPA of 2.7 on a 4.0 scale are required for admission. Applicants to the M.S.A. program must have a minimum GPA of 3.0. Prior professional work experience is a definite plus. Personal interviews are encouraged but not required.

Finances

The tuition and fees in 1997–98 for Texas residents were $1600 per semester; for non-Texas residents, they were $4100 per semester. These fees are based on a 12-hour course load. Books and supplies may cost up to $400 per semester.

Research assistantships are awarded on a competitive basis to students with outstanding academic credentials. They include stipends and a waiver of out-of-state tuition. Additional aid, primarily loan funds, is available through the University Student Financial Aid Office. Dean's scholarships are awarded to students with high GPAs and GMAT scores. In 1997–98, these provided a $1000 tuition credit and qualified the student for in-state tuition.

International Students

There is a strong international student body at Texas Tech. International student groups across campus host the weekly International Coffee Hour and the International Week. One third of the student population in the College of Business Administration graduate programs is international, representing twenty-seven countries.

Application Facts and Dates

The College of Business Administration has a rolling admission policy. Applications may be made for fall, spring, or summer terms. There are no formal application deadlines for domestic students. International students are advised to complete their applications by April 30 for fall, September 30 for spring, and by February 15 for summer. Applicants receive a decision within four to eight weeks of receipt of all the application materials.

Texas Tech University
College of Business Administration
Graduate Services Center
P.O. Box 42101
Lubbock, Texas 79409-2101
Telephone: 806-742-3184
        800-882-6220 (toll-free)
Fax: 806-742-3958
E-mail: bagrad@coba.ttu.edu
World Wide Web: http://www.ba.ttu.
    edu/www/Grad/Index.htm
For more information about the M.B.A./ M.D. joint-degree program, students should contact:

M.D./M.B.A. Program
Office of Admissions-2B116
School of Medicine
Texas Tech University Health Sciences
    Center
Lubbock, Texas 79430

THΞSEUS THESEUS Institute

International Management Institute

Sophia Antipolis, Côte d'Azur, France

AN ENGLISH-LANGUAGE M.B.A. PROGRAM IN INNOVATION, STRATEGY, INFORMATION, AND TECHNOLOGY

▶ *THESEUS' M.B.A. is built around the vision that the Information Age makes management a very different responsibility from what it has been in the past. It is not simply that some tasks have been automated by the use of computers and that the transfer of data is faster. New communication and information systems affect the way people interact to exchange information and make decisions. Referring to a question asked a few months ago in a leading academic journal: "How do you manage people you don't see?", we believe that management is losing, perhaps, one of its important features: supervision. Despite the fact that it is not yet clear what managers' main task will be in the future, in the meantime conventional business schools are still helping their students to become better "supervisors."*

We have participants from all around the world, with no dominant nationality, which is a characteristic that only a handful of business schools can claim. Likewise, our faculty members come from the four corners of the globe.

—Professor Charles Wiseman, Dean of the M.B.A. Program

Programs and Curricular Focus

THESEUS was founded by a group of forward-looking business and educational organizations to redefine management for the Information Age. The Institute is located in France in the Technology Park of Sophia Antipolis, Europe's "Silicon Valley."

THESEUS, International Management Institute and "Networked Learning Community," offers an international, multiperspective, one-year M.B.A. program for professionals with significant work experience and a desire for an integrative business education. The program emphasizes innovation, strategy, information, and technology. It seeks enterprising, boundary-crossing individuals with diverse experience and academic credentials. The language of instruction is English.

Named after the ancient Greek myth of Theseus, who subdued the minotaur and escaped from the labyrinth that contained it, the THESEUS M.B.A. prepares its participants to master the mazes and minotaurs of management, the managerial challenges of the Information Age.

Designed for those who want not only to learn the conventions of business but also to think unconventionally about them, the THESEUS M.B.A. combines academic studies, personal development activities, and team projects in a company. THESEUS developed a multidisciplinary approach toward business studies that incorporates the findings of other disciplines, such as sociology, artificial intelligence, anthropology, and philosophy.

THESEUS' multidisciplinary approach has been materialized in the creation of pedagogical units called clusters, of which there are four: thematic clusters, classic topics: management and technology, personal development skills, and consulting projects. Clusters are innovative, multidisciplinary periods of instruction lasting from four to six weeks. They address a common theme from multiple points of view and integrate material from different disciplines.

There are four thematic cluster units that weave together and highlight the essential elements of educated managerial judgment: critical analysis, management interpretation, and creative response.

The classic topics units provide participants with the basic language, ideas, and understanding needed to navigate in the various functional fields of management and technology. Systematic exposure rather than technical proficiency is the goal. These topics include, for example, information systems and networks, accounting, finance, marketing, economics (micro and macro), industry analysis, and operations management.

The personal development skills courses begin with team-building exercises in September. Working in and with groups, understanding their dynamics, and experiencing teamwork are essential aspects of managerial life; the same is true of communications, negotiation, and consulting skills.

The consulting project unit, an integral part of the M.B.A. curriculum, lasts for eight weeks and divides into two phases: one week in March and seven weeks in May and June. The consulting project enables participants to apply and develop, under faculty supervision, what they have learned in the M.B.A. courses through a real-life issue they have to face for a European or international company. The project is usually carried out in teams of 4 to 6 people. The team's final report must satisfy both the client and the supervisor. Last year, the projects were commissioned by Hewlett-Packard, ABN-AMRO Bank, Ericsson, France Telecom, Sema Telecom Group, and IBM Europe.

Students and the M.B.A. Experience

THESEUS attracts entrepreneurial participants from all over the world who are searching for a unique, cutting-edge M.B.A. program. Highly motivated and hard working, between 27 and 35 years of age, they bring to their studies a variety of educational backgrounds, proven professional experience, and a rich cultural diversity. In terms of educational background, 39 percent of the students have business degrees; 11 percent, humanities; 42 percent, sciences and engineering; and 8 percent, social sciences. The professional backgrounds of the students are as follows: banking and finance, 13 percent; consulting, 27 percent; manufacturing, 20 percent; and services, 40 percent.

A trend toward entrepreneurial and consulting activities has been observed among alumni in countries as diverse as the United States, Japan, Israel, and Azerbaijan and reflects the dynamic environment that is an integral part of the learning experience at THESEUS. Generally, candidates tend to go into high-growth sectors, including telecommunications, IT, and pharmaceuticals. Candidates come equally from science, business, and humanities backgrounds.

The average age of the THESEUS M.B.A. participant is 31, representing a range of people from 26 to 40 years of age. In a class of 20 to 30 participants, there are, on average, fifteen to nineteen nationalities represented.

The Faculty

THESEUS has a very low student-faculty ratio of 4:1. This does not include affiliate and visiting faculty members and lecturers who come from many of the world's best business schools and organizations.

The Business School Network

Many companies sponsor consulting projects, recruit, and are regular clients of THESEUS's M.B.A., public, and executive programs. Recent company programs include those for Volkswagen, General Electric, Johnson and Johnson, ABN-AMRO Bank, PPC (South Africa), and Indonesian Telecoms. M.B.A. students are often invited to meet company participants and interact with them.

Over the years, the Institute has developed a true "Networked Learning Community" of business contacts, alumni, professors, and participants who make extensive use of the Institute's e-mail server and other standard communication tools.

The College and Environs

Sophia Antipolis, Europe's largest research and development park, houses more than 1,000 multinational and smaller companies. Among them are Air France, Amadeus, Andersen Consulting, Bay Networks, Cisco Systems, Digital, France Telecom, Glaxo Welcome, NCR, Rockwell International, SEMA Group, Siemens, Texas Instruments, and VLSI Technology.

Set in the middle of a pine forest and only 4 miles from the beaches, Sophia Antipolis is in the heart of the French Riviera, in a 25-kilometer circle that includes the International Airport and the cities of Nice and Cannes, with its annual film festival and Milia, the multimedia extravaganza. The weather is particularly pleasant, and the surroundings are extremely agreeable to work in. Italy and Monaco are less than 1 hour away. Spain and Switzerland are both within a half-day's drive.

Technology Environment

If needed, each participant receives a portable computer on loan for the duration of the program, with remote access software and an Internet connection. A deposit is required. A two- to three-week technology core course is offered to all participants. There are network connections in all sections of the building, contributing to a general sense of technology ubiquity that is a major feature of the THESEUS culture.

Placement

M.B.A. participants are contacted with job offers by international executive search firms, consulting firms, and large corporations. Placement is undertaken in a focused manner, with specific persons being recommended to companies that offer the best fit for their needs. To give M.B.A. candidates exposure, many formal and informal arrangements are made with contacts in the THESEUS network of companies and visiting faculty members as well as with participants in executive programs.

According to the first answers from a recent alumni survey, the average salary increase following completion of the M.B.A. program is 37 percent. The average number of serious job offers around graduation time is five. The average starting salary after completion of the M.B.A. program is Fr 420,000 (US$70,000). The current salary figures are high and correspond to the reality of the strong demand of the technology-intensive companies that recruit most of THESEUS's students.

The value of an M.B.A. is, however, more complex than a salary increase, and, according to THESEUS alumni, there is a large place for hidden value at THESEUS, value they had not assessed at first. The issues raised in the M.B.A. program, especially in the IT area, Internet, or the networked society, are pertinent issues for the business world, and THESEUS alumni have established a clear competitive advantage in this regard.

Admission

M.B.A. applicants are expected to possess strong academic and intellectual capabilities coupled with at least four to seven years of working experience. They should be self-motivated women and men determined to fully invest the energy required to develop their managerial talent and judgment. Participants should have international experience, have shown evidence of entrepreneurial energy, and delight in exploring new environments of ideas, practices, and people.

In making its admission decision, THESEUS takes into account a candidate's educational credentials, professional background, and personal skills; GMAT scores are also required. Applicants should demonstrate an aptitude for independent study and a desire to participate in team activities. Candidates also have international experience.

Finances

The tuition fee is Fr 140,000 for individual participants and Fr 195,000 for company sponsored participants, including taxes (the current VAT rate is 20.6 percent). Participants may arrange to pay their fee in three installments with the last due on December 31, four months after their enrollment in the M.B.A. program. The tuition fee covers all course materials, use of portable computers (for which there is a deposit), and access credit to international databases.

International Students

Non–European Union (EU) candidates, including Americans, are urged to apply early for visa reasons. M.B.A. participants must enter France with a student visa and not a tourist or business visa or visa-waiver, particularly if they are not EU citizens.

Once at THESEUS, students are assisted by staff members who help participants obtain their residency permit. Participants form a very international student body. Typically, 15 percent of the students are French, 40 percent anglophone (Canadian, Australian, American, British, etc.), 20 percent Asian, and 20 percent are northern European.

Application Facts and Dates

The selection process starts after a candidate's completed application packet is received. As part of the process, THESEUS faculty members and/or an alumnus interview applicants. The Admission Committee meets regularly starting on December 15th, 1998, until April 30th, 1999.

For more information, students should contact:

Mr. Eddy Travia
THESEUS Institute
M.B.A. Admissions Office
BP 169 - rue Albert Einstein
06903 Sophia Antipolis cedex
France
Telephone: +33 4 92 94 51 00
Fax: +33 4 93 65 38 37
E-mail: admissions@theseus.fr
WWW: http://www.theseus.fr

Thunderbird, The American Graduate School of International Management

Master's Program in International Management

Glendale, Arizona

> ### CITIZENS OF THE WORLD
>
> *Our students often tell me that Thunderbird is one of the few places where they have found people who think like they do. These students are truly "Citizens of the World," and theirs is a global perspective. Many of them have traveled in several countries and speak several languages. Others, however, may never have owned a passport. Yet for all of them, it is their global viewpoint that sets them apart. If you are seeking a community of internationalists and you thrive on intellectual challenge, I invite you to be a part of the Thunderbird experience. It will change your life.*
>
> —Roy A. Herberger Jr., President

Programs and Curricular Focus

Thunderbird's three-part curriculum provides an interrelated program of instruction in three departments—International Studies, Modern Languages, and World Business—leading to the Master of International Management (M.I.M.) degree. This successful educational concept is based on the proven fact that an ability to understand and adapt to the global business environment is a major reason for executive success in international operations.

The curriculum of the Department of International Studies focuses on the international business environment and is designed to acquaint students with foreign areas and their cultural management styles. This curriculum also provides the student with a conceptual framework for informed analysis of an international milieu.

The Department of Modern Languages offers courses in ten languages: Arabic, Chinese, French, German, Italian, Japanese, Portuguese, Russian, Spanish, and English as a Second Language. The three-level sequence stresses oral proficiency and heavily emphasizes business vocabulary and usage. In addition, many advanced commercial and issues-oriented courses are also offered.

The Department of World Business offers a far wider range of international courses than traditional graduate schools of business. Courses have a strong international practical orientation. There is heavy reliance on group teamwork and the use of computer simulation games.

The School has long enjoyed a reputation for teaching excellence, featuring an approach that is pragmatic and student-focused.

Thunderbird has developed dual-degree programs with Arizona State University, Arizona State University West, the University of Arizona, Case Western Reserve University, the University of Colorado Denver, Drury College, the University of Florida, the University of Houston, the University of Texas at Arlington, and ESADE in Spain.

Thunderbird also offers a Master of International Health Management (M.I.H.M.) degree, a Master of International Management for Latin America (M.I.M.L.A.), a Master of International Management of Technology (I.M.O.T.) degree, and a post-M.B.A./M.I.M degree for individuals who hold an AACSB–The International Association for Management Education-accredited M.B.A.

Students and the M.B.A. Experience

The School's 1,400 students come from every state in the union. By design, 45 percent are from outside the U.S.; usually sixty to seventy countries are represented. The mean student age is 28 years, and approximately 35 percent are women. Students have an average of 3½ years of full-time postbaccalaureate work experience. Diversity is a Thunderbird student trademark. More than 130 undergraduate college majors are represented, from more than 500 undergraduate colleges and universities worldwide.

Thunderbird was established in 1946. More than 30,000 alumni occupy executive offices in multinational enterprises around the world. The bond that unites them is a combination of elements that make up the "Thunderbird Experience." It starts on the Thunderbird campus and extends around the world.

It is a group of alumni living, working, and making business contacts in every state in the United States and nearly 140 countries. It is the "First Tuesday" tradition in New York, Omaha, Paris, Mexico City, Taipei, and 157 other cities around the world where alumni meet to develop social and business relationships. It is strangers who become instant friends when both are T'birds. It is a team spirit that grows from the many challenges of a demanding curriculum. It is the cacophony of students practicing language dialogues in the dining hall. It is an on-campus camaraderie where everyone knows everyone, and lifelong friendships transcend international barriers.

❖ Global Focus

Every year nearly one third of Thunderbird's students study on campuses around the globe in special international programs designed to augment their degree program, improve their language skills, and intensify their exposure to other cultures. Semester and/or summer programs are located in Europe, Asia, and Latin America.

The School has established its own campuses in Japan and in France, near Geneva. In addition, a ten-week session is held each summer in Guadalajara, Mexico.

Students may also avail themselves of exchange opportunities in China, Costa Rica, Finland, Germany, Korea, Norway, and Spain.

Special Features

Each January, Thunderbird presents Winterim, a three-week program of seminars that incorporate the newest international business theories along with practical problem-solving tools.

This unique educational opportunity arises from the mutual collaboration of Thunderbird faculty members with distinguished business and government professionals, many of whom are involved in the highest levels of strategic policy planning.

Past Winterim seminars have included Marketing to U.S. Hispanics; International Consumer Marketing Management;

Counter Trade/Offset and Barter; International Banking Symposium; Johnson & Higgins International Insurance and Risk Management Conference; The Corporate Executive Officer; Women Leaders of Today; Competitive Response of U.S. Business; Asia/Pacific Rim Management and Investment; Doing Business in Eastern Europe and Russia; Privatization; Cross-Cultural Communication for International Managers; Opportunity and Risk in the New International Business Order; International Management of Technology; Managing in a Borderless World; and Issues in International Health Care Management.

Winterim courses are also held in numerous international locations, including Austria, Brazil, Central Europe, Chile/Peru, Costa Rica/Nicaragua, Cuba, France, Germany, Kuwait, Mexico, Russia, Saudi Arabia, South Africa, Spain/Portugal, and the United Arab Emirates. In the U.S., Thunderbird offers U.S. Foreign Policy and the New Global Environment, which is held in Washington, D.C., and Winterim on Wall Street.

The Faculty

Thunderbird's faculty combines strong academic credentials with significant international and corporate experience. Among the more than 100 full-time professors are individuals from more than two dozen countries—a truly global representation. The Modern Language faculty features native speakers and scholars. Members of the International Studies Department have spent long periods abroad in diplomatic and economic development assignments. World Business faculty members are involved in international consulting. All are hired for their ability to communicate their knowledge to students.

The Business School Network

Thunderbird has an unparalleled network of more than 30,000 alumni working internationally in more than 130 countries around the globe. The School also has its own exclusive electronic forum on CompuServe, available only to Thunderbird students, alumni, faculty, and staff. Online conversations, conferences, and reunions occur regularly, linking alumni around the world. In addition, many of the School's library and career resources are available on the School's World Wide Web site.

The College and Environs

Thunderbird is located in the Sun Belt area of the Southwest in a suburb of Phoenix, Arizona, America's sixth-largest city. The Phoenix metropolitan area has numerous cultural resources typical of a major urban center.

Technology Environment

Thunderbird's technology environment and infrastructure are headed by a Chief Information Officer. Students have on-campus access to approximately 180 computer terminals throughout the campus. CompuServe, Dialog, LEXIS/NEXIS, and the Internet are on-line services available to M.I.M. students. Standard business application software training and software packages are available for student use in the Lincoln Computer Center. Bibliographic services provided to students in the IBIC include NEXIS, Datastar, Dialog, ABI/Inform, Global Vantage, Predicasts F&S, Business Dateline, Datastream, Moody's, Hoovers, Investext, Info South, Emerging Markets, and newspaper abstracts.

Multimedia support through the Multimedia Center is also available to students, and access to worldwide news programming is provided through the SCOLA satellite system. A center for distance learning was recently completed on campus, and students regularly use telconferencing facilities for job interviews.

Placement

Thunderbird's commitment to the success of its graduates extends well beyond the classroom. More than 700 employers recruit Thunderbird graduates for full-time and internship positions in a typical year, including more than 270 visits on campus. Each student is assisted in creating a Personal Business Plan that takes full advantage of the skills, experiences, and knowledge that come with a Thunderbird education. Off-campus recruiting events are arranged in major cities in the U.S., and alumni career volunteers are available to help graduates access the 30,000 alumni who are working in global assignments throughout the world. Thunderbird utilizes the latest technology, including an electronic resume database and the Thunderbird Alumni Forum on CompuServe, to distribute candidate information and link graduates to opportunities in the global market. Several hundred employers around the world are visited each year by Career Services staff to ensure that employers have personalized access to candidates and understand the distinctive capabilities of the Thunderbird graduate.

The Thunderbird Graduate Management Internship program offers credit-bearing full-time and part-time internships to satisfy diverse employer needs and to formally integrate a student's academic study with meaningful, professional experience. Both international and

domestic internships are available, based on employer needs and candidate qualifications.

Previous internships have included positions with AT&T, CNN International, Daimler-Benz (Germany), Kellogg, Rhone-Poulenc (France), American Business Center (Moscow), Disney Consumer Products, Johnson & Johnson, Merck, Miles, Citibank, U.S. Department of Commerce, U.S. & Foreign Commercial Service, Coca-Cola, General Motors, M&M Mars, Seiko, Sony, Suntory, and Teledyne. Internship assignments have included locations in Europe, Asia, and Latin America as well as in corporate centers through the U.S. and Canada.

Admission

A bachelor's degree from an accredited college or university is required for acceptance into the M.B.A. program. Students must submit a minimum GMAT test score of 500 and must have a minimum 3.0 college GPA. International students must submit a TOEFL score of no less than 550. Two to five years of work experience, international travel or living experience, and proficiency in a foreign language are strongly encouraged.

Finances

Tuition and fees for 1997–98 were approximately $9970 per semester and $7315 for the summer term. Books and instructional supplies run about $500 per semester.

The School estimates that living expenses for a single student living in the residence halls are approximately $1190 for lodging and $1500 for board per semester. Off-campus expenses may be slightly higher. The School requires students to have an IBM or IBM-compatible personal computer. This cost is additional.

Application Facts and Dates

The deadline for summer and fall entrance is January 31; for Winterim and spring entrance, July 31; for summer and fall scholarship applications, March 1; and for Winterim and spring scholarship applications, October 1. For more information, applicants should contact:

Office of Admissions
Thunderbird Campus
American Graduate School of
    International Management
15249 North 59th Avenue
Glendale, Arizona 85306-9903
Telephone: 602-978-7210
        800-848-9084 (toll-free)
        (admissions inquiries only)
Fax: 602-439-5432
E-mail: tbird@t-bird.edu
World Wide Web: http://www.t-bird.edu

Truman State University

Division of Business and Accountancy

Kirksville, Missouri

NEW DIRECTIONS FOR THE ACCOUNTING PROFESSION

The passage of the "150-hour" requirement to sit for the Uniform CPA examination by most states is resulting in new directions for entry into the accounting profession. Technology is changing the role of accountants, particularly in the larger public accounting firms. As future accountants assume more professional consulting responsibilities, it is necessary for them to have a broad background in the liberal arts and sciences, in the functional areas of business and economics, and in technical accounting knowledge. The accounting programs at Truman State provide the necessary knowledge and skills to equip students as lifelong learners in a global society.

—Robert A. Dager, Head, Division of Business and Accountancy

Program of Study

Truman State University offers instruction at the master's level in the area of accounting. The Master of Accountancy is designed to prepare graduates to enter the fields of public accounting, industrial accounting, government accounting, and accounting education. General objectives of the Master of Accountancy program are to provide students with a well-rounded body of professional knowledge based on a strong liberal arts and sciences undergraduate education; to provide the decision-making tools necessary for handling futuristic problems in a pluralistic and ever-changing society; to build the theoretical foundation necessary for analyzing complex problems in a systematic manner; to promote understanding of an environment that has impacted the evolution of accounting thought and practice; to develop skills in utilizing information databases and in researching the professional accounting and/or tax literature; to develop the leadership skills necessary for making independent and informed professional judgments; to prepare students for admission to and success in a doctoral or other graduate professional program; and to prepare students for successful careers in public, management, and governmental accounting or as accounting educators.

The Master of Accountancy program is structured for qualified individuals with a baccalaureate degree in accounting and business administration but also accommodates those who hold degrees in nonbusiness fields. Total graduate credit hours required for the degree range from 30 to 42, depending on the student's background. A 9-hour tax concentration is also available.

Students who finish the program demonstrate knowledge of the following as measured by a test in the various courses and a rigorous comprehensive examination: accounting theory, familiarity and knowledge of accounting pronouncements, cost and managerial cost with expanded analysis, and a specialty area dependent on the student's focus of study.

Student Group

Sixty percent of the students at Truman State have undergraduate degrees in accounting. Other students have degrees in such fields as business, math, English, economics, and sociology. Fifty percent of the students are from the Midwest; others are from states such as Colorado, California, Oklahoma, Kentucky, Michigan, and Washington. One fourth have full-time work experience and 20 percent are international students.

The Faculty

The primary responsibility of every faculty member at Truman State is to become an effective and dedicated classroom teacher. The majority of their efforts are on effective teaching, advising, and student-centered activities. In support of their primary responsibility, each faculty member is expected to continue his/her intellectual and professional growth with scholarly activities and professional service that contributes to the improvement of teaching or the develop-

ment and dissemination of ideas within his/her academic discipline or professional area of study.

The Business School Network

The Division of Business and Accountancy maintains strong ties with the

FACULTY LIST

Stephen L. Allen, Associate Professor of Business Administration, Ph.D. Quantitative methods.

Michael W. Blum, Assistant Professor of Business Administration, Ph.D. Human resource management.

Debra Cartwright, Assistant Professor of Business Administration, Ph.D. candidate. Marketing.

Robert A. Dager, Professor of Business; Head, Division of Business and Accountancy, Ed.D.

Paul G. Fellows, Associate Professor of Business Administration, Ph.D. Finance.

Sandra Fleak, Associate Professor of Accounting, Ph.D., CPA. Financial accounting.

Scott R. Fouch, Associate Professor of Accounting, Ph.D., CPA. Tax.

Neil D. Gilchrist, Associate Professor of Business Administration, Ph.D. Strategic management.

Mary Giovannini, Associate Professor of Business Administration, Ph.D., CPS. Systems.

Pyung Eui Han, Associate Professor of Business Administration, Ed.D. Management.

Keith E. Harrison, Assistant Professor of Accounting, Ph.D. candidate, CPA. Auditing and systems.

Bryce J. Jones II, Professor of Business Administration, J.D., Ph.D. Law.

Debra K. Kerby, Associate Professor of Accounting, Ph.D., CPA, CMA. Managerial accounting.

Steven H. Klein, Associate Professor of Accounting, M.S., CPA. Tax.

Jia-yuan (Jason) Lin, Associate Professor of Business Administration, Ph.D. Finance.

Kyung C. (Andrew) Mun, Assistant Professor of Business Administration, Ph.D. Finance.

John R. Perrachione, Associate Professor of Business Administration, Ph.D. Marketing.

Jeffrey Romine, Associate Professor of Accounting, Ph.D., CPA. Auditing and systems.

Sandra L. Weber, Associate Professor of Accounting, Ph.D., CPA, CMA. Managerial and financial accounting.

business community and alumni. Various alumni chapters provide input to the business programs, networking opportunities for job searches, support for classroom speakers, and program sponsors. The Bentele/Mallingckrodt Executive-in-Residence Program is sponsored by the IMCERA Group and Mallinckrodt, Inc. The program provides for two visiting executives to spend two to three days on campus each year. The executives make class presentations and spend time with students in both formal and informal settings.

The College and Environs

Truman State University, formerly Northeast Missouri State University, is the statewide public liberal arts and sciences university for Missouri. Founded in 1867 as a school to educate teachers, Truman State began its historic new mission in 1986. Truman State is recognized nationally and internationally for its Value-Added Model of Assessment, a comprehensive testing and surveying program used to monitor student progress and the University's educational success.

The University is situated in Kirksville, which has a population of approximately 17,000. The city is located 30 miles south of Iowa; 70 miles west of Quincy, Illinois; and 3 to 4 hours from Kansas City, St. Louis, and Des Moines, Iowa. The Kirksville College of Osteopathic Medicine, the birthplace of osteopathic medicine, is also located in Kirksville. The Kirksville area features a 3,250-acre state park and a 700-acre lake for camping, fishing, swimming, sailing, boating, skiing, and picnicking. Thousand Hills State Park and Forest Lake are located within 10 miles of the campus.

Facilities

Pickler Memorial Library has a book collection of more than 350,000 volumes, augmented by subscriptions to approximately 1,750 journals and periodicals, 1 million microforms, and both U.S. and Missouri document depositories. In addition to an expanding collection of books, periodicals, and microforms and to increasing online access to networks and databases, the library contains several special collections.

Technology Environment

Pickler Memorial Library is a member of the On-line Computer Library Center (OCLC), a worldwide library database, and has implemented the fully automated Northwestern Total Integrated Library System (NOTIS). The Office of Computer Services provides centralized computing for large-scale research, online information systems, and online interactive computing capability for all interested students, faculty, and staff.

Placement

The University Career Center (UCC) offers a full range of job search and placement services. In addition to on-campus interviews, the UCC provides students opportunities for mock interviews, resume reviews, job fairs, employment bulletin subscriptions, and a resume referral service.

Admission

Applicants for the Master of Accountancy program must have a baccalaureate degree from an accredited institution. The GMAT must be taken prior to acceptance. Admission decisions depend heavily on prior undergraduate work and GMAT scores.

Finances

In-state tuition is $151 per credit hour, and out-of-state tuition is $268 per credit hour for the 1998–99 academic year. Living expenses are estimated at $8000 per year.

Graduate teaching and research assistantships are available for a limited number of students. The assistantships pay a cash stipend of $5000 per academic year, and the recipients' tuition is waived for a maximum of 9 credit hours per semester. All books and supplies and any special course fees are the responsibility of the recipient. Recipients are expected either to teach one class each semester or to assist in research for the same number of hours. To be considered for an assistantship, the student must have a 3.0 minimum undergraduate grade point average, a score above the 50th percentile on the GMAT, enrollment in a minimum of 15 graduate hours per academic year, and maintenance of a 3.5 graduate grade point average. Graduate teaching/research assistantships are awarded annually and all applications are due by February 15. Various grants and loans are also available.

Application Facts and Dates

Applications are accepted throughout the year, and students may begin their program at the start of the fall, spring, or summer semester.

To request an informational brochure and application, students should contact:

Dr. Scott R. Fouch
Coordinator of Graduate Studies in Accounting
Division of Business and Accountancy
Truman State University
Kirksville, Missouri 63501
Telephone: 816-785-4371
E-mail: bu58@truman.edu
World Wide Web: http//www.truman.edu

Tulane University

A. B. Freeman School of Business

New Orleans, Louisiana

FREEMAN: A DYNAMIC M.B.A. EXPERIENCE

▶ *The mission of the Freeman School is to develop tomorrow's leaders through innovative education, a team focus, and individual attention. As one of America's oldest and most respected business schools, Freeman offers the opportunity to join a select group of students in a dynamic learning experience.*

The M.B.A. program provides a global business perspective in America's most international city. The Freeman M.B.A. will enhance your leadership and management skills. We encourage you to take advantage of this outstanding educational opportunity. It will provide you with the academic tools to assist you in the realization of your goals.

—James W. McFarland, Dean

Programs and Curricular Focus

The Freeman program is designed to maximize the skills needed to manage in the future. Students enter the program via a module that expands their concepts of management and the M.B.A. The global representation of the student body becomes clear as a student gets to know classmates from around the world. A first-year core curriculum emphasizes teamwork and analytical skills. Ten elective courses provide the breadth of the Freeman M.B.A. while allowing students to focus on subjects of value to their careers.

Students participate in career development programs, organizational activities, and a range of School- and community-sponsored events concurrently with the program.

In addition to the full-time M.B.A. program, the Freeman School offers three joint-degree programs and several other degree options. The M.B.A./Juris Doctor allows students to complete both law and business degrees in four years. The M.B.A./Master of Public Health is a 93-credit-hour program. The M.B.A./Master of Arts in Latin American Studies requires 75 credit hours. A Master of Accounting program, Professional (part-time) M.B.A. Program, Executive M.B.A. Program, and Ph.D. program complete the range of degree options possible at the Freeman School.

Students and the M.B.A. Experience

Freeman students join one of the most diverse and talented peer groups to be found. Classmates share this perspective through the first year of intensive interpersonal experience. With a third of the student body made up of international students and 70 percent of the domestic student body multilingual, Freeman students enjoy a truly global perspective.

Professional backgrounds also contribute to the diversity of Freeman students. Students enjoy peers who have worked as consultants for international firms, engineers for multinational corporations, and entrepreneurs, which are among the many careers in private, public, and nonprofit enterprises evident in the Freeman student body.

Special Features

The most striking feature of the Freeman School is its people. Faculty members, renowned in their fields, participate actively in unique class and project settings, and an alumni network includes more than 2,000 contacts who are ready to lend their expertise in career planning. With these features, Freeman students participate in an active and innovative learning experience.

At Freeman, institutes augment the traditional classroom discussion with centers for specific interests. The Goldring Institute focuses on international business, the Levy-Rosenblum Institute focuses on entrepreneurship, and the Burkenroad Institute centers on the study of leadership and ethics in management. The institutes provide a facility for students, faculty members, and the business community to participate in interactive programs and research. Each year, dozens of business leaders and

academics come to the Freeman School to participate in the institute's programs.

The Faculty

The Freeman School faculty designed the innovative curriculum to make the best use of its expertise and the students' own abilities and interests. A combination of teaching styles is used throughout the curriculum, with an emphasis on teamwork. While the first year is more theoretical, the second year relies heavily on the case method. The size of the program is intentionally small. Freeman students have easy access to their professors. The faculty consists of internationally recognized scholars in many business fields.

The Business School Network

Prominent business leaders visit Freeman regularly to address student organizations, to serve as Executives-in-Residence, and to participate in career development and placement programs. The School enjoys tremendous support from its more than 7,000 graduates.

The College and Environs

Tulane is one of the major private research universities in the United States. With its eleven schools and colleges that range from the liberal arts to the sciences and a full spectrum of professional schools, Tulane offers a breadth of experience equaled by only six other private universities in the United States. Tulane's history dates back to the Medical College of Louisiana, founded in 1834. Tulane offered the South's first schools of architecture, business, and social work. The University offers a lively academic atmosphere, while each school focuses on the needs and abilities of the individual student.

Tulane is located in a residential, parklike setting in one of America's first great cities, New Orleans. Founded by the French in the early 1700s, New Orleans offers its own unique food, music, architecture, and lifestyle. As the nation's largest port, New Orleans plays a critical role in North America's expanding commerce with Latin America, Europe, and Africa. Annual events such as Mardi Gras, the Jazz and Heritage Festival, and the Sugar Bowl make New Orleans an international tourist destination.

Facilities

The Freeman School is housed in Goldring/Woldenberg Hall, a seven-story complex designed and built for the needs of management education. All business school classes are located in the building, as are an auditorium, group study rooms, faculty offices, and the library. Classrooms seat up to 60 and are designed to foster an interactive learning environment. State-of-the-art classroom technologies include computer ports and presentation equipment. A computer classroom adds to the available technology. The Turchin Library is one of the most modern business libraries in the area. More than a dozen electronic sources complement the 35,000 volumes and more than 700 journals available through the library.

Technology Environment

From state-of-the-art classrooms to a complete television studio, the Freeman School offers the latest in business technologies. The building features its own in-house network (accessible by modem), computer classrooms, and computer labs.

Placement

The School's in-house placement center reviews the abilities of entering students and prepares career development strategies for future graduates annually. Through seminars and individual counseling, students are provided with the resources to define objectives, explore career options, and identify potential employers. Last year, 97 percent of the class was placed within three months of graduation, with salaries ranging between $32,000 and $115,000.

Admission

Diversity among the student body is an integral part of the Freeman experience. The Admissions Committee actively seeks applicants from all over the world and encourages candidates with degrees from accredited institutions in all major fields of study. The committee considers all credentials presented by the candidate. Undergraduate performance and results of the Graduate Management Admission Test (GMAT) are used to assess verbal and quantitative abilities. An essay, letters of recommendation, and a personal interview provide the committee with further information on candidates' abilities, skills, motivation, and career focus. The Test of English as a Foreign Language (TOEFL) score is required of all applicants for whom English is not the native language or who have graduated from a university in which all or most of the instruction is not in English. Emphasis is given to the breadth of professional experience, academic ability, and fit with Freeman programs in the selection of students.

Finances

For the 1998–99 academic year, tuition is $21,720. University fees are $1280, and there is a health center fee of $304. Estimated costs for books are $800. The estimated housing and living expenses are $10,500.

International Students

An international flavor permeates New Orleans and the Freeman School. More than a third of the entering class come from outside the United States, representing more than twenty-five countries. International programs at the University and within the School highlight the diversity of experiences and cultures within the community. A number of M.B.A. activities and University services focus on the international dimension and the needs of the international business community.

Application Facts and Dates

Admission to the Freeman School is on a rolling basis. Applications are evaluated as early as September of the preceding year. Decisions are issued approximately four weeks after the receipt of completed applications.

All full-time applicants are automatically considered for fellowships during the application process. Assistantships are held by approximately 40 percent of the first-year students and 60 percent of the second-year students. Assistantship positions are arranged by students at the beginning of the semester.

Mr. John C. Silbernagel
Assistant Dean of Admissions
    and Financial Aid
A. B. Freeman School of Business
Tulane University
7 McAlister Drive, Suite 400
New Orleans, Louisiana 70118
Telephone: 504-865-5410
Fax: 504-865-6770
E-mail: admissions@freeman.tulane.
    edu
World Wide Web: http://freeman.
    tulane.edu

Union College

ANALYTICAL PROBLEM SOLVING IN MANAGEMENT

The Union College M.B.A. program has dedicated itself to analytical problem solving in management, based on the tradition of a small, select liberal arts and engineering college. The program rests on three pillars. For one, we believe that management is human intervention. Good managers must understand leadership, teamwork, and motivation. Secondly, we believe that management can only achieve its goals when it is based on measurable facts. Finally, we believe that management is interdisciplinary, system-oriented, and global.

Our faculty members dedicate themselves to teaching and supporting students. We seek interaction with and among students. We invite our students to collaborate with us on state-of-the-art research. Our overall aim is to challenge students to achieve individual growth, strong analytical skills, and sharpened global perspectives. We seek to reinforce the intellectual tradition taught in a high-quality college.

—Joseph Zolner, Director

Programs and Curricular Focus

Union College's Graduate Management Institute offers M.B.A. students an opportunity to study in the attractive environment of a liberal arts campus, where students get to know both the faculty and their peers. Union's M.B.A. curriculum blends theory with practice in a well-balanced approach consisting of lectures, case studies, written reports, computer models, and business games. For curricular development, the Institute benefits from the advice of a distinguished council that includes prominent leaders from business, government, and education. Union management students learn problem-solving techniques directly applicable to a progressive decision-making environment.

Union's M.B.A. programs develop the traditional knowledge of accounting, economics, finance, operations, marketing, and organizational behavior. The programs provide a foundation for effective team building, quantitative decision making, creative problem solving, and total quality management process skills. Students are assigned group projects in a number of core courses. These groups are carefully selected to include students with diverse educational and work experiences.

In addition to the M.B.A. in management, Union offers three other M.B.A. programs. The M.B.A. in accounting program at Union includes an internship at one of the "Big Six" accounting firms.

This program also prepares students to sit for the first section of the CPA examination. The M.B.A. in health systems administration includes a paid residency at a health-care institution during the summer between the two years of the program. This program, fully accredited by the Accrediting Commission on Education for Health Services Administration (ACEHSA), prepares graduates for management positions in health services delivery and related institutions.

Union has added a new option beginning in fall 1996, the M.B.A. in international management. This program prepares students for careers in both private and public international and multinational organizations. Students must demonstrate proficiency in at least one foreign language. An international internship is normally required, but students may substitute an approved graduate study-abroad program.

Union also offers a combined M.B.A./J.D. program with the Albany Law School of Union University. Students in this program can earn their M.B.A. degree in management, accounting, or health systems along with their J.D. degree in four academic years.

Students and the M.B.A. Experience

The Graduate Management Institute includes both full- and part-time students with very diverse backgrounds and work experiences. Full- and part-time students take the same classes. They are offered the flexibility to transfer between full-time and part-time status as personal and professional circumstances dictate. Women comprise approximately 40 percent of the student population, and international and minority students comprise 10 percent of the full-time students.

Approximately 25 percent of the students have undergraduate degrees in business or finance. Another 25 percent come from engineering or technical disciplines, with the remaining 50 percent coming from science, social science, humanities, and other disciplines. About 10 percent of the students are pursuing a joint degree in law and business.

The Faculty

Faculty ideas and attitudes make one institution different from another. The composition of GMI's faculty attests to Union's concern with providing a comprehensive education that remains relevant in the future. Every full-time member of the faculty is engaged in research, and all publish regularly in national journals. Research allows faculty members to remain current in their fields, and classroom teaching translates this expertise into an educational experience.

The adjunct faculty members are all either researchers in industry or successful in business in their field. They bring practical experience and diversity to all programs.

The Business School Network
Corporate Partnerships

The Graduate Management Institute has recently begun a Corporate Fellowship Program. This is a joint venture between GMI and various companies that provides opportunities for talented students to receive a scholarship from GMI and the sponsoring company and to work for the sponsoring company for 10 hours per week during the school year and 40 hours per week during the summer. Students are paid by the company for this work. Students in this program increase their work experience during the educational process. Permanent employment opportunities may result from these fellowships.

GMI's Advisory Council consists of business leaders in industry and in the fields of health and accounting as well as alumni and faculty members. This council functions to advise GMI on the changing needs in the corporate, health, and accounting industries. Council members are also encouraged to visit classes and to meet with students informally.

A series of lectures features prominent business leaders who address Union's graduate students on current business issues. In addition to these lectures, each term a colloquium series is featured. The guests for this series generally address specific functional areas of business. Students are encouraged to attend these functions as part of their educational experience.

The College and Environs

In 1795, Union College became the first college chartered by the Regents of the State of New York. Since its beginnings, Union has been committed to innovative education, offering scientific studies in the early nineteenth century. In 1845, Union became the first liberal arts college to offer engineering. In the 1950s, the College established programs that cut across the barriers separating the traditional academic disciplines. It was in this spirit that the Graduate Management Institute evolved as a center that builds on the values of a broad education.

The Graduate Management Institute offers its programs on the Union College grounds, a campus of some 100 acres located on a hill overlooking Schenectady, a city founded by the Dutch in 1661. The campus, designed by the French architect Joseph Jacques Ramée in 1813, is recognized as a historic landmark in the development of the American college campus.

Technology Environment

Housed in the Stanley G. Peschel Center for Computer Science and Information Systems, Union's computer center is the home of a distributed network that provides access to various computer resources, including a cluster of four VAX computers and a DEC system 5000/200 running UNIX. There are more than 700 personal computers (and workstations) and 100 terminals on campus. All students have access to national and international resources of the Internet through the College's member-

ship in the NYSERnet. There is no charge for a student computer account. The on-line catalog in Schaffer Library is accessible from any point on the network.

Schaffer Library houses some 490,000 volumes and 1,600 current periodical subscriptions. It operates on the open stack plan and offers bibliographic instruction, interlibrary loan services, on-line bibliographic retrieval services, document delivery, CD-ROM workstations, and public-use computer terminals connected to the campus computer center. Automated circulation of books and other library materials as well as the on-line catalogs are in place. The library has been a depository for federal government documents since 1901. Professional reference service is offered during nearly all hours that the library is open.

Placement

The Career Development Center offers a variety of services for graduate students, including career planning, resume writing, and interviewing skills. On-campus recruiting generally takes place during the fall and winter terms. In addition, the Graduate Management Institute has a strong alumni network to help with placement for its graduates.

Admission

The Graduate Management Institute requires all students to submit official transcripts from all undergraduate and graduate schools, GMAT scores, three letters of recommendation, and an essay. The average GMAT score for enrolling M.B.A. students is 570, with a range of 500 to 700. The average undergraduate GPA is 3.2.

TOEFL results are required for all students for whom English is not the native language. A score of 550 to 600 is required. International students must present proof of adequate funds to cover two full years. International students are considered for assistantships based on academic merit.

There are no specific prerequisite courses except for precalculus. Basic skills in writing and computing are expected. Students who have not taken precalculus may take a two-course sequence in precalculus and calculus at the Graduate Management Institute, but only one of these courses may be applied toward the degree.

Students with appropriate undergraduate backgrounds may waive up to four courses. These students may complete the program in one calendar year.

All students must provide proof of immunization for measles and rubella. This is a New York State Health Law requirement. Health insurance is available from the College at a very reasonable price.

Finances

Tuition for the 1998–99 academic year is $13,000. Books and fees cost approximately $1500 per year.

There is no on-campus housing provided for graduate students at Union College, but housing is plentiful within walking distance of the campus. The cost of housing, utilities, and living expenses is estimated to be approximately $7000 per year. Students are not required to purchase a computer, but it is strongly encouraged.

A number of M.B.A. assistantships are available, and candidates applying for the program are considered if they request this on their application. The awards are based on academic merit and may be awarded to international students.

International Students

Approximately 15 percent of the full-time student population are international students. They are encouraged to attend the orientation held for international students prior to the beginning of classes in September. Graduate international students are also encouraged to participate in the International Club on Union's campus.

Application Facts and Dates

The Graduate Management Institute has a rolling admission process, and students may begin during any of the trimesters or summer sessions. However, most full-time students begin in the fall. For full-time students who wish to be considered for assistantships or fellowships, completed applications must be received no later than March 31. For more information, students should contact:

Carolyn J. Micklas, Coordinator for Recruiting and Admissions
Graduate Management Institute
Union College
Schenectady, New York 12308
Telephone: 518-388-6239
Fax: 518-388-6754
E-mail: micklasc@union.edu
World Wide Web: http://gmi.union.edu

The University of Alabama

Manderson Graduate School of Business

Tuscaloosa, Alabama

> ### A COMPLETE BUSINESS EDUCATION
>
> *With a long-standing reputation and backed with strong traditions of excellence, the University of Alabama provides students with a unique M.B.A. experience. Our program provides the highest-quality students with a complete business education that emphasizes applied practical learning. The quality of the education, the support of fifty years of loyal alumni, and the satisfaction of spending two years as part of a very special group make the Alabama M.B.A. program what it is. It is distinguished not by its quality alone but also by its relatively low cost and its focus on the education of excellent students. In all of this, the University of Alabama is a unique experience, educating leaders for the twenty-first century.*
>
> *—J. Barry Mason, Dean, Culverhouse College of Commerce and Business Administration*

Programs and Curricular Focus

The Alabama M.B.A. program is designed to provide bright, energetic, and ambitious students a solid business education that focuses on current topics and business concerns, with a strong underlying core of business theory and practices. From the first day of orientation, students embark on a two-year experience that lasts far beyond the classroom. Students are constantly challenged and encouraged to push the limit through course work, case studies, and hands-on projects involving regional and national corporations.

In the past few years, the Alabama program has undergone a fundamental change that is culminating in a revised curriculum and improved placement and career development opportunities. The curriculum at Manderson is innovative, with traditional semester-long courses being replaced by "resource modules." The goal is simple—equip the students with the tools and resources needed to contribute to an organization immediately upon graduation. The first year of the program focuses on foundation tools—accounting, marketing, finance, organizational behavior, economics, statistics, production and operations management, communication skills, and business strategy. These core topics are interwoven throughout the fall and spring semesters as students are faced with the challenge of identifying and solving complex business problems. During the second year of the program, students complete a concentration pertaining to their career objectives.

The University of Alabama also offers a joint M.B.A./J.D. degree program that combines the work for both degrees into a four-year program. Individual applications must be submitted to both the M.B.A. program and the Law School. Both the GMAT and the LSAT are required for admission purposes.

Students and the M.B.A. Experience

The hallmark of the Alabama M.B.A. program is teamwork. Students are organized into teams of 4 to 5 students during orientation, and work together in and outside of the classroom throughout the first year. Teams are also utilized in the second year within the concentrations and are often called upon to work on projects for corporations and other organizations. Students also work individually, complementing the team experiences in learning about time and conflict management, leadership skills, ethical decision making, analysis and problem solving, and interpersonal relations.

Students in the program have diverse backgrounds, bringing a wide range of experiences and interests to the classroom. About 50 percent have undergraduate degrees in liberal arts and sciences, and 20 percent have engineering degrees. Each fall, about 60 students begin the M.B.A. program. Small class sizes and a diverse student population foster a sense of mutual respect and responsibility. Faculty and staff members work closely with the students throughout the two-year program through informal and formal channels such as the Faculty Mentor Program.

Special Features

The Alabama M.B.A. program begins with a one-week orientation program in which students participate in individual, leadership, and team-building activities. These are designed to foster a sense of corporate leadership and responsibility. From this, a foundation is formed for the remainder of the two-year business education.

Throughout the first year, students are involved in a professional development program for which topics have ranged from art, music, and theater appreciation to sexual harassment awareness.

Along with these formal programs, students are involved in many out-of-class activities, including community service, intramural sports, and clubs such as the MBA Association and the Alabama Student Government. Once a year, the students sponsor MBA Week, which includes career development seminars, student/faculty sports competitions, keynote speakers, and an annual MBA Golf Outing that attracts current students, alumni, and prominent corporate executives.

The Faculty

Alabama's faculty is among the best in the business. Those faculty members chosen to work with the M.B.A. program are men and women of widely diverse backgrounds and experience united by a shared love of teaching and an appreciation for the need to have useful knowledge immediately upon entering the workplace. Each is a recognized scholar in his or her chosen field, but, as a cohesive and complementary M.B.A. staff member, each is part of a team dedicated to the future of the Alabama student. Each faculty member is actively engaged in real-world research, consulting, and related activities along with his or her pure academic pursuits.

Mary Hewell Alston Hall, central to the Manderson Graduate School, houses several state-of-the-art classrooms, offices, and the Insurance Hall of Fame.

The Business School Network

M.B.A. alumni are active in all phases of the Alabama M.B.A. experience. From placement opportunities to classroom visits and service on the College's Advisory Boards, Alabama M.B.A. alumni bring a vital practitioner's viewpoint to the operations of the college. Traditionally spread throughout the Southeast and more recently along the whole of the eastern seaboard to New York, Alabama alumni form a deep and dedicated pool of practical knowledge and resources on which the college, its faculty, and ultimately each student depends. Since its establishment in the early 1950s, the University of Alabama's M.B.A. program has graduated more than 1,500 men and women, each of whom is a valuable and loyal member of the Alabama family.

The College and Environs

The University of Alabama is located in Tuscaloosa, Alabama, which is 60 minutes from Birmingham and near Atlanta, New Orleans, Nashville, and Memphis. With its attractive countryside and location near the Black Warrior River, the town has a historic quality. The University has about 20,000 students, 380 of whom are graduate business students. Tuscaloosa, with about 170,000 residents, is a pleasant town that is growing into a thriving business center. The climate is usually comfortable, and favorite pastimes include outdoor activities such as waterskiing, fishing, camping, biking, and jogging. Nationally and internationally known performers often come to campus to perform, and the local community is very supportive of the arts.

Facilities

The College of Commerce and Business Administration is the proud home of Bidgood Hall, Mary Hewell Alston Hall, and the 65,000-square-foot Angelo Bruno Business Library and Sloan Y. Bashinsky Computer Center. All three buildings house state-of-the-art classrooms and facilities. Alston Hall includes faculty and departmental offices along with the Insurance Hall of Fame. Bidgood Hall, reopened after a beautiful refurbishing, houses multimedia classrooms and areas for graduate students, as well as several research centers and the Manderson Graduate School of Business. The Bruno-Bashinsky Library and Computer Center houses more than 200 computer terminals for student use, group study rooms, and computerized library reference systems.

Placement

The Manderson Graduate School recognizes that career education and development is of utmost importance to the students. Numerous opportunities are available to students, including career conferences, participation in the Southeast MBA Consortium, in-house interviewing and placement services, and personalized career search assistance. Workshops in areas such as employment search strategies and interviewing skills are offered through MBA Career Services, as well as the University Placement Office. Summer internships are strongly encouraged, many of which result in offers of postgraduation employment.

Admission

Application requirements include the completion of an undergraduate degree at an accredited U.S. college or its international equivalent, submission of scores from the General Management Admissions Test (GMAT), and completion of the application materials. Letters of recommendation, transcripts, essays, and an interview are also required and are integral in the admissions decision process. All international students must also submit scores from the TOEFL.

Finances

The costs for tuition at Alabama have been cited by a leading business publica-

tion as offering the "best bang for your buck." Full-time tuition is $2954 per academic year for residents and $6808 per academic year for nonresidents, plus an addtional $200 fee for each of ten core courses. This fee totals $2000 over the two-year program. Living expenses may include an estimated rent for an off-campus apartment of between $300 and $550 per month. Additional bills for water, cable, telephone, and power can vary according to use. University dorms or apartments are also available.

Individuals who wish to be considered for any fellowships, scholarships, or assistantships offered by the University of Alabama's M.B.A. program must first apply to the program, be unconditionally accepted, and have competitive academic credentials. All students who are accepted unconditionally into Alabama's M.B.A. program are considered for all academic awards. There are no additional forms that must be submitted.

Application Facts and Dates

Applicants are encouraged to submit their applications to the University of Alabama as early as possible. The application process begins on October 1 of the year prior to the year applicants wish to start. The final application deadline is May 14. Students who wish to be considered for scholarships, fellowships, or assistantships should apply by February 12. All University of Alabama offices are open between 8 a.m. and 4:45 p.m. Central Standard Time. Students with any questions regarding international applications and requirements should contact:

Mrs. Edwina Crawford
The University of Alabama Graduate School
Box 870118, 102 Rose Administration Building
Tuscaloosa, Alabama 35487-0118
Telephone: 205-348-5921

Students may also contact:

Coordinator of Graduate Recruiting
The University of Alabama
Manderson Graduate School of Business
Box 870223, 101 Bidgood Hall
Tuscaloosa, Alabama 35487-0223
Telephone: 205-348-6517
888-863-2622 (toll-free in the United States)
E-mail: mba@alston.cba.ua.edu

The University of Arizona

INNOVATIVE MANAGEMENT EDUCATION—THE ELLER SCHOOL APPROACH

The goal of the Eller School M.B.A. program is to provide the foundation for a lifetime of development so that each student can maximize his or her potential for success. We accomplish this by providing a curriculum that combines the benefits of education based in the business disciplines with the relevance of dealing with real business problems. When you finish our program, you will be able to identify and formulate business problems, to specify and locate the information needed to solve them, and to develop and implement practical solutions. In short, you will know what questions to ask, where to go for information, and how to use that information to make effective managerial decisions. These are the keys to success in business, and they are the cornerstones of our program. We promise you hard work, a measure of fun, a friendly and supportive learning environment, and the knowledge and skills to be an effective business leader when you graduate. Join us for an unmatched learning experience!

—Christopher P. Puto, Associate Dean and Director of the M.B.A. Program

Programs and Curricular Focus

The Eller School's philosophy is that successful business leaders must have a solid understanding of business concepts and how they are interrelated in the overall business system.

The M.B.A. curriculum is based on two years of full-time study, with an optional internship in industry during the summer between the first and second years. The first year comprises the M.B.A. Core. Ten courses (plus the three communications modules) are designed to introduce students to crucial concepts and skills for professional managers.

The second-year curriculum offers students the opportunity to pursue their professional interests and goals through a wide selection of electives. Individual majors are not required in the Eller School M.B.A. program. By planning elective choices carefully, students can achieve functional depth and interdisciplinary breadth.

This combination of flexibility and structure lets students customize their individual course of study while ensuring that each student leaves the program with the knowledge and skills required to identify, create, and deliver superior customer value in his or her chosen career. Areas of study and concentration include highly ranked MIS and marketing departments, a nationally recognized entrepreneurship program, and an

expanded finance concentration. The final semester of the second year also includes a required business policy course, which serves as the capstone for the program.

Students and the M.B.A. Experience

Communications skills are vital for successful managers. To ensure relevance for business, the Eller School communications component is directly connected to and completely integrated with the first-year core courses. Each oral and written business communications activity has a theoretical and a practical component that relates directly to a corresponding business topic.

Similarly, team building and teamwork are vital aspects of business success. Because these skills are essential to long-term success, M.B.A. students in the Eller School are taught the theoretical underpinnings of good teamwork, and they are coached in the practical methods for achieving it.

The Eller School is deliberately kept small (approximately 100 full-time students are enrolled each year) so that students can grow and develop in a friendly, professional environment. A variety of opportunities for interactions with faculty and staff members in both academic and social settings results in a friendly, supportive atmosphere in which

each individual can feel comfortable and confident. Where competition exists, such as in the simulation, it is good-natured and focused on mutual goals of learning and success.

Social life in the M.B.A. program is plentiful and varied. The close-knit, team-oriented nature of the program produces deep and lasting friendships. This past year, students participated in a tour of regional wineries, hiking and camping in the surrounding mountains, intramural sports, and the Eller Cup semiannual golf tournament.

Special Features

Classroom activities alone are not sufficient to prepare students for leadership roles when they finish the program. Dealing with real business situations and having the opportunity to confront issues, make decisions, and see the results is one way to enhance the learning experience for M.B.A. students. At the Eller School, a unique approach has been developed for introducing students to the real world of business and integrating the material of the first-year curriculum. It is called The Management Experience. Beginning in the third week of the first semester, students are organized into teams of 4 to 6 individuals, who compete in an advanced, highly complex computerized business simulation. As the semester progresses, students make weekly decisions regarding market opportunities, product development, marketing strategy, production planning, and strategic positioning. They receive weekly feedback in the form of sales results, market-share data, stock prices, and bottom-line profits. Students have the opportunity to apply their classroom knowledge in a controlled, but highly competitive, environment. They sharpen their analytical, team-building, and communications skills while they learn how the various components of a business system combine to form a successful enterprise. The results of the simulation are then stored until the fourth semester, when they are revisited in the capstone course. Second-year M.B.A. students recruit and form their own teams, who then bid to take over the

management of their former companies. Using the knowledge and skills developed in the first three semesters of their M.B.A. program, these fourth-semester students then have the opportunity to demonstrate their abilities to successfully operate a business. When students complete this activity, they leave the program with a level of maturity, competence, and business savvy that is well beyond what is typically learned in a classroom setting. This activity, and the level of interaction generated among the M.B.A. students, is one of the highlights of the Eller School M.B.A. program. It is the only major M.B.A. program in the country that applies this advanced learning system in this manner.

The Faculty

Faculty members serve as mentors and coaches to students entering a new realm of experience. All are highly credentialed scholars who bring their extensive research, consulting, and business backgrounds to the classroom experience. Representing a full range of management disciplines, Eller School faculty members have received national attention for the quality, originality, and leadership of their work. In addition to advancing the state of knowledge in traditional fields, they are pioneering new areas such as judgment and decision making and group decision support systems.

The Business School Network

M.B.A. students find a ready source of mentoring and helpful support in the M.B.A. Student Association (MBASA). One special aspect of the MBASA is the student consulting group. Student consultants work with area businesses to help

them solve real business problems. Recent clients include the Tucson Urban League, which retained the MBASA Consulting Group to instruct minority businesspeople in the business planning process.

The College and Environs

The University of Arizona is located in Tucson, a city of more than 650,000 in the southeastern corner of the state. Surrounded by mountains and blessed with an eternally blue sky, the high Sonoran Desert is a delightful place to live and to learn. Housing is readily available and reasonably priced.

Technology Environment

The routine use of the computer is incorporated throughout the curriculum. Students regularly use group collaboration software, e-mail, statistical analysis, word processing, and presentation software packages. Because information technologies are a pervasive component of the M.B.A. program, students should enter with a reasonable comfort with either a Windows or Macintosh computing environment and familiarity with a spreadsheet package (such as Microsoft Excel) and a word processing package (such as Microsoft Word). The Business School Information Technology Service (BITS) offers refresher courses in each of these areas throughout the semester for those students who wish to brush up or expand their skills. BITS also offers courses in the popular statistical packages, so it is not necessary for students to know this material prior to the start of school. Access to computers is available throughout the campus, and graduate student labs are available during the hours when McClelland Hall is open. If individual resources permit, it is recommended that students own a notebook computer with a modem to facilitate 24-hour access to technology.

Placement

The Eller School Graduate Placement Office assists students in developing career plans and job search strategies and actively markets the School and the students to regional and national employers. In addition to on-campus interviews for full-time positions and summer internships, the Eller School participates in the West Coast M.B.A. Consortium, an annual recruiting event held in Irvine, California, and has recently utilized videoconference technology to enable employers to conduct live video interviews with Eller School students. The EllerNet Alumni Network enables

students to make contacts with M.B.A. alumni across the country.

Admission

Applicants for admission to the M.B.A. program must submit transcripts from all undergraduate and graduate institutions attended, essays in response to specific questions, a resume, GMAT scores, application forms, and a nonrefundable application fee. International students must submit TOEFL scores (minimum of 600) and evidence of financial resources. Mathematics prerequisites for admission include calculus.

The entering class in the fall of 1997 had an average GMAT score of 610, average GPA of 3.39 (on a 4.0 scale), average age of 29, and an average of six years of work experience.

Finances

The 1998–99 registration fee for full-time in-state students is $4162 per year. Tuition and fees for full-time nonresident students total $11,114 per year. In-state part-time students pay $2644 per year for registration fees; part-time nonresident students, $5584 per year. Room and board cost approximately $5470 per year. Students should budget $1000 for books, software, and photocopying for the first year of study and approximately $800 for the second year. They should also budget $600 for insurance and $2500 for miscellaneous expenses per year.

Merit-based financial aid is available through the Eller School for full-time students only. This includes waivers of nonresident tuition, graduate assistantships, waivers of registration fees, and donor-funded scholarships. Loans are available through the Office of Student Financial Aid.

Application Facts and Dates

Applications for fall admission are processed as they are received. Deadlines are February 1 for financial aid and for international students and March 1 for domestic students. Decision letters are mailed within four to six weeks after receipt of completed applications. For more information, students should contact:

Ms. Susan K. Salinas Wong
Director of Admissions
Eller Graduate School of Management
210 McClelland Hall
P.O. Box 210108
The University of Arizona
Tucson, Arizona 85721-0108
Telephone: 520-621-3915
Fax: 520-621-2606
E-mail: ellernet@bpa.arizona.edu

University of Arkansas

Fayetteville, Arkansas

WINNING IN THE NEXT MILLENNIUM—THE ARKANSAS M.B.A.

Through our new, competency-based M.B.A. program, University of Arkansas (UA) M.B.A. students develop the necessary skills and knowledge to be change agents in the global environment of the twenty-first century. We emphasize an integrated perspective to business problems through our modular core curriculum, concentrations, and Partners in Progress program.

Our program combines the strengths of individuals in numerous team-based, real-world projects. You will find that our students are competitive in nature but cooperative with each other.

From their first exposure to the exceptional beauty of the Ozark Mountains, Arkansas M.B.A. students gain new friendships and experiences that underscore lifelong personal and business success. We will prepare you to manage, lead, and change the business environment for the next millennium.

—Doyle Z. Williams, Dean

Programs and Curricular Focus

The University of Arkansas Master of Business Administration program is designed to produce graduates with a broad view of the issues confronting managers in cutting-edge organizations. In a departure from the traditional collection of 3-hour courses, the Arkansas M.B.A. program is organized around a collection of coordinated modules. UA M.B.A. students are involved in classes and projects that ensure students possess the following five competencies upon graduation: the skills, knowledge, and ability to lead change; the ability to approach problems from a managerial perspective; the ability to manage and work in teams; the ability to write and speak persuasively, based upon a comprehensive analysis of situations facing managers; and self-confidence grounded in one's ability.

Both the full-time and the managerial (part-time) programs comprise five primary blocks: preparatory work, foundations, core modules, a partnering project, and a concentration in one of five areas: strategic retail alliances, finance, entrepreneurship and strategic innovation, global business, or a customized concentration. The customized concentration is designed by the student and can be completed with either business administration courses and/or courses outside of the College. Joint-degree programs are available with several colleges at the University of Arkansas.

The UA M.B.A. program is a one-year program for all students, regardless of their undergraduate degree. Through extensive self-study with preparatory materials, participation in prematriculation workshops, and completion of the foundations module, all students should have sufficient background to pursue the rigorous 38-hour, lock-step curriculum. The managerial program is a two-year (minimum) program. Initial matriculation is around July 1 for the full-time program and around May 20 for the managerial program.

Students and the M.B.A. Experience

The UA M.B.A. experience is different from the experience found in large M.B.A. programs. Arkansas' small program size allows frequent and substantial contact among students and between students and faculty members. A very active graduate business student association plans and carries out community outreach work, professional development activities, and social functions.

Arkansas M.B.A. students have widely varying backgrounds. More than twenty states and fifteen countries are represented in the M.B.A. student body. Students average 27 years of age and possess, on average, three years of professional work experience prior to joining the program. Approximately 40 percent of students are women and 10 percent are members of minority groups.

The M.B.A. program is open to any undergraduate degree student; majors have included business, biology, liberal arts, history, psychology, political science, and other social sciences. Nearly 15 percent of students possess undergraduate degrees and work experience in chemical, civil, industrial, mechanical, or electrical engineering.

Special Features

UA M.B.A. students have the opportunity to participate in numerous international programs and courses. Jointly taught summer classes are offered with the University of Quebec at Montreal and Monterey Institute of Technology in Mexico. A dual master's degree program with ESC Toulouse in France allows French-speaking students to complete one year of study at the University of Arkansas and a second year of study in France, with degrees from both institutions being awarded at the completion of the second year. Many M.B.A. students choose to participate in College of Business Administration classes in Costa Rica, Greece, and Italy.

Future entrepreneurs can participate in the Students Acquiring Knowledge through Enterprise (SAKE) course. SAKE is a retail operation that offers high-quality, unique merchandise for the college market. Profits from the business are used to fund international travel; in the past year, students have traveled to Hong Kong, China, and Costa Rica.

The Faculty

Arkansas M.B.A. faculty members possess extensive experience in corporate problem solving for a variety of businesses and government agencies. Twenty-one percent of the graduate faculty comprises women and members of minority groups. Graduate faculty members have received doctoral degrees from major research institutions, including Carnegie Mellon, Duke, Georgia, Harvard, Indiana, Michigan, Michigan State, North Carolina, Pennsylvania, Purdue, Tennessee, and Texas. Faculty members are active in research and professional publications.

The Business School Network

The Dean's Executive Advisory Board utilizes its experience and expertise to assist

Expectations of excellence; performance to match.

the College of Business Administration in defining and realizing its goals. The board consists of 31 corporate leaders, 26 of whom are chairmen, CEOs, presidents, or division presidents of large regional, national, or international corporations, including Wal-Mart Stores, Inc.; Tyson Foods, Inc.; J. B. Hunt Transport, Inc.; Entergy Corporation; ALLTEL Corporation; Beverly Enterprises; J. C. Penney Company; Frito-Lay, Inc.; and Southwestern Bell Telephone. These corporate leaders provide valuable insight and contacts and play an integral part of the M.B.A. experience, bridging academic learning with hands-on professional training.

The College also utilizes the services of the Business Alumni Advisory Council members. Council members serve as ambassadors to advance the presence of the College throughout the nation. The council comprises 26 members, all of whom are graduates of the University of Arkansas. Each member is a business leader in his or her field of expertise.

The College and Environs

The University of Arkansas, Fayetteville, serves as the major center of liberal and professional education and as the primary land-grant campus for the state. The University offers graduate education leading to the master's degree in more than eighty-two fields and to the doctoral degree in more than thirty carefully selected areas.

The entire UA student population is approximately 15,000. The College of Business Administration enrolls approximately 2,300 undergraduate students and approximately 300 graduate students.

The University is located in Fayetteville, a community of 60,000 residents. It is situated in the northwestern corner of the state in the heart of the Ozark Mountains at an elevation of 1,400

feet. Fayetteville is a 2-hour drive from Tulsa, a 4-hour drive from Kansas City, and a 5-hour drive from Dallas and St. Louis. A regional airport offering daily flights to Chicago, Dallas, St. Louis, and Memphis services the city.

Facilities

All M.B.A. classes are taught in state-of-the-art, dedicated rooms that allow technology to be fully integrated into classroom discussions. A separate graduate computer lab with the latest computer software supplements the laptop computers that are required of all M.B.A. students. A graduate lounge is available for student use for team meetings, study, and socializing. In fall 1999, the Donald W. Reynolds Center for Enterprise Development will be available for student use.

For students' living needs, both on- and off-campus housing (within walking distance of the campus) is available. For on-campus housing, application should be made at least three months prior to the summer enrollment date. A mass transit system is available to all students for transportation in and around the surrounding areas. Transportation fees are nominal and are included as part of the total tuition fee expense.

Placement

The College of Business Administration has a full-time placement director dedicated to supporting the career development needs of master's degree students. In addition, the University of Arkansas lends placement support through the Career Planning and Placement Office. Services that are provided include resume preparation, counseling, career workshops, employer information services, and employment search assistance. UA M.B.A. graduates have been successful in finding jobs with partnering firms and with Fortune 500 companies. Ninety percent of Arkansas M.B.A. graduates are in career positions or continue additional studies within three months of graduation.

Admission

Admission to the Master of Business Administration program is competitive and limited. Successful applicants are expected to rank in the 80th percentile on the Graduate Management Admission Test (GMAT) and possess a cumulative undergraduate grade point average of 3.4. International applicants must score a minimum of 550 on the Test of English as a Foreign Language (TOEFL), and a TOEFL score of 600 is strongly recommended.

Although work experience is not required for the full-time program, applicants with a minimum of two years of professional work experience are given preference. Applicants to the managerial program must possess two

years of full-time work experience prior to graduation. Letters of recommendation from those familiar with the applicant's aptitude for graduate-level work in business and essays from the applicant are weighted heavily in admission decisions.

Finances

Tuition fees for one semester of the 1998–99 academic year are $1932 for Arkansas residents and $4596 for nonresidents for 12 hours of graduate-level studies. In addition, students enrolled in 6 or more hours are assessed $175 for health, activity, technology, recreation, transportation, and facilities fees. International students must show proof of health insurance and are required to pay a nonimmigrant student service fee of $50 per semester.

Fayetteville consistently has been selected as one of the best cities in which to live in the United States. The area has a relatively low cost of living; students can expect to pay approximately $9000 a year for living expenses, including room, board, books, supplies, and personal expenses.

Students may apply for graduate assistantships, which currently offer a tuition waiver and pay a stipend of $5200 for nine months. Students who are awarded graduate assistantships are required to work 20 hours per week to support the instructional or research needs of the faculty in the College of Business Administration.

Application Facts and Dates

International applicants, all applicants without an undergraduate business degree, and applicants who completed an undergraduate degree in business more than three years ago should submit their completed application materials by November 15. Admission decisions for early applicants are made by December 15, giving the successful applicant sufficient time to complete the preparatory work prior to matriculation in the summer. Preference in admission and financial aid is given to applicants who submit their application prior to February 15. All applications received after February 15 are processed on a space-available basis. In no case is an applicant admitted after May 15.

For additional information, students should contact:

M.B.A. Director
Graduate Studies Office
CBA Suite 475
College of Business Administration
University of Arkansas
Fayetteville, Arkansas 72701
Telephone: 501-575-2851
Fax: 501-575-8721
E-mail: gso@comp.uark.edu
World Wide Web: http://www.uark.
    edu/depts/mba/public_html/

University of Baltimore

Robert G. Merrick School of Business

Baltimore, Maryland

MERRICK—YOUR CAREER ADVANTAGE

Recognizing the changing needs of today's workforce, the Merrick School offers a high-quality program that prepares students for a successful career in a highly competitive marketplace. An up-to-date curriculum helps students develop knowledge and skills in managing people, information, and technology, crucial resources for every organization in today's global business environment.

Sensitive to the time constraints of students with work and family responsibilities, we have developed three modes of delivering the M.B.A. program. The Saturday M.B.A., in which students attend classes only on Saturdays and complete studies in twenty-three months; the Advantage M.B.A., a full-time day program that allows students to graduate in one calendar year; and a traditional FLEX M.B.A., the part-time evening option for students who need more flexibility in class meeting days and times.

We believe that a high-quality program delivered to students at convenient times is the key to a good graduate business education in a changing world. Our students and alumni agree.

—John D. Hatfield, Dean

Programs and Curricular Focus

The hallmark of the M.B.A. at the Merrick School is flexibility, developing skills applicable to career goals and transferable to future employment opportunities. With an emphasis on teamwork and the case study approach, students learn from real-world business problems and successes. Students in all three M.B.A. programs may select a personal mentor from the Merrick Advisory Board or the UB Alumni Association. Mentors work with new students, providing access to a vast network of Baltimore business leaders.

Depending on a student's academic background, 30 to 51 credits are required in the FLEX M.B.A. evening program. Preparatory courses covering a basic knowledge of business functions account for up to 21 credits, which can be taken as part of the undergraduate program or in the graduate school. Of the 30 credits in the M.B.A. program, 18 consist of cross-functional areas of business practice. The remaining 12 credits are selected from electives. Students may create their own grouping of elective credits from the following areas: decision technologies, entrepreneurship, finance, health-care management, human resource management, international business, marketing, management information systems, and service and manufacturing operations.

The Advantage M.B.A. (AMBA), a fixed 48-credit, one-year, full-time program, allows students to complete a concentrated program with a cohesive cohort of students who work together on a team project within a regional business. This fast-track program provides opportunities to network with peers and the business community and matches students with mentors from business leaders.

The two-year Saturday M.B.A., also a 48-credit program, gives students an opportunity to finish the M.B.A. on a fixed schedule. Classes are offered in ten-week modules, with a three-week break between each ten-week term. As a cohort, students benefit from working within their group and may have the advantage of individual networking opportunities within the business community.

The following joint programs are also available: J.D./M.B.A., M.B.A./M.S. in nursing, M.B.A./Ph.D. in nursing, and M.B.A./Pharm.D. (pharmacy).

Students and the M.B.A. Experience

Merrick School students are a mature and diverse population. The average age is 30, and 85 percent have work experience prior to entering the M.B.A. program. Merrick School students are employed at Fortune 500 companies such as Lockheed Martin, Black and Decker, Northrup Grumman, USF&G, AT&T, and BEG as well as regional financial services, government, and business organizations.

In the most recent academic year, women made up 38 percent of the entering M.B.A. class. International students come from such countries as India, China, Israel, Brazil, Turkey, the Ukraine, Kenya, Thailand, France, Greece, and Japan. While some 48 percent completed an undergraduate business degree, others have backgrounds in engineering, science, liberal arts, and the humanities.

The Faculty

The most important resource of any business school is its faculty. Merrick School professors combine a dedication to teaching with significant research, professional, and community service activities. Many Merrick School faculty members have earned national reputations in their fields, both for research and classroom innovations. They are published in leading scholarly journals, including the *Harvard Business Review,* the *Journal of Finance,* and *JAMA* (the *Journal of the American Medical Association*). The faculty includes the founder and president of the international Production and Operations Management Society (POMS) and the former president and current board member of the Consumer Federation of America. At the same time, faculty members have designed new courses for the M.B.A. curriculum that have received recognition from professional groups throughout the region.

Many professors are graduates of prestigious institutions, such as Harvard, MIT, Michigan, and Wharton. As a group, they have nearly 300 years of full-time professional work experience with business, government, and nonprofit organizations. This combination of academic expertise and real-world experience translates into a unique and rewarding experience for students.

Of the 55 full-time faculty members, 95 percent have terminal degrees, 23 percent are female, and 28 percent are international or members of minority groups.

The Business School Network

The ties between the Merrick School and the region's business leaders are strong. The Merrick Advisory Board comprises 85 senior executives who represent a broad spectrum of companies and industries, both national and international. Faculty members work closely with business leaders to ensure program and course relevance. The School's corporate partners emphasize continuous improvement in academic programs to prepare students for the competitive marketplace. They also support student career development and placement efforts.

Members of the Advisory Board and the UB Alumni Association serve as mentors for all M.B.A. students, providing an opportunity to observe and interact with seasoned professionals, business owners, and entrepreneurs. They meet on a regular basis with the students, arrange for informational interviews with colleagues, and introduce students to the Baltimore business community. In addition, Advantage M.B.A. students work on an intensive one-semester project submitted by local businesses in the Baltimore-Washington area.

Advisory Board members have sponsored internships for Merrick students and serve on panels for student classroom presentations. In addition, they have been active in revising the curriculum, reviewing issues of customer service, and developing systems to track students from inquiry to graduation.

The College and Environs

The University of Baltimore is located in Baltimore, Maryland, a city of 600,000, less than an hour from Washington, D.C., and three hours by car or train from New York. The Baltimore metropolitan area serves as a regional center for the operations of many businesses and nonprofit organizations.

The University is located in the city's revitalized cultural district. Five minutes south of the campus is Baltimore's famous Inner Harbor, which features shopping, restaurants, and entertainment attractions.

The School of Business was named in honor of Robert G. Merrick, a pioneer in the Baltimore financial services industry. The Merrick School is accredited by AACSB–The International Association for Management Education.

Facilities

The Thumel Business Center, home of the Merrick School of Business, includes classrooms, case rooms, seminar rooms, offices, and labs linked together by high-speed digital networks that tie together an array of information technology and facilitate communication within the building, around the campus, and worldwide via the Internet. A Group Decision Support Lab, a Multimedia Lab, and a Microcomputing Lab allow students to work individually or in groups.

The Langsdale Library and School of Law Library house more than 400,000 bound volumes, microform and CD-ROM holdings, government documents, and periodicals. Interlibrary loan programs with area libraries and the thirteen University System of Maryland institutions expand the resources available to UB students. All card catalogs in the system and across the state are accessible from the students' homes via computer and modem.

Placement

The Career Center offers a variety of services to help students and alumni attain their career goals. In individual and group sessions, professional career counselors address such issues as resume writing, job search, and networking. In addition, counselors administer and interpret traditional and computerized self-assessment tools. Job-related services include a job bank and resume referral to employers (both Web-based) and assistance with paid and unpaid internships. Each semester the Career Center sponsors specialized workshops, networking programs for graduating seniors, and career and job fairs.

In support of placement activities, the Merrick School of Business offers students the opportunity to be mentored by a regional business leader and, in addition, sponsors career-related programs specific to academic specializations.

Admission

Students apply by submitting an application, GMAT score, two letters of recommendation, resume, letter of intent explaining reasons for pursuing the master's degree, and official transcripts of undergraduate work. New fall 1996 and spring 1997 registrants had an average GMAT score of 530 and an average GPA of 3.2. Applicants with foreign transcripts should arrange for an evaluation of their academic records and must submit a TOEFL score of at least 550.

Finances

Graduate business tuition for the 1997–98 academic year for in-state students was $223 per credit. Tuition for out-of-state students was $333 per credit. The University also applies some flat and some per-credit fees. Thus, a 3-credit course for in-state residents cost $761, while out-of-state charges were $1091. All charges for graduate business courses are on a per-credit basis. No separate scale is used for full-time study.

Merit scholarships are available for all M.B.A. students. Thumel Scholarships provide approximately one half of the tuition for AMBA students. The France and Merrick Scholarships are also available for Saturday M.B.A. and FLEX M.B.A. students.

Graduate students are eligible for graduate assistantships, which cover tuition and include a small stipend.

Applications for scholarships are due by March 1 each year, and applications for financial aid are due by April 1.

International Students

The Merrick School of Business welcomes applicants from outside the U.S. In fall 1996, international students accounted for nearly 12 percent of the graduate enrollment in the Merrick School. The International Services Office provides admission advisement, visa assistance, and orientation services to prospective and enrolled students at the University of Baltimore.

Application Facts and Dates

Applications are accepted for the FLEX M.B.A. program for fall, spring, and summer semesters. The Advantage M.B.A. class enters in May; the Saturday M.B.A. class begins in the summer and in the winter. Applications are processed on a rolling or continuous basis. Early application is recommended for all programs, especially the Advantage and Saturday programs.

Recommended deadlines for the FLEX program are July 15 for the fall semester, December 1 for the spring semester, and April 1 for the summer semester.

Inquiries and requests for application materials should be directed to:

Ms. Tracey M. Jamison
Coordinator of Graduate Admission
University of Baltimore
1420 North Charles Street
Baltimore, Maryland 21201-5779
Telephone: 410-837-4777
Fax: 410-837-4820
E-mail: admissions@ubmail.ubalt.edu

University of Bridgeport

Bridgeport, Connecticut

ADDRESSING THE GLOBAL PERSPECTIVE

The School of Business offers a master of business administration degree program in general administration. It features a combination of courses from accounting, finance, international business, management, marketing, and information systems. Degree completion normally requires two years of full-time or three to five years of part-time study. Accelerated study is available for qualified students who have recently completed a business degree from an accredited college. On alternate weekends, a weekend M.B.A. program is available at the University's Stamford campus.

The M.B.A. program begins with a focus on analysis and evaluation of the control of an organization and of the environment for leadership. Courses include accounting, decision theory, economics, the Organization and Management of Finance, production and marketing, and the Socio-Cultural Aspects of People in Organizations. Advanced courses expand and integrate topics explored in introductory courses and provide a strong focus on the global perspective necessary for contemporary management. The School is accredited by the Association of Collegiate Business Schools and Programs (ACBSP).

—Glenn Bassett, Director

Programs and Curricular Focus

The M.B.A. program at the University of Bridgeport develops effective and responsible leaders for business, industry, and government in the global market. It not only emphasizes traditional management skills but also stresses the technical and cultural preparation necessary to understand the increasingly complex international environment.

The M.B.A. requires between 30 and 54 semester credit hours of study, depending on the student's academic background and level of academic achievement. The curriculum is designed to recognize substantial diversity in preparation and experience for students entering M.B.A. study, as well as different goals and expectations of students.

Core courses provide the management tools for analysis, decision making and communications; concepts, theory, and current practice in the major functional areas of operation; and the opportunity to study continuing and contemporary problems of management responsibility. The core is central to M.B.A. study, providing a base of knowledge for additional study in electives and a specific professional discipline. The M.B.A. core courses (24 credits) are as follows: Accounting Concepts, Economic Analysis, Financial Management, Organizational Behavior, Operations Management, Marketing Concepts, Management Science and Linear Programming, Management Information Systems, Decision Theory.

Listed below are the advanced courses for which the M.B.A. core is only a prerequisite: Accounting for Managers, International Accounting, International Trade and Finance, Advanced Financial Management and Policy, the Financial Management of Financial Institutions, Management Theory, Small Business Entrepreneurship, Advanced Operations Management, Buyer Analysis, Global Market Management and Strategy Planning, Advanced Statistical Decision Theory, Business Simulation, Business and Society, and Business Policy. The Global Management group of electives comprises International Issues and Languages. The Experiential Learning group comprises Leadership and Organizational Change, Business Games, and internships. Teaching methods include a mix of lecture, case study, experiential learning, and an analysis of international social-political issues.

Students and the M.B.A. Experience

M.B.A. program participants represent thirty-five nationalities. Five percent are from Europe, 50 percent are from North America, and 45 percent from other countries. Thirty-five percent of the students have a degree background in sciences/technology, 40 percent in economics, 2 percent in law, and 23 percent in other majors. Student GMAT scores range from 375 to 650; the average is 500. International student TOEFL scores average 575. Women comprise 45 percent of the student population. Student ages range from 27 to

55. The average age is 27. The average length of student work experience is three to five years.

Special Features

The program features a flexible course of study to meet the convenience of all kinds of students; a strong emphasis on global business to prepare for the twenty-first century business world; experiential learning in a small group setting; a diverse student body composed of domestic and international students; and a systematic understanding of discipline, value, and an ethical code of behavior in business.

The Faculty

The faculty is as diverse as the student body. It is composed of domestic and international members with superb academic qualifications and corporate business experience. Faculty members are active in research, authoring books, journals, and conference papers. They pride themselves on excellence in teaching as a primary goal of their profession.

The Business School Network

The University of Bridgeport's 86-acre campus is situated on Long Island Sound. Located in Fairfield County, the area is home to one of the nation's largest multinational corporate headquarters and provides students with excellent opportunities for jobs, internships, and co-op training. Through the Director's Advisory Board, the School interfaces with many executives from corporations, who give advice and direction as well as instruction in the classroom.

The University's Stamford Center is conveniently located in Stamford, Connecticut, and is easily accessible to working professionals from southern Fairfield and Westchester counties, New York, and New Jersey.

Corporate Partnerships

Through the Trefz Center for Venture Management, which is housed in the School of Business, the School sponsors a number of activities that link the School with the business community. Components of Trefz Center of Venture Management include The Business Development Institute, which assists potential entrepreneurs and small business persons in

start-up, business organization, finance, marketing, staffing and management, and evaluating technology and development planning. The Bridgeport Foreign Trade Institute sponsors monthly international business seminars and conferences; develops networks of international business firms; provides consultation services to those individuals and organizations who attempt to enter international business; and assists local governments in promoting local businesses and products made in the state of Connecticut for foreign markets and investors. The Urban Management Institute studies socioeconomic issues in the region and recommends appropriate policy initiatives. The Special Projects Unit promotes activities especially targeted for small business people in the region through conferences, seminars, and special events.

The College and Environs

Founded in 1927, the University of Bridgeport is a private, nonsectarian, comprehensive, coeducational, urban university located in Bridgeport, Connecticut, just one hour (50 miles) from New York City and three hours (160 miles) from Boston. The University has a long-standing partnership with the local community to provide its employees with excellent educational opportunities that lead to degrees and career advancement.

There are approximately 1,000 graduate students enrolled at the University, representing a diverse group of interests, professions, nationalities, and ages. The University maintains an international focus, with 19 percent of its students coming from outside the U.S.

Facilities

The Wahlstrom Library contains more than 275,000 bound volumes (including bound journals, indexes/abstracts), more than 1,000,000 microforms, and sub-

scribes to more than 1,500 periodicals and other serials. Online database searching is available on the Internet, DIALOG, First Search, EBSCO's Academic Search Full Text 1,000, and LEXIS/NEXIS. CD-ROM databases include ERIC, Moody's Company Data, Medline, reQuest, Books in Print Plus, and the National Trade DataBank.

Placement

Most of the University's students are already employed and seek M.B.A. study on a part-time basis. However, because of the University's location in Fairfield county, where sixty-five of Connecticut's Fortune 500 companies are located, students have access to a number of employment opportunities.

Admission

As a professional program, the M.B.A. is designed to build upon undergraduate study in the arts, humanities, science, engineering, or other disciplines. No specific undergraduate curriculum is expected or preferred before entry to M.B.A. study. Admission is based on a bachelor's degree or equivalent in any discipline, scores on the Graduate Management Admission Test (GMAT), and two letters of recommendation. Provisional admission may be granted to a limited number of students, pending GMAT scores, provided that the undergraduate records are exceptionally strong and the applicant has at least three years of management experience. If a student is admitted provisionally, the GMAT must be taken during the first semester. For students whose native language is not English, a TOEFL score of 575 is required.

Finances

For the program, tuition costs $350 per credit (1–12 credits) or $6700 per

semester (13 or more credits). Room and board cost $6810 per year, and students should have approximately $1600 allotted for miscellaneous expenses, excluding travel. There is a $40 application fee for domestic students ($50 for international students).

Financial aid is available to U.S. citizens in the form of Federal Stafford Student Loans and graduate assistantships. International students must demonstrate that they have sufficient funds to finance their studies in the United States.

International Students

The focus on a global perspective at the University of Bridgeport offers the international student the opportunity to obtain vital training in a specialized field of study, to enrich his or her life by experiencing another culture, and to gain new perspective on the world and to develop contacts, interpersonal skills, and knowledge necessary to those who work in the international community as technicians, scholars, businessmen, politicians, and scientists.

The University's English Language Institute (ELI) is located on the campus of the University of Bridgeport. ELI offers intensive instruction in English as a second language as well as trips and activities designed to introduce the student to America and its people.

The University's Office of International Affairs provides services and assistance to international students with immigration, personal, and other nonacademic concerns.

Application Facts and Dates

Applications must be submitted two months prior to the date of intended entry. Electronic applications may be made through the University of Bridgeport's Web site and Polaris. Students may enter in the fall, spring, and summer. For more information, students should contact:

Office of Admissions
University of Bridgeport
126 Park Avenue
Bridgeport, Connecticut 06601
Telephone: 203-576-4552
          800-EXCEL-UB
          (392-3582) (toll-free)
Fax: 203-576-4941
E-mail: admit@cse.bridgeport.edu
World Wide Web: http://www.
   bridgeport.edu

M.B.A. Program
School of Business
University of Bridgeport
230 Park Avenue
Bridgeport, Connecticut 06601
Telephone: 203-576-4363
Fax: 203-576-4388

University of Bristol

> ### MANAGING CULTURAL DIVERSITY IN THE GLOBAL MARKETPLACE
>
> *An M.B.A. in International Business whose ethos and origin are international and global, delivered to a wide international mix of students, by an international faculty . . . the University of Bristol's M.B.A. in International Business is truly international. We are committed to incorporating a global dimension into our strategic thinking and to developing a creative, innovative, and entrepreneurial approach to our work. Successful managers of the future will be working strategically and operationally across national and cultural boundaries. Managing diversity while maintaining cultural sensitivity in the environment of the market economy is the challenge to be faced by today's managers.*
>
> —Catherine Cunningham, Director

Programs and Curricular Focus

The M.B.A. in international business is both international and entrepreneurial. The University of Bristol is committed to academic excellence and is at the forefront of international research and higher education. The program is accredited by the Association of MBA's, the United Kingdom's foremost accrediting body.

In collaboration with the Graduate School of International Business at the Ecole Nationale Des Ponts et Chaussees in Paris, the University of Bristol's Graduate School of International Business offers the opportunity for selected groups of highly motivated people who intend to pursue an international career to acquire an M.B.A. in international business by full-time or extended study.

Postgraduate diploma and certificate programs are also available based on the full-time curriculum.

Research students wishing to gain a Ph.D. by research in areas of international business, such as Globalisation and Emerging Markets; Innovation, Organisation and Business Processes in the International Context; and International Management Development were accepted beginning in 1996.

The full-time program accepts 60 students each year from more than twenty different countries. Students take eight core modules then select seven electives from a wide-ranging menu of choices. The M.B.A. is completed with a four- to six-month international work placement project from which is written a 10,000-word dissertation.

Students and the M.B.A. Experience

Graduates are managers who understand the workings of the international marketplace, are sensitive to other cultures and capable of working in international teams, are comfortable with and capable of managing diversity, have developed strategic skills and adaptability, and have good language skills.

Students, with an average of 5 years of work experience, come from a wide variety of backgrounds with degrees in engineering, business and administration, economics, and finance. The average age of the student body is 28, and most students speak at least one other language. About 30 percent of the students are recruited from the Far East, 30 percent from Europe and the U.K., and 30 percent from the Americas.

Students are encouraged to develop their own initiatives in relation to the program. Selection of modules is made in accordance with participants' own personal and professional goals. They work within a multicultural environment in which they begin to appreciate and understand the differences in conducting business around the world. An emphasis is placed on teamwork, and many of the assessments and presentations are done in multicultural groups.

❖ Global Focus

Its international nature is reflected in every aspect of the program. Students can select from a wide variety of electives delivered in four major areas of the

world, in Eastern or Central Europe, the Far East, and the Americas. The School works closely with Ecole des Ponts et Chaussees, Paris; University of Ljubljana, Slovenia; University of Katowice, Poland; and the University of Hong Kong, and study trips are made annually to Prague, Japan, and Malaysia.

Special Features

The international experience is enhanced not only by the overseas options described above but also by the opportunity for a four- to six-month placement in a company anywhere in the world. A placement manager assists students in focusing on a desired area of work and in devising a strategic plan to attain the placement of their choice. The project undertaken during this placement is the subject of a written 10,000-word dissertation that is presented to an assessment team made up of international specialists in the area of research.

The Faculty

Faculty members are drawn from the University of Bristol's strongest departments: economics, law, and engineering. They work alongside visiting faculty members who teach at the best universities in the world, such as Harvard, Stanford, and MIT in the United States and other leading institutions in the United Kingdom, Europe, and the Far East. In order to expose students to the latest business practices, some modules are led by businessmen from international companies, and the University's faculty members also bring their consultancy experience to the program.

The Business School Network

Guest speakers range from financial experts from London to entrepreneurs who operate across the global marketplace. Representatives of major international companies contribute to the program either as part of a taught module or in more informal events involving students. The School's Industrial Advisory Board, chaired by Lord Cairns of BAT Industries, works with the School to assist students with obtaining placements.

The large, modern Arts and Social Sciences Library is nearby, and business databases are available online. The Students' Union houses a swimming pool and M.B.A. students will find themselves close to the sports and gymnasium facilities. Students are assisted by the accommodation office to find rental accommodations close to the School in the City Centre.

Placement

The professional placement is for a four- to six-month period and is facilitated by the placements manager. Many students convert this into a full-time, permanent job opportunity. The University's careers office is nearby, and students are exposed to a variety of visiting speakers from commerce and industry for opportunities for job placements.

Admission

Admissions requirements are a university degree or equivalent, three references, an interview in person or by telephone, and English language fluency (TOEFL 650 or IELTS 7). Two years of full-time work experience or the equivalent is preferred for the full-time program, and the part-time program preference is for at least five years of work experience.

The School recruits highly intelligent, intellectually curious, and ambitious students from around the world. An individual's potential contribution to the program is assessed using the above criteria alongside other detailed information required on the application form.

Finances

Full-time tuition for the M.B.A. in International Business program for the 1998–99 academic year is £12,500. It is £14,000 for part-time studies.

Application Facts and Dates

For a full prospectus or an informal interview, students should call:

Judy Denham
Administrative Director
University of Bristol
Graduate School of International
    Business
10 Woodland Road, Clifton, Bristol
    BS8 1UQ
England
Telephone: (44)117 973 7683
Fax: (44)117 973 7687
E-mail: gsintbus@bristol.ac.uk
World Wide Web: http://www.bris.ac.
    uk/Depts/MBA/

The Graduate School's expertise in international business is recognized by global organizations who benefit from programs tailor-made for specialist groups of employees and resulting in accreditation from this prestigious University.

The College and Environs

Founded in 1876, Bristol is one of the most prestigious of British universities. It ranks in the top ten nationwide and is recognized for it's high standards of teaching and research. It is the second-most sought-after University in England and is in the center of a thriving modern city. Bristol is the capital of England's West Country, approximately an hour west by train from London, which has its own international airport connecting

daily, in under 2 hours, with Amsterdam and other European capitals. Bristol is one of Britain's oldest and most beautiful cities and, at the same time, is a thriving and modern center with major industries in aerospace and defense, communications, technology, and banking. Its maritime past is reflected in its architecture and newly developed leisure areas in the docklands.

Facilities

The University is based across a large, city-center campus, providing lecture rooms and student facilities of many shapes and sizes. The Graduate School has its own computer laboratory, but students are encouraged to use facilities elsewhere on campus when necessary.

University of British Columbia

Vancouver, British Columbia, Canada

NEW DIRECTIONS FOR UBC'S M.B.A.

In the complex and competitive business environment of the 90s, the generalist training traditionally associated with an M.B.A. needs to be supported by in-depth specialist knowledge. Not only is competence across the range of key business disciplines, such as finance, accounting, and marketing, essential, but also the interconnections between these disciplines need to be clearly understood.

Our redesigned M.B.A. program, launched in September 1995, commences with a highly integrated core centred on current business situations. Following this, students develop an area of expertise by selecting from a wide range of specializations. Through projects and internships, students analyze existing business problems and are exposed to leading practitioners.

Our approach to management education stresses the development of graduates with broad management skills complemented by expert knowledge in one area of business.

—Derek Atkins, Acting Dean

Programs and Curricular Focus

The M.B.A. program at the University of British Columbia (UBC) is rigorous and challenging, offering both structure and flexibility. Students complete the integrated core, after which they choose the specialization that meets their career objectives. Both the core and the specializations are supported and strengthened through business applications in internships, projects, and a professional development program. UBC offers small classes and a balance of instructional techniques, including lecture, case discussion, simulations, and group projects. The program starts in September, lasts fifteen continuous months, and is offered full-time only.

The program is centred on a four-month integrated core, which provides students with a foundation in finance, marketing, human resources, accounting, statistics, economics, and information systems. The core is a team-taught seminar in which these topics are taught from a multidisciplinary perspective, rather than individual functional areas. This innovative approach has been implemented to emulate more closely the multidimensional problems encountered in business.

Following the core, students select one of the following six specializations: entrepreneurship, finance, marketing, information technology and management, strategic management, and supply chain management. In addition, international business may be offered adjunct to any of the above specializations. Students may

also choose from a range of electives, including organizational behaviour, human resources management, logistics, transportation, not-for-profit management, real estate and urban development, and technology management.

Additional opportunities at UBC include a combined M.B.A./LL.B. program. Also offered are a Master of Science in Business Administration (M.Sc.Bus.Admin.) and a Doctor of Philosophy (Ph.D.) in business administration for students wishing to pursue research in business.

Students and the M.B.A. Experience

Students are one of the Faculty's greatest resources. M.B.A. classmates have diverse professional, cultural, and academic backgrounds, which create a unique and dynamic learning environment. On average, students are 28 years of age with four years of full-time work experience. The class is 34 percent women.

❖ Global Focus

UBC is committed to offering students unique international educational experiences. A global perspective is gained through specialized international courses, interaction with the multicultural student body and faculty, and UBC's extensive exchange program. Exchanges are available with twenty-eight leading universities located in twenty countries in

Asia, Australia, Europe, the Middle East, Great Britain, and Latin America.

Special Features

Internships and projects are a key part of UBC's M.B.A. program. During the specialization component, students have the opportunity to apply their knowledge in either an internship or an industry-related project directly related to their area of specialization.

Throughout the M.B.A. program, several weeks are devoted to developing professional skills in areas such as communications, teamwork, negotiation, technology, and leadership.

Students are required to have an adequate general knowledge of economics, statistics, accounting, and computers. In addition, students should attend UBC's Pre-core Program, designed to refresh these skills, prior to the start of the M.B.A. program.

The Faculty

UBC is committed to excellence in teaching. The M.B.A. program has a large number of outstanding instructors, some of whom have received national and international recognition for their contributions to teaching. UBC's revised program has a strong focus on teaching innovation and course development.

In addition, the Faculty's reputation for research excellence is unmatched by any other Canadian business school. Exceptional work is ongoing in many areas, such as international business and trade policy, entrepreneurship, nonprofit marketing, decision making and creative problem solving, and strategic thinking in negotiating and bargaining.

The Business School Network

Corporate Partnerships

Strong linkages have been developed between UBC and the corporate community. The Dean's Advisory Council, which assists the Dean in developing and evaluating commerce initiatives, consists of senior representatives from government, labour, and the private sector.

The corporate community provides opportunities for students to apply their busi-

ness knowledge through projects, internships, and industry field trips. In addition, M.B.A. students interact directly with prominent business leaders in UBC's CEO speakers series and by participating in a wide range of professional and social events.

Prominent Alumni

Alumni of the Faculty of Commerce and Business Administration have excelled in business and include individuals in the private and public sectors. UBC alumni have held the titles of President and/or Chief Executive Officer of the Hongkong Bank of Canada, Procter & Gamble, Scotiabank, and the Hudson's Bay Company. They have also been well represented in the major accounting firms in the capacity of senior partners. UBC alumni have used their entrepreneurial skills to develop companies such as the Great Canadian Railtour Company and the Savolite Group. In addition, alumni have led prestigious business schools, including Harvard, Queen's at Kingston, and UBC.

The College and Environs

The University of British Columbia is located in Vancouver, one of the world's most beautiful cities. Vancouver is Canada's third-largest and fastest-growing city. Major economic activities include tourism, forestry, fishing, and mining. Situated equally between Europe and Asia, Vancouver is ideally located for international business, and its economic potential is extremely promising. In addition, Vancouver offers a

wonderful lifestyle in which people can ski, sail, cycle, and stroll along the beach all year round.

UBC is Canada's third-largest university, with more than 30,000 academic students. The campus, a few kilometres from the city centre, is on a 1,000-acre forested peninsula overlooking the Pacific Ocean and the Coastal Mountain range. Students find that the campus offers an exceptional variety of cultural and recreational facilities.

Facilities

At UBC, the Faculty of Commerce and Business Administration is committed to providing the highest quality student services. This is accomplished by the professional staff in the Commerce Masters' Programs Office, the Commerce Career Centre, the Study Abroad and Exchange Office, the David Lam Management Research Library, and the Computer Lab.

Placement

Students' job searches are supported by the Commerce Career Centre, which is instrumental in marketing UBC graduates to major national and international corporations. Each year, on-campus information and recruiting sessions are held for more than 200 companies. Career Centre staff members also organize seminars in resume writing, interviewing techniques, and job search strategies to assist M.B.A. students in the competitive job market.

Admission

The admissions committee assesses undergraduate performance, GMAT scores, full-time work experience, extracurricular involvement, and demonstrated leadership. Specific minimum academic requirements are outlined in the M.B.A. application. A TOEFL score is required from an applicant whose prior degree is from a country other than Canada, the United States, the United Kingdom, Ireland, Australia, New Zealand, Kenya, South Africa, and the English-speaking countries of the West Indies. A minimum TOEFL score of 600 is required.

Applicants are not required to complete prerequisite courses to be eligible to apply, but a basic level of knowledge in economics, financial accounting, statistics, and computers is required prior to the start of the program.

Finances

Estimated program fees for 1999–2000 are Can$15,000 for Canadian citizens and landed immigrants and Can$20,000 for non-Canadian students for the complete fifteen-month program. Annual costs for books and materials are approximately Can$1500. The University estimates room and board for a single student living off campus at Can$900 per month.

All applicants are considered for merit-based awards and fellowships at the time of admission.

Application Facts and Dates

Application deadlines are March 31 for international applicants and April 30 for applicants from the United States and Canada. Application materials are available at UBC's Web site (address below). For additional information, students should contact:

Commerce Masters' Programs Office
102-2053 Main Mall
University of British Columbia
Vancouver, British Columbia V6T 1Z2
Canada
Telephone: 604-822-8422
Fax: 604-822-9030
E-mail: masters.programs@commerce.ubc.ca
World Wide Web: http://www.commerce.ubc.ca

▰UCD·GSM University of California, Davis

Graduate School of Management

Davis, California

> ### DEVELOPING MANAGERIAL POTENTIAL
>
> *At the Graduate School of Management at UC Davis, we believe that students learn best in a supportive, cooperative learning environment that encourages them to stretch intellectually. To create this environment, we've developed a rigorous program that features small classes, faculty members committed to teaching excellence, and opportunities to work closely with faculty members and a select group of bright and energetic students. We then guide you to test your new knowledge and creative thinking in real-world business situations. I invite you to take advantage of an outstanding opportunity to fully develop your managerial potential and leadership skills.*
>
> —Robert H. Smiley, Dean

Programs and Curricular Focus

The UC Davis Graduate School of Management is accredited by AACSB–The International Association for Management Education. Conceived just over seventeen years ago, the program has gained greater stature each year. It is recognized for the high quality of its graduates, its world-class faculty, and the excellence of its overall program.

The UC Davis M.B.A. program cultivates each student's ability to deal successfully with the challenges of a continually changing, increasingly complex business environment. The program's strengths come from a managerial approach to the basic business disciplines; a student-faculty ratio of 10:1; a curriculum that integrates the social, political, economic, and ethical aspects of business; and a variety of teaching methodologies, including case studies, lectures, class discussions, computer simulations, team projects, and real-world applications.

The program is twenty-four classes (72 quarter units). Joint degrees are available in engineering (M.B.A./M.Eng.), law (M.B.A./J.D.), medicine (M.B.A./M.D.), and agricultural economics (M.B.A./M.S.). All students spend their first year in core classes mastering the curriculum, which provides a common foundation of fundamental management knowledge and skill. Elective concentrations are available either in the full-time day program or in the evening M.B.A. Program for Working Professionals in accounting, agricultural management, environmental and natural resources management, finance, general manage-

ment, general resources management, health services management, information systems, international management, management science, marketing, and technology management. Students can also design a customized concentration. The second-year capstone course, Management Policy and Strategy, places students in teams and gives them an opportunity to apply their decision-making and problem-solving skills by developing a strategic plan for real "client" businesses.

Students and the M.B.A. Experience

UC Davis M.B.A. students bring to the School a wide variety of academic and work experiences, and the School's personalized focus and hands-on teaching approach is augmented by this diversity. While 25 percent of the student body reflects preparation in business and economics, the School is also traditionally very attractive to students from engineering and the sciences because of the strong emphasis in technology management. Many members of the 1997 entering class came from undergraduate majors in the humanities and social sciences as well. The 1997 entering class represents more than thirty-three undergraduate institutions.

The average full-time student is 27 years old, with 4½ years of full-time work experience. Women make up 26 percent of the student population, and international students, 10 percent. The School sponsors several international student exchange programs.

Special Features

The School encourages prospective students to take advantage of the Visitation Program. While visiting the School, prospective students are able to talk one-on-one with current students and professors and can attend one of their classes. To enhance preparation for the job market, the School requires that students participate in a videotaped mock interview with one of several volunteer executives from both the public and private sectors. This program gives students a unique chance to meet top executives in a one-on-one situation, as well as dramatically improve interviewing skills. The annual Alumni Day, created to provide current students with the "inside track" on up-to-date industry information and career opportunities from alumni volunteers, also provides a valuable networking activity.

The Faculty

Faculty members of the UC Davis Graduate School of Management represent doctoral preparation from many of the most prestigious schools in the country and excel both as teachers and researchers. Their current consulting projects keep them in touch with managerial concerns of leading U.S. corporations as well as federal and state agencies. One of the most distinctive features of the faculty is the close relationships members forge with students. The School recognizes the academic value students receive when given the opportunity to work closely and individually with faculty members and offers many formal and informal chances to do so.

The Business School Network

Business and government leaders are frequent visitors to campus, serving as guest lecturers in classes, resources for career development, or speakers at frequent School-sponsored forums and lectures. Through these important contacts, students can gain a pragmatic viewpoint that balances the academic and theoretical perspective they find in the classroom.

The Executive-in-Residence program gives students and faculty members alike a unique opportunity to work closely with a top business leader during the executive's quarter-long visit to the School.

The Dean's Advisory Council, made up of many of California's top business leaders, provides the School with one of its strongest connections to the business community. The School's Business Partnership program offers companies a special series of benefits when they make an annual contribution to the School, and students have the opportunity to network with representatives from major corporations.

The College and Environs

In the 1998 rankings by *U.S. News & World Report*, the UC Davis Graduate School of Management tied for thirteenth in the nation among public M.B.A. programs and tied for thirty-first overall, making UC Davis's the youngest public M.B.A. program ever to be nationally ranked.

The city of Davis is one of California's last remaining "college towns." Close-by Sacramento, the state capital, offers all the amenities expected in a major metropolitan area. It is home to an expanding high-technology manufacturing industry and a community of data processing enterprises. A couple hours east lies the stunning Sierra Nevada. An hour's drive west is the beautiful Napa Valley wine country. A short distance to the west is the cosmopolitan San Francisco Bay Area and the booming Silicon Valley.

Facilities

Academic resources include a library of 2.3 million volumes, ranked among the top research libraries in North America. A full-time business reference librarian is available to assist students with the latest information-gathering strategies, including several online services. The School's newly remodeled classrooms feature state-of-the-art multimedia instructional support.

Technology Environment

The School maintains a 24-hour computer lab, with all necessary business software, networking to library services, and access to the Internet. Each student is issued a University computer account, which includes electronic mail.

Placement

The Career Services Center begins offering support and personal guidance to students in the first week of the program. Through workshops, on-campus recruiting, mock interviews, and an emphasis on internships, the Career Services Center provides students with the tools to build long-term relationships with the corporate community. In addition to several national databases that provide students with job openings and recruiter information, M.B.A. students participate in career fairs, company information sessions, and on-site company tours. Approximately 55 percent of UC Davis's M.B.A. students were placed in high-technology industries, with positions in finance, marketing, consulting, and technology management. The School also actively participates in the West Coast M.B.A. Consortium recruiting event to give students an additional avenue for seeking career employment. Over the past few years, an average of 94 percent of the School's M.B.A. graduates have been placed within three months of graduation, with an average starting salary of $60,000.

Admission

Admission to the UC Davis Graduate School of Management is highly selective. Applicants are evaluated on the basis of demonstrated academic achievement, performance on the Graduate Management Admission Test (GMAT), and interest in professional management. Full-time business experience is considered an asset. No particular area of undergraduate preparation is required, but the University requires the completion of a bachelor's degree from an accredited college or university. The 1997 entering class had an average GMAT score of 660, an average undergraduate GPA of 3.2, and an average of 4½ years of work experience.

Finances

The estimated fees for 1998–99 for full-time study are $10,468 per year for California residents and $19,452 for nonresidents. These fees are subject to change. The 1998–99 cost of the M.B.A. Program for Working Professionals is $1150 per class. Many reasonably priced apartments are within biking distance. Monthly rents range from $553 for a one-bedroom apartment to $700 for a two-bedroom apartment. Student-family housing monthly rents range from $427 to $559. Need-based grants, loans, and fee offsets are available, as is the merit-based GSM Scholar's Grant.

International Students

The School encourages applications from international students. International students must earn a score of 600 or better on the TOEFL to be eligible for admission to the program. For visa purposes, international students must provide a statement of finances showing at least $31,000 to cover tuition and fees for their first year.

Application Facts and Dates

Application deadlines are February 1 (full-time program priority deadline), April 1 (full-time program final deadline), and May 15 (M.B.A. Program for Working Professionals) for fall quarter admission. Applicants should contact:

Office of Admissions
Graduate School of Management
University of California, Davis
One Shields Avenue
Davis, California 95616-8609
Telephone: 530-752-7399
Fax: 530-752-2924
E-mail: gsm@ucdavis.edu
World Wide Web: http://www.gsm.ucdavis.edu

University of California, Irvine

Graduate School of Management

Irvine, California

ANSWERS FOR THE FUTURE

GSM is a school with a sharp focus and an innovative attitude. We are constantly looking for ways to give our students that extra advantage, whether they are in the full-time M.B.A. program or in one of our three degree programs for practicing executives and professionals. This is the nature of our school, and it also is the nature of the dynamic, Tech Coast business community in Orange County and southern California.

We believe that business will be fundametally changed by those men and women who have a solid understanding of the constantly changing technology that helps us collect, analyze, disseminate, and use information. Our graduates are recognized for their ability to step into situations where they are using information and technology to bring the customer closer to the supplier, to develop partnerships between vendors and manufacturers, or to create a world-wide network that gives companies the competitive edge. Our graduates are able to develop solutions. No wonder they are in such demand by consulting firms, financial institutions, industrial and customer companies, and others that know that continuous innovation is necessary for success.

GSM is a school that is on the move. What exists now will be changed somewhat tomorrow. Programs will be introduced and revised as appropriate. Our faculty and staff are innovators. We experiment with the new while holding firmly to the rigor and demands of a first-rate M.B.A. program. In other words, we live the change for which we are preparing our students to lead.

—David H. Blake, Dean

Programs and Curricular Focus

The Graduate School of Management (GSM) offers four M.B.A. degree options, three of which are designed for the working professional, and a Ph.D. program. The curriculum for the M.B.A. programs is a broad-based, integrative, and comprehensive one that responds to the needs of the high-tech, international, and global economic environment.

The full-time M.B.A. program takes two years to complete. The first year of study incorporates ten of the twelve core courses; the second year is primarily electives of the students' choosing. Functional areas of study include accounting, marketing, information systems, strategy, operations and decision technologies, health care, public policy, finance, and organizational behavior. UCI's new Information Technology Management Track within the full-time M.B.A. program comprehensively integrates the teaching of information technology into all facets of the curriculum. Participants in the ITM Track, which is comprised of students from all functional areas with a variety of backgrounds, learn how technology affects organizations and markets, and how to use

information to create new strategic options and gain a lasting competitive advantage.

The Executive M.B.A. is a two-year program designed for managers and working professionals. The Fully Employed M.B.A. Program is a thirty-three-month program intended for working professionals who require a program conducted entirely outside of regular working hours. The Health Care Executive M.B.A. program is a twenty-four month program designed primarily for health-care professionals. It meets one weekend per month.

The doctoral program prepares individuals for teaching and scholarly positions in academic and other institutions where demonstrated ability to do original research is required. It is neither course- nor unit-based and consists of three separate and distinct phases. It is also a small and highly individualized program and allows students to pursue their own areas of interest.

Students and the M.B.A. Experience

GSM makes a special effort to admit a diverse group of students each year who

represent a wide range and variety of academic, cultural, and professional backgrounds. The average age for the class of 1999 is 27, with about five years of work experience. Women comprise approximately 30 percent of the student population, and international students comprise about 25 percent.

Special Features

As part of their educational experience, GSM students are also offered the opportunity to supplement their course work through the International and Intercampus Exchange Programs. A joint M.D./M.B.A. program is also offered with the College of Medicine. Research units associated with the School and its faculty members include the Center for Research on Information Technology and Organizations (CRITO), the only site in the country funded by the National Science Foundation studying the impact of technology on organizations and markets.

The Faculty

The faculty members of the Graduate School of Management at UCI are scholars from some of the most esteemed institutions nationally and internationally. They are a diverse group, and their composition is perhaps one of the most international in all business schools. Due to the smaller size and nature of the program, students also have the opportunity to work closely with faculty members throughout the program.

The Business School Network

Corporate Partnerships

The Corporate Partners program actively brings together GSM students and faculty members with the business community through activities such as the Corporate Partners/M.B.A. Roundtable series, Day-on-the-Job, Corporate Speakers Series, and Management Practicum. Companies such as IBM, KPMG Peat Marwick, Hewlett-Packard, Taco Bell Corporation, Western Digital, Monex International, Merrill Lynch, American Airlines, and Manufacturers Bank are just a few represented within the ranks of GSM's Corporate Partners.

The College and Environs

UCI is located midway between Los Angeles and San Diego and is in the center of Orange County, one the nation's fastest-growing regions. It is also one of the most prolific and dynamic seedbeds for entrepreneurial, high-growth, and high-technology companies. The area provides easy access to professional theater, first-run movies, and dance companies, as well as a rich diversity of international cuisine at world-class restaurants. Other advantages include proximity to the mountains and beaches, which offer a variety of recreational opportunities such as water and snow skiing, hang gliding, bicycling, tennis, hiking, sailing, golf, and surfing on a year-round basis.

Technology Environment

The ability to use and manage electronic resources plays a significant role in today's information age. All GSM students are connected to electronic mail and the GSM Intranet, and every seat in GSM's largest classrooms has a network connection, enabling the student to maximize productivity within the classroom setting. Notebook computers are also required of all incoming students.

Placement

The Graduate School of Management provides a full range of placement and career services designed to assist M.B.A. students. Along with the career services director, faculty and staff members work collectively to provide graduates with employment opportunities and contacts with major business and governmental units. Services offered include on-campus recruitment visits, career expo events, resume books, interview skills workshops, and the latest in electronic candidate identification databases. A variety of internship and part-time positions are also available. Graduates receive starting salaries at or above the national average.

Admission

Admission for the M.B.A. and Ph.D. programs is offered each fall and is on a rolling basis. The deadline for the full-time program is May 1; for the Executive and Fully Employed M.B.A. programs, June 15; for the Health Care Executive M.B.A., October 1; and for the Ph.D. program, April 1. Admissions decisions for the M.B.A. programs are based on an overall evaluation of undergraduate GPA, GMAT scores (required), letters of recommendation, statement of purpose, and work experience. A minimum TOEFL score of 600 is required for international applicants whose native language is not English, and proof of adequate funds to cover two years of study is necessary. Introductory courses in calculus and statistics with probability are required prior to beginning the M.B.A. program.

Finances

The 1998–99 fees for the full-time M.B.A. program are $3670 per quarter for California residents (three academic quarters per year); $6800 per quarter for non-California residents. Costs for on-campus room and board range from $5382 to $7074; off-campus costs for room and board are approximately $8485.

Primary sources of financial aid for the full-time program include loans, grants, and fellowships. The School also has an on-site financial aid director to assist and guide students in this process. To be considered for the full range of financial aid programs, applicants are strongly encouraged to meet the institutional financial aid deadline of March 1.

Ph.D. applicants may also be considered for Regent's, Chancellor's, and tuition fellowships, in addition to teaching and research assistant positions. To be considered for the full range of financial aid programs, applicants are strongly encouraged to meet the institutional financial aid deadline of March 1. Financial aid is awarded only to citizens or permanent residents of the United States.

Application Facts and Dates

The M.B.A. and Ph.D. programs can be contacted directly by telephone: the M.B.A. program (telephone: 949-UCI-4MBA) and the Ph.D. program (telephone: 949-824-8318).

University of California, Irvine
MBA Admissions Office
350 GSM
Irvine, California 92697-3125
E-mail (M.B.A. Program): gsm-mba@
  uci.edu
World Wide Web: http://www.gsm.uci.
  edu

FACULTY LIST

Dennis J. Aigner, Ph.D., Berkeley. Applied econometrics.

David H. Blake, Dean of the Graduate School of Management; Ph.D., Rutgers. International management.

Yannis Bakos, Ph.D., MIT. Management information systems.

Thomas C. Buchmueller, Ph.D., Wisconsin–Madison. Health care/economics.

Nai-fu Chen, Ph.D., Berkeley; Ph.D., UCLA. Finance.

Imran S. Currim, Ph.D., Stanford. Marketing.

Marta M. Elvira, Ph.D., Berkeley. Organizational behavior.

Paul J. Feldstein, Ph.D., Chicago. Health care/economics.

Mary Gilly, Ph.D., Houston. Marketing.

Daniel Givoly, Ph.D., NYU. Accounting.

John Graham, Ph.D., Berkeley. Marketing.

Vijay Gurbaxani, Ph.D., Rochester. Management information systems.

Robert A. Haugen, Ph.D., Illinois at Urbana-Champaign. Finance.

Joanna L. Ho, Ph.D., Texas at Austin. Accounting.

Philippe Jorion, Ph.D., Chicago. Finance.

L. Robin Keller, Ph.D., UCLA. Operations and decision technologies.

John Leslie King, Ph.D., California, Irvine. Management information systems.

Kenneth L. Kraemer, Ph.D., USC. Management information systems.

Richard B. McKenzie, Ph.D., Virginia Tech. Public policy.

Barrie Nault, Ph.D., British Columbia. Management information systems.

Peter Navarro, Ph.D., Harvard. Public policy.

Paul Olk, Ph.D., Pennsylvania (Wharton). Organizational behavior.

Jone L. Pearce, Ph.D., Yale. Organizational behavior.

Cornelia Pechmann, Ph.D., Vanderbilt. Marketing.

Lyman W. Porter, Ph.D., Yale. Organizational behavior.

Judy B. Rosener, Ph.D., Claremont. Public policy.

Carlton H. Scott, Ph.D., New South Wales (Australia). Operations and decision technologies.

Claudia B. Schoonhaven, Ph.D., Stanford. Organizational behavior.

Kut C. So, Ph.D., Stanford. Operations and decision technologies.

Jing-Sheng Song, Ph.D., Columbia. Operations and decision technologies.

Neal M. Stoughton, Ph.D., Stanford. Finance.

Eli Talmor, Ph.D., North Carolina at Chapel Hill. Finance.

Robert J. Town, Ph.D., Wisconsin–Madison. Health-care/economics.

Rajeev Tyagi, Ph.D., Pennsylvania (Wharton). Marketing.

Alladi Venkatesh, Ph.D., Syracuse. Marketing.

James S. Wallace, Ph.D., Washington (Seattle). Accounting.

Margarethe F. Wiersema, Ph.D., Michigan. Business strategy.

William F. Wright, Ph.D., Berkeley. Accounting.

University of California, Los Angeles

Los Angeles, California

THE ANDERSON SCHOOL—CREATING INTELLECTUAL CAPITAL AND ENTREPRENEURIAL LEADERS FOR THE GLOBAL INFORMATION AGE

▶ *The Anderson School at UCLA has long been a leader and innovator in management education. Driven by superior research as well as an astute responsiveness to indicators and trends in the ever-expanding business environment, The Anderson School is preparing the management leaders who will define success in the years to come.*

These leaders will have a strong fundamental grounding in contemporary management and business theory, they will have a thorough knowledge of the role of technology in business, and they will understand the intricacies of global business relations and be skilled in working with people from widely differing personal and professional backgrounds.

If you aspire to the highest levels of managerial success, we invite you to take your place now among the leaders of the future; we invite you to join The Anderson School M.B.A. Program.

—John Mamer, Interim Dean

Programs and Curricular Focus

The Anderson School M.B.A. Program is designed for highly motivated, exceptional students and is structured to ensure that each graduate leaves with a leadership-level knowledge of all key management disciplines as well as the conceptual and analytical frameworks underlying those disciplines. Consisting of three components—the management core, advanced electives, and the management field study—the curriculum is regularly updated to address the evolving challenges today's business managers must meet.

The Anderson School's M.B.A. program has a general management focus, which enables students to tailor individual discipline-based programs of study rather than declare a major or a concentration. There are nine specialized areas of study and several interdisciplinary studies.

All students are required to take the management core, a set of eight courses that provides the base knowledge for the major functional fields of management. The management core provides the first building blocks on which advanced study in a variety of areas can be developed. The eight core courses are integrated and sequential, so that each successive course builds upon the knowledge gained in prior courses.

Two thirds (fourteen courses) of the M.B.A. curriculum are composed of advanced electives, which are chosen from any of the nine disciplines: accounting, business economics, decision sciences, finance, human resources and organizational behavior, information systems, marketing, operations and technology management, and strategy and organization as well as the interdisciplinary areas of study: entrepreneurial studies, international business and comparative management, and real estate.

The ratio of electives to core courses and the flexibility that students can practice in choosing electives adds breadth to each student's program of study.

The Management Field Study is the capstone requirement of the M.B.A. program and is conducted during the second year of the program. In this project, students integrate and apply their knowledge and skills in a professional setting outside the classroom.

The Anderson School provides two M.B.A. programs for individuals whose professional goals require that they remain employed while completing their M.B.A. degree. The Fully Employed M.B.A. Program is targeted toward emerging managers, typically junior-level professionals averaging 30 years of age and 6 years of work experience. The Executive M.B.A. Program is an intensive twenty-four-month program designed for professionals who have demanding jobs with a high level of responsibility and who seek a high-quality global management education while continuing in their professional roles.

Students and the M.B.A. Experience

The Anderson School at UCLA has a vibrant student body whose extraordinary intellectual, cultural, social, and athletic energies spill out of the classroom into a plethora of nonacademic activities. The average full-time student is 27 years old, with just over four years of full-time work experience. Women comprise 26 percent of the student population, members of minority groups make up 24 percent, and international students make up 23 percent.

From day one, The Anderson School teaches students how to work effectively with others to transform ideas into realities. Teamwork is part of everyday life at Anderson. Students work together in study groups or on class assignments or Field Study and other projects.

❖ Global Focus

The Anderson School offers students a wide range of exciting opportunities to increase their international perspectives, from working on group projects with peers from among the forty-eight countries represented at Anderson to studying abroad and from enrolling in the International Management Fellows Program to touring a factory in Prague.

The Anderson School encourages students to become involved in academic exchange programs with universities located abroad. Currently, the School participates in more than thirty academic foreign exchange programs.

The Faculty

The renowned Anderson faculty, whose members are widely acclaimed for their expertise and compelling research, teaches advanced management theory and practice in a contemporary and vibrant interactive model of course work and field-based study. The Anderson School has a total of 142 faculty members and twenty-seven endowed chaired professorships.

The Business School Network

Corporate Partnerships

The Anderson School Board of Visitors comprises successful entrepreneurs and business executives from a broad range of national and international industries and professions. Among them are John E. Anderson, the School's namesake and President of Topa Equities, Ltd.; Jeffrey Berg, Chairman and CEO of International Creative Management; B. Kipling Hagopian, founder of venture capitalist firm Brentwood Associates; Lester B. Korn, founder of Korn/Ferry International; and Zuisho Hayashi, President and Chairman of the Board of the Japan-based HUMAX Corporation.

Prominent Alumni

Anderson alumni comprise an eclectic body of talented business leaders and research professionals, from corporate executives to entrepreneurs and from consultants to film producers. Anderson alumni form a valuable management network that spans the globe. This list includes Fred D. Anderson, CFO of Apple Computer; Jill Barad, CEO of Mattel, Inc.; and George Montgomery, President and CEO of Taylor Made Golf.

The College and Environs

Strolling to classes through the serene gardens on UCLA's campus, it is easy to forget that The Anderson School is located in the middle of the second-largest city in the United States. For Anderson students, Los Angeles offers the best of many worlds. Beach, mountain, and desert recreation areas are plentiful and easily accessible by car. Los Angeles

museums and theaters offer the world's most acclaimed entertainment. In addition, Westwood Village, which adjoins the UCLA campus to the south, offers shopping, dining, and a wide range of services.

Facilities

The Anderson School's management education complex is a testament to the School's vision of the growing importance of superior management education. Continuing its reputation as a national leader in the use of technology in M.B.A. instruction, the eleven specially designed case study rooms have data ports at each seating station to integrate the instructional program of each faculty member with the School's central computing facility in the Rosenfeld Library.

Placement

Career planning begins before students enter The Anderson School and becomes increasingly focused during the M.B.A. program. Starting with Orientation Week and continuing throughout graduation, Anderson's MBA Career Management Center (CMC) helps students define their career objectives, identify resources, strategize opportunities, hone interviewing skills, and make critical connections. The center's skilled professional staff helps Anderson students attain career goals across a broad span of interests that range from not-for-profit enterprises to Wall Street investment banking. Anderson's class of 1997 had nearly 99 percent placement success. The average salary was $75,000, and signing bonuses averaged $25,000. CMC's many valuable services and resources include

employer briefings and receptions, a campus interview program, videoconferencing interviews, resume books, vacancy listings, counseling and advising, workshops, a career connection program, a career resource center, and online resources.

Admission

The Anderson School admissions policy emphasizes academic ability, leadership, work experience, and breadth of life experiences. Anderson students come from diverse backgrounds yet share important qualities such as superior intelligence, the ability to think broadly and analytically, strong interpersonal skills, and a desire to solve complex problems. The Admissions Committee evaluates applicants' prospects as future leaders and their projected ability to succeed and profit from the M.B.A. program. The committee carefully considers biographical and academic background information, GMAT and TOEFL (for most international applicants) scores, achievements, awards and honors, employment history, letters of recommendation, and college and community involvement, especially where candidates have served in a leadership capacity.

Finances

The cost of attending the UCLA M.B.A. program during the 1997–98 academic year was $32,463 for California residents and $41,447 for nonresidents. Students can expect 1998–99 costs to increase from 10 percent to 20 percent over 1997–98 costs. Fellowships and scholarships are available, and, upon admission, students automatically receive a financial aid application packet.

Application Facts and Dates

Applicants may apply for fall 1999 admission from October 1, 1998, through April 3, 1999. The Admissions Committee begins considering applications in December of each year. For more information, students should contact:

Ms. Linda Baldwin
Director of M.B.A. Admissions
The Anderson School at UCLA
110 Westwood Plaza, Suite B201
Box 951481
Los Angeles, California 90095-1481
Telephone: 310-825-6944
Fax: 310-825-8582
E-mail: mba.admissions@anderson.
  ucla.edu
World Wide Web: http://www.
  anderson.ucla.edu/

University of California–Riverside

The A. Gary Anderson Graduate School of Management

Riverside, California

BALANCING THE ART AND SCIENCE OF MANAGEMENT

At the A. Gary Anderson Graduate School of Management (AGSM), our M.B.A. curriculum provides a balance of the art and science of management. This recognition of the dual challenges that face today's manager permeates one's educational experience at AGSM. The Anderson School offers an intimate educational environment where classes are small by typical M.B.A. standards, professors are accessible to students, and the business community is very supportive and closely involved with the School's myriad activities.

—David Mayers, Interim Dean of Academic Affairs

Programs and Curricular Focus

The M.B.A. curriculum balances the art and science of management, with a particular emphasis on managing through information, and recognizes the global context of management. The program stresses the essential interdependencies that exist across functional areas, emphasizing the development of superior management skills as well as theoretical foundations. Great importance is placed on teamwork, relationships, and communication.

The core courses provide the foundation in analytical and managerial skills. The twelve-course core culminates in an integrative case course that synthesizes the various functional area approaches to managerial issues. After a required internship experience, which may be based on current employment, students proceed to study elective topics in greater depth. Most students choose nine elective courses from areas including accounting, entrepreneurial management, finance, general management, human resources management/organizational behavior, international management, management information systems, management science, marketing, and production/ operations management. Students conclude the twenty-three-course, 92-unit program with a capstone strategic management course and a case analysis. There is a thesis option for students who wish to do significant research on a special topic.

The program is designed to accommodate the unique requirements of both career professionals and full-time students. Sufficient sections of courses are offered in the evenings to permit career professionals to complete the M.B.A. on a part-time basis. In this way,

full-time and part-time students take classes together, enriching the educational experience of both.

Students and the M.B.A. Experience

Diverse backgrounds and experiences are characteristic of students in the AGSM M.B.A. program. The average age of students is 27, with an age range from 21 to 49. Approximately 45 percent are women, and 27 percent are minority students. Sixty-five percent of the students have an average of three years' work experience in fields ranging from medicine to manufacturing; 35 percent come directly from undergraduate programs. In recent classes, 45 percent of the student body has come from the Western United States, 15 percent from the Northeast and South, and 10 percent from the Midwest. Approximately 35 percent are international students. Forty percent of AGSM's students have undergraduate degrees in business or economics, 30 percent have degrees in science or engineering, and 30 percent have backgrounds in the humanities or social sciences.

❖ Global Focus

Most AGSM required courses include a global perspective, with recognition of the international issues that affect each functional area. In addition, electives in many of the functional areas provide opportunities for in-depth study of international topics. The campus maintains liaison with most of the networks offering international internships, and overseas study options are available in thirty countries through the University of California Education Abroad Program.

Special Features

The management synthesis course at the end of the first year of study and the required internship are key elements of the AGSM M.B.A. program. The synthesis course is a team-taught, integrative, cross-functional case course that places students in actual managerial decision situations. The required internship enables students to apply their academic background to real-world projects, where they learn to perfect their professional, interpersonal, and communication skills.

The Faculty

The A. Gary Anderson Graduate School of Management has a renowned, multicultural faculty, representing excellence in its respective areas. Faculty members have doctorates from world-class universities and publish research in top journals in their fields. Faculty members also have industry and consulting experience and teach in executive programs and workshops.

The Business School Network

Relationships with the corporate community are an integral part of the AGSM M.B.A. program. The AGSM Advisory Council assists the School with developing and maintaining a relevant curriculum and interacts with M.B.A. students at numerous events. Every year, the School also names two distinguished business leaders as AGSM Fellows. Each Fellow spends one day each quarter speaking to classes and consulting with M.B.A. students. In the spring, a contemporary issues seminar series brings 8 to 10 corporate executives to the School to discuss emerging issues with M.B.A. students. These and other activities ensure that each M.B.A. student has the opportunity to develop a network of business contacts prior to graduation.

The College and Environs

The 1,200-acre Riverside campus of the University of California is conveniently located some 50 miles east of Los Angeles, within easy driving distance of most of the major cultural and recreational offerings in southern California. Enrollment at UCR is approximately 9,700, nearly 20 percent of whom are graduate students. The campus,

with its modern classroom buildings, its beautiful commons, and its 161-foot Carillon Tower, is designed to support the academic and research programs that are part of its assigned mission as a campus in the University of California system.

A city of 250,000, Riverside has several major shopping malls, a symphony orchestra, an opera association, two community theaters, an art center, and many restaurants in proximity to the campus.

Facilities

The University library is the focal point of research and study at UCR. The collection includes more than 1.8 million bound volumes, 13,300 serial subscriptions, and 1.5 million microforms. The collections are arranged and staffed to support programs of instruction and research for faculty and students.

The M.B.A. program is housed in Anderson Hall. M.B.A. students have access to the latest computing equipment, including both Macintosh and PC platforms, as well as powerful UNIX workstations.

UCR offers graduate students several affordable housing options both on and off campus. Campus housing includes Bannockburn Village, University Plaza Apartments, and Canyon Crest Married Student Housing.

Technology Environment

The AGSM Microcomputer Facility consists of fifty Intel-based microcomputers. The facility is connected to the campus network and to the Internet. It is centrally located in the A. Gary Anderson Hall, south wing, and is staffed by student lab consultants and a manager.

The facility offers major software packages in the areas of word processing, spreadsheets, presentation graphics, databases, and statistics.

Within the School, the facility is utilized for teaching, class demonstrations, theses, statistical analysis and faculty research projects and as a tool for effective management decisionmaking.

One of AGSM's goals is to graduate students with wide-ranging computer skills that help them become successful in the modern business world.

Placement

A full range of career planning and placement services is offered through the M.B.A. Career Services Center. The center is staffed by professional counselors to address the specific career needs of graduate business students. Services available include on-campus interviews, career seminars and workshops, individual counseling, an alumni career network, a resume directory, and an extensive career library including computerized employment databases. The school participates in the West Coast M.B.A. Consortium and also sponsors a career night, which provides M.B.A. candidates the opportunity to meet with local and national corporate representatives.

Admission

Admission is open to eligible students from all undergraduate majors. Admission is based on several criteria, including the quality of previous academic work as measured by GPA for the last two years of undergraduate work, scores on the Graduate Management Admission Test (GMAT), letters of recommendation, and potential for success in the program. In recent years, the average GPA for entering students has been approximately 3.3 and the average GMAT score has been 560–565. Applicants whose first language is not English are required to score a minimum of 550 on the TOEFL.

Basic accounting and quantitative methods are prerequisites to the program.

Students may be admitted without these courses but must meet these requirements during their first two quarters in residence.

Finances

Tuition and fees for 1997–98 for full-time students were $4866 for California residents and $13,854 for nonresidents. An additional $5000 per year professional school fee is also assessed, although in 1997–98, AGSM provided grants to all M.B.A. students to cover 50 percent of this fee. Annual fees for part-time students in 1997–98 ranged from $3602 to $4375 for California residents, including the professional school fee. Approximate costs for books and supplies are $900 per year. Living expenses, including housing and personal expenses, are estimated to be $6500 to $7500 per year.

Several kinds of financial assistance are available. These include fellowships, teaching assistantships, and research assistantships. Applicants indicate interest in support on the application form. Loans and work study may be applied for through the UCR Financial Aid Office.

International Students

Approximately 30 percent of AGSM's M.B.A. students are international students. The International Services Center provides special assistance to international students and their dependents. An orientation program is held at the beginning of each quarter to help new students adjust to their new environs and the campus. Throughout the year, workshops, excursions, and individual advising sessions are offered. In addition, language workshops tailored to the needs of the international M.B.A. students are available.

Application Facts and Dates

Application deadlines for domestic students are May 1 for fall quarter, September 1 for winter quarter, and December 1 for spring quarter. Deadlines for international students are February 1 for fall, July 1 for winter, and October 1 for spring. Applications are processed on a rolling basis, and decisions are made when files are complete. For further information, applicants should contact:

Gary J. Kuzas
Director of M.B.A. Admissions
The A. Gary Anderson Graduate
    School of Management
University of California
Riverside, California 92521-0203
Telephone: 909-787-4551
Fax: 909-787-3970
E-mail: agsmmba@ucrac1.ucr.edu
World Wide Web: http://www.agsm.
    ucr.edu

University of Chicago

Chicago, Illinois

THE CHOICE IS YOURS!

As you plan your business education, I invite you to consider one of the world's premier institutions of general management and business leadership education: the University of Chicago Graduate School of Business (GSB).

Since it was founded in 1898, Chicago has been a focal point of cutting-edge business research as well as innovative educational methods. Our flexible curriculum puts you in charge by allowing you to tailor your business education according to your personal experience, interests, and career plans. The wealth of programs within the School and its integral relationship with the rest of the University offer wide choices from which you can create the course of study most appropriate for you.

—Robert S. Hamada, Dean and Edward Eagle Brown Distinguished Service Professor of Finance

Programs and Curricular Focus

The M.B.A. curriculum is designed to prepare students for significant careers in management. It encompasses both the basic disciplines that underlie management and the operational areas specific to business. The courses are designed to provide the understanding of the components of managerial decision making while furnishing perspective on the role of business as an economic, political, and social institution.

Chicago's curriculum has long emphasized freedom of choice and flexibility, allowing students to develop a program that suits their own needs. Compared to other M.B.A. programs, Chicago has a short list of requirements and a long list of electives. Students have unparalleled flexibility in their choice of courses, professors, and activities.

The curriculum students design for themselves complements their individual backgrounds, interests, and abilities and is targeted to each student's specific career goals. Students are encouraged to build on their previous education and experience rather than repeat work mastered elsewhere. They may take as many as six courses in other University departments and study with some of the world's most renowned scholars in such fields as economics, law, languages, philosophy, or literature. Or they may fashion a joint-degree course of study that combines business with international relations, area studies, law, public policy, or medicine. At Chicago, the ultimate responsibility

for learning and attaining a student's particular educational goals rests with the student.

The Graduate School of Business also includes five alternative programs to meet everyone's needs: the International M.B.A., Evening M.B.A., Weekend M.B.A., Executive M.B.A., and International Executive M.B.A. (Barcelona, Spain).

Students and the M.B.A. Experience

Each of the students plays a critical role in defining the culture, values, and direction of the GSB. The best and the brightest students are chosen from around

the world because they will have an impact on the School and on their chosen profession. From the moment they arrive on campus, the active involvement of all students, both at work and play, is promoted.

The Business Students Association (BSA) and its elected officers coordinate social events, conferences, and professional and special interests groups. Students may participate in a wide variety of organizations and activities that draw people with similar interests and goals.

The Faculty

Intellectual freedom, flexibility, and respect for the individual are hallmarks of Chicago's academic tradition. Faculty members are free, indeed encouraged, to develop innovative ways of presenting and teaching material and to introduce new courses based on cutting-edge research or changing demands from the business community. The result is a wide and lively mix of teaching styles and conceptual frameworks as well as philosophies that add to the richness and diversity of the Chicago experience. Students have the opportunity to study with Nobel Prize winners (Merton Miller, 1990; Robert Fogel, 1993), a former chairman of the President's Council of Economic Advisers, or a senior examiner for the Malcom Baldrige National Quality Award.

The Business School Network

The M.B.A. experience is not restricted to the classroom at Chicago. Although the Graduate School of Business is not a case study institution, a substantial percentage of the course work, depending on the student's choice of classes, consists of various kinds of cases and applied analysis. Because of the School's location in one of the world's major commercial centers, students meet business, economic, labor, and political leaders at the numerous lecture and seminar series held on campus and through alumni and friends in the Chicago business community. A host of companies sponsor numerous laboratory courses at the GSB, including Merrill Lynch & Co., Inc.; A. T. Kearney, Inc.; Kraft General Foods; and the Amoco Corporation.

The College and Environs

Established in 1898, the Graduate School of Business is the second-oldest business school in the United States and one of its most distinguished. The core of the University of Chicago's 175-acre campus, one of the most beautiful urban universi-

ties in the country, is a collection of neo-Gothic buildings clustered around quadrangles. Surprises abound. Rockefeller Chapel, the site of graduation and other official events, turns out to be closer in size to a cathedral. Tiny ivy-covered Bond Chapel, barely visible under a canopy of trees, stuns visitors with dazzling stained-glass windows and intricate wood carvings and is a favorite spot for weddings.

Placement

Employers actively seek to hire University of Chicago M.B.A.'s. In 1997–98, 288 employers recruited Graduate School of Business graduates and interns, conducting approximately 12,500 interviews in the School's on-campus recruiting facilities. The Office of Career Services offers individual counseling and career planning resources as well as lecture series and job search workshops. In addition, student professional interest groups bring corporate speakers to campus to discuss their jobs and their industries.

Admission

Prerequisites for admission include completion of an undergraduate degree from an accredited U.S. institution or the equivalent from another country, the results of the GMAT (or GRE), and the GSB's application. A TOEFL score is required of all applicants for whom English is not their native language. Interviews are highly recommended but not required. Applicants are evaluated individually based on their professional experience, academic background, and personal qualities.

Finances

The Graduate School of Business is committed to identifying financial resources for students who require assistance in meeting the costs of the M.B.A. program. The School provides scholarship awards, loan assistance, and college work-study employment to students who demonstrate financial need. Scholarship awards are based on academic excellence, demonstrated qualities of leadership, and financial need. Awards are granted to first-year students, with a few renewable for the second year. Scholarships are awarded only to students who are entering the campus M.B.A. program.

Application Facts and Dates

The Graduate School of Business has three deadlines for admission for the programs beginning in fall 1999: November 20, 1998; January 8, 1999; and March 19, 1999. Applicants should apply by the January 8 deadline for full scholarship consideration. A decision takes approximately eight weeks from the deadline, but more detailed information is available in the application packet. For more information, students should contact:

Director of Admissions and Financial
 Aid
Graduate School of Business
University of Chicago
6030 South Ellis Avenue
Chicago, Illinois 60637
Telephone: 773-702-7369
Fax: 773-702-9085
E-mail: admissions@gsb.uchicago.edu
World Wide Web: http://www-gsb.
 uchicago.edu

Developing
The
Leaders of
Tomorrow

College of Business
& Administration

University of Colorado at Boulder

Graduate School of Business Administration

Boulder, Colorado

▶ **DEVELOPING THE LEADERS OF TOMORROW**

AT CU–Boulder, we develop the leaders of tomorrow. Our M.B.A. program not only provides students with business skills; we educate them for the rapidly changing marketplace of the new millennium. Our strategy in this effort is twofold. First, by partnering with the region's dynamic business community, we provide students with hands-on experience through internships and course projects. A host of entrepreneurial and high-tech firms reside nearby, as do major corporations, including Coors, Hewlett Packard, and Lucent Technologies. Second, our professors educate students on the most critical issues facing world business. This crucial balance of pragmatic experience and academic rigor positions our talented graduates at the forefront of tomorrow's business leadership.

—Larry Singell, Dean

Programs and Curricular Focus

As the premier M.B.A. program in the region, the University of Colorado at Boulder (CU–Boulder) prepares its high-quality students for success in the marketplace. Teamwork, leadership, and communication skills prepare graduates for management roles within the international economy. Majoring in entrepreneurship, finance, marketing, organization management, real estate, or technology and innovation management, students graduate with the background necessary to compete globally. Students also take advantage of other nationally ranked programs by pursuing a self-designed major.

For students focusing on the global marketplace, a certificate in international business is available. This program offers international courses in finance, marketing, and management and is supplemented by professional experiences, including international internships, participation in the College's London Seminar in Business or other study-abroad experiences, or domestic internships focusing on global issues.

As the marketplace becomes more specialized, a demand for legal and high-technology experience drives the economy. For those interested in law or telecommunications, the program offers J.D./M.B.A. and M.B.A./M.S. in telecommunications double-degree programs. These programs provide an ideal balance of management expertise and technical focus.

Students and the M.B.A. Experience

Students in the program come from all over the world. Sharing their experiences from countries such as Brazil, Germany, India, Japan, Korea, and Turkey, students gain from the multicultural dialogue that takes place within and beyond the classroom. The class of 1999 is 26 percent women. The average student is 27 years old and has nearly five years of professional experience. Students' areas of expertise include marketing and sales (24 percent), engineering/computers (15 percent), management (14 percent), finance/accounting/banking (14 percent), real estate/construction management (12 percent), military/government (8 percent), law or education (8 percent), and scientific research or other (5 percent).

Special Features

The Colleges of Business and Engineering responded to the country's growth in small business by founding the Center for Entrepreneurship. The center features outstanding professors and leading entrepreneurs who teach students to initiate the creativity to launch and manage new ventures and practice the risk required to effectively compete in the entrepreneurial community. The entrepreneurship program, which is ranked in *Success* magazine's top twenty-five, emphasizes hands-on learning and facilitates interaction with Boulder County's community through field projects and lectures. Ranked as one of *Inc.* magazine's top entrepreneurial

communities, Boulder provides great opportunities for the entrepreneurially inclined.

The Center for Real Estate, established as a partnership between the College of Business and the CU Real Estate Council, emphasizes a multidisciplinary approach to real estate education. With the 150-member council of real estate executives actively involved in curriculum development, mentoring, internships, and job placement, the center provides students with the skills demanded by the marketplace. Transcending traditional real estate education, this program encourages students to take courses from the College of Architecture and Planning, the College of Engineering's construction management department, and the School of Law. The program's environmental focus is particularly appropriate given Boulder's commitment to its natural resources and its strength in growth management.

As a telecommunications hub, Colorado is headquarters for industry leaders, including Tele-Communications, Inc. (TCI), U S West, Level 3 Communications, and Jones Intercable, Inc. Responding to the community's strengths, the Colleges of Business and Engineering created the M.B.A./M.S.-telecommunications degree. CU–Boulder is one of the few universities to offer this unique program, and students are given the opportunity to combine their management expertise with the outstanding resources of the engineering college's telecommunications programs.

The Faculty

As leaders in business education, the faculty combines pragmatic management experience with innovative research. CU's nationally recognized faculty spearheads the cutting-edge curriculum, preparing graduates to become high-level managers in a challenging and evolving international marketplace. Courses incorporate case studies, group projects, team teaching, lectures, discussions, simulations, and the Internet. Issues such as ethics, technology, communication, and the global marketplace are integrated throughout the curriculum to enhance students' learning experiences.

The University of Colorado at Boulder, nestled in the foothills of the Rocky Mountains, offers a beautiful environment in which to pursue a graduate education.

The Business School Network

Advisory boards, composed of prominent executives, work with students to provide mentoring and support. In addition to the College's Business Advisory Council, each College division (accounting and information systems, finance and economics, management, and marketing), as well as the entrepreneurship and real estate centers, have advisory boards. Members talk to students about new developments in their field, internships, and industry contacts.

In addition to working with board members, M.B.A. students benefit from pursuing their degrees in a high-growth economic region. Students gain pragmatic experience by interacting with regional and international firms. The area's unique business environment provides a setting in which established corporations enjoy success and entrepreneurial ventures also flourish. The region has business niches in the computer, biotechnology, finance, lifestyle and vision, and entrepreneurial fields.

The College and Environs

As the flagship university in the region, CU–Boulder ranks tenth among public research universities and third among rising research universities in the public sector according to a 1997 study. The campus is strategically located near the mountains and city, and students can take a 20-mile drive and be atop the Continental Divide or drive 30 miles to Denver.

Acres of protected open space surround Boulder, providing beautiful hiking, biking, and riding trails. The city of Boulder hosts cultural and recreational activities, including the Shakespeare Festival, the Colorado Music Festival, and the Bolder Boulder 10K run.

Technology Environment

Technology, a critical dimension of the business world and of an M.B.A. education, is a vital component of CU's academic experience. Students are acquainted with the School's computing environment at the MBA Leadership Forum at the onset of their program, where they are introduced to the College's Web-based information system that maximizes internship and placement opportunities.

The MBA Business Center provides a computing environment for master's students in which they can research course assignments and create presentations using multimedia equipment in an isolated working environment. The College's PepsiCo Case Room is equipped with laptop computer workstations as well as multimedia and distance learning capabilities. Classrooms and computer labs house computers and the latest software, state-of-the-art projection systems, and multimedia capabilities.

Master's students use the M.B.A. Forum, a Web-based bulletin board system, to browse the latest information about their classes and group projects and to access the M.B.A. calendar. E-mail accounts and home pages are also established for all M.B.A. students.

Placement

The M.B.A. Career Placement Office helps position students for business success. Facilitating internships, forums, panels, and executive luncheons, the placement office establishes networking opportunities that enable students to discuss career and business issues with executives.

The placement office enhances students' job opportunities through workshops, a career guidebook, videotaped mock interviews, industry forums, resume books, employer briefings, a career resource library, and on-campus recruiting. An online database of student resumes is also available to employers to match their needs with student interests. Students benefit from an online database that lists internships and job vacancies. In addition to internal resources, the M.B.A. program is involved with the Rocky Mountain M.B.A. Consortium, which hosts national employers who are seeking employees.

Admission

The M.B.A. program admits high-achieving individuals who demonstrate the ability to lead and manage in today's evolving international marketplace. Ideal candidates work as team players and demonstrate initiative in the workplace. The candidate's academic credentials, GMAT scores, work history, and recommendations are all weighed for admission consideration.

Finances

Full-time tuition per semester in 1997–98 was $1855 for residents and $7335 for nonresidents. Students paid semester fees of approximately $420. Half of CU-Boulder's students receive financial aid, which is available to graduate students through fellowships, loans, grants, and work-study.

Application Facts and Dates

For additional information, students should contact:

M.B.A. Program
Campus Box 419
University of Colorado at Boulder
Boulder, Colorado 80309-0419
Telephone: 303-492-1831
Fax: 303-492-1727
E-mail: busgrad@spot.colorado.edu
World Wide Web: http://www-bus.
colorado.edu/

University of Colorado at Denver

Denver, Colorado

FLEXIBLE PROGRAMS...BUSINESS PARTNERSHIPS... WORLD-CLASS TEACHING AND RESEARCH

The University of Colorado at Denver (CU-Denver) offers future business leaders a unique combination of flexibility in program schedules, including our new 11-Month M.B.A.; faculty committed to excellence in both teaching and research; and close relationships with the Denver business community. This, combined with the vast cultural, recreational, and networking opportunities the thriving downtown Denver environment offers, makes CU-Denver an ideal place for graduate business education. I cordially invite you to learn more about us. Call for further information or consult our home page on the World Wide Web (see the last section of this description).

—Yash Gupta, Dean

Programs and Curricular Focus

The Graduate School of Business Administration at the University of Colorado at Denver is recognized as one of the premier graduate business programs in the Rocky Mountain region. Graduate programs include a number of flexible options for pursuing the Master of Business Administration (M.B.A.) degree: the Individualized M.B.A., the innovative 11-Month Accelerated M.B.A., and the Cohort M.B.A. In addition, Master of Science (M.S.) degrees in seven focused fields of study are offered. All management programs are nationally accredited by AACSB—The International Association for Management Education. The Master of Science in Health Administration (M.S.H.A.) program is also accredited by the Accrediting Commission on Education for Health Services Administration (ACEHSA).

The sixteen-course, 48-credit-hour M.B.A. program consists of eleven core courses that provide an introduction to all functional areas of business management. The emphasis is on integrating the functional area courses through application of theory to real business problems. Skills in both qualitative and quantitative methods of analysis are taught, since both are important for making competitive business decisions. In addition to the functional core, students take elective and special topics courses along with one required international business course.

The innovative 11-Month M.B.A. is new for fall 1998. This accelerated, full-time program enables highly motivated students to complete all

M.B.A. requirements in five 8-week sessions. The accelerated program allows students to minimize time spent away from work yet provides students with all of the strategic management skill taught in the Individual and Cohort programs. The program begins in late August, and the degree is completed in mid-July of the following year. Enrollment is limited to approximately 40 students.

For a more specialized business program, students may choose the Master of Science degree in one of seven fields of study: accounting, finance, health services administration, information systems, international business, marketing, or organization and management. Dual-degree programs are available, combining the M.B.A. with any Master of Science degree plan. Selected graduate study in other schools within the University also may be combined with the M.B.A. for a dual degree. In addition, the Graduate School of Business offers a dual Master of Business Administration/ Master of International Management (M.B.A./M.I.M.) degree in cooperation with Thunderbird, The American Graduate School of International Management in Glendale, Arizona.

The University of Colorado Executive M.B.A. program is taught in downtown Denver. The executive program invites business executives to participate in a specialized program of seminars with prominent business faculty members from all three University of Colorado campuses. Classes meet once a week, alternating Fridays and Saturdays, for two academic years.

Students and the M.B.A. Experience

M.B.A. students at CU-Denver are adult learners with an average age of 30; many have five to ten years of work experience. More than half continue to be employed full-time as they complete their degree programs. The Graduate School of Business Administration seeks diversity in the student body. Approximately 12 percent of the students represent more than thirty countries around the world. Denver is a recognized center of international business, and, as an integral part of the greater Denver community, CU-Denver is committed to including international perspectives in all programs. Services to international students, including assistance with arrival, housing, orientation, and immigration concerns, are provided through the Office of International Education. A team of graduate advisers assists all students in the M.B.A. and M.S. programs with degree planning and registration.

The Faculty

M.B.A. and M.S. programs are designed to help students achieve learning and career objectives through interaction with a high-quality, internationally diverse faculty committed to teaching and research. More than 60 full-time faculty members, along with distinguished business professionals, work with students to create a dynamic learning environment. CU-Denver faculty members rank among the top business scholars in the country, conducting leading research directly related to the courses they teach. As a group, the faculty is on the cutting edge of business knowledge, publishing an average of 100 articles a year in scholarly business journals. Several faculty members have written textbooks used by universities around the world, and many are reviewers or editors for scholarly journals.

CU-Denver's business students also learn from the faculty's extensive managerial and consulting experience. In addition, the faculty members of the graduate school of business rank among the best teachers on campus. Several business faculty members have received

the prestigious "Outstanding Teacher of the Year" award from CU-Denver.

The Business School Network

The undergraduate College of Business Administration and the Graduate School of Business Administration are privileged to have the support of a 45-member Board of Advisors, comprising CEOs and senior executives from the greater Denver business community, many of whom are graduates of the program. The board serves in an advisory capacity to the dean and the faculty on matters concerning curriculum; outreach programs, such as mentoring and internships; and the development of strong ties with the local business community.

The College and Environs

The University of Colorado at Denver is in the Auraria Higher Education Consortium. The Auraria campus is safe and vibrant and is located in downtown Denver. The mild climate and the city's proximity to the Rocky Mountains contribute to Denver's status as one of the most beautiful and dynamic cities in the country.

Students in CU-Denver's Graduate School of Business benefit from close ties to Colorado's business community. Through CU-Denver's Executive-in-Residence Program, the CU-in-Class Program, the prestigious Celebration of Success dinner, and the monthly Dean's Business Breakfast lecture series, CU-Denver students stay linked with the business community while they complete their program of study.

Technology Environment

Four computer labs on campus (one reserved exclusively for business students) are equipped with IBM-compatible computers that are part of a local area network and linked to the Internet. The Auraria Library houses more than 750,000 books, videos, government publications, and me-

dia items, with subscriptions to more than 3,500 journals, magazines, and newspapers. Hundreds of periodicals are accessible full-text via the Auraria Online Information System. Within the library, students have access to more than 300 online and CD-ROM commercial databases and the Internet. With a PC, registered students and faculty and staff members may access many of these databases from home. The library is a depository of Colorado and U.S. government publications.

Placement

A full-service career planning and internship advisory office is available on campus to all students at CU-Denver. The Career Center offers information and support to students seeking internships with companies in the greater Denver area; it also provides career counseling and workshops on resume preparation and interview techniques. The Career Center serves as a clearinghouse for employer connections and job vacancy announcements. A computer-assisted resume referral service allows prospective employers to review the qualifications of students and graduates registered with the program and informs students of job openings on the Web.

Admission

The Graduate School of Business Administration admits qualified students for the fall and spring semesters and for the summer session. A two-part application form, optional resume, personal essay, required GMAT score, two original transcripts in sealed envelopes, directly from each institution of higher education attended, and an application fee (M.B.A., $50; M.B.A./M.S. dual degree, $80; and international students, $80) must be submitted by published deadlines. International students whose native language is not English must submit TOEFL scores. Letters of recommendation are required for all international

students and M.S. in health services administration applicants.

Finances

In 1997–98, Colorado resident students in business paid $222 per graduate credit hour; nonresidents in business paid $752 per credit hour. Full-time graduate business tuition (covering a tuition "window" of 9 to 15 credit hours) was $1853 for Colorado residents and $6274 for nonresidents. Required student fees totaled approximately $150 per semester. Student health insurance purchased through the University group policy, required for international students, was $710 per calendar year.

Single students should budget approximately $1000 per month for housing, food, books, and moderate entertainment expenses. CU-Denver provides no on-campus housing, but reasonably priced accommodations are available in nearby neighborhoods.

Financial aid may be available to U.S. citizens through the Financial Aid Office. In addition, graduate scholarships are available to graduate students in business administration through the M.B.A. program or through one of the seven specialized Master of Science programs. Students should request scholarship assistance when they apply for admission.

Application Facts and Dates

The Graduate School of Business Administration welcomes applications on an ongoing basis for admission in the fall or spring semester and the summer session. The 11-Month M.B.A. accepts applications for the fall semester only.

Regular application deadlines for admission to a graduate program in business administration are July 1 for the fall semester, November 1 for spring, and April 1 for summer. International applications should be received by March 1 (fall enrollment), July 1 (spring), and December 1 (summer). Completed applications for the 11-Month M.B.A. program must be received by June 15. CU-Denver's programs are competitive; early application is encouraged. Application materials and all program information may be accessed through the World Wide Web. For further information, students should contact:

Graduate School of Business
   Administration
Campus Box 165
University of Colorado at Denver
P.O. Box 173364
Denver, Colorado 80217-3364
Telephone: 303-556-5900
Fax: 303-556-5904
E-mail: lori_cain@maroon.cudenver.
   edu
World Wide Web: http://www.
   cudenver.edu/public/business

University of Connecticut

QUALITY AND THE M.B.A. PROGRAM

You will invest a significant amount of time and money in working toward an M.B.A. degree. The program you select should provide you with a multidimensional and integrated series of challenging learning experiences that prepare you for a business leadership position. Concern for quality is a key consideration in choosing an M.B.A. program. The "Connecticut M.B.A." has a well-established tradition of excellence in four essential areas: the quality and diversity of our students, the quality of our faculty, the quality of the curriculum, and the quality of the support services. Our students' geographic and cultural diversity creates a supportive learning environment for all. The faculty members have a strong commitment to teaching, and they bring relevant research and consulting experience to their classes. The curriculum gives you many choices and provides flexibility in selecting electives for a concentration. Finally, the support services, including the library, computer labs, and counseling and placement services, provide the support you need, when you need it.

—Thomas G. Gutteridge, Dean

Programs and Curricular Focus

The M.B.A. curriculum requires a total of nineteen courses (57 credits) to earn the degree, which typically takes two academic years. By taking courses during intersessions or summer, students can complete the entire program in only sixteen months. Students with previous academic course work in core subjects may be able to substitute electives for two or three required courses, which adds to the choices and flexibility in selecting courses. Concentrations are available in accounting, finance, health-care management, international business, management, management of technology, marketing, and real estate.

The UConn M.B.A. Program integrates international business into the curriculum and provides several opportunities for students to study and work overseas. M.B.A. students may concentrate in international business or in any of the functional areas or they may complete a double concentration in international business and one of the functional areas. M.B.A. courses taught in English, French, and German are available as part of the study overseas, dual-degree, and exchange programs in France, Germany, and the Netherlands. Students are expected to take advantage of the diversity of backgrounds in their classes to develop the perspectives and skills that are critically relevant to managing in this increasingly complex and ever-shrinking world.

Students and the M.B.A. Experience

The class of 107 students who entered the program in the fall of 1997 included 40 international students representing nineteen countries. Many noninternational students have studied foreign languages or traveled extensively abroad. The average age of the entering class was 26, with a range from age 20 to over 40. Most of the students were in their mid-20s, and most of them had between two and six years of work experience. This diversity of geographic, cultural, and work backgrounds is a key ingredient to the success of the UConn M.B.A. Program.

The Graduate Business Association (GBA) is an important and integral part of the learning experience. The GBA is student-run, and it sponsors the Executive Speaker Series, career and interviewing workshops with alumni, and the annual Career Interview Conference. One of the elected officers of the GBA, the Vice President of International Affairs, must be an international student.

Many of the students obtain paid internships during the summer, both to earn money and to obtain work experience that is relevant to their choice of career. Other students extend the length of their M.B.A. studies to take advantage of internship opportunities that occur during the academic year. One M.B.A. student is working on an internship in Morocco, as one of only 16 chosen by the U.S. Agency for International Development for its Free Market Advisers Program. Several M.B.A. students are working as paid interns for Connecticut-based companies. Another M.B.A.

UConn M.B.A. students attending one of many placement functions.

The University of Connecticut's main campus in Storrs, Connecticut.

student is working as a part-time intern in the area of foreign trade for the U.S. Department of Commerce. When combined with an independent study, internships can also be done for academic credit.

The Faculty

With very few exceptions, all of the faculty members who teach in the full-time M.B.A. program have earned their Ph.D. or the equivalent terminal degree in their field. The faculty members have very diverse academic backgrounds, with alma maters that include Harvard, Yale, and MIT. They also have equally interesting and diverse cultural backgrounds, including professors from Australia and from countries in Africa, South America, and Asia. New electives are introduced almost every semester, and teaching assignments for required core courses are rotated frequently so that students benefit from the latest developments in research and consulting conducted by the faculty. Many faculty members conduct research, consult, teach, or maintain professional contacts in other countries. At UConn, the world is in the classroom.

The Business School Network

Connecticut is the "Insurance Capital of the World," a major center for financial services, a major manufacturing area with a strong involvement in international trade, and the incredible retail market for the highest per capita income population of any state. This very diverse corporate

community provides the context and, ultimately, the resources by which the School of Business Administration maintains its preeminence within the state. Essentially all of the major corporations, as well as many small and medium-size companies in the corporate corridor connecting New York City and Boston, employ the School's alumni. This greatly facilitates both placement and maintenance of a state-of-the-art curriculum.

The College and Environs

Centrally located in the "corporate corridor" between New York and Boston, Connecticut is one of the most commercially diverse states in the country. The University of Connecticut is a large, multifaceted institution with nationally recognized professional schools of business, dentistry, engineering, law, and medicine. The University is one of the nation's major public research universities, with 25,000 students, 95,000 alumni, and 120 major buildings on 3,100 acres at the main campus in Storrs. In 1998, UConn was ranked among the top 20 national public universities by *U.S. News & World Report* and is also ranked the top public university in New England.

All of the academic, library, computer, social, and cultural opportunities and facilities of a major university are readily available to all M.B.A. students. The immediate area surrounding the main campus is rural, with the bucolic charm of New England. Compared to most major universities, the University campus is a safe and very scenic environment. The cost of living is substantially less than in most metropolitan areas. However, many internship and employment opportunities are available nearby. The capital and metropolitan area of Hartford is a ½-hour, Boston is a 1½-hour, and New York City is a 3-hour drive. One third of the Fortune 500 companies, and hundreds of small and medium-size firms, have their corporate headquarters in this unique corporate corridor.

Placement

For most M.B.A. students, building and developing a challenging and satisfying management career is their primary purpose in attending an M.B.A. program. The University of Connecticut M.B.A. Program provides the education, training, support, and opportunities to advance toward this goal. Activities in career planning begin during orientation and continue throughout the two academic years. Coaching and opportunities to

practice specific skills, such as developing effective resumes and cover letters, interview techniques, arranging interviews, and networking, are available to all M.B.A. students. Mock interviews with supportive but tough alumni executives make a significant difference in preparing students for successful interviews. Many M.B.A. students acquire new and relevant work experience through summer internships or semester co-ops. These experiences augment the academic program and develop skills that make effective managers. Internships can also provide a very important source of financial support.

Admission

The minimum requirements for admission include a 3.0 GPA, out of a possible 4.0, or the equivalent and a total GMAT score of at least 530. However, applicants who do not meet all these requirements may be considered for admission based on strengths in other areas of their application. For international students whose native language is not English, a TOEFL score of at least 550 is required.

Finances

Total costs for students attending the University of Connecticut M.B.A. Program are approximately $23,000 per academic year. Financial aid in the form of scholarships and graduate assistantships is available to students who are U.S. citizens; it is also available to international students on a very limited basis. Scholarships and graduate assistantships are more available to international students during their second year in the program.

Application Facts and Dates

Admission decisions are made on a rolling basis as completed applications are received, so there is no rigid deadline for submitting an application. However, the size of the entering class is limited, and very few applications from international students submitted after April are approved for admission. Early application is strongly advised. International applicants are encouraged to submit their application prior to taking the GMAT. Admission is available only for the fall semester. For additional information, students should contact:

UConn M.B.A. Program
368 Fairfield Road, U-41MBA
Storrs, Connecticut 06269-2041
Telephone: 860-486-2872
Fax: 860-486-5222

University of Dallas

THE GRADUATE SCHOOL OF MANAGEMENT IN THE GLOBAL ARENA

▶ *The Graduate School of Management is a real-world and performance-oriented graduate business school. We believe the best education for business leadership is a high-quality, global, applied, action-oriented, and customer-driven academic curriculum tied to the realities of the world in which we live and work. In that regard, we made a commitment to "internationalize" a significant portion of our academic program long before it became fashionable. We plan to do even more in the global arena in order to be totally prepared for the future.*

—Paula Ann Hughes, Dean

Programs and Curricular Focus

The Master of Business Administration programs of the Graduate School of Management (GSM) provide multiple options to suit a variety of career paths. Students seeking a generalist approach may select the M.B.A. in business management, which provides the broadest management education.

Students who wish to develop more specific skills or focus on a particular business environment may select from the following concentrations or tracks within the M.B.A. program: entrepreneurship, marketing management, consumer marketing, business-to-business marketing, international marketing, corporate finance, international finance, corporate investment analysis, engineering management, industrial management, operations management, materials management, quality management, logistics management, purchasing and contract management, financial and estate planning, investment management, financial services management, health services management, human resource management, international human resource management, international management, inter-Americas trade, information systems management, applications development, and telecommunications management.

The curriculum for each M.B.A. program includes a set of core courses designed to provide a strong business foundation and a set of specialized courses unique to each concentration.

M.B.A. programs require the completion of 49 credit hours (sixteen courses). This may be reduced to a minimum of 37 credit hours (twelve courses) for students who have courses transferred from another graduate institution or waived on the basis of undergraduate course work. On GSM's thirteen-week trimester system, most full-time M.B.A. students can complete their degree requirements in three or four trimesters.

Students who have already earned an M.B.A. may pursue a second master's degree, the Master of Management. This degree requires the completion of 30 credit hours (ten courses) in the selected area of concentration.

GSM's noncredit Pre-M.B.A. and intensive English programs allow international students to prepare for graduate studies in business while becoming acclimated to life in the United States.

The Pre-M.B.A. program is an intensive, thirteen-week preparatory program that is designed to enhance communication skills, improve GMAT scores, and teach fundamental business concepts. This program is specifically designed to meet the needs of international students who wish to improve their GMAT score or who may not have an undergraduate degree in business.

The full-time intensive English program utilizes the "focal skills" method of instruction, allowing students to progress at their own pace through classes in listening, reading, writing, and immersion, which focuses on all skill areas. Students continuing to GSM may take a business fluency course designed to prepare them for oral presentations and writing research papers.

Students and the M.B.A. Experience

The Graduate School of Management attracts mature students who have substantial professional experience. The average GSM student is 32 years old and has seven years of work experience. The student body includes 40 percent women, 18 percent minorities, and 25 percent international students from more than fifty countries. Nineteen percent of GSM students have engineering degrees, 16 percent were science majors, and 18 percent have various undergraduate degrees, including liberal arts and social sciences. Fourteen percent already hold graduate degrees. This mature, diverse student body is one of the GSM's outstanding educational resources.

❖ Global Focus

The Graduate School of Management has long recognized the importance of global education. The M.B.A. in international management program at GSM is one of the ten largest in the United States and has recently been expanded to include a specialization in inter-Americas trade. Travel courses, which include faculty-guided study in international business capitals, are offered between trimesters.

Special Features

The Graduate School of Management was the first business school in the region to assign students to real consulting projects for local, national, and international firms. These strategic planning projects allow students to apply the concepts and methods taught in their previous courses to real business problems.

The Faculty

GSM's faculty provides a rare mix of competence in both the theoretical aspects of management and the applied working knowledge of its practical aspects. The faculty is organized into a relatively small resident group and a larger adjunct group. The resident faculty members are full-time instructors with extensive backgrounds in business, teaching, applied research, and consulting. The adjunct faculty consists of practicing managers, attorneys, accountants, consultants, and other professionals, who

their job search and offers workshops on resume preparation and interviewing skills. Students participate in job fairs on- and off-campus, and many corporations come to GSM to select students for professional internships.

Admission

Applicants must have a bachelor's degree from an accredited institution. Other admission criteria include an undergraduate GPA of at least 3.0, a satisfactory score on the GMAT, and a work history of professional managerial work experience. International students whose native language is not English must submit satisfactory TOEFL scores; for immigration purposes, these students must show the availability of $22,000 for each year of study.

Finances

Tuition for the Graduate School of Management in 1998–99 is $380 per credit hour. Books and supplies cost approximately $150 per class. Living expenses, including housing, meals, utilities, and miscellaneous expenses, average $850 per month. Mandatory health insurance is $192 each trimester. Students should plan to purchase a car for local transportation.

International Students

International students comprise over 23 percent of the GSM student body. International students become members of the International Student Association, and many join a regional or country-specific student organization.

teach part-time. GSM students enjoy the best of both the academic and the practical worlds.

The Business School Network

Over the years, GSM has developed significant alliances and corporate partnerships. Each concentration has an advisory board made up of prominent professionals in related fields who assist the program directors in the development of their programs. Through the Management Lecture Series, world business leaders visit the University to lecture to GSM students. In their capstone courses, all GSM students have the opportunity to work on a real project for a corporation.

The College and Environs

The University of Dallas was founded in 1956 as an independent Catholic university dedicated to the pursuit of excellence in its educational programs. The current total enrollment in undergraduate and graduate programs exceeds 2,500 students.

The Graduate School of Management was founded in 1966 as an evening graduate school for individuals who were already employed in business and the professions. Over the years, the school's educational scope has broadened to serve a diverse student population, while its programs have remained focused on the practical realities of managerial life.

The University of Dallas is located in the suburban community of Irving, Texas,

a part of the Dallas–Fort Worth metroplex, and is within 10 miles of downtown Dallas and the Dallas–Fort Worth International Airport. The scenic campus, on more than 600 acres of rolling hills, is directly adjacent to Texas Stadium, home of the Dallas Cowboys football team.

The Dallas–Fort Worth metroplex has 3.4 million people and is one of the fastest-growing population centers in the country. Its diversified economy includes important industries in electronics, aerospace, insurance, and banking. The moderate climate and abundance of lakes and parks in the surrounding area offer numerous recreational opportunities. The metroplex also provides rich cultural and entertainment opportunities.

Technology Environment

Faulkner's Communications Infodisk, Computer Select, the National Trade Data Base, Compact Disclosure, and the ABI-Inform full text system are a few of the technical resources available in the University of Dallas Blakley Library. Students also have access to the resources of many other public and university libraries in north Texas.

Computer facilities are available to all students. The on-campus computer center provides access to personal computers and the University's Prime superminicomputer.

Placement

The University of Dallas Career Counseling Center assists M.B.A. students with

The University of Delaware

Newark, Delaware

THE VALUE OF A DELAWARE M.B.A.

Earning an M.B.A. degree is a significant undertaking that requires considerable dedication, energy, and time. We put powerful resources behind our program to make sure students receive a superlative business education. Consequently, at the University of Delaware, you will find an academically accomplished faculty, a demanding and exciting curriculum, and—because of our commitment to admissions quality—highly accomplished classmates. Because we believe that students develop their critical problem-solving and decision-making skills from each other, as well as from the faculty, you will be in a classroom of no more than 35 students, immersing you in a highly concentrated and learning-supportive environment.

—Dana J. Johnson, Dean

Programs and Curricular Focus

The College of Business and Economics offers rigorous programs for superior students leading to the M.B.A. and the M.A./M.B.A. degrees. The special combination of academically accomplished faculty, highly qualified students, and ideal location—a small university town in the midst of the large eastern megalopolis—provides the necessary ingredients for an outstanding experience in graduate business education. The Delaware M.B.A. program is accredited by AACSB-The International Association for Management Education.

The Delaware M.B.A. curriculum includes courses that focus on capable leadership, effective team building, group decision making, strategic use of technology, power negotiating, creative problem-solving techniques, international concerns, coordinating an effective total quality management process, and ethical considerations. The new courses complement the traditional courses in accounting, economics, finance, operations, and marketing. Students who wish to pursue more in-depth course work are offered the option of concentrating in accounting, business economics, finance, information technology, international business, leadership and management of museums, management, marketing, operations, or technology and innovation management. Internships are also available to supplement the student's academic program.

The 48-credit M.B.A. program can normally be completed in eighteen to twenty-one months. Up to 12 credits may be waived for students with prior

instruction in accounting, business, and/or economics, making it possible for some individuals to complete the program in twelve months. The program can also be completed on a part-time basis, taking between three and five years. An Executive M.B.A. program allows students with at least five years of professional experience to complete the degree in nineteen months by taking classes Friday evenings and Saturdays. The combination of small class sizes, classroom theory, and students' practical experiences creates a stimulating environment for the analysis of today's business world.

Students and the M.B.A. Experience

For fall 1998, the average length of work experience for entering M.B.A. students was four years, the average age was 26, and the average GMAT score was 605. In 1998–99, approximately 550 students were enrolled in all M.B.A. programs, of whom 37 percent were women, 7 percent were members of minority groups, and 7 percent were international students (20 percent of the full-time student body), including students from China, France, Germany, Iceland, India, Norway, Singapore, and Venezuela. The diversity of the student body adds to the interactive learning environment in the classroom.

Special Features

All Delaware M.B.A. students are given an account on the Internet and are introduced to its many tools during the

new student orientation program. The M.B.A. program has its own Usenet news group and Web site that are used for information sharing. Some M.B.A. classes also use news groups and the World Wide Web as additional learning environments. E-mail is the preferred form of communication between students, faculty members, and administrators.

The Faculty

The faculty members who teach M.B.A. classes hold doctoral degrees in their disciplines. Through widely respected research and publishing efforts, they have earned national reputations in their fields of study. M.B.A. faculty members have also enhanced their respective skills through consulting positions with major national and international corporations, a good number of which are headquartered a short distance from the University.

The Business School Network

Because of the excellent reputation of the Delaware M.B.A., positive program relations exist with members of the corporate community, including DuPont, MBNA America, Bank of New York, J. P. Morgan Delaware, ICI America, and Zeneca. For example, M.B.A. classes are currently offered on-site at DuPont and MBNA America. These relationships have fostered the development of internship opportunities for Delaware M.B.A. students at these and other firms (e.g., Hewlett-Packard, First USA Bank, Arco, and Cyanamid). The College has also developed an innovative corporate associates program that partners with the corporate community to provide a mutually beneficial financial aid package for full-time students.

The College's Visiting Board, composed of high-ranking corporate executives from major corporations, serves as an advisory group to the dean of the College on various matters, including those pertaining to the M.B.A. program.

The activities of an M.B.A. alumni network are supported by the regular publication of the M.B.A. Alumni Resource Directory, which is available to all M.B.A. students and alumni. The directory is a key resource for M.B.A. career planning and placement.

The College and Environs

The University of Delaware, founded in 1743 as a small liberal arts school, now ranks among the finest of the nation's medium-sized universities, with approximately 14,000 undergraduate and 3,000 graduate students. Included in the College of Business and Economics are four departments: accounting, business administration, economics, and finance.

The University of Delaware is located in Newark, a suburban community of approximately 30,000 residents. Newark is situated in the northwest corner of Delaware within 3 miles of the Pennsylvania and Maryland borders. It is located within easy driving distance of Philadelphia (45 miles), Baltimore (50 miles), Washington, D.C. (100 miles), and New York City (130 miles). Newark is also less than 100 miles from the Delaware and New Jersey beaches. Nearby Wilmington is a major center for credit banking and the chemical industry. Eighty percent of all Fortune 500 companies are incorporated in Delaware, which allows the College to maintain strong ties with the corporate sector.

Facilities

The University library is a modern research facility with more than 2 million volumes, is a member of the Association of Research Libraries, and is a depository for U.S. government documents and patents.

Mainframe computer facilities include an extensive array of both hardware and software. Sun Workstations operating under UNIX are used for research, course work, text processing, and communication. The College has a computer laboratory that focuses on business applications, as well as a state-of-the-art local area network.

Placement

In addition to M.B.A. job fairs and on-campus interviews, the Delaware M.B.A. program participates in two

M.B.A. Consortia in Philadelphia and Washington, D.C. Along with graduates from other top M.B.A. schools, Delaware's M.B.A. graduates network and arrange interviews with a number of prospective employers. The average annual salary for 1997 graduates of the full-time program was $45,000. Employers of recent full-time graduates include Andersen Consulting, Arthur Andersen, Colgate Palmolive, DuPont, IBM, Lockheed Martin, MBNA America, Stanley Works, and W. L. Gore.

Admission

A student must submit official copies of all undergraduate and graduate transcripts, GMAT scores, and two letters of recommendation. For qualified applicants, a personal interview is also required. Delaware M.B.A. students are a highly accomplished group. For fall 1998, the mean GMAT score of entering students was 605 and the mean undergraduate GPA was 3.1. A score of 585 is required on the TOEFL for all students for whom English is not the native language. No prior work experience is required, although it is strongly recommended. Although no prerequisite courses are required, applicants are assumed to possess basic skills in written and oral communication, mathematics, and computer use.

Finances

In 1998–99, the yearly tuition for full-time M.B.A. students is $12,250 ($5360 for Delaware residents). Part-time study was $298 per credit hour for Delaware residents and $681 per credit hour for nonresident students. Rental costs for shared occupancy in a graduate student complex were $350 per month. University and privately owned apartments, furnished and unfurnished, are available at costs ranging from $350 to $900 per month.

Numerous financial aid packages are available to superior full-time M.B.A. students. These include graduate assistantships, corporate assistantships, and tuition grants that are awarded on a competitive basis regardless of nationality or financial

need. Awards to first-year students are based on prior experience and academic performance. Awards to second-year students are based on academic performance in the program.

A typical aid package may include a $4000 per year stipend and/or a 50 percent waiver of tuition. These awards are administered by the M.B.A. Programs Office. Information on other possible sources of aid can be obtained by writing to the University's Office of Scholarships and Student Financial Aid.

International Students

More than 30 percent of the full-time student body is international. The Cosmopolitan Club provides activities for international students that help them understand the American culture as well as the cultures of other countries. International students are also oriented to the needs placed on them in a highly interactive M.B.A. classroom. The University of Delaware also offers a Pre-MBA Program for international students via the English Language Institute.

Countries represented by the international students include Colombia, England, Ethiopia, France, Germany, Ghana, Greece, India, Malaysia, the Netherlands, the People's Republic of China, Singapore, South Africa, Sweden, Taiwan, Turkey, and Venezuela.

Application Facts and Dates

Applications for the fall semester must be submitted by May 1. Students seeking financial aid should submit their applications by February 15. For more information, students should contact:

Kathy Kuck, Admissions
M.B.A. Programs
College of Business and Economics
103 MBNA America Hall
University of Delaware
Newark, Delaware 19716
Telephone: 302-831-2221
Fax: 302-831-3329
E-mail: mba@udel.edu
World Wide Web: http://www.mba.udel.edu

University of Denver

Daniels College of Business

Denver, Colorado

PREPARING YOU FOR BUSINESS LEADERSHIP

At the Daniels College of Business, we are committed to your success—as a highly competent professional, as a team builder and leader, and as a valued member of your community. Founded in 1908, the Daniels College of Business is the nation's eighth-oldest accredited collegiate business school and a leader in management education. With one of the nation's premier M.B.A. programs, we put you at the cutting edge of knowledge, present an educational experience that prepares you for a lifetime of leadership, and provide our commitment to your career placement and development. We do all this in a classic campus setting located in Denver, a wonderful city that symbolizes the dynamic business environment of the Rocky Mountain West.

—James R. Griesemer, Dean

Programs and Curricular Focus

The Daniels College of Business M.B.A. program presents a forward-thinking, integrated curriculum that challenges students through an active learning environment. The core curriculum incorporates experiential elements in leadership, case studies, and group work in addition to traditional methods of learning. Through this exciting experience, students learn technical business knowledge, refine skills that are key to managerial excellence, and gain an appreciation for values-based leadership.

Mirroring the cross-functional involvement of management decision-making, the core courses combine the business technical fundamentals and management skills into a more applications-oriented format from which students develop a comprehensive view of business the way it actually operates. Included in the experience are an outdoor leadership and team-building program, opportunities for volunteer participation, and a team field-study project in which students work with Denver-based organizations.

Starting in cohort groups of approximately 35, students move through the core into elective or specialization courses that provide focus to their degree. Specializations in accounting, entrepreneurship, finance, marketing, information technology, electronic commerce, real estate, and construction management are available, or students may create their own specializations from courses offered at the University.

A part-time M.B.A. program is available. Other options include an M.B.A./J.D. joint-degree program, a flexible dual-degree program that allows students to combine their M.B.A. degree with programs from other schools and departments within the University of Denver, and the Mountain M.B.A. program, which is taught on site in Summit County and Vail.

The Executive M.B.A. program is an eighteen-month program designed to strengthen the management skills and leadership abilities of middle- and upper-level managers and managing professionals. Intensive course work, creative problem solving, and an international cultural travel seminar provide firsthand knowledge of management, international, and emerging business opportunities.

Students and the M.B.A. Experience

Daniels College of Business students have a wide range of academic and professional backgrounds and represent more than twenty countries around the world. Insights and skills from an average of more than six years of professional experience and undergraduate majors such as business, engineering, international studies, history, and economics provide diverse perspectives that add to dynamic classroom environments and group projects. Of the approximately 425 M.B.A. students, 35 percent are working professionals in the evening program, 36 percent are women, and 24 percent are international students.

❖ Global Focus

The Daniels College of Business's M.B.A. program emphasizes international business and a global understanding of cultures and perspectives. A core course focuses on global perspectives and elective courses include international marketing, comparative management, and multinational finance. In addition, courses in international politics, economics, and policy analysis are available from the University's Graduate School of International Studies, a designated U.S. Department of Education Resource Center.

Special Features

The integrated curriculum helps develop creative critical thinking and decision making through courses that focus on applying business tools in an interrelated format. Exciting core courses have replaced traditional individual function courses to combine tools and skills as students use them.

A three-day outdoor leadership experience provides an arena for students to learn key elements of communication skills, team building, and consensus problem solving and to learn about one another. Added to the managerial excellence focus are negotiation skills and Myers-Briggs testing.

The Faculty

The Daniels College of Business's 75 full-time faculty members have a balance of industry experience and academic dedication, providing a classroom environment that is diverse and exciting. They have developed the curriculum with outside business leaders and continue to refine the program as well as maintain their excellence in teaching, research, and consulting. They are recognized worldwide for their industry knowledge and work with educational organizations such as the Fulbright Foundation.

The Business School Network

Corporate Partnerships

The Daniels College of Business works with corporate advisers in a multitude of program areas. The curriculum continues to be shaped by faculty members and

The Daniels College of Business and picturesque University of Denver campus provide easy access to the thriving city of Denver, Colorado, and the Rocky Mountains.

corporate advisers. The Career Placement Center works with executives in operations and panel discussions, and the team field study course, Integrative Challenge, is a partnership with Denver-area corporations and businesses who utilize Daniels students to address management problems. In addition, the Career Placement Center mentor program provides contacts with alumni in a wide range of industries and positions for placement counseling and assistance.

Prominent Alumni

Prominent alumni include Peter Coors, CEO, Coors Brewing Company; June Travis, Executive Vice President, National Cable Television Association; Andy Daly, President, Vail Associates; and Gareth Flora, Vice President of Business Development/Launch Systems, Lockheed Martin Astronautics.

The College and Environs

The University of Denver is the largest independent private university in the Rocky Mountain region, with more than 8,700 students from more than 100 countries. Founded in 1864 by John Evans, the Colorado Territory Governor for Abraham Lincoln, the 125-acre University of Denver campus is located in a quiet neighborhood in Denver, Colorado, providing students an academic atmosphere with access to the cosmopoli-

tan population, activities, and lifestyle of Denver, with the Rocky Mountains nearby.

Facilities

Computer facilities include labs with forty-five networked microcomputers supporting word processing, spreadsheet, and visual presentation software; VAX mainframes providing statistical packages; and Internet and information research database access.

Penrose Library houses a total collection of more than 1 million volumes, is a founding member of the Colorado Alliance Research Libraries, and provides students access to major library collections in the Denver Metro area and to other major university libraries through the online Public Access Catalog System.

Placement

The Daniels Career Placement Center helps students assess career choices and develop effective career strategies using a wide range of resources. Workshops and personal counseling are available to help students enhance job search skills, techniques, and knowledge. Career forums, job fairs, alumni networking events, regional consortium events, computerized job and internship listing databases, a research library, and an

alumni mentor program provide access to employers from around the nation.

Admission

The Daniels College of Business enrolls students in September and March. Applications are reviewed on a rolling basis through a comprehensive process that evaluates previous academic performance and completion of a four-year undergraduate degree or the equivalent from a regionally accredited college or university, results of the Graduate Management Admission Test (GMAT) or Graduate Record Examinations (GRE), professional work experience, responses to essay questions, two letters of recommendation, and a completed application form. International students whose primary language is not English are required to submit TOEFL results. Interviews are encouraged but are not always required.

Finances

For the academic year 1998–99, tuition for full-time students attending three quarters is $18,216. Books, supplies, fees, and housing and meal expenses vary, depending on number of courses taken per quarter and extracurricular activities. Even though Denver is the largest city in the Rocky Mountain region, the cost of living is well below other major U.S. cities.

Application Facts and Dates

Applications are evaluated on a rolling basis as they are received and completed, with a decision response within three weeks of completion. The deadline for September enrollment is May 1, and the deadline for March enrollment is January 1. Applications received after these dates are reviewed on a space-available basis. For inquiries, students should contact:

Office of Student Services
Daniels College of Business
University of Denver
2020 South Race Street, BA-122
Denver, Colorado 80208
Telephone: 303-871-3416
        800-622-4723 (toll-free)
Fax: 303-871-4466
E-mail: dcb@du.edu
World Wide Web: http://www.dcb.du.
    edu

University of Detroit Mercy

College of Business Administration

Detroit, Michigan

DEVELOPING VALUE-ORIENTED BUSINESS LEADERS

The College of Business Administration provides professional education in business and related fields, recognizing the importance of a liberalizing education as a foundation for a career of continuing self-education. The College aims to instill in its students, through a personalized educational process, a sense of personal integrity, a high measure of intellectual curiosity, and a deep awareness of personal and social values in contemporary society. One of the hallmarks of the University of Detroit Mercy is the ability to offer individualized education in small classes. Graduate business students are able to tailor their programs to specific needs and interests and build on their current bases of knowledge and work experiences. Students benefit from personal contact with our highly experienced faculty members, many of whom serve as consultants in the private and public sectors. We look forward to helping you achieve your career objectives.

—Bahman Mirshab, Acting Dean

Programs and Curricular Focus

In the program's current format, the number of credit hours required for completion ranges from a minimum of 36 to a maximum of 60. Courses in the curriculum are divided into three groups: precore (24 credit hours), core (24 credit hours), and postcore (12 credit hours). The precore consists of eight foundation courses, which may be waived depending on the individual's academic background. The core consists of eight courses that are required for all students. The postcore is composed of a required capstone course and three electives that allow students to individualize their programs in specific areas of management, marketing, finance, accounting, economics, international business, decision analysis, or computer information systems. Depending upon academic background, it is possible to complete the degree requirements in one year on a full-time basis. In addition, a joint M.B.A./J.D. program is offered, which enables students to complete both degrees in approximately four years.

Students and the M.B.A. Experience

Students at the University of Detroit Mercy bring a wide variety of work experiences and academic and cultural diversity to the M.B.A. program. The average age of the student body is about 30; approximately 30 percent are women, 20 percent are members of minority groups, and 10 percent are international students. The average length of work experience is seven to eight years. Ninety-five percent of the students matriculate on a part-time basis.

❖ Global Focus

In response to the importance of globalization in the business world, the College offers students intensive courses during the summer in England, Ireland, China, Brazil, and Mexico for up to 6 hours of credit.

Special Features

Detroit Mercy is one of eleven members of a consortium with other Jesuit institutions across the United States, whereby courses taken at one institution are accepted by the others.

To accommodate students who cannot take classes during the week, Saturday classes are offered. In addition to the fourteen-week fall and winter semesters, two accelerated seven-week summer sessions are offered, which allow students to move more quickly through the program.

The Faculty

The College of Business Administration has highly qualified faculty members with superb academic and professional backgrounds. Many have lived, worked, and studied abroad, bringing global perspectives to the classroom.

A faculty-student ratio of 1:17 keeps classes small and ensures individual attention. Faculty members often act as academic advisers to students and assist with their research projects and career objectives.

The Business School Network

The University has an excellent reputation in the metropolitan Detroit business community. More than 275 business and professional organizations are represented in the graduate business program. An independent study conducted by Dun & Bradstreet revealed that there are more graduates from Detroit Mercy in top management positions with Michigan firms than from any other private college or university in the state. Strong ties between the College and corporate leaders in the area continuously contribute to the success and excellence of the program.

The College and Environs

In 1990, the University of Detroit consolidated with Mercy College of Detroit and formed the University of Detroit Mercy. The University is an independent Catholic institution of higher education that is sponsored by the Religious Sisters of Mercy and the Society of Jesus.

The University of Detroit Mercy's M.B.A. program is one of the oldest graduate business programs in the United States. Instituted in 1948, it was given full recognition by AACSB–The International Association for Management Education in 1963. It was among the first sixty universities in the United States to be so accredited. The College is the second-oldest M.B.A. program in Michigan that is accredited by AACSB–The International Association for Management Education. The mission of the College is to offer an integrated, value-oriented, high-quality business education within the Jesuit and Mercy traditions that will enable students to utilize and expand their knowledge and skills to improve and serve the organizations in which they work and the society in which they live.

The University's environment is highly conducive to learning. The Graduate Business Programs Office is located on the attractive 70-acre McNichols campus in the College Park area of northwest Detroit. The city offers a world-famous symphony orchestra, an opera company, numerous theatrical and dance groups, and a host of art, science, and history museums. The city is home to professional baseball, basketball, football, and hockey teams.

Technology Environment

In addition to various computer laboratory locations across the campus, the College has two state-of-the-art computer labs. A rich library of software packages is available to students. Computer integration is an essential feature of the graduate program.

Placement

The Professional Practice and Career Development Office offers full service to graduate students. Opportunities for practical training, seminars, and on-campus recruiting are all available through this office. After completion of the appropriate credit hours, students are eligible for career-related assignments. Students are provided the opportunity to select full-time assignments, alternating semesters of work and study, or part-time assignments with parallel semesters of work and study.

Admission

Admission decisions are based on a combination of the score attained on the required Graduate Management Admission Test (GMAT), undergraduate GPA, work experience, and any other supporting material. The average GMAT score of accepted students is 520; the average GPA is 3.1.

It is not necessary for international students to take the TOEFL because English proficiency will be established on campus. However, a TOEFL score of 600 and a TWE score of 4.0 will exempt an individual from testing. International students must apply through International Services at the University of Detroit Mercy.

Finances

The current tuition rate for graduate business courses is $448 per credit hour. The registration fee each term is $50 for a part-time student and $75 for a full-time student. There is also an activities fee of $5 per term. The University estimates that the average cost per month for on-campus room and board is $700. Off-campus living expenses range from $600 to $1000 per month. Since the University is located in a large metropolitan area, a variety of living arrangements are available.

A limited number of graduate assistantships are available each term. Normally, applications are accepted after the individual has completed one semester of course work. Students should contact the Financial Aid Office for other kinds of assistance that may be available.

International Students

The Detroit area was ranked in the top six "most desirable metropolitan international living areas" by a recent international study reported in *Asia Week*. The University offers many specialized services, such as a weekly international coffee hour, a free American studies class about living in the United States, international housing, student organizations, and a dedicated international service staff. Assistantships are open to international students after one semester of study.

Application Facts and Dates

Application deadlines for international students are Term I, May 1; Term II, September 1; and Summer I and Summer II, January 1. Application deadlines for all others are four weeks prior to the start of each particular term. Deviations from these deadlines are possible through the approval of the Director of Graduate Business Programs. Usually decision letters are mailed within a week of receipt of all required documents. For more information, students should contact:

Bahman Mirshab
Director, Graduate Business Programs
College of Business Administration
University of Detroit Mercy
P.O. Box 19900
Detroit, Michigan 48219-0900
Telephone: 313-993-1202 or 1203
Fax: 313-993-1052
E-mail: mirshabb@udmercy.edu

University of Edinburgh

A TOP M.B.A. IN SCOTLAND'S CAPITAL

The University of Edinburgh is consistently rated amongst the top three or four universities in the United Kingdom and amongst the top universities in the world. The Edinburgh M.B.A. is therefore obtained at one of the UK's top management schools.

Our students are drawn from all over the world and bring to the course their extensive experience and working knowledge. We add to this our knowledge and experience, gained from being the first Scottish university to introduce the study of business and management, and our current faculty members, who are highly rated for their teaching and research. This powerful combination provides an outstanding learning environment in a school dedicated to postgraduate management education. Our M.B.A. provides a demanding and exciting learning experience, which the hardworking will thrive upon and which will advance their careers.

—Professor James Fleck, Director, The Management School

Programs and Curricular Focus

The Edinburgh International M.B.A. is a general management course that covers all the main management disciplines and provides for specialisation in marketing, finance, operations management, and entrepreneurship.

The full-time course runs for one calendar year, starting in October with a foundation term that covers business policy, economics and quantitative methods, accounting and finance, human behaviour at work, marketing, and operations management. In the second and third terms, students can choose any four of fifty optional subjects to study alongside the core course in strategic management. In addition, there are optional language and outdoor education components to the course, with a parallel programme of communication and presentation skills. The summer term provides for completion of a thesis or project, which can take a number of forms, including a research study, a business plan, or a company-based project. Success in the M.B.A. degree is based on assessment through course work and examinations at the end of the third term and then completion of the M.B.A. thesis or project.

Students and the M.B.A. Experience

The student body in each full-time M.B.A. program is genuinely interna-

tional. The composition of the 1997 class (100 people) included representatives from thirty different countries, with 30 percent drawn from the British Isles and no more than 7 or 8 percent from any other single country. The average age is about 30, with the youngest being 24; two students are over 40. The average work experience of the students is around seven years, with most having already held career management positions. In this year, 26 percent of students are women. Students spend a considerable amount of time in the second and third terms working in different syndicate groups, both on class case studies and out-of-school projects.

Special Features

A major element of the course is the requirement in the spring to carry out a team consultancy project for a local company. The project can be based in a small local company, many of which are developing new technologies, or a division of a larger company. Many students base their dissertation on project work with a company, and, in collaboration with the British Council, the University has developed opportunities for overseas students to take up an internship with major Scottish trading companies that have international interests.

The Faculty

There are more than 60 teaching staff members in the Management School, drawn from twelve different countries. Staff members are active in industry-based research and consultancy for both commercial organisations and government. This research work feeds directly into the quality of the teaching to M.B.A. students and also provides opportunities for student dissertations as part of their course.

The Business School Network

The School advisory board includes leading business figures from the city of Edinburgh. In addition, a number of research centres associated with the School involve leading businesspeople. In particular, Connect—a programme that arranges the start-up and growth of high-technology companies—is at the centre of a Scotland-wide network of leading companies, investment organisations, and corporate advisers.

Leading business figures are regular guest speakers at the School, and several, such as Alex Trotman, Chairman and Chief Executive of the Ford Motor Company, are appointed as visiting faculty members. Their teaching and informal contact with students provide a direct insight into current management and business practice.

The College and Environs

The Management School is at the heart of the University campus, in the city centre of the capital of Scotland. Edinburgh is an attractive city, one of the safest in Britain, with the best cultural facilities outside London. The School is opposite the city opera house within a 10-minute walk of the Castle, Holyrood Palace, theatres and concert halls, and the central business district.

Facilities

The School is situated in a city centre building used exclusively by postgraduate management students, researchers, and executive course participants. The purpose-built premises have a large computer lab and other specialised

Edinburgh University's campus in the spring.

facilities for M.B.A. students, all of whom have international e-mail accounts. The building has secure 24-hour access to provide for independent student learning and international Internet contact and the opportunity to work with colleagues at convenient times. It is close to the main University library, one of the best in the country, and to the National Library of Scotland, which has a specialised business information service and where students have automatic membership.

The University has a wide range of accommodation, ranging from full catering to self-contained flats solely for postgraduates. Most students live within the heart of the city in accommodations that are within a few hundred meters of the School.

Technology Environment

The University and the School are part of one of the most powerful area networks in the British university system; there are facilities for videoconferencing and high-speed data transfer. Several elective classes from a number of courses specifically build upon the use of these facilities, and much course work integrates the use of multimedia materials. Hardware connected to the network is updated each year, and the computer system provides remote student access to personal computers if necessary.

Placement

The induction week for the M.B.A. program starts with a focus on career development, which is fully integrated into all parts of the programme. The Career Management Advisor provides advice and support for careers placement. Many students have gone on to highly successful careers in industry (Mercedes-Benz), consultancy (PA, McKinsey), and finance (First National of Chicago). The University maintains a career book for current and former M.B.A.'s, which is readily accessed by employers through the regularly updated Web site rather than the more traditional printed form.

Admission

Candidates generally are required to have a first degree and good work experience and therefore to be at least 25 years old. All candidates must complete an application statement that explains why they want to pursue an M.B.A. degree and prepare other written work. An interview may be scheduled. A GMAT test score is required. Students are required to have a good command of English (minimum TOEFL score of 580 [6.5 ELTS]); the University offers preparatory courses in English in the weeks just before the M.B.A. program starts for those who need language support.

Finances

The courses have the highest possible level of accreditation, which ensures that students are able to access loan schemes and grants from their own host country. Some scholarships and grants are available through the School. (Details are sent to all applicants.) Fees for students from outside the European Union are £9900 in 1998–99 for the academic year and include all costs related to study. Living costs for students vary according to individual circumstances and may also be about £9500 for a full year.

International Students

Welcome sessions are provided for overseas students, and an active M.B.A. student social committee provides entertainment and social events for all students.

Each year there are a number of overseas students funded by their own government agencies and through British scholarships, including Chevening scholarships. These are processed through the local representative of the British Council.

Application Facts and Dates

Applications are dealt with on a rolling basis, although the latest recommended application date is August of each year. The turnaround for applications is within two or three weeks of receiving all documentation.

Course Director
M.B.A. Programme
University of Edinburgh Management School
University of Edinburgh
7 Bristo Square
Edinburgh EH8 9AL
Scotland
Telephone: 44 0 131 650 6339
Fax: 44 0 131 650 8077
E-mail: management.school@ed.ac.uk
World Wide Web: http://www.ems.ed.ac.uk

University of Florida

Gainesville, Florida

THE FLORIDA M.B.A.: THE NEXT 50 YEARS

For more than fifty years, the University of Florida (UF) has developed successful leaders and managers to meet the challenges of a rapidly changing business environment. We carry that commitment into the next century, with increased emphasis on promoting academic excellence, creating innovative programs, and fostering a collegial environment.

Innovative new programs and curricular enhancements provide improved accessibility and greater flexibility for all students. Small class sizes, a low student-faculty ratio, and expanded program staff ensure that individual needs are met throughout the program. Tremendous value results from the combination of our nationally ranked M.B.A. program, comparatively low cost of attendance, and Gainesville's high quality of life.

We look toward a bright future with renewed focus, ambition, and spirit. We invite you to join the dynamic Florida M.B.A. community.

—John Kraft, Dean

Florida M.B.A. students attend classes in the heart of the University of Florida's historic campus.

Programs and Curricular Focus

A variety of program options makes the Florida M.B.A. degree highly accessible. The two-year Traditional Program and the 11-Month Accelerated Program cater to students who wish to study full-time. The Managers, Weekend, and Executive Programs, which meet on campus only one time per month, allow busy professionals to earn their degrees without interrupting successful careers. The new Internet-based Flexible Program incorporates leading-edge interactive technology, a weeklong international trip, and only eight extended weekends on campus to deliver a high-caliber graduate degree via distance education. Other graduate programs in business are also available.

The modular curriculum of the in-residence programs allows greater flexibility and multiple concentrations. After completing the core curriculum, students may choose from fourteen different concentrations, including security analysis, marketing, competitive strategy, and global management. Sixteen international exchange opportunities are available in more than ten countries during the summer or fall following the first year of the Traditional Program. The four programs for working professionals provide a broad general management education.

Six joint-degree programs enable students to combine their M.B.A. with another UF degree in law, health administration, engineering, sports

management, biotechnology, or pharmacy. Dual-degree programs with The American Graduate School of International Management (Thunderbird) and Nijenrode University take three years or less to complete. Students are awarded the Master of International Management from Thunderbird or the International Master of Business Administration from Nijenrode in addition to the Florida M.B.A.

A balanced mix of lectures, case studies, group projects, presentations, simulations, and fieldwork challenges students to hone their analytical, decision-making, and leadership skills. The Professional Development Program helps students develop skills in written and oral communication, computers, career management, networking, and community involvement.

Students and the M.B.A. Experience

The Florida M.B.A. programs integrate a distinguished faculty, talented students, a dedicated staff, and successful alumni to form a cooperative, team-oriented, and supportive community. Students share their outstanding personal and professional experience with classmates from around the world.

The Florida M.B.A. programs enroll a diverse class, with about 18 percent of the students coming from outside the U.S. and 11 percent from underrepresented ethnic groups; 27 percent are women.

These candidates average more than five years of work experience and come from a variety of academic disciplines ranging from philosophy to engineering. Each of the programs offers a distinctive learning environment for students with diverse backgrounds and different levels of experience.

Besides the academic challenges, students benefit from the professional interaction provided by extracurricular activities such as the M.B.A. Association, the Network for Careers in Consulting, the Investment Club, Toastmasters, Graduate Women in Business, and the Sports and Entertainment Marketing Association. Students also enjoy participating in the many social and recreational opportunities the University and the surrounding community provide.

The Faculty

Florida M.B.A. faculty members possess exceptional credentials and are recognized by their peers and industry leaders for their contributions in various areas of expertise. The Departments of Accounting, Marketing, Finance, and Management are consistently ranked among the top twenty-five in the country. National awards have honored individual faculty members for research and teaching in accounting, finance, marketing, management, economics, insurance, and real estate.

Faculty members serve as editors of major scholarly journals in marketing, finance, accounting, management, and business law. They also direct the school's thirteen research centers, which explore emerging trends in economics, business ethics, accounting, public policy, consumer research, decision sciences, entrepreneurship, insurance, human resources, public utilities, real estate, and retailing. Florida M.B.A. faculty members are not only leading researchers, but also outstanding teachers. The 6:1 student-faculty ratio ensures that students are able to frequently interact with these accomplished scholars.

The Business School Network
Corporate Partnerships
Corporate leaders are an integral part of the business school community. The program is shaped largely by the contributions of its executive advisory board, corporate recruiters, and alumni. Numerous speakers and guest lecturers visit the University either through the Distinguished Speaker Series or by invitation from various professors. Last year, 176 companies recruited M.B.A. students on campus for full-time employment and internships.

Prominent Alumni
Prominent alumni include John Dasburg, CEO, Northwest Airlines; Allen Lastinger, former President and COO, Barnett Banks; Judith Rosenblum, Chief Learning Officer, Coca Cola Company; and Chris Verlander, President and COO, American Heritage Life.

The College and Environs
The University of Florida is a comprehensive, public research university that traces its roots to 1853. Today, with about 42,000 students, it is among the ten largest universities in the nation. A member of the prestigious Association of American Universities, UF has a long history of established programs in international education, research, and service.

Facilities
Three buildings and the courtyard they surround comprise the "Business Triangle." Bryan Hall houses the Graduate Computer Lab, the M.B.A. team-study area, a student information center, and program staff. Classrooms, faculty offices, and academic research centers are located in the other two buildings. The business school is adjacent to the main library, important University

The Florida M.B.A. programs provide a close-knit, team-oriented community.

offices, and a small commercial district. Florida's 2,000-acre campus provides two state-of-the-art fitness centers, swimming pools, a golf course, and numerous athletic facilities. Also on campus, students enjoy the performing arts center, wildlife sanctuary, and several museums.

Technology Environment
All University of Florida students are required to have personal computers beginning with fall 1998 enrollment. The Internet-based Flexible Program helps introduce leading-edge interactive technologies, such as streaming audio and video, group-discussion software, and multimedia courseware, into the other programs. M.B.A. students use Microsoft Windows, Microsoft Office, Netscape Navigator, and Lotus Notes to communicate and collaborate with classmates and faculty and staff members from school, home, or work. Forty workstations in the computer lab and team-study area are reserved exclusively for graduate business students. The business school network is accessed through laptop connections in the classrooms and team-study area.

Placement
Dedicated career services professionals assist students with skills assessment, career planning, resume preparation, and mock interviews. The staff also develops corporate relationships, coordinates recruiting events, and maintains job postings for positions in major cities. Students have access to the University's Career Resource Center (CRC), which is one of the nation's finest. The CRC provides an extensive career resource

library and videoconferencing capabilities. Recent graduates have pursued challenging careers in consulting, investments, marketing, and finance.

Admission
Candidates are evaluated based on demonstrated academic ability, professional experience, community involvement, and personal character. Applicants must have a bachelor's degree from an accredited U.S. institution or its equivalent. Additional requirements include at least two years of significant work experience, official GMAT scores, official transcripts, two career progress reports, four essays, completed application forms, and a personal interview. The Accelerated and Managers Programs also require an undergraduate business degree. Official TOEFL scores are usually required for applicants whose native language is not English. Requirements vary by program. Students should request an application packet for details.

Finances
The Florida M.B.A. is consistently rated as one of the best buys in business education. Nationally ranked academic programs, low cost of attendance, and Gainesville's high quality of life provide outstanding value. Tuition rates for each program vary based on the student's Florida residency status. A limited number of M.B.A. fellowships, graduate minority fellowships, and graduate assistantships may help students reduce educational expenses.

Application Facts and Dates
The Traditional and Executive Programs students enroll each August, the Managers and Weekend Programs start in January, and the Accelerated and Flexible Programs begin in May. Students should refer to the application packet or the Web site for specific admissions deadlines, program calendars, and student budgets. Candidates receive a decision within six to eight weeks of submitting a completed application. An online inquiry and application system is available through the Florida M.B.A. Web site. For more information, students should contact:

Florida M.B.A. Programs
University of Florida
134 Bryan Hall
P.O. Box 117152
Gainesville, Florida 32611-7152
Telephone: 352-392-7992
Fax: 352-392-8791
E-mail: floridamba@notes.cba.ufl.edu
World Wide Web: http://www.
floridamba.ufl.edu

University of Georgia

Athens, Georgia

PREPARING STUDENTS FOR THE FUTURE

The M.B.A. experience at the University of Georgia combines rigorous course work with opportunities for skill development in areas such as leadership and communication. The program attracts outstanding students and fosters a close-knit community feeling by emphasizing teamwork and positive competition. In fall 1997, we opened Sanford Hall, our new $8-million classroom building that contains the latest in educational computer technology. Each of the 900 seats in the hall is wired to the Internet. We have made significant changes in our curriculum to fully utilize the new technology and are truly entering a new era of excellence in M.B.A. education at Terry College.

—P. George Benson, Dean

Programs and Curricular Focus

Acknowledging that no one program can be all things to all people, the Georgia M.B.A. is a program that has a broad-based appeal. From finance to entrepreneurship, marketing to real estate, Georgia offers across-the-board excellence. Flexibility to build a program of study that reflects a student's personal goals and objectives is a highlight of the M.B.A. program.

The College's approach to instruction encompasses a mixture of lecture and case-study methods. Each is used in a manner that accomplishes the goals of a given class. Both are integral parts of the program objectives, which are to provide the basic analytical tools required by managers, including fundamental concepts and principles from the various functional areas; develop skills in using these tools in an imaginative, problem-solving capacity; create the ability to make and carry out decisions; develop a basis for dealing effectively with others, with both written and oral communication; instill a thorough understanding of today's economic, political, and social environment; and encourage continuous learning from experience.

In addition to its traditional two-year program, Georgia offers a one-year M.B.A. program designed to meet the needs of students with undergraduate degrees in business from institutions accredited by AACSB–The International Association for Management Education. The program consists of 41 semester hours (three academic semesters) of full-time study with summer-quarter matriculation. This program offers

eligible candidates a unique opportunity to lower the cost associated with getting an M.B.A. degree without sacrificing the quality of their education.

In the two-year program, the first year of study consists of course work designed to provide students with the basic analytical, functional, and managerial skills necessary to deal with both short- and long-term business problems. It also serves to prepare students for the selection of their individual areas of specialization. During the second year, students develop a high degree of competence in their chosen fields via sequence and elective course work.

A four-year J.D./M.B.A. degree program is also available.

Students and the M.B.A. Experience

The students in the M.B.A. program at Georgia are a blend of individuals with varied educational and professional experiences. They are a select group that represents undergraduate majors as diverse as biology, civil engineering, public relations, and sociology. Students come from areas that span the continent and the globe, from California to Connecticut and from France to China.

The majority of students have two years or more of full-time work experience, with a class average of four years of prior experience. The average age of the students is 26½. Approximately one quarter of the students are women, 10 percent are members of minority groups, and one quarter are international. All one-year M.B.A.'s are business under-

graduates. Sixty-five percent of two-year students have engineering, science, humanities, or social science backgrounds.

Special Features

Students build on their classroom experiences through the MBA P.L.U.S. Program. The mission of the MBA P.L.U.S. Program is to enhance the quality of the M.B.A. experience by linking the technical skills learned in the classroom with skills required for success in the business world. This task is accomplished through challenging, interrelated, experiential learning and interactions with business and community leaders.

The Progressive Partners Program is a bottom-line commitment to ethnic diversity created by the Georgia M.B.A. Program. In partnership with several leading companies, including Merck, Union Camp, and Wachovia Bank of Georgia, the Georgia M.B.A. Program is dedicated to providing educational and potential career opportunities for highly motivated and talented individuals belonging to ethnic minority groups.

A dual-degree program with Nijenrode University in the Netherlands allows candidates the potential to spend their second year abroad in a one-year international management program.

The Faculty

The faculty members in the Terry College of Business are recognized worldwide for their contributions to both the business and academic communities. The College has endowed chairs that are used to attract and retain academic leaders in all disciplines. Many faculty members hold prominent positions with leading academic publications and are recognized as leading contributors to some of the most heralded journals. Faculty members employ instruction methods that include lecture, group and individual projects, case studies and competitions, and other methods deemed appropriate for accomplishment of class objectives.

The Business School Network

Corporate Partnerships

Corporate executives serve as guest lecturers in the classroom and frequent guest-speakers in association with the MBA P.L.U.S. Program. The CEO Breakfast Program allows students to visit corporations and discuss business trends and issues with senior executives of the company. Participating companies include Delta Airlines, Home Depot, UPS, Georgia-Pacific, BellSouth Corp., and Wachovia.

Prominent Alumni

The Terry College of Business is represented by outstanding alumni, including Daniel P. Amos, President and CEO, AFLAC, Inc.; James H. Blanchard, Chairman and CEO, Synovus Financial Corporation; A.D. "Pete" Correll, Chairman and CEO, Georgia-Pacific Corporation; M. Douglas Ivestor, Chairman and CEO, the Coca-Cola Company; and Charles S. Sanford Jr., Former Chairman and CEO, Bankers Trust.

The College and Environs

Situated in Athens, Georgia (population 90,000), 70 miles northeast of Atlanta, in the rolling wooded-hill country of northeast Georgia, the University of Georgia enters its third century of progress as one of the finest teaching and research institutions in America. As the state's largest and most comprehensive and diversified educational institution, the University of Georgia sets the pace for educational excellence and creates a climate of intellectual and cultural development within and beyond the state of Georgia. The campus is situated on 532 carefully landscaped acres and is home to more than 30,000 students from all over the world.

Technology Environment

The Terry College of Business provides operational and network support for some of the most advanced computing facilities in the country. As of fall 1997, networked facilities include Sanford Hall, a new classroom facility that provides laptop connectivity from every classroom seat in the building. M.B.A.'s have 24-hour lab access that includes the most up-to-date multimedia PCs, laser printers, and high-speed Internet connectivity. Students are expected to enter the program with a high degree of computer proficiency.

Placement

Career Services (CS) provides a complete range of opportunities, from self-assessment to on-campus interviewing. Opportunities include individual and group counseling/seminars/workshops in the areas of effective resume writing, executive correspondence, and interview skills/behavioral interviewing; career-area interest testing and feedback; networking and negotiation; and mock interviewing. CS publishes the *MBA Employment & Internship Directory* of current M.B.A. students, which is sent to prospective employers nationwide. CS participates in the National MBA Consortium at Chicago, the Southern Alliance, the Capital MBA Consortium, and the International MBA Consortium Employment Conference.

Admission

Enrollment is twice a year: summer for accelerated one-year program candidates and fall for two-year program candidates. Selection includes a review of academic transcripts, work experience, GMAT scores, essays, collegiate/professional honors and activities, and recommendation letters. On-campus interviews are recommended. The TOEFL is required of all applicants whose native language is not English and who have not graduated from an English-speaking undergraduate or graduate institution within the past two years.

Finances

Tuition and required University fees for the 1998–99 academic year are $3290 for residents and $11,300 for nonresidents. Students on a graduate assistantship (approximately 50 percent of the class) pay reduced tuition and fees of $670 per year. Room, board, books, and personal expenses vary greatly based on marital status and type of accommodations but should range from $7600 to $11,000 per academic year.

International Students

The University of Georgia and the Terry College of Business are represented by a strong and diverse international student population. For the 1998–99 year, countries represented in the M.B.A. program include Bulgaria, China, Colombia, France, Germany, India, Italy, Korea, and Turkey.

Application Facts and Dates

Candidates are encouraged to apply no later than six months prior to the quarter they intend to enroll. The early application deadline is December 1. Admission decisions are mailed approximately six weeks after receipt of a completed application. The admission decision schedule, which includes deadline dates, is listed on the World Wide Web and in the application materials.

Mr. Donald R. Perry Jr.
Director, M.B.A. Admissions
Terry College of Business
346 Brooks Hall
University of Georgia
Athens, Georgia 30602-6264
Telephone: 706-542-5671
Fax: 706-542-5351
E-mail: ugamba@cba.uga.edu
World Wide Web: http://www.cba.uga.edu/mba/

University of Hawai'i at Mānoa

Honolulu, Hawai'i

WHAT WILL IT TAKE TO LEAD IN THE TWENTY-FIRST CENTURY?

The College of Business Administration (CBA) offers students an enriching and stimulating education designed to expand intellectual processes and broaden global perspectives. As we approach the twenty-first century, the College has focused its efforts on preparing managers and executives with the skills and abilities to succeed in the Asia-Pacific region and the world. With the continued rapid economic development of the Asia-Pacific region, businesses worldwide will find that an in-depth understanding of the languages, cultures, and economic realities of this region will be necessary in order to become a winner in the new economic marketplace.

—Chuck Gee, Interim Dean

Programs and Curricular Focus

The College of Business Administration offers the Master of Business Administration (M.B.A.) and Master of Accounting (M.Acc.) degrees. Both are primarily evening programs and may be pursued on either a full-time or a part-time basis. An Executive M.B.A. program, a Japan-focused M.B.A. program, and a China-focused M.B.A. program are also available.

With its close ties to the Hawai'i community, the College provides internships and study-abroad programs that afford students the opportunity to gain practical experience in solving real business problems. The College provides the only M.B.A., M.Acc., and B.B.A. programs in the state of Hawai'i that are accredited by AACSB–The International Association for Management Education.

The M.B.A. is a 42- to 48-credit hour program with either a thesis or a nonthesis option. The core consists of four basic modules, followed by six elective courses and the capstone experience, which consists of business policy and strategy and field studies in the enterprise.

The M.Acc. program is a 30-credit-hour program designed to prepare students for careers in professional accounting.

The Japan-focused M.B.A., now in its ninth year, and the new companion China-focused M.B.A. are fifteen-month cohort programs that provide intensive study in the language and culture of Japan and China, respectively. As the capstone of these programs, a three-month internship/field study experience with major corporations in Japan or China provides exposure to and

practical application of Japanese or Chinese management and allows the student to gain valuable real-world experiences, Asian-style.

The Executive M.B.A. program is a twenty-two-month, accredited, intensive Master of Business Administration degree program. The accelerated format is structured as an intensive one-week residential session held in August prior to the first semester, with the balance of the classes meeting full days on Fridays and Saturdays of alternating weeks.

The CBA also provides access to dual-degree programs with other disciplines within the University, such as law, economics, and public health. The Ph.D. in international management program admits its first students in fall 1998. Admission to this program is in the fall only.

Professional development programs and activities are available through the Asia-Pacific Center for Executive Development, the Pacific Asian Management Institute (PAMI), the Pacific Business Center Program, and the Pacific Research Institute for Information Systems and Management. These programs draw participants from major corporations in Hawai'i, the mainland United States, the Pacific Basin, and Asia.

Students and the M.B.A. Experience

Proximity to the United States mainland, Asia, and the Pacific has made Hawai'i, with its population of 1.1 million people on seven major islands, a gateway between the East and West. Reflecting its history as a "gathering place," the city of Honolulu and

the University of Hawai'i at Mānoa are among the most multicultural populations in the world. One in every 5 of the 20,000 students studying at the University of Hawai'i at Mānoa is of Japanese ancestry; 1 in 10 is of Chinese ancestry; 1 in every 6 is Filipino, and approximately 12 percent are Hawaiian or part-Hawaiian.

Total enrollment in the M.B.A. program is approximately 350; 25–30 students are enrolled in the Japan-focused M.B.A. One half are women, and 70 percent are part-time students, most of whom work full-time. The average M.B.A. student is 28 years old with four years of work experience.

❖ Global Focus

The College believes that no business student should graduate in today's world without a true appreciation and competency in both international business and the utilization of information systems technology. The international business programs at the College have been ranked fifth among graduate programs in the United States. Study-abroad opportunities are also available in Japan and Denmark.

Special Features

PAMI's International Summer Program offers a certificate in international business or management. Students must complete either three PAMI courses or two PAMI courses and one related area studies or language course. Each summer, up to 25 business students have the opportunity to observe first-hand, factories and boardrooms of Asia through the PAMI Asian field study program. In addition, 6 to 8 students are selected each year to participate in summer internships in partnership with Northern Marianas College. Interns are assigned to a business incubator in Saipan and work with business development specialists on a variety of development projects.

The Faculty

All full-time M.B.A. faculty members hold doctoral degrees. Students are kept apprised of current business developments as a result of the research and consulting done by the faculty. Many faculty members have completed and/or are currently conducting research on the nations of Asia and the Pacific.

Teaching methods include case analysis, lectures, independent research, and simulation exercises. The interaction of students in group projects is an important part of the M.B.A. experience.

The Business School Network
The University of Hawai'i M.B.A. Alumni Group was established in 1975 by University of Hawai'i College of Business graduates who saw the benefits of forming a network to broaden their career opportunities.

The College and Environs
The University of Hawai'i at Mānoa was founded in 1907. Today's enrollment of approximately 20,000 includes 4,600 graduate students. The College of Business Administration was founded in 1949 and awarded its first M.B.A. degree in 1951. The central campus of the University covers 300 acres in the Mānoa Valley, a residential area close to the heart of Honolulu. Honolulu is an international center with cultural activities that include Pacific Island and Asian festivals as well as symphony concerts, ballet, theater, and opera. Hawai'i and its university are positioned and prepared to play a significant role in the emerging Pacific Century.

Facilities
The University library collections total more than 2 million volumes and more than 35,000 currently received serials. Materials from other libraries in Hawai'i and the mainland are available through interlibrary loan. The Asian Collection in Hamilton Graduate Library has a heavy concentration of materials related to statistics in South and Southeast Asia. Business information on these countries is available in the collection. More than 150 databases can be searched for references.

Technology Environment
Graduate students have access to eighty personal computers in two microcomputer labs at the CBA. An extensive library of software for business applications is available. Use of the IBM ES/9000 is provided by the mainframe lab of the CBA. Mainframe terminals are also available at other locations.

Placement
Career Services offers students and alumni year-round assistance in their career searches. Services include workshops in resume design, letters of application, and interviewing techniques; Dial-a-Job, the University of Hawai'i at Mānoa's automated round-the-clock employment hot line; a career-oriented research library; career fairs and panel discussions; and personal counseling and credential file development.

Admission
The ideal student entering the M.B.A. program at the University of Hawai'i has a record of strong academic performance, high test scores, outstanding motivation, and well-thought-out career goals. Admission to the M.B.A. program is competitive and is based upon a "package" of capabilities indicated by the applicant's grade point average, GMAT scores, work experience, and professional objectives.

For admission into graduate programs, the CBA prefers applicants to have a GMAT score of 500 or above and a grade point average of 3.0 or higher (on a 4.0 scale) in the last two years of undergraduate course work and all past post-baccalaureate work. Applicants from countries where English is not the primary language are re-

quired to take TOEFL. The minimum score is 500. Work experience is not required but is preferred. A resume and official transcripts are required of all applicants. Translations of transcripts not in English must be certified.

Finances
Full-time graduate tuition per semester in 1998–99 is $1956 for residents and $4920 for nonresidents. Part-time tuition is $164 per credit hour for residents and $410 for nonresidents. Fees total $50 to $60 per semester. Costs for books and materials comes to approximately $300.

The 1998–2000 Executive M.B.A. program costs $19,400, and the 1998–99 Japan- and China-focused M.B.A. programs cost approximately $29,000. These rates include tuition, fees, and all books and materials.

International Students
There is a strong international student community at the University of Hawai'i College of Business that comprises approximately 15 percent of the M.B.A. student body. The majority of international students come from Asian-Pacific countries. The University's International Student Services Office helps students become acclimated to American university life.

Application Facts and Dates
For the M.B.A. program, students are admitted in either the fall or the spring semester; for the M.Acc. program, students are admitted in the fall semester only. Application deadlines are May 1 for fall and November 1 for spring. Application deadlines and admission criteria for the Executive M.B.A. program differ from the M.B.A. and M.Acc. programs. Specifics on these programs can be obtained from the addresses below.

For M.B.A. and M.Acc. programs:

Graduate Programs
Office of Student Academic Services
College of Business Administration
University of Hawai'i at Mānoa
2404 Maile Way
Honolulu, Hawai'i 96822-2282
Telephone: 808-956-8266
Fax: 808-956-9890
World Wide Web: http://www.cba.
    hawaii.edu

For the Executive M.B.A. program:

Executive M.B.A. Programs
College of Business Administration
University of Hawai'i at Mānoa
2404 Maile Way, Room C305
Honolulu, Hawai'i 96822-2282
Telephone: 808-956-3260
Fax: 808-956-3261
World Wide Web: http://www.cba.
    hawaii.edu/emba/

University of Houston

Houston, Texas

GETTING THE BEST EDUCATION POSSIBLE

The University of Houston (UH) College of Business Administration (CBA) is a comprehensive institution with an excellent undergraduate major; several tracks in the M.B.A. program, including professional and executive programs; doctoral programs; and executive education programs. The CBA's strong ties to the national and international markets, as well as the Houston community, reflect an ongoing desire to stay on the cutting edge of business education. The CBA offers students the opportunity to get an education that will help them achieve their goals with a talented and diverse student body. Our students have the desire to get the best education possible.

—Sara M. Freedman, Dean

Programs and Curricular Focus

The Master of Business Administration program at the UH College of Business Administration is designed to enhance work experience and academic accomplishments while focusing on the global economy and the international arena. As business changes, the demand increases for professionals with courage, knowledge, and skills to effectively and proactively manage change. M.B.A. students who choose the CBA have the advantage of studying in the fourth-largest city in the nation, an international center of finance and home to the energy, aerospace, health care, and computer industries. This location makes employment and internship opportunities available in some of the most innovative corporations in the world.

The M.B.A. program offers concentrations in accountancy, finance, international business, management, management information systems, marketing, operations management, statistics and operations research, and taxation. The M.B.A. program can be pursued on a full-time or part-time basis with day or evening classes. All M.B.A. programs are accredited by AACSB–The International Association for Management Education.

Joint M.B.A. programs offer the advantage of earning two graduate degrees in less time than it would take to pursue them separately. Joint M.B.A. programs include an M.B.A./Doctor of Jurisprudence (J.D.) degree with the Law Center; M.B.A./Master of Arts in Spanish (M.A.) with the UH College of Humanities, Fine Arts and Communication; M.B.A./Master of Hospitality Management (M.H.M.) with the UH Conrad Hilton College of Hotel and Restaurant

Management; M.B.A./Master of Industrial Engineering (M.I.E.) with the UH Cullen College of Engineering; M.B.A./Master of International Management (M.I.M.) in cooperation with the American Graduate School of International Management (Thunderbird in Glendale, Arizona); and M.B.A./Master of Social Work (M.S.W.) with the UH Graduate School of Social Work.

The CBA also offers M.B.A. options for business professionals: a two-year Executive M.B.A., a three-year Professional M.B.A., and, for business professionals with an undergraduate degree in business administration, a one-year Executive M.B.A.

Students and the M.B.A. Experience

UH is ranked in the top twenty in the nation in international student population. Learning side-by-side with international students gives CBA students a unique perspective. Total enrollment in the M.B.A. program is more than 1,000. Of those, one third attend full-time. The average M.B.A. student is 28 years old, with four years of full-time work experience. Students with undergraduate degrees in fields other than business, including education, engineering, liberal arts, social sciences, physical sciences, and others, find the M.B.A. degree from the CBA beneficial.

Special Features

The CBA has several centers and institutes designed to support and promote academic activities in a number of business areas. These include the A. A. White Dispute Resolution Institute; the Center for Entrepreneurship and Innovation; the Center for

Executive Development; the Center for Global Manufacturing; the Energy Institute; the Fixed Income Research Program; the Information Systems Research Center; the Institute for Business, Ethics, and Public Issues; the Institute for Corporate Environmental Management; the Institute for Diversity and Cross-Cultural Management; the Institute for Health Care Marketing; the Small Business Development Center; and the Southwest Center for International Business.

The Faculty

Leadership, expertise, and experience are the most important things CBA faculty members offer to their students. The CBA has attracted an excellent faculty from a broad range of disciplines dedicated to preparing students to succeed in a competitive world. The CBA faculty is made up of teachers, researchers, consultants, advisers, experienced business leaders, and widely published authors who share their diverse perspectives with their students. The faculty is composed of experts in such fields as accountancy and taxation, entrepreneurship, finance, international business, management, management information systems, marketing, operations management, and statistics.

The CBA also has a number of executive professors who serve as valuable resources. These business leaders from top corporations in the Houston business community share their knowledge with CBA students and faculty.

The Business School Network
Corporate Partnerships

The urban location of the CBA provides a number of advantages, including the availability of business leaders willing to visit classrooms, teach, work on committees, coordinate special projects, help faculty members and graduate students establish research contacts, and offer advice to the dean and other administrators. Students gain valuable experience as they interact with the various management styles within a metropolitan business community. Students also have access to real-world work experiences through internships and projects.

Melcher Hall, opened in 1986, houses the College of Business Administration.

located in Houston, which offer internship and special project opportunities to students. All of these available sources account for more than 85 percent of the M.B.A. students who are employed within three months of graduation.

Admission

Admission to the CBA is highly competitive. The admission process involves a comprehensive review of past academic accomplishments, GMAT scores, career goals, and work experience. International applicants whose native language is not English must also submit official TOEFL scores with their M.B.A. application.

Finances

Tuition and fees for the 1998–99 academic year are $2570 for Texas residents and $7129 for out-of-state and international students. Tuition is based on 12 hours for two semesters and is subject to change. The CBA offers a variety of entrance, study-abroad, and major-specific scholarships. More than $500,000 per year is awarded to about 300 outstanding graduate and undergraduate students. Students admitted to the M.B.A. program may apply for scholarship funds by submitting a CBA Scholarship Application Form. The application deadline is March 1 for awards for the following academic year.

International Students

The International Student Services Office works with new students on enrollment, legal status of immigration documents, and orientation. Students who are not U.S. citizens, are nonnative speakers of English, and have a nonimmigrant visa (F-1 or J-1) are classified as international students.

Prominent Alumni

The CBA recognizes a number of prominent alumni, including Sam P. Douglas, Chairman, Equus International; LeRoy Melcher, Chairman of the Board and CEO (retired), Fairmont Foods; Gene McDavid, President, *Houston Chronicle;* Kenneth W. Reese (deceased), Executive Vice President, Tenneco, Inc.; Elizabeth D. Rockwell, Executive Director, CIBC Oppenheimer; Lane Sloan, Regional Coordinator East and Australasia, Shell Oil; Jack Valenti, President, Motion Picture Association of America; Kathryn J. Whitmire, former Mayor of Houston and Director of the Academy of Leadership, University of Maryland; and Melvyn Wolff, President and CEO, Star Furniture.

The College and Environs

The UH campus consists of ninety-two modern classroom and laboratory buildings spread over 556 acres of woodlands and open spaces in the heart of the nation's fourth-largest city. This world-class city offers students concerts; nightclubs; major symphony orchestra, opera, and ballet companies; shopping; country and western dance halls; comedy clubs; museums; and professional sporting events. Blue skies and sunshine are the rule. The Gulf Coast beaches at historic Galveston, Freeport, and Bolivar Peninsula lie an hour to the south. The beautiful hill country is northwest of the University, and to the northeast there are piney woods and lakes to fulfill all recreational needs.

Facilities

The UH M. D. Anderson Library boasts more than 1.4 million volumes, supplemented by professional libraries in art, architecture, law, music, optometry, and pharmacy. The libraries add more than 50,000 volumes and microtexts to their collections annually and subscribe to more than 14,000 periodicals. The business collection holds 85,250 bound volumes, 600 periodicals, and eleven CD-ROMs and offers access to Dialog, Legislate, ABI Inform, Compustat, and other business online services.

Technology Environment

With access to more than 175 computers within the business school, the CBA offers M.B.A. students computing resources that rank among the finest anywhere. Internet online services are available at no charge. As businesses begin to apply the technology base of the information superhighway, M.B.A. graduates from UH will be prepared.

Placement

UH Career Services and the CBA's own Elizabeth D. Rockwell Career Services Center located in Melcher Hall offer individualized career management programs, educational resources, and job search opportunities for CBA students and alumni. Nearly 200 employers from around the country recruited M.B.A. students on-campus during the last academic year. Most M.B.A. students also take advantage of the large number of international corporations

Application Facts and Dates

A resume or statement of career goals, application, two official transcripts, official GMAT scores, and a nonrefundable application fee are required. Deadlines are May 1 for the fall semester and October 1 for spring.

For more information, students should contact:

Office of Student Services
College of Business Administration
University of Houston
Houston, Texas 77204-6282
Telephone: 713-743-4900
Fax: 713-743-4942
World Wide Web: http://www.cba.uh.edu

The University of Illinois at Chicago

PREPARING FOR OPPORTUNITY

▶ *UIC has both full-time and evening M.B.A. programs as well as joint-degree programs at the master's level in accounting, economics, nursing, and public health. Our programs are accredited by AACSB–The International Association for Management Education, making us one of only five universities in Chicago to carry that distinction. Both programs also have innovative professional topics courses, which cover nontraditional subjects and often bring corporate executives into the classroom. UIC faculty members are nationally known for their research and work on public policy. One of our strong points is entrepreneurship. UIC is consistently rated as one of the top schools in the country in this area. Our proximity to downtown is ideal for students seeking corporate internships, while our exchange and foreign internship programs provide students with the opportunity to study and work around the world before completing their degree. As Dean, I invite M.B.A. students to meet in my office to hear their viewpoints. Also, the Director of the M.B.A. program and I join students in the classroom to exchange ideas. I invite you to learn more about our programs and I look forward to seeing you in the class in the near future.*

—Lawrence H. Officer, Interim Dean

Programs and Curricular Focus

The UIC/M.B.A. programs offer innovative full-time and evening curricula for students who are preparing themselves for advanced managerial responsibility. The full-time program is a comprehensive two-year program that begins with a year of core courses taught in integrated modules. Students attend the Professional Topics Sequence (PTS), a series of workshops, seminars, and lectures that focus on areas of skill acquisition and managerial practice not covered in traditional academic courses. In addition, students have the option of studying abroad at partner institutions in Great Britain, France, or Austria. "Know Europe," an intensive interactive course, is taught in Europe every summer by faculty members from around the world. For those students who want to gain international work experience, many opportunities exist for internships with top multinational firms.

In the second year of the full-time program, students complete at least six advanced courses offered in the following areas: accounting, economics, entrepreneurship, finance, health administration, human resource management, international business, management information systems, marketing, operations management, statistical methodology for business, and industry and pharmacy

administration. Students can also tailor their curriculum by taking courses through UIC's other graduate programs.

UIC's evening M.B.A. program is designed for working professionals who are preparing themselves to take on increased managerial responsibility. Beyond the traditional academic courses, UIC also offers PTS electives in the evening program.

Joint degrees are offered together with master's degree programs in economics, public health, nursing, and accounting, or through the Normandy Business School in France.

The UIC/M.B.A. Programs are fully accredited by AACSB—The International Association for Management Education.

Students and the M.B.A. Experience

The UIC/M.B.A. Programs have approximately 300 evening students and 100 full-time students. The full-time class of 1997 is 45 percent international, 10 percent minority, and 48 percent women. Undergraduate business majors comprise 27 percent of the class, with the rest of the class having diverse backgrounds. The median GPA is 3.2 on a 4.0 scale, and the mean GMAT is 550. The mean age of full-time students entering the program is 26.5, and they average three years of full-time work experience.

Special Features

Students can study and/or work abroad through one of many international options. With the appropriate language skills, students can opt to study at top European business schools in France, Austria, and Great Britain. The UIC International Student Exchange Program (IESEP) allows students the opportunity to spend three to six months working abroad as an intern at a major international company.

The College of Business Administration supports several centers that offer students opportunities for research including the Center for Research in Information Management, the Center for Urban Business, the Family Business Council, the Office for Advanced Financial Research, the Office of Entrepreneurial Studies, and the Office of Governmental Accounting.

The Faculty

The graduate business faculty is a leader in academic productivity and research. Faculty members have Ph.D. degrees from leading institutions and conduct research in topical business areas.

The Business School Network

The Business Advisory Council, the College of Business Administration's board of advisors (from large and small companies within the Chicago area), sponsors interns, lunches with first year students, participates in the Professional Topics Sequence, and advises on and develops curriculum. Students also interact with corporate executives who come to speak, sit on panels, and lead seminars. With alumni working throughout the states and internationally, M.B.A. students have a ready network of contacts in all industries and firm sizes.

The College and Environs

UIC is an academic institution that commands international attention, and is the largest institution of higher learning in the city of Chicago. In recognition of the depth and scope of the academic programs, UIC has been identified by the Carnegie Foundation for the Advancement of teaching as one of eighty-eight

"Research I" institutions. The University is located close to the Loop, Chicago's commercial and social hub. With the resources of Chicago at the University's doorstep, students have exceptional opportunities to experience the energy of the city's neighborhoods, and a range of cultural, intellectual, and recreational activities that few other cities can match.

Facilities

The UIC Library system comprises more than 2.1 million books and periodicals, 18,000 current journal and serial subscriptions, and 1.5 million other items. Catalog information is accessible through UIC's automated data network from campus terminals or through a modem from home. UIC offers a wide variety of recreational and fitness facilities. A comprehensive intramural sports program offers opportunities for organized competition throughout the academic year. All students have access to the complete range of sports and fitness options.

Technology Environment

The UIC Computer Center offers a wealth of resources for students, including access to an IBM 3090 mainframe computer, UNIX operating systems, PC labs with both Windows and Macintosh workstations, and full Internet and Web access. The College of Business Administration computer lab features common software such as the Microsoft Office suite and Perfect Office Suites. The M.B.A. Programs Office operates an

e-mail network for program students that is used extensively for communication by students, faculty and placement personnel. Some M.B.A. professors use the Web as an outlet for retrieving lecture notes and class assignments.

Placement

The UIC M.B.A. program has a strong record of providing career services that assist students in pursuing managerial careers in a wide variety of settings and fields. The M.B.A. Placement Director coaches full-time M.B.A. students in the job search and career management process and facilitates contact with prospective employers. The director also coordinates on-campus interviews. The M.B.A. Placement Library has a CD-ROM research terminal and maintains files of internship and full-time position announcements. The College of Business Career Center is another source for internship and job leads. The University career center also provides on-campus interviewing, job fairs, career seminars and a career library.

Admission

The UIC/M.B.A. program seeks individuals with proven academic ability and strong managerial potential. The ideal candidate is one who demonstrates both the ability to lead and to be a team member; conceptualizes issues from several perspectives; and analyzes complex problems and formulates solutions. Academic credentials, which include previous course work and GMAT

scores, are reviewed for evidence of strong analytic and quantitative skills.

Finances

Full-time tuition and fees for the 1998–99 academic year are $10,436 for residents and $16,878 for nonresidents. M.B.A. program scholarships are awarded on the basis of academic and professional qualifications and are available to full-time domestic and international students. Evening tuition is contingent upon the number of courses taken: for state residents, tuition and fees for the 1998–99 academic year are $982 for one course and $1649 for two courses.

Application Facts and Dates

For full-time enrollment, the priority deadline for financial aid is February 1. The application deadline is March 26 for international applicants and June 16 for U.S. citizens and permanent residents. For part-time enrollment in the fall semester, the application deadline is July 14; for the spring semester, November 17; and for the summer term, April 4. For further information, students should contact:

The M.B.A. Program
The University of Illinois at Chicago (M/C 077)
815 West Van Buren Street, Suite 220
Chicago, Illinois 60607
Telephone: 312-996-4573
Fax: 312-413-0338
E-mail: mba@uic.edu
World Wide Web: http://www.uic.edu/cba/mba

University of Illinois at Urbana-Champaign

Urbana, Illinois

THE ILLINOIS M.B.A.—A NEW STANDARD IN BUSINESS EDUCATION

The new Illinois M.B.A. curriculum has been in place for a year now. The results are outstanding: There is excitement and teamwork in the classroom; students are tackling in-depth consulting and management projects; and communication between students, faculty, and administration has increased dramatically thanks to our computer net. It's all about partnerships. We are forging partnerships with the supercomputing and engineering centers on campus; our students are heavily involved in transferring groundbreaking technologies from the lab to the marketplace. We consider the students to be partners as well. They have an investment in the success of the Illinois M.B.A., and we have an investment in their success. The Illinois M.B.A. will be the standard against which all others are measured.

—Howard Thomas, Dean and James F. Towey
Professor of Strategic Management

Programs and Curricular Focus

The Illinois M.B.A. curriculum focuses on teamwork, integration of functional areas and course assignments, hands-on business experience, and quick feedback and response mechanisms.

For the first year of the program, students work in teams within four 7-week core course modules that guide them step-by-step through the processes of establishing or managing a business. Faculty members also work in teams and present particular business problems from their own functional perspectives—such as finance, accounting, and marketing. The faculty teams coordinate their assignments and case studies so student teams can integrate the different perspectives and provide comprehensive solutions. The assignments also require students to utilize the vast resources of the University, including the nation's third-largest academic library and a world-leading research center for supercomputer applications, virtual reality environments, and network software. The faculty and student teams remain in constant contact using First Class networking software, which allows students to receive quick responses to questions or raise issues about the curriculum.

In addition to the course modules, students participate in a weeklong Applying Business Perspectives seminar once every semester. Applying Business Perspectives seminars are in-depth computer simulations or case studies that require students to analyze and apply their functional knowledge, exercise leadership and motivational skills, and formulate effective solutions under tight time constraints. They must then present their results to a panel of judges selected from the world's leading firms.

During the second year of the Illinois M.B.A., each student focuses on a Professional Track that teaches skills specific to his or her chosen career. Students can select from eighteen tracks, which include entrepreneurship and new venture creation or technology systems management, or design one of their own. Alternately, they can enroll in a Joint Degree Program with any of several other outstanding programs at the University; these programs include engineering, law, and medicine, among others. A capstone course at the end of the second year pulls together all the lessons students have learned and provides them with an overview of contemporary business and its future.

Students and the M.B.A. Experience

Computerworld magazine ranked the Illinois M.B.A. eleventh in its December 1995 rating of the top twenty-five techno M.B.A. programs. That ranking reflects the technological and entrepreneurial focus of many students in the program.

Forty percent of Illinois M.B.A. students have technological backgrounds, and more than 50 percent have expressed interest in starting their own company after graduation. The Illinois M.B.A. class of 1999 is 51 percent U.S. citizens and 49 percent international students; 31 percent are women. Twenty percent of the class are members of racial or ethnic minorities. The average student is 26 years old and brings nearly four years of work experience to the program. Of the 550 students in the M.B.A. program, nearly 100 are pursuing joint degrees.

The Faculty

The Illinois M.B.A. faculty members are intimately involved and invested in the new curriculum. For three years, faculty members worked closely with administrators and focus groups to develop the curriculum's structure and content. Throughout the semester, the faculty team members communicate extensively with students and among themselves to ensure that learning objectives and student needs are met.

The Business School Network

The University of Illinois is home to a world-renowned engineering program and the Beckman Institute for Advanced Science and Technology. The Illinois M.B.A. has built strategic partnerships with these groups by developing an Office for Strategic Business Initiatives (OSBI). Through the OSBI, students consult with researchers about the commercial applications of new technologies and software. Some of these "technology transfer" projects can even lead to key management positions in start-up companies based on the new technologies.

The OSBI also offers students opportunities to get involved with a project in a business incubation laboratory, participate in FAST-trac entrepreneurship training, or manage a venture capital fund. A project could involve helping a local business get off the ground, or it could mean developing licensing and marketing strategies for a new software product straight out of the National Center for Supercomputing Applications.

Illinois M.B.A. students relax between classes on the business campus of the University of Illinois.

The College and Environs

Located within a 3-hour drive of Chicago, St. Louis, and Indianapolis, the University of Illinois and the twin cities of Urbana and Champaign form a thriving community rich in social, cultural, and recreational opportunities. Each year, the Krannert Center for the Performing Arts presents more than 350 plays, concerts, ballets, and operas. The University's Krannert Art Museum is second only to Chicago's Art Institute among Illinois public museums. The Division of Campus Recreation administers one of the most comprehensive recreational programs in the world. In addition to an array of intramural athletics, the division operates facilities for year-round basketball, tennis, squash, racquetball, and swimming.

Placement

Six staff members and several graduate assistants are fulfilling the Career Services Office's mission: to provide Illinois M.B.A. students with the tools and resources they need for their career development and provide employers with information on how to recruit on campus and identify Illinois M.B.A. students who meet their staffing needs. Allied Signal, Arthur Andersen, Citibank, Dow Chemical, Eaton Corporation, Ernst & Young, Ford Motor Company, and Pillsbury are some of the major corporations recruiting Illinois M.B.A. students.

Among the most innovative services the office offers are an online job posting system and a developing World Wide Web site. The Web site will feature links to corporate sites and online career search services and will soon include student resume posting, job fair notices, and other resources. The Career Services Office has also integrated career skills development into the communications portion of the Illinois M.B.A. curriculum. For example, a writing assignment that might otherwise be unfocused is now a chance to write a resume or cover letter. A speaking assignment develops skills and themes that a student can ultimately use in an interview situation.

Admission

Admission to the Illinois M.B.A. is based on undergraduate grade point average over the last 60 credit hours, GMAT results, verbal and written communication skills demonstrated in essays and interviews, TOEFL and TSE scores for nonnative speakers of English, demonstrated leadership qualities, professional work experience, analytical ability, and letters of recommendation. The average GMAT score for the class of 1999 was 610, and the average GPA was 3.3 on a 4.0 scale.

Applicants should hold a bachelor's degree from an accredited U.S. college or university or the equivalent from another country. Prior academic experience in business is not required. Students should have a minimum grade of B in at least one semester of calculus.

Finances

Tuition and fees for Illinois residents enrolling in fall 1998 are $10,700 for the academic year. Nonresident tuition and fees are $17,400. Students can expect to spend about $1500 for books, $8000 for room and board, and $2000 for personal expenses.

The Illinois M.B.A. offers a Student Management Leadership Grant program. The grants are based on merit, not financial need. During their second year of study, students receive grant assignments that allow them to assist in the management of this largely student-run program. The application for admittance to the Illinois M.B.A. is used in choosing recipients.

Application Facts and Dates

The application deadline is April 1, but early application is encouraged. Students are also encouraged to download an application from the Illinois M.B.A. Web site at the World Wide Web address listed below. To order an application by mail or for additional information, students can contact:

Illinois M.B.A. Admissions
410 David Kinley Hall
1407 West Gregory Drive
Urbana, Illinois 61801
Telephone: 217-244-7602
          800-MBA-UIUC (toll-free
          in the U.S. only)
Fax: 217-333-1156
E-mail: mba@uiuc.edu
World Wide Web: http://mba.cba.uiuc.edu

The University of Iowa

School of Management

Iowa City, Iowa

LEARNING AND WORKING TOGETHER

The Iowa M.B.A. program is designed for people who like to learn and work together. Often, assignments are completed by students working in teams, and group presentations are the rule rather than the exception. The program is small enough so that our students get to know our faculty and staff members and each other very well.

The Pappajohn Building is a high-tech, state-of-the-art environment complete with Bloomberg financial markets technology, Dow Jones markets, LEXIS-NEXIS, and a real-time trading room. But it's also our students' home base; so, in addition to all the desirable learning tools, we have some of the comforts of home, such as study areas with upholstered chairs, meeting rooms for small groups of students working together, lockers, an ATM machine, parking under the building after 4:30 p.m. on weekdays and all weekend, and an in-house restaurant.

The unique combination of a top-notch M.B.A. program situated in a safe and cosmopolitan small city make The University of Iowa School of Management an excellent choice for anyone.

—Gary Fethke, Dean

Programs and Curricular Focus

The University of Iowa M.B.A. program provides students with a solid foundation for future growth and flexibility in business management. The curriculum is rigorous, but learning takes place in a collaborative environment that builds teamwork while encouraging independent problem solving.

Students tailor individual course portfolios to combine analytical skills, broad-based knowledge, and professional experiences into a package that will advance their personal career goals.

Concentrations are available in accounting, finance, management information systems, marketing, entrepreneurship, human resources/organizational performance, operations management, and product development and management. Students may also create their own concentration, incorporating courses from the University's other colleges, or pursue a dual-degree program in hospital and health administration, nursing, law, or library and information science.

Students and the M.B.A. Experience

IMPACT, a weeklong orientation program for entering M.B.A. students, links students with one another and with faculty even before course work begins. This collaborative atmosphere is sustained throughout the pro-

gram through team projects, student organization activities, alumni functions, corporate visits, and daily communication. Dedicated and diverse, Iowa M.B.A. students come from top undergraduate institutions worldwide and hold degrees and honors in disciplines ranging from English to engineering.

The average student is 27 years old and has three years of professional experience. Women comprise 30 percent of the student population, and minority students make up 10 percent.

Fifty percent of students come from the Midwest, and 36 percent are international students.

❖ Global Focus

The University of Iowa M.B.A. program offers many opportunities for developing a global business perspective. Corporate partners include Fortune 100 companies with multinational operations and middle-market businesses with extensive import/export activities. These companies provide internship and consulting opportunities and willingly share their vast knowledge of global markets and emerging economies.

Iowa M.B.A. students gain international experience in other ways as well. For the past several years, students have traveled to the Czech and Slovak Republics to work with local business executives. Recently, summer internships

in Argentina have been added to the international opportunities available to Iowa M.B.A. students.

Special Features

Information technology is dramatically altering the way most business is conducted. Managers now have nearly instantaneous access to information about changing financial markets, customer demand, and competitive conditions in international and domestic markets. In addition to a state-of-the-art computer lab and trading room, Iowa M.B.A. students and faculty members benefit from the program's substantial investment in information technology: real-time electronic links to more than 130 financial markets worldwide; online access to major business periodicals, investment analysts' research reports, and consumer demographics databases. Videoconferencing facilities provide communication with business leaders throughout the world.

The Faculty

Iowa M.B.A. faculty members are accomplished, dynamic, and dedicated to providing a comprehensive business education to students. Holding Ph.D.'s from some of the world's top educational institutions, all can apply practical experiences gained in such places as Tenneco, Inc.; Andersen Consulting; Citicorp; General Motors; and the Commodity Futures Trading Commission to the M.B.A. classroom.

Beyond their impressive credentials, Iowa M.B.A. faculty members are dedicated professionals who share a passion for teaching. They are enthusiastic about challenging students to excel, and they interact with students both inside and outside the classroom. This personal approach to management education is not often available to students in larger M.B.A. programs.

The Business School Network

Corporate Partnerships

The University of Iowa School of Management is fortunate to have excellent ties to and communication with the business community—regionally, nationally, and globally. Prominent business leaders often visit

The Pappajohn Building is designed to provide a conducive learning environment.

campus to talk about issues facing their industries. Internship opportunities are plentiful, and many classes routinely involve students on consulting projects with the University's corporate partners, who span the globe and include companies representing every economic sector.

The College and Environs
Iowa City is a uniquely wonderful community. Here, students, faculty, and townspeople work and play together harmoniously.

The University of Iowa is the very heart of Iowa City, both in fact and spirit. The oldest of Iowa's three state universities, it includes, in addition to the College of Business Administration, the Colleges of Dentistry, Education, Engineering, Law, Liberal Arts, Medicine, Nursing, and Pharmacy. There are approximately 28,000 students, of whom 6,000 are pursuing graduate study.

Chicago, Minneapolis, St. Louis, and Kansas City are almost equidistant from the Iowa campus, providing urban advantages when desired. The Iowa City community itself offers an impressive array of cultural and recreational diversions.

Facilities
The M.B.A. program is housed in the John Pappajohn Business Administration Building, a beautiful, functional, and up-to-date setting that fosters interpersonal and technological interactions. The facility's classrooms, restaurant, and informal spaces encourage one-on-one communication, group discussion, and the impromptu exchange of ideas between students and faculty. Completed in 1994, the John Pappajohn Building provides an ideal learning environment for M.B.A. study.

Technology Environment
In addition to the global information and videoconferencing capabilities of the Pappajohn Building, the facility houses the largest student computing facility on the University of Iowa campus. Three computing classrooms, available for M.B.A. student use, complement a laboratory of nearly 100 workstations. Technology in the computer laboratory, library, and classrooms provides direct links to the global community, ranging from real-time national and international stock market feeds and information databases to a full spectrum of electronic resources.

Placement
The M.B.A. career services staff provides everything from resources to referrals. Beginning early in a student's program, staff members help develop a resume, research companies, and explore career options. Through a far-reaching alumni network, brokering services, and videoconferencing capabilities, Iowa M.B.A. career services personnel work with students to find internships and employment opportunities in the students' chosen fields and geographic locations. Interviews are arranged at on-campus locations, employer offices, and national job fairs. The Career Resource Center, exclusively for M.B.A. student use, provides access to career development information and employer databases, plus computer, telephone, fax, and copier equipment, to facilitate the job search process.

Admission
Each applicant's entire portfolio is considered. The admissions committee reviews each file individually and in full, looking for candidates who are a good match with the Iowa program. Students are asked to submit a completed application form, transcripts of all undergraduate and graduate

work, a resume, responses to essay questions, GMAT scores, three references, and an application fee. Work experience is a key factor. Admission is only available for the fall term (mid-August). April 15 is both the priority consideration date and the application deadline for international applicants. Applications received between April 15 and July 15 are reviewed on a space-available basis. Application reviews begin in January.

A minimum score of 600 on the TOEFL is required for all students for whom English is not the native language. International students must present proof of adequate funds to cover the full two years of study.

Finances
Tuition and fees for 1998–99 are $4130 for Iowa residents and $11,246 for nonresidents. Books and supplies cost approximately $1362 per year. Estimates provided by the Office of Student Financial Aid suggest that M.B.A. students budget approximately $575 per month for room and board.

Merit-based scholarships and fellowships are available to M.B.A. students. All applicants are considered for these competitive awards. Awards are based on information found within the application portfolio (including GMAT scores, GPA, and work experience). Students are also encouraged to apply for need-based financial assistance through the University Office of Student Financial Aid. Second-year students are eligible for assistantships in the College of Business.

International Students
International students and issues are integrated into the Iowa M.B.A. program as critical elements of the learning process. Built-in global connections occur within the classroom when discussion takes place between international and domestic students under the direction of knowledgeable faculty members who weave global issues into the fabric of their courses.

Application Facts and Dates
Admission preference for the full-time program (fall entrance) will be given to those applications completed by April 15. Electronic applications are available through the M.B.A. Web site.

School of Management
The University of Iowa
108 Pappajohn Business
    Administration Building, Suite
    C140
Iowa City, Iowa 52242
Telephone: 319-335-1039
        800-622-4692 (toll-free)
E-mail: iowamba@uiowa.edu
World Wide Web: http://www.biz.
  uiowa.edu/mba

University of Kansas

Graduate School of Business

Lawrence, Kansas

THE ROAD TO THE TWENTY-FIRST CENTURY

In today's business world, it is no longer enough to plan only for the short term, compete only against domestic firms, or accept today's technology as the final word. The realities of achieving success in business today are that we must learn to plan strategically for the long term as well as the short term, we must learn to compete globally as well as domestically, and we must continuously improve our product lines and our productivity by developing new technologies and more efficient methods of getting the job done. These truths of today will be even more true tomorrow and into the next century. At the University of Kansas, we teach our M.B.A. students critical and systems thinking, problem-solving skills, communications, leadership, teamwork, and the importance of lifelong learning—skills that will lead to success in the business world of tomorrow. If you are equal to the challenges ahead and would like to take your first step on the road to the twenty-first century in an environment of excellence, join our team today and learn the skills you'll need for tomorrow.

—Tom Sarowski, Dean

Programs and Curricular Focus

The new, improved full-time M.B.A. program retains the best of the traditional program—strong quantitative skills development; a solid base in marketing, finance, accounting, and human resources; and an outstanding spectrum of electives—with some striking innovations. Team building is stressed throughout the program, Immersion Weeks focus on critical new areas of business, and nine concentrations include finance, marketing, international business, information technology, and human resources management.

A top-notch faculty, an excellent placement record, actively supportive alumni, and the resources of a world-class university give the University of Kansas (KU) M.B.A. great value. This program is 60 credit hours long and takes two years to complete, full-time. Students are required to take an internship, study abroad, or participate in a similarly meaningful experience that complements first-year studies during the summer between the first and second years. Study-abroad opportunities include sites in Italy, France, England, Brazil, and Japan.

The part-time M.B.A. program offers the same faculty and academic excellence as the full-time program and can be completed in three years (48 credit hours). At least two years of meaningful work experience are required for

admission. This program, taught at the Edwards Campus in Overland Park, Kansas (near Kansas City), features an enriched classroom environment. Students have an average of seven years of work experience.

Students and the M.B.A. Experience

KU's M.B.A. students represent a diverse cross section of the population. The current M.B.A. class consists of 37 percent women, more than 6 percent domestic members of minority groups, and nearly 20 percent international students from ten countries. The average age of the students is 25 years, and the average length of full-time work experience is nearly two years.

❖ Global Focus

Each summer, many KU M.B.A. students study abroad in one of several programs. Students can choose to travel to Italy, France, England, Brazil, or Japan for this option. There is also an exchange program with ESC Clermont-Ferrand, France, which includes the exchange of both faculty members and students. International internships are also possible. This year, students are interning in France, Germany, and India.

The Faculty

KU's 53 faculty members bring a mix of practical experience and theory to the

classroom and provide a rich educational experience fostered by excellence in research. Members of the faculty publish nationally recognized textbooks, serve as editors of national publications, and perform consulting and research services for corporate entities. The faculty is diverse, consisting of 15 percent women and 15 percent members of minority groups, bringing additional perspectives and insights to the students.

The Business School Network

The KU School of Business draws extensively upon alumni and business professionals to serve as members of the Board of Advisors. These executives help to shape the future of the School and also volunteer to serve as mentors for the M.B.A. students, exposing them to the practical, real-time issues and management solutions being used in the corporate world today. These same executives help to identify internships for the students in their respective industries and are often a part of the students' networking and job search processes in their final year of M.B.A. study.

The College and Environs

The University of Kansas is a major educational and research institution with more than 27,000 students, including about 6,000 graduate students, and 1,900 faculty members. The School of Business is housed in Summerfield Hall, located in the heart of campus. The main campus occupies 1,000 acres of forested, rolling hills on and around Mount Oread in the city of Lawrence, a growing community of 68,000. Located only 35 miles west of Kansas City, historic Lawrence combines the atmosphere of a small college town with the cosmopolitan flavor of a major city. Shopping areas, restaurants, entertainment, and recreational facilities are easily accessible from campus.

Placement

The KU School of Business has its own Career Services Office where students can input resumes into an electronic database that is automatically screened for each employer's criteria. More than

A team of M.B.A. students works on a group assignment.

Finances

Tuition and fees for Lawrence Campus courses for the 1998–99 academic year are $100 per credit hour plus a semester fee of $214 for in-state residents; $328.75 per credit hour plus a semester fee of $214 for out-of-state residents and international students. Tuition and fees for courses taken on Edwards Campus are $196 per credit hour, regardless of residency. Double- or single-occupancy rooms in residence halls cost approximately $3500–$4500 per academic year and include nineteen meals per week. Limited scholarship assistance, based on academic credentials, is available for both domestic and international students through the School of Business.

1,700 on-campus interviews with more than 200 companies were scheduled last year. Of the graduate students who completed their business degrees last year, 95 percent were placed within six weeks of graduation. The average starting salary for KU's M.B.A. graduates was $44,500.

Admission

Admission requirements include the equivalent of a four-year college degree in any major, completion of a semester of college algebra (or higher math), a nonrefundable $50 application fee, and scores from the Graduate Management Admission Test (GMAT). International students must also provide scores from the Test of English as a Foreign Language (TOEFL). The average GMAT score for students admitted to the program is 600. Ideally, students have two or more years of meaningful full-time work experience and strong academic credentials and show evidence of leadership, strong interpersonal skills, and potential for success in the business world.

Application Facts and Dates

The application deadline is May 1 to begin the full-time M.B.A. program in Lawrence in August. The part-time M.B.A. program deadline is May 1 (for fall), October 1 (for spring), and March 1 (for summer).

School of Business
206 Summerfield Hall
University of Kansas
Lawrence, Kansas 66045-2003
Telephone: 785-864-4254
E-mail: grad@bschool.wpo.ukans.edu
World Wide Web: http://www.bschool. ukans.edu

University of Kentucky

Lexington, Kentucky

STRAIGHT TALK ABOUT THE M.B.A.

▶ *The M.B.A. program at the Carol Martin Gatton College of Business and Economics is widely recognized as offering a quality education at a relatively modest cost. A distinguished faculty, excellent learning environment, flexible curriculum, state-of-the-art computer facilities, and a superior library, plus a variety of internships and opportunities for study abroad, all add up to an M.B.A. degree that gives those seeking advancement and professional success that significant extra edge in today's highly competitive business environment. The curriculum is demanding. It challenges students to synthesize a large and diverse set of concepts and ideas, while gaining not only mastery and understanding of the technology needed for a business enterprise to succeed in a global economy but also a solid foundation in the ethical principles that must underlie any business operation. The program is deliberately selective and limited in size to ensure personal attention and guidance from the faculty as well as to facilitate networking and teamwork. In short, our M.B.A. graduates are well prepared to meet the present and future demands made of them by society and the world of business.*

—Richard W. Furst, Dean

Programs and Curricular Focus

The largest single gift in the history of the University of Kentucky (UK) has resulted in the renaming of the former College of Business and Economics after Carol Martin Gatton, a distinguished alumnus. Graduate programs offered include the Ph.D. in business administration, Ph.D. in economics, M.B.A., M.S. in accounting, and M.S. in economics. Joint-degree programs include B.S.in Eng./M.B.A. and M.B.A./J.D.

The M.B.A. program enrolls approximately 100 new students each year; the entering class size is deliberately limited to ensure personal contact with graduate faculty and individualized attention. The program is designed to provide students with the education needed to prepare them for upper-level managerial responsibilities. Two 36-hour programs are offered: one is for those with an undergraduate degree in business who desire more specialized skills, the other is for students without an undergraduate degree in business but who are interested in acquiring a broad-based management training. A basic common core of seven courses provide an understanding of business enterprise, an understanding of quantitative methods and the applications of analysis to business decision making, development of leadership skills, the ability to solve complicated and realistic business problems, and an understanding

of managing a business enterprise in a global environment. For the business undergraduate, the remaining courses are electives that permit the development of skills in a particular area. Concentrations are offered in accounting and corporate finance; finance, real estate, and banking; international business; management information systems; and marketing and distribution. For the nonbusiness undergraduate, the remaining required courses provide an understanding of problems encountered in business enterprise as related to organizational behavior, production, marketing, and finance.

Students and the M.B.A. Experience

In 1997–98, the College enrolled approximately 380 graduate students, of whom 270 are M.B.A. students. Of the 1997 incoming M.B.A. class, women represented 37 percent, international students 17 percent, and minorities 12 percent of the student body. Thirty percent of the students are part-time and 44 percent have a nonbusiness undergraduate degree. The average age of students was 26. Degrees of work experience include seasoned managers of many years to those without significant work experience in a managerial capacity. The program offers a judicious mix of teamwork and individual projects, case

study, and lectures, designed to improve analytic, technical, and communications skills. Students are selected on the basis of proven academic excellence and a commitment to succeed. A significant percentage of full-time M.B.A. students have internships.

❖ Global Focus

Students seeking an understanding of the global business environment find that the curriculum and the program supplies them with this opportunity. A core course on global business management provides the essential foundation, which can be supplemented by appropriate electives. The concentration in international business is available for those wishing to specialize. Study abroad is made possible by exchange agreements with premier institutions in Europe and Asia. There are a number of opportunities to interact with the many visiting faculty and business experts from abroad who come to the college to share their expertise and culture with their U.S. counterparts. Facility in foreign language can be acquired or improved through the many courses offered at the University.

The Faculty

The College, headed by Dean Richard W. Furst and Associate Dean Michael G. Tearney, consists of three divisions; the School of Accountancy, with 18 faculty members under the direction of Dr. Stuart Keller; the School of Management, incorporating the areas of decision sciences and information systems, finance, management, and marketing, with a total of 40 faculty members under the direction of Dr. Steven Skinner; and the Department of Economics, with 26 faculty members under the chairmanship of Dr. Glenn Blomquist. Faculty members have achieved both national and international recognition for excellence in teaching and research as well as for service to the commonwealth of Kentucky and the business community. Many of the faculty members are presently actively engaged in joint research projects with faculty at institutions around the world including Austria, England, China, Indonesia, Kazakhstan, Sweden, and Croatia.

The Business School Network

Corporate Partnerships

The College's University of Kentucky Business Partnership Foundation consists of prominent individuals in the business and academic communities. The Board of Directors of the Foundation fulfills an important role in assessing the present and future needs of the business world and in advising the College on how to provide the education necessary to meet those needs in a manner consistent with the College's missions of excellence in teaching, research, and service. Local businesses provide scholarships and internships for M.B.A. students. Guest speakers from the business community visit the college on a regular basis throughout the year.

Prominent Alumni

There are more than 1,300 M.B.A. alumni in all fifty states and in twenty-two other countries. Prominent alumni of the College include the presidents and CEOs of numerous corporations including public companies listed on the NYSE. Inductees into the College's Hall of Fame include former State Governor Edward T. Breathitt; Carl F. Pollard, former Chairman and CEO of Columbia Healthcare, Inc.; James E. Rogers, Chairman, President, and CEO, PSI Holdings, Inc.; Warren W. Rosenthal; Chris Sullivan, CEO, Outback Steakhouse; Paul Chellgren, CEO, Ashland Oil, Inc.; and Carol Martin Gatton.

The College and Environs

The UK campus and the Carol Martin Gatton College of Business and Economics are close to the heart of downtown Lexington, a city with a population of 230,000, where many of the cultural and recreational amenities of a large city are combined with the charm and traditions of a small town. Famed for its horse farms, Lexington lies within a 500-mile radius of nearly three fourths of the manufacturing, employment, retail sales, and population of the United States. Established in 1865, the University of Kentucky has more than 24,000 students, of whom approximately 6,400 are graduate students. Founded in 1925 as the College of Commerce, the AACSB-accredited Carol Martin Gatton College of Business and Economics occupies a modern building with all the facilities needed to fulfill the mission of excellence in teaching, research, and service.

Technology Environment

As befits a Carnegie Foundation Research University of the first class, the Univer-sity of Kentucky has excellent facilities. The M. I. King Library contains more than 2.5 million volumes and receives more than 27,000 periodical and serial titles; the new $58-million William T. Young library opened in spring 1998. The Computing Center has several high-level systems supporting research and network-ing needs. Within the College are the electronic Business Information Center for state-of-the-art business database access and seven centers of research that serve as resources to the state, local, and international business community. At sites throughout the campus, computer workstations cater to the computing needs of all students.

Placement

The M.B.A. program has its own placement office and a Placement Director who provides placement assistance and organizes programs and workshops on the skills needed for finding the right job. Each year, the M.B.A. resume book is sent to selected business enterprises and corporate recruiters. The College is an active member of the SEMBA consortium of Business Colleges. At an annual meeting held in Atlanta, MBA students interview with company recruiters. At the annual Career Day, students meet with recruiters to research companies and discuss job opportunities. In 1996–97, 71 percent of program graduates had jobs immediately upon graduation; 100 percent had jobs within six months of graduation.

Admission

Admission to the full-time program is for the fall semester only. Admission to the part-time program is possible in spring for students who already have an undergraduate degree in business. An undergraduate degree with a minimum GPA of 2.5 is required, together with the following course work: two principles of accounting courses (financial, manage-rial), two principles of economics courses (micro, macro), a course in statistics and probability, and an elementary calculus course. All prerequisite courses should be equivalent to at least 3 semester hours. Applicants must also submit a GMAT, and international applicants must also present a minimum TOEFL score of 550 overall and a minimum Test of Written English (TWE) score of 4.5. Academic background, GMAT score, personal recommendations, and the applicant's statement of purpose are all considered in the evaluation for admission. Demon-strated academic ability and potential for subsequent success in the business world are qualities that are looked for in applicants.

Finances

The College and Graduate School offer merit-based scholarships and fellowships. Approximately 35 percent of the fall 1997 entering class received some form of college-based aid, including scholar-ships for minority and disadvantaged students. Students of outstanding merit are nominated for Graduate School Fellowships. Eligible students may also obtain on-campus employment through the UK STEPS service and the UK workstudy program.

The University of Kentucky operates on the semester system. For 1997–98, in-state graduate tuition for a full-time student was $1320 per semester, part-time students paid $147 per credit hour. Nonresident full-time graduate tuition was $3960 per semester; part-time nonresident tuition was $440 per credit hour. The registration fee for full-time students is $168 per semester; part-time students pay $6 per credit hour. A full-time nonresi-dent student can expect to pay approxi-mately $8800 for tuition, fees, and books for an academic year.

On-campus housing rents range from $318 to $540 per month. A single student living frugally needs approximately $5200 in housing and living expenses for an academic year.

Application Facts and Dates

Admission to the College's graduate business programs is achieved by applying both to the Graduate School and the College. For fall admission to the M.B.A. program, the application deadline for U.S. citizens is July 1; international applicants must apply by February 1. March 1 is the deadline for financial aid consideration. Successful applicants are generally notified within two weeks of receipt of all required documentation. For admission advice and information, students should contact:

Ms. Marilyn Underwood
Graduate Center
Carol Martin Gatton College of
    Business and Economics
University of Kentucky
Lexington, Kentucky 40506
Telephone: 606-257-7722
Fax: 606-257-3923
E-mail: mleste00@pop.uky.edu

For application materials, students should contact:

Ms. Donna Ballos
Graduate Center
Carol Martin Gatton College of
    Business and Economics
University of Kentucky
Lexington, Kentucky 40506
Telephone: 606-257-3592
Fax: 606-257-3923
E-mail: drball01@pop.uky.edu

UofL The University of Louisville

Louisville, Kentucky

THE M.B.A.: FUTURE TRENDS AND DIRECTIONS

Managers and leaders face unprecedented challenges in our rapidly changing world. The global marketplace is creating new structures and processes for business and government. To be competitive, the required skills and attitudes are innovation in solving complex problems, self-knowledge and confidence in making a difference, and a comprehensive understanding of theory and practice.

The University of Louisville (U of L) M.B.A. program is designed to meet these challenges and your needs. Our faculty have current business experience, state-of-the-art research, and a sincere commitment to teaching excellence. They will help you discover your potential.

We believe that U of L offers you one of the best opportunities to study, learn, and experience the world of organizations—whether they be large industrial firms, small entrepreneurial businesses, or government and not-for-profit agencies. Our goal is to help you succeed.

—Robert L. Taylor, Dean

Programs and Curricular Focus

The mission of the University of Louisville College of Business and Public Administration is to provide high-quality education and professional development in business, public administration, and urban policy that meets the special needs of an urban constituency. Teaching, research, and service reflect innovation and responsiveness to a rapidly changing global environment. Undergraduate and graduate education are complemented with continuing education and training programs, scholarly activity, student involvement, and community outreach. Faculty and staff members are committed to programs that reflect continuing intellectual growth, pragmatism, and the importance of human values.

Entrepreneurship is a particular focus of the business program with the Integrative M.B.A. and Executive B.S.B.A. having this as a specific theme. In addition, faculty members work with a few select undergraduate and graduate students each year to help them actually launch a new venture. Students successfully completing New Venture Creation, Entrepreneurship I and II courses are assigned an experienced faculty mentor who helps them take a business plan to practical reality. Thus far, 14 businesses have been created through this initiative in the past five years. For technology-based ideas, the Telecommunications Research Center is used as an incubator where students and recent graduates

receive ongoing technical and business support for a limited period after graduation. Finally, a spirit of entrepreneurship pervades all of the curricula as a philosophy of thinking about business and careers.

In addition to entrepreneurship, the College offers 12-hour concentrations in healthcare administration and technology. The technology concentration is offered in cooperation with the Engineering School to students simultaneously enrolled in the Master of Engineering and M.B.A. programs.

A student's degree program is 36 semester credit hours, possibly more, depending upon undergraduate preparation and placement test results. The M.B.A. program's 36-hour core curriculum consists of eight requisite 600-level courses and three approved electives. Serving as the academic common body of knowledge for the M.B.A. core requirements, the foundation core of 500-level courses provides those students with less extensive undergraduate business backgrounds a means toward preparing for the M.B.A. core courses.

All required 600-level courses are offered in the fall and spring semesters, along with a variety of elective courses. A smaller selection of 600-level courses is offered during the two summer sessions. The foundation core's 500-level course offerings are split between the fall and spring semesters and normally are not part of the summer course schedule.

Two-year advanced course schedule planners are available to assist students in planning their curriculum and avoiding unforeseen delays in degree completion.

In order to foster international expertise, the College of Business and Public Administration provides frequent opportunities for M.B.A. students to learn the international aspects of business administration, including cross-cultural perspectives. Such opportunities consist of courses, seminars, exchange programs, and independent study. M.B.A. students are strongly encouraged to take advantage of these opportunities. In addition, the College offers M.B.A. programs in Athens, San Salvador, Hong Kong, and Singapore, with full-time faculty members teaching modules in the host countries. This offers additional international experience for faculty and selected students.

Students and the M.B.A. Experience

The M.B.A. students at U of L bring a wide variety of work experiences and academic diversity to the program. With approximately two thirds of the students pursuing their graduate degrees on a part-time basis, classes benefit from a wealth of current and diverse real-world business experiences. In addition, the program is proud of its progress in attracting women and students of diverse ethnic and cultural backgrounds.

The M.B.A. program is primarily an evening program in which an individual can enroll as either a part-time or full-time student. During the fall and spring semesters, courses typically are offered Monday through Thursday, one evening per week, from 5:30 to 8:15 p.m. During the summer session, there are two successive six-week sessions in which classes meet three evenings per week: Monday, Tuesday, and Thursday. Although the majority of the program's student population enrolls on a part-time basis, courses are scheduled so that a student may pursue the program on a full-time basis of 9 hours per semester.

The M.B.A./J.D. program is offered jointly by the College of Business and Public Administration and the School of

Law. The program combines the two-year M.B.A. program and the three-year Juris Doctor (J.D.) program into one four-year, full-time program. Upon successful completion of the program, the student is awarded both the M.B.A. and J.D. degrees. Requests for further information regarding this program should be directed to the M.B.A. coordinator.

The Faculty

The College's faculty members offer exceptional teaching ability, applied business research, and individualized, high-quality interactions with students. Diversity, commitment, and professionalism characterize the faculty. Like the curriculum itself, the more than 70 faculty members reflect the changing nature of the workforce.

Ninety-five percent of the M.B.A. course work is taught by doctorally qualified faculty members who enrich the learning experience by providing a balance of theory and application. Faculty members enlist a wide variety of classroom approaches, including lectures, case studies, computer simulation, group projects, and discussions. In addition, the development and demonstration of appropriate oral and written communication skills are an integral part of M.B.A. course objectives.

The Business School Network

Corporate Partnerships

While preparing individuals to add value to the community, the College of Business and Public Administration recognizes its role as an active partner in the development and growth of organizations in the region. The M.B.A. program is committed to working with the regional business community through applied research, consulting, and training. On a continual basis, M.B.A. students are offered special opportunities to meet and learn from some of the region's most dynamic and successful business leaders.

Prominent Alumni

The College notes among its alumni a number of the region's most distinguished business leaders, including Malcolm Chancey Jr., Chairman, Banc One Kentucky Corporation, Louisville; Dan Ulmer, former chairman of Citizen's Fidelity Bank (now PNC Bank), Louisville; David Jones, Chairman of the Board, Humana, Inc.; Gene Gardner, retired president of a major Louisville company and co-owner of the Louisville Redbirds AAA baseball organization; Charles McCarty, retired president,

BATUS Industries; and James Patterson, fast-food executive, Long John Silver's, Chi Chi's, Wendy's, and Rally's.

The College and Environs

The University of Louisville is an urban educational institution that celebrates its bicentennial in 1998. Consisting of thirteen academic units and spanning three campuses, the University became part of the Kentucky state system of higher education in 1970.

The College of Business and Public Administration is located on the 140-acre Belknap campus in the historic Old Louisville section of the city. Kentucky's largest urban center, Louisville offers some of the region's most diverse, enjoyable cultural surroundings and events. From the Kentucky Derby and its weeklong festival to the Kentucky Center for the Arts, "the river city" offers enough variety in cultural, recreational, and sports opportunities to rival cities three times its size.

Technology Environment

The College of Business and Public Administration provides an outstanding computer and technology environment. A computer classroom and lab, with over fifty networked workstations dedicated for use by business faculty members and students, supports the latest software applications. In addition, the building houses the University's North Computing Center, containing seventy additional workstations. Multimedia applications, electronic mail, interactive television, and LANs comprise an integral part of the M.B.A. curriculum.

Placement

The College works aggressively to build strong ties with regional organizations and on-campus recruiters in order to help students construct a network of professional contacts. Regional, national, and international companies visit regularly to recruit for full-time and internship positions.

Admission

Admission into the M.B.A. program is competitive. Entering M.B.A. candidates at the University of Louisville are in the top third of all entering M.B.A. candidates nationwide.

Applicants must submit a completed graduate application, along with a nonrefundable $25 application fee. In addition, applicants must have sent to the University Admissions Office official transcripts, GMAT results, and two letters

of recommendation from individuals familiar with the applicant's academic performance.

International applicants are required to take the TOEFL if English is not their native language. Though optional, a written personal statement is highly recommended for applicants with marginal GMAT scores, undergraduate grade point averages, or both.

Finances

Estimated tuition and fees for full-time students in 1998–99 are $1585 for Kentucky residents and $4525 for nonresidents. For part-time residents, courses cost approximately $175 per semester hour, while nonresidents pay $502 per semester hour. University fees are subject to approval of the Board of Trustees and may be changed without prior notice.

Although many graduate students live off campus, the University provides some graduate dormitory rooms and apartments. The Housing/Resident Administration maintains a referral file of off-campus rooms and apartments. Housing costs in Louisville are lower than in most other metropolitan areas.

A limited number of graduate research assistantships are available to full-time students. These grants require students to work up to 20 hours per week as research aides to departmental faculty members and provide living stipends plus tuition. The University's Financial Aid Office and Student Employment Office also provide four types of assistance: scholarships, grants, educational loans, and part-time employment.

Application Facts and Dates

The College employs a rolling application deadline. For students wishing to begin course work in either the fall or spring semester, all application materials must be received at least 120 days prior to the semester's start. Those students planning to begin in the summer term must have all materials submitted at least eighty days before the start of course work in mid-May. For more information, applicants should address inquiries to:

M.B.A. Coordinator
Student Academic Support Services Office
College of Business and Public Administration
University of Louisville
Louisville, Kentucky 40292
Telephone: 502-852-7439

University of Maine

The Maine Business School

Orono, Maine

LEADERSHIP IN THE GLOBAL ECONOMY

The University of Maine (UM) Business School serves as the primary source of management education, research, and service in the state of Maine. Through the integration of research, teaching, and extensive interactions with the business community, the Maine Business School develops and communicates knowledge, prepares students for successful careers in a global economy, and contributes to the economic development of the region.

Maine's M.B.A. program affords the benefits of small classes and close interaction with the faculty and staff. Our diversity provides an optimal learning environment with students from a wide range of backgrounds and cultures. The combination of a committed teaching faculty and high-quality students has resulted in an outstanding M.B.A. program.

—Virginia R. Gibson, Dean

Programs and Curricular Focus

The University of Maine M.B.A. program equips candidates with the concepts, analytical tools, and executive skills required for competent and responsible management. Built-in course and program flexibility enables the School to meet the needs of the individual student. Students have the opportunity to take up to 30 percent of their graduate course work in electives in order to meet their own career goals. Full-time students with an undergraduate degree in business administration can usually complete the 30-hour graduate program in one calendar year. Required courses include business, government, and society; behavioral analysis for administrative decisions; quantitative methods for business decisions; financial management; marketing management; management information systems; and management policy. Students are expected to be proficient in college algebra and the use of word processing and spreadsheet software. Students with no business course work can complete requirements in two years of full-time study. Undergraduate core courses include introduction to accounting, principles of management and organization, business finance, marketing, macroeconomics, and production and operations management.

Both the undergraduate and graduate programs in business administration are accredited by AACSB–The International Association for Management Education.

Students and the M.B.A. Experience

The current M.B.A. class is a heterogeneous group, with representatives from more than forty undergraduate colleges and universities and more than forty different undergraduate majors. In 1997, thirteen countries were represented. More than 50 percent of the class have undergraduate preparation in fields other than business administration. The average age of entering students is 28. Women comprise 30 percent of the enrollment. Of the 9,000 University students, more than 2,000 are graduate students. Academic rigor, emphasis on teamwork, and esprit de corps among students and faculty are noted by many alumni as key components of their experience at UM.

The Faculty

Faculty members are actively engaged in scholarly work and public service activities, offering seminars and workshops for business practitioners and providing consulting services both nationally and internationally, greatly enriching the classroom experience.

The Business School Network

Since 1965, more than 900 M.B.A. alumni have achieved positions of significant authority and responsibility in many organizations locally, nationally, and internationally. Many serve as mentors through the Maine Mentor Program.

The College and Environs

Students at the University of Maine benefit from the advantages of both rural and urban environments. Located just a 1- to 2-hour drive from Mount Katahdin, state parks, ski slopes, and the Maine coast, the University is a 4-hour drive on Interstate 95 from Boston. Bangor International Airport, located 8 miles from campus, provides service to many major U.S. and international cities. The 1,100-acre campus is the site of a dynamic modern university, encompassing five colleges, various schools and academic programs, and a graduate school. The M.B.A. degree has been offered since 1965. In 1993, the $7-million Donald P. Corbett Business Building opened with several high-technology, seminar, and case classrooms. The Maine Center for the Arts provides cultural focus for the University campus, the communities of the region, and all Maine citizens. Musical, dance, and theatrical performances and lectures by distinguished speakers are presented in the 1,628-seat Hutchins Concert Hall. The center also includes the Hudson Museum and Palmer Gallery.

Facilities

The UM M.B.A. program exposes students to state-of-the-art systems for management decision support. Both mainframe and microcomputer facilities on the Orono campus are excellent. The central computing facility for the entire University of Maine System is located on the Orono campus. Public access microcomputer clusters are available in Fogler Library and the Student Union. The Fogler Library houses more than 900,000 volumes, subscribes to more than 5,600 journals, and is a tristate regional federal depository for publications of the U.S. government and a selective depository for Canadian government documents.

Technology Environment

The Business School supports two labs of networked 486 and Pentium-class microcomputers. Students have access to an extensive software library as well as the Internet and World Wide Web, the library, and the mainframe.

Placement

The University's Career Center provides a variety of services to assist students in obtaining positions following graduation. Services include individual career counseling, career information for exploring options, the mentor program, resume/vita critiques, job search workshops, mock interviews, job listings, employer information, and assistance in identifying potential employers.

Admission

All applicants must hold a four-year baccalaureate degree from a regionally accredited college or university. Consideration is given to an applicant's official transcript(s), GMAT scores, three letters of recommendation on forms provided in the application material, and potential for leadership in business. The mean GMAT score of entering students is 535. All applicants whose native language is not English must submit official TOEFL scores. The minimum score required is 550. Although work experience is not required, the majority of students have three or more years of work experience. Students can apply for fall, spring, or summer admission.

Finances

In 1997–98, tuition charges for one course per semester were $1593 for nonresidents and $564 for residents. The room and board (full meal plan included) cost was $2453 per semester. A comprehensive fee for 7 to 11 credit hours was $101 and for 1 to 6 credit hours, no charge. Other fees included a student activity fee of $17.50, a communications fee of $10, a recreation fee of $12.50, and a technology fee of $3 per credit hour. In addition, all international students and their dependents must purchase health insurance through the University unless they are sponsored by agencies providing comparable insurance coverage. Financial aid is extremely limited and highly competitive when available.

International Students

International students currently in the M.B.A. program represent thirteen countries; campuswide, seventy countries are represented. More than 100 international students have graduated with an M.B.A. degree since 1980. The relatively small size of graduate classes permits students a one-on-one working relationship with faculty members. The International Programs Office assists with immigration matters and offers intercultural opportunities. The friendliness of fellow students makes the learning experience at UM positive. Classes with both full-time and part-time students add to the international student experience. Classmates are academic resources and constitute a network of professional contacts and allies for the future. For students who have completed the undergraduate core courses, the program can be completed within one calendar year.

Application Facts and Dates

For program information, students should call 207-581-1973. It is recommended that all application material be received by February 15 for fall admission. Applications must be submitted no later than six weeks prior to the beginning of the semester. All official transcripts, test scores, letters of recommendation, and the $50 application fee must be on file prior to a review being made. Application fees cannot be waived. Application material should be sent directly to:

Graduate School
5782 Winslow Hall
University of Maine
Orono, Maine 04469-5782
Telephone: 207-581-1973
Fax: 207-581-3232
E-mail: mba@maine.maine.edu
World Wide Web: http://www.maine.
edu/~gibson/umocba.html

The University of Manitoba

Winnipeg, Manitoba, Canada

MBA MANITOBA—A FULLY INTEGRATED ONE-YEAR M.B.A. PROGRAM

MBA MANITOBA is a newly designed program targeted for individuals with a minimum of three years of full-time managerial experience. In addition to a curriculum designed for today's and tomorrow's managers operating in a global, competitive economy, MBA MANITOBA offers a complete M.B.A. degree in eleven months of full-time, concentrated study. The new curriculum is the product of in-depth research with alumni and businesspeople to identify the skills and knowledge that are desirable in M.B.A. graduates.

MBA MANITOBA is an integrated program rather than a collection of courses. This means that the participants experience a managed curriculum with each part complementing the other parts. Courses are offered in a modular format, which gives increased flexibility in the design of course topics.

We believe this new curriculum and format will set the standard for all M.B.A. programs in the future. In today's competitive job market, traditional two-year programs often present insurmountable opportunity costs in lost income and foregone career progression. A complete, fully qualified M.B.A. curriculum offered on an eleven-month basis presents a unique educational opportunity for midcareer individuals.

—J. L. Gray, Dean

Programs and Curricular Focus

MBA MANITOBA is unique because it was designed to be a program, not merely a collection of courses. Through the collaborative efforts of faculty members, students, business leaders, and alumni, a powerful new curriculum was developed to enable participants to earn their M.B.A. in eleven months of intense exposure to the most current ideas and practices in international management education. The curriculum of MBA MANITOBA is cross-disciplinary—in each course, resources are pulled together from all functional and skill development areas to emphasize the importance of the "big picture" to managers. Ideas and concepts are never considered in isolation but are always integrated with the participant's previous learning and experience. This approach combines the application of practical knowledge with real business problems and always emphasizes how all aspects of management are interconnected.

The curriculum is divided into three phases: Foundations, Functions, and Strategy and Implementation. The Foundations courses are designed to provide participants with the necessary tools for general managers. Topics such as Understanding Financial Statements and Essential Financial Con-

cepts for Managers help managers to assess the financial position of their firms, while courses such as Designing Fast Response Operations and Using Information Technology help managers move their firms into the twenty-first century. In the Functions phase, participants explore ways in which the functional areas of business interconnect. They are exposed to topics such as Managing for Strategic Market Advantage and Global Operations Strategy, which are designed to change the way they think about business problems and to encourage the adoption of the general manager's cross-disciplinary viewpoint. The Strategy and Implementation phase serves as the integrative core of the curriculum. The sum of each participant's knowledge is refined in courses such as Strategy Implementation and Strategic Leadership and Managing Change and then shared with the entire class in projects ranging from repositioning a company in a strategic cluster to developing an exit strategy from an industry.

By the end of the program, students are thinking like strategists—planning for long-term competitive advantage, identifying the forces that shape their industry, understanding how short-term functions impact on long-term strategic plans, and exploring some of the weaknesses of conventional strategic planning.

Students and the M.B.A. Experience

All MBA MANITOBA participants enter the program after working several years instead of immediately after their undergraduate degree, and few have previous education in the field of business. The result is that the learning experience of all participants is vastly enriched by the variety of backgrounds and by the depth of experience each participant brings to the classroom. Participants come from most Canadian provinces, international participants typically constitute 20 percent of the class, and approximately 30 percent are women.

MBA MANITOBA participants work as a cohesive unit since all participants proceed through the program as a cohort. From the beginning, a great deal of learning takes place in small groups, and through these experiences participants quickly discover that they can achieve more as part of the group than on their own. They also learn the leadership skills necessary to build and maintain productive group processes, an essential managerial capability.

The collaborative atmosphere in the classroom results in the development of a strong sense of community among the participants. Throughout the eleven months, they work together, socialize together, and gradually build an environment in which they feel confident enough to experiment, take risks, and interact with complete freedom.

Special Features

A unique feature of MBA MANITOBA is the emphasis on enrichment experiences. Throughout the eleven months, participants complete not only the normal M.B.A. course work but are also exposed to a series of "extras" that guarantee that their leadership and managerial capabilities are developed and refined to the maximum of their potential. Two international trips are integrated into the core of the curriculum to provide the international focus necessary for managers in the twenty-first century. Throughout the program, themes such as international competition, shifting alliances, and new trade agreements are interwoven with functional topics, resulting in a truly global perspective.

A special managerial communications course is integrated into the core of the program and ensures that all participants will emerge with enhanced abilities to relate with groups and individuals by developing strong writing, speaking, presentation, and interpersonal skills.

The public service project allows participants and local nonprofit organizations to work together, giving the participants hands-on experience as they share in the daily workings of agencies in the public sector, usually those concerned with the less advantaged of society.

Numerous professional and leadership seminars are utilized to further improve the participants' abilities to understand themselves, to understand others, and to understand leading-edge, critical themes in the business world; in short, to manage effectively in the changing business environment. Topics such as diversity, ethics, the legal responsibilities of directors and officers, and the effective management of high and low performers are some of the seminar titles.

The Faculty

The Faculty of Management consists of 60 full-time faculty members, supplemented by adjunct professors who are brought in for specialized expertise. Ninety percent of the faculty members have Ph.D.'s. The MBA MANITOBA teaching faculty members are selected specifically for their experience and skill in developing a learning environment for M.B.A. participants. Previous business experience, consulting activities, and/or executive development experience are all prerequisites for teaching in the program. In addition to the regular teaching faculty, the Core Teaching Team monitors the course development and integration of course materials.

The Business School Network

The Associates Program of the Faculty of Management is Canada's largest business school support group. With more than 200 members and chapters in Winnipeg, Vancouver, and Toronto, the Associates Program provides financial, administrative, and academic support to the Faculty. The Associates' membership consists of the leading businesspeople across Canada, many of whom are graduates of the Faculty of Management. Interaction between the Associates and M.B.A. participants occurs at numerous functions held throughout the year, as well as at the popular "M.B.A. for a Day" program in which members of the Associates Program spend a day on campus taking classes with the M.B.A. participants.

In 1982 the Faculty of Management, in cooperation with the Associates Program, initiated the International Distinguished Entrepreneur Award (IDEA), which honours a businessperson who has made world-renowned contributions to the quality of business and community life. The presentation is made annually at the IDEA Dinner held in Winnipeg. Some of the recipients are H. Ross Perot, Chairman and CEO, The Ross Perot Group; Akio Morita, Chairman and CEO, Sony Corporation; Paul Desmarais, Chairman and CEO, Power Corporation of Canada; and Roberto Goizueta, Chairman and CEO, The Coca-Cola Company.

The Faculty of Management's Executive-in-Residence Program is one of several strategies used to integrate the academic programs with the activities of the business community. The Executive-in-Residence is an individual who joins the Faculty on a full-time basis to serve as a resource to participants and faculty members. The present Executive-in-Residence is Mr. Charles Curtis, former Deputy Minister of Finance, Province of Manitoba.

The College and Environs

The University of Manitoba, established in 1877, is the oldest university in western Canada. The main campus is located on a 677-acre site in south Winnipeg. The University has more than 25,000 students and offers programs in sixty-four disciplines. More than 120,000 students have graduated from the University during its 120-year history.

The Faculty of Management's origins go back to 1937 when a complete business curriculum was first established at the University of Manitoba. Since that time the Faculty has grown to offer bachelor's, master's, Ph.D., and executive programs in a variety of business disciplines.

Winnipeg, Manitoba, is the fifth-largest city in Canada, with a population of more than 600,000. Located in the centre of Canada, Winnipeg is an ethnically diverse city and has a broadly diversified economy led by such major industries as aerospace, agriculture, banking, insurance, and tourism. Winnipeg sees more hours of sunshine per year than any other Canadian city and enjoys hot, dry summers and crisp, bright winters. Within an hour's drive of the city are numerous white sand beaches along one of the world's best freshwater lakes. Only 63 miles from the U.S. border, Winnipeg is easily reached by highway, rail, and major airlines. Winnipeg is a clean, safe, comfortable city and was recently named by the *Toronto Globe and Mail Report on Business* as "one of Canada's best cities for business."

Facilities

The Faculty of Management is housed in the Drake Centre for Management Education, one of the most modern business education facilities in Canada. The building also houses the Asper Centre for Entrepreneurship, the Centre for Accounting Research and Education, the Transport Institute, the Warren Centre for Actuarial Sciences, the Centre for International Business Studies, the Albert D. Cohen Library, and three separate computer facilities for students.

Placement

The Career Services Centre is a major career resource centre devoted exclusively to the use of graduates of the Faculty of Management. The Centre organizes visits by corporate recruiters and assists participants in preparing for job interviews. Seminars on career planning, resume writing, and interviewing skills are offered on a regular basis.

Admission

The factors considered in the admission decision are undergraduate grades, work and managerial experience, GMAT score, references, leadership potential, entrepreneurial potential, and career goals. A TOEFL score is required of all participants for whom English is a second language, and the CANTEST must be taken upon arrival at the University. GMAT scores of participants typically average 575–600. Occasionally, participants without undergraduate degrees are admitted if they show outstanding accomplishments and potential in other areas of qualification.

Finances

Tuition fees for the 1998–99 academic year are Can$17,600. Books, participant fees, living expenses, and the international study trips are not included in the tuition fee. Living costs for participants vary with lifestyle, but Winnipeg is noted for having living costs among the lowest of the major Canadian cities. All applicants are automatically considered for financial aid. Decisions are based upon admission qualifications.

Application Facts and Dates

The application deadline for MBA MANITOBA is May 1, although applications will be considered after this date if space permits. Admission decisions are made once the applicant's file is complete. Application fees are Can$50. For more information and application forms, students should contact:

MBA MANITOBA
Faculty of Management
The University of Manitoba
Winnipeg, Manitoba R3T 5V4
Canada
Telephone: 204-474-8448
          800-MBA-6296 (toll-free)
Fax: 204-474-7529
E-mail: mbamb@ms.umanitoba.ca

University of Maryland, College Park

College Park, Maryland

AN INCOMPARABLE EDUCATIONAL VALUE

▶

The Robert H. Smith School of Business has put together a unique combination of resources that will provide you with an incomparable educational value. As you learn about our program, you should glean three primary elements that allow us to provide you with a great experience: quality, reasonable cost, and location.

Our implementation of a cutting-edge curriculum and the use of state-of-the-art information technologies is the keystone to the quality education that we provide. The Robert H. Smith School of Business is about half the cost of other top thirty M.B.A. programs, and our program is in a prime location that is just 35 minutes from both Baltimore and Washington, D.C.

Please visit us to learn why the Maryland M.B.A. deserves its place among the top 4 percent of all M.B.A. programs in the United States.

—Mark Wellman, Assistant Dean

Programs and Curricular Focus

The Robert H. Smith School of Business has put together an exceptional combination of resources that provides students with an incomparable educational value. Some of the many strengths of the Robert H. Smith School of Business are the top-quality and cutting-edge master's programs, a location that is minutes from Washington, D.C., financial aid for international students, and an M.B.A. that costs about half the amount of other top M.B.A. programs. Accredited by AACSB–The International Association for Management Education and a full member of the Graduate Management Admission Council, the Robert H. Smith School of Business is a leader in the field of graduate management education.

The Master of Business Administration (M.B.A.) program has a fully integrated experience-based curriculum designed to create the type of graduate that business has long demanded. The first half of the curriculum is spent gaining the fundamental skills and judgment necessary to succeed in a contemporary management team. Learning Modules (LMs) and course work ensure that new skills are applied in and out of the classroom.

LMs are intensive, experience-based courses that focus on specific topics, such as interaction with the federal government in Washington, D.C.; an international business simulation; and an exploration of ethics in the business environment. These courses provide the student with experi-ence in areas often ignored by other American M.B.A. programs.

The second year allows the student to specialize in a particular area of business and to participate in a Group Field Project. Group Field Projects assign teams of students to work as consultants to an American organization for a semester. The teams address specific concerns within the organization and make recommendations regarding those concerns to the management staff of the client organization. This program is required of all second-year, full-time students.

The Master of Science (M.S.) program requires a strong quantitative background. There are several areas of concentration available: information systems, operations research, statistics, logistics, transportation, and finance. The M.S. program can be completed in two to five semesters, depending on previously completed course work.

The doctoral (Ph.D.) program is designed to develop outstanding research scholars and teachers in the management-related disciplines. Specializations include accounting, finance, human resource management and labor relations, information systems, management science and statistics, management strategy and policy, marketing, organizational behavior, and transportation and logistics.

Students and the M.B.A. Experience

The student population of the M.B.A. program consists of about 430 full-time M.B.A. students, 35 M.S. students, and 100 Ph.D. students. Of the 1997 incoming class, 34 percent were international students and about 40 percent were women.

Special Features

The Robert H. Smith School of Business maintains formal and informal exchange arrangements with graduate business programs in seven countries around the world. Students spend one semester of their second year at their exchange school.

The Faculty

There are 80 full-time faculty members assigned to M.B.A. programs, all of whom hold doctoral-level degrees. The following is a listing of chairpersons and their corresponding department areas of research.

Accounting: Dr. James Beddingfield, Chair.

Department research: Management accounting, accounting for regulated industries, government contract accounting, capital budgeting, decision support systems, financial accounting, accounting information systems, tax, auditing, accounting ethics.

Finance: Dr. Lemma W. Senbet, Chair.

Department research: Corporate finance, financial institutions, investments, futures and options contracts, investment analysis, portfolio management, capital asset pricing theory, international finance, portfolio analysis, capital market theory, commercial banking, financial theory, agency theory.

Decision and Information Technologies: Arjand Assad, Co-Chair; Dr. Michael Ball, Co-Chair.

Department research: End-user computing, information systems analysis and design, knowledge-based systems, production management systems, database systems, network analysis, information technology in the workplace, software design and development, statistical quality control, multivariate process control, time-series analysis, vehicle routing and scheduling, large-scale systems modeling, network optimization, electronic commerce, virtual organizations, applied mathematical programming, decision support systems.

Management and Organization: Dr. Susan Taylor, Chair.

Department research: Performance appraisal and compensation design, management by objectives systems, executive leadership, strategy implementation, labor relations, goal setting, employee motivation, organizational staffing, teamwork, organizational life cycles, competitive strategy.

Marketing: Dr. Richard Durand, Chair.

Department research: New product development, marketing strategy, international marketing, business-to-business marketing, consumer behavior, advertising.

Transportation, Business and Public Policy: Dr. Curtis Grimm, Chair.

Department research: Deregulation, international aviation, airline pricing and competition, carrier management, government policies toward business, international business regulation, global management strategies, international trade policies, international joint ventures, public utility pricing.

The College and Environs

The University of Maryland, College Park is the flagship institution of the University of Maryland System. The enrollment of approximately 34,000, of whom about 9,000 are graduate students, supports nearly 100 doctoral and master's programs. The University is a member of the prestigious fifty-eight-member Association of American Universities. The University of Maryland is further recognized as having more than a dozen

programs rated among the ten best at public universities in the United States by the National Academy of Sciences and other prestigious organizations.

Nine miles from the White House, the Robert H. Smith School of Business is located on a 1,300-acre campus. This location affords students the benefits of a suburban setting while maintaining the cultural and employment opportunities of Washington, D.C., and Baltimore. In fact, the concert halls, museums, art galleries, and restaurants are a short 15-minute subway ride away in Washington, D.C.

Facilities

Classified as a Research I facility by the Carnegie Foundation (its highest ranking), the research facilities at the University of Maryland are among the best in the world. With the addition of National Archives II, the main repository of information for the government of the United States of America, Maryland offers access to one of the world's most complete collections of research material right in College Park. The University proper offers an outstanding library collection of about 2 million volumes, state-of-the-art laboratories, a network of campus research centers, and excellent microcomputing and mainframe computing facilities. Beyond the facilities at College Park, students have access, within minutes, to other world-class research facilities at sites such as the Library of Congress, the Smithsonian Institution, the Federal Reserve, and the National Libraries of Medicine and Agriculture, to name a few.

Admission

Application to the M.B.A. program is open to individuals holding a four-year bachelor's degree or its equivalent from an accredited college or university. Submission of a GMAT score is required.

International students must submit a minimum score of 600 on the TOEFL, provide proof of adequate funds, and provide proof of immunizations.

Finances

Students are eligible for merit-based financial aid that is awarded as fellowships, which provide a waiver of all tuition plus a stipend for living expenses, and as graduate and teaching assistantships, which cover almost all tuition charges.

The low cost of the University of Maryland is a benefit to both domestic and international students. For the 1998–99 academic year, full-time tuition is $9558 for in-state students and $14,184 for out-of-state students.

Living expenses in the Washington, D.C., area are comparable to those of other metropolitan areas in the United States. Students live both on and off campus, and the average cost for room and board is about $10,000 per academic year.

Application Facts and Dates

The decision to admit an applicant is based on a thorough evaluation of the candidate's managerial and leadership potential, ability to add perspective to the class, and evidence of academic excellence. Admission to the M.B.A. program is for fall only. Applicants should make inquiries to:

Director of M.B.A./M.S. Admission
2308 Van Munching Hall
University of Maryland
College Park, Maryland 20742
Telephone: 301-405-2278
Fax: 301-314-9862
E-mail: mba_info@rhsmith.umd.edu
World Wide Web: http://www.rhsmith.umd.edu

The University of Memphis

Fogelman College of Business and Economics

Memphis, Tennessee

AN INVITATION TO LEARNING

The Fogelman College of Business and Economics offers outstanding graduate education and a range of choices to meet a broad spectrum of professional interests and career aspirations. Graduate programs benefit from instruction from high-quality and dedicated instructors and generous support from the business community in terms of scholarships, internships, and full- and part-time job opportunities.

Our International M.B.A. program combines graduate training in other languages, geographic area studies, and culture and leads to a semester-long business internship abroad. The program benefits from a thriving international business community and support from the Wang Center for International Business (one of only twenty-six centers nationwide with a prestigious CIBER grant). Our Executive M.B.A. program provides strategic-level decision making skills to corporate leaders in the region. I invite you to join our learning community here at The University of Memphis.

—Donna M. Randall, Dean

Programs and Curricular Focus

As one of the 5 percent of AACSB—The International Association for Management Education schools that have achieved all levels of accreditation, the Fogelman College of Business and Economics strives for excellence in every program. These include programs leading to the Master of Business Administration (M.B.A.), with concentrations in accounting, economics, finance, insurance and real estate, management, management information systems, management science, and marketing; the Master of Science (M.S.) in accounting; the Master of Science (M.S.) in business administration; and the Master of Arts (M.A.) in economics. A joint M.B.A./J.D. program is offered in conjunction with the School of Law. An Executive M.B.A. program meets over a twenty-two-month period and allows successful managers to obtain the M.B.A. degree without interrupting their careers. The Ph.D. in business administration is also offered with many different concentration areas.

The International M.B.A. program incorporates language, cultural, and geographic area studies with business instruction in a full-time twenty-two-month program. It offers rigorous, intensive, and challenging international business education and five language tracks (German, French, Spanish, Chinese, and English) for highly qualified students. The I.M.B.A. program features a semester-long, University-arranged internship in the country or region of the student's language track, personalized faculty involvement, and scholarships or assistantships for superior applicants.

Students and the M.B.A. Experience

The student body is international, highly competent, and talented. Students enjoy living in Memphis and bring a unique richness to the University that builds on tradition and history.

The average student has a mean undergraduate GPA of 3.2 and an average GMAT score of 530. The total number of master's students in the Fogelman College of Business and Economics is 700, and there are more than 100 students working toward the Ph.D. degree.

Special Features

The Robert Wang Center for International Business was established in 1988 through the support of Mr. Robert Wang, an alumnus of the University and president of Wang International. The activities of the Wang Center for International Business greatly enrich the learning environment of the I.M.B.A. program.

The Center for International Business Education and Research (CIBER), one of only twenty-six in the U.S., was established in 1990 when the University received a major grant from the U.S. Department of Education. The University received a renewal of the grant in 1993 and again in 1996. Housed in the Wang Center, CIBER provides national leadership on international business issues. The combined efforts of the centers support the innovative International M.B.A. program and the richness of its interdisciplinary and cross-cultural components.

The Faculty

The Fogelman College has more than 100 full-time faculty members, with more than 80 percent involved in graduate programs. The faculty members teaching at Fogelman College hold the highest possible degrees in their areas of expertise. They continuously generate and disseminate new knowledge about global management issues of today and tomorrow.

The Business School Network

Memphis is known nationally as "America's Distribution Center." It is also a primary medical, educational, communication, and transportation center. The University of Memphis enjoys close ties to these local and regional businesses. In addition, faculty members receive national and international recognition from the business and academic communities. Thus, students are able to utilize many resources, including those available to the University as one of only twenty-six CIBERs nationally.

Because of these factors, the University is able to organize excellent internship opportunities, especially for the International M.B.A. students, who intern in other countries such as Brazil, France, Germany, and Mexico. Additional connections with the business community of benefit to M.B.A. students include outstanding speakers from local and regional businesses who regularly address students, a Dean's Executive Advisory Council composed of 75 highly placed executives from the regional business community, and an active Executive in Residence program.

The College and Environs

The University of Memphis was founded in 1912 and has a student population of

20,000. Instruction is offered in six colleges and one school in more than 100 fields. Fogelman College of Business and Economics has an enrollment of about 3,000 students.

With a population of 1 million, Memphis is one of the South's largest and most attractive cities. As a primary medical, communication, and transportation center, Memphis offers a full range of research opportunities and cultural experiences. The city, known for its musical heritage, has many fine restaurants, museums, and theaters. Built on a bluff that towers over the Mississippi River, Memphis is devoted to preserving its heritage while it builds for the future.

Technology Environment

The Fogelman College of Business and Economics has contemporary business research facilities. Six computer laboratories are devoted to microcomputer instruction and research, and several classrooms have integrated video-computer facilities, enabling students and faculty members to develop state-of-the-art case presentations. The College is known for its information systems capability and its market research laboratory.

Placement

University Placement Services are provided to assist graduating students and alumni in locating career employment in business and industry, government, and service organizations. Students are encouraged to register with University Placement Services three semesters prior to graduation. Services that are offered include state-of-the-art computerized resume referral and job notification systems, on-campus interviews, job-seeking skill development programs, an employer information library, and comprehensive career fairs. In addition,

professional staff members are available by appointment to assist students with all aspects of their job search.

Admission

A bachelor's degree from an accredited college or university is required for admission to the M.B.A. program. Students should have an acceptable college GPA and must submit an adequate GMAT score for admission consideration. International students must have a minimum score of 550 on the Test of English as a Foreign Language (TOEFL), provide proof of adequate funds, and submit proof of immunizations. Up to 6 graduate credit hours from an AACSB-accredited program may be transferred.

Finances

The 1998–99 tuition for students who are Tennessee residents is $147 per credit hour; tuition for out-of-state students is $348 per credit hour. All students must pay an activities fee of $34 per semester. Estimated rates for residence halls on campus for 1998–99 range from $770 to $1435 per semester. The University has 126 apartments for student families on the south campus, with some units constructed specifically for handicapped students. Rates for these apartments range from $350 to $500 per month. Students are responsible for the cost of utilities. Numerous housing facilities are available off campus.

A number of graduate research and teaching assistantships are available each year. These assistantships, which provide a monthly stipend, are granted on the basis of GMAT scores, GPA, and personal interviews. Recipients of assistantships are granted in-state tuition status. A student must be fully admitted to the graduate program by mid-July to be considered for an assistantship. Other

sources of aid may be coordinated through the Office of Student Aid at the University.

International Students

All applicants who plan to attend The University of Memphis on a student visa must have achieved a minimum score of 550 on the TOEFL. Scores must be sent directly from the testing agency to The University of Memphis.

Application Facts and Dates

Applications may be obtained from the Office of Graduate Admissions or from the address below. Completed forms must be returned with a $5 nonrefundable application fee ($30 for international students). Application deadlines are August 1 for the fall semester, December 1 for the spring semester, and May 1 for the summer term (three months earlier for international students). The International M.B.A. and Executive M.B.A. programs accept students only for the fall semester, and applicants are encouraged to submit their materials in the preceding spring to ensure a place in the class. GMAT scores must be submitted for the M.B.A., M.S., and Ph.D. programs; GRE scores are acceptable for the M.A. program. All scores must be sent directly from the testing agency to The University of Memphis, Office of Graduate Admissions, 216 Administration Building, Memphis, Tennessee 38152. For further information on all graduate programs, applicants should write or call:

Graduate Programs Office
Fogelman College of Business and
  Economics
The University of Memphis
Memphis, Tennessee 38152
Telephone: 901-678-3721
Fax: 901-678-4705
E-mail: fcbegp@cc.memphis.edu

University of Miami

Coral Gables, Florida

> ### M.B.A. PROGRAMS AT THE UNIVERSITY OF MIAMI
>
> *The School of Business Administration is rapidly becoming a premier school for business education. Should you enroll as a student, you can look forward to classmates from all over the world whose diverse backgrounds and perspectives will enhance your learning. Your classes will be taught by our renowned faculty members, leading educators, and consultants to major corporations. Job placement is a priority at the University of Miami (UM). Our modern placement center provides personalized career development, on-campus interviews, career fairs, and forums. Join us . . . the business ideas and skills you'll acquire at UM will benefit you for a lifetime.*
>
> —Dr. Paul K. Sugrue, Dean

Programs and Curricular Focus

The School of Business Administration's M.B.A. program is accredited by AACSB–The International Association for Management Education. Meeting these accreditation standards is a measure of a school's excellence. The School has the distinction of having complete accreditation for its baccalaureate, master's, and accounting programs.

There are two program tracks offered. Track I is a one-year M.B.A. program for business undergraduates who have earned their degree within the past five years from a school accredited by AASCB–The International Association for Management Education. This track contains 36 credits, 24 of which are electives. Track II is a two-year track offered for all other students that includes 61 credits, 24 of which are also electives. The duration of the two-year program may be reduced to nineteen months by attending summer classes. Some required courses may be waived, depending on the individual's undergraduate background. Full-time students can choose to take three, four, or five courses per semester, all during the day or a mix of day and evening classes.

The curriculum is flexible and customizable. Students may choose from twenty-six specializations: applied statistics, computer information systems, controllership, corporate finance, economics, finance, financial markets and banking, human resource management, international business, international finance, investments, leadership, legal implications, logistics, management, management information systems, management science, management science applications, marketing, operations research, personal financial planning, political science, professional accounting, quality management, taxation, and telecommunications.

Students and the M.B.A. Experience

Located in a major hub of international trade and commerce, the School of Business Administration has been acclaimed for the global orientation and diversity of its faculty, student body, and curriculum. A third of the students are international, and more than a third are women. Approximately half of the students' undergraduate majors are from areas other than business. As of the fall 1997 semester, there were approximately 550 students enrolled in the regular, full-time M.B.A. program. Entering students average 25 years of age, with three years of work experience.

Special Features

The School of Business Administration offers several programs. The J.D./M.B.A. degrees can be earned in a full-time three-year program. The MIBS program earns the student an M.B.A. and a certificate in international business. This is a two-year program that features additional language training in French, German, Portuguese, or Spanish and a four-month, University-arranged, paid corporate internship. Typically, students whose second language is English intern with a company in the United States; students whose first language is English are generally placed overseas in the country where their second language is spoken. Prior work experience is necessary. A second master's degree in computer information systems, management science, or taxation may be earned with as few as 15 credits beyond the M.B.A. degree.

There is an active graduate business student association (GBSA) that organizes social and professional activities. Executives representing south Florida businesses act as guest speakers. Social events include beach parties, barbecues, and football tailgate parties. The Mentor Program provides personal interaction with experienced professionals.

The Faculty

Dean Paul Sugrue states, "Fine teaching is a necessary condition for the success of a faculty member at the School of Business Administration. It is proven by the ability to create and disseminate meaningful knowledge about the practice of business." Faculty members at the University of Miami's School of Business Administration are characterized by their strong commitment to the students. Their courses offer a blend of case studies and theory and emphasize practical application to the modern business world. They are recognized experts in their fields. All full-time, tenured faculty members hold a doctorate or the highest degree in their fields.

The Business School Network

Corporate Partnerships

The School of Business Administration maintains close ties to the Florida and international business communities. Miami is strategically located as a gateway between the United States, Latin America, and the Caribbean. Miami has emerged as a critical node in the global business network, and the strong feeling of excitement and growth in this area add significant value to the learning experience. Corporate affiliate–sponsored events are open to all graduate students. Students use these opportunities to meet and visit with top corporate executives in small-group and seminar settings. Through an annual membership commitment, participating corporations provide valuable support to the School.

The Mentor Program pairs University of Miami alumni and other professionals with graduate business students. These mentors are willing to assist with the personal and professional development of the M.B.A. students. Mentors serve as advisers, supporters, sponsors, tutors, and coaches. These relationships provide a link between academic theories and the realities of the business world. The program bolsters the students' sense of confidence by increasing their knowledge of the careers they are about to enter. It also creates a feeling of greater involvement with the community and provides students with a benchmark to strive for and, eventually, attain.

The College and Environs

Founded in 1925, the University of Miami is a private, independent, international research university. The first Master of Business Administration degree was offered in 1948. The University of Miami's School of Business Administration offers state-of-the-art facilities located on a lushly landscaped, 260-acre campus in Coral Gables, Florida, minutes from metropolitan Miami.

There are more than 13,650 degree-seeking students in approximately 110 undergraduate, ninety-five master's, fifty-five doctoral, and two professional areas of study. There are currently 1,856 full-time faculty members, whose ranks include Guggenheim Fellows, Fulbright Scholars, and National Science Foundation award recipients. Of this distinguished faculty, 96 percent hold doctorates or the highest degree in their fields.

Technology Environment

Computer facilities are located both in the School of Business Administration complex and at the University's Ungar Computer Center. The Ungar Computer Center houses a DEC VAX cluster with two VAX 4000-600 systems and an IBM 9672-R42. In addition, the information resources department supports all data communications network requirements, including dial-up access facilities and an instructional support facility with three computer laboratories that house twenty-two terminals, thirty-six personal computers, and eleven Macintosh computers. IBM-compatible and Macintosh computers can also be found in many other academic buildings as well as in the residential colleges.

The combined University libraries, which can accommodate special research requests from students, contain more than 2.1 million volumes, 20,353 serial subscriptions, and 3.1 million microforms. More than 18,250 current periodical and serial publications are received. The Otto B. Richter Library is the heart of the library system and is also a Federal Government Documents Depository.

Placement

The Sanford L. Ziff Placement Center is dedicated to assisting students realize their career goals. After all, the most important reason to earn a graduate business degree is to prepare for a future in business. Offering a variety of services, from career counseling to resume preparation, the professional staff at the Ziff placement center assists and actively promotes graduate business students exclusively. During the 1997–98 academic year, the placement center arranged 104 corporate visits that yielded 1,040 interviews. The average starting salary for graduates was $47,800, with a high of $70,000.

Admission

The Graduate Admissions Committee welcomes applications from individuals whose undergraduate degrees are from accredited colleges or universities. Attendance at orientation prior to the beginning of the student's first term is mandatory. Students are admitted for programs starting in August and January.

A completed application file contains an application form, a nonrefundable $35 application fee, GMAT scores (less than five years old), and academic credentials, including an official transcript from each college or university attended (including summer school, part-time study, or postgraduate work—even for only one course). An additional final transcript showing the degree conferred and date of graduation should be sent after completion of any course work still in progress at the time of admission. Work experience is not required for admission. Recommendations are optional. Applicants from foreign institutions should provide statements by the officials of the institutions attended indicating the courses taken, grades earned, and classification of degree. If not in English, foreign credentials must be accompanied by certified translations. International applicants whose native language is not English and/or who did not earn an undergraduate degree from an English-speaking institution must submit a TOEFL

score with their application. The TOEFL should have been taken within two years prior to application for admission; a minimum score of 550 is required.

Finances

Tuition for 1998–99 is $815 per credit hour. Living expenses are estimated at $10,600. There are a limited number of merit-based graduate assistantships. Typically, a graduate assistantship is for 60 percent to 75 percent of the student's tuition and includes a stipend of $1500 per semester. The student is assigned to a particular department and is expected to carry at least 12 credit hours and work 15 hours per week on assigned research or special projects. Early application is recommended for those requesting a graduate assistantship.

Students applying for need-based assistance must submit the Free Application for Federal Student Aid (FAFSA). Federal Perkins Loans, Federal Stafford Student Loans, and the Federal Work-Study Program are based upon the financial need of applicants and the availability of funds. Federal Stafford loans are available to students enrolled in 5 or more credit hours. The Unsubsidized Stafford Loan is a non-need-based federal loan program. The FAFSA must be completed and submitted to the processors by students requesting this loan, even if no need is demonstrated.

Application Facts and Dates

Decisions for admission are made on a rolling admission basis until the programs are closed. Because applications received early are evaluated first, applicants are urged to file a complete application as soon as possible. Applications should be received at least two months prior to the beginning of classes to provide sufficient time for processing. For questions regarding admission requirements or the status of an application, students should contact:

Graduate Business Programs
School of Business Administration
University of Miami
221 Jenkins Building
P.O. Box 248505
Coral Gables, Florida 33124-6524
Telephone: 305-284-4607
          800-531-7137 (toll-free,
          U.S. only)
Fax: 305-284-1878
E-mail: gba@sba.miami.edu
World Wide Web: http://www.bus.
    miami.edu/grad

University of Michigan–Flint

Flint, Michigan

THE CHALLENGE OF THE UNIVERSITY OF MICHIGAN–FLINT M.B.A.

Accepting the challenge of the University of Michigan–Flint (UM–Flint) is an important decision. We seek bright, energetic men and women eager to accept the challenge of a modern program that encourages participants—students and faculty members—to think in new and creative ways. The UM–Flint M.B.A. challenges you to be an active learner. You will work and learn with diverse, highly qualified student and faculty colleagues who bring rich talents, backgrounds, and professional experiences to the program. The program will enhance your current knowledge and experience and provide many of the tools you will need for leadership positions. You will broaden your perspectives so you can approach problems not only from multiple function viewpoints, but from global and ethical perspectives as well.

I invite you to accept the challenge of our M.B.A. program. I am confident you will find it one of the most exciting and rewarding professional experiences of your life.

—Fred E. Williams, Dean

Programs and Curricular Focus

The University of Michigan–Flint School of Management is an upper-division professional school offering programs leading to the Master of Business Administration (M.B.A.) degree. The M.B.A. program (accredited by AACSB–The International Association for Management Education) is designed for those individuals who have distinguished themselves in their previous college studies, show a high aptitude for management studies, and have, or soon may have, responsible positions in management.

The program is designed as a part-time 48-credit program that takes three years (thirty-three months) to complete. Classes meet in the evening, with students taking two courses in each fall and winter semester and one course in the spring session. The program is atypical of evening offerings, in that an entering group will stay together throughout. Students can profit not only from close relationships with faculty members, but also from extended associations with other students. The M.B.A. program is designed to educate individuals to think effectively about solutions for management problems. Its emphasis is on learning and applying the principles of problem solving, which leads to effective decision making. Accounting, organization, and management studies highlight

the first year, with analysis, economics, and management studies hallmarks of the second year. Finance, management, and a focus elective are major components of the third year. Students can select additional course work in fields such as finance, operations, management, and marketing and can reduce their course load to one class a semester or temporarily withdraw. UM–Flint requires that M.B.A. candidates complete degree requirements within seven years of the date of their first course. Accommodations may be made if job requirements affect class attendance.

Students and the M.B.A. Experience

More than 250 of UM–Flint's 6,444 students are presently in the M.B.A. program. The average graduate student is 29.5 years of age. Twenty-nine percent are women, and 11 percent are members of minority groups. The fall 1997 mean GPA was 3.1, and the mean GMAT was 530. Of those applying, 90 percent were accepted. Students in the program represent a variety of about twenty-five undergraduate degrees, including zoology, engineering, political science, and education. The average student has six years work experience. The program prides itself on flexibility, its policy of keeping an entering group together, and promotion of close communication among students and faculty members.

Special Features

Entering students are part of a group called a cohort, which allows each student to quickly develop a strong professional network for personal and professional development that lasts beyond their time in the M.B.A. program. It also offers classes via UM–Flint's Lansing program, at Lansing Catholic High School, for students who find that location more convenient. Classes are usually small, averaging 25

to 40 students, making the program's goal of close group support possible.

The Faculty

The 17 members of the School of Management's M.B.A. faculty are a diverse group who all hold doctoral degrees. Fields of specialization include marketing, accounting, quantitative methods, management, finance, and industrial/organizational psychology.

The Business School Network

The School of Management maintains close ties with many Michigan corporations. As part of its outreach program, the University has a Business Development Center that offers technical assistance, business plan assistance, and an Enterprise Community Database. There are also community development and service learning programs. Students are able to take advantage of the University of Michigan's ProNet program, a database that matches skills and availability of graduating students with corporations looking to fill positions.

The College and Environs

The UM–Flint campus is located on a 70-acre riverfront campus in an urban setting on the south bank of the Flint River. The campus, with skywalks connecting most major buildings, is a pleasing, comfortable environment that encourages academic success. There are major open spaces, including Wilson Park on the south edge. The Harding Mott University Center houses student activity offices, Clint's Cafe, and many areas in which students can study or relax. The University Pavilion is the focal point for food services and student services. The Recreation Center features a variety of physical fitness areas and an indoor pool, whirlpool, and sauna. UM-Flint also operates WFUM-TV and WFUM-FM in the Mott Memorial Building. Flint's business district is adjacent to the campus, making students' access to the downtown area, Flint's College and Cultural Center, Mott Community College, Sloan Museum, the Flint Public Library, and additional city attractions easy.

Facilities

The Classroom Office Building is the setting for many general-purpose classrooms and faculty offices and is connected to the theater. An Adult Resource and Women's Center is maintained in the University Pavilion.

Students have full use of the Frances Wilson Thompson Library, which opened in 1994. Funded by donations from the Thompson family and others, it holds 147,000 volumes, 111,000 government documents, and 21,000 periodicals. CD-ROM players and a microfilm collection in excess of 500,000 items are also maintained. It also contains several special collections, including the Genesee County Historical Collection, and the Henry H. Crapo Room and the Coleman J. and Lois R. Ross Learning Resource Center.

Technology Environment

Microcomputer labs for students are located in both the Classroom Office Building and William R. Murchie Science Building. The labs and classrooms contain 140 computers with differing types of display and memory. Local area networks (LANs) provide additional storage. UNIX machines provide e-mail and other computerized services. Campus users can connect to the Internet through the MichNet Computer System.

Placement

UM–Flint's Cooperative Education and Career Center has a wide array of programs for career exploration. The career advising staff provides up-to-date information on employment trends and salary statistics and offers vocational testing, resume preparation, and individual career counseling. Equally important to the school's M.B.A. program is the Adult Resource and Women's Center, which supports the older students returning to college after several years with help in course planning, financial aid, child care, study skills, career planning, and test-taking skills.

Admission

Suitability for a candidate for the M.B.A. program is based on a review of job experience, prior educational background, scores on the Graduate Management Admission Test (GMAT), and letters of recommendation. One year of college mathematics, including college algebra and either finite math or calculus, is required as are three letters of recommendation, one academic and two from employers. Applicants must have a bachelor's degree from an accredited college or university and submit a resume showing job history.

Finances

Tuition for the 1997–98 year, following the thirty-three-month program, was $1983.75 for 6 credit hours, which included a registration fee ($43.50), an activity fee ($10), and technical fee ($10.75). The first credit hour was $357 and each additional credit hour was $312.50. Financial aid is available in the form of grants and scholarships as well as various loans. The School is committed to not allowing the cost of a college education to stand between a student and a degree. Students should contact the Financial Aid Office (810-762-3444) for information on how it might be able to fill their needs.

Application Facts and Dates

Deadline for winter admission is November 1; for fall admission, July 1. Applications for both winter and fall admission are accepted for the Flint program, while only winter admission is available for the Lansing program. Applications received after the deadlines will be reviewed if class space is available. For more information, students should contact:

Janet McIntire
Interim Program Coordinator
M.B.A. Program
School of Management
Flint, Michigan 48502-2186
Telephone: 810-762-3163
Fax: 810-762-3282
E-mail: jmcintir@flint.umich.edu

University of Mississippi

Oxford, Mississippi

BUSINESS AT THE NEXT LEVEL

Since 1946, when the first M.B.A. degree was awarded at the University of Mississippi, the M.B.A. Program has held a reputation for producing capable and qualified graduates. The program is known for its emphasis on practical knowledge and real-world experience while maintaining a high level of academic rigor. These traditional strengths now form the foundation for an entirely new M.B.A. program designed to give students the competitive edge in the global, cross-functional, and technologically intensive environment that will dominate the business world in the twenty-first century. Consider joining this exciting new program so that you can experience what is proudly referred to as "Business at the Next Level."

—W. Randy Boxx, Dean

Programs and Curricular Focus

The M.B.A. curriculum is designed to develop effective cross-functional decision-making skills in an environment that emphasizes practical applications and real-world experience.

The first year begins in July with an intensive orientation session that precedes the beginning of the fall semester. In this session, students develop essential skills in statistics, finance, computer usage, and communications. Students move through the fall and spring semesters as a cohort. Skills courses in both semesters develop advanced capabilities in math, statistics, communication, and computer applications. Three cross-functional courses are also taken in the fall semester: Mobilizing Technology in the Modern Business, the Business Environment, and Business Decision Making. Business Decision Making, which emphasizes the development of practical solutions to real business problems using cases and team projects, is continued in the spring semester. Two other core courses, Managing Operations Through the Life Cycle and the M.B.A. Project Course, are also taken in the spring.

Attendance in the second summer session is optional. Students who do attend take courses in their area of specialization and may be able to complete the program in December. Others complete the program in May. In the fall semester of the second year, all students take an integrative capstone course and courses in their area of specialization. Students who did not attend the summer session take specialization courses in the spring semester.

Students and the M.B.A. Experience

A diverse student body from all regions of the country, as well as many other countries, is an important resource of the program. Students with nonbusiness undergraduate degrees find the program to be well suited to their needs. The curriculum focuses on developing the analytical skills and breadth of judgment that are essential elements of effective decision making in any organization. A thorough understanding of the functional areas of business is built from the required courses. In addition, the program allows the flexibility to specialize in an area that serves the individual needs of the student. Instructional methods include lectures, cases, team projects, and group presentations. Some courses are team taught and most are cross-functional and highly integrative. The effective use of computer and information technology is emphasized throughout the program.

The Faculty

M.B.A. students benefit from close and personal contact with faculty members who come from leading universities across the nation and who have extensive research and consulting records. Many have several years of management experience as well. A number of the faculty members have international reputations in areas that define the cutting edge of business education and practice,

such as economics, finance, management, marketing, MIS, and international business. These excellent teachers and researchers bring a wealth of academic and business experience into their classes, and they are accessible to and genuinely interested in all of their students.

The Business School Network

The School of Business Administration benefits in enormous measure from the loyalty and generosity of the Business Alumni Chapter and the Business Advisory Council. Both groups serve the School and its students by providing employment and internship opportunities, personal referrals and contacts, and opportunities for class projects. The Hearin Distinguished Lecture Series, the Otho Smith Fellows Program, and the Sam and Mary Carter Lecture Series bring prominent business leaders and scholars to campus on a regular basis to serve as guest lecturers in classes and to lead discussion forums with students. Business leaders from the local region are also frequent participants in classes, projects, and site visits.

The College and Environs

The University of Mississippi (Ole Miss) was founded in 1848 and its School of Business Administration opened its doors in 1917. The first Master of Business Administration (M.B.A.) degree was awarded in 1946. The M.B.A. program is AACSB-accredited. Commonly ranked as one of the best places to live in the United States, Oxford is famous as the home of William Faulkner and, more recently, John Grisham. Nestled in the hills and forests of northern Mississippi, the University of Mississippi offers unsurpassed natural beauty and small-town Southern charm.

Facilities

The entirely new Business/Accountancy Building Complex, completed in the summer of 1998, defines a new level of business education, bringing students and faculty members together in an environment that is designed to promote efficient learning and personal interaction. It

1102

The new Business/Accountancy Building Complex features a student-oriented design and outstanding instructional facilities. Construction, completed in the summer of 1998, provides one of the most technologically advanced learning environments in the country.

incorporates the most advanced instructional technology available, including multimedia presentation facilities, distance learning classrooms, videoconferencing capabilities, and computer classrooms and labs. Other campus facilities, including the recently expanded library, offer students one of the best learning and living environments anywhere.

Technology Environment

The School of Business Administration has been on the cutting edge of information and instructional technology usage for many years. The new building complex described above contains more than 2,000 network connections, allowing students to attach to the LAN from anywhere in the building to communicate with faculty members and classmates, access online resources, and receive or submit assignments.

Placement

An aggressive and expanding program of placement and career services provides students with an extensive schedule of employment interviews throughout the academic year. Career planning seminars, resume workshops, mock interviews, and other services give students valuable experience in job search techniques. The use of online resources is encouraged. Semiannual career fairs attract many companies to campus. Professors actively cultivate career opportunities with

potential employers and help students develop career plans and objectives. The Business Advisory Council, composed of more than 50 top-level executives from prominent companies, serves as an important resource for internships, career opportunities, and personal contacts.

Admission

Admission is competitive and cohort size is limited. Applicants are evaluated based on their academic qualifications, GMAT score, work experience, and other personal attributes. Minimum requirements for admission in full standing include completion of an undergraduate program in an accredited U.S. college or its international equivalent with at least a 3.0 GPA on the last 60 semester hours of academic course work, an acceptable GMAT score, and two letters of recommendation. A TOEFL score of at least 600 is required for international applicants whose native language is not English. Work experience is helpful but not required. All students must have completed at least one semester of economics, statistics, and calculus prior to beginning the program. Familiarity with personal computers and standard business software applications is assumed, and all students are required to have a laptop computer. Admission may not be deferred. All students must begin the program in July.

Finances

The 1998–99 tuition is $1527 per semester for Mississippi residents and

$3078 per semester for nonresidents. International students pay additional fees for insurance and other services. On-campus housing is approximately $930 per semester. Meal plans are available at additional cost. All costs vary over time. Off-campus housing is plentiful and reasonably priced. The John N. Palmer Assistantship and Fellowship Program provides financial aid and practical experience to students who have excelled in their undergraduate programs and who possess the academic and leadership skills to become successful business executives or entrepreneurs. Palmer Assistantships and Fellowships provide $1500 to $2000 per semester and a waiver of tuition charges.

Application Facts and Dates

The application deadline is April 15. However, application evaluations and admission decisions begin in February. Applications are considered in the order in which they are received complete with all required materials. For additional information, students should contact:

M.B.A. Program Director
School of Business Administration
253 Holman Hall
The University of Mississippi
University, Mississippi 38677
Telephone: 601-232-5820
Fax: 601-232-5821
E-mail: mbainfo@bus.olemiss.edu
World Wide Web: http://www.bus.
    olemiss.edu

University of Missouri–Columbia

Columbia, Missouri

THE MISSOURI M.B.A.—DESIGNED TO MEET YOUR GOALS

Besides being challenging and contemporary, the Missouri M.B.A. program is flexible and friendly, with small class sizes and individualized attention from faculty and staff members. Our format allows you the flexibility to join the program at a time that better fits your schedule and the freedom to tailor your program of study to satisfy your personal interests and career goals. Missouri M.B.A. candidates are top caliber. Our admission standards are high and the curriculum is rigorous; you'll graduate with the knowledge, skills, and values necessary for success in the business world. Our M.B.A. program, with classes taught by the College's award-winning faculty, will provide the foundation you need to realize your professional goals.

—Bruce J. Walker, Dean

Programs and Curricular Focus

Flexibility and individuality are the hallmark of the M.B.A. program at the University of Missouri (MU). The MU M.B.A. provides graduate professional management education to students from diverse backgrounds while allowing them to prepare for specific career paths. A student may enter the program at three times during the year. Foundation courses provide training in basic business functions; however, they may be waived for students having equivalent prior course work. Students may concentrate electives in the business areas of finance, marketing, and management, or they may individualize their programs with outside course work in areas as diverse as law, engineering, journalism, public relations, health-services management, sports administration, or computer science. To complement the foundation and electives, the Missouri M.B.A. offers skill-enhancing experiences in communication, leadership, and teamwork. A professional perspective is infused through small group meetings with executives, summer internships, real-world case experiences, and professional development seminars designed specifically for M.B.A. students.

The Missouri M.B.A. program permits broad flexibility in the second year, enabling students to tailor programs of study to meet their specific needs and interests. Students complete a minimum of 33 and a maximum of 55 semester hours, assuming completion of prerequisite course work in business calculus, basic and intermediate statistics, and microeconomic theory, which must be

accomplished prior to or concurrent with entering the program. A typical program is 46 semester hours. Joint-degree programs are also available for students wishing to pursue an M.B.A. degree simultaneously with a J.D., Master of Health Administration, or Master of Science in Industrial Engineering degree.

Students and the M.B.A. Experience

Admission to the Missouri M.B.A. program is selective; students admitted to the program are committed to and capable of academic and professional success. The program is kept relatively small, enrolling between 80 and 120 students a year. MU's M.B.A. students typically represent more than sixty colleges in twenty states and fifteen countries; they hold undergraduate degrees in more than thirty different disciplines. Managerial experience is not a prerequisite for admission.

❖ Global Focus

Students can study abroad through MU's formal relationships with various foreign universities and selected exchange programs. Currently, MU's Business and Public Administration (B&PA) faculty members are assisting in the development of a Business Management Program at the University of Sibiu in Romania. Through this program, several MU M.B.A. students have had the opportunity to visit Romania to work as interns. MU M.B.A. students who are interested in international business can attend summer

class in Asolo, Italy, as part of an International Business Studies Consortium. B&PA recently offered its M.B.A. program at Nanjing University in the People's Republic of China and cooperates in several M.B.A. exchanges. The MU M.B.A. network of alumni stretches to nations all around the globe.

Special Features

Beginning with the orientation, students have the opportunity to know their instructors and actively participate in and out of class. They might attend a reception at the home of a faculty member, have lunch with a visiting executive, help design a business plan for a small local business, or intern with a large company or maybe a start-up firm. Students gain real-world experience in team case project and consulting case courses, which require consultation with a local or regional business. By becoming a member of the student-led M.B.A. Association, a student has frequent social opportunities. MU M.B.A. students participate in an MBA's Make a Difference service project and frequently socialize with fellow M.B.A. students after an executive presentation. These opportunities promote personal involvement in the M.B.A. program and provide a personal touch difficult to find in larger, lock-step programs.

The Faculty

Effective teaching is a priority among B&PA faculty members, many of whom have won national and campus awards in recognition of their teaching. Innovative classroom techniques, computer technology, and effective class materials strengthen the learning process. In addition to the high quality of its classroom instruction, the College's faculty, which includes a large number of young, doctorally qualified instructors along with well-known senior professors, is recognized for its research productivity.

The Business School Network

Corporate Partnerships

Interaction between business leaders and M.B.A. students is facilitated through the

College's Executive-in-Residence, Professor-for-a-Day, and M.B.A. seminar programs. Held each year, M.B.A. Consulting Week invites business leaders to offer special seminars and presentations centered around a selected theme.

Prominent Alumni
The College's more than 21,000 alumni contribute their expertise to organizations in every state and a multitude of other countries. *Business Week* magazine ranked MU as the number-one producer of corporate CEOs in both the state of Missouri and the Midwest, while *Fortune* ranked MU in the top fifteen nationally. The College has six advisory boards that bring CEOs, CFOs, and other top officials from Fortune 500 companies back to 'Mizzou' for regular visits and support.

The College and Environs
MU is the oldest state university west of the Mississippi River and the largest of the four campuses of the University of Missouri System. The University, which enrolls more than 22,500 students, offers many cultural and sports events. Columbia is a warm, friendly, cosmopolitan, and safe college community with a population in excess of 75,000. Columbia's growing economy and low unemployment rate offer job opportunities for student family members. The community includes a large number private apartment complexes oriented to both students and professionals conveniently located near MU. Sidewalk restaurants, pubs, coffeehouses, and the quaint downtown shopping district are within three blocks of MU and help make the community a very pleasant place to live.

Facilities
Ellis Library houses more than 1.5 million volumes, 4.8 million microforms, and nearly 18,000 serial titles. Friendly, professional staff are available to answer questions, help solve research problems, and support numerous on-line and CD-ROM databases. MU has excellent recreational facilities as well as residence

halls for men and women students. Over 300 unfurnished University apartments are available for married student families and single graduate students.

Technology Environment
Middlebush Hall, which houses B&PA, contains a computer lab and classroom with a help desk staffed by user consultants. Networked PCs in Middlebush classrooms and computer labs provide access to the mainframe and the Internet as well as to a variety of up-to-date business software. On-line database access available to students includes the BRIDGE System for real-time stock market data, LEXIS/NEXIS, Dow Jones News/Retrieval Service, ABI/Inform, Compact Disclosure SEC and Worldscope, Extell, and Compustat PC+. The B&PA Research Center also provides computer support services, including COMPUSTAT, Census, CRSP, FDIC, and Citibank files.

Placement
The College's Career Services office brings more than 180 recruiting firms to campus each year. Recent graduates have accepted employment throughout the United States, with annual starting salaries ranging from $32,000 to $65,000. Internships allow many students the opportunity to preview positions and companies prior to accepting employment offers. The Career Services office also sponsors a career fair each fall, coordinates and schedules on-campus interviews, maintains a job listing service for employers, and holds career development workshops and seminars.

Admission
Admission depends primarily upon the quality of the undergraduate work and the score received on the Graduate Management Admission Test (GMAT). The average entering grade point average is 3.3, and the average GMAT score ranges between 585 and 600. The Test of English as a Foreign Language (TOEFL) is required of applicants whose native

language is other than English and who do not have a degree from an institution in the United States.

Finances
Missouri residents and out-of-state graduate students enrolled are required to pay educational fees of $162.60 and $489.10 per credit hour, respectively. Other miscellaneous fees of approximately $300 per semester are also assessed. Fees are subject to change without notice. M.B.A. assistantships are widely available to academically qualified students. These assistantships typically involve 10 hours of work per week at a rate of $1924 per semester and may be accompanied by a complete or partial waiver of tuition fees. Scholarships that may waive out-of-state tuition charges are also available to students with outstanding academic credentials. Scholarships, grants, and loans are also available through the MU Financial Aid Office. International students enrolled at MU can apply for a Curator's Grant-in-Aid that allows them to remit educational fees at the in-state rate.

Application Facts and Dates
Students may enter the M.B.A. program in the fall semester (August), winter semester (January), or summer session (June). Application deadlines are August 1, December 1, and May 1, respectively. Exceptions to deadlines are possible if GMAT scores and transcripts are available. For more information, applicants should contact:

Ms. Barbara Schneider
Senior Academic Advisor
Graduate Studies in Business
College of Business and Public
  Administration
303D Middlebush Hall
University of Missouri
Columbia, Missouri 65211
Telephone: 573-882-2750
Fax: 573-882-0365
E-mail: grad@bpa.missouri.edu
World Wide Web: http://tiger.bpa.
  missouri.edu

University of Navarra

IESE M.B.A. Program

Barcelona, Spain

IESE—A UNIQUE CENTER OF HIGHER EDUCATION

IESE is an international graduate school of management with a professional approach to management education, a humanistic view, and a true university character. IESE concentrates its research and teaching activities in the field of general management. The school is not theory oriented but directed toward the needs of the practicing professional, providing students the opportunity to acquire the most advanced knowledge and to develop the necessary skills and attitudes vital to today's top-level executives. IESE believes management is essentially a "people affair." Decision making takes place with people and through people. Accordingly, our faculty emphasizes the human and ethical connotations of any business decision.

—Professor Carlos Cavallé, Dean

Program and Curricular Focus

The bilingual M.B.A. program is designed to develop the knowledge and decision-making ability of a select group of university graduates aspiring to key positions in management. IESE considers the practical focus fundamental. The extensive use of the case method, backed up by lectures, discussions, presentations, group projects, and simulation exercises, provides a well-rounded educational experience.

The twenty-one-month program differentiates itself by the extent to which it is complete, thorough, and rigorous. The first year of the program is complete in that it dedicates nine months to fifteen required courses that cover the five areas of business administration: accounting, finance, marketing, organizational behavior, and production. The second year of the program is thorough in that an additional nine months are dedicated to one core course and fourteen elective courses that allow the students time for in-depth study of areas of particular interest. The entire program is rigorous in that a high standard of both objective and subjective criteria creates a demanding and challenging academic environment.

The ten- to twelve-week Corporate Internship between the first and second years of the program is a distinguishing characteristic of the IESE experience. IESE is one of the few schools that requires participation in such a program, offering students an ideal opportunity to apply their newly acquired skills and knowledge to a real business experience. Companies from around the world hire interns to solve specific problems or complete special projects.

Students and the M.B.A. Experience

In today's global economy, managers increasingly find themselves working in a multicultural environment. IESE helps students to meet this challenge with its emphasis on teamwork with participants from a wide range of academic and professional backgrounds who represent a large number of countries. A cooperative spirit of team effort and friendship is fomented through daily meetings and group projects and reports.

❖ Global Focus

The international character of IESE and, specifically, the bilingual M.B.A. program is clearly demonstrated by all facets of the school's activities, the content of the programs, and the diversity of its participants. The International Exchange Program is an excellent opportunity for M.B.A. students to spend a term at one of the top universities in North America, Asia, or Latin America. In addition, IESE places particular value on the diversity of nationalities represented in its student body, with more than half of the class coming from outside Spain.

Special Features

In 1980 IESE became the first school in the world to offer a bilingual M.B.A. program. The unique structure of the program allows students to completely immerse themselves in what may be a completely new culture. During the first year, classes may be taken entirely in English. Included in the tuition and fees is the monthlong Intensive Spanish Course, which is taken before M.B.A. studies begin. Daily life in Spain combined with formal language training enable students to gain a working knowledge of Spanish by the end of the M.B.A. program.

The Faculty

IESE's 109 faculty members bring an array of academic and professional backgrounds to the classroom. Professors maintain an active presence in the world

of management through consulting projects, research, and the creation of teaching materials. IESE's faculty members publish the second-largest number of cases in the world after the Harvard Business School and the largest number in the Spanish language.

The Business School Network

Corporate Partnerships

IESE's International Advisory Board is composed of chairmen and presidents of some of the world's most important multinational companies, including KLM, Repsol, Siemens, Pomodès, Nissan Motor Co. Ltd., La Caixa, and Henkel. Its objective is to advise IESE's Board of Governors on the state of the international economy and developments in management.

The College and Environs

IESE's campus is located in Barcelona, the capital of Catalonia, an autonomous region in northeastern Spain that currently has the nation's strongest economy. Its rich history, art, and fascinating architecture and a vigorous, multifaceted cultural life make Barcelona a rewarding and exciting place to be.

IESE's compact and attractive campus is located in Pedralbes, a primarily residential area of Barcelona overlooking the center of the city and within easy walking distance of public transportation.

Placement

IESE's Career Management Center has been very successful over the years in identifying employment opportunities for graduates of the bilingual M.B.A. program. More than 75 percent of the students find their first job after graduation through IESE's efforts. The center provides services such as career advisement, interview training, and on-campus recruitment.

Admission

Applicants should hold the minimum of a bachelor's degree. Other requirements include the Graduate Management Admission Test (GMAT), the Test of English as a Foreign Language (TOEFL) for those applicants for whom English is not their native language, the IESE application form, original university transcripts, and two letters of recommendation. The Admissions Committee evaluates each applicant based on personal qualities, academic background, and personal experience.

Finances

The tuition fee for the academic year 1998–99 is 2,300,000 pesetas per year. Charges for the monthlong Intensive Spanish Course, health insurance, and virtually all course materials are included in this fee.

Application Facts and Dates

Applications should be submitted before April 30 for the M.B.A. program beginning the following fall. Applications are evaluated in the order in which they are received. Therefore, applicants are encouraged to apply as early as possible. For more information, students should contact:

IESE International Graduate School of Management
University of Navarra
M.B.A. Admissions Department
Avenida Pearson, 21
08034 Barcelona
Spain
Telephone: 34-93-253-4229
Fax: 34-93-253-4343
E-mail: mbainfo@iese.edu
World Wide Web: http://www.iese.edu

UNLV University of Nevada, Las Vegas

College of Business

Las Vegas, Nevada

EDUCATION FOR LIFE'S CAREER

At the University of Nevada, Las Vegas (UNLV), we have taken the position that the best education package we can offer to our students is a broad educational experience. Most professional managers are faced with a dynamic business environment that changes frequently. M.B.A. graduates from UNLV are prepared to accept and meet the business challenges that will come to them.

We make every effort to challenge all students to magnify their talents in such a way that they will be ready to face the exciting challenges of a global economy.

—Elvin C. Lashbrooke Jr., Dean

Programs and Curricular Focus

The M.B.A. program at the College of Business at UNLV is designed for those who seek global career and leadership opportunities. Today's business leaders face challenges that are quite different from those of a generation ago. Faced with a global competitive business environment and supported by new information and communication technologies, organizational structures are changing. Success in the new marketplace requires teams of executives working across functions and across borders.

The innovative M.B.A. program at UNLV prepares students to succeed in today's business environment by providing them with the needed skills, knowledge, and tools to become visionary and creative leaders. The program, 30 credit hours of core and 18 credit hours of elective concentrations, focuses on ethics and critical thinking, business communications, the role of the firm and its goals and markets, firms' strategic planning and positioning, value chain management approach, international business culture, technology management, integration of curriculum, and teamwork. The faculty is committed to continuous quality improvement of the curriculum and teaching, to increased vertical and horizontal integration of course material, and to team teaching and team learning. To achieve the best outcome, the faculty embraces no one teaching method but rather employs a combination of methods best suited to the particular objectives of the course. Lectures, group discussions, seminars, case studies, computer simulations, and individual and group research projects are frequently used within courses and across the curriculum.

The College of Business at UNLV, including the M.B.A. program, is fully accredited by AACSB–The International Association for Management Education.

Students and the M.B.A. Experience

Since UNLV has taken the position that an M.B.A. candidate is best served with a broad general education, it follows that students from all academic majors are welcome in the program. The only prerequisites for students with a good academic record are that they come into the program with good computer, math, and English skills.

An M.B.A. education is much more meaningful if the student has had pertinent work experience. An M.B.A. is not an extension of undergraduate education but rather a degree allowing the student to become a scholar with specific career goals in mind.

The average age of students entering the program is 29 years, with five years of full-time work experience. The age range is 24 to 52 years. Women make up 30 percent of the student body, members of minority groups represent 10 percent, international students make up 12 percent of entering students, and 6 percent of the students already have advanced degrees.

Special Features

The highlights of the M.B.A. program include a holistic approach to business management that starts with the role of the firm, its goals and markets, its strategic planning and positioning, and value chain management; integrative course modules across the functional areas, including accounting and finance, as well as marketing and operations;

major course modules with team teaching using cross-departmental faculty and a greater emphasis on student teamwork; explicit emphasis on a framework for analysis of ethical issues and critical thinking; a greater emphasis on international studies through a specific course in international business and cross-cultural perspective, a greater internationalization of other courses, and international elective and concentration courses; an integrative Capstone Experience to integrate important issues in the M.B.A. core and to provide students with a live business team case; accommodating the needs of both full-time and part-time students by offering courses during nontraditional hours (early morning, late afternoon, and evening); maximizing students' learning and credit-hour load by offering courses in full- and half-semester (sixteen- and eight-week) models; and a dual concentration (18 hours of electives) that provides greater flexibility in tailoring programs of study to each student's needs and interests.

The Faculty

UNLV values outstanding classroom instruction and provides a rich learning environment that will motivate young scholars. All faculty members teaching in the M.B.A. program have doctoral degrees and are outstanding in their field of expertise. The faculty members have extensive experience in their chosen areas of instruction. The faculty includes professors with training and experience from many nations. Every M.B.A. candidate is assigned a faculty member to serve as his or her adviser and guide.

The Business School Network

Many of the faculty members consult with businesses in an attempt to find solutions to various problems confronting modern mangers. As a result, the faculty has established networks that are beneficial to students, faculty members, and the businesses. Many faculty members invite business leaders to visit and/or lecture in their classes. Many business executives provide support to the University and look at UNLV as their institution.

The College and Environs

While the University is relatively young, it has experienced rapid growth in recent years. The student enrollment is about 21,000, with approximately 6,500 graduate students. Las Vegas is one of the fastest-growing cities in the United States and is the primary shopping and business district for more than 1.2 million people.

The University is located within the city, so students have easy access to all city services. The airport is less than 2 miles from the campus. The airport is one of the busiest in the United States, with easy connection to any location. Las Vegas is only a half-day automobile ride from Los Angeles or Phoenix.

Millions of international visitors come to Las Vegas, which indirectly provides opportunities for the students. There are many ethnic restaurants and grocery stores. Las Vegas is located on the edge of the desert, where the residents enjoy hot summers and mild winters. There are also large lakes and high mountains nearby, which provide students with the opportunity to appreciate the beauties of nature and to enjoy many forms of outdoor recreation.

Facilities

For the single student, there is excellent campus housing available. There are six new dormitories in which 2 students share each room. There are a few rooms available for single occupants, but this requires an additional fee. The dormitory room and board cost varies from $2700 to $3000 per semester. There are hundreds of apartments available near the University, with prices starting at $400 per month. There is a fine health facility on campus to provide emergency medical services. All students must purchase the Comprehensive Student Health Plan offered by UNLV.

For additional information on housing, students should contact the Office of Residential Life, 4760 Gym Road, Las Vegas, Nevada 89119 (telephone: 702-895-3489; fax: 702-895-4332).

Technology Environment

The College of Business has excellent computer facilities available for student use, including computer labs and electronic information centers. UNLV is one of the few universities in the world that has a Cray Supercomputer.

The College also sponsors research centers that make extensive use of modern facilities, such as the Center for Business and Economic Research and the Small Business Development Center.

Placement

The University has a very active student placement office on campus, offering numerous services to students. These include career workshops, resume preparation assistance, placement file services for current or future use, counseling, and information on job expectations and the employment outlook.

Admission

The College of Business at UNLV welcomes applications from college graduates in all fields. No specific undergraduate major is preferred. Applicants must hold a bachelor's degree from an accredited college or university. Applicants are evaluated based upon demonstrated academic ability as evidenced by a strong undergraduate record, a strong performance on the Graduate Management Admission Test (GMAT), maturity, motivation, leadership, communication skills, and interest in professional management. The requirements for admission include a grade point average (GPA) of 3.0 or higher on a 4.0 scale and a GMAT score of 550 or higher. The test score should be reflective of general, verbal, and quantitative aptitude, with each component over the 25th percentile. GMAT scores over five years old are not accepted. Applicants with a GPA of less than 3.0 but not lower than 2.75 or a GMAT score not lower than 520 may be admitted as provisional students provided that (GPA x 200) + GMAT score is not less than 1,150.

International students must also have a minimum score of 550 on the Test of English as a Second Language.

Finances

UNLV is relatively inexpensive because it is a state-supported institution. Estimated fees and living expenses per semester for 1998–99 include $97 per semester credit hour, a nonresident fee of $2885, $2700 for dormitory and meals, $300 for books and supplies, $300 for student health insurance, and $500 for personal expenses. Assuming the student takes 9 credit hours, the total per semester cost is approximately $7500.

If a student chooses to live off campus, food and housing are relatively inexpensive compared to that of many other states.

Students may apply for graduate assistant positions. These positions are very competitive and are filled on the basis of student merit and University needs.

International Students

All international students are required to register with the Office of International Student Services (OISS). This office exists only to serve the students and to make their adjustment to campus life pleasant and productive. If necessary, an OISS representative can meet new students at the McCarran Airport upon arrival. For additional information regarding the OISS, students should call 702-895-3221.

There are more than 800 international students on campus representing more than fifty countries. Residence hall, alumni, and student organizations provide important support groups for international students interested in affiliating with social and business organizations.

For students who need to reinforce their language skills, the University provides education through the Center for English Language Studies. Beginning-, intermediate-, and advanced-level courses are offered.

Application Facts and Dates

Application deadlines are June 1 for the fall semester and November 15 for the spring semester. All international application materials must be completed and received by May 1 for the fall semester and October 1 for the spring semester.

For additional information, students should contact:

Nasser Daneshvary, Associate Dean
University of Nevada, Las Vegas
4505 Maryland Parkway
P.O. Box 456031
Las Vegas, Nevada 89154-6031
Telephone: 702-895-3655
Fax: 702-895-4090
E-mail: daneshva@ccmail.nevada.edu

University of Nevada, Reno

Reno, Nevada

A PIONEER IN BUSINESS PROGRAMS

The pioneering history of the College of Business Administration at the University of Nevada, Reno, mirrors that of the state of Nevada. Ours was one of the first universities in the United States to offer business and related programs, with courses taught as early as 1888. The present-day College of Business Administration was officially founded in 1956. Our Bachelor of Science and Master of Business Administration (M.B.A.) programs have been accredited by AACSB–The International Association for Management Education continuously since 1961, and we were among the first to receive separate accreditation for our accounting program. Our College is one of the most rapidly growing units of the University of Nevada, combining the excitement of testing new ideas with a commitment to achieving excellence in teaching.

—Mike Reed, Dean

Programs and Curricular Focus

The Master of Business Administration (M.B.A.) program is designed for people with a variety of backgrounds working in business and industry, government, or the nonprofit sector, particularly those who already hold management or executive positions. Students have flexibility in tailoring a program that meets their needs. The program offers a variety of industry or professional specializations, such as logistics and gaming, in addition to the traditional functional specializations, such as management and finance. All appropriate courses have international and computer components. The program is flexible to meet the needs of those presently in managerial and professional positions.

A typical class size is approximately 25 students. The program offers a mix of team-based assignments and individual projects. The style of instruction is also diverse and includes case study analysis, lecture, and seminar. Many students pursue independent study projects, and internships are available. The Logistics Management summer internship program has been particularly successful, with students being placed in major corporations throughout the United States.

The curriculum has been designed to promote understanding of the basic tools and techniques needed to manage effectively in a changing global marketplace. An M.B.A. from the University of Nevada, Reno, enables a manager or executive to perform a wide range of managerial functions, including managing human and material resources in a culturally diverse and rapidly changing technological world, making decisions based on complex accounting and financial information, using state-of-the-art information technology to support the operation and management of organizations, and marketing products and services with a clear understanding of the economic and socioeconomic trends of greatest importance. Graduates understand the implications of an increasingly global economy and the changing legal, ethical, cultural, and political environments of business and are able to develop business policies and strategies that are responsive to rapid change.

Students and the M.B.A. Experience

The College enrolls approximately 200 graduate students, of whom 150 are M.B.A. students. Approximately 30 percent of the students are full-time. The remaining 70 percent work full-time and attend classes in the evening. Women make up approximately 43 percent of the students in the program. Members of minority groups and international students represent 11 percent and 10 percent of the student body, respectively. The average age at admission is 29 years, with the range being 22 to 48. All students entering the program are required to have a minimum of two years of professional work experience. In a recent class, the average years of work experience was ten. The professional backgrounds of the students are quite diverse. Many have realized significant accomplishments and have already moved into managerial positions, while others have only recently begun their careers. Students bring their professional experience to the classroom. This creates a stimulating environment where academic theories are critically examined for their applicability to the real world.

The Faculty

The faculty of the College of Business Administration is an accomplished, dynamic group of professionals dedicated to providing the highest quality business education possible. The faculty members hold Ph.D.'s from some of the world's leading institutions and most have practical work experience in their fields. They are active in research and professional service and many have achieved national and international prominence in their fields. The M.B.A. faculty also has a high degree of international diversity. Its members are natives of many different countries, including Mauritius, England, Taiwan, Korea, Brazil, India, Iran, China, and Germany. An international faculty provides a global focus that is difficult to achieve in any other way.

The Business School Network

The College has excellent ties to the business community, both locally and nationally. The Dean's advisory board is an active, energetic group of senior executives and successful entrepreneurs who interact with the students and faculty in a variety of ways. The College also has several specialized organizations with which M.B.A. students can become involved. The Center for Logistics Management was established in 1988 to combine the resources of the business community and the University to focus on the field of logistics management. The center is aggressively utilizing this alliance by providing companies throughout the United States with a pool of graduates with specialized training in logistics, continuing education programs to train current employees, and ongoing research efforts to address the challenge ahead in one of today's fastest moving fields—logistics.

The Institute for the Study of Gambling and Commercial Gaming was formed in 1989 with the mission of broadening the base of knowledge and understanding of gaming and public policy in Nevada, the United States, and throughout the world. The institute has been actively involved in coordinating and sponsoring international conferences on gaming, publishing books and studies related to gaming and the commercial gaming industry, facilitating educational programs and courses dealing with various facets of gaming, and acting as an information gathering and dissemination center for current developments in gaming and public policy.

The Nevada Small Business Development Center (NSBDC) is a cooperative effort between the University and the United States Small Business Administration. Counselors provide services to existing and new small business enterprises throughout the state by helping them through all individual service areas, including assistance with business start-up, sources of capital, marketing, financial analysis, invention assessment, planning for growth, computer systems, and personnel issues.

The Bureau of Business and Economic Research (BBER), founded in 1956, is the applied research unit of the College of Business Administration. It provides a broad array of research services, publications, and consulting for private, local, state, and national business and governmental entities. The bureau operates on a statewide basis, matching the expertise of consultants, students, faculty experts, and databases with the needs of organizations outside the University.

The College and Environs

The University of Nevada, Reno, Nevada's land-grant institution, is the state's oldest university. It has an enrollment of approximately 12,100 students, of whom more than 25 percent are enrolled in graduate programs. The Reno area, at an altitude of 4,500 feet, has more than 290 days of sunshine a year. Warm, clear days are plentiful in spring, summer, and early fall. Late fall and winter are crisp, but mostly sunny. The city's valley location allows its residents and visitors to enjoy the scenic beauty of the high desert and the outdoor activities available in the spectacular Sierra Nevada Mountains and the incomparable Lake Tahoe, all less than an hour away. The city is also a short drive from more than a dozen prominent ski resorts, Yosemite National Park, the Pacific Crest Trail, San Francisco, and the Napa and Sonoma Valleys.

The area's 294,290 residents create an economy of diversity and entrepreneurial spirit. In addition to being a major

recreational and gaming destination, Reno has become an important distribution center for many of the nation's top companies. The city enjoys extensive community support for the Reno Philharmonic, the Nevada Opera, the Reno Chamber Orchestra, and the Nevada Festival Ballet. In addition, the 56-year-old Reno Little Theater and the Nevada Repertoire Company offer traditional avant-garde entertainment year-round.

Facilities

The College of Business Administration is in the Nazir Ansari Business Building, a modern, six-story building. The building encourages students to interact in a relaxed, informal atmosphere in its student lounges and restaurant. Many of the classrooms have Internet connections, audio and video projection systems, and built-in podiums containing such equipment as electronic presenters, microcomputers, VCR/CD players, and connections for personal laptop computers.

Technology Environment

The College maintains several information technology laboratories available to M.B.A. students. These include the general purpose microcomputer lab, the Internet development lab, the networking and telecommunications lab, and the telecommuting lab. These networked facilities are all connected to the Internet, house approximately 100 microcomputers and other devices, and provide access to a wide variety of software applications and databases. The University library is highly automated and supports electronic access (from campus and through remote dial-up) to additional database resources and powerful bibliographic search tools.

Placement

The College's Office of Career Services works closely with students, the faculty, and the administration to integrate career assistance into the overall M.B.A. program, centralize career planning resources, and create a positive image for the program within the business community. The office currently maintains relationships with more than seventy major organizations who recruit regularly at the College. As a result of recent on-campus interviews, M.B.A. students have received job offers from organizations such as Electronic Data Systems, Ford Motor, Chrysler Corporation, Coca-Cola, Intel, Ernst and Young, DSC Logistics, American Micro Devices, Pepsi, Deloitte and Touche, and Kraft Foods.

Admission

Individuals holding baccalaureate degrees from accredited four-year institutions of higher education are encouraged to apply. Any academic background is acceptable, but students holding degrees in fields

other than business may find the degree particularly beneficial. Fitness for graduate study in business is determined by previous higher education experience as determined by transcripts, results of the GMAT, letters of recommendation, and a personal statement of goals and objectives. International applicants are required to submit TOEFL results unless they received a degree from an institution where English is the language of instruction. The admissions committee also considers each applicant's personal and professional accomplishments as determined by a detailed resume. Applicants are required to have a minimum of two years of meaningful work experience at the time of admission. The committee seeks to admit men and women representing diverse geographic, racial, and religious groups.

Finances

Residents of the state of Nevada pay $93 per graduate credit in tuition and fees. Nonresidents and international students, pay an additional $97 per credit for 1–6 credits or $2885 for 7 credits or more. All students pay a mandatory $57 per semester for health center fees. International students are required to pay a one-time registration fee of $75 and an annual fee for international student insurance of $202.

The College of Business Administration and the Graduate School award graduate assistantships (GAs) on a competitive basis. Students awarded a GA receive $9500 per ten-month academic year and $73 per credit toward their tuition and fees. Nonresident tuition is waived for students who receive a GA. In addition, all M.B.A. students are eligible for scholarships offered by the College and Graduate School.

Application Facts and Dates

Students are admitted into the M.B.A. program for both the fall and spring semesters. To be considered for the fall semester, all application materials must be received by February 1; for spring admission, application materials must be received by October 1. Applications received after the deadlines will be considered on a space-available basis.

For additional information, students should contact:

M.B.A. Program
College of Business Administration/024
University of Nevada, Reno
Reno, Nevada 89557
Telephone: 702-784-4912
Fax: 702-784-1773
E-mail: bowman@unr.edu
World Wide Web: http://www.unr.edu

University of New Hampshire

Durham, New Hampshire

THE NEW M.B.A. IN THE GLOBAL ECONOMY

The mission of the Whittemore School of Business and Economics is to be a distinguished professional school in which the liberal arts are the basic foundation and the management of change in a global economic community is the major emphasis. In order to achieve this mission, the school is committed to a broad set of goals that preserves our commitment to excellence in critical thought, verbal and written communications, quantitative skills, computer literacy and ethical reasoning.

Our environment fosters collegiality and fairness through continuous interaction with business and other external entities. The promotion of international awareness and cross-cultural understanding is an essential component of the educational student experience at The Whittemore School.

—Lyndon E. Goodridge, Dean of the Whittemore School

Programs and Curricular Focus

The M.B.A. program is intentionally small (approximately 30 to 40 students) to foster a close association between students and faculty. Although each incoming M.B.A. class has its own particular blend of individuals with a wide range of experiences, the small size allows classes to be informal and maximizes student involvement with the program.

A sequence of thirteen required and seven elective courses can only be started in September and requires two years of full-time study to complete. During the first year, ten required courses make up a common schedule for the entire entering class. The first-year curriculum is both demanding and highly structured.

During the second year, M.B.A. students complete their last three required courses. The remainder of the year is allocated for electives that can develop and expand areas of individual career interest. Elective classes in the second year of study can take the form of traditional classroom experiences, off-campus consulting opportunities, or team project work. A mixture of experiences is often chosen to allow a gradual transition to the workplace.

Other program opportunities offered at the Whittemore School include joint B.A./M.B.A. programs, which allow highly qualified students to complete both degrees in five years instead of the traditional six years. An M.A. and Ph.D. program in economics is offered both on a full-time and part-time framework to

those students who are interested in research and academic careers. For the corporate managers who wish to mix full-time work with graduate study, the University offers a highly acclaimed twenty-two-month Executive M.B.A. and a residential three-week Executive Development Program. A new evening, part-time M.B.A. program, with the same curriculum as the full-time model, began in 1995.

Students and the M.B.A. Experience

While 4 out of every 10 students in the M.B.A. program are from the local region, the remaining 6 are split almost evenly between other New England regions, the rest of the United States, and other countries. The academic background of each class also varies significantly. Half of the students are prepared in the liberal arts and social science disciplines, while a quarter of each entering class have been prepared in the physical sciences and business and economics. The mix of men to women is two thirds to one third, with the average age of an entering class at 27.

❖ Global Focus

The Whittemore School's M.B.A. program encourages student development in the international arena via a mixture of classroom, study-abroad, and international residential experiences. In the second year of study, elective courses are offered with a purely international orientation,

courses such as international business and international finance and international management are regularly part of the second-year offerings. In addition, courses may include international residence; for example, a recent course in international management had a mandatory residence in Quebec, Canada.

Special Features

The Whittemore School M.B.A. Investment Fund allows students who are interested in a career in the investment field an opportunity to try their hands at managing a real fund portfolio. With funds provided by alumni, two teams of selected students are allowed to actually invest funds over an eighteen-month period.

A team of Whittemore School M.B.A. students is selected each year to represent the School in an international case competition held in Montreal, Canada. This exciting program is fully funded by corporate sponsors.

M.B.A. students who desire an entrepreneurial concentration may participate in the Holloway Entrepreneurial Competition. This program encourages individual and small-group projects that are reviewed first by a faculty panel and then by a panel of distinguished corporate representatives in an open forum. The finalists receive cash awards intended to serve as seed money for new ventures.

The Faculty

Unlike many other institutions, all of the faculty members of the Whittemore School are researchers and teachers; they perform both at a high level of excellence. The 53 faculty members in the school support the business management, economics, and hospitality management programs. Frequently, practitioners are invited into the classrooms as guest lecturers, and on occasion the University has invited top-notch practitioners to teach a course in their fields of specialty. The Whittemore School does not use graduate assistants to teach in any of its masters or doctoral programs.

The Business School Network

Corporate Partnerships

The Whittemore School Executive Board is made up of 40 senior officers from many of the top businesses in the Northeast and Atlantic regions of the United States. These senior officers interact with the schools' leadership and students to provide an educational experience that is both up-to-date and real-world. Many members of the Executive Board fund corporate fellowships in their companies' name. These fellowships provide M.B.A. students with financial support, as well as summer research opportunities. All M.B.A. students have an opportunity to meet these corporate leaders and compete for the summer work opportunities provided by their companies.

The College and Environs

The University of New Hampshire, founded in 1866, is located in Durham—a small town in a semirural area that retains many traces of its colonial past. The 200-acre campus is surrounded by more than 3,000 acres of fields, farms, and woodlands owned by the University. A stream running through a large wooded area in the middle of the campus enhances a sense of openness and natural beauty. The University enrolls more than 12,000 students in both its undergraduate and graduate programs and as such is the largest academic institution in the state. The accessibility of Boston's cultural opportunities (65 miles south); the skiing, hiking, and scenery of the White Mountains (60 miles north); and the sandy beaches and rocky coast of New Hampshire and Maine (10 miles east) make it an ideal location to live and study.

Placement

The University maintains a comprehensive full-time career planning and placement staff for the benefit of all graduate students. In addition to the on-campus interview system, the office maintains an active alumni file for those students interested in career networking. In cooperation with Career Services, the Whittemore School conducts a number of workshops throughout the year that include resume writing, interviewing techniques, salary negotiations, and overviews of the current job market.

Admission

The crucial requirement for admission to the M.B.A. program is a history that demonstrates that the applicant has the potential and desire for graduate study in business. All students must have completed a bachelor's degree before beginning the M.B.A. program. The focus of the applicants' undergraduate studies is of less importance than evidence of academic ability and potential for becoming a responsible manager and leader. The GMAT exam is required of all applicants, along with the TOEFL exam for all international applicants. In recent years, the average GMAT score was 570 and the average grade point average was 3.1. The minimum TOEFL score is 550.

Finances

Yearly tuition for the M.B.A. program in 1997–98 was $13,760 for out-of-state applicants and $4900 for in-state applicants. Mandatory fees were $790. Babcock House is the graduate student residence for single students, where a single room costs $2978 per school year. Students may remain in Babcock during summer at reduced rates. Limited on-campus housing is available for married students in Forest Park. Prices for efficiencies and one- and two-bedroom apartments range from $352 to $468 per month. Graduate assistantships and tuition scholarships are competitive and awarded to applicants of high academic achievement and promise.

Application Facts and Dates

Application deadlines are July 1 for U.S. nationals and April 1 for international applicants. For information, applicants should contact:

George Abraham
Director of Graduate Programs
The Whittemore School of Business
Box PI, McConnell Hall
University of New Hampshire
15 College Road
Durham, New Hampshire 03824-3593
Telephone: 603-862-1367
Fax: 603-862-4468
E-mail: wsbe.grad.program@unh.edu

University of New Haven

AN UPDATED M.B.A. FOR TODAY'S PROFESSIONAL

The working environment is changing, becoming more global and competitive. Information technology has revolutionized the way we do business. New service-based corporations and industries are forming, and established industries such as banking, health care, and energy are being reshaped. Professional success in today's world requires knowledge and skills in all of the basic business functional areas plus the ability to lead in a multicultural society, to build effective functionally integrated teams, and, most importantly, to successfully manage constant change. Because of these changes in the business environment and the increasingly robust economy, employers are intensifying their recruitment of M.B.A. graduates. The job market for new hires is expanding, and the possibilities for advancement abound. Now is the time to prepare for these new opportunities.

Upon graduation, you will join more than 15,000 alumni from the University of New Haven (UNH) School of Business who work in businesses throughout the world.

—Linda R. Martin, Ph.D., Dean

Programs and Curricular Focus

The primary objective of the M.B.A. program at the University of New Haven is the development of leadership skills and the global perspective required in today's complex business environment. Additional objectives include strong coverage of analytical tools and specializations required for effective performance in a range of organizations, from entrepreneurial to high technology and global. Many courses require cases, group projects, and in-class presentations. Since many students in the program are currently working in high-technology and multinational firms operating in Connecticut, class discussions reflect this rich mix.

The M.B.A. curriculum has three components that include a total of seventeen courses (51 credits). Students with prior studies in business might be able to reduce their requirements to as little as eleven courses (33 credits). Full-time students can complete their studies within twelve to twenty-two months. Part-time students typically take three to four years.

The first component is six courses covering core competencies. Although some students will need all six, those with a strong coverage of core undergraduate business studies may be able to waive most.

The second component is courses in seven required areas (communication, product creation, valuation, global issues, organizational change, business and society, and strategic vision).

The concluding component is four advanced electives. These may be used to explore a mix of interests or may be used to form a concentration from one of several areas (accounting, business policy, computer science, finance, health-care management, human resources, international business, logistics, organizational management, marketing, operations research, public relations, sports industry, technology management, and telecommunications).

Computer applications are included in most courses. Labs, Internet connections, and projection equipment are available as needed.

Students and the M.B.A. Experience

Nearly 500 students, many holding full-time jobs, are enrolled in the M.B.A. program at the University of New Haven. Most students are from the Northeastern United States, but the University has made a strong commitment to maintain a diverse student body. Women comprise 40 percent of the student population, and 10 percent are international students, representing approximately fifty countries.

Special Features

Trimester scheduling allows students to accelerate progress toward their degree,

and, while a complete curriculum is available to full-time students, there are evening and weekend classes suitable for working adults.

Students can enrich their personal and professional competences by selecting a concentration in a particular discipline, and some departments offer students the opportunity to obtain additional credit and practical experience by participation in an internship program.

The Faculty

The highly qualified faculty represents a combination of full-time academics who hold doctoral degrees in their specialties from a variety of prestigious institutions and part-time faculty members chosen from managers who have demonstrated a high degree of leadership and who have received national recognition for their applied research. Each brings practical insight and experience to the classroom.

Class size within the Graduate School is relatively small, averaging less than 25 students. Classes are kept small to allow for interaction and personal attention. The faculty members at UNH get to know students and act as sounding boards in discussions about business decisions and plans for personal and professional growth and development. UNH faculty members have international, national, and regional reputations in their fields through outstanding accomplishments in research and writing and as visiting lecturers.

The Business School Network

Most students in the M.B.A program hold full-time positions in regional businesses and nonprofit corporations; that experience allows the classroom to become a mechanism for extending students' learning into varied practical environments. Ongoing interaction with the business community also occurs throughout the Business School Advisory Board, composed of leaders from private and public sectors; the Institute for Business Evolution; the Center for Family Business; and a vast network of alumni. Additional networking occurs through students' participation in the recently chartered chapter of Sigma Beta Delta, the National Honor Society in Business, Management, and Administration.

Each fall and spring, the Bartels' Fellowship Lecture Series brings a successful CEO or entrepreneur to campus to lecture and interact with faculty and students. Some Distinguished Bartels' Fellows have been David Beckerman, President of Starter Corporation; Robert Beavers Jr., Senior Vice President of McDonald's Corporation; Francis Freidman, former CEO of GCI Group, Grey Advertising; Ronald G. Shaw, President and CEO of Pilot Pen; and William J. Weisz, former CEO of Motorola, Inc.

The College and Environs

The University's 73-acre campus is located in south-central Connecticut, on a hillside in West Haven that overlooks Long Island Sound and downtown New Haven. The area is semisuburban and is easily accessible by car, bus, train, or plane. The campus, located near the intersection of interstate highways 95 and 91, is 75 miles northeast of New York City and 135 miles southwest of Boston.

New Haven, just 10 minutes away from campus, is a city where arts and cultural activities flourish and coexist with science and business. Settled in the early 1600s and rich in history and heritage, the New Haven area is proud of its past, prouder of its present, and actively planning for its future. The city, considered by many as the "Gateway to New England," is a manufacturing center, a deep-water port, a major art center, and a college town with seven colleges and universities in the immediate area.

Facilities

The University of New Haven provides facilities for a full complement of student services, including career development and placement services; academic, vocational, and personal counseling;

alumni relations; health services; housing; international student services; veterans' affairs; minority affairs; and services for students with disabilities. In addition, there are athletic facilities and a campus store for the students' use and convenience.

Both on-campus and off-campus housing is available for graduate students.

Technology Environment

The UNH Center for Computing Services provides both administrative and academic computing support. Clusters of terminals and personal computers for student use are spread throughout the campus. A PC and Internet lab is located in the business building. Access to the Internet, graphics terminals, printing and plotting devices, laser printing, and a wide variety of data files and software and simulation packages are available.

Placement

The University of New Haven provides career development and placement services as well as academic, vocational, and personal counseling.

Admission

Admission decisions are based primarily on an applicant's undergraduate record. In support of their applications, students should submit scores from the Graduate Management Admission Test (GMAT).

Students for whom English is not their native language must present a TOEFL score of at least 500. International students must submit official, certified documents showing sufficient financial support from personal or sponsor's funds or a scholarship.

Finances

For the 1998–99 academic year, the tuition rate was $1080 per 3-credit course. There are no other regular fees;

however, there is a nonrefundable application fee of $50 and an additional nonrefundable acceptance fee of $200 for international students not on scholarship. Students should calculate additional expenses for books, supplies, and housing.

Financial aid is available for domestic students in a variety of forms, including loans, grants-in-aid, work-study, fellowships, and assistantships. Financial aid is not available for international students.

International Students

Qualified international students are welcome in the M.B.A. program at the University of New Haven. Ten percent of the students currently enrolled are from approximately fifty countries outside the United States. To qualify, a prospective student must have completed an acceptable undergraduate degree program. All transcripts must be submitted in English.

The University has an Office of International Student Services that provides a full range of support services for international students.

To facilitate preparation for admission by international students, a branch of an internationally known English as a second language (ESL) school is located on campus.

Application Facts and Dates

For more information or applications, students should contact:

Joseph F. Spellman
Director of Graduate Admissions
University of New Haven
West Haven, Connecticut 06516-1999
Telephone: 203-932-7133
            800-DIAL-UNH ext. 7133
            (toll-free)
E-mail: dharma@charger.newhaven.
    edu
World Wide Web: http://www.mba.
    newhaven.edu

 # University of North Carolina at Greensboro

SCHOOL OF BUSINESS AND ECONOMICS

Joseph M. Bryan School of Business and Economics

Greensboro, North Carolina

LEADERSHIP IN A NEW ERA

At the Bryan School, we have a vision for the future: we want to become a focal point for international business education, research, and public service. We are internationalizing our programs, because we think this is the most effective way to serve our students and the business community. Our graduates must have the fundamental knowledge and skills of business enhanced by an international perspective. They must understand global markets and have the skills and knowledge to function in them.

We believe that our new initiatives related to student development, such as career planning and placement activities, faculty development, and enhancement of information technology capabilities, will take us to the next level in pursuing the internationalization of all programs in the Bryan School and will best serve the interests of our students.

—James K. Weeks, Dean

Programs and Curricular Focus

The Bryan M.B.A. prepares men and women for leadership roles in business and the community. It is designed to develop general managers who think and act strategically and who will lead in a global economy. Students are challenged throughout their experience to think; to understand a broad, long-range perspective; and to act decisively.

The program is designed for qualified students from all academic backgrounds and consists of 48 semester hours of course work—33 hours of required courses and a 15 elective hours. Through the required courses, students obtain a standard of understanding that all M.B.A.'s should possess. The elective courses provide a richer knowledge in different areas of management activity.

The heart of the program is a modular, flexible curriculum that enables students to take courses at their own pace and adjust their course load accordingly. The curriculum focuses on business strategy. The core curriculum is highly integrated and reflects concerns with today's pressing issues—environmental concerns, global business operations, and changing work forces and markets.

All M.B.A. classes are scheduled in the evening to meet the needs of students working full-time as well as to accommodate full-time students who are fulfilling assistantship and internship opportunities or who work part-time with regional firms. Classes are offered during fall and

spring semesters as well as during two six-week summer sessions.

The Bryan School of Business and Economics is the largest of the University of North Carolina at Greensboro's (UNCG) six professional schools. Its undergraduate and graduate programs are among the 25 percent of all business programs nationwide that are accredited by AACSB–The International Association for Management Education.

Students and the M.B.A. Experience

A major benefit of the Bryan M.B.A. program is the interaction with fellow students. Ninety percent of the students work full-time and attend classes on a part-time basis. This provides many opportunities for students to meet and get to know other professionals with a wide variety of business backgrounds and adds greatly to their depth of understanding of business issues. Students work in teams with colleagues who bring an abundance of personal experience to the subject matter of each class.

Thirty-three percent of the students have undergraduate degrees in business; 32 percent have training in science and engineering. Sixteen percent have backgrounds in the humanities and social sciences. The typical student is 30 years old and has six years of work experience. Approximately one third of the students are women, and 13 percent are members

of minority groups. Five percent of students enrolled in the program are international.

❖ Global Focus

The Bryan School's curriculum has a strong international component and is strengthened by core-level courses on global operations strategy as well as elective courses on aspects of international commerce. The Bryan M.B.A. program also offers exchange programs with several international business schools and opportunities to develop foreign language and management skills pertinent to individual regions.

The newly established Center for Global Business Education and Research is positioned to become a focal point for international business education, research, and public service in the region.

Special Features

The Center for Global Business Education and Research is an integral part of the University's efforts to prepare students and business professionals to function effectively in the global economy. One of the program's goals is to make international study experiences available for all students in the Bryan School, with twenty-five to thirty partnerships with business schools in other countries.

The Faculty

The faculty of UNCG's Bryan School is committed to excellence in teaching. In a recent survey of students, the students rated the faculty as the most commendable feature of the M.B.A. program. Students recognize the commitment of the faculty to contributing to learning and appreciate the ease of access to the faculty.

National recruiting has brought together a staff of highly qualified academics whose teaching, scholarship, and work experience complement the M.B.A. program. Many have significant managerial and executive experience; several provide consulting services for individual clients and companies. A large number of faculty members are nationally

and internationally recognized for their research accomplishments.

The Business School Network

Corporate Partnerships

The Business Advisory Board, a group of local and regional executives, fosters closer interaction between the School and the professional and business community. In addition to providing sound advice and counsel to the dean and faculty, they play an integral part of the review process for curriculum and other program innovations.

In addition, relationships with local, national, and international corporations lead to field consulting projects and internships for students and to employment opportunities for graduates.

The College and Environs

The institution that is now the University of North Carolina at Greensboro was chartered in 1891 to provide higher education for women. Formerly The Women's College—one of the three original institutions of the Consolidated University of North Carolina—it has been highly regarded for more than a century for both its strong liberal arts tradition and its excellent professional preparation for careers.

Among the approximately 500 full-time faculty members are nationally known scholars whose research and creative work regularly contribute new knowledge to their fields.

The city of Greensboro is rich in culture and history, and is considered one of the most progressive cities in North Carolina. The current metropolitan population of the Piedmont Triad is 1.3 million, and Greensboro, with 280,000 residents, combines the resources and activities of a large metropolitan center with the amenities of a human-sized environment where one can get to know and care about one's neighbors.

Facilities

All M.B.A. classes are taught in the evening in the Bryan School of Business and Economics Building. The building's modern design accommodates the teaching and research needs of approximately 60 faculty members and 250 students.

Jackson Library, a modern nine-story structure, contains more than 2 million items, including government documents and microtext. The library subscribes to more than 6,100 newspapers, periodicals, and other serials. In addition, all M.B.A. students can utilize the inter-library loan system to access materials that are available in other libraries across the nation.

Technology Environment

Instructional and Research Computing provides comprehensive computing support and resources for campus users. The campus supports a highly distributed network supported by Novell file servers, network printers, SUN-based Solaris for UNIX support, and a large DEC VAX-cluster, including a VAX 6000-610. UNCG is an Internet node, including access to the N.C. Supercomputing Center. Microcomputer labs are readily available, including three in the Bryan Building.

Placement

Most placement services are coordinated by the Graduate Placement Office, which acts as a liaison between graduate students and prospective employers. Services include career counseling and planning, career placement, and an electronic job bank. Often there are informal gatherings and contacts between area employers and students, which are facilitated by the Bryan School.

Admission

Admission decisions are based on a combination of the undergraduate academic record, GMAT scores, an admission essay, relevant managerial experience, and recommendations. International student applicants whose native language is not English must also demonstrate English language proficiency. A minimum TOEFL score of 550 is required, along with proof of health and proof of adequate funds. Each application is reviewed on its own merits and is not compared with an applicant pool.

Finances

Tuition for 1998–99 for M.B.A. students is estimated at $976 per semester for in-state students and $5135 per semester for out-of-state students. There are a limited number of assistantships and tuition waivers available. Competitively awarded Bryan Fellowships, with the opportunity to work with a faculty mentor, are also available.

Application Facts and Dates

Because of processing requirements, an admission for decision for the fall semester cannot be guaranteed unless all credentials are received before July 1; for spring semester, by November 1; and for summer session, by April 1. For international students, admissions application deadlines are May 1 for fall and October 1 for spring; admissions are coordinated through the International Student Office.

For further information, students should contact:

M.B.A. Program
220 Bryan Building
University of North Carolina at
   Greensboro
Greensboro, North Carolina 27412
Telephone: 336-334-5390
Fax: 336-334-4209
E-mail: mba@uncg.edu

University of Notre Dame

NEW M.B.A. INITIATIVES

▶ *The College of Business Administration prepares its students for a journey for which they can't buy a ticket— visiting new frontiers in technology and world markets, developing new and better products, anticipating creative marketing strategies to integrate into a changing world, looking at how we work as individuals and as a team, and devising systems to make the world better for us all. Our students graduate with the preparation they need to face this increasingly difficult but exciting journey that is filled with many possibilities.*

—Carolyn Y. Woo, Dean

Programs and Curricular Focus

The University of Notre Dame's M.B.A. program is solidly based on the vision of its founders—to help develop the student's fullest potential and send him or her forth to make a difference in the world. This is accomplished by developing in the student the following portfolio of skills: critical thinking, teamwork, effective communication, a global business perspective, and the manager's ability to make practical and ethical business decisions. With more than eighty elective courses, fourteen concentration tracks, and two programs of study, the Notre Dame M.B.A. program provides students with a challenging and flexible educational experience.

The Two-Year program is designed for students with little or no academic background in business. In the first year of the program, students study the core business disciplines. The curriculum is tightly integrated so that students learn to analyze situations from the vantage point of each of the functional areas. The second year allows students to select the concentration track that furthers their interests and future prospects. Students are required to complete 63 credit hours of work over four semesters.

The One-Year program is designed for students who have an undergraduate degree in business. This program enables students to begin study in June and graduate the following May. Beginning with a ten-week summer semester, students attend intensive sessions in the core disciplines that are normally explored during the first year of the Two-Year program. After the summer semester, students move directly into the second year of the Two-Year program. They take a course in corporate strategy and elective courses in both international business and ethics while customizing the remainder

of their elective courses by choosing from one of the fourteen concentration tracks. Students must complete 44 credit hours of work over eleven months.

Students may also pursue a joint Master of Business Administration/Juris Doctor (M.B.A./J.D.) degree program that is offered jointly by the College of Business Administration and the Notre Dame Law School. Students can complete both degrees in a total of four years. Students must apply to each school separately.

Students and the M.B.A. Experience

Notre Dame attracts high-caliber students from more than 170 undergraduate institutions and nearly thirty countries. Approximately 30 percent of the student body is international students, 28 percent is from the Midwest, 20 percent is from the East, and 15 percent is from the West. The Two-Year students at Notre Dame represent a varied mix of undergraduate majors, including business, engineering, economics, math, science, and humanities. Notre Dame M.B.A. students range in age from 21 to 37 years, and they enter the program with nearly four years of meaningful work experience. Nearly 30 percent of the students are women, and roughly 10 percent are members of minority groups.

❖ Global Focus

At Notre Dame, students can learn global perspectives firsthand and diversify their portfolio by studying in London, England; Santiago, Chile; or Monterrey, Mexico or through international internships.

At Notre Dame's London program, M.B.A. students learn from distinguished British professors who hail from prestigious

institutions in the United Kingdom. Courses are conducted at the technologically updated and renovated Notre Dame London Centre, which includes computer labs with instant Internet access. Students gain exposure to the European business environment through planned tours and professional networking opportunities.

Students who choose to study in Santiago begin with a two-week orientation during which they are immersed in the Spanish language and the cultural norms and traditions of South America. Courses are conducted in English at the Instituto Latino Americano de Doctrina y Estudios Sociales (ILADES) by eminent Chilean business faculty members. Chile serves as an ideal laboratory for learning about developing economies. Included in the program are visits to the Ministry of Finance and the stock exchange as well as tours of nearby copper mines and vineyards.

Notre Dame offers students the opportunity to learn about the economic and social infrastructure of Mexico through seminars at the Monterrey Institute of Technology. Students tour neighboring corporations and small businesses and meet face-to-face with top corporate executives.

In 1998, Notre Dame M.B.A. students launched a summer internship initiative in South Africa that combines service with valuable business experience. Through this outreach, students spend eight weeks in the townships of South Africa where they help small-business owners and entrepreneurs develop marketing and business plans.

Special Features

The Notre Dame M.B.A. experience begins with the Becoming Irish orientation. During this orientation program, students engage in team-building exercises and attend two-week math and accounting review workshops as well as a Microsoft Excel workshop.

The Faculty

Notre Dame's faculty members are highly regarded, stand at the top of their fields, and are engaged in the business world. The professors have a passion for teaching and make an impact in their fields. The 4:1 student to faculty ratio ensures each student accessibility and personal attention.

The Business School Network

Notre Dame's alumni network is one of the most extensive in higher education, with more than 100,000 members in 240 alumni clubs worldwide. These clubs are actively involved in promoting the University and extending its learning community. Notre Dame also has active Asian Pacific, Black, and Hispanic alumni clubs.

Every year, Notre Dame attracts corporate executives who speak on campus through a variety of lecture series and classroom visits. Some of the most interesting networking discussions take place in small classroom settings where students work directly with corporate executives on classroom projects. For example, Corporate Strategy students connect with managers located in Germany using two-way videoconferencing, while students in Entrepreneurship work directly with local start-ups to develop a business plan for their product or service ideas. Because of the small class size, students have unique opportunities to meet with executives over breakfast, lunch, or at small receptions.

The College and Environs

Notre Dame was founded in 1842 by Rev. Edward Frederick Sorin and 6 brothers of the French religious community known as the Congregation of Holy Cross. The University's 1,250-acre campus is situated immediately north of the city of South Bend, Indiana. Its twin lakes and many wooded areas provide a setting of natural beauty for more than 100 University buildings. The total University enrollment is about 10,200 students, of whom approximately 7,850 are enrolled at the undergraduate level. The Law School, the graduate division of the College of Business Administration, and the Graduate School have a combined enrollment of 2,350 students.

With a population of approximately 250,000, South Bend has a familiar hometown feel yet is large and diverse enough to provide students with a myriad of cultural, shopping, and entertainment opportunities. The area is served by numerous city parks, golf courses, and county facilities that offer a variety of outdoor recreational activities. Medical and religious needs are adequately met by three hospitals and more than 220 churches and synagogues of all major denominations.

Facilities

Notre Dame's state-of-the-art College of Business Administration complex, opened in 1995, features a multimedia amphitheater, a computer lab, a two-story M.B.A. lounge, team rooms equipped with networked computers, and Media-on-Call classrooms with computer controls and a fiber-optic network that provides faculty members with access to satellite feeds from major international networks.

Technology Environment

Notre Dame is a campus without boundaries. Whether in London or South Bend, every student is linked to the University's advanced computer network and has instant desktop access to the latest versions of leading business application software. The Thomas J. Mahaffey Jr. Business Information Center (BIC) provides students with easy online access to complete electronic business resources, such as Dow Jones News Retrieval Service, LEXIS-NEXIS, General BusinessFile ASAP, and Bridge real-time investment information. The College of Business Administration's new Management Information Systems (MIS) laboratory enables students to develop software applications, test innovative hardware and software configurations, and explore entrepreneurial opportunities that are based on information technology applications.

Placement

The Doermer Family M.B.A. Career Development Center schedules interviews for full-time positions and summer internships with a variety of companies and organizations that recruit M.B.A.'s on campus each year. Placement professionals also receive and pass along numerous job postings for M.B.A.'s each year, many of which are received from supportive alumni. M.B.A. students also have contact with nearly 400 companies that come to campus each year to recruit undergraduate students, and, through participation in the National M.B.A. Consortium, students have the opportunity to interview with a large number of companies at the annual consortium in Chicago. International students are invited to take part in two international placement consortiums that are held annually in major cities, and students from minority groups are invited to attend professional development conferences that are sponsored by the National Black MBA Association and the National Society of Hispanic MBAs.

Admission

The University of Notre Dame's M.B.A. program seeks highly qualified and well-rounded applicants. Typically, there are three characteristics of incoming students that have proven to be reliable gauges of success in the Notre Dame M.B.A. program: a demonstrated history and aptitude for academic success, at least two years of meaningful work experience, and leadership qualities that prove the student will be an active participant in the M.B.A. community. Because Notre Dame seeks well-rounded candidates, students are encouraged to apply even if their profile is atypical. The Graduate Management Admission Test (GMAT) is required for all applicants to the M.B.A. program. Average GMAT scores and GPA are 613 and 3.2,

respectively, for the class entering in fall 1998. The Test of English as a Foreign Language (TOEFL) is required for all applicants whose native language is not English.

Finances

Tuition for the 1998–99 academic year is $21,500. Tuition for the 1998 ten-week summer semester is $8600. Books and supplies average $925 per year. Living expenses, including room, board, and personal expenses, total approximately $6000 per academic year for an average single student living on or off campus. Married students should expect to increase their living expenses by about $150 a month.

Fellowships are awarded primarily on merit and are open to all domestic and international applicants. All applicants are considered for fellowship awards if they mark the appropriate box on the application. Loans and campus employment opportunities are available to qualified students through the University's Financial Aid Office.

International Students

Because 30 percent of students enrolled in the Two-Year program are international, they have a notable influence on the program's learning environment. To ease their transition into the academic environment and enhance their educational success at Notre Dame, international students are required to attend a two-week language and culture workshop prior to orientation. The University's Office of International Student Affairs offers support, activities, and a newsletter specific to international students' concerns. Also, the M.B.A. Association's international student affairs committee attends to issues unique to international M.B.A. students and their families.

Application Facts and Dates

Admission decisions are made on a rolling basis. Applicants to the Two-Year program must submit all application materials on or before April 16, 1999, with a decision being mailed four to six weeks after the application is completed. The deadline for applicants to the One-Year program is March 6, 1999. For additional information regarding the University of Notre Dame M.B.A. program, students should contact:

MBA Admissions
College of Business Administration, Suite 276
University of Notre Dame
P.O. Box 399
Notre Dame, Indiana 46556-0399
Telephone: 800-631-8488 (toll-free within the U.S.)
219-631-8488
Fax: 219-631-8800
E-mail: mba.1@nd.edu
World Wide Web: http://www.nd.edu/~mba

University of Oklahoma

Norman, Oklahoma

NEW DIRECTIONS FOR THE M.B.A.

The faculty members and students of the Price College of Business are excited about the new directions of our M.B.A. program. As you look through our descriptive material I think you will sense the strong team spirit among us all.

With the amenities offered by an urban area; a modern, friendly, and beautiful campus; and outstanding faculty members (several of whom are nationally recognized in their fields), the University of Oklahoma (OU) M.B.A. is a program on the rise, welcoming students from diverse disciplines and backgrounds to our full-time, integrated lockstepped program or to our late afternoon and evening program. The former consists primarily of high-performing students who have recently earned their baccalaureate degrees, while the latter includes primarily more experienced students who, because of their jobs, need the flexibility offered by such a program.

If you are interested in the intellectual stimulation and rigor of an outstanding program, we invite you to seek additional information about the Oklahoma M.B.A.

—Richard A. Cosier, Dean and Fred E. Brown Chair

Programs and Curricular Focus

Michael F. Price, renowned Wall Street fund manager and 1973 OU College of Business alumnus, presented the College with an $18-million endowment in May 1997. This was one of the largest single donations to a public university in the United States in 1997 and among the top five received by a nationally accredited business school. This gift resulted in the renaming of the former College of Business after Michael F. Price, one of the most respected and influential business leaders in America.

The M.B.A. program enrolls approximately 100 new students each year, thus allowing personal contact with the graduate faculty members and individualized attention. In addition to students with business experience, undergraduate students who enroll directly from nonbusiness programs, such as engineering, the sciences, and the humanities, are welcomed. Recognizing the needs of students with limited experience, the program strives to offer internships and international exchange opportunities to students needing practical experience.

The traditional 3-credit-hour, one-semester course format is not sacred in the Oklahoma M.B.A. full-time program. The program features a 3-credit-hour integration and applications course each semester and a series of courses that continue across semesters. The program

focuses on teamwork and globalization. It spans the needs of small and global businesses, with careful attention to the issues of concern to contemporary managers.

The part-time M.B.A. program is designed to cater to the needs of the full-time employee/part-time student. Because of the time constraints placed on working people, convenient late afternoon and evening M.B.A. classes are offered. The program focuses on leadership and teamwork, with careful attention to issues of concern to contemporary managers. The part-time students receive the same high quality of classroom attention as the full-time students, but in smaller doses and spread out over a longer period of time. In short, students in the part-time program receive a nationally respected M.B.A. degree in a time frame that fits their schedule.

Concentrations are offered in accounting, management information systems, finance, marketing, international business, human resource management, and general management. In recognition of the strong demand for interdisciplinary expertise in many settings, the Price College of Business, in cooperation with other academic units within the University, offers several dual-degree programs. While dual-degree programs require fewer total hours than two separate degree programs, applicants must be

admitted to each program independently. The most popular dual-degree program is the J.D./M.B.A.

Students and the M.B.A. Experience

Students in the M.B.A. program come from the U.S. and many other countries. In 1997–98, the M.B.A. program enrolled approximately 100 graduate students, of whom 70 were full-time. Of the class, women represented 35 percent; international students, 25 percent; and members of minority groups, 12 percent. The average age of students was approximately 24 in the full-time program and 28 in the part-time program. Degrees of work experience include managers with many years to students without any previous work experience.

The Faculty

The faculty members are an integrated team with excellent research and teaching skills. Both the University of Oklahoma and the Price College of Business share the conviction that strong research and ongoing relations with business are essential for a faculty member. The faculty members give students the vision to see things from new perspectives and inspire them to apply teamwork to problem-solving and decision-making processes. The College's business advisers and team approach bring to the classroom a rich mixture of academic theory and practical application.

The Business School Network

Price College of Business M.B.A.'s can acquire a good deal of hands-on experience in the classroom. Two courses, both initiated in 1996, have been huge success stories for students and faculty members. In the first, the Price College of Business partnered with Fleming Company to offer a unique course on Marketing Channels. Representatives from Fleming Company and its suppliers, along with OU faculty members, offered the course at Fleming's training center to OU M.B.A. students. The College has continued to offer the course to rave reviews.

For the second, Michael F. Price, renowned Wall Street fund manager and 1973 OU College of Business alumnus, initiated an investment class in which students have $100,000 of real money to invest in stocks. Students get hands-on experience in performing stock analysis, study various stock picking strategies, and actually make the transaction. This has been an astoundingly positive experience for the students who participate, and the program is in the process of being expanded.

Relationships between the Oklahoma M.B.A. students and faculty members and the corporate community are strong. OU M.B.A. faculty members are consultants to business and organizations in the Southwest, across the nation, and throughout the world. The Michael F. Price College of Business Corporate Relation Executives link the M.B.A. students with influential alumni and corporate executives to provide internships, co-ops, and networking relationships.

The College and Environs

The University of Oklahoma is located in Norman, approximately 20 miles south of Oklahoma City. The diversity of Oklahoma's Frontier Country is reflected in the varied range of things to see and do in Norman, from rustic wilderness areas to high-tech industries and from prehistoric artifacts to contemporary art and drama. For the outdoor enthusiast, Norman includes a major recreational lake, a state park, and an urban wilderness area.

The Norman campus is home to two of the Southwest's premier museums: the Fred Jones Jr. Museum of Art and the Sam Noble Oklahoma Museum of Natural History. The Fred Jones Jr. Museum of Art is nationally recognized as one of the finest university art museums. It offers some of the most interesting exhibitions of contemporary art. The Sam Noble Oklahoma Museum of Natural History, scheduled for completion in 1999 on a 40-acre site, will be the nation's largest university-based museum of natural history. The museum's collection holds more than 5-million artifacts and specimens, including dinosaur fossils, American Indian art, and Greek and Roman antiquities.

Facilities

Research facilities available to graduate students include an extensive University library, the Bass Business History Collection, the Oklahoma University Research Institute, the Center for Economic and Management Research, and extensive computer facilities.

The Price College of Business has five microcomputer laboratories; four are available for instruction and one for research. The four instructional laboratories are open for student use when a class is not in session. All computers are networked to a 90 MHz Pentium file server using the Novell Netware 4.11 Operating System.

Placement

The Oklahoma M.B.A. places emphasis on the success of its graduates. Ninety percent of 1997 Oklahoma graduates were placed at graduation. Many graduates accept positions in the Southwest: Dallas, Houston, Oklahoma City, and Tulsa, where business is strong, the cost of living is less, and the quality of life unsurpassed.

Admission

Admission is open to qualified individuals holding a bachelor's degree from an accredited college or university who show high promise of success in graduate study. Applicants should note that a GMAT score of 600 and an undergraduate grade point average of at least 3.4 is representative of students currently in the program. International applicants for whom English is not the primary language must have an official TOEFL score of 550 or higher.

Part-time students may enter the fall semester beginning in late August; the spring semester, beginning early January; or the eight-week summer session, beginning early in June. Students may only enter the full-time M.B.A. program in the fall semester.

Finances

Tuition in 1997–98 for full-time state residents was $91 per credit hour; nonresident students paid $266 per credit hour. Books and supplies are estimated at $800 per academic year, and other fees are approximately $75 per semester.

Graduate assistantships, special instructorships, fellowships and scholarships, and fee-waiver scholarships are available for qualified graduate students. Graduate assistantships may include a waiver of out-of-state fees.

Application Facts and Dates

For admission advice and information, students should contact:

Graduate Programs Office
Price College of Business
University of Oklahoma
Norman, Oklahoma 73019
Telephone: 405-325-4107
Fax: 405-325-1957
E-mail: awatkins@ou.edu
World Wide Web: http://www.ou.edu/business/oumba

University of Otago

Dunedin, New Zealand

MANAGEMENT FOR THE NEW MILLENNIUM

The new millennium brings forth many opportunities and significant challenges for those involved in the management process. Organisations are continuously being delayered, markets are accessible on a global basis, and the external environment is chaotic and unpredictable.

New Zealand has a small population of 3.7 million people on an island the size of Britain. This means that we are dependent on overseas trade and have, as a country, more than 100 years of experience dealing in international markets.

Our M.B.A. focuses on management in an international context, with team problem solving and decision making. We concentrate on developing leaders who focus on business from a general management perspective.

We have a superb campus and great facilities. In effect, Dunedin is a campus town, far away from the hustle and bustle. It is a great opportunity to refresh and prepare for the new millennium.

I extend to you the warmest welcome and encourage you to put the Otago M.B.A. on your serious list of options.

—Professor Geoffrey Lorigan

Programs and Curricular Focus

The Advanced Business Programme (ABP) is part of New Zealand's oldest and one of its most reputable universities. The University has a long and distinguished history and a reputation for innovation and excellence. The Advanced Business Programme is proud to be a part of this and not only lives up to the overall image of the University but also adds to it through the strong international reputation of its M.B.A. programme.

The Otago M.B.A. programme has been successfully developing the business leaders of the future for more than twenty years, and their outstanding performances are testimony to the high quality of the programme and the Otago M.B.A. experience.

The M.B.A. is delivered in five modules, with each module building upon the learning outcomes of the previous ones.

The central core of the Otago M.B.A. is a series of integrative and strategic management courses designed to promote and develop critical thinking in a relevant and innovative manner. There is no specialisation in any of the functional areas of management—a student does not gain an in-depth knowledge in any of the traditional management disciplines. Rather, courses in all functional areas serve to support and underpin the core

strategic and integrative papers that provide the necessary tools an effective manager must have.

In this way, the integration between functions and disciplines is ongoing, and students use these tools and practical skills to make connections in critically evaluating and solving business problems.

In addition to the integrative nature of the curriculum, one of the distinguishing features of the Otago M.B.A. is the intensive nature of the teaching. Each class consists of only 25 students, and a significant proportion of the work undertaken is highly interactive and conducted in small groups of 5 people. The experiential learning process is vital to the acquisition of knowledge, the development of skills, and the building of lifelong relationships. Dedicated staff members are able to adopt a significant mentoring role in their relationships with the students, and time is devoted to the individual in order to ensure a personalised learning environment and opportunity for personal development.

Students and the M.B.A. Experience

The Otago full-time M.B.A. candidate is typically a midcareer achiever, 28 to 35 years of age, who has already demonstrated leadership qualities either at work or at other pursuits. Many have impres-

sive corporate or entrepreneurial track records and now seek a broader range of skills and experiences to create a more strategic big-picture approach.

Approximately 40–50 percent of participants are from outside New Zealand, including the United States, the United Kingdom, Brazil, and India, as well as from other countries in the Pacific Rim area, including Australia, China, and Korea. As the business world has adapted to globalisation, the Otago M.B.A. has developed a more international focus while still remaining relevant to New Zealand's particular situation. The combination of international students, faculty members, and perspectives highlights yet another strength of the Otago M.B.A.

The Faculty

The Advanced Business Programme is part of the Division of Commerce, one of the four divisions of the University of Otago. There are 4 full-time teaching faculty members in the ABP who are committed to mentoring the M.B.A. students. As a department within the Division of Commerce, the ABP also benefits from a large pool of academic staff members from which to choose the teachers for the M.B.A. programme.

In addition, the Otago M.B.A. obtains many contributors to the programme from the New Zealand and international business communities. The careful choice of teaching staff members ensures that the Otago M.B.A. remains on the cutting edge of theory and practice, with the accent heavily on the relevant and useful.

The Business School Network

The Otago M.B.A. is not only about earning a degree. Of more importance is the Otago reputation and the network of relationships formed with students, University staff members, and members of the business community.

The Otago M.B.A. has woven an established network of alumni and business contacts. Activities such as the Live Case Studies, where the benefits to the students flow directly back to the organisations under scrutiny, increase the programme's value to the community in

general. The M.B.A. program also hosts a number of events, such as the annual Burns Supper, where existing networks are strengthened and new relationships are forged.

The College and Environs

The University of Otago, founded in 1869, is located in the heart of Dunedin, a town steeped in history, nestled on the shores of a natural harbour on the spectacular east coast of New Zealand's South Island. Dunedin has some of the most beautiful scenery in the world, and the area is also home to many native animals and birds, including the royal albatross, yellow-eyed penguin, and New Zealand fur seal.

Facilities

The M.B.A. programme occupies dedicated space in the Advanced Business Programme. This comprises two purpose-built, fully equipped lecture theatres, several small-group teaching rooms/ syndicate rooms, an M.B.A. reading room and resource room, a student common room, and offices. All student areas are equipped with telephones and computer facilities with Internet access, and the resource room gives students access to fax, printing, and binding facilities. Twenty-four-hour access to the ABP is controlled by a swipe-card system, which ensures that the facilities remain for the sole use of M.B.A. students and staff members.

Admission

Candidates for admission to the programme should have the following minimum entry criteria: an undergraduate degree or professional equivalent, a minimum of three years of management experience, an impressive track record, a good balanced GMAT score, and fluency in English. The selection process requires that candidates complete an Otago M.B.A. application form that includes, among other things, five 1-page essays. Two references are also required, and candidates must undergo a personal interview.

Finances

The 1999 tuition fees for the full-time programme, including all texts and teaching and resource materials, will be NZ$20,000 for New Zealand citizens and permanent residents and NZ$33,000 for international students.

Application Facts and Dates

The M.B.A. programme is a sixteen-month programme that starts in mid-January of each year. Applications are processed on an ongoing basis; therefore, early application is an advantage. Continuous processing ensures that applications can be dealt with quickly and decisions about individual cases can be made and communicated without the need to wait for closing dates. It is unlikely that candidates would be accepted into the programme without an interview, but interviews can be arranged in the candidate's home country. For further information and an application packet, students should contact:

M.B.A. Admissions
Advanced Business Programme
University of Otago
P.O. Box 56
Dunedin, New Zealand
Telephone: 64 3 479 8046
Fax: 64 3 479 8045
E-mail: mbainfo@commerce.otago.ac.nz
World Wide Web: http://divcom.otago.
    ac.nz:800/mba

University of Pennsylvania

Philadelphia, Pennsylvania

ONE WORLD, TWO DEGREES

Superb management skills merely open the door to a career as an international manager. To excel, individuals also need a solid grasp of the global environment of business and a finely tuned understanding of the language, culture, business practices, history, and politics of the regions in which they will work. The Joseph H. Lauder Institute of Management & International Studies provides this blend through a unique program that integrates two critical degrees: the Wharton M.B.A. and the M.A. in international studies from the School of Arts & Sciences. The Lauder Institute is a pioneer in integrating management education, international studies, and language and cross-cultural competencies.

—Dr. Stephen J. Kobrin, Director and William H. Wurster Professor of Multinational Management

Programs and Curricular Focus

The curriculum is an intensive, twenty-four-month program that integrates three essentials for the global manager. The first is a superior management education. The Wharton M.B.A. provides a foundation in the disciplines vital to the practice of professional development. The second essential is focused international studies. An integrated sequence of courses prepares Lauder students to understand the international political, economic, and social contexts in which their organizations will operate. The third is high-level language and cross-cultural courses. Mastery of a second language and detailed attention to regional, cultural, and managerial perspectives provide an essential base for future success.

All students complete the core management curriculum for the Wharton M.B.A. They also pursue a disciplinary concentration in any of Wharton's fields, such as strategic management, multinational management, marketing, finance, or operations management. Lauder students fulfill all requirements for the Wharton M.B.A. degree.

For the M.A. degree, students pursue an international studies course sequence in the social sciences and humanities with School of Arts & Sciences faculty as well as courses in their regional and language specialization. Several courses, such as Area History and International Political Economy, were designed particularly for the Lauder program.

The advanced language and cultural perspectives program develops students' knowledge of another language and culture for use in professional settings. Students must attain superior proficiency in a second language to graduate. They live and study in the region of their specialization during the first summer's cultural immersion program and typically arrange an Executive Internship in an international environment during their second summer. Students select from the following region and language options: East Asia (Mandarin Chinese or Japanese), Europe (French, German, or Russian), Latin America (Portuguese or Spanish), or North America (English). Upon graduation, students are competent to function independently and conduct business in their selected language.

Students and the Program Experience

With a student body of approximately 120 students, the Lauder Institute is a small community of people devoted to international studies. All students enter the program with previous experience living, working, or studying outside their home countries. Eighty percent of the class has worked abroad for six or more months. All Lauder students are fluent in a second language, and 80 percent are fluent in a third language. Of an average of 60 students entering Lauder each May, 37 percent are women, 13 percent are members of minority groups, and 27 percent are international students from approximately thirteen countries.

❖ Global Focus

Lauder students do not just study a world region, they experience it. At least 20 percent of their time is spent abroad, where they are immersed in a region's language, economics, history, politics, law, religion, business, and culture.

Special Features

During their first summer abroad, students experience life and business in major cosmopolitan centers and regional areas. They gain in-depth appreciation for the country's history, society, politics, business, theater, art, and literature through the local language. Housing varies from country to country, ranging from university quarters to apartments to rooms in homes. Corporate visits, a highlight of the summer program, are conducted in the native language and give students a firsthand look into the operations and cultures of foreign businesses. These visits to both multinational and indigenous companies provide opportunities for field projects associated with core courses in the M.B.A. program.

Executive Internships during the second summer provide the opportunity to work in a business setting rooted in another culture. Students take the lead in obtaining internships, with support from the Wharton School and the Lauder Institute. Over the years, Lauder students have held Executive Internships in 260 companies in thirty-eight countries. Students live and work in a country for twelve weeks, learning to apply their expertise in meaningful positions. Companies benefit from the advanced management and language skills the students bring. Often, internships lead to offers of permanent employment following graduation.

The Faculty

The Wharton School is ranked as the nation's premier school in management education and research. Today, the Wharton School comprises eleven departments and eighteen research centers. With a faculty of nearly 500 and a student body of more than 2,000, the Graduate Division of the University of Pennsylvania's School of Arts & Sciences is one of the world's leading graduate programs in the liberal arts. The school has thirty-four programs with some of the world's finest scholars on its faculty, contributing to the school's reputation for strong interdisciplinary research and instruction.

The Business School Network

Students benefit from a diverse, supportive, and dedicated community of classmates who enter the program from countries all over the world. Upon graduation, they join a still broader network of alumni in management positions around the globe. Lauder Institute graduates belong to a worldwide network of more than 650 alumni working in more than forty countries. Lauder alumni offer one another valuable international experience and contacts and frequently open doors to a wide array of opportunities.

Students enjoy exposure to senior executives of companies around the world through the International Executive Lecture Series. Members of the Institute's Board of Governors, an impressive body of global corporate leaders, visit the campus each year and are dedicated to helping Lauder students become the global business leaders of the future.

The College and Environs

The University of Pennsylvania was founded in 1740 by Benjamin Franklin. The 260-acre Ivy League campus is located in University City, which contains several colleges, business and government offices, and one of the largest urban research parks in the nation. The University includes twelve leading graduate schools and serves more than 22,000 undergraduate, master's, and doctoral students.

Facilities

In addition to the vast resources of the Wharton School, the University of Pennsylvania, and the greater Philadelphia region, Lauder students enjoy many special benefits, including a modern building, simultaneous translation facilities, satellite reception of world broadcasts, and the international camaraderie they find in the Lauder Lounge.

Placement

In addition to access to the Wharton Career Development and Placement Office, Lauder students benefit from a supportive and intimate network of alumni. Lauder Institute graduates belong to a worldwide network of more than 650 alumni working in more than forty countries. They remain in touch through personal friendship and ongoing support from the Institute, including newsletters, address lists, a regularly updated resume book, reunions, and alumni events in connection with summer immersion projects. Lauder graduates go out of their way to help one another, and they frequently speak of the bond they feel for fellow graduates. Lauder graduates have hired students for summer internships and full-time positions. As Edgar Bronfman Jr., President and CEO of Joseph E. Seagram & Sons, Inc., states, "Companies around the world recognize the value created in those who graduate from the Lauder Institute. There's no better business preparation, and graduates are positioned ideally for international management." Paul Fribourg, Chairman and CEO of Continental Grain Company, states, "Companies that want to build a worldwide business come here to hire. They know they'll find a concentrated group of very high-level people."

Admission

The Lauder Institute enrolls approximately 60 students into its M.B.A./M.A. program annually, all of whom have advanced knowledge of at least one nonnative language and are, by virtue of their experience and interests, strongly committed to international management careers. Admission to the Lauder Institute is highly competitive, and applicants are strongly encouraged to apply early. Applicants must complete both the regular Wharton M.B.A. application for admission and the Lauder Institute application. An international career focus, interest in enhancing their cross-cultural understanding, and exceptional leadership potential are the common denominators of most successful applicants. Students are required to submit results of the

Graduate Management Admission Test (GMAT), for which no minimum score is required, and a TOEFL score is required of all applicants for whom English is not the native language, unless they have earned a degree from an English-speaking university. After the application materials have been submitted, candidates will be tested by telephone for oral proficiency in the language for which they have applied.

Finances

Over the course of the Institute's twenty-four-month program, in addition to the regular M.B.A. tuition, Lauder students pay an Institute fee. The current Lauder fee for the twenty-four-month program is $16,000, subject to change. A limited number of scholarships and partial fellowships, need-based aid, and international student assistance is available to Lauder students.

Application Facts and Dates

The Lauder program begins in early May, and applications must be postmarked by the end of the first week of February. Although the final deadline for application to the Lauder Institute's dual-degree program is the first week of February, both Wharton and Lauder use a rolling admission process and begin to evaluate applications and make admissions decisions in the middle of the previous November. Applicants receive a decision approximately eight weeks after Lauder and Wharton both receive a completed application.

For more information, students should contact:

Ms. Natacha Davis Keramidas
Associate Director for Admissions and Recruiting
The Lauder Institute
256 South 37th Street, 2nd Floor
Philadelphia, Pennsylvania 19104-6330
Telephone: 215-898-1215
Fax: 215-898-2067
E-mail: lauderinfo@wharton.upenn.edu
World Wide Web: http://lauder.wharton.upenn.edu

Wharton University of Pennsylvania

The Wharton School
University of Pennsylvania

The Wharton School

Philadelphia, Pennsylvania

WHAT WILL IT TAKE TO LEAD IN THE TWENTY-FIRST CENTURY?

Modern organizations are undergoing fundamental transformations. As companies become more dynamic, more global, and more entrepreneurial, business leaders will need both broader and deeper skills to succeed.

From its founding in 1881 as the world's first school of management, Wharton has always been the leader in extending the frontiers of management education. Our new M.B.A. curriculum takes that leadership into the next century. The program builds upon Wharton's substantial strengths—our expertise across the widest range of areas, our extensive global initiatives, and our long-standing commitment to innovation and entrepreneurship. It breaks new ground to provide the new skills and perspectives that forward-thinking business leaders have identified as critical to success today and in the future.

The evolving business environment presents great challenges. The Wharton M.B.A. program is equally demanding. But both also offer tremendous opportunities for those with the insights, skills, and drive to succeed.

—Thomas P. Gerrity, Dean

Programs and Curricular Focus

Wharton's curriculum is designed to generate innovative ideas and creative thinking and to instill an excitement about learning. Students are challenged through their core courses, case studies, and leadership course work to formulate and solve problems.

The first year focuses on Wharton's business core, providing fundamental skill, knowledge, and perspectives. Traditional semesters are replaced by four tightly focused six-week quarters to expose students to the greatest number of subjects and to allow faculty to coordinate material across courses. Cohorts of 60 students, who take core courses together in the first year, form a strong social and academic group. Clusters of three cohorts form "a class within a class."

The second year allows students to choose electives from one of the largest selections of courses of any business school; this selection allows students to pursue one of two dozen majors or create joint majors and individualized programs. Students work individually and in 5-person learning teams to examine issues of self-awareness, teamwork, ethics, communication, effective negotiation, managing differences, managing careers, and power and authority.

The Lauder Institute offers a twenty-four-month joint-degree program to prepare future leaders to operate effectively and comfortably in a language and culture other than their own. This program leads to an M.B.A. from Wharton and an M.A. in international studies from the University's School of Arts and Sciences.

Wharton also offers joint-degree programs, which generally require one less year of study, in the areas of communication, engineering, law, medical sciences, dental, veterinary, nursing, social work, and Wharton doctoral programs.

The Wharton Executive M.B.A. program enables individuals with full-time job responsibilities in the private and public sectors to gain an M.B.A. degree without interrupting their careers. Experienced executives and highly promising managers nominated by their organizations enroll in the program. Classes meet all day Friday and Saturday on alternate weekends for two years.

Students and the M.B.A. Experience

Wharton students have outstanding records of professional achievement and bring a wide range of experience, insights, and interests to the classroom and to campus. Drawing on their experiences throughout the world, students offer diverse cultural viewpoints on business issues. They bring perspectives from undergraduate majors that range from English to engineering and work experience that extends from non-profit management to marketing to corporate finance. Wharton M.B.A. students help shape the intellectual atmosphere of challenge and collaboration that is a central part of a Wharton education.

About 45 percent of incoming students have liberal arts and science degrees, and 20 percent have training in engineering. Almost all have had significant work experience in private, public, or nonprofit enterprises. Of an average class of 750 students entering Wharton each fall, about 29 percent are women, 18 percent are members of minority groups, and 30 percent are foreign nationals from more than sixty countries.

❖ Global Focus

Wharton's curriculum has a strong international perspective, reinforced by a core course on global strategic management and a range of electives that provide insights into global business. In addition, the Wharton Global Immersion Program option offers four weeks of intense, hands-on experience and education abroad, following six weeks of classroom study. Recent groups have traveled to China, Europe, Latin America, and the ASEAN countries. Wharton also offers two international joint-degree programs, exchange programs with ten leading international business schools, and opportunities to develop foreign language skills.

Special Features

A four-week preterm program ensures that students from diverse backgrounds begin the M.B.A. program on equal academic footing. The program includes an introduction to accounting, microeconomics, and statistics and optional courses in humanities and business history. The program ends with a two-day team-building retreat.

Beyond cohorts and learning teams, students pursue individual interests through more than 125 professional, social, and academic affairs clubs and task forces. Wharton also offers opportunities to work on service projects with area students and community organizations.

The Faculty

Wharton's 183 standing faculty members bring a diversity of perspectives, both theoretical and practical, to the classroom. They have earned worldwide recognition for excellence in both teaching and research. Their work has extended the frontiers of many fields—from conducting groundbreaking studies in international finance to developing one of the most widely used methods of marketing research to creating the first center for the study of entrepreneurship. Wharton professors have received numerous awards, including the Nobel Prize in Economic Sciences and honors from the White House and the National Science Foundation.

The Business School Network

Corporate Partnerships

An advisory board of executives as well as corporate recruiters and alumni help shape the future development of the curriculum. In addition, more than 200 guest executive lecturers and speakers visit Wharton each year. In addition to contact with senior executives as guest lecturers in the classroom and in presentations and professional clubs, Wharton students have the opportunity to interact in a more intimate and informal context with business leaders through the Zweig Executive Dinner Series.

Prominent Alumni

Prominent alumni include the Hon. Walter H. Annenberg, a former ambassador and publisher; the Hon. William Brennan, a former chief justice; Charles S. Sanford Jr., Chairman, Bankers Trust; Reginald Jones, Chairman Emeritus, General Electric; Lewis Platt, Chairman and CEO, Hewlett-Packard; Yataro Kobayashi, Chairman and CEO, Fuji Xerox; Robert Crandall, CEO, American Airlines; John Sculley, former CEO,

Apple Computer; and Stanley R. Jaffe, COO, Paramount Communications.

The College and Environs

The University of Pennsylvania was founded in 1740 by Benjamin Franklin. The 260-acre Ivy League campus is located in University City, which contains several colleges, business and government offices, and one of the largest urban research parks in the nation. The University includes twelve leading graduate schools and serves more than 22,000 undergraduate, master's, and doctoral students.

Facilities

In addition to a University library with nearly 3.6 million volumes, students use Wharton's Lippincott Library, which contains approximately 200,000 volumes and 3,500 periodical titles specifically related to business, as well as copies of 5,000 corporate annual reports. Wharton's library computing center offers access to a variety of business, news, and information databases on optical disk and on line.

Technology Environment

Computing facilities available to M.B.A. students include a cluster of Digital VAX 6400 mainframes, more than 125 microcomputers in student labs, and a Schoolwide data communications network accessible by modem. Wharton also offers training courses, user documentation, and consulting services.

Placement

The Wharton Career Development and Placement Office coordinates more than thirty-five different programs for students, from identifying potential career areas and developing effective job search strategies to interviewing, negotiating, and evaluating offers. Programs include

career management classes in the first year, alumni career panels, videotaped interview training, and seminars on negotiating offers.

Admission

Prerequisites for admission include completion of an undergraduate program in an accredited U.S. college or its equivalent in another country, results of the Graduate Management Admission Test (GMAT) for which no minimum score is required, and completion of the Wharton application. A TOEFL score is required of all applicants for whom English is not the native language. Applicants are evaluated based on their personal qualities, academic background, and professional experience. Personal interviews are strongly encouraged but not required.

Finances

The 1998–99 educational budget for first-year students is $43,036. This cost includes tuition and fees, room and board, books and supplies, miscellaneous fees, and preterm expenses. Preterm fees apply only in the first year and vary, depending on the program components in which a student enrolls.

International Students

There is a strong international student community at Wharton, with resources and programs to meet social, cultural, and professional interests. International students make up one third of the M.B.A. student body, and they represent more than sixty nationalities. Many of the campus club activities are generated by the cultural interests of M.B.A. students.

Application Facts and Dates

Although the final deadline for application is in early April, Wharton begins to evaluate applications and make admissions decisions in the middle of the previous November. Wharton uses a rolling admission process, evaluating applications in order of their receipt and completion. Applicants receive a decision approximately eight to twelve weeks after Wharton receives a completed application.

Mr. Robert Alig
Director of M.B.A. Admissions
The Wharton School
University of Pennsylvania
3733 Spruce Street
Philadelphia, Pennsylvania 19104-6361
Telephone: 215-898-6182
Fax: 215-898-0120
E-mail: mba.admissions@wharton.upenn.edu
World Wide Web: http://www.wharton.upenn.edu/

University of Pittsburgh

Pittsburgh, Pennsylvania

Programs and Curricular Focus

The Katz Graduate School of Business offers a unique eleven-month full-time M.B.A. program. The program begins each year in mid-July and is completed in mid-June. The program includes student participation in team-building exercises, learning organizations, capability assessments, and career evaluations. The curriculum provides a global management perspective in every phase of the program; emphasizes interrelationships across business functions; incorporates continuous quality improvement in theory and methods; focuses on teamwork, interpersonal skills, and the empowerment process; and applies leading-edge management theory to real-world problems and issues by emphasizing today's set of challenges.

Seven concentrations are offered, from accounting to strategic planning. Forty-four percent of the full-time M.B.A. program's credits are elective. In addition to traditional courses, students may also participate in project courses, internships, practicums, and independent studies.

The Katz School also offers an M.B.A. degree program that meets in the evenings and Saturdays to accommodate students who are employed full-time.

The Center for Executive Education offers a Master of Business Administration (E.M.B.A.) that is completed in two years. Classes are conducted on alternating Fridays and Saturdays. Also offered is the FLEX-M.B.A., which is completed in two years with only fourteen weeks of in-residence classes.

Students and the M.B.A. Experience

Students in the Katz M.B.A. program bring to their studies an exciting variety of talents, backgrounds, and interests. Eighty-four percent of enrolling students have, on average, 4½ years of work experience, in areas that include accounting, consulting, finance, information systems, manufacturing, and marketing and sales. About one third of the class generally have technical and engineering backgrounds. Students have worked in a wide variety of industries, from accounting to banking to manufacturing to health care. There is also a significant representation of students from abroad—representing approximately thirty countries—adding their experiences to the forum of ideas. A typical M.B.A. class generally includes students with degrees from as many as 150 undergraduate institutions. Undergraduate majors encompass the natural sciences and humanities, economics, business, engineering, the liberal arts and the performing arts, and virtually every other broad discipline. The varied perspectives of the students create a stimulating environment for interaction.

❖ Global Focus

The full-time M.B.A. class is divided into group learning organizations with diverse memberships. These groups study together, prepare together, and form rotating teams as the basis for case discussions and group projects in many courses. This simulates what it is like to be in a real organization and helps students learn and practice trust building, communication, teamwork, conflict management, negotiation, and problem management skills.

Special Features

Full-time students ease into a rigorous academic schedule through the Transition Module. The Transition Module provides a series of workshops that integrate the basics of management while introducing the instructional environment at the Katz School. In addition, students have the opportunity to meet classmates during a series of social events, professional workshops, and classroom settings.

The Faculty

The faculty of the Katz School is internationally respected for its pioneering research and corporate consulting. The 68 full-time faculty members include recognized authorities in accounting, economics, finance, marketing, international business, behavioral science, quantitative methods, human resources management, operations management, management information systems, organizational studies, public and social policy, and strategic planning and policy. Corporations, governmental agencies, and not-for-profit groups commission research by the faculty members. The knowledge gained through faculty members' research and consulting becomes part of the experience of the M.B.A. student in the classroom.

The Business School Network

Corporate Partnerships

A city as important to the nation's economy as Pittsburgh is provides a wide range of opportunities for M.B.A. students. The Katz School takes advantage of these opportunities by offering an unparalleled series of activities that bring many of America's leading executives to the Katz School on a regular basis.

Through the American Assembly Dialogue, some of the country's highest-ranking executives gather on campus each spring to discuss the significant economic and social issues of the day in response to an agenda prepared by Pittsburgh M.B.A. students. The Katz School is the only school in the country to hold this annual event, which has been co-sponsored by the New York–based American Assembly since 1971.

The Executive Briefings series also fosters ties between students and business leaders. Two or three times each month, chief executives from major Pittsburgh and national corporations come to the Katz School to share their thoughts on those issues of most concern to them, then open the sessions to questions from students.

Through the Executives-in-Residence program, top executives are available on campus for one or two days, lecturing in classes and, just as importantly, mingling with students after class.

The Associates Program includes 200 corporations that support and cooperate with the School, providing fellowships for M.B.A. students, student internships, and employment opportunities for M.B.A. graduates.

Prominent Alumni

The University of Pittsburgh counts among its alumni Donald R. Beall, Chairman and CEO, Rockwell International; Thomas E. Frank, President and CEO, Hickory Farms, Inc.; Robert H. Hood Jr., President, McDonnell Douglas Corporation; James J. Howard, Chairman and CEO, Northern States Power Company; Samuel A. McCullough,

Chairman and CEO, Meridian Bancorp, Inc.; John M. Peterson, President and CEO (Retired), Erie Insurance Group; David M. Roderick, Chairman and CEO (Retired), USX Corporation; Charles Russell, President and CEO (Retired), Visa International; John J. Shea, President and CEO, Speigel, Inc.; and Raymond W. Smith, Chairman and CEO, Bell Atlantic.

The College and Environs

Founded in 1787, the University of Pittsburgh is one of the oldest institutions of higher education in the United States. The Pittsburgh campus consists of ninety buildings on 132 acres. The campus includes the forty-two-story Cathedral of Learning, with its ornate Gothic architecture, which is the tallest school building in the Western world.

The city of Pittsburgh is the hub of the Eastern business wheel, equidistant from the major economic centers of New York and Chicago and only an hour's plane ride from other primary business points such as Philadelphia, Boston, Toronto, Montreal, Detroit, Atlanta, and Washington, D.C. Pittsburgh has a diverse economic base developed through both phases of its heralded renaissance, and it is a prominent transportation, technological, medical, commercial, and communications center as well as an international industrial leader. It is one of the country's largest corporate headquarters. Pittsburgh is an attractive city with a rich mixture of bustling industry and colorful neighborhoods. This combination of vital business and comfortable living is unusually compelling. Pittsburgh is consistently cited as one of the most livable cities in the United States.

Facilities

Mervis Hall, the home of the Katz Graduate School of Business, is sleek in appearance and represents the best in contemporary architecture and the forward-looking Pittsburgh corporate community. All M.B.A. classes are held here, which fosters a sense of unity among the M.B.A. students. The building's tiered classrooms and unique behavior science laboratory accommodate a variety of teaching modes, from case discussions and lectures to small-group exercises. Video cameras and playback systems as well as other contemporary audio and visual aids are a regular part of student learning.

Mervis Hall offers a computer and communications system that provides hands-on access to the Katz School's comprehensive internal and external data environment. The building incorporates state-of-the-art fiber optics that enable the school to have a complete communications system, including e-mail. The complex also includes a 9,000-square-foot library, interview rooms, a career library, and a videotape area. The facility also houses faculty and administrative offices, student lounges, and offices for the School's research institutes.

Placement

The Career Services Center begins its work with each new M.B.A. class shortly after students arrive on campus. The initial step is individual counseling, which gives the student an opportunity to investigate career opportunities with the assistance of a placement officer. To enhance this phase of the placement process, the placement office sponsors lunchtime seminars in which middle- and upper-level managers from major companies meet with groups of students to speak informally about their jobs and careers. The Career Services Center schedules career seminars on topics such as writing effective resumes and cover letters, interviewing skills, and job search strategies. Students participate in mock interview sessions that are videotaped and analyzed by placement staff. The placement office maintains a comprehensive, up-to-date placement library with handbooks, business reviews, annual reports, and a database of contact persons for hundreds of companies and organizations. The placement office also compiles an M.B.A.-student resume directory, which is distributed to some 500 companies nationwide. Last year, more than 100 companies participated in on-campus interviewing, which began in November and continued through June.

Admission

The Katz School has developed an application procedure managed by the applicant. The School uses a system of rolling admissions, so early application is encouraged. The Admissions Committee reviews applications every four to six weeks. All applicants are required to have earned an undergraduate degree or, for international applicants, the equivalent of a U.S. bachelor's degree. Applicants need not have had prior business course work to be eligible for admission. Applicants are required to have completed at least introductory college-level work in integral and differential calculus prior to enrollment in the M.B.A. program. All applicants are required to have taken the GMAT. The Test of English as a Foreign Language (TOEFL) is required if the applicant's native language is not English. The Admissions Committee reviews and evaluates each applicant's academic record, GMAT score, letters of recommendation, essays, professional work history, and other information presented by the candidate on the application. International applicants must submit their applications by February 15. Applicants who request scholarship aid should submit their applications by February 15.

Finances

Tuition for 1997–98 full-time Pennsylvania residents was $15,375 for the year of study. Tuition for 1997–98 full-time non-Pennsylvania residents was $26,190 for the year of study. Tuition for 1997–98 for part-time/evening students was $446 per credit for Pennsylvania residents and $834 per credit for non-Pennsylvania residents.

For full-time study, students should budget a minimum of $14,000 for the year—in addition to tuition and fees—for room, board, and miscellaneous expenses. This is a baseline estimate, since individual needs and preferences create a wide variance in actual living costs.

The primary source of financial assistance is tuition fellowships, which are awarded in various dollar amounts and applied against tuition charges. These fellowships are awarded primarily on the basis of academic merit, with financial need as a secondary consideration. Teaching fellowships and assistantships are not offered through the Katz School for students studying at the master's level. Because of the amount of course work students must undertake in the M.B.A. program, there is insufficient time to commit to a teaching fellowship.

International Students

Approximately 40 percent of the M.B.A. class are international students. The University of Pittsburgh's Office of International Services provides assistance with admissions and advising on personal, social, immigration, and financial matters.

Application Facts and Dates

Generally, applications are reviewed and decision notification is sent within a four- to six-week time frame from the date the completed application with all required documentation is received. Applicants requesting scholarship aid should submit their complete applications to the full-time M.B.A. program by February 15. The deadline for international applicants is February 15. Part-time/evening applicants should submit their completed applications one or two months prior to the preferred term of entry.

Office of Admissions
276 Mervis Hall
Joseph M. Katz Graduate School of
  Business
University of Pittsburgh
Pittsburgh, Pennsylvania 15260
Telephone: 412-648-1700
Fax: 412-648-1659
E-mail: mba-admissions@katz.
  business.pitt.edu
World Wide Web: http://www.pitt.edu/
  ~business/

THE BUSINESS SCHOOL
FOR FINANCIAL MARKETS

University of Reading

ISMA Centre

Reading, England

> ### THE BUSINESS SCHOOL FOR FINANCIAL MARKETS
>
> *The value of any program of education and training in finance is the recognition it receives from the financial community at large. The market leaders who have given their support to ISMA Centre programs include Reuters, Bridge Telerate, Bloomberg, the London Stock Exchange, ISMA, and, of course, the member firms of ISMA themselves. Our graduates have been employed by well over 100 securities companies, including J. P. Morgan, Bankers Trust, D. E. Shaw, Citibank, C. S. First Boston, SBC Warburg Dillon Read, Union Bank of Switzerland, Barclays Capital, Nomura, and Merrill Lynch. If you are seeking a qualification in finance that includes an international dimension, then the ISMA Centre is the premier location in Europe for such programs.*
>
> —Professor Brian Scott-Quinn, Director, University of Reading ISMA Centre

Programs and Curricular Focus

The M.Sc. in international securities, investment, and banking is a specialized postgraduate degree program that combines the theory of international financial markets, investments, and banking with a large element of professional securities and investment industry training.

This nine-month full-time program is both academically and intellectually rigorous and is designed for those wishing to enter or those who are already in the international securities industry. It covers all financial markets and is equally suited to those who wish to work in U.S., European, Asian, or Australasian markets.

The unique INVEST dealing rooms have fifty Reuters 3000 dealing positions with live datafeeds, spreadsheet valuation models, computer-based derivative securities valuation, and portfolio management simulations. Students also have access to Bloomberg terminals in the brand-new, purpose-built $5-million teaching facility.

The degree program is divided into three terms of ten weeks each. The first term provides a general introduction to the international securities industry, including industry training sessions, and develops the core concepts of corporate finance. Fixed income, equity, and derivative securities are then analyzed. The first term ends in early January with an examination on topics covered up to that time. The options in the second term include financial engineering, portfolio management, operations management, risk management, corporate control, financial regulation, and mergers and acquisitions.

Although this course has many innovations in its content, delivery, and use of industry software, it has been designed to ensure that the topics covered also include the major areas required by many of the world's professional examination bodies, such as the Chartered Financial Analysts of America (CFA/AIMR). In addition, the Director of Professional Education has arranged for training to be provided to allow participants to undertake examinations such as the NYSE/NASDAQ Series examinations.

To supplement the existing M.Sc., a new master's degree in finance, regulation, and risk management has been developed. This is designed for students with a first degree in law, for example, as well as for those with a first degree in business. The Centre also awards Doctoral Scholarships in finance to suitably qualified candidates.

Students and the M.Sc. Experience

The ISMA Centre's programs are designed both for those who have recently graduated with a first degree in economics, accounting, or business and also for those with a first degree in other disciplines, such as computer studies, mathematics, physics, chemistry, or law. Students who have already had employment experience and have a good GMAT score are also welcome.

The master's degree provides individuals with the core competencies and skills required by firms operating in the international securities market.

This M.Sc. degree program is a large and very successful program in international securities and investment. Although 120 places are available each year, there are more than 800 applicants. Because of this, the program can only accept those who are well qualified.

Students enter the program from more than thirty-five different countries. Many are from continental and Eastern Europe as well as the U.K., with more than 15 percent of applicants coming from the

The new purpose-built ISMA Centre building.

One of the dealing rooms at the ISMA Centre.

Americas. There are also students from the Middle East, Asia, and Australasia.

Special Features

The ISMA Centre is supported by the International Securities Market Association (ISMA), which serves as the market regulator and trade association of what has now become the largest capital market in the world after domestic government bond markets. The members of ISMA are the securities houses that trade international securities and meet the investment needs of their clients. There are currently about 780 member firms from fifty-two countries, clear evidence of the Association's international character.

ISMA, whose head office is in Zurich, Switzerland, has donated $5 million to the University for the construction of a purpose-built facility on campus exclusively for these programs and related international securities courses.

The Faculty

The ISMA Centre is part of the Business and Management Group in the Department of Economics, which was awarded an official research ranking of fourth out of 100 business and management units in British universities.

Every member of the full-time ISMA Centre teaching staff has a doctorate and is actively researching their specialist area of finance. They work alongside visiting professors who teach part-time on their specialist subject and have been involved professionally in the international securities industry as well as in financial research.

In addition to the academic staff members, the Centre enjoys weekly presentations from industry professionals from the City of London financial markets.

The Business School Network

Supported by ISMA, the Centre enjoys a privileged position in the provision of education and research in international securities, investment, and banking. Proximity to London allows representatives of the member firms working in the City of London to contribute their expertise and guidance to the program. As a partner of the Centre for the Study of Financial Innovation (CSFI), a London-based body financed by the securities industry, the ISMA Centre benefits from weekly presentations from city practitioners. The Centre is also one of the partners of Carnegie Mellon University in Pittsburgh in the Financial Analysis and Securities Trading (FAST) trading and investment simulation program.

The College and Environs

The University of Reading has more than a century of history. It was originally an extension college of Oxford University and received its Royal Charter in 1926. With student numbers exceeding 12,000, it is one of Britain's largest and most successful traditional universities, providing excellence in teaching and research.

The landscaped campus is situated on its own 300-acre site on the outskirts of Reading, which provides a central focus for academic, social, and recreational aspects of University life.

Reading is an outer commuter suburb of London located between Oxford and Windsor. London's Heathrow International Airport is conveniently nearby.

Facilities

The ISMA Centre is centrally situated on the University Campus and has its own high-specification facility comprising a 120-seat lecture theater, seminar rooms, catering facilities, resource and computer rooms, and unique INVEST dealing rooms with Bloomberg terminals and fifty Reuters 3000 dealing positions.

Students are also able to make use of the facilities elsewhere on campus, including the large University library, which offers CD-ROM databases and Internet services as well as the usual selection of books, periodicals, archives, and audiovisual materials.

The University of Reading has many residence halls, some with full en-suite facilities, which are conveniently situated on campus. Most sports, including American football, are supported by the University.

Placement

The Centre has excellent links with employers and selection firms and provides an assessment and career advisory service. Career opportunities are assisted by the distribution to employers of profiles of all the students in the program. The Centre's graduates benefit from recruitment visits from many of the international banks and securities houses based in the city.

Admission

Admission requirements are a minimum GPA of 3.3 or an upper second class honours degree or equivalent, two academic references, and an academic transcript. GMAT scores higher than 600 are preferred. There should be evidence of a high level of numeracy and English language fluency (minimum TOEFL score of 590 or minimum IELTS score of 7).

Those applying are expected to demonstrate an interest in a career in the fields of corporate finance, portfolio management, investment banking, securities, mergers and acquisitions, risk management, market regulation, and compliance or corporate treasury.

Finances

Full-time tuition for the M.Sc. program during the 1998–99 academic year is £8500 (approximately $13,900 U.S. dollars). The estimate of a year's living costs for 1998–99 is £5600 (approximately $9200 U.S. dollars).

Application Facts and Dates

For an explanatory brochure and application form, students should contact:

Zoë Lewsley
University of Reading
ISMA Centre
Whiteknights
P.O. Box 242
Reading RG6 6BA
England
Telephone: 011 44 118 931 6675
Fax: 011 44 118 931 4741
E-mail: admin@ismacentre.reading.ac.uk
World Wide Web: http://www.ismacentre.reading.ac.uk

University of Rochester

William E. Simon Graduate School of Business Administration

Rochester, New York

A SIMON SCHOOL EDUCATION—PREPARATION FOR A LIFETIME CAREER IN MANAGEMENT

The Simon School's integrated, cross-functional approach to management is enhanced by our small size and significant international composition. The school's small size promotes communication among faculty members and students that is very difficult to achieve in a large, departmentalized school. The international student body, combined with the School's emphasis on student teams, brings the global workplace to life for the Simon School student.

—Charles I. Plosser, Dean

Programs and Curricular Focus

The Simon School's M.B.A. programs are designed to train individuals to solve management problems as team members in a study-team structure. The curriculum emphasizes learning the principles of economics and effective decision making through a mix of lecture, case study, and project courses. The degree program requires 67 hours (twenty quarter courses) and can be completed in six quarters of full-time study. Five core courses are required in the underlying disciplines of economics, applied statistics, accounting, and computers and information systems. One course must be taken in each of the functional areas of finance, marketing, operations management, and organization theory. A 2-credit course in business communications and a Practicum in Management capstone course are required of all full-time students. Ten elective courses are required, of which five or more may form a sequence of concentration, although a concentration is not required for graduation. The thirteen areas of concentration offered are corporate accounting, public accounting, accounting and information systems, business environment and public policy, computers and information systems, entrepreneurship, finance, health-care management, international management, marketing, operations management–manufacturing, operations management–services, and organizations and markets. Students may select an individualized double-concentration to customize their course of study in preparation for specific career objectives.

Students and the M.B.A. Experience

Each September approximately 170 students enter the Simon community as members of four cohorts (class teams). Another 60 students join their classmates in January as cohort number five. Each cohort takes all core classes together. September entrants complete the first-year core courses during the fall, winter, and spring quarters; the majority of January entrants complete core courses during the winter, spring, and summer quarters. Within each cohort, students are assigned to a study team of 4 or 5 members. Due to the large number of students from outside the United States (44 percent), the study-team structure at the Simon School takes on special significance. Each team always includes representatives from at least three countries.

Simon students enter the program with a wide range of educational, professional, and geographic backgrounds. In the class of 1999, 124 undergraduate institutions and twenty-two countries are represented. Undergraduate majors include economics, humanities, social sciences, business and commerce, engineering, and math and science. Prior full-time work experience averages five years, and the average age is 27. Women comprise 23 percent of the class. Thirteen percent of Simon students are members of American minority groups.

❖ Global Focus

Of the leading business schools, the Simon School is one of the most geographically diverse. More than 40 percent of its students come from outside the United States. Approximately one third of its alumni reside and work outside of the United States, and about one third of its tenure-track faculty members have non-U.S. backgrounds. The Simon School emphasizes the high percentage of international students because the success of its hands-on approach to global management education depends in part on the cultural, geographic, and professional composition of the student management teams. The benefits of such a richly internationalized student and alumni population are obvious. A Simon School education combines rigorous training in the business disciplines and functions with cross-cultural training and lifelong professional contact with an international alumni network.

During the Broaden Your Horizons seminar series, students present lunch hour seminars about their various countries' cultures, economies, political environments, and business protocols. Exchange programs are offered with schools in eight countries, each approved by a faculty committee for compatibility with Simon M.B.A. program objectives. Interested students pursue study abroad during one quarter of their second year of study.

Special Features

VISION: A Partnership for Developing Future Managers is the student-managed portion of the Simon School's M.B.A. program. Designed each year by a committee of second-year M.B.A. students, the VISION program consists of sixteen teaching modules that supplement and enhance the academic curriculum. Student managers use the human resources and expertise of corporate sponsors—in partnership with Simon administrators, faculty members, and other students—to present required (and some optional) modules covering such topics as time management, team building, negotiation skills, leadership training, and ethics. Past corporate partners have included AT&T, IBM, Levi-Strauss, PepsiCo, Wells Fargo Bank, and Xerox Corporation, among others.

To ensure that Simon School graduates possess effective oral and written communication skills, they are required to complete a management-communication sequence comprising two courses, Presentation Skills and Business Writing and Editing.

The Faculty

The Simon School faculty is known internationally for leading scholarship in management education. There is a long tradition at Simon of coordinating teaching and research, as well as integrating knowledge from all of the functional areas into the curriculum. Faculty accessibility is a specific benefit of a Simon education. Teaching awards for the best teachers are presented annually by each M.B.A. class, and teaching is improved continuously through a formal faculty peer-review. Leading-edge research is intrinsic to teaching the basic scientific principles of management. Many research findings used by the Simon faculty in classroom study have served as foundations for corporate practices in use today. Simon faculty members serve as editors on six major academic journals, and six recent studies of research productivity rank them among the top five faculties in the United States.

The Business School Network

Corporate Partnerships

The Frederick Kalmbach Executive Seminar Series, jointly sponsored by the Simon School and the Graduate Business Club, features senior corporate executives who lecture annually on current issues in management. Each year a number of the series' speakers include members or professional associates of Simon's internationally prominent Executive Advisory Committee. Simon students participate in an annual marketing-case competition sponsored by Johnson & Johnson, and, through the VISION program described above, students interact directly with the employees of top international corporate partners. Students work directly with local worldwide corporations, such as Bausch & Lomb and Eastman Kodak Company, in project courses offered as part of the regular academic curriculum.

Prominent Alumni

The long list of successful Simon alumni includes Richard T. Bourns, Senior Vice President, Eastman Kodak Company; Paul A. Brands, Chief Executive Officer, American Management Systems; W. Scott Gould, Chief Financial Officer, United States Department of Commerce; Mark B. Grier, Executive Vice President, Financial Management, The Prudential Insurance Company of America; Charles R. Hughes, President, Land Rover of North America, Inc.; John C. MacDonald, Managing Director, Lehman Brothers; R. Kae Robertson, Partner, Ernst & Young; and Joseph T. Willett, Chief Operating Officer, Merrill Lynch Europe, Middle East and Africa (MLEMEA), Merrill Lynch & Co., Inc.

The College and Environs

The Simon School is part of the ivy-clad University of Rochester, an independent, leading research university offering graduate study in approximately fifty fields to about 2,700 of its 8,700 students. Situated near Lake Ontario, one of the Great Lakes, the metropolitan Rochester area (population 1 million) is home to many major international industries and entrepreneurial ventures, including Eastman Kodak Company, Bausch & Lomb, and Xerox Corporation's marketing group. Numerous cultural and recreational opportunities include the Rochester Philharmonic Orchestra and the University's own Eastman School of Music.

Facilities

Schlegel Hall, opened in 1991, is the Simon School's classroom and student services building. It contains case-style classrooms equipped with state-of-the-art technology and rear projection equipment, study rooms, a student lounge, and its own Computing Center. The center supports student-accessible IBM-compatible and Macintosh personal computers linked for data sharing and laser printing via local area networks and access to several external data sources, such as Bloomberg, Business News, and Dow Jones, as well as e-mail services on the Internet. On-campus graduate housing, both high-rise apartments and town houses, is available to Simon students. Off-campus housing is also available.

Placement

The hallmark of the Career Services Office is personalized support for the internship and full-time M.B.A. job search. Campus interviews are the leading source of offers (27 percent), with off-site recruiting events in New York City and Atlanta, Georgia; resume referrals; *The Hire Authority* (job listing newsletter for Simon students); videoconferencing; and resume books accounting for another 33 percent annually. The mean total offer package for 1998 graduates was $76,699.

Admission

A Simon School Admissions Committee reads each application individually and evaluates recommendations, teamwork and communication skills, the nature and scope of prior work experience, the undergraduate academic record, GMAT scores, TOEFL scores as an indicator of English-language skills, evidence of leadership and maturity, and career focus. English language proficiency is critically important for successful interaction in the Simon School's geographically diversified

study-team structure. Potential contributions to Simon classmates and to the world's business community are carefully considered. All undergraduate majors are represented in the program.

Finances

In addition to the $75 application fee, tuition is $792 per credit hour, or $23,760 per year, for 1998–99. The cost of books and supplies averages $1300 a year, and living expenses (rent, food supplies, personal expenses, and health insurance) are estimated at less than $10,000 for the 1998–99 academic year. Both U.S. and international applicants are eligible for merit awards. The deadline for applying for merit-scholarship assistance is March 1 for September applicants and November 15 for January applicants.

International Students

There is an active program of support for international students in Rochester. In addition to Simon International, a graduate business school student organization, the University of Rochester's International Student Affairs Office provides professional guidance to incoming international students. They are assisted by an independent, but University-affiliated, community volunteer group, the Rochester International Friendship Council, which locates host families for interested Simon students and helps students' spouses in language instruction and acculturation. Social outings and employment and cultural adjustment workshops are offered during late August orientation for all University international students. Instruction in English as a second language and orientation to U.S. culture are also available through the Simon Summer Advantage Program, offered each August.

Application Facts and Dates

Application deadlines are March 1 (for merit-scholarship consideration) and June 1 for September enrollment, November 15 for January enrollment. Students are notified of admissions decisions on a rolling basis. For additional information, students should contact:

Pamela Black-Colton
Assistant Dean for M.B.A. Admissions
 and Administration
William E. Simon Graduate School of
 Business Administration
University of Rochester
Rochester, New York 14627-0107
Telephone: 716-275-3533
Fax: 716-271-3907
E-mail: mbaadm@mail.ssb.rochester.
 edu
World Wide Web: http://www.ssb.
 rochester.edu

University of St. Thomas

Minneapolis and St. Paul, Minnesota

DECISION MAKING IN AN ETHICAL FRAMEWORK

The Graduate School of Business at the University of St. Thomas has more than 3,000 students in nine graduate degree programs and is one of the five largest graduate schools of business in the U.S. Our programs are known for their excellence in teaching and their emphasis on an applications orientation.

Decision making under an ethical framework is a theme that runs throughout the M.B.A. programs' curricula. Class size is kept to 25 students or fewer to ensure appropriate interaction among students and the instructor. As a result, the classroom experience is dynamic and stimulating.

Through its excellence in teaching and service to the community and through the success of its alumni, the St. Thomas M.B.A. and other graduate business degree programs have gained the reputation of being among the best in the United States. We invite you to join us and help us add to that reputation.

—Theodore L. Fredrickson, Dean and McNeely Chair Professor

Programs and Curricular Focus

St. Thomas's Graduate School of Business offers a comprehensive array of educational resources encompassing nine degree programs and thirteen professional development centers and institutes. These are specifically designed to meet the needs of adult learners, with a strong theory-based and practitioner-oriented approach and curriculum. Students benefit from the enhanced knowledge that derives from immediately applying what they learn in the classroom to the challenges they experience in the workplace, with valuable real-world guidance and feedback from faculty members with extensive business and academic backgrounds.

The Evening M.B.A. program provides working professionals with a comprehensive business management education, beginning with a base of foundation and core courses tailored to students' individual needs. Students complete a minimum of four concentration courses, and the program culminates with one of four integrative capstone courses. Areas of concentration include accounting, environmental management, finance, financial services management, franchise management, health-care management, human resource management, information management, management, manufacturing systems, marketing, nonprofit management, real estate, risk and insurance management, sports and entertainment management, and venture management. Graduate-level certificates

are also available in some concentrations for students who choose not to earn a degree, but wish to gain expertise at an accelerated pace.

St. Thomas' newest program, the Day M.B.A., was launched in fall 1997. Designed for recent college graduates and career changers, it provides students with the business knowledge and skills they need to get their careers off to a strong start through an innovative curriculum with extensive experiential components.

Other master's programs offered by the Graduate School of Business include the Accounting M.B.A., a full-time, fifteen-month program for recent liberal arts and sciences graduates and those seeking a career change to the accounting profession; the Executive M.B.A., with an integrative focus for experienced managers; the Master of Business Communication, for professional communicators who wish to broaden their business knowledge and enhance their technical skills; the Master of International Management, for managers wishing to develop or extend a career in international business in the U.S. or abroad; the M.B.A. in Human Resource Management Program, for human resource professionals wishing to develop specific competencies; the M.B.A. in Medical Group Management Program, for health-care professionals and those wishing to develop a management career in that field; and the M.S. in Real Estate Appraisal Program, for real estate

appraisers who are involved in complex appraisal assignments.

Students and the M.B.A. Experience

St. Thomas's Graduate School of Business is the fourth-largest in the United States, with an enrollment of more than 3,000 students in its nine degree programs. Students come from a wide range of educational and professional backgrounds, with most from the region around the Twin Cities. The student body is composed of 55 percent men and 45 percent women; 5 percent are members of minority groups, and 4 percent are international students. Ages vary somewhat by program, ranging from the 20s to 40s and beyond. Postundergraduate work experience varies accordingly, and current students are employed at more than 2,000 companies. This diversity in the student body greatly enhances the educational experience through the different perspectives brought to team projects, classroom discussions, and other activities.

❖ Global Focus

International issues are addressed in the curricula of almost all the degree programs, and the Master of International Management program is specifically designed to provide the necessary business skills, foreign language proficiency, and cultural sensitivity needed to compete successfully in the global marketplace. In addition, students can take advantage of several study-abroad and exchange programs with affiliate schools in Europe, Asia, Canada, and South America.

The Faculty

St. Thomas's full-time and adjunct faculty members, many of whom are leaders in their industries, bring a wealth of business and academic experience to the classroom. This unique mixture of expertise results in leading-edge curricula and the real-world applied approach that makes a University of St. Thomas degree so valued in the business community. Students benefit from this expertise through the accessibility that results from small class sizes and the advisory or mentoring roles assumed by many faculty members.

The Business School Network

The Graduate School of Business is highly regarded in the business community and benefits from the support and involvement of leaders in multiple sectors of that community in a variety of ways. Many teach as adjunct faculty members, serve as guest lecturers, sponsor internships, or host students at their facilities. In addition, many serve on boards advising the school and its various degree programs and concentrations, thus ensuring a dialogue between the school and its corporate partners that results in curricula and programming that truly meet the demands of a competitive, rapidly changing marketplace. Several companies have sponsored endowed chairs in business ethics, family business, risk and insurance management, international management, management, and entrepreneurship. The Executive Fellows of the Graduate School of Business comprise distinguished retired CEOs and senior managers who remain active in both the business and academic communities, bringing their counsel and expertise to the school through a variety of special projects and initiatives. The Graduate School of Business also has thirteen professional development centers and institutes that have strong affiliations with many companies and professional organizations through advice and consulting services and sponsorship of custom and joint programming. St. Thomas's Small Business Institute, in affiliation with the Small Business Administration and the local business community, offers students opportunities to consult for growing small businesses. Finally, students have access, through various networking initiatives, to many of the more than 17,000 business alumni who have gone on to distinguished careers and leadership roles in thousands of companies.

The College and Environs

Founded in 1885, the University of St. Thomas is an independent, coeducational, comprehensive university with more than 10,000 students, half of whom are graduate students. The main campus is located in St. Paul, while the Minneapolis campus, built in 1991, is home to the Graduate School of Business. Classes are also held on the St. Paul campus and at five other convenient locations in and around the Twin Cities metropolitan area. Both the Minneapolis and St. Paul campuses are centrally located and easily accessible using public transportation.

Facilities

Students have access to more than 150 computing stations, which, in turn, provide access to the Internet, VAX network, e-mail system, electronic databases, and other library resources. Comprehensive library resources, with more than 300,000 volumes, are located on both the St. Paul and Minneapolis campuses, and the school also is a member of local seven-library consortium that provides computerized access to more than 1 million volumes. Distance learning facilities also exist on most campuses.

Placement

The University of St. Thomas Counseling and Career Services office is available to all students. Services range from self-assessment counseling to resume and interviewing skill workshops, complemented by a comprehensive library of directories and employment-related books and periodicals. This office also coordinates career fairs, recruitment visits by employers, resume referrals, and job listings. In addition, the Graduate School of Business has an extensive alumni network available for students to use as a resource and publishes listings of employment and internship opportunities available to students and alumni.

Admission

Admission requirements vary somewhat by degree program, especially with regard to previous work or managerial experience (many programs require at least two years of postundergraduate work experience) and requirements for a personal essay and letters of recommendation. In general, programs require GMAT scores above the 50th percentile, and TOEFL scores of at least 550. The Executive M.B.A. program requires the Miller Analogies Test. The average undergraduate GPA of incoming students is 3.0, based upon receipt of official transcripts from applicants' schools.

Finances

Tuition for 1998–99 is $416 per credit hour for all programs except the Executive M.B.A. program, which is $585 per credit hour. Book expenses vary by program and course. Financial aid is available through a variety of private, institutional, and federal programs, both need-based and non-need-based.

International Students

International students are welcomed at the University of St. Thomas, and the International Student Services Office has several programs to assist with counseling and support services, housing, visa services, and ESL courses, as well as many other special needs. Programs are available to help students become quickly acclimated to the school and the local community, and to make the most of their educational experience.

Application Facts and Dates

Applications are considered on a rolling basis; most programs adhere to a semester schedule, but cohort programs, such as the Accounting M.B.A., the Day M.B.A., the Executive M.B.A., and the M.B.A. in Medical Group Management Program, may have different start times. For specific information and application materials, students should contact:

Graduate School of Business
University of St. Thomas
1000 LaSalle Avenue, MPL251
Minneapolis, Minnesota 55403-2005
Telephone: 612-962-4200
              800-328-6819 Ext. 2-4200
              (toll-free)
Fax: 612-962-4260
E-mail: mba@stthomas.edu
World Wide Web: http://www.gsb.
    stthomas.edu

U🜊D University of San Diego

School of Business Administration

San Diego, California

▶ DEVELOPING GLOBAL BUSINESS LEADERS

The School of Business Administration at the University of San Diego (USD) is a dynamic institution with regional and global influence. Our mission statement sets the benchmark for our strategic thrusts: The School of Business is committed to improving global business practices through applied research and innovative, personalized education to develop socially responsible leaders. Faculty task forces interact with business leaders to continuously improve the M.B.A. and M.I.B. programs and to bring applied learning opportunities to our students. Students can participate in global learning experiences through USD programs in Mexico, Great Britain, France, Germany, and Hong Kong. USD is a community infused with values, where faculty members and students learn together.

—Dr. Curtis W. Cook, Dean

Programs and Curricular Focus

The Master of Business Administration (M.B.A.) and the Master of International Business (M.I.B.) programs are 60 units in length and are designed for students with no prior academic background in business. Students with prior course work in the core business subjects may waive up to 30 units. The cornerstone of the degree programs at USD is flexibility. It is the student's choice whether to seek the M.B.A. degree or the M.I.B. degree. Students may begin their studies in the fall, spring, or summer. They may attend full-time or part-time, days or evenings. The students choose whether to focus their studies in such fields as finance, international business, management, marketing, new venture management, project management, real estate, or supply management, or simply to obtain a broad-based general M.B.A. or M.I.B. degree. Students choose which elective courses to take, and in which semester, and whether to avail themselves of contact with local firms and well-placed alumni, whether to participate in internship programs here or abroad, or whether to experience foreign cultures through study abroad opportunities.

Students and the M.B.A. Experience

To meet the challenges of a new century, the student in the Master of Business Administration and Master of International Business programs at the University of San Diego receives comprehensive training in theory and case analysis. This develops technical and financial skills, fosters global and strategic thinking, and provides a philosophy that stresses corporate responsibility and the interconnection of all the stakeholders of the business enterprise. These skills are reinforced through extensive team exercises and group projects in classes averaging just 25 students, and through interaction with businesses and business leaders locally, nationally, and internationally.

❖ Global Focus

USD's Master of International Business program is now one of the largest in the United States. The primary objective of the M.I.B. program is to prepare individuals to meet the special challenges of a global marketplace. Foreign language competency, international internships, and mentor programs are components of the program.

USD's John Ahlers Center for International Business hosts guest speakers from around the world. It provides summer courses abroad in cities such as Paris, Hong Kong, Munich, and London. Exchange programs have been established with universities in Mexico, Argentina, and France. International internships are available with companies in San Diego, nationwide, and abroad. A new dual-degree program with Monterrey Institute of Technology (ITESM) in Mexico allows students to earn degrees from both USD and ITESM. With fluency in Spanish and English, students pursue internships and learn the business culture of the United States and Mexico.

Special Features

The School of Business Administration offers joint-degree programs in several areas that allow students the opportunity to complete two separate degrees in a timely manner. The joint programs include M.B.A./J.D. and M.I.B./J.D. in conjunction with the School of Law, an M.B.A./Master of Science in Nursing with the School of Nursing, and an M.I.B./Master of International Relations with the Department of Political Science. There is also a new dual-degree program with the Monterrey Institute of Technology in Mexico, which allows students to earn degrees from both USD and ITESM.

The Faculty

The University of San Diego School of Business Administration has been able to attract highly qualified faculty members with degrees from well-recognized universities around the world. Among the faculty members are 3 Fulbright scholars, more than a dozen certified in their professions, and more than 20 who have authored books in their fields. All faculty members are doctorally qualified, or the equivalent, and remain current in their research and professional fields. Most faculty members are regularly invited to speak at conferences, seminars, and dinner meetings both in the U.S. and abroad, and maintain regular contact with the business community. Faculty publications are frequent and recognized for their contribution to the business world as well as academia. The primary focus of members of the faculty remains educating students about the applicability of proven management theory.

The Business School Network

The University of San Diego Graduate School of Business enjoys a strong relationship with the corporate community. There are three advisory boards, the Accountancy Advisory Board, the Ahlers Center for International Business Board, and the Real Estate Finance Board. Each contributes its expertise and also advise on the planning and implementation of long-range programs.

A substantial number of graduate courses require practical projects working on current problems for local companies. The internship program places graduate students for three to six months with companies both in San Diego and overseas to work on major business projects. These projects and internships provide mutual benefit and positive interactions with the business community.

The School actively supports an Executives in Residence program in which corporate professionals work and teach at the University for a year. These business leaders bring the real and practical world into the classroom. Furthermore, other classes host guest speakers on current and relevant topics.

Finally, the Ahlers Center for International Business provides various programs that interrelate with the corporate community. They host a Breakfast Briefing Series as well as half- and full-day seminars. The School actively nurtures this multidimensional relationship with the corporate community.

The College and Environs

The University of San Diego is an independent, Roman Catholic university founded in 1949. The 180-acre hilltop campus, known for its graceful Spanish Renaissance architecture, overlooks Missions Bay with breathtaking views of the Pacific Ocean and San Diego Bay. The campus is located in the nation's sixth-largest city; ideally close to cultural, business, residential, and recreational areas of the city.

Facilities

The Helen K. and James C. Copley Library houses more than 360,000 books and bound periodicals and includes subscriptions to 2,200 journals and collections of reference works, government documents, pamphlets, newspapers in many languages, and rare books.

In addition to its own collection, Copley Library has network connections with most academic and large public libraries in North America and with major national bibliographic and informational databases available to USD students and faculty. Many databases are directly accessible to students from computer terminals in the library. SALLY, the online catalog of the campus libraries and

Media Center, can be accessed by computer from home. More than 700 study spaces are available in group study areas, quiet carrels, and reading rooms.

Technology Environment

USD has several minicomputer systems for campus use. E-mail accounts are available to all M.B.A. and M.I.B. students allowing for enhanced communications between students and faculty members and provides access to the information superhighway to all students. Several student computer labs exist on campus for PC and Mac users. The School of Business Administration lab is designed primarily for users of IBM-compatible microcomputers. A Novell network serves more than thirty workstations and includes laser printers. There are also a limited number of Macintosh stations with access to print facilities. Terminal access to the minicomputers as well as a high-speed line printer is also available. Virtually all workstations in academic computing labs are tied to the University's network, allowing users to access processors in remote locations.

Placement

Career Services works to support the professional development of students and alumni. Coordinating with the School of Business, the center offers a number of resources and services. Each semester, training workshops in the areas of resume writing, interviewing, and networking are conducted. The Resource Library includes multimedia holdings that range from employer information to job and internship listings. Career Services partners with the Alumni Office and the School of Business in sponsoring events such as the Career Night & Networking Forum. Individualized assistance with job search strategy is available to all, and the Alumni Career Network is an active resource for student use. In addition, faculty and career advisers strongly support students' job seeking efforts through direct contact with corporate professionals.

Admission

Matriculation into the M.B.A. and M.I.B. programs is possible in the fall semester,

spring semester, or summer session allowing students to enter whenever they are ready. By utilizing a rolling admissions process, applications are evaluated individually as received, providing feedback to the applicant in a timely manner. Qualification for admission is based upon prior academic achievement, acceptable performance on the GMAT, three letters of recommendation, and a current resume. Additional requirements for international applicants includes a detailed evaluation of all foreign transcripts, a declaration of finances, and a minimum TOEFL score of 580 and a minimum score of 4.5 on the Test of Written English (TWE) for all applicants who are nonnative speakers of English.

Finances

The tuition for the 1998–99 year is $585 per credit. The total cost of the program will vary, depending on the number of courses required for each individual student to complete the degree.

The Office of Financial Aid Services provides information, counseling, and application processing for students who need assistance in meeting their educational and living expenses. Financial assistance consists of fellowships, scholarships, assistantships, employment (contact the Office of Human Resources or Student Employment Center), grants, and loans. Each type of aid has different application forms, requirements, and deadlines. For applications and more information, students should contact the Office of Financial Aid Services at 619-260-4514.

Application Facts and Dates

Admission is open for the fall and spring semesters and the summer session. The priority filing date for applications is May 1 for the fall, November 15 for the spring, and March 15 for the summer.

For an application and more information, students should contact:

Office of Graduate Admissions
University of San Diego
5998 Alcala Park
San Diego, California 92110
Telephone: 619-260-4524
          800-248-4873 (toll-free)
E-mail: grads@acusd.edu

University of San Francisco

San Francisco, California

POSITION YOURSELF AT THE CUTTING EDGE

Located on the edge of entrepreneurial and corporate opportunities in California's Silicon Valley and also on the edge of Pacific Rim cultures and markets, the McLaren School of Business prepares men and women of richly diverse backgrounds for leadership positions in the global business environment of the twenty-first century.

—Gary Williams, Dean

Programs and Curricular Focus

The McLaren M.B.A. program is fully accredited by AACSB–The International Association for Management Education and enjoys a reputation for excellence regionally, nationally, and internationally. The curriculum is designed to strengthen the analytical, practical, and interpersonal skills essential for success in the international marketplace.

Five integrative themes (communication skills, leadership dynamics, creative problem solving, global perspectives, and ethical action) are highlighted in each course to develop broadly experienced, visionary managers. Small classes (rarely larger than 25) ensure the individual attention necessary to develop first-rate communication skills and allow direct participation in cases and discussions focusing on current and future management and organizational issues.

The M.B.A. core curriculum comprises 33 units (thirteen courses). In addition, students choose 12 units (four courses) of electives and a capstone course for a total of 48 units. The core curriculum challenges students to diagnose and solve a wide variety of managerial problems. Through the use of case studies, guest speakers, computer simulations, and faculty-student interaction, course content closely mirrors real-world business experience.

The advanced elective courses enable the student to choose a study emphasis in one of five concentrations: finance, international business, management, marketing, and telecommunications.

Other programs include an Executive M.B.A. (E.M.B.A.) program for working professionals. Classes for the E.M.B.A. meet on alternating Fridays and Saturdays for twenty-two months. Applicants must have completed ten years of work experi-

ence, with at lest five years of significant managerial experience.

Students and the M.B.A. Experience

USF's 1997 M.B.A. class of 248 included representatives from dozens of countries. The average age for the group was 28, with an average of five years' work experience. Corporations sponsoring employees for M.B.A. study included Andersen Consulting, Bank of America, Bechtel, Citibank, Clorox, Genentech, Hewlett Packard, Hitachi, Sun Microsystems, and many others.

Special Features

The Graduate Business Association (GBA) is a student organization committed to enhancing the quality of campus life for M.B.A. students. The GBA provides social and professional programs, faculty/course guides for students, and representation in the administration of the School.

The USF Consulting Group, open to all M.B.A. students, is a large club offering valuable consulting services to San Francisco–area businesses. The organization comprises five operational teams: Community Outreach, Database Management, Marketing, Quality Assurance, and Executive Board.

The *USF Business Journal* is published monthly by M.B.A. students. It features student-written articles about business topics and events, including information about M.B.A. activities and career opportunities as well as student/faculty profiles.

Many other organizations are eager to involve new student members. Several faculty-led international trips are scheduled each year on a for-credit basis.

The Faculty

All faculty members of the McLaren School of Business are committed above all

to the personal and professional development of their students. More than 90 percent of the faculty members have earned doctorates at outstanding universities and are well-known as scholars and authors in their fields. They bring to the classroom an innovative enthusiasm for motivational education and up-to-date expertise in current business realities, gained in part through their consulting relationships with major corporations. In and out of the classroom, students find their professors deeply interested in their perspectives and in their progress in the program.

The Business School Network

The McLaren School of Business and its students benefit from the guidance of a distinguished domestic and international Advisory Council made up of outstanding business leaders. In addition, the network of alumni built up over the University's 143-year history gives M.B.A. students a rich resource for internships and career opportunities.

The College and Environs

The University of San Francisco, the city's largest private university, overlooks an urban area of incredible beauty, diversity, and opportunity. As America's gateway to the Pacific Rim, San Francisco is well-positioned to benefit from expanding trade with Asian and Latin American countries as well as the United States' traditional European partners.

This vibrant international trade center is also alive with the humanities, including theater, film, dance, musical performances, and fine art exhibitions.

Placement

The Career Services Center assists students in job placement and career planning. On-campus recruiting is conducted year-round and features such companies as Sprint, Wells Fargo, Eastman Kodak, and Andersen Consulting.

Admission

Admission to the McLaren M.B.A. program is available to individuals who fulfill the criteria listed in the Application for Admission, including records of undergraduate

preparation, acceptable GMAT scores, letters of recommendation, and a personal essay.

Finances

Tuition for the 1998–99 academic year is $658 per unit. (Students typically take 12 to 15 units per semester.) Average yearly expenses (books, room and board, transportation, and personal expenses) are approximately $16,000. A wide variety of financial aid programs are available, including

McLaren Graduate Fellowships, University Tuition Grants, and several student loan programs.

International Students

With students from more than fifty countries in recent years, the University of San Francisco is well prepared to meet the special needs of international students. English classes, housing advice, visa information, and other services are available. As an international trade center celebrating its ethnic

diversity, San Francisco offers a welcoming study and leisure environment for virtually all international students.

Application Facts and Dates

Students are admitted into the M.B.A. program for the fall, spring, and summer semesters. Admission decisions are made on a rolling basis. Applicants can expect a decision within four to five weeks of the date that their application is complete. For fall admission, the GMAT should be taken no later than May, with the application due by June 1. For spring admission, the GMAT should be taken no later than October, with the application due by November 10. For summer admission, the GMAT should be taken no later than February, with the application due by April 1.

Students' questions and requests for an application package are welcomed. Applicants should contact:

McLaren School of Business
Graduate School of Management
University of San Francisco
2130 Fulton Street
San Francisco, California 94117-1080
Telephone: 415-422-6314
          415-422-6665 (for
             applications only)
Fax: 415-422-2502
E-mail: mbausf@usfca.edu
World Wide Web: http://www.usfca.
  edu/usf/mclaren

FACULTY LIST

Steven Alter, Professor of Information Systems and Decision Sciences; Ph.D., MIT, 1975.

Richard Babcock, Professor of Management; Ph.D., UCLA, 1970.

Jonathan Barsky, Associate Professor of Hospitality Management; Ph.D., Golden Gate, 1991.

Michael Becker, Professor of Organizational Psychology; Ph.D., Brigham Young, 1975.

Arthur Bell, Professor of Management; Ph.D., Harvard, 1973.

Rex Bennett, Professor of Marketing; Ph.D., North Carolina at Chapel Hill, 1972.

Keqian Bi, Professor of Finance; Ph.D., Florida, 1989.

Daniel L. Blakley, Professor of Applied Economics and Quantitative Methods; Ph.D., Duke, 1981.

Karl A. Boedecker, Professor of Marketing; Ph.D., Michigan State, 1974; J.D., San Francisco, 1982.

Stephen D. Calvert, Professor of Marketing; Ph.D., Cincinnati, 1979.

Rodger (Rongxin) Chen, Assistant Professor of Management; Ph.D., Texas at Dallas, 1996.

Thomas Costello, Associate Professor and Director of Hospitality Management; M.A., Saint Louis, 1972.

Barry W. Doyle, Professor of Finance; Ph.D., Oregon, 1984.

Alev M. Efendioglu, Professor of Management; Ph.D., LSU, 1978.

Shenzhao Fu, Professor of Marketing; Ph.D., Indiana, 1989.

Leslie A. Goldgehn, Professor of Marketing; Ph.D., Northwestern, 1982.

Oren Harari, Professor of Management; Ph.D., Berkeley, 1978.

Heather E. Hudson, Professor of Telecommunications Management and Policy and Director of Telecommunications Program; Ph.D., Stanford, 1974.

Stephen J. Huxley, Professor of Business Administration; Ph.D., California, San Diego, 1975.

Nicholas Imparato, Professor of Business Administration; Ph.D., Bowling Green State, 1970.

Kathleen Kane, Professor of Management; Ph.D., Claremont, 1990.

John Koeplin, S. J., Associate Professor of Accounting; Ph.D., North Texas, 1998.

Zhan Li, Assistant Professor of Marketing; D.B.A., Boston University, 1994.

Byungha Lim, Assistant Professor of Management Information Systems; Ph.D., Iowa, 1996.

Paul Lorton, Professor of Information Systems; Ph.D., Stanford, 1973.

Robert N. Mefford, Professor of International Business and Operations Management; Ph.D., Berkeley, 1983.

Michael R. Middleton, Professor of Information Systems and Decision Sciences; Ph.D., Stanford, 1979.

Luis Murillo, Assistant Professor of Management; Ph.D., Berkeley, 1993.

L. W. Murray Jr., Professor of Finance; Ph.D., Clark, 1973.

Eugene Muscat, Professor of Management Information Systems and Associate Dean; Ed.D., USC, 1974.

Denis Neilson, Professor of Accounting and Associate Dean; Ph.D., Berkeley, 1974.

Joel Oberstone, Professor of Decision Sciences; Ph.D., USC, 1972.

Richard Puntillo, Professor of Finance; M.B.A., Berkeley, 1969.

Diane Roberts, Associate Professor of Accounting; Ph.D., California, Irvine, 1994.

David G. Scalise, Professor of Business Law; J.D., San Francisco, 1973.

Edwin J. Shapiro, Professor of Quantitative Methods; Ph.D., Pittsburgh, 1962.

Dayle Smith, Professor of Management; Ph.D., USC, 1986.

Peggy Takahashi, Assistant Professor of International Management; Ph.D., Berkeley, 1998.

Manuel Tarrazo, Associate Professor of Finance; Ph.D., SUNY at Albany, 1992.

Philip Taylor, Professor of Information Systems and Decision Sciences; Ph.D., Ohio State, 1975.

Heinz Weihrich, Professor of International Business and Management; Ph.D., UCLA, 1973.

David P. Weiner, Professor of Accounting; Ph.D., Michigan, 1972; CPA (New York).

Gary Williams, Professor of Management and Dean, McLaren School of Business; Ph.D., Stanford, 1966.

University of South Carolina

Columbia, South Carolina

GLOBALIZATION—MEETING BUSINESS NEEDS IN THE NEXT MILLENNIUM

The University of South Carolina's College of Business Administration is an innovator in preparing students for careers in the global marketplace. We offer three distinct programs with opportunities for preparation that stress an international focus. Each program is based on a strong grounding in needed business skills supplemented by options that include a concentration in international business topics. Each program offers in-depth training leading to competency in one of eight languages, six-month in-country internships, a unique study-abroad program, and internationally oriented consulting opportunities. The College's innovative approaches to preparing students for the global marketplace have earned it international recognition. Such innovation is essential for business students who will be operating in a world of few boundaries and constant change.

—David L. Shrock, Dean

Programs and Curricular Focus

The College offers a Master of International Business Studies (M.I.B.S.) program, a Master of Business Administration (M.B.A.) program, and an International Master of Business Administration (I.M.B.A.) program.

The M.I.B.S. core curriculum spans all of the traditional disciplines in business administration, but with courses that are fully international in scope. Core courses are taught in four- to eight-week integrated modules, as well as some full-semester core and elective courses. Students start in the summer (June) or fall term, depending on undergraduate degree and foreign language proficiency. The M.I.B.S. program currently offers the following language tracks for U.S. nationals: Chinese, French, German, Italian, Japanese, Portuguese, Russian, and Spanish. Chinese and Japanese are three-year language tracks, and all others are two-year language tracks. All foreign national applicants are carefully screened for English language skills and enter the two-year foreign national (English) track. All M.I.B.S. students are required to learn a foreign language and to develop that language as well as cultural understanding through a six-month internship in a country where that language is spoken (foreign nationals intern in the United States).

The M.B.A. core curriculum of thirteen courses (39 hours) focuses on the fundamentals of business administration

and starts in the fall of each year. In addition, five elective courses (15 hours) enable students to further develop their skills in a variety of areas or to specialize in a particular area of their choice. All eighteen of these courses are taught in four traditional sixteen-week semesters. The required summer (between first and second year) field consulting project (6 hours) places teams of students in a consulting environment with corporations, nonprofit organizations, or government agencies. Study abroad as a part of the M.B.A. program is also encouraged. The combined 60-hour program prepares students from all educational backgrounds to assume managerial positions.

The International Master of Business Administration (I.M.B.A.) program, the College's most recent innovation in graduate business education, is a joint venture with Austria's most prestigious business school, the Wirtschaftsuniversität Wien (WU-Wien), more commonly known as the Vienna University of Economics and Business Administration. Through this partnership, the College is able to offer a fifteen-month, 48-credit-hour, all English language program of instruction leading to the I.M.B.A. degree. The I.M.B.A. core curriculum is a combination of the traditional M.B.A. and M.I.B.S. programs, with the first seven months of instruction in Vienna and the next eight months at USC. The curriculum includes twelve months of intensive business course work followed by a

three-month project in management consulting. The instruction in Vienna is conducted by faculty from both WU-Wien and USC, while the instruction in Columbia is conducted by USC faculty. The program starts at WU-Wien each May, with two terms of highly integrated business course modules. After completing this core curriculum in Vienna, the students come to USC for a semester of four electives and a capstone course on strategy and policy in a global enterprise. I.M.B.A. students then complete their curriculum with the field consulting project.

Students and the M.B.A. Experience

The students in USC's graduate business programs come from a wide variety of backgrounds, with qualifications varying from program to program. The total enrollment for all three programs for fall 1996 was 544 students. Women represent 34 percent of this student population, while minorities represent 5 percent. Foreign national students make up 25 percent of the student body; this adds greatly to the global perspective in business, as these students bring their experiences to the classroom. The typical entering student is 26 years old and has approximately three years of work experience.

The Faculty

The faculty of USC's College of Business Administration has strong research interests that have won national and international visibility. Faculty members have nearly 100 articles and more than a dozen books published in a typical year and they stay on the cutting edge of the various academic disciplines represented in the College.

The Business School Network

The College's ties to the business community are strong, and these ties play several critical roles in the educational process. Relationships with local, national, and international corporations lead to field consulting projects for M.B.A. and I.M.B.A. students, to

The H. William Close and Francis M. Hipp buildings comprise the College of Business Administration's nine-story complex.

internships for M.I.B.S. students, and to employment opportunities for all graduates. The USC-Business Partnership Foundation is composed of business and academic leaders who play an active leadership role for the College and are an integral part of the review process for curriculum and other program innovations.

The College and Environs

Founded in 1801, the University of South Carolina's main campus (and the College of Business Administration) is located in downtown Columbia, the state's capital. The University has a total enrollment of more than 38,000 students, including USC's two other four-year campuses and five regional campuses. USC is a progressive, comprehensive institution committed to excellence in education and public service. On the Columbia campus, eleven colleges offer seventy-nine undergraduate degree programs. The commitment extends to the continued development and support of graduate education, and research is a priority. This commitment has led to growth in the variety and number of graduate programs available. Currently, USC enrolls more than 11,000 graduate students.

The city of Columbia is the seat of state government, is rich in culture and

history, and is considered one of the most progressive cities in the Southeast. The current metropolitan population of 453,000 is expected to rise to 510,700 by the year 2000. The state's economy is flourishing, thanks to the tourism industry, international and domestic business, and industry giants. Government and industry are working together to provide excellent employment opportunities throughout the state.

South Carolinians appreciate the fine arts and are committed to the cultivation of the arts throughout the state. Columbia is the home of several outstanding museums and the nationally ranked Riverbanks Zoo. Diverse vacation spots are abundant throughout the state, including ocean resorts, historic cities, and the Blue Ridge Mountains.

Facilities

The College of Business Administration is housed in the H. William Close and Francis M. Hipp buildings. The twin towers of the complex symbolize the working partnership between the College and the business community. Within the complex, the College is relatively self-sufficient with its business library, computer center, classrooms, and faculty offices. The library features a circulation collection that includes business and industrial directories and publications, with approximately 100 current subscriptions and back issues of selected magazines and newspapers and nearly 500 journals in microfilm format. Students also have access to the University's main library, which seats 2,500 users at one time and allows access to more than 7 million volumes, microfilm entries, manuscripts, and periodicals. The computer center has 150 interactive workstations accessing a large open-system network comprising multiple Novell and UNIX servers, with 650 clients and more than 32 billion characters of online storage. Through the campus network, users also have access to numerous software packages and mainframe processing.

Placement

Most placement services are coordinated by the College's Graduate Placement Office, which acts as a liaison between graduate students and prospective employers. In addition to on-campus

interviewing opportunities, students benefit from the following available resources: a resume book, correspondence recruiting, placement referral network, career development seminars, and the M.I.B.S. alumni job bank.

Admission

Every applicant's complete file, including his or her academic record, resume, required essays, and GMAT scores, is evaluated through comparison with the current applicant pool for the appropriate program. Average GMAT scores and GPAs vary for the different programs, with M.I.B.S. being the most selective (a 1997 average GMAT score of 611 and an average GPA of 3.3). The College looks for reasons to admit students, not a reason to decline them.

Finances

Tuition for 1998–99 for all M.B.A. and M.I.B.S. students is estimated at $1862 per semester for in-state students and $3817 per semester for out-of-state students. There is a one-time, nonrefundable enrichment fee for the M.B.A. program of $2900 for in-state students and $4400 for out-of-state students. The M.I.B.S. program enrichment fee is estimated at $5000 in-state and $8800 out-of-state. Tuition and fees for the I.M.B.A. program are $25,000 total cost, with no enrichment fees.

A number of graduate assistantships and fellowships are available. Applications for these awards are considered in February, and the awards are based on merit, not need.

Application Facts and Dates

For best consideration, applications for all programs should be submitted by February 1. All applications for assistantships and fellowships must be received by February 1. Applications for all programs will be considered until the program is full or until approximately one month prior to the start of the program. For more information or an application package, students should contact:

Graduate Division, PGG98
College of Business Administration
University of South Carolina
Columbia, South Carolina 29208
Telephone: 803-777-4346
Fax: 803-777-0414

University of Southern California

Los Angeles, California

> ### THE MARSHALL M.B.A.—A BUSINESS EDUCATION FOR THE REAL WORLD
>
> *The Marshall M.B.A. Program is characterized by a real-world focus and a heritage of innovation and change. Faculty and students explore business problems from a multidisciplinary perspective while emphasizing interpersonal skills designed to build global awareness, improve technological sophistication, and develop talents in leadership and entrepreneurial areas.*
>
> *Working with one of the largest alumni networks of any business school in the world, we have an environment that fosters innovative ways of understanding and improving business today. Teams of students are assigned to tackle tough, real-world issues by applying theoretical concepts to real-time business problems in both profit and nonprofit settings. The Marshall M.B.A. provides a business education for the 21st century.*
>
> —Randolph W. Westerfield, Dean

Programs and Curricular Focus

The Marshall M.B.A. Program prepares men and women to become leaders at all levels of organizations in all sectors of the economy. Intellectual and practical in nature, the two-year M.B.A. program provides grounding in the functional business disciplines, hones analytic tools required to address management problems, and develops the interpersonal and communication skills necessary to lead. Along with the program's real-world focus, an emphasis on teamwork and the development of interpersonal skills are key elements of the Marshall M.B.A. Program.

In 1997, the Marshall School of Business sent its entire first-year class to study abroad in China, Japan, or Mexico through its Pacific Rim Education Program (PRIME). The Marshall School is the only major business school to do this, and the program is now a required part of the curriculum.

A new module of study for first-year students, Electronic Commerce, has been added to the core curriculum. The new course integrates changes taking place in all disciplines due to increasing technology. A team-taught module, it focuses on marketing, finance, communications, and operations.

Year one is structured around a set of required courses designed to establish a basis for assuming the role of general manager. These courses are arranged in a new structure for the Core program built around three major themes during the first year: Theme I—Foundations for the General Manager; Theme II—Management Functions; and Theme III—Integration and Implementation.

Flexibility in year two allows students to tailor a course of study to their individual needs and long-term career objectives. In the second year, students can choose from courses in high growth areas such as technology and international business along with specialized courses in specific industries.

In addition to the full-time M.B.A., the Marshall School offers an M.B.A. for Professionals and Managers (M.B.A.-PM), a one-year International M.B.A. (IBEAR), an Executive M.B.A. (E.M.B.A.), a Ph.D., and dual degree programs with the schools of law, urban planing, pharmacy, real estate development, nursing, gerontology, dental surgery, information systems, and engineering as well as in East Asian studies. Master's degrees in accounting and business taxation are also offered.

Students and the M.B.A. Experience

The Marshall M.B.A. Program enrolls approximately 300 students each year. The average Marshall M.B.A. student is 27 years of age, with 4.5 years of work experience. International students comprise approximately 25 percent of the student population and represent more than twenty countries from around the world. Twenty-five percent of the students are women.

Every geographic region and major ethnic group of the United States is represented.

Special Features

At orientation, the entering class, second-year M.B.A. students, and core faculty and staff members engage in a series of intellectual and physical exercises aimed at demonstrating the power of teams to accomplish challenging tasks in high-quality ways. Sustained project teams, established at orientation, return to campus and become responsible for collaborative work in selected first-year classes. Throughout the fall and the early spring semester, these groups are evaluated and receive feedback on not only their completed projects but also their teamwork skills.

The Faculty

There are more than 170 faculty members in the Marshall School of Business, with expertise in such areas as international business, accounting, entrepreneurship, real estate, consulting, finance, human resources management, marketing, operations, information systems, business economics, and leadership. They are noted for their cutting-edge research, a constant drive to apply the business theories they develop to the real world, teaching excellence in the classroom, and an open-door policy toward students.

The Business School Network

The more than 50,000 alumni of the Marshall School of Business form a renowned global network and have achieved remarkable success in the national and international business community. Dedicated alumni encourage their companies to recruit Marshall M.B.A. students and regularly return to campus to speak about careers, act as mentors, and provide consulting opportunities. In addition, alumni are actively involved with students in planning recruiting trips to major cities such as San Francisco and New York.

The College and Environs

Located on USC's main campus on 150 park-like acres south of the downtown Los Angeles, the Marshall School is well positioned in a city where the diversity of manufacturing, financial, telecommunica-

tions, entertainment, and international trade activities rivals that of many countries. USC is committed to diversity and has one of the largest populations of international students of any private university in the United States. In addition, Los Angeles is a multicultural city that serves as America's gateway to the Pacific Rim.

Technology Environment

Each classroom is equipped as a multimedia instructional environment with full Internet access. More than 225 state-of-the-art microcomputers and numerous laser printers are available within the School for student use. Workshops provide training on the large array of applications accessible through the School's network software library. In addition, a large collection of instructional videotapes and an inventory of presentation graphics equipment are maintained for student use. The business libraries offer electronic gateways to LEXIS-NEXIS, the major research information repositories of the world, and

to a collection of more than 150 informational databases. Popovich Hall, a 55,000-square-foot facility for M.B.A. students, will be ready for fall 1999.

Placement

The Office of Career Services is designed specifically to assist graduate-level students in the career planning and placement process. It provides services such as seminars and workshops, career counseling, job data and resources, resume books, on-site visits by corporate recruiters, and opportunities to sharpen interviewing and negotiating skills. In addition, events such as Brown Bag Lunches, Industry Nights, and Days-on-the-Job offer students opportunities to meet and exchange information with prospective employers in informal settings.

Admission

The Admissions committee considers all qualified applicants who hold a bachelor's degree from an accredited undergraduate institution. The application is evaluated based upon prior academic performance, previous work experience,

GMAT score, essay questions, letters of recommendation, and ability to demonstrate leadership and interpersonal skills. A TOEFL score is required for applicants for whom English is not their native language. Interviews are encouraged though not required and may be conducted by alumni as well as staff members.

Finances

Tuition and fees for the 1998–99 academic year are approximately $23,600. Scholarships are available and awarded at the discretion of the Admissions Committee to competitive applicants.

International Students

USC has one of the largest populations of international students of any private university in the U.S., adding a unique perspective to classroom and teamwork experiences. International students represented 26 percent of the class of 1998, representing countries from Asia, Europe, Africa, and the Americas. International students are required to attend the M.B.A. International Institute prior to the start of classes. The Institute offers assistance in settling into Los Angeles, developing a supportive network and obtaining necessary documentation for such essentials as driving, banking, housing, and health insurance.

Application Facts and Dates

Application deadlines begin in the fall, with a final deadline of April 1. Early application is encouraged. International applicants are encouraged to apply by February 8. For application materials and information, students should contact:

Marshall School of Business
M.B.A. Admissions
University of Southern California
Bridge Hall 101
Los Angeles, California 90089-1421
Telephone: 213-740-7846
Fax: 213-749-8520
E-mail: uscmba@marshall.usc.edu
World Wide Web: http://www.
    marshall.usc.edu

University of Southern California

Los Angeles, California

AN M.B.A. FOR THE PACIFIC CENTURY

▶ *USC's IBEAR M.B.A. Program is a unique undertaking in international management education. To successfully lead organizations today, one must know not only how to apply management skills in the international workplace but also how to cultivate and communicate with diverse peoples and create a globally informed vision of the opportunities that lie ahead. The IBEAR M.B.A. Program provides that knowledge base. Its practical, Pacific Rim–oriented international business curriculum, the teamwork that participants must demonstrate to complete real-world projects and consulting assignments, and the rich diversity of cultural and work experience that the participants themselves bring to discussions make the IBEAR M.B.A. Program the soundest of springboards for managers who want to lead business in the Pacific Century.*

—Randolph W. Westerfield, Dean

Programs and Curricular Focus

USC's IBEAR M.B.A. Program is the only one-year international M.B.A. program in North America that is accredited by AACSB–The International Association for Management Education. Designed for high-potential, midcareer managers, the program emphasizes business in and between Asia and the Americas.

Completing the equivalent of two years of course work in just one year requires intense dedication and focus but permits participants to minimize time away from the workplace and maximize their gains from the time invested.

Classes begin in mid-August with a three-week transition program in microcomputing and business communication, followed by four 11-week terms of M.B.A. classes. The curriculum consists of nineteen integrated courses, including Management in a Global Economy, Global Marketing Strategies, International Financial Management, Global Strategic Planning, International Trade, The National and International Economy, and Business Environment and Management Practices in the Pacific Rim. All courses emphasize international business issues.

The faculty members work closely to integrate course work across disciplines. They emphasize practical, team-based, project-based, and case-based learning.

Students and the M.B.A. Experience

The IBEAR M.B.A. Program is noted for the maturity of its participants and their diversity in terms of both culture and work experience. By working together every day for a year in the classroom and on many project teams, participants gain experiential understanding of cultural differences in business practice.

Enrollment in each class is limited to 48 participants. They average 33 years of age and ten years of work experience. Ages range from 26 to the mid-40s. Typically, fourteen or more countries are represented. Current participants come from Argentina, Australia, Brazil, Canada, China, Colombia, France, India, Indonesia, Japan, Korea, Peru, Singapore, Switzerland, Taiwan, and the United States. In its twenty years, IBEAR has served 734 participants from forty-six countries. Approximately 50 percent of IBEAR M.B.A. Program participants have corporate sponsors; the rest are self-sponsored.

Special Features

A key feature of the program, the inclusion of international consulting projects for major multinational firms, ensures each participant meaningful real-world experience in international business. From March to July, participants work in 4-member teams to complete an international consulting project on an issue of pressing practical concern for a sponsor company. The consulting projects focus on such challenges as country-focused market entry or expansion strategy, regional business development strategy, offshore manufacturing feasibility, international sourcing, cross-border acquisitions, or the establishment of joint-venture operations. The IBEAR teams work closely with a project manager at their sponsor firm. Most of the projects require international travel.

Other special features of the IBEAR M.B.A. Program include the transition program, which emphasizes computing, team-building, and presentation skills, and a team-development retreat and enrollment in the annual three-day Asia/Pacific Business Outlook Conference hosted at USC in March, sponsored by IBEAR and the U.S. Department of Commerce International Trade Administration and attended by 400 executives from U.S. and international firms, the Senior Commercial Officers of every U.S. Embassy in the Asia/Pacific region, and experts from government, business, and academe who serve on the conference faculty.

The Faculty

IBEAR faculty members are selected from among the most respected of the 170 full-time faculty members in USC's Marshall School of Business. *U.S. News & World Report* recently ranked USC's international business faculty and programs among the strongest in the United States. The Marshall School of Business was ranked twenty-first nationally. IBEAR faculty members are devoted to intellectual and social interactions with program participants.

The Business School Network

In July, the new IBEAR graduates join an influential, global network of more than 700 IBEAR alumni who hold senior positions in many of the most respected firms in the Pacific Rim and around the world. The bonds are strong in this extended IBEAR family. Alumni return regularly to campus to speak about their careers, serve as mentors, and provide consulting opportunities for students and faculty members. They help facilitate links between USC and the business and academic communities abroad, and they encourage their companies to recruit IBEAR graduates. The network is perhaps most valuable to the alumni themselves.

When an alumnus or alumna needs information, a referral, to test an idea, or to see something from a new perspective, they often call on IBEAR colleagues around the globe. IBEAR publishes a quarterly newsletter and maintains a database with current contact information on all of its alumni. IBEAR graduates also join a dynamic network of 50,000 business school alumni and 240,000 USC alumni.

IBEAR's network also includes many nonalumni friends in the business and public sectors around the world. USC has embarked on a strategic initiative to strengthen the University's international ties, especially with the countries in Asia and Latin America. IBEAR serves as a focal point for the promotion of teaching and research in international business. In addition to the M.B.A. Program, IBEAR sponsors faculty research on international business and trade and provides a variety of nonexecutive education programs at USC and abroad. IBEAR also helps coordinate the business school's relationships with international businesses, governments, and academic institutions.

The College and Environs

The IBEAR Program is housed in the Marshall School of Business on USC's parklike 150-acre main campus, just 3 miles south of Los Angeles' downtown business center. Founded in 1880, USC is the oldest and largest private university in the western United States. It offers degrees in 198 fields of study and eighteen professional schools. Its 28,000 students come from all fifty states and 105 countries. The University is strategically located in a city with a population of 7 million and a diversity of high-technology manufacturing, financial, telecommunications, and trade activities to rival many countries. As America's most important gateway to the Pacific Basin, Los Angeles provides an outstanding learning laboratory for managers interested in expanding their international horizons.

Technology Environment

IBEAR and the Marshall School of Business are committed to remaining at the forefront of computing for their

program participants and faculty members. Each seat in the IBEAR classroom is wired for e-mail and the Internet. The IBEAR lounge is also wired for laptop use. All IBEAR participants and faculty members are connected to the business school communications system from their homes, which permits virtual group work and Internet communication worldwide. Assignments, data distribution, substantive discussions, and program and social announcements are handled on the IBEAR e-mail bulletin board system. The business libraries offer electronic gateways to LEXIS-NEXIS and to a collection of more than 150 informational databases. Study carrels are wired into the network for laptop computer use. The Experiential Learning Center uses state-of-the-art video and multimedia equipment in five simulation rooms designed to improve presentation and negotiation skills.

Placement

The Career Resource Center provides personalized job search counseling and assistance to self-sponsored participants. Services include industry nights, networking opportunities, workshops, resume and interview preparation, and access to IBEAR's alumni and business networks.

Admission

Applicants must have completed their undergraduate studies and have five or more years of full-time work and/or military experience. All applicants must submit official GMAT results. International applicants must also submit official TOEFL scores.

Finances

The total education fee for the 1999–2000 academic year will be $44,750, including $34,750 in University tuition for 56 units (nineteen courses) and $10,000 for the IBEAR professional program fee. The program fee supports the cost of the orientation and transition programs; a package of preparatory material; tutorial assistance; communication consulting; special seminars and workshops; optional language classes in Mandarin, Japanese, and Spanish; guest executive lunches;

faculty research and development; dissemination of research and program news; a participant-managed social fund for participants and their families; off-campus organization business lunches, dinners, and seminars; a team-building retreat; and job search services for self-sponsored participants. Living expenses for a single participant range from $1250 to $2000 per month, depending on choice of housing and transportation. IBEAR can assist participants in resolving their housing needs. Costs may be slightly higher in 1999–2000.

Scholarships of $10,000 to $25,000 are available to high-potential U.S. and international applicants.

International Students

IBEAR's objective is to build a diverse community of participants each year who come from the western or eastern Pacific Rim or who have an interest in doing business in the Pacific Rim. Ideally, half of the participants come from Asia, 25 percent from the United States, and the balance from Canada, Mexico, Central and South America, and other regions of the world. IBEAR provides financial assistance to high-potential foreign nationals who have limited funding for graduate education. Diversity of cultural background and work experience within each class enhances the educational experience and strengthens the IBEAR network long after participants receive their degrees.

Application Facts and Dates

Admission decisions begin in October. IBEAR follows a rolling admission procedure and reviews applications as soon as all materials are received. For more information, students should contact:

Fujiko Terayama, Director of
    Admissions and Administration
IBEAR M.B.A. Program
Marshall School of Business
University of Southern California
Los Angeles, California 90089-1421
Telephone: 213-740-7140
Fax: 213-740-7559
E-mail: ibear@usc.edu

The University of Tampa

ACHIEVING YOUR PERSONAL BEST

There are many reasons to get your M.B.A. from The University of Tampa (UT), but three in particular stand out. We care about you as an individual, and when you enroll, you join a family, not just an institution or a Web site chatroom. We care about teaching, and our professors are both qualified and dedicated to helping you progress in the classroom. We care about technology and use it to enhance our teaching. The result is a school on the move taking the lead in business education.

You can get a generic M.B.A. degree anywhere if all you want is a storefront certificate. But we believe there's more to it than that. Personal attention and teaching excellence are what set UT apart from the competition. Call, visit, or better yet, apply to The University of Tampa M.B.A. program. It will be one of the best decisions you ever make.

—Alfred N. Page, Ph.D., Dean

Programs and Curricular Focus

The accredited M.B.A. program consists of 39 hours of course work (for those applicants holding a bachelor's degree in business or related areas), 30 hours of which are required upper-level core courses. The remaining 9 elective hours may be used to investigate special areas of interest or, with an additional 3 hours, can be applied toward one of the following concentrations: accounting, finance, health services administration, information systems management, international business, leadership in human resources management, marketing management, or quality management. These concentrations provide the opportunity to combine an area of specialization with knowledge of the business world to enhance career options. This approach keeps the curriculum up to date so as to reflect the topics and skills essential to business success.

Students and the M.B.A. Experience

Approximately 80 percent of The University of Tampa's M.B.A. students work full-time in the Tampa Bay community (an area with a population of 2.2 million). The remaining 20 percent are full-time students. The average student is 31 years old and has seven years of working experience. Fourteen percent of the M.B.A. students are international. This mix enlivens the classroom and provides students with a

wide variety of perceptions and backgrounds. The increasing contingent of international students is typically full-time, and many serve as graduate assistants to faculty members.

❖ Global Focus

Today, virtually all professionals are involved in international business. An educational foundation infused with a global perspective has therefore become essential. In response to this challenge, The University of Tampa's M.B.A. faculty has thoroughly integrated its core curriculum with global business perspectives and has developed a separate concentration in international business. Students develop an appreciation for and an understanding of how to manage in today's international arena.

Special Features

Required M.B.A. courses help students develop an understanding of the operating systems in business enterprises and develop a broad strategic perspective. It is this perspective that is ultimately necessary to effect change and to lead an organization. Students learn to examine business processes from a cross-functional perspective, which in turn helps them avoid departmental narrowsightedness and make better top-level managerial decisions. Pre-M.B.A. courses (a lower-level core) are available for students requiring preparatory work prior to starting the upper-level core of M.B.A. courses.

The Faculty

All of the faculty members teaching in The University of Tampa's M.B.A. program have earned doctorates in their fields of expertise. Just as importantly, they were recruited to teach at The University of Tampa because of their teaching competence and real-world practical experience. Teaching excellence is the primary focus. A significant majority of every faculty member's performance evaluation is based upon excellence in teaching. Love of teaching is an essential characteristic of The University of Tampa faculty.

The Business School Network

Hundreds of community-based internships in practically every field enrich the historical partnership between the University and the business community and balance the concepts of learning by thinking and learning by doing. Further cementing the historical partnership, The University of Tampa faculty and staff members and students are involved in hundreds of community volunteer projects each year.

The College and Environs

Symbolically and geographically, The University of Tampa lies at the heart of the city of Tampa, one of the country's most exciting growth areas of the last decade. Tampa is Florida's west coast center for banking, commerce, government, law, manufacturing, and real estate. The campus, made up of thirty-seven buildings plus athletic facilities, open spaces, and park lands, covers 70 acres stretching along the banks of the Hillsborough River in the midst of Tampa's booming downtown.

Facilities

Although the College of Business considers the faculty and staff members and students its most valuable assets, other learning resources available include several unique elements. Through these, The University of Tampa's M.B.A. program offers innovative teaching and support not typically found in graduate programs. The Decision Support Center houses a range of software products, packages for financial and statistical analysis, international databases, and graphics presentation software. Computer labs, both Macintosh and IBM, are available. UT has three outstanding centers: the Center for Ethics, the Center for Quality, and the Center for Leadership. These centers assist students and business leaders in making ethical decisions, developing leadership and management skills, and applying total quality management concepts. An Applied Strategic Analysis project helps local businesses and provides students with the opportunity to study and apply what they learn through a consulting role. The Merl Kelce Library houses a number of research and study aids, including such user-friendly retrieval databases as ABI-INFORM, LEXIS-NEXIS, Disclosure, and the National Trade Data Bank.

Placement

The University provides a full range of career placement services, including testing, resume preparation, career opportunities, career days, interview opportunities, and industry trends.

Admission

Admission to UT's M.B.A. program is competitive and is based on a number of important factors, including a student's undergraduate grade point average, GMAT scores, and two letters of recommendation. Admission decisions cannot be made unless official copies of both transcripts and test scores are available in the Office of Graduate Admissions. Applications are processed on a rolling basis and admission can be effective in either the fall, spring, or summer s

University of Tennessee, Knoxville

College of Business Administration

Knoxville, Tennessee

THE WHOLE IS GREATER THAN THE SUM OF THE PARTS: INTEGRATED LEARNING

The University of Tennessee M.B.A. program immerses students in an integrated environment like no other. Running their own businesses, working in teams, making decisions about problems as they arise, students learn business by doing business.

The result is an exciting new curriculum with an emphasis on applied learning, teamwork, integration across business functions, massive use of technology, and exposure to global issues.

The University of Tennessee is proud to be breaking the rules and setting new standards in graduate management education.

—C. Warren Neel, Dean

Programs and Curricular Focus

Students in the University of Tennessee, Knoxville (UTK), M.B.A. program learn how to learn, the most critical factor for success in a time as dynamic as ours. Tennessee M.B.A. students master the business fundamentals in a highly applied environment, work in teams to solve complex problems via conventional methods and new tools from information technology, and are prepared to enter a world of global competition fueled by information technology and led by an increasingly diverse workforce.

In the first year, the core curriculum immerses students in the most highly integrated and applied learning environment in existence. In a way it is "not like school at all," but is instead like working at a high level in a dynamic organization. In management teams of 5 peers, students run a hypothetical company. They learn how to assess what customers value, how to finance their operations, how to reengineer their processes, how to align personnel systems and operational processes, and how the business skills they are learning apply to companies they will be joining, creating, or working for in the future. The year ends with an intensive, integrated computer simulation game, The MarketPlace, which brings into sharp focus all of the skills and concepts students have learned throughout the year.

In the second year, students complete elective and concentration courses. In addition to such established concentrations as economics, finance, management, and marketing, the University of Tennes-

see offers innovative concentrations in entrepreneurism, environmental management, global business, logistics and transportation, management science, manufacturing management engineering, and statistics. The goal of the second year is to round out the students' management education and to equip them with a specialty that will give them an edge in the job market.

Between the first and second years, students complete a summer internship. With the assistance of a career management specialist, students research careers, make contacts, and secure an internship for the summer. Tennessee M.B.A. students have consistently secured internships with some of the most renowned and progressive national and international companies.

UTK also offers two joint programs: the J.D./M.B.A. degree, which allows students to complete both degrees in one to two semesters less than each degree requires separately, and an M.S./M.B.A. degree in manufacturing management and engineering, which allows students to complete both degrees in two years, including one summer session.

Students and the M.B.A. Experience

Diversity defines the student profile of the UTK M.B.A. student. Tennessee M.B.A. students bring a wealth of experiences, both professional and personal, which enrich the learning environment. The average student has 4½ years of professional work experience; 92

percent have more than one year of experience. Their professional experiences include the private, public, and nonprofit domain with a number of students also having been entrepreneurs.

About 38 percent have backgrounds in the arts and sciences with 12 percent having engineering degrees. The average class size is 85; about 30 percent are women, 10 percent are members of minority groups, and 11 percent are foreign nationals who represent seven countries.

❖ Global Focus

Throughout their M.B.A. careers, students apply what they learn to a global context. In the first year, they complete a major international project. In the second year, students can select a concentration in global business and get deep exposure to international management, finance, marketing, logistics, and related issues. In addition, the UTK M.B.A. program has partnerships with programs in France and Chile enabling students to travel abroad to study international business and international business education.

Special Features

During the summer, students utilize an interactive multimedia CD-ROM-based course to begin or strengthen their skills in spreadsheets, word processing, and database management.

There are also numerous student organizations that add great value to the students' M.B.A. education, and students are encouraged to join several. The Tennessee Organization of M.B.A.'s (TOMBA) is a must. Other organizations include New Ventures Now for aspiring entrepreneurs; the Global Business Club for students with international experience or aspirations; an investment club for students with their sights set on Wall Street; Corporate Connections, an organization that puts M.B.A. students in front of leaders of major businesses to describe the vitality and value of the UTK M.B.A. program and its students; Community Connections, an organization of M.B.A. students committed to public service; and numerous others.

The Faculty

Faculty members who teach in the M.B.A. program are selected for their outstanding teaching, research, and experience working with corporations. Many of the UTK M.B.A. faculty members are instructors in the executive education programs delivered through the Management Development Center. Working with corporate leaders, faculty members learn the kinds of skills and talents companies currently value and what they are likely to need in the future. They bring these concepts into the classroom to more accurately prepare M.B.A. students for the competitive world they will enter after graduation.

The Business School Network

Faculty, administration, and students are committed to maintaining active relationships with the local, national, and international business communities. M.B.A. administrators work closely with the chancellor of the University as well to maintain strong business and industry partnerships.

Corporate Partnerships

The UTK M.B.A. program is enriched by the close ties held with the College's Management Development Center, which trains approximately 1,000 corporate executives yearly, as well as the close ties held with the executive M.B.A. program, which enrolls close to 40 international executives each year. More than 30 guest executives visit UT annually as part of the Executive-in-Residence classes offered to M.B.A. students. The Dean maintains an Advisory Board consisting of executives from many national companies who meet with students and faculty once a year to assess the status and currency of the M.B.A. curriculum. In addition, a select group of M.B.A. students are chosen each year to serve on the Corporate Connections team, which serves as a means to market the M.B.A. program to the national business community.

The College and Environs

The University of Tennessee, Knoxville, a federal land-grant institution that began its tradition of service in 1794, is one of the nation's twenty largest universities, enrolling approximately 25,000 students, including 6,500 graduate students. The College of Business Administration is the second-largest college of the University, enrolling 3,900 students.

Knoxville lies within a metropolitan area of approximately 600,000 that houses major corporate headquarters and numerous industrial and commercial operations. Many cultural and entertainment activities are available year-round, and the nearby Great Smoky Mountains National Park offers year-round recreational opportunities. Knoxville is consistently rated as one of the top ten cities in the country in providing gracious amenities and a high quality of life.

Facilities

The University of Tennessee is the home of one of the finest library facilities in the nation. The Hodges Library has more than 2 million volumes and subscribes to 19,000 journals. In addition, the library has state-of-the-art electronic resources available for student research, communication, and information retrieval. M.B.A. classes are generally held in two classrooms specially reserved for the M.B.A. program. The University itself also has excellent cultural, recreational, fitness, and sports facilities.

Technology Environment

The chancellor of the University of Tennessee has challenged the school to become the "information university" for the state of Tennessee. Accordingly, the campus has an excellent information infrastructure for the M.B.A. program to use. Given the intense use of information technology in the M.B.A. program, each student is required to have his/her own computer for document preparation, spreadsheet analysis, database design, computer graphics, and Internet and e-mail connections.

Placement

The UTK M.B.A. Program Placement Office coordinates with the campuswide Career Services Office for on-campus interviews and interviews via video teleconferencing. Additional services delivered exclusively to M.B.A. students include resume referrals for both intern and full-time searches, membership and participation in three University-business consortia, resume writing workshops, videotaped interviews, and three career management seminars aimed at developing students' skills in such areas as job/intern search strategies, salary negotiation techniques, and dressing for success.

Admission

Applications are accepted for fall semester only. Applicants must have completed at least one college-level calculus course with a grade of B or better within the past five years. The Admission Committee considers the applicant's academic record, with particular emphasis on the last two years of undergraduate work and any previous graduate studies; scores on the GMAT and TOEFL (if applicable); work experience and other activities that demonstrate leadership potential. Personal interviews are strongly recommended but not required.

Finances

The 1998–99 educational expense for first-year students is approximately $11,000–$14,000, including $3154 annually for in-state tuition and $8210 annually for out-of-state tuition. (The total amount quoted includes M.B.A.-specific fees, books, supplies, room, board, and other miscellaneous costs.) Merit-based fellowships and assistantships are awarded by the college. Assistantships carry a full tuition waiver and a monthly stipend. Federal and state programs for student loans and grants and the Student Employment Service are administered by the Office of Financial Aid, 115 Student Services Building, 423-974-3131. The priority deadline is March 1.

International Students

There is a significant international student population at the University of Tennessee, Knoxville. (The M.B.A. program has 11 percent international students, with seven nationalities represented.) The University's Center for International Education and the International House provide resources and programs to meet the cultural, social, and professional interests of the international students.

Application Facts and Dates

The M.B.A. program application deadline (fall entrance only) for domestic and international applicants is March 1. Admission decisions are made on a rolling basis. Applicants receive a decision approximately four to six weeks after the M.B.A. Program Office receives a completed application. For additional information, students should contact:

Donna L. Potts
M.B.A. Admissions Director
University of Tennessee, Knoxville
527 Stokely Management Center
Knoxville, Tennessee 37996-0552
Telephone: 423-974-5033
Fax: 423-974-3826
World Wide Web: http://mba.bus.utk.edu

The University of Texas at Arlington

College of Business Administration

Arlington, Texas

EDUCATIONAL FOCUS FOR THE GLOBAL VILLAGE

The M.B.A. program welcomes all students who are intently focused on making professional contributions to today's dynamic global village. Our location in the center of the dynamic Dallas/Fort Worth Metroplex helps provide an enriched and seldom matched educational opportunity for both full-time and part-time students. Students are encouraged to design programs that prepare them for a specific functional area, level of management, or industry environment and that empower them to successfully deal with the related market uncertainty, social and technological change, and leadership and/or management demands. Our students are intently focused, broadly educated, keenly aware of market opportunities, and eager to accept the challenges in today's global economy.

—Dan Worrell, Interim Dean

Programs and Curricular Focus

Students from a wide variety of academic backgrounds choose the University of Texas at Arlington's (UTA) M.B.A. program because of its flexibility and academic rigor. Students with limited or no business background may begin their studies in fall, spring, or summer and complete up to 18 hours of core courses. Students with high-quality academic backgrounds in business (within ten years) may waive core and deficiency courses (similar courses with a B or better grade), and complete their advanced studies on a full-time basis in as little as sixteen months. Courses are offered in the afternoons and evenings and on Saturdays for convenience. The M.B.A. program provides students the opportunity to tailor their 36-hour advanced programs such that they include skills-building electives appropriate for their chosen functional areas, levels, and industries. They may select a very broad program of study or one that provides functional expertise in one of these concentrations: accounting, economics, finance, information systems, management, management science, marketing, production and operations management, or real estate. Each approach may be modified to provide a heightened emphasis in international business topics. Students with professional degrees may design a high-tech M.B.A. by taking their outside electives in their professional areas such as engineering, science, environmental, or other areas. Students wishing to expand their expertise in a business area of study may complete four

to seven business courses beyond the M.B.A. and earn an Advanced Studies certificate, or complete reduced requirements for a dual (second) degree in business, engineering, architecture, nursing, social work, or urban affairs. The College also provides a dual degree with Thunderbird, The American Graduate School of International Management, that allows students to earn an M.B.A. from UTA and a Master of International Management (MIM) degree from Thunderbird. Students may take advantage of UTA's reasonable cost and excellent business curriculum and Thunderbird's specialized international studies. Through waivers and transfer credit, students can substantially reduce the overall number of hours required for both degrees.

The M.B.A. curriculum provides students with a competitive advantage through their expanded ability to effectively perform on challenging teams, consulting, or leadership assignments that must deal with advanced technologies, organizational change, and emerging markets.

Students and the M.B.A. Experience

The student body in fall 1997 consisted of 491 students, with 190 pursuing their studies on a full-time basis. Approximately 90 percent of the students have industry experience, with the average being five years. Slightly less than half of the students have degrees outside of business, with engineering and science

making up the largest group (26 percent). The student diversity makes the M.B.A. experience an innovative approach to learning about business teams in the global village. Thirty-three percent of the students are women, 22 percent come from forty-one different countries on every continent, and more than 12 percent are members of minority groups. Every year, students may participate in exchange programs in Australia, England, France, Germany, Korea, Mexico, or Norway, as well as participate in other study-abroad opportunities. These experiences allow students to perform at a broader level in the global village and be less restricted by parochial views.

Special Features

Students participate, on an optional basis, in a comprehensive careers program that begins with a careers class (BUS4 5338) that provides extensive individual assessment, skills for analyzing career options, and networking with key people in possible career alternatives. Once a career orientation is chosen, the student is advised on recommended electives and encouraged to discuss options with advisers, key faculty, and alumni. Students are then assisted in locating paid internships that will provide excellent experiences in their chosen fields.

The Faculty

The College has 124 full-time equivalent faculty members, of whom 112 are full-time. More than 76 percent of full-time faculty members hold doctoral degrees from some of the most prestigious business schools in the U.S. Full-time faculty members are growing in both number and diversity; currently, they include 26 women and 21 members of minority groups. Faculty members are assigned to six departments.

The Business School Network

The College of Business Administration has seven advisory councils and boards that serve as advocacy groups for the College, providing advice and support on such matters as curriculum, internship programs, facilities enhancements, career services for students, and staff and faculty recruitment. A special program developed by the founder of Banctec partners successful executives and entrepreneurs with faculty to assist in the development and conduct of select courses. The Small Business Institute also helps match the research needs of small businesses with M.B.A. students' interests and academic experience. Each year the college hosts "Business Week," featuring guest speakers from top corporations. These councils, boards, and events provide personal contacts between the members of the College and the business community, which greatly assists in the shaping of our programs and the leaders of tomorrow.

The College and Environs

The Dallas/Fort Worth Metroplex is a large market and distribution center, a major convention site, a growing financial and cultural center, and the tenth-largest market in the U.S. Arlington, located midway between these larger cities, is a busy suburban city of 300,000 that contains many of the top entertainment sites in the state and boasts of one of the safest community environments among all major cities. The University, located on a peaceful 333-acre campus, has flourished for more than 100 years and has grown to become one of the top 100 universities based on enrollment in the U.S. The College of Business Administration, one of the largest in the nation with more than 4,600 graduate and undergraduate students, is housed in a modern facility that contains research centers, numerous computer labs, electronic classrooms, special libraries, and modern advising facilities.

Facilities

Much of a student's library research can be conducted from his or her PC and modem. Business research librarians provide, during the new-student orientation, a roadmap to the electronic research

superhighway that contains hundreds of databases and electronic links to high-quality research sources. Students may also attend a high-tech tour of the library or an Internet seminar; both help expedite research efforts.

Technology Environment

In the College there are eight laboratory facilities with 146 computers and related software libraries. Visual Basic, Power Builder, the COOL GEN CASE tool, Microsoft Office Suites, and the Netscape web browser, as well as DOS, OS/2, and Windows operating systems are available for use by students. All students have a VAX computer account and access to the Internet and are able to complete advising by e-mail. The College designed and implemented the first CyberAdvising program in the nation.

Placement

The Dallas/Fort Worth Metroplex provides a fertile lab for the exploration and pursuit of hundreds of career alternatives. The University annually hosts one of the largest "career day events" in Texas, which attracts top employers throughout the region. This event helps maintain one of the nation's largest student employment services, which offers daily 8,000–10,000 part-time jobs, co-ops, and internships. A core of career professionals participate in a comprehensive M.B.A. careers program and present an array of seminars designed to enhance the candidate's circle of opportunities. Traditional on-campus interviews are complemented by cooperative career fairs, extended electronic job listings, and an interactive resume data bank.

Admission

Applicants seeking admission should have a wide variety of skills and experience relevant to the modern business arena. While managerial or supervisory experience is preferred, it is not required. Prerequisites for admission to this program include a bachelor's degree from an accredited university, a satisfactory GMAT score, past academic performance that demonstrates the potential for graduate work, three letters of recommendation that reflect an ability to perform at a high level, and a personal essay that persuasively outlines the student's academic goals, strengths, and weaknesses. An entering class of students will normally have an average GMAT score of 550 and an average GPA of 3.2.

Finances

Modest tuition rates and fees make this M.B.A. a great selection for students seeking the biggest "bang for the buck." Annual tuition for the 1997–98 year for 30 semester hours of graduate course work was $3691 for in-state residents and $10,411 for out-of-state residents. Annual mandatory fees were approximately $384. The annual cost for textbooks and supplies was approximately $900. The annual costs (twelve months) for room, board, and incidentals may cost an additional $8700 (lower if shared living). A vehicle may be necessary to take full advantage of internships and work opportunities. Students are encouraged to participate in the M.B.A. loans program when necessary.

International Students

A growing array of international students from every continent are participating in the M.B.A. program. The University provides a Graduate English Skills Program that helps international students adjust to the culture and helps polish verbal skills that are vital to success in the M.B.A. classroom. International students should have a TOEFL score of at least 550.

Application Facts and Dates

Applications may be submitted for fall, spring, and summer semesters. Application deadlines are generally as follows:

For U.S. students for fall semester the deadline is mid-June; for spring semester the deadline is mid-October; and for summer semester the deadline is mid-March. For international students, the deadline for fall semester is April 1; for spring semester the deadline is September 1; and for summer semester, the deadline is January 1.

Detailed information on application requirements and steps to take after acceptance are all explained on the University's World Wide Web Home Page at http://www.uta.edu/gradbiz/gradweb.htm. Application material may also be requested using the information listed below.

Graduate Business Programs
University of Texas at Arlington
UTA Box 19376
Arlington, Texas 76019-0376
Telephone: 817-272-3005
Fax: 817-272-5799
E-mail: admit@uta.edu
World Wide Web: http://www.uta.edu/gradbiz/gradweb.htm

The University of Texas at Austin

Graduate School of Business

Austin, Texas

A REPUTATION FOR QUALITY AND EXCELLENCE

As you peruse our information, we are confident that you will find us to be a top-ranked program offering you the opportunity to differentiate yourself in a competitive market for M.B.A. talent that places a premium on executive and leadership potential. We offer you this opportunity at an extraordinary value.

As a professional program that's been part of The University of Texas (UT) at Austin for seventy-five years, our ultimate goal is your success and satisfaction. To this end, the Texas M.B.A. Program is devoted to providing you with the best educational experience and support services in graduate business education.

When you choose the Texas M.B.A. Program, you have our commitment that we will live up to our reputation for quality and excellence. This commitment also extends to the way the program does business. We will provide you with an education, not merely training; we build our entire experience on the foundation of individual student's backgrounds and interests. We will work together to creatively and analytically challenge the management assumptions and practices of today.

—Dr. Ramesh K. S. Rao, Associate Dean for Graduate Programs and Director of the M.B.A. Program

Programs and Curricular Focus

The Texas M.B.A program is a full-time, two-year, 60-hour program. The seven-course (21-hour) core curriculum provides a broad, cross-functional perspective followed by thirteen electives. Concentrations include one of several information and/or technology management tracks, entrepreneurship, a strong array of finance tracks, accounting, operations management, human resource, marketing, and environmental and natural resource management. Students are encouraged to create their own customized concentrations or divide their time between two or more concentrations.

The Texas M.B.A. program offers one-semester exchange programs with seventeen international business schools (nine of which are English-language programs). New programs are being developed continually, the most recent with Pontifica Universidad Catolica in Santiago, Chile. The Texas M.B.A. Language Track in Spanish is a one-year, three-course sequence specifically tailored for business students. In addition to enhanced language proficiency, students gain an understanding of Latin American economic structures, business practices, and protocols.

Students and the M.B.A. Experience

The student-selection equation is simple: Quality inputs produce quality outputs. For that reason, the program's standards are highly competitive. The Texas M.B.A. program requires intelligent, experienced, and professional applicants. The most recent class hails from widely varying cultural, geographic, national, educational, and professional backgrounds. Talent and motivation are the only shared traits among all Texas M.B.A. students. The average M.B.A. student has a GMAT score of 670, a GPA of 3.42, and five years of full-time work experience. The average age is 28. The class profile includes 26 percent women, 8 percent members of minority groups, and 25 percent international students. More than thirty-five countries are represented in the international population.

Each class is divided into a number of cohorts selected to create a diverse blend of academic, professional, and cultural backgrounds. The rigorous core curriculum fills most of the first year. In the core courses, students study administrative and behavioral concepts, general quantitative methods, and individual functional areas of business. This survey of "the organization"—its many forms, influences, and surroundings—grounds every Texas M.B.A. student in a similarly excellent

framework and provides a strong base for later, more focused course work.

Special Features

Responding to the rapid changes taking place in the energy industry, including the development of a deregulated, competitive electricity market, The University of Texas at Austin and Enron have teamed up to launch the nation's first Energy Finance Program and to create an Enron MBA Excellence Scholarship Fund. UT will seek support from other leading energy firms to join in the development of the Energy Finance Program, creating an unprecedented partnership between education and industry.

Enron has funded a $3-million grant, part of which will be used to create the new Energy Finance curriculum, which will enable M.B.A. students to learn innovative ways in which commodities such as electricity and natural gas can be traded, much like equity stocks. Enron has pioneered and continues to lead risk management practices in the energy field, offering its customers innovative financing alternatives for long-term contracts related to domestic and international energy projects. The grant also will fund scholarships for students exhibiting both academic excellence and leadership capabilities.

The International Entrepreneurial Challenge of the MOOT CORP Program is a new venture competition in which graduate business students develop a detailed, growth-oriented business plan and then match their efforts against those of their peers from other top business schools. Originated by the Graduate School of Business (GSB) at The University of Texas at Austin, the program combines cutting-edge academic theories with the most effective business practices. It enables business school disciplines to be applied to actual entrepreneurial ventures in an integrated fashion. Aspiring entrepreneurs gain the opportunity not only to learn every facet of developing a business plan but also to experience the process of creating a venture and seeking the money to launch it.

The Faculty

The faculty members (17 percent women, 16 percent international) are unusually committed to the development of their students on both personal and professional levels. This fact manifests itself in an extraordinary accessibility to business students. The faculty's close connections with the corporate world give its members a realistic, informed perspective on modern business, thus ensuring that the classroom remains as relevant as possible.

The Business School Network

Corporate Partnerships
The Texas M.B.A. program has outstanding relationships with such corporations as EDS, Enron, Andersen Consulting, and Dell Computer Corporation. The corporate partners have joined with the Texas M.B.A. program to develop such lasting programs as the EDS Financial Technology and Trading Center, the Enron Energy Finance Program and Excellence Fund, the Center for Customer Insight with Anderson Consulting, and a recent laptop initiative with Dell Computers and Cisco.

Prominent Alumni
Texas M.B.A. alumni are prominent leaders in many industries in the United States and abroad. They are dedicated and loyal supporters of the School who give generously of their time, experience, and counsel to current students and faculty members. Alumni are eager to speak with prospective students.

The College and Environs
The Graduate School of Business at The University of Texas at Austin is internationally recognized in the areas of information technology, entrepreneurship, accounting, and global collaboration, with a special focus toward Central and South America. Austin, in addition to being the state capital of Texas, is noted for its excellent quality of life, progressive and friendly attitude, thriving high-technology industries, and high levels of education among its citizens. It is one of the most livable and affordable cities in the U.S. Located in central Texas along the banks of the Colorado River, this area features an abundance of outdoor recreational opportunities and entertainment venues.

Facilities
The business school encompasses a three-building complex on the main campus of

The University of Texas at Austin. The complex includes the Graduate School of Business, the College of Business Administration (CBA), and the University Teaching Center. Executive-style classrooms are used for M.B.A. core curriculum instruction. Faculty offices are also housed within the CBA/GSB complex.

A career services facility is provided for all business school students. A new 10,000-square-foot corporate interviewing suite opened in February 1998. A single, point-of-service reception foyer fronts the suite of forty-two interview rooms equipped with laptop ports and computers.

The University of Texas at Austin library is ranked ninth in the nation for holdings of research libraries. The library has more than 7.4 million volumes and 515 permanent staff members. ABI/Inform, LEXIS-NEXIS, Moody's, and many other online databases are available for student use. The library is located directly adjacent to the business school complex.

Technology Environment
Starting in the fall of 1998, all incoming graduate students are required to buy or lease at least a corporate model 233 MHz PC laptop, specially configured with Microsoft Windows NT 4.0 and a wealth of collaborative tools. The School is committed to keeping its technology current, becoming an early adopter of Windows NT 5.0 and other corporate standardized operations.

Placement
M.B.A. services include on-campus interview programs, individual career counseling, career panels, professional development seminars, and skill-building workshops. Also provided are resume referrals to prospective employers, publication of job announcements and resume books, salary information, assistance with company receptions, and the comprehensive Graduate Career Library. More than 260 companies from across the nation and around the world come to the UT campus to interview, while several hundred more hire through the computer Jobline. The Career Services Office has recently added the 1000th company to its On Campus Recruiter database. This past year, 93

percent of M.B.A. graduates had accepted employment offers by August 1.

Admission
The M.B.A. program offers full-time fall semester admission only. To be admitted to the program, applicants must submit letters of recommendation, official GMAT and TOEFL (for international students) scores, and transcripts from any undergraduate institutions.

Finances
The estimated cost of attendance for 1998–99 includes tuition, $3240 (first year, for 30 semester hours); fees, $2754 (including M.B.A., general University, and other fees); books and supplies, $1000 (per year); and living expenses, $9450; for an estimated annual total of $16,444.

For information about financial assistance opportunities and application deadlines for the M.B.A. program, interested students should contact Ms. Mary Gielstra, Financial Assistance Coordinator (telephone: 512-471-7607, fax: 512-471-4131; e-mail: mgielstra@ mail.utexas.edu).

International Students
International students comprise 25 percent of the M.B.A. population and represent thirty-five countries. A career counselor assists international students with their specific job search needs.

Application Facts and Dates
For the Master of Business Administration program (fall admission only), the early application due date is January 1, the international (non-U.S. citizens) due date is February 1, and the domestic (U.S. citizens and permanent residents) due date is April 15. For more information, students should contact:

Dr. Carl Harris
Director of Admission, M.B.A.
   Programs
Graduate School of Business
The University of Texas at Austin
P.O. Box 7999
Austin, Texas 78713-7999
Telephone: 512-471-7612
Fax: 512-471-4243 or 4131
E-mail: texasmba@bus.utexas.edu
World Wide Web: http://texasinfo.bus.
   utexas.edu/

The University of Texas at Dallas

Dallas, Texas

> ### MANAGEMENT EDUCATION—A HIGH PRIORITY
>
> *There are many distinguishing features to the University of Texas at Dallas (UT Dallas). First, we have a very talented group of faculty members, many of whom have achieved national and international recognition, and we are recruiting the very best junior and senior faculty members. Second, we are located in a dynamic and growing area populated with many global and vibrant companies, offering the School a unique competitive advantage. We have an active industry Advisory Board, and we are committed to further strengthening our relationships with industry. Finally, we are part of a young but high-quality university that has identified management education as an area of high priority. All these features provide an environment in which we can deliver the highest quality education to our students.*
>
> —Hasan Pirkul, Dean

Programs and Curricular Focus

The School of Management's mission is to meet the challenges of a rapidly changing, technology-driven, global society by partnering with the business community to deliver high-quality management education to a diverse group of undergraduate and graduate students and practicing executives, and to develop and continuously improve programs advancing management education and practice and conduct research that enhances management knowledge. These programs address the multidimensional needs of a dynamic modern society driven by the development, diffusion, understanding, and management of advanced technologies.

The University of Texas at Dallas School of Management offers the following graduate degrees: the Master of Business Administration (M.B.A.), the Master of Arts in international management studies (M.A.), the Master of Science in accountancy (M.S.), and the Master of Science in business administration (M.S.).

Two specialized M.B.A.'s are offered in the School, both of which are 48-hour degrees. The M.B.A. is the largest program and is offered both in a lockstep format and on a part-time basis with classes primarily in the evenings, designed to provide students with full-time jobs the opportunity to earn a graduate degree at nontraditional times. Now in its fifth year, the Executive M.B.A. program (EMBA) focuses on "managing for change." The curriculum stresses the knowledge, skills, perspectives, and attitudes necessary to lead in the twenty-first century. The EMBA program is

a lockstep, two-year program with classes on Friday and Saturday every other weekend. Participants in the program have at least ten years of business experience.

The Cohort M.B.A. Program focuses on developing "management skills for the information age." The curriculum stresses the ideas and concepts that will provide the knowledge and skills necessary to gain an edge in managing in the next century. The Cohort M.B.A. is offered in a full-time day format; classes begin each fall. Students age in range from 22 to 30 and have three to five years of management experience.

The part-time M.B.A. program, like the EMBA and Cohort M.B.A., is a 48-hour degree. The curriculum is similar in focus to the specialized M.B.A.'s in that it allows the student the opportunity to specialize in finance, international management, management information systems, managerial economics, marketing, operations management, and organizations and strategy.

Both the M.A. and M.S. programs are 36-hour degrees offered on a full-time or part-time basis. Classes are primarily at night and allow specialization in accounting, decision sciences, finance and managerial economics, international management, marketing, and organizations and strategies.

Entrance to any master's program does not require a previous business degree.

Students and the M.B.A. Experience

Participants in the School of Management's graduate programs are primarily students with full-time jobs with a mini-

mum of five years of managerial experience. Approximately 90 percent are pursuing degrees on a part-time basis while working locally at the many high-technology corporations that surround the campus complex. They range in age from 28 to 50+. Almost half of the student body of the University is female. Approximately 38 percent of the master's students are female. The minority population represents about 25 percent of the University's population. Approximately 22 percent of the School of Management's students are members of minority groups. International students comprise 32.2 percent of the total student population.

There is a consistent international emphasis in the programs. It is driven by the faculty and the participants. Programs include opportunities for field-based projects. Technology and its use is a primary focus of all graduate programs.

Special Features

The Master's in International Management Studies (MIMS) is a flextime, distance learning curriculum designed for executives. Successful completion of the MIMS curriculum (24 hours) and business core (12 hours) earns a Master of Arts in International Management Studies. The MIMS program is ideal for professionals seeking to acquire or upgrade global management skills.

Approximately half of the content of the seven organized MIMS courses, offered sequentially over the one-year course period, is delivered during four 2-day retreats on the UT Dallas campus and during one foreign study tour. The other half of the curriculum is delivered to students using a variety of instructional technologies, such as groupware accessed via the Internet and audio cassettes. The MIMS program begins every January and takes one year to complete. For additional information about this program, interested students should locate http://www.utdallas.edu/dept/mgmt/mims/mims.html on the World Wide Web.

New this year is an additional executive education program entitled Program/Project Management, designed primarily for certification of project managers. This certificate program can also lead to an

M.S. degree by taking an additional 12 hours. Offered once a month on a Thursday, Friday, and Saturday schedule, it is ideal for busy executives.

The School of Management also announces an alliance with The University of Texas Southwestern Medical School to begin offering, in May 1998, a Master of Medical Management designed for physicians and physician executives. The modular format will run every three months for 5½ days and can be noncredit or CME credit and/or academic credit. The program will be taught jointly by School of Management faculty and UT Southwestern medical faculty.

The Faculty

The University of Texas at Dallas School of Management has strong, committed faculty members who teach all of the master's programs. All faculty members have extensive experience in master's education, consulting, and/or practical experience both domestically and internationally. Some are leading scholars. Many serve as editors of professional journals. Others have received awards for teaching excellence. At times, faculty members join together to team-teach selected courses. The faculty is supplemented in selected courses by outstanding UT Dallas faculty members from outside the School. All graduate courses are taught by faculty members with Ph.D.'s from universities across the nation, such as Stanford, Berkeley, Harvard, Carnegie Mellon, University of Minnesota, Rochester, and the University of Chicago. One highlight of the program is the addition of local corporate executives who supplement faculty teaching and who often provide case problems for student participation.

The Business School Network

The School of Management enjoys great support and counsel from the business community through its Advisory Council and President's Leadership Circle. Members of the council provide essential feedback for the various programs within the School. Business leaders are frequent speakers in the classroom, are included in all graduate retreats, and often work together with executive graduate students to resolve case problems. The School of Management, located in the north Dallas high-technology region, is fortunate to have Fortune 500 companies as employers of its students.

The College and Environs

Prior to becoming the University of Texas at Dallas in 1969, the University operated as the privately funded Southwest Center for Advanced Studies (SCAS). By act of the 61st Texas legislature, SCAS was transferred to the state of Texas. Graduate programs were expanded and enrollment for junior and senior undergraduate students began in September 1975. When the University opened its new campus buildings that year, the existing academic programs were organized into the Schools of Natural Sciences and Mathematics, Management, and Human Development. New programs were introduced through the Schools of Arts and Humanities, General Studies, and Social Sciences.

Facilities

UT Dallas is located between Richardson and Plano, two populous suburbs of almost 400,000 that are still growing rapidly. For the most part, the housing (apartments) available is less than 20 years old. For those who prefer to be on campus, the University has the Waterview Park Apartments, a series of low-rise, garden-style apartments run by a private company. These apartments have a long list of amenities, including kitchens, washer/dry-

ers, alarm systems, and access to swimming and other recreational facilities.

Admission

Prerequisites for all graduate admissions include completion of an undergraduate calculus class and personal computer proficiency; spreadsheet proficiency is a must. Completion of a baccalaureate degree from an accredited institution is required; previous undergraduate work in business is not a requirement. Additional criteria for admission include the GMAT, completion of an application, and three recent letters of reference. A TOEFL score is required of all applicants for whom English is not the native language. Applicants are evaluated based on their personal qualities and academic background; GMAT scores are evaluated using the formula designated by the AACSB to evaluate admission criteria and professional experience. Personal interviews are not required. To download an application, applicants can send e-mail to grad-admission@utdallas.edu.

Finances

Resident tuition for 1997–98 was $1379 for full-time students and $527 per 3 credits for part-time students; nonresident tuition was $3305 for full-time students and $1169 per course for part-time students.

International Students

The School of Management at UT Dallas has a strong international graduate community. 32.2 percent of the graduate population is international, representing twenty nationalities. India, People's Republic of China, and Taiwan are the largest sources of international students.

Application Facts and Dates

The final deadline for fall admission is July 15 of each year; however, admission decisions are made in the order of application receipt and completion. Part-time students are admitted to the master's programs on a semester-by-semester basis. The deadline for spring admission is December 1; summer is May 1. The deadline for the Cohort M.B.A. and other specialized master's programs is July 15. For information, students should contact:

Dr. Gary Horton, Head of Advising
Advising Office
University of Texas at Dallas
Richardson, Texas 75083-0688
Telephone: 972-883-2701
Fax: 972-883-6425
E-mail: grad-admission@utdallas.edu
World Wide Web: http://www.utdallas.edu/dept/mgmt

The University of Texas at San Antonio

San Antonio, Texas

A PLACE TO BUILD YOUR BUSINESS PORTFOLIO

Business educators and practitioners have come to understand that building your personal business portfolio is a lifelong process. At The University of Texas at San Antonio (UTSA) we have developed a variety of high-quality business program options. Choices range from the traditional M.B.A., International M.B.A., Weekend M.B.A., and an M.B.A. with concentration options to a number of Master of Science (M.S.) degrees in business related disciplines. We also have a new and unique Executive M.B.A. focused on personal leadership development and self-organizing systems for the more seasoned executives. Our graduate students can take classes either in the new and technologically sophisticated Business Building on the main campus or at the modern UTSA Downtown Campus. Our College has an ongoing commitment to provide the graduate programs needed to either establish or keep current your personal business portfolio.

—James F. Gaertner, Dean

Programs and Curricular Focus

The College of Business is accredited by AACSB–The International Association for Management Education, placing it in the top 25 percent of business schools across the nation. The high quality of programs is ensured by AACSB standards, which address curriculum issues, credentials of professors, student-teacher ratio issues, and educational resources such as library and computer facilities.

Catering to the demand for a broad range of advanced-degree offerings, recently developed M.B.A. and graduate options include:
Executive M.B.A. program for professionals with ten or more years of increasing managerial experience
Weekend and evening M.B.A.'s for working professionals
M.S. in management of technology for those with technical undergraduate training
M.B.A. in international business for those with a global business interest
M.S. in accounting
Master of Taxation
UTSA also offers the traditional M.B.A. with concentrations in business economics, finance, employee relations, healthcare management, information systems, management accounting, management of technology, management science, and taxation.

There are three new degrees under development: an M.S. in finance, an M.S. in information technology, and an M.A. in economics. A new M.B.A. concentra-

tion in marketing management is also under development. Approval of these new degrees and concentration is pending.

Students and the M.B.A. Experience

UTSA has an average business graduate enrollment of 500. The students' average age is 30, with a 34 percent female enrollment. Twenty-five percent of the students are members of minority groups, and 17 percent are international students. Seventy-five percent attend graduate school part-time and work at least part-time. Students recently admitted to the programs have an average GMAT of 522 and a 3.0 average GPA.

❖ Global Focus

Located in San Antonio, the College has enjoyed a strategic edge in offering opportunities to integrate global business issues. Special relationships have been developed with the La Universidad Nacional Autónoma de México (UNAM) in Mexico City, The University of Calgary in Canada, and others in Europe and Asia. Attention has been primarily focused on business in Mexico and business issues related to the North American Free Trade Agreement. There is an M.B.A. in international business option as well as special exchange program opportunities coordinated

through both the College's and the University's International Program Offices.

Special Features

As a large business school, UTSA has the latitude to offer a large number of program choices and scheduling plans for virtually anyone who is seriously interested in pursuing a business graduate education. Programs have been developed to cater to the top-level executive looking for a challenging peer group experience and to the mid-level manager returning for the tools necessary for promotion as well as to the more traditional full-time graduate student. A strong student organization, the M.B.A. Association is only one of the many opportunities available for graduate students to enrich their academic experience.

The Faculty

Over the past several years, UTSA has built an outstanding business faculty with Ph.D.'s from leading business schools nationwide. Forty-two percent of the faculty members are female or members of minority groups. Successful recruiting has created a broad and diverse faculty with a balanced approach to teaching, research, and service. The majority of business classes are taught by full-time professors, many whom have practical business experience. Highly qualified professionals from the business community supplement them for special topic categories.

The Business School Network

The College enjoys an extensive corporate community network. A variety of opportunities are provided for interaction. A formal Business Advisory Council, comprising 45 top-level executives from the business community, routinely participates in the many social and academic activities. In addition to this advisory council and its subcommittees, other, more discipline-focused groups have been formed to interact with both faculty members and students. The College's Center for Professional Excellence provides yet another venue for business executives to gather and reflect, away from their typical work environment.

The College and Environs

San Antonio, Texas, is one of the nation's ten largest cities—a city rich in history and culture. Tourism and the medical and military industries, along with a growing communications and technology sector, make for a dynamic business community. The University, with an enrollment of approximately 17,500, is respected as an energetic, growing metropolitan university and a leading provider of Hispanic graduates. The campus is located in the flourishing area of northwest San Antonio and neighbors the famous Texas Hill Country. The College of Business was recently lauded by its accrediting agency, AACSB–The International Association of Business Education, as a college with entrepreneurial spirit, responsive to the needs of the business community, with a faculty focused on innovation and student success.

Facilities

In January 1997 the College moved into the new 205,000-square-foot, $30-million Business Building. Students enrolled at UTSA have the benefit of many new academic buildings and facilities. Since 1994, UTSA has built four new major buildings, including the first phase of a new Downtown Campus. The second phase will be completed in fall 1998. In addition, a new health, wellness, and recreation center is scheduled to open by 2000.

Technology Environment

The University has recently made capital investments in equipment, created ways for students to retrieve information more quickly and easily, and expanded its training, distance-learning, and computer support programs. About $4 million alone was dedicated to equip the Business Building with the latest in teaching and learning technologies. Distance education and teleconference facilities, an advanced computer projects lab, two 30-station networked computer classrooms, and an

additional 200-station general student computing facility are all part of the technology available in the Business Building. A complex of organizational behavior policy classrooms and break-out rooms are equipped with mirrored observation windows, video monitors, and audio capabilities that allow faculty/student project interaction and instruction on group behavior. Each classroom is equipped with a custom-designed instructor podium that provides direct access to all of the instructional technology available.

Placement

In addition to the University Career Services Office, the College of Business provides direct access to a counselor. This M.B.A. counselor facilitates placement in permanent part-time or internship positions.

Admission

A bachelor's degree from an accredited institution is the basic requirement for admission to graduate study at UTSA. For admission to the M.B.A. program, applicants must meet University-wide graduate admission requirements and the following College of Business requirements: an approximate overall grade point average of at least 3.0 (on a 4.0 scale) in all work completed at the undergraduate level and an approximate composite score of at least 500 (with no component less than the 20th percentile) on the GMAT. The GMAT results will only be accepted if the test has been taken no more than five years before the date of application. International students are also required to show proof of adequate funds, and proof of health/immunizations is recommended. International students whose native language is not English must submit TOEFL results with a minimum score of 500.

Finances

Full-time tuition (9 semester hours) and fees for residents are $1230. For nonresidents, they are $3147. Tuition and fee amounts are subject to change by Legislative action or by action of the Board of Regents of The University of

Texas System. Changes in tuition and fees will be effective upon the date of enactment. Refer to each semester's Schedule of Classes for current tuition and fee amounts.

Financial aid is available in the form of fellowships, research assistantships, grants, scholarships, work-study, and loans. Financial aid is available to international students.

International Students

Services and facilities for international students include the international student office, international student center, international student housing, visa services, ESL courses, and counseling/support services.

Application Facts and Dates

For domestic applicants, applications and any required documents for the master's degree programs should be filed by July 1 for the fall semester, December 1 for the spring semester, and May 1 for the summer sessions. Deadlines for international students submitting applications for admission are June 1 for the fall semester, October 15 for the spring semester, and March 1 for the summer sessions.

Students should contact the office below for applications and instructions for completion:

Office of Graduate Studies and
  Research
College of Business
The University of Texas at San
  Antonio
6900 North Loop 1604 West
San Antonio, Texas 78249
Telephone: 210-458-4641
Fax: 210-458-4398
E-mail: mbainfo@lonestar.utsa.edu
World Wide Web: http://cobweb.utsa.
  edu

International students should contact:

Assistant Director for International
  Student Admissions
The University of Texas at San
  Antonio
6900 North Loop 1604 West
San Antonio, Texas 78249
Telephone: 210-458-4530
Fax: 210-458-4187

University of the Pacific

Stockton, California

EDUCATING INNOVATIVE LEADERS

The University of the Pacific M.B.A. program is committed to cultivating the leadership ability and innovative spirit of our students, in addition to training them in state-of-the-art technical business skills.

Our unique curriculum includes a heavy emphasis on experience in the workplace, which we achieve through class consulting projects, internships, and a mentor program that teams each full-time student with a senior business executive. Our small, highly interactive classes also encourage close working relationships between students and faculty, enabling faculty to challenge students to achieve their full potential.

Whether you are interested in the general M.B.A. or the entrepreneurship track, the University of the Pacific M.B.A. is designed for students who want to make a difference.

—Mark Plovnick, Dean

Programs and Curricular Focus

The focus of the M.B.A. programs at the University of the Pacific is on training future business leaders to be competitive in the twenty-first century. The course work is challenging and provides a firm grounding in various academic disciplines yet goes beyond the traditional business school curriculum to emphasize critical leadership skills and a global perspective. The classes are small to encourage close student-faculty relationships.

There are two M.B.A. programs offered through the Eberhardt School of Business (ESB): the one-year, full-time day program and the evening program, which can be completed on a full- or part-time basis. The one-year M.B.A. is a unique, customized program that enables a limited number of students, with sufficient previous course work in business, to complete the M.B.A. program in ten months. The team begins the program in August, taking a three-week class called Leadership and Change that involves off-campus activities that can include outdoor adventure challenges, corporate visits, and other experiential assignments. The curriculum for the fall semester includes corporate finance, business and public policy, strategic marketing, and technology and innovation.

In January, the entire cohort travels overseas to take the Global Business Competition course. This includes classroom work, corporate visits, and cultural events. The entire experience provides students with the opportunity to actually live the culture and to attain the international per-

spective that is critical for M.B.A. degree holders today. Recent classes have been held in Seoul, Singapore, Kuala Lumpur, and Santiago, Chile. The spring semester includes Managing Productivity and Quality and Strategic Management, as well as the flexibility to choose a concentration with two elective courses. Students in the full-time day program are also matched with a senior manager from the business community who acts as a mentor and helps guide them through the M.B.A. program. Internships and consulting projects round out the workplace exposure emphasized by the M.B.A. program.

The evening program curriculum is divided into two phases totaling 54 semester units. Phase One includes eight courses covering basic business skills; these courses can be waived if similar courses have been successfully completed with a grade of B or better at the undergraduate or graduate level. Phase Two embodies the heart of the M.B.A. program, with two tracks—the general management M.B.A. and the entrepreneurship M.B.A. In each track, students take two courses that develop leadership and innovation skills, four courses that integrate the foundation course work into a managerial framework, and four elective courses that allow students to explore their areas of interest, such as finance, marketing, or accounting.

The University also offers a joint M.B.A./J.D. degree program with the School of Law. This accelerated program allows students to complete both degrees in four years. The Master's International

Program is offered in conjunction with the Peace Corps. This program allows individuals to complete their M.B.A. while also fulfilling a two-year Peace Corps service experience abroad.

Students and the M.B.A. Experience

The M.B.A. students at the University of the Pacific come from a wide variety of academic institutions, with diverse academic credentials. Geographically, a high percentage of students are from California, although there are students from throughout the United States and many other countries. Women comprise about 45 percent of the program's students, and approximately 30 percent of the students identify themselves as members of underrepresented groups. The average age of the students is 30, with six years of full-time work experience.

Special Features

The University of the Pacific M.B.A. program is unique in its overall emphasis on integrating the classroom experience with the business world and its focus on the personal as well as academic development of each student. The M.B.A. program offers an international travel option each January for full-time students. The Global Business Competition course meets one week on campus and then travels overseas for a two-week period. The entrepreneurship M.B.A. program is a specialized course of study that complements the general management M.B.A. program and provides students with an intensified and rigorous exposure to the principles, tools, and ideas needed to succeed in entrepreneurial pursuits. Also available is the one-year M.B.A. program, which provides an unusual opportunity for a small group of students to experience an innovative fast-track M.B.A.

The Faculty

The Eberhardt School of Business is committed to teaching excellence. Teaching is the primary responsibility of the faculty. Research complements the teaching mission and enables faculty to offer instruction that is relevant and current, providing a high-quality learning experience for every student. While the faculty members have earned their academic credentials from the finest universities, most have significant experience in management or consulting; they integrate such experience into their course work.

The Business School Network

Corporate Partnerships

The University of the Pacific ESB has built strong relationships with the corporate community and strives to integrate the classroom experience with the business world in a variety of ways, including the Pacific Business Forum, which brings nationally and internationally recognized corporate or government leaders to campus several times a year to speak about current issues in the world today; the Westgate Center for Management Development, which provides management training for the regional business community; the Institute for Family Business, which assists family-owned businesses in finding and developing solutions to their unique business challenges; the Community Consulting Corps, which brings students together with managers of nonprofit organizations to work in a client-consultant relationship to solve business problems; the Business Advisory Board, which includes 30 execu-

tives from local, regional, and national businesses who work closely with the dean and faculty at integrating the business school and the business world; the Mentorship Program, in which every student in the full-time program is matched with an executive to help him or her make decisions regarding classes, careers, and the job search; and the Internship Program, which provides business exposure for students, either on an individual basis or as part of a consulting team.

The College and Environs

The University of the Pacific, with its redbrick buildings and ivy-covered walls, is now in its 147th year. California's first chartered university, the University of the Pacific was established in 1851, one year after California became a state. The main campus spreads more than 170 acres along the Calaveras River. Stockton is a short drive from San Francisco, Yosemite National Park, Lake Tahoe, the Napa and Sonoma wine country, Sierra skiing, and the state capitol in Sacramento. The University also has a dental school in San Francisco and a law school in Sacramento.

Technology Environment

The University has substantial academic computing resources available for students, with multiple laboratories distributed across the campus and a network linking the labs, personal computers, and the campus mainframe. The computer lab in the ESB has a Novell LAN with twenty-one 200-MHz computers, each equipped with CD-ROM capabilities and 32 MB of RAM. All graduate students are expected to take advantage of the University's electronic mail system and the Internet.

Placement

The Office of Career Services facilitates career decision making and job search assistance for all students on an individual basis and in small group sessions. It annually coordinates an on-campus recruiting program and a career fair, in addition to a variety of workshops and special programs. The office also maintains a Career Advisory Network, which links students to alumni of the University to help build their professional connections. In addition to the work of Career Services, the faculty and staff in the Eberhardt School of Business work with alumni and corporations to secure internships and full-time positions for M.B.A. students.

Admission

Qualified candidates are admitted to the part-time evening program on a rolling basis for the fall semester, spring semester, and summer session. The one-year full-time day program is limited to 25 students per class, and that class is admitted each

year and begins in August as a cohort. Each candidate's file is evaluated on the basis of academic record, scores on the required Graduate Management Admission Test (GMAT), a personal essay, and three letters of recommendation. Although the entire "package" is considered for each applicant, the typical undergraduate GPA considered is 3.0 or higher. GMAT scores are generally 500 and above. A score of 550 or better on the TOEFL is required for all students for whom English is not the native language. International students must present proof of adequate funds to cover expenses for the entire M.B.A. program.

Finances

The annual expenses for an M.B.A. student at the University of the Pacific depend on a variety of factors. The 1998–99 tuition for the one-year program is $17,820. In the part-time program, costs are based on the number of courses a student takes (at $1782 per course in 1998–99). The cost of living in Stockton is relatively low, and students can find housing for about $380 to $500 per month. Room and board on campus are approximately $5800 per year, depending on the housing and meal plan options chosen. Full-time students must also pay a health services fee, which is approximately $250, and a University Center fee of $50. Financial assistance is available through scholarships, assistantships, and loans. Merit-based scholarships and teaching and research assistantships are available directly from the Eberhardt School of Business. These awards are generally determined by June 30, so students should submit applications by March 1 to be considered.

Application Facts and Dates

Application deadlines are May 1 for the fall semester, November 1 for the spring semester, and April 1 for the summer session. Since the one-year M.B.A. program is limited to 25 students per year, applicants to this program are advised to submit their applications by March 1 to guarantee consideration. M.B.A. admission decisions are made on a rolling basis, and applicants are notified immediately when decisions have been made. To ensure a quick response, application packages should be complete. For more information, contact:

Director of Student Recruitment
Eberhardt School of Business
Weber Hall-Room 206
University of the Pacific
3601 Pacific Avenue
Stockton, California 95211
Telephone: 209-946-2629
Fax: 209-946-2586
E-mail: mba@uop.edu
World Wide Web: http://www.uop.edu/
esb/docs/mba/index.htm

University of the Witwatersrand

Johannesburg, South Africa

A UNIQUE LEARNING EXPERIENCE

Established in 1968, the Wits Business School (WBS) has proven to be highly effective in empowering individuals to handle local and global business challenges and continues to produce a significant number of the country's most outstanding business leaders.

The Wits M.B.A. offers a blend of a deeply relevant South African orientation to management practice with a critical component of international exposure and experience.

The Wits M.B.A. is a focused, practical, and future-oriented programme designed to give students a leading edge in the changing business environment. Market surveys and feedback from companies show that the Wits M.B.A. remains the most highly respected qualification of its kind in the country.

—Professor Mike Ward, Director, Wits Business School

Programs and Curricular Focus

Three formats are available for the Wits M.B.A. The twelve-month full-time programme offers classes six days per week and on some evenings. In the three-year part-time programme, students are required to attend lectures on two evenings each week and a few Saturday mornings. The eighteen-month programme allows students to complete the first half of the M.B.A. in six months of full-time study and the second half of the programme (electives and research report) over a period of twelve months of part-time study.

The curriculum for the M.B.A. degree consists of a core course in business administration, four elective courses, a compulsory course in research methodology, and a research report on any relevant subject or business aspect.

Topics for the course in business administration are grouped into three teaching areas: general management; informatics, finance and operations; and human resources. Topics include the domestic and global economy, analytical methods, the global and local environment of business, financial accounting, organisational behavior, management of operations and technology, industrial relations, marketing management, creating corporate and human competence, management accounting, corporate finance, entrepreneurship, information and knowledge management, strategic management, and international business.

The four electives are chosen from a selection of approximately twenty topics. The research report requires the student

to work independently on an unstructured problem and to present the findings in a formal report.

Students and the M.B.A. Experience

Students come from a wide range of academic backgrounds that include commerce, engineering, science, arts, and law. The average age of students is 32, with an average of nine years' work experience. Students bring to the classrooms their own wealth of experience and views on management practice.

While the student body is still predominantly white, enrollment is steadily changing to more closely reflect South Africa's broad cultural diversity. The ratio of white to black and Asian students is currently 8:3:1. Approximately one fifth of the class are women.

Each year, a few international students register for the Wits M.B.A., and several more exchange students join the class for electives. The tremendous diversity of the students interacting in the classrooms is an exceedingly valuable experience.

The WBS's approach to teaching is highly interactive and maximizes student involvement. Extensive use is made of case studies, individual and syndicate projects, class presentations, and multimedia technology.

Special Features

Beginning in 1998, the international business component of the Wits M.B.A. includes a compulsory overseas experience for all students. The School

organises a selection of four study trips of ten days to two weeks to Western and Eastern Europe, Southeast Asia, China, South America, and Africa.

The Faculty

The faculty is staffed by academics who are recognized authorities in their fields. Most of the lecturers have extensive experience in the private sector and continue to make important contributions to South Africa's top companies through their consulting work. A number of lecturers have taught in foreign business schools.

The WBS also invites international faculty members to teach in its M.B.A. programme on a regular basis. Prominent lecturers include Professor Peter Brews (Fuqua School of Business, Duke University), Stuart Chambers (Warwick Business School), Professor Nigel Slack (Warwick Business School), Professor Tan Chin Tiong (School of Management, National University of Singapore), and Professor Patrick McGowan (Arizona State University).

The Business School Network

The WBS enjoys an ongoing working relationship with the South African business community. Specialist representatives from the private sector are invited to teach in the M.B.A. programme, and the School's advisory board comprises some of the country's most prominent business leaders and decision makers.

The WBS relies on the business community for assistance in funding new facilities and two chairs. The Chairs of Marketing and of International Business

FACULTY LIST

Mike Ward, Associate Professor of Finance and Director; Ph.D.

Russell Abratt, First National Bank Chair of Marketing and Area Head of General Management; D.B.S.

Neil Duffy, Professor of Management Information Systems and Area Head of Informatics, Finance and Operations; D.B.L.; FCSSA.

Paul Semark, Senior Lecturer in Human Resources Management and Area Head of Human Resources Management; B.Sc., B.A.

The shady quad, the historical centre of the Wits Business School, is a popular gathering place for students.

have been sponsored by First National Bank and South African Breweries, respectively. In a recent survey conducted among South Africa's leading companies, WBS emerged as the most admired business school in the country.

The Wits Business School Association (WBSA) is an active alumni association with branches overseas. The WBSA aims to provide continuing opportunities for the exchange of knowledge between business leaders, faculty members, and former students as well as to promote an ongoing relationship among its members.

The WBS boasts many prominent business people among its alumni. Currently, South Africa's largest management consultancies are all headed by Wits M.B.A. graduates.

The College and Environs

The Wits Business School is located in Johannesburg in the heart of South Africa's business community.

Although an integral part of the University of the Witwatersrand, the School has its own campus in the leafy suburb of Parktown. The gracious old mansion bought by the University in 1968 to house its new Graduate School of Business Administration remains the centre of the WBS, although many new buildings have been added. The School's attractive landscaping and extensive green areas provide a tranquil setting for study, and its location is only a short distance from the commercial centre of Johannesburg and its burgeoning northern suburbs.

Facilities

Lecturing facilities include a new 230-seat auditorium and a recently refurbished 98-seat auditorium. Both are fully equipped with technologically up-to-date audiovisual facilities. There are also three 75-seat lecture

rooms and thirty syndicate rooms for group discussions. All facilities are designed to stimulate interaction between students and lecturers.

The John S. Schlesinger Library, known as the Faculty of Management Library, contains more than 15,000 volumes and subscribes to more than 200 journals.

Technology Environment

The WBS's computer facilities rank among the best in the country for academic institutions. The School operates on a Novell LAN attached to the University's fibre-optic backbone for access to the Internet. A well-equipped computer laboratory with thirty 586 super VGA computers is available to students, and most of the syndicate rooms are equipped with a computer linked to the network. The School uses Microsoft Office Suite software in the Windows environment as well as several specialist software packages and online databases.

Placement

The WBS recently opened a specialized on-campus Career Management Centre. Services offered include career counselling, employment-related consultations, and interview simulations. Resources include the WBS Career Management home page, company documentation, career management–related books and videos, and the Graduate Recruitment Notice Board. The centre also runs a series of workshops and guest lectures during the year, which are designed to equip students with essential skills, such as curriculum vitae formulation and interview techniques. This programme culminates in the Graduate Recruitment Drive.

Admission

Applicants to the Wits M.B.A. are required to have a bachelor's degree or

higher from a recognized university as well as at least four years of post-university experience. They are expected to be well motivated and conversant with the content of the M.B.A. programme.

Local applicants are required to take the Admissions Test, an aptitude test designed to measure a student's abilities in the areas of reading comprehension, written English, and general, arithmetic, and cognitive reasoning.

Overseas applicants may submit recent GMAT test results. Where English is not the spoken language, international students are required to submit proof of proficiency in English.

Finances

For the 1999–2000 academic year, students can expect to spend R45,000 for the complete M.B.A. programme. This cost includes approximately R27,000 for tuition, R15,000 for the overseas study trip, and R3000 for books.

Fully catered accommodation costs approximately R11,000 per annum, and self-catering accommodation costs approximately R6000 per annum.

The University offers financial aid packages to needy and high-achieving South African students, but international students are not eligible.

International Students

Students in the M.B.A. programme comprise approximately 2 percent from Europe, 2 percent from North America, 2 percent from Asia, and 94 percent from Africa.

Wits University's International Office assists international students with registration, study permits, and accommodation. The WBS has a dedicated member of the staff to provide further information and assistance.

Application Facts and Dates

Applications for the part-time M.B.A. programme that begins in January 1999 must be submitted by August 1998. Applications for the full-time M.B.A. programme that begins in June 1999 must be submitted by February 1999.

Applicants receive notification of their application status approximately three weeks after receipt of the application. Completed applications should be forwarded to:

The Assistant Registrar
Faculty of Management
Graduate School of Business
    Administration
University of the Witwatersrand
P.O. Box 98
Wits 2050
South Africa
Telephone: 011 27 11 488 5661 or
    5581
Fax: 011 27 11 643 2336
World Wide Web: http://www.wits.ac.
    za/wbs

The University of Toledo

Toledo, Ohio

DEVELOPING BUSINESS LEADERS

At the University of Toledo (UT), we understand what it takes to succeed. After all, we have been educating and developing business leaders since 1933. Our rigorous M.B.A. curriculum skillfully integrates academic theory with real-world application. And like the business community we serve, we are committed to continuous improvement to keep our program in the forefront of business thought and practice. Our commitment to this philosophy is reflected in our faculty's superior records of accomplishment in mentoring, teaching, research, and consulting. The quality of our faculty, combined with our small class size, state-of-the-art facilities, and beautiful suburban setting, makes for a memorable and fulfilling learning experience that provides students with the needed skills and knowledge to succeed in an increasingly competitive environment.

—Dr. James Pope, Dean

Programs and Curricular Focus

The basic principles underlying managerial decision making are the main focus of the Master of Business Administration program. This program gives the students a grasp of the techniques and the fundamentals of management as well as the breadth necessary to prepare students for general management responsibility. Students can elect a broad (general) program or one with special emphasis on related areas in which they have particular interest. Specializations are offered in accounting, administration (general), finance, human resource management, information systems, international business, management, marketing, and operations management. Students may attend on either a full-time or part-time basis. No business experience is required for admission. An accelerated program is also available to qualifying students.

The graduate curriculum may be built upon a bachelor's degree in business administration or any other baccalaureate degree. The length of the program varies depending on the nature of the undergraduate degree.

The Master of Business Administration degree is granted to students who satisfactorily complete a minimum of 30 semester hours of graduate course work in business administration beyond a bachelor's in business administration with a GPA of 3.0 or better. The required graduate program for all students consists of basic core courses, advanced core courses, and specialization courses. Students who have an undergraduate

degree in business administration are able to waive some or all of the basic core courses. No business experience is required for admission.

Students and the M.B.A. Experience

Variety best describes The University of Toledo. Students at UT come from around the United States and around the world and bring with them rich and varied backgrounds. The profile of an average student in the program in 1997–98 was a 29-year-old with approximately five years of experience. Approximately 20 percent of the students in the program are full-time. Women account for more than a third of the students, while minority students account for 12 percent. International students account for approximately 25 percent.

Special Features

In addition to traditional classwork, M.B.A. students can get hands-on experience through the Office of Professional Experience Programs (OPEP), the Small Business Institute, the Institute for International Studies, and the award-winning UT Center for Family Business.

The Faculty

UT's faculty provides students with a dynamic and challenging learning environment. The faculty members in the College of Business Administration hold advanced degrees from a variety of distinguished institutions. Many are

nationally and internationally recognized researchers whose articles have appeared in leading business and academic publications.

The Business School Network
Corporate Partnerships

The distinguished members of the College of Business Administration's Business Advisory Council (BAC) serve as a vital link to the corporate world. The BAC provides the College with valuable direction and advice, ensuring that a UT business education addresses current issues in today's business world. In addition, the College's Visiting Executives Program exposes students to executives from a variety of business backgrounds and helps to complement and build on students' classroom experiences. Business leaders in the program share their thoughts with students in designated classes on issues of concern to them and business in general. Several students are also selected to join the visiting executive and the dean of the College for either breakfast or lunch.

Prominent Alumni

The UT-M.B.A. Program provides individuals with the high-quality graduate business education they need to succeed. The results speak for themselves. Many UT-M.B.A. graduates hold leadership positions in the business world. Among the school's prominent alumni are Ora Alleman, Executive Vice President, National City Bank; William Ammann, Vice President, Administration, Aeroquip-Vickers, Inc.; Michael Durik, Executive Vice President, The Limited Stores Inc.; Marvin Herb, CEO, Coca-Cola Bottling Company, Chicago; Julie Higgins, Executive Vice President, The Trust Company of Toledo; Donald Saunders, Vice Chairman, Toledo Edison; and Mark Tincher, Senior Portfolio Manager, Chase Manhattan Bank.

The College and Environs

Founded in 1872, The University of Toledo is Ohio's fourth-largest state-assisted university, with more than 21,000 students. Through its eight different colleges and schools, UT offers nearly 150 different aca-

Stranahan Hall, which won an award for its unique architectural design, is the home of the College of Business Administration at the University of Toledo.

demic majors. Located in a tree-lined suburban area 6 miles from downtown Toledo, the more than 200-acre main campus combines classic architecture with beautifully landscaped grounds to make learning a truly enjoyable experience. As Ohio's fourth-largest city, Toledo also offers a host of business, industrial, social, and cultural opportunities. Toledo houses the headquarters of several Fortune 500 companies and features the Toledo Symphony, the Toledo Zoo, and the Toledo Museum of Art, one of the world's leading museums.

Facilities
The College of Business Administration's classrooms, computer labs, and faculty and administrative offices are located in Stranahan Hall. The main University library contains more than 1.5 million volumes and more than 1.4 million microform items. In addition, the library is a U.S. government documents depository and contains materials from the Census Bureau and the Department of Commerce. An online computer system allows students to access the catalog and serial records as well as databases, abstracts, and periodical indexes.

Technology Environment
Students in the College of Business Administration have access to computer facilities at many points on campus. In addition to the 115 networked Pentium PCs located in the four microcomputer labs in the College of Business Administration, there are approximately 400 more PCs located in various buildings across the campus. All machines on campus are

networked. Students have access to the terminal software, the mainframe, VAX, and the campuswide network. This provides for direct access to the library, among other locations, from any terminal on campus.

Placement
The University of Toledo's Office of Career Services offers M.B.A. students a broad support system throughout their program. Advising, workshops, and other programs are offered to enhance students' job-seeking skills and to help students make the contacts necessary to compete effectively for jobs in today's competitive job market. Assistance in assessing career goals and employment objectives is provided through individual counseling, workshops, seminars, and videotapes. The placement and career services also bring organizational representatives from both profit and nonprofit firms and health, education, and government agencies for on-campus interviews. In addition, students have access to computerized employment databases for job referrals in the tristate region and nationwide.

Admission
Admission is granted to individuals showing high promise of success in graduate business study. Applicants are considered for admission based on their undergraduate record; scores on the Graduate Management Admission Test (GMAT); managerial, professional, and leadership potential as exhibited by extracurricular activities, job experience, and community service;

and a statement of purpose describing long-term goals and objectives. The GMAT score for students accepted into the M.B.A. program has averaged between 500 and 525. The average undergraduate GPA is approximately 3.1.

Finances
Tuition and fees for full-time enrollment for 1997–98 were approximately $5505 for Ohio residents and $10,790 for nonresidents. Graduate students live in off-campus housing.

The College of Business Administration offers graduate assistantships, tuition scholarships, and fellowships based primarily on achievement or merit. Most forms of assistance are awarded to students beginning their program in the fall.

Application Facts and Dates
Application deadlines are August 1 for fall semester, November 15 for spring semester, and April 15 for summer. Admission decisions typically take one to two weeks once a student's admission file is complete. For more information, students should contact:

Dr. Bruce Kuhlman, M.B.A. Director
Office of Graduate Studies in Business
College of Business Administration
The University of Toledo
Toledo, Ohio 43606-3390
Telephone: 419-530-2775
Fax: 419-530-7260
E-mail: bkuhlma@pop3.utoledo.edu

University of Toronto

> ### ACCESS TO THE MOST REWARDING CAREERS
>
> *If your bottom line is an M.B.A. degree from a leading business school that gives you the access to the most rewarding careers, you should check out the University of Toronto Rotman School of Management. The reason: Toronto M.B.A. students are being actively recruited and hired by North America's top companies.*
>
> —Hugh Gunz, Associate Dean, Programs

Programs and Curricular Focus

The University of Toronto M.B.A. Program brings together outstanding young men and women from Canada and other nations. They are immersed in a demanding, innovative management curriculum taught by the most distinguished business school faculty in Canada. The program makes creative use of the world-class Toronto business community to enrich the M.B.A. learning experience.

Top global firms actively recruit Toronto M.B.A. graduates, who are supported in their job search by a professional Career Management Service. Whether a student wants to work for a multinational corporation or a smaller company, or start one of his or her own, the comprehensive, flexible Toronto M.B.A. curriculum provides the knowledge and the skills to succeed. High-calibre classmates dramatically enhance the learning experience and provide a lifetime network of friends who will someday occupy leadership positions in the global economy. The Toronto M.B.A. degree carries the name of the Canadian university recognized worldwide for excellence.

The Rotman School of Management at the University of Toronto offers a variety of graduate programs in management designed to meet the needs of managers, professionals, and scholars at various stages of their careers. The options include the Full-Time M.B.A. Program, which is twenty months (two 8-month academic periods or four semesters total) with a four-month summer break for internships and/or other work experience. It begins in September and admits 120 students each fall. The Part-Time M.B.A. Program, which admits 60 students per year and begins in January, offers evening classes, usually completed over ten terms that stretch over 3⅓ years.

The M.B.A./LL.B. Program is a four-year, joint-degree program offered by the Schools of Management and Law. It begins in September. The Master of Management and Professional Accounting Program is designed to educate students to become leaders of the accounting profession. It is a seven term co-op program over twenty-seven months (twenty-four or sixteen months with advanced standing entry). Two of the terms are spent working in an accounting environment.

The Executive M.B.A. Program is for individuals who have the potential for senior management and eight or more years of work experience, including three at the management level. The program, which begins in August, runs twenty months, with classes held one day a week on alternating Fridays and Saturdays.

Students and the M.B.A. Experience

University of Toronto M.B.A. students are talented, intelligent, and high-achieving young men and women who have the potential to become exceptional managers and leaders. The program purposefully seeks students who have done something interesting with their lives after their undergraduate education. These are students who have worked in the real world for two, three, or more years. The range of previous professional and academic experience is wide, from the entrepreneur running a local construction company to the manager of a large multinational manufacturing firm to the investment banker to the physician specializing in genetics. Academic backgrounds run across all disciplines, from business to the arts and from engineering to the sciences. The most recent Toronto M.B.A. classes have average GMAT scores that rank well above 650, placing the program among the top tier of business schools.

❖ Global Focus

The Toronto M.B.A. Program emphasizes international content throughout the M.B.A. curriculum. Students are continually exposed to a global perspective of management beginning in the first year. They are also engaged in several team projects for cross-cultural communications and skills development. A range of second-year elective courses focuses specifically on international management.

Toronto M.B.A. students may also participate in graduate exchange programs with a number of top management schools in Europe and Asia to add an even greater international dimension to the M.B.A. education. Students can elect to go abroad for international study for one term in the second year of the M.B.A. Program.

Special Features

The Toronto M.B.A. has been designed to provide students with the tools to adapt to constantly changing circumstances in business and in individual careers. Full-time M.B.A. students begin their studies with a mandatory four-day orientation session at a resort north of Toronto. Orientation consists of an intense program of academic, social, and recreational activities designed to emphasize teamwork and class spirit. Students are also assigned to six-member study groups that work together through the first year. M.B.A. core courses are delivered in an integrated approach, with each course building on previous learning. Intensive focus is given to leadership and team building skills and international business. In the second year, students are free to choose areas of specialization from a wide range of options, including more than forty-five elective courses offered each year—many of them innovative. The Rotman School of Management was the first business school in the world to offer a course in derivatives. Students are also free to take electives from the vast, rich course offerings of the University of Toronto.

The Faculty

Roger L. Martin, a prominent international management consultant, has been appointed Dean of the Rotman School of Management, effective September 1, 1998. He is a senior partner of the Massachusetts-based Monitor Company, which he joined in 1985. He has served as Co-Head of the company and was responsible for its day-to-day activities and more than 700 consultants worldwide. He has also helped to develop Monitor's customized business education programs for leading corporations.

Toronto M.B.A. students are taught by a management faculty that is recognized around the world for its scholarly achievements in management. One indication of why this faculty is second to none in Canada is that 4 of the 5 Fellows of the prestigious Royal Society of Canada teaching at Canadian business schools are professors at the University of Toronto Rotman School of Management.

The Business School Network

Corporate Partnerships

The Toronto M.B.A. Program, located adjacent to downtown Toronto, takes full advantage of its proximity by drawing on Canadian business leaders as instructors in classrooms and as speakers at numerous special events. Group projects in the M.B.A. program use local businesses as the focal point for their activities. The Dean's Advisory Council comprises the top business leaders in Canada, who regularly meet at the school to offer their advice and assistance.

Prominent Alumni

The Toronto M.B.A. Program has produced more than 4,000 high-achieving graduates who occupy significant leadership positions in business and other organizations throughout Canada and elsewhere. They comprise part of the growing University of Toronto management alumni network of business contacts and friends, which is now some 14,000 members strong. It includes graduates of the University of Toronto Bachelor of Commerce Program and other management programs. Among the alumni are Joseph L. Rotman, Canadian entrepreneur and CEO of Clairvest Group; Richard Lint, Vice Chairman, Scotia Capital Markets; John Cassaday, President and CEO, Shaw Media; Leslie Dan, founder, Chairman, and CEO of Novopharm Group of Companies; Eric Weider, President and COO, Weider Health and Fitness; Michael Wilson, former Canadian Minister of Industry; Ira Gluskin, Gluskin Sheff & Assoc.; F. Ross Johnson, former CEO, RJR Nabisco; William Farlinger, Chairman, Ontario Hydro; and Ned Goodman, Chairman and CEO, Dundee Bancorp, Inc.

The College and Environs

The University of Toronto enjoys an international reputation for excellence of its faculty members, students, and graduates. As Canada's foremost research university, the University of Toronto receives more research grants than any other university in the country. Four of Canada's Nobel Prizes have been associated with the University. The entire University of Toronto campus is open to M.B.A. students. With more than 53,000 students and a faculty of more than 1,700 members, the University of Toronto

offers an unmatched diversity of opportunities. Students have access to some of the best thinkers in the world, first-rate libraries, and gymnasiums and other leisure-time facilities and programs.

Toronto, the heart of the Canadian business community, was named by *Fortune* magazine in 1995 as the seventh-best city in the world in which to do business. Not surprisingly, Toronto is also a terrific place to learn about business. With a metropolitan population of 4.5 million and with its safe, clean streets, vibrant culture and entertainment, and diverse population from around the world, Toronto is the financial, commercial, and sporting centre of Canada. Toronto has great restaurants and lots of live theatre, music, film, and dance and often has some trend-setting examples. Toronto is also home to all of Canada's major banks, trust companies, brokerage houses, insurance companies, and advertising agencies.

Facilities

The home of the Toronto M.B.A. Program is the Joseph L. Rotman Centre for Management, a spectacular, state-of-the-art teaching and research facility that features cutting-edge computer technology for the use of students and faculty and staff members. Opened in 1995, the Rotman Centre was described as "a gem" by the *Toronto Star*. Configured around a beautiful enclosed central atrium, the building houses all of the school's academic programs and the offices of professors. With its technologically advanced classrooms, attractive study spaces, a business library, and underground parking, the building is as comfortable as it is convenient.

Placement

The Career Management Service actively helps Toronto M.B.A. students prepare themselves for the job search and recruitment process and teaches them how to manage their careers. The service offers individual career counseling, resume clinics, mock interview sessions, a career resource library, a job listing service, and special information sessions on various career paths and industries. Moreover, with an active on-campus recruiting program, students are able to interview with prospective employers from a variety of industries for jobs in a wide range of functional areas. This year, more than 95 percent of graduates found jobs by graduation time, with an average starting salary of Can$78,400.

Admission

Candidates for admission are evaluated on a total portfolio of previous performance, personal characteristics, and life experiences, as well as professional and academic references. Candidates must have a recognized undergraduate degree with a minimum mid-B average in their final year

(75 percent or a 3.0 GPA); GMAT results (scores above 550 preferred); two years of full-time work experience (or its equivalent) preferred (five years for the part-time program); demonstrated evidence of leadership, initiative, and a superior capacity for high-level work productivity; and three professional or academic reference letters. A very good command of both written and spoken English is essential for all incoming graduate students.

Finances

Tuition for the 1998–99 academic year for domestic, full-time M.B.A. students is Can$7390. International students pay Can$13,610 for the full-time program. Students should contact the Rotman School for information about part-time program fees, which over the course of part-time study equal the total fee of the full-time program. In addition to tuition, a full-time student spends approximately Can$1000 per year on University fees, case materials, and supplies. Living expenses, food, lodging, and personal expenses are minimally estimated to be Can$1000 per month for eight months, or Can$8000 for the academic year. Some financial assistance is available to qualified applicants. Scholarships and awards are generally made to the top 20 percent of the incoming M.B.A. class.

International Students

Diversity in the Toronto M.B.A. Program means a rich mix of cultural and ethnic backgrounds of M.B.A. students. The M.B.A. Program enrolls about 30 percent of each class from more than thirty different countries outside Canada, including Japan, Russia, China, France, Hong Kong, and the United States.

Application Facts and Dates

Applicants to the full-time program are admitted only in September of each year and must forward complete application credentials by one of the two application deadlines: January 3 or April 30, at the latest. Applicants to the part-time program are admitted only in January of each year and must forward complete application credentials by September 30. For more information, students should contact:

Toronto M.B.A. Programs
Rotman School of Management
University of Toronto
105 St. George Street
Toronto, Ontario M5S 3E6
Canada
Telephone: 416-978-3499
Fax: 416-978-5812
E-mail: mbaprog@fmgmt.mgmt.
    utoronto.ca
World Wide Web: http://www.mgmt.
    utoronto.ca

TSM Business School University of Twente

International Institute for Management of Technology & Business Development

TSM Business School

Enschede, the Netherlands

BECOMING A WORLD LEADER

In a rapidly shrinking world that is made ever smaller by the increasing pace of technological developments, skilled managers who have a solid background in technique are in demand. For technologically driven companies, a great many of the core competencies are held by the engineers and design and technical people. TSM Business School is striving, through its M.B.A. programs, in-company training programs, international programs, and research projects, to be a world leader in the management of technology, entrepreneurship, and innovation.

—Dr. Richard C. Kaehler, Dean

Programs and Curricular Focus

TSM Business School was founded in 1987 and is the postgraduate management institute of the Universities of Eindhoven, Twente, and Groningen, the Netherlands. It uses results-oriented approaches from industry to effectively manage and deploy the capabilities and knowledge within universities. In doing so, TSM Business School is the industrial gateway to a large and rich capacity of research and educational resources. Besides the lecturers and researchers from these institutes, TSM Business School selects lecturers and researchers from businesses and consulting firms and from partners within the international network of business schools and universities.

TSM Business School is specialized in the multidisciplinary field of technology management. TSM Business School supports companies in acquiring and strengthening the three organizational requirements for knowledge-based competition: technological competence, which is the ability of an enterprise to master the particular technologies that are relevant to its need; entrepreneurial attitude, which is the ability to generate and implement a strategy for the use of new technologies; and learning ability, which is the capacity to adapt organizationally and culturally in order to accommodate technological change.

There are two M.B.A. programs offered at the School. The full-time M.B.A. is an international results-oriented program for engineers who want to become managers working with the interface of business and technology. Engineers and university graduates in

beta-disciplines (technology-oriented sciences) who prove to have management potential in intellectual and personal perspectives are eligible. The program extends over one academic year and is followed by a business assignment lasting six months.

The executive part-time M.B.A. is an international program that is specifically designed for managers in technology-intensive companies. Engineers and university graduates in beta-disciplines with at least three years of working experience are eligible. The program consists of nineteen 4-day seminars, which are spread over twenty-two months. It includes a final thesis project that is conducted within the participant's company.

Students and the M.B.A. Experience

The program consists of lectures, group assignments, case studies, and projects. Groups are deliberately kept small, which enhances interaction among participants and between participants and lecturers. In this high-quality intensive program, it is results that count; results in the knowledge acquired, results in terms of personal development, and results in linking theory and practice.

❖ Global Focus

TSM Business School has partners within the international network of business schools and universities. Exchange programs with many international business schools and universities have long been a mainstay of the M.B.A.

experience. The State University of New York at Buffalo and the Georgia Institute of Technology (U.S.A.), Grenoble ESC (France), and Pepperdine University (Los Angeles, U.S.A.) are just a few of the many alliance partners that TSM Business School cooperates with on many levels. This cooperation includes exchanges of students and faculty members, combined research and management development projects, and combining resources through strategic alliances.

Special Features

Management skills can be acquired through intuition and a great deal of practice. In order to build the skills of the participants, the School has structured a carefully designed program of training courses to develop interpersonal and other essential management skills.

In order to assess students' personal strengths and weaknesses, their (potential) management skills are tested at the beginning of the program. These skills include factors such as persuasiveness, empathy, and the ability to lead. The assessment, carried out in cooperation with Assessment Development Consult (ADC Ltd.), serves as the basis for drawing up a personal development plan, which provides a guideline for the development of skills during the entire full-time M.B.A. program. A personal coach is assigned to each participant to guide the candidate on his or her development path.

The Faculty

The international core faculty of TSM Business School is specialized in designing results-oriented programs and studies that integrate the know-how of researchers and lecturers from different disciplines. This faculty, with members from the member universities and from alliance business schools and industries, contributes to the knowledge creation process that is a core competency of the School.

The Business School Network

The alliance of three of the best universities in the Netherlands, the Technical

University of Eindhoven, the State University of Groningen, and the University of Twente, where TSM is physically located, ensures both the high quality of education and the availability of rich resources.

The College and Environs

TSM is the only business school in the Netherlands, and one of the few in Europe, that is located on a beautifully wooded campus, the former Drienerlo estate. The parklike atmosphere fosters concentration and creativity. The campus has many faculty and general-use libraries, a computer center, and numerous lecture theaters. Furthermore, it offers just about any amenity one can think of, including a bank, a supermarket, a book shop, sports facilities, restaurants, cafés, theaters, a hairdresser, and a hotel. For several years, TSM Business School has had exclusive lodging facilities for many of the full-time participants.

Placement

Career services available to graduate students include the Alumni Network, which is an active association of graduates in every area of management. Other career services include career assessment and individual career counseling.

Admission

The selection criteria for full-time M.B.A. candidates include a master's degree in a technology-oriented science, or so-called "beta-studies," from universities and polytechnics; high motivation; possess an entrepreneurial attitude, good communication and interpersonal skills, and a wide scope of interests; good results in all former education; 0 to 5 years of work experience; acceptable GMAT scores; and an acceptable TOEFL score (meaning fluency in the English language) for nonnative speakers of English.

Finances

The total course fee for the full-time M.B.A. program is DFL 34,500. The part-time executive program is DFL 67,500. In addition, books, syllabi, and other course materials carry an estimated cost of about DFL 2,200 for the entire program.

TSM Business School has contacts with several banks who are willing to supply loans at reasonable rates. TSM Business School has working relationships with many of the major banks of the Netherlands, including ING Bank, ABN Amro, and Rabobank. All of these banks have staff members familiar with the School and its programs.

Full sponsoring, which is a combination of a company sponsor and a Dutch state scholarship, is available to a few Central and Eastern European candidates. Selection depends on their background (technical discipline and further curriculum vitae). In such a case, it may be requested that the student execute his or her final assignment for the sponsoring company and possibly be available to be employed by it afterwards. Of course, a sponsoring company may supply the student with additional funds equivalent to the bank loan as well. Even though candidates are encouraged to look for sponsors themselves, TSM Business School has a wide network of company contacts and interested parties with sponsoring possibilities.

Application Facts and Dates

The programs start every year in August. For application forms and additional information, students should contact:

Leo J. Salazar
TSM Business School
P.O. Box 217
7500 AE Enschede
The Netherlands
Telephone: 31 53 489 8009
Fax: 31 53 489 4848
E-mail: mba@tsm.utwente.nl
World Wide Web: http://www.tsm.nl

University of Utah

Salt Lake City, Utah

BUILDING FOUNDATIONS FOR BUSINESS LEADERSHIP

The educational mission of the David Eccles School of Business is building foundations for business leadership. In these times of accelerating technological change, globalization of markets, and increasing diversity in the workforce, business leaders are faced with a unique set of challenges. The profile attributes we have outlined for our graduates define the distinctive set of skills and knowledge that business leaders will need to create and lead organizations now and in the decades ahead.

We are proud of our program and equally proud of our graduates. I invite you to join us. We offer you our best professors, our personal attention, and our commitment to your personal success. With our program as the cornerstone, you will build a strong foundation for business leadership.

—John W. Seybolt, Ph.D., Dean

Programs and Curricular Focus

The educational mission of the David Eccles School of Business is centered on developing these profile attributes in its graduates: a solid foundation in the basic functional areas of business; the ability to take the initiative and to exercise creativity in solving business problems; well-developed communication skills; an understanding and appreciation of the economic, social, political, environmental, technological, and business issues in a dynamic environment; an understanding of historical, literary, philosophical, scientific, and artistic events and achievements; and an understanding of and motivation for lifelong learning.

The program begins with courses that teach the fundamental skills of teamwork, leadership, and effective communication. Group projects and oral presentations, integrated throughout the program, give students opportunities to strengthen interpersonal and oral communication skills. As students work through case analyses, they perfect their skills in problem identification, analysis, and decision making. Finally, an extensive field-study experience brings classroom theory to life as students integrate the knowledge and skills they have developed and apply them to real-world business problems.

Because the program places significant emphasis on effective communication and leadership skills, students are expected to make contributions to the learning environment by daily participation in class discussions.

Students earn M.B.A. degrees through one of three programs of study. A traditional two-year day program serves students with nonbusiness undergraduate backgrounds. Students with bachelor's degrees in business from nationally accredited schools may be eligible for an accelerated one-year M.B.A. program. A three-year part-time evening program meets the unique needs of working professionals who wish to continue their full-time employment while pursuing an M.B.A. degree.

Students may choose one of the three optional study specializations—the International Emphasis with Foreign Language Proficiency Certificate, Health Services Administration, or Management of Technology. Joint programs of study available are the M.B.A./J.D. and the M.B.A./Master of Architecture.

Students and the M.B.A. Experience

Students who entered the program in 1997 represent fifteen states and fifteen countries on six continents. Twenty-nine percent were women, 6 percent were members of ethnic minority groups, and 18 percent were international students. The 87 students who entered the two-year day and three-year evening programs have degrees in forty-three different majors: 45 percent in science and engineering, 20 percent in behavioral sciences, and 19 percent in arts, humanities, education, and health. Ninety-four percent of day students and 100 percent

of evening students have full-time work experience; day students have an average of just more than five years' experience, and evening students average eight years' experience.

❖ Global Focus

Students in the M.B.A. program have a rich proficiency in foreign language skills. Roughly 53 percent of students speak a second language, and 70 percent have experience abroad. Building on this unique strength, the program is designed to teach students to conduct business in a global environment. The School supports international field-study projects, internships, and study exchanges in which students expand their horizons and apply their language skills in a business environment.

The Faculty

The School's faculty members have earned their degrees at some of the nation's most prestigious institutions. Their research interests allow students the opportunity to develop a broad background and experience diverse viewpoints.

The Business School Network

Corporate Partnerships

The School supports many programs with ties to the corporate community. Partnerships with numerous regional, national, and worldwide companies provide valuable field-study opportunities for students. The Business at Breakfast lecture series provides a lively forum of exchange for faculty members, students, and members of Utah's vibrant business community. National Advisory Board members provide input on regular curricular reviews as well as guidance and resources for special projects, including diversity recruitment, scholarship development, and internships.

Prominent Alumni

Prominent alumni include David L. Gorham, Chief Financial Officer of *The New York Times;* J. Willard Marriott Jr., Chief Executive Officer of Marriott International; Dr. Steven R. Covey,

The University of Utah is nestled at the foot of the majestic Wasatch Mountains.

Chairman and Founder of the Covey Leadership Center; Spencer F. Eccles, Chairman and Chief Executive Officer of First Security Corporation; Jake Garn, Vice Chairman of Huntsman Chemical Corporation and former U.S. Senator; and Jerry C. Atkin, President and Chief Executive Officer of Skywest Airlines.

The College and Environs
The University of Utah was founded in 1850. The 1,500-acre campus, located on the northeastern edge of Salt Lake City, reaches to the foothills of the majestic Wasatch Mountains. The University is a major research institution, with more than 1,500 projects in progress at any time. This level of research consistently ranks Utah among the country's top twenty-five public universities in attracting funding for research.

Salt Lake City, host of the 2002 Olympic Winter Games, is a city that blends subtle sophistication with the comfortable pace and friendliness of the West. Culture flourishes on the same scale as that of much larger cities. The Utah Symphony, Ballet West, and the

Utah Opera Company are major attractions. NBA basketball, AAA baseball, and IHL hockey cater to sports enthusiasts. Rugged mountains, four distinct seasons, and ready access to outdoor recreation are enticing features of the University's location. Visitors and residents alike enjoy snow skiing at seven world-class ski resorts, all within 45 minutes of campus.

Facilities
This year, the School plans to break ground for the new C. Roland Christensen Center, a student-centered educational environment that features discussion-method classrooms, a state-of-the-art computer technology center, student team discussion rooms, and a commons area designed to foster conversation and lively interaction.

Placement
Through the personalized attention of the M.B.A. Career Services Office, in conjunction with the central University Career Services Office, students have

excellent assistance in securing positions in regional, national, and international companies and organizations.

Through the Career Services Office, students have access to several programs and job-search opportunities, including career-search courses; personalized service in the areas of self-assessment, skill development, and job-search strategies; the West Coast M.B.A. Consortium; international career fairs; and AlumNet, an alumni career advisory network.

Admission
Students are admitted during just one admission cycle each academic year. The goal of admissions is to admit academically strong applicants who show the greatest potential for completing the program and succeeding in a career and whose backgrounds contribute to the academic excellence and the demographic, educational, and experiential diversity of each class.

The average GMAT score for those admitted in the 1997–98 admission cycle was 590. International applicants are required to have a minimum TOEFL score of 570 and a minimum TSE score of 50.

Finances
In 1998–99, yearly expenses are $13,800 for residents and $20,100 for nonresidents. This includes tuition and fees, books and supplies, campus room and board, and general miscellaneous expenses such as personal costs and insurance.

The School of Business awards numerous privately funded scholarships to students based on need or academic merit. The School also supports several fellowships, which are awarded to individuals who enhance the ethnic, gender, or geographic diversity of the student body.

Application Facts and Dates

All applicants receive notification of an admission decision by April 30. For application deadlines and more information, students should contact:

Master's Programs Office
1645 East Campus Center Drive, Room 101
David Eccles School of Business
University of Utah
Salt Lake City, Utah 84112-9301
Telephone: 801-581-7785
Fax: 801-581-3666
E-mail: masters@business.utah.edu
World Wide Web: http://www.business.utah.edu/masters

University of Washington

PRIDE IN PARTNERSHIP

At the University of Washington, we believe that partnership is a pathway to excellence. Today's competitive business market values managers who are team players as well as high individual achievers. This idea guides every aspect of our operations and curriculum. We select entering students with impressive records of personal accomplishment, and we challenge them to navigate rigorous course work while sharpening their team-building skills. M.B.A.'s learn to work in partnership with each other and with the members of the faculty, administration, and staff. Their input and energy enliven the curriculum and have a lasting impact on the School.

—William D. Bradford, Dean

Programs and Curricular Focus

The University of Washington M.B.A. program is designed to prepare graduates for success in today's fast-paced and rapidly changing business climate. The M.B.A. is a two-year, full-time program, combining thorough study of business fundamentals with focused course work in specialized fields of study.

The curriculum emphasizes intellectual challenge, teamwork, leadership, and application of classroom concepts to actual business problems. Students take an active role in their education, giving life to the course material. M.B.A.'s with prior work experience varying from financial analysis to software design bring a wide range of perspectives to class discussions.

The program consists of a year-long M.B.A. core, followed by a year of self-designed elective work. The core consists of a sequence of three integrated courses taught by teams of faculty members representing all the major business disciplines. M.B.A.'s take core classes in sections of 55 students, which in turn are divided into 5- or 6-person study teams. By emphasizing leadership skills, these teams are able to integrate multidisciplinary approaches to forge innovative solutions.

In the second year, students design a course of elective study and gain expertise in one or more fields of interest. In a typical year, students can choose from nearly 100 electives in fourteen different business disciplines, and they may select up to four courses outside the business school to apply toward the M.B.A. degree. Students have the option

of completing special study programs in the areas of entrepreneurship and international management. M.B.A.'s may also earn concurrent master's degrees with the Schools of Law, Health Administration, Engineering, and International Studies.

Students and the M.B.A. Experience

The University of Washington attracts students with diverse professional experience and strong leadership abilities. Each class possesses unique strengths as well as impressive academic and professional qualifications. More than 30 percent of the M.B.A.'s have undergraduate liberal arts degrees; 27 percent have science and technical backgrounds. Almost all entering M.B.A.'s have substantial professional work experience. Cultural diversity abounds—the program attracts students from forty-one states and twenty-three countries. The class of 1999 profile includes 37 percent women, 15 percent students who are members of minority groups, and 24 percent international students.

❖ Global Focus

The University of Washington is a recognized leader in global management education, with both a federally funded Center for International Business Education and Research and a membership in the M.B.A. Enterprise Corps. All students are required to take international management as part of the first-year core, and international business concepts are integrated throughout the curriculum. In

addition to the many courses with international business components, the program offers a range of electives focused on global management issues. Beyond the regular curriculum, students can also study abroad in fourteen different exchange programs, pursue international internships, complete overseas language programs and study tours, and participate in weekly, on-campus, foreign language conversation sessions.

Special Features

The overwhelming majority of M.B.A.'s participate in student clubs and organizations. Students interact closely with members of the faculty and administration, and student input is actively solicited in shaping school policies. Faculty-sponsored programs include projects in global telecommunication, entrepreneurship, and business and economic development.

Many first-year students join the Business Diagnostic Center, a student-run volunteer group that sends teams of M.B.A.'s on consulting assignments with local businesses. Other groups bring together students interested in technology, consulting, marketing, public speaking, environmental issues, and socially responsible business practices. M.B.A. students are also extremely active in charitable organizations, such as Challenge for Charity.

The Faculty

The University of Washington M.B.A. philosophy emphasizes a partnership between students and faculty members. Professors at the University of Washington business school have achieved high recognition for both teaching and research. At the same time, M.B.A.'s have high praise for the faculty's active involvement in student learning and their integration of research and teaching. Professors take a personal interest in their students and, in return, they demand a high level of student effort and commitment.

The Business School Network

Corporate Partnerships

The M.B.A. program enjoys an increasingly strong relationship with the business community. Prominent business leaders and entrepreneurs function as guest speakers and foster relationships between students and the School. Guest lecturers, including the former CEO of Seafirst Bank and the Chairman and CEO of Immunex Corporation, teach real-world classes, such as "Leadership and the Board of Directors." Lecture series, small business nights, consulting and business plan competitions, and networking events also bring students and executives together. In addition, an active alumni network offers students the chance to hear from M.B.A.'s in a wide range of fields and geographical areas.

The College and Environs

The University of Washington is one of the nation's leading universities, achieving international recognition in both teaching and research. Since 1975, the University has ranked first among public institutions in the number of federal grants and contracts awarded to its faculty members. Its sixteen schools and colleges provide education to 34,000 students, who can choose from more than 100 academic disciplines and 5,000 courses. Of course, the University's prominence is assisted by its location in one of the fastest-growing regions of the country. The Puget Sound region is home to a large number of well-known companies, including Microsoft, Boeing, Nordstrom, REI, and Weyerhauser. Ranked as one of the country's most livable cities, Seattle also boasts world-renowned opera, ballet, and theater productions as well as an array of hiking, climbing, biking, and water activities.

Facilities

The University of Washington library system is the twelfth largest in the nation and houses more than 5.4 million volumes. The Business School's Foster Library, located in the new Seafirst Executive Center, holds a comprehensive collection of books, periodicals, reference materials, newspapers, pamphlets, CD-ROMs, videotapes, microfiche, and

corporate annual reports. The library also offers a multitude of online search services and worldwide databases.

Technology Environment

The School fosters relationships with high-tech companies, such as Hewlett-Packard and Intel, and each of these companies has awarded technology grants to the School. Computer resources for the School of Business Administration include computer labs, overnight laptop checkout services, mainframe computer facilities, research databases, and full Internet access. The M.B.A. program requires all students to own a computer, and the new library provides laptop ports for students. In addition, use of information technology is heavily incorporated into academic course work, and a variety of training courses are offered for M.B.A.'s who want to enhance their skills or learn new ones.

Placement

The Business Career Center offers an array of services for M.B.A. students, including training in personal assessment, evaluating the job market, and developing search strategies as well as self-presentation in resumes, cover letters, and interviews. One-on-one interview coaching, videotaped mock interviews, individualized career counseling, and a comprehensive library of career resources are also available. The center sponsors numerous recruiting events and coordinates visits by the many hiring companies that recruit on campus.

Admission

To be eligible for admission, students must have completed a college-level calculus course and have a four-year undergraduate degree. To apply, candidates should submit the University of Washington M.B.A. application and take the Graduate Management Admission Test (GMAT). The TOEFL is required for non-U.S. citizens and permanent residents whose undergraduate course work was not conducted in English. In addition, interviews are strongly recommended. (Alumni interviews are also available.)

Finances

The University of Washington is one of the best values in management education.

Tuition for the 1998–99 academic year is $5424 for Washington State residents and $13,470 for nonresidents. (Domestic nonresidents may petition for Washington residency in their second year of study.) Books cost approximately $1200 per year. Financial aid is available for U.S. citizens and permanent residents. The M.B.A. Program offers need-based scholarships to qualified students. Applicants for scholarships and financial aid must fill out the Free Application for Federal Student Aid (FAFSA) by February 28, 1999.

International Students

International students comprise approximately 24 percent of the entering M.B.A. class, representing fifteen different countries. The University has a variety of active student groups and resources for international students, including the International Services Office, various international and cultural organizations, and English as a second language courses, which are designated specifically for graduate students in business and law.

Application Facts and Dates

The University of Washington has a cyclical admissions process with four filing dates. For priority consideration, candidates are strongly encouraged to submit their completed applications by December 1. International students should submit their materials by February 15. Personal interviews are strongly recommended. Appointments must be made before the application deadline and be accompanied by a complete application. For more information, applicants should contact:

Master of Business Administration
    Program Office
School of Business Administration
110 Mackenzie Hall
Box 353200
University of Washington
Seattle, Washington 98195
Telephone: 206-543-4661
Fax: 206-616-7351
E-mail: mba@u.washington.edu
World Wide Web: http://weber.u.
    washington.edu/~bschool

IVEY The University of Western Ontario

London, Ontario, Canada

INTEGRATED AND FOCUSED

The Ivey M.B.A. has long been regarded as one of the leading M.B.A. programs in the world. The Ivey program is highly integrated and focuses on the leadership skills and perspectives essential for success in a global marketplace. Our faculty members are dedicated to teaching and creating an intense and "real world" learning environment. As the second-largest producer of teaching cases in the world, Ivey utilizes a variety of interactive and experiential learning methods that capitalize on the rich base of experience in the class.

Our general management focus and global perspective have led Ivey to be ranked repeatedly as the best business school in Canada by Canadian Business *and among the top in the world by* Business Week, The Economist Intelligence Unit, *and* Asian Business *and* Asia, Inc.

—L. G. Tapp, Dean

Programs and Curricular Focus

The M.B.A. program is two years in length. The first year is the same for all students, while the second year allows selection from an array of options.

The LL.B./M.B.A. program is a four-year limited-enrollment program offered jointly by the Business School and the Faculty of Law to train students for careers in which business and law overlap.

The executive M.B.A. and videoconferencing executive M.B.A. programs are for managers with exceptional potential and a minimum of eight years of work experience. The Ph.D. program provides advanced training in research and teaching and advanced substantive work in a specialized field.

Students and the M.B.A. Experience

The students in the M.B.A. program are distinguished by the diversity of their educational and professional backgrounds and their history of outstanding achievement. On average, they are 28 years of age, with four years of full-time work experience. They come from more than twenty countries worldwide. About 40 percent have substantial work or educational experience outside Canada, and about one third speak at least two languages.

❖ Global Focus

Ivey's programs help students to develop a global perspective—to work in a

business environment that increasingly transcends national boundaries. A multinational student body, faculty members with international experience as consultants and teachers, specialized international courses, and the integration of global issues in all core courses work to foster this perspective. The School also offers several special opportunities.

International exchanges are arranged with top business schools in Australia, Austria, Brazil, Denmark, France, Germany, Hong Kong, Italy, Japan, Korea, Mexico, the Netherlands, the Philippines, Singapore, Spain, Sweden, Switzerland, and other countries.

Each year, approximately 50 M.B.A. students travel to Eastern Europe and China to teach basic management skills to managers and entrepreneurs as part of the LEADER and China projects.

Ivey students have won case competitions in the United States and Hong Kong against teams from around the world.

In the second year, courses covering various international and entrepreneurial topics such as "Doing Business in Asia, Latin America, or Europe" and "Entrepreneurial Creativity" are available.

Special Features

Learning at Ivey is highly interactive. Although there are some lectures, most of the classes rely heavily on case discussions, computer simulations, and role plays. Ivey is especially well known for its business cases. A case presents an actual business situation rather than

theories about business. Usually it describes a particular manager's problem that must be resolved. Students first analyze the case individually, trying to reach a decision, and then meet in a small study group to compare approaches. Finally, students meet with the entire class to discuss the case and its implications for management. During this time, students are also interacting frequently with executives and managers from various organizations. The whole process is designed to help students become effective decision makers. An essential part of Ivey's learning process is the study group. With organizational activity increasingly taking place in teams, this experience is critical for every effective manager.

In the first year, students are also exposed to an intensive workshop in managing diversity to help them understand the impact of greater diversity on management and how to harness that diversity to achieve better organizational performance.

The Faculty

Ivey's faculty members are renowned as excellent teachers. With degrees from esteemed universities, they welcome the challenge of creating a stimulating learning environment. As a result, they can be found as guest professors in universities around the world. And since their research centers on the practical problems of managers, they consult widely with diverse national and international businesses.

The Business School Network

Corporate Partnerships

The corporate community plays a significant role in the educational experience at Ivey. Class projects undertaken with corporations allow companies to show future managers how major institutions operate and implement key strategic changes. This interaction with executives and managers results in a strong integration of material in the first year of the program.

A board of advisers, consisting of key players in the Canadian business community, is also actively involved in maintaining the M.B.A. program's relevance in an increasingly demanding global environment.

A program of industry tours, seminars, and guest speakers features prominent business and government leaders, many of whom are Ivey Business School graduates.

Prominent Alumni

The Ivey experience does not end when the program is over. Students join a network of more than 11,000 men and women who have gone on to occupations in almost every place imaginable. Some of the prominent Business School alumni include Robert Nourse, once voted entrepreneur of the year by *Inc.* magazine and president of the Bombay Company; Laurie Campbell, president of Morgan Stanley; David Thomas, president of Lloyds Bank Brazil; Raymond Verdon, president of Nabisco; and more than 1,000 other presidents and chief executive officers in companies around the world.

The College and Environs

Since it was founded in 1878, the University of Western Ontario has established a tradition of excellence in teaching and research. One of Canada's oldest and largest universities, Ivey consists of seventeen faculties in the sciences, arts, social sciences, and professions, serving a body of over 22,000. The University is particularly well known nationally and internationally for its professional schools, which include Business, Dentistry, Law, and Medicine.

London is called the Forest City in recognition of the many trees that line the streets and add beauty to its parks. With a population of 320,000, London is a university city as well as a center of services, light industry, and commerce.

The city is small enough to have a sense of community but sufficiently large and diverse to have many of the cultural, entertainment, and recreational amenities of a big city. Beyond the city, the beaches and parks of two of the Great Lakes are within an hour's drive. It is just 2 hours by car or train to both Toronto and Detroit.

Facilities

Students have access to all the University's libraries, including a specialized and well-stocked business library. The School operates its own computer facility and student laboratories with PCs that are accessible 24 hours a day. The National Centre for Management Research and Development undertakes full-time research on major challenges facing management today.

Placement

The Career Services Department helps students plan their job search, write resumes, and develop interviewing skills. The office organizes on-campus visits by major corporations and helps both those corporations and students "make the match." Each fall, Career Services sends hundreds of employers resume books containing profiles of all second-year students. These companies may then invite students for an interview. The office also coordinates the activities of over 400 organizations from across Canada and around the world that contact students for employment in a variety of fields.

The records show that Ivey graduates are highly valued in the job market—companies want the kinds of insights, perspectives, and skills that students develop in the program. Ivey graduates have achieved success in a wide range of careers. Many have become CEOs of major corporations. Other Ivey M.B.A. graduates are top civil servants, leading consultants, deans of other business schools, and entrepreneurs. Many decide to spend a few years in the corporate world and then start their own business.

Admission

Students must normally hold an undergraduate degree with high academic standing from an accredited university. The applicant's leadership skills, achievements, undergraduate grades, GMAT score, TOEFL score (600 minimum), full-time work experience, and extracurricular involvement are all carefully considered. Ivey looks for applicants who have thoughtfully analyzed their personal and career goals and have demonstrated the potential to become leaders. Ivey is interested in individuals whose accomplishments indicate an ability to benefit from and contribute to the Business School. A few applicants without an undergraduate degree, who have at least seven years of challenging work experience, some university courses with high standing, and other strong management qualities, may also gain admission. Ivey encourages applications from international students and members of minority groups.

Finances

The estimated tuition fee for international students is Can$14,000 and for Canadian citizens, Can$12,000. The application fee is Can$100.

Costs for housing, medical insurance, food, transportation, and personal items range from Can$13,000 to Can$18,000 for single students and from Can$20,000 to Can$25,000 for a family of four. The cost of books and supplies ranges from Can$1500 to Can$2000 per year.

Well-qualified students are automatically considered for scholarships and awards.

International Students

With the globalization of trade, there is an increasing need for businesspeople to see beyond their own geographic boundaries. At Ivey, students will find outstanding people from diverse educational and cultural backgrounds working in an intense environment.

Students will discover the global economic, political, and technological factors that shape business activity in Canada and around the world. Students will also tap into the powerful network of Canadian business alumni.

Application Facts and Dates

Because the class fills early, students should submit an application as soon as possible. Files are evaluated on a rolling basis starting in November, and this process continues until May. The deadline for applications from outside Canada and the United States is April 1. The deadline for applications from Canada and the United States is May 15. For more information, applicants should contact:

Larysa Gamula, Admissions Director
Ivey Business School
University of Western Ontario
London, Ontario N6A 3K7
Canada
Telephone: 519-661-3212
Fax: 519-661-3431
E-mail: admiss@ivey.uwo.ca
World Wide Web: http://www.ivey. uwo.ca

University of Wisconsin–Madison

> ## A SPECIAL SCHOOL IN A SPECIAL CITY
>
> *The University of Wisconsin–Madison School of Business offers a unique package to graduate students—the resources of a large, top-notch public research institution; one of the finest business school facilities in the nation; faculty noted for outstanding teaching and research; and a superb track record in placing our graduates. Best of all, we are located in the heart of Madison, Wisconsin, long recognized as one of America's most livable cities.*
>
> —Andrew J. Policano, Dean

Programs and Curricular Focus

The M.B.A. program at the University of Wisconsin–Madison School of Business seeks to equip candidates with the broad business background, major specialization, and analytical skills necessary to make sound management decisions. To gain expertise in these areas, the curriculum combines traditional lecture-style delivery with case analysis, project work, team interaction, and hands-on/practical experience in the business community. Located in a technologically advanced facility, the School of Business offers intensive study in small, personalized classes.

The Wisconsin approach to graduate business education combines a solid foundation in core areas of business management in a flexible, tailored curriculum. The Fast Track M.B.A. option permits those with an undergraduate background in business to complete the M.B.A. in a calendar year or three semesters of full-time study.

The program also embodies the marriage of analytical skills to pragmatic managerial problems. Manufacturing and technology students, for example, work closely with counterparts in the University's College of Engineering. Real estate students regularly travel to Asia, Latin America, and Eastern Europe for investment and appraisal seminars. Applied security analysis program students manage actual securities portfolios valued at more than $11.9 million.

Students and the M.B.A. Experience

Academic diversity marks graduate business students at Wisconsin. Approximately 45 percent of entering master's students come from nonbusiness backgrounds, including 25 percent from engineering, mathematics, and science, with the remainder from social sciences, humanities, and fine arts. More than 100 undergraduate institutions from more than twenty-five different countries are represented.

In the fall entering class of 188 students, 34 percent were women, 27 percent were international, and 13 percent were from underrepresented groups. The class possessed an average of 3.8 years of work experience. Their average scores on the GMAT and TOEFL were 596 and 618, respectively, with an average GPA of 3.31.

Students are encouraged to go beyond the boundaries of the School of Business. The University of Wisconsin–Madison is a world-class center of research and learning. It provides an unparalleled opportunity to enrich a business student's knowledge and understanding in a variety of fields.

Special Features

The School of Business attempts to integrate an international perspective into all of its courses. In addition, it currently offers twelve semester-long study-abroad opportunities specifically designed to enhance students' understanding of the international business environment. Students may also choose to participate in shorter international experiences offered during the summer and spring breaks. In the past, such short courses have been offered in China, the Czech Republic, France, Hungary, Indonesia, Thailand, and the United Kingdom.

The Faculty

Close interaction between faculty members and students is a hallmark of the UW–Madison School of Business. More than 80 professors teach and conduct research. Many are leaders in their academic disciplines. In recent years, School of Business faculty members have been elected presidents of a variety of prestigious professional organizations, including the American Accounting Association, the American Academy of Management, and the American Risk and Insurance Association. Business school faculty members have also been recognized for the caliber of their teaching, winning University and national teaching awards.

The Business School Network

Corporate Partnership

The University of Wisconsin–Madison School of Business is well known for responding to the business community's need for high-quality programs in emerging fields.

Invaluable input from businesses is provided to the School in a variety of ways: advisory boards, mentor programs, internships, and an extensive program to bring top executives into the classroom to share their experience with students.

Prominent Alumni

The School of Business has many nationally recognized business leaders among its more than 28,000 alumni, including Paul J. Collins, Vice Chairman, Citibank, N.A.; John P. Morgridge, Chairman of the Board, Cisco Systems, Inc.; and Arthur C. Nielsen Jr., former Chairman and CEO, A. C. Nielsen Company.

The College and Environs

The University of Wisconsin–Madison and the city of Madison provide a rich, multicultural experience. The city's population, including the growing suburbs, is approaching 250,000 and has a growing ethnic population. In addition, UW–Madison's 40,000-member student population is one of the most diverse in the nation. This diversity in ethnic heritages and nationalities of students, faculty, staff, and visiting scholars creates unique cultural and educational benefits to complement the strong academic base.

In 1998, Madison was voted best city in the country in which to live by *Money* magazine; Madison also received this honor from *Life* and *USA Today* in recent years. Situated along the shores of Lake Mendota, one of five lakes within the

In Madison, Wisconsin, one of the most attractive and liveable cities in the U.S., M.B.A. students meet on the terrace outside UW's Grainger Hall.

city's borders, Madison is considered one of the most picturesque college campuses in the country. It offers hilly terrain, scattered parks, and woodlands to augment the urban setting with a friendly neighborhood atmosphere. The capital city is also home to American Family Insurance, Oscar Mayer Foods, Rayovac Corporation, CUNA Credit Union, and several banks and research and technology parks.

UW–Madison is a university of Nobel Prize winners, recipients of the National Medal of Science, and members of the National Academies of Science, Engineering, and Education. It routinely ranks among the top five universities in the nation in terms of funded research.

Facilities

The UW–Madison School of Business is housed in Grainger Hall. The $40-million facility incorporates leading-edge instructional technology throughout its 260,000 square feet. It is one of the most visually appealing and technologically advanced business school facilities in the country.

The two lower levels of the building house thirty modern, spacious classrooms with the latest teaching technology, including an auditorium and two large lecture halls. The upper three levels contain continuing education facilities and offices for research and career services as well as for members of the faculty and administration. The library offers electronic access to specialized databases across campus and around the world.

The School has several instructional computer labs, including a dedicated lab for graduate students, computer classrooms, its own research computer, and a building-wide network of computer outlets to allow students to use laptop computers in almost every corner of the building.

A state-of-the-art videoconferencing room allows School of Business faculty members and students to interact with employers, industry experts, and business leaders, in real time, anywhere in the world.

Grainger Hall was designed from the ground up to be "student friendly," offering student lockers, a graduate student lounge, mailboxes for students, and several other special features.

Placement

UW–Madison is known for the strength of its career development and placement assistance. In 1997–98, more than 250 employers interviewed on campus for graduate students seeking internships and full-time employment opportunities. In addition, more than 1,000 job listings are received and posted each year.

The staff of the Business Career Center (BCC) includes an adviser dedicated to providing assistance and resources to master's students.

The BCC offers a comprehensive array of services to help graduate students achieve their career goals. Utilizing resources available in the BCC and the Career Information Library, Wisconsin students learn about different career options/opportunities and develop essential search skills required to make informed choices throughout their professional careers.

In addition to the Career Focus Seminars offered each fall, the BCC sponsors a career fair, employer briefings, mock interviews, video teleconferencing/interviewing, and roundtable discussions, and a variety of workshops on career-related topics. These activities, coupled with individual career plans, employment strategies, and career counseling, help ensure UW students are able to find the positions they are looking for. In 1998, the average starting salary for graduate students with four years of experience was $57,403.

Admission

The School of Business seeks well-rounded students who possess a solid undergraduate education coupled with strong work experience. To this end, applicants should possess two years of full-time work experience, along with a strong undergraduate GPA.

In addition to academic credentials, test scores (GMAT and TOEFL), and work experience, personal achievements, motivation, leadership, communication skills (written and oral), international exposure, and recommendation letters are considered in the application process. Also, all international applicants are required to submit proof of financial resources along with the application for admission.

Although the School of Business does not require an interview, applicants are encouraged to visit Grainger Hall to see the state-of-the-art teaching, research, and computer facilities. Arrangements are made through the Graduate Programs Office. During the visit, prospective students can meet with an admissions representative to discuss the application process, admission criteria, file status, financial aid/scholarship opportunities, degree plans, and career placement. They can also sit in on a graduate class to see the interaction between faculty members and students and to experience the learning environment. They also have the chance to speak with current graduate students to learn about student life, activities, and experiences.

Finances

Tuition for the 1997–98 school year was $5666 for Wisconsin residents and $15,380 for nonresidents. Housing, books, and incidentals accounted for an additional $10,600.

More than one third of incoming students receive merit-based financial assistance in the form of scholarships and graduate assistantships. Fellowships for African-American, Hispanic American, and Native American students are available through the Consortium for Graduate Study in Management, the Wisconsin Investment Scholarship Program, and the Advanced Opportunity Fellowship. The deadline for merit-based financial assistance from the School of Business is February 15. Other University-wide fellowship opportunities may have earlier deadlines.

Application Facts and Dates

Application deadlines are May 1 for September enrollment and October 1 for January enrollment.

For more information, to schedule a visit, or speak with an admissions representative, students should contact:

Graduate Programs Office
School of Business
2266 Grainger Hall
University of Wisconsin–Madison
975 University Avenue
Madison, Wisconsin 53706-1323
Telephone: 608-262-1555 or 1556
Fax: 608-265-4192
E-mail: uwmadmba@bus.wisc.edu
World Wide Web: http://www.wisc.edu/bschool/

Villanova University

EDUCATING INDIVIDUALS TO PROSPER IN THE GLOBAL ECONOMY OF THE 21ST CENTURY

As technology races ahead and American businesses face the traumas created by the globalization of many markets, graduate programs must determine the type of educational experience that will be required to ensure that their students will have a competitive advantage as managers. The Villanova M.B.A. program provides a broad educational experience that enables its graduates to assume managerial responsibilities at all levels of business, government, and nonprofit organizations.

Just as important, however, Villanova adheres to its American, Catholic, and Augustinian tradition by emphasizing to students in its M.B.A. program the importance of creating strategies, making decisions, and executing plans within a framework of value judgments and ethical considerations.

Villanova's M.B.A. program is one of approximately 250 in the nation accredited by AACSB.

—Thomas F. Monahan, Ph.D., Dean

Programs and Curricular Focus

Villanova University's College of Commerce and Finance offers an M.B.A. program that target toward professionals who seek to improve their managerial and leadership skills. The intensive workday demands faced by the program's students necessitate that all course offerings be scheduled in the evenings and occasionally on Saturdays. The goals of the program include providing the student with the knowledge and understanding of the fundamental disciplines involved in business decision making; providing current and future managers with the ability to identify problems, obtain relevant information, devise and evaluate alternative approaches, and choose and implement decisions; ensuring the development of moral, competent, and innovative managers who understand their responsibility to promote the welfare of society; and increasing the capacity of managers to adapt to a rapidly changing domestic and global environment.

The M.B.A. course work is organized into three levels: basic core, advanced core, and elective. A student initially takes courses at the basic core level. The number of required courses in the basic core varies from student to student, depending upon the area studied at the undergraduate level, the number of years since the undergraduate degree was earned, and qualifying examinations.

Individual work experience does not qualify for academic credit.

After satisfying the requirements of the basic core, the student starts the course work leading to the M.B.A. degree. Eleven courses beyond the basic core are required, including seven advanced core courses and four elective courses. Students may choose to develop expertise in an area by selecting a concentration (three elective courses) in finance, management information systems, or marketing. For those who do not wish to specialize in one of these areas, they may tailor their M.B.A. degree by selecting those electives most appropriate for their career goals. All degree requirements beyond the basic core level must be completed within seven years from the date of registration for the first management core course.

Villanova University also offers a joint J.D./M.B.A. program that enables students to work simultaneously in the College of Commerce and Finance and in the Villanova School of Law to obtain a joint degree.

Students and the M.B.A. Experience

In order to uphold the quality of both the candidates and the program, the student population is maintained at approximately 650. Nearly 85 percent of applicants who are accepted by the college enroll. About 90 percent of the current enrollment are part-time students, with degrees from more than 100 different undergraduate schools. Their average age at admission is 27 years, with an average of five years of work experience in fields that include communications, banking, engineering, medicine, accounting, information systems, and law. Women comprise 36 percent of the student population. The undergraduate majors of the current M.B.A. candidates include business (58 percent), engineering (18 percent), science (11 percent), and liberal arts (13 percent).

❖ Global Focus

Villanova's M.B.A. program recognizes the importance of providing a curriculum that enables a student to learn how American business can best compete in the international arena. To that end, the program includes the study of issues relevant to international competition at both the basic core and advanced core levels. In addition, students must select one international course from a wide range of elective courses that focus on issues relating to competition in global environments.

Special Features

The unique features of Villanova's M.B.A. program include small classes—class size is limited in order to maintain a personalized learning environment; full-time faculty instructors—more than 95 percent of all M.B.A. classes are taught by full-time faculty members; and a solid foundation—the program is built on the base of an undergraduate program which enjoys an excellent national reputation and has been in existence since 1922.

The Faculty

Practical experience in business, government, and the professions, in addition to a strong academic background, is characteristic of a faculty with more than 94 percent holding Ph.D. or equivalent degrees from more than 40 different academic institutions. The faculty members' commitment to teaching

excellence is documented by the fact that a sizeable percentage of the College of Commerce and Finance's 85 faculty members have been awarded the prestigious Lindback Award for Teaching Excellence. The faculty members are also deeply engaged in research activities and have published in many premier academic and professional journals.

The Business School Network

Corporate Partnerships

An advisory board of executives and alumni help shape the future development of the curriculum. In addition, guest lecturers and speakers address the students each year, both on campus and in professionals organizations.

The College and Environs

Founded in 1842 under the leadership of the Order of St. Augustine, Villanova University has witnessed significant growth not only in its student population but also in its position in the academic community. This has been chronicled by a national survey showing Villanova as one of the nation's best comprehensive educational institutions.

Since 1900, the University has added to the original College of Liberal Arts and Sciences a College of Engineering (1905), a Science division for the College of Liberal Arts and Sciences (1915), the University College (1918), the College of Commerce and Finance (1922), the College of Nursing (1953), and the School of Law (1953). Today the student

population is approximately 11,500, of which approximately 30 percent are engaged in graduate study.

Located on a tree-lined, 222-acre campus in the suburbs of Philadelphia, Villanova is close (by private or public transportation) to one of the oldest cities in the country—a city which offers the finest in ballet, theater, music, and art. It is also accessible (within a 2- or 3-hour drive) to New York City, Washington, D.C., and Baltimore, Maryland.

Facilities

The Falvey Memorial Library provides resources and facilities for study and research by graduate and undergraduate students, faculty members, and visiting scholars. The total seating capacity is more than 2,000 with a book capacity of more than 500,000 volumes. Annual reports for top corporations are readily available to M.B.A. candidates. The library also offers on-line access to a variety of databases.

Technology Environment

The University's computer center is located in Mendal Hall. Satellite computing centers are available in a number of other locations, including Bartley Hall, which is the home of the College of Commerce and Finance and the M.B.A. program. These centers are equipped with terminals, microcomputers, and reference materials and are staffed by professionals from University Information Technologies (UNIT). In addition, several classrooms

in Bartley Hall are equipped with computers for courses from various business disciplines that integrate the use of computers into course work. In addition, three classrooms are complete multimedia facilities.

Admission

Applicants must possess a baccalaureate degree from an accredited college or university. An applicant need not possess an undergraduate degree in business or have taken any business courses to be considered for admission. The applicant must submit documentation that includes a completed application, two essays, and two letters of recommendation along with a nonrefundable $25 application fee; official undergraduate and, if applicable, graduate transcripts for all institutions attended; and official test results from the Graduate Management Admission Test (GMAT). International applicants whose native language is not English are required to take the Test of English as a Foreign Language (TOEFL) and submit proof of adequate financial resources. Admission to the program is competitive. Applications are reviewed by an admissions committee comprised of faculty members.

Finances

Tuition and fees for the 1998–99 academic year are $490 per credit or $1470 per course. Information regarding financial assistance available to graduate students may be obtained from the University's financial assistance office. In addition, the M.B.A. has a number of positions for graduate research assistants to work for faculty members engaged in research activities.

Application Facts and Dates

Students are admitted for enrollment in the fall and spring of each year. Applications should be submitted as far in advance as possible for the following deadlines: June 30 for the fall semester and November 15 for the spring semester. For additional information, students should contact:

Melinda B. German
Director of Graduate Studies in
  Business
Room 112-Bartley Hall
Villanova University
800 Lancaster Avenue
Villanova, Pennsylvania 19085-1699
Telephone: 610-519-4336
Fax: 610-519-6273
E-mail: mba@email.vill.edu

Virginia Tech

Virginia Polytechnic Institute and State University

Pamplin College of Business

Blacksburg, Virginia

WHY THE PAMPLIN COLLEGE OF BUSINESS?

Besides being one of the Southeast's top business schools, we are Virginia's largest business school, accounting for 20 percent of all business degrees awarded from the state's fifteen public senior institutions. Our M.B.A. and other degree programs are all accredited by AACSB–The International Association for Management Education, which is the nationally recognized accrediting agency for graduate and undergraduate business programs.

We are committed to providing top-quality business education through outstanding teaching by full-time faculty members who are nationally recognized in theoretical and applied research. We are also committed to developing a global perspective in our students so that they may better understand the interdependence of nations in the world economy and how cultural differences can become the basis of strength. We are preparing our students for global business challenges with core courses that include the global context of business, international summer internships, and faculty-led study-abroad programs.

—Richard E. Sorensen, Dean

Programs and Curricular Focus

The Master of Business Administration degree at the Pamplin College of Business requires the completion of 48 semester credit hours. The program consists of a twofold educational process. First, through program prerequisites and a set of required courses, students gain proficiency in the basic disciplines of accounting, finance, management, marketing, and production/operations management. Students also acquire an understanding of the quantitative, economic, behavioral, and statistical tools required of a competent manager and a contributing team member.

Next, students are given an opportunity to strengthen their knowledge in a particular area through the careful selection of elective courses. They may concentrate in financial risk management, information and decision support systems, human resource management, leadership, finance, management, management science, marketing, and global business. They may also select a broader range of electives and not declare a formal concentration. Students are thus given some flexibility to put together an M.B.A. program that is tailored to their individual professional goals.

The two-year, full-time program has two program prerequisites. These requirements can be fulfilled by completing at least one college-level course in differential calculus and one college-level course each in microeconomics and macroeconomics. Students should also be familiar with matrix algebra.

The program provides a strong theoretical base, vital to the foundation of a future manager. A solid understanding of business functions and a sensitivity to the needs of organizational stakeholders enable managers to better understand and adapt to change. The classroom procedures offer students a blend of case study, lectures, role play, individual and group presentations, and simulation exercises.

Students and the M.B.A. Experience

The M.B.A. program has about 220 full-time students on campus. The students represent a diversity of ages, work experiences, undergraduate studies, nationalities, cultural backgrounds, and career interests. About one quarter of the students obtained their undergraduate degrees from out-of-state institutions, with approximately another quarter having undergraduate degrees from universities outside the United States. The students come from about twenty-five countries. Business undergraduate majors comprise about 45 percent of the students; engineering or technical majors represent just under 30 percent. The average age of the entering students is 26. Students typically have more than two years of work experience. Men account for 65 percent of the students; women, 35 percent.

The College seeks to attract a cross-section of highly qualified individuals from different cultural and career backgrounds. Because diversity is a reality in today's workplace and in the global economy, students are encouraged to be open to and embrace differing views and interpretations of the world.

Special Features

The College also enrolls about 325 part-time students in its off-campus M.B.A. programs, offered in northern Virginia and, by satellite downlink, in other sites around the state.

The Northern Virginia M.B.A. Program has been fully accredited since 1971. The program offers professionals in the Washington, D.C., area an opportunity to earn an M.B.A. without interrupting their careers. Of the approximate 240 students enrolled in this program, more than 95 percent have full-time careers in engineering, computer applications, accounting, finance, human resources, and marketing.

The M.B.A. Program via Satellite Downlink provides courses that are received at sites through live satellite telecast plus a two-way audio connection via telephone lines—permitting students at various locations to interact with the instructor and with students in classrooms at other sites.

The Faculty

The College has about 125 full-time faculty members, many of whom are nationally recognized teachers and scholars with practical business experience. As a result of their dedication to advancing leading-edge business concepts, the faculty members have been involved with instituting nationally recognized research entities, such as the Center for Study of Futures and Options Markets, Center for Wireless Telecommunications, Center for Relationship Development, and the Business/Technology Center.

The Business School Network

The Pamplin Advisory Council is a select group of 65 prominent business and government leaders from across the country who meet with College administrators to provide guidance on College programs, fund-raising, and ties with industry and government.

Alumni volunteers assist students in various capacities, including information interviews, networking referrals, referring resumes in their respective companies, and advising students seeking jobs within the alumni's specific geographic areas.

The alumni return to their alma mater to share their work experiences and to discuss factors for success that go beyond their technical knowledge.

Experienced recruiters conduct panel discussions and practice interviews for first-year students. M.B.A. students receive straightforward feedback on how they performed during the mock interviews, how they were perceived by recruiters, and what they can do to prepare for live interviews during their second year.

The College and Environs

Virginia Polytechnic Institute and State University, commonly known as Virginia Tech, was founded in 1872 as a land-grant college. Its recent history is one of rapid, well-planned growth. Virginia Tech is the largest university in the state in terms of full-time enrollment.

Virginia Tech, ranked in the nation's top fifty in terms of research expenditures, conducts a \$121-million-a-year research program supporting more than 3,500 research projects. The Virginia Tech Corporate Research Center offers businesses the opportunity to establish close working relationships with the University.

Facilities

The Pamplin M.B.A. Program is housed in Pamplin Hall, a state-of-the-art academic facility. An atrium, combining large skylights with natural foliage, forms a creative yet relaxing environment for both students and faculty to interact.

Virginia Tech's Newman Library currently contains more than 1.7 million bound volumes, 5.2 million microforms, 5,000 videos and films, 6,700 cassettes and recordings, and more than 13,000 journals and periodicals. Access to the collection is provided through an online computer system, VTLS, which is an integrated system used by more than seventy-five other libraries around the world.

Technology Environment

The Pamplin College of Business is committed to providing its students with the best educational experience possible. Pamplin has two computer labs equipped with Pentium PCs and Power Macs; labs also make available some of the latest peripherals such as flatbed color scanners, laser printers, and multimedia. Students have unlimited access to the Internet. This virtual connection with the program allows students to download full-text articles from the library, register for classes, and download assignments. These and other time-saving activities allow students to focus on and devote more time to studies. Blacksburg and Virginia Tech are also the home of Blacksburg Electronic Village (BEV), the oldest and most connected Internet community in the world. With the growing importance of information and computer technologies, the program prepares students for a competitive and changing world.

Placement

The M.B.A. career service's mission is to help students identify and capitalize on their distinctive talents and focus on how their career objectives fit their personal and professional priorities. Individual counseling focuses on customizing the career planning and marketing process for each student. Two courses are offered to assist students: Career Marketing and Planning and the Job Search Strategy Seminar. Corporate briefings and alumni career events occur throughout the year.

Admission

Applicants to the Pamplin M.B.A. Program must take the Graduate Management Admission Test (GMAT) and have the official scores reported to Virginia Tech. In addition, each applicant is required to submit an application for admission, official transcripts of all past course work, two letters of recommendation, and a current resume.

Undergraduate grades (particularly those from the junior and senior years), GMAT scores, work experience, and letters of recommendation are all important, although each is only one measure of an individual's potential to pursue graduate study. Considered collectively, however, this information helps to determine which applicants are most likely to succeed in the program.

Finances

Estimated in-state tuition for the 1998–99 academic year is \$4122. The out-of-state student rate is \$6354. Estimated living expenses are \$6700, and miscellaneous expenses are estimated at \$1100 for both in-state and out-of-state students. Travel expenses are not included.

Merit-based financial aid is available for students with outstanding academic background, GMAT scores, work experience, leadership skills, and references. Financial aid is available for graduate students in the form of fellowships, instructional fee waivers, and graduate assistantships.

Need-based financial aid is based primarily on demonstrated financial need. In order to be considered, students must submit a Free Application for Federal Student Aid (FAFSA) for the appropriate year no later than February 15. The University will advise applicants of their financial aid awards by August 1.

International Students

Approximately twenty-five countries are represented in the M.B.A. program, and international students comprise about 25 percent of the program's student body. At the university level, there are thirty-five international student organizations and an international center, the Cranwell International Center, which is a focal point for cultural, social, and educational programs with a global focus. Films, dinners, lectures, parties, orientation programs, and community contacts are facilitated throughout the center.

Application Facts and Dates

Applications for admission are accepted at any time. Admission decisions are made within six to eight weeks after the application file is complete. Although most students enter the program in August, students may also enter in January (spring semester). Application materials should be received at least eight weeks before the beginning of the semester for which enrollment is requested. For more information, students should contact:

Associate Dean for Graduate and
    International Programs
1044 Pamplin Hall
Virginia Polytechnic Institute and
    State University
Blacksburg, Virginia 24061-0209
Telephone: 540-231-6152
Fax: 540-231-4487
E-mail: mbainfo@vt.edu

Wake Forest University

Babcock Graduate School of Management

Winston-Salem, North Carolina

THE SCHOOL OF FIRST CHOICE

Exciting developments are taking place to make Babcock the 'school of first choice' for an increasing number of outstanding students. Babcock's recent strategic initiative—the 3/38 Plan (3 sections of 38 students)—provides the smallest first-year class sections of any major graduate business school in the nation. In the second year, you can tailor your studies for optimal learning with one of Babcock's thirteen newly developed career concentrations. Even after graduation, your education at Babcock will continue through new lifelong learning options.

The M.B.A. curriculum will give you a personalized and experiential learning experience, access to innovative technology in a modern facility, extensive team-based and cross-functional learning opportunities, a global management perspective, and the chance to acquire depth in your chosen career area.

Investment in the M.B.A. degree will be one of the most important decisions of your life. I invite you to visit and see firsthand why you should make the Babcock School your 'school of first choice.'

—Charlie Moyer, Dean

Programs and Curricular Focus

Babcock's curriculum stresses the integrated, global, and strategic nature of management. Students gain a broad managerial perspective, functional competence, and enhanced communication skills. Other hallmarks of the Babcock School are the state-of-the-art facilities, leading-edge technology, close interaction with faculty members, teamwork, emphasis on practical application, and dedication to lifelong learning.

Babcock's cross-functional first-year curriculum enables students to learn and apply knowledge across all management disciplines. Knowledge and problem-solving skills acquired in one class are applied to situations in another, and integrative exercises reinforce this approach. Also, knowledge builds as first-year students progress through three distinct modules: Business Foundations, Functional and Cross-Functional Applications, and Strategic Perspectives.

The first-year class, composed of 114 students, is divided into three sections of 38 students and study teams of 5 or 6 members with diverse academic and work-experience backgrounds. The first-year core courses include accounting, analysis and communications, financial management, international business management, international competitive policy, law and ethics, macroeconomics, management information systems,

managerial economics, marketing management, operations management, organizational behavior, and quantitative methods.

Second-year students may choose to concentrate in one of thirteen newly developed career concentrations: four in finance, three in marketing, three in operations, one in consulting, one in entrepreneurship and family business, and one that can be custom designed. This gives each student the opportunity to design an individualized curriculum to fit specific career needs. An integral part of the second year is the Field Study Program, which offers consulting projects that provide experiential learning.

The Babcock School offers two joint-degree programs: a J.D./M.B.A. degree program that takes four years to complete and a full-time M.D./M.B.A. degree program, which takes five years to complete.

Students and the M.B.A. Experience

Students benefit from the diverse backgrounds of their fellow classmates. The average incoming student is 26 years old with 3½ years of full-time work experience. Thirty percent of the class are women, 21 percent is international, and minority students comprise 8 percent of the class. The entering class represents every region of the United States as well as

ten other countries. Babcock students have undergraduate degrees in business/accounting (38 percent), engineering/natural sciences (19 percent), economics (14 percent), social sciences (10 percent), and liberal arts/other degrees (19 percent).

❖ Global Focus

Multinational studies are interlaced throughout the curriculum. More than 80 percent of the faculty members have international experience.

Babcock offers three 2-week international study programs in China/Hong Kong; Japan; and Oxford, England, and a semester abroad of study can be arranged in Europe or Latin America. In addition, an international summer internship is an option through Babcock's International Internship Program in Asia, Europe, and Latin America.

Special Features

A hallmark of the Babcock School is the personal attention students receive. The program is small enough for close relationships with other students and professors yet large enough for students to experience different cultures and academic and work backgrounds. The personalized approach is inherent in all aspects of the program, from faculty advisers for study groups to the career services staff making corporate calls on an individual student's behalf to the Mentor Program. The Babcock School's Mentor Program offers students a real-world perspective through one-on-one relationships with business professionals.

The Faculty

Babcock faculty members are excellent teacher-scholars and are experienced managers. They know how academic theory relates to conditions in practice. The faculty members take an interest in students' professional development and quickly come to know students as individuals.

Faculty members are actively engaged in research and publication for leading scholarly journals. Many develop cases, textbooks, and other classroom materials, supporting the schoolwide emphasis on teaching excellence. Faculty members also engage in consulting to stay abreast of current managerial practices.

The Business School Network

Babcock values its partnerships with corporate leaders, who support the School in many ways. Corporate leaders assist with career development by participating in the Mentor Program and the Career Symposium, a half-day event in which business leaders from twelve different functional areas come to share their business experiences and advice. Prominent business leaders volunteer to speak to classes and clubs or to participate in one of two lecture series, sharing their views on the current business environment. The Babcock School's Board of Visitors is an advisory body of business leaders who provide strategic counsel to the School. Members are available to help students with career networking, and, along with other individuals and businesses, have generously provided scholarships for incoming students.

The College and Environs

Wake Forest University was founded in 1834 and is one of the oldest institutions of higher learning in North Carolina. The University is consistently ranked in Tier One of national colleges and universities. Total enrollment in the University is 6,015, with one third of these students enrolled in graduate or professional programs.

Wake Forest University is located in North Carolina's Piedmont Triad region, with a population that exceeds 1.2 million. Winston-Salem has a well-established reputation as the "city of the arts," with numerous museums, galleries, concerts, and organizations. Students also take advantage of Atlantic Coast Conference action, minor league baseball, and many philanthropic, club, and Student Government Association activities.

Technology Environment

Opened in 1993, the Worrell Professional Center for Law and Management is one of the most outstanding business school facilities in the United States. Babcock is committed to providing students with leading-edge technologies in information systems. As a result, the building is well equipped for studying, with each study room, study carrel, and most classrooms containing connections to link the students' ThinkPads to the computer network. Every student receives an IBM ThinkPad as part of tuition. Through the network, students can access the Professional Center Library, the Internet, and libraries and databases throughout the world. Students have dial-in capability from home for activities such as checking e-mail or accessing the Intranet or professors' shared data files. Classrooms also include integrated computer and audiovisual equipment.

Placement

Babcock graduates are competitive in the marketplace. The Career Services Office builds close working relationships with corporations, alumni, and other business professionals. Babcock students have access to top multinational companies through on-campus interviews and recruiting events in New York and Atlanta. Babcock also takes part in two international career conferences. The School's career planning assistance includes individual counseling, group seminars covering self-assessment and career management topics, videotaped practice job interviews with interview consultants, the Career Symposium, first- and second-year resume books, a resume referral service, and interviews through the VIEWnet teleconferencing system. At the class of 1998's graduation, 94 percent of Babcock M.B.A. graduates had employment offers, and based on previous years, it is anticipated that between 97 and 98 percent will have offers by September 1, 1998. The median annual salary, exclusive of bonuses, commissions, and other benefits, was $60,000.

Admission

Applicants must hold a bachelor's degree or its equivalent from an accredited college or university. Applicants are primarily evaluated on three criteria: academic record, GMAT scores, and work experience. Babcock's entering class has an average GPA of 3.2, an average GMAT score of 639, and an average of 3½ years of work experience. Ninety percent of the incoming class has full-time postgraduate work experience. Additionally, the Admissions Committee looks for evidence of leadership ability, teamwork skills, a strong sense of values, and unique talents, skills, or achievements. International students must submit a satisfactory score on the TOEFL and a certificate of finances, proving the availability of funds to cover two years of expenses. Interviews are only required for individuals lacking postgraduate work experience but are strongly recommended for every applicant. There are no requisite courses for admission, but students need to have a working knowledge of statistics, accounting, and economics, plus sound spreadsheet skills.

Finances

The estimated student budget for the 1998–99 school year is $33,000, which includes the following expenses: tuition, $20,400; books/supplies, $1500; room, $3600; board, $2000; utilities, $850; personal expenses, $2235; insurance (health and renter's), $675; transportation, $1640; and an SGA fee of $100. These expense estimates are based on a nine-month academic year for single students living off campus. There is limited on-campus housing for married couples and international students. Scholarship awards are made on the basis of merit and are awarded on a first-come, first served basis. Applicants who wish to be considered for merit-based scholarships should apply by March 1, and those who wish to be considered for the ten Babcock Scholars full-tuition scholarships must apply by February 15. Both U.S. citizens and international students are eligible for scholarships. The School also assists students with obtaining federally sponsored loans.

International Students

International students must arrive for the international student orientation program one week prior to general orientation. This program introduces international students to U.S. business and culture. Housing is available for international students in the Wake Forest International House on a space-available basis. The house is located within walking distance of the Babcock School.

Application Facts and Dates

Babcock makes admission decisions on a rolling basis, and decisions are made within one month of receipt of a completed application. The early admission deadline is December 1. Applications received after April 1 are considered on a space-available basis. Admission is for the fall semester only. For more information, students should contact the admissions office.

Admissions and Financial Aid
Babcock Graduate School of
    Management
Wake Forest University
P.O. Box 7659
Winston-Salem, North Carolina 27109
Telephone: 336-758-5422
        800-722-1622 (toll-free)
Fax: 336-758-5830
E-mail: admissions@mail.mba.wfu.edu
World Wide Web: http://www.mba.
    wfu.edu

Walsh College of Accountancy and Business Administration

Troy, Michigan

EDUCATING TOMORROW'S BUSINESS LEADERS

Walsh College is one of the ten largest business schools serving part-time students in the nation. A leader in business education for seventy-five years, Walsh will offer the traditional M.B.A. with a unique twist beginning fall 1998. Case studies and a focus on the entire business enterprise tailor this graduate program. Walsh also offers a Master of Science in Management (M.S.M.) program grounded in the practical approach. In addition to providing core management skills, the M.S.M. affords students a chance to develop specialized skills through four program concentrations. Program instructors are business practitioners as well as subject matter experts.

—Dr. Michael Wood, Dean

Programs and Curricular Focus

Rapidly advancing technology, the global marketplace, and changing organizational structures pose significant challenges for tomorrow's managers. Walsh College's M.B.A. and M.S.M. programs are designed to help managers meet these challenges and become true leaders in their fields.

More businesses, in particular those in the service industries, require or recommend graduate education for employee advancement. The M.B.A. and M.S.M. programs were developed with all managers and aspiring managers in mind.

The 36-credit-hour programs include eight to nine core courses. The M.B.A. requires an additional four electives, while the M.S.M. requires an additional three courses in one area of concentration. The four concentrations are business operations, human resources, marketing, and international management.

In addition to providing a high-quality education, Walsh demonstrates its commitment to the students through convenient class scheduling, with evening and weekend classes currently offered at two locations in southeast Michigan; extended office hours for student services; tutoring; faculty mentoring; and state-of-the-art technology.

Walsh College also offers Master of Science degrees in finance, information management and communication, professional accountancy, and taxation.

Students and the M.B.A. Experience

Business professionals, professionals with a technical background, and even those with a liberal arts degree find that the M.B.A. and M.S.M. programs prepare them for the challenges of being a manager. Many of the students are engineers, automotive field employees, health-care professionals, business owners, or aspiring managers.

The majority of the 483 students enrolled in the Master of Science in Management program at Walsh College are working professionals, often with family responsibilities. The average student is 35 years old. Forty-eight percent of the students are women, 10 percent are members of minority groups, and 4 percent are international students. These individuals bring a broad range of experience to the classroom.

The Faculty

The faculty comprises business professionals holding master's and doctoral degrees. They include CPAs, attorneys, and marketing managers and analysts who bring "real-world" experience into the classroom and provide a network between students and business. Currently, there are 3 full-time and 30 part-time faculty members teaching in the M.S.M. program.

The Business School Network

Walsh College students are provided networking opportunities through internships, contact with faculty members and classmates holding professional positions, alumni activities, and student clubs, including the Student Government, Walsh College Accounting Club, and Finance/Economics Club. In addition, students are encouraged to join professional organizations with college chapters at Walsh, including the Association of Information Technology Professionals, American Marketing Association, and the National Association of Black Accountants, Inc.

The College and Environs

Walsh College of Accountancy and Business Administration is a private upper-division institution with an enrollment of nearly 3,340 students. The College offers bachelor's and master's degree programs in business administration and related fields. Walsh College was established on December 31, 1968, as a successor to Walsh Institute of Accountancy. The Institute was founded in 1922 by Mervyn B. Walsh, a prominent certified public accountant.

Facilities

Walsh College offers classes at four convenient locations in southeast Michigan, including Troy, Novi, Port Huron, and the University Center in Clinton Township. The M.B.A. and M.S.M. programs are offered at the Troy and Novi campuses.

The main campus is located in Troy, Michigan, approximately 17 miles north of downtown Detroit. The campus is strategically placed to serve commuting students within the Detroit metropolitan area. The Troy main campus is located on 20 acres. No housing facilities are available on campus. Walsh College facilities are modern and exemplify a professional learning environment. At the main campus, students can attend classes during the day, in the evening, and on Saturdays.

The Novi campus opened in fall 1993. A new building will open in September 1998.

Technology Environment

Student labs are equipped with Pentiums that run Windows and Microsoft Office Professional. The library features an electronic card catalog, automated administration system, network-based CD-ROM, and Internet access.

Placement

Walsh College's Career Services Office assists current students and alumni in securing full-time, part-time, internship, or co-op positions either while attending the College or after graduation.

A wide range of services is offered, including workshops and programs such as on-campus recruiting in the spring and fall, job listings that are updated daily and posted at all four campuses, resume referrals, career days, and mock interview sessions. In addition, specific career development needs are addressed in individual appointments, providing assistance with resume preparation, job search techniques, interviewing skills, career planning, and career-related assessment. Finally, Career Services and the library have numerous resources, including more than 1,200 annual reports, industry-specific journals, online company databases, and corporate recruiting brochures.

Admission

Admission requirements for the M.B.A. program include an evaluation of undergraduate academic achievement, work experience, and GMAT score. In order to be prepared for the M.S.M. curriculum, students need two years of work experience and an academic background in accounting, economics, statistics, and microcomputers. The GMAT is not required for the M.S.M. program. Students needing preparation in specific areas of business study may complete prerequisite course work at Walsh.

Finances

Tuition for 1997–98 was $263 per semester credit hour. A $75 nonrefundable registration fee is assessed each semester. The minimum registration deposit is $400. In addition, books for each course cost approximately $100.

Students interested in financial aid should complete and mail the Free Application for Federal Student Aid (FAFSA) to the Federal Processing Center before September 1. Graduate students who are Michigan residents and who demonstrate financial need through the information provided on the FAFSA may qualify for a Michigan Tuition Grant, which offers up to $2500 toward tuition costs, or a Federal Family Education Loan (FFEL) with an annual maximum of $18,500.

Merit scholarships are available to new and continuing students based upon high academic achievement, as demonstrated by a grade point average of 3.5 or higher.

International Students

Six percent of the student population at Walsh College comprises international students representing thirty-two countries, with the majority coming from Canada and Europe. Students typically have family and friends living and working in southeast Michigan.

Application Facts and Dates

Students may begin their studies at the beginning of any academic semester. Applications for admission in a given semester are accepted until the beginning of that semester. However, students living overseas should make application to the College no later than six months before the start of classes. In addition, international applicants whose native language is not English must demonstrate a sufficient proficiency in English by attaining a score of 550 or better on the Test of English as a Foreign Language (TOEFL) or a score of 80 or better on the Michigan English Language Assessment Battery (MELAB). All classes at Walsh College are conducted entirely in English. Upon receipt of the application, Walsh College requests the official transcripts for the applicant to be sent from all other colleges previously attended. After evaluation, a letter is sent to the applicant regarding admission. For more information, students should contact:

Sherree Hyde, Director of Enrollment
    Services
Walsh College
P.O. Box 7006
Troy, Michigan 48007-7006
Telephone: 810-689-8282
Fax: 810-524-2520
E-mail: mkt@walshcol.edu

Waseda University

Graduate School of Asia-Pacific Studies

Tokyo, Japan

ASIA-PACIFIC FOCUS

In July 1997, Waseda University opened a new center called the Waseda Institute of Asia-Pacific Studies (WIAPS), which offers research and education programs and activities that focus on the Asia-Pacific region. The Graduate School of Asia-Pacific Studies (GSAPS), with a concentration in international relations and international management, cooperates with this new center in offering master's degree programs to educate professionals and executives in the public and private sectors to function as experts and researchers. GSAPS programs began in April 1998.

—Ken'ichi Goto, Dean, GSAPS

Program and Curricular Focus

Waseda University's M.B.A. program is a full-time intensive program intended to provide talented professionals with the necessary specialized international management skills to perform successfully in positions of responsibility in business administration in Asia-Pacific firms and organizations. The curriculum stresses not only knowledge-based techniques and methods in business and management but also infrastructure-related topics (such as business ethics, intercultural studies, comparative industry theory, environmental problems, ecology, negotiation, and methodologies, including system analysis, system design, and paradigm shifts). Students are required to complete a minimum of eighteen months of study, 30 credits, and a thesis based upon a research project or internship program.

This program also offers internship and field study. Students are involved in a research project and are expected to accomplish a thesis related to the project. Also, students are offered opportunities to study a natural language intensively (Japanese, English, Mandarin, Korean, Thai, Pilipino, Malay, Indonesian, Vietnamese, or Spanish).

One of the characteristics of the graduate education program is the "Triangle Method," which consists of interaction among research, education, and society. The intention of WIAPS is to receive, then to research projects commissioned by governments, local authorities, and companies and to organize students to work on these projects. Students are educated through problem-solving and practice-oriented

curricula. Multimedia education is also emphasized. The language of instruction is English and Japanese, and the course is offered through four terms.

Students and the M.B.A. Experience

Students are required to have earned a B.A. degree (or the equivalent) following the completion of sixteen years of school education in a country other than Japan and have at least three years' working

experience. The University welcomes applications from international students.

❖ Global Focus

In addition to the International Management Program, GSAPS offers the International Relations Program, which is tailored to meet the needs of global business leaders.

The Faculty

One half of all faculty members are executives of major corporations, specialists, and central and local government officials from both Japan and throughout the world. The University also invites visiting professors from prestigious business schools as guest speakers.

The Business School Network

Waseda University has a student and faculty member exchange agreement with 126 institutions of higher education all over the world. GSAPS uses this global network for maximizing results of international business education.

GSAPS is located in Waseda University's Nishiwaseda Building.

In addition, WIAPS' International Advisory Board (IAB), consisting of distinguished members such as CEOs of leading Japanese companies, leaders of the global business world, and a former president, will provide valuable guidance and consultation for this program.

The College and Environs

In 1882, Shigenobu Okuma, one of the leading political figures of the Meiji Era, founded Tokyo College for Technical Studies (Tokyo-senmon-gakko) with the aim of upholding independence of learning, promoting the practical utilization of knowledge, and fostering good citizenship. In 1902, this institution became Waseda University.

Waseda University, located in the center of Tokyo, now consists of nine undergraduate schools, ten graduate schools, and various affiliated research institutions. It has about 1,500 full-time faculty members and about 50,000 students.

Waseda University is one of the most prestigious and most respected private universities in Japan in terms of its history, tradition, the number and achievements of its graduates, and the standard of its teaching and research.

Facilities

Central Library, which is located next to GSAPS's building, with a capacity of more than 4 million collections and a fully equipped audiovisual auditorium, offers an ideal environment for study and research. Waseda University also has an International Conference Center and a unique theater museum built in 1928 and devoted to the study of the history of drama.

Technology Environment

Waseda University provides full Internet access for every student, which includes an e-mail account and access to the NetNews and the World Wide Web.

Waseda University's Okuma Auditorium.

To ensure that this environment can be used optimally, technical support is also given to students who are less familiar with computers. Students are also offered the chance to study artificial language (computer and Internet). The Media Network Center currently holds more than 2,000 PCs and 100 servers.

Waseda University's integrated network system enables students to reach a wide range of databases not only from international database providers but also from major newspapers.

Placement

The Career Development Office provides assistance to help graduating students in finding employment as well as individual counseling. It has on file information on almost 30,000 companies. It also publishes *Employment Guidance* and designs employment seminars that consider actual social and economic conditions as well as character of students based on rich data and long-time experience.

Admission

New students are admitted in either April or September. The Admissions Office is considering accepting applicants based on either documentation screening, a language proficiency test (either Japanese or English), or an interview.

The academic calendar is as follows: spring term, April (new enrollment) to mid-July; summer session, late July to late August; fall term, early September (new enrollment) to late December; and winter term, early January to March.

For further details, students should contact the GSAPS Admissions Office mentioned below.

Finances

For the academic year 1998–99, the tuition fee is ¥1,300,000 plus a special program fee (first year only) of ¥400,000.

International Students

International students are encouraged to apply. Forty percent of the student body are international students who come from twelve countries, including China, Indonesia, Korea, and the U.S. The goal is for up to one half of all students to come from abroad. Students can take a degree in either Japanese or English (not all courses are given in English). The GSAPS Office helps students to adjust to life in Tokyo. It offers counseling on immigration regulations as well as academic, finance, and personal concerns.

Application Facts and Dates

Students should address all correspondence to:

Admissions Office
Graduate School of Asia-Pacific
   Studies
Waseda University
1-21-1 Nishi-waseda, Shinjuku-ku
Tokyo 169-0051, Japan
Telephone: 011-81-3-5286-3877
Fax: 011-81-3-5272-4533
E-mail: gsaps@mn.waseda.ac.jp
World Wide Web: http://www.waseda.
   ac.jp/gsaps/e-b/f.html

Washburn University of Topeka

Topeka, Kansas

> ### DEVELOPING BUSINESS LEADERS FOR THE 21ST CENTURY
>
> *Any successful organization must have leaders who know how to motivate people to get things done in a rapidly changing, highly competitive world. The Washburn program is designed for men and women who want to sharpen their managerial and leadership skills while continuing on the job; the objective is to help the student learn concepts and decision-making tools that are directly relevant to the work place. Washburn University is intimately connected to the business community it serves. We are committed to the highest standards of quality and professionalism. If you have the drive, the intellect, and the perseverance to maximize your managerial potential, come and look us over.*
>
> *—Lawrence E. McKibbin, Dean and Professor of Management*

Programs and Curricular Focus

The Washburn M.B.A. curriculum combines opportunities to develop one's skills in communication, quantitative analysis, computer technology, and teamwork with study of accountancy, economics, finance, information systems, general management, marketing, legal and ethical issues, production and operations management, and international business in the context of domestic and global enterprise. Students with a prior business degree and proficiency in quantitative methods may attain the M.B.A. by completing 30 semester hours (ten courses). For the nonbusiness undergraduate, as many as 55 semester hours (nineteen courses) may be required. The typical student requires 36 semester hours; full-time students can normally complete the 55-semester-hour program in two years.

Electives beyond the required curriculum are available for those who wish to focus on a particular area of interest. Up to 9 hours of upper-level M.B.A. courses from accredited business schools or American Bar Association–accredited law schools may be transferred in by petition.

Students and the M.B.A. Experience

Washburn's current graduate student population of about 200 students consists of approximately 80 percent part-time, working professionals drawn from local industry and government and 20 percent full-time international students from many countries. Class sizes are small, ranging from 6 to 20 students for foundation and elective courses and between 30 and 40 students for upper-level required courses. Classes are conveniently scheduled on weekday evenings and occasionally on Saturday mornings.

The Faculty

Washburn's full-time graduate faculty members all have doctoral degrees. They are dedicated professors whose professional interests include teaching, practical research, and consulting with businesses, government, and educational organizations. Their job is to be on the cutting edge, to know best practices and relevant trends.

The Business School Network
Corporate Partnerships

The Topeka business and professional community includes a wide array of nationally and internationally prominent firms and government agencies. Prominent organizations include Payless ShoeSource, Hills Pet Nutrition, Southwestern Bell Telephone, Western Resources, Frito-Lay, Goodyear, Security Benefit Group, Hallmark Cards, Burlington Northern Santa Fe, and a wide variety of smaller firms. Topeka is a regional medical and financial services center, including the world-famous Menninger Foundation. The experience brought into the classroom by practicing professionals enriches the program and helps to insure its practical, applied focus.

Prominent Alumni

Washburn graduates have attained prominence in many organizations throughout the United States and in many countries. Notables include Richard Davidson, CEO of Union Pacific Railroad; Ronald Richey, CEO of Torchmark Corporation; Greg Brenneman, COO of Continental Airlines; and Steve Kitchen, CFO of Western Resources.

Reciprocal relationships connect metropolitan Topeka and the Washburn M.B.A.'s as they engage the global market place.

An Executive-in-Residence debates strategy with Washburn M.B.A.'s.

The College and Environs

Washburn University, founded in 1865, is a comprehensive public urban university of 6,500 students. Its major academic units include the College of Arts and Sciences and four professional schools— the Schools of Nursing, Applied Studies, Law, and Business. The University is fully accredited by the Commission on Institutions of Higher Education of the North Central Association of Colleges and Schools and other specialized accrediting agencies. The city of Topeka, just one hour's drive from Kansas City by interstate highway, is small enough to radiate Midwestern friendliness, yet large enough to provide regional shopping, cultural events, and entertainment. The parklike campus is located 2 miles from downtown and is surrounded by well-established picturesque residential neighborhoods that afford reasonable and comfortable housing for Washburn students.

Facilities

With modern and attractive buildings, indoor and outdoor sports facilities, state-of-the-art library and computer centers, a television station (KTWU) serving northeast Kansas, and a student union housing dining, recreation, and bookstore facilities, Washburn University provides a complete, friendly, and well-maintained campus. M.B.A. students have full access to all University facilities and student services, including athletic and cultural activities and health services.

Admission

Admission is granted to students showing high promise of success in postgraduate business study. To be considered, an applicant must hold a baccalaureate degree from a regionally accredited institution of higher education, complete forms for application to Washburn University and to the Graduate Program

in Business, take the Graduate Management Admission Test (GMAT), submit official transcripts from all previously attended institutions, and arrange for two letters to be submitted by academicians, employers, or other persons who can attest to the applicant's potential for success in graduate study in business. International applicants must hold a university credential that is equivalent to a U.S. baccalaureate degree, submit GMAT and TOEFL scores, and submit two letters of recommendation along with transcripts. Transcripts from foreign institutions submitted as part of an application for graduate study in the School of Business must be evaluated by Educational Credentials Evaluators, Inc.

Finances

Tuition for the 1998–99 academic year is $135 per credit hour for Kansas residents and $278 per credit hour for nonresidents. Most M.B.A. courses are 3 credit hours.

Application Facts and Dates

Priority deadlines for applications are November 15 for spring semester, May 1 for summer session, and July 1 for fall semester. Application materials are available from:

Director of Graduate Programs
School of Business
Washburn University
1700 S.W. College Avenue
Topeka, Kansas 66621
Telephone: 785-231-1010 Ext. 1307
Fax: 785-231-1063
E-mail: mba@washburn.edu
World Wide Web: http://www.
  washburn.edu/sobu/mba

FACULTY LIST

W. Gary Baker, Professor of Finance; Ph.D., Nebraska, 1975.

Gary Cameron, Associate Professor of Management; Ph.D., Nebraska, 1979.

Novella Noland Clevenger, Associate Professor of Taxation; LL.M., William and Mary, 1987; CPA, CFE, CGFM.

Thomas Benton Clevenger, Associate Professor of Accounting; D.B.A., Memphis, 1987; CPA.

Martha Crumpacker, Associate Professor of Management; D.B.A., Louisiana Tech, 1980.

James Eck, Professor of Finance; Ph.D., Illinois, 1979.

Robert L. Gustavson, Professor of Economics; Ph.D., Colorado, 1976.

Mary Alice Hines, C.W. King Professor of Real Estate and Finance; Ph.D., Ohio State, 1967.

Robert M. Hull, Associate Professor of Finance; Ph.D., Kansas, 1990.

Robert B. Kerchner, Associate Professor of Economics; Ph.D., Missouri-Columbia, 1973.

Aron M. Levin, Assistant Professor of Marketing; Ph.D., Kentucky, 1997.

Teresita S. Leyell, Associate Professor of Business Administration; Ph.D., Kansas, 1983.

Juliann Mazachek, Associate Professor of Accounting; Ph.D., Kansas, 1993.

Lawrence E. McKibbin, Dean and Professor of Management; Ph.D., Stanford, 1968.

Darryl W. Miller, Assistant Professor of Marketing; Ph.D., Kent State, 1994.

Richard A. Moellenberndt, Professor of Accounting; Ph.D., Nebraska, 1973; CPA.

Kanalis A. Ockree, Associate Professor of Accounting; Ph.D., Kansas, 1993; CPA.

Richard E. Olson, Professor of Economics and Business Administration; Ph.D., Nebraska, 1965; J.D., Alabama, 1978.

William L. Roach, Professor of Business Administration; Ph.D., Michigan, 1973.

Ray D. Siehndel, Associate Professor of Business Law; LL.M., Missouri–Kansas City, 1977.

Russell E. Smith, Director of Graduate Programs, School of Business, and Associate Professor of Economics; Ph.D., Illinois, 1984.

Linda L. Woolf, Associate Professor of Economics; Ph.D., Kansas State, 1979.

Gene C. Wunder, Associate Dean, School of Business, and Associate Professor of Marketing; Ph.D., Arkansas, 1987.

Wayne State University

Detroit, Michigan

THE WAYNE STATE M.B.A.—A PROGRAM FOR YOUR FUTURE

The M.B.A. program at Wayne State University is one of the oldest in the United States and, we believe, one of the finest. The School has assembled graduate faculty members who publish regularly in their discipline's most prestigious journals and who are dedicated to the highest teaching standards. The fine academic credentials and impressive professional backgrounds of the students in the M.B.A. program serve not only to attract and retain our fine faculty but also to enrich the educational experience in the program through the insights they bring to the classroom.

The faculty and staff members of the School of Business Administration have worked hard to make the graduate study of business an enjoyable and exciting experience for our M.B.A. students. Thank you for taking a closer look!

—Harvey Kahalas, Dean

Programs and Curricular Focus

Wayne State University's Master of Business Administration emphasizes the dynamic, global nature of modern business. It is intended to prepare men and women for leadership and management positions in business, government, and other types of organizations. The core and elective requirements for the program consist of 36 semester hours of study (twelve courses). Applicants with a baccalaureate degree in business administration usually meet all of the program's foundation requirements. Applicants with baccalaureate degrees in fields other than business administration may have to complete certain foundation requirements in the following areas: accounting, economics, finance, management, management information systems, marketing, mathematics, production management, and statistics. Special accelerated foundation courses have been developed to help entering M.B.A. students to meet these requirements.

In addition to taking six core courses, the M.B.A. student may select from an extensive number of elective courses in accounting, business economics, finance, industrial relations, international business, management and organization behavior, management information systems, marketing, personnel/human resources management, quality management, and taxation. Graduate-level courses in other schools and colleges of the University may also be elected with special approval of the M.B.A. program director. Students

interested in pursuing a J.D./M.B.A. should contact an adviser in the Office of Student Services.

The academic year is divided into two 15-week semesters and a split spring/summer semester; a full schedule of graduate courses is offered each term. Courses are taught in convenient suburban locations as well as on campus.

Students and the M.B.A. Experience

Wayne State M.B.A. students bring cross-cultural diversity and a broad range of employment experiences to the program. More than 93 percent of the students are employed full- or part-time, with an average of three years of work experience. Half of the M.B.A. students hold supervisory positions within their corporations.

The average student is 27 years old, with women making up 36 percent of the student base. International students comprise 10 percent of the M.B.A. population, bringing to the program valued input on business in their regions of the world.

Students in the Wayne State M.B.A. program find its strength to be the real-world experience their peers bring to classroom discussions and projects, combined with relevant business theory presented by the faculty. While 55 percent of current M.B.A. students hold undergraduate degrees in business, the

remaining half are made up of engineering, liberal arts, fine arts, and science graduates.

The Faculty

Faculty members of Wayne State's School of Business Administration are recruited from the finest graduate programs both in America and abroad, and the excellent quality of both the graduate and undergraduate students has proven to be a powerful force in retaining this talented group. The business school faculty members publish more than 200 books, journal articles, and scholarly papers each year. They are regular contributors to the finest academic journals in the business disciplines.

In addition, the School is proud of the energetic group of business executives who teach as adjunct faculty members in the M.B.A. program. These experienced professional managers are consistently well-received by their graduate students.

The Business School Network

Corporate Partnerships

Among the strong partnerships that have been established between the School of Business Administration and prominent local and international corporations are relationships with ANR Pipeline Company, Comerica, EDS, Federal Mogul, Ford Motor Company, and Kmart Corporation.

Prominent Alumni

The School of Business Administration at Wayne State University counts among its alumni a number of notable business leaders, including Victor J. Fryling, president, CMS Energy Corporation, and vice president, Consumers Power Company; Dennis O. Green, chief auditor, Citicorp and Citibank, N.A.; Eric Mittelstadt, president and CEO, GMFanuc Robotics Corporation; and Anne Regling, executive vice president, operations, Children's Hospital of Michigan.

The College and Environs

Tracing its origins to 1868, Wayne State occupies a 185-acre campus that is graced by open courtyards and malls and whose

105 buildings represent a blend of traditional and ultramodern architecture. The modern University campus is a distinctive element in Detroit's expansive cultural center, which includes the Fisher Theater, Detroit Institute of Arts, Historical Museum, Science Center, Public Library, and four University Theaters. Also near the campus are the Engineering Society of Detroit, the Detroit Medical Center, the Merrill Palmer Institute, and the General Motors World Headquarters. Detroit and south-eastern Michigan provide extensive opportunities for study, research, cultural enjoyment, and employment.

Facilities

Wayne State, with three mainframe computers, operates one of the largest computing centers in the Detroit area. Links with MichNet provide users with access to the Internet (NSFNET), SprintNet, AutoNet, and Datapac networks. The University is also linked to the BITNET academic network. The total system is available 24 hours a day.

Currently, 300 terminals and 128 dial-up lines are available for student use. Students use terminals and microcomputers in the School's six microcomputer classrooms and laboratories as an integral part of many graduate courses.

Wayne State University is the host institution for Detroit Area Library Network (DALNET), made up of twelve local libraries. Through computer terminals in the libraries, users can access more than 7.8 million volumes, representing the majority of holdings in the area's educational institutions.

Placement

Working together with the School of Business Administration, the WSU Placement Office regularly places M.B.A.

students in permanent positions locally, nationally, and internationally. The School of Business Administration annually offers a Career Day, providing students with an opportunity to meet recruiters from dozens of national and international manufacturing and service corporations; "How to Prepare for Your Business Career" is an annual conference for students interested in learning where to find the best jobs; and the M.B.A. Student Association publishes a resume book for annual corporate distribution. The University's Placement Reference Center offers information on major corporations, job searching, interviewing, and resume writing.

Admission

Admission to the Master of Business Administration program is open to students who have a baccalaureate degree in any discipline from a regionally accredited institution and who demonstrate high promise of success in the graduate study of business. A minimum 2.5 overall undergraduate honor point average (HPA) or 2.75 honor point average in the last half of the undergraduate program is required. In addition, a minimum GMAT score of 450 is required. No decision regarding a student's admission will be made without the GMAT results.

International students must have completed an appropriate four-year university-level program and, in addition to the above requirements, achieve a minimum score of 550 on the Test of English as a Foreign Language (TOEFL) or a score of at least 95 on the Michigan English Language Assessment Battery (MELAB).

Finances

The Office of Scholarships and Financial Aid provides students with information

regarding sources of funds. Graduate research assistantships are offered through the School's academic departments. Stipends for 1997–98 averaged $10,030 for nine-month appointments. University graduate and professional scholarships are also available.

Tuition per semester in 1997–98for Michigan residents was $387–$1182 (part-time) and $1341–$1977 (full-time). Non-Michigan residents paid $751–$2456 (part-time) and $2797–$4161 (full-time).

International Students

International students constitute 10 percent of the M.B.A. student body. The International Services Office offers assistance to all students with their new surroundings. The International Business Association also offers students an opportunity to know their fellow class-mates and develop international networks through special events and business functions.

Application Facts and Dates

Application deadlines for graduate admission are August 1 for the fall term, December 1 for the winter term, and April 1 for the spring/summer term. International students must provide required materials four months prior to the beginning of the term. For more information, students should address inquiries to:

Office of Student Services
School of Business Administration
Wayne State University
Detroit, Michigan 48202
Telephone: 313-577-4510
       800-910-EARN (toll-free)
Fax: 313-577-5299
World Wide Web: http://www.busadm.
  wayne.edu

West Chester University

West Chester, Pennsylvania

THE BUSINESS SCHOOL FOR FINANCIAL MARKETS

Innovative, flexible, challenging, rewarding, convenient, progressive, pragmatic, and cost-effective. These are just some of the words that I have recently heard our students use to describe the Master of Business Administration (M.B.A.) program at West Chester University (WCU). We have significantly changed the M.B.A. program during the last few years, modernizing and expanding the M.B.A. course work and giving our students a variety of format opportunities from which to choose the right program for their personal needs. The program continues to evolve. Because of the everchanging global and technological business climate, M.B.A. students must be prepared to cope with change. M.B.A. Director and Professor James Hamilton noted that because of the modifications "we are able to send more individuals back into the community as leaders equipped with increased knowledge to cope with change." Our M.B.A. graduates are people who are prepared to become actively involved in their communities and who care about the values and roles of business, their families, our society, and our government.

—Dr. Christopher M. Fiorentino, Dean

Program and Curricular Focus

West Chester University's Master of Business Administration is designed for professional growth and career advancement in today's changing business climate. It is a multidisciplinary program offering concentrations in economics/finance, management, and general business (individualized). The program consists of 30 semester hours of core courses plus 6 semester hours of courses selected from the concentration. WCU's M.B.A. program is uniquely flexible, with three options available for attending classes: accelerated, executive, and evening. Courses are the same for all options, but format, location, and admission requirements differ. On-site corporate programs are also available to organizations with sufficient student enrollment.

The accelerated program is held at Cabrini College in Radnor, Pennsylvania. It is open to candidates who have three or more years of business experience. The program takes twenty-three months to complete and consists of six 10-week sessions. Classes meet Wednesday and Friday evenings and half days on Saturday in a rotating format of two weeks on and one week off.

The evening program, held on the main campus, allows students to enroll in one, two, or three weekly classes each semester (fall, spring, and summer).

Classes are generally offered Monday through Thursday. Students progress through the program at their own pace.

The executive option is a cohort process, with class startup in the fall semester on the main campus. Classes meet every three weeks on Thursday and Friday evenings and all day on Saturday. Students are required to take 6 credit hours of classes each semester, including the summer, and complete the program in two years. Typically, participants in this program are middle- and upper-level managers who already have significant professional and/or management responsibilities. The admission process includes a personal interview with the M.B.A. director and attendance at an information session.

Students and the M.B.A. Experience

Classes are composed of individuals from diverse backgrounds and experiences. Typical classes have included engineers, doctors, certified public accountants, entrepreneurs, public employees, international students, biomedical researchers, and environmentalists. Many applicants have nonbusiness undergraduate degrees, including liberal arts. Some have graduate degrees, including doctorates and master's degrees from a variety of disciplines.

The Faculty

The greatest resource of the M.B.A. program at West Chester University is its faculty. The professors are eminently capable of teaching and advising working professionals. Predominantly full-time professors with earned doctorates, they have made a firm commitment to their department and to their students. In addition, many of them work closely with companies and institutions in the Philadelphia area, staying in close touch with the needs and developments of the companies that employ their students. The faculty members continually strive toward integrating their academic expertise with practical needs in the workplace. They relate the theoretical understanding that they bring to the classroom to actual business situations from the surrounding community. The case-study approach used by several professors is an extremely effective way to achieve such integration. The theoretical is never far from a practical setting in the M.B.A. classroom at West Chester University.

The Business School Network

All three M.B.A. program formats enjoy pragmatic relationships with area corporations, thus developing students' technical and professional leadership qualities. Opportunities for student interaction and networking with area business and industry are keystones of WCU's M.B.A. program.

The College and Environs

West Chester University is a comprehensive, multipurpose institution with the largest graduate enrollment in the Pennsylvania State System of Higher Education. West Chester is accredited by the Middle States Association of Colleges and Schools. Since 1959, graduate programs at West Chester University have provided full- and part-time students with opportunities to enhance their professional skills, obtain new knowledge, and engage in research and creative activities. WCU offers strong academic programs, an excellent faculty, and affordable tuition.

Approximately 2,000 current graduate students are enrolled in master's degree and certification programs in more than fifty areas of study. Most M.B.A. students work full-time and pursue their degrees on a part-time basis.

West Chester University is located in the borough of West Chester, 25 miles west of Philadelphia. With a population of 20,000, West Chester offers the environment and amenities of a traditional small town while also providing a full array of services. Because of the borough's proximity to Philadelphia and Wilmington, Delaware, excellent libraries, museums, performing arts centers, and other cultural resources are close by. West Chester is part of the expanding suburban complex of Philadelphia and offers many opportunities for employment.

Facilities

The Francis Harvey Green Library collection includes more than 524,000 volumes, 2,600 periodicals, and a micromedia collection representing more than 350,000 titles. The library also holds a number of special collections. Library services include reference advice, computerized online literature searches, and photo duplication. West Chester University is a member of the Tri-State College Library Cooperative and the Pennsylvania Academic Library Connectivity Initiative, which provide students with library privileges at many other libraries.

Technology Environment

The University's extensive state-of-the-art computer facilities include an IBM 4381 mainframe and more than 400 IBM and Apple workstations that are available to students. The University has Braille printers, translators, and speech synthesizers for its visually impaired students. Students can use the computing facilities 16 hours a day. Each student also has his or her own e-mail account and access to the World Wide Web.

Placement

Services at the University's Career Development Center include access to on-campus job fairs, individual career counseling, a careers library job bank, resume preparation, and referrals. Workshops are offered on resume writing, interviewing, and job-search techniques.

Admission

West Chester University's M.B.A. program seeks motivated individuals with diverse backgrounds who have demonstrated a high-quality performance as an undergraduate. Special provisions are available for candidates who do not have accounting and/or statistical course exposure. Individuals with management experience or professional experience are encouraged to apply.

The following materials should be submitted to the Office of Graduate Studies: a completed application form, including a goals statement; transcripts demonstrating high-quality performance in the major area of study; scores on the Graduate Management Admission Test (GMAT); a current resume (two copies); and two letters of recommendation.

Finances

In-state tuition and fees for 1998–99 are $678 per 3-credit course. Out-of-state students pay $1137 per 3-credit course. Graduate assistantships are available to qualified full- and part-time graduate students. In return for a 20-hour weekly service assignment to an academic department or administrative office, a full-time graduate assistant receives tuition remission and a stipend of $5000 for the academic year. Half-time assistants work 10 hours per week and receive a tuition remission for 6 credits plus a stipend of $2500 for the academic year.

Application Facts and Dates

Students are admitted for enrollment beginning in each semester. Applicants are considered throughout the calendar year on a space-available basis.

For more information, students should contact the addresses below.

Office of Graduate Studies and
    Sponsored Research
102 McKelvie Hall
West Chester University
West Chester, Pennsylvania 19383
Telephone: 610-436-2943
Fax: 610-436-2763
E-mail: gradstudy@wcupa.edu
World Wide Web: http://www.wcupa.edu
or

M.B.A. Program Director
Telephone: 610-436-2608
Fax: 610-436-3458
E-mail: mba@wcupa.edu

Widener University

Chester, Pennsylvania

THE PHILOSOPHY BEHIND THE PROGRAM

The Graduate Program in Business Administration is designed to provide aspiring and practicing managers with the skills, social sensitivity, and interdisciplinary perspective needed to assume leadership roles in society. The core curriculum and electives deal equally with theoretical concepts and their practical applications. This results in a program that offers an integrated and comprehensive exposure to the knowledge believed to be of essential and lasting value to the business or institutional professional.

—Joseph A. DiAngelo Jr., Dean

Programs and Curricular Focus

Widener's School of Business Administration provides graduate and professional programs that are accredited by AACSB–The International Association for Management Education and focus on the self-paced graduate student and the special needs of the part-time student, so that Widener's commitment to taking the education of students personally is fulfilled. The program is designed to take full advantage of the working status of the majority of its students. Unlike the full-time student, the student/employee is immersed daily in the realities of organizational life. This concurrent relationship provides students with immediate opportunities to test and validate the relevancy of classroom learning. The blending of directed classroom study and daily work-related experience reinforces learning while supplementing it with the fuller understanding of how theoretical principles must be modified and adapted to fit particular environments.

The curriculum consists of a core program comprising key elements of economic and administrative theories that underlie managerial and entrepreneurial activity and advanced courses in functional areas. The core program includes course work in accounting; economic analysis; finance; marketing; operations of technology; quantitative methods and behavioral aspects of management; social, ethical, and global issues; and strategic management. Elective course work is available in accounting, economics, environmental management, finance, human resources, international business, marketing, management information systems, and taxation.

Graduate transfer credit must be approved by the dean of the School of Business Administration and may be permitted subject to various restrictions.

The specific degree programs that are offered are the Master of Business Administration (M.B.A.); the Saturday M.B.A.; the M.B.A./CFP® track; the Master of Business Administration, Health and Medical Services Administration (M.B.A./HMSA); Master of Health Administration (M.H.A.); Master of Science in accounting; and Master of Science in taxation/CFP® track. Dual-degree programs offered are the J.D./M.B.A. in conjunction with the School of Law; M.E./M.B.A. with the School of Engineering; B.S./M.B.A. and B.S./M.S. through the School of Business Administration's undergraduate and graduate programs; Psy.D./M.B.A.(HMSA) and Psy.D./M.H.A. with Graduate Clinical Psychology; and M.D./M.H.A. and M.D./M.B.A.(HMSA) in conjunction with Jefferson Medical College of Thomas Jefferson University.

Widener also offers a Master of Public Administration degree program in the College of Arts and Sciences and, through the School of Law, LL.M. programs in corporate law and finance and health law.

Students and the M.B.A. Experience

More than 600 students, mostly in their late twenties or early thirties, are currently enrolled in a Widener part-time evening graduate business program. Classes are conveniently held in the evening between 6:30 and 9:30 and are also available on Saturdays in a seminar format. Some students choose to take as

many as three courses, which is considered a full-time program. While attending Widener, most are fully employed in a cross section of business environments, from small to large in size, encompassing manufacturing, the service industries, government, and nonprofit organizations.

❖ Global Focus

A senior executive from an international corporation has a two-year appointment as the School of Business Administration's Executive in Residence. The Executive in Residence maintains an office on campus and teaches courses. Students have the opportunity to meet with the Executive in Residence on a one-on-one basis during office hours.

Special Features

Learning by experience is incorporated into the programs in several ways. Some of the programs require clerkships, management and career development seminars, and residency experience. These are designed as vehicles to gain actual on-the-job learning and integration of academic theory with practice. Students are also invited to attend the

Widener University is located on a 100-acre suburban campus. The eighty-five buildings include a mixture of modern and Victorian architecture.

banking and finance lecture series and the Nobel Laureate lecture series.

The Faculty

The unique blend of faculty talents combines state-of-the-art education with doctorally prepared as well as industry- and public administration–experienced professionals. The primary interest of each faculty member is teaching while simultaneously developing his or her own potential through ongoing research. Teaching style focuses not only on theory but also on the practical application of this material in the workplace. Widener is proud of its mandate as a teaching institution, featuring personal attention for each student at both the undergraduate and graduate level.

The Business School Network

Widener M.B.A. students are employed by such companies and organizations as Aetna U.S. Healthcare; A. I. DuPont Institute; ARCO; Arthur Andersen & Company; Bell of Pennsylvania; Blue Cross/Blue Shield; Boeing; Campbell Soup; Chase Manhattan Bank; CIGNA; Coopers & Lybrand; Department of Defense; E. F. Hutton; General Electric; Honeywell; KPMG Peat Marwick; McNeil Lab; PECO; PFPC; PNC; RCA; QVC; SmithKline Beckman; SMS; Springfield School District; State of Delaware; Texaco; Upjohn; Vanguard; Xerox; and Zeneca.

The College and Environs

Widener University is recognized nationally and internationally as a distinguished private educational institution. An accredited university chartered in Pennsylvania and Delaware, Widener is today a three-campus university offering ninety-five programs of study leading to associate, baccalaureate, master's, or doctoral degrees.

Founded in Wilmington, Delaware, in 1821, the University is composed of eight schools and colleges that offer liberal arts and sciences, professional, and preprofessional curricula. The University's schools include the College of Arts and Sciences, the School of Engineering, the School of Hospitality Management, the School of Human Service Professions, the School of Business Administration, the School of Nursing, the School of Law, and University College.

Facilities

Graduate business students may take advantage of the variety of facilities and services offered on both the main (Chester, Pennsylvania) campus and the Delaware Campus. Classes average fewer than 25 students each in Kapelski Learning Center or Academic Center North on the main campus and in Polishook Hall on the Delaware Campus.

Libraries are equipped with online computer indexing and personal computer labs for class or individual use. Bookstores, accessible parking, and evening advisers are available on both campuses.

Placement

Graduate advisers are present each evening to help merge career goals with programs offered. To assist those who are relocating in the job market, there is a professionally staffed Career Advising and Placement Service (CAPS) on the main campus.

Admission

Admission to any of the graduate business programs involves completing the application and paying the nonrefundable application fee, submitting two letters of recommendation, and possessing a bachelor's degree. In addition, various programs require GMAT, GRE, or MAT scores, and the M.S. degree programs in taxation and accounting require the GMAT or documentation of CPA, CIA, or CMA certification. International students from non-English-speaking countries must take the Test of English as a Foreign Language (TOEFL).

Finances

For the 1997–98 academic year, students in the M.B.A. programs paid a tuition fee of $470 per credit.

Graduate assistantships are available for full-time students (up to three courses per semester). Graduate assistants aid the faculty in research projects and work approximately 20 hours per week. Assistantships are awarded to students on campus. Assistantships are compensated by a stipend and tuition remission for up to three courses.

Application Facts and Dates

Applications must be received for fall semester entrance by July 1, spring semester by December 1, and for the summer semester by April 1. Applications from international students must be received two months prior to the dates given.

For more information, students should contact:

Graduate Programs
School of Business Administration
Widener University
One University Place
Chester, Pennsylvania 19013
Telephone: 610-499-4305
Fax: 610-499-4615

Wilfrid Laurier University

School of Business and Economics

Waterloo, Ontario, Canada

CHANGING THE FACE OF BUSINESS

The speed of innovation, competitiveness, and technical complexity in all business sectors has increased dramatically. A business education cannot guarantee success in this new world. Nothing can. But obtaining a solid grounding in the functional business disciplines and mixing this with case studies, simulations, and real business activities can make a big difference. At Laurier, we seek to develop leaders. The programs emphasize strategic thinking and problem solving. The Laurier experience encourages teamwork, enthusiasm, innovation, and competitiveness.

Laurier Business and Economics is a vibrant and dynamic school. The face of business is rapidly changing, and we want to ensure that our graduates are not just another face in the crowd.

—A. Scott Carson, Ph.D., Dean

Programs and Curricular Focus

The Laurier M.B.A. program stresses the skills and abilities required to take effective action and to develop managers, not just people who know about management. Central to this philosophy is the belief that management must be problem centred and opportunity centred. While it is essential that managers know the theories and concepts of management, it is in the solving of problems that their contributions are measured.

The learning environment at Laurier enables students to develop the skills needed to be effective decision makers. The presentation and defence of one's ideas, the exchange of ideas, and the critical evaluation by one's peers form an important part of the classroom process.

Three M.B.A. programs are offered at Laurier. They provide a broad overview of the major areas of business activities and consist of ten required half-credit courses as well as ten half-credit elective courses.

The core component of the full-time program is delivered in an integrated format. The program begins in mid-August and continues for twelve months.

The part-time program, offered through late afternoon and evening courses, normally consists of two courses per term for three terms per year. It takes approximately three years to complete.

The community-based programs are offered Friday evenings and Saturdays on alternate weekends over a three-year period. The academic cycle begins in

April. Sessions are not held during the summer or from mid-December to January.

Laurier's School of Business and Economics also offers an M.A. in Business Economics that prepares economists for a career in the private sector.

Students and the M.B.A. Experience

The Laurier M.B.A. program is one of the most selective in Canada. It has the country's highest overall level of prior work experience (averaging 8.5 years) and draws students from a diverse array of academic and employment backgrounds. Coming from across Canada and around the world, fifteen percent of the students are international. Women comprise more than one third of the class. The average age of the students is 33, and all enter with a successful track record at work and a technical background in their chosen fields.

❖ Global Focus

Students have the opportunity to be involved in projects that prepare them to manage in the complexities of the global marketplace. International Study Tours offer an opportunity to combine field study with in-class components. Prior to the field-study component, students conduct background research into the country's economic, regulatory, and political environments. The experience

culminates in a two-week international excursion to the region under investigation.

Special Features

Laurier initiated Canada's first one-year M.B.A. program in 1986, recognizing a need for innovation in business education programming. The resulting integrative approach emulates the multidimensional nature of the business world. The community-based programs allow participants to enjoy the convenience of attending classes close to work and home.

The Faculty

Faculty members at Laurier are committed to the interplay between teaching and research. The combination of current research and innovative teaching provides Laurier Business and Economics students with an engaging, dynamic environment that stimulates learning. It also provides industry partners with valuable competitive intelligence.

Because Laurier boasts one of the largest business and economics faculties in Canada, it offers tremendous breadth and depth in research and teaching expertise. More than 90 faculty members publish and consult worldwide, bringing industry experience and global perspective to the classroom. This in turn strongly positions students for future business endeavours and teaches them to capitalize on new, relevant, and late-breaking business trends.

The Business School Network

Strong ties have been developed between Laurier and the corporate community. Whether through research centres, an Integrated Case Exercise, a Speaker Series, the MBA Industry Dinner, or the Laurier Business Leader of the Year Award, Laurier provides students with opportunities to connect and build relationships with local, national, and international business leaders.

The Dean's Advisory Council, consisting of distinguished CEOs, leading academics, and senior government representatives, offers advice and networks to support the strategic planning and implementation of Laurier's programs.

Students take advantage of the University's connections and partnerships when choosing applied research projects. The "Adopt-A Company" initiative provides students with an opportunity to apply the techniques they have learned in the classroom to solve practical strategic management issues.

The Laurier Institute offers customized management development programs and open enrolment, as well as self-employment programs and case competitions.

The College and Environs

Located in the hub of Canada's Technology Triangle, one of the most prosperous areas in the country, and only an hour away from metropolitan Toronto, Laurier is ideally situated. Laurier's main campus is located in the city of Waterloo in the province of Ontario, Canada. The twin cities of Kitchener-Waterloo, with a combined population of approximately 275,000, are located 112 kilometers west of Toronto and 128 kilometers northwest of Niagara Falls. Throughout the region of Waterloo, the rich history, vigorous industry, and the high quality of life are readily apparent. Community-based campuses are located in southwestern Ontario (Sarnia) as well as in Toronto.

Established in 1910 as Waterloo Lutheran Seminary, the institution later became known as Waterloo Lutheran University. In 1973, Wilfrid Laurier University became one of Ontario's provincially funded universities.

Technology Environment

First-class computing facilities are provided through a voluntary student-funded organization. All labs are equipped with Pentium and 486 computers and have Internet access. The School also provides notebook computers for overnight/weekend sign out. Through corporate assistance, an extensive upgrading of all classroom facilities within Laurier Business and Economics has resulted in full multimedia capabilities.

Placement

Career Services provide assistance to all students both on an individual and group basis. The services are part of students' activities from their first term through graduation and beyond (with the Alumni Referral Service).

Throughout the academic year, a number of workshops are offered on a regular basis. These include resume writing, job search techniques, and networking and informational interviewing. As well, programs and special events are scheduled throughout the academic year. These include an annual M.B.A. Fair and Employer Information Sessions. Each fall and winter semester, representatives from business, industry, government, and social services visit the campus to interview for permanent employment available following graduation. Job postings, application deadlines, and interview dates are posted in Career Services. Many small and medium-sized employers as well as large corporations take advantage of the popular service.

Admission

Admission to the M.B.A. program is competitive and is based on the following criteria: a recognized undergraduate degree (or its equivalent), with a minimum B average in the final year of study (72 percent, a 3.0 GPA, or second class honours); GMAT results (scores above 550 preferred); full-time work experience (two years or its equivalent); and three letters of reference (normally one academic and two professional). Applicants whose language of instruction during the undergraduate degree was not English must furnish evidence of proficiency in English; a minimum of 550 on the TOEFL exam, or its equivalent, is required.

Finances

Tuition for the 1998–99 academic year for Canadian full-time M.B.A. students is Can$4860 and Can$2628 for part-time students. International students pay Can$10,500 for the full-time program. Fees, books, case materials, and supplies are approximately Can$2560 per year for full-time students and Can$1500 per year for part-time students.

The total tuition for community-based programs is currently Can$22,000, with an additional material and services fee that ranges between Can$4000-Can$6000 for the total program. Fees are payable on an installment basis, three times per year.

Financial assistance is available to qualified applicants.

Application Facts and Dates

Applications for the full- and part-time programs are considered for the fall term only. Students are encouraged to submit a completed application early in the year in order to be considered for the first round of offers. The final date to apply is May 1. Applications for the community-based programs should be received by February 15 for an April start.

For further information, students should contact:

Dianne Hotson
Program Administrator
SBE Graduate Programs Office
Wilfrid Laurier University
75 University Avenue
Waterloo, Ontario N2L 3C5
Canada
Telephone: 519-884-0710 Ext. 2544
Fax: 519-886-6978
E-mail: wlumba@wlu.ca
World Wide Web: http:/www.wlu.ca/
~wwwsbe

Willamette University

Salem, Oregon

A QUALITY LEARNING EXPERIENCE

The education and professional development of Atkinson students are the top priority of Atkinson faculty and staff.

Our focus on teaching, integration, and the practical application of knowledge builds the perspective, experience, and decision-making skills needed for successful managerial careers, and our collegial atmosphere helps students develop the confidence and team skills of successful managers.

Our learning environment has already earned national recognition for the Atkinson School, and we remain firmly committed to providing a distinctive graduate management education—an education that offers the strategic benefits of professional growth, real-world experience, and confidence to meet the managerial challenges of today and tomorrow.

—Steven M. Maser, Interim Dean

Programs and Curricular Focus

The Master of Management (M.M.) program prepares students for careers in business, government, and not-for-profit organizations. The M.M. enhances understanding of management decision making through an integrated curriculum, global perspective, and emphasis on the practical application of knowledge. The Atkinson School M.M. degree is the only program in the U.S. to be accredited for both business administration (AACSB—The International Association for Management Education) and public affairs/administration (NASPAA).

The program is two academic years in length and is composed of 30 credits of core curriculum (ten courses) and 30 credits of elective curriculum (ten courses). The balance of required and elective courses ensures a broad understanding of the functions of management and the flexibility to pursue career goals. Cocurricular seminars enhance teamwork, strategic career management, and communication skills.

The core curriculum is project based, experiential, and cross-functional in nature; it also crosses sectors by integrating the legal, international, negotiation, and ethical issues of management. The integrated and project-based curriculum helps students apply their knowledge to changing environments and recognize the internal and external factors that influence managerial decisions.

The elective curriculum provides the opportunity to pursue a generalist perspective or greater knowledge in an area of interest, including accounting, finance, general management, human resource management, international management, marketing, organizational analysis, public management, and quantitative analysis/management science.

Teaching methods include lecture, case study, team projects, consulting projects with organizations, group discussions, simulations, student presentations, internships, and independent study/research.

An accelerated, waiver-based M.M. program is available for qualified students. Willamette University also offers a four-year joint degree in law and management (J.D./M.M.).

Students and the M.B.A. Experience

The Atkinson student profile is characterized by a diversity of age and experience common in organizations. The average student is 26 years of age and has three years of work experience. Thirty percent of the student population are women, 25 percent are international students, and 10 percent are minority students. Although generally from the Western United States, students come from twent-two states and twenty-one countries. Most Atkinson students have undergraduate degrees in social science, liberal arts, or business. Most enter the program with experience in business, government, or not-for-profit organizations, but some enter directly after their undergraduate education.

The School's size and exclusive focus on the master's level of study facilitates a high degree of accessibility and interaction between faculty and students. The learning environment is collegial and emphasizes teamwork and the practical application of knowledge. The program demands approximately 60 hours of academic work per week.

❖ Global Focus

The core curriculum integrates international issues of management, and the elective curriculum supports career interests in international management.

Special Features

Each year begins with Compass Week, a program of teamwork, strategic career management, academic review, and perspectives on important issues of management.

The core curriculum includes an extensive "hands-on" management project in which teams of students create a business, make a profit, close the business, and use the profits to provide a not-for-profit service.

The Faculty

The Atkinson School faculty members are excellent teachers and nationally and internationally respected scholars. They are recipients of awards for outstanding teaching and research; leaders of professional and community organizations; authors of books, articles, software, and simulations; and consultants to business and government.

One hundred percent of the full-time faculty members have the doctorate. Ninety-one percent have worked, consulted, or completed academic work internationally. Seventy-three percent have received awards for outstanding teaching/research. Eighteen percent are women.

Three endowed faculty chairs (business, public policy, and international management) provide additional resources for faculty to pursue teaching innovation and scholarly research.

The Business School Network

Corporate Partnerships

Interaction with leaders of business, government, and not-for-profit organiza-

tions is frequent and occurs through class projects, faculty/student consulting projects, internships, the visiting executive program, guest speakers, career services seminars, and site visits.

Prominent Alumni

The average alumnus is 37 years old and pursuing a career in small to large businesses, entrepreneurial ventures, government service, or not-for-profit organizations. Seventy percent of Atkinson alumni live and work in the Pacific Northwest. Thirty percent are located throughout the United States and internationally.

Information regarding titles and employers of Atkinson alumni will be provided on request.

The College and Environs

Willamette University is an independent coeducational university with a total of 2,200 students enrolled in the College of Liberal Arts (1,500), College of Law (400), Atkinson Graduate School of Management (180), and the School of Education (80). The University was founded in 1842 and is recognized for excellence and innovation in academic and professional education. Willamette University is located in Salem, Oregon. Salem, the state capital of Oregon, is recognized as one of the most livable cities in the United States and has been named an "All America City." Acclaimed for its balance of career opportunities and quality of life, the Pacific Northwest is one of the fastest-growing areas of the United States.

Technology Environment

Atkinson students have 24-hour-a-day access to the computer laboratory, which provides Macintosh and IBM-compatible personal computers. A local network provides all standard word processing, spreadsheet, and graphics applications. The Internet provides access to worldwide information services and electronic mail. University library resources include books, periodicals, journals, and specialized computerized information databases, such as ABI/INFORM, CD-ROM Compact Disk Disclosure, CD-ROM National Trade Data Bank, and CD-ROM Predicast F&S.

Placement

The Atkinson School works with employers to provide a complete program of services connecting students and alumni with employment opportunities. Career service programs help students develop strategic career management skills, improve job search skills, and obtain internships and employment. Services include workshops, internship programs, on-campus interviews, employment opportunity postings, national employment databases, individual counseling, mentoring programs, the West Coast MBA Consortium interview program with national employers, and the Pacific Northwest MBA Career Fair.

Admission

The Atkinson School welcomes applicants with diverse career objectives and experiences. Admission is based on academic ability and managerial potential. All applicants must submit an application for admission, the application fee, a personal statement of experience and professional goals, two letters of reference, official transcripts of all undergraduate and graduate course work, and official GMAT or GRE scores. International students for whom English is not the first language must also submit a minimum TOEFL score of 550 and provide documentation of funds sufficient to cover two years of educational and living expenses.

The average GMAT score is between 540 and 560. The undergraduate GPA is 3.2. There are no specific prerequisite courses for admission, but students should have a solid understanding of mathematical principles and well-developed writing skills. Previous experience with economics, accounting, and personal computers (word processing and spreadsheet applications) is helpful.

Finances

Tuition for 1998–99 is $15,450. Books and supplies cost approximately $1000. Room and board expenses range from $4500 to $6800 per year, depending on personal choice of accommodations and lifestyle. Approximately 50 percent of full-time students receive merit-based scholarship assistance ranging from 25 percent to 75 percent of tuition. Loans and work-study are available to eligible students.

Application Facts and Dates

Applications completed by March 31 receive priority consideration in admission and scholarship decisions. Applicants are notified by mail when their application materials are received and are notified of the admission decision within three weeks after completion of the application process. For further information, contact:

Director of Admission
Atkinson Graduate School of
　Management
Willamette University
Salem, Oregon 97301
Telephone: 503-370-6167
Fax: 503-370-3011
E-mail: agsm-admission@willamette.
　edu
World Wide Web: http://www.
　willamette.edu/agsm/

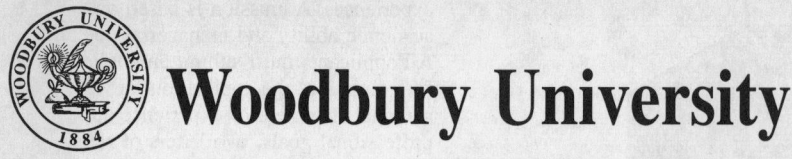

Woodbury University

Burbank, California

PREPARING BUSINESS LEADERS WITH ENTREPRENEURIAL SKILLS TO COPE WITH THE GLOBALIZATION OF BUSINESS

It has been said, "The world is like a drum; you strike it anywhere, and it resounds everywhere." This is certainly true in the world of business today. Political barriers are being erased in favor of commercial and economic flows that enhance global interaction, competition, and collaboration. The challenge for higher education is to provide our students with the entrepreneurial skills, vision, and creativity needed to lead business enterprises into the twenty-first century.

With its 114-year heritage in business education, Woodbury University has been preparing business leaders to cope with the realities of the present and to meet the challenges of the future. We are committed to preparing M.B.A. candidates with skills that support flexibility, critical thinking, and pragmatic problem solving.

—Richard King, Dean

FACULTY LIST

Tahmoures A. Afshar, M.B.A., Ph.D.
Frank Benson, CPA, CIA, CMA, CFP, Ph.D.
David R. Black, M.B.A.
Ray Briant, M.A.
John Charnay, J.D.
Inoh Choi, Ph.D.
Satinder Dhiman, M.B.A., Ed.D. (Chair of Business)
Joel Fisher, Ph.D.
Eugene B. Gendel, Ph.D.
John Gleiter, M.B.A.
Judith Heineman, M. of Human Resources and Organization
Norman Kaderlan, Ph.D.
Rauf Kahn, M.P.A., Ll.B, M.B.A., D.B.A.
Karen Kaigler-Walker, Ph.D. (Chair of Marketing)
William H. Kraus, M.P.A., D.P.A.
William Lieberman, Ph.D.
Horst J. Liebl, Ph.D.
Kenneth H. Marcus, M.B.A., Ph.D.
Qadir Mohiuddin, Ph.D.
Sheila J. Moore, M.B.A., Ph.D.
Gwynda J. Myers, M.B.A., Ph.D.
Jon W. Myers, CPA, M.B.A. (Chair of Accounting)
J. U. Overall IV, Ph.D.
Marvin J. Richman, M.U.P., M.B.A.
Alexandra Saba, Ph.D.
Kailas C. Sahu, Ph.D.
Mohammad A. Sangeladji, CPA, CMA, CCA, M.B.A., Ph.D.
Robert A. Schultz, Ph.D. (Chair of Computer Information Systems)
Sameer Shah, M.I.M.
Xiaochuan Song, M.A., M.S.
Hamid Taheri, M.B.A., CPA
Vivian A. Terr, J.D.
Ravi Tripuraneni, M.B.A., Ph.D.

Programs and Curricular Focus

The high quality of course work in Woodbury University's M.B.A. program is affirmed by the school's accreditation by the Association of Collegiate Business Schools and Programs (ACBSP). The courses in accounting, computer information systems, finance, international business, management, and marketing all emphasize teamwork and presentation skills. Designed primarily for those fully employed, classes are scheduled on weekends and evenings. More than 30 percent of the M.B.A. students are international and attend Woodbury's M.B.A. program full-time.

The M.B.A. curriculum has a comprehensive management core that provides the basic foundation for understanding the various business disciplines and prepares the student for further study in general or specific interest areas. Areas of emphasis provide the opportunity for students to study more intensively according to their goals. Accounting covers major areas required for the CPA examination. Computer information systems includes systems design and development, communication networks, the Internet, and Web site development. Finance includes financial institutions, corporate finance, mergers and acquisitions, investment analysis, and capital markets. International business includes finance, economics, marketing, world business area studies, and comparative management. Management includes organizational behavior/human relations, policy studies, organizational theory, management systems, strategic planning, entrepreneurship, and strategy formulation. Marketing includes international marketing, advertising, contemporary marketing problems, and market research.

Woodbury courses are offered on the semester system. Candidates for the degree must complete 36 units or a total of twelve 3-unit courses. Students who hold undergraduate degrees in a discipline other than business may have to complete additional preparatory courses called the Common Professional Component, which may be waived through testing or work experience or taken as electives. Up to 6 units may be transferred from another accredited institution.

The program's flexibility allows for scheduling variations. A person in full-time employment typically takes two courses per term and can complete the degree in two years. Full-time students may complete the program within a year. There is no pressure, however, to conform to a particular schedule.

Students and the M.B.A. Experience

Professional men and women are drawn to the Woodbury M.B.A. program from a variety of industries in the United States and abroad. Often sponsored by their home governments or multinational corporations, international students come to Woodbury's program from Brazil, China, Egypt, Indonesia, Chile, Nigeria, and Thailand as well as thirty other nations. Approximately 40 per-cent have undergraduate business degrees; the remaining 60 percent have done their undergraduate work in such fields as engineering, humanities, and the social sciences.

The Woodbury M.B.A. program does not lock candidates into one particular peer group. Instead, students get the opportunity to work with many different students as they explore each new subject area. In addition to strengthening the key business skill of team building, this structure allows an M.B.A. candidate to acquire the widest possible interaction with fellow students and professors. Class sizes are small, with an average of 18 students.

The Faculty

The Woodbury M.B.A. program augments its forward-looking orientation with faculty members who are leaders in their respective fields. A combination of full-time academics and seasoned professionals, Woodbury's M.B.A. professors have excellent academic credentials, which are complemented with current corporate executive and management experience. They come to Woodbury from the management ranks of major corporations and from entrepreneurial efforts in fields such as artificial intelligence and global management consulting, as well as from the most distinguished academic institutions, including Berkeley, Harvard, Stanford, and the Wharton School of Business.

The Business School Network

Corporate Partnerships

Ties between Woodbury's M.B.A. program and the southern California business community are strengthened by a large number of faculty members who are active participants in the day-to-day world of free enterprise. Teaching professionals come to Woodbury from such firms as The Walt Disney Company, Pacific Bell, and NASA.

Prominent Alumni

Woodbury graduates join a network of professionals who are business leaders in every part of the world—from a regional manager for a multinational oil company in Bangkok to an international banker from Mexico to an information systems director in Toronto. In Los Angeles, Woodbury alumni are found in the major accountancy firms and investment houses and in the entertainment industry, as well

as in the fields of health care, information systems, and multimedia.

Alumni forums and a mentor program provide opportunities to solidify business relationships formed in the classroom.

The College and Environs

Situated in the hills of Burbank, the northernmost suburb of Los Angeles and media capital of the world, Woodbury offers students easy access to beaches, mountains, and deserts; it is within a 20-minute drive of downtown Los Angeles. Art, history, and science museums; professional sports events; and world-class entertainment are activities readily accessible to Woodbury students.

One of the largest cities in the United States, Los Angeles serves as a worldwide business and financial center. The University is linked to the international business, financial, design, and commercial communities, providing networking and career development opportunities for students who choose to take advantage of the wealth of business opportunities in southern California.

Facilities

Housed in a relaxing, cathedral-style building, Woodbury's Los Angeles Times Library provides a valuable resource for M.B.A. students to study either on campus or from wherever they may be with their personal computers. Multiple databases are available over the Internet via student passwords and offer access to more than 6,000 journals through online subscriptions, including LEXIS-NEXIS and Proquest Direct. The library houses a comprehensive collection of books, periodicals, CD-ROMs, and technical and year-end reports that are selected to meet the curricular needs of the students.

Woodbury also provides a modern online computer resource center that features sixty Windows PC and Macintosh computers with the latest in business and graphics software plus printers and scanners.

On-campus housing is available in two residence halls, which accommodate up to 189 students. Residential areas surrounding Woodbury also provide plenty of options for off-campus housing.

Placement

The Office of Career Services offers students individual, personal career counseling. In addition to annual career fairs and online job search facilities, the office coordinates mentor seminars, internships, job referrals, and career and resume development workshops.

Admission

M.B.A. candidates may begin study during any term. A bachelor's degree from an accredited institution and a minimum GPA of 2.5 are required for admission. Students with undergraduate degrees from institutions outside the United States may submit transcripts for individual consideration. The completed application should be submitted with a $35 fee ($50 for international students), transcripts from all colleges attended, TOEFL score (if applicable), and two letters of recommendation from professors or employers. The GMAT must be taken within the first two terms at Woodbury, but is not required for admission.

Finances

Tuition for the academic year 1998–99 is $550 per unit, making the tuition for the twelve-course M.B.A. program $19,800. Each semester, the University charges a services fee of $150 per semester plus the M.B.A. Association fee of $30. To approximate other costs, the University uses the California Student Aid Commission estimate of at least $9144 for two semesters for food, housing, transportation, books, and miscellaneous expenses.

Financial aid in the form of federal government subsidized and unsubsidized loans is available to U.S. citizens; international students may take out loans through private lending.

Application Facts and Dates

For applications, students may contact:

Master of Business Administration
Woodbury University
7500 Glenoaks Boulevard
Burbank, California 91510-7846
Telephone: 818-767-0888 Ext. 261
Fax: 818-767-0032
E-mail: mba@vaxb.woodbury.edu
World Wide Web: http://www.
woodburyu.edu

Worcester Polytechnic Institute

> ### THE MANAGEMENT OF TECHNOLOGY
>
> *An exciting opportunity in graduate management education is available at WPI, the nation's third-oldest private technological university. With our mission to educate students to contribute meaningfully to the management of organizations in a global, technical, and competitive environment, we prepare our graduates to address the key issues facing business today and in the future.*
>
> *A New England location, small college environment, dedicated faculty, outstanding facilities, and superior record of graduates' successes make WPI one of the nation's most respected names in technology-based education.*
>
> —McRae C. Banks, Harry G. Stoddard Professor of Management and Department Head

Programs and Curricular Focus

Worcester Polytechnic Institute (WPI) offers a variety of graduate management programs focusing on the management of technology. WPI's Master of Business Administration (M.B.A.) program is a highly integrated, applications-oriented M.B.A. program. The WPI M.B.A. provides students with both the "big picture" perspective required of successful upper-level managers and the hands-on knowledge needed to meet the daily demands of the workplace. WPI's focus on the management of technology comes from the recognition that rapidly changing technology is driving the pace of business. WPI ensures that its students understand leading and managing in high technology organizations, converting technology into new products and services that the market values, and integrating technology into the workplace. The program's strong emphasis on behavior skills prepares students to be leaders in any organization, and the global threads throughout the curriculum ensure that students understand the global imperative facing all businesses.

WPI's M.B.A. program features a 16-credit core of five cross-functional courses designed to give students a larger framework for understanding disciplinary material that is critical for managers in a globally competitive technological world. Core courses include interpersonal and leadership skills for technological managers, creating and implementing strategy for technological organizations, creating processes in technological organizations, business analysis for technological managers, and legal and ethical context of technological organizations. Each core course, with

the exception of legal and ethical context of technological organizations, has prerequisite requirements from within an 18-credit foundation. The purpose of the foundation is to ensure that students have a solid understanding of the basic functions carried out in organizations and of the environment in which they operate as well as an introduction to the tools used to analyze business problems. Foundation courses consist of the following nine 2-credit courses, each of which covers a major functional area of business: financial accounting, finance, organizational behavior, production/operations management, quantitative methods, principles of marketing, management information systems, economics of the firm, and domestic and global economic environment of business. Foundation-level courses are potentially waivable based on prior graduate or undergraduate course work.

The M.B.A. program also features a capstone Graduate Qualifying Project (GQP), which provides students with a hands-on, real-world opportunity to apply and enhance their classroom experience.

M.B.A. students are required to complete 12 credit hours of free elective course work, which may be taken within the Department of Management or within other academic departments at WPI. In addition, students have a 6-credit Option for Specialization, which requires 6 additional credits in a particular functional area in combination with at least 6 credits of the free electives in the chosen area.

WPI also offers two highly specialized 30-credit Master of Science (M.S.) programs specifically designed for individuals seeking advanced academic training in a

particular area. These include the M.S. in marketing and technological innovation and the M.S. in operations and information technology.

All graduate management degree programs provide internship, thesis, and independent study options. Part-time students typically complete the M.B.A. program in three to five years, dependent upon prior academic background, while full-time students may complete the M.B.A. program in as little as one year, dependent upon prior academic background. An M.S. degree program is typically completed in two to four years part-time or one year full-time.

Students and the M.B.A. Experience

Approximately 225 students are currently enrolled in WPI's graduate management programs. The majority are working professionals pursuing their degrees part-time in the evening. WPI students average seven years of prior full-time work experience when they commence their programs. Many students are practicing managers from the region's leading high-technology employers, creating a dynamic peer-to-peer educational experience as well as presenting outstanding networking opportunities. Students bring to class their experiences in the computer, electronics, biotechnology, machine tool, chemical, software, and defense industries, to name but a few, facilitating in-class discussions grounded in real-world experience.

Twenty-three countries are represented in WPI's Graduate Management Programs. Women comprise 25 percent of the student population. Students range in age from 21 to 56, with an average age of 33.

Special Features

Tailored to meet the challenges of working professionals, WPI offers full- and part-time graduate management study at its campuses in Worcester and Waltham, Massachusetts, as well as worldwide via its Advanced Distance Learning Network (ADLN).

Since 1979, WPI's Department of Management has been a leader in distance education. Courses are delivered worldwide to students via individual videocassettes. Students then participate in the course via electronic means (Internet, e-mail, phone, or fax). The complete WPI M.B.A. may be earned via distance education.

The Faculty

The WPI management faculty is dedicated to academic excellence through scholarship and teaching. Faculty members approach the study of management from both theoretical and applications-oriented perspectives and use the classroom as a forum for exploring traditional management principles and practices and current management topics. Case studies, lectures, discussions, and computer simulations all contribute to a stimulating and challenging instructional program.

In addition to teaching, the Department of Management's faculty members are involved in a variety of sponsored research and consulting work. A sampling of current research includes quality control in information-handling processes, supply chain management, financial distress, environmentally conscious manufacturing, international accounting differences, strategy and new venture teams, and reengineering business education.

The Business School Network

Prominent Alumni

Numerous national and international business leaders are from the ranks of WPI alumni, including Steve Anderson, chief engineer, Neles-Jamesbury; Raymond Baker, vice president of manufacturing, Uvex Safety; Neil Buske, director of division engineering, Niagara Mohawk Power; Thomas Copp, president, Spectrum Wire; Leonard Devanna, president, Commonwealth Energy Enterprises; Robert Flaherty, first vice president for investments, Prudential Securities; Robert Foley, site operations manager, Texas Instruments; Charles Gordon, senior vice president, Swank; Ira Gregorman, vice president information systems, State Street Bank; Eric Gulliksen, vice president marketing, Koehler Manufacturing; David Holt, vice president of engineering, New England Electric; Michael Horgan, area operations manager, NYNEX; James Montagnino, North American operations manager, Data General; David Oberhauser, senior scientist, Polaroid; and David White, president, R. H. White Construction.

The College and Environs

WPI is set on an 80-acre hilltop campus situated in a residential section of Worcester, Massachusetts, a city of 170,000. Located in the heart of New England, Worcester is the second-largest city in the six-state region. WPI is located near many national and international businesses and industries and enjoys close working relationships with a number of major firms.

Worcester is well known for its many colleges and for such cultural centers as the Worcester Art Museum, which houses one of the finest collections in the country, and the world-renowned American Antiquarian Society, both of which are adjacent to WPI. Also nearby is the historic Higgins Armory Museum and the New England Science Center. Music is well represented by several excellent choruses, a symphony orchestra, and concerts performed by internationally recognized artists in the beautifully restored Mechanics Hall, one of the finest concert halls in the U.S. The city is home to several theater companies, and the 15,500-seat Worcester Centrum and the new Worcester Convention Center host a wide variety of entertainment events and meetings.

The city is within an easy drive of many historical sites, cultural centers, and recreational facilities. These include Boston's Freedom Trail, Old Sturbridge Village (a living museum depicting the 1830s rural village life), the beaches of Cape Cod and Maine, the ski slopes of New Hampshire and Vermont, the splendid country charm of the Berkshires, and several major metropolitan areas featuring world-class museums, concert halls, and professional sports teams.

Facilities

WPI's Computer Center (CCC) provides a full range of services and access to computer resources for the WPI community. Computer facilities are accessible from a wide variety of locations on campus, by modem, or from around the world via the Internet. The CCC workstation room houses twenty-four UNIX workstations. A PC file server drives laser printers in both the CCC and the Advanced Document Preparation (ADP) Lab and provides file service for several software packages, including PC-based desktop publishing and a scientific typesetting system. The microcomputer lab for the Department of Management, located in the Washburn Shops, currently includes thirteen high-end IBM-compatible microcomputers and is regularly updated to support state-of-the-art business software. In all, more than 350 personal computers are available for student use in general-access laboratories, computer classrooms, and specialized laboratories.

WPI's Gordon Library is home to more than 345,000 bound volumes and subscribes to more than 1,200 periodicals, supporting all graduate areas. The library provides online search services to hundreds of databases, interlibrary loan services, technical support, Internet access, CD-ROM databases, and a variety of other research support services.

Placement

The services of WPI's Career Development Center (CDC) are available to all WPI students and alumni. In a typical year, recruiters from more than 300 organizations, including large and small industrial firms, government, and civic and professional organizations, visit the campus. The CDC maintains a large reference library for WPI students and alumni. The CDC is also involved in on-campus recruiting, hot line job listings, resume referral, and corporate presentations.

Admission

Admission to WPI's graduate management programs is competitive. Admission is granted to applicants whose academic and professional records indicate the likelihood of success in a challenging academic program and whose career aspirations are in line with the focus of the specific degree program.

Applicants should have the analytic aptitude and academic preparation necessary to complete a technology-oriented management program. This includes a minimum of three semesters of college-level math or two semesters of college-level calculus. Applicants are also required to have an understanding of computer systems.

Current students have an average GMAT score of 560 and an average undergraduate CQPA of 3.1. The minimum TOEFL requirement is 550.

Finances

The estimated tuition and fees for full-time graduate students are $12,000 per academic year. Books and supplies average $900 per year. Local apartment rentals average $400 per month. The 1998–99 tuition rate is $636 per credit hour.

A limited number of fellowships are available for full-time students. Students should contact the Director of Graduate Management Programs for details.

Application Facts and Dates

Applicants are required to submit a formal application, a nonrefundable $50 application fee (waived for WPI alumni), official transcripts of all college work, three recommendations, a GMAT report (GRE may be substituted for M.S. applicants), and a TOEFL score if applicable. Applicants are accepted on a rolling admissions basis. Applicants should contact:

Norman D. Wilkinson
Director of Graduate Management
  Programs
Worcester Polytechnic Institute
100 Institute Road
Worcester, Massachusetts 01609

Telephone: 508-831-5218
Fax: 508-831-5720
E-mail: wpigmp@wpi.edu

Wright State University

College of Business and Administration

Dayton, Ohio

STRIVING FOR EXCELLENCE

The College of Business and Administration at Wright State University is proud to be part of a major metropolitan university that cherishes and embraces its neighboring communities. Wright State University's mission includes a ". . . commitment to providing leadership addressing the educational, social, and cultural needs of the Greater Miami Valley and to promoting the economic and technological development of the region through a strong program of basic and applied research and professional service. Wright State desires to create an intellectually exciting community and encourages all students and faculty to strive for excellence." The College of Business and Administration, which is endowed with a rich tradition of academic excellence, is an integral part of this exciting endeavor and is committed to playing a critically important role in meeting the business and educational challenges in our region and beyond.

As the dean of the College of Business and Administration, I am proud to serve as the articulator and facilitator for many new and challenging initiatives as we embark on the twenty-first century. The faculty, students, and staff form a collaborative team that is involved in moving our college into the future. New initiatives focus on quality in education, leadership through teamwork, economic development, globalization, faculty and staff development, new program and new process developments, and developing networking relationships with businesses and other professional organizations.

—Rishi Kumar, Dean

Programs and Curricular Focus

The Wright State M.B.A. program provides a high-quality education that is both broad-based and professionally relevant. The program addresses the diverse needs of students through a three-stage curriculum. The first stage provides preparatory business course work for those individuals who lack such preparation or who need to update their background. The second stage gives the student a broad business base, utilizing quantitative tools and teamwork within the case method approach. Stage three allows students to pursue an area of study of particular interest to them.

Roughly 50 percent of the students entering the Wright State M.B.A. program do not have any undergraduate business courses, and others need to update or upgrade their knowledge. The first stage of the program consists of a series of survey courses. The courses provide the students with the necessary academic background to be successful in the program. The courses entail accountancy, computer work, economics, finance, management, management science, marketing, mathematics, and statistics. The focus of the courses is to

relate material that the student will need to better understand and master the advanced M.B.A. course work. Students with a strong undergraduate background in business may not need to take any of these courses.

The second phase of the program, common to all students, entails advanced study of business, including an integration of the business disciplines. There is a significant case study and teamwork component in this stage of the course work. Cases from business in the areas of accountancy, finance, management, operations, and marketing are analyzed by individuals within their team of students and presented to the class. The students thus apply their knowledge of the discipline to real-world situations, while developing their communication skills. Approximately 50 percent of the courses, including economics, management science, and operations management, utilize quantitative methods. This helps students further develop their analytical skills.

The third stage of the students' study has a concentrated focus. Students can choose areas from business economics, finance, financial administration, health-

care management, international business, logistics management, management, management information systems, marketing, operations management, and project management. This stage of study is planned with faculty advisers.

Students may choose to complete an additional degree while pursuing the M.B.A. degree. Degrees in social and applied economics and nursing are available.

Students and the M.B.A. Experience

The M.B.A. student body is one of the program's greatest strengths. The diversity of backgrounds enriches the educational experience of all. Upon admission to the program, almost 50 percent of the students have an undergraduate degree in business, another 25 percent studied engineering, around 15 percent were in mathematics and the sciences, and the remaining 10 percent studied the humanities, nursing, education, and other disciplines. More than 6 percent of the students have already earned another advanced degree. Although 57 percent of the students graduated from Midwestern colleges, almost 10 percent attended colleges in the South, another 10 percent in the West, and 5 percent in the Northeast. Nearly 15 percent of the students earned their degree from a non-U.S. institution.

Students bring with them a wealth of work experience, averaging about six years of full-time work experience from a wide array of industries and occupations. About 18 percent of admitted students have no full-time work experience. Women comprise 40 percent of the student body. This diverse student body contributes to lively classroom discussion and enhances the analyzing of cases by student teams.

The Faculty

The 59 graduate faculty members of the College also have very diverse backgrounds. Over 90 percent (54) hold a doctoral degree in their area of teaching responsibilities. Sixty percent of the degrees were earned at Midwestern institutions, over 15 percent from institutions in the West, over 10 percent at schools in the South, and the remainder from universities in the Northeast or overseas. Almost 15 percent (8) are women. Although research is important, the emphasis is on the application of knowledge. A number of the faculty members have been employed outside of academia in full-time jobs and as consultants. They bring this wealth of experience to the classroom to bring theory to life.

The Business School Network

The College's Board of Advisors are respected leaders from the greater Dayton area. They come from manufacturing, banking, retailing, consulting, and nonprofit and governmental organizations. The board advises the College on a wide range of important issues, such as curricula and faculty development.

The College and Environs

Wright State University, founded in the mid-1960s, is located in suburban Dayton, Ohio. Over 16,000 students (more than 3,000 graduate students) from almost fifty different countries are pursuing studies in approximately 100 undergraduate majors and more than 30 graduate programs. The 557-acre campus has twenty-two major buildings, including a 10,632- to 13,000-seat multipurpose sports and entertainment complex, while also maintaining a 200-acre biological preserve.

The campus in Dayton is 75 minutes from Cincinnati and Columbus. Students can take advantage of cultural, entertainment, sports, and educational events in all three of these cities. The climate in southwestern Ohio allows one to enjoy all four seasons, with the average normal temperature ranging from 80°F in the summer to 20°F in the winter.

Placement

Wright State's placement activities are centralized in the Office of Career Services. This office assists undergraduate and graduate students from all degree programs in finding internship and co-op positions during their education and employment after graduation. Individual and group career counseling and planning are available. The office offers a job search course, resume preparation assistance, and resume referral (electronic and paper); it also arranges interviews and conducts successful career fairs. The office has available many publications that can assist students with their job search and career planning.

Admission

The College considers a number of factors in making admission decisions.

All applicants must hold a baccalaureate degree from a regionally accredited institution (individuals graduating from a non-U.S. institution must hold the equivalent of a four-year U.S. baccalaureate), submit official transcripts from all postsecondary institutions attended, have official scores on the Graduate Management Admission Test (GMAT) sent, and pay a $25 application fee. International students need to send official scores on the Test of English as a Foreign Language (TOEFL).

Students who have met all standards for admission to the program will be considered for admission on a regular basis and without conditions. Students with an admission index (AI) of 1000 using the overall undergraduate grade point average (UGPA) or an AI of 1050 using the last half UGPA are eligible for regular admission but are not guaranteed this status. The AI is computed by multiplying the UGPA by 200 and adding the total GMAT score. Applicants who have completed graduate-level course work must have a 3.0 graduate GPA to be considered for regular admission. International applicants must meet the 550 minimum acceptable score on the TOEFL. Once these thresholds are met, the College's admission committee reviews the application materials and makes its recommendation to the School of Graduate Studies for a final determination.

Admission is granted for each quarter: fall, winter, spring, and summer. Approximately 740 students were admitted to the M.B.A. program during 1996 and 1997. The average UPGA was 3.1, and the average GMAT score was 524. The average age was 30, the average length of full-time work experience was five years (although about 15 percent had none), more than 40 percent were women, approximately 10 percent were members of minority groups, and 20 percent were international. They held degrees in a wide array of disciplines, with 5 percent having previously earned another graduate degree.

Finances

For 1997–98, the cost of 1 to 10½ credit hours was $148 per credit hour for Ohio residents and $263 for nonresidents. For 11 to 18 credit hours, it was $1563 per quarter for Ohio residents and $2799 per quarter for nonresidents. The international student fee was $52 per quarter. On-campus room and board (double occupancy) averaged $475 per month per

person; off-campus room and board (double occupancy) averaged $450 per month per person. The approximate cost of books and supplies was estimated at $80 per course.

Graduate assistantships and fellowships are available to M.B.A. students, including first-year students, in addition to other traditional student loan programs. The Office of Financial Aid, E136 Student Union, administers the campus-based aid and student loan programs; there is an April 1 application deadline. The College administers the graduate fellowship program for full-time students. The fellowships are academically based and cover all tuition costs. The College administers the graduate assistantship (GA) program. GA applications are circulated to the departments for a decision approximately two months prior to the requested starting quarter. Over 40 GAs are employed by the College. A monthly (September through June) stipend of $360 (minimum) plus tuition waiver is paid in exchange for the student working an average of 20 hours per week for the College.

Application Facts and Dates

Admission application decisions are made up to and including the first week of classes for a quarter. The School of Graduate Studies notifies students of the admission decision by mail within a week after the decision is made. To obtain information and application materials for the M.B.A. program, students should contact:

James Crawford
College of Business and
    Administration
110 Rike Hall
Wright State University
Dayton, Ohio 45435
Telephone: 937-775-2437
Fax: 937-775-3545
E-mail: jcrawford@wright.edu

Students should send all admission application materials to:

School of Graduate Studies
106 Oelman Hall
Wright State University
Dayton, Ohio 45435
Telephone: 937-775-2975

For information regarding international student admission, students should contact:

Office of International Student
    Programs
E190 Student Union
Wright State University
Dayton, Ohio 45435
Telephone: 937-775-5745
Fax: 937-775-5795

Xavier University

Williams College of Business Administration

Cincinnati, Ohio

AN M.B.A. WITH ENDURING VALUES

The manager-leader is an artisan of business: Simultaneously applying skills and resources from a variety of disciplines. Seeing patterns where others see confusion. Creating momentum. Sustaining progress and direction amid resistance and change. Filtering data through the insights of logic and situational consideration. Such a person has command of known business tools, yet also possesses the perspective and courage to address the unknown.

The Xavier M.B.A. degree prepares students for the business of the world. A thorough curriculum of technical skills enhancement balanced with training in multifunctional application of those skills provides the management depths and dexterity so necessary in today's dynamic business environment. Yet it is the timeless, enduring values taught here—unchanging truths for changing times— that enable graduates to become leaders in the organizations they serve and in the society in which they live.

—Dr. Michael Webb, Dean

Programs and Curricular Focus

Just as today's business environment calls for greater flexibility and product customization, so too has Xavier responded to the diverse needs of students and sponsoring organizations. This is evident in Xavier's offering of the M.B.A. in three distinct formats. Each of these AACSB–The International Association for Management Education-accredited programs delivers the required education and core attributes in a manner that addresses the needs of each student. The result is the opportunity for a highly pertinent and valuable educational experience for all Xavier M.B.A. candidates.

The Master's Program has specific features that distinguish it from the other two delivery processes described below. A central feature of this program is its focus on the individual needs of each participant, including the ability to tailor the course sequence to the participant's own academic needs. Offering flexible class scheduling, including evenings and Saturdays, the program is easily adaptable to part-time or full-time students. A highly integrated, team-based curriculum forms the basis for an especially useful degree with relevance for today and for the future. On average, part-time students earn their degrees in 2½ years.

Designed to fulfill the unique educational needs of the highly experienced executive or professional, the Executive Program is a concentrated,

nineteen-month course that includes an international field experience. Limited class sizes allow individual focus, interaction with many of Xavier's strongest faculty members, and a team environment. Each class, representing a variety of occupational and professional backgrounds, begins and completes the program together—often resulting in professional relationships with value beyond that of the M.B.A. degree itself. Course scheduling is designed to complement the participants' business responsibilities.

Xavier's On-Site Program is designed to benefit student groups and sponsoring organizations with assurance of consistency and convenience. The course provides flexible scheduling options and, if desired, certain opportunities for tailoring of course material to the individual needs of the organization. The On-Site Program is an excellent way for an organization to promote focused team-building through team learning. The program is designed for participants to earn the M.B.A. degree in two years.

Xavier M.B.A. programs require the completion of between 36 and 51 semester credit hours.

Students and the M.B.A. Experience

More than 95 percent of Xavier's M.B.A. students are working professionals who represent diverse industrial sectors such

as financial services, health care, engineering, advertising, manufacturing, and consumer products. A demographically diverse student population contributes to the depth and breadth of perspective so highly valued at Xavier. In a typical class, 35 percent are women, 10 percent members of minority groups, and 8 percent are international students.

Special Features

Both operationally and substantively, the Xavier M.B.A. program is built upon a highly integrated, team-based design with an emphasis on continuous quality improvement. The opportunity to achieve significant depth in a specific skill area is balanced by education in the effective cross-functional application of many business disciplines. The result is an M.B.A. degree that stresses broad-based leadership skills and integration of business segments into whole systems for addressing today's complex business issues.

Xavier participates in a unique partnership with approximately eighteen other accredited Jesuit M.B.A. programs located in many major metropolitan areas. This partnership allows the receiving university to accept all comparable course work completed at the original institution with a grade of B or better. The degree is awarded by the university at which more than half the core program was completed.

The Faculty

The Xavier M.B.A. faculty is made up of exceptionally skilled classroom teachers whose daily focus is to provide a consistent, effective, and meaningful class experience for all students. Faculty members regularly engage in research and other scholarly pursuits at Xavier, activities which contribute to the quality and depth of the classroom teaching approach. The M.B.A. faculty members draw from real world experiences as business managers, owners, or consultants to bring classroom topics to life with substance and perspective.

The Business School Network

The Business Advisory Council, composed of business leaders in the local

Professionals can easily balance career and family obligations while in pursuit of their M.B.A. degrees.

community, was formed in 1975 to address questions of policy planning and direction for the College of Business Administration. Its vision and involvement help assure that Xavier's M.B.A. curriculum remains closely aligned with the actual demands of business.

Prominent Alumni

Throughout the Midwest region, among any group of assembled business leaders, there is a high probability that several are Xavier M.B.A. alumni. But the Xavier alumni community extends well beyond the Midwest. Alumni occupy leadership positions across the U.S. and around the world. Whether American or international, the skills and qualities that were honed in their Xavier M.B.A. studies serve them well in any location and any position. This ability to make a difference in business, in society, and in their own lives is a reflection of the values-based leadership principles and skills for which the M.B.A. program stands.

The College and Environs

Established in 1831, Xavier University was the first Catholic institution of higher learning in the Northwest Territory. In 1841, Xavier offered its first night course, beginning a long tradition of serving the unique needs and schedules of profession-

als in and around Cincinnati. The M.B.A. degree was founded in 1952 and today is awarded to an average of 275 students each year.

Xavier University's 100-acre, terraced campus is situated in an established residential district just 5 miles north of downtown Cincinnati. The convenient, centralized location is within 15 minutes of most major business centers in the area as well as in proximity to major highways. Busy working professionals find access to and from as well as on the Xavier campus to be predictable and efficient—an important feature to individuals balancing career, educational, family, and other life interests.

Placement

The Career Services Center provides essential career development, job search, and job success information and education. Career counselors assist in developing necessary job search skills, including resume writing, interviewing, employer identification, and research. The Career Services Center also sponsors the Professional Experience Program, which provides excellent part-time or summer work experience. Additional services include on-campus interviews, resume referral, a job hotline, and a yearly employment fair.

Admission

Students are accepted throughout the year and may begin in the fall, spring, or summer semester. Each applicant is evaluated on a variety of criteria to determine sound scholarship, management, and leadership potential. These criteria include undergraduate (and graduate) transcripts, GMAT results, a job resume, and letters of recommendation.

Finances

Tuition for 1998–99 is $400 per semester hour. Financial aid is available in the form of grants, graduate assistantships, payment plans, and low-interest loans. International students qualify for most financial programs.

International Students

Xavier has a strong international program with students from all parts of the global community. The TOEFL (minimum score of 550) is required of applicants for whom English is not the native language unless they hold a bachelor's degree or higher from an accredited U.S. college or university. Xavier offers an exceptional English as a second language (ESL) program for students who wish to increase their English language proficiency prior to applying for the M.B.A. program.

Application Facts and Dates

There is no formal deadline; however, it is suggested that students apply by the following dates to assure timely processing and class registration: for fall, August 1; for spring, December 1; and summer, April 15. Applications are reviewed after all materials have arrived. Once accepted, students have up to one year to enroll, after which time they must reapply.

Dr. James D. Brodzinski
Associate Dean
College of Business Administration
Xavier University
3800 Victory Parkway
Cincinnati, Ohio 45207-3221
Telephone: 513-745-3525
Fax: 513-745-2929
E-mail: xumba@admin.xu.edu

York University

Schulich School of Business

Toronto, Ontario, Canada

> ### ▶ PROGRAMS OFFERING THE BEST OF BOTH WORLDS
>
> *Established in 1966, York's Schulich School of Business (formerly the Faculty of Administrative Studies) is Canada's largest graduate school of management. We have built a strong reputation, both at home and abroad, for richly diverse, creative, real-world programs. Our students have the best of both worlds— innovation and tradition, both of which are kept in balance through a dynamic process of continuous improvement in programming and program delivery. In addition to becoming strong generalists, Schulich students have rich opportunities for multiple specializations and for the development of critical leadership, entrepreneurial, group, and negotiation skills. The School's combination of relevance, opportunity, and choice permits our graduates to build successful careers in the private, public, and nonprofit sectors.*
>
> *—Dezsö J. Horváth, Dean*

Programs and Curricular Focus

At the master's level, the Schulich School offers three degrees: the Master of Business Administration (M.B.A.), the Master of Public Administration (M.P.A.), and the International M.B.A. (I.M.B.A.). Entry to the M.B.A. and M.P.A. programs is in September or January. According to an applicant's educational background, the minimum length of these programs can vary from eight to sixteen months of full-time study. Part-time study is also possible. The I.M.B.A. is a full-time, six-semester program limited to 60 students entering in September. Schulich also offers a Ph.D. program.

Revised and restructured in the mid-1990s, York's M.B.A. degree prepares students to turn the challenges of a constantly changing business environment to advantage. Schulich's traditional strengths are a breadth and flexibility of programming, diversity of student body and faculty, a real-world focus, and its location at the centre of corporate Canada. To these have been added an increased emphasis on relevance, a more applied focus, the integration of international aspects of business across courses, a broader frame of reference for decision making that includes business issues such as ethics and entrepreneurism, the development of a wide range of essential competencies such as communication and interpersonal skills, and increased specialization options.

Those in full-time studies are assigned to a cohort of 50 to 55 students with whom they take their first-year core courses. The average size of elective courses is 25. In all courses, much of the work is completed in smaller groups of 5 to 6 people.

In the first year of all master's-level programs, students become strong generalists after completing a core of required Foundations of Management courses. In the final second-year required course (the strategy field study), small groups of students complete a six-month detailed analysis of an actual organization. They present their findings and recommendations for improved performance to the organization's senior management. The course applies and integrates knowledge and skills acquired throughout the degree program.

The balance of the M.B.A.'s second year consists of elective courses selected from the School's more than 100 offerings from eighteen existing areas of specialization. These include management functions such as finance and marketing; industry sectors, including financial services, arts and media, and real property; and special management topics such as international business, entrepreneurism, financial engineering, business and the environment, public management, nonprofit management and leading, and business ethics.

Students and the M.B.A. Experience

The Schulich student body is composed of Canadian and international students from a variety of educational and work-related backgrounds who are bright, dynamic, and culturally diverse. The average student is 29 years of age. Of the total full-time and part-time master's-level complement of 1,250 students, 38 percent are women and 30 percent are international students. Their average work experience prior to admission is nearly 5½ years.

As a large, urban-centred institution, York University offers Schulich students the many benefits of its location in Toronto, one of the world's most cosmopolitan cities and the corporate and banking centre of Canada. In particular, this means students have access to expertise related to every kind of organization—large, small, domestic, global, family-owned, entrepreneurial, public, private, and nonprofit.

❖ Global Focus

Schulich has become a global business school, with a broad range of strategic alliances in more than forty-five countries around the world. International business issues are integrated into all Foundations of Management core courses. Schulich students gain first-hand international experience by spending a semester overseas at one of twenty-nine of the world's leading management schools located in twenty countries in the Americas, Asia, and Europe. This academic partnership network is continually being expanded.

Special Features

Schulich offers an exceptional range of programming choices resulting in rich opportunities for individualized career planning. The School has pioneered master's-level niche programs in a number of specialized areas. In 1992, Schulich introduced Canada's first International M.B.A. program, in which students develop specialized region and country expertise, master a foreign language, and spend up to six months working and studying abroad.

The School also offers a growing number of joint and dual degrees. It was the first in Canada to offer a joint M.B.A./LL.B. degree. Schulich offers a joint M.B.A. degree with Laval University in Quebec and a dual degree with ESC Lyon in France. In fall 1999, it will offer a new joint Master of Fine Arts (M.F.A.) and M.B.A. degree.

Schulich is committed to providing lifelong learning opportunities to practicing managers. It recently launched a unique M.B.A. Certificate in Advanced Management for graduates of recognized M.B.A. programs. The School's Division of Executive Development is the largest in Canada and is ideally situated in the heart of Toronto's financial district at King and Bay Streets in the Miles S. Nadal Management Centre.

The Faculty

Schulich has recruited its faculty internationally. There are currently 80 full-time faculty members. They have graduated from the world's top business schools, and applied and pure research are as fundamental to their mandate as educating tomorrow's corporate leaders. Teaching and research blend rigour and relevance in national and international contexts.

The Business School Network

The Schulich School has traditionally fostered strong ties to the business community in Canada and abroad. The Dean's Advisory Council, the International Advisory Council, and eight other advisory boards consisting of close to 200 distinguished CEOs, leading academics, and senior government representatives offer their advice and networks to support the strategic planning and implementation of Schulich programs.

Throughout the school year, prominent executives deliver talks and attend student-sponsored conferences. The School's York Consulting Group provides consulting services for small and medium-sized businesses and an action-learning opportunity for students. In addition, the Schulich Alumni Mentorship Program matches graduate-level students with alumni to help them find windows into their fields of interest.

The College and Environs

York University is the third-largest university in Canada, located in Toronto, Ontario—the country's industrial, commercial, and financial heartland.

York's main campus is situated on a 600-acre site at the northwest perimeter of the city. With a population of 40,000 students, York has all the necessary amenities and facilities typical of a large urban university campus. York is accessible by bus or car. The majority of business students commute, although many of the full-time students live in apartment-like housing on campus.

Technology Environment

Although approximately 90 percent of Schulich students have their own computers, they also have exclusive use of more than fifty computer access points and some forty machines (Intel-based standard and multimedia 486 IBM machines as well as multimedia Pentiums) in three labs within the School. Experienced staff members assist students during PC lab hours. More than 200 dial-up lines and remote connectivity software allow remote access to e-mail, the Internet (using Netscape), and the School's computer networks.

Placement

The Schulich Business Career Services unit offers placement services geared specifically to the needs of its students. These services are part of students' activities from their first term through graduation and beyond. The services include a career day, on-campus company information sessions, on-campus recruiting, a Company and Career Information Library, an Immediate Opening Service, individual and group counselling, a graduate directory, a summer employment program, and instruction self-assessment, resume writing, interviewing, and job search techniques. An effort is made to include in the job search process not only the large multinational companies but also the small to medium-size firms. Job opportunities are posted on the Career Services Web site.

Admission

An applicant must possess an undergraduate degree from a recognized university and submit scores for the GMAT (Graduate Management Admission Test). Normally, an applicant will be accepted only if he or she has achieved a B average or better in the last two full years (or equivalent) of academic work and achieved a set of acceptable scores on all three GMAT measurements. In addition, the applicant's work experience, demonstrated leadership qualities, communication skills, and apparent creativity and innovation are considered. In lieu of a degree, a nonbaccalaureate candidate must have at least eight years of high-quality management experience and must have demonstrated a strong upward progression in his or her career.

Finances

At the master's level, students pay fees each semester, according to whether they are enrolled on a full-time or part-time basis. The 1998–99 full-time tuition is approximately Can$2200 per semester for Canadian residents and approximately Can$8700 per term for non-Canadian residents.

Application Facts and Dates

Application deadlines for regular M.B.A. or M.P.A. programs are May 1 for the fall term and October 15 for the winter term. The application deadlines for the M.B.A./LL.B. program (for September only) are November 1 (of the previous year) for the law application and April 1 (of the previous year) for the M.B.A. application. The application deadline for the I.M.B.A. (for September only) is May 1. Applications must be submitted to:

Division of Student Affairs
Room 106, SSB
Schulich School of Business
York University
4700 Keele Street
Toronto, Ontario M3J 1P3
Canada
Telephone: 416-736-5060
Fax: 416-736-5687
E-mail: admissions@bus.yorku.ca
World Wide Web: http://www.bus. yorku.ca

Indexes

There are two indexes in this section. The first, **School Index,** is arranged alphabetically and gives page references for all colleges and universities in the guide. The second, **Areas of Concentration Index,** lists schools in alphabetical order under the specific areas of study available within the MBA program.

School Index

In this index the page locations of the profiles are printed in regular type, announcements in italic type, and In-Depth Descriptions in bold type.

School Index

Butler University, College of Business Administration (IN) 227

California Baptist College, Graduate Program in Business Administration (CA) 107

California Lutheran University, School of Business Administration (CA) 108, *108*

California Polytechnic State University, San Luis Obispo, College of Business (CA) 109

California State Polytechnic University, Pomona, College of Business (CA) 109

California State University, Bakersfield, School of Business and Public Administration (CA) 110

California State University, Chico, College of Business (CA) 110

California State University, Dominguez Hills, School of Management (CA) 111

California State University, Fresno, Sid Craig School of Business (CA) 111

California State University, Fullerton, School of Business Administration and Economics (CA) 112

California State University, Hayward, School of Business and Economics (CA) 113

California State University, Long Beach, College of Business Administration (CA) 114

California State University, Los Angeles, School of Business and Economics (CA) 114

California State University, Northridge, College of Business Administration and Economics (CA) 115

California State University, Sacramento, School of Business Administration (CA) 116

California State University, San Bernardino, School of Business and Public Administration (CA) 116

California State University, San Marcos, Graduate Program in Business Administration (CA) 117

California State University, Stanislaus, School of Business Administration (CA) 117

California University of Pennsylvania, School of Graduate Studies and Research (PA) 450

Cambridge College, Program in Management (MA) 283

Cameron School of Business
See University of North Carolina at Wilmington

Cameron School of Business
See University of St. Thomas

Cameron University, School of Graduate and Professional Studies (OK) 436

Campbell School of Business
See Berry College

Campbell University, Lundy-Fetterman School of Business (NC) 402

Canisius College, Wehle School of Business (NY) 368

Capital University, Graduate School of Administration (OH) 420

Cardinal Stritch University, College of Business and Management (WI) 558

Carleton University, School of Business (Canada) 588, *589*

Carlson School of Management
See University of Minnesota, Twin Cities Campus

Carnegie Mellon University, Graduate School of Industrial Administration (PA) 450, **740**

Carol Martin Gatton College of Business and Economics
See University of Kentucky

Case Western Reserve University, Weatherhead School of Management (OH) 420, **742**

The Catholic University of America, Department of Economics and Business (DC) 165

Central Connecticut State University, School of Business (CT) 153

Central Michigan University, College of Business Administration (MI) 297

Central Missouri State University, College of Business and Economics (MO) 326

Chadron State College, Department of Business and Economics (NE) 341

Chaminade University of Honolulu, School of Business (HI) 200

Chapman University, School of Business and Economics (CA) 118, **744**

Charles H. Kellstadt Graduate School of Business
See DePaul University

Charles H. Lundquist College of Business
See University of Oregon

Charleston Southern University, Graduate Program in Business (SC) 478

Chatham College, Program in Management (PA) 451

The Chinese University of Hong Kong, Faculty of Business Administration (Hong Kong) 624

Christian Brothers University, School of Business (TN) 486

Chulalongkorn University, Sasin Graduate Institute of Business Administration (Thailand) 659, **746**

The Citadel, College of Graduate and Professional Studies (SC) 479

City University, Graduate School of Business and Management Professions (WA) 548

City University, Business School (United Kingdom) 662

Claremont Graduate University, Peter F. Drucker Graduate School of Management (CA) 118, *119*, **748**

Clarion University of Pennsylvania, College of Business Administration (PA) 452, **750**

Clark Atlanta University, School of Business Administration (GA) 189

Clarke College, Business Department (IA) 237

Clarkson University, School of Business (NY) 369, **752**

Clark University, Graduate School of Management (MA) 284, **754**

Clemson University, College of Business and Public Affairs (SC) 480, **756**

Cleveland State University, James J. Nance College of Business Administration (OH) 422, **758**

Coleman College, Information Systems Department, Graduate Division (CA) 120

College for Financial Planning, Program in Financial Planning (CO) 146

College of Insurance, Business Programs (NY) 370

College of Notre Dame, Business Programs (CA) 120

College of Notre Dame of Maryland, Center for Graduate Studies (MD) 268

College of St. Catherine, Business Programs (MN) 313

The College of Saint Rose, School of Business (NY) 370, **760**

College of St. Scholastica, Program in Management (MN) 313

College of Santa Fe, Department of Business Administration (NM) 362

College of William and Mary, Graduate School of Business Administration (VA) 537, **762**

Colorado State University, College of Business (CO) 146, **764**

Colorado Technical University, Management Department (CO) 147

Columbia College, Department of Management (IL) 206

Columbia College, Program in Business Administration (MO) 326

Columbia University, Columbia Business School (NY) 371, **766**

Columbus State University, Abbott Turner College of Business (GA) 190

Concordia University, Faculty of Commerce and Administration (Canada) 589, **768**

Concordia University Wisconsin, Business Programs (WI) 559

Copenhagen Business School, Faculty of Economics and Business Administration (Denmark) 611

Cornell University, Johnson Graduate School of Management (NY) 372, **770**

Cranfield School of Management
See Cranfield University

Cranfield University, Cranfield School of Management (United Kingdom) 663, **772**

Creighton University, College of Business Administration (NE) 342

Crummer Graduate School of Business
See Rollins College

Cumberland University, Business and Economics Division (TN) 487

Curtin University of Technology, Graduate School of Business (Australia) 574

Czech Management Center, Graduate School of Business (Czech Republic) 611

Dahlkemper School of Business
See Gannon University

Dalhousie University, Faculty of Management (Canada) 590, **774**

Dallas Baptist University, Graduate School of Business (TX) 499, *499*

Daniels College of Business
See University of Denver

Darden Graduate School of Business Administration
See University of Virginia

Dartmouth College, Amos Tuck School of Business Administration (NH) 347, **776**

David Eccles School of Business
See University of Utah

Deakin University, Faculty of Business and Law (Australia) 574

DeBusk School of Business
See Lincoln Memorial University

Delaware State University, School of Management (DE) 161

Delta State University, School of Business (MS) 320

De Montfort University, Leicester Business School (United Kingdom) 664

DePaul University, Charles H. Kellstadt Graduate School of Business (IL) 206, **778**

Dominican College of San Rafael, School of Business and International Studies (CA) 120, **780**

Dominican University, Graduate School of Business (IL) 207, **782**

Dowling College, School of Business (NY) 373, **784**

Drake University, College of Business and Public Administration (IA) 238

Drexel University, College of Business and Administration (PA) 452, **786**

Drury College, Breech School of Business Administration (MO) 327

Duke University, The Fuqua School of Business at Duke University (NC) 403

DuPree College of Management
See Georgia Institute of Technology

Duquesne University, Graduate School of Business Administration (PA) 453, *453*, **788**

Duxx Graduate School of Business Leadership, Business Programs (Mexico) 633

EAP-European School of Management, Business School (Spain) 651

EAP-European School of Management, Business Programs (United Kingdom) 664

EAP-European School of Management, School of Management (France) 613

East Carolina University, School of Business (NC) 404, **790**

Eastern College, Graduate Business Programs (PA) 454, **792**

Eastern Connecticut State University, Program in Organizational Management (CT) 154

Eastern Illinois University, Lumpkin College of Business and Applied Science (IL) 208

Eastern Kentucky University, College of Business (KY) 252

Eastern Michigan University, College of Business (MI) 298, *298*, **794**

Eastern New Mexico University, College of Business (NM) 362

Eastern Washington University, College of Business Administration and Public Administration (WA) 548

East Tennessee State University, College of Business (TN) 487

East Texas Baptist University, Program in Business Administration (TX) 500

Eberhardt School of Business
See University of the Pacific

Eberly College of Business
See Indiana University of Pennsylvania

École des Hautes Études Commerciales, Master of Business Administration Program (Canada) 591, **796**

École Nationale des Ponts et Chaussées, ENPC Graduate School of International Business (France) 614

École Supérieure de Commerce de Rouen, Business Programs (France) 615

École Supérieure des Sciences Économiques et Commerciales, ESSEC School of Management (France) 615

Edgewood College, Program in Business (WI) 559

Edith Cowan University, Faculty of Business (Australia) 575

Edwin L. Cox School of Business
See Southern Methodist University

EGADE School of Business
See Instituto Tecnológico y de Estudios Superiores de Monterrey, Campus Querétaro

E. J. Ourso College of Business Administration
See Louisiana State University and Agricultural and Mechanical College

Eli Broad Graduate School of Management
See Michigan State University

Elon College, Martha and Spencer Love School of Business (NC) 404

Else School of Management
See Millsaps College

Embry-Riddle Aeronautical University, Department of Aviation Business Administration (FL) 170, **798**

Embry-Riddle Aeronautical University, Extended Campus, College of Career Education (FL) 170

Emerson College, School of Communication, Management and Public Policy (MA) 284, **800**

E. M. Lyon, Cesma MBA (France) 616, **802**

Emmanuel College, Center for Adult Studies (MA) 285

Emory University, Roberto C. Goizueta Business School (GA) 190, **804**

Emporia State University, School of Business (KS) 244, **806**

Erasmus University Rotterdam, Rotterdam School of Management (Netherlands) 638, **808**

Erivan K. Haub School of Business
See Saint Joseph's University

Escola d'Alta Direcció i Administració (EADA), Business Programs (Spain) 651

Escuela de Administracion de Negocios para Graduados, Programa Magister (Peru) 645

Escuela Superior de Administración y Dirección de Empresas (ESADE), Business School (Spain) 652

European University, International Center for Management Studies (Belgium) 586, **810**

Fairfield University, School of Business (CT) 154, **812**

Fairleigh Dickinson University, Samuel J. Silberman College of Business Administration (NJ) 351, **814**

Fayetteville State University, Program in Business Administration (NC) 405

Ferris State University, Graduate Programs, College of Business (MI) 299, **816**

Fielding Institute, Graduate Programs—Organizational Design and Effectiveness (CA) 121

Fisher Graduate School of Business Management
See Monterey Institute of International Studies

Fitchburg State College, Division of Graduate and Continuing Education (MA) 285, **818**

Florida Agricultural and Mechanical University, School of Business and Industry (FL) 171

Florida Atlantic University, College of Business (FL) 171

Florida Institute of Technology, School of Business (FL) 172

Florida International University, College of Business Administration (FL) 173, **820**

Florida Metropolitan University-Tampa College, Business and Computer Information Division (FL) 173

Florida Metropolitan University-Orlando College, North, Graduate Program (FL) 174

Florida Southern College, Department of Business and Economics (FL) 174

Florida State University, College of Business (FL) 175

Fogelman College of Business and Economics
See The University of Memphis

Fontbonne College, Business Department (MO) 327

Fordham University, Graduate School of Business Administration (NY) 373, **822**

Fort Hays State University, College of Business (KS) 244

Foster College of Business Administration
See Bradley University

Framingham State College, Program in Business Administration (MA) 286

Franciscan University of Steubenville, Business Programs (OH) 422

Francis Marion University, School of Business (SC) 480

Frank G. Zarb School of Business
See Hofstra University

Frank H. Sobey Faculty of Commerce
See Saint Mary's University

Franklin P. Perdue School of Business
See Salisbury State University

Franklin University, Graduate School of Business (OH) 423

Frank Sawyer School of Management
See Suffolk University

Fresno Pacific University, Fresno Pacific Graduate School (CA) 122

Friends University, Graduate Programs (KS) 245

Frostburg State University, School of Business (MD) 269

Fudan University, School of Management (China) 610

The Fuqua School of Business at Duke University
See Duke University

F. W. Olin Graduate School of Business
See Babson College

Gannon University, Dahlkemper School of Business (PA) 455

Gardner-Webb University, School of Business (NC) 405

George Fox University, Department of Business and Economics (OR) 444

George H. Atkinson Graduate School of Management
See Willamette University

The George L. Graziadio School of Business and Management
See Pepperdine University

George Mason University, School of Management (VA) 538, **824**

Georgetown University, School of Business (DC) 165, **826**

The George Washington University, School of Business and Public Management (DC) 166, **828**

Georgia College and State University, J. Whitney Bunting School of Business (GA) 191

Georgia Institute of Technology, DuPree College of Management (GA) 192, **830**

Georgian Court College, Program in Business Administration (NJ) 351

Georgia Southern University, College of Business Administration (GA) 193

Georgia Southwestern State University, School of Business (GA) 193

Georgia State University, College of Business Administration (GA) 194, **832**

Gladys A. Kelce School of Business and Economics
See Pittsburg State University

Golden Gate University, School of Business (CA) 122, **834**

Goldey-Beacom College, Office of Graduate Studies (DE) 162, *162*

Gonzaga University, School of Business Administration (WA) 549

Göteborg University, School of Economics and Commercial Laws (Sweden) 655

Governors State University, College of Business and Public Administration (IL) 208

The Graduate School of America, Management Field (MN) 314

Graduate School of Business Administration Zürich, Business Programs (Switzerland) 656

Graham School of Management
See Saint Xavier University

Grand Canyon University, College of Business (AZ) 98

Grand Valley State University, Seidman School of Business (MI) 300

Groupe CERAM, Ceram ESC Nice School of Management (France) 617

Groupe ESC Clermont, Clermont Graduate School of Management (France) 617

Groupe ESC Nantes Atlantique, Groupe ESC Nantes Atlantique Business Programs (France) 617

Groupe ESC Toulouse, ESC Toulouse Graduate School of Management (France) 618

Grove City College, Program in Accounting (PA) 455

Haas School of Business
See University of California, Berkeley

Hagan School of Business
See Iona College

Hampton University, School of Business (VA) 539

Hankamer School of Business
See Baylor University

Harry F. Byrd, Jr. School of Business
See Shenandoah University

Harry W. Block School of Public Administration
See University of Missouri-Kansas City

Harvard University, Graduate School of Business Administration (MA) 286

Hasan School of Business
See University of Southern Colorado

Hawaii Pacific University, Center for Graduate Studies (HI) 201, **836**

Haworth College of Business
See Western Michigan University

Hebrew University of Jerusalem, Jerusalem School of Business Administration (Israel) 630

HEC Graduate School of Management, Institute Supérieur des Affaires (France) 619

Heidelberg College, Graduate Studies in Business (OH) 424

School Index

Helsinki School of Economics and Business Administration, International Center (Finland) 613

Henderson State University, School of Business Administration (AR) 102

Henley Management College, Business Programs (United Kingdom) 665

Heriot-Watt University, Edinburgh Business School (United Kingdom) 665

High Point University, Graduate Studies (NC) 406

H.L. McLaughlin One-Year MBA Program
See St. Ambrose University

Hofstra University, Frank G. Zarb School of Business (NY) 374, **838**

Holy Names College, Department of Business Administration and Economics (CA) 123

Hong Kong Baptist University, School of Business (Hong Kong) 625

The Hong Kong University of Science and Technology, School of Business and Management (Hong Kong) 626

Hood College, Department of Economics and Management (MD) 270

Hope International University, Graduate Management Program (CA) 123

Houston Baptist University, College of Business and Economics (TX) 500

Howard University, School of Business (DC) 167

Humboldt State University, School of Business and Economics (CA) 124

Huron University, School of Business (SD) 485

Huron University USA in London, MBA Program (United Kingdom) 666, *666,* **840**

Husson College, Graduate Studies Division (ME) 265

IADE, Instituto Universitario de Administracion de Empresas (Spain) 653

Idaho State University, College of Business (ID) 203

IESE International Graduate School of Management
See University of Navarra

Illinois Institute of Technology, Stuart School of Business (IL) 209, **842**

Illinois State University, College of Business (IL) 210, **844**

Imperial College, Management School (United Kingdom) 667

Indiana State University, School of Business (IN) 228

Indiana University Bloomington, Kelley School of Business (IN) 229, *229,* **846**

Indiana University Kokomo, Division of Business and Economics (IN) 229

Indiana University Northwest, Division of Business and Economics (IN) 230

Indiana University of Pennsylvania, Eberly College of Business (PA) 456

Indiana University-Purdue University Fort Wayne, School of Business and Management Sciences (IN) 231

Indiana University-Purdue University Indianapolis, Kelley School of Business (IN) 231

Indiana University South Bend, Division of Business and Economics (IN) 232

Indiana Wesleyan University, Division of Adult and Professional Studies (IN) 232

INSEAD (The European Institute of Business Administration), Business Programs (France) 619, **848**

INCAE (Instituto Centroamericano de Administración de Empresas), Graduate Program (Costa Rica) 610

Instituto de Empresa, Business School (Spain) 653

Instituto Empresarial Portuense, Business School (Portugal) 646

Instituto Tecnológico y de Estudios Superiores de Monterrey, Graduate School of Business Administration and Leadership (Mexico) 634

Instituto Tecnológico y de Estudios Superiores de Monterrey, Campus Estado de México, Graduate Division (Mexico) 634

Instituto Tecnológico y de Estudios Superiores de Monterrey, Campus Guadalajara, Program in Business Administration (Mexico) 634

Instituto Tecnológico y de Estudios Superiores de Monterrey, Campus Laguna, Graduate School (Mexico) 635

Instituto Tecnológico y de Estudios Superiores de Monterrey, Campus León, Program in Business Administration (Mexico) 635

Instituto Tecnológico y de Estudios Superiores de Monterrey, Campus México City, Programs in Business (Mexico) 635

Instituto Tecnológico y de Estudios Superiores de Monterrey, Campus Querétaro, EGADE School of Business (Mexico) 636

Instituto Tecnológico y de Estudios Superiores de Monterrey, Campus Toluca, Graduate Programs (Mexico) 636

Institut Pengembangan Manajemen Indonesia, Business Programs (Indonesia) 627

Institut Superieur de Gestion, ISG International School of Business (France) 620

Inter American University of Puerto Rico, Metropolitan Campus, Division of Economics and Business Administration (PR) 569

Inter American University of Puerto Rico, San Germán Campus, Department of Business Administration (PR) 569

International College of the Cayman Islands, Graduate Studies Program (Cayman Islands) 609

International Executive Development Center, School of Business Administration (Slovenia) 649

International Institute for Management Development (IMD), Business Programs (Switzerland) 657, **850**

The International Management Institute of St. Petersburg, Marketing Department (Russian Federation) 648

International School of Information Management, Programs in Information Management and Business Administration (CO) 148

International University of Business Agriculture and Technology (IUBAT), College of Business Administration (Bangladesh) 585

International University of Japan, Graduate School of International Management (Japan) 632, *632,* **852**

Iona College, Hagan School of Business (NY) 375, **854**

Iowa State University of Science and Technology, College of Business (IA) 239, **856**

ISMA Centre
See University of Reading

Jack C. Massey Graduate School of Business
See Belmont University

Jackson State University, School of Business (MS) 321

Jacksonville State University, College of Commerce and Business Administration (AL) 87

Jacksonville University, College of Business (FL) 176

James J. Nance College of Business Administration
See Cleveland State University

James Madison University, College of Business (VA) 539

Jesse H. Jones Graduate School of Management
See Rice University

Jesse H. Jones School of Business
See Texas Southern University

J. L. Kellogg Graduate School of Management
See Northwestern University

John A. Walker College of Business
See Appalachian State University

John Carroll University, John M. and Mary Jo Boler School of Business (OH) 424

John E. Simon School of Business
See Maryville University of Saint Louis

John F. Kennedy University, School of Management (CA) 125

John M. and Mary Jo Boler School of Business
See John Carroll University

John M. Olin School of Business
See Washington University in St. Louis

Johns Hopkins University, School of Continuing Studies, Division of Business and Management (MD) 270, **858**

Johnson & Wales University, Alan Shawn Feinstein Graduate School (RI) 476, **860**

Johnson Graduate School of Management
See Cornell University

John W. Weems Graduate School
See Meredith College

Jones-Benedum Division of Business
See The University of Charleston

Joseph A. Butt, SJ, College of Business Administration
See Loyola University New Orleans

Joseph L. Rotman School of Management
See University of Toronto

Joseph M. Bryan School of Business and Economics
See University of North Carolina at Greensboro

Joseph M. Katz Graduate School of Business
See University of Pittsburgh

J. Whitney Bunting School of Business
See Georgia College and State University

Kansas Newman College, Program in Organizational Leadership (KS) 245

Kansas State University, College of Business Administration (KS) 245, **862**

Kansas Wesleyan University, MBA Program (KS) 246

Karl Eller Graduate School of Management
See University of Arizona

Katholieke Universiteit Leuven, Department of Applied Economic Sciences (Belgium) 587

Kean University, School of Business, Government, and Technology (NJ) 352

Keller Graduate School of Management, Master of Business Administration Program (IL) 211, **864**

Kelley School of Business
See Indiana University Bloomington

Kenan-Flagler Business School
See University of North Carolina at Chapel Hill

Kennesaw State University, Michael J. Coles College of Business (GA) 195, *195,* **866**

Kent State University, Graduate School of Management (OH) 425

Kettering University, Graduate Studies and Extension Services (MI) 300

King's College, William G. McGowan School of Business (PA) 456

Kingston University, Kingston Business School (United Kingdom) 667

Kogod College of Business Administration
See American University

Krannert Graduate School of Management
See Purdue University

Kutztown University of Pennsylvania, College of Business (PA) 457

Kyiv State University of Economics, MBA Program (Ukraine) 660

LaGrange College, Division of Business Administration and Economics (GA) 195

Lahore University of Management Sciences, Graduate School of Business Administration (Pakistan) 644

Lake Erie College, Division of Management Studies (OH) 425

The University of Findlay, Business Programs (OH) 432

University of Florida, Warrington College of Business Administration (FL) 182, *182*, **1070**

University of Georgia, Terry College of Business (GA) 199, **1072**

University of Glasgow, University of Glasgow Business School (United Kingdom) 680

University of Guam, College of Business and Public Administration (GU) 569

University of Guelph, Business Programs (Canada) 600

University of Hartford, Barney School of Business and Public Administration (CT) 158

University of Hawaii at Manoa, College of Business Administration (HI) 201, **1074**

University of Hong Kong, University of Hong Kong School of Business (Hong Kong) 626

University of Houston, College of Business Administration (TX) 518, **1076**

University of Houston-Clear Lake, College of Business and Public Administration (TX) 519

University of Houston-Victoria, Division of Business Administration (TX) 519

University of Hull, School of Management (United Kingdom) 681

University of Idaho, College of Business and Economics (ID) 204

University of Illinois at Chicago, College of Business Administration (IL) 222, **1078**

University of Illinois at Springfield, School of Business and Management (IL) 223

University of Illinois at Urbana-Champaign, Illinois MBA (IL) 224, **1080**

University of Indianapolis, Graduate Business Programs (IN) 235

The University of Iowa, School of Management (IA) 241, **1082**

University of Judaism, Lieber School of Graduate Studies (CA) 140

University of Kansas, School of Business (KS) 248, **1084**

University of Kentucky, Carol Martin Gatton College of Business and Economics (KY) 255, **1086**

University of La Verne, School of Business and Global Studies (CA) 141

University of Limerick, College of Business (Ireland) 629

University of London, London Business School (United Kingdom) 681

University of Louisville, College of Business and Public Administration (KY) 256, **1088**

University of Maine, The Maine Business School (ME) 266, **1090**

The University of Manchester, Manchester Business School (United Kingdom) 682

University of Manitoba, Faculty of Management (Canada) 600, **1092**

University of Mary, Business Division (ND) 416

University of Mary Hardin-Baylor, School of Business (TX) 520

University of Maryland, College Park, Robert H. Smith School of Business (MD) 274, **1094**

University of Maryland University College, Graduate School of Management and Technology (MD) 275

University of Massachusetts Amherst, School of Management (MA) 292

University of Massachusetts Boston, College of Management (MA) 292

University of Massachusetts Dartmouth, College of Business and Industry (MA) 293

University of Massachusetts Lowell, College of Management (MA) 294

University of Melbourne, Melbourne Business School (Australia) 579

The University of Memphis, Fogelman College of Business and Economics (TN) 492, **1096**

University of Miami, School of Business Administration (FL) 183, **1098**

University of Michigan, University of Michigan Business School (MI) 308

University of Michigan-Dearborn, School of Management (MI) 309

University of Michigan-Flint, School of Management (MI) 310, **1100**

University of Minnesota, Duluth, School of Business and Economics (MN) 317

University of Minnesota, Twin Cities Campus, Carlson School of Management (MN) 317, *318*

University of Mississippi, School of Business Administration (MS) 323, **1102**

University of Missouri-Columbia, College of Business and Public Administration (MO) 335, **1104**

University of Missouri-Kansas City, Harry W. Block School of Public Administration (MO) 335

University of Missouri-St. Louis, School of Business Administration (MO) 336, *336*

University of Mobile, School of Business (AL) 92

The University of Montana-Missoula, School of Business Administration (MT) 340

University of Navarra, IESE International Graduate School of Management (Spain) 654, *654*, **1106**

University of Nebraska at Kearney, College of Business and Technology (NE) 343

University of Nebraska at Omaha, College of Business Administration (NE) 343, *343*

University of Nebraska-Lincoln, College of Business Administration (NE) 344, *344*

University of Nevada, Las Vegas, College of Business (NV) 345, **1108**

University of Nevada, Reno, College of Business Administration (NV) 346, **1110**

University of New Brunswick, Faculty of Administration (Canada) 602

University of New Brunswick, Faculty of Business (Canada) 601

University of Newcastle, Graduate School of Business (Australia) 580

University of Newcastle upon Tyne, School of Management (United Kingdom) 682

University of New Hampshire, Whittemore School of Business and Economics (NH) 350, **1112**

University of New Haven, School of Business (CT) 159, **1114**

University of New Mexico, Robert O. Anderson Graduate School of Management (NM) 364

University of New Orleans, College of Business Administration (LA) 263

University of New South Wales, Australian Graduate School of Management (Australia) 581

University of North Alabama, College of Business (AL) 93

University of North Carolina at Chapel Hill, Kenan-Flagler Business School (NC) 410

The University of North Carolina at Charlotte, The Belk College of Business Administration (NC) 410, *411*

University of North Carolina at Greensboro, Joseph M. Bryan School of Business and Economics (NC) 411, **1116**

The University of North Carolina at Pembroke, Graduate Studies (NC) 412

University of North Carolina at Wilmington, Cameron School of Business (NC) 413

University of North Dakota, College of Business and Public Administration (ND) 417

University of Northern Iowa, College of Business Administration (IA) 242

University of North Florida, College of Business Administration (FL) 184

University of North Texas, College of Business Administration (TX) 521

University of Northumbria, Newcastle Business School (United Kingdom) 683

University of Notre Dame, College of Business Administration (IN) 235, **1118**

University of Nottingham, School of Management and Finance (United Kingdom) 683

University of Oklahoma, Michael F. Price College of Business (OK) 442, **1120**

University of Oregon, Charles H. Lundquist College of Business (OR) 447, *447*

University of Oslo, Department of Economics (Norway) 644

University of Otago, Advanced Business Programme (New Zealand) 641, **1122**

University of Ottawa, Faculty of Administration (Canada) 602

University of Oxford, School of Management Studies (United Kingdom) 684

University of Pennsylvania, Wharton School (PA) 469, **1124, 1126**

University of Phoenix, Department of Graduate Business (AZ) 101

University of Pittsburgh, Joseph M. Katz Graduate School of Business (PA) 470, **1128**

University of Plymouth, Business School (United Kingdom) 685

University of Portland, School of Business Administration (OR) 447

University of Puerto Rico, Mayagüez Campus, College of Business Administration (PR) 570

University of Puerto Rico, Río Piedras, Graduate School of Business Administration (PR) 571

University of Reading, ISMA Centre (United Kingdom) 686, **1130**

University of Redlands, Alfred North Whitehead College (CA) 141

University of Regina, Faculty of Administration (Canada) 603

University of Rhode Island, College of Business Administration (RI) 478

University of Richmond, The Richard S. Reynolds Graduate School (VA) 544

University of Rochester, William E. Simon Graduate School of Business Administration (NY) 401, *401*, **1132**

University of Saint Francis, Department of Business Administration (IN) 236

University of St. Francis, College of Graduate Studies (IL) 225, *225*

University of St. Gallen, Business School (Switzerland) 658

University of St. Thomas, Cameron School of Business (TX) 521

University of St. Thomas, Graduate School of Business (MN) 318, **1134**

University of Salford, Management School (United Kingdom) 686

University of San Diego, School of Business Administration (CA) 142, **1136**

University of San Francisco, McLaren School of Business (CA) 143, **1138**

University of Sarasota, College of Business Administration (FL) 185

University of Saskatchewan, College of Commerce (Canada) 603

University of Scranton, Program in Business Administration (PA) 471

University of Sheffield, Management School (United Kingdom) 687

University of South Alabama, College of Business and Management Studies (AL) 93

University of South Carolina, College of Business Administration (SC) 483, *483*, **1140**

University of South Dakota, School of Business (SD) 485

University of Southern California, Marshall School of Business (CA) 143, *143*, **1142, 1144**

University of Southern Colorado, Hasan School of Business (CO) 152

School Index

University of Southern Europe, Monaco Graduate
School (Monaco) 637
University of Southern Indiana, School of
Business (IN) 237
University of Southern Maine, School of Business
(ME) 267
University of Southern Mississippi, College of
Business Administration (MS) 324
University of Southern Queensland, Faculty of
Business (Australia) 581
University of South Florida, College of Business
Administration (FL) 185
University of Southwestern Louisiana, Graduate
School (LA) 264
University of Stirling, School of Management
(United Kingdom) 687
University of Strathclyde, Strathclyde Graduate
Business School (United Kingdom) 688
The University of Sydney, Graduate School of
Business (Australia) 582
The University of Tampa, College of Business
(FL) 186, **1146**
University of Technology, Sydney, Graduate
School of Business (Australia) 582
University of Tennessee at Chattanooga, School of
Business Administration (TN) 493, *493*
The University of Tennessee at Martin, School of
Business Administration (TN) 494
University of Tennessee, Knoxville, College of
Business Administration (TN) 494, *495*, **1148**
The University of Texas at Arlington, College of
Business Administration (TX) 522, **1150**
University of Texas at Austin, Graduate School of
Business (TX) 523, **1152**
The University of Texas at Brownsville, School of
Business (TX) 524
University of Texas at Dallas, School of
Management (TX) 525, *525*, **1154**
University of Texas at El Paso, College of
Business Administration (TX) 526
University of Texas at San Antonio, College of
Business (TX) 526, **1156**
University of Texas at Tyler, School of Business
Administration (TX) 527
University of Texas of the Permian Basin, School
of Business (TX) 528
University of Texas-Pan American, College of
Business Administration (TX) 528
University of the District of Columbia, College of
Professional Studies (DC) 168
University of the Incarnate Word, College of
Professional Studies (TX) 529
University of the Pacific, Eberhardt School of
Business (CA) 144, *145*, **1158**
University of the Sacred Heart, Business School
(PR) 571
University of the Virgin Islands, Division of
Business Administration (VI) 572
University of the West of England, Bristol, Bristol
Business School (United Kingdom) 689
University of the Witwatersrand, Graduate School
of Business Administration (South Africa) 650,
1160
University of Toledo, College of Business
Administration (OH) 433, **1162**
University of Toronto, Joseph L. Rotman School
of Management (Canada) 604, **1164**
University of Tulsa, College of Business
Administration (OK) 443
University of Twente, TSM Business School
(Netherlands) 640, **1166**
University of Ulster at Jordanstown, Ulster
Business School (United Kingdom) 689
University of Utah, David Eccles School of
Business (UT) 532, **1168**
University of Vermont, School of Business
Administration (VT) 536, *536*
University of Victoria, Faculty of Business
(Canada) 605

University of Virginia, Darden Graduate School of
Business Administration (VA) 545
University of Waikato, School of Management
Studies (New Zealand) 642
University of Wales, Business School (United
Kingdom) 690
University of Warwick, Warwick Business School
(United Kingdom) 690
University of Washington, School of Business
Administration (WA) 552, **1170**
University of Waterloo, School of Accountancy
(Canada) 605
The University of Western Australia, Graduate
School of Management (Australia) 583
The University of Western Ontario, Richard Ivey
School of Business (Canada) 606, *606*, **1172**
University of Western Sydney, Macarthur, Faculty
of Business and Technology (Australia) 584
University of West Florida, College of Business
(FL) 187
University of Westminster, Business School
(United Kingdom) 691
University of Windsor, Faculty of Business
Administration (Canada) 607
University of Wisconsin-Eau Claire, School of
Business (WI) 562
University of Wisconsin-Green Bay, Program in
Administrative Sciences (WI) 563
University of Wisconsin-La Crosse, College of
Business Administration (WI) 563
University of Wisconsin-Madison, School of
Business (WI) 564, **1174**
University of Wisconsin-Milwaukee, School of
Business Administration (WI) 565
University of Wisconsin-Oshkosh, College of
Business Administration (WI) 565
University of Wisconsin-Parkside, School of
Business and Administrative Science (WI) 566
University of Wisconsin-Stout, Program in
Training and Development and Program in
Management Technology (WI) 566
University of Wisconsin-Whitewater, College of
Business and Economics (WI) 567
University of Wyoming, College of Business
(WY) 568
Upper Iowa University, Program in Business
Leadership (IA) 243
Utah State University, College of Business (UT)
533
Valdosta State University, College of Business
Administration (GA) 200
Vanderbilt University, Owen Graduate School of
Management (TN) 495
Victoria University of Wellington, Graduate
School of Business and Government
Management (New Zealand) 642
Vienna University of Economics and Business
Administration, Business Program/International
MBA (Austria) 584
Villanova University, College of Commerce and
Finance (PA) 471, **1176**
Virginia Commonwealth University, School of
Business (VA) 545
Virginia Polytechnic Institute and State University,
Pamplin College of Business (VA) 546, **1178**
Virginia State University, School of Business (VA)
547
Wagner College, Department of Economics and
Business Administration (NY) 402
Wake Forest University, Babcock Graduate School
of Management (NC) 413, **1180**
Wallace E. Carroll Graduate School of
Management
See Boston College
Walsh College of Accountancy and Business
Administration, College of Accountancy and
Business Administration (MI) 311, **1182**
Walsh University, Program in Management (OH)
433

Walter E. Heller College of Business
Administration
See Roosevelt University
Warren P. Williamson Jr. College of Business
Administration
See Youngstown State University
Warrington College of Business Administration
See University of Florida
Waseda University, Graduate School of Asia-
Pacific Studies (Japan) 633, **1184**
Washburn University of Topeka, School of
Business (KS) 249, **1186**
Washington State University, College of Business
and Economics (WA) 553
Washington University in St. Louis, John M. Olin
School of Business (MO) 337
W. Averell Harriman School for Management and
Policy
See State University of New York at Stony
Brook
Wayland Baptist University, Graduate Studies
Office (TX) 529
Waynesburg College, Graduate Program in
Business Administration (PA) 472
Wayne State College, Division of Business (NE)
345
Wayne State University, School of Business
Administration (MI) 311, *311*, **1188**
Weatherhead School of Management
See Case Western Reserve University
Weber State University, College of Business and
Economics (UT) 534
Webster University, School of Business and
Technology (MO) 338
Wehle School of Business
See Canisius College
Wesley J. Howe School of Technology
Management
See Stevens Institute of Technology
West Chester University of Pennsylvania, School
of Business and Public Affairs (PA) 472, **1190**
Western Carolina University, College of Business
(NC) 414
Western Connecticut State University, Ancell
School of Business and Public Administration
(CT) 160
Western Illinois University, College of Business
and Technology (IL) 225
Western International University, Graduate
Programs in Business (AZ) 101, *101*
Western Michigan University, Haworth College of
Business (MI) 312
Western New England College, School of Business
(MA) 294
Western New Mexico University, Department of
Business Administration (NM) 365
Western Washington University, College of
Business and Economics (WA) 553
Westminster College of Salt Lake City, Bill and
Vieve Gore School of Business (UT) 534
West Texas A&M University, T. Boone Pickens
College of Business (TX) 530
West Virginia University, College of Business and
Economics (WV) 556
West Virginia Wesleyan College, Faculty of
Business (WV) 557
W. Fielding Rubel School of Business
See Bellarmine College
W. Frank Barton School of Business
See Wichita State University
Wharton School
See University of Pennsylvania
Wheeling Jesuit University, Graduate Business
Program (WV) 557
Whittemore School of Business and Economics
See University of New Hampshire
Whitworth College, Whitworth Graduate School of
International Management (WA) 554
WHU Koblenz, Otto-Beisheim Graduate School of
Management (Germany) 623

1220

Peterson's Guide to MBA Programs 1999

Areas of Concentration Index

In this index the page locations of the profiles are printed in regular type, announcements in italic type, and In-Depth Descriptions in bold type.

Florida Southern College, Department of Business and Economics (FL) 174

Florida State University, College of Business (FL) 175

Fordham University, Graduate School of Business Administration (NY) 373, **822**

Fort Hays State University, College of Business (KS) 244

Franciscan University of Steubenville, Business Programs (OH) 422

Gannon University, Dahlkemper School of Business (PA) 455

George Mason University, School of Management (VA) 538, **824**

The George Washington University, School of Business and Public Management (DC) 166, **828**

Georgia College and State University, J. Whitney Bunting School of Business (GA) 191

Georgia Institute of Technology, DuPree College of Management (GA) 192, **830**

Georgia Southern University, College of Business Administration (GA) 193

Georgia State University, College of Business Administration (GA) 194, **832**

Golden Gate University, School of Business (CA) 122, **834**

Goldey-Beacom College, Office of Graduate Studies (DE) 162, *162*

Governors State University, College of Business and Public Administration (IL) 208

Graduate School of Business Administration Zürich, Business Programs (Switzerland) 656

Grand Canyon University, College of Business (AZ) 98

Groupe CERAM, Ceram ESC Nice School of Management (France) 617

Groupe ESC Clermont, Clermont Graduate School of Management (France) 617

Grove City College, Program in Accounting (PA) 455

Hawaii Pacific University, Center for Graduate Studies (HI) 201, **836**

Hebrew University of Jerusalem, Jerusalem School of Business Administration (Israel) 630

HEC Graduate School of Management, Institute Supérieur des Affaires (France) 619

Henderson State University, School of Business Administration (AR) 102

Hofstra University, Frank G. Zarb School of Business (NY) 374, **838**

Hong Kong Baptist University, School of Business (Hong Kong) 625

The Hong Kong University of Science and Technology, School of Business and Management (Hong Kong) 626

Hood College, Department of Economics and Management (MD) 270

Houston Baptist University, College of Business and Economics (TX) 500

IADE, Instituto Universitario de Administracion de Empresas (Spain) 653

Illinois State University, College of Business (IL) 210, **844**

Indiana State University, School of Business (IN) 228

Indiana University Northwest, Division of Business and Economics (IN) 230

Instituto de Empresa, Business School (Spain) 653

Institut Superieur de Gestion, ISG International School of Business (France) 620

Inter American University of Puerto Rico, Metropolitan Campus, Division of Economics and Business Administration (PR) 569

Inter American University of Puerto Rico, San Germán Campus, Department of Business Administration (PR) 569

International Executive Development Center, School of Business Administration (Slovenia) 649

International School of Information Management, Programs in Information Management and Business Administration (CO) 148

Iowa State University of Science and Technology, College of Business (IA) 239, **856**

Jacksonville State University, College of Commerce and Business Administration (AL) 87

John Carroll University, John M. and Mary Jo Boler School of Business (OH) 424

Johnson & Wales University, Alan Shawn Feinstein Graduate School (RI) 476, **860**

Kansas State University, College of Business Administration (KS) 245, **862**

Katholieke Universiteit Leuven, Department of Applied Economic Sciences (Belgium) 587

Keller Graduate School of Management, Master of Business Administration Program (IL) 211, **864**

Kennesaw State University, Michael J. Coles College of Business (GA) 195, *195,* **866**

King's College, William G. McGowan School of Business (PA) 456

Lakeland College, Graduate Studies Division (WI) 559

Lamar University, College of Business (TX) 500

Lancaster University, Management School (United Kingdom) 668

La Salle University, School of Business Administration (PA) 458

La Sierra University, School of Business and Management (CA) 125

Le Moyne College, Department of Business (NY) 376

Lewis University, College of Business (IL) 212

Lindenwood University, Department of Business Administration (MO) 328

Long Island University, Brooklyn Campus, School of Business and Public Administration (NY) 376

Long Island University, C.W. Post Campus, College of Management (NY) 377

Louisiana State University and Agricultural and Mechanical College, E. J. Ourso College of Business Administration (LA) 257

Louisiana Tech University, College of Administration and Business (LA) 258

Loyola College, Sellinger School of Business and Management (MD) 271, **874**

Loyola Marymount University, College of Business Administration (CA) 126, *126,* **876**

Loyola University Chicago, Graduate School of Business (IL) 212, **878**

Loyola University New Orleans, Joseph A. Butt, SJ, College of Business Administration (LA) 258, *259*

Manchester College, Department of Accounting (IN) 233

Manchester Metropolitan University, Faculty of Management and Business, Department of Management (United Kingdom) 670

Marist College, School of Management (NY) 379, **882**

Marquette University, College of Business Administration (WI) 561

Maryville University of Saint Louis, John E. Simon School of Business (MO) 329

McMaster University, Michael G. DeGroote School of Business (Canada) 593

Mercer University, Cecil B. Day Campus, Stetson School of Business and Economics (GA) 196

Metropolitan State University, Management and Administration Program (MN) 314

Miami University, Richard T. Farmer School of Business Administration (OH) 427

Michigan State University, Eli Broad Graduate School of Management (MI) 303

Middlesex University, Business School (United Kingdom) 670

Middle Tennessee State University, College of Business (TN) 488

Millsaps College, Else School of Management (MS) 321, *321*

Mississippi College, School of Business (MS) 322

Mississippi State University, College of Business and Industry (MS) 323, **886**

Monash University, Monash Mt. Eliza Business School (Australia) 577

Montana State University-Bozeman, College of Business (MT) 339

Montclair State University, School of Business Administration (NJ) 353

Mount Saint Mary's College and Seminary, Graduate Program of Business (MD) 272

Murdoch University, School of Business (Australia) 577

Murray State University, College of Business and Public Affairs (KY) 253

Nanyang Technological University, Nanyang Business School (Republic of Singapore) 647

National University, School of Management and Technology (CA) 128, **890**

National University of Singapore, Graduate School of Business (Republic of Singapore) 648

New Hampshire College, Graduate School of Business (NH) 348, **892**

New Jersey Institute of Technology, School of Industrial Management (NJ) 354

New York Institute of Technology, School of Management (NY) 382, **896**

New York University, Leonard N. Stern School of Business (NY) 382, **898**

Niagara University, Graduate Division of Business Administration (NY) 383

Nichols College, Graduate School of Business (MA) 288

North Carolina Central University, School of Business (NC) 407

North Carolina State University, College of Management (NC) 408, **902**

North Dakota State University, College of Business Administration (ND) 416

Northeastern Illinois University, College of Business and Management (IL) 214

Northwestern University, J. L. Kellogg Graduate School of Management (IL) 216

Nova Southeastern University, School of Business and Entrepreneurship (FL) 177, **912**

Oakland University, School of Business Administration (MI) 305, *305*

Oglethorpe University, Division of Business Administration (GA) 197

The Ohio State University, Max M. Fisher College of Business (OH) 427

Oklahoma City University, Meinders School of Business (OK) 437

Oklahoma State University, College of Business Administration (OK) 438

Old Dominion University, College of Business and Public Administration (VA) 541

Oral Roberts University, School of Business (OK) 439

Pace University, Lubin School of Business (NY) 384, **916**

Pennsylvania State University University Park Campus, Mary Jean and Frank P. Smeal College of Business Administration (PA) 463, **922**

Philadelphia College of Textiles and Science, School of Business Administration (PA) 464, **926**

Pittsburg State University, Gladys A. Kelce School of Business and Economics (KS) 247

Providence College, Graduate Business Program (RI) 476

Purdue University, Krannert Graduate School of Management (IN) 234, **934**

Quinnipiac College, School of Business (CT) 155, **938**

Radford University, College of Business and Economics (VA) 542

Areas of Concentration Index

University of Illinois at Urbana-Champaign,
Illinois MBA (IL) 224, **1080**
The University of Iowa, School of Management
(IA) 241, **1082**
University of Limerick, College of Business
(Ireland) 629
University of Louisville, College of Business and
Public Administration (KY) 256, **1088**
The University of Manchester, Manchester
Business School (United Kingdom) 682
University of Maryland, College Park, Robert H.
Smith School of Business (MD) 274, **1094**
University of Michigan, University of Michigan
Business School (MI) 308
University of Minnesota, Twin Cities Campus,
Carlson School of Management (MN) 317, *318*
University of Missouri-Kansas City, Harry W.
Block School of Public Administration (MO)
335
University of Newcastle upon Tyne, School of
Management (United Kingdom) 682
University of New Mexico, Robert O. Anderson
Graduate School of Management (NM) 364
University of New South Wales, Australian
Graduate School of Management (Australia)
581
University of North Carolina at Chapel Hill,
Kenan-Flagler Business School (NC) 410
University of North Carolina at Wilmington,
Cameron School of Business (NC) 413
University of Nottingham, School of Management
and Finance (United Kingdom) 683
University of Oregon, Charles H. Lundquist
College of Business (OR) 447, *447*
University of Rochester, William E. Simon
Graduate School of Business Administration
(NY) 401, *401,* **1132**
University of San Diego, School of Business
Administration (CA) 142, **1136**
University of South Carolina, College of Business
Administration (SC) 483, *483,* **1140**
University of Southern California, Marshall School
of Business (CA) 143, *143,* **1142**
University of South Florida, College of Business
Administration (FL) 185
University of Stirling, School of Management
(United Kingdom) 687
University of Tennessee at Chattanooga, School of
Business Administration (TN) 493, *493*
University of Tennessee, Knoxville, College of
Business Administration (TN) 494, *495,* **1148**
University of Texas at Austin, Graduate School of
Business (TX) 523, **1152**
University of the Pacific, Eberhardt School of
Business (CA) 144, *145,* **1158**
University of the West of England, Bristol, Bristol
Business School (United Kingdom) 689
University of the Witwatersrand, Graduate School
of Business Administration (South Africa) 650,
1160
University of Toledo, College of Business
Administration (OH) 433, **1162**
University of Twente, TSM Business School
(Netherlands) 640, **1166**
University of Ulster at Jordanstown, Ulster
Business School (United Kingdom) 689
University of Victoria, Faculty of Business
(Canada) 605
University of Washington, School of Business
Administration (WA) 552, **1170**
The University of Western Ontario, Richard Ivey
School of Business (Canada) 606, *606,* **1172**
University of Western Sydney, Macarthur, Faculty
of Business and Technology (Australia) 584
University of Wisconsin-Madison, School of
Business (WI) 564, **1174**
Utah State University, College of Business (UT)
533
Wake Forest University, Babcock Graduate School
of Management (NC) 413, **1180**

Waseda University, Graduate School of Asia-
Pacific Studies (Japan) 633, **1184**
Wayne State University, School of Business
Administration (MI) 311, *311,* **1188**
Western Illinois University, College of Business
and Technology (IL) 225
Wichita State University, W. Frank Barton School
of Business (KS) 250, *250*
William Carey College, School of Business (MS)
325
Woodbury University, School of Business and
Management (CA) 145, **1198**
Worcester Polytechnic Institute, Graduate
Management Programs (MA) 295, *295,* **1200**
Xavier University, Williams College of Business
Administration (OH) 435, **1204**
York University, Schulich School of Business
(Canada) 608, **1206**

ENVIRONMENTAL ECONOMICS/MANAGEMENT

Bentley College, Graduate School of Business
(MA) 279, *280,* **722**
Brigham Young University, Marriott School of
Management (UT) 531, **736**
Clark University, Graduate School of Management
(MA) 284, **754**
Dalhousie University, Faculty of Management
(Canada) 590, **774**
National University, School of Management and
Technology (CA) 128, **890**
Norwegian School of Management, Graduate
School (Norway) 643
Open University, Business School (United
Kingdom) 671
Rensselaer at Hartford, Lally School of
Management and Technology (CT) 155
Rensselaer Polytechnic Institute, Lally School of
Management and Technology (NY) 386, **942**
University of Bath, School of Management
(United Kingdom) 675
University of Houston-Clear Lake, College of
Business and Public Administration (TX) 519
University of Illinois at Urbana-Champaign,
Illinois MBA (IL) 224, **1080**
University of Maryland University College,
Graduate School of Management and
Technology (MD) 275
University of Massachusetts Boston, College of
Management (MA) 292
University of St. Thomas, Graduate School of
Business (MN) 318, **1134**
University of Texas at Austin, Graduate School of
Business (TX) 523, **1152**
University of Wales, Business School (United
Kingdom) 690
University of Western Sydney, Macarthur, Faculty
of Business and Technology (Australia) 584
Widener University, School of Business
Administration (PA) 473, **1192**

EUROPEAN BUSINESS STUDIES

Aston University, Aston Business School (United
Kingdom) 662
Brigham Young University, Marriott School of
Management (UT) 531, **736**
EAP-European School of Management, Business
Programs (United Kingdom) 664
EAP-European School of Management, School of
Management (France) 613
École Nationale des Ponts et Chaussées, ENPC
Graduate School of International Business
(France) 614
Groupe ESC Toulouse, ESC Toulouse Graduate
School of Management (France) 618
Institut Superieur de Gestion, ISG International
School of Business (France) 620
Katholieke Universiteit Leuven, Department of
Applied Economic Sciences (Belgium) 587

Open University of the Netherlands, Business
Programs (Netherlands) 639
Sheffield Hallam University, Business School
(United Kingdom) 673
University of Brighton, Center for Management
Development (United Kingdom) 677
University of Bristol, Graduate School of
International Business (United Kingdom) 678,
1040
University of Connecticut, School of Business
Administration (CT) 158, **1058**
University of Glasgow, University of Glasgow
Business School (United Kingdom) 680
University of the West of England, Bristol, Bristol
Business School (United Kingdom) 689
The University of Western Ontario, Richard Ivey
School of Business (Canada) 606, *606,* **1172**

FINANCE

Adelphi University, School of Management and
Business (NY) 366, **696**
Alabama Agricultural and Mechanical University,
Department of Business Administration (AL)
85
Allentown College of St. Francis de Sales,
Business Programs (PA) 449
American International College, School of
Business Administration (MA) 276
American University, Kogod College of Business
Administration (DC) 164, **702**
Anna Maria College, Graduate Program in
Business Administration (MA) 277
Antioch University Seattle, Graduate Management
Program (WA) 547
Arizona State University, College of Business
(AZ) 96, **704**
Armstrong University, Graduate School (CA) 106,
706
Ashridge Management College, Ashridge
Executive MBA Program (United Kingdom)
661
Assumption College, Department of Business
Studies (MA) 278, *278*
Aston University, Aston Business School (United
Kingdom) 662
Auburn University, College of Business (AL) 85,
710
Auburn University Montgomery, School of
Business (AL) 86
Avila College, Department of Business and
Economics (MO) 325
Ball State University, College of Business (IN)
226
Bangkok University, Graduate School (Thailand)
659
Bar-Ilan University, S. Daniel Abraham Center of
Economics and Business, The Graduate School
of Business (Israel) 630
Barry University, School of Business (FL) 169
Baruch College of the City University of New
York, Zicklin School of Business (NY) 367,
718
Baylor University, Hankamer School of Business
(TX) 498, **720**
Benedictine University, Graduate Programs (IL)
205
Bentley College, Graduate School of Business
(MA) 279, *280,* **722**
Bilkent University, School of Business
Administration (Turkey) 660
Boise State University, College of Business and
Economics (ID) 202, **724**
Bond University, School of Business (Australia)
573
Boston College, Wallace E. Carroll Graduate
School of Management (MA) 280, **726**
Boston University, School of Management (MA)
281, **728**
Bradley University, Foster College of Business
Administration (IL) 206

FINANCIAL ECONOMICS

FINANCIAL INFORMATION SYSTEMS

McMaster University, Michael G. DeGroote
School of Business (Canada) 593
Mercer University, Cecil B. Day Campus, Stetson
School of Business and Economics (GA) 196
Millsaps College, Else School of Management
(MS) 321, *321*
Morehead State University, College of Business
(KY) 253
Mount Saint Mary's College and Seminary,
Graduate Program of Business (MD) 272
National University, School of Management and
Technology (CA) 128, **890**
New Hampshire College, Graduate School of
Business (NH) 348, **892**
New Mexico State University, College of Business
Administration and Economics (NM) 364
New York Institute of Technology, School of
Management (NY) 382, **896**
Northeast Louisiana University, College of
Business Administration (LA) 261
Northwestern University, J. L. Kellogg Graduate
School of Management (IL) 216
Nova Southeastern University, School of Business
and Entrepreneurship (FL) 177, **912**
Oklahoma City University, Meinders School of
Business (OK) 437
Old Dominion University, College of Business and
Public Administration (VA) 541
Pennsylvania State University Great Valley
Graduate Center, School of Graduate
Professional Studies (PA) 462, **920**
Pennsylvania State University University Park
Campus, Mary Jean and Frank P. Smeal
College of Business Administration (PA) 463,
922
Philadelphia College of Textiles and Science,
School of Business Administration (PA) 464,
926
Quinnipiac College, School of Business (CT) 155,
938
Rensselaer at Hartford, Lally School of
Management and Technology (CT) 155
Rider University, College of Business
Administration (NJ) 355
Rivier College, Department of Business
Administration (NH) 349
Robert Morris College, Graduate Programs in
Business and Related Professional Areas (PA)
465, **948**
Roosevelt University, Walter E. Heller College of
Business Administration (IL) 219, **954**
Royal Melbourne Institute of Technology,
Graduate School of Business (Australia) 578
Rutgers, The State University of New Jersey,
Camden, School of Business (NJ) 356
Sacred Heart University, College of Business (CT)
156, **958**
Saint Francis College, Business Administration
Program (PA) 466
Saint Joseph's University, Erivan K. Haub School
of Business (PA) 467, **966**
Saint Mary College, Department of Business,
Economics and Information Technology (KS)
248
Saint Mary's University of Minnesota, School of
Graduate Studies/School of Business and
Social Sciences (MN) 316
St. Thomas University, Department of Business
Administration (FL) 179, **974**
Saint Xavier University, Graham School of
Management (IL) 219
Shenandoah University, Harry F. Byrd, Jr. School
of Business (VA) 543
Silver Lake College, Program in Management and
Organizational Behavior (WI) 562
Southeastern University, College of Graduate
Studies (DC) 167
Stanford University, Graduate School of Business
(CA) 134

State University of New York at Buffalo, School
of Management (NY) 394, **1000**
State University of New York at Stony Brook, W.
Averell Harriman School for Management and
Policy (NY) 396, **1002**
State University of New York Institute of
Technology at Utica/Rome, School of Business
(NY) 398
Stephens College, Program in Business
Administration (MO) 333
Temple University, School of Business and
Management (PA) 468, *468*, **1010**
Texas A&M University-Corpus Christi, College of
Business Administration (TX) 511
Texas Tech University, College of Business
Administration (TX) 514, *515*, **1018**
Université Laval, Faculty des Sciences de
l'Administration (Canada) 597
University of Alberta, Faculty of Business
(Canada) 597
University of Arizona, Karl Eller Graduate School
of Management (AZ) 100, **1032**
University of Auckland, Executive Programs (New
Zealand) 640
University of Baltimore, Robert G. Merrick School
of Business (MD) 274, **1036**
University of Colorado at Denver, Graduate
School of Business Administration (CO) 150,
1056
University of Connecticut, School of Business
Administration (CT) 158, **1058**
University of Dallas, Graduate School of
Management (TX) 517, **1060**
University of Denver, Daniels College of Business
(CO) 151, *151*, **1064**
The University of Findlay, Business Programs
(OH) 432
University of Houston-Clear Lake, College of
Business and Public Administration (TX) 519
University of Illinois at Chicago, College of
Business Administration (IL) 222, **1078**
University of Illinois at Urbana-Champaign,
Illinois MBA (IL) 224, **1080**
University of La Verne, School of Business and
Global Studies (CA) 141
University of Louisville, College of Business and
Public Administration (KY) 256, **1088**
University of Mary, Business Division (ND) 416
University of Maryland University College,
Graduate School of Management and
Technology (MD) 275
University of Massachusetts Amherst, School of
Management (MA) 292
University of Massachusetts Boston, College of
Management (MA) 292
University of Missouri-Kansas City, Harry W.
Block School of Public Administration (MO)
335
University of New Haven, School of Business
(CT) 159, **1114**
University of Oklahoma, Michael F. Price College
of Business (OK) 442, **1120**
University of Pennsylvania, Wharton School (PA)
469, **1124**
University of Plymouth, Business School (United
Kingdom) 685
University of Rochester, William E. Simon
Graduate School of Business Administration
(NY) 401, *401*, **1132**
University of St. Francis, College of Graduate
Studies (IL) 225, *225*
University of St. Thomas, Graduate School of
Business (MN) 318, **1134**
University of Sarasota, College of Business
Administration (FL) 185
University of South Florida, College of Business
Administration (FL) 185
University of Southwestern Louisiana, Graduate
School (LA) 264

The University of Tampa, College of Business
(FL) 186, **1146**
University of Technology, Sydney, Graduate
School of Business (Australia) 582
University of Tennessee at Chattanooga, School of
Business Administration (TN) 493, *493*
University of Texas at San Antonio, College of
Business (TX) 526, **1156**
University of Utah, David Eccles School of
Business (UT) 532, **1168**
University of Wisconsin-Milwaukee, School of
Business Administration (WI) 565
University of Wisconsin-Whitewater, College of
Business and Economics (WI) 567
Upper Iowa University, Program in Business
Leadership (IA) 243
Wayland Baptist University, Graduate Studies
Office (TX) 529
Webster University, School of Business and
Technology (MO) 338
Western Connecticut State University, Ancell
School of Business and Public Administration
(CT) 160
Western International University, Graduate
Programs in Business (AZ) 101, *101*
Western New England College, School of Business
(MA) 294
Westminster College of Salt Lake City, Bill and
Vieve Gore School of Business (UT) 534
Widener University, School of Business
Administration (PA) 473, **1192**
William Carey College, School of Business (MS)
325
Wilmington College, Business Programs (DE) 163
Wright State University, College of Business and
Administration (OH) 434, **1202**
York College of Pennsylvania, Department of
Business Administration (PA) 474

HUMAN RESOURCES
Adelphi University, School of Management and
Business (NY) 366, **696**
Alabama Agricultural and Mechanical University,
Department of Business Administration (AL)
85
American University, Kogod College of Business
Administration (DC) 164, **702**
Antioch New England Graduate School,
Department of Organization and Management
(NH) 347
Antioch Southern California/Los Angeles, Program
in Organizational Management (CA) 105
Antioch Southern California/Santa Barbara,
Graduate Program in Organizational
Management (CA) 105
Antioch University Seattle, Graduate Management
Program (WA) 547
Ashridge Management College, Ashridge
Executive MBA Program (United Kingdom)
661
Assumption College, Department of Business
Studies (MA) 278, *278*
Aston University, Aston Business School (United
Kingdom) 662
Athabasca University, Centre for Innovative
Management (Canada) 588, *588*
Auburn University, College of Business (AL) 85,
710
Auburn University Montgomery, School of
Business (AL) 86
Azusa Pacific University, School of Business and
Management (CA) 107, *107*
Baker College Center for Graduate Studies, Center
for Graduate Studies (MI) 297, **714**
Ball State University, College of Business (IN)
226
Bangkok University, Graduate School (Thailand)
659
Baruch College of the City University of New
York, Zicklin School of Business (NY) 367,
718

INSURANCE

INTERNATIONAL AND AREA BUSINESS STUDIES

Areas of Concentration Index

Vienna University of Economics and Business Administration, Business Program/International MBA (Austria) 584
Virginia Polytechnic Institute and State University, Pamplin College of Business (VA) 546, **1178**
Wagner College, Department of Economics and Business Administration (NY) 402
Washington State University, College of Business and Economics (WA) 553
Washington University in St. Louis, John M. Olin School of Business (MO) 337
Wayne State University, School of Business Administration (MI) 311, *311*, **1188**
Webster University, School of Business and Technology (MO) 338
Western Illinois University, College of Business and Technology (IL) 225
Western International University, Graduate Programs in Business (AZ) 101, *101*
Western New England College, School of Business (MA) 294
Westminster College of Salt Lake City, Bill and Vieve Gore School of Business (UT) 534
Widener University, School of Business Administration (PA) 473, **1192**
Woodbury University, School of Business and Management (CA) 145, **1198**
Wright State University, College of Business and Administration (OH) 434, **1202**
Xavier University, Williams College of Business Administration (OH) 435, **1204**
York University, Schulich School of Business (Canada) 608, **1206**

INTERNATIONAL DEVELOPMENT MANAGEMENT
Curtin University of Technology, Graduate School of Business (Australia) 574
Eastern College, Graduate Business Programs (PA) 454, **792**
Graduate School of Business Administration Zürich, Business Programs (Switzerland) 656
Groupe ESC Toulouse, ESC Toulouse Graduate School of Management (France) 618
Hope International University, Graduate Management Program (CA) 123
McGill University, Faculty of Management (Canada) 592, **884**
Naval Postgraduate School, Department of Systems Management (CA) 128
School for International Training, Program in International and Intercultural Management (VT) 535
University of Arizona, Karl Eller Graduate School of Management (AZ) 100, **1032**
University of Plymouth, Business School (United Kingdom) 685
University of Texas at Dallas, School of Management (TX) 525, *525*, **1154**

INTERNATIONAL ECONOMICS
Baylor University, Hankamer School of Business (TX) 498, **720**
Bocconi University, SDA Bocconi (Italy) 631
Brandeis University, Graduate School of International Economics and Finance (MA) 282, *282*, **734**
The Catholic University of America, Department of Economics and Business (DC) 165
École Nationale des Ponts et Chaussées, ENPC Graduate School of International Business (France) 614
Graduate School of Business Administration Zürich, Business Programs (Switzerland) 656
IADE, Instituto Universitario de Administracion de Empresas (Spain) 653
Lancaster University, Management School (United Kingdom) 668

Marquette University, College of Business Administration (WI) 561
Monterey Institute of International Studies, Fisher Graduate School of Business Management (CA) 127, **888**
Murdoch University, School of Business (Australia) 577
Naval Postgraduate School, Department of Systems Management (CA) 128
Radford University, College of Business and Economics (VA) 542
Stockholm School of Economics, Department of Business Administration (Sweden) 655
University of Arizona, Karl Eller Graduate School of Management (AZ) 100, **1032**
University of Bristol, Graduate School of International Business (United Kingdom) 678, **1040**
University of California, Los Angeles, The Anderson School at UCLA (CA) 138, **1048**
University of Georgia, Terry College of Business (GA) 199, **1072**
University of Illinois at Urbana-Champaign, Illinois MBA (IL) 224, **1080**
University of Washington, School of Business Administration (WA) 552, **1170**
University of Western Sydney, Macarthur, Faculty of Business and Technology (Australia) 584
Utah State University, College of Business (UT) 533

INTERNATIONAL FINANCE
American University, Kogod College of Business Administration (DC) 164, **702**
Ashridge Management College, Ashridge Executive MBA Program (United Kingdom) 661
Brandeis University, Graduate School of International Economics and Finance (MA) 282, *282*, **734**
Brigham Young University, Marriott School of Management (UT) 531, **736**
City University, Business School (United Kingdom) 662
DePaul University, Charles H. Kellstadt Graduate School of Business (IL) 206, **778**
Dowling College, School of Business (NY) 373, **784**
École Nationale des Ponts et Chaussées, ENPC Graduate School of International Business (France) 614
École Supérieure des Sciences Économiques et Commerciales, ESSEC School of Management (France) 615
Erasmus University Rotterdam, Rotterdam School of Management (Netherlands) 638, **808**
George Mason University, School of Management (VA) 538, **824**
Graduate School of Business Administration Zürich, Business Programs (Switzerland) 656
HEC Graduate School of Management, Institute Supérieur des Affaires (France) 619
Huron University USA in London, MBA Program (United Kingdom) 666, *666*, **840**
IADE, Instituto Universitario de Administracion de Empresas (Spain) 653
Imperial College, Management School (United Kingdom) 667
Instituto Tecnológico y de Estudios Superiores de Monterrey, Campus México City, Programs in Business (Mexico) 635
International Executive Development Center, School of Business Administration (Slovenia) 649
International University of Japan, Graduate School of International Management (Japan) 632, *632*, **852**
Katholieke Universiteit Leuven, Department of Applied Economic Sciences (Belgium) 587

Loyola Marymount University, College of Business Administration (CA) 126, *126*, **876**
McGill University, Faculty of Management (Canada) 592, **884**
Monterey Institute of International Studies, Fisher Graduate School of Business Management (CA) 127, **888**
Murdoch University, School of Business (Australia) 577
Nijenrode University, Netherlands Business School (Netherlands) 638, **900**
Oklahoma City University, Meinders School of Business (OK) 437
Open University of the Netherlands, Business Programs (Netherlands) 639
Radford University, College of Business and Economics (VA) 542
Richmond, The American International University in London, School of Business (United Kingdom) 672, **946**
Royal Melbourne Institute of Technology, Graduate School of Business (Australia) 578
St. John's University, College of Business Administration (NY) 390, **964**
San Francisco State University, College of Business (CA) 132
Sheffield Hallam University, Business School (United Kingdom) 673
Thunderbird, The American Graduate School of International Management, Master's Program in International Management (AZ) 99, **1022**
Universidade do Porto, Graduate School of Business (Portugal) 646
University of Arizona, Karl Eller Graduate School of Management (AZ) 100, **1032**
University of Bristol, Graduate School of International Business (United Kingdom) 678, **1040**
University of California, Los Angeles, The Anderson School at UCLA (CA) 138, **1048**
University of Glasgow, University of Glasgow Business School (United Kingdom) 680
University of Illinois at Urbana-Champaign, Illinois MBA (IL) 224, **1080**
University of Maryland University College, Graduate School of Management and Technology (MD) 275
University of Nottingham, School of Management and Finance (United Kingdom) 683
University of Plymouth, Business School (United Kingdom) 685
University of South Carolina, College of Business Administration (SC) 483, *483*, **1140**
The University of Texas at Arlington, College of Business Administration (TX) 522, **1150**
University of the West of England, Bristol, Bristol Business School (United Kingdom) 689
University of Washington, School of Business Administration (WA) 552, **1170**
University of Western Sydney, Macarthur, Faculty of Business and Technology (Australia) 584
Walsh College of Accountancy and Business Administration, College of Accountancy and Business Administration (MI) 311, **1182**
Waseda University, Graduate School of Asia-Pacific Studies (Japan) 633, **1184**
York University, Schulich School of Business (Canada) 608, **1206**

INTERNATIONAL LOGISTICS
City University, Business School (United Kingdom) 662
Copenhagen Business School, Faculty of Economics and Business Administration (Denmark) 611
École Supérieure des Sciences Économiques et Commerciales, ESSEC School of Management (France) 615

Areas of Concentration Index

Areas of Concentration Index

MANAGEMENT INFORMATION SYSTEMS
(continued)

Massachusetts Institute of Technology, Sloan School of Management (MA) 288

McMaster University, Michael G. DeGroote School of Business (Canada) 593

Mercer University, Cecil B. Day Campus, Stetson School of Business and Economics (GA) 196

Metropolitan State University, Management and Administration Program (MN) 314

Miami University, Richard T. Farmer School of Business Administration (OH) 427

Michigan State University, Eli Broad Graduate School of Management (MI) 303

Middle Tennessee State University, College of Business (TN) 488

Mississippi State University, College of Business and Industry (MS) 323, **886**

Monash University, Monash Mt. Eliza Business School (Australia) 577

Montclair State University, School of Business Administration (NJ) 353

Nanyang Technological University, Nanyang Business School (Republic of Singapore) 647

National University of Singapore, Graduate School of Business (Republic of Singapore) 648

Naval Postgraduate School, Department of Systems Management (CA) 128

New Hampshire College, Graduate School of Business (NH) 348, **892**

New Jersey Institute of Technology, School of Industrial Management (NJ) 354

New Mexico State University, College of Business Administration and Economics (NM) 364

New York Institute of Technology, School of Management (NY) 382, **896**

New York University, Leonard N. Stern School of Business (NY) 382, **898**

North Carolina State University, College of Management (NC) 408, **902**

North Central College, Department of Business Administration (IL) 214, *214*

Northern Arizona University, College of Business Administration (AZ) 98

Northern Kentucky University, College of Business (KY) 254

Nova Southeastern University, School of Business and Entrepreneurship (FL) 177, **912**

Oakland University, School of Business Administration (MI) 305, *305*

The Ohio State University, Max M. Fisher College of Business (OH) 427

Oklahoma City University, Meinders School of Business (OK) 437

Oklahoma State University, College of Business Administration (OK) 438

Old Dominion University, College of Business and Public Administration (VA) 541

Pace University, Lubin School of Business (NY) 384, **916**

Pennsylvania State University Great Valley Graduate Center, School of Graduate Professional Studies (PA) 462, **920**

Pennsylvania State University Harrisburg Campus of the Capital College, School of Business Administration (PA) 462

Pennsylvania State University University Park Campus, Mary Jean and Frank P. Smeal College of Business Administration (PA) 463, **922**

Philadelphia College of Textiles and Science, School of Business Administration (PA) 464, **926**

Purdue University, Krannert Graduate School of Management (IN) 234, **934**

Quinnipiac College, School of Business (CT) 155, **938**

Regis University, School for Professional Studies (CO) 148

Reims Graduate Business School, Reims Business School (France) 621

Rensselaer at Hartford, Lally School of Management and Technology (CT) 155

Rensselaer Polytechnic Institute, Lally School of Management and Technology (NY) 386, **942**

Rhodes University, Management Department (South Africa) 649

Rice University, Jesse H. Jones Graduate School of Management (TX) 503, **944**

Robert Morris College, Graduate Programs in Business and Related Professional Areas (PA) 465, **948**

Rochester Institute of Technology, College of Business (NY) 388, **950**

Roosevelt University, Walter E. Heller College of Business Administration (IL) 219, **954**

Rutgers, The State University of New Jersey, Camden, School of Business (NJ) 356

Rutgers, The State University of New Jersey, Newark, Graduate School of Management (NJ) 357

Sacred Heart University, College of Business (CT) 156, **958**

St. Ambrose University, H.L. McLaughlin One-Year MBA Program (IA) 240, **962**

St. Edward's University, School of Business (TX) 504

St. John's University, College of Business Administration (NY) 390, **964**

Saint Joseph's University, Erivan K. Haub School of Business (PA) 467, **966**

Saint Louis University, School of Business and Administration (MO) 331, *331*, **968**

Saint Michael's College, Prevel School Graduate Program in Administration and Management (VT) 535

Saint Peter's College, Graduate Business Programs (NJ) 359, **972**

Salve Regina University, Graduate School (RI) 477

San Diego State University, Graduate School of Business (CA) 131

San Francisco State University, College of Business (CA) 132

Santa Clara University, Thomas and Dorothy Leavey School of Business and Administration (CA) 133, **978**

Seattle Pacific University, School of Business and Economics (WA) 550, **982**

Seattle University, Albers School of Business and Economics (WA) 551, **984**

Seton Hall University, W. Paul Stillman School of Business (NJ) 359, **986**

Sheffield Hallam University, Business School (United Kingdom) 673

Shenandoah University, Harry F. Byrd, Jr. School of Business (VA) 543

Simon Fraser University, Faculty of Business Administration (Canada) 595

Southern Illinois University at Carbondale, College of Business and Administration (IL) 220, **990**

Southern Illinois University at Edwardsville, School of Business (IL) 221, *221*, **992**

Southern Methodist University, Edwin L. Cox School of Business (TX) 506, **994**

Southern Polytechnic State University, School of Management (GA) 198

Southwest Missouri State University, College of Business Administration (MO) 333, *333*

State University of New York at Albany, School of Business (NY) 392, **996**

State University of New York at Binghamton, School of Management (NY) 393, **998**

State University of New York at Buffalo, School of Management (NY) 394, **1000**

State University of New York at Stony Brook, W. Averell Harriman School for Management and Policy (NY) 396, **1002**

Strayer University, Graduate School (DC) 168

Suffolk University, Frank Sawyer School of Management (MA) 291, **1004**

Tarleton State University, College of Business Administration (TX) 508

Tel Aviv University, Leon Recanati Graduate School of Business Administration (Israel) 630

Temple University, School of Business and Management (PA) 468, *468*, **1010**

Tennessee Technological University, College of Business Administration (TN) 490

Texas A&M University, Lowry Mays Graduate School of Business (TX) 510, **1014**

Texas A&M University Commerce, College of Business and Technology (TX) 511

Texas Tech University, College of Business Administration (TX) 514, *515*, **1018**

Troy State University Dothan, School of Business (AL) 89

Troy State University Montgomery, Division of Business (AL) 90

Tulane University, A. B. Freeman School of Business (LA) 262, **1026**

Université du Québec à Montréal, École des Sciences de la Gestion (Canada) 597

Université Laval, Faculty des Sciences de l'Administration (Canada) 597

University College Cork, Faculty of Commerce (Ireland) 627

University College Dublin, The Michael Smurfit Graduate School of Business (Ireland) 628

University College, Galway, Faculty of Commerce (Ireland) 629

University of Akron, College of Business Administration (OH) 430

The University of Alabama, Manderson Graduate School of Business (AL) 90, **1030**

University of Arizona, Karl Eller Graduate School of Management (AZ) 100, **1032**

University of Arkansas, College of Business Administration (AR) 103, **1034**

University of Baltimore, Robert G. Merrick School of Business (MD) 274, **1036**

University of Bath, School of Management (United Kingdom) 675

University of Bridgeport, School of Business (CT) 157, **1038**

University of Brighton, Center for Management Development (United Kingdom) 677

University of British Columbia, Faculty of Commerce and Business Administration (Canada) 598, *598*, **1042**

The University of Calgary, Faculty of Management (Canada) 599

University of California, Berkeley, Haas School of Business (CA) 136

University of California, Davis, Graduate School of Management (CA) 137, **1044**

University of California, Los Angeles, The Anderson School at UCLA (CA) 138, **1048**

University of California, Riverside, A. Gary Anderson Graduate School of Management (CA) 139, **1050**

University of Canterbury, Department of Management (New Zealand) 641

University of Central Florida, College of Business Administration (FL) 181

University of Central Oklahoma, College of Business Administration (OK) 442

University of Central Texas, Division of Management, Business and Technology (TX) 517

University of Colorado at Colorado Springs, Graduate School of Business Administration (CO) 150, *150*

University of Colorado at Denver, Graduate School of Business Administration (CO) 150, **1056**

University of Dallas, Graduate School of Management (TX) 517, **1060**

University of Dayton, School of Business Administration (OH) 431

University of Denver, Daniels College of Business (CO) 151, *151,* **1064**

University of Detroit Mercy, College of Business Administration (MI) 308, **1066**

University of Georgia, Terry College of Business (GA) 199, **1072**

University of Hartford, Barney School of Business and Public Administration (CT) 158

University of Houston, College of Business Administration (TX) 518, **1076**

University of Houston-Clear Lake, College of Business and Public Administration (TX) 519

University of Illinois at Chicago, College of Business Administration (IL) 222, **1078**

The University of Iowa, School of Management (IA) 241, **1082**

University of Kentucky, Carol Martin Gatton College of Business and Economics (KY) 255, **1086**

University of Maryland, College Park, Robert H. Smith School of Business (MD) 274, **1094**

University of Maryland University College, Graduate School of Management and Technology (MD) 275

University of Massachusetts Boston, College of Management (MA) 292

University of Massachusetts Lowell, College of Management (MA) 294

University of Melbourne, Melbourne Business School (Australia) 579

The University of Memphis, Fogelman College of Business and Economics (TN) 492, **1096**

University of Miami, School of Business Administration (FL) 183, **1098**

University of Michigan, University of Michigan Business School (MI) 308

University of Mississippi, School of Business Administration (MS) 323, **1102**

University of Missouri-Columbia, College of Business and Public Administration (MO) 335, **1104**

University of Missouri-Kansas City, Harry W. Block School of Public Administration (MO) 335

University of Missouri-St. Louis, School of Business Administration (MO) 336, *336*

University of Nebraska-Lincoln, College of Business Administration (NE) 344, *344*

University of Newcastle, Graduate School of Business (Australia) 580

University of New Mexico, Robert O. Anderson Graduate School of Management (NM) 364

University of New Orleans, College of Business Administration (LA) 263

University of North Carolina at Wilmington, Cameron School of Business (NC) 413

University of North Texas, College of Business Administration (TX) 521

University of Northumbria, Newcastle Business School (United Kingdom) 683

University of Notre Dame, College of Business Administration (IN) 235, **1118**

University of Nottingham, School of Management and Finance (United Kingdom) 683

University of Oklahoma, Michael F. Price College of Business (OK) 442, **1120**

University of Pittsburgh, Joseph M. Katz Graduate School of Business (PA) 470, **1128**

University of Redlands, Alfred North Whitehead College (CA) 141

University of Rhode Island, College of Business Administration (RI) 478

University of Rochester, William E. Simon Graduate School of Business Administration (NY) 401, *401,* **1132**

University of St. Thomas, Cameron School of Business (TX) 521

University of Salford, Management School (United Kingdom) 686

University of Sarasota, College of Business Administration (FL) 185

University of Scranton, Program in Business Administration (PA) 471

University of South Carolina, College of Business Administration (SC) 483, *483,* **1140**

University of South Dakota, School of Business (SD) 485

University of Southern California, Marshall School of Business (CA) 143, *143,* **1142**

University of Southern Mississippi, College of Business Administration (MS) 324

University of South Florida, College of Business Administration (FL) 185

University of Stirling, School of Management (United Kingdom) 687

The University of Tampa, College of Business (FL) 186, **1146**

The University of Texas at Arlington, College of Business Administration (TX) 522, **1150**

University of Texas at Austin, Graduate School of Business (TX) 523, **1152**

University of Texas at Dallas, School of Management (TX) 525, *525,* **1154**

University of Texas at San Antonio, College of Business (TX) 526, **1156**

University of the Sacred Heart, Business School (PR) 571

University of the West of England, Bristol, Bristol Business School (United Kingdom) 689

University of the Witwatersrand, Graduate School of Business Administration (South Africa) 650, **1160**

University of Toledo, College of Business Administration (OH) 433, **1162**

University of Ulster at Jordanstown, Ulster Business School (United Kingdom) 689

University of Washington, School of Business Administration (WA) 552, **1170**

University of Wisconsin-Madison, School of Business (WI) 564, **1174**

University of Wisconsin-Milwaukee, School of Business Administration (WI) 565

University of Wisconsin-Oshkosh, College of Business Administration (WI) 565

University of Wisconsin-Whitewater, College of Business and Economics (WI) 567

Vanderbilt University, Owen Graduate School of Management (TN) 495

Villanova University, College of Commerce and Finance (PA) 471, **1176**

Walsh University, Program in Management (OH) 433

Washington State University, College of Business and Economics (WA) 553

Wayland Baptist University, Graduate Studies Office (TX) 529

Wayne State University, School of Business Administration (MI) 311, *311,* **1188**

Western Illinois University, College of Business and Technology (IL) 225

Western International University, Graduate Programs in Business (AZ) 101, *101*

Western Michigan University, Haworth College of Business (MI) 312

Western New England College, School of Business (MA) 294

West Texas A&M University, T. Boone Pickens College of Business (TX) 530

Widener University, School of Business Administration (PA) 473, **1192**

Worcester Polytechnic Institute, Graduate Management Programs (MA) 295, *295,* **1200**

Wright State University, College of Business and Administration (OH) 434, **1202**

Xavier University, Williams College of Business Administration (OH) 435, **1204**

York University, Schulich School of Business (Canada) 608, **1206**

MANAGEMENT SCIENCE

Arthur D. Little School of Management, One-Year Master of Science in Management Program (MA) 277, *277,* **708**

Assumption College, Department of Business Studies (MA) 278, *278*

California State University, Fullerton, School of Business Administration and Economics (CA) 112

California State University, Hayward, School of Business and Economics (CA) 113

California State University, Northridge, College of Business Administration and Economics (CA) 115

Columbia University, Columbia Business School (NY) 371, **766**

Copenhagen Business School, Faculty of Economics and Business Administration (Denmark) 611

Drexel University, College of Business and Administration (PA) 452, **786**

Edith Cowan University, Faculty of Business (Australia) 575

The George Washington University, School of Business and Public Management (DC) 166, **828**

Houston Baptist University, College of Business and Economics (TX) 500

IADE, Instituto Universitario de Administracion de Empresas (Spain) 653

Illinois Institute of Technology, Stuart School of Business (IL) 209, **842**

Instituto Tecnológico y de Estudios Superiores de Monterrey, Campus México City, Programs in Business (Mexico) 635

International University of Business Agriculture and Technology (IUBAT), College of Business Administration (Bangladesh) 585

Kean University, School of Business, Government, and Technology (NJ) 352

Lancaster University, Management School (United Kingdom) 668

Loyola University Chicago, Graduate School of Business (IL) 212, **878**

Massachusetts Institute of Technology, Sloan School of Management (MA) 288

McMaster University, Michael G. DeGroote School of Business (Canada) 593

Metropolitan State University, Management and Administration Program (MN) 314

Naval Postgraduate School, Department of Systems Management (CA) 128

Pace University, Lubin School of Business (NY) 384, **916**

Pennsylvania State University University Park Campus, Mary Jean and Frank P. Smeal College of Business Administration (PA) 463, **922**

Regis University, School for Professional Studies (CO) 148

Rensselaer Polytechnic Institute, Lally School of Management and Technology (NY) 386, **942**

Rutgers, The State University of New Jersey, Newark, Graduate School of Management (NJ) 357

San Diego State University, Graduate School of Business (CA) 131

Sheffield Hallam University, Business School (United Kingdom) 673

Simon Fraser University, Faculty of Business Administration (Canada) 595

State University of New York Institute of Technology at Utica/Rome, School of Business (NY) 398

Areas of Concentration Index

ORGANIZATIONAL BEHAVIOR/DEVELOPMENT

Areas of Concentration Index

University of Missouri-Columbia, College of Business and Public Administration (MO) 335, **1104**
University of New South Wales, Australian Graduate School of Management (Australia) 581
University of Redlands, Alfred North Whitehead College (CA) 141
University of Salford, Management School (United Kingdom) 686
University of South Florida, College of Business Administration (FL) 185
The University of Tampa, College of Business (FL) 186, **1146**
University of Western Sydney, Macarthur, Faculty of Business and Technology (Australia) 584
University of Wisconsin-Madison, School of Business (WI) 564, **1174**
University of Wisconsin-Milwaukee, School of Business Administration (WI) 565
Upper Iowa University, Program in Business Leadership (IA) 243
Wayne State University, School of Business Administration (MI) 311, *311,* **1188**
Xavier University, Williams College of Business Administration (OH) 435, **1204**

QUANTITATIVE ANALYSIS

Ashridge Management College, Ashridge Executive MBA Program (United Kingdom) 661
Aston University, Aston Business School (United Kingdom) 662
Bangkok University, Graduate School (Thailand) 659
Baruch College of the City University of New York, Zicklin School of Business (NY) 367, **718**
Bentley College, Graduate School of Business (MA) 279, *280,* **722**
Bilkent University, School of Business Administration (Turkey) 660
Brigham Young University, Marriott School of Management (UT) 531, **736**
Carnegie Mellon University, Graduate School of Industrial Administration (PA) 450, **740**
City University, Business School (United Kingdom) 662
Copenhagen Business School, Faculty of Economics and Business Administration (Denmark) 611
Curtin University of Technology, Graduate School of Business (Australia) 574
Emory University, Roberto C. Goizueta Business School (GA) 190, **804**
Fairleigh Dickinson University, Samuel J. Silberman College of Business Administration (NJ) 351, **814**
Hong Kong Baptist University, School of Business (Hong Kong) 625
IADE, Instituto Universitario de Administracion de Empresas (Spain) 653
Instituto de Empresa, Business School (Spain) 653
Katholieke Universiteit Leuven, Department of Applied Economic Sciences (Belgium) 587
Louisiana Tech University, College of Administration and Business (LA) 258
Monash University, Monash Mt. Eliza Business School (Australia) 577
New York University, Leonard N. Stern School of Business (NY) 382, **898**
Providence College, Graduate Business Program (RI) 476
Reims Graduate Business School, Reims Business School (France) 621
Rensselaer Polytechnic Institute, Lally School of Management and Technology (NY) 386, **942**
Roosevelt University, Walter E. Heller College of Business Administration (IL) 219, **954**

San Francisco State University, College of Business (CA) 132
Santa Clara University, Thomas and Dorothy Leavey School of Business and Administration (CA) 133, **978**
Seton Hall University, W. Paul Stillman School of Business (NJ) 359, **986**
Université Laval, Faculty des Sciences de l'Administration (Canada) 597
University College, Galway, Faculty of Commerce (Ireland) 629
University of Brighton, Center for Management Development (United Kingdom) 677
University of Bristol, Graduate School of International Business (United Kingdom) 678, **1040**
University of Canterbury, Department of Management (New Zealand) 641
University of Cincinnati, Graduate Business Program (OH) 431
University of Detroit Mercy, College of Business Administration (MI) 308, **1066**
University of Edinburgh, Edinburgh University Management School (United Kingdom) 679, **1068**
University of Georgia, Terry College of Business (GA) 199, **1072**
University of Houston, College of Business Administration (TX) 518, **1076**
University of Mississippi, School of Business Administration (MS) 323, **1102**
University of Missouri-Kansas City, Harry W. Block School of Public Administration (MO) 335
University of Newcastle, Graduate School of Business (Australia) 580
University of New South Wales, Australian Graduate School of Management (Australia) 581
University of Puerto Rico, Río Piedras, Graduate School of Business Administration (PR) 571
University of the West of England, Bristol, Bristol Business School (United Kingdom) 689
University of the Witwatersrand, Graduate School of Business Administration (South Africa) 650, **1160**
University of Washington, School of Business Administration (WA) 552, **1170**
Utah State University, College of Business (UT) 533
Walsh University, Program in Management (OH) 433
Willamette University, George H. Atkinson Graduate School of Management (OR) 448, **1196**

REAL ESTATE

American University, Kogod College of Business Administration (DC) 164, **702**
Brigham Young University, Marriott School of Management (UT) 531, **736**
California State Polytechnic University, Pomona, College of Business (CA) 109
California State University, Sacramento, School of Business Administration (CA) 116
City University, Business School (United Kingdom) 662
Cleveland State University, James J. Nance College of Business Administration (OH) 422, **758**
Columbia University, Columbia Business School (NY) 371, **766**
Duquesne University, Graduate School of Business Administration (PA) 453, *453,* **788**
The George Washington University, School of Business and Public Management (DC) 166, **828**
Georgia State University, College of Business Administration (GA) 194, **832**

Johns Hopkins University, School of Continuing Studies, Division of Business and Management (MD) 270, **858**
Louisiana State University and Agricultural and Mechanical College, E. J. Ourso College of Business Administration (LA) 257
Mississippi State University, College of Business and Industry (MS) 323, **886**
Northwestern University, J. L. Kellogg Graduate School of Management (IL) 216
The Ohio State University, Max M. Fisher College of Business (OH) 427
Pennsylvania State University University Park Campus, Mary Jean and Frank P. Smeal College of Business Administration (PA) 463, **922**
Royal Melbourne Institute of Technology, Graduate School of Business (Australia) 578
Rutgers, The State University of New Jersey, Newark, Graduate School of Management (NJ) 357
St. Cloud State University, College of Business (MN) 315
San Diego State University, Graduate School of Business (CA) 131
Southern Methodist University, Edwin L. Cox School of Business (TX) 506, **994**
Temple University, School of Business and Management (PA) 468, *468,* **1010**
Texas A&M University, Lowry Mays Graduate School of Business (TX) 510, **1014**
Université du Québec à Montréal, École des Sciences de la Gestion (Canada) 597
University of British Columbia, Faculty of Commerce and Business Administration (Canada) 598, *598,* **1042**
University of California, Berkeley, Haas School of Business (CA) 136
University of California, Los Angeles, The Anderson School at UCLA (CA) 138, **1048**
University of Central Florida, College of Business Administration (FL) 181
University of Cincinnati, Graduate Business Program (OH) 431
University of Colorado at Boulder, Graduate School of Business Administration (CO) 149, **1054**
University of Connecticut, School of Business Administration (CT) 158, **1058**
University of Denver, Daniels College of Business (CO) 151, *151,* **1064**
University of Florida, Warrington College of Business Administration (FL) 182, *182,* **1070**
University of Georgia, Terry College of Business (GA) 199, **1072**
The University of Memphis, Fogelman College of Business and Economics (TN) 492, **1096**
University of Michigan, University of Michigan Business School (MI) 308
University of Mississippi, School of Business Administration (MS) 323, **1102**
University of New Orleans, College of Business Administration (LA) 263
University of North Carolina at Chapel Hill, Kenan-Flagler Business School (NC) 410
University of North Texas, College of Business Administration (TX) 521
University of Pennsylvania, Wharton School (PA) 469, **1124**
University of St. Thomas, Graduate School of Business (MN) 318, **1134**
University of San Diego, School of Business Administration (CA) 142, **1136**
University of Southern California, Marshall School of Business (CA) 143, *143,* **1142**
The University of Texas at Arlington, College of Business Administration (TX) 522, **1150**
University of Wisconsin-Madison, School of Business (WI) 564, **1174**

Areas of Concentration Index

TAXATION (continued)

Case Western Reserve University, Weatherhead School of Management (OH) 420, **742**

The College of Saint Rose, School of Business (NY) 370, **760**

Colorado State University, College of Business (CO) 146, **764**

Copenhagen Business School, Faculty of Economics and Business Administration (Denmark) 611

DePaul University, Charles H. Kellstadt Graduate School of Business (IL) 206, **778**

Drexel University, College of Business and Administration (PA) 452, **786**

Duquesne University, Graduate School of Business Administration (PA) 453, *453,* **788**

EAP-European School of Management, Business School (Spain) 651

Edith Cowan University, Faculty of Business (Australia) 575

Escuela Superior de Administración y Dirección de Empresas (ESADE), Business School (Spain) 652

Fairfield University, School of Business (CT) 154, **812**

Fairleigh Dickinson University, Samuel J. Silberman College of Business Administration (NJ) 351, **814**

Florida Atlantic University, College of Business (FL) 171

Florida International University, College of Business Administration (FL) 173, **820**

Florida State University, College of Business (FL) 175

Fordham University, Graduate School of Business Administration (NY) 373, **822**

The George Washington University, School of Business and Public Management (DC) 166, **828**

Hofstra University, Frank G. Zarb School of Business (NY) 374, **838**

Kennesaw State University, Michael J. Coles College of Business (GA) 195, *195,* **866**

King's College, William G. McGowan School of Business (PA) 456

Long Island University, Brooklyn Campus, School of Business and Public Administration (NY) 376

Long Island University, C.W. Post Campus, College of Management (NY) 377

Michigan State University, Eli Broad Graduate School of Management (MI) 303

Mississippi College, School of Business (MS) 322

Mississippi State University, College of Business and Industry (MS) 323, **886**

Murdoch University, School of Business (Australia) 577

New Hampshire College, Graduate School of Business (NH) 348, **892**

New York University, Leonard N. Stern School of Business (NY) 382, **898**

Nova Southeastern University, School of Business and Entrepreneurship (FL) 177, **912**

Pace University, Lubin School of Business (NY) 384, **916**

Philadelphia College of Textiles and Science, School of Business Administration (PA) 464, **926**

Quinnipiac College, School of Business (CT) 155, **938**

Robert Morris College, Graduate Programs in Business and Related Professional Areas (PA) 465, **948**

Royal Melbourne Institute of Technology, Graduate School of Business (Australia) 578

Rutgers, The State University of New Jersey, Newark, Graduate School of Management (NJ) 357

St. Cloud State University, College of Business (MN) 315

St. John's University, College of Business Administration (NY) 390, **964**

St. Mary's University of San Antonio, School of Business and Administration (TX) 505

San Diego State University, Graduate School of Business (CA) 131

San Francisco State University, College of Business (CA) 132

Southeastern University, College of Graduate Studies (DC) 167

State University of New York at Albany, School of Business (NY) 392, **996**

Suffolk University, Frank Sawyer School of Management (MA) 291, **1004**

Texas A&M University, Lowry Mays Graduate School of Business (TX) 510, **1014**

Texas Tech University, College of Business Administration (TX) 514, *515,* **1018**

Thomas College, Programs in Business (ME) 266

Truman State University, Division of Business and Accountancy (MO) 334, **1024**

Tulane University, A. B. Freeman School of Business (LA) 262, **1026**

University of Akron, College of Business Administration (OH) 430

University of Baltimore, Robert G. Merrick School of Business (MD) 274, **1036**

University of Colorado at Boulder, Graduate School of Business Administration (CO) 149, **1054**

University of Georgia, Terry College of Business (GA) 199, **1072**

University of Hartford, Barney School of Business and Public Administration (CT) 158

University of Houston, College of Business Administration (TX) 518, **1076**

University of Kansas, School of Business (KS) 248, **1084**

The University of Memphis, Fogelman College of Business and Economics (TN) 492, **1096**

University of Miami, School of Business Administration (FL) 183, **1098**

University of Minnesota, Twin Cities Campus, Carlson School of Management (MN) 317, *318*

University of Missouri-St. Louis, School of Business Administration (MO) 336, *336*

University of New Mexico, Robert O. Anderson Graduate School of Management (NM) 364

The University of North Carolina at Charlotte, The Belk College of Business Administration (NC) 410, *411*

University of North Florida, College of Business Administration (FL) 184

University of Notre Dame, College of Business Administration (IN) 235, **1118**

University of South Carolina, College of Business Administration (SC) 483, *483,* **1140**

University of Southern California, Marshall School of Business (CA) 143, *143,* **1142**

University of South Florida, College of Business Administration (FL) 185

The University of Texas at Arlington, College of Business Administration (TX) 522, **1150**

University of Texas at Austin, Graduate School of Business (TX) 523, **1152**

University of Texas at San Antonio, College of Business (TX) 526, **1156**

University of the Sacred Heart, Business School (PR) 571

University of the West of England, Bristol, Bristol Business School (United Kingdom) 689

University of Utah, David Eccles School of Business (UT) 532, **1168**

University of Washington, School of Business Administration (WA) 552, **1170**

The University of Western Ontario, Richard Ivey School of Business (Canada) 606, *606,* **1172**

University of Wisconsin-Madison, School of Business (WI) 564, **1174**

University of Wisconsin-Milwaukee, School of Business Administration (WI) 565

Utah State University, College of Business (UT) 533

Virginia Commonwealth University, School of Business (VA) 545

Walsh College of Accountancy and Business Administration, College of Accountancy and Business Administration (MI) 311, **1182**

Washington State University, College of Business and Economics (WA) 553

Wayne State University, School of Business Administration (MI) 311, *311,* **1188**

Weber State University, College of Business and Economics (UT) 534

Western Illinois University, College of Business and Technology (IL) 225

Widener University, School of Business Administration (PA) 473, **1192**

Xavier University, Williams College of Business Administration (OH) 435, **1204**

TECHNOLOGY MANAGEMENT

Ashridge Management College, Ashridge Executive MBA Program (United Kingdom) 661

Auburn University, College of Business (AL) 85, **710**

Benedictine University, Graduate Programs (IL) 205

Bentley College, Graduate School of Business (MA) 279, *280,* **722**

Bond University, School of Business (Australia) 573

Brigham Young University, Marriott School of Management (UT) 531, **736**

Case Western Reserve University, Weatherhead School of Management (OH) 420, **742**

City University, Business School (United Kingdom) 662

Cleveland State University, James J. Nance College of Business Administration (OH) 422, **758**

The College of Saint Rose, School of Business (NY) 370, **760**

Copenhagen Business School, Faculty of Economics and Business Administration (Denmark) 611

Creighton University, College of Business Administration (NE) 342

EAP-European School of Management, School of Management (France) 613

École des Hautes Études Commerciales, Master of Business Administration Program (Canada) 591, **796**

École Nationale des Ponts et Chaussées, ENPC Graduate School of International Business (France) 614

Edith Cowan University, Faculty of Business (Australia) 575

E. M. Lyon, Cesma MBA (France) 616, **802**

Franklin University, Graduate School of Business (OH) 423

The George Washington University, School of Business and Public Management (DC) 166, **828**

Georgia Institute of Technology, DuPree College of Management (GA) 192, **830**

Groupe ESC Toulouse, ESC Toulouse Graduate School of Management (France) 618

Helsinki School of Economics and Business Administration, International Center (Finland) 613

IADE, Instituto Universitario de Administracion de Empresas (Spain) 653

INCAE (Instituto Centroamericano de Administración de Empresas), Graduate Program (Costa Rica) 610

Instituto Tecnológico y de Estudios Superiores de Monterrey, Campus México City, Programs in Business (Mexico) 635

Areas of Concentration Index